DEBORAH EDWARDS SAKACH
TIFFANY CROSSWY

Published By

The Bed & Breakfast Encyclopedia

Every effort has been made to produce a dependable reference guide based on information gathered from innkeepers. American Historic Inns, Inc. makes no representations or warranties with respect to the establishments listed herein and specifically disclaims any warranties of fitness for any particular purpose. We recommend that you contact each inn and B&B to verify information prior to making reservations. Although every attempt was made to be as accurate as possible, American Historic Inns, Inc. does not make any representation that this book is free from error. Information included in this publication has been checked for accuracy prior to publication. Since changes do occur, American Historic Inns, Inc. cannot be responsible for any variations from the information printed.

American Historic Inns, Inc. supports reforestation projects and volunteer tree planting and maintenance programs as a contributor to the National Tree Trust in Washington, D.C., and its America's Treeways Program. More than 600 trees have been planted by American Historic Inns.

Front Cover:

From upper left clockwise:
Guest room photo – Photo by Lucy Poshek
Joshua Wilton House, Harrisonburg, Va. – Photo by American Historic Inns
Red Brook Inn, Old Mystic, Conn. – Photo by American Historic Inns
Green Gables Inn Breakfast Room, Pacific Grove, Calif. – Photo by Grant Huntington
Dessert at The Carter House, Eureka, Calif. – Photo by Patricia Brabant
Scofield House B&B, Sturgeon Bay, Wis. – Photo by American Historic Inns

Back Cover:

Top to bottom:
Welbourne, Middleburg, Va. – Photo by American Historic Inns
Hillbrook Inn, Charles Town, W.V. – Photo by American Historic Inns
Great Oak Manor, Chestertown, M.D. – Photo by American Historic Inns

Cover Design:
David Sakach

Database Manager:
Sandy Imre

Database Assistants:
Melanie Hackett, Joyce Roll, Elizabeth Spehart

Editorial Assistants:
Alex Murashko, Lucy Poshek, Stephen Sakach

Programming and cartography:
Tim Sakach

Publisher's Cataloging in Publication Data

Sakach, Deborah Edwards
Crosswy, Tiffany
American Historic Inns, Inc.
Bed & Breakfasts and Country Inns

1. Bed & Breakfast Accommodations - United States, Directories, Guide Books.
2. Travel - Bed & Breakfast Inns, Directories, Guide Books.
3. Bed & Breakfast Accommodations - Historic Inns, Directories, Guide Books.
4. Hotel Accommodations - Bed & Breakfast Inns, Directories, Guide Books.
5. Hotel Accommodations - United States, Directories, Guide Books.
I. Title. II. Author. III. Bed & Breakfast, Bed & Breakfasts and Country Inns.

American Historic Inns is a trademark of American Historic Inns, Inc.
ISBN: 1-888050-00-4
Softcover
Printed in the United States of America.

10 9 8 7 6 5 4 3 2 1

TABLE OF CONTENTS

For Crispin & Rebecca Crosswy
in appreciation of a lifetime of love, support and encouragement

INTRODUCTION

As our family sat around the breakfast table, entranced by stories of Yosemite National Park, we knew we'd discovered something unique.

It was our first time at a bed & breakfast, and, for this journey, we'd chosen to stay in the home of a Yosemite park ranger and his wife. Now, 16 years afterwards, our family still recalls the experiences made possible by their advice ... the large brown trout caught at the secret crook in the Merced River ... swinging from the rope that hung from a branch of an old oak bent over a secluded swimming hole ... listening to bear stories, great hikes and rescue adventures in Yosemite that the innkeepers shared with us at night. Since that time, Yosemite has become a specially loved place, visited often by all the members of my family.

That was back in 1981. Since then we've visited hundreds of bed & breakfasts, country inns and homestays. The impact of these excursions has so touched our lives, that it has inspired us to share our experiences with others.

Here at American Historic Inns, Inc. we hear similar stories every day from those who use our books to roam the countryside. One of our recent favorites was a call from the couple who told us that when they get time off, they open our B&B guide, choose a state, close their eyes and point — and that's where they go. They raved about the many great places they would not otherwise have visited.

Over the years, we've watched the inn industry change and flourish. Where once only a few thousand inns dotted the landscape, there are now more than 15,000 (some say 20,000) B&Bs and country inns throughout the United States and Canada. This morning, 15,000 tables are being set, some with fine china and candles, in walnut-paneled Victorian dining rooms, others on antique sideboards in 250-year-old colonials or in hand-crafted log houses with mountaintop views. At bed & breakfasts overlooking sandy ocean beaches, rolling vineyards, woodlands and waterfalls, thousands of innkeepers have been up before dawn grinding coffee beans, preparing muffins and scones, creating savory frittatas and decorating tables with fresh flowers. Thousands of guests are sitting down to a morning meal filled not just with excellent cuisine but with the camaraderie of other travelers.

It is this type of experience that sets the inn apart from the generic hotel or motel. Even a Ritz-Carlton cannot compare to nestling into a nine-foot-tall carved antique French bed topped with a mounded feather bed, across from a lit fireplace in a grand Victorian mansion overlooking the Pacific Ocean.

Seasoned innkeepers, sometimes the fourth or fifth generation of their family to have lived in the house, are armed with experience and knowledge about their community. Aside from staying in a B&B or country inn, there are few other ways to travel that allow us to so totally immerse ourselves into the local culture.

Two of us recently had a chance to take a historic lodging tour of Montana. Had we stayed in a motel, we would have had a parallel experience to others driving through the state. By lodging with the innkeepers of small country inns and B&Bs, we experienced much more of what Montana has to offer. We spent one memorable night in a copper baron's mansion where we were entertained during a four-course feast with stories of miners, a drunken dog named Otto and the fascinating history of the house. After dinner, our innkeepers suggested several off-the-beaten-path taverns, and our group headed out for a taste of local flavor. We mingled with the locals, we heard their stories and brought those memories home with us to share with our own families.

Most of us live complex lives. We balance the pressures, needs and expectations of work, parents, mates and children.

Sometimes we are so engulfed it's hard to see how to pull away. But when we do, we come back rejuvenated and passionate once again. From a distance we can reorder our priorities. Sometimes, we're simply refreshed and inspired by the adventure we've had and our new awareness of another place.

Bed & breakfast inns allow us to have these kinds of adventures in small doses, taking advantage of the windows of opportunity we find to break away. A four-week vacation is not so easily accomplished these days, though none of us doubt its benefit. But we can still manage a quick getaway to a lighthouse off the coast of Maine, a vineyard manor in California, a South Carolina plantation or perhaps a farmhouse tucked into the Pennsylvania Dutch country.

Because of knowledgeable, adventure-craving travelers such as yourself, more and more historic properties are being renovated, and newly designed country inns are being constructed in extraordinarily scenic locations. In our own state of California, small inns are sometimes allowed to be built on blufftops overlooking the Pacific Ocean where a Marriott or Hilton would not have been permitted. The small inn, with its low environmental impact, can open up beautiful areas for exploration.

When a historic building is readied for use as a country inn or bed & breakfast — usually an enormous undertaking — the property is bequeathed at least another 75 to 100 years of life. Most innkeepers we know continue to improve their buildings, putting profits into the continuing restoration and refinement of the property. Now, in every region of North America, historic treasures continue to be opened up to the traveling public. The demand of travelers who appreciate heritage homes has prevented thousands of buildings from being turned into multi-unit apartments, fraternity houses and parking lots.

We are grateful to have encouraged so many thousands of innkeepers and hundreds of thousands of guests to enjoy these opportunities. When we first started publishing information about B&Bs, most travelers and many travel writers had not yet stayed at inns and didn't yet understand their lure. But travelers like you pushed open the doors to more of these travel adventures. The first time our material was mentioned in the *New York Times* in 1982, we received 4,000 letters asking for our information on country inns and B&Bs. Those requests from travelers set us strongly on our course to provide the best information possible for inn travelers.

Back in 1981, when we first started helping travelers find B&Bs, the industry had barely begun. But experienced travelers were eager to discover B&Bs and small country inns such as those they had enjoyed in Europe. Most of the homes open then were what we now term "homestays" - primarily a family home but with one or two rooms for paying guests. We could visit an area such as Charleston, and by staying with the people who lived there, immerse ourselves in the history and culture. If we stayed another night or two at a nearby plantation or at an old seaside cottage, we broadened our understanding of the Charleston area even further.

We have learned to relish the tiny things that make up the character of a place. Innkeepers have guided us to discover everything from offbeat local eateries to nests of baby eagles. Often, after returning home, we also realized we had made new friends. And we now felt a connection to a place that would stay in our memory as though we had taken our first trip abroad with a well-traveled European friend.

B&Bs make new travel adventures easy because so many of them are close at hand. Kathleen Laragy, a reader from Grand Rapids, Mich., called us today while we were writing these pages. "I just walked in the door from our B&B trip. It was only two hours away but it was like being in a different world. I felt as if I was on a great escape and didn't realize how close to home I really was."

In these pages, there's room for every kind of adventure - whether full-blown or bite-sized. Just open the guide and choose. Whatever the experience, you'll return rejuvenated and ready to re-enter your world.

HOW TO USE THIS BOOK

Welcome! You hold in your hands the most comprehensive bed & breakfast and country inn guidebook on the market today. We have chosen an expansive selection of some of North America's most fascinating lodging establishments. In addition to the more than 2,000 individual inn listings, you'll find comprehensive state maps, an index to more than 13,000 inns, favorite recipes from innkeepers and special sections detailing inns of interest, bed & breakfast hot spots, inns that welcome families, how to start your own B&B and much more.

Accommodations

Among the listings, you'll find B&Bs and country inns in converted schoolhouses, lighthouses, 18th-century farmhouse, Queen Anne Victorians, adobe lodges and a variety of other unique places, both new and old.

The majority of inns included in this book were built in the 17th, 18th, 19th or early 20th centuries. We have stated the date each building was constructed at the beginning of each description. Many of the inns are steeped in the traditions of Colonial America, the Victorian Era, The Civil War, Spanish colonization or the Old West. Some are listed in the National Register of Historic Places.

A Variety of Inns

A **Country Inn** generally serves both breakfast and dinner and may have a restaurant associated with it. Many have been in operation for years; some since the 18th century as you will note in our "Inns of Interest" section. Although primarily found on the East Coast, a few country inns are in other regions of the nation.

A **Bed & Breakfast** facility's primary focus is lodging. It can have from three to 20 rooms or more. The innkeepers often live on the premises. Breakfast usually is the only meal served and can be a full-course, gourmet breakfast or a simple buffet. B&B owners often pride themselves on their culinary skills.

As with Country Inns, many B&Bs specialize in providing historic, romantic or gracious atmospheres with amenities such as canopied beds, fireplaces, spa tubs, afternoon tea in the library and scenic views.

Some give great attention to recapturing a specific historic period, such as the Victorian or Colonial eras. Many display antiques and other furnishings from family collections.

A **Homestay** is a room available in a private home. It may be an elegant stone mansion in the best part of town or a charming country farm. Homestays have one to three guest rooms. Because homestays are often operated as a hobby-type business and open and close frequently, only a very few such properties are included in this publication.

A Note About Innkeepers

Your innkeepers are a tremendous resource. Most knowledgeable innkeepers enjoy sharing regional attractions, local folklore, area history, and pointing out favorite restaurants and other special features of their areas. Unlike hotel and motel operators, innkeepers often bring much of themselves into creating an experience for you to long remember. Many have personally renovated historic buildings, saving them from deterioration and often, the bulldozer. Others have infused their inns with a unique style and personality to enliven your experience with a warm and inviting environment.

How to Use This Book

Note: We try to keep the use of codes to a minimum, but they do help us create a more comprehensive listing for each of the inns and B&Bs. We encourage to read this entire section, as it will help plan a getaway that is just right for you.

Area Codes

Although we have made every effort to update area codes throughout the book, new ones do pop up from time to time. The phone companies do provide recordings for several months after a change, but beyond that point, it can be difficult to reach an inn or B&B. Although they are listed by state or province, the new codes were added only in certain sections of the state or province. For example, the 310 area code in California applies only to certain areas in southern Los Angeles. The following list includes the most recent area code changes that were available at press time.

State/Province	Old Code	New Code	Effective Date of Change
Illinois	312	773	10/12/96
British Columbia	604	250	10/20/96
Texas	713	281	11/2/96
California	310	562	1/2/97
California	619	760	3/22/97
California	818	626	1997

Baths

Not all bed & breakfasts and country inns provide a private bath for each guest room. We have included the number of rooms and the number of private baths in each facility. The code *"PB,"* indicates how many guest rooms include a private bath. If you must have a private bath, make sure the room reserved for you provides this facility. If a listing indicates that there are suites available, one should assume that a suite includes a private bath. Most cottages also include a private bath, sometimes more than one, but be sure to inquire with the innkeeper about facilities in these units.

Beds

K, Q, D, T, R indicates King, Queen, Double, Twin or Rollaway beds available at the inn. A **C** indicates that a crib is available.

Children

This is always a sensitive subject. We do not list whether children are allowed at inns or B&Bs in this guide because it is illegal in several states to discriminate against persons of any age. However, occasionally innkeepers do "discourage" children as guests. Some innkeepers consider their inn a place for romance or solitude, and often do not think younger guests fit into this scheme. Also, many inns are filled with fine antiques and collectibles, so it may be an inappropriate place for very small children. Some innkeepers discourage children simply because they are not set up to accommodate the needs of a family.

If you plan to bring your children, always ask your innkeeper if children are welcome, and if so, at what age. Many innkeepers go out of their way to provide a wonderful atmosphere for families. In fact, more and more inns are catering to families.

Meals

Continental breakfast: Coffee, juice and toast or pastry.

Continental-plus breakfast: A continental breakfast plus a variety of breads, cheeses and fruit.

Full breakfast: Coffee, juice, breads, fruit and an entree.

Gourmet breakfast: May be a four-course candlelight offering or especially creative cuisine.

Teas: Usually served in the late afternoon with cookies, crackers or other in-between-meal offerings.

Meal Plans

AP: American Plan. All three meals may be included in the price of the room. Check to see if the rate quoted is for two people (double occupancy) or per person (single occupancy).

MAP: Modified American Plan. Breakfast and dinner may be included in the price of the room.

EP: European Plan. No meals are included. We have listed only a few historic hotels that operate on an EP plan.

Always find out what meals, if any, are included in the rates. Not every establishment in this guidebook provides breakfast, although most do. Please do not assume meals are included in the rates featured in the book. Occasionally, an innkeeper has indicated *MAP* and *AP* when she or he actually means that both programs are available and you must specify in which program you are interested.

Payments

MC: MasterCard
VISA
DS: Discover
AX: American Express
DC: Diner's Club
CB: Carte Blanche
TC: Traveler's Cheques
PC: Personal Checks

Pets Allowed

Under some listings, you will note that pets are allowed. Despite this, it is always wise to inform the innkeeper that you have a pet. Some innkeepers charge a fee for pets or only allow certain types and sizes of animals. The innkeeper also may have set aside a specific room for guests with pets, so if this room is booked, you may not be able to bring your pet along this trip.

Rates

Rates are usually listed in ranges, i.e., $45-105. The LOWEST rate is almost always available during off-peak periods and may only apply to the least expensive room. Rates are always subject to change and are not guaranteed. You should always confirm the rates when making the reservations. Rates for Canadian listings usually are listed in Canadian dollars. Rates are quoted for double occupancy.

Breakfast and other meals MAY or MAY NOT be included in the rates.

Minimum stays

Many inns require a two-night minimum stay on weekends. A three-night stay often is required during holiday periods.

Cancellations

Cancellation policies are individual for each bed & breakfast. It is not unusual to see 7- to 14-day cancellation periods or more. Please verify the inn's policy when making your reservation.

Rooms

Under some listings, you will note that suites are available. We typically assume that suites include a private bath.

Additionally, under some listings, you will note a reference to cottages. A cottage may be a rustic cabin tucked in the woods, a seaside cottage or a private apartment-style accommodation.

Fireplaces

When fireplaces are mentioned in the listing they may be in guest rooms or in common areas. A few have fireplaces that are non-working because of city lodging requirements. Please verify this if you are looking forward to an evening in front of a crackling fire.

Special Discounts

Under many listings, you may note the heading *"Special Discounts."* Although many are, please do not assume these discounts are valid throughout the year. Always be sure to tell the innkeeper you are interested in one of the discounts while you are making a reservation.

Smoking

The majority of country inns and B&Bs, especially those located in historic buildings, prohibit smoking; therefore, if you are a smoker, we advise you to call and specifically check with each inn to see if and how they accommodate smokers.

State maps

The state maps have been designed to help travelers find an inn's location quickly and easily. Each city shown on the maps contains one or more inns. As you browse through the guide, you will notice coordinates next to each city name, i.e. *"C3."* The coordinates designate the location of inns on the state map.

Media coverage

Some inns have provided us with copies of magazine or newspaper articles written by travel writers about their establishments and we have indicated that in the listing. Articles written about the inns may be available either from the source as a reprint, through libraries or from the inn itself.

Comments from guests

Over the years, we have collected reams of guest comments about thousands of inns. Our files are filled with these documented comments. At the end of some descriptions, we have included a guest comment received about that inn.

Descriptions

This book contains descriptions of more than 2,000 inns, and each establishment was reviewed carefully prior to being approved for this guide. Although we do charge a listing fee, this is never a guarantee that an inn or B&B will appear in the guide. Many inns and B&Bs were turned away from this guide because they did not meet our standards. We also do not allow innkeepers to write their own descriptions. Our descriptions are created from visits to the inns, interviews with innkeepers and a bulk of other information from ratings to guest comments to articles from top magazines and newspapers.

Inspections

Each year we travel across the country visiting inns. Since 1981, we have had a happy, informal team of inn travelers and prospective innkeepers who report to us about new bed & breakfast discoveries and repeat visits to favorite inns.

Although our staff usually sees hundreds of inns each year, inspecting inns is not the major focus of our travels. We visit as many as possible, photograph them and meet the innkeepers. Some inns are grand mansions filled with classic, museum-quality antiques. Others are rustic, such as reassembled log cabins or renovated barns or stables. We have enjoyed them all and cherish our memories of each establishment, pristine or rustic.

Only rarely have we come across a truly disappointing inn, poorly kept or poorly managed. This type of business usually does not survive because an inn's success depends upon repeat guests and enthusiastic word-of-mouth referrals from satisfied guests. We do not promote these types of establishments.

Traveler or tourist

Travel is an adventure into the unknown, full of surprises and rewards. A seasoned "traveler" learns that even after elaborate preparations and careful planning, travel provides the new and unexpected. The traveler learns to live with uncertainty and considers it part of the adventure.

To the "tourist," whether "accidental" or otherwise, new experiences are disconcerting. Tourists want no surprises. They expect things to be exactly as they had envisioned them. To tourists we recommend staying in a hotel or motel chain where the same formula is followed from one locale to another.

We have found that inngoers are travelers at heart. They relish the differences found at these unique bed & breakfasts and country inns. This is the magic that makes traveling from inn to inn the delightful experience it is.

What if the inn is full?

Ask the innkeeper for recommendations. They may know of an inn that has recently opened or one nearby but off the beaten path. Call the local Chamber of Commerce in the town you hope to visit. They may also know of inns that have recently opened. Please let us know of any new discoveries you make.

We want to hear from you!

We've always enjoyed hearing from our readers and have carefully cataloged all letters and recommendations. If you wish to participate in evaluating your inn experiences, use the Inn Evaluation Form in the back of this book. You might want to make copies of this form prior to departing on your journey.

We hope you will enjoy this book so much that you will want to keep an extra copy or two on hand to offer to friends and family. Many readers have called to purchase our books for hostess gifts, birthday presents, or for seasonal celebrations. It's a great way to introduce your friends to America's enchanting country inns and bed & breakfasts.

HOW TO READ AN INN LISTING

Anytown

❶ G6

An American Historic Inn

❷ 123 S Main St
Anytown, VT 12345-6789
(123)555-1212 (800)555-1212
Fax:(123)555-2121

❸ E-mail:ahii@ix.netcom.com

❹ **Rates:** $125-185. MAP
❺ **Payment:** MC VISA AX DC CB DS PC TC.
Innkeeper(s): Candice & Sterling Christopher
Circa: 1907.

❻ **Rooms:** 13 rooms with PB, 4 with FP. 1 suite. 1 conference room.
❼ **Beds:** KQDT.

❽ Every inch of this breathtaking inn offers something special. The interior is decorated to the hilt with lovely furnishings, plants, beautiful rugs and warm, inviting tones. Rooms include four-poster and canopy beds combined with the modern amenities such as two-person Jacuzzi tubs, fireplaces, wet bars and stocked refrigerators. Enjoy a complimentary full breakfast at the inn's gourmet restaurant. The chef offers everything from a light breakfast of fresh fruit, cereal and a bagel to heartier treats such as whole grain French toast stuffed with Brie and sundried peaches served with fresh fruit and crisp bacon.

❿ 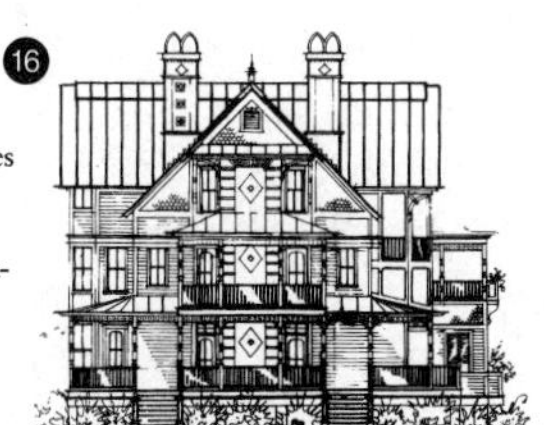

❾ Breakfast and afternoon tea included in rates. Types of meals: full breakfast, gourmet breakfast and early coffee/tea. Dinner, picnic lunch, gourmet lunch, banquet service, catering service and room service available. Air conditioning, turn-down service, ceiling fan and cable TV in room. VCR, fax, copier and bicycles on premises. Handicap access. Weddings, small meetings, family reunions and seminars hosted. English and Dutch spoken. Antiques, fishing, parks, shopping, theater and watersports nearby. TAC10. ❿

⓫ **Pets Allowed:** With advanced notice.

⓬ **Location:** One-half mile from Historic Route 1A.

⓭ **Publicity:** *Anytown News, Southern Living, Country Inns, US Air.*

⓮ **Special Discounts:** 10% off midweek January-March

⓯ *"You have captured a beautiful part of our history."*

① ***Map coordinates***
Easily locate an inn on the state map using these coordinates.

② ***Inn address***
Mailing or street address and all phone numbers for the inn.

③ ***E-mail address***
Contact the inn via the Internet.

④ ***Rates***
Rates are quoted for double occupancy. The rate range includes off-season rates and is subject to change.

⑤ ***Payment types accepted***
MC-MasterCard, VISA, DS-Discover, AX-American Express, DC-Diner's Club, CB-Carte Blanche, TC-Traveler's Check, PC-Personal Check.

⑥ ***Rooms***
Number and types of rooms available. PB=Private Bath

⑦ ***Beds***
King, Queen, Double, Twin, Rollaway, Crib

⑧ ***Description of inn***
Descriptions of inns are written by experienced travel writers based on visits to inns, interviews and information collected from inns.

⑨ ***Amenities and activities***
Information included here describes the meals that might be included in the rates and other amenities or services available at the inn. Nearby activities are also included.

⑩ ***Travel agent commission***
Number represents a percentage. Example: TAC10=10%

⑪ ***Pets allowed***
Indicates the inn's policy on pets.

⑫ ***Location***
Location of inn in relation to local landmarks.

⑬ ***Publicity***
Newspapers, magazines and other publications which have featured articles about the inn.

⑭ ***Special discounts***
Indicates special packages or discounts that may be available. Always verify availability of discount with innkeeper.

⑮ ***Guest comments***
Comments about the inn from guests.

⑯ ***Drawing of inn***
Many listings include artistic renderings.

NOTES

Alabama

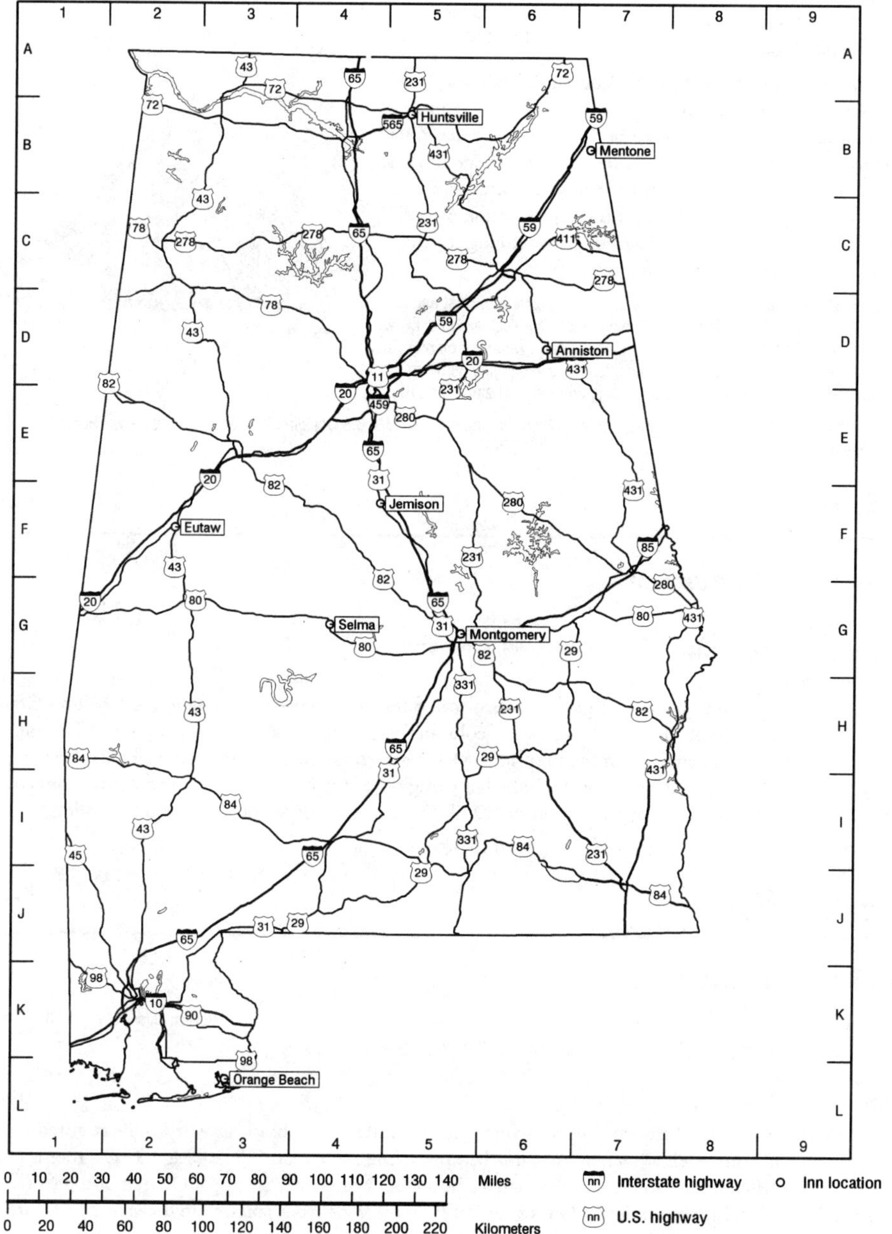
Huntsville
Mentone
Anniston
Jemison
Eutaw
Selma
Montgomery
Orange Beach
0 10 20 30 40 50 60 70 80 90 100 110 120 130 140 Miles
0 20 40 60 80 100 120 140 160 180 200 220 Kilometers
Interstate highway
U.S. highway
Inn location

Anniston D6

The Victoria, A Country Inn & Restaurant

1604 Quintard Ave #2213
Anniston, AL 36201-3849
(205)236-0503 (800)260-8781
Fax:(205)236-1132
E-mail: jao619@aol.com

Rates: $64-225. EP.
Payment: MC VISA AX DC CB DS TC.
Innkeeper(s): Beth & Fain Casey, Jean Ann Oglesby.
Circa: 1887.

Rooms: 60 rooms with PB, 4 with FP. 1 cottage. 4 conference rooms.
Beds: KQD.

This Victorian estate, an Alabama landmark, occupies almost an entire square block on Quintard Avenue, Anniston's major thoroughfare. The first floor of the main house has four dining rooms, a piano lounge and a glass-enclosed veranda. The guest rooms and suites here are furnished with antiques, while those in the new Victorian annex feature reproduction pieces. Covered walkways, verandas and gazebos flow among the massive hardwoods, gardens, courtyard and pool.

Breakfast included in rates. Types of meals: continental-plus breakfast and early coffee/tea. Banquet service, catering service and room service available. EP. Air conditioning and cable TV in room. VCR, fax, copier and swimming on premises. Handicap access. Weddings, small meetings, family reunions and seminars hosted. Amusement parks, antiques, parks, shopping and theater nearby. TAC10.

Publicity: *Southern Living, New York Times, Anniston Star, Birmingham Post Herald, Decatur Daily, Birmingham News, Good Housekeeping.*

Eutaw F2

Kirkwood Plantation

111 Kirkwood Dr
Eutaw, AL 35462-1101
(205)372-9009

Rates: $75.
Innkeeper(s): Mary Swayze.

Rooms: 4 rooms.

Located on more than eight acres of green lawns, pecan trees and azaleas, this is a stately antebellum Greek Revival plantation house. There are eight Ionic columns on the front and side of the house and inside, Italian Carrarra marble mantels adorn the fireplaces. Massive mirrors and a Waterford crystal chandelier add to the elegance of the inn's furnishings, most of which are original to the house. The innkeeper gives tours of the plantation along with a mini history lesson on the Civil War and its influence on Kirkwood Plantation.

Breakfast included in rates. Type of meal: full breakfast. Air conditioning in room.

Huntsville B5

Stockton House B&B

310 Greene St Se
Huntsville, AL 35801-4215
(205)539-3195
Fax:(205)539-9752

Rates: $70-110.
Innkeeper(s): Nannette Laughlin.
Circa: 1910.

Rooms: 3 rooms, 2 with PB.
Beds: KD.

This brick Queen Anne Victorian features white columns and just one block away from the restored Alabama Constitution Village where Alabama became a state more than 175 years ago. Guest rooms overlook either the 1819 Weeden House Museum across the street, or the 1859 Episcopal Church of the Nativity, a National Historic Landmark, next door. Guests can relax on the wide front porch with its wicker furniture or in the big swing.

Breakfast included in rates. Type of meal: continental-plus breakfast. Antiques, fishing and theater nearby.

Publicity: *Huntsville Times, Birmingham News.*

"Charm and true southern hospitality are understatements when used for Stockton/Laughlin House. This is my favorite."

Jemison

F4

The Jemison Inn

212 Hwy 191
Jemison, AL 35085
(205)688-2055

Rates: $55-60.
Payment: MC VISA AX DC CB DS.
Innkeeper(s): Nancy Ruzicka.
Circa: 1930.

Rooms: 3 rooms, 1 with PB, 1 with FP.
Beds: T.

Heirloom quality antiques fill this gabled brick house. A Victorian decor predominates. Casseroles, sausage, cheese grits and muffins comprise the inn's hearty breakfast.

Breakfast and afternoon tea included in rates. Type of meal: full breakfast. Picnic lunch available.

Location: Midway between Birmingham and Montgomery in the heart of horse country.

"I've never had a better breakfast anywhere."

Mentone

B7

Mentone Inn

Hwy 117, PO Box 290
Mentone, AL 35984
(205)634-4836 (800)455-7470

Rates: $60-125.
Payment: MC VISA AX TC.
Innkeeper(s): Frances & Karl Waller.
Circa: 1927.

Rooms: 11 rooms with PB.
Beds: QT.

Mentone is a refreshing stop for those in search of the cool breezes and natural air conditioning of the mountains. Here antique treasures mingle with modern-day conveniences. A sun deck and spa complete the experience. Sequoyah Caverns, Little River Canyon and DeSoto Falls are moments away. The inn has its own hiking trails.

Breakfast and afternoon tea included in rates. Types of meals: continental breakfast, continental-plus breakfast, full breakfast and early coffee/tea. Dinner, evening snack, picnic lunch, lunch, banquet service and catering service available. Air conditioning and ceiling fan in room. Cable TV, VCR, spa and bicycles on premises. Weddings, small meetings, family reunions and seminars hosted. Antiques, fishing, parks, downhill skiing and watersports nearby.

Location: On Lookout Mountain in northeast Alabama.

Publicity: *Birmingham News.*

Montgomery

G5

Red Bluff Cottage B&B

551 Clay St, PO Box 1026
Montgomery, AL 36104
(334)264-0056
Fax:(334)263-3054

Rates: $65.
Payment: MC VISA AX DS PC TC.
Innkeeper(s): Anne & Mark Waldo.
Circa: 1987.

Rooms: 4 rooms with PB. 1 suite.
Beds: QT.

This raised cottage sits high above the Alabama River in Montgomery's historic Cottage Hill District. Guest rooms are on the first floor, while the kitchen, dining room, living room, sitting room and music room with piano and harpsichord are on the second floor. An upstairs porch has a panoramic view of the river plain, downtown Montgomery and the state Capitol building. Each of the guest rooms is furnished with family antiques.

Breakfast included in rates. Types of meals: full breakfast and early coffee/tea. Air conditioning and ceiling fan in room. Cable TV, VCR and library on premises. Small meetings hosted. Antiques, parks, shopping and theater nearby. TAC10.

Location: Convenient to the Alabama Shakespeare Festival and Montgomery Museum of Fine Arts.

"This was our first time to a bed and breakfast and I dare say it won't be our last after this wonderful experience."

Orange Beach

L3

The Original Romar House Inn

23500 Perdido Beach Blvd
Orange Beach, AL 36561
(334)974-1625 (800)487-6627
Fax:(334)974-1163

Rates: $79-120.
Payment: MC VISA AX PC.
Innkeeper(s): Darrell Finley & Beverly Lane.
Circa: 1924.

Rooms: 6 rooms with PB. 1 suite. 1 cottage. 1 conference room.
Beds: Q.

From the deck of the Purple Parrot Bar, guests at this seaside inn can enjoy a cocktail and a view of the Gulf of Mexico. Each of the guest rooms is named and themed after a local festival and decorated with authentic Art Deco furnishings. Stained- and beveled-glass windows add to the romantic atmosphere. A full Southern breakfast is served each morning, and in the evening, wine and cheese is served in the Purple Parrot Bar.

Breakfast included in rates. Type of meal: full breakfast. Air conditioning, turn-down service and ceiling fan in room. Cable TV, VCR, spa, swimming, bicycles and library on premises. Weddings, small meetings and family reunions hosted. Amusement parks, antiques, fishing, parks, shopping and watersports nearby. TAC10.

Selma

G4

Grace Hall B&B Inn

506 Lauderdale St
Selma, AL 36701-4527
(334)875-5744
Fax:(334)875-9967

Rates: $79-99.
Payment: MC VISA AX DS.
Innkeeper(s): Joey & Coy Dillon.
Circa: 1857.

Rooms: 6 rooms with PB. 1 conference room.

The first-floor rooms of this antebellum mansion open up to a New Orleans-style garden with ferns, fountains, and stone walls. Larger, more opulent rooms can be found upstairs. A wood-burning fireplace in each room adds a romantic touch to an inn that has all the ambiance of 1860, but all the modern-day conveniences. The inn is located in one of three historic districts, and walking and driving tours are available to museums, cemeteries and quaint shopping and antiquing.

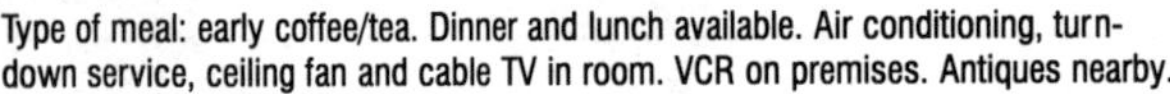

Type of meal: early coffee/tea. Dinner and lunch available. Air conditioning, turn-down service, ceiling fan and cable TV in room. VCR on premises. Antiques nearby.

Farmer's Cheese Dip

The Inn at Bethlehem
Bethlehem, Indiana.

- 1 cup cottage cheese (4% fat)
- ½ cup mayonnaise
- ¼ cup sour cream
- 2 t chopped fresh parsley
- 1 t chopped fresh dill
- 1 clove garlic, mashed into a paste
- ½ t seasoned salt
- 1 t chives, chopped
- Dash of Tabasco sauce
- 1 t Worcestershire sauce

Mix all ingredients will in a medium bowl. Cover and refrigerate overnight.

Yields 2 cups.

Alaska

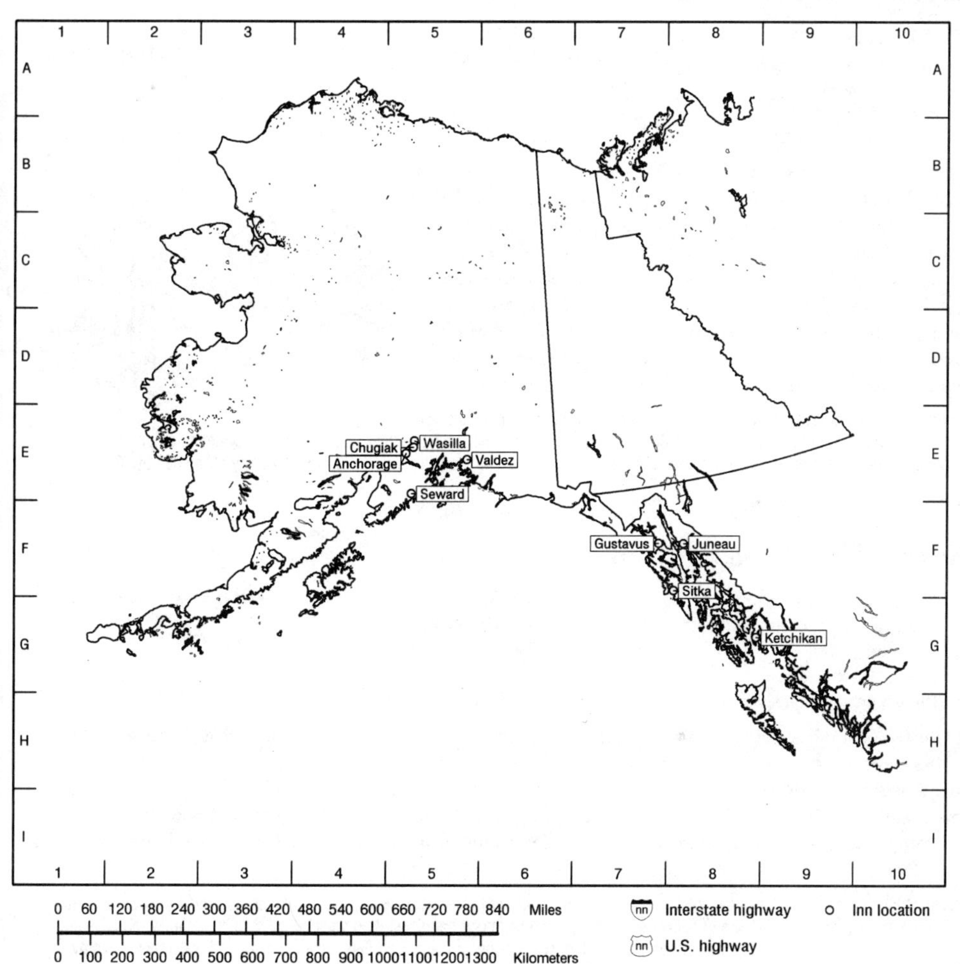

Anchorage

E5

A Garden House B&B

1511 Woo Blvd
Anchorage, AK 99515-3216
(907)344-3312
Fax:(907)344-3312

Rates: $65-95.
Payment: MC VISA PC TC.
Innkeeper(s): Hersh & Karen Kendall.
Circa: 1974.

Rooms: 3 rooms, 1 with PB.
Beds: KQD.

This contemporary redwood home is surrounded by more than an acre of spruce and birch trees, as well as a garden. Moose occasionally stop by to enjoy the fragrance of the flowers. The home is a quiet, secluded spot, yet within minutes to the airport, shopping, restaurants, golfing and the zoo. Each room has a floral theme, from the Garden Room to the smaller Rose and Forget-Me-Not rooms. In season, fresh-from-the-garden berries and smoked salmon appear on the breakfast table. Reindeer sausage, quiche and orange-cranberry bread are other possibilities.

Breakfast and evening snack included in rates. Types of meals: full breakfast, gourmet breakfast and early coffee/tea. Cable TV in room. VCR, fax, copier, sauna and bicycles on premises. Family reunions hosted. Fishing, parks, shopping, downhill skiing, cross-country skiing, sporting events, theater and watersports nearby. TAC10.

"Beautiful surroundings, warmth and kindness, soft bed and great food."

Alaskan Frontier Gardens

PO Box 24-1881
Anchorage, AK 99524-1881
(907)345-6556
Fax:(907)562-2923
E-mail: afg@alaska.net

Rates: $75-175.
Payment: MC VISA AX DC DS PC TC.
Innkeeper(s): Rita Gittins.
Circa: 1982.

Rooms: 5 rooms, 2 with PB, 1 with FP. 2 suites. 1 conference room.
Beds: KQDT.

Secluded on three scenic acres of woods, manicured lawns and gardens, this lodge-style home offers privacy, yet is less than half an hour from downtown Anchorage. The two suites include Jacuzzi tubs, and the Ivory Suite also has a sauna and fireplace. Furnishings are contemporary and comfortable, and guests are encouraged to enjoy the house and relax. The innkeepers can store camping and fishing gear and have a freezer for fish and game. Freshly made Belgian waffles, reindeer sausage, gourmet coffee and homemade pastries are often part of the breakfast fare.

Breakfast included in rates. Types of meals: full breakfast, gourmet breakfast and early coffee/tea. Ceiling fan, cable TV and VCR in room. Fax, copier, spa, sauna, bicycles, library and pet boarding on premises. Weddings, small meetings and family reunions hosted. Parks, shopping, downhill skiing and cross-country skiing nearby. TAC10.

Pets Allowed.

Aurora Winds B&B Resort

7501 Upper Omalley Rd
Anchorage, AK 99516-1176
(907)346-2533
Fax:(907)346-3192
E-mail: awbnb@alaska.net

Rates: $75-165.
Innkeeper(s): James Montgomery.
Circa: 1984.

Rooms: 5 rooms with PB, 1 with FP. 1 conference room.
Beds: KQT.

Situated on a hillside above Anchorage, this inn offers many amenities and features that the seasoned traveler has come to expect at the most luxurious accommodations. Guests can relax in an eight-person Jacuzzi after a workout in the exercise room. Other areas of enjoyment include a sauna, billiard room, two family rooms and three fireplaces. The inn is close to downtown, the airport, cross-country and downhill skiing. A full complement of culinary delights or an expanded continental breakfast is available in the dining room or at your door.

Breakfast and evening snack included in rates. Types of meals: continental-plus breakfast, full breakfast, gourmet breakfast and early coffee/tea. Ceiling fan, cable TV and VCR in room. Fax, spa and sauna on premises. Weddings, small meetings, family reunions and seminars hosted. Fishing, parks, shopping, downhill skiing, cross-country skiing, sporting events, theater and watersports nearby. TAC10.

Pets Allowed: On approval.

Glacier Bear B&B

4814 Malibu Rd
Anchorage, AK 99517-3274
(907)243-8818
Fax:(907)248-4532
E-mail: 76602.505@compuserve.com

Rates: $59-95.
Payment: MC VISA AX DS PC TC.
Innkeeper(s): Marge Brown & Georgia Taton.
Circa: 1986.

Rooms: 5 rooms, 3 with PB, 1 with FP.
Beds: KQT.

This cedar-sided contemporary home is located just a mile and a half from the world's largest float plane lake. The B&B is decorated with a mix of Oriental and Victorian pieces. One bedroom includes a pencil canopy bed, while another offers an antique king bed and a fireplace. The landscaped grounds include an eight-person spa surrounded by ferns, trees and wild berry bushes. The innkeepers offer both a hearty full breakfast or continental fare. Freshly ground coffee, tea, soft drinks and freshly baked cookies are available throughout the day. The innkeepers provide a courtesy van to and from the airport.

Breakfast included in rates. Types of meals: full breakfast, gourmet breakfast and early coffee/tea. Evening snack available. Cable TV, VCR, fax, spa, bicycles and library on premises. Weddings and family reunions hosted. Antiques, fishing, parks, shopping, downhill skiing, cross-country skiing, sporting events and watersports nearby. TAC10.

Lynn's Pine Point B&B

3333 Creekside Dr
Anchorage, AK 99504-4026
(907)333-2244
Fax:(907)333-1043

Rates: $75-90.
Payment: MC VISA AX DS PC TC.
Innkeeper(s): Rich & Lynn Stouff.
Circa: 1981.

Rooms: 3 rooms, 2 with PB.
Beds: Q.

For outdoor enthusiasts, this rustic cedar home is within walking distance to a bicycle path and fitness trail. For those who wish to explore Anchorage, the home is located nine miles from the downtown area. Rooms are comfortably furnished with some antiques and decorated in country style. Guest rooms include the modern amenities of a coffee maker and two also have microwaves. The innkeepers provide continental-plus fare for early risers and at 8 a.m., full breakfast is available. Crepes, blueberry pancakes, savory egg dishes and freshly baked muffins prepare guests for a day of activity. Hors d'oeuvres are sometimes served in the inn's gazebo in the afternoons.

Breakfast included in rates. Types of meals: continental-plus breakfast and full breakfast. Cable TV and VCR in room. Fax and spa on premises. Antiques, fishing, parks, shopping, downhill skiing, cross-country skiing, sporting events and theater nearby. TAC10.

"The breakfasts were very special and started the day off on a good note."

North Country Castle B&B

PO Box 111876, 14600
Joanne Circle
Anchorage, AK 99511
(907)345-7296
Fax:(907)345-7296

Rates: $74-134.
Payment: PC TC.
Innkeeper(s): Cindy & Wray Kinard.
Circa: 1986.

Rooms: 3 rooms, 1 with FP. 1 suite.
Beds: QT.

While this modern, Victorian cottage-style home is not actually a castle, guests are treated like royalty. The innkeepers offer two rooms with mountain views, and the Turnagain View Suite, which features a fireplace, double Jacuzzi and private deck. The home, which is surrounded by woods, rests in the foothills of the Chugach Mountains. The innkeepers serve a hearty, traditional breakfast with muffins, French toast, egg dishes, fresh fruit, juice and reindeer sausage.

Breakfast included in rates. Types of meals: continental breakfast, continental-plus breakfast, full breakfast and gourmet breakfast. Turndown service in room. Fax, copier and library on premises. Weddings hosted. Some Spanish and German spoken. Fishing, parks, shopping, downhill skiing, cross-country skiing, sporting events and theater nearby. TAC10.

Special Discounts: $5 per night discount with 3 or more nights in a row; family rates.

The Oscar Gill House

1344 W 10th Ave
Anchorage, AK 99501-3245
(907)258-1717
Fax:(907)258-6613

Rates: $75-95.
Payment: MC VISA AX PC.
Innkeeper(s): Mark & Susan Lutz.
Circa: 1913.

Rooms: 3 rooms, 1 with PB.
Beds: QDT.

This clapboard, Craftsman-style home was built in Knik, Alaska, but later disassembled and moved to Anchorage in 1916. The home is the city's oldest, and the innkeepers have kept the decor simple and comfortable, with antiques here and there, as well as vintage furnishings from the '30s and '40s. Down comforters and bathrooms stocked with toiletries are a few of the special touches guests will find. Breakfasts are served up in the cheery dining room, which features panoramic photos of Anchorage and the home in its original location. Innkeeper Susan Lutz prepares a variety of entrees for the morning meal, including items such as sourdough French toast Mexican egg casseroles accompanied by freshly ground coffee, a selection of teas and homemade hot chocolate.

Breakfast included in rates. Type of meal: full breakfast. Fax, bicycles and child care on premises. Small meetings and family reunions hosted. Fishing, parks, downhill skiing, cross-country skiing, sporting events and theater nearby. TAC5.

Chugiak E5

Peters Creek B&B

22626 Chambers
Chugiak, AK 99567
(907)688-3465 (800)405-3465
Fax:(907)688-3466
E-mail: pcbnb@anc.ak.net

Rates: $85.
Payment: MC VISA AX DS PC TC.
Innkeeper(s): Bob & Lucy Moody.
Circa: 1994.

Rooms: 4 rooms, 3 with PB. 1 suite. 1 conference room.
Beds: KQDT.

This bed & breakfast is located just off the shore of its namesake creek. The home itself is contemporary, but filled with many Victorian antiques. Guest rooms have amenities such as fluffy robes, irons and refrigerators. There is a recreation room with exercise equipment. Breakfast entrees such as omelets and reindeer sausage are accompanied by selections of beverages, yogurt, fruit and oven-fresh muffins. The home is located in between Anchorage and the Mat-Su Valley.

Breakfast and evening snack included in rates. Types of meals: full breakfast and gourmet breakfast. Cable TV and VCR in room. Fax, copier, bicycles and library on premises. Handicap access. Small meetings, family reunions and seminars hosted. Spanish spoken. Antiques, fishing, parks, shopping, downhill skiing, cross-country skiing, sporting events, theater and watersports nearby. TAC10.

Pets Allowed: In outdoor accommodations.

Gustavus F7

Glacier Bay Country Inn

PO Box 5
Gustavus, AK 99826-0005
(907)697-2288
Fax:(907)697-2289

Rates: $260. AP.
Payment: MC VISA AX DS.
Innkeeper(s): Ponch and Sandi Marchbanks.
Circa: 1986.

Rooms: 10 rooms, 9 with PB. 3 cottages.
Beds: QDT.

The innkeepers assure guests that although a trip to their remote lodge is a bit of a challenge (reached by bush plane or Alaska Airlines shuttle), it is definitely worthwhile. Set in a clearing, and surrounded by a lush, green forest and a mountain backdrop, the inn's design was derived from fairy-tale cottages. Its unique architecture includes multi-angled roofs, dormer windows, log-beamed ceilings and large porches. Take glacier tours, or go whale watching or kayaking. The inn has a charter boat available for day and overnight fishing cruises for some of the best halibut and salmon around. All meals are included in the rate.

Breakfast, dinner and lunch included in rates. AP. 160 acres. Weddings, small meetings, family reunions and seminars hosted. Fishing nearby.

Juneau F8

Pearson's Pond Luxury Inn & Gardens

4541 Sawa Cir
Juneau, AK 99801-8723
(907)789-3772
Fax:(907)789-6722
E-mail: pearsons.pond@juneau.com

Rates: $79-169.
Payment: MC VISA AX DC CB PC TC.
Innkeeper(s): Steve & Diane Pearson.
Circa: 1985.

Rooms: 3 rooms with PB, 2 with FP. 2 suites.
Beds: Q.

From this award-winning, B&B resort, guests can view glaciers, visit museums and chance their luck at gold-panning streams, or simply soak in a hot tub surrounded by a lush forest and nestled next to a picturesque duck pond. Blueberries hang over the private decks of the guest rooms. A full, self-serve breakfast is provided each morning in the kitchenettes. Nearby trails offer excellent hiking, and the Mendenhall Glacier is within walking distance. The sportsminded will enjoy river rafting or angling for world-class halibut and salmon.

Breakfast, afternoon tea and evening snack included in rates. Types of meals: continental-plus breakfast and early coffee/tea. Cable TV and VCR in room. Fax, copier, spa, bicycles and library on premises. Weddings, small meetings, family reunions and seminars hosted. Antiques, fishing, parks, shopping, downhill skiing, cross-country skiing, theater and watersports nearby. TAC10.

Location: Three miles to airport and ferry terminal.

"A definite 10!"

Ketchikan G8

D & W's "Almost Home" B&B

412 D 1 Loop Rd N
Ketchikan, AK 99901-9202
(907)225-3273 (800)987-5337
Fax:(907)247-5337
E-mail: krs@ktn.net

Rates: $75.
Payment: MC VISA AX DC CB DS PC TC.
Innkeeper(s): Darrell & Wanda Vandergriff.
Circa: 1986.

Rooms: 2 cottages.
Beds: KDT.

These rural B&B accommodations, located a few minutes' drive north of Ketchikan, provide guests with a completely outfitted two-bedroom apartment that sleeps six. A special welcome is extended to fishing parties. Ketchikan is known for its excellent salmon and halibut fishing and offers several fishing derbies each summer. A gas barbecue grill on the deck outside your room comes in handy for the catch of the day.

Breakfast included in rates. Type of meal: continental-plus breakfast. Ceiling fan and cable TV in room. Fax on premises. Small meetings and family reunions hosted. Fishing, parks, shopping, theater and watersports nearby. TAC10.

Seward E5

The White House B&B

PO Box 1756
Seward, AK 99664-1756
(907)224-3614
Fax:(907)224-3615

Rates: $60-100.
Payment: MC VISA AX PC TC.
Innkeeper(s): Nathan & Alicia Tuning.
Circa: 1978.

Rooms: 8 rooms, 6 with PB.
Beds: QDTR.

Enjoy views of mountains and forests at this Alaskan bed & breakfast, just a few miles from the main portion of historic Seward and Resurrection Bay. Each of the country-style guest rooms offers a view of the wilderness. The Iditarod Trail is nearby, offering cross-country skiing during the winter months.

Breakfast included in rates. Type of meal: continental-plus breakfast. Cable TV on premises. Small meetings and family reunions hosted. Fishing, parks, shopping and cross-country skiing nearby. TAC5.

Special Discounts: 10% discount - clergy.

Sitka F8

Alaska Ocean View B&B

1101 Edgecumbe Dr
Sitka, AK 99835-7122
(907)747-8310
Fax:(907)747-8310

Rates: $79-139.
Payment: MC VISA AX PC TC.
Innkeeper(s): Carole & Bill Denkinger.
Circa: 1986.

Rooms: 3 rooms with PB. 2 suites. 1 conference room.
Beds: KQDT.

This Alaska-style all-cedar home is located in a quiet neighborhood just one block from the seashore and the Tongass National Forest. Witness the spectacular Alaska sunsets over Sitka Sound and surrounding islands. On clear days, view Mt. Edgecumbe, which is an extinct volcano located on Kruzoff Island and looks like Mt. Fuji. Binoculars are kept handy for guests who take a special treat in viewing whales and eagles.

Breakfast, afternoon tea and evening snack included in rates. Types of meals: continental-plus breakfast, full breakfast, gourmet breakfast and early coffee/tea. Turn-down service, ceiling fan, cable TV and VCR in room. Fax, copier, spa and library on premises. Small meetings hosted. Antiques, fishing, parks, shopping, theater and watersports nearby. TAC10.

Pets Allowed: Kept outdoors in kennel only.

Valdez

E5

Downtown B&B Inn

PO Box 184, 113 Galena Dr
Valdez, AK 99686-0184
(907)835-2791 (800)478-2791
Fax:(907)835-5406

Rates: $40-110.
Payment: MC VISA AX DS PC TC.
Innkeeper(s): Glen & Sharon Mills.
Circa: 1989.

Rooms: 31 rooms, 21 with PB.
Beds: QDT.

At first glance, this bed & breakfast appears as a little chalet tucked in the Swiss Alps. Window boxes dot the exterior and the mountains provide wonderful scenery. Inside, accommodations are simple, comfortable and modern. Some rooms offer views of the bay or mountains. The inn's location is ideal, a block from the small harbor, a museum, restaurants and shops. A 10-minute walk will take you to the ferry. There's plenty to do in the area, including fishing, hiking, whitewater rafting and viewing glaciers.

Breakfast included in rates. Types of meals: continental-plus breakfast and early coffee/tea. Cable TV in room. Fax on premises. Handicap access. Spanish spoken. Fishing, parks, shopping, downhill skiing, cross-country skiing and watersports nearby. TAC10.

Wasilla

E5

Yukon Don's B&B Inn

1830 E Parks Hwy # 386
Wasilla, AK 99654-7374
(907)376-7472 (800)478-7472
Fax:(907)376-6515
E-mail: 102737.3133@compuserve.com

Rates: $75-125.
Payment: MC VISA AX DS PC TC.
Innkeeper(s): Don & Kristan Tanner.
Circa: 1971.

Rooms: 7 rooms, 3 with PB. 3 suites. 1 cottage. 1 conference room.
Beds: QT.

Decorated with an Alaskan theme, this comfortable bed & breakfast boasts a second-floor room with a spectacular 360-degree view of the Matanuska Valley. Guests can partake of continental breakfast bar each morning and also enjoy use of a sauna and exercise room. The inn is about an hour from Anchorage and is on the direct route to Denali National Park, Fairbanks and Valdez. Among its distinctions, Wasilla is the home of the International Iditarod Dog Sled Race, the Reindeer Farm and the Matanuska and Knik glaciers.

Breakfast included in rates. Type of meal: continental-plus breakfast. Ceiling fan, cable TV and VCR in room. Fax, copier, sauna and library on premises. Weddings, small meetings, family reunions and seminars hosted. Antiques, fishing, parks, shopping, downhill skiing, cross-country skiing and sporting events nearby. TAC10.

Pets Allowed: Limited.

Special Discounts: 10% for specific programs.

Arizona

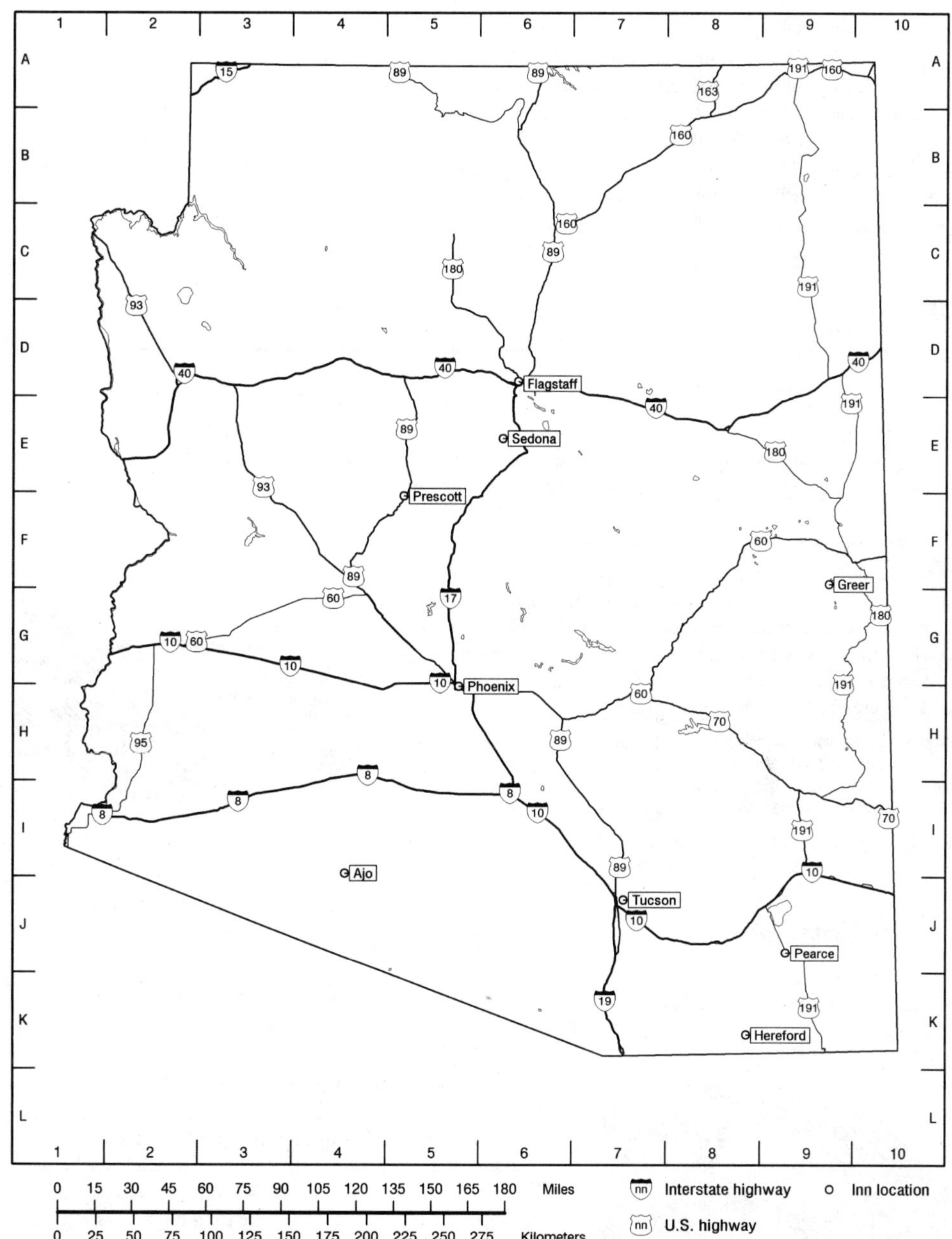
Flagstaff
Sedona
Prescott
Phoenix
Greer
Ajo
Tucson
Pearce
Hereford
0 15 30 45 60 75 90 105 120 135 150 165 180 Miles
0 25 50 75 100 125 150 175 200 225 250 275 Kilometers
Interstate highway
U.S. highway
Inn location

Ajo **I4**

The Mine Manager's House Inn B&B

1 W Greenway Dr
Ajo, AZ 85321-2713
(520)387-6505
Fax:(520)387-6508

Rates: $69-105.
Payment: MC VISA TC.
Innkeeper(s): Jean & Micheline Fournier.
Circa: 1919.

Rooms: 5 rooms with PB. 3 suites.
Beds: QT.

Overlooking the Southwestern Arizona desert and a mile-wide copper mine pit, the Mine Manager's is a large Craftsman home situated on three acres. Built by the local copper mining industry, it has 10-inch thick walls. A library, coin laundry and gift shop are on the premises. The Greenway Suite features a marble tub and shower and one other suite has two queen-size beds. A full breakfast is served in the formal dining room.

Breakfast and evening snack included in rates. Type of meal: full breakfast. Air conditioning and ceiling fan in room. Cable TV, VCR, fax and spa on premises. Handicap access. Small meetings and family reunions hosted. French spoken. Parks and shopping nearby. TAC10.

Publicity: *Arizona Daily Star, Tucson Citizen, Catalina-Oracle, Arizona Sun, Arizona Highways-Sunset.*

"The hospitality is what makes this place so inviting! A palace at the top of the hill with service to match."

Flagstaff **D6**

Birch Tree Inn

824 W Birch Ave
Flagstaff, AZ 86001-4420
(520)774-1042 (888)774-1042
Fax:(520)774-8462
E-mail: birch@flagstaff.az.us

Rates: $55-99.
Payment: MC VISA AX PC TC.
Innkeeper(s): Donna & Rodger Pettinger, Sandy & Ed Znetko.
Circa: 1917.

Rooms: 5 rooms, 3 with PB.
Beds: KQT.

This bungalow is surrounded by a wraparound veranda supported with Corinthian columns. Southwestern and antique decor is featured including shaker pine and white wicker. Nature lovers and ski enthusiasts will appreciate the Ponderosa Pine Forest nearby. Adjacent to the inn, cross-country ski trails are especially popular. A full breakfast and afternoon refreshments are served.

Breakfast and afternoon tea included in rates. Types of meals: full breakfast and early coffee/tea. Air conditioning in room. Cable TV, fax, copier and spa on premises. Family reunions hosted. Antiques, fishing, parks, shopping, downhill skiing, cross-country skiing, sporting events and theater nearby. TAC10.

Publicity: *Daily Sun, Desert Sun, San Francisco Chronicle, Phoenix Gazette.*

"Charming hosts and wonderful food."

Comfi Cottages

1612 N Aztec St
Flagstaff, AZ 86001-1106
(520)774-0731
Fax:(520)779-1008

Rates: $65-195.
Payment: MC VISA DS.
Innkeeper(s): Patricia Wiebe.
Circa: 1920.

Rooms: 5 cottages.
Beds: KQDT.

Each of the five cottages has been refurbished and features a variety of styles. One cottage is decorated in a Southwestern motif, while the others feature antiques and English Country decor. Four cottages include fireplaces and all include kitchens stocked with equipment. They also have the added luxury of a washer and dryer. Bicycles are available for guest use, as well as picnic tables, a barbecue grill and picnic baskets. The Grand Canyon and national parks are close by, and the cottages are in the perfect location to enjoy all Flagstaff has to offer.

Breakfast included in rates. Type of meal: full breakfast. Ceiling fan, cable TV and

VCR in room. Bicycles and tennis on premises. Small meetings and family reunions hosted. French spoken. Antiques, fishing, parks, shopping, downhill skiing, cross-country skiing, sporting events, theater and watersports nearby. TAC10.

Special Discounts: AAA: 10%.

"Beautiful and relaxing. A port in the storm."

Inn at Four Ten

410 N Leroux St
Flagstaff, AZ 86001-4502
(520)774-0088 (800)774-2008
Fax:(520)774-6354

Rates: $100-165.
Payment: MC VISA PC TC.
Innkeeper(s): Howard & Sally Krueger.
Circa: 1894.

Rooms: 9 rooms with PB, 7 with FP. 4 suites.
Beds: KQT.

Built by a wealthy banker, businessman and cattle rancher, this inn was first a stately family residence. Now fully renovated and elegantly decorated with antiques, stained glass and lace, the inn is a great home base for your Northern Arizona getaway. Two rooms include a Jacuzzi tub. It's an easy jaunt to the Grand Canyon, volcanic and meteor craters, ancient Pueblo ruins, Hopi and Navajo villages, the Painted Desert, the red rocks of Sedona and Oak Creek Canyon.

Breakfast and evening snack included in rates. Type of meal: gourmet breakfast.
Air conditioning and ceiling fan in room. Library on premises. Handicap access. Weddings, small meetings and family reunions hosted. Antiques, parks, shopping, downhill skiing, cross-country skiing and theater nearby. TAC10.

Publicity: *Westways, Arizona Daily Sun.*

"It was a joy to discover that the Inn embodied the finest qualities of what make a Bed and Breakfast our first choice when staying out of town."

Greer F9

White Mountain Lodge

PO Box 143
Greer, AZ 85927-0143
(520)735-7568
Fax:(520)735-7498

Rates: $65-95.
Payment: PC TC.
Innkeeper(s): Charles & Mary Bast.
Circa: 1892.

Rooms: 7 rooms with PB. 3 cottages.
Beds: KQDT.

With the White Mountains as its backdrop, this rustic, 19th-century lodge offers panoramic views of the Greer Valley. The Little Colorado River runs along the edge of the property. The guests rooms are comfortable, with country furnishings and Southwestern touches. The Lodge's living room is an ideal place to relax with its stone fireplace. While dining on the homemade breakfasts, guests not only are treated to entrees such as blueberry pancakes or a Swiss omelet casserole, they also enjoy a view from the picture window. In the afternoon, beverages and homemade cookies or cake are served. Small pets are allowed, although certain restrictions apply. The innkeepers also host several murder-mystery events throughout the year. The inn is near excellent hiking trails.

Breakfast and evening snack included in rates. Types of meals: full breakfast and early coffee/tea. Cable TV, VCR, fax, copier and library on premises. Small meetings and family reunions hosted. Spanish spoken. Antiques, fishing, shopping, downhill skiing and cross-country skiing nearby.

Pets Allowed: One small pet per unit. Must not be left unattended in room.

Special Discounts: One day free on a seven day stay, September-May.

Hereford

K8

Ramsey Canyon Inn

31 E Ramsey Canyon Rd
Hereford, AZ 85615-9613
(520)378-3010
Fax:(520)378-0487

Rates: $90-105.
Payment: TC.
Innkeeper(s): Ron & Shirlene DeSantis.
Circa: 1988.

Rooms: 6 rooms with PB.
Beds: KQD.

A stream winds its way through this 12-acre spread tucked up in the Huachuca mountains. The innkeepers offer accommodations in the rustic main house and in two creekside cottages. The cottages include a bedroom, sofa bed in the living room and fully stocked kitchen. Guests in the main house are treated to a full breakfast accompanied by home-baked breads and homemade jellies and jams from fruit in the inn's orchard. More than a dozen varieties of hummingbirds call Ramsey Canyon their home and during a morning walk, guests are sure to find a few hummers and other wildlife.

Breakfast, afternoon tea and evening snack included in rates. Types of meals: gourmet breakfast and early coffee/tea. Ceiling fan in room. 12 acres. Weddings, small meetings, family reunions and seminars hosted. Antiques, parks and shopping nearby.

Pearce

J9

Grapevine Canyon Ranch

PO Box 302
Pearce, AZ 85625-0302
(520)826-3185 (800)245-9202
Fax:(520)826-3636

Rates: $130-255. AP.
Payment: MC VISA AX DS.
Innkeeper(s): Eve & Gerry Searle.

Rooms: 12 rooms.
Beds: KQD.

Guests can ride 64,000 acres of range at this working cattle ranch. Horseback riding is included in the rates, and there are a variety of different ride options, including trips to old Apache lookouts, deserted ghost towns and abandoned mining camps. The owners also offer riding lessons. Experienced equestrians also may take part in the seasonal cattle work if they wish. The ranch's casitas include a bedroom, sitting area, private bath and a private porch or sundeck. Cabins include a private bathroom and porch, as well. Both lodging choices include amenities such as coffee pots and refrigerators. Aside from horseback riding, guests can take part in hiking or birdwatching. The grounds include a heated swimming pool. There are laundry facilities on the premises.

Breakfast, lunch and dinner included in rates. Type of meal: full breakfast. AP. Air conditioning and ceiling fan in room. VCR, fax, copier, swimming and library on premises. Weddings, small meetings, family reunions and seminars hosted. TAC12.

Phoenix

H5

La Estancia B&B Inn

4979 E Camelback Rd
Phoenix, AZ 85018-2900
(602)808-9924 (800)410-7655
Fax:(602)808-9925

Rates: $125-195. EP.
Payment: MC VISA AX DC DS TC.
Innkeeper(s): Ruth & Richard Maloblocki.
Circa: 1929.

Rooms: 5 rooms with PB.
Beds: KQ.

Three of the guest rooms at this historic Monterey Revival home are named for the views guests enjoy from the windows. All of the guest quarters have whirlpool tubs and include romantic iron and poster beds dressed in elegant linens. The home is listed in the National Register and still maintains original light fixtures and scored cement floors. Before heading out to dinner, guests are treated to afternoon wine and cheese. There is a rooftop deck and heated swimming pool on the premises.

Breakfast and afternoon tea included in rates. Types of meals: gourmet breakfast and early coffee/tea. Picnic lunch, lunch and catering service available. EP. Air conditioning, turn-down service and ceiling fan in room. VCR, fax, copier, swimming, bicycles and library on premises. Weddings and small meetings hosted. Antiques, parks, shopping, sporting events and theater nearby. TAC10.

Maricopa Manor

15 W Pasadena Ave
Phoenix, AZ 85013
(602)274-6302 (800)292-6403
Fax:(602)266-3904
E-mail: mmanor@getnet.com

Rates: $79-179.
Payment: MC VISA AX DS PC TC.
Innkeeper(s): Mary Ellen & Paul Kelley.
Circa: 1928.

Rooms: 5 suites, 2 with FP.
Beds: KQ.

AZ

The secluded Maricopa Manor stands amid palm trees on an acre of land. The Spanish-styled house features four graceful columns in the entry hall, an elegant living room with a marble mantel and a music room. The spacious suites are decorated with satins, lace, antiques and leather-bound books. Guests may relax on the deck, on the patio, by the pool or in the gazebo spa.

Breakfast included in rates. Type of meal: continental-plus breakfast. Air conditioning, ceiling fan and cable TV in room. VCR, fax, copier, spa and swimming on premises. Handicap access. Weddings, small meetings, family reunions and seminars hosted. Antiques, parks, shopping, sporting events and theater nearby. TAC10.

Location: North central Phoenix near museums, theaters.

Publicity: *Arizona Business Journal, Country Inns, AAA Westways, San Francisco Chronicle, Focus, Sombrero.*

"I've stayed 200+ nights at B&Bs around the world, yet have never before experienced the warmth and sincere friendliness of Maricopa Manor."

Prescott F5

Juniper Well Ranch

PO Box 11083
Prescott, AZ 86304-1083
(520)442-3415

Rates: $105.
Payment: MC VISA AX DS PC TC.
Innkeeper(s): David Bonham.
Circa: 1991.

Rooms: 3 cottages with PB, 3 with FP.
Beds: QDT.

A working horse ranch sits on the front 15 acres of this 50-acre, wooded property, which is surrounded by the Prescott National Forest. Guests are welcome to feed the horses, and children have been known to take a ride on a tractor with innkeeper David Bonham. Two log cabins and the ranch house sit farther back on the land where families can enjoy nature, "unlimited" hiking and seclusion. A summer house, which can be reserved by guests staying at the ranch, has no walls, a sloping roof with skylight, and an eight-foot hot tub. Guest pets, including horses, are welcome on an individual basis.

Breakfast included in rates. Type of meal: full breakfast. Ceiling fan in room. Spa on premises. Handicap access. 50 acres. Weddings, small meetings, family reunions and seminars hosted. Antiques, fishing, parks, shopping, cross-country skiing and theater nearby. TAC10.

Pets Allowed: Well mannered guest pets, including horses, welcome on an individual basis.

Special Discounts: Multiple night discounts.

Mount Vernon Inn

204 N Mount Vernon Ave
Prescott, AZ 86301-3108
(520)778-0886
Fax:(520)778-7305
E-mail: mtvrnon@primenet.com

Rates: $90-120.
Payment: MC VISA DS TC.
Innkeeper(s): Michele & Jerry Neumann.
Circa: 1900.

Rooms: 4 rooms with PB. 3 cottages.
Beds: QDT.

The inn is nestled among towering shade trees in the center of the Mt. Vernon Historical District, Arizona's largest Victorian neighborhood. The architecture of this grand house with its turret, gables, pediments and Greek Revival porch can best be described as whimsical. Cottages that once served as the carriage and tack houses also are available.

Breakfast included in rates. Types of meals: full breakfast and early coffee/tea. Ceiling fan in room. Cable TV, fax and library on premises. Handicap access. Weddings, small meetings and family reunions hosted. Antiques, parks, shopping and theater nearby. TAC10.

Special Discounts: 10% discount Sunday-Thursday for AAA, AARP, Nov. 1-April 30.

Prescott Pines Inn

901 White Spar Rd
Prescott, AZ 86303-7231
(520)445-7270 (800)541-5374
Fax:(520)778-3665

Rates: $59-199. EP.
Payment: MC VISA PC.
Innkeeper(s): Jean Wu & Michael Acton.
Circa: 1902.

Rooms: 13 rooms with PB, 3 with FP. 3 suites. 4 cottages.
Beds: KQ.

A white picket fence beckons guests to the veranda of this comfortably elegant country Victorian inn, originally the Haymore Dairy. There are masses of fragrant pink roses, lavenders and delphiniums, and stately ponderosa pines tower above the inn's four renovated cottages, which were once shelter for farmhands. The acre of grounds includes a garden fountain and romantic tree swing.

Breakfast included in rates. Types of meals: full breakfast and early coffee/tea. EP. Air conditioning, ceiling fan and cable TV in room. Fax and copier on premises. Small meetings, family reunions and seminars hosted. Antiques, parks, shopping and theater nearby.

Location: One-and-a-third miles south of Courthouse Plaza.

Publicity: *Sunset, Arizona Republic News.*

Special Discounts: AAA discount, Sunday-Thursday, excluding holidays.

"The ONLY place to stay in Prescott! Tremendous attention to detail."

Sedona **E6**

B&B at Saddle Rock Ranch

255 Rock Ridge Dr
Sedona, AZ 86336
(520)282-7640
Fax:(520)282-6829

Rates: $125-145.
Payment: PC TC.
Innkeeper(s): Fran & Dan Bruno.
Circa: 1926.

Rooms: 3 rooms with PB, 3 with FP. 1 cottage.
Beds: KQT.

Romance and elegance highlight your stay at this historic ranch, which was featured in movies depicting the Old West and Sedona. The unique interior features flagstone floors, beamed ceilings, rock and adobe walls, and 14-foot view windows in the guest parlor. Antique-filled rooms include romantic items such as canopied beds, teddy bears, deluxe linens, woodburning fireplaces and soft, fluffy robes. Coffee, tea, ice and a guest refrigerator are available around the clock. Strolling the grounds, one will be taken in by the beautiful views, gardens and wildlife. Guests have use of a pool and relaxing spa. The innkeepers offer a free concierge service, jeep tours and romance packages.

Type of meal: full breakfast. Afternoon tea and catering service available. Air conditioning, ceiling fan and cable TV in room. Fax, copier, computer, spa and swimming on premises. Weddings, small meetings and family reunions hosted. Antiques, fishing, parks, shopping, theater and watersports nearby.

Location: On three acres of hillside, one mile from the center of Sedona in the heart of Red Rock Country.

Publicity: *Arizona Republic, Longevity, Sedona Red Rock News, Esquire, Phoenix Home & Garden, ABC, NBC, CBS.*

Special Discounts: Complimentary Jeep tour with five-night stay.

"Thank you for sharing your ranch with us. It has been the highlight of our trip."

Canyon Villa B&B Inn

125 Canyon Trl #204
Sedona, AZ 86351-7705
(520)284-1226 (800)453-1166
Fax:(520)284-2114

Rates: $125-205.
Payment: MC VISA PC TC.
Innkeeper(s): Chuck and Marion Yadon.
Circa: 1992.

Rooms: 11 rooms with PB, 4 with FP.
Beds: KQT.

Canyon Villa was carefully designed by Chuck and Marion Yadon with maximum guest comfort and privacy in mind. The inn faces the famous red rocks of Sedona, and the tall windows of the living and dining rooms take full advantage of the magnificent view. All ten bedrooms, decorated in eclectic themes, have private patios or balconies with unobstructed views. Many rooms feature fireplaces and whirlpool tubs. Afternoon refreshments are served by the swimming pool, and the full breakfast is graciously served with selections from the inn's cookbook, "Red Rocks and Cinnamon Rolls."

Breakfast and evening snack included in rates. Types of meals: gourmet breakfast and early coffee/tea. Air conditioning, turn-down service, ceiling fan and cable TV in room. VCR, fax, copier, swimming, bicycles and library on premises. Handicap access. Spanish spoken. Antiques, parks and shopping nearby. TAC10.

Publicity: *Scottsdale Scene, Phoenix Home and Garden, Sedona.*

"Your hotel ranks with the very best."

The Graham B&B Inn

150 Canyon Circle Dr
Sedona, AZ 86351-8676
(520)284-1425 (800)228-1425
Fax:(520)284-0767
E-mail: rogerr@sedona.net

Rates: $109-219.
Payment: MC VISA DS PC TC.
Innkeeper(s): Roger & Carol Redenbaugh.
Circa: 1985.

Rooms: 6 rooms with PB, 4 with FP. 3 suites. 1 conference room.
Beds: KQT.

If the stunning Sedona scenery isn't enough to draw you to this popular Arizona getaway spot, this four-star, four-diamond bed & breakfast should do the trick. Guest rooms and suites are decorated in a variety of styles from Southwest to Victorian to Art Deco. Rooms and suites include amenities such as Jacuzzis, private balconies or patios, fireplaces. Bathrooms are stocked with bubble bath and lotions, and there are irons, hair dryers, curling irons and robes. The innkeepers get the day off to a perfect start with a bountiful breakfast. The creative breakfast menus include items such as fanned pears with orange/almond sauce, a Southwestern green chili casserole, night-grain toast with homemade jam, fresh juice and freshly brewed coffee. In the afternoon, refreshments are served.

Breakfast, afternoon tea and evening snack included in rates. Types of meals: full breakfast, gourmet breakfast and early coffee/tea. Air conditioning, turn-down service, ceiling fan, cable TV and VCR in room. Fax, copier, spa, swimming, bicycles and library on premises. Weddings, small meetings, family reunions and seminars hosted. Spanish and South African spoken. Antiques, fishing, parks, shopping and theater nearby.

The Inn on Oak Creek

556 Hwy 179
Sedona, AZ 86336-6145
(520)282-7896 (800)499-7896
Fax:(520)282-0696

Rates: $130-225.
Payment: MC VISA AX DS PC TC.
Innkeeper(s): Rick Morris & Pam Harrison.
Circa: 1973.

Rooms: 11 rooms with PB, 11 with FP. 1 suite.
Beds: KQDT.

With the red rocks of Oak Creek Canyon as its backdrop and the gentle sounds of water meandering down Oak Creek, guests enjoy a serene experience at this contemporary-style inn. Each room offers a fireplace. After a day of exploring Sedona or hiking through scenic canyons, guests can relax in a whirlpool tub. Many rooms also offer private decks with water views. Homemade pastries and granola, gourmet coffee, fresh fruit and creative entrees such as a spinach and cheese frittata, a Southwestern-style artichoke and salsa bake or German apple pancakes make waking up a treat. Guests may enjoy breakfast in bed if they prefer. The inn is within walking distance to galleries, shops and restaurants.

Breakfast and evening snack included in rates. Types of meals: gourmet breakfast and early coffee/tea. Picnic lunch available. Air conditioning, cable TV and VCR in room. Fax, copier, swimming and library on premises. Handicap access. Weddings, small meetings and family reunions hosted. Antiques, fishing, parks, shopping, downhill skiing, theater and watersports nearby. TAC10.

The Lodge at Sedona

125 Kallof Pl
Sedona, AZ 86336-5566
(520)204-1942 (800)619-4467
Fax:(520)204-2128
E-mail: lodge@sedona.net

Rates: $120-225.
Payment: MC VISA PC.
Innkeeper(s): Barb & Mark Dinunzio.
Circa: 1959.

Rooms: 10 rooms with PB, 3 with FP. 3 suites. 1 conference room.
Beds: KQT.

This charming lodge, surrounded by the natural wonders of Sedona's red rock and pine trees, was built by the town's first doctor to house his large family. Red rock walls and rough-hewn beamed ceilings add to the rustic atmosphere of the lodge, which features a glassed-in morning porch, atrium and several fireplaces to enjoy. Expansive, gourmet fare is served each morning and hors d'oeuvres and desserts are provided later in the day for hungry guests. The Grand Canyon is a two-hour day trip, and the area offers many hiking trails and jeep tours of the surrounding canyons.

Breakfast and evening snack included in rates. Types of meals: gourmet breakfast and early coffee/tea. Picnic lunch available. Air conditioning and ceiling fan in room. Cable TV, VCR, fax, copier and library on premises. Handicap access. Small meetings, family reunions and seminars hosted. Antiques, fishing, parks, shopping, downhill skiing, cross-country skiing and theater nearby. TAC10.

Publicity: *Arizona Republic, Sedona, Red Rock News, San Francisco Examiner, Country Register, New York Post, Sedona Magazine*

"A place of such beauty and grace that feels safe and warm."

Southwest Inn at Sedona

3250 W Hwy 89a
Sedona, AZ 86336-4918
(520)828-3344 (800)483-7422
Fax:(520)282-0267
E-mail: info@swinn.com

Rates: $89-195.
Payment: MC VISA AX DS TC.
Innkeeper(s): Joel & Sheila Gilgoff.
Circa: 1994.

Rooms: 28 rooms with PB, 28 with FP. 4 suites. 1 conference room.
Beds: KQ.

The adobe-style exterior of this intimate, Southwestern hotel is an ideal complement to the red rock and mountains that serve as the scenery. Rooms are bright with contemporary, Southwestern decor and kiva fireplaces. There are plenty of amenities here, including refrigerators, hair dryers, coffeemakers and jacks for a modem. The inn has earned four diamonds from AAA.

Breakfast included in rates. Type of meal: continental-plus breakfast. Air conditioning, turn-down service, ceiling fan, cable TV and VCR in room. Fax, copier, spa and swimming on premises. Handicap access. Weddings, small meetings, family reunions and seminars hosted. Antiques, fishing, parks, shopping, downhill skiing, cross-country skiing, sporting events, theater and watersports nearby. TAC10.

Territorial House, An Old West B&B

65 Piki Dr
Sedona, AZ 86336-4345
(520)204-2737 (800)801-2737
Fax:(520)204-2230

Rates: $95-155.
Payment: MC VISA AX.
Innkeeper(s): John & Linda Steele.
Circa: 1970.

Rooms: 4 rooms with PB, 1 with FP. 1 suite.
Beds: KQ.

This red rock and cedar two-story ranch home, nestled in the serene setting of Juniper and Cottonwood, is a nature lover's delight. Guests can see families of quail march through the landscape of cacti, plants and red rock or at night hear the call of coyotes. The territorial decor includes Charles Russell prints collected from taverns throughout the Southwest. More than 40 western movies were filmed in Sedona.

Breakfast and evening snack included in rates. Type of meal: full breakfast. Air conditioning in room. Cable TV, VCR, spa and bicycles on premises. Antiques, fishing, parks, shopping, downhill skiing, theater and watersports nearby.

Tucson *J7*

Adobe Rose Inn

940 N Olsen Ave
Tucson, AZ 85719-4951
(520)318-4644 (800)328-4122
Fax:(520)325-0055

Rates: $45-115.
Payment: MC VISA PC TC.
Innkeeper(s): Diana Graham.
Circa: 1933.

Rooms: 5 rooms with PB, 2 with FP. 2 cottages.
Beds: KQT.

This three-diamond rated inn is located in the historic Sam Hughes neighborhood just a few blocks from the University of Arizona campus. Airy guest rooms are decorated with a romantic, Southwestern flavor. The Arizona Room includes a fireplace and a huge hand-painted tile tub. The Rainbow's End, which overlooks the pool, offers a beehive fireplace. The innkeepers also offer two cottages, one with a refrigerator and toaster oven and another with a galley kitchen.

Breakfast and evening snack included in rates. Types of meals: full breakfast, gourmet breakfast and early coffee/tea. Air conditioning, ceiling fan, cable TV and VCR in room. Spa and swimming on premises. Small meetings, family reunions and seminars hosted. Amusement parks, antiques, parks, shopping, downhill skiing, sporting events, theater and watersports nearby. TAC10.

Casa Alegre B&B

316 E Speedway Blvd
Tucson, AZ 85705-7429
(520)628-1800 (800)628-5654
Fax:(520)792-1880

Rates: $55-95.
Payment: MC VISA DS PC TC.
Innkeeper(s): Phyllis Florek.
Circa: 1915.

Rooms: 5 rooms with PB, 1 with FP. 1 conference room.
Beds: QT.

AZ

Innkeeper Phyllis Florek decorated the interior of this Craftsman-style home with artifacts reflecting the history of Tucson, including Native American pieces and antique mining tools. Wake to the aroma of fresh coffee and join other guests as you enjoy fresh muffins, fruit and other breakfast treats, such as succulent cheese pancakes with raspberry preserves. The Arizona sitting room opens onto serene gardens, a pool and a Jacuzzi. A two-bedroom suite, complete with kitchen privileges, is also available in the neighboring historic Buchanan House. An abundance of shopping and sightseeing are found nearby.

Breakfast included in rates. Types of meals: full breakfast and gourmet breakfast. Ceiling fan in room. VCR, fax, spa and swimming on premises. Weddings, small meetings and family reunions hosted. Antiques, parks, shopping, sporting events and theater nearby. TAC10.

Location: West University Historic District.

Publicity: *Arizona Times, Arizona Daily Star, Tucson Weekly.*

"Enjoyed your excellent care."

Catalina Park Inn

309 E 1st St
Tucson, AZ 85705-7821
(520)792-4541 (800)792-4885
Fax:(520)792-0838

Rates: $90-115.
Payment: MC VISA TC.
Innkeeper(s): Paul Richard & Mark Hall.
Circa: 1927.

Rooms: 4 rooms with PB. 1 suite. 1 cottage.
Beds: Q.

Classical Music sets the mood as guests linger in front of a roaring fireplace at this inn located in Tucson's West University Historic District. The main house offers a spacious room with mountain views and two rooms with private porches that overlook Catalina Park. Colorful rooms are furnished with antiques and other unique pieces. A bounty of patterned linens, down pillows and comforters dress the beds. The inn is just a few blocks from the University of Arizona and the eclectic shops and restaurants that line Fourth Avenue.

Breakfast and afternoon tea included in rates. Types of meals: gourmet breakfast and early coffee/tea. Air conditioning and cable TV in room. Fax on premises. Antiques, parks, sporting events and theater nearby. TAC10.

Publicity: *Dateline Downtown, Arizona Daily Star, Arizona Illustrated, Tucson Weekly.*

"Our stay here in your beautiful home was wonderful and your hospitality was unsurpassed. Can't wait to return!"

The El Presidio B&B Inn

297 N Main Ave
Tucson, AZ 85701-8219
(602)623-6151 (800)349-6151

Rates: $70-115.
Innkeeper(s): Patti Toci.
Circa: 1886.

Rooms: 3 suites, 1 with FP. 1 conference room.
Beds: Q.

The cobblestone courtyards, fountains, and lush gardens surrounding El Presidio are filled with an old-world Southwestern ambiance. The inn is comprised of a Victorian-Territorial adobe built around a traditional zaguan, or large central hall, plus separate suites in the former carriage house and gate house. Innkeepers Jerry and Patti Toci conducted a 10-year, award-winning restoration of this inn. Rooms are immaculate, romantic and richly appointed. Gourmet breakfasts are served in a dining room that overlooks the patio. This inn was voted the "Best B&B in Tucson" for 1995-96. Restaurants and museums are nearby.

Breakfast and afternoon tea included in rates. Bicycles on premises. Antiques and theater nearby.

Location: Near downtown Tucson in El Presidio Historic District.

Publicity: *Gourmet, Travel and Leisure, Glamour, Tucson Home and Garden, Arizona Highways, Innsider.*

"Thank you again for providing such a completely perfect, pampering, relaxing, delicious, gorgeous vacation 'home' for us."

Gable House

2324 N Madelyn Cir
Tucson, AZ 85712-2621
(520)326-1150 (800)756-4846

Rates: $55-95.
Payment: MC VISA AX.
Innkeeper(s): Al & Phyllis Cummings.
Circa: 1930.

Rooms: 3 rooms, 1 with PB, 1 with FP.
Beds: K.

After his wife, actress Carole Lombard died in 1942, actor Clark Gable chose this rustic, Southwestern-style home as a place for solitude. Guests are sure to enjoy the same peace and tranquility Gable found within the walls of this bed & breakfast, which features Santa Fe Pueblo Indian and Mexican influences. The guest rooms, named the Nina, Pinta and Santa Maria, are spacious and airy. The Santa Maria also includes a fireplace. The innkeepers prepare a continental-plus breakfast with a healthy touch.

Breakfast included in rates. Type of meal: continental-plus breakfast. Air conditioning, ceiling fan and VCR in room. Cable TV and spa on premises. Some Spanish spoken. Amusement parks, antiques, parks, shopping, downhill skiing, sporting events, theater and watersports nearby. TAC10.

"You helped us with an immediate need. Gable House was wonderful, perfect, and better than we could have hoped."

La Posada Del Valle

1640 N Campbell Ave
Tucson, AZ 85719-4313
(602)795-3840
Fax:(602)795-3840

Rates: $65-135.
Payment: MC VISA PC TC.
Innkeeper(s): Karin Dennen.
Circa: 1929.

Rooms: 5 rooms with PB. 1 cottage.
Beds: QT.

This Southwestern adobe has 18-inch thick walls, which wraparound to form a courtyard. Ornamental orange trees surround the property, which is across the street from the University Medical Center. All the rooms have outside entrances and open to the patio or overlook the courtyard and fountain. Furnishings include antiques and period pieces from the '20s and '30s. Afternoon tea is served.

Breakfast and afternoon tea included in rates. Type of meal: gourmet breakfast. Air conditioning in room. Cable TV, VCR, fax and library on premises. Weddings, small meetings and family reunions hosted. German spoken. Antiques, parks, shopping, downhill skiing, sporting events and theater nearby. TAC10.

Location: Walking distance to the University of Arizona.

Publicity: *Gourmet, Los Angeles Times, USA Today, Travel & Leisure.*

Special Discounts: Summer rates.

"Thank you so much for such a beautiful home, romantic room and warm hospitality."

Arkansas

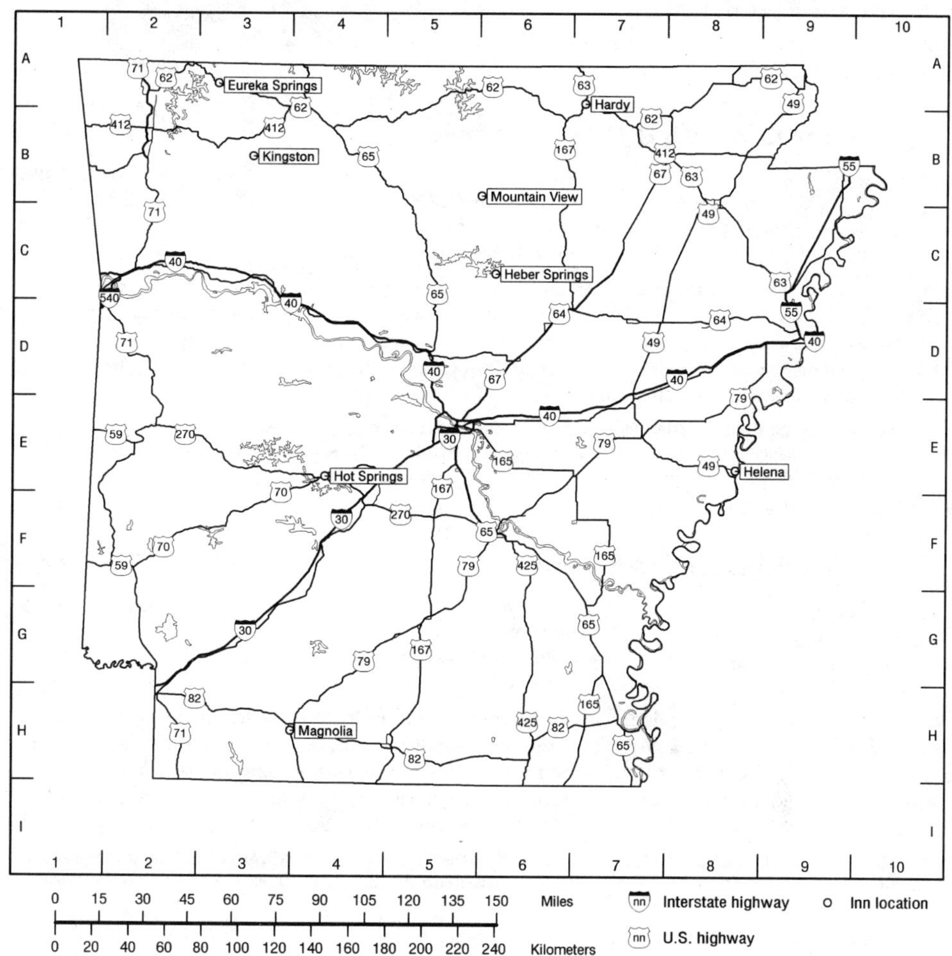

Eureka Springs A3

5 Ojo Inn B&B

5 Ojo St
Eureka Springs, AR 72632
(501)253-6734 (800)656-6734

Rates: $64-139.
Payment: MC VISA PC TC.
Innkeeper(s): Paula Adkins.
Circa: 1891.

Rooms: 10 rooms with PB, 2 with FP. 3 suites. 2 cottages. 1 conference room.
Beds: Beds: KDT.

Guests at 5 Ojo choose between lodging in cottages or in one of two restored Victorian homes, the Ojo House and the Sweet House. Rooms are decorated with antiques, but include modern amenities such as refrigerators and coffee makers. Several rooms include whirlpool tubs and two offer fireplaces. The Carriage House Cottage and the Anniversary Suite are ideal places for honeymooners or those celebrating a special

occasion. Among its romantic amenities, the Anniversary Suite includes a private porch with a swing. Gourmet breakfasts are served in the Sweet House's dining room, but private dining can be arranged.

Breakfast included in rates. Type of meal: full breakfast. Air conditioning, ceiling fan and cable TV in room. VCR, spa and library on premises. Weddings, small meetings and family reunions hosted. Amusement parks, antiques, fishing, parks, shopping, sporting events, theater and watersports nearby. TAC10.

Special Discounts: $60 mid-week; Stay Sunday-Thursday nights and Wednesday is free.

"Thank you for another lovely stay."

The Arbour Glen B&B & Guesthouse

7 Lema St
Eureka Springs, AR 72632
(501)253-9010 (800)515-GLEN

Rates: $65-125.
Payment: MC VISA AX DS PC TC.
Innkeeper(s): Jeffrey Beeler.
Circa: 1879.

Rooms: 5 rooms with PB, 2 with FP. 3 suites. 2 cottages.
Beds: Q.

One might say romance is in the air at Arbour Glen. Guest rooms are decorated in Victorian style with antiques, handmade quilts, luxurious linens and fresh flowers, which create a warm, intimate atmosphere. Some rooms also have double Jacuzzi tubs. There are wraparound verandas to enjoy, and from the porch swing, guests can take in a view of woods and the town's historic district. Gourmet breakfasts are served on the veranda on tables set with china and silver.

Breakfast and afternoon tea included in rates. Types of meals: continental-plus breakfast and gourmet breakfast. Air conditioning, ceiling fan, cable TV and VCR in room. Spa on premises. Weddings and family reunions hosted. Antiques, fishing, parks, shopping, sporting events, theater and watersports nearby. TAC10.

Special Discounts: Three nights or more, 15% off.

Arsenic & Old Lace B&B Inn

60 Hillside Ave
Eureka Springs, AR 72632
(501)253-5454 (800)243-5223
Fax:(501)253-2246

Rates: $76-150.
Payment: MC VISA AX DS PC TC.
Innkeeper(s): Gary & Phyllis Jones.
Circa: 1992.

Rooms: 5 rooms with PB, 2 with FP. 2 suites.
Beds: KQ.

This bed & breakfast is a meticulous reproduction of Queen Anne Victorian style, and offers five guest rooms decorated with antique Victorian furnishings. Popular with honeymooners, the three upper-level guest rooms offer whirlpool tubs, balconies and fireplaces. One ground-floor room also has a whirlpool tub. The inn's gardens complement its attractive exterior, which includes a wraparound veranda and stone wall. Its location in the historic district makes it an excellent starting point for a sightseeing stroll or shopping.

Breakfast and evening snack included in rates. Types of meals: full breakfast and gourmet breakfast. Air conditioning, ceiling fan, cable TV and VCR in room. Fax on premises. Weddings and family reunions hosted. Antiques, fishing, parks, shopping, theater and watersports nearby. TAC10.

Special Discounts: Free day with three-night stay.

Bridgeford House

263 Spring St
Eureka Springs, AR 72632
(501)253-7853
Fax:(501)253-5497

Rates: $85-105.
Payment: MC VISA.
Innkeeper(s): Denise McDonald.
Circa: 1884.

Rooms: 4 rooms, 3 with PB. 1 suite.
Beds: QT.

This peach-colored Victorian delight is nestled in the heart of the Eureka Springs Historic District. Rooms feature antiques and are decorated in a wonderfully charming Victorian style with private entrances. Guests will enjoy the fresh, hot coffee and selection of teas in their suites, and the large gourmet breakfast is the perfect way to start the day. Enjoy the horse-drawn carriage rides down Eureka Springs' famed boulevard with its stately homes.

Breakfast and afternoon tea included in rates. Types of meals: full breakfast, gourmet breakfast and early coffee/tea. Evening snack and room service available. Air conditioning, ceiling fan and cable TV in room. VCR on premises. Weddings, small meetings, family reunions and seminars hosted. Antiques, fishing, shopping, theater and watersports nearby.

Location: North one mile on 62B in Eureka Springs Historic District.

Publicity: *Times Echo Flashlight, Arkansas National Tour Guide, The American Country Inn & Bed and Breakfasts Cookbook, The Bed and Breakfast Cookbook.*

"You have created an enchanting respite for weary people."

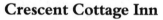

Cliff Cottage & The Place Next Door, A Bed & Breakfast Inn

42 Armstrong St
Eureka Springs, AR 72632
(501)253-7409 (800)799-7409

Rates: $99-140.
Payment: MC VISA PC.
Innkeeper(s): Sandra Smith.
Circa: 1892.

Rooms: 5 rooms with PB. 3 suites.
Beds: KQ.

In the heart of Historic Downtown, this Painted Lady Eastlake Victorian is listed in the National Register of Historic Places. A favorite among honeymooners, accommodations also are available in a Victorian replica named The Place Next Door. Guest rooms include a double Jacuzzi, mini-refrigerator stocked with complimentary champagne and beverages and private decks. The inn offers gourmet candlelight dinners, Victorian picnic lunches and sunset dinner cruises served aboard a 24-foot pontoon boat, which explores the area's romantic coves. Guests enjoy golf and tennis privileges at Holiday Island, which is located five miles away.

Breakfast included in rates. Types of meals: gourmet breakfast and early coffee/tea. Evening snack, picnic lunch and room service available. Air conditioning, ceiling fan, cable TV and VCR in room. Weddings, small meetings, family reunions and seminars hosted. French, Spanish and German spoken. Antiques, fishing, parks, shopping, theater and watersports nearby. TAC10.

Publicity: *Arkansas Democrat Gazette, Country Inns*

Crescent Cottage Inn

211 Spring St
Eureka Springs, AR 72632
(501)253-6022 (800)223-3246
Fax:(501)253-6234

Rates: $90-130.
Payment: MC VISA DS PC TC.
Innkeeper(s): Ralph & Phyllis Becker.
Circa: 1881.

Rooms: 4 rooms with PB, 2 with FP. 1 suite.
Beds: Q.

This Victorian inn was home to the first governor of Arkansas after the Civil War. Two long verandas overlook a breathtaking valley and two mountain ranges. The home is graced by a beautiful tower, spindlework and coffered ceilings. A huge arch joins the dining and living rooms, which, like the rest of the inn, are filled with antiques. Three of the guest rooms feature whirlpool spas, and two have a fireplace. The inn is situated on the quiet, residential end of the historic loop. A five-minute walk into town takes guests past limestone cliffs, tall maple trees, gardens and refreshing springs. Try a ride on the steam engine train that departs nearby.

Breakfast included in rates. Types of meals: full breakfast and early coffee/tea. Air conditioning, ceiling fan, cable TV and VCR in room. Fax and copier on premises. Weddings and family reunions hosted. Spanish, some Portuguese and little German spoken. Amusement parks, antiques, fishing, parks, shopping, sporting events, theater and watersports nearby. TAC10.

Publicity: *Country Homes, Country Inns, Minneapolis Tribune, Fort Lauderdale News, America's Painted Ladies.*

Special Discounts: 15% off third night; 4 or more nights: 10% of all nights Sunday-Thursday, November-April.

"You gave us a piece of heaven. We will never forget, what we dreamed of."

Dairy Hollow House

515 Spring St
Eureka Springs, AR 72632
(501)253-7444 (800)562-8650
Fax:(501)253-7223
E-mail: 74762.1652@compuserve.com

Rates: $135-205.
Payment: MC VISA AX DC CB DS PC TC.
Innkeeper(s): Ned Shank & Crescent Dragonwagon.
Circa: 1888.

Rooms: 6 rooms with PB, 6 with FP. 3 suites. 1 conference room.
Beds: KQD.

Dairy Hollow House, the first of Eureka Springs' bed & breakfast inns, consists of a restored Ozark vernacular farmhouse and a 1940s bungalow-style cottage, both in a national historic district. Stenciled walls set off a collection of Eastlake Victorian furnishings. Outstanding "Nouveau 'zarks" cuisine is available by reservation on six special-occasion dinners a year. Innkeeper Crescent Dragonwagon is the author of more than 40 cookbooks and children's books, including the award-winning Dairy Hollow House Cookbook and the new Soup and Bread Cookbook, and was called upon to cater President Clinton's inaugural brunch in Washington, D.C.

Breakfast and evening snack included in rates. Types of meals: full breakfast and early coffee/tea. Restaurant on premises. Air conditioning in room. Fax, copier and spa on premises. Handicap access in restaurant. Weddings, small meetings, family reunions and seminars hosted. Limited French spoken. Amusement parks, antiques, fishing, parks, shopping, theater and watersports nearby. TAC10.

Location: At the junction of Spring & Dairy Hollow Road.

Publicity: *Innsider, Christian Science Monitor, L.A. Times, Gourmet, Southern Living, Bon Appetit, Country, Country Living, Conde Nast Traveler.*

"The height of unpretentious luxury."

Heart of The Hills Inn

5 Summit
Eureka Springs, AR 72632
(501)253-7468 (800)253-7468

Rates: $64-109.
Payment: MC VISA PC.
Innkeeper(s): Fred Janney.
Circa: 1883.

Rooms: 4 rooms, 3 with PB. 1 suite. 1 cottage.
Beds: KQDT.

Three suites and a Victorian cottage comprise this antique-furnished homestead located just four blocks from downtown. The Victorian Room is furnished with a white iron bed, dresser, antique lamp and antique pedestal sink. Evening dessert is served. The honeymoon suite has a double Jacuzzi. The village trolley stops at the inn.

Breakfast and evening snack included in rates. Types of meals: gourmet breakfast and early coffee/tea. Air conditioning, turn-down service, ceiling fan and cable TV in room. Library on premises. Handicap access. Small meetings and family reunions hosted. Antiques, fishing, shopping, theater and watersports nearby.

Location: On the historic loop.

Publicity: *Carroll County Tribune's Peddler.*

"It was delightful — the bed so comfortable, room gorgeous, food delicious and ohhh those chocolates."

The Heartstone Inn & Cottages

35 King's Hwy
Eureka Springs, AR 72632
(501)253-8916 (800)494-4921
Fax:(501)253-6821

Rates: $65-120.
Payment: MC VISA AX DS PC TC.
Innkeeper(s): Iris & Bill Simantel.
Circa: 1903.

Rooms: 12 rooms with PB, 1 with FP. 3 suites. 2 cottages.
Beds: KQ.

Described as a "pink and white confection," this handsomely restored Victorian with its wraparound verandas is located in the historic district. The award-winning inn is filled with antiques and artwork from the innkeeper's native England. Live music is featured: in May a fine arts festival and in September, a jazz festival.

Afternoon refreshments are available on the sunny deck overlooking a wooded ravine. Pink roses line the picket fence surrounding the inviting garden.

Breakfast included in rates. Type of meal: gourmet breakfast. Air conditioning, ceiling fan and cable TV in room. Fax and spa on premises. Weddings, small meetings, family reunions and seminars hosted. Amusement parks, antiques, fishing, parks, shopping, theater and watersports nearby. TAC10.

Location: Northwest Arkansas, Ozarks.

Publicity: *Insider, Arkansas Times, New York Times, Arkansas Gazette, Southern Living, Country Home, Country Inns.*

Special Discounts: 10% discount on stays of four or more days.

"Extraordinary! Best breakfasts anywhere!"

Sleepy Hollow Inn

92 S Main
Eureka Springs, AR 72632
(501)253-5561

Rates: $110.
Payment: MC VISA DS PC.
Circa: 1904.

Rooms: 3 rooms, 1 with PB. 1 suite.
Beds: D.

This three-story Victorian cottage with gingerbread trim serves as an ideal accommodation for honeymooners or those in search of privacy and romance. There are two bedrooms, the main suite and a guest room with antique furnishings. The cottage is rented to one group or couple at a time, so they are free to relax and enjoy the home. Guests can take a soak in the antique clawfoot tub or snuggle up on the romantic porch swing. There is a well-equipped kitchen, stocked with beverages, pastries and other treats. Chilled champagne and fresh flowers can be provided for those celebrating a special occasion. The one-acre grounds are dotted with gardens. The village's historical museum is across the street, and restaurants, galleries and shops are just a short walk away.

Types of meals: continental breakfast and early coffee/tea. Air conditioning, ceiling fan, cable TV and VCR in room. Antiques, fishing, parks, shopping, theater and watersports nearby.

Special Discounts: Wedding room packages available for honeymooners.

Hardy — A7

Hideaway Inn

RR 1 Box 199
Hardy, AR 72542-9749
(501)966-4770

Rates: $50-125.
Payment: MC VISA AX DS PC TC.
Innkeeper(s): Julia Baldridge.
Circa: 1980.

Rooms: 5 rooms, 3 with PB. 1 cottage.
Beds: Q.

For those seeking solitude, this contemporary home is an ideal place to hide away, surrounded by more than 370 acres of Ozark wilderness. There are walking trails, a private fishing pond, swimming pool and a playground area on the premises for guests to enjoy. There are three guest rooms in the house, and for those needing even more privacy, the innkeeper offers a private log cabin with two bedrooms, two bathrooms and a room that serves as a living, dining and kitchen area. The gourmet breakfasts include such items as homemade granola, freshly baked breakfasts and peach upside-down French toast. For those celebrating a special occasion, the innkeeper can create special packages.

Breakfast and evening snack included in rates. Types of meals: continental breakfast, gourmet breakfast and early coffee/tea. Ceiling fan in room. VCR and swimming on premises. 376 acres. Antiques, fishing, parks, shopping, theater and watersports nearby.

"This is a great place to look at the stars without the interference of the city lights."

The Olde Stonehouse B&B Inn

511 Main St
Hardy, AR 72542-9034
(501)856-2983 (800)514-2983
Fax:(501)856-4036

Rates: $59-95.
Payment: MC VISA AX DS PC TC.
Innkeeper(s): Peggy Johnson.
Circa: 1928.

Rooms: 9 rooms with PB, 2 with FP. 2 suites.
Beds: QDT.

The stone fireplace which graces the comfortable living room of this former banker's home is set with fossils and unusual stones, including an Arkansas diamond. Lace tablecloths, china and silver make breakfast a special occasion. Each room is decorated to keep the authentic feel of the roaring '20s. The bedrooms have antiques and ceiling fans. Aunt Jenny's room boasts a claw-foot tub and a white iron bed, while Uncle Buster's room is filled with Depression-era furniture. Spring River is only one block away and offers canoeing, boating and fishing. Old Hardy Town caters to antique and craft lovers. The innkeepers offer "Secret Suites," located in a nearby historic home. These romantic suites offer plenty of amenities, breakfasts in a basket are delivered to the door each morning. The home is listed in the National Register.

Breakfast and evening snack included in rates. Types of meals: full breakfast, gourmet breakfast and early coffee/tea. Picnic lunch available. Air conditioning, ceiling fan and VCR in room. Fax, copier, bicycles and library on premises. Antiques, fishing, parks, shopping, theater and watersports nearby. TAC10.

Location: In a historic railroad town.

Publicity: *Memphis Commercial Appeal, Jonesboro Sun, Vacations*

"For many years we had heard about 'Southern Hospitality' but never thought it to be this good .. this was the best!"

Heber Springs C6

The Anderson House Inn

201 E Main St
Heber Springs, AR 72543
(501)362-5266 (800)264-5279
Fax:(501)362-2326
E-mail: jhildebr@cswnet.com

Rates: $75-105.
Payment: MC VISA AX DS PC TC.
Innkeeper(s): Jim & Susan Hildebrand.
Circa: 1880.

Rooms: 16 rooms with PB, 1 with FP. 2 conference rooms.
Beds: QDT.

The original section of this welcoming two-story inn was built by one of Heber Springs' founding citizens. The main structure of the inn was built to house a theater, and the home also has enjoyed use as a schoolhouse, doctor's clinic and, when the second story was added, a hotel. Rooms are decorated in a cozy, country motif with bright colors and floral prints. Many of the antiques that fill each room are available for purchase. Historic Spring Park is just across the street offering pleasant scenery for the inn's guests as well as a variety of activities.

Breakfast included in rates. Types of meals: full breakfast and early coffee/tea. Banquet service available. Air conditioning and ceiling fan in room. Cable TV, VCR, fax, spa and library on premises. Small meetings, family reunions and seminars hosted. French spoken. Antiques, fishing, parks, shopping and watersports nearby. TAC10.

Special Discounts: Special packages including lodging, meals and special events available.

Oak Tree Inn & Little Red River Cottages

1802 W Main St
Heber Springs, AR 72543
(501)362-7731 (800)959-3857

Rates: $75-165.
Payment: MC VISA DS.
Innkeeper(s): Freddie Lou & Jerry Quist.
Circa: 1983.

Rooms: 4 rooms with PB. 3 cottages.
Beds: Q.

Fishing and boating enthusiasts will appreciate the proximity to Greers Ferry Lake and the Little Red River. The inn, a modern Colonial Revival home, offers four guest rooms. River cottages also are available. Each of the inn's rooms is named for a prominent citizen who contributed to the growth of Cleburne County.

Rooms feature whirlpool baths, ceiling fans, fireplaces, and wooden floors. Heber Springs is an easy getaway from Little Rock.

Breakfast included in rates. Type of meal: gourmet breakfast. Air conditioning and ceiling fan in room. Swimming and tennis on premises. Antiques, fishing and shopping nearby.

Location: In the Ozark Mountains, near 45,000 acre Greers Ferry Lake.

Publicity: *USA Today, Brides Magazine, Vacation Magazine.*

Helena E8

Edwardian Inn

317 S Biscoe
Helena, AR 72342
(501)338-9155 (800)598-4749
Fax:(501)572-9105

Rates: $59-85.
Payment: MC VISA AX DC CB DS PC TC.
Innkeeper(s): Marjorie Hornbeck & Julie Brown.
Circa: 1904.

Rooms: 12 rooms with PB. 5 suites. 1 conference room.
Beds: KD.

In his book Life on the Mississippi, Mark Twain wrote, "Helena occupies one of the prettiest situations on the river." William Short, cotton broker and speculator, agreed and built his stately home here. The Edwardian Inn boasts a large rotunda and two verandas wrapping around both sides of the house. Inside are wood carpets and floor designs imported from Germany that are composed of 36 pieces of different woods arranged in octagon shapes. Polished-oak paneling and woodwork are set off with a Victorian-era decor.

Breakfast included in rates. Types of meals: full breakfast and early coffee/tea. Evening snack and catering service available. Air conditioning, ceiling fan and cable TV in room. VCR, fax, copier and library on premises. Weddings, small meetings, family reunions and seminars hosted. Antiques, fishing, parks, shopping and watersports nearby. TAC10.

Publicity: *Arkansas Times Magazine, The Dallas Morning News*

"The Edwardian Inn envelopes you with wonderful feelings, smells and thoughts of the Victorian era."

Hot Springs E4

Vintage Comfort B&B Inn

303 Quapaw Ave
Hot Springs, AR 71901
(501)623-3258 (800)608-4682

Rates: $65-90.
Payment: MC VISA AX PC TC.
Innkeeper(s): Helen Bartlett.
Circa: 1907.

Rooms: 4 rooms with PB.
Beds: QDT.

This two-story Victorian provides large, comfortable rooms with a charming atmosphere. Honeymooners and romantics will appreciate a getaway package that includes champagne, roses, breakfast, and dinner and dancing on the Belle of Hot Springs. A trip to the Hot Springs Mountain Tower is also included. The Family Reunion Package includes the use of all four bedrooms and a catered dinner. Innkeeper Helen Bartlett conducts innkeeping seminars for guests who want to learn the trade.

Breakfast and evening snack included in rates. Type of meal: full breakfast. Catering service available. Cable TV, VCR and fax on premises. Weddings, small meetings, family reunions and seminars hosted. Antiques, fishing, parks, shopping, theater and watersports nearby. TAC12.

Location: Located within Hot Springs National Park.

"Our only disappointment, we couldn't stay longer."

Kingston

B3

Fool's Cove Ranch B&B

HCR 30 Box 198
Kingston, AR 72742-9608
(501)665-2986
Fax:(501)665-2372
E-mail: klobster@nwark.com

Rates: $55-75.
Payment: MC VISA AX DC CB DS PC TC.
Innkeeper(s): Mary Jo & Bill Sullivan.
Circa: 1979.

Rooms: 4 rooms, 1 with PB.
Beds: QD.

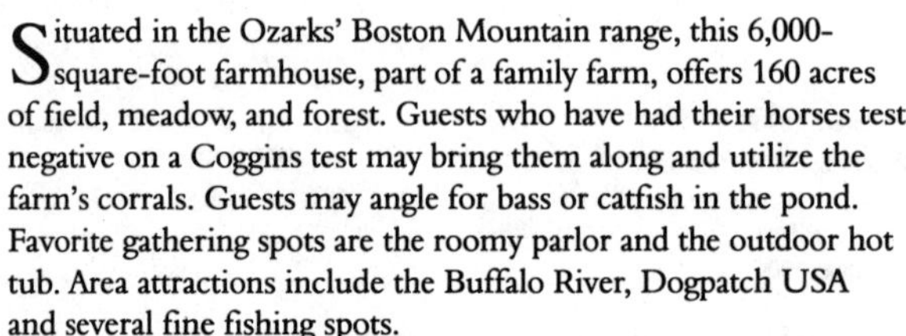

Situated in the Ozarks' Boston Mountain range, this 6,000-square-foot farmhouse, part of a family farm, offers 160 acres of field, meadow, and forest. Guests who have had their horses test negative on a Coggins test may bring them along and utilize the farm's corrals. Guests may angle for bass or catfish in the pond. Favorite gathering spots are the roomy parlor and the outdoor hot tub. Area attractions include the Buffalo River, Dogpatch USA and several fine fishing spots.

Breakfast included in rates. Types of meals: full breakfast and early coffee/tea. Evening snack available. Air conditioning, turn-down service and ceiling fan in room. Cable TV, VCR, fax, copier, spa, library and pet boarding on premises. Handicap access. 130 acres. Small meetings and family reunions hosted. Amusement parks, antiques, fishing, parks, shopping, sporting events, theater and watersports nearby.

Pets Allowed: Must make prior arrangements.

Magnolia

H4

Magnolia Place B&B

510 E Main St
Magnolia, AR 71753
(501)234-6122 (800)237-6122
Fax:(501)234-1254

Rates: $89-99.
Payment: MC VISA AX DC DS.
Innkeeper(s): Carolyne Hawley & Ray Sullivent.
Circa: 1910.

Rooms: 5 rooms with PB. 1 suite. 1 conference room.
Beds: Q.

A prominent Magnolia attorney and his wife were the first to reside in this gracious home, and it remained in the family for three generations. The Four-Square-style home is surely as elegant now as it was in its early days. Polished wood floors, original light fixtures, posh draperies and elegant decor enhance the period furnishings, some of which are family heirlooms. Breakfasts are a formal affair served on a beautiful 1820s table once used by President Harding. Entrees such as eggs Benedict get guests off to a good start, and after breakfast, there's plenty to see and do in Magnolia. Guests can tour historic homes or a historic courthouse, and Lake Columbia, Logoly State Park, a unique artificial marsh designed by NASA, museums, restaurants and shops are nearby.

Breakfast and evening snack included in rates. Types of meals: full breakfast and early coffee/tea. Air conditioning, ceiling fan and cable TV in room. Library on premises. Small meetings hosted. Antiques, fishing, parks, shopping, sporting events and watersports nearby. TAC10.

Mountain View

B6

Ozark Country Inn

PO Box 1201
Mountain View, AR 72560
(501)269-8699 (800)379-8699

Rates: $55-65.
Payment: MC VISA.
Innkeeper(s): G.W. & Glenna Northern.
Circa: 1906.

Rooms: 6 rooms with PB.
Beds: QDT.

This historic two-story Federal-style inn is located within a block of Courthouse Square and downtown eateries and shops. A full breakfast is served at 8 a.m. before guests head out to explore the many attractions offered in the surrounding area, including Blanchard Springs Caverns and the Ozark Folk Center.

Breakfast included in rates. Type of meal: full breakfast. Air conditioning and cable TV in room. VCR on premises. Weddings and family reunions hosted. Antiques, fishing, shopping and watersports nearby.

Wildflower B&B

100 Washington St,
PO Box 72
Mountain View, AR 72560
(501)269-4383 (800)591-4879

Rates: $42-71.
Payment: MC VISA AX DS.
Innkeeper(s): Andrea Budy.
Circa: 1918.

Rooms: 8 rooms, 6 with PB. 3 suites.
Beds: DT.

AR

The inn's wraparound porches are a gathering place for local musicians who often play old-time music. If you sit long enough, you're likely to see an impromptu hootenanny in the Courthouse Square across the street. Since there are no priceless antiques, children are welcome.

Breakfast included in rates. Types of meals: continental-plus breakfast and early coffee/tea. Air conditioning, turn-down service and ceiling fan in room. Small meetings, family reunions and seminars hosted. Antiques, fishing, parks, shopping, sporting events, theater and watersports nearby.

Location: In the Ozarks.

Publicity: *New York Times, Dan Rather & CBS, Midwest Living, National Geographic Traveler, Travel Holiday.*

"It's the kind of place you'll look forward to returning to."

Bean and Barley Soup Bourguignon

Dairy Hollow House
Eureka Springs, Ark.

Cooking spray
½ cup dried baby lima beans
½ cup dried regular lima beans
1 cup dried red beans
2 qts. vegetable or chicken stock
1 bay leaf
1 t dried basil
1 t dried sage
1 t dried oregano
¼ cup pearl barley
2 cloves garlic, peeled and finely chopped
salt & pepper to taste
1 large onion, chopped
2 medium carrots, peeled and diced
2 ribs celery, diced
½ lb. Green beans, trimmed and sliced ½-inch thick
1 can (15 ounces) whole tomatoes with juice
1 ½ cups hearty red wine
¼ cup tomato paste
2 T peanut butter, creamy or chunky
1 T honey
1 T Pickapeppa or Worcestershire sauce
2 to 4 T red wine vinegar

Spray a large heavy pot with cooking spray, and in it soak the limas and red beans in enough stock to cover overnight. (If using chicken stock, refrigerate.)

The next day add enough of the remaining stock to cover the beans by two inches, then drop in the bay leaf and herbs. Bring to a boil, then turn down the heat to very low and let simmer, covered, until the beans are nearly done, about one hour. Add more stock if necessary to keep the beans covered.

Stir in the barley and garlic, and continue to simmer until the beans are very tender and the barley is almost done, about 30 minutes. Season with salt and pepper.

Add the onion, carrots, celery and green beans. Simmer, covered, until the vegetables are nearly done, about 15 minutes.

Place the tomatoes, with their juice, in a food processor and coarsely puree. Add the red wine, tomato paste, peanut butter, honey and Pickapeppa or Worcestershire. Buzz until blended.

Stir this mixture into the soup and simmer over very low heat, about 15 minutes longer. Stir in vinegar to taste and serve hot.

Serves six to eight as an entree.

California

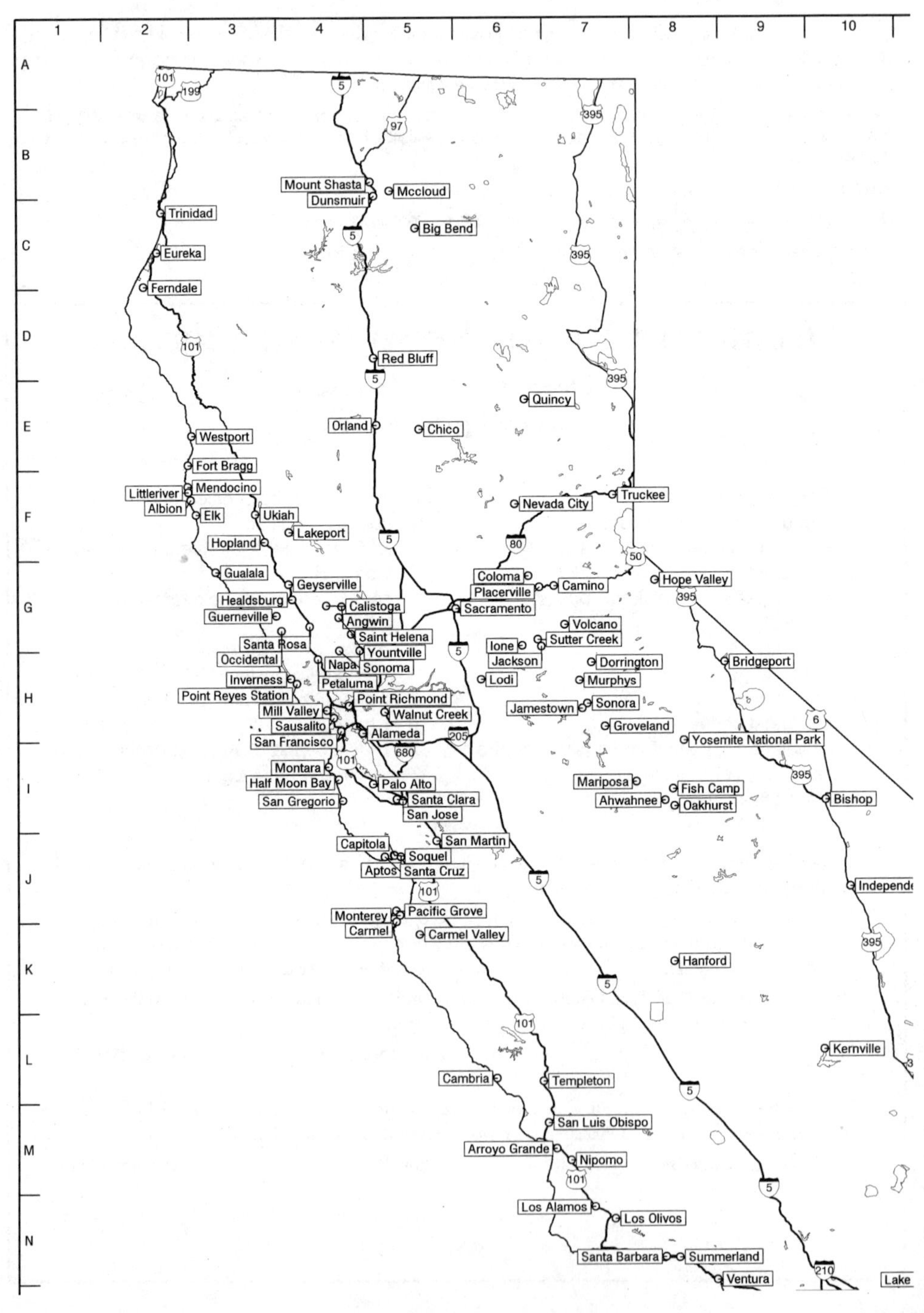

1
2
3
4
5
6
7
8
9
10
A
B
C
D
E
F
G
H
I
J
K
L
M
N
Mount Shasta
Dunsmuir
Mccloud
Trinidad
Big Bend
Eureka
Ferndale
Red Bluff
Quincy
Westport
Orland
Chico
Fort Bragg
Littleriver
Mendocino
Albion
Elk
Ukiah
Nevada City
Truckee
Lakeport
Hopland
Gualala
Geyserville
Coloma
Camino
Placerville
Hope Valley
Healdsburg
Calistoga
Sacramento
Guerneville
Angwin
Volcano
Saint Helena
Sutter Creek
Santa Rosa
Yountville
Ione
Occidental
Napa
Sonoma
Jackson
Dorrington
Bridgeport
Inverness
Lodi
Murphys
Petaluma
Point Reyes Station
Point Richmond
Mill Valley
Walnut Creek
Jamestown
Sonora
Sausalito
Groveland
Alameda
San Francisco
Yosemite National Park
Montara
Half Moon Bay
Palo Alto
Mariposa
Fish Camp
Santa Clara
Ahwahnee
Oakhurst
Bishop
San Gregorio
San Jose
Capitola
San Martin
Soquel
Aptos
Santa Cruz
Monterey
Pacific Grove
Carmel
Carmel Valley
Hanford
Kernville
Cambria
Templeton
San Luis Obispo
Arroyo Grande
Nipomo
Los Alamos
Los Olivos
Santa Barbara
Summerland
Ventura
Lake

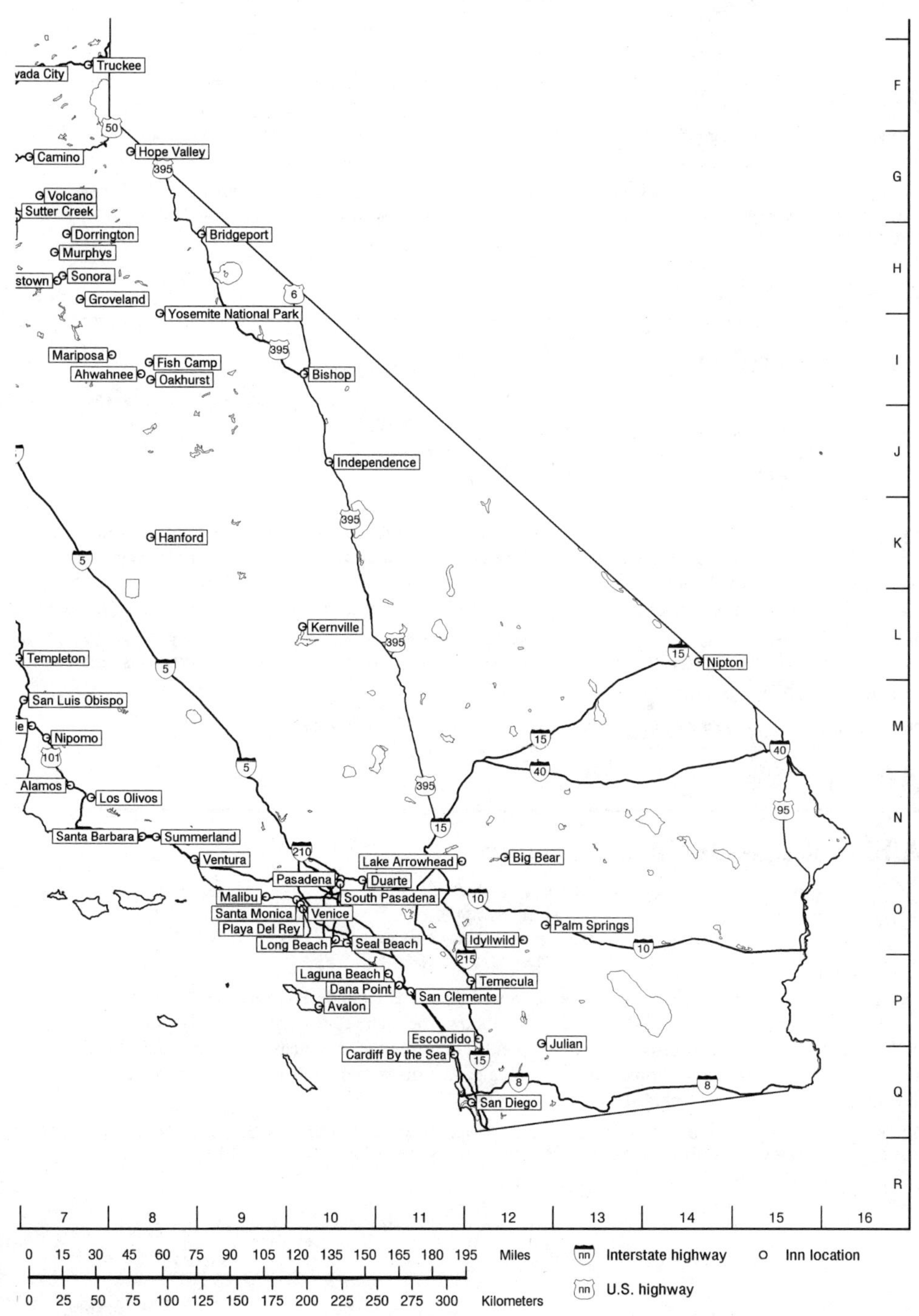
Truckee
vada City
Hope Valley
Camino
Volcano
Sutter Creek
Dorrington
Bridgeport
Murphys
stown
Sonora
Groveland
Yosemite National Park
Mariposa
Fish Camp
Ahwahnee
Oakhurst
Bishop
Independence
Hanford
Kernville
Templeton
Nipton
San Luis Obispo
Nipomo
Alamos
Los Olivos
Santa Barbara
Summerland
Ventura
Lake Arrowhead
Big Bear
Pasadena
Duarte
Malibu
South Pasadena
Santa Monica
Venice
Playa Del Rey
Palm Springs
Idyllwild
Long Beach
Seal Beach
Laguna Beach
Temecula
Dana Point
San Clemente
Avalon
Escondido
Julian
Cardiff By the Sea
San Diego
F
G
H
I
J
K
L
M
N
O
P
Q
R
7
8
9
10
11
12
13
14
15
16
0 15 30 45 60 75 90 105 120 135 150 165 180 195 Miles
0 25 50 75 100 125 150 175 200 225 250 275 300 Kilometers
Interstate highway
Inn location
U.S. highway

Ahwahnee I8

Apple Blossom Inn B&B

44606 Silver Spur Tr
Ahwahnee, CA 93601
(209)642-2001
E-mail: lhays@sierranet.net.

Rates: $55-130.
Payment: MC VISA AX DS TC.
Innkeeper(s): Lance, Lynn & Jenny Hays.
Circa: 1991.

Rooms: 3 rooms, 2 with PB.
Beds: QD.

A bountiful organic apple orchard surrounds this inn, an attractive country cottage a short distance from Yosemite National Park. Visitors choose either the Red Delicious Room, with its two double beds and private entrance, or the Granny Smith Room, with queen bed and private balcony. Both rooms feature ceiling fans, private bath and sitting areas. Guests enjoy the inn's woodburning stove and the spa overlooking the woods.

Breakfast, afternoon tea and evening snack included in rates. Types of meals: full breakfast and early coffee/tea. Air conditioning, turndown service, ceiling fan and VCR in room. Spa on premises. Antiques, fishing, parks, shopping, downhill skiing, cross-country skiing, theater and watersports nearby. TAC10.

Alameda H4

Garratt Mansion

900 Union St
Alameda, CA 94501-4143
(510)521-4779
Fax:(510)521-6796

Rates: $75-125.
Payment: MC VISA AX DC PC TC.
Innkeeper(s): Royce & Betty Gladden.
Circa: 1893.

Rooms: 7 rooms, 5 with PB, 1 with FP. 1 suite. 1 conference room.
Beds: QDT.

This handsome, 27-room Colonial Revival mansion was built for industrialist W.T. Garratt. It features walnut and oak paneling, crystal windows and ornate-manteled fireplaces. The staircase rises three stories with hundreds of gleaming Jacobean turned balusters. A set of stained-glass windows encircles a bay at the stairwell landing. The elegance of the mansion is matched by the warmth of its proprietress, Betty Gladden.

Breakfast and evening snack included in rates. Types of meals: full breakfast and early coffee/tea. Ceiling fan in room. Cable TV, VCR, fax and library on premises. Weddings and small meetings hosted. Antiques, parks, sporting events, theater and watersports nearby. TAC10.

Publicity: *Alameda Times Star, Denver Post.*

"I can't wait to return as I found an exception to the saying, 'there's no place like home'."

Albion F3

Albion Ridge Huckleberry House

29381 Albion Ridge Rd
Albion, CA 95410-9701
(707)937-2374 (800)482-5532
Fax:(707)937-1644

Rates: $100-150.
Payment: MC VISA PC.
Innkeeper(s): Jon & Sally Geller.
Circa: 1995.

Rooms: 4 rooms, 3 with FP. 2 suites. 1 cottage.
Beds: Q.

Acres of Redwood and huckleberry bushes surround this romantic hideaway tucked just off the Mendocino coast. The grounds offer a pond stocked with rainbow trout. The suites include fireplaces and private decks, and the tower room affords a view of the pond. Three guest rooms include the amenities of coffee, tea and a refrigerator stocked with drinks. In the evening gaze at the stars or grab a movie from the house library. The innkeepers also offer a secluded cottage.

Breakfast included in rates. Types of meals: full breakfast, gourmet breakfast and early coffee/tea. VCR in room. Fax on premises. Small meetings, family reunions and seminars hosted. Antiques, fishing, parks, shopping, theater and watersports nearby.

Albion River Inn

3790 Hwy 1N, PO Box 100
Albion, CA 95410-0100
(707)937-1919 (800)479-7944
Fax:(707)937-2604

Rates: $160-250. EP.
Payment: MC VISA AX.
Innkeeper(s): Linda Lee.
Circa: 1919.

Rooms: 20 rooms with PB, 20 with FP.
Beds: KQ.

CA

The Albion River Inn is located on ten acres along a spectacular bluffside. All guest rooms are distinguished by a dramatic view of the ocean and Albion Cove. The dining room is among the finest on the Northern California coast.

Breakfast included in rates. Types of meals: full breakfast, gourmet breakfast and early coffee/tea. Dinner available. EP. Handicap access. 10 acres. Weddings and seminars hosted. Antiques, fishing, parks, shopping and theater nearby.

Publicity: *California, San Francisco Chronicle.*

"Warm hospitality and wonderful cuisine."

Fensalden Inn

PO Box 99
Albion, CA 95410-0099
(707)937-4042 (800)959-3850

Rates: $80-145.
Payment: MC VISA.
Innkeeper(s): Scott & Frances Brazil.
Circa: 1860.

Rooms: 8 rooms with PB, 6 with FP. 3 suites. 2 conference rooms.
Beds: KQ.

Originally a stagecoach station, Fensalden looks out over the Pacific Ocean as it has for more than 100 years. The Tavern Room has witnessed many a rowdy scene and if you look closely you can see bullet holes in the original redwood ceiling. The inn provides 20 acres for walks, whale-watching, viewing deer and bicycling. Relax with wine and hors d'oeuvres in the evening.

Breakfast and afternoon tea included in rates. Types of meals: full breakfast and early coffee/tea. Ceiling fan in room. Handicap access. 20 acres. Weddings, small meetings, family reunions and seminars hosted. Antiques, fishing, parks, shopping, theater and watersports nearby. TAC10.

Location: Seven miles south of Mendocino on Hwy 1.

Publicity: *Sunset, Focus, Peninsula, Country Inns.*

"Closest feeling to heaven on Earth."

Angwin G4

Forest Manor

415 Cold Springs Rd
Angwin, CA 94508-9657
(707)965-3538 (800)788-0364
Fax:(707)965-3303

Rates: $149-239.
Payment: MC VISA PC.
Innkeeper(s): Dr. Harold & Corlene Lambeth.
Circa: 1981.

Rooms: 4 suites, 3 with FP.
Beds: K.

Aside from the wineries, shops, restaurants and scenic beauty of Napa Valley, Forest Manor offers yet another reason to visit this land of vineyards. The English Tudor home is situated on a wooded 20-acre estate about a half-hour drive from Napa. The interior is decorated with a mix of traditional furnishings and pieces collected from around the world. Beds are topped with down comforters, and rooms include amenities such as refrigerators, coffeemakers, hot drinks, fruit baskets and fluffy robes. Some have a Jacuzzi tub, and three include a fireplace. Guests can take their full breakfasts either in the privacy of their quarters, on the veranda or in the dining room. In the afternoons, freshly baked cookies and tea are served. Aside from the hundreds of wineries in the area, guests can take a hot air balloon ride or glider flight, shop for antiques, visit a candle factory, fish, play golf and more.

Breakfast and afternoon tea included in rates. Types of meals: full breakfast and gourmet breakfast. Room service available. Air conditioning, ceiling fan and VCR in room. Fax, copier, spa, swimming and library on premises. 20 acres. Antiques, parks, shopping and watersports nearby. TAC10.

Aptos

J5

Apple Lane Inn

6265 Soquel Dr
Aptos, CA 95003-3117
(408)475-6868 (800)649-8988
Fax:(408)464-5790

Rates: $95-150.
Innkeeper(s): Doug & Diana Groom.
Circa: 1870.

Rooms: 5 rooms with PB. 3 suites.
Beds: QDT.

Ancient apple trees border the lane that leads to this Victorian farmhouse set on two acres of gardens and fields. Built by the Porter brothers, founding fathers of Aptos, the inn is decorated with Victorian wallpapers and hardwood floors. The original wine cellar still exists, as well as the old barn and apple-drying shed used for storage after harvesting the orchard. Miles of beaches are within walking distance. The innkeepers were married at the inn and later purchased it.

Breakfast and evening snack included in rates. Types of meals: continental breakfast, continental-plus breakfast, full breakfast, gourmet breakfast and early coffee/tea. Afternoon tea available. Turn-down service, ceiling fan and cable TV in room. Fax, copier, library and pet boarding on premises. Handicap access. Weddings, small meetings, family reunions and seminars hosted. Antiques, parks, shopping, sporting events, theater and watersports nearby. TAC10.

Pets Allowed: Horses in stables, 1 guest room for dogs.

Location: One mile from the beach, five minutes south of Santa Cruz.

Publicity: *Santa Barbara Times, 1001 Decorating Ideas, New York Times.*

"Our room was spotless and beautifully decorated."

Bayview Hotel

8041 Soquel Dr
Aptos, CA 95003-3928
(408)688-8654 (800)422-9843
Fax:(408)688-5128
E-mail: pobrien@bluespruce.com

Rates: $90-150.
Payment: MC VISA AX TC.
Innkeeper(s): Gwen Burkhard.
Circa: 1878.

Rooms: 11 rooms with PB, 2 with FP. 1 suite. 1 conference room.
Beds: KQD.

This Victorian hotel is the oldest operating inn on the Monterey Coast. Each of the rooms is decorated with local art, antiques, fireplaces and sitting areas. The inn is just a half a mile from beautiful beaches and a redwood forest is nearby. This inn is an ideal spot for those seeking relaxation or those on a coastal trip. Monterey and San Jose are less than an hour from the hotel, and San Francisco is 90 miles north. Hearty breakfasts are served in the inn's dining room, and the inn also has an on-site restaurant.

Breakfast included in rates. Types of meals: gourmet breakfast and early coffee/tea. Afternoon tea available. Turn-down service, cable TV and VCR in room. Fax and copier on premises. Weddings, small meetings, family reunions and seminars hosted. Amusement parks, antiques, parks, shopping and watersports nearby.

Location: Santa Cruz County.

Publicity: *Mid-County Post, Santa Cruz Sentinel.*

"Thank you so much for all of your tender loving care and great hospitality."

Arroyo Grande

M7

Arroyo Village Inn

407 El Camino Real
Arroyo Grande, CA 93420
(805)489-5926

Rates: $80-195. AP.
Payment: MC VISA AX DS.
Innkeeper(s): Chuck & Louise Holden.
Circa: 1984.

Rooms: 7 rooms, 2 with PB. 5 suites.
Beds: KQ.

The travel section of the Los Angeles Times has featured many rare reviews of this country Victorian. Rooms feature extras such as balconies and window seats. Laura Ashley prints complement the antiques.

Day trips from the inn include Hearst Castle, wineries and mineral springs. Guests can test the water of local beaches on foot or ride up the coast on horseback. Breakfast features specialities such as homemade granola and breads, fresh fruit, omelets and French toast with caramel sauce and apple slices. A late afternoon tea provides wine and cheese or cookies and tea.

Breakfast and evening snack included in rates. Type of meal: early coffee/tea. AP. Air conditioning in room. Cable TV and fax on premises. TAC10.

Publicity: *Los Angeles Times.*

"Absolutely all the essentials of a great inn."

CA

Avalon

P10

Catalina Island Seacrest Inn

PO Box 128,
201 Claressa Ave
Avalon, CA 90704-0128
(310)510-0800
Fax:(310)510-1122

Rates: $65-185.
Payment: MC VISA DC CB DS TC.
Innkeeper(s): Michele Prevatt & Kathy Connelly.
Circa: 1910.

Rooms: 8 rooms with PB, 4 with FP. 6 suites.
Beds: KQ.

The unique and romantic setting of Catalina Island is home to this inn, just a block from the ocean. The inn enjoys tremendous popularity with honeymooners, who love the in-room whirlpools and tubs for two offered in many of the guest rooms. The inn often hosts weddings and offers special packages, including round-trip transportation to the island and many other extras. Many guests enjoy exploring Avalon's shops and sights.

Breakfast included in rates. Type of meal: continental breakfast. Air conditioning, ceiling fan, cable TV and VCR in room. Fax on premises. Weddings and family reunions hosted. Fishing, parks, shopping and watersports nearby. TAC10.

Special Discounts: 10% off Monday-Thursday, holidays excluded.

The Inn on Mt. Ada

PO Box 2560
Avalon, CA 90704-2560
(310)510-2030

Rates: $170-490.
Payment: MC VISA AX.
Innkeeper(s): Susie Griffin & Marlene McAdam.
Circa: 1921.

Rooms: 6 rooms with PB, 4 with FP. 1 conference room.
Beds: QD.

This Georgian mansion was built by the famous Wrigley family. Wrigley brought the Chicago Cubs to Avalon for spring training and watched them from his house. Once the summer White House for Presidents Coolidge and Harding, the inn's breathtaking ocean and bay views are framed by a multitude of wide windows and terraces. Weekends are booked six months ahead.

Types of meals: full breakfast and gourmet breakfast.

Location: Catalina Island.

Publicity: *Los Angeles Times, Chicago Tribune, Los Angeles Magazine.*

"Mere words cannot describe this place! The breath-taking views, beautifully appointed rooms and marvelous cuisine surpass any I have enjoyed anywhere!"

Big Bear

N12

Gold Mountain Manor Historic B&B

1117 Anita, PO Box 2027
Big Bear, CA 92314
(909)585-6997
Fax:(909)585-0327
E-mail: goldmtn@bigbear.com

Rates: $75-190.
Payment: MC VISA DS.
Innkeeper(s): Robert Angilella, Gloria Oren & Jose Tapia.
Circa: 1928.

Rooms: 7 rooms, 4 with PB, 6 with FP. 2 suites. 3 cottages. 1 conference room.
Beds: Q.

This spectacular log mansion was once a hideaway for the rich and famous. Eight fireplaces provide a roaring fire in each room in fall and winter. The Lucky Baldwin Room offers a hearth made from stones of gold gathered in the famous Lucky Baldwin mine nearby. In the Clark Gable room is the fireplace Gable and Carole Lombard enjoyed on their honeymoon. Gourmet country breakfasts and afternoon hors d'oeuvres are served. In addition to the guest rooms, there are three cabins.

Afternoon tea and evening snack included in rates. Types of meals: full breakfast, gourmet breakfast and early coffee/tea. Ceiling fan in room. Cable TV, VCR, fax, spa, bicycles and library on premises. Weddings, small meetings, family reunions and seminars hosted. Spanish spoken. Fishing, parks, downhill skiing, cross-country skiing, sporting events and watersports nearby. TAC10.

Location: Two hours northeast of Los Angeles and Orange counties.

Publicity: *Best Places to Kiss, Fifty Most Romantic Places, Kenny G holiday album cover.*

Special Discounts: Sunday - Thursday, 25% off second day.

"A majestic experience! In this magnificent house, history comes alive!"

Bishop

I10

The Matlick House

1313 Rowan Ln
Bishop, CA 93514-1937
(619)873-3133 (800)898-3133

Rates: $79-89.
Payment: MC VISA AX DS TC.
Innkeeper(s): Ray & Barbara Showalter.
Circa: 1906.

Rooms: 5 rooms with PB.
Beds: QT.

This lovely gray and pink home with a double veranda was built by Alan Matlick, one of the area's pioneers. The spacious parlor features a clawfoot settee with massive curved arms, antique recliner, European burled-wood armoire and original cherry-wood fireplace. Rooms boast special pieces such as the white iron bed, Eastlake chair and quilted settee in the Lenna room. Guests will enjoy the home's views of both the Sierra Nevadas and the White Mountains. A hearty American breakfast with eggs, bacon and homemade biscuits is served in the dining room. The Eastern Sierras provide a wealth of activities, year-round catch-and-release fly fishing is within 20 minutes from the home.

Breakfast and evening snack included in rates. Types of meals: continental-plus breakfast, full breakfast and early coffee/tea. Picnic lunch, lunch and catering service available. Air conditioning and ceiling fan in room. Cable TV, VCR and fax on premises. Weddings, small meetings, family reunions and seminars hosted. Antiques, fishing, parks, shopping, downhill skiing and cross-country skiing nearby. TAC10.

Publicity: *Inyo Register, Sunset.*

"Like sleeping on a nice pink cloud after our Rock Creek Horse drive."

Bridgeport H9

The Cain House

340 Main St, PO Box 454
Bridgeport, CA 93517
(619)932-7040 (800)433-2246
Fax:(619)932-7419

Rates: $80-135.
Payment: MC VISA AX DC CB DS PC TC.
Innkeeper(s): Chris & Marachal Gohlich.
Circa: 1920.

Rooms: 7 rooms with PB.
Beds: KQ.

CA

The grandeur of the Eastern Sierra Mountains is the perfect setting for evening refreshments as the sun sets, turning the sky into a fiery, purple canvas. The innkeeper's experiences while traveling around the world have influenced The Cain House's decor to give the inn a European elegance with a casual western atmosphere. Travelers can take a short drive to the ghost town of Bodie where 10,000 people once lived in this gold-mining community. Outdoor enthusiasts can find an abundance of activity at Lake Tahoe, which is an hour-and-a-half away.

Breakfast and evening snack included in rates. Type of meal: full breakfast. Air conditioning and cable TV in room. Fax on premises. Family reunions hosted. Fishing and shopping nearby. TAC10.

Location: Eastern Sierra Mountains.

Calistoga G4

Calistoga Wayside Inn

1523 Foothill Blvd
Calistoga, CA 94515-1619
(707)942-0645 (800)845-3632
Fax:(707)942-4169

Rates: $95-145.
Payment: MC VISA AX DS PC TC.
Innkeeper(s): Cora Freitas.
Circa: 1928.

Rooms: 3 rooms with PB.
Beds: KQ.

The woodsy grounds at this Spanish-style hacienda include a waterfall, which cascades into a picturesque pond. Guests can enjoy the soothing sounds of water fountains from their rooms, which are decorated in a garden theme. The Delaney Room includes a private balcony with wicker furnishings. Down comforters, special soaps and robes are a few of the thoughtful amenities. The two-course, country breakfast is a perfect start to a day touring the popular Napa Valley. Wine and cheese is served in the afternoon. The Wayside Inn is within walking distance to Calistoga's famed spas. The innkeepers can help guests plan wine-tasting tours as well as glider or hot air balloon rides.

Breakfast included in rates. Types of meals: full breakfast and early coffee/tea. Air conditioning and ceiling fan in room. Fax and library on premises. Weddings, small meetings and family reunions hosted. Antiques, parks and shopping nearby. TAC10.

Special Discounts: Three nights, $115 per night, in-week, in-season.

"This was my first stay at a B&B and now, certainly the first of many."

The Elms

1300 Cedar St
Calistoga, CA 94515-1608
(707)942-9476 (800)235-4316
Fax:(707)942-9479

Rates: $105-175.
Payment: MC VISA PC TC.
Innkeeper(s): Stephen & Karla Wyle.
Circa: 1871.

Rooms: 7 rooms with PB, 6 with FP.
Beds: KQ.

This white three-story Victorian has a French-style mansard roof and is located on a quiet street close to the main part of town. Romantic, antique-filled rooms have extras such as bathrobes, coffeemakers and chocolates. Down comforters, feather beds, fireplaces and whirlpools are featured. In the afternoon, wine and cheese are served.

Breakfast and evening snack included in rates. Type of meal: gourmet breakfast. Air conditioning, ceiling fan and cable TV in room. VCR, fax and copier on premises. Family reunions hosted. French and German spoken. Antiques, fishing, parks, shopping, sporting events, theater and watersports nearby.

Foothill House

3037 Foothill Blvd
Calistoga, CA 94515-1225
(707)942-6933 (800)942-6933
Fax:(707)942-5692

Rates: $135-250.
Payment: MC VISA AX DS PC TC.
Innkeeper(s): Doris & Gus Beckert.
Circa: 1892.

Rooms: 4 suites, 4 with FP.
Beds: KQT.

This country farmhouse overlooks the western foothills of Mount St. Helena. Graceful old California oaks and pockets of flowers greet guests. Each room features country antiques, a four-poster bed, a fireplace and a small refrigerator. Breakfast is served in the sun room or is delivered personally to your room in a basket. Three rooms offer private Jacuzzi tubs.

Breakfast and evening snack included in rates. Types of meals: full breakfast, gourmet breakfast and early coffee/tea. Air conditioning, turn-down service, ceiling fan, cable TV and VCR in room. Fax, copier and library on premises. Weddings, small meetings and family reunions hosted. Amusement parks, antiques, fishing, parks, shopping and watersports nearby. TAC10.

Location: Napa Valley.

Publicity: *Herald Examiner, Baltimore Sun, Sunset, San Francisco Examiner.*

"Gourmet treats served in front of an open fire. Hospitality never for a moment flagged."

Scarlett's Country Inn

3918 Silverado Trl
Calistoga, CA 94515-9611
(707)942-6669
Fax:(707)942-6669
E-mail: scarletts@aol.com

Rates: $95-150.
Payment: PC.
Innkeeper(s): Scarlett Dwyer.
Circa: 1900.

Rooms: 3 rooms with PB, 1 with FP. 2 suites. 1 cottage.
Beds: Q.

Formerly a winter campground of the Wappo Indians, the property now includes a restored farmhouse. There are green lawns and country vistas of woodland and vineyards. Each room has a private entrance. Breakfast is often served beneath the apple trees or poolside.

Breakfast and afternoon tea included in rates. Types of meals: full breakfast, gourmet breakfast and early coffee/tea. Room service available. Air conditioning and turn-down service in room. Cable TV, fax, copier and swimming on premises. Small meetings and family reunions hosted. Spanish spoken. Antiques, fishing, parks, shopping and watersports nearby. TAC10.

Location: Napa Valley wine country.

Publicity: *Daily News.*

"Wonderful, peaceful, serene."

Trailside Inn

4201 Silverado Trl
Calistoga, CA 94515-9605
(707)942-4106
Fax:(707)942-4702

Rates: $95-150.
Payment: MC VISA AX DS.
Innkeeper(s): Randy & Lani Gray.
Circa: 1932.

Rooms: 3 suites, 3 with FP.
Beds: QDT.

This secluded valley farmhouse overlooks Three Palms Vineyard and the distant Sterling Winery. Each accommodation is a tastefully decorated suite with its own porch, private entrance, small kitchen, private bath and fireplace. Furnished with country antiques and old quilts, two suites have an extra bedroom to accommodate a family of four. House specialties are banana and blueberry breads, freshly baked and brought to your room.

Breakfast included in rates. Type of meal: continental-plus breakfast. Antiques and watersports nearby.

Location: Napa Valley.

Publicity: *San Francisco Examiner, Wine Country Review.*

"If Dorothy and Toto were to click their heals together they would end up at the Trailside Inn."

Blue Whale Inn

6736 Moonstone Beach Dr
Cambria, CA 93428-1814
(805)927-4647
Fax:(805)927-4647

Rates: $155-195.
Payment: MC VISA.
Innkeeper(s): Bob & Karleen Hathcock.
Circa: 1990.

Rooms: 6 rooms with PB, 6 with FP.
Beds: KQ.

This oceanfront inn of shiplap redwood is surrounded by gardens and has a pond and waterfall. Each guest room affords ocean views and boasts a canopy bed, fireplace and garden view from the bath. English floral fabrics, armoires, love seats and small refrigerators add to the luxury. From the picture windows of the breakfast room, guests look out to the ocean where sea lions lounge on the rocks.

Breakfast and afternoon tea included in rates. Types of meals: full breakfast and early coffee/tea. Ceiling fan and cable TV in room. Fax, copier and library on premises. Antiques, fishing, parks, shopping, theater and watersports nearby.

The J. Patrick House

2990 Burton Dr
Cambria, CA 93428-4002
(805)927-3812 (800)341-5258

Rates: $110-160.
Payment: MC VISA AX DS PC.
Innkeeper(s): Barbara & Mel Schwimmer.
Circa: 1983.

Rooms: 8 rooms with PB, 8 with FP. 1 suite.
Beds: KQ.

This charming log cabin bed & breakfast is nestled in the woods overlooking Cambria's east village. The picturesque grounds include a garden area that separates the main house from the redwood cabin, where all but one of the guest rooms are located. Each of the guest rooms includes a wood-burning fireplace. Rooms are decorated in a romantic style with hand-stitched quilts and feather-filled duvet covers atop the beds. Wine and hors d'oeuvres are served each evening in the main house's fireplaced living room. Fresh fruits, home-made granola and freshly baked breads and muffins are among the fare during the morning meal. Be sure to request one of the innkeeper's "killer" chocolate chip cookies.

Breakfast and evening snack included in rates. Types of meals: continental-plus breakfast and early coffee/tea. Family reunions hosted. Antiques, fishing, parks and shopping nearby. TAC10.

Special Discounts: Winter packages.

Olallieberry Inn

2476 Main St
Cambria, CA 93428-3406
(805)927-3222
Fax:(805)927-0202

Rates: $72-165.
Payment: MC VISA PC TC.
Innkeeper(s): Peter & Carol Ann Irsfeld.
Circa: 1873.

Rooms: 9 rooms with PB, 6 with FP. 1 suite.
Beds: KQ.

This restored Greek Revival home features rooms decorated with fabrics and wall coverings and furnished with period antiques. Six of the guest rooms feature fireplaces. Butterfly and herb gardens and a 110-year-old redwood grace the front yard. The cheery gathering room boasts a view of the Santa Rosa Creek. Full breakfast with fresh breads, fruits and a special entree start off the day, and wine and hors d'oeuvres are served in the afternoon. The inn is within walking distance to restaurants and shops.

Breakfast and evening snack included in rates. Types of meals: full breakfast, gourmet breakfast and early coffee/tea. Fax on premises. Handicap access. Weddings, small meetings, family reunions and seminars hosted. Antiques, fishing, shopping and watersports nearby. TAC10.

Location: Central coast wine country.

Publicity: *Los Angeles Times, Elmer Dills Radio Show.*

"Our retreat turned into relaxation, romance and pure Victorian delight."

Pickford House B&B

2555 MacLeod Way
Cambria, CA 93428-4302
(805)927-8619

Rates: $89-130.
Payment: MC VISA PC TC.
Innkeeper(s): Anna Larsen.
Circa: 1983.

Rooms: 8 rooms with PB, 3 with FP.
Beds: KQ.

Just a few miles from Hearst Castle, Pickford House pays a tribute to the many actors and actresses who visited the publisher's opulent estate during its early 20th-century heyday. Pictures of Jean Harlow, John Barrymore, and, of course, Mary Pickford are just a few of the movie memorabilia guests will encounter. Antiques fill guest rooms, which are named for movie stars of the '20s and '30s. The innkeeper is full of interesting stories about the area and Hearst Castle. Although the home was built in 1983, the innkeeper decorated her combination dining room and tavern with a massive 1860s bar fashioned from mahogany. The bar was first used at the Hilton in Buffalo, N.Y. The breakfast specialty is aebleskive, Danish pancakes topped with fruit sauce.

Ceiling fan and cable TV in room. Weddings, small meetings and family reunions hosted. Fishing, parks, shopping and watersports nearby.

The Squibb House

4063 Burton Dr
Cambria, CA 93428-3001
(805)927-9600

Rates: $95-140.
Payment: MC VISA PC TC.
Innkeeper(s): Martha Carolyn.
Circa: 1877.

Rooms: 5 rooms with PB.
Beds: Q.

A picket fence and large garden surround this Victorian inn with its Italianate and Gothic Revival architecture. Guests may relax in the main parlor, stroll the gardens or sit and rock on the porch. The home was built by a Civil War veteran and young school teacher. The downstairs once was used as a classroom while an addition was being made in the town's school. Each guest room has a firestove.

Breakfast and afternoon tea included in rates. Type of meal: continental-plus breakfast. Small meetings hosted. Antiques, fishing, parks, shopping, theater and watersports nearby. TAC10.

Publicity: *Cambrian.*

Camino G7

The Camino Hotel-Seven Mile House

4103 Carson Rd,
PO Box 1197
Camino, CA 95709
(916)644-7740 (800)200-7740
Fax:(916)644-7740

Rates: $65-95. AP.
Payment: MC VISA AX DS PC TC.
Innkeeper(s): Paula Norbert & John Eddy.
Circa: 1888.

Rooms: 9 rooms, 3 with PB. 1 conference room.
Beds: QDT.

Once a barracks for the area's loggers, this inn now caters to visitors in the state's famed gold country. Just east of Placerville, historic Camino is on the Old Carson Wagon Trail. Nine guest rooms are available, including the E.J. Barrett Room, a favorite with honeymooners. Other rooms feature names such as Pony Express, Stage Stop and Wagon Train. The family-oriented inn welcomes children, and a local park offers a handy site for their recreational needs. Popular area activities include antiquing, hot air ballooning and wine tasting.

Breakfast and evening snack included in rates. Types of meals: full breakfast and early coffee/tea. Afternoon tea, picnic lunch and banquet service available. AP. Turn-down service and ceiling fan in room. Fax, copier and library on premises. Weddings, small meetings, family reunions and seminars hosted. Antiques, fishing, parks, shopping, downhill skiing, cross-country skiing, theater and watersports nearby. TAC15.

Location: In the Apple Hill area of California's Gold Country.

Special Discounts: Midweek $55-75 (Sunday-Thursday)

Capitola-By-The-Sea

The Inn at Depot Hill

250 Monterey Ave
Capitola-By-The-Sea, CA
95010-3358
(408)462-3376 (800)572-2632
Fax:(408)462-3697

Rates: $165-250.
Payment: MC VISA AX TC.
Innkeeper(s): Suzie Lankes & Dan Floyd.
Circa: 1901.

Rooms: 8 rooms with PB, 8 with FP. 4 suites.
Beds: KQ.

CA

Once a railroad depot, this inn offers rooms with themes to represent different parts of the world-a chic auberge in St. Tropez, a romantic hideaway in Paris, an Italian coastal villa, a summer home on the coast of Holland, and a traditional English garden room. Five rooms have garden patios boasting hot tubs. The rooms have many amenities which include a fireplace, white marble bathrooms and featherbeds. Guests are greeted with fresh flowers in their room.

Breakfast and evening snack included in rates. Types of meals: full breakfast and gourmet breakfast. Afternoon tea and room service available. Turn-down service, cable TV and VCR in room. Fax and spa on premises. Handicap access. Weddings, small meetings, family reunions and seminars hosted. Amusement parks, antiques, fishing, parks, shopping, theater and watersports nearby.

Publicity: *Country Inn, Santa Cruz Sentinel, McCalls, Choices & Vacation, San Jose Mercury News, Fresno & Sacramento Bee, San Francisco Focus, American Airline Flight.*

"The highlight of our honeymoon. Five stars in our book!"

Cardiff-By-The-Sea Q11

Cardiff-By-The-Sea Lodge

142 Chesterfield Dr
Cardiff-By-The-Sea, CA
92007-1922
(760)944-6474
Fax:(760)944-6841

Rates: $89-350.
Payment: MC VISA AX DS TC.
Innkeeper(s): James & Jeanette Statser.
Circa: 1991.

Rooms: 17 rooms with PB, 5 with FP.
Beds: Q.

Each of the guest rooms at this romantic seaside retreat features an individual theme. For instance, the Santa Fe room is decorated with a whitewashed, four-poster log bed, a handcrafted fireplace and a large Roman tub. This ocean view room also includes a wet bar. The Sweetheart room, with its hand-carved bed, a heart-shaped whirlpool tub, a fireplace and ocean view is a perfect place for romantics. Other rooms feature themes such as "Garden View," "Victorian," "Summer" and "Paradise." This inn, which offers convenient access to San Diego, is listed in "The Best Places to Kiss in Southern California."

Breakfast included in rates. Type of meal: continental-plus breakfast. Air conditioning and cable TV in room. Fax, copier, spa and library on premises. Handicap access. Weddings, small meetings and family reunions hosted. Amusement parks, antiques, fishing, parks, shopping, sporting events, theater and watersports nearby. TAC10.

Carmel J5

Cobblestone Inn

PO Box 3185
Carmel, CA 93921-3185
(408)625-5222 (800)833-8836
Fax:(408)625-0478

Rates: $95-175.
Innkeeper(s): Suzi Russo.

Rooms: 24 rooms with PB, 24 with FP.

An exterior of wood and cobblestone gathered from the Carmel River provide a friendly facade for visitors to this bed & breakfast located two blocks from the heart of Carmel. Each guest room has its own cobblestone fireplace. The inn's English country decor is enhanced with quilts, a colorful antique carousel horse and other early American antiques. In addition to breakfast and afternoon tea, evening wine and hors d'oeuvres are served. Guests can borrow one of the inn's bicycles to explore the area. The beach and shopping are nearby. Cobblestone is one of the Four Sisters Inns.

Breakfast and afternoon tea included in rates. Types of meals: gourmet breakfast and early coffee/tea. Picnic lunch available. Fax and copier on premises.

Publicity: *Country Inns, Honeymoons.*

Special Discounts: Celebration package available.

The Stonehouse Inn

PO Box 2517, 8th Below
Monte Verde
Carmel, CA 93921-2517
(408)624-4569 (800)748-6618

Rates: $89-199.
Payment: MC VISA AX.
Innkeeper(s): Ad Navailles.
Circa: 1906.

Rooms: 6 rooms, 1 with PB.
Beds: KQDT.

This quaint Carmel country house boasts a stone exterior, made from beach rocks collected and hand shaped by local Indians at the turn of the century. The original owner, "Nana" Foster, was hostess to notable artists and writers from the San Francisco area, including Sinclair Lewis, Jack London and Lotta Crabtree. The romantic Jack London room features a dramatic gabled ceiling, a brass bed and a stunning view of the ocean. Conveniently located, the inn is a short walk from Carmel Beach and two blocks from the village.

Breakfast included in rates. Type of meal: full breakfast. Weddings and family reunions hosted. Fishing, parks, shopping, theater and watersports nearby. TAC10.

Location: Two blocks to downtown, 4 blocks to beach.

Publicity: *Travel & Leisure, Country Living.*

"First time stay at a B&B — GREAT!"

Vagabond's House Inn

PO Box 2747, Dolores & 4th
Carmel, CA 93921-2747
(408)624-7738 (800)262-1262
Fax:(408)626-1243

Rates: $68-165.
Payment: MC VISA AX PC TC.
Innkeeper(s): Honey Spence.
Circa: 1940.

Rooms: 11 rooms with PB, 9 with FP.
Beds: KQD.

Shaded by the intertwined branches of two California live oaks, the stone-paved courtyard of the Vagabond's House sets the tone of this romantic retreat. The inn is comprised of a cluster of white stucco cottages built into a slope. Some include kitchens, but all feature a fireplace and an antique clock. In the morning continental breakfast is delivered to you near the camellias or in the privacy of your room.

Type of meal: continental-plus breakfast. Cable TV in room. Fax and copier on premises. Weddings hosted. Spanish and Korean spoken. Antiques, fishing, parks, shopping and theater nearby. TAC10.

Pets Allowed: $10 per night - pet policy.

Location: 4th & Dolores.

Publicity: *Diversion, Cat Fancy.*

"Charming & excellent accommodations and service. Very much in keeping with the character and ambiance of Carmel's historic setting."

Carmel Valley K5

Robles Del Rio Lodge

200 Punta Del Monte
Carmel Valley, CA 93924
(408)659-3705 (800)833-0843
Fax:(408)659-5157

Rates: $89-250.
Payment: MC VISA AX TC.
Innkeeper(s): Ron Gurries Family.
Circa: 1928.

Rooms: 33 rooms with PB, 5 with FP. 2 suites. 5 cottages. 1 conference room.
Beds: KQT.

Situated among nine acres of oaks on a romantically secluded ridge above Carmel Valley, this lodge provides accommodations with hilltop views in guestrooms in the main house. There are also private cottages with fireplaces. The unpretentious lodge look of board-and-batten or rustic French countryside motifs mark the decor. Make a dinner reservation for sunset at Ridge Restaurant at the lodge. It has evolved to become one of the premier eateries on the Monterey Peninsula.

Breakfast included in rates. Type of meal: continental-plus breakfast. Picnic lunch, lunch, gourmet lunch, banquet service and catering service available. Ceiling fan and cable TV in room. Fax, copier, spa, swimming, sauna and tennis on premises. Handicap access. Weddings, small meetings, family reunions and seminars hosted. Fishing, parks, shopping and theater nearby. TAC10.

Location: Perched high in the hills above Carmel Valley, inland of the coastal fog.

Publicity: *Peninsula, Sacramento Bee Final, Five Cities Times, San Francisco Focus, Country Inns of America, Los Angeles, Front Nine Golf Monthly, San Francisco Examiner, Travel & Leisure, Lifestyle, San Jose Mercury.*

"Your staff did many things to make our meeting there so wonderful. It's BETTER than the brochure..no false advertising about this place!"

Chico — E5

Music Express Inn

1091 El Monte Ave
Chico, CA 95928-9153
(916)345-8376
Fax:(916)893-8521
E-mail: icobeen@aol.com

Rates: $55-85.
Payment: MC VISA AX DS PC TC.
Innkeeper(s): Barney & Irene Cobeen.
Circa: 1977.

Rooms: 9 rooms with PB. 1 suite. 1 cottage. 2 conference rooms.
Beds: KQDT.

Music lovers will delight in this inn's warmth and charm. Nine air-conditioned guest rooms, all with private bath and cable TV, provide country-style comfort to those visiting the college town of Chico. Guests will awake to the smell of homemade bread or rolls. Visitors are welcome to tickle the ivories of the inn's Steinway grand piano. The innkeeper, a music teacher, is adept at many instruments and plays mandolin in a local band. The inn's library also lures many guests, and those who explore the surrounding area will find plenty of opportunities for antiquing and fishing.

Breakfast included in rates. Type of meal: full breakfast. Air conditioning, ceiling fan, cable TV and VCR in room. Fax, copier and library on premises. Handicap access. Weddings, small meetings, family reunions and seminars hosted. Antiques, fishing, parks, shopping, sporting events, theater and watersports nearby. TAC5.

Coloma — G6

Coloma Country Inn

PO Box 502
Coloma, CA 95613-0502
(916)622-6919

Rates: $90-130.
Payment: PC TC.
Innkeeper(s): Alan & Cindi Ehrgott.
Circa: 1852.

Rooms: 8 rooms, 4 with PB. 2 suites. 2 cottages. 1 conference room.
Beds: QD.

Guests at this country farmhouse will want to take advantage of the nearby American River for whitewater rafting. Innkeeper Alan Ehrgott is a veteran hot air balloon pilot and offers flights down the river year-round. Bed, Breakfast and Balloon packages are available at the inn, along with whitewater rafting packages. The inn is situated on five, private acres in the middle of the 300-acre Gold Discovery State Park and guests will feel like they've gone back to the Gold Rush days. A duck pond and gazebo are part of the inn's charm, coupled with antique beds, stenciling and country decor.

Breakfast and afternoon tea included in rates. Types of meals: full breakfast and early coffee/tea. Picnic lunch and catering service available. Air conditioning and ceiling fan in room. Bicycles on premises. Weddings, small meetings, family reunions and seminars hosted. Spanish spoken. Antiques, fishing, parks, downhill skiing, theater and watersports nearby. TAC10.

Location: Heart of the Gold Country, Coloma, where the Gold Rush began.

Publicity: *Country Living, Los Angeles Times, Country Inns, Sunset, Motorland, New York Times.*

Special Discounts: 10% off midweek, November-January.

Dana Point

P11

Blue Lantern Inn

34343 Street of
The Blue Lantern
Dana Point, CA 92629
(714)661-1304 (800)950-1236
Fax:(714)496-1483

Rates: $135-350.
Payment: MC VISA AX TC.
Innkeeper(s): Lin McMahon.
Circa: 1990.

Rooms: 29 rooms with PB, 29 with FP. 3 conference rooms.
Beds: KQD.

The four-diamond inn is situated high on a blufftop overlooking a stunning coastline and the blue waters of Dana Point harbor with its pleasure craft, fishing boats and the tall ship, Pilgrim. Each guest room features both a fireplace and a whirlpool tub and many offer private sundecks. Afternoon tea, evening turndown service and bicycles are just a few of the amenities available. In the evening, wine and hors d'oeuvres are served. Shops, restaurants and beaches are nearby, and popular Laguna Beach is just a few miles to the north. Blue Lantern is one of the Four Sisters Inns.

Breakfast and afternoon tea included in rates. Type of meal: gourmet breakfast. Picnic lunch available. Turn-down service in room. Fax and bicycles on premises. Handicap access. Weddings, small meetings and family reunions hosted. Amusement parks, antiques, fishing, parks, shopping and watersports nearby. TAC10.

Location: Overlooking yacht harbor near Laguna Beach.

Publicity: *Los Angeles Magazine, Glamour, Oregonian, Orange County Register.*

Special Discounts: Honeymoon packages.

Dorrington

H7

The Dorrington Hotel & Restaurant

3431 Hwy 4, PO Box 4307
Dorrington, CA 95223
(209)795-5800

Rates: $85.
Payment: MC VISA PC TC.
Innkeeper(s): Bonnie Saville.
Circa: 1860.

Rooms: 5 rooms.
Beds: Q.

This historic hotel was built by Dorrington's town founders as a hotel and restaurant for those traveling through the area on stagecoach. More than a century later, it still serves that purpose. Guest rooms are decorated in country style with antiques and brass beds topped with handmade quilts. The innkeepers want their guests to have a relaxing stay, free from the modern world, so there are no televisions or phones in guest rooms. Continental fare in the mornings, and Northern Italian cuisine nightly in the restaurant. According to legend, the ghost of the hotel's former mistress sometimes walks the hallways.

Breakfast included in rates. Types of meals: continental breakfast and early coffee/tea. Dinner and room service available. 38 acres. Weddings and small meetings hosted. Antiques, fishing, parks, shopping, downhill skiing, cross-country skiing, theater and watersports nearby.

"The Dorrington has always existed in the dreams of all those out there that love romance."

Duarte

O10

White Horse Estate, B&B Inn

330 Las Lomas Rd
Duarte, CA 91010-1335
(818)358-0798 (800)653-8886
Fax:(818)793-6409

Rates: $75-150.
Payment: MC VISA AX PC.
Innkeeper(s): Christine & Steven Pittard.
Circa: 1906.

Rooms: 6 rooms with PB. 1 conference room.
Beds: QD.

An acre of gardens surround this turn-of-the-century Queen Anne home. The six-room bed & breakfast is decorated in Victorian style and much of the home's original architectural features have been preserved. The continental-plus breakfasts, which include fresh fruits, baked goods, cereals and specialty coffees and tea, are served on the veranda or in the formal dining room. The inn is within walking distance of Royal Oaks Park, and it's a short drive to horse racing at Santa Anita, Old Town Pasadena and the Rose Bowl.

Breakfast and afternoon tea included in rates. Type of meal: continental-plus breakfast. Air conditioning in room. Handicap access. Small meetings, family reunions and seminars hosted. TAC10.

Dunsmuir B5

Dunsmuir Inn

5423 Dunsmuir Ave
Dunsmuir, CA 96025-2011
(916)235-4543 (888)386-7684
Fax:(916)235-4154

Rates: $55-65.
Payment: MC VISA AX DC CB DS PC TC.
Innkeeper(s): Jerry & Julie Iskra.
Circa: 1925.

Rooms: 4 rooms with PB. 1 suite.
Beds: KDT.

Set in the Sacramento River Valley, this country-style inn may serve as a base for an assortment of outdoor activities. At the end of the day, guests can enjoy an old-fashioned soda or ice cream cone. Fishing, available in the crystal-clear waters of the Upper Sacramento River, is within walking distance. The innkeepers can suggest hiking trails and driving tours to mountain lakes, waterfalls, the Castle Crags State Park and Mt. Shasta.

Breakfast included in rates. Types of meals: full breakfast and early coffee/tea. Evening snack and picnic lunch available. Air conditioning, turn-down service and ceiling fan in room. Cable TV, VCR and fax on premises. Family reunions hosted. Antiques, fishing, parks, downhill skiing, cross-country skiing and watersports nearby. TAC10.

Location: Sacramento River Valley.

Elk F3

Elk Cove Inn

6300 S Hwy 1, PO Box 367
Elk, CA 95432
(707)877-3321 (800)275-2967
Fax:(707)877-1808

Rates: $29-298.
Payment: MC VISA AX PC.
Innkeeper(s): Elaine Bryant & Jim Carr.
Circa: 1883.

Rooms: 14 rooms with PB, 7 with FP. 4 suites. 4 cottages. 1 conference room.
Beds: KQ.

This mansard-style Victorian home was built as a guest house for lumber baron L. E. White. Operated as a full-service country inn for more than 27 years, Elk Cove Inn commands a majestic view from atop a scenic bluff. Four cabins and an addition to the house feature large bay windows, skylights and Victorian fireplaces. Most rooms have an ocean view. Antiques, hand-embroidered linens and down comforters add to the amenities. Below the inn is an expansive driftwood-strewn beach. Gourmet breakfasts are served in the ocean-view dining rooms. Coffee makers with fresh ground coffee, teas, cider and hot chocolate are available in the rooms.

Breakfast included in rates. Type of meal: gourmet breakfast. VCR and fax on premises. Handicap access. Weddings, small meetings, family reunions and seminars hosted. Antiques, fishing, parks, shopping, theater and watersports nearby.

Location: 15 miles south of Mendocino.

Special Discounts: Mid-week off season (December-April) specials.

"Quiet, peaceful, romantic, spiritual. This room, the inn, and the food are all what the doctor ordered."

Sandpiper House Inn

5520 S Hwy 1
Elk, CA 95432
(707)877-3587

Rates: $110-215. MAP.
Payment: MC VISA AX DS PC TC.
Innkeeper(s): Claire & Richard Melrose.
Circa: 1916.

Rooms: 5 rooms with PB, 3 with FP. 1 suite.
Beds: Q.

A garden path leads Sandpiper guests to a bluff overlooking the California coast. The path continues onward to a private beach. The historic home was built out of redwood by the local lumber company. Guest quarters are appointed to look like rooms in an English country manor. Canopied beds, Oriental rugs and polished wood floors create a romantic ambiance. Rooms offer either ocean or wilderness views, and three have a fireplace. Gourmet breakfasts are served on tables set with lace and fresh flowers.

Breakfast and afternoon tea included in rates. Types of meals: full breakfast, gourmet breakfast and early coffee/tea. MAP. Fishing, parks, shopping, theater and watersports nearby.

Escondido — P12

Zosa Gardens B&B

9381 W Lilac Rd
Escondido, CA 92026
(619)723-9093
Fax:(619)723-3460

Rates: $100-175.
Payment: MC VISA AX DS PC TC.
Innkeeper(s): Connie Vlasis.
Circa: 1971.

Rooms: 9 rooms, 5 with PB, 1 with FP. 1 suite. 1 cottage. 1 conference room.
Beds: KQD.

Escondido, located in northern San Diego County, is the setting for this Spanish Hacienda. The home rests on 22 well-landscaped acres atop a bluff in the Monserate Mountains. Rooms bear flowery themes. For angel lovers try the Angel Room. The Master Suite includes a fireplace. The innkeeper is an accomplished chef, and her cuisine has been featured on the TV Food Network, as well as in Bon Appetit. She serves a full customized breakfast for her guests. In the evenings, gourmet ti dbits are served with a selection of local wines. Guests are free to enjoy the grounds. There is an outside grill and billiards and massages are available. Golf courses, restaurants and other sites are just minutes away.

Breakfast and evening snack included in rates. Type of meal: full breakfast. Picnic lunch, catering service and room service available. Air conditioning and turn-down service in room. Cable TV, VCR, fax, copier, spa, swimming and tennis on premises. Handicap access. 22 acres. Weddings, small meetings, family reunions and seminars hosted. Spanish and Filapino spoken. Amusement parks, antiques, fishing, parks, shopping, downhill skiing, cross-country skiing, sporting events, theater and watersports nearby. TAC10.

Special Discounts: Corporate guests: 20% off; Seniors: 10% off.

Eureka — C2

"An Elegant Victorian Mansion" Bed & Breakfast

1406 C St
Eureka, CA 95501-1765
(707)444-3144
Fax:(707)442-5594

Rates: $95-185. EP.
Payment: MC VISA.
Innkeeper(s): Doug & Lily Vieyra.
Circa: 1888.

Rooms: 4 rooms, 2 with PB. 1 suite. 1 conference room.
Beds: Q.

One of Eureka's leading lumber barons built this picturesque home from 1,000-year-old virgin redwood. Original wallpapers, wood carpets and antique light fixtures create a wonderfully authentic Victorian ambiance. A tuxedoed butler and your hosts, decked in period attire, greet guests upon arrival. Croquet fields and Victorian gardens surround the inn. The hosts can arrange horse-drawn carriage rides or boat cruises. Old-fashioned ice cream sodas are served and to top it all off, each morning guests partake in a multi-course gourmet breakfast feast. The beds in the well-appointed guest quarters are topped with custom-made mattresses. There a video library of vintage silent films. The inn has been host to many historic personalities, including actresses Lillie Langtry and Sarah Bernhardt, and many senators and representatives.

Breakfast, afternoon tea and evening snack included in rates. Types of meals: gourmet breakfast and early coffee/tea. EP. Air conditioning and turn-down service in room. Cable TV, VCR, fax, copier, sauna, bicycles, tennis and library on premises. Small meetings and seminars hosted. French, Dutch and German spoken. Amusement parks, antiques, fishing, parks, shopping, sporting events, theater and watersports nearby. TAC10.

Special Discounts: Multiple night (three or more) 10% discount off "in season" rate.

"A magnificent masterpiece, both in architecture and service. Four-star service and regal opulence."

The Carter House Victorians

301 L St
Eureka, CA 95501
(707)444-8062 (800)404-1390
Fax:(707)444-8067
E-mail: carter52@humboldt1.com

Rates: $95-275. MAP, AP, EP.
Payment: MC VISA AX DC CB DS PC TC.
Innkeeper(s): Mark & Christi Carter.
Circa: 1884.

Rooms: 31 rooms with PB, 15 with FP. 15 suites. 1 cottage. 2 conference rooms.
Beds: KQDT.

The Carters found a pattern book in an antique shop and built this inn according to the architectural plans for an 1890 San Francisco Victorian. (The architect, Joseph Newsom, also designed the Carson House across the street.) Three open parlors with bay windows and marble fireplaces provide an elegant backdrop for relaxing. Guests are free to visit the kitchen in quest of coffee and views of the bay. The inn is famous for its three-course breakfast, including an Apple Almond Tart featured in Gourmet magazine.

Breakfast and afternoon tea included in rates. Types of meals: continental breakfast, continental-plus breakfast, full breakfast, gourmet breakfast and early coffee/tea. Dinner, evening snack and room service available. MAP, AP, EP. Air conditioning, turn-down service, cable TV and VCR in room. Fax, copier and spa on premises. Handicap access. Weddings, small meetings, family reunions and seminars hosted. Italian, Spanish and French spoken. Antiques, fishing, parks, shopping, sporting events, theater and watersports nearby. TAC10.

Location: Corner of Third & L streets in Old Town.

Publicity: *Sunset, U.S. News & World Report, Country Home, Country Living, Bon Appetit, San Francisco Focus, Northwest Palate, Gourmet, Art Culinare, San Francisco Chronicle.*

"We've traveled extensively throughout the U.S. and stayed in the finest hotels. You've got them all beat!!"

The Daly Inn

1125 H St
Eureka, CA 95501-1844
(707)445-3638 (800)321-9656
Fax:(707)444-3636

Rates: $80-140.
Payment: MC VISA AX DS PC TC.
Innkeeper(s): Sue & Gene Clinesmith.
Circa: 1905.

Rooms: 5 rooms, 3 with PB, 1 with FP. 2 suites.
Beds: QT.

This 6,000-square-foot Colonial Revival mansion is located in the historic section of Eureka. Enjoy the Belgian antique bedstead, fireplace and view of fish pond and garden from Annie Murphy's Room, or try the former nursery, Miss Martha's Room, with bleached pine antiques from Holland. Breakfast is served fireside in the inn's formal dining room or in the breakfast parlor or garden patio.

Breakfast and evening snack included in rates. Types of meals: gourmet breakfast and early coffee/tea. Turn-down service in room. Cable TV, VCR, fax, copier and library on premises. Weddings, small meetings, family reunions and seminars hosted. Antiques, fishing, parks, shopping, sporting events and theater nearby. TAC10.
Location: California's north coast.
"A genuine delight."

Old Town B&B Inn

1521 3rd St
Eureka, CA 95501-0710
(707)445-3951 (800)331-5098
Fax:(707)268-0231
E-mail: otb-b@humboldt1.com

Rates: $75-150.
Payment: MC VISA AX DC CB DS.
Innkeeper(s): Leigh & Diane Benson.
Circa: 1871.

Rooms: 6 rooms, 4 with PB, 1 with FP.
Beds: KQDT.

This early Victorian/Greek Revival was the original family home of Lumber Baron William Carson. It was constructed of virgin redwood and Douglas fir. (Redwood from the Carson's mill was used to build a significant portion of San Francisco.) Try to time your stay on a day when the Timber Beast breakfast menu is served, and be sure to take home a copy of the inn's cookbook.

Breakfast, afternoon tea and evening snack included in rates. Types of meals: continental breakfast, continental-plus breakfast, full breakfast, gourmet breakfast and early coffee/tea. Family reunions hosted. Spanish and Italian spoken. Antiques, fishing, parks, shopping, downhill skiing, sporting events, theater and watersports nearby.

Location: Heart of the Redwood Empire on the Pacific Coast, north of San Francisco.

Publicity: *Times-Standard, Country, San Francisco Chronicle, Sunset.*

"From the moment you opened the door, we knew we had chosen a special place to stay."

Ferndale C2

Gingerbread Mansion Inn

PO Box 40, 400 Berding St
Ferndale, CA 95536-1380
(707)786-4000 (800)952-4136
Fax:(707)786-4381
E-mail: kenn@humboldt1.com

Rates: $120-350.
Payment: MC VISA AX PC TC.
Innkeeper(s): Ken Torbert.
Circa: 1899.

Rooms: 10 rooms with PB, 5 with FP. 5 suites.
Beds: KQT.

Built for Dr. H.J. Ring, the Gingerbread Mansion is now the most photographed of Northern California's inns. Near Eureka, it is in the fairy-tale Victorian village of Ferndale (a California Historical Landmark). Outside the inn are formal English gardens. Gingerbread Mansion is a unique combination of Queen Anne and Eastlake styles with elaborate gingerbread trim. Inside are spacious and elegant rooms including two suites with "his" and "her" bathtubs. There are four parlors.

Breakfast and afternoon tea included in rates. Types of meals: full breakfast and early coffee/tea. Turn-down service in room. Library on premises. Small meetings and family reunions hosted. Antiques, fishing, parks, shopping and theater nearby. TAC10.

Location: Five miles west off Hwy 101; 30 minutes south of Eureka.

Publicity: *Stockton Record, San Francisco Focus, Los Angeles Times, Sunset.*

Special Discounts: Call for special corporate rates.

"Absolutely the most charming, friendly and delightful place we have ever stayed."

Fish Camp I8

Karen's B&B Yosemite Inn

PO Box 8
Fish Camp, CA 93623-0008
(209)683-4550

Rates: $90.
Innkeeper(s): Karen Bergh.
Circa: 1988.

Rooms: 3 rooms.

This contemporary country house enjoys a setting of pine, oak and cedar trees at 5,000 feet. The Rose Room features wicker furniture and a rose motif on quilts and pillows. There's a porch to relax on and in the evening guests enjoy watching raccoons come by for their evening snacks. Cottage-fried potatoes and fresh-baked muffins are a sample of the country breakfast. It's a three-minute drive to the southern gate of Yosemite National Park.

Breakfast included in rates. Type of meal: full breakfast. Parks nearby.

Location: One mile south of Yosemite National Park.

Publicity: *Contra Costa Times.*

Fort Bragg

E2

CA

Avalon House

561 Stewart St
Fort Bragg, CA 95437-3226
(707)964-5555 (800)964-5556

Rates: $70-140.
Payment: MC VISA AX DS PC TC.
Innkeeper(s): Anne Sorrells.
Circa: 1905.

Rooms: 6 rooms with PB, 4 with FP.
Beds: QDT.

This redwood California Craftsman house was extensively remodeled in 1988, and furnished with a mixture of antiques and willow furniture. Some rooms feature fireplaces, whirlpool tubs, or ocean views and decks. The inn is in a quiet residential area, three blocks from the Pacific Ocean, one block west of Hwy. 1, and two blocks from the Skunk Train depot.

Breakfast included in rates. Types of meals: full breakfast and early coffee/tea. Cable TV and VCR on premises. Weddings, small meetings and family reunions hosted. Antiques, fishing, parks, shopping, theater and watersports nearby. TAC10.

Location: 150 miles northwest of San Francisco.

Publicity: *Advocate News.*

Special Discounts: 20% off Monday through Thursday except holidays, year round.

"Elegant, private and extremely comfortable. We will never stay in a motel again."

Grey Whale Inn

615 N Main St
Fort Bragg, CA 95437-3240
(707)964-0640 (800)382-7244
Fax:(707)964-4408
E-mail: gwhale@mcn.org

Rates: $90-180.
Payment: MC VISA AX DS PC TC.
Innkeeper(s): John & Colette Bailey.
Circa: 1915.

Rooms: 14 rooms with PB, 3 with FP. 2 conference rooms.
Beds: KQDT.

As the name implies, whales can be seen from many of the inn's vantage points during the creatures' migration season along the West Coast. The stately four-story redwood inn features airy and spacious guest rooms with ocean views. Some rooms include a fireplace, whirlpool tub for two or private deck. Near the heart of downtown Fort Bragg, it's an easy walk to the Skunk Train, shops, galleries and restaurants. There is also a fireside lounge, TV-VCR room and a recreation area with pool table.

Breakfast included in rates. Type of meal: full breakfast. Cable TV, VCR, fax, copier and library on premises. Handicap access. Weddings, small meetings, family reunions and seminars hosted. German, Spanish and Dutch spoken. Antiques, fishing, parks, shopping, theater and watersports nearby. TAC10.

Location: Almost in the heart of downtown Fort Bragg on the Mendocino Coast Highway.

Publicity: *Inn Times, San Francisco Examiner, Travel, Fort Bragg Advocate News, Mendocino Beacon, Los Angeles Times, Sunset.*

Special Discounts: Variable AAA rates available.

"We are going to return each year until we have tried each room. Sunrise room is excellent in the morning or evening."

Geyserville

G4

Campbell Ranch Inn

1475 Canyon Rd
Geyserville, CA 95441-9641
(707)857-3476 (800)959-3878
Fax:(707)857-3239

Rates: $100-165.
Payment: MC VISA AX PC TC.
Innkeeper(s): Mary Jane & Jerry Campbell.
Circa: 1968.

Rooms: 5 rooms with PB, 1 with FP. 1 cottage.
Beds: K.

Perched atop a 35-acre hilltop, this inn affords views of local vineyards within Sonoma County's Alexander Valley and Dry Creek wine regions. Rooms are spacious with comfortable, contemporary decor. Three rooms offer balconies with views, and the private cottage includes a fireplace and a deck. Guests enjoy use of a swimming pool, tennis court, hot tub, bicycles and there are gardens as well. The innkeepers authored "The

Campbell Ranch Inn Cookbook," serves her delicious recipes during the morning meal, and she also serves homemade pie each evening.

Breakfast and evening snack included in rates. Type of meal: full breakfast. VCR, fax, copier, spa, swimming, bicycles and tennis on premises. 35 acres. Weddings, small meetings, family reunions hosted. Antiques, fishing, parks, shopping, watersports nearby. TAC10.

Publicity: *Sunset, Country, Healdsburg Tribune, San Francisco Examiner*

"The best of all possible worlds."

Hope-Merrill House

21253 Geyserville Ave
Geyserville, CA 95441-9637
(707)857-3356 (800)825-4233
Fax:(707)857-4673

Rates: $95-140.
Payment: MC VISA AX PC TC.
Innkeeper(s): Rosalie Hope.
Circa: 1885.

Rooms: 12 rooms with PB, 3 with FP. 1 suite.
Beds: Q.

The Hope-Merrill House is a classic example of the Eastlake Stick style that was so popular during Victorian times. Built entirely from redwood, the house features original wainscoting and silk-screened wallcoverings. A swimming pool, vineyard and gazebo are favorite spots for guests to relax. The Hope-Bosworth House, on the same street, was built in the Queen Anne style by an early Geyserville pioneer who lived in the home until the 1960s. The front picket fence is covered with roses. Period details include oak woodwork, sliding doors, polished fir floors and antique light fixtures. Guests will enjoy innkeeper Rosalie Hope's prize-winning breads with their full breakfasts.

Breakfast included in rates. Types of meals: full breakfast, gourmet breakfast and early coffee/tea. Picnic lunch available. Ceiling fan in room. Fax and copier on premises. Weddings, small meetings and family reunions hosted. Spanish spoken. Antiques, parks, shopping and watersports nearby. TAC10.

Publicity: *San Diego Union, Country Homes, Sunset, Sacramento Union, Los Angeles Times.*

Special Discounts: Pick & Press wine event.

"Innkeepers extraordinaire" — Leisure and Outdoor Guide.

Gilroy J5

Country Rose Inn - B&B

PO Box 2500
Gilroy, CA 95021
(408)842-0441
Fax:(408)842-6646

Rates: $89-189.
Payment: MC VISA PC.
Innkeeper(s): Rose Hernandez.
Circa: 1920.

Rooms: 5 rooms with PB, 2 with FP. 1 suite. 2 conference rooms.
Beds: KQDT.

Amid five wooded acres, a half-hour's drive south of San Jose, sits the aptly named Country Rose Inn. A roomy Dutch Colonial manor, this inn was once a farmhouse on the Lucky Hereford Ranch. Every room features a rose theme, including wallpaper and quilted bedspreads. Each window offers a relaxing view of horses grazing, fertile fields, or the tranquil grounds, which boast magnificent 100-year-old oak trees.

Breakfast and afternoon tea included in rates. Types of meals: full breakfast and early coffee/tea. Picnic lunch available. Air conditioning and turn-down service in room. Fax and library on premises. Weddings, small meetings and seminars hosted. Spanish spoken. Antiques, parks, shopping and theater nearby. TAC10.

Location: Masten Avenue exit off Hwy 101 in San Martin, north of Gilroy.

"The quiet, serene country setting made our anniversary very special. Rose is a delightful, gracious hostess and cook."

Grass Valley

Murphy's Inn

318 Neal St.
Grass Valley, CA 95945
(916)273-6873 (800)895-2488
Fax:(916)272-1716

Rates: $76-140.
Payment: MC VISA AX TC PC.
Innkeeper(s): Ted & Nancy Daus
Circa: 1866.

Rooms: 8 rooms with PB. 3 suites.
Beds: KQT.

This Victorian was built by gold baron Edward Coleman for his new bride. Rooms are decorated in period style. Four of the antique-filled guest rooms have wood stoves, and several have skylights or four-poster beds. Century-old ivy decorates the home's exterior, as does a 140-year old giant sequoia.

Breakfast included in rates. Types of meals: full breakfast, gourmet breakfast and early coffee/tea. Air conditioning and cable TV in room. Fax and library on premises. Small meetings, family reunions hosted. Antiques, parks, fishing, skiing, shopping and watersports nearby.

Groveland H7

The Groveland Hotel

18767 Main St, PO Box 481
Groveland, CA 95321
(209)962-4000 (800)273-3314
Fax:(209)962-6674
E-mail: peggy@groveland.com

Rates: $95-175.
Payment: MC VISA AX DC CB DS PC TC.
Innkeeper(s): Peggy A. & Grover C. Mosley.
Circa: 1849.

Rooms: 17 rooms with PB, 3 with FP. 3 suites. 1 conference room.
Beds: QT.

CA

Located 23 miles from Yosemite National Park, the newly restored hotel features both an 1849 adobe building with 18-inch-thick walls constructed during the Gold Rush and a 1914 building erected to house workers for the Hetch Hetchy Dam. Both feature two-story balconies. There is a Victorian parlor, a gourmet restaurant and a Western saloon. Guest rooms feature European antiques and down comforters. The feeling is one of casual elegance.

Breakfast included in rates. Types of meals: continental-plus breakfast and early coffee/tea. Picnic lunch, banquet service, catering service and room service available. Air conditioning and ceiling fan in room. Cable TV, VCR, fax, copier, computer, library, pet boarding and child care on premises. Handicap access. Weddings, small meetings, family reunions and seminars hosted. Antiques, fishing, parks, shopping, downhill skiing, cross-country skiing and watersports nearby. TAC10.

Publicity: *Sonora Union Democrat, Peninsula, Sunset, Stockton Record, Country Inns.*

"Hospitality is outstanding."

Gualala G3

North Coast Country Inn

34591 S Hwy 1
Gualala, CA 95445
(707)884-4537 (800)959-4537

Rates: $135.
Payment: MC VISA AX PC TC.
Innkeeper(s): Loren & Nancy Flanagan.
Circa: 1951.

Rooms: 4 rooms with PB, 4 with FP.
Beds: Q.

Overlooking the Pacific Ocean, the four suites that comprise North Coast Country Inn are tucked into a pine and redwood covered hillside. Each is furnished with a four-poster bed and includes a wood-burning fireplace, wet-bar kitchenette and private ocean-view deck. There is a hot tub on the hillside or you may relax in the gazebo. A full breakfast is brought to your room so you can continue to enjoy your seclusion. Barking sea lions are often heard in the distance.

Breakfast included in rates. Type of meal: full breakfast. Spa and library on premises. Fishing, parks and shopping nearby. TAC10.

Location: On the Mendocino Coast.

Publicity: *Wine Trader, Motortrend, Los Angeles Times, San Francisco Chronicle.*

"Thank you so much for a very gracious stay in your cozy inn. We have appreciated all the special touches."

Guerneville G3

Ridenhour Ranch

12850 River Rd
Guerneville, CA 95446-9276
(707)887-1033
Fax:(707)869-2967

Rates: $95-130.
Payment: MC VISA AX PC TC.
Innkeeper(s): Fritz & Diane Rechberger.
Circa: 1906.

Rooms: 8 rooms with PB, 1 with FP. 1 suite. 1 conference room.
Beds: QD.

Located on a hill overlooking the Russian River, this ranch house is shaded by redwoods, oaks and laurels. There are seven guest rooms and a cottage overlooking the rose garden. The innkeepers are former restaurateurs from Southern California and provide a changing dinner menu for their guests. The Korbel Champagne cellars are nearby and it's a five-minute walk to the river.

Breakfast included in rates. Types of meals: full breakfast and early coffee/tea. Catering service available. Ceiling fan and cable TV in room. Fax and spa on premises. Handicap access. Weddings, small meetings, family reunions and seminars hosted. German spoken. Antiques, fishing, parks, shopping, theater and watersports nearby. TAC10.

Location: Thirty minutes from Santa Rosa and 75 minutes north of San Francisco.

Publicity: *Los Angeles Times, Orange County Register, Los Altos Town Crier.*

Special Discounts: 20% off midweek-winter.

"Your hospitality and food will ensure our return!"

Half Moon Bay 14

Old Thyme Inn

779 Main St
Half Moon Bay, CA 94019
(415)726-1616
Fax:(415)726-6394

Rates: $85-220.
Payment: MC VISA PC.
Innkeeper(s): George & Maria Dempsey.
Circa: 1899.

Rooms: 7 rooms with PB, 4 with FP. 1 suite. 1 conference room.
Beds: Q.

Located on the historic Main Street of Old Town, this Queen Anne Victorian has a flower and herb garden surrounding it. Seven rooms are named after various herbs that are found in the garden. Guests receive a complimentary book on herbs with each reservation. Most of the rooms have whirlpool baths and/or fireplaces. Resident teddy bears help keep guests in good company. The inn is within walking distance to beaches, restaurants, shops and art galleries.

Breakfast included in rates. Cable TV and VCR in room. Computer and spa on premises. Small meetings and family reunions hosted. Spanish & French spoken. Antiques, fishing, parks, shopping, sporting events, theater and watersports nearby.

Location: Five minutes from ocean.

Publicity: *California Weekends, Los Angeles, San Mateo Times, San Jose Mercury News, Herb Companion, San Francisco Examiner.*

Special Discounts: Call for special promotions.

"Furnishings, rooms and garden were absolutely wonderful. Delicious breakfast and great coffee .. loved the peaceful neighborhood."

Zaballa House

324 Main St
Half Moon Bay, CA 94019
(415)726-9123
Fax:(415)726-3921

Rates: $75-250.
Payment: MC VISA AX DS PC TC.
Innkeeper(s): Simon Lowings & Kerry Pendergast.
Circa: 1858.

Rooms: 12 rooms with PB, 6 with FP. 3 suites. 1 conference room.
Beds: Q.

The Zaballa House is the oldest building still standing in Half Moon Bay. The inn features an elegant reception room, a breakfast nook and a parlor with comfortable Victorian-style chairs. Guest rooms have such amenities as 10-foot ceilings, vaulted ceilings, fireplaces, clawfoot tubs and garden views. Some rooms have double size whirlpool tubs. They have private entrances and kitchenettes.

Breakfast and evening snack included in rates. Type of meal: full breakfast. Ceiling fan and cable TV in room. Fax and copier on premises. Small meetings, family reunions and seminars hosted. Antiques, fishing, parks, shopping, theater and watersports nearby. TAC10.

Pets Allowed: Must be clean, confined to bedroom during meals, $10 extra.

Publicity: *Half Moon Bay Review, San Francisco Examiner, Los Angeles Times.*

Special Discounts: May is nurse appreciation month, $79 for fireplace/jacuzzi room mid-week for nurses.

"The hospitality extended to us made us feel very welcome."

Camellia Inn

211 North St
Healdsburg, CA 95448
(707)433-8182 (800)727-8182
Fax:(707)433-8130
E-mail: info@cameliainn.com

Rates: $75-150.
Payment: MC VISA AX.
Innkeeper(s): Ray, Del and Lucy Lewand.
Circa: 1869.

Rooms: 9 rooms with PB, 4 with FP. 1 suite.
Beds: QD.

An elegant Italianate Victorian townhouse, the Camellia Inn has twin marble parlor fireplaces and an ornate mahogany dining room fireplace. Antiques fill the guest rooms, complementing Palladian windows and classic interior moldings. The award-winning grounds feature 30 varieties of camellias and are accentuated with a swimming pool which guests may use in summer.

Breakfast included in rates. Type of meal: full breakfast. Fax on premises. Antiques and fishing nearby.

Location: Heart of the Sonoma Wine Country, 50 wineries within 10 miles.

Publicity: *Sunset, Travel & Leisure, New York Times, San Fernando Valley Daily News, San Diego Union, Sacramento Bee, Healdsburg Tribune.*

"A bit of paradise for city folks."

Grape Leaf Inn

539 Johnson St
Healdsburg, CA 95448
(707)433-8140

Rates: $90-150.
Payment: MC VISA DS PC TC.
Innkeeper(s): Terry & Karen Sweet.
Circa: 1900.

Rooms: 7 rooms with PB.
Beds: KQ.

This magnificently restored Queen Anne home was built in what was considered the "Nob Hill" of Healdsburg. It was typical of a turn-of-the-century, middle-class dream house. It is situated near the Russian River and the town center. Seventeen skylights provide an abundance of sunlight, fresh air, and stained glass. Five guestrooms offer whirlpool tubs or showers for two. The innkeepers make the most of their wine country location, hosting a wine tasting each evening with a display of at least five Sonoma County wines. Each guest room is named for a wine variety, such as Zinfandel or Merlot. The inn is just four blocks from many of Healdsburg's restaurants and shops.

Breakfast included in rates. Type of meal: full breakfast. Air conditioning in room. Antiques, fishing, shopping and watersports nearby. TAC10.

"Reminds me of my grandma's house."

Haydon Street Inn

321 Haydon St
Healdsburg, CA 95448
(707)433-5228 (800)528-3703
Fax:(707)433-6637

Rates: $95-165.
Payment: MC VISA DS PC TC.
Innkeeper(s): Joanne Claus.
Circa: 1912.

Rooms: 8 rooms with PB, 1 with FP. 1 cottage. 1 conference room.
Beds: QD.

Architectural buffs will have fun naming the several architectural styles found in the Haydon House. It has the curving porch and general shape of a Queen Anne Victorian, the expansive areas of siding and unadorned columns of the Bungalow style, and the exposed roof rafters of the Craftsman. The decor is elegant and romantic, with antiques. The Turret Room includes a clawfoot tub and a fireplace. Two rooms are located in the inn's Victorian Cottage. Both have whrilpool tubs, the Pine Room offers a pencil post bed with a Battenburg lace canopy, while the Victorian Room includes fine antiques and Ralph Lauren wicker bed.

Breakfast, afternoon tea and evening snack included in rates. Types of meals: full breakfast, gourmet breakfast and early coffee/tea. Air conditioning and ceiling fan in room. Cable TV, VCR and fax on premises. Family reunions and seminars hosted. Antiques, fishing, parks, shopping and watersports nearby. TAC10.

Location: Western Sonoma County, heart of the wine country.

Publicity: *Los Angeles.*

Special Discounts: 10% off for corporate, senior guests; Midweek rates available December through June to all.

"Adjectives like class, warmth, beauty, thoughtfulness with the right amount of privacy, attention to details relating to comfort, all come to mind. Thank you for the care and elegance."

The Honor Mansion

14891 Grove St
Healdsburg, CA 95448
(707)433-4277 (800)554-4667
Fax:(707)431-7173

Rates: $120-160.
Payment: MC VISA DS.
Innkeeper(s): Cathi Fowler.
Circa: 1883.

Rooms: 5 rooms with PB, 1 with FP.
Beds: Q.

This Italianate manor was built by Dr. Herbert Honor and remained in his family for more than a century. The acre of grounds are pleasant with century-old trees, flowers, a koi pond and waterfall. The interior is decorated with antiques, many of which the innkeeper acquired at an auction. Fresh fruit topped with whipped cream sauce, a vegetable frittata and cranberry orange scones might be among the breakfast treats. Downtown Healdsburg is within walking distance.

Breakfast and afternoon tea included in rates. Types of meals: full breakfast, gourmet breakfast and early coffee/tea. Air conditioning, turn-down service and ceiling fan in room. Cable TV, swimming and sauna on premises. Antiques, fishing, parks, shopping, theater and watersports nearby. TAC10.

Pets Allowed: Yes.

Madrona Manor, A Country Inn

PO Box 818
Healdsburg, CA 95448
(707)433-4231 (800)258-4003
Fax:(707)433-0703

Rates: $140-240.
Payment: MC VISA AX DC CB DS PC TC.
Innkeeper(s): John & Carol Muir.
Circa: 1881.

Rooms: 21 rooms with PB, 17 with FP. 3 suites. 1 cottage. 2 conference rooms.
Beds: KQDT.

The inn is comprised of four historic structures in a national historic district. Surrounded by eight acres of manicured lawns and terraced flower and vegetable gardens, the stately mansion was built for John Paxton, a San Francisco businessman. Embellished with turrets, bay windows, porches, and a mansard roof, it provides a breathtaking view of surrounding vineyards. Elegant antique furnishings and a noteworthy restaurant add to the genuine country inn atmosphere. The Gothic-style Carriage House offers more casual lodging.

Breakfast included in rates. Type of meal: gourmet breakfast. Dinner and picnic lunch available. Air conditioning in room. Fax, copier, computer and swimming on premises. Handicap access. Weddings, small meetings, family reunions and seminars hosted. Antiques, fishing, parks, shopping, sporting events, theater and watersports nearby. TAC10.

Pets Allowed: In select buildings.

Location: In the heart of the wine country, Sonoma County.

Publicity: *Gourmet, Woman's Day Home Decorating Ideas, Travel & Leisure, US News, Diversions, Money, Good Housekeeping.*

Special Discounts: Sunday-Thursday, $140 rate on all rooms upgrades.

"Our fourth visit and better every time."

Raford House

10630 Wohler Rd
Healdsburg, CA 95448
(707)887-9573 (800)887-9503
Fax:(707)887-9597

Rates: $95-140.
Payment: MC VISA AX DS.
Innkeeper(s): Carole & Jack Vore.
Circa: 1880.

Rooms: 7 rooms with PB. 1 suite.
Beds: Q.

CA

Situated on more than four acres of rose gardens and fruit trees, this classic Victorian country estate originally was built as a summer home and ranch house in the 1880s. Just 70 miles north of San Francisco, Raford House is nestled in the heart of the Sonoma County wine country, minutes away from award-winning wineries and many fine restaurants. Located close to the Russian River, between Healdsburg and the beautiful Northern California coast, the area has scenic country roads and rugged coastlines.

Breakfast and evening snack included in rates. Types of meals: full breakfast and early coffee/tea. Fax on premises. Weddings, small meetings and family reunions hosted. Antiques, fishing, parks, shopping, theater and watersports nearby. TAC10.

Publicity: *Los Angeles Times, Travel & Leisure, Country.*

"Truly a 'serendipity' experience! Wonderful, welcoming ambiance, great food, lovely hosts. I am 'renewed'."

Hope Valley G8

Sorensen's Resort

14255 Hwy 88
Hope Valley, CA 96120
(916)694-2203 (800)423-9949

Rates: $65-350.
Payment: MC VISA AX DS PC TC.
Innkeeper(s): John & Patty Brissenden.
Circa: 1876.

Rooms: 30 rooms, 28 with PB, 21 with FP. 28 cottages. 2 conference rooms.
Beds: QD.

Where Danish sheepherders settled in this 7,000-foot-high mountain valley, the Sorensen family built a cluster of fishing cabins. Thus began a century-old tradition of valley hospitality. The focal point of Sorensen's is a "stave" cabin — a reproduction of a 13th-century Nordic house. Now developed as a Nordic ski resort, a portion of the Mormon-Emigrant Trail and Pony Express Route pass near the inn's 165 acres. In the summer, river rafting, fishing, pony express re-rides, and llama treks are popular Sierra pastimes. Lake Tahoe lies 20 miles to the north. Breakfast is included in the rates for bed & breakfast units only, all the cabins are equipped with kitchens.

Types of meals: continental-plus breakfast, full breakfast and early coffee/tea. Dinner, picnic lunch, lunch and banquet service available. Copier, sauna and library on premises. Handicap access. 165 acres. Weddings, small meetings, family reunions and seminars hosted. Spanish spoken. Antiques, fishing, parks, downhill skiing, cross-country skiing and watersports nearby. TAC10.

Publicity: *Sunset, San Francisco Chronicle, Los Angeles Times, Motorland, Outside.*

"In one nights stay, I felt more comfortable, relaxed, and welcome than any vacation my 47 years have allowed. Thank you for the happiness you have given my children."

Hopland F3

Thatcher Inn

13401 S Hwy 101
Hopland, CA 95449
(707)744-1890 (800)266-1891
Fax:(707)744-1219

Rates: $100-155.
Payment: MC VISA AX PC TC.
Innkeeper(s): Carmen Gleason.
Circa: 1890.

Rooms: 20 rooms with PB. 2 suites. 1 conference room.
Beds: KQT.

Elegant Victorian furnishings fill the rooms at this late Victorian manor. The Fireside Library with its rich, wood bookshelves, marble fireplace and highback chairs is an inviting place to enjoy a good book. Each of the guest rooms is individually decorated with antiques and reproductions. A full, country breakfast is served each morning, and the inn offers dinner service in the well-appointed dining room. The dinner fare ranges from traditional items such as filet mignon to special pasta and seafood dishes. The Lobby Bar, where guests can enjoy an evening cocktail, is stocked with a vast collection of various single malt whiskies. The innkeepers offer a romantic, weekday getaway package, and can help guests plan visits to local wineries or the Hopland brewery.

Breakfast included in rates. Types of meals: full breakfast, gourmet breakfast and early coffee/tea. Dinner, lunch, gourmet lunch and banquet service available. Air conditioning and ceiling fan in room. Cable TV, VCR, fax, copier, swimming and library on premises. Small meetings, family reunions and seminars hosted. Antiques, fishing, parks and watersports nearby. TAC10.

Special Discounts: Group rates of ten rooms or more.

"We appreciate your attention to details and efforts which made our visit so pleasant."

Idyllwild O12

The Pine Cove Inn

23481 Hwy 243,
PO Box 2181
Idyllwild, CA 92549
(909)659-5033 (888)659-5033
Fax:(909)659-5034

Rates: $70-100.
Payment: MC VISA AX PC TC.
Innkeeper(s): Bob & Michelle Bollmann.
Circa: 1935.

Rooms: 10 rooms, 9 with PB, 6 with FP. 3 suites. 1 conference room.
Beds: QT.

These rustic, A-frame cottages offer a variety of amenities in a natural, mountain setting. Refrigerators and microwaves have been placed in each unit, several of which include a wood-burning fireplace. A full breakfast is served in a separate lodge which dates back to 1935. The village of Idyllwild is three miles down the road, and the surrounding country offers a variety of activities.

Breakfast included in rates. Type of meal: full breakfast. Ceiling fan in room. Cable TV, VCR and fax on premises. Weddings, small meetings, family reunions and seminars hosted. Antiques, fishing, parks, shopping, cross-country skiing and theater nearby. TAC10.

Special Discounts: Midweek discounts, Sunday-Thursday, units $55-$85 per night, no minimum stay.

Strawberry Creek Inn

PO Box 1818
Idyllwild, CA 92549-1818
(909)659-3202 (800)262-8969
Fax:(909)659-4707

Rates: $70-135.
Payment: MC VISA DS PC TC.
Innkeeper(s): Jim Goff & Diana Dugan.
Circa: 1941.

Rooms: 9 rooms with PB, 6 with FP. 1 cottage.
Beds: KQ.

Each of the rooms at this country inn is individually decorated with its own theme. Six of the guest rooms include fireplaces. Skylights, window seats and mini refrigerators are a few of the other items guest might find in their room. The innkeepers also offer a private cottage with a whirlpool tub, river rock fireplace, fully-equipped kitchen, a bedroom, living area and two bathrooms. The full breakfasts are served in the glassed-in porch where guests can enjoy Idyllwild's scenery. The one-acre grounds include outdoor decks and hammocks.

Breakfast included in rates. Type of meal: gourmet breakfast. VCR in room. Fax, copier and library on premises. Handicap access. Small meetings hosted. Antiques, fishing, parks, shopping and cross-country skiing nearby.

Wilkum Inn B&B

26770 Hwy 243
PO Box 1115
Idyllwild, CA 92549-1115
(909)659-4087 (800)659-4086

Rates: $75-100.
Payment: PC TC.
Innkeeper(s): Barbara Jones & Annamae Chambers.
Circa: 1938.

Rooms: 6 rooms, 4 with PB, 2 with FP. 1 cottage.
Beds: KQDT.

CA

Situated among tall pines and oaks, this mountain village inn provides European-style hospitality. The Eaves is a two-room suite with queen bed, open-beam ceiling and a view of the pines. Nearby, the Idyllwild School of Music and the Arts hosts presentations and exhibitions year-round.

Breakfast and evening snack included in rates. Types of meals: continental-plus breakfast, gourmet breakfast and early coffee/tea. Handicap access. Antiques, parks, shopping and theater nearby. TAC10.

Location: Three-fourths of a mile south of village center.

Publicity: *Los Angeles Times, Westways, Odyssey, Los Angeles Magazine.*

Special Discounts: Less $10 for stays of 2 or more nights, Less $5 for single.

"Your inn really defines the concept of country coziness and hospitality."

Independence J10

Winnedumah Inn

PO Box 147
Independence, CA 93526
(619)878-2040

Rates: $40-59.
Payment: MC VISA.
Innkeeper(s): Marvey Chapman.
Circa: 1927.

Rooms: 22 rooms, 18 with PB.
Beds: QDT.

This old hotel was built in a Spanish Colonial style with arches, stucco and a front portico. Its location is at the foot of the Eastern Sierra in Owens Valley. Independence offers a trout-filled steam, majestic scenery and nearby hiking and fishing. The inn's restaurant will provide box lunches for these excursions.

Breakfast included in rates. Types of meals: continental-plus breakfast and early coffee/tea. Banquet service and catering service available. Air conditioning in room. Cable TV, VCR, fax, copier, bicycles and library on premises. Handicap access. Weddings, small meetings, family reunions and seminars hosted. Spanish spoken. Fishing, downhill skiing, cross-country skiing and watersports nearby. TAC10.

Special Discounts: 10% for groups with 10 rooms or more.

Inverness H4

Golden Hinde Inn & Marina

12938 Sir Francis Drake,
PO Box 295
Inverness, CA 94937
(415)669-1389 (800)339-9398
Fax:(415)669-1128

Rates: $60-125.
Payment: MC VISA AX TC.
Innkeeper(s): Jeanne & Craig Schuller.
Circa: 1962.

Rooms: 35 rooms with PB, 18 with FP. 2 suites.
Beds: QD.

Many of the guest rooms at Golden Hinde offer views of Tomales Bay, and 18 also have a fireplace. Midweek guests enjoy continental breakfast service, and there is a restaurant on the premises. Fresh seafood and oysters are a specialty. The inn is located on the Point Reyes National Seashore, and plenty of outdoor activities are nearby.

Breakfast included in rates. Types of meals: continental breakfast and early coffee/tea. Cable TV in room. Fax, copier, swimming and library on premises. Handicap access. Small meetings hosted. Limited Spanish spoken. Antiques, fishing, shopping and watersports nearby. TAC10.

Special Discounts: Winter first night full price, second night one half price.

Laurel Ridge

217 Laurel St, PO Box 38
Inverness, CA 94937
(415)663-1286 (800)853-2074
Fax:(415)663-9418

Rates: $125-150.
Payment: PC TC.
Innkeeper(s): Rita & Bill Landis.
Circa: 1992.

Rooms: 1 cottage.
Beds: QT.

This cottage is surrounded by two acres of forest adjacent to Point Reyes National Seashore. Although the cottage generally is rented to one couple at a time, it can accommodate two couples or a small family. There is a wood stove and a deck with comfortable chairs. The owners provide wild bird seed. Baked goods, croissants, juices, cereals, eggs, coffee and tea are provided so guests can make their own breakfast. The cottage has no telephone, but the innkeepers do have a main office where messages and faxes can be received.

Breakfast included in rates. Types of meals: continental-plus breakfast and early coffee/tea. Cable TV in room. Fax, copier, library and child care on premises. Antiques, fishing, parks and shopping nearby.

Location: Bordering the Point Reyes National Seashore.

Special Discounts: Sunday-Thursday, $115-125 (call); Vacations negotiable.

Rosemary Cottage

PO Box 273
Inverness, CA 94937-0273
(415)663-9338 (800)808-9338

Rates: $150-170.
Payment: PC TC.
Innkeeper(s): Suzanne Storch.
Circa: 1986.

Rooms: 3 cottages with PB, 3 with FP.
Beds: QT.

From the windows in this secluded cottage, guests can enjoy views of a wooded canyon and hillside in the Point Reyes National Seashore park. The cottage is a cozy, self-contained unit with a well-equipped kitchen, bedroom, library and a living room with a wood-burning stove. The decor is French country, highlighting the wood beams, red oak floors and terra cotta tiles. There is a hot tub in the garden.

Breakfast included in rates. Type of meal: full breakfast. Spa on premises. Small meetings hosted. Antiques, fishing, parks, shopping and watersports nearby. TAC10.

Pets Allowed: Yes.

Special Discounts: November-May, Sunday-Thursday, 20% discount or stay three nights, pay for two.

Ten Inverness Way

10 Inverness Way,
PO Box 63
Inverness, CA 94937
(415)669-1648
Fax:(415)669-7403
E-mail: tiw@nbn.com

Rates: $110-160.
Payment: MC VISA PC TC.
Innkeeper(s): Mary Davies & Barbara Searles.
Circa: 1904.

Rooms: 5 rooms with PB.
Beds: Q.

Shingled in redwood, this handsome bed & breakfast features a stone fireplace, good books, a guitar, piano and access to a wonderful hiking area. The view from the breakfast room invites you to include a nature walk in your day's plans. The innkeepers provide inside information on hiking and biking the 100 square miles of wilderness and nearby beaches at Point Reyes National Seashore. A hot tub is offered for weary travelers.

Breakfast and afternoon tea included in rates. Types of meals: full breakfast and early coffee/tea. Evening snack available. Fax, spa and library on premises. Some French. spoken. Antiques, fishing, parks and watersports nearby.

Location: Near Point Reyes National Seashore.

Publicity: *Los Angeles Times, New York Times, Travel & Leisure, Sunset, Gourmet.*

Special Discounts: "Early Birders Special" November-March, Sunday - Thursday, excluding holidays.

Ione

G6

The Heirloom

214 Shakeley Ln,
PO Box 322
Ione, CA 95640-9572
(209)274-4468

Rates: $60-92.
Payment: MC VISA AX PC TC.
Innkeeper(s): Melisande Hubbs & Patricia Cross.
Circa: 1863.

Rooms: 6 rooms, 4 with PB, 3 with FP. 2 cottages.
Beds: KQDT.

A two-story Colonial with columns, balconies and a private English garden, the antebellum Heirloom is true to its name. It has many family heirlooms and a square grand piano once owned by Lola Montez. The building was dedicated by the Native Sons of the Golden West as a historic site.

Breakfast and afternoon tea included in rates. Types of meals: full breakfast, gourmet breakfast and early coffee/tea. Room service available. Air conditioning in room. Library on premises. Weddings, small meetings, family reunions and seminars hosted. Antiques, fishing, parks, shopping, theater and watersports nearby. TAC10.

Location: California Gold Country - halfway between Yosemite and Lake Tahoe.

Publicity: *San Francisco Chronicle, Country Living.*

"Hospitality was amazing. Truly we've never had such a great time."

Jackson

G6

Gate House Inn

1330 Jackson Gate Rd
Jackson, CA 95642-9539
(209)223-3500 (800)841-1072
Fax:(209)223-1299
E-mail: info@gatehouseinn.com

Rates: $81-135.
Payment: MC VISA AX DS PC TC.
Innkeeper(s): Keith & Gail Sweet.
Circa: 1902.

Rooms: 5 rooms with PB, 3 with FP. 1 suite. 1 cottage.
Beds: Q.

This striking Victorian inn is listed in the National Register of Historic Places. Set on a hillside amid lovely gardens, the inn is within walking distance of a state historic park and several notable eateries. The inn's country setting, comfortable porches and swimming pool offer many opportunities for relaxation. Accommodations include three rooms, a suite and a romantic cottage with wood stove and whirlpool tub. All of the guest rooms feature queen beds and elegant furnishings. Nearby are several lakes, wineries and golf courses.

Breakfast included in rates. Types of meals: full breakfast and early coffee/tea. Afternoon tea available. Air conditioning and ceiling fan in room. Fax, copier and swimming on premises. Weddings, small meetings and family reunions hosted. Antiques, fishing, parks, shopping, downhill skiing, cross-country skiing, theater and watersports nearby. TAC10.

"Most gracious, warm hospitality."

Wedgewood Inn

11941 Narcissus Rd
Jackson, CA 95642-9600
(209)296-4300 (800)933-4393
Fax:(209)296-4301
E-mail: wedgewd@cdepot.net

Rates: $90-155.
Payment: MC VISA AX DS PC TC.
Innkeeper(s): Vic & Jeannine Beltz.
Circa: 1987.

Rooms: 6 rooms with PB, 4 with FP. 1 suite. 1 cottage.
Beds: Q.

Located in the heart of Sierra gold country on a secluded, five acres, this charming Victorian replica is crammed full of sentimental family heirlooms and antiques. Each room has been designed with careful attention to detail. A baby grand piano rests in the parlor. The carriage house is a separate cottage with its own private entrance. It boasts four generations of family heirlooms, a carved canopy bed, a wood-burning stove and a two-person Jacuzzi tub. The innkeepers' 1921 Model-T "Henry," is located in its own special showroom. Gourmet breakfasts are served on bone china and include specialties such as cheese-filled blintzes, fruit and baked goods. Breakfast is available in selected guest rooms by request.

Breakfast and evening snack included in rates. Types of meals: gourmet breakfast and early coffee/tea. Air conditioning and turn-down service in room. Fax and copier on premises. Antiques, fishing, parks, shopping, downhill skiing, cross-country skiing, theater and watersports nearby. TAC10.

Special Discounts: Midweek two-for-one dinner certificates.

Jamestown H7

The Historic National Hotel B&B

77 Main St, PO Box 502
Jamestown, CA 95327
(209)984-3446 (800)894-3446
Fax:(209)984-5620

Rates: $80.
Payment: MC VISA AX DC CB DS PC TC.
Innkeeper(s): Pamela & Stephen Willey.
Circa: 1859.

Rooms: 11 rooms, 5 with PB. 1 conference room.
Beds: QT.

One of the 10 oldest continuously operating hotels in California, the inn maintains its original redwood bar where thousands of dollars in gold dust were spent. Electricity and plumbing were added for the first time when the inn was restored a few years ago. It is decorated with Gold Rush period antiques, brass beds and handmade quilts. The restaurant is considered to be one of the finest in the Mother Lode.

Breakfast included in rates. Types of meals: continental-plus breakfast and early coffee/tea. Dinner, evening snack, picnic lunch, lunch, gourmet lunch, banquet service and catering service available. Air conditioning and cable TV in room. VCR and fax on premises. Weddings, small meetings, family reunions and seminars hosted. Spanish spoken. Antiques, fishing, parks, downhill skiing, cross-country skiing, theater and watersports nearby. TAC10.

Pets Allowed: By arrangement - credit card or cash deposit required.

Location: Center of town.

Publicity: *Bon Appetit, California Magazine, Focus, San Francisco Magazine, Gourmet.*

"Excellent, wonderful place!"

The Palm Hotel B&B

10382 Willow St
Jamestown, CA 95327-9761
(209)984-3429
Fax:(209)984-4929
E-mail: palmbb@sonnet.com

Rates: $65-135.
Payment: MC VISA AX TC.
Innkeeper(s): Rick & Sandy Allen.
Circa: 1890.

Rooms: 9 rooms, 5 with PB. 2 suites.
Beds: KQD.

Enjoy Gold Country at this Victorian, which was home to Albert and Amelia Hoyt, publishers of the Mother Lode Magnet. In the 1890s, the home served as a boarding house. Today, it offers nine guest rooms with lacy curtains, fresh flowers, clawfoot tubs, bubble baths and robes. The innkeepers also have a soda fountain bar in the parlor. A full, buffet breakfast is served each morning along with The Palm's special blend of coffee. The inn is located two-and-a-half hours from San Francisco and about an hour from Yosemite Valley, and is within walking distance of Main Street, boutiques, galleries, restaurants and Railtown State Park.

Breakfast included in rates. Type of meal: full breakfast. Air conditioning, ceiling fan and cable TV in room. Fax and copier on premises. Handicap access. Small meetings and family reunions hosted. Antiques, fishing, parks, shopping, downhill skiing, cross-country skiing, theater and watersports nearby. TAC10.

"The simple elegance of our room and ambiance of the Palm in general was a balm for our souls."

Royal Hotel

PO Box 219, 18239 Main St
Jamestown, CA 95327-9748
(209)984-5271
Fax:(209)984-1675

Rates: $45-85.
Payment: MC VISA AX TC.
Innkeeper(s): Robert & Nancy Bosich.
Circa: 1922.

Rooms: 21 rooms, 19 with PB. 4 suites. 3 cottages. 1 conference room.
Beds: QT.

Guests can experience a bit of the old west at the Royal Hotel, which was built in the early '20s to provide luxurious lodging for travelers. The hotel originally had a ballroom and restaurant, and for those who preferred to ignore prohibition, there was a secret "back bar." Rooms are decorated in Victorian style with turn-of-the-century antiques. In addition to the guest rooms, there are two suites and a honeymoon cottage. There is a coffee-house on the premises as well as plenty of old movies and train memorabilia to enjoy. Jamestown is California's second oldest gold mining town and has been the site of more than 150 movies and television shows. Jamestown offers shops, antique stores, restaurants and gold mining attractions. The innkeepers can arrange for steam train rides.

Breakfast included in rates. Types of meals: continental-plus breakfast and early coffee/tea. Air conditioning and ceiling fan in room. Cable TV, fax, copier and library on premises. Handicap access. Small meetings and seminars hosted. Antiques, fishing, parks, shopping, downhill skiing, theater and watersports nearby. TAC10.

Julian **P12**

Julian Gold Rush Hotel

2032 Main St, PO Box 1856
Julian, CA 92036
(619)765-0201

Rates: $72-160.
Payment: MC VISA AX PC TC.
Innkeeper(s): Steve & Gig Ballinger.
Circa: 1897.

Rooms: 14 rooms with PB, 1 with FP. 1 suite. 2 cottages. 1 conference room.
Beds: QDT.

The dream of a former slave and his wife lives today in this sole surviving hotel in Southern California's "Mother Lode of Gold Mining." This Victorian charmer is listed in the National Register of Historic Places and is a designated State of California Point of Historic Interest (#SDI-09). Guests enjoy the feeling of a visit to Grandma's and a tradition of genteel hospitality.

Breakfast and afternoon tea included in rates. Type of meal: full breakfast. Weddings, small meetings and seminars hosted. Antiques, fishing, parks and theater nearby. TAC10.

Location: Center of town.

Publicity: *San Diego Union, PSA.*

Special Discounts: 15% discount for Seniors and Corporate.

"Any thoughts you have about the 20th century will leave you when you walk into the lobby of this grand hotel," Westways Magazine.

Julian White House

3014 Blue Jay Dr,
PO Box 824
Julian, CA 92036-9208
(619)765-1764 (800)948-4687

Rates: $90-135.
Payment: MC VISA PC TC.
Innkeeper(s): Mary & Alan Marvin.
Circa: 1979.

Rooms: 4 rooms with PB. 1 suite.
Beds: Q.

Towering white pillars greet this inn's guests, who may feel they have traveled back in time to a Southern plantation. The attractive Colonial-style inn offers four luxurious guest rooms, including the Honeymoon Suite. The French Quarter Room features a New Orleans theme and Mardi Gras memorabilia, and the popular East Room boasts a goose down mattress and Laura Ashley linens on a queen-size Victorian-style brass bed. Guests often enjoy an evening at the Pine Hills Dinner Theatre, an easy walk from the inn.

Breakfast and evening snack included in rates. Types of meals: full breakfast and early coffee/tea. Air conditioning and ceiling fan in room. Library on premises. Weddings and family reunions hosted. Antiques, fishing, parks, cross-country skiing, theater and watersports nearby. TAC10.

Publicity: *San Diego Home/Garden, San Diego Union Tribune, HGTV, Elmer Dills KABC-TV, KABC Talk radio.*

Orchard Hill Country Inn

2502 Washington St,
PO Box 425
Julian, CA 92036-0425
(619)765-1700
(800)71-ORCHARD
Fax:(619)765-0290

Rates: $140-195.
Payment: MC VISA AX PC TC.
Innkeeper(s): Darrell & Pat Straube.
Circa: 1994.

Rooms: 22 rooms with PB, 11 with FP. 2 conference rooms.
Beds: KQ.

This charming Craftsman-style inn is a perfect country getaway for those seeking solace from the city lights. Expansive, individually appointed guest suites offer amenities such as fireplaces, whirlpool tubs, hand-knitted afghans and down comforters all surrounded by warm, country decor. Gourmet coffee, tea and cocoas also are provided in each suite, as are wet bars. The innkeepers also offer more than 100 games to help pass the time. Guests can enjoy a breakfast of fruits, muffins and a special egg dish in the dining room. Wine and hors d'oeuvres are provided each afternoon. The expansive grounds boast a variety of gardens highlighting native plants and flowers.

Breakfast and evening snack included in rates. Types of meals: full breakfast and early coffee/tea. Dinner, picnic lunch, lunch, gourmet lunch, banquet service and catering service available. Air conditioning, ceiling fan, cable TV and VCR in room. Fax and copier on premises. Handicap access. Small meetings and seminars hosted. Antiques, fishing, parks, shopping and theater nearby. TAC10.

Publicity: *San Diego Union Tribune, Los Angeles Times, Orange County Register, Orange Coast, San Francisco Chronicle, San Bernadino Sun, Oceanside Blade-Citizen.*

Special Discounts: Call for mid-week special.

"The quality of the rooms, service and food were beyond our expectations."

Random Oaks Ranch

3742 Pine Hills Rd,
PO Box 454
Julian, CA 92036
(619)765-1094 (800)262-4344

Rates: $120-160.
Payment: MC VISA.
Innkeeper(s): Shari Foust-Helsel.
Circa: 1987.

Rooms: 2 cottages with PB.
Beds: Q.

Guests at this inn, which doubles as a thoroughbred horse ranch, choose from two elegant cottages. The English Squire Cottage features a marble fireplace, Queen Anne furniture and a half-canopy queen bed. The Victorian Garden Cottage offers a custom-manteled fireplace, Victorian cherry bed and sliding French doors. Both cottages sport private decks with spas, wet bars, microwave ovens and small refrigerators. Breakfast is served in the privacy of the cottages. The charming town of Julian is just two miles from the inn.

Breakfast included in rates. Types of meals: continental breakfast and full breakfast. Antiques, shopping and theater nearby.

Kernville *L10*

Kern River Inn B&B

119 Kern River Dr
Kernville, CA 93238
(619)376-6750 (800)986-4382
Fax:(619)376-6643

Rates: $79-99.
Payment: MC VISA AX PC TC.
Innkeeper(s): Jack & Carita Prestwich.
Circa: 1991.

Rooms: 6 rooms with PB, 3 with FP.
Beds: KQ.

Located across from Riverside Park and the Kern River, this country-style inn boasts a wraparound porch with views and sounds of the river. The Whiskey Flat, Whitewater and Piute rooms include fireplaces. The

Big Blue and Greenhorn rooms offer whirlpool tubs. All rooms afford river views. Breakfasts includes the inn's renowned giant home-baked cinnamon rolls, egg and cheese dishes or sweetheart waffles.

Breakfast and afternoon tea included in rates. Types of meals: full breakfast and early coffee/tea. Air conditioning and ceiling fan in room. Cable TV, VCR, fax, copier and library on premises. Weddings, small meetings and family reunions hosted. Fishing, downhill skiing, cross-country skiing and watersports nearby. TAC10.

Location: In the southern Sierra Nevada Mountains.

Publicity: *Kern Valley Sun, Los Angeles Times, Valley News, Westways*

Special Discounts: AAA, $10 off.

"For us, your place is the greatest. So romantic."

CA

Laguna Beach

P11

Carriage House

1322 Catalina
Laguna Beach, CA 92651
(714)494-8945

Rates: $95-150.
Payment: PC TC.
Innkeeper(s): Dee & Thom Taylor.
Circa: 1920.

Rooms: 6 suites.
Beds: KQDT.

A Laguna Beach historical landmark, this inn has a Cape Cod clapboard exterior. It housed an art gallery and a bakery before it was converted into apartments with large rooms and kitchens. Now as a cozy inn, each room has a private parlor. Outside, the courtyard fountain is shaded by a large carrotwood tree with hanging moss.

Breakfast and evening snack included in rates. Type of meal: continental-plus breakfast. Cable TV in room. Antiques, fishing, parks, shopping, theater and watersports nearby. TAC10.

Pets Allowed: Housebroken & quiet.

Location: Two & one-half blocks from the ocean.

Publicity: *Glamour, Los Angeles Times, Orange County Register, Sunset.*

"A true home away from home with all the extra touches added in. Reminds me of New Orleans."

Lake Arrowhead

N11

Prophet's Paradise

PO Box 2116
Lake Arrowhead, CA 92352
(909)336-1969 (800)987-2231

Rates: $90-160.
Payment: MC VISA DS PC.
Innkeeper(s): LaVerne & Tom Prophet Jr.
Circa: 1992.

Rooms: 4 rooms with PB, 2 with FP. 2 suites.
Beds: QD.

Lake Arrowhead, a popular getaway spot for Southern Californians, is the site of this Mountain Tudor home. Stained and leaded glass, antiques and comfortable furnishings create a warm environment. The Wintergreen Suite offers both a queen-size feather bed and a day bed, a fireplace and a Jacuzzi. Two other rooms also include feather beds. Breakfasts are served in the dining area or on the deck when weather permits. Special frittatas, fresh fruit and homemade muffins are selections from the morning fare. Hors d'oeuvres and beverages are a special treat for Saturday-night guests.

Breakfast and evening snack included in rates. Types of meals: gourmet breakfast and early coffee/tea. Room service available. Cable TV, VCR and bicycles on premises. Weddings hosted. Amusement parks, antiques, fishing, parks, shopping, downhill skiing, cross-country skiing and watersports nearby. TAC10.

Pets Allowed: Yes.

"Paradise doesn't quite say all that is here."

Lakeport **F4**

Forbestown B&B Inn

825 N Forbes St
Lakeport, CA 95453
(707)263-7858
Fax:(707)263-7878

Rates: $65-150.
Payment: MC VISA AX PC TC.
Innkeeper(s): Jack & Nancy Dunne.
Circa: 1863.

Rooms: 4 rooms, 1 with PB. 1 cottage.
Beds: KQ.

Located in the downtown area, this early California farmhouse is two blocks from the lake. Wisteria drape the front porch, overlooking the inn's yard. The dining room, where gourmet breakfasts are served, has a wall of French windows looking out to the back garden with a tall redwood tree and handsome flagstone swimming pool. Clear Lake is fed by rain and underground sulfur and soda springs. The area has been acknowledged as having the cleanest air in California.

Breakfast, afternoon tea and evening snack included in rates. Types of meals: full breakfast, gourmet breakfast and early coffee/tea. Catered breakfast available. Turn-down service and ceiling fan in room. Cable TV, VCR, fax, copier, spa, swimming and library on premises. Weddings, small meetings, family reunions and seminars hosted. Antiques, fishing, parks, shopping and watersports nearby. TAC10.

Little River **F2**

The Victorian Farmhouse

7001 N Hwy 1
Little River, CA 95456
(707)937-0697 (800)264-4723

Rates: $65-160.
Payment: MC VISA AX.
Innkeeper(s): Carole Molnar.
Circa: 1877.

Rooms: 11 rooms with PB.
Beds: KQT.

Built as a private residence, this Victorian farmhouse is located on two-and-a-half acres in Little River. Two miles south of the historic village of Mendocino, the inn offers a relaxed country setting with deer, quail, flower gardens, an apple orchard and a running creek (School House Creek). A short walk will take you to the shoreline.

Breakfast and afternoon tea included in rates. Type of meal: full breakfast. Small meetings hosted. Amusement parks, antiques, fishing, parks, shopping, theater and watersports nearby. TAC10.

Pets Allowed: Yes.

"This morning when we woke up at home we really missed having George deliver breakfast. You have a lovely inn and you do a super job."

Lodi **H6**

Wine & Roses Country Inn

2505 W Turner Rd
Lodi, CA 95242-4643
(209)334-6988
Fax:(209)334-6570

Rates: $99-145.
Payment: MC VISA AX CB DS.
Innkeeper(s): Del & Sherri Smith.
Circa: 1902.

Rooms: 10 rooms with PB. 4 suites. 1 conference room.
Beds: Q.

A 75-foot-long hedge of old-fashioned, pink Princess roses border the entrance to this cottage-style inn. The romantically landscaped six acres include white latticed arches, manicured lawns and wide borders of impatiens. Rooms are furnished with antiques, and the restaurant offers excellent dining in a garden setting. Although the inn enjoys popularity with honeymooners and business people, its location five miles off I-5 makes it an ideal midway stop between Los Angeles and San Francisco.

Breakfast included in rates. Types of meals: full breakfast, gourmet breakfast and early coffee/tea. Evening snack, picnic lunch, banquet service, catering service, catered breakfast and room service available. Air conditioning and ceiling fan in room. Fax, copier and child care on premises. Handicap access. Weddings, small meetings, family reunions and seminars hosted. Antiques, fishing, shopping, sporting events, theater and watersports nearby.

Publicity: *Los Angeles, Business Tribune, Country Inns.*

"Hospitality here exceeds Southern hospitality. I feel as if I am somewhere in time."

Long Beach — O10

Kennebec Corner Inn

2305 E 2nd St
Long Beach, CA 90803
(310)439-2705
Fax:(310)518-0616

Rates: $95-140.
Payment: PC TC.
Innkeeper(s): Michael & Marty Gunhus.
Circa: 1923.

Rooms: 1 suite.
Beds: K.

This California Craftsman-style home offers a large four-room suite with a sitting room, office, fireplace, bathroom with a double sunken tub and a bedroom with a king-size bed. There is an outdoor spa available in the home's courtyard. The innkeepers deliver the morning paper and a tray with coffee or tea to your door an hour prior to breakfast. On weekdays, a healthy California or continental breakfast is served, and on weekends, guests enjoy a full, gourmet meal. The home is located in Bluff Park, a city historic district.

Breakfast included in rates. Types of meals: continental-plus breakfast, gourmet breakfast and early coffee/tea. Picnic lunch available. Cable TV, VCR, fax, spa, bicycles and library on premises. Antiques, fishing, parks, shopping, sporting events, theater and watersports nearby. TAC20.

Los Alamos — N7

Union Hotel & Victorian Mansion

PO Box 616
Los Alamos, CA 93440
(805)344-2744 (800)230-2744
Fax:(805)344-3125
E-mail: unionhtl@silcom.com

Rates: $60-242. AP.
Payment: MC VISA AX DS TC.
Innkeeper(s): Bill & Vivian Bubbel.
Circa: 1880.

Rooms: 20 rooms, 9 with PB, 7 with FP. 1 conference room.
Beds: KQDT.

The casual Western facade of the Union Hotel is in sharp contrast with its intensely decorated interiors. Richly upholstered and carved furnishings, Egyptian burial urns and an enormous Tiffany grandfather clock furnish the parlor. Fantasy guest rooms in the Victorian mansion include the Egyptian room, entered through a one-ton stone door. An enormous pillared bed is draped in white, and there is a private soaking tub, fireplace and King Tut statue.

Breakfast included in rates. Types of meals: full breakfast and early coffee/tea. Dinner, evening snack, picnic lunch, banquet service, catering service and room service available. AP. Air conditioning, cable TV and VCR in room. Fax, copier, spa, swimming, library and child care on premises. Weddings, small meetings, family reunions and seminars hosted. German and Spanish spoken. Antiques, fishing, parks, shopping, sporting events, theater and watersports nearby. TAC10.

Location: Santa Barbara County.

Publicity: *Los Angeles Times, The Good Life, Pacific Coast.*

"The entire weekend was a fairy tale turned into a reality by you and the rest of your staff."

Los Olivos N7

Los Olivos Grand Hotel

2860 Grand Ave
Los Olivos, CA 93441
(805)688-7788 (800)446-2455
Fax:(805)688-1942

Rates: $160-325.
Payment: MC VISA AX.
Innkeeper(s): Ken Mortensen.
Circa: 1985.

Rooms: 21 rooms with PB, 21 with FP. 1 suite. 3 conference rooms.
Beds: KQ.

This four-star, four-diamond inn is ideally located in the Santa Ynez Valley, with its picturesque vineyards and rolling hills. Each guest room is decorated with the artwork of a different western or classic impressionist artist. There are fireplaces in all rooms, and many rooms also offer Jacuzzi tubs. Down comforters, room service, laundry service and in-room mini refrigerators are among the many amenities, and the hotel offers plenty of items to help business travelers. A full breakfast and afternoon tea are served daily, and on the weekends, brunch is served. The hotel's Remington Restaurant features an extensive dinner menu. Cocktails are available at Le Saloon, located in the lounge. There is a heated swimming pool and Jacuzzi on the premises, and guests enjoy complimentary use of bicycles for touring the countryside. Los Olivos is one of the Four Sisters Inns.

Breakfast and afternoon tea included in rates. Types of meals: full breakfast and gourmet breakfast. Picnic lunch, lunch and room service available. Air conditioning and turn-down service in room. Fax, copier, spa, swimming and bicycles on premises. Weddings, small meetings, family reunions and seminars hosted. Antiques, fishing, parks, shopping and watersports nearby. TAC10.

Special Discounts: Grand Getaway - $199 includes dinner for two and a king fireplace suite.

Malibu O9

Malibu Country Inn

6506 Westward Beach Rd
Malibu, CA 90265-4147
(310)457-9622 (800)386-6787
Fax:(310)457-1349

Rates: $95-155.
Payment: MC VISA AX DC CB DS TC.
Innkeeper(s): Mohsen Abrahim.
Circa: 1943.

Rooms: 16 rooms with PB, 1 with FP. 5 suites.
Beds: KQD.

This Cape Cod-style home is located near the famed beaches of Malibu. The location—beneath a blufftop on the ocean side of Pacific Coast Highway—of this former motel has contributed to its on-going transformation into a bed & breakfast inn. Guest rooms are airy with a mixture of country furnishings and floral prints, and several offer garden views. Rooms are full of amenities, such as refrigerators, coffee makers and a basket with snacks. The daily continental fare is served in the poolside breakfast room.

Breakfast included in rates. Types of meals: continental breakfast and full breakfast. Lunch, banquet service, catering service and room service available. Ceiling fan, cable TV and VCR in room. Fax, swimming and child care on premises. Weddings, small meetings and family reunions hosted. Spanish spoken. Fishing, parks, shopping, sporting events and watersports nearby. TAC10.

"We make the Malibu Country Inn part of our vacation plan every year."

Mariposa I8

Finch Haven

4605 Triangle Rd
Mariposa, CA 95338-9649
(209)966-4738
Fax:(209)966-4738

Rates: $75.
Payment: PC TC.
Innkeeper(s): Bruce & Carol Fincham.
Circa: 1980.

Rooms: 2 rooms with PB.
Beds: QT.

This bed and breakfast is surrounded by nine acres located in the heart of the California gold country. Birds, deer and wildlife are common sites at this peaceful stopping place less than a hour out of Yosemite National Park. Historic Mariposa is a 10-minute drive and offers shops and a museum showcasing Native American, mining and pioneer memorabilia. The innkeeper is a former Yosemite Park Ranger. For guests with gold fever, the area boasts a gold mine tunnel. Horse-drawn carriage rides take guests on a relaxing tour of the town.

Breakfast included in rates. Type of meal: continental-plus breakfast. Air conditioning in room. Cable TV, VCR and fax on premises. Spanish spoken. Antiques, fishing, parks, shopping, downhill skiing, cross-country skiing and watersports nearby. TAC10.

Location: In the heart of the California gold country.

"Now we know where to come for a relaxing vacation."

McCloud

B5

McCloud Hotel B&B

408 Main St, PO Box 730
McCloud, CA 96057-0730
(916)964-2822 (800)964-2823
Fax:(916)964-2844
E-mail: mchotel@telis.org

Rates: $68-130.
Payment: MC VISA.
Innkeeper(s): Marilyn & Lee Ogden.
Circa: 1915.

Rooms: 18 rooms with PB. 4 suites. 1 conference room.
Beds: QT.

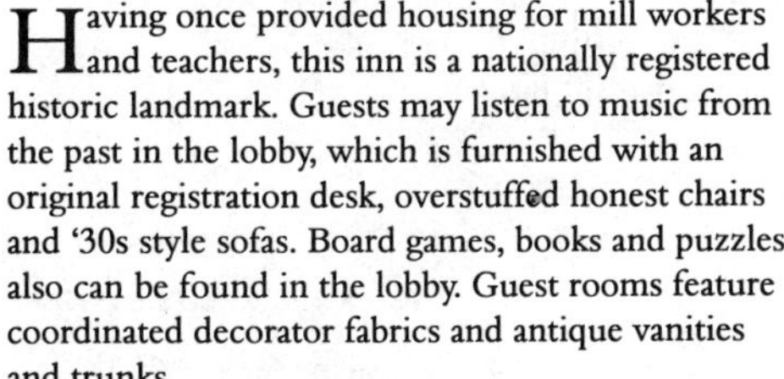

Having once provided housing for mill workers and teachers, this inn is a nationally registered historic landmark. Guests may listen to music from the past in the lobby, which is furnished with an original registration desk, overstuffed honest chairs and '30s style sofas. Board games, books and puzzles also can be found in the lobby. Guest rooms feature coordinated decorator fabrics and antique vanities and trunks.

Breakfast and afternoon tea included in rates. Types of meals: full breakfast and early coffee/tea. Room service available. Ceiling fan in room. Cable TV, fax and copier on premises. Handicap access. Weddings, small meetings, family reunions and seminars hosted. Fishing, shopping, downhill skiing, cross-country skiing and watersports nearby. TAC10.

Publicity: *Sunset, PBS California Gold, Redding Searchlight, Mount Shasta Herald.*

Mendocino

F2

Blair House

PO Box 1608,
45110 Little Lake St
Mendocino, CA 95460-1608
(707)937-1800 (800)699-9296
Fax:(707)937-2444

Rates: $80-155.
Payment: MC VISA TC.
Innkeeper(s): Ming & Geoffrey Hart.
Circa: 1888.

Rooms: 5 rooms, 2 with PB, 1 with FP. 1 suite. 1 cottage.
Beds: Q.

"Murder, She Wrote," fans will recognize this Cape Cod-style inn as the home of TV sleuth Jessica Fletcher. Although the home lies on the West Coast, and not in Fletcher's Maine town, guests enjoy equally picturesque scenery. Ironically the builder of the 19th-century home was a Maine native, Elisha Warren Blair. Polished wood floors, made from Douglas fir and walls of Redwood have created a sturdy, yet elegant Victorian manor. Guest rooms are decorated with Swedish and American antiques. Featherbeds, handmade quilts and comforters add a cozy, country touch. Angela's Suite, an opulent two-room chamber, includes a fireplace, bay window and stencilled walls. Other rooms offer stunning views of the ocean or village of Mendocino. A cottage also is available. For special occasions, the innkeepers can prepare a package with flowers, champagne or other gifts.

Breakfast included in rates. Ceiling fan in room. Library and pet boarding on premises. Weddings and small meetings hosted. Chinese and Japanese spoken. Antiques, fishing, theater and watersports nearby.

Pets Allowed: Yes.

The Headlands Inn

PO Box 132
Mendocino, CA 95460-0132
(707)937-4431 (800)354-4431
Fax:(707)937-1400

Rates: $105-195.
Payment: MC VISA AX DS PC.
Innkeeper(s): David & Sharon Hyman.
Circa: 1868.

Rooms: 6 rooms with PB, 6 with FP. 1 cottage.
Beds: KQ.

Originally a small barbershop on Main Street, the building later became the elegant "Oyster and Coffee Saloon" in 1884. Finally, horses pulled the house over log rollers to its present location. The new setting provides a spectacular view of the ocean, the rugged coastline, and breathtaking sunsets. Antiques, featherbeds, and wood-burning fireplaces warm each guest room. There is a romantic honeymoon cottage, an English-style garden, and a parlor. A full gourmet breakfast is brought directly to your room.

Breakfast and afternoon tea included in rates. Type of meal: gourmet breakfast. Fax on premises. Antiques, fishing, parks, shopping, theater and watersports nearby.

Location: Two blocks from the village center, within historic preservation district.

Publicity: *Los Angeles Times, New York Times, Innsider, Oakland Tribune, Orange County Register, Contra Costa Times, Palo Alto Times.*

"If a Nobel Prize were given for breakfasts, you would win hands down. A singularly joyous experience!!"

John Dougherty House

571 Ukiah St, PO Box 817
Mendocino, CA 95460
(707)937-5266 (800)486-2104
E-mail: jdhbmw@mcn.org

Rates: $95-185.
Payment: MC VISA DS PC TC.
Innkeeper(s): David & Marion Wells.
Circa: 1867.

Rooms: 6 rooms with PB, 6 with FP. 3 suites.
Beds: Q.

Early American furnishings and country-style stenciling provide the decor at this welcoming inn. Four rooms have outstanding water views, including the Captain's Room. The water tower room has an 18-foot ceiling and wood-burning stove. The inn's grounds sparkle with an array of beautiful flowers. The inn has been featured on the cover of Country Homes.

Breakfast included in rates. Types of meals: gourmet breakfast and early coffee/tea. Cable TV in room. Family reunions hosted. Antiques, fishing, parks, shopping, theater and watersports nearby. TAC10.

Location: Historic District.

Publicity: *Mendocino Beacon, Country Home, Los Angeles Times, San Francisco Times/Tribune.*

Special Discounts: Winter rates.

"A treasure chest of charm beauty and views."

Joshua Grindle Inn

PO Box 647
Mendocino, CA 95460-0647
(707)937-4143 (800)474-6353
E-mail: joshgrin@mcn.org

Rates: $90-180.
Payment: MC VISA PC TC.
Innkeeper(s): Arlene & Jim Moorehead.
Circa: 1879.

Rooms: 10 rooms with PB, 6 with FP.
Beds: QT.

The town banker, Joshua Grindle, built this New England-style home on two acres. The decor is light and airy, with Early American antiques, clocks and quilts. In addition to lodging in the house, there are rooms in the water tower and in an adjacent cottage. Six of the guest rooms have fireplaces. Some have views over the town to the ocean.

Breakfast and evening snack included in rates. Types of meals: full breakfast and gourmet breakfast. Fishing, parks, shopping and theater nearby. TAC10.

Location: On the Pacific Ocean at the edge of the village.

Publicity: *Peninsula, Copley News Service.*

"We are basking in the memories of our stay. We loved every moment."

CA

Reed Manor

Palette Dr, PO Box 127
Mendocino, CA 95460
(707)937-5446
Fax:(707)937-5407

Rates: $175-350.
Payment: MC VISA PC TC.
Innkeeper(s): Barbara & Monte Reed.
Circa: 1990.

Rooms: 5 rooms with PB, 5 with FP. 1 suite.
Beds: KQ.

This elegant, four-diamond inn rests on a hilltop overlooking the seaside village of Mendocino. Guest rooms and the suite are individually appointed, some offer decks, others have secluded garden areas. All have fireplaces, whirlpool tubs and romantic decor. Continental breakfasts are served in the privacy of your room. Refrigerators, answering machines and VCRs are some of the in-room amenities guests will find. The innkeepers keep a stock of local menus on hand. Guests often enjoy making their dinner decision while relaxing in the fireplaced parlor.

Breakfast included in rates. Type of meal: continental breakfast. Afternoon tea available. Cable TV and VCR in room. Fax and spa on premises. Small meetings hosted. Antiques, fishing, parks, shopping and theater nearby.

Mill Valley H4

Mountain Home Inn

810 Panoramic Hwy
Mill Valley, CA 94941-1765
(415)381-9000
Fax:(415)381-3615

Rates: $131-239.
Payment: MC VISA AX PC TC.
Innkeeper(s): Lynn Saggese.
Circa: 1912.

Rooms: 10 rooms with PB, 5 with FP. 1 conference room.
Beds: QD.

At one time the only way to get to Mountain Home was by taking the train up Mount Tamalpais. With 22 trestles and 281 curves, it was called "the crookedest railroad in the world." Now accessible by auto, the trip still provides a spectacular view of San Francisco Bay. Each guest room has a view of the mountain, valley or bay.

Breakfast included in rates. Type of meal: full breakfast. Picnic lunch and lunch available. Fax and copier on premises. Weddings, small meetings and family reunions hosted. Parks and shopping nearby. TAC10.

Location: Mt. Tamalpais.

Publicity: *San Francisco Examiner, California.*

"A luxurious retreat. Echoes the grand style and rustic feeling of national park lodges — Ben Davidson, Travel & Leisure."

Montara I4

The Goose & Turrets B&B

835 George St, PO Box 937
Montara, CA 94037-0937
(415)728-5451
Fax:(415)728-0141
E-mail: rhmgt@montara.com

Rates: $85-120.
Payment: MC VISA AX DC DS PC TC.
Innkeeper(s): Raymond & Emily Hoche-Mong.
Circa: 1908.

Rooms: 5 rooms with PB, 3 with FP.
Beds: KQDT.

In the peaceful setting of horse ranches, strawflower farms and an art colony, this Italian villa features beautiful gardens surrounded by a 20-foot-high cypress hedge. The gardens include an orchard, vegetable garden, herb garden, rose garden, fountains, a hammock, swing and plenty of spots to enjoy the surroundings. The large dining and living room areas are filled with art, collectibles and classical music plays during afternoon tea. Among its many previous uses, the Goose & Turrets once served as Montara's first post office, the town hall, a Sunday school and a grocery store.

Breakfast and afternoon tea included in rates. Turn-down service in room. Library on premises. French spoken. Antiques, fishing, parks and watersports nearby. TAC10.

Location: One-half mile from the Pacific Ocean, 20 minutes from San Francisco airport.

Publicity: *San Jose Mercury News, Half Moon Bay Review, Peninsula Times Tribune, San Mateo Times, Los Angeles Times, Tri-Valley Herald, Contra Costa Times.*

Special Discounts: 15% discount AARP, ASU and Prodigy, Monday-Thursday.

"Lots of special touches. Great Southern hospitality — we'll be back."

Monterey J5

The Jabberwock

598 Laine St
Monterey, CA 93940-1312
(408)372-4777
Fax:(408)655-2946

Rates: $105-190.
Payment: MC VISA.
Innkeeper(s): Joan & John Kiliany.
Circa: 1911.

Rooms: 7 rooms, 3 with PB, 1 with FP. 2 suites.
Beds: KQ.

Set in a half-acre of gardens, this Victorian inn provides a fabulous view of Monterey Bay and its famous barking seals. When you're ready to settle in for the evening, you'll find huge Victorian beds complete with lace-edged sheets and goose-down comforters. In the late afternoon, hors d'oeuvres and aperitifs are served in an enclosed veranda. After dinner, guests are tucked into bed with cookies and milk.

Types of meals: gourmet breakfast and early coffee/tea. Evening snack available. Fax, copier and library on premises. Weddings, small meetings and family reunions hosted. Antiques, fishing, parks, shopping, theater and watersports nearby.

Location: Four blocks above Cannery Row, the beach and Monterey Bay Aquarium.

Publicity: *Sunset, Travel & Leisure, Sacramento Bee, San Francisco Examiner, Los Angeles Times, Country Inns, San Francisco Chronicle, Diablo, Elmer Dill's KABC-Los Angeles TV.*

"Words are not enough to describe the ease and tranquility of the atmosphere of the house, rooms, owners and staff of Jabberwock."

Mount Shasta B5

Mount Shasta Ranch B&B

1008 W.a. Barr Rd
Mount Shasta, CA 96067
(916)926-3870
Fax:(916)926-6882
E-mail: alpinere@snowcrest.net

Rates: $50-95.
Payment: MC VISA AX DS PC TC.
Innkeeper(s): Bill & Mary Larsen.
Circa: 1923.

Rooms: 9 rooms, 4 with PB. 1 cottage. 1 conference room.
Beds: Q.

This large two-story ranch house offers a full view of Mt. Shasta from its 60-foot-long redwood porch. Spaciousness abounds from the 1,500-square-foot living room with a massive rock fireplace to the large suites with private bathrooms that include large tubs and roomy showers. A full country breakfast may offer cream cheese-stuffed French toast or fresh, wild blackberry crepes. Just minutes away, Lake Siskiyou boasts superb fishing, sailing, swimming, and 18 hole golf course with public tennis courts.

Breakfast included in rates. Types of meals: full breakfast and early coffee/tea. Afternoon tea available. Air conditioning, ceiling fan and cable TV in room. VCR, fax, copier, spa and library on premises. Small meetings, family reunions and seminars hosted. Antiques, fishing, parks, shopping, downhill skiing, cross-country skiing and watersports nearby.

Pets Allowed: Yes.

Murphys H7

CA

Dunbar House, 1880

271 Jones St, PO Box 1375
Murphys, CA 95247-1375
(209)728-2897 (800)692-6006
Fax:(209)728-1451
E-mail: dunbarhs@goldrush.com

Rates: $115-165.
Payment: MC VISA AX PC TC.
Innkeeper(s): Bob & Barbara Costa.
Circa: 1880.

Rooms: 4 rooms with PB, 4 with FP. 1 suite.
Beds: KQ.

A picket fence frames this Italianate home, built by Willis Dunbar for his bride. The porch, lined with rocking chairs, is the perfect place to take in the scenery of century-old gardens decorated by fountains, birdhouses and swings. A collection of antiques, family heirlooms and comfortable furnishings fill the interior. The two-room garden suite includes a bed dressed with fine linens and a down comforter and a two-person Jacuzzi spa. Guests can enjoy the morning fare in the dining room, garden or opt for breakfast in their room.

Breakfast and afternoon tea included in rates. Types of meals: full breakfast, gourmet breakfast and early coffee/tea. Room service available. Air conditioning, turn-down service, ceiling fan, cable TV and VCR in room. Fax, copier and library on premises. Antiques, fishing, parks, shopping, downhill skiing, cross-country skiing, theater and watersports nearby. TAC10.

Location: Two blocks from the center of town.

Publicity: *Los Angeles Times, Gourmet, Victorian Homes, Country Inns, Travel & Leisure.*

"Your beautiful gardens and gracious hospitality combine for a super bed & breakfast."

Redbud Inn

402 Main St
Murphys, CA 95247-9695
(209)728-8533 (800)827-8533
Fax:(209)728-9123

Rates: $225. MAP.
Payment: MC VISA DS PC TC.
Innkeeper(s): Pam & Steve Hatch.
Circa: 1993.

Rooms: 14 rooms with PB, 5 with FP. 1 suite. 1 cottage. 1 conference room.
Beds: KQD.

Guests traveling along Murphys' Main Street are sure to notice this Victorian-style country inn. Each guest room has a special theme, such as the Carousel, with its collection of carousel horses, woodstove and a four-poster bed. Opi's Cabin, decorated to look like a miner's cabin, which includes distressed pine floors and a pressed tin ceiling. Five rooms have fireplaces, and some offer whirlpool tubs and balconies. A V.I.P. suite was recently added with a fireplace, Jacuzzi, wet bar and porch. Murphys is a quaint, Gold Rush town offering more than 70 historic buildings and homes. Guests can enjoy a ride around town in a horse-drawn wagon or surrey.

Breakfast and evening snack included in rates. Types of meals: full breakfast and early coffee/tea. Afternoon tea, picnic lunch and catering service available. MAP. Air conditioning in room. Cable TV, VCR, fax and copier on premises. Handicap access. Weddings, small meetings, family reunions and seminars hosted. Antiques, fishing, parks, shopping, downhill skiing, cross-country skiing, theater and watersports nearby.

Napa H4

Beazley House

1910 1st St
Napa, CA 94559-2351
(707)257-1649 (800)559-1649
Fax:(707)257-1518
E-mail: jbeaz@aol.com

Rates: $105-195.
Payment: MC VISA.
Innkeeper(s): Carol, Jim & Scott Beazley.
Circa: 1902.

Rooms: 11 rooms with PB, 6 with FP. 5 suites.
Beds: KQDT.

Nestled in green lawns and gardens, this graceful shingled mansion is frosted with white trim on its bays and balustrades. Stained-glass windows and polished-wood floors set the atmosphere in the parlor. There are six rooms in the main house and the carriage house features five more, many with fireplaces and whirlpool tubs. The venerable Beazley House was Napa's first bed & breakfast inn.

Breakfast and afternoon tea included in rates. Types of meals: full breakfast and early coffee/tea. Air conditioning and ceiling fan in room. Fax on premises. Handicap access. Weddings and small meetings hosted. Spanish and French spoken. Antiques, fishing, parks and shopping nearby. TAC10.

Location: In the historic neighborhood of Old Town Napa, at the south end of Napa Valley.

Publicity: *Los Angeles Times, USA Today, Yellow Brick Road, Emergo, Sacramento Bee.*

"There's a sense of peace & tranquility that hovers over this house, sprinkling magical dream dust & kindness."

Blue Violet Mansion

443 Brown St
Napa, CA 94559-3349
(707)253-2583 (800)959-2583
Fax:(707)257-8205

Rates: $145-285.
Payment: MC VISA AX DC DS PC TC.
Innkeeper(s): Kathy & Bob Morris.
Circa: 1886.

Rooms: 14 rooms with PB, 11 with FP. 3 suites. 1 conference room.
Beds: KQ.

English lampposts, a Victorian gazebo, and a rose garden welcome guests to this blue and white Queen Anne Victorian. Listed in the National Register, the house was originally built for a tannery executive. There are three-story bays, and from the balconies guests often view hot air balloons in the early morning. Eight rooms feature two-person spas and 11 have fireplaces. A full breakfast is served in the dining room. The innkeepers offer room service by request. Nearby is the wine train and restaurants.

Breakfast and evening snack included in rates. Types of meals: full breakfast and early coffee/tea. Dinner, picnic lunch, banquet service, catering service, catered breakfast and room service available. Air conditioning, turn-down service and ceiling fan in room. Cable TV, VCR, fax, copier, spa and swimming on premises. Handicap access. Weddings, small meetings, family reunions and seminars hosted. Amusement parks, antiques, fishing, parks, shopping, theater and watersports nearby. TAC10.

Churchill Manor

485 Brown St
Napa, CA 94559-3349
(707)253-7733
Fax:(707)253-8836

Rates: $75-145.
Payment: MC VISA AX DS PC TC.
Innkeeper(s): Joanna Guidotti & Brian Jenson.
Circa: 1889.

Rooms: 10 rooms with PB, 3 with FP. 3 suites. 3 conference rooms.
Beds: KQ.

Each room of this stately Napa Valley manor contains something special. The Bordello Room, a must for a romantic getaway, features a red and black Jacuzzi spa, a huge king-size brass bed, and a carved 10-foot French armoire. Three rooms have fireplaces, and the bath tiles and fireplaces in Edward's Room and Rose's Room are trimmed with 24-karat gold. Guests are treated to delicious breakfasts, freshly baked cookies and refreshments in the afternoons. Each evening there is a two-hour wine and cheese reception. The innkeepers add the Victorian flavor by keeping tandem bicycles and a croquet set on hand for their guests. Napa Wine Train and balloon ride packages are available to make any vacation memorable.

Breakfast, afternoon tea and evening snack included in rates. Types of meals: full breakfast, gourmet breakfast and early coffee/tea. Catering service available. Air conditioning in room. Cable TV, VCR, fax, copier, bicycles and library on premises. Handicap access. Weddings, small meetings, family reunions and seminars hosted. Spanish, French and Italian spoken. Amusement parks, antiques, fishing, parks, shopping, theater and watersports nearby. TAC10.

Publicity: *Napa County Record, Food & Beverage Journal, ABC-KGO TV, San Francisco Bay Guardian*

"Retaining the ambiance of the 1890s yet providing comfort for the 1990s."

Country Garden Inn

1815 Silverado Trl
Napa, CA 94558-3735
(707)255-1197
Fax:(707)255-3112
E-mail: innkeep@countrygardeninn.com

Rates: $120-210.
Payment: MC VISA AX PC TC.
Innkeeper(s): Lisa & George Smith.
Circa: 1860.

Rooms: 10 rooms with PB, 4 with FP.
Beds: KQ.

This historic carriage house is situated on the Napa River and one-and-a-half acres of woodland. A circular rose garden with a lily pond and fountain add to the natural beauty of the location. Many of the guest rooms have spas, canopy beds, fireplaces, or private decks looking out over the water. English innkeepers serve hors d'oeuvres in the early evening and desserts later.

Breakfast, afternoon tea and evening snack included in rates. Types of meals: full breakfast, gourmet breakfast and early coffee/tea. Air conditioning, turn-down service and ceiling fan in room. Fax on premises. Antiques, fishing, parks and watersports nearby. TAC10.

Location: South end of Napa Valley.

Publicity: *Los Angeles Times, San Francisco Examiner.*

"I felt goose bumps all over the moment we arrived and saw our beautiful room and surroundings."

The Hennessey House B&B

1727 Main St
Napa, CA 94559-1844
(707)226-3774
Fax:(707)226-2975

Rates: $85-160.
Payment: MC VISA AX DS.
Innkeeper(s): Andrea LaMar.
Circa: 1889.

Rooms: 10 rooms with PB, 4 with FP.
Beds: KQT.

This gracious Queen Anne Eastlake Victorian was once home to Dr. Edwin Hennessey, a Napa County physician. Pristinely renovated, the inn features stained-glass windows and a curving wraparound porch. A handsome hand-painted, stamped-tin ceiling graces the dining room. All rooms are furnished in antiques. The four guest rooms in the carriage house boast whirlpool baths, fireplaces or patios.

Breakfast included in rates. Type of meal: full breakfast. Air conditioning, ceiling fan and cable TV in room. Fax, spa and sauna on premises. Weddings, small meetings, family reunions and seminars hosted. Antiques and shopping nearby. TAC10.

Location: One hour from San Francisco.

Publicity: *AM-PM Magazine.*

"Thank you for making our stay very pleasant."

Napa Inn

1137 Warren St
Napa, CA 94559-2302
(707)257-1444 (800)435-1144

Rates: $100-190.
Payment: MC VISA AX DS PC TC.
Innkeeper(s): Ann & Denny Mahoney.
Circa: 1899.

Rooms: 6 rooms with PB, 2 with FP. 2 suites.
Beds: KQ.

Herb and flower gardens frame this Queen Anne Victorian nestled in the heart of a serene wine country neighborhood. Furnished with antiques, the inn has a sitting room with a fireplace. Shaded parks, gourmet and family restaurants are a short stroll from the inn.

Breakfast and evening snack included in rates. Types of meals: full breakfast and early coffee/tea. Air conditioning in room. Weddings, small meetings and family reunions hosted. Amusement parks, antiques, fishing, parks, shopping and theater nearby. TAC10.

Location: In the historic district.

Publicity: *San Francisco Examiner.*

"You made this a very memorable honeymoon—perhaps we can stay again on our anniversary."

Old World Inn

1301 Jefferson St
Napa, CA 94559-2412
(707)257-0112

Rates: $115-150.
Payment: MC VISA AX DS PC TC.
Innkeeper(s): Diane Dumaine.
Circa: 1906.

Rooms: 8 rooms with PB.
Beds: KQ.

The decor in this exquisite bed & breakfast is second to none. In 1981, Macy's sought out the inn to showcase a new line of fabrics inspired by Scandinavian artist Carl Larrson. Each romantic room is adorned in bright, welcoming colors and includes special features such as canopy beds and clawfoot tubs. The Garden Room boasts three skylights, and the Anne Room is a must for honeymoons and romantic retreats. The walls and ceilings are painted in a warm peach and blue, bows are stenciled around the perimeter of the room. A decorated canopy starts at the ceiling in the center of the bed and falls downward producing a curtain-like

effect. A buffet breakfast is served each morning and a delicious afternoon tea and wine and cheese social will curb your appetite until dinner. After sampling one of Napa's gourmet eateries, return to the inn where a selection of desserts await you.

Breakfast and afternoon tea included in rates. Spa and bicycles on premises. Antiques nearby. TAC10.

Publicity: *Napa Valley Traveller.*

"Excellent is an understatement. We'll return."

Stahlecker House B&B Country Inn & Gardens

1042 Easum Dr
Napa, CA 94558-5525
(707)257-1588 (800)799-1588
Fax:(707)224-7429

Rates: $95-185.
Payment: MC VISA AX TC.
Innkeeper(s): Ron & Ethel Stahlecker.
Circa: 1947.

Rooms: 4 rooms with PB, 4 with FP. 1 suite.
Beds: QT.

This country inn is situated on the banks of tree-lined Napa Creek. The acre and a half of grounds feature rose and orchard gardens, fountains and manicured lawns. Guests often relax on the sun deck. There is an antique refrigerator stocked with soft drinks and lemonade. Full, gourmet breakfasts are served by candlelight in the glass-wrapped dining room. In the evenings, coffee, tea and freshly made chocolate chip cookies are served. The Napa Wine Train station is five minutes away. Wineries, restaurants, antique shops, bike paths and hiking all are nearby.

Breakfast and evening snack included in rates. Types of meals: full breakfast, gourmet breakfast and early coffee/tea. Afternoon tea available. Air conditioning and turn-down service in room. Library on premises. Antiques, fishing, parks, shopping, theater and watersports nearby. TAC10.

Publicity: *Napa Valley Traveler.*

Special Discounts: Active military - 10%.

"Friendly hosts and beautiful gardens."

❑ **For additional inns in the Napa Valley, please see the map.**

Nevada City F6

Downey House

517 W Broad St
Nevada City, CA 95959
(916)265-2815 (800)258-2815

Rates: $75-100.
Payment: MC VISA.
Innkeeper(s): Miriam Wright.
Circa: 1870.

Rooms: 6 rooms with PB.
Beds: QD.

This Eastlake Victorian house is one of Nevada City's noted Nabob Hill Victorians. There are six sound-proofed guest rooms, a curved veranda, and in the garden, a pond and restored red barn. One can stroll downtown where the evening streets are lit by the warm glow of gas lights.

Breakfast, afternoon tea and evening snack included in rates. Types of meals: full breakfast, gourmet breakfast and early coffee/tea. Small meetings hosted. Antiques, fishing, parks, shopping, downhill skiing, cross-country skiing, theater and watersports nearby.

Location: On Nabob Hill close to the Historic District.

Publicity: *San Francisco Examiner, Country Living.*

"The best in Northern California."

Emma Nevada House

528 E Broad St
Nevada City, CA 95959
(916)265-4415 (800)916-3662
Fax:(916)265-4416
E-mail: emmanev@oro.net

Rates: $90-150.
Payment: MC VISA AX DC PC TC.
Innkeeper(s): Ruth Ann Riese.
Circa: 1856.

Rooms: 6 rooms with PB, 1 with FP.
Beds: Q.

What is considered the childhood home of 19th-century opera star Emma Nevada now serves as an attractive Queen Anne Victorian inn. English roses line the white picket fence in front, and the forest-like back garden has a small stream with benches. The Empress' Chamber is the most romantic room with ivory Italian linens atop a French antique bed, a bay window and a massive French armoire. Some rooms have whirlpool baths. Guests enjoy relaxing in the hexagonal sunroom and on the inn's wraparound porches. Empire Mine State Historic Park is nearby.

Breakfast and afternoon tea included in rates. Types of meals: full breakfast and early coffee/tea. Air conditioning in room. Fax and library on premises. Weddings and small meetings hosted. Antiques, fishing, parks, shopping, downhill skiing, theater and watersports nearby. TAC10.

Publicity: *Country Inns, Los Angeles Times, San Jose Mercury News.*

"A delightful experience: such airiness and hospitality in the midst of so much history. We were fascinated by the detail and the faithfulness of the restoration. This house is a quiet solace for city-weary travelers. There's a grace here."

The Red Castle Inn

109 Prospect St
Nevada City, CA 95959
(916)265-5135 (800)761-4766

Rates: $100-125.
Payment: MC VISA PC TC.
Innkeeper(s): Conley & Mary Louise Weaver.
Circa: 1860.

Rooms: 7 rooms with PB. 3 suites.
Beds: QD.

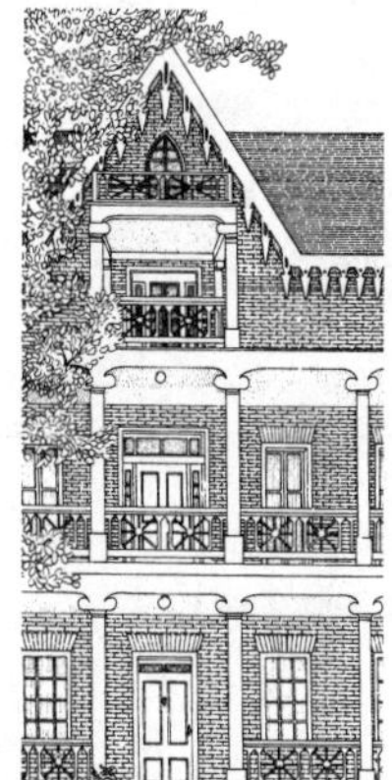

The Smithsonian has lauded the restoration of this four-story brick Gothic Revival known as "The Castle" by townsfolk. Its roof is laced with wooden icicles and the balconies are adorned with gingerbread. Within, there are intricate moldings, antiques, Victorian wallpapers, canopy beds and woodstoves. Verandas provide views of the historic city through cedar, chestnut and walnut trees, and of terraced gardens with a fountain pond.

Breakfast and afternoon tea included in rates. Types of meals: full breakfast, gourmet breakfast and early coffee/tea. Catering service available. Air conditioning and turn-down service in room. Library on premises. Weddings, small meetings and family reunions hosted. Antiques, fishing, parks, shopping, downhill skiing, cross-country skiing, theater and watersports nearby. TAC10.

Location: Within the Nevada City historic district overlooking the town.

Publicity: *Sunset, Gourmet, Northern California Home and Garden, Sacramento Bee, Los Angeles Times, Travel Holiday, Victorian Homes, Innsider, U.S. News and World Report, USAir, McCalls, New York Times.*

"The Red Castle Inn would top my list of places to stay. Nothing else quite compares with it-Gourmet."

Nipomo M7

The Kaleidoscope Inn

130 E Dana St
Nipomo, CA 93444-1297
(805)929-5444

Rates: $80.
Payment: MC VISA AX.
Innkeeper(s): Patty & Bill Linane.
Circa: 1887.

Rooms: 3 rooms with PB. 1 conference room.
Beds: KQ.

The sunlight that streams through the stained-glass windows of this charming Victorian creates a kaleidoscope effect and thus the name. The inn is surrounded by gardens. Each romantic guest room is decorated with antiques and the library offers a fireplace. Fresh flowers add a special touch. Breakfast is either served in the dining room, or in the gardens or in your room.

Breakfast included in rates. Types of meals: full breakfast, gourmet breakfast and early coffee/tea. Room service available. Turn-down service and ceiling fan in room. Cable TV, VCR and library on premises. Weddings, small meetings and family reunions hosted. Antiques, fishing, parks, shopping, theater and watersports nearby. TAC10.

Location: Twenty miles south of San Luis Obispo, near Pismo Beach.

Publicity: *Santa Maria Times, Los Angeles Times, Country.*

"Beautiful room, chocolates, fresh flowers, peaceful night's rest, great breakfast."

Nipton

L14

Hotel Nipton

HC1, Box 357, 107355
Nipton Rd
Nipton, CA 92364
(619)856-2335
E-mail: seeniptonc@aol.com

Rates: $50.
Payment: MC VISA DS.
Innkeeper(s): Gerald & Roxanne Freeman.
Circa: 1904.

Rooms: 4 rooms.
Beds: DT.

This Southwestern-style adobe hotel with its wide verandas once housed gold miners and Clara Bow, wife of movie star Rex Bell. It is decorated in period furnishings and historic photos of the area. A 1920s rock and cactus garden blooms, and an outdoor spa provides the perfect setting for watching a flaming sunset over Ivanpah Valley, the New York Mountains and Castle Peaks. Later, a magnificent star-studded sky appears undimmed by city lights.

Breakfast included in rates. Types of meals: continental breakfast and early coffee/tea. Air conditioning in room. Fax and library on premises. 40 acres. Weddings, small meetings, family reunions and seminars hosted. Amusement parks, fishing, parks, shopping, sporting events, theater and watersports nearby. TAC7.

Location: Mojave National Preserve.

Publicity: *National Geographic Traveler, Town & Country, U.S. News & World Report.*

Special Discounts: 10% discount when occupying entire hotel (4 rooms)

"Warm, friendly, unpretentious, genuine. The hotel's historical significance is well-researched and verified."

Oakhurst

I8

Chateau Du Sureau

PO Box 577
Oakhurst, CA 93644-0577
(209)683-6860
Fax:(209)683-0800

Rates: $360-430.
Payment: MC VISA AX.
Innkeeper(s): Erna Kubin-Clanin & Lucy Royse.

Rooms: 9 rooms with PB.
Beds: K.

One of United States' three inns awarded five diamonds, this elegant estate is superb in both lodging and cuisine. Set back from the road off the Southern entrance to Yosemite, the French country estate features a gathering room with a Monticello-like domed performance area with floor-to-ceiling palladian windows and grand piano, fireplace, beamed ceiling and oak and tile floors. Finely decorated guest rooms may include a canopy bed, whirlpool for two overlooking a garden, antique desk or a fireplace. Beds are dressed in Italian linens and down comforters. There are formal rose gardens, and herb gardens. Erna's Elderbery House Restaurant is on the premises but in a separate building.

Breakfast included in rates. Swimming on premises. Fishing and downhill skiing nearby.

Occidental

G4

The Inn at Occidental

3657 Church St
Occidental, CA 95465
(707)874-1047 (800)522-6324
Fax:(707)874-1078
E-mail: innkeeper@innatoccidental.com

Rates: $95-195.
Payment: MC VISA AX DC DS PC TC.
Innkeeper(s): Dee Wickham.
Circa: 1877.

Rooms: 8 rooms with PB, 4 with FP. 1 conference room.
Beds: KQT.

CA

Stencilled walls, shiny woodwork and a gracious collection of American and European antiques create the warm, idyllic environment at this 19th-century Victorian. Four of the guest rooms offer fireplaces, and all eight overlook the garden. There are plenty of places to relax, from a wicker-filled veranda to a manicured courtyard with a fountain as its centerpiece. The innkeepers serve gourmet country breakfasts, afternoon refreshments and in the evenings, local wines. The inn offers convenient access to wineries, Point Reyes National Seashore, Bodega Bay and canoeing, swimming and fishing at the Russian River.

Breakfast, afternoon tea and evening snack included in rates. Types of meals: full breakfast and early coffee/tea. Cable TV in room. Fax and copier on premises. Handicap access. Weddings, small meetings, family reunions and seminars hosted. Limited French and limited Spanish spoken. Antiques, fishing, parks, shopping, cross-country skiing, sporting events, theater and watersports nearby. TAC10.

Location: Wine country village near Sonoma Coast and Russian River.

Publicity: *Art, Antiques and Collectibles.*

Orland

E5

The Inn at Shallow Creek Farm

4712 County Road DD
Orland, CA 95963-9336
(916)865-4093 (800)865-4093

Rates: $55-75.
Payment: MC VISA PC.
Innkeeper(s): Mary & Kurt Glaeseman.
Circa: 1900.

Rooms: 4 rooms, 2 with PB. 1 suite.
Beds: QT.

This vine-covered farmhouse was once the center of a well-known orchard and sheep ranch. The old barn, adjacent to the farmhouse, was a livery stop. The citrus orchard, now restored, blooms with 165 trees. Apples, pears, peaches, apricots, persimmons, walnuts, figs, and pomegranates are also grown here. Guests can meander to examine the Polish crested chickens, silver guinea fowl, Muscovy ducks and African geese. The old caretaker's house is now a four-room guest cottage. Hundreds of narcissus grow along the creek that flows through the property.

Breakfast included in rates. Types of meals: continental-plus breakfast and early coffee/tea. Air conditioning and ceiling fan in room. Library on premises. French, German and Spanish spoken. Antiques, fishing, parks and theater nearby.

Location: Northern California, 3 miles off Interstate 5.

Publicity: *Adventure Road, Orland Press Register, Focus, Chico Enterprise Record, Minneapolis Star*

"Now that we've discovered your country oasis, we hope to return as soon as possible."

Pacific Grove

J5

Centrella B&B Inn

612 Central Ave
Pacific Grove, CA 93950
(408)372-3372 (800)233-3372
Fax:(408)372-2036
E-mail: centrella@aol.com

Rates: $95-195.
Payment: MC VISA.
Innkeeper(s): Maurine Diaz.
Circa: 1886.

Rooms: 26 rooms, 16 with PB, 6 with FP. 5 suites. 5 cottages.
Beds: KQDT.

Pacific Grove was founded as a Methodist resort in 1875, and this home, built just after the town's incorporation, was billed by a local newspaper as, "the largest, most commodious and pleasantly located boarding house in the Grove." Many a guest is still sure to agree. The rooms are well-appointed in a comfortable, Victorian style. Six guest rooms include fireplaces. The Honeymooner's Hideaway has a private entrance, fireplace, wet bar, Jacuzzi tub and a canopy bed topped with designer linens. Freshly baked croissants or pastries and made-to-order waffles are common fare at the inn's continental buffet breakfast. The inn is within walking distance of the Monterey Bay Aquarium, the beach and many Pacific Grove shops.

Breakfast and evening snack included in rates. Types of meals: continental-plus breakfast and early coffee/tea. Cable TV, VCR, fax, copier and library on premises. Handicap access. Spanish, French, German, Italian, Japanese and Korean spoken. Antiques, fishing, parks, shopping, sporting events and watersports nearby. TAC10.

Special Discounts: Romance package available.

Gosby House Inn

643 Lighthouse Ave
Pacific Grove, CA 93950
(408)375-1287 (800)527-8828
Fax:(408)655-9621

Rates: $90-150.
Payment: MC VISA AX TC.
Innkeeper(s): Tess Arthur.
Circa: 1887.

Rooms: 22 rooms, 20 with PB, 11 with FP.
Beds: KQD.

Built as an upscale Victorian inn for those visiting the old Methodist retreat, this sunny yellow mansion features an abundance of gables, turrets and bays. During renovation the innkeeper slept in all the rooms to determine just what antiques were needed and how the beds should be situated. Eleven of the romantic rooms include fireplaces and many offer canopy beds. The Carriage House rooms include fireplaces, decks and spa tubs. Gosby House, which has been open to guests for more than a century, is in the National Register. Gosby House is one of the Four Sisters Inns. The Monterey Bay Aquarium is nearby.

Breakfast and afternoon tea included in rates. Types of meals: gourmet breakfast and early coffee/tea. Picnic lunch available. Turn-down service in room. Fax, copier and bicycles on premises. Handicap access. Antiques and shopping nearby. TAC10.

Location: Six blocks from Monterey Bay.

Publicity: *San Francisco Chronicle, Oregonian, Los Angeles Times, Travel & Leisure.*

Special Discounts: Celebration package with champagne, truffles and teddy bear.

Green Gables Inn

104 5th St
Pacific Grove, CA 93950
(408)375-2095 (800)722-1774
Fax:(408)375-5437

Rates: $110-160.
Payment: MC VISA AX TC.
Innkeeper(s): Emily Frew.
Circa: 1888.

Rooms: 11 rooms, 7 with PB, 7 with FP. 1 suite.
Beds: KQD.

This half-timbered Queen Anne Victorian appears as a fantasy of gables overlooking spectacular Monterey Bay. The parlor has stained-glass panels framing the fireplace and bay windows looking out to the sea. A favorite focal point is an antique carousel horse. Most of the guest rooms have panoramic views of the ocean, fireplaces, gleaming woodwork, soft quilts and teddy bears. Across the street is the Monterey Bay paved oceanfront cycling path. (Mountain bikes may be borrowed from the inn.) Green Gables is one of the Four Sisters Inns.

Breakfast and afternoon tea included in rates. Type of meal: gourmet breakfast. Picnic lunch available. Turn-down service in room. Fax, copier and bicycles on premises. Handicap access. Antiques, shopping and theater nearby.

Location: On Monterey Bay four blocks from Monterey Bay Aquarium.

Publicity: *Travel & Leisure, Country Living.*

Martine Inn

255 Ocean View Blvd
Pacific Grove, CA 93950
(408)373-3388 (800)852-5588
Fax:(408)373-3896

Rates: $125-230.
Payment: MC VISA AX DS PC TC.
Innkeeper(s): Marion & Don Martine, Tracey Harris.
Circa: 1890.

Rooms: 20 rooms with PB, 13 with FP. 3 suites. 6 conference rooms.
Beds: KQD.

This turn-of-the-century oceanfront manor sits atop a jagged cliff overlooking the coastline of Monterey Bay. Bedrooms are furnished with antiques and each room contains a fresh rose and a silver Victorian bridal basket filled with fresh fruit. Thirteen rooms also boast fireplaces. Some of the museum-quality antiques were exhibited in the 1893 Chicago World's Fair. Other bedroom sets include furniture that belonged to Edith Head, and there is an 1860 Chippendale Revival four-poster bed with a canopy and side curtains. Innkeeper Don Martine has a collection of old MGs, three on display for guests. Twilight wine and hors d'oeuvres are served, and Godiva mints accompany evening turndown service. The inn is a beautiful spot for romantic getaways and weddings.

Breakfast included in rates. Types of meals: full breakfast and early coffee/tea.
Picnic lunch available. Turn-down service in room. Cable TV, fax, copier, spa and library on premises. Handicap access. Weddings, small meetings, family reunions and seminars hosted. Antiques, fishing, parks, shopping, sporting events, theater and watersports nearby. TAC10.

Location: On Monterey Bay, five miles from Monterey airport.

Publicity: *Sunday Oregonian, Bon Appetit, Innsider, Country Inns.*

"Wonderful, can't wait to return."

Old St. Angela Inn

321 Central Ave
Pacific Grove, CA 93950
(408)372-3246 (800)748-6306
Fax:(408)372-8560

Rates: $90-115.
Payment: MC VISA DS PC TC.
Innkeeper(s): Lewis Shaefer & Susan Kuslis.
Circa: 1910.

Rooms: 8 rooms, 5 with PB.
Beds: QDT.

Formerly a convent, this Cape-style inn has been restored and includes a glass solarium where breakfast is served. The ocean is a block away and it's just a short walk to the aquarium or fisherman's wharf.

Breakfast, afternoon tea and evening snack included in rates. Types of meals: full breakfast, gourmet breakfast and early coffee/tea. Fax and spa on premises. Small meetings and family reunions hosted. Antiques, fishing, parks, shopping, theater and watersports nearby. TAC10.

Pets Allowed: Small animals limited to rooms with private entrances.

Special Discounts: AAA 10%.

"Outstanding inn and outstanding hospitality."

Seven Gables Inn

555 Ocean View Blvd
Pacific Grove, CA 93950
(408)372-4341

Rates: $125-225.
Payment: MC VISA.
Innkeeper(s): The Flatley Family.
Circa: 1886.

Rooms: 14 rooms with PB.
Beds: Q.

At the turn of the century, Lucie Chase, a wealthy widow and civic leader from the East Coast, embellished this Victorian with gables and verandas, taking full advantage of its spectacular setting on Monterey Bay. All guest rooms feature ocean views, and there are elegant antiques, intricate Persian carpets, chandeliers and beveled-glass armoires throughout. Sea otters, harbor seals and whales often can be seen from the inn.

Breakfast included in rates. Type of meal: full breakfast. Afternoon tea and picnic lunch available. Antiques, fishing, theater and watersports nearby.

Publicity: *Travel & Leisure, Country Inns.*

"Our stay was everything your brochure said it would be, and more."

Casa Cody Country Inn

175 S Cahuilla Rd
Palm Springs, CA 92262
(619)320-9346 (800)231-2639
Fax:(619)325-8610

Rates: $49-199.
Payment: MC VISA AX DC CB DS PC TC.
Innkeeper(s): Elissa Goforth.
Circa: 1920.

Rooms: 23 rooms, 24 with PB, 10 with FP. 8 suites. 2 cottages.
Beds: KQT.

Casa Cody, built by a relative of Wild Bill Cody and situated in the heart of Palm Springs, is the town's oldest continuously operating inn. The San Jacinto Mountains provide a scenic background for the tree-shaded spa, the pink and purple bougainvillea and the blue waters of the inn's two swimming pools. Each suite has a small kitchen and features red and turquoise Southwestern decor. Several have wood-burning fireplaces. There are Mexican pavers, French doors and private patios. The area offers many activities, including museums, a heritage center, boutiques, a botanical garden, horseback riding and golf.

Breakfast included in rates. Type of meal: continental-plus breakfast. Air conditioning, ceiling fan and cable TV in room. Fax, copier, spa, swimming and library on premises. Weddings, small meetings, family reunions and seminars hosted. French, Dutch and limited German & Spanish spoken. Antiques and theater nearby. TAC10.

Pets Allowed.

Publicity: *New York Times, Washington Post, Los Angeles Times, San Diego Union Tribune, Seattle Times, Portland Oregonian, Los Angeles, San Diego Magazine, Pacific Northwest Magazine, Sunset, Westways, Alaska Airlines Magazine*

Special Discounts: Summer and shoulder season midweek discounts.

"Outstanding ambiance, friendly relaxed atmosphere."

Palo Alto

I5

Adella Villa

PO Box 4528
Palo Alto, CA 94309-4528
(415)321-5195
Fax:(415)325-5121

Rates: $110.
Payment: MC VISA AX DC CB PC TC.
Innkeeper(s): Tricia Young.
Circa: 1923.

Rooms: 5 rooms with PB. 1 conference room.
Beds: KQT.

This Italian villa is located in an area of one-acre estates five minutes from Stanford University. Two guest rooms feature whirlpool tubs, three guest rooms have showers. The music room boasts a 1920 mahogany Steinway grand piano. There is a solar-heated swimming pool set amid manicured gardens.

Breakfast and afternoon tea included in rates. Types of meals: full breakfast, gourmet breakfast and early coffee/tea. Evening snack available. Ceiling fan and cable TV in room. VCR, fax, copier, swimming, bicycles and library on premises. Small meetings and seminars hosted. Spanish & German spoken. Amusement parks, antiques, fishing, parks, shopping, sporting events, theater and watersports nearby. TAC10.

Location: Twenty-five miles south of San Francisco at the tip of Silicon Valley.

Publicity: *Los Angeles Times.*

"This place is as wonderful, gracious and beautiful as the people who own it!"

The Victorian on Lytton

555 Lytton Ave
Palo Alto, CA 94301-1538
(415)322-8555
Fax:(415)322-7141

Rates: $112-220. EP.
Payment: MC VISA AX.
Innkeeper(s): Susan & Maxwell Hall.
Circa: 1896.

Rooms: 10 rooms with PB, 1 with FP.
Beds: KQ.

This Queen Anne home was built for Hannah Clapp, a descendant of Massachusetts Bay colonist Roger Clapp. The house has been graciously restored and each guest room features its own sitting area. Most rooms boast a canopy or four-poster bed. Stanford University is within walking distance.

Breakfast and evening snack included in rates. Types of meals: continental-plus breakfast and early coffee/tea. EP. Air conditioning and cable TV in room. Fax on premises. Handicap access. Antiques, parks, shopping and sporting events nearby. TAC10.

Publicity: *USA Today.*

"A beautiful inn! My favorite."

Pasadena O10

Pasadena Hotel B&B

76 N Fair Oaks Ave
Pasadena, CA 91103-3610
(818)568-8172 (800)653-8886
Fax:(818)793-6409

Rates: $79-165.
Payment: MC VISA AX.
Innkeeper(s): John Tsern.
Circa: 1904.

Rooms: 12 rooms, 1 with PB. 1 suite.
Beds: Q.

The turn-of-the-century building that houses the Pasadena hotel once served as the town's courthouse. Located in Old Town Pasadena, the inn is similar to a European pension with accommodations sharing baths. All but one of the guest rooms have shared baths. The hotel's parlor and guest rooms offer comfortable furnishings, some antiques, skylights, phones and television. A light continental breakfast is served in the back lounge. There is a courtyard surrounded by several restaurants and sports bars.

Breakfast and afternoon tea included in rates. Type of meal: continental breakfast. Catering service and room service available. Restaurant on premises. Air conditioning in room. Fax and copier on premises. Weddings, small meetings, family reunions and seminars hosted. Spanish and Chinese spoken. Antiques, parks, shopping, sporting events and theater nearby.

Special Discounts: Government employees; group rates; extended stays.

Petaluma H4

Cavanagh Inn

10 Keller St
Petaluma, CA 94952-2939
(707)765-4657
Fax:(707)769-0466

Rates: $70-125.
Payment: MC VISA AX PC.
Innkeeper(s): Ray & Jeanne Farris.
Circa: 1902.

Rooms: 7 rooms, 5 with PB. 1 conference room.
Beds: KQDT.

Embrace turn-of-the-century California at this picturesque Georgian Revival manor. The garden is filled with beautiful flowers, plants and fruit trees. Innkeeper Jeanne Farris is an award-winning chef and prepares the mouthwatering breakfasts. A typical meal might start off with butterscotch pears and fresh muffins with honey butter. This starter would be followed by an entree, perhaps eggs served with rosemary potatoes. The innkeepers also serve afternoon refreshments. The parlor and library, which boasts heart-of-redwood panelled walls, is an ideal place to relax. Cavanagh Inn is located at the edge of Petaluma's historic district, and close to shops and the riverfront, including the Petaluma Queen Riverboat.

Breakfast and evening snack included in rates. Type of meal: gourmet breakfast. Turn-down service in room. Cable TV, VCR, fax and library on premises. Small meetings, family reunions and seminars hosted. Spanish spoken. Antiques, parks, shopping and theater nearby. TAC10.

Special Discounts: 10% for five days or more in some rooms.

Placerville G6

Chichester-McKee House B&B

800 Spring St
Placerville, CA 95667-4424
(916)626-1882 (800)831-4008

Rates: $80-90.
Payment: MC VISA AX DS PC TC.
Innkeeper(s): Doreen & Bill Thornhill.
Circa: 1892.

Rooms: 3 rooms.
Beds: QT.

D.W. Chichester, a partner in the local sawmill, built this house for his wife and the Victorian manor is said to be the first home in Placerville with built-in plumbing. The house is full of places to explore and admire, including the lovely parlor, library and a conservatory. Guest rooms are filled with family treasures and antiques, and the home is decorated with charming fireplaces and stained glass. Breakfast at the inn includes freshly baked goods and delicious entrees. Evening refreshments are a treat and the special blends of morning coffee will wake your spirit. Ask the innkeepers about the discovery of a gold mine beneath the dining room floor.

Breakfast and evening snack included in rates. Types of meals: full breakfast, gourmet breakfast and early coffee/tea. Cable TV, VCR and library on premises. Small meetings and family reunions hosted. Antiques, fishing, parks, shopping, downhill skiing, cross-country skiing, theater and watersports nearby. TAC10.

Publicity: *Hi Sierra, Mount Democrat.*

"The most relaxing and enjoyable trip I've ever taken."

Playa del Rey — O10

Inn at Playa del Rey

435 Culver Blvd
Playa del Rey, CA 90293
(310)574-1920
Fax:(310)574-9920
E-mail: playainn@aol.com

Rates: $95-225.
Payment: MC VISA AX DS PC.
Innkeeper(s): Susan Zolla.
Circa: 1995.

Rooms: 22 rooms with PB, 9 with FP. 2 suites.
Beds: KQT.

Relax and enjoy the view of a 350-acre bird sanctuary from this restful Cape Cod-style inn, located just a few blocks from the ocean. The individually appointed rooms are designed for relaxation. The hosts keep the bathrooms stocked with thick towels, fluffy robes and plenty of bubble bath. Some rooms include private decks, others offer fireplaces, Marina views or Jacuzzi tubs. Two of the rooms offer the romantic amenity of a fireplace in the bathroom. The third-floor suite, with its fireplace, private deck, Jacuzzi tub, living room and scenic view, is a perfect place to celebrate a romantic occasion. Guests are treated to a hearty breakfast, and after a day combing the beach, the guests are offered wine and cheese. There are bicycles available to tour the area, and a hot tub is located in the inn's private garden.

Breakfast and afternoon tea included in rates. Types of meals: full breakfast and early coffee/tea. Air conditioning, cable TV and VCR in room. Fax, copier, spa, bicycles and library on premises. Handicap access. 300 acres. Small meetings hosted. French, Spanish and Japanese spoken. Amusement parks, antiques, fishing, parks, shopping, sporting events, theater and watersports nearby. TAC10.

Point Reyes Station — H4

Carriage House

325 Mesa Rd, PO Box 1239
Point Reyes Station,
CA 94956
(415)663-8627
Fax:(415)663-8431

Rates: $110-160.
Innkeeper(s): Felicity Kirsch.
Circa: 1960.

Rooms: 1 room, 2 with PB, 2 with FP. 2 suites.
Beds: QT.

This recently remodeled home boasts a view of Inverness Ridge. One guest rooms and two suites are furnished in antiques and folk art with a private parlor, television, VCR and a fireplace. Children are welcome and cribs and daybeds are available. Point Reyes National Seashore has 100 miles of trails for cycling, hiking or horseback riding. Breakfast items such as freshly squeezed juice, muffins and breads are stocked in your room, so guests may enjoy it at leisure.

Breakfast included in rates. Type of meal: continental-plus breakfast. Cable TV and VCR in room. Bicycles and child care on premises. Small meetings, family reunions and seminars hosted. Antiques, fishing, parks and shopping nearby.

Location: Near Point Reyes National Seashore and Tomales Bay State Park.

"What a rejuvenating getaway. We loved it. The smells, sounds and scenery were wonderful."

CA

Ferrando's Hideaway

12010 Hwy 1, PO Box 688
Point Reyes Station,
CA 94956
(415)663-1966 (800)337-2636
Fax:(415)663-1825
E-mail: ferrando@nbn.com

Rates: $110-220.
Payment: MC VISA PC TC.
Innkeeper(s): Doris & Greg Ferrando.
Circa: 1972.

Rooms: 3 rooms with PB. 2 cottages.
Beds: K.

This modern home is secluded on three acres, offering decks, flower and vegetable gardens and a hot tub. Guests can opt for one of three guest rooms in the main house or stay in one of two cottages. The Garden Cottage includes a loft with a king-size bed, wood stove, a fully-equipped kitchen and a deck offering views of rolling hills. Alberti Cottage is located a short distance from the inn and offers its own hot tub, a fully equipped kitchen, a private patio, TV, VCR and a stereo. Both cottages are stocked with farm-fresh eggs, breads, muffins, cheeses, coffee, herbal teas and juice. Bed & breakfast guests enjoy a morning meal with fresh juice, egg dishes and fresh baked goods.

Breakfast and afternoon tea included in rates. Types of meals: full breakfast and early coffee/tea. Cable TV and VCR in room. Fax, spa and sauna on premises. Small meetings and family reunions hosted. German spoken. Antiques, fishing, parks, shopping and watersports nearby. TAC5.

Special Discounts: Nov. 1 to March 31, mid-week, Monday-Thursday, three nights for price of two.

Holly Tree Inn

3 Silverhills Rd, PO Box 642
Point Reyes Station,
CA 94956
(415)663-1554
Fax:(415)663-8566

Rates: $110-200.
Payment: MC VISA AX PC TC.
Innkeeper(s): Diane & Tom Balogh.
Circa: 1939.

Rooms: 4 rooms with PB, 4 with FP. 3 cottages.
Beds: KQ.

Innkeepers Diane and Tom Balogh have created an environment to please any guest at their elegant bed & breakfast inn. Located on 19 acres adjoining the Point Reyes National Seashore, the inn is ideal for families. The Vision Cottage is a perfect place for parents and children. The cottage includes two bedrooms, each with a queen-size pine bed dressed with handmade quilts and down comforters. Extra futons are available for children, and there's a wood-burning fireplace and a kitchen. For honeymooners or those seeking solitude, the innkeepers offer Sea Star Cottage, a romantic hamlet for two. The cottage sits at the end of a 75-foot dock on Tomales Bay. Both cottages are several miles from the main inn, but guests also can opt for four, well-appointed rooms in the main inn or the Cottage in the Woods.

Breakfast included in rates. Types of meals: full breakfast and early coffee/tea. Afternoon tea available. Fax, spa and library on premises. 19 acres. Small meetings and seminars hosted. Limited Spanish and limited French spoken. Antiques, fishing, parks, shopping, theater and watersports nearby. TAC10.

Thirty-Nine Cypress

39 Cypress St, Box 176
Point Reyes Station,
CA 94956
(415)663-1709

Rates: $110-130.
Innkeeper(s): Julia Bartlett.

The lures of the country and seashore are combined at this charming redwood home. Three guest rooms, all filled with country touches, feature patios with views of the bay and the peninsula. Julia, who was in charge of the natural history program at the Point Reyes National Seashore, will be happy to aid guests in planning their excursions. And Flora, the inn's well-behaved Australian cattle dog, will greet all comers, maybe even showing them the spa, cozily situated down the bluff with a view of the marsh below. Guests often enjoy eating breakfast at an outdoor table, overlooking the valley and its varied wildlife.

Cable TV on premises. Small meetings, family reunions and seminars hosted. Antiques nearby.

Pets Allowed: Well-behaved dogs by arrangement, $10 per night.

Point Richmond H4

East Brother Light Station Inc

117 Park Pt
Point Richmond, CA 94801
(415)233-2385

Rates: $250.
Innkeeper(s): Pat Diamond, Linda & Leigh Hurley.
Circa: 1873.

Rooms: 4 rooms, 2 with PB.

Managed by a non-profit organization, this lighthouse inn is located on an acre of island. Guest quarters, furnished simply, are situated in the outbuildings and on the second story of the innkeeper's Victorian house. The light has been automated since 1969.

Type of meal: continental-plus breakfast.

Location: Ten minutes from dock.

Publicity: *Uncommon Lodgings.*

Quincy E6

The Feather Bed

542 Jackson St
PO Box 3200
Quincy, CA 95971-9412
(916)283-0102 (800)696-8624

Rates: $75-120.
Payment: MC VISA AX DC DS PC TC.
Innkeeper(s): Bob & Jan Janowski.
Circa: 1893.

Rooms: 7 rooms with PB, 4 with FP. 1 suite. 2 cottages. 1 conference room.
Beds: QT.

Englishman Edward Huskinson built this charming Queen Anne house shortly after he began his mining and real estate ventures. Ask for the secluded cottage with its own deck and clawfoot tub. Other rooms in the main house overlook downtown Quincy or the mountains. Check out a bicycle to explore the countryside.

Breakfast and evening snack included in rates. Types of meals: full breakfast, gourmet breakfast and early coffee/tea. Air conditioning, ceiling fan, cable TV and VCR in room. Fax, copier, bicycles and library on premises. Handicap access. Small meetings hosted. Antiques, fishing, parks, shopping, cross-country skiing, theater and watersports nearby. TAC10.

Location: In the heart of Plumas National Forest.

Publicity: *Focus, Reno Gazette, San Francisco Chronicle.*

Special Discounts: 10% discount third night.

"After living and traveling in Europe where innkeepers are famous, we have found The Feather Bed to be one of the most charming in the U.S. and Europe!"

Red Bluff D5

Faulkner House

1029 Jefferson St
Red Bluff, CA 96080-2725
(916)529-0520 (800)549-6171
Fax:(916)527-4970

Rates: $65-90.
Payment: MC VISA AX.
Innkeeper(s): Harvey & Mary Klingler.
Circa: 1890.

Rooms: 4 rooms with PB.
Beds: QD.

This Queen Anne Victorian stands on a quiet, tree-lined street in the Victorian town of Red Bluff. Furnished in antiques, the house has original stained-glass windows, ornate molding, and eight-foot pocket doors separating the front and back parlors. The Tower Room is a cozy spot or choose the Rose Room with its brocade fainting couch and queen bed.

Breakfast included in rates. Type of meal: full breakfast. Antiques, fishing, parks and cross-country skiing nearby.

Location: Three and one-half hours north of San Francisco near Lassen National Park.

Publicity: *Red Bluff Daily News.*

"Enjoyed our stay at your beautiful home."

Sacramento G6

Abigail's

2120 G St
Sacramento, CA 95816
(916)441-5007 (800)858-1568
Fax:(916)441-0621

Rates: $105-165.
Payment: MC VISA AX DC CB DS PC TC.
Innkeeper(s): Susanne & Ken Ventura.
Circa: 1912.

Rooms: 5 rooms with PB. 1 conference room.
Beds: KQ.

CA

This Colonial Revival inn, on an elm-lined street just minutes from the capitol building and convention center, offers gracious surroundings to both business and weekend getaway travelers. The inn's five guest rooms include The Margaret Room, with its four-poster, canopy queen bed, and the maroon and gray "country gentleman" Uncle Albert Room, with marble-floor bathroom and a queen bed. The inn's secluded garden spa is a favorite spot to relax after a busy day exploring California's capital city and its surrounding area.

Breakfast and evening snack included in rates. Types of meals: full breakfast and early coffee/tea. Catered breakfast available. Air conditioning and ceiling fan in room. Fax, copier and spa on premises. Small meetings hosted. Amusement parks, antiques, fishing, parks, shopping, sporting events and theater nearby. TAC10.

Publicity: *The Times Picayune.*

"Thank you so much for inviting us to rest in your garden of hospitality once again. Each time we visit we find yet another reason to return."

Saint Helena G4

Bartels Ranch & Country Inn

1200 Conn Valley Rd
Saint Helena, CA 94574
(707)963-4001
Fax:(707)963-5100

Rates: $115-350.
Payment: MC VISA AX DC CB DS PC TC.
Innkeeper(s): Jami Bartels.
Circa: 1979.

Rooms: 4 rooms with PB, 4 with FP. 1 suite. 1 conference room.
Beds: KQ.

A tree-lined drive leads up to this rock and redwood home, located on 60 acres of Napa Valley countryside. Guest rooms include furnishings such as antique brass or canopy beds, fluffy robes, coffee service, bubble bath and other amenities. The Blue Valley Room features a private deck with a view. Relaxation is a priority here; breakfasts are served until noon allowing guests time to sleep late. Guests enjoy breakfast on the decks in sunny weather and during winter months, by candlelight in the formal dining room. The inn is a short drive from wineries, shops and restaurants.

Breakfast, afternoon tea and evening snack included in rates. Types of meals: full breakfast and early coffee/tea. Catering service and room service available. Air conditioning, ceiling fan, cable TV and VCR in room. Fax, copier, spa, sauna, bicycles, library, pet boarding and child care on premises. Handicap access. 60 acres. Weddings, small meetings and family reunions hosted. Amusement parks, antiques, fishing, parks, shopping, theater and watersports nearby. TAC10.

Location: In the heart of Napa Valley Wine Country.

Publicity: *Chicago Tribune, National Geographic Traveler, Gourmet Arts, La Jolla News, Dallas Morning News.*

Cinnamon Bear B&B

1407 Kearney St
Saint Helena, CA 94574
(707)963-4653 (888)963-4600
Fax:(707)963-0251

Rates: $115-155.
Payment: MC VISA AX.
Innkeeper(s): Cathye Raneri.
Circa: 1904.

Rooms: 3 rooms with PB.
Beds: Q.

This Craftsman bungalow, originally home to a town mayor, has broad wraparound porches with inviting bent-willow furniture. The decor includes antiques, original light fixtures, hardwood floors, teddy bears and quilts. The innkeeper's husband is a local Napa Valley chef, so the gourmet breakfasts are a treat. There are plenty of restaurants nearby, and the inn is also near the West Coast campus of the famed Culinary Institute of America.

Breakfast included in rates. Type of meal: gourmet breakfast. Evening snack and catering service available. Air conditioning in room. Cable TV, VCR, fax and copier on premises. Family reunions hosted. Antiques, parks and shopping nearby. TAC10.

Location: Two blocks from town.

Publicity: *Napa Register.*

Special Discounts: Midweek stays of three days or more $85-$115.

"Just like home, only better."

Deer Run Inn

PO Box 311 3995 Spring Mountain Rd
Saint Helena, CA 94574
(707)963-3794 (800)843-3408
Fax:(707)963-9026

Rates: $125-155.
Payment: MC VISA AX PC TC.
Innkeeper(s): Tom & Carol Wilson.
Circa: 1929.

Rooms: 4 rooms with PB, 3 with FP. 1 suite. 1 cottage.
Beds: KQ.

This secluded mountain home is located on four forested acres just up the road from the house used for the television show "Falcon Crest." A fir-tree-shaded deck provides a quiet spot for breakfast while watching birds and deer pass by. Your host, Tom, was born on Spring Mountain and knows the winery area well. There is a watercolorist in residence.

Breakfast included in rates. Types of meals: gourmet breakfast and early coffee/tea. Air conditioning and ceiling fan in room. Fax, copier and swimming on premises. Amusement parks, antiques, fishing, parks, shopping, sporting events, theater and watersports nearby. TAC10.

Location: Napa Valley.

Publicity: *Forbes, Chicago Tribune, Napa Record.*

"The perfect honeymoon spot! We loved it!"

Villa St. Helena

2727 Sulphur Springs Ave
Saint Helena, CA 94574
(707)963-2514
Fax:(707)963-2614
E-mail: villash@aol.dam

Rates: $145-245.
Payment: MC VISA AX TC.
Innkeeper(s): Ralph & Carolyn Cotton.
Circa: 1941.

Rooms: 3 suites.
Beds: KQ.

In the hills of the Mayacamas Mountains, the 20 secluded acres of this large Mediterranean-style estate offer guests panoramic views of the area's famed vineyards and Mt. St. Helena. A three-quarter mile drive leads up to the estate. Architect Robert M. Carrere designed the 12,000-square-foot villa with classic Mexican, European and American influences, when combined created what became a prototype of the California ranch house style. Included are Mexican tile floors, a mission tile roof, thick walls of sand-cast bricks, rambling verandas, a courtyard, and a variety of wings and levels. Scenes for Falcon Crest were filmed in the living room with its beamed ceiling and large stone fireplace. A French country decor includes an eclectic collection of period-style furnishings.

Breakfast included in rates. Type of meal: continental-plus breakfast. Turn-down service and ceiling fan in room. Fax and library on premises. 20 acres. Antiques, parks and shopping nearby. TAC10.

Wine Country Inn

1152 Lodi Ln
Saint Helena, CA 94574
(707)963-7077
Fax:(707)963-9018
E-mail: romance@winecountryinn.com

Rates: $125-248.
Payment: MC VISA PC TC.
Innkeeper(s): Jim Smith.
Circa: 1975.

Rooms: 24 rooms with PB, 14 with FP. 3 suites. 1 conference room.
Beds: KQ.

Rolling hills and vineyards create a peaceful setting at this inn. Many guest rooms have fireplaces and several have balconies offering views of vineyards. The innkeepers prepare a breakfast buffet, and in the afternoon, wine and appetizers are served. Three rooms offer a private hot tub, but there is a pool and Jacuzzi for all guests to enjoy. The area has hundreds of wineries and most are within a half hour of the inn.

Breakfast and evening snack included in rates. Type of meal: full breakfast. Air conditioning in room. Cable TV, fax, copier, spa, swimming and library on premises. TAC10.

Special Discounts: Seasonal discounts available.

San Clemente

P11

Casa De Flores B&B

184 Ave La Cuesta
San Clemente, CA 92672
(714)498-1344

Rates: $75-100.
Payment: PC.
Innkeeper(s): Marilee Arsenault.
Circa: 1974.

Rooms: 2 suites, 1 with FP.
Beds: K.

Located a mile from the Pacific, you can enjoy a 180-degree view of the ocean, harbor and hills from this home. In a residential area, it was designed by your hostess. The Private Patio room offers skylights, a private spa and an ocean view. More than 1,000 orchid plants are grown on the grounds. Grab a sand chair and towel and head for your own stretch of the five miles of San Clemente beaches. Whale watching and fishing charters are available at the Dana Point Harbor, 10 minutes away.

Breakfast included in rates. Type of meal: gourmet breakfast. Cable TV and VCR in room. Library on premises. Amusement parks, antiques, fishing, parks, shopping and watersports nearby. TAC20.

Location: South of the Dana Point Harbor.

San Diego

Q12

Heritage Park Inn

2470 Heritage Park Row
San Diego, CA 92110-2803
(619)299-6832 (800)995-2470
Fax:(619)299-9465

Rates: $90-225. MAP.
Payment: MC VISA TC.
Innkeeper(s): Nancy & Charles Helsper.
Circa: 1889.

Rooms: 10 rooms with PB. 1 suite. 1 conference room.
Beds: KQT.

Situated on a seven-acre Victorian park in the heart of Old Town, this inn two of seven preserved classic structures. The main house offers a variety of beautifully appointed guest rooms, decked in traditional Victorian furnishings and decor. The opulent Manor Suite includes two bedrooms, a Jacuzzi tub and sitting room. Several rooms offer ocean views, and guest also can see the nightly fireworks show at nearby Sea World. A collection of classic movies is available, and a different movie is shown each night in the inn's parlor. Guests are treated to a light afternoon tea and the breakfast are served on fine china on candlelit tables. The home is within walking distance to the many sites, shops and restaurants in the historic Old Town. A small antique shop and Victorian toy store also are located in the next door to the inn.

Breakfast and afternoon tea included in rates. Types of meals: gourmet breakfast and early coffee/tea. Picnic lunch and catering service available. MAP. Turn-down service and ceiling fan in room. VCR, fax and copier on premises. Small meetings, family reunions and seminars hosted. Amusement parks, antiques, fishing, parks, shopping, sporting events, theater and watersports nearby.

Location: In historic Old Town.

Publicity: *Los Angeles Herald Examiner, Innsider, Los Angeles Times, Orange County Register, San Diego Union, In-Flight, Glamour, Country Inns.*

"A beautiful step back in time. Peaceful and gracious."

Alamo Square Inn

719 Scott St
San Francisco, CA 94117
(415)922-2055 (800)345-9888
Fax:(415)931-1304

Rates: $85-295.
Payment: MC VISA AX TC.
Innkeeper(s): Wayne M. Corn & Klaus E. May.
Circa: 1890.

Rooms: 9 rooms with PB, 3 with FP. 5 suites. 1 conference room.
Beds: KQDT.

These two, adjacent Victorians have been graciously restored and appointed in period style. The interiors and exteriors both are charming, as is the location in a historic San Francisco neighborhood filled with restored Victorians. Three of the antique-filled guest rooms have wood-burning fireplaces, and several offer memorable views of parks, Alamo Square or the city lights. There are several well-appointed parlors, which can be used for relaxing or reserved for small meetings and gatherings. Freshly-squeezed orange juice, home-made breads and fresh fruit accompany breakfast entrees such as omelets or French toast. The inn is near many of San Francisco's sites and easily accessible to the freeway.

Breakfast included in rates. Type of meal: full breakfast. Fax and copier on premises. Weddings, small meetings, family reunions and seminars hosted. German, Mandarin and Spanish spoken. Parks and shopping nearby. TAC10.

The Amsterdam Hotel

749 Taylor St
San Francisco, CA 94108
(415)673-3277 (800)637-3444
Fax:(415)673-0453

Rates: $69-89.
Payment: MC VISA AX TC.
Innkeeper(s): Harry Hainf.
Circa: 1909.

Rooms: 32 rooms, 31 with PB.
Beds: KQD.

This brick Victorian has the feel of a small European hotel. All San Francisco attractions are easily reached from the inn's downtown location. The cable cars are two blocks away and Union Square is three blocks away. Guests staying on business as well as pleasure are accommodated with clean spacious rooms, direct dial phone and a fax machine on premises.

Breakfast included in rates. Types of meals: continental breakfast and early coffee/tea. Cable TV in room. VCR, fax, copier and sauna on premises. Amusement parks, antiques, parks, shopping and theater nearby. TAC10.

Casa Arguello

225 Arguello Blvd
San Francisco, CA 94118
(415)752-9482
Fax:(415)681-1400
E-mail: 103221.3126@compuserve.com

Rates: $58-85.
Payment: MC VISA AX DS PC TC.
Innkeeper(s): Marina, Jim & Pete McKenzie.
Circa: 1920.

Rooms: 4 rooms, 2 with PB. 1 suite.
Beds: KDT.

This Edwardian flat is located conveniently between San Francisco's Richmond district and Pacific Heights. Public transportation as well as a variety of shops and restaurants are within walking distance. A mix of antiques and contemporary furnishings decorate the rooms, which boast city views. A continental-plus breakfast with fresh fruit, cereals and pastry is served in the dining room.

Breakfast included in rates. Type of meal: continental-plus breakfast. Cable TV on premises. Spanish spoken. Antiques, parks, shopping, sporting events, theater and watersports nearby.

The Chateau Tivoli

1057 Steiner St
San Francisco, CA 94115
(415)776-5462

Rates: $80-200.
Payment: MC VISA AX.
Innkeeper(s): Chris Clarke & Sonny Coatar.
Circa: 1892.

Rooms: 8 rooms, 4 with PB, 2 with FP.
Beds: KQD.

Built for lumber magnate Daniel Jackson, this 10,000-square-foot mansion is painted in 22 colors with highlights of glimmering gold leaf accentuating its turrets and towers. It has been named "The Greatest Painted Lady in the World" by Elizabeth Pomada and Michael Larson, authors of the Painted Ladies series. Antiques and art from the estates of Cornelius Vanderbilt, Charles de Gaulle and J. Paul Getty are featured throughout. Canopy beds, marble baths, fireplaces and balconies are all reminiscent of San Francisco's Golden Age of Opulence. Chateau Tivoli holds the California Heritage Council's 1989 award for best restoration of a Victorian house in California. During the week, guests are served continental-plus fare. On weekends, a champagne brunch is served.

Breakfast included in rates. Type of meal: continental-plus breakfast. Fax and copier on premises. Antiques and theater nearby.

Location: Alamo Square historic district, 1 block from geographical center of San Francisco.

Publicity: *Bay City Guide, Elle Decor, Northern California Jewish Bulletin, Country Inns.*

"The romance and charm has made Chateau Tivoli the place to stay whenever we are in San Francisco."

CA

Dockside Boat & Bed

Pier 39
San Francisco, CA 94133
(510)444-5858 (800)436-2574
Fax:(510)444-0420

Rates: $95-275.
Payment: MC VISA AX DS TC.
Innkeeper(s): Rob & Mollie Harris.
Beds: QDT.

Enjoy views of San Francisco's skyline at this unique bed & breakfast, which offers dockside lodging aboard private motor or sailing yachts. The 14 private yachts vary in size from a 35-foot vessel to a 60-foot yacht. Each boat includes staterooms, galleys, bathrooms and living/dining areas. A continental breakfast is served each morning. Private charters and catered, candlelight dinners can be arranged. The yachts are docked at Pier 39 in San Francisco and Jack London Square in Oakland. Both locations are convenient to restaurants, shops and other attractions.

Breakfast included in rates. Type of meal: continental breakfast. Picnic lunch and catering service available. VCR in room. Fax and copier on premises. Weddings, small meetings, family reunions and seminars hosted. Antiques, fishing, parks, shopping, sporting events, theater and watersports nearby.

Location: On San Francisco Bay.

Publicity: *People, San Jose Mercury News, San Francisco Chronicle, Portland Oregonian, Denver Post, Washington Post.*

Special Discounts: Multiple night stay discounts.

Golden Gate Hotel

775 Bush St
San Francisco, CA 94108
(415)392-3702 (800)835-1118
Fax:(415)392-6202

Rates: $65-99.
Payment: MC VISA AX DC PC TC.
Innkeeper(s): John & Renate Kenaston.
Circa: 1913.

Rooms: 23 rooms, 14 with PB.
Beds: QDT.

News travels far when there's a bargain. Half of the guests visiting this four-story Edwardian hotel at the foot of Nob Hill are from abroad. Great bay windows on each floor provide many of the rooms with gracious spaces at humble prices. An original bird cage elevator kept in working order floats between floors. Antiques, fresh flowers, and afternoon tea further add to the atmosphere. Union Square is two-and-a-half blocks from the hotel.

Breakfast and afternoon tea included in rates. Type of meal: continental breakfast. Cable TV in room. Fax and child care on premises. Family reunions hosted. French, German and Spanish spoken. Amusement parks, antiques and theater nearby. TAC10.

Pets Allowed: Prior notification $10.00 additional.

Publicity: *Los Angeles Times, Melbourne Sun (Australia), Sunday Oregonian, Globe & Mail.*

"Stayed here by chance, will return by choice!"

The Inn San Francisco

943 S Van Ness Ave
San Francisco, CA 94110
(415)641-0188 (800)359-0913
Fax:(415)641-1701

Rates: $75-195.
Payment: MC VISA AX DC CB DS PC TC.
Innkeeper(s): Marty Neely & Connie Wu.
Circa: 1872.

Rooms: 22 rooms, 17 with PB, 4 with FP. 3 suites. 1 cottage.
Beds: QD.

Built on one of San Francisco's earliest "Mansion Rows" this 27-room Italianate Victorian is located near the civic and convention centers, close to Mission Dolores. Antiques, marble fireplaces and Oriental rugs decorate the opulent grand double parlors. Most rooms have featherbeds, Victorian wallcoverings and desks, while deluxe rooms offer private spas, fireplaces or bay windows. There is a rooftop deck offering a panoramic view.

Breakfast included in rates. Type of meal: gourmet breakfast. Afternoon tea available. Fax and spa on premises. Antiques, parks, shopping, sporting events and theater nearby. TAC10.

Pets Allowed.

Publicity: *Innsider.*

"..in no time at all you begin to feel a kinship with the gentle folk who adorn the walls in their golden frames."

No Name Victorian B&B

847 Fillmore St
San Francisco, CA 94117
(415)479-1913
Fax:(415)921-2273
E-mail: bbsf@linex.com

Rates: $69-125.
Payment: MC VISA AX PC TC.
Innkeeper(s): Eva Strakova.
Circa: 1890.

Rooms: 5 rooms, 3 with PB, 4 with FP. 1 suite.
Beds: QT.

Located in the historic district of Alamo Square, this Second Empire Victorian sits close to the Civic Center, Opera House, Davies Symphony Hall and Union Square. An 1830s wedding bed from mainland China adorns the honeymoon room. The massive hand-carved bed is believed to bring good spirits and luck to the couple who spend their wedding night there. Chinese antiques, a wood-burning fireplace, a city view and Chinese robes also are included. There's a family accommodation with a private entrance, full kitchen and a crib.

Breakfast included in rates. Types of meals: full breakfast and early coffee/tea. Cable TV, fax, spa and child care on premises. Weddings and family reunions hosted. Parks, shopping, sporting events and theater nearby. TAC10.

Location: In the heart of San Francisco.

Special Discounts: Third night complimentary, Sunday-Thursday.

Petite Auberge

863 Bush St
San Francisco, CA 94108
(415)928-6000 (800)365-3004
Fax:(415)775-5717

Rates: $110-220.
Payment: MC VISA AX TC.
Innkeeper(s): Brian Larsen.
Circa: 1917.

Rooms: 26 rooms with PB, 17 with FP. 1 suite.
Beds: KQ.

This five-story hotel features an ornate baroque design with curved bay windows. Now transformed to a French country inn, there are antiques, fresh flowers and country accessories. Most rooms also have working fireplaces. It's a short walk to the Powell Street cable car. In the evenings, wine and hors d'oeuvres are served. Petite Auberge is one of the Four Sisters Inns.

Breakfast and afternoon tea included in rates. Types of meals: gourmet breakfast and early coffee/tea. Picnic lunch available. Turn-down service in room. Fax and copier on premises. Handicap access. Antiques, parks, shopping, sporting events and theater nearby. TAC10.

Location: Two-and-a-half blocks from Union Square.

Publicity: *Travel & Leisure, Oregonian, Los Angeles Times, Brides.*

Special Discounts: Celebration package including champagne and truffles.

"Breakfast was great, and even better in bed!"

Spencer House

1080 Haight St
San Francisco, CA 94117
(415)626-9205
Fax:(415)626-9230

Rates: $105-165.
Payment: MC VISA AX.
Innkeeper(s): Barbara Chambers.
Circa: 1887.

Rooms: 6 rooms with PB.
Beds: KQD.

CA

This opulent mansion, which sits on three city lots, is one of San Francisco's finest examples of Queen Anne Victorian architecture. Ornate parquet floors, original wallpapers, gaslights, and antique linens are featured. Breakfast is served with crystal and silver in the elegantly paneled dining room.

Types of meals: full breakfast and early coffee/tea. Antiques and theater nearby.

Location: Ten minutes from the wharf.

Stanyan Park Hotel

750 Stanyan St
San Francisco, CA 94117
(415)751-1000
Fax:(415)668-5454
E-mail: info@stanyan.com

Rates: $85-185.
Payment: MC VISA AX DC CB DS TC.
Innkeeper(s): John Brockelhurst.
Circa: 1904.

Rooms: 36 rooms, 30 with PB. 6 suites.
Beds: QT.

Many of the guest rooms of this restored Victorian inn overlook Golden Gate Park. The turret suites and bay suites are popular, but all rooms are decorated in a variety of antiques and color schemes. Museums, horseback riding and biking are available in the park, as well as the Japanese Tea Garden.

Fax, copier and bicycles on premises. Handicap access. Weddings, small meetings, family reunions and seminars hosted. Parks, shopping, sporting events and theater nearby. TAC10.

Publicity: *Metropolitan Home, New York Times.*

The Inn at Union Square

440 Post St
San Francisco, CA 94102
(415)397-3510 (800)288-4346
Fax:(415)989-0529
E-mail: inn@unionsquare.com

Rates: $140-350.
Payment: MC VISA AX DC DS PC TC.
Innkeeper(s): Brooks Bayly.
Circa: 1920.

Rooms: 30 rooms with PB, 2 with FP. 7 suites.
Beds: KQDT.

This elegant small hotel is tucked away only one-half block from Union Square. The emphasis here is on comfort and European service, from valet parking, to breakfast in bed, to polished shoes at your door each morning. Each room is individually decorated with fine fabrics, Georgian furniture, and lion-head door knockers. The penthouse suite has a whirlpool bath, sauna, fireplace, and wet bar. Each floor features its own lounge and fireplace where breakfast is served. Afternoon tea includes scones, cakes, and cucumber sandwiches, followed by evening wine and hors d'oeuvres.

Breakfast, afternoon tea and evening snack included in rates. Types of meals: continental-plus breakfast and early coffee/tea. Picnic lunch and room service available. Turn-down service and cable TV in room. VCR, fax, copier, sauna and bicycles on premises. Handicap access. Antiques, parks, shopping, sporting events and theater nearby. TAC10.

Location: In the heart of San Francisco.

Publicity: *Denver Post, Los Angeles Times, Contra Costa Times, Good Housekeeping.*

"My private slice of San Francisco. I'll always stay here."

Victorian Inn on The Park

301 Lyon St
San Francisco, CA 94117
(415)931-1830 (800)435-1967
Fax:(415)931-1830

Rates: $99-164.
Payment: MC VISA AX DC CB DS PC TC.
Innkeeper(s): Lisa & William Benau.
Circa: 1897.

Rooms: 12 rooms with PB, 3 with FP. 2 suites.
Beds: QT.

This grand three-story Queen Anne inn, built by William Curlett, has an open belvedere turret with a teahouse roof and Victorian railings. Silk-screened wallpapers, created especially for the inn, are accentuated by intricate mahogany and redwood paneling. The opulent Belvedere Suite features French doors opening to a Roman tub for two. Overlooking Golden Gate Park, the inn is 10 minutes from downtown.

Breakfast included in rates. Types of meals: continental-plus breakfast and early coffee/tea. Cable TV, fax, library and child care on premises. Small meetings and family reunions hosted. Russian and Spanish spoken. Antiques, parks, sporting events and theater nearby. TAC10.

Location: Adjacent to Golden Gate Park.

Publicity: *Innsider, Country Inns, Good Housekeeping, New York Times, Good Morning America, Country Inns USA, Great Country Inns of America.*

Special Discounts: Romantic special Sunday-Thursday fireplace room with champagne $125.

"The excitement you have about your building comes from the care you have taken in restoring and maintaining your historic structure."

White Swan Inn

845 Bush St
San Francisco, CA 94108
(415)775-1755 (800)999-9570
Fax:(415)775-5717

Rates: $145-250.
Payment: MC VISA AX TC.
Innkeeper(s): Brian Larsen.
Circa: 1915.

Rooms: 26 rooms with PB, 26 with FP. 3 suites. 1 conference room.
Beds: KQT.

This four-story inn is near Union Square and the Powell Street cable car. Beveled-glass doors open to a reception area with granite floors, an antique carousel horse and English artwork. Bay windows and a rear deck contribute to the feeling of an English garden inn. The guest rooms are decorated with bold English wallpapers and prints. All rooms have fireplaces. Turndown service and complimentary newspapers are included, and in the evenings, wine and hors d'oeuvres are served. White Swan is a Four Sisters Inns.

Breakfast and afternoon tea included in rates. Types of meals: gourmet breakfast and early coffee/tea. Picnic lunch available. Turn-down service in room. Fax and copier on premises. Small meetings hosted. Antiques, parks, shopping, sporting events and theater nearby. TAC10.

Location: In the heart of downtown.

Publicity: *Travel & Leisure, Victoria, Wine Spectator.*

Special Discounts: Celebration package available.

"Wonderfully accommodating. Absolutely perfect."

San Gregorio

I4

Rancho San Gregorio

5086 San Gregorio Rd,
Box 54
San Gregorio, CA 94074
(415)747-0810
Fax:(415)747-0184
E-mail: rsgleebud@aol.com

Rates: $75-145.
Payment: MC VISA AX DS PC TC.
Innkeeper(s): Bud & Lee Raynor.
Circa: 1971.

Rooms: 4 rooms with PB, 3 with FP. 1 conference room.
Beds: KQDT.

CA

Built in the Mission style, this home appropriately rests on 15 acres that were part of an old Spanish land grant. Beamed redwood ceilings, terra cotta floors and Spanish furnishings reflect the old Spanish era. Fruits trees and gardens are sprinkled along the ranch's paths. Guests often find their way to the creek just below the inn where there is a picnic table. A barn on the property is more than 100 years old and is said to have been the site for many local dances when the Raynor family originally settled here in the late 1800s. San Francisco is 40 miles to the north.

Breakfast and evening snack included in rates. Types of meals: full breakfast and early coffee/tea. VCR in room. Fax and library on premises. 15 acres. Weddings, small meetings, family reunions and seminars hosted. Antiques, fishing, parks, shopping and theater nearby. TAC10.

Publicity: *Innsider Magazine, Country Magazine, Los Angeles Times, San Francisco Examiner.*

Special Discounts: 10% weekdays over four days.

"A little bit of paradise."

San Jose

I5

The Hensley House

456 N 3rd St
San Jose, CA 95112-5250
(408)298-3537 (800)498-3537
Fax:(408)298-4676

Rates: $79-175.
Payment: MC VISA AX.
Innkeeper(s): Sharon Layne.
Circa: 1884.

Rooms: 5 rooms with PB. 1 suite.
Beds: Q.

This colorful Queen Anne-style, shingled home is topped off with a Witches' cap. Decorated in rich burgundies and blues, rooms are complemented with lacy curtains, chandeliers, dark woodwork and fine furnishings. Each of the well-appointed rooms is unique with special light fixtures, stained glass and beautiful wall coverings. The Judge's Chamber includes a feather bed, fireplace and the modern amenities of a wet bar and whirlpool bath. Breakfast begins with an assortment of coffee, espresso and cappuccino and is followed by fresh fruit and muffins, croissants and an entree. The innkeepers serve a proper high tea on Thursday and Saturday, and wine, teas and hors d'oeuvres are daily afternoon fare.

Breakfast included in rates. Type of meal: full breakfast. Afternoon tea, dinner, picnic lunch, lunch, catering service and room service available. Antiques, fishing and theater nearby.

Publicity: *Mercury News, New York Times, Metro, Business Journal.*

"Can we move in! Wonderful staff, homey atmosphere, very accommodating. Everything was perfect, breakfast was royal."

San Luis Obispo

M7

Apple Farm Inn

2015 Monterey St
San Luis Obispo, CA
93401-2617
(805)544-2040 (800)255-2040

Rates: $95-225.
Innkeeper(s): Katy & Bob Davis.
Circa: 1988.

Rooms: 69 rooms with PB, 69 with FP. 1 conference room.

Each of the guest rooms at Apple Farm is decorated in a burst of color in bright, romantic tones and offers fireplaces and canopy or brass beds. Apple Farm guests can stay either in one of 69 rooms in the elegant inn or the Trellis Court, which is located in a single-story, motel-style building. The four-diamond-rated inn is understandably a favorite of guests traveling the California coast. Trellis Court guests enjoy a complimentary continental breakfast. Aside from lodging, Apple Farm includes a restaurant featuring American cuisine, a gift shop and the Millhouse. At the Millhouse, guests are welcome to watch as the 14-foot paddle wheel creates the energy that grinds the mill's wheat, presses cider and churns homemade ice cream. Try the restaurant's apple specialties during your visit.

Air conditioning, turndown service and cable TV in room. Fax, spa and swimming on premises. Handicap access.

Garden Street Inn

1212 Garden St
San Luis Obispo,
CA 93401-3962
(805)545-9802
Fax:(805)545-9403

Rates: $90-160.
Payment: MC VISA AX.
Innkeeper(s): Kathy & Dan Smith.
Circa: 1887.

Rooms: 13 rooms with PB, 5 with FP. 4 suites. 2 conference rooms.
Beds: KQ.

Innkeepers Dan and Kathy Smith restored this elegant home, paying meticulous attention to detail. Each room has a special theme. The Field of Dreams room, dedicated to Kathy Smith's father, includes memorabilia from his sports reporting days, toy figures from various baseball teams and framed pictures of antique baseball cards. The Cocoon room displays dozens of beautiful butterfly knickknacks. Situated downtown, the inn is within walking distance of shops and restaurants and the San Luis Obispo Mission. Pismo Beach and Hearst Castle are also nearby attractions.

Breakfast and afternoon tea included in rates. Types of meals: full breakfast, gourmet breakfast and early coffee/tea. Air conditioning and turn-down service in room. Fax on premises. Handicap access. Weddings, small meetings and seminars hosted. Antiques, fishing, parks, shopping, sporting events, theater and watersports nearby. TAC10.

Publicity: *Times-Press-Recorder, Telegram-Tribune, San Francisco Chronicle, Los Angeles Times, Orange County Register, Los Angeles Daily News.*

"We appreciate your warmth and care."

Santa Barbara

N8

Bath Street Inn

1720 Bath St
Santa Barbara, CA 93101
(805)682-9680 (800)341-2284
Fax:(805)569-1281

Rates: $80-195.
Payment: MC VISA AX PC.
Innkeeper(s): Susan Brown.
Circa: 1890.

Rooms: 10 rooms with PB, 4 with FP. 1 suite.
Beds: KQT.

Overlooking the Victorian front veranda, a semi-circular "eyelid" balcony on the second floor seems to wink, beckoning guests to come in for an old-fashioned taste of hospitality provided by innkeeper Susan Brown. Originally the home of a merchant tailor, the inn is within a few blocks of the heart of Old Santa

Barbara. Guest chambers upstairs have polished hardwood floors, floral wallpapers and antiques. The back garden deck surrounded by wisteria and blossoming orange trees and the more formal dining room are the locations available for enjoying breakfast, afternoon tea and wine and cheese. The Summer House was recently converted to guest rooms which offer Jacuzzis and fireplaces.

Breakfast, afternoon tea and evening snack included in rates. Types of meals: full breakfast and early coffee/tea. Air conditioning, ceiling fan, cable TV and VCR in room. Fax and copier on premises. Handicap access. Family reunions hosted. Antiques, fishing, parks, shopping, sporting events, theater and watersports nearby. TAC10.

Publicity: *Sunset.*

"Like going to the home of a favorite aunt. Country Inns."

Blue Dolphin Inn

420 W Montecito St
Santa Barbara, CA 93101
(805)965-2333
Fax:(805)962-4907

Rates: $65-185. EP.
Payment: MC VISA AX DC DS PC TC.
Innkeeper(s): Byria O'Hayon-Crosby.
Circa: 1870.

Rooms: 9 rooms with PB, 6 with FP. 3 suites.
Beds: KQT.

It's a short walk to the beach and harbor from this Victorian inn, which offers accommodations in the main house and adjacent carriage house. Guest rooms are decorated in period style with antiques. Brass beds, tapestry pillows, and fluffy comforters add a romantic touch. Several rooms include fireplaces, Jacuzzi tubs or private balconies and terraces. Fresh fruit salads, croissants, homemade breads and quiche highlight the breakfast fare. With prior notice and for an extra cost, the innkeepers can arrange in-room gourmet dinners.

Breakfast and afternoon tea included in rates. Types of meals: gourmet breakfast and early coffee/tea. Picnic lunch and room service available. EP. Ceiling fan, cable TV and VCR in room. Fax and library on premises. Handicap access. Weddings, small meetings, family reunions and seminars hosted. French and Spanish spoken. Antiques, fishing, parks, shopping, sporting events, theater and watersports nearby. TAC10.

Special Discounts: Inquire for off-season rates, special packages.

Casa Del Mar Inn

18 Bath St
Santa Barbara, CA 93101
(805)963-4418 (800)433-3097
Fax:(805)966-4240
E-mail: mikedmont@aol.com

Rates: $69-209.
Payment: MC VISA AX DC DS PC TC.
Innkeeper(s): Mike & Becky Montgomery.
Circa: 1929.

Rooms: 21 rooms with PB, 6 with FP. 6 suites.
Beds: KQ.

This Mediterranean-style inn offers grounds with gardens and a courtyard with a Jacuzzi. Guest can choose from spacious, private rooms or one- and two-room suites with kitchens and fireplaces. Business travelers will appreciate the fax service and modem hook-ups. The inn hosts a special social hour each evening with wine and cheese. An all-you-can-eat buffet breakfast is a perfect start to a day enjoying the Santa Barbara area. The inn is within easy walking distance of shops and restaurants.

Breakfast included in rates. Type of meal: continental-plus breakfast. Ceiling fan and cable TV in room. Fax, copier and spa on premises. Handicap access. Weddings and family reunions hosted. German spoken. Antiques, parks and watersports nearby. TAC10.

Pets Allowed: Small, must not be left alone in room.

Cheshire Cat Inn

36 W Valerio St
Santa Barbara, CA 93101
(805)569-1610
Fax:(805)682-1876

Rates: $100-270.
Payment: MC VISA PC TC.
Innkeeper(s): Christine Dunstan.
Circa: 1894.

Rooms: 14 rooms, 10 with PB. 4 suites. 1 conference room.
Beds: KQT.

The Eberle family built two graceful houses side by side, one a Queen Anne, the other a Colonial Revival. President McKinley was entertained here on a visit to Santa Barbara. There is a pagoda-like porch, a square and a curved bay, rose gardens, grassy lawns and a gazebo. Laura Ashley wallpapers are featured here and in the owner's other inn, a 12th-century manor in Scotland. Large English flower gardens, new deck with sitting areas and fountains, were recently added.

Breakfast included in rates. Type of meal: full breakfast. Room service available. Ceiling fan and cable TV in room. Spa on premises. Weddings, small meetings, family reunions and seminars hosted. Amusement parks, antiques, fishing, shopping, sporting events, theater and watersports nearby.

Location: Downtown.

Publicity: *Two on the Town, KABC, Los Angeles Times, Santa Barbara, American In Flight, Elmer Dills Recommends.*

"Romantic and quaint."

Glenborough Inn

1327 Bath St
Santa Barbara, CA 93101
(805)966-0589 (800)962-0589
Fax:(805)564-8610
E-mail: glenboro@silcom.com

Rates: $100-250.
Payment: MC VISA AX DC CB DS PC TC.
Innkeeper(s): Michael Diaz & Steve Ryan.
Circa: 1906.

Rooms: 11 rooms with PB, 6 with FP. 4 suites. 1 cottage.
Beds: KQD.

This Craftsman-style inn recreates a turn-of-the-century atmosphere in the Main house and White house. There is also an 1880s cottage reminiscent of the Victorian era. Inside are antiques, rich wood trim and elegant fireplace suites with canopy beds. There's always plenty of hospitality and an open invitation to the secluded garden hot tub. Breakfast is homemade and has been written up in "Bon Appetit" and "Chocolatier."

Breakfast included in rates. Types of meals: continental breakfast, full breakfast, gourmet breakfast and early coffee/tea. Dinner, picnic lunch and gourmet lunch available. Ceiling fan in room. Fax and spa on premises. Weddings, small meetings and family reunions hosted. Spanish and Sign spoken. Antiques, fishing, parks, shopping, sporting events, theater and watersports nearby. TAC10.

Publicity: *Houston Post, Los Angeles Times, Horizon, Los Angeles, Pasadena Choice.*

"A delightful, elegant and charming suite.."

The Old Yacht Club Inn

431 Corona Del Mar
Santa Barbara, CA 93103
(805)962-1277 (800)676-1676
Fax:(805)962-3989

Rates: $140-185.
Payment: MC VISA AX DS.
Innkeeper(s): Nancy Donaldson.
Circa: 1912.

Rooms: 10 rooms with PB. 1 conference room.
Beds: KQ.

This California Craftsman house was the home of the Santa Barbara Yacht Club during the Roaring '20s. It was opened as Santa Barbara's first B&B and has become renowned for its gourmet food and superb hospitality. Innkeeper Nancy Donaldson is the author of The Old Yacht Club Inn Cookbook.

Breakfast included in rates. Types of meals: full breakfast, gourmet breakfast and early coffee/tea. Dinner available. Cable TV, fax, copier and bicycles on premises. Small meetings and seminars hosted. Antiques, fishing, shopping, sporting events, theater and watersports nearby.
Location: East Beach.
Publicity: *Los Angeles, Valley.*
"Donaldson is one of Santa Barbara's better-kept culinary secrets."

Olive House Inn

1604 Olive St
Santa Barbara, CA 93101
(805)962-4902 (800)786-6422
Fax:(805)899-2754
E-mail: olivehse@aol.com

Rates: $110-180.
Payment: MC VISA AX DS.
Innkeeper(s): Lois Gregg & Bharti Singh.
Circa: 1904.

Rooms: 6 rooms with PB, 1 with FP.
Beds: KQ.

The Craftsman-style home is located a short walk from Santa Barbara's Mission and downtown. The living room is decorated with bay windows, redwood paneling, a fireplace and a studio grand piano. Two guest rooms have a hot tub. Guests can enjoy city and ocean views from private decks and hot tubs. In the afternoon, wine is offered and in the evening, tea, cookies and sherry are presented.

Breakfast included in rates. Types of meals: full breakfast, gourmet breakfast and early coffee/tea. Evening snack available. Cable TV and fax on premises. Small meetings, family reunions and seminars hosted. Antiques, parks, shopping, sporting events and theater nearby.

"Thank you for providing not only a lovely place to stay but a very warm and inviting atmosphere."

Secret Garden Inn and Cottages

1908 Bath St
Santa Barbara, CA 93101
(805)687-2300 (800)676-1622
Fax:(805)687-4576

Rates: $110-195.
Payment: MC VISA AX PC TC.
Innkeeper(s): Jack Greenwald, Christine Dunstan.
Circa: 1908.

Rooms: 10 rooms with PB, 1 with FP. 3 suites. 4 cottages.
Beds: KQ.

The main house and adjacent cottages surround the lovely gardens and are decorated in American and English-Country style. The Hummingbird is a large cottage guest room with a queen-size white iron bed and a private deck with a hot tub for your exclusive use. The three suites have private outdoor hot tubs. Wine and light hors d'oeuvres are served in the late afternoon, and hot apple cider is served each evening.

Breakfast, afternoon tea and evening snack included in rates. Types of meals: full breakfast and early coffee/tea. Cable TV, fax, copier and bicycles on premises. Weddings, small meetings, family reunions and seminars hosted. Antiques, fishing, shopping, theater and watersports nearby. TAC10.

Location: Quiet residential area near town and the beach.

Publicity: *Los Angeles Times, Santa Barbara, Independant*

Special Discounts: 10% Monday-Thursday January-April & October-December.

"A romantic little getaway retreat that neither of us will be able to forget. It was far from what we expected to find."

Simpson House Inn

121 E Arrellaga St
Santa Barbara, CA 93101
(805)963-7067 (800)676-1280
Fax:(805)564-4811

Rates: $140-315.
Payment: MC VISA AX DS.
Innkeeper(s): Linda & Glyn Davies.
Circa: 1874.

Rooms: 14 rooms with PB, 7 with FP. 5 suites. 1 conference room.
Beds: KQ.

If you were one of the Simpson family's first visitors, you would have arrived in Santa Barbara by stagecoach or by ship. The railroad was not completed for another 14 years. A stately Italianate Victorian house, the inn is situated on an acre of English gardens hidden behind a 20-foot-tall eugenia hedge. Wine and hors d'oeuvres are served in the early evening, and they are particularly enjoyable under the shade of the magnolia trees.

Breakfast and afternoon tea included in rates. Fax, copier and bicycles on premises. Handicap access. Antiques, fishing, theater and watersports nearby.

Location: Five-minute walk to downtown Santa Barbara and the historic district.

Publicity: *Country Inns, Santa Barbara, L.A. Magazine, Avenues.*

"Perfectly restored and impeccably furnished. Your hospitality is warm and heartfelt and the food is delectable. Whoever said that 'the journey is better than the destination' couldn't have known about the Simpson House."

The Upham Hotel & Garden Cottages

1404 De La Vina St
Santa Barbara, CA 93101
(805)962-0058 (800)727-0876
Fax:(805)963-2825

Rates: $125-365.
Payment: MC VISA AX DC CB DS TC.
Innkeeper(s): Jan Martin Winn.
Circa: 1871.

Rooms: 50 rooms with PB, 8 with FP. 4 suites. 4 cottages. 4 conference rooms.
Beds: KQD.

Antiques and period furnishings decorate each of the inn's guest rooms and suites. The inn is the oldest continuously operating hostelry in Southern California. Situated on an acre of gardens in the center of downtown, it's within easy walking distance of restaurants, shops, art galleries and museums. The staff is happy to assist guests in discovering Santa Barbara's varied attractions. Garden cottage units feature porches or secluded patios and several have gas fireplaces.

Breakfast and evening snack included in rates. Types of meals: continental-plus breakfast and early coffee/tea. Banquet service available. Ceiling fan and cable TV in room. VCR, fax and copier on premises. Small meetings, family reunions and seminars hosted. Spanish spoken. Antiques, fishing, parks, shopping, sporting events, theater and watersports nearby. TAC10.

Publicity: *Los Angeles Times, Santa Barbara, Westways, Santa Barbara News-Press.*

Special Discounts: 10% off for seniors staying Sunday-Thursday.

"Your hotel is truly a charm. Between the cozy gardens and the exquisitely comfortable appointments, The Upham is charm itself."

Santa Clara *I5*

Madison Street Inn

1390 Madison St
Santa Clara, CA 95050
(408)249-5541 (800)491-5541
Fax:(408)249-6676
E-mail: madstinn@aol.com

Rates: $60-85.
Payment: MC VISA AX DC DS PC TC.
Innkeeper(s): Theresa & Ralph Wigginton.
Circa: 1890.

Rooms: 6 rooms, 4 with PB.
Beds: QD.

This Queen Anne Victorian inn still boasts its original doors and locks, and "No Peddlers or Agents" is engraved in the cement of the original carriageway. Guests, however, always receive a warm and gracious welcome to high-ceilinged rooms furnished in antiques, Oriental rugs and Victorian wallpaper.

Breakfast, afternoon tea and evening snack included in rates. Types of meals: continental breakfast, continental-plus breakfast, full breakfast, gourmet breakfast and early coffee/tea. Picnic lunch, gourmet lunch, banquet service, catering service and catered breakfast available. Ceiling fan in room. Cable TV, VCR, fax, spa, swimming and bicycles on premises. Weddings, small meetings, family reunions and seminars hosted. Amusement parks, antiques, parks, sporting events, theater and watersports nearby. TAC10.

Pets Allowed.

Location: Ten minutes from San Jose airport.

Publicity: *Discovery.*

"We spend many nights in hotels that look and feel exactly alike whether they are in Houston or Boston. Your inn was delightful. It was wonderful to bask in your warm and gracious hospitality."

Santa Cruz *J5*

Babbling Brook B&B Inn

1025 Laurel St
Santa Cruz, CA 95060-4237
(408)427-2437 (800)866-1131
Fax:(408)427-2457

Rates: $85-165.
Payment: MC VISA AX DC CB DS TC.
Innkeeper(s): Helen King.
Circa: 1909.

Rooms: 12 rooms with PB, 10 with FP.
Beds: KQ.

This inn was built on the foundations of an 1870 tannery and a 1790 grist mill. Secluded, yet within the city, the inn features a cascading waterfall, historic waterwheel and meandering creek on one acre of gardens and redwoods. Country French decor, cozy fireplaces, and deep-soaking whirlpool tubs are luxurious amenities of the Babbling Brook. In the evenings, complimentary wine and cheese are served.

Breakfast, afternoon tea and evening snack included in rates. Types of meals: full breakfast, gourmet breakfast and early coffee/tea. Room service available. Cable TV in room. Fax, computer and spa on premises. Handicap access. Weddings hosted. Spanish and limited French spoken. Amusement parks, antiques, fishing, parks, shopping, sporting events, theater and watersports nearby. TAC10.
Location: North end of Monterey Bay.
Publicity: *Country Inns, Yellow Brick Road, Times-Press-Recorder.*
"We were impressed with the genuine warmth of the inn. The best breakfast we've had outside our own home!"

CA

Chateau Victorian

118 1st St
Santa Cruz, CA 95060-5402
(408)458-9458

Rates: $110-140.
Payment: MC VISA PC.
Innkeeper(s): Alice June.

Rooms: 7 rooms with PB, 7 with FP. 1 suite. 1 cottage.
Beds: Q.

This charming, rose-colored Victorian is within a block of the waterfront. No wonder so many of the inn's guests choose the romantic Ocean View Room, which offers a marble fireplace, clawfoot tub, and, of course, the beautiful Monterey Bay just out the window. Breakfasts, including a variety of tempting fruits and bread can be enjoyed in a variety of settings, on the front terrace, the patio, dining room or on the secluded side deck. After a day of exploring Santa Cruz and its surroundings, evening refreshments are a perfect touch. The inn is within walking distance to downtown, the wharf, a variety of restaurants and the Boardwalk Amusement Park.

Breakfast included in rates. Type of meal: continental-plus breakfast. Evening snack available. Small meetings hosted. Amusement parks, antiques, fishing, parks, shopping, theater and watersports nearby.

Location: One block from the beach.

Publicity: *Times Tribune, Santa Cruz Sentinel, Good Times.*

Special Discounts: 7th night free, accumulative 6 nights.

"Certainly enjoyed our most recent stay and have appreciated all of our visits."

Cliff Crest B&B

407 Cliff St
Santa Cruz, CA 95060-5009
(408)427-2609 (800)427-2609
Fax:(408)427-2710
E-mail: innkpr@cliffcrestinn.com

Rates: $95-165.
Payment: MC VISA AX DS PC TC.
Innkeeper(s): Sharon & Bruce Taylor.
Circa: 1887.

Rooms: 5 rooms with PB, 2 with FP.
Beds: KQ.

Warmth, friendliness and comfort characterize this elegantly restored Queen Anne Victorian home. An octagonal solarium, tall stained-glass windows, and a belvedere overlook Monterey Bay and the Santa Cruz Mountains. The mood is airy and romantic. The spacious gardens were designed by John McLaren, landscape architect for Golden Gate Park. Antiques and fresh flowers fill the rooms, once home to William Jeter, lieutenant governor of California.

Breakfast and evening snack included in rates. Types of meals: full breakfast and early coffee/tea. Fax on premises. Amusement parks, antiques, fishing, parks, shopping, theater and watersports nearby. TAC10.

Location: Two-and-a-half blocks from the beach and boardwalk.

Publicity: *Los Angeles Times.*

"Delightful place, excellent food and comfortable bed."

Valley View B&B

600 Hacienda Dr
Santa Cruz, CA 95066-3310
(415)321-5195
Fax:(415)325-5121

Rates: $195.
Payment: MC VISA AX DC CB PC TC.
Innkeeper(s): Tricia Young.
Circa: 1962.

Rooms: 2 rooms with PB.
Beds: KQ.

This Frank Lloyd Wright-style house was built by one of the famed architect's students. It is offered as an unhosted two bedroom house for couples. Located in the mountains outside Santa Cruz, it offers panoramic views from its wide circular deck and vast stretches of floor-to-ceiling windows. There is an unusual massive circular

fireplace. Guests prepare their own breakfast from the stocked refrigerator. The privacy, pleasant contemporary decor and the setting makes it well worthwhile.

Breakfast included in rates. Type of meal: continental-plus breakfast. Cable TV in room. VCR and spa on premises. Amusement parks, antiques, fishing, parks, shopping, sporting events, theater and watersports nearby. TAC10.

Santa Monica O10

Channel Road Inn

219 W Channel Rd
Santa Monica, CA 90402
(310)459-1920
Fax:(310)454-9920
E-mail: channel@village.ios.com

Rates: $95-225.
Payment: MC VISA AX PC TC.
Innkeeper(s): Kathy Jensen.
Circa: 1910.

Rooms: 12 rooms with PB, 2 with FP. 2 suites.
Beds: KQDT.

This shingle-clad building is a variation of the Colonial Revival Period, one of the few remaining in Los Angeles. The abandoned home was saved from the city's wrecking crew by Susan Zolla, with the encouragement of the local historical society. The rooms feature canopy beds, fine linens, custom mattresses and private porches. Chile Cheese Puff served with salsa, is a popular breakfast speciality. The Pacific Ocean is one block away, and guests often enjoy borrowing the inn's bicycles to pedal along the 30-mile coastal bike path. In the evening, the inn's spectacular cliffside spa is popular.

Breakfast, afternoon tea and evening snack included in rates. Types of meals: full breakfast and early coffee/tea. Room service available. Ceiling fan, cable TV and VCR in room. Fax, copier, computer, spa and bicycles on premises. Handicap access. Amusement parks, antiques, fishing, parks, shopping, sporting events, theater and watersports nearby. TAC10.

Location: One block from the ocean.

Publicity: *Los Angeles Magazine, New York Times, Brides.*

"One of the most romantic hotels in Los Angeles."

Santa Rosa G4

The Gables Inn

4257 Petaluma Hill Rd
Santa Rosa, CA 95404-9796
(707)585-7777 (800)422-5376
Fax:(707)584-5634

Rates: $110-190.
Payment: MC VISA AX DS.
Innkeeper(s): Michael & Judy Ogne.
Circa: 1877.

Rooms: 8 rooms with PB, 4 with FP. 1 suite. 1 cottage.
Beds: KQT.

Fifteen gables accentuate this striking Gothic Revival house with a French influence situated on three-and-a-half acres in the Sonoma Wine Country. Inside, there are 12-foot ceilings, a winding staircase with ornately carved balustrades, and three marble fireplaces. The Brookside Suite overlooks Taylor Creek and is decorated in an Edwardian theme. Other rooms feature views of the sequoias, meadows and the barn.

Breakfast and afternoon tea included in rates. Types of meals: gourmet breakfast and early coffee/tea. Handicap access. Antiques, fishing, parks, shopping, sporting events, theater and watersports nearby. TAC10.

Publicity: *Press Democrat.*

"You all have a warmth about you that makes it home here. "

Melitta Station Inn

5850 Melita Rd
Santa Rosa, CA 95409-5641
(707)538-7712 (800)504-3099

Rates: $70-95.
Payment: MC VISA.
Innkeeper(s): Diane Crandon & Vic Amstadter.
Circa: 1890.

Rooms: 6 rooms, 4 with PB. 1 suite.
Beds: QD.

Originally built as a stagecoach stop, this rambling structure became a freight depot for the little town of Melitta. Basalt stone quarried from nearby hills was sent by rail to San Francisco where it was used to

pave the cobblestone streets. Still located down a country lane, the station has been charmingly renovated. Oiled-wood floors, a rough-beam cathedral ceiling and French doors opening to a balcony are features of the sitting room. Wineries and vineyards stretch from the station to the town of Sonoma.

Breakfast included in rates. Types of meals: gourmet breakfast and early coffee/tea. Family reunions hosted. Antiques, fishing, parks and theater nearby.

Publicity: *Los Angeles Times, New York Times, Press Democrat.*

"Warm welcome and great food."

CA

Pygmalion House B&B Inn

331 Orange St
Santa Rosa, CA 95401-6226
(707)526-3407
Fax:(707)526-3407

Rates: $75-95.
Payment: MC VISA PC TC.
Innkeeper(s): Caroline Berry.
Circa: 1880.

Rooms: 6 rooms with PB. 1 suite.
Beds: KQD.

This historic Victorian, which has been restored to its 19th-century grandeur, is just a few blocks from Santa Rosa's Old Town and many antique shops, cafes, coffeehouses and restaurants. The home is filled with a unique mix of antiques, many of which belonged to famed stripper, Gypsy Rose Lee. Each of the Victorian guest rooms includes a bath with a clawfoot tub. Five different varieties of coffees are prepared each morning for breakfast service, which includes homemade entrees, freshly baked breads and fresh fruit.

Breakfast included in rates. Types of meals: full breakfast and early coffee/tea. Afternoon tea and evening snack available. Air conditioning and cable TV in room. Fax and copier on premises. Family reunions and seminars hosted. Antiques, parks, shopping, sporting events, theater and watersports nearby.

Vintners Inn

4350 Barnes Rd
Santa Rosa, CA 95403-1514
(707)575-7350 (800)421-2584
Fax:(707)575-1426

Rates: $128-205.
Payment: MC VISA AX DC CB TC.
Innkeeper(s): John & Cindy Duffy.
Circa: 1984.

Rooms: 44 rooms, 39 with PB, 23 with FP. 5 suites. 2 conference rooms.
Beds: Q.

This inn, developed after touring the French countryside, consists of several red tile-roofed buildings gathered around a village-like courtyard with a fountain. The inn's 45-acre vineyard features Chardonnay and Sauvignon Blanc grapes, and there are 100-year-old French Columbard vines. Antique French-country furnishings, beamed ceilings and fireplaces are found in many of the rooms, and all have balconies or patios to enjoy the wine country setting. The inn is popular for small gatherings, and it also offers a four-diamond restaurant.

Breakfast included in rates. Type of meal: continental-plus breakfast. Lunch, banquet service and room service available. Air conditioning, turn-down service and cable TV in room. VCR, fax, copier and spa on premises. Handicap access. 50 acres. Small meetings hosted. Spanish spoken. Antiques, parks, shopping and theater nearby. TAC10.

Sausalito H4

Casa Madrona Hotel

801 Bridgeway
Sausalito, CA 94965-2186
(415)332-0502 (800)567-9524
Fax:(415)332-2537

Rates: $125-245. MAP.
Payment: MC VISA AX DC DS TC.
Innkeeper(s): John W. Mays.
Circa: 1885.

Rooms: 35 rooms with PB. 3 suites. 4 cottages. 1 conference room.
Beds: KQT.

This Victorian mansion was first used as a lumber baron's mansion. As time went on, additional cottages were added, giving it a European look. A registered Sausalito Historical Landmark, it is the oldest building in town. Each room has a unique name, such as "Lord Ashley's Lookout" or "Kathmandu," and the appointments are as varied as the names. The inn faces San Francisco Bay, enabling guests to enjoy the barking seals, the evening fog and the arousing sunsets. Rooms have fireplaces and decks overlooking the bay.

Breakfast and evening snack included in rates. Type of meal: continental-plus breakfast. Banquet service, catering service and room service available. MAP. Turn-down service and cable TV in room. VCR, fax, copier and spa on premises. Weddings, small meetings and family reunions hosted. Parks, shopping, sporting events, theater and watersports nearby. TAC10.

Location: Downtown Sausalito.

Publicity: *Los Angeles Times, Orange County Register.*

"Had to pinch myself several times to be sure it was real! Is this heaven? With this view it, sure feels like it."

Seal Beach — O10

The Seal Beach Inn & Gardens

212 5th St
Seal Beach, CA 90740-6115
(562)493-2416 (800)HIDEAWAY
Fax:(562)799-0483

Rates: $118-185. AP.
Payment: MC VISA AX DC CB DS TC.
Innkeeper(s): Marjorie B. & Harty Schmaehl.
Circa: 1923.

Rooms: 23 rooms with PB, 4 with FP. 11 suites.
Beds: KQ.

This historic Southern California inn has lush gardens and the look of an oceanside estate. It's a short walk to the Seal Beach pier, shops and restaurants. Major attractions in Orange County and the Los Angeles area are within short driving distances. Business travelers can plan meetings in rooms where 24 people can sit comfortably. The inn has a Mediterranean villa ambiance, and no two rooms are alike.

Breakfast and evening snack included in rates. Types of meals: full breakfast and early coffee/tea. Afternoon tea available. AP. Turn-down service in room. Fax and copier on premises. Weddings, small meetings, family reunions and seminars hosted. Amusement parks, antiques, fishing, parks, shopping, sporting events, theater and watersports nearby.

Location: 300 yards from the ocean, five minutes from Long Beach.

Publicity: *Brides, Country Inns, Glamour, Country, Long Beach Press Telegram, Orange County Register, Los Angeles Times.*

"The closest thing to Europe since I left there. Delights the senses and restores the soul."

Soda Springs — C5

Royal Gorges Rainbow Lodge

9411 Hillside Dr, PO Box 1100,
Soda Springs, CA 95728
(916)426-3871 (800)500-3871
Fax:(916)426-9221
E-mail: royalg@ix.netcom.com

Rates: $79-109. AP.
Payment: MC VISA TC.
Innkeeper(s): Jacqui James.
Circa: 1920.

Rooms: 32 rooms, 10 with PB. 2 suites. 1 conference room.
Beds: QDT.

Located on a bend of the Yuba River, this old mountain lodge offers a picturesque site to enjoy the area's fishing, hiking and skiing. The lodge is decorated with pictures of Donner Summit and the railroad. The lounge offers an area for playing games. The Historic Rainbow Bar has been refurbished.

Breakfast included in rates. Types of meals: full breakfast and gourmet breakfast. Dinner, lunch, gourmet lunch and banquet service available. AP. Cable TV and fax on premises. Weddings, small meetings, family reunions and seminars hosted. Antiques, fishing, parks, shopping, downhill skiing, cross-country skiing, sporting events and watersports nearby.

Sonoma Hotel

110 W Spain St
Sonoma, CA 95476-5696
(707)996-2996 (800)468-6016
Fax:(707)996-7014

Rates: $60-125.
Payment: MC VISA AX DC PC TC.
Innkeeper(s): Dorene & John Musilli.
Circa: 1879.

Rooms: 17 rooms, 5 with PB. 1 suite.
Beds: DT.

Originally built as a two-story adobe, a third story was added in the '20s and it became the Plaza Hotel. The first floor now boasts an award-winning restaurant. The top two floors contain antique-filled guest rooms. The Vallejo Room is furnished with a massive carved rosewood bedroom suite. In room 21, Maya Angelou wrote "Gather Together in My Name." A short walk from the tree-lined plaza are several wineries.

Breakfast included in rates. Types of meals: continental breakfast and early coffee/tea. Gourmet lunch available. Fax and copier on premises. Weddings and family reunions hosted. Italian spoken. Antiques, parks, shopping and theater nearby. TAC5.

Publicity: *Americana, House Beautiful, Press Democrat, California Getaway Guide.*

"Great food and service! I was so pleased to see such a warm and lovable place."

Starwae Inn

21490 Broadway
Sonoma, CA 95476-8204
(707)938-1374 (800)793-4792
Fax:(707)935-1159

Rates: $125-185. EP.
Payment: MC VISA TC.
Innkeeper(s): John Curry & Janice Crow.
Circa: 1930.

Rooms: 4 suites. 2 cottages. 1 conference room.
Beds: QD.

There are two cottages at this inn, divided somewhat like a duplex. Each side of the cottages has a suite with a separate entrance, bathroom and bedroom. The innkeepers, both local artists live on the property and their studios are on the grounds as well. The cottages feature original artwork and pottery, and guest rooms also feature some furnishings handcrafted by one of the innkeepers. Individual quiche, fresh fruit and scones are among the treats served for breakfast.

Breakfast included in rates. Type of meal: continental-plus breakfast. EP. Air conditioning and cable TV in room. Fax, copier and bicycles on premises. Small meetings and seminars hosted. Antiques, fishing, parks, shopping and theater nearby.

Trojan Horse Inn

19455 Sonoma Hwy
Sonoma, CA 95476-6416
(707)996-2430 (800)899-1925

Rates: $125-145.
Payment: MC VISA AX.
Innkeeper(s): John & Doris Leonard.
Circa: 1887.

Rooms: 6 rooms with PB, 1 with FP. 1 conference room.
Beds: Q.

This blue Victorian home rests on one acre on the banks of Sonoma Creek. Recently restored, the pristine interiors offer antiques and a romantic country decor. The Bridal Veil Room has a canopied bed, wood-burning stove and windows overlooking a magnolia tree, while a private Jacuzzi tub is a popular feature in the Grape Arbor Room. Bicycles, an additional outdoor Jacuzzi, flower gardens and grand old bay and spruce trees add to the experience.

Types of meals: full breakfast and early coffee/tea. Air conditioning and ceiling fan in room. Spa and bicycles on premises. Handicap access. Small meetings and family reunions hosted. Antiques, shopping and theater nearby.

Location: In the heart of California's world famous Wine Country. On the banks of the Sonoma Creek just a mile from the historic Sonoma Square.

Publicity: *Contra Costa Times, Mobil Travel Guide, Sonoma Index Tribune.*

"We came for one night and stayed for four."

Sonora H7

Lavender Hill B&B

683 Barretta St
Sonora, CA 95370-5132
(209)532-9024

Rates: $75-95.
Payment: MC VISA AX.
Innkeeper(s): Jean & Charles Marinelli.

Rooms: 4 rooms with PB.

In the historic Gold Rush town of Sonora is this Queen Anne Victorian inn. Its four guest rooms include the Lavender Room, which has a mini-suite with desk, sitting area and clawfoot tub and shower. After a busy day fishing, biking, river rafting or exploring nearby Yosemite National Park, guests may relax in the antique-filled parlor or the sitting room. Admiring the inn's gardens from the wraparound porch is also a favorite activity. Be sure to ask about dinner theater packages.

Breakfast included in rates. Types of meals: full breakfast and early coffee/tea. Air conditioning, turn-down service and ceiling fan in room. Cable TV on premises. Weddings, small meetings, family reunions, seminars hosted. Antiques, skiing, sporting events, theater nearby.

Ryan House, 1855

153 S Shepherd St
Sonora, CA 95370-4736
(209)533-3445 (800)831-4897
Fax:(209)532-0277

Rates: $85-175.
Payment: MC VISA AX PC TC.
Innkeeper(s): Nancy & Guy Hoffman.
Circa: 1855.

Rooms: 4 rooms with PB, 1 with FP. 1 suite.
Beds: Q.

This restored homestead is set well back from the street in a quiet residential area. Green lawns and gardens with 35 varieties of roses surround the house. Each room is individually decorated with handsome antiques. A suite is available that includes a private parlor with stove and a bathroom with a two-person tub. An antique-style cookstove sets the mood for a country breakfast served in the dining room.

Breakfast and afternoon tea included in rates. Types of meals: full breakfast, gourmet breakfast and early coffee/tea. Air conditioning and ceiling fan in room. Cable TV, VCR and library on premises. Small meetings and family reunions hosted. Antiques, fishing, parks, shopping, skiing, theater and watersports nearby. TAC10.

Location: Two blocks from the heart of historic Sonora.

Publicity: *Home and Garden, Union Democrat, California, Sunset, L.A. Style.*

"Everything our friends said it would be: warm, comfortable and great breakfasts. You made us feel like long-lost friends the moment we arrived."

Serenity - A B&B Inn

15305 Bear Cub Dr
Sonora, CA 95370-9696
(209)533-1441 (800)426-1441

Rates: $90-125.
Payment: MC VISA AX PC TC.
Innkeeper(s): Fred & Charlotte Hoover.

Rooms: 4 rooms with PB, 2 with FP.
Beds: KQT.
Circa: 1984.

A glorious old-fashioned veranda wraps around three sides of this white clapboard inn, designed in a "Gold Rush Colonial" style. The guest rooms are decorated simply in floral themes and feature handmade quilts and lace-trimmed linens. Serenity was rebuilt after a fire and is located on six acres of ponderosa pines and wildflowers near the Stanislaus National Forest.

Breakfast and evening snack included in rates. Types of meals: full breakfast and early coffee/tea. Air conditioning, turn-down service and ceiling fan in room. Library on premises. Antiques, fishing, parks, shopping, skiing, theater and watersports nearby. TAC10.

Location: Six miles east of downtown.

Publicity: *Country Inns.*

"We have already advertised to all our friends the wonderful extras that come with a stay at Serenity."

Soquel J5

Blue Spruce Inn

2815 S Main St
Soquel, CA 95073-2412
(408)464-1137 (800)559-1137
Fax:(408)475-0608
E-mail: pobrien@got.net

Rates: $85-150.
Payment: MC VISA AX PC TC.
Innkeeper(s): Patricia & Tom O'Brien.
Circa: 1875.

Rooms: 6 rooms with PB, 5 with FP. 1 conference room.
Beds: QT.

Near the north coast of Monterey Bay, this old farmhouse has been freshly renovated and refitted with luxurious touches. The Seascape is a favorite room with its private entrance, wicker furnishings and bow-shaped Jacuzzi for two. The Carriage House offers skylights above the bed, while a heart decor dominates Two

Hearts. Local art, Amish quilts and featherbeds are featured throughout. Brunch enchiladas are the inn's speciality. Santa Cruz is four miles away.

Breakfast and evening snack included in rates. Types of meals: full breakfast, gourmet breakfast and early coffee/tea. Turn-down service, cable TV and VCR in room. Fax and library on premises. Small meetings and seminars hosted. Spanish spoken. Amusement parks, antiques, fishing, parks, shopping, theater and watersports nearby. TAC10.

Location: At the edge of Soquel Village, mid-Santa Cruz County, north shore of the Monterey Bay.

Publicity: *Village View.*

"You offer such graciousness to your guests and a true sense of welcome."

CA

South Pasadena **O10**

The Artists' Inn B&B

1038 Magnolia St
South Pasadena,
CA 91030-2518
(818)799-5668 (888)799-5668
Fax:(818)799-3678

Rates: $100-130.
Payment: MC VISA AX PC TC.
Innkeeper(s): Leah & Scott Roberts.
Circa: 1895.

Rooms: 5 rooms with PB. 1 suite.
Beds: KQDT.

A poultry farm once surrounded this turn-of-the-century home. Today the streets are lined with trees and a variety of beautiful homes. Interior designer Janet Marangi restored the historic ambiance of the cheery, yellow home, filling it with antiques and original artwork. Each of the guest rooms captures a different artistic style. Soft, soothing colors enrich the Impressionist room, which includes a clawfoot tub and brass bed. The Italian Suite is decorated in rich hues and includes an adjoining sunroom. The 18th Century English room is filled with pieces by Gainsborough, Reynolds and Constable and includes a romantic, canopied bed. Innkeeper Leah Roberts creates a breakfast menu with freshly made breads, homemade granola, fruit and a special entree. The home is just a few blocks from South Pasadena's many shops, boutiques, cafes and restaurants.

Breakfast and afternoon tea included in rates. Types of meals: continental breakfast, continental-plus breakfast, full breakfast, gourmet breakfast and early coffee/tea. Dinner, picnic lunch, gourmet lunch, catered breakfast and room service available. Air conditioning and ceiling fan in room. Cable TV, fax and library on premises. Weddings, small meetings and family reunions hosted. Amusement parks, antiques, parks, shopping, sporting events and theater nearby. TAC10.

Publicity: *Pasadena Star News, San Marino Tribune, Stanford, Pasadena Weekly, South Pasadena Review, Recommended by Elmer Dills, Travel & Leisure.*

Summerland **N8**

The Inn on Summer Hill

2520 Lillie Ave
Summerland, CA 93067
(805)969-9998 (800)845-5566
Fax:(805)565-9946

Rates: $165-295.
Payment: MC VISA AX DS.
Innkeeper(s): Verlinda Richardson.
Circa: 1989.

Rooms: 16 rooms with PB. 1 suite.
Beds: KQ.

Although recently constructed, the inn is a stunning example of early Craftsman-style architecture. Each of the guest rooms boasts a view of the Pacific Ocean. The incredible rooms are filled to the brim with beautiful furnishings, fluffy pillows, comforters and an eclectic mix of colors. Sumptuous gourmet breakfasts are followed later in the day with hors d'oeuvres and wine and the day is topped off with fresh baked cookies and desserts in the candlelit dining room. Try out one of the inn's many unique packages. The Gourmet Grape Escape features a wine sampler gift basket, wine tasting on nearby Santa Barbara's wharf and a romantic dinner for two. The Polo in Paradise includes tickets to a polo match and picnic lunch, while the Pedal and Paddle package takes guests on a two-hour guided bicycling or kayaking tour with a gourmet picnic lunch. The inn is adjacent to the freeway, which will take guests the short distance into Santa Barbara.

Breakfast included in rates. Type of meal: full breakfast. Picnic lunch, catering service and room service available. Antiques, fishing, theater and watersports nearby. TAC10.

Publicity: *Country Inns, Victoria, Brides.*

"This inn is outstanding. The four star rating should be a five. We have not stayed at any inn that compares to this one."

The Gold Quartz Inn

15 Bryson Dr
Sutter Creek, CA 95685
(209)267-9155 (800)752-8738
Fax:(209)267-9170
E-mail: 6quartz@cdepot.net

Rates: $80-150.
Payment: MC VISA AX DS PC TC.
Innkeeper(s): Wendy Woolrich.
Circa: 1988.

Rooms: 24 rooms with PB. 2 suites. 1 conference room.
Beds: KDT.

A small footbridge leads to the wrap-around porch and entrance to this gabled inn, set among the hills above Sutter Creek. In the parlor are antique sofas in pastel fabrics, delicate wallpapers and a pink marble fireplace mantel. The bridal suite features a lavish, lace-topped, four-poster bed and a deep antique clawfoot tub.

Breakfast and afternoon tea included in rates. Types of meals: full breakfast and early coffee/tea. Catering service available. Air conditioning, ceiling fan and cable TV in room. VCR, fax and copier on premises. Handicap access. Small meetings, family reunions and seminars hosted. Antiques, fishing, shopping, downhill skiing, cross-country skiing, theater and watersports nearby. TAC10.

Grey Gables B&B Inn

161 Hanford St,
PO Box 1687
Sutter Creek, CA 95685
(209)267-1039 (800)473-9422
Fax:(209)267-0998

Rates: $85-135.
Payment: MC VISA AX DS PC TC.
Innkeeper(s): Roger & Susan Garlick.
Circa: 1897.

Rooms: 8 rooms with PB, 8 with FP.
Beds: KQT.

The innkeepers of this Victorian home offer poetic accommodations both in the delightful decor and by the names of their guest rooms. The Keats, Bronte and Tennyson rooms afford garden views, while the Byron and Browning rooms include clawfoot tubs. The Victorian Suite, which encompasses the top floor, affords views of the garden, as well as a historic churchyard. All of the guest rooms boast fireplaces. Stroll down brick pathways through the terraced garden or relax in the parlor. A proper English tea is served with cakes and scones. Hors d'oeuvres and libations are served in the evenings.

Breakfast, afternoon tea and evening snack included in rates. Types of meals: gourmet breakfast and early coffee/tea. Air conditioning and ceiling fan in room. Fax and copier on premises. Handicap access. Antiques, fishing, parks, shopping, downhill skiing, cross-country skiing, theater and watersports nearby. TAC10.

The Hanford House

61 Hanford St, Hwy 49
Sutter Creek, CA 95685
(209)267-0747 (800)871-5839
Fax:(209)267-1825
E-mail: bobkat@hanfordhouse.com

Rates: $89-139.
Payment: MC VISA DS TC.
Innkeeper(s): Bob & Karen Tierno.
Circa: 1929.

Rooms: 10 rooms with PB, 2 with FP. 1 conference room.
Beds: Q.

When Karen and Bob Tierno purchased this unique Gold Country inn, they were determined to maintain the former innkeepers' standards for hospitality. Karen and Bob went a step further and added many new amenities for their guests, including a conference room, fax machine and providing computer access. While these touches are perfect for the business traveler, the inn is still a place to relax. The inn offers a shaded outdoor patio, charming parlor and a roof-top sundeck. Guests are greeted with freshly baked cookies upon check-in, treated to a homemade breakfast each morning and invited to partake in afternoon refreshments. Wineries, antiquing and historic sites are nearby.

Breakfast, afternoon tea and evening snack included in rates. Types of meals: full breakfast, gourmet breakfast and early coffee/tea. Catering service available. Air conditioning and ceiling fan in room. Fax on premises. Handicap access. Weddings, small meetings, family reunions and seminars hosted. Antiques and parks nearby.

Temecula **P12**

Loma Vista B&B

33350 La Serena Way
Temecula, CA 92591-5049
(909)676-7047
Fax:(909)676-0077

Rates: $95-135.
Payment: MC VISA DS PC TC.
Innkeeper(s): Betty & Dick Ryan.
Circa: 1987.

Rooms: 6 rooms with PB.
Beds: KQT.

This California Mission-style home offers vineyard views from its balconies. Each guest room is named for a variety of wine. The Fume Blanc, Zinfandel, Sauvignon Blanc and Chardonnay rooms include private balconies where guests can take in the view. Champagne breakfasts get the day off to a good start, and evening wine and cheese is served. After dinner, relax in the inn's hot tub. The area is full of activities, including winery tours, shopping and hot air ballooning. Temecula is an hour from San Diego and about 90 miles from Los Angeles.

Breakfast and evening snack included in rates. Types of meals: gourmet breakfast and early coffee/tea. Air conditioning and ceiling fan in room. Cable TV, fax, spa, bicycles and library on premises. Weddings, small meetings and family reunions hosted. Antiques, fishing and parks nearby. TAC10.

Location: Wine country, 5 miles from Lake Skinner.

Publicity: *Sunset, Bride's Magazine, Los Angeles Times, Los Angeles Magazine.*

Special Discounts: Mid-week.

Templeton **L6**

Country House Inn

91 S Main St
Templeton, CA 93465-8701
(805)434-1598 (800)362-6032

Rates: $85-95.
Payment: MC VISA DS PC.
Innkeeper(s): Dianne Garth.
Circa: 1886.

Rooms: 5 rooms with PB, 1 with FP. 1 suite.
Beds: KQT.

This Victorian home, built by the founder of Templeton, is set off by rose-bordered gardens. It was designated as a historic site in San Luis Obispo County. All of the rooms are decorated with antiques and fresh flowers. Hearst Castle and six wineries are nearby.

Breakfast included in rates. Types of meals: full breakfast, gourmet breakfast and early coffee/tea. Afternoon tea available. Ceiling fan in room. Weddings, small meetings and family reunions hosted. Antiques, fishing, parks, shopping, theater and watersports nearby. TAC10.

Location: Twenty miles north of San Luis Obispo on Hwy 101.

"A feast for all the senses, an esthetic delight."

Trinidad **C2**

The Lost Whale Inn B&B

3452 Patricks Point Dr
Trinidad, CA 95570-9782
(707)677-3425 (800)677-7859
Fax:(707)677-0284
E-mail: lmiller@northcoast.com

Rates: $100-160.
Payment: MC VISA AX DS PC TC.
Innkeeper(s): Susanne Lakin & Lee Miller.
Circa: 1989.

Rooms: 8 rooms with PB. 2 cottages. 1 conference room.
Beds: QDT.

The view from this Cape Cod-style inn is one of the best in Northern California. Rugged coastline and an endless sea, dotted from time to time with whales, is what guests enjoy from the inn's relaxing porch. Several guest rooms offer ocean views. Innkeepers Susanne Lakin and Lee Miller are an artist and musician, respectively, and their creative energy has formed a wonderful sense of romance throughout the inn. However, there is a family atmosphere prevalent as well. The innkeepers offer several sleeping lofts for children, a playground area and a variety of animals to pet.

Breakfast and afternoon tea included in rates. Types of meals: gourmet breakfast and early coffee/tea. Fax, copier, spa and library on premises. Small meetings, family reunions and seminars hosted. Antiques, fishing, parks, shopping, cross-country skiing, sporting events, theater and watersports nearby. TAC10.

Special Discounts: Mid-week winter discounts.

Trinidad B&B

PO Box 849
Trinidad, CA 95570-0849
(707)677-0840

Rates: $99-155.
Payment: MC VISA PC TC.
Innkeeper(s): Carol & Paul Kirk.
Circa: 1949.

Rooms: 4 rooms with PB, 1 with FP. 2 suites.
Beds: KQ.

Enjoy ocean views from your room at this New England Cape Cod-style home, which is located on Northern California's beautiful coast. The memorable full breakfasts include items such as baked apples and sausages, fresh fruit topped with yogurt and locally made cheeses. Guests in two of the inn's four rooms can enjoy breakfast delivered to their door. Redwood National Park is just 15 minutes from the inn.

Breakfast, afternoon tea and evening snack included in rates. Types of meals: full breakfast and early coffee/tea. Antiques, fishing, parks and theater nearby.

"We went away with wonderful memories of the warmth you extended."

Truckee F7

Richardson House

PO Box 2011
Truckee, CA 96160-2011
(916)587-5388
Fax:(916)587-0927

Rates: $80-125.
Payment: MC VISA AX DS.
Innkeeper(s): Jeannine Karnofsky.
Circa: 1886.

Rooms: 8 rooms, 6 with PB, 3 with FP.
Beds: KQT.

This Victorian bears the name of the prominent lumber baron who built it. It remained in the Richardson family until 1940, eventually becoming a boarding house. The owners are continually restoring and renovating the property. Each of the guest rooms is individually appointed with antiques and Victorian decor and beds are topped with fine linens and down comforters. Some rooms offer mountain views while others have views of the inn's garden. Three rooms include a fireplace, and some also have clawfoot tubs. The inn's garden has a gazebo and hot tub, which guests are welcome to use. Inside, the parlor is set up for relaxation with a player piano, television, VCR and a stereo.

Breakfast and evening snack included in rates. Types of meals: continental-plus breakfast and early coffee/tea. Air conditioning, turn-down service and cable TV in room. Fax, copier and spa on premises. Handicap access. Weddings, small meetings, family reunions and seminars hosted. Antiques, fishing, parks, shopping, downhill skiing, cross-country skiing, sporting events, theater and watersports nearby.

Ukiah F3

Vichy Hot Springs Resort & Inn

2605 Vichy Springs Rd
Ukiah, CA 95482-3507
(707)462-9515
Fax:(707)462-9516

Rates: $130-175.
Payment: MC VISA AX DC CB DS PC TC.
Innkeeper(s): Gilbert & Marjorie Ashoff.
Circa: 1854.

Rooms: 17 rooms with PB, 3 with FP. 3 cottages. 2 conference rooms.
Beds: QT.

This famous spa once attracted guests such as Jack London, Mark Twain and Teddy Roosevelt. Seventeen rooms and three redwood cottages have been renovated for bed & breakfast, while the 1860s naturally warm and sparkling mineral baths remain unchanged. A hot spa and Olympic-size pool await your arrival. A magical waterfall is a 30-minute walk along a year-round stream.

Breakfast included in rates. Type of meal: continental-plus breakfast. Catering service available. Air conditioning in room. Fax, copier, computer, spa and swimming on premises. Handicap access. 700 acres. Small meetings, family reunions and seminars hosted. Spanish spoken. Antiques, fishing, parks, shopping, theater and watersports nearby. TAC10.

Location: Three miles east of US Hwy 101 in Ukiah, Mendocino County.

Publicity: *Sunset, Sacramento Bee, San Jose Mercury News, Gulliver (Japan), Oregonian, Contra Costa Times, New York Times, San Francisco Chronicle, San Francisco Examiner*

"Very beautiful grounds and comfortable accommodations. Thanks for your gracious hospitality and especially the opportunity to meet such good friends ... and the water's great!" - Attorney General State of California, Dan Lungren. "Great place! Good for Presidents and everyone else." - Ex-Governor California, Jerry Brown.

Venice **O10**

Venice Beach House

15 30th Pl
Venice, CA 90291-0043
(310)823-1966
Fax:(310)823-1842

Rates: $85-165.
Payment: MC VISA AX PC TC.
Innkeeper(s): Leslie Smith.
Circa: 1911.

Rooms: 9 rooms, 5 with PB, 1 with FP. 2 suites.
Beds: KQDT.

This California Craftsman house was the summer home of relatives Warren Wilson and Abbot Kinney and their families. Wilson found the Los Angeles Daily News, and Kinney founded the town of Venice, a popular L.A. hot spot for those in search of surf, sand, shopping, food or people watching. The home has been fully restored to its original state. Guest rooms are individually decorated. James Peasgood's Room is especially suite for guests in search of romance. It offers a king-size bed, balcony and a double Jacuzzi tub. The Pier Suite is another idyllic choice, offering an ocean view, a fireplace and sitting room.

Breakfast and afternoon tea included in rates. Type of meal: full breakfast. Cable TV in room. Fax, swimming and library on premises. Weddings, small meetings, family reunions and seminars hosted. Amusement parks, antiques, fishing, parks, shopping, sporting events, theater and watersports nearby. TAC10.

Location: One-half block from the famous Venice beach boardwalk.

Publicity: *Independent Journal, Sunset, The Argaunant, Daily News, Herald Examiner.*

"To stay at the Venice Beach House is to stay with a friendly family - a 'home away from home' (except the breakfasts are a lot better!) We've stayed in four different rooms, each better than the last."

Ventura **N8**

La Mer European B&B

411 Poli St
Ventura, CA 93001-2614
(805)643-3600
Fax:(805)653-7329

Rates: $105-155.
Payment: MC VISA AX.
Innkeeper(s): Gisela Baida.
Circa: 1890.

Rooms: 5 rooms.
Beds: KQ.

This three-story Cape Cod Victorian overlooks the heart of historic San Buenaventura and the spectacular California coastline. Each room is decorated to capture the feeling of a specific European country. French, German, Austrian, Norwegian and English-style accommodations are available. Gisela, your hostess, is a native of Siegerland, Germany. Midweek specials include romantic candlelight dinners, therapeutic massages and a mineral spa in the country. Horse-drawn antique carriage rides and island cruises are also available.

Breakfast included in rates. Types of meals: full breakfast and early coffee/tea.
Ceiling fan in room. Cable TV, fax, copier, library and child care on premises. Family reunions hosted. Antiques, fishing, shopping, theater and watersports nearby. TAC10.

Location: Second house west of City Hall.

Publicity: *Los Angeles Times, California Bride, Los Angeles Magazine, Westways, The Tribune, Daily News.*

Special Discounts: Midweek packages.

"Where to begin? The exquisite surroundings, the scrumptious meals, the warm feeling from your generous hospitality! What an unforgettable weekend in your heavenly home."

Volcano G7

St. George Hotel

16104 Pine Grove, PO Box 9
Volcano, CA 95689-0009
(209)296-4458
Fax:(209)296-4458

Rates: $71-77. MAP.
Payment: MC VISA AX.
Innkeeper(s): Marlene & Chuck Inman.
Circa: 1862.

Rooms: 20 rooms, 6 with PB. 1 conference room.
Beds: QDT.

This handsome old three-story hotel in the National Register features a double-tiered wraparound porch. There is a dining room, full bar and lounge area with fireplace. It is situated on one acre of lawns. An annex built in 1961 provides rooms with private baths. Volcano is a Mother Lode town that has been untouched by supermarkets and modern motels and remains much as it was during the Gold Rush. Modified American Plan (breakfast and dinner) available.

Breakfast included in rates. Type of meal: full breakfast. Dinner available. MAP. Fax and copier on premises. Weddings, small meetings, family reunions and seminars hosted. Antiques, fishing, parks, shopping, downhill skiing, cross-country skiing, theater and watersports nearby.

Location: Sixty-one miles from Sacramento.

"What is so precious about the hotel is its combination of graciousness and simplicity."

Walnut Creek H5

The Mansion at Lakewood

1056 Hacienda Dr
Walnut Creek, CA 94598
(510)945-3600 (800)477-7898
Fax:(510)945-3608

Rates: $135-300.
Payment: MC VISA AX DS.
Innkeeper(s): Sharyn McCoy.

Rooms: 7 rooms.

Secluded acres with garden paths, fountains and a gazebo surround this Victorian hideaway. Guests are pampered with flowers, fluffy robes, bath salts and rooms scented with potpourri. Heart-shaped chocolates and poetry books restored many weary guests' tired spirits. The grounds were part of an old Spanish land grant, and the home was built by an early Walnut Creek settler. The old-fashioned chandeliers and antiques add to the historical charm. The Juliet Suite includes a balcony with a garden view. Another room offers a Jacuzzi tub, and still others include fireplaces, four-poster beds and canopies.

Breakfast included in rates. Type of meal: continental-plus breakfast.

Westport E3

Howard Creek Ranch

40501 N Hwy One,
PO Box 121
Westport, CA 95488
(707)964-6725
Fax:(707)964-1603

Rates: $55-145.
Payment: MC VISA AX.
Innkeeper(s): Charles & Sally Grigg.
Circa: 1871.

Rooms: 11 rooms, 9 with PB, 5 with FP. 3 suites. 3 cottages.
Beds: KQD.

First settled as a land grant of thousands of acres, Howard Creek Ranch is now a 40-acre farm with sweeping views of the Pacific Ocean, sandy beaches and rolling mountains. A 75-foot bridge spans a creek that flows past barns and outbuildings to the beach 200 yards away. The farmhouse is surrounded by green lawns, an award-winning flower garden, and grazing cows and horses. This rustic rural location offers antiques, a hot tub and sauna.

Breakfast included in rates. Types of meals: full breakfast, gourmet breakfast and early coffee/tea. Ceiling fan in room. Fax, spa, swimming, sauna and library on premises. 40 acres. German and Spanish spoken. Antiques, fishing, parks, shopping and theater nearby.

Pets Allowed: By prior arrangement.

Location: Mendocino Coast on the ocean.

Publicity: *California, Country, Vacations.*

"Of the dozen or so inns on the West Coast we have visited, this is easily the most enchanting one."

CA

Yosemite National Park

I8

Yosemite West High Sierra B&B

7460 Henness Ridge Rd
Yosemite National Park,
CA 95389-9100
(209)372-4808

Rates: $90-150.
Payment: MC VISA.
Innkeeper(s): Bob & Karen Kosarowich.
Circa: 1995.

Rooms: 3 rooms with PB.
Beds: QT.

This mountain home is located midway between Yosemite Valley and Wawona inside Yosemite National Park. The forested setting is a peaceful place to relax after a day exploring the park. Gaze at a sky filled with stars or simply relax in front of the fireplace. One guest room includes a two-person, Jacuzzi tub. A hearty breakfast with items such as whole-wheat French toast topped with sauteed fruit is served daily. The innkeepers are happy to help guests plan excursions in the park.

Breakfast included in rates. Types of meals: full breakfast and early coffee/tea. Ceiling fan in room. VCR and library on premises. Antiques, fishing, parks, shopping, downhill skiing, cross-country skiing, theater and watersports nearby. TAC10.

"We were treated as long-lost friends and we shall remember you fondly."

Yountville

G4

Maison Fleurie

6529 Yount St
Yountville, CA 94599-1278
(707)944-2056 (800)788-0369
Fax:(707)944-9342

Rates: $110-200.
Payment: MC VISA AX TC.
Innkeeper(s): Roger Asbill.
Circa: 1894.

Rooms: 13 rooms with PB, 7 with FP.
Beds: KQD.

Vines cover the two-foot thick brick walls of the Bakery, the Carriage House and the Main House of this French country inn. One of the Four Sisters Inns, it is reminiscent of a bucolic setting in Provence. Rooms are decorated in a warm, romantic style, some with vineyard and garden views. Rooms in the Old Bakery have fireplaces. A pool and outdoor spa are available and you may borrow bicycles for wandering the countryside. In the evenings, wine and hors d'oeuvres are served. Yountville, just north of Napa, offers close access to the multitude of wineries and vineyards in the valley.

Breakfast and afternoon tea included in rates. Type of meal: gourmet breakfast. Turn-down service in room. Fax, spa and bicycles on premises. Handicap access. Weddings hosted. Antiques nearby.

"Peaceful surroundings, friendly staff."

Colorado

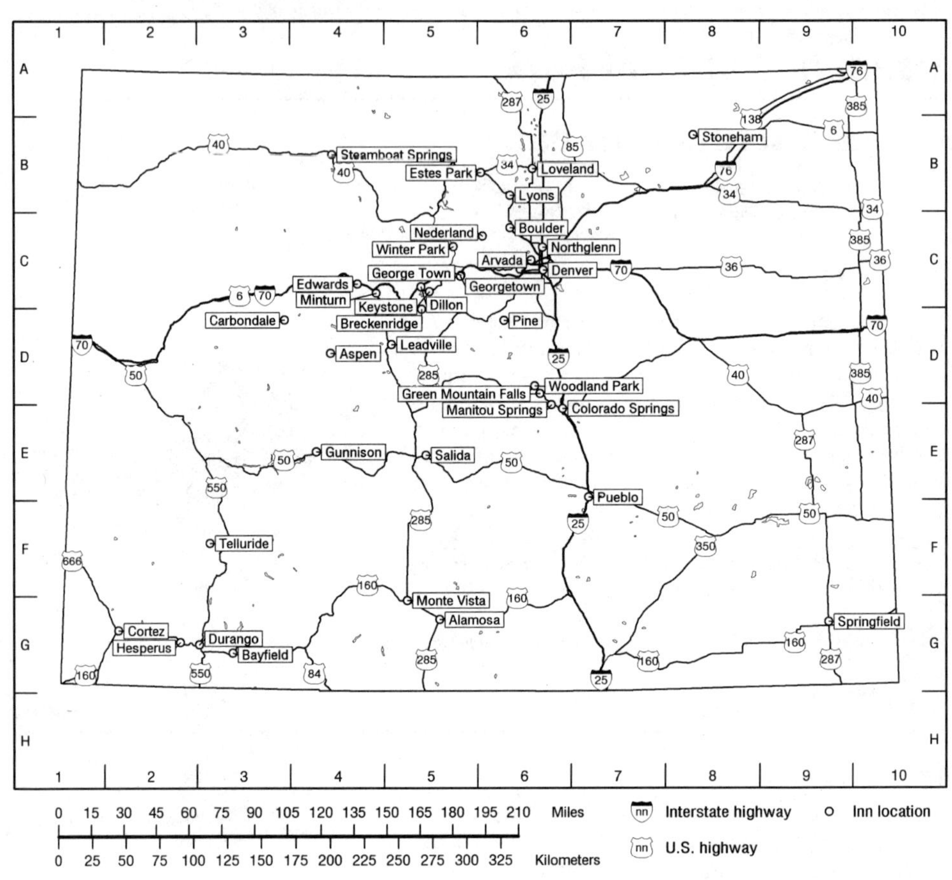

Alamosa

G5

Cottonwood Inn

123 San Juan Ave
Alamosa, CO 81101-2547
(719)589-3882 (800)955-2623
Fax:(719)589-6437
E-mail: julie@csn.org

Rates: $48-85.
Payment: MC VISA AX DC CB DS PC TC.
Innkeeper(s): Julie Mordecai & George Sellman.
Circa: 1908.

Rooms: 7 rooms, 2 with PB. 3 suites.
Beds: KQTD.

This refurbished Colorado bungalow is filled with antiques and paintings by local artists. The dining room set once belonged to Billy Adams, a Colorado governor in the 1920s. Blue-corn blueberry pancakes and flaming Grand Marnier omelets are the inn's specialties. A favorite day trip is riding the Cumbres-Toltec Scenic Railroad over the La Magna Pass, site of an Indiana Jones movie.

Breakfast and evening snack included in rates. Types of meals: full breakfast, gourmet breakfast and early coffee/tea. Afternoon tea and catered breakfast available. Cable TV, VCR, fax and copier on premises. Small meetings, family reunions and seminars hosted. Spanish and French spoken. Antiques, parks and downhill skiing nearby.

Pets Allowed: In two of our suites with wood floors. Must be well behaved. Guests pay for all damages.

Location: Close to Great Sand Dunes National Monument.

Publicity: *Rocky Mountain News, Country Inns, Denver Post, Milwaukee Journal.*

Special Discounts: 10% off if guests arrive on bicycles.

"My husband wants to come over every morning for blueberry pancakes and strawberry rhubarb sauce."

Arvada C6

The Tree House

6650 Simms St
Arvada, CO 80004-2534
(303)431-6352
Fax:(303)456-1414
E-mail: thetreehou@aol.com

Rates: $59-99.
Payment: MC VISA.
Innkeeper(s): LeAnne & Todd Thomas.
Circa: 1940.

Rooms: 5 rooms with PB, 4 with FP.
Beds: KQT.

Each of the guest rooms at this modern, chalet-style bed & breakfast offers something special. Four of the rooms have a wood-burning fireplace, and the fifth guest room includes a bay window and a king-size brass bed topped with cozy quilts. There are 10 acres to wander, including wooded trails, and a after a refreshing walk, guests can return and enjoy a soak in the outdoor Jacuzzi or just relax on the deck. Denver is less than 30 minutes from the home.

Breakfast and afternoon tea included in rates. Types of meals: full breakfast and gourmet breakfast. Air conditioning in room. Fax and spa on premises. 10 acres. Small meetings, family reunions and seminars hosted. Amusement parks, antiques, fishing, parks, downhill skiing, cross-country skiing, sporting events and theater nearby. TAC10.

Aspen D4

Sardy House

128 E Main St
Aspen, CO 81611-1714
(970)920-2525

Rates: $120-575.
Innkeeper(s): Jayne Poss.
Circa: 1892.

Rooms: 20 rooms with PB. 1 conference room.
Beds: KQT.

This Queen Anne Victorian was built by J. William Atkinson, an owner of the Little Annie Mine and Aspen's first freight company. The mansion is built with thick brick walls, sandstone detailing, and wood ornamental trim. A Colorado blue spruce on the grounds is more than 90 feet tall, the tallest in Aspen. There are deluxe guest rooms and six suites. Dinner is available nightly. At the Sardy House guests enjoy the ultimate in pampered luxury.

Type of meal: full breakfast. Spa and sauna on premises.

Publicity: *Country Inns.*

"I was overwhelmed by your attention to details. A job well done!"

Bayfield G3

Wit's End Guest Ranch

254 Country Rd 500
Bayfield, CO 81122
(970)884-4113 (800)236-9483
Fax:(940)884-3261

Rates: $2352-3380. AP.
Payment: MC VISA AX DS PC TC.
Innkeeper(s): Jim & Lynn Custer.
Circa: 1870.

Rooms: 2 rooms with PB. 35 cottages. 1 conference room.
Beds: Q.

When the owners of this Adirondack guest ranch bill their place as "luxury at the edge of the wilderness," it isn't just a snappy slogan, it's true. If 550 acres and views of snow capped mountain peaks don't entice you, the historic lodge's interior should. It's difficult to describe, but picture polished exposed beams and wood paneled or log walls, a mix of Victorian and country French furnishings and just enough antlers to create that rustic, lodge atmosphere. Each guest room includes a stone fireplace. There are also an assortment of cabins to consider, some more than a century old. The cabins include a living room, stone fireplace, kitchen and some have a private porch or deck. There is a full-service restaurant and a tavern often hosting live musical groups from nearby Durango. There's also little shortage of things to do here. Guided wilderness hikes, hayrides, mountain biking, dogsled rides, showshoeing, sleigh rides and watersports are literally just a few of the possibilities. Horseback and trail riding, of course, are a major part of the fun. The ranch offers a full children's program, with many interesting activities. As is typical of dude ranches, rates are quoted for weekly visits.

Breakfast, dinner, evening snack and picnic lunch included in rates. Types of meals: continental-plus breakfast, full breakfast and gourmet breakfast. Lunch, gourmet lunch, banquet service, catering service, catered breakfast and room service available. AP. Turn-down service and VCR in room. Cable TV, fax, copier, spa, swimming, stables, bicycles, tennis and library on premises. Handicap access. 550 acres. Weddings, small meetings, family reunions and seminars hosted. Spanish, French, Italian and German spoken. Antiques, fishing, parks, shopping, downhill skiing, cross-country skiing, sporting events, theater and watersports nearby. TAC10.

Publicity: *Jeopardy, Wheel of Fortune, Quicksilver, Family Feud, Country Inns, Country Living*

Boulder C6

Briar Rose B&B

2151 Arapahoe Ave
Boulder, CO 80302-6601
(303)442-3007
Fax:(303)786-8440

Rates: $89-139.
Payment: MC VISA AX DC PC TC.
Innkeeper(s): Bob & Margaret Weisenbach.
Circa: 1896.

Rooms: 9 rooms with PB, 2 with FP.
Beds: QDT.

Known locally as the McConnell House, this English-style brick house is situated in a neighborhood originally composed of bankers, attorneys, miners and carpenters. The inn recently received the Award of Excellence from the City of Boulder. Fresh flowers, handmade feather comforters and turndown service with chocolates add to the atmosphere.

Breakfast and afternoon tea included in rates. Types of meals: continental-plus breakfast and early coffee/tea. Air conditioning, turn-down service and ceiling fan in room. Cable TV, fax and copier on premises. Weddings, small meetings and family reunions hosted. French, Spanish and American Sign Language spoken. Antiques, fishing, parks, shopping, downhill skiing, cross-country skiing, sporting events and theater nearby. TAC10.

Special Discounts: 10% five days or more.

"It's like being at Grandma's; the cookies, the tea, the welcoming smile."

Breckenridge D5

The Evans House B&B

102 S French St,
PO Box 387
Breckenridge, CO 80424
(970)453-5509

Rates: $55-95.
Payment: PC TC.
Innkeeper(s): Pete & Georgette Contos.
Circa: 1886.

Rooms: 4 rooms, 2 with PB.
Beds: KQDT.

A view of the famed Breckenridge ski slopes are visible from the windows of this former miner's home. A cornucopia of activities are available to guests who have a love for the outdoors, including rafting, boating and an alpine slide. A ski shuttle is available at the front door and on site parking. This 150-year-old mining town offers many interesting shops and restaurants. In the heart of a historical district with 120 circa 1860-1890 buildings and three museums, tours are available daily.

Breakfast and afternoon tea included in rates. Type of meal: full breakfast. Cable TV and VCR on premises. Greek and French spoken. Amusement parks, antiques, fishing, parks, shopping, downhill skiing, cross-country skiing, sporting events, theater and watersports nearby.

Location: In the Breckenridge historic district.

Publicity: *Denver Post.*

"Very clean, outstanding hospitality."

Hunt Placer Inn

275 Ski Hill Rd,
PO Box 4898
Breckenridge, CO 80424
(970)453-7573 (800)472-1430
Fax:(970)453-2335
E-mail: hpi@colorado.net

Rates: $95-185.
Payment: MC VISA AX DC CB DS PC TC.
Innkeeper(s): Carl & Gwen Ray.
Circa: 1994.

Rooms: 8 rooms with PB, 3 with FP. 1 conference room.
Beds: QT.

Set among woods in a historic, gold-mining town, this delightful mountain chalet is located on what was an actual mining claim. Guest rooms are decorated in a variety of styles, from Southwestern to European, each with an elegant flair. The room and suite names reflect the decor, such as the Bavaria Suite or the Gold Rush Room. The morning menu changes daily, offering items such as Swiss muesli, fresh fruit, pancakes topped with praline sauce, creme brulee and quiche. A free shuttle takes wintertime guests to the nearby ski slopes and alpine slide.

Breakfast and afternoon tea included in rates. Types of meals: full breakfast, gourmet breakfast and early coffee/tea. Cable TV, VCR and fax on premises. Handicap access. Weddings, small meetings, family reunions and seminars hosted. German spoken. Antiques, fishing, parks, shopping, downhill skiing, cross-country skiing, theater and watersports nearby. TAC10.

Breckenridge (Dillion)

Swan Mountain Inn

16172 Hwy 9
Breckenridge (Dillion), CO 80424
(970)453-7903 (800)578-3687

Rates: $40-100.
Payment: MC VISA DS PC TC.
Innkeeper(s): Steve Gessner.
Circa: 1986.

Rooms: 4 rooms, 3 with PB. 1 suite.

Less than seven miles from the outstanding ski areas of Keystone, Breckenridge and Copper Mountain, this log home is a cozy, warm place to enjoy a mountain getaway. After a day enjoying nature, guests can dine by candlelight at the inn's dining room or enjoy a drink at the fireside bar. Relax in the glassed-inn sun porches, the decks or on a comfortable hammock.

Breakfast and afternoon tea included in rates. Types of meals: full breakfast and gourmet breakfast. Dinner and gourmet lunch available. Cable TV and VCR in room. Spa on premises. Handicap access. Weddings, small meetings, family reunions and seminars hosted. Antiques, fishing, parks, shopping, downhill skiing, cross-country skiing and watersports nearby. TAC10.

Special Discounts: Off season dinner specials.

Carbondale — *D3*

Ambiance Inn

66 N 2nd St
Carbondale, CO 81623
(970)963-3597 (800)350-1515
Fax:(970)963-3130

Rates: $60-100.
Payment: MC DS PC.
Innkeeper(s): Norma & Robert Morris.
Circa: 1976.

Rooms: 4 rooms with PB. 1 suite.
Beds: Q.

This contemporary chalet-style home is located in the beautiful Crystal Valley between Aspen and Glenwood Springs. Year-round activities are numerous in the area, but ski buffs will be excited to know that Aspen and Snowmass are only a 30-minute drive away. Glenwood Springs and the world's largest hot springs are just 15 minutes away. Custom picnic baskets for outings are available with two days' advance notice. The New Orleans Library is adjacent to all three guest rooms on the second floor.

Breakfast included in rates. Types of meals: full breakfast and early coffee/tea. Ceiling fan and cable TV in room. VCR on premises. Weddings, small meetings, family reunions and seminars hosted. Antiques, fishing, parks, shopping, downhill skiing, cross-country skiing and sporting events nearby. TAC10.

Cheyenne Canon Inn

2030 W Cheyenne Blvd
Colorado Springs,
CO 80906
(719)633-0625 (800)633-0625
Fax:(800)633-8826

Rates: $75-175.
Payment: MC VISA AX DS PC TC.
Innkeeper(s): John, Barbara & Josh Starr.
Circa: 1921.

Rooms: 9 rooms with PB, 3 with FP. 3 suites. 1 cottage. 2 conference rooms.
Beds: KQT.

World travelers Barbara and John Starr have filled this rustic home with interesting finds from their many visits to foreign lands. The home was built by the wife of a Manitou Springs sheriff and originally served as an upscale casino, and more infamously, a bordello. During the home's heyday as an inn, guests included the Marx Brothers and Lon Cheney. The massive home features more than 100 windows, all boasting beautiful views, original stained glass and silver wall sconces. Each of the seven guest rooms and two cottages captures an unique international flavor. The innkeepers recently added "Le Petit Chateau," a romantic cottage tucked beneath 50-foot tall pines trees. Spend the night tucked away in a room reminiscent of a Swiss chalet or enjoy the atmosphere of an Oriental tea room in another guest quarter. The second-floor hot tub affords a view of Cheyenne Mountain. The innkeepers have created a relaxing retreat, but also offer many amenities for the business traveler including in-room phones and modem outlets.

Types of meals: full breakfast and early coffee/tea. Turn-down service, ceiling fan, cable TV and VCR in room. Fax, copier, spa and library on premises. Weddings, small meetings and seminars hosted. French spoken. Antiques, fishing, parks, shopping, downhill skiing, cross-country skiing, sporting events and theater nearby. TAC10.

Publicity: *Denver Post, Colorado Source, Beacon.*

"It truly was 'home away from home.' You have made it so welcoming and warm. Needless to say our breakfasts at home will never come close to the Cheyenne Canon Inn!!"

Holden House-1902 B&B Inn

1102 W Pikes Peak Ave
Colorado Springs, CO
80904-4347
(719)471-3980
E-mail: holdenhous@aol.com

Rates: $105-115.
Payment: MC VISA AX DC CB DS PC TC.
Innkeeper(s): Sallie & Welling Clark.
Circa: 1902.

Rooms: 5 suites.
Beds: Q.

Built by the widow of a prosperous rancher and businessman, this Victorian inn has rooms named after the many Colorado towns the Holdens owned mining interests in. The main house, adjacent carriage house and Victorian house next door include the Leadville, Cripple Creek, Aspen, Silverton, Goldfield and Independence rooms. The inn's suites boast fireplaces and oversized tubs for two. Guests can relax in the living room with fireplace, front parlor with TV, or veranda with mountain views.

Breakfast included in rates. Types of meals: gourmet breakfast and early coffee/tea. Afternoon tea available. Air conditioning, turn-down service and ceiling fan in room. Cable TV, VCR, fax and copier on premises. Handicap access. Seminars hosted. Antiques, fishing, parks, shopping, sporting events and theater nearby. TAC10.

Location: Near the historic district, "Old Colorado City."

Publicity: *Denver Post, Rocky Mountain News, Victorian Homes, Pikes Peak Journal, Glamour.*

"Your love of this house and nostalgia makes a very delightful experience."

Room at The Inn B&B

618 N Nevada Ave
Colorado Springs, CO
80903-1006
(719)442-1896 (800)579-4621
Fax:(719)442-6802

Rates: $85-125.
Payment: MC VISA AX DC CB DS PC TC.
Innkeeper(s): Chick, Jan & Kelly McCormick.
Circa: 1896.

Rooms: 7 rooms with PB, 3 with FP. 2 suites. 1 cottage. 1 conference room.
Beds: Q.

CO

A Colorado pioneer built this Queen Anne Victorian, a delightful mix of turret, gables and gingerbread trim. While restoring their century-old Victorian, the innkeepers discovered several hand-painted murals had once decorated the interior. Original fireplace mantels and a collection of antiques add to the nostalgic ambiance. Fresh flowers, turn-down service and a bountiful breakfast are just a few of the amenities. Several rooms include a fireplace or double whirlpool tub.

Breakfast, afternoon tea and evening snack included in rates. Types of meals: continental breakfast, full breakfast and early coffee/tea. Air conditioning and turn-down service in room. Cable TV, VCR, fax and copier on premises. Handicap access. Weddings, small meetings, family reunions and seminars hosted. Antiques, fishing, parks, shopping, sporting events and theater nearby. TAC10.

Special Discounts: $10 off in November, April, January; Sunday-Thursday, no holidays.

Cortez G2

Kelly Place B&B

14663 County Road G
Cortez, CO 81321-9575
(970)565-3125 (800)745-4885
Fax:(970)565-3540

Rates: $69-99.
Payment: MC VISA PC TC.
Innkeeper(s): Rodney & Kristie Carriker.
Circa: 1965.

Rooms: 8 rooms with PB. 1 cottage. 1 conference room.
Beds: QT.

With more than two dozen Anasazi archaeological sites to explore, guests at this Southwestern-style adobe have little trouble finding an interesting activity. Guests can take self-guided tours of the scenic, 180-acre grounds or take part in actual archaeological digs, finding bits of history from the Anasazi's past. The innkeepers offer packages that include horseback riding, archaeological programs, Anasazi pottery reproduction and guided hikes. Innkeeper Kristie Carriker starts off these busy days with bountiful breakfasts of fresh fruit, homemade granola, freshly baked breads and a special, daily entree. Families are welcome here, and both parents and children alike enjoy exploring the grounds and learning about the Anasazi.

Breakfast included in rates. Types of meals: full breakfast and early coffee/tea. Afternoon tea, dinner, evening snack, picnic lunch, lunch, gourmet lunch, banquet service, catering service and catered breakfast available. Air conditioning and ceiling fan in room. Fax, copier, stables and library on premises. 180 acres. Weddings, small meetings, family reunions and seminars hosted. Antiques, fishing, parks, shopping, downhill skiing, cross-country skiing and watersports nearby. TAC10.

Special Discounts: 10% discount if staying three nights or longer.

Denver C6

Capitol Hill Mansion

1207 Pennsylvania St
Denver, CO 80203-2504
(303)839-5221 (800)839-9329
Fax:(303)839-9046

Rates: $90-165.
Payment: MC VISA AX DS.
Innkeeper(s): Kathy Robbins.
Circa: 1891.

Rooms: 8 rooms with PB. 3 suites.
Beds: KQ.

Although only open a few years, owner Kathy Robbins has mastered the art of innkeeping at this beautiful, red sandstone mansion. High turrets, balconies and soaring chimneys create a romantic, elegant almost castle-like appearance. Each of the guest rooms is uniquely decorated. The Gold Banner Suite features a queen

brass bed, a fireplace and cozy sitting area. The Pasqueflower Room boasts a six-foot, round whirlpool tub located in the alcove of one of the home's turrets. Enjoy breakfast downstairs or in the privacy of your own room.

Breakfast and afternoon tea included in rates. Type of meal: continental-plus breakfast. Antiques, fishing, downhill skiing, cross-country skiing, theater and watersports nearby.

Publicity: *Yellow Brick Road, Life on Capitol Hill, Journal Constitution, Denver Post, Rocky Mountain News.*

Castle Marne - A Luxury Urban Inn

1572 Race St
Denver, CO 80206-1308
(303)331-0621 (800)926-2763
Fax:(303)331-0623

Rates: $85-220.
Payment: MC VISA AX DC CB DS.
Innkeeper(s): The Peiker Family.
Circa: 1889.

Rooms: 9 rooms with PB. 2 suites. 1 conference room.
Beds: KQDT.

This 6,000-square-foot fantasy was designed by William Lang and is in the National Register. It is constructed of hand-hewn rhyolite stone. Inside, polished oak, maple and black ash woodwork enhance the ornate fireplaces, period antiques and opulent Victorian decor. For special occasions ask for the Presidential Suite with its tower sitting room, king-size tester bed, whirlpool tub in the solarium and private balcony.

Breakfast and afternoon tea included in rates. Type of meal: full breakfast. Fax and copier on premises. Antiques, fishing, downhill skiing, cross-country skiing, theater and watersports nearby.

Publicity: *Denver Post, Innsider, Rocky Mountain News, Los Angeles Times, New York Times, Denver Business Journal, Country Inns, Brides, U.S. Air.*

"The beauty, service, friendliness, delicious breakfasts - everything was so extraordinary! We'll be back many times."

The Merritt House

941 E 17th Ave
Denver, CO 80218-1407
(303)861-5230
Fax:(303)861-9009

Rates: $95-115.
Payment: MC VISA AX DC DS PC TC.
Innkeeper(s): Mary & Thomas E. Touris.
Circa: 1889.

Rooms: 10 rooms with PB.
Beds: Q.

Colorado Senator Elmer Merritt was this home's first resident, and through the years it found use as a boarding house, office building, apartment house and the Denver office for the United Steel Workers of America. The innkeepers, however, refurbished the Queen Anne Victorian back to the glorious state it was in when the Merritt family called it home. Beautiful elements such as the carved wood panelling and leaded-glass windows have either been restored or authentic reproductions have been added. A mix of turn-of-the-century Victorian furnishings completes the look. Each guest room, as the innkeepers say, features modern amenities such as Mr. Bell's latest invention, Mr. Edison's electric filament lighting and a private water closet. Some of the "private water closets" include a whirlpool tub. Breakfast is a splendid affair, as guests choose their own combination of treats from a wide menu that includes omelets, pancakes, savory meats and more. Downtown Denver, the state capitol and the U.S. mint all are close by.

Breakfast included in rates. Type of meal: full breakfast. Air conditioning and cable TV in room. Fax and copier on premises. Small meetings hosted. Amusement parks, antiques, parks, shopping, sporting events and theater nearby. TAC10.

Victoria Oaks Inn

1575 Race St
Denver, CO 80206-1307
(303)355-1818 (800)662-6257
Fax:(303)331-1095

Rates: $60-85.
Payment: MC VISA AX DC CB DS PC TC.
Innkeeper(s): Clyde & Ric.
Circa: 1897.

Rooms: 9 rooms, 7 with PB, 2 with FP.
Beds: QD.

CO

In a quiet neighborhood of historic Capitol Hill, this large Four Square style Victorian is within walking distance to Denver's zoo, museum of Natural History, the Laserium and Imax. A hanging staircase, leaded-glass windows, oak woodwork and tile fireplaces establish the settled tone of the inn. Restored antiques, wood floors and panoramic views of the city are additional appreciated amenities.

Breakfast included in rates. Type of meal: continental-plus breakfast. Ceiling fan in room. Cable TV and fax on premises. Weddings hosted. Amusement parks, antiques, fishing, parks, shopping, downhill skiing, cross-country skiing, sporting events, theater and watersports nearby. TAC10.

Dillon C5

Paradox Lodge

5040 Montezuma Rd
Dillon, CO 80435-7644
(970)468-9445
Fax:(970)262-6466
E-mail: 71501,530@compuserve.com

Rates: $55-110.
Payment: MC VISA AX DC DS PC TC.
Innkeeper(s): George & Connie O'Bleness.
Circa: 1987.

Rooms: 4 rooms. 3 cottages. 1 conference room.
Beds: KQT.

Guests choose from comfortable rooms in a mountain lodge home or cabins at this woodsy retreat, located within Arapahoe National Forest. The lodge rooms are set up for two, and the cabins can sleep five comfortably. Guests enjoy use of a wood-fired, outdoor hot tub. The lodge offers close access to many seasonal activities. Rafting, hiking, an alpine slide, sleigh rides, snowmobile tours, cross-country skiing and ice fishing are just a few of the area's offerings.

Breakfast included in rates. Types of meals: continental-plus breakfast and early coffee/tea. VCR, fax and library on premises. 37 acres. Small meetings, family reunions and seminars hosted. Antiques, parks, shopping, downhill skiing and cross-country skiing nearby. TAC10.

Pets Allowed: In cabins only.

Snowberryhill B&B

PO Box 2910
Dillon, CO 80435-2910
(970)468-8010

Rates: $75-105.
Payment: MC VISA PC TC.
Innkeeper(s): Kristi & George Blincoe.
Circa: 1984.

Rooms: 1 room.
Beds: QT.

Delectable Belgian waffles topped with fresh berries get the day off to the right start at this contemporary mountain home, warmed with antiques. Snowberryhill is just 10 minutes from Keystone Ski Area and within half an hour of Arapahoe Basin, Breckenridge, Copper Mountain and Loveland Ski Area. The innkeepers can store skis in a special locker. Guests have the run of the entire first floor during their stay, which includes use of a full kitchen and laundry facilities. The guest quarters also include

a private bedroom and a living area with additional bedding. The suite accommodates up to four comfortably, and a crib or other baby equipment can be requested.

Breakfast included in rates. Type of meal: gourmet breakfast. Cable TV and VCR in room. Fishing, shopping, downhill skiing, cross-country skiing, theater and watersports nearby.

"Thank you for sharing your little bit of paradise with us."

Durango G3

Apple Orchard Inn

7758 County Road 203
Durango, CO 81301-8643
(970)247-0751 (800)426-0751

Rates: $75-150.
Payment: MC VISA DS PC TC.
Innkeeper(s): Celeste & John Gardiner.
Circa: 1994.

Rooms: 10 rooms with PB, 4 with FP. 6 cottages. 1 conference room.
Beds: KQ.

As one might assume from the name, this elegant inn and cabins are ideally situated in an apple orchard. The main house is a welcoming farmhouse, and the innkeepers continue the country look inside as well. Guest rooms offer featherbeds, some with canopies. Four rooms also include fireplaces and Jacuzzi tubs. Hearty, fresh-from-the-oven breakfasts are accompanied with fresh fruits. In the evenings, refreshments are served, and special gourmet dinners are sometimes available upon request.

Breakfast and evening snack included in rates. Types of meals: full breakfast, gourmet breakfast and early coffee/tea. Afternoon tea, dinner, picnic lunch, lunch and gourmet lunch available. Ceiling fan and cable TV in room. Spa on premises. Handicap access. Weddings, small meetings and family reunions hosted. Portuguese & Italian spoken. Fishing, parks, shopping, downhill skiing, cross-country skiing, theater and watersports nearby. TAC10.

Special Discounts: 10% AAA.

"A must stay anytime we are in the area."

Leland House

721 E 2nd Ave
Durango, CO 81301-5435
(970)385-1920 (800)664-1920
Fax:(970)385-1967

Rates: $85-135.
Payment: MC VISA AX DS PC TC.
Innkeeper(s): Kirk & Diane Komick.
Circa: 1927.

Rooms: 10 rooms with PB. 6 suites.
Beds: QD.

Each room of this two-story brick building is named after a historic figure associated with the Leland House, which has ties to a well-known builder, lumber company magnate, wool merchant and railroad executive. Gourmet breakfasts include the inn specialties of home-cooked granola and cranberry scones. Also, daily entrees include Southwestern burritos, filled French toast, pancakes or waffles topped with fresh fruit. Guests can tour the historic districts of Durango and browse through many fine shops, galleries and outlet stores.

Breakfast and afternoon tea included in rates. Types of meals: full breakfast and gourmet breakfast. Picnic lunch and catering service available. Restaurant on premises. Air conditioning, ceiling fan and cable TV in room. VCR, fax and copier on premises. Weddings, small meetings, family reunions and seminars hosted. Spanish spoken. Antiques, fishing, parks, shopping, downhill skiing, cross-country skiing, theater and watersports nearby. TAC10.

Special Discounts: Winter ski packages.

Lightner Creek Inn Bed & Breakfast

999 County Rd 207
Durango, CO 81301
(970)259-1226
Fax:(970)259-0732

Rates: $75-150.
Payment: MC VISA DS PC TC.
Innkeeper(s): Richard & Julie Houston.
Circa: 1903.

Rooms: 8 rooms, 6 with PB, 1 with FP. 1 cottage.
Beds: KQ.

With a tree-covered hillside as its backdrop, this French Country estate is a picturesque site to arriving guests. The elegant interior is an uncluttered mix of country and Victorian styles. The turn-of-the-century home has been well restored, and maintains many of its original elements. Guests who opt for the romantic Carriage House enjoy a spacious suite with a sitting area, king-size featherbed and a pellet stove. After a restful sleep, guests enjoy a gourmet breakfast that starts off with a well-presented medley of fruit. From there, a baked egg dish is served, followed by yet another treat, such as stuffed French toast or gingerbread pancakes topped with lemon sauce.

Breakfast and afternoon tea included in rates. Types of meals: full breakfast, gourmet breakfast and early coffee/tea. Cable TV, VCR, fax, copier and bicycles on premises. Handicap access. 20 acres. Weddings, small meetings and family reunions hosted. Antiques, fishing, parks, shopping, downhill skiing, cross-country skiing, sporting events, theater and watersports nearby. TAC10.

The Rochester Hotel

721 E Second Ave
Durango, CO 81301
(970)385-1920 (800)664-1920
Fax:(970)385-1967

Rates: $125-185.
Payment: MC VISA AX DS PC TC.
Innkeeper(s): Kirk & Diane Komick.
Circa: 1892.

Rooms: 15 rooms with PB. 2 suites. 2 conference rooms.
Beds: KQ.

This Federal-style inn's decor is inspired by many Western movies filmed in and around the town. The inn is located one block from the Historic Main Avenue District and three blocks from the Durango-Silverton Narrow Gauge Railroad. Conveniently located in a beautifully landscaped downtown setting, the building is an authentically restored late-Victorian hotel, fully furnished with antiques from the period.

Breakfast included in rates. Types of meals: full breakfast and gourmet breakfast. Afternoon tea, picnic lunch and catering service available. Air conditioning, ceiling fan and cable TV in room. VCR, fax and copier on premises. Handicap access. Weddings, small meetings, family reunions and seminars hosted. Spanish spoken. Antiques, fishing, parks, shopping, downhill skiing, cross-country skiing, theater and watersports nearby. TAC10.

Pets Allowed: Small pets, prior permission needed.

Publicity: *Conde Nast Traveler.*

Special Discounts: Winter ski packages.

"In a word — exceptional! Far exceeded expectations in every way."

Scrubby Oaks B&B

PO Box 1047,
1901 Florida Rd
Durango, CO 81302-1047
(970)247-2176

Rates: $65-75.
Innkeeper(s): Mary Ann Craig.
Circa: 1959.

Rooms: 7 rooms, 3 with PB.
Beds: KQDT.

This Monterey-style inn sits on ten acres overlooking the Animas River Valley. The house is decorated with family antiques and photos, artwork and books found in all the rooms. Guests are invited to relax and enjoy the gardens from one of the patios. The home is open for guests from the end of April to the end of October. Although secluded on scenic grounds, the home is just three miles from downtown Durango.

Breakfast included in rates. Types of meals: full breakfast and early coffee/tea. Cable TV, VCR and sauna on premises. 10 acres. Weddings, small meetings, family reunions and seminars hosted. Antiques, fishing, shopping, downhill skiing, cross-country skiing, sporting events, theater and watersports nearby.

Publicity: *Scrubby Oaks Spirit.*

"What a beautiful place, tons of character, amazing view and wonderful food."

The Verheyden Inn/Logwood B&B

35060 Us Hwy 550 N
Durango, CO 81301
(303)259-4396 (800)369-4082

Rates: $65-90.
Innkeeper(s): Debby & Greg Verheyden.
Circa: 1988.

Rooms: 7 rooms, 6 with PB. 1 suite.

Large windows of this Western red cedar log structure make for great viewing of the upper Animas Valley. Deer often pass through this 15-acre property with a stream, varieties of mountain trees and animal life. The perfect place to nap is a hammock for two under oaks 50 feet away from the inn. All of the guest rooms are furnished with colorful home-stitched quilts to match the inn's Western decor. Breakfast menus range from hearty country fare to gourmet specialty dishes like quiche, casseroles and coffee cakes.

Breakfast and afternoon tea included in rates. Type of meal: full breakfast. Turn-down service in room. Cable TV and VCR on premises. 15 acres. Small meetings, family reunions and seminars hosted. Fishing, shopping, downhill skiing, cross-country skiing, sporting events and theater nearby.

Publicity: *Denver Post, Log Home Living, Durango Magazine, New York News.*

"You made our visit to Durango another glorious experience. You are a class act."

Edwards — C4

The Lazy Ranch B&B

PO Box 404
Edwards, CO 81632-0404
(970)926-3876 (800)655-9343
Fax:(970)926-3876

Rates: $60-125.
Payment: MC VISA DS TC.
Innkeeper(s): Buddy & Linda Calhoun.
Circa: 1886.

Rooms: 4 rooms, 1 with PB, 1 with FP. 1 suite.
Beds: QD.

Enjoy a taste of the Old West at this working horse ranch. The Lazy Ranch is the only original homestead left in the Vail Valley. A variety of animals, including chickens, peacocks, Porkchop the pig, rabbits, dogs and cats create the authentic farm atmosphere. Hearty country breakfasts are served with farm-fresh eggs. The innkeepers offer bonfires, barbecues and barn dances to make your country vacation complete. Couples might enjoy moonlight horseback rides accompanied by a romantic dinner. Innkeeper Buddy Calhoun's "Cowboy" artwork is displayed in a converted bunk house, which now serves as an art studio.

Breakfast included in rates. Types of meals: full breakfast and early coffee/tea. Picnic lunch, catering service and catered breakfast available. Turn-down service in room. Cable TV, VCR, fax, copier, stables and pet boarding on premises. 60 acres. Weddings, small meetings, family reunions and seminars hosted. Fishing, shopping, downhill skiing, cross-country skiing and watersports nearby. TAC10.

Pets Allowed: $15.00/day.

"As weekends go, they just don't get any better than the one spent at Lazy Ranch. Thank you so much for the hospitality."

Estes Park — B6

Anniversary Inn

1060 Mary's Lake Rd,
Moraine Rt
Estes Park, CO 80517
(970)586-6200

Rates: $90-140.
Payment: MC VISA PC TC.
Innkeeper(s): Harry & Norma Menke.
Circa: 1890.

Rooms: 4 rooms with PB, 1 with FP. 1 cottage.
Beds: Q.

High in the Colorado Rockies, at 7,600 feet, this authentic log home is surrounded by spectacular views. There are two acres with a pond and river nearby. An exposed-log living room is dominated by a massive mossrock fireplace. The guest rooms boast stenciled walls and other country accents. Sunset refreshments are timed to coincide with the daily stroll of deer through the property. The inn specializes in honeymoons and anniversaries and features a honeymoon cottage.

Breakfast included in rates. Types of meals: full breakfast and early coffee/tea. Evening snack available. Turn-down service in room. Cable TV, VCR and library on premises. Antiques, fishing, parks, shopping, cross-country skiing and theater nearby. TAC10.

Publicity: *Denver Post, Columbus Dispatch, Rocky Mountain News.*

"The splendor and majesty of the Rockies is matched only by the warmth and hospitality you showed us during our stay."

The Baldpate Inn

PO Box 4445
Estes Park, CO 80517-4445
(970)586-6151
E-mail: baldpatein@aol.com

Rates: $75-125.
Payment: MC VISA DS PC TC.
Innkeeper(s): Mike, Lois, Jenn & MacKenzie Smith.
Circa: 1917.

Rooms: 12 rooms, 2 with PB. 3 cottages. 1 conference room.
Beds: KQDT.

This National Register inn is nestled on the side of Twin Sisters Mountain, adjacent to Rocky Mountain National Park. The front porch affords a spectacular view. Guest rooms and private cabins feature country decor with quilts and down comforters. The lobby and library are ideal places to relax, each is flanked with a massive native stone fireplace. The inn also boasts a unique collection of more than 15,000 keys as well as a notable photo collection. Three-course breakfasts are served, as well as lunch and dinner in the inn's dining room.

Breakfast and evening snack included in rates. Types of meals: full breakfast, gourmet breakfast and early coffee/tea. Picnic lunch and banquet service available. VCR and library on premises. Weddings, small meetings and seminars hosted. Fishing, parks, shopping and watersports nearby. TAC7.

Publicity: *The Discover Channel, Rocky Mountain News, Country Living.*

Special Discounts: Returning customer 7%.

"This place unlocked my heart!"

Black Dog Inn B&B

PO Box 4659,
650 S Saint Vrain Ave
Estes Park, CO 80517-4659
(970)586-0374

Rates: $70-140.
Payment: MC VISA PC TC.
Innkeeper(s): Pete & Jane Princehorn.
Circa: 1910.

Rooms: 4 rooms with PB, 2 with FP. 2 suites.
Beds: Q.

Imagine relaxing in a private whirlpool bath enjoying a warm fire while surrounded by the majestic Rocky Mountains. Travelers are sure to enjoy this romantic getaway and mountain retreat. All rooms have private baths with two tubs and marble showers. Tasteful family antiques decorate each room, reminding visitors of the charm of yesteryear while they can enjoy the comforts of today. The innkeepers invite guests to visit often to enjoy the many seasons of the Rockies.

Breakfast and evening snack included in rates. Types of meals: full breakfast, gourmet breakfast and early coffee/tea. Ceiling fan in room. Cable TV, VCR and library on premises. Weddings, small meetings, family reunions and seminars hosted. Antiques, fishing, parks, shopping, downhill skiing, cross-country skiing, sporting events, theater and watersports nearby. TAC10.

Special Discounts: Winter packages and midweek specials.

"The peace and tranquility are so refreshing."

Henderson House

5455 Hwy 36, PO Box 3134
Estes Park, CO 80517
(970)586-4639 (800)798-4639

Rates: $110-175.
Payment: MC VISA PC TC.
Innkeeper(s): Vicki & Carl Henderson.
Circa: 1989.

Rooms: 4 rooms with PB. 1 suite.
Beds: K.

Although this house is just a few years old, it has many Victorian touches, including a carved staircase and rich woodwork. The decor is also Victorian and rooms feature flowery wallpapers, lacy curtains and country furnishings. Two rooms have double whirlpool tubs. The English Rose Garden Suite is especially suited for those celebrating a special occasion. The suite includes romantic decor, a sitting room, bedroom and stairs up to an efficiency kitchen. The plentiful breakfasts are worth waking for with an array of treats, from homemade waffles to souffles to succulent casseroles.

Breakfast included in rates. Types of meals: continental breakfast, full breakfast and early coffee/tea. Turn-down service in room. Cable TV, VCR and spa on premises. 11 acres. Fishing, parks and cross-country skiing nearby.

Georgetown C5

The Hardy House

605 Brownell St, Box 156
Georgetown, CO 80444
(303)569-3388 (800)490-4802
E-mail: hardyhousebb@usa.pipeline.com

Rates: $73-88.
Payment: MC VISA PC.
Innkeeper(s): Carla & Mike Wagner.
Circa: 1880.

Rooms: 4 rooms with PB, 1 with FP. 2 suites.
Beds: QT.

With its late 19th-century charm, this red and white Victorian is nestled in a quaint mining town and is close to many major ski areas. In the summer you can tour historic Georgetown on the inn's bicycles, hike to the summits of nearby 14,000-foot-high peaks and picnic in alpine meadows or by mountain streams. Guests can relax by the pot-bellied stove or outdoors in the hot tub and when its time to bed down, sleep under feather comforters.

Breakfast and afternoon tea included in rates. Types of meals: full breakfast, gourmet breakfast and early coffee/tea. Turn-down service, ceiling fan, cable TV and VCR in room. Spa and bicycles on premises. Antiques, fishing, parks, shopping, downhill skiing, cross-country skiing, sporting events and theater nearby. TAC10.

Publicity: *Metro, Country, Colonial Life.*

Green Mountain Falls D6

Outlook Lodge B&B

6975 Howard St, PO Box 5
Green Mountain Falls,
CO 80819
(719)684-2303

Rates: $60-95.
Payment: MC VISA DS PC.
Innkeeper(s): Patrick & Hayley Moran.
Circa: 1889.

Rooms: 8 rooms with PB. 1 conference room.
Beds: KQD.

Outlook Lodge was originally the parsonage for the historic Little Church in the Wildwood. Hand-carved balustrades surround a veranda that frames the alpine village view, and inside are many original parsonage furnishings. Iron bedsteads topped with patchwork quilts add warmth to the homey environment. This secluded mountain village is nestled at the foot of Pikes Peak.

Breakfast and evening snack included in rates. Types of meals: full breakfast and early coffee/tea. Cable TV on premises. Weddings, small meetings, family reunions and seminars hosted. Amusement parks, antiques, fishing, parks, shopping, downhill skiing, cross-country skiing, sporting events and theater nearby. TAC10.

Publicity: *Colorado Springs Gazette.*

"Found by chance, will return with purpose."

Gunnison E4

Mary Lawrence Inn

601 N Taylor St
Gunnison, CO 81230-2241
(970)641-3346
Fax:(970)641-3346

Rates: $69-89.
Payment: MC VISA.
Innkeeper(s): Pat & Jim Kennedy.
Circa: 1885.

Rooms: 5 rooms with PB. 2 suites.
Beds: KQT.

A local entrepreneur and saloon owner built this Italianate home in the late 19th century, but the innkeepers named their home in honor of Mary Lawrence, a later resident. Lawrence, a teacher and administrator for the local schools, used the building as a boarding house. The innkeepers have created an inviting interior with touches such as patchwork quilts, antique furnishings and stencilled walls. The innkeepers

serve a variety of treats each morning for breakfast, and keep the cookie jars full. The inn offers convenient access to the area's bounty of outdoor activities.

Breakfast included in rates. Types of meals: full breakfast, gourmet breakfast and early coffee/tea. Fax, copier and library on premises. Family reunions hosted. Fishing, parks, shopping, downhill skiing, cross-country skiing, theater and watersports nearby. TAC10.

Publicity: *Rocky Mountain News, Denver Post, Gunnison Country.*

Special Discounts: Ski packages, special weekends.

"You two are so gracious to make our stay a bit of 'heaven' in the snow."

CO

Hesperus G2

Blue Lake Ranch

16000 Hwy 140
Hesperus, CO 81326
(970)385-4377
Fax:(970)385-4088

Rates: $65-245.
Payment: PC TC.
Innkeeper(s): David & Shirley Alford.
Circa: 1910.

Rooms: 4 rooms with PB, 4 with FP. 2 suites. 1 conference room.
Beds: KQDT.

Built by Swedish immigrants, this renovated Victorian farmhouse is surrounded by spectacular flower gardens. The inn is filled with comforts such as down quilts, vases of fresh flowers and family antiques. The property is designated as a wildlife refuge and there is a cabin overlooking trout-filled Blue Lake, cottage on the river and uninterrupted mountain views. Enjoy a European/Southwest buffet breakfast.

Breakfast and afternoon tea included in rates. Types of meals: gourmet breakfast and early coffee/tea. Turn-down service, ceiling fan and VCR in room. Fax, copier and swimming on premises. Handicap access. 100 acres. Weddings, small meetings, family reunions and seminars hosted. German spoken. Antiques, fishing, parks, shopping, downhill skiing, cross-country skiing, theater and watersports nearby. TAC10.

Location: Twenty minutes from Durango.

Publicity: *Colorado Home & Lifestyles, Durango Herald, Conde Nast Traveler, Country Inns, Beautiful Gardens, Sunset.*

Special Discounts: 10% week or more stay.

"What a paradise you have created. We would love to return!!"

Keystone C5

Ski Tip Lodge

PO Box 38, 0764
Montezuma Rd
Keystone, CO 80435-0038
(970)468-4202 (800)222-0188

Rates: $44-198.
Payment: MC VISA AX DC CB DS TC.
Innkeeper(s): Erin Clark Gilchrist.
Circa: 1860.

Rooms: 9 rooms, 7 with PB. 2 suites.
Beds: DT.

This Bavarian inn served as a stagecoach stop in the 1860s and in the 1940s, it became the first ski lodge in Colorado. The inn is a restful, relaxing place so guests won't find clanging phones or television sets in their rooms. The common areas are welcoming places to relax or socialize with other guests. Each common room offers a stone hearth fireplace. Be sure to make a reservation, as there is a full-service restaurant on the premises serving gourmet, four-course dinners for guests and the public alike. Lunch service also is available, and during winter months, a buffet luncheon is prepared. Both cross-country and downhill ski areas are nearby.

Breakfast and afternoon tea included in rates. Lunch available. Spa on premises. Weddings and family reunions hosted. Fishing, downhill skiing and cross-country skiing nearby. TAC10.

The Apple Blossom Inn Victorian B&B

120 W 4th St
Leadville, CO 80461-3630
(719)486-2141 (800)982-9279

Rates: $59-79. MAP.
Payment: MC VISA AX PC TC.
Innkeeper(s): Maggie Senn & Sara Stutes.
Circa: 1879.

Rooms: 6 rooms, 2 with PB, 1 with FP.
Beds: KQDT.

Originally the home of Leadville banker Absalom Hunter, who lived here with his wife Estelle until 1918, the inn offers a glimpse into the good life of the late 19th century. Brass lights, beautiful crystal, fireplaces with Florentine tile, beveled mirrors, maple and mahogany inlaid floors, and stained-glass windows including one in a front window that gives The Apple Blossom Inn its name, are evidence to Hunter's prosperity. Innkeeper Maggie Senn invites guests to raid her cookie jar, which can include fresh brownies and chocolate chip cookies.

Breakfast and evening snack included in rates. Types of meals: continental breakfast, continental-plus breakfast, full breakfast, gourmet breakfast and early coffee/tea. Afternoon tea, dinner, picnic lunch, lunch, gourmet lunch and catered breakfast available. MAP. Weddings, small meetings and family reunions hosted. Antiques, fishing, parks, shopping, downhill skiing, cross-country skiing, theater and watersports nearby. TAC10.

The Ice Palace Inn & Antiques

813 Spruce St
Leadville, CO 80461-3555
(719)486-8272 (800)754-2840

Rates: $69-129.
Payment: MC VISA AX DS PC TC.
Innkeeper(s): Giles & Kami Kolakowski.
Circa: 1901.

Rooms: 3 rooms with PB.
Beds: QDT.

Innkeeper Kami Kolakowski was born in this historic Colorado town, and it was her dream to one day return and run a bed & breakfast. Now with husband Giles, she has created a restful retreat out of this turn-of-the-century home built with lumber from the famed Leadville Ice Palace. Giles and Kami have filled the home with antiques and pieces of history from the Ice Palace and the town. Guests are treated to a mouth-watering gourmet breakfast with treats such as stuffed French toast or German apple pancakes. As the name suggests, an antique shop is located on the premises.

Breakfast, afternoon tea and evening snack included in rates. Types of meals: gourmet breakfast and early coffee/tea. Catering service and room service available. Turn-down service and ceiling fan in room. Cable TV, VCR and library on premises. Weddings, small meetings, family reunions and seminars hosted. Antiques, fishing, parks, shopping, downhill skiing, cross-country skiing, theater and watersports nearby. TAC10.

Wood Haven Manor

PO Box 1291, 809 Spruce
Leadville, CO 80461-1291
(719)486-0109 (800)748-2570
Fax:(719)486-0210

Rates: $59-95.
Payment: MC VISA AX DS PC TC.
Innkeeper(s): Bobby & Jolene Wood.
Circa: 1898.

Rooms: 8 rooms, 7 with PB. 2 suites.
Beds: QDT.

Located on the town's Banker's Row, this Victorian inn is located in a winter wonderland, with cross-country and downhill skiing nearby, snowmobiling and back country outings. Gourmet breakfasts include freshly baked bread, sourdough pancakes or eggs Santa Fe, in-season fruits and cool fruit smoothies.

Breakfast, afternoon tea and evening snack included in rates. Types of meals: full breakfast, gourmet breakfast and early coffee/tea. Cable TV, VCR, fax, copier and library on premises. Weddings, small meetings, family reunions and seminars hosted. Amusement parks, antiques, fishing, parks, shopping, downhill skiing, cross-country skiing, theater and watersports nearby. TAC5.

Location: Historic "Bankers Row."

Publicity: *Country Traditional, Country Almanac, Country Decorating Ideas.*

"The room, the food and the hospitality were truly wonderful."

Loveland **B6**

The Lovelander B&B Inn

217 W 4th St
Loveland, CO 80537-5524
(970)699-0798 (800)459-6694
Fax:(970)699-0797

Rates: $83-125.
Payment: MC VISA AX DS PC TC.
Innkeeper(s): Marilyn Wiltgen, Sandy Strauss, Annmarie Arbo.
Circa: 1902.

Rooms: 11 rooms with PB, 1 with FP. 1 conference room.
Beds: KQDT.

CO

Prepare to be pampered at the Lovelander. Chocolate turndown service, fresh flowers, whirlpool tubs and bubble bath are just a few of the idyllic touches. Guest rooms are appointed in an uncluttered and romantic Victorian style. Three rooms include a fireplace and whirlpool tub. Enjoy the gentle sounds of a waterfall in the garden or sit back and relax on the wraparound porch. If weather permits, gourmet breakfasts can be enjoyed on the veranda or in the garden. Specialties such as pumpkin apple waffles topped with caramel pecan sauce are the reason why guests will be pleased to note that the inn now offers four-course dinners on Friday and Saturday nights. The inn's memorable cuisine has been featured on the TV shows "Inn Country USA" and "Inn Country Chefs." In addition to these more romantic amenities, there is a fax and copier available, a concierge and tour planning service, and conference facilities, which are located across the street.

Breakfast included in rates. Types of meals: full breakfast, gourmet breakfast and early coffee/tea. Picnic lunch available. Air conditioning and turn-down service in room. Cable TV, fax, copier and library on premises. Weddings, small meetings, family reunions and seminars hosted. Antiques, parks, shopping and cross-country skiing nearby. TAC10.

Lyons **B6**

The Inn at Rock 'n River: B&B and Trout Pond Fishing

16858 N Saint Vrain Dr
Lyons, CO 80540-9036
(303)443-4611 (800)448-4611

Rates: $68-159.
Payment: MC VISA AX DS TC.
Innkeeper(s): Marshall & Barbara McCrummen.
Circa: 1890.

Rooms: 9 rooms with PB, 1 with FP. 1 conference room.
Beds: KQDT.

Drive under a covered bridge to reach this scenic inn surrounded by woods, ponds, waterfalls and mountain views, all along the banks of the North Saint Vrain River. For lodge guests, pay-by-the-inch trout fishing is the catch of the day at this relaxing retreat. Bait, tackle and license are provided at no extra charge. They'll even clean the catch and show you various ways to cook the fish on an outdoor grill, if desired. The innkeepers ship their gourmet smoked trout throughout the year and it is available for purchase at the inn. Flowers dot the landscape, and guest rooms are filled with comfortable furnishings. The two-story carriage house boasts a fireplace and private two-person Jacuzzi, and every room offers full kitchens and beautiful views. After a restful night's sleep, awake to the scent of fresh coffee and enjoy a home-cooked breakfast before heading out for a day of exploring, fishing or antique shopping.

Breakfast included in rates. Type of meal: full breakfast. 18 acres. Weddings, small meetings, family reunions and seminars hosted. Amusement parks, antiques, fishing, parks, shopping, cross-country skiing, sporting events and theater nearby. TAC10.
Publicity: *Country.*

"Tremendous food and fantastic service. Our favorite place to visit in Colorado. I've been coming here for six years and best food and service we've had."

Manitou Springs

E6

Red Crags B&B

302 El Paso Blvd
Manitou Springs,
CO 80829-2308
(719)685-1920 (800)721-2248
Fax:(719)685-1073
E-mail: redcrags@databahn.net

Rates: $75-150.
Payment: MC VISA AX DS PC TC.
Innkeeper(s): Howard & Lynda Lerner.
Circa: 1870.

Rooms: 6 rooms with PB, 5 with FP. 3 suites.
Beds: K.

Well-known in this part of Colorado, this unique, four-story Victorian mansion sits on a bluff with a combination of views that includes Pikes Peak, Manitou Valley, Garden of the Gods and the City of Colorado Springs. The formal dining room features a rare cherrywood Eastlake fireplace. Outside, guests can walk through beautifully landscaped gardens or enjoy a private picnic area with a barbecue pit and a spectacular view.

Breakfast, afternoon tea and evening snack included in rates. Types of meals: continental breakfast, gourmet breakfast and early coffee/tea. Fax, spa and bicycles on premises. Weddings, small meetings, family reunions and seminars hosted. Antiques, parks, shopping and theater nearby. TAC10.

Publicity: *Bridal Guide, Denver Post, Los Angeles Times, Springs Woman.*

Minturn

C4

Eagle River Inn

PO Box 100
Minturn, CO 81645-0100
(970)827-5761 (800)344-1750
Fax:(970)827-4020
E-mail: eri@vail.net

Rates: $85-180.
Payment: MC VISA AX PC TC.
Innkeeper(s): Patty Bidez.
Circa: 1894.

Rooms: 12 rooms with PB.
Beds: KT.

Earth red adobe walls, rambling riverside decks, mature willow trees and brilliant flowers enhance the secluded backyard of this Southwestern-style inn. Inside, the lobby features comfortable Santa Fe furniture, an authentic beehive fireplace and a ceiling of traditional latilas and vegas. Baskets, rugs and weavings add warmth. Guest rooms found on two floors have views of the river or mountains. The innkeepers hold a wine tasting with appetizers each evening. Minturn, which had its beginnings as a stop on the Rio Grande Railroad, is the home of increasingly popular restaurants, shops and galleries.

Breakfast and evening snack included in rates. Type of meal: full breakfast. Cable TV in room. Fax and bicycles on premises. Weddings, small meetings and family reunions hosted. Fishing, shopping, downhill skiing, cross-country skiing and sporting events nearby. TAC10.

Location: Vail Valley.

Publicity: *Rocky Mountain News, Country Accents, Travel Holiday, Resorts, Vail Valley.*

"We love this place and have decided to make it a yearly tradition!"

Monte Vista

G5

The Windmill B&B

4340 W Hwy 160
Monte Vista, CO 81144
(719)852-0438 (800)467-3441

Rates: $65-99.
Payment: MC VISA PC.
Innkeeper(s): Sharon & Dennis Kay.
Circa: 1959.

Rooms: 4 rooms with PB.
Beds: KQT.

This Southwestern-style inn affords panoramic views of the surrounding Sangre De Cristo and San Juan mountain ranges. The 22-acre grounds still include the namesake windmill that once was used to irrigate water in the yard and garden. Now it stands guard over the hot tub. Each of the guest rooms is decorated in a different theme, with a few antiques placed here and there. The plentiful country breakfast are served in a dining room with mountain views.

Breakfast and evening snack included in rates. Types of meals: full breakfast, gourmet breakfast and early coffee/tea. Turn-down service in room. 22 acres. Family reunions hosted. Antiques, fishing, parks, shopping, downhill skiing, cross-country skiing and theater nearby.

Nederland C6

Goldminer Hotel

601 Klondike Ave
Nederland, CO 80466-9542
(303)258-7770 (800)422-4629
Fax:(303)258-3850

Rates: $69-129.
Payment: MC VISA AX TC.
Innkeeper(s): Scott Bruntjen.
Circa: 1897.

Rooms: 8 rooms, 4 with PB, 1 with FP. 1 suite. 1 cottage. 1 conference room.
Beds: KDT.

CO

This turn-of-the-century hotel is a highlight in the Eldora National Historic District. Suites and rooms are decorated with period antiques. The inn provides packages that include guided jeep, horseback, hiking and fishing tours in the summer and back-country ski tours in the winter.

Breakfast included in rates. Types of meals: full breakfast and early coffee/tea. Cable TV, VCR, fax, copier, computer, spa and library on premises. Handicap access. Weddings, small meetings, family reunions and seminars hosted. Antiques, fishing, parks, shopping, downhill skiing, cross-country skiing and sporting events nearby.

Pets Allowed: Cottage only.

Location: Eldora National Historic District.

Publicity: *Daily Camera, Mountain Ear.*

Northglenn C6

Country Gardens B&B

1619 East 136th Ave,
PO Box 33765
Northglenn, CO 80233
(303)451-1724 (800)475-1724

Rates: $65-105.
Payment: MC VISA PC TC.
Innkeeper(s): Arlie & Donna Munsie.
Circa: 1979.

Rooms: 4 rooms, 3 with PB. 1 suite.
Beds: KQ.

Nestled on four acres, this country Victorian offers three guest rooms and a suite all furnished with country antiques and family heirlooms. Handmade crafts enhance the country decor. The suite includes a private sitting area and a whirlpool situated beneath a stained-glass bay window. Other guest rooms include items such as a four-poster bed or a doll collection. The grounds offer a gazebo, gardens and an outdoor hot tub. Guests can stroll the grounds or relax on the veranda. Homemade breakfasts are served either in the dining room, sundeck or in the gazebo.

Breakfast, afternoon tea and evening snack included in rates. Types of meals: full breakfast and early coffee/tea. Air conditioning in room. Cable TV, VCR, spa and library on premises. Weddings, small meetings and family reunions hosted. Amusement parks, antiques, fishing, parks, shopping, downhill skiing, cross-country skiing, sporting events and theater nearby. TAC10.

Pine D6

Meadow Creek B&B Inn

13438 Hwy 285
Pine, CO 80470
(303)838-4167

Rates: $89-180.
Payment: MC VISA.
Innkeeper(s): Pat & Dennis Carnahan.
Circa: 1929.

Rooms: 7 rooms with PB. 3 suites.
Beds: KQ.

This marvelous stone structure, shrouded by pines and aspens, was built as a summer home for Italian Prince Balthasar Gialma Odescalchi, a descendant of rulers of the Holy Roman Empire. Enjoy views of the surrounding mountains as you breath in Colorado' s cool, clean air. The lush 55-acre grounds include the main house, barns, a smoke house and a cabin. Although Meadow Creek has been home to royalty, it had been vacant for some time when the current innkeepers found and restored their little treasure. Their restoration efforts have created a truly memorable inn. Rooms are filled with country charm, gracious furnishings and little extras such as teddy bears, flowers, beautiful quilts and lacy curtains. Grandma's Attic, a secluded loft bedroom, offers a sitting area and views at tree-top level. The Colorado Sun Suite offers the modern amenities of

a bar, microwave, coffee pot and refrigerator, combined with the romantic amenities of a private sitting room and a Jacuzzi underneath a skylight, perfect for stargazing. Some rooms boast fireplaces, and all guests are pampered with stocked cookie jars and refreshments available throughout the day. A luscious full breakfast with unique entrees, home-baked breads and other treats is served each morning, and dinners can be arranged.

Breakfast and evening snack included in rates. Types of meals: full breakfast and early coffee/tea. Dinner available. 35 acres. Weddings, small meetings, family reunions and seminars hosted. Antiques, fishing, shopping and cross-country skiing nearby.

Pueblo

E7

Abriendo Inn

300 W Abriendo Ave
Pueblo, CO 81004-1814
(719)544-2703
Fax:(719)542-6544

Rates: $58-110.
Payment: MC VISA AX DC PC.
Innkeeper(s): Kerrelyn & Chuck Trent.
Circa: 1906.

Rooms: 10 rooms with PB, 1 with FP. 1 suite.
Beds: KQ.

This three-story, 7,000-square-foot foursquare-style mansion is embellished with dental designs and wide porches supported by Ionic columns. Elegantly paneled and carved oak walls and woodwork provide a gracious setting for king-size brass beds, antique armoires and Oriental rugs. Breakfast specialties include raspberry muffins, Italian strada and nut breads. Ask for the music room with its own fireplace and bay window.

Breakfast included in rates. Types of meals: continental breakfast, gourmet breakfast and early coffee/tea. Evening snack and room service available. Air conditioning in room. Cable TV, fax and copier on premises. Weddings and small meetings hosted. Antiques, fishing, parks, shopping, cross-country skiing, sporting events and watersports nearby. TAC10.

Publicity: *Pueblo Chieftain, Rocky Mountain News.*

"Thank you for warm hospitality, cozy environment and fine cuisine! Outstanding!"

Salida

E5

Thomas House

307 E 1st St
Salida, CO 81201-2801
(719)539-7104

Rates: $45-65.
Payment: MC VISA PC TC.
Innkeeper(s): Tammy & Steve Office.
Circa: 1888.

Rooms: 5 rooms with PB. 1 suite.
Beds: QDT.

This home was built as a boarding house to help accommodate the thousands of railroad workers and travelers that passed through Salida. Today, the home still serves as a restful place for weary travelers drawn to the Colorado wilderness. The inn is decorated with antiques, collectibles and contemporary furnishings. Each guest room is named for a mountain. The Mt. Princeton suite includes a bedroom, private bath with an antique clawfoot tub and a separate sitting area. The innkeepers keep reading materials on hand, and there is an outdoor hot tub as well. Breakfasts are continental, yet hearty, with a variety of freshly baked breads and muffins, yogurt, granola, cheese and fruit.

Breakfast included in rates. Types of meals: continental breakfast and early coffee/tea. Ceiling fan and cable TV in room. Spa and library on premises. Small meetings and family reunions hosted. Antiques, fishing, parks, shopping, downhill skiing, cross-country skiing, theater and watersports nearby. TAC10.

Special Discounts: 10-20% for seven night or more, depending on the season.

Springfield G9

Plum Bear Ranch

PO Box 241, 29461 CR 21
Springfield, CO 81073
(719)523-4344
Fax:(719)523-4324

Rates: $40-50.
Payment: MC VISA PC TC.
Innkeeper(s): Wendy & Rory Lynch.
Circa: 1995.

Rooms: 6 rooms, 2 with PB. 1 conference room.
Beds: QD.

CO

Guests at the Plum Bear, which is set on a rustic 257-acre spread, are witnesses to history in the making. Although the lodging is located in a modern home, the grounds include a variety of unique, historic buildings that are being or recently have been restored. The grounds include two restored barns and the homestead house, on which the innkeepers are still working. The early 20th-century house will be filled with some of its original furnishings. There is antique farm equipment on the premises too. The ranch was a dream of Edna Minnick's, whose parents built and settled this homestead. She donated the ranch to the Colorado Boys Ranch. Minnick wanted guests to get an idea of what it might have been like as a pioneer on a dusty, Colorado ranch. Each of the guest rooms is decorated with a different theme, such as the Cowboy Room, which sleeps four people and includes a double bed and two bunk beds. Several other rooms also can sleep up to four. Full breakfasts are served family-style, but continental fare is available for those who prefer something lighter.

Breakfast and evening snack included in rates. Types of meals: continental breakfast, continental-plus breakfast and full breakfast. VCR, fax, copier, stables and pet boarding on premises. 257 acres. Weddings, small meetings, family reunions and seminars hosted. Antiques nearby.

Pets Allowed: Dogs-current rabies tag, livestock-current health traveling papers.

Steamboat Springs B4

Steamboat Valley Guest House

PO Box 773815
Steamboat Springs, CO
80477-3815
(970)870-9017 (800)530-3866
Fax:(970)879-0361

Rates: $73-148.
Payment: MC VISA AX DC CB DS PC TC.
Innkeeper(s): George & Alice Lund.
Circa: 1957.

Rooms: 4 rooms with PB, 1 with FP. 1 suite.
Beds: Q.

Enjoy a sleigh ride across snow-covered hills or take in the mountain view from the hot tub at this rustic Colorado home. Logs from the town mill and bricks from an old flour mill were used to construct the home, which features rooms with exposed wooden beams, high ceilings and country furnishings. Beds are covered with fluffy comforters, and several guest rooms afford magnificent views of this skiing resort town. The innkeepers prepare a varied breakfast menu with staples such as Irish oatmeal to the more gourmet, such as a puffy souffle. The home is located in the Steamboat Springs' historic Old Town area.

Breakfast and afternoon tea included in rates. Types of meals: full breakfast and early coffee/tea. Cable TV, VCR, fax, copier, spa and library on premises. Fishing, parks, shopping, downhill skiing, cross-country skiing, theater and watersports nearby. TAC10.

Special Discounts: 25% discount on a two night stay Monday-Thursday, some restrictions apply.

Stoneham B8

Elk Echo Ranch Country B&B

47490 WCR 155
Stoneham, CO 80754
(970)735-2426
Fax:(970)735-2427

Rates: $89-99.
Payment: MC VISA PC TC.
Innkeeper(s): Craig & Noreen McConnell.
Circa: 1994.

Rooms: 4 rooms with PB. 1 conference room.
Beds: KQD.

A heard of elk and a buffalo call this 2,000-acre ranch their home. A tour of the ranch is included in the rates, and guests on these tours can often get close enough to pet an elk. Prize hunting trophies of deer, elk and moose are displayed in the great room. Guest rooms are paneled with natural wood and each has a theme.

The Buffalo Bungalow includes a whirlpool tub and buffalo decor. Guests also can request to sleep in the enormous teepee that rests just a few yards from the main house. The ranch is an ideal place for families, and children are welcome. Hearty breakfasts include treats such as crispy French toast topped with strawberries and whipped cream.

Breakfast and evening snack included in rates. Type of meal: full breakfast. Picnic lunch, lunch and banquet service available. Air conditioning, ceiling fan and VCR in room. Fax and copier on premises. Handicap access. 2000 acres. Weddings, small meetings, family reunions and seminars hosted. Antiques, fishing, parks, shopping and watersports nearby. TAC10.

Pets Allowed: $20 refundable deposit required for pets.

Telluride — F3

Alpine Inn B&B

440 W Colorado Ave,
PO Box 2398
Telluride, CO 81435
(970)728-6282 (800)707-3344
Fax:(970)728-3424
E-mail: johnw@alpineinn.com

Rates: $60-220.
Payment: MC VISA PC TC.
Innkeeper(s): John & Denise Weaver.
Circa: 1903.

Rooms: 8 rooms, 6 with PB. 1 suite. 1 cottage.
Beds: KQDT.

Located in the heart of the historic district, this inn is within walking distance of the ski lifts. While enjoying the gourmet breakfast, guests also can take in the spectacular mountain view. Guest bedrooms feature a Victorian decor with antiques. The deluxe room has a fireplace and private balcony. After an active day, relax in the hot tub, which also has a wonderful view. Telluride, along with its famed outdoor activities, offers galleries, restaurants and gift shops.

Breakfast included in rates. Type of meal: full breakfast. Cable TV in room. Fax and library on premises. Fishing, parks, shopping, downhill skiing, cross-country skiing and theater nearby. TAC10.

"Wonderful, quaint and beautifully decorated."

New Sheridan Hotel

231 W Colorado Ave, PO Box 980
Telluride, CO 81435
(970)728-4351 (800)200-1891
Fax:(970)728-5024

Rates: $65-285.
Payment: MC VISA AX TC.
Innkeeper(s): John Coyle.
Circa: 1895.

Rooms: 32 rooms, 24 with PB. 6 suites.
Beds: KQ.

This charming hotel reflects the Victorian ambiance of a historic mining town. The building was redecorated recently to its former glory and is the only remaining original Victorian hotel and bar in Telluride. Much of the bar's interior is original, including a cherrywood back bar with carved lions imported from Austria. The adjoining Sheridan Opera House hosted such stars as Sarah Bernhardt, Lillian Gish and William Jennings Bryan. Guests can relax in their cozy guests rooms or in the library or parlor. Fluffy terry robes, in-room ceiling fans, a fitness room, rooftop Jacuzzi and evening wine and hors d'oeuvres await to pamper you. The hotel, one of the Four Sisters Inns, is a five-minute walk from ski lifts.

Breakfast included in rates. Type of meal: full breakfast. Picnic lunch available. Turn-down service in room. Fax, copier and bicycles on premises. Handicap access. Small meetings, family reunions and seminars hosted. Antiques, fishing, parks, shopping, downhill skiing, cross-country skiing, theater and watersports nearby. TAC10.

Publicity: *Bon Appetit, In Style, San Francisco Examiner, Sunset, Arizona Republic*

Special Discounts: Celebration package available.

San Sophia

330 W Pacific Ave,
PO Box 1825
Telluride, CO 81435
(303)728-3001 (800)537-4781
Fax:(970)728-6226

Rates: $114-260.
Payment: MC VISA AX PC.
Innkeeper(s): Keith & Alicia Hampton.
Circa: 1988.

Rooms: 16 rooms with PB. 1 conference room.
Beds: KQD.

CO

An observation tower rises gingerly from the inn's gabled roofline, providing 360-degree views from the valley floor to the 13,000-foot peaks of the Saint Sophia Ridge. Rooms are decorated with antiques, brass beds and wallpapers, and feature soaking tubs and bay windows or balconies. The two-story windows of the dining room reveal views of waterfalls plunging from the peaks on one side and ski slopes on the other.

Breakfast and afternoon tea included in rates. Type of meal: full breakfast. Cable TV in room. Fax, copier, computer and spa on premises. Fishing, shopping, downhill skiing and cross-country skiing nearby.

Publicity: *Rocky Mountain News, Snow Country, Country Inns, Glamour, New York Times.*

"Telluride is a great town and your bed and breakfast is part of the charm and beauty of the entire area."

Winter Park C5

Alpen Rose

244 Forest Tr, PO Box 769
Winter Park, CO 80482
(970)726-5039 (800)531-1373
Fax:(970)726-0993

Rates: $65-125.
Payment: MC VISA AX DS PC TC.
Innkeeper(s): Robin & Rupert Sommerauer.
Circa: 1960.

Rooms: 6 rooms with PB, 1 with FP.
Beds: KQT.

The innkeepers of this European-style mountain B&B like to share their love of the mountains with guests. There is a superb view of the James and Perry Peaks from the large southern deck where you can witness spectacular sunrises and evening alpen glows. The view is enhanced by lofty pines, wildflowers and quaking aspens. Each of the bedrooms is decorated with treasures brought over from Austria, including traditional featherbeds for the queen-size beds. The town of Winter Park is a small, friendly community located 68 miles west of Denver.

Breakfast and afternoon tea included in rates. Types of meals: gourmet breakfast and early coffee/tea. Cable TV, VCR, fax, copier and spa on premises. Weddings and family reunions hosted. German spoken. Antiques, fishing, parks, shopping, downhill skiing, cross-country skiing and watersports nearby. TAC10.

The Bear Paw Inn

871 Bear Paw Dr,
PO Box 334
Winter Park, CO 80482
(970)887-1351 (800)474-0091
Fax:(970)887-1351

Rates: $85-135.
Payment: MC VISA PC TC.
Innkeeper(s): Rick & Sue Callahan.
Circa: 1989.

Rooms: 3 rooms, 2 with PB. 1 suite.
Beds: Q.

This hand-hewn log home is exactly the type of welcoming retreat one might hope to enjoy on a vacation in the Colorado wilderness, and the panoramic views of the Continental Divide and Rocky Mountain National Park are just one reason. The cozy interior is highlighted by wood beams, log walls and antiques. There are three guest rooms, including one with a Jacuzzi tub and a private deck with a

swing. All guests can snuggle up in feather beds topped with down comforters. Winter Park is a Mecca for skiers, and ski areas are just a few miles from the Bear Paw, as is ice skating, snow mobiling and other winter activities. For summer guests, there is whitewater rafting, golfing, horseback riding and bike trails.

Breakfast included in rates. Types of meals: gourmet breakfast and early coffee/tea. Turn-down service in room. Cable TV, VCR, fax and copier on premises. Weddings, small meetings, family reunions and seminars hosted. Antiques, fishing, shopping, downhill skiing, cross-country skiing, theater and watersports nearby. TAC5.

Publicity: *Cape Cod Life, Boston Globe, Los Angeles Times.*

Special Discounts: 10% Sunday-Thursday to airline employees, senior citizens and teachers.

"Outstanding hospitality."

Candlelight Mountain Inn

148 Fern Way, PO Box 600
Winter Park, CO 80482
(970)887-2877 (800)546-4846

Rates: $45-85.
Payment: PC TC.
Innkeeper(s): Kim & Tim Onnen.
Circa: 1978.

Rooms: 4 rooms, 2 with PB.
Beds: QDT.

Stroll down a candlelit lane to reach this mountainside inn, surrounded by woods. Relax in a glider swing as you gaze at a campfire and mountain views, or soak in the hot tub as you watch shooting stars. The innkeepers have created a relaxing environment at their comfortable inn, which includes a common area with a recreation room, toy room, dining area and guest kitchen. The inn is a perfect place to relax after a busy day of skiing, skating, biking, golfing or hiking. Other popular area activities include white-water rafting, jeep tours and taking in the scenery from a hot air balloon. The Rocky Mountain National Park is just 30 minutes from the inn.

Breakfast and evening snack included in rates. Type of meal: full breakfast. VCR and pet boarding on premises. Small meetings and family reunions hosted. Antiques, fishing, parks, shopping, downhill skiing, cross-country skiing and theater nearby.

Pets Allowed: With prior arrangements.

Woodland Park D6

Pikes Peak Paradise

236 Pinecrest Rd,
PO Box 5760
Woodland Park, CO 80863
(719)687-6656 (800)728-8282
Fax:(719)687-9008
E-mail: woodlandco@aol.com

Rates: $95-195.
Payment: MC VISA AX DS PC TC.
Innkeeper(s): Priscilla, Martin & Tim.
Circa: 1987.

Rooms: 6 rooms, 2 with PB, 3 with FP. 4 suites.
Beds: KQ.

This three-story Georgian Colonial with stately white columns rises unexpectedly from the wooded hills west of Colorado Springs. The entire south wall of the inn is made of glass to enhance its splendid views of Pikes Peak. A sliding glass door opens from each room onto a patio. Eggs Benedict and Belgian waffles are favorite breakfast dishes.

Breakfast included in rates. Type of meal: gourmet breakfast. Ceiling fan in room. VCR, fax and spa on premises. Handicap access. Weddings and family reunions hosted. Amusement parks, antiques, fishing, parks, shopping, cross-country skiing, sporting events, theater and watersports nearby. TAC10.

Pets Allowed: Small pets with prior approval.

Location: West of Colorado Springs, 25 minutes.

Publicity: *Rocky Mountain News.*

Special Discounts: Sunday-Thursday $25 off.

Connecticut

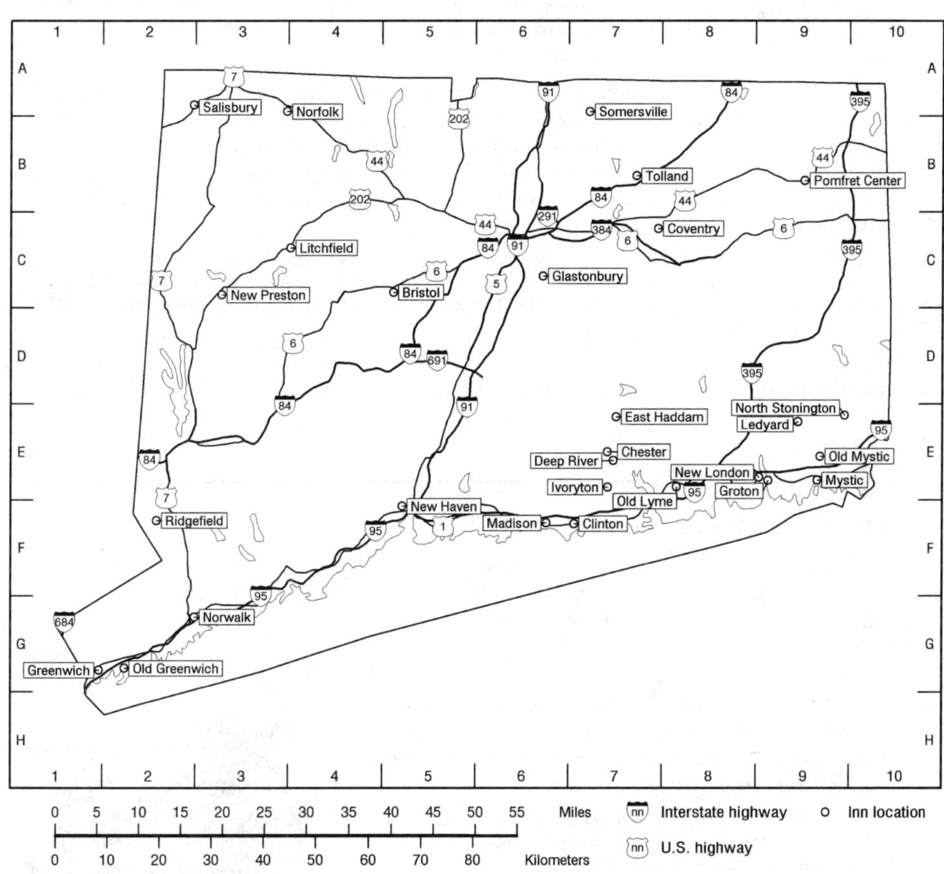

Bristol C5

Chimney Crest Manor

5 Founders Dr
Bristol, CT 06010-5209
(860)582-4219

Rates: $75-150.
Payment: MC VISA AX.
Innkeeper(s): Dante & Cynthia Cimadamore.
Circa: 1930.

Rooms: 5 rooms with PB, 2 with FP. 3 suites. 1 conference room.
Beds: KQ.

This 32-room Tudor mansion possesses an unusual castle-like arcade and a 45-foot living room with a stone fireplace at each end. Many of the rooms are embellished with oak paneling and ornate plaster ceilings. The inn is located in the Federal Hill District, an area of large colonial homes.

Breakfast included in rates. Types of meals: full breakfast and early coffee/tea. Afternoon tea and evening snack available. Air conditioning, ceiling fan and cable TV in room. VCR and library on premises. Weddings and small meetings hosted. Amusement parks, parks and cross-country skiing nearby. TAC10.

Publicity: *Record-Journal.*

"Great getaway — unbelievable structure. They are just not made like this mansion anymore."

Chester E7

The Inn at Chester

318 W Main St
Chester, CT 06412-1026
(860)526-9541 (800)949-7829
Fax:(860)526-4387

Rates: $88-205.
Payment: MC VISA AX.
Innkeeper(s): Deborah Moore.
Circa: 1778.

Rooms: 42 rooms with PB, 2 with FP. 1 suite. 3 conference rooms.
Beds: KQDT.

More than 200 years ago, Jeremiah Parmelee built a clapboard farmhouse along a winding road named the Killingworth Turnpike. The Parmelee Homestead stands as a reflection of the past and is an inspiration for the Inn at Chester. Each of the rooms is individually appointed with Eldred Wheeler Reproductions. The Lincoln Suite has a sitting room with a fireplace. Enjoy lively conversation or live music while imbibing your favorite drink at the inn's tavern, Dunk's Landing. Outside Dunk's Landing a 30-foot fireplace soars into the rafters.

Breakfast and dinner included in rates. Type of meal: continental-plus breakfast. Lunch and banquet service available. Air conditioning and cable TV in room. VCR, fax, copier, sauna, bicycles, tennis, library and pet boarding on premises. Handicap access. 12 acres. Weddings, small meetings, family reunions and seminars hosted. Antiques, fishing, parks, shopping, downhill skiing, cross-country skiing, theater and watersports nearby.

Pets Allowed.

Publicity: *New Haven Register, Hartford Courant, Pictorial Gazette, Discover Connecticut, New York Times.*

Clinton F7

Captain Dibbell House

21 Commerce St
Clinton, CT 06413-2054
(860)669-1646
Fax:(860)669-1646

Rates: $60-95.
Payment: MC VISA.
Innkeeper(s): Helen & Ellis Adams.
Circa: 1866.

Rooms: 4 rooms with PB.
Beds: KQT.

Built by a sea captain, this graceful Victorian house is only two blocks from the harbor where innkeeper Ellis Adams used to sail his own vessel. A ledger of household accounts dating from the 1800s is on display, and there are fresh flowers in each guest room.

Breakfast included in rates. Type of meal: full breakfast. Air conditioning, turn-down service and ceiling fan in room. Cable TV and bicycles on premises. Antiques, fishing, parks, shopping, theater and watersports nearby. TAC10.

Location: Exit 63 & I-95, south on Rt. 81 to Rt. 1, east for 1 block, right on Commerce.

Publicity: *Clinton Recorder, New Haven Register, Hartford Courant.*

"This was our first experience with B&Bs and frankly, we didn't know what to expect. It was GREAT!"

Coventry C7

Bird-In-Hand

2011 Main St
Coventry, CT 06238-2034
(860)742-0032

Rates: $70-90.
Payment: PC TC.
Innkeeper(s): Donald & Joanna Harte.
Circa: 1731.

Rooms: 3 rooms with PB, 3 with FP. 1 cottage.
Beds: Q.

Prepare for a remarkable journey back in time at this 18th-century home, part of which was built in 1731. Rooms still include original work, including fireplaces, and the innkeepers have added romantic canopy beds and hot tubs. According to legend, a man was burned in effigy in the home, and a secret closet in one of the bedrooms hid slaves during the days of the Underground Railroad. The innkeepers have in the past recreated a traditional, colonial meal cooked at the hearth, in full costume. On weekends they serve a hearty, country breakfast. The inn is near plenty of antique shops and restaurants, as well as the University of Connecticut and Eastern University. Caprilands Herb Farm is a fun trip just down the road.

Breakfast and afternoon tea included in rates. Types of meals: continental-plus breakfast, full breakfast and early coffee/tea. Turn-down service and ceiling fan in room. Cable TV, VCR, fax and spa on premises. Weddings, small meetings, family reunions and seminars hosted. Amusement parks, antiques, fishing, parks, shopping, cross-country skiing, sporting events, theater and watersports nearby.

Special Discounts: 20% discount on stays over 5 days.

"We were delighted then, to find such a jewel in the Bird-In-Hand."

CT

Maple Hill Farm B&B

365 Goose Ln
Coventry, CT 06238-1215
(860)742-0635 (800)742-0635

Rates: $55-75.
Payment: MC VISA PC TC.
Innkeeper(s): Anthony Felice, Jr. & Marybeth Gorke-Felice.
Circa: 1731.

Rooms: 4 rooms, 1 with PB.
Beds: DT.

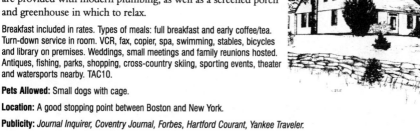

This historic farmhouse still possesses its original kitchen cupboards and a flour bin used for generations. Family heirlooms and the history of the former home owners are shared with guests. There is a three-seat outhouse behind the inn. Visitors, of course, are provided with modern plumbing, as well as a screened porch and greenhouse in which to relax.

Breakfast included in rates. Types of meals: full breakfast and early coffee/tea. Turn-down service in room. VCR, fax, copier, spa, swimming, stables, bicycles and library on premises. Weddings, small meetings and family reunions hosted. Antiques, fishing, parks, shopping, cross-country skiing, sporting events, theater and watersports nearby. TAC10.

Pets Allowed: Small dogs with cage.

Location: A good stopping point between Boston and New York.

Publicity: *Journal Inquirer, Coventry Journal, Forbes, Hartford Courant, Yankee Traveler.*

"Comfortable rooms and delightful country ambiance."

Deep River E7

Riverwind

209 Main St
Deep River, CT 06417-2022
(860)526-2014

Rates: $95-165.
Payment: MC VISA AX.
Innkeeper(s): Barbara Barlow & Bob Bucknall.
Circa: 1790.

Rooms: 8 rooms with PB.
Beds: QD.

Chosen "most romantic inn in Connecticut" by Discerning Traveler Newsletter, this inn features a wraparound gingerbread porch filled with gleaming white wicker furniture. A happy, informal country decor includes antiques from Barbara's Virginia home. There are fireplaces everywhere, including a 12-foot cooking fireplace in the keeping room.

Breakfast included in rates. Type of meal: full breakfast. Weddings hosted. Antiques and theater nearby.

Publicity: *Hartford Courant, Country Living, Country Inns, Country Decorating, New York, Travel & Leisure, New York Times, Boston Globe, Los Angeles Times.*

"Warm, hospitality, a quiet homey atmosphere, comfortable bed, well thought-out and delightful appointments, delicious light hot biscuits — a great find!"

East Haddam E7

Bishopsgate Inn

Goodspeed Landing,
PO Box 290
East Haddam, CT 06423
(860)873-1677
Fax:(860)873-3898

Rates: $85-120. MAP.
Payment: MC VISA PC.
Innkeeper(s): Kagel Family.
Circa: 1818.

Rooms: 6 rooms with PB, 4 with FP. 1 suite. 1 conference room.
Beds: QDT.

This Colonial house is furnished with period antiques, and each floor of the inn has a sitting area where guests often relax with a good book. Four of the guest rooms include a fireplace and a suite has a sauna. The innkeepers serve a hearty breakfast, and for an additional charge, can prepare picnic lunches and five-course dinners. Although secluded on two acres, the inn is a short walk to the Goodspeed Opera House and shopping.

Breakfast and afternoon tea included in rates. Types of meals: continental breakfast, full breakfast, gourmet breakfast and early coffee/tea. Dinner, evening snack, picnic lunch, lunch and room service available. MAP. Air conditioning in room. Small meetings and family reunions hosted. Antiques, fishing, parks, shopping, downhill skiing, cross-country skiing, theater and watersports nearby.

Publicity: *The Discerning Traveler, Adventure Road, The Manhattan Cooperator.*

Special Discounts: Corporate and long stay rates negotiable.

"... Attention to detail, ambiance and amenities ... Bishopsgate is truly outstanding."

Glastonbury C6

Butternut Farm

1654 Main St
Glastonbury, CT 06033
(860)633-7197
Fax:(860)659-1758

Rates: $70-90.
Payment: AX PC TC.
Innkeeper(s): Don Reid.
Circa: 1720.

Rooms: 4 rooms with PB, 3 with FP. 2 suites.
Beds: DT.

This Colonial house sits on two acres of landscaped grounds amid trees and herb gardens. Prize-winning goats, pigeons and chickens are housed in the old barn on the property. Eighteenth-century Connecticut antiques, including a cherry highboy and cherry pencil-post canopy bed, are placed throughout the inn, enhancing the natural beauty of the pumpkin-pine floors and eight brick fireplaces.

Breakfast included in rates. Type of meal: full breakfast. Air conditioning and VCR in room. Fax on premises. Family reunions hosted. Antiques, fishing, parks, shopping, downhill skiing, cross-country skiing, sporting events and theater nearby.

Location: South of Glastonbury Center, 1.6 miles, 10 minutes to Hartford.

Publicity: *New York Times, House Beautiful, Yankee, Antiques.*

Greenwich G1

Stanton House Inn

76 Maple Ave
Greenwich, CT 06830-5622
(203)869-2110

Rates: $65-135.
Payment: MC VISA AX DS TC.
Innkeeper(s): Tog & Doreen Pearson.
Circa: 1900.

Rooms: 24 rooms, 22 with PB, 2 with FP. 1 conference room.
Beds: KQDT.

It took 150 years for one of the Saketts to finally build on the land given them in 1717. The manor they built was remodeled on a grand scale at the turn-of-the-century under architect Sanford White. In the '40s, the house became a tourist home and received visitors for many years. Renovated recently, it now offers spacious rooms decorated in a traditional, country inn style.

Breakfast included in rates. Type of meal: continental breakfast. Air conditioning and cable TV in room. Fax, copier and swimming on premises. Weddings, small meetings and family reunions hosted. French and Spanish spoken. Antiques, parks, shopping and theater nearby. TAC10.

Publicity: *Foster's Business Review.*

"For a day, or a month or more, this is a special place."

Ivoryton **E7**

The Copper Beech Inn

46 Main St
Ivoryton, CT 06442-1004
(860)767-0330
Fax:(860)767-7840

Rates: $118-190.
Payment: MC VISA AX DC CB PC TC.
Innkeeper(s): Eldon & Sally Senner.
Circa: 1887.

Rooms: 13 rooms with PB. 1 conference room.
Beds: KQDT.

The Copper Beech Inn was once the home of ivory importer A.W. Comstock, one of the early owners of the Comstock Cheney Company, producer of ivory combs and keyboards. The village took its name from the ivory trade centered here. An enormous copper beech tree shades the property. Each room in the renovated Carriage House boasts a whirlpool bath and French doors opening onto a deck. The wine list and French country cuisine at the inn's restaurant have received numerous accolades.

Breakfast included in rates. Type of meal: continental-plus breakfast. Banquet service available. Air conditioning and cable TV in room. Library on premises. Handicap access. Weddings, small meetings and seminars hosted. Limited Spanish and Portuguese spoken. Antiques, fishing, parks, shopping, theater and watersports nearby.

Location: Lower Connecticut River valley.

Publicity: *Los Angeles Times, Bon Appetit, Connecticut, Travel & Leisure, Discerning Traveler.*

"The grounds are beautiful .. just breathtaking .. accommodations are wonderful."

Ledyard **E9**

Applewood Farms Inn

528 Colonel Ledyard Hwy
Ledyard, CT 06339-1649
(860)536-2022
Fax:(860)536-6015
E-mail: rsdp66a@prodigy.com

Rates: $115-270.
Payment: MC VISA AX PC TC.
Innkeeper(s): Frankie & Tom Betz.
Circa: 1826.

Rooms: 6 rooms, 4 with PB, 4 with FP. 1 suite.
Beds: KDT.

Five generations of the Gallup family worked this farm near Mystic. The classic center-chimney Colonial, furnished with antiques and early-American pieces, is situated on 33 acres of fields and meadows. Stone fences meander through the property and many of the original outbuildings remain. It is in the National Register, cited as one of the best surviving examples of a 19th-century farm in Connecticut.

Breakfast included in rates. Types of meals: full breakfast and early coffee/tea. Air conditioning and turn-down service in room. Cable TV, VCR, fax and copier on premises. 33 acres. Weddings, small meetings and family reunions hosted. Amusement parks, antiques, fishing, parks, shopping, cross-country skiing, sporting events, theater and watersports nearby. TAC10.

Pets Allowed.

Publicity: *Country, New Woman, Travel Host.*

"This bed & breakfast is a real discovery."

Litchfield C4

Tollgate Hill Inn

Rt 202 & Tollgate Rd,
Box 1339
Litchfield, CT 06759
(860)567-4545 (800)445-3903
Fax:(860)567-8397

Rates: $90-175. EP.
Payment: AX DC CB DS PC TC.
Innkeeper(s): Ferdinand J. Zivic.
Circa: 1745.

Rooms: 21 rooms with PB, 9 with FP. 6 suites. 2 conference rooms.
Beds: QDT.

Formerly known as the Captain Bull Tavern, the inn underwent extensive renovations in 1983. Listed in the National Register, features include Indian shutters, wide pine-paneled walls, a Dutch door fireplace, and an upstairs ballroom. Next door is a historic schoolhouse that contains four of the inn's guest rooms.

Breakfast included in rates. Type of meal: continental breakfast. Dinner, picnic lunch, lunch, gourmet lunch, banquet service, catering service, catered breakfast and room service available. EP. Air conditioning and cable TV in room. VCR, fax, copier and pet boarding on premises. Handicap access. 10 acres. Weddings, small meetings, family reunions and seminars hosted. Amusement parks, antiques, fishing, parks, shopping, downhill skiing, cross-country skiing, sporting events, theater and watersports nearby. TAC6.

Pets Allowed.

Publicity: *Food & Wine, Travel & Leisure, The New York Times, Bon Appetit.*

Madison F6

Tidewater Inn

949 Boston Post Rd
Madison, CT 06443-3236
(203)245-8457

Rates: $80-160.
Payment: MC VISA AX PC TC.
Innkeeper(s): Jean Foy & Rich Evans.
Circa: 1840.

Rooms: 10 rooms, 9 with PB, 2 with FP. 1 cottage.
Beds: KQDT.

Long ago, this 19th-century home was no doubt a welcome site to travelers needing a rest after a bumpy stagecoach ride. Although its days as a stagecoach stop have long since past, the inn is still a welcoming place for those needing a romantic getaway. The rooms are elegantly appointed with items such as four-poster or canopy beds, Oriental rugs and fine furnishings. The inn's sitting area is a cozy place to relax, with its fireplace and exposed beams. The one-and-a-half-acre grounds include an English garden. The inn is within walking distance to many of Madison's sites, and beaches are just a couple of miles away.

Breakfast included in rates. Types of meals: continental breakfast, full breakfast and early coffee/tea. Air conditioning and cable TV in room. Antiques, fishing, parks, shopping, theater and watersports nearby.

Mystic E9

The Whaler's Inn

20 E Main St
Mystic, CT 06355-2646
(860)536-1506 (800)243-2588
Fax:(860)572-1250

Rates: $69-135.
Payment: MC VISA AX TC.
Innkeeper(s): Richard Prisby.
Circa: 1901.

Rooms: 41 rooms with PB. 1 suite. 1 conference room.
Beds: KQD.

This classical revival-style inn is built on the historical site of the Hoxie House, the Clinton House and the U.S. Hotel. Just as these famous 19th-century inns offered, the Whaler's Inn has the same charm and convenience for today's visitor to Mystic. Once a booming ship-building center, the town's connection to the sea is ongoing and the sailing schooners still pass beneath the Bascule Drawbridge in the center of town. The inn has indoor and outdoor dining available and more than 75 shops and restaurants are within walking distance.

Type of meal: early coffee/tea. Dinner, lunch and gourmet lunch available. Air conditioning and cable TV in room. Fax, copier and child care on premises. Handicap access. Weddings, small meetings, family reunions and seminars hosted. Antiques, fishing, parks, shopping and watersports nearby.

New Haven

F5

Three Chimneys Inn

CT

1201 Chapel St
New Haven, CT 06511-4701
(203)789-1201
Fax:(203)776-7363
E-mail: chimneysnh@aol.com

Rates: $150-165.
Payment: MC VISA AX DS PC TC.
Innkeeper(s): Fay Carrow.
Circa: 1870.

Rooms: 10 rooms with PB, 2 with FP. 2 conference rooms.
Beds: KQ.

Located only one block from the campus of Yale University and three blocks from New Haven's best dining and entertainment area, Three Chimneys offers an elegant setting for enjoying the area. Georgian and Federal period furnishings fill the inn and there are Oriental rugs, desks, and four-poster beds in the guest rooms. Additional features include a grand staircase, oak fireplaces, two parlors, a club room and a library with two fireplaces. A veranda overlooks the inn's garden. Nearby are the Shubert, Yale Repertory Theater and the Palace Theater.

Breakfast included in rates. Air conditioning and cable TV in room. Fax and copier on premises. Small meetings and seminars hosted. Parks, shopping, sporting events and theater nearby. TAC10.

Location: Downtown, one block from the Yale campus.

Publicity: *New York Times, Business Digest of Greater New Haven.*

New London

E9

Queen Anne Inn

265 Williams St
New London, CT 06320
(860)447-2600 (800)347-8818

Rates: $89-185.
Payment: MC VISA AX DS PC TC.
Innkeeper(s): Ed Boncich & Janet Moody.
Circa: 1903.

Rooms: 10 rooms, 7 with PB, 2 with FP. 1 suite.
Beds: KQDT.

Several photographers for historic house books have been attracted to the classic good looks of the Queen Anne Inn. The traditional tower, wraparound verandas and elaborate frieze invite the traveler to explore the interior with its richly polished oak walls and intricately carved alcoves. Stained-glass windows curve around the circular staircase landing. Period furnishings include brass beds and some rooms have their own fireplace.

Breakfast and afternoon tea included in rates. Types of meals: full breakfast and early coffee/tea. Picnic lunch available. Air conditioning and cable TV in room. Library on premises. Small meetings and family reunions hosted. Amusement parks, antiques, fishing, parks, shopping, cross-country skiing, sporting events, theater and watersports nearby. TAC10.

Publicity: *New London Day Features.*

"Absolutely terrific — relaxing, warm, gracious — beautiful rooms and delectable food."

New Preston

C3

Boulders Inn

East Shore Rd, Rt 45
New Preston, CT 06777
(203)868-0541
Fax:(203)868-1925

Rates: $125-300. MAP.
Payment: MC VISA AX TC.
Innkeeper(s): Kees & Ulla Adema.
Circa: 1895.

Rooms: 17 rooms with PB, 11 with FP. 6 suites. 1 conference room.
Beds: KQD.

Outstanding views of Lake Waramaug and its wooded shores can be seen from the living room and many of the guest rooms and cottages of this country inn. The terrace is open in the summer for cocktails, dinner and sunsets over the lake. Antique furnishings, a basement game room, a beach house with a hanging wicker swing and a tennis court are all part of Boulders Inn.

Breakfast, afternoon tea and dinner included in rates. Types of meals: full breakfast, gourmet breakfast and early coffee/tea. Banquet service available. MAP. Air conditioning, turn-down service and ceiling fan in room. Cable TV, fax, copier and bicycles on premises. Handicap access. 27 acres. Weddings, small meetings and family reunions hosted. Antiques, fishing, parks, shopping, downhill skiing, cross-country skiing, theater and watersports nearby.

Location: Lake Waramaug.

Publicity: *New York Times, Travel & Leisure, Country Inns.*

"Thank you for a welcome respite from the daily hurly-burly. "

Noank-Mystic

Palmer Inn

25 Church St
Noank-Mystic, CT 06340
(860)572-9000

Rates: $105-215. EP.
Payment: MC VISA AX DS PC TC.
Innkeeper(s): Patricia Ann White.
Circa: 1907.

Rooms: 6 rooms with PB, 1 with FP. 2 conference rooms.
Beds: KQDT.

This gracious seaside mansion was built for shipbuilder Robert Palmer Jr. by shipyard craftsmen. It features a two-story grand columned entrance, mahogany beams, mahogany staircase, quarter-sawn oak floors and 14-foot ceilings. The Lincrusta wallcovering, original light fixtures and nine stained-glass windows remain. The inn is located two miles to downtown Mystic, and one block to the water in the historic fishing village of Noank.

Breakfast and afternoon tea included in rates. Types of meals: continental-plus breakfast and early coffee/tea. EP. Air conditioning, turn-down service and ceiling fan in room. Library on premises. Small meetings and seminars hosted. Amusement parks, antiques, fishing, parks, shopping, theater and watersports nearby.

Location: Two miles from Mystic.

Publicity: *Boston Globe, Yankee, Norwalk Hour, Discerning Traveler, Companion, Day, Coastal Cruising, Historic Preservation.*

Special Discounts: 10% off weekly stays.

"Your Inn is gracious, yet it has the atmosphere of a warm and lovely home."

Norfolk

A3

Greenwoods Gate B&B Inn

Greenwoods Rd E,
PO Box 491
Norfolk, CT 06058
(860)542-5439

Rates: $175-235.
Payment: PC TC.
Innkeeper(s): George & Marian Schumaker.
Circa: 1797.

Rooms: 4 suites.
Beds: QDT.

Luxurious is perhaps the best way to describe this inn. From little touches like fresh flowers and soft, fluffy bath robes to the beautiful interior, the innkeepers pamper each guest. Enjoy gourmet breakfast in the formal dining room and refreshments in the late afternoon. Each of the four suites offers something unique. The three-level Levi Thompson Suite offers a romantic sitting area and tiered canopy bed. The E.J. Trescott Suite is full of antiques and doll collections. The Lillian Rose Suite is perfect for couples traveling together as it offers two bedrooms and a library room with a fireplace. A private stairway leads up to the Captain Darius Phelps Suite.

Breakfast, afternoon tea and evening snack included in rates. Types of meals: gourmet breakfast and early coffee/tea. Air conditioning and ceiling fan in room. Cable TV, VCR and library on premises. Antiques, fishing, parks, shopping, downhill skiing, cross-country skiing, theater and watersports nearby. TAC10.

Publicity: *Yankee, Ladies Home Journal, Country Inns, National Geographic Traveler.*

Special Discounts: Less 10% Monday-Thursday, mid-November-May.

Manor House

69 Maple Ave
Norfolk, CT 06058-0447
(860)542-5690
Fax:(860)542-5690

Rates: $85-190.
Payment: MC VISA AX DS PC TC.
Innkeeper(s): Hank & Diane Tremblay.
Circa: 1898.

Rooms: 8 rooms with PB, 2 with FP. 1 suite. 1 conference room.
Beds: KQDT.

CT

Charles Spofford, designer of London's subway, built this home with many gables, exquisite cherry paneling and grand staircase. There are Moorish arches and Tiffany windows. Guests can enjoy hot-mulled cider after a sleigh ride, hay ride, or horse and carriage drive along the country lanes nearby. The inn was named by "Discerning Traveler" as Connecticut's most romantic hideaway.

Breakfast and afternoon tea included in rates. Types of meals: full breakfast, gourmet breakfast and early coffee/tea. Catering service, catered breakfast and room service available. Ceiling fan in room. Cable TV, fax, computer and library on premises. Weddings, small meetings, family reunions and seminars hosted. French spoken. Antiques, fishing, parks, shopping, downhill skiing, cross-country skiing, sporting events, theater and watersports nearby. TAC10.

Location: Close to the Berkshires.

Publicity: *Boston Globe, Philadelphia Inquirer, Innsider, Rhode Island Monthly, Gourmet, National Geographic Traveler, Good Housekeeping.*

Special Discounts: 10-20%, subject to availability.

"Queen Victoria, eat your heart out."

North Stonington

E9

Antiques & Accommodations

32 Main St
North Stonington,
CT 06359-1709
(860)535-1736 (800)554-7829

Rates: $169-229.
Payment: MC VISA.
Innkeeper(s): Ann & Tom Gray.
Circa: 1861.

Rooms: 5 rooms, 6 with PB. 2 suites.
Beds: Q.

Set amongst the backdrop of an acre of herb, edible flower, perennial and cutting gardens, this Victorian treasure offers a romantic location for a weekend getaway. Rooms filled with antiques boast four-poster canopy beds and fresh flowers surrounded by a soft, pleasing decor. Honeymooners or couples celebrating an anniversary are presented with special amenities such as balloons, champagne and heart-shaped waffles for breakfast. Candlelit breakfasts include unique items such as edible flowers along with the delicious entrees. Historic Mystic Seaport and Foxwood's Casino are just minutes from the inn.

Breakfast included in rates. Type of meal: full breakfast. Air conditioning, cable TV and VCR in room. Antiques and fishing nearby.

Publicity: *Country Inns, Woman's Day, New London Day*

Special Discounts: Mid-week package.

"The building's old-fashioned welcome-all decor made us feel comfortable the moment we stepped in."

Arbor House at Kruger's Old Maine Farm

75 Chester Maine Rd
North Stonington, CT 06359
(860)535-4221
Fax:(860)535-4221

Rates: $75-150. AP.
Payment: MC VISA PC TC.
Innkeeper(s): Allen & Michelle Kruger.
Circa: 1900.

Rooms: 4 rooms, 2 with PB. 2 suites.
Beds: Q.

From this restored, turn-of-the-century farmhouse, guests enjoy a view of Connecticut's coastline and picturesque countryside. Spacious guest rooms are decorated in an uncluttered, country style. The farmhouse is surrounded by 37 acres, which includes a vineyard. The old barn has been converted into a winery. Three-course breakfasts are served each morning in the dining room.

Breakfast and afternoon tea included in rates. Types of meals: full breakfast and early coffee/tea. AP. Air conditioning, turn-down service and cable TV in room. VCR, fax, stables and pet boarding on premises. 37 acres. Weddings, small meetings, family reunions and seminars hosted. Antiques, fishing, parks, shopping, cross-country skiing and watersports nearby. TAC5.

Pets Allowed: Outside.

Norwalk G2

Silvermine Tavern

194 Perry Ave
Norwalk, CT 06850-1123
(203)847-4558
Fax:(203)847-9171

Rates: $90-110.
Payment: MC VISA AX DC CB PC TC.
Innkeeper(s): Frank Whitman, Jr.
Circa: 1790.

Rooms: 10 rooms with PB.
Beds: DT.

The Silvermine consists of the Old Mill, the Country Store, the Coach House and the Tavern itself. Primitive paintings and furnishings, as well as family heirlooms, decorate the inn. Guest rooms and dining rooms overlook the Old Mill, the waterfall and swans gliding across the millpond. Some guest rooms offer items such as canopy bed or private decks. In the summer, guests can dine al fresco and gaze at the mill pond.

Breakfast included in rates. Type of meal: continental breakfast. Dinner, lunch, banquet service and catering service available. Air conditioning in room. VCR, fax and copier on premises. Weddings, small meetings, family reunions and seminars hosted. Antiques, fishing, parks and shopping nearby. TAC10.

Publicity: *Advocate, Greenwich Time.*

Special Discounts: Special rates for guests staying longer than one week.

Old Greenwich G2

Harbor House Inn

165 Shore Rd
Old Greenwich, CT 06870
(203)637-0145
Fax:(203)698-0943

Rates: $79-139.
Payment: MC VISA AX TC.
Innkeeper(s): Rosemarie Stuttig & Dawn Browne.
Circa: 1890.

Rooms: 23 rooms, 17 with PB. 1 conference room.
Beds: QDT.

This turn-of-the-century home is decorated with unique, Old World flair. Guest rooms, decorated with wood-paneled walls feature poster beds and sturdy, comfortable furnishings. Each room includes a mini refrigerator and a coffee maker, and there are laundry facilities on the premises. Business travelers will appreciate the availability of a fax machine and copier, and the inn offers a conference room. Restaurants and shops are nearby, and the inn is 45 minutes by train from New York City. The innkeepers offer more accommodations on River Road in Cos Cob.

Breakfast included in rates. Type of meal: continental breakfast. Air conditioning and VCR in room. Cable TV, fax, copier and bicycles on premises. Weddings, small meetings and family reunions hosted. Amusement parks, antiques, fishing, parks, shopping and theater nearby. TAC10.

Old Lyme E8

Bee and Thistle Inn

100 Lyme St
Old Lyme, CT 06371-1426
(860)434-1667 (800)622-4946
Fax:(860)434-3402

Rates: $75-215. EP.
Payment: MC VISA AX DC PC TC.
Innkeeper(s): Bob, Penny, Lori and Jeff Nelson.
Circa: 1756.

Rooms: 11 rooms with PB, 1 with FP. 1 cottage.
Beds: KQDT.

CT

This stately inn is situated along the banks of the Lieutenant River. There are five and one-half acres of trees, lawns and a sunken English garden. The inn is furnished with Chippendale antiques and reproductions. A guitar duo plays in the parlor on Friday, and a harpist performs on Saturday evenings. Bee and Thistle was voted the most romantic inn in the state, the most romantic dinner spot, and for having the best Restaurant in the state by readers of "Connecticut Magazine."

Type of meal: gourmet breakfast. Afternoon tea and lunch available. EP. Air conditioning and ceiling fan in room. Weddings, small meetings and family reunions hosted. Antiques, fishing, parks, shopping, theater and watersports nearby. TAC10.

Location: Historic district next to Florence Griswold Museum.

Publicity: *Countryside, Country Living, Money, New York, U.S. Air, New York Times, Country Traveler.*

Old Mystic E9

The Old Mystic Inn

52 Main St, Box 634
Old Mystic, CT 06372-0634
(860)572-9422

Rates: $95-145.
Payment: MC VISA AX PC TC.
Innkeeper(s): Peter & Mary E. Knight.
Circa: 1794.

Rooms: 8 rooms with PB, 3 with FP. 1 suite.
Beds: Q.

Charles Vincent ran the Old Mystic Bookstore from this house for 35 years. Although it once housed 20,000 old books and maps, it has been renovated to a bed and breakfast inn. The old maps and drawings hung around the stairwell have been preserved. There are stone fireplaces in all the rooms and wide board floors. Furnishings include replica Colonial period pieces.

Breakfast and afternoon tea included in rates. Types of meals: full breakfast and early coffee/tea. Air conditioning in room. Cable TV, fax, copier, bicycles and library on premises. Weddings, small meetings, family reunions and seminars hosted. Antiques, parks and watersports nearby. TAC10.

Publicity: *New Jersey Monthly, New London Day.*

"A real delight and the breakfast was sumptuous!"

Red Brook Inn

2800 Gold Star Hwy,
PO Box 237
Old Mystic, CT 06372-0237
(860)572-0349

Rates: $95-189.
Payment: MC VISA AX DS PC TC.
Innkeeper(s): Ruth Keyes.
Circa: 1740.

Rooms: 10 rooms with PB, 7 with FP. 3 conference rooms.
Beds: QDT.

If there was no other reason to visit Old Mystic, a charming town brimming with activities, the Red Brook Inn would be reason enough. The Crary Homestead features two unique rooms, both with working fireplaces, while the Haley Tavern offers guest rooms with canopy beds and fireplaces. Innkeeper Ruth Keyes has selected a beautiful array of antiques to decorate her inn. Guests are sure to enjoy Keyes wonderful authentic Colonial breakfasts. A special winter meal takes three days to complete and Keyes prepares it over an open hearth. The aquarium, Mystic Seaport Museum, a cider mill, casinos and many charming shops are only minutes away.

Breakfast, afternoon tea and evening snack included in rates. Type of meal: full breakfast. Air conditioning in room. Cable TV, VCR and library on premises. Small meetings, family reunions and seminars hosted. Amusement parks, antiques, fishing, parks, shopping, sporting events, theater and watersports nearby.

Location: Off route 184 (Gold Star Highway).

Publicity: *Travel & Leisure, Yankee, New York, Country Decorating, Philadelphia Inquirer, National Geographic Traveler, Discerning Traveler.*

"The staff is wonderful. You made us feel at home. Thank you for your hospitality."

Pomfret Center **B9**

Clark Cottage at Wintergreen

354 Pomfret St
Pomfret Center, CT 06259
(860)928-5741
Fax:(860)928-1591
E-mail: qurq@necca.com

Rates: $70-80.
Payment: MC VISA PC TC.
Innkeeper(s): Stan & Doris Geary.
Circa: 1888.

Rooms: 4 rooms, 2 with PB, 2 with FP. 1 suite.
Beds: KQT.

Built for a landscape designer with seven children, this Victorian estate includes more than seven acres of flower and vegetable gardens and 100-year-old towering trees. Innkeeper Doris Geary can help you with your itinerary, which should include a visit to Sturbridge Village. The Williamsburg-like town, a 30-minute drive away, is steeped in Colonial lifestyle with authentic homes and traditional cooking. Doris will prepare breakfast to order if given the request the night before.

Breakfast included in rates. Type of meal: full breakfast. Air conditioning, ceiling fan, cable TV and VCR in room. Fax, bicycles and library on premises. Small meetings, family reunions and seminars hosted. Antiques, shopping and cross-country skiing nearby.

Ridgefield **F2**

West Lane Inn

22 West Ln
Ridgefield, CT 06877-4914
(203)438-7323
Fax:(203)438-7325

Rates: $110-165.
Payment: MC VISA AX DC CB.
Innkeeper(s): Maureen Mayer.
Circa: 1849.

Rooms: 20 rooms with PB, 2 with FP.
Beds: KQ.

This National Register Victorian mansion on two acres features an enormous front veranda filled with white whicker chairs and tables overlooking a manicured lawn. A polished oak staircase rises to a third-floor landing and lounge. Chandeliers, wall sconces and floral wallpapers help to establish an intimate atmosphere. Although the rooms do not have antiques, they feature amenities such as heated towel racks, extra-thick towels, air conditioning and desks. The inn holds a AAA four-diamond award.

Breakfast included in rates. Type of meal: continental breakfast. Evening snack and room service available. Air conditioning and ceiling fan in room. Handicap access. Small meetings hosted. Antiques, fishing, shopping, cross-country skiing and theater nearby.

Publicity: *Stanford-Advocate, Greenwich Times, Home & Away Connecticut.*

"Thank you for the hospitality you showed us. The rooms are comfortable and quiet. I haven't slept this soundly in weeks."

Salisbury **A2**

Under Mountain Inn

482 Under Mountain Rd
Salisbury, CT 06068-1104
(860)435-0242
Fax:(860)435-2379

Rates: $160-195.
Innkeeper(s): Peter & Marged Higginson.
Circa: 1732.

Rooms: 7 rooms with PB.
Beds: KQD.

Situated on three acres, this was originally the home of iron magnate Jonathan Scoville. A thorned locust tree, believed to be the oldest in Connecticut, shades the inn. Paneling that now adorns the pub was discovered hidden between the ceiling and attic floorboards. The boards were probably placed there in violation of a Colonial law requiring all wide lumber to be given to the king of England. British-born Peter Higginson was happy to reclaim it in the name of the Crown.

Breakfast, afternoon tea and dinner included in rates. Air conditioning in room. VCR and fax on premises. Weddings and small meetings hosted. TAC10.

Publicity: *Travel & Leisure, Country Inns, Yankee, Connecticut, Country Accents.*

"You're terrific!"

Somersville A7

The Old Mill Inn B&B

63 Maple St
Somersville, CT 06072
(860)763-1473

Rates: $85-95.
Payment: PC TC.
Innkeeper(s): Jim & Stephanie D'Amour.
Circa: 1860.

Rooms: 5 rooms.
Beds: KD.

Giant maples and landscaped grounds create a private, peaceful ambiance at this Greek Revival home, secluded along the banks of the Scantic River. There is a hammock set up for those hoping for a nap among the trees, or perhaps you'd prefer a trip up the river on the inn's canoe. The grounds also are decorated with a gazebo. Rooms feature romantic decor, with snugly comforters, fine linens and furnishings such as a brass bed or a wicker loveseat. In the evenings, hors d'oeuvres and beverages are served in the fireplaced parlor. One of your innkeepers is an accomplished chef and professional cake decorator, so guests should expect something wonderful during the gourmet breakfast service. The innkeepers provide bicycles for those who wish to tour the area, and there is a spa on premises. The inn is often the site of weddings, parties and family reunions.

Types of meals: gourmet breakfast and early coffee/tea. Spa and bicycles on premises. Weddings and family reunions hosted. Antiques, fishing and shopping nearby.

Location: Five miles east of Exit 47E on I-91, 1 block south of Rt. 190.

"We loved staying here! You are both delightful. P.S. We slept like a log."

Tolland B7

Old Babcock Tavern

484 Mile Hill Rd
Tolland, CT 06084-3606
(860)875-1239

Rates: $70-85.
Payment: PC TC.
Innkeeper(s): Barb & Stu Danforth.
Circa: 1720.

Rooms: 3 rooms with PB, 1 with FP. 1 suite.
Beds: D.

This 18th-century post and beam home is listed in the National Register. The innkeepers have decorated their historic gem in a warm, inviting style with Early American furnishings, and they are happy to share their vast knowledge of restoration upon request. Rich wood panels and polished floors add to the interior's charm. Breakfasts are served by candlelight to the pleasant sounds of classical music. The innkeepers offer a morning feast with juice, coffee, tea, freshly baked muffins, herbed potatoes, eggs, turkey ham, fruit and homemade apple pie. The inn is close to many attractions, including an herb farm, historic jail, Old Sturbridge village and plenty of antique shops.

Breakfast included in rates. Types of meals: full breakfast, gourmet breakfast and early coffee/tea. Cable TV on premises. Antiques, fishing, parks, shopping, sporting events and theater nearby.

Special Discounts: Three days or more 10% off.

Tolland Inn

63 Tolland Green,
PO Box 717
Tolland, CT 06084
(860)872-0800
Fax:(860)870-7958
E-mail: tollandinn@aol.com

Rates: $60-120.
Payment: MC VISA AX DC CB DS PC TC.
Innkeeper(s): Susan & Stephen Beeching.
Circa: 1790.

Rooms: 7 rooms with PB, 2 with FP. 2 suites. 1 conference room.
Beds: KQDT.

This white clapboard house on the village green originally provided lodging for travelers on the old Post Road between New York and Boston. After extensive renovation, the Tolland Inn has been opened once again and has been refurbished with antiques and many furnishings made by the innkeeper. Nearby is the town hall and the Old Jail Museum.

Breakfast and afternoon tea included in rates. Types of meals: full breakfast, gourmet breakfast and early coffee/tea. Cable TV, VCR, fax, spa and library on premises. Small meetings, family reunions and seminars hosted. Antiques, fishing, parks, shopping, cross-country skiing, sporting events and theater nearby. TAC10.

Location: On the village green, 1/2 mile to exit 68 & I-84.

Publicity: *Journal Inquirer, Hartford Courant, Tolland County Times.*

Special Discounts: Seasonal, inquire.

"The rooms are very clean, the bed very comfortable, the food consistently excellent and the innkeepers very courteous."

Grandview Chocoholic Tart

Grandview Lodge
Waynesville, N.C.

Crust:
1 ¾ cup flour
⅓ cup cocoa
¼ cup sugar
¼ cup shortening
½ cup butter or margarine
⅓ cup to ½ cup ice water

Filling:
12 oz. bittersweet chocolate or semi-sweet chocolate chips
⅔ cup sugar
1 T chocolate or coffee liqeuer
1 T instant coffee powder
2 T milk
2 eggs
1 cup coarsely chopped walnuts

In a mixing bowl, combine first three ingredients. Using a pastry blender or two knives, cut shortening and butter into flour mixture until it resembles coarse meal. Add water slowly, mixing with a fork. Add only enough water to gather dough into a ball. Wrap in plastic wrap and chill. This dough is stickier than ordinary pie pastry. Roll out between 2 pieces of floured waxed paper. Line an 11" false bottom pan with pastry.

In top of double boiler or in a heavy saucepan, melt chocolate. Stir in remaining ingredients except nuts. Pour into prepared pastry. Sprinkle with nuts. Bake in preheated 375-degree oven for 30-35 minutes until set in center. Filling will puff up slightly and crack. Cool on wire rack. Remove sides of pan. Cut into 12 or 16 pie-shaped slices. It's very rich, so a small slice is sufficient.

Serves 12 to 16.

Delaware

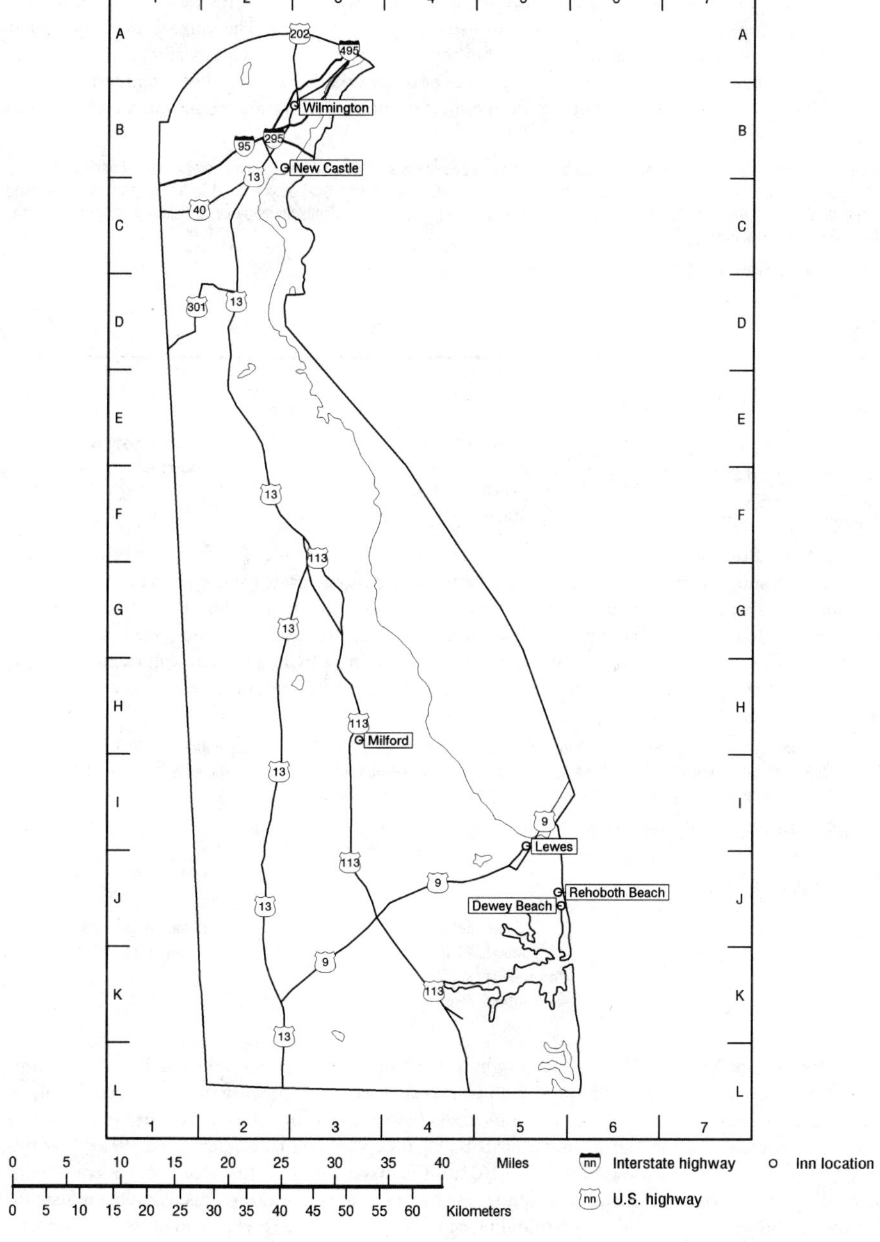
Wilmington
New Castle
Milford
Lewes
Rehoboth Beach
Dewey Beach
202
495
95
295
13
40
301
113
9
0 5 10 15 20 25 30 35 40 Miles
0 5 10 15 20 25 30 35 40 45 50 55 60 Kilometers
nn Interstate highway
nn U.S. highway
o Inn location

Dewey Beach

J5

Barry's Gull Cottage B&B

116 Chesapeake St
Dewey Beach, DE 19971
(302)227-7000
Fax:(302)227-7000

Rates: $75-135.
Payment: PC TC.
Innkeeper(s): Vivian & Bob Barry.
Circa: 1962.

Rooms: 6 rooms. 1 suite. 1 cottage.
Beds: KQD.

It's only a block to the beach from this Nantucket-style home, which also affords views of a lake. Rooms feature antiques, beds covered in quilts, wicker furnishings and stained glass. The innkeepers pamper guests with treats throughout the day, beginning with a healthy breakfast. Afternoon tea is served, and the evening is topped off with sherry, port wine, coffee and luscious chocolate cake. Relax in the hot tub illuminated by candlelight. The area offers plenty of shopping, from outlets to antiques, and good restaurants are close to this beach retreat.

Breakfast, afternoon tea and evening snack included in rates. Types of meals: full breakfast, gourmet breakfast and early coffee/tea. Air conditioning, turn-down service, ceiling fan and cable TV in room. VCR, fax, copier, spa, bicycles and library on premises. Weddings, small meetings, family reunions and seminars hosted. German and Polish spoken. Amusement parks, antiques, fishing, parks, shopping, theater and watersports nearby.

Special Discounts: Five days 10%.

Lewes

I5

The Bay Moon B&B

128 Kings Hwy
Lewes, DE 19958-1418
(302)644-1802
Fax:(302)644-1802

Rates: $75-145. EP.
Payment: MC VISA PC TC.
Innkeeper(s): Laura Beth Kelly.
Circa: 1887.

Rooms: 4 rooms with PB. 1 suite.
Beds: KQ.

The exterior of this three-story, cedar Victorian is mysterious and unique. The front veranda is shrouded by the flowers and foliage that decorate the front walk. The custom-made, hand-crafted beds in the guest rooms are topped with feather pillows and down comforters. Cordials are placed in the room and there is a champagne turndown service. During a nightly cocktail hour, appetizers and wine are served. The innkeeper offers plenty of amenities. Each room is stocked with cable TV and a VCR, and there's an extensive library as well. Beach supplies and an outdoor shower are helpful for guests who want to enjoy the ocean, which is about one mile from the inn.

Breakfast and evening snack included in rates. Types of meals: continental-plus breakfast and early coffee/tea. EP. Turn-down service, ceiling fan and cable TV in room. VCR, fax, library and child care on premises. Handicap access. Weddings, small meetings and family reunions hosted. Antiques, fishing, parks, shopping, sporting events, theater and watersports nearby.

Special Discounts: Stay three days or more, get 10% off.

Wild Swan Inn

525 Kings Hwy
Lewes, DE 19958-1421
(302)645-8550
Fax:(302)645-8550

Rates: $85-120.
Payment: PC TC.
Innkeeper(s): Michael & Hope Tyler.
Circa: 1900.

Rooms: 3 rooms with PB.
Beds: Beds: Q.

This Queen Anne Victorian is a whimsical sight, painted in pink with white, green and burgundy trim. The interior is dotted with antiques and dressed in Victorian style. A full, gourmet breakfast and freshly ground coffee are served each morning. The innkeepers have placed many musical treasures in their inn, including an early Edison phonograph and a Victrola. Michael often serenades guests on a 1912 player piano during breakfast. Lewes, which was founded in 1631, is the first town in the first state. Wild Swan is within walking distance of downtown where several fine restaurants await you. Nearby Cape Heinlopen State Park offers hiking and watersports, and the surrounding countryside is ideal for cycling and other outdoor activities.

Breakfast and evening snack included in rates. Types of meals: gourmet breakfast and early coffee/tea. Air conditioning and turn-down service in room. Fax, swimming, bicycles and library on premises. Antiques, fishing, parks, shopping, theater and watersports nearby.

Milford

H3

The Towers B&B

101 NW Front St
Milford, DE 19963-1022
(302)422-3814 (800)366-3814

Rates: $95-125.
Payment: MC VISA.
Innkeeper(s): Daniel Bond.
Circa: 1783.

Rooms: 6 rooms, 4 with PB. 2 suites.
Beds: QD.

Once a simple colonial house, this ornate Steamboat Gothic fantasy features every imaginable Victorian architectural detail, all added in 1891. There are 10 distinct styles of gingerbread as well as towers, turrets, gables, porches and bays. Inside, chestnut and cherry woodwork, window seats and stained-glass windows are complemented with American and French antiques. The back garden boasts a gazebo, porch and swimming pool. Ask for the splendid Tower Room or Rapunzel Suite.

Breakfast included in rates. Air conditioning and ceiling fan in room. Swimming and bicycles on premises. Russian spoken. Antiques, fishing, parks, shopping, theater and watersports nearby. TAC15.

Location: In the historic district. A short drive to Delaware Bay & the Atlantic Ocean.

Publicity: *Washington Post, Baltimore Sun, Washingtonian, Mid-Atlantic Country.*

"I felt as if I were inside a beautiful Victorian Christmas card, surrounded by all the things Christmas should be."

New Castle

B2

Armitage Inn

2 The Strand
New Castle, DE 19720-4826
(302)328-6618
Fax:(302)324-1163

Rates: $105-135.
Payment: MC VISA AX DS.
Innkeeper(s): Stephen & Rina Marks.
Circa: 1732.

Rooms: 4 rooms with PB, 2 with FP.
Beds: KQ.

The oldest portion of this historic home was constructed in the early 1730s, but the back room of the inn's main floor may have been constructed in the 17th century. For centuries, the Armitage has been a place of elegance and its current state as a country inn is no exception. Deluxe bed linens, fluffy towels, canopy beds and whirlpool tubs are just a few of the romantic amenities guests might find in their quarters. Gourmet coffee and teas accompany the breakfasts of fruit, cereal, yogurt, homemade baked goods and a special entree.

Breakfast included in rates. Type of meal: gourmet breakfast. Air conditioning, ceiling fan and cable TV in room. VCR, fax, copier, tennis and library on premises. Weddings, small meetings and family reunions hosted. Antiques, fishing, parks, shopping and theater nearby. TAC10.

"I could not have dreamed of a lovelier place to wake up on Christmas morning."

The Jefferson House B&B

5 The Strand
New Castle, DE 19720-4825
(302)325-1025

Rates: $54-85.
Payment: MC VISA PC TC.
Innkeeper(s): Brenda.
Circa: 1790.

Rooms: 3 rooms with PB, 1 with FP. 2 suites.
Beds: D.

Overlooking the Strand and the Delaware River, The Jefferson House served as a hotel, a rooming house and a shipping-company office during Colonial times. On the side lawn is a "William Penn landed here" sign. The inn features heavy paneled doors, black marble mantels over the fireplaces and a fanlight on the third floor. There is private access to the river, and a spa beckons guests after a long day of sightseeing. Cobblestone streets add to the quaintness of the first capital city of the colonies.

Breakfast included in rates. Type of meal: continental breakfast. Air conditioning, ceiling fan and cable TV in room. Spa on premises. Antiques, fishing, parks, shopping, cross-country skiing, sporting events and watersports nearby. TAC10.

Location: Mid-Atlantic region.

Publicity: *Roll Call.*

"I loved sleeping on an old brass bed, in a room filled with antiques and charm, just feet from where William Penn landed in New Castle."

Rehoboth Beach J5

Tembo B&B

100 Laurel St
Rehoboth Beach, DE
19971-2246
(302)227-3360

Rates: $75-125.
Payment: PC TC.
Innkeeper(s): Don & Gerry Cooper.
Circa: 1935.

Rooms: 6 rooms, 1 with PB.
Beds: KQDT.

A railroad conductor built this cottage, which now is decorated with Early American furnishings. The innkeepers also have a large assortment of elephant collectibles and artwork displayed in the bed & breakfast. Homemade scones, fruit salads and muffins highlight the buffet-style, continental breakfasts. Guests enjoy use of the kitchen and a picnic table, and there is a place to lock up bicycles.

Breakfast included in rates. Types of meals: continental-plus breakfast and early coffee/tea. Air conditioning and ceiling fan in room. Library on premises. Amusement parks, antiques, fishing, parks, shopping and watersports nearby.

Wilmington B3

The Boulevard B&B

1909 Baynard Blvd
Wilmington, DE 19802-3915
(302)656-9700
Fax:(302)656-9701

Rates: $60-75.
Payment: MC VISA AX PC TC.
Innkeeper(s): Judy & Charles Powell.
Circa: 1913.

Rooms: 6 rooms, 4 with PB.
Beds: QDT.

Located in a Wilmington historic district, this red brick, Colonial Revival home greets guests with an entrance flanked by carved columns. The columns and architecture add an elegant feel to this home, which is decorated in a simple, traditional style with antiques and four generations of family pieces. Each guest room is decorated in a different style, with names such as the Blue Room or the Gold Room. The honeymoon suite offers a whirlpool tub. Breakfasts include made-to-order egg dishes, fresh fruit, muffins, sweet breads and other treats. A variety of museums and historic homes are nearby.

Breakfast, afternoon tea and evening snack included in rates. Type of meal: full breakfast. Air conditioning, ceiling fan and cable TV in room. VCR, fax, copier and library on premises. Weddings, small meetings, family reunions and seminars hosted. Antiques, parks, shopping, sporting events and theater nearby.

Special Discounts: Book the entire house for two nights, receive a special discount.

Florida

FL

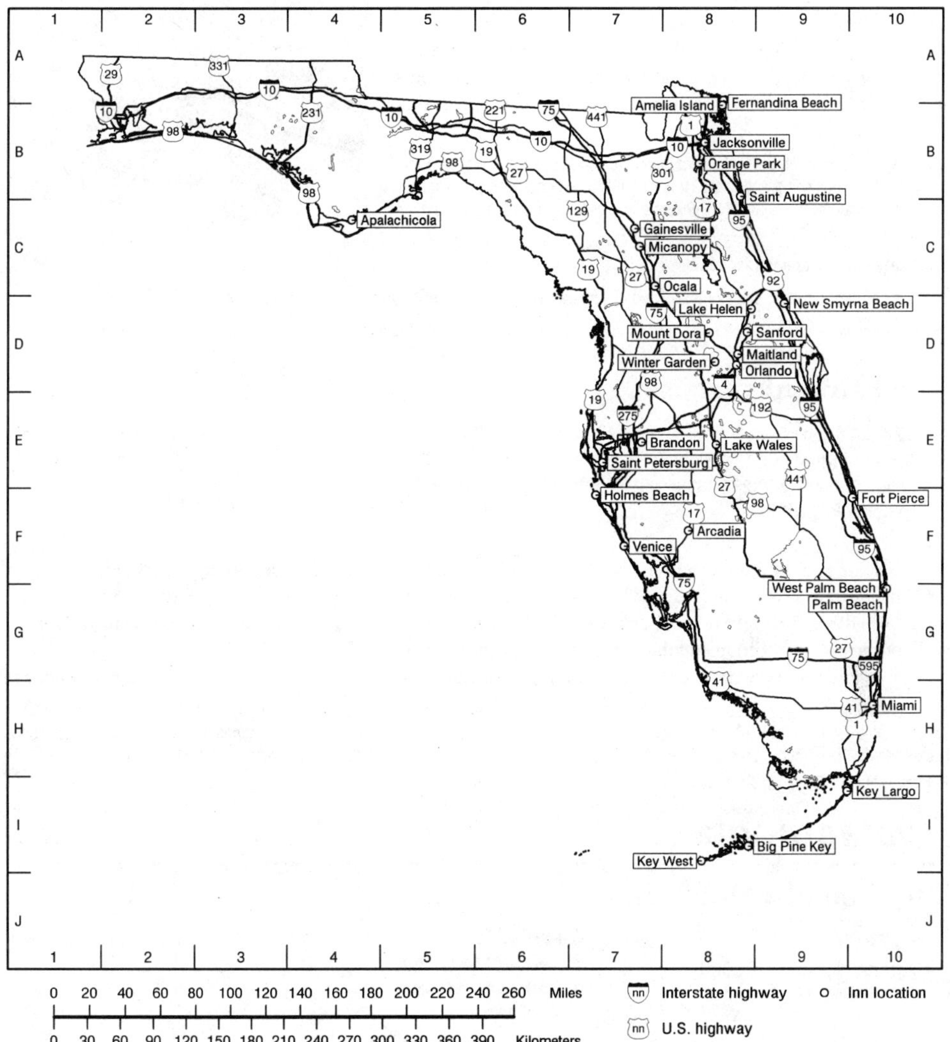

Amelia Island
Fernandina Beach
Jacksonville
Orange Park
Saint Augustine
Apalachicola
Gainesville
Micanopy
Ocala
New Smyrna Beach
Lake Helen
Mount Dora
Sanford
Maitland
Winter Garden
Orlando
Brandon
Lake Wales
Saint Petersburg
Holmes Beach
Fort Pierce
Arcadia
Venice
West Palm Beach
Palm Beach
Miami
Key Largo
Big Pine Key
Key West
0 20 40 60 80 100 120 140 160 180 200 220 240 260 Miles
0 30 60 90 120 150 180 210 240 270 300 330 360 390 Kilometers
Interstate highway
U.S. highway
Inn location

Elizabeth Point Lodge

98 S Fletcher Ave
Amelia Island, FL 32034
(904)277-4851 (800)772-3359
Fax:(904)277-6500

Rates: $100-175.
Payment: MC VISA AX DS.
Innkeeper(s): David & Susan Caples.
Circa: 1991.

Rooms: 25 rooms with PB. 8 suites. 1 conference room.
Beds: KQ.

Situated directly on the ocean, this newly constructed inn is in an 1890s Nantucket shingle-style design. Guest rooms feature king-size beds and oversized tubs. Two rooms have private whirlpools. Lemonade is served on the porch, which is filled with rockers for viewing the sea and its treasures of pelicans, dolphins and sea birds. Touring bikes, beach equipment and airport pickup are available.

Breakfast included in rates. Picnic lunch, lunch, catering service and room service available. Air conditioning and cable TV in room. Fax and copier on premises. Weddings, small meetings, family reunions and seminars hosted. Antiques, fishing, shopping, theater and watersports nearby.

Location: Oceanfront on Barrier Island.

Publicity: *Money, Country, Ladies Home Journal, Florida Living, Elegant Bride, United Air's Hemispheres.*

"The innkeeper's labor of love is evident in every detail. Outstanding. Superb accommodations and service."

The Fairbanks House

227 S 7th St
Amelia Island, FL 32034
(904)277-0500 (800)261-4838
Fax:(904)277-3103

Rates: $95-165. EP.
Payment: MC VISA AX DS.
Innkeeper(s): Nelson & Mary Smelker.
Circa: 1885.

Rooms: 12 rooms with PB, 9 with FP. 3 suites. 3 cottages. 1 conference room.
Beds: KQT.

The living and dining room fireplace tiles of this Italianate-style mansion bring to life scenes from Shakespeare's works and "Aesop's Fables." Other features include polished hardwood floors, intricately carved moldings and eight other fireplaces that grace spacious rooms. Each of the guest rooms is furnished with a four-poster or canopied king, queen or twin bed, Jacuzzi and clawfoot tubs or showers. Guests can step outside to enjoy an inviting courtyard, swimming pool and gardens bursting with roses, palms and magnolias.

Breakfast included in rates. Types of meals: gourmet breakfast and early coffee/tea. Picnic lunch available. EP. Air conditioning, ceiling fan and cable TV in room. VCR, fax, copier, swimming and bicycles on premises. Handicap access. Weddings, small meetings and seminars hosted. Amusement parks, antiques, fishing, parks, shopping, sporting events, theater and watersports nearby. TAC10.

Publicity: *Florida Times Union, Florida Living, Amelia Now, Islander, Country Inns.*

Apalachicola C4

The Coombs House Inn

80 6th St
Apalachicola, FL 32320
(904)653-9199

Rates: $89-115.
Payment: MC VISA AX PC TC.
Innkeeper(s): Marilyn & Charlie Schubert.
Circa: 1905.

Rooms: 18 rooms with PB. 3 suites. 1 conference room.
Beds: KQDT.

This Victorian manor was built for James N. Coombs, a wealthy lumber baron who served in the Union Army. Despite his Yankee roots, Coombs was an influential figure in Apalachicola. The home has been lovingly restored to reflect its previous grandeur. Co-owner Lynn Wilson is a renown interior designer and her talents accent the inn's high ceilings, tiled fireplaces and period antiques. Bright English fabrics decorate windows and oriental rugs accentuate the hardwood floors.

Breakfast included in rates. Types of meals: continental breakfast and early coffee/tea. Catering service available. Air conditioning, ceiling fan and cable TV in room. Copier and bicycles on premises. Handicap access. Weddings, small meetings, family reunions and seminars hosted. German spoken. Antiques, fishing, parks, shopping and watersports nearby.

Pets Allowed: With prior arrangements.

Arcadia

F8

Historic Parker House

427 W Hickory St
Arcadia, FL 34266-3703
(941)494-2499 (800)969-2499

Rates: $60-75.
Payment: MC VISA AX TC.
Innkeeper(s): Bob & Shelly Baumann.
Circa: 1895.

Rooms: 4 rooms, 2 with PB, 2 with FP. 1 conference room.
Beds: QDT.

FL

Period antiques, including a wonderful clock collection, grace the interior of this turn-of-the-century home, which was built by a local cattle baron. Along with two charming rooms and a bright, "yellow" suite, innkeepers Shelly and Bob Baumann recently added the spacious Blue Room, which offers a white iron and brass bed and clawfoot bathtub. An expanded continental breakfast with pastries, fresh fruits, cereals, muffins and a variety of beverages is offered each morning, and afternoon teas can be prepared on request.

Breakfast and afternoon tea included in rates. Types of meals: continental-plus breakfast and early coffee/tea. Room service available. Air conditioning, ceiling fan and cable TV in room. Small meetings and family reunions hosted. Antiques, fishing, parks, shopping and watersports nearby.

Publicity: *Tampa Tribune, Desoto Sun Herald, Florida Travel & Life, Miami Herald (Palm Beach Edition), WINK-TV News.*

"Everything was first class and very comfortable."

Big Pine Key

I8

Deer Run B&B on the Atlantic

PO Box 431, Long Beach Dr
Big Pine Key, FL 33043
(305)872-2015

Rates: $95-110.
Payment: TC.

This oceanfront home offers a unique setting that includes a beachfront spa and Key deer strolling along the beach. Antiques, wicker and rattan along with Bahama fans and French doors enhance the tropical atmosphere. The inn's veranda overlooks the water and is the location of choice for breakfast. Popular activities include diving in Looe Key, fishing the flats, deep sea fishing and enjoying the beaches of nearby Bahia Honda State Park.

Breakfast included in rates. Air conditioning and ceiling fan in room. Fishing, theater and watersports nearby.

"The beautiful view, the lovely breezes, the peacefulness and the adorable key deer will never be forgotten."

Brandon

E7

Behind the Fence B&B Inn

1400 Viola Dr at
Countryside
Brandon, FL 33511-7327
(813)685-8201 (800)448-2672

Rates: $59-79.
Payment: PC TC.
Innkeeper(s): Larry & Carolyn Yoss.
Circa: 1976.

Rooms: 5 rooms, 3 with PB. 1 suite. 1 cottage. 1 conference room.
Beds: DT.

Experience the charm of New England on Florida's west coast at this secluded country inn surrounded by tall pines and oaks. Although the frame of the home was built in the mid-1970s, the innkeepers searched Hillsborough County for 19th century and turn-of-the-century artifacts, including old stairs, doors, windows, a pantry and the back porch. Guests can stay either in the main house or in a two-bedroom cottage. All rooms are filled with antique Amish-county furniture. The innkeepers serve fresh popcorn on cool nights in front of the fireplace. Breakfast includes fresh fruit, cereals, juices, coffees and delicious Amish sweet rolls.

Breakfast, afternoon tea and evening snack included in rates. Types of meals: continental-plus breakfast and early coffee/tea. Air conditioning, cable TV and VCR in room. Swimming on premises. Small meetings and seminars hosted. Amusement parks, antiques, fishing, parks, shopping, sporting events, theater and watersports nearby. TAC7.

Publicity: *Brandon News, Travel Host, Country Living.*

Special Discounts: 10% AAA or extended stay 7 nights or more.

"One of the best kept secrets in all of Tampa! Thanks again!"

Bailey House

28 S 7th St
Fernandina Beach, FL
32034-3960
(904)261-5390 (800)251-5390
Fax:(904)321-0103

Rates: $85-125. AP.
Payment: MC VISA AX PC.
Innkeeper(s): Tom & Jenny Bishop.
Circa: 1895.

Rooms: 5 rooms with PB, 3 with FP.
Beds: KQD.

This elegant Queen Anne Victorian was a wedding present that steamship agent Effingham W. Bailey gave to his bride. He shocked the locals by spending the enormous sum of $10,000 to build the house with all its towers, turrets, gables and verandas. The parlor and dining room open to a fireplace in a reception hall with the inscription "Hearth Hall - Welcome All." A spirit of hospitality has reigned in this home from its beginning.

Breakfast included in rates. Type of meal: full breakfast. AP. Air conditioning, ceiling fan and cable TV in room. Fax, copier and bicycles on premises. Handicap access. Weddings hosted. Antiques, fishing, parks, shopping and watersports nearby. TAC10.

Location: In historic district on Amelia Island.

Publicity: *Innsider, Southern Living, Victorian Homes Magazine, Saint Petersburg Times, Jacksonville.*

"Well, here we are back at Mickey Mouse land. I think we prefer the lovely Bailey House!"

Fort Pierce F10

Mellon Patch Inn

3601 N A-1-A
Fort Pierce, FL 34949
(407)461-5231 (800)656-7824
Fax:(407)464-6463

Rates: $80-120.
Payment: MC VISA AX DC PC TC.
Innkeeper(s): Andrea & Arthur Mellon.
Circa: 1994.

Rooms: 4 rooms with PB. 1 conference room.
Beds: KQ.

Mellon Patch guests enjoy close access to the ocean and Indian River, both just a few yards away. There is a private dock at this North Hutchinson Island respite where guests may fish, or embark down the Indian River on the inn's canoe. The home is appointed in contemporary style, but each guest quarter has been individually appointed. The innkeepers hired a local artist to help decorate the guest rooms which offer water views. Guests are pampered with a hearty breakfast of freshly squeezed orange juice, home-baked breads, fresh fruit salads and entrees such as baked, stuffed French toast, blueberry pancakes or cheese souffle stuffed with spinach. In the late afternoons, guests can enjoy the water view and refreshments from the inn's patio.

Breakfast and afternoon tea included in rates. Types of meals: gourmet breakfast and early coffee/tea. Picnic lunch available. Air conditioning, ceiling fan and cable TV in room. Fax, copier and tennis on premises. Handicap access. Weddings, small meetings and family reunions hosted. Antiques, fishing, parks, shopping, sporting events, theater and watersports nearby. TAC10.

Special Discounts: AAA.

Gainesville

C7

Magnolia Plantation

309 SE 7th St
Gainesville, FL 32601-6831
(352)375-6653
Fax:(352)338-0303

Rates: $75-125. AP.
Payment: MC VISA AX.
Innkeeper(s): Joe & Cindy Montalto.
Circa: 1885.

Rooms: 5 rooms with PB, 5 with FP. 1 cottage.
Beds: Q.

FL

This restored French Second Empire Victorian is in the National Register. Magnolia trees surround the house. Six guest rooms are filled with family heirlooms. All bathrooms feature clawfoot tubs and candles. Guests may enjoy the gardens, reflecting pool with waterfalls, and gazebo. Bicycles are also available. Evening wine and snacks are included. The inn is two miles from the University of Florida.

Breakfast, afternoon tea and evening snack included in rates. Types of meals: full breakfast and early coffee/tea. AP. Air conditioning, turn-down service and ceiling fan in room. Cable TV, VCR, fax, bicycles and library on premises. Antiques, parks, shopping, sporting events and theater nearby. TAC10.

"This has been a charming, once-in-a-lifetime experience."

Holmes Beach

F7

Harrington House Beachfront B&B

5626 Gulf Dr N
Holmes Beach, FL 34217
(941)778-5444
Fax:(941)778-0527

Rates: $109-225.
Payment: MC VISA.
Innkeeper(s): Jo & Frank Davis.
Circa: 1925.

Rooms: 13 rooms with PB.
Beds: KQDT.

A mere 40 feet from the water, this gracious home is set among pine trees and palms. Constructed of 14-inch-thick coquina blocks, the house features a living room with a 20-foot-high beamed ceiling, fireplace, '20s wallpaper and French doors. Many of the guest rooms have four-poster beds, antique wicker furnishings and French doors opening onto a deck overlooking the swimming pool and Gulf of Mexico. Kayaks are available for dolphin watching.

Breakfast included in rates. Type of meal: full breakfast. Air conditioning, ceiling fan, cable TV and VCR in room. Computer on premises. Handicap access. Weddings, small meetings, family reunions and seminars hosted. Amusement parks, antiques, fishing, shopping, sporting events, theater and watersports nearby.

Publicity: *Sarasota Herald Tribune, Island Sun, Palm Beach Post, Tampa Tribune, Glamour, Atlantic Monthly.*

"Elegant house and hospitality."

Jacksonville

B8

House on Cherry St

1844 Cherry St
Jacksonville, FL 32205
(904)384-1999
Fax:(904)384-5013

Rates: $85.
Payment: MC VISA PC TC.
Innkeeper(s): Carol Anderson.
Circa: 1909.

Rooms: 4 suites.
Beds: QT.

Seasonal blooms fill the pots that line the circular entry stairs to this Federal-style house on tree-lined Cherry Street. It was moved in two pieces to its present site on St. Johns River in the historic Riverside area. Traditionally decorated rooms include antiques, collections of hand-carved decoy ducks and old clocks that chime and tick. Most rooms overlook the river. Your hosts are a social worker and family doctor.

Breakfast and evening snack included in rates. Type of meal: gourmet breakfast. Air conditioning and ceiling fan in room. Cable TV, VCR, fax, copier and bicycles on premises. Weddings, small meetings, family reunions and seminars hosted. Antiques, fishing, parks, shopping, sporting events, theater and watersports nearby. TAC10.

Location: Historic Avondale.

Publicity: *Florida Wayfarer, Tampa Tribune, New York Times.*

Key Largo

I9

Jules' Undersea Lodge

51 Shoreland Dr
Key Largo, FL 33037
(305)451-2353
Fax:(305)451-4789

Rates: $390-590.
Payment: MC VISA AX DS TC.
Innkeeper(s): Agnes Newcomer.
Circa: 1972.

Rooms: 2 rooms.
Beds: D.

If you aren't claustrophobic, can scuba dive and are looking for a lifetime memory, this is the adventure for you. Originally built as a research lab, the futuristic undersea space was turned into a hotel in 1986.Once the La Chalupa research habitat, the structure was used off the coast of Puerto Rico in 105 feet of water during the '70s. Forty-two-inch round windows provide deep-sea views of Emerald Lagoon, five fathoms down. Request dinner and a "mer chef" will dive down to prepare a filet mignon or lobster tail meal. If you don't dive, take a short course and an instructor will dive with you into the lodge.

Breakfast, dinner and evening snack included in rates. Types of meals: continental breakfast, continental-plus breakfast, full breakfast, gourmet breakfast and early coffee/tea. Lunch and room service available. Cable TV and VCR in room. Fax, copier and swimming on premises. Weddings hosted. Fishing, parks and watersports nearby. TAC10.

Key West

I8

Blue Parrot Inn

916 Elizabeth St
Key West, FL 33040-6406
(305)296-0033 (800)231-2473
Fax:(305)296-5697
E-mail: bluparotin@aol.com

Rates: $70-160.
Payment: MC VISA AX DC CB TC.
Innkeeper(s): Larry Rhinard & Frank Yaccino.
Circa: 1884.

Rooms: 10 rooms with PB.
Beds: QDT.

This Bahamian-style inn is decorated in a pleasing, tropical style. The grounds are lush and peaceful. Continental-plus breakfasts of fresh fruit, bagels, muffins and quiche are served poolside. There is plenty of space to relax and tan around the pool, but for those who prefer, the innkeepers also offer a private, clothing-optional sun deck. The inn is located in a historic neighborhood and is near shops and restaurants. The ocean is just a few blocks away.

Breakfast included in rates. Type of meal: continental breakfast. Air conditioning, ceiling fan and cable TV in room. Fax, copier, swimming and bicycles on premises. Handicap access. Weddings, small meetings and family reunions hosted. Antiques, fishing, parks, shopping, theater and watersports nearby. TAC10.

Cypress House

601 Caroline St
Key West, FL 33040-6674
(305)294-6969 (800)525-2488
Fax:(305)296-1174
E-mail: cypress@key.net

Rates: $80-220.
Payment: MC VISA AX DC DS PC TC.
Innkeeper(s): Arthur Kelley.
Circa: 1888.

Rooms: 16 rooms, 6 with PB. 1 suite.
Beds: KQD.

There's much to see and do in popular Key West, and Cypress House is an ideal place for those visiting the area. The National Register inn was built by one of Key West's first settlers, and it still maintains many original features. Guest rooms are airy and spacious, decorated in a variety of styles. A continental breakfast with quiche, croissants, blintzes, muffins, fresh fruit and more is served poolside. A cocktail hour also is included in the rates. The inn is just a block from Duval Street, which offers shops, galleries, eateries and plenty of nightlife.

Breakfast included in rates. Type of meal: continental-plus breakfast. Air conditioning and ceiling fan in room. Cable TV, fax and swimming on premises. Weddings, small meetings, family reunions and seminars hosted. Antiques, fishing, parks, shopping, theater and watersports nearby. TAC10.

FL

Duval House

815 Duval St
Key West, FL 33040-7405
(305)294-1666 (800)223-8825
Fax:(305)292-1701

Rates: $80-260.
Payment: MC VISA AX DC DS TC.
Innkeeper(s): Richard Kamradt.
Circa: 1890.

Rooms: 25 rooms. 4 suites.
Beds: QD.

The Duval House's seven Victorian houses surround a garden and a swimming pool. French doors open onto the tropical gardens. Guests may relax on the balconies. Continental Plus breakfast is served in the pool lounge. Rooms have wicker and antique furniture and Bahamian fans.

Breakfast included in rates. Air conditioning and ceiling fan in room. Swimming on premises. Antiques, fishing, shopping and watersports nearby. TAC10.

Publicity: *Newsday, Palm Beach Post, Cleveland Plain-Dealer, Roanoke Times, Brides, Vacations.*

Special Discounts: 10% AAA discount.

"You certainly will see us again."

Eden House

1015 Fleming St
Key West, FL 33040-6962
(305)296-6868 (800)533-5397
Fax:(305)294-1221
E-mail: eden@key.net

Rates: $55-250. EP.
Payment: MC VISA TC.
Circa: 1924.

Rooms: 42 rooms, 26 with PB. 6 suites.
Beds: QDT.

This charming art deco hotel was once a hot spot for writers, intellectuals and European travelers. Innkeeper Mike Eden improved the home, adding a 10-person Jacuzzi, decks and gazebos. Ceiling fans and wicker furniture complete the tropical atmosphere found in each room. The home was the site for the Goldie Hawn movie, "Criss Cross." Next door, Martin's Cafe boasts delicious cuisine by chef and owner Martin Busam. Breakfast is not included in the room price, but the restaurant offers gourmet entrees such as Shrimp Eggs Benedict and cinnamon coffee. For lunch and dinner, enjoy the "Island" and German-style cuisine. Guests are served cold refreshments upon arrival, and there is a complimentary happy hour.

EP. Air conditioning and ceiling fan in room. Cable TV, fax, spa, swimming and bicycles on premises. French, German and Spanish spoken. Fishing, shopping and watersports nearby.

Pets Allowed: Restrictions apply.

Publicity: *Chicago Tribune, Woman's Day, Southern Living, Miami Herald.*

"We feel lucky to have found such a relaxing place, and we look forward to returning."

Island City House

411 William St
Key West, FL 33040-6853
(305)294-5702 (800)634-8230
Fax:(305)294-1289

Rates: $95-210.
Payment: MC VISA DC CB DS TC.
Innkeeper(s): Stanley & Janet Corneal.
Circa: 1889.

Rooms: 24 suites.
Beds: KQD.

This house was built for a wealthy Charleston merchant who later converted it to a small hotel, anticipating the arrival of the railroad in 1912. Restored by two active preservationists, Island City House and Arch House provide apartments in beautifully restored environs with turn-of-the-century decor. Private porches and ceiling fans are historical amenities that remain.

Breakfast included in rates. Type of meal: continental-plus breakfast. Air conditioning, ceiling fan and cable TV in room. VCR, fax, copier, spa, swimming and bicycles on premises. Weddings hosted. Antiques, fishing, parks, shopping, theater and watersports nearby. TAC10.

Pets Allowed.

Publicity: *Palm Beach Daily News, London Times, Miami Herald, Palm Beach Post.*

"We really enjoyed our stay and have decided we're going to visit the Keys every year and stay at our new-found 'home,' apartment #4."

Merlinn Guest House

811 Simonton St
Key West, FL 33040-7445
(305)296-3336 (800)642-4753
Fax:(305)296-3524
E-mail: merlinnc@aol.com

Rates: $68-150.
Payment: MC VISA AX DS TC.
Innkeeper(s): (Ms) Pat Hoffman.
Circa: 1948.

Rooms: 18 rooms with PB. 2 suites. 5 cottages.
Beds: KQDT.

This tropical guest house is located in the heart of a Key West historic district. Accommodations include guest rooms, suites, apartments and guest cottages. All of the accommodations are decorated with modern, tropical furnishings. The Tree House and Tea House cottages each have a private deck or patio. The apartments include kitchens, and for an additional charge, some pets may be allowed in these units.

Breakfast included in rates. Type of meal: continental-plus breakfast. Air conditioning, ceiling fan and cable TV in room. Fax, copier, swimming, library and pet boarding on premises. Handicap access. Weddings hosted. Antiques, fishing, shopping, theater and watersports nearby. TAC10.

Pets Allowed: In apartment units only.

Publicity: *Palm Beach Post.*

Special Discounts: Free seventh night during summer/early fall.

Nassau House

1016 Fleming St
Key West, FL 33040-6908
(305)296-8513 (800)296-8513
Fax:(305)293-8423
E-mail: 102050.1161@compuserve.com

Rates: $75-200.
Payment: MC VISA AX TC.
Innkeeper(s): Damon Leard.
Circa: 1894.

Rooms: 9 rooms, 7 with PB. 2 suites.
Beds: KQD.

This century-old home, located in Key West's historic Old Town, has been completely restored. The grounds are beautifully landscaped and the area around the pool is a tropical delight. The porch is lined with wicker rockers and loveseats topped with pillows, and paddle fans provide added comfort. Guest rooms are elegant, yet comfortable with wicker and fine linens. The Treetop Suites also include living rooms and kitchens.

Breakfast and evening snack included in rates. Type of meal: continental-plus breakfast. Air conditioning, ceiling fan and cable TV in room. VCR, fax, copier, spa, swimming, bicycles, library and pet boarding on premises. Handicap access. Weddings and small meetings hosted. German and Dutch spoken. Fishing, shopping, theater and watersports nearby. TAC10.

Pets Allowed: Small dogs only.

"Our stay has been absolutely delightful!"

Paradise Inn

819 Simonton St
Key West, FL 33040-7445
(305)293-8007 (800)888-9648
Fax:(305)293-0807
E-mail: ssegel3403@aol.com

Rates: $160-475.
Payment: MC VISA AX DC CB DS TC.
Innkeeper(s): Shel Segel & William Kemp.
Circa: 1995.

Rooms: 18 suites. 3 cottages.
Beds: K.

Although this inn was constructed recently, its Bahamian architecture is reminiscent of Key West's early days. Rooms are open and spacious, decorated with elegant, contemporary furnishings, such as king-size sleigh beds. Jacuzzi tubs and a bar with a refrigerator are a few of the in-room amenities. There is a fountain-fed pool, Jacuzzi and koi pond on the premises, too. In addition to the modern accommodations, guests also may stay in one of the historic cigar-makers cottages. The cottages are ideal for families, and each has two bedrooms and two bathrooms. The inn is located in a Key West historic district, and is close to the many shops, restaurants and nightclubs on Duval Street.

Breakfast included in rates. Type of meal: continental breakfast. Catering service and room service available. Air conditioning, ceiling fan, cable TV and VCR in room. Fax, copier, spa and swimming on premises. Handicap access. Weddings, small meetings, family reunions and seminars hosted. Spanish, Portuguese and Czech spoken. Antiques, fishing, parks, shopping, theater and watersports nearby. TAC10.

Lake Helen D8

Clauser's B&B

201 E Kicklighter Rd
Lake Helen, FL 32744-3514
(904)228-0310 (800)220-0310
Fax:(904)228-2337
E-mail: clauserinn@totcon.com

Rates: $65-120.
Payment: MC VISA AX DS PC TC.
Innkeeper(s): Tom & Marge Clauser, Janet Watson.
Circa: 1890.

Rooms: 8 rooms with PB, 1 with FP.
Beds: KQ.

This three-story, turn-of-the-century vernacular Victorian inn is surrounded by a variety of trees in a quiet, country setting. The inn is listed in the national, state and local historic registers, and offers eight guest rooms, all with private bath. Each room features a different type of country decor, such as Americana, English and prairie. Guests enjoy hot tubbing in the Victorian gazebo or relaxing on the inn's porches, which feature rockers, a swing and cozy wicker furniture. Borrow a bike to take a closer look at the historic district. Stetson University, fine dining and several state parks are nearby.

Breakfast and evening snack included in rates. Types of meals: full breakfast and early coffee/tea. Air conditioning and ceiling fan in room. Cable TV, VCR, fax, copier, spa, bicycles and library on premises. Handicap access. Small meetings, family reunions and seminars hosted. Amusement parks, antiques, fishing, parks, sporting events, theater and watersports nearby. TAC10.

Lake Wales E8

Chalet Suzanne Country Inn & Restaurant

3800 Chalet Suzanne Dr
Lake Wales, FL 33853-7060
(941)676-6011 (800)433-6011
Fax:(941)676-1814

Rates: $135-195.
Payment: MC VISA AX DC CB DS TC.
Innkeeper(s): Carl & Vita Hinshaw.
Circa: 1924.

Rooms: 30 rooms with PB.
Beds: KQDT.

Situated on 70 acres adjacent to Lake Suzanne, this country inn's architecture includes gabled roofs, balconies, spires and steeples. The superb restaurant has a glowing reputation, and places of interest on the property include the Swiss Room, Wine Dungeon, Gift Boutique, Autograph Garden, Chapel Antiques, Ceramic Salon, Airstrip and the Soup Cannery. The inn has been transformed into a village of cottages and miniature chateaux, one connected to the other seemingly with no particular order.

Breakfast included in rates. Types of meals: full breakfast and early coffee/tea. Dinner, lunch and room service available. Air conditioning, ceiling fan and cable TV in room. VCR, fax, copier, swimming and library on premises. Handicap access. 70 acres. Weddings, small meetings, family reunions and seminars hosted. German spoken. Amusement parks, antiques, fishing, parks, shopping, sporting events, theater and watersports nearby. TAC10.

Pets Allowed: $20 per night.

Location: Four miles north of Lake Wales. US Hwy 27 & Chalet Suzanne Rd.

Publicity: *Southern Living, Country Inns, National Geographic Traveler. Uncle Ben's 1992 award.*

"I now know why everyone always says, 'Wow!' when they come up from dinner. Please don't change a thing."

Maitland

D8

Thurston House

851 Lake Ave
Maitland, FL 32751-6306
(407)539-1911 (800)843-2721
Fax:(407)539-0365
E-mail: jball54@aol.com

Rates: $100.
Payment: MC VISA AX.
Innkeeper(s): Carole Ballard.
Circa: 1885.

Rooms: 4 rooms with PB.
Beds: Q.

Just minutes from busy Orlando and the many attractions found nearby, this classic Queen Anne Victorian inn boasts a lakefront, countryside setting. Two of the inn's screened porches provide views of Lake Eulalia. Two parlors provide additional relaxing spots, and many guests like to stroll the grounds, which feature fruit trees and several bountiful gardens.

Breakfast and evening snack included in rates. Types of meals: continental-plus breakfast and early coffee/tea. Air conditioning and ceiling fan in room. Cable TV, VCR, fax, copier and library on premises. Antiques, fishing, parks, shopping, sporting events and theater nearby. TAC10.

Publicity: *Fort Lauderdale Sun Sentinel, Orlando Sentinel, Florida Living, Country Almanac.*

"Gracious hosts. What a jewel of a place. We couldn't have enjoyed ourselves more!"

Miami

H10

Banyantree B&B

7436 SW 117 Ave, Box 160
Miami, FL 33183
(305)271-5422
Fax:(305)279-7744

Rates: $50-85.
Payment: TC.
Innkeeper(s): Earleen Beck.

Rooms: 8 rooms with PB. 3 suites.
Beds: KQT.

Despite its Miami address, Banyantree is surrounded by five lush, peaceful acres. Staying here is more akin to a private, island retreat than a city inn. The ranch home's elegant atmosphere is created by cathedral ceilings, marble floors and antiques. There are three guest rooms in the main house, and three additional apartments also are available. Guests in the ranch house enjoy full use of the main kitchen. The apartments include kitchens and amenities such as a private lanai or bi-level deck, answering machine, sitting areas, canopy beds and more. Laundry facilities are available to all guests. Restaurants, shops and attractions are just a few minutes away.

Breakfast included in rates. Types of meals: continental breakfast, continental-plus breakfast and early coffee/tea. Air conditioning, ceiling fan, cable TV and VCR in room. Fax, copier, spa, stables and bicycles on premises. Amusement parks, antiques, fishing, parks, shopping, sporting events, theater and watersports nearby. TAC20.

Micanopy C7

Herlong Mansion

402 Ne Cholokka Blvd,
PO Box 667
Micanopy, FL 32667
(352)466-3322 (800)437-5664
Fax:(352)466-3322

Rates: $50-150.
Payment: MC VISA AX.
Innkeeper(s): H.C. (Sonny) Howard, Jr.
Circa: 1845.

Rooms: 12 rooms with PB, 6 with FP. 4 suites. 2 cottages. 1 conference room.
Beds: KQD.

FL

This mid-Victorian mansion features four two-story carved-wood Roman Corinthian columns on its veranda. The mansion is surrounded by a garden with statuesque old oak and pecan trees. Herlong Mansion features leaded-glass windows, mahogany inlaid oak floors, 12-foot ceilings and floor-to-ceiling windows in the dining room. Guest rooms have fireplaces and are furnished with antiques.

Breakfast and evening snack included in rates. Types of meals: full breakfast and early coffee/tea. Catering service available. Air conditioning and ceiling fan in room. Cable TV, VCR, fax, copier and bicycles on premises. Handicap access. Weddings, small meetings, family reunions and seminars hosted. Antiques, fishing, parks, sporting events and watersports nearby. TAC10.

Publicity: *Country Inns, Travel & Leisure, National Geographic Traveler, Southern Living, Florida Living.*

Special Discounts: Call for corporate or government rates.

Mount Dora D8

Lakeside Inn

100 N Alexander St
Mount Dora, FL 32757-5570
(352)383-4101 (800)556-5016
Fax:(352)735-2642

Rates: $80-160.
Payment: MC VISA AX DC DS TC.
Innkeeper(s): Tom Fultz.
Circa: 1883.

Rooms: 88 rooms with PB. 17 suites. 5 conference rooms.
Beds: KDT.

A stay at the Lakeside Inn is like being transported back in time to a grand old hotel. The inn was a hot spot during the roaring 20s and has served guests since its creation in 1883. Set on the water's edge, many of the historic hotel's guests enjoy simply taking in the view on the veranda while lounging in a rocker. The hotel offers tennis courts, a pool, lakefront rooms, verandas and courtyard gardens. Gourmet chefs prepare delectable meals featuring an abundance of seasonal fare and a popular Sunday brunch. The Lakeside Inn hosts many special events including tea dances and sunset cruises on Lake Dora. Only 25 miles from Orlando, the village of Mount Dora offers plenty of shops, galleries, flea markets and antiquing.

Breakfast included in rates. Types of meals: continental breakfast, continental-plus breakfast, full breakfast, gourmet breakfast and early coffee/tea. Afternoon tea, dinner, evening snack, picnic lunch, lunch, gourmet lunch, banquet service, catering service, catered breakfast and room service available. Air conditioning, cable TV and VCR in room. Fax, copier, swimming, tennis and child care on premises. Handicap access. Weddings, small meetings, family reunions and seminars hosted. Dutch, German, French and Spanish spoken. Amusement parks, antiques, fishing, parks, shopping, sporting events, theater and watersports nearby. TAC10.

Publicity: *Orvis, AAA World, AAA Going Places.*

Special Discounts: Call for package information.

Magnolia Inn

347 E 3rd Ave
Mount Dora, FL 32757-5654
(352)735-3800 (800)776-2112
Fax:(352)735-0258

Rates: $90-160.
Payment: MC VISA AX PC TC.
Innkeeper(s): Gerry & Lolita Johnson.
Circa: 1926.

Rooms: 4 rooms with PB.
Beds: KQT.

This Mediterranean-style inn in Central Florida offers elegant accommodations to its guests, who will experience the Florida Boom furnishings of the 1920s. Guests will enjoy the convenience of early coffee or tea before sitting down to the inn's full breakfasts. Guests can take a soak in the inn's spa, relax in the hammock by the garden wall or swing beneath the magnolias. Lake Griffin State Recreational Area and Wekiwa Springs State Park are within easy driving distance. Just an hour from Disneyworld and the other Orlando major attractions, Mount Dora is the antique capital of Central Florida. Known as the Festival City, it is also recommended by "Money" Magazine as the best retirement location in Florida and is the site of Renninger's Winter Antique Extravaganzas. Romantic carriage rides and historic trolley tours of the downtown, two blocks from the inn, are available.

Breakfast included in rates. Types of meals: full breakfast and early coffee/tea. Air conditioning and ceiling fan in room. Cable TV, VCR, fax, copier and spa on premises. Weddings hosted. Amusement parks, antiques, fishing, parks, shopping, theater and watersports nearby. TAC10.

Publicity: *Mount Dora Topic.*

Special Discounts: Three or more midweek nights at $100 per night.

"I love the way you pamper your guests."

New Smyrna Beach **D9**

Little River Inn B&B

532 N Riverside Dr
New Smyrna Beach, FL
32168-6741
(904)424-0100

Rates: $79-119.
Payment: MC VISA AX.
Innkeeper(s): Wendy Maclean.

Rooms: 6 rooms, 4 with PB. 1 conference room.
Beds: KQ.

Located on two acres of cobblestone paths, gardens and oak trees, this historic house offers wide, wraparound brick verandas. Guests enjoy views of Indian River and the blue herons and manatees that take refuge in the nature preserve. Rooms are appointed pleasantly and each has a separate theme. Breakfasts are served in the dining room. There is a tennis court, hammock and fishing dock, and nearby New Smyrna Beach offers antique shops and the beach, which harbors sea turtles.

Breakfast and evening snack included in rates. Types of meals: full breakfast, gourmet breakfast and early coffee/tea. Afternoon tea and picnic lunch available. Air conditioning, ceiling fan and cable TV in room. VCR, fax, copier, spa, bicycles and tennis on premises. Handicap access. Weddings, small meetings, family reunions and seminars hosted. Amusement parks, antiques, fishing, parks, shopping, theater and watersports nearby.

"Our retreat turned into relaxation, romance and pure Victorian delight."

Night Swan Intracoastal B&B

512 S Riverside Dr
New Smyrna Beach, FL
32168-7345
(904)423-4940 (800)465-4261
Fax:(904)427-2814
E-mail: nightswanb@aol.com

Rates: $65-129.
Payment: MC VISA AX DS TC.
Innkeeper(s): Martha & Chuck Nighswonger.
Circa: 1906.

Rooms: 8 rooms with PB. 4 suites. 1 conference room.
Beds: KQ.

From the 140-foot dock at this waterside bed & breakfast, guests can gaze at stars, watch as ships pass or perhaps catch site of dolphins. The turn-of-the-century home is decorated with period furnishings, including an antique baby grand piano, which guests are invited to use. Several guest rooms afford views of the Indian River, which is part of the Atlantic Intracoastal Waterway. The innkeepers have created several special packages, featuring catered gourmet dinners, boat tours or romantic baskets with chocolate, wine and flowers.

Breakfast and evening snack included in rates. Types of meals: full breakfast and early coffee/tea. Catering service available. Air conditioning, ceiling fan, cable TV and VCR in room. Fax and library on premises. Weddings, small meetings, family reunions and seminars hosted. Antiques, fishing, parks, shopping, theater and watersports nearby. TAC10.

Ocala — C7

Seven Sisters Inn

820 SE Fort King St
Ocala, FL 34471-2320
(352)867-1170
Fax:(352)867-5266

Rates: $105-135.
Innkeeper(s): Ken Oden & Bonnie Morehardt.
Circa: 1888.

Rooms: 8 rooms with PB, 3 with FP. 4 suites. 1 conference room.
Beds: KQT.

This highly acclaimed Queen Anne-style Victorian is located in the heart of the town's historic district. In 1986, the house was judged "Best Restoration Project" in the state by Florida Trust Historic Preservation Society. Guests may relax on the large covered porches or visit with other guests in the club room. A gourmet breakfast features a different entree daily which include blueberry French bread, three-cheese stuffed French toast, egg pesto and raspberry-oatmeal pancakes.

Breakfast, afternoon tea and evening snack included in rates. Types of meals: full breakfast, gourmet breakfast and early coffee/tea. Dinner and picnic lunch available. Air conditioning, turn-down service, ceiling fan and cable TV in room. Fax, copier and pet boarding on premises. Weddings, small meetings, family reunions and seminars hosted. Amusement parks, antiques, fishing, parks, shopping, sporting events, theater and watersports nearby.

Pets Allowed.

Publicity: *Southern Living Feature, Glamour, Conde Nast Traveler, Country Inns (one of twelve best).*

Orange Park — B8

The Club Continental Suites

2143 Astor St
Orange Park, FL 32073
(904)264-6070 (800)877-6070
Fax:(904)264-4044

Rates: $65-145.
Payment: MC VISA AX PC TC.
Innkeeper(s): Caleb Massee & Karrie Stevens.
Circa: 1923.

Rooms: 22 rooms with PB, 2 with FP. 4 suites. 2 conference rooms.
Beds: KQ.

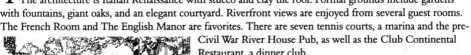

This lavish waterfront estate was constructed for the Palmolive family and overlooks the St. Johns River. The architecture is Italian Renaissance with stucco and clay tile roof. Formal grounds include gardens with fountains, giant oaks, and an elegant courtyard. Riverfront views are enjoyed from several guest rooms. The French Room and The English Manor are favorites. There are seven tennis courts, a marina and the pre-Civil War River House Pub, as well as the Club Continental Restaurant, a dinner club.

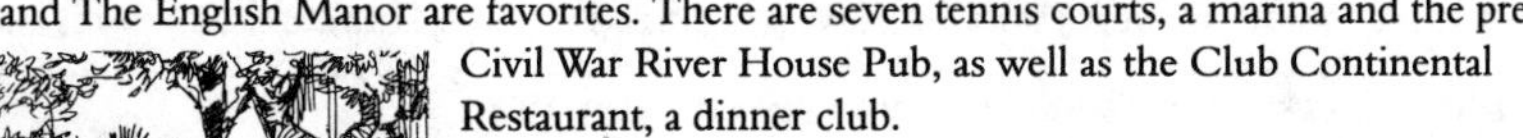

Breakfast included in rates. Type of meal: continental breakfast. Dinner and gourmet lunch available. Air conditioning, ceiling fan and cable TV in room. Fax, copier, swimming and tennis on premises. Weddings, small meetings, family reunions and seminars hosted. Antiques, fishing, parks, shopping, sporting events and theater nearby. TAC10.

Pets Allowed: In two rooms only.

Location: On the St. Johns River, 20 miles to many Florida beaches and 30 miles to St. Augustine.

Publicity: *Miami Herald, Sun Sentinel, Tampa Tribune.*

"Superb dining with spectacular grounds."

Orlando

D8

Perrihouse B&B

10417 Centurion Ct
Orlando, FL 32836
(407)876-4830 (800)780-4830
Fax:(407)876-0241
E-mail: perrihse@iag.net

Rates: $79-95.
Payment: MC VISA AX DS PC TC.
Innkeeper(s): Nick & Angi Perretti.
Circa: 1990.

Rooms: 8 rooms with PB.
Beds: KQT.

Although adjacent to Walt Disney World, this inn is secluded on 20 acres that serve as bird sanctuary and wildlife refuge. For those who wish to enjoy the tranquil grounds, there is a pool and a spa. The home is cheerful place, guest rooms have flowery prints and poster beds. Breakfast is served buffet-style and includes muffins, pastries, cereals and other continental fare. All of Orlando and Lake Buena Vista's popular attractions are nearby.

Breakfast included in rates. Types of meals: continental-plus breakfast and early coffee/tea. Air conditioning and ceiling fan in room. Fax, copier, spa, swimming and library on premises. 20 acres. Small meetings and family reunions hosted. Amusement parks, antiques, fishing, parks, shopping, sporting events, theater and watersports nearby. TAC10.

Special Discounts: 10% discount for weekly stays; AAA, AARP, seniors.

Orlando (Winter Garden)

Meadow Marsh B&B

940 Tildenville School Rd
Orlando (Winter Garden),
FL 34787
(407)656-2064 (888)656-2064

Rates: $95-195.
Payment: MC VISA TC.
Innkeeper(s): Cavelle & John Pawlack.
Circa: 1877.

Rooms: 2 suites, 1 with FP.
Beds: QD.

Meadow Marsh is located on 12 acres just outside the quiet village of Winter Garden, an Orlando suburb. One of the town's settlers built the Victorian manor, which is highlighted by verandas on the first and second stories. The home remained in the original family until the 1980s. Today guest rooms appear much as they probably did in the 19th century, filled with country Victorian pieces. However, there have been some pleasant additions, including Jacuzzi tubs in each of the two suites. A three-course breakfast is served, as is afternoon tea. The innkeeper owns a local gift shop and tea room.

Breakfast, afternoon tea and evening snack included in rates. Dinner, picnic lunch, lunch and catering service available. Air conditioning, turn-down service and ceiling fan in room. Cable TV, VCR, fax, copier and library on premises. 12 acres. Weddings hosted. Amusement parks, antiques, parks, sporting events, theater and watersports nearby. TAC6.

"What a beautiful home with such warm, gracious Southern hospitality."

Palm Beach

G10

Palm Beach Historic Inn

365 S County Rd
Palm Beach, FL 33480-4472
(407)832-4009
Fax:(407)832-6255

Rates: $75-150.
Payment: MC VISA AX DC CB DS TC.
Innkeeper(s): Brenda Lee Inniss.
Circa: 1923.

Rooms: 9 rooms with PB. 4 suites.
Beds: KQDT.

Visitors are welcomed into a lobby with the look of an elegant European parlor. Intimate, comfortable, meticulously clean accommodations with every modern convenience await each guest. Besides choice lodging, travelers will enjoy being just one block from the beach. Also a few short steps away are a variety of entertainment options, gift and antique shopping, spectacular dining experiences and tours of legendary mansions and art galleries. Recreational activities range from horseback riding, tennis and golf to snorkeling, scuba diving or fishing. Ask the concierge for advice in exploring this tropical paradise.

Breakfast included in rates. Type of meal: continental breakfast. Air conditioning and cable TV in room. VCR, fax, copier, library and child care on premises. Family reunions hosted. Fishing, parks, shopping, sporting events, theater and watersports nearby. TAC10.

Publicity: *PB Today, PB Society.*

Saint Augustine **B8**

FL

Alexander Homestead B&B

14 Sevilla St
Saint Augustine, FL 32084
(904)826-4147 (800)555-4147
Fax:(904)823-9503

Rates: $95-150.
Payment: MC VISA AX DS PC TC.
Innkeeper(s): Bonnie Alexander.
Circa: 1888.

Rooms: 4 rooms with PB, 2 with FP.
Beds: Q.

Green pastel hues, dotted with white, create a fanciful, tropical look at this Victorian bed & breakfast. Polished wood floors, colorful rugs and a mix of antiques and family pieces set the stage for a nostalgic getaway. Oversized tubs, lace, scented sachets and fresh flowers are just a few treats awaiting guests. The plentiful breakfasts are served in the elegant dining room. In the evening, guests also may enjoy a cordial in the Victorian parlor. The inn is located in St. Augustine's downtown historic area, so there is plenty of nearby activity.

Breakfast included in rates. Types of meals: gourmet breakfast and early coffee/tea. Air conditioning and cable TV in room. Fax on premises. Weddings, small meetings and family reunions hosted. Antiques, fishing and shopping nearby. TAC10.

Special Discounts: Extended stays will be discounted (5 days and over).

"Thanks so much for another wonderful 'mental health' weekend at your B&B."

Carriage Way B&B

70 Cuna St
Saint Augustine, FL 32084
(904)829-2467 (800)908-9832
Fax:(904)826-1461

Rates: $69-125.
Payment: MC VISA AX DS TC.
Innkeeper(s): Bill & Diane Johnson.
Circa: 1883.

Rooms: 9 rooms with PB, 1 with FP.
Beds: QD.

A two-story veranda dominates the facade of this square Victorian. Painted creamy white with blue trim, the house is located in the heart of the historic district. It's within a four-block walk to restaurants and shops and the Intracoastal Waterway. Guest rooms reflect the charm of a light Victorian touch, with brass, canopy and four-poster beds. Many furnishings have been in the house for 60 years. On Saturday evenings the dining-room table is laden with scrumptious desserts and coffee. A full gourmet breakfast is provided in the morning.

Breakfast and evening snack included in rates. Types of meals: full breakfast and early coffee/tea. Dinner and picnic lunch available. Air conditioning and ceiling fan in room. Cable TV, fax, copier and bicycles on premises. Weddings, small meetings and family reunions hosted. Amusement parks, antiques, fishing, parks, shopping, sporting events, theater and watersports nearby.

Location: Heart of historic district.

Publicity: *Miami Herald, Florida Times Union, Palm Beach Post, Sunday Oklahoman.*

"Charming in every detail."

Casa De La Paz

22 Avenida Menendez
Saint Augustine, FL 32084
(904)829-2915 (800)929-2915

Rates: $79-159.
Payment: MC VISA AX PC TC.
Innkeeper(s): Bob & Donna Marriott.
Circa: 1915.

Rooms: 6 rooms with PB, 1 with FP.
Beds: Q.

Overlooking Matanzas Bay, Casa de la Paz was built after the devastating 1914 fire leveled much of the old city. An ornate stucco Mediterranean Revival house, it features clay barrel tile roofing, bracketed eaves, verandas and a lush walled courtyard. The home is listed in the National Register of Historic Places. Guest rooms offer ceiling fans, central air, hardwood floors, antiques, a decanter of sherry, chocolates and complimentary beverages and snacks.

Breakfast and afternoon tea included in rates. Types of meals: full breakfast and early coffee/tea. Air conditioning, ceiling fan and cable TV in room. Bicycles on premises. Family reunions hosted. Antiques, fishing, parks, shopping, sporting events, theater and watersports nearby.

Publicity: *Innsider, US Air Magazine.*

"We will always recommend your beautifully restored, elegant home."

Casa De Solana, B&B Inn

21 Aviles St
Saint Augustine, FL 32084
(904)824-3555 (800)760-3556
Fax:(904)824-3316
E-mail: solana@aug.com

Rates: $125.
Payment: MC VISA AX DS PC.
Innkeeper(s): Faye' Lang-McMurray.
Circa: 1776.

Rooms: 4 suites.
Beds: KQD.

Spanish military leader Don Manuel Solana built this home in the early European settlement, and Spanish records show that a Solana child was the first child born in America. The thick coquina-shell walls (limestone formed of broken shells and corals cemented together), high ceilings with dark, hand-hewn beams and polished hand-pegged floors are part of the distinctive flavor of this period. Two working Majorcan fireplaces are in the carriage house. A southern breakfast is served at an elegant 10-foot-long mahogany table.

Breakfast included in rates. Type of meal: full breakfast. Air conditioning and cable TV in room. Fax on premises. Amusement parks, antiques, fishing, parks, shopping, sporting events, theater and watersports nearby.

Location: In the Historic District.

Publicity: *House Beautiful, Palm Beach Post.*

Cedar House Inn

79 Cedar St
Saint Augustine, FL 32084
(904)829-0079 (800)233-2746
Fax:(904)825-0916
E-mail: russ@aug.com

Rates: $79-150.
Payment: MC VISA DS PC.
Innkeeper(s): Russ & Nina Thomas.
Circa: 1893.

Rooms: 6 rooms with PB, 3 with FP. 1 suite. 1 conference room.
Beds: Q.

A player piano entertains guests in the parlor of this restored Victorian, which offers plenty of relaxing possibilities. Enjoy refreshments on the veranda or simply curl up with a good book in the library. Innkeepers Russ and Nina Thomas have preserved the home's luxurious heart-of-pine floors and 10-foot ceilings. They highlighted this architectural treasure with period furnishings and reproductions. Guests rooms are decked in Victorian decor and boast either clawfoot or Jacuzzi tubs. The innkeepers also offer an outdoor Jacuzzi spa. Elegant breakfasts are served either in the dining room or on the veranda. Guests may borrow bicycles perfect for exploring historic Saint Augustine or nearby beaches.

Breakfast and evening snack included in rates. Types of meals: gourmet breakfast and early coffee/tea. Dinner and picnic lunch available. Air conditioning and ceiling fan in room. Fax, spa and bicycles on premises. Weddings, small meetings, family reunions and seminars hosted. Antiques, fishing, parks, shopping, theater and watersports nearby. TAC5.

Special Discounts: 15-20% discount Monday-Thursday.

"What a special 'home' to spend our honeymoon! Everything was terrific! We feel this is our place now and will be regular guests here! Thank you!"

Kenwood Inn

38 Marine St
Saint Augustine, FL 32084
(904)824-2116
Fax:(904)824-1689

Rates: $85-150.
Payment: MC VISA DS PC TC.
Innkeeper(s): Mark & Kerrianne Constant.
Circa: 1865.

Rooms: 14 rooms with PB. 4 suites.
Beds: KQD.

Originally built as a summer home, the Kenwood Inn has taken in guests for more than 100 years. Early records show that it was advertised as a private boarding house as early as 1886. Rooms are decorated in periods ranging from the simple Shaker decor to more formal colonial and Victorian styles.

Breakfast included in rates. Type of meal: continental breakfast. Air conditioning and ceiling fan in room. Cable TV, fax and swimming on premises. Antiques, fishing, shopping, theater and watersports nearby.

Location: One block from the bay front.

Publicity: *Palm Beach Post, Florida Living, Southern Living, Seabreeze.*

"It's one of my favorite spots for a few days of relaxation and recuperation."

St. Francis Inn

279 Saint George St
Saint Augustine, FL 32084
(904)824-6068 (800)824-6062
Fax:(904)810-5525

Rates: $75-165.
Payment: MC VISA AX PC.
Innkeeper(s): Joseph Finnegan, Jr.
Circa: 1791.

Rooms: 14 rooms, 8 with PB, 4 with FP. 6 suites. 1 cottage. 2 conference rooms.
Beds: KQDT.

Long noted for its hospitality, the St. Francis Inn is nearly the oldest house in town. A classic example of Old World architecture, it was built by Gaspar Garcia who received a Spanish grant to the plot of land. Coquina was the main building material. A buffet breakfast is served. Some rooms have whirlpool tubs. The city of Saint Augustine was founded in 1565.

Breakfast included in rates. Type of meal: early coffee/tea. Air conditioning, ceiling fan and cable TV in room. Fax, copier, swimming and bicycles on premises. Weddings, small meetings, family reunions and seminars hosted. American Sign Language spoken. Antiques, fishing, parks, shopping, sporting events and watersports nearby. TAC10.

Location: In the Saint Augustine Historic District, the nation's oldest city.

Publicity: *Orlando Sentinel.*

"We have stayed at many nice hotels but nothing like this. We are really enjoying it."

Saint Petersburg — E7

Bayboro House B&B on Old Tampa

1719 Beach Dr SE
Saint Petersburg, FL 33701
(813)823-4955
Fax:(813)823-4955

Rates: $85-145.
Payment: MC VISA PC TC.
Innkeeper(s): Antonia Powers.
Circa: 1905.

Rooms: 4 rooms with PB. 1 suite.
Beds: QD.

Victorian decor and beautiful antique furnishings fill the Bayboro House, a charming turn-of-the-century manor. The veranda is set up for relaxation with a variety of rockers, swings, wicker chairs and chaise lounges. Breakfasts, served in the formal dining room, feature what every Florida breakfast should, freshly squeezed juices and in-season fruits. Before heading out to one of St. Petersburg's many restaurants, relax and sip a glass of wine in the parlor.

Breakfast and afternoon tea included in rates. Type of meal: continental-plus breakfast. Air conditioning, ceiling fan and VCR in room. Fax on premises. Amusement parks, antiques, fishing, parks, shopping, sporting events, theater and watersports nearby.

Location: Off exit 9 (I-275), downtown Saint Petersburg.

Publicity: *Miami Herald, Sun Sentinal.*

"Made our anniversary very special; got the feeling I could be a new bride, a celebrity or even a princess."

Sanford D8

The Higgins House

420 S Oak Ave
Sanford, FL 32771-1826
(407)324-9238 (800)584-0014

Rates: $85-145.
Payment: MC VISA AX DS PC TC.
Innkeeper(s): Walter & Roberta Padgett.
Circa: 1894.

Rooms: 3 rooms. 1 cottage.
Beds: QD.

This inviting blue Queen Anne-style home features cross gables with patterned wood shingles, bay windows and a charming round window on the second floor. Pine floors, paddle fans and a piano in the parlor, which guests are encouraged to play, create Victorian ambiance. The second-story balcony affords views not only of a charming park and Sanford's oldest church, but of Space Shuttle launches from nearby Cape Canaveral. The Queen Anne room looks out over a Victorian box garden, while the Wicker Room features a bay window sitting area. The Country Victorian room boasts a 19th-century brass bed. Guests also can opt to stay in Cochran's Cottage, which features two bedrooms and baths, a living room, kitchen and porch. Nature lovers will enjoy close access to Blue Spring State Park, Ocala National Forest, Lake Monroe and the Cape Canaveral Wildlife Refuge. And of course, Walt Disney World, Seaworld and Universal Studios aren't far away.

Breakfast and evening snack included in rates. Types of meals: continental-plus breakfast and early coffee/tea. Picnic lunch available. Air conditioning, turn-down service and ceiling fan in room. Cable TV, VCR, spa and bicycles on premises. Weddings, small meetings, family reunions and seminars hosted. Antiques, fishing, parks, shopping and watersports nearby. TAC10.

Location: In the historic district.

Publicity: *Southern Living, Sanford Herald, Connecticut Traveler, LifeTimes, Orlando Sentinel, Southern Accents, Country Inns.*

"The Higgins House is warm and friendly, filled with such pleasant sounds, and if you love beauty and nature, you're certain to enjoy the grounds."

Tampa E8

Gram's Place

3109 N Ola Ave
Tampa, FL 33603-5744
(813)221-0596
Fax:(813)221-0596

Rates: $55-75.
Payment: MC VISA AX TC.
Innkeeper(s): Mark Holland.
Circa: 1945.

Rooms: 7 rooms, 4 with PB.
Beds: QF.

These two cottages offer a variety of amenities, including lush grounds with a Jacuzzi, waterfall, sundeck and courtyard. The innkeepers named their relaxing home after singer Gram Parsons. The home and comfortable guest rooms feature a mix of European and modern decor with a few simple, country touches. The home is just a few miles from downtown Tampa.

Breakfast included in rates. Types of meals: continental breakfast and continental-plus breakfast. Air conditioning, ceiling fan, cable TV and VCR in room. Fax and spa on premises. Amusement parks, antiques, fishing, parks, shopping, sporting events, theater and watersports nearby.

Venice F7

Banyan House

519 Harbor Dr S
Venice, FL 34285-2812
(941)484-1385
Fax:(941)484-8032

Rates: $70-120.
Payment: MC VISA TC.
Innkeeper(s): Ian & Suzie Maryan.
Circa: 1926.

Rooms: 4 rooms with PB. 5 suites.
Beds: KQT.

FL

Spanish and Mediterranean influences are prominent in the design of this European-style inn. The grounds are lush, sporting tropical plants, trees and flowers. There is a hot tub tucked beneath a banyan tree, and the first swimming pool built in Venice. The innkeepers offer bicycles for those who wish to explore the area, and there are plenty of nearby activities, including the beach, shops and restaurants. There are laundry facilities on the premises.

Breakfast included in rates. Type of meal: continental-plus breakfast. Afternoon tea available. Air conditioning, ceiling fan and cable TV in room. Fax, copier, spa, swimming, bicycles and library on premises. Weddings, small meetings and family reunions hosted. Amusement parks, antiques, fishing, parks, shopping, theater and watersports nearby.

West Palm Beach G10

Hibiscus House

501 30th St
West Palm Beach, FL
33407-5121
(407)863-5633 (800)203-4927
Fax:(407)863-5633

Rates: $55-160.
Payment: MC VISA AX DC PC TC.
Innkeeper(s): Raleigh Hill.
Circa: 1922.

Rooms: 5 rooms with PB, 1 with FP. 1 suite. 1 cottage.
Beds: Q.

Built for John Dunkle, once the mayor of West Palm Beach, the Hibiscus House offers guest rooms individually decorated with antiques. There is a poolside cottage which can accommodate six people and includes a kitchen. Two-course breakfasts are served either by the pool or in the formal dining room, and at sunset, complimentary cocktails are served.

Breakfast included in rates. Type of meal: full breakfast. Air conditioning, turn-down service, ceiling fan and cable TV in room. Fax, swimming, bicycles and library on premises. Weddings, small meetings, family reunions and seminars hosted. Antiques, fishing, parks, shopping, sporting events, theater and watersports nearby. TAC10.

Publicity: *Ft. Lauderdale-Sun Sentinel.*

Special Discounts: 20% off for weekly stays.

"You have such a warm and beautiful home. We have told everyone of our stay there."

Georgia

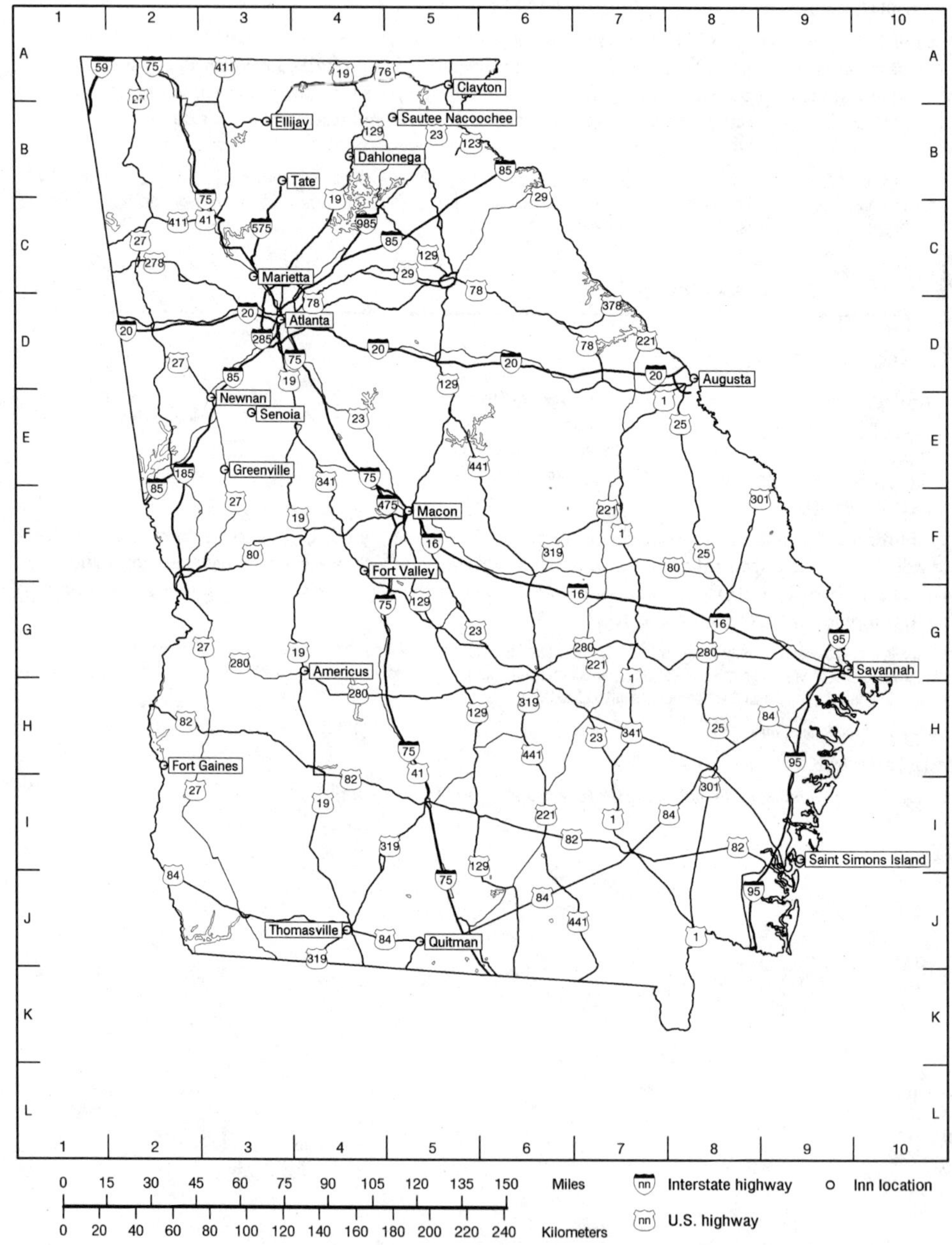

Clayton
Ellijay
Sautee Nacoochee
Dahlonega
Tate
Marietta
Atlanta
Augusta
Newnan
Senoia
Greenville
Macon
Fort Valley
Americus
Savannah
Fort Gaines
Saint Simons Island
Thomasville
Quitman
0 15 30 45 60 75 90 105 120 135 150 Miles
0 20 40 60 80 100 120 140 160 180 200 220 240 Kilometers
Interstate highway
U.S. highway
Inn location

Americus G4

The Pathway Inn B&B

501 S Lee St
Americus, GA 31709-3919
(912)928-2078 (800)889-1466
Fax:(912)928-2078

Rates: $70-117.
Payment: MC VISA AX DS PC TC.
Innkeeper(s): Sheila & David Judah.
Circa: 1906.

Rooms: 5 rooms with PB, 2 with FP. 1 conference room.
Beds: KQ.

This turn-of-the-century inn is located along the Andersonville Trail and not far from the city of Andersonville, a Civil War village. The gracious, wraparound porch is a perfect spot for relaxation. The innkeepers plan the breakfast times around their guests' schedules, serving up a country breakfast with freshly baked breads. The guest rooms offer romantic amenities such as whirlpools and snug down comforters. Two of the rooms are named in honor of Jimmy and Rosalynn Carter, whose hometown is just a short distance down the road. Late afternoons are reserved for wine and refreshments.

GA

Breakfast included in rates. Types of meals: gourmet breakfast and early coffee/tea. Evening snack and room service available. Air conditioning, ceiling fan, cable TV and VCR in room. Fax and copier on premises. Small meetings hosted. Antiques, parks and theater nearby. TAC10.

Pets Allowed: With prior approval.

Atlanta D3

Beverly Hills Inn

65 Sheridan Dr NE
Atlanta, GA 30305-3121
(404)233-8520 (800)331-8520
Fax:(404)233-8659
E-mail: mit-bhi@mindspring.com

Rates: $90-160.
Payment: MC VISA AX DC DS PC TC.
Innkeeper(s): Mit Amin.
Circa: 1929.

Rooms: 18 suites.
Beds: QD.

Period furniture and polished-wood floors decorate this inn located in the Buckhead neighborhood. There are private balconies, kitchens and a library with a collection of newspapers and books. The governor's mansion, Neiman-Marcus, Saks and Lord & Taylor are five minutes away.

Breakfast included in rates. Type of meal: continental-plus breakfast. Air conditioning and cable TV in room. Small meetings and family reunions hosted. French, Italian and Spanish spoken. Antiques, parks and shopping nearby. TAC10.

Pets Allowed: With kennels.

Location: North on Peachtree 15 minutes then one-half block off Peachtree.

Publicity: *Country Inns, Southern Living, Time.*

"Our only regret is that we had so little time. Next stay we will plan to be here longer."

The Gaslight Inn B&B

1001 Saint Charles Ave NE
Atlanta, GA 30306-4221
(404)875-1001
Fax:(404)876-1001

Rates: $95-195.
Payment: MC VISA AX DS PC TC.
Innkeeper(s): Jim Moss, Shannon DeLaney.
Circa: 1913.

Rooms: 6 rooms with PB, 3 with FP. 3 suites. 2 cottages. 1 conference room.
Beds: KQ.

Flickering gas lanterns outside, original gas lighting inside and five working fireplaces add to the unique quality of this inn. Beautifully appointed guest rooms offer individual decor. The Ivy Cottage is a romantic bungalow with a living room and kitchen. The regal English Suite boasts a four-poster bed covered in rich blue hues and a private deck. The Rose Room features a fireplace and four-poster bed covered with lace. Located in the Virginia Highlands neighborhood, the inn is approximately five minutes from downtown and is served by Atlanta's public transportation system.

Breakfast included in rates. Types of meals: continental-plus breakfast and early coffee/tea. Air conditioning, ceiling fan, cable TV and VCR in room. Fax, copier, spa, sauna and library on premises. Handicap access. Weddings, small meetings, family reunions and seminars hosted. Amusement parks, antiques, parks, shopping, sporting events and theater nearby. TAC10.

Publicity: *Travel Channel.*

"Best B&B I've ever stayed in."

Oakwood House B&B Inn

951 Edgewood Ave NE
Atlanta, GA 30307-2582
(404)521-9320
Fax:(404)688-6034

Rates: $75-145.
Payment: MC VISA AX DS PC TC.
Innkeeper(s): Judy & Robert Hotchkiss.
Circa: 1911.

Rooms: 5 rooms with PB, 1 with FP. 1 suite. 2 conference rooms.
Beds: KQDT.

This post-Victorian house has seen duty as a boarding house, travel agency and psychologists' offices. The inviting interior includes original moldings, stained glass, exposed brick and traditional furnishings. A mantel, which once graced an old-style movie theater, now makes its home at the inn. Bookworms will appreciate the innkeepers' large collection of books. The inn, located in Atlanta's charming Inman Park Historic District, is full of beautiful old homes. Guests are only a few minutes from the World Congress Center, stadiums, Underground Atlanta and shopping in exclusive Buckhead. The Jimmy Carter Library and Martin Luther King Jr. Tomb also are nearby. A subway station is only one a one half blocks away.

Breakfast included in rates. Types of meals: continental-plus breakfast and early coffee/tea. Air conditioning, turn-down service and ceiling fan in room. Fax, copier and library on premises. Handicap access. Small meetings and family reunions hosted. Amusement parks, antiques, parks, shopping, sporting events and theater nearby. TAC10.

Location: Two miles east of downtown.

Publicity: *CBS, Style, Inn Times, Los Angeles Times, Men's Journal, Women's Health & Fitness, Style, Inn Times*

Special Discounts: Government at per diem, free theater tickets (in season) two-night stay required.

"Thank you for a wonderful stay."

Augusta D8

The Partridge Inn

2110 Walton Way
Augusta, GA 30904-6905
(706)737-8888 (800)476-6888
Fax:(706)731-0826

Rates: $89-125. AP.
Payment: MC VISA AX DC DS.
Innkeeper(s): Joel & Gerrie Sobel.
Circa: 1836.

Rooms: 155 rooms with PB. 43 suites. 7 conference rooms.
Beds: KQD.

The original structure of this inn was built prior to the Civil War, and it was Morris Partridge who purchased the house in the 1890s and transformed it into an inn. By 1929, the inn had blossomed into a 129-room hostelry with a quarter-mile of porches and balconies. Throughout its history, the inn has hosted prominent personalities, such as senators, actors and even a president. Guests are greeted with a welcome beverage and led to their elegantly appointed room, decorated in traditional, Southern style. For those on an extended stay, some rooms offer small kitchens. Guests enjoy use of an on-site swimming pool as well as a nearby health spa. There are plenty of dining options here as well. The Bar & Grill is a popular spot for lunch or an informal dinner, and often is host to jazz ensembles. The inn's Dining Room is the place for a romantic, gourmet meal, and The Veranda offers a variety of light fare. Inn guests are treated to a full Southern-style breakfast each morning.

Breakfast included in rates. Types of meals: full breakfast and early coffee/tea. Afternoon tea, dinner, evening snack, picnic lunch, lunch, banquet service, catering service, catered breakfast and room service available. AP. Air conditioning and cable TV in room. Fax, copier and swimming on premises. Handicap access. Weddings, small meetings, family reunions and seminars hosted. Amusement parks, antiques, parks, shopping and sporting events nearby. TAC10.

Special Discounts: Group rates available; AARP, AAA, Travel Agent.

The Telfair Inn - A Victorian Village

326 Greene St
Augusta, GA 30901-1619
(706)724-3315 (800)241-2407
Fax:(706)823-6623

Rates: $77-147.
Payment: MC VISA AX DC CB DS PC TC.
Innkeeper(s): Herb Upton.
Circa: 1988.

Rooms: 61 rooms with PB, 45 with FP. 23 suites. 1 cottage. 3 conference rooms.
Beds: KQD.

Telfair is a collection of 15 Victorian houses in the heart of historic Olde Town. Each one has been renovated and decorated with four-poster beds, fireplaces, whirlpool baths, antiques and gleaming hardwood floors. There is also a large conference center.

Types of meals: full breakfast and early coffee/tea. Dinner, lunch and room service available. Restaurant on premises. Air conditioning and cable TV in room. VCR, fax, copier, swimming and tennis on premises. Handicap access. Weddings, small meetings, family reunions and seminars hosted. Antiques, fishing, parks, shopping, sporting events, theater and watersports nearby. TAC10.

Pets Allowed: $50.00-$150.00 pet fee.

"A great experience! Thanks for everything. The service here is excellent!"

Clayton — A5

English Manor

Hwy 76 E
Clayton, GA 30525
(706)782-5789 (800)782-5780
Fax:(706)782-5789

Rates: $69-169.
Payment: PC TC.
Innkeeper(s): Juanita Shope.
Circa: 1912.

Rooms: 42 rooms with PB, 14 with FP. 7 suites.
Beds: KQD.

Seven wooded acres serve as the location for this unique collection of inns. The main inn was actually purchased as a kit from a Sears Roebuck catalog and assembled on the property. The remaining six inns are just under a decade old. All seven have individually decorated guest rooms filled with antiques. Suites offer the added amenity of a Jacuzzi tub, and 14 rooms have fireplaces. There is a pool and oversized hot tub for guest use and verandas lined with rockers. The innkeepers host conferences, seminars and murder-mystery weekends. Well-mannered pets are welcome with prior arrangement.

Breakfast and evening snack included in rates. Types of meals: gourmet breakfast and early coffee/tea. Catering service available. Air conditioning and cable TV in room. Copier, swimming and library on premises. Handicap access. Weddings, small meetings, family reunions and seminars hosted. Spanish and French spoken. Antiques, fishing, parks, shopping and watersports nearby. TAC10.

Pets Allowed: Yes.

Dahlonega — B4

The Smith House

84 Chestatee St SE
Dahlonega, GA 30533-1612
(706)867-7000 (800)852-9577
Fax:(706)864-7564

Rates: $65-150.
Payment: MC VISA AX DS TC.
Innkeeper(s): Freddy & Shirley Welch.
Circa: 1885.

Rooms: 16 rooms with PB. 1 conference room.
Beds: KQD.

This inn in the Blue Ridge Mountains stands on a vein of gold. (In 1884 the landowner tried, without success, to get permission from city officials to set up a mining operation.) The inn features original woodwork, dry-rock fireplaces and a large wrap-around porch with rocking chairs. Some guest rooms have porches. Family-style dining is offered.

Breakfast included in rates. Type of meal: continental breakfast. Dinner and lunch available. Air conditioning, ceiling fan and cable TV in room. Fax, copier and swimming on premises. Small meetings and family reunions hosted. Antiques, parks, shopping and theater nearby.
Location: One block south of town square.
Publicity: *Gainesville Times, Atlanta Constitution, Atlanta Magazine.*

Ellijay

B3

Home of Gardener Fatness, A B&B

59 River St
Ellijay, GA 30540-1230
(706)276-7473

Rates: $65-100.
Payment: MC VISA PC TC.
Innkeeper(s): Susan Hough.
Circa: 1910.

Rooms: 4 rooms.
Beds: QDT.

Gardner Fatness, an elusive character, is never actually seen at this turn-of-the-century home, but his presence is always felt. At least that's the way innkeeper Susan Hough sees it. She named her bed & breakfast after Gardener, her childhood imaginary friend. Susan's fun, whimsical nature doesn't just stop at the home's name, she has created a theme for each of the four guest rooms. The Wild West Room sports a cowboy theme, while the Ivy Plantation Room celebrates Georgia's Southern heritage. The town of Ellijay is known for its apple orchards, so Susan is sure to add an apple dish to the hearty full breakfasts. The inn also houses a Peace Officers' Museum with a collection of badges, handcuffs and unique pieces from around the world.

Breakfast and afternoon tea included in rates. Types of meals: full breakfast and early coffee/tea. Air conditioning, turn-down service, cable TV and VCR in room. Handicap access. Weddings, small meetings and family reunions hosted. Antiques, fishing, parks, shopping, theater and watersports nearby.

Fort Gaines

H2

John Dill House

PO Box 8, 102 S
Washington St
Fort Gaines, GA 31751
(912)768-2338
Fax:(912)768-2338

Rates: $50-70.
Payment: PC TC.
Innkeeper(s): Philip & Ramona Kurland.
Circa: 1820.

Rooms: 9 rooms with PB, 9 with FP.
Beds: Q.

This stately homestead, once a stagecoach stop, is just two blocks from the Chattahoochee River in the state's Southwest region. The inn, listed with the national, state and local historic registers, boasts a fireplace in each of its nine guest rooms, have a queen size bed and a private bath, all tastefully furnished in Adams mantels, imported Italian tile, cypress wainscotting and hand-carved antiques. Features include a 600-square-foot kitchen and more than $500,000 worth of antiques. Proceeds of the Elizabeth Dill Gift Shop, also on the grounds, go toward the costs of restoring the inn.

Breakfast included in rates. Type of meal: gourmet breakfast. Catering service available. Turn-down service in room. Cable TV, VCR and fax on premises. Handicap access. Weddings, small meetings and family reunions hosted. Antiques, fishing, parks and watersports nearby.

Fort Valley

F4

The Evans-Cantrell House

300 College St
Fort Valley, GA 31030-3415
(912)825-0611

Rates: $75-95.
Payment: MC VISA AX PC TC.
Innkeeper(s): Norman & Cyriline Cantrell.
Circa: 1916.

Rooms: 4 rooms with PB. 1 suite.
Beds: QD.

Innkeepers Norman and Cyriline Cantrell are only the second owners of this majestic home which was constructed by A.J. Evans, who built an empire reaching into agriculture, commerce and finance. The Italian Renaissance Revival-style architecture is the perfect package for what guests discover inside. Brightly painted walls, traditional furnishings and glorious woodwork create an atmosphere reminiscent of early America. The dining room boasts the table and chairs that were built originally for the home. A beautiful mahogany-stained staircase leads up to the guest rooms, each of which is named for one of A.J. Evans' children. Morning meals, either a light continental or hearty southern fare, are served in the cheerful breakfast room with its arched windows.

Breakfast, afternoon tea and evening snack included in rates. Type of meal: early coffee/tea. Dinner available. Air conditioning, turn-down service, ceiling fan and cable TV in room. Amusement parks, antiques and shopping nearby.

Publicity: *Georgia Journal, Macon.*

"Award Winning! We must get your efforts a Georgia Trust Award!! Keep up the good work!!!"

Greenville E3

Samples Plantation

PO Box 648
Greenville, GA 30222-0648
(706)672-4765
Fax:(706)672-4765

Rates: $149-289.
Payment: MC VISA PC TC.
Innkeeper(s): Marjorie Samples.
Circa: 1832.

Rooms: 7 suites, 6 with FP.
Beds: KQDT.

The romance of the South lives on at this Antebellum mansion. The manor originally was part of the Render Plantation, and among the Render family were a Georgia governor, a congressman and a Supreme Court justice. Each guest room has been individually decorated with antiques, lace, satin and romance in mind. Guests are pampered with a homemade plantation-style breakfast. Shopping and other attractions, including Franklin Roosevelt's Little White House, are nearby. Atlanta is 50 miles away, and Callaway Gardens are 17 miles away.

Breakfast, afternoon tea, evening snack and picnic lunch included in rates. Types of meals: full breakfast and early coffee/tea. Air conditioning, turn-down service and ceiling fan in room. Cable TV, VCR, fax, copier, bicycles and library on premises. 25 acres. Weddings hosted. Amusement parks, antiques, fishing, parks, shopping, sporting events, theater and watersports nearby. TAC10.

Publicity: *Columbia Ledger, Atlanta Journal.*

"Outstanding."

Macon F5

1842 Inn

353 College St
Macon, GA 31201-1651
(912)741-1842 (800)336-1842
Fax:(912)741-1842

Rates: $95-135.
Payment: MC VISA AX.
Innkeeper(s): Phillip Jenkins & Richard Meils.
Circa: 1842.

Rooms: 21 rooms with PB, 8 with FP. 1 conference room.
Beds: KQDT.

Judge John J. Gresham, cotton merchant and founder of the Bibb Manufacturing Company, built this antebellum Greek Revival house. It features graceful columns, elaborate mantels, crystal chandeliers and oak parquet floors inlaid with mahogany. Guest rooms boast cable television discreetly tucked into antique armoires. There are whirlpool baths available in the main house and in an adjoining Victorian cottage. All rooms are accented with fine English antiques, oriental rugs and working fireplaces.

Breakfast included in rates. Type of meal: continental-plus breakfast. Afternoon tea and room service available. Copier and spa on premises. Handicap access. Antiques and theater nearby.

Publicity: *Christian Science Monitor, Southern Living, Daily News, Touring USA, Country Inns.*

"The best B&B we've seen! Deserves all four stars!"

Marietta C3

Whitlock Inn

57 Whitlock Ave
Marietta, GA 30064-2343
(770)428-1495
Fax:(770)919-9620

Rates: $85.
Payment: MC VISA AX DS.
Innkeeper(s): Alexis Edwards.
Circa: 1900.

Rooms: 5 rooms with PB. 3 conference rooms.
Beds: KQT.

This cherished Victorian has been recently restored and is in a National Register Historic District, located one block from the Marietta Square. Amenities even the Ritz doesn't provide are in every room and you can rock on the front verandas. An afternoon snack also is served. There is a ballroom grandly suitable for weddings and business meetings.

Breakfast included in rates. Type of meal: continental-plus breakfast. Air conditioning, ceiling fan and cable TV in room. Fax and copier on premises. Weddings, small meetings, family reunions and seminars hosted. Amusement parks, antiques, parks, shopping, sporting events and theater nearby. TAC10.

Publicity: *Marietta Daily Journal.*

"Your inn is beautiful. It was a great experience."

Newnan

E3

The Old Garden Inn

51 Temple Ave
Newnan, GA 30263
(770)304-0594 (800)731-5011
Fax:(770)304-9003

Rates: $75-89.
Payment: MC VISA AX PC TC.
Innkeeper(s): Patty & Ron Gironda.
Circa: 1904.

Rooms: 4 rooms with PB, 2 with FP. 1 cottage.
Beds: KQ.

This turn-of-the-century Greek Revival home boasts more than 100 panels of beveled glass in its dramatic grand hall. The innkeepers commissioned a renowned stencil artist to create a unique "garden" inside the house, and it's in this mural-painted area where guests first are greeted. Each guest bath is themed after a special scent, such as raspberry. Two guest rooms include a fireplace. Gourmet breakfasts are memorable with menus such as a goat cheese and tomato frittata, accompanied by potatoes and cheesy grits with chives or a succulent dish of berries topped with black currant liqueur, whipped cream and edible flowers.

Breakfast included in rates. Types of meals: gourmet breakfast and early coffee/tea. Evening snack available. Air conditioning, turn-down service, ceiling fan and cable TV in room. VCR, fax and copier on premises. Family reunions hosted. Antiques, fishing, parks, shopping and sporting events nearby. TAC10.

Quitman

J5

Malloy Manor

401 W Screven St
Quitman, GA 31643-1917
(912)263-5704 (800)239-5704

Rates: $55-85.
Payment: MC VISA AX PC TC.
Innkeeper(s): Wendall & Gail Way.
Circa: 1905.

Rooms: 5 rooms, 3 with PB, 5 with FP.
Beds: QDT.

This three-story Victorian displays many of the romantic features that make that era's architecture so transfixing, including carved woodwork, polished hardwood floors, leaded-glass windows and high ceilings. The innkeepers have decorated the home in a simple, country Victorian style. Bedrooms include four-poster canopied beds and lacy touches and each has a working fireplace. The Victorian look is enhanced by an upright piano in the music room and a victrola in the manor's parlor. Malloy Manor is within a short drive of antique shops, a factory outlet mall, museums and historic Remerton Mill Village.

Breakfast and evening snack included in rates. Types of meals: full breakfast, gourmet breakfast and early coffee/tea. Room service available. Air conditioning, turn-down service and cable TV in room. Fishing, parks, shopping and theater nearby.

Pets Allowed: If well-behaved.

Saint Simons Island

I9

Little St. Simons Island

PO Box 21078
Saint Simons Island, GA
31522-0578
(912)638-7472
Fax:(912)634-1811
E-mail: 102063.467@compuserve.com

Rates: $275-500. AP.
Payment: MC VISA PC.
Innkeeper(s): Debbie & Kevin McIntyre.
Circa: 1917.

Rooms: 11 rooms with PB. 1 suite. 1 conference room.
Beds: KQT.

GA

Once a part of Butler Plantation, Little St. Simons Island was purchased at the turn of the century by the Berolzheimer family. Deer roam freely and eagles soar over 10,000 acres of pristine forests, fresh water ponds, isolated beaches, and marshland. There are more than 200 species of birds, and guests can enjoy horseback riding on miles of private trails. The Hunting Lodge, filled with books and memorabilia, is the gathering spot for the island.

Breakfast, dinner, evening snack and picnic lunch included in rates. Types of meals: full breakfast and early coffee/tea. Lunch available. AP. Ceiling fan in room. Fax, copier, swimming, stables and bicycles on premises. Handicap access. Weddings, small meetings, family reunions and seminars hosted. Fishing nearby.

Location: A privately owned island 20 minutes offshore from St. Simons.

Publicity: *Meeting Destinations, Savannah Magazine, Chattanooga News Free Press, Gourmet.*

Special Discounts: Family and corporate packages available.

"The staff is unequaled anywhere."

Sautee

B5

The Stovall House

1526 Hwy 255 N
Sautee, GA 30571
(706)878-3355

Rates: $60-75.
Payment: MC VISA PC TC.
Innkeeper(s): Ham Schwartz.
Circa: 1837.

Rooms: 5 rooms with PB.
Beds: KQDT.

This house, built by Moses Harshaw and restored in 1983 by Ham Schwartz, has received two state awards for its restoration. The handsome farmhouse has an extensive wraparound porch providing vistas of 28 acres of cow pastures, meadows and creeks. High ceilings, polished walnut woodwork and decorative stenciling provide a pleasant backdrop for the inn's collection of antiques. Victorian bathroom fixtures include pull-chain toilets and pedestal sinks. The inn has its own restaurant.

Breakfast included in rates. Type of meal: continental breakfast. Dinner and catering service available. Ceiling fan in room. Library on premises. 26 acres. Weddings, small meetings and family reunions hosted. Amusement parks, antiques, fishing, parks, shopping, theater and watersports nearby.

Publicity: *Atlanta Journal.*

Special Discounts: Discount for stays of three or more nights.

"Great to be home again. Very nostalgic and hospitable."

Savannah

G9

Forsyth Park Inn

102 W Hall St
Savannah, GA 31401-5519
(912)233-6800

Rates: $115-185.
Payment: MC VISA AX DS PC TC.
Innkeeper(s): Hal & Virginia Sullivan.
Circa: 1893.

Rooms: 10 rooms, 9 with PB, 8 with FP. 1 cottage.
Beds: KQT.

This graceful yellow and white three-story Victorian features bay windows and a large veranda overlooking Forsyth Park. Sixteen-foot ceilings, polished parquet floors of oak and maple, and a handsome oak stair-

way provide an elegant background for the guest rooms. There are several whirlpool tubs, marble baths, four-poster beds, fireplaces and there is a walled garden courtyard.

Breakfast included in rates. Type of meal: continental breakfast. Air conditioning in room. French spoken. Antiques, fishing, parks, shopping, theater and watersports nearby.

Location: Savannah's historic district, opposite Forsyth Park.

Publicity: *Savannah Morning News, Land's End Catalog, United Airlines, Vis-A-Vis, Learning Channel.*

"Breathtaking, exceeded my wildest dreams."

Kehoe House

123 Habersham St
Savannah, GA 31401-3820
(912)232-1020 (800)820-1020
Fax:(912)231-1587

Rates: $175-300.
Payment: MC VISA AX DC CB DS TC.
Innkeeper(s): Maureen Horvath & Brenda Giffin.
Circa: 1892.

Rooms: 15 rooms with PB. 2 suites. 1 conference room.
Beds: KQT.

A wealthy Irish businessman built this Renaissance Revival manor. The interior has been impeccably restored and decorated in Victorian style with antiques, reproductions and original artwork. In honor of the original owner, the individually decorated guest rooms are named for a county in Ireland. Each day begins with a gourmet, Southern-style breakfast. Fresh fruit, freshly squeezed orange juice and home-baked breads accompany such entrees as eggs Savannah, bacon, grits and potatoes. The staff is always happy to assist guests and can direct you to fine restaurants, shops and attractions in the Savannah area. This inn has received both a four-diamond rating from AAA and four stars from Mobil.

Breakfast and evening snack included in rates. Types of meals: full breakfast, gourmet breakfast and early coffee/tea. Afternoon tea, picnic lunch, lunch and catered breakfast available. Air conditioning, turn-down service, ceiling fan, cable TV and VCR in room. Fax and copier on premises. Handicap access. Small meetings hosted. Dutch and Spanish spoken. Antiques, fishing, parks, shopping, theater and watersports nearby. TAC10.

Remshart-Brooks House

106 W Jones St
Savannah, GA 31401-4508
(912)234-6928

Rates: $75.
Payment: PC TC.
Innkeeper(s): Anne & Ewing Barnett.
Circa: 1853.

Rooms: 1 suite.
Beds: Q.

Guests at this Savannah-style home enjoy complete privacy as the single accommodation is a spacious terrace-garden suite. The home is the second house of a four-house row that was constructed for William Remshart and his family, and is surrounded by a neighborhood of restored homes. The furnishings include country antiques gathered from Virginia and Georgia. The suite offers a bedroom, living room, private bath and kitchen.

Breakfast included in rates. Type of meal: continental breakfast. Air conditioning and cable TV in room. Antiques, fishing, parks, shopping, sporting events, theater and watersports nearby.

Location: Center of historic district.

Senoia

E3

Culpepper House B&B

35 Broad St
Senoia, GA 30276
(770)599-8182
Fax:(770)599-8182

Rates: $85.
Payment: MC VISA AX PC.
Innkeeper(s): Maggie Armstrong & Barb Storm.
Circa: 1871.

Rooms: 3 rooms with PB, 2 with FP.
Beds: KQT.

GA

This Queen Anne Victorian was built by a Confederate veteran and later occupied for 50 years by Dr. Culpepper. With original moldings, stained-glass windows and mantelpieces, the house is decorated in cozy Victorian style. The inn offers guests Southern hospitality at its finest.

Breakfast included in rates. Type of meal: gourmet breakfast. Air conditioning and turn-down service in room. Cable TV, VCR, fax, copier, bicycles and library on premises. Weddings, small meetings and family reunions hosted. Antiques, parks and shopping nearby. TAC5.

Publicity: *Newman Times-Herald, Woman of Greater Atlanta.*

"Thank you for your generous hospitality."

The Veranda

252 Seavy St, PO Box 177
Senoia, GA 30276-0177
(770)599-3905
Fax:(770)599-0806

Rates: $95-115.
Payment: MC VISA AX DS PC TC.
Innkeeper(s): Jan & Bobby Boal.
Circa: 1906.

Rooms: 9 rooms with PB. 1 conference room.
Beds: KQ.

Doric columns adorn the verandas of this 9,000-square-foot Neoclassical hotel. William Jennings Bryan stayed here, and it is said that Margaret Mitchell, who wrote 'Gone With the Wind' came here to interview Georgia veterans of the Civil War who held their annual reunion at the hotel. Furnishings include walnut bookcases owned by President William McKinley and a rare Wurlitzer player piano-pipe organ. There are Victorian collections of hair combs, walking canes, books and one of the largest assortments of kaleidoscopes in the Southeast.

Types of meals: gourmet breakfast and early coffee/tea. Afternoon tea and evening snack available. Air conditioning and turn-down service in room. VCR, fax and copier on premises. Handicap access. Weddings, small meetings, family reunions and seminars hosted. Amusement parks and antiques nearby. TAC10.

Location: Thirty miles south of Atlanta airport.

Publicity: *Atlanta, Glamour, Southern Homes, Southern Living, Atlanta Journal Constitution.*

"The mystique and reality of The Veranda are that you're being elaborately entertained by friends in their private home."

Tate

B3

Tate House

PO Box 33
Tate, GA 30177-0033
(770)735-3122

Rates: Call for rates.
Circa: 1926.

Rooms: 13 rooms, 9 with FP. 4 suites. 9 cottages.

The white columned, Greek-Revival-style Tate House is locally known as the Pink Marble Mansion and was built by the president of the Georgia Marble company. The exterior of the National Register mansion is of Etowah marble and there are marble floors, baths and fireplaces. Marble walkways, statues and fountains are incorporated into the gardens of the 27-acre estate, as well. The cabins boast fireplaces and hot tubs, but you may prefer the historic main house's suites. Tennis courts and a pool are available, and there is a camping area.

Swimming on premises. 27 acres. Weddings, small meetings, family reunions and seminars hosted.

Serendipity Cottage

339 E Jefferson St
Thomasville, GA 31792
(912)226-8111
Fax:(912)226-2656

Rates: $75.
Payment: PC TC.
Innkeeper(s): Kathy & Ed Middleton.
Circa: 1906.

Rooms: 3 rooms with PB, 2 with FP.
Beds: QD.

A wealthy Northerner hand picked the lumber used to build this Four-Square house for his family. The home still maintains its original oak pocket doors and leaded-glass windows. The decor in guest rooms ranges from Victorian with antiques to rooms decorated with wicker furnishings. Honeymooners will find a bottle of champagne placed in the room. Breakfasts are hearty and made from scratch, including freshly baked breads and homemade jams. The home is located in a neighborhood of historic houses, and guests can take a walking or driving tour of the town's many historic sites.

Breakfast included in rates. Types of meals: continental breakfast, full breakfast and early coffee/tea. Air conditioning, turn-down service, ceiling fan, cable TV and VCR in room. Bicycles on premises. Antiques, fishing, parks, shopping, sporting events and theater nearby. TAC10.

"Thank you for the wonderful weekend at Serendipity Cottage. The house is absolutely stunning and the food delicious."

Melissa Kelly's Rubbed Rack of Lamb

Old Chatham Sheepherding Company
Old Chatham, N.Y.

- 1 ½ t sea salt or to taste
- 2 t dried oregano
- 1 t dried rosemary
- 1 T caraway seeds
- 1 t cumin seeds
- ½ t ground turmeric
- 2 T extra-virgin olive oil
- 1 T roasted garlic (about 2 large roasted cloves, mashed; ½ T garlic paste may be substituted)
- 2 T prepared harissa (North African hot sauce, sold at gourmet and Middle Eastern food shops) or Tomato paste seasoned with ground red pepper
- 2 racks of lamb, frenched

Combine the salt, oregano, rosemary, caraway, cumin and turmeric in a mortar, spice grinder or blender, and process until fairly well ground. Transfer to a small dish, and work in 1 ½ T of the olive oil plus the garlic and the harissa or tomato paste mixture. Rub the lamb with the mixture and set aside to marinate at room temperature, at least 3 hours.

Preheat oven to 450 degrees.

Shortly before serving, heat a heavy oven proof saute pan on top of the stove and brush with remaining olive oil. Add the lamb, and sear for a couple of minutes on each side. Turn the lamb so it sits bone side up and place the pan with the lamb in the oven for about 15 minutes, or until a meat thermometer registers 125 degrees for medium-rare. Carve each rack into four double chops.

Serves 4.

Hawaii

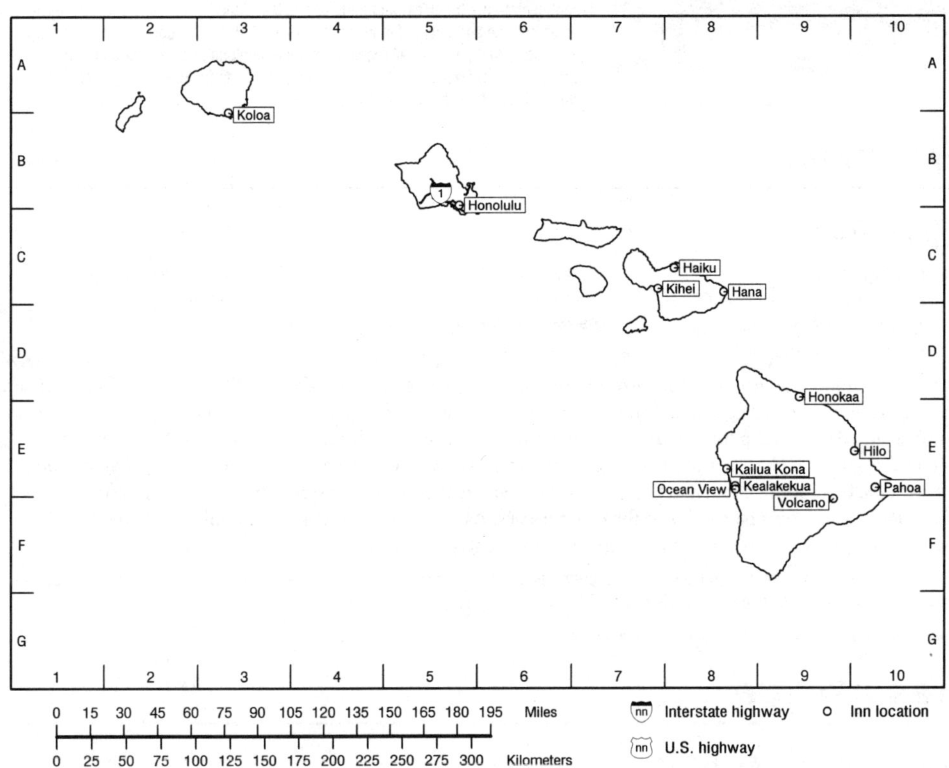

HAWAII (BIG ISLAND)

Hilo E10

Shipman House

131 Ka'iulani St
Hilo, HI 96720
(808)934-8002 (800)627-8447
Fax:(808)934-8002
E-mail: bighouse@bigisland.com

Rates: $130.
Payment: MC VISA AX TC.
Innkeeper(s): Barbara & Gary Andersen.
Circa: 1899.

Rooms: 5 rooms, 4 with PB. 1 cottage. 2 conference rooms.
Beds: QT.

Locals know Shipman House as "The Castle," no doubt because of both its size and grandeur. The manor, a mix of Italianate and Queen Anne styles, is listed on both the state and national historic registers. The home's former mistress, Mary Shipman, not only was the daughter of a Hawaiian chiefess, but a friend of Queen Lili'uokalani. Jack London and his wife once stayed here as a guest of the Shipmans. The grounds still feature many of the plants, palms and flowers nurtured by the Shipmans. Inside, the innkeeper has decorated the home with a mix of antiques and traditional furnishings. There is a cottage available as well, secluded by trees and foliage. A lavish, continental-plus breakfast buffet is served on the home's lanai offering such items as

homemade granola, local fruit (and there are 20 different varieties of fruit trees on the property), freshly baked breads, homemade passionfruit butter and pancakes, waffles or French toast. With advance notice, the innkeeper is happy to accommodate any special dietary needs.

Breakfast, afternoon tea and evening snack included in rates. Types of meals: continental-plus breakfast and early coffee/tea. Banquet service available. Turndown service and ceiling fan in room. Cable TV, VCR, fax, copier and library on premises. Weddings, small meetings, family reunions and seminars hosted. Limited French spoken. Antiques, fishing, parks, shopping, sporting events, theater and watersports nearby. TAC10.

Honokaa — *D9*

Hale Kukui

PO Box 5044
Honokaa, HI 96727-5044
(808)775-7130 (800)444-7130
Fax:(808)775-7130

Rates: $85-125.
Payment: PC TC.
Innkeeper(s): Bill & Sarah McCowatt.
Circa: 1992.

Rooms: 2 suites. 1 cottage.
Beds: Q.

From the four-acre grounds that surround this snug cottage, guests can take in a 20-mile view of spectacular Hawaii coastline. The grounds feature a stream and a variety of tropical foliage, including palms, plantains, bamboo and African tulip trees. During the early months of the year, humpback whales choose the waters below as a spot to frolic. Half of the cottage is devoted to a two-bedroom suite, which features a living room, kitchenette, bathroom and private lanai. The other section encompasses a studio unit, a compact version of the suite. These rooms can be combined for larger parties. As the nearest store is several miles away, the hosts provide a variety of continental fare for the first morning's stay.

Ceiling fan and VCR in room. Fax and swimming on premises. Handicap access. Weddings, small meetings, family reunions and seminars hosted. Fishing, parks and watersports nearby. TAC15.

Special Discounts: 5% off to members of environmental groups.

Kealakekua — *E8*

Kealakekua Bay B&B

PO Box 1412, 82-6002
Napoopoo Rd
Kealakekua, HI 96750-1412
(808)328-8150 (800)328-8150
Fax:(808)328-8150

Rates: $85-190.
Payment: PC TC.
Innkeeper(s): Michael Sisk.
Circa: 1991.

Rooms: 3 rooms, 2 with PB. 1 suite. 1 cottage.
Beds: KQ.

This mediterranean villa is situated on a tropical fruit farm with a magnificent view of the ocean. Hawaiian ambiance abounds in the main house where guests have their own private entry from a large lanai and in the Polynesian-style hale, which has a fully equipped kitchen, laundry, dining room and living room. Two of the inn's five acres are planted in avocados, mangoes, citrus, bananas, papayas and other fruit. Three beaches are within walking distance and a National Park, which contains exhibits of the old Hawaiian culture, is a five-minute drive away.

Breakfast included in rates. Types of meals: continental-plus breakfast and early coffee/tea. Ceiling fan in room. Cable TV, VCR, fax, copier and library on premises. Weddings and family reunions hosted. Limited French spoken. Fishing, parks, shopping, theater and watersports nearby. TAC10.

"What a pleasure to experience Aloha."

Merryman's B&B

PO Box 474
Kealakekua, HI 96750-0474
(808)323-2276 (800)545-4390
Fax:(808)323-3749
E-mail: merryman@ilhawaii.net

Rates: $75-95.
Payment: MC VISA DS PC TC.
Innkeeper(s): Penny & Don Merryman.
Circa: 1982.

Rooms: 4 rooms, 2 with PB.
Beds: QD.

A lush, garden setting is the site of this tropical bed & breakfast. Fresh flowers brighten guest rooms, several of which boast garden or ocean views. The Lanai Room has its own private deck overlooking the emerald lawn and gardens. In the morning, fresh papaya and pineapple accompany items such as Hawaiian sweet bread French toast topped with bananas grown on the property. Guests may borrow snorkeling gear and beach supplies. Merryman's is about 20 miles south of Keahole Airport and the village of Kailua-Kona is a short drive as well.

HI

Breakfast included in rates. Type of meal: full breakfast. Cable TV in room. Fax, copier and spa on premises. Family reunions and seminars hosted. Antiques, fishing, parks, shopping, theater and watersports nearby. TAC10.

"Your place is brilliantly designed and built. The gardens are absolutely beautiful and compliment the house wonderfully!"

Kailua-Kona

E8

Kailua Plantation House

75-5948 Alii Dr
Kailua-Kona, HI 96740-1324
(808)329-3727

Rates: $145-205.
Payment: MC VISA AX TC.
Innkeeper(s): Danielle Berger.
Circa: 1990.

Rooms: 5 rooms with PB. 1 conference room.
Beds: QT.

This oceanfront bed and breakfast sets on a promontory of black lava which descends into the Pacific ocean. The guest rooms boast private lanais, the perfect location to watch spinner dolphins, whales and the spectacular Hawaii sunsets. The rooms feature a tropical decor and each contains amenities such as refrigerators and in-room hot beverage equipment. The fresh fruit breakfast includes specialty muffins and features Kona coffee, of course. It is served in the bright, well-furnished living area with its high ceilings and exposed beams. The beach is about 100 yards away.

Breakfast included in rates. Types of meals: full breakfast and gourmet breakfast. Air conditioning, ceiling fan and cable TV in room. Spa and swimming on premises. Small meetings and family reunions hosted. French spoken. Fishing, parks, shopping, downhill skiing, theater and watersports nearby. TAC10.

Publicity: *Chicago Tribune, Vis A Vis, Conde Nast Traveler.*

Special Discounts: Internet rates $125-$190.

Kehena Beach

Kalani Oceanside Eco Resort

RR2 Box 4500
Kehena Beach, HI 96778
(808)965-7828 (800)800-6886
Fax:(808)965-9613
E-mail: kh@ilhawaii.net

Rates: $70-145. AP.
Payment: MC VISA AX DC PC TC.
Innkeeper(s): Richard, Dotty, Carol and Delton.
Circa: 1982.

Rooms: 37 rooms, 17 with PB. 9 cottages. 5 conference rooms.
Beds: KQDT.

Kalani's is more a resort than a bed & breakfast, but it is unique in that it's the only lodging accommodation within the state's largest conservation area. The magnificent surroundings and gracious hospitality are two of the many reasons why guests choose this spot for relaxation and rejuvenation. The 113 acres include a black sand beach, and guests can snorkel in tidepools, bicycle or hike along a coastal road, visit rainforests or enjoy one of nearly a dozen on-site activities. There are plenty of themed retreats scheduled throughout the year, including couples seminars, dance festivals, lesbian and gay retreats, a marine ecotourism workshop and many more. For a minimal extra charge, guests can include all three meals in their stay. The resort serves a variety of vegetarian specialties, utilizing the native bounty of tropical produce.

Breakfast, afternoon tea, dinner, evening snack and picnic lunch included in rates. Types of meals: continental-plus breakfast, full breakfast, gourmet breakfast and early coffee/tea. Lunch and gourmet lunch available. AP. Turn-down service and ceiling fan in room. VCR, fax, copier, spa, swimming, sauna, stables, bicycles, tennis, library and child care on premises. Handicap access. 113 acres. Weddings, small meetings, family reunions and seminars hosted. Hawaiian, German, French, Spanish and Japanese spoken. Antiques, fishing, parks, shopping, downhill skiing, cross-country skiing, sporting events, theater and watersports nearby. TAC10.

Special Discounts: Discounts for groups, also 10% off for stays of 7 or more nights for travel professionals and senior citizens.

"Being here has taught me a lot about Hawaii and the Aloha spirit."

Ocean View — E8

Bougainvillea B&B

PO Box 6045
Ocean View, HI 96737-6045
(808)929-7089 (800)688-1763
Fax:(808)929-7089
E-mail: peaceful@interpac.net

Rates: $59.
Payment: MC VISA AX DC CB DS PC TC.
Innkeeper(s): Martie Jean & Don Nitsche.
Circa: 1980.

Rooms: 4 rooms with PB.
Beds: Q.

Visitors to this Hawaiian Plantation-style home will be treated to the expertise of an innkeeper who has an extensive background in travel as the owner of an agency and as a teacher. All ground arrangements can be made through her. While using the inn as your base, you can enjoy the Hawaii of old as well as all the diversity the Big Island has to offer. The inn is located in a historic area near Volcano National Park.

Breakfast included in rates. Types of meals: continental-plus breakfast and gourmet breakfast. Ceiling fan and VCR in room. Fax, copier, spa, swimming and bicycles on premises. Family reunions hosted. Fishing, parks, theater and watersports nearby. TAC10.

Special Discounts: For one week or more; check when booking.

Volcano — F9

Chalet Kilauea - The Inn at Volcano

PO Box 998
Volcano, HI 96785-0998
(808)967-7786 (800)937-7786
Fax:(808)967-8660
E-mail: bchawaii@aol.com

Rates: $125-395.
Payment: MC VISA AX DS PC.
Innkeeper(s): Lisha & Brian Crawford.
Circa: 1945.

Rooms: 5 rooms with PB, 1 with FP. 2 suites. 6 cottages. 2 conference rooms.
Beds: KQT.

From elegant guest rooms to private cottages and vacation homes, this collection of properties offers something for everyone. The vacation homes are perfect for families. The inn itself offers five rooms, each with a special theme. The rooms sport names such as the Out of Africa, Treehouse or Oriental Jade. The Bridal and Treehouse suites include Jacuzzi tubs. Inn guests are treated to a two-course, gourmet breakfast served by candlelight.

Breakfast and afternoon tea included in rates. Type of meal: gourmet breakfast. Catering service available. Ceiling fan, cable TV and VCR in room. Fax, copier, spa and library on premises. Weddings, small meetings, family reunions and seminars hosted. French, Dutch and Spanish spoken. Antiques, fishing, parks, shopping, theater and watersports nearby. TAC10.

"Your attention to detail is what makes Chalet Kilauea special to all who stay here. Everything from the mints on the bed to the tea service set you apart from other establishments. Thank you for the enjoyable and relaxing atmosphere."

Hale Ohia Cottages

PO Box 758
Volcano, HI 96785-0758
(808)967-7986 (800)455-3803
Fax:(808)967-8610

Rates: $75-95.
Payment: MC VISA DC CB DS PC TC.
Innkeeper(s): Michael Tuttle.
Circa: 1931.

Rooms: 2 rooms with PB, 2 with FP. 1 suite. 3 cottages. 1 conference room.
Beds: QDT.

These country cottages, nestled in the quaint Volcano Village area, are surrounded by Hawaiian gardens and lush forest. You can stroll the serene property on paths made of lava rock and enjoy the many orchids and native plants. The gardens are some of the finest in Volcano. Volcano National Park is only one mile from the cottage.

Breakfast included in rates. Type of meal: continental breakfast. VCR, fax, copier and spa on premises. Handicap access. Weddings, small meetings, family reunions and seminars hosted. Antiques, fishing, parks, shopping, theater and watersports nearby. TAC10.

Publicity: *National Geographic Traveler, New York Times, Hawaii Bride, Pacific Connection.*

"The hospitality and accommodations couldn't have been better. A beautiful cottage in a peaceful, tropical garden."

Kilauea Lodge

PO Box 116
Volcano, HI 96785-0116
(808)967-7366
Fax:(808)967-7367
E-mail: k-lodge@aloha.net

Rates: $95-225.
Payment: MC VISA PC TC.
Innkeeper(s): Lorna & Albert Jeyte.
Circa: 1938.

Rooms: 11 rooms with PB, 7 with FP. 3 suites. 2 cottages.
Beds: KQT.

HI

Guests are pampered at this gorgeous tropical paradise, only a mile from the entrance to Volcanoes National Park. Fluffy towels, cozy, comfortable beds and rich decor create a feeling of warmth and romance in each of the guest rooms. Fresh flowers and original art add to the majesty of the lodge. The wonderful, gourmet meals are served in front of the lodge's historic Fireplace of Friendship, which is decked with all sorts of artifacts. The innkeepers offer truly memorable meals, praised by such publications as Bon Appetit. The inn has an interesting history, built as a YMCA, it later was used during World War II as offices and a military bivouac.

Breakfast included in rates. Type of meal: full breakfast. Dinner available. VCR and library on premises. Handicap access. 10 acres. Weddings and family reunions hosted. German spoken. Antiques, shopping and theater nearby.

Publicity: *National Geographic Traveler, Bon Appetit, Pacific Business News, Conde Nast.*

"Your rooms were outstanding both for cleanliness and decor. As to the dinner we had, it was superb, and as far as I'm concerned the best four-course dinner I have ever eaten."

The Lodge at Volcano

PO Box 998, Ama Uma U
Volcano, HI 96785
(808)967-7244 (800)736-7140
Fax:(808)967-8660
E-mail: bchawaii@aol.com

Rates: $85-125.
Payment: MC VISA AX DS PC TC.
Innkeeper(s): Brian & Lisha Crawford.
Circa: 1993.

Rooms: 6 rooms, 5 with PB, 1 with FP. 1 suite.
Beds: KQT.

Located in upcountry Volcano on 30 acres that include a native fern forest, this B&B is in a ranch-style house. The master guest room has a woodstove, double sunken tub with garden views and a king bed. A wraparound deck has a Jacuzzi for eight people. Breakfast features local fruits, cereals, muffins and Kona coffee.

Breakfast included in rates. Type of meal: continental breakfast. Catering service available. Cable TV and VCR in room. Spa and library on premises. 30 acres. Weddings, small meetings, family reunions and seminars hosted. Fishing, parks, shopping, theater and watersports nearby. TAC10.

Volcano B&B

PO Box 998
Volcano, HI 96785-0998
(808)967-7779 (800)736-7140
Fax:(800)577-1849
E-mail: bchawaii@aol.com

Rates: $45-65.
Innkeeper(s): Brian & Lisha Crawford.
Circa: 1912.
Rooms: 6 rooms.

This three-story historic home, one of Volcano's oldest, has been renovated into a relaxing bed & breakfast. The six, comfortable guest rooms are decorated in a casual, country style. Tropical fruit and sweet breads highlight the continental buffet. The inn is just five minutes from Volcano National Park.

KAUAI

Poipu Beach

Poipu B&B Inn & Gallery

2720 Hoonani Rd,
Poipu Beach
Kauai, HI 96756
(808)742-1146 (800)552-0095
Fax:(808)742-6843
E-mail: poipu@aloha.net

Rates: $80-350.
Payment: MC VISA AX DC CB DS PC TC.
Innkeeper(s): Dotti Cichon.
Circa: 1933.

Rooms: 9 rooms with PB. 2 suites. 3 cottages.
Beds: KQT.

This restored plantation house preserves the character of old Kauai, while providing for every modern convenience. The handcrafted wood interiors and old-fashioned lanais provide the perfect backdrop for the ornate white Victorian wicker, carousel horses, pine antiques and tropical color accents. Local art and handcrafts abound as one of the innkeepers is an avid collector and artist. The beach is one block away and the innkeepers can help you arrange every detail of your stay including helicopter tours, short-term health spa membership and dinner reservations.

Breakfast and afternoon tea included in rates. Types of meals: continental-plus breakfast and early coffee/tea. Ceiling fan, cable TV and VCR in room. Fax, copier and library on premises. Weddings, small meetings, family reunions and seminars hosted. French and German spoken. Fishing, parks, shopping and watersports nearby. TAC10.

Location: Poipu Beach.

Publicity: *Travel & Leisure, Smart Money, Country Inns, Travel-Holiday.*

Special Discounts: AAA, seniors; immediate space available 30%, within 48 hours 20%; seven nights or longer when prepaid 10%, 14 nights or longer when prepaid 15%.

"Thank you for sharing your home as well as yourself with us. I'll never forget this place, it's the best B&B we've stayed at."

Koloa **B3**

Victoria Place B&B

3459 Lawailoa Ln
Koloa, HI 96756-9646
(808)332-9300
Fax:(808)332-9465

Rates: $60-111.
Payment: PC TC.
Innkeeper(s): Edee Seymour.
Circa: 1970.

Rooms: 3 rooms with PB. 1 suite.
Beds: KQDT.

Three guest rooms open out to a pool area surrounded by hibiscus, gardenia and bougainvillea. The light and cheerful rooms are tiny but filled with native plants and flowers such as ginger and bird of paradise. For more spacious accommodations request the apartment. Innkeeper Edee Seymour loves to share her island secrets with guests and can direct you to hidden beaches off the tourist track. (She has received an award for being the friendliest person on the island.)

Breakfast included in rates. Type of meal: continental-plus breakfast. Cable TV, VCR, fax, copier, swimming and library on premises. Handicap access. Parks, shopping, theater and watersports nearby. TAC10.

MAUI

Haiku C8

Haikuleana B&B Inn, Plantation Style

555 Haiku Rd
(formerly 69 Haiku Rd)
Haiku, HI 96708-5884
(808)575-2890
Fax:(808)575-9177

Rates: $95-100.
Payment: PC TC.
Innkeeper(s): Ralph H. & Jeanne Elizabeth Blum.
Circa: 1850.

Rooms: 4 rooms with PB. 1 suite.
Beds: KQDT.

HI

A true plantation house, the Haikuleana sits in the midst of pineapple fields and Norfolk pine trees. With high ceilings and a tropical decor, the inn has all of the flavor of Hawaiian country life. The porch looks out over exotic gardens. Beaches and waterfalls are nearby.

Breakfast included in rates. Types of meals: full breakfast, gourmet breakfast and early coffee/tea. Picnic lunch available. Ceiling fan in room. Cable TV, VCR, fax, copier, spa, swimming, sauna and library on premises. Weddings, small meetings, family reunions and seminars hosted. Russian, French, Italian, German and Spanish spoken. Antiques, fishing, parks, shopping, theater and watersports nearby. TAC10.

Location: Twelve miles east of Kahului. One mile from Hana Highway and northshore beaches.

Publicity: *Honolulu Advertiser, Maui News, Los Angeles Times, Portland Oregonian.*

Special Discounts: 10% local Hawaiians, 10% on stays over two weeks.

"Great, great, extra great! Maui is paradise thanks to your daily guidance, directions and helpful hints."

Halfway to Hana House

PO Box 675
Haiku, HI 96708-0675
(808)572-1176
Fax:(808)572-3609

Rates: $65.
Innkeeper(s): Gail Pickholz.

Rooms: 1 room.
Beds: D.

This guest studio offers a covered, outdoor patio with a spectacular ocean view. In addition to the sleeping area and bathroom, there is a kitchenette. Decor is tropical, with modern furnishings, wicker and bright floral arrangements. White sand beaches, fresh water pools, horseback riding and hiking trails all are nearby. The host is a longtime Maui resident, and is happy to advise guests on the best of her beautiful island.

Breakfast included in rates. Shopping and watersports nearby.

Hana C8

Kaia Ranch & Co

PO Box 404
Hana, HI 96713-0404
(808)248-7725

Rates: $75.
Innkeeper(s): John & Jo Loyce Kaia.

Rooms: 1 room with PB. 2 suites.
Beds: QT.

This Hawaiian country farm consists of 27 acres that include a tropical botanical garden, fruit trees and flowers. If you stay in the Flower or Marine studio, you will enjoy your own kitchen and lanai. There are dogs and cats on the property. Also offered is a cedar chalet near Volcano National Park on the Big Island. The chalet features two, keyed rooms, each decorated in an individual theme, a shared kitchenette and a sitting room with a fireplace.

Type of meal: continental breakfast.

Kihei

C7

Aloha Pualani

15 Wailana Pl
Kihei, HI 96753-9054
(808)874-9265 (800)782-5264
Fax:(808)874-9127

Rates: $69-109. EP.
Payment: MC VISA AX PC TC.
Innkeeper(s): Marina & Keith Dinsmoor.
Circa: 1978.

Rooms: 5 suites.
Beds: QT.

Guests need only step out the door and take a short walk across the street to reach Maalaea Bay and one of Maui's longest stretches of sandy beach. The innkeepers have prepared their five suites with plenty of amenities, including kitchens and laundry facilities. From the private lanais of three suites, guests enjoy an ocean view. There is a swimming pool on premises, and it is here that the innkeepers host weekly pupu parties. The nearby bay is renowned for its windsurfing and a host of watersports, golf and tennis are close by, as well as restaurants and shops.

Type of meal: continental-plus breakfast. EP. Air conditioning, ceiling fan and cable TV in room. Fax and swimming on premises. Family reunions hosted. Russian spoken. Fishing, parks, shopping, sporting events, theater and watersports nearby. TAC10.

Lahaina

The Lahaina Inn

127 Lahainaluna Rd
Lahaina, HI 96761-1502
(808)661-0577 (800)669-3444
Fax:(808)667-9480

Rates: $89-129.
Payment: MC VISA AX DS.
Innkeeper(s): Ken Eisley.
Circa: 1938.

Rooms: 12 rooms with PB. 3 suites.
Beds: KQDT.

After a fire in 1963, the hotel was rebuilt in a frontier storefront style. Recently renovated by Rick Ralston, founder of Crazy Shirts, the inn has been appointed in furnishings chosen from Ralston's warehouse of 12,000 antiques. Each of the stunning guest rooms boast balconies with views of the harbor or mountains. The 12 rooms each feature individual decor with coordinating bed covers and linens, Oriental rugs, antique beds made from iron, brass or wood, and ceiling fans. An antique sideboard outside the guest rooms is stocked each morning with steaming Kona coffee, and continental breakfasts are served on the veranda. The inn's restaurant, David Paul's Lahaina Grill, is well recommended and features a variety of gourmet fare.

Breakfast included in rates. Type of meal: continental breakfast. Fax and copier on premises. Antiques, fishing and watersports nearby.

Publicity: *Tour & Travel News, Hawaii Magazine, Honolulu, Pacific Business News, Glamour.*

"Outstanding lodging and service. Ahhh! Paradise. Fantastic. Excellent. Exquisite."

OAHU

Honolulu

B5

The Manoa Valley Inn

2001 Vancouver Dr
Honolulu, HI 96822-2451
(808)947-6019 (800)535-0085
Fax:(808)946-6168
E-mail: marc@aloha.net

Rates: $99-190.
Payment: MC VISA AX DC TC.
Innkeeper(s): Herb Fukushima.
Circa: 1915.

Rooms: 8 rooms, 3 with PB. 1 suite. 1 cottage.
Beds: KQD.

This exquisite home offers the best of two worlds, a beautiful, country home surrounded by a tropical paradise. Each restored room features lavish decor with ornate beds, ceiling fans and period furniture. Little amenities such as the his and her robes create a romantic touch. Breakfasts with kona coffee, juices and fresh fruits are served, and after a day of sightseeing, evening wine and cheese are served. The inn's common rooms offer unique touches such as nickelodeon and antique Victrola. The Manoa Valley is a perfect location to enjoy Hawaii and is only blocks away from the University of Hawaii.

Breakfast and evening snack included in rates. Type of meal: continental breakfast. Ceiling fan in room. Cable TV, fax, copier and library on premises. Weddings, small meetings and seminars hosted. Fishing, parks, shopping, sporting events, theater and watersports nearby. TAC10.

Location: On the island of Oahu.

Publicity: *Travel & Leisure, LA Style.*

"A wonderful place!! Stepping back to a time of luxury!"

HI

Salmon Potato Cakes with Hollandaise Sauce

Shelburne Inn
Seaview, Wash.

½ yellow onion, chopped
1 ½ T butter
4 large potatoes, peeled, cooked, drained & mashed
2 ½ lbs Salmon filet, baked, skin & bones removed
⅓ cup heavy cream
3 T melted butter
¼ t mace
¼ t nutmeg
¾ t salt
½ t freshly ground black pepper
1 egg
2 T fresh dill, chopped
1 ½ cup fresh bread crumbs, seasoned with salt, freshly ground black pepper, paprika and cayenne pepper to taste
butter for re-heating

Sauté onion in butter until tender. Add to mashed potatoes

Next, add the salmon, heavy cream, melted butter, mace, nutmeg, salt, black pepper, egg and fresh dill. Mix these ingredients together.

Now prepare the bread crumb mixture.

Form 4-inch-wide patties by hand and dip each side into the seasoned bread crumbs and refrigerate until ready for use.

Melt a little butter over medium heat in a sauté pan and place patties in it until heated through, turning once.

Serve with a poached egg and the following Hollandaise Sauce.

Hollandaise Sauce:

6 egg yolks
2 T freshly squeezed lemon juice
½ lb. unsalted butter, melted
½ t salt
⅛ t cayenne pepper

Put the egg yolks and lemon juice in a 2-quart stainless steel bowl. Place over very hot, but not boiling water, making sure the bowl does not touch the water. Whip with a wire whisk until the yolks are the consistency of heavy cream.

Very slowly, whisk in the melted butter until the sauce thickens even more. As you add more butter (at first in small quantities) and the sauce thickens, you can begin to add it a little faster.

Finally, add the salt and cayenne pepper.

Idaho

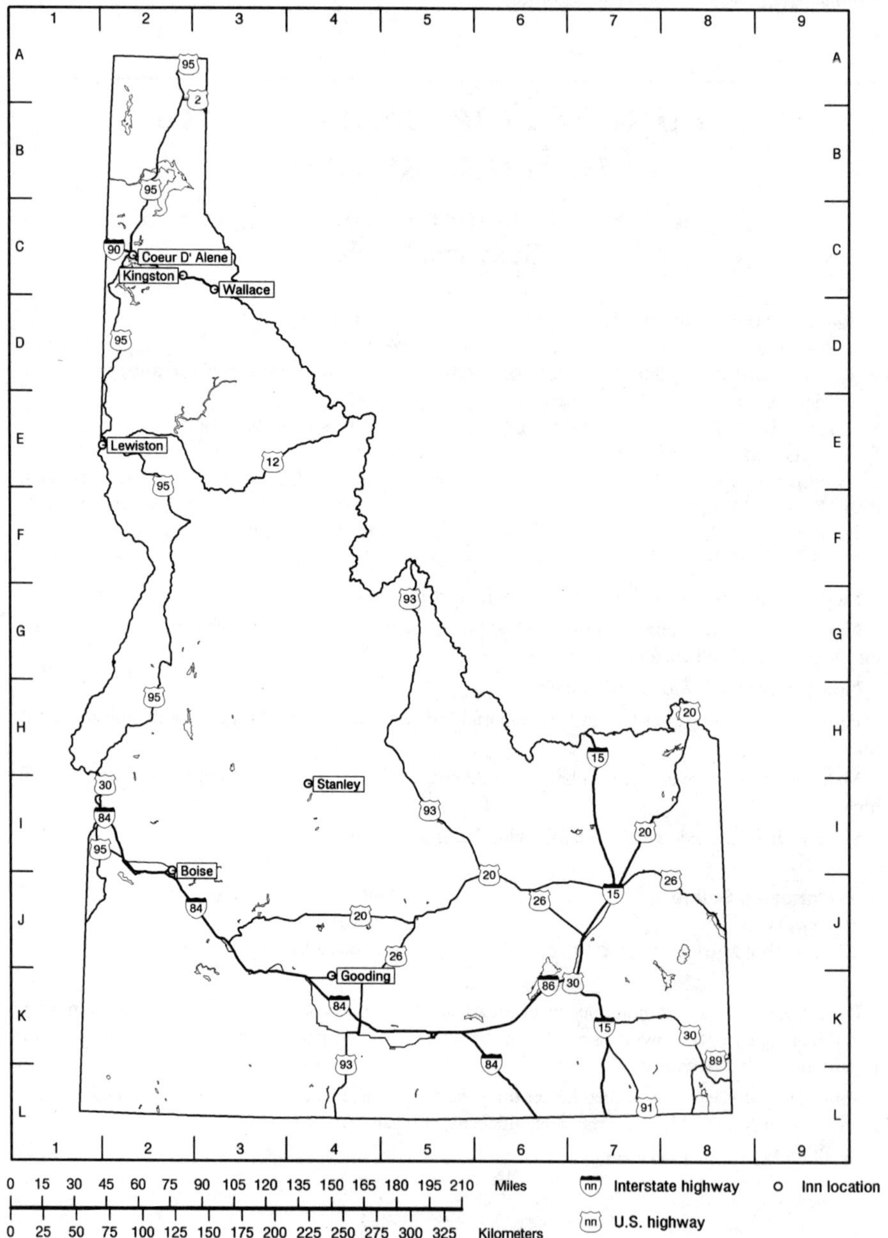
1
2
3
4
5
6
7
8
9
A
B
C
D
E
F
G
H
I
J
K
L
95
2
90
Coeur D' Alene
Kingston
Wallace
Lewiston
12
93
20
15
30
84
Stanley
Boise
26
86
Gooding
89
91
0 15 30 45 60 75 90 105 120 135 150 165 180 195 210 Miles
0 25 50 75 100 125 150 175 200 225 250 275 300 325 Kilometers
nn Interstate highway
nn U.S. highway
o Inn location

Boise
I2

Idaho Heritage Inn

109 W Idaho St
Boise, ID 83702-6122
(208)342-8066
Fax:(208)343-2325

Rates: $60-95.
Payment: MC VISA AX DS PC TC.
Innkeeper(s): Phyllis Lupher.
Circa: 1904.

Rooms: 6 rooms with PB. 2 suites. 1 cottage.
Beds: Q.

This Colonial Revival home, set back on a tree-lined street near downtown, was once the home of Senator Frank Church and is in the National Register. Because of its location in the historic Warm Springs district, geothermal water is used for heating and bathing. Period furnishings and wall coverings are found throughout. Bicycles are available for enjoying the nearby greenbelt which winds along the Boise River.

ID

Breakfast included in rates. Types of meals: full breakfast, gourmet breakfast and early coffee/tea. Air conditioning and cable TV in room. VCR, fax and bicycles on premises. Antiques, fishing, parks, shopping, downhill skiing, cross-country skiing and watersports nearby. TAC10.

Location: Six blocks from downtown.

Publicity: *The Idaho Statesman, The American West, The Idaho Business Review.*

"Thanks so much for the hospitality and warmth."

Coeur d'Alene
C2

Baragar House B&B

316 Military Dr
Coeur d'Alene, ID 83814
(208)664-9125 (800)615-8422
Fax:(208)765-2427
E-mail: baragar@dmi.net

Rates: $95-125.
Payment: MC VISA AX DS PC TC.
Innkeeper(s): Bernie & Carolyn Baragar.
Circa: 1926.

Rooms: 3 rooms, 1 with PB.
Beds: Q.

This Craftsman-style bungalow was built by a lumber baron. Each of the rooms is casually and individually decorated. The spacious Honeymoon Suite is especially appealing with its oversized bathroom offering a clawfoot tub, bay window and Victorian decor. The Country Cabin room is comfortable and rustic, with a wilderness scene decorating one of the walls. Flowery wallcoverings brighten the Garden Room. The innkeeper takes pride in preparing a creative morning meal, and is happy to accommodate special dietary needs.

Breakfast and evening snack included in rates. Types of meals: full breakfast, gourmet breakfast and early coffee/tea. Air conditioning, ceiling fan, cable TV and VCR in room. Fax, spa, sauna and library on premises. Amusement parks, antiques, fishing, parks, shopping, downhill skiing, cross-country skiing, sporting events, theater and watersports nearby. TAC10.

"Thank you for the hospitality and most exquisite honeymoon setting."

Berry Patch Inn B&B

N 1150 Four Winds Rd
Coeur d'Alene, ID 83814
(208)765-4994
Fax:(208)664-0374

Rates: $125-150.
Payment: MC VISA PC TC.
Innkeeper(s): Ann M. Caggiano.
Circa: 1976.

Rooms: 3 rooms with PB.
Beds: KQ.

Two acres of pines provide the secluded setting at this chalet bed & breakfast. Rooms have views of woods or Mt. Spokane. Guests enjoy healthy, but hearty breakfasts in the dining room or deck, which affords a

view of mountains and the valley. Spokane is about an hour away, and the home is less than two miles from the headwaters of the Spokane River and Lake Coeur d'Alene.

Breakfast and afternoon tea included in rates. Type of meal: gourmet breakfast. Air conditioning in room. VCR, fax, copier and library on premises. Small meetings hosted. Amusement parks, antiques, fishing, parks, shopping, downhill skiing, cross-country skiing, theater and watersports nearby. TAC10.

"Perfect place to stay while touring America's countryside," Country Magazine.

Country Ranch

1495 S Greenferry Rd
Coeur d'Alene, ID 83814
(208)664-1189
Fax:(208)664-1189

Rates: $85-95.
Payment: MC VISA PC TC.
Innkeeper(s): Ann & Harry Holmberg.

Rooms: 2 suites.
Beds: Q.

Surrounded by almost 30 acres of woods and rolling hills, this serene retreat is an ideal spot to escape from life's hectic pace. Explore the hillside on a nature walk and guests are sure to find a variety of birds and other wildlife, perhaps deer and elk. Each of the guest suites is decorated with a queen-size poster bed. The Valley View Suite includes a sitting room with a mini-library. The Jacuzzi tub in the Mountain View Suite overlooks the ranch's orchard. The scent of freshly baked breads and gourmet coffee entices guests to the glass-enclosed morning room or formal dining room for a full, gourmet breakfast. In the evenings, hors d'oeuvres are served. There is a sports court on the premises. Spokane is 30 minutes away.

Breakfast included in rates. Types of meals: gourmet breakfast and early coffee/tea. Evening snack available. Air conditioning in room. VCR, fax and library on premises. 29 acres. Amusement parks, antiques, fishing, parks, shopping, downhill skiing, cross-country skiing, theater and watersports nearby.

Gooding — *K4*

Gooding Hotel B&B

112 Main St
Gooding, ID 83330-1102
(208)934-4374

Rates: $35-55. AP.
Payment: MC VISA AX DS PC TC.
Innkeeper(s): Lauren & Elsa Freeman.
Circa: 1906.

Rooms: 8 rooms, 1 with PB.
Beds: QDT.

Travelers will appreciate the handy location of this Colonial Revival inn, between Boise and Twin Falls, just off Interstate 84. The historic hotel is listed in the National Register. Guests may avail themselves of the inn's two sitting rooms. Many attractions are found within a one-hour drive of the inn, including Malad Gorge State Park, Shoshone Falls, Shoshone Ice Caves, Snake River Canyon and Sun Valley.

Breakfast included in rates. Types of meals: continental breakfast, continental-plus breakfast, full breakfast, gourmet breakfast and early coffee/tea. Room service available. AP. Air conditioning and ceiling fan in room. Cable TV, copier and bicycles on premises. Small meetings hosted. Antiques, fishing, parks, shopping, downhill skiing and cross-country skiing nearby. TAC10.

Pets Allowed: $25 deposit on pets.

Kingston C2

Kingston 5 Ranch B&B

42297 Silver Valley Rd
Kingston, ID 83839-0130
(208)682-4862 (800)443-3505
Fax:(208)682-4862

Rates: $99-125.
Payment: MC VISA PC TC.
Innkeeper(s): Walter & Pat Gentry.
Circa: 1930.

Rooms: 2 rooms with PB, 1 with FP. 1 suite.
Beds: Q.

With the Coeur d'Alene Mountains as its backdrop, this picturesque country farmhouse is a wonderful place to escape and relax. Lazy mornings begin as the scent of freshly ground coffee wafts through the home. Then a hearty country breakfast is served with cured ham, bacon, Belgian waffles topped with fresh fruit, omelets and plenty of other treats. Many of the ingredients are grown on the farm. The original owners built a garage on the property first and lived there until the Pennsylvania Dutch barn and the farmhouse were built. Innkeepers Walt and Pat Gentry have refurbished the home completely, filling the guest rooms with lace, down comforters and charming furnishings. Rooms also offer romantic amenities such as mountain views, a four-poster bed, private veranda, jetted tub or a private deck with an outdoor hot tub.

Breakfast included in rates. Types of meals: full breakfast and early coffee/tea. Evening snack available. Air conditioning, turn-down service, ceiling fan and cable TV in room. VCR, fax, copier, spa, stables and bicycles on premises. Small meetings hosted. Amusement parks, antiques, fishing, parks, shopping, downhill skiing, cross-country skiing, theater and watersports nearby. TAC10.

Special Discounts: Multiple night discount: $99 per night for more than two nights.

"The food was fabulous and so much!"

Lewiston E2

Shiloh Rose B&B

3414 Selway Dr
Lewiston, ID 83501-9671
(208)743-2482

Rates: $75.
Payment: MC VISA PC.
Innkeeper(s): Dorthy A. Mader.
Circa: 1980.

Rooms: 1 room.
Beds: Q.

From the deck of this contemporary ranch home, guests enjoy views of the Lewis & Clark Valley. The decor is country Victorian with fresh roses placed about the home in season. The innkeeper prepares an abundant breakfast with seasonal fruits, freshly baked breads, breakfast meats, eggs, waffles and the like. The area is full of activities, among the more interesting is a day-long jet boat trip through the Northwest's deepest gorge, Hells Canyon.

Breakfast and afternoon tea included in rates. Type of meal: full breakfast. Air conditioning in room. Cable TV, VCR and library on premises. Small meetings hosted. Antiques, fishing, parks, shopping, downhill skiing, cross-country skiing, sporting events, theater and watersports nearby. TAC10.

"The only thing more outstanding than the delicious breakfasts was your hospitality."

Stanley I4

Idaho Rocky Mountain Ranch

HC 64 Box 9934
Stanley, ID 83278-9602
(208)774-3544
Fax:(208)774-3477

Rates: $130-224. MAP.
Payment: MC VISA DS PC TC.
Innkeeper(s): Bill & Jeana Leavell.
Circa: 1930.

Rooms: 21 rooms with PB, 17 with FP. 17 cottages.
Beds: QT.

This large cattle ranch is situated at the 6,600-foot level in the Sawtooth Valley. A rustic lodge dining room overlooks the Salmon River, a mile away, to the spectacular ragged ridges of the Sawtooth Mountains. Near the edge of the river, the inn has a pool constructed from a natural hot springs. Rustic accommoda-

tions in lodgepole pine cabins feature handmade log furniture and fieldstone fireplaces. The lodge and cabins recently were listed in the National Register of Historic Places.

Breakfast and dinner included in rates. Type of meal: full breakfast. Picnic lunch available. MAP. Fax, copier, computer, swimming, stables, bicycles and library on premises. 1000 acres. Spanish spoken. Fishing, parks, downhill skiing, cross-country skiing and watersports nearby.

Location: Fifty miles north of Sun Valley.

Publicity: *Washington Post.*

"We had such a great time! The kids loved it! Can't you adopt us so we can stay longer?"

Wallace C3

The Beale House

107 Cedar St
Wallace, ID 83873-2115
(208)752-7151

Rates: $75-125.
Payment: PC TC.
Innkeeper(s): Jim & Linda See.
Circa: 1904.

Rooms: 5 rooms, 1 with PB, 1 with FP.
Beds: DT.

This attractive, three-story Colonial Revival home is listed in the National Register, as is the town of Wallace. Original parquet wood floor, antiques and memorabilia combine to lend an authentic aura of the past. Each of the five guest rooms offers a unique feature, such as a fireplace, balcony or wall of windows. The innkeepers are well versed in their home's history and guests are welcome to look over a photographic record of the house and its former owners. A backyard hot tub provides views of the mountains and creek. Recreational activities abound in the vicinity, famous for its silver mines.

Breakfast included in rates. Types of meals: continental breakfast, full breakfast and early coffee/tea. Turn-down service in room. Cable TV, VCR, spa and library on premises. Weddings hosted. Antiques, fishing, parks, shopping, downhill skiing, cross-country skiing, theater and watersports nearby. TAC10.

Publicity: *Shoshone News Press, Spokesman Review, Silver Valley Voice.*

"Thank you for the fine hospitality."

Wild Mushroom and Shallot Muffins

The Inn at Bethlehem
Bethlehem, Indiana

- 2 cups unbleached all-purpose flour
- 1 T sugar
- 1 T baking powder
- ¾ t salt
- ¼ t freshly ground black pepper
- ⅓ cup butter, melted
- 1 egg, beaten
- 1 cup whole milk
- 1½ cups chopped fresh mushrooms (morel, shiitake or portobella)
- 1 large or 2 small shallots, minced

Sift first five ingredients. Stir in butter, egg and milk until just moistened. Fold in mushrooms and shallots.

Coat a muffin tin with cooking spray and pour in batter. Bake at 400 degrees for 20 minutes.

Yields 12 muffins.

Illinois

IL

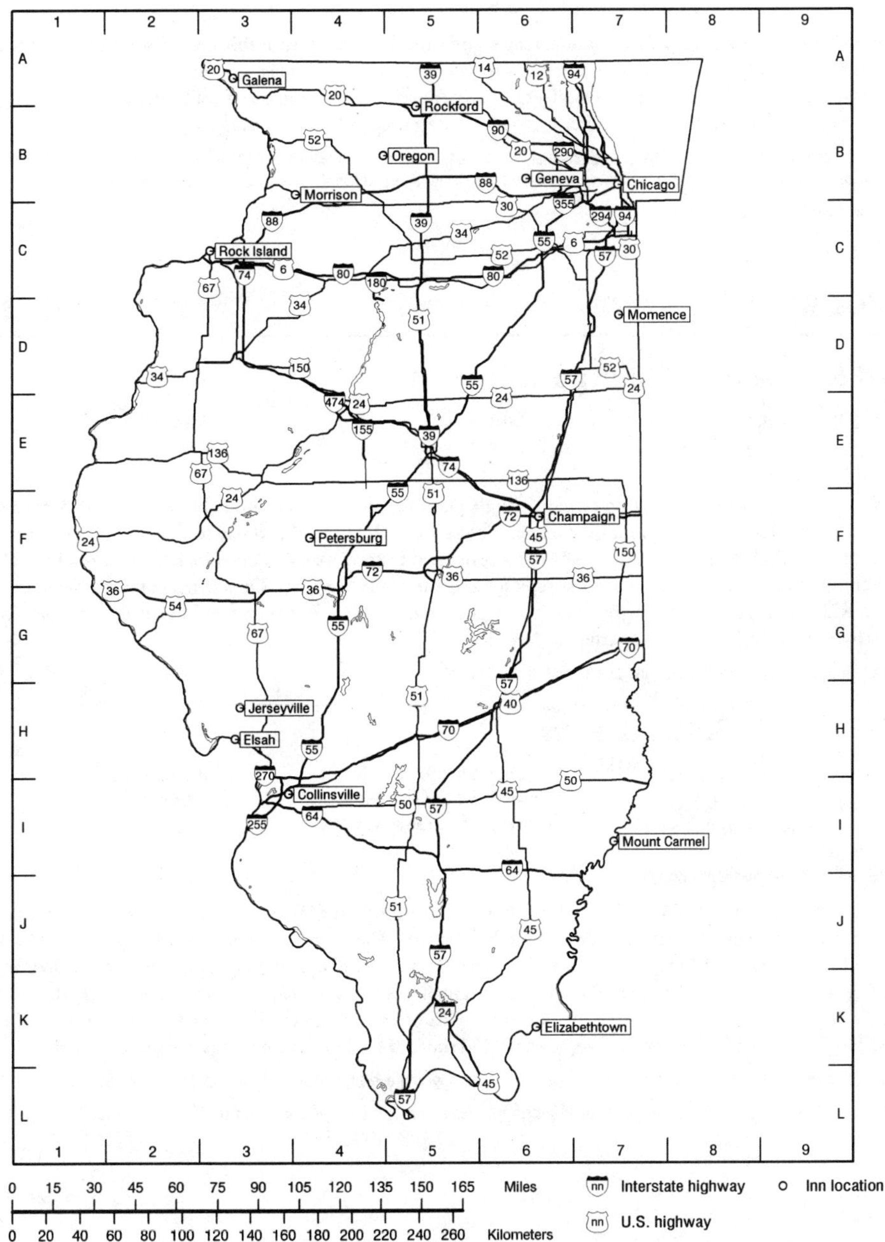

Galena
Rockford
Oregon
Geneva
Chicago
Morrison
Rock Island
Momence
Champaign
Petersburg
Jerseyville
Elsah
Collinsville
Mount Carmel
Elizabethtown
Miles
Kilometers
Interstate highway
U.S. highway
Inn location

Champaign

F6

The Golds B&B

2065 County Road 525 E
Champaign, IL 61821-9521
(217)586-4345

Rates: $45-50.
Payment: PC TC.
Innkeeper(s): Rita & Bob Gold.
Circa: 1874.

Rooms: 3 rooms, 1 with PB.
Beds: QDT.

Visitors to the University of Illinois area may enjoy a restful experience at this inn, west of town in a peaceful farmhouse setting. Antique country furniture collected by the innkeepers over the past 25 years is showcased in the inn and is beautifully offset by early American stenciling on its walls. An apple tree and garden are on the grounds, and seasonal items are sometimes used as breakfast fare.

Breakfast included in rates. Types of meals: continental-plus breakfast and early coffee/tea. Air conditioning in room. Cable TV and VCR on premises. Antiques, fishing, parks, shopping, cross-country skiing, sporting events, theater and watersports nearby. TAC10.

Location: near University of Illinois.

Publicity: *News Gazette.*

Chicago

B7

Bed & Breakfast/Chicago

PO Box 14088
Chicago, IL 60614-0088
(312)951-0085

Rates: $50-80.
Payment: MC VISA AX.

Rooms: 75 rooms.
Beds: QDT.

The 70 listings of this reservation service include guest rooms in private family homes and self-contained apartments located throughout the Greater Chicago area. If you'd like to stay in the Gold Coast, just north of Magnificent Mile, a popular choice is a converted historic mansion one block from Lake Shore Drive. It offers apartments with wood-burning fireplaces and antique furnishings. Or you may prefer a high-rise condo with a panoramic city view or a handsome guest room with a four-poster bed in a charming Old Town house where the host is a local reporter.

Types of meals: continental breakfast and continental-plus breakfast.

Wooded Isle Suites & Apts

5750 S Stony Island Ave
Chicago, IL 60637-2051
(312)288-6305 (800)290-6844
Fax:(312)288-6305
E-mail: chavenswi@aol.com

Rates: $69-102.
Payment: MC VISA AX DS PC.
Innkeeper(s): Charlie Havens & Sara Pitcher.
Circa: 1914.

Rooms: 9 suites.
Beds: Q.

Although neither bed & breakfast nor country inn, this collection of two- and three-room apartment suites serve as a convenient, relaxing alternative to hotel travel. The suites are located in Chicago's Hyde Park area and are convenient to the many museums, shops, restaurants and attractions in the downtown area and Lake Michigan. The early 20th-century complex originally served as housing for employees of the Illinois Central Railroad Hospital. Each suite includes a long list of practical amenities, such as a kitchen stocked with pots, pans, dishes, coffee makers, coffee, tea bags and more. The decor is a pleasant, contemporary style.

Air conditioning, ceiling fan and cable TV in room. Fishing, parks, sporting events, theater and watersports nearby. TAC10.

"We have all had very positive experiences at Wooded Isle. Everyone has been pleasant and tuned in to our joy."

Collinsville

I3

Maggie's B&B

2102 N Keebler Ave
Collinsville, IL 62234-4713
(618)344-8283

Rates: $37-80.
Payment: PC TC.
Innkeeper(s): Maggie Leyda.
Circa: 1900.

Rooms: 5 rooms, 3 with PB, 2 with FP. 1 suite. 1 conference room.
Beds: QDT.

A rustic two-acre wooded area surrounds this friendly Victorian inn, once a boarding house. Rooms with 14-foot ceilings are furnished with exquisite antiques and art objects collected on worldwide travels. Downtown St. Louis, the Gateway Arch and the Mississippi riverfront are just 10 minutes away.

Breakfast included in rates. Types of meals: full breakfast and early coffee/tea. Air conditioning, turn-down service, ceiling fan, cable TV and VCR in room. Spa and library on premises. Handicap access. Weddings, small meetings and family reunions hosted. Amusement parks, antiques, fishing, parks, shopping, sporting events and theater nearby.

Publicity: *Collinsville Herald Journal, Innsider, Belleville News, Democrat, Saint Louis Homes & Gardens.*

"We enjoyed a delightful stay. You've thought of everything. What fun!"

IL

Elizabethtown

K6

River Rose Inn B&B

1 Main St PO Box 78
Elizabethtown, IL 62931
(618)287-8811

Rates: $53-90.
Payment: MC VISA PC TC.
Innkeeper(s): Don & Elisabeth Phillips.
Circa: 1914.

Rooms: 5 rooms with PB, 1 with FP. 1 cottage.
Beds: Q.

Large, shade trees veil the front of this Greek Gothic home, nestled along the banks of the Ohio River. From the grand front entrance, guests look out to polished woodwork and a staircase leading to shelves of books. Rooms are cheerful and nostalgic, decorated with antiques. Each guest room offers something special. One has a four-poster bed, another offers a fireplace. The Scarlet Room has its own balcony, and the Rose Room has a private patio. The Magnolia Cottage is ideal for honeymooners and includes a whirlpool tub for two, fireplace and a deck that overlooks the river. Breakfasts are served either in the dining room or in the glass atrium room, where guests can enjoy the water views.

Breakfast included in rates. Types of meals: gourmet breakfast and early coffee/tea. Air conditioning, ceiling fan and cable TV in room. VCR, swimming and library on premises. English, French and German spoken. Antiques, fishing, parks, shopping and watersports nearby.

Special Discounts: February: first night full price second night half price with champagne and chocolates.

Elsah

H3

Green Tree Inn

15 Mill St
Elsah, IL 62028
(618)374-2821 (800)701-8003

Rates: $69-105.
Payment: MC VISA PC.
Innkeeper(s): Michael Pitchford.
Circa: 1985.

Rooms: 10 rooms with PB. 1 conference room.
Beds: QDT.

Located in a New England-style village, this red clapboard inn is just a short walk from the Mississippi River. Opening onto a large front porch, the first floor provides an 1850s country store with Victorian linens, lace, hand-blown glass, dried flowers, herbs and teas for sale. Each room is decorated in a period style and features a private porch. Monthly seminars offer insight into 19th-century perennial and herb gardening. Bicycles are provided so guests may enjoy the 16-mile Vadalabene bike trail that winds along the river and offers views of sailboats and the Delta Queen, and in winter, an occasional bald eagle.

Breakfast included in rates. Types of meals: full breakfast and early coffee/tea. Air conditioning in room. Bicycles and library on premises. Handicap access. Weddings, small meetings, family reunions and seminars hosted. Amusement parks, antiques, fishing, parks, shopping, sporting events, theater and watersports nearby.

Publicity: *Midwest Living, Chicago Tribune, Good Morning America.*

Special Discounts: Call for specials.

"Thank you for the wonderful stay at your inn."

Galena

A3

Captain Gear Guest House

1000 S Bench St,
PO Box 1040
Galena, IL 61036-1040
(815)777-0222 (800)794-5656
Fax:(815)777-3210

Rates: $135-175.
Payment: MC VISA DS PC.
Innkeeper(s): Susan Pettey.
Circa: 1855.

Rooms: 3 rooms with PB, 3 with FP. 1 suite.
Beds: KQ.

Lead miner Captain Hezekiah H. Gear chose this picturesque spot overlooking the Galena River Valley to build his gracious estate. The lush, four-acre grounds create a secluded, country atmosphere paralleled by the romantic, country guest rooms, each of which contains a fireplace and a view of the grounds. One room also includes a whirlpool tub. The home has been carefully decorated with carved rosewood and mahogany furnishings. The formal breakfasts at this National Register home are served on silver and china in the dining room.

Breakfast included in rates. Type of meal: full breakfast. Air conditioning and VCR in room. Antiques, parks, shopping, downhill skiing, cross-country skiing, theater and watersports nearby.

Cottage at Amber Creek

PO Box 5
Galena, IL 61036-0005
(815)777-9320 (800)781-9530
Fax:(815)777-9476

Rates: $75-175.
Payment: MC VISA AX DC DS PC TC.
Innkeeper(s): Kate Freeman.
Circa: 1840.

Rooms: 1 room with PB.
Beds: Q.

This horse farm is set on 300 acres of woods, meadows and hilly countryside. There is a secluded cottage tucked in the woods. The cottage once served as the summer kitchen for the farm's main house, which was built in the 1840s. The cozy haven includes a small kitchen, fireplace, living room, bedroom and bathroom with a whirlpool tub. The antique four-poster bed is covered with down comforters and fluffy pillows. Firewood, towels and linens all are provided. For an extra charge, the hosts will provide flowers or champagne.

Breakfast included in rates. Type of meal: continental breakfast. Air conditioning in room. 300 acres. Antiques, fishing, parks, shopping, downhill skiing, cross-country skiing and theater nearby. TAC15.

Pets Allowed: Advance notice and deposit required.

Special Discounts: Off-season discounts.

Hellman Guest House

318 Hill St
Galena, IL 61036-1836
(815)777-3638

Rates: $89-149.
Payment: MC VISA DS PC.
Innkeeper(s): Merilyn Tommaro.
Circa: 1895.

Rooms: 4 rooms with PB.
Beds: Q.

A corner tower and an observatory turret rise above the gabled roof line of this Queen Anne house built of Galena brick. The house was constructed from designs drawn by Schoppel of New York. An antique telescope in the parlor is a favorite of guests who wish to view the town. Stained glass, pocket doors and antique

furnishings add to the inn's charms. The Tower Room with its brass bed and village views is recommended.

Breakfast included in rates. Types of meals: full breakfast and early coffee/tea. Air conditioning in room. Library on premises. Small meetings and family reunions hosted. Amusement parks, antiques, parks, shopping, downhill skiing, cross-country skiing, theater and watersports nearby.

Publicity: *Innsider, Midwest Living, Chicago Tribune.*

"We found your home a treasure, the breakfast delicious and your company superb."

Park Avenue Guest House

208 Park Ave
Galena, IL 61036-2306
(815)777-1075

Rates: $85-105.
Payment: MC VISA AX DS PC TC.
Innkeeper(s): Sharon & John Fallbacher.
Circa: 1893.

Rooms: 4 rooms with PB, 3 with FP. 1 suite.
Beds: QT.

IL

A short walk from Grant Park sits this attractive Queen Anne Victorian with turret and wraparound porch. Gardens and a gazebo add to this peaceful neighborhood charm, as does the original woodwork throughout. The Helen Room features a gas fireplace, TV, tub and shower, while Miriam Room's brass bed highlights a cheerful floral decor and a fireplace. The Anna Suite also has a fireplace and boasts a comfortable sitting room in the inn's turret area and the Lucille Room is tastefully furnished in mauve, gray and white tones. The holiday decorations, including eight Christmas trees, are not to be missed.

Evening snack included in rates. Types of meals: continental-plus breakfast and early coffee/tea. Air conditioning, ceiling fan and cable TV in room. VCR on premises. Weddings, small meetings and family reunions hosted. Antiques, fishing, shopping, downhill skiing, cross-country skiing and theater nearby.

Publicity: *Country Inns.*

Special Discounts: $10 midweek only.

Geneva

B6

The Herrington

15 S River Ln
Geneva, IL 60134-2251
(630)208-7433
Fax:(630)208-8930

Rates: $135-215. EP.
Payment: MC VISA AX DS.

Rooms: 40 rooms with PB, 40 with FP. 1 conference room.
Beds: KD.

An enclosed gazebo rests near the banks of the Fox River just a few hundred yards from this inn, an eclectic mix of architecture, which once served as the Geneva Rock Cremery. The interior is charming, elegant and just a bit rustic, with stone floors and natural woodwork. Each of the guest rooms at this four-diamond inn is well appointed and includes a fireplace, whirlpool tub, minibar and a terrace looking out to the river. The on-premise restaurant, Atwater's, serves a mouthwatering assortment of gourmet specialties. Guests might start with jumbo sea scallops with toasted saffron pine nut polenta or perhaps a bleu cheese and escargot purse with grilled portabella mushrooms. From there an assortment of salads are available, and with main dish choices such as oven-roasted breast of Moullard, goat cheese and spinach stuffed salmon or a veal chop, there's something sure to please everyone.

Breakfast and evening snack included in rates. Types of meals: continental breakfast, continental-plus breakfast, full breakfast and early coffee/tea. Afternoon tea, dinner, lunch, banquet service, catering service, catered breakfast and room service available. Restaurant on premises. EP. Air conditioning and turn-down service in room. Fax, copier and spa on premises. Handicap access. Weddings, small meetings, family reunions and seminars hosted. Antiques, fishing, parks, shopping, cross-country skiing, sporting events and theater nearby. TAC10.

Jerseyville

H3

The Homeridge B&B

1470 N State St
Jerseyville, IL 62052-1127
(618)498-3442

Rates: $65-75.
Payment: MC VISA AX PC TC.
Innkeeper(s): Sue & Howard Landon.
Circa: 1867.

Rooms: 4 rooms with PB.
Beds: KDT.

This red brick Italianate Victorian features ornate white trim, a stately front veranda and a cupola where guests often take in views of sunsets and the surrounding 18 acres. The home was constructed by Cornelius Fisher, just after the Civil War. In 1891, it was purchased by Senator Theodore Chapman and remained in his family until the 1960s. The innkeepers have filled the 14-room manor with traditional and Victorian furnishings, enhancing the high ceilings and ornate woodwork typical of the era. Guests are invited to take a relaxing dip in the inn's swimming pool or relax with a refreshment on the veranda.

Breakfast included in rates. Types of meals: full breakfast and early coffee/tea. Afternoon tea available. Air conditioning and ceiling fan in room. Cable TV, VCR, copier, swimming, bicycles and library on premises. 20 acres. Weddings, small meetings, family reunions and seminars hosted. Amusement parks, antiques, fishing, parks, shopping, cross-country skiing, sporting events, theater and watersports nearby.

"A most beautiful, entertaining, snow-filled few days."

Momence

D7

Wikstrom Manor B&B

304 W 2nd St
Momence, IL 60954-1403
(815)472-3156

Rates: $55-65.
Payment: PC TC.
Innkeeper(s): Tony & Evalyn Surprenant.
Circa: 1892.

Rooms: 3 rooms, 1 with PB, 1 with FP. 1 suite.
Beds: KQD.

This Eastlake-style home was built to lodge Swedish dignitaries who came to the area to visit the 1892 World's Fair in Chicago. From the 1920s to 1964, the home served as a boarding school. Three years later, the innkeepers bought the home, eventually turning it into a bed & breakfast. Guests choose from three rooms, one a private suite with a sitting area and a fireplace.

Breakfast included in rates. Types of meals: continental breakfast, continental-plus breakfast, full breakfast and early coffee/tea. Air conditioning, turn-down service, ceiling fan, cable TV and VCR in room. Library on premises. Antiques, fishing, parks, shopping, sporting events, theater and watersports nearby.

Morrison

B4

Hillendale B&B

600 W Lincolnway
Morrison, IL 61270-2058
(815)772-3454 (800)349-7702
Fax:(815)772-7023

Rates: $55-150.
Payment: MC VISA AX DC DS TC.
Innkeeper(s): Barb & Mike Winandy.
Circa: 1891.

Rooms: 10 rooms with PB.
Beds: KQ.

Guests at Hillendale don't simply spend the night in the quaint town of Morrison, Ill., they spend the night in France, Italy, Hawaii or Africa. Each of the guests rooms in this Tudor manor reflects a different theme from around the world. Travelers and innkeepers Barb and Mike Winandy cleverly decorated each of the guest quarters. The Kimarrin room reflects Mayan culture with photographs of antiquities. The Outback, a private cottage, boasts a fireplace and whirlpool spa along with its Australian decor. The Failte room includes a rococo Victorian antique highback bed,

fireplace and Irish-themed decor. And these are just a few of the possibilities. Barb creates wonderful breakfasts full of muffins, breads and special entrees. Stroll the two-acre grounds and you'll encounter a three-tier water pond, which sits in front of a teahouse, built by the original owner after a trip to Japan. One of the tiers houses Japanese Koi and another a water garden. The area has riverboat gambling and plenty of outdoor activities. Carriage, hay and sleigh rides can be arranged.

Breakfast included in rates. Type of meal: full breakfast. Air conditioning, ceiling fan, cable TV and VCR in room. Fax and copier on premises. Small meetings hosted. Antiques, fishing, parks, cross-country skiing and theater nearby.

Publicity: *New York Times, Sterling Gazette, Whiteside News Sentinel, Midwest Living.*

"We've never been any place else that made us feel so catered to and comfortable. Thank you for allowing us to stay in your beautiful home. We feel very privileged."

Mount Carmel I7

IL

The Poor Farm B&B

Poor Farm Rd
Mount Carmel, IL 62863
(618)262-4663 (800)646-3276
Fax:(618)262-8199
E-mail: poorfarm@midwest.net

Rates: $45-85.
Payment: MC VISA AX DS PC TC.
Innkeeper(s): Liz & John Stelzer.
Circa: 1915.

Rooms: 5 rooms with PB, 2 with FP. 2 suites. 2 conference rooms.
Beds: QDT.

This uniquely named inn served as a home for the homeless for more than a century. Today, the stately Federal-style structure hosts travelers and visitors to this area of Southeast Illinois. An antique player piano and VCRs add to guests' comfort, and the inn also has bicycles available for those wishing to explore the grounds. The Poor Farm B&B sits adjacent to a recreational park with a well-stocked lake and is within walking distance of an 18-hole golf course and driving range. Riverboat gambling is 45 minutes away in Evansville, Ind.

Breakfast included in rates. Types of meals: full breakfast and early coffee/tea. Afternoon tea, dinner, evening snack, lunch, banquet service and catering service available. Air conditioning, turn-down service, ceiling fan and VCR in room. Fax, copier, bicycles and library on premises. Handicap access. Weddings, small meetings, family reunions and seminars hosted. Amusement parks, antiques, fishing, parks, shopping, cross-country skiing, sporting events, theater and watersports nearby. TAC10.

Pets Allowed: None inside-outside enclosure.

Special Discounts: Seventh night free.

"Delightful. Oatmeal supreme. Best in Illinois. Enjoyed every moment. Hi Yo Silver!"

Oregon B4

Pinehill B&B

400 Mix St
Oregon, IL 61061-1113
(815)732-2061

Rates: $65-195.
Payment: PC TC.
Innkeeper(s): Sharon Burdick.
Circa: 1874.

Rooms: 5 rooms with PB, 3 with FP. 1 conference room.
Beds: KQD.

This Italianate country villa is listed in the National Register. Ornate touches include guest rooms with Italian marble fireplaces and French silk-screened mural wallpaper. Outside, guests may enjoy porches, swings and century-old pine trees. Seasonal events include daily chocolate tea parties featuring the inn's own exotic homemade fudge collection.

Breakfast and afternoon tea included in rates. Types of meals: gourmet breakfast and early coffee/tea. Air conditioning, turn-down service and ceiling fan in room. Library on premises. Weddings, small meetings, family reunions and seminars hosted. Antiques, parks, shopping, sporting events and watersports nearby. TAC10.

Publicity: *Fox Valley Living, Victorian Sampler, Freeport Journal.*

"We enjoyed our stay at Pine Hill, your gracious hospitality and the peacefulness. Our thanks to you for a delightful stay. We may have to come again, if just to get some fudge."

Petersburg

F4

The Oaks Bed & Breakfast

510 W Sheridan St
Petersburg, IL 62675-1358
(217)632-5444

Rates: $70-115.
Payment: MC VISA DS PC TC.
Innkeeper(s): Susan & Ken Rodger.
Circa: 1875.

Rooms: 5 rooms, 3 with PB.
Beds: QD.

More than three acres of manicured gardens and grand oak trees surround this brick Italianate Victorian, complete with tower and gables. Inside, a three-story walnut staircase with finely carved newel post, seven fireplaces, ornate plasterwork, walnut woodwork and interior shutters set an elegant tone. The Edward Laning Suite provides an excellent view of historic Petersburg and the Sangamon River. A fireplace and antique furnishings complement its black, gold and ivory decor. Seven-course dinners and picnic lunches are available with advance arrangement. Nearby is Lincoln's New Salem with its reconstructed 1830s village.

Breakfast and afternoon tea included in rates. Type of meal: gourmet breakfast. Dinner and picnic lunch available. Spa and library on premises. Weddings, small meetings, family reunions and seminars hosted. Antiques, fishing, parks and watersports nearby.

Rock Island

C3

Potter House B&B

1906 7th Ave
Rock Island, IL 61201-2633
(309)788-1906 (800)747-0339
Fax:(309)794-3947

Rates: $65-100.
Payment: MC VISA AX TC.
Innkeeper(s): Maribeth & Frank Skradski.
Circa: 1907.

Rooms: 7 rooms with PB. 1 cottage.
Beds: QDT.

This Colonial Revival mansion is in the National Register. Embossed leather wall coverings, mahogany woodwork and stained- and leaded-glass windows are special features. There is a solarium with a tile and marble floor and there are six fireplaces. A white Chinese carpet, antique beds and a round-tiled shower are features of the Palladian Room. Nearby are the riverboat casinos and a number of excellent restaurants.

Breakfast and afternoon tea included in rates. Types of meals: continental-plus breakfast, full breakfast and early coffee/tea. Evening snack available. Air conditioning, turn-down service, ceiling fan and cable TV in room. Fax, bicycles and library on premises. Weddings, small meetings, family reunions and seminars hosted. Antiques, fishing, parks, shopping, downhill skiing, cross-country skiing, sporting events, theater and watersports nearby. TAC10.

Publicity: *Chicago Sun Times, Quad City Times, Vacations.*

Special Discounts: Government rates available.

"We love your home and you were so gracious and hospitable."

Rockford

B5

Victoria's B&B

201 N 6th St
Rockford, IL 61107-4161
(815)963-3232

Rates: $59-225.
Payment: MC VISA AX DS PC TC.
Innkeeper(s): Martin Lewis.
Circa: 1897.

Rooms: 5 suites. 1 conference room.
Beds: KQ.

This turn-of-the-century mansion features a parlor with eight different hand-painted wallpapers. Guests may relax on the front-porch swing, the outside benches or in the Victorian parlor by a cozy fire. Breakfast is served in the second-floor parlor.

Breakfast included in rates. Type of meal: gourmet breakfast. Air conditioning, turn-down service, ceiling fan, cable TV and VCR in room. Spa on premises. Weddings, small meetings, family reunions and seminars hosted. Amusement parks, antiques, fishing, parks, shopping, cross-country skiing, sporting events, theater and watersports nearby.

Publicity: *Midwest Living.*

"The house is magnificent from canaries to creaks in the floor!"

Indiana

IN

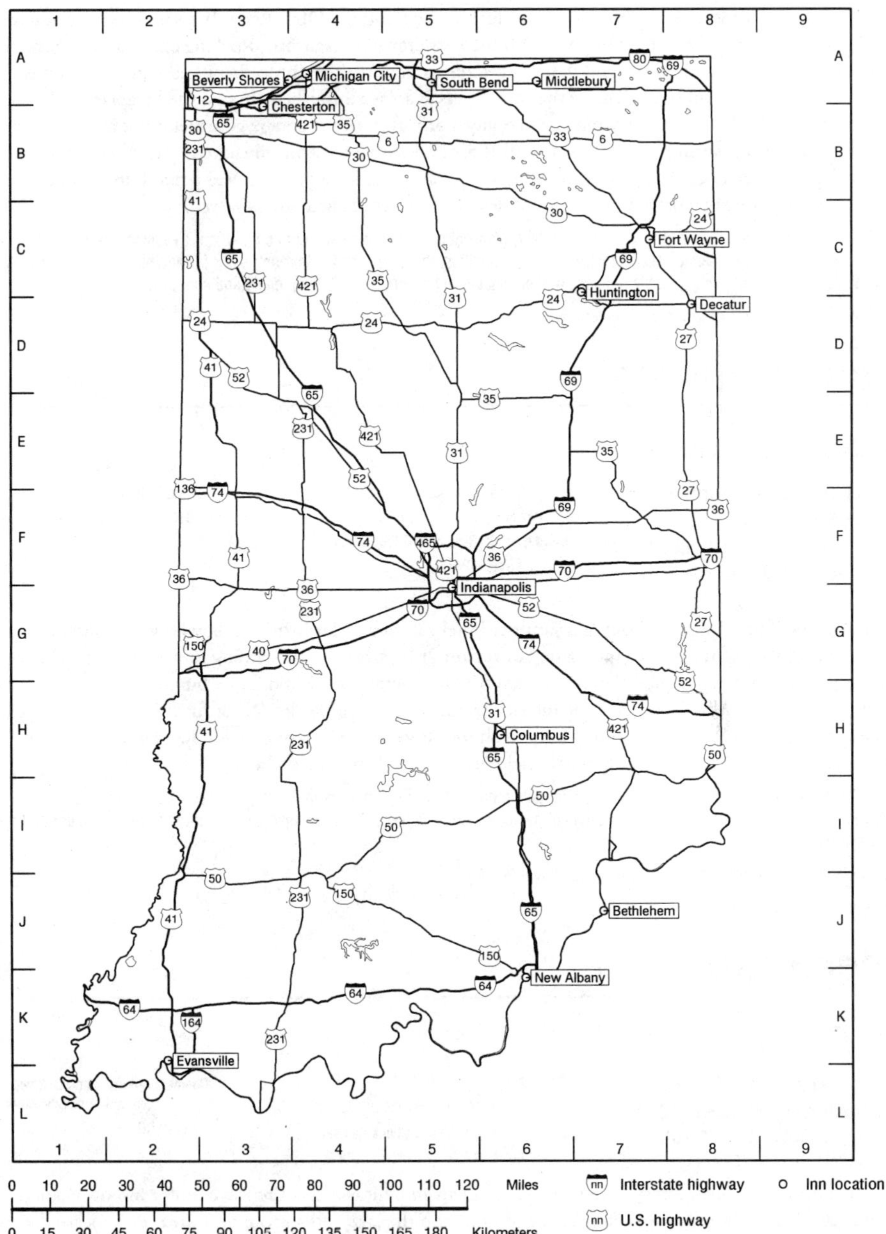

Beverly Shores
Michigan City
South Bend
Middlebury
Chesterton
Fort Wayne
Huntington
Decatur
Indianapolis
Columbus
Bethlehem
New Albany
Evansville
Miles
Kilometers
Interstate highway
U.S. highway
Inn location

Bethlehem

J7

Inn at Bethlehem

Walnut and Riverview
Bethlehem, IN 47104
(812)293-3975

Rates: $60-150. MAP, AP.
Payment: MC TC.
Innkeeper(s): Lawrence & Debbie Llana.
Circa: 1830.

Rooms: 10 rooms with PB. 1 suite. 2 conference rooms.
Beds: KQDT.

This two-story, Federal-style inn sits atop a bluff overlooking the Ohio River. In its long history, it has seen uses as a grocery, jail and possibly a stop on the Underground Railroad. Rocking chairs and hammocks are ready for those who wish to relax, and there's 26 acres to explore. The inn is furnished with elegant pieces, including some period antiques. One of the innkeepers is an accomplished chef, so the breakfasts are a treat. Guests who stay Friday or Saturday night, can enjoy a prix-fixe, multi-course gourmet dinner. Your menu might include saffron shrimp bisque, garden salad dressed with a balsamic vinaigrette, an appetizer of wild mushroom cream in a beggars purse, then bourbon pecan chicken or perhaps beef tenderloin wrapped in smoky bacon and finished off with a succulent dessert. Sunday brunch also is served.

Breakfast included in rates. Types of meals: full breakfast, gourmet breakfast and early coffee/tea. Dinner, evening snack, picnic lunch, gourmet lunch and banquet service available. MAP, AP. Air conditioning and ceiling fan in room. VCR, fax and bicycles on premises. 26 acres. Weddings, small meetings, family reunions and seminars hosted. Antiques, fishing, parks and shopping nearby. TAC10.

"We love this place! It is now our little getaway."

Beverly Shores

A4

Dunes Shore Inn

33 Lakeshore County Rd,
Box 807
Beverly Shores, IN 46301
(219)879-9029

Rates: $50-60.
Payment: PC TC.
Innkeeper(s): Rosemary & Fred Braun.
Circa: 1946.

Rooms: 12 rooms. 1 suite.
Beds: DT.

The Dunes Shore Inn started out as a summer hotel catering to Lithuanian folk who were fond of the area because of its resemblance to the Baltic Sea region. It later became a boarding house for national park employees of the Indiana Dunes National Lakeshore. A concrete-block and frame building, the inn is located one block from Lake Michigan. Its rustic interior features an eclectic collection of furnishings. Guests gather in one of the upstairs lounges or around a Swedish tile stove in the knotty-pine lobby. The innkeepers have an apartment available May to October, which includes a private bath and kitchen.

Breakfast included in rates. Type of meal: continental-plus breakfast. Ceiling fan in room. Library on premises. Small meetings and family reunions hosted. German spoken. Amusement parks, antiques, fishing, parks, shopping, cross-country skiing, theater and water-sports nearby.

Publicity: *Milwaukee Journal, Chicago Sun-Times, Travel Holiday.*

"The setting was so perfect. Thank you."

Chesterton

B3

The Gray Goose

350 Indian Boundary Rd
Chesterton, IN 46304-1511
(219)926-5781 (800)521-5127
Fax:(219)926-4845

Rates: $80-148.
Payment: MC VISA AX DS PC TC.
Innkeeper(s): Tim Wilk & Chuck Ramsey.
Circa: 1939.

Rooms: 8 rooms with PB, 3 with FP. 3 suites. 1 conference room.
Beds: KQ.

Situated on 100 wooded acres, just under one hour from Chicago, this English country inn overlooks a private lake. Guests can see Canadian geese and ducks on the lake and surrounding area. Rooms are decorated in 18th-century English, Shaker and French country styles. Some of the rooms feature fireplaces and poster beds. Complimentary snacks, soft drinks, coffee and tea are available throughout the day. Strains of Mozart or Handel add to the ambiance.

Breakfast, afternoon tea and evening snack included in rates. Types of meals: full breakfast, gourmet breakfast and early coffee/tea. Air conditioning, ceiling fan and VCR in room. Fax, copier and library on premises. 100 acres. Weddings, small meetings, family reunions and seminars hosted. Antiques, fishing, parks, shopping, downhill skiing, cross-country skiing, sporting events, theater and watersports nearby.

Publicity: *Innsider, Post-Tribune, Glamour, Country Inns, Midwest Living.*

"Extremely gracious!"

Columbus H6

The Columbus Inn

445 5th St
Columbus, IN 47201-6206
(812)378-4289
Fax:(812)378-4289

Rates: $96.
Payment: MC VISA AX DC CB DS PC TC.
Innkeeper(s): Paul A. Staublin.
Circa: 1895.

Rooms: 34 rooms with PB. 5 suites. 3 conference rooms.
Beds: QD.

IN

Dances, basketball games and poultry shows once convened in the auditorium of the old Columbus City Hall during its years as the focal point of town. The original terra-cotta floors, enormous brass chandeliers and hand-carved oak woodwork now welcome overnight guests. Lavishly decorated rooms feature reproduction antiques such as cherry sleigh beds. Twelve-foot-high windows and 21-foot ceilings grace the Charles Sparrell Suite with its separate sleeping level. A horse and buggy stops at the inn's front door. Awarded AAA four-diamond rating.

Breakfast and evening snack included in rates. Types of meals: full breakfast, gourmet breakfast and early coffee/tea. Afternoon tea, dinner, picnic lunch, lunch, gourmet lunch, banquet service and catering service available. Air conditioning, turn-down service, cable TV and VCR in room. Fax, copier, computer, library and child care on premises. Handicap access. Weddings, small meetings, family reunions and seminars hosted. Amusement parks, antiques, fishing, parks, shopping, downhill skiing, sporting events, theater and watersports nearby.

Publicity: *Chicago Sun-Times, Country Inns, Home & Away, The Cincinnati Enquirer, Glamour, Innsider, InnReview*

"A delicious and beautifully served breakfast was the crowning glory of our stay."

Decatur D8

Cragwood Inn B&B

303 N 2nd St
Decatur, IN 46733-1329
(219)728-2000

Rates: $60-65.
Payment: MC VISA PC TC.
Innkeeper(s): George & Nancy Craig.
Circa: 1900.

Rooms: 4 rooms, 2 with PB, 2 with FP. 1 conference room.
Beds: QDT.

This Queen Anne Victorian with four porches, gingerbread frosting, a turret and a graceful bay facade was built by a Decatur banker. Finely carved oak is magnificently displayed in the paneled ceilings, staircase and pillars of the parlor. Ornate tin ceilings, leaded-glass windows and a crystal chandelier are among other highlights. The wicker bed in the Garden Room looks out through a Palladian window. Two other rooms have their own fireplace. The innkeepers host weekend workshops for those interesting in learning how to do fine needlework, including Battenburg lace and ribbon work. The also have chocolate lovers' weekends in March and October.

Breakfast and evening snack included in rates. Types of meals: full breakfast, gourmet breakfast and early coffee/tea. Air conditioning in room. VCR, bicycles and library on premises. Weddings and small meetings hosted. Antiques and parks nearby.

Location: South of Fort Wayne.

Publicity: *Inside Chicago, Great Lakes Getaway, Christmas Victorian Craft.*

"Your wonderful hospitality, beautiful home and company made my trip that much more enjoyable."

Evansville K2

Coolbreeze Estate B&B

1240 SE 2nd St
Evansville, IN 47713-1304
(812)422-9635

Rates: $75.
Payment: AX DC CB DS PC TC.
Innkeeper(s): Katelin & David Hills.
Circa: 1906.

Rooms: 4 rooms with PB. 2 suites. 2 conference rooms.
Beds: QD.

This prairie school home, is surrounded by more than an acre of grounds, ideal for those in search of peace and quiet. Truck and automobile maker Joseph Graham once lived here, as well as philanthropist Giltner Igleheart. One room features the wallpaper mural, "Scenic America." The same mural was chosen by Jacqueline Kennedy to decorate the White House. The sunny rooms have names such as Margaret Mitchell or Bronte. A zoo, art museum and riverboat casino are among the nearby attractions.

Breakfast included in rates. Type of meal: full breakfast. Air conditioning in room. Cable TV, VCR and library on premises. Weddings, small meetings, family reunions and seminars hosted. Antiques, parks, shopping, sporting events, theater and watersports nearby.

Pets Allowed: Must be well trained.

Location: Old Ohio River city.

Publicity: *Evansville Courier, Midwest Living.*

"It was so much like discovering something wonderful from the past and disappearing into the warmth of childhood again."

Fort Wayne C7

The Carole Lombard House B&B

704 Rockhill St
Fort Wayne, IN 46802-5918
(219)426-9896

Rates: $55-65.
Payment: MC VISA DS PC TC.
Innkeeper(s): Bev Fiandt.
Circa: 1895.

Rooms: 4 rooms with PB.
Beds: KQDT.

Jane Alice Peters, a.k.a. Carole Lombard, spent her first six years in this turn-of-the-century home located in Ft. Wayne's historic West-Central neighborhood. The innkeepers named two guest rooms in honor of Lombard and her second husband, Clark Gable. Each of these rooms features memorabilia from the Gable-Lombard romance. A video library with a collection of classic movies is available, including many of Lombard's films. The innkeepers provide bicycles for exploring Fort Wayne and also provide information for a self-guided architectural tour of the historic area.

Breakfast included in rates. Types of meals: full breakfast and early coffee/tea. Air conditioning and cable TV in room. VCR and bicycles on premises. Small meetings hosted. Antiques, parks, sporting events and theater nearby. TAC5.

Special Discounts: Genealogy Special, three nights (Sunday-Thursday) $99.

Huntington C7

Purviance House

326 S Jefferson St
Huntington, IN 46750-3327
(219)356-4218

Rates: $45-55.
Payment: MC VISA DS TC.
Innkeeper(s): Bob & Jean Gernand.
Circa: 1859.

Rooms: 5 rooms, 2 with PB, 2 with FP. 2 conference rooms.
Beds: DT.

This Italianate-Greek Revival house is listed in the National Register of Historic Places. The inn features a winding cherry staircase, parquet floors, original interior shutters, tile fireplaces, antique faucets, ornate ceiling designs, antiques and period reproductions. The gold parlor offers well-stocked bookshelves.

Breakfast and evening snack included in rates. Types of meals: full breakfast and early coffee/tea. Banquet service and room service available. Air conditioning and ceiling fan in room. Library on premises. Weddings, small meetings, family reunions and seminars hosted. Antiques, fishing, parks, shopping and watersports nearby. TAC5.

Location: One-half hour from Ft. Wayne.

Publicity: *Huntington County TAB, Purdue Alumnus, Richmond Palladium-Item.*

Special Discounts: 10% off second consecutive night.

"A completely delightful experience!"

Indianapolis G5

Hoffman House

PO Box 906
Indianapolis, IN 46206-0906
(317)635-1701
Fax:(317)635-1701
E-mail: tag906@aol.com

Rates: $60-100.
Payment: MC VISA PC.
Innkeeper(s): Laura A. Arnold.
Circa: 1903.

Rooms: 2 rooms, 1 with FP.
Beds: DT.

IN

This homestay bed & breakfast, a turn-of-the-century home, offers two well-appointed bedrooms. The Peach Room includes a beautiful, carved bed and an ornate fireplace mantel. The innkeeper offers several amenities for business travelers, including a fax and access to a modem. The house dog, Pluto, is happy to accompany guests on a morning walk or jog.

Breakfast included in rates. Types of meals: continental-plus breakfast, full breakfast and early coffee/tea. Picnic lunch and catering service available. Air conditioning in room. Cable TV, VCR, fax, copier and library on premises. Small meetings hosted. Antiques, parks, shopping, sporting events and theater nearby. TAC10.

Pets Allowed: Pet care available across the street.

Special Discounts: Weekday business discount for two plus nights.

The Nuthatch B&B

7161 Edgewater Pl
Indianapolis, IN 46240-3020
(317)257-2660
Fax:(317)257-2677
E-mail: bbmorri@indyvax.iupu

Rates: $80-95.
Payment: MC VISA AX DS PC TC.
Innkeeper(s): Joan & Bernie Morris.
Circa: 1928.

Rooms: 2 rooms with PB, 1 with FP.
Beds: Q.

"Breakfast." That's the only word it should take to draw guests to this 1920s, cottage-like home. Innkeeper Joan Morris is a cooking instructor and creator of the inn's memorable breakfasts. Each morning brings with it a different culinary style, from down-home fare to a goat-cheese omelet with peppers and shitake mushrooms or poached pears with rosemary honey. The two guest rooms are decorated with an eclectic mix of styles. Guests walk down a circular staircase to reach The Adirondack Suite, which includes a fireplace and a greenhouse. The Wren's Nest is decorated with stained glass and a wren motif, and the bath includes a clawfoot tub.

Breakfast, afternoon tea and evening snack included in rates. Types of meals: full breakfast, gourmet breakfast and early coffee/tea. Air conditioning, turn-down service and ceiling fan in room. Fax and library on premises. Yiddish and some Spanish spoken. Antiques, fishing, parks, shopping, cross-country skiing, sporting events, theater and watersports nearby. TAC10.

Pets Allowed: In one room only, must be crated, crate provided.

Special Discounts: Special events frequently higher.

"We had a wonderful night for our sixth anniversary."

Old Northside B&B

1340 N Alabama St
Indianapolis, IN 46202-2524
(317)635-9123 (800)635-9127
Fax:(317)635-9243
E-mail: oldnorth@indy.net

Rates: $85-165.
Payment: MC VISA AX DS PC TC.
Innkeeper(s): Susan Berry.
Circa: 1885.

Rooms: 5 rooms, 4 with PB, 2 with FP. 1 suite. 1 conference room.
Beds: KQ DT.

This Romanesque Revival mansion is fashioned out of bricks, and the grounds are enclosed by a rod iron fence. Border gardens and an English side garden complete the look. Rooms are decorated with a theme in mind. The Literary Room, which includes a fireplace and Jacuzzi tub, is decorated to honor Indiana authors. Another room honors the state's racing tradition. The home has many modern conveniences, yet still retains original maple floors and hand-carved, mahogany woodwork. Candlelit breakfasts are served in the formal dining room or on the patio. Guests can walk to many city attractions.

Breakfast included in rates. Types of meals: gourmet breakfast and early coffee/tea. Catering service available. Air conditioning, turndown service, cable TV and VCR in room. Fax and copier on premises. Weddings, small meetings, family reunions and seminars hosted. Spanish and French spoken. Antiques, fishing, parks, shopping, cross-country skiing, sporting events, theater and watersports nearby. TAC10.

Special Discounts: Discounts for extended stays, Seniors, midweek/corporate.

Renaissance Tower Historic Inn

230 E 9th St
Indianapolis, IN 46204-1151
(317)261-1652 (800)676-7786
Fax:(317)262-8648

Rates: $75-85.
Payment: MC VISA AX PC TC.
Innkeeper(s): Jeffrey Bowling.
Circa: 1922.

Rooms: 80 suites.
Beds: QD.

Nestled in the heart of one of Indianapolis' most historic areas, this inn is listed in the National Register of Historic Places. The inn features distinctive construction details. Guest rooms have cherry four-poster beds, Queen Anne furniture, elegant sitting rooms and scenic bay windows. Each suite has a European-style fully equipped kitchen.

Air conditioning and cable TV in room. Fax and copier on premises. Shopping, sporting events and theater nearby. TAC10.

Publicity: *Indianapolis Business Journal, New York Times, Indianapolis Star, Muncie Star, TWAs Ambassador.*

Special Discounts: AAA, AARP, QUEST.

"We were so pleased with your lovely decor in the rooms."

The Tranquil Cherub

2164 N Capitol Ave
Indianapolis, IN 46202-1251
(317)923-9036

Rates: $55-85.
Payment: MC VISA AX.
Innkeeper(s): Thom & Barb Feit.
Circa: 1904.

Rooms: 4 rooms, 1 with PB. 1 suite.
Beds: KQ.

Visitors to the bustling Indianapolis area will appreciate the quiet elegance of the Tranquil Cherub, a Greek Revival home. The morning routine begins with freshly brewed coffee and juice served prior to breakfast, which is eaten in the oak-paneled dining room or on a back deck overlooking a pond. Guests may choose from the blue and white Victorian Room, with its antique wicker furniture and lace curtains, or the Gatsby Room, highlighted by its Art Deco-era four-poster cannonball bed. The jade green and navy Rogers Room features stained glass and an oak bedroom set that originated in an old Chicago hotel.

Breakfast and evening snack included in rates. Types of meals: gourmet breakfast and early coffee/tea. Air conditioning and ceiling fan in room. Cable TV and VCR on premises. Weddings and small meetings hosted. Antiques, shopping and theater nearby.

Michigan City

A4

The Hutchinson Mansion Inn

220 W 10th St
Michigan City, IN 46360
(219)879-1700

Rates: $65-135.
Payment: MC VISA AX.
Innkeeper(s): Ben & Mary DuVal.
Circa: 1875.

Rooms: 10 rooms with PB. 5 suites.
Beds: QD.

Built by a lumber baron in 1875, this grand, red-brick mansion features examples of Queen Anne, Classic Revival and Italianate design. The mansion boasts 11 stained-glass panels and the front parlor still has its original plaster friezes, ceiling medallion and a marble fireplace. The dining room's oak-paneled walls include a secret panel. The library is stocked with interesting books and games, and classical compositions and Victorian parlor music are piped in. The second floor offers a host of places perfect for relaxation, including a small game room, mini library and a sun porch. Rooms are filled with antiques and unusual pieces such as the Tower Suite's octagon, Gothic-style bed. The carriage house suites include a sitting room, refrigerator and either a whirlpool or large, soaking tub.

Breakfast included in rates. Antiques, fishing, shopping, cross-country skiing and theater nearby.

Publicity: *Midwest Living, Midwest Motorist, Heritage Country, Indianapolis Star, Michigan Living.*

"Beautiful, romantic inn, exceptional hospitality, your breakfasts were fabulous."

Middlebury

A6

Bee Hive B&B

PO Box 1191
Middlebury, IN 46540-1191
(219)825-5023
Fax:(219)825-5023

Rates: $52-68.
Payment: MC VISA PC TC.
Innkeeper(s): Herb & Treva Swarm.
Circa: 1985.

Rooms: 4 rooms, 1 with PB. 1 cottage.
Beds: QD.

This comfortable home was built with native timber. Red oak beams and a special loft add ambiance and a homey feel. Rooms include country decor and snuggly quilts, which are handmade locally. Guests can spend the day relaxing or visit the nearby Amish communities. There are local craft shops and other attractions, which include flea markets and the Shipshewana auction. The bed & breakfast is only four miles from the oldest operating mill in Indiana.

Breakfast and evening snack included in rates. Types of meals: full breakfast and early coffee/tea. Air conditioning and ceiling fan in room. VCR, fax and copier on premises. 40 acres. Small meetings and family reunions hosted. Antiques, fishing, parks, shopping, downhill skiing, cross-country skiing, sporting events, theater and watersports nearby.

Location: In Amish Country.

"What a great place to rest the mind, body and soul."

IN

Varns Guest House

PO Box 125
Middlebury, IN 46540-0125
(219)825-9666 (800)398-5424

Rates: $65-80.
Payment: MC VISA DS PC.
Innkeeper(s): Carl & Diane Eash.
Circa: 1898.

Rooms: 5 rooms with PB.
Beds: QT.

Built by the innkeepers' great-grandparents, this home has been in the family for nearly a century. Recently restored, it is located on the town's tree-shaded main street. Guests enjoy gliding on the front porch swing while they watch Amish horses and buggies clip-clop past the inn. The Kinder Room features a whirlpool tub.

Breakfast included in rates. Type of meal: continental-plus breakfast. Air conditioning and cable TV in room. Weddings, small meetings and family reunions hosted. Parks and shopping nearby. TAC10.

Publicity: *Heritage Country, Midwest Living.*

"In terms of style, decor, cleanliness and hospitality, there is none finer!"

New Albany — K6

Honeymoon Mansion B&B & Wedding Chapel

1014 E Main St
New Albany, IN 47150-5843
(812)945-0312 (800)759-7270

Rates: $70-140.
Payment: MC VISA PC TC.
Innkeeper(s): J. Franklin & Beverly Dennis.
Circa: 1850.

Rooms: 6 rooms, 4 with PB, 1 with FP. 1 suite. 2 conference rooms.
Beds: Q.

The innkeepers at Honeymoon Mansions can provide guests with the flowers, wedding chapel and honeymoon suite. All you need to bring is a bride or groom. An ordained minister is on the premises and guests can marry or renew their vows in the inn's Victorian wedding chapel. However, one need not be a newlywed to enjoy this bed & breakfast. Canopy beds, stained-glass windows and heart-shaped rugs are a few of the romantic touches. Several suites include marble Jacuzzis flanked on four sides with 8-foot-high marble columns, creating a dramatic and elegant effect. The home itself, a pre-Civil War Italianate-style home listed in the state and national historic registers, boasts many fine period features. Gingerbread trim, intricate molding and a grand staircase add to the Victorian ambiance. Guests are treated to an all-you-can-eat country breakfast with items such as homemade breads, biscuits and gravy, eggs, sausage and potatoes.

Breakfast included in rates. Type of meal: full breakfast. Catering service available. Air conditioning, ceiling fan, cable TV and VCR in room. Copier on premises. Handicap access. Weddings, small meetings, family reunions and seminars hosted. Amusement parks, antiques, fishing, parks, shopping, downhill skiing, cross-country skiing, sporting events, theater and watersports nearby. TAC10.

Publicity: *Indianapolis Star, Courier-Journal, Evening News, Tribune.*

Special Discounts: 10% off Sunday-Thursday.

The Book Inn B&B

508 W Washington St
South Bend, IN 46601-1528
(219)288-1990
Fax:(219)234-2338
E-mail: bookinn@aol.com

Rates: $80-120.
Payment: MC VISA AX PC TC.
Innkeeper(s): Peggy & John Livingston.
Circa: 1872.

Rooms: 5 rooms with PB. 2 suites. 1 conference room.
Beds: KQT.

Hand-hewn, butternut woodwork and 12-foot ceilings accentuate the rich decor at this Second Empire-style home. Among the many impressive architectural features are entry doors with double leaf wood and applied decorations. The Cushing Suite boasts a bay window, hand-painted walls and four-poster bed. Other rooms, which are named in honor of famous female authors, feature delightful decor. Bookworms will delight not only in the name of this inn, but also the inn's own used bookstore.

Breakfast included in rates. Types of meals: continental-plus breakfast and early coffee/tea. Air conditioning in room. VCR, fax, copier and library on premises. Small meetings, family reunions and seminars hosted. Antiques, fishing, parks, shopping, cross-country skiing, sporting events, theater and watersports nearby. TAC10.

IN

Oliver Inn

630 W Washington St
South Bend, IN 46601-1444
(219)232-4545
Fax:(219)288-9788

Rates: $85-175.
Payment: MC VISA AX DS TC.
Innkeeper(s): Richard & Venera Monahan.
Circa: 1886.

Rooms: 8 rooms with PB, 2 with FP. 3 suites. 1 conference room.
Beds: KQT.

This stately Queen Anne Victorian sits amid 30 towering maples and was once home to Josephine Oliver Ford, daughter of James Oliver, of chilled plow fame. Located in South Bend's historic district, this inn offers a comfortable library and eight inviting guest rooms, some with built-in fireplaces. The inn is within walking distance of downtown, and public transportation is available.

Breakfast and evening snack included in rates. Types of meals: continental-plus breakfast and early coffee/tea. Air conditioning, turn-down service, ceiling fan and cable TV in room. Fax on premises. Handicap access. Weddings, small meetings, family reunions and seminars hosted. Antiques, fishing, parks, shopping, cross-country skiing, sporting events, theater and watersports nearby.

Queen Anne Inn

420 W Washington St
South Bend, IN 46601-1526
(219)234-5959 (800)582-2379

Rates: $70-105.
Payment: MC VISA AX.
Innkeeper(s): Pauline & Bob Medhurst.
Circa: 1893.

Rooms: 6 rooms with PB, 1 with FP. 1 suite. 1 conference room.
Beds: KQDT.

Samuel Good, a local who made his fortune from the Gold Rush, built this Queen Anne, Neo-Classical home which was later moved to its present neighborhood. Frank Lloyd Wright-designed bookcases, oak floors and panelling, crystal chandeliers, hand-painted silk wallpaper, and a mirrored, mahogany buffet enhance the warm, rich interior. Special teas are served on Thursdays and Saturdays. Amenities are available for business travelers.

Breakfast included in rates. Types of meals: full breakfast and early coffee/tea. Afternoon tea, picnic lunch, banquet service and catering service available. Air conditioning in room. Cable TV, VCR, fax, copier, bicycles and library on premises. Weddings, small meetings, family reunions and seminars hosted. Antiques and watersports nearby. TAC8.

Location: Near downtown.

Publicity: *Romantic Getaways.*

Iowa

0 15 30 45 60 75 90 105 120 135 150 165 180 Miles

0 25 50 75 100 125 150 175 200 225 250 275 Kilometers

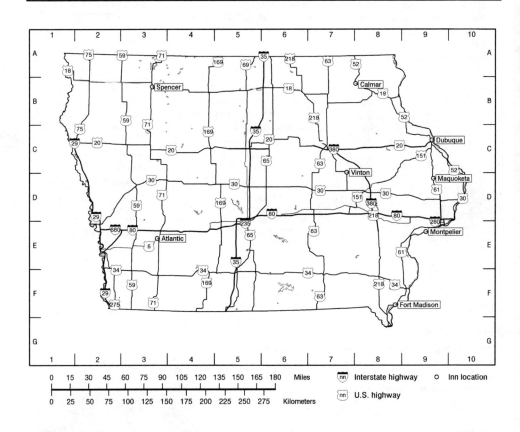

nn Interstate highway
nn U.S. highway
o Inn location

Atlantic — E3

Chestnut Charm B&B

1409 Chestnut St
Atlantic, IA 50022-2547
(712)243-5652

Rates: $75-115.
Payment: MC VISA PC.
Innkeeper(s): Barbara Stensvad.
Circa: 1898.

Rooms: 5 rooms with PB. 1 suite.
Beds: KQD.

The charm doesn't end at this richly appointed bed & breakfast. Guests first will be taken by the expansive manicured lawn and the charming Victorian design of the manor. Inside, natural hardwood floors, ornate woodwork and original, hand-painted linen wall coverings are exquisite. Relax in one of the sunrooms, or enjoy the view by the fountained patio or on the romantic gazebo. Each of the rooms features something fun and unique, from the private sunroom in the Master Suite to the Battenburg lace and ruffles in Tabitha's Quarters. The innkeepers offer upscale suites in a newly remodeled carriage

house, as well. The wafting scent of fresh coffee leads hungry guests into the dining room for a delectable breakfast. Formal dinners are available with prior reservations.

Breakfast included in rates. Type of meal: gourmet breakfast. Dinner available. Air conditioning in room. Library on premises. Antiques, fishing, parks and shopping nearby. TAC10.

Location: Halfway between Omaha, Nebraska and Des Moines, Iowa.

Publicity: *Atlantic News Telegraph, Midwest Living, Iowan, Women's Edition, Iowa Lady, Home & Away.*

"We truly had a wonderful weekend. Your hospitality was unsurpassed!"

Calmar

B8

Calmar Guesthouse

RR 1 Box 206
Calmar, IA 52132-9801
(319)562-3851

Rates: $45-50.
Payment: MC VISA PC TC.
Innkeeper(s): Lucile Kruse.
Circa: 1890.

Rooms: 5 rooms, 1 with PB.
Beds: Q.

IA

This beautifully restored Victorian home was built by John B. Kay, a lawyer and poet. Stained-glass windows, carved moldings, an oak-and-walnut staircase and gleaming woodwork highlight the gracious interior. A grandfather clock ticks in the living room. In the foyer, a friendship yellow rose is incorporated into the stained-glass window pane. Breakfast is served in the formal dining room. The Laura Ingalls Wilder Museum is nearby in Burr Oak. Smoking is not permitted.

Breakfast included in rates. Types of meals: full breakfast and early coffee/tea. Air conditioning and cable TV in room. VCR, bicycles and library on premises. Small meetings hosted. Antiques, fishing, parks, shopping, downhill skiing, cross-country skiing, sporting events, theater and watersports nearby.

Publicity: *Iowa Farmer Today, Calmar Courier, Minneapolis Star-Tribune, Home and Away, Iowan.*

"What a delight it was to stay here. No one could have made our stay more welcome or enjoyable."

Dubuque

C9

The Hancock House

1105 Grove Ter
Dubuque, IA 52001-4644
(319)557-8989
Fax:(319)583-0813

Rates: $75-150.
Payment: MC VISA AX DS PC TC.
Innkeeper(s): Chuck & Susan Huntley.
Circa: 1891.

Rooms: 9 rooms with PB, 3 with FP. 1 suite. 1 cottage.
Beds: Q.

Victorian splendor can be found at The Hancock House, one of Dubuque's most striking examples of Queen Anne architecture. Rooms feature period furnishings and offer views of the Mississippi River states of Iowa, Illinois and Wisconsin. The Hancock House, listed in the National Register, boasts several unique features, including a fireplace judged blue-ribbon best at the 1893 World's Fair in Chicago. Visitors also will enjoy the inn's authentic bathrooms, featuring clawfoot tubs and pull-chain water closets.

Breakfast included in rates. Type of meal: full breakfast. Air conditioning and cable TV in room. Fax, copier and spa on premises. Family reunions hosted. Antiques, fishing, parks, shopping, downhill skiing, cross-country skiing, theater and watersports nearby. TAC10.

Special Discounts: Extended stays.

The Mandolin Inn

199 Loras Blvd
Dubuque, IA 52001-4857
(319)556-0069 (800)524-7996
Fax:(319)556-0587

Rates: $60-110.
Payment: MC VISA AX DS PC TC.
Innkeeper(s): Jan Oswald.
Circa: 1908.

Rooms: 8 rooms, 4 with PB. 2 conference rooms.
Beds: KQD.

This three-story brick Edwardian with Queen Anne wrap-around veranda boasts a mosaic-tiled porch floor. Inside are in-laid mahogany and rosewood floors, bay windows and a turret that starts in the parlor and ascends to the second-floor Holly Marie Room, decorated in a wedding motif. This room features a seven-piece French Walnut bedroom suite and a crystal chandelier. A three-course gourmet breakfast is served in the dining room with Italian tile depicting women's work at the turn-of-the-century. There is an herb garden outside the kitchen. A church is across the street and riverboat gambling is 12 blocks away.

Breakfast included in rates. Types of meals: gourmet breakfast and early coffee/tea. Air conditioning, ceiling fan and cable TV in room. Fax on premises. Weddings, small meetings, family reunions and seminars hosted. Antiques, fishing, parks, shopping, downhill skiing, cross-country skiing, sporting events, theater and watersports nearby. TAC10.

"From the moment we entered the Mandolin, we felt at home. I know we'll be back."

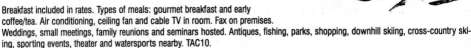

Fort Madison **F8**

Kingsley Inn

707 Avenue H (Hwy 61)
Fort Madison, IA 52627
(319)372-7074 (800)441-2327
Fax:(319)372-7096

Rates: $65-115.
Payment: MC VISA AX DC DS.
Innkeeper(s): Nannette Evans.
Circa: 1858.

Rooms: 14 rooms with PB. 1 conference room.
Beds: KQD.

Overlooking the Mississippi River, this century-old inn is located in downtown Fort Madison. Though furnished with antiques, all 14 rooms offer modern amenities and private baths (some with whirlpools) as well as river views. A riverboat casino and a variety of shops are within a few blocks of the inn. There is a restaurant, Alphas on the Riverfront, and a gift shop on the premises.

Breakfast included in rates. Types of meals: continental-plus breakfast and early coffee/tea. Air conditioning and cable TV in room. Fax on premises. Handicap access. Weddings, small meetings, family reunions and seminars hosted. Antiques, fishing, shopping and theater nearby.

Location: US Highway 61 in downtown Fort Madison.

Publicity: *Hawkeye.*

"Wow, how nice and relaxing, quiet atmosphere, great innkeeper so personal kind and friendly."

Mississippi Rose & Thistle Inn

532 Avenue F
Fort Madison, IA 52627
(319)372-7044

Rates: $65-90.
Payment: MC VISA AX DS PC TC.
Innkeeper(s): Bill & Bonnie Saunders.
Circa: 1881.

Rooms: 4 rooms with PB. 1 suite. 1 conference room.
Beds: KQ.

Gourmet suppers and picnics are available to guests with advance reservations at this beautiful, red brick Victorian inn. Breakfast specialties cooked by the innkeeper, a gourmet chef, include creamy scrambled eggs with sausage and vegetables in a buttery crustade and B.J.'s Sticky Buns. There are three parlors including a game room. The first fort built west of the Mississippi is two blocks away. Also, two blocks away is the

Catfish Bend Casino River Boat and not too much farther is the longest swing-span bridge in the world.

Breakfast included in rates. Types of meals: gourmet breakfast and early coffee/tea. Afternoon tea, dinner, picnic lunch, lunch and gourmet lunch available. Air conditioning and turn-down service in room. Cable TV, VCR and library on premises. Weddings, small meetings, family reunions and seminars hosted. Antiques, fishing, parks, shopping, sporting events, theater and watersports nearby. TAC10.

Publicity: *Daily Democrat.*

"The very best, we've never been so pampered. Thanks for a memorable stay."

Maquoketa D9

Squiers Manor B&B

418 W Pleasant St
Maquoketa, IA 52060-2847
(319)652-6961

Rates: $75-185.
Payment: MC VISA AX.
Innkeeper(s): Virl & Kathy Banowetz.
Circa: 1882.

Rooms: 8 rooms with PB. 3 suites.
Beds: KQT.

Innkeepers Virl and Kathy Banowetz are ace antique dealers, who along with owning one of the Midwest's largest antique shops, have refurbished this elegant, Queen Anne Victorian. The inn is furnished with period antiques that are beyond compare. Guest rooms boast museum-quality pieces such as a Victorian brass bed with lace curtain wings and inlaid mother-of-pearl or an antique mahogany bed with carved birds and flowers. Four guest rooms include whirlpool tubs, and one includes a unique Swiss shower. The innkeepers restored the home's original woodwork, shuttered-windows, fireplaces, gas and electric chandeliers and stained and engraved-glass windows back to their former glory. They also recently renovated the mansion's attic ballroom into two luxurious suites. The Loft, which is made up of three levels, features pine and wicker furnishings, a sitting room and gas-burning wood stove. On the second level, there is a large Jacuzzi, on the third, an antique queen-size bed. The huge Ballroom Suite boasts 24-foot ceilings, oak and pine antiques, gas-burning wood stove and a Jacuzzi snuggled beside a dormer window. Suite guests enjoy a breakfast basket delivered to their rooms. Other guests feast on an array of mouth-watering treats, such as home-baked breads, seafood quiche and fresh fruits. Evening desserts are served by candlelight.

Breakfast and evening dessert included in rates. Types of meals: full breakfast and gourmet breakfast. Weddings and small meetings hosted. Antiques, fishing, parks, shopping, downhill skiing, cross-country skiing and watersports nearby.

Publicity: *Des Moines Register Datebook, Daily Herald.*

"We couldn't have asked for a more perfect place to spend our honeymoon. The service was excellent and so was the food! It was an exciting experience that we will never forget!"

Montpelier E9

Varners' Caboose

204 E 2nd, Box 10
Montpelier, IA 52759
(319)381-3652

Rates: $55.
Payment: PC.
Innkeeper(s): Bob & Nancy Varner.
Circa: 1958.

Rooms: 1 room with PB.
Beds: QT.

Located halfway between Davenport and Muscatine, this original Rock Island Lines caboose rests on its own track behind the Varners' home, the former Montpelier Depot. The caboose is decorated in simple, country style. The innkeepers prepare a full breakfast and deliver it to their guests. Llamas, ducks and geese are available for petting.

Breakfast included in rates. Type of meal: full breakfast. Air conditioning in room. Fishing and parks nearby.

Pets Allowed.

Location: Located on Route 22 half way between Davenport and Muscatine.

Spencer
B3

The Hannah Marie Country Inn

4070 Highway 71
Spencer, IA 51301-2033
(712)262-1286 (800)972-1286
Fax:(712)262-3294

Rates: $70-110.
Payment: MC VISA DS PC TC.
Innkeeper(s): Mary Nichols.
Circa: 1907.

Rooms: 6 rooms with PB. 1 conference room.
Beds: Q.

Enjoy the romance of the country at Hannah Marie's, tucked just off a rural highway in the midst of golden fields of corn. Feather beds topped with down comforters, double whirlpool tubs, soften water and bubble bath are some of the luxurious amenities. Each guest room has a special theme. Guests are given parasols for strolling along the grounds with herb, flower and vegetable gardens. The innkeepers host themed tea parties, children's etiquette lunches, herb workshops and afternoon tea. Guests can mingle with the Queen of Hearts tea or perhaps Queen Elizabeth at a garden party. The full breakfasts are served by candlelight, or guests can opt for lighter fare delivered to their guest room door in a basket. Early evening refreshments also are included in the rates.

Breakfast and evening snack included in rates. Types of meals: continental breakfast, gourmet breakfast and early coffee/tea. Afternoon tea and gourmet lunch available. Air conditioning and ceiling fan in room. Library on premises. Weddings, small meetings and seminars hosted. Sign spoken. Amusement parks, antiques, fishing, parks, shopping, theater and watersports nearby. TAC10.

Pets Allowed: Outside.

Location: Five miles south of Spencer.

Publicity: *Midwest Living, Partners, Des Moines Register, Sioux City Journal, Home and Away.*

"Best bed & breakfast in Iowa." - Des Moines Register.

Vinton
C7

Lion & The Lamb B&B

913 - 2nd Ave
Vinton, IA 52349
(319)472-5086 (800)808-5262
Fax:(319)472-9115
E-mail: lionlamb@fyiowa.infi

Rates: $55-75.
Payment: MC VISA PC TC.
Innkeeper(s): Richard & Rachel Waterbury.
Circa: 1892.

Rooms: 4 rooms, 2 with PB, 2 with FP. 2 conference rooms.
Beds: QT.

This Queen Anne Victorian, a true "Painted Lady," boasts a stunning exterior with intricate chimneys, gingerbread trim, gables and turrets. The home still maintains its original pocket doors and parquet flooring, and antiques add to the nostalgic flavor. One room boasts a 150-year-old bedroom set. Breakfasts, as any meal in such fine a house should, are served on china. Succulent French toast topped with powdered sugar and a rich strawberry sauce is a specialty. In the evenings, desserts are served.

Breakfast and evening snack included in rates. Types of meals: full breakfast and early coffee/tea. Room service available. Air conditioning and ceiling fan in room. VCR, fax and bicycles on premises. Weddings, small meetings, family reunions and seminars hosted. Antiques, fishing, parks, shopping, cross-country skiing and theater nearby. TAC10.

Kansas

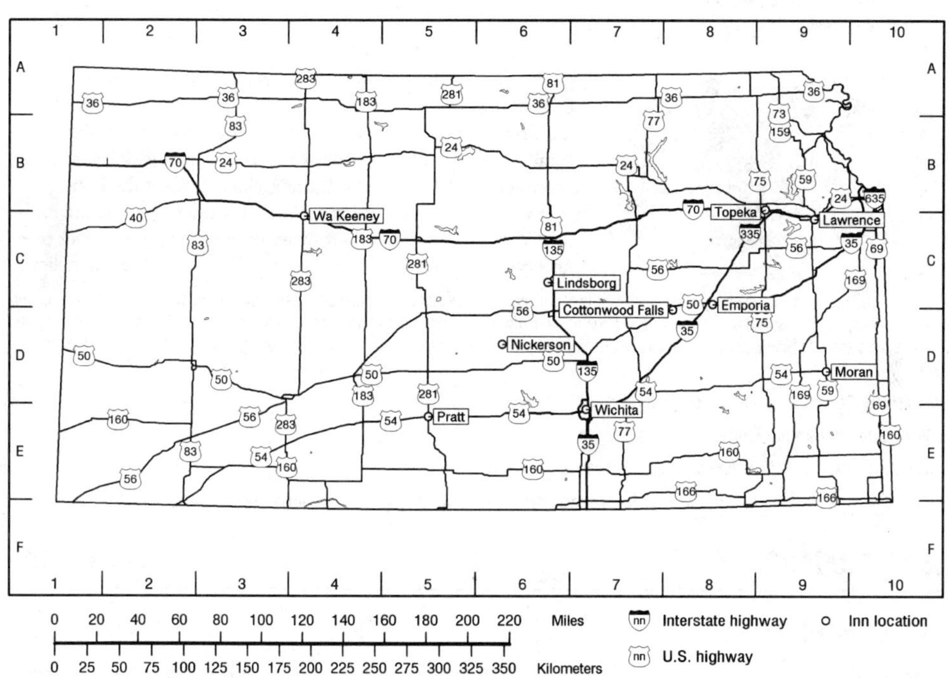

KS

Cottonwood Falls **D8**

Stonehouse B&B on Mulberry Hill

Rt 1, Box 67A
Cottonwood Falls, KS 66845
(316)273-8481
Fax:(316)273-8481
E-mail: 5hmh1874@aol.com

Rates: $60-75.
Payment: MC VISA TC.
Innkeeper(s): Dan & Carrie Riggs.
Circa: 1874.

Rooms: 3 rooms with PB.
Beds: KQT.

More than 100 acres surround this historic home, which is one of the state's oldest native stone homes that is still in use. Each guest room offers something special. The Rose Room includes a sleigh bed, while the Blue Room and Yellow Room offer views either of the quarry pond or the Flint Hills. Explore the property and you'll see wildlife, an old stone barn and corral ruins. The Cottonwood River runs through the property at one point, offering fishing. The innkeepers can arrange for guests to fish in a stocked pond, too.

Breakfast included in rates. Types of meals: continental breakfast, full breakfast and gourmet breakfast. Air conditioning and ceiling fan in room. VCR, fax, copier and library on premises. 120 acres. Antiques, fishing, parks, shopping and watersports nearby.

Pets Allowed: Kennel for dogs.

"I have never felt so pampered. Our walk around the countryside was so peaceful and beautiful."

Emporia C8

Plumb House B&B

628 Exchange St
Emporia, KS 66801-3008
(316)342-6881

Rates: $65-80.
Payment: MC VISA AX PC TC.
Innkeeper(s): Barbara Stoecklin.
Circa: 1910.

Rooms: 5 rooms, 3 with PB, 1 with FP. 1 suite. 1 conference room.
Beds: KQDT.

Named for former owners of this restored Victorian Shingle home, the Plumb House offers elegant touches of that period's finery throughout its attractive interior. Try the Rosalie Room, with its pink roses and white lace or the Horseless Carriage Room with old-fashioned tub and rocking chair or the Loft, a suite with not only a view, but all the amenities of home, including TV, refrigerator and microwave. Be sure to inquire about the inn's two-hour Tea Party, available for that extra-special occasion.

Breakfast, afternoon tea and evening snack included in rates. Types of meals: continental breakfast, full breakfast, gourmet breakfast and early coffee/tea. Room service available. Air conditioning, turn-down service and ceiling fan in room. Cable TV, VCR and spa on premises. Weddings, small meetings, family reunions and seminars hosted. Antiques, fishing, parks, shopping, sporting events and theater nearby. TAC10.

Pets Allowed: Pet boarding off premises, but nearby.

Publicity: *Emporia Gazette, KSNW-TV, Wichita, Kansas.*

Special Discounts: 10% off for corporate guests, seniors.

"This is the most elegant place I have ever had the pleasure to stay in. It's beautiful Victorian decor has refreshed my soul."

Lawrence C9

Halcyon House

1000 Ohio St
Lawrence, KS 66044-2972
(913)841-0314
Fax:(913)843-7273

Rates: $45-85.
Payment: MC VISA AX.
Innkeeper(s): Constance Wolfe.
Circa: 1895.

Rooms: 9 rooms, 3 with PB, 1 with FP. 3 suites.
Beds: KQDT.

This remodeled Victorian house is located within three blocks of the University of Kansas. Polished oak floors in the parlor lead to an expansive kitchen featuring a vaulted ceiling, brick floor and floor-to-ceiling window walls. Guest rooms are brightly painted with an eclectic mix of cheerful furnishings. The master suite features a circular bathtub and skylights.

Breakfast included in rates. Type of meal: full breakfast. Air conditioning, cable TV and VCR in room. Fax on premises. Weddings and family reunions hosted. Antiques, parks, shopping, sporting events and theater nearby.

Location: Twenty-five miles west of Kansas City.

Publicity: *University Daily Kansan, Midwest Living, Kansas Business News.*

"I enjoyed it so much I am planning to bring my parents up for a shopping trip before Christmas."

Lindsborg C6

Swedish Country Inn

112 W Lincoln St
Lindsborg, KS 67456-2319
(913)227-2985 (800)231-0266

Rates: $50-61.
Payment: MC VISA AX DS PC TC.
Innkeeper(s): Becky Anderson.
Circa: 1904.

Rooms: 19 rooms with PB. 2 suites.
Beds: QD.

Founded in the 1860s by Swedish immigrants, the town of Lindsborg is still known as "Little Sweden," maintaining its heritage through a variety of cultural events, festivals, galleries, shops and restaurants. The

Swedish Country Inn adds to the town's ethnic flavor. All the furnishings have been imported from Sweden. Bright, airy rooms feature pine furnishings, hand-made quilts and hand-painted cupboards. A Swedish-style buffet breakfast is served each morning, with items such as meatballs, lingonberries, herring, knackebread, fruit, cheese, cold meats and fresh baked goods. The Christmas season is an especially festive time to visit this inn and picturesque small town.

Breakfast, afternoon tea and evening snack included in rates. Types of meals: full breakfast, gourmet breakfast and early coffee/tea. Air conditioning and cable TV in room. Sauna and bicycles on premises. Weddings, small meetings, family reunions and seminars hosted. Antiques, parks and shopping nearby.

Special Discounts: Group rates.

Moran — D9

Hedgeapple Acres B&B

4430 US 54 Hwy
Moran, KS 66755-9500
(316)237-4646

Rates: $58-65.
Payment: MC VISA AX DS PC TC.
Innkeeper(s): Jack & Ann Donaldson.
Circa: 1974.

Rooms: 6 rooms with PB, 1 with FP. 1 conference room.
Beds: K.

KS

Nestled on 80-acres of farmland, this country home offers comfortable furnishings and plenty of places to relax. One of the bedchambers boasts a whirlpool tub, while another includes a fireplace. Guests not only enjoy a hearty country breakfast, but supper as well. Spend the day exploring the area, which includes historic Fort Scott, or grab your rod and reel and try out the farm's two stocked ponds.

Breakfast, dinner and evening snack included in rates. Types of meals: full breakfast and early coffee/tea. Banquet service and catering service available. Air conditioning and ceiling fan in room. Cable TV, VCR, fax and library on premises. Handicap access. 80 acres. Weddings, small meetings, family reunions and seminars hosted. Antiques, fishing, parks, shopping and theater nearby. TAC10.

Nickerson — D6

Hedrick's Exotic Animal Farm and B&B

7910 N Roy L Smith Rd
Nickerson, KS 67561-9049
(316)422-3245 (800)618-9577

Rates: $59-100.
Payment: MC VISA DS PC TC.
Innkeeper(s): Joe & Sondra Hedrick.
Circa: 1993.

Rooms: 7 rooms with PB. 1 suite. 2 conference rooms.
Beds: Q.

There are few places where one can say they've been properly greeted by a giraffe, and Hedrick's is one of them. You may reread the first sentence if you wish. That's right, a giraffe is among the many unusual animals that inhabit the grounds at this exotic animal farm. Guests are welcome to pet camels, kiss giraffes, hop with kangaroos or hug a llama. Even the exterior of this bed & breakfast is entrancing. The whole place appears as the facade of an Old West town. The rooms are a wild, exotic mix of decor, that is both whimsical and strangely elegant at the same time. Local artists have painted murals in each of the themed guest quarters, and each room is named in honor of one of the animals who reside at the farm. The innkeepers offer vacation options for groups, and this farm is an ideal place for a family vacation. Children can enjoy pony rides and even help bottle feed baby animals.

Breakfast and evening snack included in rates. Types of meals: full breakfast and early coffee/tea. Banquet service, catering service and catered breakfast available. Air conditioning and ceiling fan in room. VCR and copier on premises. Handicap access. Weddings, small meetings, family reunions and seminars hosted. Antiques, fishing, parks, shopping and sporting events nearby.

"This is fantastic—great service, food, animals, room—just everything!"

Pratt E5

Pratt Guest House B&B Inn

PO Box 326
Pratt, KS 67124-0326
(316)672-1200

Rates: $50-90.
Payment: MC VISA PC.
Innkeeper(s): Marguerite Flanagan.
Circa: 1910.

Rooms: 5 rooms with PB.
Beds: KQD.

This three-story Colonial Revival was built by Samuel Gebhart, who not only founded a town newspaper, but also served as a mayor and councilman. The innkeeper painstakingly restored the three-story manor, which is the only property in Pratt listed in both the state and national historic registers. William Jennings Bryan was once a guest here. Family heirlooms and antiques are the furnishings that decorate the interior, giving the home a nostalgic atmosphere. However, two of the rooms include the modern amenity of a whirlpool tub. Stuffed French toast or a frittata are among the breakfast specialties, served along with freshly ground coffee, fruit and homemade muffins or breads.

Breakfast and evening snack included in rates. Types of meals: full breakfast, gourmet breakfast and early coffee/tea. Air conditioning in room. Weddings, small meetings and family reunions hosted. Antiques, fishing, parks and shopping nearby.

"Beautiful B&B. A+ from a couple of school folks."

Topeka B9

Heritage House

3535 SW 6th Ave
Topeka, KS 66606-1985
(913)233-3800 (800)582-1937
Fax:(913)233-9793

Rates: $79-159.
Payment: MC VISA AX DC DS.
Innkeeper(s): Mike Guernsey.
Circa: 1880.

Rooms: 10 rooms with PB. 1 suite. 1 conference room.
Beds: KQD.

This was the original Midwestern farm home of the Menninger Clinic. A wide porch that wraps around the front is filled with wicker furnishings. Each room was decorated by a different design firm when the inn appeared as a designer showcase home. Dr. Karl's Study is popular with its luminous paneling and desk. The bridal suite boasts a four-poster bed and whirlpool.

Breakfast included in rates. Types of meals: full breakfast and gourmet breakfast. Dinner, lunch, catering service and room service available. Fax and copier on premises. Antiques, fishing and theater nearby.

Publicity: *Adventure Road.*

"The meal served, the service and the setting were second to none."

Wakeeney C4

Thistle Hill B&B

RR 1 Box 93
Wakeeney, KS 67672-9736
(913)743-2644

Rates: $55-65.
Payment: MC VISA PC TC.
Innkeeper(s): Dave & Mary Hendricks.
Circa: 1950.

Rooms: 3 rooms with PB.
Beds: QD.

This modern cedar farmhouse has a unique, "older" feel, aided mainly by its porch, which is reminiscent of the Old West. The interior features an oak-floored dining room and views of the inn's gardens, farm and prairie. The second-story guest rooms include the Prairie Room, with a queen-size bed; the Sunflower Room, which boasts a handmade Kansas sunflower quilt and a view of the farm's working windmill; and the Oak

Room, which offers a queen-size handmade fence post bed and a hide-a-bed for extra family members. Guests may explore a 60-acre prairie-wildflower restoration, which attracts many species of birds.

Breakfast and afternoon tea included in rates. Types of meals: full breakfast, gourmet breakfast and early coffee/tea. Air conditioning and ceiling fan in room. Spa, stables and library on premises. 620 acres. Small meetings and family reunions hosted. Antiques, fishing, parks and shopping nearby. TAC10.

Pets Allowed: Outside only.

Location: Half-way between Denver and Kansas City. Sternberg Museum, Cottonwood Ranch and Castle Rock nearby.

Publicity: *Kansas Weekend Guide, Kansas City Star, Country, Denver Post.*

Wichita

E7

The Inn at The Park

3751 E Douglas Ave
Wichita, KS 67218-1002
(316)652-0500 (800)258-1951
Fax:(316)652-0610

Rates: $75-135.
Payment: MC VISA AX DS.
Innkeeper(s): Lynda Weixelman.
Circa: 1910.

Rooms: 12 rooms with PB, 8 with FP. 3 suites. 1 conference room.
Beds: KQ.

KS

This popular three-story brick mansion offers many special touches, including unique furnishings in each of its 11 guest rooms, three of which are suites. Some of the rooms feature fireplaces, refrigerators or hot tubs. The inn's convenient location makes it ideal for business travelers or those interested in exploring Wichita at length. The inn's parkside setting provides additional opportunities for relaxation or recreation. Ask for information about shops and restaurants in Wichita's Old Town.

Breakfast included in rates. Types of meals: continental-plus breakfast and early coffee/tea. Catering service available. Air conditioning, turn-down service, cable TV and VCR in room. Fax, copier, computer and spa on premises. Weddings, small meetings and seminars hosted. Antiques, shopping and theater nearby.

Publicity: *Wichita Business Journal.*

"This is truly a distinctive hotel. Your attention to detail is surpassed only by your devotion to excellent service."

Wine and Cheese Strata

Henderson House
Estes Park, Colo.

Note: The innkeeper suggests serving this dish with an appetizer of fresh fruit and a side of asparagus.

½ loaf French bread, cubed
2 cups shredded Swiss cheese
1 cup shredded Monterey Jack cheese
½ cup grated Parmesan cheese
¾ cup ham, cubed
2 green onions, sliced
6 eggs
2 cups half and half
1 pint sour cream
2 t Dijon mustard
⅛ t pepper
¼ cup dry white wine

Spray 9-by-13" baking dish. Cover bottom with cubed bread. Top bread with shredded Swiss and Jack cheeses, ham and green onion.

In a large mixing bowl, combine eggs, half and half, wine, mustard and pepper. Beat until thoroughly mixed. Pour over dry mixture in baking dish. Press lightly with back of spoon to soak bread with liquid. Cover and refrigerate overnight.

Preheat oven to 325 degrees. Bake covered for 40 to 45 minutes, until puffed and knife inserted comes out clean.

Combine sour cream and Parmesan cheese in sauce pan and allow to simmer. Let strata cool 10 minutes. Cut into squares. Top each serving with sour cream mixture.

Kentucky

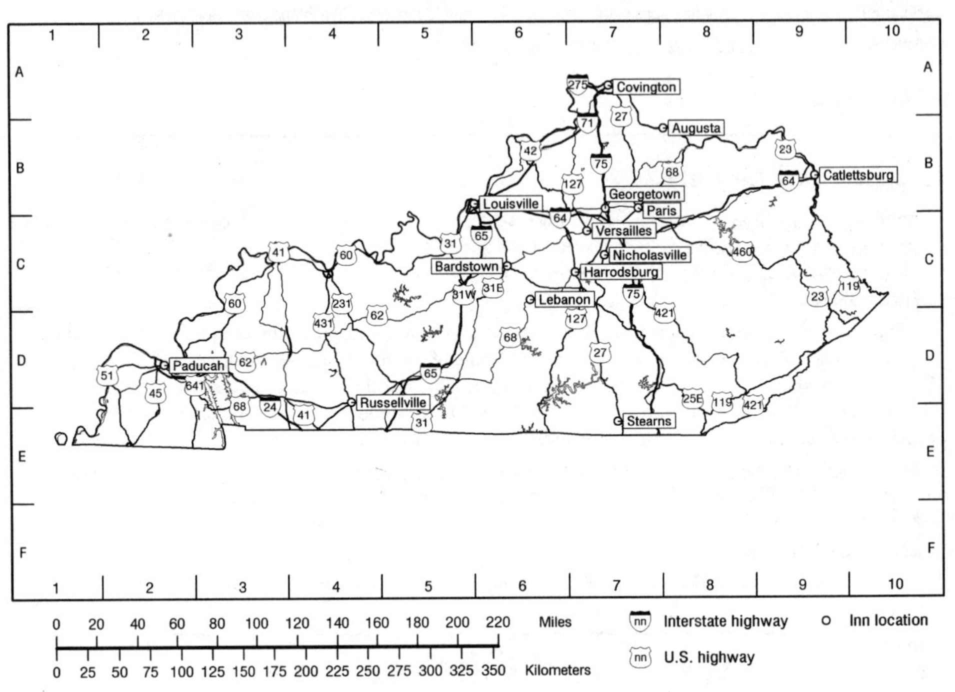

Augusta

B8

Augusta Ayre

201 W 2nd St
Augusta, KY 41002-1004
(606)756-3228

Rates: $65-90.
Payment: DS.
Innkeeper(s): Maynard Krum.
Circa: 1840.

Rooms: 2 rooms, 2 with FP.
Beds: D.

This Federal-style home was built by a freed slave and offers close access to the Ohio River and a city park. Each of the guest rooms includes a fireplace, and the sitting room is the perfect place to curl up and enjoy a book or old movie. Augusta offers many historic homes and antique shops to visit.

Breakfast included in rates. Types of meals: full breakfast and early coffee/tea. Air conditioning and ceiling fan in room. Cable TV and VCR on premises. Small meetings, family reunions and seminars hosted. Antiques, fishing, parks and watersports nearby.

Pets Allowed.

"Thank you for your generous hospitality and all the special touch surprises! A wonderful home away from home."

Bardstown

C6

Jailer's Inn

111 W Stephen Foster Ave
Bardstown, KY 40004-1415
(502)348-5551 (800)948-5551
Fax:(502)348-1852

Rates: $65-95.
Payment: MC VISA AX DS PC TC.
Innkeeper(s): Paul McCoy.
Circa: 1819.

Rooms: 6 rooms with PB. 1 conference room.
Beds: KQD.

This old jail was constructed of native limestone. There were two cells and an upstairs dungeon to house prisoners. The back building, sometimes referred to as the new jail, is completely surrounded by a stone wall. A former women's cell serves as a suite. Antiques and heirlooms fill the rooms now. Two rooms have double Jacuzzi tubs. Only one of the inn's rooms resembles a jail cell, complete with two of the original bunks.

Breakfast included in rates. Types of meals: full breakfast and early coffee/tea. Evening snack available. Air conditioning, turn-down service, ceiling fan and cable TV in room. VCR on premises. Weddings, small meetings and family reunions hosted. Antiques, parks, shopping and theater nearby. TAC10.

Location: South of Louisville 35 miles.

Publicity: *Vacations, New Choices, Kentucky Standard, USA Weekend.*

"Wonderful experience! A very special B&B."

KY

Catlettsburg

B9

Levi Hampton House B&B

2206 Walnut St, Rt 23
Catlettsburg, KY 41129
(606)739-8118
Fax:(606)739-6148

Rates: $60-80.
Payment: MC VISA PC TC.
Innkeeper(s): Dennis & Kathy Stemen.
Circa: 1847.

Rooms: 4 rooms, 3 with PB, 4 with FP.
Beds: QT.

Levi J. Hampton, was one of the area's first settlers, and he built this pre-Civil War, Italianate-style home. Guest rooms are decorated with poster beds, candles and just a touch of lace. The innkeepers offer plenty of amenities for their business travelers, including computer jacks and fax or copier service. Guests enjoy early morning coffee or tea service in their rooms before joining the hosts for a full breakfast with treats such as homemade breads and perhaps a Southwestern-style quiche with tomatoes and salsa.

Breakfast and afternoon tea included in rates. Types of meals: full breakfast and early coffee/tea. Air conditioning in room. Cable TV, VCR, fax, copier and bicycles on premises. Weddings and small meetings hosted. Amusement parks, antiques, fishing, parks and shopping nearby. TAC10.

"We will leave with delightful memories of this wonderful home."

The Licking Riverside Historic B&B

516 Garrard St
Covington, KY 41011-2561
(606)291-0191 (800)483-7822
Fax:(606)291-0939
E-mail: freelyn@aol.com

Rates: $79-129.
Payment: MC VISA AX PC TC.
Innkeeper(s): Lynda L. Freeman.
Circa: 1870.

Rooms: 2 rooms. 1 suite.
Beds: Q.

What once was a home for aged and indigent women now offers two suites decked in Victorian decor. One suite offers period furnishings, a sitting area, fireplace and raised Jacuzzi, which boasts a river view. The other suite features a wrought iron four-poster bed, sitting room, dining area and wet bar. Breakfasts of homemade muffins, breads and cakes are delivered to the suites each morning along with juices, coffee and tea.

Breakfast included in rates. Type of meal: continental-plus breakfast. Picnic lunch available. Air conditioning, cable TV and VCR in room. Fax and copier on premises. Weddings, small meetings and seminars hosted. Amusement parks, antiques, fishing, parks, shopping, sporting events, theater and watersports nearby.

Publicity: *Kentucky Post.*

"We loved your B&B and plan on returning. Your home is lovely and the cheesecake was delicious."

Sandford House B&B

1026 Russell St
Covington, KY 41011-3065
(606)291-9133
E-mail: danrrmiles@aol.com

Rates: $55-85.
Payment: MC VISA PC TC.
Innkeeper(s): Dan & Linda Carter.
Circa: 1820.

Rooms: 5 rooms with PB. 1 suite. 1 cottage.
Beds: QT.

Originally a fine example of Federal architecture, the inn underwent reconstruction after a fire in the 1880s and changed to a more Victorian style. The inn once served as a finishing school for young ladies, and was the President's home for the Western Baptist Theological Seminary. The home now offers two full apartments, a suite and one guest room. Guests enjoy a gourmet breakfast. The inn is in the heart of the Old Seminary Historic District, listed in the National Register. Just two blocks away is the Basilica.

Breakfast included in rates. Type of meal: gourmet breakfast. Ceiling fan, cable TV and VCR in room. Weddings, small meetings, family reunions and seminars hosted. Amusement parks, antiques, parks, shopping, sporting events, theater and watersports nearby. TAC10.

Pets Allowed.

Publicity: *Cincinnati Post.*

Special Discounts: Fourth night free.

Georgetown B7

Jordan Farm

4091 Newtown Pike
Georgetown, KY 40324
(502)863-1944
Fax:(502)868-9002

Rates: $75.
Payment: PC TC.
Innkeeper(s): Harold & Becky Jordan.
Circa: 1992.

Rooms: 3 suites. 1 cottage.
Beds: Q.

Spend the night at a working horse farm at this bed & breakfast. Guest rooms feature Jacuzzi tubs and traditional decor. There is a private fishing lake on the 100-acre farm, which guests are invited to use. The continental-plus breakfasts include items such as country ham and homemade breads.

Breakfast included in rates. Type of meal: continental-plus breakfast. Air conditioning in room. Bicycles on premises. 100 acres. Amusement parks, antiques, fishing, parks, shopping, sporting events and theater nearby.

KY

Harrodsburg C7

Shakertown at Pleasant Hill

3500 Lexington Rd
Harrodsburg, KY 40330
(606)734-5411

Rates: $45-85. EP.
Innkeeper(s): Ann Voris.
Circa: 1805.

Rooms: 81 rooms with PB. 1 conference room.
Beds: DT.

A non-profit organization preserves this 19th-century Shaker village set atop a pleasant meadow. Guest rooms are in 15 restored buildings. The old road running through the village is a National Landmark and is restricted to foot traffic. Reproductions of authentic Shaker furnishings fill the guest rooms. Air conditioning is hidden, and there are no closets. Instead, clothes (and sometimes chairs and lamps) are hung on Shaker pegs spaced one foot apart on all four walls. Costumed interpreters in the craft buildings describe Shaker culture and craft.

Type of meal: gourmet breakfast. EP. Fax on premises.

Location: Twenty-five miles southwest of Lexington on US Hwy 68.

Publicity: *Southern Living, Traveler, Richmond Times-Dispatch.*

"We can't wait to return! We treasure our memories here of peaceful, pleasant days."

Lebanon C6

Myrtledene B&B

370 N Spalding Ave
Lebanon, KY 40033-1563
(502)692-2223 (800)391-1721

Rates: $65.
Payment: MC VISA PC TC.
Innkeeper(s): James F. Spragens.
Circa: 1833.

Rooms: 4 rooms, 1 with FP. 1 conference room.
Beds: DT.

Once a Confederate general's headquarters at a point during the Civil War, this pink brick inn, located at a bend in the road, has greeted visitors entering Lebanon for more than 150 years. When General John Hunt Morgan returned in 1863 to destroy the town, the white flag hoisted to signal a truce was flown at Myrtledene. A country breakfast usually features ham and biscuits as well as the innkeepers' specialty, peaches and cream French toast.

Breakfast included in rates. Types of meals: full breakfast, gourmet breakfast and early coffee/tea. Afternoon tea available. Air conditioning and turn-down service in room. Cable TV, VCR and library on premises. Weddings, small meetings, family reunions and seminars hosted. Antiques, fishing, parks, shopping, theater and watersports nearby. TAC10.

Publicity: *Lebanon Enterprise, Louisville Courier-Journal, Lebanon/Marion County Kentucky.*

"Our night in the Cabbage Rose Room was an experience of another time, another culture. Your skill in preparing and presenting breakfast was equally elegant! We'll be back!"

Louisville **B6**

Ashton's Victorian Secret B&B

1132 S 1st St
Louisville, KY 40203-2804
(502)581-1914
E-mail: sroosa@ix.netcom.com

Rates: $48-89.
Payment: PC.
Innkeeper(s): Nan & Steve Roosa.
Circa: 1883.

Rooms: 4 rooms, 1 with PB, 4 with FP. 1 suite.
Beds: KQD.

This three-story Queen Anne Victorian has 11 fireplaces. Antiques and period furnishings are featured throughout the brick inn, located in Historic Old Louisville. Guest amenities include sundecks, washer-dryer facilities and a workout room with a bench press, rowing machine and stationary bicycle.

Breakfast included in rates. Type of meal: continental-plus breakfast. Air conditioning and ceiling fan in room. VCR on premises. Small meetings and family reunions hosted. Amusement parks, antiques, parks, shopping, downhill skiing, sporting events and theater nearby. TAC7.

Special Discounts: Call.

Inn at The Park

1332 S 4th St
Louisville, KY 40208-2314
(502)637-6930 (800)700-7275
Fax:(502)637-2796
E-mail: innatpark@aol.com

Rates: $79-119.
Payment: MC VISA AX PC TC.
Innkeeper(s): John & Sandra Mullins.
Circa: 1886.

Rooms: 7 rooms, 6 with PB, 3 with FP. 1 suite.
Beds: KQ.

An impressive sweeping staircase is one of many highlights at this handsome Richardsonian Romanesque inn, in the historic district of Old Louisville. Guests also will appreciate the hardwood floors, 14-foot ceilings and stone balconies on the second and third floors. The six guest rooms offer a variety of amenities and a view of Central Park. Guests may enjoy breakfast in their rooms or in the well-appointed central dining area.

Breakfast included in rates. Types of meals: full breakfast and early coffee/tea. Air conditioning, ceiling fan and cable TV in room. VCR and fax on premises. Small meetings and seminars hosted. German spoken. Amusement parks, antiques, parks, shopping, sporting events and theater nearby. TAC10.

Old Louisville Inn

1359 S 3rd St
Louisville, KY 40208-2378
(502)635-1574
Fax:(502)637-5892

Rates: $65-195.
Payment: MC VISA PC TC.
Innkeeper(s): Marianne Lesher.
Circa: 1901.

Rooms: 11 rooms, 6 with PB, 1 with FP. 2 suites.
Beds: KQDT.

This 10,000-square-foot, three-story Beaux Arts inn boasts massive ornately carved mahogany columns in the lobby. Rooms are filled with antiques gathered from local auctions and shops. The third-floor Celebration Suite, with its whirlpool bath, fireplace and king-size canopy bed, offers perfect honeymoon accommodations. The morning meal, including the inn's famous popovers, is served in the breakfast room, courtyard or in the guest rooms. The inn's location, in the heart of Louisville's Victorian district, makes sightseeing inviting.

Breakfast and afternoon tea included in rates. Type of meal: gourmet breakfast. Air conditioning in room. VCR, fax and copier on premises. Weddings, small meetings, family reunions and seminars hosted. Antiques, parks, shopping, sporting events and theater nearby.

"My most enjoyable, relaxed business trip!"

Nicholasville C7

Sandusky House & O'Neal Log Cabin B&B

1626 Delaney Ferry Rd
Nicholasville, KY 40356
(606)223-4730

Rates: $75-95.
Payment: MC VISA PC.
Innkeeper(s): Jim & Linda Humphrey.
Circa: 1855.

Rooms: 3 rooms with PB. 1 cottage.
Beds: D.

This Greek Revival inn rests in the tree-lined countryside, surrounded by horse farms and other small farms. Its tranquil setting offers a perfect getaway from busy nearby Lexington. The inn, which is listed on Kentucky's state register, boasts six porches, seven fireplaces and impressive brick columns. The three guest rooms feature desks, private baths and turndown service. The innkeepers also offer lodging in a two-bedroom, 180-year-old log cabin. Although historic, the National Register cabin includes modern amenities such as a full kitchen and whirlpool tub. Area attractions include Asbury College, Keeneland Race Course, the Mary Todd Lincoln House and the University of Kentucky.

KY

Breakfast included in rates. Types of meals: full breakfast and early coffee/tea. Air conditioning and turn-down service in room. Cable TV and VCR on premises. 10 acres. Amusement parks, antiques, fishing, parks, shopping, sporting events and theater nearby.

Special Discounts: Seventh day free.

Paducah D2

The 1857's B&B

PO Box 7771
Paducah, KY 42001-0789
(502)444-3960 (800)264-5607
Fax:(502)444-3960

Rates: $65-95.
Payment: MC VISA PC TC.
Innkeeper(s): Deborah Bohnert.
Circa: 1857.

Rooms: 3 rooms. 1 suite.
Beds: KQDT.

Paducah's thriving, history-rich commercial district is home to this Folk Victorian inn, located in Market House Square. Guests choose from rooms such as the Master Bedroom, a suite featuring a king-size, four-poster bed or perhaps the Hunt Room, which includes a four-poster, queen-size canopy bed. The popular third-floor game room boasts an impressive mahogany billiard table. There is an outdoor hot tub on the deck. The Ohio River is an easy walk from the inn, and guests also will enjoy an evening stroll along the gas-lit brick sidewalks. The inn occupies the second and third floors of a former clothing store, with an Italian restaurant at street level.

Breakfast included in rates. Types of meals: continental-plus breakfast and early coffee/tea. Room service available. Air conditioning, ceiling fan and cable TV in room. VCR, fax, copier and library on premises. Small meetings and family reunions hosted. Antiques, fishing, shopping, theater and watersports nearby. TAC10.

Paris B7

Rosedale B&B

1917 Cypress St
Paris, KY 40361-1220
(606)987-1845 (800)644-1862

Rates: $65-100.
Payment: MC VISA PC TC.
Innkeeper(s): Katie & Jim Haag.
Circa: 1862.

Rooms: 4 rooms, 2 with PB. 2 suites.
Beds: DT.

Once the home of Civil War General John Croxton, this low-roofed Italianate inn was voted prettiest B&B in the Bluegrass area by the Lexington Herald-Leader in 1994. The four decorated guest rooms feature Colonial touches and are filled with antiques and paintings. Fresh flowers, down comforters and ceiling fans add to the rooms' comfort and charm. The Henry Clay Room, with its twin four-poster beds, is one option for visitors. Guests may relax with a game of croquet, bocce, horseshoes on one of the benches found on the

inn's three-acre lawn, or on the screened porch. Duncan Tavern Historic Shrine is nearby, as well as beautiful horse farms.

Breakfast and evening snack included in rates. Types of meals: full breakfast and early coffee/tea. Air conditioning and ceiling fan in room. Cable TV, VCR and library on premises. Small meetings, family reunions and seminars hosted. Antiques, fishing, parks, shopping, sporting events and theater nearby.

"Your hospitality has been lovely and your home is a fine example of tradition and comfort."

Russellville **D4**

The Log House

2139 Franklin Rd
Russellville, KY 42276-9410
(502)726-8483
Fax:(502)726-2270
E-mail: 731333,647@compuserve.com

Rates: $85-95.
Payment: MC VISA AX DS PC TC.
Innkeeper(s): Allison & Richard Dennis.
Circa: 1976.

Rooms: 4 rooms with PB, 2 with FP.
Beds: QDT.

This ideal log cabin retreat was built from hand-hewn logs from old cabins and barns in the area. Rooms are full of quilts, early American furnishings and folk art from around the world. The log walls and hardwood floors create an unparalleled atmosphere of country warmth. An impressive kitchen is decorated with an old-fashioned stove and crammed with knickknacks. Innkeeper Allison Dennis creates hand-woven garments and accessories in an adjacent studio. Nashville and Opryland are about an hour's drive, and the local area boasts a number of antique shops.

Breakfast included in rates. Type of meal: gourmet breakfast. Room service available. Air conditioning in room. VCR, fax, copier, spa and library on premises. 15 acres. Weddings and small meetings hosted. Amusement parks, antiques, fishing, parks, shopping, sporting events, theater and watersports nearby.

Stearns **E7**

Marcum-Porter House

#35 Home Dr, PO Box 369
Stearns, KY 42647-0369
(606)376-2242
Fax:(502)875-3421

Rates: $55-65.
Payment: MC VISA PC TC.
Innkeeper(s): Charles & Sandra Porter, Patricia Porter Newton.
Circa: 1902.

Rooms: 4 rooms, 1 with PB.
Beds: D.

This two-story frame home once housed employees of the Stearns Coal & Lumber Company. Many guests like to wander the gardens of the historic inn. Golfers will enjoy a nearby nine-hole course, believed to be the second-oldest course in the state. Be sure to take a ride on the Big South Fork Scenic Railway during your stay. Area attractions include Big South Fork National Recreation Area, Cumberland Falls State Park and Yahoo Falls.

Breakfast, afternoon tea and evening snack included in rates. Types of meals: full breakfast, gourmet breakfast and early coffee/tea. Ceiling fan in room. Cable TV, VCR and library on premises. Handicap access. Weddings, small meetings and family reunions hosted. Antiques, fishing, parks, shopping and watersports nearby.

Special Discounts: 10% off for multiple rooms and nights.

B&B at Sills Inn

270 Montgomery Ave
Versailles, KY 40383-1427
(606)873-4478 (800)526-9801
Fax:(606)873-7099
E-mail: sillsinn@aol.com

Rates: $59-129.
Payment: MC VISA AX DS TC.
Innkeeper(s): Tony Sills.
Circa: 1911.

Rooms: 12 rooms with PB. 9 suites. 30 cottages. 2 conference rooms.
Beds: KQ.

Innkeeper Tony Sills didn't miss a detail with this restored Victorian Inn, located only a short distance from the state capital and many other attractions, including the Keeneland race course, a restored Shaker village and plenty of interesting shops, cafes and art studios. A fully stocked guest kitchen is available to guests craving a midnight snack and three of the suites feature wet bars. Breakfast is served on fine china and crystal in the sun porch. There are plenty of places to relax, including three common areas and a wraparound porch.

Breakfast and evening snack included in rates. Type of meal: gourmet breakfast. Air conditioning, ceiling fan, cable TV and VCR in room. Fax, copier and library on premises. Handicap access. Small meetings, family reunions and seminars hosted. Antiques, fishing, parks, shopping, sporting events and theater nearby. TAC10.

KY

Huevos Santa Barbara

Simpson House Inn
Santa Barbara, Calif.

For each serving:
2 T Mexican salsa
2 T cooked black beans
1 whole egg
2 T sharp white cheddar cheese
5-6 black olives (chopped)

Beans:
1 lb. black beans
¼ medium onion, chopped
2 T chili powder
1 tomato, chopped
Oil

Garnish:
Sour cream
Salsa
Fresh cilantro

Saute onion, chili powder and tomato in oil until tender. Set aside. Cook beans by placing 1 lb. of beans in a covered pot. Cover beans with water and add 1 T salt. Cover and bring to a boil. Reduce heat and simmer until beans are cooked through, approximately two hours. When beans are cooked , drain thoroughly.

Lightly oil individual-size ramekins and in the following order, place each ingredient in a ramekin: Salsa , beans, egg, cheese and olives. Bake at 375 degrees for 12-15 minutes or microwave covered, 2 minutes for each egg.

Serve with a dollop of sour cream, salsa and a sprig of fresh cilantro.

Louisiana

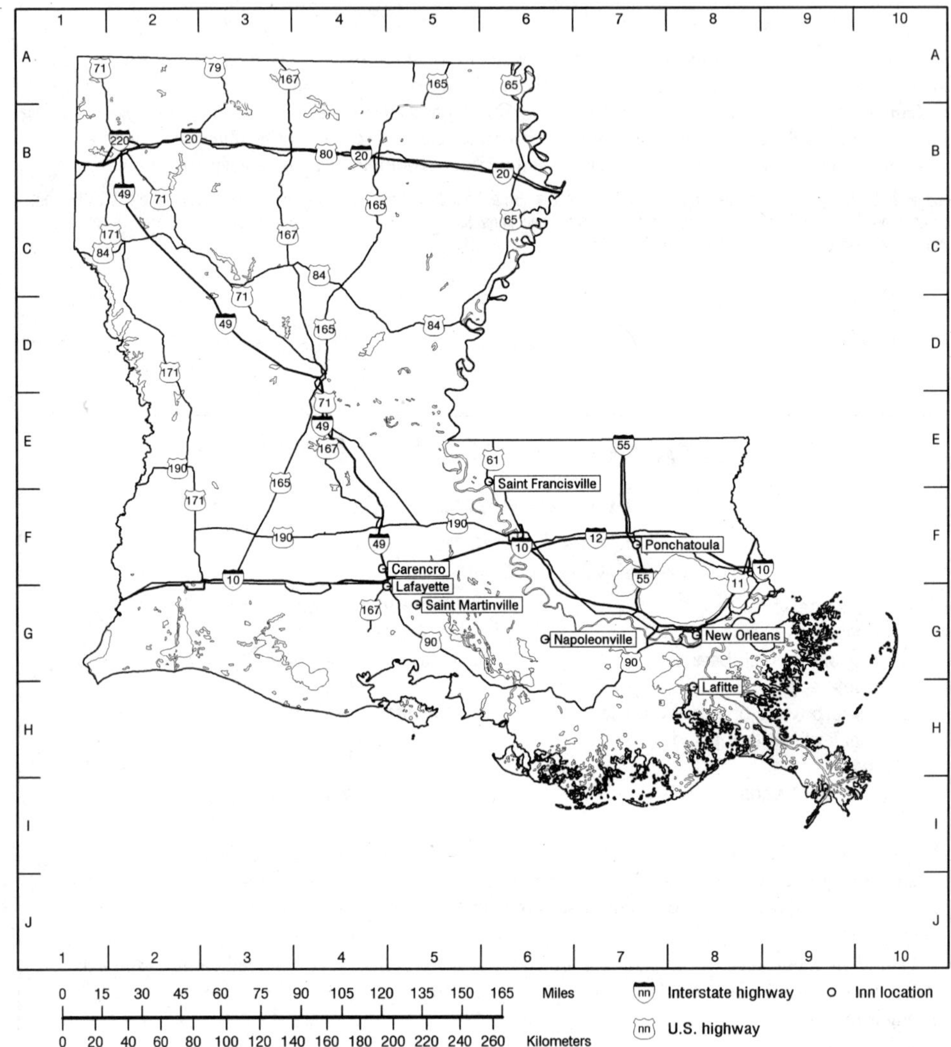

Saint Francisville
Ponchatoula
Carencro
Lafayette
Saint Martinville
Napoleonville
New Orleans
Lafitte
Miles
Kilometers
Interstate highway
U.S. highway
Inn location

Carencro

F4

La Maison De Campagne, Lafayette

825 Kidder Rd
Carencro, LA 70520-9119
(318)896-6529 (800)895-0235
Fax:(318)896-1494

Rates: $100-140. AP.
Payment: MC VISA AX DS PC TC.
Innkeeper(s): Joeann & Fred McLemore.
Circa: 1871.

Rooms: 4 rooms with PB. 1 cottage.
Beds: KQD.

Built by a successful plantation owner, this turn-of-the-century Victorian has once again found a new life with innkeepers Fred and Joeann McLemore. The McLemores turned what was an almost dilapidated old home into a welcoming B&B, surrounded by nine acres of manicured lawns dotted with flowers and trees. The home is filled with antiques and treasures Joeann collected during Fred's three decades of military service, which took them around the world. Fine Victorian pieces are accented by lace and Oriental rugs. The innkeepers offer accommodations in the main house, or for longer stays, in an adjacent sharecropper's cottage. The cottage includes kitchen and laundry facilities. Joeann prepares the Cajun-style breakfasts. Several different homemade breads or pastries accompany items such as banana-strawberry soup, sweet potato biscuits, spicy Cajun eggs souffles or a potato and sausage quiche.

Breakfast and evening snack included in rates. Types of meals: continental breakfast, gourmet breakfast and early coffee/tea. AP. Air conditioning, turn-down service and ceiling fan in room. Cable TV, fax, copier and swimming on premises. Small meetings hosted. Cajun French spoken. Antiques, fishing, parks, shopping, sporting events, theater and watersports nearby. TAC10.

LA

Location: Heart of Cajun Country.

Publicity: *Los Angeles Times, Boston Globe, Country, Texas Monthly, Country Inn.*

Lafayette

G4

Alida's, A B&B

2631 SE Evangeline
Thruway, Lafayette, LA
70508-2168
(318)264-1191 (800)922-5867
Fax:(318)264-1415
E-mail: alidas@iamerica.net

Rates: $75-125.
Payment: MC VISA AX DS PC TC.
Innkeeper(s): Tanya & Doug Greenwald.
Circa: 1902.

Rooms: 4 rooms with PB. 1 conference room.
Beds: QD.

This home is named for teacher Alida Martin, who along with once owning this Queen Anne house, was responsible for educating many Lafayette citizens, including a few civic leaders. Alida taught at the house until a one-room schoolhouse was constructed. The innkeepers named a room for Alida, decorated with a 19th-century walnut bed and matching armoire. The bath still features the original clawfoot tub. Other rooms include special antiques, Bavarian collectibles and clawfoot tubs. After breakfast, guest can trek to nearby sites such as the Tabasco Plant and Live Oak Gardens on Jefferson Island.

Breakfast and evening snack included in rates. Types of meals: full breakfast and gourmet breakfast. Air conditioning and ceiling fan in room. VCR, fax and copier on premises. Small meetings hosted. French spoken. Antiques, fishing, parks, shopping and sporting events nearby. TAC10.

Lafitte H8

Victoria Inn

Hwy 45, Box 545B
Lafitte, LA 70067
(504)689-4757 (800)689-4797
Fax:(504)689-3399

Rates: $75-125.
Payment: MC VISA AX DS.
Innkeeper(s): Roy & Dale Ross.
Circa: 1884.

Rooms: 7 rooms, 5 with PB. 3 suites.
Beds: QDT.

This enchanting West Indies-style home features fanciful, unique decor done up in bright hues. The Rose Room is a country retreat with a quilt and lacy curtains. Other rooms are decorated in a more tropical style. The Magnolia Suite is furnished with Eastlake antiques and heirloom linens. The inn lies on the banks of Bayou Barataria, and several rooms afford water views. The galleries and grounds offer several relaxing possibilities. Guests can enjoy a national park, swamp tours and cajun music and food, all of which are nearby.

Breakfast included in rates. Types of meals: full breakfast and early coffee/tea. Fishing and watersports nearby.

Publicity: *Times Picayune, Shreveport Times, San Francisco Examiner.*

"You contributed greatly to the fine memories of our 35th wedding anniversary."

Napoleonville G6

Madewood Plantation

4250 Highway 308
Napoleonville, LA 70390
(504)369-7151 (800)375-7151
Fax:(504)369-9848

Rates: $175. MAP.
Payment: MC VISA AX DS.
Innkeeper(s): Keith Marshall.
Circa: 1846.

Rooms: 8 rooms with PB, 1 with FP. 2 suites. 1 conference room.
Beds: QDT.

Six massive ionic columns support the central portico of this striking Greek Revival mansion, a national historic landmark. Framed by live oaks and ancient magnolias, Madewood, on 20 acres, overlooks Bayou Lafourche. It was designed by Henry Howard, a noted architect from Cork, Ireland. Elegant double parlors, a ballroom, library, music room and dining room are open to guests. Breakfast and dinner are included.

Breakfast and dinner included in rates. Type of meal: full breakfast. MAP. Copier on premises.

Location: Seventy-five miles from New Orleans.

Publicity: *Travel & Leisure, Southern Living, Los Angeles Times, Country Home, Country Inns (1 of 12 best inns in 1993).*

"We have stayed in many hotels, other plantations and English manor houses, and Madewood has surpassed them all in charm, hospitality and food."

New Orleans G8

A Hotel, The Frenchman

417 Frenchmen St
New Orleans, LA 70116
(504)948-2166 (800)831-1781
Fax:(509)948-2258

Rates: $59-245.
Payment: MC VISA AX PC TC.
Innkeeper(s): Brent A. Kovach.
Circa: 1860.

Rooms: 27 rooms with PB. 6 suites.
Beds: QDT.

Two town houses built by Creole craftsmen have been totally renovated, including the slave quarters. The original site was chosen to provide convenient access to shops and Jackson Square. The location today is still prime. Historic homes, quaint shops, and fine restaurants are immediately at hand. The Old Mint and

French Market are across the way. Most rooms are furnished with period antiques. There is a hot tub and swimming pool on the premises, and free limited parking is available.

Breakfast included in rates. Types of meals: continental breakfast and continental-plus breakfast. Air conditioning, ceiling fan and cable TV in room. Swimming on premises. Amusement parks, antiques, fishing, parks, sporting events and theater nearby. TAC10.

Location: The French Quarter.

"Still enjoying wonderful memories of my stay at your charming hotel...such a delightful respite from the frantic pace of the Quarter."

Beau Sejour

1930 Napoleon Ave
New Orleans, LA 70115
(504)897-3746
Fax:(504)897-3746

Rates: $95-175.
Payment: PC.
Innkeeper(s): Gilles & Kim Gagnon.
Circa: 1906.

Rooms: 6 rooms, 5 with PB. 1 suite.
Beds: KQT.

On an avenue lined with grand, live oaks hung with Spanish moss, Beau Sejour recently has undergone a complete renovation. Its uptown location places the inn in a neighborhood of grand mansions. Stained-glass, an ornate staircase, 12-foot ceilings and elegant fireplaces fill the three-story house, which once held seven apartments. Original moldings, floor-to-ceiling windows and gleaming wood floors provide the background for the four-poster beds and American and European antiques. During Mardi Gras more than 12 parades pass by and guest line the inn's balconies to watch. Several fine New Orleans restaurants are nearby, and a short ride on the St. Charles Avenue streetcar will take you to the French Quarter. The innkeepers are local preservationists and are also knowledgeable about area activities such as bayou swamp tours and visiting Mississippi River Road plantations.

LA

Breakfast included in rates. Type of meal: continental-plus breakfast. Antiques, fishing, parks, theater and watersports nearby.

"You have a very friendly and warm inn and we enjoyed getting to know you. We'll be back."

Fairchild House

1518 Prytania St
New Orleans, LA 70130
(504)524-0154 (800)256-8096
Fax:(504)568-0063

Rates: $75-125.
Payment: MC VISA AX TC.
Innkeeper(s): Rita Olmo & Beatriz Aprigliano.
Circa: 1841.

Rooms: 7 rooms with PB. 1 suite.
Beds: KQDT.

Situated in the oak-lined Lower Garden District of New Orleans, this Greek Revival home was built by architect L.H. Pilie. The maintains its Victorian ambiance with elegantly appointed guest rooms. Wine and cheese is served upon guests' arrival. Excluding holidays and Sundays, afternoon tea can be served upon request. The inn, which is on the Mardi Gras parade route, is 17 blocks from the French Quarter and eight blocks from the convention center. Streetcars are nearby, as are many local attractions, including paddleboat cruises, Canal Place and Riverwalk shopping, an aquarium, zoo, the Charles Avenue mansions and Tulane and Loyola universities.

Breakfast included in rates. Type of meal: continental-plus breakfast. Air conditioning and ceiling fan in room. Fax and copier on premises. Weddings and family reunions hosted. Antiques, shopping and theater nearby.

Location: Lower garden district.

"Accommodations were great; staff was great...Hope to see ya'll soon!"

Glimmer Inn

1631 7th St
New Orleans, LA 70115
(504)897-1895

Rates: $55-90.
Payment: PC TC.
Innkeeper(s): Sharon Agiewich & Cathy Andros.
Circa: 1891.

Rooms: 6 rooms, 3 with FP. 1 cottage.
Beds: KQDT.

This is a simple Victorian house embellished with a two-story bay, a front porch and balcony. Eclectically appointed, there are antiques, modern furnishings and art. Rooms are spacious with 12-foot-high coved ceilings. St. Charles Avenue and the street car are one block away.

Breakfast included in rates. Type of meal: continental-plus breakfast. Air conditioning and ceiling fan in room. Cable TV and VCR on premises. Antiques, fishing, parks, shopping and theater nearby.

"We had a fantastic time and the accommodations were superb."

The House on Bayou Road

2275 Bayou Rd
New Orleans, LA 70119
(504)945-0992 (800)882-2968
Fax:(504)945-0993
E-mail: hobr@aol.com

Rates: $125-245.
Payment: MC VISA AX TC.
Innkeeper(s): Cynthia Reeves.
Circa: 1798.

Rooms: 8 rooms, 6 with PB, 2 with FP. 2 suites. 2 cottages.
Beds: KQT.

Romantic guest rooms, gourmet cuisine and beautiful two-acre grounds dotted with ponds, herb and flower gardens await guests at this elegant Creole Plantation home. The home was built as the main house to an indigo plantation just prior to the turn of the 19th century. The lush surroundings are a distraction from city life, yet this restful inn is just a few blocks from the French Quarter. The guest quarters are beautifully appointed with fine linens and elegant furnishings. Breakfast is a don't-miss, three-course event. The innkeeper is co-director of a New Orleans cooking school. Guests with a flair for the gourmet might consider signing up for the school's popular Grand or Mini classes, which include tuition and lodging.

Breakfast included in rates. Types of meals: full breakfast and gourmet breakfast. Air conditioning, turn-down service, ceiling fan and cable TV in room. VCR, fax, copier, spa and swimming on premises. Weddings and small meetings hosted. Spanish and French spoken. Antiques, fishing, parks and theater nearby. TAC10.

Publicity: *Southern Living, Travel & Leisure*

Special Discounts: Corporate rates - 10 to 20% discount. 10 to 20% discount for stays over 7 days.

La Maison a l'Avenue Jackson

1740 Jackson Ave
New Orleans, LA 70113
(504)522-1785

Rates: $125-250.
Innkeeper(s): Jessie Smallwood.
Circa: 1858.

Rooms: 4 suites.
Beds: QT.

Enjoy the excitement of New Orleans at this four-suite townhouse on the Carnival parade route. Guest quarters include private entrances and dining and kitchen facilities where guests enjoy a breakfast of cereals, fresh breads, fruit and coffee and tea while reading through the newspaper. Fresh flowers and high ceilings brighten the large guest suites, which can sleep two to four people comfortably. The French Quarter is only 10 minutes away as are many of New Orleans famed restaurants, jazz clubs and shops.

Breakfast included in rates. Type of meal: continental breakfast. Antiques, shopping and theater nearby.

Publicity: *Times Picayune/States Item, Essence, American Vision.*

"The service was lovely and all the small finishing touches just added to our stay."

Lamothe House

621 Esplanade Ave
New Orleans, LA 70116
(504)947-1161 (800)367-5858
Fax:(504)943-6536

Rates: $75-250.
Payment: MC VISA AX PC TC.
Innkeeper(s): Carol Chauppette.
Circa: 1830.

Rooms: 20 rooms with PB, 1 with FP. 9 suites. 2 cottages. 1 conference room.
Beds: QTD.

A carriageway that formerly cut through the center of many French Quarter buildings was enclosed at the Lamothe House in 1866, and is now the foyer. Splendid Victorian furnishings enhance moldings, high ceilings, and hand-turned mahogany stairway railings. Gilded opulence goes unchecked in the Mallard and Lafayette suites. Registration takes place in the second-story salon above the courtyard.

Breakfast included in rates. Type of meal: continental-plus breakfast. Afternoon tea available. Air conditioning, turn-down service, ceiling fan and cable TV in room. VCR, fax, copier, swimming and child care on premises. Weddings, small meetings and family reunions hosted. Amusement parks, antiques, fishing, parks, shopping, sporting events and theater nearby. TAC10.

Publicity: *Houston Post, Travel & Leisure.*

Special Discounts: Summer one-week special.

The Melrose Mansion

937 Esplanade Ave
New Orleans, LA 70116
(504)944-2255
Fax:(504)945-1794

Rates: $225-425.
Payment: MC VISA AX DS PC TC.
Innkeeper(s): Melvin & Rosemary Jones.
Circa: 1884.

Rooms: 8 rooms with PB. 4 suites.
Beds: KQT.

LA

It's little wonder why this dramatic Italianate Victorian has been named a top accommodation. Aside from its gracious exterior, the interior has been carefully restored and filled with the finest of furnishings. Antique-filled guest rooms offer amenities such as down pillows, private patios, fresh flowers, whirlpool tubs and bathrooms stocked with fine soaps. Despite the elegance, guests are encouraged to relax and enjoy the New Orleans' tradition of hospitality. Fresh fruit laced with cognac and a regional favorite, Creole "lost bread" are among the memorable breakfast fare. The National Register Home is located in the French Quarter.

Breakfast included in rates. Types of meals: gourmet breakfast and early coffee/tea. Air conditioning, ceiling fan and cable TV in room. Fax, copier and swimming on premises. Antiques, fishing, parks, shopping, sporting events and theater nearby. TAC10.

"The Melrose Mansion is more than a hotel. It is a rare sanctum of style and grace, the personification of true southern gentility."

St. Peter House

1005 Saint Peter St
New Orleans, LA 70116
(504)524-9232 (800)535-7815
Fax:(504)523-5198

Rates: $49-225.
Payment: MC VISA AX PC TC.
Innkeeper(s): Brent Kovach.
Circa: 1800.

Rooms: 28 rooms with PB. 11 suites.
Beds: KQDT.

The St. Peter House, which is ideally situated in the middle of the French Quarter, offers a delightful glance at New Orleans French heritage and 18th-century charm. From the lush courtyards to the gracious balconies, guests will enjoy the view of the busy quarter. Rooms are individually appointed with period antiques.

Breakfast included in rates. Type of meal: continental-plus breakfast. Air conditioning, turn-down service, ceiling fan and cable TV in room. Fax on premises. Amusement parks, antiques, fishing, parks, shopping and theater nearby. TAC10.

Special Discounts: Off season lengthy stay.

Sully Mansion - Garden District

2631 Prytania St
New Orleans, LA 70130
(504)891-0457
Fax:(504)899-7237

Rates: $78-175.
Payment: MC VISA AX DS PC TC.
Innkeeper(s): Maralee Prigmore.
Circa: 1890.

Rooms: 7 rooms with PB.
Beds: KQT.

This handsome Queen Anne Victorian, designed by its namesake, Thomas Sully, maintains many original features common to the architecture. A wide veranda, stained-glass, heart-of-pine floors and a grand staircase are among the notable items. Rooms are decorated in a comfortable mix of antiques and more modern pieces. This is a place where people can relax and enjoy New Orleans' Garden District.

Breakfast included in rates. Type of meal: continental-plus breakfast. Air conditioning in room. Fax on premises. Antiques and parks nearby. TAC10.

"I truly enjoyed my stay at Sully Mansion—the room was wonderful, the pastries memorable and so enjoyed your conversation."

Sun Oak Inn B&B

2020 Burgundy St
New Orleans, LA 70116
(504)945-0322
Fax:(504)945-0322

Rates: $75-175.
Payment: PC TC.
Innkeeper(s): Eugene D. Cizek & Lloyd L. Sensat, Jr.
Circa: 1836.

Rooms: 2 rooms with PB. 1 conference room.
Beds: D.

This historic home was restored to its former glory as an early 19th-century manor by innkeeper Eugene Cizek. Cizek heads the preservation program at Tulane University and has won awards for historic preservation. His expertise has turned a dilapidated home into a beautiful showplace. Rooms feature a variety of French, Creole, Acadian and mid-French Louisiana antiques, oriental rugs, ceiling fans, fine fabrics and beautiful light fixtures. Behind the home lie lush, landscaped patios, gardens and the Sun Oak tree.

Breakfast included in rates. Type of meal: continental breakfast. Air conditioning and ceiling fan in room. Fax and library on premises. Weddings, small meetings, family reunions and seminars hosted. Some Spanish spoken. Antiques, fishing, parks, shopping, sporting events, theater and watersports nearby. TAC10.

Publicity: *Colonial Homes, Better Homes & Gardens, Traditional Home.*

"From A-Z we loved our visit to Sun Oak. The house is so warm and charming."

Ponchatoula **F7**

Bella Rose Mansion

225 N 8th St
Ponchatoula, LA 70454
(504)386-3857
Fax:(504)386-3857

Rates: $125-225.
Payment: MC VISA.
Innkeeper(s): Rose James & Michael-Ray Britton.
Circa: 1942.

Rooms: 4 rooms with PB. 2 suites.
Beds: KQ.

This Georgian-style mansion boasts a three-story spiral staircase which rises up to a stained-glass dome. Master craftsmen detailed this luxurious manor with mahogany paneling, parquet floors, Waterford crystal chandeliers and a marble-walled solarium with a fountain. The home once served as a monastery for Jesuit priests. The mansion includes an indoor terrazzo shuffleboard court and heated swimming pool. Gourmet breakfasts feature entrees such as Eggs Benedict complemented with fresh fruits and juices. Ponchatoula's many antique shops have earned its nickname as America's Antique City.

Breakfast included in rates. Type of meal: gourmet breakfast. Air conditioning and ceiling fan in room. VCR, fax, copier, swimming, bicycles and library on premises. Antiques, fishing, parks, shopping, sporting events, theater and watersports nearby. TAC10.

Publicity: *Houston Chronicle, Sunday Star.*

"What a fabulous place! Your warmth is truly an asset. The peacefulness is just what we needed in our hectic lives."

Saint Francisville

E6

Barrow House Inn

9779 Royal, Drawer 2550
Saint Francisville, LA 70775
(504)635-4791
Fax:(504)635-4769
E-mail: staff@topteninn.com

Rates: $85-135.
Payment: MC VISA PC.
Innkeeper(s): Shirley Dittloff.
Circa: 1800.

Rooms: 8 rooms with PB. 3 suites.
Beds: KQDT.

This salt box with a Greek Revival addition was built during Spanish colonial times. Antiques dating from 1840-1860 include a Mississippi plantation bed with full canopy and a massive rosewood armoire crafted by the famous New Orleans cabinet-maker Mallard. One room has a Spanish-moss mattress, traditional Louisiana bedding material used for more than 200 years. Six near-by plantations are open for tours.

Breakfast included in rates. Types of meals: continental breakfast, full breakfast, gourmet breakfast and early coffee/tea. Dinner available. Air conditioning in room. VCR, fax and copier on premises. Weddings, small meetings and family reunions hosted. Antiques, parks and shopping nearby. TAC10.

LA

Publicity: *Louisiana Life, Chicago Tribune, Southern Living.*

"This was the icing on the cake."

Saint Martinville

G5

The Old Castillo Hotel

PO Box 172
Saint Martinville, LA 70582
(318)394-4010 (800)621-3017
Fax:(318)394-7983

Rates: $50-80.
Payment: MC VISA AX.
Innkeeper(s): Peggy Hulin.
Circa: 1825.

Rooms: 5 rooms with PB. 3 suites. 1 conference room.
Beds: QD.

Ionic columns and a second-story veranda grace the exterior of this Greek Revival home, which was used originally as an inn. From the turn of the century until the mid 1980s, the home served as a Catholic girls' school. Today, the home once again serves travelers, both as hotel and restaurant. Guest rooms are furnished with antiques and reproductions. The restaurant serves up Bayou favorites such as fried alligator, catfish, craw-fish, frog legs, as well as other seafood and steak specialties.

Breakfast included in rates. Types of meals: continental breakfast, continental-plus breakfast, full breakfast and early coffee/tea. Dinner and lunch available. Air conditioning in room. Fax on premises. Small meetings, family reunions and seminars hosted. French spoken. Amusement parks, antiques, fishing, parks, shopping, sporting events, theater and watersports nearby. TAC10.

Special Discounts: Mention listing with American Historic Inns - 10%.

Maine

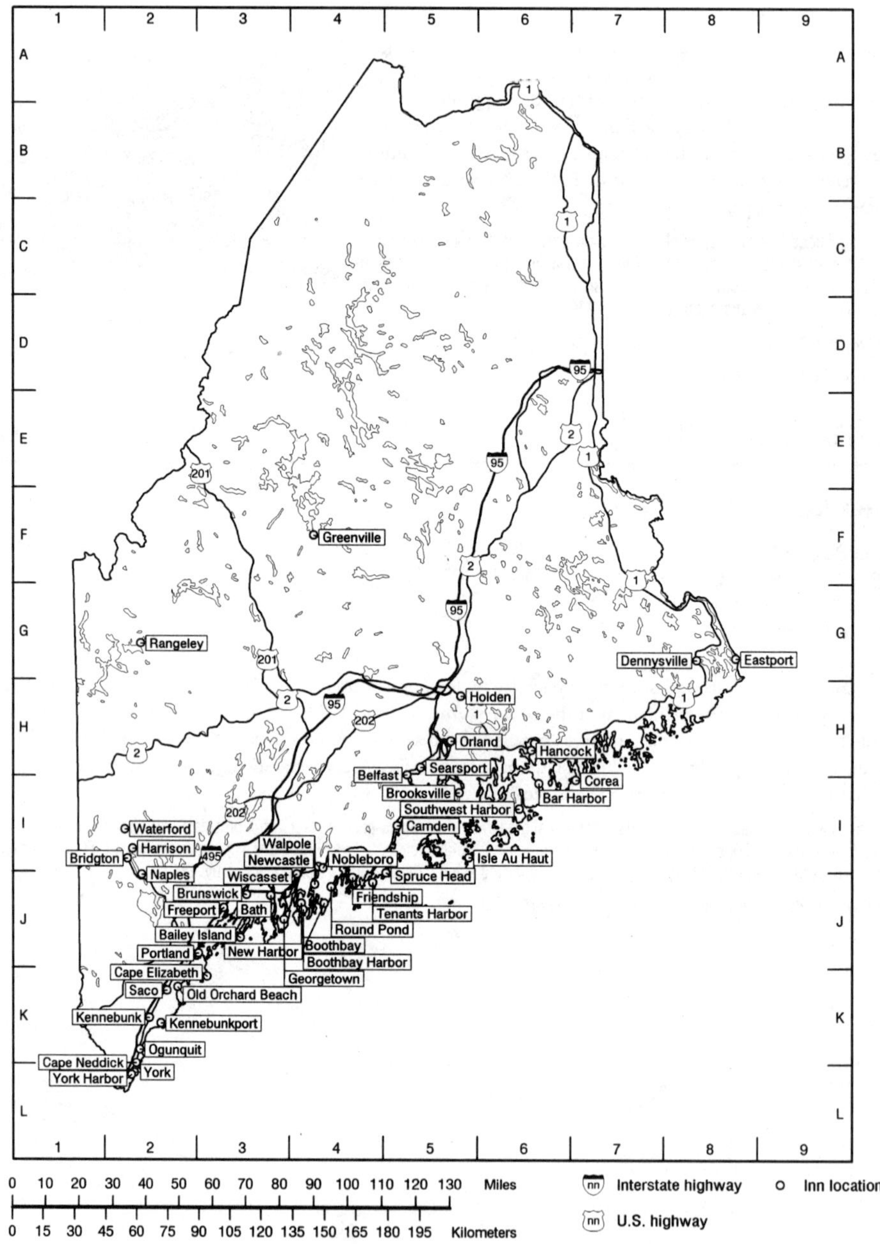

Greenville
Rangeley
Holden
Orland
Hancock
Searsport
Belfast
Brooksville
Corea
Bar Harbor
Southwest Harbor
Camden
Waterford
Harrison
Bridgton
Naples
Walpole
Newcastle
Nobleboro
Wiscasset
Spruce Head
Isle Au Haut
Brunswick
Freeport
Bath
Friendship
Tenants Harbor
Round Pond
Bailey Island
Portland
New Harbor
Boothbay
Boothbay Harbor
Cape Elizabeth
Georgetown
Saco
Old Orchard Beach
Kennebunk
Kennebunkport
Ogunquit
Cape Neddick
York
York Harbor
Dennysville
Eastport
Miles
Kilometers
Interstate highway
U.S. highway
Inn location

Bailey Island J3

Captain York House B&B

Route 24
Bailey Island, ME 04003
(207)833-6224
E-mail: 104502.1272@compuserve.com

Rates: $64-85.
Payment: PC TC.
Innkeeper(s): Charles & Ingrid Divita.
Circa: 1906.

Rooms: 4 rooms, 2 with PB.
Beds: QT.

Bailey Island is the quaint fisherman's village of stories, poems and movies. Guests cross the world's only cribstone bridge to reach the island, where beautiful sunsets and dinners of fresh Maine lobster are the norm. This shingled, turn-of-the-century, Mansard-style home was the home of a famous Maine sea captain, Charles York. Now a homestay-style bed & breakfast, the innkeepers have restored the home to its former glory, filling it with many antiques. Guests at Captain York's enjoy water views from all the guest rooms. Wild Maine blueberries often find a significant place on the breakfast menu.

Breakfast included in rates. Type of meal: full breakfast. Cable TV and VCR on premises. Weddings, small meetings, family reunions and seminars hosted. Antiques, parks, shopping, sporting events, theater and watersports nearby. TAC10.

ME

Special Discounts: Length of stay discounts.

"Bailey Island turned out to be the hidden treasure of our trip and we hope to return for your great hospitality again."

Bar Harbor I6

Balance Rock Inn on The Ocean

24 Albert Mdws
Bar Harbor, ME 04609-1702
(207)288-2610 (800)753-0494
Fax:(207)288-5534

Rates: $135-425.
Payment: MC VISA AX DS PC TC.
Innkeeper(s): Mike & Nancy Cloud.
Circa: 1903.

Rooms: 14 rooms with PB, 6 with FP. 3 suites.
Beds: KQ.

Built for a Scottish railroad tycoon, the Shingle-style structure was designed by a prestigious Boston architectural firm often used by wealthy summer residents of Bar Harbor. The inn is set on a secluded tree-covered property with views of the islands and Frenchman's Bay. Bar Harbor is two short blocks away. Off the back veranda, overlooking the pool, and past nearly an acre of sweeping lawns is the Historic Shore Path that winds its way around the waterfront.

Breakfast included in rates. Types of meals: full breakfast and early coffee/tea. Afternoon tea available. Air conditioning, turn-down service and cable TV in room. VCR, fax, swimming and pet boarding on premises. Weddings hosted. Antiques, parks, theater and watersports nearby. TAC10.

Pets Allowed.

Black Friar Inn

10 Summer St
Bar Harbor, ME 04609-1424
(207)288-5091
Fax:(207)288-4197
E-mail: blackfriar@acadia.net

Rates: $55-140.
Payment: MC VISA DS PC TC.
Innkeeper(s): Perry & Sharon Risley & Falke.
Circa: 1900.

Rooms: 7 rooms with PB, 1 with FP. 1 suite.
Beds: KQ.

When this three-story house was renovated in 1981, the owners added mantels, hand-crafted woodwork and windows gleaned from old Bar Harbor mansions that had been torn down. Victorian and country furnishings are accentuated with fresh flowers and soft carpets. Breakfast is presented in the greenhouse, a room that boasts cypress panelling and embossed tin recycled from an old country church.

Breakfast and afternoon tea included in rates. Type of meal: gourmet breakfast. Air conditioning and ceiling fan in room. Cable TV and VCR on premises. Antiques, fishing, parks, shopping, cross-country skiing, theater and watersports nearby.

"A great place and great innkeepers!"

Breakwater

45 Hancock St
Bar Harbor, ME 04609-1700
(207)288-2313 (800)238-6309
Fax:(207)288-2377

Rates: $145-325.
Payment: MC VISA AX PC TC.
Innkeeper(s): Margaret Eden.
Circa: 1904.

Rooms: 6 rooms with PB, 6 with FP. 2 cottages. 2 conference rooms.
Beds: KQ.

This is an oceanfront English Tudor estate on more than four acres of lawns, gardens and woods. It is located at the end of Bar Harbor's historic Shore Path. There are plenty of common areas and 11 working fireplaces. Bedchambers feature queen beds, walk-in closets and most have ocean views. Guests may play billiards in the library.

Breakfast, afternoon tea and evening snack included in rates. Type of meal: full breakfast. Banquet service available. Turn-down service in room. Fax and library on premises. Weddings, small meetings and family reunions hosted. Antiques, parks, shopping, cross-country skiing, theater and watersports nearby. TAC10.

Publicity: *Country Inns, Down East, Discerning Traveler, B&B of the Year.*

"There's no place like home, unless it's here at Breakwater! It was beautiful, delicious, and our every 'want' was anticipated by the outstanding staff. The most outstanding inn we've ever visited."

The Inn at Canoe Point

Rt 3 Box 216R - Hull's Cove
Bar Harbor, ME 04644
(207)288-9511

Rates: $55-175.
Innkeeper(s): Tom & Nancy.
Circa: 1889.

Rooms: 5 rooms with PB, 1 with FP. 1 conference room.
Beds: KQT.

This oceanfront inn has served as a summer residence for several generations of families escaping city heat. Guests are treated to the gracious hospitality of the past, surrounded by the ocean and pine forests. They can relax on the deck overlooking Frenchman's Bay, or pursue outdoor activities in the National Park.

Type of meal: full breakfast.

Publicity: *The New York Times, Travel-Holiday Magazine.*

Graycote Inn

40 Holland Ave
Bar Harbor, ME 04609-1432
(207)288-3044
Fax:(207)288-2719
E-mail: jgraycote@acadia.net

Rates: $65-150.
Payment: MC VISA DS PC TC.
Innkeeper(s): Pat & Roger Samuel.
Circa: 1881.

Rooms: 12 rooms with PB, 3 with FP.
Beds: KQ.

This Victorian inn was built by the first rector of St. Saviour's Episcopal Church. Some of the guest rooms have fireplaces, while others have sun porches or balconies. A full breakfast is served on a sunny, glass-enclosed porch with tables set for two or four. Afternoon refreshments also are served. The inn is located on a one-acre lot with lawns, large trees, flower gardens, a croquet court and a double-size hammock. Guest can also relax on the veranda, which is furnished with wicker. The innkeepers are happy to make activity and dining recommendations. Guests can walk to restaurants, and Acadia National Park is nearby.

Breakfast included in rates. Type of meal: full breakfast. Air conditioning and ceiling fan in room. Small meetings and seminars hosted. Antiques, parks, shopping, cross-country skiing, theater and watersports nearby.

Location: Bar Harbor and Acadia National Park.

Publicity: *Victorian Decorating & Lifestyle.*

"Thank you for the honeymoon of our dreams! The decor and the atmosphere combine to make this one of the most romantic places we've ever been."

ME

Ledgelawn Inn

66 Mount Desert St
Bar Harbor, ME 04609-1324
(207)288-4596 (800)274-5334
Fax:(207)288-9968

Rates: $65-250.
Payment: VISA AX.
Innkeeper(s): Nancy & Mike Cloud.
Circa: 1904.

Rooms: 33 rooms with PB. 1 suite.
Beds: KQD.

Gables, bays, columns and verandas are features of this rambling three-story summer house located on an acre of wooded land within walking distance to the waterfront. The red clapboard structure sports black shutters and a mansard roof. Filled with antiques and fireplaces the inn features a sitting room and library.

Breakfast included in rates. Types of meals: full breakfast and early coffee/tea. Afternoon tea available. Turn-down service and cable TV in room. Fax, swimming, pet boarding and child care on premises. Family reunions hosted. Antiques, parks, theater and watersports nearby.

Pets Allowed.

Publicity: *New York Times.*

"A lovely place to relax and enjoy oneself. The area is unsurpassed in beauty and the people friendly."

Manor House Inn

106 West St
Bar Harbor, ME 04609-1856
(207)288-3759 (800)437-0088
Fax:(207)288-2974

Rates: $50-175.
Payment: MC VISA.
Innkeeper(s): Mac Noyes.
Circa: 1887.

Rooms: 14 rooms, 7 with PB, 6 with FP. 7 suites.
Beds: KQT.

Colonel James Foster built this 22-room Victorian mansion, now in the National Register. It is an example of the tradition of gracious summer living for which Bar Harbor was and is famous. In addition to the main house, there are several charming cottages situated in the extensive gardens on the property.

Breakfast and afternoon tea included in rates. Types of meals: full breakfast and early coffee/tea. Ceiling fan in room. Cable TV, fax and copier on premises. Weddings, small meetings, family reunions and seminars hosted. Antiques, fishing, parks, shopping and watersports nearby. TAC10.

Location: Close to Acadia National Park.

Publicity: *Discerning Traveler.*

"Wonderful honeymoon spot! Wonderful inn, elegant, delicious breakfasts, terrific innkeepers. We loved it all! It's our fourth time here and it's wonderful as always."

The Maples Inn

16 Roberts Ave
Bar Harbor, ME 04609-1820
(207)288-3443
Fax:(207)288-0356

Rates: $60-150.
Payment: MC VISA DS PC TC.
Innkeeper(s): Susan Sinclair.
Circa: 1903.

Rooms: 6 rooms with PB, 1 with FP. 1 suite.
Beds: QT.

This Victorian "summer cottage" once served wealthy summer visitors to Mt. Desert Island. Located on a quiet residential street, away from Bar Harbor traffic, it has been tastefully restored and filled with Victorian furnishings. The inn is within walking distance of shops, boutiques and restaurants. Acadia National Park is five minutes away. Hiking, kayaking and cycling are among the nearby activities.

Breakfast and afternoon tea included in rates. Types of meals: gourmet breakfast and early coffee/tea. Cable TV, fax and library on premises. Weddings, small meetings, family reunions and seminars hosted. Antiques, fishing, parks, shopping, cross-country skiing, sporting events, theater and watersports nearby.

Location: Within two blocks of the ocean.

Publicity: *San Diego Tribune, New York Times, Gourmet, Bon Appetit, Los Angeles Times.*

"What a wonderful place this is. Warm, comfortable, friendly, terrific breakfasts, great tips for adventure around the island. I could go on and on."

Mira Monte Inn & Suites

69 Mount Desert St
Bar Harbor, ME 04609-1327
(207)288-4263 (800)553-5109
Fax:(207)288-3115
E-mail: mburns@acadia.net

Rates: $86-180.
Payment: MC VISA AX DS TC.
Innkeeper(s): Marian Burns.
Circa: 1864.

Rooms: 16 rooms, 15 with PB, 11 with FP. 3 suites.
Beds: KQT.

A gracious 18-room Victorian mansion, the Mira Monte has been newly renovated in the style of early Bar Harbor. It features period furnishings, pleasant common rooms, a library and wraparound porches. Situated on estate grounds, there are sweeping lawns, paved terraces, and many gardens. The inn was one of the earliest of Bar Harbor's famous summer cottages. The two-room suites each feature canopy beds, two-person whirlpools, a parlor with a sleeper sofa, fireplace and kitchenette. The two-bedroom suite includes a full kitchen, dining area and parlor. The suites boast private decks with views of the gardens.

Breakfast and afternoon tea included in rates. Types of meals: full breakfast and early coffee/tea. Air conditioning, cable TV and VCR in room. Fax and library on premises. Handicap access. Small meetings hosted. Antiques, fishing, parks, shopping and theater nearby. TAC10.

Location: Five-minute walk from the waterfront, shops and restaurants.

Publicity: *Los Angeles Times.*

Special Discounts: Spring, late fall and honeymoon packages.

"On our third year at your wonderful inn in beautiful Bar Harbor. I think I enjoy it more each year. A perfect place to stay in a perfect environment."

The Ridgeway Inn

11 High St
Bar Harbor, ME 04609-1816
(207)288-9682

Rates: $60-150.
Payment: MC VISA PC TC.
Innkeeper(s): Lucie Rioux Hollfelder.
Circa: 1890.

Rooms: 5 rooms with PB. 2 suites.
Beds: KQ.

Located on a quiet, tree-lined street, this Victorian B&B is a welcome sight for weary travelers. Each of the guest rooms is individually decorated and named after the cottages of the wealthy who made Bar Harbor their summer vacation spot. Many of these homes were destroyed in a 1947 fire, but the innkeepers have preserved their memory. Beds are covered with down comforters. One room includes a Jacuzzi tub, while another offers a private deck. The innkeepers serve an expansive, multi-course breakfast on fireside tables illuminated by candlelight. Freshly baked breads, scones and muffins are followed by a fruit recipe, which all precedes the daily entree.

ME

Breakfast and afternoon tea included in rates. Types of meals: full breakfast, gourmet breakfast and early coffee/tea. Weddings hosted. French spoken. Amusement parks, antiques, fishing, parks, shopping, cross-country skiing, theater and watersports nearby.

The Tides

119 West St
Bar Harbor, ME 04609-1430
(207)288-4968

Rates: $85-275. AP.
Payment: MC VISA PC TC.
Innkeeper(s): Joe & Judy Losquadro.
Circa: 1887.

Rooms: 4 rooms with PB, 2 with FP. 3 suites.
Beds: Q.

As innkeeper Joe Losquadro might explain, The Tides has endurance. The gracious Victorian survived a 10-day firestorm that destroyed more than 17,000 acres and 60 of Mt. Desert Island's grand summer homes. The Tides still stands as testament to local resilience. Each of the suites offers something special. The Master Suite includes a four-poster bed and working fireplace, while the Ocean Suite boasts water views from every window, including the bath. The room includes a parlor with a working fireplace and a balcony. Guests in the Captain's Suite enjoy a bubble bath in a clawfoot tub and the view of the historic, tree-lined West Street as well as the bay. Joe has been an innkeeper on the island for more than five years and is full of local information and plenty of ideas for vacationers.

Breakfast included in rates. Types of meals: full breakfast and early coffee/tea. Afternoon tea, evening snack and catering service available. AP. Ceiling fan and cable TV in room. Weddings, small meetings and family reunions hosted. Antiques, parks, shopping, cross-country skiing, theater and watersports nearby.

"Your hospitality made us feel very welcome. Thank you once again."

Bath — *J3*

Elizabeth's B&B

360 Front St
Bath, ME 04530-2749
(207)443-1146

Rates: $45-65.
Payment: PC TC.
Innkeeper(s): Elizabeth A. Lindsay.
Circa: 1820.

Rooms: 4 rooms, 2 with FP.
Beds: KQDT.

This early Federal house was built by a family of shipbuilders. From its location on the Kennebec River, Elizabeth's provides a relaxing atmosphere with country antiques and "Mr. T," the resident cat. The dining room features stenciled walls and flagstone and brick floors. Choose the Captain's Quarters for a king-size bed, wide-pine flooring, window seat and river view.

Breakfast included in rates. Afternoon tea available. Cable TV on premises. Family reunions hosted. Antiques, fishing, parks, shopping and theater nearby.

Publicity: *Times Record.*

"It was truly a warming experience to feel so at home, away from home."

Fairhaven Inn

RR 2 Box 85, N Bath Rd
Bath, ME 04530
(207)443-4391

Rates: $80-120.
Payment: MC VISA DS PC TC.
Innkeeper(s): Susie & Dave Reed.
Circa: 1790.

Rooms: 8 rooms, 6 with PB. 1 suite. 1 cottage. 1 conference room.
Beds: KQT.

With its view of the Kennebec River, this site was so attractive that Pembleton Edgecomb built his Colonial house where a log cabin had previously stood. His descendants occupied it for the next 125 years. Antiques and country furniture fill the inn. Meadows and lawns, and woods of hemlock, birch and pine cover the inn's 16 acres.

Breakfast included in rates. Types of meals: full breakfast and early coffee/tea. Cable TV, fax and library on premises. 16 acres. Small meetings and family reunions hosted. Antiques, parks, shopping, cross-country skiing, sporting events, theater and watersports nearby. TAC10.

Publicity: *The State, Coastal Journal.*

"The Fairhaven is now marked in our book with a red star, definitely a place to remember and visit again."

The Galen C. Moses House

1009 Washington St
Bath, ME 04530-2759
(207)442-8771

Rates: $65-95.
Payment: MC VISA PC TC.
Innkeeper(s): James Haught, Larry Kieft.
Circa: 1874.

Rooms: 4 rooms with PB.
Beds: QDT.

This Victorian mansion is filled with beautiful architectural items, included stained-glass windows, wood-carved and marble fireplaces and a grand staircase. The innkeepers have filled the library, a study, morning room and the parlor with antiques. A corner fireplace warms the dining room, overlooking the lawns and gardens. There is a formal drawing room where tea is presented.

Breakfast and afternoon tea included in rates. Types of meals: continental breakfast and gourmet breakfast. Turn-down service in room. Cable TV, VCR and library on premises. Family reunions and seminars hosted. Antiques, fishing, parks, shopping, cross-country skiing, theater and watersports nearby.

Publicity: *Philadelphia, Back Roads USA.*

"For our first try at B&B lodgings, we've probably started at the top, and nothing else will ever measure up to this. Wonderful food, wonderful home, grounds and wonderful hosts!"

Packard House

45 Pearl St
Bath, ME 04530-2746
(207)443-6069 (800)516-4578

Rates: $60-90.
Payment: MC VISA PC TC.
Innkeeper(s): Debby & Bill Hayden.
Circa: 1790.

Rooms: 3 rooms with PB. 1 suite.
Beds: KQT.

Shipbuilder Benjamin F. Packard restored this handsome home in 1870, and the inn still reflects the Victorian influence so prominent in Bath's busy shipbuilding years. The Packard family has allowed several family pieces to remain in the home. Period furnishings, authentic colors and shipbuilding memorabilia recapture the romantic past of Bath. The Kennebec River is just a block away.

Breakfast included in rates. Type of meal: full breakfast. Cable TV and library on premises. Family reunions hosted. Some French spoken. Antiques, parks, shopping, theater and watersports nearby.

Location: Historic district.

Publicity: *Times Record, Maine Sunday Telegram, Coastal Journal.*

Special Discounts: Seventh night always free, we give frequent guest cards.

"Thanks for being wonderful hosts."

Belfast

H5

The Jeweled Turret Inn

40 Pearl St
Belfast, ME 04915-1907
(207)338-2304 (800)696-2304

Rates: $70-95.
Payment: MC VISA PC TC.
Innkeeper(s): Cathy & Carl Heffentrager.
Circa: 1898.

Rooms: 7 rooms with PB, 1 with FP.
Beds: QDT.

This grand Victorian is named for the staircase that winds up the turret, lighted by stained- and leaded-glass panels and jewel-like embellishments. It was built for attorney James Harriman. Dark pine beams adorn the ceiling of the den, and the fireplace is constructed of bark and rocks from every state in the Union. Elegant antiques furnish the guest rooms. Guests can relax in one of the inn's four parlors, which are furnished with period antiques, wallpapers, lace and boast fireplaces. The verandas feature wicker and iron bistro sets and views of the historic district. The inn is within walking distance of the town and its shops, restaurants and the harbor.

Breakfast and afternoon tea included in rates. Types of meals: full breakfast and early coffee/tea. Ceiling fan in room. Small meetings and family reunions hosted. Antiques, fishing, shopping, downhill skiing, cross-country skiing, theater and watersports nearby. TAC10.

ME

Publicity: *Republican Journal, Waterville Sentinel, Los Angeles Times, Country Living, Victorian Homes.*

"The ambiance was so romantic that we felt like we were on our honeymoon."

The Thomas Pitcher House B&B

19 Franklin St
Belfast, ME 04915-1105
(207)338-6454

Rates: $65-85.
Payment: MC VISA PC TC.
Innkeeper(s): Fran & Ron Kresge.
Circa: 1873.

Rooms: 4 rooms with PB.
Beds: QD.

This richly appointed home was considered state-of-the-art back in 1873 for it was one of only a few homes offering central heat and hot or cold running water. Today, innkeepers have added plenty of modern amenities, but kept the ambiance of the Victorian Era. Each room is unique, some vanities include original walnut and marble, while another bathroom includes tin ceilings and a step-down bath. Some rooms have cozy reading areas. Guests enjoy a full breakfast each morning with menus that feature specialties such as Maine blueberry buttermilk pancakes or a French toast puff made with homemade raisin bread.

Breakfast included in rates. Types of meals: gourmet breakfast and early coffee/tea. Cable TV, VCR and library on premises. German and limited French spoken. Antiques, fishing, parks, shopping, downhill skiing, cross-country skiing, theater and watersports nearby. TAC10.

Publicity: *Republican Journal, Boston Herald, Jackson Clarion-Ledger, Toronto Sunday Sun.*

"A home away from home."

Boothbay

J4

Kenniston Hill Inn

Rt 27, PO Box 125
Boothbay, ME 04537-0125
(207)633-2159 (800)992-2915
Fax:(207)633-2159

Rates: $60-110.
Payment: MC VISA DS PC TC.
Innkeeper(s): Susan & David Straight.
Circa: 1786.

Rooms: 10 rooms with PB, 5 with FP. 1 cottage.
Beds: KQDT.

The elegant clapboard home is the oldest inn at Boothbay Harbor and was occupied by the Kenniston family for more than a century. Five of the antique-filled bedrooms have fireplaces. After a walk through the beautiful gardens or woods, warm up in the parlor next to the elegant, open-hearthed fireplace. Boothbay

Harbor offers something for everybody, including whale-watching excursions and dinner theaters.

Breakfast and afternoon tea included in rates. Types of meals: full breakfast, gourmet breakfast and early coffee/tea. Ceiling fan in room. Cable TV, VCR and fax on premises. Weddings and family reunions hosted. Antiques, fishing, parks, shopping, downhill skiing, cross-country skiing, theater and watersports nearby. TAC10.

Publicity: *Boothbay Register.*

Special Discounts: Discounts for repeat guests - introductory offer for others.

"England may be the home of the original bed & breakfast, but Kenniston Hill Inn is where it has been perfected!"

Boothbay Harbor — J4

Admiral's Quarters Inn

105 Commercial St
Boothbay Harbor, ME
04538-1003
(207)633-2474

Rates: $65-125.
Payment: MC VISA DS TC.
Innkeeper(s): Les & Deb Hallstrom.
Circa: 1830.

Rooms: 6 rooms with PB. 4 suites.
Beds: KQT.

Set on a rise looking out to the sea, this handsome sea captain's house commands a splendid harbor view. The inn is decorated with white wicker and antiques and each accommodation features French doors or sliding glass doors that open to a private deck or terrace to take advantage of the view of the harbor. Guests may walk a short distance to the wharf.

Breakfast and afternoon tea included in rates. Ceiling fan and cable TV in room. Library on premises. Family reunions hosted. Amusement parks, antiques, fishing, parks, shopping, theater and watersports nearby.

Location: On the point of Commercial, facing up the harbor.

Publicity: *Franklin Business Review.*

"If you're looking to put down stakes in the heart of Boothbay Harbor, the Admiral's Quarters Inn provides an eagle's eye view on land and at sea.-Yankee Traveler"

Harbour Towne Inn on The Waterfront

71 Townsend Ave
Boothbay Harbor, ME
04538-1158
(207)633-4300 (800)722-4240
Fax:(207)633-4300

Rates: $69-150.
Payment: MC VISA AX DS PC TC.
Innkeeper(s): George Thomas.
Circa: 1890.

Rooms: 11 rooms with PB. 1 conference room.
Beds: KQDT.

This waterfront Victorian inn boasts 11 guest rooms and one suite. Most rooms offer a private deck and the Penthouse has an astonishing view of the harbor. Breakfast is served in the inn's Sunroom, and guests also may relax in the parlor, which has a fireplace. The inn's meticulous grounds include flower gardens and well-kept shrubs and trees. It's an easy walk to the village and its art galleries, restaurants and shops. Special off-season packages are available. The Ft. William Henry Fisherman's Memorial is nearby.

Breakfast included in rates. Type of meal: continental-plus breakfast. Cable TV in room. Fax and copier on premises. Handicap access. Weddings, small meetings, family reunions and seminars hosted. Antiques, fishing, parks, shopping, downhill skiing, cross-country skiing, theater and watersports nearby. TAC10.

Topside

McKown Hill
Boothbay Harbor, ME 04538
(207)633-5404
E-mail: footbridge@wiscasset.net

Rates: $60-100.
Payment: MC VISA PC TC.
Innkeeper(s): Newell J. & Faye Wilson.
Circa: 1850.

Rooms: 9 rooms with PB.
Beds: KQD.

From various points at this mid-19th-century former sea captain's home, guests can watch as boats traverse in and out of the harbor or enjoy the view of a picturesque seaside village. Because of its ideal hilltop location, the home was selected in World War I and II as a Navy look-out to guard the harbor if necessary. The home is filled with many antiques, but guests also have the modern amenities of a coffee maker and mini refrigerator in their rooms. The inn is open during Maine's warmer months, from Memorial Day until Columbus Day.

Type of meal: early coffee/tea. Library on premises. Weddings, small meetings and family reunions hosted. Antiques, fishing, theater and watersports nearby.

"This spot is a pure joy in every way, and beautiful besides."

Bridgton *I2*

ME

Noble House

PO Box 180
Bridgton, ME 04009-0180
(207)647-3733
Fax:(207)647-3733

Rates: $64-120.
Payment: MC VISA AX.
Innkeeper(s): The Starets Family.
Circa: 1903.

Rooms: 9 rooms, 6 with PB. 3 suites.
Beds: QDT.

This inn is tucked among three acres of old oaks and a grove of pine trees, providing an estate-like view from all guest rooms. The elegant parlor contains a library, grand piano and hearth. Bed chambers are furnished with antiques, wicker and quilts. Three rooms have whirlpool tubs, and family suites are available. A hammock placed at the water's edge provides a view of the lake and Mt. Washington. The inn's lake frontage also allows for canoeing at sunset and swimming. Restaurants are nearby.

Breakfast included in rates. Type of meal: full breakfast. Antiques, fishing, downhill skiing, cross-country skiing, theater and watersports nearby.

Location: Forty miles northwest of Portland.

Publicity: *Bridgton News.*

"It's my favorite inn."

Brooksville *I5*

Oakland House Seaside Inn & Cottages

Herrick Rd, RR1 Box 400
Brooksville, ME 04617
(207)359-8521 (800)359-7352

Rates: $51-172. MAP.
Payment: PC TC.
Innkeeper(s): Jim & Sally Littlefield.

Rooms: 10 rooms, 7 with PB, 2 with FP. 15 cottages. 2 conference rooms.
Beds: QDT.

Guests at this seaside getaway spot enjoy the best of Maine, from the half-mile of private ocean front to the miles of hiking trails. The innkeeper is a descendant of John Billings, who received the property's original land grant from King George of England in the 18th century, and the land has remained in the family since that time. Bed & Breakfast guests stay at a more recent addition to the property, Shore Oaks, a 1907 Craftsman-style home. The interior of this bed & breakfast is decorated with Craftsman-style furnishings and

Victorian pieces. The living room has a large stone fireplace, original wicker furnishings, huge multi-paned windows and offers a panoramic view of Penobscot Bay. Breakfasts are served in the dining room, and dinner is served in the on-premises hotel dining rooms. In addition to the bed & breakfast rooms in Shore Oaks, more than a dozen cottages dot the 50-acre property, offering from one to five bedrooms. Many of the cottages include amenities such as kitchenettes and living rooms with fireplaces, and most boast panoramic views of Penobscot Bay. Each of the cottages are unique, a few are more than 100 years old. In-season guests at Shore Oaks are treated to both breakfast and dinner.

Breakfast and dinner included in rates. Types of meals: continental breakfast, continental-plus breakfast, full breakfast and early coffee/tea. Picnic lunch, banquet service, catering service and catered breakfast available. MAP. VCR, fax, copier, swimming and library on premises. 50 acres. Weddings, small meetings, family reunions and seminars hosted. Antiques, fishing, parks, shopping, cross-country skiing and watersports nearby.

Pets Allowed: In some cottages.

Publicity: *Country Living, Down East.*

Special Discounts: Stay six days, get seventh free; corporate group rates available.

"We thoroughly enjoyed the peace, quiet and wonderful smells of pines and salt water. Thanks again for a wonderful get-away place!"

Brunswick — J3

Bethel Point B&B

RR 5 Bethel Point Rd
Box 2387
Brunswick, ME 04011
(207)725-1115

Rates: $60-95.
Payment: MC VISA PC.
Innkeeper(s): Peter & Betsy Pachard.
Circa: 1830.

Rooms: 3 rooms, 1 with PB, 1 with FP. 1 suite.
Beds: DT.

Nestled at the edge of Casco Bay, this pre-Civil War home is a fine example of Federal-style architecture. Even before the construction of paved roads, the home served as an inn for those traveling by boat on their way to Portland and points south. The home affords views of the bay and islands, and guests are sure to see seals playing in their natural habitat. There is an outdoor hot tub on the premises, and an abundance of seasonal activities nearby, including ocean swimming and cross-country skiing. Boudoin College and the L.L. Bean store are some of the nearby attractions.

Breakfast included in rates. Type of meal: full breakfast. VCR and spa on premises. Weddings and small meetings hosted. Antiques, fishing, shopping, downhill skiing, cross-country skiing and theater nearby.

"Magnificent. Your maniac hospitality and sense of humor warmed our souls. We'll be back! A delightful retreat."

Camden — I5

Castleview By The Sea

59 High St
Camden, ME 04843-1733
(207)236-2344 (800)272-8439

Rates: $75-185.
Payment: MC VISA PC TC.
Innkeeper(s): Bill Butler.
Circa: 1856.

Rooms: 3 rooms with PB.
Beds: KQ.

Located on an acre, this classic American cape house is on the waterside of Camden's historic district, 500 feet from the ocean. Guest rooms feature wide pine floors, beamed ceilings, stained glass, and some have private porches. Take in the sun and sea and the view of two castles from the favorite place at the inn, the ocean view decks. A healthy breakfast includes locally grown items, organic juices and eggs.

Breakfast included in rates. Types of meals: continental-plus breakfast and full breakfast. Air conditioning, ceiling fan, cable TV and VCR in room. Tennis and library on premises. Family reunions hosted. Antiques, fishing, parks, shopping, downhill skiing, cross-country skiing, theater and watersports nearby. TAC10.

Edgecombe-Coles House

64 High St, HCR 60 Box 3010
Camden, ME 04843
(207)236-2336
Fax:(207)236-6227

Rates: $80-180.
Payment: MC VISA AX DC CB DS.
Innkeeper(s): Terry & Louise Price.
Circa: 1800.

Rooms: 6 rooms with PB, 1 with FP.
Beds: KQT.

Admiring the view of Penobscot Bay, Chicago lawyer Chauncey Keep built this house on the foundation of a sea captain's house. By 1900, his 22-room cottage was too small and he built a 50-room mansion up the hill, retaining this as a guest house. Country antiques set the tone and many rooms command a spectacular ocean view.

Breakfast and afternoon tea included in rates. Type of meal: full breakfast. Antiques, fishing, downhill skiing, cross-country skiing and theater nearby.

Location: North of Camden Harbor on Highway 1.

Publicity: *Uncommon Lodgings, Yankee Traveler.*

"A beautiful view, beautiful decor and a lovely hostess make this a very special place," Shelby Hodge, Houston Post.

Hartstone Inn

41 Elm St
Camden, ME 04843-1910
(207)236-4259 (800)788-4823

Rates: $60-125.
Payment: MC VISA AX PC TC.
Innkeeper(s): Sunny & Peter Simmons.
Circa: 1835.

Rooms: 10 rooms with PB, 2 with FP. 2 suites.
Beds: KQDT.

ME

A third story, mansard roof and large bay windows were added to this house at the turn-of-the-century, changing it to a stately Victorian. Both the parlor and dining room feature fireplaces. A carriage house with barn beams, kitchen, skylights and sleeping loft is available as well as the comfortable rooms in the main house. Located in the village, the inn is a block away from the harbor with its fleet of windjammers.

Breakfast included in rates. Types of meals: full breakfast, gourmet breakfast and early coffee/tea. Afternoon tea available. Air conditioning in room. Cable TV and library on premises. Weddings, small meetings and family reunions hosted. Antiques, fishing, parks, shopping, downhill skiing, cross-country skiing, theater and watersports nearby. TAC10.

Publicity: *Bangor Daily News, Newsday.*

Special Discounts: Two-night dinner package November-May $195 per couple for three days or more.

"When can I move in?"

Hawthorn Inn

9 High St
Camden, ME 04843-1610
(207)236-8842
Fax:(207)236-6181
E-mail: hawthorn@midcoast.com

Rates: $80-185.
Payment: MC VISA AX PC TC.
Innkeeper(s): Nicholas & Patricia Wharton.
Circa: 1894.

Rooms: 10 rooms with PB, 3 with FP.
Beds: QDT.

This handsome yellow and white turreted Victorian sits on an acre and a half of sloping lawns with a view of the harbor. The interior boasts a grand, three-story staircase and original stained-glass windows. The carriage house offers additional rooms with private decks, double Jacuzzi tubs and fireplaces. Some rooms in the main house offer harbor views and some look out onto Mt. Battie. Breakfasts with fresh fruit, coffeecakes and egg dishes are served. During warm weather guests are invited to eat on the deck overlooking the harbor.

Breakfast included in rates. Types of meals: full breakfast and early coffee/tea. VCR in room. Fax on premises. Small meetings hosted. Antiques, fishing, parks, shopping, downhill skiing, cross-country skiing, theater and watersports nearby. TAC10.

Publicity: *Glamour, Country Inns, Outside, Yankee, Down East, Cleveland Plain Dealer, Minneapolis Tribune.*

Lord Camden Inn

24 Main St
Camden, ME 04843-1704
(207)236-4325 (800)336-4325
Fax:(207)236-7141
E-mail: lordcam@midcoast.com

Rates: $88-178.
Payment: MC VISA PC.
Innkeeper(s): Stuart Smith.
Circa: 1893.

Rooms: 31 rooms with PB. 4 suites. 2 conference rooms.
Beds: KQD.

Located in a restored brick building on the town's Main Street, the inn is decorated in American country antiques. A friendly staff will be happy to suggest some of the many activities in the area. Day sails and island picnics can be arranged and bicycle rentals are available for inland rides or to tour islands after a short ferry ride. Most guest rooms offer balconies with spectacular views of Camden Harbor, the village or the hills.

Breakfast included in rates. Types of meals: continental-plus breakfast and early coffee/tea. Air conditioning and cable TV in room. Fax and copier on premises. Weddings, small meetings, family reunions and seminars hosted. Antiques, fishing, parks, shopping, downhill skiing, cross-country skiing, theater and watersports nearby. TAC10.

The Maine Stay Inn

22 High St
Camden, ME 04843-1735
(207)236-9636

Rates: $55-115.
Payment: MC VISA AX.
Innkeeper(s): Peter & Donny Smith & Diana Robson.
Circa: 1802.

Rooms: 8 rooms, 4 with PB, 4 with FP.
Beds: QDT.

The innkeepers of this treasured colonial, which is one of the oldest of the 66 houses which comprise the High Street Historic District, take great pleasure in making guests feel at home. One of the trio of innkeepers is known for his "down-east" stories told in a heavy "down-east" accent. Antiques from the 17th, 18th and 19th centuries adorn the rooms. The center of the village and the Camden Harbor are a short five-minute walk away.

Breakfast included in rates.

Publicity: *Miami Herald, Lewiston Sun-Journal, Country Inns, Glamour, Country Living, Rand McNally's Best B&Bs, Discerning Traveler, Bazaar.*

"We've traveled the East Coast from Martha's Vineyard to Bar Harbor and this is the only place we know we must return to."

Spouter Inn

Rt 1, PO Box 270
Camden, ME 04849
(207)789-5171

Rates: $65-150.
Payment: MC VISA AX DS PC TC.
Innkeeper(s): Lippman Family.
Circa: 1832.

Rooms: 6 rooms with PB, 5 with FP. 2 suites.
Beds: KQD.

From the porch of this early 19th-century Colonial, guests can gaze out at Penobscot Bay. Several of the inn's antique-filled guest rooms also boast ocean views. The guest quarters are elegantly appointed with romantic touches, such as four-poster beds and stained glass. Most rooms offer ocean or mountain views, and several include fireplaces or Jacuzzi tubs. The gourmet breakfasts at this three-diamond rated inn include delectables such as baked glazed pears, puffed pancakes topped with a caramel sauce, homemade sausages, freshly baked muffins or breads, quiche and eggs Benedict. The inn is within walking distance from the beach, restaurants, shops and antiquing.

Breakfast included in rates. Types of meals: full breakfast, gourmet breakfast and early coffee/tea. Air conditioning and ceiling fan in room. Cable TV, bicycles and library on premises. Small meetings and family reunions hosted. Antiques, fishing, parks, shopping, downhill skiing, cross-country skiing, theater and watersports nearby.

Special Discounts: Stay seven days, get one night free.

The Swan House

49 Mountain St
Camden, ME 04843-1635
(207)236-8275 (800)207-8275
Fax:(207)236-0906

Rates: $65-120.
Payment: MC VISA PC TC.
Innkeeper(s): Lyn & Ken Kohl.
Circa: 1870.

Rooms: 6 rooms with PB. 1 suite.
Beds: QD.

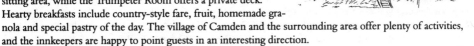

Nestled on just under an acre of wooded grounds at the foot of Mt. Battie, this Victorian is a welcoming site inside and out. Antique-filled guest rooms are comfortable, each named for a different variety of swan. Four of the rooms offer private entrances. The Lohengrin Suite is a spacious room with its own sitting area, while the Trumpeter Room offers a private deck. Hearty breakfasts include country-style fare, fruit, homemade granola and special pastry of the day. The village of Camden and the surrounding area offer plenty of activities, and the innkeepers are happy to point guests in an interesting direction.

Breakfast included in rates. Types of meals: full breakfast and early coffee/tea. Afternoon tea available. Fax on premises. Small meetings and family reunions hosted. Antiques, fishing, parks, shopping, downhill skiing, cross-country skiing, theater and watersports nearby.

"We loved our stay at the Swan House and our breakfast there was by far the most excellent breakfast we have ever had."

Victorian B&B

PO Box 1385
Camden, ME 04843
(207)236-3785 (800)382-9817
Fax:(207)236-0017
E-mail: victbb@midcoast.com

Rates: $95-245.
Payment: MC VISA AX.
Innkeeper(s): Ray & Marie Donner.
Circa: 1881.

Rooms: 6 rooms with PB, 5 with FP. 2 suites.
Beds: Q.

This Queen Anne combines a Victorian setting of green lawns and colorful gardens with an ocean view. These elements most commonly are enjoyed from the wraparound porch and gazebo. The decor is on the elegant side, and in keeping with the Victorian house. Many of the guest rooms have fireplaces. Breakfast is served on the porch.

Breakfast and evening snack included in rates. Types of meals: full breakfast and early coffee/tea. Turn-down service and ceiling fan in room. Fax on premises. Weddings, small meetings and family reunions hosted. Antiques, parks, shopping, downhill skiing, cross-country skiing, theater and watersports nearby. TAC10.

"You really spoiled us with your warm hospitality. This vacation will stay with us for a long time."

Windward House B&B

6 High St
Camden, ME 04843-1611
(207)236-9656
Fax:(207)230-0433
E-mail: windward@coastalmaine.com

Rates: $85-170.
Payment: MC VISA AX PC TC.
Innkeeper(s): Tim & Sandy La Plante.
Circa: 1854.

Rooms: 8 rooms with PB, 3 with FP.
Beds: Q.

Each guest room at this charming Greek Revival home has been individually decorated and sport names such as the Carriage Room, Trisha Romance Room or Brass Room. The Mount Battie room offers a mountain view and a skylight, so guests can stargaze as they relax on a queen-size bed. The rooms include antiques and romantic amenities such as candles and fine linens. The innkeepers further pamper guests with a hearty breakfast featuring a variety of juices, freshly ground coffee and teas, homemade muffins and breads, raspberry sour cream coffee cake and perhaps a gourmet frittata, featherbed eggs or Belgian waffles topped with fresh Maine blueberries. After the morning meal, guests are sure to enjoy a day exploring Camden, noted as the village where "the mountains meet the sea." The inn is open year-round.

Breakfast and afternoon tea included in rates. Types of meals: gourmet breakfast and early coffee/tea. Ceiling fan in room. Fax, copier and library on premises. Small meetings hosted. Antiques, fishing, parks, shopping, downhill skiing, cross-country skiing, theater and watersports nearby. TAC10.

Cape Elizabeth

K3

Inn By The Sea

40 Bowery Beach Rd
Cape Elizabeth, ME 04107
(207)799-3134 (800)888-4287
Fax:(207)799-4779

Rates: $100-390. EP.
Payment: MC VISA AX DS TC.
Innkeeper(s): Maureen McQuade.
Circa: 1986.

Rooms: 43 suites, 6 with FP. 2 conference rooms.
Beds: KQD.

This cottage-style resort is like a modern version of the hotels and inns that dotted Maine's coast in its heyday as a summer spot. The inn has its own private boardwalk leading to Crescent Beach. Guests can enjoy swimming, tennis and shuffleboard without leaving the inn's grounds, which also offer a tea garden and gazebo. The well-appointed rooms are elegant, but not imposing, with Chippendale furnishings, wicker and floral chintz. Guests opting for one of the inn's cozy garden suites can grab a book from the inn's library and enjoy it from a rocker on their own private porch. Cuisine at the inn's gourmet Audubon Room is full of memorable items. In the summer months, the inn opens its outdoor West End Cafe and Pool Bar.

Type of meal: full breakfast. Dinner, picnic lunch, banquet service, catering service and room service available. EP. Turn-down service, ceiling fan, cable TV and VCR in room. Fax, copier and bicycles on premises. Weddings, small meetings, family reunions and seminars hosted. Amusement parks, antiques, fishing, parks, shopping, downhill skiing, cross-country skiing, sporting events, theater and watersports nearby.

Pets Allowed: Yes.

Cape Neddick

K2

Cape Neddick House

1300 Rt 1, PO Box 70
Cape Neddick, ME 03902
(207)363-2500
Fax:(207)363-4499

Rates: $65-95.
Payment: PC TC.
Innkeeper(s): Dianne & John Goodwin.
Circa: 1885.

Rooms: 5 rooms with PB, 1 with FP. 1 suite.
Beds: D.

As the scent of freshly baked muffins and brewing coffee drifts upward, guests at this Victorian farmhouse are sure to relish waking. The meal itself, which always includes a special daily entree accompanied by fruits and fresh breads, is only part of the fun. The home has been in the Goodwin family since its construction in 1885, and the innkeepers, eighth-generation Goodwins themselves, are full of interesting stories about the house, their family and Cape Neddick. The home features polished wood floors, high ceilings and carved woodwork enhanced by the Oriental rugs, antiques and country pieces that decorate the rooms. A turn-of-the-century post office building is on the premises. The home is a short distance from beaches, Rachel Carson Wildlife Sanctuary, York Village's historic homes, shops, factory outlet stores, horseback riding, skiing and more.

Breakfast included in rates. Types of meals: full breakfast, gourmet breakfast and early coffee/tea. Air conditioning in room. Cable TV, VCR, fax and library on premises. 10 acres. Small meetings, family reunions and seminars hosted. Amusement parks, antiques, fishing, parks, shopping, cross-country skiing, theater and watersports nearby.

Special Discounts: Packages available.

"A wonderful vacation from all. Breakfast was super."

Corea

I7

The Black Duck Inn on Corea Harbor

PO Box 39
Corea, ME 04624-0039
(207)963-2689
Fax:(207)963-7495
E-mail: bduck@acadia.net

Rates: $60-125.
Payment: MC VISA PC TC.
Innkeeper(s): Barry Canner & Bob Travers.
Circa: 1890.

Rooms: 4 rooms, 2 with PB. 1 suite. 2 cottages.
Beds: QDT.

Two of the guest rooms at this turn-of-the-century farmhouse boast harbor views, while another offers a wooded scene out its windows. The innkeepers have decorated the home in an eclectic mix of old and new with antiques and contemporary pieces. There are two waterfront cottages for those who prefer more privacy. The full, gourmet breakfasts include house specialties, such as "eggs Black Duck" or items such as orange glazed French toast, blintzes or perhaps eggs Benedict.

Breakfast included in rates. Types of meals: gourmet breakfast and early coffee/tea. Cable TV, VCR, fax, bicycles and library on premises. 12 acres. Weddings and family reunions hosted. Danish spoken. Antiques, fishing, parks, shopping, cross-country skiing and watersports nearby. TAC10.

"Never could we have known how warmly received we would all four feel and how really restored we would be by the end of the week."

Damariscotta Mills

Mill Pond Inn

50 Main St, Damariscotta Mills, ME 04555
(207)563-8014

Rates: $80.
Innkeeper(s): Bobby & Sherry Whear.
Circa: 1780.

Rooms: 6 rooms with PB, 3 with FP. 1 suite.
Beds: KQT.

The one acre of grounds surrounding this 18th-century home are packed with scenery. A pond with a waterfall flows into the adjacent Damariscotta Lake and trees offer plenty of shade. Rooms are decorated in a whimsical country style, some offer lake views, and fresh flowers are placed in each bedchamber. Breakfasts are served in a room that overlooks the pond and grounds. Innkeeper Bobby Whear is a registered Maine guide, and the innkeepers offer private fishing trips.

ME

Breakfast and afternoon tea included in rates. Types of meals: full breakfast and early coffee/tea. Cable TV, VCR, fax, copier and bicycles on premises. Weddings, small meetings, family reunions and seminars hosted. Antiques, fishing, parks, shopping, downhill skiing, cross-country skiing, sporting events, theater and watersports nearby.

Dennysville G8

Lincoln House Country Inn

Rts 1 & 86
Dennysville, ME 04628
(207)726-3953
Fax:(207)726-0654

Rates: $68-85.
Payment: MC VISA PC TC.
Innkeeper(s): Mary & Jerry Haggerty.
Circa: 1787.

Rooms: 6 rooms, 2 with PB, 2 with FP. 1 conference room.
Beds: QDT.

Theodore Lincoln, son of General Benjamin Lincoln, who accepted the sword of surrender from Cornwallis after the American Revolution, built this house. The four-square Colonial looks out to the Dennys River and its salmon pools. John James Audubon stayed here on his way to Labrador. He loved the house and family so much that he named the Lincoln Sparrow in their honor.

Breakfast included in rates. Types of meals: full breakfast, gourmet breakfast and early coffee/tea. Dinner available. Library on premises. 100 acres. Antiques, fishing, parks, shopping, cross-country skiing and watersports nearby. TAC10.

Location: On the Dennys River.

Publicity: *Good Housekeeping, Washington Post, New York Times.*

Special Discounts: Third night lodging free.

"The food was delicious, the ambiance special."

The Inn at Eastport

13 Washington St
Eastport, ME 04631-1324
(207)853-4307
Fax:(207)853-6143

Rates: $40-65.
Payment: MC VISA DS PC TC.
Innkeeper(s): Robert & Brenda Booker.
Circa: 1840.

Rooms: 4 rooms with PB.
Beds: QD.

Skin-divers consider the waters near this Federal-style inn among the best in the United States. The innkeepers are more than happy to assist guests with their sightseeing efforts in America's most northeasterly city. The inn's antique furnishings, hardwood floors and black marble hearths will please visitors. Enjoy a soak in the inn's outdoor hot tub. The gourmet breakfasts may include wild blueberry pancakes. New Brunswick is just a 15-minute ferry ride away.

Breakfast and afternoon tea included in rates. Type of meal: full breakfast. Turn-down service in room. Cable TV, VCR and fax on premises. Small meetings hosted. Antiques, fishing, parks, shopping and theater nearby.

Pets Allowed: If well behaved.

"Thanks for the great Northern hospitality! It was the best B&B experience we've ever had!"

The Milliken House

29 Washington St
Eastport, ME 04631-1324
(207)853-2955

Rates: $40-60.
Payment: MC VISA AX PC TC.
Innkeeper(s): Joyce Weber.
Circa: 1846.

Rooms: 5 rooms. 1 conference room.
Beds: QT.

Formerly known as the Artists Retreat, this stately Victorian is furnished with ornately carved, marble-topped furniture. The builder maintained a wharf on Eastport's waterfront from which he serviced the tall trading ships that used the harbor as a port of entry to the United States. Much of the furniture is original, brought to the United States for Benjamin Milliken's bride.

Breakfast included in rates. Type of meal: full breakfast.

Weston House

26 Boynton St
Eastport, ME 04631-1305
(207)853-2907 (800)853-2907

Rates: $55-70.
Payment: TC.
Innkeeper(s): Jett & John Peterson.
Circa: 1810.

Rooms: 5 rooms, 1 with FP. 1 suite. 1 conference room.
Beds: KQDT.

Jonathan Weston, an 1802 Harvard graduate, built this Federal-style house on a hill overlooking Passamaquoddy Bay. John Audubon stayed here as a guest of the Westons while awaiting passage to Labrador in 1833. Each of the guest rooms are furnished with antiques and Oriental rugs. The Weston and Audubon rooms boast views of the bay and gardens. Breakfast menus vary, including such delectables as heavenly pancakes with hot apricot syrup or freshly baked muffins and coddled eggs. Seasonal brunches are served on weekends and holidays. The area is full of outdoor activities, including whale watching. Nearby Saint Andrews-by-the-Sea offers plenty of shops and restaurants.

Breakfast and afternoon tea included in rates. Type of meal: gourmet breakfast. Picnic lunch and catering service available. Cable TV in room. Weddings, small meetings and family reunions hosted. Fishing, shopping and theater nearby.

Publicity: *Downeast Magazine, Los Angeles Times, Boston Globe, Boston Magazine.*

"The most memorable bed & breakfast experience we have ever had."

Captain Josiah Mitchell House

188 Main St
Freeport, ME 04032-1407
(207)865-3289

Rates: $52-82.
Payment: MC VISA PC TC.
Innkeeper(s): Alan & Loretta Bradley.
Circa: 1789.

Rooms: 7 rooms with PB.
Beds: DT.

Captain Josiah Mitchell was commander of the clipper ship "Hornet." In 1866, en route from New York to San Francisco it caught fire, burned and was lost. The passengers and crew survived in three longboats, drifting for 45 days. When the boats finally drifted into one of the South Pacific Islands, Samuel Clemens was there, befriended the Captain and wrote his first story under the name under the name of Mark Twain about the captain. The diary of Captain Mitchell parallels episodes of "Mutiny on the Bounty." Flower gardens and a porch swing on the veranda now welcome guests to Freeport and Captain Mitchell's House.

Breakfast included in rates. Type of meal: full breakfast. Air conditioning and ceiling fan in room. Amusement parks, antiques, fishing, parks, shopping, downhill skiing, cross-country skiing, sporting events and theater nearby. TAC10.

Publicity: *Famous Boats and Harbors.*

"Your wonderful stories brought us all together. You have created a special place that nurtures and brings happiness and love. This has been a dream!"

ME

Country at Heart B&B

37 Bow St
Freeport, ME 04032-1519
(207)865-0512

Rates: $65-85.
Payment: MC VISA PC TC.
Innkeeper(s): Roger & Kim Dubay.
Circa: 1870.

Rooms: 3 rooms with PB.
Beds: QDT.

This cozy country home is decorated with handmade crafts and antiques. The Shaker Room has a hand-stenciled border with Shaker accents throughout. A Shaker peg rack surrounds the room. The Quilt Room has a heart stenciled border with quilt related wall hangings and antique quilts. The Teddy Bear Room is full of, you guessed it, bears of all shapes and sizes. Breakfast is served on an eight-foot oak dining room table.

Breakfast and afternoon tea included in rates. Types of meals: full breakfast and early coffee/tea. Ceiling fan in room. Cable TV and VCR on premises. Antiques, fishing, parks, shopping, cross-country skiing, sporting events, theater and watersports nearby. TAC10.

Special Discounts: Stay six nights, seventh night is free.

"Thank you for your genuine hospitality! Wonderful breakfast too!"

Kendall Tavern B&B

213 Main St
Freeport, ME 04032-1411
(207)865-1338 (800)341-9572

Rates: $70-120.
Payment: MC VISA AX DS TC.
Circa: 1800.

Rooms: 7 rooms with PB.
Beds: QT.

Kendall Tavern is a welcoming farmhouse painted in a cheerful, creamy yellow hue with white trim. The interior is appointed in an elegant New England country style. Each of the parlors has a fireplace. One parlor includes an upright piano and is a perfect place to curl up with a book, the other has a television and VCR. Breakfasts are creative and plentiful. The morning meal might start off with poached pears topped with a French vanilla yogurt sauce and accompanied by blueberry muffins. From there, guests enjoy a broccoli and mushroom quiche, grilled ham and home fries. Another menu might include baked apples stuffed with cranberries, cream cheese raspberry coffeecake, blueberry pancakes, scrambled eggs and crisp bacon. Whatever the menu, the breakfast is always a perfect start to a day of shopping in outlet stores, hiking, sailing or cross-country skiing, all of which are nearby.

Breakfast included in rates. Types of meals: full breakfast and gourmet breakfast. Cable TV, VCR, fax, copier and spa on premises. Small meetings hosted. Antiques, fishing, parks, shopping, cross-country skiing, theater and watersports nearby.

"What a wonderful introduction to your beautiful country."

Friendship J4

Outsiders' Inn B&B

Box 521A,
Corner Rt 97 & Rt 220
Friendship, ME 04547
(207)832-5197

Rates: $50-75.
Payment: MC VISA PC TC.
Innkeeper(s): Debbie & Bill Michaud.
Circa: 1830.

Rooms: 5 rooms, 2 with PB. 1 cottage.
Beds: D.

Window boxes filled with flowers dot the second story windows of this Colonial home, which was built by a sea captain. For nearly half a century, it was known as the village doctor's house. Period furnishings and country decor create a warm, friendly atmosphere. The home is near many attractions, including museums, beaches, restaurants and antique shops. The innkeepers can outfit guests for a day of sea kayaking, and they offer kayak rentals, clinics and tours from a registered Maine guide.

Breakfast included in rates. Types of meals: full breakfast and early coffee/tea. Sauna on premises. Weddings, small meetings, family reunions and seminars hosted. Antiques, shopping, theater and watersports nearby.

"A fabulous Maine farmhouse in a fabulous Maine town. You made our visit extra special."

Georgetown J3

Coveside-Five Islands B&B

HCR 33 Box 462, North End Rd
Georgetown, ME 04548
(207)371-2807
Fax:(207)371-2572
E-mail: jte@maine.com

Rates: $65-115.
Payment: MC VISA PC TC.
Innkeeper(s): Tom & Judy Ewing.
Circa: 1880.

Rooms: 3 rooms with PB. 2 suites.
Beds: KQT.

Guest rooms at this farmhouse look out to the cove where the Sheepscot River merges with the Atlantic Ocean. The rooms are decorated in a simple, comfortable style. Guests are invited to lounge on the deck, stroll the five acres or take the innkeeper's canoe out and explore the island. Breakfasts start off with fresh fruit and muffins, followed by an entree. French toast topped with strawberry sauce is one pleasing example. Carriage house suites also are available. The suites can sleep four, and each includes a bedroom, bathroom, living room and a kitchen/eating area.

Breakfast included in rates. Types of meals: full breakfast and early coffee/tea. Fax on premises. Antiques, fishing, parks, shopping, cross-country skiing and theater nearby. TAC10.

The Grey Havens

PO Box 308
Georgetown, ME 04548
(207)371-2616
Fax:(207)371-2274

Rates: $100-195.
Payment: MC VISA PC TC.
Innkeeper(s): Bill & Haley Eberhart.
Circa: 1904.

Rooms: 12 rooms with PB. 1 suite. 1 conference room.
Beds: KQD.

For more than 20 summers, members of the Texas-based Hardcastle family have returned to welcome guests to this handsome shingle-style hotel on Georgetown Island. From the wraparound porch and many of the rooms, guests may view the harbor, the inn's deep water dock and rowboats, islands, lighthouses and the open ocean. The lounge features a huge rock fireplace and a 12-foot-tall window. Furnishings are antique. Ask for one of the four turret rooms for a 180-degree ocean view. Reid State Park, Bath, the Maine Maritime Museum and Freeport are nearby.

Breakfast and evening snack included in rates. Types of meals: continental-plus breakfast and early coffee/tea. Fax, copier and bicycles on premises. Weddings, small meetings, family reunions and seminars hosted. Antiques, fishing, parks, shopping and watersports nearby.

Greenville F4

Greenville Inn

Norris St, PO Box 1194
Greenville, ME 04441
(207)695-2206 (888)695-6000
Fax:(207)695-2206

Rates: $85-185.
Payment: MC VISA DS PC TC.
Innkeeper(s): Elfi, Michael and Susie Schnetzer.
Circa: 1895.

Rooms: 5 rooms, 6 with PB, 2 with FP. 1 suite. 6 cottages.
Beds: KQDT.

The Greenville Inn sits on a hill, one block from town. It's also one block from the shore line of Moosehead Lake, the largest lake completely contained in any one state. A wealthy lumber family built the house. Ten years were needed to complete the cherry and mahogany paneling. There are six fireplaces with carved mantels and mosaics. From the dining room, guests have an excellent water view.

Type of meal: continental-plus breakfast. Dinner available. Weddings, small meetings and family reunions hosted. German & French spoken.

Location: Moosehead Lake, Greenville.

Publicity: *Maine Times, Portland Monthly, Bangor Daily News, Grays Sporting Journal.*

"The fanciest place in town. It is indeed a splendid place."

ME

Hancock H6

Crocker House Country Inn

Hancock Point Rd
Hancock, ME 04640
(207)422-6806
Fax:(207)422-3105
E-mail: crocker@acadia.net

Rates: $75-120.
Payment: MC VISA AX DS PC TC.
Innkeeper(s): Richard S. Malaby.
Circa: 1884.

Rooms: 11 rooms with PB. 1 conference room.
Beds: KQ.

For more than a century, guests have been enjoying Crocker House. The inn has changed hands many times, and legend has it that the ghost of one former owner, Baroness Olga Szabo, still roams the house on occasion. The elegant guest rooms are decorated with warm, country furnishings, with an emphasis on the romantic. Guests are treated to a full breakfast, and there is a restaurant on the premises serving dinner specialties such as Crocker House scallops or roast tenderloin of pork stuffed with basil, pinenuts and roasted red peppers. The inn's cheesecake is a must for dessert.

Breakfast included in rates. Type of meal: gourmet breakfast. Catering service available. Cable TV, VCR, fax, spa, bicycles and library on premises. Weddings, small meetings, family reunions and seminars hosted. Amusement parks, fishing, parks, theater and watersports nearby.
Pets Allowed.
Special Discounts: Fall and April, May $109 per night includes dinner for two.
"Very nice. Our third stay."

Harrison I2

Harrison House B&B

RR 2 Box 2035
Harrison, ME 04040-9529
(207)583-6564

Rates: $55-90.
Payment: PC TC.
Innkeeper(s): Sheila Baxter & Cathy McMahon.

Rooms: 5 rooms, 4 with PB. 2 suites.
Beds: QDT.
Circa: 1867.

Built just after the Civil War, this red-roofed farmhouse offers lake views from each guest room. Featherbeds, poster beds and handmade quilts decorate the quarters. Breakfasts include fresh fruit platters, homemade breads and a special daily entree. Nearby Long Lake provides many activities.

Breakfast included in rates. Types of meals: full breakfast and early coffee/tea. Ceiling fan in room. Cable TV, VCR and swimming on premises. Weddings, small meetings and family reunions hosted. Antiques, fishing, shopping, downhill skiing, cross-country skiing, theater and watersports nearby.
Special Discounts: Stay two nights get second night half price (limited offers)

Holden

H5

Tether's End B&B

12 Church Rd
Holden, ME 04429-9626
(207)989-7886
E-mail: tethers@agate.net

Rates: $45-65.
Payment: MC VISA PC TC.
Innkeeper(s): Judy Madson.
Circa: 1890.

Rooms: 3 rooms, 2 with PB.
Beds: QDT.

With a half-acre of lush, garden-covered grounds to enjoy, this cozy, little bed & breakfast is a relaxing place to enjoy nearby Bangor, just 10 minutes away. The innkeeper prepares a gourmet feast for breakfast with traditional items such as fruit, muffins and coffeecake and more unique dishes such as a cheesy breakfast apple pie, gingerbread pancakes and locally made lamb sausage. In the afternoon, coffee and tea is served on the large front porch. Champagne is available for those celebrating anniversaries or a honeymoon.

Breakfast included in rates. Types of meals: gourmet breakfast and early coffee/tea. Afternoon tea available. Air conditioning and ceiling fan in room. Cable TV, VCR and library on premises. German spoken. Antiques, fishing, parks, shopping, sporting events, theater and watersports nearby. TAC10.

Special Discounts: Five-night stay, pay for four nights, fifth night free.

"Had a unique experience. Felt like I was visiting friends."

Isle Au Haut

I5

The Keeper's House

PO Box 26
Isle Au Haut, ME 04645
(207)367-2261

Rates: $250-285.
Payment: PC TC.
Innkeeper(s): Jeff & Judi Burke.
Circa: 1907.

Rooms: 6 rooms. 1 cottage.
Beds: D.

Designed and built by the U.S. Lighthouse Service, the handsome 48-foot-high Robinson Point Light guided vessels into this once-bustling island fishing village. Guests arrive on the mailboat. Innkeeper Judi Burke, whose father was a keeper at the Highland Lighthouse on Cape Cod, provides picnic lunches so guests may explore the scenic island trails. Dinner is served in the keeper's dining room. The lighthouse is adjacent to the most remote section of Acadia National Park. It's not uncommon to hear the cry of an osprey, see deer approach the inn, or watch seals and porpoises cavorting off the point. Guest rooms are comfortable and serene, with stunning views of the island's ragged shore line, forests and Duck Harbor.

Breakfast, dinner and picnic lunch included in rates. Types of meals: full breakfast, gourmet breakfast and early coffee/tea. Afternoon tea, lunch and gourmet lunch available. Swimming, bicycles and library on premises. Weddings, small meetings, family reunions and seminars hosted. Spanish spoken. Parks and shopping nearby.

Location: A small island six miles south of Stonington, reached by mailboat.

Publicity: *New York Times, USA Today, Los Angeles Times, Ladies Home Journal, Christian Science Monitor, Down East, New York Woman, Philadelphia Inquirer, McCalls, Country, Men's Journal, Travel & Leisure.*

"Simply one of the unique places on Earth."

Arundel Meadows Inn

PO Box 1129
Kennebunk, ME 04043
(207)985-3770

Rates: $65-125.
Innkeeper(s): Mark Bachelder & Murray Yaeger.
Circa: 1827.

Rooms: 7 rooms with PB, 3 with FP. 2 suites.
Beds: KQDT.

This expansive farmhouse features seven bedrooms, each with their own sitting areas. Three rooms boast fireplaces. A gourmet breakfast is prepared by innkeeper Mark Bachelder, who studied under Madeleine Kamman, a popular chef on PBS. Mark's freshly baked delicacies also are served during afternoon teas. Antiques and paintings by innkeeper Murray Yaeger decorate the house. Nearby Kennebunkport provides excellent shopping at factory outlets, antique galleries and a variety of restaurants.

Breakfast and afternoon tea included in rates. Type of meal: full breakfast. Antiques, theater and watersports nearby.

Publicity: *York County Coast Star.*

"The room was beautiful. Breakfast wonderful."

ME

Lake Brook Bed & Breakfast

PO Box 762
Kennebunk, ME 04043
(207)967-4069

Rates: $80-100.
Payment: MC VISA.
Innkeeper(s): Carolyn A. McAdams.
Circa: 1900.

Rooms: 3 rooms with PB. 1 suite.
Beds: QD.

This pleasant old farmhouse is situated on a tidal brook. Comfortable rockers offer an inviting rest on the wrap-around porch where you can enjoy the inn's flower gardens that trail down to the marsh and brook. Gourmet breakfasts are served. Walk to Kennebunkport's Dock Square and lower village to visit fine galleries, shops and restaurants.

Breakfast included in rates. Types of meals: gourmet breakfast and early coffee/tea. Ceiling fan in room. Small meetings and family reunions hosted. Spanish spoken. Antiques, fishing, parks, shopping, cross-country skiing, theater and watersports nearby. TAC10.

"Truly wonderful atmosphere."

Sundial Inn

48 Beach Ave
Kennebunk, ME 04043
(207)967-3850
Fax:(207)967-4719
E-mail: sundial@lamere.net

Rates: $65-185.
Payment: MC VISA AX DC CB TC.
Innkeeper(s): Kenny Family.
Circa: 1893.

Rooms: 34 rooms with PB.
Beds: KQDT.

This yellow and white clapboard house faces the ocean and Kennebunk Beach. The inn is decorated with country Victorian antiques, and some rooms have a whirlpool bath. An elevator makes for easy access. Beachcombing for sand dollars, sea shells and sea urchins is a popular pastime, along with enjoying splendid views from the porch rockers and guest rooms.

Breakfast included in rates. Type of meal: continental-plus breakfast. Air conditioning and cable TV in room. Fax, copier and library on premises. Handicap access. Weddings, small meetings, family reunions and seminars hosted. Amusement parks, antiques, fishing, parks, shopping, cross-country skiing, sporting events, theater and watersports nearby.

Location: Beach Avenue #48.

Publicity: *New England Travel, LL Bean.*

"We've been here in a blizzard and on an idyllic summer day. Love it always (all ways). Thanks!"

Kennebunk Beach

The Ocean View

72 Beach Ave
Kennebunk Beach, ME
04043-2524
(207)967-2750
Fax:(207)967-5418

Rates: $90-195.
Payment: MC VISA DS TC.
Innkeeper(s): Carole & Bob Arena.
Circa: 1900.

Rooms: 9 rooms with PB. 4 suites.
Beds: KQDT.

This brightly painted Victorian is literally just steps to the beach. The oceanfront guest quarters are located either in the turn-of-the-century Victorian or in the Ocean View Too, a separate guest house with four suites. The suites include cable TV, VCR, wet bar, refrigerator and a small terrace. A continental breakfast is delivered to these suite guests. Guests in the main house are pampered with a full meal in the oceanfront breakfast room. Guests might partake of a baked pineapple with a brown sugar glaze and a Belgian waffle topped with seasonal fruits or other tempting fare. The village of Kennebunkport is just one mile away.

Breakfast and afternoon tea included in rates. Types of meals: full breakfast, gourmet breakfast and early coffee/tea. Ceiling fan, cable TV and VCR in room. Fax and library on premises. French spoken. Amusement parks, antiques, fishing, parks, shopping, cross-country skiing, sporting events, theater and watersports nearby.

Kennebunkport

K2

The Captain Lord Mansion

Corner Pleasant & Green,
PO Box 800
Kennebunkport, ME 04046
(207)967-3141
Fax:(207)967-3172
E-mail: captain@briddefond.com

Rates: $100-350.
Payment: MC VISA DS.
Innkeeper(s): Bev Davis & Rick Litchfield.
Circa: 1812.

Rooms: 16 rooms with PB, 15 with FP. 2 conference rooms.
Beds: KQ.

In the National Register, the Captain Lord Mansion was built during the War of 1812 and is one of the finest examples of Federal architecture on the coast of Maine. A four-story spiral staircase winds up to the cupola where one can view the town and the Kennebunk River and Yacht Club. The inn is furnished with elegant antiques. Many bed chambers have working fireplaces and there's a room with a fireplace in the bathroom. A family-style breakfast is served in the country kitchen.

Breakfast included in rates. Types of meals: full breakfast and early coffee/tea. Afternoon tea available. Air conditioning in room. Cable TV, fax, copier and library on premises. Small meetings, family reunions and seminars hosted. Antiques, fishing, shopping, cross-country skiing and theater nearby. TAC7.

Publicity: *Andrew Harper's Hideaway Report, Colonial Homes, Yankee, New England Getaways.*

"A showcase of elegant architecture. Meticulously clean and splendidly appointed. It's a shame to have to leave."

Cove House

11 S Maine St
Kennebunkport, ME 04046
(207)967-3704

Rates: $70-90.
Payment: MC VISA PC TC.
Innkeeper(s): Katherine Jones.
Circa: 1793.

Rooms: 3 rooms with PB. 1 cottage.
Beds: QT.

This roomy Colonial Revival farmhouse overlooks Chick's Cove on the Kennebunk River. The inn's peaceful setting offers easy access to beaches, shops and the town. Three guest rooms serve visitors of this antique-filled home. Guests enjoy full breakfasts, which often include the inn's famous blueberry muffins, in the Flow Blue dining room. A popular gathering spot for guests is the book-lined living room/library. Bicycles may be borrowed for a leisurely ride around the town. A cozy, secluded cottage with a screened front porch is another lodging option.

Breakfast and afternoon tea included in rates. Types of meals: full breakfast and early coffee/tea. Cable TV, VCR, bicycles and library on premises. Small meetings hosted. Antiques, fishing, parks, shopping, cross-country skiing, theater and watersports nearby. TAC10.

English Meadows Inn

141 Port Rd
Kennebunkport, ME 04043
(207)967-5766 (800)272-0698
Fax:(207)967-5766

Rates: $75-108.
Payment: MC VISA AX DS PC TC.
Innkeeper(s): Charles Doane.
Circa: 1860.

Rooms: 13 rooms with PB. 1 suite. 1 cottage.
Beds: KQDT.

Bordered by century-old lilac bushes, this Queen Anne Victorian inn and attached carriage house offer 13 guest rooms. The inn's well-tended grounds, which include apple trees, gardens and lush lawns, invite bird-lovers or those who desire a relaxing stroll. Four-poster beds, afghans and handsewn quilts are found in many of the guest rooms, and visitors also will enjoy the talents of local artists, whose works are featured throughout the inn. Guests may eat breakfast in bed before heading out to explore Kennebunkport.

Breakfast and afternoon tea included in rates. Types of meals: full breakfast and early coffee/tea. Room service available. Cable TV and fax on premises. Small meetings and family reunions hosted. Amusement parks, antiques, fishing, parks, shopping, cross-country skiing, theater and watersports nearby.

"Thanks for the memories! You have a warm Yankee hospitality here!"

The Inn at Harbor Head

41 Pier Rd
Kennebunkport, ME 04046
(207)967-5564
Fax:(207)967-1294

Rates: $105-250.
Payment: MC VISA PC TC.
Innkeeper(s): Joan & David Sutter.
Circa: 1890.

Rooms: 5 rooms with PB, 2 with FP. 2 suites.
Beds: KQ.

This shingled saltwater farmhouse is located directly on the water in historic Cape Porpoise — a fishing village where lobstermen have worked for generations. Sounds of sea gulls and bellbuoys blend with the foghorn from the lighthouse nearby. There are outstanding views of the harbor, ocean and islands. Guest rooms feature antiques, paddle fans and down comforters. A gourmet breakfast is served in the stenciled dining room amidst collections of pewter and crystal.

Breakfast, afternoon tea and evening snack included in rates. Types of meals: full breakfast, gourmet breakfast and early coffee/tea. Air conditioning, turn-down service and ceiling fan in room. Fax, swimming and library on premises. Weddings, small meetings, family reunions and seminars hosted. Amusement parks, antiques, fishing, shopping, cross-country skiing, theater and watersports nearby.

Location: On the rocky shore of Cape Porpoise Harbor.

Publicity: *Boston Globe, Country Inns, Los Angeles Times, Morning Sentinal.*

"Your lovely home is our image of what a New England B&B should be. Unbelievably perfect! So glad we found you."

Harbor Inn

Ocean Ave, PO Box 538A
Kennebunkport, ME 04046
(207)967-2074

Rates: $75-140.
Payment: MC VISA PC TC.
Innkeeper(s): Charlotte & Bill Massmann.
Circa: 1903.

Rooms: 8 rooms with PB, 1 with FP. 2 suites. 1 cottage.
Beds: QDT.

This welcoming inn lies behind a white iron, Victorian fence. A yellow canopy covers the stairs leading to the large, rocker-lined veranda, a perfect place to relax and enjoy the sea air and an early morning cup of coffee. Period antiques and oriental rugs decorate the well-appointed guest rooms. The innkeepers also offer Woodbine Cottage, which includes a private patio. A full breakfast is served buffet style in the formal dining room and garden room. After the morning meal, guests can take a short walk to the ocean or enjoy a leisurely stroll to the town's shopping area, about a half-mile from the inn.

Breakfast included in rates. Types of meals: full breakfast, gourmet breakfast and early coffee/tea. Cable TV on premises. Antiques, fishing, parks, shopping, theater and watersports nearby.

Publicity: *Country Inns, Yankee Travel Guide.*

"Everything is beautifully done. It's the best we've ever been to."

Kennebunkport Inn

1 Dock Sq
Kennebunkport, ME 04046
(207)967-2621 (800)248-2621
Fax:(207)967-3705

Rates: $69-239. MAP, AP, EP.
Payment: MC VISA AX PC TC.
Innkeeper(s): Rick & Martha Griffin.
Circa: 1899.

Rooms: 34 rooms with PB, 1 with FP. 1 suite.
Beds: KQDT.

The Kennebunkport Inn offers a wonderful combination of elegance and relaxation. The main lounge is furnished with velvet loveseats and chintz sofas. Guest rooms are decorated with mahogany queen-sized beds, wing chairs and Queen Anne writing desks. Innkeeper Martha Griffin is graduate of Paris' prestigious La Varenn Ecole de Cuisine and London's Elizabeth Pomeroy Cooking School. Her culinary creations are unforgettable and award-winning. Maine lobster is a dinner staple, but save room for dessert. The inn also includes a firelit lounge with a piano bar.

Type of meal: full breakfast. Dinner and lunch available. MAP, AP, EP. Air conditioning and cable TV in room. Fax, copier and swimming on premises. Small meetings hosted. Amusement parks, antiques, fishing, shopping, cross-country skiing, theater and watersports nearby. TAC10.

Location: In the center of Kennebunkport.

Publicity: *Getaways for Gourmets, Coast Guide.*

Special Discounts: Special packages May-October.

"From check-in, to check-out, from breakfast through dinner, we were treated like royalty."

Maine Stay Inn & Cottages

PO Box 500-A
Kennebunkport, ME 04046
(207)967-2117 (800)950-2117
Fax:(207)967-8757
E-mail: copeland4@cybertours.com

Rates: $85-225.
Payment: MC VISA AX PC TC.
Innkeeper(s): Carol & Lindsay Copeland.
Circa: 1860.

Rooms: 17 rooms with PB, 7 with FP. 4 suites. 11 cottages.
Beds: QDT.

In the National Register, this is a square-block Italianate contoured in a low hip-roof design. Later additions reflecting the Queen Anne period include a suspended spiral staircase, crystal windows, ornately carved mantels and moldings, bay windows and porches. A sea captain built the handsome cupola that became a favorite spot for making taffy. In the '20s, the cupola was a place from which to spot offshore rumrunners. Guests enjoy afternoon tea with stories of the Maine Stay's heritage. One suite and one room in the main building and five of the cottage rooms have working fireplaces.

Breakfast and afternoon tea included in rates. Types of meals: full breakfast and early coffee/tea. Air conditioning and cable TV in room. Fax, copier, computer and child care on premises. Weddings, small meetings, family reunions and seminars hosted. Amusement parks, antiques, fishing, shopping, cross-country skiing, theater and watersports nearby. TAC10.

Location: In the Kennebunkport National Historic District.

Publicity: *Boston Globe, Discerning Traveler, Montreal Gazette, Innsider, Tourist News, Down East, Staten Island Advance, Birmingham News, Delaware County Times, Family Travel Times.*

Special Discounts: Off season: two night packages.

"We have traveled the East Coast from Martha's Vineyard to Bar Harbor, and this is the only place we know we must return to."

Old Fort Inn

Old Fort Ave, PO Box M 1
Kennebunkport, ME 04046
(207)967-5353 (800)828-3678
Fax:(207)967-4547

Rates: $95-260.
Payment: MC VISA AX DS PC TC.
Innkeeper(s): Sheila & David Aldrich.
Circa: 1880.

Rooms: 16 rooms with PB. 1 conference room.
Beds: KQD.

The Old Fort Inn is a luxurious country inn located in a secluded setting, minutes away from Kennebunkport's shops, art galleries and beaches. The inn's gracious interiors feature antiques, canopy and four-poster beds. There is an antique shop, a tennis court and a fresh-water pool on the property. The ocean is just a block away.

Breakfast included in rates. Type of meal: full breakfast. Air conditioning and cable TV in room. Fax, copier, swimming and tennis on premises. 15 acres. Small meetings hosted. Antiques, fishing, parks, shopping and theater nearby. TAC10.

Publicity: *Country Inns.*

"My husband and I have been spending the last two weeks in August at the Old Fort Inn for years. It combines for us a rich variety of what we feel a relaxing vacation should be."

The Inn on South Street

PO Box 478A
Kennebunkport, ME 04046
(207)967-5151 (800)963-5151

Rates: $90-199.
Payment: MC VISA.
Innkeeper(s): Jacques & Eva Downs.
Circa: 1806.

Rooms: 4 rooms with PB, 2 with FP. 1 suite.
Beds: QT.

This early 19th-century Greek Revival manor is within walking distance of Kennebunkport's many shops, restaurants and the ocean. A unique "Good Morning" staircase will be one of the first items guests will notice upon entering the inn. Richly appointed rooms are full of beautiful furnishings, lovely window dressings and accented by the pine plank floors. Guests will enjoy such amenities as telephones, fireplaces and fresh flowers in the guest rooms. Breakfasts are a treat, served up in the second-floor or country kitchen with views of the river and ocean, and special dishes featuring herbs from the inn's own herb garden.

ME

Breakfast and afternoon tea included in rates. Types of meals: gourmet breakfast and early coffee/tea. German, Spanish and Russian spoken. Antiques, fishing, parks, theater and watersports nearby.

Publicity: *Summertime, Country Inns, Down East.*

"Superb hospitality. We were delighted by the atmosphere and your thoughtfulness."

Naples

J2

Augustus Bove House

Corner Rts 302 & 114,
RR 1 Box 501
Naples, ME 04055
(207)693-6365 (800)693-6365

Rates: $49-125.
Payment: MC VISA AX DS PC TC.
Innkeeper(s): David & Arlene Stetson.
Circa: 1830.

Rooms: 11 rooms, 7 with PB. 1 suite.
Beds: KQT.

A long front lawn nestles up against the stone foundation and veranda of this house, once known as the Hotel Naples, one of the area's summer hotels in the 1800s. The guest rooms are decorated in a Colonial style and modestly furnished with antiques. Many rooms provide a view of Long Lake. A fancy country breakfast is provided.

Breakfast and afternoon tea included in rates. Types of meals: full breakfast and early coffee/tea. Air conditioning and cable TV in room. VCR, fax and spa on premises. Weddings, small meetings and family reunions hosted. Antiques, fishing, parks, shopping, downhill skiing, cross-country skiing, theater and watersports nearby. TAC10.

Pets Allowed.

Location: Corner of routes 302 & 114.

Publicity: *Brighton Times.*

"Beautiful place, rooms, and people."

Inn at Long Lake

Lake House Rd, PO Box 806
Naples, ME 04055
(207)693-6226 (800)437-0328

Rates: $55-130.
Payment: MC VISA DS PC TC.
Innkeeper(s): Maynard & Irene Hincks.
Circa: 1906.

Rooms: 16 rooms with PB. 2 suites. 1 conference room.
Beds: QDT.

Reopened in 1988, the inn housed the overflow guests from the Lake House resort about 90 years ago. Guests traveled to the resort via the Oxford-Cumberland Canal, and each room is named for a historic canal boat. The cozy rooms offer fluffy comforters and a warm, country decor in a romantic atmosphere. Warm up in front of a crackling fire in the great room, or enjoy a cool Long Lake breeze on the veranda while watching horses in nearby pastures. Murder-mystery weekends offer a spooky alternative to your getaway plans.

Breakfast included in rates. Types of meals: continental-plus breakfast and early coffee/tea. Air conditioning in room. Library on premises. Weddings, family reunions and seminars hosted. Spanish and French spoken. Antiques, fishing, parks, shopping, downhill skiing, cross-country skiing and watersports nearby. TAC10.

Location: Sebago Lakes Region.

Publicity: *Bridgton News, Portland Press Herald.*

Special Discounts: AAA 10% discount; midweek discounts depending on length of stay.

"Convenient location, tastefully done and the prettiest inn I've ever stayed in."

Lamb's Mill Inn

RR 1, Box 676,
Lambs Mill Rd
Naples, ME 04055
(207)693-6253
E-mail: lambsmill@aol.com

Rates: $75-95.
Payment: MC VISA PC TC.
Innkeeper(s): Laurel Tinkham & Sandy Long.
Circa: 1800.

Rooms: 6 rooms with PB.
Beds: KQ.

This cheery, yellow farmhouse offers six guest rooms, each filled with comfortable furnishings. Guests are pampered with down comforters, a hot tub and 20 peaceful acres of woods, fields and perennial gardens. Fresh vegetable frittata with items picked from the garden and raspberry Belgian waffles are among the breakfast entrees. Evening snacks are served as well. The home is close to cross-country and alpine skiing, golf, tennis, parasailing, shopping, restaurants and antiquing.

Breakfast, afternoon tea and evening snack included in rates. Types of meals: gourmet breakfast and early coffee/tea. Turn-down service in room. Cable TV, VCR, fax, spa, stables and library on premises. 20 acres. Weddings and family reunions hosted. Antiques, fishing, parks, shopping, downhill skiing, cross-country skiing, theater and watersports nearby. TAC10.

Special Discounts: Stay 5 nights receive 6th free or 15% discount mid-week Monday-Thursday.

"We really enjoyed our week in your lovely home."

New Harbor — J4

Gosnold Arms

Chamberlain Rd, Rt 32
New Harbor, ME 04554
(207)677-3727
Fax:(207)677-2662

Rates: $50-125.
Payment: MC VISA PC TC.
Innkeeper(s): The Phinney Family.
Circa: 1840.

Rooms: 26 rooms with PB.
Beds: QDT.

Located on the historic Pemaquid peninsula, the Gosnold Arms includes a remodeled, saltwater farmhouse situated on a rise above the harbor. There are several cottages and many accommodations with views. A cozy lounge offers two large stone fireplaces and a glassed-in dining porch overlooking the water.

Breakfast included in rates. Type of meal: full breakfast. Dinner available. Antiques, fishing and theater nearby.

Publicity: *New York, Down East.*

Newcastle — I4

The Newcastle Inn

River Rd, RR 2 Box 24
Newcastle, ME 04553-9802
(207)563-5685 (800)832-8669
Fax:(207)563-6877
E-mail: newcastinn@aol.com

Rates: $70-200.
Payment: MC VISA AX PC.
Innkeeper(s): Howard & Rebecca Levitan.
Circa: 1860.

Rooms: 15 rooms with PB, 4 with FP. 1 suite. 1 conference room.
Beds: KQDT.

The Newcastle Inn is a Federal-style colonial picturesquely situated on a lawn that slopes down to the Damariscotta River. Most rooms feature antique beds and water views. Honeymooners like the room with the old-fashioned canopy bed. Breakfast consists of four courses and may include eggs with caviar on puff pastry, or brioche with lemon curd. A three- or five-course dinner is available.

Breakfast included in rates. Types of meals: full breakfast and early coffee/tea. Afternoon tea and banquet service available. Fax, copier and library on premises. Weddings, small meetings, family reunions and seminars hosted. French and limited Spanish spoken. Antiques, parks, shopping, downhill skiing, cross-country skiing, sporting events, theater and watersports nearby.

Location: Tidal Damariscotta River.

Publicity: *Yankee Magazine, Downeast Magazine, Romantic Hideaways.*

"To eat and stay here is to know life to the fullest."

Ogunquit K2

Chestnut Tree Inn

PO Box 2201
Ogunquit, ME 03907-2201
(207)646-4529 (800)362-0757

Rates: $35-125.
Payment: MC VISA AX TC.
Innkeeper(s): Cynthia Diana & Ronald St. Laurent.
Circa: 1870.

Rooms: 33 rooms, 15 with PB. 1 suite.
Beds: QDT.

Gable roofs peak out from the top of this Victorian inn, which has greeted guests for more than a century. A smattering of antiques and Victorian decor creates a 19th-century atmosphere. Guests can relax on the porch or head out for a stroll on Marginal Way, a mile-long path set along Maine's scenic coastline. The beach, shops, Ogunquit Playhouse and a variety of restaurants are just a few minutes down the road.

ME

Types of meals: continental breakfast and continental-plus breakfast. Air conditioning and cable TV in room. Family reunions hosted. French spoken. Amusement parks, antiques, fishing, parks, shopping, downhill skiing, cross-country skiing, sporting events, theater and watersports nearby. TAC10.

Special Discounts: Seventh night free with weekly stay.

Old Orchard Beach K2

Atlantic Birches Inn

20 Portland Ave Rt 98
Old Orchard Beach, ME 04064-2212
(207)934-5295 (888)934-5295
E-mail: dancyn@aol.com

Rates: $45-89. EP.
Payment: MC VISA AX DS TC.
Innkeeper(s): Dan & Cyndi Bolduc.
Circa: 1903.

Rooms: 8 rooms with PB.
Beds: KQDT.

The front porch of this Shingle-style Victorian is shaded by white birch trees. Badminton and croquet are set up on the lawn. The house is a place for relaxation and enjoyment, an uncluttered, simple haven filled with comfortable furnishings. The guest rooms are decorated with a few antiques and pastel wallcoverings. Maine's coast offers an endless amount of activities, from boating to whale watching.

Breakfast included in rates. Type of meal: continental-plus breakfast. EP. Air conditioning and ceiling fan in room. Cable TV, VCR, copier, swimming and library on premises. Small meetings and family reunions hosted. French spoken. Amusement parks, antiques, fishing, parks, shopping, sporting events and watersports nearby. TAC10.

Orland H5

Alamoosook Lodge

PO Box 16
Orland, ME 04472-0016
(207)469-6393

Rates: $56-85.
Innkeeper(s): Jan & Doug Gibson.
Circa: 1960.

Rooms: 6 rooms with PB.

This country lodge is a comfortable, inviting place from which to enjoy a Maine getaway. Rooms are decorated in country style, and beds are topped with quilts. Each guest room's entrance opens out onto the grounds, which border Alamoosook Lake. The innkeepers have chairs set up lakeside for those who wish to relax and enjoy the view. On a chilly day, guests can relax in the wood-paneled common room, which offers a warming wood stove. Breakfasts include homemade muffins or pastries and a choice of entrees, such as blueberry waffles or an omelet. The morning meal is served in a dining room overlooking the lake.

"The food is scrumptious. A beautiful place by the lake."

Portland

J3

Andrews Lodging B&B

417 Auburn St
Portland, ME 04103-2109
(207)797-9157
Fax:(207)797-9040
E-mail: 74232.116@compuserve.com

Rates: $55-155.
Payment: MC VISA AX TC.
Innkeeper(s): Douglas & Elizabeth Andrews.
Circa: 1780.

Rooms: 6 rooms, 1 with PB. 1 suite.
Beds: QT.

Innkeepers Douglas and Elizabeth Andrews offer plenty of activities to keep guests busy at their Colonial inn. The grounds include badminton, croquet and volleyball areas, and during winter months guests can use the inn's ice rink. Rooms are cozy, decorated with bright prints and a collection of antiques. The suite includes a whirlpool tub. There is a kitchen for guest use. Well-behaved pets are welcomed, as Douglas is also a veterinarian. The Freeport Factory Outlets and L.L. Bean store are just a few miles away, as is the coast.

Breakfast included in rates. Types of meals: continental-plus breakfast and early coffee/tea. Catered breakfast available. Cable TV in room. Fax and bicycles on premises. Weddings, small meetings, family reunions and seminars hosted. Antiques, fishing, parks, shopping, downhill skiing, cross-country skiing, sporting events, theater and watersports nearby.

Pets Allowed: Yes.

Inn on Carleton

46 Carleton St
Portland, ME 04102-3226
(207)775-1910 (800)639-1779
Fax:(207)761-2160

Rates: $75-115.
Payment: MC VISA DS PC TC.
Innkeeper(s): Phil & Sue Cox.
Circa: 1869.

Rooms: 7 rooms, 4 with PB. 1 suite.
Beds: QDT.

This Victorian townhouse is located in a historic Portland neighborhood just a short walk to an art museum, art center and the city's business district. Rooms are decorated in a comfortable, Victorian style with antiques. Several bathrooms include a clawfoot tub. The innkeepers have placed their collection of clocks throughout the home, and there is a variety of artwork on display. The full breakfasts include cereals, fresh fruit, yogurt, muffins and items such as blueberry pancakes.

Breakfast included in rates. Types of meals: full breakfast and early coffee/tea. Air conditioning and ceiling fan in room. Cable TV, VCR and fax on premises. Weddings and small meetings hosted. Amusement parks, antiques, fishing, parks, shopping, cross-country skiing, sporting events, theater and watersports nearby.

West End Inn

146 Pine St
Portland, ME 04102-3541
(207)772-1377 (800)338-1377

Rates: $79-169.
Payment: MC VISA AX PC.
Innkeeper(s): Teri Dizon.
Circa: 1871.

Rooms: 6 rooms with PB.
Beds: KQT.

Located in Portland's Western Promenade Historic District, this Georgian-style inn is one of many lovely Victorian-era homes found there. Rooms are decorated with four-poster, canopy beds. The inn's full, New England-style breakfasts include such items as blueberry pancakes, sausages, eggs, fruit and more, the menu changes daily. Guests may opt for lighter fare if they choose. An afternoon tea also is served, and provides a perfect opportunity to relax after an activity-filled day. The inn also offers facilities for meetings, reunions and wedding receptions. The Museum of Art and the University of South Maine are nearby.

Breakfast included in rates. Type of meal: full breakfast. Ceiling fan and cable TV in room. Bicycles and library on premises. Small meetings hosted. Spanish spoken. Antiques, fishing, parks, shopping, downhill skiing, cross-country skiing, sporting events, theater and watersports nearby. TAC10.

Rangeley

G2

Northwoods

PO Box 79
Rangeley, ME 04970-0079
(207)864-2440 (800)295-4968

Rates: $60-90.
Payment: MC VISA PC TC.
Innkeeper(s): Janice Thorp.
Circa: 1912.

Rooms: 4 rooms, 3 with PB.
Beds: QDT.

This immaculate Colonial Revival home, which has all the original woodwork intact, has a magnificent view of Rangeley Lake. Inside, guests can find a doll house museum filled with porcelain dolls and antiques. Still largely unspoiled, the surrounding mountain and lake region offers a variety of activities and moose can be seen grazing and walking through the area. The inn's formal and prominent character is part of the unique residential architecture of the town. Although centrally located in Rangeley Village, Northwoods has a peaceful and lofty quality.

Breakfast included in rates. Type of meal: full breakfast. Cable TV and VCR on premises. Weddings, small meetings, family reunions and seminars hosted. Antiques, fishing, downhill skiing, cross-country skiing, theater and watersports nearby. TAC10.

ME

Round Pond

J4

The Briar Rose B&B

Rt 32, Box 27
Round Pond, ME 04564
(207)529-5478

Rates: $50-85.
Payment: PC TC.
Innkeeper(s): Anita & Fred Palsgrove.
Circa: 1850.

Rooms: 4 rooms, 3 with PB. 1 suite.
Beds: QDT.

At the turn of the century, this house served the village of Round Pond as the Harbor View Hotel and hosted vacationers and those working with the busy shipping trade that once filled the tiny harbor. Guest rooms are large and airy with views of the harbor. Parlors are filled with books, magazines, games and other rainy-day entertainment. The winter parlor also offers a wood stove for chilly evenings. Within walking distance are country stores, antique shops, galleries and the working studios of local craftspeople. Sample fresh lobster picnic-style at the dock or in a waterfront restaurant.

Breakfast included in rates. Types of meals: full breakfast, gourmet breakfast and early coffee/tea. Picnic lunch available. Library on premises. Antiques, fishing, parks, shopping, downhill skiing, cross-country skiing, theater and watersports nearby.

Publicity: *Westways, Best Places to Kiss in New England, Boston Magazine, Travel & Holiday, Berlitz.*

Special Discounts: 5 nights or more, $5 off each night.

"We have found a New England Treasure—thank you for sharing it with us."

Saco

K2

Crown 'n' Anchor Inn

121 North St, PO Box 228
Saco, ME 04072-0228
(207)282-3829 (800)561-8865
Fax:(207)282-7495

Rates: $60-95.
Payment: MC VISA AX PC TC.
Innkeeper(s): John Barclay & Martha Forester.
Circa: 1827.

Rooms: 5 rooms with PB, 2 with FP.
Beds: KQDT.

This Greek Revival house features both Victorian baroque and colonial antiques. A collection of British coronation memorabilia displayed throughout the inn includes 200 items. Guests gather in the Victorian parlor or the formal library. The innkeepers, a college librarian and an academic bookseller, lined the shelves with several thousand volumes, including extensive Civil War and British royal family collections and travel, theater and nautical books. Royal Dalton china, crystal and fresh flowers create a festive breakfast setting.

Breakfast included in rates. Types of meals: full breakfast, gourmet breakfast and early coffee/tea. Afternoon tea available. Cable TV in room. VCR and library on premises. Weddings, small meetings, family reunions and seminars hosted. Limited French spoken. Amusement parks, antiques, fishing, parks, shopping, downhill skiing, cross-country skiing, sporting events, theater and watersports nearby. TAC10.

Pets Allowed: Small or caged.

Publicity: *Lincoln County News, Yankee, Saco, Biddeford, Old Orchard Beach Courier, Country, Portland Press Herald.*

Searsport H5

Brass Lantern Inn

PO Box 407, 81 W Main St
Searsport, ME 04974-3501
(207)548-0150
(800)691-0150
E-mail: brasslan@brasslan.sdi.agate.net

Rates: $60-85.
Payment: MC VISA PC TC.
Innkeeper(s): Pat Gatto & Lee Anne Lee.
Circa: 1850.

Rooms: 4 rooms with PB.
Beds: DT.

This Victorian inn is nestled at the edge of the woods on a rise overlooking Penobscot Bay. Showcased throughout the inn are many collectibles, antiques and family heirlooms, including an extensive doll collection. Enjoy breakfast in the dining room with its ornate tin ceiling, where you'll feast on Maine blueberry pancakes and other sumptuous treats. Centrally located between Camden and Bar Harbor, Searsport is known as the antique capital of Maine. There are many local attractions, including the Penobscot Marine Museum, fine shops and restaurants, as well as a public boat facility.

Breakfast included in rates. Type of meal: full breakfast. Cable TV and library on premises. Small meetings and family reunions hosted. Antiques, fishing, parks, shopping, cross-country skiing and theater nearby. TAC5.

Publicity: *Country Living, Republication Journal, Travel Today*

"Very elegant surrounding, cozy atmosphere. Truly caring, thoughtful, friendly, people sharing their house."

Homeport Inn

RR 1 Box 647
Searsport, ME 04974-9728
(207)548-2259 (800)742-5814

Rates: $55-85.
Payment: MC VISA AX DS.
Innkeeper(s): Dr. & Mrs. F. George Johnson.
Circa: 1861.

Rooms: 10 rooms, 6 with PB.
Beds: QT.

Captain John Nickels built this home on Penobscot Bay. On top of the two-story historic landmark is a widow's walk. A scalloped picket fence frames the property. Fine antiques, black marble fireplaces, a collection of grandfather clocks and elaborate ceiling medallions add to the atmosphere. Landscaped grounds sweep out to the ocean's edge. Some rooms have an ocean view.

Breakfast included in rates. Type of meal: full breakfast. Cable TV on premises. Handicap access. Small meetings and family reunions hosted. Antiques, fishing, parks, shopping, downhill skiing, cross-country skiing, sporting events and theater nearby.

Publicity: *Yankee, Down East.*

"Your breakfast is something we will never forget."

Thurston House B&B

PO Box 686, 8 Elm St
Searsport, ME 04974-3368
(207)548-2213 (800)240-2213
E-mail: thurston@acadia.net

Rates: $45-65.
Payment: MC VISA.
Innkeeper(s): Carl Eppig.
Circa: 1831.

Rooms: 4 rooms, 2 with PB, 2 with FP. 1 suite.
Beds: DT.

The innkeepers of this Colonial home proudly serve their "Forget About Lunch" breakfast, which consists of three courses, fresh prepared fruit, baked hot breads and then a sumptuous entree course. Special diets are happily accommodated as well. Stephen Thurston was the pastor of the first Congregational Church in

Searsport for the heart of the 19th century. He was one of the town's most prominent citizens as well. In 1853, the 242-ton brig named after Thurston was launched.

Breakfast included in rates. Types of meals: full breakfast and early coffee/tea. Afternoon tea available. Small meetings hosted. Antiques, fishing, shopping, downhill skiing, cross-country skiing, sporting events, theater and watersports nearby.

Publicity: *Yankee, The Evening Times-Globe, The Clarion-Ledger*

Special Discounts: Varies.

"When we again travel in the Maine area, there is no doubt that we will make certain to stay at Thurston House. They deserve the best accolades!"

Searsport (Waldo County)

Watchtide

190 W Main St
Searsport (Waldo County), ME 04974-3514
(207)548-6575 (800)698-6575
E-mail: watchtyd@agate.net

Rates: $55-85.
Payment: MC VISA DS PC TC.
Innkeeper(s): Nancy-Linn Nellis & Jack Elliott.
Circa: 1795.

Rooms: 4 rooms, 2 with PB.
Beds: DT.

ME

Built for a sea captain, this New England Cape-style inn with its nearly four acres of lawns and gardens, has a spectacular view of Penobscot Bay. Breakfast is served on the wicker furnished porch which overlooks the inn's bird sanctuary and the bay. An antique shop, with a large collection of angels made by the resident artist, is located in the adjacent barn. Guests can receive a discount at this shop.

Breakfast and afternoon tea included in rates. Types of meals: gourmet breakfast and early coffee/tea. Turn-down service in room. Cable TV and library on premises. Limited French spoken. Antiques, fishing, parks, shopping, downhill skiing, cross-country skiing, sporting events, theater and watersports nearby. TAC15.

Publicity: *Republican Journal, Daily Item, Courier Weekend, Bangor Daily News, Pilot Tribune, Clarion-Ledger, Sunday Patriot News, Sunday Herald-Times.*

"We'd felt like being back to the 19th-century, with lovely furnished rooms and warm hospitality."

Southwest Harbor *I6*

Harbour Woods

PO Box 1214
Southwest Harbor, ME 04679-1214
(207)244-5388
Fax:(207)244-7156

Rates: $55-115.
Payment: MC VISA PC TC.
Innkeeper(s): Joseph & Christine Titka.
Circa: 1840.

Rooms: 3 rooms, 14 with PB. 11 cottages.
Beds: Q.

This gracious Maine farmhouse offers pleasant views of the harbor and its three-acre grounds, which include a pond. The atmosphere is warm and inviting, rooms are decorated with a collection of family keepsakes, antiques and flowers. The guest rooms include amenities such as fireplaces, fluffy towels, luxury bath soaps and hair dryers. The full breakfasts are served by candlelight. Guests have use of a common room with TV, VCR, a collection of books, a stocked cookie jar and refrigerator filled with soft drinks. Guests also can reserve the inn's indoor spa. Seasonally, the innkeepers offer 11 cottages for their guests, ranging in size from cozy studios to two-bedroom facilities. Each of the cottages includes a kitchenette. The home, located on historic Mount Desert Island, is across the street from Great Harbor Marina and surrounded by the beauty of Acadia National Park.

Breakfast and afternoon tea included in rates. Type of meal: full breakfast. Cable TV, VCR and spa on premises. Antiques, fishing, shopping and watersports nearby.

Location: Across the street from the Harbor on the edge of the village of Southwest Harbor at Acadia National Park.

Special Discounts: Discount for stays of seven nights or longer.

"Thanks for the friendly greeting, good guidance and beautiful room!"

The Lamb's Ear B&B

60 Clark Point Rd,
PO Box 30
Southwest Harbor, ME 04679
(207)244-9828
Fax:(207)244-9924

Rates: $85-165.
Payment: MC VISA PC TC.
Innkeeper(s): Elizabeth, Monique & Darrell Hoke.
Circa: 1857.

Rooms: 8 rooms with PB, 2 with FP. 1 suite.
Beds: QDT.

This stately colonial inn was built by Captain Mayo, one of the town's earliest settlers. Guests can view lobster boats, sailing ships and all the other activities of Southwest Harbor. The harbor is surrounded by Acadia National Park with its pristine pine forests, lakes and mountains. Breakfasts at the inn are known to be as artistic as they are excellent.

Breakfast and afternoon tea included in rates. Types of meals: gourmet breakfast and early coffee/tea. Cable TV in room. Fax on premises. Amusement parks, antiques, fishing, parks, shopping, cross-country skiing, theater and watersports nearby.

"The food is delicious, the presentation is beautiful."

The Moorings

Shore Rd, PO Box 744
Southwest Harbor, ME 04679
(207)244-5523 (800)596-5523

Rates: $55-100.
Payment: PC TC.
Innkeeper(s): S. Leslie & Betty King.

Rooms: 19 rooms with PB, 4 with FP. 7 suites. 3 cottages.
Beds: KDT.

Maine's Mt. Desert Island is a spectacular place to visit, from its picturesque harbor towns to Acadia National Park. The Moorings, a rambling New England-style farmhouse, is a nice spot from which to enjoy the sites. There are comfortably furnished accommodations in the main house, the Pilot House cottage, three suites in Lookout Cottage and three rooms in what is called the Lighthouse View Wing. The latter three rooms have an outside deck, refrigerator and microwave. Many rooms in the main house also have outside decks and some have waterfront views. The Lookout Cottage rooms have kitchens or kitchenettes and two have living room areas. About a mile from the main complex, there are two cottages available. Each have two bedrooms, a kitchen, a fireplace and view either of the water or the inner harbor and mountains. Coffee, juice and doughnuts are available in the mornings. The Moorings Restaurant, although not operated by the inn, is adjacent to the complex.

Breakfast included in rates. Type of meal: continental breakfast. Cable TV, VCR and bicycles on premises. Small meetings and family reunions hosted. Antiques, fishing, parks, shopping and watersports nearby.

"It's such a nice feeling to know that we can go somewhere to get away from it all and be treated like family."

Spruce Head — J5

Craignair Inn

533 Clark Island Rd
Spruce Head, ME 04859
(207)594-7644 (800)320-9997
Fax:(207)596-7124

Rates: $74-102.
Payment: MC VISA AX PC TC.
Innkeeper(s): Theresa E. Smith.
Circa: 1930.

Rooms: 24 rooms, 8 with PB.
Beds: KDT.

Craignair originally was built to house stonecutters working in nearby granite quarries. Overlooking the docks of the Clark Island Quarry, where granite schooners once were loaded, this roomy, three-story inn is tastefully decorated with local antiques.

Breakfast included in rates. Types of meals: full breakfast and early coffee/tea. Banquet service, catering service and catered breakfast available. Ceiling fan in room. Fax, copier and swimming on premises. Weddings, small meetings, family reunions and seminars hosted. Antiques, fishing, parks, shopping, downhill skiing, cross-country skiing, theater and watersports nearby. TAC10.

Pets Allowed.

Location: Clark Island ocean view.

Publicity: *Boston Globe, Free Press, Tribune.*

"A coastal oasis of fine food and outstanding service with colonial maritime ambiance!"

Tenants Harbor J4

East Wind Inn & Meeting House

Mechanic St, PO Box 149
Tenants Harbor, ME 04860
(207)372-6366 (800)241-8439
Fax:(207)372-6320

Rates: $64-150. EP.
Payment: MC VISA AX DC DS PC TC.
Innkeeper(s): Tim Watts.
Circa: 1860.

Rooms: 26 rooms, 8 with PB. 3 suites. 1 cottage. 1 conference room.
Beds: DT.

Because of its proximity to the ocean, each of the inn's guest rooms has a view of the harbor. The inn was once a sail loft and the Meeting House was a captain's house. Spacious porches also afford a view, where guests can read and smell the salt air. Enjoy the beaches, tidal pools, berry picking and wildflowers. The nearby Farnsworth Art Museum has a permanent Wyeth collection, and another attraction is the Shore Village Lighthouse Museum.

ME

Breakfast included in rates. Types of meals: continental breakfast and full breakfast. Dinner, lunch and banquet service available. EP. Cable TV, VCR, fax, copier, swimming, tennis and library on premises. Weddings, small meetings, family reunions and seminars hosted. Antiques, fishing, parks, shopping, downhill skiing, cross-country skiing and watersports nearby. TAC10.

Pets Allowed: By arrangement.

Walpole J4

Brannon-Bunker Inn

349 S State Rt 129
Walpole, ME 04573
(207)563-5941 (800)563-9225

Rates: $60-70.
Payment: MC VISA AX PC TC.
Innkeeper(s): Joe & Jeanne Hovance.
Circa: 1820.

Rooms: 8 rooms, 5 with PB. 1 suite.
Beds: QDT.

This Cape-style house has been a home to many generations of Maine residents, one of whom was captain of a ship that sailed to the Arctic. During the '20s, the barn served as a dance hall. Later, it was converted into comfortable guest rooms. Victorian and American antiques are featured and there are collections of military and political memorabilia.

Breakfast included in rates. Type of meal: continental-plus breakfast. VCR, library and child care on premises. Handicap access. 28 acres. Weddings, small meetings and family reunions hosted. Antiques, fishing, parks, shopping, cross-country skiing, theater and watersports nearby. TAC10.

Publicity: *Times-Beacon Newspaper.*

"Wonderful beds, your gracious hospitality and the very best muffins anywhere made our stay a memorable one."

Waterford I2

Kedarburn Inn

Rt 35 Box 61
Waterford, ME 04088
(207)583-6182
Fax:(207)583-6424

Rates: $71-125.
Payment: MC VISA AX DS PC TC.
Innkeeper(s): Margaret & Derek Gibson.
Circa: 1858.

Rooms: 7 rooms, 3 with PB. 1 suite. 1 conference room.
Beds: KQDT.

The innkeepers of this Victorian establishment invite guests to try a taste of olde English hospitality and cuisine at their inn, nestled in the foothills of the White Mountains in Western Maine. Located in a historic village, the inn sits beside the flowing Kedar Brook, which runs to the shores of Lake Keoka. Each of the spacious rooms is decorated with handmade crocheted pillows, embroidered curtains, hand-sewn linens and arrangements of dried flowers. A variety of tea sandwiches, beverages, pastries, English biscuits and other tasty items are served for afternoon tea.

Breakfast included in rates. Types of meals: full breakfast and early coffee/tea. Afternoon tea, dinner, evening snack, banquet service, catering service, catered breakfast and room service available. Restaurant on premises. Air conditioning in room. Cable TV, VCR, fax and pet boarding on premises. Weddings, small meetings, family reunions and seminars hosted. Antiques, fishing, shopping, downhill skiing, cross-country skiing, theater and watersports nearby.

Pets Allowed.

Location: In the White Mountains.

Publicity: *Maine Times.*

Special Discounts: Three days or more 5% off. 2% off for cash payment.

West Boothbay Harbor

Lawnmeer Inn

PO Box 505
West Boothbay Harbor, ME 04575-0505
(207)633-2544 (800)633-7645
Fax:(207)633-2544

Rates: $50-170.
Payment: MC VISA.
Innkeeper(s): Lee & Jim Metzger.
Circa: 1899.

Rooms: 32 rooms with PB. 1 suite. 1 cottage.
Beds: KQD.

This pleasant inn sits by the shoreline, providing a picturesque oceanfront setting. Located on a small, wooded island, it is accessed by a lift bridge. Family-oriented rooms are clean and homey, and there is a private honeymoon cottage in the Smoke House. The dining room is waterside and serve continental cuisine with an emphasis on seafood. Boothbay Harbor is two miles away.

Types of meals: full breakfast and early coffee/tea. Dinner and banquet service available. Computer on premises. Weddings, small meetings and family reunions hosted. Antiques, fishing, shopping, theater and watersports nearby. TAC10.

Pets Allowed: Small pets-one per room.

Publicity: *Los Angeles Times, Getaways for Gourmets.*

"Your hospitality was warm and gracious and the food delectable."

Wiscasset J4

The Squire Tarbox Inn

RR 2 Box 620
Wiscasset, ME 04578-9659
(207)882-7693

Rates: $85-166. MAP.
Payment: MC VISA AX DS PC TC.
Innkeeper(s): Bill & Karen Mitman.
Circa: 1763.

Rooms: 11 rooms with PB, 4 with FP.
Beds: DT.

North of Bath, deep into the country and woods, Squire Tarbox built his rambling farmhouse around a building originally constructed in 1763. Today, the rooms are warm and comfortable in the inn and in the remodeled hayloft. The innkeepers raise Nubian goats, all photogenic, that have become part of the entertainment (milking and goat cheese). A house-party atmosphere pervades the inn.

Breakfast included in rates. Types of meals: full breakfast and early coffee/tea. Afternoon tea and dinner available. MAP. Air conditioning in room. Bicycles and library on premises. 12 acres. Antiques, fishing, parks, shopping and theater nearby. TAC10.

Location: Route 144, 8 1/2 miles on Westport Island.

Publicity: *Washington Post, New York Times, Yankee, Bon Appetit.*

"Your hospitality was warm, friendly, well-managed and quite genuine. That's a rarity, and it's just the kind we feel best with."

York

L2

Dockside Guest Quarters

PO Box 205
York, ME 03909-0205
(207)363-2868
Fax:(207)363-1977

Rates: $73-149.
Payment: MC VISA DS PC.
Innkeeper(s): Lusty Family.
Circa: 1900.

Rooms: 21 rooms, 2 with FP. 6 suites. 1 conference room.
Beds: KQDT.

This small resort provides a panoramic view of the Atlantic Ocean and harbor activities. Guest rooms are located in the classic, large New England home, which is the Maine House, and modern multi-unit cottages. Most rooms have private balconies or porches with unobstructed views of the water. Some suites have fireplaces. The resort is available for weddings. The on-premise restaurant is bi-level with floor to ceiling windows, affording each table a view of the harbor. Child care services are available.

Types of meals: continental-plus breakfast and early coffee/tea. Afternoon tea and lunch available. Cable TV in room. Fax, bicycles, library and child care on premises. 635 acres. Weddings, small meetings and family reunions hosted. French spoken. Amusement parks, antiques, fishing, parks, shopping, cross-country skiing, theater and watersports nearby. TAC10.

Location: York Harbor, Maine Rt. 103.

Publicity: *Boston Globe.*

Special Discounts: Off season rates and packages.

"We've been back many years. It's a paradise for us, the scenery, location, maintenance, living quarters."

ME

York Harbor

L2

Bell Buoy B&B

570 York St
York Harbor, ME 03911
(207)363-7264

Rates: $60-85.
Payment: PC TC.
Innkeeper(s): Wes & Kathie Cook.
Circa: 1884.

Rooms: 4 rooms, 3 with PB. 1 suite.
Beds: KQDT.

Just a short walk to Long Sands Beach, this Victorian inn is located in prestigious York Harbor. You may want to stroll the Marginal Way along the ocean shore or catch the scenic trolley that stops across the street and takes you to points of interest while giving you a narrative about the town. After your day of enjoying the area, check out one of the many outstanding restaurants in the area, some just a walking distance away. Breakfasts can be relished in the family dining room or on the porch.

Breakfast included in rates. Types of meals: full breakfast and early coffee/tea. Turn-down service and ceiling fan in room. Cable TV and VCR on premises. Amusement parks, antiques, fishing, parks, shopping, theater and watersports nearby.

Special Discounts: 10% discount for stays 7 nights or longer.

The Inn at Harmon Park

415 York St
York Harbor, ME 03911
(207)363-2031
Fax:(207)351-2948

Rates: $49-99.
Payment: PC TC.
Innkeeper(s): Sue Antal.
Circa: 1899.

Rooms: 5 rooms with PB, 1 with FP. 1 suite.
Beds: KQDT.

The innkeeper of this turn-of-the-century inn has worked hard to maintain the home's Victorian ambiance. Rooms are decorated with wicker furnishings and ceiling fans. Fresh flowers add extra color. The inn includes several fireplaces, one of which is found in a guest room. The inn is within walking distance of York Harbor Beach.

Breakfast included in rates. Types of meals: full breakfast and early coffee/tea. Ceiling fan in room. Cable TV, VCR, fax, copier, bicycles and library on premises. Weddings, small meetings, family reunions and seminars hosted. Amusement parks, antiques, fishing, parks, shopping, cross-country skiing, sporting events, theater and watersports nearby. TAC10.

Location: Three-block walk to beaches and historic district.

York Harbor Inn

PO Box 573, Rt 1A
York Harbor, ME 03911
(207)363-5119 (800)343-3869
Fax:(207)363-3545
E-mail: garyinkeep@aol.com

Rates: $89-195. MAP.
Payment: MC VISA AX DC CB PC TC.
Innkeeper(s): Joseph & Garry Dominguez.
Circa: 1800.

Rooms: 33 rooms with PB, 4 with FP. 1 suite. 4 conference rooms.
Beds: KQD.

The core building of the York Harbor Inn is a small log cabin constructed on the Isles of Shoals. Moved and reassembled at this dramatic location overlooking the entrance to York Harbor, the cabin is now a gathering room with a handsome stone fireplace. There is an English-style pub in the cellar, a large ballroom and five meeting rooms. The dining room and some guest rooms overlook the ocean. Several guest rooms have ocean view decks, working fireplaces, and Jacuzzi spas. One three-room suite is available.

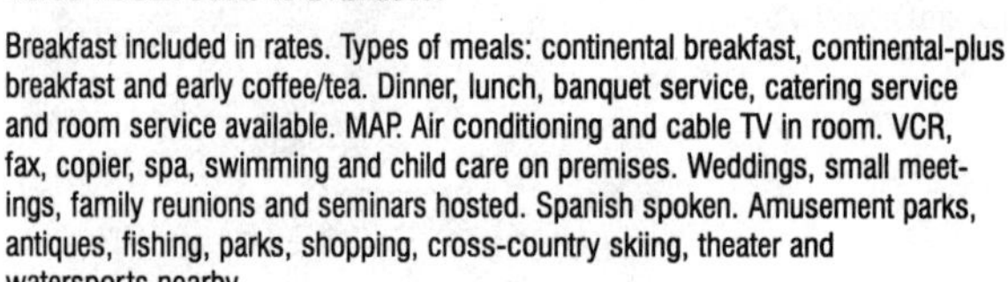

Breakfast included in rates. Types of meals: continental breakfast, continental-plus breakfast and early coffee/tea. Dinner, lunch, banquet service, catering service and room service available. MAP. Air conditioning and cable TV in room. VCR, fax, copier, spa, swimming and child care on premises. Weddings, small meetings, family reunions and seminars hosted. Spanish spoken. Amusement parks, antiques, fishing, parks, shopping, cross-country skiing, theater and watersports nearby.

Location: York Harbor's historic district.

Publicity: *New York Times, Down East, Food & Wine.*

Special Discounts: Package rates one & two nights available.

"It's hard to decide where to stay when you're paging through a book of country inns. This time we chose well."

Great Granola-Misty River Style

Misty River Bed & Breakfast
Ripley, Ohio

- 5 cups rolled oats
- 1 cup pecans
- 1 cup sliced almonds
- ½ cup light brown sugar, packed
- 1 T grated orange peel
- 2 t ground cinnamon
- ½ t ground nutmeg
- 1 cup butter, melted
- ⅓ cup maple syrup
- 1 cup toasted flaked coconut
- ½ cup golden raisins
- ½ cup diced dried apricots

Stir together first seven ingredients. Add melted butter and syrup and gently mix. Press into a buttered 10-by-15" baking pan and bake in a 350-degree oven until golden brown (about 30 minutes). Let cool. Break into chunks and stir with coconut, raisins and apricots. Put in 200-degree oven for 10 or 15 minutes. Cool and store in airtight container for up to one month.

Maryland

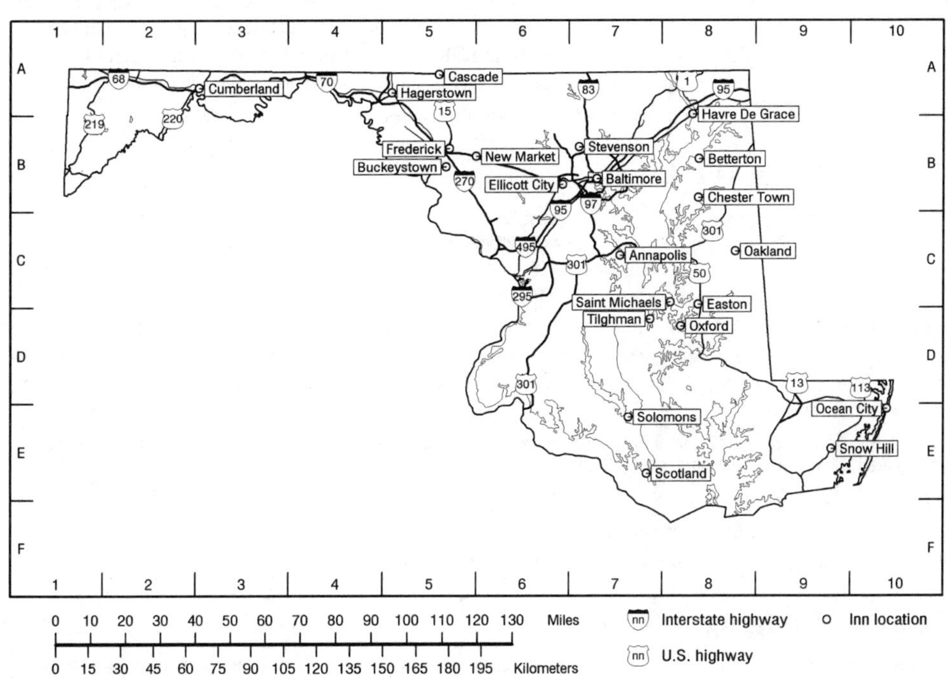

MD

Annapolis C7

The Barn on Howard's Cove

500 Wilson Rd
Annapolis, MD 21401-1052
(410)266-6840
Fax:(410)266-7293
E-mail: gdgutsche5@aol.com

Rates: $85-90.
Payment: PC.
Innkeeper(s): Graham & Libbie Gutsche.
Circa: 1850.

Rooms: 2 rooms with PB.
Beds: Q.

This renovated 1850 horse barn is located just outside Annapolis on a cove of the Severn River. The six-and-a-half acre grounds create a restful environment. The two guest rooms, which are decorated with antiques and handmade quilts, offer water and garden views. A private balcony adjoins one guest room. The innkeepers, a U.S. Naval Academy professor and an artist also keep a unique Noah's Ark collection on display. The innkeepers have canoes on the premises.

Breakfast and afternoon tea included in rates. Types of meals: continental breakfast and full breakfast. Air conditioning and ceiling fan in room. Cable TV, fax and swimming on premises. Small meetings hosted. Antiques, fishing, parks, shopping, sporting events, theater and watersports nearby. TAC10.

Publicity: *Baltimore Sun.*

Special Discounts: $10 reduction for stays over three nights.

"Thank you so much for your gracious hospitality and for making our wedding night special."

Chesapeake Bay Lighthouse B&B

1423 Sharps Point Rd
Annapolis, MD 21401-6139
(410)757-0248

Rates: $95-149.
Payment: MC VISA AX.
Innkeeper(s): Janice & Bill Costello.
Circa: 1923.

Rooms: 3 rooms.

Each of the guest rooms in this cottage-style working lighthouse boasts water views of scenic Chesapeake Bay. The innkeepers built their unique B&B from designs found in the National Archives. Grab a pair of binoculars and enjoy the sites of the Bay Bridge, Thomas Point Lighthouse or Annapolis harbor entrance and a 300-foot pier. The lighthouse is only six miles from Annapolis, which is full of historic attractions, shops and restaurants.

Breakfast included in rates. Type of meal: continental-plus breakfast. Air conditioning in room.

Duke & Duchess B&B

151 Duke of Gloucester St
Annapolis, MD 21401-2504
(410)268-6323

Rates: $85-150.
Payment: MC VISA PC TC.
Innkeeper(s): Doris Marsh.
Circa: 1850.

Rooms: 2 rooms with PB. 1 suite.
Beds: KQT.

Built prior to the Civil War, this Italianate Victorian still retains its original heart-of-pine flooring and carved staircase. Each of the guest rooms includes antiques and original artwork. The homestay bed & breakfast is located in Annapolis' historic district a few blocks from the city's dock, the U.S. Naval Academy, shops and restaurants.

Breakfast included in rates. Type of meal: full breakfast. Air conditioning, cable TV and VCR in room. Antiques, fishing, parks, shopping, sporting events, theater and watersports nearby. TAC10.

Pets Allowed: With some restrictions.

Special Discounts: 10% discount on weekday rates.

"Beautiful suite, delicious breakfast and gracious host. We would recommend it."

Gibson's Lodgings

110 Prince George St
Annapolis, MD 21401-1704
(410)268-5555

Rates: $68-125.
Payment: MC VISA AX TC.
Innkeeper(s): Claude & Jeanne Schrift.
Circa: 1786.

Rooms: 21 rooms, 7 with PB. 2 suites. 2 conference rooms.
Beds: QDT.

This Georgian house in the heart of the Annapolis Historic District was built on the site of the Old Courthouse, circa 1680. Two historic houses make up the inn and there was a new house built in 1988. All the rooms, old and new, are furnished with antiques. Only a few yards away is the City Dock Harbor and within two blocks is the Naval Academy visitor's gate. Parking on premises.

Breakfast, afternoon tea and evening snack included in rates. Type of meal: continental-plus breakfast. Air conditioning, ceiling fan and cable TV in room. Fax on premises. Handicap access. Weddings, small meetings, family reunions and seminars hosted. Antiques, fishing, parks, shopping, sporting events, theater and watersports nearby. TAC10.

Publicity: *Mid Atlantic Country, New York.*

Special Discounts: 40% discount Sunday through Thursday, January and February.

"We had a delightful stay! We enjoyed the proximity to the waterfront, the fun atmosphere and the friendly people."

Jonas Green House B&B

124 Charles St
Annapolis, MD 21401-2621
(410)263-5892
Fax:(410)263-5892

Rates: $65-95.
Payment: MC VISA AX DS PC TC.
Innkeeper(s): Randy & Dede Brown.
Circa: 1690.

Rooms: 3 rooms, 1 with PB, 2 with FP.
Beds: KDT.

For those seeking a truly historic vacation, Jonas Green House is a perfect starting place. The kitchen building of this historic home was completed in the 1690s and still houses the original cooking fireplace and an original crane. From this point, more was added until its completion sometime in the 1740s. Much of the home's original floors, wainscoting, fireplace surroundings and a corner cabinet with original glass has survived through the years. The home is named for one of innkeeper Randy Brown's relatives, who was a colonial patriot and printer. Jonas Green brought his bride to Annapolis and in 1738 settled at the home where the current innkeeper's family has resided ever since. Restoration of the home uncovered many interesting artifacts which guests are sure to enjoy. Traditional furnishings fill the home, adding to its historic flavor. The innkeepers have kept the decor simple and authentic.

Breakfast included in rates. Type of meal: continental-plus breakfast. Air conditioning in room. Copier on premises. Small meetings hosted. Danish spoken. Antiques, fishing, parks, shopping, sporting events, theater and watersports nearby.

Pets Allowed: Stay with owner in room.

Publicity: *Annapolitan, Capital, Washington Post, National Geographic Traveler, New York Times*

Special Discounts: Five or more night at 10% discount.

"Thank you for your hospitality in a wonderful house so full of personal and American history."

Prince George Inn

232 Prince George St
Annapolis, MD 21401-1632
(410)263-6418
Fax:(410)626-0009

Rates: $85-110.
Payment: MC VISA PC.
Innkeeper(s): Janet & Dennis Coughlin.
Circa: 1884.

Rooms: 4 rooms, 2 with PB.
Beds: KQT.

MD

The Prince George Inn is a three-story brick town house comfortably furnished with antiques. The guest parlor, breakfast room, porch and courtyard offer areas for relaxing. In the heart of the colonial city, the inn is near restaurants, museums, shops and the City Dock. The Naval Academy is two blocks away.

Breakfast included in rates. Type of meal: gourmet breakfast. Air conditioning, turn-down service, ceiling fan, cable TV and VCR in room. Fax and copier on premises. Antiques, fishing, shopping, sporting events, theater and watersports nearby. TAC10.

Location: Historic District of Annapolis.

Publicity: *WMAR TV, Country Inns, Annapolitan.*

"Thoroughly enjoyed our six days in your lovely home!"

Baltimore B7

Bauernschmidt Manor B&B

2316 Bauernschmidt Dr
Baltimore, MD 21221-1713
(410)687-2233

Rates: $75-125.
Innkeeper(s): Suzanne Gerard.

Rooms: 3 rooms.

This historic home was the summer residence of the son of George Bauernschmidt family, who started a beer brewing company in 1860. In its heyday, the brewery was one of the world's leading producers of beer. The turn-of-the-century home is believed to have been built from bricks from the Baltimore fire of 1904. The antique-filled home boasts four fireplaces and a fourth-floor cupola, which affords a beautiful view of the bay. One of the fireplaces is found in the charming Bauernschmidt Room, which also includes a Jacuzzi. The innkeepers offer special theater and boating packages.

Breakfast included in rates. Type of meal: full breakfast.

Betsy's B&B

1428 Park Ave
Baltimore, MD 21217-4230
(410)383-1274 (800)899-7533
Fax:(410)728-8957
E-mail: amandars@aol.com

Rates: $85.
Payment: MC VISA AX DS PC TC.
Innkeeper(s): Betsy Grater.
Circa: 1870.

Rooms: 3 rooms with PB.
Beds: KQ.

This four-story townhouse features a hallway floor laid with alternating strips of oak and walnut, ceiling medallions, large windows and marble mantels. Walls are decked with family heirlooms and other collectibles. Breakfast is served in the formal dining room, with a unique carved marble mantel. Each of the comfortably decorated guest rooms is spacious, with a private bath.

Breakfast included in rates. Type of meal: full breakfast. Air conditioning in room. Cable TV, VCR, fax, copier and computer on premises. Weddings hosted. Antiques, parks, shopping, sporting events and theater nearby. TAC10.

Location: Inner Harbor, about 1.5 miles north.

Publicity: *Peabody Reflector, Nation's Business, Times Herald, Baltimore Sun, Working Woman, WJZ-TV.*

Special Discounts: $65 single Sunday through Thursday, $75 double.

"What hotel room could ever compare to a large room in a 115-year-old house with 12-foot ceilings and a marble fireplace with hosts that could become dear longtime friends?"

The Paulus Gasthaus

2406 Kentucky Ave
Baltimore, MD 21213-1014
(410)467-1688
Fax:(410)467-1688

Rates: $80.
Payment: PC TC.
Innkeeper(s): Lucie & Ed Paulus.
Circa: 1927.

Rooms: 2 rooms, 1 with PB.
Beds: QDT.

The Gasthaus serves as a comfortable home base from which to enjoy Baltimore. The three-story home is simply furnished, and fresh flowers and chocolates pamper guests. German and American specialties are prepared for the morning meal. Mass transit is just a block away, as is Johns Hopkins University and the football stadium.

Breakfast, afternoon tea and evening snack included in rates. Type of meal: gourmet breakfast. Air conditioning and ceiling fan in room. Fluent German and some French spoken. Antiques, parks, shopping, sporting events and theater nearby. TAC10.

Location: Four and one half miles from Inner Harbor.

"We felt at home from the first moment and enjoyed every minute of the stay."

Union Square House B&B

23 S Stricker St
Baltimore, MD 21223-2423
(410)233-9064
Fax:(410)233-4046

Rates: $85-120.
Payment: MC VISA AX DS TC.
Innkeeper(s): Joseph & Patrice Debes.
Circa: 1870.

Rooms: 4 rooms with PB, 3 with FP. 1 suite. 1 conference room.
Beds: D.

This restored Victorian Italianate townhouse is situated in "Millionaires' Row" of the Union Square Historic District. It faces Union Square Park with its gardens, trees, gracious domed gazebo and fountain. Rooms feature original plaster moldings, handsome woodwork and period furnishings. The University of Maryland, B&O Railroad Museum, Convention Center and the Inner Harbor are just a few blocks away.

Breakfast and afternoon tea included in rates. Types of meals: continental-plus breakfast, full breakfast and early coffee/tea. Air conditioning in room. Fax on premises. Weddings and small meetings hosted. Antiques, parks, shopping, sporting events, theater and watersports nearby. TAC10.

Pets Allowed: Seeing eye dogs only.

"It is apparent that much care and thoughtfulness have gone into making your house a memorable and delightful place for your guests."

Betterton

B8

Lantern Inn

115 Ericsson Ave,
PO Box 29
Betterton, MD 21610-9746
(410)348-5809 (800)499-7265

Rates: $70-90.
Payment: MC VISA.
Innkeeper(s): Ken & Ann Washburn.
Circa: 1904.

Rooms: 13 rooms, 4 with PB.
Beds: KDT.

Framed by a picket fence and a wide front porch, this four-story country inn is located one block from the nettle-free public beach on Chesapeake Bay. Comfortable rooms are furnished with antiques and handmade quilts. The surrounding area is well-known for its wildlife preserves. Antique shops and restaurants are nearby. Kent County offers plenty of cycling possibilities, and there are detailed maps available at the inn for trips that start at the inn and go for 10 to 90 miles. Tennis courts are two blocks away.

Breakfast included in rates. Type of meal: continental-plus breakfast. Antiques and fishing nearby.

Location: On the Chesapeake Bay.

Publicity: *Richland Times-Dispatch, North Carolina Outdoorsman, Washingtonian, Mid-Atlantic Country.*

"Thanks for your warm hospitality."

Buckeystown

B5

MD

The Inn at Buckeystown

3521 Buckeystown Pike
Gen Del,
Buckeystown, MD 21717
(301)874-5755 (800)272-1190

Rates: $225-300. MAP.
Payment: MC VISA AX.
Innkeeper(s): Daniel R. Pelz & Chase Barnett.
Circa: 1897.

Rooms: 7 rooms, 3 with PB, 3 with FP. 4 suites. 1 conference room.
Beds: QDT.

Gables, bay windows and a wraparound porch are features of this grand Victorian mansion located on two-and-a-half acres of lawns and gardens (and an ancient cemetery). Nearby St. John's Reformed Church, built in 1884, has been refurbished as a cottage. The inn features a polished staircase, antiques and elegantly decorated guest rooms. Ask for the Winter Suite, which boasts a lavish queen oak bed. At dinner, cream of garlic brie, German duck and ginger cream cake are house specialties. The village of Buckeystown is in the National Register.

Breakfast, afternoon tea and dinner included in rates. Types of meals: full breakfast and early coffee/tea. MAP. Air conditioning, cable TV and VCR in room. Spa on premises. Weddings, small meetings, family reunions and seminars hosted. Antiques, fishing, shopping, downhill skiing, cross-country skiing, sporting events and watersports nearby.

Publicity: *Mid-Atlantic, Innsider, The Washingtonian, Washington Post.*

"The courtesy of you and your staff were the glue that bound the whole experience together."

Catoctin Inn & Antiques

3613 Buckeystown Pike
Buckeystown, MD 21717
(301)874-5555 (800)730-5550

Rates: $85-150.
Payment: MC VISA AX DS PC.
Innkeeper(s): Terry & Sarah MacGillivray.
Circa: 1780.

Rooms: 16 rooms with PB, 12 with FP. 8 suites. 3 cottages. 3 conference rooms.
Beds: KQ.

The inn's four acres of dogwood, magnolias, maples and sweeping lawns overlook the village and the Catoctin Mountains range. Some special features of the inn include a library with marble fireplaces and a handsome wraparound veranda. A gazebo marks the site for weddings, showers and receptions for up to 150

guests. Twelve of the guest rooms include a fireplace and a whirlpool tub. An antique shop on the property is housed in a two-story Victorian carriage house. Nearby villages to visit include Harper's Ferry, Antietam and New Market. Buckeystown's Monocacy River provides canoeing and fishing.

Breakfast and afternoon tea included in rates. Type of meal: full breakfast. Catering service available. Air conditioning, turn-down service, cable TV and VCR in room. Library and child care on premises. Weddings, small meetings, family reunions and seminars hosted. Antiques, fishing, shopping, downhill skiing, cross-country skiing, sporting events and theater nearby.

Cascade — A5

Bluebird on The Mountain

14700 Eyler Ave
Cascade, MD 21719-1938
(301)241-4161 (800)362-9526

Rates: $105-125.
Payment: MC VISA AX PC.
Innkeeper(s): Eda Smith-Eley.
Circa: 1900.

Rooms: 5 rooms, 3 with PB, 3 with FP. 2 suites.
Beds: KQT.

In the mountain village of Cascade, this gracious shuttered Georgian manor is situated on two acres of trees and wildflowers. Three suites have double whirlpool tubs. There is an outdoor hot tub as well. The Rose Garden Room and Mt. Magnolia suites have fireplaces and porches overlooking the back garden. The inn is appointed with antiques, lace and white linens, and white wicker.

Breakfast included in rates. Types of meals: continental-plus breakfast, full breakfast, gourmet breakfast and early coffee/tea. Room service available. Air conditioning, turn-down service, ceiling fan, cable TV and VCR in room. Spa on premises. Small meetings, family reunions and seminars hosted. French and Spanish spoken. Antiques, fishing, parks, shopping, downhill skiing, sporting events, theater and watersports nearby. TAC10.

Publicity: *Warm Welcomes, Baltimore Sun, Frederick News.*

Special Discounts: Midweek rates $95-$115.

"A wonderful balance of luxury and at-home comfort."

Chestertown — B8

Brampton Inn

25227 Chestertown Rd
Chestertown, MD 21620
(410)778-1860
Fax:(410)778-1805
E-mail: brampton@friend.ly.net

Rates: $95-155. MAP.
Payment: MC VISA AX PC TC.
Innkeeper(s): Michael & Danielle Hanscom.
Circa: 1860.

Rooms: 10 rooms, 8 with PB, 8 with FP. 2 suites. 2 cottages.
Beds: KQDT.

Situated on 35 acres of gardens, meadows and woodland on Maryland's Eastern Shore between the Chester River and Chesapeake Bay, Brampton is a graceful three-story brick, Greek Italianate Revival house. Swiss innkeeper Danielle Hanscom selected family antiques to furnish the parlor and dining room. A massive walnut staircase winds to the upstairs where spacious rooms feature canopied beds, antiques and reproductions. A full country breakfast is served.

Breakfast and afternoon tea included in rates. Types of meals: full breakfast, gourmet breakfast and early coffee/tea. MAP. Air conditioning and ceiling fan in room. Fax, copier and library on premises. Handicap access. 35 acres. French and German spoken. Antiques, shopping, theater and watersports nearby. TAC10.

Publicity: *Washington Post, New York Times.*

"A stately beauty that exudes peace and tranquility."

Great Oak Manor

10568 Cliff Rd
Chestertown, MD 21620
(410)778-5943 (800)504-3098
Fax:(410)778-5943

Rates: $76-145.
Payment: MC VISA AX DS PC TC.
Innkeeper(s): Don & Dianne Cantor.
Circa: 1938.

Rooms: 11 rooms with PB, 5 with FP. 1 suite. 2 conference rooms.
Beds: KT.

This elegant Georgian mansion anchors vast lawns at the end of a long driveway. Situated directly on the Chesapeake Bay, it is a serene and picturesque country estate. A library with fireplace, den and formal parlors are available to guests. With its grand circular stairway, bayside gazebo, and nearby beach and marina, the Manor is a remarkable setting for events such as weddings and reunions. Chestertown is eight miles away.

Breakfast included in rates. Types of meals: continental-plus breakfast and early coffee/tea. Air conditioning in room. VCR, fax, copier, bicycles and library on premises. 12 acres. Weddings, small meetings, family reunions and seminars hosted. Antiques, fishing, parks, shopping, sporting events, theater and watersports nearby. TAC10.

Publicity: *Country Inns.*

Special Discounts: 20% off all rooms (Sunday through Thursday).

"The charming setting, professional service and personal warmth we experienced at Great Oak will long be a pleasant memory. Thanks for everything!"

MD

Lauretum Inn B&B

954 High St
Chestertown, MD 21620
(410)778-3236 (800)742-3236
Fax:(410)778-1922

Rates: $60-115.
Payment: MC VISA AX DS PC.
Innkeeper(s): Peg Sites.
Circa: 1870.

Rooms: 5 rooms, 3 with PB. 2 suites.
Beds: QDT.

At the end of a long winding driveway this massive Queen Anne Victorian commands a hilltop setting on six acres just outside of town. Inviting parlors and a porch are available to guests. Spacious guest rooms overlook the inn's lawns, often visited by deer in the early morning. Peg, the mother of 16 children, once plied the intracoastal waters on her 40-foot boat and can help you plan your stay in the area.

Breakfast, afternoon tea and evening snack included in rates. Types of meals: continental-plus breakfast and early coffee/tea. Air conditioning in room. VCR and fax on premises. Small meetings and family reunions hosted. Antiques, fishing, parks, shopping, sporting events, theater and watersports nearby. TAC10.

The Inn at Mitchell House

8796 Maryland Pkwy
Chestertown, MD 21620
(410)778-6500

Rates: $75-110.
Payment: MC VISA.
Innkeeper(s): Tracy Stone.
Circa: 1743.

Rooms: 6 rooms, 5 with PB, 2 with FP. 2 suites.
Beds: KQ.

This pristine 18th-century manor house sits as a jewel on 12 acres overlooking Stoneybrook Pond. The guest rooms and the inn's several parlors are preserved and appointed in an authentic Colonial mood, heightened by handsome polished wide-board floors. Eastern Neck Island National Wildlife Refuge, Remington Farms, St. Michaels, Annapolis and nearby Chestertown are all delightful to explore. The Inn at Mitchell House is a popular setting for romantic weddings and small corporate meetings.

Breakfast included in rates. Types of meals: full breakfast and early coffee/tea. Afternoon tea and gourmet lunch available. Air conditioning and turn-down service in room. VCR on premises. 12 acres. Weddings, small meetings, family reunions and seminars hosted. Antiques, fishing, shopping, sporting events, theater and watersports nearby.

Publicity: *Washingtonian, New York, Glamour, Philadelphia Inquirer, Baltimore Sun, Kent County News, Ten Best Inns in the Country.*

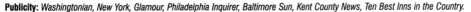

Cumberland

A3

The Inn at Walnut Bottom

120 Greene St
Cumberland, MD 21502
(301)777-0003 (800)286-9718
Fax:(301)777-8288

Rates: $69-160. MAP.
Payment: MC VISA AX DS PC TC.
Innkeeper(s): Grant M. Irvin & Kirsten O. Hansen.
Circa: 1820.

Rooms: 12 rooms, 8 with PB. 2 suites.
Beds: KQDT.

Two historic houses comprise the Inn at Walnut Bottom: the 1815 Cowden House and the 1890 Dent house. There are two guest parlors. Country antiques and reproduction furnishings decorate the old-fashioned rooms. The Oxford House Restaurant serves meals Monday through Saturday.

Breakfast included in rates. Types of meals: continental breakfast, full breakfast and early coffee/tea. Lunch and room service available. MAP. Air conditioning, ceiling fan and cable TV in room. Fax, copier and bicycles on premises. Weddings, small meetings, family reunions and seminars hosted. Danish, German and French spoken. Antiques, fishing, parks, shopping, downhill skiing, cross-country skiing and theater nearby.

Publicity: *Washington Post, Mid-Atlantic Country, Southern Living.*

Easton

C8

Gross' Coate Plantation 1658

11300 Gross' Coate Rd
Easton, MD 21601-5458
(410)819-0802 (800)580-0802
Fax:(410)819-0803

Rates: $295-495.
Payment: MC VISA AX DS PC.
Innkeeper(s): Jon & Molly Ginn.
Circa: 1760.

Rooms: 8 suites, 6 with FP. 1 conference room.
Beds: KQDT.

Lord Baltimore granted this expansive property to Roger Gross in 1658, and the plantation home, a classic example of Georgian architecture, dates back to 1760. The innkeepers purchased the home in 1983 and after extensive renovation have restored the manor and several other buildings to their original glory. The innkeepers also added a swimming pool and four ponds for waterfowl and wildlife conservation. The dining room floor was built in 1850 from walnut trees which fell during a hurricane. The south parlor still features the home's original mantel with hand-carved reeded pilasters, rope carving and tabour fluting.

Breakfast and afternoon tea included in rates. Types of meals: continental-plus breakfast, gourmet breakfast and early coffee/tea. Turndown service in room. VCR, fax, copier, swimming, bicycles, library and pet boarding on premises. 60 acres. Small meetings hosted. Antiques, fishing, parks, shopping, sporting events, theater and watersports nearby. TAC10.

Pets Allowed.

Location: On Chesapeake Bay.

Publicity: *Chesapeake Current, Garden Design, Mid Atlantic, Southern Living, Washingtonian, Washington Post Weekend, Homes of the Cavaliers.*

"Your inn is beautiful and so peaceful, relaxing, we will most definitely return and look forward to your gracious hospitality in the future."

Ellicott City B6

Wayside Inn

4344 Columbia Rd
Ellicott City, MD 21042-5910
(410)461-4636
Fax:(410)750-2070

Rates: $70-90.
Payment: MC VISA AX PC TC.
Innkeeper(s): Margo & John Osantowski.
Circa: 1800.

Rooms: 4 rooms, 2 with PB, 2 with FP. 2 suites.
Beds: QD.

This stone farmhouse is situated on two acres and has a small pond. A parlor and music room are available for guests. The Pierpont Suite has a queen-size bed with a flat-top canopy and its own sitting room. The innkeepers continue the tradition of lighting a candle in each window where a room is still available for the night.

Breakfast and evening snack included in rates. Types of meals: continental-plus breakfast, gourmet breakfast and early coffee/tea. Air conditioning and turn-down service in room. Fax and copier on premises. Small meetings hosted. Antiques, parks, shopping and theater nearby. TAC10.

Publicity: *Mid-Atlantic, Howard County Sun, Maryland.*

"Thank you! So much for such a wonderful experience! You make your guests feel extra special!"

Frederick B5

MD

"Spring Bank," A B&B Inn

7945 Worman's Mill Rd
Frederick, MD 21701
(301)694-0440 (800)400-4667

Rates: $75-90.
Payment: MC VISA AX DS PC TC.
Innkeeper(s): Beverly & Ray Compton.
Circa: 1880.

Rooms: 5 rooms, 1 with PB.
Beds: D.

Both Gothic Revival and Italianate architectural details are featured in this National Register brick Victorian. High ceilings accommodate 10-foot arched windows. The original interior shutters remain. The parlor has a marbleized slate fireplace and there is original hand-stenciling and a plaster fresco in the Billiards Room. Victorian furnishings and Oriental rugs have been collected from the family's antique shop. Black birch, pine, maple and poplar trees dot the inn's 10 acres.

Breakfast included in rates. Type of meal: continental-plus breakfast. Air conditioning in room. Cable TV, VCR and library on premises. 10 acres. Antiques, fishing and theater nearby. TAC7.

Special Discounts: Increasing discounts for stays of four days or longer.

Middle Plantation Inn

9549 Liberty Rd
Frederick, MD 21701-3246
(301)898-7128

Rates: $95-110.
Payment: MC VISA PC TC.
Innkeeper(s): Shirley & Dwight Mullican.
Circa: 1988.

Rooms: 4 rooms with PB.
Beds: QD.

The innkeepers at this unique Colonial log house built around the original 1810 structure to create their inn, which offers four guest rooms. The house still includes the authentic, early 19th-century hardwood floors, the stone and log frame and wood beams. These original features give the inn a cozy, rustic feel. Guest rooms are decorated with quilts, stenciling and country furnishings, include a lace-covered canopy bed. Guests are welcome to relax in the Keeping Room, which offers comfortable furnishings, stained-glass windows, sky-lights and a huge, stone fireplace. The 26-acre grounds include a garden and a brook. The home is located just a few miles to the east of Frederick.

Breakfast included in rates. Type of meal: continental-plus breakfast. Air conditioning, ceiling fan and cable TV in room. 26 acres. Antiques, fishing, parks and shopping nearby. TAC10.

Publicity: *Baltimore Magazine, Frommer's, Innsider.*

Special Discounts: $15 discount without breakfast; special weekday and business rates.

"Inn was furnished elegantly with authentic antiques. Blueberry muffins were a heavenly delight that melted in my mouth."

Hagerstown

A5

Beaver Creek House B&B

20432 Beaver Creek Rd
Hagerstown, MD 21740
(301)797-4764

Rates: $75-95.
Payment: MC VISA AX PC TC.
Innkeeper(s): Donald & Shirley Day.
Circa: 1905.

Rooms: 5 rooms with PB. 1 conference room.
Beds: DT.

History buffs enjoy this turn-of-the-century inn located minutes away from Antietam and Harpers Ferry National Historical Parks. The surrounding villages house antique shops and some hold weekend auctions. The inn features a courtyard with a fountain and a country garden. Innkeepers Don and Shirley Day furnished the home with family antiques and memorabilia. Guests can sip afternoon tea or complimentary sherry in the elegant parlor or just relax on the porch and take in the view of South Mountain.

Breakfast included in rates. Types of meals: full breakfast, gourmet breakfast and early coffee/tea. Air conditioning and ceiling fan in room. Copier on premises. Small meetings, family reunions and seminars hosted. Amusement parks, antiques, fishing, parks, shopping, downhill skiing, cross-country skiing, sporting events, theater and watersports nearby. TAC10.

Publicity: *Baltimore Sun, Hagerstown Journal, Herald Mail, Washington Post, Frederick.*

"Thanks so much for your hospitality. You're wonderful hosts and breakfast was delicious as usual. Don't change a thing."

Havre De Grace

A8

Spencer Silver Mansion

200 S Union Ave
Havre De Grace, MD 21078
(410)939-1097 (800)780-1485

Rates: $65-125.
Payment: MC VISA AX DS PC TC.
Innkeeper(s): Carol & Jim Nemeth.
Circa: 1896.

Rooms: 5 rooms, 3 with PB, 1 with FP. 1 cottage.
Beds: QDT.

This elegant granite Victorian mansion is graced with bays, gables, balconies, a turret and a gazebo veranda. The Victorian decor, with antiques and Oriental rugs, complements the house's carved-oak woodwork, fireplace mantels and parquet floors. The Concord Point Lighthouse (oldest continuously operated lighthouse in America) is only a walk away. In addition to the four rooms in the main house, a romantic carriage house suite is available, featuring an in-room fireplace, TV, whirlpool bath and kitchenette.

Breakfast included in rates. Types of meals: full breakfast and early coffee/tea. Air conditioning, turn-down service and cable TV in room. Weddings, small meetings and family reunions hosted. German spoken. Antiques, fishing, parks, shopping and watersports nearby. TAC10.

Pets Allowed: In Carriage House only.

Location: In the heart of the historic district, 2 blocks from the waterfront.

Publicity: *Mid-Atlantic Country, Maryland.*

Special Discounts: $10 off any room, Monday-Thursday nights.

"A fabulous find. Beautiful house, excellent hostess. I've stayed at a lot of B&Bs, but this house is the best."

McDaniel

Wades Point Inn on The Bay

1090 Wades Point Rd
McDaniel, MD 21647
(410)745-2500

Rates: $84-180. AP.
Payment: MC VISA PC TC.
Innkeeper(s): Betsy & John Feiler.
Circa: 1819.

Rooms: 24 rooms, 15 with PB. 1 suite. 1 conference room.
Beds: QDT.

This beautiful waterfront estate is located on 120 acres and was named for Zachary Wade who received the land grant in 1657. Thomas Kemp, a ship builder, built the house and his families' burial grounds are adjacent to the inn's mile-long walking trail. The trail passes the farm's crops and cultivated flowers and fishing ponds. Deer rabbit, fox, raccoons, bald eagles, blue heron, swans and osprey are often seen. There is a boat dock and fishing pier. Rooms are available in the main house and in a pretty new building with balconies and screened porches overlooking the Chesapeake.

Breakfast included in rates. Types of meals: continental-plus breakfast and early coffee/tea. Catering service available. AP. Air conditioning and ceiling fan in room. Fax, copier and library on premises. Handicap access. 120 acres. Small meetings, family reunions and seminars hosted. Antiques, fishing, parks, shopping, sporting events, theater and watersports nearby.

Special Discounts: $107 for three nights or longer. 15% Seniors discount Sunday-Thursday.

MD

New Market B6

National Pike Inn

PO Box 299
New Market, MD 21774
(301)865-5055

Rates: $75-125.
Payment: MC VISA PC TC.
Innkeeper(s): Tom & Terry Rimel.
Circa: 1796.

Rooms: 6 rooms, 4 with PB, 3 with FP. 1 suite. 1 conference room.
Beds: QD.

This red shuttered brick Federal-style home is one of the few inns remaining on the National Pike, an old route that carried travelers from Baltimore to points west. The inn's Colonial decor includes wingback chairs, Oriental rugs and four-poster beds. Azalea gardens border a private courtyard and fountain. New Market, founded in 1793, offers more than 30 antique shops and other charming points of interest, including an old-fashion general store, all within walking distance of the inn.

Breakfast included in rates. Type of meal: full breakfast. Air conditioning in room. Cable TV and VCR on premises. Small meetings hosted. Antiques, shopping, sporting events and theater nearby.

Location: Exit 62 off interstate 70, 6 miles east of Frederick, Maryland.

Publicity: *Mid-Atlantic Country, Country.*

Special Discounts: Rates are $65-95 weekdays, Monday-Thursday.

"A total joy! A relaxed, charming and romantic setting."

Oakland C8

Harley Farm B&B

16766 Garrett Hwy
Oakland, MD 21550-4036
(301)387-9050 (888)231-3276
Fax:(301)387-9050
E-mail: kgillespie@harleyfarmbb.com

Rates: $70-100.
Payment: MC VISA AX DS PC TC.
Innkeeper(s): Wayne & Kam Gillespie.
Circa: 1990.

Rooms: 7 rooms with PB. 1 suite.
Beds: QD.

From the drive, this B&B appears as an unassuming, albeit charming, farmhouse surrounded by acres of rolling hills. Inside, the innkeepers have added many elegant touches, transforming the home into a gracious retreat with Chinese carpets, tapestries and European furnishings. The innkeepers host a variety of classes and workshops throughout the year, with subjects ranging from yoga, art, leadership and management. Guests can sign up for seasonal programs as well, one workshop teaches guests how to create their own Williamsburg Christmas, while another instructs guests on how to prepare fresh apple and pumpkin butter. Croquet, badminton and volleyball courts are set up on the grounds, and summertime brings hay rides and barn dances.

Breakfast included in rates. Type of meal: full breakfast. Air conditioning and ceiling fan in room. Cable TV, VCR, spa, bicycles and library on premises. Weddings, small meetings, family reunions and seminars hosted. German, limited French and limited Spanish spoken. Antiques, fishing, parks, shopping, downhill skiing, cross-country skiing and watersports nearby. TAC8.

Ocean City E10

Atlantic House

501 N Baltimore Ave
Ocean City, MD 21842-3926
(410)289-2333

Rates: $55-145.
Payment: MC VISA AX DS TC.
Innkeeper(s): Paul & Debi Cook.
Circa: 1927.

Rooms: 14 rooms, 8 with PB. 1 suite. 1 conference room.
Beds: QD.

From the front porch of this bed & breakfast, guests can partake in ocean views. The rooms are decorated in a casual, beach style with simple furnishings. The morning breakfast buffet includes such items as freshly baked breads, fruit, egg casseroles, cereals and yogurt. In the afternoons, light refreshments also are served. The inn is a short walk to the beach, boardwalk and shopping.

Breakfast, afternoon tea and evening snack included in rates. Types of meals: full breakfast and early coffee/tea. Air conditioning, ceiling fan and cable TV in room. Spa and swimming on premises. Weddings, small meetings, family reunions and seminars hosted. Amusement parks, antiques, fishing, parks, shopping, sporting events, theater and watersports nearby. TAC10.

Special Discounts: Beach retreat; entire B&B including full kitchen/breakfast, capacity 35 people.

"We were anxious to see if we made the right choice, we definitely did."

Oxford D8

The Robert Morris Inn

314 S Morris St PO Box 70
Oxford, MD 21654-1311
(410)226-5111
Fax:(410)226-5744

Rates: $50-220. EP.
Payment: MC VISA PC.
Innkeeper(s): Jay Gibson.
Circa: 1710.

Rooms: 35 rooms with PB.
Beds: DT.

Once the home of Robert Morris Sr., a representative of an English trading company, the house was constructed by ship carpenters with wooden-pegged paneling, ship's nails and hand-hewn beams. Bricks brought to Oxford as ballast in trading ships were used to build the fireplaces. Robert Morris Jr., a partner in a Philadelphia law firm, used his entire savings to help finance the Continental Army. He signed The Declaration of Independence, The Articles of Confederation and The United States Constitution. The inn is closed on Tuesdays for breakfast and lunch.

Type of meal: full breakfast. Dinner and lunch available. EP. Air conditioning in room. Fax, copier and library on premises. Handicap access. Small meetings and seminars hosted. Antiques, fishing, parks, shopping, theater and watersports nearby. TAC10.

Publicity: *Southern Accents, The Evening Sun, Maryland, Mid-Atlantic Country.*

"Impressed! Unbelievable!"

Saint Michaels C8

Kemp House Inn

412 Talbot St, PO Box 638
Saint Michaels, MD 21663
(410)745-2243

Rates: $65-105.
Payment: MC VISA DS.
Innkeeper(s): Diane M. Cooper.
Circa: 1807.

Rooms: 8 rooms, 6 with PB, 4 with FP.
Beds: QDT.

This two-story Georgian house was built by Colonel Joseph Kemp, a shipwright and one of the town forefathers. The inn is appointed in period furnishings accentuated by candlelight. Guest rooms include patchwork quilts, a collection of four-poster rope beds and old-fashioned nightshirts. There are several working fireplaces. Robert E. Lee is said to have been a guest.

Breakfast included in rates. Types of meals: continental breakfast and early coffee/tea. Catered breakfast available. Air conditioning in room. Antiques, fishing, shopping and watersports nearby.

Pets Allowed.

Location: Historic town on the eastern shore of the Chesapeake.

Publicity: *Gourmet, Philadelphia.*

"It was wonderful. We've stayed in many B&Bs, and this was one of the nicest!"

Parsonage Inn

210 N Talbot St
Saint Michaels, MD 21663
(410)745-5519 (800)394-5519

Rates: $90-145.
Payment: MC VISA PC TC.
Innkeeper(s): Marcie Stalter.
Circa: 1883.

Rooms: 8 rooms with PB, 3 with FP.
Beds: KQD.

A striking Victorian steeple rises next to the wide bay of this brick residence, once the home of Henry Clay Dodson, state senator, pharmacist and brickyard owner. The house features brick detail in a variety of patterns and inlays, perhaps a design statement for brick customers. Porches are decorated with filigree and spindled columns. Laura Ashley linens, late Victorian furnishings, fireplaces and decks add to the creature comforts. Four bikes await guests who wish to ride to Tilghman Island or to the ferry that goes to Oxford. Gourmet breakfast is served in the dining room.

Breakfast included in rates. Types of meals: full breakfast and gourmet breakfast. Air conditioning and ceiling fan in room. Cable TV and bicycles on premises. Handicap access. Small meetings and family reunions hosted. Antiques, fishing, shopping and watersports nearby. TAC10.

Location: In the historic district.

Publicity: *Wilmington, Delaware News Journal, Philadelphia Inquirer.*

Special Discounts: 10% off mid-week (except June-September)

"Striking, extensively renovated."

MD

Scotland

E7

St. Michael's Manor B&B

50200 St Michael's Manor
Way, Scotland, MD 20687
(301)872-4025
Fax:(301)872-4025

Rates: $45-70.
Payment: PC TC.
Innkeeper(s): Joe & Nancy Dick.
Circa: 1805.

Rooms: 4 rooms.
Beds: QDT.

Twice featured on the Maryland House and Garden Tour, St. Michael's Manor is located on Long Neck Creek, a half-mile from Chesapeake Bay. The original hand-crafted woodwork provides a handsome backdrop for the inn's antique collection. A three-acre vineyard and swimming pool are on the property.

Breakfast included in rates. Types of meals: full breakfast and early coffee/tea. Air conditioning in room. Cable TV, fax, swimming and bicycles on premises. 10 acres. Weddings, small meetings, family reunions and seminars hosted. Antiques, fishing, parks, shopping, cross-country skiing, sporting events, theater and watersports nearby.

Location: Near Point Lookout State Park.

Publicity: *Washington Post.*

Special Discounts: Lower rates Monday-Thursday.

"Your B&B was so warm, cozy and comfortable."

Snow Hill

E9

Chanceford Hall Inn

209 W Federal St
Snow Hill, MD 21863-1159
(410)632-2231

Rates: $115-135.
Payment: PC TC.
Innkeeper(s): Michael & Thelma C. Driscoll.
Circa: 1759.

Rooms: 5 rooms with PB, 4 with FP. 1 suite.
Beds: Q.

This pre-Revolutionary War inn is listed in the National Register and Smithsonian's "Guide to Historic America." The home maintains many original features, including woodwork, floors and mantels. Rooms feature romantic, canopy beds and the home boasts 10 wood-burning fireplaces and Oriental rugs throughout. Wine and hors d'oeuvres are served after guests check in, and a full breakfast is served each morning in the inn's formal dining room. Spend the day exploring the Snow Hill area, or simply relax by the lap pool. The innkeepers offer bicycles for their guests.

Breakfast included in rates. Types of meals: full breakfast, gourmet breakfast and early coffee/tea. Air conditioning in room. Cable TV, VCR, copier, swimming and bicycles on premises. Antiques, fishing, parks, shopping, sporting events and watersports nearby. TAC10.

River House Inn

201 E Market St
Snow Hill, MD 21863-2000
(410)632-2722
Fax:(410)632-2866

Rates: $110-160.
Payment: MC VISA AX TC.
Innkeeper(s): Larry & Susanne Knudsen.
Circa: 1860.

Rooms: 8 rooms with PB, 6 with FP. 1 suite. 1 cottage.
Beds: KQT.

This picturesque Gothic Revival house rests on the banks of the Pocomoke River and boasts its own dock. Its two acres roll down to the river over long tree-studded lawns. Lawn furniture and a hammock add to the invitation to relax as do the inn's porches. Some guest rooms feature marble fireplaces. The 17th-century village of Snow Hill boasts old brick sidewalks and historic homes. Canoes can be rented a block from the inn or you may wish to take a river cruise on the innkeeper's pontoon boat.

Breakfast and evening snack included in rates. Types of meals: full breakfast and early coffee/tea. Air conditioning and ceiling fan in room. Cable TV, VCR, fax, copier, bicycles, library and child care on premises. Handicap access. Weddings, small meetings and family reunions hosted. Amusement parks, antiques, fishing, shopping and watersports nearby. TAC10.

Publicity: *Daily Times*

Special Discounts: Packages with biking, golf, canoeing.

"Thank you for making our first B&B an exceptional one."

Solomons

E7

Back Creek B&B

PO Box 520
Solomons, MD 20688-0520
(410)326-2022
Fax:(410)326-2946

Rates: $75-140.
Payment: MC VISA PC TC.
Innkeeper(s): Lin Cochran & Carol Pennock.
Circa: 1880.

Rooms: 7 rooms with PB, 2 with FP. 2 suites. 1 cottage. 1 conference room.
Beds: KQD.

This delightful inn serves as a perfect respite for those visiting the charming village of Solomon's. Located along the banks of Back Creek, the grounds offer water views and gardens. Guests are encouraged to enjoy the grounds, which include an outdoor spa. Many guests stroll along the creek banks to watch the sunset. A country garden theme permeates the inn, with handmade quilts and bouquets of herbs and flowers decorating guest rooms. The innkeepers take pride in their well-presented breakfasts, which often include what they call "one-of-a-kind" omelets topped with homemade salsa, waffled French toast with sausage or perhaps Back Creek "Eggs Benny." On Sunday, a buffet breakfast is presented. Guests are welcome to borrow a bicycle and explore the country side.

Breakfast and evening snack included in rates. Types of meals: continental breakfast, continental-plus breakfast, full breakfast and early coffee/tea. Afternoon tea and picnic lunch available. Air conditioning, ceiling fan and cable TV in room. VCR, fax, spa and bicycles on premises. Handicap access. Small meetings, family reunions and seminars hosted. Antiques, fishing, parks, shopping, sporting events, theater and watersports nearby.

Solomons Island

Solomons Victorian Inn

125 Charles Street
Solomons Island, MD 20688
(410)326-4811
Fax:(410)326-0133

Rates: $90-165.
Payment: MC VISA PC.
Innkeeper(s): Richard & Helen Bauer.
Circa: 1906.

Rooms: 6 rooms with PB. 1 suite.
Beds: KQ.

The Davis family, renowned for their shipbuilding talents, constructed this elegant Queen Anne Victorian at the turn of the century. Each of the inn's elegant common rooms and bedchambers boast special touches such as antiques, oriental rugs and lacy curtains. The home affords views of Solomons Harbor and its entrance into the picturesque Chesapeake Bay. Guests are treated to an expansive breakfast in a dining room, which overlooks the harbor.

Breakfast and evening snack included in rates. Types of meals: full breakfast and early coffee/tea. Air conditioning in room. Cable TV, fax and library on premises. Small meetings hosted. Antiques, fishing, parks, shopping, theater and watersports nearby.

"Instead of guests at a place of lodging, you made us feel like welcome friends in your home."

Stevenson

B7

Gramercy B&B

1400 Greenspring Valley Rd, Box 119
Stevenson, MD 21153-0119
(410)486-2405
Fax:(410)486-1765

Rates: $145-250.
Payment: MC VISA AX DS PC TC.
Innkeeper(s): Anne & Cristin Pomykala.
Circa: 1902.

Rooms: 10 rooms, 5 with PB, 3 with FP. 2 suites. 2 conference rooms.
Beds: KD.

MD

This beautiful English Tudor mansion was built as a wedding present for the daughter of Alexander Cassatt, president of Pennsylvania Railroad and brother to Mary Cassatt, famous impressionist. A mother and daughter team runs the B&B. There is a music room, library and parlors, all decorated with antiques and Oriental rugs. Most of the guest rooms have fireplaces and a few have Jacuzzi baths. Cookie, the inn's collie, loves taking guests on nature walks along the woodland trails to flush deer and fox out for viewing. There are commercial herb gardens, an orchard, a stream and flower gardens. The house was featured as the Decorator Showhouse to benefit the Baltimore Symphony. The inn is known for its delectable breakfasts.

Breakfast and evening snack included in rates. Types of meals: full breakfast and gourmet breakfast. Air conditioning, turn-down service and VCR in room. Fax, copier, swimming, tennis and library on premises. 45 acres. Weddings, small meetings, family reunions and seminars hosted. Antiques, parks and shopping nearby.

Location: 20 minutes from Baltimore Inner Harbor.

Publicity: *Mid-Atlantic B&B Guide, Washington Post.*

"The hospitality, atmosphere, food, etc. were top-notch."

Tilghman

D7

Black Walnut Point Inn

Black Walnut Rd,
PO Box 308
Tilghman, MD 21671
(410)886-2452
Fax:(410)886-2053

Rates: $120-140.
Payment: MC VISA PC TC.
Innkeeper(s): Tom & Brenda Ward.
Circa: 1843.

Rooms: 7 rooms with PB. 2 cottages. 1 conference room.
Beds: Q.

Located on 57 beautiful acres set aside as a wildlife sanctuary, this handsome Colonial Revival manor commands waterfront views from its private peninsula location. Charter fishing and island river cruises can be arranged by the innkeepers. From its bayside hammock to its nature walk, swimming pool and lighted tennis court, the inn provides an amazingly private getaway. Accommodations are in the main house as well as the Riverside Cottage. The Cove Cottage has its own kitchen and screened porch facing the river.

Breakfast included in rates. Types of meals: continental-plus breakfast and early coffee/tea. Air conditioning in room. Fax, copier, spa, swimming, bicycles, tennis and library on premises. 57 acres. Small meetings, family reunions and seminars hosted. Antiques, fishing, parks, shopping and watersports nearby.

Special Discounts: Meeting groups $100.

Massachusetts

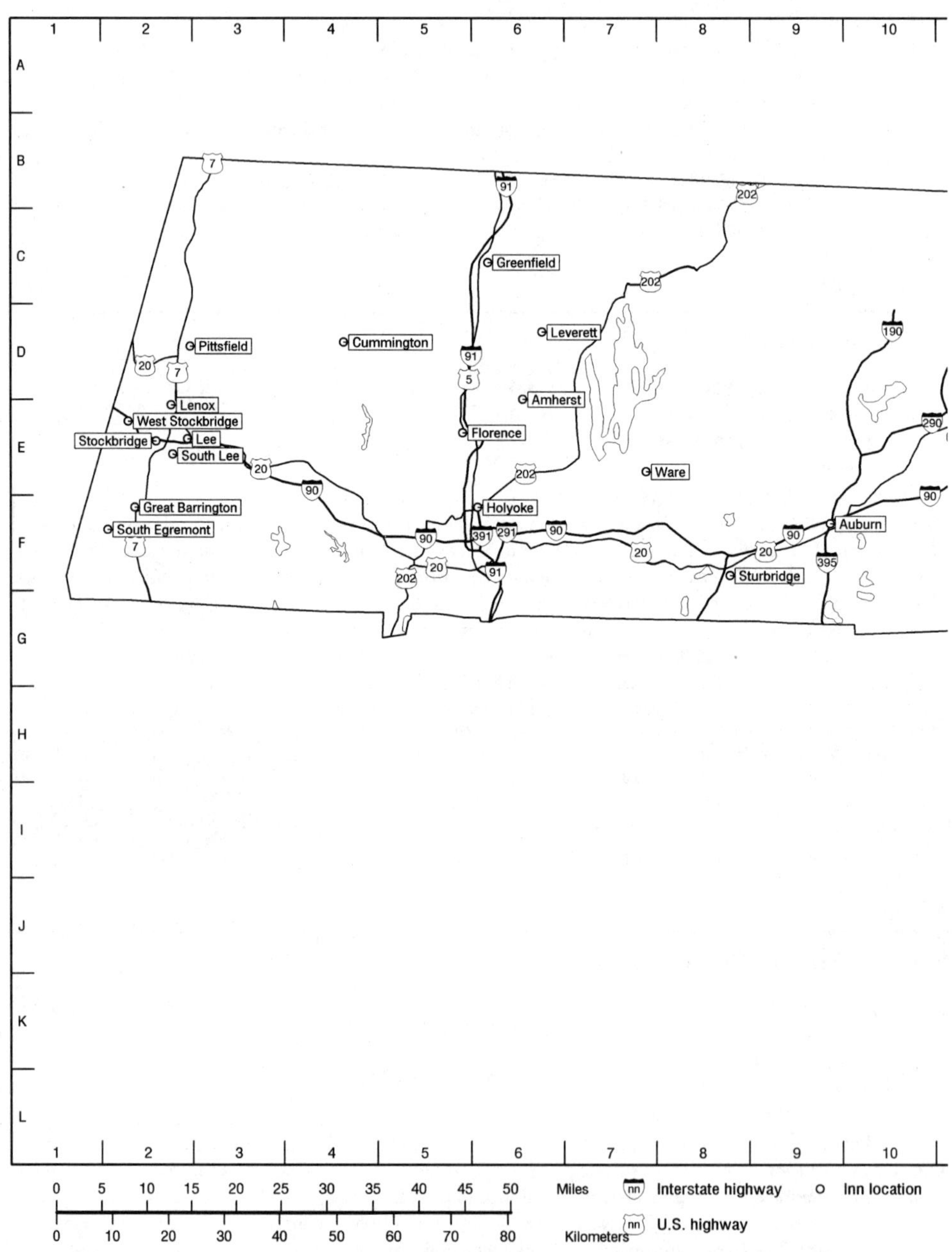

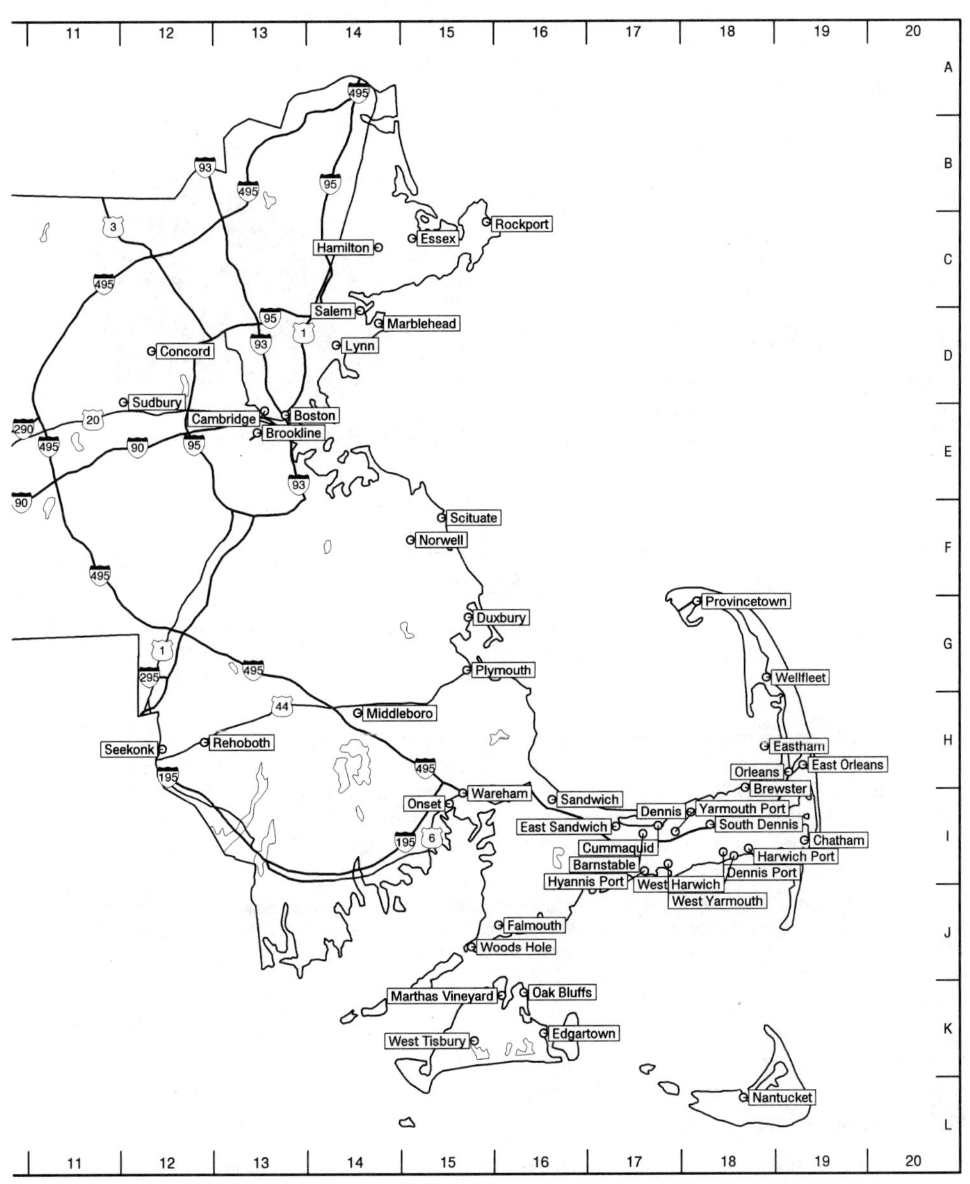

11
12
13
14
15
16
17
18
19
20
A
B
C
D
E
F
G
H
I
J
K
L
Rockport
Essex
Hamilton
Salem
Marblehead
Lynn
Concord
Sudbury
Cambridge
Boston
Brookline
Scituate
Norwell
Provincetown
Duxbury
Plymouth
Wellfleet
Middleboro
Seekonk
Rehoboth
Eastham
East Orleans
Orleans
Brewster
Wareham
Sandwich
Onset
Dennis
Yarmouth Port
East Sandwich
South Dennis
Chatham
Cummaquid
Harwich Port
Barnstable
Dennis Port
Hyannis Port
West Harwich
West Yarmouth
Falmouth
Woods Hole
Marthas Vineyard
Oak Bluffs
Edgartown
West Tisbury
Nantucket
495
93
95
3
1
20
290
90
44
295
195
6

Amherst

D6

Allen House Victorian Inn

599 Main St
Amherst, MA 01002-2409
(413)253-5000

Rates: $55-115. MAP, AP, EP.
Payment: MC VISA AX DS PC TC.
Innkeeper(s): Alan & Ann Zieminski.
Circa: 1886.

Rooms: 7 rooms with PB.
Beds: QDT.

This stick-style Queen Anne is much like a Victorian museum with guest rooms that feature period reproduction wallpapers, pedestal sinks, carved golden oak and brass beds, painted wooden floors and plenty of antiques. Among its many other treasures include Eastlake fireplace mantels. Unforgettable breakfasts include specialties such as Eggs Benedict or French toast stuffed with rich cream cheese. Afternoon tea is a treat, and the inn offers plenty of examples of poetry from Emily Dickinson, whose home is just across the street from the inn.

Breakfast, afternoon tea and evening snack included in rates. Types of meals: full breakfast, gourmet breakfast and early coffee/tea. MAP, AP, EP. Air conditioning and ceiling fan in room. Cable TV and library on premises. Amusement parks, antiques, fishing, parks, shopping, downhill skiing, cross-country skiing, sporting events, theater and watersports nearby.

Publicity: *New York Times, Boston Globe, Bon Appetit, Yankee Travel.*

"Our room and adjoining bath were spotlessly clean, charming, and quiet, with good lighting. Our meals were delicious and appetizing, and the casual, family-like atmosphere encouraged discussions among the guests."

Auburn

F9

Captain Samuel Eddy House B&B

609 Oxford St S
Auburn, MA 01501-1811
(508)832-7282

Rates: $65-85.
Payment: TC.
Innkeeper(s): Diedre & Mike Meddaugh.
Circa: 1765.

Rooms: 5 rooms, 4 with PB. 1 suite. 1 conference room.
Beds: KQDT.

This Georgian-style house was once the home of a Revolutionary War captain. The B&B is decorated in period style with handmade quilts, antiques, stenciling, hooked rugs and four-poster beds in the guest rooms. The Captain's Attic Suite has a king-size bed and couch in one room and Chinese decor. The suite also has a double bed with brass headboard and an antique maple twin bed in the other room. The Common Room is a popular place for guests to relax, especially in front of a warm fire. The sunroom is another relaxing spot, boasting views of woods, a pond and the garden.

Breakfast and afternoon tea included in rates. Types of meals: full breakfast, gourmet breakfast and early coffee/tea. Air conditioning in room. Cable TV, VCR, bicycles and library on premises. Weddings, small meetings and family reunions hosted. Antiques, fishing, parks, shopping, downhill skiing, cross-country skiing, sporting events and theater nearby. TAC10.

Publicity: *Boston Herald, Auburn News, New York Times, Country.*

"Like stepping back in time."

Barnstable

I17

Beechwood Inn

2839 Main St, Rt 6A
Barnstable, MA 02630-1017
(508)362-6618 (800)609-6618
Fax:(508)362-0298

Rates: $90-150.
Payment: MC VISA AX PC TC.
Innkeeper(s): Debbie & Ken Traugot.
Circa: 1853.

Rooms: 6 rooms with PB, 2 with FP.
Beds: KQD.

Beechwood is a beautifully restored Queen Anne Victorian offering period furnishings, some rooms with fireplaces or ocean views. Its warmth and elegance make it a favorite hideaway for couples looking for a peaceful and romantic return to the Victorian Era. The inn is named for rare old beech trees that shade the veranda.

Breakfast and afternoon tea included in rates. Types of meals: full breakfast and early coffee/tea. Fax, copier, bicycles and library on premises. Weddings, small meetings and family reunions hosted. French spoken. Antiques, fishing, parks, shopping, sporting events, theater and watersports nearby. TAC10.

Location: Cape Cod's historic North Shore.

Publicity: *National Trust Calendar, New England Weekends, Rhode Island Monthly.*

Special Discounts: Off-season, midweek discounts.

"Your inn is pristine in every detail. We concluded that the innkeepers, who are most hospitable, are the best part of Beechwood."

Crocker Tavern B&B

3095 Main St
Barnstable, MA 02630-1119
(508)362-5115 (800)773-5359
Fax:(508)362-5562

Rates: $70-105.
Payment: MC VISA PC TC.
Innkeeper(s): Sue & Jeff Carlson.
Circa: 1754.

Rooms: 5 rooms with PB, 2 with FP.
Beds: QD.

This historic Cape Cod inn once served as a headquarters for the Whigs during the Revolutionary Era. The inn is part of the Olde Kings Highway Historic District, and also is listed on the National Register. Visitors choose from five guest rooms in this two-story, Georgian-style inn, each with a four-poster or canopy bed, sitting area and antiques. Several rooms include working fireplaces. Many of this homes Colonial elements have been beautifully restored, such as the wood plank floors, exposed beams, window seats and the elegant woodwork. The inn's continental breakfasts are served on candlelit tables set with china and crystal. The B&B is within walking distance to restaurants, antique shops, historic sites and the harbor, where guests sign up for whale-watching excursions.

Breakfast and evening snack included in rates. Types of meals: continental-plus breakfast and early coffee/tea. Afternoon tea available. Air conditioning in room. Fax and library on premises. Handicap access. Small meetings and family reunions hosted. Antiques, fishing, parks, shopping, cross-country skiing, theater and watersports nearby. TAC10.

Publicity: *Cape Cod Times, Society for the Preservation of New England Antiquities.*

"Thank you so much for your wonderful hospitality. You have a lovely home, and your attention to detail made our stay all the more pleasant. We will always remember fondly our stay at Crocker Tavern."

The Lamb & Lion

2504 Main St, Rt 6A,
PO Box 511
Barnstable, MA 02630
(508)362-6823
Fax:(508)362-0227

Rates: $85-150.
Payment: MC VISA AX DS.
Innkeeper(s): Donald P. McKeag.

Rooms: 12 rooms, 4 with PB, 3 with FP. 4 suites. 2 cottages.
Beds: KQDT.

This rambling collection of Cape-style buildings sits on four acres overlooking the Old King's highway. Newly decorated, the inn offers a feeling of casual elegance. The Innkeeper's Pride is a romantic suite with sunken tub, fireplace, kitchenette and a deck overlooking a garden and woods. The Barn-stable, is one of the original buildings and now offers three bedrooms, a living and dining area and French doors to a private patio. A large central courtyard houses a generous sized pool.

Breakfast included in rates. Type of meal: continental-plus breakfast. Afternoon tea and catering service available. Air conditioning and cable TV in room. VCR, fax, swimming and library on premises.

Barnstable, Cape Cod

Ashley Manor Inn

3660 Olde Kings Hwy
PO Box 856, Barnstable,
Cape Cod, MA 02630
(508)362-8044

Rates: $115-175.
Payment: MC VISA AX PC TC.
Innkeeper(s): Donald & Fay Bain.
Circa: 1699.

Rooms: 6 rooms with PB, 5 with FP. 4 suites. 1 cottage.
Beds: KQD.

This beautiful rustic home has lived through a succession of expansions, the first addition being built in 1750. The final effect is wonderful and mysterious. The inn, thought to be a hiding place for Tories during the Revolutionary War, features huge open-hearth fireplaces with beehive ovens and a secret passageway connecting the upstairs and downstairs suites. The inn, reminiscent of a gracious English country house, is filled with Oriental rugs and antiques. Each of the guest rooms boast fireplaces. Two acres of manicured lawns include a regulation-size tennis court. Nature lovers will enjoy the landscape, dotted with cherry and apple trees. The romantic gazebo is the perfect location to view the fountain garden. A full gourmet breakfast is served on the brick terrace or fireside in the formal dining room.

Breakfast included in rates. Type of meal: gourmet breakfast. Air conditioning in room. Bicycles, tennis and library on premises. French spoken. Antiques, fishing, parks, theater and watersports nearby. TAC10.

Location: In the heart of Cape Cod's historic district.

Publicity: *Chicago Tribune, Boston Globe, Bon Appetit, Tennis, New York Times, Pittsburgh Press, Gourmet, GBH.*

"This is absolutely perfect! So many very special, lovely touches."

Boston E13

Beacon Hill B&B

27 Brimmer St
Boston, MA 02108-1013
(617)523-7376

Rates: $125-175.
Payment: TC.
Innkeeper(s): Susan Butterworth.
Circa: 1869.

Rooms: 3 rooms with PB.
Beds: QD.

This six-story Victorian rowhouse overlooks the Charles River in a quiet residential area of downtown Boston. Rooms are spacious and each has a fireplace. Two of the comfortably furnished guest rooms and the dining room have views of the river. There's an elevator for toting luggage. The Boston Common and Freedom Trail, Quincy Market, conference hotels and the Back Bay are all within easy walking distance. The neighborhood can't be beat, but you'll have to pay extra for parking a few blocks away.

Breakfast included in rates. Type of meal: full breakfast. Air conditioning in room. French spoken. Antiques, parks, shopping, sporting events and theater nearby.

"Enjoyed your lovely home, your cooking, your friendliness and the vibrant, alive decor."

Host Homes of Boston

PO Box 117-Waban Branch
Boston, MA 02168-0001
(617)244-1308

Rates: $68-125.
Payment: MC VISA AX PC.
Innkeeper(s): Marcia Whittington.
Circa: 1864.
Beds: KQDT.

One of the many fine homes available through this reservation service includes a stately townhouse on Commonwealth Avenue in Boston's chic Back Bay, less than one block away from the Boston Common and a short walk to Copley Square. Host Homes offers a variety of vacation possibilities throughout the Boston area and its suburbs. Some are inland, others, including a lakefront townhouse in New Hampshire, are close to the ocean.

Breakfast included in rates. Type of meal: continental-plus breakfast. Handicap access. Amusement parks, antiques, fishing, parks, shopping, downhill skiing, cross-country skiing, sporting events, theater and watersports nearby.

Location: Additional homes in Beacon Hill, Back Bay, Cambridge, Greater Boston.

Publicity: *Changing Times, USA Today, What's Doing in Boston, BBC Holiday, Marie Claire.*

"Very special. I have never stayed at such an excellent, elegant B&B. Our hosts were delightful, the place, magnificent!"

Brewster H18

The Beechcroft Inn

1360 Main St
Brewster, MA 02631-1724
(508)896-9534

Rates: $55-145. MAP, AP.
Payment: MC VISA AX DC CB DS PC TC.
Innkeeper(s): Celeste & Bob Hunt.
Circa: 1828.

Rooms: 10 rooms with PB.
Beds: KQDT.

This Greek Revival structure originally served as the First Universalist Church, but opened its doors to inngoers more than a century ago. Today, it offers 10 relaxing guest rooms, decorated in a comfortable, country style. There is a pub on the premises where guests can enjoy an evening cocktail in front of a crackling fire. The inn's restaurant, The Beechcroft Inn Bistro, serves delectables such as Wellfleet Quahog chowder, baked brie with grilled vegetables, gourmet pizzas, pasta, seafood and more.

MA

Breakfast included in rates. Types of meals: full breakfast and early coffee/tea. Afternoon tea, dinner, banquet service and catering service available. MAP, AP. Cable TV, VCR, bicycles and library on premises. Weddings, small meetings, family reunions and seminars hosted. Antiques, fishing, parks, shopping, theater and watersports nearby. TAC10.

Bramble Inn & Restaurant

Rt 6A 2019 Main St
Brewster, MA 02631
(508)896-7644
Fax:(508)896-9332

Rates: $95-125.
Payment: MC VISA AX DS PC TC.
Innkeeper(s): Ruth & Cliff Manchester.
Circa: 1861.

Rooms: 8 rooms with PB, 1 with FP.
Beds: QD.

The venerable Bramble Inn is comprised of three buildings. The main house containing a restaurant and lodging, and the house next door with five guest rooms, are of Greek Revival architecture. The Captain Bangs Pepper House on the other side of the main house of the Federal style, built in 1793. Williamsburg and Laura Ashley fabrics and wall coverings decorate the inn.

Breakfast included in rates. Types of meals: full breakfast and gourmet breakfast. Picnic lunch and catering service available. Restaurant on premises. Air conditioning in room. Cable TV, VCR, fax and copier on premises. Weddings, small meetings and family reunions hosted. Antiques, fishing, parks, shopping, cross-country skiing, theater and watersports nearby.

Location: Walking distance to the ocean.

Publicity: *Boston Globe, Boston Herald, Bon Appetit.*

Brookline E13

The Bertram Inn

92 Sewall Ave
Brookline, MA 02146-5327
(617)566-2234 (800)295-3822
Fax:(617)277-1887

Rates: $59-164.
Payment: MC VISA PC TC.
Innkeeper(s): Bryan Austin.
Circa: 1907.

Rooms: 13 rooms, 11 with PB, 2 with FP.
Beds: KQDT.

Antiques and authenticity are the rule at this turn-of-the-century Gothic Revival inn, found on a peaceful, tree-lined street. Innkeeper Bryan R. Austin is well-versed in the restoration of historical properties and furniture. That knowledge is evident at the Bertram Inn, with its old-English stylings and Victorian decor.

Boston College, Boston University, Fenway Park and the F.L. Olmstead National Historic Site all are nearby. Shops and restaurants are within walking distance.

Breakfast included in rates. Type of meal: continental-plus breakfast. Afternoon tea available. Air conditioning, ceiling fan and cable TV in room. Fax on premises. German, French and Spanish spoken. Antiques, parks, shopping, sporting events and theater nearby. TAC10.

Pets Allowed.

"This B&B is just wonderful, I can't imagine a nicer place. Thank you for your warm generosity, a fine substitute for home."

Cambridge E13

A Cambridge House B&B Inn

2218 Massachusetts Ave
Cambridge, MA 02140-1836
(617)491-6300 (800)232-9989
Fax:(617)868-2848

Rates: $89-225.
Payment: MC VISA AX DS TC.
Innkeeper(s): Ellen Riley & Tony Femmino.
Circa: 1892.

Rooms: 16 rooms, 13 with PB, 2 with FP.
Beds: QDT.

Listed in the National Register, Cambridge House has been restored to its turn-of-the-century elegance. A remarkable carved cherry fireplace dominates the den, and some rooms have four-poster canopy beds and fireplaces. The library is often the setting for mulled cider, wine or tea served fireside on brisk afternoons. Parking is available and the subway is four blocks away.

Breakfast included in rates. Types of meals: full breakfast and gourmet breakfast. Air conditioning and cable TV in room. Fax and copier on premises. Weddings, small meetings, family reunions and seminars hosted. Antiques, parks, shopping, sporting events and theater nearby.

Location: Minutes from downtown Boston.

Publicity: *Evening, Glamour, Los Angeles Times, Entrepreneur.*

"I'm afraid you spoiled us quite badly! Your home is elegant, charming and comfortable. Breakfasts were delicious and beautifully served."

Chatham I19

The Cranberry Inn at Chatham

359 Main St
Chatham, MA 02633-2425
(508)945-9232 (800)332-4667
Fax:(508)945-3769

Rates: $85-240.
Payment: MC VISA AX DS PC TC.
Innkeeper(s): Ray & Brenda Raffurty.
Circa: 1830.

Rooms: 18 rooms with PB, 8 with FP. 2 suites.
Beds: QDT.

Continuously operating for over 150 years, this inn was originally called the Traveler's Lodge, then the Monomoyic after a local Indian tribe. A cranberry bog adjacent to the property inspired the current name. Recently restored, the inn is located in the heart of the historic district. It's within walking distance of the lighthouse, beaches, shops and restaurants. Guest rooms feature four-poster beds, wide-planked floors and coordinated fabrics. A tap room is on the premises.

Breakfast and afternoon tea included in rates. Type of meal: full breakfast. Air conditioning and cable TV in room. VCR, fax and library on premises. Weddings and family reunions hosted. Antiques, fishing, parks, shopping, theater and watersports nearby. TAC10.

Location: Near many Cape Cod attractions.

Publicity: *Detroit Free Press, Cape Cod Chronicle, Goodtimes.*

Cyrus Kent House

63 Cross St
Chatham, MA 02633-2207
(508)945-9104 (800)338-5368
Fax:(508)945-9104

Rates: $85-175.
Payment: MC VISA.
Innkeeper(s): Sharon Mitchell-Swan.
Circa: 1877.

Rooms: 10 rooms with PB.
Beds: QD.

A former sea captain's home, the Cyrus Kent House was built in the Greek Revival style. The award-winning restoration retained many original features such as wide pine floorboards, ceiling rosettes, and marble fireplaces. Although furnished with antiques and reproductions, all modern amenities are available. Most bedrooms have four-poster beds. Suites feature sitting rooms with fireplaces. Chatham's historic district is a short stroll away.

Breakfast and afternoon tea included in rates. Types of meals: continental-plus breakfast and early coffee/tea. Cable TV in room. Fax on premises. Weddings, small meetings, family reunions and seminars hosted. Antiques, fishing, shopping and watersports nearby.

Location: Located on a quiet side street within easy walking distance of the historic village of Chatham.

Publicity: *Country Inns.*

MA

Old Harbor Inn

22 Old Harbor Rd
Chatham, MA 02633-2315
(508)945-4434 (800)942-4434
Fax:(508)945-2492

Rates: $105-195.
Payment: MC VISA DC CB DS PC TC.
Innkeeper(s): Judy & Ray Braz.
Circa: 1932.

Rooms: 8 rooms with PB, 2 with FP. 1 conference room.
Beds: KQT.

This pristine New England bed & breakfast was once the home of "Doc" Keene, a popular physician in the area. A meticulous renovation has created an elegant, beautifully appointed inn offering antique furnishings, designer linens and lavish amenities in an English country decor. A buffet breakfast, featuring Judy's homemade muffins, is served in the sunroom or on the deck. The beaches, boutiques and galleries are a walk away and there is an old grist mill, the Chatham Lighthouse, and a railroad museum. Band concerts are offered Friday nights in the summer at Kate Gould Park.

Breakfast included in rates. Types of meals: continental-plus breakfast and early coffee/tea. Afternoon tea available. Air conditioning and ceiling fan in room. Small meetings hosted. Antiques, fishing, parks, shopping, theater and watersports nearby. TAC10.

Location: On the elbow of Cape Cod.

Publicity: *Cape Cod Life, Country Inns, Cape Cod Travel Guide, Yankee.*

Special Discounts: 10% discount on seven or more nights stay.

Port Fortune Inn

201 Main St
Chatham, MA 02633-2423
(508)945-0792 (800)750-0792
Fax:(508)945-0792

Rates: $80-170.
Payment: MC VISA.
Innkeeper(s): Michael & Renee Kahl.
Circa: 1930.

Rooms: 14 rooms with PB.
Beds: QDT.

The front of this charming Cape Cod home is decorated with colorful flowers and plants. The interior is elegant and inviting with traditional furnishings, and some guest rooms are decorated with poster beds. The grounds include perennial gardens and a patio set up with furniture for those who wish to relax and catch a few sea breezes. The inn is the only lodging in the neighborhood, which is Chatham's oldest.

Breakfast included in rates. Type of meal: continental-plus breakfast. Air conditioning in room. Cable TV on premises. Antiques, fishing, parks, shopping, sporting events, theater and watersports nearby.

"Excellent. The entire experience was wonderful as usual."

Concord D12

Colonel Roger Brown House

1694 Main St
Concord, MA 01742-2831
(508)369-9119 (800)292-1369
Fax:(508)369-1305

Rates: $75-95.
Payment: MC VISA AX DC PC TC.
Innkeeper(s): Lauri Berlied.
Circa: 1775.

Rooms: 5 rooms with PB. 1 suite.
Beds: QDT.

This house was the home of Minuteman Roger Brown who fought the British at the Old North Bridge. The frame for this center-chimney Colonial was being raised on April 19, the day the battle took place. Some parts of the house were built as early as 1708. The adjacent Damon Mill houses a fitness club available to guests. Both buildings are in the National Register.

Breakfast and afternoon tea included in rates. Type of meal: continental-plus breakfast. Air conditioning in room. Fax, copier, computer, spa, swimming, sauna and library on premises. Family reunions and seminars hosted. Antiques, fishing, parks, shopping, downhill skiing, cross-country skiing, theater and watersports nearby. TAC10.

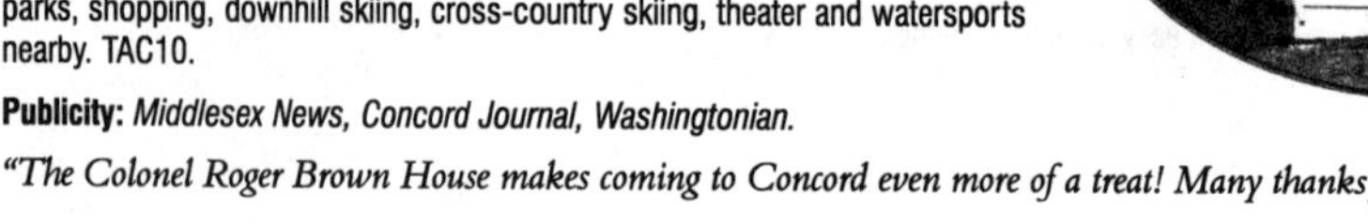

Publicity: *Middlesex News, Concord Journal, Washingtonian.*

"The Colonel Roger Brown House makes coming to Concord even more of a treat! Many thanks for your warm hospitality."

Hawthorne Inn

462 Lexington Rd
Concord, MA 01742-3729
(508)369-5610
Fax:(508)287-4949

Rates: $140-215.
Payment: MC VISA AX DS PC TC.
Innkeeper(s): Marilyn Mudry & Gregory Burch.
Circa: 1870.

Rooms: 7 rooms with PB.
Beds: QDT.

The Hawthorne Inn is situated on land that once belonged to Ralph Waldo Emerson, the Alcotts and Nathaniel Hawthorne. It was here that Bronson Alcott planted his fruit trees, made pathways to the Mill Brook, and erected his Bath House. Hawthorne purchased the land and repaired a path leading to his home with trees planted on either side. Two of these trees still stand. Across the road is Hawthorne's House, The Wayside. Next to it is the Alcott's Orchard House, and Grapevine Cottage where the Concord grape was developed. Nearby is Sleepy Hollow Cemetery where Emerson, the Alcotts, the Thoreaus, and Hawthorne were laid to rest.

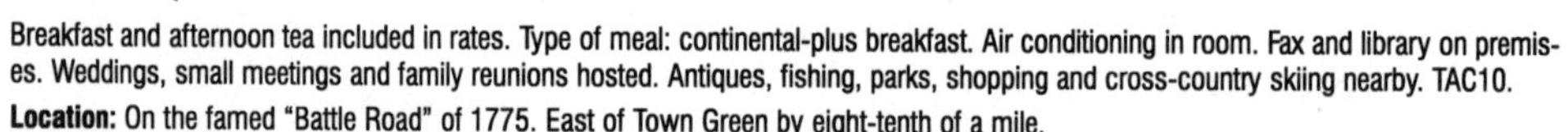

Breakfast and afternoon tea included in rates. Type of meal: continental-plus breakfast. Air conditioning in room. Fax and library on premises. Weddings, small meetings and family reunions hosted. Antiques, fishing, parks, shopping and cross-country skiing nearby. TAC10.

Location: On the famed "Battle Road" of 1775. East of Town Green by eight-tenth of a mile.

Publicity: *New York Times, Boston Globe, Yankee.*

"Surely there couldn't be a better or more valuable location for a comfortable, old-fashioned country inn."

Cummaquid I17

The Acworth Inn

4352 Old Kings Hwy,
PO Box 256
Cummaquid, MA 02637
(508)362-3330 (800)362-6363

Rates: $75-95.
Payment: MC VISA AX DS PC TC.
Innkeeper(s): Cheryl & Jack Ferrell.
Circa: 1860.

Rooms: 6 rooms with PB, 1 with FP.
Beds: QDT.

This inn, located on the Olde Kings Highway on the north side of Cape Cod, offers a strategic midway point for those exploring the area. The historic Cape-style farmhouse features six guest rooms, each with a private bath. Hand-painted, restored furniture adds charm to the inn's interior. Guests select from the

Cummaquid, Chatham, Yarmouth Port, Barnstable, Wellfleet and Orleans rooms, all named for Cape Cod villages. Visitors will find the shore just a half-mile from the inn.

Breakfast and afternoon tea included in rates. Types of meals: continental-plus breakfast and early coffee/tea. Turn-down service in room. Cable TV and library on premises. German spoken. Antiques, fishing, parks, shopping, theater and watersports nearby. TAC10.

Publicity: *Boston Magazine.*

Special Discounts: Seven day stay 10% discount.

"...great accommodations, food, tour guiding, local flavor, etc...We will be back."

Cummington D4

Windfields Farm

154 Windsor Bush Rd
Cummington, MA 01026
(413)684-3786

Rates: $70.
Payment: PC TC.
Innkeeper(s): Carolyn & Arnold Westwood.
Circa: 1830.

Rooms: 2 rooms.
Beds: QD.

This homestay bed & breakfast is located in a charming Federal-style farmhouse, which dates back to the early 19th century. Some of the home's original post and beams still are visible. The two rooms are decorated comfortably with modern Danish pieces and a selection of antiques, and one room includes a four-poster bed. The innkeepers prepare a mouth-watering breakfast, using prize-winning organic produce and fresh-from-the-farm eggs.

MA

Breakfast and afternoon tea included in rates. Types of meals: full breakfast and early coffee/tea. Copier, swimming and library on premises. 100 acres. Weddings and family reunions hosted. Antiques, fishing, parks, shopping, downhill skiing, cross-country skiing and theater nearby.

Special Discounts: 10% discount Monday-Thursday.

"We could not have imagined a more peaceful retreat from city life! We love the blue room."

Deerfield C6

Deerfield Inn

81 Old Main St
Deerfield, MA 01342-9706
(413)774-5587 (800)926-3865
Fax:(413)773-8712

Rates: $99-141.
Payment: MC VISA AX.
Innkeeper(s): Jane Sabo.
Circa: 1884.

Rooms: 23 rooms with PB. 1 conference room.
Beds: QT.

Deerfield was settled in 1670. Farmers in the area still unearth bones and ax heads from an ancient Indian massacre. Now 50 beautifully restored colonial and Federal homes line mile-long The Street, considered by many to be the loveliest street in New England. Twelve of these houses are museums open to the public. The inn is situated at the center of this peaceful village and is filled with antiques from historic Deerfield's remarkable collection. The village has been designated a National Historic Landmark.

Breakfast and afternoon tea included in rates. Type of meal: full breakfast. Dinner and lunch available. Fax and copier on premises. Handicap access. Antiques, fishing, cross-country skiing and theater nearby.

Location: Middle of historic village.

Publicity: *Travel Today, Country Accents, Colonial Homes, Country Living.*

"We've stayed at many New England inns, but the Deerfield Inn ranks among the best."

Dennis

I18

Isaiah Hall B&B Inn

152 Whig St
Dennis, MA 02638-1917
(508)385-9928 (800)736-0160
Fax:(508)385-5879

Rates: $85-145.
Payment: MC VISA AX TC.
Innkeeper(s): Marie Brophy.
Circa: 1857.

Rooms: 9 rooms, 10 with PB, 1 with FP. 1 suite.
Beds: QDT.

Adjacent to the Cape's oldest cranberry bog is this Greek Revival farmhouse built by Isaiah Hall, a cooper. His brother was the first cultivator of cranberries in America and Isaiah designed and patented the original barrel for shipping cranberries. In 1948, Dorothy Gripp, an artist, established the inn. Many examples of her artwork remain.

Breakfast included in rates. Types of meals: continental-plus breakfast and early coffee/tea. Air conditioning in room. Cable TV and fax on premises. Weddings, small meetings, family reunions and seminars hosted. Antiques, fishing, parks, shopping, theater and watersports nearby.

Location: Cape Cod.

Publicity: *Cape Cod Life, New York Times, Golf.*

"Your place is so lovely and relaxing."

Dennisport

I18

Rose Petal B&B

152 Sea St PO Box 974
Dennisport, MA 02639-2404
(508)398-8470

Rates: $52-92.
Payment: MC VISA AX.
Innkeeper(s): Gayle & Dan Kelly.
Circa: 1872.

Rooms: 3 rooms, 2 with PB.
Beds: QT.

This Cape Cod-style home was built for Almond Wixon, whose seafaring family was among the original settlers of Dennisport. In 1918, Wixon was lost at sea with all on board. The Wixon homestead was completely restored in 1986. Surrounded by a white picket fence and attractively landscaped yard, the Rose Petal is situated in the heart of Cape Cod, a short walk from the beach. Home-baked pastries highlight a full breakfast in the dining room.

Breakfast included in rates. Types of meals: gourmet breakfast and early coffee/tea. Air conditioning in room. Cable TV on premises. Family reunions hosted. Some French spoken. Antiques, fishing, parks, shopping, theater and watersports nearby. TAC10.

"Perfect. Every detail was appreciated."

Duxbury

G15

The Winsor House Inn

390 Washington St
Duxbury, MA 02332-4552
(617)934-0991
Fax:(617)934-5955

Rates: $105-125.
Payment: MC VISA AX DS PC TC.
Innkeeper(s): Mr & Mrs David M O'Connell.
Circa: 1803.

Rooms: 3 rooms with PB, 3 with FP. 1 suite.
Beds: QT.

A visit to this inn is much like a visit back in time to our early Colonial days. The early 19th-century home was built by prominent sea captain and merchant Nathaniel Winsor as a wedding gift for his daughter, Nancy. With an eye for the authentic, the innkeepers have restored parts of the inn to look much the way it might have when the young bride and groom took up residence. Rooms are decorated with Colonial furnishings, canopied beds, fresh flowers, and each has a fireplace. The Carriage House offers lunch fare, and guests might enjoy a drink at the inn's English-style pub. For a romantic dinner, try the inn's Dining Room, which serves everything from roasted venison with a juniper berry and mushroom crust to herb-seared salmon with plum tomato saffron vinaigrette.

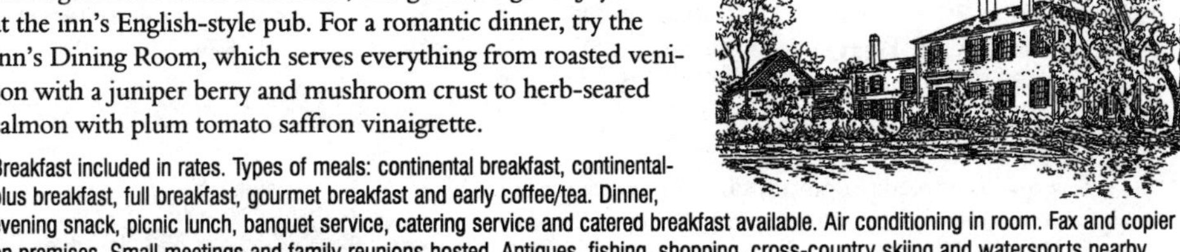

Breakfast included in rates. Types of meals: continental breakfast, continental-plus breakfast, full breakfast, gourmet breakfast and early coffee/tea. Dinner, evening snack, picnic lunch, banquet service, catering service and catered breakfast available. Air conditioning in room. Fax and copier on premises. Small meetings and family reunions hosted. Antiques, fishing, shopping, cross-country skiing and watersports nearby.

East Orleans — H19

The Nauset House Inn

143 Beach Rd, PO Box 774
East Orleans, MA 02643
(508)255-2195

Rates: $65-115.
Payment: MC VISA PC TC.
Innkeeper(s): Al & Diane Johnson, John & Cindy Vessella.
Circa: 1810.

Rooms: 14 rooms, 8 with PB. 1 cottage.
Beds: KQDT.

Located a short distance from the water, the Nauset House is a renovated farmhouse set on three acres, which include an old apple orchard. A Victorian conservatory was purchased from a Connecticut estate and reassembled here, then filled with wicker furnishings, Cape flowers and stained glass. Hand-stenciling, handmade quilts, antiques and more bouquets of flowers decorate the rooms. The breakfast room features a fireplace, brick floor and beamed ceiling. For an extra charge, guests can partake in a continental or country breakfast, which includes treats such as ginger pancakes or waffles with fresh strawberries. Wine and cranberry juice are served in the evenings.

Afternoon tea included in rates. Types of meals: continental breakfast, full breakfast and early coffee/tea. Antiques, fishing, parks, shopping, sporting events, theater and watersports nearby.

Publicity: *Country Living, Glamour, West Hartford News, Travel & Leisure.*

"The inn provided a quiet, serene, comforting atmosphere."

The Parsonage Inn

202 Main St, PO Box 1501
East Orleans, MA 02643
(508)255-8217
Fax:(508)255-8216

Rates: $65-105.
Payment: MC VISA AX.
Innkeeper(s): Ian & Elizabeth Browne.
Circa: 1770.

Rooms: 8 rooms with PB. 2 suites.
Beds: QDT.

Originally a parsonage, this Cape-style home is now a romantic inn nestled in the village of East Orleans and only a mile and a half from Nauset Beach. Rooms are decorated with antiques, quilts, Laura Ashley fabrics and stenciling, and include the original pine floors and low ceilings. Freshly baked breakfasts are served either in the dining room or on the brick patio. The innkeepers keep a selection of menus from local restaurants on hand and serve appetizers and refreshments each evening while guest peruse their dining choices. The Parsonage is the perfect location to enjoy nature, with the national seashore, Nickerson State Park and whale-watching opportunities available to guests.

Breakfast included in rates. Air conditioning and ceiling fan in room. Fax on premises. Family reunions hosted. Antiques, shopping, theater and watersports nearby. TAC10.

Publicity: *Conde' Nast Traveler.*

"Your hospitality was as wonderful as your home. Your home was as beautiful as Cape Cod. Thank you!"

Ship's Knees Inn

186 Beach Rd, PO Box 756
East Orleans, MA 02643
(508)255-1312
Fax:(508)240-1351

Rates: $45-110.
Payment: MC VISA.
Innkeeper(s): Jean & Ken Pitchford.
Circa: 1820.

Rooms: 11 rooms with PB, 3 with FP.
Beds: KQDT.

This 175-year-old restored sea captain's home is a three-minute walk from the ocean. Rooms are decorated in a nautical style with antiques. Several rooms feature authentic ship's knees, hand-painted trunks, old clipper ship models and four-poster beds. Some rooms boast ocean views and the Master Suite has a working fireplace. The inn offers swimming and tennis facilities on the grounds. About three miles away, the innkeepers also offer a one-bedroom efficiency apartment and two heated cottages on the Cove. Head into town or spend the day basking in the beauty of Nauset Beach with its picturesque sand dunes.

Breakfast included in rates. Type of meal: continental breakfast. Weddings, small meetings and family reunions hosted. Amusement parks, antiques, fishing, parks, shopping, theater and watersports nearby.

Location: One-and-a-half hours from Boston.

Publicity: *Boston Globe.*

"Warm, homey and very friendly atmosphere. Very impressed with the beamed ceilings."

East Sandwich — I17

Wingscorton Farm Inn

Rt 6A, Olde Kings Hwy
East Sandwich, MA 02537
(508)888-0534

Rates: $115-150.
Payment: MC VISA AX PC TC.
Innkeeper(s): Sheila Weyers & Richard Loring.
Circa: 1763.

Rooms: 7 rooms, 7 with FP. 4 suites. 2 cottages.
Beds: QDT.

Wingscorton is a working farm on seven acres of lawns, gardens and orchards. It adjoins a short walk to a private ocean beach. This Cape Cod manse, built by a Quaker family, is a historical landmark on what once was known as the King's Highway, the oldest historical district in the United States. All the rooms are furnished with antiques and working fireplaces (one with a secret compartment where runaway slaves hid). Breakfast features fresh produce with eggs, meats and vegetables from the farm's livestock and gardens. Pets and children welcome.

Breakfast included in rates. Types of meals: full breakfast and gourmet breakfast. Swimming, library and child care on premises. 13 acres. Weddings, small meetings, family reunions and seminars hosted. Antiques, fishing, parks, shopping, downhill skiing, cross-country skiing, sporting events, theater and watersports nearby. TAC10.

Pets Allowed.

Location: North Side of Cape Cod, off Route 6A.

Publicity: *Boston Globe, New York Times.*

"Absolutely wonderful. We will always remember the wonderful time."

Eastham — H18

Over Look Inn, Cape Cod

3085 County Rd,
PO Box 771
Eastham, MA 02642
(508)255-1886
Fax:(508)240-0345

Rates: $75-145.
Payment: MC VISA AX DC CB DS.
Innkeeper(s): Ian & Nan Aitchison.
Circa: 1869.

Rooms: 10 rooms with PB. 1 conference room.
Beds: QDT.

Schooner Captain Barnabus Chipman built this three-story home for his wife. In 1920 it opened as an inn and was frequented by author and naturalist Henry Beston as he wrote "The Outermost House." Located on three acres of grounds, the inn is furnished with Victorian antiques. A collection of Winston

Churchill books fills the inn's library. The Aitchisons, from Edinburgh are known for their warm Scottish charm and occasional bagpipe serenades.

Breakfast and afternoon tea included in rates. Type of meal: full breakfast. Antiques, fishing, parks, theater and watersports nearby.

Location: Across from Cape Cod National Seashore on the bike trail.

Publicity: *Conde Nast Traveler, Victorian Homes, New York Times, Cape Code Life, Outside.*

"A delightful experience—Max Nichols, Oklahoma City Journal Record."

Penny House Inn

4885 County Rd,
PO Box 238
Eastham, MA 02651
(508)255-6632 (800)554-1751
Fax:(508)255-4893

Rates: $85-165.
Payment: MC VISA AX DS PC TC.
Innkeeper(s): Margaret Keith.
Circa: 1690.

Rooms: 11 rooms with PB, 3 with FP. 1 conference room.
Beds: KQDT.

Captain Isaiah Horton built this house with a shipbuilder's bow roof. Traditional wide-planked floors and 200-year-old beams buttress the ceiling of the public room. The Captain's Quarters, the largest guest room with its own fireplace, bears the motto: Coil up your ropes and anchor here, Til better weather doth appear.

Breakfast and afternoon tea included in rates. Types of meals: full breakfast and early coffee/tea. Air conditioning and ceiling fan in room. Cable TV, VCR, fax, copier and library on premises. Weddings, small meetings, family reunions and seminars hosted. Antiques, fishing, parks, shopping, theater and watersports nearby. TAC10.

Location: One mile from National Seashore, Cape Cod.

Publicity: *Cape Cod Life, Cape Codder.*

"Enjoyed my stay tremendously. My mouth waters thinking of your delicious breakfast."

MA

The Whalewalk Inn

220 Bridge Rd
Eastham, MA 02642-3261
(508)255-0617
Fax:(508)240-0017

Rates: $120-190.
Payment: MC VISA PC TC.
Innkeeper(s): Carolyn & Richard Smith.
Circa: 1830.

Rooms: 12 rooms with PB, 6 with FP. 5 suites.
Beds: KQDT.

Three acres of meadow and lawn surround the Whalewalk, originally a whaling captain's house. An old picket fence frames the elegant house and there is a widow's walk. In addition to the main house, suites are available in a separate guest house, a renovated barn and a salt-box cottage. Common rooms boast 19th-century antiques from England, France and Denmark, and guest rooms boast wooden and brass beds, country furnishings and lovely linens. Start off the day with a delectable full breakfast including crepes, waffles or Grand Marnier French toast. The inn is within walking distance of Cape Cod's bayside beaches and the Cape Cod Rail Trail, a 27-mile bike path.

Breakfast and evening snack included in rates. Types of meals: full breakfast, gourmet breakfast and early coffee/tea. Air conditioning in room. Fax, copier, bicycles and library on premises. Small meetings, family reunions and seminars hosted. Antiques, fishing, shopping, theater and watersports nearby. TAC10.

Location: Near the warm bay-side beaches, but only a 10-minute drive to the Atlantic side.

Publicity: *New York Times, Glamour, Yankee Traveler, Conde Nast Traveler.*

"Your hospitality will long be remembered."

The Arbor

222 Upper Main St,
PO Box 1228
Edgartown, MA 02539
(508)627-8137

Rates: $75-145.
Payment: MC VISA PC TC.
Innkeeper(s): Peggy Hall.
Circa: 1880.

Rooms: 10 rooms, 8 with PB. 1 cottage.
Beds: QD.

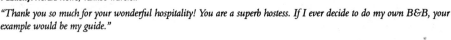

Originally built on the adjoining island of Chappaquiddick, this house was moved over to Edgartown on a barge at the turn of the century. Located on the bicycle path, it is within walking distance from downtown and the harbor. Guests may relax in the hammock, have tea on the porch, or walk the unspoiled island beaches of Martha's Vineyard.

Breakfast and afternoon tea included in rates. Type of meal: continental breakfast. Air conditioning in room. Antiques, fishing, shopping, theater and watersports nearby. TAC10.

Location: Martha's Vineyard.

Publicity: *Herald News, Yankee Traveler.*

"Thank you so much for your wonderful hospitality! You are a superb hostess. If I ever decide to do my own B&B, your example would be my guide."

Colonial Inn of Martha's Vineyard

38 N Water St, PO Box 68
Edgartown, MA 02539-0068
(508)627-4711 (800)627-4701
Fax:(508)627-5904

Rates: $65-235.
Payment: MC VISA AX PC TC.
Innkeeper(s): Linda Malcouronne.
Circa: 1911.

Rooms: 43 rooms with PB. 4 suites. 3 conference rooms.
Beds: QD.

This impressive Colonial structure has served as an inn since opening its doors in 1911. Somerset Maugham and Howard Hughes were among the regulars at the inn. Guests at Colonial Inn can sit back and relax on a porch lined with rockers as they gaze at the harbor and enjoy refreshing sea breezes. Flowers, an atrium and courtyards decorate the grounds. The inn has a full-service restaurant and seven boutiques on the premises. Some guest rooms boast harbor views, and all are decorated in an elegant country style. The inn is located in the heart of the town's historic district.

Breakfast included in rates. Type of meal: continental-plus breakfast. Dinner and lunch available. Air conditioning and cable TV in room. Fax, library and child care on premises. Handicap access. Small meetings and seminars hosted. Portuguese, Spanish and German spoken. Antiques, fishing, parks, shopping, theater and watersports nearby. TAC10.

Location: Overlooking the harbor.

Publicity: *Glamour.*

Special Discounts: Seniors: 5% discount, Sunday-Thursday.

"Everyone very friendly and very efficient."

Point Way Inn

PO Box 128
Edgartown, MA 02539-0128
(508)627-8633
Fax:(508)627-8579

Rates: $75-260.
Payment: MC VISA AX PC TC.
Innkeeper(s): Ben & Linda Smith.
Circa: 1850.

Rooms: 15 rooms with PB, 10 with FP. 1 suite.
Beds: QDT.

The reception area of Point Way Inn is papered with navigational charts from a 4,000-mile cruise the innkeepers made with their two daughters. After the voyage, they discovered this old sea captain's house. They completely renovated it, filling it with New England antiques, period wallpapers, and canopied beds. There are working fireplaces and French doors opening onto private balconies. Complimentary laundry service and a guest car are available.

Breakfast and afternoon tea included in rates. Types of meals: continental-plus breakfast and early coffee/tea. Air conditioning, turn-down service and ceiling fan in room. Fax and copier on premises. Weddings, small meetings, family reunions and seminars hosted. Antiques, fishing, parks, shopping, theater and watersports nearby.

Location: Martha's Vineyard.

Publicity: *Boston Herald American.*

"One of the most pleasant old New England inns around."

Essex

C15

George Fuller House

148 Main St # 133
Essex, MA 01929-1304
(508)768-7766 (800)477-0148
Fax:(508)768-6178

Rates: $75-135.
Payment: MC VISA AX DC DS PC.
Innkeeper(s): Cindy & Bob Cameron.
Circa: 1830.

Rooms: 7 rooms with PB, 4 with FP. 2 suites.
Beds: KQDT.

This three-story, Federal-style home is situated on a lawn that reaches to the salt marsh adjoining the Essex River. Original Indian shutters and Queen Anne baseboards remain. All the guest accommodations boast Boston rockers, and some feature canopy beds and fireplaces. For a view of the water, ask for the Andrews Suite. Belgian waffles and cranberry muffins are a house specialty. Many of the town's 50 antique shops are within walking distance of the inn.

Breakfast and afternoon tea included in rates. Type of meal: full breakfast. Air conditioning and cable TV in room. VCR and fax on premises. Weddings, small meetings, family reunions and seminars hosted. Antiques, fishing, shopping, cross-country skiing, theater and watersports nearby. TAC10.

MA

Publicity: *Gloucester Times, Yankee Traveler, Discerning Traveler.*

"Thank you for the wonderful time we had at your place. We give you a 5-star rating!"

Falmouth

J16

"Inn On The Sound"

313 Grand Ave
Falmouth, MA 02540-3434
(508)457-9666 (800)564-9668
Fax:(508)457-9631

Rates: $60-140.
Payment: MC VISA AX DS PC TC.
Innkeeper(s): Renee Ross & David Ross.
Circa: 1875.

Rooms: 10 rooms with PB.

As the name suggests, this inn treats guests to a beautiful view of Vineyard Sound. Most guest quarters offer ocean views. Guests are encouraged to relax, either in the fireplaced sitting room or on the inn's large deck. The breakfasts feature blended juices, fresh fruit, three homemade breads and daily entrees, such as a spinach souffle. For those celebrating special occasions, the innkeepers spice up the festivities with champagne, fresh flowers and other treats. The inn offers convenient access to the Martha's Vineyard ferry, shopping and the beach.

"Great food, great music, great company, great everything. What an elegant, relaxed weekend."

Captain Tom Lawrence House

75 Locust St
Falmouth, MA 02540-2658
(508)540-1445 (800)266-8139
Fax:(508)457-1790

Rates: $85-135.
Payment: MC VISA PC TC.
Innkeeper(s): Barbara Sabo-Feller.
Circa: 1861.

Rooms: 6 rooms with PB. 1 suite.
Beds: KQT.

After completing five whaling trips around the world, each four years in length, Captain Lawrence retired at 40 and built this house. There is a Steinway piano here now and elegantly furnished guest rooms, some with canopied beds. The house is near the beach, bikeway, ferries and bus station. Freshly ground organic grain is used to make Belgian waffles with warm strawberry sauce, crepes Gisela and pancakes. German is spoken here.

Breakfast included in rates. Types of meals: full breakfast and early coffee/tea. Air conditioning and ceiling fan in room. Fax and bicycles on premises. Family reunions hosted. German spoken. Antiques, fishing, parks, shopping, theater and watersports nearby.

Location: Cape Cod.

Publicity: *Country Inns.*

Special Discounts: During off season.

"This is our first B&B experience. Better than some of the so-called 4-star hotels!! We loved it here."

Mostly Hall B&B Inn

27 Main St
Falmouth, MA 02540-2652
(508)548-3786 (800)682-0565

Rates: $90-130.
Payment: MC VISA AX DS PC TC.
Innkeeper(s): Caroline & Jim Lloyd.
Circa: 1849.

Rooms: 6 rooms with PB.
Beds: Q.

Albert Nye built this Southern plantation house with wide verandas and a cupola to observe shipping in Vineyard Sound. It was a wedding gift for his New Orleans bride. Because of the seemingly endless halls on every floor (some 30 feet long), it was whimsically called Mostly Hall. All rooms have queen-size canopy beds. Bicycles are available for guest use.

Breakfast and afternoon tea included in rates. Types of meals: full breakfast, gourmet breakfast and early coffee/tea. Air conditioning and ceiling fan in room. Cable TV, VCR, fax, bicycles and library on premises. Small meetings and family reunions hosted. German spoken. Antiques, fishing, parks, shopping, theater and watersports nearby.

Location: In the historic district across from the village green.

Publicity: *Bon Appetit, Boston Globe.*

Special Discounts: Honeymoon package.

"Of all the inns we stayed at during our trip, we enjoyed Mostly Hall the most. Imagine, Southern hospitality on Cape Cod!!"

The Inn at One Main Street

1 Main St
Falmouth, MA 02540-2652
(508)540-7469 (800)281-6246

Rates: $70-110.
Payment: MC VISA PC TC.
Innkeeper(s): Karen Hart & Mari Zylinski.
Circa: 1892.

Rooms: 6 rooms with PB.
Beds: QT.

In the historic district where the road to Woods Hole begins is this shingled Victorian with two-story turret, an open front porch and gardens framed by a white picket fence. It first became a tourist house back in the '50s. Cape Cod cranberry pecan waffles and gingerbread pancakes with whipped cream are favorite specialties. Within walking distance, you'll find the Shining Sea Bike Path, beaches, summer theater, tennis, ferry shuttle and bus station. The innkeepers are Falmouth natives and are available to offer their expertise on the area.

Breakfast included in rates. Type of meal: full breakfast. Air conditioning and ceiling fan in room. Cable TV on premises. Family reunions hosted. Antiques, shopping, theater and watersports nearby.

Special Discounts: Off season corporate rates available.

"The art of hospitality in a delightful atmosphere, well worth traveling 3,000 miles for."

Palmer House Inn

81 Palmer Ave
Falmouth, MA 02540-2857
(508)548-1230 (800)472-2632
Fax:(508)540-1878

Rates: $70-175.
Payment: MC VISA AX DC CB DS PC TC.
Innkeeper(s): Ken & Joanne Baker.
Circa: 1901.

Rooms: 13 rooms with PB. 1 suite.
Beds: KQDT.

MA

Just off the village green in Falmouth's historic district, lies this turn-of-the-century Victorian and its adjacent guest house. The polished woodwork, stained-glass windows and collection of antiques tie the home to a romantic, bygone era. Innkeeper Joanne Baker prepares an opulent feast for the morning meal, which is served in traditional Victorian style, by candelight on tables set with fine china and crystal. Finnish pancakes with strawberry soup and chocolate-stuffed French toast are two of the reasons why the cuisine has been featured in Gourmet and Bon Appetit. Joanne also offers heart-healthy fare for those monitoring their fat and cholesterol. Afternoon refreshments quell those before-dinner hunger pangs.

Breakfast and evening snack included in rates. Types of meals: gourmet breakfast and early coffee/tea. Afternoon tea available. Air conditioning, turn-down service, ceiling fan and cable TV in room. Fax, copier and bicycles on premises. Handicap access. Weddings, small meetings, family reunions and seminars hosted. Antiques, fishing, parks, shopping, cross-country skiing, theater and watersports nearby. TAC10.

Location: In the historic district of Falmouth.

Publicity: *Country Inns, Gourmet, Runners World, Yankee Traveler, Bon Appetit.*

Special Discounts: 10% discount on stays of 5 or more nights.

"Exactly what a New England inn should be!"

Village Green Inn

40 Main St
Falmouth, MA 02540-2667
(508)548-5621 (800)237-1119
Fax:(508)457-5051

Rates: $85-145.
Payment: MC VISA AX PC TC.
Innkeeper(s): Diane & Don Crosby.
Circa: 1804.

Rooms: 5 rooms with PB, 2 with FP. 1 suite.
Beds: Q.

The inn, listed in the National Register, originally was built in the Federal style for Braddock Dimmick, son of Revolutionary War General Joseph Dimmick. Later, "cranberry king" John Crocker moved the house onto a granite slab foundation, remodeling it in the Victorian style. There are inlaid floors, large porches and gingerbread trim.

Breakfast and afternoon tea included in rates. Types of meals: full breakfast and early coffee/tea. Air conditioning, ceiling fan and cable TV in room. Bicycles on premises. Family reunions hosted. Antiques, fishing, parks, shopping, sporting events, theater and watersports nearby.

Location: Falmouth's historic village green.

Publicity: *Country Inns, Cape Cod Life, Yankee.*

Special Discounts: Less 10% for seven nights or more stay.

"Like we've always said, it's the innkeepers that make the inn!"

Woods Hole Passage B&B Inn

186 Woods Hole Rd
Falmouth, MA 02540-1670
(508)548-9575 (800)790-8976
Fax:(508)540-4771
E-mail: whpassage@ccsnet.com

Rates: $75-115.
Payment: MC VISA AX DC DS PC TC.
Innkeeper(s): Todd & Robin Norman.
Circa: 1890.

Rooms: 5 rooms with PB.
Beds: QD.

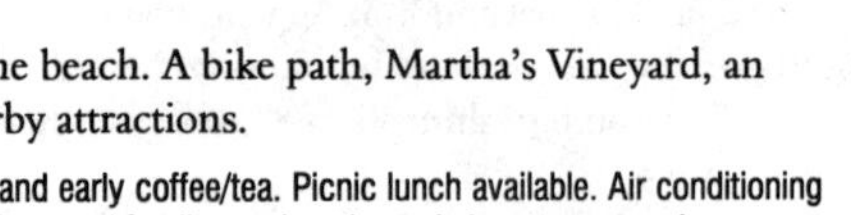

This Cape Cod-style carriage house was moved more than 50 years ago to its present site, surrounded by trees and wild berry bushes. The home's common area is decorated in a Southwestern, contemporary style, while guest quarters feature country decor. Breakfasts often are served on the patio, which overlooks the one-and-a-half-acre grounds or in the garden. Items such as homemade breads, fresh fruit and quiche are among the fare. It's just a short walk through the woods to the beach. A bike path, Martha's Vineyard, an aquarium, shopping and restaurants are just a few of the nearby attractions.

Breakfast and afternoon tea included in rates. Types of meals: full breakfast and early coffee/tea. Picnic lunch available. Air conditioning and ceiling fan in room. Fax, bicycles, tennis and library on premises. Weddings and family reunions hosted. Amusement parks, antiques, fishing, parks, shopping, theater and watersports nearby. TAC10.

Falmouth Heights

Grafton Inn

261 Grand Ave S
Falmouth Heights, MA
02540-3784
(508)540-8688 (800)642-4069
Fax:(508)540-1861

Rates: $75-149.
Payment: MC VISA AX DS TC.
Innkeeper(s): Liz & Rudy Cvitan.
Circa: 1870.

Rooms: 11 rooms with PB.
Beds: KQDT.

If you want to enjoy grand ocean views while staying at an inn in Cape Cod, this is the place. Oceanfront and within walking distance to the ferries, you can hop on board and spend a day on Nantucket Island or Martha's Vineyard and return that evening to relax and watch the moon over the ocean from your bedroom window. Snacks of wine, cheeses, teas and cookies are served in the afternoon. The inn is often seen on TV and ESPN because of its unique location at the final leg of the Falmouth Road Race.

Breakfast and afternoon tea included in rates. Types of meals: gourmet breakfast and early coffee/tea. Picnic lunch available. Air conditioning and ceiling fan in room. Cable TV, VCR, fax, swimming and library on premises. Small meetings hosted. Antiques, fishing, parks, shopping, theater and watersports nearby. TAC10.

Publicity: *Enterprise, At Your Leisure, Cape Cod Life.*

"You have certainly created a lovely inn for those of us who wish to escape the city and relax in luxury."

Florence E5

Lupine House

PO Box 60483,
185 N Main St
Florence, MA 01060-0483
(413)586-9766 (800)890-9766

Rates: $70.
Payment: MC VISA PC TC.
Innkeeper(s): Evelyn & Gil Billings.
Circa: 1900.

Rooms: 3 rooms with PB.
Beds: QDT.

This turn-of-the-century Colonial offers a comfortable setting for those enjoying a New England getaway. Rooms are simply furnished, antiques add to the ambiance. Light, continental-plus fare is served in the mornings, including homemade granola, fresh fruit, cereals, breads and muffins. The B&B is a short drive from downtown Northampton and many area schools, including Amherst, Smith, Hampshire and Mount Holyoke colleges and the University of Massachusetts.

Breakfast included in rates. Types of meals: continental-plus breakfast and early coffee/tea. Cable TV and library on premises. Antiques, fishing, parks, shopping, downhill skiing, cross-country skiing, sporting events and theater nearby.

Special Discounts: $5 less for consecutive nights; discount for more than one room.

Great Barrington F2

Baldwin Hill Farm B&B

121 Baldwin Hill Rd N/S
Great Barrington, MA
01230-9061
(413)528-4092

Rates: $70-94.
Payment: MC VISA PC TC.
Innkeeper(s): Richard & Priscilla Burdsall.
Circa: 1840.

Rooms: 4 rooms, 2 with PB, 1 with FP. 2 conference rooms.
Beds: KDT.

Several barns, dating back to the mid-18th century are still to be found on this 450-acre farm. The main house, a Victorian-style, New England farmstead, features a screened-in front porch where guests can enjoy the tranquil scenery of hills, fields, valleys, mountains, gardens and orchards. As the home has been in the family since 1912, the four guest rooms include many family antiques. Homemade country breakfasts are served in the formal dining room. The inn is 30 minutes or less from many attractions, including museums, golf courses, ski areas, Tanglewood and antique shops.

Breakfast and afternoon tea included in rates. Type of meal: full breakfast. Cable TV, VCR, copier, swimming, stables and library on premises. 450 acres. Weddings, small meetings and family reunions hosted. Antiques, fishing, parks, shopping, downhill skiing, cross-country skiing, sporting events, theater and watersports nearby. TAC10.

Special Discounts: 10% discount 4 or more nights.

"We enjoyed your home immensely - from the wonderful views to your beautiful perennial flower beds to your sumptuous breakfasts."

Seekonk Pines

142 Seekonk Cross Rd
Great Barrington, MA
01230-1571
(413)528-4192 (800)292-4192

Rates: $80-125.
Payment: MC VISA PC.
Innkeeper(s): Bruce, Roberta & Rita Lefkowitz.
Circa: 1832.

Rooms: 6 rooms with PB.
Beds: QTT.

Known as the Crippen Farm from 1835-1879, Seekonk Pines Inn now includes both the original farmhouse and a Dutch Colonial wing. Green lawns, gardens and meadows surround the inn. The name

"Seekonk" was the local Indian name for the Canadian geese which migrate through this part of the Berkshires. The inn is an easy drive to Tanglewood.

Breakfast included in rates. Types of meals: full breakfast and early coffee/tea. VCR, swimming, bicycles and library on premises. Family reunions hosted. Antiques, parks, shopping, downhill skiing, cross-country skiing and theater nearby.

Location: Near Tanglewood.

Publicity: *Los Angeles Times, Boston Sunday Globe, Country Inns.*

"Of all the B&Bs we trekked through, yours was our first and most memorable! This has been our best ever Berkshire escape..thanks to your wonderful B&B."

Windflower Inn

684 S Egremont Rd
Great Barrington, MA
01230-1932
(413)528-2720 (800)992-1993
Fax:(413)528-5147

Rates: $110-160. MAP.
Payment: AX PC TC.
Innkeeper(s): Barbara & Gerald Liebert, Claudia & John Ryan.
Circa: 1870.

Rooms: 13 rooms with PB, 6 with FP.
Beds: KQT.

This country manor is situated on 10 acres shaded by giant oaks and maples. Early American and English antiques fill the spacious guest rooms. There is a piano room with shelves of books, and a clock collection is featured throughout. The inn's dinners have received excellent reviews and feature herbs, vegetables and berries from the garden. Guests may cross the street for tennis and golf at the country club.

Breakfast and afternoon tea included in rates. Types of meals: full breakfast and early coffee/tea. MAP. Air conditioning in room. Fax, copier, swimming and library on premises. 10 acres. Weddings, small meetings, family reunions and seminars hosted. Antiques, parks, shopping, downhill skiing, cross-country skiing, theater and watersports nearby.

Publicity: *Los Angeles Times, Boulevard, Redbook, Country Inns, Countryside, Road Best Traveled, Discerning Traveler.*

Special Discounts: By special arrangement.

"Every creative comfort imaginable, great for heart, soul and stomach."

Greenfield C6

The Brandt House

29 Highland Ave
Greenfield, MA 01301-3605
(413)774-3329 (800)235-3329
Fax:(413)772-2908
E-mail: brandt@crocker.com

Rates: $90-165.
Payment: MC VISA AX DS TC.
Innkeeper(s): Phoebe Compton.
Circa: 1890.

Rooms: 8 rooms, 6 with PB, 2 with FP. 1 suite. 1 conference room.
Beds: KQT.

Three-and-a-half-acre lawns surround this impressive three-story Colonial Revival house, situated hilltop. The library and pool room are popular for lounging. A full breakfast often includes homemade scones. There is a clay tennis court, nature trails, badminton, horseshoes and in winter, lighted ice skating at a nearby pond. Historic Deerfield is within five minutes.

Breakfast included in rates. Types of meals: continental-plus breakfast, full breakfast and early coffee/tea. Gourmet lunch available. Air conditioning, ceiling fan and cable TV in room. VCR, fax, copier, tennis and library on premises. Weddings, small meetings, family reunions and seminars hosted. Antiques, fishing, parks, shopping, downhill skiing, cross-country skiing, sporting events, theater and watersports nearby. TAC10.

Pets Allowed: Call for approval.

Special Discounts: Extend your weekend-book Friday and Saturday and get Thursday or Sunday at 50%.

"Ensconced deep in a featherbed under mounds of snow eiderdown, surrounded by a rich tapestry of childhood yesteryear, is like a foretaste of heaven."

Hamilton C14

Miles River Country Inn

823 Bay Rd, Box 149
Hamilton, MA 01936
(508)468-7206
Fax:(508)468-3999

Rates: $84-155.
Payment: MC VISA AX PC TC.
Innkeeper(s): Gretel & Peter Clark.
Circa: 1789.

Rooms: 8 rooms, 5 with PB, 4 with FP. 1 suite. 2 conference rooms.
Beds: QDT.

This rambling colonial inn sits on more than 30 acres of magnificent curving lawns bordered by trees and formal gardens that lead to the Miles River. There are meadows, woodlands and wetlands surrounding the property and available for exploring. The river flows through the property, which is a haven for a wide variety of wildlife. Many of the inn's 12 fireplaces are in the guest rooms. Family heirloom antiques compliment the interior.

Breakfast and afternoon tea included in rates. Types of meals: full breakfast and early coffee/tea. Cable TV, VCR, fax, copier, bicycles and library on premises. 30 acres. Weddings, small meetings, family reunions and seminars hosted. Spanish, French and German spoken. Antiques, fishing, parks, shopping, downhill skiing, cross-country skiing, sporting events, theater and watersports nearby.

Publicity: *Boston Globe, Beverly Times, Salem Evening News.*

Harwich Port I18

MA

Augustus Snow House

528 Main St
Harwich Port, MA 02646
(508)430-0528 (800)320-0528
Fax:(508)432-7995

Rates: $105-160.
Payment: MC VISA AX DS PC TC.
Innkeeper(s): Joyce & Steve Roth.
Circa: 1901.

Rooms: 5 rooms with PB, 1 with FP.
Beds: KQ.

This gracious, Queen Anne Victorian is a turn-of-the-century gem, complete with a wide, wraparound veranda, gabled windows and a distinctive turret. Victorian wallpapers, stained glass and rich woodwork complement the interior, which is appropriately decorated in period style. Each of the romantic guest quarters offers something special. One room has a canopy bed and a fireplace, while another includes a relaxing claw-foot tub. Three rooms have Jacuzzi tubs. The king-size beds are dressed in fine linens. As is the Victorian way, afternoon refreshments are served each day. The breakfasts include delectables, such as banana chip muffins, baked pears in raspberry cream sauce or, possibly, baked French toast with layers of homemade cinnamon bread, bacon and cheese.

Breakfast included in rates. Types of meals: gourmet breakfast and early coffee/tea. Afternoon tea available. Air conditioning, ceiling fan and cable TV in room. Fax and copier on premises. Weddings, small meetings and family reunions hosted. Antiques, fishing, parks, shopping and watersports nearby.

Special Discounts: Mid week: Stay three nights, third night free. Stay two nights, second night half off. (Oct. 1-Memorial Day)

"Being able to walk to the beach early in the morning before breakfast was the perfect start to our stay. Breakfast was more than we ever thought we could eat."

Dunscroft By The Sea Inn & Cottage

24 Pilgrim Rd
Harwich Port, MA 02646
(508)432-0810 (800)432-4345
Fax:(508)432-5134

Rates: $95-225. MAP.
Payment: MC VISA AX PC.
Innkeeper(s): Alyce & Wally Cunningham.
Circa: 1920.

Rooms: 9 rooms with PB, 2 with FP. 1 suite. 1 cottage. 1 conference room.
Beds: KQ.

This gambrel-roofed house sits behind a split-rail fence at the end of a winding brick driveway. Inside the handsome columned entrance is an extensive library and a living room with a piano. Best of all are the candlelit bed chambers with turned-down bed and the music of ocean waves rolling onto the private beach on Nantucket Sound, 300 feet from the inn.

Breakfast included in rates. Types of meals: full breakfast and gourmet breakfast. Catering service available. MAP. Air conditioning, turn-down service, ceiling fan and cable TV in room. Fax, copier, swimming, tennis and library on premises. Handicap access. Weddings, small meetings, family reunions and seminars hosted. Amusement parks, antiques, fishing, parks, shopping, cross-country skiing, sporting events, theater and watersports nearby. TAC10.

Location: One-and-a-half hours from Providence, R.I., and Boston on Cape Cod.

Publicity: *Cape Codder.*

"A quaint and delightful slice of New England. Your generous hospitality is greatly appreciated. Your place is beautiful."

Harbor Breeze

326 Lower County Rd
Harwich Port, MA 02646
(508)432-0337 (800)272-4343
Fax:(508)432-1276
E-mail: dvangeld@capecod.net

Rates: $75-120.
Payment: MC VISA AX DS PC TC.
Innkeeper(s): Kathleen & David Van Gelder.
Circa: 1945.

Rooms: 9 rooms with PB, 1 with FP. 1 suite.
Beds: KQT.

Ideally located across the street from picturesque Allens Harbor and only a short walk from the Brooks Road beach, this inn is a classic Cape Cod home. A rambling connection of cedar shake additions, nestled in an attractive pine setting, surround a garden courtyard to form a guest wing. Flowered walkways lead to nine guest rooms, which are furnished in wicker, woods and country floral. There are restful sitting areas amid the pines and a swimming pool where you can enjoy the ocean breezes. A short walk down a shady tree-lined street brings you to a sandy beach on Nantucket Sound.

Breakfast included in rates. Types of meals: continental-plus breakfast and early coffee/tea. Cable TV in room. Fax and swimming on premises. Family reunions hosted. Antiques, fishing, parks, shopping, theater and watersports nearby. TAC10.

Special Discounts: Midweek/off season-two nights for $99.

Holyoke F6

Yankee Pedlar Inn

1866 Northampton St
Holyoke, MA 01040-1921
(413)532-9494
Fax:(413)536-8877

Rates: $60-115.
Payment: MC VISA AX DC TC.
Innkeeper(s): The Clayton Family.
Circa: 1875.

Rooms: 30 rooms with PB. 12 suites.
Beds: KQT.

Five buildings comprise this Pioneer Valley inn, located in western Massachusetts. In addition to the inn's restaurant, the Oyster Bar & Grill Room, there are seven banquet facilities and a lounge where guests can enjoy lighter fare and live entertainment. Each of the guest rooms has been redecorated recently with fine antiques, rich draperies and new carpeting. Museums, shopping and the volleyball and basketball halls of fame are among the many nearby attractions.

Breakfast included in rates. Types of meals: continental breakfast and early coffee/tea. Dinner, lunch, gourmet lunch, banquet service and catering service available. Air conditioning and cable TV in room. VCR, fax and copier on premises. Handicap access. Weddings, small meetings, family reunions and seminars hosted. Amusement parks, antiques, fishing, parks, shopping, downhill skiing, cross-country skiing, sporting events, theater and watersports nearby. TAC10.

Hyannis Port I17

The Simmons Homestead Inn

288 Scudder Ave
Hyannis Port, MA 02647
(508)778-4999 (800)637-1649
Fax:(508)790-1342

Rates: $80-160.
Payment: MC VISA AX DS TC.
Innkeeper(s): Bill Putman.
Circa: 1820.

Rooms: 10 rooms with PB.
Beds: KQT.

This former sea captain's home features period decor and includes huge needlepoint displays and lifelike ceramic and papiermache animals that give the inn a country feel. Some rooms boast canopy beds and each is individually decorated. Traditional full breakfasts are served in the formal dining room. Evening wine helps guests relax after a day of touring the Cape. There is a billiard room on the premises.

Breakfast included in rates. Type of meal: full breakfast. Ceiling fan in room. Cable TV, fax, copier and bicycles on premises. Small meetings and family reunions hosted. Antiques, fishing, parks, shopping and watersports nearby. TAC10.

Location: In heart of Cape Cod.

Publicity: *Bon Appetit, Cape Code Life, Yankee.*

"I want to say that part of what makes Cape Cod special for us is the inn. It embodies much of what is wonderful at the Cape. By Sunday, I was completely rested, relaxed, renewed, and restored."

MA

Lee E2

Applegate

279 W Park St
Lee, MA 01238-1718
(413)243-4451 (800)691-9012
Fax:(413)243-4451

Rates: $85-225.
Payment: MC VISA PC TC.
Innkeeper(s): Richard & Nancy Begbie-Cannata.
Circa: 1920.

Rooms: 6 rooms with PB, 2 with FP. 1 cottage.
Beds: KQD.

This romantic bed & breakfast is an ideal accommodation for those visiting the Berkshires. Well-dressed, four-poster beds rest atop polished wood floors. Gracious furnishings, Oriental rugs and soft lighting add to the ambiance. Two guest rooms offer fireplaces, and several offer views of woods or gardens. Fresh flowers, brandy and Godiva chocolates are just a few extras that await guests. In the early evening, wine and cheese is served. Breakfasts are served by candlelight, with crystal stemware and antique china.

Breakfast included in rates. Type of meal: continental-plus breakfast. Air conditioning in room. Cable TV, VCR, fax, copier, swimming, bicycles and library on premises. Weddings, small meetings, family reunions and seminars hosted. Antiques, parks, shopping, downhill skiing, cross-country skiing, theater and watersports nearby.

Special Discounts: Winter/spring - two-night packages; 10% off stays of 7 nights or more; wine tasting and dinner weekends.

"The house is decorated beautifully—cozy dolls decorate all the little nooks and crannies."

Devonfield

85 Stockbridge Rd
Lee, MA 01238-9308
(413)243-3298 (800)664-0880
Fax:(413)243-1360

Rates: $70-260.
Payment: MC VISA AX DS PC TC.
Innkeeper(s): Sally & Ben Schenck.
Circa: 1800.

Rooms: 10 rooms with PB, 4 with FP. 4 suites. 1 cottage.
Beds: KQT.

The original section of this Colonial inn was built by a Revolutionary War soldier. Guest rooms are spacious with charming furniture and patterned wallcoverings. Three of the rooms feature fireplaces. The one-bedroom cottage features both a fireplace and an efficiency kitchen. Guests are treated to a light breakfast of juices, cereals and fresh baked goods. Midnight snacks are available in the guest pantry. One need not wander far from the grounds to find something to do. The innkeepers offer a tennis court, swimming pool and bicycles for guests, and a nine-hole golf course is just across the way. Inside, guests can relax in the living room with its fireplace and library or in the television room. The area is full of boutiques, antique shops and galleries to explore, as well as hiking, fishing and skiing.

Air conditioning in room. Cable TV, fax, copier, swimming, bicycles, tennis and library on premises. 40 acres. TAC10.

Publicity: *Discerning Traveler.*

"A special thank you for your warm and kind hospitality. We feel as though this is our home away from home."

Lenox

E2

Birchwood Inn

7 Hubbard St, Box 2020
Lenox, MA 01240-2329
(413)637-2600 (800)524-1646
Fax:(413)637-2600

Rates: $60-199.
Payment: MC VISA AX DC CB DS.
Innkeeper(s): Joan, Dick & Dan Toner.
Circa: 1767.

Rooms: 12 rooms, 10 with PB, 6 with FP. 2 suites. 1 conference room.
Beds: KQDT.

This inn, which is the only privately owned Lenox building listed in the National Register, is situated on a hilltop and overlooks the village. The gardens and lawns are surrounded by old New England stone fences. Guests can enjoy the wood burning fireplaces and large library. Full international breakfasts are changed daily and include items such as Eggs Benedict, huevos rancheros, omelets and New England pancakes. For a small fee, the innkeepers can arrange for guests to use a local health club, which includes tennis courts and a swimming pool.

Breakfast included in rates. Types of meals: full breakfast and early coffee/tea. Evening snack available. Ceiling fan and cable TV in room. VCR on premises. Small meetings, family reunions and seminars hosted. Antiques, fishing, shopping, downhill skiing, cross-country skiing, theater and watersports nearby.

Pets Allowed.

Location: Berkshires.

"Inn-credible! Inn-viting! Inn-spiring! Inn-comparable! Our ultimate getaway. Wonderful ambiance, great food and the finest hosts we ever met."

Blantyre

16 Blantyre Rd, PO Box 995
Lenox, MA 01240
(413)637-3556
Fax:(413)637-4282

Rates: $225-585.
Payment: MC VISA AX DC DS.
Innkeeper(s): Roderick Anderson.
Circa: 1902.

Rooms: 23 rooms, 7 with FP. 5 suites. 1 conference room.
Beds: KQDT.

Situated on manicured lawns near Tanglewood, this Tudor manor is entered through a massive portico. Grandly-sized rooms include the Great Hall and an elegantly paneled dining room. Breakfast is graciously served in the conservatory. Formal grounds offer four tennis courts, two championship croquet courts, a pool and carriage house.

Types of meals: continental breakfast, full breakfast and gourmet breakfast. Dinner, picnic lunch, lunch and room service available. Fax, copier, spa and sauna on premises. Antiques, fishing, theater and watersports nearby.

Publicity: *Hideaway Report, Country Inns, Conde Nast Traveler.*

"There was not a single aspect of our stay with you that was not worked out to total perfection."

Brook Farm Inn

15 Hawthorne St
Lenox, MA 01240-2404
(413)637-3013 (800)285-7638
Fax:(413)637-4751

Rates: $75-185.
Payment: MC VISA DS PC TC.
Innkeeper(s): Joe & Anne Miller.
Circa: 1870.

Rooms: 12 rooms with PB, 6 with FP.
Beds: KQDT.

Brook Farm Inn is named after the original Brook Farm, a literary commune that sought to combine thinker and worker through a society of intelligent, cultivated members. In keeping with that theme, this gracious Victorian inn offers poetry and writing seminars and has a 650-volume poetry library. Canopy beds, Mozart and a swimming pool tend to the spirit.

Breakfast and afternoon tea included in rates. Types of meals: full breakfast and early coffee/tea. Air conditioning and ceiling fan in room. Fax, copier and swimming on premises. Family reunions hosted. Antiques, fishing, parks, shopping, downhill skiing, cross-country skiing, sporting events, theater and watersports nearby.

Location: In the heart of Berkshire County.

Publicity: *Berkshire Eagle, Country Inns, Travel & Leisure, Boston.*

"We've been traveling all our lives and never have we felt more at home."

The Gables Inn

81 Walker St, Rt 183
Lenox, MA 01240-2719
(413)637-3416 (800)382-9401

Rates: $80-195.
Payment: MC VISA DS PC TC.
Innkeeper(s): Mary & Frank Newton.
Circa: 1885.

Rooms: 18 rooms with PB, 15 with FP. 3 suites.
Beds: Q.

At one time, this was the home of Pulitzer Prize-winning novelist, Edith Wharton. The Queen Anne-style Berkshire cottage features a handsome eight-sided library and Mrs. Wharton's own four-poster bed. An unusual indoor swimming pool with spa is available in warm weather.

Breakfast included in rates. Air conditioning, cable TV and VCR in room. Fax, swimming and tennis on premises. Family reunions hosted. Antiques, fishing, parks, shopping, downhill skiing, cross-country skiing, sporting events, theater and watersports nearby.

Location: Within walking distance to Tanglewood, summer home of the Boston Symphony Orchestra.

Publicity: *P.M. Magazine, New York Times.*

"You made us feel like old friends and that good feeling enhanced our pleasure. In essence it was the best part of our trip."

MA

Garden Gables Inn

PO Box 52
Lenox, MA 01240-0052
(413)637-0193
Fax:(413)637-4554
E-mail: gardeninn@aol.com

Rates: $80-250.
Payment: MC VISA AX DS PC TC.
Innkeeper(s): Mario & Lynn Mekinda.
Circa: 1780.

Rooms: 18 rooms with PB, 8 with FP. 2 suites. 4 cottages.
Beds: KQFT.

Several distinctive gables adorn this home set on five wooded acres. Deer occasionally wander into the garden to help themselves to fallen apples. Breakfast is served in the dining room, which overlooks tall maples, flower gardens and fruit trees. The swimming pool was the first built in the county, and is still the longest. Guests will find many special amenities including in-room phones, fireplaces and whirlpool tubs. There is Baby Grand Steinway Piano in the living room.

Breakfast and afternoon tea included in rates. Types of meals: full breakfast and early coffee/tea. Air conditioning and cable TV in room. VCR, fax, computer and swimming on premises. Weddings, small meetings, family reunions and seminars hosted. French and German spoken. Antiques, fishing, parks, shopping, downhill skiing, cross-country skiing, theater and watersports nearby.

Location: In the Berkshires.

Publicity: *National Geographic Traveler, Berkshire Eagle, Los Angeles Times, Long Island News.*

"Charming and thoughtful hospitality. You restored a portion of my sanity and I'm very grateful" —Miami Herald.

The Kemble Inn

2 Kemble St
Lenox, MA 01240-2813
(413)637-4113 (800)353-4113

Rates: $75-295.
Payment: MC VISA DC CB DS PC TC.
Innkeeper(s): J. Richard & Linda Reardon.
Circa: 1881.

Rooms: 15 rooms with PB, 6 with FP.

Named for a famous 19th-century actress, Fanny Kemble, this three-story Georgian-style inn boasts an incredible view of the Berkshires. The inn's 12 luxurious guest rooms are named for American authors, including Nathaniel Hawthorne, Henry Wadsworth Longfellow, Herman Melville, Mark Twain and Edith Wharton. The impressive Fanny Kemble Room, which boasts mountain views, includes two fireplaces, a Jacuzzi tub and a king-size, four-poster bed. The inn is within minutes of five major ski areas, and Tanglewood is less than two miles away.

Breakfast included in rates. Type of meal: continental breakfast. Air conditioning and cable TV in room. Handicap access. Antiques, fishing, parks, shopping, downhill skiing, cross-country skiing, theater and watersports nearby.

Publicity: *Country Inns.*

Special Discounts: Two night special packages available Nov. 1-April.

"Kemble Inn was a showcase B&B - just what we had hoped for."

Lilac Inn

PO Box 2294
Lenox, MA 01240-5294
(413)637-2172
Fax:(413)637-2172
E-mail: aliceatlilacinn@msn.com

Rates: $130-195.
Payment: PC.
Innkeeper(s): Alice Maleski.
Circa: 1895.

Rooms: 3 rooms with PB. 2 suites.
Beds: KQT.

Aptly named for a flower, this Victorian inn features guest rooms that appear much like a garden. Flowery prints, wicker furnishings and views of Lilac Park enhance this cheerful atmosphere. Guests are treated to afternoon refreshments, with a proper mix of savory and sweet tidbits. Breakfasts are bountiful and delicious, yet surprisingly healthy with low-fat, vegetarian versions of treats such as banana nut bread, French toast, and vegetable quiche. The library is stocked with books and the living room, which has a fireplace, is a good place to curl up and relax.

Breakfast and afternoon tea included in rates. Types of meals: gourmet breakfast and early coffee/tea. Turn-down service and ceiling fan in room. Cable TV, VCR, fax, copier and library on premises. Small meetings and family reunions hosted. French, Hebrew and Lithuanian spoken. Antiques, fishing, parks, shopping, downhill skiing, cross-country skiing, theater and watersports nearby.

Special Discounts: Week-long packages, including Friday, Saturday and five days, $775-$975.

"We are really looking forward to shamelessly overindulging in your breakfasts, and being carried away by the music, the time and the place."

Rookwood Inn

11 Old Stockbridge Rd
PO Box 1717
Lenox, MA 01240-2415
(413)637-9750 (800)223-9750

Rates: $80-275.
Payment: MC VISA AX PC.
Innkeeper(s): Amy & Stephen Lindner-Lesser.
Circa: 1885.

Rooms: 21 rooms with PB, 8 with FP. 2 suites. 2 conference rooms.
Beds: KQTD.

This turn-of-the-century Queen Anne Victorian inn offers 21 elegant guest rooms, including two suites. Among the amenities in the air-conditioned guest rooms are ceiling fans and fireplaces. The inn's size makes it perfect for small meetings, reunions and weddings. The beautiful Berkshires are famous for cultural and recreational opportunities, including the Chesterwood Museum, cross-country and downhill skiing, fishing, Jacob's Pillow Dance Festival, the Mount, the Norman Rockwell Museum and numerous other performing arts attractions.

Breakfast and afternoon tea included in rates. Type of meal: full breakfast. Air conditioning and ceiling fan in room. Cable TV, library and child care on premises. Handicap access. Weddings, small meetings, family reunions and seminars hosted. Antiques, fishing, parks, shopping, downhill skiing, cross-country skiing, theater and watersports nearby. TAC5.

Location: One-half block from town center. Walk to shops and dining.

Publicity: *New York Times, Boston Globe, London Times.*

Summer Hill Farm

950 East St
Lenox, MA 01240-2205
(413)442-2059 (800)442-2059

Rates: $55-150.
Payment: MC VISA AX PC.
Innkeeper(s): Sonya & Michael Wessel.
Circa: 1840.

Rooms: 7 rooms with PB, 2 with FP. 1 cottage.
Beds: KQDT.

Situated on a scenic 19 acres, this Colonial home was once part of a 300-acre farm deeded to the Steven family just after the French & Indian War. Several rooms include fireplaces or brass beds. The Loft and Mountain View rooms both offer views. The Cottage, an old hay barn, includes a bedroom as well as sitting, dining and cooking areas. Fresh fruit, homemade granola, and home-baked bread accompany the morning's special breakfast entree. After a hearty breakfast, guests should have no trouble finding something to do. Arts and sports activities are nearby, as are museums, Hancock Shaker Village, antique shops, Tanglewood and many other cultural attractions.

Breakfast included in rates. Type of meal: full breakfast. Air conditioning and cable TV in room. VCR, stables and library on premises. 19 acres. Family reunions hosted. Limited French and limited Spanish spoken. Antiques, fishing, parks, downhill skiing, cross-country skiing, sporting events, theater and watersports nearby. TAC10.

Special Discounts: Up to 15% for midweek, further 18% for whole week.

"You and your home are wonderfully charming."

Walker House

64 Walker St
Lenox, MA 01240-2718
(413)637-1271 (800)235-3098
Fax:(413)637-2387

Rates: $60-180.
Payment: PC.
Innkeeper(s): Peggy & Richard Houdek.
Circa: 1804.

Rooms: 8 rooms with PB, 5 with FP. 1 conference room.
Beds: QDT.

MA

This beautiful Federal-style house sits in the center of the village on three acres of graceful woods and restored gardens. Guest rooms have fireplaces and private baths. Each is named for a favorite composer such as Beethoven, Mozart, or Handel. The innkeepers' musical backgrounds include associations with the San Francisco Opera, the New York City Opera, and the Los Angeles Philharmonic. Walker House concerts are scheduled from time to time. The innkeepers offer film and opera screenings nightly on a seven-foot screen. With prior approval, some pets may be allowed.

Breakfast and afternoon tea included in rates. Types of meals: continental-plus breakfast and early coffee/tea. Air conditioning in room. Cable TV, VCR, fax, copier and library on premises. Handicap access. Weddings, small meetings and family reunions hosted. French and Spanish spoken. Antiques, fishing, parks, shopping, downhill skiing, cross-country skiing, theater and watersports nearby.

Pets Allowed: With prior approval.

Location: Route 183 & 7A.

Publicity: *Boston Globe, PBS, Los Angeles Times, New York Times.*

Special Discounts: 10% off single occupancy off season.

"We had a grand time staying with fellow music and opera lovers! Breakfasts were lovely."

Whistler's Inn

5 Greenwood St
Lenox, MA 01240-2029
(413)637-0975
Fax:(413)637-2190

Rates: $70-200.
Payment: MC VISA AX DS PC TC.
Innkeeper(s): Richard & Joan Mears.
Circa: 1820.

Rooms: 12 rooms with PB, 2 with FP. 3 conference rooms.
Beds: KQDT.

Whistler's Inn is an English Tudor home surrounded by eight acres of woodlands and gardens. Inside, elegance is abundant. In the impressive Louis XVI music room you'll find a Steinway piano, chandeliers, and gilt palace furniture. There is an English library with chintz-covered sofas, hundreds of volumes of books, and a fireplace of black marble. Here, guests have sherry or tea and perhaps engage in conversation with their well-traveled hosts, both authors. A baronial dining room features a Baroque candelabrum.

Breakfast included in rates. Types of meals: full breakfast and gourmet breakfast. Afternoon tea available. Air conditioning and ceiling fan in room. Cable TV, VCR, fax, copier and library on premises. Weddings, small meetings, family reunions and seminars hosted. Antiques, fishing, parks, shopping, downhill skiing, cross-country skiing, theater and watersports nearby. TAC10.

Publicity: *Berkshire Book.*

Leverett — D6

Hannah Dudley House Inn

114 Dudleyville Rd
Leverett, MA 01054-9713
(413)367-2323

Rates: $125-185.
Payment: MC VISA PC TC.
Innkeeper(s): Erni & Daryl Johnson.
Circa: 1797.

Rooms: 4 rooms with PB, 2 with FP. 1 suite.
Beds: QD.

Each season brings with it a new reason to visit this 18th-century Colonial, which is named for a member of the first family to inhabit this home. In autumn, the home's 110 acres explode in color. In winter, snowcapped pines adds to the festive atmosphere, and guests snuggle up in front of a roaring fire. Two guest rooms include fireplaces, and the house offers four others. The guest room refrigerators are always stocked with drinks. At certain times of the year, dinner specials are available. During warm months, guests enjoy use of a barbecue grill and swimming pool. Stroll the grounds and you'll find plenty of wildlife, including two ponds inhabited by ducks, goldfish, trout and bullfrogs. During the winter months, the pond transforms into the inn's skating rink.

Breakfast and evening snack included in rates. Types of meals: full breakfast and early coffee/tea. Dinner available. Turn-down service in room. Swimming and library on premises. 110 acres. Weddings, small meetings, family reunions and seminars hosted. Antiques, fishing, parks, shopping, downhill skiing, cross-country skiing, sporting events and theater nearby.

Special Discounts: Occasional specials, business rates, please inquire.

Lynn D14

Diamond District Breakfast Inn

142 Ocean St
Lynn, MA 01902-2007
(617)599-4470 (800)666-3076
Fax:(617)595-2200

Rates: $76-150.
Payment: MC VISA AX DC CB DS PC TC.
Innkeeper(s): Sandra & Jerry Caron.
Circa: 1911.

Rooms: 8 rooms, 4 with PB. 1 conference room.
Beds: QDT.

This 17-room Georgian house was built for shoe manufacturer P.J. Harney-Lynn. The Charles Pinkham family (son of Lydia Pinkham, a health tonic producer) later purchased it. Many of the original fixtures remain, and the inn is suitably furnished with Oriental rugs and antiques. The parlor features a collection of antique musical instruments. There are several views of the ocean from the house, but the porch is the most popular spot for sea gazing. Breakfast is served in the dining room or on the porch. Fresh fruits, homemade breads and hot coffee, tea or cider start off the meal, followed by a special entree.

Breakfast included in rates. Type of meal: full breakfast. Air conditioning and ceiling fan in room. Fax, copier and computer on premises. Small meetings hosted. Russian spoken. Antiques, fishing, cross-country skiing and watersports nearby. TAC10.

Pets Allowed: Small dogs prior arrangement.

"The room was spectacular and breakfast was served beautifully. Bed and breakfast were both outstanding! Thanks so much for your hospitality."

Marblehead D14

Brimblecomb Hill

33 Mechanic St
Marblehead, MA 01945
(617)631-3172

Rates: $60-80.
Payment: MC VISA.
Innkeeper(s): Gene Arnould.
Circa: 1721.

Rooms: 3 rooms, 1 with PB.
Beds: QD.

This gracious pre-Revolutionary War Colonial home is fun place to soak in New England's history and charm. The home was host to a variety tradesman including a cooper and a wigmaker, not to mention a friend of Benjamin Franklin. The bed & breakfast is only about 20 miles from Boston and the town of Marblehead offers many fine galleries, shops and restaurants, and of course, Marblehead Harbor.

Breakfast included in rates. Types of meals: continental breakfast and continental-plus breakfast. Air conditioning in room. Antiques, fishing, theater and watersports nearby.

"Thank you for such wonderful hospitality. We really enjoyed our stay & loved the B&B atmosphere! We will definitely plan a trip back!"

The Guest House at Lavender Gate

1 Summer St
Marblehead, MA 01945
(617)639-0400

Rates: $85-100.
Payment: MC VISA PC TC.
Innkeeper(s): Nash Robbins & Cate Olson.
Circa: 1714.

Rooms: 2 rooms with PB.
Beds: QDT.

There's no need to bring along a book to this Colonial inn. The Much Ado Bookstore, located on the premises, offers more than 35,000 used and rare books. Booklovers are sure to enjoy the literary connections. The gardens are filled with flowers and plants highlighted in Shakespearean plays, and the innkeepers have a variety of authors' portraits and autographs decorating the walls. The two suites are decorated with a flair for the British, and there are plenty of British magazines and newspapers on hand. The early, 18th-century home is located in a Marblehead historic district.

Breakfast and evening snack included in rates. Type of meal: continental-plus breakfast. Air conditioning in room. Weddings, small meetings and seminars hosted. French and German spoken. Antiques, fishing, parks, shopping, theater and watersports nearby.

Special Discounts: 10% off 7 days or more rate.

Harborside House B&B

23 Gregory St
Marblehead, MA 01945
(617)631-1032
E-mail: swliving@shore.net

Rates: $65-85.
Payment: PC TC.
Innkeeper(s): Susan Livingston.
Circa: 1840.

Rooms: 2 rooms.
Beds: DT.

Enjoy the Colonial charm of this home, which overlooks Marblehead Harbor on Boston's historic North Shore. Rooms are decorated with antiques and period wallpaper. A third-story sundeck offers excellent views. A generous continental breakfast of home-baked breads, muffins and fresh fruit is served each morning in the well-decorated dining room or on the open porch. The village of Marblehead provides many shops and restaurants. Boston and Logan airport are 30 minutes away.

Breakfast, afternoon tea and evening snack included in rates. Type of meal: continental-plus breakfast. Bicycles on premises. Antiques, parks, shopping and watersports nearby. TAC10.

Publicity: *Marblehead Reporter.*

Special Discounts: One night free with six night booking.

"Harborside Inn is restful, charming, with a beautiful view of the water. I wish we didn't have to leave."

Martha's Vineyard K16

Captain Dexter House of Edgartown

35 Pease's Point Way,
Box 2798
Martha's Vineyard, MA 02539
(508)693-6564
Fax:(508)693-8448

Rates: $85-175.
Payment: MC VISA AX PC TC.
Innkeeper(s): Rick Fenstemaker.
Circa: 1843.

Rooms: 8 rooms with PB, 2 with FP. 1 suite.
Beds: QD.

Located just three blocks from Edgartown's harbor and historic district, this black-shuttered sea merchant's house has a graceful lawn and terraced flower gardens. A gentle Colonial atmosphere is enhanced by original wooden beams, exposed floorboards, working fireplaces, old-fashioned dormers and a collection of period antiques. Luxurious canopy beds are featured, and some rooms include fireplaces.

Breakfast included in rates. Type of meal: continental-plus breakfast. Afternoon tea available. Air conditioning and ceiling fan in room. Fax on premises. Weddings, small meetings, family reunions and seminars hosted. Antiques, fishing, parks, theater and watersports nearby. TAC10.

Location: On a tree-lined residential street in downtown Edgartown on the island of Martha's Vineyard.

Publicity: *Island Getaways, Vineyard Gazette, Martha's Vineyard Times, Cape Cod Life.*

"Since we were on our honeymoon, we were hoping for a quiet, relaxing stay, and the Captain Dexter House was perfect!"

Captain Dexter House of Vineyard Haven

100 Main St, PO Box 2457
Martha's Vineyard, MA
02568
(508)627-7289
Fax:(508)627-3382

Rates: $95-195.
Payment: MC VISA AX PC TC.
Innkeeper(s): Rick Fenstemaker.
Circa: 1840.

Rooms: 11 rooms with PB, 4 with FP.
Beds: QD.

Captain Dexter House was the home of sea captain Rodolphus Dexter. Authentic 18th-century antiques and reproductions are among the inn's appointments. There are Count Rumford fireplaces and hand-stencilled walls in several rooms. Located on a street of historic homes, the inn is a short stroll to the beach, town and harbor. The innkeepers offer an evening aperitif and in the summer, lemonade is served.

Breakfast included in rates. Type of meal: continental-plus breakfast. Afternoon tea available. Air conditioning and ceiling fan in room. Fax on premises. Weddings, small meetings, family reunions and seminars hosted. Antiques, fishing, parks, shopping, theater and watersports nearby. TAC10.

Location: Martha's Vineyard.

Publicity: *Martha's Vineyard Times, Cape Cod Life.*

"The house is sensational. Your hospitality was all one could expect. You've made us permanent bed & breakfast fans."

Nancy's Auberge

102 Main St, PO Box 4433
Martha's Vineyard, MA 02568
(508)693-4434

Rates: $68-108.
Payment: MC VISA.
Innkeeper(s): Nancy Hurd.
Circa: 1840.
Rooms: 3 rooms.

This 1840 Greek Revival home affords harbor views from its spot in a historic neighborhood once home to early settlers and whaling captains. Three of the antique-filled rooms include fireplaces, and one of the bedchambers boasts a harbor view. The inn is just a few blocks from the local ferry. Bicycle paths and beaches are nearby, as well as restaurants and a variety of shops.

Breakfast included in rates. Type of meal: continental-plus breakfast. VCR on premises. Family reunions hosted. Antiques, shopping and theater nearby.

MA

Thorncroft Inn

278 Main St, PO Box 1022
Martha's Vineyard, MA 02568
(508)693-3333 (800)332-1236
Fax:(508)639-3333

Rates: $129-349.
Payment: MC VISA AX DC CB DS.
Innkeeper(s): Karl & Lynn Buder.
Circa: 1918.
Rooms: 13 rooms with PB, 9 with FP. 1 suite.
Beds: QD.

The Thorncroft Estate is a classic craftsman bungalow with a dominant roof and neo-colonial details. It was built by Chicago grain merchant John Herbert Ware as the guest house of a large oceanfront estate. Most guest rooms include working fireplaces and canopied beds. Some also boast two-person whirlpool tubs or private 300-gallon hot tubs. The inn is situated on three-and-one-half acres of lawns and woodlands. Full breakfasts and afternoon teas are served in the dining rooms, but guests can opt for a continental breakfast served in their room.

Breakfast and afternoon tea included in rates. Types of meals: full breakfast and gourmet breakfast. Room service available. Fax, copier and spa on premises. Antiques, fishing, theater and watersports nearby.

Location: Martha's Vineyard Island.

Publicity: *Cape Cod Life, New England Travel, Glamour.*

"It's the type of place where we find ourselves falling in love all over again."

❑ **See the map for more inns in the Martha's Vineyard area.**

Middleboro H14

On Cranberry Pond B&B

43 Fuller St
Middleboro, MA 02346
(508)946-0768
Fax:(508)947-8221
E-mail: ocpbandb@aol.com

Rates: $65-125.
Payment: MC VISA AX DC CB PC TC.
Innkeeper(s): Jeannine LaBossiere & Tim Dombrowski.
Circa: 1989.
Rooms: 6 rooms, 3 with PB, 2 with FP. 2 suites. 1 conference room.
Beds: QDT.

Nestled in the historic "cranberry capital of the world," this modern farmhouse rests on a working berry bog by the shores of its namesake tarn. There are two miles of trails to meander, and during berry picking season, guests can watch as buckets of the fruit are collected. The rooms are decorated with knickknacks and flowers, the Master Suite includes a working fireplace. Innkeeper Jeannine LaBossiere creates the breakfasts, which begin with fresh coffee, muffins, cookies and scones.

Breakfast and evening snack included in rates. Types of meals: full breakfast, gourmet breakfast and early coffee/tea. Afternoon tea and banquet service available. Air conditioning, turn-down service, ceiling fan, cable TV and VCR in room. Fax, copier, stables, bicycles, library and pet boarding on premises. Weddings, small meetings, family reunions and seminars hosted. Amusement parks, antiques, fishing, parks, shopping, downhill skiing, theater and watersports nearby. TAC10.

Pets Allowed: Must stay in crate all night. Guests are totally responsible for all damages.

Special Discounts: Weekend getaways two nights between $150-$300.

"Your dedication to making your guests comfortable is above and beyond. You are tops in your field."

Nantucket

L18

The Carlisle House Inn

26 N Water St
Nantucket, MA 02554-3548
(508)228-0720
Fax:(508)228-6074

Rates: $60-175.
Payment: MC VISA AX PC TC.
Innkeeper(s): Peter Conway.
Circa: 1765.

Rooms: 14 rooms, 10 with PB, 4 with FP.
Beds: KQDT.

For more than 100 years, the Carlisle House has served as a notable Nantucket lodging establishment. Three floors of picture-perfect rooms provide accommodations from the simple to the deluxe. Hand stenciling, polished wide-board floors, handsome color schemes and carpets fill each room. Special candelight dinners are occasionally served at a harvest table in the kitchen. The ferry is a five-minute walk.

Breakfast and afternoon tea included in rates. Type of meal: continental-plus breakfast. Air conditioning, ceiling fan and cable TV in room. Fax, copier and library on premises. Weddings, small meetings, family reunions and seminars hosted. Antiques, shopping, theater and watersports nearby.

Publicity: *Cape Cod Life, Boston Globe, Los Angeles Times.*

"Outstanding hospitality."

Corner House

49 Center St, PO Box 1828
Nantucket, MA 02554-3666
(508)228-1530
E-mail: cornerhs@nantucket.net

Rates: $65-185. AP.
Payment: MC VISA TC.
Innkeeper(s): John & Sandy Knox-Johnston.
Circa: 1790.

Rooms: 15 rooms with PB, 3 with FP. 2 suites. 1 conference room.
Beds: QDT.

The Corner House is a charming 18th-century village inn. Architectural details such as the original pine floors, paneling and fireplaces have been preserved. A screened porch overlooks the English perennial garden, where guests often take afternoon tea. Many of the romantically appointed bed chambers feature canopy beds.

Breakfast and afternoon tea included in rates. Type of meal: continental-plus breakfast. AP. Air conditioning and cable TV in room. Fax and library on premises. Limited French and German spoken. Antiques, fishing, theater and watersports nearby.

Publicity: *Detroit Free Press, Atlanta Journal, Newsday, Gourmet, Elle Decor.*

Special Discounts: Off season third night half price or 4th night free.

"The most beautiful place we've ever been to and the most comfortable!!"

Four Chimneys

38 Orange St
Nantucket, MA 02554-3755
(508)228-1912

Rates: $150-225.
Payment: MC VISA AX.
Innkeeper(s): Bernadette Mannix.
Circa: 1855.

Rooms: 10 rooms with PB, 5 with FP. 1 conference room.
Beds: Q.

The Four Chimneys is located on famous Orange Street where 126 sea captains built mansions. Captain Frederick Gardner built this Greek Revival, one of the largest houses on Nantucket Island. The Publick Room is a double parlor with twin fireplaces. Porches stretch across three levels of the house providing views of the harbor and beyond.

Type of meal: continental-plus breakfast. Fax and copier on premises.

Publicity: *Country Home, Gourmet*

House of The Seven Gables

32 Cliff Rd
Nantucket, MA 02554-3644
(508)228-4706

Rates: $65-175.
Payment: MC VISA AX.
Innkeeper(s): Suzanne Walton.
Circa: 1865.

Rooms: 10 rooms, 8 with PB.
Beds: KQF.

Originally the annex of the Sea Cliff Inn, one of the island's oldest hotels, this three-story Queen Anne Victorian inn offers 10 guest rooms. Beaches, bike rentals, museums, restaurants, shops and tennis courts are all found nearby. The guest rooms are furnished with king or queen beds and period antiques. Breakfast is served each morning in the guest rooms, and often include homemade coffee cake, muffins or Portuguese rolls.

Breakfast included in rates. Type of meal: continental breakfast. Cable TV on premises. Antiques, fishing, shopping, theater and watersports nearby.

"You have a beautiful home and one that makes everyone feel relaxed and at home."

MA

Martin House Inn

61 Centre St PO Box 743
Nantucket, MA 02554
(508)228-0678

Rates: $65-160.
Payment: MC VISA AX PC TC.
Innkeeper(s): Channing & Cecilia Moore.
Circa: 1803.

Rooms: 13 rooms, 9 with PB, 3 with FP.
Beds: QDT.

Known as Wonoma Inn in the '20s, this shingled mariner's house in the historic district is tucked behind a picket fence. In summer, roses climb to the six-over-six windows and the hammock gently sways on the side veranda. Authentic period pieces include Chippendale chests, Windsor rockers and Victorian settlers, and there are four-poster and canopy beds in the guest rooms. The cobblestone streets of Nantucket's Main Street are a stroll away.

Breakfast included in rates. Types of meals: continental-plus breakfast and early coffee/tea. Cable TV and library on premises. Weddings and family reunions hosted. Antiques, fishing, parks, shopping, theater and watersports nearby.

Publicity: *Cape Cod Life.*

"A wonderful weekend filled with warm hospitality. We enjoyed it all."

Seven Sea Street Inn

7 Sea St
Nantucket, MA 02554-3545
(508)228-3577
Fax:(508)228-3578
E-mail: seast7@nantucket.net

Rates: $85-245.
Payment: MC VISA AX.
Innkeeper(s): Matthew & Mary Parker.
Circa: 1987.

Rooms: 10 rooms, 12 with PB. 2 suites.
Beds: Q.

Romance flourishes at this country inn located in the heart of Nantucket. Fishnet canopy beds, hardwood floors and Colonial furnishings create a cozy, elegant ambience. Spend breakfast in bed enjoying home-baked breads and muffins with fresh juice and fruits. Relax in the Jacuzzi or take in the view of Nantucket from the inn's widow walk deck. Enjoy a stroll down the cobblestone Main Street as you head to the wharf. The village is abound with galleries, boutiques and restaurants.

Breakfast included in rates. Types of meals: continental-plus breakfast and early coffee/tea. Air conditioning and cable TV in room. VCR, fax, spa and library on premises. Antiques, fishing, parks, shopping, theater and watersports nearby.

Publicity: *New York Times, First Magazine, Nantucket Journal.*

Special Discounts: 10% discount off season midweek.

"We loved your inn and had the most restful and relaxed time on Nantucket."

The Woodbox Inn

29 Fair St
Nantucket, MA 02554-3798
(508)228-0587

Rates: $140-230.
Payment: PC TC.
Innkeeper(s): Dexter Tutein.
Circa: 1709.

Rooms: 9 rooms with PB, 6 with FP. 6 suites.
Beds: KQDT.

Nantucket's oldest inn was built by Captain George Bunker. In 1711, the captain constructed an adjoining house. Eventually, the two houses were made into one by cutting into the sides of both. Guest rooms are furnished with period antiques. The inn's gourmet dining room features an Early American atmosphere with low-beamed ceilings and pine-paneled walls.

Type of meal: full breakfast. Weddings, small meetings and family reunions hosted. French, German and Spanish spoken. Antiques, fishing, parks, shopping, theater and watersports nearby.

Location: Historic district.

Publicity: *Wharton Alumni, Cape Cod Life, Boston Magazine.*

"Best breakfast on the island, Yesterday's Island."

Norwell F15

1810 House B&B

147 Old Oaken Bucket Rd
Norwell, MA 02061-1320
(617)659-1810
E-mail: tuttle1810@aol.com

Rates: $75-85.
Payment: PC TC.
Innkeeper(s): Susanne & Harold Tuttle.
Circa: 1810.

Rooms: 3 rooms, 2 with PB. 1 suite.
Beds: QT.

Exposed beams, original to this early 19th-century house, add a rustic touch to the 1810 House. Guest rooms are simply furnished in a traditional country decor. One includes a canopy bed and another offers an antique spool bed. Savory New England breakfasts with fresh fruit, yogurt, muffins, egg dishes, sausage, bacon and ham are served in the fireside dining room or on the screened-in porch. Guests can take a tour of the village via the innkeeper's restored 1915 Model T. The 1810 house is located midway between Plymouth and Boston.

Breakfast included in rates. Types of meals: full breakfast and early coffee/tea. Air conditioning, turn-down service and ceiling fan in room. Cable TV, VCR and copier on premises. Antiques, fishing, shopping, theater and watersports nearby. TAC10.

"We will remember the warmth of your welcome and hospitality."

Oak Bluffs (Martha's Vineyard)

Tivoli Inn, Martha's Vineyard

222 Circuit Ave,
PO Box 1033
Oak Bluffs (Martha's Vineyard), MA 02557
(508)693-7928

Rates: $50-130.
Payment: MC VISA AX.
Innkeeper(s): Lori & Lisa Katsounakis.
Circa: 1890.

Rooms: 6 rooms, 3 with PB.
Beds: QDT.

With a flowery balcony and wraparound latticed porch, this inn provides the perfect setting for a relaxing stay. A hearty continental breakfast is served on the porch during the summer season. Town beaches, ferries, main street shops and night life are all within walking distance. The inn is newly renovated and visitors will enjoy the island charm along with the clean friendly atmosphere. Vacation homes also are available, and both the inn and homes are open all year.

Cable TV on premises. Small meetings and family reunions hosted. Antiques, fishing, parks, shopping and watersports nearby. TAC10.

Publicity: *Boston Magazine.*

Special Discounts: Weekly rentals get their seventh night for free.

"I will recommend your inn to all who wish a pleasant stay at the Vineyard."

Onset I15

Onset Pointe Inn

9 Eagle Way, PO Box 1450
Onset, MA 02558
(508)295-8442 (800)356-6738
Fax:(508)295-5241

Rates: $45-150.
Payment: MC VISA AX DS PC TC.
Innkeeper(s): Debi & Joe Lopes.
Circa: 1880.

Rooms: 15 rooms with PB. 6 suites. 2 cottages. 1 conference room.
Beds: QDT.

This restored Victorian mansion is surrounded by the ocean on a sandy part of Onset Point. Its casually elegant decor is enhanced by sea views, sunlight, bright colors and florals. Spacious verandas, an enclosed circular sun porch and a bayside gazebo are available to guests. Accommodations are divided among the main house and two cottages. A full breakfast is served in a waterfront dining room. The inn received the National Trust first prize for preservation in their B&B category.

Breakfast included in rates. Cable TV, fax, copier and swimming on premises. Handicap access. Weddings, small meetings, family reunions and seminars hosted. Antiques, fishing, parks, shopping, theater and watersports nearby.

Location: Village of Onset, at the gateway to Cape Cod.

Special Discounts: Call for details, changes by season.

"We've found the B&B we've been looking for!"

MA

Orleans H19

The Farmhouse at Nauset Beach

163 Beach Rd
Orleans, MA 02653-2732
(508)255-6654

Rates: $42-105.
Payment: MC VISA PC.
Innkeeper(s): Dorothy Standish.
Circa: 1870.

Rooms: 8 rooms with PB, 1 with FP.
Beds: KQD.

Feel the intimacy of Orleans and capture the flavor of Cape Cod at this quiet country inn resting in a seashore setting. Rooms in this Greek Revival-style inn are comfortably furnished to depict their 19th-century past. Some rooms offer ocean views. Guests enjoy the "at home" feeling with morning coffee and freshly baked muffins or coffee cake. Nauset Beach is a short walk away. Spend a day charter fishing in Cape Cod Bay or the Atlantic. To make your stay complete, your itinerary can include antiquing, shopping, exploring quiet country lanes or a day at the beach. The inn is open year-round.

Breakfast included in rates. Type of meal: continental-plus breakfast. Ceiling fan and cable TV in room. Family reunions hosted. Antiques, fishing, shopping, theater and watersports nearby.

Special Discounts: 5% teachers, seven nights 10%.

Pittsfield D2

Olde White Horse Inn

378 South St
Pittsfield, MA 01201-6804
(413)442-2512

Rates: $95-160.
Payment: MC VISA AX DC CB DS TC.
Innkeeper(s): Joe & Linda Kalisz.
Circa: 1902.

Rooms: 8 rooms with PB.
Beds: QD.

Innkeeping runs in the family at the Olde White Horse, which features an elegant Colonial exterior set on an acre of manicured lawn. The current innkeeper's grandparents also were innkeepers and two rooms are named in honor of them. The Colonial theme continues on into the home and the eight guest rooms, decorated with antiques and beds topped with cozy comforters. The innkeepers' daughters also pitch in and help run the inn; the oldest prepares the breakfasts. The morning meal includes such items as quiche, pancakes, homemade muffins or breads and fresh fruit.

Breakfast included in rates. Types of meals: full breakfast and early coffee/tea. Evening snack available. Air conditioning and turn-down service in room. Cable TV, VCR, fax and copier on premises. Weddings, small meetings and family reunions hosted. Antiques, fishing, parks, shopping, downhill skiing, cross-country skiing, sporting events, theater and watersports nearby.

"White Horse Inn is absolutely the best place to stay."

Plymouth G15

Foxglove Cottage

101 Sandwich Rd
Plymouth, MA 02360-2503
(508)747-6576 (800)479-4746
Fax:(508)747-7622

Rates: $80.
Payment: DS PC TC.
Innkeeper(s): Mr. & Mrs. Charles K. Cowan.
Circa: 1820.

Rooms: 3 rooms with PB, 3 with FP.
Beds: QT.

Follow tree-lined Sandwich Road, the original Colonial highway to Boston, as it meanders to Foxglove Cottage, a pink Cape-style house. There are 40 acres of meadow and woodland, and a lawn with rhododendron and parts of an old stone fence. Across the street, horses graze in a pasture. Wideboard floors, Victorian antiques, fireplaces and coordinating fabrics and wallpapers create a warm, welcoming environment. Ask for the Rose Room for a handsomely decorated retreat with a four-poster canopy bed or the Canopy Room for two twin-size canopy beds. Baked French toast with blueberries or a sausage, egg and cheese casserole are popular breakfast items. Plimoth Plantation is nearby.

Breakfast and afternoon tea included in rates. Type of meal: full breakfast. Air conditioning in room. Cable TV, VCR, fax, copier and bicycles on premises. 45 acres. Antiques, fishing, parks, shopping, theater and watersports nearby. TAC10.

"A very charming place."

Provincetown G18

Land's End Inn

22 Commercial St
Provincetown, MA 02657
(508)487-0706 (800)276-7088

Rates: $87-285.
Payment: MC VISA PC TC.
Innkeeper(s): Anthony Arakelian.
Circa: 1904.

Rooms: 16 rooms with PB.
Beds: QD.

Built as a shingle-style summer cottage for Boston merchant Charles Higgins, Land's End stands high on a hill overlooking Provincetown and all of Cape Cod Bay. Part of the Higgins' collection of Oriental wood carvings and stained glass is housed at the inn. Furnished lavishly in a Victorian style, the inn offers a comforting atmosphere for relaxation and beauty.

Breakfast included in rates. Types of meals: continental breakfast and early coffee/tea. Ceiling fan in room. Cable TV, VCR and bicycles on premises. Weddings, small meetings, family reunions and seminars hosted. Antiques, fishing, parks, shopping, theater and watersports nearby.

Location: At the tip of Cape Cod.

Publicity: *Herald News, Travel Magazine, Cape Cod Review.*

White Wind Inn

174 Commercial St
Provincetown, MA 02657
(508)487-1526
Fax:(508)487-3985
E-mail: wwinn@capecod.net

Rates: $75-180.
Payment: MC VISA AX TC.
Innkeeper(s): Sandra Rich, Russell Dusablon.
Circa: 1845.

Rooms: 11 rooms with PB, 2 with FP. 1 suite.
Beds: KQD.

This white Victorian house is located across the street from the beach and some rooms have water views. There are TVs and small refrigerators, and some air conditioners. A few rooms have fireplaces and balconies, as well as four-poster beds. Breakfast is continental during the season. Most of the town's offerings may be reached within a five-minute walk.

Breakfast included in rates. Type of meal: continental breakfast. Air conditioning, ceiling fan, cable TV and VCR in room. Fax on premises. Antiques, fishing, parks, shopping, theater and watersports nearby. TAC10.

Pets Allowed: Must be approved by manager.

Rehoboth *H12*

Five Bridge Farm

PO Box 462, 154 Pine St
Rehoboth, MA 02769-0462
(508)252-3190
Fax:(508)252-3190

Rates: $50-80.
Payment: MC VISA AX DC CB DS PC TC.
Innkeeper(s): Ann & Harold Messenger.
Circa: 1987.

Rooms: 6 rooms, 2 with PB, 1 with FP. 1 suite. 1 conference room.
Beds: KQT.

MA

This Georgian Colonial is centered on 70 acres of New England countryside. The grounds are decorated with English herb and flower gardens and a screened gazebo, where the morning meal is served during warmer months. The decor is that of understated elegance. Polished antiques, chandeliers and a few, simple knickknacks complete the look. The farm includes a tennis court, lap pool, jogging track, hiking trails and llamas. Riding stables are located adjacent to the property. However, the hosts provide many places to simply sit and relax.

Air conditioning and ceiling fan in room. VCR, fax, copier, spa, swimming, bicycles, tennis, library, pet boarding and child care on premises. Handicap access. 70 acres. Weddings, small meetings, family reunions and seminars hosted. Antiques, fishing, parks, shopping, cross-country skiing, sporting events, theater and watersports nearby. TAC10.

Pets Allowed: Yes.

Gilbert's Tree Farm B&B

30 Spring St
Rehoboth, MA 02769-2408
(508)252-6416
E-mail: jeanneg47@aol.com

Rates: $45-50.
Payment: PC TC.
Innkeeper(s): Jeanne & Martin Gilbert.
Circa: 1835.

Rooms: 3 rooms.
Beds: KDT.

This country farmhouse sits on 100 acres of woodland that includes an award-winning tree farm. Cross-country skiing, hiking, and pony-cart rides are found right outside the door. If they choose to, guests can even help with the farm chores, caring for horses and gardening. A swimming pool is open during summer. Three antique-filled bedrooms share a second-floor sitting room. The nearby town of Rehoboth is 350 years old.

Breakfast, afternoon tea and evening snack included in rates. Types of meals: full breakfast and early coffee/tea. VCR, copier, swimming, stables, bicycles, library and pet boarding on premises. 100 acres. Antiques, fishing, parks, shopping, cross-country skiing, sporting events, theater and watersports nearby. TAC10.

Location: Twelve miles east of Providence.

Publicity: *Attleboro Sun Chronicle, Country, Somerset Spectator, Country Gazette, Pawtucket Times.*

"This place has become my second home. Thank you for the family atmosphere of relaxation, fun, spontaneity and natural surroundings."

Richmond

A B&B In The Berkshires

1666 Dublin Rd
Richmond, MA 01254-9620
(413)698-2817 (800)795-7122
Fax:(413)698-3164

Rates: $85-125.
Innkeeper(s): Doane Perry.
Circa: 1963.

Rooms: 3 rooms with PB.

This modern ranch home, with its striking views, offers easy access to the area's many attractions. Guests choose from three air-conditioned guest rooms, all with cable TV, king or queen beds, phones, private bath, turndown service and VCRs. Bousque Ski Area, Pleasant Valley Wildlife Sanctuary and Tanglewood all are within easy driving distance of the inn. Hancock Shaker Village and the Norman Rockwell Museum are other nearby attractions.

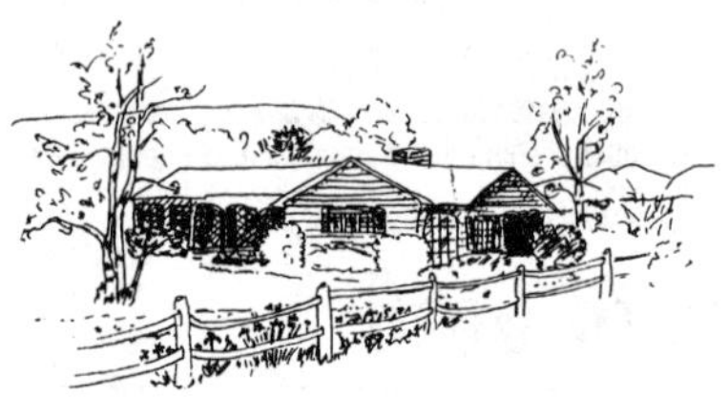

Types of meals: full breakfast and early coffee/tea. Air conditioning, turn-down service, cable TV and VCR in room. Small meetings and family reunions hosted. Antiques, shopping, downhill skiing, cross-country skiing and theater nearby.

Rockport **C15**

Addison Choate Inn

49 Broadway
Rockport, MA 01966-1527
(508)546-7543 (800)245-7543
Fax:(508)546-7638

Rates: $70-120.
Payment: MC VISA DS PC TC.
Innkeeper(s): Knox & Shirley Johnson.
Circa: 1851.

Rooms: 7 rooms with PB. 1 suite. 2 cottages.
Beds: KQT.

Antiques and reproductions decorate the interior of this mid-19th-century home. The guest rooms feature antique and wicker furnishings, artwork and polished, pine floors. Specialty coffee, freshly baked breads, fruit and cereals are served each morning in the inn's dining room, which still contains the original fireplace and beehive oven. If weather permits, breakfasts are served on the inn's wraparound porch, offering a view of the garden. Parking is within walking distance, as are shops, restaurants and other sites.

Breakfast and afternoon tea included in rates. Types of meals: continental-plus breakfast, full breakfast and early coffee/tea. Air conditioning, ceiling fan and cable TV in room. VCR, fax, copier and swimming on premises. Antiques, fishing, parks, shopping, theater and watersports nearby. TAC10.

Publicity: *Los Angeles Times, Detroit Free Press, Gloucester Daily Times.*

Special Discounts: Two nights winter $150 or $190 including tax.

"Lovely! Charming and quaint."

The Inn on Cove Hill

37 Mount Pleasant St
Rockport, MA 01966-1727
(508)546-2701

Rates: $45-101.
Payment: MC VISA PC TC.
Innkeeper(s): John & Marjorie Pratt.
Circa: 1791.

Rooms: 11 rooms, 9 with PB.
Beds: QDT.

Pirate gold found at Gully Point paid for this Federal-style house. A white picket fence and granite walkway welcome guests. Inside, an exquisitely crafted spiral staircase, random-width, pumpkin-pine floors and hand-forged hinges display the original artisan's handiwork. Furnishings include family heirlooms, four-poster canopy beds, and paintings by area artists. Muffin Du Jour is baked fresh each day by John. Bicycles can be delivered to your door by a local rental company or you can enjoy whale watching, fishing the local waters, or simply strolling the antique shops and village streets.

Breakfast included in rates. Types of meals: continental breakfast and early coffee/tea. Air conditioning in room. Antiques, fishing, parks and theater nearby.

Linden Tree Inn

26 King St
Rockport, MA 01966-1444
(508)546-2494 (800)865-2122
E-mail: ltree@shore.net

Rates: $73-105.
Payment: MC VISA PC TC.
Innkeeper(s): Dawn & Jon Cunningham.
Circa: 1840.

Rooms: 18 rooms with PB. 1 suite.
Beds: KQDT.

The breakfasts at this lovely Victorian-style inn keep guests coming back year after year. Guests feast on home-baked treats such as pumpkin chocolate chip bread, blueberry cake or Sunday favorites, lemon nut bread and sour cream chocolate chip coffee cake. Each of the bedchambers features individual decor, and the innkeepers offer a formal living room and sun room for relaxation. The cupola affords a view of Mill Pond and Sandy Bay.

Breakfast and afternoon tea included in rates. Types of meals: continental breakfast and continental-plus breakfast. Air conditioning, ceiling fan and cable TV in room. VCR and copier on premises. Weddings, small meetings, family reunions and seminars hosted. Antiques, fishing, parks, shopping, theater and watersports nearby. TAC10.

Publicity: *Gloucester Daily Times.*

Special Discounts: Off season groups.

"Great coffee! Love that apple walnut bread. Thank you for making this home."

Ralph Waldo Emerson Inn

Phillips Ave
Rockport, MA 01966
(508)546-6321
Fax:(508)546-7043
E-mail: emerson@cove.com

Rates: $85-137. EP.
Payment: MC VISA DS PC TC.
Innkeeper(s): Gary Wemyss.
Circa: 1840.

Rooms: 36 rooms with PB. 3 suites. 3 conference rooms.
Beds: KQDT.

MA

This Greek Revival inn's namesake once called the place, "the proper summer home." As it is the oldest continuously operated inn on Cape Ann, decades of travelers agree with his sentiment. The guest rooms are comfortable, yet tastefully furnished, some boast ocean views. The grounds include a heated, saltwater swimming pool as well as a sauna and whirlpool. Although breakfasts are not included in the rates, guests can enjoy the morning meal or dinner at the inn's dining room, an area added to the 19th-century inn in 1912.

Types of meals: continental breakfast, continental-plus breakfast, full breakfast and early coffee/tea. Afternoon tea, dinner, catered breakfast and room service available. EP. Air conditioning in room. Cable TV, VCR, fax, copier, spa, swimming and sauna on premises. Handicap access. Weddings, small meetings, family reunions and seminars hosted. Antiques, fishing, parks, theater and watersports nearby. TAC10.

Special Discounts: April & November - $68-$100.

"We were very impressed with every aspect of the Emerson Inn."

Romantik Hotel Yankee Clipper Inn

PO Box 2399
Rockport, MA 01966-3399
(508)546-3407 (800)545-3699
Fax:(508)546-9730

Rates: $109-249. MAP.
Payment: MC VISA AX DS PC TC.
Innkeeper(s): Robert & Barbara Ellis.
Circa: 1840.

Rooms: 26 rooms with PB. 6 suites. 1 cottage. 1 conference room.
Beds: KQDT.

This white clapboard oceanfront mansion features sweeping views of the sea and the rocky shoreline. Gleaming mahogany woodwork and fireplaces combined with fine antiques create an old-fashioned, elegant ambiance in the main building. Some accommodations offer canopy beds and balconies. The Bulfinch House, a Greek Revival building housing extra guest rooms, is situated away from the water uphill from the main inn. A heated salt-water pool is in view of the ocean.

Breakfast included in rates. Types of meals: continental-plus breakfast, full breakfast and gourmet breakfast. Dinner and room service available. MAP. Air conditioning in room. Cable TV, VCR, fax, copier, swimming and library on premises. Weddings, small meetings, family reunions and seminars hosted. German spoken. Antiques, fishing, parks, shopping, theater and watersports nearby. TAC10.

Publicity: *Gloucester Daily Times, L.A. Times, North Shore Life, Country Living, Discerning Traveler, Country Inns, Travel Holidays.*

Special Discounts: Packages-see brochure.

"The rooms were comfortable, the views breathtaking from most rooms, and the breakfasts delicious, with prompt and courteous service."

Seacrest Manor

131 Marmion Way
Rockport, MA 01966-1927
(508)546-2211

Rates: $84-136.
Payment: PC TC.
Innkeeper(s): Leighton Saville & Dwight MacCormack, Jr.
Circa: 1911.

Rooms: 8 rooms, 6 with PB.
Beds: KQDT.

After more than two decades of serving guests, the innkeepers at this estate inn have achieved "ace" status, welcoming travelers with well-polished hospitality. Their inn was once summer home to a prominent restaurateur and looks out to the sea. The two-and-a-half acres include gardens to stroll through, and inside there is a well-stocked library. Fresh flowers are placed in each guest room, and some rooms are further enhanced with decorative fireplaces. Various types of berry pancakes, Irish oatmeal topped with dates, corn fritters and French toast are just a few of the items that might be found on the morning table.

Breakfast and afternoon tea included in rates. Types of meals: full breakfast, gourmet breakfast and early coffee/tea. Turn-down service and cable TV in room. Bicycles and library on premises. French spoken. Antiques, fishing, parks, shopping, theater and watersports nearby.

Special Discounts: 5% for two consecutive weeks or longer.

"We'll always have many fond memories."

Tuck Inn

17 High St
Rockport, MA 01966-1644
(508)546-7260 (800)789-7260

Rates: $47-107.
Payment: MC VISA PC TC.
Innkeeper(s): Liz & Scott Wood.
Circa: 1790.

Rooms: 11 rooms with PB. 1 suite.
Beds: KQDT.

Two recent renovations have served to make this charming Colonial inn all the more enticing. Period antiques and paintings by local artists are featured throughout the spacious inn. A favorite gathering spot is the living room with its fireplace, wide pine floors, tasteful furnishings and a piano available for guest use. Buffet breakfasts feature homemade breads, muffins, cakes and scones, granola accompanied by fresh fruit and yogurt. Guests may take a dip in the swimming pool or at local beaches. Within easy walking distance are the many art galleries, restaurants and shops of Bearskin Neck. A nearby train station offers convenient access to Boston.

Breakfast included in rates. Types of meals: continental-plus breakfast and early coffee/tea. Afternoon tea available. Air conditioning, ceiling fan and cable TV in room. VCR, swimming, bicycles and library on premises. Small meetings and family reunions hosted. Antiques, fishing, parks, shopping, downhill skiing, cross-country skiing, sporting events, theater and watersports nearby.

Publicity: *Fall River Herald News, North Shore News, Cape Ann Weekly.*

Special Discounts: Winter special 11/1-4/30, 2 nights for $98 per room DO.

"Wonderful people, lovely scenery, and great food, all good for the soul! Your hospitality and service was wonderful and we look forward to returning very soon!"

Amelia Payson Guest House

16 Winter St
Salem, MA 01970-3807
(508)744-8304

Rates: $65-105.
Payment: MC VISA AX.
Innkeeper(s): Ada & Donald Roberts.
Circa: 1845.

Rooms: 4 rooms with PB.
Beds: QT.

This elegantly restored two-story house features four white columns and is a prime example of Greek Revival architecture. Period antiques and wallpapers decorate the guest rooms and the formal dining room. Located in the heart of the Salem Historic District, it is a short walk to shops, museums, Pickering Wharf and waterfront restaurants. Train service to Boston is four blocks away. This is a non-smoking establishment.

Breakfast included in rates. Type of meal: continental-plus breakfast. Antiques and watersports nearby.

Location: Thirteen miles north of Boston.

"Your hospitality has been a part of my wonderful experience."

The Salem Inn

7 Summer St
Salem, MA 01970-3315
(508)741-0680 (800)446-2995
Fax:(508)744-8924

Rates: $99-175.
Payment: MC VISA AX DC CB DS TC.
Innkeeper(s): Richard & Diane Pabich.
Circa: 1834.

Rooms: 33 rooms with PB, 14 with FP. 5 suites. 1 conference room.
Beds: KQT.

MA

This picturesque Federal-style inn is located in the heart of Salem's historic district, which features galleries, antiques, museums and the wharf and harbor. Many of the spacious guest rooms feature Jacuzzi tubs, fireplaces and canopy beds. Families will appreciate the two-room suites, which include kitchenettes. The dining area, with its brick walls and cozy atmosphere, is the perfect place to enjoy a light breakfast.

Breakfast included in rates. Type of meal: early coffee/tea. Air conditioning and cable TV in room. Fax on premises. Weddings and small meetings hosted. Antiques, fishing, parks, shopping, sporting events, theater and watersports nearby. TAC10.

Pets Allowed.

Location: Historic downtown.

Publicity: *New York Times, Boston Sunday Globe.*

"Delightful, charming. Our cup of tea."

The Inn at Seven Winter Street

7 Winter St
Salem, MA 01970-3806
(508)745-9520
Fax:(508)745-5052

Rates: $95-165.
Payment: MC VISA AX.
Innkeeper(s): D.L. and Jill Cote, Sally Flint.
Circa: 1871.

Rooms: 10 rooms with PB. 2 suites.
Beds: QDT.

Historic sites, museums, the waterfront, unique shops and quaint restaurants are all within walking distance of this French Second Empire Victorian manor. Some of the guest rooms have a working marble fireplace, canopy bed, Victorian bath, Jacuzzi, or open onto a large sundeck overlooking the inn's gardens. Breakfast is served in the main parlor and evening tea is served fireside.

Breakfast and afternoon tea included in rates. Type of meal: continental-plus breakfast. Air conditioning and cable TV in room. Antiques, fishing, shopping, cross-country skiing, sporting events, theater and watersports nearby.

Bay Beach B&B

1-3 Bay Beach Ln
Sandwich, MA 02563
(508)888-8813 (800)475-6398
Fax:(508)888-5416

Rates: $150-195.
Payment: VISA PC TC.
Innkeeper(s): Emily & Reale Lemieux.

Rooms: 6 rooms with PB. 3 suites.
Beds: KD.

Beautiful grounds bursting with gardens and a heavenly view of the sea attract many guests to this peaceful Cape Cod bed & breakfast, located in historic Sandwich. Rooms are tastefully appointed with contemporary furnishings and include amenities such as ceiling fans, mini refrigerators stocked with a few choice refreshments and private decks. The inn has received a four-diamond rating from AAA.

Breakfast and afternoon tea included in rates. Type of meal: continental-plus breakfast. Air conditioning, turn-down service, ceiling fan and cable TV in room. Fax, copier, swimming, bicycles and library on premises. French spoken. Antiques, fishing, parks, shopping, theater and watersports nearby.

Captain Ezra Nye House

152 Main St
Sandwich, MA 02563-2232
(508)888-6142 (800)388-2278
Fax:(508)833-2897
E-mail: captnye@aol.com

Rates: $75-100.
Payment: MC VISA AX DS PC TC.
Innkeeper(s): Elaine & Harry Dickson.
Circa: 1829.

Rooms: 6 rooms with PB, 1 with FP. 1 suite.
Beds: QDT.

Captain Ezra Nye built this house after a record-shattering Halifax to Boston run, and the stately Federal-style house reflects the opulence and romance of the clipper ship era. Hand-stenciled walls and museum-quality antiques decorate the interior. Within walking distance are the Doll Museum, the Glass Museum, restaurants, shops, the famous Heritage Plantation, the beach and marina.

Breakfast included in rates. Types of meals: full breakfast, gourmet breakfast and early coffee/tea. Cable TV, VCR, fax and library on premises. Small meetings and family reunions hosted. Spanish spoken. Antiques, fishing, parks, shopping, theater and watersports nearby. TAC10.

Location: In the heart of Sandwich Village, the oldest town on Cape Cod.

Publicity: *Glamour, Innsider, Cape Cod Life, Toronto Life, Yankee.*

"The prettiest room and most beautiful home we have been to. We had a wonderful time."

The Dunbar House

1 Water St.
Sandwich, MA 02563
(508)833-2485
Fax:(508)833-2485
E-mail: captnye@aol.com

Rates: $65-95.
Payment: MC VISA PC TC.
Innkeeper(s): Michael & Mary Bell.
Circa: 1741.

Rooms: 3 rooms with PB, 3 with FP.
Beds: QT.

This Colonial-style house overlooks a pond in the charming setting of Cape Cod's oldest town. The three guest rooms are appointed in Colonial style, and all boast a view of the pond. The Ennerdale room has a four-poster bed. Each morning, guests are pampered with a homemade breakfast, and afternoon tea is served in the innkeeper's English tea shop. The inn is within walking distance of many historic sites.

Breakfast and afternoon tea included in rates. Types of meals: continental breakfast, continental-plus breakfast, full breakfast, gourmet breakfast and early coffee/tea. Lunch available. Restaurant on premises. VCR, fax, copier, bicycles and library on premises. Weddings, seminars, small meetings and family reunions hosted. Antiques, fishing, parks, shopping, theater and watersports nearby. TAC10.

Publicity: *Cape Cod Times.*

"A romantic getaway with a relaxing Colonial atmosphere."

The Summer House

158 Main St
Sandwich, MA 02563-2232
(508)888-4991

Rates: $65-85.
Payment: MC VISA AX DS PC TC.
Innkeeper(s): Marjorie & Kevin Huelsman.
Circa: 1835.

Rooms: 5 rooms with PB, 4 with FP.
Beds: KQT.

The Summer House is a handsome Greek Revival in a setting of historic homes and public buildings. (Hiram Dillaway, one of the owners, was a famous mold maker for the Boston & Sandwich Glass Company.) The house is fully restored and decorated with antiques and hand-stitched quilts. Four of the guest rooms have black marble fireplaces. The porch overlooks an old-fashioned perennial garden, antique rose bushes, and a 70-year-old rhododendron hedge.

Breakfast and afternoon tea included in rates. Types of meals: full breakfast, gourmet breakfast and early coffee/tea. Library on premises. Weddings, small meetings and family reunions hosted. Antiques, fishing, parks, shopping, cross-country skiing, theater and watersports nearby.

Location: Center of village, Cape Cod.

Publicity: *Country Living, Boston, Cape Cod Times.*

"An absolutely gorgeous house and a super breakfast. I wish I could've stayed longer! Came for one night, stayed for three! Marvelous welcome."

Sandwich (Cape Cod)

MA

Isaiah Jones Homestead

165 Main St
Sandwich (Cape Cod), MA 02563-2283
(508)888-9115 (800)526-1625

Rates: $75-155.
Payment: MC VISA AX DS PC TC.
Innkeeper(s): Shirley & Bud Lamson.
Circa: 1849.

Rooms: 5 rooms with PB, 3 with FP.
Beds: QDT.

This fully restored Victorian homestead is situated on Main Street in the village. Eleven-foot ceilings and two bay windows are features of the Gathering Room. Guest rooms contain antique Victorian bedsteads such as the half-canopy bed of burled birch in the Deming Jarves Room where there is an over-sized whirlpool tub and a fireplace. Candlelight breakfasts are highlighted with the house speciality, freshly baked cornbread, inspired by nearby Sandwich Grist Mill.

Breakfast and afternoon tea included in rates. Types of meals: full breakfast and early coffee/tea. Cable TV on premises. Weddings, small meetings, family reunions and seminars hosted. Antiques, fishing, parks, shopping, theater and watersports nearby. TAC10.

Publicity: *Cape Cod Life, New England Travel, National Geographic Travel.*

Special Discounts: Four days or more 10% discount.

"Excellent! The room was a delight, the food wonderful, the hospitality warm & friendly. One of the few times the reality exceeded the expectation."

Scituate F15

Allen House

18 Allen Pl
Scituate, MA 02066-1302
(617)545-8221
Fax:(617)545-8221

Rates: $69-179.
Payment: MC VISA AX DS PC TC.
Innkeeper(s): Christine & Iain Gilmour.
Circa: 1905.

Rooms: 6 rooms with PB. 1 conference room.
Beds: KQD.

Originally a prosperous merchant's home, the Allen House was converted into a bed & breakfast by English owners Iain and Christine Gilmour. Christine, also a caterer, likes to embellish her breakfasts with flowers and herbs. English afternoon tea, classical music and two resident cats provide a cozy, civilized ambiance. Some guest rooms have views of Scituate (pronounced "Situate") harbor, where the famous New England lobsters are landed. The town was established more than 350 years ago.

Breakfast and afternoon tea included in rates. Type of meal: early coffee/tea. Air conditioning and turn-down service in room. Cable TV and fax on premises. Handicap access. Weddings, small meetings and family reunions hosted. Some French & German spoken. Antiques and fishing nearby. TAC10.

Location: Two-minute walk from harbor.

Publicity: *Kent Life.*

"I wish we could have stayed a week."

Seekonk — H12

Historic Jacob Hill Farm B&B

120 Jacob St
Seekonk, MA 02771
(508)336-9165 (888)336-9165
Fax:(508)336-0951

Rates: $65-135.
Payment: MC VISA DS PC TC.
Innkeeper(s): Bill & Eleonora Rezek.
Circa: 1722.

Rooms: 7 rooms, 5 with PB, 3 with FP. 2 suites.
Beds: KQDT.

This historic Colonial home overlooks 50 acres and is located three miles outside Providence. In the '20s and '30s, it was the Jacob Hill Hunt Club and hosted the Vanderbilts during hunts and horse shows. Beamed ceilings, wall paintings of horse and hunting scenes and rare Southern longleaf pine floors create the gracious setting. Guest rooms may include a canopy bed, fireplace or whirlpool tub. Enjoy the inn's stable of horses or take a riding lesson, then relax in the gazebo at sunset. Stuffed French toast with whipped cream and strawberries is often served in the original kitchen area with its large beehive fireplace.

Breakfast, afternoon tea and evening snack included in rates. Types of meals: full breakfast, gourmet breakfast and early coffee/tea. Air conditioning and turn-down service in room. Cable TV, VCR, fax, swimming, stables and tennis on premises. Weddings, small meetings and family reunions hosted. Polish spoken. Amusement parks, antiques, fishing, parks, shopping, downhill skiing, cross-country skiing, sporting events, theater and watersports nearby. TAC10.

South Dennis — I18

Captain Nickerson Inn

333 Main St
South Dennis, MA 02660
(508)398-5966 (800)282-1619

Rates: $60-90.
Payment: MC VISA DS PC.
Innkeeper(s): Pat & Dave York.
Circa: 1828.

Rooms: 5 rooms, 3 with PB.
Beds: QDT.

This Queen Anne Victorian inn originally was built by a sea captain. Guests can relax on the front porch with white wicker rockers and tables. The guest rooms are decorated with period four-poster or white iron queen beds and 'Oriental' or hand-woven rugs. The dining room has a fireplace and a stained-glass picture window. The Cape Cod bike Rail Trail, which is more than 20 miles long, is less than a mile away.

Breakfast included in rates. Type of meal: full breakfast. Air conditioning and ceiling fan in room. Cable TV, VCR, fax and bicycles on premises. Small meetings and family reunions hosted. Antiques, fishing, parks, shopping, theater and watersports nearby. TAC10.

Special Discounts: 10% discount for AAA members.

"Your inn is great!"

South Egremont

F2

Egremont Inn

Old Sheffield Rd
South Egremont, MA 01258
(413)528-2111 (800)859-1780
Fax:(413)528-3284

Rates: $80-165. MAP.
Payment: MC VISA AX PC TC.
Innkeeper(s): Karen & Steven Waller.
Circa: 1780.

Rooms: 20 rooms with PB. 1 suite. 1 conference room.
Beds: KQDT.

This three-story inn was once a stagecoach stop. Guest rooms are furnished with country antiques. Dinner is available Wednesday through Sunday in the formal dining room, and there is a historic tavern room. Five fireplaces are found in the common rooms. A wraparound porch, tennis courts and a swimming pool are on the premises.

Breakfast included in rates. Type of meal: continental-plus breakfast. Dinner available. MAP. Air conditioning and ceiling fan in room. VCR, swimming, tennis and library on premises. Weddings, small meetings, family reunions and seminars hosted. Antiques, fishing, parks, shopping, downhill skiing, cross-country skiing, sporting events and theater nearby. TAC10.

Location: In the heart of the Berkshires.

"All the beauty of the Berkshires without the hassle, the quintessential country inn."

MA

Stockbridge

E2

Arbor Rose B&B

8 Yale Hill, Box 114
Stockbridge, MA 01262
(413)298-4744

Rates: $60-150.
Payment: MC VISA AX PC TC.
Innkeeper(s): Christina Alsop.
Circa: 1810.

Rooms: 5 rooms, 2 with PB. 1 conference room.
Beds: KQT.

This large, white farmhouse overlooks an 1800s mill, millpond and gardens with the mountains as a backdrop. Floral wallpapers, paintings and antiques occupy sunny rooms. After a day on the slopes or on cross-country paths, skiers can warm themselves next to the fireplace in the front parlor. Guests can walk to the Berkshire Theatre and Stockbridge Center. The Norman Rockwell Museum, Tanglewood Music Festival, ski areas, antique and other shops are all within a seven-mile radius.

Breakfast included in rates. Types of meals: full breakfast, gourmet breakfast and early coffee/tea. Ceiling fan in room. Cable TV and VCR on premises. Weddings, small meetings, family reunions and seminars hosted. French spoken. Antiques, parks, shopping, downhill skiing, cross-country skiing and theater nearby. TAC10.

Location: One-half mile from center of Stockbridge.

Publicity: *Yankee Traveler.*

Special Discounts: Rent two rooms midweek, get one room free; or two nights, get one free midweek off season.

"If houses really do exude the spirit of events and feelings stored from their history, it explains why a visitor feels warmth and joy from the first turn up the driveway."

Broad Meadows

N Church St, PO Box 485
Stockbridge, MA 01262
(413)298-4972

Rates: $95-115.
Payment: PC TC.
Innkeeper(s): Ted Spencer & Associates.
Circa: 1902.

Rooms: 5 rooms with PB.
Beds: QDT.

Surrounded by an old stone wall, this large yellow house was once a summer estate. Set back on a gentle hill, the veranda provides views of the inn's gardens, meadows and forests. The library with a grand piano is a popular spot for guests.

Types of meals: full breakfast and early coffee/tea. VCR and library on premises. 50 acres. Weddings, small meetings and family reunions hosted. Antiques, parks, shopping and theater nearby.

Special Discounts: 10% off for stays of four nights or more.

"Thank you for your gracious hospitality."

The Inn at Stockbridge

PO Box 618
Stockbridge, MA 01262
(413)298-3337
Fax:(413)298-3406

Rates: $85-235.
Payment: MC VISA AX PC TC.
Innkeeper(s): Alice & Lenny Schiller.
Circa: 1906.

Rooms: 8 rooms with PB. 2 suites.
Beds: DT.

Giant maples shade the drive leading to this Southern-style Georgian Colonial with its impressive pillared entrance. Located on 12 acres, the grounds include a reflecting pool, a fountain, meadows and woodland as well as wide vistas of the rolling hillsides. The guest rooms feature antiques and handsome 18th-century reproductions. Breakfast is graciously presented with fine china, silver and linens.

Breakfast and evening snack included in rates. Types of meals: full breakfast, gourmet breakfast and early coffee/tea. Air conditioning in room. Cable TV, VCR, fax, copier, swimming and library on premises. 12 acres. Weddings, small meetings, family reunions and seminars hosted. Antiques, fishing, parks, shopping, downhill skiing, cross-country skiing, theater and watersports nearby. TAC10.

Publicity: *Vogue, New York, New York Daily News, Country Inns Northeast, Arts & Antiques.*

Special Discounts: Winter weekend $169-$259 two nights two people.

"Classy & comfortable."

Stockbridge (South Lee)

Merrell Historic Inn

1565 Pleasant St, Rt 102
Stockbridge, MA 01260
(413)243-1794 (800)243-1794
Fax:(413)243-2669
E-mail: merey@bcn.net

Rates: $55-135.
Payment: MC VISA.
Innkeeper(s): Pam Hurst.
Circa: 1794.

Rooms: 9 rooms with PB, 3 with FP.
Beds: QDT.

This elegant stagecoach inn was carefully preserved under supervision of the Society for the Preservation of New England Antiquities. Architectural drawings of Merrell Inn have been preserved by the Library of Congress. Eight fireplaces in the inn include two with original beehive and warming ovens. An antique circular birdcage bar serves as a check-in desk. Comfortable rooms feature canopy and four-poster beds with Hepplewhite and Sheraton-style antiques.

Breakfast included in rates. Type of meal: full breakfast. Air conditioning in room. Cable TV, fax and copier on premises. Family reunions and seminars hosted. Antiques, fishing, parks, shopping, cross-country skiing and theater nearby.

Publicity: *Americana, Country Living, New York Times, Boston Globe, Country Accents, Travel Holiday.*

"We couldn't have chosen a more delightful place to stay in the Berkshires. Everything was wonderful. We especially loved the grounds and the gazebo by the river."

Sturbridge F8

Commonwealth Cottage

11 Summit Avenue
Sturbridge, MA 01566-1225
(508)347-7708

Rates: $85-145.
Payment: PC TC.
Innkeeper(s): Robert & Wiebke Gilbert.
Circa: 1873.

Rooms: 5 rooms, 4 with PB.
Beds: QDT.

This 16-room Queen Anne Victorian house, on an acre near the Quinebaug River, is just a few minutes from Old Sturbridge Village. Both the dining room and parlor have fireplaces. The Baroque theme of the Sal Raciti room makes it one of the guest favorites and it features a queen mahogany bed. Breakfast may be offered on the gazebo porch or in the formal dining room. It includes a variety of homemade specialties, such as freshly baked breads and cakes.

Types of meals: full breakfast and early coffee/tea. Evening snack available. Ceiling fan in room. Library on premises. Weddings and family reunions hosted. German spoken. Antiques, fishing, parks, shopping, theater and watersports nearby.

MA

Publicity: *Long Island Newsday, Villager.*

"Your home is so warm and welcoming we feel as though we've stepped back in time. Our stay here has helped to make the wedding experience extra special!"

Publick House Historic Inn & Country Motor Lodge

PO Box 187, Common
Route 131
Sturbridge, MA 01566-0187
(800)PUBLICK
Fax:(508)347-5073

Rates: $74-155.
Payment: MC VISA AX DC CB PC TC.
Innkeeper(s): Lenora Bowen.
Circa: 1771.

Rooms: 14 rooms with PB. 7 suites.
Beds: KQDT.

This property includes four lodging facilities, three restaurants, 12 meeting rooms and 60 acres of countryside. Many special events take place throughout the year, including a New England Lobster Bake, a Beer and Wine Maker's Dinner, Harvest Weekend, Yankee Winter Weekends and Murder-Mystery Weekends. All the rooms in the main building are decorated with period furnishings.

Types of meals: continental breakfast, continental-plus breakfast, full breakfast, gourmet breakfast and early coffee/tea. Afternoon tea, dinner, evening snack, picnic lunch, lunch, gourmet lunch, banquet service, catering service, catered breakfast and room service available. Restaurant on premises. Air conditioning and cable TV in room. VCR, fax and swimming on premises. Handicap access. 60 acres. Weddings, small meetings, family reunions and seminars hosted. Spanish and French spoken. Antiques, fishing, parks, shopping, cross-country skiing, sporting events and theater nearby. TAC10.

Sturbridge Country Inn

PO Box 60, 530 Main St
Sturbridge, MA 01566-0060
(508)347-5503
Fax:(508)347-5319

Rates: $59-159.
Payment: MC VISA AX DS PC TC.
Innkeeper(s): Patricia Affenito.
Circa: 1840.

Rooms: 9 rooms with PB, 9 with FP. 1 suite. 1 conference room.
Beds: KQ.

Shaded by an old silver maple, this classic Greek Revival house boasts a two-story columned entrance. The attached carriage house now serves as the lobby and displays the original post-and-beam construction and exposed rafters. All guest rooms have individual fireplaces and whirlpool tubs. They are gracefully appointed in reproduction colonial furnishings, including queen-size, four-posters. A patio and gazebo are favorite summertime retreats.

Breakfast included in rates. Types of meals: continental breakfast and early coffee/tea. Room service available. Air conditioning, ceiling fan, cable TV and VCR in room. Fax, copier and spa on premises. Weddings, small meetings, family reunions and seminars hosted. Spanish spoken. Antiques, fishing, parks, shopping, downhill skiing, cross-country skiing, theater and watersports nearby. TAC10.

Location: Near Old Sturbridge Village.

Publicity: *Southbridge Evening News, Worcester Telegram & Gazette.*

"Best lodging I've ever seen."

Sudbury D12

Longfellow's Wayside Inn

Wayside Inn Rd
Sudbury, MA 01776
(508)443-1776
Fax:(508)443-8041

Rates: $53.
Circa: 1702.

Rooms: 10 rooms with PB. 1 conference room.
Beds: TD.

Henry Ford endowed the non-profit corporation that manages the Wayside Inn in 1944, to preserve it as a historic and literary shrine. The inn's second owner is known to have led the colonists of Sudbury on the march to Concord on April 19, 1775, toward the Old North Bridge. Originally opened as How's Tavern in 1702, it later became Red Horse Tavern. Finally, in 1897, a new owner, acknowledging the popular association with Longfellow's poem, Tales of a Wayside Inn, changed the name. The Old Barroom, Longfellow's Parlor, the pianoforte and grandfather clock are all here. A reproduction Grist Mill, and the Redstone Schoolhouse are open for touring. Allow six to twelve months ahead for reservations.

Ware E7

The Wildwood Inn

121 Church St
Ware, MA 01082-1203
(413)967-7798 (800)860-8098

Rates: $50-85.
Payment: MC VISA AX DC PC TC.
Innkeeper(s): Fraidell Fenster & Richard Watson.
Circa: 1880.

Rooms: 9 rooms, 7 with PB. 1 suite. 2 conference rooms.
Beds: KQDT.

This yellow Victorian has a wraparound porch and a beveled-glass front door. American primitive antiques include a collection of New England cradles and heirloom quilts, a saddlemaker's bench, and a spinning wheel. The inn's two acres are dotted with maple, chestnut and apple trees. Through the woods you'll find a river.

Breakfast and afternoon tea included in rates. Types of meals: full breakfast and early coffee/tea. Banquet service, catering service and catered breakfast available. Air conditioning, turn-down service and ceiling fan in room. Bicycles, tennis and library on premises. Handicap access. Weddings, small meetings, family reunions and seminars hosted. Amusement parks, antiques, fishing, parks, shopping, downhill skiing, cross-country skiing, sporting events and theater nearby. TAC10.

Publicity: *Boston Globe, National Geographic Traveler, Country, Worcester Telegram-Gazette.*

Special Discounts: Stays of 10 days or more, beginning at 10% off, to maximum of 50% off.

"Excellent accommodations, not only in rooms, but in the kind and thoughtful way you treat your guests. We'll be back!"

The Cranberry Rose B&B

105 High St
Wareham, MA 02571-2053
(508)295-5665 (800)269-5665

Rates: $60-75.
Payment: MC VISA PC TC.
Innkeeper(s): Sue & Chris Makepeace.
Circa: 1903.

Rooms: 3 rooms with PB.
Beds: KQDT.

Innkeeper Chris Makepeace's family built this sturdy, New England home. The house eventually was sold to another family, but Chris and wife, Sue, bought the home several years ago and renovated it into a bed & breakfast. Chris and Sue also have continued the Makepeace tradition as cranberry farmers. During the harvest, the two will prepare picnics and tours of their cranberry bogs. Sue has created several cranberry recipes, some of which she serves in the afternoon along with wine and sherry. Her recipe for Cranberry Bars was featured in Bon Appetit. The home is decorated in a cozy, country style with quilts, ceiling fans and antiques from an 18th-century boarding house.

Breakfast and afternoon tea included in rates. Type of meal: early coffee/tea. Air conditioning and ceiling fan in room. Cable TV, VCR, fax, copier and bicycles on premises. Weddings and family reunions hosted. Antiques, fishing, parks, shopping, cross-country skiing, sporting events, theater and watersports nearby.

"My family found the Cranberry Rose to be the finest and very charming."

Mulberry B&B

257 High St
Wareham, MA 02571-1407
(508)295-0684
Fax:(508)291-2909

Rates: $50-65.
Payment: MC VISA AX DS PC TC.
Innkeeper(s): Frances Murphy.
Circa: 1847.

Rooms: 3 rooms.
Beds: KDT.

MA

This former blacksmith's house is in the historic district of town and has been featured on the local garden club house tour. Frances, a former school teacher, has decorated the guest rooms in a country style with antiques. A deck, shaded by a tall mulberry tree, looks out to the back garden.

Breakfast included in rates. Type of meal: full breakfast. Afternoon tea available. Air conditioning and turn-down service in room. Cable TV and VCR on premises. Antiques, fishing, parks, shopping, cross-country skiing, sporting events, theater and watersports nearby. TAC10.

Publicity: *Brockton Enterprise, Wareham Courier.*

Special Discounts: 15% for stays of seven days or longer - cash or check.

"Thank you for your hospitality. The muffins were delicious."

Wellfleet G18

The Inn at Duck Creeke

70 Main St, PO Box 364
Wellfleet, MA 02667-0364
(508)349-9333
Fax:(508)349-0234

Rates: $50-100.
Payment: MC VISA AX PC TC.
Innkeeper(s): Bob Morrill & Judy Pihl.
Circa: 1815.

Rooms: 25 rooms, 17 with PB. 1 conference room.
Beds: QDT.

The five-acre site of this sea captain's house features both a salt water marsh and a duck pond. The Saltworks house and the main house are appointed in an old-fashioned style with antiques, and the rooms are comfortable and cozy. Some have views of the nearby salt marsh or the pond. The inn is favored for its two restaurants; Sweet Seasons and the Tavern Room. The latter is popular for its jazz performances.

Breakfast included in rates. Types of meals: continental-plus breakfast and early coffee/tea. Dinner available. Ceiling fan in room. Weddings, small meetings, family reunions and seminars hosted. Antiques, fishing, parks, shopping, theater and watersports nearby.

Publicity: *New York Times, Provincetown, Providence Journal, Cape Cod Life, Conde Nast Traveler.*

"Duck Creeke will always be our favorite stay!"

West Harwich I18

The Gingerbread House

141 Division St
West Harwich, MA 02671
(508)432-1901 (800)788-1901

Rates: $45-105.
Payment: MC VISA TC.
Innkeeper(s): Stacia & Les Kostecki.
Circa: 1883.

Rooms: 5 suites, 1 with FP. 1 conference room.
Beds: Q.

This rambling Queen Anne Victorian is decked with ornate, gingerbread trim and gables. The innkeepers, of Polish descent, have added European flavor to their inn with a collection of Polish art, crystal and crafts. Aside from the scrumptious breakfasts, the innkeepers offer dinner service at the inn's restaurant. Proper afternoon teas are served in the Tea Room, which is located in the Carriage House. Sandwiches, freshly baked goods and scones are accompanied by Devon clotted cream and a selection of teas. The inn is near many of Cape Cod's shops and restaurants.

Breakfast and afternoon tea included in rates. Types of meals: continental breakfast, continental-plus breakfast, full breakfast, gourmet breakfast and early coffee/tea. Dinner, evening snack, picnic lunch, gourmet lunch and room service available. Ceiling fan and cable TV in room. VCR and child care on premises. Handicap access. Weddings and small meetings hosted. Antiques, fishing, parks, shopping and theater nearby.

Lion's Head Inn

186 Belmont Rd
West Harwich, MA 02671
(508)432-7766 (800)321-3155

Rates: $60-120.
Payment: MC VISA PC TC.
Innkeeper(s): Marilyn & Tom Hull.
Circa: 1804.

Rooms: 6 rooms with PB. 2 cottages.
Beds: KQT.

This Cape-style house was built by Thomas Snow, a sea captain of Orient-bound schooners. Recently renovated, the inn has retained its colonial feeling with its fireplace and the Captain's Staircase, a steep stairway that is original to the house. The inn is decorated with period antiques and traditional furnishings, highlighting the pine floors. Several antique maps hang in the Map Room, once used as a study for Captain Snow.

Breakfast included in rates. Type of meal: continental-plus breakfast. Air conditioning in room. Cable TV, VCR, swimming and bicycles on premises. Weddings, small meetings, family reunions and seminars hosted. Antiques, fishing, parks, shopping, sporting events, theater and watersports nearby.

Publicity: *Harwich Oracle, Suburban Spotlight.*

Special Discounts: Group discounts for party booking more than three rooms.

"The best innkeepers we have met on the Cape!"

West Stockbridge E2

Card Lake Inn

PO Box 38
West Stockbridge, MA
01266-0038
(413)232-0272
Fax:(413)232-0272

Rates: $60-140.
Payment: MC VISA AX DS.
Innkeeper(s): Ed & Lisa Robbins.
Circa: 1880.

Rooms: 8 rooms.
Beds: KQ.

Located in the center of town, this Colonial Revival inn features a popular local restaurant on the premises. Norman Rockwell is said to have frequented its tavern. Stroll around historic West Stockbridge then enjoy the inn's deck cafe with its flower boxes and view of the sculpture garden of an art gallery across the street. Original lighting, hardwood floors and antiques are features of the inn. Chesterwood and Tanglewood are within easy driving distance.

Breakfast included in rates. Types of meals: continental breakfast and early coffee/tea. Restaurant on premises. Air conditioning and ceiling fan in room. Cable TV and VCR on premises. Weddings, small meetings, family reunions and seminars hosted. Amusement parks, antiques, shopping and sporting events nearby.

Williamsville Inn

Rt 41, West Stockbridge, MA 01266
(413)274-6118
Fax:(413)274-3539

Rates: $105-185.
Payment: MC VISA AX PC.
Innkeeper(s): Gail & Kathleen Ryan.
Circa: 1797.

Rooms: 16 rooms with PB, 2 with FP. 1 suite. 1 conference room.
Beds: KQDT.

At the foot of Tom Ball Mountain is this Federal-style inn, formerly the Tom Ball farm. Some guest rooms feature fireplaces or woodstoves. The inn's grounds sport gardens, a swimming pool and tennis court. Guests often enjoy relaxing in a swing that hangs from an ancient elm. Chesterwood, Mission House, Old Corner House and Tanglewood are within easy driving distance.

Breakfast included in rates. Type of meal: full breakfast. Dinner available. Air conditioning in room. Fax, copier, swimming and tennis on premises. 10 acres. Weddings, small meetings, family reunions and seminars hosted. Spanish, French and Some Japanese spoken. Antiques, fishing, parks, shopping, downhill skiing, cross-country skiing, theater and watersports nearby. TAC10.

Pets Allowed.

Location: Heart of the Berkshires.

West Tisbury K15

MA

Bayberry Inn

PO Box 654, Old Courthouse Rd
West Tisbury, MA 02575
(508)693-1984 (800)693-9960
Fax:(508)693-4505

Rates: $125-175.
Payment: MC VISA AX PC TC.
Innkeeper(s): Rosalie H. Powell.

Rooms: 5 rooms, 3 with PB.
Beds: KQDT.

Apple trees shade the lawn of this Cape-style house, built on land first settled in 1642. (The innkeeper is a descendant of Martha's Vineyard's first settler, Thomas Mayhew.) The house is filled with antiques and hooked rugs. A favorite guest room features a canopied bed with a view of meadows and woods. Breakfast is festively served with blue and white Staffordshire china and fine table linens.

Breakfast and afternoon tea included in rates. Types of meals: full breakfast, gourmet breakfast and early coffee/tea. Cable TV, VCR and fax on premises. Weddings and family reunions hosted. Antiques, fishing, parks, shopping, theater and watersports nearby. TAC10.

Publicity: *Enterprise, Martha's Vineyard Times, Capital Entertainment.*

"Darling, delightful, delicious."

West Yarmouth I17

Manor House

57 Maine Ave
West Yarmouth, MA 02673
(508)771-3433 (800)962-6679

Rates: $58-108.
Payment: MC VISA AX PC TC.
Innkeeper(s): Rick & Liz Latshaw.
Circa: 1920.

Rooms: 6 rooms with PB.
Beds: QD.

This bed & breakfast is located on Cape Cod's south shore overlooking Lewis Bay. The beach and a boat ramp are within walking distance. The quiet neighborhood also is near whale watching, golf and fine dining. Take a ferry to one of the islands or just relax in the comfort of your own room. The fireplaced sitting room is a great place to finish a book.

Breakfast and afternoon tea included in rates. Types of meals: continental-plus breakfast and early coffee/tea. Air conditioning and turn-down service in room. Cable TV, VCR and library on premises. Antiques, fishing, parks, shopping, theater and watersports nearby. TAC10.

"An experience I am anxious to repeat."

Woods Hole

J15

The Marlborough B&B

PO Box 238
Woods Hole, MA 02543
(508)548-6218 (800)320-2322
Fax:(508)457-7519

Rates: $65-125.
Payment: MC VISA AX PC.
Innkeeper(s): Diana Smith.
Circa: 1942.

Rooms: 5 rooms, 6 with PB. 1 cottage.
Beds: QD.

This is a faithful reproduction of a Cape-style cottage complete with picket fence and rambling roses. An English paddle-tennis court and swimming pool are popular spots in summer. In winter, breakfast is served beside a roaring fire. The inn is the closest bed & breakfast to the ferries to Martha's Vineyard and Nantucket.

Breakfast included in rates. Types of meals: gourmet breakfast and early coffee/tea. Air conditioning in room. Cable TV, fax, swimming and tennis on premises. Antiques, fishing, shopping, theater and watersports nearby. TAC10.

Location: Near Falmouth historic district.

Publicity: *Cape Cod Life.*

"Our stay at the Marlborough was a little bit of heaven."

Yarmouth Port

I17

Colonial House Inn

Rt 6A, 277 Main St
Yarmouth Port, MA 02675
(508)362-4348 (800)999-3416
Fax:(508)362-8034

Rates: $70-95. MAP, AP, EP.
Payment: MC VISA AX DS PC TC.
Innkeeper(s): Malcolm Perna.
Circa: 1730.

Rooms: 21 rooms with PB, 3 with FP. 2 suites. 3 conference rooms.
Beds: KQDT.

Although the original structure was built in pre-revolutionary times, a third floor was later added and another section was shipped in from Europe. The innkeepers renovated the carriage house, creating 10 new rooms. Dining areas include the Colonial Room with hand-stenciled walls and a fireplace, and the Common Room, a recent glass-enclosed addition with a view of the veranda and town green. A traditional Thanksgiving dinner is served every year, and guests may enjoy other specialties, including murder-mystery, Las Vegas and wine-tasting weekends.

Breakfast and dinner included in rates. Type of meal: continental breakfast. MAP, AP, EP. Air conditioning and ceiling fan in room. VCR, fax, copier, spa, swimming, sauna, library and child care on premises. Handicap access. Weddings, small meetings, family reunions and seminars hosted. French, Spanish and Italian spoken. Antiques, fishing, parks, shopping, cross-country skiing, sporting events, theater and watersports nearby. TAC10.

Pets Allowed: Certain rooms.

Publicity: *New York Times, Yankee, Cape Cod Life, Boston Globe, Newsday.*

Special Discounts: For $10 additional two people may get dinner included.

"The nicest place I've ever stayed."

One Centre Street Inn

1 Center St
Yarmouth Port, MA 02675
(508)362-8910

Rates: $65-110.
Payment: MC VISA PC TC.
Innkeeper(s): Karen Iannello.
Circa: 1824.

Rooms: 6 rooms, 4 with PB, 1 with FP.
Beds: QDT.

A rustic cookstove warms the dining room where such items as freshly baked scones, homemade granola and orange French toast topped with a strawberry-Grand Marinier sauce get the morning off to a perfect start. This National Register inn was used as a church parsonage when it was built in the 1820s. Four-poster or brass

beds decorated the guest rooms, appointed in a mix of styles, from Queen Anne to Colonial.

Breakfast included in rates. Types of meals: full breakfast and gourmet breakfast. Bicycles on premises. Small meetings and family reunions hosted. Antiques, fishing, parks, shopping, theater and watersports nearby. TAC10.

Special Discounts: Stay two nights, get third night free from Oct. 15 - May 15, excluding holidays.

Wedgewood Inn

83 Main St
Yarmouth Port, MA 02675
(508)362-5157
Fax:(508)362-5851

Rates: $95-160.
Payment: MC VISA AX DC PC TC.
Innkeeper(s): Milt & Gerrie Graham.
Circa: 1812.

Rooms: 6 rooms with PB, 4 with FP. 2 suites.
Beds: QT.

This three-story Greek Revival home was built for a maritime attorney and was the first architecturally designed home in town. A built-in hallway clock is written up in the town's local history. Wide-board floors, pencil-post beds, antiques, fireplaces and private porches create a romantic ambiance. Afternoon tea is served.

Breakfast and afternoon tea included in rates. Types of meals: full breakfast and early coffee/tea. Air conditioning in room. Cable TV and fax on premises. Small meetings and seminars hosted. Antiques, fishing, shopping, theater and watersports nearby. TAC10.

Publicity: *Cape Cod Life, Fine Life of America (Japanese), Colonial Home.*

"Fabulous — wonderful little getaway. We'll be back. Great romantic getaway."

MA

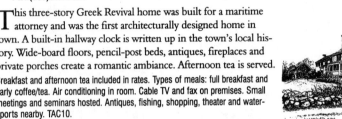

Shitake Mushrooms with Vermicelli

The Inn at Little Washington
Washington, Va.

2 ½ cups cubed tomatoes, fresh or canned
¼ cup tomato paste
1 T balsamic vinegar
2 ½ t dried thyme
½ t herbes de Provence (optional)
3 T sugar
Salt, freshly ground pepper to taste
¼ t Tabasco
1 cup plus 2 T olive oil
2 cups thinly sliced onions, loosely packed
2 ¼ t finely minced garlic
1 ¼ lbs. shitake mushrooms
¼ lb. vermicelli or capellini
2 T finely chopped scallions or chives
1 ½ t sesame oil
1 t soy sauce
¼ t grated fresh ginger
⅛ t five-spice powder

Combine tomatoes, tomato paste, vinegar, thyme, herbes de Provence, sugar, salt, pepper and Tabasco in a saucepan. Bring to a boil.

Heat ¼ cup of the olive oil in a heavy skillet and add onions. Cook, stirring until wilted. Add to tomato mixture and cook, stirring, about 30 minutes or until sauce is quite thick. Add 2 teaspoons of the garlic and stir.

Cut mushrooms into thin slices. Heat ¾ cup olive oil in a large, heavy skillet. Add half of the mushrooms, salt and pepper and cook, stirring often, until mushrooms are crisp. Drain, but reserve oil, returning it to the skillet to cook the remaining mushrooms, adding more oil if necessary. Drain.

Add mushrooms to tomato sauce, stir to blend. Let stand until room temperature.

Bring a large quantity of water to boil and add some salt. Add vermicelli or capellini and cook about 3 minutes, or to desired degree of doneness. Drain and run under cold water until chilled. Drain thoroughly, pour into bowl, add remaining olive oil, scallions or chives, sesame oil, soy sauce, remaining garlic, ginger and five-spice powder. Toss to blend well. Serve with tomato-mushroom sauce.

Serves 8 or more.

Michigan

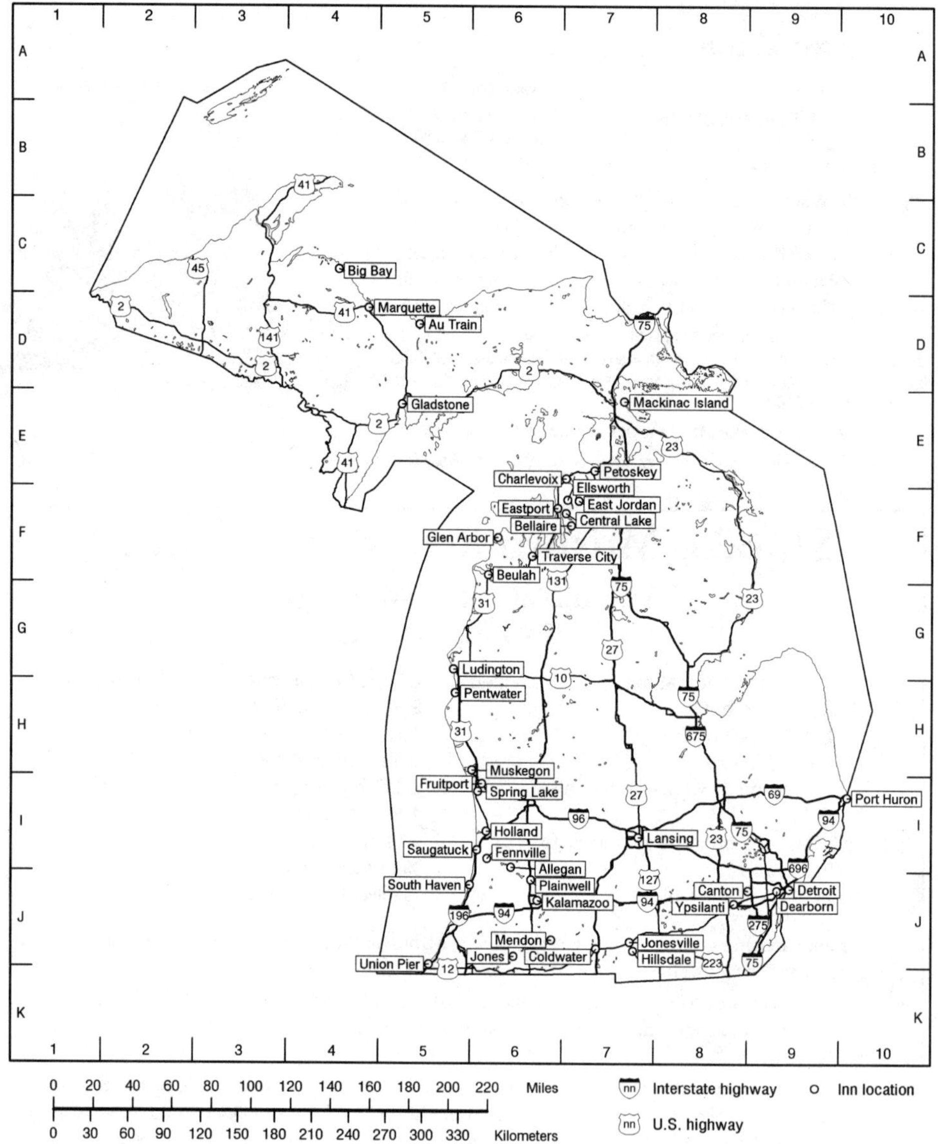

Big Bay
Marquette
Au Train
Gladstone
Mackinac Island
Petoskey
Charlevoix
Ellsworth
East Jordan
Eastport
Central Lake
Bellaire
Glen Arbor
Traverse City
Beulah
Ludington
Pentwater
Muskegon
Fruitport
Spring Lake
Port Huron
Holland
Lansing
Saugatuck
Fennville
Allegan
Plainwell
South Haven
Canton
Detroit
Kalamazoo
Ypsilanti
Dearborn
Mendon
Jonesville
Union Pier
Jones
Coldwater
Hillsdale
0 20 40 60 80 100 120 140 160 180 200 220 Miles
0 30 60 90 120 150 180 210 240 270 300 330 Kilometers
Interstate highway
U.S. highway
Inn location

Allegan

I6

Winchester Inn

524 Marshall St M-89
Allegan, MI 49010-1632
(616)673-3620 (800)582-5694

Rates: $70-90.
Payment: MC VISA AX PC TC.
Innkeeper(s): Denise & Dave Ferber.
Circa: 1864.

Rooms: 4 rooms with PB.
Beds: KQD.

This neo-Italian Renaissance mansion was built of double-layer brick and has been restored to its original beauty. Surrounded by a unique, hand-poured iron fence, the inn is decorated with period antiques, including antique toys and trains. The innkeeper's love for Christmas and other holidays is evident. Many christmas decorations, including a 10-foot Victorian tree remain up throughout the year. The tree in the dining room is decorated for whatever holiday is near. For instance, around Halloween, pumpkins and gourds decorate the tree. Three guest rooms are decorated in a Christmas theme with trees, and another guest room's decor rotates in honor of the most current holiday.

Breakfast included in rates. Types of meals: continental-plus breakfast, full breakfast and early coffee/tea. Ceiling fan in room. Cable TV on premises. Weddings, small meetings and family reunions hosted. Antiques, fishing, parks, shopping, downhill skiing, cross-country skiing, sporting events, theater and watersports nearby. TAC10.

Location: Near Grand Rapids, Kalamazoo, Holland, Saugatuck and Lake Michigan State Forest.

Publicity: *Architectural Digest, Home and Away, Midwest Living, Detroit Free Press, Cleveland Plain Dealer, Grand Rapids Press.*

"This is one of Michigan's loveliest country inns."

MI

Au Train

D5

Pinewood Lodge

PO Box 176
Au Train, MI 49806-0176
(906)892-8300
Fax:(906)892-8510

Rates: $75-105.
Payment: MC VISA DS TC.
Innkeeper(s): Jenny & Jerry Krieg.
Circa: 1989.

Rooms: 7 rooms, 3 with PB. 2 suites.
Beds: Beds: QDT.

This rustic log lodge is surrounded by two picturesque acres of Norway pines. This is a place for those who wish to commune with nature or simply relax, so furnishings are casual and comfortable. The great room offers a large, granite fireplace to enjoy a crackling fire. The area is full of seasonal activities, including hiking, the beach, bicycling and cross-country skiing. There are cross-country, snowshoe and snowmobile trails right out the front door.

Breakfast included in rates. Types of meals: full breakfast and early coffee/tea. Ceiling fan and VCR in room. Fax, swimming and sauna on premises. Weddings, small meetings, family reunions and seminars hosted. Antiques, fishing, parks, shopping, downhill skiing, cross-country skiing, sporting events and watersports nearby. TAC10.

"This was definitely the highlight of our Upper Peninsula vacation."

Bellaire

F7

Grand Victorian B&B Inn

402 N Bridge St
Bellaire, MI 49615-9591
(616)533-6111 (800)336-3860
Fax:(616)533-8197

Rates: $90-125.
Payment: MC VISA AX.
Innkeeper(s): Jill Watson.
Circa: 1895.

Rooms: 4 rooms with PB.
Beds: QD.

It's hard to believe that anything but joy has ever been associated with this beautiful Queen Anne Victorian inn, but its original owner, who built it in anticipation of his upcoming nuptials, left town broken-hearted when his wedding plans fell through. The eye-pleasing inn, with its gables, square corner towers, bays and overhangs, is listed in the National Register of Historic Places. There is much to do in this popular area of Northern Michigan, with its famous nearby skiing and fishing spots, but the inn's impressive interior may entice guests to stay on the premises. Guest rooms are well-appointed with period antiques and lavish touches. Visitors may borrow a bicycle built for two for a relaxing tour of town.

Breakfast and afternoon tea included in rates. Types of meals: full breakfast and early coffee/tea. Picnic lunch available. Air conditioning and VCR in room. Cable TV on premises. Weddings, small meetings, family reunions and seminars hosted. Antiques, fishing, shopping, downhill skiing, cross-country skiing and watersports nearby.

Publicity: *Featured on Nabisco Crackers/Cookies Boxes Promotion, Midwest Living, Country Inns.*

"We certainly enjoyed our visit to the Grand Victorian. It has been our pleasure to stay in B&Bs in several countries, but never one more beautiful and almost never with such genial hosts."

Beulah F6

Brookside Inn

115 N Michigan, PO Box 506
Beulah, MI 49617
(616)882-9688

Rates: $195-250. MAP.
Payment: MC VISA AX.
Innkeeper(s): Pam & Kirk Lorenz.
Circa: 1939.

Rooms: 20 rooms with PB, 19 with FP. 1 conference room.
Beds: KW.

Antiques and country furnishings decorate the interior of Brookside Inn, located by Crystal Lake. King-size canopy waterbeds, Polynesian spas, wood-burning stoves and saunas are just a few of the romantic amenities. Both breakfast and dinner are included in the rates, and guests may dine on the outdoor deck or by the fireplace. The inn's seven-acre grounds include a bridge to an herb and flower garden.

Type of meal: full breakfast. MAP. Spa and sauna on premises. Handicap access.

Publicity: *Detroit Free Press.*

"Michigan's romantic retreat..works a spell," Rick Sylvain, Detroit Free Press.

Big Bay C4

The Big Bay Point Lighthouse B&B

3 Lighthouse Rd
Big Bay, MI 49808
(906)345-9957
E-mail: Compuserve 72324,262

Rates: $85-155.
Payment: PC TC.
Innkeeper(s): Linda & Jeff Gamble.
Circa: 1896.

Rooms: 7 rooms with PB. 2 suites.
Beds: QD.

With 4,500 feet of frontage on Lake Superior, this landmark lighthouse commands 534 acres of forests and a five-acre lawn. The interior of the lighthouse features a brick fireplace. Several guest rooms look out to the water. The tower room on the top floor offers truly unforgettable views. Breakfast is light, so pack some extra food.

Breakfast and evening snack included in rates. Types of meals: full breakfast and early coffee/tea. Ceiling fan in room. VCR, fax, copier and sauna on premises. 40 acres. Antiques, fishing, parks, shopping, downhill skiing, cross-country skiing, sporting events, theater and watersports nearby. TAC10.

Location: Four miles northeast of Big Bay.

Publicity: *Los Angeles Times, USA Today.*

Canton J9

Willow Brook Inn

44255 Warren Rd
Canton, MI 48187-2147
(313)454-0019 (888)454-1919

Rates: $75-105.
Payment: MC VISA DS.
Innkeeper(s): Bernadette & Michael Van Lenten.
Circa: 1929.

Rooms: 4 rooms, 2 with PB. 1 suite.
Beds: KQDT.

Willow Brook winds its way through the backyard of this aptly named inn, situated on a lush, wooded acre. Innkeepers Bernadette and Michael Van Lenten filled their home with oak and pine country antiques and beds covered with soft quilts. They also added special toys and keepsakes from their own childhood to add a homey touch. After a peaceful rest, guests are invited to partake in the morning meal either in the "Teddy Bear" dining room, in the privacy of their rooms or in the sun room. Breakfasts consist of luscious treats such as homemade breads, scones topped with devon cream and a rich, egg dish.

Breakfast and evening snack included in rates. Types of meals: gourmet breakfast and early coffee/tea. Afternoon tea, picnic lunch and catering service available. Turn-down service, ceiling fan and VCR in room. Fax, copier, bicycles, pet boarding and child care on premises. Weddings, small meetings and family reunions hosted. French spoken. Antiques, parks, shopping, cross-country skiing, sporting events, theater and watersports nearby. TAC10.

Pets Allowed: Not permitted in bedrooms.

Publicity: *Canton Observer, Canton Eagle, Detroit News.*

"I love the Dolls Dollhouse Room. Really enjoyed my visit. Wonderful, warm, family feeling. Great scones!"

MI

Central Lake F7

Bridgewalk B&B

2287 S Main, PO Box 399
Central Lake, MI 49622
(616)544-8122

Rates: $75-85.
Payment: MC VISA PC TC.
Innkeeper(s): Janet & Tom Meteer.
Circa: 1895.

Rooms: 5 rooms with PB. 1 suite.
Beds: KQT.

Secluded on a wooded acre, this three-story Victorian is accessible by crossing a foot bridge over a stream. Guest rooms are simply decorated with Victorian touches, floral prints and fresh flowers. The Garden Suite includes a clawfoot tub. Much of the home's Victorian elements have been restored, including pocket doors and the polished woodwork. Breakfasts begin with such items as a cold fruit soup, freshly baked muffins or scones accompanied with homemade jams and butters. A main dish, perhaps stuffed French toast tops off the meal.

Breakfast included in rates. Types of meals: full breakfast and early coffee/tea. Ceiling fan in room. Small meetings hosted. Antiques, fishing, parks, shopping, downhill skiing, cross-country skiing and watersports nearby. TAC10.

Charlevoix E7

Bridge Street Inn

113 Michigan Ave
Charlevoix, MI 49720-1819
(616)547-6606
Fax:(616)547-1812

Rates: $56-110.
Payment: MC VISA PC TC.
Innkeeper(s): Vera & John McKown.
Circa: 1895.

Rooms: 9 rooms, 3 with PB.
Beds: QT.

This three-story Colonial Revival structure recalls the bygone era when Charlevoix was home to many grand hotels. Originally a guest "cottage" of one of those large hotels, this inn boasts nine gracious guest rooms, many of which are available with private bath. The rooms sport antique furnishings, floral rugs and wooden floors and offer stunning views of the surrounding lakes. Guests are within walking distance of Lake

Michigan's beaches, Round Lake's harbor and Lake Charlevoix's boating and fishing. Be sure to inquire in advance about the inn's many discounts and special rate for small groups.

Breakfast included in rates. Type of meal: continental-plus breakfast. Ceiling fan in room. Cable TV, VCR and fax on premises. Family reunions hosted. German spoken. Antiques, fishing, parks, shopping, downhill skiing, cross-country skiing, sporting events, theater and watersports nearby. TAC10.

Coldwater J7

Batavia Inn

1824 W Chicago Rd
Coldwater, MI 49036-9331
(517)278-5146

Rates: $64-104.
Payment: MC VISA DS PC TC.
Innkeeper(s): Fred Marquardt.
Circa: 1872.

Rooms: 5 rooms with PB.
Beds: KQDT.

Today the Batavia Inn serves as a getaway spot for travelers, but its original purpose was the home of a hotel owner, his wife and their 10 children. The home was built using walnut and butternut wood found on the property. The inn still boasts its original etched and beveled windows. The innkeepers named the guest rooms in honor of families that have lived in the home. A hand-painted mural graces the Bristol Room, which overlooks the garden. The Wiggans Room features heirloom needlework and lace-canopied bed. Other rooms include special antiques, such as the 8-foot canopy bed in the Marquardt Room. The innkeepers also include seasonal decor in the guest rooms. For instance, December visitors will find a Christmas tree in their room.

Breakfast included in rates. Types of meals: full breakfast, gourmet breakfast and early coffee/tea. Air conditioning in room. Swimming, stables, bicycles and library on premises. 15 acres. Weddings, small meetings, family reunions and seminars hosted. German spoken. Antiques, fishing, parks, shopping, cross-country skiing, theater and watersports nearby. TAC10.

Location: West of I-69 on US 12.

Chicago Pike Inn

215 E Chicago St
Coldwater, MI 49036-2001
(517)279-8744

Rates: $80-165.
Payment: MC VISA AX PC TC.
Innkeeper(s): Becky Schultz.
Circa: 1903.

Rooms: 8 rooms with PB, 1 with FP. 2 suites. 1 conference room.
Beds: QT.

This exquisite colonial mansion was built by an architect who designed many of the homes on Mackinac Island. Furnished with period antiques, the inn features chandeliers, stained glass, parquet flooring and a stunning cherry staircase. Its name is derived from Coldwater's midway location on the old Detroit-Chicago turnpike. Guests will enjoy exploring Coldwater's historic buildings or perhaps a visit to the Victorian-style Tibbits Opera House built in 1882.

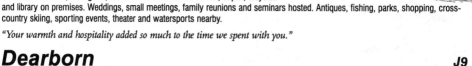

Breakfast included in rates. Types of meals: full breakfast and early coffee/tea. Turn-down service, ceiling fan, cable TV and VCR in room. Fax, copier, bicycles and library on premises. Weddings, small meetings, family reunions and seminars hosted. Antiques, fishing, parks, shopping, cross-country skiing, sporting events, theater and watersports nearby.

"Your warmth and hospitality added so much to the time we spent with you."

Dearborn J9

Dearborn B&B

22331 Morley Ave
Dearborn, MI 48124-2131
(313)563-2200 (888)959-0900
Fax:(313)277-2962

Rates: $85-165.
Payment: MC VISA AX DS PC TC.
Innkeeper(s): Nancy Siwik & Rick Harder.
Circa: 1927.

Rooms: 4 rooms, 3 with PB. 1 suite.
Beds: D.

The innkeepers at Dearborn painstakingly restored their Victorian, which is listed in the state historical register. During the renovation process, the home's original mahogany, oak, poplar, birch and pine woodwork was uncovered. Fine antiques, including a unique 1815 Empire sofa, decorate the home. Three guest quarters are named for the type of wood furniture included in the room, such as the Mahogany Room filled with turn-of-the-century pieces, or the Walnut Room with its Eastlake walnut bed. Along with a continental-plus breakfast, guests also receive free tickets to the Henry Ford Museum and Greenfield Village.

Breakfast, afternoon tea and evening snack included in rates. Types of meals: continental-plus breakfast and early coffee/tea. Air conditioning, ceiling fan and cable TV in room. VCR, fax, copier, swimming and library on premises. Weddings, small meetings and family reunions hosted. Antiques, fishing, parks, shopping, sporting events and theater nearby. TAC10.

Detroit J9

The Blanche House Inn

506 Parkview Dr
Detroit, MI 48214-2968
(313)822-7090
Fax:(313)822-7090

Rates: $60-115.
Payment: MC VISA AX DC CB TC.
Innkeeper(s): Lesa Bucceri.
Circa: 1902.

Rooms: 11 rooms, 8 with PB, 1 with FP. 1 suite. 1 conference room.
Beds: QD.

This massive "White House"-style Victorian mansion has two-story columns supporting a rotunda entrance. Located on the Stanton Canal, a block from the Detroit River, the inn provides an expansive view of Detroit's waterways. Polished wood floors, etched glass, Pewabic tile, gleaming woodwork and antiques fill the inn's 10,000 square feet. The home was built by Marvin Stanton, former overall manufacturer and Detroit lighting commissioner. In the '20s this house and adjoining "Castle" served as a private boys' school where Henry Ford II attended.

Breakfast included in rates. Types of meals: continental-plus breakfast, full breakfast and early coffee/tea. Afternoon tea, banquet service and catering service available. Air conditioning, cable TV and VCR in room. Fax and copier on premises. Weddings, small meetings, family reunions and seminars hosted. Antiques, fishing, parks, shopping, sporting events, theater and watersports nearby.

MI

Location: Three miles east of downtown on the canal.

Publicity: *Detroit Monthly, Crain's Detroit Business.*

East Jordan F7

Easterly Inn

209 Easterly, PO Box 366
East Jordan, MI 49727
(616)536-3434

Rates: $65-85.
Payment: MC VISA PC TC.
Innkeeper(s): Joan Martin.
Circa: 1906.

Rooms: 4 rooms with PB.
Beds: QD.

Finely crafted woodwork of cherry, birds-eye maple and oak are hints that this turn-of-the-century Victorian was built for a lumber merchant. Its three stories and 18 rooms have been carefully restored and furnished with fine antiques and period wallcoverings which enhance its gleaming hardwood floors and leaded windows. Guest rooms include the Turret Room, which offers a tall, carved walnut and burl queen bed, and the Romantic Lace Room, with Victorian rose prints and a queen canopy bed. Breakfast is served in the semi-circular dining room.

Breakfast included in rates. Type of meal: full breakfast. Ceiling fan in room. Cable TV and library on premises. Small meetings and family reunions hosted. Antiques, fishing, parks, shopping, downhill skiing, cross-country skiing and watersports nearby.

"A wonderful inn, full of history and romance. Thank you for sharing yourself with us."

Eastport F6

Torch Lake Sunrise B&B

Box 52, 3644 Blasen Shores Ln
Eastport, MI 49627-0052
(616)599-2706

Rates: $75-110.
Payment: PC.
Innkeeper(s): Betty A. Collins.
Circa: 1980.

Rooms: 3 rooms with PB.
Beds: KQ.

This house is located in the village and overlooks Torch Lake, considered by many to be one of the three most beautiful lakes in the world. Each room is furnished with antiques and has a private deck. In summer, guests may borrow the canoe or rowboat. Eggs Benedict and strawberry pancakes are specialties of the innkeeper.

Breakfast included in rates. Types of meals: full breakfast, gourmet breakfast and early coffee/tea. Ceiling fan, cable TV and VCR in room. Swimming and bicycles on premises. Handicap access. Weddings, small meetings and family reunions hosted. Amusement parks, antiques, fishing, parks, shopping, downhill skiing, cross-country skiing, sporting events, theater and watersports nearby. TAC10.

Pets Allowed: Seeing eye dogs only.

Location: Fifteen miles north of Elk Rapids.

Publicity: *Detroit Free Press.*

Ellsworth F7

The House on The Hill

9661 Lake St, PO Box 206
Ellsworth, MI 49729
(616)588-6304

Rates: $105-125.
Payment: MC VISA PC TC.
Innkeeper(s): Julie & Buster Arnim.
Circa: 1900.

Rooms: 7 rooms with PB, 3 with FP. 1 cottage.
Beds: QT.

From the spacious veranda of this homey Victorian, guests can relax and enjoy a view of the lake and surrounding 51 acres. Guests opting for the Carriage House also enjoy views of woods and meadows. Rooms are filled with period antiques, and three also offer fireplaces. The innkeepers are native Texans and enjoy serving fiery fare for breakfast, including Texas toast and a curious dish named, "Eggs from Hell."

Breakfast included in rates. Types of meals: gourmet breakfast and early coffee/tea. Catering service available. Ceiling fan in room. Cable TV and child care on premises. Handicap access. 51 acres. Weddings, small meetings, family reunions and seminars hosted. Antiques, fishing, parks, shopping, downhill skiing, cross-country skiing and watersports nearby.

Special Discounts: Dining/lodging winter package: Two nights $375.

"We cannot thank you enough for the wonderful weekend our family spent in your home. You made us all feel so welcome."

Fennville I6

The Kingsley House

626 W Main St
Fennville, MI 49408-9442
(616)561-6425

Rates: $80-145.
Payment: MC VISA AX DS PC TC.
Innkeeper(s): Gary & Kari King.
Circa: 1886.

Rooms: 8 rooms with PB, 3 with FP. 3 suites.
Beds: KQD.

Construction of this Queen Anne Victorian, with a three-story turret, was paid for in silver bricks by the Kingsley family. Mr. Kingsley is noted for having introduced the apple tree to the area. In recognition of him, guest rooms are named Dutchess, Golden Delicious, Granny Smith, McIntosh and Jonathan. The Northern Spy, complete with hot tub, is nestled in the third-floor suite. A winding oak staircase leads to the antique-filled guest chambers. Family heirlooms and other period pieces add to the inn's elegance.

Breakfast and evening snack included in rates. Types of meals: continental-plus breakfast, full breakfast and early coffee/tea. Picnic lunch available. Air conditioning, ceiling fan and cable TV in room. Fax, bicycles and library on premises. Small meetings and seminars hosted. Antiques, fishing, parks, shopping, downhill skiing, cross-country skiing, sporting events, theater and watersports nearby. TAC10.

Location: 196 South of Holland to Exit 34 then East 5 miles.

Publicity: *Innsider, Battle Creek Enquirer, Fennville Herald, Commercial Record, Glamour, Country.*

Special Discounts: Off season specials and special packages.

"It was truly enjoyable. You have a lovely home and a gracious way of entertaining."

Fruitport

I6

Village Park B&B

60 Park St
Fruitport, MI 49415-9668
(616)865-6289 (800)469-1118

Rates: $60-95.
Payment: MC VISA PC TC.
Innkeeper(s): John Hewett.
Circa: 1873.

Rooms: 6 rooms with PB.
Beds: KDT.

Located in the midst of Western Michigan's Tri-Cities area, this inn's small-town village location offers comfort and relaxation to those busy partaking of the many nearby activities. This farmhouse-style inn overlooks Spring Lake and a park where guests may picnic, play tennis, use a pedestrian/bike path and boat launch. There also is a hot tub and exercise room on the premises. The inn offers six guest rooms, all with private bath. A library is just across the street. P.J. Hoffmaster State Park, the Gillette Nature Center and Pleasure Island water park are nearby. Be sure to inquire about the inn's Wellness Weekends with massage.

Breakfast included in rates. Types of meals: continental breakfast, continental-plus breakfast, full breakfast and early coffee/tea. Air conditioning in room. Cable TV, VCR, fax, spa, sauna, bicycles and tennis on premises. Small meetings and family reunions hosted. Amusement parks, antiques, fishing, parks, shopping, cross-country skiing, theater and watersports nearby. TAC10.

Gladstone

E5

Cartwrights' Birdseye Inn B&B

1020 Minnesota Ave
Gladstone, MI 49837-1502
(906)428-3997

Rates: $58-128.
Payment: MC VISA PC TC.
Innkeeper(s): Joyce & Beau Cartwright.
Circa: 1904.

Rooms: 5 rooms, 2 with PB.
Beds: KQD.

MI

This turn-of-the-century home, formerly a boarding house, was named because of the abundance of bird's eye maple within it, both in the furnishings and polished floors. In fact, the innkeepers own one of the largest collections of birdseye maple antiques and accessories. A variety of amenities await to pamper you, including turndown service, fluffy robes, fresh flowers and a basket of toiletries. Guests offer high praise for the gourmet breakfasts, which include seasonal fruit, freshly baked breads and specialty entrees. Guests choose their complete meal and the seating time. Dinners, for parties of six or more, can be arranged.

Breakfast and evening snack included in rates. Types of meals: gourmet breakfast and early coffee/tea. Turn-down service and ceiling fan in room. Cable TV, VCR and bicycles on premises. Antiques, fishing, parks, shopping, cross-country skiing, theater and watersports nearby. TAC10.

Special Discounts: Family rate (adult regular/children half) and group discount.

"More pampering than we've ever had. The hospitality and comfort were great."

Glen Arbor

F6

The Sylvan Inn

PO Box 648,
6680 Western (M-109)
Glen Arbor, MI 49636-0309
(616)334-4333

Rates: $60-120.
Payment: MC VISA PC TC.
Innkeeper(s): Jenny & Bill Olson.
Circa: 1885.

Rooms: 14 rooms, 7 with PB. 1 suite.
Beds: QT.

During restoration, innkeepers Jenny and Bill Olson worked diligently to maintain their 19th-century farmhouse's historic flavor. The older portion of the inn is furnished with antiques, and guest rooms feature brass or iron beds dressed with fine linens and down comforters. In the newer "Great House," there are six additional guest rooms with more contemporary decor and furnishings. There are plenty of things to see and do in the Glen Arbor area, including winery tours, activities at Lake Michigan, hiking, skiing, golf and more.

Breakfast included in rates. Types of meals: continental-plus breakfast and early coffee/tea. Ceiling fan and cable TV in room. Spa and sauna on premises. Handicap access. Weddings and family reunions hosted. Antiques, fishing, parks, shopping, downhill skiing, cross-country skiing, theater and watersports nearby. TAC10.

Special Discounts: Discounts for stays longer than five days.

"Your wonderful service and luxurious accommodations helped to make our wedding a very memorable occasion."

Hillsdale J7

Bluebird Trails B&B

8591 Blount Rd
Hillsdale, MI 49242-9524
(517)254-4754

Rates: $60.
Payment: PC TC.
Innkeeper(s): Larry & Emilie Dasch.
Circa: 1900.

Rooms: 2 rooms, 1 with PB. 1 cottage.
Beds: QT.

This comfortable country cottage contains two bedrooms, a bathroom and a woodstove. The cottage is an ideal place for families with children as the house is set on a 320-acre nature preserve. Guests can help feed sheep and chickens or pick apples and berries. The grounds include groomed walking trails, where guests are sure to encounter a variety of birds and possibly a deer or two. Breakfasts are homemade with ingredients from the property, including farm-fresh eggs. During snowy months, guests are invited to bring along their ice skates or cross-country skis.

Breakfast included in rates. Types of meals: full breakfast and early coffee/tea. 320 acres. Antiques, fishing and cross-country skiing nearby.

"Wonderful scenery, the kids liked the animals, enjoyed our walk, delicious breakfast."

Holland I6

Dutch Colonial Inn

560 Central Ave
Holland, MI 49423-4846
(616)396-3664
Fax:(616)396-0461

Rates: $75-150.
Payment: MC VISA AX DS PC.
Innkeeper(s): Linda Lutke.
Circa: 1928.

Rooms: 5 rooms with PB, 2 with FP. 2 suites. 1 conference room.
Beds: KQ.

Romantic rooms at this Dutch-inspired home include the Hideaway Room with a Brattenberg lace coverlet and whirlpool for two. Another choice is the Jenny Lind Room with a king canopy bed and raspberry and creme decor. A few prized family heirlooms from the Netherlands are featured. A sun porch overlooks part of the inn's lawns.

Breakfast included in rates. Types of meals: full breakfast and early coffee/tea. Air conditioning and cable TV in room. VCR and fax on premises. Weddings, small meetings and seminars hosted. Antiques, fishing, parks, shopping, downhill skiing, cross-country skiing and watersports nearby.

Publicity: *Shoreline Living, Country Folk Art.*

"Thank you again for your generous hospitality, Dutch cleanliness and excellent breakfasts."

The Parsonage 1908

6 E 24th St
Holland, MI 49423-4817
(616)396-1316

Rates: $80-100.
Payment: PC TC.
Innkeeper(s): Bonnie McVoy-Verwys.
Circa: 1908.

Rooms: 3 rooms, 2 with PB.
Beds: DT.

Members of Prospect Park Christian Reformed Church built this American four-square structure as their parsonage. Over the years, it housed seven different pastors and their families. Rich oak woodwork, antique furnishings and leaded glass are found throughout the bed & breakfast. There are two sitting rooms, a formal dining room, garden patio and summer porch. The inn flies a B&B flag designed by the hosts.

Breakfast included in rates. Types of meals: full breakfast and gourmet breakfast. Air conditioning, turn-down service and ceiling fan in room. VCR and library on premises. Antiques, fishing, parks, shopping, cross-country skiing, sporting events, theater and watersports nearby. TAC10.

Location: Close to Hope College.

Publicity: *Detroit Free Press Travel Tales, Midwest Living.*

Special Discounts: Single rates and discount for longer stays.

"Charming. We slept so well! Thank you again for a pleasant visit to a beautiful city in Michigan. And our special thanks to Ms. Verwys and her wonderful home."

Jones

J6

The Sanctuary at Wildwood

58138 M-40
Jones, MI 49061-9713
(616)244-5910 (800)249-5910
Fax:(616)496-8403

Rates: $139-179.
Payment: MC VISA AX DS PC TC.
Innkeeper(s): Dick & Dolly Buerkle.
Circa: 1972.

Rooms: 11 suites. 3 cottages. 1 conference room.
Beds: Q.

Travelers in search of relaxation and a little solitude will enjoy the serenity of this estate, surrounded by 95 forested acres. A stroll down the hiking trails introduces guests to a variety of wildlife, but even inside, guests are pampered by the inn's natural setting. One room, named Medicine Hawk, is adorned with a mural depicting a woodland scene. A mural of a pine forest graces the Quiet Solace room. The Keeper of the Wild Room includes a rustic birch headboard. Each of the rooms includes a fireplace, Jacuzzi and service bar. There also are three cottage suites, situated around a pond. From the dining and great rooms, guests can watch the abundant wildlife. The innkeeper offers a variety of interesting packages. A swimming pool is available during the summer months. Wineries are nearby, and the inn is a half hour from Notre Dame and Shipshewana.

Breakfast included in rates. Air conditioning in room. Handicap access. 95 acres. Weddings, small meetings, family reunions and seminars hosted. Antiques, fishing, shopping, downhill skiing and cross-country skiing nearby. TAC10.

Special Discounts: Special introductory rates from November until April.

Jonesville

J7

Horse & Carriage B&B

MI

7020 Brown Rd
Jonesville, MI 49250-9720
(517)849-2732
Fax:(517)849-2732

Rates: $50-75.
Payment: PC.
Innkeeper(s): Keith L. Brown & family.
Circa: 1898.

Rooms: 3 rooms, 1 with PB. 1 suite.
Beds: QT.

Families are treated to a winter horse drawn sleigh ride at this early 18th-century home, which is surrounded by a 700-acre dairy farm. In the warmer months, horse drawn carriage rides pass down an old country lane past Buck Lake. The innkeepers' family has lived on the property for more than 150 years. The home itself was built as a one-room schoolhouse. A mix of contemporary and country furnishings decorate the interior. The Rainbow Room, a perfect place for children, offers twin beds and a playroom. Guests are treated to hearty breakfasts made with farm-fresh eggs and cream from the farm's cows.

Breakfast and evening snack included in rates. Types of meals: continental breakfast, continental-plus breakfast, full breakfast, gourmet breakfast and early coffee/tea. Picnic lunch and catered breakfast available. Air conditioning in room. Fax and copier on premises. 700 acres. Small meetings and family reunions hosted. Portuguese spoken. Antiques, fishing, parks, shopping, cross-country skiing, sporting events, theater and watersports nearby.

Kalamazoo

J6

Hall House

106 Thompson St
Kalamazoo, MI 49006-4537
(616)343-2500

Rates: $85-109.
Payment: MC VISA.
Innkeeper(s): Jerry & Joanne Hofferth.
Circa: 1923.

Rooms: 5 rooms with PB, 1 with FP. 2 suites.
Beds: KQDT.

This Georgian Colonial Revival-style house was constructed by builder H.L. Vander Horst as his private residence. During the Depression when the construction slowed, Mr. Vander Horst busied himself painting the vaulted ceiling with a Dutch landscape now much admired. Other special features of the house include a 10-head shower, an early intercom system and secret drawers. The hillside campus of Kalamazoo College and the city center are nearby.

Breakfast and afternoon tea included in rates. Types of meals: continental-plus breakfast, full breakfast and early coffee/tea. Air conditioning, ceiling fan and cable TV in room. Library on premises. Weddings, small meetings and family reunions hosted. Antiques, fishing, parks, shopping, downhill skiing, cross-country skiing, sporting events and theater nearby.

Publicity: *Canton Observer, Encore.*

"A step into the grace, charm and elegance of the 19th century but with all the amenities of the 20th century right at hand."

Lansing **I7**

Ask Me House

1027 Seymour Ave
Lansing, MI 48906-4836
(517)484-3127 (800)ASK-ME-41
Fax:(517)484-4193
E-mail: mekiener@aol.com

Rates: $65-95.
Payment: MC VISA PC TC.
Innkeeper(s): Mary Elaine Kiener & Alex Kruzel.
Circa: 1991.

Rooms: 4 rooms. 1 cottage.
Beds: DT.

This early 20th-century home still includes its original hardwood floors and pocket doors. A hand-painted mural was added to the dining room in the 1940s. Guests can enjoy the unique art during the breakfasts, which are served on antique Limoges china and Depression glass. The innkeepers offer a quaint honeymoon cottage along with the guest rooms. The home is near a variety of museums, theaters, a historical village and Michigan State University.

Breakfast included in rates. Types of meals: full breakfast, gourmet breakfast and early coffee/tea. Ceiling fan in room. Cable TV, VCR and fax on premises. Weddings, small meetings, family reunions and seminars hosted. Polish spoken. Antiques, parks, sporting events and theater nearby. TAC10.

Special Discounts: 10% off for seniors, corporate guests.

Ludington **G5**

Lamplighter B&B

602 E Ludington Ave
Ludington, MI 49431-2223
(616)843-9792
Fax:(616)845-6070
E-mail: catsup@aol.com

Rates: $75-125.
Payment: MC VISA AX DS.
Innkeeper(s): Judy & Heinz Bertram.

Rooms: 5 rooms with PB.
Beds: Q.

This Queen Anne home offers convenient access to Lake Michigan's beaches, the Badger Car Ferry to Wisconsin and Michigan state parks. A collection of European antiques and original paintings and lithographs by artists such as Chagall and Dali, decorate the inn. The home's centerpiece, a golden oak curved staircase, leads guests up to their rooms. The innkeepers have created a mix of hospitality and convenience that draws both vacationers and business travelers. A full, gourmet breakfast is served each morning. Freddy, the inn's resident cocker spaniel, is always available for a tour of the area. The innkeepers are fluent in German.

Breakfast included in rates. Types of meals: gourmet breakfast and early coffee/tea. Air conditioning, turn-down service and cable TV in room. VCR on premises. Small meetings and seminars hosted. Antiques, shopping and cross-country skiing nearby.

The Inn at Ludington

701 E Ludington Ave
Ludington, MI 49431-2224
(616)845-7055 (800)845-9170

Rates: $65-85.
Payment: MC VISA AX PC TC.
Innkeeper(s): Diane Shields & David Nemitz.
Circa: 1890.

Rooms: 6 rooms with PB, 2 with FP. 1 suite.
Beds: QD.

This Queen Anne Victorian was built during the heyday of Ludington's lumbering era by a local dentist. Despite its elegant exterior with its three-story turret, the innkeepers stress relaxation at their inn. The rooms are filled with comfortable, vintage furnishings. Guests can snuggle up with a book in front of a warming fireplace or enjoy a soak in a claw-foot tub. A hearty, buffet-style breakfast is served each morning. The innkeepers take great pride in their cuisine and are always happy to share some of their award-winning recipes with guests. After a day of beachcombing, antiquing, cross-country skiing or perhaps a bike ride, guests return to the inn to find a chocolate atop their pillow. Don't forget to ask about the innkeepers' murder-mystery weekends.

Breakfast included in rates. Types of meals: full breakfast and early coffee/tea. Picnic lunch available. Air conditioning, turn-down service and ceiling fan in room. Cable TV, copier and library on premises. Weddings, small meetings and seminars hosted. Amusement parks, antiques, fishing, parks, shopping, downhill skiing, cross-country skiing, theater and watersports nearby. TAC10.

Location: Near Lake Michigan.

Publicity: *Ludington Daily News, Detroit Free Press, Chicago Tribune, Country Accents.*

"Loved the room and everything else about the house."

Snyder's Shoreline Inn

903 W Ludington Ave
Ludington, MI 49431-2035
(616)845-1261
Fax:(616)843-4441

Rates: $65-209.
Payment: MC VISA AX DS.
Innkeeper(s): Angela Snyder & Kate Whitaker.
Circa: 1955.

Rooms: 44 rooms with PB. 8 suites.
Beds: KQD.

This casual, country inn is located on the shores of Lake Michigan. Private balconies, canopy beds and in-room spas are some of the amenities. The innkeepers offer a variety of off-season packages.

Breakfast included in rates. Type of meal: continental breakfast. Air conditioning, ceiling fan, cable TV and VCR in room. Fax, copier, spa, swimming and library on premises. Handicap access. Small meetings and seminars hosted. Antiques, fishing, parks, shopping, theater and watersports nearby.

Mackinac Island — *E7*

MI

Cloghaun

PO Box 203
Mackinac Island, MI 49757
(906)847-3885

Rates: $70-110.
Payment: PC.
Innkeeper(s): James Bond.
Circa: 1884.

Rooms: 10 rooms, 8 with PB.
Beds: QD.

Built big enough to house Thomas and Bridgett Donnelly's large Irish family, this handsome Victorian home is still owned and operated by their descendants today. Its name, pronounced "Clah hahn," is Gaelic for "land of little stones" in reference to Mackinac Island's beaches. Guests can enjoy watching horse-drawn carriages pass by as they relax on the large front porch and balconies. Guest privileges at the nearby Grand Hotel are included.

Breakfast included in rates. Types of meals: continental breakfast and continental-plus breakfast. Cable TV, VCR and library on premises. Weddings, small meetings, family reunions and seminars hosted. Parks and shopping nearby.

Publicity: *Detroit Metropolitan Woman.*

Haan's 1830 Inn

PO Box 123
Mackinac Island, MI 49757
(906)847-6244

Rates: $64-122.
Innkeeper(s): Nicholas & Nancy Haan.
Circa: 1830.

Rooms: 7 rooms, 5 with PB. 2 suites.
Beds: QD.

The clip-clopping of horses is still heard from the front porches of this inn as carriages and wagons transport visitors around the island. In the Michigan Register of Historic Places, Haan's 1830 Inn is the oldest Greek Revival-style home in the Northwest Territory. It is behind a picket fence and just across the street from Haldiman Bay. Victorian and early American antiques include a writing desk used by Colonel Preston, an officer at Fort Mackinac at the turn of the century, and a 12-foot breakfast table formerly used by Amish farmers when they harvested each other's crops. The inn is open from May to October.

Breakfast included in rates. Types of meals: continental-plus breakfast and early coffee/tea. Cable TV on premises. Weddings, small meetings and family reunions hosted. Antiques, fishing and shopping nearby.

Publicity: *Detroit Free Press, Chicago Tribune, Innsider, Chicago Sun-Times, Good Housekeeping.*

"The ambiance, service and everything else was just what we needed."

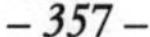

Marquette D4

The Bayou Place

2361 US 41 South
Marquette, MI 49855
(906)249-3863

Rates: $55-125.
Payment: MC VISA PC TC.
Innkeeper(s): Chet & Kim Taylor.
Circa: 1857.

Rooms: 4 rooms, 2 with PB, 1 with FP. 1 conference room.
Beds: QD.

This home was built by the man who engineered the first above-ground rail system in Chicago and New York. The rooms are decorated with antiques, and one suite offers a Jacuzzi tub and fireplace. Turndown service, evening desserts, fluffy robes, a sauna and a hot tub are a few of the amenities. There is an exercise room on the premises and the innkeepers offer a concierge service. Plenty of seasonal activities are nearby, from cross-country and downhill skiing in the winter, to canoeing and fishing in the warmer months.

Breakfast and evening snack included in rates. Types of meals: full breakfast, gourmet breakfast and early coffee/tea. Air conditioning and turn-down service in room. Cable TV, VCR, spa, swimming and sauna on premises. Small meetings, family reunions and seminars hosted. Antiques, fishing, parks, shopping, downhill skiing, cross-country skiing, sporting events, theater and watersports nearby. TAC10.

Mendon J6

The Mendon Country Inn

PO Box 98
Mendon, MI 49072-9502
(616)496-8132 (800)304-3366
Fax:(616)496-8403
E-mail: wildwoodinns@voyager.net

Rates: $69-159.
Payment: MC VISA AX DS PC TC.
Innkeeper(s): Dick & Dolly Buerkle.
Circa: 1873.

Rooms: 18 rooms with PB, 14 with FP. 9 suites. 2 cottages. 2 conference rooms.
Beds: QD.

This two-story stagecoach inn was constructed with St. Joseph River clay bricks fired on the property. There are eight-foot windows, high ceilings and a walnut staircase. Country antiques are accentuated with woven rugs, collectibles and bright quilts. The nine suites include a fireplace and Jacuzzi tub. Depending on the season, guests may also borrow a tandem bike or arrange for a canoe trip. Special events are featured throughout the year. A rural Amish community and Shipshewana are nearby.

Breakfast included in rates. Types of meals: continental-plus breakfast and early coffee/tea. Air conditioning and ceiling fan in room. Fax, sauna, bicycles and library on premises. Handicap access. 14 acres. Seminars hosted. Antiques, fishing, shopping, downhill skiing and cross-country skiing nearby. TAC10.

Location: Halfway between Chicago and Detroit.

Publicity: *Innsider, Country Home.*

"A great experience. Good food and great hosts. Thank you."

Muskegon H6

Port City Victorian Inn

1259 Lakeshore Dr
Muskegon, MI 49441-1659
(616)759-0205 (800)274-3574
Fax:(616)759-0205

Rates: $65-150.
Payment: MC VISA AX.
Innkeeper(s): Fred & Barbara Schossau.
Circa: 1877.

Rooms: 5 rooms, 2 with PB. 2 suites.
Beds: QD.

Lumber baron Alexander Rodgers, Sr. built this Queen Anne-style home. Among its impressive features are the grand entryway with a natural oak staircase and paneling, carved posts and spindles. The leaded-glass windows in the inn's parlor offer a view of Muskegon Lake. Beveled-glass doors enclose the natural wood fireplace in the sitting room, and high ceilings, intricate molding, polished oak floors and antiques further enhance the charm of this house. Guest rooms offer views of the lake, as well as double whirlpool tubs. The full breakfasts are served either on the sun porch, in the dining room or guests can enjoy the meal in the privacy of their room.

Breakfast included in rates. Types of meals: full breakfast and early coffee/tea. Air conditioning and turn-down service in room. Cable TV, VCR, fax, copier and bicycles on premises. Amusement parks, fishing, parks, shopping, cross-country skiing, theater and watersports nearby. TAC10.

Special Discounts: For long term stays, business rates are available.

"The Inn offers only comfort, good food and total peace of mind."

Pentwater H5

Pentwater Inn

180 E Lowell Box 98
Pentwater, MI 49449
(616)869-5909
Fax:(616)869-7002

Rates: $65-85.
Payment: MC VISA PC TC.
Innkeeper(s): Quintus & Donna Renshaw.
Circa: 1869.

Rooms: 5 rooms with PB.
Beds: QD.

After six years in England, innkeepers Quintus and Donna Renshaw purchased this Victorian inn and opened the home for guests, pampering them with European hospitality. A collection of British and American antiques highlight the rooms, many pieces were collected during the Renshaw's travels. Evening snacks often take on a British flair with freshly baked scones and a pot of tea. The innkeepers host a variety of theme weekends, including a Chocolate Lover's Weekend, where guests enjoy a multitude of sweet snacks throughout their stay. The inn offers close access to Lake Michigan, and within walking distance (bikes also are available for guests) of shops and Mears State Park. German and French are spoken here.

Breakfast, afternoon tea and evening snack included in rates. Types of meals: full breakfast and gourmet breakfast. Ceiling fan in room. Cable TV, VCR, fax, spa, bicycles and library on premises. Family reunions hosted. German and French spoken. Antiques, fishing, parks, shopping, cross-country skiing, theater and watersports nearby. TAC10.

Petoskey E7

Stafford's Perry Hotel

Bay & Lewis Streets
Petoskey, MI 49770
(616)347-4000 (800)456-1917
Fax:(616)347-0636

Rates: $65-175. EP.
Payment: MC VISA AX.
Innkeeper(s): Judy Honor.
Circa: 1899.

Rooms: 80 rooms with PB. 2 conference rooms.
Beds: KQD.

This gracious, Victorian Italianate hotel has been welcoming guests since the turn of the century. At one point in its history, the hotel almost was converted into a hospital. It has remained a place for hospitality instead. Some of the pleasant, period-style guest rooms boast balconies overlooking Little Traverse Bay. Guests can enjoy live music, from jazz to folk, at the hotel's Noggin Room Pub. The H.O. Rose Room serves breakfast, lunch and dinner, and The Salon serves appetizers in the afternoon and evening. For guests seeking relaxation after a day exploring the area, there is a hot tub on the premises.

Types of meals: continental breakfast, continental-plus breakfast, full breakfast and early coffee/tea. Dinner, evening snack, picnic lunch, lunch, banquet service, catering service, catered breakfast and room service available. EP. Air conditioning and cable TV in room. VCR, fax, copier, spa and library on premises. Handicap access. Weddings, small meetings, family reunions and seminars hosted. Antiques, fishing, parks, shopping, downhill skiing, cross-country skiing, theater and watersports nearby. TAC10.

Special Discounts: AARP and AAA: 10% off; $55-65 for corporate guests.

Plainwell J6

The 1882 John Crispe House

404 E Bridge St
Plainwell, MI 49080-1802
(616)685-1293

Rates: $65-110.
Payment: MC VISA PC.
Innkeeper(s): Nancy E. Lefever & Family.
Circa: 1882.

Rooms: 3 rooms with PB. 2 suites.
Beds: DT.

Sunburst gables, a cast-iron roof cresting and bay windows accentuate this stick-style inn. Butternut and walnut woodwork, pocket doors, and original gaslight fixtures add to the historic, Victorian ambiance. Candlelit breakfasts are served on fine china, silver and crystal. The morning meal begins with juices, fresh

fruits and freshly baked muffins, topped off with a delectable entree. The home is situated above the Kalamazoo River and affords views not only of the river, but the historic neighborhood. A carriage house with flowers and vegetable gardens offers guests the opportunity to relax under a canopy of maple trees.

Breakfast included in rates. Types of meals: full breakfast and gourmet breakfast. Air conditioning in room. Small meetings hosted. Antiques, fishing, parks, downhill skiing, cross-country skiing, sporting events, theater and watersports nearby.

Publicity: *Kalamazoo Gazette.*

Special Discounts: Midweek days or long term up to thirty days $45.00 single $55.00 double.

"Real Victorian charm without being overly heavy or formal; attractive setting."

Port Huron I10

Victorian Inn

1229 7th St
Port Huron, MI 48060-5303
(810)984-1437

Rates: $65-75.
Payment: MC VISA AX DC CB DS PC TC.
Innkeeper(s): Kelly Lozano.
Circa: 1896.

Rooms: 4 rooms, 2 with PB, 2 with FP. 1 suite.
Beds: QDT.

This finely renovated Queen Anne Victorian house has both an inn and restaurant. Gleaming carved-oak woodwork, leaded-glass windows and fireplaces in almost every room reflect the home's gracious air. Authentic wallpapers and draperies provide a background for carefully selected antiques. At the Pierpont's Pub & Wine Cellar, Victorian-inspired menus include such entrees as partridge with pears and filet of beef Africane, all served on antique china.

Breakfast included in rates. Room service available. Air conditioning in room. Cable TV on premises. Weddings and small meetings hosted. Antiques, fishing, parks, shopping, cross-country skiing, theater and watersports nearby.

Publicity: *Detroit Free Press.*

"In all of my trips, business or pleasure, I have never experienced such a warm and courteous staff."

Saugatuck I6

The Park House

888 Holland St
Saugatuck, MI 49453-9607
(616)857-4535 (800)321-4535
Fax:(616)857-1065

Rates: $60-150.
Payment: MC VISA AX DS PC TC.
Innkeeper(s): Lynda & Joe Petty, Linda Matzen.
Circa: 1857.

Rooms: 8 rooms with PB, 6 with FP. 3 suites. 6 cottages.
Beds: KQT.

This Greek Revival-style home is the oldest residence in Saugatuck and was constructed for the first mayor. Susan B. Anthony was a guest here for two weeks in the 1870s, and the local Women's Christian Temperance League was established in the parlor. A country theme pervades the inn, with antiques, old woodwork and pine floors. A cottage with a hot tub and a river-front guest house are also available.

Breakfast included in rates. Types of meals: full breakfast and early coffee/tea. Air conditioning, cable TV and VCR in room. Fax and copier on premises. Handicap access. Small meetings, family reunions and seminars hosted. Antiques, fishing, parks, shopping, cross-country skiing, theater and watersports nearby. TAC10.

Publicity: *Detroit News, Innsider, Gazette, South Bend Tribune.*

"Thanks again for your kindness and hospitality during our weekend."

The Red Dog B&B

132 Mason St
Saugatuck, MI 49453
(616)857-8851

Rates: $60-110.
Payment: MC VISA AX DC DS PC TC.
Innkeeper(s): Patrick & Kristine Clark.
Circa: 1879.

Rooms: 7 rooms, 5 with PB, 1 with FP. 1 suite.
Beds: QD.

This comfortable, two-story farmhouse is located in the heart of downtown Saugatuck and is just a short walk away from shopping, restaurants and many of the town's seasonal activities. Rooms are furnished with a combination of contemporary and antique furnishings. One room includes a fireplace and Jacuzzi tub for two. Guests can relax and enjoy views of the garden from the B&B's second-story porch, or warm up next to the fireplace in the living room. The full breakfast, which is served in the formal dining room, includes treats such as baked apple cinnamon French toast or a ham and cheese strata. The innkeepers offer special golf and off-season packages.

Breakfast included in rates. Types of meals: full breakfast and early coffee/tea. Air conditioning, ceiling fan and cable TV in room. VCR, fax and copier on premises. Weddings, small meetings and family reunions hosted. Antiques, fishing, parks, shopping, cross-country skiing, theater and watersports nearby. TAC10.

Publicity: *South Bend Trio, Michigan Cyclist, Restaurant and Institutions.*

Special Discounts: Golf packages and off-season specials.

Sherwood Forest B&B

938 Center St, PO Box 315
Saugatuck, MI 49453
(800)838-1246
Fax:(616)857-1996

Rates: $60-140.
Payment: MC VISA DS PC.
Innkeeper(s): Keith & Susan Charak.
Circa: 1904.

Rooms: 4 rooms with PB, 1 with FP. 1 cottage. 1 conference room.
Beds: Q.

MI

As the name suggests, this gracious Victorian is surrounded by woods and flanked with a large wraparound porch. Each guest room features antiques, one room offers a Jacuzzi and another an oak-manteled fireplace with a unique mural that transforms the room into a tree-top loft. A breakfast of delicious coffees or teas and homemade treats can be enjoyed either in the dining room or on the porch. The heated pool includes a mural of dolphins riding on ocean waves. White-sand beaches and the eastern shore of Lake Michigan are only a half block away.

Breakfast and afternoon tea included in rates. Types of meals: continental-plus breakfast and early coffee/tea. Catering service available. Air conditioning and ceiling fan in room. Cable TV, VCR, fax, swimming and bicycles on premises. Weddings, small meetings, family reunions and seminars hosted. Antiques, fishing, parks, shopping, cross-country skiing, theater and watersports nearby. TAC10.

Publicity: *Commercial Record, Chicago SunTimes.*

"Staying at Sherwood Forest was like staying at my best friend's house. The house itself is quaint and beautiful."

Twin Gables Country Inn

PO Box 881, 900 Lake St
Saugatuck, MI 49453-0881
(616)857-4346 (800)231-2185

Rates: $54-98.
Payment: MC VISA AX DS.
Innkeeper(s): Michael & Denise Simcik.
Circa: 1865.

Rooms: 14 rooms with PB. 3 cottages.
Beds: KQDT.

This rustic inn includes the only remaining original mill left in the area, a reminder of the busy lumbering days of Saugatuck's past. Among its other uses, the home has served as a brewery icehouse, a tannery and a boat building factory. On warm evenings, guests might lounge on the veranda, and winter guests will appreciate the indoor Jacuzzi. Rooms feature wallpapers or stenciling, and some include the polished hardwood floors that also grace the breakfast and common rooms. The inn is within walking distance to the many shops in Saugatuck and is a good base for those hoping to take in the variety of outdoor activities. The innkeepers also offer use of a heated swimming pool.

Breakfast included in rates. Type of meal: continental-plus breakfast. Antiques, fishing, parks, cross-country skiing, theater and watersports nearby.

"Thank you so much for your hospitality and kindness!"

Twin Oaks Inn

PO Box 867, 227 Griffith St
Saugatuck, MI 49453-0867
(616)857-1600

Rates: $65-105.
Payment: MC VISA DS TC.
Innkeeper(s): Jerry & Nancy Horney.
Circa: 1860.

Rooms: 7 rooms with PB. 3 suites. 1 conference room.
Beds: KQ.

This large Queen Anne Victorian inn was a boarding house for lumbermen at the turn of the century. Now an old-English-style inn, it offers a variety of lodging choices, including three suites. One room has a Jacuzzi. Guests also may stay in the inn's cozy cottage, which boasts an outdoor hot tub. There are many diversions at Twin Oaks, including a collection of videotaped movies numbering more than 700. An English garden with a pond and fountain provides a relaxing setting, and guests also may borrow bicycles or play horseshoes on the inn's grounds.

Breakfast and evening snack included in rates. Types of meals: continental-plus breakfast, full breakfast and early coffee/tea. Air conditioning, cable TV and VCR in room. Weddings, small meetings and family reunions hosted. Antiques, fishing, parks, shopping, cross-country skiing, theater and watersports nearby.

Location: Downtown.

Publicity: *Home & Away, Cleveland Plain Dealer, South Bend Tribune, Shape Magazine.*

South Haven — J5

The Seymour House

1248 Blue Star Hwy
South Haven, MI 49090
(616)227-3918
Fax:(616)227-3918
E-mail: seymour@cybers.com

Rates: $75-129.
Payment: MC VISA PC TC.
Innkeeper(s): Tom & Gwen Paton.
Circa: 1862.

Rooms: 5 rooms with PB, 2 with FP. 1 cottage.
Beds: KQD.

Less than a mile from the shores of Lake Michigan, this pre-Civil War, Italianate-style home rests upon 11 acres of grounds, complete with nature trails and a stocked, fishing pond. Each of the guest rooms is named for a state significant in the innkeepers' lives. The Arizona Suite, popular with honeymooners, includes a Jacuzzi tub. Poached pears with raspberry sauce, buttermilk blueberry pancakes and locally made sausages are a few of the items that might appear on the breakfast menu. The inn is midway between Saugatuck and South Haven, which offer plenty of activities. Beaches, Kal-Haven Trail, shopping, horseback riding and winery tours are among the fun destination choices.

Breakfast and evening snack included in rates. Types of meals: gourmet breakfast and early coffee/tea. Picnic lunch available. Air conditioning, ceiling fan and VCR in room. Cable TV, fax, copier and swimming on premises. 11 acres. Antiques, fishing, parks, shopping, downhill skiing, cross-country skiing, theater and watersports nearby. TAC10.

Special Discounts: Winter rates Nov. 1-May 1.

"Enjoyed our stay and the wonderful hospitality, Beware! We shall return."

Spring Lake — I6

The Royal Pontaluna Inn B&B

1870 Pontaluna Rd
Spring Lake, MI 49456-9614
(616)798-7271 (800)865-3545
Fax:(616)798-7271

Rates: $85-135.
Payment: MC VISA AX DS PC TC.
Innkeeper(s): Charles & Di Beacham.
Circa: 1978.

Rooms: 5 rooms with PB, 1 with FP. 1 suite. 2 conference rooms.
Beds: Q.

This bed & breakfast is located on 27 acres. There is a tennis court, a whirlpool, sauna and indoor pool to keep guests busy, but travelers are welcome to simply sit and relax in front of the stone fireplace or stroll the wooded grounds. As the innkeepers are named Charles and Di, the two appointed their inn with a regal name. The Royal Suite is a romantic haven with a fireplace and Jacuzzi tub. Three other rooms also include Jacuzzi tubs. Although there is plenty to do at the inn, the area has many lake-related activities, shops, museums and state parks to visit.

Breakfast included in rates. Types of meals: full breakfast and early coffee/tea. Catering service available. Air conditioning, cable TV and VCR in room. Fax, copier, spa, swimming, sauna and tennis on premises. 27 acres. Weddings, small meetings, family reunions and seminars hosted. Amusement parks, antiques, fishing, parks, shopping, cross-country skiing, theater and watersports nearby. TAC10.

Victoriana 1898

622 Washington St
Traverse City, MI 49686
(616)929-1009

Rates: $60-80.
Payment: PC.
Innkeeper(s): Flo & Bob Schermerhorn.
Circa: 1898.

Rooms: 3 rooms with PB, 1 with FP. 1 suite.
Beds: QD.

Egbert Ferris, a partner in the European Horse Hotel, built this Italianate Victorian manor and a two-story carriage house. Later, the bell tower from the old Central School was moved onto the property and now serves as a handsome Greek Revival gazebo. The house has three parlors, all framed in fretwork. Etched and stained glass is found throughout. Guest rooms are furnished with family heirlooms. The house speciality is Belgian waffles topped with homemade cherry sauce.

Breakfast and afternoon tea included in rates. Types of meals: gourmet breakfast and early coffee/tea. Air conditioning and turn-down service in room. Cable TV, VCR, fax and library on premises. Antiques, fishing, parks, shopping, downhill skiing, cross-country skiing, theater and watersports nearby. TAC10.

Publicity: *Midwest Living, Oakland Press.*

"In all our B&B experiences, no one can compare with the Victoriana 1898. You're 100% in every category!"

MI

Union Pier J5

Pine Garth B&B

15790 Lakeshore Rd
Union Pier, MI 49129-9340
(616)469-1642
Fax:(616)469-1642

Rates: $80-150.
Payment: MC VISA DS PC.
Innkeeper(s): Paula & Russ Bulin.
Circa: 1905.

Rooms: 7 rooms with PB, 1 with FP. 5 cottages. 1 conference room.
Beds: Q.

The seven rooms and five guest cottages at this charming bed & breakfast inn are decorated in a country style and each boasts something special. Some have a private deck and a wall of windows that look out to Lake Michigan. Other rooms feature items such as an unusual twig canopy bed, and several have whirlpool tubs. The deluxe cottages offer two queen-size beds, a wood-burning fireplace, VCR, cable TV and an outdoor tub on a private deck with a gas grill. Rates vary for the cottages. The inn has its own private beach and there are sand dunes, vineyards, forests and miles of beaches in the area.

Breakfast included in rates. Types of meals: full breakfast and gourmet breakfast. Afternoon tea, evening snack and banquet service available. Ceiling fan and VCR in room. Cable TV, fax, copier, swimming, bicycles and library on premises. Shopping nearby.

Location: On the shores of Lake Michigan with private beach.

"Your warm and courteous reception, attentiveness and helpfulness will never be forgotten."

The Inn at Union Pier

9708 Berrien
Union Pier, MI 49129-0222
(616)469-4700
Fax:(616)469-4720

Rates: $110-185.
Payment: MC VISA DS PC TC.
Innkeeper(s): Joyce & Mark Pitts.
Circa: 1920.

Rooms: 16 rooms with PB, 12 with FP. 2 suites. 1 conference room.
Beds: KQT.

Set on a shady acre across a country road from Lake Michigan, this inn features unique Swedish ceramic fireplaces, a hot tub and sauna, a veranda ringing the house and a large common room with comfortable overstuffed furniture and a grand piano. Rooms offer such amenities as private balconies and porches, whirlpools, views of the English garden and furniture dating from the early 1900s. Breakfast includes fresh fruit and homemade jams made of fruit from surrounding farms.

Breakfast and evening snack included in rates. Types of meals: continental breakfast, full breakfast, gourmet breakfast and early

coffee/tea. Catering service available. Air conditioning and ceiling fan in room. Cable TV, VCR, fax, copier, spa, swimming, sauna, bicycles and library on premises. Handicap access. Weddings, small meetings, family reunions and seminars hosted. Antiques, fishing, parks, cross-country skiing, sporting events, theater and watersports nearby.

Publicity: *Chicago Tribune, USA Today, Detroit News, Chicago, Midwest Living, Chicago Sun Times.*

Special Discounts: Sunday-Thursday, discounted packages available.

"The food, the atmosphere, the accommodations, and of course, the entire staff made this the most relaxing weekend ever."

Ypsilanti

J8

Parish House Inn

103 S Huron St
Ypsilanti, MI 48197-5421
(313)480-4800 (800)480-4866
Fax:(313)480-7472

Rates: $85-115.
Payment: MC VISA AX PC TC.
Innkeeper(s): Mrs. Chris Mason.
Circa: 1893.

Rooms: 9 rooms with PB, 2 with FP. 1 conference room.
Beds: DT.

This Queen Anne Victorian was named in honor of its service as a parsonage for the First Congregational Church. The home remained a parsonage for more than 50 years after its construction and then served as a church office and Sunday school building. It was moved to its present site in Ypsilanti's historic district in the late 1980s. The rooms are individually decorated with Victorian-style wallpapers and antiques. One guest room includes a two-person Jacuzzi tub. Those in search of a late-night snack need only venture into the kitchen to find drinks and the cookie jar. For special occasions, the innkeepers can arrange trays with flowers, non-alcoholic champagne, chocolates, fruit or cheese. The terrace overlooks the Huron River.

Breakfast and evening snack included in rates. Types of meals: continental breakfast, full breakfast, gourmet breakfast and early coffee/tea. Afternoon tea, picnic lunch, catering service and catered breakfast available. Air conditioning, ceiling fan, cable TV and VCR in room. Fax and library on premises. Handicap access. Small meetings, family reunions and seminars hosted. Amusement parks, antiques, fishing, parks, shopping, cross-country skiing, sporting events, theater and watersports nearby. TAC10.

Special Discounts: Sunday-Thursday, 15% off double occupancy.

Eggs Callahan

Bear Paw Inn
Winter Park, Colo.

- 6-8 oz package frozen shredded hash browns, thawed
- ½ cup melted butter (or a little less)
- 2 cups cheddar cheese, shredded
- ½ lb Italian sausage (cooked)
- 2 cups mushrooms, diced
- 1 cup yellow pepper
- 1 cup red pepper
- 5 eggs
- ½ cup milk
- Seasoning to taste

Press thawed hash browns between paper towels to remove moisture. Spray quiche pan with cooking spray. Press hash browns into pan forming crust. Brush with butter, bake at 450 degrees for 30 minutes.

Remove from oven, sprinkle with cheddar cheese. Add sausage pepper and mushrooms. Beat together eggs with milk. Add seasoning to taste, pour over baking dish.

Bake uncovered at 350 degrees for 30-40 minutes. Slice and serve with sliced tomatoes, avocado and salsa on the side.

Note: Vegetarians may omit the sausage.

Minnesota

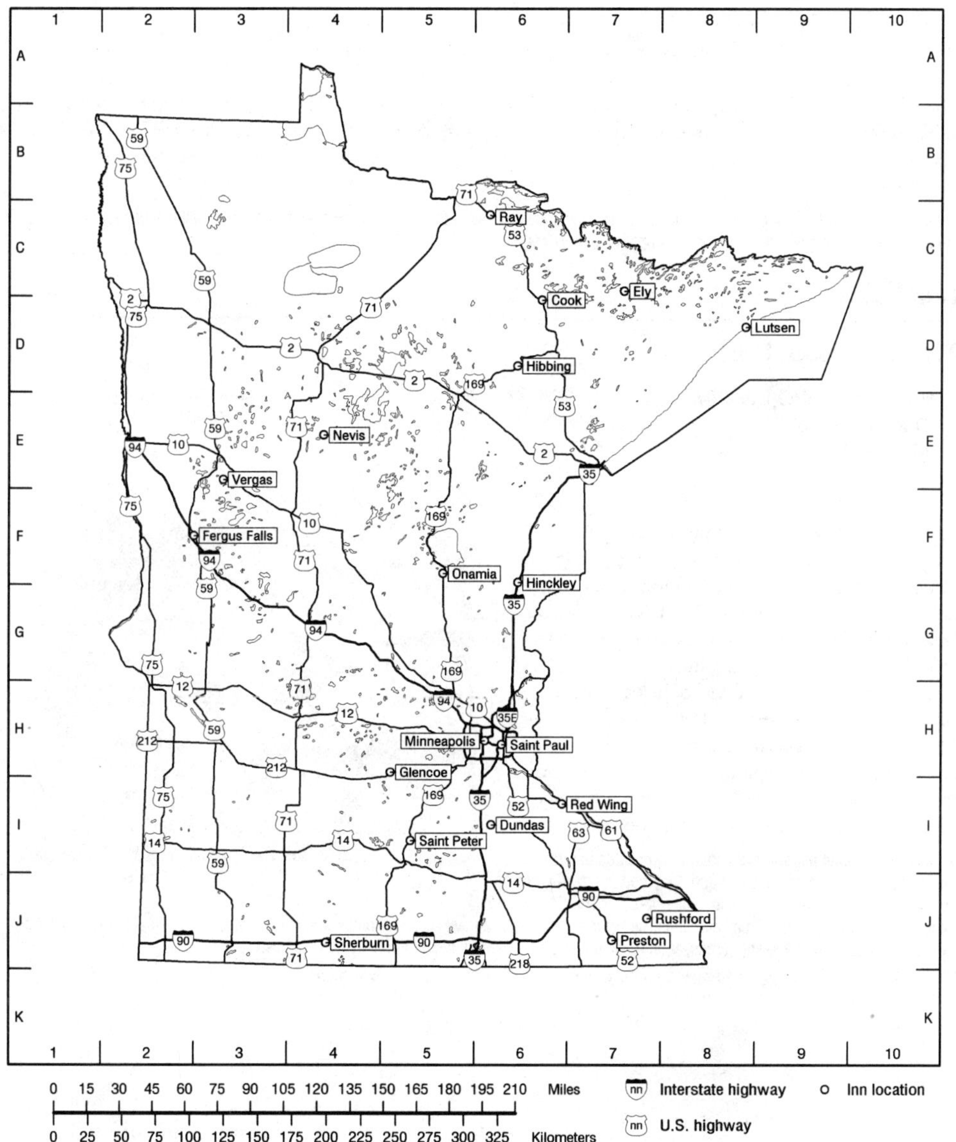

MN

Cook D6

Ludlow's Island Lodge

PO Box 1146
Cook, MN 55723-1146
(218)666-5407 (800)537-5308
Fax:(218)666-2488
E-mail: ludlowsl@aol.com

Rates: $165-190.
Payment: MC VISA AX DS PC TC.
Innkeeper(s): Mark & Sally Ludlow.
Circa: 1945.

Rooms: 51 rooms. 18 cottages. 2 conference rooms.
Beds: KDT.

A collection of 18 rustic cabins are spread across two shores of the lake and a private island. They range in style and size and are from one to five bedrooms. All have fireplaces, kitchens and outdoor decks. Most cabins have more than one bath and are equipped with tubs and showers. This resort is very private with many activities on property that are free of charge including tennis, racquetball, canoeing and sailboating. A 24-hour convenience grocery store is also on property. Children may enjoy watching movies that are shown every evening in the lodge.

Dinner available. VCR, fax, copier, swimming, sauna, tennis, library and child care on premises. Weddings, small meetings and family reunions hosted. Antiques, fishing, parks, shopping and watersports nearby. TAC10.

Dundas I6

Martin Oaks B&B

107 First St, PO Box 207
Dundas, MN 55019
(507)645-4644

Rates: $55-79. MAP.
Payment: MC VISA PC TC.
Innkeeper(s): Marie & Frank Gery.
Circa: 1869.

Rooms: 3 rooms.
Beds: DT.

The rich lilac exterior and picket fence at this prairie Victorian conjure up nostalgic images of yesteryear. Antiques, flowers, handmade quilts and candles add to the homey, cozy feel. Multi-course breakfasts of fresh fruit, home-baked breads and special entrees are served on china. Guests will return in the evenings to find not just the usual chocolate turn-down service, but rather a rich, fudge brownie or other special treat decoratively arranged on a plate atop a fluffy pillow. Bubble bath and soft robes are just a few of the many extras guests enjoy. The innkeepers can arrange teas or gourmet dinners.

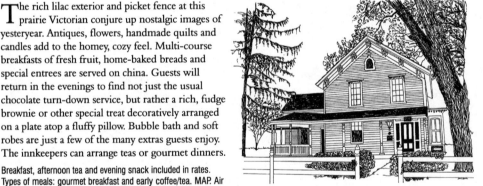

Breakfast, afternoon tea and evening snack included in rates. Types of meals: gourmet breakfast and early coffee/tea. MAP. Air conditioning, turn-down service and ceiling fan in room. Cable 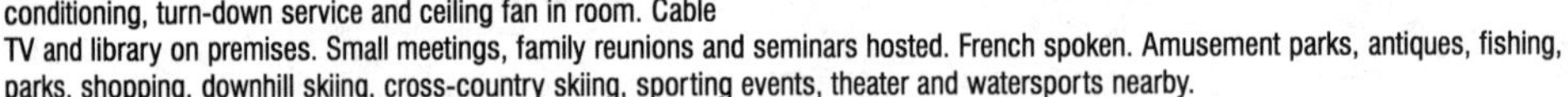 TV and library on premises. Small meetings, family reunions and seminars hosted. French spoken. Amusement parks, antiques, fishing, parks, shopping, downhill skiing, cross-country skiing, sporting events, theater and watersports nearby.

"It's been wonderful living in fantasy land for a few days. Thanks for the enchantment."

Ely

C7

Burntside Lodge

2755 Burntside Lodge Rd
Ely, MN 55731-8402
(218)365-3894

Rates: $90-165. MAP, EP.
Payment: MC VISA AX DS PC TC.
Innkeeper(s): Lou & Lonnie LaMontagne.
Circa: 1913.

Rooms: 24 cottages.
Beds: KDT.

"Staying here is like taking a vacation 60 years ago," states innkeeper Lou LaMontagne. Families have come here for more than 70 years to enjoy the waterfront and woodside setting. The lodge and its cabins are in the National Register and much of the original hand-carved furnishings remain from the jazz age. Fishing, listening to the cry of the loon and boating around the lake's 125 islands are popular activities. Breakfast and dinner are available in the waterside dining room.

Types of meals: full breakfast and early coffee/tea. Dinner and lunch available. MAP, EP. VCR, fax, copier, swimming, sauna and library on premises. 20 acres. Weddings, small meetings, family reunions and seminars hosted. Antiques, fishing, parks, shopping and watersports nearby. TAC5.

Location: Six miles southwest of Ely.

Special Discounts: Early season 20% discount (minimum stay of two days); $78 per day (requires full week stay).

"Unforgettable."

Fergus Falls

F3

MN

Bakketopp Hus

RR 2 Box 187A
Fergus Falls, MN 56537
(218)739-2915 (800)739-2915

Rates: $65-95.
Payment: MC VISA DS PC TC.
Innkeeper(s): Dennis & Judy Nims.
Circa: 1976.

Rooms: 3 rooms with PB.
Beds: Q.

From the decks of this wooded home, guest can enjoy the scenery of Long Lake and catch glimpses of wildlife. Antiques, handmade quilts and down comforters decorate the cozy guest rooms. One room includes a private spa and draped canopy bed. Another room includes a fireplace. A bounty of nearby outdoor activities are sure to please nature lovers, and antique shops and restaurants are nearby.

Breakfast, afternoon tea and evening snack included in rates. Types of meals: gourmet breakfast and early coffee/tea. Air conditioning, ceiling fan and cable TV in room. VCR and swimming on premises. Small meetings and seminars hosted. Amusement parks, antiques, fishing, parks, shopping, downhill skiing, cross-country skiing, theater and watersports nearby.

Publicity: *Minneapolis Tribune.*

Glencoe

H5

Glencoe Castle B&B

831 13th St E
Glencoe, MN 55336-1503
(320)864-3043 (800)517-3334
E-mail: rschoeneck@gnn.com

Rates: $65-175.
Payment: MC VISA AX DS PC.
Innkeeper(s): Becky & Rick Schoeneck.
Circa: 1895.

Rooms: 4 rooms, 1 with PB, 1 with FP.
Beds: KD.

Glencoe Castle was built as a wedding promise to lure a bride from New York to Minnesota. She would move to Glencoe only if her husband built her a castle. This grand manor did the trick, with its carved woodwork, stained glass and ornate wood floors. The third floor was originally built as a ballroom. The home is decorated with antiques, Oriental and country pieces. Guests are treated to a lavish candlelight breakfast with such items as baked eggs in cream and Havarti cheese, Canadian bacon, Blueberry French toast, homemade bread, pastries and fresh fruit. In the evenings, tea and dessert are served. There is a Victorian gift shop on the premises. For an extra charge, guests can arrange small meetings, parties, group teas, dinner or teas for two. The teas range from a light breakfast tea to the more extravagant Victorian High Tea. Murder Mystery events also can be arranged.

Breakfast and evening snack included in rates. Types of meals: full breakfast and gourmet breakfast. Afternoon tea available. Air conditioning in room. Cable TV, VCR, fax and copier on premises. Weddings and small meetings hosted. Amusement parks, antiques, fishing, parks, shopping, downhill skiing, cross-country skiing, sporting events and theater nearby.

Pets Allowed: Yes.

Hibbing D6

The Adams House

201 E 23rd St
Hibbing, MN 55746-1915
(218)263-9742 (888)891-9742

Rates: $48-53.
Innkeeper(s): Marlene & Merrill Widmark.
Circa: 1927.

Rooms: 5 rooms, 2 with PB.
Beds: DT.

This Tudor-style home gives guests a touch of England, complete with pleasing decor. The house's unique look, with slanted roof and windows of leaded glass, has been recognized by the city's historical society, and guests will enjoy its large bedrooms and antique-filled interior. Downtown shopping and several of the area's churches are within walking distance, and Hibbing is well-known for its recreational offerings, including boating, fishing and skiing.

Breakfast included in rates. Type of meal: continental-plus breakfast. Afternoon tea available. Cable TV on premises. Weddings and small meetings hosted. Antiques, fishing, shopping, downhill skiing, cross-country skiing, theater and watersports nearby.

"A little bit of England in Northern Minnesota."

Hinckley F6

Dakota Lodge B&B

Rt 3 Box 178
Hinckley, MN 55037-9418
(320)384-6052
Fax:(320)384-6052

Rates: $58-135.
Payment: MC VISA DS PC TC.
Innkeeper(s): Mike Schmitz & Tad Hilborn.
Circa: 1976.

Rooms: 5 rooms with PB, 4 with FP. 1 cottage.
Beds: KQ.

Although this inn is situated between Minneapolis and Duluth on six scenic acres, the innkeepers named their B&B in honor of their birthplace: North Dakota. The guest rooms are named after little known Dakota towns. The Medora and Kathryn rooms include whirlpools and fireplaces. Other rooms include lacy curtains, quilts and special furnishings. The country breakfasts are expansive with egg and meat dishes, fruit and a daily entree. Hinckley offers a variety of activities, including a 32-mile bike trail, a casino and antique shops.

Breakfast included in rates. Types of meals: full breakfast and early coffee/tea. Air conditioning and ceiling fan in room. VCR, fax, copier and library on premises. Antiques, fishing, parks, cross-country skiing and watersports nearby. TAC10.

Lutsen D8

Cascade Lodge

HC 3 Box 445
Lutsen, MN 55612-9705
(218)387-1112 (800)322-9543
Fax:(218)387-1113

Rates: $40-170. MAP, EP.
Payment: MC VISA AX DS PC TC.
Innkeeper(s): Gene & Laurene Glader.
Circa: 1938.

Rooms: 28 rooms with PB, 9 with FP. 1 suite. 11 cottages. 1 conference room.
Beds: QDT.

A main lodge and 10 cabins (including log cabins), a four-unit motel and a nearby house, comprise Cascade Lodge, tucked away in the midst of Cascade River State Park, which overlooks Lake Superior. Cascade Creek meanders between the cabins toward the lake. The lodge has a natural-stone fireplace and the living room and restaurant areas are decorated with hunting trophies of moose, coyote, wolves and bear. Canoeing,

hiking to Lookout Mountain, walking along Wild Flower Trail and watching the sunset from the lawn swing are favorite summer activities. The lodge is open all year.

Type of meal: early coffee/tea. MAP, EP. VCR, fax, copier, computer, bicycles and library on premises. 14 acres. Small meetings, family reunions and seminars hosted. German spoken. Antiques, fishing, parks, shopping, downhill skiing, cross-country skiing, theater and watersports nearby. TAC10.

Location: Overlooking Lake Superior on Highway 61.

Publicity: *Country Inns, Lake Superior.*

"We needed to get away and recharge ourselves. This was the perfect place."

Lindgren's B&B on Lake Superior

County Rd 35, PO Box 56
Lutsen, MN 55612-0056
(218)663-7450

Rates: $85-125.
Payment: MC VISA PC.
Innkeeper(s): Shirley Lindgren.
Circa: 1926.

Rooms: 4 rooms with PB, 1 with FP.
Beds: KDT.

This '20s log home is in the Superior National Forest on the north shore of Lake Superior. The inn features massive stone fireplaces, a baby grand piano, wildlife decor and a Finnish-style sauna. The living room has tongue-and-groove, Western knotty cedar wood paneling and seven-foot windows offering a view of the lake. The innkeeper's homemade jams, freshly baked breads and entrees such as French Toast topped with homemade chokecherry syrup, eggs Benedict or Danish pancakes get the day off to a pleasant start. In addition to horseshoes and a volleyball court, guests can gaze at the lake on a swinging love seat.

MN

Breakfast included in rates. Types of meals: full breakfast and early coffee/tea. Afternoon tea, evening snack and picnic lunch available. VCR, sauna and library on premises. Antiques, fishing, parks, shopping, downhill skiing, cross-country skiing, theater and watersports nearby. TAC10.

Location: On the Lake Superior Circle Tour.

Publicity: *Brainerd Daily Dispatch, Duluth News-Tribune, Tempo, Midwest Living, Minnesota Monthly, Lake Superior.*

"Thanks so much for providing a home base for us as we explored the North Country."

Minneapolis H6

The LeBlanc House

302 University Ave Ne
Minneapolis, MN 55413
(612)379-2570

Rates: $85-105.
Payment: MC VISA AX PC.
Innkeeper(s): Barb Zahasky & Bob Shulstad.
Circa: 1896.

Rooms: 3 rooms, 1 with PB.
Beds: Q.

Visitors to the University of Minnesota area should look no further than the LeBlanc House. The restored Queen Anne Victorian offers guests a historical perspective of life in the 1800s. The inn's convenient location also provides easy access to the Metrodome and downtown Minneapolis, while giving its guests a chance to relax in style after exploring the area. Amelia's Room has a view of the city lights and visitors may be treated to gourmet specialties such as pistachio quiche or rum raisin French toast.

Breakfast included in rates. Type of meal: full breakfast. Air conditioning, turn-down service and ceiling fan in room. Amusement parks, antiques, fishing, parks, shopping, downhill skiing, cross-country skiing, sporting events, theater and watersports nearby. TAC10.

Nan's B&B

2304 Fremont Ave S
Minneapolis, MN 55405
(612)377-5118
E-mail: zosel@mn.mcad.edu

Rates: $50.
Payment: MC VISA AX DC PC TC.
Innkeeper(s): Nan & Jim Zosel.
Circa: 1895.

Rooms: 3 rooms.
Beds: QDR.

Guests at Nan's enjoy close access to downtown Minneapolis, including the Guthrie Theatre, shopping and restaurants. The Lake of the Isles with its scenic walking paths is just four blocks away, and a bus stop is just down the street. The late Victorian home is furnished with antiques and decorated in a country Victorian style. The innkeepers are happy to help guests plan their day-to-day activities.

Breakfast included in rates. Type of meal: full breakfast. Air conditioning in room. Antiques, fishing, shopping, cross-country skiing, theater and watersports nearby.

"I had a wonderful stay in Minneapolis, mostly due to the comfort and tranquility of Nan's B&B."

Nevis — *E4*

The Park Street Inn

RR 1 Box 254
Nevis, MN 56467-9704
(218)652-4500 (800)797-1778

Rates: $60-90.
Payment: MC VISA PC TC.
Innkeeper(s): Irene & Len Hall.
Circa: 1912.

Rooms: 3 rooms with PB. 1 suite.
Beds: D.

This late Victorian home was built by one of Minnesota's many Norwegian immigrants, a prominent businessman. He picked an ideal spot for the home, which overlooks Lake Belle Taine, and sits across from a town park. The three comfortable guest rooms feature country antiques and beds topped with quilts. Homemade fare such as waffles, pancakes, savory meats, egg dishes and French toast are served during the inn's daily country breakfast.

Breakfast included in rates. Types of meals: full breakfast and early coffee/tea. VCR, bicycles and library on premises. Weddings, small meetings and family reunions hosted. Antiques, fishing, parks, shopping, cross-country skiing and watersports nearby. TAC10.

Pets Allowed: By arrangement only.

"Our favorite respite in the Heartland, where the pace is slow, hospitality is great and food is wonderful."

Onamia — *F5*

Cour Du Lac B&B

10654 390th St
Onamia, MN 56359
(320)532-4627

Rates: $85-110.
Payment: MC VISA.
Innkeeper(s): Frank & Susan Courteau.
Circa: 1989.

Rooms: 3 rooms with PB, 1 with FP.
Beds: QD.

From the outside, Cour Du Lac appears as a friendly lakeside country home with a welcoming front porch and manicured two-acre grounds. Inside polished woodwork and country French furnishings enhance this welcoming ambiance. The innkeepers have placed a bit of stenciling here and there, bringing bits of the garden inside. The Benjamin Wallace Room offers two sitting areas and a fireplace, in addition to the four-poster bed, window seat and lake or garden views. The two other guest quarters are individually decorated as well. There is a sitting room overlooking the lake where guests often curl up with a good book, and there are plenty of volumes to enjoy. The innkeepers prepare hearty, seasonal breakfast menus. In the summer, guests might enjoy fresh fruit and a garden quiche. In the autumn or winter months, items such as pumpkin-cranberry muffins or apple cinnamon sausage might appear on the menu. There are 18 miles of biking and ski trails nearby, as well as golf, a casino and Mille Lacs Indian Museum.

Breakfast included in rates. Types of meals: full breakfast and gourmet breakfast. Turn-down service and ceiling fan in room. Cable TV, swimming and library on premises. Antiques, fishing, parks, shopping and cross-country skiing nearby.

"Our first experience at a B&B, you made it wonderful. We'll definitely be back."

Preston J7

The Jail House Historic Inn

109 Houston 3 NW
Preston, MN 55965
(507)765-2181
Fax:(507)765-2558

Rates: Call for rates.
Circa: 1869.

Rooms: 3 suites.

The Old Fillmore County Jail is better known these days as the Jail House Inn. The current "jailers" are anything but gruff to their guests, who are treated to one of the Midwest's most unique inn settings. The striking Italianate structure, featured in the National Register of Historic Places, offers authentic Victorian decor in its 12 fascinating rooms, including the Cell Block, where guests actually sleep behind bars, the Detention Room and Master Bedroom, with a china tub weighing nearly half a ton. After guests are sprung for the day, they are free to explore the state's historic bluff country. Tours of nearby caves and a fish hatchery are just a few of the activities available.

Breakfast included in rates. Lunch and catering service available. Air conditioning, ceiling fan and cable TV in room. Weddings, small meetings, family reunions and seminars hosted. Antiques, shopping, downhill skiing and theater nearby.

Ray C6

Bunt's B&B Inns

12497 Burma Rd,
Lake Kabetogama
Ray, MN 56669
(218)875-2691 (888)741-1020
Fax:(218)875-3008

Rates: $48-140.
Payment: MC VISA AX DS PC TC.
Innkeeper(s): Bob Buntrock.
Circa: 1916.

Rooms: 9 rooms, 7 with PB. 2 suites. 2 cottages. 1 conference room.
Beds: KQDT.

MN

Outdoor lovers don't need to settle for dreary lodgings when visiting the Voyageurs National Park area. Bunt's provides a wide range of options for guests with regard to privacy and comfort. A brand-new facility, the Kab-Inn, joins three existing B&B options at Bunt's. Bunt's variety of accommodations allows for family reunions and business groups. Lake Kabetogama is well known for its walleye fishing while other nearby lakes provide additional opportunities for boating and canoeing enthusiasts.

Breakfast included in rates. Types of meals: continental-plus breakfast, full breakfast and early coffee/tea. Air conditioning, ceiling fan, cable TV and VCR in room. Fax, copier, spa, swimming, sauna, library and child care on premises. Handicap access. 80 acres. Weddings, small meetings, family reunions and seminars hosted. Antiques, fishing, parks, shopping, downhill skiing, cross-country skiing, sporting events, theater and watersports nearby. TAC10.

Special Discounts: 20% off three nights or more; 10% AARP; 10% AAA. Only one discount at a time.

Red Wing I6

St. James Hotel

406 Main St
Red Wing, MN 55066-2325
(612)388-2846 (800)252-1875
Fax:(612)388-5226

Rates: $100-155. EP.
Payment: MC VISA AX DC CB DS TC.
Innkeeper(s): E.F. Foster.
Circa: 1875.

Rooms: 60 rooms with PB. 13 conference rooms.
Beds: QT.

The historic St. James provides a glimpse back to the exciting Mississippi riverboat era. The elegant Italianate structure, listed in the National Register, is filled with classy Victorian touches. Just a block from the riverfront, the St. James has at its back door a city park, providing a restful setting for guests. The inn's rooms, some of which boast river views, sport names such as Samuel Clemens, LaCrosse Queen and Huck Finn, and a third of them carry non-smoking designations. Guests will appreciate the distinctive and period-authentic room furnishings and the detail-oriented staff.

Types of meals: continental breakfast, full breakfast and early coffee/tea. Dinner, lunch, banquet service and room service available. EP. Air conditioning, turn-down service and cable TV in room. VCR, fax, copier, spa and child care on premises. Handicap access. Weddings, small meetings, family reunions and seminars hosted. Antiques, fishing, parks, shopping, downhill skiing, cross-country skiing, theater and watersports nearby.

Publicity: *Midwest Living.*

Rushford J7

Meadows Inn

RR 2 Box 221
Rushford, MN 55971-9528
(507)864-2378
Fax:(507)864-7501

Rates: $50-120.
Payment: MC VISA DS PC TC.
Innkeeper(s): Nancy Johnson.
Circa: 1993.

Rooms: 5 rooms with PB, 1 with FP. 1 suite. 1 conference room.
Beds: KQD.

This European-style, two-story stucco home offers panoramic views of the hills and meadows that surround the village of Rushford. The inn's Chateauesque exterior is complemented by its custom French and European-country interior. French reproduction furnishings decorate the guest rooms, and the romantic Bridal Chamber also includes a Jacuzzi. The inn offers close access to Root River State Bike and Ski Trail as well as other outdoor activities.

Breakfast included in rates. Types of meals: continental breakfast and full breakfast. Dinner and catering service available. Air conditioning in room. Cable TV, VCR, spa, tennis and library on premises. 10 acres. Weddings, small meetings, family reunions and seminars hosted. Antiques, fishing, parks, shopping, downhill skiing, cross-country skiing, sporting events, theater and watersports nearby. TAC10.

Special Discounts: Two nights for one - midweek and off season.

Saint Paul H6

The Garden Gate B&B

925 Goodrich Ave
Saint Paul, MN 55105-3127
(612)227-8430 (800)967-2703

Rates: $65-75.
Payment: PC TC.
Innkeeper(s): Miles & Mary Conway.
Circa: 1907.

Rooms: 4 rooms.
Beds: QT.

One of the most striking of the city's Victoria Crossing neighborhood homes is this recently redecorated Prairie-style Victorian. The large duplex features guest rooms named Gladiolus, Rose and Delphinium, and the rooms are as lovely as they sound. Visitors to the Garden Gate will be enthralled with the treats within walking distance, including other beautiful neighborhood homes, and the well-known shops and restaurants on Grand and Summit avenues. After a busy day of exploring, guests may want to request a therapeutic massage or soak in a clawfoot tub.

Breakfast included in rates. Types of meals: continental-plus breakfast and early coffee/tea. Air conditioning in room. Family reunions hosted. Amusement parks, antiques, fishing, parks, shopping, cross-country skiing, sporting events, theater and watersports nearby.

"I couldn't have felt more at home!"

Saint Peter **I5**

Engesser House

1202 S Minnesota Ave
Saint Peter, MN 56082-2208
(507)931-9594 (800)688-2646
Fax:(507)931-9622
E-mail: jstorm@ic.st-peter.mn.us

Rates: $65-85.
Payment: MC VISA AX DS PC TC.
Innkeeper(s): Chuck & Julie Storm.
Circa: 1880.

Rooms: 4 rooms with PB. 1 suite.
Beds: KQT.

This brick and stone home was built by local brewer Joseph Engesser and features Eastlake design with some Queen Anne influences. Inside, the innkeepers have decorated the house with artwork and pieces collected on their many travels. Gourmet breakfasts are served in the formal dining room. Guest rooms feature elegant touches such as canopy beds, lace and quilts. The innkeepers also offer plenty of amenities for the business traveler, including fax and copy machines, a typewriter and a Macintosh computer.

Breakfast included in rates. Types of meals: gourmet breakfast and early coffee/tea. Evening snack and catering service available. Air conditioning, turn-down service, ceiling fan, cable TV and VCR in room. Fax, copier, bicycles and library on premises. Weddings, small meetings, family reunions and seminars hosted. Antiques, fishing, parks, shopping, downhill skiing, cross-country skiing, sporting events, theater and watersports nearby. TAC10.

Publicity: *Saint Peter Herald, Mankato Free Press.*

"The fine wines, interesting conversations, the wonderful breakfast, the graciousness of you both made for a memorable weekend."

MN

Sherburn **J4**

Four Columns Inn

RR 2 Box 75
Sherburn, MN 56171-9732
(507)764-8861

Rates: $55-75.
Payment: PC TC.
Innkeeper(s): Norman & Pennie Kittleson.
Circa: 1884.

Rooms: 4 rooms with PB.
Beds: KQ.

This Greek Revival home rests on a 320-acre working farm, with 10 acres of flowers, trees and lawns surrounded by wrought iron and wood fences. The four guest rooms are decorated with antiques. Rooms are furthered adorned with wicker, Tiffany lamps, stained-glass windows and decorative fireplaces. Guests can relax in the redwood hot tub or take a look at the greenhouse filled with flowers. The innkeepers have an ice cream parlor on the premises, as well. For those celebrating a special occasion, try the Bridal Suite, which offers a rooftop deck with a view of the peaceful countryside. Hearty breakfasts are served either in the formal dining room, on the balcony, in the greenhouse, gazebo or perhaps in front of a crackling fire in the kitchen. There are music rooms with a player piano, phonographs, an antique pump organ and a jukebox. The inn is located two miles north of I-90 in between Chicago and the Black Hills.

Breakfast and afternoon tea included in rates. Types of meals: gourmet breakfast and early coffee/tea. Evening snack available. Air conditioning and ceiling fan in room. 320 acres. Weddings, small meetings and family reunions hosted. Amusement parks, antiques, fishing, parks, shopping, downhill skiing, cross-country skiing, theater and watersports nearby. TAC10.

"I think I'm in heaven. This has been so enjoyable."

The Log House & Homestead on Spirit Lake

PO Box 130
Vergas, MN 56587-0130
(218)342-2318 (800)342-2318

Rates: $85-135.
Payment: MC VISA AX DS PC TC.
Innkeeper(s): Yvonne & Lyle Tweten.
Circa: 1889.

Rooms: 5 rooms with PB, 3 with FP. 1 suite. 1 conference room.
Beds: KQ.

Either a 19th-century family log house or a turn-of-the-century homestead greets guests at this inn, situated on 115 acres of woods and fields. The inn overlooks Spirit Lake in the heart of Minnesota's lake country. Both houses have been carefully restored in a romantic, country style. Guest rooms are light and airy with colorful quilts, poster beds and elegant touches. The innkeepers recently added a penthouse suite, perfect for a romantic getaway. During the summer months, guests enjoy use of small boats and a canoe, and in the winter, snowshoes are available. Guests are welcomed with a tray filled with goodies. For an additional charge, the innkeepers offer a picnic lunch.

Breakfast included in rates. Types of meals: gourmet breakfast and early coffee/tea. Picnic lunch available. Air conditioning and ceiling fan in room. Swimming on premises. 115 acres. Weddings, small meetings and seminars hosted. French spoken. Antiques, parks, shopping, cross-country skiing, sporting events, theater and watersports nearby.

Publicity: *Forum, News Flashes, Minneapolis/St. Paul, Minnesota Monthly, House To Home, Pioneer Press.*

"Our stay here has made our anniversary everything we hoped for! The romance and solitude is exactly what we needed!"

Blackberry Cream Cheese Coffee Cake

Apple Blossom Inn
Ahwahnee, Calif.

Cake:
2 ¼ cups flour
¾ cup butter
½ t baking soda
¾ cup sour cream
1 egg
¾ cup sugar
½ t baking powder
¼ t salt
1 t almond extract

Preheat oven to 350 degrees. Grease and flour 9" or 10" springform pan. Lightly spoon flour into measuring cup; level off. In large bowl, combine flour and sugar. Using pastry blender, cut in butter until mixture resembles coarse crumbs. Reserve 1 cup of crumb mixture. To remaining crumb mixture, add the rest of above ingredients; blend well. Spread batter over bottom and 2" up sides of pan. (Batter should be about ¼" thick on sides.)

Filling:
8 oz. package cream cheese, softened
¼ cup sugar
½ cup blackberry preserves
1 egg
½ cup sliced almonds

In small bowl, combine cream cheese, ¼ cup sugar and egg; blend well. Pour over batter. Spoon preserves carefully and evenly over cream cheese mixture. In small bowl, combine reserved crumb mixture and sliced almonds. Sprinkle over preserves.

Bake at 350 degrees for 45 to 55 minutes or until cream cheese filling is set and crust is golden brown. Cool 15 minutes. Remove sides of pan. Serve warm or cool, cut into wedges. Refrigerate leftovers.

Mississippi

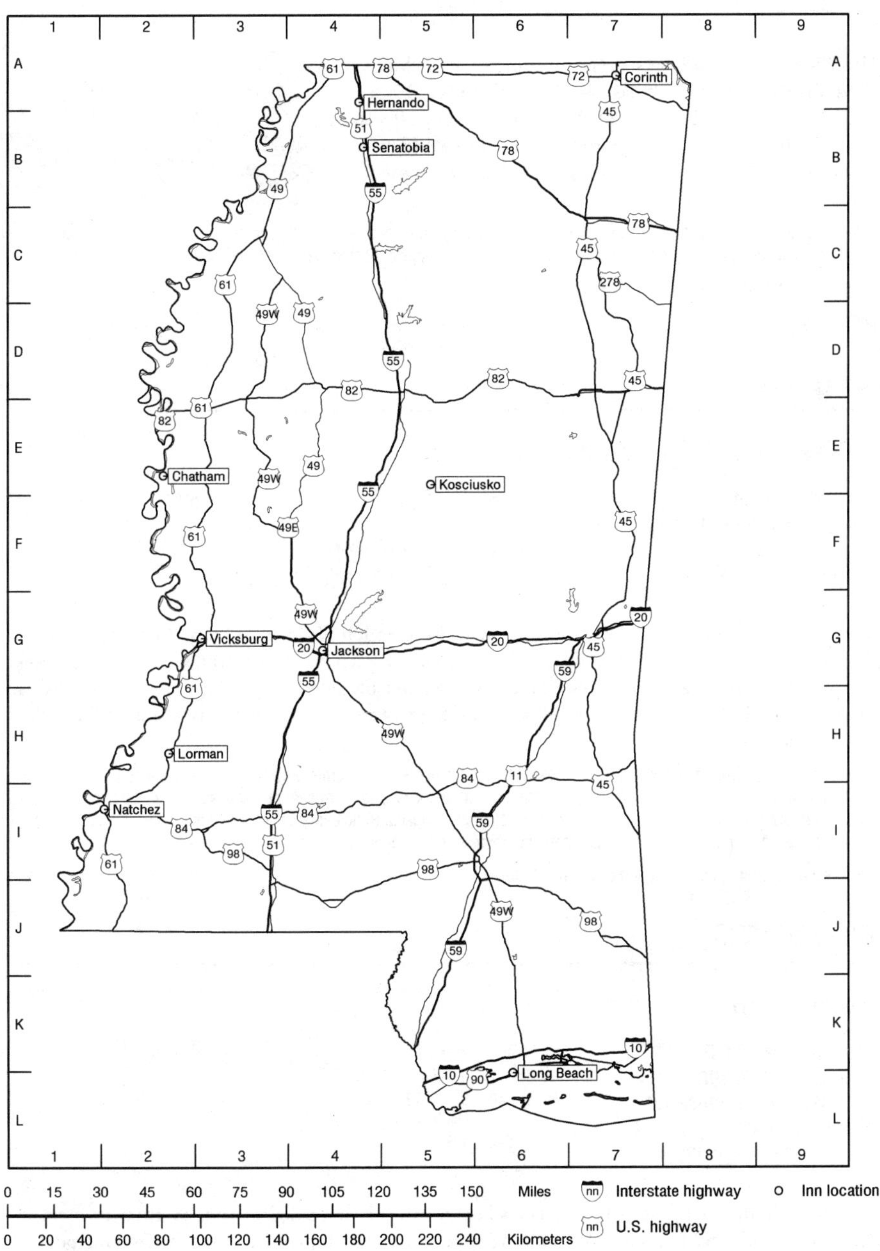

MS

Chatham E2

Mount Holly Plantation Inn

HC 63 Box 140
Chatham, MS 38731-9601
(601)827-2652
Fax:(601)827-5661

Rates: $65-150.
Payment: MC VISA DS PC TC.
Innkeeper(s): Ann Woods.
Circa: 1855.

Rooms: 7 rooms, 4 with PB, 4 with FP. 1 suite. 1 conference room.
Beds: KQDT.

This 20-room mansion, on six acres fronting Lake Washington, is in the Italianate style. It has 24-inch-thick walls of brick. Most of the rooms are 25 by 25 feet. All bedrooms open off a large second-floor ballroom, including a room with a 12-foot-high canopy bed. Antique furnishings, bordered ceilings, and chandeliers decorate the interior.

Breakfast included in rates. Types of meals: full breakfast and early coffee/tea. Air conditioning and ceiling fan in room. Fax on premises. Weddings, small meetings, family reunions and seminars hosted. Antiques, fishing, parks and watersports nearby. TAC10.

Location: On Lake Washington, close to Greenville.

Publicity: *Southern Living.*

Corinth A7

The Generals' Quarters B&B

924 Fillmore St
Corinth, MS 38834-4125
(601)286-3325
Fax:(601)287-8188

Rates: $75-85.
Payment: MC VISA DS TC.
Innkeeper(s): Charlotte Brandt & Luke Doehner.
Circa: 1872.

Rooms: 5 rooms with PB, 4 with FP. 2 suites. 1 conference room.
Beds: KQDT.

History buffs will enjoy this inn, located 22 miles from Shiloh National Military Park, and in the historic district of Corinth, a Civil War village. Visitors to this Queen Anne Victorian, with its quiet, tree-lined lot, enjoy a full breakfast and grounds decorated with a pond and flowers. Three guest rooms and two suites are available. Fort Robinette and Corinth National Cemetery are nearby. The inn is within walking distance to shops, museums, historic sites, restaurants and more.

Breakfast and evening snack included in rates. Types of meals: full breakfast, gourmet breakfast and early coffee/tea. Dinner, picnic lunch, gourmet lunch, banquet service, catering service, catered breakfast and room service available. Air conditioning, turn-down service, ceiling fan, cable TV and VCR in room. Fax and bicycles on premises. Handicap access. Weddings, small meetings, family reunions and seminars hosted. Antiques, fishing, parks, shopping, theater and watersports nearby.

Special Discounts: Group, corporate and government rates.

Hernando A4

Sassafras Inn

785 Highway 51 S
Hernando, MS 38632-8149
(601)429-5864 (800)882-1897
Fax:(601)429-4591
E-mail: sassyinn@mem.net

Rates: $80-175.
Payment: MC VISA AX DS PC TC.
Innkeeper(s): Dennis & Francee McClanahan.
Circa: 1985.

Rooms: 4 rooms, 3 with PB. 1 suite. 1 cottage.
Beds: QD.

This modern inn offers guests to the state's Northwest corner a delightful respite from their travels or from the hustle and bustle of Memphis, 10 miles south. An impressive indoor swimming pool and spa are guest favorites and visitors also enjoy the cabana room for reading or lounging, or the recreation room with billiards, darts and ping pong. A romantic honeymoon cottage also is available. Arkabutla Lake is an easy drive from the inn.

Breakfast, afternoon tea and evening snack included in rates. Types of meals: full breakfast and early coffee/tea. Air conditioning, turn-down service, ceiling fan, cable TV and VCR in room. Fax, copier, spa, swimming and library on premises. Weddings, small meetings and family reunions hosted. Limited Spanish spoken. Antiques, parks and watersports nearby. TAC10.

Location: Near Graceland, 25 minutes from downtown Memphis.

Jackson G4

Fairview Inn

734 Fairview St
Jackson, MS 39202-1624
(601)948-3429 (800)888-1908
Fax:(601)948-1203

Rates: $115-165. EP.
Payment: MC VISA AX DS PC TC.
Innkeeper(s): Carol & William Simmons.
Circa: 1908.

Rooms: 8 rooms with PB. 5 suites. 4 conference rooms.
Beds: KQ.

There's little question why this magnificent Colonial Revival mansion has been chosen as one of the United States' premiere inns. Designed by an associate of Frank Lloyd Wright, the home boasts unforgettable polished hardwood floors, a beautiful marble floor, fine furnishings and tasteful decor. The innkeepers Carol and William Simmons pamper guests with a plentiful cook-to-order breakfast, fresh flowers and have hosted many a wedding reception and party. History buffs will appreciate William's knowledge of Mississippi's past. There are helpful business amenities here, including in-room dataports.

Breakfast included in rates. Types of meals: continental breakfast, full breakfast, gourmet breakfast and early coffee/tea. Dinner, evening snack, lunch, gourmet lunch, banquet service, catering service and catered breakfast available. EP. Air conditioning, turn-down service, ceiling fan, cable TV and VCR in room. Fax, copier and library on premises. Handicap access. Weddings, small meetings, family reunions and seminars hosted. French spoken. Antiques, parks, shopping, sporting events and theater nearby. TAC10.

MS

Publicity: *Country Inns.*

"Elegant and comfortable."

Kosciusko E5

The Redbud Inn

121 N Wells St
Kosciusko, MS 39090-3647
(601)289-5086 (800)379-5086
Fax:(601)289-5086

Rates: $70-100.
Payment: MC VISA AX DS PC TC.
Innkeeper(s): Maggie Garrett & Ruth Aldridge.
Circa: 1884.

Rooms: 5 rooms, 4 with PB. 1 suite. 1 conference room.
Beds: QT.

Kosciusko, the birthplace of Oprah Winfrey, is also home to this striking Queen Anne Victorian inn, which boasts a long and distinguished history as a traveler's haven. Beautiful woodwork and an impressive square staircase highlight the inn's interior, and its architectural details have made it a well-known local landmark. Five guest rooms are available, all filled with antiques. An antique shop/tea room is on the premises.

Breakfast and afternoon tea included in rates. Types of meals: full breakfast and early coffee/tea. Gourmet lunch, banquet service and catering service available. Air conditioning, turn-down service, ceiling fan and cable TV in room. Fax on premises. Handicap access. Weddings, small meetings and family reunions hosted. French spoken. Antiques, parks and sporting events nearby. TAC10.

Publicity: *Colonial Homes, Southern Living.*

Long Beach L6

Red Creek Inn, Vineyard & Racing Stables

7416 Red Creek Rd
Long Beach, MS 39560
(601)452-3080 (800)729-9670
Fax:(601)452-4450

Rates: $59-89.
Payment: PC.
Innkeeper(s): Karl & "Toni" Mertz.
Circa: 1899.

Rooms: 5 rooms, 3 with PB, 1 with FP. 1 suite. 1 conference room.
Beds: DT.

This inn was built in the raised French cottage-style by a retired Italian sea captain, who wished to entice his bride to move from her parents' home in New Orleans. There are two swings on the 64-foot front porch and one swing that hangs from a 300-year-old oak tree. Magnolias and ancient live oaks, some registered with the Live Oak Society of the Louisiana Garden Club, dot 11 acres. The inn features a parlor, six fireplaces, ceiling fans and antiques, including a Victorian organ, wooden radios and a Victrola.

Breakfast included in rates. Types of meals: continental-plus breakfast and early coffee/tea. Air conditioning in room. Cable TV, VCR, fax, copier, stables and library on premises. 11 acres. Weddings, small meetings, family reunions and seminars hosted. Spanish spoken. Amusement parks, antiques, fishing, parks, shopping, theater and watersports nearby. TAC15.

Publicity: *Jackson Daily News, Innviews, TV Channel 13.*

"We loved waking up here on these misty spring mornings. The Old South is here."

Lorman H2

Rosswood Plantation

Hwy 552 East
Lorman, MS 39096
(601)437-4215 (800)533-5889
Fax:(601)437-6888
E-mail: whylander@aol.com

Rates: $99-125.
Payment: MC VISA AX DS PC TC.
Innkeeper(s): Jean & Walt Hylander.
Circa: 1857.

Rooms: 4 rooms with PB, 4 with FP.
Beds: QDT.

Rosswood is a stately, columned mansion in an original plantation setting. Here, guests may find antiques, buried treasure, ghosts, history of a slave revolt, a Civil War battleground, the first owner's diary and genuine southern hospitality. Voted the "prettiest place in the country" by Farm & Ranch Living, the manor is a Mississippi Landmark and is in the National Register.

Breakfast included in rates. Types of meals: gourmet breakfast and early coffee/tea. Air conditioning, ceiling fan and VCR in room. Fax, copier, spa, swimming and library on premises. 100 acres. Weddings hosted. Antiques, fishing, parks and shopping nearby. TAC10.

Publicity: *Southern Living, The New York Times, Mississippi Magazine, Conde Nast Traveler, Inn Country USA.*

Natchez I2

The Burn

712 N Union St
Natchez, MS 39120-2951
(601)442-1344

Rates: $75-125.
Payment: MC VISA AX DC CB DS.
Innkeeper(s): Loveta & Tony Byrne.
Circa: 1834.

Rooms: 6 rooms with PB, 4 with FP. 1 conference room.
Beds: QDT.

White Doric columns support the front portico of this Greek Revival gem set in four blossoming acres of dogwoods, magnolias and camellias. An extensive antique collection graces the inn with gaslight chandeliers, Belgian draperies and finely carved woodwork adding to the genteel setting. The lavish Pink Room features an exquisite antique four-poster bed built by master craftsman Prudent Mallard and canopied with swagged damask draperies. Further pampering is provided with a plantation breakfast served at a polished mahogany dining table set with crystal and silver. The innkeeper served for 20 years as mayor of Natchez.

Type of meal: full breakfast. Fax on premises.

Publicity: *Country Inns, Bon Appetit.*

"We are still basking in the pleasures we found at The Burn."

Dunleith

84 Homochitto St
Natchez, MS 39120-3905
(601)446-8500 (800)433-2445

Rates: $85-130.
Payment: MC VISA DS TC.
Innkeeper(s): Nancy Gibbs.
Circa: 1856.

Rooms: 11 rooms with PB, 11 with FP. 1 conference room.
Beds: QDT.

This Greek Revival plantation house is listed as a National Historic Landmark. During the Civil War the Davis family raised thoroughbred horses here, and the story goes that when they heard Union officers were coming to take their horses, they hid their favorites in the cellar under the dining room. The officers ate dinner and heard nothing so the horses were saved. Rare French Zuber mural wallpaper decorates the dining room.

Breakfast included in rates. Type of meal: full breakfast. Air conditioning and cable TV in room. 40 acres. Antiques nearby.

Publicity: *Southern Accents, Unique Homes, Good Housekeeping, Country Inns.*

"The accommodations at the mansion were wonderful. Southern hospitality is indeed charming and memorable!"

Glen Auburn

300 S Commerce St
Natchez, MS 39120
(601)442-4099 (800)833-0170

Rates: $110-195.
Innkeeper(s): Dick & Carolyn Boyer.
Circa: 1875.

Rooms: 7 rooms with PB, 5 with FP. 5 suites. 1 conference room.

This grand Victorian mansion is a stunning example of Second Empire architecture. The National Register home has been restored to its original grandeur and the skillfully crafted millwork, ornamental plaster and a stenciled ceiling still remain. The innkeepers have filled the historic home with period antiques. Five of the guest suites offer fireplaces, and all include Jacuzzi tubs. Turndown service and a full Southern-style breakfast await guests. Apple-smoked bacon, a mushroom and pepper omelet and homemade blackberry coffeecake are typical items on the breakfast menu. The inn is located in downtown Natchez, a unique Victorian gem in a town sporting a more antebellum influence.

Highpoint

215 Linton Ave
Natchez, MS 39120-2315
(601)442-6963 (800)283-4099

Rates: $80-125.
Payment: PC TC.
Innkeeper(s): Frank Bauer, John Davis.
Circa: 1890.

Rooms: 3 rooms with PB, 2 with FP.
Beds: KQT.

This Queen Anne Victorian is just a block from the Mississippi River. The home was the first residence built in the state's first planned subdivision. Guests enjoy a tour of the historic home upon arrival. A plentiful, plantation-style breakfast is served each morning.

Breakfast and evening snack included in rates. Types of meals: full breakfast, gourmet breakfast and early coffee/tea. Air conditioning and turn-down service in room. Cable TV and library on premises. Small meetings and family reunions hosted. Antiques, shopping and theater nearby. TAC10.

Monmouth Plantation

36 Melrose Ave
Natchez, MS 39120-4005
(601)442-5852 (800)828-4531
Fax:(604)446-7762

Rates: $115-225.
Payment: MC VISA AX DC CB DS PC TC.
Innkeeper(s): Lani Riches.
Circa: 1818.

Rooms: 27 rooms with PB, 18 with FP. 13 suites. 4 cottages. 1 conference room.
Beds: KQDT.

Monmouth was the home of General Quitman who became acting Governor of Mexico, Governor of Mississippi, and a U. S. Congressman. In the National Register, the inn features antique four-poster and canopy beds, turn-down service, and an evening cocktail hour. Guests Jefferson Davis and Henry Clay enjoyed the same acres of gardens, pond and walking paths available today.

Breakfast included in rates. Types of meals: full breakfast and early coffee/tea. Dinner available. Air conditioning, turn-down service and cable TV in room. Fax and copier on premises. 26 acres. Weddings, small meetings, family reunions and seminars hosted. French spoken. Antiques and shopping nearby.

"The best historical inn we have stayed at anywhere."

Oakland Plantation

1124 Lower Woodville Rd
Natchez, MS 39120-8657
(800)824-0355 (800)824-0355
Fax:(601)442-5182

Rates: $65-75. AP.
Payment: MC VISA AX TC.
Innkeeper(s): Jean & Andy Peabody.
Circa: 1785.

Rooms: 3 rooms, 2 with PB, 3 with FP. 1 conference room.
Beds: KT.

Andrew Jackson courted his future wife Rachel Robards at this gracious 18th-century home. This working cattle plantation includes nature trails and a game preserve, fishing ponds, a tennis court and canoeing. Rooms are filled with antiques, and the innkeepers provide guests with a tour of the main home and plantation. They also will arrange tours of Natchez.

Breakfast included in rates. Type of meal: full breakfast. AP. Air conditioning in room. Cable TV and tennis on premises. 360 acres. Small meetings hosted. Antiques, fishing, parks, theater and watersports nearby. TAC10.

Publicity: *Southern Living, Country Inns.*

"Best kept secret in Natchez! Just great!"

Senatobia B4

Spahn House B&B

401 College St
Senatobia, MS 38668-2128
(601)562-9853 (800)400-9853
Fax:(601)562-8160

Rates: $60-110.
Payment: MC VISA PC TC.
Innkeeper(s): Daughn & Joe Spahn.
Circa: 1904.

Rooms: 3 rooms with PB. 1 suite. 5 conference rooms.
Beds: Q.

Originally built by a cotton and cattle baron, this 5,000-square-foot Neoclassical house sits on two acres and is listed in the National Register. Professionally decorated, it features fine antiques and luxuriously furnished rooms with elegant bed linens and Jacuzzi tubs. Be sure not to miss the 3 p.m. chocolate-covered strawberries and champagne. Private candlelight dinners are available by advance request. Breakfasts feature gourmet cuisine as the inn also manages a full-time catering business. (Guests sometimes are invited to sample food in the kitchen before it makes its way to local parties and events.) Memphis is 30 minutes south.

Breakfast included in rates. Types of meals: continental breakfast, continental-plus breakfast, full breakfast, gourmet breakfast and early coffee/tea. Afternoon tea, dinner, evening snack, picnic lunch, lunch, gourmet lunch, banquet service, catering service, catered breakfast and room service available. Air conditioning, ceiling fan and cable TV in room. VCR, fax and library on premises. Weddings, small meetings, family reunions and seminars hosted. Limited French, German and Spanish spoken. Amusement parks, antiques, fishing, parks, shopping, sporting events, theater and watersports nearby. TAC10.

Special Discounts: $150 private candlelight dinner, room rental, gourmet breakfast, flowers.

Vicksburg G3

Anchuca

1010 First East St
Vicksburg, MS 39180-2513
(601)631-6800 (800)469-2597

Rates: $75-135.
Payment: MC VISA AX DC CB DS.
Innkeeper(s): May C. Burns.
Circa: 1830.

Rooms: 6 rooms, 5 with FP. 1 suite.
Beds: QD.

This early Greek Revival mansion rises resplendently above the brick-paved streets of Vicksburg. It houses magnificent period antiques and artifacts and features gas-burning chandeliers. Confederate President Jefferson Davis once addressed the townspeople from the balcony while his brother was living in the home during the Civil War. The turn-of-the century guest cottage has been transformed into an enchanting hideaway and rooms in the mansion are appointed with formal decor and four-poster beds. A swimming pool and Jacuzzi are modern amenities.

Breakfast included in rates. Types of meals: full breakfast and gourmet breakfast. Afternoon tea available. Spa on premises.

Location: Historic District.

Publicity: *Times Herald, Southern Living, Innsider, Country Inns.*

"The 'Southern Hospitality' will not be forgotten. The best Southern breakfast in town."

Annabelle

501 Speed St
Vicksburg, MS 39180-4065
(601)638-2000 (800)791-2000
Fax:(601)636-5054

Rates: $75-125.
Payment: MC VISA AX DC CB DS PC TC.
Innkeeper(s): Carolyn & George Mayer.
Circa: 1868.

Rooms: 7 rooms with PB, 2 with FP. 1 suite. 1 cottage.
Beds: KQ.

From the outside, Annabelle looks like a friendly mix of Victorian and Italianate architecture set on an unassuming lawn of magnolias and pecan trees. It is the gracious interior and hospitality that has earned this bed & breakfast consistently high ratings. Walls are painted in deep, rich hues, highlighting the polished wood floors, Oriental rugs and beautiful antiques. Some of the furnishings are family heirlooms. Innkeepers George and Carolyn Mayer spent many years in the restaurant business and offer delicious Southern fare during the morning meal. George, a native of Moravia, speaks German, Portuguese and some Spanish.

Breakfast and afternoon tea included in rates. Types of meals: gourmet breakfast and early coffee/tea. Air conditioning, turn-down service and cable TV in room. Fax, swimming and library on premises. Handicap access. Family reunions hosted. German and Portuguese spoken. Amusement parks, antiques, fishing, parks, shopping, theater and watersports nearby. TAC10.

Pets Allowed: Small.

"You have a beautiful home. The history and decor really give the place flavor."

Belle of The Bends

508 Klein St
Vicksburg, MS 39180-4004
(601)634-0737 (800)844-2308

Rates: $95-135.
Payment: MC VISA AX DS.
Innkeeper(s): Wallace & Josephine Pratt.
Circa: 1876.

Rooms: 4 rooms with PB.
Beds: KQDT.

MS

Located in Vicksburg's Historic Garden District, this Victorian, Italianate mansion was built by Mississippi State Senator Murray F. Smith and his wife, Kate, and is nestled on a bluff overlooking the Mississippi River. The decor includes period antiques, Oriental rugs and memorabilia of the steamboats that plied the river waters in the 1880s and early 1900s. Two bedrooms and the first- and second-story wraparound verandas provide views of the river. A plantation breakfast is served and a tour of the house and history of the steamboats owned by the Morrissey Line is given. A tour of the Victorian Gardens also is available to guests.

Breakfast and afternoon tea included in rates. Type of meal: full breakfast. Air conditioning, cable TV and VCR in room. Antiques nearby.

Publicity: *Natchez Trace News Explorer, Victorian Style, America's Painted Ladies.*

"Thank you for the personalized tour of the home and area. We greatly enjoyed our stay. This house got us into the spirit of the period."

Cedar Grove Mansion Inn

2200 Oak St
Vicksburg, MS 39180-4008
(601)636-1000 (800)862-1300
Fax:(601)634-6126

Rates: $68-165.
Payment: MC VISA AX DS TC.
Innkeeper(s): Rhonda Abraham.
Circa: 1840.

Rooms: 28 rooms with PB, 3 with FP. 11 suites. 8 cottages. 4 conference rooms.
Beds: KQDT.

It's easy to relive "Gone With the Wind" at this grand antebellum estate built by John Klein as a wedding present for his bride. Visitors sip mint juleps and watch gas chandeliers flicker in the finely appointed parlors. The children's rooms and master bedroom contain their original furnishings. Although Cedar Grove survived the Civil War, a Union cannonball is still lodged in the parlor wall. There is a magnificent view of the Mississippi from the terraces and front galleries. Four acres of gardens include fountains and gazebos. There is a bar, and the inn's restaurant opens each evening at 6 p.m.

Breakfast included in rates. Type of meal: full breakfast. Banquet service and room service available. Restaurant on premises. Air conditioning, turn-down service and cable TV in room. Fax, copier, swimming, bicycles, tennis and library on premises. Handicap access. Weddings, small meetings and family reunions hosted. Amusement parks, antiques, fishing, parks, shopping, theater and watersports nearby. TAC10.

Publicity: *Vicksburg Post, Southern Living, Victorian Homes, Country Inns.*

Special Discounts: AAA members 10% discount.

"Love at first sight would be the best way to describe my feelings for your home and the staff."

Floweree Cottage

2309 Pearl St
Vicksburg, MS 39180-4013
(601)638-2704 (800)262-6315
Fax:(601)636-0052

Rates: $85-119.
Payment: MC VISA DS PC.
Innkeeper(s): Skippy & Gayle Tuminello.
Circa: 1873.

Rooms: 8 rooms with PB, 3 with FP. 2 suites.
Beds: KQT.

"Cottage" is an unassuming way to describe this majestic estate adorned by ornate, Post Bellum plasterwork, which was created by Bavarian immigrants. The home is named for Charles Conway-Floweree, the youngest colonel in the Confederate Army and a leader in Pickett's charge at Gettysburg. The innkeeper is an architect and his restoration efforts have recreated the grand era of this Italianate manor, which is listed in the National Register as well as the Historic American Building Survey. The lush grounds include a swimming pool and greenhouse, and the area offers many outdoor activities.

Breakfast included in rates. Types of meals: continental-plus breakfast and full breakfast. Air conditioning, ceiling fan and cable TV in room. VCR and swimming on premises. Small meetings hosted. Amusement parks, antiques, fishing, parks, shopping, theater and watersports nearby. TAC10.

Publicity: *1,001 Ideas, Southern Living.*

Stained Glass Manor - Oak Hall

2430 Drummond St
Vicksburg, MS 39180
(601)638-8893 (800)771-8891
(888)VICKBNB
Fax:(601)636-3055
E-mail: vickbnb@magnolia.net

Rates: $60-165.
Payment: MC VISA AX DS TC.
Innkeeper(s): Bill & Shirley Smollen.
Circa: 1902.

Rooms: 6 rooms, 4 with PB, 10 with FP. 1 suite. 1 cottage. 3 conference rooms.
Beds: KQDT.

Billed by the innkeepers as "Vicksburg's historic Victorian inn," this restored, Mission-style manor boasts 38 stained-glass windows, original woodwork and light fixtures. Period furnishings create an authentic Victorian flavor. George Washington Maher, who employed a young draftsman named Frank Lloyd Wright, designed the home, which was built in 1902. Later additions were made by 1908. The home's first owner, Fannie Vick Willis Johnson, was a descendant of the first Vick in Vicksburg. All but one guest room has a fireplace, and all are richly appointed with antiques, reproductions and Oriental rugs. "New Orleans" breakfasts begin with cafe au lait. Freshly baked breads, quiche and other treats follow.

Breakfast included in rates. Types of meals: continental-plus breakfast, gourmet breakfast and early coffee/tea. Air conditioning and cable TV in room. VCR, fax and library on premises. Weddings, small meetings, family reunions and seminars hosted. Amusement parks, antiques, fishing, parks, shopping, theater and watersports nearby. TAC10.

Pets Allowed: If kept under control.

Missouri

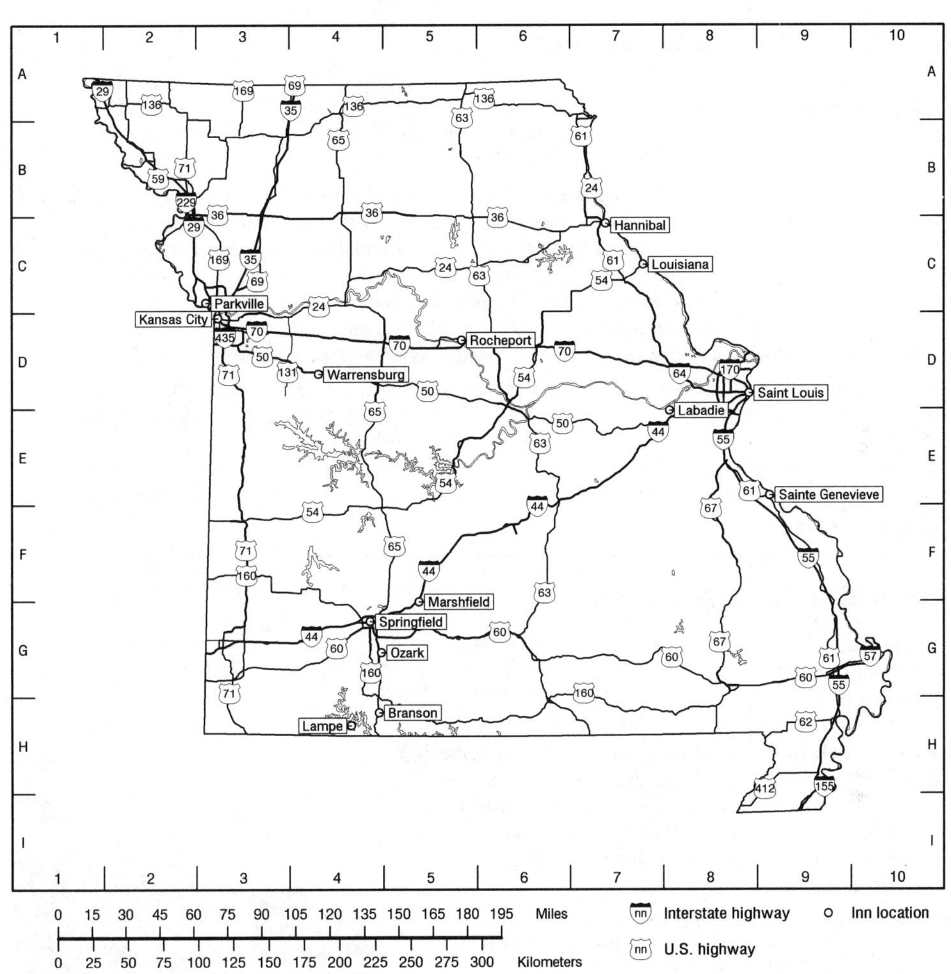

Branson **H4**

Aunt Sadie's Garden Glade

163 Fountain St
Branson, MO 65616-9194
(417)335-4063 (800)944-4250
Fax:(417)336-6992

Rates: $70-95.
Payment: MC VISA AX DS PC TC.
Innkeeper(s): Linda & Richard Hovell.
Circa: 1963.

Rooms: 4 rooms with PB, 2 with FP. 1 suite. 2 cottages.
Beds: KQDT.

This secluded home is nestled in a wooded glade, just five minutes from Branson's many activities. The modern ranch home offers two guest rooms in the main house, a cottage that sleeps up to five adults and a private honeymoon suite. Both the Paisley and Rose rooms have private hot tubs, and the Paisley also has a fireplace. Suite Infinity offers a king bed, fireplace and a two-person, heart-shaped whirlpool tub. All rooms have private entrances and some include modern amenities such as coffee makers, refrigerators and microwaves. The inn's big country breakfast, served family style, includes homemade biscuits and gravy, several entrees, fruit and pastry. A large outdoor deck is the perfect place for birdwatching, relaxing or socializing.

Breakfast and evening snack included in rates. Types of meals: full breakfast and early coffee/tea. Air conditioning, turn-down service, ceiling fan and cable TV in room. Child care on premises. Family reunions hosted. Amusement parks, antiques, fishing, parks, shopping, theater and watersports nearby. TAC10.

Josie's Peaceful Getaway B&B

HC 1 Box 1104
Branson, MO 65616-9613
(417)338-2978 (800)289-4125

Rates: $60-110.
Payment: MC VISA AX DS PC.
Innkeeper(s): Bill & JoAnne Coats.
Circa: 1978.

Rooms: 4 rooms, 3 with PB, 1 with FP. 1 suite.
Beds: KQ.

With 300 feet of Table Rock Lake shoreline to call its own, as well as more than an acre of grounds, this contemporary home is ideal for travelers hoping to enjoy all the Ozarks has to offer. For those who love country music, Branson's own version of Music Row beckons with brightly lit nightclubs. At Josie's, rooms are decorated in Victorian style with quilt-topped beds and lacy curtains. One room includes a whirlpool tub for two, while another offers its own outdoor Jacuzzi. Romantic breakfasts are served by candlelight on crystal and china. The innkeepers also have a private "tree house" condo, which offers lake views, two bedrooms, two bathrooms and a swimming pool. There are packages for honeymooners and those celebrating special occasions.

Breakfast included in rates. Types of meals: continental breakfast, full breakfast and early coffee/tea. Air conditioning and cable TV in room. Swimming on premises. Family reunions hosted. Amusement parks, antiques, fishing, parks, shopping, theater and watersports nearby. TAC10.

"We have found Branson's best kept secret!"

Hannibal C7

Garth Woodside Mansion

RR 3 Box 578
Hannibal, MO 63401-9634
(573)221-2789

Rates: $67-107.
Payment: MC VISA.
Innkeeper(s): Irv & Diane Feinberg.
Circa: 1871.

Rooms: 8 rooms with PB, 4 with FP.
Beds: QD.

This Italian Renaissance mansion is set on 39 acres of meadow and woodland. Original Victorian antiques fill the house. An unusual flying staircase with no visible means of support vaults three stories. Best of all, is the Samuel Clemens Room where Mark Twain slept. Afternoon beverages are served, and there are nightshirts tucked away in your room.

Breakfast and afternoon tea included in rates. Types of meals: gourmet breakfast and early coffee/tea. Air conditioning and turn-down service in room. 39 acres. Small meetings hosted. Amusement parks, antiques, fishing, parks and theater nearby.

Location: Along the Mississippi River just off highway 61.

Publicity: *Country Inns, Chicago Sun-Times, Glamour, Victorian Homes, Midwest Living, Innsider, Country Living, Conde Nast Traveler, Bon Appetit.*

"So beautiful and romantic and relaxing, we forgot we were here to work—Jeannie and Bob Ransom, Innsider."

Kansas City D3

The Doanleigh Inn

217 E 37th St
Kansas City, MO 64111
(816)753-2667
Fax:(816)531-5185

Rates: $90-135.
Payment: MC VISA AX DS PC TC.
Innkeeper(s): Terry Maturo & Cynthia Brogdon.
Circa: 1907.

Rooms: 5 rooms with PB, 2 with FP. 1 suite. 1 conference room.
Beds: KQ.

This three-story Georgian inn overlooks Hyde Park, and is a perfect spot to enjoy the best of Kansas City. American and European antiques grace the guest rooms. Jacuzzis, fireplaces and decks are among the amenities. A gourmet breakfast is served each morning, and in the evenings, wine and cheese are served.

Breakfast and evening snack included in rates. Types of meals: gourmet breakfast and early coffee/tea. Air conditioning, turn-down service, cable TV and VCR in room. Fax and copier on premises. Weddings, small meetings, family reunions and seminars hosted. Antiques, parks, shopping, sporting events, theater and watersports nearby.

Location: Five minutes from Crown Center and Country Club Plaza.

Southmoreland on The Plaza

116 E 46th St
Kansas City, MO 64112
(816)531-7979
Fax:(816)531-2407

Rates: $110-150.
Payment: MC VISA AX PC TC.
Innkeeper(s): Susan Moehl & Penni Johnson.
Circa: 1913.

Rooms: 12 rooms with PB, 3 with FP. 2 conference rooms.
Beds: KQ.

Located on the perimeter of the illustrious Country Club Plaza, this Colonial Revival mansion features a carriage house and three courtyards. Paired glass doors flank the foyer and original stair designs and fireplaces have been restored. Guests can explore the elegant shops that line the Plaza or visit Crown Center, an elaborate enclosed area featuring specialty shops and gourmet restaurants. A drive to nearby Mission Hills displays beautiful tudor-style mansions, including that of candy-maker Russel Stover and the Hall family, owners of Hallmark corporation.

Breakfast included in rates. Types of meals: full breakfast and gourmet breakfast. Air conditioning, turn-down service, ceiling fan and cable TV in room. VCR, fax, copier and computer on premises. Handicap access. Small meetings hosted. Antiques, parks, shopping, sporting events and theater nearby.

Publicity: *Inn Business Review.*

"Southmoreland on the Plaza goes beyond just setting new standards for an emergent class of inns in the European tradition. It is a uniquely Kansas City interpretation of an ancient form of roadside respite," Lawrence Goldblatt, Kansas City Business Journal.

MO

Labadie E8

Hunter's Hollow Inn & Restaurant

Washington & Front Streets,
PO 127, Labadie, MO 63055
(314)458-3326
Fax:(314)742-4820

Rates: $120-130.
Payment: MC VISA AX DS PC TC.
Innkeeper(s): Don L. Wolfsberger.
Circa: 1987.

Rooms: 3 rooms. 1 suite. 2 cottages.
Beds: KQ.

Just under an hour from the hustle and bustle of St. Louis, guests will find this unique accommodation. The Victorian Country Suite includes two well-appointed bedrooms, a living room and a formal dining room. The Fox and Hounds cottage is a historic dwelling once inhabited by the town's blacksmith and his family. Among the two-story cabin's romantic touches include hand-painted walls, a four-poster bed and a Victorian sitting porch. Finally, there is The Complete Angler, a masculine, 60-year-old cabin decorated in a fishing motif. All the accommodations are testament to the innkeeper's flair for design and creativity. Aside from the cabins and suite, the Hunter's Hollow Restaurant is a popular venue, heralded by many a food critic for its fine, American country classic cuisine.

Breakfast included in rates. Type of meal: continental-plus breakfast. Air conditioning and cable TV in room. Weddings, small meetings and family reunions hosted. Amusement parks, antiques, fishing, parks and shopping nearby. TAC10.

Special Discounts: Longer than two days, week's stay, etc.

"Enjoyed the atmosphere, food and hospitality."

Lampe H4

Grandpa's Farm B&B

HCR 1, PO Box 476
Lampe, MO 65681-0476
(417)779-5106 (800)280-5106

Rates: $65-85.
Payment: MC VISA DS PC TC.
Innkeeper(s): Keith & Pat Lamb.
Circa: 1891.

Rooms: 4 rooms with PB. 3 suites. 1 conference room.
Beds: KD.

This limestone farmhouse in the heart of the Ozarks offers guests a chance to experience country life in a relaxed farm setting. Midway between Silver Dollar City and Eureka Springs, Ark. and close to Branson, the inn boasts several lodging options, including a duplex with suites and honeymoon suite. The innkeepers are known for their substantial country breakfast and say guests enjoy comparing how long the meal lasts before they eat again. Although the inn's 186 acres are not farmed extensively, domesticated farm animals are on the premises.

Breakfast included in rates. Type of meal: full breakfast. Air conditioning and ceiling fan in room. VCR, fax and spa on premises. Handicap access. 116 acres. Small meetings, family reunions and seminars hosted. Amusement parks, antiques, fishing, parks, shopping, theater and watersports nearby. TAC10.

Special Discounts: Retreats $30 per person for two nights, one free evening meal.

Louisiana C7

Meadowcrest Bed & Breakfast

RR NN
Louisiana, MO 63353
(573)754-6594
Fax:(573)754-5406

Rates: $65-75.
Payment: PC TC.
Innkeeper(s): John & Karen Stoeckley.
Circa: 1970.

Rooms: 2 rooms, 1 with PB.
Beds: QD.

Art lovers will enjoy a stay at this cozy bed & breakfast, the home of Missouri Historian artist John Stoeckley. Along with his own pieces, he and wife, Karen, have decorated the home with other fine artwork and a collection of furnishings acquired on world travels, as well as antiques and family heirlooms. There are 12 wooded acres to explore here, with hiking trails. Guests often relax in the sitting room, where a warming fire is often crackling away. There is a fireplace and classic billiard table in the home's billiard room, as well. If weather permits, breakfasts, perhaps French toast, country bacon, herbed potatoes, fruit and homemade muffins, are served in the pavilion. The innkeepers also have a gallery in town located in an 1837 stagecoach stop. Guests receive a key for the gallery, so they are free to let themselves in at their leisure. John's artwork, as well as other Missouri artists are on display. For an extra charge, special dinners can be arranged at the gallery, and there is a small conference room there, as well.

Breakfast and evening snack included in rates. Type of meal: full breakfast. Air conditioning and ceiling fan in room. Sauna on premises. 12 acres. Weddings and small meetings hosted. Antiques, fishing, parks, shopping and watersports nearby.

"What a house. What a gallery. What a meal. We love this place."

Marshfield G5

Dickey House

331 S Clay St
Marshfield, MO 65706-2114
(417)468-3000
Fax:(417)859-5478

Rates: $55-95.
Payment: MC VISA DS PC TC.
Innkeeper(s): William & Dorothy Buesgen.
Circa: 1913.

Rooms: 6 rooms with PB. 2 suites. 1 cottage.
Beds: KQD.

This Greek Revival mansion is framed by ancient oak trees and boasts eight massive two-story Ionic columns. Burled woodwork, beveled glass and polished hardwood floors accentuate the gracious rooms. Interior columns soar in the parlor, creating a suitably elegant setting for the innkeeper's outstanding collec-

tion of antiques. A queen-size canopy bed, fireplace and balcony are featured in the Heritage Room. Some rooms offer amenities such as Jacuzzi tubs, a fireplace and cable TV.

Breakfast included in rates. Types of meals: full breakfast and gourmet breakfast. Air conditioning, ceiling fan and VCR in room. Cable TV, fax, copier and library on premises. Handicap access. Weddings, small meetings, family reunions and seminars hosted. TAC10.

Special Discounts: 10% AAA discount.

"Thanks so much for all that you did to make our wedding special."

Ozark

G4

Dear's Rest Bed & Breakfast

1408 Cap Hill Ranch Rd
Ozark, MO 65721-6149
(417)581-3839 (800)588-2262

Rates: $75.
Payment: MC VISA PC.
Innkeeper(s): Linda & Allan Schilter.
Circa: 1988.

Rooms: 1 suite.
Beds: DT.

Amish craftsmen fashioned this cedar house in a beautiful, secluded wooded setting that is close to Southwest Missouri's many attractions. The B&B only accommodates one party at a time, providing guests extraordinary comfort and privacy. A fireplace and outdoor hot tub add to the allure. The surrounding area abounds with wildlife and many guests enjoy hiking along nearby Bull Creek in the Mark Twain National Forest. Branson and Springfield are 45 minutes away.

Breakfast and evening snack included in rates. Type of meal: full breakfast. Air conditioning, ceiling fan and VCR in room. Spa and swimming on premises. 35 acres. Weddings, small meetings and family reunions hosted. Amusement parks, antiques, fishing, parks, shopping, sporting events, theater and watersports nearby.

Publicity: *Voice and View, Ozark Headliner.*

"You have a little bit of heaven here and to share it with others is very generous of you."

Parkville

C3

Down to Earth Lifestyles

12500 NW Crooked Rd
Parkville, MO 64152-1482
(816)891-1018

Rates: $75.
Payment: PC TC.
Innkeeper(s): Lola & Bill Coons.
Circa: 1982.

Rooms: 4 rooms with PB.
Beds: DT.

This unusually named bed & breakfast is located about 30 minutes north of Kansas City on a 86-acre spread. The name itself is a bit of a pun, the bed & breakfast is in what is known as an earth-integrated home. The home is contemporary in style, with four pleasing guest rooms, decorated in country style. There are woods and pastures to enjoy, two stocked fishing ponds and a heated, indoor pool. Guests select their breakfast menu from a long list of choices, which include eggs, biscuits and gravy, waffles, pancakes, French toast, breakfast meats and Lola's Fruit n' Cakes, a mouthwatering recipe of crepes stuffed with cream cheese and topped with warm fruit sauce and whipped cream.

Breakfast included in rates. Types of meals: continental-plus breakfast, full breakfast, gourmet breakfast and early coffee/tea. Air conditioning and turn-down service in room. VCR, swimming and library on premises. Handicap access. 86 acres. Small meetings, family reunions and seminars hosted. Amusement parks, antiques, fishing, parks, shopping, sporting events, theater and watersports nearby.

"A delightful place! But even more than that, it's an atmosphere of comfort."

Rocheport D5

School House B&B Inn

504 Third St
Rocheport, MO 65279
(573)698-2022

Rates: $85-150.
Payment: MC VISA.
Innkeeper(s): Penny Province.
Circa: 1914.

Rooms: 10 rooms with PB. 1 suite. 1 conference room.
Beds: KQDT.

This three-story brick building was once a schoolhouse. Now luxuriously appointed as a country inn, it features 13-foot-high ceilings, small print wallpapers and a bridal suite with Victorian furnishings and a private spa. The basement houses an antique shop. Nearby is a winery and a trail along the river providing many scenic miles for cyclists and hikers.

Breakfast and evening snack included in rates. Types of meals: continental breakfast, continental-plus breakfast, full breakfast, gourmet breakfast and early coffee/tea. Afternoon tea available. Air conditioning and ceiling fan in room. Cable TV, VCR, bicycles and library on premises. Small meetings and family reunions hosted. Antiques, fishing, parks, shopping, sporting events and theater nearby. TAC10.

Publicity: *Midwest Motorist, Missouri Wein Press, Successful Farming, Hallmark Greeting Cards.*

"We are still talking about our great weekend in Rocheport. Thanks for the hospitality, the beautiful room and delicious breakfasts, they were really great."

Saint Louis D8

Fleur-de-Lys Inn, Mansion at The Park

3500 Russell Blvd
Saint Louis, MO 63104
(314)773-3500 (888)969-3500
Fax:(314)773-6546

Rates: $85-175.
Payment: MC VISA AX DC CB DS PC TC.
Innkeeper(s): Kathryn Leep.
Circa: 1912.

Rooms: 2 rooms with PB. 3 suites. 1 conference room.
Beds: KQD.

The innkeepers at Fleur-de-Lys are ace decorators, creating bed chambers that are both warm and inviting, yet bright and cheerful at the same time. The Botanical Garden room features creamy yellow walls, a bed piled high with pillows and dressed with a puffy comforter and yellow gingham bed skirt. Another room, the Reservoir Park, is highlighted by a carved, four-poster plantation bed and masculine hues of burgundy and pale green. Other rooms include a king-size, antique iron and brass bed and a huge double bath, while another has a double Jacuzzi tub. Guests are pampered with amenities such as Turkish towels placed on heated towel racks, fresh flowers and a hot tub. There is a library, a cigar porch, a parlor and a gallery featuring works for sale by local artists. The inn is perfect for those seeking romance, but there are plenty of amenities for the business traveler. Fax, copying and printing services are available, as well as same-day dry cleaning, desks in each guest room and a selection of national and local papers available daily. Guests enjoy a gourmet breakfast, and in the evenings, hors d'oeuvres. Downtown St. Louis and many area attractions are five minutes away.

Breakfast and evening snack included in rates. Types of meals: gourmet breakfast and early coffee/tea. Dinner available. Air conditioning, turn-down service, ceiling fan, cable TV and VCR in room. Fax, copier, spa and library on premises. Small meetings hosted. Amusement parks, antiques, parks, shopping, sporting events and theater nearby. TAC10.

Lafayette House

2156 Lafayette Ave
Saint Louis, MO 63104
(314)772-4429 (800)641-8965
Fax:(314)664-2156

Rates: $55-85.
Payment: MC VISA AX DC CB DS PC TC.
Innkeeper(s): Nancy Buhr, Anna Millet.
Circa: 1876.

Rooms: 5 rooms, 1 with PB. 1 suite.
Beds: QDT.

Captain James Eads, designer and builder of the first trussed bridge across the Mississippi River, built this Queen Anne mansion as a wedding present for his daughter Margaret. The rooms are furnished in

antiques, and there is a suite with a kitchen on the third floor. The house overlooks Lafayette Park.

Breakfast included in rates. Types of meals: gourmet breakfast and early coffee/tea. Air conditioning and cable TV in room. VCR, fax and copier on premises. Weddings, small meetings, family reunions and seminars hosted. Antiques, parks, shopping, sporting events and theater nearby. TAC10.

Pets Allowed: Check with innkeepers, cats on premises.

Location: In the center of St. Louis.

"We had a wonderful stay at your house and enjoyed the furnishings, delicious breakfasts and friendly pets."

Lehmann House B&B

10 Benton Pl
Saint Louis, MO 63104
(314)231-6724

Rates: $60-75.
Payment: MC VISA AX DC DS PC TC.
Innkeeper(s): Marie & Michael Davies.
Circa: 1893.

Rooms: 4 rooms, 2 with PB, 3 with FP. 2 conference rooms.
Beds: KQDT.

This National Register manor's most prominent resident, former U.S. Attorney General Frederick Lehmann, hosted Presidents Taft, Theodore Roosevelt and Coolidge at this gracious home. Several key turn-of-the-century literary figures also visited the Lehmann family. The inn's formal dining room, complete with oak panelling and a fireplace, is a stunning place to enjoy the formal breakfasts. Antiques and gracious furnishings dot the well-appointed guest rooms. The home is located in St. Louis' oldest historic district.

Breakfast included in rates. Types of meals: full breakfast and early coffee/tea. Catering service available. Air conditioning, ceiling fan and VCR in room. Library on premises. Weddings, small meetings, family reunions and seminars hosted. Antiques, parks, shopping, sporting events and theater nearby. TAC10.

Special Discounts: Seven-plus days: 10% off.

The Winter House

3522 Arsenal St
Saint Louis, MO 63118
(314)664-4399
Fax:(314)776-6261

Rates: $75-110.
Payment: MC VISA AX DC CB DS PC TC.
Innkeeper(s): Kendall Winter.
Circa: 1897.

Rooms: 3 rooms with PB. 1 suite.
Beds: KQDR.

Original brass hardware, three fireplaces and a turret provide ambiance at this turn-of-the-century brick Victorian. Embossed French paneling adds elegance. The suite features a balcony, and the bedroom has a pressed-tin ceiling. The Rose Room is decorated with its namesake flower and a king-size bed. The home is ideally located three miles from the downtown area. Exotic restaurants are within walking distance. Breakfast is served on antique Wedgewood china and includes hand-squeezed orange juice, gourmet coffees, teas and a full breakfast.

Breakfast included in rates. Type of meal: full breakfast. Air conditioning and ceiling fan in room. Amusement parks, antiques, fishing, parks, shopping, sporting events and theater nearby. TAC10.

Publicity: *Innsider, Saint Louis Post Dispatch.*

Special Discounts: 10% off after second night.

"A delightful house with spotless, beautifully appointed rooms, charming hosts. Highly recommended."

Inn St. Gemme Beauvais

78 N Main St
Sainte Genevieve, MO
63670-1336
(573)883-5744 (800)818-5744
Fax:(573)883-3899

Rates: $69-125. AP.
Payment: MC VISA PC TC.
Innkeeper(s): Janet Joggerst.
Circa: 1848.

Rooms: 7 rooms with PB, 1 with FP. 5 suites. 2 conference rooms.
Beds: QDT.

This three-story, Federal-style inn is an impressive site on Ste. Genevieve's Main Street. The town is one of the oldest west of the Mississippi River, and the St. Gemme Beauvais is the oldest operating Missouri inn. The rooms are nicely appointed in period style, but there are modern amenities here, too. The Jacuzzi tubs in some guest rooms are one relaxing example. There is an outdoor hot tub as well. Guests are pampered with all sorts of cuisine, from full breakfasts to luncheons with sinfully rich desserts, and in the late afternoons, wine, hors d'oeuvres and refreshments are served.

Breakfast and afternoon tea included in rates. Types of meals: full breakfast, gourmet breakfast and early coffee/tea. Evening snack, picnic lunch, lunch, gourmet lunch, banquet service, catering service, catered breakfast and room service available. AP. Air conditioning, turn-down service, ceiling fan and cable TV in room. VCR, fax, copier, spa and bicycles on premises. Weddings, small meetings, family reunions and seminars hosted. Antiques, parks and shopping nearby.

Main Street Inn

221 North Main St, Sainte Genevieve, MO 63670
(573)883-9199 (800)918-9199

Rates: $70-115.
Payment: MC VISA AX DS PC TC.
Innkeeper(s): Ken & Karen Kulberg.
Circa: 1883.

Rooms: 7 rooms with PB.
Beds: QDT.

This exquisite inn is one of Missouri's finest bed & breakfast establishments. Built as the Meyer Hotel, the inn has welcomed guests for almost a century. Each of the individually appointed rooms is stocked with amenities, such as bubble bath, lace and flowers. Many of the inn's antiques were used during the inn's days as the Meyer Hotel. One room features stencilled walls, while another includes a whirlpool tub. Beds are topped with vintage quilts, linens and bedspreads. The morning meal is served in a beautiful brick kitchen, which features an unusual blue cookstove. The menu changes from day to day, caramelized French toast is one of the inn's specialties.

Breakfast and evening snack included in rates. Types of meals: full breakfast, gourmet breakfast and early coffee/tea. Air conditioning and ceiling fan in room. Cable TV, VCR, copier and library on premises. Small meetings, family reunions and seminars hosted. Antiques, parks and shopping nearby. TAC10.

The Southern Hotel

146 S 3rd St
Sainte Genevieve, MO
63670-1667
(573)883-3493 (800)275-1412
Fax:(573)883-9612

Rates: $80-125.
Payment: MC VISA PC TC.
Innkeeper(s): Mike & Barbara Hankins.
Circa: 1790.

Rooms: 8 rooms with PB, 4 with FP. 1 conference room.
Beds: KQD.

This Federal building is the largest and oldest brick home west of the Mississippi. It features a long front porch, large parlors and a spacious dining room. Highlights of the guest rooms include cedar bedposts carved in the shape of Old Man River, a hand-painted headboard and a delicately carved Victorian bed. The clawfoot tubs are hand-painted. Guests are invited to add their names to a quilt-in-progress, which is set out in the parlor.

Breakfast included in rates. Types of meals: full breakfast, gourmet breakfast and early coffee/tea. Air conditioning and ceiling fan in room. Bicycles on premises. Small meetings, family reunions and seminars hosted. Antiques, fishing, parks and shopping nearby.

Publicity: *Innsider, St. Louis Gourmet, River Heritage Gazette.*

"I can't imagine ever staying in a motel again! It was so nice to be greeted by someone who expected us. We felt right at home."

Springfield G4

The Mansion at Elfindale

1701 S Fort Ave
Springfield, MO 65807-1280
(417)831-5400

Rates: $50-125.
Payment: MC VISA AX DC DS.
Innkeeper(s): Jef Wells.
Circa: 1800.

Rooms: 13 rooms with PB, 2 with FP. 1 conference room.
Beds: KQDT.

The Mansion at Elfindale once served as the St. de Chantel Academy for girls. The gray stone structure features a turret observation room, ornate fireplaces, stained-glass windows, vaulted ceilings, marble-finish furnishings, wicker furniture and antiques. Breakfast includes foods from around the world.

Breakfast included in rates. Dinner, banquet service and catering service available. Handicap access. Weddings, small meetings, family reunions and seminars hosted. Antiques, shopping and sporting events nearby. TAC10.

"Many thanks for your warm hospitality."

Virginia Rose B&B

317 E Glenwood St
Springfield, MO 65807-3543
(417)883-0693 (800)345-1412

Rates: $50-90.
Payment: MC VISA DS PC TC.
Innkeeper(s): Jackie & Virginia Buck.
Circa: 1906.

Rooms: 5 rooms, 3 with PB. 1 suite.
Beds: QD.

Three generations of the Botts family lived in this home before it was sold to the current innkeepers, Virginia and Jackie Buck. The grounds still include the rustic red barn. Comfortable, country rooms are named after Buck family members and feature beds covered with quilts. The innkeepers also offer a two-bedroom suite, the Rambling Rose, which is decorated in a sportsman theme in honor of the nearby Bass Pro. Hearty breakfasts are served in the dining room and the innkeepers will provide low-fat fare on request.

Breakfast included in rates. Types of meals: full breakfast and early coffee/tea. Evening snack and picnic lunch available. Air conditioning and turn-down service in room. Cable TV, VCR and fax on premises. Weddings, small meetings, family reunions and seminars hosted. Amusement parks, antiques, fishing, parks, shopping, sporting events, theater and watersports nearby. TAC10.

Publicity: *Auctions & Antiques.*

Special Discounts: 10% AARP.

"The accommodations are wonderful and the hospitality couldn't be warmer."

Walnut Street Inn

900 E Walnut St
Springfield, MO 65806-2603
(417)864-6346 (800)593-6346
Fax:(417)864-6184

Rates: $65-150.
Payment: MC VISA AX DC DS.
Innkeeper(s): Gary & Paula Blankenship.
Circa: 1894.

Rooms: 12 rooms with PB, 6 with FP. 5 suites.
Beds: QD.

This three-story Queen Anne gabled house has cast-iron Corinthian columns and a veranda. Polished wood floors and antiques are featured throughout. Upstairs you'll find the gathering room with a fireplace. Ask for the McCann guest room with two bay windows. A full breakfast is served, including items such as peach-stuffed French toast.

Breakfast included in rates. Types of meals: gourmet breakfast and early coffee/tea. Afternoon tea available. Air conditioning, ceiling fan, cable TV and VCR in room. Fax and copier on premises. Handicap access. Amusement parks, antiques, fishing, parks, shopping, downhill skiing, sporting events, theater and watersports nearby.

Publicity: *Midwest Living, Victoria, Country Inns, Innsider, Glamour, Midwest Motorist, Missouri, Saint Louis Post, KC Star, USA Today.*

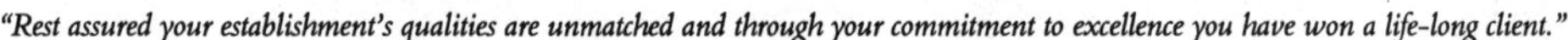

"Rest assured your establishment's qualities are unmatched and through your commitment to excellence you have won a life-long client."

Warrensburg D4

Cedarcroft Farm B&B

431 SE Y Hwy
Warrensburg, MO 64093
(816)747-5728 (800)368-4944
E-mail: bwayne@cedarcroft.com

Rates: $75-85.
Payment: MC VISA AX DS PC TC.
Innkeeper(s): Sandra & Bill Wayne.
Circa: 1867.

Rooms: 1 room.
Beds: D.

John Adams, a Union army veteran, and Sandra's great grandfather, built this house. There are 80 acres of woodlands, meadows and creeks where deer, fox, coyotes and wild turkeys still roam. Two original barns remain. Guests stay in a private, two-bedroom suite, which can accommodate couples or families. Bill participates in Civil War reenactments and is happy to demonstrate clothing, weapons and customs of the era. Sandra cares for her quarter horses and provides the home-baked, full country breakfasts.

Breakfast and evening snack included in rates. Type of meal: full breakfast. Air conditioning in room. Cable TV and VCR on premises. 80 acres. Antiques, fishing, parks, shopping and theater nearby. TAC10.

Location: About six miles southeast of Warrensburg, Mo., 60 miles from Kansas City.

Publicity: *Kansas City Star, Higginsville Advance, Midwest Motorist, KCTV, KMOS TV, Territorial Small Farm Today, Country America, Entrepreneur.*

"We enjoyed the nostalgia and peacefulness very much. Enjoyed your wonderful hospitality and great food."

Audubon Lodge Sausage-Cheese Breakfast Bread

Audubon Lodge
Dayton, Texas

- 1 lb hot pan sausage
- ½ cup chopped onions
- ¾ cup grated Parmesan cheese
- 1 cup grated Swiss cheese
- 1 egg, beaten
- ¼ t hot sauce
- 2 T chopped parsley
- 1 ½ t salt
- 2 cups Bisquick mix
- ⅔ cup milk
- ¼ cup mayonnaise

Cook hot sausage and chopped onions together until sausage is brown and onions are soft. Drain grease and cool. Mix all other ingredients. Add the sausage onion mixture, it will be stiff.

Butter or spray with cooking spray a 9-by-13" pan and press dough in and bake, uncovered at 400 degrees for 25 to 30 minutes.

Cool slightly before cutting into squares and serving with jalapeno jelly and fresh fruit. May be reheated in the microwave or regular oven.

Serves 12 (approximately).

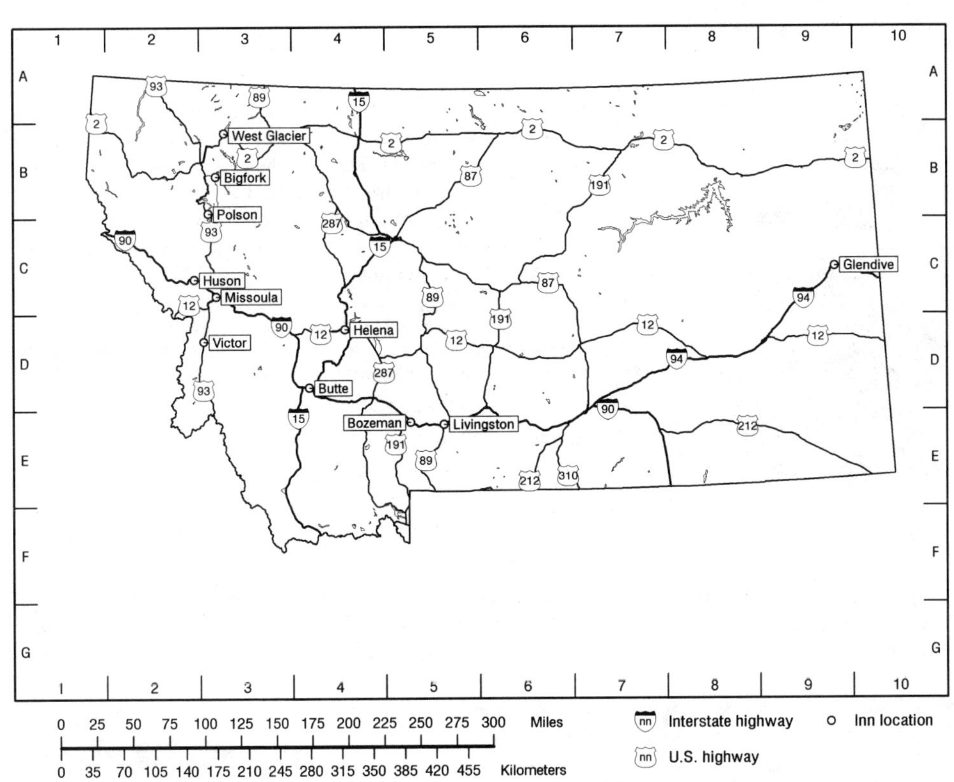

Bigfork B3

Burggraf's Countrylane B&B

Rainbow Drive on Swan Lake
Bigfork, MT 59911
(406)837-4608 (800)525-3344
Fax:(406)837-2468

Rates: $85-100. AP.
Payment: MC VISA PC TC.
Innkeeper(s): Natalie & RJ Burggraf.
Circa: 1984.

Rooms: 6 rooms with PB.
Beds: KQT.

This contemporary log home on Swan Lake, minutes from Flathead Lake in the Rockies, offers fine accommodations in one of America's most beautiful settings. Upon arrival, visitors enjoy hors d'oeuvres, chilled wine, and fresh fruit. Ceiling fans, clock radios and turndown service are amenities. Picnic baskets are available and would be ideal for taking along on a paddle boat lake excursion. Excellent skiing and snowmobiling opportunities await winter visitors, and all will enjoy the inn's seven scenic acres.

Breakfast and evening snack included in rates. Types of meals: full breakfast, gourmet breakfast and early coffee/tea. Picnic lunch available. AP. Ceiling fan, cable TV and VCR in room. Fax, copier, swimming, library and pet boarding on premises. Handicap access. Weddings, small meetings and family reunions hosted. Antiques, fishing, parks, shopping, downhill skiing, cross-country skiing, sporting events, theater and watersports nearby. TAC10.

Torch & Toes B&B

309 S 3rd Ave
Bozeman, MT 59715-4636
(406)586-7285 (800)446-2138

Rates: $80-90.
Payment: MC VISA PC TC.
Innkeeper(s): Ron & Judy Hess.
Circa: 1906.

Rooms: 4 rooms with PB.
Beds: KQT.

This Colonial Revival home, three blocks from the center of town, boasts an old-fashioned front porch with porch swing and a carriage house. Antique furnishings in the dining room feature a Victrola and a pillared and carved oak fireplace. Ron is a professor of architecture at nearby Montana State University and Judy is a weaver. Her loom and some of her colorful work are on display at this artisan's inn.

Breakfast included in rates. Types of meals: full breakfast and gourmet breakfast. Ceiling fan in room. Cable TV and VCR on premises. Small meetings, family reunions and seminars hosted. Antiques, fishing, parks, shopping, downhill skiing, cross-country skiing, sporting events, theater and watersports nearby. TAC10.

Location: North of Yellowstone National Park.

Publicity: *Bozeman Chronicle, San Francisco Peninsula Parent, Northwest.*

"Thanks for your warm hospitality."

Voss Inn

319 S Willson Ave
Bozeman, MT 59715-4632
(406)587-0982
Fax:(406)585-2964

Rates: $85-95.
Payment: MC VISA AX PC TC.
Innkeeper(s): Bruce & Frankee Muller.
Circa: 1883.

Rooms: 6 rooms with PB.
Beds: KQ.

The Voss Inn is a restored two-story house with a large front porch and a Victorian parlor. Old-fashioned furnishings include an upright piano and chandelier. A full breakfast is served, with fresh baked rolls kept in a unique warmer that's built into an ornate 1880s radiator. Day trips and overnight trips into Yellowstone Park are conducted by the owner, who has had extensive experience leading Safaris in Africa.

Breakfast and afternoon tea included in rates. Types of meals: full breakfast and gourmet breakfast. Picnic lunch available. Air conditioning in room. Cable TV and fax on premises. Weddings, small meetings and family reunions hosted. Spanish and some Dutch spoken. Antiques, fishing, parks, shopping, downhill skiing, cross-country skiing and watersports nearby. TAC7.

Location: Four blocks south of downtown.

Publicity: *Sunset, Cosmopolitan, Gourmet, Countryside.*

"First class all the way."

Butte

D4

Copper King Mansion

219 W Granite St
Butte, MT 59701-9235
(406)782-7580

Rates: $55-95.
Payment: MC VISA AX DS.
Innkeeper(s): Maria Sigl.
Circa: 1884.

Rooms: 4 rooms.

This turn-of-the-century marvel was built, as the name indicates, by W.A. Clark, one of the nation's leading copper barons. In the early 1900s, Clark made millions each month hauling copper out of Butte's vast mines. Stained-glass windows, gold leafing on the ceilings and elaborate woodwork are just a few of the opulent touches. Clark commissioned artisans brought in from Germany to carve the intricate staircase, which graces the front hall. The mansion is decked floor to ceiling in antiques collected by the innkeeper's mother and grandmother, who purchased the home from Clark's relatives. A three-room master suite includes two fireplaces, a lavish bedroom, a sitting room and a huge bathroom with a clawfoot tub.

Breakfast included in rates. Type of meal: full breakfast.

Publicity: *Sunset Magazine.*

Glendive C9

The Hostetler House B&B

113 N Douglas St
Glendive, MT 59330-1619
(406)365-4505 (800)965-8456
Fax:(406)365-8456

Rates: $50.
Payment: MC VISA DS PC TC.
Innkeeper(s): Craig & Dea Hostetler.
Circa: 1912.

Rooms: 2 rooms.
Beds: D.

Casual country decor mixed with handmade and heirloom furnishings are highlights at this two-story inn. The inn features many comforting touches, such as a romantic hot tub and gazebo, enclosed sun porch and sitting room filled with books. The two guest rooms share a bath, and are furnished by Dea, an interior decorator. The full breakfasts may be enjoyed on Grandma's china in the dining room or on the deck or sun porch. The Yellowstone River is one block from the inn and downtown shopping is two blocks away. Makoshika State Park, home of numerous fossil finds, is nearby.

Breakfast included in rates. Types of meals: gourmet breakfast and early coffee/tea. Air conditioning and ceiling fan in room. Cable TV, VCR, fax, spa and library on premises. Small meetings hosted. German spoken. Antiques, fishing, parks, shopping, cross-country skiing, sporting events, theater and watersports nearby. TAC10.

MT

Publicity: *Ranger Review.*

Special Discounts: 10% discount, length of stay; senior citizens.

"Warmth and loving care are evident throughout your exquisite home. Your attention to small details is uplifting. Thank you for a restful sojourn."

Helena D4

Appleton Inn B&B

1999 Euclid Ave,
Hwy 12 West
Helena, MT 59601-1908
(406)449-7492 (800)956-1999
Fax:(406)449-1261

Rates: $50-105. AP.
Payment: MC VISA AX DS PC TC.
Innkeeper(s): Tom Woodall & Cheryl Boid.
Circa: 1890.

Rooms: 5 rooms, 3 with PB. 2 suites.
Beds: Q.

Montana's first resident dentist called this Victorian his home. It remained in his family until the 1970s when it was transformed into apartments. Fortunately, the innkeepers bought and restored the home, bringing back the original beauty. The innkeepers have their own furniture-making company and have created many of the pieces that decorate the guest rooms. Rooms range from the spacious Master Suite, with its oak, four-poster bed and bath with a clawfoot tub, to the quaint and cozy Attic Playroom. The inn is a convenient place to enjoy the Helena area, and there are mountain bikes on hand for those who wish to explore.

Breakfast included in rates. Afternoon tea and picnic lunch available. AP. Air conditioning in room. Cable TV, VCR, fax, copier and bicycles on premises. Weddings, small meetings, family reunions and seminars hosted. Antiques, fishing, parks, shopping, downhill skiing, cross-country skiing, sporting events, theater and watersports nearby. TAC10.

Pets Allowed: Need prior approval.

Publicity: *Philadelphia, Back Roads USA.*

Special Discounts: 10% senior rates.

"For our first try at B&B lodgings, we've probably started at the top, and nothing else will ever measure up to this. Wonderful food, wonderful home, grounds and wonderful hostess!"

The Sanders - Helena's Bed & Breakfast

328 N Ewing St
Helena, MT 59601-4050
(406)442-3309
Fax:(406)443-2361

Rates: $85-105.
Payment: MC VISA AX PC TC.
Innkeeper(s): Bobbi Uecker & Rock Ringling.
Circa: 1875.

Rooms: 7 rooms with PB, 1 with FP. 2 conference rooms.
Beds: Q.

This historic inn is filled with elegantly carved furnishings, paintings and collections that are original to the house. Wilbur Sanders, an attorney and a Montana senator, built his house near the Governor's Mansion, in the heart of Helena. The three-story house features a front and side porch, and balconies and bay windows that provide views of the mountains and downtown Helena. In addition to the rich interior and hospitality, guests are pampered with gourmet breakfasts, featuring such items as freshly ground, organically grown coffee, orange-banana juice, Grand Marinier French toast and mixed fruit topped with a yogurt-nutmeg sauce.

Breakfast included in rates. Types of meals: full breakfast, gourmet breakfast and early coffee/tea. Afternoon tea, catering service and room service available. Air conditioning, turn-down service and ceiling fan in room. Fax and library on premises. Weddings, small meetings, family reunions and seminars hosted. Antiques, fishing, parks, shopping, downhill skiing, cross-country skiing, sporting events, theater and watersports nearby.

Publicity: *Philadelphia, Back Roads USA.*

"For our first try at B&B lodgings, we've probably started at the top, and nothing else will ever measure up to this. Wonderful food, wonderful home, grounds and wonderful hostess!"

Huson C2

The Schoolhouse and The Teacherage

Remound Rd-9 Mile
Huson, MT 59846
(406)626-5879

Rates: $60.
Payment: PC TC.
Innkeeper(s): Les & Hanneke Ippisch.
Circa: 1893.

Rooms: 5 rooms. 1 cottage.
Beds: QDT.

Built by the Anaconda Company for the area's school children, the original building became the teachers house (now the Teacherage) and a second, the Schoolhouse. Folk art collections fill the inn and guest rooms sport Amish, Swedish, Montana and Dutch themes, all with featherbeds and handmade quilts. Deer often may be viewed from the porch, grazing in nearby fields. Apple trees on the property include a rare snowapple tree. The historic 9 Mile Ranger Station, an old forest service mule station, is a mile away. Guests enjoy area hiking and cross-country skiing, as well as fishing and whitewater rafting at Clark Fork River. Glacier Park is within a three-hour drive.

Breakfast included in rates. Types of meals: full breakfast and gourmet breakfast. Picnic lunch available. Weddings, small meetings and family reunions hosted. Swedish and Dutch spoken. Fishing, parks, shopping, downhill skiing, cross-country skiing, sporting events and theater nearby.

Livingston E5

The River Inn on The Yellowstone

4950 Hwy 89 S
Livingston, MT 59047
(406)222-2429

Rates: $45-85.
Payment: MC VISA.
Innkeeper(s): Dee Dee VanZyl & Ursula Neese.
Circa: 1895.

Rooms: 3 rooms with PB. 1 cottage.
Beds: QDT.

Crisp, airy rooms decorated with a Southwestern flavor are just part of the reason why this 100-year-old farmhouse is an ideal getaway. There are five acres to meander, including more than 500 feet of riverfront, and close access to a multitude of outdoor activities is yet another reason. Each of the three guest rooms offers a wonderful view. Two rooms have decks boasting views of the river, and the third offers a canyon view. Guests also can stay in Calamity Jane's, a rustic riverside cabin. For an unusual twist, summer guests can opt for Spangler's Wagon and experience life as it was on the range. This is a true, turn-of-the-century sheep-herders' wagon and includes a double bed and woodstove. The innkeepers guide a variety of interesting hikes, bike and canoe trips in the summer and fall. The inn is close to many outdoor activities. Don't forget to check out Livingston, just a few miles away. The historic town has been used in several movies and maintains an authentic Old West spirit.

Breakfast included in rates. Types of meals: full breakfast, gourmet breakfast and early coffee/tea. Picnic lunch available. VCR and bicycles on premises. Weddings, small meetings, family reunions and seminars hosted. Limited Spanish spoken. Antiques, fishing, parks, shopping, downhill skiing, cross-country skiing, sporting events, theater and water-sports nearby. TAC10.

Pets Allowed: Horses, possibly dogs and cats by arrangement well in advance.

Missoula C3

Goldsmith's B&B

809 E Front St
Missoula, MT 59802-4704
(406)721-6732

Rates: $69-119.
Payment: MC VISA AX TC.
Innkeeper(s): Dick & Jeana Goldsmith.
Circa: 1911.

Rooms: 7 rooms with PB, 2 with FP. 4 suites.
Beds: QD.

Missoula, made famous for its "A River Runs Through It" connection, is the site of this Four-Square-style home. It would be difficult for the inn to offer a better view of the Clark Fork River, the waterway is just a few feet from the home's front door. Guest quarters are a mixture of turn-of-the-century country and romantic whimsy with bright flowery patterns and quilts dressing the sleigh, pewter, porcelain or wicker beds. Several rooms boast river views. There is a full-service restaurant in an adjoining building, and guests are treated to a memorable full breakfast. Omelets and ice cream batter pancakes are famed specialties of the house. The restaurant includes a bagel bakery and has homemade ice cream.

Breakfast included in rates. Types of meals: full breakfast and early coffee/tea. Lunch available. Air conditioning, ceiling fan and cable TV in room. Library on premises. Small meetings, family reunions and seminars hosted. Fishing, parks, shopping, downhill skiing, cross-country skiing, sporting events and theater nearby. TAC10.

Special Discounts: Single Sunday night through Thursday night; special rates for the whole house.

MT

Polson B3

Hidden Pines

792 Lost Quartz Rd
Polson, MT 59860-9428
(406)849-5612 (800)505-5612

Rates: $50-60.
Payment: PC TC.
Innkeeper(s): Emy & Earl Atchley.
Circa: 1976.

Rooms: 4 rooms, 2 with PB.
Beds: QD.

Relax on the porch of this secluded, quiet home and the only sounds you'll hear are birds chirping and the breezes that blow across the wooded grounds. Hidden Pines borders Flathead Lake, where guests will enjoy swimming and boating. The innkeepers offer picnic tables and lawn chairs for those who want to soak up the natural surroundings. The home's hot tub is a great place to end the day. The innkeepers prepare a hearty breakfast, but lighter fare is available. Each of the comfortable guest rooms features individual decor. The Deckside room has a private entrance onto the deck and hot tub area.

Breakfast and picnic lunch included in rates. Types of meals: full breakfast and early coffee/tea. Ceiling fan and VCR in room. Spa on premises. Family reunions hosted. Antiques, fishing, parks, shopping, theater and watersports nearby.

Pets Allowed: Small, very well behaved.

Victor

D3

Bear Creek Lodge

1184 Bear Creek Trl
Victor, MT 59875-9680
(406)642-3750 (800)270-5550
Fax:(406)642-6847
E-mail: bearcrik@montananet.com

Rates: $200-250.
Payment: MC VISA AX DS PC.
Innkeeper(s): Roland & Elizabeth Turney.
Circa: 1991.

Rooms: 8 rooms with PB. 1 conference room.
Beds: QDT.

There are many reasons to visit Montana, not the least of which is Bear Creek Lodge. The lodge was built from logs harvested after the vicious fires that ripped through Yellowstone National Park in 1988. Its secluded location makes the lodge a perfect place to commune with nature and gaze at starry skies. Guests can spend the day enjoying the wilderness on a hike or horseback trip. For those who wish to fish, there is private access to Bear Creek. A hot tub, exercise room and sauna are on the premises as well. Guests are pampered with three hearty meals each day, hors d'oeuvres in the late afternoon, fresh baked goods and beverages, all of which are included in the rates.

Cable TV, VCR, fax, copier, spa, sauna, stables, bicycles and library on premises. 72 acres. Weddings, small meetings, family reunions and seminars hosted. Limited Spanish spoken. Antiques, fishing, parks, downhill skiing and cross-country skiing nearby. TAC10.

Pets Allowed: No cats; dogs would have to have prior approval.

Special Discounts: Whole lodge for $1500 per night for first 12 people, $75 thereafter (off season - $1200-$50).

"We'll long remember our wonderful stay with you nice,nice folks."

West Glacier

B3

Mountain Timbers Lodge

PO Box 94
West Glacier, MT 59936
(406)387-5830 (800)841-3835
Fax:(406)387-5835

Rates: $55-125.
Payment: MC VISA.
Innkeeper(s): Karen Schweitzer.
Circa: 1973.

Rooms: 7 rooms, 4 with PB. 1 conference room.
Beds: QDT.

With the wilderness of Glacier National Park as its backdrop, this rustic, log home is designed for nature lovers. The grounds include miles of professionally designed cross-country ski trails, and guests on a morning walk shouldn't be surprised if they encounter deer or elk sharing the countryside. The inviting interior complements the spectacular scenery. The huge living room is warmed by a rock and stone fireplace and decorated with Southwestern style furnishings. For those who prefer to simply relax and curl up with a good book, the innkeepers offer a well-stocked library. Beds are topped with down comforters, and guests are further pampered with an outdoor hot tub.

Breakfast included in rates. Type of meal: full breakfast. Fax, copier and spa on premises. Fishing nearby.

Location: One mile outside Glacier National Park.

Nebraska

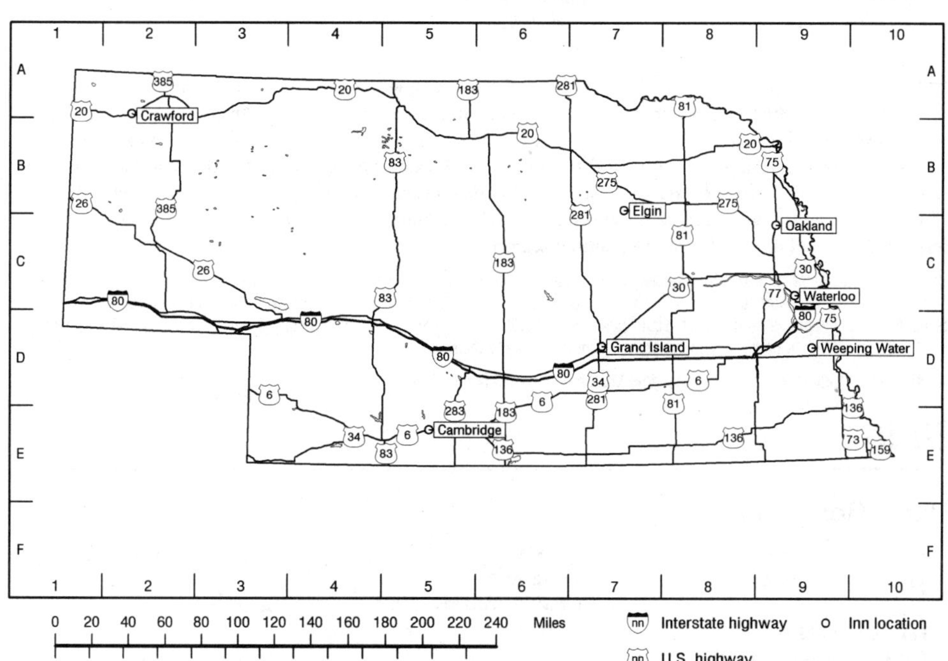

Cambridge E5

The Cambridge Inn

606 Parker, PO Box 239
Cambridge, NE 69022
(308)697-3220

Rates: $50-75.
Payment: MC VISA.
Innkeeper(s): Mike & Elaine Calabro.

Rooms: 5 rooms, 3 with PB.

The Prairie Lakes region of Southwest Nebraska is known for its abundant outdoor activities, and the Cambridge Inn offers an ideal setting for those exploring the area. A beautiful, historic Neoclassical home, the inn features both Ionic and Corinthian columns supporting its stories. Handsome woodwork is found throughout, and authentic decor such as a clawfoot tub, pedestal sink and stained glass add to the charm. Breakfasts are served in the formal dining room, and guests may relax in the parlor and library. The Ivy Court room offers a sitting area and a writing desk.

Breakfast included in rates. Dinner and lunch available.

Crawford

A2

Fort Robinson Inn

PO Box 392
Crawford, NE 69339-0392
(308)665-2900
Fax:(308)665-2906

Rates: $26-520.
Payment: MC VISA PC TC.
Innkeeper(s): Steve Kemper.
Circa: 1909.

Rooms: 23 rooms. 32 cottages. 1 conference room.
Beds: QDT.

This collection of lodge rooms, cabins, adobes and a ranch-style home are located within Fort Robinson State Park. Accommodations are comfortable and simple, available from early April until the third weekend in November. The real draw here is the park, which was an active military post from 1884 to 1948. The area was the site of several Indian wars, and served as a POW camp during World War II. Horseback and jeep tours as well as stagecoach rides are available, as well as fishing and camping. Some activities are scheduled for summer months only. Some accommodations have kitchen facilities and the Fort Robinson Inn provides breakfast, lunch and dinner during the summer season.

Types of meals: continental breakfast, continental-plus breakfast, full breakfast and early coffee/tea. Afternoon tea, dinner, picnic lunch, lunch, banquet service, catering service and catered breakfast available. Air conditioning and ceiling fan in room. Fax, copier, swimming, stables, bicycles and tennis on premises. Handicap access. 22,000 acres. Weddings, small meetings, family reunions and seminars hosted. Antiques, fishing, parks, shopping, cross-country skiing and theater nearby.

Pets Allowed: In cabins, not permitted in lodge. Must be on leash when outside.

Elgin

B7

Plantation House

401 Plantation St
Elgin, NE 68636-9301
(402)843-2287
Fax:(402)843-2287
E-mail: bdclark@juno.com

Rates: $35-60.
Payment: PC TC.
Innkeeper(s): Merland & Barbara Clark.
Circa: 1916.

Rooms: 5 rooms, 2 with PB. 1 cottage. 2 conference rooms.
Beds: QT.

This historic mansion sits adjacent to Elgin City Park, and guests will marvel at its beauty and size. Once a small Victorian farmhouse, the Plantation House has evolved into a 20-room Greek Revival treasure. Visitors will be treated to a tour and a large family-style breakfast, and may venture to the park to play tennis or horseshoes. The antique-filled guest rooms include the Stained Glass Room, with a queen bed and available twin-bed anteroom, and the Old Master Bedroom, with clawfoot tub and pedestal sink.

Breakfast included in rates. Types of meals: full breakfast and early coffee/tea. Banquet service available. Air conditioning and ceiling fan in room. Cable TV, VCR, fax, copier and library on premises. Weddings, small meetings, family reunions and seminars hosted. Antiques, fishing, parks and shopping nearby. TAC10.

Publicity: *Omaha World Herald, Norfolk Daily News, Home & Away, Midwest Living.*

Special Discounts: Multi-night stay $5 discount except for certain weekends.

"Gorgeous house! Relaxing atmosphere. Just like going to Mom's house."

Grand Island

D7

Kirschke House B&B

1124 W 3rd St
Grand Island, NE 68801
(308)381-6851 (800)381-6851

Rates: $55-145.
Payment: MC VISA AX DS PC TC.
Innkeeper(s): Lois Hank & Kiffani Smith.
Circa: 1902.

Rooms: 5 rooms, 2 with PB. 1 cottage.
Beds: QDT.

A steeply sloping roofline and a two-story tower mark this distinctive, vine-covered brick Victorian house. Meticulously restored, there are polished wood floors, fresh wallpapers and carefully chosen antiques. The Roses Roses Room is a spacious accommodation with a lace canopy bed, wicker rocking chair and decorating accents of roses and vines. In the old brick wash house is a wooden hot tub. In winter and spring, the area is popular for viewing the migration of sandhill cranes and whooping cranes.

Breakfast included in rates. Types of meals: gourmet breakfast and early coffee/tea. Lunch and room service available. Air conditioning and ceiling fan in room. Cable TV, VCR, spa and library on premises. Weddings, small meetings and family reunions hosted. Antiques, fishing, parks, shopping and watersports nearby. TAC10.

Location: In the historic district near downtown.

Publicity: *Grand Island Daily Independent.*

"We have been to many B&Bs in England, Canada and America. The Kirschke House ranks with the finest we've stayed in."

Oakland

C9

NE

Benson B&B

402 N Oakland Ave
Oakland, NE 68045-1135
(402)685-6051

Rates: $47-55.
Payment: PC TC.
Innkeeper(s): Stan & Norma Anderson.
Circa: 1905.

Rooms: 3 rooms.
Beds: QD.

This inn is on the second floor of the Benson Building, a sturdy, turreted brick structure built of walls nearly 12 inches thick. Decorated throughout in mauve, blue and cream, the Benson B&B features three comfortable guest rooms, and a restful, small-town atmosphere. Guests may visit the Swedish Heritage Center and a nearby city park. An 18-hole golf course is a five-minute drive away. Check out the craft and gift store on the building's lower level, the inn's collection of soft drink memorabilia, and be sure to ask about the Troll Stroll.

Breakfast and evening snack included in rates. Types of meals: full breakfast and early coffee/tea. Cable TV, VCR, spa and library on premises. Small meetings and family reunions hosted. Antiques, parks, shopping and sporting events nearby. TAC10.

Omaha

Offutt House

140 N 39th St
Omaha, NE 68131-2307
(402)553-0951

Rates: $55-85.
Payment: MC VISA AX.
Innkeeper(s): Jeannie & Arthur Swoboda.
Circa: 1894.

Rooms: 9 rooms, 10 with PB. 2 suites. 1 conference room.
Beds: KQD.

This two-and-a-half-story, 14-room house is built like a chateau with a steep roof and tall windows. During the 1913 tornado, although almost every house in the neighborhood was leveled, the Offutt house stood firm. It is said that a decanter of sherry was blown from the dining room to the living room without anything spilling. The large parlor features a handsome fireplace, a wall of books and an inviting sofa. A bridal suite is tucked under the gables of the third floor.

Breakfast included in rates. Types of meals: continental-plus breakfast and full breakfast. Catering service available. Antiques, fishing and theater nearby.

Pets Allowed.

Location: One block from downtown.

Publicity: *Midwest Living, Innsider, Bon Appetit, Innovations.*

"Hospitable, comfortable, lovely. A wonderful place to stay and great central location."

Waterloo C9

J.C. Robinson House B&B

102 Lincoln St, PO Box 190
Waterloo, NE 68069-2004
(402)779-2704

Rates: $50-75.
Innkeeper(s): John Clark.
Circa: 1905.

Rooms: 4 rooms. 1 conference room.

A short drive from Omaha, the Journey's End is an elegant, Neoclassical Greek Revival home boasting two impressive Ionic columns. The inn, surrounded by large trees, is listed in the national and state historic registers. Antiques, including a stunning clock collection, are found throughout the attractive interior, and the Gone With the Wind Room offers a garden and orchard view. The home, built by seed company founder J.C. Robinson, also features a guest room in his name. Fishing and canoeing are a short walk away or guests may decide to soak up the village's relaxed atmosphere.

Breakfast included in rates. Types of meals: full breakfast and early coffee/tea. Dinner, evening snack, gourmet lunch and banquet service available.

Weeping Water D9

Lauritzen's Danish-American

1002 E Eldora Ave
Weeping Water, NE 68463
(402)267-3295

Rates: $45-65.
Payment: MC VISA PC TC.
Innkeeper(s): Ken & Alice Lauritzen.
Circa: 1901.

Rooms: 2 rooms, 1 with PB.
Beds: Q.

This late Victorian home offers two bedrooms, decorated with American and Danish antiques. Enjoy small town atmosphere or quiet times on the porch swing and in the beautifully landscaped yard. The innkeepers serve American and Danish items during the breakfast hour. For an additional charge, they can prepare a special dinner. Their traditional Danish dinner is a specialty.

Breakfast and evening snack included in rates. Types of meals: gourmet breakfast and early coffee/tea. Afternoon tea and dinner available. Air conditioning and ceiling fan in room. Cable TV, VCR and bicycles on premises. Antiques, fishing, parks, shopping, cross-country skiing, sporting events and theater nearby. TAC10.

Nevada

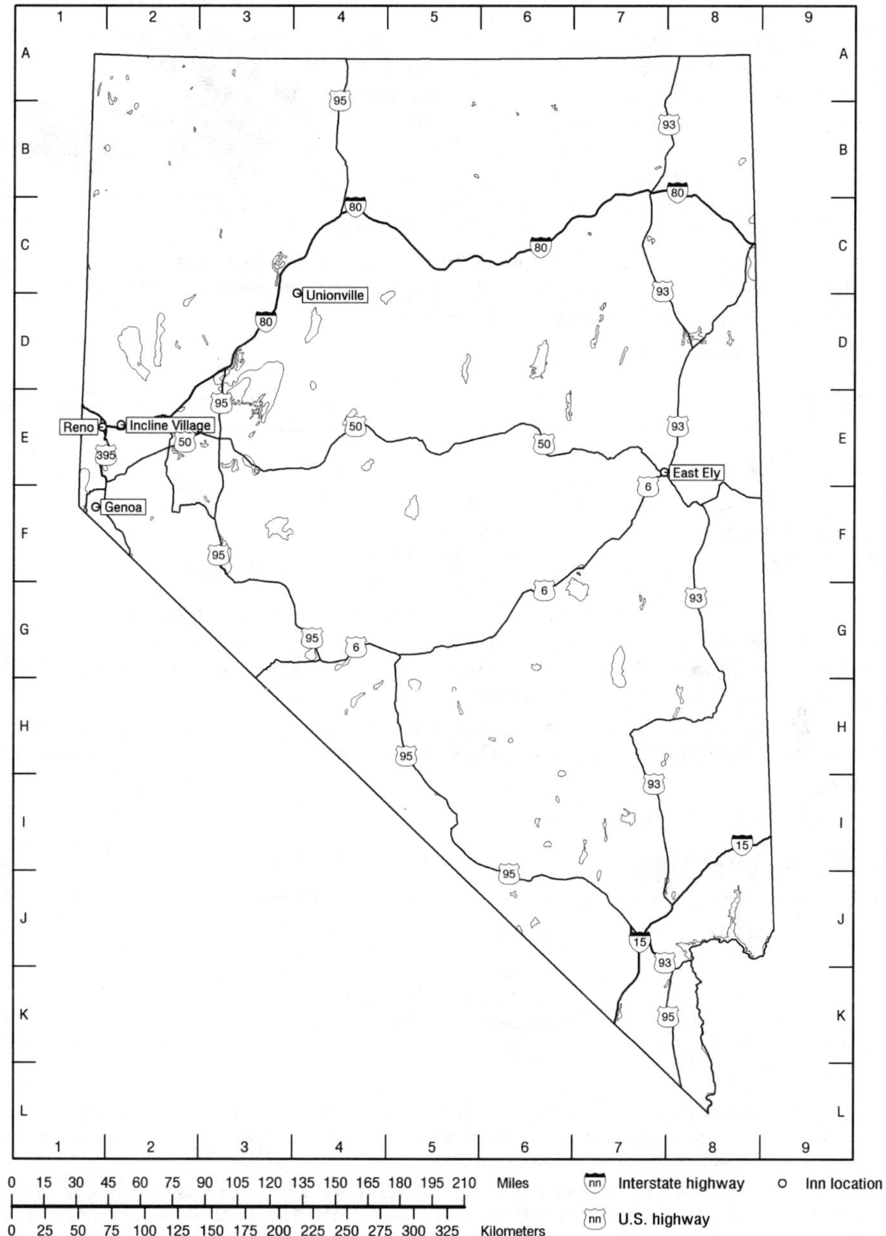

1
2
3
4
5
6
7
8
9
A
B
C
D
E
F
G
H
I
J
K
L
Unionville
Reno
Incline Village
East Ely
Genoa
95
93
80
50
395
6
15
0 15 30 45 60 75 90 105 120 135 150 165 180 195 210 Miles
0 25 50 75 100 125 150 175 200 225 250 275 300 325 Kilometers
nn Interstate highway
nn U.S. highway
Inn location

NV

East Ely
E7

Steptoe Valley Inn

220 E 11th St
East Ely, NV 89315-1110
(702)289-8687

Rates: $79-85.
Payment: MC VISA AX PC TC.
Innkeeper(s): Jane & Norman Lindley.
Circa: 1907.

Rooms: 5 rooms with PB. 1 conference room.
Beds: QT.

Originally a grocery store at the turn of the century, this inn has been lovingly reconstructed to resemble a Victorian country cottage. Five uniquely decorated guest rooms are named for local pioneers. The rooms also have views of the inn's scenic surroundings, and three of them feature queen beds. A nearby railroad museum offers train rides and Great Basin National Park is 70 miles away. Guests may rent a jeep at the inn for exploring the area's back country. This inn is open from June to October. During the off-season, guests may inquire about the inn at (702) 435-1196.

Breakfast and evening snack included in rates. Type of meal: full breakfast. Air conditioning, ceiling fan and cable TV in room. VCR and library on premises. Weddings, small meetings and family reunions hosted. Spanish spoken. Fishing and parks nearby. TAC10.

Publicity: *Las Vegas Review Journal, Great Getaways, Yellow Brick Road.*

"Everything was so clean and first-rate."

Genoa
F1

Wild Rose Inn

2332 Main St, PO Box 256
Genoa, NV 89411
(702)782-5697

Rates: $95-125.
Payment: MC VISA.
Innkeeper(s): Sandi & Joe Antonucci.
Circa: 1989.

Rooms: 5 rooms with PB.
Beds: Q.

Located 15 miles from Lake Tahoe in Nevada's oldest settlement, this newly built Victorian is resplendent with gables, porches and a two-story turret. The Garden Gate Room is housed in the tower and features five windows overlooking the valley and the Sierras. Among the antiques is a collection of old toys. Freshly baked orange rolls are prepared often for breakfast.

Types of meals: full breakfast and early coffee/tea. Air conditioning, turn-down service, ceiling fan and cable TV in room. Spa and sauna on premises. Small meetings and family reunions hosted. Antiques, shopping, downhill skiing and cross-country skiing nearby.

Publicity: *Sacramento Bee.*

"We enjoyed our stay so much. The room was great!"

Incline Village
E2

Haus Bavaria

PO Box 3308,
593 N Dyer Cir
Incline Village, NV 89450
(702)831-6122 (800)731-6222
Fax:(702)831-1238

Rates: $110-145.
Payment: MC VISA AX DS PC TC.
Innkeeper(s): Bick Hewitt.
Circa: 1980.

Rooms: 5 rooms with PB. 1 conference room.
Beds: KQ.

This Bavarian mountain house is located one mile from Lake Tahoe. In summer, window boxes are filled with petunias and the patio is bordered with snapdragons, pansies and peonies. Every guest room has its own balcony with views of the pine trees and mountains.

Breakfast included in rates. Types of meals: full breakfast and early coffee/tea. Cable TV, VCR, fax and copier on premises. Weddings, small meetings, family reunions and seminars hosted. Fishing, parks, shopping, downhill skiing, cross-country skiing, sporting events, theater and watersports nearby.

Publicity: *Sunset Magazine.*

Special Discounts: 10% off for seniors; $99 corporate rates.

"Great fun!"

Reno

E1

Bed and Breakfast: South Reno

136 Andrew Ln
Reno, NV 89511-9740
(702)849-0772

Rates: $75-85.
Payment: MC VISA AX PC.
Innkeeper(s): Caroline Walters & Robert McNeill.
Circa: 1948.

Rooms: 3 rooms, 2 with PB. 1 suite.
Beds: QT.

Steamboat Valley, the location of this B&B, is ten miles from Reno. There are three acres of landscaped lawns, 40 trees, a pool and several patios and decks for relaxing and enjoying neighboring ranchscapes and views of Mount Rose and Slide Mountain. Early American furnishings include four-poster beds and wing chairs. Caroline's egg souffle and hot baked apple-nut cake are frequent breakfast items. Nearby Washoe Lake offers windsurfing, and it's 15 miles to good skiing, sledding and snowmobiling areas.

Breakfast included in rates. Types of meals: gourmet breakfast and early coffee/tea. Turn-down service, cable TV and VCR in room. Swimming and library on premises. Weddings and seminars hosted. Amusement parks, antiques, fishing, parks, shopping, downhill skiing, cross-country skiing, sporting events, theater and watersports nearby. TAC5.

Unionville

D4

Old Pioneer Garden Guest Ranch

2805 Unionville Rd
Unionville, NV 89418-8204
(702)538-7585

Rates: $65-75.
Innkeeper(s): Mitzi & Lew Jones.
Circa: 1861.

Rooms: 12 rooms, 4 with PB, 1 with FP. 1 suite. 1 conference room.
Beds: D.

NV

Once a bustling silver mining town, Unionville now has only a handful of citizens, and Old Pioneer Garden Guest Ranch is just down the road from town. Accommodations are in a renovated blacksmith's house, a farmhouse and across the meadow in the Hadley House. A Swedish-style gazebo rests beside a bubbling stream, and there are orchards, grape arbors, vegetable gardens, sheep and goats. A country supper is available.

Breakfast included in rates. Types of meals: full breakfast, gourmet breakfast and early coffee/tea. Dinner, picnic lunch, lunch, gourmet lunch, banquet service and catering service available. Handicap access. 114 acres. Antiques and fishing nearby.

Location: 139 miles east of Reno.

Publicity: *Denver Post.*

"An array of charm that warms the heart and delights the soul."

New Hampshire

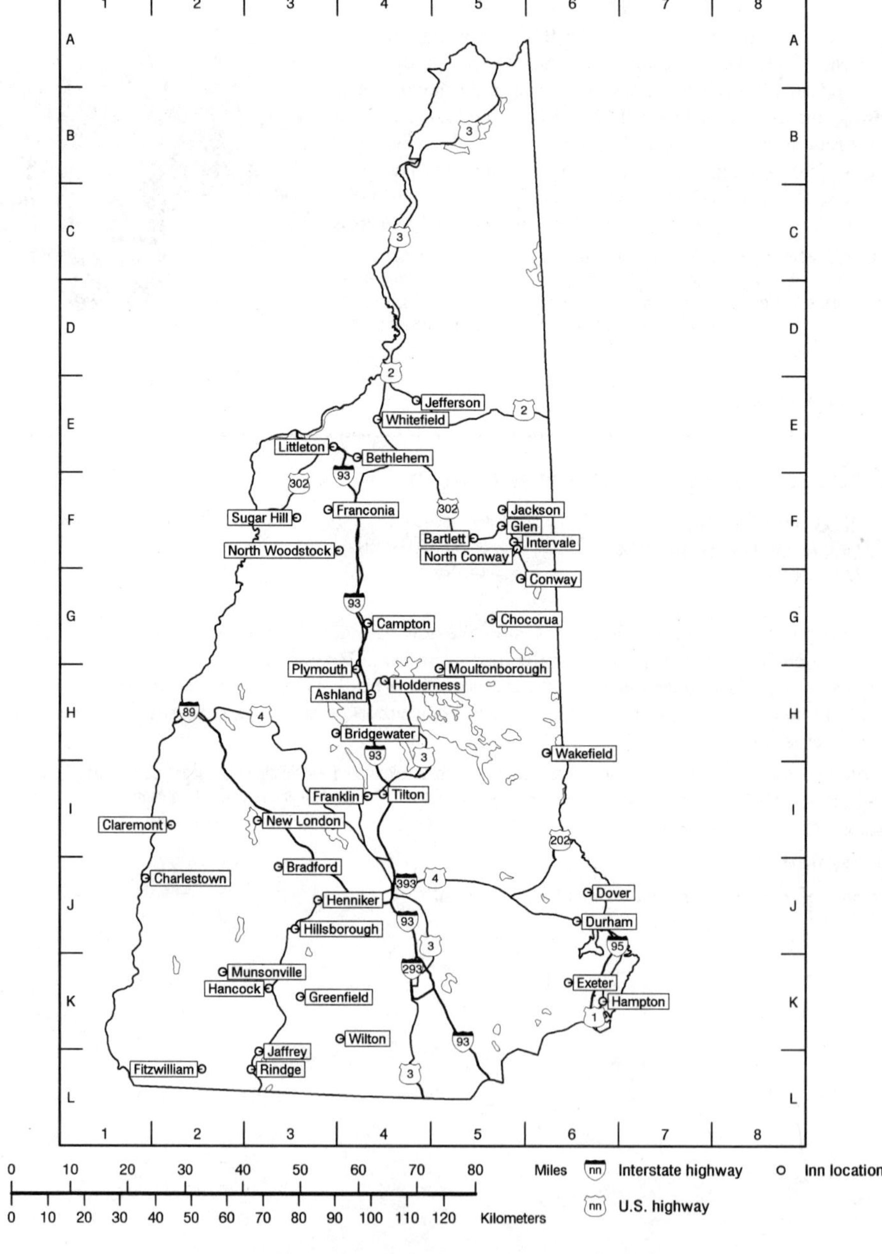

Ashland

H4

Glynn House Inn

43 Highland St, PO Box 719
Ashland, NH 03217-0719
(603)968-3775 (800)637-9599
Fax:(603)968-3129

Rates: $65-150.
Payment: MC VISA AX DC PC TC.
Innkeeper(s): Karol & Betsy Paterman.
Circa: 1895.

Rooms: 8 rooms with PB, 3 with FP. 2 suites. 1 conference room.
Beds: KQDT.

A three-story turret, gables and verandas frosted with Queen Anne gingerbread come together in an appealing mass of Victoriana in the Glynn House. Carved-oak woodwork and pocket doors accentuate the foyer. Period furnishings and ornate Oriental wall coverings decorate the parlor. The village of Ashland is a few minutes from "On Golden Pond" (Squam Lake) and the White Mountains.

Circa 1895

Breakfast included in rates. Types of meals: full breakfast, gourmet breakfast and early coffee/tea. Banquet service available. Air conditioning, turn-down service, cable TV and VCR in room. Fax and computer on premises. Weddings, small meetings, family reunions and seminars hosted. Amusement parks, antiques, fishing, parks, shopping, downhill skiing, cross-country skiing, sporting events and watersports nearby. TAC10.

Location: Two hours from Boston.

"Boston was fun, but the Glynn House is the place we'll send our friends."

Bethlehem

E4

Adair - A Country Inn

80 Guider Lane
Bethlehem, NH 03574
(603)444-2600 (800)441-2606
Fax:(603)444-4823

Rates: $135-220.
Payment: MC VISA AX PC TC.
Innkeeper(s): Hardy, Pat & Nancy Banfield.
Circa: 1927.

Rooms: 9 rooms with PB, 3 with FP. 1 suite.
Beds: KQ.

Adair represents all that a New England country inn is supposed to be. From its Georgian Colonial architecture to its elegant decor to rooms warmed by fireplaces, the inn is picturesque enough that Sears chose to highlight its exterior on the cover of the 1995 Wish Book. The four-diamond rated inn originally served as wedding gift from Frank Hogan to his daughter Dorothy Adair Hogan. Dorothy hosted many famed guests at her home, among them were presidents, Supreme Court justices and actors. Freshly baked popovers start off the morning fare, followed by fresh fruit, granola and specialty dishes such as eggs Benedict accompanied by hash brown potatoes and a fried tomato. Cakes and cookies are served during the complimentary afternoon tea service. The inn also offers dinner service at Tim-Bir Alley restaurant, but be sure to make advance reservations as the dining room is open to the public as well.

Breakfast and afternoon tea included in rates. Types of meals: full breakfast and early coffee/tea. Cable TV, VCR, fax, copier, tennis and library on premises. 200 acres. Small meetings, family reunions and seminars hosted. Antiques, shopping, downhill skiing, cross-country skiing and theater nearby. TAC10.

Special Discounts: Corporate rate $80 single occupancy Sunday-Thursday.

"What can we say, we expected a lot - and got much more."

The Mulburn Inn

2370 Main St, Rt 302
Bethlehem, NH 03574
(603)869-3389 (800)457-9440
Fax:(603)869-5633
E-mail: the.mulburn.inn@connriver.net

Rates: $55-85.
Payment: MC VISA AX DS PC TC.
Innkeeper(s): The Skeels Family.
Circa: 1908.

Rooms: 7 rooms with PB.
Beds: KQDT.

This summer cottage was known as the Ivie Estate, and many of the Ivie and Woolworth (as in the famed five and dime store) family members vacationed here in summer. Cary Grant and Barbara Hutton spent their honeymoon at the mansion. Polished oak staircases and stained-glass windows add to the atmosphere.

Breakfast and afternoon tea included in rates. Types of meals: full breakfast and early coffee/tea. Cable TV, VCR and copier on premises. Amusement parks, antiques, fishing, parks, downhill skiing, cross-country skiing and theater nearby.

Publicity: *The Record, Yankee, Boston Globe.*

"You have put a lot of thought, charm, beauty and warmth into the inn. Your breakfasts were oh, so delicious!!"

Bradford J3

The Rosewood Country Inn

67 Pleasant View Rd
Bradford, NH 03221-9109
(603)938-5253
Fax:(603)938-5253

Rates: $79-140.
Payment: MC VISA PC TC.
Innkeeper(s): Lesley & Dick Marquis.
Circa: 1850.

Rooms: 7 rooms with PB. 1 suite. 1 conference room.
Beds: QDT.

This three-story country Victorian inn in the Sunapee Region treats its guests to a candlelight and crystal breakfast and elegant accommodations that manage to avoid being stuffy. The inn prides itself on special touches. The innkeepers like to keep things interesting with ideas such as theme weekends and special breakfast fare, including cinnamon apple pancakes with cider sauce. Mount Sunapee Ski Area and Lake Sunapee are less than 8 minutes away.

Breakfast included in rates. Types of meals: gourmet breakfast and early coffee/tea. Cable TV and fax on premises. Handicap access. 12 acres. Weddings, small meetings, family reunions and seminars hosted. French spoken. Antiques, fishing, shopping, downhill skiing, cross-country skiing, sporting events, theater and watersports nearby. TAC10.

Special Discounts: Third night free Sunday-Thursday (except August, October and Monday holidays)

Bridgewater H3

The Inn on Newfound Lake

1030 Mayhew Tpke
Bridgewater, NH 03222
(603)744-9111 (800)745-7990
Fax:(603)744-3894

Rates: $55-105. MAP, AP.
Payment: MC VISA AX DS.
Innkeeper(s): Phelps C. Boyce II.
Circa: 1840.

Rooms: 31 rooms, 23 with PB. 2 suites.
Beds: QT.

This inn was the mid-way stop on the stage coach route from Boston to Montreal and formerly was known as the Pasquaney Inn. A full veranda overlooks the lake with its spectacular sunsets. Located in the foothills of the White Mountains, the inn is situated on more than seven acres of New Hampshire countryside.

Breakfast included in rates. Type of meal: continental breakfast. Dinner, picnic lunch and lunch available. MAP, AP. Antiques, fishing, downhill skiing, cross-country skiing and watersports nearby.

Publicity: *The Record Enterprise.*

"The rooms were quaint and cozy with just the right personal touches, and always immaculate. The bed and pillows were so comfortable, it was better than sleeping at home! The inn itself is magnificent, elegance never felt so warm and homey."

Campton G4

Mountain-Fare Inn

Mad River Rd, PO Box 553
Campton, NH 03223
(603)726-4283

Rates: $65-95. MAP, EP.
Innkeeper(s): Susan & Nick Preston.
Circa: 1820.

Rooms: 10 rooms, 8 with PB.
Beds: QDT.

This white farmhouse is surrounded by flower gardens in the summer and unparalleled foliage in the fall. Ski teams, family reunions and other groups often enjoy the outdoors here with Mountain-Fare as a base. In the winter everyone seems to be a skier, and in the summer there are boaters and hikers. The inn is decorated in a casual New Hampshire-style country decor. The hearty breakfast is a favorite of returning guests.

Breakfast and afternoon tea included in rates. Type of meal: full breakfast. MAP, EP. Cable TV, VCR and child care on premises. Weddings, small meetings and family reunions hosted. Antiques, fishing, parks, downhill skiing, cross-country skiing, sporting events, theater and watersports nearby.

Location: Two hours from Boston in the White Mountains.

Publicity: *Ski, Skiing, Snow Country.*

"Thank you for your unusually caring attitude toward your guests."

Charlestown J1

Maplehedge B&B

355 Main St, PO Box 638
Charlestown, NH 03603
(603)826-5237 (800)962-7539
Fax:(603)826-5237
E-mail: 103571.2355@compuserve.com

Rates: $80-100.
Payment: MC VISA PC.
Innkeeper(s): Joan & Dick DeBrine.
Circa: 1815.

Rooms: 5 rooms with PB. 1 suite.
Beds: QT.

This elegantly restored home is set among acres of lawn and 200-year-old maple trees. The bed & breakfast boasts five distinctive bedrooms. The Beale Room is named for the innkeeper's grandparents and is full of sentimental treasures such as milk bottles from her grandfather's dairy and family photos. The Butterfly Suite is filled with white wicker, including an antique, glass-topped hamper and Victorian butterfly trays. The rooms are furnished in antiques, including some of the linens. A delectable three-course breakfast is served and may include fresh fruit salads and scones. Evening refreshments include California wine with New Hampshire cheese. Guests can go on antiquing tours or attend country auctions, and many historical attractions are nearby.

Breakfast and evening snack included in rates. Types of meals: gourmet breakfast and early coffee/tea. Air conditioning and turn-down service in room. Fax, copier and library on premises. Small meetings and family reunions hosted. Antiques, fishing, shopping, theater and watersports nearby. TAC10.

Location: Connecticut River Valley.

Publicity: *Los Angeles Times, Buffalo News, Country Living, Yankee Traveler.*

"The highlight of my two weeks in New England. A breakfast worth jumping out of bed for."

Chocorua

G5

Riverbend Country Inn

PO Box 288
Chocorua, NH 03817-0288
(603)323-7440 (800)628-6944
Fax:(603)323-7554

Rates: $60-125.
Payment: MC VISA AX PC TC.
Innkeeper(s): Noreen Bullock/Russ Stone.
Circa: 1966.

Rooms: 9 rooms, 5 with PB.
Beds: KQD.

A secluded, wooded lane leads up to the two, adjacent buildings that combine to create this country inn. The 14 forested acres allow for privacy, and the inn's tasteful, yet comfortable decor encourages relaxation. There is a deck overlooking the river, and plenty of space to relax inside. Two parlors have fireplaces and there also is a reading room. French toast almondine, eggs Benedict and souffles are among the morning specialties.

Breakfast included in rates. Types of meals: gourmet breakfast and early coffee/tea. Fax, copier and library on premises. 14 acres. Weddings, small meetings and family reunions hosted. Antiques, fishing, parks, shopping, downhill skiing, cross-country skiing, sporting events, theater and watersports nearby.

"We can't wait to see all four seasons here. Thank you for all the extra touches."

Claremont

I2

Goddard Mansion B&B

25 Hillstead Rd
Claremont, NH 03743-3399
(603)543-0603 (800)736-0603
Fax:(603)543-0001

Rates: $65-105.
Payment: MC VISA AX DC CB DS PC TC.
Innkeeper(s): Debbie Albee.
Circa: 1905.

Rooms: 10 rooms, 3 with PB. 1 suite. 2 conference rooms.
Beds: QDT.

This English-style manor house and adjacent garden tea house is surrounded by seven acres of lawns and gardens. Each of the guest rooms is decorated in a different style. One features French Country decor, another sports a Victorian look. The living room with its fireplace, window seats and baby grand piano is a perfect place to relax. Homemade breakfasts are made using natural ingredients and fresh produce, such as souffles, pancakes, freshly baked muffins and fruit. The hearty meals are served in wood paneled dining room highlighted by an antique Wurlitzer jukebox.

Breakfast included in rates. Types of meals: continental-plus breakfast, full breakfast and gourmet breakfast. Air conditioning and turn-down service in room. Cable TV, VCR, fax, bicycles and library on premises. Weddings, small meetings, family reunions and seminars hosted. Antiques, fishing, parks, shopping, downhill skiing, cross-country skiing and theater nearby.

Publicity: *Eagle Times.*

"Our trip would not have been as enjoyable without having stayed at your inn."

Conway

G5

Mountain Valley Manner

PO Box 1649
Conway, NH 03818-1649
(603)447-3988

Rates: $55-110.
Payment: MC VISA DS PC TC.
Innkeeper(s): Bob & Lynn Lein.
Circa: 1885.

Rooms: 3 rooms with PB. 1 suite.
Beds: KQDT.

This historic Victorian, surrounded by an acre of scenic New Hampshire countryside, offers a charming view of two historic, covered "kissing" bridges. Antiques and country pieces decorate the interior, guest rooms include carved, four poster or canopy beds. In addition to the country breakfasts, afternoon snacks are served, and there's always a cup of tea or hot chocolate available for those needing a nightcap. The inn is conveniently located near many attractions within White Mountain National Forest. The innkeepers also provide a complimentary cassette guided tour of the Central Notch for guests booking two or more nights.

Breakfast, afternoon tea and evening snack included in rates. Types of meals: full breakfast and early coffee/tea. Air conditioning in room. Cable TV, VCR, computer and swimming on premises. Amusement parks, antiques, fishing, parks, shopping, downhill skiing, cross-country skiing, theater and watersports nearby. TAC10.

Special Discounts: Discounts for multi-day stays. Complimentary Central Notch Tour cassette with two nights.

"Accommodations excellent, hospitality better than the Ritz, surroundings very nice, meals way above expectation."

Dover

J6

Silver Street Inn

103 Silver St
Dover, NH 03820-3923
(603)743-3000
Fax:(603)749-5673

Rates: $69-89.
Payment: MC VISA DC CB DS TC.
Innkeeper(s): Lorene Cook.
Circa: 1880.

Rooms: 10 rooms, 9 with PB. 1 suite.
Beds: QDT.

For nearly a century this stately Victorian remained in the Frank B. Williams family, owners of the I.B. Williams Belt & Lace Factory. They decorated their mansion with imported Honduran mahogany, Italian slate, and Austrian crystal, all of which remains intact today. Ornate molded plaster ceilings, covered boiserie wall panels, and Oriental rugs further enhance the classic European elegance. Original fixtures such as pedestal sinks and clawfoot tubs have been preserved in some of the bedrooms, but all modern conveniences have been added.

Breakfast included in rates. Type of meal: full breakfast. Air conditioning and cable TV in room. Fax and copier on premises. Weddings and small meetings hosted. Antiques, parks and theater nearby.

"Extremely pleasant atmosphere, quiet and clean."

Durham

J6

The Pines Guest House

47 Dover Rd, Rt 108
Durham, NH 03824
(603)868-3361

Rates: $45-85.
Payment: MC VISA AX PC TC.
Innkeeper(s): Roger & Mary Margaret Jaques.
Circa: 1870.

Rooms: 4 rooms, 2 with PB, 3 with FP. 1 suite.
Beds: QDT.

This rambling Victorian manor is surrounded by 15 acres of countryside, including a pond. The home has remained in the same family for five generations, and many of the furnishings are family pieces. The screened-in porches are set up with wicker furniture for those who wish to relax. Three of the guest rooms include a fireplace. Breakfasts are served in a dining room decorated with period furniture. Tables are set with antique china and silver. The University of New Hampshire is a half-mile from the home.

Breakfast included in rates. Types of meals: continental-plus breakfast and early coffee/tea. Air conditioning and cable TV in room. VCR and library on premises. 15 acres. French spoken. Antiques, fishing, parks, shopping, cross-country skiing, sporting events, theater and watersports nearby. TAC10.

Special Discounts: Discount for extended stay.

"What a beautiful setting with these towering pines."

Inn By The Bandstand

4 Front St
Exeter, NH 03833-2737
(603)772-6352
Fax:(603)778-0212

Rates: $89-145.
Payment: MC VISA AX TC.
Innkeeper(s): George & Muriel Simmons.
Circa: 1809.

Rooms: 8 rooms with PB, 7 with FP.
Beds: QT.

This Federal-style inn was built by the son of Revolutionary War General George Sullivan, and the during the mid-19th century, it served as the Squamscott Hotel. A century later, this landmark was saved from demolition by the town's historic society, and now the inn is listed in the National Register. Eclectic is the best way to describe the guest rooms, which offer furnishings such as curtained, four-poster beds, and seven rooms have a fireplace. One especially romantic room is decorated with a wrought-iron bed draped with a chiffon canopy. Antiques, an English boudoir sink and a fireplace add to its ambiance. Guests will find fluffy robes, down pillows, and special bath toiletries in their rooms. The morning mimosas and freshly baked pastries can be enjoyed in the parlor or in the privacy of your room. The inn is a stop on the town's historic walking tour.

Breakfast included in rates. Types of meals: continental breakfast and early coffee/tea. Air conditioning and cable TV in room. Fax, copier, library, pet boarding and child care on premises. Handicap access. Weddings, small meetings, family reunions and seminars hosted. Amusement parks, antiques, fishing, parks, shopping, cross-country skiing, sporting events, theater and watersports nearby. TAC10.

Location: Ninety miles north of New York City.

Publicity: *Newsday, New York Post.*

Inn of Exeter

90 Front St
Exeter, NH 03833-2723
(603)772-5901 (800)782-8444
Fax:(603)778-8757

Rates: $89-97.
Payment: MC VISA AX DC CB DS TC.
Innkeeper(s): Carl G. Jensen.
Circa: 1932.

Rooms: 47 rooms with PB, 1 with FP. 1 suite. 7 conference rooms.
Beds: KQDT.

For more than 60 years, guests have been enjoying New England hospitality at this inn. A mix of fine antiques and reproductions are found in the traditionally appointed guest rooms. The inn is often the site of weddings and receptions, as well as business meetings. Although meals are not included in the rates, the inn's restaurant serves breakfast, lunch, dinner and Sunday brunch. The location is within walking distance of museums, historical sites and shops.

Types of meals: continental breakfast, continental-plus breakfast, full breakfast, gourmet breakfast and early coffee/tea. Dinner, evening snack, picnic lunch, lunch, gourmet lunch and banquet service available. Air conditioning and cable TV in room. VCR, fax, copier and sauna on premises. Handicap access. Weddings, small meetings, family reunions and seminars hosted. Danish and Italian spoken. Antiques, fishing, parks, shopping, cross-country skiing, sporting events, theater and watersports nearby. TAC10.

Fitzwilliam L2

Amos A. Parker House

PO Box 202
Fitzwilliam, NH 03447-0202
(603)585-6540

Rates: $80-90.
Payment: PC TC.
Innkeeper(s): Freda B. Houpt.
Circa: 1780.

Rooms: 4 rooms with PB, 3 with FP. 2 suites.
Beds: KQDT.

An antique liberty pole is attached to the original part of this appealing Federal house. (Liberty poles were used to identify meeting places for Revolutionaries.) Situated on three acres, with mountain views, the house is bordered by green lawns and perfect flower beds. Antiques, Spode china, beautiful stenciling and Oriental carpet collections add grace and style to the rooms. Freda, a former travel agent from Chicago, exudes enthusiasm for all New Hampshire's sights and is an expert on the area. Hopefully, your arrival will coincide with a breakfast menu of spinach souffle with mushroom Newburg sauce or "Praline French Toast."

Breakfast and afternoon tea included in rates. Types of meals: full breakfast and early coffee/tea. VCR on premises. Antiques, fishing, parks, shopping, downhill skiing, cross-country skiing, theater and watersports nearby. TAC7.

Publicity: *New York Times, Washington Post, Tampa Tribune-Times, Boston Globe, Christian Science Monitor.*

"Care and solicitation is what makes staying here more the experience of visiting a wealthy and hospitable relative in the country than simply staying at an inn or hotel."

Bungay Jar

PO Box 15, Easton Valley Rd
Franconia, NH 03580-0015
(603)823-7775
Fax:(603)444-0110

Rates: $70-150.
Payment: MC VISA AX DS PC TC.
Innkeeper(s): Kate Kerivan.
Circa: 1967.

Rooms: 7 rooms, 5 with PB, 2 with FP. 3 suites. 1 cottage.
Beds: KQDT.

An 18th-century barn was taken down and moved piece by piece to Easton Valley, six miles from Franconia. A post-and-beam, barn-style-home was constructed on 12 wooded acres with a stream nearby and the White Mountains in view. The two-story living room, reminiscent of a hay loft, is decorated with antique country furnishings, as are all the guest rooms. Your host, a landscape architect, has planted herb and perennial gardens, featured in national magazines. Rates are higher during foliage.

Breakfast and afternoon tea included in rates. Sauna on premises. 12 acres. Small meetings, family reunions and seminars hosted. Antiques, fishing, parks, shopping, downhill skiing, cross-country skiing, theater and watersports nearby.

Publicity: *Country Accents, Discerning Traveler, Yankee, Birds & Bloom, Brides, American Homestyle.*

Special Discounts: Group & extended stay rates available on request.

"Such a perfect spot with such a great view."

Franconia Inn

1300 Easton Rd
Franconia, NH 03580-4921
(603)823-5542 (800)473-5299
Fax:(603)823-8078

Rates: $75-135. MAP, EP.
Payment: MC VISA AX.
Innkeeper(s): Alec Morris.
Circa: 1934.

Rooms: 34 rooms, 29 with PB, 3 with FP. 4 suites. 1 conference room.
Beds: KQDT.

NH

Beautifully situated on 117 acres below the White Mountain's famous Franconia Notch, this white clapboard inn is three stories high. An oak-paneled library, parlor, rathskeller lounge and two verandas offer relaxing retreats. The inn's rooms are simply decorated in a pleasing style and there is a special honeymoon suite with private Jacuzzi. Bach, classic wines and an elegant American cuisine are featured in the inn's unpretentious dining room. There's no shortage of activity here. The inn offers four clay tennis courts, horseback riding, a heated swimming pool, croquet, fishing, cross-country ski trails and glider rides among its outdoor amenities.

Breakfast included in rates. Types of meals: gourmet breakfast and early coffee/tea. Dinner, picnic lunch and catering service available. MAP, EP. VCR, copier, spa, swimming, bicycles, tennis and child care on premises. 107 acres. Weddings, small meetings, family reunions and seminars hosted. Amusement parks, antiques, fishing, parks, shopping, downhill skiing, cross-country skiing, sporting events and theater nearby.

Location: Exit 38 off I-93, two-and-a-half miles south on Route 116.

Publicity: *Philadelphia Inquirer, Boston Globe, Travel & Leisure, Powder.*

"The piece de resistance of the Franconia Notch is the Franconia Inn." — Philadelphia Inquirer.

The Inn at Forest Hills

Rt 142, PO Box 783
Franconia, NH 03580
(603)823-9550 (800)280-9550
Fax:(603)823-8701
E-mail: innfhills@connriver.net

Rates: $85-145.
Payment: MC VISA AX DC PC TC.
Innkeeper(s): Gordon & Joanne Haym.
Circa: 1890.

Rooms: 7 rooms with PB.
Beds: KQ.

This Tudor-style inn in the White Mountains offers a solarium, a living room with fireplace and a large common room with fireplace and cathedral ceilings. Breakfast is served with a quiet background of classical music in the dining room, where in the winter there's a blazing fireplace, and in summer the French doors

open to the scenery. Guest rooms feature a casual country decor with quilts, flowered wall coverings and some four-poster beds. Cross-country ski for free on the inn's property and at the local touring center. Downhill facilities are found at Bretton Woods, Cannon or Loon Mountain. Nearby Franconia Notch Park and the White Mountains feature trails designed for cycling and hiking. The innkeeper is a justice of the peace, and will do weddings or a renewal of vows.

Breakfast included in rates. Type of meal: full breakfast. Evening snack available. Cable TV, VCR, fax, tennis and library on premises. Weddings, small meetings, family reunions and seminars hosted. Antiques, fishing, parks, shopping, downhill skiing, cross-country skiing and watersports nearby.

Special Discounts: Sunday-Thursday during November 1-April 30: stay two nights & get third night free (some weekends & holidays excluded).

"What a delightful inn! I loved the casual country elegance of your B&B and can understand why you are so popular with brides and grooms."

Franklin — I4

Maria W. Atwood Inn

RFD 2, Rt 3A
Franklin, NH 03235
(603)934-3666
Fax:(603)934-6949

Rates: $80-90.
Payment: MC VISA AX DC CB DS PC TC.
Innkeeper(s): Phil & Irene Fournier.
Circa: 1830.

Rooms: 7 rooms with PB, 4 with FP.
Beds: QDT.

Candles in the windows welcome guests to this brick Colonial, which was built by Henry Greenleaf. The home maintains many original features, including Indian shutters, old locks, Count Rumford fireplaces, and wide-plank wood floors. The innkeepers have filled the rooms with their antique collection and many artworks.

Breakfast, afternoon tea and evening snack included in rates. Types of meals: full breakfast and early coffee/tea. Cable TV and fax on premises. Small meetings and family reunions hosted. French and Greek spoken. Antiques, fishing, parks, shopping, downhill skiing, cross-country skiing and theater nearby. TAC10.

Publicity: *Concord, Alumni.*

"Wouldn't stay anywhere else."

Glen — F5

Bernerhof Inn

Rt 302, PO Box 240
Glen, NH 03838-0240
(603)383-4414 (800)548-8007
Fax:(603)383-0809
E-mail: bhofenxi.com

Rates: $69-139. MAP.
Payment: MC VISA AX DS PC TC.
Innkeeper(s): Hollie Smith.
Circa: 1894.

Rooms: 9 rooms with PB. 2 suites.
Beds: KQD.

This historic inn is located in the foothills of the Green Mountains. Several of the nine guest rooms include a double whirlpool tub. Guests can dine on gourmet cuisine at the inn's award-winning restaurant. The inn's Black Bear Pub is a perfect place for a more casual meal, including a taste from the pub's ample beer selection. Novice chefs should try the inn's "Taste of the Mountains Cooking School," where they can pick up many tricks of the trade.

Breakfast included in rates. Type of meal: full breakfast. Dinner, lunch, catering service and room service available. MAP. Air conditioning, ceiling fan and cable TV in room. Fax and copier on premises. 10 acres. Weddings, small meetings and family reunions hosted. Amusement parks, antiques, fishing, parks, shopping, downhill skiing, cross-country skiing and theater nearby.

Publicity: *Bon Appetit, New Hampshire Profiles, Boston Globe, Yankee, Skiing, National Geographic Traveler.*

"When people want to treat themselves, this is where they come."

Greenfield

K3

The Greenfield Inn

Forest Rd at Rts 31 N & 136
Greenfield, NH 03047
(603)547-6245
Fax:(603)547-2418
E-mail: bnbreakfast@aol.com

Rates: $49-119.
Payment: MC VISA AX PC TC.
Innkeeper(s): Barbara & Vic Mangini.
Circa: 1817.

Rooms: 11 rooms, 8 with PB. 2 suites. 1 cottage. 1 conference room.
Beds: KQDT.

In the 1850s this inn was purchased by Henry Dunklee, innkeeper of the old Mayfield Inn across the street. When there was an overflow of guests at his tavern, Mr. Dunklee accommodated them here. This totally renovated Victorian mansion features veranda views of Crotched, Temple and Monadnock Mountains. The comfortable interiors and gracious innkeepers have been enjoyed by many well-traveled guests including Dolores and Bob Hope.

Breakfast included in rates. Type of meal: full breakfast. Air conditioning, ceiling fan and VCR in room. Fax, copier and library on premises. Small meetings, family reunions and seminars hosted. Antiques, fishing, parks, shopping, downhill skiing, cross-country skiing, theater and watersports nearby. TAC10.

Location: Southern New Hampshire, 90 minutes from Boston.

Publicity: *Manchester Union Leader, Innsider.*

"I'm coming back for more of this New Hampshire therapy,"—Bob Hope.

Hampton

K6

The Inn at Elmwood Corners

252 Winnacunnet Rd
Hampton, NH 03842-2726
(603)929-0443 (800)253-5691

Rates: $65-85.
Payment: MC VISA TC.
Innkeeper(s): John & Mary Hornberger.
Circa: 1870.

Rooms: 7 rooms, 2 with PB. 2 suites.
Beds: QT.

NH

This old sea captain's house boasts a wide wraparound porch, filled with wicker in the summer. The inn is decorated with stenciled walls, braided rugs and collections such as thimbles and dolls. Mary has stitched the quilts that top the beds. The library is jammed and guests may borrow a book and finish reading it at home. A favorite breakfast is John's poached brook trout or Eggs Benedict. Dinner available upon request.

Breakfast included in rates. Air conditioning in room. Cable TV and library on premises. Weddings and family reunions hosted. Limited French spoken. Amusement parks, antiques, fishing, parks, shopping, cross-country skiing, theater and watersports nearby.

Location: Three miles east of I-95, one mile west of the ocean.

Publicity: *Portsmouth Herald, Hampton Union, Boston Globe, Country.*

Special Discounts: Reduced rates three plus days.

"Very hospitable, can't think of a thing you need to add."

Hancock

K3

The Hancock Inn

33 Main St
Hancock, NH 03449
(603)525-3318 (800)525-1789
Fax:(603)525-9301

Rates: $98-150. MAP, AP, EP.
Payment: MC VISA AX DC CB DS PC TC.
Innkeeper(s): Linda & Joe Johnston.
Circa: 1789.

Rooms: 11 rooms with PB.
Beds: QDT.

Travelers have enjoyed this old inn, now in the National Register of Historic Places, since the days it served as a stagecoach stop more than 200 years ago. Canopied beds are found in some rooms and there are hooked rugs, wing-back chairs and rockers. The Mural Room boasts a pastoral mural painted in 1825. All

rooms have hand-sewn quilts and antique appointments. The fireplaced common room has comfortable chairs and couches with a small bar.

Breakfast included in rates. Types of meals: full breakfast and early coffee/tea. Afternoon tea, dinner, picnic lunch and banquet service available. MAP, AP, EP. Air conditioning in room. Cable TV, fax and library on premises. Small meetings, family reunions and seminars hosted. Antiques, fishing, parks, shopping, downhill skiing, cross-country skiing, theater and watersports nearby.

Publicity: *Country Inns, Boston Globe, Keene Sentinel, Yankee Homes.*

"The warmth you extended was the most meaningful part of our visit."

Henniker

J3

Colby Hill Inn

3 The Oaks, PO Box 779
Henniker, NH 03242-0779
(603)428-3281 (800)531-0330
Fax:(603)428-9218
E-mail: colbyhillinn@conknet.com

Rates: $85-165.
Payment: MC VISA AX DC CB DS PC TC.
Innkeeper(s): Ellie, John & Laurel Day.
Circa: 1797.

Rooms: 16 rooms with PB, 2 with FP. 3 suites. 1 conference room.
Beds: KQDT.

This 18th-century Colonial and its surrounding five acres is a classic example of an old New England Farm. There are still old barns on the grounds, as well as a restored carriage house. Stroll the grounds and you'll also find gardens, a swimming pool and a picturesque gazebo. Antiques fill the guest rooms, each of which is individually appointed in an elegant, traditional style. Two rooms include fireplaces. Guests can enjoy a romantic dinner by candlelight at the inn's dining room. Specialties of the house include items such as baked brie with toasted almonds, poached salmon in a mustard cream sauce and rich desserts, including maple walnut pie.

Breakfast included in rates. Types of meals: gourmet breakfast and early coffee/tea. Dinner, evening snack, banquet service and room service available. Air conditioning in room. Cable TV, VCR, fax, copier and swimming on premises. Weddings, small meetings, family reunions and seminars hosted. Antiques, fishing, parks, downhill skiing and cross-country skiing nearby. TAC10.

The Meeting House Inn & Restaurant

35 Flanders Rd
Henniker, NH 03242-3313
(603)428-3228
Fax:(603)428-6334
E-mail: 71233.255@compuserve.com

Rates: $65-105.
Payment: MC VISA AX DS PC TC.
Innkeeper(s): June & Bill Davis, Peter & Cheryl Bakke.
Circa: 1770.

Rooms: 6 rooms with PB. 2 suites.
Beds: QDT.

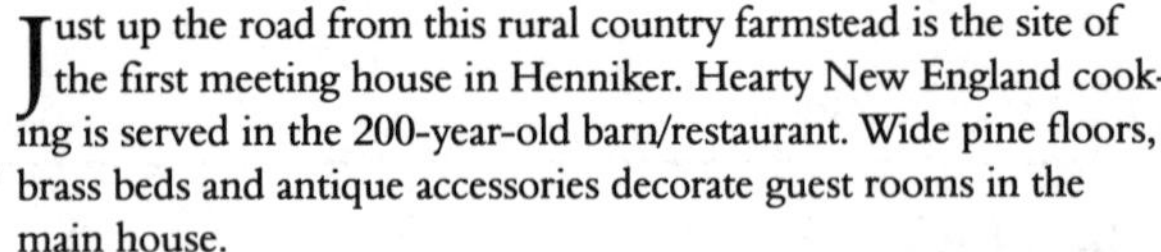

Just up the road from this rural country farmstead is the site of the first meeting house in Henniker. Hearty New England cooking is served in the 200-year-old barn/restaurant. Wide pine floors, brass beds and antique accessories decorate guest rooms in the main house.

Breakfast included in rates. Types of meals: continental breakfast, full breakfast and gourmet breakfast. Room service available. Air conditioning in room. Cable TV, VCR, fax, copier, spa and sauna on premises. Weddings, small meetings, family reunions and seminars hosted. Antiques, fishing, parks, shopping, downhill skiing, cross-country skiing, sporting events, theater and watersports nearby. TAC10.

Location: Off 114S, 2 miles from Henniker Center.

Publicity: *Boston Globe, Manchester Union Leader.*

Special Discounts: After third night, 15%.

"Thank you for giving us a honeymoon worth waiting eleven years for."

Hillsborough

J3

The Inn at Maplewood Farm

447 Center Rd, PO Box 1478
Hillsborough, NH 03244
(603)464-4242 (800)644-6695
Fax:(603)464-5401

Rates: $75-125. EP.
Payment: MC VISA AX DS PC TC.
Innkeeper(s): Laura & Jayme Simoes.
Circa: 1794.

Rooms: 4 suites. 1 conference room.
Beds: KQDT.

Antique-lovers will enjoy this historic inn, which not only features attractive American and European pieces, but a location in the heart of antique and auction country. An 1880s barn has been renovated to include guest rooms, and the inn's gift shop is located in the original 1794 tavern room. The innkeepers rebroadcast vintage radio programs, such as "Inner Sanctum," to the antique radios found in guest rooms. The inn borders scenic Fox State Forest and historic Hillsborough Center is just up the road.

Breakfast included in rates. Types of meals: full breakfast and early coffee/tea. Picnic lunch available. EP. Air conditioning, turn-down service and ceiling fan in room. VCR, fax and library on premises. 14 acres. Small meetings, family reunions and seminars hosted. Portuguese and Spanish spoken. Antiques, fishing, parks, shopping, downhill skiing, cross-country skiing and watersports nearby. TAC10.

Publicity: *New York Times, Boston Globe, Chicago Tribune, Yankee, Boston Herald, Baltimore Sun.*

"Your house is charming and you are both very hospitable."

Holderness

H4

The Inn on Golden Pond

Rt 3, PO Box 680
Holderness, NH 03245
(603)968-7269

Rates: $85-135.
Payment: MC VISA AX.
Innkeeper(s): Bill & Bonnie Webb.
Circa: 1879.

Rooms: 9 rooms with PB. 2 suites.
Beds: KQT.

NH

Framed by meandering stone walls and split-rail fences more than 100 years old, this inn is situated on 50 acres of woodlands. Most rooms overlook picturesque countryside and nearby is Squam Lake, setting for the film "On Golden Pond." An inviting, 60-foot screened porch provides a place to relax during the summer.

Breakfast included in rates. Types of meals: full breakfast and early coffee/tea. Turn-down service in room. Cable TV on premises. 50 acres. Antiques, fishing, shopping, downhill skiing, cross-country skiing, sporting events, theater and watersports nearby. TAC10.

Location: In the lakes region, close to Squam Lake.

Publicity: *Boston Globe, Baltimore Sun, Los Angeles Times.*

"Another sweet flower added to my bouquet of life."

Intervale

F5

The Forest - A Country Inn

PO Box 37
Intervale, NH 03845-0037
(603)356-9772 (800)448-3534
Fax:(603)356-5652
E-mail: wguppy@aol.com

Rates: $60-169.
Payment: MC VISA AX DS PC TC.
Innkeeper(s): Bill & Lisa Guppy.
Circa: 1830.

Rooms: 12 rooms, 10 with PB, 5 with FP. 2 suites. 3 cottages.
Beds: QDT.

This spacious Second Empire Victorian offers easy access to the many attractions of the Mt. Washington Valley. The inn's 11 guest rooms are uniquely decorated with country antique furnishings. Honeymooners often enjoy the privacy of the inn's turn-of-the-century stone cottage. A stream runs through the inn's 25 wooded acres, and guests may cross-country ski right on the property. The inn also boasts a built-in swimming

pool. Breakfast fare could include apple pancakes, cinnamon French toast or spiced Belgian waffles. Heritage New Hampshire and Story Land are nearby.

Breakfast and evening snack included in rates. Type of meal: full breakfast. Ceiling fan in room. Cable TV, fax and swimming on premises. 25 acres. Family reunions and seminars hosted. Amusement parks, antiques, fishing, parks, shopping, downhill skiing, cross-country skiing, sporting events, theater and watersports nearby. TAC10.

Jackson **F5**

Dana Place Inn

RR 16, Pinkham Notch Rd
Jackson, NH 03846
(603)383-6822 (800)537-9276
Fax:(603)383-6022

Rates: $75-135. MAP, AP.
Payment: MC VISA AX DC CB DS PC TC.
Innkeeper(s): The Levine Family.
Circa: 1860.

Rooms: 31 rooms with PB. 4 suites.
Beds: KQDT.

The original owners received this Colonial farmhouse as a wedding present. The warm, cozy atmosphere of the inn is surpassed only by the spectacular mountain views. During autumn, the fall leaves explode with color, and guests can enjoy the surroundings while taking a hike or bike ride through the area. The beautiful Ellis River is the perfect place for an afternoon of fly-fishing or a picnic. After a scrumptious country breakfast, winter guests can step out the door and into skis for a day of cross-country skiing.

Breakfast and afternoon tea included in rates. Types of meals: continental-plus breakfast and full breakfast. Dinner and picnic lunch available. MAP, AP. Cable TV in room. VCR, fax, copier, spa, swimming, tennis and library on premises. Weddings, small meetings, family reunions and seminars hosted. French and Spanish spoken. Antiques, parks, shopping, downhill skiing, cross-country skiing and watersports nearby. TAC10.

Pets Allowed: Exterior rooms.

Location: At the base of Mt. Washington, White Mountain National Forest.

Publicity: *Travel & Leisure, Inn Spots, Bon Appetit, Country Journal.*

Special Discounts: AAA, AARP, AMC.

"We had such a delightful time at Dana Place Inn. We will recommend you to everyone."

Ellis River House

Rt 16, Box 656
Jackson, NH 03846
(603)383-9339 (800)233-8309
Fax:(603)383-4142
E-mail: 76073,1435@compuserve.com

Rates: $79-229. MAP.
Payment: MC VISA AX DC CB DS PC TC.
Innkeeper(s): Barry & Barbara Lubao.
Circa: 1893.

Rooms: 20 rooms with PB, 13 with FP. 4 suites. 1 cottage. 1 conference room.
Beds: KQDT.

Andrew Harriman built this farmhouse, as well as the village town hall and three-room schoolhouse where the innkeepers' children attended school. Classic antiques and Laura Ashley prints decorate the guest rooms and riverfront "honeymoon" cottage, and each window reveals views of magnificent mountains, the vineyard or spectacular Ellis River. In 1993, the innkeepers added 18 rooms, 13 of which feature fireplaces and three offer two-person Jacuzzis. They also added four family suites, a heated, outdoor pool, an indoor Jacuzzi and a sauna.

Breakfast included in rates. Types of meals: full breakfast and early coffee/tea. Afternoon tea, dinner and picnic lunch available. MAP. Air conditioning and cable TV in room. Fax, spa, swimming and sauna on premises. Handicap access. Weddings, small meetings, family reunions and seminars hosted. Polish spoken. Amusement parks, antiques, fishing, parks, shopping, downhill skiing, cross-country skiing, sporting events, theater and watersports nearby. TAC5.

Location: White Mountain area.

Publicity: *Philadelphia Inquirer.*

Special Discounts: Seventh night free year-round. March, third night free. April, May, June, fourth night free.

"We have stayed at many B&Bs all over the world and are in agreement that the beauty and hospitality of Ellis River House is that of a world-class bed & breakfast."

The Inn at Jackson

PO Box 807, Main St at
Thorn Hill R
Jackson, NH 03846
(603)383-4321 (800)289-8600
Fax:(603)383-4085

Rates: $69-169.
Payment: MC VISA AX DC CB DS PC TC.
Innkeeper(s): Lori Tradewell.
Circa: 1902.

Rooms: 14 rooms with PB, 3 with FP.
Beds: KQT.

Architect Stanford White built this inn overlooking the village and White Mountains. The atmosphere is comfortable and inviting, and breakfast is served in a glassed-in porch which provides a panoramic view. In winter, sleigh rides can be arranged and in summer, hay rides and horseback riding. Miles of cross-country skiing are just out the door.

Breakfast included in rates. Type of meal: full breakfast. Air conditioning in room. Cable TV, VCR, fax, spa and library on premises. Fishing, parks, shopping, downhill skiing, cross-country skiing and theater nearby. TAC10.

"We had a terrific time and found the inn warm and cozy and most of all relaxing."

Nestlenook Farm Resort

Dinsmore Road
Jackson, NH 03846
(603)383-9443 (800)659-9443
Fax:(603)383-4515

Rates: $125-270.
Payment: MC VISA DS.
Innkeeper(s): Robert & Nancy Cyr.
Circa: 1790.

Rooms: 7 rooms with PB, 1 with FP.
Beds: KQ.

This 200-year-old Victorian is decorated with white gingerbread trim on windows, balustrades and porches. Each guest room has its own Jacuzzi and antique furnishings. In the dining room is a handsome Victorian bird cage complete with two love birds. The Murdoch Suite boasts a double Jacuzzi, original art and views of the inn's 65 acres of grounds. Sleigh rides and mountain bikes are available.

Breakfast included in rates. Type of meal: full breakfast. Evening snack available. Fax, copier, swimming, stables and bicycles on premises. 65 acres. Weddings hosted. Antiques, fishing, parks, shopping, downhill skiing, cross-country skiing, theater and watersports nearby. TAC10.

NH

Location: Cross the historic Jackson covered bridge then take the first right onto Dinsmore Road. In the Mount Washington Valley.

Publicity: *Ski, Friends, Manage Quebec, Discerning Traveler.*

The Inn at Thorn Hill

Thorn Hill Rd, PO Box A
Jackson, NH 03846-0800
(603)383-4242 (800)289-8990
Fax:(603)383-8062
E-mail: thornhll@ncia.net

Rates: $150-275. MAP.
Payment: MC VISA AX DC DS PC TC.
Innkeeper(s): Jim & Ibby Cooper.
Circa: 1895.

Rooms: 19 rooms with PB. 3 suites. 3 cottages. 1 conference room.
Beds: KQD.

Follow a romantic drive through the Honeymoon Covered Bridge to Thorn Hill Road where this country Victorian stands, built by architect Stanford White. Its 10 acres are adjacent to the Jackson Ski Touring trails. Inside, the decor is Victorian and a collection of antique light fixtures accentuates the guest rooms, pub, drawing room, and parlor.

Breakfast, afternoon tea and dinner included in rates. Types of meals: full breakfast and early coffee/tea. Picnic lunch available. MAP. Air conditioning and turn-down service in room. Cable TV, fax, copier, swimming and library on premises. Weddings, small meetings, family reunions and seminars hosted. Antiques, fishing, parks, shopping, downhill skiing, cross-country skiing and theater nearby. TAC10.

Location: In the heart of the White Mountains on the edge of White Mountain National Forest.

Publicity: *Mature Outlook, Reporter, Bon Appetit, Gourmet, Ski, Washington Post, Toledo Blade, GEO, Good Housekeeping, Mirabella.*

"Magnificent, start to finish! The food was excellent but the mountain air must have shrunk my clothes!"

Village House

Rt 16A Box 359
Jackson, NH 03846
(603)383-6666 (800)972-8343
Fax:(603)383-6464

Rates: $55-145.
Payment: MC VISA DS PC TC.
Innkeeper(s): Robin Crocker.
Circa: 1860.

Rooms: 15 rooms, 13 with PB. 2 suites. 1 conference room.
Beds: KQDT.

Village House was built as an annex to the larger Hawthorne Inn which eventually burned. It is a colonial building, with a porch winding around three sides. The Wildcat River flows by the inn's seven acres, and there is a swimming pool, outdoor Jacuzzi, clay tennis court and shuffleboard set in view of the White Mountains.

Breakfast and afternoon tea included in rates. Types of meals: continental-plus breakfast, full breakfast and early coffee/tea. Evening snack and picnic lunch available. Cable TV, fax, copier, spa, swimming and tennis on premises. Weddings, small meetings, family reunions and seminars hosted. Antiques, fishing, parks, shopping, downhill skiing, cross-country skiing, theater and watersports nearby. TAC10.

Pets Allowed: In one building, security deposit required.

Publicity: *Foxboro Reporter.*

Special Discounts: Group rates available; specials in April, May, June & November.

"Your hospitality and warmth made us feel right at home. The little extras, such as turn-down service, flowers and baked goods are all greatly appreciated."

Whitneys' Inn

Rt 16B, PO Box 822
Jackson, NH 03846
(603)383-8916 (800)677-5737
Fax:(603)383-6886

Rates: $64-166. MAP.
Payment: MC VISA AX DS PC TC.
Innkeeper(s): Kevin Martin.
Circa: 1842.

Rooms: 29 rooms with PB, 3 with FP. 9 suites. 2 cottages. 1 conference room.
Beds: KQDT.

This country inn offers romance, family recreation and a lovely setting at the base of the Black Mountain Ski Area. The inn specializes in recreation, as guests enjoy cookouts, cross-country and downhill skiing, hiking, lawn games, skating, sledding, sleigh rides, swimming and tennis. Homemade corned beef hash is one of the breakfast specialties. Popular nearby activities include trying out Jackson's two golf courses and picnicking at Jackson Falls.

Breakfast and dinner included in rates. Type of meal: full breakfast. Afternoon tea, picnic lunch and banquet service available. MAP. Cable TV, VCR, swimming, tennis and library on premises. 14 acres. Weddings, small meetings, family reunions and seminars hosted. Amusement parks, antiques, fishing, parks, downhill skiing, cross-country skiing, theater and watersports nearby. TAC10.

Pets Allowed.

Jaffrey **L3**

The Benjamin Prescott Inn

Rt 124 E, 433 Turnpike Rd
Jaffrey, NH 03452
(603)532-6637
Fax:(603)532-6637

Rates: $65-140. EP.
Payment: MC VISA AX PC TC.
Innkeeper(s): Jan & Barry Miller.
Circa: 1853.

Rooms: 9 rooms with PB. 2 suites. 1 conference room.
Beds: KQDT.

Colonel Prescott arrived on foot in Jaffrey in 1775, with an ax in his hand and a bag of beans on his back. The family built this classic Greek Revival many years later. Now, candles light the windows, seen from the stonewall-lined lane adjacent to the inn. Each room bears the name of a Prescott family member and is furnished with antiques.

Breakfast included in rates. Type of meal: full breakfast. EP. Ceiling fan in room. VCR, fax and library on premises. Weddings, small meetings, family reunions and seminars hosted. Antiques, fishing, parks, shopping, downhill skiing, cross-country skiing, sporting events, theater and watersports nearby. TAC10.

"The coffee and breakfasts were delicious and the hospitality overwhelming."

Woodbound Inn

Woodbound Rd
Jaffrey, NH 03452
(603)532-8341 (800)688-7770
Fax:(603)532-8341
E-mail: woodbound@aol.com

Rates: $79-135. MAP, EP.
Payment: MC VISA AX PC.
Innkeeper(s): Kohlmorgen Family.
Circa: 1819.

Rooms: 38 rooms, 34 with PB, 6 with FP. 5 suites. 5 cottages. 5 conference rooms.
Beds: QDT.

Vacationers have enjoyed the Woodbound Inn since its opening as a year-round resort in 1892. The main inn actually was built in 1819, and this portion offers 19 guest rooms, all appointed with classic-style furnishings. The innkeepers offer more modern accommodations in the Edgewood Building, and there are several cabins available. The one- and two-bedroom cabins rest along the shore of Lake Contoocok. The inn's 162 acres include a private beach, fishing, hiking and nature trails, tennis courts, a volleyball court, a game room and a golf course. There is a full service restaurant, a cocktail lounge and banquet facilities on premises. If for some reason one would want to venture away from the inn, the area is full of activities, including ski areas, more golf courses and Mount Monadnock.

Breakfast included in rates. Type of meal: full breakfast. Dinner, lunch, banquet service and catering service available. MAP, EP. Air conditioning in room. VCR, copier, swimming, tennis, library and child care on premises. Handicap access. 162 acres. Weddings, small meetings, family reunions and seminars hosted. Amusement parks, antiques, fishing, parks, shopping, downhill skiing, cross-country skiing, theater and watersports nearby. TAC10.

Pets Allowed: In cabins only.

Special Discounts: Long term packages. Corporate rate, $59-$69; Seniors, 10% discount.

Jefferson *E4*

Applebrook B&B

Rt 115A, PO Box 178
Jefferson, NH 03583-0178
(603)586-7713 (800)545-6504
E-mail: applebrk@aol.com

Rates: $40-75.
Payment: MC VISA AX PC TC.
Innkeeper(s): Sandra Conley & Martin Kelly.
Circa: 1797.

Rooms: 14 rooms, 7 with PB. 1 conference room.
Beds: KQDT.

Panoramic views surround this large Victorian farmhouse nestled in the middle of New Hampshire's White Mountains. Guests can awake to the smell of freshly baked muffins made with locally picked berries. A comfortable, fire-lit sitting room boasts stained glass, a goldfish pool and a beautiful view of Mt. Washington. Test your golfing skills at the nearby 18-hole championship course, or spend the day antique hunting. A trout stream and spring-fed rock pool are nearby. Wintertime guests can ice skate or race through the powder at nearby ski resorts or by way of snowmobile, finish off the day with a moonlight toboggan ride. After a full day, guests can enjoy a soak in the hot tub under the stars, where they might see shooting stars or the Northern Lights.

Breakfast included in rates. Types of meals: full breakfast and early coffee/tea. Ceiling fan in room. Spa and library on premises. 35 acres. Weddings, small meetings, family reunions and seminars hosted. Amusement parks, antiques, fishing, parks, shopping, downhill skiing, cross-country skiing, theater and watersports nearby. TAC10.

Pets Allowed: Two rooms kept pet-free; $5.00/night per pet-half of which is donated to Lancaster Humane Society.

Publicity: *PriceCostco Connection, New Hampshire Outdoor Companion.*

"We came for a night and stayed for a week."

Jefferson Inn

RR 1 Box 68A
Jefferson, NH 03583
(603)586-7998 (800)729-7908
Fax:(603)586-7808
E-mail: jeffinn@moose.ncia.net

Rates: $65-150. EP.
Payment: MC VISA AX DS PC TC.
Innkeeper(s): Marla Mason & Don Garretson.
Circa: 1896.

Rooms: 11 rooms, 9 with PB. 2 suites.
Beds: KQDT.

This rambling Victorian house features a turret, gables and wraparound verandas. Nestled in the White Mountain National Forest, the inn overlooks the Jefferson Meadows to Franconia Notch, Mt. Washington and the northern Presidential range. All rooms have views and period antiques. Trails for Mt. Waumbek and Starr King lead from the inn. Nearby, the Weathervane Summer Theater provides nightly entertainment. An afternoon tea with homemade baked goods is served daily.

Breakfast, afternoon tea and evening snack included in rates. Types of meals: full breakfast, gourmet breakfast and early coffee/tea. EP. Fax, copier and swimming on premises. Handicap access. Weddings, family reunions and seminars hosted. German spoken. Amusement parks, antiques, parks, downhill skiing, cross-country skiing, theater and watersports nearby.

"Marvelous breakfast and a warm, comfortable atmosphere."

Littleton E3

Beal House Inn

2 W Main St
Littleton, NH 03561-3502
(603)444-2661
Fax:(603)444-6224
E-mail: beal.house.inn@connriver.net

Rates: $60-85.
Payment: MC VISA AX DS.
Innkeeper(s): Ted & Barbara Snell.
Circa: 1833.

Rooms: 14 rooms, 8 with PB. 1 suite. 1 conference room.
Beds: QDT.

This Federal Renaissance farmhouse has been an inn since 1938. The original barn still stands, now covered with white clapboard. The inn is furnished with handsome antiques, canopy beds and down comforters. Candlelight breakfasts are served fireside and often includes homemade muffins and Belgian waffles. Beal House is a Main Street landmark.

Breakfast and afternoon tea included in rates. Type of meal: full breakfast. Fax on premises. Small meetings hosted. Antiques, fishing, parks, shopping, downhill skiing, cross-country skiing, theater and watersports nearby.

Location: In the heart of the White Mountains.

Publicity: *Country Inn, Glamour, Le Soleil, Star Ledger, New Jersey, Yankee.*

"These innkeepers know and understand people, their needs and wants. Attention to cleanliness and amenities, from check-in to check-out, is a treasure."

Moultonborough H5

Olde Orchard Inn

RR 1 Box 256, Lees Rd. &
Lees Mill, Moultonborough,
NH 03254-9502
(603)476-5004 (800)598-5845
Fax:(603)476-5419
E-mail: innkeep1@aol.com

Rates: $70-125.
Payment: MC VISA PC TC.
Innkeeper(s): Jim & Mary Senner.
Circa: 1790.

Rooms: 8 rooms with PB, 3 with FP. 1 suite. 1 cottage.
Beds: QDT.

This farmhouse rests next to a mountain brook and pond in the midst of an apple orchard. Eight guest rooms and one family suite are available, all with private baths. After enjoying a large country breakfast, guests may borrow a bicycle for a ride to Lake Winnipesaukee, just a mile away. The inn is within an hour's drive of five downhill skiing areas, and guests also may cross-country ski nearby. The Castle in the Clouds and the Ossipee Ski Area are nearby.

Breakfast included in rates. Type of meal: full breakfast. Air conditioning in room. Cable TV, VCR, fax and child care on premises. 12 acres. Small meetings, family reunions and seminars hosted. Antiques, fishing, parks, shopping, downhill skiing, cross-country skiing, theater and watersports nearby. TAC10.

Pets Allowed: In cottage or kennel/barn.

Special Discounts: Third night free during certain periods off season.

Munsonville K2

The Old Mill House B&B

RR 9, Box 224
Munsonville, NH 03457
(603)847-3224

Rates: $45.
Innkeeper(s): Walter & Susan Lawton.
Circa: 1833.

Rooms: 7 rooms.
Beds: DT.

Built in the early 1800s to house workers from a nearby mill, the inn offers peace and relaxation in bedrooms that house hand-made quilts, afghans and teddy bears. The surrounding area offers many sites, including a childrens museum and historic Fort No. 4. A drive through the fall foliage is recommended or climb up nearby Mount Monadnock. In winter, guests can try their hand at ice fishing or spend the afternoon skating or snowmobiling.

NH

Breakfast included in rates. Type of meal: full breakfast. VCR on premises. Antiques, fishing, parks, shopping, cross-country skiing and theater nearby.

New London I3

Pleasant Lake Inn

125 Pleasant St,
PO Box 1030
New London, NH 03257
(603)526-6271 (800)626-4907

Rates: $65-100.
Payment: MC VISA PC TC.
Innkeeper(s): Margaret & Grant Rich.
Circa: 1790.

Rooms: 11 rooms with PB. 1 suite.
Beds: KQDT.

In its early days, this inn served as a farmhouse. By the late 1870s, it was serving guests as a summer resort. Its tradition of hospitality continues today with relaxing guest rooms, decorated in a country style with Oriental rugs and four-poster or brass beds. The grounds include a spring-fed lake with a private beach. Meander over wooded trails and you'll find a footbridge over a pleasant little brook. Guests are invited to bring their own row boat or canoe to use on the lake, but the innkeepers will also lend theirs if requested. Innkeepers Margaret and Grant Rich share the kitchen duty. Grant prepares mouthwatering breakfasts with treats such as blueberry pan-

cakes, while Margaret creates the Friday and Saturday night dinners with fresh garden salads, hearty soups, rich desserts and specialty entrees. The cranberry chicken is a favorite. The area is bursting with things to do. Golfing, tennis, fishing, theater, craft shops and state parks all are nearby.

Breakfast included in rates. Types of meals: full breakfast and early coffee/tea. Dinner available. Ceiling fan in room. Cable TV, copier and swimming on premises. Family reunions hosted. Antiques, fishing, shopping, downhill skiing, cross-country skiing, sporting events and theater nearby. TAC10.

"What a perfect setting for our first ever visit to New England."

North Conway F5

The 1785 Inn

3582 White Mountain Hwy
North Conway, NH 03860
(603)356-9025 (800)421-1785
Fax:(603)356-6081
E-mail: the1785inn@aol.com

Rates: $69-169.
Payment: MC VISA AX DC CB DS PC TC.
Innkeeper(s): Becky & Charles Mallar.
Circa: 1785.

Rooms: 17 rooms, 12 with PB. 1 suite. 2 conference rooms.
Beds: KQD.

The main section of this center-chimney house was built by Captain Elijah Dinsmore of the New Hampshire Rangers. He was granted the land for service in the American Revolution. Original hand-hewn beams, corner posts, fireplaces, and a brick oven are still visible and operating.

Breakfast included in rates. Types of meals: full breakfast, gourmet breakfast and early coffee/tea. Dinner, evening snack, banquet service and room service available. Air conditioning in room. Cable TV, VCR, fax, copier, swimming, library and child care on premises. Weddings, small meetings, family reunions and seminars hosted. French spoken. Amusement parks, antiques, fishing, parks, shopping, downhill skiing, cross-country skiing, theater and watersports nearby. TAC10.

Location: Two miles north of North Conway in the White Mountains.

Publicity: *Valley Visitor, Bon Appetit, Ski, Travel Holiday, Connecticut Magazine.*

"Occasionally in our lifetimes is a moment so unexpectedly perfect that we use it as our measure for our unforgettable moments. We just had such an experience at The 1785 Inn."

Buttonwood Inn

Mount Surprise Rd
North Conway, NH 03860
(603)356-2625 (800)258-2625
Fax:(603)356-3140
E-mail: button_w@moose.ncia.net

Rates: $70-150.
Payment: MC VISA AX DS PC TC.
Innkeeper(s): Claudia & Peter Needham.
Circa: 1820.

Rooms: 9 rooms, 5 with PB, 1 with FP. 2 suites. 1 conference room.
Beds: KQDT.

This center-chimney, New England-style inn was once a working farm of more than 100 acres on the mountain. Of the original outbuildings, only the granite barn foundation remains. Through the years, the house has been extended to a total of 20 rooms.

Breakfast and afternoon tea included in rates. Types of meals: full breakfast, gourmet breakfast and early coffee/tea. Cable TV, VCR, fax, swimming, bicycles and library on premises. Weddings, small meetings, family reunions and seminars hosted. Amusement parks, antiques, fishing, parks, shopping, downhill skiing, cross-country skiing, theater and watersports nearby. TAC10.

Location: Tucked away on Mt. Surprise, two miles from town.

Publicity: *Northeast Bound, Skiing, Boston Globe, Yankee Travel, The Mountain Ear.*

"The very moment we spotted your lovely inn nestled midway on the mountainside in the moonlight, we knew we had found a winner."

Cranmore Mt Lodge

859 Kearsarge Rd,
PO Box 1194
North Conway, NH 03860
(603)356-2044 (800)356-3596
Fax:(603)356-8963
E-mail: helfandd@nxi.com

Rates: $69-125.
Payment: MC VISA AX DC DS PC TC.
Innkeeper(s): Judy & Dennis Helfand.
Circa: 1860.

Rooms: 21 rooms, 15 with PB. 1 suite.
Beds: KQDT.

Babe Ruth was a frequent guest at this old New England farmhouse when his daughter was the owner. There are many rare Babe Ruth photos displayed in the inn and one guest room is still decorated with his furnishings. The barn on the property is held together with wooden pegs and contains dorm rooms.

Breakfast included in rates. Types of meals: full breakfast and early coffee/tea. Air conditioning, ceiling fan and cable TV in room. VCR, fax, copier, spa, swimming and tennis on premises. Weddings and family reunions hosted. Danish spoken. Amusement parks, antiques, fishing, parks, shopping, downhill skiing, cross-country skiing, theater and watersports nearby. TAC10.

Location: Village of Kearsarge.

Publicity: *Ski Magazine, Snow Country, Montreal Gazette, Newsday.*

Special Discounts: 10% AAA.

"Your accommodations are lovely, your breakfasts delicious."

Merrill Farm Resort

428 White Mountain Hwy,
Rt 16
North Conway, NH 03860
(603)447-3866 (800)445-1017
Fax:(603)447-3867
E-mail: merrilfarm@aol.com

Rates: $59-109.
Payment: MC VISA AX DC CB DS TC.
Innkeeper(s): Lynn T. McArdle.
Circa: 1792.

Rooms: 60 rooms with PB, 8 with FP. 11 cottages. 3 conference rooms.
Beds: QDT.

This picturesque patch of farmland was settled by the Merrill family, some of the area's earliest settlers. The 200-year-old farmhouse is decorated in a rustic, period style with antiques and country furnishings. All but five of the guest rooms include small refrigerators that are stocked daily with complimentary sodas. Despite the 18th-century ambiance, some accommodations include whirlpool tubs. There's plenty to do at the inn. Canoeing, volleyball, badminton, ice skating and sledding are some of the options. There also is a heated outdoor pool, sauna and hot tub on the premises. The farm has the only maple sugaring house in the Mount Washington Valley, and it is this facility that creates the homemade maple butter, offered during the breakfast service.

NH

Breakfast and afternoon tea included in rates. Types of meals: continental-plus breakfast and early coffee/tea. Air conditioning, ceiling fan, cable TV and VCR in room. Fax, copier, spa, swimming, sauna, bicycles and library on premises. Handicap access. Weddings, small meetings, family reunions and seminars hosted. French and German spoken. Amusement parks, antiques, fishing, parks, shopping, downhill skiing, cross-country skiing, theater and watersports nearby. TAC10.

Special Discounts: Canadian cash at par 80% of year; 10% AAA and Senior.

Nereledge Inn

River Rd, Off Main St,
PO Box 547
North Conway, NH 03860
(603)356-2831
Fax:(603)356-7085

Rates: $9-109.
Payment: MC VISA AX DS.
Innkeeper(s): Valerie & Dave Halpin.
Circa: 1787.

Rooms: 11 rooms, 5 with PB. 1 suite.
Beds: QDT.

This big white house is decorated simply in a New England style featuring cozy English eiderdowns and rocking chairs in many of the guest rooms. Woodstoves warm the breakfast room and the sitting room. There is an English-style pub room with a fireplace, darts and backgammon. For breakfast you may be served apple crumble with ice cream as a dessert after the main course. Innkeeper Valerie Halpin grew up in Burnley, England. The area is bursting with activity for those who wish to bask in the outdoors. The river, a perfect place to enjoy swimming, canoeing and fishing, is within walking distance, as are shopping and restaurants in the village. The area boasts wonderful rock and ice climbing.

Breakfast included in rates. Type of meal: full breakfast. Antiques, fishing, downhill skiing, cross-country skiing and theater nearby.

Location: In the heart of Mt. Washington Valley.

Publicity: *White Mountain Region Magazine, Outside.*

"Not the fanciest, but by far the most hospitable."

Stonehurst Manor

Rt 16, North Conway,
NH 03860-1937
(603)356-3113 (800)525-9100
Fax:(603)356-3217

Rates: $106-176. MAP.
Payment: MC VISA AX PC TC.
Innkeeper(s): Peter Rattay.
Circa: 1876.

Rooms: 24 rooms, 22 with PB, 7 with FP.
Beds: KQDT.

This English-style manor stands on lush, landscaped lawns and 30 acres of pine trees. It was built as the summer home for the Bigelow family, founder of the Bigelow Carpet Company. Inside the tremendous front door is an elegant display of leaded and stained-glass windows, rich oak woodwork, a winding staircase and a massive, hand-carved oak fireplace.

Breakfast and dinner included in rates. Type of meal: full breakfast. MAP. Air conditioning, ceiling fan and cable TV in room. Fax, copier, spa, swimming and tennis on premises. Handicap access. 33 acres. Weddings, small meetings, family reunions and seminars hosted. German spoken. Antiques, fishing, shopping, downhill skiing, sporting events, theater and watersports nearby.

Location: In White Mountains.

Publicity: *Boston Globe, New York Daily News, Bon Appetit, Boston Magazine, Gourmet.*

"An architecturally preserved replica of an English country house, a perfect retreat for the nostalgic-at-heart," —Phil Berthiaume, Country Almanac.

North Woodstock **F4**

Three Rivers House

RR 1 Box 72
North Woodstock, NH
03262-9710
(603)745-2711 (800)241-2711
Fax:(603)745-2773

Rates: $58-128.
Payment: MC VISA DS PC TC.
Innkeeper(s): Brian A Crete & Diane Brisson.
Circa: 1875.

Rooms: 15 rooms with PB, 7 with FP. 4 suites.
Beds: QDT.

Situated at a choice spot on the banks of the Moosalauki River, this is the only hotel remaining in the area from the 1800s. Original tin ceilings and cobblestone fireplaces were first enjoyed when visitors came for the summer, taking carriage rides through the mountains. Unique rock formations along the river behind the inn are called the "mummies" and tourists have explored them for more than a century.

Breakfast and afternoon tea included in rates. Types of meals: full breakfast and early coffee/tea. Room service available. Air conditioning and cable TV in room. Fax, copier and library on premises. French spoken. Antiques, fishing, parks, shopping, downhill skiing, cross-country skiing, theater and watersports nearby.

Publicity: *Outlook.*

"Last of the grand inns when guests were dropped off by train right across the road."

Plymouth

H4

Colonel Spencer Inn

RR 1, Box 206
Plymouth, NH 03264
(603)536-3438

Rates: $45-65.
Payment: PC TC.
Innkeeper(s): Carolyn & Alan Hill.
Circa: 1764.

Rooms: 7 rooms with PB. 1 suite.
Beds: D.

This pre-Revolutionary Colonial boasts Indian shutters, gleaming plank floors and a secret hiding place. Joseph Spencer, one of the house's early owners, fought at Bunker Hill and with General Washington. Within view of the river and the mountains, the inn is now a cozy retreat with warm Colonial decor. A suite with a kitchen is also available.

Breakfast and evening snack included in rates. Type of meal: full breakfast. Small meetings and family reunions hosted. Amusement parks, antiques, fishing, parks, shopping, downhill skiing, cross-country skiing, sporting events, theater and watersports nearby. TAC10.

Location: Near lake and mountain district.

"You have something very special here and we very much enjoyed a little piece of it!"

Rindge

L3

Cathedral House B&B

63 Cathedral Entrance
Rindge, NH 03461
(603)899-6790

Rates: $45-125.
Payment: MC VISA PC.
Innkeeper(s): Donald & Shirley Mahoney.
Circa: 1850.

Rooms: 5 rooms.
Beds: QDT.

This pre-Civil War, Colonial-style farmhouse is surrounded by 450 acres with meadows, a fishing pond, nature trails and scenic vistas. The five, comfortable bedrooms have been decorated in Colonial style, with artwork and fresh flowers in season. Rooms offer views of mountains or Emerson Pond. A hearty country breakfast is served. The bed & breakfast is located on the grounds of the Cathedral of the Pines, a non-denominational place of worship which offers solitude in natural surroundings. The grounds originally were selected by a young pilot and his wife as a location for their home upon his return from World War II. The pilot was killed in the line of duty, and his parents created the Cathedral of the Pines in his memory and others who served. The site has been recognized by the U.S. Congress as a national memorial.

Breakfast included in rates. Type of meal: full breakfast. Library on premises. 450 acres. Antiques, fishing, parks, shopping, downhill skiing, cross-country skiing, sporting events, theater and watersports nearby.

Special Discounts: 10% Veterans, Valentines and Mother/daughter weekends.

"Thank you for making our wedding day such a success and for making our family feel so welcome."

Sanbornville

Wakefield Inn

2723 Wakefield Rd
Sanbornville, NH 03872
(603)522-8272 (800)245-0841

Rates: $50-75.
Payment: MC VISA PC TC.
Innkeeper(s): Harry & Lou Sisson.
Circa: 1804.

Rooms: 7 rooms with PB.
Beds: QDT.

Early travelers pulled up to the front door of the Wakefield Inn by stagecoach and while they disembarked, their luggage was handed up to the second floor. It was brought in through the door which is still visible over the porch roof. A spiral staircase, ruffled curtains, wallpapers and a wraparound porch all create the romantic ambiance of days gone by. In the dining room an original three-sided fireplace casts a warm glow on dining guests as it did more than 190 years ago.

Breakfast included in rates. Types of meals: full breakfast and early coffee/tea. Ceiling fan in room. VCR on premises. Antiques, fishing, shopping and cross-country skiing nearby.

Location: Historic district.

Special Discounts: Off season weekend packages.

"Comfortable accommodations, excellent food and exquisite decor highlighted by your quilts."

Sugar Hill

F3

The Hilltop Inn

Main St
Sugar Hill, NH 03585
(603)823-5695 (800)770-5695
Fax:(603)823-5518
E-mail: mike.hern@hilltopinn.com

Rates: $70-230.
Payment: MC VISA DS PC TC.
Innkeeper(s): Meri & Mike Hern.
Circa: 1895.

Rooms: 6 rooms with PB, 1 with FP. 3 suites. 1 cottage.
Beds: KQD.

This rambling Victorian guest house is located on the quiet main street of town. The rooms are decorated with antiques, and there are several cozy common rooms, decks and porches for relaxing after a day of canoeing, horseback riding or skiing. A spacious deck provides views of the sunsets. Pets are welcome.

Breakfast and afternoon tea included in rates. Types of meals: full breakfast, gourmet breakfast and early coffee/tea. Picnic lunch and catering service available. Ceiling fan in room. Cable TV, VCR, fax, copier, library and pet boarding on premises. Weddings, small meetings, family reunions and seminars hosted. Amusement parks, antiques, fishing, parks, shopping, downhill skiing, cross-country skiing, theater and watersports nearby.

Pets Allowed: Yes. **Location:** White Mountain National Forest area.

Publicity: *Boston Globe, Littleton Courier, Baltimore Sun, Philadelphia Herald, Yankee, Outside Magazine, Victoria.*

"Relaxing and comforting, better than being home!"

Sunset Hill House

Sunset Hill Rd
Sugar Hill, NH 03585
(603)823-5522 (800)786-4455
Fax:(603)823-5738

Rates: $80-150. MAP.
Payment: MC VISA AX DS TC.
Innkeeper(s): Michael & Tricia Coyle.
Circa: 1882.

Rooms: 30 rooms with PB. 2 suites. 3 conference rooms.
Beds: KQDT.

This Second Empire Victorian has views of two mountain ranges. Three parlors, all with cozy fireplaces, are favorite gathering spots. The inn's lush grounds offer many opportunities for recreation or relaxing, and guests often enjoy special events, such as fly-fishing lessons and maple-sugar tours. The Cannon Mountain Ski Area and Franconia Notch State Park are nearby, and there is 30 kilometers of cross-country ski trails at the inn. Be sure to inquire about golf and ski packages.

Breakfast included in rates. Types of meals: full breakfast and early coffee/tea. Dinner, picnic lunch, lunch, banquet service and catering service available. MAP. Ceiling fan in room. Cable TV and fax on premises. Handicap access. 680 acres. Weddings, small meetings, family reunions and seminars hosted. Antiques, fishing, parks, shopping, downhill skiing, cross-country skiing, theater and watersports nearby.

Publicity: *Yankee, Courier, Caledonia Record, Boston Globe.*

"I have visited numerous inns and innkeepers in my 10 years as a travel writer, but have to admit that few have impressed me as much as yours and you did."

Tilton

I4

Tilton Manor

40 Chestnut St
Tilton, NH 03276-5546
(603)286-3457

Rates: $60-70.
Payment: MC VISA AX DS PC TC.
Innkeeper(s): Chip & Diane.
Circa: 1884.

Rooms: 4 rooms, 2 with PB, 1 with FP. 2 suites.
Beds: KDT.

This turn-of-the-century Folk Victorian inn is just two blocks from downtown Tilton. The inn's comfortable guest rooms are furnished with antiques and sport handmade afghans. Guests are treated to a hearty country breakfast featuring freshly baked muffins, and dinner is available with advance reservations. Visitors enjoy relaxing in the sitting room, where they may play games, read or watch TV after a busy day exploring the historic area. Gunstock and Highland ski resorts are nearby and the Daniel Webster Birthplace and Shaker Village are within easy driving distance. Shoppers will enjoy Tilton's latest addition — an outlet center.

Breakfast included in rates. Type of meal: full breakfast. Cable TV, library and child care on premises. Weddings, small meetings, family reunions and seminars hosted. Antiques, fishing, shopping, downhill skiing, cross-country skiing and watersports nearby.

Pets Allowed: Small pets with responsible owners.

"A home away from home."

Whitefield E4

Spalding Inn & Club

Mountain View Rd
Whitefield, NH 03598
(603)837-2572 (800)368-8439
Fax:(603)837-3062
E-mail: mflinder@Moose.ncia.

Rates: $109-119.
Payment: MC VISA PC TC.
Innkeeper(s): Diane,April Cockrell,Mike Flinder.
Circa: 1865.

Rooms: 36 rooms with PB, 6 with FP. 6 suites. 6 cottages. 2 conference rooms.
Beds: KT.

For 131 years, guests have enjoyed New England hospitality at this charming country inn. Guest rooms are located in the main inn and in the carriage house. There are several private cottages as well, each with one or more bedrooms, a living room, fireplace and private bath. Laura Ashley decor and antiques create a romantic atmosphere. The inn is noted for its cuisine, but the dining room's mountain views are memorable, too. Breakfasts won't leave you hungry, a variety of country goodies are prepared. Dinners, served by candlelight, feature a menu which changes daily. The innkeepers offer a variety of packages, with golf, tennis, family vacation and theater lovers' as themes.

Breakfast included in rates. Types of meals: full breakfast and early coffee/tea. Afternoon tea and banquet service available. VCR, fax, copier, swimming, tennis, library and child care on premises. 220 acres. Weddings, small meetings and family reunions hosted. Amusement parks, antiques, fishing, parks and theater nearby. TAC15.

Pets Allowed: In cottages only.

Special Discounts: Group rate available.

"A special spot in an enchanting setting."

Wilton Center

Stepping Stones B&B

Bennington Battle Tr
Wilton Center, NH 03086
(603)654-9048

Rates: $50-55.
Payment: PC TC.
Innkeeper(s): D. Ann Carlsmith.
Circa: 1790.

Rooms: 3 rooms, 1 with PB.
Beds: QDT.

Decks and terraces overlook the enormous gardens of this Greek Revival house, in the local historic register. Guest rooms feature white-washed pine, cherry or Shaker-style country pieces accented with botanical prints. Poached eggs on asparagus with hollandaise sauce, blueberry Belgian waffles and jumbo apple muffins with streusel topping are guests' favorite breakfast choices. The innkeeper is both a garden designer and weaver.

Breakfast included in rates. Types of meals: full breakfast and early coffee/tea. Afternoon tea available. Library on premises. Weddings and family reunions hosted. Antiques, parks, shopping, downhill skiing, cross-country skiing and theater nearby.

Pets Allowed: If well-behaved.

Special Discounts: Weekly rate with seventh night free.

"A very relaxing and beautiful get away. The color and fragrance of the gardens is stunning."

New Jersey

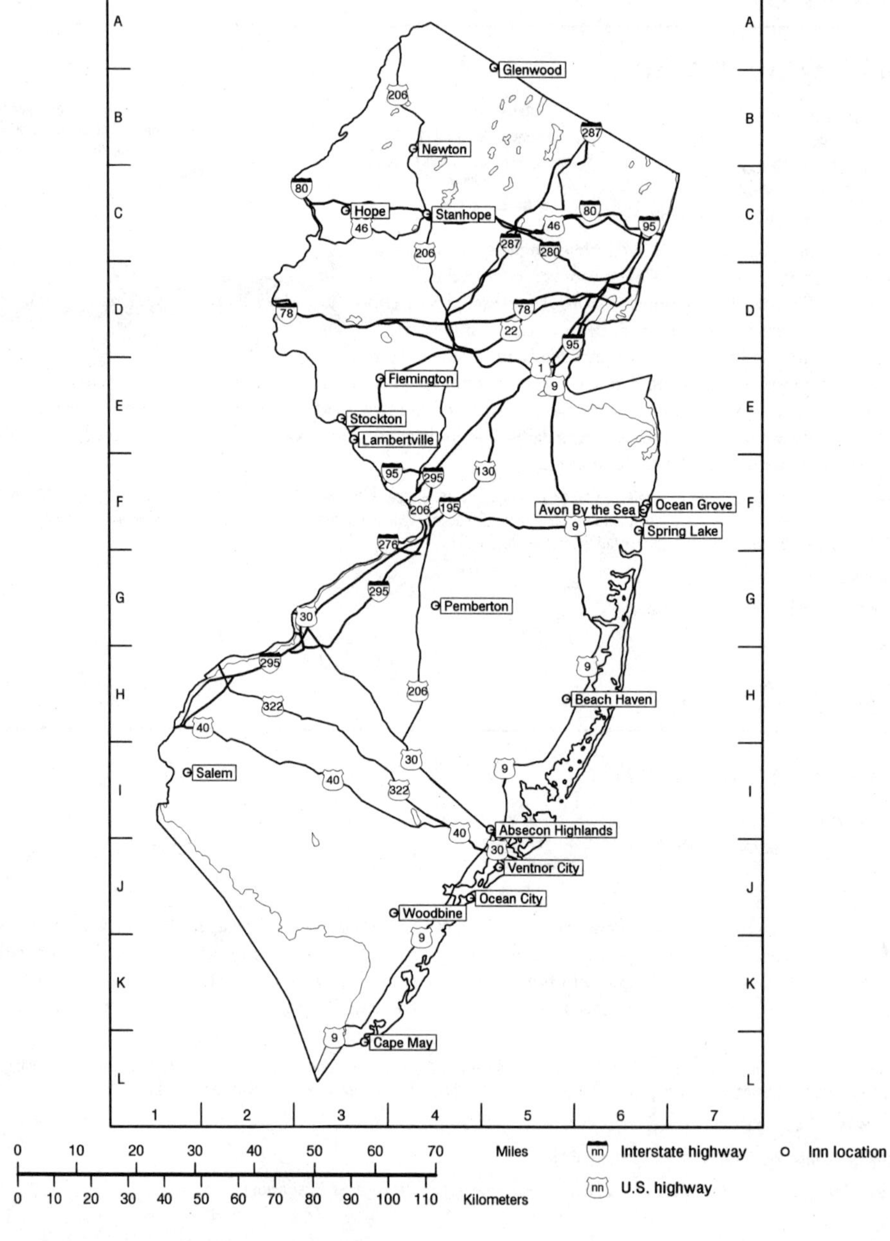

Glenwood
Newton
Hope
Stanhope
Flemington
Stockton
Lambertville
Avon By the Sea
Ocean Grove
Spring Lake
Pemberton
Beach Haven
Salem
Absecon Highlands
Ventnor City
Ocean City
Woodbine
Cape May
Miles
Kilometers
Interstate highway
U.S. highway
Inn location

Absecon Highlands I5

White Manor Inn

739 S 2nd Ave
Absecon Highlands, NJ
08201-9542
(609)748-3996
Fax:(609)652-0073

Rates: $48-85.
Payment: PC TC.
Innkeeper(s): Anna Mae & Howard R. Bensel Jr.
Circa: 1932.

Rooms: 7 rooms, 5 with PB. 1 suite. 1 conference room.
Beds: QDT.

This quiet country inn was built by the innkeeper's father and includes unique touches throughout, many created by innkeeper Howard Bensel himself, who became a master craftsman from his father's teachings and renovated the home extensively. Beautiful flowers and plants adorn both the lush grounds and the interior of the home. Everything is comfortable and cozy at this charming B&B, a relaxing contrast to the glitz of nearby Atlantic City.

Breakfast and evening snack included in rates. Types of meals: continental breakfast, continental-plus breakfast and early coffee/tea. Air conditioning and ceiling fan in room. VCR on premises. Small meetings, family reunions and seminars hosted. Amusement parks, antiques, fishing, parks, shopping, sporting events, theater and watersports nearby.

"We felt more like relatives than total strangers. By far the most clean inn that I have seen — spotless!"

Avon By The Sea F6

Atlantic View Inn

20 Woodland Ave
Avon By The Sea, NJ
07717-1435
(908)774-8505
Fax:(908)775-3206

Rates: $80-160.
Payment: MC VISA AX TC.
Innkeeper(s): Cathy & Bill Dey.
Circa: 1900.

Rooms: 13 rooms, 11 with PB, 2 with FP. 3 suites.
Beds: KQ DT.

NJ

This inn does, indeed, offer splendid ocean views. In fact, guests often are treated to their morning meal on the open porch, which overlooks the sea. The turn-of-the-century home includes many Victorian features, including high ceilings and delicate, carved mantels. Guest quarters are decorated in a romantic, English country style. Two rooms offer a fireplace and some boast ocean views. The inn often serves as a romantic site for honeymooners and intimate weddings.

Breakfast and afternoon tea included in rates. Types of meals: full breakfast, gourmet breakfast and early coffee/tea. Air conditioning and ceiling fan in room. Cable TV, fax, swimming and library on premises. Weddings, small meetings, family reunions and seminars hosted. Amusement parks, antiques, fishing, parks, shopping, theater and watersports nearby. TAC10.

"Your place is quaint and beautiful. The food is delicious."

Beach Haven H5

Green Gables Inn, Restaurant & Tea Room

212 Centre St
Beach Haven, NJ 08008
(609)492-3553 (800)492-0492
Fax:(609)492-2507

Rates: $85-135.
Payment: MC VISA AX DC TC.
Innkeeper(s): Rita & Aldolfo De Martino.
Circa: 1880.

Rooms: 6 rooms, 2 with PB.
Beds: D.

This Queen Anne Victorian located in the Beach Haven Historic District is in the National Register. Decorated in an elegant Victorian style, the inn's dining room provides romantic candlelight dinners rated "four-star" by many. (If you plan to dine here, be sure and make reservations at the same time you reserve your room.) Among some guest favorites are enjoying the inn's flower gardens from front porch rockers, strolling on the beach a block and a half away, and walking to shops, concerts in the park and nearby clubs. New Broadway plays may be seen at the summer stock theater, Surflight, just around the corner.

Breakfast included in rates. Types of meals: continental-plus breakfast and early coffee/tea. Afternoon tea, picnic lunch, lunch, gourmet lunch and catering service available. Ceiling fan in room. Handicap access. Weddings, small meetings, family reunions and seminars hosted. Italian and French spoken. Amusement parks, antiques, fishing, parks, shopping, sporting events, theater and watersports nearby.

Cape May *L3*

The Abbey Bed & Breakfast

34 Gurney St at Columbia Ave
Cape May, NJ 08204
(609)884-4506
Fax:(609)884-2379

Rates: $90-275.
Payment: MC VISA DS PC TC.
Innkeeper(s): Jay & Marianne Schatz.
Circa: 1869.

Rooms: 14 rooms with PB. 2 suites. 2 conference rooms.
Beds: KQD.

This inn consists of two buildings, one a Gothic Revival villa with a 60-foot tower, Gothic arched windows and shaded verandas. Furnishings include floor-to-ceiling mirrors, ornate gas chandeliers, marble-topped dressers and beds of carved walnut, wrought iron and brass. The cottage adjacent to the villa is a Second Empire-style home with a mansard roof. A full breakfast is served in the dining room in spring and fall and on the veranda in the summer. Late afternoon refreshments and tea are served each day at 5 p.m. The beautiful inn is featured in the town's Grand Christmas Tour.

Breakfast and afternoon tea included in rates. Types of meals: full breakfast and early coffee/tea. Weddings, small meetings and seminars hosted. Antiques, fishing, parks, shopping, theater and watersports nearby.

Location: In the heart of Cape May's historic district.

Publicity: *Richmond Times-Dispatch, New York Times, Glamour, Philadelphia Inquirer, National Geographic Traveler.*

"Staying with you folks really makes the difference between a 'nice' vacation and a great one!"

Alexander's Inn

653 Washington St
Cape May, NJ 08204-2324
(609)884-2555
Fax:(609)884-8883

Rates: $90-160.
Payment: MC VISA AX DC CB DS PC TC.
Innkeeper(s): Larry & Diane Muentz.
Circa: 1883.

Rooms: 7 rooms with PB. 1 conference room.
Beds: QD.

This mansard-roofed Victorian has been recently renovated and fitted with sprinkler system, private baths and central air conditioning, yet the inn still maintains its elegant Victorian atmosphere. There are Oriental rugs, antiques and oil paintings in abundance. The gourmet dining room provides white-glove service with silver, crystal, linen and lace. Located on Washington Street are the trolley tours, horse-and-carriage rides, bicycle rentals, museums and shops. Saturday night guests at the inn are treated to a five-course Sunday brunch. During the rest of the week guests are pampered with a continental-plus breakfast and buffet-style afternoon tea service.

Breakfast and afternoon tea included in rates. Type of meal: continental-plus breakfast. Dinner and banquet service available. Air conditioning and ceiling fan in room. Fax and copier on premises. Weddings, small meetings, family reunions and seminars hosted. Antiques, fishing, shopping, theater and watersports nearby.

Barnard-Good House

238 Perry St
Cape May, NJ 08204-1447
(609)884-5381

Rates: $90-145.
Payment: MC VISA PC.
Innkeeper(s): Nan & Tom Hawkins.
Circa: 1865.

Rooms: 5 rooms with PB. 2 suites.
Beds: KQD.

The Barnard-Good House is a Second Empire Victorian with a mansard roof and original shingles. A wraparound veranda adds to the charm of this lavender, blue and tan cottage along with the original picket fence and a concrete-formed flower garden. The inn was selected by New Jersey Magazine as the No. 1 spot for breakfast in New Jersey, and breakfasts are special, a four-course, gourmet feast.

Breakfast included in rates. Types of meals: full breakfast and gourmet breakfast. Air conditioning and ceiling fan in room. Antiques, fishing, parks, shopping, theater and watersports nearby.

Publicity: *New York Times, New Jersey Monthly, McCalls, Philadelphia Inquirer.*

"Even the cozy bed can't hold you down when the smell of Nan's breakfast makes its way upstairs."

Bedford Inn

805 Stockton Ave
Cape May, NJ 08204-2446
(609)884-4158
Fax:(609)884-0533

Rates: $95-195.
Payment: MC VISA AX PC.
Innkeeper(s): Cindy & Al Schmucker.
Circa: 1880.

Rooms: 11 rooms, 8 with PB, 1 with FP. 3 suites.
Beds: QDT.

The Bedford, decked in gingerbread trim with verandas on both of its two stories, has welcomed guests since its creation in the 19th century. Electrified gaslights, period wallcoverings and rich, Victorian furnishings create an air of nostalgia. The inn is close to many of Cape May's shops and restaurants, as well as the beach, which is just half a block away. Guests are pampered with breakfasts of quiche, gourmet egg dishes, French toast and freshly baked breads.

Breakfast and afternoon tea included in rates. Type of meal: gourmet breakfast. Air conditioning, ceiling fan and cable TV in room. Library on premises. Weddings hosted. Antiques, fishing, parks, theater and watersports nearby. TAC10.

Special Discounts: Mid-week September to June 15.

Captain Mey's B&B Inn

202 Ocean St
Cape May, NJ 08204-2322
(609)884-7793

Rates: $75-210.
Payment: MC VISA AX PC TC.
Innkeeper(s): George & Kathleen Blinn.
Circa: 1890.

Rooms: 8 rooms with PB. 1 suite.
Beds: QT.

Named after Dutch explorer Capt. Cornelius J. Mey, who named the area, the inn displays its Dutch heritage with table-top Persian rugs, Delft china and imported Dutch lace curtains. The dining room features chestnut and oak Eastlake paneling and a fireplace. The charming exterior is painted in shades of lavender and cream. A hearty breakfast is served by candlelight, or on the wraparound veranda in the summertime.

Breakfast and afternoon tea included in rates. Type of meal: full breakfast. Air conditioning and ceiling fan in room. Cable TV on premises. Small meetings and family reunions hosted. Amusement parks, antiques, fishing, parks, shopping, theater and watersports nearby. TAC10.

Publicity: *Atlantic City, Americana, Country Living, New Jersey Monthly.*

"The innkeepers pamper you so much you wish you could stay forever."

The Carroll Villa B&B

19 Jackson St
Cape May, NJ 08204-1417
(609)884-9619
Fax:(609)884-0264

Rates: $75-160.
Payment: MC VISA PC.
Innkeeper(s): Mark Kulkowitz & Pamela Ann Huber.
Circa: 1882.

Rooms: 22 rooms with PB. 1 conference room.
Beds: QD.

This Victorian hotel is located one-half block from the ocean on the oldest street in the historic district of Cape May. Breakfast at the Villa is a memorable event, featuring dishes acclaimed by the New York Times and Frommer's. Homemade fruit breads, Italian omelets and Crab Eggs Benedict are a few specialties. Meals are served in the Mad Batter Restaurant on a European veranda, a secluded garden terrace or in the skylit Victorian dining room. The decor of this inn is decidedly Victorian with period antiques and wallpapers.

Breakfast included in rates. Type of meal: early coffee/tea. Dinner, lunch, banquet service, catering service and catered breakfast available. Air conditioning and ceiling fan in room. Cable TV, VCR, fax, copier and computer on premises. Weddings, small meetings, family reunions and seminars hosted. Amusement parks, antiques, fishing, parks, shopping and theater nearby. TAC10.

Location: One-half block from the ocean.

Publicity: *Atlantic City Press, Asbury Press, Frommer's, New York Times, Washington Post.*

Special Discounts: 10% AAA Sunday-Thursday off season.

"Mr. Kulkowitz is a superb host. He strives to accommodate the diverse needs of guests."

The Chalfonte

301 Howard St, PO Box 475
Cape May, NJ 08204-2430
(609)884-8409
Fax:(609)884-4588

Rates: $58-170. MAP.
Payment: MC VISA.
Innkeeper(s): Anne LeDuc & Judy Bartella.
Circa: 1876.

Rooms: 108 rooms, 11 with PB. 2 cottages. 1 conference room.
Beds: KQDT.

This 108-room hotel has a rambling veranda. Rooms are simple and the cooking is Southern. Children of all ages are welcome and there is a children's dining room, library and special children's programs. Much of the hotel's restoration and preservation is accomplished by dedicated volunteers who have adopted the hotel as their own. Painting workshops, Elderhostel educational programs and children's playshops are popular.

Breakfast and dinner included in rates. Banquet service and catering service available. MAP. Ceiling fan in room. Cable TV, VCR, fax, library and child care on premises. Handicap access. Weddings, small meetings, family reunions and seminars hosted. Amusement parks, antiques, fishing, shopping, theater and watersports nearby. TAC10.

Location: Centrally located in the historic district, three blocks from beaches.

Publicity: *Travel & Leisure, Philadelphia Inquirer, New York Times, Country Inns, Richmond Times, Mid-Atlantic Country, Star and Wave, Virginian Pilot & Ledger-Star.*

Special Discounts: Group packages available.

"The well-loved building, enthusiastic innkeepers, great food and friendly atmosphere made the weekend a success."

Dormer House

800 Columbia Ave
Cape May, NJ 08204-2310
(609)884-7446 (800)884-5052

Rates: $80-180.
Payment: MC VISA AX PC TC.
Innkeeper(s): Lucille & Dennis Doherty.
Circa: 1899.

Rooms: 10 rooms with PB, 1 with FP. 1 suite. 2 cottages.
Beds: QDT.

This Colonial Revival estate is three blocks from the ocean and the historic walking mall. It was built by marble-dealer John Jacoby and retains much of the original marble and furniture. Several years ago the inn was converted into guest suites with kitchens.

Breakfast and afternoon tea included in rates. Types of meals: full breakfast and early coffee/tea. Air conditioning, ceiling fan and cable TV in room. Bicycles on premises. Weddings and family reunions hosted. Amusement parks, antiques, fishing, parks, shopping, theater and watersports nearby.

Location: Corner of Franklin & Columbia in the historic district.

Publicity: *Cape May Star & Wave.*

"Our 7th year here. We love it."

Duke of Windsor Inn

817 Washington St
Cape May, NJ 08204-1651
(609)884-1355 (800)826-8973

Rates: $70-185.
Payment: MC VISA PC TC.
Innkeeper(s): Bruce & Fran Prichard.
Circa: 1896.

Rooms: 10 rooms, 8 with PB.
Beds: QDT.

This Queen Anne Victorian was built by Delaware River boat pilot Harry Hazelhurst and his wife Florence. They were both six feet tall, so the house was built with large open rooms and doorways, and extra-wide stairs. The inn has a carved, natural oak open staircase with stained-glass windows at top and bottom. Five antique chandeliers grace the dining room. Beach tags and parking on premises.

Breakfast and afternoon tea included in rates. Types of meals: full breakfast and early coffee/tea. Air conditioning and ceiling fan in room. Antiques, fishing, parks, shopping, theater and watersports nearby.

Publicity: *Philadelphia Inquirer, Innsider, Mainline Magazine.*

"Tom and I loved staying in your home! We certainly appreciate all the hard work you put into renovating the house."

Gingerbread House

28 Gurney St
Cape May, NJ 08204
(609)884-0211

Rates: $65-190.
Payment: MC VISA PC TC.
Innkeeper(s): Fred & Joan Echevarria.
Circa: 1869.

Rooms: 6 rooms, 2 with PB. 1 suite.
Beds: QD.

The Gingerbread is one of eight original Stockton Row Cottages, summer retreats built for families from Philadelphia and Virginia. It is a half-block from the ocean and breezes waft over the wicker-filled porch. The inn is listed in the National Register and is decorated with period antiques and a fine collection of paintings.

Breakfast and afternoon tea included in rates. Type of meal: full breakfast. Ceiling fan in room. Small meetings and family reunions hosted. Antiques, fishing, parks, shopping, theater and watersports nearby.

Location: Historic District, one-half block from the beach.

Publicity: *Philadelphia Inquirer, New Jersey Monthly, Atlantic City Press Newspaper.*

Special Discounts: Weekly stays - 10% discount.

"The elegance, charm and authenticity of historic Cape May, but more than that, it appeals to us as `home'."

NJ

The Henry Sawyer Inn

722 Columbia Ave
Cape May, NJ 08204-2332
(609)884-5667 (800)449-5667

Rates: $80-160.
Payment: PC TC.
Innkeeper(s): Mary & Barbara Morris.
Circa: 1877.

Rooms: 5 rooms, 3 with PB, 1 with FP. 2 suites. 1 conference room.
Beds: KQT.

This fully restored three-story white Victorian home boasts a gingerbread embellished veranda, burgundy shutters and green trim. Inside, the parlor features Victorian antiques, a marble fireplace, polished wood floors, an Oriental rug, formal wallcoverings, a crystal chandelier and fresh flowers. Guest rooms have been decorated with careful attention to a romantic and fresh Victorian theme, as well. Ask for the Mary Sawyer room.

Breakfast and afternoon tea included in rates. Types of meals: full breakfast, gourmet breakfast and early coffee/tea. Air conditioning, ceiling fan, cable TV and VCR in room. Small meetings and family reunions hosted. Antiques, fishing, parks, shopping, theater and watersports nearby. TAC10.

Humphrey Hughes House

29 Ocean St
Cape May, NJ 08204-2411
(609)884-4428 (800)582-3634

Rates: $85-215.
Payment: MC VISA PC.
Innkeeper(s): Lorraine & Terry Schmidt.
Circa: 1903.

Rooms: 7 rooms with PB. 4 suites.
Beds: KQ.

Stained-glass windows mark each landing of the staircase, and intricately carved American chestnut columns add to the atmosphere in this 30-room mansion. The land was purchased by the Captain Humphrey Hughes family in the early 1700s and remained in the family until 1980. Dr. Harold Hughes' majestic grandfather clock remains as one of many late-Victorian antiques.

Breakfast and afternoon tea included in rates. Air conditioning and ceiling fan in room. Handicap access. Antiques, shopping, theater and watersports nearby.

Publicity: *New York Times.*

"Thoroughly enjoyed our stay."

John Wesley Inn

30 Gurney St
Cape May, NJ 08204
(609)884-1012

Rates: $75-165.
Payment: PC TC.
Innkeeper(s): John & Rita Tice.
Circa: 1869.

Rooms: 6 rooms, 4 with PB. 2 cottages. 1 conference room.
Beds: QD.

The innkeepers of this graciously restored Carpenter Gothic home have won awards for their captivating exterior Christmas decorations, and holidays at the inn are a seasonal delight. The interior decor preserves the Victorian Era so treasured in this seaside village. Antiques are set in rooms decorated with bright, patterned wallpapers and windows decked in lace. The innkeepers also offer a restored carriage house, featuring the same period decor, but the modern amenity of a stocked kitchen.

Breakfast included in rates. Type of meal: continental-plus breakfast. Air conditioning and ceiling fan in room. Weddings, small meetings, family reunions and seminars hosted. Amusement parks, antiques, fishing, parks, shopping, theater and watersports nearby.

The King's Cottage

9 Perry St
Cape May, NJ 08204-1460
(609)884-0415

Rates: $95-225.
Payment: MC VISA PC.
Innkeeper(s): Tony & Pat Marino.
Circa: 1878.

Rooms: 9 rooms with PB.
Beds: QDT.

Enjoy the beautiful ocean views as you relax on antique wicker on the wrap-around verandas at this architectural gem, designed by Frank Furness for a wealthy New York couple. The railings boast ceramic tiles that were part of a Japanese exhibition from the Philadelphia Centennial of 1876, and a measured drawing is recorded in the Library of Congress. Many of the guest rooms afford ocean views and all feature unique period decor and antiques. Breakfasts are served in the formal dining room on tables set with china, crystal and silver. Afternoon tea is served on the veranda or in the formal garden.

Breakfast and afternoon tea included in rates. Types of meals: full breakfast and early coffee/tea. Air conditioning and ceiling fan in room. Cable TV, VCR and library on premises. Weddings, small meetings, family reunions and seminars hosted. Amusement parks, antiques, fishing, parks, shopping, theater and watersports nearby.

"Thanks so much again for your incredible hospitality, scrumptious food and impeccable lodging, the experience is without sufficient words! Hope to see you again soon."

Mainstay Inn

635 Columbia Ave
Cape May, NJ 08204-2305
(609)884-8690

Rates: $95-245.
Payment: PC TC.
Innkeeper(s): Tom & Sue Carroll.
Circa: 1872.

Rooms: 16 rooms with PB, 4 with FP. 7 suites.
Beds: KQDT.

This was once the elegant and exclusive Jackson's Clubhouse popular with gamblers. Many of the guest rooms and the grand parlor look much as they did in the 1870s. Fourteen-foot-high ceilings, elaborate chandeliers, a sweeping veranda and a cupola add to the atmosphere. Tom and Sue Carroll received the annual American Historic Inns award in 1988 for their preservation efforts, and have been making unforgettable memories for guests for 25 years. A writer for Conde Nast Traveler once wrote, "architecturally, no inn, anywhere, quite matches the Mainstay."

Breakfast and afternoon tea included in rates. Types of meals: continental breakfast, continental-plus breakfast, full breakfast, gourmet breakfast and early coffee/tea. Catered breakfast available. Air conditioning, ceiling fan, cable TV and VCR in room. Library on premises. Handicap access. Small meetings and seminars hosted. Amusement parks, antiques, fishing, parks, shopping, sporting events, theater and watersports nearby.

Location: Cape May National Landmark District.

Publicity: *Washington Post, Good Housekeeping, New York Times, Conde Nast Traveler, Smithsonian, Americana, Travel & Leisure, National Geographic Traveler.*

"By far the most lavishly and faithfully restored guesthouse..run by two arch-preservationists,"—Travel & Leisure.

The Inn on Ocean

25 Ocean St
Cape May, NJ 08204-2411
(609)884-7070 (800)304-4477
Fax:(609)884-1384

Rates: $99-295.
Payment: MC VISA AX DC CB DS PC TC.
Innkeeper(s): Jack & Katha Davis.
Circa: 1880.

Rooms: 4 rooms with PB. 1 suite.
Beds: KQ.

NJ

Pansies and petunias blossom in front of this Second Empire Victorian and accentuate the green, white and yellow color scheme and strawberry pink roof. Inside, a light Victorian decor creates a bright and airy, yet elegant atmosphere. The inn boasts the only Victorian billiard room in town.

Breakfast and afternoon tea included in rates. Types of meals: full breakfast and early coffee/tea. Air conditioning, ceiling fan and cable TV in room. Small meetings and seminars hosted. Antiques, fishing, parks, shopping, theater and watersports nearby. TAC10.

Publicity: *Delta Airlines In-Flight Magazine, Washington Post Sunday Magazine.*

"The food was fabulous and served with a delicate flair. We enjoyed the family warmth and Victorian elegance."

Perry Street Inn B&B & Motel

29 Perry St
Cape May, NJ 08204-1460
(609)884-4590 (800)297-3779

Rates: $55-145.
Payment: MC VISA AX DS TC.
Innkeeper(s): John & Cynthia Curtis.
Circa: 1902.

Rooms: 20 rooms with PB. 10 suites. 2 conference rooms.
Beds: KDT.

The Perry Street Inn was first home to a large, turn-of-the-century Victorian family. The home was designed not in the town's predominant Victorian style, but as a comfortable family home instead. Some rooms include air conditioning. Guests also will appreciate the free, on-site parking. A buffet breakfast is served, beginning with homemade breads and coffee. Guests enjoy the meal either in the dining room, with its stained-glass windows, or on the porch, which offers an ocean view. The innkeepers offer special packages, including a murder mystery weekend and ecology tours. The inn, located in a historic district, is within easy walking distance of shops, restaurants and the beach, all less than a block away. Lighthouses, museums, tennis, Atlantic City also are nearby. The innkeepers also offer accommodations at the Perry Street Inn Motel, which include air-conditioned efficiency suites that can accommodate up to six people.

Breakfast included in rates. Types of meals: full breakfast and early coffee/tea. Afternoon tea and picnic lunch available. Air conditioning and ceiling fan in room. Cable TV on premises. Small meetings, family reunions and seminars hosted. Amusement parks, antiques, parks and theater nearby. TAC10.

Special Discounts: Early reservations; 65 years or old; five-day midweek stay.

Poor Richard's Inn

17 Jackson St
Cape May, NJ 08204-1417
(609)884-3536

Rates: $59-135. EP.
Payment: MC VISA.
Innkeeper(s): Richard Samuelson.
Circa: 1882.

Rooms: 9 rooms, 8 with PB. 2 suites.
Beds: QDT.

The unusual design of this Second-Empire house has been accentuated with five colors of paint. Arched gingerbread porches tie together the distinctive bays of the house's facade. The combination of exterior friezes, ballustrades and fretwork has earned the inn an individual listing in the National Register. Some rooms sport an eclectic country Victorian decor with patchwork quilts and pine furniture, while others tend toward a more traditional turn-of-the-century ambiance. A few apartment suites are available.

Breakfast included in rates. Types of meals: continental-plus breakfast and early coffee/tea. EP. Air conditioning and cable TV in room. Copier on premises. Small meetings and family reunions hosted. Amusement parks, antiques, fishing, parks, theater and watersports nearby.

Publicity: *Washington Post, New York Times, National Geographic Traveler, New Jersey.*

Special Discounts: Sept. 15-May 15, Monday-Thursday: stay one night full price, get one night free.

"Hold our spot on the porch. We'll be back before you know it."

The Queen Victoria

102 Ocean St
Cape May, NJ 08204-2320
(609)884-8702

Rates: $90-260. EP.
Payment: PC.
Innkeeper(s): Joan & Dane Wells.
Circa: 1881.

Rooms: 23 rooms with PB, 2 with FP. 7 suites. 2 cottages.
Beds: QD.

Christmas is a special festival at these beautifully restored Victorians. Special tours, Charles Dickens' feasts and costumed carolers crowd the calendar. The rest of the year, well-stocked libraries, and long porches lined with antique rocking chairs provide for more sedate entertainment. "Victorian Homes" featured 23 color photographs of The Queen Victoria. Amenities include afternoon tea and mixers, a fleet of bicycles, and evening turndown service. The innkeepers also offer complimentary beach tags and towels for their summer guests. Suites feature a whirlpool tub, fireplace or private porch. Guest rooms are spread among three, adjacent Victorian homes, all beautifully appointed in Victorian country style.

Breakfast and afternoon tea included in rates. Types of meals: full breakfast and early coffee/tea. Room service available. EP. Air conditioning, turn-down service and ceiling fan in room. Cable TV, VCR, bicycles, library and child care on premises. Handicap access. Weddings, small meetings, family reunions and seminars hosted. French spoken. Amusement parks, antiques, fishing, parks, shopping, theater and watersports nearby.

Location: In the heart of the historic district, one block from the beach.

Publicity: *Discerning Traveler, New York, Cover Girl, Washington Post, Victorian.*

Special Discounts: $25 per night off for summer stays of 4 or more nights.

"Especially impressed by the relaxed atmosphere and the excellent housekeeping."

The Queen's Hotel

601 Columbia Ave
Cape May, NJ 08204-2305
(609)884-1613

Rates: $60-240.
Payment: PC.
Innkeeper(s): Don Pettifer.
Circa: 1876.

Rooms: 9 rooms with PB. 2 suites.
Beds: QD.

This charming Victorian hotel is located just a block from the beach in the center of Cape May's historic district. Period decor graces the luxurious guest rooms. The historic hotel is full of history. Originally, the building was used for commercial purposes, and a large, second-story room once served as a gambling casino with rumors of ghostly visitors. The feeling is distinctly historic, but one suite does include a modern and romantic double whirlpool tub. Other amenities include hair dryers, coffemakers and mini refrigerators. As this is a hotel, meals are not included in the rates; however, a multitude of restaurants and cafes are within walking distance.

Air conditioning, ceiling fan and cable TV in room. Bicycles on premises. Weddings, small meetings and family reunions hosted. Amusement parks, antiques, fishing, parks, theater and watersports nearby.

Special Discounts: Discounted weekday rates fall, winter and spring. $25 per night off for summer stays of four or more nights.

Sea Holly B&B Inn

815 Stockton Ave
Cape May, NJ 08204-2446
(609)884-6294
Fax:(609)884-5157

Rates: $80-180.
Payment: MC VISA AX TC.
Innkeeper(s): Christy Lacey-Igoe.
Circa: 1875.

Rooms: 8 rooms with PB. 2 suites.
Beds: KQ.

The home-baked cuisine at this charming three-story Gothic cottage is an absolute delight. Innkeeper Christy Igoe began her love for baking in childhood and at 12, she created her own chocolate chip cookie recipe and now has her own cookbook. Her goodies are served at breakfast and in the afternoons with tea and sherry. The beautiful home is decorated with authentic Renaissance Revival and Eastlake antique pieces. Some rooms boast ocean views. The inn is a wonderful place for a special occasion, and honeymooners or those celebrating an anniversary receive complimentary champagne. In addition to the romantic amenities, the innkeeper provides practical extras such as hair dryers, irons and ironing boards in each room or suite.

circa 1875

Breakfast and afternoon tea included in rates. Types of meals: full breakfast and early coffee/tea. Air conditioning and ceiling fan in room. Fax on premises. Weddings and family reunions hosted. Amusement parks, antiques, fishing, parks, shopping, theater and watersports nearby.

Publicity: *Mid-Atlantic Newsletter, New Jersey Monthly.*

"You have shown us what a real B&B is supposed to be like."

NJ

Seventh Sister Guesthouse

10 Jackson St
Cape May, NJ 08204-1418
(609)884-2280
Fax:(609)898-9899

Rates: $75-135. EP.
Payment: MC VISA AX PC TC.
Innkeeper(s): Bob & JoAnne Myers.
Circa: 1888.

Rooms: 6 rooms, 1 with PB.
Beds: D.

Most of the Seventh Sister's guest rooms have ocean views. The inn is listed in the National Register. The artist/architect innkeepers have original art collections on display. Wicker and original antique furnishings fill the rooms. The home's three floors are joined by a spectacular central circular staircase. The center of town is a one-block walk, and the beach is just 100 feet away.

EP. Fax and library on premises. Small meetings hosted. Amusement parks, antiques, fishing, parks, shopping, theater and watersports nearby.

Publicity: *New York Times, 1001 Decorating Ideas.*

Special Discounts: 5% off for one week. Students of art & architecture always discounted in our smaller room.

Stetson B&B Inn

725 Kearney Ave
Cape May, NJ 08204-2450
(609)884-1724

Rates: $80-135.
Payment: MC VISA AX PC TC.
Innkeeper(s): Carol & Lou Elwell.
Circa: 1915.

Rooms: 7 rooms with PB.
Beds: QD.

This bed & breakfast features country English and Victorian decor with stenciling and hardwood floors. There are two porches and a sitting room with fireplace available to guests. Breakfast is served in a sunny dining room. Located one block from the beach, the inn has a dressing room and beach shower for you to use on your last day when you wish to stay at the beach, past check-out time.

Breakfast included in rates. Types of meals: full breakfast and early coffee/tea. Air conditioning in room. Cable TV and VCR on premises. Amusement parks, antiques, fishing, parks, shopping, theater and watersports nearby. TAC10.

Special Discounts: Midweek discounts spring and fall.

White Dove Cottage

619 Hughes St
Cape May, NJ 08204-2317
(609)884-0613 (800)321-3683

Rates: $80-190.
Innkeeper(s): Frank & Sue Smith.
Circa: 1866.

Rooms: 4 rooms, 6 with PB, 2 with FP. 2 suites.
Beds: KQD.

The beautiful octagonal slate on the Mansard roof of this Second Empire house is just one of the inn's many handsome details. Bright sunny rooms are furnished in American and European antiques, period wallpapers, paintings, prints and handmade quilts. Breakfast is served to the soft music of an antique music box and boasts heirloom crystal, fine china and lace. Located on a quiet, gas-lit street, the inn is two blocks from the beach, restaurants and shops. Ask about mystery weekends and the inn's Honeymoon and Romantic Escape packages.

Breakfast and afternoon tea included in rates. Types of meals: full breakfast, gourmet breakfast and early coffee/tea. Antiques, fishing, shopping, theater and watersports nearby.

Location: Center of historic Cape May.

Windward House

24 Jackson St
Cape May, NJ 08204-1465
(609)884-3368
Fax:(609)884-1575

Rates: $85-176.
Payment: MC VISA PC TC.
Innkeeper(s): Owen & Sandy Miller.
Circa: 1905.

Rooms: 8 rooms with PB. 2 suites.
Beds: KQ.

All three stories of this blue Edwardian-style cottage contain antique-filled guest rooms. Beveled and stained glass cast rainbows of flickering light from the windows and French doors, while gleaming chestnut and oak paneling set off a collection of museum-quality antiques and collectibles. The Eastlake and Empire rooms offer a glimpse of the ocean. All rooms have ceiling fans, air-conditioning, TVs and mini refrigerators.

Breakfast and afternoon tea included in rates. Types of meals: gourmet breakfast and early coffee/tea. Air conditioning, ceiling fan and cable TV in room. Fax, bicycles and library on premises. Small meetings and family reunions hosted. Antiques, fishing, parks, shopping, theater and watersports nearby.

Location: Southern New Jersey shore region.

Publicity: *New Jersey Monthly, Delaware Today, Mid-Atlantic Country, Country Inns, Victorian Homes, Innsider, Mainline Magazine.*

"The loveliest and most authentically decorated of all the houses we visited."

Flemington

E3

The Cabbage Rose Inn

162 Main St
Flemington, NJ 08822-1616
(908)788-0247
E-mail: cabbageros@aol.com

Rates: $80-125.
Payment: MC VISA AX DS PC TC.
Innkeeper(s): Pam Venosa & Al Scott.
Circa: 1891.

Rooms: 5 rooms with PB, 1 with FP.
Beds: QD.

This pink and white Victorian mansion boasts a three-story turret with an open gingerbread porch on the tower's third floor. Oriental rugs, antiques and fabrics with large cabbage rose motifs are featured throughout. "Romance and Roses" is a package that offers a queen-size room, champagne, a box of Cabbage Rose Inn chocolates, long-stemmed red roses, and a four-course fireside dinner.

Breakfast included in rates. Types of meals: full breakfast and early coffee/tea. Room service available. Air conditioning and ceiling fan in room. Cable TV and fax on premises. Small meetings and family reunions hosted. Antiques, fishing, parks, shopping, cross-country skiing, theater and watersports nearby.

Location: Midway between New York and Philadelphia.

Publicity: *Innsider Magazine, New Jersey Monthly, New York Post.*

"Incredible hospitality. Made our stay in New Jersey wonderful."

Jerica Hill B&B Inn

96 Broad St
Flemington, NJ 08822-1604
(908)782-8234
Fax:(908)782-8234

Rates: $95-110.
Payment: MC VISA AX PC TC.
Innkeeper(s): Judith Studer-Hamilton.
Circa: 1901.

Rooms: 5 rooms with PB.
Beds: KQD.

This Queen Anne Victorian is decorated in a bright and airy decor with four-poster beds, bay windows, ceiling fans and flowers. Breakfast is served on a mahogany breakfront. The innkeeper has several romantic packages available to guests. Her "Country Winery Tour" package includes a wine tour, tastings and a wicker basket filled with a country picnic and wine tasting glasses.

Breakfast, afternoon tea and evening snack included in rates. Types of meals: continental-plus breakfast and early coffee/tea. Picnic lunch available. Air conditioning in room. Fax and copier on premises. Small meetings, family reunions and seminars hosted. Antiques, fishing, parks, shopping, downhill skiing, cross-country skiing, sporting events, theater and watersports nearby. TAC10.

Publicity: *Mid-Atlantic Country, New York Times, Country Inns.*

"If you've been searching for an inn that's homey and unpretentious - then I've found the place for you: Jerica Hill."

NJ

Glenwood

A5

Apple Valley Inn B&B and Antiques

Corner Rts 517 & 565,
PO Box 302
Glenwood, NJ 07418-0302
(201)764-3735
Fax:(201)764-1050

Rates: $70-90.
Payment: MC VISA PC TC.
Innkeeper(s): Mitzi & John Durham.
Circa: 1804.

Rooms: 7 rooms, 2 with PB.
Beds: DT.

This three-story Colonial farmhouse is set on three acres with its own apple orchard (more than 40 trees) and in-ground pool. A brook running next to the house is a great trout-fishing spot. The innkeeper is an avid antique collector and guest rooms (named after varieties of apples) include American antiques. Try the

Red Delicious room. Across the street is a popular pick-your-own-fruit farm. Check with the innkeeper to find when the strawberries, peaches, cherries and apples are ripe so you can gather your favorites. Action Park, ski slopes, and the Appalachian Trail are nearby.

Breakfast and afternoon tea included in rates. Types of meals: full breakfast and early coffee/tea. Picnic lunch available. Air conditioning and ceiling fan in room. Cable TV, VCR, fax, copier, swimming, bicycles and library on premises. Weddings, small meetings, family reunions and seminars hosted. Amusement parks, antiques, fishing, parks, shopping, downhill skiing, cross-country skiing, sporting events and theater nearby.

Publicity: *Cleveland Plain Dealer, Appalachian Trail News, New Jersey Herald, Country Living.*

Special Discounts: Multi-night discount.

Hope C3

The Inn at Millrace Pond

PO Box 359, Rt 59 at Millbrook Rd
Hope, NJ 07844-0359
(908)459-4884 (800)786-4673
Fax:(908)459-5276

Rates: $85-165.
Payment: MC VISA AX DC TC.
Innkeeper(s): Cordie & Charles Puttkammer.
Circa: 1769.

Rooms: 17 rooms with PB, 1 with FP. 1 suite. 1 conference room.
Beds: Q.

The former grist mill buildings house an authentically restored Colonial inn, set in the rolling hills of Northwestern New Jersey. Decorated in the Colonial period, many of the rooms feature original wide-board floors, antiques and Oriental rugs. Rooms in the limestone Grist Mill, a building listed in the National Register of Historic Places, boast hand-crafted American primitive reproductions and braided rugs. The inn's restaurant features the original millrace room, complete with running water. A former wheel chamber has a staircase that leads to the Tavern Room with its own walk-in fireplace and grain chute.

Breakfast included in rates. Type of meal: continental-plus breakfast. Evening snack and banquet service available. Air conditioning and cable TV in room. Fax, copier and bicycles on premises. Handicap access. 23 acres. Weddings, small meetings, family reunions and seminars hosted. Amusement parks, antiques, fishing, parks, shopping and cross-country skiing nearby.

"The most interesting thing of all is the way these buildings have been restored."

Lambertville E3

Chimney Hill B&B

207 Goat Hill Rd
Lambertville, NJ 08530
(609)397-1516
Fax:(609)397-9353

Rates: $75-175.
Payment: MC VISA AX PC.
Innkeeper(s): Terry Ann & Richard Anderson.
Circa: 1820.

Rooms: 8 rooms with PB, 5 with FP. 1 conference room.
Beds: KQD.

Chimney Hill is a grand display of stonework, designed with both Federal and Greek Revival-style architecture. The inn's stone sunroom is particularly appealing, with its stone walls, fireplaces and windows looking out to the lush, eight-acre grounds. Five of the guest rooms include a fireplace, and some have canopy beds. The innkeepers offer adventure, romance and special interest packages for their guests. There's plenty of seasonal activities nearby, from kayaking to skiing.

Breakfast and evening snack included in rates. Types of meals: continental-plus breakfast, full breakfast, gourmet breakfast and early coffee/tea. Air conditioning in room. VCR, fax and copier on premises. Weddings, small meetings, family reunions and seminars hosted. Antiques, fishing, parks, shopping, downhill skiing, cross-country skiing, sporting events, theater and watersports nearby.

"We would be hard pressed to find a more perfect setting to begin our married life together."

Newton

B4

The Wooden Duck B&B

140 Goodale Rd,
Andover Township
Newton, NJ 07860-2788
(201)300-0395
Fax:(201)300-0141

Rates: $90-110.
Payment: MC VISA AX DS PC TC.
Innkeeper(s): Bob & Barbara Hadden.
Circa: 1978.

Rooms: 5 rooms with PB.
Beds: Q.

Guests enjoy exploring the 17 acres of wooded grounds and fields that surround this country farmhouse. The innkeepers keep their home filled with things to do. Guests can watch movies, play games or enjoy a good book as they snuggle up next to the huge, double hearth fireplace in the inn's game room. During warm months, guest can use the outdoor pool. Rooms are comfortable and cozy, decorated in country style. The innkeepers display their unique collectibles throughout the home.

Breakfast and evening snack included in rates. Type of meal: full breakfast. Air conditioning, cable TV and VCR in room. Fax, copier, swimming and library on premises. 18 acres. Small meetings, family reunions and seminars hosted. Amusement parks, antiques, fishing, parks, shopping, downhill skiing, cross-country skiing, sporting events, theater and watersports nearby.

Ocean City

J4

Northwood Inn B&B

401 Wesley Ave
Ocean City, NJ 08226-3961
(609)399-6071
Fax:(609)398-5553

Rates: $80-150.
Payment: MC VISA AX PC.
Innkeeper(s): Marj & John Loeper.
Circa: 1894.

Rooms: 8 rooms with PB. 1 suite.
Beds: QT.

This gracious three-story Queen Anne Victorian with Colonial Victorian touches has been restored recently by the innkeeper, who is a wooden boat builder and custom-home builder. There are gleaming plank floors, a sweeping staircase and library. The Tower Room in the turret is a favorite as is the Lotus Blossom Suite with a separate sitting room. The inn is within walking distance of the beach and boardwalk. The innkeepers offer bicycles and beach tags to their guests.

Types of meals: continental-plus breakfast and full breakfast. Air conditioning in room. Cable TV, VCR, fax and library on premises. Weddings and small meetings hosted. Amusement parks, antiques, fishing, parks, shopping, theater and watersports nearby.

Publicity: *Philadelphia Magazine.*

Special Discounts: Reserve one week one day free; midweek three nights deduct $10.00 per night.

"Our only regret was that we couldn't have visited longer! It was our 55th wedding anniversary and you helped to make it a very happy time for us."

NJ

Scarborough Inn

720 Ocean Ave
Ocean City, NJ 08226-3749
(609)399-1558 (800)258-1558
Fax:(609)399-4472

Rates: $85-149.
Payment: MC VISA AX DS PC TC.
Innkeeper(s): Gus & Carol Bruno.
Circa: 1895.

Rooms: 24 rooms with PB. 3 suites.
Beds: KQDT.

Painted in wedgewood, rose, and soft creams, the Scarborough Inn is a familiar Victorian landmark in this seaside resort. Family-owned and operated, the inn is filled with the innkeepers' artwork collection and an upright piano for informal singalongs. A continental breakfast is served in a cozy, plant-filled parlor or on the wraparound porch. The beach and boardwalk are a short stroll from the inn.

Breakfast and afternoon tea included in rates. Types of meals: continental-plus breakfast and early coffee/tea. Catering service available. Air conditioning and ceiling fan in room. Cable TV, VCR, fax and library on premises. Small meetings and family reunions hosted. Italian spoken. Amusement parks, antiques, fishing, parks, shopping, sporting events, theater and watersports nearby. TAC10.

Location: One-and-one-half blocks to beach and boardwalk.

Publicity: *Country Inns Bed & Breakfast, Pittsburgh Press.*

Special Discounts: 20% mid-week special, Sunday through Thursday.

"Your hospitality is truly unsurpassed..anywhere. A million thanks."

Serendipity B&B

712 E 9th St
Ocean City, NJ 08226-3554
(609)399-1554 (800)842-8544
Fax:(609)399-1527

Rates: $70-120.
Payment: MC VISA AX DS PC TC.
Innkeeper(s): Clara & Bill Plowfield.
Circa: 1912.

Rooms: 6 rooms, 2 with PB.
Beds: KQDT.

The beach and boardwalk are less than half a block from this renovated inn. Healthy full breakfasts are served, and the innkeepers offer dinners by reservation with a mix of interesting, vegetarian items. In the summer, breakfasts are served on a vine-shaded veranda. The guest rooms are decorated in pastels with wicker pieces.

Breakfast and evening snack included in rates. Type of meal: full breakfast. Dinner available. Air conditioning, ceiling fan and cable TV in room. Library on premises. Amusement parks, antiques, fishing, parks, shopping, theater and watersports nearby. TAC10.

Special Discounts: 10% military discount.

Ocean Grove F6

The Cordova

26 Webb Ave
Ocean Grove, NJ 07756
(908)774-3084 summer season
(212) 751 9577 winter season

Rates: $46-160.
Payment: PC.
Innkeeper(s): Doris A. Chernik.
Circa: 1885.

Rooms: 20 rooms, 5 with PB. 2 cottages.
Beds: KQDT.

This Victorian community was founded as a Methodist retreat. Ocean-bathing and cars were not allowed until a few years ago, so there are no souvenir shops along the white sandy beach and wooden boardwalk. The inn has hosted Presidents Wilson, Cleveland and Roosevelt who were also speakers at the Great Auditorium with its 7,000 seats. The kitchen, lounge, picnic and barbecue areas make this a popular place for family reunions. Two cottage apartments also are available.

Breakfast included in rates. Type of meal: continental-plus breakfast. TV, VCR, bicycles and library on premises. Antiques and fishing nearby. TAC10.

Publicity: *New Jersey, Asbury Park Press, St. Martin's Press, "O'New Jersey" by Robert Heide and John Gilman.*

Special Discounts: Weekday three nights for price of two; week stay seven nights for the price of five.

"Warm, helpful and inviting, homey and lived-in atmosphere."

Pemberton G4

Isaac Hilliard House B&B

31 Hanover St
(Towne Centre)
Pemberton, NJ 08068
(609)894-0756 (800)371-0756

Rates: $50-125.
Payment: MC VISA AX PC TC.
Innkeeper(s): Marian & Dan Michaels.
Circa: 1750.

Rooms: 4 rooms with PB, 1 with FP. 1 suite.
Beds: Q.

A wrought-iron fence sets off this two-story green and white Victorian. The inn is filled with antique bric-a-brac and collections such as plates and books. There's an antique bridal gown in one of the guest rooms. One suite includes a gas fireplace, sitting room and a bathroom with a garden tub. Walk two minutes to the canoe rental, then paddle along the Rancocas River. The Grist Mill Village Antiques is within walking distance, and several other antique shops and fine restaurants are close by.

Breakfast included in rates. Type of meal: full breakfast. Air conditioning, turn-down service, ceiling fan, cable TV and VCR in room. Swimming, bicycles and library on premises. Weddings and small meetings hosted. Amusement parks, antiques, fishing, parks, theater and watersports nearby.

Publicity: *New Jersey Travel Guide, New Jersey Monthly.*

Special Discounts: 10% military discount.

"Every little detail was made so kind and warm. For even a short time, we both felt as if we traveled abroad. Your home is kept gorgeous and so tasteful."

Salem I1

Brown's Historic Home B&B

41-43 Market St
Salem, NJ 08079
(609)935-8595
Fax:(609)935-6573

Rates: $55-100.
Payment: MC VISA AX DS TC.
Innkeeper(s): William & Margaret Brown.
Circa: 1738.

Rooms: 3 rooms, 2 with PB, 1 with FP.
Beds: DT.

Brown's Historic Home originally was built as a Colonial house. About 1845 the house was modernized to the Victorian Era. The inn is furnished with antiques and heirlooms, including a handmade chess set and quilt. The fireplaces are made of King of Prussia marble. The backyard garden features a lily pond, wildflowers and a waterfall.

Breakfast included in rates. Types of meals: full breakfast and early coffee/tea. Air conditioning, ceiling fan and cable TV in room. Fax on premises. Small meetings and family reunions hosted. Antiques, fishing, parks, shopping, theater and watersports nearby.

Pets Allowed: Kennel nearby.

Location: Fifteen minutes from Delaware Memorial Bridge.

Publicity: *Newsday, Mid-Atlantic Country, Early American Life, Today's Sunbeam.*

"Down-home-on-the-farm breakfasts with great hospitality."

NJ

Spring Lake F6

Ashling Cottage

106 Sussex Ave
Spring Lake, NJ 07762
(908)449-3553 (888)274-5464

Rates: $70-165.
Payment: PC TC.
Innkeeper(s): John Stewart.
Circa: 1877.

Rooms: 10 rooms, 8 with PB.
Beds: Q.

Surrounded by shady sycamores on a quiet residential street, this three-story Victorian residence features a mansard-and-gambrel roof with hooded gambrel dormers. One of the two porches has a square, pyramid-roofed pavilion which has been glass-enclosed and screened. Guests can watch the sun rise over the ocean one block away or set over Spring Lake. A full buffet breakfast can be enjoyed in the plant- and wicker-filled pavilion.

Breakfast and afternoon tea included in rates. Types of meals: full breakfast and early coffee/tea. Air conditioning and ceiling fan in room. Cable TV, VCR, bicycles and library on premises. Weddings, small meetings, family reunions and seminars hosted. Limited German spoken. Amusement parks, antiques, fishing, parks, shopping, sporting events, theater and watersports nearby.

Location: Six miles from exit 98.

Publicity: *New York Times, New Jersey Monthly, Town & Country, Country Living, New York, Harrods of London.*

Special Discounts: Special rates can be offered.

La Maison

404 Jersey Ave
Spring Lake, NJ 07762
(908)449-0969 (800)276-2088
Fax:(908)449-4860

Rates: $110-235.
Payment: MC VISA AX DC DS PC TC.
Innkeeper(s): Barbara Furdyna & Peter Oliver.
Circa: 1870.

Rooms: 5 rooms, 8 with PB. 2 suites. 1 cottage.
Beds: QT.

A French Victorian with a wide wraparound veranda, this historic inn is located four blocks from the water. The French influence is repeated in romantic furnishings such as French beds, Jacuzzis, French country and Louis Philippe pieces. At breakfast, Creme Brulee French toast is often served. A cottage is popular in summer for families with children.

Breakfast included in rates. Types of meals: gourmet breakfast and early coffee/tea. Air conditioning and cable TV in room. Fax and bicycles on premises. Weddings, small meetings, family reunions and seminars hosted. Limited French spoken. Antiques, fishing, parks, shopping, theater and watersports nearby. TAC10.

Pets Allowed: In small cottage only.

Victoria House

214 Monmouth Ave
Spring Lake, NJ 07762
(908)974-1882
Fax:(908)974-9702

Rates: $90-185.
Payment: MC VISA AX DS PC TC.
Innkeeper(s): Louise & Robert Goodall.
Circa: 1882.

Rooms: 9 rooms, 7 with PB, 1 with FP. 1 suite.
Beds: KQD.

Queen Victoria surely would have enjoyed a trip to this bed & breakfast, as well as to Spring Lake, a pleasant village on the Jersey Shore. Each of the guest rooms is individually decorated with pieces such as an antique Eastlake armoire and wicker or brass beds. Several bathrooms include clawfoot tubs. The beach is within walking distance, and the innkeepers provide beach passes for their guests. Shops and restaurants are nearby as well.

Breakfast included in rates. Types of meals: full breakfast and early coffee/tea. Air conditioning in room. Cable TV, fax and bicycles on premises. Small meetings and seminars hosted. Amusement parks, antiques, fishing, parks, shopping, sporting events, theater and watersports nearby. TAC10.

Special Discounts: Sweetheart weekend, winter get away specials, summer midweek specials.

"A very charming stay. We enjoyed your hospitality."

Stanhope C4

Whistling Swan Inn

110 Main St
Stanhope, NJ 07874-2632
(201)347-6369
Fax:(201)347-3391
E-mail: wswan@worldnet.att.net

Rates: $85-135.
Payment: MC VISA AX DS PC TC.
Innkeeper(s): Joe Mulay & Paula Williams.
Circa: 1905.

Rooms: 10 rooms with PB. 1 suite. 1 conference room.
Beds: Q.

This Queen Anne Victorian has a limestone wraparound veranda and a tall, steep-roofed turret. Family antiques fill the rooms and highlight the polished ornate woodwork, pocket doors and winding staircase. It is a little more than a mile from Waterloo Village and the International Trade Zone.

Breakfast included in rates. Type of meal: full breakfast. Air conditioning and ceiling fan in room. Cable TV, VCR, fax, copier and bicycles on premises. Seminars hosted. Antiques, fishing, parks, shopping, sporting events, theater and watersports nearby.

Location: East of the Pocono Mountains. Forty-five miles west of New York City in the scenic Skylands tourism region.

Publicity: *Sunday Herald, New York Times, New Jersey Monthly, Mid-Atlantic Country, Star Ledger, Daily Record, Philadelphia, Country, Chicago Sun Times.*

"Thank you for your outstanding hospitality. We had a delightful time while we were with you and will not hesitate to recommend the inn to our listening audience, friends and anyone else who will listen!" —Joel H. Klein, Travel Editor, WOAI AM.

Stockton

E3

Woolverton Inn

6 Woolverton Rd
Stockton, NJ 08559-2147
(609)397-0802 (888)AN-INN-4U
Fax:(609)397-4936

Rates: $100-180.
Payment: MC VISA AX.
Innkeeper(s): Michael & Elizabeth Palmer.
Circa: 1792.

Rooms: 10 rooms with PB, 2 with FP. 2 suites.
Beds: KQD.

This stone Colonial inn rests above the Delaware River and is surrounded by 10 bucolic acres, which include set-ups for croquet and horseshoes as well as resident sheep. Family antiques decorate guest rooms, and some have the added amenity of a fireplace or Jacuzzi tub. The front porch is lined with comfortable, wicker rockers. A full country breakfast of fresh fruits, juices, a basket of freshly baked breads and a daily entree is served each morning, and refreshments are served in the afternoons.

Breakfast and afternoon tea included in rates. Types of meals: full breakfast, gourmet breakfast and early coffee/tea. Catering service available. Air conditioning in room. Fax on premises. Handicap access. 10 acres. Weddings, small meetings, family reunions and seminars hosted. Antiques, fishing, parks, shopping, theater and watersports nearby.

Publicity: *New York Magazine, Colonial Homes.*

"Thank you for providing a perfect setting and relaxed atmosphere for our group. You're terrific."

Ventnor City

J5

Carisbrooke Inn

105 S Little Rock Ave
Ventnor City, NJ 08406
(609)822-6392
Fax:(609)822-9710

Rates: $65-205.
Payment: MC VISA PC.
Innkeeper(s): Lori Beckley.
Circa: 1918.

Rooms: 9 rooms, 7 with PB. 1 suite.
Beds: KQD.

The inn was named for a Ventnor City hotel, once the grand centerpiece of this seaside town. Fresh flowers and lacy curtains add a romantic touch to the guest rooms. The innkeeper offers a huge breakfast with a mix of healthy and decadent treats. Multi-grain pancakes, banana waffles, cheddar potato pie and a basil-tomato frittata are some of the main dishes accompanied by freshly baked muffins, bagels and fruit. There is a game room in the basement offering board games, a TV, VCR and books. The beach and boardwalk are within walking distance.

NJ

Breakfast and afternoon tea included in rates. Types of meals: full breakfast, gourmet breakfast and early coffee/tea. Picnic lunch and room service available. Air conditioning, ceiling fan and cable TV in room. VCR, fax and copier on premises. Weddings, small meetings and family reunions hosted. Amusement parks, antiques, fishing, parks, shopping, theater and watersports nearby. TAC10.

"You have a beautiful, elegant inn. My stay here was absolutely wonderful."

Woodbine

J4

Henry Ludlam Inn

1336 Route 47
Woodbine, NJ 08270-3608
(609)861-5847

Rates: $85-125.
Payment: MC VISA PC TC.
Innkeeper(s): Chuck & Pat DeArros.
Circa: 1804.

Rooms: 5 rooms with PB, 3 with FP.
Beds: QD.

This country inn borders picturesque Ludlam Lake. Canoeing, birding, biking and fishing are popular activities, and the innkeepers make sure you enjoy these at your peak by providing you with a full country breakfast. Some of the bedrooms have fireplaces, and all feature antique double and queen beds topped with handmade quilts.

Breakfast included in rates. Types of meals: full breakfast, gourmet breakfast and early coffee/tea. Air conditioning and ceiling fan in room. Library on premises. Small meetings hosted. Antiques, fishing, parks, shopping, cross-country skiing, theater and watersports nearby. TAC10.

Location: Cape May County.

Publicity: *Atlantic City Press, New Jersey Outdoors, National Geographic Traveler.*

"An unforgettable breakfast. Enjoy a piece of history!"

New Mexico

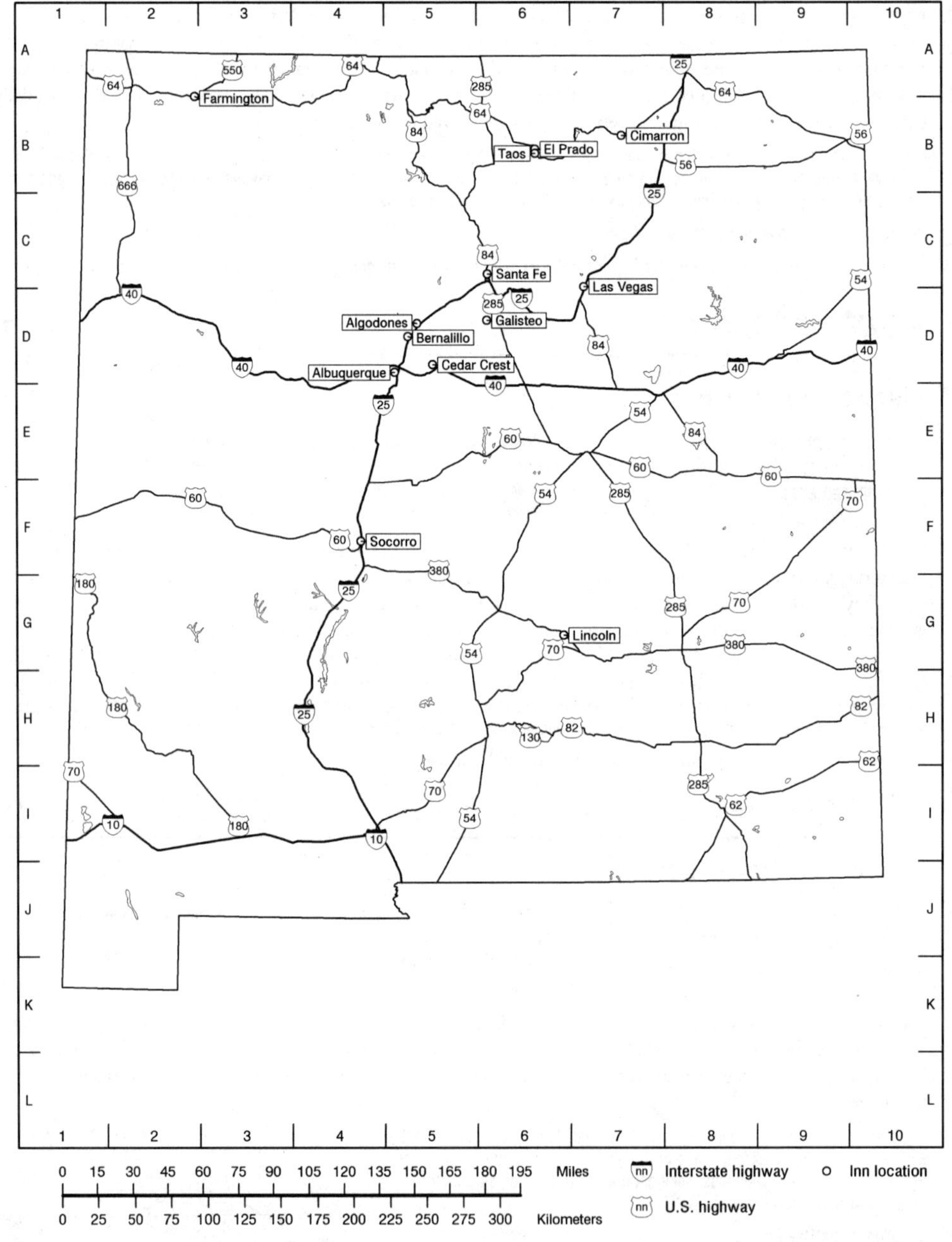

Farmington
Taos
El Prado
Cimarron
Santa Fe
Las Vegas
Galisteo
Algodones
Bernalillo
Albuquerque
Cedar Crest
Socorro
Lincoln
Miles
Kilometers
Interstate highway
U.S. highway
Inn location

Bottger Mansion B&B

110 San Felipe NW,
Old Town
Albuquerque, NM 87104
(505)243-3639
Fax:(505)243-3639

Rates: $79-109.
Payment: MC VISA AX PC TC.
Innkeeper(s): Patsy Garcia.
Circa: 1912.

Rooms: 7 rooms with PB. 1 suite.
Beds: KQT.

Just steps from the plaza in historic Old Town, this four-square Victorian mansion is a slight departure from the surrounding adobe architecture. The seven guest rooms feature brass, oak, cherry and mahogany four-poster beds. Evening wine and hors d'oeuvres are served. A soda fountain and coffee and tea bar are available at all times.

Breakfast, afternoon tea and evening snack included in rates. Types of meals: continental breakfast, continental-plus breakfast, full breakfast, gourmet breakfast and early coffee/tea. Catered breakfast available. Air conditioning and ceiling fan in room. Cable TV, fax and copier on premises. Weddings, small meetings and family reunions hosted. Spanish and English spoken. Amusement parks, antiques, fishing, parks, shopping, downhill skiing, cross-country skiing, sporting events, theater and watersports nearby. TAC10.

Location: In historic Old Town.

"Yours ranks with the best for ambiance and location."

Hacienda Antigua B&B

6708 Tierra Dr NW
Albuquerque, NM 87107
(505)345-5399 (800)201-2986

Rates: $95-125.
Payment: MC VISA AX DS PC TC.
Innkeeper(s): Ann Dunlap & Melinda Moffitt.
Circa: 1780.

Rooms: 5 rooms, 4 with PB, 5 with FP. 1 suite.
Beds: KQT.

In the more than 200 years since this Spanish Colonial-style hacienda was constructed, the current innkeepers are only the fourth owners. Once a stagecoach stop on the El Camino Real, it also served as a cantina and mercantile store. It was built by Don Pablo Yrisarri, who was sent by the King of Spain to search the area for gold. The home is elegant, yet maintains a rustic, Spanish charm with exposed beams, walls up to 30 inches thick, tile floors and kiva fireplaces. Along with a sitting room and kiva fireplace, the Don Pablo Suite includes a "ducking door" that leads onto the courtyard. Other rooms have clawfoot tubs, antique iron beds or a private patio. The cuisine is notable and one of the inn's recipes appeared in Culinary Trends magazine. Guests might sample a green chile souffle along with bread pudding and fresh fruit.

NM

Breakfast included in rates. Types of meals: full breakfast and early coffee/tea. Air conditioning and ceiling fan in room. Cable TV, VCR, fax, spa and swimming on premises. Family reunions and seminars hosted. Antiques, fishing, parks, shopping, downhill skiing, cross-country skiing, sporting events and theater nearby. TAC10.

Special Discounts: Four nights or more less $10 per night.

The W.J. Marsh House Victorian B&B

301 Edith Blvd SE
Albuquerque, NM 87102
(505)247-1001 (888)956-2774

Rates: $90-120.
Payment: MC VISA TC.
Innkeeper(s): Janice Lee Sperling, MD.
Circa: 1892.

Rooms: 6 rooms, 1 with FP. 1 cottage.
Beds: QDT.

This three-story brick Queen Anne mansion is located in the Huning Highland Historic District. Original redwood doors and trim, porcelain fixtures and an ornate hand-carved fireplace are highlighted by high Victorian decor. A friendly ghost is said to inhabit the house, occasionally opening drawers and rearranging the furniture. The inn is listed in the National and State Historic Registers.

Breakfast included in rates. Types of meals: full breakfast and gourmet breakfast. Picnic lunch available. Air conditioning in room. Library on premises. Weddings, small meetings, family reunions and seminars hosted. French and Spanish spoken. Amusement parks, antiques, fishing, parks, shopping, downhill skiing, cross-country skiing, sporting events, theater and watersports nearby. TAC10.

Location: In one of Albuquerque's four historic districts, Huning Highland.

Publicity: *Albuquerque Monthly.*

Special Discounts: 10% off seven nights or more, 10% AARP.

Algodones D5

Hacienda Vargas

PO Box 307
Algodones, NM 87001-0307
(505)867-9115 (800)261-0006
Fax:(505)867-1902
E-mail: hacvar@aol.com

Rates: $79-149.
Payment: MC VISA PC TC.
Innkeeper(s): Paul & Jule De Vargas.
Circa: 1800.

Rooms: 7 rooms with PB, 7 with FP. 4 suites.
Beds: QT.

Nestled among the cottonwoods and mesas of the middle Rio Grande Valley, Hacienda Vargas has seen two centuries of Old West history. It once served as a trading post for Native Americans as well as a 19th-century stagecoach stop between Santa Fe and Albuquerque. The grounds contain an adobe chapel, courtyard, and gardens. The main house features five kiva fireplaces, Southwest antiques, Spanish tile, a library, art gallery and suites with private Jacuzzis.

Breakfast included in rates. Type of meal: full breakfast. Air conditioning and ceiling fan in room. Fax and library on premises. Weddings and family reunions hosted. Spanish and German spoken. Antiques, fishing, shopping, downhill skiing, sporting events, theater and watersports nearby. TAC10.

Location: Twenty-two miles north of Albuquerque, 22 miles south of Santa Fe.

Publicity: *Vogue, San Francisco Chronicle, Albuquerque Journal.*

"This is the best! Breakfast was the best we've ever had!"

Bernalillo D5

La Hacienda Grande

21 Baros Ln
Bernalillo, NM 87004
(505)867-1887 (800)353-1887
Fax:(505)867-4621
E-mail: lhg@swcp.com

Rates: $89-129.
Payment: MC VISA AX DS TC.
Innkeeper(s): Shoshana Zimmerman & Daniel Buop.
Circa: 1711.

Rooms: 6 rooms with PB, 5 with FP. 1 conference room.
Beds: KQDT.

The rooms in this historic adobe inn surround a central courtyard. The first European trekked across the grounds as early as 1540. The land was part of a 1711 land grant from Spain, and owned by descendants of the original family until the innkeepers purchased it. The decor is Southwestern, and each bedchamber is filled with beautiful, rustic furnishings. One includes an iron high-poster bed and Jacuzzi tub, others offer a kiva fireplace. Breakfasts are served in a dining room decorated with wood beams and a brick floor.

Breakfast included in rates. Types of meals: full breakfast and early coffee/tea. Air conditioning in room. Cable TV, VCR, fax, copier and library on premises. Weddings, small meetings, family reunions and seminars hosted. Spanish spoken. Antiques, fishing, parks, shopping, downhill skiing, cross-country skiing, sporting events, theater and watersports nearby.

Cedar Crest D5

Elaine's, A B&B

PO Box 444
Cedar Crest, NM 87008
(505)281-2467 (800)821-3092

Rates: $85-99.
Payment: MC VISA AX TC.
Innkeeper(s): Elaine O'Neil.
Circa: 1979.

Rooms: 3 rooms with PB.
Beds: KQ.

This three-story log home is on four acres of evergreens in the forests of the Sandia Peaks. Rooms are furnished with European country antiques, and there are two fireplaces. Three varieties of hummingbirds visit the property. Guests enjoy views of the mountains from the inn's two balconies. Smoothies and raisin-cinnamon French toast are breakfast items.

Breakfast included in rates. Type of meal: full breakfast. Library on premises. Weddings, small meetings, family reunions and seminars hosted. Parks, shopping, downhill skiing and cross-country skiing nearby. TAC10.

Location: On four acres adjoining the Cibola National Forest in the Sandia Mountains.

Publicity: *Fodor's, New Mexico Magazine.*

Cimarron

B7

Casa Del Gavilan

PO Box 518
Cimarron, NM 87714-0518
(505)376-2246 (800)GAVILAN
Fax:(505)376-2247

Rates: $70-125.
Payment: MC VISA AX DS PC.
Innkeeper(s): Bob and Helen Hittle.
Circa: 1915.

Rooms: 5 rooms with PB, 1 with FP. 1 suite.
Beds: KQT.

Situated against the base of Tooth of Time Peak, in the foothills of the Sangre de Cristo Mountains, Casa del Gavilan's 18-inch-thick adobe walls have provided the setting for decades of superb hospitality. Will James and Zane Grey knew the house well, and Grey used it as the setting for his Knights of the Range. The pueblo-style house, part of the UU Bar Ranch, features 12-foot ceilings and museum-quality southwestern antiques.

Breakfast and evening snack included in rates. Types of meals: continental breakfast, full breakfast and early coffee/tea. Ceiling fan in room. Cable TV, fax and library on premises. Handicap access. Weddings, small meetings and family reunions hosted. Fishing, parks, downhill skiing and cross-country skiing nearby. TAC10.

"Thank you for the wonderful visit and great accommodations. We enjoyed the history of the Casa and the area. The food and service was outstanding and we felt totally at home. Can't wait to come back again."

El Prado-Taos

Cottonwood Inn

HCR 74 Box 24609
El Prado-Taos, NM 87529
(505)776-5826 (800)324-7120
Fax:(505)776-5826
E-mail: cottonbb@taos.newmex.com

Rates: $85-140.
Payment: MC VISA PC TC.
Innkeeper(s): Bill & Kit Owen.
Circa: 1947.

Rooms: 7 rooms with PB, 5 with FP. 3 suites. 1 conference room.
Beds: KQT.

Nestled on an acre of cottonwoods, herb gardens and perennial beds, this renovated pueblo-style adobe home is a picturesque site for vacationers to Taos. In keeping with Taos' notoriety as an artist colony, the innkeepers display a collection of original artwork. Hand-crafted furnishings also decorate the interior. Rooms are individually appointed and offer views of gardens, meadows or mountains. Five rooms include a fireplace, and some also have a whirlpool tub, sauna or steam room. Breakfasts are seasoned with herbs from the garden and include such items as fresh fruit, homemade breads, frittatas or sourdough pancakes topped with blueberry sauce. Afternoon refreshments also are served.

Breakfast and evening snack included in rates. Types of meals: gourmet breakfast and early coffee/tea. Ceiling fan in room. Cable TV, VCR, fax, copier, spa and library on premises. Handicap access. Weddings, small meetings, family reunions and seminars hosted. Spanish and German spoken. Antiques, fishing, parks, shopping, downhill skiing, cross-country skiing, theater and watersports nearby. TAC10.

Farmington

A2

Silver River Adobe Inn

3151 W Main, PO Box 3411
Farmington, NM 87499
(505)325-8219 (800)382-9251
Fax:(505)325-8219

Rates: $75-105.
Payment: MC VISA AX PC TC.
Innkeeper(s): Diana Ohlson & David Beers.
Circa: 1988.

Rooms: 3 rooms, 2 with PB. 1 suite.
Beds: QT.

Guests at this contemporary adobe house enjoy a view of the San Juan River from the patio of their room. Amenities in the suite include a dining/living room, kitchen with microwave and refrigerator, Mexican tile bathroom, phone and queen bed. Guests may take a refreshing walk in the nearby cottonwood forest, a perfect spot for birdwatching. The peaceful setting caters to those wishing to get away from it all, while those interested in sightseeing will find many opportunities in the area, such as the Aztec and Salmon ruins, Four Corners Monument and Mesa Verde and Chaco Canyon.

Breakfast included in rates. Type of meal: continental breakfast. Catering service available. Ceiling fan in room. Library on premises. Handicap access. Weddings and seminars hosted. Antiques, fishing, parks, shopping, downhill skiing, cross-country skiing, theater and watersports nearby. TAC10.

Galisteo D6

The Galisteo Inn

9 La Vega
Galisteo, NM 87540-9701
(505)466-4000
Fax:(505)466-4008
E-mail: galisteoin@aol.com

Rates: $100-175.
Payment: MC VISA DS PC TC.
Innkeeper(s): Joanna Kaufman & Wayne Aarniokoski.
Circa: 1740.

Rooms: 12 rooms, 8 with PB, 4 with FP.
Beds: KQDT.

In the historic Spanish village of Galisteo, this adobe hacienda is surrounded by giant cottonwoods. The inn features a comfortable Southwestern decor, a library and eight fireplaces. Located on eight acres, there is a duck pond and a creek (the Galisteo River) forms the boundary of the property. Sophisticated cuisine includes dishes such as chile-seared salmon with cucumber yogurt cream and tomato relish or shrimp and tortilla bisque. Chocolate espresso cheesecake is one of the mouthwatering deserts.

Breakfast included in rates. Type of meal: full breakfast. Picnic lunch available. Ceiling fan in room. Fax, copier, spa, swimming, sauna, stables, bicycles and library on premises. Handicap access. Weddings, small meetings, family reunions and seminars hosted. Shopping, downhill skiing, cross-country skiing and theater nearby. TAC10.

Pets Allowed: Horses only.

Location: Twenty-three miles southeast of Santa Fe, one block east of Hwy 41.

Publicity: *Country Living, Physicians Lifestyle, Innsider, Chicago Tribune, Boston Globe, Orange County Register, Southern Living.*

"Ahhh, what peace and perfection. Thank you so very much for this magic time in a magic space."

Las Vegas C7

Plaza Hotel

230 Old Town Plaza
Las Vegas, NM 87701
(505)425-3591 (800)328-1882
Fax:(505)425-9659

Rates: $55-130.
Payment: MC VISA AX DC DS TC.
Innkeeper(s): Wid & Kak Slick.
Circa: 1882.

Rooms: 37 rooms with PB. 4 suites. 1 conference room.
Beds: KQDT.

This brick Italianate Victorian hotel, once frequented by the likes of Doc Holliday, Big Nose Katy and members of the James Gang, was renovated in 1982. A stencil pattern found in the dining room inspired the selection of Victorian wallpaper borders in the guest rooms, decorated with a combination of contemporary and period furnishings. Guests are still drawn to the warm, dry air and the hot springs north of town.

Types of meals: continental breakfast, continental-plus breakfast, full breakfast and gourmet breakfast. Dinner, picnic lunch, lunch, gourmet lunch, banquet service, catering service, catered breakfast and room service available. Air conditioning and cable TV in room. VCR and copier on premises. Handicap access. Weddings, small meetings, family reunions and seminars hosted. Spanish/English spoken. Antiques, fishing, parks, shopping, cross-country skiing and watersports nearby. TAC10.

Pets Allowed: $10 charge.

Lincoln G6

Casa De Patron B&B Inn

PO Box 27, Hwy 380 E
Lincoln, NM 88338-0027
(505)653-4676 (800)524-5202
Fax:(505)653-4671

Rates: $79-107.
Payment: MC VISA PC.
Innkeeper(s): Jeremy & Cleis Jordan.
Circa: 1860.

Rooms: 7 rooms with PB, 2 with FP. 2 cottages. 1 conference room.
Beds: KQDT.

This historic adobe once was used to imprison Billy the Kid and played an integral part in the colorful frontier days of Lincoln County. A shaded courtyard and walled garden add to the authentic Old West atmosphere, and the comfortable rooms are supplemented by two contemporary adobe casitas. Cleis plays the inn's pipe organ and arranges soapmaking workshops for guests. Salon evenings feature classical music and Old World cookery. Dinner is available by advance reservation.

Breakfast included in rates. Types of meals: continental-plus breakfast and full breakfast. Dinner and catering service available. Ceiling fan in room. VCR, fax and copier on premises. Handicap access. Weddings, small meetings, family reunions and seminars hosted. Antiques, fishing, parks, shopping and downhill skiing nearby. TAC10.

Location: In the foothills of the Sacramento and Capitan mountain ranges, southeastern New Mexico. Located 185 miles southeast of Albuquerque and 160 miles northeast of El Paso, TX.

Publicity: *Albuquerque Journal, Preservation News, Sunset, Travelin', Rocky Mountain News, Milwaukee Journal.*

"The time with you at Casa de Patron is truly a treasure to me."

Santa Fe C6

Alexander's Inn

529 E Palace Ave
Santa Fe, NM 87501-2200
(505)986-1431
Fax:(505)982-8572
E-mail: alexandinn@aol.com

Rates: $75-150. EP.
Payment: MC VISA PC TC.
Innkeeper(s): Carolyn Lee.
Circa: 1903.

Rooms: 8 rooms, 6 with PB, 4 with FP. 1 suite. 2 cottages.
Beds: KQT.

Twin gables and a massive front porch are prominent features of this Craftsman-style brick and wood inn. Eclectic decor, stained-glass windows and a selection of antiques create a light Victorian touch. Breakfast is often served in the backyard garden. Home-baked treats are offered to guests in the afternoon, and the innkeepers keep a few bicycles on hand for those who wish to explore the neighborhood.

Breakfast and afternoon tea included in rates. Types of meals: continental-plus breakfast, gourmet breakfast and early coffee/tea. EP. Cable TV and VCR in room. Fax, spa, bicycles, library and child care on premises. Weddings and family reunions hosted. French spoken. Antiques, fishing, parks, shopping, downhill skiing, cross-country skiing, theater and watersports nearby. TAC10.

Pets Allowed: Well behaved.

Publicity: *New Mexican, Glamour, Southwest Art, San Diego Union Tribune.*

"Thanks to the kindness and thoughtfulness of the staff, our three days in Santa Fe were magical."

Casa De La Cuma B&B

105 Paseo De La Cuma
Santa Fe, NM 87501-1213
(505)983-1717 (888)366-1717
Fax:(505)988-2883

Rates: $65-145.
Payment: MC VISA PC TC.
Innkeeper(s): Arthur & Donna Bailey.
Circa: 1940.

Rooms: 8 rooms, 6 with PB. 5 suites.
Beds: KQT.

These two locations offer different types of travel experiences. The Chapelle Street Casitas has private suites with fully equipped and furnished kitchens, living rooms and bedrooms with hand-crafted Southwestern-style furniture. The Casitas is located in the heart of the historic district and is four blocks from the Plaza, which is the center of activity in Santa Fe. Casa De La Cuma B&B has three unique rooms decorated with Navajo textiles, original artwork and Southwestern-period furniture. The inn offers views of the Sangre De Cristo Mountains and is also within walking distance of the Plaza.

Breakfast and evening snack included in rates. Type of meal: continental-plus breakfast. Afternoon tea available. Air conditioning, ceiling fan and cable TV in room. Fax on premises. Spanish spoken. Antiques, parks and downhill skiing nearby. TAC10.

Publicity: *Denver Post.*

"Their pleasant nature, helpful hints for visitors and genuine hospitality were memorable and valuable to us."

Dunshee's

986 Acequia Madre
Santa Fe, NM 87501-2819
(505)982-0988

Rates: $110.
Payment: MC VISA PC TC.
Innkeeper(s): Susan Dunshee.
Circa: 1930.

Rooms: 3 rooms, 2 with PB, 3 with FP. 1 suite. 1 cottage.
Beds: QD.

Where better could one experience Santa Fe's rich history than in an authentic adobe casita or a restored adobe home? Innkeeper Susan Dunshee offers accommodations in both. Guests can stay in the adobe home's spacious suite or rent the casita by the week or month. The casita offers two bedrooms, a kitchen, a living room warmed by a rustic, Kiva fireplace, and a private patio. The antique-filled rooms are decorated in a warm, Santa Fe style, and bedrooms sport a more country look. Guests who opt for the bed & breakfast suite are treated to Southwestern breakfasts with items such as a green chile souffle. The refrigerator at the casita is stocked with treats for the guests' first morning breakfast.

Breakfast included in rates. Types of meals: continental-plus breakfast, full breakfast, gourmet breakfast and early coffee/tea. Cable TV in room. Library on premises. Weddings, small meetings and family reunions hosted. Antiques, parks, shopping, downhill skiing, cross-country skiing and theater nearby.

Special Discounts: Casita has weekly and monthly rates.

El Paradero

220 W Manhattan Ave
Santa Fe, NM 87501-2622
(505)988-1177
E-mail: elpara@trail.com

Rates: $60-130.
Payment: MC VISA.
Innkeeper(s): Ouida MacGregor & Thomas Allen.
Circa: 1820.

Rooms: 14 rooms, 10 with PB, 5 with FP. 2 suites. 1 conference room.
Beds: QT.

This was originally a two-bedroom Spanish farmhouse that doubled in size to a Territorial style in 1860, was remodeled as a Victorian in 1912, and became a Pueblo Revival in 1920. All styles are present and provide a walk through many years of history.

Breakfast and afternoon tea included in rates. Types of meals: gourmet breakfast and early coffee/tea. Air conditioning in room. Cable TV on premises. Fishing, shopping, cross-country skiing and theater nearby. TAC10.

Pets Allowed: Only by prearrangements and only in certain rooms.

Location: Downtown.

Publicity: *Innsider, Country Inns, Outside, Sunset, New York Times, Los Angeles Times, Travel & Leisure, America West, Travel & Holiday.*

Special Discounts: 5% AARP if made directly by guest; 5% AAA if made directly by guest.

"I'd like to LIVE here."

Heart Seed B&B Retreat Center and Spa

PO Box 6019
Santa Fe, NM 87502-6019
(505)471-7026

Rates: $79-89.
Payment: VISA AX DS.
Innkeeper(s): Judith Polich.
Circa: 1991.

Rooms: 4 rooms with PB. 3 suites. 2 cottages. 1 conference room.
Beds: Q.

Pinons and junipers cover the 100-acre grounds that surround this rustic retreat, which affords glorious mountain views. Pamper yourself at the center's spa with massages, herbal wraps and other decadent treats. The Desert Hearts Room is decorated in a '50s cowboy-cowgirl motif and includes two, queen-size beds. The Mountain-Sky Room boasts a wonderful view and a private deck. Studio-apartment rooms are available for guests planning a long stay in Santa Fe. The studios offer fully equipped kitchenettes and can sleep up to four guests. All rooms have mountain views. The hosts have designed special discount packages for those who wish to enjoy the spa along with their stay.

Breakfast and evening snack included in rates. Types of meals: full breakfast, gourmet breakfast and early coffee/tea. VCR, fax, copier, spa and library on premises. 100 acres. Weddings, small meetings, family reunions and seminars hosted. Antiques, fishing, shopping, downhill skiing, cross-country skiing, sporting events and theater nearby. TAC10.

Special Discounts: 5-20% discount packages all year.

Inn on The Paseo

630 Paseo De Peralta
Santa Fe, NM 87501-1957
(505)984-8200 (800)457-9045
Fax:(505)989-3979

Rates: $65-155.
Payment: MC VISA AX DC PC TC.
Innkeeper(s): Nancy & Mick Arseneault.
Circa: 1992.

Rooms: 18 rooms with PB, 1 with FP. 1 suite.
Beds: KQT.

Santa Fe is a city with many interesting lodging choices, and the Inn on the Paseo is an elegant example. It was created from two historic homes and the result is an exterior that appears as a New Mexican farmhouse with a pitched roof. Inside, sparkling guest rooms are decorated in contemporary, Southwest style. Beds are dressed with handmade quilts and down comforters. The suite, which boasts a fireplace and four-poster bed, is ideal for honeymooners. Fresh fruits, still-warm-from-the-oven muffins, coffeecake and other treats fill the daily continental breakfast buffet. The inn is located just a few blocks from historic Santa Fe Plaza.

Breakfast and afternoon tea included in rates. Types of meals: continental-plus breakfast and early coffee/tea. Air conditioning, ceiling fan and cable TV in room. Fax and library on premises. Handicap access. Spanish and French spoken. Antiques, fishing, parks, shopping, downhill skiing, cross-country skiing and theater nearby. TAC10.

Pueblo Bonito

138 W Manhattan Ave
Santa Fe, NM 87501-2620
(505)984-8001 (800)461-4599
Fax:(505)984-3155

Rates: $70-140.
Payment: MC VISA PC.
Innkeeper(s): Amy & Herb Behm.
Circa: 1880.

Rooms: 18 rooms with PB, 18 with FP. 7 suites.
Beds: QD.

A large adobe wall surrounds the grounds of this estate, once the home of a circuit judge. An original Indian oven is attached to the house. Flagstone pathways, old oak trees and a rose garden add to the atmosphere.

Breakfast and afternoon tea included in rates. Type of meal: continental-plus breakfast. Cable TV in room. Copier and spa on premises. Handicap access. Fishing, parks, shopping, downhill skiing, cross-country skiing, theater and watersports nearby. TAC10.

Location: Downtown.

Publicity: *Innsider.*

Special Discounts: 10% AARP.

"You captured that quaint, authentic Santa Fe atmosphere, yet I didn't feel as if I had to sacrifice any modern conveniences."

Socorro F4

The Historic Eaton House

403 Eaton Ave
Socorro, NM 87801-4414
(505)835-1067
Fax:(505)835-3527

Rates: $85-135.
Payment: MC VISA AX.
Innkeeper(s): Anna Appleby.
Circa: 1881.

Rooms: 5 rooms with PB, 2 with FP.
Beds: KQDT.

Birdwatchers, prepare your binoculars. Within six miles of the Eaton House, bird lovers might discover 345 species throughout the year. For those who prefer other activities, this home, which was built from native materials, offers guests plenty of other reasons to stay. Rooms are filled with antiques, artwork and furnishings built by local artisans. The Colonel Eaton Room features Victorian decor, flowered tile, lace, needlework and wood furnishings. The quaint Daughter's Room features push button switches, a clawfoot tub and twin beds designed for twin daughters 80 years ago. The innkeepers also offer two casitas during the year. Each of these rooms boasts fireplaces, high ceilings and unique decor. The innkeepers serve up gourmet breakfasts, which may include entrees such as blue-corn pancakes with walnuts or French toast marinated overnight in Grand Marinier. A special basket of goodies can be arranged for those wishing to birdwatch before breakfast is served.

Breakfast included in rates. Types of meals: gourmet breakfast and early coffee/tea. Picnic lunch available. Air conditioning and ceiling fan in room. Fax on premises. Handicap access. Small meetings hosted. Antiques, fishing, parks, shopping and theater nearby.

Publicity: *American Way in Flight, Sunset, Atlanta Constitution, NY Times, Boston Globe, Portland Oregonian, Albuquerque*

Casa Europa Inn & Gallery

HC 68, Box 3F, 840 Upper Ranchitos
Taos, NM 87571
(505)758-9798

Rates: $75-135.
Payment: MC VISA PC TC.
Innkeeper(s): Rudi & Marcia Zwicker.
Circa: 1700.

Rooms: 7 rooms with PB, 6 with FP. 2 suites. 2 conference rooms.
Beds: KQT.

Guests will appreciate both the elegance and history at work here at Casa Europa. The home is a 17th-century pueblo-adobe creation with rustic beams, walls three-feet thick and a dining room with a massive kiva fireplace. Freshly baked pastries are served in the afternoons, and during ski season, hors d'oeuvres are provided in the early evening. European antiques fill the rooms, which are decorated in an elegant, Southwestern style. The French Room offers an 1860 bed, kiva fireplace and French doors opening onto the courtyard. Other rooms include a fireplace, wood stove or whirlpool tub. The five-room Apartment Suite includes a kitchen-dining room, sitting room, bedroom, a private hot tub and a kiva fireplace. The inn is 1.6 miles from Taos Plaza.

Breakfast, afternoon tea and evening snack included in rates. Types of meals: full breakfast, gourmet breakfast and early coffee/tea. Turn-down service, ceiling fan and cable TV in room. Spa and sauna on premises. Small meetings and family reunions hosted. German and Spanish spoken. Antiques, fishing, parks, shopping, downhill skiing, cross-country skiing, theater and watersports nearby. TAC10.

Pets Allowed: Outside only.

Hacienda Del Sol

PO Box 177
Taos, NM 87571
(505)758-0287
E-mail: sunhouse@taos.newmex.com

Rates: $70-130.
Payment: PC TC.
Innkeeper(s): John & Marcine Landon.
Circa: 1810.

Rooms: 9 rooms with PB, 8 with FP. 2 suites.
Beds: KQDT.

Mabel Dodge, patron of the arts, purchased this old hacienda as a hideaway for her Native American husband Tony Luhan. The spacious adobe sits among huge cottonwoods, blue spruce, and ponderosa pines, with an uninterrupted view of the mountains across 95,000 acres of Native American Indian lands. Among Dodge's famous guests were Georgia O'Keefe, who painted here, and D. H. Lawrence. The mood is tranquil and on moonlit nights guests can hear Indian drums and the howl of coyotes.

Breakfast and evening snack included in rates. Types of meals: full breakfast and early coffee/tea. Cable TV, fax, spa and library on premises. Handicap access. Weddings, small meetings, family reunions and seminars hosted. Antiques, fishing, parks, shopping, downhill skiing, cross-country skiing, theater and watersports nearby. TAC10.

Location: North of Santa Fe at the base of Sangre de Cristo Mountains.

Publicity: *Chicago Tribune, Los Angeles Daily News, Denver Post, The Globe and Mail.*

"Your warm friendliness and gracious hospitality have made this week an experience we will never forget!"

La Posada De Taos

PO Box 1118
Taos, NM 87571-1118
(505)758-8164 (800)645-4803
Fax:(505)751-3294

Rates: $70-117.
Payment: PC TC.
Innkeeper(s): Bill & Nancy Swan.
Circa: 1907.

Rooms: 6 rooms with PB, 3 with FP. 1 conference room.
Beds: KQD.

Located within the historic district of Taos, La Posada is built in the adobe vernacular of the Southwest. Log-beamed ceilings, polished floors, Mexican headboards, and whitewashed walls contribute to the southwestern decor. A Japanese rock garden adds to the serenity. The living room library is centered around a tiled, adobe fireplace. French doors in the dining room open onto a garden with mountain views. Most of the four guest rooms and honeymoon cottage have woodburning stoves or fireplaces.

Breakfast included in rates. Type of meal: full breakfast. Ceiling fan in room. Cable TV, VCR, fax, copier and library on premises. Handicap access. Weddings, small meetings and family reunions hosted. Antiques, fishing, parks, shopping, downhill skiing, cross-country skiing, theater and watersports nearby.

Publicity: *New York Times, Bon Appetit, Country Inns, Glamour, Los Angeles Times.*

"I want to tell you how much we enjoyed our visit with you at La Posada De Taos in September. It was definitely the highlight of our trip."

Old Taos Guesthouse

1028 Witt Rd, Box 6552
Taos, NM 87571
(505)758-5448 (800)758-5448

Rates: $70-115.
Payment: MC VISA PC TC.
Innkeeper(s): Tim & Leslie Reeves.
Circa: 1850.

Rooms: 9 rooms with PB, 5 with FP. 2 suites.
Beds: KQT.

This adobe hacienda sits on a rise overlooking Taos and is surrounded by large cottonwood, blue spruce, apple, apricot and pinon trees. This estate, which offers panoramic views, originally served as a farmer's home, but later was home to an artist. As the years went by, rooms were added. Rustic rooms include special items such as kiva fireplaces, hand-woven wall hangings, dried flowers, log four-poster beds and hand-painted vanities. The Southwestern-style rooms all have private entrances. The outdoor hot tub boasts a wonderful view. Healthy, homemade breakfasts are served in a room filled with antiques. The home is set on more than seven acres, located less than two miles from the Plaza.

NM

Breakfast included in rates. Types of meals: continental-plus breakfast and early coffee/tea. Spa, stables and library on premises. Spanish and German spoken. Antiques, fishing, parks, shopping, downhill skiing, cross-country skiing and theater nearby.

Publicity: *Denver Post Travel, Inn for the Night, Travelin', Travel Age West, Country, Houston Chronicle.*

"We really enjoyed the authenticity of your guesthouse."

Orinda B&B

461 Valverde
Taos, NM 87571
(505)758-8581 (800)847-1837
Fax:(505)758-8581
E-mail: gnpiv@laplaza.taos.nm.us

Rates: $75-85.
Payment: MC VISA AX DS PC TC.
Innkeeper(s): Cary & George Pratt.
Circa: 1935.

Rooms: 4 rooms with PB, 1 with FP. 1 suite.
Beds: QDT.

Current innkeepers Cary and George Pratt are only the fourth owners of this property, which was deeded to its original owners by Abraham Lincoln. The house itself, a rustic adobe, was built some years later, and features Southwestern flair with kiva fireplaces, Mexican tile in the bathrooms and viga ceilings. Cary serves up a flavorful breakfast with treats such as scrambled eggs wrapped in a tortilla, freshly baked bread or muffins and fruit. Many of the inn's picture windows afford views of Taos Mountain.

Breakfast and evening snack included in rates. Cable TV, VCR and fax on premises. Weddings and family reunions hosted. Antiques, fishing, parks, shopping, downhill skiing and cross-country skiing nearby. TAC10.

"It really is 'a B&B paradise' with your beautiful surroundings."

Salsa Del Salto B&B Inn

#543 Taos Ski Valley Rd
Taos, NM 87529
(505)776-2422 (800)530-3097
Fax:(505)776-2422

Rates: $85-160.
Payment: MC VISA PC TC.
Innkeeper(s): Mary Hockett & Dadou Mayer.
Circa: 1970.

Rooms: 10 rooms with PB, 3 with FP.
Beds: KQT.

In the foothills eight miles from ancient Taos Pueblo, this southwestern inn welcomes guests with a flower-filled courtyard. Rooms are furnished with elegant New Mexican pieces and each has a view of either mesa or mountain. French chef and ski champion Dadou, winner of the "Fastest Chef in the US" ski race, prepares gourmet cuisine for guests and in his spare time, holds cooking schools and writes cookbooks.

Breakfast and afternoon tea included in rates. Type of meal: gourmet breakfast. Ceiling fan in room. VCR, fax, spa, swimming and tennis on premises. Small meetings and family reunions hosted. French, Spanish and German spoken. Antiques, fishing, parks, shopping, downhill skiing, cross-country skiing, theater and watersports nearby. TAC10.

Location: The foothills eight miles from ancient Taos Pueblo.

Publicity: *Los Angeles Times.*

"The warm feelings that we felt as guests only made it more difficult to leave. The laughter, the warmth, the friendship will be with us through the years."

The Willows Inn

409 Dolan St
Taos, NM 87571
(505)758-2558 (800)525-8267
Fax:(505)758-5445
E-mail: willows@taos.nex.mex.com

Rates: $95-130.
Payment: MC VISA PC TC.
Innkeeper(s): Janet & Doug Camp.
Circa: 1926.

Rooms: 5 rooms with PB, 5 with FP. 1 suite.
Beds: QD.

This authentic, Southwestern-style adobe was once home to artist E. Martin Hennings, a member of the Taos Society of Artists. Each of the rooms features a unique theme, including Henning's Studio, which was the artist's workplace. The studio boasts a seven-foot headboard, high ceilings and private patio. The Santa Fe Room is decked in contemporary, Southwestern style and has a sitting area. Each of the rooms includes a kiva fireplace. The Conquistador Room reflects old Spanish decor with an antique chest, pigskin couch and ropero. The Cowboy and Anasazi rooms include artifacts such as a cowhide rug, handmade quilts, Zuni kachinas and hand-crafted pottery. Breakfasts are highlighted by fresh items right out of the inn's herb and vegetable gardens. Afternoon refreshments are served as guests study menus from various Taos eateries.

Breakfast and evening snack included in rates. Types of meals: continental breakfast, continental-plus breakfast, full breakfast, gourmet breakfast and early coffee/tea. Afternoon tea available. Cable TV, VCR, fax, copier and library on premises. Weddings, small meetings, family reunions and seminars hosted. Spanish spoken. Antiques, fishing, parks, shopping, downhill skiing, cross-country skiing, theater and watersports nearby. TAC10.

Pets Allowed: Can be boarded at nearby vet clinic.

Publicity: *New York Times, Travel Holiday, Taos Magazine.*

French Toast With Apples and Walnuts

Mapleton Farm Bed & Breakfast
Putney, Vt.

- 6 Granny Smith apples
- ¼ cup orange juice
- ¼ cup pure Vermont maple syrup
- 1 large loaf sourdough French bread
- 8 eggs
- ¾ cup milk
- 1 t vanilla extract
- 1 t cinnamon
- ¼ t allspice
- ½ cup chopped walnuts or pecans
- 1 T vegetable oil
- ½ cup chopped walnuts or pecans
- Powdered sugar

Peel, core and slice apples into wedges. Toss with orange juice. Place apples in an oven-proof casserole dish. Drizzle maple syrup over apples. Cover and bake in a 350 degree oven for approximately 20 minutes, or until apples are fork tender (do not overcook or you will have applesauce). Keep apples warm while you prepare the toast.

Slice the sourdough French bread into thick slices. Mix the remaining ingredients, except the walnuts and powdered sugar, in a bowl.

Dip the bread in the egg mixture. Cook on a hot griddle or skillet until golden brown on each side.

Place 2-3 slices of toast on a warm plate. Top with apples. Sprinkle with chopped nuts and powdered sugar. Serve immediately.

Cottage Sticky Buns

Columbia Cottage
Vancouver, B.C.

- ½ cup light corn syrup or maple-flavored syrup
- ⅓ cup packed brown sugar
- 3 T butter, melted
- 1 T water
- ½ cup coarsely chopped walnuts or pecans
- 2 cups flour
- 2 T sugar
- 2 t baking powder
- ½ t baking soda
- ½ t salt
- ½ cup butter
- ⅔ cup buttermilk

In a saucepan, combine syrup, brown sugar, butter and water. Cook and stir over low heat until brown sugar is dissolved; DO NOT BOIL. Line a 9.5" or 10" springform pan with foil and pour in mixture. Sprinkle nuts on top.

In a mixing bowl, stir together flour, sugar, baking powder, baking soda and salt into a large bowl. Cut in the butter until it resembles irregular crumbs. Add buttermilk and stir until dough forms a cohesive mass.

Turn dough on to a floured surface and knead gently about 10 times. Roll dough into rectangle about 12" long and 8" wide.

Mix ¼ cup sugar with ½ t with ½ t cinnamon and sprinkle over dough.

Roll up jelly roll style (long side). Slice into about 12 pieces and place cut side down in prepared pan. Bake at 425 degrees for about 30 minutes or until golden.

Invert onto serving plate. Serve warm.

New York

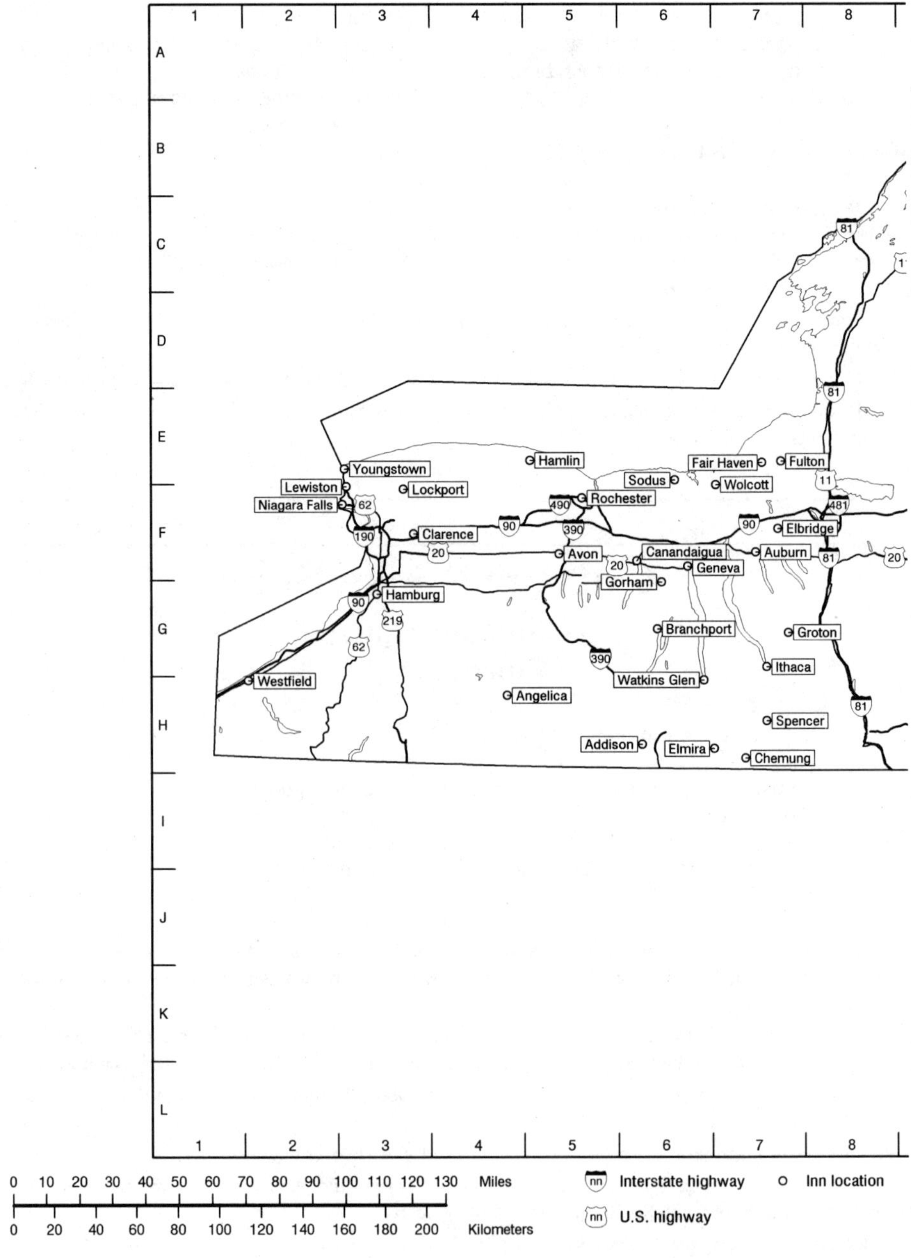

1
2
3
4
5
6
7
8
A
B
C
D
E
F
G
H
I
J
K
L
Youngstown
Lewiston
Niagara Falls
Lockport
Hamlin
Fair Haven
Fulton
Sodus
Wolcott
Rochester
Clarence
Avon
Canandaigua
Geneva
Auburn
Elbridge
Gorham
Hamburg
Branchport
Groton
Ithaca
Westfield
Watkins Glen
Angelica
Spencer
Addison
Elmira
Chemung
0 10 20 30 40 50 60 70 80 90 100 110 120 130 Miles
0 20 40 60 80 100 120 140 160 180 200 Kilometers
Interstate highway
U.S. highway
Inn location

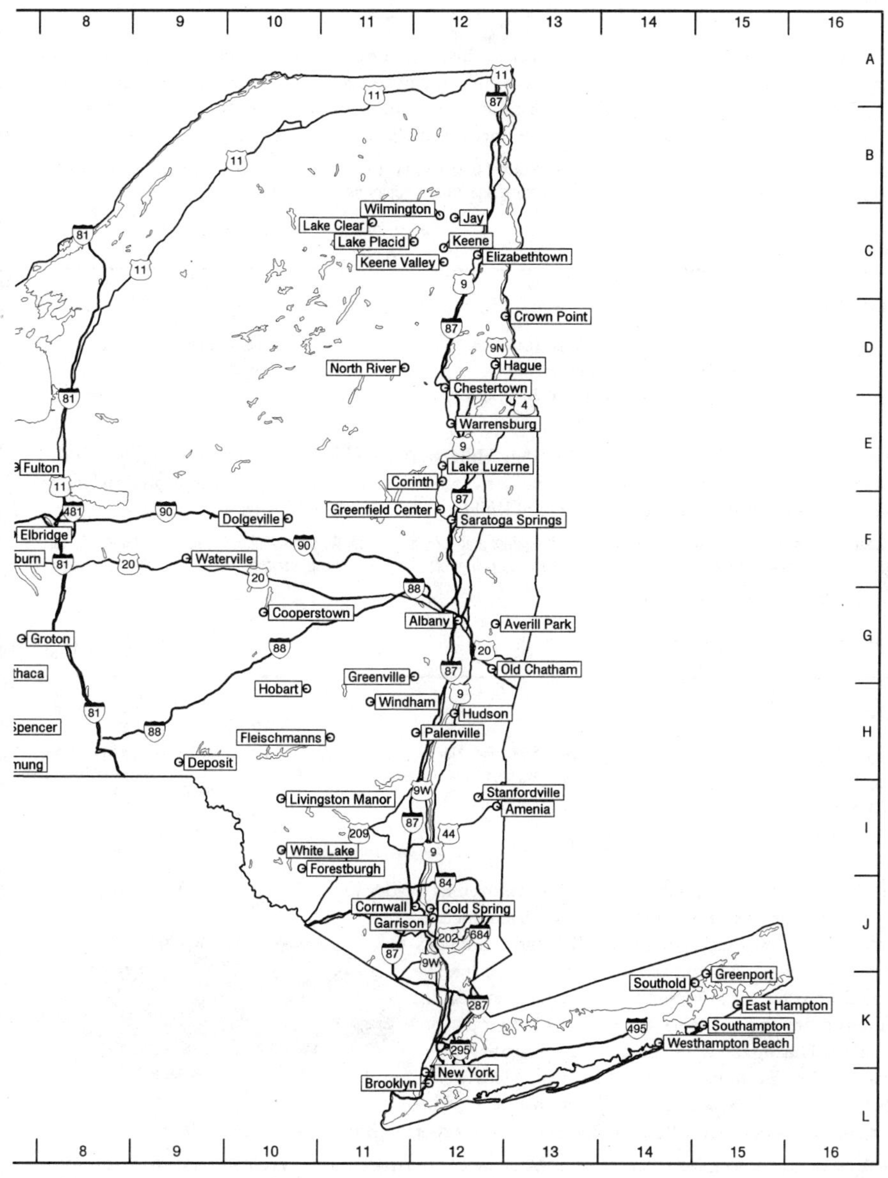

8
9
10
11
12
13
14
15
16
A
B
C
D
E
F
G
H
I
J
K
L
Wilmington
Jay
Lake Clear
Lake Placid
Keene
Keene Valley
Elizabethtown
Crown Point
North River
Hague
Chestertown
Warrensburg
Fulton
Lake Luzerne
Corinth
Greenfield Center
Saratoga Springs
Dolgeville
Elbridge
Waterville
Cooperstown
Albany
Averill Park
Groton
Old Chatham
Greenville
Hobart
Windham
Hudson
Fleischmanns
Palenville
Deposit
Stanfordville
Livingston Manor
Amenia
White Lake
Forestburgh
Cornwall
Cold Spring
Garrison
Southold
Greenport
East Hampton
Southampton
Westhampton Beach
New York
Brooklyn

NY

Addison H6

Addison Rose B&B

37 Maple St
Addison, NY 14801-1009
(607)359-4650

Rates: $65-85.
Payment: PC TC.
Innkeeper(s): William & Maryann Peters.
Circa: 1892.

Rooms: 3 rooms with PB.
Beds: DT.

Located on a scenic highway south of the Finger Lakes, this Queen Anne Victorian "painted lady" inn is an easy getaway from Corning or Elmira. The inn was built by a doctor for his bride and was presented to her on Christmas Eve, their wedding day. The three guest rooms offer authentic Victorian furnishings. Many fine examples of Victorian architecture exist in Addison. Pinnacle State Park is just east of town.

Breakfast and afternoon tea included in rates. Types of meals: gourmet breakfast and early coffee/tea. Ceiling fan in room. Library on premises. Family reunions hosted. Antiques, fishing, parks, shopping and cross-country skiing nearby.

Albany G12

Pine Haven B&B

531 Western Ave
Albany, NY 12203-1721
(518)482-1574

Rates: $64-79.
Payment: PC TC.
Innkeeper(s): Janice Tricarico.
Circa: 1896.

Rooms: 5 rooms, 2 with PB.
Beds: DT.

This turn-of-the-century Victorian is located in Pine Hills, an Albany historic district. In keeping with this history, the innkeepers have tried to preserve the home's 19th-century charm. The rooms offer old-fashioned comfort with Victorian influences. The Capitol Building and other historic sites are nearby.

Breakfast included in rates. Types of meals: continental-plus breakfast and early coffee/tea. Air conditioning in room. Weddings, small meetings, family reunions and seminars hosted. Antiques, parks, shopping, cross-country skiing, sporting events and theater nearby.

Special Discounts: Stay 7 nights, last night free.

Amenia I12

Troutbeck

Leedsville Rd
Amenia, NY 12501
(914)373-9681
Fax:(914)373-7080

Rates: $650-1050. MAP.
Payment: MC VISA AX PC TC.
Innkeeper(s): Jim Flaherty & Garret Corcoran.
Circa: 1918.

Rooms: 42 rooms, 37 with PB, 9 with FP. 8 suites. 3 conference rooms.
Beds: KQDT.

This English country estate on 422 wooded acres enjoyed its heyday in the '20s. The NAACP was conceived here and the literati and liberals of the period, including Teddy Roosevelt, were overnight guests. Weekend room rates include six meals on weekends and an open bar as well as luxurious accommodations for two. On Sundays, brunch is served. The inn has a fitness center, billiard table, outdoor and indoor pools and tennis courts. During the week the inn is a corporate retreat and has been awarded Executive Retreat of the Year. Many weddings are held here each year and a new ballroom has been added, which accommodates weddings with up to 250 guests and corporate gatherings for about 70 people.

Breakfast and dinner included in rates. Types of meals: continental breakfast, full breakfast and early coffee/tea. Evening snack, picnic lunch, banquet service, catering service and room service available. MAP. Air conditioning and turn-down service in room. Cable TV, VCR, fax, copier, computer, spa, swimming, sauna, tennis and library on premises. 20 acres. Weddings, family reunions and seminars hosted. Spanish, Portuguese and Italian spoken. Antiques, fishing, parks, shopping, downhill skiing, cross-country skiing, sporting events and theater nearby. TAC5.

Location: Foothills of the Berkshires.

Publicity: *Good Housekeeping, New York Magazine, American Express, Vogue.*

"This 1920s-style estate makes you wish all life could be this way."

Angelica

H4

Angelica Inn

64 W Main St
Angelica, NY 14709
(716)466-3295

Rates: $65-80.
Payment: MC VISA AX DC CB DS PC TC.
Innkeeper(s): Cindy & Nick Petito.
Circa: 1886.

Rooms: 7 rooms with PB, 4 with FP. 4 suites. 1 cottage. 1 conference room.
Beds: QD.

Located in the Allegany foothills, the Angelica Inn features stained glass, crystal chandeliers, parquet floors, an oak staircase, carved woodwork, antique furnishings and scented rooms. Guest rooms offer such amenities as fireplaces, a porch and a breakfast alcove area.

Breakfast included in rates. Types of meals: full breakfast and early coffee/tea. Catered breakfast available. Air conditioning, ceiling fan and cable TV in room. Copier on premises. Weddings, small meetings, family reunions and seminars hosted. Antiques, fishing, shopping, downhill skiing and cross-country skiing nearby. TAC10.

"Victorian at its best!"

Auburn

F7

The Irish Rose - A Victorian B&B

102 South St
Auburn, NY 13021-4836
(315)255-0196 (800)255-0196
Fax:(315)255-0988

Rates: $65-105.
Payment: MC VISA AX DS PC TC.
Innkeeper(s): Patricia Fitzpatrick.
Circa: 1872.

Rooms: 5 rooms, 3 with PB, 1 with FP. 1 suite. 1 conference room.
Beds: KQT.

A Victorian setting and Irish hospitality are blended at this National Register Queen Anne Victorian. The inn features cherry hardwood floors, cherry fireplace mantels, and cherry doors. An uncluttered Victorian style includes some antiques. The innkeeper, once a head chef, provides a full gourmet buffet breakfast. On the grounds are a swimming pool and rose garden.

Breakfast included in rates. Type of meal: gourmet breakfast. Picnic lunch, catering service and room service available. Air conditioning and ceiling fan in room. Cable TV, VCR, fax and copier on premises. Weddings, small meetings, family reunions and seminars hosted. Antiques, fishing, shopping, downhill skiing, cross-country skiing, sporting events, theater and watersports nearby.

Location: Fingerlakes Region.

Publicity: *Auburn Citizen, Syracuse News Times, Fingerlakes Magazine, Central New York Magazine, Echo Newspaper.*

"My first B&B experience, won't be my last. Romantic."

NY

Averill Park

G12

Ananas Hus B&B

148 South Rd
Averill Park, NY 12018-3414
(518)766-5035

Rates: $60.
Payment: AX PC.
Innkeeper(s): Clyde & Thelma Olsen Tomlinson.
Circa: 1963.

Rooms: 3 rooms.
Beds: DT.

This ranch home in the mountains east of Albany offers stunning views of the Hudson River Valley. Visitors enjoy gourmet breakfasts and relaxing afternoon teas. There are 29 acres available to guests who wish to hike or play lawn games. The surrounding area offers antiquing, downhill skiing and shopping, and the inn's location provides convenient access to the recreation and sightseeing opportunities of three states. Cherry Plain State Park is nearby.

Breakfast included in rates. Types of meals: full breakfast, gourmet breakfast and early coffee/tea. Afternoon tea available. VCR on premises. 30 acres. Norwegian spoken. Antiques, fishing, downhill skiing, cross-country skiing, theater and watersports nearby. TAC15.

Location: One mile off Rt. 43.

Publicity: *Discovery Press.*

Special Discounts: 7th day free.

The Gregory House Country Inn & Restaurant

Rt 43 PO Box 401
Averill Park, NY 12018-0401
(518)674-3774
Fax:(518)674-8916
E-mail: gregoryhse@aol.com

Rates: $80-90. EP.
Payment: MC VISA AX DC CB DS PC TC.
Innkeeper(s): Bette & Robert Jewell.
Circa: 1830.

Rooms: 12 rooms with PB. 1 conference room.
Beds: QDT.

This colonial house was built in the center of the village by stockbroker Elias Gregory. It became a restaurant in 1984. The historic section of the building now holds the restaurant, while a new portion accommodates overnight guests. It is decorated with Early American braided rugs and four-poster beds.

Breakfast included in rates. Type of meal: continental breakfast. EP. Air conditioning in room. Cable TV, VCR, fax, copier and swimming on premises. Weddings, small meetings, family reunions and seminars hosted. Amusement parks, antiques, fishing, parks, shopping, downhill skiing, cross-country skiing, sporting events, theater and watersports nearby. TAC10.

Location: Minutes from Albany.

Publicity: *Hudson Valley, Albany Times Union, Schenectady Gazette, Courier, Sunday Record.*

"We experienced privacy and quiet, lovely surroundings indoors and out, excellent service, and as much friendliness as we were comfortable with, but no more."

Avon F5

Avon Inn

55 E Main St
Avon, NY 14414-1438
(716)226-8181
Fax:(716)226-8185

Rates: $50-85.
Payment: MC VISA AX DC CB DS TC.
Innkeeper(s): Linda Reusch.
Circa: 1820.

Rooms: 15 rooms with PB.
Beds: KQD.

This Greek Revival mansion, in both the state and national historic registers, has been providing lodging for more than a century. After 1866, the residence was turned into a health center that provided water cures from the local sulphur springs. The guest registry included the likes of Henry Ford, Thomas Edison and Eleanor Roosevelt. Though the inn is no longer a health spa, guests can still relax in the garden with its gazebo and fountain or on the Grecian-pillared front porch. A full-service restaurant and conference facilities are on the premises.

Breakfast included in rates. Types of meals: continental breakfast and early coffee/tea. Picnic lunch available. Air conditioning in room. Cable TV, fax and copier on premises. Weddings, small meetings, family reunions and seminars hosted. Amusement parks, antiques, fishing, parks, shopping, downhill skiing and cross-country skiing nearby. TAC10.

Location: Nestled in the village of Avon, 20 minutes south of Rochester.

Special Discounts: 10% AAA or Senior citizen.

Branchport G6

Gone With The Wind on Keuka Lake

453 W Lake Rd, Rt 54a
Branchport, NY 14418
(607)868-4603

Rates: $70-125.
Payment: PC TC.
Innkeeper(s): Linda & Robert Lewis.
Circa: 1887.

Rooms: 11 rooms, 3 with PB, 1 with FP. 1 conference room.
Beds: KQ.

Breezes from Keuka Lake waft up to the front porch where guests often sit with a cup of coffee. The lakeside home, a Victorian, is decorated with an eclectic assortment of reproductions. Each of the bathrooms features unique decor, such as oak, brass or marble. One room includes a fireplace. There's a hot tub in the solarium, and the grounds offer a gazebo by the inn's private beach cove.

Breakfast included in rates. Types of meals: full breakfast and gourmet breakfast. Air conditioning and turn-down service in room. Fax, spa, swimming and tennis on premises. 14 acres. Weddings, small meetings, family reunions and seminars hosted. Antiques, fishing, parks, shopping, cross-country skiing and watersports nearby.

"Thanks once again for a delightful stay. You have a little bit of heaven here."

Brooklyn — L12

Bed & Breakfast on The Park

113 Prospect Park W
Brooklyn, NY 11215-3710
(718)499-6115

Rates: $100-135.
Payment: MC VISA.
Innkeeper(s): Liana Paolella.
Circa: 1895.

Rooms: 6 rooms, 4 with PB, 8 with FP.
Beds: DT.

This four-story Park Slope townhouse brims with Victorian finery — canopied beds, feather comforters, and is lavishly decorated with a family art collection, including museum quality paintings spanning from the 18th century to contemporary times. Guests may enjoy city and park views through the stained-glass windows swathed in old lace. A "convenience flat" on the garden level with a separate entrance is available. The aroma of freshly baked bread draws guests to the dining room where tables are set with Irish tablecloths, period china and flatware.

Type of meal: full breakfast. Fax on premises. Handicap access.

Location: Two miles from downtown Manhattan.

Publicity: *Kings Courier, New York Times.*

"Wonderful breakfasts, beds, rooms, conversation!"

Canandaigua — F6

The Acorn Inn

4508 Rt 64 S
Canandaigua, NY 14424
(716)229-2834
Fax:(716)229-5046

Rates: $105-165.
Payment: MC VISA AX DS PC TC.
Innkeeper(s): Joan & Louis Clark.
Circa: 1795.

Rooms: 4 rooms with PB, 2 with FP.
Beds: Q.

NY

Guests to this Federal Stagecoach inn can relax before the blazing fire of a large colonial fireplace equipped with antique crane and hanging iron pots. Guest rooms, two with a fireplace, are furnished with period antiques, canopy beds, luxury linens and bedding, and each has a comfortable sitting area. Books are provided in each guest room as well as in the libraries. After a day of visiting wineries, skiing, hiking in the Finger Lakes area and dinner at a local restaurant, guests can relax in an outdoor Jacuzzi. Beds are turned down each night and a carafe of ice water and chocolates are placed in each room.

Breakfast and afternoon tea included in rates. Types of meals: continental-plus breakfast, gourmet breakfast and early coffee/tea. Air conditioning, turn-down service, cable TV and VCR in room. Fax, copier, spa and library on premises. Weddings, small meetings and family reunions hosted. Antiques, fishing, parks, shopping, downhill skiing, cross-country skiing, theater and watersports nearby. TAC10.

Pets Allowed.

Publicity: *New York, Mid-Atlantic.*

Special Discounts: Off season, November-April, Monday-Thursday 50% off second night weekends, 10% off second night.

Enchanted Rose Inn B&B

7479 Rts 5 & 20, PO Box 128
Canandaigua, NY 14424
(716)657-6003
Fax:(716)657-4405
E-mail: enchrose@vivanet.com

Rates: $95-125.
Payment: MC VISA DS PC TC.
Innkeeper(s): Jan & Howard Buhlmann.
Circa: 1820.

Rooms: 3 rooms, 2 with PB. 1 suite.
Beds: Q.

During the restoration of this early 19th-century home, the innkeepers uncovered the many original features, including the wood floors that now glimmer. The fireplace dates back to the 1790s, part of the original log home. The present structure was built onto the original in the 1820s. The innkeepers are only the fourth owners and have returned the home to its original glory. Freshly cut flowers from the inn's gardens are placed in the guest rooms, which feature antiques and romantic decor. The dining room table is set with beautiful china, a perfect accompaniment to the gourmet breakfasts. Afternoon tea is served in the rose garden or in an inviting fireplaced parlor.

Breakfast included in rates. Types of meals: full breakfast, gourmet breakfast and early coffee/tea. Evening snack available. Air conditioning, turn-down service, cable TV and VCR in room. Fax and library on premises. Weddings, small meetings and family reunions hosted. Antiques, fishing, parks, shopping, downhill skiing, cross-country skiing, sporting events, theater and watersports nearby. TAC10.

Special Discounts: Off season promotions 20-50% off second night; in season 20% off third night.

Morgan Samuels B&B Inn

2920 Smith Rd
Canandaigua, NY 14424
(716)394-9232
Fax:(716)394-8044

Rates: $109-225.
Payment: MC VISA DS PC TC.
Innkeeper(s): Julie & John Sullivan.
Circa: 1812.

Rooms: 6 rooms with PB, 6 with FP. 1 suite. 1 conference room.
Beds: KQ.

Ivy decorates the exterior of this stone manor house, set on 46 acres of countryside. The estate is reminiscent of an English country home. Its interior is elegant and romantic and each room has its own theme. The quiet location is an ideal one for those in search of peace or romance. Guests at this four-diamond inn are pampered with a lavish breakfast, with such items as gourmet omelets and homemade sausage accompanied by breads or muffins and a huge fruit platter, with more than a dozen different varieties.

Breakfast, afternoon tea and evening snack included in rates. Types of meals: gourmet breakfast and early coffee/tea. Air conditioning and turn-down service in room. Cable TV, VCR, fax, copier, bicycles, tennis, library and child care on premises. 46 acres. Weddings, small meetings, family reunions and seminars hosted. Antiques, fishing, parks, shopping, downhill skiing, cross-country skiing, sporting events, theater and watersports nearby. TAC10.

The Sutherland House B&B

3179 Bristol Rd, Rt 21 South
Canandaigua, NY 14424
(716)396-0375 (800)396-0375
Fax:(716)396-9281

Rates: $90-165.
Payment: MC VISA AX PC.
Innkeeper(s): Cor & Diane Van Der Woude.
Circa: 1885.

Rooms: 5 rooms with PB, 1 with FP. 1 suite. 1 conference room.
Beds: KQ.

Innkeepers Cor and Diane Van Der Woude refurbished this gracious home, adding more than 40 new windows, but leaving original elements such as a winding cherry staircase and marble fireplaces. Their restoration effort has created a charming 19th-century atmosphere. Rooms feature elegant, Victorian decor, and some boast two-person whirlpool tubs. Diane serves up a bountiful breakfast each morning. The home is just a mile and a half from Main Street Canandaigua, and wineries, antique shopping and outdoor activities are nearby.

Breakfast, afternoon tea and evening snack included in rates. Types of meals: continental breakfast, continental-plus breakfast, full breakfast, gourmet breakfast and early coffee/tea. Dinner, lunch, banquet service, catered breakfast and room service available. Air conditioning, ceiling fan and VCR in room. Fax, copier and spa on premises. Weddings, small meetings, family reunions and seminars hosted. Dutch spoken. Antiques, fishing, parks, shopping, downhill skiing, cross-country skiing, sporting events, theater and watersports nearby. TAC10.

Chemung

H7

Halcyon Place B&B

197 Washington St,
PO Box 244
Chemung, NY 14825
(607)529-3544

Rates: $55-70.
Payment: PC TC.
Innkeeper(s): Douglas & Yvonne Sloan.
Circa: 1820.

Rooms: 3 rooms, 1 with PB, 1 with FP.
Beds: D.

The innkeepers chose the name "halcyon" because it signifies tranquility and a healing richness. The historic Greek Revival inn and its grounds offer just that to guests, who will appreciate the fine period antiques, paneled doors, six-over-six windows of hand-blown glass and wide plank floors. An herb garden and screen porch also beckon visitors. Full breakfasts may include omelets with garden ingredients, raspberry muffins, rum sticky buns or waffles. The inn's three guest rooms feature double beds, and one boasts a romantic fireplace. Fine antiquing and golfing are found nearby. During the summer months, the innkeepers host a Wednesday afternoon herb series and afternoon tea. Also ask about other special packages.

Breakfast included in rates. Type of meal: gourmet breakfast. Afternoon tea available. Turn-down service in room. Weddings hosted. German spoken. Antiques, parks, shopping, cross-country skiing, sporting events, theater and watersports nearby.

Publicity: *Elmira Star Gazette, Chemung Valley Reporter, Evening Star.*

Special Discounts: More than three nights stay-deduct 15%.

"We appreciate all the little touches you attend to, to make our stay special."

Chestertown

D12

The Friends Lake Inn

Friends Lake Rd
Chestertown, NY 12817
(518)494-4751
Fax:(518)494-4616

Rates: $160-250. MAP.
Payment: MC VISA AX PC TC.
Innkeeper(s): Sharon & Greg Taylor.
Circa: 1860.

Rooms: 14 rooms with PB.
Beds: Q.

NY

Formerly a boardinghouse for tanners who worked in the area, this Mission-style inn now offers its guests elegant accommodations and fine dining. Overlooking Friends Lake, the inn provides easy access to many well-known skiing areas, including Gore Mountain. Guests are welcome to borrow a canoe for a lake outing and use the inn's private beach. Guest rooms are well-appointed and include brass and iron beds. Many have breathtaking lake views. An outdoor hot tub is a favorite spot after a busy day of recreation. The new 30 km Nordic Ski Center is on site with groomed wilderness trails, lessons and rentals.

Breakfast and dinner included in rates. Type of meal: full breakfast. Picnic lunch, catering service and room service available. MAP. Air conditioning and turn-down service in room. Cable TV, VCR, fax, copier, swimming and library on premises. Handicap access. 10 acres. Weddings, small meetings, family reunions and seminars hosted. Amusement parks, antiques, fishing, parks, shopping, downhill skiing, cross-country skiing, sporting events, theater and watersports nearby. TAC10.

Special Discounts: Midweek seasonal packages.

"Everyone here is so pleasant, you end up feeling like family!"

Clarence

F3

Asa Ransom House

10529 Main St
Clarence, NY 14031-1624
(716)759-2315
Fax:(716)759-2791
E-mail: asaransom@aol.com

Rates: $85-145. MAP, EP.
Payment: MC VISA DS PC TC.
Innkeeper(s): Robert & Judy Lenz.
Circa: 1853.

Rooms: 9 rooms with PB, 7 with FP. 2 suites. 1 conference room.
Beds: KQDT.

Set on spacious lawns, behind a white picket fence, the Asa Ransom House rests on the site of the first grist mill built in Erie County. Silversmith Asa Ransom, constructed an inn and grist mill here in response to the Holland Land Company's offering of free land to anyone who would start and operate a tavern. A specialty of the dining room is "Veal Perrott" and "Pistachio Banana Muffins."

Breakfast included in rates. Types of meals: full breakfast and early coffee/tea. Dinner available. MAP, EP. Air conditioning and turn-down service in room. Fax, copier and library on premises. Handicap access. Weddings and small meetings hosted. Antiques, parks, shopping, cross-country skiing and theater nearby. TAC10.

Publicity: *Country Living.*

"Popular spot keeps getting better."

Cold Spring

J12

Hudson House

2 Main St
Cold Spring, NY 10516
(914)265-9355

Rates: $105-150.
Payment: MC VISA AX.
Innkeeper(s): Joe & Kathleen Klingelsmith.
Circa: 1832.

Rooms: 13 rooms with PB. 1 suite.
Beds: QD.

This is a restored Historic Landmark Building located on the banks of a beautiful section of the Hudson River. The inn is said to be the second oldest inn in continuous operation in New York state. It was built to accommodate the increase in passenger traffic along the river because of a new paddle steamer. The rooms are filled with antiques and many have waterfront views of West Point and the hills.

Breakfast included in rates. Type of meal: full breakfast. Air conditioning, turn-down service and ceiling fan in room. Cable TV and copier on premises. Weddings, small meetings and family reunions hosted. Antiques, fishing, parks, shopping, downhill skiing, cross-country skiing and sporting events nearby.

Location: Hudson River Valley.

Publicity: *New York Times, Conde Nast Traveler.*

Cooperstown

G10

The Inn at Cooperstown

16 Chestnut St
Cooperstown, NY 13326
(607)547-5756
Fax:(607)547-8779

Rates: $75-120.
Payment: MC VISA AX DC DS TC.
Innkeeper(s): Michael Jerome.
Circa: 1874.

Rooms: 18 rooms with PB. 1 conference room.
Beds: QT.

This three-story, Second Empire hotel features a graceful porch filled with wicker furniture and rocking chairs. The inn is located in the center of the Cooperstown National Historic District. The guest rooms are decorated tastefully and comfortably. A block from Otsego Lake, the inn is within walking distance of most of Cooperstown's attractions.

Breakfast included in rates. Type of meal: continental breakfast. Cable TV, fax and library on premises. Handicap access. Small meetings hosted. Antiques, fishing, parks, shopping, cross-country skiing, sporting events, theater and watersports nearby.

Publicity: *Cleveland Plain Dealer, New York Times, Atlanta Journal, Los Angeles Times, New York Magazine.*

"In the evenings, a quiet soothes the soul like brandy in a portly gentleman," — Travel Holiday.

Corinth

E12

Agape Farm B&B

4894 Rt 9N
Corinth, NY 12822-1704
(518)654-7777

Rates: $60-125.
Payment: MC VISA PC TC.
Innkeeper(s): Fred & Sigrid Koch.
Circa: 1870.

Rooms: 6 rooms with PB. 1 cottage.
Beds: KQDT.

Amid 33 acres of fields and woods, this Adirondack farmhouse inn is home to chickens and horses, as well as guests seeking a refreshing getaway. Visitors have their choice of six guest rooms, all with ceiling fans, phones, private baths and views of the tranquil surroundings. The inn's wraparound porch lures many visitors, who often enjoy a glass of icy lemonade. Homemade breads, jams, jellies and muffins are part of the full breakfast served here, and guests are welcome to pick berries or gather a ripe tomato from the garden. A trout-filled stream on the grounds flows to the Hudson River, a mile away.

Breakfast, afternoon tea and evening snack included in rates. Types of meals: full breakfast and early coffee/tea. Ceiling fan in room. Cable TV, VCR, library and child care on premises. Handicap access. 33 acres. Small meetings hosted. Amusement parks, antiques, fishing, parks, shopping, downhill skiing, cross-country skiing, sporting events, theater and watersports nearby. TAC5.

Pets Allowed: Housed in outside building.

Location: Between Saratoga & Lake George attractions.

Special Discounts: Church and military discount.

"Clean and impeccable, we were treated royally."

NY

Cornwall

J12

Cromwell Manor Inn B&B

Angola Rd
Cornwall, NY 12518
(914)534-7136

Rates: $120-250.
Payment: MC VISA PC.
Innkeeper(s): Dale & Barbara O'Hara.
Circa: 1820.

Rooms: 13 rooms with PB, 7 with FP. 2 suites. 1 conference room.
Beds: QD.

A descent of Oliver Cromwell built this stunning Greek Revival home, which is set on seven lush acres boasting scenic views of mountains and a 4,000-acre forest preserve. The innkeepers refurbished the manor, leaving original elements and adding period antiques and fine furnishings throughout. Relax by the fireplace or enjoy the inn's Jacuzzi and steam room. The innkeepers prepare a breakfast of home-baked treats such as muffins, quiche, omelets, fruits and specialty breads. The innkeepers also offer a romantic cottage dating back to 1764, which boasts a fireplace and country antiques.

Breakfast included in rates. Types of meals: full breakfast, gourmet breakfast and early coffee/tea. Afternoon tea, picnic lunch, catering service and room service available. Air conditioning and turn-down service in room. Cable TV, VCR and copier on premises. Handicap access. Weddings, small meetings, family reunions and seminars hosted. Antiques, fishing, parks, shopping, downhill skiing, cross-country skiing, sporting events, theater and watersports nearby. TAC10.

Publicity: *Orange Life.*

"Wonderful, great attention to detail. Immaculate, great setting. Romantic."

Crown Point

D12

Crown Point B&B

Main St, Rt 9N, PO Box 490
Crown Point, NY 12928
(518)597-3651
Fax:(518)597-4451

Rates: $60-120.
Payment: MC VISA PC TC.
Innkeeper(s): Al & Jan Hallock.
Circa: 1886.

Rooms: 5 rooms, 4 with PB. 1 suite.
Beds: QDT.

This Queen Anne Victorian inn north of Fort Ticonderoga offers a fascinating vantage point from which to view the historical area. Crown Point served as a fortress guarding Lake Champlain during the Revolutionary War. The inn, originally owned by a local banker, boasts cherry, chestnut, mahogany, oak, pine and walnut woodwork. The spacious guest rooms, furnished with period antiques, all feature private baths. The Master Bedroom Suite includes a highback walnut bed and marble-topped dresser. Three parlors are available for relaxing and socializing.

Breakfast included in rates. Type of meal: continental-plus breakfast. Turn-down service and ceiling fan in room. Cable TV, fax and copier on premises. Small meetings and family reunions hosted. Spanish on weekends spoken. Antiques, fishing, parks, shopping, cross-country skiing, theater and watersports nearby. TAC10.

Special Discounts: 10% off AARP.

De Bruce (Livingston Manor)

De Bruce Country Inn on The Willowemoc

De Bruce Road #286-A
De Bruce (Livingston Manor), NY 12758
(914)439-3900

Rates: $150-225. MAP.
Innkeeper(s): Ron & Marilyn Lusker.
Circa: 1917.

Rooms: 15 rooms with PB. 2 suites.
Beds: KQDT.

This inn is nestled along the banks of the Willowemoc River, near the spot where the first dry fly was cast in the United States. Guests at this early 20th-century retreat came for the excellent trout fishing and secluded woodlands, and its those same ingredients that draw visitors today.The inn, located in the Catskill Forest Reserve, offers wooded trails, wildlife, game, a stocked pond, whirlpool, sauna and spa. After a day enjoying the outdoors, relax in the Dry Fly Lounge, where a crackling fire will warm you. From the dining terrace, guests enjoy a view of the valley and mountains. Hearty breakfasts and romantic dinners are included in the rates.

Breakfast and dinner included in rates. Type of meal: full breakfast. MAP. Ceiling fan in room. Cable TV, VCR, fax, copier, spa, swimming, sauna and library on premises. 50 acres. Weddings, small meetings, family reunions and seminars hosted. French, limited German and limited Italian spoken. Antiques, downhill skiing, cross-country skiing and theater nearby.

Pets Allowed: At inn owners' discretion.

Deposit

H9

Chestnut Inn at Oquaga Lake

498 Oquaga Lake Rd
Deposit, NY 13754-3833
(607)467-2500 (800)467-7676
Fax:(607)467-5911

Rates: $69-199. MAP.
Payment: MC VISA AX DC DS PC TC.
Innkeeper(s): Tom Spaulding & Dale Shaw.
Circa: 1928.

Rooms: 30 rooms, 10 with PB. 6 suites. 1 cottage. 1 conference room.
Beds: KQD.

This spacious Craftsman-style inn east of Binghampton offers a variety of rooming and dining options. The family-oriented inn is well-equipped to handle meetings, receptions and weddings, and guests will find no shortage of activities or amenities. Bicycles, child care and swimming are offered. The inn features picnic lunches, perfect for a day by the lake. Oquaga Creek State Park is a short drive away.

Afternoon tea included in rates. Type of meal: full breakfast. Dinner, lunch and banquet service available. MAP. Cable TV in room. VCR, fax, copier, swimming and bicycles on premises. Weddings, small meetings, family reunions and seminars hosted. Antiques, fishing, parks, shopping, sporting events and watersports nearby. TAC10.

Dolgeville F10

Adrianna B&B

44 Stewart St
Dolgeville, NY 13329-1423
(315)429-3249 (800)335-4233

Rates: $45-65.
Payment: MC VISA PC TC.
Innkeeper(s): Adrianna Naizby.
Circa: 1965.

Rooms: 3 rooms, 1 with PB.
Beds: QDT.

In the foothills of the Adirondacks, this two-story raised ranch home awaits visitors to the central New York area. Three guest rooms are available, one with private bath and all with ceiling fans. Barney, the resident cat, often curls up in front of the fireplace, and guests are welcome to join him there for afternoon tea. The inn's swimming pool is another favorite relaxation area, especially after a day spent antiquing or touring the area's many points of interest, including Beaversprite Sanctuary and the Herkimer House. The National Baseball Hall of Fame at Cooperstown is within easy driving distance.

Breakfast included in rates. Types of meals: full breakfast and early coffee/tea. Air conditioning and ceiling fan in room. Cable TV, VCR, swimming and library on premises. Antiques, fishing, shopping, downhill skiing and cross-country skiing nearby. TAC10.

East Hampton K15

Mill House Inn

33 N Main St
East Hampton, NY 11937
(516)324-9766
Fax:(516)324-9793

Rates: $100-275.
Payment: MC VISA AX PC.
Innkeeper(s): Daniel & Katherine Hartnett.
Circa: 1790.

Rooms: 8 rooms with PB, 6 with FP.
Beds: QD.

This Colonial house is just opposite the Old Hook Windmill. It is in the center of East Hampton, which has been called "America's most beautiful village." Guest rooms are decorated with a Hampton's theme in mind, sporting names such as Sail Away or Hampton Holiday. Romantic amenities abound, including fireplaces in six of the guest rooms. Several rooms also have whirlpool tubs. Breakfasts are a gourmet delight, featuring home-baked granola bread, cranberry orange scones or sour cream coffeecake followed by entrees such as a potato and smoked salmon frittata, maple bread pudding and pumpkin pancakes.

Breakfast and afternoon tea included in rates. Types of meals: full breakfast and early coffee/tea. Air conditioning, ceiling fan, cable TV and VCR in room. Fax, copier and library on premises. Handicap access. Small meetings and family reunions hosted. Spanish spoken. Antiques, fishing, shopping, theater and watersports nearby.

Location: In the heart of East Hampton Village.

Publicity: *New York Magazine.*

"Perfect everything, it's hard to leave."

Elbridge F7

Fox Ridge Farm B&B

4786 Foster Rd
Elbridge, NY 13060-9770
(315)673-4881
Fax:(315)673-3691
E-mail: foxridg@aol.com

Rates: $55-65.
Payment: MC VISA AX DS PC TC.
Innkeeper(s): Marge Sykes.
Circa: 1910.

Rooms: 3 rooms, 1 with PB.
Beds: QD.

Guest shouldn't be surprised to encounter deer or other wildlife at this secluded country home surrounded by woods. The innkeepers have transformed the former farmhouse into a cozy inn with rooms boasting quilts, a four-poster bed and views of the woods or flower garden. Enjoy breakfasts in front of a fire in the large country kitchen. The innkeepers are happy to accommodate dietary needs. Snacks and refreshments are always available for hungry guests in the evening. Nearby Skaneateles Lake offers swimming, boating and other outdoor activities. Dinner cruises, touring wineries and antique shopping are other popular activities.

Breakfast and evening snack included in rates. Types of meals: continental-plus breakfast, full breakfast, gourmet breakfast and early coffee/tea. VCR on premises. 120 acres. Weddings hosted. Antiques, fishing, parks, shopping, downhill skiing, cross-country skiing, sporting events, theater and watersports nearby.

Special Discounts: January through March: half off second night.

Elizabethtown — C12

Stony Water B&B

RR 1 Box 69
Elizabethtown, NY 12932
(518)873-9125 (800)995-7295

Rates: $75-85.
Payment: MC VISA AX PC TC.
Innkeeper(s): Winifred Thomas & Sandra Murphy.
Circa: 1870.

Rooms: 5 rooms, 4 with PB. 1 suite. 2 cottages.
Beds: QDT.

The innkeepers at Stony Water, a 19th-century farmhouse, have created a cozy, comfortable environment perfect for those in search of relaxation. Families are welcome here, especially in the spacious Meadow Rue room and Trillium Cottage. The home's 87-acre grounds offers plenty to explore, from meadows of wildflowers to a pond and brooks. There also is a swimming pool on the premises. Robert Frost was a guest here in the 1930s, when the home was owned by Louis Untermeyer, a well-known literary figure of the time. Lake Champlain is a 15-minute drive, and Lake Placid is a half hour away.

Breakfast and afternoon tea included in rates. Types of meals: full breakfast and early coffee/tea. Ceiling fan in room. VCR and swimming on premises. Handicap access. 87 acres. Small meetings, family reunions and seminars hosted. Limited French spoken. Antiques, fishing, parks, shopping, downhill skiing, cross-country skiing, theater and watersports nearby.

Elmira — H7

Lindenwald Haus

1526 Grand Central Ave
Elmira, NY 14901-1208
(607)733-8753

Rates: $49-105.
Payment: MC VISA PC TC.
Innkeeper(s): Sharon & Michael J Dowd.
Circa: 1875.

Rooms: 17 rooms, 10 with PB. 3 suites.
Beds: QDT.

Two graceful porticos decorate the exterior of this impressive Italianate Victorian. The 48-room interior boasts 12-foot ceilings, windows stretching nearly nine feet, a grand staircase and polished wood floors. Lindenwald Haus originally served as a home for widows of Civil War veterans. A brass bed, red velvet sofa or perhaps an iron bed are among the charming, Victorian furnishings found in the guest rooms. The beds are topped by quilts handmade by the innkeeper's mother. German-style, continental-plus breakfasts are served buffet-style in the Victorian dining room, with fresh meats, cheeses, fruit, home-baked treats, cereals and plenty of juices and coffee. Elmira offers many activities, from tours of historic homes to four-star dining.

Breakfast included in rates. Type of meal: continental-plus breakfast. Air conditioning and ceiling fan in room. Cable TV, VCR, copier, swimming, bicycles and library on premises. Handicap access. Weddings, small meetings and family reunions hosted. Amusement parks, antiques, fishing, parks and shopping nearby.

"What a dream! Absolutely delightful!"

Fair Haven — E7

Black Creek Farm B&B

PO Box 390
Fair Haven, NY 13064-0390
(315)947-5282

Rates: $50-75.
Payment: MC VISA DS PC.
Innkeeper(s): Bob & Kathy Sarber.
Circa: 1888.

Rooms: 3 rooms, 1 with PB.
Beds: DT.

Pines and towering birch trees frame this Victorian farmhouse inn, filled with an incredible assortment of authentic antiques. Set on 20 acres in the countryside west of Fair Haven, this inn offers a refreshing

escape from big-city life. The inn's impressive furnishings come as no real surprise since there is an antique shop on the premises. Guests enjoy relaxing in a hammock, on the porch, or by taking a stroll along the peaceful country roads. The inn is two miles from Lake Ontario's shoreline and within easy reach of Fair Haven Beach State Park and Thorpe Vineyard.

Breakfast and afternoon tea included in rates. Types of meals: full breakfast and early coffee/tea. Evening snack available. Air conditioning in room. VCR and bicycles on premises. 20 acres. Family reunions hosted. Antiques, fishing, parks, cross-country skiing and watersports nearby.

Special Discounts: For extended stays.

Fleischmanns H11

River Run

Main St, Box D4
Fleischmanns, NY 12430
(914)254-4884

Rates: $60-95.
Payment: MC VISA PC.
Innkeeper(s): Larry Miller.
Circa: 1887.

Rooms: 10 rooms, 6 with PB. 1 suite.
Beds: KQDT.

The backyard of this large three-story Victorian slopes to the river where the Little Red Kill and the Bushkill trout streams join. Guests are invited to bring their well-behaved pets with them. (They are given a spot on the porch where there are doggie towels for wiping dusty paws before entering the inn.) Inside, stained-glass windows shine on the hardwood floors of the dining room, and there's a pleasant fireplace in the parlor. Adirondack chairs are situated comfortably on the front porch. The inn is two and a half hours out of New York City, 35 minutes west of Woodstock, and accessible by public transportation.

Breakfast and afternoon tea included in rates. Types of meals: continental-plus breakfast and early coffee/tea. Cable TV, VCR, bicycles and library on premises. Small meetings and family reunions hosted. French and German spoken. Antiques, fishing, parks, shopping, downhill skiing, cross-country skiing, theater and watersports nearby. TAC10.

Pets Allowed: Well behaved, fully trained, over one year old.

Location: Country village in the high peaks of the Catskill Mountains.

Publicity: *Catskill Mountain News, Kingston Freeman, New York Times, New York Daily News, Philadelphia Inquirer, Inn Country USA.*

Special Discounts: $10 off nightly rates midweek (Monday-Thursday); 10% single discount.

"We are really happy to know of a place that welcomes all of our family."

NY

Forestburgh I10

The Inn at Lake Joseph

400 St Josephs Rd
Forestburgh, NY 12777
(914)791-9506
Fax:(914)794-1948

Rates: $138-298. MAP, EP.
Payment: MC VISA AX PC TC.
Innkeeper(s): Ivan Weinger & Jane Stock.
Circa: 1860.

Rooms: 10 rooms with PB, 9 with FP. 3 suites. 2 conference rooms.
Beds: KQ.

This Queen Anne Victorian, listed in the National Register of Historic Places, was once the vacation home of Cardinals Hayes and Spellman. The inn rests next to a 250-acre lake by 2,000 acres of a wildlife preserve and forest. In addition to the full breakfast, an afternoon buffet and dinner are available.

Type of meal: full breakfast. Dinner available. MAP, EP. Swimming and tennis on premises. 2000 acres. Weddings, small meetings, family reunions and seminars hosted. Antiques, shopping, downhill skiing and theater nearby.

Publicity: *New York Times, New York Magazine.*

"This is a secluded spot where every detail is attended to, making it one of the country's best inns."

Fulton

E7

Battle Island Inn

2167 SR 48
Fulton, NY 13069-4132
(315)593-3699
E-mail: hzgu49a@prodigy.com

Rates: $60-95. AP.
Payment: MC VISA AX DS PC TC.
Innkeeper(s): Richard & Joyce Rice.
Circa: 1840.

Rooms: 5 rooms with PB. 1 suite.
Beds: QDT.

Topped with a gothic cupola, this family farmhouse overlooks the Oswego River and a golf course. There are three antique-filled parlors. Guest accommodations are furnished in a variety of styles including Victorian and Renaissance Revival. There are four wooded acres with lawns and gardens. Guests are often found relaxing on one of the inn's four porches and enjoying the views.

Breakfast included in rates. Types of meals: full breakfast, gourmet breakfast and early coffee/tea. AP. Ceiling fan and cable TV in room. VCR, fax and copier on premises. Handicap access. Small meetings and seminars hosted. Fishing, parks, shopping, cross-country skiing, theater and watersports nearby.

Location: Seven miles south of Oswego on Lake Ontario.

Publicity: *Lake Effect, Palladium Times, Travel, Journey, Oswego County Business, Valley News.*

"We will certainly never forget our wonderful weeks at Battle Island Inn."

Garrison

J12

The Bird & Bottle Inn

R9 Old Albany Post Rd,
R2 Box 129
Garrison, NY 10524
(914)424-3000
Fax:(914)424-3283
E-mail: birdbottle@aol.com

Rates: $210-240. MAP.
Payment: MC VISA AX PC TC.
Innkeeper(s): Ira Boyar.
Circa: 1761.

Rooms: 4 rooms with PB, 4 with FP. 1 suite. 1 cottage.
Beds: Q.

Built as Warren's Tavern, this three-story yellow farmhouse served as a lodging and dining spot on the New York-to-Albany Post Road, now a National Historic Landmark. George Washington, Hamilton, Lafayette and many other historic figures frequently passed by. The inn's eight acres include secluded lawns, a bubbling stream and Hudson Valley woodlands. Timbered ceilings, old paneling and fireplace mantels in the inn's notable restaurant maintain a Revolutionary War era ambiance. Second-floor guest rooms have canopied or four-poster beds and each is warmed by its own fireplace.

Breakfast and dinner included in rates. Type of meal: full breakfast. Lunch, banquet service and catering service available. MAP. Air conditioning in room. Cable TV, fax and copier on premises. Weddings, small meetings, family reunions and seminars hosted. Antiques, fishing, parks, shopping, cross-country skiing and theater nearby.

Publicity: *Colonial Homes, Hudson Valley, Spotlight.*

Special Discounts: Midweek specials on request.

Geneva

F6

Geneva on The Lake

1001 Lochland Rd, Rt 14S
Geneva, NY 14456-3217
(800)343-6382
Fax:(315)789-0322

Rates: $124-481.
Payment: MC VISA AX DS.
Innkeeper(s): William Schickel.
Circa: 1911.

Rooms: 30 suites. 3 conference rooms.
Beds: QDT.

This opulent world-class inn is a replica of the Renaissance-era Lancellotti Villa in Frascati, Italy. It is listed in the National Register. Although originally built as a residence, it became a monastery for Capuchin monks. Now it is one of the finest resorts in the U.S. Meticulously restored in 1979-1980 under the direction of award-winning designer William Schickel, all rooms have kitchens and there are 10 two-bedroom suites — some with views of the lake. Here, you may have an experience as fine as Europe can offer, without leaving the states. Some compare it to the Grand Hotel du Cap-Ferrat on the French Riviera. The inn has been awarded four diamonds from AAA for 14 consecutive years. Breakfast is available daily and on Sunday, brunch is served. Dinner is served Wednesday through Sunday, and in the summer, lunch is served on the terrace.

Breakfast included in rates. Type of meal: gourmet breakfast. Banquet service and room service available. Air conditioning, turn-down service, cable TV and VCR in room. Fax, copier, swimming and bicycles on premises. 10 acres. Weddings, small meetings, family reunions and seminars hosted. Antiques, parks, shopping, downhill skiing, cross-country skiing, sporting events, theater and watersports nearby. TAC10.

Location: On Seneca Lake in New York's Finger Lakes Wine District.

Publicity: *Bon Appetit, Country Inns, New York Times, Innsider, Bride's, Catholic Register, Pittsford-Brighton Post, New York, Glamour, Gourmet, Washingtonian, Toronto Star, Globe & Mail, Rochester Democrat & Chronicle.*

"The food was superb and the service impeccable."

Gorham

G6

The Gorham House

4752 E Swamp Rd
Gorham, NY 14461
(716)526-4402
Fax:(716)526-4402

Rates: $60-80.
Payment: PC TC.
Innkeeper(s): Nancy & Al Rebmann.
Circa: 1887.

Rooms: 3 rooms, 1 with PB.
Beds: QD.

NY

The Gorham House serves as a homey, country place to enjoy New York's Finger Lakes region. The five, secluded acres located between Canandaigua and Seneca lakes, include herb gardens, wildflowers and berry bushes. Part of the home dates back to the early 19th century, but it's the architecture of the 1887 expansion that accounts for the inn's Victorian touches. The interior is warm and cozy with comfortable, country furnishings. Some of the pieces are the innkeepers' family heirlooms. There are more than 50 wineries in the area, as well as a bounty of outdoor activities.

Breakfast included in rates. Types of meals: gourmet breakfast and early coffee/tea. Air conditioning in room. Library on premises. Family reunions hosted. Antiques, fishing, parks, shopping, downhill skiing, cross-country skiing, sporting events, theater and watersports nearby.

Greenfield Center F12

The Wayside Inn

104 Wilton Rd
Greenfield Center, NY
12833-1705
(518)893-7249
Fax:(518)893-2884

Rates: $60-150.
Payment: MC VISA DC DS.
Innkeeper(s): Karen & Dale Shook.
Circa: 1786.

Rooms: 3 rooms with PB. 1 suite. 2 conference rooms.

This Federal-style inn and arts center provides a unique atmosphere to visitors of the Saratoga Springs area. Situated on 10 acres amid a brook, herb gardens, pond, wildflowers and willows, the inn originally served as a stagecoach tavern. Many interesting pieces, gathered during the innkeepers' 10 years living abroad, highlight the inn's interior. Visitors select from the Colonial American, European, Far East and Middle East rooms. Migrating birds are known to frequent the inn's picturesque pond.

Breakfast included in rates. Types of meals: full breakfast and early coffee/tea. Air conditioning and ceiling fan in room. Cable TV and VCR on premises. 10 acres. Small meetings, family reunions and seminars hosted. Amusement parks, antiques, shopping, downhill skiing, cross-country skiing, sporting events and theater nearby.

Greenport K15

The Bartlett House Inn

503 Front St
Greenport, NY 11944-1519
(516)477-0371

Rates: $75-105.
Payment: MC VISA PC TC.
Innkeeper(s): Bill & Diane May.
Circa: 1908.

Rooms: 10 rooms with PB, 1 with FP. 1 suite. 1 conference room.
Beds: QDT.

A family residence for more than 60 years and then a convent for a nearby church, this large Victorian house became a bed & breakfast in 1982. Features include corinthian columns, stained-glass windows, two fireplaces and a large front porch. Period antiques complement the rich interior. The inn is within walking distance of shops, the harbor, the Shelter Island Ferry and train station.

Breakfast included in rates. Types of meals: continental-plus breakfast and early coffee/tea. Air conditioning in room. Weddings, small meetings, family reunions and seminars hosted. Amusement parks, antiques, fishing, parks, shopping and watersports nearby.

Greenville G12

Greenville Arms

South St, PO Box 659
Greenville, NY 12083
(518)966-5219
Fax:(518)966-8754
E-mail: NY1889inn@aol.com

Rates: $110-145. MAP.
Payment: MC VISA DC CB DS PC TC.
Innkeeper(s): Eliot & Letitia Dalton.
Circa: 1889.

Rooms: 14 rooms. 1 suite. 2 conference rooms.
Beds: KQDT.

William Vanderbilt had this graceful Victorian built with Queen Anne gables and cupolas. Seven acres of lush lawns are dotted with gardens and a 50 foot outdoor pool. There are floor-to-ceiling fireplaces, chestnut woodwork and wainscoting, and Victorian bead work over the doorways. Painting workshops are held in summer and fall. Dinner is served to inn guests seven nights a week.

Breakfast and afternoon tea included in rates. Types of meals: full breakfast and early coffee/tea. Dinner and lunch available. MAP. Cable TV, VCR, fax, swimming, bicycles and library on premises. Weddings, small meetings, family reunions and seminars hosted. Amusement parks, antiques, fishing, parks, shopping, downhill skiing, cross-country skiing and watersports nearby. TAC10.

Location: On SR 32, 2 1/2 hours from New York City.

Publicity: *Victorian Homes, New York, Yankee.*

"Just a note of appreciation for all your generous hospitality, and wonderful display of attention and affection!"

Groton

G7

Gale House B&B

114 Williams St
Groton, NY 13073-1136
(607)898-4904

Rates: $85-105.
Payment: MC VISA PC TC.
Innkeeper(s): Barbara Ingraham.
Circa: 1890.

Rooms: 4 rooms, 2 with PB.
Beds: Q.

Old-fashioned lace, crystal, elegant woodwork and antiques fill this beautiful Queen Anne Victorian inn. Each bedroom has its own antique bed accentuated with beautiful blankets and pillows. During the week, guests are served continental-plus fare, and weekend guests are treated to a full breakfast with cereals, yogurt, fruit, freshly baked muffins, egg dishes and an entree such as waffles or French toast. Wineries, lake cruises and ski slopes are nearby. The inn is only 20 minutes from Cornell University, Ithaca College and SUNY Cortland. If road trips aren't your style, relax in the parlor or browse through the inn's antique shop.

Breakfast and evening snack included in rates. Types of meals: continental-plus breakfast and early coffee/tea. Afternoon tea and picnic lunch available. Air conditioning, turn-down service, ceiling fan and cable TV in room. Family reunions hosted. Japanese spoken. Antiques, fishing, parks, shopping, downhill skiing, cross-country skiing, sporting events, theater and watersports nearby. TAC10.

Location: Gateway to the eastern Finger Lakes.

Special Discounts: Packages available; government rate.

"Everything about our stay was just perfect."

Hague

D12

Trout House Village Resort

PO Box 510
Hague, NY 12836-0510
(518)543-6088 (800)368-6088

Rates: $46-94. AP.
Payment: MC VISA AX DS PC TC.
Innkeeper(s): Scott & Alice Patchett.
Circa: 1934.

Rooms: 13 rooms, 11 with PB, 15 with FP. 1 suite. 15 cottages. 2 conference rooms.
Beds: QDT.

NY

On the shores of beautiful Lake George is this resort inn, offering accommodations in the lodge, authentic log cabins or cottages. Many of the guest rooms in the lodge boast lake views, while the log cabins offer jetted tubs and fireplaces. The guest quarters are furnished comfortably. The emphasis here is on the abundance of outdoor activities. Outstanding cross-country skiing, downhill skiing and snowmobiling are found nearby. The inn furnishes bicycles, canoes, kayaks, paddle boats, rowboats, sleds, skis and toboggans. Summertime evenings offer games of capture-the-flag and soccer. Other activities include basketball, horseshoes, ping pong, a putting green and volleyball.

Types of meals: continental-plus breakfast and early coffee/tea. Banquet service available. AP. Cable TV and VCR in room. Spa, swimming, bicycles, tennis, library and child care on premises. Handicap access. Weddings, small meetings, family reunions and seminars hosted. Amusement parks, antiques, fishing, parks, shopping, downhill skiing, cross-country skiing and watersports nearby. TAC10.

Pets Allowed: During off season.

"My wife and I felt the family warmth at this resort. There wasn't that coldness you get at larger resorts."

Hamburg

G3

Sharon's B&B Lake House

4862 Lake Shore Rd
Hamburg, NY 14075-5542
(716)627-7561

Rates: $100-110.
Payment: PC TC.
Innkeeper(s): Sharon & Vince De Maria.
Circa: 1935.

Rooms: 2 rooms, 1 with PB.
Beds: D.

This historic lakefront house is located 10 miles from Buffalo and 45 minutes from Niagara Falls. Overlooking Lake Erie, the West Lake Room and the Upper Lake Room provide spectacular views. The home's beautiful furnishings offer additional delights.

Breakfast included in rates. Type of meal: gourmet breakfast. Afternoon tea available. Ceiling fan and cable TV in room. VCR and swimming on premises. Fishing, parks, shopping, downhill skiing, cross-country skiing, theater and watersports nearby.

Location: On the shore of Lake Erie.

Special Discounts: Gift certificates, one promotion per month.

"Spectacular view, exquisitely furnished."

Hamlin E5

Sandy Creek Manor House

1960 Redman Rd
Hamlin, NY 14464-9635
(716)964-7528 (800)594-0400

Rates: $50-70.
Payment: MC VISA AX DS PC TC.
Innkeeper(s): Shirley Hollink & James Krempasky.
Circa: 1910.

Rooms: 4 rooms, 1 with PB.
Beds: KQDT.

Six acres of woods and perennial gardens provide the setting for this English Tudor house. Stained glass, polished woods and Amish quilts add warmth to the home. Breakfast is served on the open porch in summer. Fisherman's Landing, on the banks of Sandy Creek, is a stroll away. Bullhead, trout and salmon are popular catches. There is a gift shop on premises. Ask about murder-mystery and sweetheart dinner packages.

Breakfast, afternoon tea and evening snack included in rates. Types of meals: continental breakfast, continental-plus breakfast, gourmet breakfast and early coffee/tea. Air conditioning in room. VCR, bicycles and library on premises. Small meetings and family reunions hosted. Antiques, fishing, parks, shopping, downhill skiing, cross-country skiing, sporting events and watersports nearby. TAC10.

Pets Allowed.

Location: Four miles north of Rt 104; 25 miles northwest of Rochester; located near the Seaway Trail.

Publicity: *Rochester Times Union.*

Special Discounts: 10%-AAA; stay 7 nights, pay for 6; Senior rate.

"Delightful in every way."

Hobart H10

Breezy Acres Farm B&B

RR 1 Box 191
Hobart, NY 13788-9754
(607)538-9338

Rates: $60-75.
Payment: MC VISA AX.
Innkeeper(s): Joyce and David Barber.
Circa: 1830.

Rooms: 3 rooms with PB.
Beds: KQ.

Maple syrup, fields of corn and hay, heifers and a fruit and vegetable stand assure guests that they are truly staying at a working crop farm. The rambling farmhouse is filled with family antiques. The innkeeper, a professional home economist, serves a full country breakfast. There is a pond and the Delaware River runs past the property. Guests often enjoy hiking the farm's 300 acres, working their way up to the log cabin hideaway.

Breakfast included in rates. 300 acres. Small meetings hosted. Antiques, fishing, downhill skiing and cross-country skiing nearby.

Location: In the northern Catskill Mountains.

Publicity: *Catskill Country.*

"Nicest people you'd want to meet. Perfect! Wonderful hosts, warm, friendly atmosphere. We will be back!"

Hudson

H12

The Inn at Blue Stores

2323 Rt 9
Hudson, NY 12534-0099
(518)537-4277

Rates: $99-165.
Payment: MC VISA.
Innkeeper(s): Linda & Robert.
Circa: 1908.

Rooms: 5 rooms, 3 with PB. 1 suite.
Beds: KQT.

A rural Hudson Valley setting may seem an unusual place for a Spanish-style inn, but this former gentlemen's farm now provides a unique setting for those seeking a relaxing getaway. Visitors will enjoy the inn's clay tile roof and stucco exterior, along with its impressive interior, featuring black oak woodwork, leaded-glass entry and stained glass. Visitors are treated to full breakfasts and refreshing afternoon teas. The spacious porch and swimming pool are favorite spots for relaxing and socializing.

Breakfast included in rates. Types of meals: full breakfast and early coffee/tea. Afternoon tea available. Air conditioning and VCR in room. Fax and swimming on premises. Small meetings and seminars hosted. French spoken. Antiques, cross-country skiing, sporting events and theater nearby.

Ithaca

G7

A Slice of Home B&B

178 N Main St
Ithaca, NY 14883
(607)589-6073

Rates: $50-140.
Payment: PC.
Innkeeper(s): Bea Brownell.
Circa: 1850.

Rooms: 5 rooms, 2 with PB. 1 suite.
Beds: KQD.

This Italianate inn's location, approximately equidistant from Ithaca and Watkins Glen, offers a fine vantage point for exploring the Finger Lakes winery region. Although the area is well-known for its scenery, many recreational opportunities also are available. The innkeeper is happy to help guests plan tours, and has a special fondness for those traveling by bicycle. The inn offers five guest rooms, furnished in country decor. Guests may relax by taking a stroll on the inn's 10 acres, mountain hiking, biking or having a cookout in the inn's backyard. Guests can begin a cross-country ski excursion right from the back porch.

Breakfast and evening snack included in rates. Types of meals: full breakfast and early coffee/tea. Picnic lunch available. Air conditioning and cable TV in room. VCR, copier and bicycles on premises. 10 acres. Weddings, small meetings, family reunions and seminars hosted. Limited German spoken. Antiques, fishing, parks, shopping, downhill skiing, cross-country skiing, sporting events, theater and watersports nearby. TAC10.

Pets Allowed: Outside only.

Special Discounts: 10% off for Seniors.

The Federal House B&B

PO Box 4914
Ithaca, NY 14852-4914
(607)533-7362 (800)533-7362
Fax:(607)533-7899

Rates: $55-175.
Payment: MC VISA AX DS PC TC.
Innkeeper(s): Diane Carroll.
Circa: 1815.

Rooms: 4 rooms with PB, 2 with FP. 2 suites.
Beds: QDT.

Salmon Creek Falls, a well-known fishing spot, is yards away from the inn. The rooms are furnished with antiques, which complement the original woodwork and hand-carved fireplace mantels. Each of the suites includes a television and a fireplace.

Breakfast included in rates. Air conditioning in room. Antiques, fishing, downhill skiing, cross-country skiing, theater and watersports nearby.

Publicity: *Ithaca Journal, Cortland Paper.*

"Your inn is so charming and your food was excellent."

La Tourelle Country Inn

1150 Danby Rd, Rt 96B
Ithaca, NY 14850-9406
(607)273-2734 (800)765-1492
Fax:(607)273-4821

Rates: $75-125. EP.
Payment: MC VISA AX TC.
Innkeeper(s): Leslie Leonard.
Circa: 1986.

Rooms: 34 rooms with PB, 1 with FP. 1 conference room.
Beds: KQ.

This white stucco European-style country inn is located on 70 acres three miles from town, allowing for wildflower walks, cross-country skiing and all-season hiking. Adjacent Buttermilk Falls State Park provides stone paths, waterfalls and streams. The inn is decorated with a hint of European decor and includes fireplace suites and tower suites. A continental breakfast arrives at your door in a basket, French Provincial style, and guests often tote it to the patio or gazebo to enjoy views of the rolling countryside. There is an indoor tennis court.

Breakfast included in rates. Types of meals: continental breakfast and early coffee/tea. Evening snack, banquet service and catering service available. EP. Air conditioning, cable TV and VCR in room. Copier and tennis on premises. Handicap access. 70 acres. Weddings, small meetings, family reunions and seminars hosted. Antiques, fishing, parks, shopping, downhill skiing, cross-country skiing, sporting events, theater and watersports nearby. TAC15.

Log Country Inn - B&B of Ithaca

PO Box 581
Ithaca, NY 14851-0581
(607)589-4771 (800)274-4771
Fax:(607)589-6151
E-mail: grunberg@logtv.com

Rates: $45-75.
Payment: MC VISA AX TC.
Innkeeper(s): Wanda Grunberg.
Circa: 1969.

Rooms: 5 rooms, 3 with PB. 1 suite.
Beds: QDT.

As the name indicates, this bed & breakfast is indeed fashioned from logs and rests in a picturesque country setting surrounding by 20 wooded acres. The cozy rooms are rustic with exposed beams and country furnishings. The decor is dotted with a European influence, as is the morning meal. Guests enjoy a full breakfast with blintzes or Russian pancakes.

Breakfast and afternoon tea included in rates. Type of meal: full breakfast. Cable TV in room. VCR, fax and sauna on premises. 20 acres. Family reunions hosted. Antiques, fishing, parks, shopping, cross-country skiing, sporting events and watersports nearby.

Pets Allowed: Yes.

Rose Inn

Rt 34N, Box 6576
Ithaca, NY 14851-6576
(607)533-7905
Fax:(607)533-7908

Rates: $100-275.
Payment: MC VISA PC TC.
Innkeeper(s): Charles & Sherry Rosemann.
Circa: 1848.

Rooms: 17 rooms with PB, 2 with FP. 5 suites. 1 cottage. 1 conference room.
Beds: KQDT.

This classic Italianate mansion has long been famous for its circular staircase of Honduran mahogany. It is owned by Sherry Rosemann, a noted interior designer specializing in mid-19th-century architecture and furniture, and her husband Charles, a hotelier from Germany. On 20 landscaped acres, it is 10 minutes from Cornell University. The inn has been the recipient of many awards for its lodging and dining, including a four star rating for seven years in a row.

Breakfast included in rates. Type of meal: full breakfast. Banquet service, catering service and catered breakfast available. Air conditioning, turn-down service and ceiling fan in room. Cable TV, VCR, fax, copier and library on premises. 14 acres. Weddings, small meetings, family reunions and seminars hosted. German and Spanish spoken. Antiques, fishing, parks, shopping, downhill skiing, cross-country skiing, sporting events, theater and watersports nearby. TAC10.

Publicity: *Country Inns, New York Times, Ithaca Times, New Woman, Toronto Globe & Mail, Newsday.*

"The blending of two outstanding talents, which when combined with your warmth, produce the ultimate experience in being away from home. Like staying with friends in their beautiful home."

Jay C12

The Book & Blanket B&B

Rt 9N, PO Box 164
Jay, NY 12941-0164
(518)946-8323
Fax:(518)946-8323

Rates: $55-75.
Payment: AX PC TC.
Innkeeper(s): Kathy, Fred, Sam & Daisy the Basset Hound.
Circa: 1850.

Rooms: 3 rooms, 1 with PB.
Beds: QD.

This Adirondack bed & breakfast served as the town's post office for many years and also as barracks for state troopers. Thankfully, however, it is now a restful bed & breakfast catering to the literary set. Guest rooms are named for authors and there are books in every nook and cranny of the house. Guests may even take one book home with them. Each of the guest rooms is comfortably furnished. From the inn's porch, guests can gaze at a covered bridge which crosses the nearby river.

Breakfast and evening snack included in rates. Types of meals: full breakfast and early coffee/tea. Afternoon tea available. Cable TV, VCR, fax and library on premises. Antiques, fishing, shopping, downhill skiing, cross-country skiing and watersports nearby.

Keene C12

The Bark Eater Inn

PO Box 139
Keene, NY 12942-0139
(518)576-2221
Fax:(518)576-2071

Rates: $88-136. MAP.
Payment: MC VISA AX DS PC TC.
Innkeeper(s): Joe-Pete & Brandy Wilson.
Circa: 1830.

Rooms: 19 rooms, 6 with PB. 2 suites. 1 cottage.
Beds: KQDT.

Originally a stagecoach stop on the old road to Lake Placid, The Bark Eater (English for the Indian word "Adirondacks") has been in almost continuous operation since the 1800s. Wide-board floors, fireplaces and rooms filled with antiques create a special haven for those seeking simple but gracious accommodations and memorable dining.

Breakfast, afternoon tea and evening snack included in rates. Types of meals: full breakfast, gourmet breakfast and early coffee/tea. Dinner, picnic lunch, catering service and catered breakfast available. MAP. Cable TV, VCR, fax, copier, computer, swimming, stables and library on premises. 250 acres. Weddings, small meetings, family reunions and seminars hosted. Antiques, fishing, parks, shopping, downhill skiing, cross-country skiing, sporting events, theater and watersports nearby. TAC10.

Location: Just minutes from Lake Placid Olympic Village.

Publicity: *New York Times, Gourmet, Toronto Star.*

"Staying at a country inn is an old tradition in Europe, and is rapidly catching on in the United States.. A stay here is a pleasant surprise for anyone who travels.—William Lederer, author, Ugly American"

Keene Valley C12

High Peaks Inn

PO Box 701
Keene Valley, NY 12943
(518)576-2003

Rates: $65-80.
Payment: MC VISA PC.
Innkeeper(s): Linda & Jerry Limpert.
Circa: 1910.

Rooms: 8 rooms, 3 with PB. 2 suites.
Beds: KQDT.

This inn is experiencing its second life as a place of hospitality. The home was built by a local logger for his family, and after his death, his widow opened it to boarders. Today, guests again enjoy the welcoming accommodations. The comfortable rooms include some antiques and beds topped with quilts. The inn, located in the scenic Adirondacks, is near many seasonal activities. Guests can enjoy hiking, fishing, canoeing, sailing, rock climbing, ice skating and cross-country skiing from the inn's back door. Lake Placid is just 20 minutes away.

Breakfast and evening snack included in rates. Type of meal: full breakfast. Picnic lunch available. Cable TV, VCR and library on premises. Weddings, small meetings and family reunions hosted. Antiques, fishing, shopping, downhill skiing, cross-country skiing and sporting events nearby.

Special Discounts: 10% discount, 3 or more nights, Sunday-Thursday.

"We don't want to leave and are anxious to return."

Trail's End Inn

Trail's End Rd, HC 01,
Box 103
Keene Valley, NY 12943
(518)576-9860
Fax:(518)576-9235

Rates: $49-115.
Payment: MC VISA AX DS PC TC.
Innkeeper(s): Frank & Karen Kovacik.
Circa: 1902.

Rooms: 10 rooms, 6 with PB, 2 with FP. 1 suite. 1 cottage. 1 conference room.
Beds: KQDT.

This charming mountain inn is in the heart of the Adirondack's High Peaks. Surrounded by woods and adjacent to a small pond, the inn offers spacious guest rooms with antique furnishings and country quilts. All-you-can-eat morning meals in the glassed-in breakfast room not only provide a lovely look at the countryside, but often a close-up view of various bird species. Fresh air and gorgeous views abound, and visitors enjoy invigorating hikes, trout fishing and fine cross-country skiing. Downhill skiers will love the challenge of nearby White Mountain, with the longest vertical drop in the East.

Breakfast included in rates. Types of meals: full breakfast and early coffee/tea. Picnic lunch available. Ceiling fan and cable TV in room. VCR, fax, copier and child care on premises. Weddings, small meetings, family reunions and seminars hosted. Amusement parks, antiques, fishing, parks, shopping, downhill skiing, cross-country skiing, sporting events and watersports nearby. TAC10.

Special Discounts: 10% off for 7 days.

Lake Clear C11

The Lodge on Lake Clear

PO Box 46
Lake Clear, NY 12945-0046
(800)442-2356
E-mail: thelodge@northnet.org

Rates: $79-188.
Payment: MC VISA PC TC.
Innkeeper(s): Cathy & Ernest Hohmeyer.
Circa: 1886.

Rooms: 5 cottages with PB, 4 with FP. 1 conference room.
Beds: KQDT.

Surrounded by 25 acres of Adirondack scenery, this German-style lodge is awash in Old World ambiance. The Lodge, run by the same family for more than a century, originally accommodated those traveling along the New York to Montreal rail line. Old tracks still run through the property. The German cuisine served at the inn's restaurant is highly recommended. Knotty pine woodwork and exposed beams add to the dining room's European atmosphere. Guest rooms sport German and Adirondack decor. More private accommodations are available in the chalet or the Sunwater Guesthaus. The Guesthaus offers two units with lake views, a woodburning fireplace, kitchen, two bedrooms and a bath with a whirlpool tub. The Lodge, not far from the Lake Placid Olympic sites, is a perfect spot for those enjoying a ski vacation.

Breakfast included in rates. Types of meals: continental breakfast, continental-plus breakfast, full breakfast and gourmet breakfast. Afternoon tea, dinner, picnic lunch, banquet service, catering service, catered breakfast and room service available. VCR, fax, copier, swimming and child care on premises. 25 acres. Weddings, small meetings, family reunions and seminars hosted. German spoken. Antiques, fishing, parks, shopping, downhill skiing, cross-country skiing, sporting events, theater and watersports nearby. TAC10.

Pets Allowed: In private chalets only.

Publicity: *Skiing, Birnbaum's, Adirondack Cookbook, Discerning Traveler, National Geographic Traveler.*

"Great as it was 20 years ago."

Lake Luzerne

E12

Lamplight Inn B&B

PO Box 70, 231 Lake Ave
Lake Luzerne, NY 12846
(518)696-5294 (800)262-4668
Fax:(518)696-5256
E-mail: lampinfo@adirondack.net

Rates: $80-165.
Payment: MC VISA AX PC TC.
Innkeeper(s): Gene & Linda Merlino.
Circa: 1890.

Rooms: 17 rooms with PB, 12 with FP.
Beds: QDT.

Howard Conkling, a wealthy lumberman, built this Victorian Gothic estate on land that had been the site of the Warren County Fair. The home was designed for entertaining since Conkling was a very eligible bachelor. It has 12-foot beamed ceilings, chestnut wainscoting and moldings, and a chestnut keyhole staircase crafted in England. Four rooms boast Jacuzzi tubs.

Breakfast included in rates. Type of meal: full breakfast. Air conditioning and ceiling fan in room. Cable TV on premises. 10 acres. Small meetings and seminars hosted. Antiques, parks, shopping, downhill skiing and cross-country skiing nearby. TAC10.

Location: Northway (I-87) exit 21, Lake George/Lake Luzerne. Near Saratoga Springs.

Publicity: *New York Magazine, Newark Star-Ledger, Newsday, Country Inns, Country Victorian.*

"Rooms are immaculately kept and clean. The owners are the nicest, warmest, funniest and most hospitable innkeepers I have ever met."

Lake Placid

C12

Interlaken Inn

15 Interlaken Ave
Lake Placid, NY 12946-1142
(518)523-3180 (800)428-4369
Fax:(518)523-0117

Rates: $120-180. MAP.
Payment: MC VISA AX.
Innkeeper(s): Kathy & Jim Gonzales.
Circa: 1906.

Rooms: 11 rooms with PB. 1 suite.
Beds: KQD.

NY

The five-course dinner at this Victorian inn is prepared by innkeeper Carol Johnson and her talented staff. The high-quality cuisine is rivaled only by the rich decor of this cozy inn. Walnut paneling covers the dining room walls, which are topped with a tin ceiling. Bedrooms are carefully decorated with wallpapers, fresh flowers and luxurious bed coverings. Spend the afternoon gazing at the mountains and lakes that surround this Adirondack hideaway, or visit the Olympic venues.

Breakfast, afternoon tea and dinner included in rates. Types of meals: full breakfast and early coffee/tea. MAP. Ceiling fan in room. Cable TV, VCR and fax on premises. Weddings, small meetings and family reunions hosted. Antiques, fishing, shopping, downhill skiing, cross-country skiing, sporting events, theater and watersports nearby.

Pets Allowed.

Location: Quaint Olympic village.

Publicity: *Outside, Country Inns, Wine Trader.*

Lewiston

F3

The Cameo Inn

4710 Lower River Rd
Lewiston, NY 14092-1053
(716)745-3034

Rates: $65-115.
Innkeeper(s): Gregory Fisher.
Circa: 1875.

Rooms: 4 rooms, 2 with PB. 1 suite.
Beds: QDT.

This classic Queen Anne Victorian inn offers a breathtaking view of the lower Niagara River. Located on the Seaway Trail, the inn offers convenient access to sightseeing in this popular region. The inn's interior features family heirlooms and period antiques, and visitors choose from four guest rooms, including a three-room suite overlooking the river. Breakfast is served buffet-style, and the entrees, which change daily, may include crepes Benedict, German oven pancakes or Grand Marnier French toast. Area attractions include Old Fort Niagara, outlet malls and several state parks.

Breakfast included in rates. Type of meal: full breakfast. Ceiling fan and cable TV in room. Amusement parks, antiques, fishing, shopping, downhill skiing, cross-country skiing, sporting events, theater and watersports nearby.

Location: Five miles north of Niagara Falls.

Publicity: *Country Folk Art, Esquire, Journey, Seaway Trail, Waterways, Buffalo News.*

"I made the right choice when I selected Cameo."

Lockport F3

Hambleton House B&B

130 Pine St
Lockport, NY 14094-4402
(716)439-9507

Rates: $50-75. MAP.
Payment: MC VISA.
Innkeeper(s): Ted Hambleton.
Circa: 1850.

Rooms: 3 rooms with PB.
Beds: DT.

A carriage maker was the first owner of this mid-19th-century home, and it remained in his family for several generations. The home maintains an old-fashioned appeal with its mix of country and traditional furnishings. Main Street and the Erie Barge Canal locks are a short walk away, and Buffalo and Niagara Falls are within a half-hour drive.

Breakfast included in rates. Type of meal: continental-plus breakfast. MAP. Air conditioning in room. Cable TV on premises. Weddings, small meetings and family reunions hosted. Antiques, fishing, parks, theater and watersports nearby. TAC5.

New York L12

Broadway B&B Inn

264 W 46th St
New York, NY 10036
(212)997-9200 (800)826-6300
Fax:(212)768-2807

Rates: $85-150. AP.
Payment: MC VISA AX DC DS TC.
Innkeeper(s): Al & Gloria Milner.
Circa: 1918.

Rooms: 40 rooms with PB. 12 suites.
Beds: KQDT.

For those hoping to explore all Manhattan has to offer, this bed & breakfast is a fun lodging choice, located above an Irish pub in Times Square in the heart of the theater district and restaurant row. The inn was built out of a restored, early 20th-century hotel. Rooms are nicely appointed, with comfortable modern decor. Croissants or baguettes delivered each morning fresh from a local bakery are served with freshly squeezed orange juice. Guests can enjoy this morning fare in the inn's lobby, which has a fireplace and exposed brick walls.

Breakfast, afternoon tea and evening snack included in rates. Types of meals: continental breakfast and early coffee/tea. AP. Air conditioning and cable TV in room. Fax, copier and library on premises. French, German and Spanish spoken. TAC10.

Niagara Falls F3

The Cameo Manor North

3881 Lower River Rd
Niagara Falls, NY 14174
(716)745-3034

Rates: $75-175.
Innkeeper(s): Gregory Fisher.
Circa: 1860.

Rooms: 4 rooms.

This Colonial Revival inn offers a restful setting ideal for those seeking a peaceful getaway. The inn's three secluded acres add to its romantic setting, as does an interior that features several fireplaces. Visitors select from three suites, which feature private sun rooms, or two guest rooms that share a bath. Popular spots with guests include the library, outdoor deck and solarium. Fort Niagara and Wilson-Tuscarora state parks are nearby, and the American and Canadian Falls are within easy driving distance of the inn. The inn is actually located about six miles from Niagara Falls in the nearby village of Youngstown.

Breakfast included in rates. Type of meal: full breakfast.

Publicity: *Country Folk Art, Esquire, Journey, Seaway Trail, Waterways, Buffalo News.*

"I made the right choice when I selected Cameo."

Manchester House B&B

653 Main St
Niagara Falls, NY 14301
(716)285-5717 (800)489-3009
Fax:(716)282-2144
E-mail: 71210.65@compuserve.com

Rates: $60-80.
Payment: MC VISA TC.
Innkeeper(s): Lis & Carl Slenk.
Circa: 1903.

Rooms: 3 rooms with PB.
Beds: KQT.

This turn-of-the-century home once was used to house doctors' offices. The home, just a mile from the famous falls, and the innkeepers are full of knowledge about their famous local attraction. The home is decorated with comfortable furnishings, family pieces and antiques. Prints and posters depicting scenes of the Niagara Falls area also decorate the home.

Breakfast included in rates. Type of meal: full breakfast. Air conditioning and ceiling fan in room. Cable TV, VCR and library on premises. Weddings, small meetings, family reunions and seminars hosted. German spoken. Amusement parks, antiques, fishing, parks and shopping nearby. TAC10.

North River D11

Mary Monroe's B&B

PO Box 312
North River, NY 12856-0312
(518)251-2496

Rates: $75.
Payment: PC.
Innkeeper(s): Jennifer Delcore.
Circa: 1880.

Rooms: 4 rooms, 2 with PB.
Beds: QDT.

During the Prohibition years, this bed & breakfast was an infamous speakeasy. Throughout its hundred-plus years, the lodging has been operating off and on for guests to the Adirondacks, including those traveling by stagecoach. The current innkeeper grew up in the Adirondack region, and is happy to share her knowledge of the area with guests. The homey, comfortable guest rooms are decorated in an Adirondack style. Hearty, gourmet fare is served, such as a Shitake mushroom and onion quiche accompanied with fresh fruit, homemade granola and muffins. With each season comes new activity in this region, from dog sledding and cross-country skiing in winter, to canoeing, fishing and rock climbing in the warmer months.

Breakfast and evening snack included in rates. Types of meals: full breakfast and gourmet breakfast. Cable TV, swimming and bicycles on premises. Family reunions and seminars hosted. French spoken. Amusement parks, antiques, fishing, parks, shopping, downhill skiing, cross-country skiing, theater and watersports nearby. TAC10.

Pets Allowed: With advance notice.

Special Discounts: 10% discount on five days or more.

Old Chatham G12

Old Chatham Sheepherding Company Inn

99 Shaker Museum Rd
Old Chatham, NY 12136
(518)794-9774
Fax:(518)794-9779

Rates: $150-325.
Payment: MC VISA AX PC TC.
Innkeeper(s): George H. Shattuck III.
Circa: 1790.

Rooms: 10 rooms with PB, 4 with FP. 4 suites. 2 cottages.
Beds: QT.

Sheep graze languidly over hundreds of pastoral acres at this inn, located in an elegant, 18th-century Georgian manor house. The setting is peaceful, offering views of rolling hills dotted with trees. The decor is simple and uncluttered with tasteful furnishings, Oriental rugs and fine linens. The inn's dining room is an impressive site, appointed with beautiful furnishings, draperies and mural-painted walls. The cuisine is equally as impressive, created by chef Melissa Kelly, who graduated first in her class at the Culinary Institute of America. The specialties include locally produced items, including lamb and sheep milk fresh from the inn's farm and herbs and vegetables from the garden. The inn is host to a variety of events throughout the year, be sure to ask for a calendar. Tuesday-night lectures are followed by dinner at the inn, and there are Thursday teas, as well.

Breakfast and afternoon tea included in rates. Types of meals: continental breakfast, continental-plus breakfast and full breakfast. Picnic lunch available. Air conditioning, turn-down service and ceiling fan in room. Fax, copier and bicycles on premises. Handicap access. 500 acres. Antiques, fishing, shopping, downhill skiing, cross-country skiing, sporting events and theater nearby.

Palenville H12

Kaaterskill Creek B&B

Kaaterskill Ave, HCR 1,
Box 14, Palenville, NY 12463
(518)678-9052

Rates: $55-65.
Payment: MC VISA PC.
Innkeeper(s): Joann & Steve Murrin.
Circa: 1882.

Rooms: 4 rooms, 1 with PB.
Beds: D.

Breakfasts at this Colonial home are a hearty affair, served in the picturesque, glass-enclosed gazebo. Guest and common rooms are comfortable, decorated in a cozy, country style with a few antiques. On cool nights, guests often watch a good movie in the living room, which offers a huge, 10-foot fireplace to snuggle up to. The wicker-filled porch is an ideal place to relax after a day of skiing, hiking through the Catskills or shopping at auctions and flea markets.

Breakfast included in rates. Types of meals: gourmet breakfast and early coffee/tea. Air conditioning and VCR in room. Cable TV on premises. Amusement parks, antiques, fishing, parks, shopping, downhill skiing, cross-country skiing and watersports nearby.

Special Discounts: Three nights or more 10% discount.

Rochester F5

Dartmouth House B&B

215 Dartmouth St
Rochester, NY 14607-3202
(716)271-7872
Fax:(716)473-0778

Rates: $65-125.
Payment: MC VISA AX DS PC TC.
Innkeeper(s): Elinor & Bill Klein.
Circa: 1905.

Rooms: 4 rooms with PB.
Beds: KQT.

The lavish, four-course breakfasts served daily at this beautiful turn-of-the-century Edwardian home are unforgettable. Innkeeper and award-winning, gourmet cook Ellie Klein starts off the meal with special fresh juice, which is served in the parlor. From this point, guests are seated at the candlelit dining table to enjoy a series of delectable dishes, such as pears poached in port wine, a mouth-watering entree, a light, lemon ice and a rich dessert. And each of the courses is served on a separate pattern of depression glass. If the breakfast isn't enough, Ellie and husband, Bill, have stocked the individually decorated guest rooms with flowers, fluffy towels, bathrobes and special bath amenities. Each of the bedchambers boast antique collectibles and guests can soak in inviting clawfoot tubs. Museums, colleges, restaurants and antique shops are among the many nearby attractions.

Breakfast included in rates. Types of meals: full breakfast and early coffee/tea. Air conditioning and ceiling fan in room. Cable TV, VCR, fax, bicycles and library on premises. Antiques, parks, shopping, theater and watersports nearby. TAC10.

Publicity: *Democrat & Chronicle, DAKA, Genesee Country, Seaway Trail, Oneida News, Travelers News, Country Living.*

Special Discounts: Corporate rates depend on frequency of stay.

"The food was fabulous, the company fascinating, and the personal attention beyond comparison. You made me feel at home instantly."

Adelphi Hotel

365 Broadway
Saratoga Springs, NY 12866
(518)587-4688
Fax:(518)587-4688

Rates: $95-320.
Payment: MC VISA AX TC.
Innkeeper(s): Gregg Siefker & Sheila Parkert.
Circa: 1877.

Rooms: 37 rooms with PB. 15 suites. 1 conference room.
Beds: QD.

This Victorian hotel is one of two hotels still remaining from Saratoga's opulent spa era. A piazza overlooking Broadway features three-story columns topped with Victorian fretwork. Recently refurbished with lavish turn-of-the-century decor, rooms are filled with antique furnishings and opulent draperies and wall coverings, highlighting the inn's high ceilings and ornate woodwork. Breakfast is delivered to each room in the morning.

Breakfast included in rates. Type of meal: continental-plus breakfast. Air conditioning, turn-down service and cable TV in room. Fax, copier and swimming on premises. Weddings, small meetings and seminars hosted. Antiques, parks, shopping and theater nearby. TAC10.

Publicity: *New York Times, Country Inns, Back Roads, Conde Nast, Victorian Homes.*

The Lombardi Farm B&B

41 Locust Grove Rd
Saratoga Springs, NY 12866
(518)587-2074
Fax:(518)587-2074

Rates: $100-115.
Payment: PC TC.
Innkeeper(s): Vincent & Kathleen Lombardi.
Circa: 1840.

Rooms: 4 rooms with PB. 1 suite.
Beds: KQDT.

A surrey rests in front of this Victorian farmhouse, which is surrounded by 10 acres of scenic countryside. The innkeepers keep Nubian and French Alpine Goats on the property, and during Spring months, guests are invited to bottle feed a baby goat. A four-course, gourmet breakfast is served in the farm's Florida Room. The menu changes daily and items such as breakfast souffles, Belgian waffles, quiche, chocolate crepes and strudels are accompanied by freshly baked muffins, scones or rolls. Guests are invited to take a relaxing dip in the B&B's indoor hot tub. Equestrians will appreciate the home's close access to the Saratoga Thoroughbred Racetrack, Saratoga Harness Track and the National Museum of Racing.

Breakfast included in rates. Types of meals: gourmet breakfast and early coffee/tea. Air conditioning and ceiling fan in room. Cable TV, VCR, fax, copier, spa, bicycles and library on premises. Handicap access. 10 acres. Weddings, small meetings, family reunions and seminars hosted. Antiques, fishing, parks, shopping, cross-country skiing, theater and watersports nearby. TAC10.

Special Discounts: AAA discount.

Saratoga Bed & Breakfast

434 Church St
Saratoga Springs, NY 12866
(518)584-0920 (800)584-0920
Fax:(518)584-4500
E-mail: sarabandb@aol.com

Rates: $65-210.
Payment: MC VISA AX DS PC TC.
Innkeeper(s): Noel & Kathleen Smith.
Circa: 1850.

Rooms: 8 rooms with PB, 6 with FP. 2 suites. 1 conference room.
Beds: KQD.

This Federal-style home was built as a wedding gift to a daughter and her young groom. The seven-acre grounds are decorated with gardens, including a water garden. The home's interior is dressed in Victorian style. Six of the guest rooms include a fireplace. Aside from the historic 19th-century home, there are accommodations in a farmhouse. For those traveling to Saratoga Springs for a day or two at the races, the innkeepers can help with scheduling and parking.

Type of meal: full breakfast. Air conditioning and cable TV in room. VCR, fax, bicycles and library on premises. French spoken. Amusement parks, antiques, fishing, parks, downhill skiing and watersports nearby. TAC15.

Publicity: *New York Alive Magazine, Hudson Valley Magazine.*

Six Sisters B&B

149 Union Ave
Saratoga Springs, NY 12866
(518)583-1173
Fax:(518)587-2470

Rates: $70-250.
Payment: MC VISA AX PC TC.
Innkeeper(s): Kate Benton.
Circa: 1880.

Rooms: 4 rooms with PB. 2 suites.
Beds: KQD.

The unique architecture of this charming Victorian home, features a large second-story bay window, a hardwood front door decked with stained glass and a veranda accentuated with plants and rocking chairs. Inside, the antiques, ceiling fans and Oriental rugs create an elegant atmosphere. During racing season, guests can rise early and take a short walk to the local race track to watch the horses prepare. Upon their return, guests are greeted with the smells of a delicious breakfast. Visit Saratoga Springs' downtown area with its shops and many restaurants.

Breakfast included in rates. Types of meals: gourmet breakfast and early coffee/tea. Air conditioning, ceiling fan and cable TV in room. Fax on premises. Weddings, small meetings, family reunions and seminars hosted. Amusement parks, antiques, fishing, parks, shopping, downhill skiing, cross-country skiing, sporting events, theater and watersports nearby. TAC10.

Location: Thirty minutes north of Albany and thirty minutes south of Lake George.

Publicity: *Gourmet, Country Inns, Country Folk Art, Country Victorian.*

Special Discounts: Spa package available September through June.

"The true definition of a bed & breakfast."

Sodus E6

Maxwell Creek Inn

7563 Lake Rd
Sodus, NY 14551-9309
(315)483-2222 (800)315-2206

Rates: $65-80.
Payment: MC VISA AX DS PC TC.
Innkeeper(s): Joseph & Edythe Ann Long.
Circa: 1840.

Rooms: 8 rooms with PB. 2 suites. 1 cottage.
Beds: KQDT.

From the five acres of woodlands and orchards that surround this cobblestone inn, guests enjoy views of Lake Ontario and, of course, Maxwell Creek. There are hiking trails, a fishing stream and a tennis court on the premises. The guest quarters are furnished with antiques, quilt-topped beds and a variety of collectibles. Groups might opt for Stone Cottage, which offers four single beds as well as a sofa bed, refrigerator, outdoor grill and a picnic table. Breakfasts are served in a rustic, wood-paneled dining room, which is warmed by a unique, old fireplace.

Breakfast included in rates. Type of meal: full breakfast. Tennis and library on premises. Weddings, small meetings, family reunions and seminars hosted. Amusement parks, antiques, fishing, parks, shopping, downhill skiing, cross-country skiing and watersports nearby. TAC10.

Southampton K15

The Old Post House Inn

136 Main St
Southampton, NY 11968
(516)283-1717

Rates: $80-175.
Payment: MC VISA AX.
Innkeeper(s): Cecile & Ed Courville.
Circa: 1684.

Rooms: 7 rooms with PB. 1 conference room.
Beds: DT.

A visit to this pre-colonial home includes a lesson in Eastern Long Island history which the innkeepers are more than happy to share with their guests. The cellar has been an archaeological dig site with finds that have included several bottles of 17th- and 18th-century origin, a spoon from the early 1800s, portions of a

primitive Indian basket and part of an early Bible. Clues from this site suggest that the inn was part of the pre-Civil War Underground Railroad.

Breakfast included in rates. Type of meal: continental breakfast. Air conditioning in room. Antiques, fishing, parks, shopping, theater and watersports nearby.

"Such a lovely retreat. Nourishing beauty."

Southold K15

Goose Creek Guesthouse

1475 Waterview Dr,
PO Box 377
Southold, NY 11971-2125
(516)765-3356

Rates: $55-85.
Payment: PC TC.
Innkeeper(s): Mary Mooney-Getoff.
Circa: 1860.

Rooms: 4 rooms.
Beds: KQDT.

Grover Pease left for the Civil War from this house, and after his death, his widow, Harriet, ran a summer boarding house here. The basement actually dates from the 1780s and is constructed of large rocks. The present house was moved here and put on the older foundation. Southold has many historic homes and a guidebook is provided for visitors. The inn is close to the ferry to New London and the ferries to the South Shore via Shelter Island.

Breakfast and afternoon tea included in rates. Types of meals: full breakfast, gourmet breakfast and early coffee/tea. Picnic lunch available. Air conditioning in room. VCR and library on premises. Weddings and family reunions hosted. Spanish spoken. Amusement parks, antiques, fishing, parks, shopping, theater and watersports nearby. TAC10.

Location: One-and-one-half miles south of Rt 25 on the north fork of Long Island.

Publicity: *New York Times, Newsday.*

"We will be repeat guests. Count on it!!"

Stanfordville I12

Lakehouse Inn on Golden Pond

Shelley Hill Rd
Stanfordville, NY 12581
(914)266-8093 (800)726-3323
Fax:(914)266-4051

Rates: $125-475.
Payment: MC VISA PC.
Innkeeper(s): Judy & Rich Kohler.
Circa: 1990.

Rooms: 9 rooms with PB, 7 with FP. 7 suites. 1 cottage. 1 conference room.
Beds: KQ.

NY

Romance abounds at this secluded contemporary home, which is surrounded by breathtaking vistas of woods and Golden Pond. Rest beneath a canopy flanked by lacy curtains as you gaze out the window. Enjoy a long, relaxing bath, or take a stroll around the 22-acre grounds. Each guest room includes a fireplace and whirlpool tub, and most include decks. The decor is a mix with a hint of Victorian, some Asian influences and modern touches that highlight the oak floors and vaulted pine ceilings. The innkeepers start off the day with a gourmet breakfast delivered to your room in a covered basket. Historic mansions and wineries are among the nearby attractions.

Breakfast included in rates. Air conditioning, ceiling fan and VCR in room. Fax, copier and swimming on premises. 22 acres. Weddings, small meetings, family reunions and seminars hosted. Antiques, fishing, parks, shopping, cross-country skiing, sporting events, theater and watersports nearby. TAC10.

Location: Ninety miles north of New York City.

Publicity: *Newsday, New York Post.*

Country Road Lodge B&B

HC 1 Box 227
Hickory Hill Rd
Warrensburg, NY 12885
(518)623-2207
Fax:(518)623-4363
E-mail: parisibbmail.@netheaven.com

Rates: $55-58.
Payment: PC.
Innkeeper(s): Sandi & Steve Parisi.
Circa: 1929.

Rooms: 4 rooms, 2 with PB.
Beds: DT.

This simple, rustic farmhouse lodge is situated on 35 acres along the Hudson River at the end of a country road. Rooms are clean and comfortable. A full breakfast is provided with homemade breads and muffins. The sitting room reveals panoramic views of the river and Sugarloaf Mountain. Bird watching, hiking and skiing are popular activities. Groups often reserve all four guest rooms.

Breakfast included in rates. Types of meals: full breakfast and early coffee/tea. Ceiling fan in room. Library on premises. 35 acres. Amusement parks, antiques, fishing, parks, shopping, downhill skiing, cross-country skiing, theater and watersports nearby. TAC10.

Location: Adirondack Mountains near Lake George.

Publicity: *North Jersey Herald & News.*

"Homey, casual atmosphere. We really had a wonderful time. You're both wonderful hosts and the Lodge is definitely our kind of B&B! We will always feel very special about this place and will always be back."

House on The Hill B&B

Rt 28 Box 248
Warrensburg, NY 12885
(518)623-9390 (800)221-9390
Fax:(518)623-9396

Rates: $89-109.
Payment: MC VISA AX DC CB DS PC TC.
Innkeeper(s): Joe & Lynn Rubino.
Circa: 1750.

Rooms: 5 rooms, 1 with PB.
Beds: KQD.

This historic Federal-style inn on a hill in the six million-acre Adirondack Park offers five guest rooms. After they are treated to coffee and baked goods in their rooms, guests enjoy the inn's full breakfasts in the sunroom, which offers wonderful views of the surrounding fields and woods from its many windows. Cross-country skiing and hiking may be enjoyed on the spacious grounds, covering 176 acres. Gore Mountain Ski Area is close and Lake George is a 10-minute drive.

Breakfast included in rates. Types of meals: continental breakfast, full breakfast and early coffee/tea. Air conditioning in room. Cable TV, VCR, fax and copier on premises. Handicap access. 176 acres. Weddings, small meetings, family reunions and seminars hosted. French and Italian spoken. Amusement parks, antiques, fishing, parks, shopping, downhill skiing, cross-country skiing, sporting events, theater and watersports nearby. TAC10.

Publicity: *Chronicle, Post Star, G.F. Business Journal, Country Victorian.*

"Very favorable."

The Merrill Magee House

2 Hudson St PO Box 391
Warrensburg, NY 12885
(518)623-2449

Rates: $105-125. MAP, EP.
Payment: MC VISA AX DS TC.
Innkeeper(s): Ken & Florence Carrington.
Circa: 1839.

Rooms: 10 rooms with PB, 10 with FP. 1 cottage. 2 conference rooms.
Beds: KQDT.

This stately Greek Revival home offers beautiful antique fireplaces in every guest room. The Sage, Rosemary, Thyme and Coriander rooms feature sitting areas, and a family suite includes two bedrooms, a sitting room with a television, refrigerator and a bathroom with a clawfoot tub. The decor is romantic and distinctly Victorian. Romantic getaway packages include complimentary champagne and candlelight dinners. The local area hosts art and craft festivals, an antique car show, white-water rafting and Gore Mountain Oktoberfest. Tour the Adirondacks from the sky during September's balloon festival or browse through the world's largest garage sale in early October.

Breakfast included in rates. Types of meals: full breakfast and early coffee/tea. Dinner, lunch and banquet service available. MAP, EP. Air conditioning and turn-down service in room. Cable TV, spa, swimming and library on premises. Handicap access. Weddings, small meetings, family reunions and seminars hosted. Amusement parks, antiques, fishing, parks, shopping, downhill skiing, cross-country skiing, sporting events, theater and watersports nearby.

Location: In Adirondack State Park.

Special Discounts: Packages including dinner.

"A really classy and friendly operation—a real joy."

Waterville F9

B&B of Waterville

211 White St
Waterville, NY 13480-1149
(315)841-8295

Rates: $45-55.
Payment: MC VISA PC TC.
Innkeeper(s): Stanley & Carol Sambora.
Circa: 1871.

Rooms: 3 rooms, 1 with PB.
Beds: DT.

This two-story Victorian is in the Waterville Historic Triangle District, one block from Rt. 12 and 20 minutes away from Hamilton College and Colgate University. The hostess is an avid quiltmaker and the house is filled with her handiwork. La Petite Maison, a fine French restaurant, is a few steps away. Thirty-five antique shops are within 10 miles.

Breakfast included in rates. Type of meal: full breakfast. Air conditioning in room. Cable TV and VCR on premises. Amusement parks, antiques, fishing, parks, shopping and cross-country skiing nearby. TAC10.

Location: Near Utica.

Publicity: *Observer Dispatch.*

"Don't change a thing ever. As a hopeless romantic, I felt that your B&B was just what we needed. We have come away renewed and refreshed. It's so lovely here, love to stay forever!"

Watkins Glen H6

Clarke House Bed & Breakfast

102 Durland Ave
Watkins Glen, NY 14891
(607)535-7965

Rates: $65-75.
Payment: PC.
Innkeeper(s): Jack & Carolyn Clarke.
Circa: 1920.

Rooms: 4 rooms with PB.
Beds: QDT.

NY

Bricks from a brewery that exploded were used to create this English Tudor home. Oriental rugs cover the wood floors, and a collection of antiques decorate the comfortable rooms. A short drive will take you to the Watkins Glen International Racetrack, wineries and the Corning Glass factory. Seneca Lake, shops, restaurants and Glen State Park are within walking distance.

Breakfast and afternoon tea included in rates. Types of meals: full breakfast and early coffee/tea. Air conditioning, ceiling fan, cable TV and VCR in room. Copier on premises. Family reunions hosted. Antiques, parks, cross-country skiing and watersports nearby.

"Thank you so much for your warm hospitality."

Westfield H2

The William Seward Inn

6645 S Portage Rd
Westfield, NY 14787-9602
(716)326-4151 (800)338-4151
Fax:(716)326-4163

Rates: $85-165.
Payment: MC VISA DS.
Innkeeper(s): James & Debbie Dahlberg.
Circa: 1821.

Rooms: 14 rooms with PB, 1 with FP.
Beds: KQD.

This two-story Greek Revival estate stands on a knoll overlooking Lake Erie. Seward was a Holland Land Company agent before becoming governor of New York. He later served as Lincoln's Secretary of State and is known for the Alaska Purchase. George Patterson bought Seward's home and also became governor of New York. Most of the mansion's furnishings are dated 1790 to 1870 from the Sheraton-Victorian period.

Breakfast included in rates. Type of meal: full breakfast. Air conditioning in room. Cable TV, fax and library on premises. Handicap access. Weddings, small meetings and family reunions hosted. Amusement parks, antiques, fishing, parks, shopping, downhill skiing, cross-country skiing and watersports nearby. TAC10.

Location: Three hours from Cleveland, Pittsburgh and Toronto.

Publicity: *Intelligencer, Evening Observer, New York-Pennsylvania Collector, N.Y. Times, Pittsburgh Post-Gazette, Toronto Globe & Mail.*

"The breakfasts are delicious. The solitude and your hospitality are what the doctor ordered."

Westhampton Beach *K14*

1880 House Bed & Breakfast

PO Box 648, Westhampton Beach, NY 11978-0648
(516)288-1559 (800)346-3290
Fax:(516)288-0721

Rates: $100-200.
Payment: MC VISA AX.
Innkeeper(s): Elsie Collins.
Circa: 1880.

Rooms: 3 suites.
Beds: QD.

On Westhampton Beach's exclusive Seafield Lane, this country estate includes a pool and tennis court, and it is just a short walk to the ocean. The inn is decorated with Victorian antiques, Shaker benches, and Chinese porcelain, creating a casual, country inn atmosphere.

Breakfast included in rates. Type of meal: full breakfast. Afternoon tea available. Weddings, small meetings, family reunions and seminars hosted. Antiques and theater nearby.

Location: Ninety minutes from Manhattan.

Publicity: *Country Inns.*

"From the moment we stepped inside your charming home we felt all the warmth you sent our way which made our stay so comfortable and memorable."

White Lake *I10*

Bradstan Country Hotel

Rt 17B, PO Box 312
White Lake, NY 12786
(914)583-4114
Fax:(914)583-5106

Rates: $75-115.
Payment: MC VISA AX DS TC.
Innkeeper(s): Scott Samuelson & Edward Dudek.
Circa: 1925.

Rooms: 2 rooms with PB. 3 suites. 3 cottages. 1 conference room.
Beds: QD.

If the innkeepers start to sing, "Come to the cabaret," it's not simply because of their love for the theater. There actually is a cabaret on the premises, drawing some of the world's top performers. In addition to this unique offering, guests will admire the award-winning restoration of this historic hotel. Guest rooms and suites are decorated with antiques and vintage furnishings and there are three cottages as well. Guests often enjoy relaxing on the wicker-filled porch. After an evening at the cabaret, the audience usually wanders into the hotel's piano bar. In the mornings, a huge breakfast is served, buffet-style, with fruits, cereals, coffeecake, freshly baked muffins, eggs, quiche, savory meats and the like.

Breakfast included in rates. Type of meal: continental-plus breakfast. Air conditioning and ceiling fan in room. Cable TV, VCR, fax, copier and swimming on premises. Weddings, small meetings, family reunions and seminars hosted. Antiques, fishing, parks, shopping, downhill skiing, cross-country skiing, theater and watersports nearby.

Special Discounts: Group rates for all rooms; stays of five days or longer 10% off.

"The beautiful surroundings were ideal for a romantic getaway and we plan on returning very soon."

Wilmington C12

Willkommen Hof

Rt 86, PO Box 240
Wilmington, NY 12997
(518)946-7669 (800)541-9119
Fax:(518)946-7626
E-mail: nybandb@aol.com

Rates: $30-80. MAP.
Payment: MC VISA PC TC.
Innkeeper(s): Heike & Bert Yost.
Circa: 1925.

Rooms: 9 rooms, 2 with PB. 1 suite.
Beds: KQDT.

This turn-of-the-century farmhouse served as an inn during the 1920s, but little else is known about its past. The innkeepers have created a cozy atmosphere, perfect for relaxation after a day exploring the Adirondack Mountain area. A large selection of books and roaring fire greets guests who choose to settle down in the reading room. The innkeepers also offer a large selection of movies. Relax in the sauna or outdoor spa or simply enjoy the comfort of your bedchamber.

Breakfast and afternoon tea included in rates. Type of meal: full breakfast. MAP. Ceiling fan in room. VCR, fax, spa, sauna, bicycles and pet boarding on premises. Weddings, small meetings and family reunions hosted. German spoken. Antiques, fishing, parks, shopping, downhill skiing, cross-country skiing and watersports nearby. TAC7.

Pets Allowed: Pets must stay in kennel when guests are gone.

"Thank you for a wonderful time, FIVE STARS!"

Windham H11

Albergo Allegria B&B

Rt 296, PO Box 267
Windham, NY 12496-0267
(518)734-5560 (800)625-2374
Fax:(518)734-5570

Rates: $65-195.
Payment: MC VISA PC TC.
Innkeeper(s): Vito & Lenore Radelich.
Circa: 1876.

Rooms: 21 rooms with PB, 7 with FP. 9 suites.
Beds: KQT.

NY

Two former boarding houses were joined to create this luxurious, Victorian bed & breakfast whose name means "the inn of happiness." Guest quarters, laced with a Victorian theme, are decorated with period wallpapers and antique furnishings. One master suites has a double whirlpool tub. There are plenty of relaxing options at Albergo Allegria, including a rustic lounge with a large fireplace and overstuffed couches. A second-story library, decorated with plants and wicker furnishings, is still another location to relax with a good book. Located just a few feet behind the inn are the Carriage House Suites, each of which includes a double whirlpool tub, gas fireplaces, king-size beds and cathedral ceilings with skylights. The innkeepers came to the area to open LaGriglia, a deluxe, gourmet restaurant just across the way from the bed & breakfast. Their command of cuisine is evident each morning as guests feast on a variety home-baked muffins and pastries, gourmet omelets, waffles and other tempting treats. Albergo Allegria has been named a registered historic site.

Breakfast included in rates. Types of meals: full breakfast and gourmet breakfast. Afternoon tea, picnic lunch and gourmet lunch available. Air conditioning, turn-down service, ceiling fan, cable TV and VCR in room. Fax, copier and bicycles on premises. Handicap access. Weddings, small meetings, family reunions and seminars hosted. Italian, African and Croatin spoken. Amusement parks, antiques, fishing, parks, shopping, downhill skiing, cross-country skiing and watersports nearby.

Publicity: *Yankee.*

Special Discounts: Sunday-Thursday, non -holiday, 10% discount; AARP 10%.

"A jewel of an inn! The ambiance was elegant, yet relaxed; beautiful, yet comfortable, reflecting the nurturance of two generations of skillful, generous innkeepers."

Danske Hus

361 South St
Windham, NY 12496
(518)734-6335

Rates: $40-85.
Payment: AX DS.
Innkeeper(s): Barbara Jensen.
Circa: 1865.

Rooms: 4 rooms, 3 with PB.
Beds: KQDT.

Located just across the road from Ski Windham, this farmhouse-style inn offers countryside and mountain views to its guests. Eclectic furnishings are found throughout the inn and its four guest rooms. Breakfast may be enjoyed in the dining room or outside on a picturesque deck. Guests also enjoy a large living room, piano, sauna, TV room and woodburning fireplace. Windham Golf Course is within walking distance. The Catskills provide many other tourist attractions, including caverns, fairs and ethnic festivals, as well as shopping, antiquing and sporting activities. The innkeeper welcomes families with children, and with prior arrangement, dogs may be allowed.

Breakfast and afternoon tea included in rates. Type of meal: full breakfast. Cable TV, VCR, sauna, library, pet boarding and child care on premises. Small meetings and family reunions hosted. Danish spoken. Amusement parks, antiques, fishing, parks, shopping, downhill skiing, cross-country skiing and watersports nearby.

Pets Allowed: Dogs only.

Wolcott F7

Bonnie Castle Farm B&B

PO Box 188
Wolcott, NY 14590-0188
(315)587-2273 (800)587-4006
Fax:(315)587-4003

Rates: $75-120.
Payment: MC VISA AX PC TC.
Innkeeper(s): Eric & Georgia Pendleton.
Circa: 1887.

Rooms: 8 rooms with PB. 1 suite.
Beds: KQD.

Bonnie Castle Farm is surrounded by expansive lawns and trees which overlook the east side of Great Sodus Bay, a popular resort at the turn of the century. Accommodations include a suite and large guest room with water views. Another room features wainscoting and cathedral ceilings. A full gourmet breakfast includes cereal bar, fresh fruit and juices and an assortment of entrees such as Orange Blossom French toast, sausages, a creamy potato casserole and fresh-baked pastries topped off with teas and Irish creme coffee.

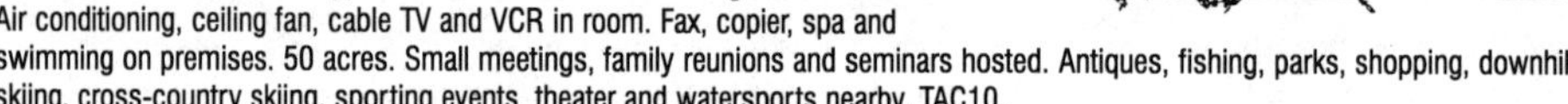

Breakfast included in rates. Types of meals: full breakfast and gourmet breakfast. Air conditioning, ceiling fan, cable TV and VCR in room. Fax, copier, spa and swimming on premises. 50 acres. Small meetings, family reunions and seminars hosted. Antiques, fishing, parks, shopping, downhill skiing, cross-country skiing, sporting events, theater and watersports nearby. TAC10.

Location: Located in Sodus Bay, N.Y., in the Finger Lakes District of upstate New York.

"We love Bonnie Castle. You have a magnificent establishment. We are just crazy about your place. Hope to see you soon."

Youngstown E3

Joanne's B&B

1380 Swann Rd
Youngstown, NY 14174
(716)754-7052 (800)484-6449

Rates: $45-65.
Payment: PC TC.
Innkeeper(s): Joanne & Larry Brennen.
Circa: 1895.

Rooms: 4 rooms.
Beds: DT.

Joanne and Larry Brennen raised a family of six in this turn-of-the-century farmhouse before turning it into a bed & breakfast. Their home is decorated with late-Victorian antiques and beds are topped with freshly ironed sheets and quilts or crocheted pillows hand-crafted by Joanne. Guests are treated like old friends, Larry will even entertain guests at night with his guitar and traditional Irish ballads. The full breakfasts begin with a fresh fruit salad, two different baked goods accompanied by homemade jam and perhaps a savory egg casserole or baked French toast.

Breakfast and evening snack included in rates. Types of meals: full breakfast and early coffee/tea. Air conditioning and ceiling fan in room. VCR on premises. Weddings, small meetings and family reunions hosted. Amusement parks, antiques, fishing, parks, shopping, cross-country skiing, sporting events, theater and watersports nearby.

Special Discounts: Special rates for family or group taking the whole house; also use of kitchen.

North Carolina

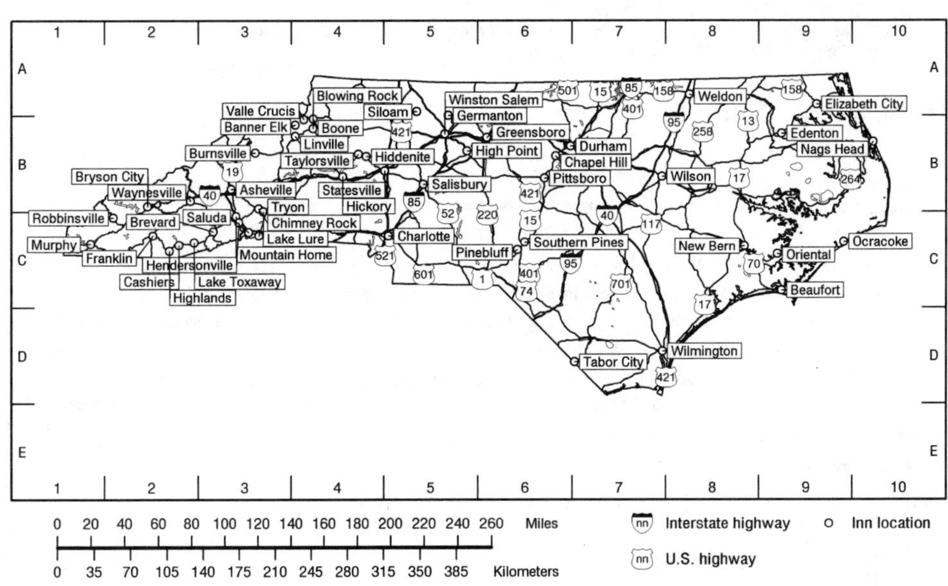

Asheville **B3**

NC

Acorn Cottage B&B

25 Saint Dunstans Cir
Asheville, NC 28803-2618
(704)253-0609 (800)699-0609
Fax:(704)258-2129

Rates: $70-95.
Payment: MC VISA DS PC TC.
Innkeeper(s): Sharon Tabor.
Circa: 1923.

Rooms: 4 rooms with PB.
Beds: Q.

This home was designed by Ronald Green, a prominent, turn-of-the-century Asheville architect, who designed many of the area's historic buildings. This Arts & Crafts period, Craftsman-style granite bungalow is found in the heart of town. The inn, with its eclectic decor and beautiful gardens, is close to many nearby attractions, including the Biltmore Estate. Guests can enjoy a cool drink while resting on the porch swing during summer afternoons or warm themselves by the fire in the living room on cool evenings. Bedrooms feature fine linens and private baths with special soaps.

Breakfast, afternoon tea and evening snack included in rates. Types of meals: full breakfast and early coffee/tea. Air conditioning and cable TV in room. VCR and fax on premises. Antiques, parks, shopping, sporting events, theater and watersports nearby. TAC10.

Albemarle Inn

86 Edgemont Rd
Asheville, NC 28801-1544
(704)255-0027 (800)621-7435

Rates: $90-150.
Payment: MC VISA DS PC TC.
Innkeeper(s): Kathy and Dick Hemes.
Circa: 1909.

Rooms: 11 rooms with PB.
Beds: KQDT.

Tall Grecian columns mark the majestic entrance to Albemarle. A wide veranda, shaded by mountain pines, welcomes guests. Inside, a carved-oak staircase and massive oak-paneled doors are polished to a high gleam. Guest rooms feature 11-foot ceilings and clawfoot tubs. The Hungarian composer Bela Bartok

is said to have written his third concerto for piano while in residence at the inn.

Breakfast and evening snack included in rates. Types of meals: full breakfast, gourmet breakfast and early coffee/tea. Air conditioning, ceiling fan and cable TV in room. Swimming on premises. Antiques, fishing, parks, shopping, sporting events, theater and watersports nearby. TAC10.

Publicity: *Stages, Atlanta Homes, Asheville Citizen-Times*

"Most outstanding breakfast I've ever had. We were impressed to say the least!"

Applewood Manor Inn

62 Cumberland Cir
Asheville, NC 28801-1718
(704)254-2244 (800)442-2197
Fax:(704)254-0899

Rates: $90-120.
Payment: MC VISA PC TC.
Innkeeper(s): Coby & Johan Verhey.
Circa: 1910.

Rooms: 4 rooms with PB, 3 with FP. 1 cottage.
Beds: Q.

This is a spacious Colonial Revival house furnished comfortably with antiques. Guests can relax in front of the wood-burning fireplace or stroll the inn's two-acre grounds. Accommodations include four guest rooms and a cottage. Cream-cheese omelets, orange French toast, blueberry pancakes or homemade waffles are some of the delectables that appear on the breakfast menu along with fresh fruits, juices and homemade breads.

Breakfast included in rates. Types of meals: full breakfast and early coffee/tea. Air conditioning and ceiling fan in room. Fax, copier and bicycles on premises. Family reunions hosted. French, German and Dutch spoken. Antiques, parks, shopping and theater nearby. TAC10.

Location: Montford Historic District.

Publicity: *Country Inns, Innsider.*

Special Discounts: Corporate rates negotiable; 10% January and February; Senior discount 10% September only.

Cedar Crest Victorian Inn

674 Biltmore Ave
Asheville, NC 28803-2513
(704)252-1389 (800)252-0310
Fax:(704)253-7667

Rates: $90-170.
Payment: MC VISA AX DC DS PC TC.
Innkeeper(s): Barbara & Jack McEwan.
Circa: 1891.

Rooms: 12 rooms with PB, 6 with FP. 3 suites. 1 cottage.
Beds: QD.

This Queen Anne mansion is one of the largest and most opulent residences surviving Asheville's 1890s boom. A captain's walk, projecting turrets and expansive verandas welcome guests to lavish interior woodwork and stained glass. All rooms are furnished in antiques with satin and lace trappings.

Breakfast and evening snack included in rates. Type of meal: full breakfast. Afternoon tea and room service available. Air conditioning and ceiling fan in room. Cable TV and fax on premises. Amusement parks, antiques, fishing, parks, shopping and theater nearby. TAC10.

Location: One quarter mile from the Biltmore Estate.

Publicity: *New Woman, Southern Living, Good Housekeeping, House Beautiful.*

"Cedar Crest is a real beauty and will hold a special place in our hearts."

Corner Oak Manor

53 Saint Dunstans Rd
Asheville, NC 28803-2620
(704)253-3525

Rates: $90-150.
Payment: MC VISA AX DS PC TC.
Innkeeper(s): Karen & Andy Spradley.
Circa: 1920.

Rooms: 4 rooms with PB, 1 with FP. 1 suite. 1 cottage.
Beds: Q.

Surrounded by oak, maple and pine trees, this English Tudor inn is decorated with many fine oak antiques and handmade items. Innkeeper Karen Spradley has handstitched something special for each room and the house features handmade items by local artisans. Breakfast delights include entrees such as Blueberry Ricotta Pancakes, Four Cheese and Herb Quiche and Orange French Toast. When you aren't enjoying local activities, you can sit on the shady deck, relax in the Jacuzzi, play a few songs on the piano or curl up with a good book.

Breakfast included in rates. Type of meal: gourmet breakfast. Air conditioning and ceiling fan in room. Family reunions hosted. Antiques, fishing, parks, shopping, downhill skiing and theater nearby.

"Great food, comfortable bed, quiet, restful atmosphere, you provided it all and we enjoyed it all!"

Dogwood Cottage

40 Canterbury Rd N
Asheville, NC 28801-1560
(704)258-9725

Rates: $95-105.
Payment: MC VISA AX PC.
Innkeeper(s): Joan & Don Tracy.
Circa: 1910.

Rooms: 4 rooms with PB, 3 with FP.
Beds: Q.

This Carolina mountain home is located a mile-and-a-half from downtown Asheville, on Sunset Mountain. The veranda, filled with white wicker and floral chintz prints, is the focal point of the inn during summer. It affords tree-top views to the Blue Ridge Mountains. Wing chairs and fresh country pieces accent the inn's gleaming hardwood floors. Breakfast is served in the formal dining room or on the covered porch.

Breakfast included in rates. Types of meals: full breakfast, gourmet breakfast and early coffee/tea. Air conditioning and ceiling fan in room. Cable TV, swimming and pet boarding on premises. Handicap access. Weddings and family reunions hosted. Antiques, fishing, parks, shopping, downhill skiing, sporting events, theater and watersports nearby. TAC10.

Pets Allowed: Yes.

"Cozy, warm and gracious."

Mountain Springs Cabins/Chalets

PO Box 6922
Asheville, NC 28816-6922
(704)665-1004
Fax:(704)667-1581

Rates: $80-125.
Payment: MC VISA TC.
Innkeeper(s): Sara & John Peltier.
Circa: 1929.

Rooms: 14 cottages with PB, 14 with FP.
Beds: D.

These rustic cabins and chalets offer a quiet, romantic lodging alternative. The secluded location sets the stage for a chorus of birds chirping or a night sky filled with stars. There are 100 acres to enjoy, with mountain trails to explore and fishing or picnicking areas. Each of the cabins and chalets includes a fireplace, kitchen and porch with rockers, and the rooms are decorated with antiques.

Cable TV in room. VCR, fax and copier on premises. 100 acres. Antiques and fishing nearby.

"We haven't stopped talking about the cabins since we have been back."

The Old Reynolds Mansion

100 Reynolds Hgts
Asheville, NC 28804
(704)254-0496

Rates: $55-125.
Payment: PC TC.
Innkeeper(s): Fred & Helen Faber.
Circa: 1855.

Rooms: 10 rooms, 8 with PB, 5 with FP. 1 cottage.
Beds: QDT.

NC

This handsome, three-story brick antebellum mansion is situated on a four-acre knoll of Reynolds Mountain. Rescued from near ruin by innkeepers Fred and Helen Faber, the home has been restored to its former glory as a gracious Southern manor. Each of the guest quarters reflects a different style from early American to Oriental. Guests can enjoy mountain views from their own room, by a wood-burning fireplace or on a rocking chair on the inn's wraparound porch. The mansion offers use of a swimming pool set among pine trees.

Breakfast and afternoon tea included in rates. Type of meal: continental-plus breakfast. Air conditioning and ceiling fan in room. Swimming and library on premises. Antiques, fishing, parks, shopping, downhill skiing, cross-country skiing, sporting events and theater nearby.

Location: Ten minutes north of downtown Asheville.

Publicity: *Greensboro News & Record, Blue Ridge Country.*

"This was one of the nicest places we have ever stayed. We spent every sundown on the porch waiting for the fox's daily visit."

Richmond Hill Inn

87 Richmond Hill Dr
Asheville, NC 28806-3912
(704)252-7313 (800)545-9238
Fax:(704)252-8726

Rates: $130-325. MAP.
Payment: MC VISA AX.
Innkeeper(s): Susan Michel.
Circa: 1889.

Rooms: 36 rooms with PB, 4 with FP. 3 suites. 1 conference room.
Beds: KQDT.

This renovated Victorian mansion was designed for the Pearson family by James G. Hill, architect of the U.S. Treasury Buildings. The elegant estate features a grand entry hall, ballroom, library and 10 master fireplaces with Neoclassical mantels. Guests may choose from accommodations in the luxurious mansion, charming cottages on a croquet court, or the garden rooms amid a striking landscape and facing a mountain waterfall. Two restaurants on the premises offer guests a choice of dining experiences. The inn is listed in the National Register of Historic Places.

Breakfast included in rates. Types of meals: full breakfast and gourmet breakfast. Dinner available. MAP. Fax, copier and spa on premises. Handicap access. Downhill skiing nearby.

Publicity: *Winston-Salem Journal, Atlanta Journal & Constitution, Asheville Citizen-Times, Courier-Tribune, Greensboro News & Record, Southern Living, USA News.*

"A great adventure into history. I am moved to tell you how grateful we are that you had the foresight and courage to rescue this wonderful place. The buildings and grounds are elegantly impressive .. and the staff superb! You have created a total experience that fulfills and satisfies."

Wright Inn & Carriage House

235 Pearson Dr
Asheville, NC 28801-1613
(704)251-0789 (800)552-5724
Fax:(704)251-0929

Rates: $90-200.
Payment: MC VISA DS PC TC.
Innkeeper(s): Carol & Art Wenczel.
Circa: 1899.

Rooms: 10 rooms with PB, 2 with FP. 1 suite. 1 cottage.
Beds: KQDT.

Located on a quiet, tree-lined street, this charming Queen Anne Victorian will take guests back in time to a more elegant, refined era. Guest rooms are furnished with antiques, family heirlooms and a bright, cheery decor. Two of the bedrooms feature fireplaces. Guests are treated to a breakfast of homemade breads, muffins, granola and tempting entrees. The Carriage House is a perfect place for families and includes a living room, dining room, kitchen, three bedrooms, two baths and the same carefully appointed decor evident in the main house.

Breakfast and afternoon tea included in rates. Types of meals: full breakfast, gourmet breakfast and early coffee/tea. Air conditioning and cable TV in room. Fax, bicycles and library on premises. Small meetings and family reunions hosted. Antiques, fishing, parks, shopping, downhill skiing, cross-country skiing, sporting events, theater and watersports nearby.

Special Discounts: Reduced winter rates.

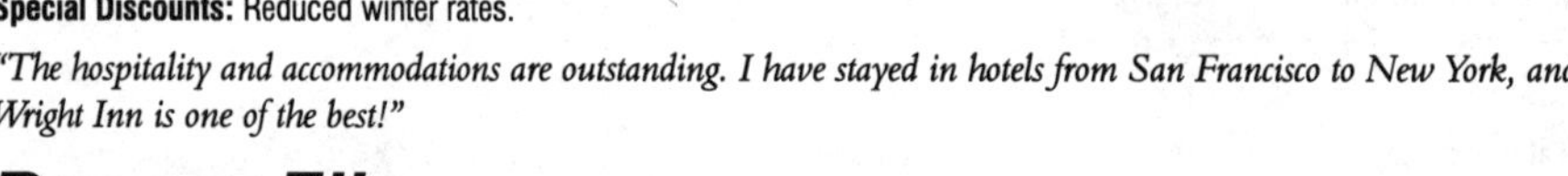

"The hospitality and accommodations are outstanding. I have stayed in hotels from San Francisco to New York, and the Wright Inn is one of the best!"

Banner Elk B4

Beech Alpen Inn

700 Beech Mountain Pkwy
Banner Elk, NC 28604-8015
(704)387-2252
Fax:(704)387-2229

Rates: $44-135.
Payment: MC VISA AX TC.
Innkeeper(s): Lisa & Taylor Rees.
Circa: 1968.

Rooms: 25 rooms with PB, 4 with FP.
Beds: KQD.

This rustic inn is a Bavarian delight affording scenic vistas of the Blue Ridge Mountains. The innkeepers offer accommodations at Top of the Beech, a Swiss-style ski chalet with views of nearby slopes. The interiors of both properties are inviting. At the Beech Alpen, several guest rooms have stone fireplaces or French

doors that open onto a balcony. Top of the Beech's great room is a wonderful place to relax with a huge stone fireplace and comfortable furnishings. The Beech Alpen Restaurant serves a variety of dinner fare.

Breakfast included in rates. Types of meals: continental breakfast and early coffee/tea. Cable TV in room. Fax and copier on premises. Weddings, small meetings, family reunions and seminars hosted. Antiques, fishing, parks, shopping, downhill skiing, cross-country skiing, sporting events and theater nearby. TAC10.

Rainbow Inn B&B

317 Old Turnpike Road
Banner Elk, NC 28604
(704)898-5611
Fax:(704)898-5611

Rates: $70-95.
Payment: PC TC.
Innkeeper(s): Tammy & Steve Rondinaro.
Circa: 1902.

Rooms: 4 rooms with PB.
Beds: QDT.

This Early American-style farmhouse, complete with a red tin roof, is located at the base of Beech Mountain. Inside, braided rugs, handmade quilts and Early American furnishings create a cozy feel. Relax in front of a roaring fire or on the home's 50-foot-long front porch. In addition to fresh fruit, a hearty cheese and sausage strata and homemade bread or muffins with jam are among the items on the breakfast table. The area is full of antique shops, and the scenic Blue Ridge Parkway is nearby.

Breakfast included in rates. Types of meals: full breakfast and early coffee/tea. Cable TV, fax and copier on premises. Small meetings hosted. Antiques, fishing, parks, shopping, downhill skiing, cross-country skiing, theater and watersports nearby.

Special Discounts: 10% discount for extended stay.

Beaufort — *C9*

Delamar Inn

217 Turner St
Beaufort, NC 28516-2140
(919)728-4300 (800)349-5823
Fax:(919)728-1471

Rates: $58-94.
Payment: MC VISA TC.
Innkeeper(s): Tom & Mabel Steepy.
Circa: 1866.

Rooms: 4 rooms with PB.
Beds: KQ.

The innkeepers, who have lived in Africa, Denmark, Hawaii and Scotland, lend an international touch to this hospitable two-story home, which boasts wide porches on each level. Each of the guest rooms is decorated to reflect a different style and period. Some of the rooms have original clawfoot tubs. The innkeepers keep plenty of coffee and tea around and stock comfortable sitting rooms with cookies and fruit for late-night snacking. They also can provide beach chairs, bicycles and box lunches for guests heading to the beach, which is less than two blocks from the inn.

Breakfast and afternoon tea included in rates. Types of meals: continental-plus breakfast and early coffee/tea. Air conditioning and ceiling fan in room. Cable TV, VCR, fax, copier and bicycles on premises. Small meetings and family reunions hosted. Antiques, fishing, parks, shopping and watersports nearby.

Publicity: *Corporate New Jersey LTD.*

"We've come back here for the last four years. It's like coming home!"

NC

Pecan Tree Inn B&B

116 Queen St
Beaufort, NC 28516-2214
(919)728-6733

Rates: $65-125.
Payment: MC VISA DS PC TC.
Innkeeper(s): Susan & Joe Johnson.
Circa: 1866.

Rooms: 7 rooms with PB. 1 suite.
Beds: KQ.

Originally built as a Masonic lodge, this state historic landmark is in the heart of Beaufort's historic district. Gingerbread trim, Victorian porches, turrets, and two-century-old pecan trees grace the exterior. Guests can relax in the parlor, on the porches, or pay a visit to the flower and herb gardens. The Bridal

Suite and "Wow" suite boast a king-size, canopied bed and two-person Jacuzzi.

Breakfast included in rates. Types of meals: continental-plus breakfast and early coffee/tea. Air conditioning and ceiling fan in room. Bicycles and library on premises. Weddings, small meetings and family reunions hosted. Amusement parks, antiques, fishing, parks, shopping and watersports nearby. TAC8.

Location: In the heart of the historic district, one-half block from the waterfront.

Publicity: *Sunday Telegram, This Week, Conde Nast Traveler, State.*

Special Discounts: Stay four days, the fifth day is free.

"After visiting B&Bs far and wide I give Pecan Tree Inn a Five-Star rating in all respects."

Blowing Rock — B4

Maple Lodge

PO Box 1236, 152 Sunset Dr
Blowing Rock, NC 28605
(704)295-3331
Fax:(704)295-9986

Rates: $78-128.
Payment: MC VISA AX DC DS PC TC.
Innkeeper(s): Marilyn & David Bateman.
Circa: 1943.

Rooms: 11 rooms with PB. 1 suite. 3 conference rooms.
Beds: KQDT.

Guests at this country B&B enjoy a 50-year tradition of innkeeping during their stay. The home was built to be a bed & breakfast, and the current innkeepers are aces at hospitality. Country antiques and family heirlooms fill the rooms. Lace, handmade quilts and down comforters create a warm, romantic atmosphere in the guest rooms, some of which include canopy beds. The buffet breakfasts are served in the unique Garden Room, which includes a wood-burning stove and stone floor.

Breakfast included in rates. Types of meals: full breakfast and early coffee/tea. Ceiling fan and cable TV in room. Fax and library on premises. Weddings, small meetings and family reunions hosted. Amusement parks, antiques, fishing, parks, shopping, downhill skiing, cross-country skiing, sporting events, theater and watersports nearby. TAC10.

The Inn at Ragged Gardens

PO Box 1927
Blowing Rock, NC 28605
(704)295-9703

Rates: $105-165.
Payment: MC VISA PC TC.
Innkeeper(s): Lee & Jama Hyett.
Circa: 1903.

Rooms: 8 rooms with PB, 8 with FP. 2 suites.
Beds: KQ.

Surrounded by rhododendron and majestic trees, this inn features guest rooms decorated with early 1900s furniture. Stone for the exterior rock columns, fireplaces and staircase was quarried from nearby Grandfather Mountain. Guest rooms and common areas are decorated with comfortable, turn-of-the-century furnishings. There are plenty of romantic amenities here, including rooms with garden views, fireplaces, whirlpool tubs or private balconies. During the morning meal, seasonal fruits, freshly baked breads, cereals and yogurt parfaits accompany a changing menu of entrees.

Breakfast included in rates. Types of meals: full breakfast and early coffee/tea. Air conditioning and ceiling fan in room. Cable TV, VCR, fax, copier and library on premises. Weddings, small meetings, family reunions and seminars hosted. Antiques, fishing, shopping, downhill skiing, cross-country skiing, theater and watersports nearby. TAC10.

Publicity: *Blowing Rocket, Lenois News-Topic, Mid-Atlantic Country, Pensacola Journal.*

Special Discounts: Corporate rates - 10% discount Monday-Thursday.

"I've never felt more welcome anywhere!"

Boone

B4

Lovill House Inn

404 Old Bristol Rd
Boone, NC 28607-7678
(704)264-4204 (800)849-9466

Rates: $85-120.
Payment: MC VISA PC TC.
Innkeeper(s): Tim & Lori Shahen.
Circa: 1875.

Rooms: 5 rooms with PB, 1 with FP.
Beds: KQT.

This traditional farmhouse was built by Capt. Edward Francis Lovill, a Civil War hero, attorney and state senator. The home stayed in the Lovill family for nearly a century. Recently restored, the rooms are elegant, yet casual enough that guests find it easy to relax. The guest rooms offer beds topped with down comforters. The innkeepers host a nightly social hour, sometimes out by the stream, other times on the front porch. In the early morning, coffee, tea and freshly baked muffins are waiting outside of each room. After this pre-breakfast fare, guests are further pampered with entrees such as Belgian waffles topped with fresh blueberries and a side of crisp bacon or perhaps a rich helping of eggs Benedict. After this feast, visitors head out to enjoy the area's activities, including golfing, fishing, hiking and antiquing.

Breakfast, afternoon tea and evening snack included in rates. Types of meals: full breakfast, gourmet breakfast and early coffee/tea. Picnic lunch available. Turn-down service, ceiling fan and cable TV in room. Bicycles and library on premises. 11 acres. Weddings, small meetings, family reunions and seminars hosted. Portuguese spoken. Amusement parks, antiques, fishing, parks, shopping, downhill skiing, cross-country skiing, sporting events, theater and watersports nearby. TAC10.

Special Discounts: Sunday-Thursday, $15 less, January, February, April, May, November.

"From the moment we walked in the door, we were treated and pampered like royalty! We will return."

Brevard

C3

The Inn at Brevard

410 E Main St
Brevard, NC 28712-3837
(704)884-2105
Fax:(704)966-9210

Rates: $65-150.
Payment: MC VISA PC TC.
Innkeeper(s): Eileen Bourget.
Circa: 1885.

Rooms: 14 rooms, 12 with PB, 3 with FP. 1 suite. 1 conference room.
Beds: QD.

General Stonewall Jackson's troops held reunion dinners at this inn in 1904 and again in 1911. The home's original owner was considered a fine Victorian lady, and her home still reflects the grace of the era. The dining room is open to the public and to guests for Friday and Saturday night dinners and Sunday brunch. Full breakfasts are served six days of the week. On Monday, continental fare is available.

Breakfast included in rates. Type of meal: full breakfast. Catering service available. Air conditioning and ceiling fan in room. Weddings, small meetings, family reunions and seminars hosted. Antiques, fishing, parks, shopping, theater and watersports nearby.

NC

Bryson City

B2

Folkestone Inn

101 Folkestone Rd
Bryson City, NC 28713-7891
(704)488-2730
Fax:(704)488-0722
E-mail: innkeeper@folkestone.com

Rates: $65-85.
Payment: MC VISA DS PC TC.
Innkeeper(s): Ellen & Charles Snodgrass.
Circa: 1926.

Rooms: 10 rooms with PB.
Beds: QD.

This farmhouse is constructed of local stone and rock. Pressed-tin ceilings, stained-glass windows and clawfoot tubs remain. The dining room, where breakfast is served, features floor-to-ceiling windows on all sides with views of the mountains. Afternoon refreshments also are served. There is a stream with a rock bridge on the property, and you can walk 10 minutes to waterfall views in the Great Smoky Mountains National Park.

Breakfast included in rates. Types of meals: full breakfast and early coffee/tea. Ceiling fan in room. Fax and copier on premises. Weddings, small meetings, family reunions and seminars hosted. Amusement parks, antiques, fishing, parks, shopping, theater and watersports nearby. TAC10.

Publicity: *Asheville Citizen-Times, Atlanta Journal, Lakeland, Palm Beach Post.*

"A charming place to spend a delightful weekend with a loved one. Wonderful breakfasts, too. Thanks!"

Nantahala Village

9400 Highway 19 W
Bryson City, NC 28713-9129
(704)488-2826 (800)438-1507
Fax:(704)488-9634

Rates: $50-70. EP.
Payment: MC VISA DS PC TC.
Innkeeper(s): John Burton & Jan Letendre.
Circa: 1948.

Rooms: 14 rooms. 4 suites. 42 cottages. 1 conference room.
Beds: KQDT.

This "village" offers guest rooms in a rustic lodge or accommodations in cabins, which are spread around 200 mountainous acres. Although breakfast is not included, the inn houses a fine restaurant with a country atmosphere. The workshop weekends feature topics such as Women's Weekend of Renewal, Making Jewelry from Paper, Landscape Design, a Painting the Smokies Watercolor Weekend, and Basket Making. Dinner concerts are another activity at this retreat. Spend the day on the tennis court or traverse the area on a mountain bike or horse. Canoeing and kayaking are some popular sports available in the area.

Type of meal: full breakfast. Dinner, picnic lunch, lunch, banquet service, catering service and catered breakfast available. EP. Air conditioning, ceiling fan and cable TV in room. VCR, fax, copier, swimming, stables, bicycles and tennis on premises. Handicap access. 200 acres. Weddings, small meetings, family reunions and seminars hosted. Antiques, fishing, parks, shopping and watersports nearby. TAC10.

Location: Adjacent to the Great Smoky Mountains National Park.

"First class, don't change anything."

Randolph House

223 Fryemont Rd,
PO Box 816
Bryson City, NC 28713-0816
(704)488-3472 (800)480-3472

Rates: $110-160. MAP.
Payment: MC VISA AX DS PC TC.
Innkeeper(s): Bill & Ruth Randolph Adams.
Circa: 1895.

Rooms: 7 rooms, 3 with PB, 2 with FP. 2 suites. 1 cottage. 1 conference room.
Beds: KQDT.

Randolph House is a mountain estate tucked among pine trees and dogwoods, near the entrance of Great Smoky Mountain National Park. Antiques, some original to the house, fill this National Register home. Each guest room is appointed in a different color scheme. The house provides an unforgettable experience, not the least of which is the gourmet dining provided on the terrace or in the dining room.

Breakfast and dinner included in rates. Types of meals: full breakfast and early coffee/tea. MAP. Air conditioning and cable TV in room. Library on premises. Handicap access. 10 acres. Small meetings, family reunions and seminars hosted. Antiques, fishing, parks, shopping and watersports nearby. TAC10.

Publicity: *Tourist News, New York Times.*

Special Discounts: Call; rates vary as to number of guests.

"Very enjoyable, great food."

Burnsville B3

The NuWray Inn

Town Square PO Box 156
Burnsville, NC 28714-0156
(704)682-2329 (800)368-9729
Fax:(704)682-6818

Rates: $75-95.
Payment: MC VISA AX DS PC TC.
Innkeeper(s): Chris & Pam Strickland.
Circa: 1833.

Rooms: 26 rooms with PB. 7 suites. 2 conference rooms.
Beds: KQDT.

This Colonial Revival home is the oldest country inn in the Western part of the state. There are featured events each month as well as theater packages in the summer season of the acclaimed Parkway Playhouse in Burnsville. Shindig-on-the-Square takes place every other weekend all summer in front of the inn, where many of the townspeople enjoy live music and street dancing. The mountains in the area offer unique beauty with the change of the seasons.

Breakfast included in rates. Types of meals: full breakfast and early coffee/tea. Dinner available. Ceiling fan and cable TV in room. Fax on premises. Handicap access. Weddings, small meetings, family reunions and seminars hosted. Antiques, fishing, parks, shopping, downhill skiing and theater nearby. TAC10.

Publicity: *Southern Living, Conde Nast Traveler, Peaks, State.*

Cashiers

C2

Millstone Inn

Hwy 64W
Cashiers, NC 28717
(704)743-2737 (888)645-5786
Fax:(704)743-0208

Rates: $99-150.
Payment: MC VISA DS PC TC.
Innkeeper(s): Paul & Patricia Collins.
Circa: 1933.

Rooms: 11 rooms, 7 with PB. 4 suites.
Beds: KQD.

The views from this inn are breathtaking, taking in both Whiteside Mountain and the surrounding valley. Inside, rustic, exposed log beams and woodsy, pine paneling complement the North Carolina wilderness. The innkeepers also offer efficiency apartments in the Garden Annex. Breakfasts are served in a glass-enclosed porch looking out to the mountains. The inn's eight acres border Natahala National Forest.

Breakfast included in rates. Types of meals: full breakfast and early coffee/tea. Ceiling fan in room. Fax and library on premises. French and Spanish spoken. Antiques, fishing, parks, shopping, downhill skiing, sporting events and watersports nearby.

Chapel Hill

B6

The Inn at Bingham School

PO Box 267
Chapel Hill, NC 27514-0267
(919)563-5583 (800)566-5583
Fax:(919)563-9826

Rates: $75-120.
Payment: MC VISA AX DS PC TC.
Innkeeper(s): Francois & Christina Deprez.
Circa: 1790.

Rooms: 5 rooms with PB, 1 with FP. 1 suite. 1 cottage. 1 conference room.
Beds: QD.

This inn served as one of the locations of the famed Bingham School. This particular campus was the site of a liberal arts preparatory school for those aspiring to attend the University at Chapel Hill. The inn is listed as a National Trust property and has garnered awards for its restoration. The property still includes many historic structures including a 1790s log home, an 1801 addition, an 1835 Greek Revival home, the headmaster's office, which was built in 1845, and a well house, smokehouse and milk house. The dining rooms and living rooms include the original pine flooring, wainscoting and milk-based paint on the ceilings. Guests can opt to stay in the Log Room, located in the log cabin, with a tightwinder staircase and fireplace. Other possibilities include Rusty's Room with two antique rope beds. Some rooms feature special mantels, an antique clawfoot tub and one offers a bedroom glassed in on three sides. A mix of breakfasts are served, from a Southern style with grits and ham to French with quiche and souffles. Gourmet coffee and tea complement each meal.

Breakfast and evening snack included in rates. Types of meals: full breakfast, gourmet breakfast and early coffee/tea. Picnic lunch available. Air conditioning in room. Cable TV, VCR, fax and library on premises. 10 acres. Weddings and small meetings hosted. Spanish and French spoken. Antiques, fishing, parks, shopping, sporting events, theater and watersports nearby. TAC10.

Publicity: *Southern Inns, Mebane Enterprise, Burlington Times, Times News, Washington Post.*

Special Discounts: Stay three nights, fourth night free, excluding weekends.

"Our stay at the inn was like a dream, another time, another place. Francois & Christina were the most hospitable, friendly hosts we've ever met."

Charlotte

C5

The Morehead Inn

1122 E Morehead St
Charlotte, NC 28204-2815
(704)376-3357 (888)667-3432
Fax:(704)335-1110

Rates: $100-150.
Payment: MC VISA AX DC PC.
Innkeeper(s): Billy Maddalon.
Circa: 1917.

Rooms: 12 rooms with PB, 1 with FP. 8 suites. 1 cottage. 3 conference rooms.
Beds: KQ.

This old-fashioned southern house is set on a huge corner lot dotted with oaks and azaleas. Guests gather in the great room, library and dining room, all furnished with English and American antiques. Balconies, canopy and four-poster beds and whirlpool tubs are among the amenities offered in some of the rooms. The Solarium Suite is a favorite choice. A two-bedroom carriage house with a stone fireplace is available for families or two couples traveling together.

Breakfast and evening snack included in rates. Types of meals: continental breakfast, continental-plus breakfast, full breakfast and gourmet breakfast. Dinner, gourmet lunch, banquet service, catering service and catered breakfast available. Air conditioning, turn-down service, ceiling fan and cable TV in room. Fax, copier, bicycles and child care on premises. Weddings, small meetings, family reunions and seminars hosted. Amusement parks, antiques, parks, shopping, sporting events and theater nearby. TAC10.

Publicity: *Business Journal, New York Times, Charlotte, Observer, Carolina Bride.*

"Thank you for your gracious attentiveness and hospitality."

Chimney Rock

B3

Esmeralda Inn

Hwy 74A PO Box 57
Chimney Rock, NC 28720
(704)625-9105

Rates: $48-75.
Payment: MC VISA AX DS TC.
Innkeeper(s): Ackie & Joanne Okpych.
Circa: 1890.

Rooms: 13 rooms, 7 with PB. 3 suites. 1 conference room.
Beds: KQD.

Nestled in the Blue Ridge Mountains, this rustic country lodge served as home base for production of several silent movies, and notables such as Mary Pickford, Gloria Swanson, Douglas Fairbanks, Clark Gable and many others used the Esmeralda as a hideout. Lew Wallace, noted author, finished the script for "Ben Hur" in room No. 9. The lobby, constructed of natural trees and filled with local artifacts, is a favorite place for visitors to take refuge and relax.

Breakfast and dinner included in rates. Picnic lunch and lunch available. Ceiling fan in room. Library on premises. Weddings, small meetings, family reunions and seminars hosted. Antiques, fishing, parks, shopping and watersports nearby.

Special Discounts: 10% if all rooms booked for reunion, business, etc.

Arrowhead Inn

106 Mason Rd
Durham, NC 27712-9106
(919)477-8430 (800)528-2207
Fax:(919)477-8430

Rates: $95-185.
Payment: MC VISA AX DC DS PC TC.
Innkeeper(s): Barb, Jerry, & Cathy Ryan.
Circa: 1775.

Rooms: 8 rooms with PB, 2 with FP. 2 suites. 1 cottage. 1 conference room.
Beds: KQD.

The home's original owners, the Lipscombe family, and later residents made several additions to this Colonial manor home, but left original features such as moldings, wainscoting, mantelpieces and heart-of-pine floors. A marker and stone arrowhead designate the land as the former location of the Great Path between mountains and Virginia, which was traveled by many Catawba and Waxhaw Indians. Rustic rooms are decorated to complement the fine woodwork. Quilts and canopy beds create a comfortable, romantic feeling. The Land Grant Cabin features rustic furnishings, a fireplace and sleeping loft set among its cozy wooden walls. The innkeepers take pride in creating a different feast every morning for breakfast. The inn is close to Duke University.

Breakfast and afternoon tea included in rates. Type of meal: full breakfast. Picnic lunch available. Air conditioning, ceiling fan and cable TV in room. Fax and copier on premises. Handicap access. Small meetings, family reunions and seminars hosted. French spoken. Antiques, parks and watersports nearby. TAC10.

Publicity: *USA Today, Food & Wine, House & Garden, Mid-Atlantic Country, Old House Journal, Southern Living.*

"I can see why you were written up in USA Today. We give you an A plus!"

Blooming Garden Inn

513 Holloway St
Durham, NC 27701-3457
(919)687-0801
Fax:(919)688-1401

Rates: $85-160.
Payment: MC VISA AX DC CB DS PC TC.
Innkeeper(s): Dolly & Frank Pokrass.
Circa: 1890.

Rooms: 4 rooms with PB, 4 with FP. 2 suites.
Beds: DT.

Blooming Garden is an apt name for this bed & breakfast. Each guest room is artfully appointed with a different, colorful theme. For instance, the Tiffany Room is accentuated with stained-glass pieces. The Moroccan Room is dressed in dramatic hues of dark green, gold and red. Each room offers a special bed, as well. Most impressive is the mid-19th-century carved Rosewood bed. In addition to the colorful interior, the exterior is dotted with a bright mix of perennials and annuals. The inn's luxury suites include a double Jacuzzi tub. Homemade ginger waffles topped with a creamy lemon curd are among the specialties served for breakfast. For guests planning an extended stay in the area, the innkeepers offer accommodations in Holly House, a restored Victorian across the street from the inn. Extended stay arrangements are possible across the street at Holly House, in a nicely furnished, restored Victorian home. The home includes a suite and three guest rooms, common areas, access to a kitchen, phone, washer and dryer. The innkeepers offer special, economical rates for those planning an extended stay. The Durham area offers many fine restaurants.

Breakfast included in rates. Types of meals: gourmet breakfast and early coffee/tea. Air conditioning, ceiling fan and cable TV in room. VCR, fax, copier and library on premises. Weddings and small meetings hosted. Antiques, parks, sporting events and theater nearby.

Special Discounts: 10% off four-six days, 20% off seven plus days.

Old North Durham Inn

922 N Mangum St
Durham, NC 27701-2229
(919)683-1885
Fax:(919)682-2645
E-mail: dvick1885@aol.com

Rates: $90-130.
Payment: MC VISA AX DS.
Innkeeper(s): Deborah Vickery.
Circa: 1906.

Rooms: 4 rooms with PB, 2 with FP. 1 suite.
Beds: QD.

The award-winning inn is a restored Colonial Revival home featuring 10-foot ceilings, six working fireplaces, brass beds, period wall coverings and furnishings. An upstairs sitting area offers an extensive reference library on Durham and North Carolina. The wraparound porch is lined with rockers, or guests can relax in the downstair's parlor before the fire and piano.

Across the street is the residence used in the movie "Bull Durham," and the innkeepers will provide guests with tickets to all Durham Bulls' home baseball games.

Breakfast and afternoon tea included in rates. Type of meal: full breakfast. Evening snack and picnic lunch available. Air conditioning, turn-down service, ceiling fan, cable TV and VCR in room. Small meetings, family reunions and seminars hosted. Antiques, shopping, sporting events and theater nearby. TAC10.

Location: Located in one of the oldest residential neighborhoods in Durham, less than a mile from Duke University, the Durham Bulls Athletic Park and the Durham Civic Center.

Publicity: *Spectator, Historic Preservation Society of Durham, News and Observer, Mid-Atlantic Country.*

"A real haven ... fresh towels as fast as you can use them, friendly and ultra solicitous hosts."

Edenton **B9**

The Lords Proprietors' Inn

300 N Broad St
Edenton, NC 27932-1905
(919)482-3641 (800)348-8933
Fax:(919)482-2432

Rates: $185-235. MAP.
Payment: PC TC.
Innkeeper(s): Arch & Jane Edwards.
Circa: 1801.

Rooms: 20 rooms with PB. 1 conference room.
Beds: KQT.

On Albemarle Sound, Edenton was one of the Colonial capitals of North Carolina. The inn consists of three houses, providing elegant accommodations in Edenton's Historic District. Breakfast and dinner are served in a separate dining room on a patio. A guided walking tour from the Visitor's Center provides an opportunity to see museum homes.

Breakfast, afternoon tea and dinner included in rates. Types of meals: gourmet breakfast and early coffee/tea. MAP. Air conditioning, ceiling fan, cable TV and VCR in room. Fax and child care on premises. Handicap access. Small meetings, family reunions and seminars hosted. Antiques, fishing and shopping nearby. TAC10.

Location: Main street of town.

Publicity: *Southern Living, Mid-Atlantic Country, House Beautiful, Washington Post.*

"One of the friendliest and best-managed inns I have ever visited."

Elizabeth City **A9**

Elizabeth City B&B

106 & 108 E Fearing St
Elizabeth City, NC 27909
(919)338-2177
Fax:(919)338-5001

Rates: $55-75.
Payment: MC VISA AX TC.
Innkeeper(s): Darla & Joseph Semonich.
Circa: 1898.

Rooms: 4 rooms with PB. 3 conference rooms.
Beds: QDT.

These two restored structures, both listed on the National Register, are located in the historic district of Elizabeth City. The L.S. Blades, Jr. House was constructed at the turn-of-the-century and features Colonial Revival architecture flanked with Victorian moldings. The other structure, which dates back to the mid-1800s, served as a fraternal lodge. Both homes are decorated with antiques. Guests are treated to innkeeper Joe Semonich's hearty full breakfast, and candlelight dinners are served in the lodge's "Secret Room" every Friday. The Pasquotank River is a short walk away. The B&B is a stop on the historic district's walking tour.

Breakfast included in rates. Type of meal: full breakfast. Dinner, banquet service and catering service available. Air conditioning, ceiling fan and cable TV in room. Fax on premises. Weddings, small meetings, family reunions and seminars hosted. Antiques, fishing, parks, shopping, theater and watersports nearby.

Special Discounts: Single corporate, Monday-Thursday $10.00-$15.00 off.

Franklin

Buttonwood Inn

50 Admiral Dr
Franklin, NC 28734-8474
(704)369-8985

Rates: $60-90.
Payment: PC TC.
Innkeeper(s): Liz Oehser.
Circa: 1927.

Rooms: 4 rooms with PB.
Beds: QDT.

Trees surround this two-story batten board house located adjacent to the Franklin Golf Course. Local crafts and handmade family quilts accent the country decor. Wonderful breakfasts are served here—often Eggs Benedict, baked peaches and sausage and freshly baked scones with homemade lemon butter. On a sunny morning enjoy breakfast on the deck and savor the Smoky Mountain vistas. Afterward, you'll be ready for white-water rafting, hiking and fishing.

Breakfast and afternoon tea included in rates. Types of meals: full breakfast and early coffee/tea. Ceiling fan in room. Cable TV on premises. Family reunions hosted. Antiques, fishing, parks and shopping nearby.

Franklin Terrace

67 Harrison Ave
Franklin, NC 28734-2961
(704)524-7907 (800)633-2431

Rates: $52-69.
Payment: MC VISA AX DS PC TC.
Innkeeper(s): Helen Henson.
Circa: 1887.

Rooms: 9 rooms with PB. 1 cottage.
Beds: KQD.

This plantation home, built originally to house a school, is listed in the National Register of Historic Places. Each of the guest rooms features period antiques. The innkeepers also offer a cottage that can sleep up to four quite comfortably. Those opting to stay in the historic home are treated to a lavish, continental-plus breakfast buffet with home-baked muffins, cereals, juices, sausages, poached eggs and several different breads. The home is within walking distance to shops, clothing boutiques and a variety of restaurants, but guests are welcome to simply sit and relax on the veranda, which is lined with wicker rocking chairs.

Breakfast included in rates. Types of meals: continental-plus breakfast and early coffee/tea. Air conditioning, ceiling fan and cable TV in room. Small meetings, family reunions and seminars hosted. Fishing, parks, downhill skiing, theater and watersports nearby. TAC5.

"We just 'discovered' this wonderful B&B on a trip home from the mountains of North Carolina. The owner maintains an antique shop on the lower floor. Guests are free to browse and raid the refrigerator late in the evening. The inn offers privacy, porches, unique rooms, comfort, cleanliness and is very pretty."

Grandfather Mountain (Linville)

Linville Cottage Bed & Breakfast

PO Box 508
Grandfather Mountain
(Linville), NC 28646-0508
(704)733-6551

Rates: $50-95.
Payment: MC VISA PC TC.
Innkeeper(s): Fran Feely.
Circa: 1910.

Rooms: 4 rooms with PB.
Beds: QD.

Just two miles from North Carolina's Grandfather Mountain rests this Victorian cottage. The innkeepers emphasize country comfort, decorating their B&B with simple antiques and collectibles. English and herb gardens surround the inn. Visit the inn's shops or simply enjoy the mountain breezes from the front porch. The area is full of scenic sites, including the Blue Ridge Parkway and Linville Caverns.

Breakfast and afternoon tea included in rates. Type of meal: continental-plus breakfast. Cable TV, VCR and library on premises. Handicap access. Weddings and family reunions hosted. Amusement parks, antiques, fishing, parks, shopping, downhill skiing, cross-country skiing, sporting events, theater and watersports nearby.

Pets Allowed: Yes.

Greensboro B6

Greenwood B&B

205 N Park Dr
Greensboro, NC 27401
(910)274-6350 (800)535-9363
Fax:(910)274-9943

Rates: $80-105.
Payment: MC VISA AX DS PC TC.
Innkeeper(s): Mike & Vanda Terrell.
Circa: 1908.

Rooms: 4 rooms with PB.
Beds: KQT.

Greenwood is a fully renovated, stick-style chalet on the park in the historic district. President W. H. Taft was once a guest here. The inn is decorated with fine western art, family heirlooms, and antiques. Turndown service and Southern cooking will make your stay unforgettable. There are two living rooms, each with a fireplace, and a swimming pool is in the backyard.

Breakfast and evening snack included in rates. Types of meals: continental breakfast, full breakfast and early coffee/tea. Air conditioning, turn-down service and ceiling fan in room. Cable TV, VCR, fax, copier, swimming and library on premises. Weddings, small meetings, family reunions and seminars hosted. Amusement parks, antiques, fishing, parks, shopping, sporting events, theater and watersports nearby. TAC10.

Location: Central Greensboro in the historic district.

Publicity: *Triad Style.*

Special Discounts: 10% off AAA.

"Your house is lovely and comfortable, but more than that it is your warmth and generous of spirit that will long be remembered."

Hendersonville C3

Claddagh Inn at Hendersonville

755 N Main St
Hendersonville, NC 28792
(704)697-7778 (800)225-4700
Fax:(704)697-8664

Rates: $79-120.
Payment: MC VISA AX DS PC TC.
Innkeeper(s): Augie & Gerri Emanuele.
Circa: 1898.

Rooms: 14 rooms with PB, 3 with FP. 2 suites.
Beds: KQDT.

Claddagh has been host for more than 90 years to visitors staying in Hendersonville. The wide, wraparound veranda is filled with rocking chairs, while the library is filled with inviting books. Many of North Carolina's finest craft and antique shops are just two blocks from the inn. Carl Sandburg's house and the Biltmore Estate are nearby, and within a short drive are spectacular sights in the Great Smoky Mountains.

Breakfast included in rates. Types of meals: full breakfast and early coffee/tea. Catering service available. Air conditioning and ceiling fan in room. Fax and library on premises. Weddings, small meetings and family reunions hosted. Antiques, fishing, parks, shopping, theater and watersports nearby. TAC10.

Location: One-half block north from 7th Avenue (US 64 W) on Main St. (US 25).

Publicity: *Country Inn, Blue Ridge Country, Southern Living.*

Special Discounts: AAA and AARP receive 10% discount; golf packages available.

"Excellent food, clean, home-like atmosphere."

The Waverly Inn

783 N Main St
Hendersonville, NC 28792
(704)693-9193 (800)537-8195
Fax:(704)692-1010
E-mail: jsheiry@aol.com

Rates: $89-139.
Payment: MC VISA AX DS PC.
Innkeeper(s): John & Diane Sheiry, Darla Olmstead.
Circa: 1898.

Rooms: 14 rooms with PB. 1 suite.
Beds: KQDT.

In the National Register, this three-story Victorian and Colonial Revival house has a two-tiered, sawn work trimmed porch and widow's walk. A beautifully carved Eastlake staircase and an original registration desk grace the inn. There are four-poster canopy beds and clawfoot tubs. Breakfast is served in the handsome dining room. The Waverly is the oldest surviving inn in Hendersonville.

Breakfast and evening snack included in rates. Type of meal: full breakfast. Picnic lunch available. Air conditioning and ceiling fan in room. Cable TV and fax on premises. Weddings and family reunions hosted. Antiques, fishing, parks, shopping, cross-country skiing and theater nearby. TAC10.

Location: Corner of 8th Ave & Main St (Rt 25 North)

Publicity: *New York Times, Country, Blue Ridge Country, Vogue, Southern Living, Travel South.*

Special Discounts: Winter specials two and three night packages starting at $169+tax.

"Our main topic of conversation while driving back was what a great time we had at your place."

Hickory B4

The Hickory B&B

464 7th St SW
Hickory, NC 28602-2743
(704)324-0548 (800)654-2961

Rates: $85.
Payment: PC TC.
Innkeeper(s): Bob & Pat Lynch.
Circa: 1908.

Rooms: 4 rooms with PB.
Beds: QT.

Bedrooms in this Georgian-style inn are decorated with antiques, collectibles and fresh flowers. There's a parlor to sit in and chat and a library to enjoy a good book or to play a game. Homemade tea and lemonade, with something from the oven are served to guests in the late afternoon. The inn is located in a city that has evolved from a furniture and textile mill town of yesteryear into a cultural arts mecca of mountain communities. From mountains to malls, Hickory satisfies the shopper as well as the sportsperson.

Breakfast included in rates. Types of meals: full breakfast and early coffee/tea. Afternoon tea available. Air conditioning and ceiling fan in room. Cable TV, VCR, swimming and library on premises. Weddings, small meetings and family reunions hosted. Antiques, fishing, parks, shopping, sporting events, theater and watersports nearby.

Publicity: *Mid-Atlantic Country, Hickory Daily News, Charlotte Observer.*

Special Discounts: Call for corporate rates.

"Now we know what Southern hospitality means. We had such a wonderful weekend with you."

Hiddenite B4

Hidden Crystal Inn

Sulphur Springs Rd
Hiddenite, NC 28636
(704)632-0063 (800)439-1639
Fax:(704)632-3562

Rates: $75-160. AP.
Payment: MC VISA AX.
Innkeeper(s): Lynn Sharpe Hill, Kim Lucas & Rita Michell.
Circa: 1945.

Rooms: 14 rooms, 12 with PB, 1 with FP. 1 cottage. 4 conference rooms.
Beds: KQDT.

NC

Set in the heart of gemstone country, gems and minerals are a natural theme at this Southern plantation-style inn. Rare specimens such as emeralds, garnets, smoky quartz, and amethysts that were unearthed nearby are displayed throughout the inn. Bedrooms are named and color-themed after local gems. Guests have access to a library, parlor, patio, swimming pool, English garden, and gazebo. Country breakfasts of ham, eggs, buttermilk biscuits, grits, and homemade pastries are accompanied by a view of the garden. The newly-added Crystal Cottage offers conference facilities.

Breakfast included in rates. Types of meals: continental breakfast and early coffee/tea. Afternoon tea, dinner, evening snack, picnic lunch, lunch, gourmet lunch, banquet service, catering service, catered breakfast and room service available. AP. Air conditioning, ceiling fan, cable TV and VCR in room. Fax, copier, swimming, bicycles and library on premises. Handicap access. Weddings, small meetings, family reunions and seminars hosted. Spanish, Thai, Mandarin Chinese and Vietnamese spoken. Antiques, fishing, parks, shopping and theater nearby. TAC10.

Publicity: *Winston-Salem Journal.*

High Point

B5

Bouldin House B&B

4332 Archdale Rd
High Point, NC 27263-3070
(910)431-4909 (800)739-1816
Fax:(910)431-4914
E-mail: lmiller582@aol.com

Rates: $85-95. MAP.
Payment: MC VISA DS PC TC.
Innkeeper(s): Larry & Ann Miller.
Circa: 1915.

Rooms: 4 rooms with PB, 4 with FP.
Beds: KT.

This home, a unique example of American Four-Square architecture, is located a few miles outside of High Point, in the nearby village of Archdale. The innkeepers are only the second owners, and have named their bed & breakfast for the family who built it. The house has been painstakingly restored and now offers four guest room, with names such as Weekend Retreat or Warm Morning. Queen Anne chairs, pocket doors or a four-poster bed are among the features guests will discover in their rooms, and all guest quarters include a fireplace. Oatmeal currant scones topped with orange butter and pecan-basil pesto omelets and sage sausage are among the tempting treats served during the gourmet breakfasts.

Breakfast and evening snack included in rates. Types of meals: gourmet breakfast and early coffee/tea. Afternoon tea available. MAP. Air conditioning and ceiling fan in room. Cable TV, VCR, fax and library on premises. Small meetings and family reunions hosted. Amusement parks, antiques, parks, shopping and sporting events nearby. TAC10.

"Great place for a honeymoon."

Highlands

C2

Colonial Pines Inn

541 Hickory St
Highlands, NC 28741-8498
(704)526-2060

Rates: $80-140.
Payment: MC VISA PC TC.
Innkeeper(s): Chris & Donna Alley.
Circa: 1937.

Rooms: 6 rooms, 7 with PB. 2 suites. 3 cottages.
Beds: KQDT.

Secluded on a hillside just half a mile from Highlands' Main Street, this inn offers relaxing porches which boast a mountain view. The parlor is another restful option, offering a TV, fireplace and piano. Rooms, highlighted by knotty pine, are decorated with an eclectic mix of antiques. The guest pantry is always stocked with refreshments for those who need a little something in the afternoon. For breakfast, freshly baked breads accompany items such as a potato/bacon casserole and baked pears topped with currant sauce. In addition to guest rooms, there are three cottages available, each with a fireplace and kitchen.

Breakfast and afternoon tea included in rates. Type of meal: full breakfast. Cable TV on premises. Antiques, fishing, parks, shopping, downhill skiing, theater and watersports nearby.

Publicity: *Greenville News, Atlanta Journal, Highlander.*

Special Discounts: January-April, second night half price, excluding holidays.

"There was nothing we needed which you did not provide."

Morning Star Inn

480 Flat Mountain Estates Rd
Highlands, NC 28741-8325
(704)526-1009
Fax:(704)526-4474

Rates: $125-140.
Payment: MC VISA PC TC.
Innkeeper(s): Pat & Pat Allen.
Circa: 1962.

Rooms: 5 rooms with PB. 1 suite.
Beds: KQ.

For anyone hoping to enjoy the serenity and scenery of North Carolina, this inn is an ideal place for that and more. Hammocks and rockers are found here and there on the two-acre grounds, dotted with gardens and fountains. There is a parlor with a stone fireplace and a wicker-filled sunporch. Rooms are decorated in a romantic and elegant style. Beds are dressed with fine linens and down comforters. To top off the amenities, one of the innkeepers is a culinary school graduate and prepares the mouthwatering cuisine guests enjoy at breakfast. On the weekends, afternoon refreshments are served. The innkeeper also is working on a cookbook, which will no doubt include tidbits such as Southwestern eggs and fresh fruit with amaretto cream sauce. For those interested in improving their culinary skills, cooking classes sometimes are available.

Breakfast and afternoon tea included in rates. Types of meals: gourmet breakfast and early coffee/tea. Evening snack available. Air conditioning, turn-down service and ceiling fan in room. Cable TV, fax and copier on premises. Small meetings hosted. Antiques, fishing, parks, shopping, downhill skiing and theater nearby. TAC10.

Ye Olde Stone House B&B

1337 S 4th St
Highlands, NC 28741
(704)526-5911

Rates: $75-130.
Payment: MC VISA PC TC.
Innkeeper(s): Jim & Rene Ramsdell.
Circa: 1938.

Rooms: 4 rooms with PB. 2 cottages.
Beds: KQDT.

Located at an elevation of 4,100 feet, this stone house with its country decor offers a place to relax and experience the natural beauty of its mountain setting. The innkeepers will be glad to help with guests' sightseeing plans, which might include a trip to nearby Dry, Glen and Bridal Veil Falls and the Cullsaja Gorge. Complimentary beverages and snacks are available and can be enjoyed in the glassed-in gazebo, porch or deck with comfortable chairs and rockers.

Breakfast included in rates. Types of meals: gourmet breakfast and early coffee/tea. Turn-down service and ceiling fan in room. Cable TV and VCR on premises. Weddings, small meetings and family reunions hosted. Antiques, fishing, parks, shopping, downhill skiing, theater and watersports nearby.

Lake Lure B3

Lodge on Lake Lure

Charlotte Dr Box 519
Lake Lure, NC 28746
(704)625-2789 (800)733-2785
Fax:(704)625-2421

Rates: $96-135.
Payment: MC VISA AX DS PC TC.
Innkeeper(s): Jack & Robin Stanier.
Circa: 1930.

Rooms: 11 rooms with PB.
Beds: KQT.

This rambling lodge features a great room with vaulted ceilings, wormy chestnut walls and hand-hewn beams. A 20-foot tall stone fireplace is highlighted with a gristmill stone. The breakfast room and the veranda, with its row of rocking chairs, provides inspirational views of the lake and mountains. Guest rooms are decorated in an elegant country style.

Breakfast included in rates. Types of meals: full breakfast and gourmet breakfast. Air conditioning and ceiling fan in room. Cable TV, VCR, fax, copier, swimming and library on premises. Small meetings and seminars hosted. Spanish spoken. Antiques, fishing, parks, shopping, theater and watersports nearby. TAC10.

Location: Located on Lake Lure, in the foothills of the Blue Ridge Mountains, 22 miles southeast of Asheville, in western NC.

Lake Toxaway C2

Greystone Inn

Greystone Ln
Lake Toxaway, NC 28747
(704)966-4700 (800)824-5766
Fax:(704)862-5689

Rates: $255-510. MAP.
Payment: MC VISA AX.
Innkeeper(s): Tim & Boo Boo Lovelace.
Circa: 1915.

Rooms: 33 rooms with PB. 3 suites.
Beds: KQD.

Guests the likes of Thomas Edison and John D. Rockefeller frequented Lake Toxaway for their summer vacations, and the magnificent scenery convinced Savannah heiress Lucy Armstrong Moltz to build her summer cottage here. Her magnificent Swiss Revival home now hosts a bounty of guests hoping to capture the atmosphere of days gone by. Gracious, elegant rooms feature beautiful antiques and reproductions. Afternoon tea is served on the wicker-filled sun porch. The innkeepers host sunset champagne cruises along Lake Toxaway on a pontoon boat. The inn boasts a restaurant on site which serves up a variety of breakfast, lunch and dinner specialties. Tennis, boating, waterskiing and canoeing are all available.

Breakfast, afternoon tea and dinner included in rates. Types of meals: full breakfast and early coffee/tea. Picnic lunch, lunch and room service available. MAP. Air conditioning, turn-down service, ceiling fan, cable TV and VCR in room. Fax, copier, spa, swimming, sauna, bicycles, tennis, library and child care on premises. Handicap access. Weddings, small meetings and family reunions hosted. Antiques, fishing, shopping, downhill skiing, theater and watersports nearby. TAC10.

Publicity: *Country Inns, Southern Living, Southern Accents.*

"Wonderful! We're already planning our next visit. We haven't felt this pampered since our last cruise."

Mountain Home C3

Mountain Home B&B

PO Box 234
Mountain Home, NC 28758
(704)697-9090 (800)397-0066

Rates: $85-195.
Payment: MC VISA PC.
Innkeeper(s): Blake & Tammie Levit, Judy Brown.
Circa: 1915.

Rooms: 7 rooms with PB, 1 with FP. 1 suite. 1 conference room.
Beds: KQD.

This home and its surrounding grounds have quite a history behind them. Although the inn itself was built in 1915, a plantation home once stood in this area, holding court over an enormous spread which included a dairy, blacksmith shop, race track and stables. The plantation home was burnt at the end of the Civil War, and it was not until the early 1900s that a hotel was built on a 640-acre parcel of the property.This, too, burnt, and in 1941, a local dentist built his family home out of the hotel's remains. Today, the guests once again travel to this picturesque spot to enjoy Southern hospitality. Rooms are romantically appointed with items such as a four-poster rice bed, sleigh bed, skylights, a fireplace or a Jacuzzi tub. The front porch is ready for those who wish to relax, offering rockers for the weary. Guests also are pampered with a hearty breakfast, raspberry stuffed French toast is a specialty. The innkeepers offer a variety of getaway packages.

Breakfast and evening snack included in rates. Types of meals: full breakfast, gourmet breakfast and early coffee/tea. Banquet service available. Air conditioning and cable TV in room. Handicap access. Small meetings, family reunions and seminars hosted. Antiques, fishing, parks, shopping and theater nearby. TAC10.

Publicity: *Arts & Entertainment.*

Special Discounts: 10% off for Seniors; other packages available.

"Thanks for showing us what 'Southern hospitality' is like."

Murphy C1

Huntington Hall B&B

500 Valley River Ave
Murphy, NC 28906-2829
(704)837-9567 (800)824-6189
Fax:(704)837-2527
E-mail: hhallbnb@grove.net

Rates: $65-95. MAP.
Payment: MC VISA AX DC CB DS PC TC.
Innkeeper(s): Kate & Bob DeLong.
Circa: 1881.

Rooms: 5 rooms with PB, 2 with FP. 1 conference room.
Beds: KQDT.

This two-story country Victorian home was built by J.H. Dillard, the town mayor and twice a member of the House of Representatives. Clapboard siding and tall columns accent the large front porch. An English country theme is highlighted throughout. Afternoon refreshments and evening turndown service are included. Breakfast is served on the sun porch. Murder-mystery, summer-theater, and white-water-rafting packages are available.

Breakfast included in rates. Types of meals: full breakfast, gourmet breakfast and early coffee/tea. MAP. Air conditioning, turn-down service, ceiling fan and cable TV in room. VCR, fax, copier, tennis and library on premises. Weddings, small meetings, family reunions and seminars hosted. Antiques, fishing, parks, shopping, theater and watersports nearby. TAC10.

Location: One block from downtown.

Publicity: *Atlanta Journal, Petersen's 4-Wheel, New York Times.*

"Your skill and attitude make it a pleasant experience to stay and rest at HH."

Nags Head

B10

First Colony Inn

6720 S Va Dare Tr
Nags Head, NC 27959
(919)441-2343 (800)368-9390
Fax:(919)441-9234

Rates: $75-225.
Payment: MC VISA AX DS PC TC.
Innkeeper(s): The Lawrences.
Circa: 1932.

Rooms: 26 rooms with PB. 6 suites. 1 conference room.
Beds: KQT.

This Shingle-style inn features two stories of continuous verandas on all four sides. It is the last of the original beach hotels built on the Outer Banks. To save it from destruction, the Lawrences moved it to family property three miles south. During the midnight move, townsfolk lined the streets cheering and clapping to see the preservation of this historic building. First Colony boasts a pool, private beach access and ocean and sound views from the second and third floors. Furnishings include antiques and traditional reproductions. There are Jacuzzis, kitchenettes, an elegant library, and a sunny breakfast room.

Breakfast and afternoon tea included in rates. Types of meals: continental-plus breakfast and early coffee/tea. Catering service and room service available. Air conditioning, turn-down service, cable TV and VCR in room. Fax, copier, swimming and library on premises. Handicap access. Weddings, small meetings, family reunions and seminars hosted. French, German, Spanish and Swedish spoken. Fishing, parks, theater and watersports nearby. TAC10.

Location: Outer banks of North Carolina.

Publicity: *Virginia News Leader, Southern Living, Carolina Style, Greensboro News & Record, Discerning Traveler, Raleigh News & Observer, Washington Post, High Point Enterprise, Lexington Dispatch, Portfolio, Coast, Norfolk Virginian-Pilot.*

Special Discounts: Thursday night free for Sunday-Thursday stays.

"Great, well done, nothing to change."

New Bern

C8

Harmony House Inn

215 Pollock St
New Bern, NC 28560-4942
(919)636-3810 (800)636-3113
Fax:(919)636-3810
E-mail: harmony@nternet.net

Rates: $85-120.
Payment: MC VISA DS PC TC.
Innkeeper(s): Ed & Sooki Kirkpatrick.
Circa: 1850.

Rooms: 9 rooms with PB, 10 with FP. 1 suite. 2 conference rooms.
Beds: KQT.

NC

Long ago, this two-story Greek Revival was sawed in half and the west side moved nine feet to accommodate new hallways, additional rooms and a staircase. A wall was then built to divide the house into two sections. The rooms are decorated with antiques, family heirlooms and collectibles. Offshore breezes sway blossoms in the lush garden. Cross the street to an excellent restaurant or take a picnic to the shore.

Breakfast and evening snack included in rates. Types of meals: full breakfast and early coffee/tea. Air conditioning, ceiling fan and cable TV in room. Fax on premises. Weddings, small meetings, family reunions and seminars hosted. Korean spoken. Antiques, parks, shopping and watersports nearby. TAC10.

Location: In the historic district, four blocks to Tyron Palace.

Publicity: *Americana.*

"We feel nourished even now, six months after our visit to Harmony House."

King's Arms Inn

212 Pollock St
New Bern, NC 28560-4943
(919)638-4409 (800)872-9306
Fax:(919)638-2191

Rates: $85-125.
Payment: MC VISA AX PC TC.
Innkeeper(s): Richard & Pat Gulley.
Circa: 1848.

Rooms: 8 rooms with PB. 1 suite.
Beds: KQD.

Three blocks from the Tryon Palace, in the heart of the New Bern Historic District, this Colonial-style inn features a mansard roof and touches of Victorian architecture. Guest rooms are decorated with antiques,

canopy and four-poster beds and decorative fireplaces. An old tavern in town was the inspiration for the name of the inn.

Breakfast and evening snack included in rates. Types of meals: continental-plus breakfast and early coffee/tea. Air conditioning, ceiling fan and cable TV in room. Fax and child care on premises. Weddings and family reunions hosted. Antiques, fishing, parks, theater and watersports nearby. TAC10.

Publicity: *Washington Post, Southern Living, Sun Journal.*

"Delightful. Wonderful breakfast. Beautiful old home. Marvelous muffins."

Ocracoke C9

The Berkley Center Country Inn

PO Box 220
Ocracoke, NC 27960-0220
(919)928-5911

Rates: $70-85.
Payment: PC.
Innkeeper(s): Wes & Ruth Egan.
Circa: 1951.

Rooms: 10 rooms, 8 with PB. 2 conference rooms.
Beds: QDT.

Once a harbor for the pirate Blackbeard, Ocracoke is a fishing village on a small island in the middle of Hattaras National Seashore, accessible only by ferry or private boat. Located on three acres in the village, the inn is framed by red and white myrtles. The weathered shingled main house boasts an enormous square tower rising from a second-story gable. The walls of the tower room are lined with windows looking out to Pamlico Sound and the Atlantic. With cedar paneling and wooden ceilings, the inn has a lodge-like atmosphere and is filled with comfortable furnishings.

Breakfast included in rates. Type of meal: continental breakfast. Air conditioning in room. Cable TV and VCR on premises. Handicap access. Weddings, small meetings, family reunions and seminars hosted. Fishing, shopping and watersports nearby. TAC10.

Publicity: *Mid-Atlantic Country, New York Times, Washington Post.*

"Outstanding hospitality, unsurpassed!"

Oriental C9

Tar Heel Inn

508 Church St, Box 176
Oriental, NC 28571
(919)249-1078
Fax:(919)249-0005
E-mail: tarheel@pamlico-nc.com

Rates: $70-90.
Payment: MC VISA PC.
Innkeeper(s): Shawna & Robert Hyde.
Circa: 1890.

Rooms: 8 rooms with PB.
Beds: KQDT.

This inn is graciously appointed in English country style, with four-poster and canopy beds dressed in fine linens. Fresh flowers, stenciling and Laura Ashley prints brighten the rooms. Before a day exploring the area, guests enjoy a gourmet breakfast. In the late afternoons, refreshments are served. Oriental, a village located at the junction of the Neuse River and Pamlico Sound, is known as a sailing capitol of the Carolinas.

Breakfast and evening snack included in rates. Types of meals: full breakfast, gourmet breakfast and early coffee/tea. Air conditioning and ceiling fan in room. Bicycles and library on premises. Small meetings and family reunions hosted. Antiques, fishing, parks, shopping, theater and watersports nearby.

Special Discounts: Fifth night free with four consecutive nights.

Pilot Mountain

The Blue Fawn B&B

3052 Siloam Rd
Pilot Mountain, NC 27047
(910)374-2064 (800)948-7716

Rates: $55-85.
Payment: MC VISA PC.
Innkeeper(s): Gino & Terri Cella.
Circa: 1892.

Rooms: 3 rooms with PB. 1 suite.
Beds: KQDT.

This Greek Revival-style house, with its four two-story columns, is bordered by an old stone fence. Located 10 minutes from town, the Blue Fawn B&B offers a friendly stay in a small tobacco farming community.

There are three porches, and one is off the second-story guest rooms, which are decorated comfortably with many quilts. Spinach blue cheese strudel, Irish soda bread and fruit or homemade biscuits served with sausage gravy, fried potatoes and baked garlic cheese grits are some of the breakfast offerings. It's a tenth of a mile to the Yadkin River.

Breakfast, afternoon tea and evening snack included in rates. Types of meals: full breakfast, gourmet breakfast and early coffee/tea. Picnic lunch, catering service and room service available. Air conditioning, turn-down service, ceiling fan and cable TV in room. VCR, bicycles and library on premises. Weddings, small meetings, family reunions and seminars hosted. Antiques, fishing, parks, shopping, theater and watersports nearby.

Special Discounts: Long term stays $25 per day.

"Words could never express how welcome and at home you have made our family feel."

Pinebluff C6

Pine Cone Manor

450 E Philadelphia Ave
Pinebluff, NC 28375
(910)281-5307

Rates: $60-65.
Payment: MC VISA PC TC.
Innkeeper(s): Virginia H. Keith.
Circa: 1912.

Rooms: 3 rooms, 2 with PB, 1 with FP. 1 cottage.
Beds: KQDT.

The family that built this home lived here for more than 60 years, finally selling it in the 1970s. Today the house is a comfortable B&B set on private, wooded acres that include a variety of the namesake pines. The front porch is an ideal place to relax, offering a collection of rockers and a swing. The area is full of interesting sites, NASCAR and horse racing tracks are just a few. The area, which offers dozens of golf courses, also includes the World Golf Hall of Fame.

Breakfast included in rates. Types of meals: continental-plus breakfast and early coffee/tea. Air conditioning, ceiling fan and cable TV in room. Library on premises. Family reunions hosted. Antiques, parks, shopping and sporting events nearby.

Pittsboro B6

The Fearrington House Inn

2000 Fearrington Village Ctr
Pittsboro, NC 27312-8502
(919)542-2121
Fax:(919)542-4202

Rates: $150-250.
Payment: MC VISA AX.
Innkeeper(s): Jenny & R.B. Fitch.
Circa: 1927.

Rooms: 24 rooms with PB, 3 with FP. 10 suites. 1 conference room.
Beds: KQT.

The Fearrington is an old dairy farm. Several of the original outbuildings, including the silo and barn, have been converted into a village with a potter's shop, bookstore, jewelry shop, and a southern garden shop. The original homestead houses an award-winning restaurant. The inn itself is of new construction and its rooms overlook pasture land with grazing sheep, as well as a courtyard. Polished pine floors, fresh floral prints and amenity-filled bathrooms are among the inn's offerings.

Breakfast and afternoon tea included in rates. Types of meals: full breakfast and gourmet breakfast. Dinner, picnic lunch, lunch, catering service and room service available. Fax and copier on premises. Handicap access. Antiques, fishing and theater nearby.

Publicity: *Gourmet, Country Inns, Living It Up, North Carolina Homes and Gardens.*

"There is an aura of warmth and caring that makes your guests feel like royalty in a regal setting!"

Robbinsville C2

Snowbird Mountain Lodge

275 Santeetlah Rd
Robbinsville, NC 28771
(704)479-3433
E-mail: snbdmtnldg@aol.com

Rates: $120-130. AP.
Payment: VISA PC TC.
Innkeeper(s): Karen & Robert Rankin.
Circa: 1940.

Rooms: 22 rooms with PB.
Beds: KQDT.

Panoramic, 40-mile views are one of the many reasons to visit this mountain-top lodge. One innkeeper is a trained chef, and the other a knowledgeable outdoorsman. So guests not only enjoy gourmet meals, but learn where to find the best hiking and nature trails in North Carolina. The lodge is decorated in a rustic style, with an emphasis on comfort. Guest rooms feature wood-paneled walls, and each room sports a different variety of wood. Furnishings have been built by local craftsman using wood native to the area. There are plenty of places to relax, from the 2,500-volume library to rooms with huge, stone fireplaces. Breakfast, lunch and dinner are included in the rates. The innkeepers offer many interesting activities, such as a dulcimer clinic, fly-fishing excursions, cooking seminars and nature walks or hikes led by experienced guides.

Breakfast, afternoon tea, dinner and evening snack included in rates. Types of meals: full breakfast and early coffee/tea. Picnic lunch and lunch available. AP. Ceiling fan in room. Fax, copier and library on premises. Handicap access. 99 acres. Weddings, small meetings, family reunions and seminars hosted. Antiques, fishing, shopping and watersports nearby.

Salisbury B5

Rowan Oak House

208 S Fulton St
Salisbury, NC 28144-4845
(704)633-2086 (800)786-0437

Rates: $85-110.
Payment: MC VISA PC TC.
Innkeeper(s): Barbara & Les Coombs.
Circa: 1901.

Rooms: 4 rooms with PB.
Beds: KQD.

This Queen Anne house, in the middle of the Salisbury Historic District, features a carved-oak front door, leaded and stained glass, meticulously carved mantels and the original ornate electric and gaslights. Guests may enjoy evening wine in the Victorian parlor or on the columned, wraparound porch overlooking gardens and fountains. Guest rooms have antiques, historic wallpaper, down comforters, fresh flowers and fruit. One room has a double Jacuzzi, and one has a double shower.

Breakfast included in rates. Type of meal: gourmet breakfast. Air conditioning in room. Weddings, small meetings, family reunions and seminars hosted. Antiques, fishing, parks, shopping, sporting events, theater and watersports nearby. TAC10.

Publicity: *Salisbury Post, Daily Independent, Country Victorian Accents.*

"A stay at the Rowan Oak House is the quintessential B&B experience. Their home is as interesting as it is beautiful, and they are the most gracious host and hostess you can imagine."

Saluda C3

Ivy Terrace B&B Inn

PO Box 639
Saluda, NC 28773-0639
(704)749-9542 (800)749-9542
Fax:(704)749-2017

Rates: $95-140.
Payment: MC VISA TC.
Innkeeper(s): Diane & Herbert McGuire & Walter Hoover.
Circa: 1890.

Rooms: 7 rooms with PB, 2 with FP. 1 conference room.
Beds: KQT.

Capt. W.G. Hinson built this two-story dwelling, surrounded by towering cedars, spruces and firs, as his summer home. The house later served as a boarding house, but today it has been lovingly transformed into an idyllic getaway. Comfortable furnishings create a homey, country atmosphere. Enjoy afternoon refresh-

ments as you take in the sounds of birds chirping away on the porches or patios. Breakfasts at Ivy Terrace won't be soon forgotten. Juices or fresh cider, pressed from locally grown apples, starts off an expansive meal with items such as hazelnut oatmeal pancakes with sauteed apples and sausage, or perhaps a cheddar French toast with maple syrup and a side of honey-marinated Canadian bacon. After the morning meal, guests can take in all the shops, outlets and craft stores in the area or head up scenic Blue Ridge Parkway. Nature lovers will enjoy the hike to Pearsons Falls.

Breakfast included in rates. Types of meals: full breakfast and early coffee/tea. Cable TV, VCR, fax and copier on premises. Handicap access. Small meetings, family reunions and seminars hosted. Antiques, fishing, parks, theater and watersports nearby.

Publicity: *SC CPA Newsletter.*

"We had a wonderful weekend, due in large part to the wonderful accommodations and surroundings of the Ivy Terrace. Be sure you will see us again!"

Southern Pines C6

Knollwood House

1495 W Connecticut Ave
Southern Pines, NC 28387
(910)692-9390
Fax:(910)692-0609

Rates: $85-170.
Payment: MC VISA PC TC.
Innkeeper(s): Dick & Mimi Beatty.
Circa: 1925.

Rooms: 6 rooms with PB, 1 with FP. 2 suites. 2 cottages.
Beds: QDT.

Fairway dreams await golfers at this English-manor-style inn where upstairs sitting rooms overlook the 14th and 15th holes of the beautiful Mid-Pines golf course. The inn's lawns roll down 100 feet or so to the course, which is a masterpiece by Scottish golf course architect Donald Ross. More than 30 golf courses are within 20 miles. There have been many celebrations under the crystal chandelier and 10-foot ceilings, and the Glenn Miller Orchestra once played on the back lawn.

Breakfast included in rates. Type of meal: gourmet breakfast. Banquet service and catering service available. Air conditioning and turn-down service in room. Cable TV, VCR, fax, copier, swimming, tennis and library on premises. Weddings, small meetings and family reunions hosted. Antiques, parks, shopping, sporting events and theater nearby. TAC10.

Statesville B5

NC

Cedar Hill Farm B&B

778 Elmwood Rd
Statesville, NC 28677-1181
(704)873-4332 (800)948-4423

Rates: $60-105.
Payment: MC VISA AX PC TC.
Innkeeper(s): Brenda & Jim Vernon.
Circa: 1840.

Rooms: 3 rooms with PB, 2 with FP. 2 cottages.
Beds: QDT.

This renovated post-and-beam farmhouse rests on a 32-acre sheep farm. Hand-hewn, heart-of-pine walls, floors and interior shutters are featured inside. Guests may stay in the converted granary, the main house or Cotswold Cottage. The air-conditioned cottages includes a full kitchen, stone fireplace, Jacuzzi, canopy bed, private deck and a window seat overlooking pastures and woods. The granary also includes a fireplace. Porches boast several swings and rockers, and there is a hammock strung between two old shade trees. Romney sheep, geese and a rooster populate the farm.

Breakfast included in rates. Type of meal: full breakfast. Air conditioning in room. Swimming on premises. 32 acres. Antiques, fishing, parks, sporting events and theater nearby.

Location: Seven miles east of Statesville.

Publicity: *Record & Landmark, Southern Living*

Special Discounts: Long term rates available in cottages.

"Gracious hospitality is an art ... we found lots of it here."

Tabor City D7

Four Rooster Inn

403 Pireway Rd Rt 904
Tabor City, NC 28463-2519
(910)653-3878 (800)653-5008
Fax:(910)653-3878

Rates: $45-75. MAP.
Payment: MC VISA AX DC DS PC TC.
Innkeeper(s): Gloria & Bob Rogers.
Circa: 1949.

Rooms: 4 rooms, 2 with PB.
Beds: QD.

This inn is surrounded by more than an acre of lush grounds, featuring camellias and azaleas planted by the innkeeper's father. Antiques, fine linens and tables set with china and crystal await to pamper you. Afternoon tea is served in the parlor. The innkeepers place a tray with steaming fresh coffee or tea and the newspaper beside your guest room door in the morning. After a good night's sleep and coffee, guests settle down to a lavish, gourmet Southern breakfast, served in the inn's formal dining room. Sherried fruit compote, yam bread and succulent French toast stuffed with cheese are just a few of the possible items guests might enjoy. Myrtle Beach offers golf courses galore, the first of which is just four miles from the inn.

Breakfast, afternoon tea and evening snack included in rates. Types of meals: gourmet breakfast and early coffee/tea. MAP. Air conditioning and turn-down service in room. Cable TV and VCR on premises. Weddings, small meetings and family reunions hosted. Amusement parks, antiques, fishing, parks, shopping, sporting events, theater and watersports nearby. TAC10.

Taylorsville B4

Barkley House B&B

2522 NC Highway 16 S
Taylorsville, NC 28681-8952
(704)632-9060 (800)474-4652

Rates: $59.
Payment: MC VISA AX DS PC TC.
Innkeeper(s): Phyllis Barkley.
Circa: 1896.

Rooms: 4 rooms, 3 with PB, 1 with FP.
Beds: KQDT.

This 19th-century home is decorated in a country Victorian motif with antiques and family heirlooms, including the wedding dress that belonged to the innkeeper's mother, which is on display in the parlor. Breakfast is lavish, Southern affair. Guests are pampered with entrees such as breakfast casseroles or stuffed French toast served with hot chocolate or hot apple cider, biscuits and gravy, grits, juice and fresh fruit. The area offers galleries, historic mansions and the Emerald Hollow Gem Mine, where guests can dig for precious gems.

Breakfast and evening snack included in rates. Types of meals: continental-plus breakfast, full breakfast, gourmet breakfast and early coffee/tea. Catered breakfast available. Air conditioning, turn-down service, ceiling fan and cable TV in room. VCR, spa and library on premises. Antiques, fishing, shopping and sporting events nearby. TAC10.

Pets Allowed: Restricted to room.

Tryon C3

Fox Trot Inn

PO Box 1561, 800 Lynn Rd
Tryon, NC 28782-2708
(704)859-9706

Rates: $75-125.
Payment: PC.
Innkeeper(s): Wim Woody.
Circa: 1915.

Rooms: 3 rooms, 1 with PB, 1 with FP. 2 suites. 1 cottage. 1 conference room.
Beds: QDT.

Located on six acres in town, this turn-of-the-century home features mountain views and large guest rooms. There is a private guest cottage with its own kitchen and a hanging deck. The rooms are furnished with antiques. The Cherry Room in the main house has a four-poster, queen-size canopy bed with a sitting area overlooking the inn's swimming pool. The Oak Suite includes a wood-paneled sitting room.

Breakfast included in rates. Type of meal: full breakfast. Air conditioning in room. Cable TV and swimming on premises. Weddings, small meetings, family reunions and seminars hosted. Antiques, fishing, parks, shopping and watersports nearby.

Pets Allowed: Yes.

Mill Farm Inn

PO Box 1251
Tryon, NC 28782-1251
(704)859-6992 (800)545-6992

Rates: $49-65.
Payment: PC TC.
Innkeeper(s): Chip, Penny & Will Kessler.
Circa: 1939.

Rooms: 8 rooms with PB. 1 suite.
Beds: KD.

The Mill Farm Inn sits on three and a half acres near the Pacolet River. The stone structure offers views of the nearby mountains. Guests may relax on the screened porch or in the living room by the fireplace. Guest rooms have traditional furnishings. A full, buffet breakfast is served.

Type of meal: full breakfast. Air conditioning and ceiling fan in room. Weddings, small meetings, family reunions and seminars hosted. French spoken. Antiques, fishing, parks, shopping and theater nearby.

Publicity: *Polk County News Journal.*

"The most well-maintained inn we've visited."

Mimosa Inn

One Mimosa Inn Ln
Tryon, NC 28782
(704)859-7688

Rates: $65.
Payment: MC VISA DS PC TC.
Innkeeper(s): Jay & Sandi Franks.
Circa: 1903.

Rooms: 9 rooms with PB. 1 conference room.
Beds: QT.

The Mimosa is situated on the southern slope of the Blue Ridge Mountains. With its long rolling lawns and large columned veranda, the inn has been a landmark and social gathering place for almost a century. There is a stone patio and outdoor fireplace. During fox hunting season there are two hunts a week in the area as well as two annual steeplechases.

Breakfast included in rates. Types of meals: full breakfast and early coffee/tea. Air conditioning in room. Cable TV and library on premises. Weddings, small meetings, family reunions and seminars hosted. Amusement parks, antiques, fishing, parks, shopping and theater nearby.

"Thanks for your hospitality. We could just feel that Southern charm."

Tryon Old South B&B

107 Markham Rd
Tryon, NC 28782-3054
(704)859-6965 (800)288-7966
Fax:(704)859-2756

Rates: $55-125.
Payment: MC VISA DS PC TC.
Innkeeper(s): Michael & Terry Cacioppo.
Circa: 1910.

Rooms: 6 rooms, 4 with PB. 2 cottages.
Beds: QDT.

NC

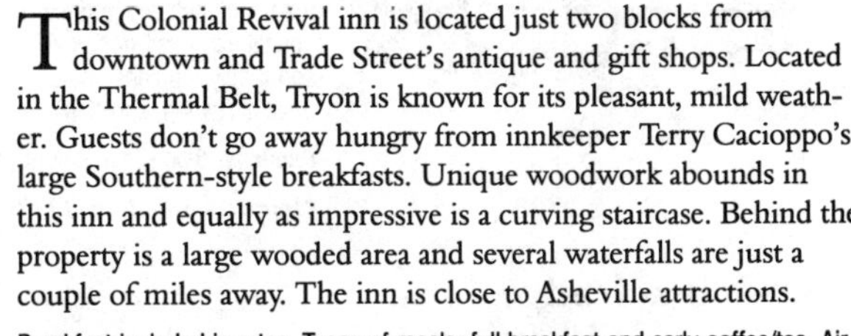

This Colonial Revival inn is located just two blocks from downtown and Trade Street's antique and gift shops. Located in the Thermal Belt, Tryon is known for its pleasant, mild weather. Guests don't go away hungry from innkeeper Terry Cacioppo's large Southern-style breakfasts. Unique woodwork abounds in this inn and equally as impressive is a curving staircase. Behind the property is a large wooded area and several waterfalls are just a couple of miles away. The inn is close to Asheville attractions.

Breakfast included in rates. Types of meals: full breakfast and early coffee/tea. Air conditioning in room. Cable TV, VCR, fax and copier on premises. Family reunions hosted. Antiques, fishing, parks, shopping and theater nearby. TAC10.

Special Discounts: Seventh night free.

Valle Crucis

B4

Mast Farm Inn

PO Box 704
Valle Crucis, NC 28691
(704)963-5857 (888)963-5857
Fax:(704)963-6404
E-mail: stay@mastfarminn.com

Rates: $75-195. MAP.
Payment: MC VISA TC.
Innkeeper(s): Wanda Hinshaw & Kay Philipp.
Circa: 1885.

Rooms: 9 rooms, 7 with PB. 4 cottages.
Beds: KQD.

Listed in the National Register of Historic Places, this 18-acre farmstead includes a main house and seven outbuildings. The inn features a wraparound porch with rocking chairs, swings and a view of the mountain valley. Homemade breads and vegetables fresh from the garden are specialties. Rooms are furnished with antiques, quilts and mountain crafts. Early morning coffee can be delivered to your room.

Breakfast included in rates. Types of meals: full breakfast and early coffee/tea. MAP. Ceiling fan in room. Fax on premises. Handicap access. 18 acres. Antiques, downhill skiing, sporting events, theater and watersports nearby.

Publicity: *Blue Ridge Country, Southern Living.*

"We want to live here!"

Waynesville

B2

Belle Meade Inn

5170 S Main St,
PO Box 1319
Waynesville, NC 28786
(704)456-3234

Rates: $65-70.
Payment: MC VISA DS PC TC.
Innkeeper(s): Gloria & Al DiNofa.
Circa: 1908.

Rooms: 4 rooms with PB, 2 with FP.
Beds: QD.

Located near Asheville in the mountains of the Western part of the state, this Craftsman-style home was named Belle Meade, a French phrase meaning "beautiful meadow." Chestnut woodwork provides the background for antiques and traditional furnishings. A fieldstone fireplace is featured in the living room. The Great Smoky Mountain Railroad ride is nearby.

Breakfast included in rates. Types of meals: full breakfast and early coffee/tea. Air conditioning, ceiling fan and cable TV in room. VCR on premises. Small meetings and family reunions hosted. Amusement parks, antiques, fishing, parks, shopping, downhill skiing, sporting events and theater nearby. TAC10.

Publicity: *Blue Ridge Magazine, Asheville Citizen Times, St. Petersburg Times.*

"Immaculately clean. Distinctively furnished. Friendly atmosphere."

Grandview Lodge

809 Valley View Cir Rd
Waynesville, NC 28786
(704)456-5212 (800)255-7826
Fax:(704)452-5432

Rates: $100-110. MAP.
Payment: PC TC.
Innkeeper(s): Stan & Linda Arnold.
Circa: 1890.

Rooms: 11 rooms, 9 with PB, 3 with FP. 2 suites.
Beds: KQDT.

Grandview Lodge is located on two-and-a-half acres in the Smoky Mountains. The land surrounding the lodge has an apple orchard, rhubarb patch, grape arbor and vegetable garden for the inn's kitchen. Rooms are available in the main lodge and in a newer addition. The inn's dining room is known throughout the region and Linda, a home economist, has written "Recipes from Grandview Lodge."

Breakfast and dinner included in rates. Types of meals: full breakfast and early coffee/tea. Lunch available. MAP. Air conditioning and cable TV in room. VCR, fax, computer and library on premises. Handicap access. Weddings, small meetings, family reunions and seminars hosted. Polish, Russian and German spoken. Amusement parks, antiques, fishing, parks, shopping, downhill skiing, sporting events, theater and watersports nearby. TAC10.

Publicity: *Asheville Citizen, Winston-Salem Journal, Raleigh News & Observer.*

"It's easy to see why family and friends have been enjoying trips to Grandview."

Hallcrest Inn

299 Hall Top Cir
Waynesville, NC 28786
(704)456-6457 (800)334-6457

Rates: $60-90. MAP.
Payment: MC VISA DC DS PC TC.
Innkeeper(s): Martin & Tesa Burson.
Circa: 1880.

Rooms: 11 rooms with PB, 6 with FP.
Beds: D.

This simple white frame farmhouse was the home of the owner of the first commercial apple orchard in western North Carolina. Atop Hall Mountain, it commands a breathtaking view of Waynesville and Balsam Mountain Range. A gathering room, a dining room, and seven guest rooms are furnished with family antiques. The side porch features four rooms with balconies. Family-style dining is offered around Lazy-Susan tables.

Breakfast and dinner included in rates. Types of meals: full breakfast and early coffee/tea. MAP. Weddings and family reunions hosted. Amusement parks, antiques, fishing, parks, shopping, sporting events and theater nearby. TAC10.

Location: US 276N from Waynesville, left on Mauney Cove Road.

Publicity: *Asheville Citizen.*

"Country charm with a touch of class."

Weldon A8

Weldon Place Inn

500 Washington Ave
Weldon, NC 27890-1644
(919)536-4582 (800)831-4470
Fax:(919)536-4708

Rates: $65-89.
Payment: MC VISA AX.
Innkeeper(s): Angel & Andy Whitby.
Circa: 1913.

Rooms: 4 rooms with PB.
Beds: D.

Sausage and cheese stuffed French toast is a pleasant way to start your morning at this Colonial Revival home. Located in a National Historic District, it is two miles from I-95. Wedding showers and other celebrations are popular here. There are beveled-glass windows, canopy beds and Italian fireplaces. Most of the inn's antiques are original to the house, including a horse-hair stuffed couch with its original upholstery. Select the Romantic Retreat package and you'll enjoy sweets, other treats, a gift bag, sparkling cider, a whirlpool tub and breakfast in bed.

Breakfast included in rates. Type of meal: full breakfast. Air conditioning and cable TV in room. VCR on premises. Weddings and small meetings hosted. Antiques, fishing, shopping and theater nearby. TAC15.

NC

Wilmington D7

Catherine's Inn

410 S Front St
Wilmington, NC 28401-5012
(910)251-0863 (800)476-0723

Rates: $75-95.
Payment: MC VISA AX.
Innkeeper(s): Catherine & Walter Ackiss.
Circa: 1883.

Rooms: 5 rooms with PB.
Beds: KQT.

This Italianate-style home features wrought iron fences and a Colonial Revival wraparound porch in the front and a two-story screened porch in the back. The 300-foot private lawn overlooks a unique sunken garden and the Cape Fear River. Antiques and reproductions fill the interior which includes 12-foot ceilings and an heirloom grand piano. Freshly brewed coffee is delivered to each room in the morning, followed by a

full breakfast served on family collections of china, crystal and sterling silver in the dining room. Turndown service and evening refreshments are some of the other amenities offered by the innkeepers.

Breakfast and afternoon tea included in rates. Antiques, fishing, theater and watersports nearby.

Publicity: *This Week, Country Inns, Encore, Mid-Atlantic, New York Times.*

"This is the best!"

James Place B&B

9 S 4th St
Wilmington, NC 28401-4534
(910)251-0999 (800)303-9444
Fax:(910)251-1150
E-mail: jamesinn@wilmington.net

Rates: $75-105.
Payment: MC VISA AX PC TC.
Innkeeper(s): Maureen & Tony Spataro.
Circa: 1909.

Rooms: 3 rooms with PB. 1 suite.
Beds: Q.

On a tree-lined street of two-story, turn-of-the-century houses, this neatly painted taupe home has gleaming white trim highlighting the porch and shutters. Each room features air conditioning and ceiling fans. Fresh coffee is available for guests in the morning, and later, a full breakfast is served downstairs. The downtown waterfront is a short stroll away.

Breakfast and evening snack included in rates. Types of meals: continental-plus breakfast and full breakfast. Air conditioning and ceiling fan in room. Cable TV, VCR, fax, copier and spa on premises. Small meetings and family reunions hosted. Amusement parks, antiques, fishing, parks, shopping, sporting events, theater and watersports nearby. TAC5.

Publicity: *Encore.*

Special Discounts: Stay six nights, seventh night free.

"An ideal setting for rejuvenation! Thanks so much for the Southern hospitality."

Taylor House Inn

14 N 7th St
Wilmington, NC 28401-4645
(910)763-7581 (800)382-9982

Rates: $95-110. MAP.
Payment: MC VISA AX PC.
Innkeeper(s): Glenda Moreadith.
Circa: 1905.

Rooms: 5 rooms with PB, 5 with FP.
Beds: KQT.

This Neo Classic Revival-style house includes five spacious guest rooms all appointed with antiques, ceiling fans and fireplaces. Three private baths feature clawfoot tubs. A full breakfast is served in the dining room. High ceilings, stained-glass windows, fireplaces, an open staircase and parquet floors add to the home's beauty. Situated in historic downtown, near antique shops and restaurants, the inn is also minutes from several beaches.

Breakfast and afternoon tea included in rates. Types of meals: gourmet breakfast and early coffee/tea. MAP. Air conditioning, turn-down service and ceiling fan in room. VCR and library on premises. Antiques, fishing, parks, shopping, sporting events, theater and watersports nearby.

Publicity: *Wilmington Morning Star.*

"It was elegant. Breakfast was terrific. The most beautiful B&B I've been in."

Wilson

B7

Miss Betty's B&B Inn

600 West Nash St
Wilson, NC 27893-3045
(919)243-4447 (800)258-2058

Rates: $60-75.
Payment: MC VISA AX DC CB DS TC.
Innkeeper(s): Betty & Fred Spitz.
Circa: 1858.

Rooms: 10 rooms with PB, 7 with FP. 3 suites.
Beds: KQDT.

Located in a gracious setting in the downtown historic district, the inn is comprised of several restored historic homes. Guests are welcomed with a bowl of chocolate kisses in their rooms. Breakfast is served in the Victorian dining room of the main house, with its walnut antique furniture and clusters of roses on the wallpaper. All the extras, such as lace tablecloths and hearty meals, conjure up the Old South. Four golf courses and many restaurants are nearby.

Breakfast included in rates. Air conditioning, ceiling fan and cable TV in room. Fax and copier on premises. Handicap access. Antiques nearby.

Location: Eastern North Carolina, near I-95.

Publicity: *Wilson Daily Times, Enterprise, Southern Living, Mid-Atlantic.*

"Yours is second to none."

Winston-Salem

B5

Augustus T. Zevely Inn

803 S Main St
Winston-Salem, NC 27101
(910)748-9299 (800)928-9299
Fax:(910)721-2211

Rates: $80-185.
Payment: MC VISA AX PC TC.
Innkeeper(s): Linda Anderson.
Circa: 1844.

Rooms: 12 rooms with PB, 3 with FP. 1 suite.
Beds: KQDT.

The Zevely Inn is the only lodging in Old Salem. Each of the rooms at this charming pre-Civil War inn boasts a view of historic Old Salem. Moravian decor permeates the decor of each of the guest quarters, some of which boast working fireplaces and whirlpool/steam baths. The home's architecture is reminiscent of many structures built in Old Salem during the second quarter of the 19th century. The formal dining room and parlor, often used for weddings and parties, offers woodburning fireplaces. A line of Old Salem furniture has been created by Lexington Furniture Industries, and several pieces were created especially for the Zevely Inn.

NC

Breakfast and evening snack included in rates. Air conditioning and cable TV in room. Fax and copier on premises. Weddings, small meetings, family reunions and seminars hosted. Antiques, shopping, sporting events and theater nearby. TAC7.

Publicity: *Washington Post Travel, Salem Star, Winston-Salem Journal, Tasteful, Country Living, National Trust for Historic Preservation, Homes and Gardens, Homes Across America.*

Special Discounts: AAA 10% discount.

"Wouldn't change one thing, service was absolutely wonderful."

Colonel Ludlow Inn

434 Summit at W 5th
Winston-Salem, NC 27101
(910)777-1887 (800)301-1887
Fax:(910)777-1890
E-mail: ludlowinn@aol.com

Rates: $99-179.
Payment: MC VISA AX DS PC TC.
Innkeeper(s): Constance Creasman.
Circa: 1887.

Rooms: 9 rooms with PB, 5 with FP.
Beds: KQ.

The innkeepers at this Queen Anne house with its graceful wraparound porches and hipped gable roof pamper guests with a bounty of amenities. Fluffy bath robes, bubble bath and fresh flowers are only a few of the offerings. More modern amenities include hair dryers and irons, small refrigerators and a stereo system with a selection of tapes. The home boasts an ornate entrance and several stained-glass windows bordering the stairway. The dining room has a gold-plated chandelier and reproduction wallpaper. The guest rooms feature Victorian antiques, antique beds and more stained-glass windows. Some rooms include two-person whirlpool tubs and fireplaces. The innkeepers also offer an extensive collection of movies to enjoy.

Breakfast included in rates. Types of meals: full breakfast and early coffee/tea. Air conditioning, ceiling fan, cable TV and VCR in room. Computer on premises. Antiques, fishing, parks, shopping, sporting events and theater nearby. TAC10.

Location: Off Hwy I-40, near downtown.

Publicity: *Charlotte Observer, Mid-Atlantic Country, Southern Living, Southern Accents, USA Today, American Way.*

"I have never seen anything like the meticulous and thorough attention to detail,"—Dannye Romine, The Charlotte Observer.

Lady Anne's B&B

612 Summit St
Winston-Salem, NC 27101
(910)724-1074

Rates: $55-155. AP.
Payment: MC VISA AX TC.
Innkeeper(s): Shelley Kirley & Steve Wishon.
Circa: 1890.

Rooms: 5 rooms with PB. 3 suites.
Beds: QD.

Like the name indicates, this bed & breakfast is decked in Victorian tradition. Victorian antiques and treasures fill the rooms. Most of the guest quarters boast stained-glass windows and high ceilings. Three rooms include a balcony, patio or glassed-in porch. Most rooms also offer modern amenities such as refrigerators, coffeemakers and stereos, double Jacuzzi tubs complete with romantic music. One offers a double garden tub perfect for viewing a romantic sunset. A Victorian-style breakfast is served in the formal dining room or on the porch. Innkeeper Shelley Kirley offers a wealth of information about the history of her inn and the surrounding area.

Breakfast and evening snack included in rates. Types of meals: full breakfast and early coffee/tea. AP. Air conditioning, ceiling fan, cable TV and VCR in room. Antiques, fishing, parks, shopping, sporting events and theater nearby.

Publicity: *Winston-Salem News.*

"We frequent B&Bs often and wanted to tell you that Lady Anne's is one of the finest that we've stayed in. We will be sure to tell all of our friends and family about your charming and friendly B&B."

Winston-Salem (Germantown)

Meadowhaven B&B

PO Box 222
Germantown, NC 27019
(910)593-3996
Fax:(910)593-3138

Rates: $70-175.
Payment: MC VISA AX DS PC TC.
Innkeeper(s): Samuel & Darlene Fain.
Circa: 1976.

Rooms: 6 rooms with PB, 2 with FP. 2 suites. 2 cottages.
Beds: QD.

This contemporary chalet is located on 25 pastoral acres in the foothills of the Blue Ridge Mountains. There are guest rooms decorated in a romantic mix of contemporary and country styles, as well as a mountain-top cottage with two bedrooms and a log cabin which offers a mountain view. Overside tubs for two, fireplaces, a spa, heated indoor pool and a sauna are just some of the amenities awaiting guests. There is a game room on the premises, and guests also have use of pedal boats. Nearby attractions include Hanging Rock State Park and Dan river perfect for canoeing or rafting. The inn is located 16 miles from Winston-Salem in the hamlet of Germantown which offers an art gallery and a winery.

Breakfast and evening snack included in rates. Types of meals: full breakfast and early coffee/tea. Picnic lunch available. Air conditioning, turn-down service, ceiling fan, cable TV and VCR in room. Fax, copier, spa, swimming and sauna on premises. 25 acres. Small meetings hosted. Antiques, fishing, parks, shopping, sporting events, theater and watersports nearby.

Special Discounts: Two night retreat packages $190 to $375 total.

"Heaven is a good name for Meadowhaven. I felt like I could relax in a home atmosphere."

North Dakota

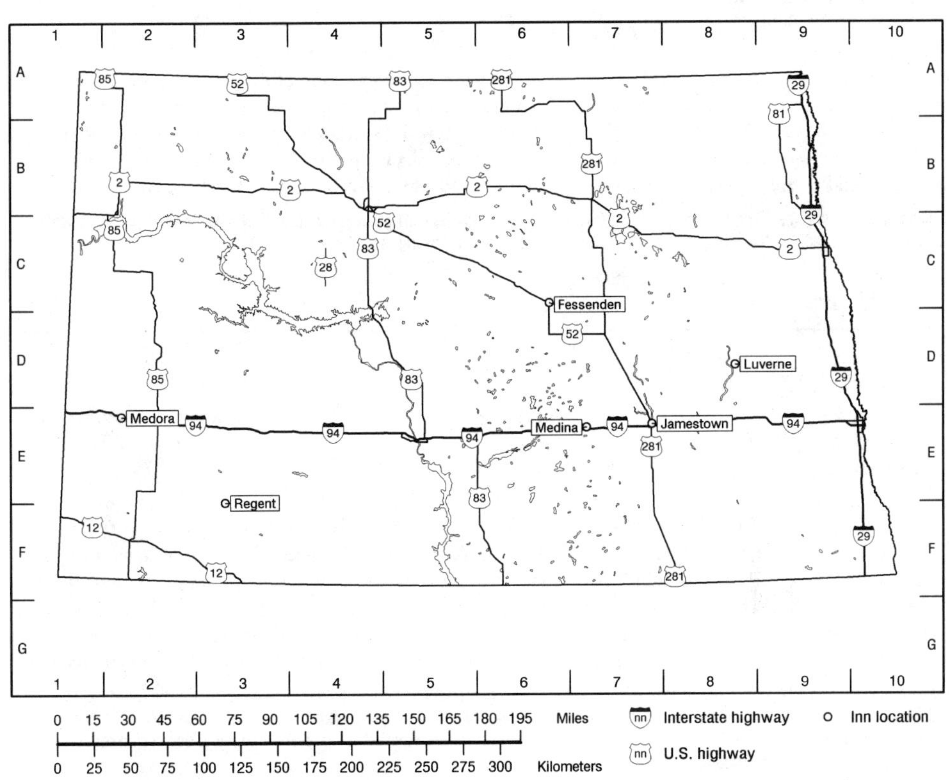

ND

Fessenden C6

Beiseker Mansion

1001 2nd St NE
Fessenden, ND 58438-7409
(701)547-3411

Rates: $55-95.
Payment: MC VISA.
Innkeeper(s): Paula & Jerry Tweton.
Circa: 1899.

Rooms: 6 rooms, 2 with PB.

Situated on nearly a city block, this 15-room Queen Anne Victorian is bordered by an old-fashioned wrought iron fence. Features include a splendid wraparound veranda and two turrets. The original golden oak woodwork is seen in the staircase, fireplace and dining room wainscoting. The turret room, with its king-size sleigh bed and marble-topped dresser, is a favorite choice. A third floor library, open to guests, contains 3,000 volumes. The house is in the National Register of Historic Places.

Type of meal: full breakfast.

Publicity: *Grand Forks Herald, Fessenden Herald Press.*

"What a beautiful house! The food and atmosphere were lovely."

Jamestown
E7

Country Charm B&B

RR 3 Box 71
Jamestown, ND 58401
(701)251-1372 (800)331-1372

Rates: $42-53.
Innkeeper(s): Ethel Oxtoby.
Circa: 1897.

Rooms: 4 rooms.

Jamestown not only offers convenience, centrally located at the intersection of the state's east-west interstate and main north-south highway, it features the Country Charm, a prairie farmhouse six miles from town and a short hop from I-94. The inn's tranquil setting is accented by the surrounding pines and cottonwood trees. The blue-dominated Patches and Lace Room features a multi-shaded patchwork quilt. Activities and places of interest abound in the Jamestown area, including Frontier Village and North Dakota's oldest courthouse.

Breakfast included in rates. Type of meal: full breakfast. Air conditioning and ceiling fan in room. VCR on premises. 12 acres. Small meetings and seminars hosted. Antiques, fishing, shopping, cross-country skiing, sporting events and theater nearby.

Luverne
D8

Volden Farm

RR 2, Box 50
Luverne, ND 58056
(701)769-2275

Rates: $50-75.
Payment: PC.
Innkeeper(s): Jim & JoAnne Wold.
Circa: 1885.

Rooms: 4 rooms. 1 suite. 1 cottage.
Beds: KDT.

Perennial gardens and a hedge of lilacs surround this redwood house with its newer addition. A favorite room is the North Room with a lace canopy bed, an old pie safe and a Texas Star quilt made by the host's grandmother. Guests enjoy soaking in the clawfoot tub while looking out to the apple and plum orchard. There is a library, music room and game room. The innkeepers also offer lodging in the Law Office, a separate little prairie house ideal for families. A stream, bordered by old oaks and formed by a natural spring, meanders through the property. The chickens here lay green and blue eggs. Supper is available by advanced arrangement.

Breakfast and evening snack included in rates. Types of meals: full breakfast, gourmet breakfast and early coffee/tea. Dinner, picnic lunch, lunch, gourmet lunch, catering service and room service available. VCR, bicycles and library on premises. 300 acres. Small meetings and seminars hosted. Limited Russian and limited Norwegian spoken. Antiques, fishing, parks, shopping, downhill skiing, cross-country skiing and watersports nearby. TAC10.

Pets Allowed: Outside.

Location: 80 miles northwest of Fargo.

Publicity: *Fargo Forum, Horizons, Grand Forks Herald.*

"Very pleasant indeed! Jim & JoAnne make you feel good. There's so much to do, and the hospitality is amazing!"

Medina
E7

Chase Lake Country Inn

2967 56th Ave SE
Medina, ND 58467-9564
(701)486-3502

Rates: $35-50.
Payment: MC VISA.
Innkeeper(s): Debra Hoffmann.

Rooms: 6 rooms. 1 suite.

Named for the national wildlife refuge just 10 miles away, this three-story farmhouse was once home to a state senator. This inn is a favorite of hunters, and the innkeepers can provide information about the area's wildlife. On the main floor, guests may stay in the handicap accessible Antique Allie. Four rooms are found on the inn's second floor, and the third level features the secluded Lover's Loft. The inn, which shares space on the property with the innkeeper's working farm, offers an exercise room and cable TV. Pets and hunting dogs may be kept on the premises.

Breakfast included in rates. Types of meals: full breakfast and early coffee/tea. Dinner, picnic lunch, lunch, banquet service, catered breakfast and room service available. Air conditioning, cable TV and VCR in room. Pet boarding on premises. 15 acres. Weddings, small meetings, family reunions and seminars hosted. Antiques, shopping, cross-country skiing and sporting events nearby.

Medora

E2

The Rough Riders Hotel B&B

Medora, ND 58645
(701)623-4444
Fax:(701)623-4494

Rates: $55.
Payment: MC VISA AX.
Innkeeper(s): Randy Hatzenbuhler.
Circa: 1865.
Rooms: 9 rooms with PB.

This old hotel has the branding marks of Teddy Roosevelt's cattle ranch as well as other brands stamped into the rough-board facade out front. A wooden sidewalk helps to maintain the turn-of-the-century cow-town feeling. Rustic guest rooms are above the restaurant and are furnished with homesteader antiques original to the area. In the summer, an outdoor pageant is held complete with stagecoach and horses. In October deer hunters are accommodated. The hotel, along with two motels, is managed by the non-profit Theodore Roosevelt Medora Foundation.

Breakfast included in rates.

Regent

F3

Prairie Vista

101 Rural Ave SW
Regent, ND 58650
(701)563-4542

Rates: $55.
Payment: PC.
Innkeeper(s): Marlys Prince.
Rooms: 7 rooms, 1 with PB.

Located on eight acres, 200 miles from Rapid City, this B&B is a brick ranch-style house. It is seventy miles to Theodore Roosevelt National Park. During hunting times, such as pheasant season, the B&B is sometimes filled with hunters. There's a heated indoor swimming pool and sauna, pool table and shuffleboard. Breakfast is eggs and sausage or apple French toast and evening meals are possible by advance request.

Breakfast included in rates. Dinner available. Swimming and sauna on premises.

Pear Pancakes

Mountain Fare Inn
Campton, N.H.

- 1 cup unbleached flour
- 1 cup whole wheat pastry flour
- 2 t baking powder
- 1 t salt
- 2 T brown sugar
- 2 eggs, beaten
- 1 ½ cup milk
- 5 T oil or melted butter
- 1 ripe pear, diced
- Dash of cinnamon & nutmeg

Mix together dry ingredients. Beat eggs until light, add milk and oil. Quickly toss the two mixtures together until mixed. Add a splash more milk if batter appears too thick. Brown on a pre-heated griddle. For a real feast, offer a variety of toppings: fruit sauces, maple syrup, cream cheese, yogurt, etc.

Ohio

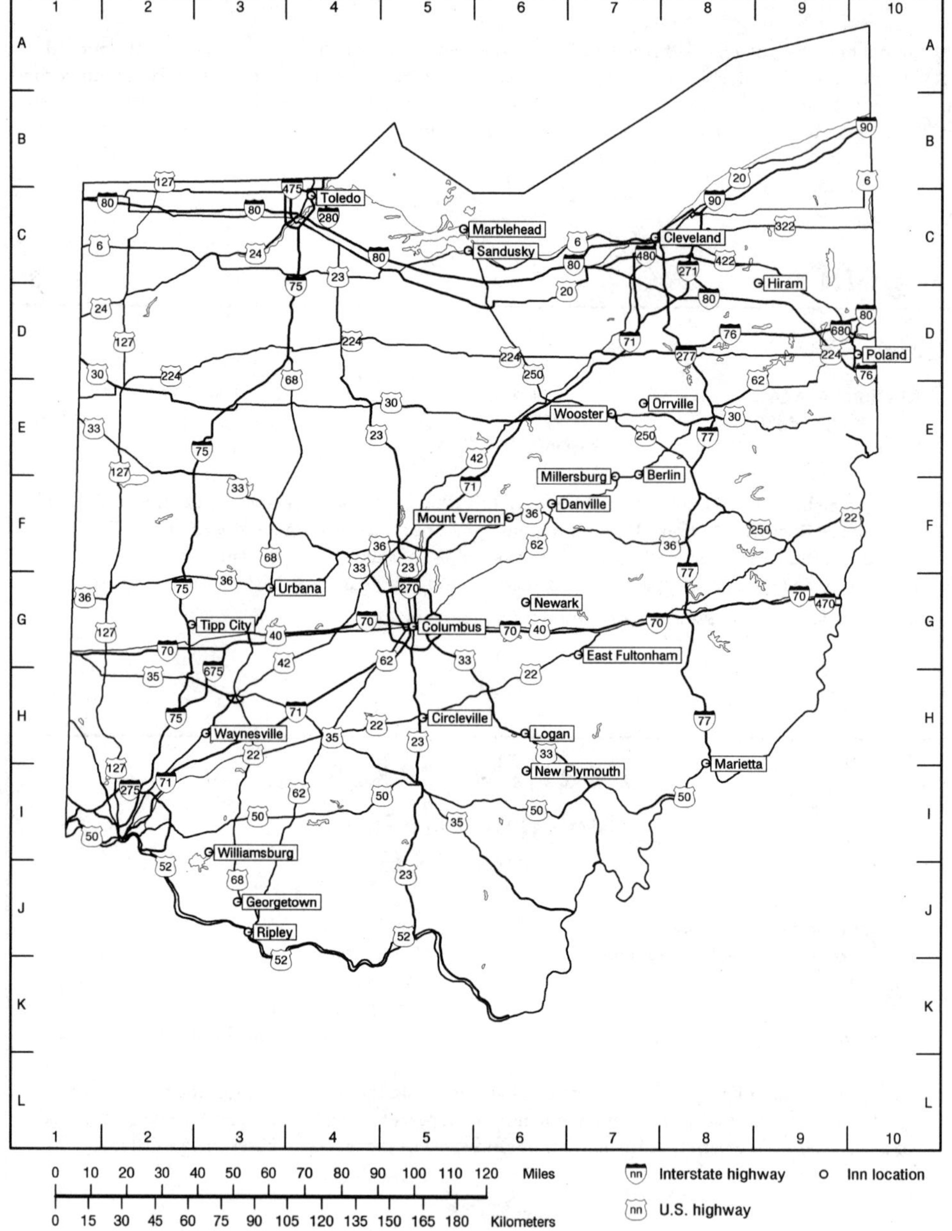
Toledo
Marblehead
Sandusky
Cleveland
Hiram
Poland
Orrville
Wooster
Millersburg
Berlin
Danville
Mount Vernon
Urbana
Newark
Tipp City
Columbus
East Fultonham
Circleville
Logan
Waynesville
New Plymouth
Marietta
Williamsburg
Georgetown
Ripley
0 10 20 30 40 50 60 70 80 90 100 110 120 Miles
0 15 30 45 60 75 90 105 120 135 150 165 180 Kilometers
Interstate highway
U.S. highway
Inn location

Berlin

E7

Donna's Country B&B

5523 Twp 358 East St
Berlin, OH 44610
(330)893-3068 (800)320-3338
Fax:(330)893-2124
E-mail: donnas@valkyrie.net

Rates: $45-225.
Payment: MC VISA DS PC.
Innkeeper(s): Johannes & Donna Marie Schlabach.
Circa: 1965.

Rooms: 8 rooms with PB. 5 cottages.
Beds: KQD.

The main, ranch-style house at this bed & breakfast was once home to an Amish family. Guests can stay in one of the eight rooms in the main house or in a collection of guest houses, ranging from a log cabin to a brick chalet. Rooms are decorated with country prints. The cottages, perfect for honeymooners or those celebrating a special occasion, include amenities such as Jacuzzi tubs, a fireplace, skylights, a TV, VCR and kitchenette. Guests in the main house enjoy an evening snack and continental-plus breakfast. Cottage guests are served a full breakfast in the privacy of their unit. Breakfast is not included for guests in the Log Cabin, which offers a full kitchen.

Breakfast included in rates. Types of meals: continental-plus breakfast and full breakfast. Evening snack available. Air conditioning, ceiling fan, cable TV and VCR in room. Pennsylvania Dutch spoken. Antiques, parks and shopping nearby.

Location: Heart of Amish Country.

Publicity: *Ohio Heartlander.*

Circleville

H5

Penguin Crossing B&B

3291 State Route 56 W
Circleville, OH 43113-9622
(614)477-6222 (800)PENGUIN
Fax:(614)477-6222

Rates: $100-175.
Payment: MC VISA DS PC TC.
Innkeeper(s): Ross & Tracey Irvin.
Circa: 1820.

Rooms: 4 rooms with PB, 1 with FP.
Beds: KQDT.

This farmhouse originally served as a stagecoach stop. Rooms include amenities such as a woodburning fireplace, clawfoot tub, brass bed or a heart-shaped whirlpool tub. Two of the guest rooms include a whirlpool tub. As the name might suggest, the innkeepers have a collection of penguins on display. Breakfasts include a selection of natural foods, and the innkeeper is happy to cater to special dietary needs.

Breakfast included in rates. Types of meals: gourmet breakfast and early coffee/tea. Air conditioning and turn-down service in room. VCR and fax on premises. Handicap access. Weddings, small meetings, family reunions and seminars hosted. Antiques, fishing, parks, shopping, theater and watersports nearby.

OH

Cleveland

C7

Glidden House

1901 Ford Dr
Cleveland, OH 44106-3923
(216)231-8900
Fax:(216)231-2130

Rates: $150-195.
Payment: MC VISA AX DC CB DS.
Innkeeper(s): Sharon Chapman.
Circa: 1910.

Rooms: 60 rooms with PB, 1 with FP. 8 suites. 1 conference room.
Beds: QD.

This eclectic French Gothic mansion is listed in the National Register of Historic Places. The inn features elaborate stone carvings, carved oak paneling, Adamesque molded ceilings, lace curtains and fireplaces with carved wood or stone mantel pieces. Guest rooms are decorated in an early-American motif.

Type of meal: continental-plus breakfast. Air conditioning and cable TV in room. Handicap access. Weddings, small meetings, family reunions and seminars hosted. Antiques, shopping, sporting events and theater nearby.

Publicity: *Plain Dealer, Vindicator, Detroit News.*

"A great place to stay and the only one we'll use in Cleveland."

Columbus

G5

50 Lincoln - A Very Small Hotel

50 E Lincoln St
Columbus, OH 43215-1516
(614)291-5056
Fax:(614)291-4924

Rates: $109-119.
Payment: MC VISA AX DS TC.
Innkeeper(s): Jeffrey C. Wilson.
Circa: 1885.

Rooms: 9 rooms with PB. 3 suites. 1 conference room.
Beds: Q.

This brick manor is just a few blocks from the center of downtown Columbus in the Short North neighborhood. The rooms are furnished with a variety of styles from Early American to contemporary with an antique tucked here and there. The expansive breakfasts include treats such as French toast created with freshly baked bread, buttermilk pancakes and homemade granola.

Breakfast included in rates. Types of meals: full breakfast, gourmet breakfast and early coffee/tea. Afternoon tea, dinner, picnic lunch, lunch, gourmet lunch, banquet service, catering service, catered breakfast and room service available. Air conditioning and cable TV in room. Fax and copier on premises. Weddings, small meetings, family reunions and seminars hosted. Antiques, parks, shopping, sporting events and theater nearby.

Shamrock B&B

5657 Sunbury Rd
Columbus, OH 43230-1147
(614)337-9849

Rates: $60.
Payment: PC TC.
Innkeeper(s): Tom L. McLaughlin.
Circa: 1961.

Rooms: 2 rooms with PB.
Beds: QT.

Guests at this homestay bed & breakfast stay in rooms decorated with original artwork and furnished with 18th-century antiques. Irish fare is served during the breakfast hour. There is more than an acre of manicured lawn to enjoy, highlighted by flower beds, more than 40 trees and a grape arbor. The modern, ranch-style home is located within 10 minutes of the airport, and offers convenient access to shopping malls, a historic village, Inniswood Botanical Gardens and more.

Breakfast and picnic lunch included in rates. Type of meal: full breakfast. Air conditioning, turn-down service and ceiling fan in room. Cable TV, VCR, copier and library on premises. Handicap access. Small meetings hosted. Antiques, parks, shopping, sporting events and theater nearby.

Special Discounts: 10%, 3 days or more.

Danville

F6

Red Fox Country Inn

26367 Danville Amity Rd
Danville, OH 43014-9769
(614)599-7369

Rates: $65-85.
Payment: MC VISA AX DS PC TC.
Innkeeper(s): Ida & Mort Wolff.
Circa: 1830.

Rooms: 4 rooms with PB.
Beds: QD.

This country inn was built originally to house those traveling on the Danville-Amity Wagon Road and later became a home. Amish woven rag rugs and antiques decorate the guest rooms. Three rooms include Amish-made oak beds and the other boasts an 1880s brass and iron double bed. A renovated horse stable serves as an antique shop with a variety of interesting pieces. Breakfasts include freshly baked pastries, fruits and coffee along with a variety of delectable entrees. For an additional charge and advance notice, guests are welcome to bring friends along for the morning meal. Special low-fat, low-cholesterol dishes are available on request. Golfing, canoeing on the Mohican River and horseback riding are a few of the area activities. Guests can visit local orchards and farm markets, and the area is host to festivals and fairs throughout the year. An Amish settlement, Malibar Farm, Roscoe Village, Mohican Park, canoeing, horseback riding, hiking and bike trails are nearby.

Breakfast included in rates. Dinner, banquet service and catering service available. Air conditioning in room. Library on premises. 15 acres. TAC10.

Publicity: *Columbus Dispatch, Mount Vernon News, Cincinnati Enquirer.*

Special Discounts: AAA 10%, Seniors 10%.

"We want to thank you again for the gracious hospitality and special kindness you showed us."

The White Oak Inn

29683 Walhonding Rd,
SR 715, Danville, OH 43014
(614)599-6107
E-mail: 74627.3717@compuserve.com

Rates: $75-140. MAP.
Payment: MC VISA AX DS PC TC.
Innkeeper(s): Yvonne & Ian Martin.
Circa: 1915.

Rooms: 10 rooms with PB, 3 with FP. 1 conference room.
Beds: QDT.

Large oaks and ivy surround the wide front porch of this three-story farmhouse situated on 13 green acres. It is located on the former Indian trail and pioneer road that runs along the Kokosing River, and an Indian mound has been discovered on the property. The inn's woodwork is all original white oak, and guest rooms are furnished in antiques. Visitors often shop for maple syrup, cheese and handicrafts at nearby Amish farms. Three cozy fireplace rooms provide the perfect setting for romantic evenings.

Breakfast and evening snack included in rates. Types of meals: full breakfast and early coffee/tea. Catering service available. MAP. Air conditioning and ceiling fan in room. Bicycles and library on premises. 14 acres. Weddings, small meetings, family reunions and seminars hosted. French spoken. Antiques, fishing, parks, shopping and watersports nearby. TAC10.

Location: Holmes County Amish area, north central Ohio.

Publicity: *Ladies Home Journal, Columbus Monthly, Cleveland Plain Dealer, Country, Glamour, Columbus Dispatch.*

Special Discounts: Packages including dinner available.

"The dinner was just fabulous and we enjoyed playing the antique grand piano."

East Fultonham G7

Hill View Acres B&B

7320 Old Town Rd
East Fultonham, OH 43735
(614)849-2728

Rates: $45-70.
Payment: MC VISA AX.
Innkeeper(s): Jim & Dawn Graham.
Circa: 1905.

Rooms: 2 rooms.
Beds: D.

Hill View Acres was an apt description for this relaxing country home, which is surrounded by more than 20 acres of rolling hills. The large deck is a wonderful place to sit and soak up the atmosphere. The grounds also include a swimming pool and spa. Innkeeper Dawn Graham has won several local cooking contests and enjoys treating her guests to a hearty country breakfast each morning. Dawn and husband Jim work out the menu with guests the night before, taking in all dietary concerns. Dawn creates luscious items accompanied by homemade jams and jellies. The home is near many attractions, including wildlife preserves, museums, outlet shopping and the Ohio Ceramic Center.

Breakfast included in rates. Types of meals: full breakfast and early coffee/tea. Dinner, evening snack, picnic lunch and lunch available. Air conditioning in room. Spa and swimming on premises. 21 acres. Antiques, fishing, parks and shopping nearby.

Georgetown

J3

Bailey House

112 N Water St
Georgetown, OH 45121
(937)378-3087

Rates: $55.
Payment: PC TC.
Innkeeper(s): Nancy Purdy & Jane Sininger.
Circa: 1830.

Rooms: 4 rooms, 2 with FP.
Beds: QD.

The stately columns of this three-story Greek Revival house once greeted Ulysses S. Grant, a frequent visitor during his boyhood when he was sent to buy milk from the Bailey's. A story is told that Grant accidentally overheard that the Bailey boy was leaving West Point. Grant immediately ran through the woods to the home of Congressman Thomas Hamer and petitioned an appointment in Bailey's place which he received, thus launching his military career. The inn has double parlors, pegged oak floors and Federal-style fireplace mantels. Antique washstands, chests and beds are found in the large guest rooms.

Breakfast and afternoon tea included in rates. Types of meals: full breakfast and early coffee/tea. Air conditioning in room. Swimming and library on premises. Weddings, small meetings, family reunions and seminars hosted. Antiques, fishing, parks, shopping and watersports nearby. TAC10.

Pets Allowed.

"Thank you for your warm hospitality, from the comfortable house to the delicious breakfast."

Hiram

C9

The Lily Ponds B&B

PO Box 322, 6720
Wakefield Rd
Hiram, OH 44234-0322
(330)569-3222 (800)325-5087
Fax:(330)569-3223

Rates: $55-75.
Payment: MC VISA.
Innkeeper(s): Marilane Spencer.
Circa: 1940.

Rooms: 3 rooms with PB.
Beds: KQT.

This homestay is located on 20 acres of woodland dotted with rhododendron and mountain laurel. There are two large ponds and an old stone bridge. Your hostess works with a tour company and has traveled around the world. The inn's decor includes her collections of Eskimo art and artifacts and a variety of antiques. Pecan waffles served with locally harvested maple syrup are a favorite breakfast. Guests enjoy borrowing the canoe or hiking the inn's trails. Sea World is a 15-minute drive away.

Breakfast included in rates. Types of meals: full breakfast and early coffee/tea. Air conditioning and cable TV in room. VCR, bicycles, library and child care on premises. 20 acres. Small meetings and family reunions hosted. Amusement parks, antiques, fishing, parks, shopping, downhill skiing, cross-country skiing and watersports nearby. TAC10.

Location: 45 minutes from downtown Cleveland.

Publicity: *Record-Courier, Record-News.*

"We felt like we were staying with friends from the very start."

Logan

H6

The Inn at Cedar Falls

21190 State Rt 374
Logan, OH 43138
(614)385-7489 (800)653-2557
Fax:(614)385-0820

Rates: $75-185.
Payment: MC VISA PC.
Innkeeper(s): Ellen Grinsfelder.
Circa: 1987.

Rooms: 14 rooms, 9 with PB, 5 with FP. 5 cottages. 1 conference room.
Beds: QT.

This barn-style inn was constructed on 60 acres adjacent to Hocking State Park and a half mile from the waterfalls. The kitchen and dining room is in a 19th-century log house with a wood-burning stove and 18-inch-wide plank floor. Accommodations in the new barn building are simple and comfortable, each furnished with antiques. There are also five, fully equipped log cabins available, each individually decorated. Verandas provide sweeping views of woodland and meadow. The grounds include organic gardens for the inn's gourmet dinners, and animals that have been spotted include bobcat, red fox, wild turkey and whitetail deer.

Breakfast included in rates. Types of meals: full breakfast, gourmet breakfast and early coffee/tea. Dinner, picnic lunch, lunch and gourmet lunch available. Air conditioning in room. Fax, copier and library on premises. Handicap access. 60 acres. Weddings, small meetings, family reunions and seminars hosted. Antiques, fishing, parks, shopping, cross-country skiing and theater nearby.

Publicity: *Post.*

"Very peaceful, relaxing and friendly. Couldn't be nicer."

Marblehead C5

Old Stone House on The Lake B&B Inn

133 Clemons St
Marblehead, OH 43440
(419)798-5922

Rates: $70-125.
Payment: MC VISA AX DS.
Circa: 1861.

Rooms: 13 rooms, 2 with PB. 1 suite. 1 conference room.
Beds: QDT.

Built by Alexander Clemons, owner of the first stone quarry in the area, the Stone House overlooks Lake Erie. Now a guest room, the enclosed Captain's Tower features a 15-foot ceiling, spindled railings around the staircase and the best view of the lake and shoreline. The inn's green lawns and gardens slope to the shore, where guests may fish from the rocks or swim.

Breakfast included in rates. Type of meal: full breakfast. Air conditioning and ceiling fan in room. Swimming on premises. Weddings, small meetings, family reunions and seminars hosted. Amusement parks, antiques, fishing, parks, shopping, theater and watersports nearby. TAC8.

Location: Marblehead Peninsula.

Publicity: *Marion Star, Cleveland Plain Dealer, The Midweek Plus.*

"Thank you so much!! Everything was wonderful!"

Marietta H8

The Buckley House

332 Front St
Marietta, OH 45750-2913
(614)373-3080
Fax:(614)373-8000

Rates: $70-80.
Payment: MC VISA DS PC TC.
Innkeeper(s): Dell & Alf Nicholas.
Circa: 1879.

Rooms: 3 rooms with PB, 1 with FP. 1 suite.
Beds: KDT.

OH

A double veranda accents this gablefront Greek Revival house and provides views of Muskingum Park and river as well as Lookout Point and the "Valley Gem," a traditional Mississippi river boat. Guests are served tea, evening aperitifs and breakfast from the inn's parlor, porches and dining room. Within a five-block area are museums, a mound cemetery, the W.P. Snyder Jr. Sternwheeler, boat rides, trolley tours and shops and restaurants.

Breakfast included in rates. Types of meals: full breakfast and early coffee/tea. Air conditioning and ceiling fan in room. Cable TV, VCR, fax, spa and library on premises. Weddings, small meetings, family reunions and seminars hosted. Antiques, fishing, parks, shopping, theater and watersports nearby.

Millersburg

F7

Bigham House

151 S Washington St
Millersburg, OH 44654-1315
(330)674-2337 (800)689-6950

Rates: $70-80.
Payment: MC VISA.
Innkeeper(s): John Henry Ellis.
Circa: 1869.

Rooms: 4 rooms, 3 with PB, 1 with FP.
Beds: Q.

Bigham House is a two-story Victorian located in the world's largest Amish settlement. Antiques and Victorian reproductions decorate the rooms. Ask for Dr. Bigham's Room and you'll enjoy stained-glass windows, a fireplace and brass ceiling fan. Nearby activities include buggy rides and the restored Ohio Central Railway.

Breakfast included in rates. Types of meals: full breakfast and gourmet breakfast. Afternoon tea available.

Location: In the heart of the largest Amish settlement in the world, Holmes County, Ohio.

Publicity: *Holmes County Traveler.*

The Inn at Honey Run

6920 Country Rd 203
Millersburg, OH 44654
(330)674-0011 (800)468-6639
Fax:(330)674-2623

Rates: $65-150. MAP.
Payment: MC VISA AX DS PC TC.
Innkeeper(s): Marjorie Stock.
Circa: 1982.

Rooms: 39 rooms with PB, 15 with FP. 2 suites. 2 cottages. 3 conference rooms.
Beds: KQT.

Located in Holmes County, the world's largest Amish area, the inn is situated on 60 wooded acres with views of bucolic pastureland dotted with sheep. The Honeycomb is a contemporary earth-shelter building dug into the hillside featuring view rooms, fireplaces and whirlpool tubs. Rooms in the main cedar and stone building have Shaker and early American furnishings as well as handmade Holmes County pieces, local art and needlework. Room comforters are filled with fleece from the inn's sheep. Picturesque Amish horses and buggies traverse the nearby country roads.

Breakfast included in rates. Types of meals: continental-plus breakfast and full breakfast. Dinner, evening snack, picnic lunch, lunch and banquet service available. MAP. Air conditioning and VCR in room. Fax, copier and library on premises. Handicap access. 66 acres. Weddings, small meetings, family reunions and seminars hosted. German spoken. Antiques and shopping nearby.

Publicity: *Country Inns, Columbus Dispatch, Lakewood Sun Press, AAA Home and Away.*

Special Discounts: Seasonal.

"The food was wonderful and the service professional."

Mount Vernon

F6

Tuck'er Inn

12059 Tucker Rd
Mount Vernon, OH 43050
(614)392-5659

Rates: $50-125.
Payment: PC TC.
Innkeeper(s): Bill & Marian Cleland.
Circa: 1969.

Rooms: 2 rooms with PB. 1 cottage.
Beds: QD.

There are 12 woodland acres to explore here. Guests can hike to ravines or enjoy the scenery around Granny Creek. There are two guest rooms in the main house, built in Colonial style. There is also a guest house in the woods with two bedrooms and a wood-burning stove. The guest house can sleep up to six people. The inn is within an hour of the sites of Amish country.

Breakfast included in rates. Type of meal: continental-plus breakfast. Air conditioning in room. VCR, bicycles and library on premises. 12 acres. Weddings, small meetings and family reunions hosted. Antiques, fishing, parks, shopping, downhill skiing, cross-country skiing, sporting events and theater nearby.

"I had such a sweet night at your inn. Many, many thanks."

New Plymouth

I6

Ravenwood Castle

Rt 1 Box 52-B
New Plymouth, OH 45654
(614)596-2606 (800)477-1541
Fax:(614)596-5818

Rates: $85-150.
Payment: MC VISA DS.
Innkeeper(s): Jim & Sue Maxwell.
Circa: 1995.

Rooms: 8 rooms with PB.
Beds: KQD.

Although this is a newer construction, the architect modeled the inn after a 12th-century, Norman-style castle, offering a glimpse back at Medieval England. A Great Hall with massive stone fireplace, an English Pub, dramatic rooms and suites with antique stained-glass windows and gas fireplaces make for a unique getaway. The castle, which overlooks Vinton County's Swan township, is surrounded by 50 acres of forest and large rock formations and is reached by a half-mile private road.

Breakfast included in rates. Types of meals: full breakfast and early coffee/tea. Afternoon tea, dinner, evening snack, picnic lunch and room service available. Air conditioning and ceiling fan in room. VCR, fax and copier on premises. Handicap access. 50 acres. Weddings, small meetings, family reunions and seminars hosted. Antiques, fishing, shopping and watersports nearby.

Publicity: *Columbus Dispatch, Cincinnati Enquirer, Athens Messenger, Southeast Ohio Traveler, Vinton County Courier, Hocking Hills Travel News, A Taste for Columbus, Country Register.*

"The atmosphere is romantic, the food excellent, the hospitality super!"

Newark

G6

Pitzer-Cooper House B&B

6019 White Chapel Rd SE
Newark, OH 43056-9245
(614)323-2680 (800)833-9536
Fax:(614)323-2680
E-mail: 74617.121@compuserve.com

Rates: $60.
Payment: PC.
Innkeeper(s): Joe & Teresa Cooper.
Circa: 1858.

Rooms: 3 rooms, 1 with PB. 1 suite.
Beds: DT.

In the National Register, this historic farmhouse boasts an elegant entry with a winding, cherry staircase among its architectural highlights. The common room has views of the pond, and there is a music room with a baby grand piano. Borrow the inn's bikes and visit the famed Dawes Arboretum a mile away. Relax on the porch swing or on a swing under a huge maple tree. Among the multitude of nearby activities are the Olde Mill Velvet Ice Cream factory and parlor, an extensive bike-trail system, Blackhand Gorge Nature Preserve and nine museums. The inn has received the Ohio Bed & Breakfast Association pineapple seal of approval.

Breakfast included in rates. Type of meal: continental breakfast. Air conditioning and turn-down service in room. Cable TV, VCR, fax, copier and bicycles on premises. 10 acres. Antiques, parks, shopping, theater and watersports nearby. TAC15.

"It was a beautiful stay, from the wooden tree swing to the soft, cool sheets."

OH

Orrville

E7

Grandma's House B&B

5598 Chippewa Rd
Orrville, OH 44667-9750
(330)682-5112

Rates: $55-90.
Payment: PC TC.
Innkeeper(s): Marilyn & Dave Farver.
Circa: 1860.

Rooms: 5 rooms, 3 with PB.
Beds: QDT.

Wheat and corn fields surround this friendly brick farmhouse. It has been in the same family for the last 60 years. The inn is furnished with antique bedsteads, homemade quilts and a collection of old rolling pins. An old-fashioned porch entices guests to relax, and behind the house is a 16-acre wooded hillside with

walking paths. Marilyn specializes in hot cinnamon rolls and home-baked breads.

Breakfast included in rates. Types of meals: continental-plus breakfast and early coffee/tea. Ceiling fan in room. Handicap access. 28 acres. Small meetings, family reunions and seminars hosted. Antiques, parks, shopping, cross-country skiing and theater nearby.

Publicity: *Wooster Daily Record, Northeast Ohio Avenues.*

Special Discounts: 30% discount on whole house Nov. 1 through April 30.

"What a delight. We will definitely be back. Perfect."

Poland

D10

The Inn at The Green

500 S Main St
Poland, OH 44514-2032
(330)757-4688

Rates: $60.
Payment: MC VISA DS.
Innkeeper(s): Ginny & Steve Meloy.
Circa: 1876.

Rooms: 4 rooms with PB, 3 with FP.
Beds: QDT.

Main Street in Poland has a parade of historic houses including Connecticut Western Reserve colonials, Federal and Greek Revival houses. The Inn at the Green is a Classic Victorian Baltimore townhouse. Two of the common rooms, the greeting room and parlor have working marble fireplaces. Interiors evoke an authentic 19th-century atmosphere with antiques and Oriental rugs that enhance the moldings, 12-foot ceilings and poplar floors.

Breakfast included in rates. Type of meal: continental breakfast. Air conditioning, cable TV and VCR in room. Bicycles and library on premises. Small meetings and family reunions hosted. Antiques, fishing, parks, shopping, cross-country skiing and theater nearby. TAC10.

Location: Seven miles southeast of Youngstown.

Publicity: *The Vindicator.*

"Thank you for a comfortable and perfect stay in your beautiful Victorian home."

Ripley

J3

Misty River B&B

206 N Front St
Ripley, OH 45167
(937)392-1556
Fax:(937)392-1556

Rates: $75.
Payment: PC TC.
Innkeeper(s): Dotty Prevost & Lanny Warren.
Circa: 1835.

Rooms: 2 rooms with PB.
Beds: D.

Ulysses S. Grant was a border here while he attended the Whittmore Private School in Ripley in the fall of 1938 and spring of 1939. The 19th-century home, located in the town's historic district, is just across the way from the Ohio River. The bed & breakfast is decorated with a comfortable mix of country and modern decor. As they partake of their full breakfast, guests also enjoy a river view. Ripley has many historic attractions, including Rankin House (of "Uncle Tom's Cabin" fame), the home of abolitionist Rev. John Rankin. Rankin and his family helped more than 1,000 slaves find their way to freedom.

Breakfast included in rates. Type of meal: full breakfast. Air conditioning in room. Cable TV, VCR and fax on premises. Antiques, fishing, parks, shopping and watersports nearby. TAC10.

Publicity: *Columbus Dispatch, Ripley Bee*

Special Discounts: Coupon for $10 off return visit.

The Signal House

234 N Front St
Ripley, OH 45167-1015
(937)392-1640

Rates: $65-75.
Payment: MC VISA DS PC TC.
Innkeeper(s): Vic & Betsy Billingsley.
Circa: 1830.

Rooms: 2 rooms, 2 with FP.
Beds: QD.

This Greek Italianate home is said to have been used to aid the Underground Railroad. A light in the attic told Rev. John Rankin, a dedicated abolitionist, that it was safe to transport slaves to freedom. Located within a 55-acre historical district, guests can take a glance back in time, exploring museums and antique shops. Twelve-foot ceilings with ornate plaster-work graces the parlor, and guests can sit on any of three porches watching paddlewheelers traverse the Ohio River.

Breakfast included in rates. Types of meals: full breakfast and early coffee/tea. Air conditioning and ceiling fan in room. Cable TV, VCR, copier and library on premises. Antiques, fishing, parks, shopping and watersports nearby. TAC10.

Publicity: *Cincinnati Enquirer, Ohio Columbus Dispatch, Ohio Off the Beaten Path, Dayton Daily News, Cincinnati Magazine.*

Special Discounts: Government rates; multi-night stays, weekdays only (three day minimum)

Sandusky

C5

The 1890 Queen Anne B&B

714 Wayne St
Sandusky, OH 44870-3507
(419)626-0391

Rates: $75-85.
Payment: MC VISA DS PC TC.
Innkeeper(s): Robert & Joan Kromer.
Circa: 1890.

Rooms: 3 rooms with PB.
Beds: KQ.

Built by John T. Mack, publisher of the city's first newspaper, the Queen Anne Bed & Breakfast is an exquisitely maintained, historical home which opened its doors to travelers in the summer of 1991. Only seven blocks away is Sandusky Bay, where travelers can book passages on local ferries to Kelleys Island, the Bass Islands, or as far away as Canada's Pelee Island. Sandusky is most popular for its summertime activities, including the largest tour destination in Ohio, Cedar Point Amusement Park. It alone attracts nearly five million visitors to the north coast each summer.

Breakfast included in rates. Type of meal: continental-plus breakfast. Air conditioning and cellIng fan in room. Cable TV, VCR and copier on premises. Amusement parks, antiques, fishing, parks, shopping, sporting events, theater and watersports nearby.

OH

Wagner's 1844 Inn

230 E Washington St
Sandusky, OH 44870-2611
(419)626-1726
Fax:(419)626-8465

Rates: $70-90.
Payment: MC VISA DS.
Innkeeper(s): Walt & Barb Wagner.
Circa: 1844.

Rooms: 3 rooms with PB, 2 with FP.
Beds: Q.

This inn originally was constructed as a log cabin. Additions and renovations were made, and the house evolved into an Italianate-style accented with brackets under the eaves and black shutters on the second-story windows. A wrought-iron fence frames the house, and there are ornate wrought-iron porch rails. A billiard room and screened-in porch are available to guests. The ferry to Cedar Point and Kelleys Island is within walking distance.

Breakfast included in rates. Type of meal: continental breakfast. Air conditioning in room. Cable TV, copier and library on premises. Amusement parks, antiques, fishing, parks and shopping nearby.

Pets Allowed: Some limitations.

Publicity: *Lorain Journal.*

"This B&B rates in our Top 10."

Tipp City

G2

Willow Tree Inn

1900 W State Rt 571
Tipp City, OH 45371-9602
(513)667-2957

Rates: $75-85.
Payment: MC VISA.
Innkeeper(s): Jolene & Chuck Sell.
Circa: 1830.

Rooms: 4 rooms with PB. 2 suites. 1 conference room.
Beds: QD.

This Federal-style mansion is a copy of a similar house in North Carolina, former home of the builders. Antique period furnishings and polished wood floors add to the atmosphere of this rambling homestead. A spring-fed pond and original out buildings adorn the premises.

Breakfast and evening snack included in rates. Type of meal: full breakfast. Banquet service and catering service available. Air conditioning, ceiling fan and VCR in room. Fax, copier and spa on premises. Handicap access. Weddings, small meetings, family reunions and seminars hosted. Amusement parks, antiques, parks, shopping and sporting events nearby. TAC10.

Publicity: *Miami Valley News, Tri-City Advocate, Tipp City Herald, Troy Daily News, Dayton News.*

"Very quiet place to stay. The grounds are beautiful, service excellent!"

Toledo

C4

The William Cummings House B&B

1022 N Superior St
Toledo, OH 43604-1961
(419)244-3219
Fax:(419)244-3219

Rates: $65-135.
Payment: PC TC.
Innkeeper(s): Lowell Greer, Lorelei Crawford.
Circa: 1857.

Rooms: 3 rooms. 1 suite.
Beds: KQDT.

This Second Empire Victorian, which is listed in the National Register, is located in the historic Vistula neighborhood. The inn's fine appointments, collected for several years, include period antiques, Victorian chandeliers, mirrors, wallcoverings and draperies. One of the innkeepers is a member of the Toledo Symphony Orchestra and sometimes the inn is the location for chamber music and other cultural events.

Breakfast and evening snack included in rates. Type of meal: continental-plus breakfast. Air conditioning, ceiling fan and VCR in room. Fax, copier and library on premises. Weddings, small meetings, family reunions and seminars hosted. Spanish spoken. Amusement parks, antiques, fishing, parks, shopping, sporting events, theater and watersports nearby.

Special Discounts: Weekly, monthly and whole house (room blocks) rates.

Urbana

G3

Northern Plantation B&B

3421 E RR 296
Urbana, OH 43078
(513)652-1782 (800)652-1782

Rates: $65-95.
Payment: MC VISA DS.
Innkeeper(s): Marsha J. Martin.
Circa: 1913.

Rooms: 4 rooms, 1 with PB.
Beds: KD.

This Victorian farmhouse, located on 100 acres, is occupied by fourth-generation family members. (Marsha's father was born in the downstairs bedroom in 1914.) The Homestead Library is decorated traditionally and has a handsome fireplace, while the dining room features a dining set and a china cabinet made by the innkeeper's great-grandfather. Most of the guest rooms have canopy beds. A large country breakfast is served. On the property is a fishing pond, corn fields, soybeans and woods with a creek. Nearby are Ohio Caverns and Indian Lake.

Breakfast included in rates. Types of meals: continental-plus breakfast and full breakfast. Evening snack available. Air conditioning in room. Cable TV, VCR and library on premises. 100 acres. Weddings, small meetings and family reunions hosted. Antiques, parks, shopping and cross-country skiing nearby.

Waynesville H3

Lakewood Farm B&B

8495 Rt 48
Waynesville, OH 45068
(513)885-9850
Fax:(513)885-9874

Rates: $60-125.
Payment: MC VISA PC TC.
Innkeeper(s): Liz & Jay Jorling.
Circa: 1834.

Rooms: 5 rooms with PB, 1 with FP. 1 suite. 1 cottage. 1 conference room.
Beds: QT.

Located on 25 acres of pasture land with tennis courts, a stable, trees and a lake, the original part of the house was built as a gristmill. It houses the Welcoming Room, Great Room, Dining Room and flower-filled courtyard. Rooms feature Victorian-type decor and a square tub, an outside porch and views of the inn's old Catalpa tree are features of The Loft Room. Some guest rooms offer views of the inn's five-acre lake, stocked with striped bass, large mouth bass and bluegill. More than 70 antique shops are located in nearby Waynesville, said to be the antique capital of the midwest.

Breakfast and evening snack included in rates. Type of meal: full breakfast. Afternoon tea, catered breakfast and room service available. Air conditioning and ceiling fan in room. Cable TV, VCR, fax, copier, swimming, stables, tennis and library on premises. Handicap access. 25 acres. Weddings and family reunions hosted. Amusement parks, antiques, fishing, parks, shopping, cross-country skiing, sporting events, theater and watersports nearby. TAC10.

Pets Allowed: If kept in kennels provided.

Williamsburg I3

The Lewis McKeever Farmhouse B&B

4475 McKeever Pike
Williamsburg, OH 45176
(513)724-7044

Rates: $65.
Payment: MC VISA PC TC.
Innkeeper(s): John & Carol Sandberg.
Circa: 1841.

Rooms: 3 rooms with PB.
Beds: Q.

Settle down with a book in front of a roaring fire in the library of this rustic, rural Italianate brick farmhouse. The pre-Civil War home was named in honor of its first resident, Lewis McKeever, a prominent landowner, farmer and horse breeder. The lush, 10-acre grounds offer walking trails and fields bursting with wildflowers. Continental breakfasts are served on the second-story porch, which affords a view of the grounds and herb garden. Guest rooms include antiques, some of which were refurbished by the innkeepers themselves. The inn is a quick drive to Cincinnati.

Breakfast included in rates. Types of meals: continental breakfast, continental-plus breakfast and early coffee/tea. Air conditioning and ceiling fan in room. Bicycles on premises. 10 acres. Weddings, small meetings, family reunions and seminars hosted. Antiques, fishing, parks, shopping, sporting events, theater and watersports nearby.

Publicity: *Community Press Journal.*

"It is a nice, peaceful getaway. You are very friendly and gracious."

OH

Wooster E7

Historic Overholt House B&B

1473 Beall Ave
Wooster, OH 44691-2303
(330)263-6300 (800)992-0643
Fax:(330)263-6300

Rates: $63-70.
Payment: MC VISA DS PC.
Innkeeper(s): Sandy Pohalski & Bobbie Walton.
Circa: 1874.

Rooms: 4 rooms with PB. 1 suite.
Beds: QD.

This burgundy Victorian with its peaked roofs and colorful trim literally was saved from the wrecking ball. Several concerned locals fought to have the home moved to another location rather than face demolition in order to make way for a parking lot. The current owners later purchased the historic home and furnished it with beautiful wall coverings, antiques and Victorian touches. The focal point of the interior is a magnificent

walnut "flying staircase" that rises three stories. The innkeepers provide plenty of ways to spend a comfortable evening. The common room is stocked with games, a player piano and reading material. Autumn and winter guests are invited to snuggle up in front of a roaring fire while sipping a hot drink and munching on homemade cookies. Candlelight dinners can be arranged by reservation. The area boasts many craft, antique and gift shops, as well as Amish country sites and activities at the College of Wooster, which is adjacent to the Overholt House.

Breakfast and evening snack included in rates. Types of meals: continental breakfast, continental-plus breakfast and early coffee/tea. Dinner available. Air conditioning, ceiling fan and cable TV in room. VCR, fax and spa on premises. Weddings and small meetings hosted. Amusement parks, antiques, parks, shopping and theater nearby.

Publicity: *Exchange, Daily Record, Pathways.*

"A real retreat. So quiet, clean and friendly. I feel pampered! An old penny always returns."

Melissa Kelly's Chocolate Hazelnut Torte

The Old Chatham Sheepherding Company
Old Chatham, N.Y.

- ½ t unsalted butter
- 6 ounces hazelnuts, toasted, skinned and chopped
- 6 ounces bittersweet chocolate, chopped fine
- Zest of 1 lemon
- Zest of 1 orange
- 6 large eggs, separated
- ½ cup granulated sugar
- Ice cream

Preheat oven to 350 degrees. Line the bottom of an 8-inch round cake pan with parchment paper, and lightly butter it.

Combine hazelnuts, chocolate, lemon zest and orange zest in a food processor. Pulse until finely ground.

Combine egg yolks and ¼ cup sugar in an electric mixer. Whisk on high speed for about 3 minutes, until light and creamy. Turn speed to low, and mix in the ground hazelnut-chocolate mixture.

Place egg whites in a clean bowl and whip at medium speed until frothy. Increase to high speed and whip until softly peaked. Continue to whip, gradually adding remaining sugar, until stiff.

Fold a third of the beaten egg whites into the batter, and when they are almost completely incorporated, fold in the rest.

Spread in prepared pan and bake for about 35 minutes until a cake tester comes out clean. Cool briefly on a rack. The cake will drop somewhat as it cools. Remove the cake from the pan and invert it. Peel off the paper. Serve while still warm with ice cream.

Serves 8.

Oklahoma

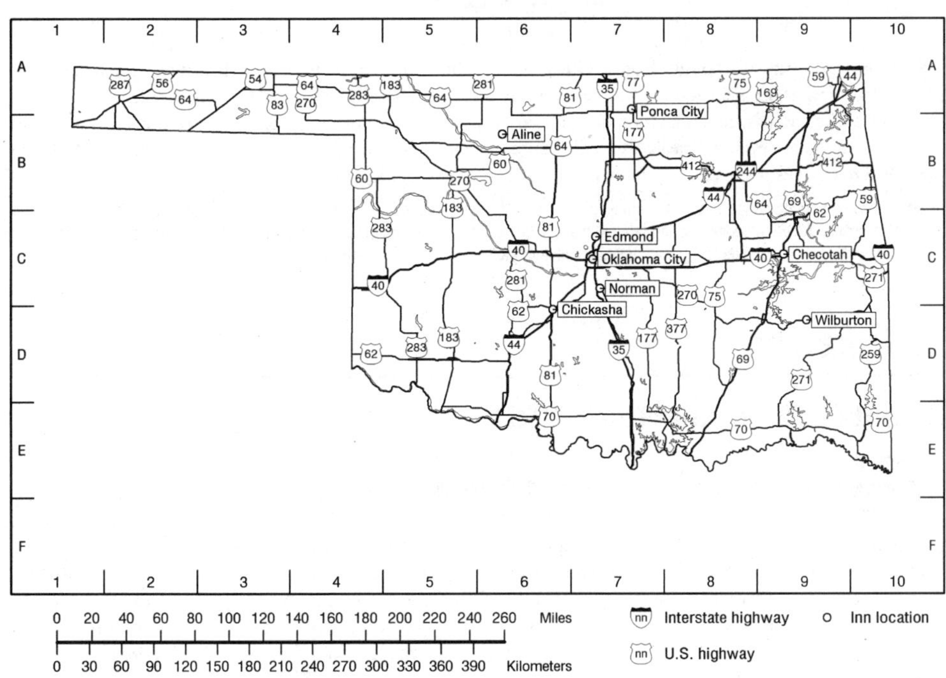

Aline **B6**

Heritage Manor

RR 3 Box 33
Aline, OK 73716-9118
(405)463-2563 (800)295-2563

Rates: $55-150.
Payment: PC TC.
Innkeeper(s): A.J. & Carolyn Rexroat.
Circa: 1903.

Rooms: 4 rooms. 2 suites. 2 conference rooms.
Beds: D.

A wonderful way to experience Oklahoma history is to stay at the Heritage Manor, two turn-of-the-century restored homes. One is an American four-square house and the other, a glorified Arts-and-Crafts-style home. Antiques were gathered from area pioneer homes and include an Edison Victrola Morning Glory Horn and a cathedral pump organ. Antique sofas and English leather chairs fill the sitting room. Mannequins dressed in pioneer clothing add to the decor. There are several fireplaces, and a widow's walk tops the main house.

Breakfast and evening snack included in rates. Types of meals: full breakfast and early coffee/tea. Afternoon tea, dinner, picnic lunch, lunch, gourmet lunch and banquet service available. Air conditioning and cable TV in room. VCR, spa and library on premises. Handicap access. 80 acres. Weddings, small meetings, family reunions and seminars hosted. Antiques, fishing, parks, shopping, sporting events, theater and watersports nearby.

Pets Allowed.

Publicity: *Country, Enid Morning News, Daily Oklahoman.*

OK

Checotah C9

Sharpe House

301 NW 2nd St
Checotah, OK 74426-2240
(918)473-2832

Rates: $35-50.
Payment: PC TC.
Innkeeper(s): Kay Kindt.
Circa: 1911.

Rooms: 3 rooms, 2 with PB. 1 suite.
Beds: D.

Built on land originally bought from a Creek Indian, this Southern plantation-style inn was a teacherage—the rooming house for single female teachers. It is furnished with heirlooms from the innkeepers' families and hand-crafted accessories. The look of the house is antebellum, but the specialty of the kitchen is Mexican cuisine. Family-style evening meals are available upon request. Checotah is located at the junction of I-40 and U.S. 69. This makes it the ideal base for your day trips of exploration or recreation in Green Country.

Breakfast included in rates. Types of meals: continental breakfast, continental-plus breakfast, full breakfast and early coffee/tea. Catered breakfast available. Air conditioning, ceiling fan and cable TV in room. Library and child care on premises. Weddings and small meetings hosted. Spanish spoken. Amusement parks, antiques, fishing, parks, shopping and watersports nearby.

Pets Allowed: Yes.

Chickasha D6

Campbell-Richison House B&B

1428 Kansas
Chickasha, OK 73018
(405)222-1754

Rates: $35-55.
Innkeeper(s): David Ratcliff.
Circa: 1909.

Rooms: 3 rooms, 1 with PB.
Beds: D.

Upon entering this prairie-style home, guests will notice a spacious entryway with a gracious stairway ascending to the second-floor guest rooms. The front parlor is a wonderful spot for relaxing, reading or just soaking up the history of the home. The dining room has a stained-glass window that gives off a kaleidoscope of beautiful colors when the morning sun shines through. A spacious yard encompasses one-quarter of a city block and has large shade trees that can be enjoyed on a swing or from the wicker-lined porch.

Breakfast included in rates. Types of meals: continental-plus breakfast and early coffee/tea. Air conditioning in room. Cable TV and VCR on premises. Small meetings hosted. Antiques, shopping and sporting events nearby.

Publicity: *Oklahoma Today, Chickasha Express, Cache Times Weekly.*

"We enjoyed our stay at your lovely B&B! It was just the getaway we needed to unwind from a stressful few weeks. Your hospitality fellowship and food were just wonderful."

Edmond C7

The Arcadian Inn B&B

328 E 1st St
Edmond, OK 73034-4543
(405)348-6347 (800)299-6347
Fax:(405)348-6347

Rates: $65-195. AP.
Payment: MC VISA AX DS TC.
Innkeeper(s): Martha & Gary Hall.
Circa: 1908.

Rooms: 6 rooms with PB. 4 suites.
Beds: KQ.

C. 1908

Unwind in the garden spa of this Victorian inn or on the wraparound porch to enjoy the Oklahoma breeze. Breakfast may be served privately in your suite or in the dining room flooded with morning sunlight, beneath the ceiling paintings of angels and Christ done by a local artisan. Located next to the University of Central Oklahoma, the inn is four blocks from downtown antique shopping. Guests will enjoy the private baths with Jacuzzis and clawfoot tubs.

Breakfast included in rates. Type of meal: full breakfast. AP. Air conditioning, ceiling fan and cable TV in room. Fax and spa on premises. Amusement parks, antiques, fishing, parks, shopping, sporting events, theater and watersports nearby.

Publicity: *Daily Oklahoman, Antique Traveler.*

Norman C7

Holmberg House B&B

766 DeBarr Ave
Norman, OK 73069-4908
(405)321-6221 (800)646-6221
Fax:(405)321-6221

Rates: $75-85.
Payment: MC VISA AX DS PC TC.
Innkeeper(s): MaryJo Meacham.
Circa: 1914.

Rooms: 4 rooms with PB.
Beds: QDT.

Professor Fredrik Holmberg and his wife Signy built this Craftsman-style home across the street from the University of Oklahoma. Each of the antique-filled rooms has its own individual decor and style. For instance, the Blue Danube Room is a romantic retreat filled with wicker, a wrought iron bed and floral accents throughout. The Bed and Bath Room boasts an old-fashioned tub next to a window seat. The parlor and front porch are perfect places to relax with friends, the lush grounds include a lovely garden. Aside from close access to the university, Holmberg House is within walking distance to more than a dozen restaurants.

Breakfast included in rates. Types of meals: gourmet breakfast and early coffee/tea. Air conditioning, ceiling fan and cable TV in room. Fax, copier and library on premises. Weddings, small meetings and family reunions hosted. Antiques, parks, shopping, sporting events and theater nearby. TAC10.

Publicity: *Metro Norman, Oklahoma City Journal Record, Norman Transcript.*

"Your hospitality and the delicious food were just super."

Montford Inn

322 W Tonhawa St
Norman, OK 73069-7124
(405)321-2200

Rates: $90-165.
Payment: MC VISA AX DS PC TC.
Innkeeper(s): Phyllis, Ron & William Murray.
Circa: 1994.

Rooms: 12 rooms with PB, 12 with FP. 1 cottage.
Beds: KQT.

Although this inn was built just a few years ago, the exterior is reminiscent of a country farmhouse, with its covered front porch lined with rockers. The interior is a mix of styles, from the decidedly Southwestern Chickasaw Rancher room to the romantic Solitude room, which includes a king-size bed canopied in Battenburg lace. Each of the guest rooms has a fireplace. The gourmet breakfasts are arranged and presented artfully, featuring succulent egg dishes, freshly baked breads and fruit smoothies.

Breakfast included in rates. Type of meal: full breakfast. Air conditioning, ceiling fan and cable TV in room. VCR, fax, copier and library on premises. Handicap access. Weddings, small meetings, family reunions and seminars hosted. Antiques, fishing, parks, shopping, sporting events, theater and watersports nearby. TAC10.

"More people should know how great a place like this can make you feel."

Oklahoma City C7

The Grandison

1200 N Shartel Ave
Oklahoma City, OK 73103
(405)232-8778 (800)240-4667
Fax:(405)521-0011

Rates: $75-150.
Payment: MC VISA AX DS PC TC.
Innkeeper(s): Claudia & Bob Wright.
Circa: 1904.

Rooms: 9 rooms with PB, 4 with FP. 3 suites. 1 conference room.
Beds: KQT.

This brick and shingled three-story house is shaded by pecan, apple and fig trees. You'll find a pond and gazebo among the lawns and gardens. The building's original Belgian stained glass remains, and the decor is an airy country Victorian. The bridal suite includes a working fireplace, white-lace curtains and a clawfoot tub, with Jacuzzi.

Breakfast and evening snack included in rates. Types of meals: continental-plus breakfast, full breakfast and early coffee/tea. Banquet service, catering service and room service available. Air conditioning, ceiling fan, cable TV and VCR in room. Fax, copier, sauna and library on premises. Handicap access. Weddings, small meetings, family reunions and seminars hosted. Antiques, parks, sporting events and theater nearby. TAC10.

Publicity: *Daily Oklahoman, Oklahoma Pride, Oklahoma Gazette, Discover Oklahoma.*

"Like going home to Grandma's!"

Rose Stone Inn

120 S 3rd St
Ponca City, OK 74601
(405)765-5699 (800)763-9922
Fax:(405)762-0240

Rates: $54-84. MAP.
Payment: MC VISA AX DC CB DS PC TC.
Innkeeper(s): David & Shirley Zimmerman.
Circa: 1994.

Rooms: 25 rooms, 22 with PB. 3 suites.
Beds: Q.

One of the first savings and loan buildings west of the Mississippi once rested where this Art Deco-style inn now resides. Some rooms lean toward Victorian decor, others are more Art Deco. A lavish breakfast buffet is served daily with homemade Southern fare such as grits and biscuits and gravy. The inn's dining room, Derricks Restaurant, offers a Scandinavian smorgasbord and lunch buffet. Many of Ponca City's historic attractions, shops and restaurants are nearby. The innkeepers offer limousine service to the local theater and amenities for business travelers.

Breakfast and evening snack included in rates. Types of meals: full breakfast and early coffee/tea. Afternoon tea, picnic lunch, lunch, gourmet lunch, banquet service, catering service and catered breakfast available. Restaurant on premises. MAP. Air conditioning, cable TV and VCR in room. Fax, copier and library on premises. Handicap access. Weddings, small meetings, family reunions and seminars hosted. Amusement parks, antiques, fishing, parks, shopping, theater and watersports nearby. TAC10.

Pets Allowed: Small animals only.

Sausage/Grits Casserole

The Decoy
Strasburg, Penn.

- 1 cup quick cooking grits
- 1 lb. bulk sausage
- 1 small onion, finely chopped
- ⅓ cup chopped green pepper
- 1 ½ cups grated cheddar cheese

Cook grits according to the directions on the box. Set aside. Cook sausage in a large frying pan. Remove sausage when done, and saute onion and green pepper until tender. Remove from grease and drain well.

Combine grits, sausage, onion and green pepper along with 1 cup of grated cheese. Spoon into a lightly greased 8" square baking pan. Bake in 350-degree oven for 15 minutes. Sprinkle top with remaining cheese and return to oven for another five minutes, or until cheese is melted and lightly browned.

Serves 8.

Oregon

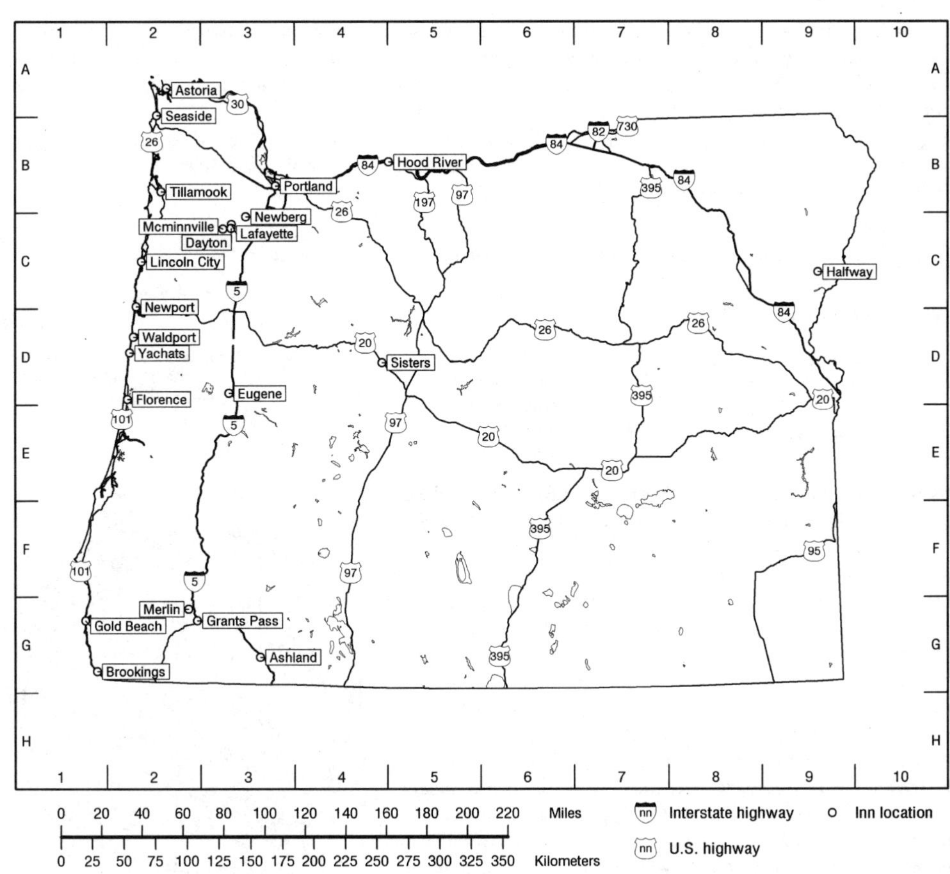

Ashland G3

Iris Inn

59 Manzanita St
Ashland, OR 97520-2615
(541)488-2286 (800)460-7650
Fax:(541)488-3709

Rates: $60-100.
Payment: MC VISA.
Innkeeper(s): Vicki Lamb.
Circa: 1905.

Rooms: 5 rooms with PB.
Beds: QDT.

The Iris Inn is a restored Victorian set on a large flower-filled yard. It features simple American country antiques. The upstairs guest rooms have views of the valley and mountains. Evening sips of wine often are taken out on the large deck overlooking a rose garden. Breakfast boasts an elegant presentation with dishes such as buttermilk scones and peaches and cream French toast.

Breakfast included in rates. Type of meal: full breakfast. Air conditioning, turn-down service and ceiling fan in room. Fax on premises. Small meetings and seminars hosted. Antiques, fishing, shopping, downhill skiing, cross-country skiing, sporting events, theater and watersports nearby.

Location: Southern Oregon.

Publicity: *Sunset, Oregonian.*

"It's like returning to home to be at The Iris Inn."

Morical House Garden Inn

668 N Main St
Ashland, OR 97520-1710
(541)482-2254 (800)208-0960
Fax:(541)482-1775
E-mail: moricalhse@aol.com

Rates: $73-160.
Payment: MC VISA AX DS PC TC.
Innkeeper(s): Gary & Sandye Moore.
Circa: 1882.

Rooms: 7 rooms with PB, 2 with FP.
Beds: KQT.

The Morical House is a mile away from the Shakespeare festival, and blooming rose gardens frame this exquisitely restored Victorian farmhouse in summer. All guest rooms are furnished with period antiques and handmade comforters, and each has a view of the Cascade Mountains. The inn's acre of grounds includes ponds, waterfalls and a large deck.

Breakfast and afternoon tea included in rates. Types of meals: gourmet breakfast and early coffee/tea. Air conditioning in room. Cable TV and fax on premises. Handicap access. Weddings, small meetings, family reunions and seminars hosted. Fishing, shopping, downhill skiing, cross-country skiing and theater nearby. TAC10.

Publicity: *Pacific Northwest Magazine.*

"Gracious hosts who spoiled us with such attention to detail and unparalleled warm hospitality."

Mt. Ashland Inn

550 Mt Ashland Ski Rd
Ashland, OR 97520-9745
(541)482-8707 (800)830-8707
Fax:(541)482-8707

Rates: $76-180.
Payment: MC VISA AX DS PC.
Innkeeper(s): Chuck & Laurel Biegert.
Circa: 1987.

Rooms: 5 rooms with PB, 3 with FP. 3 suites. 1 conference room.
Beds: KQT.

Innkeepers Chuck and Laurel Biegert truly have mastered the art of innkeeping. It doesn't hurt that the two "keep" a spectacular mountain cedar log lodge surrounded by a pine forest. During chilly months, a fire crackles in the front room's magnificent stone fireplace. Guests trample in after a day on the slopes ready to enjoy a soak in the outdoor spa and sauna under a night sky sparkling with stars. Guest rooms and suites are appointed with elegant, yet comfortable furnishings. Quilts, antiques, double whirlpool tubs and wonderful views are just some of the surprises guests will discover. The Biegerts go all out during the holiday season and from November to New Year's, the inn participates in the town's Festival of Lights. But winter isn't the only season to visit the inn, the area offers hiking, fishing, shopping, galleries, museums and more. No matter what time of year, guests are treated to a divine breakfast. The cuisine at Mount Ashland has been featured in several cookbooks, as well as Bon Appetit and Gourmet.

Breakfast included in rates. Type of meal: gourmet breakfast. Fax, copier, spa, sauna and bicycles on premises. 40 acres. Weddings hosted. Antiques, fishing, parks, shopping, downhill skiing, cross-country skiing, theater and watersports nearby. TAC10.

Location: Fourteen miles from Ashland. Six miles west of I-5 on Mount Ashland Road.

Publicity: *Pacific Northwest, Edward Carter's Travels, Snow Country, Oregon, Glamour, Travel & Leisure, Country Living, Log Home Living.*

"I've wondered where my dreams go when I can't remember them. Now I know they come here, among the snow, trees, valley, dogs, wind, sun, and dance at night around the Lodge."

Pedigrift House

407 Scenic Dr
Ashland, OR 97520-1638
(541)482-1888 (800)262-4073
Fax:(541)482-8867

Rates: $85-120.
Payment: MC VISA PC.
Innkeeper(s): Dorothy & Richard Davis.
Circa: 1888.

Rooms: 4 rooms with PB.
Beds: Q.

This Queen Anne Victorian features twin protruding bay windows and gables accentuated with bead and spindle work. The first floor's high ceilings are detailed with original trim and nine-foot-high doors, which lead into the dining room still boast their original copper finish pulls and bolt. Rooms include a mix of

traditional and antique furnishings with fluffy comforters and a French Country decor. Fresh flowers are placed in each room. A full breakfast is served either in the dining room, and a afternoon treats and beverages are available throughout day. Ashland attracts thousands of theater buffs to its world-renown Shakespeare Festival, which runs from mid-February until October. The Bard of Avon's plays are performed on an outdoor Elizabethan stage or in two indoor theaters.

Breakfast and evening snack included in rates. Types of meals: full breakfast, gourmet breakfast and early coffee/tea. Air conditioning and ceiling fan in room. Small meetings and family reunions hosted. Antiques, fishing, parks, shopping, downhill skiing, cross-country skiing, theater and watersports nearby.

Astoria A2

Grandview B&B

1574 Grand Ave
Astoria, OR 97103-3733
(503)325-5555 (800)488-3250

Rates: $39-92.
Payment: MC VISA DS.
Innkeeper(s): Charleen Maxwell.
Circa: 1896.

Rooms: 9 rooms, 7 with PB, 3 with FP. 2 suites.
Beds: QT.

To fully enjoy its views of the Columbia River, this Victorian house has both a tower and a turret. Antiques and white wicker furnishings contribute to the inn's casual, homey feeling. The Meadow Room is particularly appealing to bird lovers with its bird cage, bird books and bird wallpaper. Breakfast, served in the main-floor turret, frequently includes smoked salmon with bagels and cream cheese.

Breakfast and evening snack included in rates. Type of meal: continental-plus breakfast. Weddings, small meetings and family reunions hosted. Antiques, fishing, parks, shopping, theater and watersports nearby.

Publicity: *Pacific Northwest Magazine, Northwest Discoveries, Los Angeles Times, Oregonian, Daily Astorian.*

"We're still talking about our visit and the wonderful breakfast you served."

Brookings G1

Chetco River Inn

21202 High Prairie Rd
Brookings, OR 97415-8200
(541)670-1645

Rates: $95-135.
Payment: MC VISA PC TC.
Innkeeper(s): Sandra Brugger.
Circa: 1987.

Rooms: 4 rooms, 3 with PB.
Beds: KQT.

OR

Situated on 35 wooded acres and the Chetco River, this modern B&B offers a cedar lodge exterior and a marble- and antique-filled interior. A collection of crafts, Oriental rugs and leather sofas add to your enjoyment. Because it's 18 miles from Brookings, you may wish to arrange ahead for a dinner. Then you can enjoy the sounds of the rushing river without interruption. Trails, Kalmioposis Wilderness area and steelhead fishing are close by.

Breakfast included in rates. Types of meals: full breakfast and early coffee/tea. Dinner and evening snack available. Swimming and library on premises. Small meetings, family reunions and seminars hosted. Antiques, fishing, parks, shopping, theater and watersports nearby. TAC10.

South Coast Inn B&B

516 Redwood St
Brookings, OR 97415-9672
(541)469-5557 (800)525-9273
Fax:(541)469-6615
E-mail: scoastin@wave.net

Rates: $79-89.
Payment: MC VISA AX DS PC TC.
Innkeeper(s): Ken Raith & Keith Pepper.
Circa: 1917.

Rooms: 3 rooms with PB. 1 cottage.
Beds: Q.

Enjoy panoramic views of the Pacific Ocean at this Craftsman-style inn built by San Francisco architect Bernard Maybeck. All rooms are furnished with antiques, ceiling fans, VCRs and TVs. A floor-to-ceiling stone fireplace and beamed ceilings make the parlor a great place to gather with friends. There are sun decks, a strolling garden and an indoor hot tub and sauna. Brookings is in the warm "Banana Belt" of the South Coast.

Breakfast included in rates. Types of meals: full breakfast, gourmet breakfast and early coffee/tea. Ceiling fan, cable TV and VCR in room. Fax, spa, sauna and library on premises. Weddings, small meetings, family reunions and seminars hosted. Antiques, fishing, parks, shopping, theater and watersports nearby. TAC10.

Special Discounts: Winter package available.

Camp Sherman

Lake Creek Lodge, Inc

13173 SW Forest Service Rd 1419, Camp Sherman, OR 97730
(541)595-6331 (800)797-6331
Fax:(541)595-1016

Rates: $70-150.
Payment: PC TC.
Innkeeper(s): Velda Brust.
Circa: 1935.

Rooms: 16 cottages. 5 conference rooms.
Beds: QDT.

Since the early 1900s, families have come to this scenic 41 acres to enjoy their summer vacation. The present lodge was built in 1935, and guests stay in newly renovated cabins. The cabins can sleep up to eight people comfortably and include a living room, two or three bedrooms, bathrooms, a kitchen and a deck. During the height of the summer season, the rates include dinner, and breakfast is available. The rest of the year, the lodge's dining room is open to pre-arranged groups only. There's always something to do here, from swimming in the lodge's heated pool in the summer, to taking in a game of tennis. Guests can hike, ride on the bike paths and play pool, ping pong, horseshoes, shuffleboard or volleyball. Horseback riding and ice skating are nearby, and guests can take a trek into the mountains or go on a hunting or fishing trip. This is definitely a place children will enjoy. The lodge's stocked trout pond is available only for youngsters, and children are the first ones invited to come up and take their pick from the summer dinner buffets.

Types of meals: continental breakfast, full breakfast and early coffee/tea. Dinner available. Cable TV, fax, copier, swimming and tennis on premises. Handicap access. 41 acres. Weddings, small meetings, family reunions and seminars hosted. Fishing, shopping, downhill skiing, cross-country skiing and watersports nearby. TAC8.

Pets Allowed: Off season.

Dayton C3

Wine Country Farm

6855 NE Breyman Orchards Rd, Dayton, OR 97114-7220
(503)864-3446 (800)261-3446
Fax:(503)864-3446

Rates: $75-125.
Payment: MC VISA PC.
Innkeeper(s): Joan Davenport.
Circa: 1910.

Rooms: 5 rooms with PB, 2 with FP. 1 suite. 1 conference room.
Beds: KQDT.

Surrounded by vineyards and orchards, Wine Country Farm is an eclectic French house sitting on a hill overlooking the Cascade Mountain Range. Arabian horses are raised here and five varieties of grapes are grown. Request the master bedroom and you'll enjoy a fireplace. The innkeepers can arrange for a horse-drawn buggy ride and picnic. There are outdoor wedding facilities and a new wine tasting room. Downtown Portland and the Oregon coast are each an hour away.

Breakfast included in rates. Types of meals: full breakfast, gourmet breakfast and early coffee/tea. Picnic lunch, banquet service, catering service and room service available. Air conditioning, ceiling fan and VCR in room. Fax, copier, stables, library and pet boarding on premises. 13 acres. Weddings, small meetings, family reunions and seminars hosted. Antiques, fishing, parks, shopping, downhill skiing, cross-country skiing, sporting events, theater and watersports nearby.

Pets Allowed.
Publicity: *Wine Spectator.*

Atherton Place, A B&B Inn

690 W Broadway
Eugene, OR 97402-5216
(541)683-2674 (800)507-1354

Rates: $60-95.
Payment: PC TC.
Innkeeper(s): Marne Krozek.
Circa: 1925.

Rooms: 3 rooms, 2 with PB.
Beds: QDT.

Within a few minutes' walk of the City Center Mall, Hult Center and the University of Oregon is Atherton Place, a Dutch Colonial-style home. A library, sun room and sitting room offer cozy places to read. Crown moldings, polished oak floors and built-in cabinets attest to a craftsmanship of former days. Guest rooms have new queen beds and a casual country decor.

Breakfast and evening snack included in rates. Types of meals: gourmet breakfast and early coffee/tea. Turn-down service and ceiling fan in room. Cable TV on premises. Weddings, small meetings, family reunions and seminars hosted. Antiques, fishing, parks, shopping, sporting events, theater and watersports nearby.

Campbell House, A City Inn

252 Pearl St
Eugene, OR 97401-2366
(541)343-1119 (800)264-2519
Fax:(541)343-2258
E-mail: campbellhouse@campbellhouse.com

Rates: $72-235.
Payment: MC VISA AX DS TC.
Innkeeper(s): Myra Plant.
Circa: 1892.

Rooms: 14 rooms with PB, 3 with FP. 1 suite. 3 conference rooms.
Beds: KQDT.

An acre of grounds surrounds this Victorian inn, built by a local timber owner and gold miner. The rooms range from a ground level room featuring fly-fishing paraphernalia and knotty-pine paneling to an elegant two-room honeymoon suite on the second floor, complete with fireplace, jetted bathtub for two and a view of the mountains. The Campbell House, located in Eugene's historic Skinner Butte District, is within walking distance of restaurants, the Hult Center for the Performing Arts, the 5th Street Public Market and antique shops. Outdoor activities include jogging or biking along riverside paths.

Breakfast included in rates. Types of meals: full breakfast and early coffee/tea. Picnic lunch and room service available. Air conditioning, turn-down service, ceiling fan, cable TV and VCR in room. Fax, copier and library on premises. Handicap access. Weddings, small meetings, family reunions and seminars hosted. Antiques, fishing, parks, shopping, sporting events, theater and watersports nearby. TAC10.

Publicity: *KVAL & KAUW T.V. News, Eugene Register Guard, Country Inns, Oregonian, Sunset, B&B Innkeepers Journal.*

"I guess we've never felt so pampered! Thank you so much. The room is beautiful! We had a wonderful getaway."

OR

Kjaer's House In Woods

814 Lorane Hwy
Eugene, OR 97405-2321
(541)343-3234 (800)437-4501

Rates: $55-75.
Payment: PC TC.
Innkeeper(s): George & Eunice Kjaer.
Circa: 1910.

Rooms: 2 rooms with PB. 1 conference room.
Beds: Q.

This handsome Craftsman house on two landscaped acres was built by a Minnesota lawyer. It was originally accessible by streetcar. Antiques include a square grand piano of rosewood and a collection of antique wedding photos. The house is attractively furnished and surrounded by flower gardens.

Breakfast included in rates. Types of meals: continental breakfast, full breakfast, gourmet breakfast and early coffee/tea. Turn-down service in room. Cable TV, VCR and library on premises. Weddings, small meetings, family reunions and seminars hosted. Antiques, fishing, parks, sporting events and theater nearby. TAC10.

Publicity: *Register-Guard, Oregonian.*

"Lovely ambiance and greatest sleep ever. Delicious and beautiful food presentation."

The Oval Door

988 Lawrence St
Eugene, OR 97401-2827
(541)683-3160 (800)882-3160

Rates: $70-93.
Payment: MC VISA AX.
Innkeeper(s): Judith McLane.
Circa: 1990.

Rooms: 4 rooms with PB.
Beds: QT.

This is a New England farm-style house, complete with wraparound porch. It is located in a residential neighborhood 15 blocks from the University of Oregon. Guest rooms feature ceiling fans and antiques. There is a whirlpool room, library and parlor. Breakfast can be catered to your dietary needs.

Turn-down service and ceiling fan in room. Cable TV, VCR, fax and library on premises. TAC10.

Pookie's B&B on College Hill

2013 Charnelton St
Eugene, OR 97405-2819
(541)343-0383 (800)558-0383
Fax:(541)343-0383

Rates: $65-90. AP.
Payment: PC TC.
Innkeeper(s): Pookie & Doug Walling.
Circa: 1918.

Rooms: 3 rooms, 2 with PB. 1 suite.
Beds: KQT.

Pookie's is a charming Craftsman house with an English influence. Surrounded by maple and fir trees, the B&B is located in the College Hill neighborhood. Mahogany and oak antiques decorate the rooms. The innkeeper worked for many years in the area as a concierge and can offer you expert help with excursion planning or business needs.

Breakfast included in rates. Types of meals: continental breakfast, continental-plus breakfast, full breakfast and early coffee/tea. AP. Ceiling fan and cable TV in room. VCR, fax and copier on premises. Weddings and small meetings hosted. Antiques, fishing, parks, shopping, sporting events, theater and watersports nearby. TAC10.

Publicity: *Oregon Wine.*

"I love the attention to detail. The welcoming touches: flowers, the 'convenience basket' of necessary items... I'm happy to have discovered your lovely home."

Florence — D2

The Blue Heron Inn

6563 Hwy 126 PO Box 1122
Florence, OR 97439-0055
(541)997-4091 (800)799-6249

Rates: $55-100.
Payment: MC VISA DS PC TC.
Innkeeper(s): Doris Van Osdell & Maurice Souza.
Circa: 1940.

Rooms: 5 rooms with PB.
Beds: KQT.

From the porch of this bed & breakfast inn, guests can gaze at rolling, forested hills and watch as riverboats ease their way down the Siuslaw River. Aside from the spectacular view, the inn is located within a few yards of a marina where docking and mooring is available. The ocean and historic Florence are just minutes away as well. The Bridal Suite offers a draped, king-size bed, sitting area, whirlpool tub and view of the river and grounds. Fresh, seasonal fare highlights the breakfast menu. Treats such as fresh fruit smoothies, muffins topped with homemade blackberry jam or a smoked salmon and avocado quiche are not uncommon.

Breakfast and afternoon tea included in rates. Type of meal: full breakfast. Ceiling fan in room. VCR and library on premises. Weddings, small meetings and family reunions hosted. German spoken. Antiques, fishing, parks, shopping and watersports nearby. TAC5.

Special Discounts: $5 off after first night with total stay of three nights or more.

Gold Beach

G1

Inn at Nesika Beach

33026 Nesika Rd
Gold Beach, OR 97444
(541)247-6434

Rates: $100-130.
Payment: PC TC.
Innkeeper(s): Ann G. Arsenault.
Circa: 1992.

Rooms: 4 rooms with PB, 3 with FP.
Beds: KQT.

Although this home is new, it sports the nostalgic Victorian design so popular with inngoers. The inn rests atop a bluff overlooking the ocean, and all of the romantic guest rooms offer water views. Bed chambers are dressed with down comforters, and there are whirlpool tubs and fireplaces. In the afternoon, light snacks are served, and the innkeeper begins each day with a hearty breakfast. The inn is located a little more than five miles from the town of Gold Beach.

Breakfast and evening snack included in rates. Types of meals: gourmet breakfast and early coffee/tea. Ceiling fan in room. Cable TV and VCR on premises. Weddings, small meetings and seminars hosted. Fishing, parks and watersports nearby.

Location: One hour from the California border on ocean front property.

Publicity: *Oregon Coast Magazine.*

"What a great surprise. The jewel of Nesika Beach."

Grants Pass

G2

The Ahlf House B&B

762 NW 6th St
Grants Pass, OR 97526
(541)474-1374 (800)863-1374

Rates: $65-110.
Payment: MC VISA AX PC TC.
Innkeeper(s): Ken & Cathy Neuschafer.
Circa: 1902.

Rooms: 6 rooms with PB. 1 suite. 1 cottage.
Beds: QT.

This four-story Queen Anne Victorian stands on a hill, framed by tulip, pine and cedar trees. With 5,500 square feet, it is the largest historic house in Grants Pass. Delicately painted in three shades of blue, the house boasts a double-tiered veranda and bay with fish-scale siding. A gracious Victorian home feeling is carried out in antique decor. Stop by the gift shop for that special remembrance.

Breakfast included in rates. Types of meals: full breakfast and early coffee/tea. Air conditioning and cable TV in room. VCR and library on premises. Small meetings hosted. Antiques, fishing, parks, shopping, theater and watersports nearby. TAC15.

Publicity: *Daily Courier, Horizon Air Magazine.*

"We felt very pampered and relaxed. The atmosphere is much more than money can buy."

Lawnridge House

1304 NW Lawnridge Ave
Grants Pass, OR 97526
(541)476-8518

Rates: $55-75.
Payment: PC TC.
Innkeeper(s): Barbara Head.
Circa: 1909.

Rooms: 1 suite.
Beds: KQ.

This inn, a graceful, gabled clapboard house is shaded by 200-year-old oaks. The home features spacious rooms with comfortable antiques, canopy beds and beamed ceilings. Mini refrigerators, TVs and VCRs are among the amenities. The innkeeper serves Northwest regional cuisine for the full breakfasts. The Rogue River is five minutes away, and the Ashland Shakespearean Festival is a 45-minute drive.

Breakfast included in rates. Type of meal: full breakfast. Air conditioning in room. Antiques, fishing, theater and watersports nearby. TAC10.

Publicity: *CBS TV, Grants Pass Courier, This Week.*

"Thank you for your incredible friendliness, warmth, and energy expended on our behalf! I've never felt so nestled in the lap of luxury - what a pleasure!"

Grants Pass (Merlin)

Pine Meadow Inn

1000 Crow Rd, Grants Pass (Merlin), OR 97532
(541)471-6277 (800)554-0806
Fax:(541)471-6277

Rates: $80-110.
Payment: PC.
Innkeeper(s): Nancy & Maloy Murdock.
Circa: 1991.

Rooms: 4 rooms with PB.
Beds: Q.

Built on a wooded knoll, this handsome yellow farmhouse looks out on a four-acre meadow, which the innkeepers call their front yard. Five acres of private forest feature walking paths, gardens and private sitting areas. The home's wraparound porch offers wicker furniture, and there is a large deck and hot tub under towering pines. There also is a koi pond and waterfall where one can relax and contemplate. The inn is easily accessible from I-5, yet feels worlds away.

Breakfast included in rates. Types of meals: gourmet breakfast and early coffee/tea. Air conditioning, turn-down service and ceiling fan in room. Fax, copier, spa and library on premises. Family reunions hosted. Antiques, fishing, parks, shopping, theater and watersports nearby. TAC10.

Special Discounts: 10% for seven days or more; 10% all four rooms.

Halfway C9

Clear Creek Farm B&B

RR 1 Box 138
Halfway, OR 97834-9705
(541)742-2238 (800)742-4992
Fax:(541)742-5175

Rates: $60.
Payment: MC VISA PC TC.
Innkeeper(s): Mike & Rose Curless.
Circa: 1900.

Rooms: 4 rooms. 1 cottage. 2 conference rooms.
Beds: KQDT.

Although the area is called Hells Canyon, the scenery of mountains and meadows is more like a little view of heaven. The grounds offer plenty of hiking trails, a creek, ponds, an orchard and buffalo graze at a nearby ranch. Guests stay in rustic rooms either in the century-old farmhouse or in the renovated barn or granary. Hearty breakfasts with seasonal berries and bison sausage are served in the summer kitchen. The innkeepers keep the cookie jar stocked and offer beverages throughout the year. For an extra fee, guests can learn the tricks of the buffalo trade at the innkeeper's sister ranch, Hells Canyon Bison Ranch.

Breakfast and afternoon tea included in rates. Types of meals: full breakfast, gourmet breakfast and early coffee/tea. Ceiling fan in room. VCR, fax, copier, spa and library on premises. Handicap access. Weddings, small meetings, family reunions and seminars hosted. Antiques, fishing, parks, shopping, cross-country skiing and watersports nearby.

Pets Allowed: Well behaved only.

Special Discounts: $55 for double occupancy for three or more nights.

"Thanks for sharing your home with us and for your graciousness."

Hood River B5

Columbia Gorge Hotel

4000 Westcliff Dr
Hood River, OR 97031-9799
(541)386-5566 (800)345-1921
Fax:(541)387-5414
E-mail: cghotel@gorgenet.com

Rates: $150-275.
Payment: MC VISA AX DC CB DS TC.
Innkeeper(s): Boyd & Halla Graves.
Circa: 1921.

Rooms: 42 rooms with PB, 2 with FP. 3 conference rooms.
Beds: KQDT.

This posh hotel is a gem among gems in the National Register of Historic Places. Idyllic guest quarters offer such ornate furnishings as a hand-carved canopy bed that once was located in a French castle. The delicately landscaped grounds, turndown service with roses and chocolate and a gourmet restaurant are favorite amenities. Last, but not least, are spectacular views of the majestic Columbia River. Guests are treated to an opulent morning meal that the staff terms "a world famous farm breakfast." The hotel is close to ski areas, golfing and popular windsurfing spots.

Breakfast included in rates. Types of meals: full breakfast, gourmet breakfast and early coffee/tea. Picnic lunch, lunch, gourmet lunch, banquet service, catering service and room service available. Turn-down service and cable TV in room. VCR, fax and copier on premises. Weddings, small meetings, family reunions and seminars hosted. Spanish and French spoken. Antiques, fishing, parks, shopping, downhill skiing, cross-country skiing, theater and watersports nearby. TAC10.

Pets Allowed.

Special Discounts: Various-offered occasionally off season.

Lafayette C3

Kelty Estate B&B

675 Third St
Lafayette, OR 97127
(503)864-3740 (800)867-3740

Rates: $65-75.
Payment: PC TC.
Innkeeper(s): Ron & JoAnn Ross.
Circa: 1872.

Rooms: 2 rooms with PB.
Beds: Q.

An early pioneer couple, one a local druggist and county sheriff and the other, the first woman elected to the Lafayette School Board, built this home. The grounds are well landscaped with gardens, trees and lush plants. Guests can enjoy the tranquility from the swing on the home's front porch. There are two guest rooms, decorated in pastels. Furnishings include period antiques. Breakfasts feature fresh Oregon-grown items, with specialties such as strawberry-kiwi juice, fresh strawberries and bananas in a cream sauce, homemade breads and eggs Benedict accompanied by herbed potatoes. Wineries, a museum and antiquing are among the nearby attractions.

Breakfast and afternoon tea included in rates. Types of meals: continental breakfast, full breakfast and early coffee/tea. Cable TV, VCR and library on premises. Weddings, small meetings, family reunions and seminars hosted. Amusement parks, antiques, fishing, parks, shopping, theater and watersports nearby.

Lincoln City C2

The Enchanted Cottage

4507 SW Coast Ave
Lincoln City, OR 97367
(541)996-4101
Fax:(541)996-2682

Rates: $100-175.
Payment: MC VISA.
Innkeeper(s): Cynthia Gale Fitton.
Circa: 1945.

Rooms: 3 rooms, 2 with PB.
Beds: KQ.

This 4,000-square-foot house is 300 feet from the beach and a short walk from Siletz Bay with its herd of sea lions. Victoria's Secret is a favorite romantic guest room that features a queen canopy bed, antique furnishings and, best of all, the sounds of the Pacific surf. Ask for Sir Arthur's View if you must see and hear the ocean. This two-room suite also has a private deck and a living room with a fireplace and wet bar. Homemade breakfast casseroles are a specialty during the morning meal, which is served either in the dining room or on the deck overlooking the Pacific. Pets are allowed with some restrictions.

Breakfast included in rates. Types of meals: full breakfast and early coffee/tea. Evening snack available. Cable TV in room. VCR, fax and copier on premises. Handicap access. Weddings, small meetings, family reunions and seminars hosted. Antiques, fishing, shopping and watersports nearby.

Pets Allowed: With some restrictions.

Publicity: *Oregonian.*

McMinnville C3

Mattey House

10221 NE Mattey Ln
McMinnville, OR 97128
(503)434-5058

Rates: $75-95.
Payment: MC VISA PC TC.
Innkeeper(s): Denise & Jack Seed.
Circa: 1892.

Rooms: 4 rooms, 1 with PB.
Beds: QD.

Windows rimmed with stained glass and gingerbread trim decorate the exterior of this Queen Anne Victorian. The home is nestled on 10 acres of vineyards, orchards and stately, old cedar trees. Visitors may even pick a few of the succulent grapes. Guest rooms are decorated in period style with antiques, and each is named appropriately for a variety of wine. Upon returning from a day of sightseeing, guests are treated to late afternoon refreshments. Breakfasts are a treat, and the innkeepers serve dishes such as a baked peach with a stuffing of raspberries and cream, baked herbed eggs or perhaps an Italian frittata. Homemade scones are a specialty.

Breakfast and evening snack included in rates. Types of meals: full breakfast and early coffee/tea. Turn-down service in room. 10 acres. Family reunions hosted. German, limited French and limited Italian spoken. Antiques, fishing, parks, shopping, sporting events, theater and watersports nearby.

Special Discounts: Extended stay discounts available.

"What a lovely home and what thoughtful innkeepers you both are. We enjoyed our cozy room with all of your nice touches."

Youngberg Hill Vineyard B&B

10660 SW Youngberg Hill Rd
McMinnville, OR 97128
(503)472-2727
Fax:(503)472-1313

Rates: $120-140.
Payment: MC VISA PC.
Innkeeper(s): Jane & Martin Wright.
Circa: 1989.

Rooms: 5 rooms with PB, 2 with FP. 1 conference room.
Beds: KQ.

This pristinely constructed turn-of-the-century-style farmhouse offers panoramic views of the Willamette Valley, the Cascade Coast Range and 10 acres of pinot noir vineyards. Sheep graze on additional pasture land of the 700-acre property. There is a conference room and a parlor with glass doors that open onto a large deck. Guest rooms offer antiques, comfortable beds, down comforters, piles of pillows, fresh flowers, chocolates and the views. Eggs Benedict, scrambled eggs in puff pastry with a crab fondue, homemade blackberry muffins and ginger scones are the inn's specialties.

Breakfast and evening snack included in rates. Types of meals: full breakfast, gourmet breakfast and early coffee/tea. Air conditioning in room. Fax on premises. Handicap access. 50 acres. Weddings, small meetings and family reunions hosted. Antiques, fishing, parks and shopping nearby. TAC10.

"This is Nirvana! Second time here and certainly not the last."

Merlin G2

Morrison's Rogue River Lodge

8500 Galice Rd
Merlin, OR 97532-9722
(541)476-3825 (800)826-1963
Fax:(541)476-4953

Rates: $150-240. MAP, AP.
Payment: MC VISA DS PC TC.
Innkeeper(s): Michelle Hanten.
Circa: 1946.

Rooms: 13 rooms with PB, 9 with FP. 9 cottages.
Beds: KQDT.

Many world travelers list Morrison's as one of their favorite places. The Rogue River wilderness that surrounds this handsome waterfront lodge provides scenic adventures up and down the river. Each cottage has its own balcony and fireplace, and the lodge is particularly noted for its excellent cuisine. In summer, a four-course, gourmet dinner is served on the deck overlooking green lawns and the river. Breakfast and dinner are included in the summer rates. Breakfast, dinner and a picnic lunch are included in the fall rates.

Breakfast included in rates. MAP, AP. Air conditioning in room. Cable TV, VCR, fax, copier, spa, swimming, bicycles, tennis and library on premises. Handicap access. Weddings, small meetings, family reunions and seminars hosted.

Antiques, fishing, parks, shopping, theater and watersports nearby. TAC10.

Location: On the Rogue River in Southern Oregon.

Publicity: *Los Angeles Times, Pacific Northwest, Bon Appetit, Orvis News.*

"The tales we heard of how delicious the food would be told nothing of how it really was! We were so delighted to find such marvelous home-cooked cuisine, and the family service was terrific!"

Newberg C3

Spring Creek Llama Ranch & B&B

14700 NE Spring Creek Ln
Newberg, OR 97132-7223
(503)538-5717
Fax:(503)538-5717
E-mail: llamabb@teleport.com

Rates: $60-79.
Payment: PC TC.
Innkeeper(s): Dave & Melinda Van Bossuyt.
Circa: 1974.

Rooms: 3 rooms, 2 with PB.
Beds: QDT.

The friendly llamas at this 24-acre ranch sometimes accompany guests on a leisurely walk through wooded trails and pastures. The innkeepers are llama experts and are always happy to answer any questions you might have about their exotic animals. The accommodations include spacious guest rooms with comfortable, modern and antique furnishings. The Red Cloud Room is decorated in blue, maroon and sunset colors with a llama motif. For families with children, the Red Cloud Room can be expanded to include the Toon Room. This whimsical room is decorated with various cartoon collectibles and includes two twin beds. Guests often relax and enjoy the forest view from the patio. The ranch is located just a few miles from wineries, antique shops, restaurants, the Willamette River and Champoeg State Park.

Breakfast included in rates. Type of meal: full breakfast. Air conditioning in room. VCR, fax, copier and library on premises. 24 acres. Small meetings hosted. Spanish spoken. Fishing, parks, sporting events and watersports nearby.

Newport C2

Oar House

520 SW 2nd St
Newport, OR 97365-3907
(541)265-9571 (800)252-2358

Rates: $90-120.
Payment: MC VISA DS PC TC.
Innkeeper(s): Jan Le Brun.
Circa: 1900.

Rooms: 4 rooms with PB. 1 suite.
Beds: Q.

This Craftsman-style home was built using wood that washed ashore after a lumber schooner was abandoned by the crew during a fierce storm. It has a colorful history, serving as a boarding house and then as the Nye Beach Bordello. One of the former occupants, a young woman, may still inhabit the house in ghostly form. Rooms feature nautical names, such as Captain's Quarters and Starboard Cabin. Guests are welcome to walk up the third-floor ship's ladder to the widow's walk and enjoy a panoramic view of the ocean, beach, mountains, lighthouses and sunsets. Roasted, freshly ground coffee, freshly squeezed juice and seasonal fruit accompanies an entree, such as lemon ricotta pancakes topped with sauteed apples.

Breakfast, afternoon tea and evening snack included in rates. Types of meals: gourmet breakfast and early coffee/tea. Cable TV, VCR, sauna and library on premises. Small meetings, family reunions and seminars hosted. Spanish spoken. Antiques, fishing, parks, shopping, theater and watersports nearby.

John Palmer House Bed & Breakfast

4314 N Mississippi Ave
Portland, OR 97217-3135
(503)284-5893 (800)518-5893
Fax:(503)284-1239

Rates: $75-96.
Payment: MC VISA AX DS PC TC.
Innkeeper(s): Richard & Mary Sauter.
Circa: 1890.

Rooms: 3 rooms. 1 suite. 1 conference room.
Beds: QD.

This stunning Victorian has been restored to the height of grandeur. The interior boasts beautifully restored and preserved woodwork, pressed tin ceilings and walls, gracious chandeliers and stained glass. Rooms are decorated in ornate, Victorian style. The grounds are picturesque as well, decorated with gardens and plants. On Sundays, the innkeepers offer public tours of the home, which is listed on the National Register, followed by high tea. Catered breakfasts are available with prior arrangement. The inn is located in an urban, Portland neighborhood, convenient to many downtown sites.

Breakfast included in rates. Types of meals: continental breakfast and full breakfast. Afternoon tea available. Air conditioning in room. Cable TV, VCR, fax, copier and spa on premises. Weddings, small meetings and family reunions hosted. Antiques, fishing, parks, shopping, sporting events, theater and watersports nearby.

"Your collection of Victorian furniture is exquisite, the hospitality grand, and the food is delicious."

Mumford Manor

1130 SW King Ave
Portland, OR 97205-1116
(503)243-2443

Rates: $70-125.
Payment: MC VISA AX.
Innkeeper(s): Janis & Courtland Mumford.
Circa: 1885.

Rooms: 5 rooms, 4 with PB, 4 with FP.
Beds: KQDT.

Flowering trees and mounds of azaleas frame this Queen Anne Tudor home in the National Register. Graceful bay windows and a porch gazebo take advantage of views of the historic neighborhood. Classic Victorian pieces are found throughout the inn. Guest rooms include a spacious suite with fireplace and twin fainting couches. Goosedown comforters and fresh flowers are additional touches. Portland's famous Rose Test Garden is a walk away.

Type of meal: full breakfast.

Publicity: *Northwest Palate, Pacific Northwest.*

"If the mothers of the world opened a B&B, this would be it!"

Terwilliger Vista House

515 SW Westwood Dr
Portland, OR 97201-2791
(503)244-0602

Rates: $75-125.
Payment: MC VISA PC TC.
Innkeeper(s): Dick & Jan Vatert.
Circa: 1940.

Rooms: 5 rooms with PB, 1 with FP. 2 suites.
Beds: KQT.

Bay windows accentuate the exterior of this stately Georgian Colonial home. A mix of modern and art deco furnishings decorate the interior. The home has an airy, uncluttered feel with its polished floors topped with Oriental rugs and muted tones. There is a canopy bed and fireplace in the spacious Garden Suite, and the Rose Suite overlooks the Willamette Valley. Other rooms offer garden views, bay windows or wicker furnishings. The house is located in what will be the Historical Terwilliger Boulevard Preserve.

Breakfast and afternoon tea included in rates. Types of meals: continental breakfast, continental-plus breakfast, full breakfast, gourmet breakfast and early coffee/tea. Air conditioning and cable TV in room. Library on premises. Family reunions hosted. Antiques, parks, shopping, sporting events and theater nearby. TAC10.

"Like staying in House Beautiful."

Seaside A2

Sand Dollar B&B

606 N Holladay Dr
Seaside, OR 97138-6926
(503)738-3491 (800)738-3491

Rates: $55-100.
Payment: MC VISA AX DS TC.
Innkeeper(s): Robert & Nita Hempfling.
Circa: 1920.

Rooms: 3 rooms with PB. 1 suite. 1 conference room.
Beds: KQT.

This Craftsman-style home looks a bit like a seashell, painted in light pink with pale blue trim. In fact, one of the guest rooms bears the name Sea Shell, filled with bright quilts and wicker. The Driftwood Room can be used as a two-bedroom suite for families. As the room names suggest, the house is decorated in a beach theme, graced by innkeeper Nita Hempfling's stained glasswork. The innkeepers also offer a cottage on the banks of the Necanicum River. The cottage includes a fully equipped kitchen and living room. Before breakfast is served, coffee or tea is delivered to the rooms.

Breakfast and evening snack included in rates. Ceiling fan, cable TV and VCR in room. Bicycles on premises. Weddings and small meetings hosted. Antiques, fishing, parks, shopping and watersports nearby.

Sisters D4

Conklin's Guest House

69013 Camp Polk Rd
Sisters, OR 97759-9705
(541)549-0123 (800)549-4262

Rates: $80-110.
Payment: PC TC.
Innkeeper(s): Frank & Marie Conklin.
Circa: 1910.

Rooms: 5 rooms with PB, 1 with FP. 1 suite.
Beds: QT.

The original portion of this Craftsman-style house was constructed in 1910, with later additions in 1938 and more recent changes in 1992 and 1993. Mountain views and four-and-a-half peaceful acres invite relaxation and romance. There are several ponds on the property stocked with trout for those wanting to try their hand at catch and release fishing. There is also a swimming pool. Three guest rooms have clawfoot tubs, and the Suite and Forget-Me-Not rooms offer a pleasing view. For those in a larger group, the inn's Dormitory room includes a queen bed and five single beds, at a rate of $25 to $30 per person. Sisters' airport is across the street from the home.

Breakfast and evening snack included in rates. Types of meals: full breakfast, gourmet breakfast and early coffee/tea. Ceiling fan in room. Swimming on premises. Handicap access. Weddings, small meetings, family reunions and seminars hosted. Spanish spoken. Fishing, parks, shopping, downhill skiing, cross-country skiing and watersports nearby.

Pets Allowed: On leash.

"A wonderful and romantic time for our wedding anniversary. Thanks so much. Oh-great fishing too."

OR

Tillamook B2

Blue Haven Inn

3025 Gienger Rd
Tillamook, OR 97141-8258
(503)842-2265
Fax:(503)842-2265

Rates: $60-75.
Payment: PC TC.
Innkeeper(s): Joy Still.
Circa: 1916.

Rooms: 3 rooms, 1 with PB.
Beds: QD.

This Craftsman-style home has been refurbished and filled with antiques and collectibles. Guest rooms feature limited-edition plate series as themes. Tall evergreens, lawns and flower gardens add to the setting.

Breakfast included in rates. Types of meals: full breakfast, gourmet breakfast and early coffee/tea. Cable TV, VCR, fax, bicycles and library on premises. Antiques, fishing, parks, shopping and watersports nearby. TAC5.

Publicity: *Oakland Tribune.*

"Your home is like a present to the eyes."

Waldport D2

Cliff House

1450 Adahi Rd Box 436
Waldport, OR 97394
(541)563-2506
Fax:(541)563-4393

Rates: $120-245.
Payment: MC VISA PC TC.
Innkeeper(s): Gabrielle Duvall.
Circa: 1987.

Rooms: 4 rooms with PB, 3 with FP. 1 suite.
Beds: KQ.

Guests enjoy a beautiful view of Oregon's coast at this seaside bed & breakfast. Chairs and chaise lounges are set up on the back deck for those wishing to enjoy the ocean breezes and scenery. The inn's Bridal Suite is an unique place to spend a honeymoon or anniversary night. Wood-paneled walls, ornate gold furnishings and a chandelier create an eclectic, romantic ambiance. Beds in the guest rooms, perhaps even a canopy bed, are set up so that guests can either enjoy a mountain or ocean view or a sparkling assortment of stars from an overhead skylight. Fresh fruit compote, crab meat quiche, eggs Benedict, French toast or fruit in puffed pastry are among the specialties served during the morning meal.

Breakfast and afternoon tea included in rates. Types of meals: full breakfast, gourmet breakfast and early coffee/tea. Catering service available. Turn-down service, cable TV and VCR in room. Fax, spa, swimming, sauna and library on premises. Weddings, small meetings and family reunions hosted. Spanish spoken. Antiques, fishing, parks, theater and watersports nearby.

Yachats D2

Sea Quest

95354 Hwy 101 S
Yachats, OR 97498-9713
(541)547-3782 (800)341-4878
Fax:(541)547-3719

Rates: $125+.
Payment: MC VISA DS PC.
Innkeeper(s): George & Elaine.
Circa: 1990.

Rooms: 5 rooms with PB.
Beds: Q.

This 6,000-square-foot cedar and glass house is only 100 feet from the ocean, located on two-and-one-half acres. Each guest room has a Jacuzzi tub and outside entrance. The second-floor breakfast room is distinguished by wide views of the ocean, forest and Ten Mile Creek. Guests are often found relaxing in front of the home's floor-to-ceiling brick fireplace. More adventuresome guests may enjoy the Oregon coast and nearby aquariums.

Breakfast included in rates. Types of meals: full breakfast and early coffee/tea. Fax, spa, sauna and library on premises. Antiques, fishing, parks, shopping and watersports nearby.

Location: One hundred feet from the water, where the forest meets the sea.

Stuffed Rosemary Bread

Sooke Harbour House
Sooke, B.C.

¼ sunflower oil
1 T snipped fresh rosemary or 1 ½ t dried rosemary
1 package active dry yeast
1 ¼ cups warm water (110- to 115-degrees)
3 ¼ to 3 ¾ cups all-purpose flour
1 t salt
2 cups finely chopped red onion
4 cloves garlic, minced
2 T sunflower oil
4 cups chopped fresh spinach or kale, stems or ribs removed
Pepper
6 oz. cold smoked salmon, cut into ½-inch pieces
2 T grated Parmesan cheese
1 egg, beaten

In a small saucepan, heat ¼ cup oil over low heat for two minutes. Add rosemary; cook two minutes more. Remove from heat; cool.

In a large mixing bowl, soften yeast in warm water for five minutes.

Add one cup of the flour, mix well. Stir in 1 t salt and rosemary mixture.

Stir in as much of the remaining flour as you can with a wooden spoon.

Turn dough onto a floured surface; knead in enough remaining flour to make moderately stiff dough that is smooth and elastic (takes six to eight minutes).

Shape dough into a ball. Place in greased bowl. Turn once to grease surface.

Cover; let rise in a warm place until double, about 45 minutes.

Meanwhile, prepare the filling. In a large skillet, cook onion and garlic in 2 T hot oil, covered, over medium heat for five minutes or until tender. Stir in spinach and cook, uncovered for three minutes or until spinach is wilted and most liquid is evaporated. Stir in pepper to taste.

Remove from heat. Stir in salmon and Parmesan cheese; set aside.

Punch dough down. Turn out onto a floured surface. Divide into four portions. Cover and let rest for 10 minutes. Roll each portion into a 6-inch circle. Spoon ¼ of the filling into the center of each circle. Pick up the edge of dough and gather all edges together over the stuffing. Pinch to seal and twist top.

Place on a greased baking sheet. Brush each with mixture of 1 egg beaten with 1 T cold water. Bake in a 375-degree oven for 35 minutes or until golden. Remove and cool slightly. Serve warm.

Makes 4.

Pennsylvania

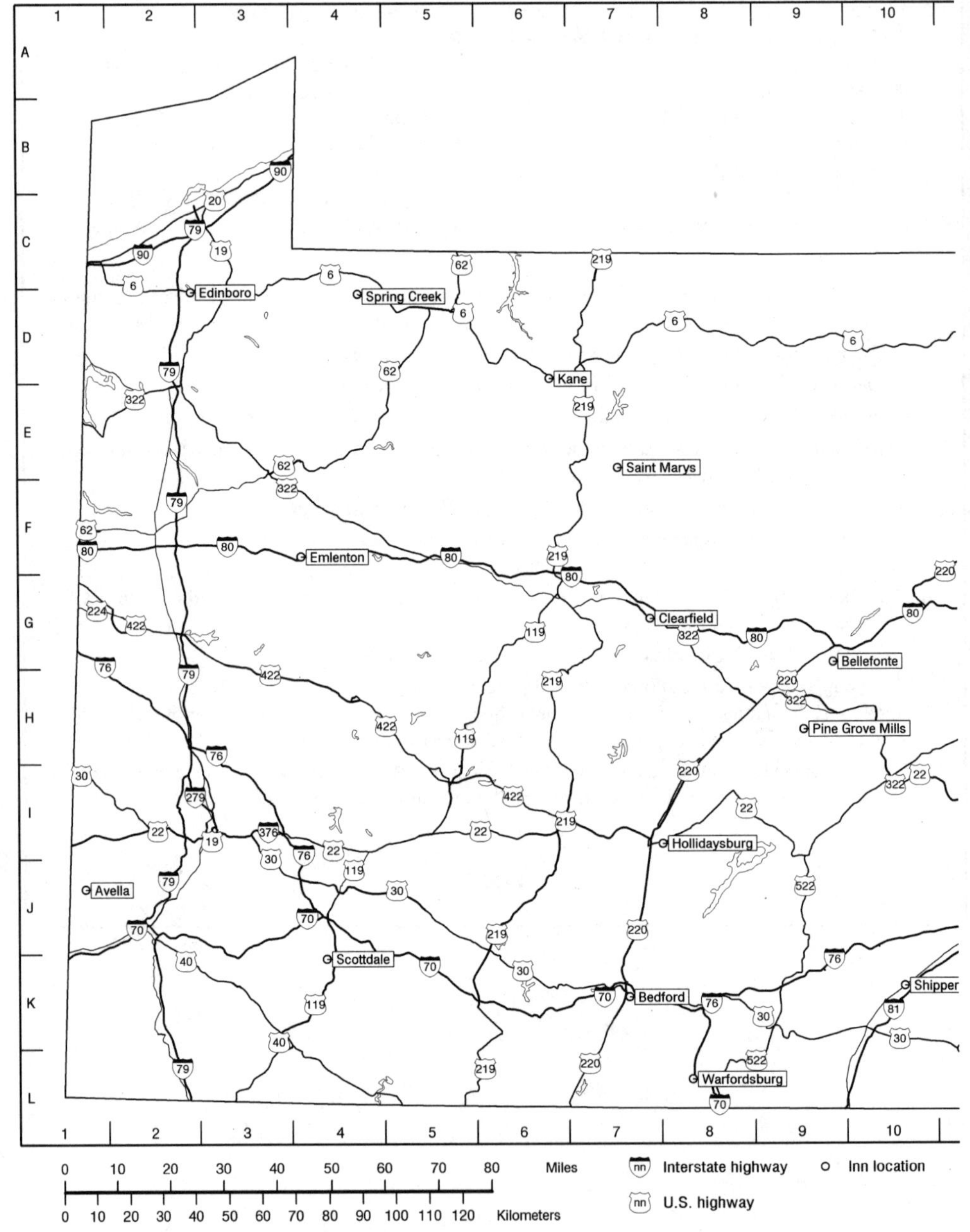

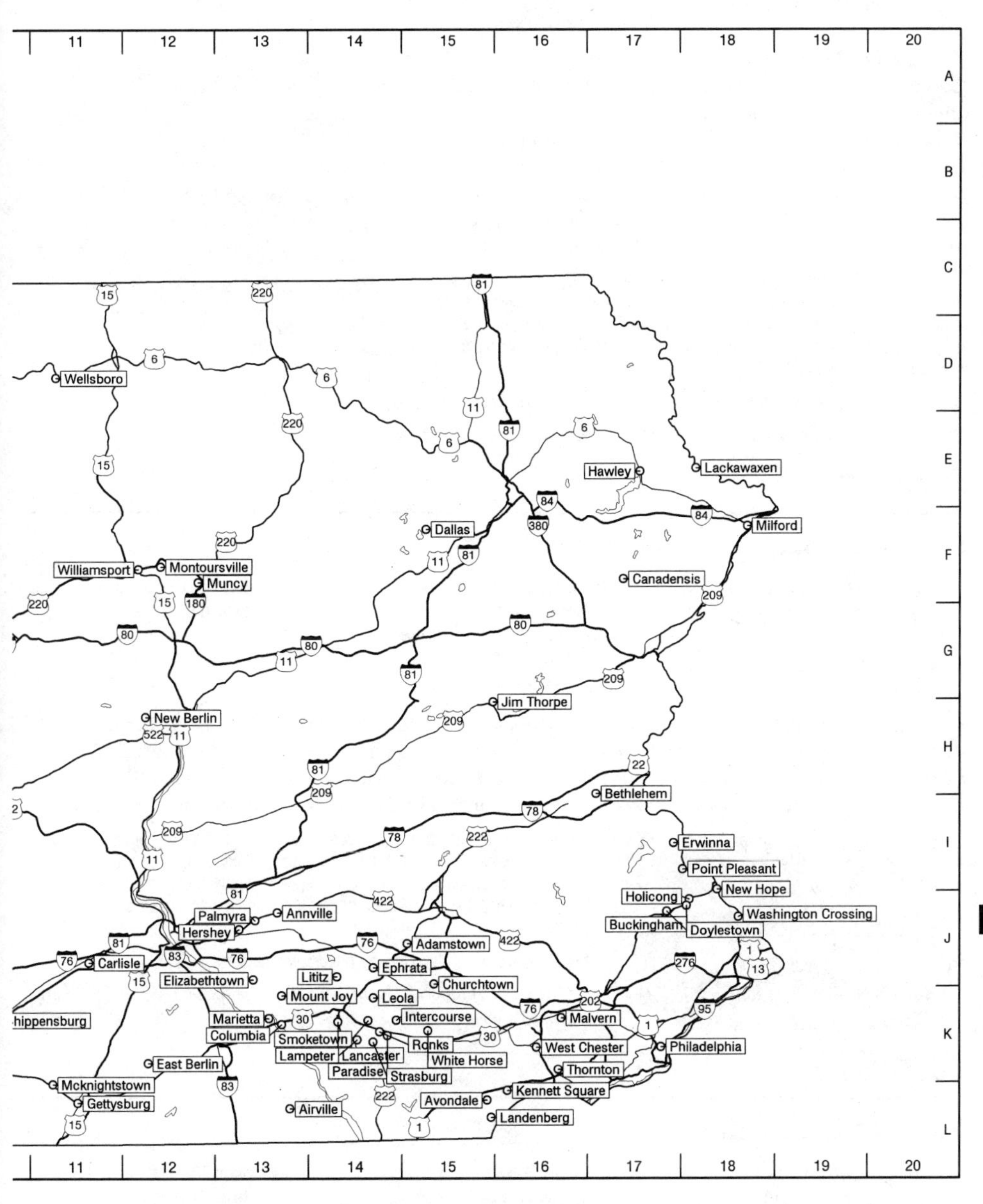

Wellsboro
Lackawaxen
Hawley
Milford
Dallas
Williamsport
Montoursville
Muncy
Canadensis
Jim Thorpe
New Berlin
Bethlehem
Erwinna
Point Pleasant
New Hope
Holicong
Washington Crossing
Buckingham
Doylestown
Palmyra
Annville
Hershey
Adamstown
Carlisle
Ephrata
Elizabethtown
Lititz
Churchtown
Mount Joy
Leola
Marietta
Intercourse
Malvern
Columbia
Smoketown
Ronks
West Chester
Philadelphia
Lampeter
Lancaster
White Horse
East Berlin
Paradise
Strasburg
Thornton
Mcknightstown
Kennett Square
Gettysburg
Avondale
Airville
Landenberg
hippensburg

PA

Adamstown

J15

Adamstown Inn

62 W Main St
Adamstown, PA 19501
(717)484-0800 (800)594-4808

Rates: $65-105.
Payment: MC VISA DS PC TC.
Innkeeper(s): Tom & Wanda Berman.
Circa: 1830.

Rooms: 4 rooms with PB, 2 with FP. 1 suite.
Beds: KQD.

This square brick house, with its 1850s pump organ found in the large parlor and other local folk art, fits right into this community (2,500 antique dealers) known as one of the antique capitols of America. Other decorations include family heirlooms, Victorian wallpaper, handmade quilts and lace curtains. Before breakfast, coffee, tea or hot chocolate is brought to your room. For outlet mall fans, Adamstown is 10 miles from Reading, which offers a vast assortment of top quality merchandise.

Breakfast, afternoon tea and evening snack included in rates. Types of meals: continental-plus breakfast and early coffee/tea. Air conditioning, ceiling fan and cable TV in room. Copier and library on premises. Small meetings, family reunions and seminars hosted. Amusement parks, antiques, fishing, parks, shopping and theater nearby. TAC10.

Publicity: *Lancaster Intelligencer, Reading Eagle, Travel & Leisure, Country Almanac.*

"Your warm hospitality and lovely home left us with such pleasant memories."

Airville

L13

Spring House

1264 Muddy Creek Forks Rd
Airville, PA 17302-9462
(717)927-6906
Fax:(717)927-8262

Rates: $60-95.
Payment: PC TC.
Innkeeper(s): Ray Hearne & Michael Schuster.
Circa: 1798.

Rooms: 4 rooms, 3 with PB. 1 cottage.
Beds: QD.

Spring House, the prominent home in this pre-Revolutionary War village located in a National Historic District, was constructed of massive stones over a spring that supplies water to most of the village. The walls are either whitewashed or retain their original stenciling. Furnished with country antiques, quilts, Oriental rugs, and paintings, the guest rooms are cozy with featherbeds in winter. The inn boasts a library and grand piano.

Breakfast and evening snack included in rates. Types of meals: full breakfast and gourmet breakfast. Fax and library on premises. Weddings, small meetings, family reunions and seminars hosted. Spanish spoken. Amusement parks, antiques, fishing, parks, shopping, cross-country skiing, theater and watersports nearby. TAC10.

Publicity: *Woman's Day, Country Decorating, Innsider.*

"What a slice of history! Thank you for your hospitality. We couldn't have imagined a more picturesque setting."

Annville

J13

Swatara Creek Inn

Box 692, Rd 2
Annville, PA 17003
(717)865-3259

Rates: $45-80.
Payment: MC VISA AX DC DS.
Innkeeper(s): Jeanette Hess.
Circa: 1860.

Rooms: 10 rooms with PB. 1 suite.
Beds: QT.

A former boys' home, this bed & breakfast now boasts canopy beds and lacy curtains. The first floor of this Victorian mansion provides a sitting room, dining room and gift shop. A full breakfast is served in the dining room, but honeymooners can request their meal in the comfort of their rooms. For chocolate lovers, nearby Hershey is a treat. Several shopping outlets are about an hour away or visit the Mount Hope Estate and Winery. For an unusual day trip, tour the Seltzer and Weaver Bologna plant in Lebanon. Each September, the town hosts a popular bologna festival. Nearby Lancaster County is the home of Amish communities.

Breakfast included in rates. Types of meals: full breakfast and early coffee/tea. Air conditioning in room. Handicap access. Small meetings and family reunions hosted. Amusement parks, antiques, fishing, parks, shopping, sporting events and theater nearby.

Publicity: *Daily News, Patriot-News.*

"Peaceful."

Avella J1

Weatherbury Farm

1061 Sugar Run Rd
Avella, PA 15312-2434
(412)587-3763
Fax:(412)587-0125

Rates: $65.
Payment: MC VISA.
Innkeeper(s): Dale, Marcy & Nigel Tudor.
Circa: 1870.

Rooms: 4 rooms with PB, 2 with FP.
Beds: KQDT.

Meadows, fields, gardens and valleys fill the 104 acres of this working farm where sheep, chickens, rabbits and cattle are raised. Stenciled walls, ceiling fans, wide-plank floors and fireplaces add to the country comforts. Peach French toast or garden vegetable eggs often are served and you may choose the garden, dining room or gazebo for your morning meal location. Enjoy porches, picnic spots, a swimming pool and the hammock.

Breakfast included in rates. Types of meals: full breakfast and early coffee/tea. Evening snack available. Air conditioning and ceiling fan in room. VCR, fax, copier, swimming, bicycles, library and child care on premises. 104 acres. Weddings and family reunions hosted. German spoken.

Publicity: *Observer, Enterprise, International Living, North Hills News Record, Pennsylvania Focus.*

"Your home and your hospitality was awesome."

Bedford K7

Bedford House

203 W Pitt St
Bedford, PA 15522-1237
(814)623-7171 (800)258-9868
Fax:(814)623-0832

Rates: $55-85.
Payment: MC VISA AX DS PC TC.
Innkeeper(s): Lyn & Linda Lyon.
Circa: 1807.

Rooms: 8 rooms with PB, 5 with FP. 1 suite. 1 cottage. 1 conference room.
Beds: KQDT.

PA

Five of the guests rooms in this beautiful 19th century home feature fireplaces. All rooms contain antiques, reproductions and family heirlooms. A full breakfast with seasonal fruits and homemade muffins, breads and entrees are served in the country kitchen. Relax on a porch that overlooks the garden or tour historic Bedford, a pre- Revolutionary War town. The inn is a five-minute walk from the Fort Bedford Museum and Park, shops and restaurants. Old Bedford Village is another popular touring attraction. Shawnee State Park and the Coral Caverns are nearby.

Breakfast included in rates. Types of meals: full breakfast and early coffee/tea. Air conditioning, cable TV and VCR in room. Fax on premises. Handicap access. Weddings, small meetings, family reunions and seminars hosted. Antiques, fishing, parks, shopping, downhill skiing, cross-country skiing, theater and watersports nearby. TAC10.

Location: Ninety-seven miles east of Pittsburgh.

Bellefonte G9

The Annie Natt House

127 W Curtin St
Bellefonte, PA 16823-1620
(814)353-1456
E-mail: dws9@psu.edu

Rates: $56-95.
Payment: AX PC.
Innkeeper(s): Doug & Wilda Stanfield.
Circa: 1882.

Rooms: 2 suites, 1 with FP.
Beds: DT.

Annie Natt was a fortunate woman. Her two daughters each married a successful iron master, and the two gentlemen built this Italianate-style home for their mother-in-law. Their own historic homes are nearby. Children are welcome here, and there is plenty of space. Each of the two suites are roomy and can accommodate up to five people comfortably. The downstairs suite includes a fireplace and kitchenette, and both have suites and sitting areas. Breakfasts are hearty with omelets, freshly baked biscuits or muffins, homemade jams, cereals and other treats served in the dining room on a table set with china and silver.

Breakfast and evening snack included in rates. Type of meal: full breakfast. Air conditioning and cable TV in room. VCR on premises. Antiques, fishing, parks, shopping, downhill skiing and sporting events nearby.

Special Discounts: Midweek discount.

"We could not have asked for a more delightful place to stay. Personal touches make any experience more pleasant and more memorable."

Reynolds Mansion B&B

101 W Linn St
Bellefonte, PA 16823-1622
(814)353-8407 (800)899-3929
E-mail: jheidt@boole.com

Rates: $75-125.
Payment: MC VISA PC.
Innkeeper(s): Joseph & Charlotte Heidt.
Circa: 1885.

Rooms: 6 rooms, 3 with PB, 2 with FP. 3 suites. 1 conference room.
Beds: KQ.

Bellefonte is a town with many impressive, historic homes, and this exquisite stone mansion is no exception. The home, a combination of late Victorian and Gothic styles, features extraordinary, hand-crafted woodwork and intricately laid wood floors, as well as eight fireplaces. Two guest rooms include a fireplace and some include a Jacuzzi tub. All enjoy a romantic atmosphere, heightened by candles, fresh flowers and the poshest of furnishings and decor. Baked stuffed French toast served with bacon or sausage is among the breakfast specialties, served with muffins, juices, cereals and a fruit compote created with more than a half dozen different fresh fruits. For a fun lunch or dinner, the innkeepers suggest the nearby Gamble Mill Tavern, a 200-year-old mill listed in the National Register.

Breakfast included in rates. Types of meals: continental-plus breakfast, full breakfast, gourmet breakfast and early coffee/tea. Cable TV, VCR, fax, copier and library on premises. Weddings, small meetings, family reunions and seminars hosted. Antiques, fishing, parks, shopping, downhill skiing, cross-country skiing, sporting events, theater and watersports nearby. TAC10.

"Your bed & breakfast is such an inspiration to us."

Bethlehem H17

Wydnor Hall

3612 Old Philadelphia Pike
Bethlehem, PA 18015-5320
(610)867-6851 (800)839-0020
Fax:(610)866-2062

Rates: $110-140.
Payment: MC VISA AX DC CB DS PC TC.
Innkeeper(s): Kristina & Charles Taylor.
Circa: 1810.

Rooms: 5 rooms with PB. 2 suites. 1 conference room.
Beds: KQD.

On the Old Philadelphia Pike, this Georgian fieldstone mansion is close to Lehigh University and the historic district. Tall trees shade the acre of grounds. Meticulously restored, the house is appointed with an English decor. Amenities include pressed linens, down comforters and terry cloth robes. The breakfast table is

set with fine china and silver. Homemade pastries, breads and cakes are served at tea time.

Breakfast included in rates. Type of meal: early coffee/tea. Afternoon tea available. Air conditioning, turn-down service, ceiling fan and cable TV in room. Fax on premises. Weddings and small meetings hosted. French and Hungarian spoken. Amusement parks, antiques and sporting events nearby. TAC10.

Publicity: *Express Times, Morning Call.*

"Wydnor Hall is warm, clean, charming, and comfortable. Your staff is cheerful, delightful and makes your guests feel graciously welcomed."

Buckingham J18

Mill Creek Farm B&B

PO Box 816, 2348 Quarry Rd
Buckingham, PA 18912
(215)794-0776 (800)562-1776
Fax:(215)794-8113

Rates: $100-140.
Payment: MC VISA AX PC TC.
Innkeeper(s): Holly Bogker.
Circa: 1730.

Rooms: 6 rooms, 4 with PB. 1 suite. 1 conference room.
Beds: Q.

One hundred Bucks Country acres surround this Federal farmhouse, a state historical site. Guest rooms are furnished with pleasing country antiques. Visit the inn's pastures and paddocks to enjoy the thoroughbred mares and yearlings. You also may wish to walk through the orchard or fish in the pond. The countryside provides lush scenery for cycling and jogging.

Breakfast and picnic lunch included in rates. Types of meals: full breakfast and early coffee/tea. Air conditioning, ceiling fan and cable TV in room. VCR, fax, copier, spa, swimming, sauna, stables, bicycles and tennis on premises. Weddings, small meetings, family reunions and seminars hosted. Amusement parks, antiques, fishing, parks, shopping, downhill skiing, cross-country skiing, theater and watersports nearby. TAC10.

Pets Allowed: Horses only.

Special Discounts: Third night: half off.

Canadensis F17

Brookview Manor B&B Inn

RR 1 Box 365
Canadensis, PA 18325-9740
(717)595-2451 (800)585-7974
Fax:(717)595-2065

Rates: $100-150.
Payment: MC VISA AX DS PC TC.
Innkeeper(s): Mary Anne Buckley.
Circa: 1911.

Rooms: 10 rooms, 9 with PB, 1 with FP. 1 suite.
Beds: QD.

PA

By the side of the road, hanging from a tall evergreen, is the welcoming sign to this forest retreat. There are brightly decorated common rooms and four fireplaces. The carriage house has three bedrooms and is suitable for small groups. The innkeepers like to share a "secret waterfall" within a 30-minute walk from the inn.

Breakfast and afternoon tea included in rates. Types of meals: full breakfast and early coffee/tea. Picnic lunch available. Air conditioning in room. Cable TV, fax and copier on premises. Weddings, small meetings and family reunions hosted. Amusement parks, antiques, fishing, parks, shopping, downhill skiing, cross-country skiing, theater and watersports nearby. TAC10.

Location: On Rt 447, Pocono Mountains.

Publicity: *Mid-Atlantic Country, Bridal Guide.*

"Thanks for a great wedding weekend. Everything was perfect."

The Merry Inn

PO Box 757, Rt 390
Canadensis, PA 18325-0757
(717)595-2011 (800)858-4182

Rates: $65-95.
Payment: MC VISA PC TC.
Innkeeper(s): Meredyth & Christopher Huggard.
Circa: 1942.

Rooms: 6 rooms.
Beds: KQDT.

Set in the picturesque Pocono Mountains, this inn is a 90-minute drive from the metropolitan New York and Philadelphia areas. The turn-of-the-century, mountainside home was built by two sisters and at one time was used as a boarding house. Current owners and innkeepers Meredyth and Chris Huggard have decorated their B&B using an eclectic mix of styles. Each guest room is individually appointed, with styles ranging from Victorian to country. Guests enjoy use of an outdoor Jacuzzi set into the mountainside. Bedroom are set up to accommodate families, and children are welcome here.

Breakfast included in rates. Type of meal: full breakfast. VCR on premises. Small meetings and family reunions hosted. Antiques, fishing, parks, shopping, downhill skiing, cross-country skiing, theater and watersports nearby.

Pets Allowed: Dogs must be trained, $25 deposit.

Carlisle

J11

Pheasant Field B&B

150 Hickorytown Rd
Carlisle, PA 17013-9732
(717)258-0717
Fax:(717)258-0717
E-mail: pheasant@pa.net

Rates: $65-95.
Payment: MC VISA AX.
Innkeeper(s): Denise Fegan.
Circa: 1800.

Rooms: 4 rooms, 2 with PB.
Beds: KQ.

Located on eight acres of central Pennsylvania farmland, this brick, two-story Federal-style farmhouse features wooden shutters and a covered front porch. An early 19th-century stone barn is on the property, and horse boarding often is available. The Appalachian Trail is less than a mile away. Fly-fishing is popular at Yellow Breeches and Letort Spring. Dickinson College and Carlisle Fairgrounds are other points of interest.

Breakfast included in rates. Types of meals: full breakfast and early coffee/tea. Air conditioning and turn-down service in room. Cable TV and VCR on premises. Weddings, small meetings and family reunions hosted. Amusement parks, antiques, fishing, downhill skiing, cross-country skiing and theater nearby.

Publicity: *Outdoor Traveler, Harrisburg Magazine.*

"You have an outstanding, charming and warm house. I felt for the first time as being home."

Churchtown

J15

Churchtown Inn B&B

2100 Main St, Rt 23
Churchtown, PA 17555
(717)445-7794

Rates: $69-95.
Payment: MC VISA DS PC TC.
Innkeeper(s): Hermine & Stuart Smith, Jim Kent.
Circa: 1735.

Rooms: 8 rooms with PB. 1 suite.
Beds: Q.

This handsome, stone Federal house with its panoramic views was once known as the Edward Davies Mansion, but was also once a tinsmith shop and rectory. It has heard the marching feet of Revolutionary troops and seen the Union Army during the Civil War. Tastefully furnished with antiques and collectables, the inn features canopy, pencil-post and sleigh beds. Breakfast is served in a lovely new glass garden room. There is music everywhere, as the innkeeper directed choruses appearing at Carnegie Hall and the Lincoln Center. By prior arrangement, guests may dine in an Amish home.

Breakfast included in rates. Type of meal: full breakfast. Air conditioning and cable TV in room. VCR on premises. Small meetings, family reunions and seminars hosted. Antiques, fishing, parks and shopping nearby.

Location: Five miles from Pennsylvania Turnpike.

Publicity: *Bon Appetit, Boston Globe, Intelligencer Journal, Innsider, Chicago Star.*

Special Discounts: Book 6 days - 7th day free.

"Magnificent atmosphere. Outstanding breakfasts. Our favorite B&B."

Clearfield G7

Christopher Kratzer House

101 E Cherry St
Clearfield, PA 16830-2315
(814)765-5024 (888)252-2632

Rates: $55-70.
Payment: MC VISA DS PC TC.
Innkeeper(s): Bruce & Ginny Baggett.
Circa: 1840.

Rooms: 4 rooms, 1 with PB.
Beds: KQT.

This inn is the oldest home in town, built by a carpenter and architect who also started Clearfield's first newspaper. The innkeepers keep a book of history about the house and town for interested guests. The interior is a mix of antiques from different eras, many are family pieces. There are collections of art and musical instruments. Several guest rooms afford views of the Susquehanna River. Refreshments and a glass of wine are served in the afternoons. The innkeeper's Bridal Suite Special includes complimentary champagne, fruit and snacks, and breakfast is served in the privacy of your room.

Breakfast, afternoon tea and evening snack included in rates. Types of meals: gourmet breakfast and early coffee/tea. Ceiling fan and cable TV in room. Library on premises. Weddings, small meetings and family reunions hosted. Antiques, fishing, parks, shopping, downhill skiing, cross-country skiing, sporting events and theater nearby.

Special Discounts: 20% discount for Lock Haven University parents/students and for all stays over three days.

Victorian Loft B&B

216 S Front St
Clearfield, PA 16830-2218
(814)765-4805 (800)798-0456
Fax:(814)765-9596
E-mail: 70724,146@compuserve.com

Rates: $45-100.
Payment: MC VISA AX DS PC TC.
Innkeeper(s): Tim & Peggy Durant.
Circa: 1894.

Rooms: 3 rooms, 1 with PB. 1 suite. 1 cottage.
Beds: QD.

Accommodations at this bed & breakfast are available in either a historic Victorian home on the riverfront or in a private, three-bedroom cabin. The white brick home is dressed with colorful, gingerbread trim, and inside, a grand staircase, stained glass and antique furnishings add to the Victorian charm. The suite is ideal for families as it contains two bedrooms, a living room, dining room, kitchen and a bath with a whirlpool tub. The cabin, Cedarwood Lodge, sleeps six and is located on eight, wooded acres near Elliot State Park. This is a favorite setting for small groups.

Breakfast included in rates. Types of meals: full breakfast and early coffee/tea. Cable TV and VCR on premises. Small meetings and family reunions hosted. Limited Spanish spoken. Antiques, fishing, parks, shopping, cross-country skiing, sporting events, theater and watersports nearby. TAC10.

Pets Allowed: By prior arrangement.

Special Discounts: 10% discount over three nights stay.

"A feeling of old fashion beauty. The elegance of roses and lace. All wrapped up into a romantic moment."

Columbia

K13

The Columbian

360 Chestnut St
Columbia, PA 17512-1156
(717)684-5869 (800)422-5869
E-mail: bedandb@aol.com

Rates: $70-89.
Payment: MC VISA PC TC.
Innkeeper(s): Chris & Becky Will.
Circa: 1897.

Rooms: 6 rooms with PB, 1 with FP. 1 suite.
Beds: QT.

This stately three-story mansion is a fine example of Colonial Revival architecture. Antique beds, a stained-glass window and home-baked breads are among its charms. Guests may relax on the wraparound sun porches.

Breakfast included in rates. Type of meal: full breakfast. Air conditioning, ceiling fan and cable TV in room. Weddings, small meetings and family reunions hosted. Amusement parks, antiques, fishing, parks, shopping, downhill skiing, cross-country skiing, sporting events, theater and watersports nearby.

Publicity: *Philadelphia Inquirer, Lancaster Intelligencer Journal, Columbia News, Washington Post, Potomac.*

Special Discounts: Winter weekend getaway, $99-$129, includes breakfast and dinner.

"In a word, extraordinary! Truly a home away from home. First B&B experience but will definitely not be my last."

Dallas

F15

Ponda-Rowland B&B Inn

RR 1 Box 349
Dallas, PA 18612-9604
(717)639-3245 (800)854-3286
Fax:(717)639-5531

Rates: $70-95.
Payment: MC VISA AX DS PC TC.
Innkeeper(s): Jeanette & Cliff Rowland.
Circa: 1850.

Rooms: 5 rooms with PB, 2 with FP.
Beds: KDT.

Situated on a 130-acre farm, this historic house overlooks a 30-acre wildlife sanctuary with six ponds, feeding stations and trails visited by whitetail deer, fox, turkeys, mallard ducks, Canadian geese and occasionally, blue herons. The home is filled with beautiful American country antiques and collections. There are beamed ceilings and a stone fireplace in the living room. The scenic setting, hospitable hosts, farm animals and hearty country breakfast make this a perfect place for a memorable vacation. Hayrides may be arranged by advance reservations.

Breakfast, afternoon tea and evening snack included in rates. Types of meals: full breakfast and early coffee/tea. Air conditioning and ceiling fan in room. Cable TV, VCR, fax, copier, stables, library, pet boarding and child care on premises. 130 acres. Amusement parks, antiques, fishing, parks, shopping, downhill skiing, cross-country skiing, sporting events, theater and watersports nearby. TAC10.

Pets Allowed: Not in inn or rooms.

"Warm and friendly people who made us feel right at home."

Doylestown

J17

Peace Valley B&B

75 Chapman Rd
Doylestown, PA 18901
(215)230-7711

Rates: $90-135.
Payment: MC VISA AX PC TC.
Innkeeper(s): Harry & Jane Beard.
Circa: 1791.

Rooms: 4 rooms with PB, 2 with FP.
Beds: KQT.

This 18th-century, stone Colonial home rests by the banks of a one-acre pond. Rooms are elegantly furnished with antiques and reproductions in traditional style. Some rooms include four-poster beds, and two have a fireplace. On weekdays, continental-plus breakfasts are served. Weekend guests enjoy a full breakfast. The bed & breakfast is adjacent to Peace Valley Park and Lake Galena, which offer nature trails.

Breakfast included in rates. Types of meals: continental-plus breakfast and full breakfast. Air conditioning and turn-down service in room. Cable TV, VCR, copier, tennis and pet boarding on premises. Small meetings hosted. Antiques, parks and shopping nearby. TAC10.

East Berlin

K12

Bechtel Mansion Inn

400 W King St
East Berlin, PA 17316
(717)259-7760 (800)331-1108

Rates: $85-150.
Payment: MC VISA AX DC DS PC TC.
Innkeeper(s): Ruth Spangler.
Circa: 1897.

Rooms: 7 rooms with PB. 2 suites. 1 conference room.
Beds: KQD.

The town of East Berlin, near Lancaster and Gettysburg, was settled by Pennsylvania Germans prior to the American Revolution. William Leas, a wealthy banker, built this many-gabled romantic Queen Anne mansion, now listed in the National Register. The inn is furnished with an abundance of museum-quality antiques and collections. Mennonite quilts top many of the handsome bedsteads.

Breakfast included in rates. Types of meals: full breakfast and early coffee/tea. Air conditioning in room. Library on premises. Weddings, small meetings and family reunions hosted. Antiques, shopping, downhill skiing, cross-country skiing and theater nearby.

Location: Located 18 miles east of Gettysburg in a National Historic District.

Publicity: *Washington Post, Richmond Times.*

"Ruth was a most gracious hostess and took time to describe the history of your handsome museum-quality antiques and the special architectural details."

Edinboro

D2

Raspberry House B&B

118 Erie St
Edinboro, PA 16412-2209
(814)734-8997

Rates: $65-70.
Payment: MC VISA PC.
Innkeeper(s): Betty & Hal Holmstrom.
Circa: 1867.

Rooms: 4 rooms with PB.
Beds: KQDT.

Raspberry gingerbread trim and stained glass are whimsical features of this early Victorian home, built by a doctor just a few years after the Civil War ended. The innkeepers painstakingly restored the home, leaving many original elements, including chandeliers, pocket doors and wooden shutters. To keep the authentic Victorian flavor, reproduction wallpapers were used. Guest quarters are decorated in an eclectic style, intermingling country and modern pieces. As one might expect from the name, items such as raspberry muffins or baked apples with raspberries often find their way onto the breakfast table. Raspberry House is located in the center of downtown Edinboro and is near the university, restaurants, shopping and Edinboro Lake.

Breakfast included in rates. Types of meals: gourmet breakfast and early coffee/tea. Air conditioning and ceiling fan in room. Cable TV, VCR and bicycles on premises. Weddings, small meetings, family reunions and seminars hosted. Amusement parks, antiques, fishing, parks, shopping, downhill skiing, cross-country skiing, sporting events, theater and watersports nearby.

Special Discounts: Winter family ski packages.

"The Raspberry House is exceptionally high on our list of pleasing and rewarding experiences."

Elizabethtown

J13

Apples Abound Inn B&B

518 S Market St
Elizabethtown, PA 17022
(717)367-3018
Fax:(717)367-9788

Rates: $70-95.
Payment: MC VISA PC TC.
Innkeeper(s): Jennifer & Jon Sheppard.
Circa: 1907.

Rooms: 5 rooms with PB.
Beds: QD.

As the name suggests, apples do abound at this early 20th-century home, which features a unique apple collection. In the local historic register, this three-story, brick Victorian has a turret and a wide, wraparound veranda. Other features include cranberry-colored glass transoms, bay windows, a stained-glass window, chestnut wood trim and doors and built-in china cabinets. Rooms are decorated with antiques and a traditional country decor. Lancaster, Harrisburg and Hershey are nearby.

Breakfast included in rates. Types of meals: full breakfast and early coffee/tea. Air conditioning, turn-down service and ceiling fan in room. Small meetings hosted. Amusement parks, antiques, fishing, parks, shopping, downhill skiing, cross-country skiing and sporting events nearby. TAC10.

Emlenton

F4

Whippletree Inn & Farm

RR 3 Box 285
Emlenton, PA 16373-9102
(412)867-9543

Rates: $50-60.
Payment: MC VISA TC.
Innkeeper(s): Warren & Joey Simmons.
Circa: 1905.

Rooms: 5 rooms, 2 with PB.
Beds: KQDT.

The 100 hilltop acres of Whippletree Farm overlook the Allegheny River, and a trail on the property leads down to the river. The restored farmhouse contains many functional antiques. If you have your own horse, you are invited to use the farm's race track. The oldest continuously operated public country club in the United States is five miles away in Foxburg and the American Golf Hall of Fame is there. The innkeepers host team penning events for 4H.

Breakfast included in rates. Types of meals: full breakfast, gourmet breakfast and early coffee/tea. Afternoon tea available. Air conditioning and ceiling fan in room. Cable TV, VCR, copier, library and pet boarding on premises. 100 acres. Weddings, small meetings, family reunions and seminars hosted. Antiques, fishing, parks, shopping and watersports nearby.

Pets Allowed: Restricted to pens.

Ephrata

J14

Martin House

265 Ridge Ave
Ephrata, PA 17522-2554
(717)733-6804 (888)651-8418
E-mail: vmartin@prolog.net

Rates: $55-115.
Payment: PC TC.
Innkeeper(s): Moses & Vera Martin.
Circa: 1990.

Rooms: 4 rooms, 3 with PB. 2 suites.
Beds: KQD.

This contemporary house offers a hint of chateau in its architecture and is set against a wooded area. This homestay has three bedrooms, including one with a waterbed. Your hosts serve eggs and sausage or quiche for breakfast. A large deck looks out to the trees.

Breakfast and evening snack included in rates. Types of meals: full breakfast and early coffee/tea. Air conditioning, ceiling fan and cable TV in room. VCR on premises. Amusement parks, antiques, fishing, parks, shopping, theater and watersports nearby.

"We're so glad we found you, it was wonderful."

Smithton Inn

900 W Main St
Ephrata, PA 17522
(717)733-6094

Rates: $75-170.
Payment: MC VISA PC TC.
Innkeeper(s): Dorothy Graybill.
Circa: 1763.

Rooms: 8 rooms with PB, 8 with FP. 1 suite.
Beds: KQD.

Henry Miller opened this inn and tavern on a hill overlooking the Ephrata Cloister, a religious society he belonged to, known as Seventh Day Baptists. Several of their medieval-style German buildings are now a museum. This is a warm and welcoming inn with canopy or four-posters beds, candlelight, fireplaces and night-shirts provided for each guest. If you're not allergic, ask for a lavish feather bed to be put in your room. All rooms boast sitting areas with reading lamps, fresh flowers and the relaxing sounds of chamber music. The grounds include wonderful gardens.

Breakfast included in rates. Type of meal: full breakfast. Air conditioning in room. Library on premises. Amusement parks, antiques, fishing, parks, shopping and theater nearby.

Pets Allowed: No cats. Dogs, obedience trained, with owners at all times.

Location: Lancaster County.

Publicity: *New York, Country Living, Early American Life.*

"After visiting over 50 inns in four countries, Smithton has to be one of the most romantic, picturesque inns in America. I have never seen its equal!"

Erwinna (Bucks County)

Evermay-On-The-Delaware

River Rd, PO Box 60, Erwinna
(Bucks County), PA 18920
(610)294-9100
Fax:(610)294-8249

Rates: $85-180.
Payment: MC VISA PC TC.
Innkeeper(s): Bill & Danielle Moffly.
Circa: 1700.

Rooms: 16 rooms with PB. 1 suite. 2 cottages. 2 conference rooms.
Beds: QD.

Twenty-five acres of Bucks County at its best — rolling green meadows, lawns, stately maples and the silvery Delaware River, surround this three-story manor. Serving as an inn since 1871, it has hosted such guests as the Barrymore family. Rich walnut wainscoting, a grandfather clock and twin fireplaces warm the parlor, scented by vases of roses or gladiolus. Antique-filled guest rooms overlook the river or gardens.

Breakfast and afternoon tea included in rates. Type of meal: continental-plus breakfast. Dinner and picnic lunch available. Air conditioning and turn-down service in room. VCR, fax, copier, computer, swimming and library on premises. Handicap access. 25 acres. Weddings, small meetings and seminars hosted. German spoken. Antiques, fishing, parks, shopping, cross-country skiing, sporting events, theater and watersports nearby. TAC10.

Publicity: *New York Times, Philadelphia, Travel & Leisure, Food and Wine, Child.*

"It was pure perfection. Everything from the flowers to the wonderful food."

Gettysburg

L11

Baladerry Inn

40 Hospital Rd
Gettysburg, PA 17325
(717)337-1342 (800)220-0025

Rates: $78-98.
Payment: MC VISA AX DC CB DS PC TC.
Innkeeper(s): Tom & Caryl O'Gara.
Circa: 1812.

Rooms: 8 rooms with PB, 2 with FP. 3 conference rooms.
Beds: KQT.

Set on the edge of the Gettysburg Battlefield, this brick country manor was used as a hospital during the Civil War. Additions were added in 1830 and 1977, and the inn has been completely restored. Guests can snuggle up with a book in their comfortable rooms or in the great room, which includes a fireplace. The spacious grounds offer gardens, a gazebo, a tennis court and dining terraces, where guests enjoy the country breakfasts. Guided tours and bicycle tours of the battlefield can be arranged, and guests also can plan a horseback riding excursion on the battlefield.

Breakfast and evening snack included in rates. Types of meals: full breakfast and early coffee/tea. Catering service available. Air conditioning in room. VCR, bicycles and tennis on premises. Weddings, small meetings, family reunions and seminars hosted. Antiques, fishing, parks, shopping, downhill skiing, cross-country skiing, sporting events and theater nearby. TAC10.

Location: Country setting at the edge of Gettysburg Battlefield.

Publicity: *Gettysburg Times, Allentown Morning Call, Pennsylvania Magazine.*

Special Discounts: Package events: Civil War ball, dinner with President Lincoln.

Battlefield B&B

2264 Emmitsburg Rd
Gettysburg, PA 17325-7114
(717)334-8804
Fax:(717)334-7330

Rates: $116-159.
Payment: MC VISA AX DS PC TC.
Innkeeper(s): Charlie & Florence Tarbox.
Circa: 1809.

Rooms: 8 rooms with PB, 2 with FP. 2 suites. 1 conference room.
Beds: QDT.

Ponds, woods and streams fill the 46 acres of this historic estate. This stone boasts four Confederate-themed guest rooms and four Union rooms. Hart's Battery provides a canopy bed and granite walls while General Merritt's Headquarters takes up an entire floor of the Cornelius Houghtelin farmhouse and includes a fireplace and sitting room. Daily programs offer history demonstrations such as handling calvary equipment, firing of artillery, hearth and fireplace cookery and Civil War gaming. Battlefield stories abound and in summer, carriage rides are offered.

Breakfast included in rates. Types of meals: full breakfast, gourmet breakfast and early coffee/tea. Air conditioning in room. VCR, fax, copier and library on premises. 46 acres. Weddings, small meetings, family reunions and seminars hosted. Antiques, parks, shopping, downhill skiing, cross-country skiing and theater nearby. TAC10.

Special Discounts: Weekend special events-event/dining/two day stays/winter.

The Brafferton Inn

44 York St
Gettysburg, PA 17325-2301
(717)337-3423

Rates: $80-125.
Payment: MC VISA AX DS PC TC.
Innkeeper(s): Jane & Sam Back.
Circa: 1786.

Rooms: 10 rooms with PB. 2 suites.
Beds: QDT.

Aside from its notoriety as the first deeded house in what became the town of Gettysburg, The Brafferton bears the mark of a bullet hole shot through the fireplace mantel during the Civil War battle. The rooms are filled with 18th- and 19th- century antiques that belong to the owners' families. The dining room boasts a unique mural painted on all four walls depicting the early town of Gettysburg. Lavish breakfasts are served in the colorful room on tables set with English china, old silver and pineapple-pattern glass goblets. Guest quarters are available in the original house or in the old carriage house across the brick atrium. Carriage house rooms feature stenciling and skylights. The garden area offers a large wooden deck to relax on as guests take in the view. The National Register inn is near to all of Gettysburg's historic attractions, including the Gettysburg National Military Park.

Breakfast included in rates. Types of meals: full breakfast and early coffee/tea. Air conditioning in room. Cable TV on premises. Weddings, small meetings and family reunions hosted. French spoken. Antiques, fishing, parks, shopping, downhill skiing, cross-country skiing, sporting events and theater nearby. TAC10.

Location: Ninety miles north of Washington, D.C.

Publicity: *Early American Life, Country Living, Gettysburg Times.*

Special Discounts: Quiet season special weekends.

"Your house is so beautiful — every corner of it — and your friendliness is icing on the cake. It was fabulous! A wonderful historical adventure!"

Brickhouse Inn

425 Baltimore St
Gettysburg, PA 17325-2623
(717)338-9337 (800)864-3464
Fax:(717)338-9265

Rates: $85-105.
Payment: MC VISA PC TC.
Innkeeper(s): Craig & Marion Schmitz.
Circa: 1898.

Rooms: 3 rooms with PB.
Beds: QD.

A veranda, dressed in gingerbread trim, decorates the exterior of this red brick Victorian. The interior still maintains its original cherry woodwork and pocket doors. Family heirlooms and antiques are featured in the guest rooms. One room offers walls in a deep burgundy hue and a bed topped with a colorful quilt. Another has a black iron bed, fine antiques and a bay window. Breakfasts with items such as a shoefly pie or baked French toast topped with blueberries are served on the brick patio, which overlooks the lawn. In the afternoons, cookies and lemonade also are served here. The home is located in Gettysburg's downtown historic district. The innkeepers keep a collection of Civil War books on hand for history buffs.

Breakfast included in rates. Type of meal: full breakfast. Air conditioning and ceiling fan in room. Fax and copier on premises. Amusement parks, antiques, fishing, parks, shopping, downhill skiing, cross-country skiing, sporting events and theater nearby.

"Beautifully presented."

The Doubleday Inn

104 Doubleday Ave
Gettysburg, PA 17325-0815
(717)334-9119

Rates: $84-104.
Payment: MC VISA DS.
Innkeeper(s): Ruth Anne & Charles Wilcox.
Circa: 1929.

Rooms: 9 rooms, 5 with PB.
Beds: DT.

This Colonial Inn is situated directly on the Gettysburg Battlefield. From its wooded grounds, flower gardens and guest patios, guests enjoy panoramic views of historic Gettysburg and the National Military Park. The innkeepers have a significant collection of Civil War relics and books on hand, and on selected evenings they feature presentations with battlefield historians. Rooms are furnished with antiques and decorated in English country style. A full, country-style breakfast is served by candlelight each morning, and the innkeepers offer a selection of teas in the afternoon.

Breakfast and afternoon tea included in rates. Types of meals: full breakfast and early coffee/tea. Picnic lunch available. Air conditioning in room. Weddings, small meetings and family reunions hosted. Amusement parks, antiques, fishing, parks, shopping, downhill skiing, cross-country skiing, sporting events and theater nearby. TAC10.

Location: On the Gettysburg Battlefield.

Publicity: *Innsider, New York, State College, Washingtonian, Potomac.*

"What you're doing for students of Gettysburg & the Civil War in general is tremendous! Our stay was wonderful!!"

PA

Keystone Inn B&B

231 Hanover St
Gettysburg, PA 17325-1913
(717)337-3888

Rates: $59-100.
Payment: MC VISA DS.
Innkeeper(s): Wilmer & Doris Martin.
Circa: 1913.

Rooms: 5 rooms, 3 with PB. 1 suite.
Beds: KQDT.

Furniture maker Clayton Reaser constructed this three-story brick Victorian with a wide-columned porch hugging the north and west sides. Cut stone graces every door and windowsill, each with a keystone. A chestnut staircase ascends the full three stories, and the interior is decorated with comfortable furnishings, ruffles and lace.

Breakfast and afternoon tea included in rates. Types of meals: full breakfast and early coffee/tea. Air conditioning in room. Library on premises. Family reunions hosted. Amusement parks, antiques, fishing, parks, shopping, downhill skiing, cross-country skiing and theater nearby.

Location: Route 116 - East Gettysburg.

Publicity: *Gettysburg Times, Hanover Sun, York Sunday News, Pennsylvania, Lancaster Sunday News, Los Angeles Times.*

Special Discounts: Weekday special four nights, Sunday through Thursday, one night free.

"We slept like lambs. This home has a warmth that is soothing."

The Old Appleford Inn

218 Carlisle St
Gettysburg, PA 17325-1305
(717)337-1711 (800)275-3373
Fax:(717)334-6228

Rates: $73-118.
Payment: MC VISA AX DS.
Innkeeper(s): John & Jane Wiley.
Circa: 1867.

Rooms: 10 rooms with PB, 2 with FP. 1 suite.
Beds: QD.

Located in the historic district, this Italianate-style brick mansion offers a taste of 19th-century charm and comfort. Among its inviting features are a plant-filled sunroom and a parlor with refurbished, 1918 grand piano. The innkeepers also display fine, linen needlework samplers and collection of antique musical instruments. As the inn was built just following the Civil War, the innkeepers have tried to keep a sense of turbulent history present. Most of the guest rooms are named for Civil War generals, another for Abraham Lincoln. Breakfasts are a fashionable affair served on fine china in the inn's Victorian dining room.

Breakfast and afternoon tea included in rates. Types of meals: full breakfast and early coffee/tea. Catering service available. Air conditioning in room. Fax and library on premises. Weddings, small meetings and family reunions hosted. Amusement parks, antiques, parks, shopping, downhill skiing and theater nearby. TAC10.

Location: Two blocks from downtown, near battlefield and historic attractions.

Publicity: *Innsider, Gettysburg Times, Baltimore Sun, Philadelphia Magazine.*

"Everything in your place invites us back."

Hawley E17

Academy Street B&B

528 Academy St
Hawley, PA 18428-1434
(717)226-3430
Fax:(201)335-5051

Rates: $65-80.
Payment: MC VISA.
Innkeeper(s): Judith Lazan.
Circa: 1863.

Rooms: 7 rooms, 4 with PB.
Beds: QDT.

This restored Civil War Victorian home boasts a mahogany front door with the original glass paneling, two large fireplaces (one in mosaic, the other in fine polished marble) and a living room with oak sideboard, polished marble mantel and yellow pine floor. The airy guest rooms have canopied brass beds. Guests are welcome to afternoon tea, which includes an array of cakes and pastries. Full, gourmet breakfast on weekends.

Breakfast and afternoon tea included in rates. Type of meal: early coffee/tea. Air conditioning, ceiling fan and cable TV in room. VCR on premises. Weddings and family reunions hosted. Amusement parks, antiques, fishing, parks, shopping, theater and watersports nearby. TAC10.

Publicity: *Wayne Independent, Citizens' Voice.*

"Truly wonderful everything!"

Settlers Inn at Bingham Park

4 Main Ave
Hawley, PA 18428-1114
(717)226-2993 (800)833-8527
Fax:(717)226-1874
E-mail: settler@prolog.pdt.net

Rates: $80-120.
Payment: MC VISA AX DS PC TC.
Innkeeper(s): Jeanne & Grant Genzlinger.
Circa: 1927.

Rooms: 18 rooms with PB. 4 suites. 2 conference rooms.
Beds: QD.

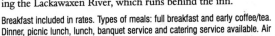

When the Wallenpaupack Creek was dammed up to form the lake, the community hired architect Louis Welch and built this Grand Tudor Revival-style hotel featuring chestnut beams, leaded-glass windows and an enormous stone fireplace. The dining room, the main focus of the inn, is decorated with antique prints, hanging plants and chairs that once graced a Philadelphia cathedral. If you're looking for trout you can try your luck fishing the Lackawaxen River, which runs behind the inn.

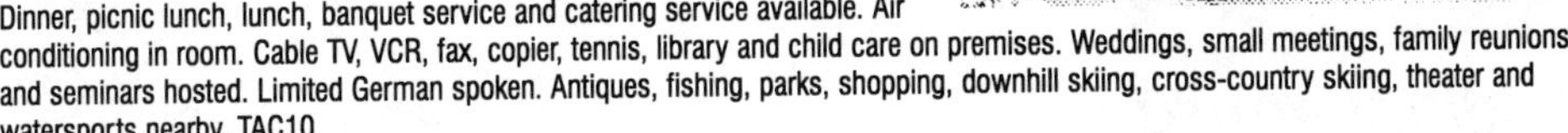

Breakfast included in rates. Types of meals: full breakfast and early coffee/tea. Dinner, picnic lunch, lunch, banquet service and catering service available. Air conditioning in room. Cable TV, VCR, fax, copier, tennis, library and child care on premises. Weddings, small meetings, family reunions and seminars hosted. Limited German spoken. Antiques, fishing, parks, shopping, downhill skiing, cross-country skiing, theater and watersports nearby. TAC10.

Publicity: *Travel Holiday, New Jersey Monthly, Philadelphia, New York Newsday, Philadelphia Inquirer.*

Special Discounts: Ask for promotional rates.

"Country cozy with food and service fit for royalty."

Hershey J13

Gibson's B&B

141 W Caracas Ave
Hershey, PA 17033-1511
(717)534-1305

Rates: $40-55.
Payment: PC TC.
Innkeeper(s): Bob, Frances & Jamie Gibson.
Circa: 1933.

Rooms: 3 rooms.
Beds: DT.

Downtown Hershey is the location for this comfortable bed & breakfast. The Cape Cod-style home is simply furnished with Early American, modern and country-style pieces. The innkeepers, a mother-father-son team, live in the home and enjoy chatting with guests and helping them plan daily excursions. Home-baked items on the breakfast menu vary from day to day, often including scones, biscuits, eggs and breakfast meats. It is half an hour to Lititz and Lancaster, and minutes to Hershey's attractions.

Breakfast included in rates. Types of meals: full breakfast and early coffee/tea. Air conditioning and ceiling fan in room. Cable TV and VCR on premises. Italian spoken. Amusement parks, antiques, parks, shopping, sporting events, theater and watersports nearby.

"Exquisite hospitality."

Hershey (Palmyra) J13

The Hen-Apple B&B

409 S Lingle Ave
Palmyra, PA 17078-9321
(717)838-8282

Rates: $55-75.
Payment: MC VISA AX TC.
Innkeeper(s): Flo & Harold Echert.
Circa: 1825.

Rooms: 6 rooms with PB.
Beds: QDT.

Located at the edge of town, this Georgian farmhouse is surrounded by an acre of lawns and gardens. There are antiques and country pieces, along with a collection of wicker in the Wicker Room. Breakfast is provided in the dining room or the screened porch. Hershey is two miles away.

Breakfast included in rates. Type of meal: full breakfast. Air conditioning and ceiling fan in room. Cable TV on premises. Amusement parks, antiques, fishing, parks, shopping, sporting events, theater and watersports nearby. TAC10.

Holicong

J18

Barley Sheaf Farm

5281 York Rd, Rt 202 Box 10
Holicong, PA 18928
(215)794-5104
Fax:(215)794-5332

Rates: $105-255.
Payment: MC VISA AX PC TC.
Innkeeper(s): Peter Suess.
Circa: 1740.

Rooms: 12 rooms with PB, 3 with FP. 4 suites. 3 conference rooms.
Beds: KQD.

Situated on part of the original William Penn land grant, this beautiful stone house with white shuttered windows and mansard roof is set on 30 acres of farmland. Once owned by noted playwright George Kaufman, it was the gathering place for the Marx Brothers, Lillian Hellman and S. J. Perlman. The bank barn, pond and majestic old trees round out a beautiful setting.

Breakfast and afternoon tea included in rates. Types of meals: full breakfast and early coffee/tea. Catering service available. Air conditioning in room. Cable TV, VCR, fax, copier and swimming on premises. Handicap access. 30 acres. Weddings, small meetings, family reunions and seminars hosted. German and French spoken. Amusement parks, antiques, fishing, parks, shopping, downhill skiing, cross-country skiing, theater and watersports nearby. TAC10.

Location: Fifty miles north of Philadelphia in Bucks County.

Publicity: *Country Living.*

Hollidaysburg

I8

Hoenstine's B&B

418 N Montgomery St
Hollidaysburg, PA 16648
(814)695-0632

Rates: $50-80.
Payment: MC VISA.
Innkeeper(s): Barbara Hoenstine.
Circa: 1839.

Rooms: 4 rooms, 1 with PB.
Beds: QDT.

This inn is an antique lover's dream, as it boasts many pieces of original furniture. Stained-glass windows and the 10-foot-high ceilings add to the atmosphere. Breakfast is served in the home's formal dining room. Guests will sleep well in the comfortable and beautifully decorated rooms, especially knowing that the house is being protected by innkeeper Barbara Hoenstine's black standard poodle, Dickens, who is a happy guide and escort around the canal-era town. The B&B is within walking distance of shops, restaurants and the downtown historic district.

Breakfast included in rates. Type of meal: full breakfast. Ceiling fan, cable TV and VCR in room. Copier on premises. Family reunions hosted. Amusement parks, antiques, fishing, parks, shopping, skiing and theater nearby.

"Thank you for a truly calm and quiet week. This was our first B&B experience and it won't be our last."

Intercourse

K14

Carriage Corner

3705 E Newport Rd,
PO Box 371
Intercourse, PA 17534-0371
(717)768-3059

Rates: $48-68.
Payment: MC VISA PC.
Innkeeper(s): Gordon & Gwen Schuit.
Circa: 1981.

Rooms: 5 rooms with PB.
Beds: QD.

Located on two acres, this is a two-story, white Colonial house. The inn is decorated with folk art and country furnishings. Homemade breads and hot cereals are served in the dining room. Walk five minutes to the village and explore shops displaying local crafts, pottery and handmade furniture. The inn is located near many Amish farms.

Breakfast included in rates. Type of meal: full breakfast. Air conditioning and cable TV in room. Small meetings and family reunions hosted. Amusement parks, antiques, parks, shopping and theater nearby.

Location: Amish farmland and tourist area.

Jim Thorpe H15

Harry Packer Mansion

Packer Hill, PO Box 458
Jim Thorpe, PA 18229
(717)325-8566

Rates: $75-390.
Payment: MC VISA TC.
Innkeeper(s): Robert & Patricia Handwerk.
Circa: 1874.

Rooms: 13 rooms, 10 with PB. 3 suites. 3 conference rooms.
Beds: QD.

This extravagant Second Empire mansion was constructed of New England sandstone, and local brick and stone trimmed in cast iron. Past ornately carved columns on the front veranda, guests enter 400-pound, solid walnut doors. The opulent interior includes marble mantels, hand-painted ceilings, and elegant antiques.

Breakfast included in rates. Types of meals: full breakfast, gourmet breakfast and early coffee/tea. Air conditioning, turn-down service and ceiling fan in room. Cable TV and VCR on premises. Weddings, small meetings, family reunions and seminars hosted. Antiques, fishing, parks, shopping, downhill skiing, cross-country skiing and watersports nearby.

Location: Six miles south of Exit 34.

Publicity: *Philadelphia Inquirer, New York, Victorian Homes.*

"The best B&B we have ever stayed at! We'll be back."

The Inn at Jim Thorpe

24 Broadway
Jim Thorpe, PA 18229-2028
(717)325-2599 (800)329-2599
Fax:(717)325-9145

Rates: $65-250. MAP.
Payment: MC VISA AX DC DS TC.
Innkeeper(s): David Drury.
Circa: 1848.

Rooms: 29 rooms with PB, 3 with FP. 5 suites. 2 conference rooms.
Beds: KQD.

This massive New Orleans-style structure, now restored, hosted some colorful 19th-century guests, including Thomas Edison, John D. Rockefeller and Buffalo Bill. All rooms are appointed with Victorian furnishings and have private baths with pedestal sinks and marble floors. Also on the premises are a Victorian dining room, Irish pub and a conference center. The inn is situated in the heart of Jim Thorpe, a quaint Victorian town that was known at the turn of the century as the "Switzerland of America."

Breakfast included in rates. Type of meal: continental-plus breakfast. Dinner, lunch and room service available. MAP. Air conditioning and cable TV in room. Fax and copier on premises. Handicap access. Weddings, small meetings, family reunions and seminars hosted. Antiques, fishing, parks, shopping, downhill skiing, cross-country skiing, theater and watersports nearby. TAC10.

Location: In the western part of the Pocono Mountains.

Publicity: *Philadelphia Inquirer, Pennsylvania, Allentown Morning Call.*

Special Discounts: Call for details on special theme weekends, ski & stay, etc.

"Thank you for having provided us a relaxing getaway."

Kane D6

Kane Manor Country Inn

230 Clay St
Kane, PA 16735-1410
(814)837-6522
Fax:(814)837-6664
E-mail: kanemanor@aol.com

Rates: $89-99.
Payment: MC VISA AX DS PC TC.
Innkeeper(s): Helen Johnson & Debra Moravcik.
Circa: 1896.

Rooms: 10 rooms, 7 with PB.
Beds: DT.

This Georgian Revival inn, on 250 acres of woods and trails, was built for Dr. Elizabeth Kane, the first female doctor to practice in the area. Many of the family's possessions dating back to the American Revolution and the Civil War remain. (Ask to see the attic.) Decor is a mixture of old family items in an unpretentious country style. There is a pub, popular with locals, on the premises. The building is in the National Register.

Breakfast and afternoon tea included in rates. Types of meals: continental breakfast, continental-plus breakfast, full breakfast and early coffee/tea. Cable TV in room. VCR, fax, copier and library on premises. Handicap access. 250 acres. Weddings, small meetings, family reunions and seminars hosted. Amusement parks, antiques, fishing, parks, shopping, downhill skiing, cross-country skiing and watersports nearby. TAC5.

Publicity: *Pittsburgh Press, News Herald, Cleveland Plain Dealer, Youngstown Indicator.*

"It's a place I want to return to often, for rest and relaxation."

Kennett Square L16

Meadow Spring Farm

201 E Street Rd
Kennett Square, PA 19348
(610)444-3903

Rates: $85.
Payment: PC TC.
Innkeeper(s): Anne Hicks.
Circa: 1836.

Rooms: 6 rooms, 4 with PB, 2 with FP.
Beds: QT.

This working, 245-acre dairy farm has more than 300 holsteins grazing in pastures beside the old red barn. The two-story, white-brick house is decorated with old family pieces and collections of whimsical animals and antique wedding gowns. A Victorian doll collection fills one room. Breakfast is hearty country style. Afterwards, guests may see the milking operation, gather eggs or pick vegetables from the garden.

Breakfast and afternoon tea included in rates. Types of meals: full breakfast and gourmet breakfast. Air conditioning and ceiling fan in room. Spa, swimming and child care on premises. Handicap access. 150 acres. Weddings, small meetings and seminars hosted. Antiques, fishing, parks, shopping, cross-country skiing and sporting events nearby. TAC10.

Location: Forty-five minutes from Philadelphia, two hours from New York.

Publicity: *Weekend GetAways, Washington Post, Country Inn.*

Kennett Square (Avondale)

B&B at Walnut Hill

541 Chandler's Mill Rd
Kennett Square (Avondale),
PA 19311-9625
(610)444-3703

Rates: $65-80.
Payment: PC TC.
Innkeeper(s): Tom & Sandy Mills.
Circa: 1840.

Rooms: 2 rooms.
Beds: KDT.

The family that built this pre-Civil War home ran a grist mill on the premises. Innkeepers Sandy and Tom Mills moved into the home as newlyweds. Today Sandy, a former caterer, serves up gourmet breakfasts, such as cottage cheese pancakes with blueberry sauce, in the formal dining room with homemade teas, lemon butter and currant jam. Her cooking expertise was recognized in Good Housekeeping's Christmas issue. The guest rooms are cozy, welcoming and filled with antiques. One room features a Laura Ashley canopy bed. Another boasts Victorian wicker. The house overlooks horses grazing in a meadow, and a nearby creek is visited by Canadian geese, deer and an occasional fox.

Breakfast and evening snack included in rates. Type of meal: gourmet breakfast. Air conditioning, turn-down service and cable TV in room. VCR, copier and spa on premises. Family reunions hosted. Limited Spanish and French spoken. Parks and shopping nearby. TAC10.

Publicity: *Times Record, Suburban Advertiser, Four Seasons of Chester County, Country Inns, Good Housekeeping.*

"The only thing left to do is move in. We came as strangers, left as friends."

Lackawaxen E18

Roebling Inn on The Delaware

Scenic Dr, PO Box 31
Lackawaxen, PA 18435
(717)685-7900
Fax:(717)685-1718

Rates: $65-95.
Payment: MC VISA AX DS TC.
Innkeeper(s): Don & JoAnn Jahn.
Circa: 1870.

Rooms: 5 rooms with PB. 1 cottage.
Beds: QDT.

This Greek Revival house is in the National Register of Historic Places and once was the home of Judge Ridgway, tallyman for the Delaware and Hudson Canal Company. Country furnishings are supplemented with some antiques, and there is a long front porch for relaxing. Full country breakfasts are provided. Afterward, ask the innkeepers for directions to nearby hidden waterfalls, or walk to the Zane Grey Museum, Roebling's Delaware Aqueduct or Minisink Battleground Park.

Breakfast included in rates. Type of meal: full breakfast. Air conditioning, ceiling fan and cable TV in room. Fax on premises. Antiques, fishing, parks, downhill skiing, cross-country skiing, theater and watersports nearby.

Publicity: *New York Magazine.*

Lampeter K14

The Australian Walkabout Inn

837 Village Rd, PO Box 294
Lampeter, PA 17537-0294
(717)464-0707
Fax:(717)464-2501

Rates: $99-199.
Payment: MC VISA AX PC TC.
Innkeeper(s): Richard & Margaret Mason.
Circa: 1925.

Rooms: 5 rooms with PB, 5 with FP. 3 suites. 1 cottage.
Beds: QT.

The Australian Walkabout Inn offers hospitality Australian-style thanks to Australian Richard Mason, one of the innkeepers. Tea is imported from down under and breakfasts are prepared from Australian recipes. From the wraparound porch, guests can watch Amish buggies pass by. Bed chambers have antique furniture, Pennsylvania Dutch quilts and hand-painted wall stencilings. Each room is named from the image stenciled on its walls.

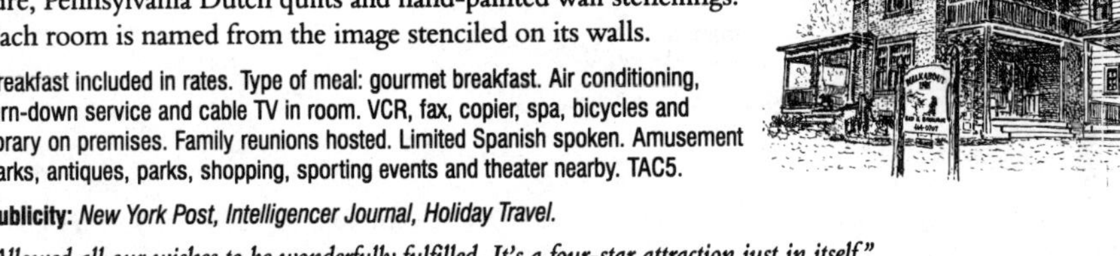

Breakfast included in rates. Type of meal: gourmet breakfast. Air conditioning, turn-down service and cable TV in room. VCR, fax, copier, spa, bicycles and library on premises. Family reunions hosted. Limited Spanish spoken. Amusement parks, antiques, parks, shopping, sporting events and theater nearby. TAC5.

Publicity: *New York Post, Intelligencer Journal, Holiday Travel.*

"Allowed all our wishes to be wonderfully fulfilled. It's a four-star attraction just in itself."

Lancaster K14

Flowers & Thyme B&B

238 Strasburg Pike
Lancaster, PA 17602-1326
(717)393-1460
E-mail: duanhar@frmail.frco.com

Rates: $70-100.
Payment: PC TC.
Innkeeper(s): Don & Ruth Harnish.
Circa: 1941.

Rooms: 3 rooms with PB. 1 suite.
Beds: QD.

This home was built by an Amishman for a Mennonite minister and his family. The innkeepers grew up among Amish and Mennonite communities and are full of knowledge about the area and its history. Fresh flowers from the inn's beautiful gardens are placed in the guest rooms in season. A country breakfast is served in the breakfast room overlooking the herb garden. The inn is only minutes away from outlet stores and plenty of outdoor activities.

Breakfast included in rates. Types of meals: full breakfast and gourmet breakfast. Air conditioning and ceiling fan in room. Cable TV and library on premises. Amusement parks, antiques, parks, shopping, sporting events, theater and watersports nearby.

Publicity: *Lancaster newspapers*

Special Discounts: 25% discount Sun. through Thurs., January through April.

"Your home is beautiful, perfectly decorated, warm and inviting and we felt so welcome. Your breakfast was delicious and served so elegantly."

Gardens of Eden

1894 Eden Rd
Lancaster, PA 17601-5526
(717)393-5179
Fax:(717)393-7722

Rates: $75-120.
Payment: MC VISA PC TC.
Innkeeper(s): Marilyn & Bill Ebel.
Circa: 1867.

Rooms: 3 rooms with PB. 1 cottage.
Beds: KQD.

Wildflowers, perennials and wooded trails cover the three-and-a-half acre grounds surrounding Gardens of Eden. The home, which overlooks the Conestoga River, is an example of late Federal-style architecture with some early Victorian touches. The innkeepers have won awards for their restoration and a room from their bed & breakfast was featured on the cover of a decorating book. The interior, laced with dried flowers, handmade quilts, baskets and country furnishings, has the feel of a garden cottage. This house is ideal for families and includes a working fireplace and an efficiency kitchen. Gardens of Eden is within minutes of downtown Lancaster. The innkeepers can arrange for personalized tours of Amish and Mennonite communities and sometimes a dinner in an Amish home.

Breakfast included in rates. Type of meal: full breakfast. Afternoon tea available. Air conditioning, turn-down service, ceiling fan, cable TV and VCR in room. Fax and copier on premises. Small meetings and family reunions hosted. Limited French spoken. Amusement parks, antiques, fishing, parks, shopping, cross-country skiing and theater nearby.

The King's Cottage, A B&B Inn

1049 E King St
Lancaster, PA 17602-3231
(717)397-1017 (800)747-8717
Fax:(717)397-3447

Rates: $80-175.
Payment: MC VISA DS.
Innkeeper(s): Karen Owens.
Circa: 1913.

Rooms: 9 rooms with PB. 1 conference room.
Beds: KQ.

This Mission Revival house features a red-tile roof and stucco walls, common in many stately turn-of-the-century houses in California and New Mexico. Its elegant interiors include a sweeping staircase, a library with marble fireplace, stained-glass windows, and a solarium. The inn is appointed with Oriental rugs and antiques and fine 18th-century English reproductions. The formal dining room provides the location for gourmet morning meals.

Breakfast and afternoon tea included in rates. Type of meal: full breakfast. Turn-down service in room. Cable TV on premises. Weddings, small meetings, family reunions and seminars hosted. Amusement parks, antiques, fishing, shopping, cross-country skiing, sporting events and theater nearby.

Location: Pennsylvania Dutch country.

Publicity: *Country, USA Weekend, Bon Appetit, Intelligencer Journal, Times.*

"I appreciate your attention to all our needs and look forward to recommending your inn to friends."

O'Flaherty's Dingeldein House B&B

1105 E King St
Lancaster, PA 17602-3233
(717)293-1723 (800)779-7765
Fax:(717)293-1947

Rates: $70-95.
Payment: MC VISA DS PC TC.
Innkeeper(s): Jack & Sue Flatley.
Circa: 1910.

Rooms: 5 rooms, 3 with PB. 1 suite.
Beds: KQDT.

This Dutch Colonial home was once residence to the Armstrong family, who acquired fame and fortune in the tile floor industry. Springtime guests will brighten at the sight of this home's beautiful flowers. During winter months, innkeepers Jack and Sue Flatley deck the halls with plenty of seasonal decorations. The hearty country breakfast might include fresh-baked muffins, fruits, the innkeepers' special blend of coffee and mouth-watering omelets, pancakes or French toast. Cozy rooms include comfortable furnishings and cheery wall coverings. The innkeepers can arrange for guests to enjoy dinner at the home of one of their Amish friends.

Breakfast included in rates. Types of meals: full breakfast, gourmet breakfast and early coffee/tea. Air conditioning and ceiling fan in room. Cable TV, VCR, fax, copier and library on premises. Family reunions hosted. Amusement parks, antiques, fishing, parks, shopping, sporting events and theater nearby.

Location: Downtown, 15 minutes from heart of Amish Country.

Publicity: *Gourmet.*

"You made our visit here very pleasant, your hospitality is what makes the stay here so wonderful."

Witmer's Tavern - Historic 1725 Inn

2014 Old Philadelphia Pike
Lancaster, PA 17602-3413
(717)299-5305

Rates: $60-90.
Payment: PC.
Innkeeper(s): Brant Hartung.
Circa: 1725.

Rooms: 7 rooms, 2 with PB, 7 with FP.
Beds: D.

This pre-Revolutionary War inn is the sole survivor of 62 inns that once lined the old Lancaster-to-Philadelphia turnpike. Immigrant Conestoga wagon trains were made up here for the Western and Southern journeys to wilderness homesteads. Designated as a National Landmark, the property is restored to its original, rustic pioneer style. There are sagging wide-board floors and antiques with original finish. History buffs will enjoy seeing the Indian escape tunnel entrance and knowing presidents Washington, Jefferson and Adams once stayed here, as well as Lafayette and Benjamin Franklin. Guest rooms feature antiques, old quilts, fresh flowers and original working fireplaces.

Breakfast included in rates. Type of meal: continental-plus breakfast. Air conditioning in room. Small meetings, family reunions and seminars hosted. Amusement parks, antiques, fishing, parks, shopping, downhill skiing, cross-country skiing, sporting events, theater and watersports nearby. TAC10.

Location: One mile east of Lancaster on Route 340.

Publicity: *Stuart News, Pennsylvania, Antique, Travel & Leisure, Mid-Atlantic, Country Living, Early American Life, Colonial Homes, USA Today.*

"Your personal attention and enthusiastic knowledge of the area and Witmer's history made it come alive and gave us the good feelings we came looking for."

PA

Lancaster County

Bed & Breakfast - The Manor

PO Box 416,
Village of Lampeter
Lancaster County, PA 17537
(717)464-9564 (800)461-6233

Rates: $79-99.
Payment: MC VISA PC TC.
Innkeeper(s): Mary Lou Paolini & Jackie Curtis.
Circa: 1939.

Rooms: 6 rooms, 4 with PB.
Beds: KQD.

The Manor, a cozy farmhouse, is located on almost five acres. Amish chairs provide a view from the front porch. Among the creative elements of the country decor, is an Amish dress and cap that hangs in one of the guest rooms. A former restaurant owner, Mary Lou prepares gourmet and low-fat breakfasts. By prior arrangement, the innkeepers will reserve a dinner for you with an Old Order Amish farm family.

Breakfast, afternoon tea and evening snack included in rates. Types of meals: gourmet breakfast and early coffee/tea. Catered breakfast and room service available. Air conditioning and ceiling fan in room. Swimming on premises. Handicap access. Weddings, small meetings, family reunions and seminars hosted. Amusement parks, antiques, parks, sporting events, theater and watersports nearby.

Special Discounts: Booking over five days 10% discount. Also, groups get a special rate 10%.

Lancaster Country (White Horse) K15

Fassitt Mansion B&B

6051 Old Philadelphia Pike,
HR 340, White Horse, PA
17527-9798
(717)442-3139 (800)653-4139

Rates: $80-125.
Payment: MC VISA TC.
Innkeeper(s): Bill & Patricia Collins.
Circa: 1845.

Rooms: 5 rooms with PB, 2 with FP.
Beds: KQDT.

Located on two acres, this Federal home is six miles from the town of Intercourse in Lancaster County. There are 12-foot-high ceilings and six fireplaces. A continental breakfast offers local butters and fruit jams, served in the dining room.

Breakfast, afternoon tea and evening snack included in rates. Types of meals: full breakfast, gourmet breakfast and early coffee/tea. Air conditioning, turn-down service and ceiling fan in room. Cable TV and VCR on premises. Antiques, fishing, shopping and theater nearby. TAC8.

Location: Lancaster County, Amish farmland.

Landenberg L15

Cornerstone B&B Inn

300 Buttonwood Rd
Landenberg, PA 19350
(610)274-2143
Fax:(610)274-0734

Rates: $75-150.
Payment: MC VISA DS PC TC.
Innkeeper(s): Linda Chamberlin & Marty Mulligan.
Circa: 1704.

Rooms: 7 rooms with PB, 5 with FP. 1 suite. 6 cottages.
Beds: KQT.

The Cornerstone is an 18th-century country manor house filled with antique furnishings. Two fireplaces make the parlor inviting. Wing chairs, fresh flowers and working fireplaces add enjoyment to the guest rooms. A water garden and swimming pool with hot tub are additional amenities. Stay in one of five guest cottages with kitchen, fireplace and living room.

Breakfast included in rates. Types of meals: continental-plus breakfast, full breakfast and early coffee/tea. Air conditioning and cable TV in room. VCR, fax, spa and swimming on premises. Small meetings and family reunions hosted. Amusement parks, antiques, parks, shopping, sporting events and theater nearby. TAC10.

Lititz J14

Alden House

62 E Main St
Lititz, PA 17543-1947
(717)627-3363 (800)584-0753
E-mail: aldenbb@ptdprolog.net

Rates: $85-120.
Payment: MC VISA PC.
Innkeeper(s): Fletcher & Joy Coleman.
Circa: 1850.

Rooms: 5 rooms with PB, 1 with FP. 3 suites.
Beds: QD.

For more than 200 years, breezes have carried the sound of church bells to the stately brick homes lining Main Street. The Alden House is a brick Victorian in the center of this historic district and within walking distance of the Pretzel House (first in the country) and the chocolate factory. A favorite room is the suite with

a loft dressing room and private bath. A full breakfast is served, often carried to one of the inn's three porches.

Breakfast included in rates. Types of meals: full breakfast and early coffee/tea. Air conditioning, ceiling fan and cable TV in room. Small meetings hosted. Amusement parks, antiques, fishing, parks, shopping and theater nearby. TAC10.

Location: Seven miles North of Lancaster.

Publicity: *Connecticut Post, Pittsburgh Post-Gazette, Travel Holiday, Rockland Journal News, Penn Dutch Traveler, Now in Lancaster County, Philadelphia Inquirer.*

"Truly represents what bed & breakfast hospitality is all about. You are special innkeepers. Thanks for caring so much about your guests. It's like being home."

Swiss Woods B&B

500 Blantz Rd
Lititz, PA 17543-9464
(717)627-3358

Rates: $60-95.
Payment: MC VISA.
Innkeeper(s): Werner & Debrah Mosimann.
Circa: 1985.

Rooms: 5 rooms with PB.
Beds: QT.

In spring, thousands of daffodils bloom in the acres of secluded woodland at the Swiss Woods Inn. The building is new and during construction heart-shaped cutouts were incorporated into the window shutters. Features include a massive sandstone fireplace, lace curtains with woven hearts, goosedown comforters, private balconies or patios and hearty Swiss breakfasts. Werner is a native of Switzerland and everyone in the family speaks Swiss German as well as English. Two rooms have spas.

Type of meal: full breakfast. Spa on premises.

Publicity: *Lancaster Intelligencer Journal.*

"A warning should be made concerning a visit to this gem of a home. If you are serious about a diet, don't bother coming. The lady of the house is not only a marvelous chef, but a genius at the baker's oven."

Marietta K13

Railroad House Restaurant B&B

280 W Front St
Marietta, PA 17547-1405
(717)426-4141

Rates: $79-99.
Payment: MC VISA TC.
Innkeeper(s): Richard & Donna Chambers.
Circa: 1820.

Rooms: 10 rooms, 8 with PB. 1 cottage. 1 conference room.
Beds: QDT.

The Railroad House, a sprawling old hotel, conjures up memories of the days when riding the rail was the way to travel. The house was built as a refuge for weary men who were working along the Susquehanna River. When the railroad finally made its way through Marietta, the rail station's waiting room and ticket office were located in what's now known as the Railroad House. The restored rooms feature antiques, Oriental rugs, Victorian decor and rustic touches such as exposed brick walls. The chefs at the inn's restaurant create a menu of American and continental dishes using spices and produce from the beautifully restored gardens. The innovative recipes have been featured in Bon Appetit. The innkeepers also host a variety of special events and weekends, including murder mysteries and clambakes serenaded by jazz bands. Carriage rides and special walking tours of Marietta can be arranged.

Breakfast included in rates. Types of meals: full breakfast, gourmet breakfast and early coffee/tea. Afternoon tea, dinner, evening snack, picnic lunch, lunch, gourmet lunch, banquet service, catering service and catered breakfast available. Air conditioning in room. Copier and bicycles on premises. Weddings, small meetings, family reunions and seminars hosted. Spanish and French spoken. Amusement parks, antiques, fishing, parks, shopping, downhill skiing, sporting events, theater and watersports nearby.

River Inn

258 W Front St
Marietta, PA 17547-1405
(717)426-2290
Fax:(717)426-2966

Rates: $60-75.
Payment: MC VISA DC CB DS PC TC.
Innkeeper(s): Joyce & Bob Heiserman.
Circa: 1790.

Rooms: 3 rooms with PB, 1 with FP.
Beds: QT.

This Colonial has more than 200 years of history within its walls. The home is listed in the National Register and located in Marietta's historic district. Herb and flower gardens decorate the grounds. Relaxing in front of a fireplace is an easy task since the inn offers six, one of which resides in a guest room. Colonial decor and antiques permeate the interior. The inn is within walking distance to the Susquhana River.

Breakfast included in rates. Types of meals: full breakfast and early coffee/tea. Picnic lunch available. Air conditioning in room. Cable TV, bicycles and library on premises. Weddings hosted. Amusement parks, antiques, fishing, parks, shopping, theater and watersports nearby. TAC10.

McKnightstown L11

Country Escape

275 Old Rt 30, PO Box 195
McKnightstown, PA 17343
(717)338-0611
Fax:(717)334-5227

Rates: $50-75.
Payment: MC VISA AX DS PC TC.
Innkeeper(s): Merry Bush & Ross Hetrick.
Circa: 1868.

Rooms: 3 rooms, 1 with PB.
Beds: Q.

This country Victorian, a brick structure featuring a porch decked in gingerbread trim, rests on the route that Confederate soldiers took on their way to nearby Gettysburg. The home itself was built just a few years after the Civil War. There are three comfortable guest rooms, decorated in country style. For an extra fee, business travelers can use the inn's typing, copying, faxing or desktop publishing services. All guests can enjoy the outdoor hot tub. There is also a children's play area outside. A traditional American breakfast is served, with such hearty items as eggs, pancakes, bacon and sausage. The inn offers close access to the famous battlefield, as well as other historic sites.

Breakfast included in rates. Type of meal: full breakfast. Air conditioning in room. Cable TV, VCR, fax, copier and spa on premises. English spoken. Antiques, parks, shopping, downhill skiing, theater and watersports nearby. TAC10.

Milford F18

Cliff Park Inn & Golf Course

RR 4 Box 7200
Milford, PA 18337-9708
(717)296-6491 (800)225-6535
Fax:(717)296-3982

Rates: $93-160. MAP, AP, EP.
Payment: MC VISA AX DC CB DS.
Innkeeper(s): Harry W. Buchanan III.
Circa: 1820.

Rooms: 18 rooms with PB. 1 conference room.
Beds: KQDT.

This historic country inn is located on a 600-acre family estate, bordering the Delaware River. It has been in the Buchanan family since 1820. Rooms are spacious with individual climate control, telephone and Victorian-style furnishings. Cliff Park features both a full-service restaurant and golf school. The inn's golf course, established in 1913, is one of the oldest in the United States. Cliff Park's picturesque setting is popular for country weddings and private business conferences. Both B&B or MAP plans are offered.

Breakfast included in rates. Types of meals: full breakfast and gourmet breakfast. Dinner, picnic lunch and lunch available. MAP, AP, EP. Fax on premises. Handicap access. Cross-country skiing and watersports nearby.

Location: In the foothills of the Pocono Mountains on the Delaware River.

"Cliff Park Inn is the sort of inn I look for in the English countryside. It has that authentic charm that comes from History."

Montoursville F12

The Carriage House at Stonegate

RR 1 Box 11A
Montoursville, PA 17754
(717)433-4340
Fax:(717)433-4653

Rates: $50-70.
Payment: PC.
Innkeeper(s): Harold & Dena Mesaris.
Circa: 1850.

Rooms: 2 rooms.
Beds: QD.

President Herbert Hoover was a descendant of the original settlers of this old homestead in the Loyalsock Creek Valley. Indians burned the original house, but the present farmhouse and numerous outbuildings date from the early 1800s. The Carriage House is set next to a lovely brook.

Breakfast included in rates. Type of meal: continental-plus breakfast. Cable TV in room. Fax, library, pet boarding and child care on premises. 30 acres. Small meetings and family reunions hosted. Amusement parks, antiques, fishing, parks, shopping, downhill skiing, cross-country skiing, sporting events, theater and watersports nearby. TAC5.

Pets Allowed.

Location: Six miles off I-180, north of Montoursville.

"A very fine B&B — the best that can be found. Gracious hosts."

Mount Joy K13

Cedar Hill Farm

305 Longenecker Rd
Mount Joy, PA 17552-8404
(717)653-4655

Rates: $65-75.
Payment: MC VISA AX DS TC.
Innkeeper(s): Russel & Gladys Swarr.
Circa: 1817.

Rooms: 5 rooms with PB.
Beds: KQDT.

Situated on 51 acres overlooking Chiques Creek, this stone farmhouse boasts a two-tiered front veranda affording pastoral views of the surrounding fields. The host was born in the house and is the third generation to have lived here since the Swarr family first purchased it in 1878. Family heirlooms and antiques include an elaborately carved walnut bedstead, a marble-topped washstand and a "tumbling block" quilt. In the kitchen, a copper kettle, bread paddle and baskets of dried herbs accentuate the walk-in fireplace, where guests often linger over breakfast. Cedar Hill is a working poultry and grain farm.

Breakfast included in rates. Types of meals: continental-plus breakfast and early coffee/tea. Air conditioning in room. VCR and computer on premises. 51 acres. Small meetings and family reunions hosted. Amusement parks, antiques, fishing, parks, shopping, cross-country skiing, sporting events, theater and watersports nearby.

Location: Midway between Lancaster and Hershey.

Publicity: *Women's World, Lancaster Farming, Philadelphia, New York Times, Ladies Home Journal.*

"Dorothy can have Kansas, Scarlett can take Tara, Rick can keep Paris — I've stayed at Cedar Hill Farm."

PA

Hillside Farm B&B

607 Eby Chiques Rd
Mount Joy, PA 17552-8819
(717)653-6697
Fax:(717)653-5233

Rates: $55-70.
Payment: MC VISA PC TC.
Innkeeper(s): Gary & Deborah Lintner.
Circa: 1863.

Rooms: 5 rooms, 3 with PB.
Beds: KQDT.

This comfortable farm has a relaxing homey feel to it. Rooms are simply decorated and special extras such as handmade quilts and antiques add an elegant country touch. The home is a true monument to the cow. Dairy antiques, cow knickknacks and antique milk bottles abound. Some of the bottles were found during the renovation of the home and its grounds. Spend the day hunting for bargains in nearby antique shops, malls and factory outlets, or tour local Amish and Pennsylvania Dutch attractions. The farm is a good vacation spot for families with children above the age of 10.

Breakfast and evening snack included in rates. Types of meals: full breakfast and early coffee/tea. Afternoon tea available. Air conditioning and ceiling fan in room. VCR, spa and library on premises. Small meetings, family reunions and seminars hosted. Amusement parks, antiques, fishing, parks, shopping, downhill skiing, cross-country skiing, theater and watersports nearby. TAC10.

Location: In the heart of Dutch/Amish country.

Special Discounts: American Historic Inn promotions, winter getaway (November-March); other packages available.

"Warm, friendly, comfortable ... feels like home."

The Olde Square Inn

127 E Main St
Mount Joy, PA 17552-1513
(717)653-4525 (800)742-3533
Fax:(717)653-0976

Rates: $65-105.
Payment: MC VISA PC TC.
Innkeeper(s): Fran & Dave Hand.
Circa: 1917.

Rooms: 4 rooms with PB.
Beds: KQDT.

Located on the town square, this Neoclassical house features handsome columned fireplaces and leaded-glass windows. The innkeeper starts off the day with breakfast items such as baked oatmeal, cherry cobbler, homemade breads and pancakes with a side of sausage. Amish farms and marketplaces are nearby. The town of Mount Joy offers restaurants, shops and parks all accessible with a short walk.

Breakfast included in rates. Types of meals: full breakfast and early coffee/tea. Air conditioning, cable TV and VCR in room. Fax on premises. Small meetings and family reunions hosted. Amusement parks, antiques, fishing, parks, shopping, sporting events and theater nearby. TAC10.

Muncy *F12*

The Bodine House B&B

307 S Main St
Muncy, PA 17756-1507
(717)546-8949
Fax:(717)546-8949

Rates: $50-125.
Payment: MC VISA AX DS PC TC.
Innkeeper(s): David & Marie Louise Smith.
Circa: 1805.

Rooms: 5 rooms with PB, 1 with FP. 1 cottage.
Beds: QDT.

This Federal-style townhouse, framed by a white picket fence, is in the National Register. Antique and reproduction furnishings highlight the inn's four fireplaces, the parlor, study and library. A favorite guest room features a walnut canopy bed, hand-stenciled and bordered walls, and a framed sampler by the innkeeper's great-great-great-grandmother. Candlelight breakfasts are served beside the fireplace in a gracious Colonial dining room. Also available is a guest cottage with kitchenette.

Breakfast included in rates. Types of meals: full breakfast and early coffee/tea. Afternoon tea available. Air conditioning, turn-down service and cable TV in room. VCR, fax, bicycles and library on premises. Small meetings and family reunions hosted. Antiques, fishing, parks, shopping, cross-country skiing and sporting events nearby. TAC10.

Publicity: *Colonial Homes, Philadelphia Inquirer.*

"What an experience, made special by your wonderful hospitality."

New Berlin

H12

The Inn at Olde New Berlin

321 Market St
New Berlin, PA 17855-0390
(717)966-0321
Fax:(717)966-9557

Rates: $80-95.
Payment: MC VISA PC TC.
Innkeeper(s): Nancy & John Showers.
Circa: 1906.

Rooms: 5 rooms with PB. 1 suite. 1 conference room.
Beds: QD.

Relax on the inviting front porch swing or in the step-down living room with its baby grand piano at this richly appointed Victorian inn. Carved woodwork and high ceilings accentuate the beautiful rooms furnished with antiques and comfortable beds covered with handmade Amish quilts. An herb garden supplies seasonings for the fine meals served at the inn's gourmet restaurant. Luscious soups, hors d'oeuvres such as smoked trout pate or stuffed mushrooms, and a variety of salads begin a dinner of scrumptious entrees and delectable desserts. Brunches are served Wednesday through Sunday with unique omelets, fruit crepes, breakfast meats and a variety of special drinks.

Breakfast and afternoon tea included in rates. Type of meal: full breakfast. Dinner, lunch and room service available. Air conditioning and turn-down service in room. Fax and copier on premises. Weddings, small meetings, family reunions and seminars hosted. Amusement parks, antiques, fishing, parks, shopping, downhill skiing, cross-country skiing, sporting events, theater and watersports nearby.

Publicity: *Susquahanna Life, Philadelphia Inquirer, Washington Post.*

"I left feeling nurtured and relaxed. You've created a very caring, rich lodging, a perfect place for regenerating."

New Hope

I18

Aaron Burr House

80 W Bridge St
New Hope, PA 18938-1303
(215)862-2520

Rates: $75-195.
Payment: MC VISA AX PC TC.
Innkeeper(s): Carl & Nadine Glassman.
Circa: 1870.

Rooms: 12 rooms with PB, 6 with FP. 6 suites. 1 cottage. 3 conference rooms.
Beds: KQT.

Aaron Burr hid in this house after his infamous duel with Alexander Hamilton. The home also is one of the Wedgewood Collection inns. A Victorian Shingle style, it is in the National Register. Its three stories, including the spacious parlor, are appointed with antiques and reproductions. Guest rooms offer amenities such as private baths, telephones, TVs and many have fireplaces. Within walking distance are fine restaurants, shops and art galleries. The grounds offer two gazebos, stately old trees, a screened-in flagstone patio and a barn perfect for bicycle storage.

PA

Breakfast, afternoon tea and evening snack included in rates. Types of meals: continental-plus breakfast and early coffee/tea. Room service available. Air conditioning, turn-down service and ceiling fan in room. VCR, fax, swimming, tennis and pet boarding on premises. Handicap access. Small meetings, family reunions and seminars hosted. Dutch, French, Spanish and Hebrew spoken. Antiques, fishing, parks, shopping, downhill skiing, cross-country skiing, sporting events, theater and watersports nearby. TAC10.

Special Discounts: Third night free.

Hollileif B&B

677 Durham Rd (Rt 413)
New Hope, PA 18940
(215)598-3100

Rates: $85-155.
Payment: MC VISA AX DS PC TC.
Innkeeper(s): Ellen & Richard Butkus.
Circa: 1700.

Rooms: 5 rooms with PB, 2 with FP.
Beds: QD.

This handsome former farmhouse sits on more than five rolling acres of scenic Bucks County countryside. The name "hollileif," which means "beloved tree," refers to the 40-foot holly trees that grace the entrance. Bedrooms are appointed with lace and fresh flowers. Afternoon refreshments in the parlor or patio are provided, as well as evening turndown service.

Breakfast and afternoon tea included in rates. Types of meals: gourmet breakfast and early coffee/tea. Air conditioning, turn-down service and ceiling fan in room. VCR, fax, copier and library on premises. Family reunions hosted. Limited spanish spoken. Antiques, fishing, parks, shopping, downhill skiing, cross-country skiing, theater and watersports nearby. TAC10.

Location: Midway between Newtown and Buckingham.

Publicity: *Trentonian, Bucks County Courier Times.*

Special Discounts: $65 available for 1 person in room, mid-week only.

"The accommodations were lovely and the breakfasts delicious and unusual, but it is really the graciousness of our hosts that made the weekend memorable."

Pineapple Hill

1324 River Rd
New Hope, PA 18938
(215)862-1790

Rates: $95-175.
Payment: MC VISA PC TC.
Innkeeper(s): Kathy & Charles "Cookie" Triolo.
Circa: 1790.

Rooms: 8 rooms, 6 with PB. 3 suites. 1 conference room.
Beds: KQD.

The pineapple always has been a sign of friendship and hospitality, and guests at Pineapple Hill are sure to experience both. The inn is secluded on five private acres, yet it's just a few miles from town, antique shops, flea markets, auctions and plenty of outdoor activities. The inviting interior is filled with Colonial-style furnishings. Guests enjoy everything from baked bananas to raspberry French toast during the romantic, candlelight breakfasts, which are served on tables set for two. Inside the ruins of an old, stone barn, is a tiled swimming pool.

Breakfast, afternoon tea and evening snack included in rates. Types of meals: full breakfast, gourmet breakfast and early coffee/tea. Air conditioning, turn-down service and cable TV in room. VCR, fax and swimming on premises. Weddings, small meetings, family reunions and seminars hosted. Amusement parks, antiques, fishing, parks, shopping, theater and watersports nearby. TAC10.

Special Discounts: Midweek discounts.

"Your rooms are spotless with great attention to historic detail."

The Whitehall Inn

1370 Pineville Rd
New Hope, PA 18938-9495
(215)598-7945

Rates: $130-190.
Payment: MC VISA AX DC CB DS.
Innkeeper(s): Mike Wass.
Circa: 1794.

Rooms: 6 rooms.

This white-plastered stone farmhouse is located on 13 country acres studded with stately maple and chestnut trees. Inside, a winding walnut staircase leads to antique-furnished guest rooms that offer widepine floors, wavy-glass windows, high ceilings and some fireplaces. An antique clock collection, Oriental rugs and late Victorian furnishings are found throughout. Afternoon tea, evening chocolates and candlelight breakfasts served with heirloom china and sterling reflect the inn's many amenities. There are stables on the property and horseback riding may be arranged.

Breakfast included in rates. Types of meals: full breakfast and early coffee/tea. Air conditioning and turn-down service in room. 13 acres. Small meetings, family reunions and seminars hosted. Amusement parks, antiques, shopping, cross-country skiing and theater nearby.

Paradise

K14

Creekside Inn

44 Leacock Rd
Paradise, PA 17562-0435
(717)687-0333
Fax:(717)687-8200

Rates: $70-120.
Payment: MC VISA.
Innkeeper(s): Catherine & Dennis Zimmermann.
Circa: 1781.

Rooms: 6 rooms, 4 with PB.
Beds: QDT.

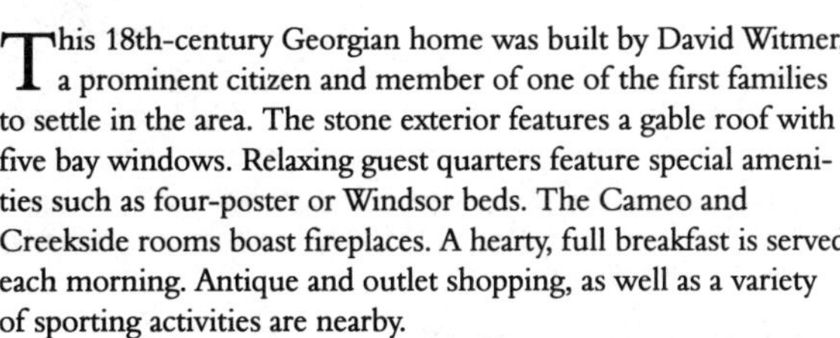

This 18th-century Georgian home was built by David Witmer, a prominent citizen and member of one of the first families to settle in the area. The stone exterior features a gable roof with five bay windows. Relaxing guest quarters feature special amenities such as four-poster or Windsor beds. The Cameo and Creekside rooms boast fireplaces. A hearty, full breakfast is served each morning. Antique and outlet shopping, as well as a variety of sporting activities are nearby.

Breakfast included in rates. Type of meal: gourmet breakfast. Afternoon tea available. Antiques, fishing and theater nearby.

Philadelphia

K17

Independence Park Inn

235 Chestnut St
Philadelphia, PA 19106
(215)922-4443
Fax:(215)922-4487

Rates: $99-155.
Payment: MC VISA AX DC CB DS.
Innkeeper(s): Terry Bompard.
Circa: 1856.

Rooms: 36 rooms with PB. 1 conference room.
Beds: KQT.

This five-story urban inn is listed in the National Register of Historic Places. The high-ceilinged guest rooms feature rich draperies and Chippendale writing tables. In the parlor lobby, guests may enjoy tea and cucumber sandwiches by the fireplace. Breakfast is served on the skylighted court. Conference rooms are available for business travelers.

Breakfast and afternoon tea included in rates. Types of meals: continental-plus breakfast and early coffee/tea. Air conditioning and cable TV in room. VCR on premises. Weddings, small meetings, family reunions and seminars hosted. French and Spanish spoken. Parks and theater nearby. TAC10.

Publicity: *Philadelphia Inquirer, Atlanta Journal, Constitution.*

"Everything possible seems to have been planned for our comfort and needs."

Thomas Bond House

PA

129 S 2nd St
Philadelphia, PA 19106
(215)923-8523 (800)845-2663
Fax:(215)923-8504

Rates: $90-160.
Payment: MC VISA AX.
Innkeeper(s): Joe Killingsworth.
Circa: 1769.

Rooms: 12 rooms with PB, 2 with FP. 2 suites. 1 conference room.
Beds: QDT.

One way to enjoy the history of Philadelphia is to treat yourself to a stay at this Colonial-period, Georgian-style residence in Independence National Historic Park. White shutters and cornices accentuate the brick exterior, often draped in red, white and blue bunting. A finely executed interior renovation provides a handsome background for the inn's collection of Chippendale reproductions, four-poster beds and dropfront desks. Working fireplaces, phones, television and whirlpool tubs provide additional comforts.

Breakfast included in rates. Types of meals: continental-plus breakfast, full breakfast and early coffee/tea. Evening snack and catering service available. Air conditioning in room. Fax and copier on premises. Weddings, small meetings, family reunions and seminars hosted. Amusement parks, antiques, fishing, parks, shopping, sporting events and theater nearby.

Location: In the Independence National Historic Park.

Publicity: *Mid-Atlantic Country, Washingtonian, Washington Post, Philadelphia Inquirer, Home & Garden, Boston Globe.*

"Your service was excellent, congenial, made us feel comfortable and welcome."

Pine Grove Mills H9

The Chatelaine at Split-Pine Farmhouse

347 W Pine Grove Rd
Pine Grove Mills, PA 16868
(814)238-2028 (800)251-2028

Rates: $80-135.
Payment: MC VISA AX DS PC TC.
Innkeeper(s): Mae McQuade.
Circa: 1830.

Rooms: 4 rooms, 2 with PB. 1 suite.
Beds: KQT.

Filled with generations of antiques layered into an English Country look, this Federal farmhouse is located a few minutes away from State College. Belleek china is used during tea time. The candlelight breakfast is served in the elegantly appointed dining room. The breakfast menu features dishes such as Mushroom Charlottes with Currant Sauce, Santa Fe Strata and Champagne Granita.

Breakfast and afternoon tea included in rates. Types of meals: gourmet breakfast and early coffee/tea. Picnic lunch available. Family reunions hosted. Amusement parks, antiques, fishing, parks, shopping, downhill skiing, cross-country skiing, sporting events, theater and watersports nearby. TAC10.

Point Pleasant I18

Tattersall Inn

16 Cafferty Rd, PO Box 569
Point Pleasant, PA 18950
(215)297-8233 (800)297-4988
E-mail: nrhg17a@prodigy.com

Rates: $70-130.
Payment: MC VISA AX DS PC TC.
Innkeeper(s): Herbert & Geraldine Moss.
Circa: 1740.

Rooms: 6 rooms with PB, 2 with FP. 2 suites. 1 conference room.
Beds: QT.

This plastered fieldstone house with its broad porches and wainscoted entry hall was the home of local mill owners for 150 years. The walls are 18 inches thick. Breakfast is usually served in the dining room where a vintage phonograph collection is on display. Breakfast can also be brought to your room. The Colonial-style common room features a beamed ceiling and walk-in fireplace. Guests gather here for apple cider, cheese and crackers and tea or coffee in the late afternoon.

Breakfast, afternoon tea and evening snack included in rates. Types of meals: full breakfast and early coffee/tea. Room service available. Air conditioning in room. Fax, copier and library on premises. Small meetings and family reunions hosted. Antiques, fishing, parks, shopping, cross-country skiing, theater and watersports nearby. TAC10.

Location: Bucks County, New Hope area.

Publicity: *Courier Times, Philadelphia, New York Times, WYOU.*

"Thank you for your hospitality and warm welcome. The inn is charming and has a wonderful ambiance."

Ronks K14

Candlelight Inn B&B

2574 Lincoln Hwy E
Ronks, PA 17572-9771
(717)299-6005 (800)772-2635
Fax:(717)299-6397

Rates: $65-105.
Payment: MC VISA DS PC TC.
Innkeeper(s): Tim & Heidi Soberick.
Circa: 1920.

Rooms: 6 rooms, 4 with PB. 1 suite.
Beds: KQT.

Located in the Pennsylvania Dutch area, this Federal-style house offers a side porch for enjoying the home's acre and a half of tall trees and surrounding Amish farmland. Guest rooms feature Victorian decor. The inn's gourmet breakfast, which might include a creme caramel French toast, is served by candlelight. Lancaster is five miles to the east.

Breakfast included in rates. Types of meals: full breakfast and gourmet breakfast. Air conditioning in room. Cable TV and fax on premises. Weddings, small meetings, family reunions and seminars hosted. French and Italian spoken. Amusement parks, antiques, fishing, parks, shopping, downhill skiing, cross-country skiing, sporting events, theater and watersports nearby. TAC10.

Special Discounts: 10% discount for four nights or more.

Saint Marys E7

Towne House Inn

138 Center St
Saint Marys, PA 15857
(814)781-1556 (800)851-9180
Fax:(814)834-4449

Rates: $59-110.
Payment: MC VISA AX DC DS PC TC.
Innkeeper(s): Burt Maki.

Rooms: 53 rooms with PB, 4 with FP. 11 suites.
Beds: KQD.

To fully enjoy the Town House Inn's historic character, be sure to request a room in the main house or in the Tudor Revival Willows house. Both of these buildings are listed in the National Register. The Victorian Bridal Suite offers a fireplace, king bed, leaded-glass windows and original bathroom fixtures. Some rooms offer whirlpool tubs. Five outstanding stained-glass windows, beamed ceiling, a fireplace and polished wood floors decorate the dining room of the inn. There is a restaurant on the premises, but the inn also offers a complimentary continental breakfast .

Types of meals: continental-plus breakfast and full breakfast. Dinner, lunch and room service available. Air conditioning, ceiling fan and cable TV in room. Fax and copier on premises. Handicap access. Small meetings and family reunions hosted. Fishing, parks, shopping, cross-country skiing and watersports nearby. TAC10.

Scottdale K4

Zephyr Glen Bed & Breakfast

205 Dexter Rd
Scottdale, PA 15683-1812
(412)887-6577
E-mail: Zephyr@hhs.net

Rates: $70-75.
Payment: MC VISA DS PC TC.
Innkeeper(s): Noreen & Gil McGurl.
Circa: 1822.

Rooms: 3 rooms with PB, 1 with FP.
Beds: D.

An inviting country theme permeates the atmosphere at this early 19th century, Federal-style farmhouse. Rooms are filled with period antiques, quilts and a few carefully placed knickknacks and musical instruments. Several rooms are decorated with stencils created by innkeeper Noreen McGurl. She and husband, Gil, also run an antique store out of their inn. Guests are treated to breakfasts of homemade granola, jams made from berries on the property, freshly baked breads and other treats. The three-acres grounds are decorated with maples, oaks, fruit trees, berry bushes, herb gardens and a fish pond. Frank Lloyd Wright's masterpiece, "Fallingwater," is nearby.

Breakfast, afternoon tea and evening snack included in rates. Types of meals: full breakfast and early coffee/tea. Picnic lunch available. Turn-down service and ceiling fan in room. Cable TV, fax and library on premises. Small meetings and seminars hosted. Amusement parks, antiques, fishing, parks, shopping, downhill skiing, cross-country skiing, theater and watersports nearby. TAC10.

"We can't stop talking about the wonderful time we had at your lovely inn."

Shippensburg K10

Field & Pine B&B

2155 Ritner Hwy
Shippensburg, PA 17257
(717)776-7179

Rates: $65-75.
Payment: MC VISA PC TC.
Innkeeper(s): Mary Ellen & Allan Williams.
Circa: 1790.

Rooms: 3 rooms, 1 with PB, 1 with FP. 1 suite.
Beds: QDT.

Local limestone was used to build this stone house, located on the main wagon road to Baltimore and Washington. Originally, it was a tavern and weigh station. The house is surrounded by stately pines, and sheep graze on the inn's 80 acres. The bedrooms are hand-stenciled and furnished with quilts and antiques.

Breakfast and evening snack included in rates. Types of meals: gourmet breakfast and early coffee/tea. Air conditioning and turn-down service in room. VCR on premises. 80 acres. Weddings, small meetings, family reunions hosted. Antiques, fishing, and parks nearby. TAC10.

Location: Twelve miles south of Carlisle, on US Rte 11.

Publicity: *Valley Times-Star.*

"Our visit in this lovely country home has been most delightful. The ambiance of antiques and tasteful decorating exemplifies real country living."

Smoketown K14

Homestead Lodging

184 E Brook Rd (Rt 896)
Smoketown, PA 17576-9701
(717)393-6927
Fax:(717)393-6927

Rates: $37-56.
Payment: MC VISA AX DS TC.
Innkeeper(s): Robert & Lori Kepiro.
Circa: 1984.

Rooms: 4 rooms with PB.
Beds: D.

An Amish farm rests adjacent to this newer brick Colonial, and from this bed & breakfast, guests can enjoy Pennsylvania Dutch country. Farmer's markets, antique shops, museums and restaurants all are nearby. Wood-paneled guest rooms are simply furnished and each includes a refrigerator and cable TV. Children are welcome.

Breakfast included in rates. Types of meals: continental breakfast and early coffee/tea. Air conditioning, ceiling fan and cable TV in room. Tennis on premises. Amusement parks, antiques, fishing, parks, shopping and theater nearby.

"Your hospitality and immaculate Lodge stay with us long after we leave."

Spring Creek D4

Spring Valley B&B

RR 1 Box 117
Spring Creek, PA 16436
(814)489-3000 (800)382-1324
Fax:(814)489-7333
E-mail: springvalley@penn.com

Rates: $75-130.
Payment: MC VISA DS PC TC.
Innkeeper(s): Jim Bird & Debora Regis.
Circa: 1820.

Rooms: 3 rooms. 2 cottages.
Beds: QD.

Although located on Pennsylvania's Allegheny Plateau, this 105-acre spread feels more like a Western-style ranch. Deer and other wildlife roam the grounds, and there are hiking and cross-country ski trails on the premises. The land is adjacent to more than 8,000 acres of state game lands. There are two suites available in the main house as well as a log and cedar cottage. The cottage sleeps six and includes a fireplace and deck overlooking the woods. Four guests can stay comfortably in the Parlor Suite, which includes a corn-burning stove and clawfoot tub. For an additional fee, guests can enjoy guided, horseback trail rides.

Breakfast included in rates. Types of meals: continental breakfast, continental-plus breakfast, full breakfast, gourmet breakfast and early coffee/tea. Evening snack, picnic lunch, lunch, gourmet lunch, catering service, catered breakfast and room service available. Ceiling fan and cable TV in room. VCR, fax, copier, stables, bicycles, library and child care on premises. Handicap access. 105 acres. Weddings, small meetings and family reunions hosted. Antiques, fishing, parks, shopping, downhill skiing, cross-country skiing, theater and watersports nearby. TAC8.

Strasburg K14

Decoy B&B

958 Eisenberger Rd
Strasburg, PA 17579-9735
(717)687-8585 (800)726-2287
Fax:(717)687-8585

Rates: $50-70.
Payment: PC.
Innkeeper(s): Debby & Hap Joy.
Circa: 1976.

Rooms: 5 rooms with PB.
Beds: KQDT.

Situated on three acres overlooking the fertile countryside of Lancaster County, this former Amish farmhouse now boasts electricity and central heat as well as five guest rooms. The innkeepers dine with guests at breakfast, which features hearty items such as meat and potato quiche, or waffles with homemade toppings. They answer questions about the area and help plan tours, often arranging dinner with an Old Order Amish family.

Breakfast included in rates. Types of meals: full breakfast and early coffee/tea. Air conditioning in room. VCR, fax, copier and library on premises. Small meetings, family reunions and seminars hosted. Amusement parks, antiques, fishing and theater nearby. TAC10.

"Thank you for all your wonderful hospitality, delicious breakfasts, helpful tour guide info, soft fluffy towels—on and on."

Thornton

K16

Pace One Restaurant and Country Inn

Thornton Rd & Glen Mills Rd
Thornton, PA 19373
(610)459-3702
Fax:(610)558-0825

Rates: $85.
Payment: MC VISA AX DC PC TC.
Innkeeper(s): Ted Pace & Jim Hunte.
Circa: 1740.

Rooms: 6 rooms with PB. 3 conference rooms.
Beds: Q.

This beautifully renovated stone barn has two-and-a-half-foot thick walls, hand-hewn wood beams, and many small-paned windows. Just in front of the inn was the Gray family home used as a hospital during the Revolutionary War when Washington's army crossed nearby Chadd's Ford.

Breakfast included in rates. Type of meal: continental-plus breakfast. Picnic lunch, lunch and banquet service available. Air conditioning in room. Fax and copier on premises. Weddings, small meetings, family reunions and seminars hosted. Antiques, fishing, parks, shopping, sporting events and theater nearby.

"Dear Ted & Staff, we loved it here!! The accommodations were great and the brunch on Sunday, fantastic. Thanks for making it a beautiful weekend."

Valley Forge

The Great Valley House of Valley Forge

110 Swedesford Rd, Rd 3
Valley Forge
(Malvern), PA 19355
(610)644-6759
Fax:(610)644-7019
E-mail: jeffbenson@unn.unisys.com

Rates: $75-90. AP.
Payment: MC VISA DS PC TC.
Innkeeper(s): Pattye Benson.
Circa: 1691.

Rooms: 3 rooms, 2 with PB.
Beds: QDT.

This 300-year-old Colonial stone farmhouse sits on four acres just two miles from Valley Forge Park. Boxwoods line the walkway and ancient trees surround the house. Each of the three guest rooms are hand-stenciled and feature canopied or brass beds topped with handmade quilts. Guests enjoy a full breakfast before a 14-foot fireplace in the "summer kitchen," the oldest part of the house. On the grounds are a swimming pool, walking and hiking trails, and the home's original smokehouse.

Breakfast included in rates. Types of meals: gourmet breakfast and early coffee/tea. Picnic lunch available. AP. Air conditioning, turndown service and cable TV in room. Fax and swimming on premises. Weddings and small meetings hosted. Spanish and French spoken. Antiques, fishing, parks, shopping, cross-country skiing, sporting events, theater and watersports nearby. TAC10.

Location: Two miles from Valley Forge National Park.

Publicity: *Main Line Philadelphia, Philadelphia Inquirer, Washington Post, New York Times, Suburban Newspaper, Phoenixville Sun.*

Special Discounts: 10% discount for four nights or longer.

"As a business traveler, Patty's enthusiasm and warm welcome makes you feel just like you're home."

Warfordsburg

L8

Buck Valley Ranch

Rt 2 Box 1170
Warfordsburg, PA 17267
(717)294-3759 (800)294-3759
Fax:(717)294-3759

Rates: $60.
Payment: MC VISA DS PC TC.
Innkeeper(s): Nadine & Leon Fox.
Circa: 1930.

Rooms: 4 rooms.
Beds: DT.

Trail riding is a popular activity on the ranch's 64 acres in the Appalachian Mountains of South Central Pennsylvania. State game lands and forests border the ranch. The guest house, decorated in a ranch/cowboy style, is a private farmhouse that can accommodate eight people. Meals are prepared using homegrown vegetables and locally raised meats. Rates also include horseback riding.

Breakfast, dinner, evening snack and picnic lunch included in rates. Types of meals: full breakfast, gourmet breakfast and early coffee/tea. Lunch and gourmet lunch available. Air conditioning in room. Fax, copier, swimming, sauna and stables on premises. 68 acres. Small meetings, family reunions and seminars hosted. Amusement parks, antiques, fishing, parks, shopping, downhill skiing, cross-country skiing and watersports nearby. TAC5.

Special Discounts: Children half price during week.

Washington Crossing — *J18*

Inn to The Woods

150 Glenwood Dr, Washington Crossing, PA 18977
(215)493-1974 (800)982-7619
Fax:(215)493-7592

Rates: $85-175.
Payment: MC VISA AX PC TC.
Innkeeper(s): Barry & Rosemary Rein.
Circa: 1978.

Rooms: 6 rooms with PB. 1 suite. 1 conference room.
Beds: KQD.

Located on 10 forested acres, this chalet offers seclusion and trails for hiking. Victorian furnishings and framed art add to the pleasingly appointed guest rooms. There is an indoor garden and fishpond. The chalet has beamed ceilings and parquet floors. On weekdays a continental breakfast is served, while on Saturday a full breakfast is provided. The fare for Sunday is a champagne brunch.

Breakfast, afternoon tea and evening snack included in rates. Types of meals: continental breakfast, continental-plus breakfast, full breakfast, gourmet breakfast and early coffee/tea. Dinner, picnic lunch, lunch, gourmet lunch, banquet service, catered breakfast and room service available. Air conditioning, ceiling fan and cable TV in room. VCR, fax, copier, bicycles and library on premises. 10 acres. Weddings, small meetings, family reunions and seminars hosted. German spoken. Amusement parks, antiques, fishing, parks, shopping, cross-country skiing, theater and watersports nearby. TAC5.

Special Discounts: Weekend packages-$195-245.

Wellsboro — *D11*

Waln Street B&B

54 Waln St
Wellsboro, PA 16901-1936
(717)724-3543

Rates: $50-70.
Payment: MC VISA.
Innkeeper(s): Catherine Casiello.
Circa: 1886.

Rooms: 4 rooms, 1 with PB.
Beds: QD.

This three-story Dutch Colonial Revival Home is decorated with lace and walnut period pieces. Guests are invited to rock away the afternoon on a sweeping wraparound porch. Evenings often are spent enjoying the sounds from a Grand piano in the drawing room. Soft beds are flanked with over-stuffed pillows and after a restful night's sleep, guests enjoy a lavish breakfast served on fine china and crystal. The bed & breakfast is located only two blocks from the quaint gaslights which decorate Wellsboro's main street.

Breakfast included in rates. Type of meal: full breakfast. Antiques, fishing, downhill skiing, cross-country skiing, theater and watersports nearby.

Pets Allowed.

Publicity: *Wellsboro Gazette, Williamsport Sun Gazette.*

"You have a beautiful presentation. Splendid."

West Chester K16

Bankhouse B&B

875 Hillsdale Rd
West Chester, PA 19382
(610)344-7388

Rates: $65-85.
Payment: TC.
Innkeeper(s): Diana & Michael Bove.
Circa: 1765.

Rooms: 2 rooms. 1 suite.
Beds: DT.

Built into the bank of a quiet country road, this 18th-century house overlooks a 10-acre horse farm and pond. The interior is decorated with country antiques, stenciling and folk art. Guests have a private entrance and porch. Two bedrooms share a common sitting room library. Hearty country breakfasts include German apple souffle pancakes, custard French toast and nearly 100 other recipes. West Chester and the Brandywine Valley attractions are conveniently close.

Breakfast and evening snack included in rates. Types of meals: full breakfast, gourmet breakfast and early coffee/tea. Ceiling fan in room. Antiques, parks, shopping, cross-country skiing, sporting events and theater nearby.

Location: In Brandywine Valley.

Publicity: *Philadelphia Inquirer, Mercury, Bucks County Town & Country Living, Chester County Living, Washington Post.*

"Everything was so warm and inviting. One of my favorite places to keep coming back to."

Williamsport F12

Reighard House

1323 E 3rd St
Williamsport, PA 17701
(717)326-3593 (800)326-8335
Fax:(717)323-4734

Rates: $58-88.
Payment: MC VISA AX DC CB PC TC.
Innkeeper(s): Sue Reighard.
Circa: 1905.

Rooms: 6 rooms with PB.
Beds: QD.

The Reighard House, a Victorian made of stone and brick, offers a formal parlor with a fireplace, music room with a grand piano, library and a formal oak-paneled dining room. Rooms are furnished with four-poster and canopy beds. Each bedroom is decorated with a different color scheme and theme and is identified by a needlepointed sign.

Breakfast included in rates. Types of meals: full breakfast and early coffee/tea. Air conditioning, cable TV and VCR in room. Fax, computer and library on premises. Antiques, fishing, parks, shopping, downhill skiing, cross-country skiing, sporting events, theater and watersports nearby.

Publicity: *Pennsylvania Business Journal.*

"I know I'm coming back!"

Rhode Island

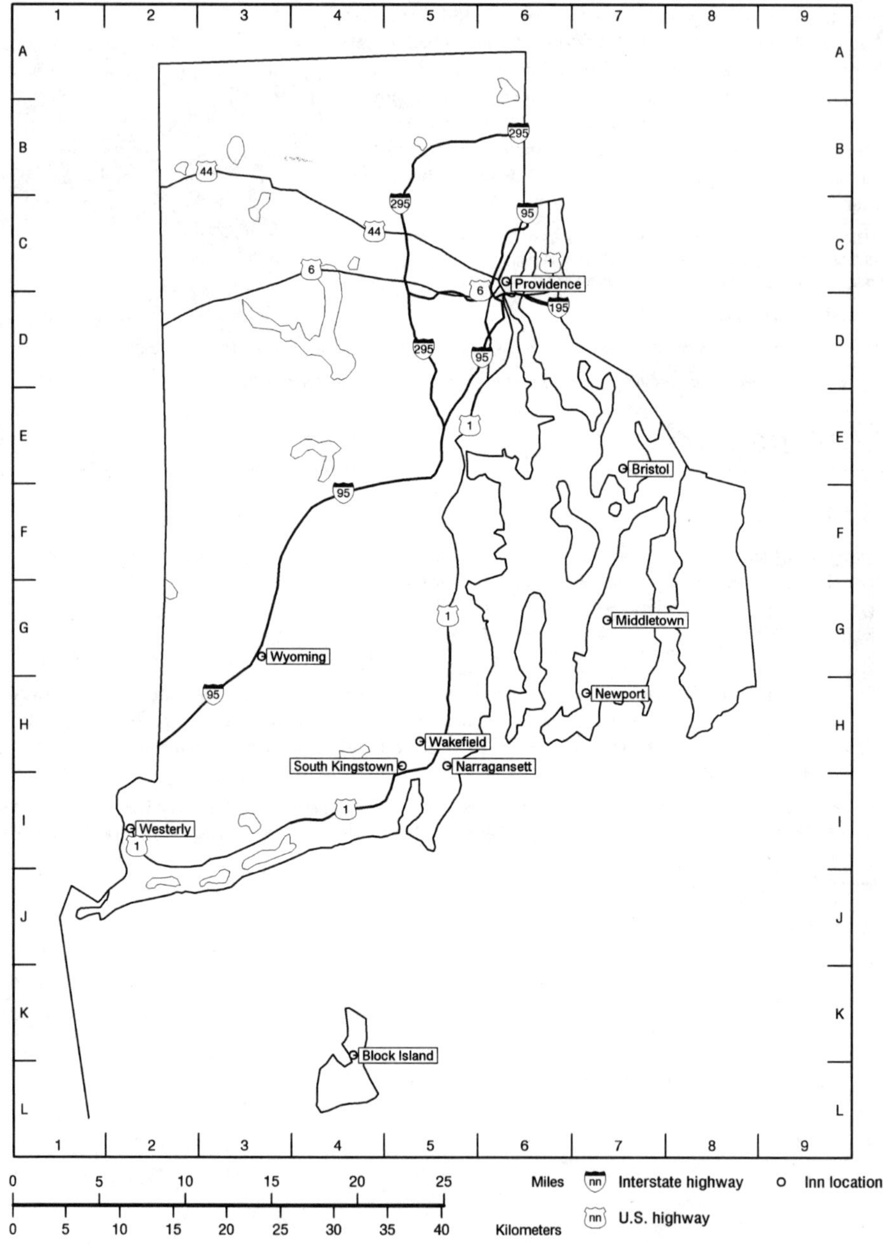

Block Island

Atlantic Inn

PO Box 188
Block Island, RI 02807-0188
(401)466-5883 (800)224-7422
Fax:(401)466-5678

Rates: $99-210.
Payment: MC VISA PC TC.
Innkeeper(s): Brad & Anne Marthens.
Circa: 1879.

Rooms: 21 rooms with PB. 1 suite. 1 conference room.
Beds: QDT.

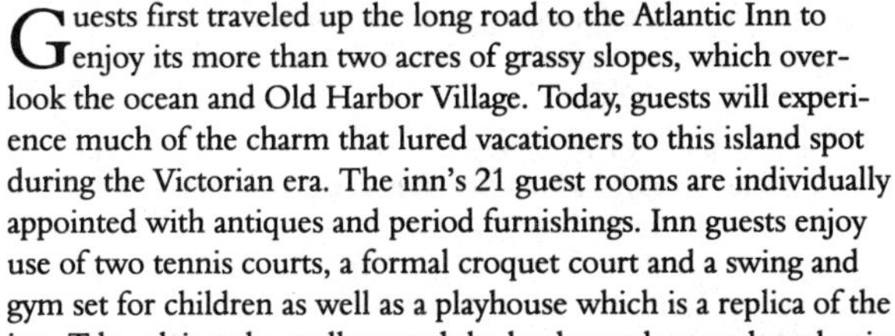

Guests first traveled up the long road to the Atlantic Inn to enjoy its more than two acres of grassy slopes, which overlook the ocean and Old Harbor Village. Today, guests will experience much of the charm that lured vacationers to this island spot during the Victorian era. The inn's 21 guest rooms are individually appointed with antiques and period furnishings. Inn guests enjoy use of two tennis courts, a formal croquet court and a swing and gym set for children as well as a playhouse which is a replica of the inn. Take a leisurely stroll around the landscaped grounds and enjoy the gardens, which provide many of the herbs and vegetables used in meals at the inn's gourmet restaurant.

Breakfast and afternoon tea included in rates. Types of meals: continental-plus breakfast and early coffee/tea. Picnic lunch available. Cable TV, fax, copier, tennis and child care on premises. Weddings, small meetings, family reunions and seminars hosted. Antiques, fishing, parks, shopping, theater and watersports nearby.

The Bellevue House

PO Box 1198, High St
Block Island, RI 02807-1198
(401)466-2912

Rates: $70-160.
Payment: MC VISA PC TC.
Innkeeper(s): Neva Flaherty.

Rooms: 5 rooms. 2 cottages.
Beds: KQD.

Offering a hilltop perch, meadow-like setting and ocean views, this Colonial Revival farmhouse inn in the Block Island Historic District has served guests for more than a century. A variety of accommodations includes five guest rooms with shared bath, five suites and two cottages. The Old Harbor Ferry, restaurants and shops are just a five-minute walk from the inn. Guests may use ferries from New London, Conn., Montauk Point, N.Y., and Newport, Point Judith and Providence, R.I., to reach the island. Beaches, Block Island National Wildlife Reserve and Rodmans Hollow Nature Area are nearby. Children are welcome.

Breakfast included in rates. Type of meal: continental breakfast. Library on premises. Family reunions hosted. Fishing, parks, shopping and watersports nearby.

Blue Dory Inn

PO Box 488, Dodge St
Block Island, RI 02807-0488
(401)466-5891 (800)992-7290
Fax:(401)466-9910

Rates: $65-195.
Payment: MC VISA AX DS PC TC.
Innkeeper(s): Ann Loedy.
Circa: 1887.

Rooms: 14 rooms with PB. 3 suites. 4 cottages. 1 conference room.
Beds: KQDT.

RI

This Shingle Victorian inn on Crescent Beach offers many guest rooms with ocean views. The Cottage, The Doll House and The Tea House are separate structures for those desiring more room or privacy. Antiques and Victorian touches are featured throughout. Year-round car ferry service, taking approximately one hour, is found at Point Judith, R.I. The island also may be reached by air on New England Airlines or by charter. Mohegan Bluffs Scenic Natural Area is nearby.

Breakfast and afternoon tea included in rates. Types of meals: continental-plus breakfast and early coffee/tea. Catered breakfast available. Cable TV, VCR, fax, copier, swimming and child care on premises. Weddings, small meetings, family reunions and seminars hosted. Antiques, fishing, parks, shopping, theater and watersports nearby. TAC10.

Pets Allowed: Restricted to certain cottages.

Special Discounts: Stay two nights-third night free midweek Sept. 15-June 15.

"The Blue Dory is a wonderful place to stay. The room was lovely, the view spectacular and the sound of surf was both restful and tranquil."

Rose Farm Inn

Roslyn Rd
Block Island, RI 02807-0895
(401)466-2034
Fax:(401)466-2053

Rates: $95-179.
Payment: MC AX DS TC.
Innkeeper(s): Robert & Judith Rose.
Circa: 1897.

Rooms: 19 rooms, 17 with PB.
Beds: KQDT.

This romantic inn is comprised of two buildings, the turn-of-the-century farmhouse and the newer Captain Rose House. Canopy beds, sitting areas and whirlpool tubs are among the elegant touches that grace the rooms at the Captain Rose House. From most rooms, either an ocean or countryside view is seen, and there's always a light sea breeze to be enjoyed from the front porch of the Farm House. A continental-plus buffet is served each morning on the enclosed sun porch, which overlooks the ocean.

Breakfast and afternoon tea included in rates. Type of meal: continental-plus breakfast. Cable TV, VCR, fax, copier and bicycles on premises. Handicap access. 20 acres. German spoken. Antiques, fishing, shopping and watersports nearby.

Sheffield House

High St, Box C-2
Block Island, RI 02807
(401)466-2494
Fax:(401)466-5067

Rates: $50-150.
Payment: VISA.
Innkeeper(s): Steve & Claire McQueeny.
Circa: 1888.

Rooms: 7 rooms, 5 with PB.
Beds: Q.

Step off the ferry and step into a by-gone era at this charming Queen Anne Victorian, which overlooks the Old Harbor district and scenic ocean vistas. Relax on the front porch or enjoy the fragrance as you stroll through the private garden. The cookie jar is always full of home-baked treats. Breakfasts are served in the quaint day room, which features a collection of milk bottles from around the world. Guests also can enjoy the morning meal in the garden surrounded by beautiful flowers and herbs. Guest rooms feature international touches, antiques and family pieces.

Breakfast, afternoon tea and evening snack included in rates. Types of meals: continental-plus breakfast and early coffee/tea. Ceiling fan in room. Cable TV, VCR and copier on premises. Weddings, small meetings, family reunions and seminars hosted. Antiques, fishing, parks, shopping and watersports nearby.

The White House

Spring St.
Block Island, RI 02807
(401)466-2653

Rates: $55-120.
Payment: MC VISA PC TC.
Innkeeper(s): Mrs. Joseph V. Connolly, Jr.
Circa: 1795.

Rooms: 2 rooms.
Beds: DT.

This Colonial-style bed & breakfast is furnished with French Provincial antiques and has sweeping views of the ocean, rolling lawns and gardens. The earliest portion of the home dates back to the 18th century. The Captain's Quarters has a bedroom-sitting room that encompasses the entire ocean side of the house. The room also has a canopied double bed and outdoor balcony. Guests have a private north portico entrance and main floor drawing room with TV. Arrangements can be made to be met at the airport or ferry.

Breakfast included in rates. Type of meal: full breakfast. Cable TV and library on premises. Weddings hosted. Fishing and shopping nearby.

"Your home is so fascinating and carries an international as well as antique filled atmosphere."

Bristol

The Joseph Reynolds House

956 Hope St
Bristol, RI 02809-1113
(401)254-0230 (800)754-0230
Fax:(401)254-2610

Rates: $49-95.
Payment: PC TC.
Innkeeper(s): Wendy & Richard Anderson.
Circa: 1684.

Rooms: 5 rooms. 2 suites.
Beds: KQDT.

The Joseph Reynolds House is a National Historic Landmark and the oldest known 17th-century, three-story wooden structure in New England. It was the military headquarters of General Lafayette in 1778. Gradually being restored to its original elegance, guest rooms are on the second and third floors. Most of the common rooms have high ceilings and were painted to look like marble. There is a Jacobean staircase, a keeping room and a great room.

Breakfast and afternoon tea included in rates. Type of meal: gourmet breakfast. Cable TV, VCR, fax, copier and library on premises. Weddings, small meetings, family reunions and seminars hosted. Antiques, fishing, parks, shopping, sporting events and theater nearby. TAC10.

Pets Allowed.

Location: Twenty-five minutes from Newport.

Publicity: *American Design, New England Colonial, New York Travel, Providence Journal, New England Magazine.*

"Wonderful, restful week after chaos."

Rockwell House Inn B&B

610 Hope St
Bristol, RI 02809-1945
(401)253-0040 (800)815-0040
Fax:(401)253-1811

Rates: $75-110.
Payment: MC VISA AX DS PC TC.
Innkeeper(s): Debra & Steve Krohn.
Circa: 1809.

Rooms: 4 rooms with PB, 2 with FP. 1 conference room.
Beds: KQT.

This Federal and Greek Revival home boasts eight-foot pocket doors, Italianate mantels and working fireplaces. Double parlors open to the dining room and its inlaid parquet floors. The sun porch features a stone turret and leaded-glass windows. Two guest rooms include working fireplaces and antiques abound in each of the elegant quarters. The inn is only one block from Narragansett Bay and a 15-mile bike path.

Breakfast and afternoon tea included in rates. Types of meals: continental-plus breakfast, full breakfast, gourmet breakfast and early coffee/tea. Catered breakfast available. Turn-down service and ceiling fan in room. VCR, fax and copier on premises. Small meetings and seminars hosted. Spanish spoken. Antiques, fishing, parks, shopping, cross-country skiing and watersports nearby. TAC10.

Special Discounts: Corporate rates Monday-Thursday.

"Next time I'll bring company. It's much too romantic to be here alone! This is such a lovely home."

William's Grant Inn

RI

154 High St
Bristol, RI 02809-2123
(401)253-4222 (800)596-4222

Rates: $65-95.
Payment: MC VISA AX DS PC TC.
Innkeeper(s): Michael Rose.
Circa: 1808.

Rooms: 5 rooms, 3 with PB, 5 with FP.
Beds: QD.

This handsome Federal Colonial home was built by Governor William Bradford for his son. There are two beehive ovens and seven fireplaces as well as original wide-board pine floors and paired interior chimneys. Antique furnishings and folk art make the guest rooms inviting. A full gourmet breakfast is served in the country kitchen.

Breakfast included in rates. Types of meals: full breakfast and gourmet breakfast. Afternoon tea available. Turn-down service and ceiling fan in room. Bicycles on premises. Small meetings hosted. Antiques, fishing, parks, shopping, sporting events and watersports nearby. TAC10.

Location: Located in the heart of Bristol's historic waterfront district.

Publicity: *New York Times, Sun Sentinal, Providence Journal, Bristol Phoenix.*

"We felt better than at home with the wonderful treats (the breakfasts were fabulous), the lovely rooms, the inn is full of inspiration and innovation.."

Middletown G7

The Inn at Shadow Lawn

120 Miantonomi Ave
Middletown, RI 02842-5450
(401)847-0902
Fax:(401)849-3574

Rates: $65-135.
Payment: MC VISA TC.
Innkeeper(s): Randy & Selma Fabricant.
Circa: 1853.

Rooms: 8 rooms with PB, 8 with FP. 2 conference rooms.
Beds: KQT.

This elegant, three-story Stick Victorian inn, listed in the National Register, offers a glimpse of fine living in an earlier age. The innkeepers' attention to detail is evident throughout, with French crystal chandeliers, stained-glass windows and parquet floors in the library as a few of the highlights. Parlors are found on each of the inn's floors. Newport's many attractions, including the Art Museum, sailing and the world famous Newport mansions are just a short drive from the inn, which also offers a daily shuttle to the city.

Breakfast included in rates. Type of meal: full breakfast. Air conditioning in room. Fax, copier and library on premises. Weddings, small meetings, family reunions and seminars hosted. Antiques nearby.

"A dream come true! Thanks for everything! We'll be back."

Lindsey's Guest House

6 James St
Middletown, RI 02842-5932
(401)846-9386

Rates: $40-75.
Payment: MC VISA AX PC TC.
Innkeeper(s): Anne T. Lindsey.
Circa: 1955.

Rooms: 2 rooms with PB.
Beds: KD.

This contemporary split-level home in a residential area features three guest rooms, including one on the ground level that boasts a private entrance and is handicap-accessible. Breakfast is served in the dining room and usually includes cereal, coffee cake, fruit, juice, muffins and jam, and coffee or beverage of choice. The innkeeper has worked in the hospitality industry for more than 30 years and is happy to offer sightseeing tips. The Norman Bird Sanctuary and Sachuest Point National Wildlife Reserve are nearby.

Breakfast included in rates. Type of meal: continental-plus breakfast. Ceiling fan in room. VCR on premises. Handicap access. Weddings, small meetings, family reunions and seminars hosted. Antiques, fishing, parks, shopping, theater and watersports nearby. TAC10.

Narragansett H5

The 1900 House B&B

59 Kingstown Rd
Narragansett, RI 02882
(401)789-7971

Rates: $65-75.
Payment: PC TC.
Innkeeper(s): Sandra & Bill Panzeri.
Circa: 1900.

Rooms: 3 rooms, 1 with PB.
Beds: D.

For more than a century, Narragansett has been a hot spot for summer vacationers. Guests at the 1900 House enjoy both close access to the town's restaurants and shops as well as a nostalgic look back at the Victorian era. The innkeepers keep a stereoscope, hat boxes filled with antique post cards and other collectibles on hand for guests to discover. You might spot the wedding certificate of the home's original owner. Waffles topped with fresh fruit and cream are typical of the rich treats served at breakfast.

Breakfast included in rates. Types of meals: full breakfast, gourmet breakfast and early coffee/tea. Antiques, fishing, parks, shopping, sporting events, theater and watersports nearby.

"Wonderful! So relaxing and lovely, lovely breakfasts."

The Brinley Victorian Inn

23 Brinley St
Newport, RI 02840-3238
(401)849-7645 (800)999-8523

Rates: $55-150.
Payment: MC VISA.
Innkeeper(s): John & Jennifer Sweetman.
Circa: 1870.

Rooms: 17 rooms, 13 with PB. 1 suite.
Beds: KQDT.

This is a three-story Victorian with a mansard roof and long porch. A cottage on the property dates from 1850. There are two parlors and a library providing a quiet haven from the bustle of the Newport wharfs. Each room is decorated with period wallpapers and furnishings. There are fresh flowers and mints on the pillows. The brick courtyard is planted with bleeding hearts, peonies and miniature roses, perennials of the Victorian Era.

Breakfast included in rates.

Location: Newport Historic District.

Publicity: *New Hampshire Times, Boston Woman, Country Victorian, Yankee.*

"Ed and I had a wonderful anniversary. The Brinley is as lovely and cozy as ever! The weekend brought back lots of happy memories."

Cliffside Inn

2 Seaview Ave
Newport, RI 02840-3627
(401)847-1811 (800)845-1811
Fax:(401)848-5850
E-mail: cliffside.inn@nccnet.com

Rates: $165-325.
Payment: MC VISA AX DC DS PC TC.
Innkeeper(s): Stephan Nicolas.
Circa: 1880.

Rooms: 13 rooms with PB, 11 with FP. 4 suites.
Beds: KQ.

The governor of Maryland, Thomas Swann, built this Newport summer house in the style of a Second Empire Victorian. It features a mansard roof and many bay windows. The rooms are decorated in a Victorian motif. Suites have marble baths, and most rooms have Jacuzzi tubs or fireplaces. The Cliff Walk is located one block from the inn.

Breakfast and afternoon tea included in rates. Types of meals: gourmet breakfast and early coffee/tea. Air conditioning, turndown service, ceiling fan, cable TV and VCR in room. Fax on premises. French spoken. Antiques, fishing, shopping, theater and watersports nearby. TAC10.

Publicity: *Country Inns, Philadelphia, Discerning Traveler, New York, Boston, Good Morning America.*

"...it captures the grandeur of the Victorian age."

Halidon Hill Guest House

Halidon Ave
Newport, RI 02840
(401)847-8318 (800)227-2130

Rates: $55-200.
Payment: AX DC DS.
Innkeeper(s): Helen & Paul Burke.
Circa: 1968.

Rooms: 2 suites.
Beds: KQDT.

This contemporary, two-story Georgian-style inn offers a convenient location and comfortable accommodations for those exploring the Newport area. The two spacious suites both boast kitchenettes. The inn is just a 10-minute walk to Hammersmith Farm and provides easy access to the area's mansions, restaurants and shopping. Guests will enjoy lounging on the roomy deck near the in-ground pool, or in front of the fireplace in cooler weather. Newport Harbor and the Tennis Hall of Fame are nearby.

Breakfast included in rates. Type of meal: full breakfast. Antiques, shopping, theater and watersports nearby.

Inntowne

6 Mary St
Newport, RI 02840-3028
(401)846-9200 (800)457-7803
Fax:(401)846-1534

Rates: $95-179.
Payment: MC VISA AX.
Innkeeper(s): Carmella Gardner.
Circa: 1935.

Rooms: 26 rooms with PB. 1 suite.
Beds: KQDT.

This Colonial-style inn is an elegant spot from which to enjoy the seaside town of Newport. Waverly and Laura Ashley prints decorate the individually appointed guest rooms, some of which have four-poster or canopy beds. The innkeepers serve an expanded continental breakfast with items such as fresh fruit, quiche and ham and cheese croissants. Afternoon tea also is served. A day in Newport offers many activities, including touring the Tennis Hall of Fame, taking a cruise through the harbor, shopping for antiques or perhaps taking a trek down Cliff Walk, a one-and-a-half-mile path offering the ocean on one side and historic mansions on the other.

Afternoon tea included in rates. Type of meal: continental-plus breakfast. Air conditioning in room. Cable TV, VCR, fax, copier and library on premises. Weddings, small meetings and family reunions hosted. Antiques, parks and shopping nearby.

Special Discounts: Midweek packages off season.

"Thank you for your excellent service with a smile."

Jailhouse Inn

13 Marlborough St
Newport, RI 02840-2545
(401)847-4638

Rates: $45-105.
Payment: DC.
Innkeeper(s): Eric Jones.
Circa: 1742.

Rooms: 22 rooms with PB. 1 conference room.
Beds: Q.

The owner of another B&B, the Yankee Peddler, has had a good bit of fun restoring and renovating the old Newport Jail. Prison-striped bed coverings and tin cups and plates for breakfast express the jailhouse motif. Guests can stay in the Cell Block, Maximum Security or Solitary Confinement, each on a separate level of the inn. Nevertheless, because guests pay for their time here, there are luxuries in abundance.

Type of meal: continental breakfast. Afternoon tea available. Handicap access. Fishing nearby.

Publicity: *Providence Journal.*

"I found this very relaxing and a great pleasure."

The Melville House

39 Clarke St
Newport, RI 02840-3023
(401)847-0640
Fax:(401)847-0956
E-mail: innkeepri@aol.com

Rates: $85-165.
Payment: MC VISA AX DS PC TC.
Innkeeper(s): Vincent DeRico & David Horan.
Circa: 1750.

Rooms: 7 rooms, 5 with PB, 1 with FP. 1 suite.
Beds: KDT.

This attractive, National Register two-story Colonial inn once housed aides to General Rochambeau during the American Revolution. Early American furnishings decorate the interior. There is also an unusual collection of old appliances, including a cherry-pitter, mincer and dough maker. A full breakfast includes Portuguese Quiche, Jonnycakes, homemade bread and Portuguese egg sandwiches. The inn is a pleasant walk from the waterfront and historic sites.

Breakfast and afternoon tea included in rates. Types of meals: full breakfast, gourmet breakfast and early coffee/tea. Picnic lunch available. Air conditioning in room. Fax and bicycles on premises. Weddings, small meetings, family reunions and seminars hosted. Antiques, fishing, parks, shopping, theater and watersports nearby. TAC10.

Location: In the heart of Newport's Historic Hill.

Publicity: *Country Inns, "Lodging Pick" for Newport, Good Housekeeping.*

Special Discounts: Discounts for long term stays.

"Comfortable with a quiet elegance."

Old Beach Inn

19 Old Beach Rd
Newport, RI 02840-3237
(401)849-3479 (888)303-5033
Fax:(401)847-1236

Rates: $75-155.
Payment: MC VISA AX DS PC TC.
Innkeeper(s): Luke & Cynthia Murray.
Circa: 1879.

Rooms: 7 rooms with PB, 4 with FP.
Beds: QD.

Stroll through the backyard at this enchanting Gothic Victorian bed & breakfast and you'll find a garden, lily pond and romantic gazebo. Innkeepers Luke and Cyndi Murray have kept a whimsical, romantic theme running inside and outside. Each of the guest rooms, two of which are located in the carriage house, bears the name of a flower. Delightful decor with bright wallcoverings and linens accent the beautiful furnishings. The Lily Room includes a 19th-century cottage bed and peach and ivory decor, while the powder blue and white Forget-Me-Not room is filled with wicker. Every item in the room is color-coordinated and features special painting and stenciling created by Cyndi. The area abounds with shops and restaurants, including a famous eatery managed by Luke.

Breakfast included in rates. Type of meal: continental-plus breakfast. Air conditioning and ceiling fan in room. Fax and copier on premises. Weddings, small meetings, family reunions and seminars hosted. Antiques, fishing, parks, shopping, theater and watersports nearby.

Publicity: *Yankee, Sun Sentinel.*

The Pilgrim House

123 Spring St
Newport, RI 02840-6805
(401)846-0040 (800)525-8373
Fax:(401)846-0357

Rates: $65-165.
Payment: MC VISA PC.
Innkeeper(s): Pam & Bruce Bayuk.
Circa: 1879.

Rooms: 10 rooms, 8 with PB. 1 conference room.
Beds: QDT.

This Victorian inn, located in the heart of Newport, has a rooftop deck with a panoramic view of the harbor. The home is within walking distance of shops, restaurants, the Cliff Walk and the Newport mansions. In the afternoon, the innkeepers serve sherry and shortbread in the living room, which often is warmed by a crackling fire.

Breakfast and afternoon tea included in rates. Types of meals: continental breakfast, continental-plus breakfast and early coffee/tea. Air conditioning in room. Cable TV, fax and copier on premises. Small meetings, family reunions and seminars hosted. Antiques, fishing, parks, shopping, theater and watersports nearby. TAC10.

Location: In the heart of the historic district, one-and-one-half blocks from Newport's harbor and wharfs.

Publicity: *The Times.*

"What can I say, it's a perfect hideaway. Great time was had by all."

RI

Villa Liberte

22 Liberty St
Newport, RI 02840-3221
(401)846-7444 (800)392-3717
Fax:(401)849-6429

Rates: $69-195.
Payment: MC VISA AX TC.
Innkeeper(s): Leigh Anne Mosco.
Circa: 1910.

Rooms: 15 rooms with PB. 4 suites. 1 conference room.
Beds: QDT.

This colorful European-style inn originally served as the site of a Bavarian restaurant. The exterior, decorated with window boxes, plants, flowers and red trim, is a pleasing site along Liberty Street. The building also has a colorful history. Among the many stories, the restaurant was a hot spot after World War I and during the 1920s, when soldiers would come here to enjoy a meal and perhaps the company of a lady. Today, guests might enter their room to find a four-poster bed dressed in deep green and paisley linens and other fine traditional furnishings. The Sunroom is a wonderful spot to relax, decorated with wicker furnishings, plants and a ceiling fan. Newport is always bustling with activities, and there are plenty of fine shops and restaurants nearby.

Breakfast and afternoon tea included in rates. Type of meal: continental-plus breakfast. Air conditioning and cable TV in room. Fax on premises. Weddings, small meetings, family reunions and seminars hosted. Antiques, fishing, parks, shopping, theater and watersports nearby.

Old Court B&B

144 Benefit St
Providence, RI 02903-1208
(401)751-2002
Fax:(401)272-4830

Rates: $75-260.
Innkeeper(s): Jon Rosenblatt.
Circa: 1863.

Rooms: 11 rooms with PB. 1 suite.
Beds: KQDT.

Adjacent to the historic Rhode Island Courthouse, this Italianate building originally served as an Episcopal rectory. Indoor shutters, chandeliers hanging from 12-foot ceilings and elaborate Italian marble mantelpieces provide the gracious setting for antique Victorian beds. Some rooms overlook the capitol. Brown University, Rhode Island School of Design and downtown Providence are a short walk away.

Breakfast included in rates. Types of meals: full breakfast and gourmet breakfast. Air conditioning in room. Fax, copier and computer on premises. Weddings and small meetings hosted. Antiques, parks, shopping, sporting events and theater nearby. TAC1.

Location: On historic Benefit Street.

Publicity: *New York Times.*

"My only suggestion is that you do everything in your power not to change it."

State House Inn

43 Jewett St
Providence, RI 02908-4904
(401)351-6111
Fax:(401)351-4261

Rates: $79-119. EP.
Payment: MC VISA AX PC TC.
Innkeeper(s): Frank & Monica Hopton.
Circa: 1889.

Rooms: 10 rooms with PB, 2 with FP.
Beds: KQ.

Shaker and Colonial furniture fill this turn-of-the-century home, located in the midst of a quaint and peaceful Providence neighborhood. The rooms provide amenities that will please any business traveler and have the country comfort and elegance of days gone by. The common room contains a small library for guest use. A famed historic district, featuring restored homes and buildings, is three blocks away, and the capitol is a five-minute walk.

Breakfast included in rates. Type of meal: full breakfast. Afternoon tea available. EP. Air conditioning and cable TV in room. Fax, copier and computer on premises. Antiques and parks nearby. TAC10.

Location: Forty minutes from Newport.

Publicity: *Providence Magazine.*

"Thank you again for the warm, comfortable and very attractive accommodations."

❑ For Providence, see also Seekonk, Mass.

South Kingstown H5

Admiral Dewey Inn

668 Matunuck Beach Rd
South Kingstown, RI 02879
(401)783-2090 (800)457-2090
Fax:(401)783-0680

Rates: $40-120.
Payment: MC VISA PC.
Innkeeper(s): Joan Lebel.
Circa: 1898.

Rooms: 10 rooms, 8 with PB.
Beds: QDT.

Although the prices have risen a bit since this inn's days as a boarding house (the rate was 50 cents per night), this stick-style home still offers hospitality and comfort. The National Register inn is within walking distance of Matunuck Beach. Guests can enjoy the sea breeze from the inn's wraparound porch. Period antiques decorate the guest rooms, some of which offer ocean views.

Breakfast included in rates. Types of meals: continental-plus breakfast and early coffee/tea. Picnic lunch available. Cable TV, VCR, fax, copier and swimming on premises. Weddings, small meetings, family reunions and seminars hosted. Polish spoken. Antiques, fishing, parks, shopping, theater and watersports nearby.

Special Discounts: Summer only weekly five nights Sunday through Thursday $399.00 plus tax.

Wakefield

H5

Larchwood Inn

521 Main St
Wakefield, RI 02879-4003
(401)783-5454 (800)275-5450
Fax:(401)783-1800

Rates: $35-110.
Payment: MC VISA AX DC CB DS.
Innkeeper(s): Francis & Diann Browning.
Circa: 1831.

Rooms: 19 rooms, 13 with PB, 3 with FP. 1 conference room.

The Larchwood Inn and its adjacent sister inn, Holly House, were both constructed in the same era. The two are sprinkled with antiques and are family-run, with 20th-century amenities. Scottish touches are found throughout the inn and the Tam O'Shanter Tavern. Three dining rooms offer breakfast, lunch and dinner. (Breakfast is an extra charge.) The tavern offers dancing on weekends. Beaches, sailing and deep sea fishing all are nearby.

Type of meal: full breakfast. Dinner, lunch, banquet service and catered breakfast available. Cable TV, fax and copier on premises. Weddings, small meetings, family reunions and seminars hosted. Antiques, shopping, downhill skiing, cross-country skiing and theater nearby.

Westerly

I2

Grandview B&B

212 Shore Rd
Westerly, RI 02891-3623
(401)596-6384 (800)447-6384
Fax:(401)596-6384

Rates: $75-95.
Payment: MC VISA AX PC TC.
Innkeeper(s): Patricia Grand.
Circa: 1910.

Rooms: 10 rooms, 4 with PB.
Beds: KDT.

An impressive wraparound stone porch highlights this majestic Shingle Victorian inn, which also boasts a lovely ocean view from its hilltop site. The inn features 10 guest rooms, a family room with cable TV, a spacious living room with a handsome stone fireplace, and a sun porch where visitors enjoy a hearty breakfast buffet. A black labrador retriever named Nike welcomes all visitors, but respectfully requests they leave their pets at home. Antiquing, fishing, golf, swimming and tennis are found nearby as are Watch Hill, Mystic and Newport. The Foxwoods and Mohegan Sun casinos also are nearby.

Breakfast included in rates. Type of meal: continental-plus breakfast. Cable TV, VCR, fax and copier on premises. Weddings, small meetings, family reunions and seminars hosted. Antiques, fishing, parks, shopping, theater and watersports nearby. TAC10.

Special Discounts: 10% Senior discount.

The Villa

190 Shore Rd
Westerly, RI 02891-3629
(401)596-1054 (800)722-9240
Fax:(401)596-6268

Rates: $75-205.
Payment: MC VISA AX TC.
Innkeeper(s): Jerry Maidrano.
Circa: 1938.

Rooms: 7 rooms with PB, 2 with FP. 6 suites.
Beds: KQD.

In a Dutch Colonial style with a Mediterranean influence, the Villa offers Italian porticos and verandas set on a lushly landscaped acre and a half. Mahogany woodwork is accented by ruby and sapphire fabrics, a queen-size bed and private sitting room in La Sala di Venezia, while the Blue Grotto features a Jacuzzi, fireplace and a natural stone wall. La Sala del Cielo has skylights and an ocean view in the distance. The outdoor Jacuzzi and Mediterranean-style pool are popular areas in summer. By request, the innkeeper will serve breakfast in bed.

Breakfast included in rates. Types of meals: continental-plus breakfast and early coffee/tea. Air conditioning, ceiling fan and cable TV in room. VCR, fax, copier, spa and swimming on premises. Weddings, family reunions and seminars hosted. Italian spoken. Antiques, fishing, parks, shopping, theater and watersports nearby. TAC10.

Pets Allowed: Well behaved pets on leash.

Special Discounts: Weekly stays 15%.

The Cookie Jar B&B

64 Kingstown Rd, Rt 138
Wyoming, RI 02898-1103
(401)539-2680 (800)767-4262

Rates: $75.
Payment: PC TC.
Innkeeper(s): Charles Sohl.
Circa: 1732.

Rooms: 3 suites.
Beds: KQDT.

The living room of this historic farmhouse inn once served as a blacksmith shop. The inn's original stone walls and wood ceiling remain, along with a granite fireplace built by an Indian stonemason after the forge, was removed. Years later, as rooms were added, the building became the Cookie Jar tea room, a name the innkeepers judged worth keeping. Visitors select their full breakfast fare from a menu listing the night before. The inn's grounds boast more than 60 fruit trees, a flower garden and a barn. Those who love the beach or fishing will find both fresh and salt water within a 20-minute drive.

Breakfast included in rates. Type of meal: full breakfast. Air conditioning and cable TV in room. VCR on premises. Small meetings and family reunions hosted. Amusement parks, antiques, fishing, shopping, downhill skiing, cross-country skiing, sporting events, theater and watersports nearby. TAC10.

Location: Boston is slightly more than an hour from the inn.

Special Discounts: 7th night is free.

"Our accommodations were so comfortable and the breakfasts delicious!"

Lavender Puff/Lavender Jelly

Spencer House
Santa Barbara, Calif.

- ¾ cup butter
- ¼ cup cream cheese
- 2 T chopped nuts (walnuts or pecans)
- 2 cups flour
- 1 cup plus 2 T water
- ½ cup plus 1 T lavender jelly
- 3 eggs

Whip together with a hand mixer on high, ¼ cup butter, the cream cheese and nuts. With mixer on low, cut in one cup of flour. Add 2 T water with a fork.

Form the dough into a round ball and divide into two parts. Pat the two pieces of dough into long strips 12-by-3" and place on two ungreased baking sheets or line the pans with cooking parchment.

Next, bring the remaining ½ cup butter and 1 cup water to a boil. Remove from heat and add 1 T lavender jelly and then beat in the remaining 1 cup of flour until smooth.

Cool the flour mixture and then add the 3 eggs, one at a time, beating well after each addition.

Divide this batter into two parts and spread over the previously prepared pastry. Bake for 60 minutes in a 350-degree oven.

Whip the ½ cup lavender jelly and spread over the warm pastry. Sprinkle with pecans or walnuts if desired.

- ½ cup fresh lavender flowers (or 3 T dried)
- 3 cups distilled water
- ¼ cup fresh lemon juice
- 4 cups sugar

First make a Lavender Infusion. Bring water to a boil and pour over flowers; steep for 15 to 20 minutes. Strain and save in a non-reactive (glass is best) container. Water also should be boiled in a non-reactive container. Glass, enamel or stainless steel may be used, but aluminum or iron should be avoided.

Take 2 cups Lavender Infusion, lemon juice and sugar and bring it to a boil, stirring constantly. Boil for one minute, stirring constantly. Remove from heat. Add blue or lavender food coloring to color.

Pour into jars and seal. Cool upright on a rack. The jelly may be stored in the refrigerator for up to one month. If you store the jelly longer or use it as a gift, process the jars in a water bath for five minutes after sealing it with canning lids.

Makes 2 pints.

South Carolina

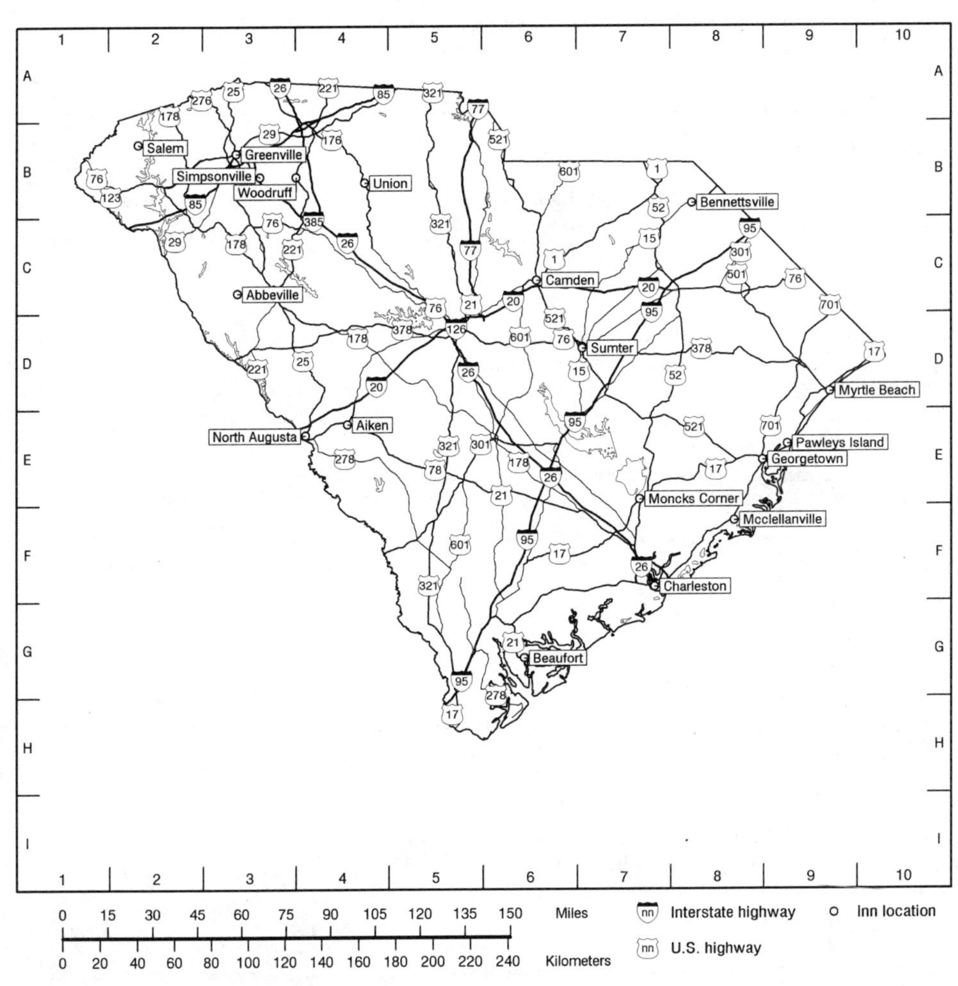

SC

Abbeville C3

Belmont Inn

106 Court Sq
Abbeville, SC 29620
(864)459-9625 (888)251-2000
Fax:(864)459-9625

Rates: $59-159.
Payment: MC VISA AX DC CB DS.
Innkeeper(s): Alan Peterson.
Circa: 1902.

Rooms: 25 rooms with PB. 2 conference rooms.
Beds: KQT.

This turn-of-the-century, Spanish-style inn was built to be one of the region's finest hotels. The richly restored building, which is listed in the National Register, displays many original elements and charming features such as an 1820s bank teller's station. Each guest room has been individually decorated. Southern cuisine with a touch of the Continental fill the menu at the inn's restaurant, a gourmet eatery where guests enjoy not only the food, but the ambiance. Formally dressed waiters attend to your every need. Guests are pampered with breakfast and afternoon tea, and with menu items such as roasted garlic and Vidalia onion cream soup, crab cakes, roast rack of lamb and succulent desserts, they'll probably want to stay for dinner.

Breakfast and afternoon tea included in rates. Types of meals: continental breakfast, continental-plus breakfast, full breakfast, gourmet breakfast and early coffee/tea. Dinner, evening snack, picnic lunch, lunch, gourmet lunch, banquet service, catering service and catered breakfast available. Air conditioning and cable TV in room. VCR, copier and bicycles on premises. Weddings, small meetings, family reunions and seminars hosted. TAC10.

"We enjoyed the wonderful southern hospitality. The food was excellent and service was outstanding."

Aiken — E4

Holley Inn

235 Richland Ave
Aiken, SC 29801
(803)648-4265
Fax:(803)648-4265

Rates: $45-95. EP.
Payment: MC VISA AX DC CB DS PC TC.
Innkeeper(s): Forrest E. Holley.
Circa: 1929.

Rooms: 35 rooms with PB, 3 with FP. 9 suites.
Beds: KQD.

This historic inn has been in operation since its opening more than half a century ago. Vintage 1930s furnishings are among the items decorating bed chambers and two-room suites. Guests have use of a pool, courtyard and lounge. Inn guests are treated to breakfast, and the inn's restaurant also serves lunch and dinner. There is a motel on the premises, too, so you may want to specifically request the main house. The inn is within two blocks of restaurants, the Alley and shops.

Breakfast included in rates. Types of meals: continental breakfast, continental-plus breakfast, full breakfast, gourmet breakfast and early coffee/tea. Afternoon tea, dinner, evening snack, picnic lunch, gourmet lunch, banquet service, catering service and room service available. EP. Air conditioning, turn-down service, ceiling fan, cable TV and VCR in room. Fax, copier, swimming and bicycles on premises. Handicap access. Weddings, small meetings, family reunions and seminars hosted. Antiques, fishing, parks, shopping, sporting events, theater and watersports nearby. TAC10.

Pets Allowed: Small.

The New Berry Inn

240 Newberry St SW
Aiken, SC 29801-3854
(803)649-2935

Rates: $60.
Payment: MC VISA AX DC DS PC TC.
Innkeeper(s): Hal & Mary Ann Mackey.
Circa: 1924.

Rooms: 5 rooms with PB, 2 with FP. 1 suite. 1 conference room.
Beds: Q.

History lovers will appreciate this inn's location, surrounded by three historic districts in the village of Old Aiken. The acre of grounds is dotted with many trees and a large gazebo, often the site for weddings. The Dutch Colonial is furnished with antiques, and two rooms include a fireplace. Omelets, breakfast meats, freshly baked breads and seasonal fruit are among the morning offerings.

Breakfast included in rates. Type of meal: full breakfast. Air conditioning, ceiling fan and cable TV in room. Weddings, small meetings, family reunions and seminars hosted. German, French and Spanish spoken. Antiques, parks, shopping, sporting events, theater and watersports nearby. TAC5.

Special Discounts: AAA, AARP, discount coupon 10%.

"You should be congratulated. Keep it up."

The Beaufort Inn

809 Port Republic St
Beaufort, SC 29901-1257
(803)521-9000
Fax:(803)521-9500

Rates: $125-185.
Payment: MC VISA AX DS PC TC.
Innkeeper(s): Russell & Debbie Fielden.
Circa: 1907.

Rooms: 13 rooms with PB, 4 with FP. 1 suite. 1 conference room.
Beds: KQ.

Every inch of this breathtaking inn offers something special. The interior is decorated to the hilt with lovely furnishings, plants, beautiful rugs and warm, inviting tones. Rooms include four-poster and canopy beds combined with the modern amenities such as two-person Jacuzzi tubs, fireplaces, wet bars and stocked refrigerators. Enjoy a complimentary full breakfast at the inn's gourmet restaurant. The chef offers everything from a light breakfast of fresh fruit, cereal and a bagel to heartier treats such as whole grain French toast stuffed with Brie and sundried peaches served with fresh fruit and crisp bacon.

Breakfast and afternoon tea included in rates. Types of meals: full breakfast, gourmet breakfast and early coffee/tea. Dinner, picnic lunch, gourmet lunch, banquet service, catering service and room service available. Air conditioning, turn-down service, ceiling fan and cable TV in room. VCR, fax, copier and bicycles on premises. Handicap access. Weddings, small meetings, family reunions and seminars hosted. English and Dutch spoken. Antiques, fishing, parks, shopping, theater and watersports nearby. TAC10.

Publicity: *Beaufort, Southern Living, Country Inns, Carolina Style, US Air.*

The Cuthbert House Inn B&B

1203 Bay St
Beaufort, SC 29902
(803)521-1315 (800)327-9275
Fax:(803)521-1314
E-mail: cuthbert@hargray.com

Rates: $90-185.
Payment: MC VISA DS PC TC.
Innkeeper(s): Gary & Sharon Groves.
Circa: 1790.

Rooms: 6 rooms with PB. 3 suites. 2 conference rooms.
Beds: KQDT.

This 18th-century Antebellum mansion, listed in the National Register, boasts a veranda overlooking Beaufort Bay. The home was built during Washington's presidency, and General W.T. Sherman was once a guest here. The home has been lovingly restored to its original grandeur. Rich painted walls are highlighted by fine molding. Hardwood floors are topped with Oriental rugs and elegant 19th-century furnishings. The morning meal is served in a breakfast room that overlooks the water. The surrounding area offers plenty of activities in every season, and for those celebrating a new marriage, a honeymoon package is available.

Breakfast included in rates. Types of meals: continental breakfast, full breakfast and early coffee/tea. Air conditioning, turn-down service, cable TV and VCR in room. Fax and library on premises. Weddings, small meetings, family reunions and seminars hosted. Antiques, fishing, parks and watersports nearby. TAC10.

TwoSuns Inn B&B

SC

1705 Bay St
Beaufort, SC 29902-5406
(803)522-1122 (800)532-4244
Fax:(803)522-1122

Rates: $105-135.
Payment: MC VISA AX PC TC.
Innkeeper(s): Ron & Carrol Kay.
Circa: 1917.

Rooms: 5 rooms with PB. 1 conference room.
Beds: KQT.

The Keyserling family built this Neoclassical Revival-style home, which was later used by the local board of education as housing for single, female teachers. The home has been completely refurbished, a difficult task, considering the home had been the victim of two fires. The U.S. Department of the Interior noted the renovation with a Historic Building Certification in 1996. Guest rooms boast bay views, and each has its own theme. Aside from the gourmet breakfast, a "Tea and Toddy Hour" is included in the rates.

Breakfast and afternoon tea included in rates. Type of meal: full breakfast. Air conditioning, ceiling fan and cable TV in room. VCR, fax, copier, computer, bicycles and library on premises. Handicap access. Small meetings and seminars hosted. Antiques, fishing, parks, shopping, theater and watersports nearby. TAC10.

Publicity: *Beaufort Gazette, Sandlapper.*

Special Discounts: AAA,AARP,Senior Citizen-10%.

"One could not wish for a better experience."

Bennettsville B8

The Breeden Inn & Carriage House

404 E Main St
Bennettsville, SC 29512
(803)479-3665

Rates: $55-65.
Payment: MC VISA PC TC.
Innkeeper(s): Wesley & Bonnie Park.
Circa: 1886.

Rooms: 7 rooms with PB, 6 with FP. 1 suite. 1 cottage. 1 conference room.
Beds: DT.

One especially bountiful cotton crop paid for the construction of this mansion, which local attorney Thomas Bouchier presented to his bride as a wedding gift. The exterior is graced with more than two dozens columns and the interior boasts a carved oak archway in the center hall. Stained and beveled glass are found throughout the home, along with original light fixtures. Breakfasts can be served in the formal dining room or on the veranda. The innkeepers also offer accommodations in a restored guest house, which includes a gathering room, kitchen and front porch lined with rocking chairs and swings.

Breakfast and afternoon tea included in rates. Types of meals: full breakfast and early coffee/tea. Air conditioning, ceiling fan and cable TV in room. VCR, fax, copier and swimming on premises. Small meetings hosted. Antiques, fishing and theater nearby. TAC10.

"We have so much enjoyed our stay here in your charming and comfortable inn."

Camden C6

Candlelight Inn

1904 Broad St
Camden, SC 29020-2606
(803)424-1057

Rates: $75-85.
Payment: MC VISA DS PC TC.
Innkeeper(s): Jo Ann & George Celani.
Circa: 1930.

Rooms: 3 rooms with PB. 1 suite.
Beds: QT.

Two acres of camellias, azaleas and oak trees surround this Cape Cod-style home. As per the name, the innkeepers keep a candle in each window, welcoming guests to this homey bed & breakfast. The decor is a delightful and tasteful mix of country, with quilts, hand-crafted samplers, poster beds, family antiques and traditional furnishings. Each of the rooms is named for someone significant in the innkeeper's life, and a picture of the special person decorates each room. Guests will enjoy the hearty breakfast, which changes daily. Several of innkeeper Jo Ann Celani's recipes have been featured in a cookbook, and one recipe won a blue ribbon at the Michigan State Fair.

Breakfast included in rates. Types of meals: full breakfast and early coffee/tea. Air conditioning and ceiling fan in room. Library on premises. Antiques, fishing, parks, shopping, theater and watersports nearby. TAC10.

Charleston F7

1837 B&B

126 Wentworth St
Charleston, SC 29401-1737
(803)723-7166

Rates: $69-129.
Payment: MC VISA AX PC TC.
Innkeeper(s): Sherri Weaver & Richard Dunn.
Circa: 1837.

Rooms: 8 rooms with PB. 1 suite.
Beds: QT.

Originally owned by a cotton planter, this three-story home and brick carriage house currently is owned by two artists and is located centrally in the Charleston Historic District. The inn is within walking distance to shops, restaurants and the convention center. Red cypress wainscoting, cornice molding and heart-of-pine floors adorn the formal parlor. A full gourmet breakfast is served in the formal dining room or on the outside piazzas. Guest rooms offer Charleston rice beds with fishnet canopies. Afternoon tea includes our homemade scones and lemon curd.

Breakfast included in rates. Afternoon tea available. Air conditioning and ceiling fan in room. Small meetings and family reunions hosted. Antiques, shopping, sporting events and theater nearby.

Location: In the historic district.

Publicity: *New York Newsday, Kansas City Star, New York Times.*

Special Discounts: $5 per night discount all year for payment by check or cash.

"This cozy room added that special touch to a much-needed weekend getaway."

Belvedere B&B

40 Rutledge Ave
Charleston, SC 29401-1702
(803)722-0973

Rates: $125.
Payment: PC TC.
Innkeeper(s): David S. Spell & Rick Zender.
Circa: 1900.

Rooms: 3 rooms with PB.
Beds: Q.

This beautiful Colonial Revival home with its semicircular portico, Ionic columns and four piazzas boasts a beautiful view of Charleston's Colonial Lake. Bright, airy rooms feature high ceilings with fans, polished wood floors, fireplaces, antique furnishings and Oriental rugs. Relax and enjoy the view on the piazzas or one of the inn's public rooms. Belvedere B&B is close to many wonderful restaurants and shops.

Breakfast included in rates. Type of meal: continental-plus breakfast. Air conditioning and ceiling fan in room. Cable TV and VCR on premises. Weddings hosted. Antiques, fishing, parks, shopping, sporting events, theater and watersports nearby.

Publicity: *Discerning Traveler, Southern Brides.*

Country Victorian B&B

105 Tradd St
Charleston, SC 29401-2422
(803)577-0682

Rates: $75-115.
Payment: PC TC.
Innkeeper(s): Diane Deardurff Weed.
Circa: 1820.

Rooms: 2 rooms with PB.
Beds: TD.

Filled with country-style collections and early American, country furnishings, this B&B has braided rugs, old quilts and iron and brass beds. There are clawfoot bathtubs. Cookies and ice tea are available during the summer. A continental breakfast is delivered to your room on a wicker tray.

SC

Breakfast and afternoon tea included in rates. Types of meals: continental-plus breakfast and early coffee/tea. Air conditioning, turn-down service and ceiling fan in room. Antiques, fishing, parks, shopping, sporting events, theater and watersports nearby.

Fulton Lane Inn

202 King St
Charleston, SC 29401-3109
(803)720-2600 (800)720-2688
Fax:(803)720-2940

Rates: $105-255. EP.
Payment: MC VISA DC.
Innkeeper(s): Randall Felkel.
Circa: 1870.

Rooms: 27 rooms with PB, 8 with FP. 4 suites. 2 conference rooms.
Beds: KQ.

Confederate blockade runner John Rugheimer built this charming brick home a few years after the Civil War ended. Bright cheery decor and fine furnishings highlight the architecture, which includes cathedral ceilings and several fireplaces. The inn affords views of the city skyline, full of historic sites and gracious,

Southern buildings. Guest rooms boast canopy beds draped with hand-strung netting and large, whirlpool tubs. The innkeepers include a stocked refrigerator in each room, and deliver breakfast on a silver tray. Wine and sherry are served in the lobby, and don't be surprised to find chocolates atop your pillow after you return from one of Charleston's many fine restaurants.

Breakfast included in rates. Type of meal: continental-plus breakfast. Room service available. EP. Air conditioning, turn-down service and cable TV in room. Fax and child care on premises. Handicap access. Weddings, small meetings, family reunions and seminars hosted. Antiques, fishing, parks, shopping, theater and watersports nearby. TAC10.

Publicity: *Southern Accents*

Hayne House B&B

30 King St
Charleston, SC 29401-2733
(803)577-2633 (800)948-1680
Fax:(803)577-6677

Rates: $70-165. AP.
Payment: MC VISA PC TC.
Innkeeper(s): Ben Chapman & Margaret Baumer.
Circa: 1755.

Rooms: 5 rooms, 4 with PB. 1 cottage.
Beds: QDT.

Located one block from the Battery, this handsome clapboard house is in the National Register of Historic Places. Surrounded by a wrought-iron garden fence, it has an 1820 addition. It was built three stories tall to capture the harbor breeze. The inn is furnished in antiques, and there is an appealing back porch with rockers and a swing.

Breakfast and evening snack included in rates. Types of meals: continental breakfast, continental-plus breakfast, full breakfast and early coffee/tea. Catered breakfast available. AP. Air conditioning in room. Fax, copier and library on premises. Antiques, fishing, parks, shopping, sporting events and theater nearby. TAC10.

"A fantasy realized. What a wonderful gift of hospitality."

John Rutledge House Inn

116 Broad St
Charleston, SC 29401-2437
(803)723-7999 (800)476-9741
Fax:(803)720-2615

Rates: $150-310. EP.
Payment: MC VISA AX DC.
Innkeeper(s): Linda Bishop.
Circa: 1763.

Rooms: 19 rooms with PB, 8 with FP. 3 suites. 2 cottages. 1 conference room.
Beds: KQD.

John Rutledge, first governor of South Carolina, Supreme Court Justice, and author and signer of the Constitution of the United States, wrote first drafts of the document in the stately ballroom of his Charleston home. In 1791 George Washington dined in this same room. Both men would be amazed by the house's recent restoration, which includes three lavish suites with elaborately carved Italian marble fireplaces, personal refrigerators, spas, air conditioning and televisions along with fine antiques and reproductions. Exterior ironwork on the house was designed in the 19th century and features palmetto trees and American eagles to honor Mr. Rutledge's service to the state and country.

Breakfast and afternoon tea included in rates. Types of meals: continental-plus breakfast and full breakfast. Room service available. EP. Air conditioning, turn-down service and cable TV in room. Fax and child care on premises. Handicap access. Weddings, small meetings, family reunions and seminars hosted. Spanish spoken. Antiques, fishing, parks, shopping, theater and watersports nearby. TAC10.

Publicity: *Innsider, Colonial Homes, New York Times, Southern Living, Southern Accents, Gourmet.*

"Two hundred years of American history in two nights; first-class accommodations, great staff. John Rutledge should've had it so good!"

King George IV Inn & Guests

32 George St, Historic District
Charleston, SC 29401-1416
(803)723-9339 (888)723-1667

Rates: $70-135.
Payment: MC VISA PC TC.
Innkeeper(s): Debbie, BJ, Mike.
Circa: 1792.

Rooms: 10 rooms, 8 with PB, 10 with FP. 3 suites. 1 conference room.
Beds: KQDT.

This inn is a Federal-style home with a Greek Revival parapet-style roofline. There are four stories with three levels of Charleston porches. All the rooms have fireplaces, 10-foot ceilings and six-foot windows. Several fireplaces and moldings are the original Adamesque architectural detail. The house had been lived in for many years by Peter Freneau, who was a prominent Charleston journalist, merchant, ship owner and Jeffersonian politician. The inn is within one minute's walk to shopping and restaurants.

Breakfast and afternoon tea included in rates. Types of meals: continental-plus breakfast and early coffee/tea. Air conditioning in room. Fax on premises. Small meetings and family reunions hosted. Antiques, fishing, parks, shopping, sporting events, theater and watersports nearby.

Kings Courtyard Inn

198 King St
Charleston, SC 29401-3109
(803)723-3000 (800)845-6119
Fax:(803)720-2608

Rates: $110-230. EP.
Payment: MC VISA AX DC.
Innkeeper(s): Laura Fox.
Circa: 1853.

Rooms: 41 rooms with PB, 13 with FP. 4 suites. 1 conference room.
Beds: KQD.

Having a Greek Revival style with unusual touches of Egyptian detail, this three-story building was designed by architect Francis D. Lee. The inn originally catered to plantation owners, shipping interests and merchant guests. Some of the rooms have fireplaces, canopied beds and views of the two inner courtyards or the garden. The building is one of historic King Street's largest and oldest structures and is at the center of Charleston's historic district.

Breakfast included in rates. Types of meals: continental-plus breakfast and full breakfast. Room service available. EP. Air conditioning, turn-down service and cable TV in room. Fax, copier, spa and child care on premises. Handicap access. Weddings, small meetings, family reunions and seminars hosted. Antiques, fishing, parks, shopping, theater and watersports nearby. TAC10.

Location: In the historic district.

Publicity: *Southern Living, USA Today, Insider, Travel Holiday.*

The Kitchen House

126 Tradd St
Charleston, SC 29401-2420
(803)577-6362
Fax:(803)797-1107

Rates: $95-195.
Payment: MC VISA.
Innkeeper(s): Lois Evans.
Circa: 1732.

Rooms: 2 rooms with PB.
Beds: QT.

This elegant, pre-Revolutionary War house was once home to Dr. Peter Fayssoux, who served as Surgeon General in the Continental Army during the Revolutionary War. The home was passed down to his daughter, and her sons became Confederate generals, one of whom bestowed the nickname of "Stonewall" to General Stonewall Jackson. The kitchen building has been restored around its four original fireplaces using original and other antique materials. The pantry is stocked with goodies, and guests are sure to find juice, fresh fruit, muffins, gourmet jams and coffees awaiting them in the refrigerator. Afternoon sherry awaits guests on arrival and a concierge service is offered.

Breakfast included in rates. Type of meal: full breakfast. Afternoon tea available. Air conditioning and cable TV in room. VCR on premises. Weddings hosted. Antiques, fishing, parks, shopping, sporting events, theater and watersports nearby.

Publicity: *New York Times, Colonial Homes.*

Special Discounts: Honeymoon packages.

"By all comparisons, one of the very best."

Loundes Grove Inn

266 Saint Margaret St
Charleston, SC 29403-3561
(803)723-8438 (800)723-8520
Fax:(803)723-0444

Rates: $75-130.
Payment: MC VISA PC TC.
Innkeeper(s): Martha & Chuck Craven.
Circa: 1786.

Rooms: 9 rooms, 7 with PB, 6 with FP. 1 conference room.
Beds: KQDT.

SC

Located on the Ashley River, this formal Greek Revival plantation is set off majestically by more than five acres of lawns and gardens, a favorite place for elegant weddings. A second-story, columned veranda stretches across the front of the mansion. In the National Register, the house played a prominent role during the Revolutionary War, and was the site for the 1901 exhibition when Teddy Roosevelt was a visitor. The inn is elegantly appointed in a style suited to its fine architecture and cultural significance to the community. Breakfast might include shrimp and grits, eggs, and bagels with cream cheese. The Citadel Military College is two blocks away.

Breakfast included in rates. Type of meal: full breakfast. Air conditioning in room. Fax, copier and swimming on premises. Handicap access. 15 acres. Weddings, small meetings, family reunions and seminars hosted. Antiques, parks, shopping and theater nearby.

Planters Inn

112 N Market St
Charleston, SC 29401-3118
(803)722-2345 (800)845-7082
Fax:(803)577-2125

Rates: $95-225.
Payment: MC VISA AX DC DS.
Innkeeper(s): Larry Spelts, Jr.
Circa: 1844.

Rooms: 41 rooms with PB.
Beds: KQ.

Prepare for a getaway of romance, elegance and history at this opulent, four-diamond-rated inn, located in historic Charleston. Built decades prior to the Civil War, the inn has watched Charleston grow and change. The interior displays the height of Southern elegance and charm. Rooms are decorated with rich wallcoverings, elegant furnishings and four-poster beds topped with the finest of linens. Breakfasts are delivered to your door on a silver tray set with crystal, china and silver. The inn's restaurant, Planters Cafe, features cuisine by a chef whose creations have appeared in the likes of Gourmet and Bon Appetit. Guests, if they choose, may dine al fresco in a landscaped courtyard. If you need even more pomp and circumstance, the innkeepers offer romance and history packages.

Breakfast included in rates. Dinner and lunch available. Air conditioning and turn-down service in room. Fax and copier on premises. Small meetings hosted. Antiques, shopping and theater nearby.

The Thomas Lamboll House

19 King St
Charleston, SC 29401-2734
(803)723-3212
Fax:(803)724-6350

Rates: $95-130.
Payment: MC VISA DS PC TC.
Innkeeper(s): Marie & Emerson Read.
Circa: 1740.

Rooms: 2 rooms with PB, 2 with FP. 1 suite.
Beds: QT.

A Colonial South Carolina judge, Thomas Lamboll, was the first resident of this impressive Colonial, located in Charleston's historic district. The home features two stories of piazzas set up with wicker furnishings, where guests can catch a cool breeze in the afternoon. The rooms are appointed with fine antiques, including Chippendale chairs and an early 19th-century sideboard in the dining room. There are two guest rooms, each with French doors leading to the piazzas, that overlook rooftops and the river in the distance.

Breakfast included in rates. Type of meal: continental breakfast. Air conditioning, ceiling fan and cable TV in room. Handicap access. Amusement parks, antiques, fishing, parks, shopping, sporting events, theater and watersports nearby.

Twenty Seven State Street B&B

27 State St
Charleston, SC 29401-2812
(803)722-4243

Rates: $85-145.
Payment: PC TC.
Innkeeper(s): Paul & Joye Craven.
Circa: 1804.

Rooms: 2 suites.
Beds: Q.

Located in Charleston's distinctive French Quarter, this inn offers comfort and the height of elegance at the same time. Rooms are skillfully decorated with wallcoverings, draperies and fine furnishings. Polished, wood floors are topped with Oriental rugs. Some rooms offer fireplaces, and some have four-poster beds. The suites in the carriage house overlook the courtyard, and the rustic interior features exposed brick walls, antiques and reproductions. Although the inn does lend itself more toward romance, the innkeepers happily provide for well-behaved children in two of the suites. Breakfast is optional.

Type of meal: continental-plus breakfast. Air conditioning and cable TV in room. Bicycles and library on premises. Antiques, parks, shopping, sporting events and theater nearby. TAC10.

Location: In the heart of historic Charleston.

"We won't soon forget such a lovely retreat."

Two Meeting Street Inn

2 Meeting St
Charleston, SC 29401-2799
(803)723-7322

Rates: $95-140.
Innkeeper(s): Karen B. Spell.
Circa: 1892.

Rooms: 9 rooms with PB.
Beds: QD.

Located directly on the Battery, horses and carriages carry visitors past the inn, perhaps the most photographed in Charleston. In the Queen Anne style, this Victorian has an unusual veranda graced by several ornate arches. The same family has owned and managed the inn since 1946 with no lapse in gracious Southern hospitality. Among the elegant amenities are original Tiffany stained-glass windows, English oak paneling and exquisite collections of silver and antiques. Continental breakfast is served in the formal dining room or side garden and sherry enjoyed in the rocking chairs on the front piazza every afternoon.

Type of meal: continental breakfast.

Location: On the Battery.

Publicity: *Innsider, Southern Bride.*

"A magnificent Queen Anne mansion, Southern Bride."

Victoria House Inn

208 King St
Charleston, SC 29401-3149
(803)720-2944 (800)933-5464
Fax:(803)720-2930

Rates: $115-225. EP.
Payment: MC VISA DC.
Innkeeper(s): Mary Kay Smith.
Circa: 1898.

Rooms: 18 rooms with PB, 4 with FP. 4 suites. 1 conference room.
Beds: KD.

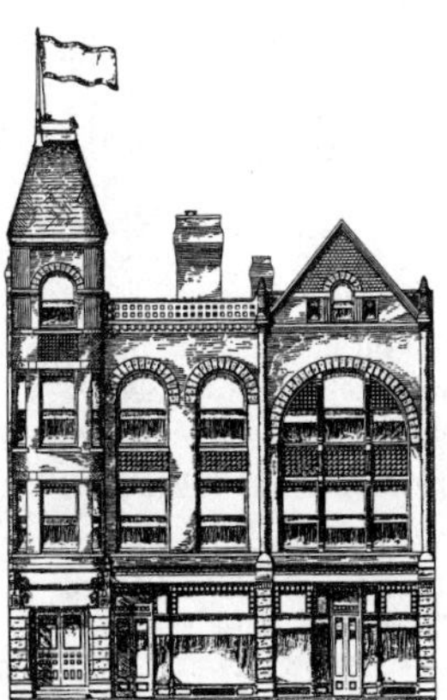

Enjoy the gracious decor of the Victorian Era while staying at this beautiful Romanesque-style inn, located in the heart of Charleston's historic district along King Street's famed Antique Row. Some rooms boast working fireplaces, while others feature romantic whirlpool baths. Champagne breakfasts are delivered to the bedchambers each morning, and the nightly turndown service includes chocolates on your pillow. Enjoy a glass of sherry before heading out to one of Charleston's many fine restaurants. The Victoria House Inn is close to a variety of antique shops and fashionable boutiques.

Breakfast included in rates. Type of meal: continental-plus breakfast. Room service available. EP. Air conditioning, turn-down service and cable TV in room. Fax, copier and child care on premises. Handicap access. Weddings, small meetings, family reunions and seminars hosted. Antiques, fishing, parks, shopping, theater and watersports nearby. TAC10.

Publicity: *Washington Post, Great Country Inns*

Villa De La Fontaine B&B

138 Wentworth St
Charleston, SC 29401-1734
(803)577-7709

Rates: $100-120.
Payment: PC TC.
Innkeeper(s): Bill & Aubrey Hancock.
Circa: 1838.

Rooms: 4 rooms with PB. 1 cottage.
Beds: KQT.

SC

This magnificent Greek Revival manor is among Charleston's finest offerings. The grounds are lush with gardens and manicured lawns, and the ionic columns adorn the impressive exterior. The innkeeper is a retired interior designer, and his elegant touch is found throughout the mansion, including many 18th-century antiques. A fully trained chef prepares the gourmet breakfasts, which are served in a solarium with a hand-painted mural and 12-foot windows. The chef's recipe for cornmeal waffles was featured in a Better Homes & Gardens' cookbook.

Breakfast included in rates. Types of meals: full breakfast and gourmet breakfast. Air conditioning in room. Antiques, fishing, parks, shopping, sporting events, theater and watersports nearby.

"What a wonderful vacation we had as recipients of your lavish hospitality."

1790 House B&B Inn

630 Highmarket St
Georgetown, SC 29440
(803)546-4821 (800)890-7432

Rates: $65-125.
Payment: MC VISA AX DS PC TC.
Innkeeper(s): John & Patricia Wiley.
Circa: 1790.

Rooms: 6 rooms with PB, 1 with FP. 1 cottage.
Beds: QT.

Located in the heart of a historic district, this beautifully restored West Indies Colonial just celebrated its 200th birthday. The spacious rooms feature 11-foot ceilings and seven fireplaces, three in the guest bedrooms. The inn decor reflects the plantations of a bygone era. Guests can stay in former slave quarters, renovated to include a queen bedroom and sitting area. Each of the romantic rooms feature special touches, such as the red and deep blue decor of the Indigo Room, and the antique white iron and brass bed in the Prince George Suite. The Dependency Cottage is a perfect honeymoon hideaway with a private entrance enhanced with gardens and a patio, and the room also includes a Jacuzzi tub.

Breakfast and evening snack included in rates. Type of meal: gourmet breakfast. Picnic lunch available. Air conditioning, ceiling fan and cable TV in room. VCR and bicycles on premises. Weddings, small meetings and family reunions hosted. Antiques, fishing, parks, shopping and theater nearby. TAC10.

Publicity: *Georgetown Times.*

Special Discounts: Long term rates-inquire; AAA 10%.

"The 1790 House always amazes me with its beauty."

Du Pre House

921 Prince St
Georgetown, SC 29442
(803)546-0298 (800)921-3877
Fax:(803)520-0771

Rates: $70-95.
Payment: MC VISA PC TC.
Innkeeper(s): Marshall Wile.
Circa: 1740.

Rooms: 5 rooms with PB.
Beds: Q.

The lot upon which this pre-Revolutionary War gem stands was partitioned off in 1734, and the home built six years later. Three guest rooms have fireplaces, and all are decorated with a poster bed. A full breakfast is prepared featuring such items as egg or grit casseroles, fresh fruit and home-baked muffins. For those who love history, Georgetown, South Carolina's third oldest city, offers more than 60 registered National Historic Landmarks.

Breakfast, afternoon tea and evening snack included in rates. Types of meals: continental-plus breakfast, full breakfast and early coffee/tea. Picnic lunch available. Air conditioning, turn-down service and ceiling fan in room. Cable TV, fax, copier, spa, swimming and library on premises. Weddings, small meetings and family reunions hosted. Amusement parks, antiques, fishing, parks, shopping, theater and watersports nearby.

King's Inn at Georgetown

230 Broad St
Georgetown, SC 29440
(803)527-6937 (800)251-8805
Fax:(803)527-6937

Rates: $75-115.
Payment: MC VISA AX.
Innkeeper(s): Marilyn & Jerry Burkhardt.
Circa: 1825.

Rooms: 7 rooms with PB.
Beds: KQDT.

Union troops seized this house and used it as headquarters during the Civil War. The gracious, Federal-style home displays the height of Southern elegance, with richly appointed common areas and guest quarters. Family heirlooms, antiques and reproductions decorate the inn. Turndown service and early morning coffee placed near your door await to pamper you. Gourmet breakfasts are served at individual tables set with fine linens, silver, china and crystal. Guests also are treated to afternoon tea and sherry. The inn offers a lap pool and croquet area. The beach and Brookgreen, one of the world's largest outdoor sculpture gardens, are nearby.

Breakfast and afternoon tea included in rates. Types of meals: full breakfast and early coffee/tea. Picnic lunch available. Cable TV, VCR, bicycles and child care on premises. Weddings, small meetings, family reunions and seminars hosted. Antiques, fishing, parks, shopping, sporting events and theater nearby.

"Wonderful effect in every room with the brilliant use of color."

The Shaw House B&B

613 Cypress Ct
Georgetown, SC 29440
(803)546-9663

Rates: $55-70.
Payment: PC TC.
Innkeeper(s): Mary & Joe Shaw.
Circa: 1985.

Rooms: 3 rooms with PB.
Beds: KQT.

Near Georgetown's historical district is the Shaw House. It features a beautiful view of the Willowbank marsh, which stretches out for more than 100 acres. Sometimes giant turtles come up and lay eggs on the lawn. Guests enjoy rocking on the inn's front and back porches and identifying the large variety of birds that live here. A Southern home-cooked breakfast often includes grits, quiche and Mary's heart-shaped biscuits.

Breakfast included in rates. Types of meals: full breakfast and early coffee/tea. Evening snack available. Air conditioning, turn-down service, ceiling fan and cable TV in room. Bicycles and library on premises. Small meetings and family reunions hosted. Amusement parks, antiques, fishing, parks, shopping, theater and water-sports nearby. TAC10.

Publicity: *Charlotte Observer, Country.*

Special Discounts: AAA 10%.

"Your home speaks of abundance and comfort and joy."

Winyah Bay B&B

403 Helena St
Georgetown, SC 29440
(803)546-9051 (800)681-6176

Rates: $65-100.
Payment: MC VISA TC.
Innkeeper(s): Peggy Wheeler.
Circa: 1984.

Rooms: 2 suites. 1 cottage.
Beds: KD.

Enjoy the breezes from the bay as you stroll down the longest private dock in South Carolina. A small private island is on the premises, as well. The innkeepers have decorated the rooms in bold, vibrant colors, and each room boasts a view overlooking the bay and a bathroom with skylights. The cupboards are stocked with breakfast goodies and guests have access to a refrigerator, microwave and coffeemaker.

Breakfast and evening snack included in rates. Type of meal: continental-plus breakfast. Picnic lunch available. Air conditioning, ceiling fan, cable TV and VCR in room. Amusement parks, antiques, fishing, shopping and theater nearby.

Greenville B3

Pettigru Place B&B

302 Pettigru St
Greenville, SC 29601-3113
(864)242-4529
Fax:(864)242-1231

Rates: $85-155.
Payment: MC VISA AX DS PC TC.
Innkeeper(s): Gloria Hendershot & Janice Beatty.
Circa: 1920.

Rooms: 5 rooms with PB, 1 with FP. 1 suite.
Beds: KQD.

SC

Former classmates Gloria Hendershot and Janice Beatty reunited after two decades apart and created a charming bed & breakfast out of this Georgian Federalist home. Their labor of love created an inviting atmosphere full of color and comfort. Gloria, a professional caterer, creates the gourmet breakfasts, and Janice tends to the beautiful English garden. After a day of meetings or sightseeing, afternoon refreshments are a welcome treat. The innkeepers offer plenty of amenities for the business travelers and plenty of romantic touches. Rooms feature special touches such as ceiling fans, feather mattresses and writing desks. The suite includes a fireplace and separate sitting area. Some baths include whirlpool or clawfoot tubs. The Greenville area, with its close access to Clemson, Furman and Bob Jones Universities, offers plenty of activities from outdoor excursions to cultural events.

Breakfast and afternoon tea included in rates. Types of meals: gourmet breakfast and early coffee/tea. Air conditioning, ceiling fan and cable TV in room. Fax and copier on premises. Antiques, parks, shopping, sporting events and theater nearby.

McClellanville F8

Laurel Hill Plantation

8913 N Highway 17
McClellanville, SC 29458
(803)887-3708

Rates: $85-95.
Payment: MC VISA AX DC PC TC.
Innkeeper(s): Jackie & Lee Morrison.

Rooms: 4 rooms with PB.
Beds: QT.

From the large wraparound porch of this plantation house is a view of salt marshes, islands and the Atlantic Ocean. A nearby creek is the perfect location for crabbing, and there is a fresh-water pond for fishing. The home was destroyed by Hurricane Hugo, but has been totally reconstructed in its original Low Country style. It is furnished with antiques, local crafts and folk art. The inn has a gift shop that features books, antiques and decorative items.

Types of meals: full breakfast and early coffee/tea. Evening snack available. Air conditioning and ceiling fan in room. Cable TV and VCR on premises. 80 acres. Antiques, fishing, parks, shopping and watersports nearby. TAC10.

Location: Thirty minutes north of Charleston on Hwy 17.

Publicity: *Country Living, Seabreeze, Pee Dee, State.*

"The total privacy yet friendliness was very much appreciated."

Moncks Corner E7

Rice Hope Plantation Inn

206 Rice Hope Dr
Moncks Corner, SC 29461
(803)761-4832 (800)569-4038
Fax:(803)884-0223

Rates: $60-80.
Payment: MC VISA AX.
Innkeeper(s): Doris Kasprak.
Circa: 1929.

Rooms: 5 rooms, 3 with PB. 1 conference room.
Beds: QD.

Resting on 11 acres of natural beauty, the inn is set among live oaks on a bluff overlooking the Cooper River. On the property are formal gardens that boast 200-year-old camellias and many old varieties of azaleas and other trees and plants. Nearby attractions include the Trappist Monastery at Mepkin Plantation, Francis Marion National Forest, Cypress Gardens and historic Charleston. Outdoor occasions are great because of the inn's formal gardens and the Cooper River backdrop.

Breakfast included in rates. Types of meals: continental-plus breakfast, full breakfast, gourmet breakfast and early coffee/tea. Afternoon tea, lunch, gourmet lunch, banquet service and catering service available. Air conditioning and ceiling fan in room. Cable TV, VCR and child care on premises. 12 acres. Weddings, small meetings, family reunions and seminars hosted. Antiques and fishing nearby.

Location: Forty-five miles from Historic Charleston.

Myrtle Beach D9

Chesterfield Inn

700 N Ocean Blvd
PO Box 218
Myrtle Beach, SC 29578
(803)448-3177 (800)392-3869
Fax:(803)626-4736

Rates: $65-143. MAP.
Payment: MC VISA AX TC.
Innkeeper(s): Barry, Chong & Patrick O'Leary.
Circa: 1946.

Rooms: 58 rooms with PB. 9 suites. 1 conference room.
Beds: D.

For half a century, Chesterfield Inn has been serving guests who come to this popular seaside town in search of golf, tennis or simple relaxation. The inn, the oldest in town, has always been family owned and operated, and for most of its history by the Brittain family. Now the O'Leary family runs the show, maintaining the inn's Southern charm. Guests are treated to both an all-you-can-eat breakfast and a hearty dinner in the inn's dining room, which overlooks the ocean. The fare has a true "comfort food" appeal, especially with the desserts, which might include homemade pecan pie, a banana split cake or a rich cherry cobbler.

Breakfast and dinner included in rates. Type of meal: full breakfast. MAP. Air conditioning, ceiling fan and cable TV in room. Fax, copier and swimming on premises. Weddings, small meetings, family reunions and seminars hosted. Korean, Spanish and Southern spoken. Amusement parks, antiques, fishing, parks, shopping, sporting events, theater and watersports nearby. TAC10.

Special Discounts: Weekly, AAA, AARP, Spring, Fall, Winter Specials.

North Augusta

E4

Rosemary & Lookaway Halls

804 Carolina Ave
North Augusta, SC 29841
(803)278-6222 (800)531-5578
Fax:(803)278-4877

Rates: $125-250.
Payment: MC VISA AX DC CB DS PC TC.
Innkeeper(s): N. Wago & Geneva Robinson.
Circa: 1902.

Rooms: 23 rooms with PB. 2 conference rooms.
Beds: KQDT.

These historic homes are gracious examples of Southern elegance and charm. Manicured lawns adorn the exterior of both homes, which appear almost as a vision out of "Gone With the Wind." The Rosemary Hall boasts a spectacular heart-of-pine staircase. The homes stand as living museums, filled to the brim with beautiful furnishings and elegant decor, all highlighted by stained-glass windows, chandeliers and lacy touches. Some guest rooms include Jacuzzis, while others offer verandas. A proper afternoon tea is served each afternoon at Rosemary Hall. The Southern hospitality begins during the morning meal. The opulent gourmet fare might include baked orange-pecan English muffins served with Canadian bacon, or perhaps a Southern strata with cheese and bacon. The catering menu is even more tasteful, and many weddings, showers and parties are hosted at these inns.

Breakfast and evening snack included in rates. Types of meals: continental-plus breakfast, full breakfast and early coffee/tea. Air conditioning, turn-down service, cable TV and VCR in room. Fax and copier on premises. Handicap access. Weddings, small meetings, family reunions and seminars hosted. Japanese spoken. Antiques, fishing, parks, shopping, sporting events and watersports nearby. TAC10.

Pawleys Island

E9

Litchfield Plantation

King's River Rd,
PO Box 290
Pawleys Island, SC 29585
(803)237-9121 (800)869-1410
Fax:(803)237-8558

Rates: $115-195.
Payment: MC VISA AX DS TC.
Innkeeper(s): Tracey Weaver & Matt Willson.
Circa: 1750.

Rooms: 24 rooms with PB, 7 with FP. 10 suites. 7 cottages. 3 conference rooms.
Beds: KQT.

Live oaks line the drive that leads up to this Antebellum mansion, and in one glance, guests can almost imagine a time when this 600-acre estate was a prosperous rice plantation. The interior boasts many original features, and although the decor is more modern than it was in 1750, it still maintains charm and elegance. Four-poster and canopy beds, as well as a collection of traditional furnishings, grace the guest rooms, which are located in a variety of lodging options. Guests can stay in a plantation house suite or opt for a room in the Guest House. Their are two- and three-bedroom cottages available too. The cottages are particularly suited to families or couples traveling together and include amenities such as a fireplace, kitchen and washer and dryer. The inn's dining room, located in the Carriage House, is a wonderful place for a romantic dinner. Start off with appetizers such as petite corn cakes topped with sour cream and caviar, followed by a Caesar salad and an entree such as medallions of pork or shrimp and pasta pomodoro. Guests enjoy privileges at the oceanfront Pawleys Island Beach House, and there are tennis courts and a swimming pool on the plantation premises. Many golf courses are nearby. Be sure to ask about the inn's romance packages.

Breakfast included in rates. Type of meal: continental-plus breakfast. Banquet service and catering service available. Air conditioning and cable TV in room. Fax, copier, swimming, stables, tennis and library on premises. 600 acres. Weddings, small meetings, family reunions and seminars hosted. Amusement parks, antiques, fishing, parks, shopping, theater and watersports nearby. TAC10.

Special Discounts: Cottage summer special; seventh night free.

"I look forward to spending more vacations at Litchfield Plantation."

Sea View Inn

PO Box 210
Pawleys Island, SC 29585
(803)237-4253

Rates: $70-120.
Payment: PC TC.
Innkeeper(s): Pat Saunders & Jim Tatom.
Circa: 1937.

Rooms: 20 rooms.
Beds: DT.

In simple low-country style, this inn rests on Pawley's Island, a narrow barrier island with the ocean on one side and a salt marsh on the other. In summer, you may not need your shoes again till you leave for home. You'll settle in as if this is the family guest house, with comfortable painted vacation cottage furnishings, wood decks set atop seagrass and ocean or marsh front rooms. Sausage, eggs, toast and grits are often served for breakfast. Three meals are included in your room rate, and the main meal is served at 1:15 p.m. Cajun Green Gumbo, Low Country Crab Cakes with basil mustard, Pecan-Pepper Rice, Carolina Cornbread with scallion butter and Savannah Cream Cake are samples from the mid-day menu. In the evening, pasta, oyster pie, minestrone soup or deviled crab may be offered. All rates are per person. During the summer, reservations are weekly with rates from $460-795.

Type of meal: full breakfast. Dinner and lunch available. Air conditioning, turn-down service and ceiling fan in room. Library on premises. Shopping and watersports nearby.

Salem B2

Sunrise Farm B&B

PO Box 164, 325 Sunrise Dr
Salem, SC 29676-0164
(864)944-0121

Rates: $55-95.
Payment: MC VISA AX TC.
Innkeeper(s): Jean Webb.
Circa: 1890.

Rooms: 3 rooms. 2 cottages.
Beds: QD.

Situated on the remaining part of a 1,000-acre cotton plantation, this country Victorian features large porches with rockers and wicker. Guest rooms are furnished with period antiques, thick comforters, extra pillows and family heirlooms. The "corn crib" cottage is located in the original farm structure used for storing corn. It has a fully equipped kitchen, sitting area and bedroom with tub and shower. The June Rose Garden Cottage includes a river rock fireplace and full kitchen, as well as offering views of pastoral and mountain views.

Breakfast and evening snack included in rates. Types of meals: continental-plus breakfast and full breakfast. Air conditioning and ceiling fan in room. Antiques, fishing, parks, sporting events and watersports nearby. TAC10.

"Saying thank you doesn't do our gratitude justice."

Simpsonville B3

Hunter House Antiques & B&B

201 E College St
Simpsonville, SC 29681
(864)967-2827 (800)815-4561

Rates: $65-95.
Payment: PC TC.
Innkeeper(s): Dianne & Earl Neely.
Circa: 1906.

Rooms: 2 rooms. 1 suite. 1 conference room.
Beds: QD.

Stained-glass windows, hand-carved woodwork, pine staircase and 12-foot ceilings are a few of the features that make this Victorian inn a pleasant place to stay. The innkeepers will be happy to assist you with special-occasion arrangements such as catering, floral decorations, photography, live music or even a horse-drawn carriage. The wood-paneled hallway leads to the Victorian parlor, with its French doors, piano and pump organ. Guests need not go far for antiquing because there's an antique shop on the premises.

Breakfast and evening snack included in rates. Type of meal: full breakfast. Catering service available. Air conditioning, turn-down service, ceiling fan and cable TV in room. Weddings, small meetings, family reunions and seminars hosted. Antiques, parks, shopping, sporting events and theater nearby.

Sumter D7

Calhoun Street B&B

302 W Calhoun St
Sumter, SC 29150-4512
(803)775-7035 (800)355-8119
Fax:(803)778-0934
E-mail: calhounst-bb@sumter.net

Rates: $65-85.
Payment: MC VISA DS PC TC.
Innkeeper(s): David & Mackenzie Sholtz.
Circa: 1890.

Rooms: 4 rooms with PB, 1 with FP.
Beds: QT.

This home was built by innkeeper Mackenzie Sholtz's great-uncle, and she is the third generation to live in the clapboard Victorian. Guest rooms are well appointed with fine furnishings. For instance, the Audubon Room includes a canopy bed, a Victorian chair and loveseat and a polished hardwood floor topped with an Oriental rug. In the afternoon, refreshments are served, and in the mornings, guests enjoy a hearty, full breakfast. Eggs Calhoun, a unique twist on eggs Benedict, is a specialty served along with freshly squeezed orange juice and homemade breads or muffins. A phone, fax machine and copier are available for business travelers. Located in the historic district, this home borders a city park, and golfing and shopping are nearby.

Breakfast and evening snack included in rates. Types of meals: gourmet breakfast and early coffee/tea. Air conditioning and ceiling fan in room. Cable TV, VCR, fax and copier on premises. Weddings, small meetings, family reunions and seminars hosted. German and Italian spoken. Antiques, fishing, parks, shopping and theater nearby.

"This house gave us a good impression of uncompromised 1800s elegance."

Union B4

The Inn at Merridun

100 Merridun Pl
Union, SC 29379-2200
(864)427-7052 (888)892-6020
Fax:(864)429-0373

Rates: $85-125.
Payment: MC VISA AX DS PC TC.
Innkeeper(s): Jim & Peggy Waller.
Circa: 1855.

Rooms: 5 rooms with PB. 3 conference rooms.
Beds: KQT.

Nestled on nine acres of wooded ground, this Greek Revival inn is in a small Southern college town. During spring, see the South in its colorful splendor with blooming azaleas, magnolias and wisteria. Sip an iced drink on the inn's marble verandas and relive memories of a bygone era. Soft strains of Mozart and Beethoven, as well as the smell of freshly baked cookies and country suppers, fill the air of this antebellum country inn.

Breakfast included in rates. Types of meals: gourmet breakfast and early coffee/tea. Afternoon tea, dinner, picnic lunch, lunch, gourmet lunch, banquet service, catering service, catered breakfast and room service available. Air conditioning, ceiling fan and cable TV in room. VCR, fax, copier and library on premises. Weddings, small meetings, family reunions and seminars hosted. Amusement parks, antiques, fishing, parks, shopping, sporting events and watersports nearby. TAC10.

Special Discounts: Military and corporate.

Woodruff B4

The Nicholls-Crook Plantation House B&B

120 Plantation Dr
Woodruff, SC 29388-9476
(864)476-8820
Fax:(864)476-8820

Rates: $85-150.
Payment: AX TC.
Innkeeper(s): Suzanne & Jim Brown.
Circa: 1793.

Rooms: 3 rooms, 2 with PB. 1 suite.
Beds: KDT.

SC

The innkeepers at this 18th-century home have restored the historic house with warmth and charm in mind. Period antiques, original mantels and the widest chimney in the state create a charming, rustic environment. The grounds boast 18th-century flowers, a white-rock courtyard and a pecan grove with one of the largest pecan trees in South Carolina. Innkeepers Jim and Suzanne are full of information about the home's family history and the residents' ties to Revolutionary War heroes. A rich, plentiful breakfast is the perfect way to start off a day full of sightseeing and shopping or enjoying the area's many outdoor activities.

Breakfast included in rates. Type of meal: continental breakfast. Air conditioning and turn-down service in room. Fax on premises. Weddings and small meetings hosted. Antiques and shopping nearby. **Publicity:** *Herald Journal News, Country, Sandlapper.*

"A beautiful, restful experience."

South Dakota

Spearfish
Deadwood
Rapid City
Custer
Hot Springs
Canova
Freeman
Yankton

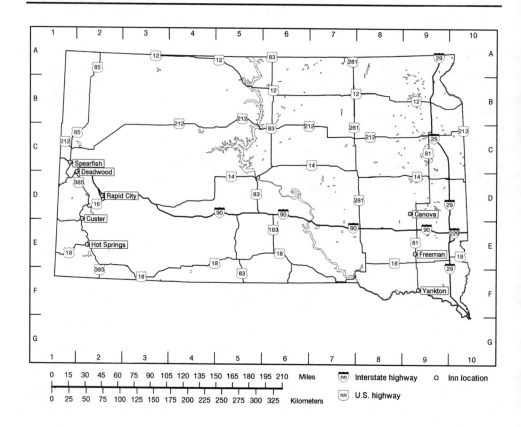

0 15 30 45 60 75 90 105 120 135 150 165 180 195 210 Miles

0 25 50 75 100 125 150 175 200 225 250 275 300 325 Kilometers

(nn) Interstate highway

(nn) U.S. highway

o Inn location

Canova — D9

B&B at Skoglund Farm

Rt 1 Box 45
Canova, SD 57321-9726
(605)247-3445

Rates: $60.
Payment: PC.
Innkeeper(s): Alden & Delores Skoglund.
Circa: 1917.

Rooms: 4 rooms.
Beds: QDT.

This is a working farm on the South Dakota prairie. Peacocks stroll around the farm along with cattle, chickens and other fowl. Guests can enjoy an evening meal with the family. The innkeepers offer special rates for families with children.

Breakfast and dinner included in rates. Types of meals: full breakfast and early coffee/tea. Evening snack available. VCR and library on premises. Antiques, fishing, parks, shopping, sporting events and watersports nearby.

Pets Allowed.

Location: Southeast South Dakota.

"Thanks for the down-home hospitality and good food."

Custer

D2

State Game Lodge

HC 83 Box 74
Custer, SD 57730-9705
(605)255-4541

Rates: $65-310. EP.
Payment: MC VISA AX DS.
Innkeeper(s): Pat Azinger.
Circa: 1923.

Rooms: 67 rooms with PB, 3 with FP.
Beds: QDT.

The State Game Lodge is listed in the National Register of Historic Places. It served as the summer White House for presidents Coolidge and Eisenhower. Although not a bed and breakfast, the lodge boasts a wonderful setting in the Black Hills. Ask for a room in the historic lodge building. (There are cottages and motel units, as well.) A favorite part of the experience is rocking on the front porch while watching deer graze. Breakfast is paid for separately in the dining room, where you may wish to order a pheasant or buffalo entree in the evening.

Type of meal: gourmet breakfast. EP.

Publicity: *Bon Appetit, Midwest Living, Sunset.*

"Your staff's cheerfulness and can-do attitude added to a most enjoyable stay."

Deadwood

D2

Black Hills Hideaway B&B

HCR 73 Box 1129
Deadwood, SD 57732-9712
(605)578-3054
Fax:(605)578-3054

Rates: $59-139.
Payment: MC VISA TC.
Innkeeper(s): Ned & Kathy Bode.
Circa: 1975.

Rooms: 9 rooms with PB, 8 with FP. 1 suite.
Beds: KQ.

Guests enjoy the privacy of 67 wooded acres and views of mountain peaks at this bed & breakfast. The nine guest rooms are tucked into a mountain chalet-style home with cathedral ceilings and natural wood interior. The home is located on what once was a wagon trail in the late 19th century. The decor is comfortable and there's a huge brick fireplace to enjoy. Each guest room has its own theme, including Western and European themes with antiques. Most rooms have a fireplace and whirlpool or hot tubs. The innkeepers also offer a housekeeping cabin south of Pactola Lake. The home is about 40 miles from Mt. Rushmore and the Crazy Horse Monument. A gold mine, the Passion Play, Spearfish Canyon and other attractions are nearby. Deadwood, a national historic landmark, is 17 miles away.

Breakfast and evening snack included in rates. Types of meals: continental breakfast, full breakfast and early coffee/tea. Picnic lunch available. Turn-down service and ceiling fan in room. Cable TV, VCR, fax, copier, bicycles and library on premises. Handicap access. 67 acres. Weddings, small meetings, family reunions and seminars hosted. Antiques, fishing, downhill skiing and cross-country skiing nearby. TAC10.

Freeman

E9

Farmer's Inn B&B

RR 2, Box 39W
Freeman, SD 57029
(605)925-7580

Rates: $42-65.
Innkeeper(s): Russell & MarJean Waltner.
Circa: 1914.

Rooms: 4 rooms with PB. 1 suite.
Beds: QDT.

Each of the guest rooms at this prairie home is decorated with a different theme. Guest rooms have names such as the Southwestern or Country rooms. The Victorian Suite includes an antique iron bed, stenciled walls, an eating area with a refrigerator and a sitting room with a TV, VCR and a daybed. The Attic Hideaway room includes a whirlpool tub. The home is furnished with many antiques and artwork from local artists. Farmer's Inn is close to many area attractions, and guest can arrange tours of local farms or Hutterite colonies.

Breakfast included in rates. Type of meal: gourmet breakfast. Dinner and lunch available. VCR, sauna and library on premises. Small meetings and family reunions hosted. German spoken. Antiques and shopping nearby.

Hot Springs

E2

Villa Theresa Guest House

801 Almond St
Hot Springs, SD 57747
(605)745-4633

Rates: $60-109.
Payment: MC VISA AX DS.
Innkeeper(s): Susan Watt.

Rooms: 7 rooms with PB.
Beds: QD.

This turn-of-the-century guesthouse has a two-story octagonal living room topped off with a lookout room. The living room has a beautiful wooden stenciled ceiling. Guest rooms feature such amenities as hardwood floors, four-poster beds, stenciled floors and pedestal sinks. The Fanny Butler Room has a picture window with a view of the city.

Breakfast included in rates. Type of meal: full breakfast. Fishing and parks nearby.

Rapid City

D2

Abend Haus Cottages & Audrie's B&B

23029 Thunderhead Falls Rd
Rapid City, SD 57702-8524
(605)342-7788

Rates: $95-145.
Payment: PC TC.
Innkeeper(s): Hank & Audry Kuhnhauser.
Circa: 1973.

Rooms: 9 rooms with PB, 4 with FP. 6 suites. 3 cottages.
Beds: KQ.

Whether guests stay in the innkeeper's country home, a historic powerhouse or in private cottages, they're sure to enjoy both the spectacular scenery and the comfortable, rooms furnished with simple, European antiques. The Old Powerhouse dates back to 1910 and was used to generate hydroelectricity. Its two suites both include a private hot tub. The suites in Abend Haus Cottage feature furnishings such as a mahogany sleigh bed and private hot tubs. The rustic, log cottages and Cranbury House are other cozy options, also with hot tubs. Guests are provided with a full breakfast, which they can heat and enjoy in the privacy of their own suite and at their convenience. With all this pampering, one shouldn't forget to mention the five acres of woods, a creek and mountain views.

Breakfast included in rates. Type of meal: full breakfast. Air conditioning, turn-down service, ceiling fan, cable TV and VCR in room. Bicycles on premises. Antiques, fishing, parks, shopping, downhill skiing, cross-country skiing and watersports nearby.

"I don't want to leave so I'm staying a few days longer! This is a wonderful place."

Spearfish

C1

Eighth Street Inn

735 N 8th St
Spearfish, SD 57783-2147
(605)642-9812 (800)642-9812

Rates: $55-85.
Payment: MC VISA TC.
Innkeeper(s): Brad & Sandy Young.
Circa: 1900.

Rooms: 5 rooms, 1 with PB. 1 suite.
Beds: QD.

A mix of country furnishings and antiques, some of which are family heirlooms, create the warm, welcoming environment prevalent at this National Register home. Beds are covered with quilts and rooms showcase the innkeepers' old family photos. Guest rooms are named in honor of the innkeepers' grandparents. Breakfast are hearty, but include healthy offerings such as lean meats, fresh fruits and homemade breads.

Breakfast included in rates. Type of meal: full breakfast. VCR and spa on premises. Amusement parks, antiques, fishing, parks, shopping, downhill skiing, cross-country skiing, theater and watersports nearby.

The Mulberry Inn

512 Mulberry St
Yankton, SD 57078-4120
(605)665-7116

Rates: $35-52.
Payment: MC VISA.
Innkeeper(s): Mildred Cameron.
Circa: 1873.

Rooms: 6 rooms, 2 with PB, 1 with FP.
Beds: KQDT.

In the National Register of Historic Places, this red brick Victorian mansion has an unusual architectural style reminiscent of Gothic Revival. In a historic neighborhood, the inn has 18 rooms that feature high ceilings, walnut paneling, marble fireplaces and parquet floors. A Laura Ashley decor prevails. A full breakfast is available by advance arrangement. A walk away is the Missouri River, where visitors enjoy the riverfront parks, boating and fishing. In winter ice fishing and skating are popular.

Breakfast included in rates. Type of meal: continental breakfast.

Publicity: *South Dakota, Yankton Press and Dakotan, Midwest Living.*

"Gorgeous house. Thank you for your hospitality. It made the evening perfect."

Blueberry Gingerbread

Sea Holly Bed & Breakfast
Cape May, N.J.

- ½ cup cooking oil
- 1 cup sugar
- 3 T molasses
- 2 eggs
- 2 ¼ cups flour
- 1 t ginger
- 2 t cinnamon
- ½ t nutmeg
- 1 t baking soda
- 1 cup buttermilk
- 1 cup blueberries, fresh or frozen
- 8 ounces lemon yogurt

Preheat oven to 350. Grease and flour an 11-by-7" baking dish.

In a large bowl, with electric mixer, beat oil, sugar and molasses. Beat in eggs. Dust blueberries with a little flour, then put the rest in a medium bowl.

Add spices and soda to flour; stir to combine. Add flour mixture and buttermilk alternately to oil mixture, beating well after each addition.

Stir in blueberries. Pour into baking dish, bake 35 to 45 minutes. Serve warm with lemon yogurt over the top or on the side.

Serves 8.

SD

Tennessee

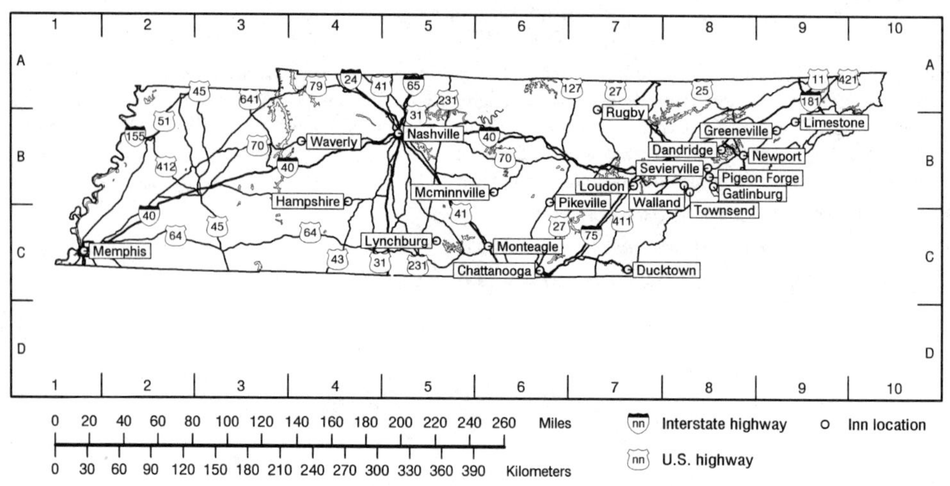

Chattanooga

C6

Adams Hilborne

801 Vine St
Chattanooga, TN 37403
(423)265-5000
Fax:(423)265-5555

Rates: $75-275.
Payment: MC VISA AX TC.
Innkeeper(s): Wendy & Dave Adams.
Circa: 1889.

Rooms: 10 rooms with PB, 4 with FP. 3 suites.
Beds: KQD.

This former Mayor's mansion is of Tudor and Romanesque design, the inside of this gracious home boasts 16-foot ceilings and floors patterned from three different woods. The large entrance hall features carved cornices, a coiffured ceiling and a fireplace at its end. Every corner offers something special, from the Tiffany windows and beveled glass to the home's 13 fireplaces and luxurious ballroom. The home has been named as a centerpiece of the Fortwood Historic District, Chattanooga's finest historic residential area.

Breakfast and lunch included in rates. Types of meals: continental-plus breakfast and early coffee/tea. Dinner, banquet service, catered breakfast and room service available. Air conditioning, turn-down service, cable TV and VCR in room. Fax, copier and library on premises. Handicap access. Weddings, small meetings, family reunions and seminars hosted. Amusement parks, antiques, fishing, parks, shopping, sporting events, theater and watersports nearby. TAC10.

Publicity: *Chattanooga Times, Chattanooga News Free Press, Monteagle Messenger.*

The Historic Milton House B&B

508 Fort Wood Pl
Chattanooga, TN 37403
(423)265-2800
Fax:(423)756-5191

Rates: $85-150.
Payment: MC VISA AX DS TC.
Innkeeper(s): Susan Mehlen.
Circa: 1915.

Rooms: 4 rooms with PB, 2 with FP. 1 suite. 1 conference room.
Beds: QD.

Ionic columns, pilasters and a slate gabled roof accent this elegant Greek Revival mansion in the National Register. Features include three pillared fireplace mantels and an American Gothic window highlighting the grand winding staircase. Maple and heart pine floors provide a sparkling background for the Victorian, Eastlake and Renaissance antiques that fill the inn. It's a few blocks to the University of Tennessee at Chattanooga, the

Tennessee River and the Tennessee Aquarium, the world's largest fresh-water aquarium. Rooms offer amenities such as a private porch, private phone, cable TV, fireplace or Jacuzzi for two.

Breakfast included in rates. Types of meals: continental-plus breakfast and early coffee/tea. Air conditioning, ceiling fan and cable TV in room. Fax, copier and spa on premises. Weddings, small meetings, family reunions and seminars hosted. Amusement parks, antiques, parks and watersports nearby. TAC10.

Publicity: *Chattanooga Free Press.*

Special Discounts: Weekly and monthly.

Dandridge B8

Mountain Harbor Country Inn

1199 Hwy 139
Dandridge, TN 37725-6049
(423)397-3345
Fax:(423)397-0264

Rates: $60-135.
Payment: MC VISA AX DS TC.
Innkeeper(s): Jim & Shirley McEwan, Rich & Patrice Steinaway.
Circa: 1947.

Rooms: 13 rooms, 4 with PB. 9 suites.
Beds: KQT.

The innkeepers, former Michigan residents, patterned this inn to look like a smaller version of the famous Grand Hotel, located on Northern Michigan's Mackinac Island. The inn's exterior is not the only "grand" element at work here. The location, nestled at the banks of Lake Douglas, provides for some truly wonderful scenery. Antiques and beds topped with quilts decorate the guest rooms. Lake or mountain views are featured. The inn's chef prepares the full breakfasts, and guests can dine at the inn's lakeside dining room. For guests planning to enjoy Lake Douglas and its 550 miles of shoreline, there is a boat dock and boat launch available. The inn is almost equidistant between Gatlinburg and Pigeon Forge.

Breakfast included in rates. Types of meals: continental-plus breakfast, full breakfast and early coffee/tea. Afternoon tea, dinner, evening snack, picnic lunch, lunch, catering service, catered breakfast and room service available. Air conditioning, ceiling fan and cable TV in room. Fax, copier and swimming on premises. Weddings, small meetings, family reunions and seminars hosted. Amusement parks, antiques, fishing, parks, shopping, downhill skiing, sporting events, theater and watersports nearby.

Pets Allowed: Yes.

Ducktown C7

White House B&B

104 Main St, PO Box 668
Ducktown, TN 37326
(423)496-4166 (800)775-4166
Fax:(423)496-4166

Rates: $60-70.
Payment: MC VISA DS PC TC.
Innkeeper(s): Dan & Mardee Kauffman.
Circa: 1898.

Rooms: 3 rooms, 1 with PB.
Beds: QT.

This Queen Anne Victorian boasts a wraparound porch with a swing. Rooms are decorated in traditional style with family antiques. Innkeepers pamper their guests with Tennessee hospitality, a hearty country breakfast and a mouth-watering sundae bar in the evenings. The innkeepers also help guests plan daily activities, and the area is bursting with possibilities. Hiking, horseback riding, panning for gold and driving tours are only a few choices. The Ocoee River is the perfect place for a river float trip or take on the challenge of roaring rapids. The river has been selected as the site of the 1996 Summer Olympic Whitewater Slalom events.

TN

Breakfast, afternoon tea and evening snack included in rates. Types of meals: full breakfast and early coffee/tea. Catering service and catered breakfast available. Air conditioning and ceiling fan in room. Cable TV, VCR, fax and library on premises. Weddings, small meetings and family reunions hosted. Antiques, fishing, parks, shopping and watersports nearby. TAC10.

Publicity: *Southern Living*

"Thank you so very much for your hospitality. We were very comfortable and felt very much at home. And I better not forget to mention a most delicious breakfast."

7th Heaven Log Inn on The Golf Resort

3944 Castle Rd
Gatlinburg, TN 37738-6321
(423)430-5000 (800)248-2923
Fax:(423)436-7748
E-mail: xg5f91a@prodigy.com

Rates: $87-137.
Payment: MC VISA PC TC.
Innkeeper(s): Cheryl & Donald Roese.
Circa: 1991.

Rooms: 5 rooms with PB. 1 suite.
Beds: KQD.

Wake up to Eggs Benedict Mountain Style served on the deck among the tree tops and you'll start to understand the inn's name. There are views of the golf course, dogwood trees, wild ducks and hummingbirds. Decks stretch for two stories all around the inn. Across the road is the Smoky Mountain National Park. Ride America's largest aerial tram, try the 1,800-foot Alpine Slide or hike and picnic in the Smoky Mountain National Park.

Breakfast and evening snack included in rates. Types of meals: full breakfast and early coffee/tea. Air conditioning and ceiling fan in room. Cable TV, VCR, fax, copier and sauna on premises. Weddings, small meetings, family reunions and seminars hosted. Amusement parks, antiques, fishing, parks, shopping, downhill skiing, sporting events, theater and watersports nearby. TAC10.

Location: A short putt from the 7th green of Bent Creek Golf Resort.

Special Discounts: Call for group rates.

"Five days was not enough. We'll be back."

Buckhorn Inn

2140 Tudor Mountain Rd
Gatlinburg, TN 37738-6014
(423)436-4668
Fax:(423)436-5009

Rates: $95-250.
Payment: MC VISA DS PC TC.
Innkeeper(s): Rachael Young.
Circa: 1938.

Rooms: 14 rooms, 12 with PB. 6 cottages.
Beds: KDT.

Set high on a hilltop, Buckhorn is surrounded by more than 30 acres of woodlands and green lawns. There are inspiring mountain views and a spring-fed lake on the grounds. Original paintings enhance the antique-filled guest rooms and the cottages have working fireplaces.

Breakfast included in rates. Types of meals: full breakfast and early coffee/tea. Afternoon tea, picnic lunch, lunch and catered breakfast available. Air conditioning in room. Cable TV, VCR, fax, copier and library on premises. 35 acres. Weddings, small meetings, family reunions and seminars hosted. Amusement parks, antiques, fishing, parks, shopping, downhill skiing, cross-country skiing, sporting events, theater and watersports nearby.

Location: One mile from the Great Smoky Mountains National Park.

Publicity: *Atlanta Journal & Constitution, Country, Brides, British Vogue, Birmingham News, New York Times.*

"This is as close to heaven as I have ever been, it's so peaceful and so relaxing, if God ever takes a vacation I bet he stays here."

Butcher House In The Mountains

1520 Garrett Ln
Gatlinburg, TN 37738-9802
(423)436-9457
Fax:(423)436-9884

Rates: $79-119.
Payment: MC VISA AX PC TC.
Innkeeper(s): Hugh & Gloria Butcher.
Circa: 1982.

Rooms: 4 rooms with PB. 1 suite. 1 conference room.
Beds: KQ.

From the balcony of Butcher House there is a spectacular view of the Great Smoky Mountains, especially scenic during the autumn months when the trees explode in color. The innkeepers have created an inviting place to enjoy all the natural beauty. Their decor is a comfortable, yet elegant mix of styles. Victorian and country pieces are balanced with other, more European furnishings. Guests are served a three-course breakfast, beginning with homemade mini muffins and followed by a fresh fruit compote topped with cashew granola and strawberry yogurt. From there, a daily entree is served, always a special and delicious creation.

Breakfast and evening snack included in rates. Types of meals: full breakfast, gourmet breakfast and early coffee/tea. Air conditioning, ceiling fan and cable TV in room. Small meetings hosted. Italian spoken. Amusement parks, antiques, fishing, parks, shopping, downhill skiing and theater nearby.

Olde English Tudor Inn B&B

135 W Holly Ridge Rd
Gatlinburg, TN 37738-3414
(423)436-7760 (800)541-3798
Fax:(423)430-7308
E-mail: tudorinn@smoky-mtns.com

Rates: $75-105.
Payment: MC VISA AX DS PC TC.
Innkeeper(s): Larry & Kathy Schuh.
Circa: 1946.

Rooms: 7 rooms with PB, 1 with FP.
Beds: KQ.

Mountain views and touches of Old World ambiance work in a pleasant combination at this English Tudor inn. The comfortable bedrooms feature simple, country furnishings, and one includes a fireplace. Several rooms offer mountain views, and guests can take in the scenery from the home's balcony. The breakfasts, served either in the dining room or on the outside patio, include traditional items such as French toast, cherry nut bread and fresh fruit.

Breakfast and afternoon tea included in rates. Types of meals: full breakfast and early coffee/tea. Air conditioning, ceiling fan and cable TV in room. VCR, fax and library on premises. Weddings and family reunions hosted. Amusement parks, antiques, fishing, parks, shopping, downhill skiing, theater and watersports nearby. TAC10.

Special Discounts: Fifth night is free.

"Home away from home is how we can describe it best here."

Tennessee Ridge Inn B&B

507 Campbell Lead Rd
Gatlinburg, TN 37738-3045
(423)436-4068 (800)737-7369

Rates: $75-150.
Payment: MC VISA PC TC.
Innkeeper(s): Dar Hullander.
Circa: 1970.

Rooms: 7 rooms with PB, 4 with FP. 1 suite. 1 conference room.
Beds: K.

It would be somewhat dismissive to simply say this lodge provides a nice view of the Great Smoky Mountains. The scenery, as a light fog drifts slowly across emerald mountains covered with forests, is spectacular. Stone fireplaces, whirlpool tubs and private balconies are some of the amenities available in the contemporary-style guest rooms. The Southern-style breakfasts with fruit, biscuits and gravy, egg dishes and other treats are served on china in a room full of windows, allowing guests to enjoy both the view and the food. Although the inn's mountain-top location feels secluded, it's just a four-minute drive into Gatlinburg.

Breakfast included in rates. Types of meals: full breakfast, gourmet breakfast and early coffee/tea. Afternoon tea available. Air conditioning and turn-down service in room. Cable TV, VCR, fax and swimming on premises. Small meetings, family reunions and seminars hosted. Amusement parks, antiques, fishing, parks, shopping, downhill skiing and sporting events nearby. TAC10.

Special Discounts: Four nights or more.

Greeneville B9

TN

Hilltop House B&B

6 Sanford Cir
Greeneville, TN 37743-4022
(423)639-8202

Rates: $70-75.
Payment: MC VISA AX PC TC.
Innkeeper(s): Denise Ashworth.
Circa: 1920.

Rooms: 3 rooms with PB.
Beds: KQD.

Situated on a bluff overlooking the Nolichuckey River valley, this manor home boasts mountain views from each of the guest rooms. The Elizabeth Noel room, named for the original owner, includes among its treasures a canopy bed, sitting room and a private veranda, a perfect spot to watch the sunsets. After a hearty breakfast, take a stroll across the beautifully landscaped grounds. Innkeeper Denise Ashworth is a landscape architect and guests will marvel at her wonderful gardens. Ashworth sponsors several gardening workshops each year at the inn, covering topics such as flower arranging, Christmas decorations and landscaping your home grounds.

Breakfast and afternoon tea included in rates. Types of meals: full breakfast, gourmet breakfast and early coffee/tea. Dinner, gourmet lunch and catering service available. Air conditioning, turn-down service, cable TV and VCR in room. Library on premises. Small meetings, family reunions and seminars hosted. Antiques, fishing, parks, shopping, theater and watersports nearby. TAC10.

Publicity: *Country Inns.*

"Peaceful and comfortable, great change of pace."

Hampshire B4

Ridgetop B&B

Hwy 412 W, PO Box 193
Hampshire, TN 38461-0193
(615)285-2777 (800)377-2770
E-mail: natcheztrace@worldnet.att.net

Rates: $65-85.
Payment: MC VISA PC TC.
Innkeeper(s): Bill & Kay Jones.
Circa: 1979.

Rooms: 1 room with PB, 1 with FP. 2 cottages.
Beds: DT.

This contemporary Western cedar house rests on 20 cleared acres along the top of the ridge. A quarter-mile below is a waterfall. Blueberries grow in abundance on the property and guests may pick them in summer. These provide the filling for luscious breakfast muffins, waffles and pancakes year-round. There are 170 acres in all, mostly wooded. Picture windows and a deck provide views of the trees and wildlife: flying squirrels, birds, raccoons and deer. The inn is handicap-accessible. The innkeepers will help guests plan excursions on the Natchez Trace, including biking trips.

Breakfast included in rates. Types of meals: full breakfast and early coffee/tea. Air conditioning and ceiling fan in room. Handicap access. 170 acres. Small meetings hosted. Antiques, fishing, parks, shopping and watersports nearby. TAC10.

Pets Allowed: In outbuilding.

Publicity: *Columbia Daily Herald.*

"What a delightful visit! Thank you for creating such a peaceful, immaculate, interesting environment for us!"

Limestone B9

Snapp Inn B&B

1990 Davy Crockett Park Rd
Limestone, TN 37681-6026
(423)257-2482

Rates: $65.
Payment: PC TC.
Innkeeper(s): Ruth & Dan Dorgan.
Circa: 1815.

Rooms: 2 rooms with PB.
Beds: D.

From the second-story porch of this brick Federal, guests enjoy views of local farmland as well as the sounds of Big Limestone Creek. The Smoky Mountains are seen from the back porch. Decorated with locally gathered antiques, the home is within walking distance of Davy Crockett Birthplace State Park. A full country breakfast often includes Ruth's homemade biscuits.

Breakfast included in rates. Types of meals: full breakfast and early coffee/tea. Air conditioning in room. Cable TV, VCR and library on premises. Antiques, fishing, parks, shopping, theater and watersports nearby. TAC10.

Pets Allowed.

Publicity: *Greenville Sun.*

Special Discounts: Fifth day free.

Loudon B7

The Mason Place B&B

600 Commerce St
Loudon, TN 37774-1101
(423)458-3921

Rates: $96-120.
Payment: PC TC.
Innkeeper(s): Bob & Donna Siewert.
Circa: 1865.

Rooms: 5 rooms with PB, 5 with FP.
Beds: QD.

In the National Register, Mason Place received an award for its outstanding restoration. In the Greek Revival style, the inn has a red slate roof, graceful columns and a handsome double-tiered balcony overlooking three acres of lawns, trees and gardens. There are 10 working fireplaces, a Grecian swimming pool, gazebo and wisteria-covered arbor. A grand entrance hall, fine antiques and tasteful furnishings make for an elegant decor, suitable for the mansion's 7,000 square feet.

Breakfast included in rates. Types of meals: gourmet breakfast and early coffee/tea. Afternoon tea and picnic lunch available. Air conditioning in room. Cable TV, VCR, swimming, bicycles, tennis and library on premises. Weddings, small meetings and seminars hosted. Amusement parks, antiques, fishing, parks, shopping, downhill skiing, cross-country skiing, sporting events, theater and watersports nearby.

Location: Smoky Mountains Cherokee National Forest.

Publicity: *Country Inn, Country Side, Country Travels, Tennessee Cross Roads, Antiquing in Tennessee, Knox-Chattanooga, Oak Ridge, Detroit Magazine.*

"Absolutely wonderful in every way. You are in for a treat! The best getaway ever!"

Lynchburg C5

Lynchburg B&B

Mechanic St, PO Box 34
Lynchburg, TN 37352-0034
(615)759-7158

Rates: $55-65.
Payment: MC VISA.
Innkeeper(s): Mike & Virginia Tipps.
Circa: 1877.

Rooms: 2 rooms with PB.
Beds: QD.

Antiques and a variety of elements original to this 19th-century home create an air of nostalgia. The exterior, flanked by an arch, columns, red roof and second-story porch, is charming. The innkeeper serves home-baked treats such as a country sausage muffin or banana bread during the continental breakfast service. Several of her recipes have been featured in a cookbook. The home is near many Lynchburg sites, and, for those so inclined, the bed & breakfast is within walking distance of the famous Jack Daniels distillery.

Type of meal: continental-plus breakfast. Air conditioning and cable TV in room. Antiques, parks and shopping nearby.

"Thank you for your wonderful southern hospitality."

McMinnville B6

Falcon Manor

2645 Faulkner Springs Rd
McMinnville, TN 37110
(615)668-4444
Fax:(615)815-4444
E-mail: falconmanor@blomand.net

Rates: $75-105.
Payment: MC VISA.
Innkeeper(s): George & Charlien McGlothin.
Circa: 1896.

Rooms: 6 rooms, 2 with PB.
Beds: KD.

TN

Victorian glory is the theme at this glorious restored manor, right down to the period clothing worn by the innkeepers during tours of their bed & breakfast. Museum-quality period furnishings fill each of the unique rooms, which are decorated in traditional Victorian style. High ceilings, a sweeping staircase, chandeliers and white oak hardwood floors accent the decor. Relax on the wraparound porch with its comfortable rockers or learn of home's past from innkeepers George and Charlien McGlothin, who can tell a few ghost

stories along with providing ample historical detail. Glorious full breakfasts are served each morning and evening refreshments and desserts are offered.

Breakfast included in rates. Type of meal: full breakfast. Catering service available. Antiques, fishing, theater and watersports nearby.

Publicity: *Tennessee Magazine, Tempo, Southern Standard, Huntsville Times, Chattanooga Free Press, Country Extra.*

"The parlor talk and your visit with us at breakfast was true Southern hospitality."

Monteagle C6

Adams Edgeworth Inn

Monteagle Assembly
Monteagle, TN 37356
(615)924-4000
Fax:(615)924-3236

Rates: $70-195. MAP, EP.
Payment: MC VISA AX.
Innkeeper(s): Wendy Adams.
Circa: 1896.

Rooms: 12 rooms with PB, 4 with FP. 1 suite. 1 conference room.
Beds: KQDT.

This National Register Victorian inn recently has been refurbished in an English-manor style. Original paintings, sculptures and fine English antiques are found throughout. Wide verandas are filled with white wicker furnishings and breezy hammocks, and there's a prize-winning rose garden. You can stroll through the 96-acre Victorian village that surrounds the inn and enjoy rolling hills, creeks and Victorian cottages. Waterfalls, natural caves and scenic overlooks are along the 150 miles of hiking trails of nearby South Cumberland State Park.

Breakfast included in rates. Types of meals: continental breakfast, gourmet breakfast and early coffee/tea. Dinner, picnic lunch, lunch and gourmet lunch available. MAP, EP. Air conditioning, ceiling fan and cable TV in room. VCR, fax and copier on premises. Handicap access. Weddings, small meetings, family reunions and seminars hosted. Antiques, fishing, parks, shopping, sporting events and theater nearby.

Location: On top of the Cumberland Mountains between Nashville & Chattanooga on I-24.

Publicity: *Country Inns, Chattanooga News Free Press, Tempo, Gourmet, Victorian Homes, Brides, Tennessean, Southern Living, PBS Crossroads, ABC TV, CBS TV.*

"Leaving totally rejuvenated. Incredibly beautiful accommodations, welcome and gracious hosts, awesome food."

Nashville B5

The Hillsboro House

1933 20th Ave S
Nashville, TN 37212-3711
(615)292-5501

Rates: $75-85.
Payment: MC VISA AX DS.
Innkeeper(s): Andrea Beaudet.
Circa: 1904.

Rooms: 4 rooms, 3 with PB.
Beds: Q.

The Hillsboro House is a cozy home base for guests wanting to experience the sites and sounds of Nashville. Vanderbilt University and famed Music Row are within walking distance from this Victorian home. After a dreamy night's sleep snuggled in a feather bed, guests are served a hearty homemade breakfast and head out for a day in Nashville, which offers a multitude of shops, outdoor activities and restaurants to explore.

Breakfast included in rates. Type of meal: continental breakfast. Antiques and theater nearby.

Pets Allowed.

"This is the real thing, as fresh and welcoming as the ingredients in your fabulous breakfasts."

Newport

B8

Christopher Place Country Inn

1500 Pinnacles Way
Newport, TN 37821-7308
(423)623-6555 (800)595-9441
Fax:(423)623-6555

Rates: $89-195.
Payment: MC VISA PC TC.
Innkeeper(s): Drew Ogle.
Circa: 1976.

Rooms: 9 rooms with PB, 3 with FP. 1 suite. 2 cottages. 1 conference room.
Beds: KQD.

Although it was built in the mid-1970s, this mansion has the appearance of a great Antebellum estate. The inn is surrounded by more than 200 acres and offers views of the Great Smoky Mountains. The inn's interior, as well as its reputation for hospitality and service, earned it a four-diamond award. Country Inns magazine and Waverly chose Christopher Place's Stargazer as the 1995 Room of the Year. Each of the guest rooms is decorated with a different theme in mind. The Roman Holiday room is a romantic retreat with an iron canopy bed draped with a sheer, dramatic canopy. There is a fireplace and a whirlpool tub for two. The Old Bearskin is a rustic room with a hand-carved bed, antique bathtub and a fireplace. In addition to the inn's transfixing decor, guests are further pampered with on-site tennis courts, a sauna, swimming pool, billiards and library. As well, Gatlinburg and Pigeon Forge aren't far away.

Pigeon Forge

B8

Hilton's Bluff B&B Inn

2654 Valley Heights Dr
Pigeon Forge, TN 37863
(423)428-9765 (800)441-4188

Rates: $69-129.
Payment: MC VISA AX TC.
Innkeeper(s): Jack & Norma Hilton.
Circa: 1989.

Rooms: 10 rooms with PB. 1 cottage. 1 conference room.
Beds: KQT.

On a wooded hilltop, this newly built country inn boasts wide decks overlooking the mountains and trees. Scents of dogwoods and honeysuckle enhance the country decor. Amenities include heart-shaped whirlpool tubs and large four-poster beds. Each room opens to a private balcony or deck. French toast, filled with strawberry and cream cheese, is a favorite breakfast item. By advance reservation, picnic baskets are available for an excursion into Great Smoky Mountains National Park or nearby Dollywood.

Breakfast, evening snack and and snacks included in rates. Types of meals: gourmet breakfast and early coffee/tea. Ask about picnic baskets. Air conditioning and ceiling fan in room. Cable TV, VCR and library on premises. Small meetings, family reunions and seminars hosted. Amusement parks, antiques, fishing, parks, shopping, downhill skiing, theater and watersports nearby. TAC10.

Pikeville

B6

Fall Creek Falls B&B

RR 3 Box 298B
Pikeville, TN 37367-9803
(423)881-5494
Fax:(423)881-5040

Rates: $65-130.
Payment: MC VISA AX DS PC TC.
Innkeeper(s): Doug & Rita Pruett.
Circa: 1981.

Rooms: 7 rooms with PB, 1 with FP. 1 suite.
Beds: QDT.

TN

An abundance of gables marks the architecture of this 6,000-square-foot country manor, surrounded by 40 acres of woodland and meadow. Victorian and country furnishings are found in rooms such as the Sweet Heart Room, which offers a heart-shaped, red whirlpool tub. Breakfast is served in the dining room or the Florida room overlooking the fields and deer trails. Stuffed French Toast Strata with apple cider syrup is a specialty. The Wild Rose Suite features a heart-shaped whirlpool and a gas log fireplace. Fall Creek Falls State Park is a mile away where you can hike trails that meander past scenic waterfalls. An 18-hole championship golf course is nearby.

Breakfast and evening snack included in rates. Types of meals: full breakfast and early coffee/tea. Picnic lunch available. Air conditioning in room. VCR, fax and copier on premises. 40 acres. Fishing, parks and watersports nearby. TAC10.

Rugby

A7

Newbury House at Historic Rugby

Hwy 52, PO Box 8
Rugby, TN 37733
(423)628-2430
Fax:(423)628-2266

Rates: $62-72.
Payment: MC VISA PC TC.
Innkeeper(s): Historic Rugby.
Circa: 1880.

Rooms: 5 rooms, 3 with PB. 2 cottages.
Beds: D.

Mansard-roofed Newbury House first lodged visitors to this English village when author and social reformer Thomas Hughes founded Rugby. Filled with authentic Victorian antiques, the inn includes some furnishings that are original to the colony. There are also several restored cottages on the property.

Breakfast and afternoon tea included in rates. Types of meals: full breakfast and early coffee/tea. Dinner, picnic lunch, lunch and banquet service available. Air conditioning and ceiling fan in room. Library on premises. Weddings, small meetings, family reunions and seminars hosted. Antiques, fishing, parks, shopping and watersports nearby.

Publicity: *New York Times, Americana, USA Weekend, Tennessean, Southern Living, Atlanta Journal Constitution, Victorian Homes.*

"I love the peaceful atmosphere here and the beauty of nature surrounding Rugby."

Sevierville

B8

Calico Inn B&B

757 Ranch Way
Sevierville, TN 37862-4729
(423)428-3833 (800)235-1054

Rates: $85-95.
Payment: MC VISA PC.
Innkeeper(s): Lill & Jim Katzbeck.
Circa: 1989.

Rooms: 3 rooms with PB.
Beds: Q.

Exposed beams, a stone fireplace and country furnishings are some of the special features of this rustic, log home. The private location is secluded on 25 wooded acres with a panoramic view of the Great Smoky Mountains. Guests are pampered with a full, country breakfast as well as other treats throughout the day. The front porch has rockers and a swing for those who wish to relax and enjoy the wonderful scenery. The home is minutes from Great Smoky Mountains National Park, Dollywood and other area attractions.

Breakfast and evening snack included in rates. Types of meals: full breakfast, gourmet breakfast and early coffee/tea. Air conditioning and ceiling fan in room. VCR on premises. 25 acres. Weddings, small meetings, family reunions and seminars hosted. Amusement parks, antiques, fishing, parks, shopping, downhill skiing, cross-country skiing, sporting events, theater and watersports nearby. TAC10.

Special Discounts: Off season discount rates offered.

"Outstanding, as usual."

Little Greenbrier Lodge

3685 Lyon Springs Rd
Sevierville, TN 37862-8257
(423)429-2500 (800)277-8100

Rates: $65-110.
Payment: MC VISA DS.
Innkeeper(s): Charles & Susan LeBon.
Circa: 1939.

Rooms: 10 rooms, 8 with PB. 1 conference room.
Beds: QDT.

The spectacular, forested setting at Little Greenbrier is worth the trip. The rustic lodge is set on five, wooded acres less than a quarter mile from Great Smoky Mountains National Park. Rooms have valley or mountain views and are decorated with Victorian-style furnishings and antiques. The lodge served guests from 1939 until the 1970s when it became a religious retreat. When the innkeepers purchased it in 1993, they tried to preserve some of its early history, including restoring original sinks and the first bathtub ever installed in the valley. A copy of the lodge's original "house rules" is still posted. Within 30 minutes are Dollywood, outlet malls, antiquing, craft stores and plenty of outdoor activities.

Breakfast, afternoon tea and evening snack included in rates. Type of meal: full breakfast. Air conditioning in room. VCR on premises. Weddings, small meetings, family reunions and seminars hosted. Amusement parks, antiques, fishing, parks, shopping, downhill skiing, sporting events and theater nearby. TAC10.

"We had a relaxing holiday. Little Greenbrier is very special and we plan to return sometime soon."

Von-Bryan Inn

2402 Hatcher Mountain Rd
Sevierville, TN 37862-8635
(423)453-9832 (800)633-1459
Fax:(423)428-8634

Rates: $90-135.
Payment: MC VISA AX DS PC TC.
Innkeeper(s): The Vaughn Family.
Circa: 1986.

Rooms: 6 rooms with PB. 1 cottage.
Beds: KQDT.

Where else in the Smokies would you be able to sit in a kidney-shaped swimming pool, enjoy a surrounding English garden and a spectacular 360-degree view of the Great Smoky Mountain peaks and foothills? Inside, the chalet-style log house, the vaulted ceiling and stone fireplace provide a warm welcome. Whirlpool tubs, large canopy beds, antiques and a country decor compete with the rocking-chair-filled front porch for your attention. A two-bedroom log chalet is available for families who prefer a separate accommodation. Full country breakfasts provide the fuel for vigorous hiking or Gatlinburg sight-seeing.

Breakfast and evening snack included in rates. Types of meals: full breakfast and early coffee/tea. Picnic lunch available. Air conditioning in room. Cable TV, VCR, fax, copier, spa, swimming and library on premises. Weddings, small meetings, family reunions and seminars hosted. Amusement parks, antiques, fishing, parks, shopping, downhill skiing, sporting events, theater and watersports nearby. TAC10.

Publicity: *Country, Country Inns, Discovery.*

Townsend B8

Richmont Inn

220 Winterberry Ln
Townsend, TN 37882-3623
(423)448-6751
Fax:(423)448-6480

Rates: $85-135.
Innkeeper(s): Jim & Susan Hind.
Circa: 1991.

Rooms: 10 rooms with PB. 1 suite.
Beds: KQ.

This inn, just a few minutes from the Great Smoky Mountains, is located in a Appalachian barn and is filled with 18th-century English antiques. French artwork adds further decoration. Guest rooms include such amenities as balconies, sitting areas, woodburning fireplaces or a whirlpool tub for two. The breakfast fare is highlighted by French and Swiss specialties. Delectable desserts and gourmet coffees are served by candlelight in the evenings. The inn has won high praise from both Gourmet and Country Inns magazines.

Breakfast included in rates. Types of meals: full breakfast and early coffee/tea. Air conditioning in room. VCR on premises. 11 acres. Small meetings and seminars hosted. Antiques, fishing, shopping, downhill skiing and cross-country skiing nearby.

Publicity: *Country Inns, National Geographic, Great Country Kitchens, Diversions.*

Terrapin Point Retreat

426 Cameron Rd
Townsend, TN 37882-6113
(423)448-6010

Rates: $59-98.
Payment: PC TC.
Innkeeper(s): Marga Lacy.
Circa: 1991.

Rooms: 3 rooms, 1 with PB. 1 suite. 2 conference rooms.
Beds: KDT.

With views of the Great Smoky Mountains, pastures, wooded acres and Carr Creek Valley to delight in, this glass-walled, contemporary solar home is a tribute to its environment. The suite includes a private spa tub room with beautiful views. The home is decorated with modern furnishings, antiques and plenty of plants. A hearty breakfast is prepared, featuring such items as fruit ambrosia, freshly baked muffins, omelets and apple cider.

Breakfast included in rates. Type of meal: gourmet breakfast. Catering service available. Air conditioning and turn-down service in room. Bicycles and library on premises. Weddings, small meetings and seminars hosted. Amusement parks, antiques, fishing, parks, shopping, downhill skiing, cross-country skiing, sporting events, theater and watersports nearby.

Special Discounts: Six nights, seventh night free.

"This is how everyone dreams of living, but hardly anyone ever does."

Walland

B8

The Inn at Blackberry Farm

1471 W Millers Cove Rd
Walland, TN 37886-2649
(615)984-8166 (800)862-7610
Fax:(615)983-5708

Rates: $250-495.
Payment: MC VISA AX.
Innkeeper(s): Keith A. Izydore.
Circa: 1939.

Rooms: 29 rooms with PB.
Beds: KQDT.

Gracious furnishings, spectacular scenery and gourmet cuisine are three of the reasons why guests return to Blackberry Farm. The 1,100 lush acres offer miles of nature to enjoy, complete with areas perfect for hiking, biking and fishing. The front terrace is lined with rocking chairs perfect for relaxing and enjoying the wonderful views. Guests are treated to deluxe breakfasts, lunches and dinners. The innkeepers also keep a pantry stocked with snacks and beverages. The rooms are exquisitely decorated and furnished with glorious attention to detail. After a few days of being mercilessly pampered, guests won't want to leave.

Breakfast, dinner and picnic lunch included in rates. Type of meal: full breakfast. Afternoon tea, lunch and room service available. Fishing and watersports nearby.

Publicity: *Country Inns, Town & Country, Travel & Leisure, Southern Living, Conde Nast Traveler, Andrew Harper's Hideway Report.*

"Everything was spectacular! A wonderful weekend getaway!"

Waverly

B4

Nolan House Inn

375 Hwy 13 N
Waverly, TN 37185
(615)296-2511

Rates: $60-75.
Payment: PC TC.
Innkeeper(s): Linda & Patrick O'Lee.
Circa: 1870.

Rooms: 3 rooms with PB, 3 with FP. 1 conference room.
Beds: QD.

This National Register home was built by prominent businessman James Nolan, who among his many occupations ran the Nolan House Hotel. The innkeepers have maintained Nolan's reputation for excellent hospitality at their Victorian-style inn, which features 19th-century furnishings throughout the home. The grounds boast walking trails, an old-fashioned stone fountain, gazebo and flower gardens.

Breakfast included in rates. Types of meals: continental-plus breakfast and early coffee/tea. Afternoon tea available. Air conditioning in room. Cable TV on premises. Weddings, small meetings, family reunions and seminars hosted. Antiques, parks and shopping nearby.

Pets Allowed: Animals not preferred, but limited to small pets.

Special Discounts: 10% AARP.

Burgundy Poached Pears

Blue Spruce Inn
Soquel, Calif.

- 8 pears
- 2 cups Burgundy wine
- 2 T lemon juice
- 2 t cinnamon
- 1 t vanilla
- Mint leaves
- zest of one lemon

In a sauce pan, bring the wine, lemon juice, sugar, cinnamon, lemon zest and vanilla to a boil.

Peel pears, then cut them in half and core.

Place the pears in a large skillet with a lid. Pour the liquid over the pears and simmer slowly, basting occasionally, until tender. It will take 10 to 30 minutes depending on the ripeness of the fruit.

Carefully remove pears to individual serving dishes and boil the liquid down until reduced to half. Pour sauce over the pears. Garnish with a mint leaf.

Texas

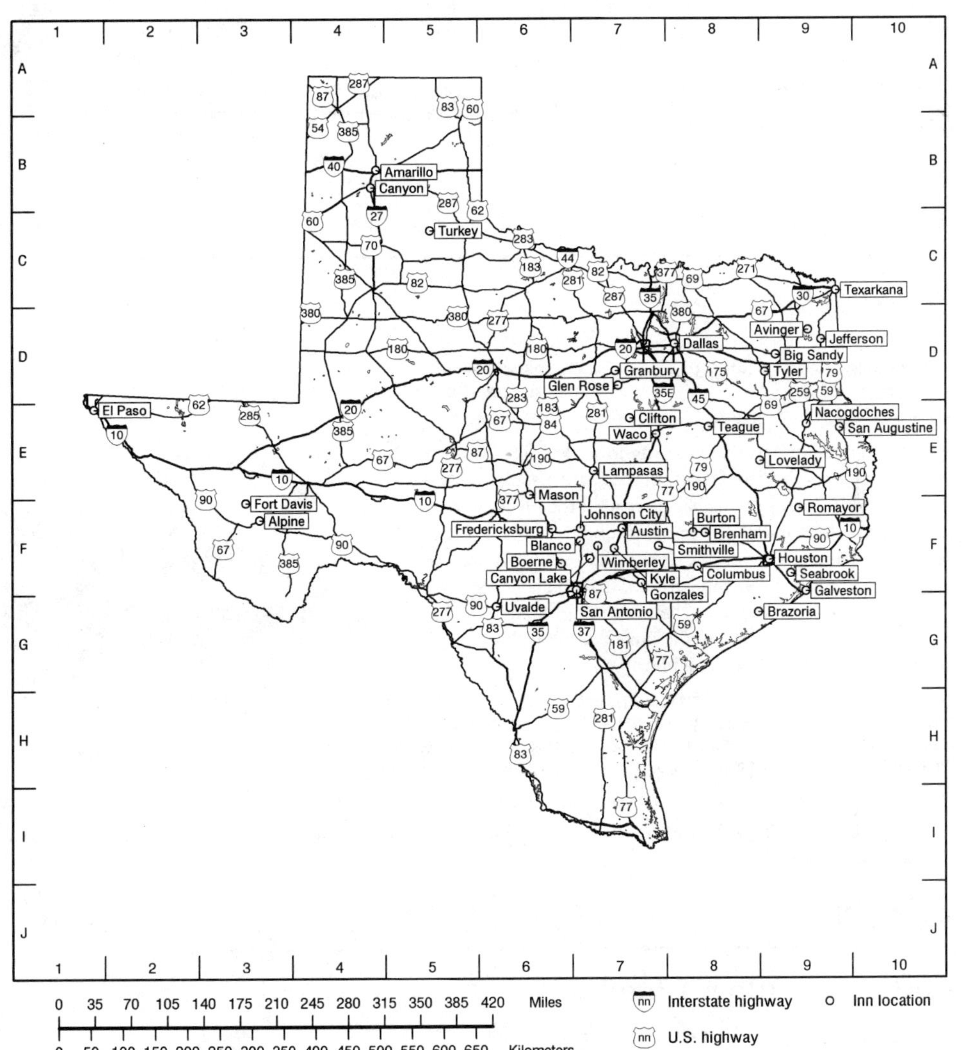
Amarillo
Canyon
Turkey
Texarkana
Avinger
Jefferson
Dallas
Big Sandy
Tyler
Granbury
Glen Rose
El Paso
Clifton
Waco
Teague
Nacogdoches
San Augustine
Lovelady
Lampasas
Mason
Fort Davis
Alpine
Johnson City
Burton
Brenham
Romayor
Fredericksburg
Austin
Blanco
Smithville
Houston
Boerne
Wimberley
Kyle
Columbus
Seabrook
Canyon Lake
Gonzales
Galveston
Uvalde
San Antonio
Brazoria
0 35 70 105 140 175 210 245 280 315 350 385 420 Miles
0 50 100 150 200 250 300 350 400 450 500 550 600 650 Kilometers
Interstate highway
U.S. highway
Inn location

TX

Alpine

F3

The Corner House

801 E Avenue E
Alpine, TX 79830-5016
(915)837-7161 (800)585-7795
Fax:(915)837-3638

Rates: $55-65.
Payment: MC VISA AX PC TC.
Innkeeper(s): Jim Glendinning.
Circa: 1937.

Rooms: 9 rooms, 7 with PB, 1 with FP.
Beds: KQDT.

The innkeeper of this bed & breakfast is an author of travel guides, as well as a world traveler. His expertise extends to the local area, and he can point guests in the direction of what to do and where to go. There are nine comfortable guest rooms. Guests enjoy a full breakfast with items such as freshly brewed coffee, homemade breads, marmalade and perhaps an "Egg in the Hole," with a potato cake on the side.

Breakfast included in rates. Type of meal: full breakfast. Air conditioning in room. Cable TV and library on premises. Weddings, small meetings, family reunions and seminars hosted. French, German and Spanish spoken. Parks, shopping, sporting events and theater nearby. TAC10.

Pets Allowed: Yes.

Amarillo

B4

Parkview House B&B

1311 S Jefferson St
Amarillo, TX 79101-4029
(806)373-9464
E-mail: dia1311@aol.com

Rates: $65-105.
Payment: MC VISA AX PC TC.
Innkeeper(s): Carol & Nabil Dia.
Circa: 1908.

Rooms: 5 rooms, 3 with PB. 1 suite. 1 cottage.
Beds: Beds: QD.

Ionic columns support the wraparound wicker-filled front porch of this prairie Victorian. Herb and rose gardens, highlighted by a statuary and Victorian gazing ball, surround the property. Antique mahogany, walnut and oak pieces are found throughout. The French, Colonial, Dutch and Victorian Rose rooms all feature draped bedsteads and romantic decor. Sticky buns, homemade granola and fruits are served in kitchen or dining room. Guests can enjoy a soak under the stars in the inn's hot tub or borrow a bicycle for a tour of the historic neighborhood.

Breakfast included in rates. Types of meals: continental breakfast, continental-plus breakfast, gourmet breakfast and early coffee/tea. Evening snack available. Air conditioning in room. Cable TV, VCR, fax, computer and bicycles on premises. Weddings and small meetings hosted. Arabic spoken. Amusement parks, antiques, parks, shopping, theater and watersports nearby. TAC10.

Publicity: *Lubbock Avalanche, Amarillo Globe News, Accent West, Sunday Telegraph Review.*

"You are what give B&B's such a wonderful reputation. Thanks very much for the wonderful stay! The hospitality was warm and the ambiance incredible."

Austin

F7

Austin's Wildflower Inn B&B

1200 W 22 1/2 St
Austin, TX 78705-5304
(512)477-9639
Fax:(512)474-4188
E-mail: kjackson@io.com

Rates: $69-89.
Payment: MC VISA AX PC TC.
Innkeeper(s): Kay Jackson.
Circa: 1936.

Rooms: 4 rooms, 2 with PB.
Beds: QD.

This Colonial-style home fits right into its woodsy street, located in a quiet Austin neighborhood just a few blocks from the University of Texas. Three of the rooms are named for relatives of innkeeper Kay Jackson, who is related to a former president of the Republic of Texas. Lacy curtains, stenciling, pedestal sinks, quilts and antiques create a homey country atmosphere. One room has a canopy bed, another includes a four-

poster, oak bed. Each morning, a new Wildflower specialty is served at breakfast, along with homemade breads or muffins and fresh fruit. The State Capitol Complex is a few minutes from the home.

Breakfast included in rates. Types of meals: full breakfast and early coffee/tea. Air conditioning and ceiling fan in room. Cable TV and fax on premises. Antiques, fishing, parks, shopping, sporting events, theater and watersports nearby.

"I was enchanted by your very friendly reception and personal care for my well-being."

Carrington's Bluff

1900 David St
Austin, TX 78705-5312
(512)479-0638 (800)871-8908
Fax:(512)476-4769

Rates: $69-99.
Payment: MC VISA AX DC CB DS PC TC.
Innkeeper(s): Lisa & Edward Mugford.
Circa: 1877.

Rooms: 8 rooms, 6 with PB. 1 suite. 1 cottage. 1 conference room.
Beds: KQDT.

Situated on a tree-covered bluff in the heart of Austin, this inn sits next to a 500-year-old oak tree. The innkeepers, one a Texan, the other British, combine down-home hospitality with English charm. The house is filled with English and American antiques and handmade quilts. Rooms are carefully decorated with dried flowers, inviting colors and antique beds, such as the oak barley twist bed in the Martha Hill Carrington Room. After a hearty breakfast, relax on a 35-foot-long porch that overlooks the bluff. The Austin area is booming with things to do.

Breakfast and evening snack included in rates. Types of meals: full breakfast, gourmet breakfast and early coffee/tea. Air conditioning, ceiling fan and cable TV in room. VCR, fax, copier, library and child care on premises. Weddings, small meetings, family reunions and seminars hosted. Amusement parks, antiques, fishing, parks, shopping, sporting events, theater and watersports nearby.

Location: Downtown.

Publicity: *PBS Special.*

"Victorian writer's dream place."

Chequered Shade B&B

2530 Pearce Rd
Austin, TX 78730-4255
(512)346-8318
Fax:(512)346-7495

Rates: $89-99.
Payment: MC VISA AX PC.
Innkeeper(s): Millie Scott.
Circa: 1977.

Rooms: 3 rooms, 2 with PB.
Beds: KQT.

Family treasures decorate this German Hill Country-style home, which is just a short walk away from Lake Austin, a fishing creek and a city park. Downtown Austin, the university, Johnson Library and many other sites are about eight miles from the home. A hearty, full breakfast is served each morning in true Texas style, featuring chili cheese puffs with salsa, a sausage-stuffed mushroom or other spicy fare. With advance notice, the innkeeper is happy to prepare breakfast trays for those who want to enjoy a more private meal.

Breakfast included in rates. Types of meals: full breakfast, gourmet breakfast and early coffee/tea. Air conditioning, ceiling fan, cable TV and VCR in room. Library on premises. Family reunions hosted. Antiques, parks, shopping, sporting events and watersports nearby.

Fairview

1304 Newning Ave
Austin, TX 78704-1841
(512)444-4746 (800)310-4746
Fax:(512)444-3494

Rates: $89-139.
Payment: MC VISA AX DC CB PC TC.
Innkeeper(s): Duke & Nancy Waggoner.
Circa: 1910.

Rooms: 3 suites.
Beds: KQDT.

Surrounded by huge live oak trees, this Texas Revival-style home has been designated an Austin historic landmark. Each of the four large guest rooms on the second floor have impressive antique beds and private baths. Some rooms also feature clawfoot tubs, screened porches and sun rooms. Two suites are offered in the Carriage House. Each has a private entrance, sitting room, full kitchen, eating area, bedroom and bath.

Breakfast included in rates. Types of meals: full breakfast and early coffee/tea. Air conditioning, ceiling fan and cable TV in room. Fax, copier and library on premises. Amusement parks, antiques, fishing, parks, shopping, sporting events, theater and watersports nearby. TAC10.

Location: Near downtown, convention center.

Publicity: *Texas Monthly, Austin, Gulliver's, Italian Travel.*

"The meal was fantastic, the tour wonderful and your hospitality gracious."

Governors' Inn

611 W 22nd St
Austin, TX 78705-5115
(512)479-0638
Fax:(512)479-0638

Rates: $69-99.
Payment: MC VISA AX DC CB DS TC.
Innkeeper(s): Lisa & Edward Mugford.
Circa: 1897.

Rooms: 10 rooms with PB, 5 with FP. 1 conference room.
Beds: KQF.

This Neo-Classical Victorian is just a few block from the University of Texas campus, and once served as a fraternity . Guest can enjoy the view of two acres of trees and foliage from the porches which decorate each story of the inn. The innkeepers have decorated the guest rooms with antiques and named them after former Texas governors. Several of the bathrooms include clawfoot tubs.

Breakfast, afternoon tea and evening snack included in rates. Types of meals: full breakfast, gourmet breakfast and early coffee/tea. Picnic lunch, banquet service and catering service available. Air conditioning, turn-down service, ceiling fan and cable TV in room. VCR, fax and copier on premises. Handicap access. Weddings, small meetings, family reunions and seminars hosted. Amusement parks, antiques, fishing, parks, shopping, sporting events, theater and watersports nearby.

Pets Allowed.

The McCallum House

613 W 32nd St
Austin, TX 78705-2219
(512)451-6744
Fax:(512)451-4752

Rates: $70-119.
Payment: MC VISA.
Innkeeper(s): Nancy & Roger Danley.
Circa: 1907.

Rooms: 5 rooms, 3 with PB. 2 suites.
Beds: QT.

This two-story Princess Anne Victorian was built by school superintendent A.N. McCallum and designed by his wife Jane. As Mrs. McCallum raised her five children she assumed a leadership position in the women's suffrage movement and led the "Petticoat Lobby" advancing human service reforms in Texas. In 1926 she became secretary of state for Texas. In addition to four rooms in the main house with private porches, all suites come with kitchens. It is an eight-block walk to the University of Texas.

Breakfast included in rates. Type of meal: full breakfast. Air conditioning, ceiling fan and VCR in room. Fax and copier on premises. Amusement parks, antiques, fishing, parks, shopping, sporting events, theater and watersports nearby. TAC10.

Publicity: *Austin American Statesman, Texas Monthly, Dallas Morning News.*

"What a special home and history.. We would like to thank you again for our wonderful stay in Jane's Loft and all your help Easter Sunday with our dead battery."

Southard House

908 Blanco St
Austin, TX 78703-4914
(512)474-4731

Rates: $69-169.
Payment: MC VISA AX DC CB DS PC TC.
Innkeeper(s): Jerry & Rejina Southard.
Circa: 1880.

Rooms: 16 rooms with PB, 6 with FP. 7 suites.
Beds: QD.

This house, an Austin historic landmark, originally had a single story, but was raised to accommodate an additional level at the turn of the century. Eleven-foot ceilings provide a background for antiques and paintings. Several guest rooms include fireplaces or clawfoot tubs, and all the rooms are graciously appointed with antique pieces. On weekdays, the innkeepers serve continental fare, but a more expansive meal is served to weekend guests. The home is within walking distance of shops, antiquing, galleries and specialty boutiques.

Breakfast included in rates. Types of meals: continental breakfast and full breakfast. Air conditioning, ceiling fan and cable TV in room. Fax and swimming on premises. Small meetings, family reunions and seminars hosted. Spanish spoken. Antiques, parks, shopping and theater nearby. TAC10.

Location: Twelve blocks from the Capitol and within walking distance of the river.

Publicity: *Southern Living, New York Times, US Air, Austin Home & Garden, Austin American-Statesman.*

"A memory to be long cherished. We especially enjoyed the home atmosphere and the lovely breakfasts in the garden."

Woodburn House B&B

4401 Avenue D
Austin, TX 78751-3714
(512)458-4335
Fax:(512)458-4319
E-mail: woodburn@iamerica.net

Rates: $79-89.
Payment: MC VISA AX PC TC.
Innkeeper(s): Herb & Sandra Dickson.
Circa: 1909.

Rooms: 4 rooms with PB.
Beds: KQ.

This stately home was named for Bettie Hamilton Woodburn, who bought the house in 1920. Hamilton's father was once the provisional governor of Texas and a friend of Abraham Lincoln. The home once was slated for demolition and saved in 1979 when George Boutwell bought the home for $1 and moved it to its present location. A friendly dog greets guests who will be taken immediately by the warmth of the home surrounded by old trees. The home is furnished with period antiques. Breakfasts are served formally in the dining room.

Breakfast included in rates. Types of meals: gourmet breakfast and early coffee/tea. Air conditioning and ceiling fan in room. Cable TV, VCR and fax on premises. Spanish spoken. Antiques, fishing, parks, shopping, sporting events and theater nearby. TAC10.

Publicity: *Austin Chronicle, Dallas Morning News.*

"The comfort, the breakfasts and the hospitality were excellent and greatly appreciated."

Big Sandy — D9

Annie's B&B

106 N Tyler
Big Sandy, TX 75755-2203
(903)636-4355 (800)222-6643
Fax:(903)636-5163

Rates: $50-115.
Payment: MC VISA AX PC TC.
Innkeeper(s): Clifton & Kathy Shaw.
Circa: 1901.

Rooms: 12 rooms, 10 with PB. 3 suites. 4 conference rooms.
Beds: QDT.

Annie's Attic, a well-known craft and pattern company, renovated this Victorian house, creating a showplace for fine antiques, imported rugs, outstanding handmade quilts and stitchery items. The inn is surrounded by a white picket fence and detailed gingerbread decorates the porches and balconies.

Breakfast and evening snack included in rates. Types of meals: full breakfast, gourmet breakfast and early coffee/tea. Afternoon tea, dinner, gourmet lunch and catering service available. Air conditioning, ceiling fan, cable TV and VCR in room. Fax and copier on premises. Handicap access. 10 acres. Weddings, small meetings, family reunions and seminars hosted. Antiques, fishing, parks, shopping and watersports nearby.

Location: Ten miles from I-20 in northeast Texas. The inn is an hour and 15 minutes east of Dallas on Hwy 80.

Blanco — F7

TX

Creekwood Country Inn

PO Box 1357, CR 411
Blanco, TX 78606-1357
(210)833-2248

Rates: $75-85.
Payment: PC TC.
Innkeeper(s): Charlotte Dorsey.
Circa: 1971.

Rooms: 2 rooms with PB.
Beds: QT.

It's not unusual to see deer meandering around the six-acre spread that surrounds this farmhouse. The home overlooks a creek, where younger guests often enjoy spending time. Adults often opt to relax on the rocker-lined porch or take a stroll across the grounds. There are two guest rooms, each appointed with antiques.

Freshly baked apple muffins and an egg, sausage and cheese strata are some of the items that might appear on the breakfast menu. Blanco is five miles away, and sites in Fredericksburg, Austin and San Antonio are less than an hour from the home.

Breakfast included in rates. Types of meals: gourmet breakfast and early coffee/tea. Air conditioning and ceiling fan in room. Handicap access. Amusement parks, antiques, fishing, parks, shopping, sporting events and watersports nearby. TAC10.

Pets Allowed: Well-behaved, leased for walking.

Boerne F6

Ye Kendall Inn

128 W Blanco Rd
Boerne, TX 78006-2014
(210)249-2138 (800)364-2138

Rates: $80-125.
Payment: MC VISA AX TC.
Innkeeper(s): Manuel Garcia.
Circa: 1859.

Rooms: 13 rooms, 9 with PB. 4 suites. 1 conference room.
Beds: KQT.

A mother and son discovered and restored this historic gem, which once served as a stagecoach stop. During the renovation, many original features were restored, and although modern bathrooms had to be added, the owners acquired clawfoot tubs to maintain the inn's historical flavor. Guests snuggle under canopies in individually appointed rooms, decorated with American and European antiques. Continental-plus fare, including croissants, specialty breads, quiche and fresh fruit, start off the day.

Breakfast included in rates. Type of meal: continental-plus breakfast. Catering service available. Air conditioning and cable TV in room. Fax and copier on premises. Weddings, small meetings, family reunions and seminars hosted. Spanish spoken. Amusement parks, antiques and shopping nearby.

Brazoria G8

Roses & The River

7074 CR 506
Brazoria, TX 77422
(409)798-1070 (800)610-1070
Fax:(409)798-1070

Rates: $125.
Payment: MC VISA PC TC.
Innkeeper(s): Mary Jo & Dick Hosack.
Circa: 1980.

Rooms: 3 rooms with PB.
Beds: Q.

This Texas farmhouse rests beside the banks of the San Bernard River. There is a sweeping veranda, lined with rockers, and the two acre grounds are well landscaped with an impressive rose garden. Each of the three guest rooms has been decorated with a special theme in mind. Rooms have names such as New Dawn or Rainbow's End. The Rise 'n Shine room offers a river view. Breakfasts include unique treats such as a "blushing orange cooler," grapefruit baked Alaska, homemade sweet rolls and savory egg dishes. The area offers many attractions, including two wildlife refuges, include Sea Center Texas, where guests can learn about marine life, the Center for the Arts and Sciences, two wildlife refuges and several historical sites.

Breakfast and evening snack included in rates. Type of meal: gourmet breakfast. Air conditioning, turn-down service, ceiling fan, cable TV and VCR in room. Fax and copier on premises. Weddings, small meetings, family reunions and seminars hosted. Amusement parks, antiques, fishing, parks, shopping, sporting events, theater and watersports nearby.

"Thank you so much for providing a memorable place . . . to spend our honeymoon night."

Brenham F8

Ant Street Inn

107 W Commerce St
Brenham, TX 77833-3635
(409)836-7393 (800)481-1951
Fax:(409)836-7595

Rates: $85-160.
Payment: MC VISA AX.
Innkeeper(s): Tommy & Pam Traylor.
Circa: 1899.

Rooms: 13 rooms with PB. 3 conference rooms.
Beds: QD.

It seemed a shame to Ant Street's innkeepers to let this historic, Renaissance Revival building go to waste. So, out of what once served as a commercial building, saloon and gambling hall, there is now an elegant inn. From the exterior, it's easy to conjure up images of life in turn-of-the-century Brenham. The interior also has a nostalgic feel, with rooms decorated in elegant antiques, including a selection of beautifully crafted beds. Exposed brick walls, stained glass and 12-foot ceilings are other special features. In addition to the fine antiques and Oriental rugs, modern amenities include cable TV, data ports and individual climate control. Breakfast is an Epicurean's delight. A typical morning menu might sound something like Canadian bacon, Brie quiche and freshly baked blueberry and peach coffeecake. There is much to see and do in Brenham, but one must make a trek out to the Blue Bell Creameries, for a taste of the famed Blue Bell ice cream.

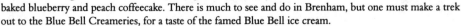

Breakfast included in rates. Types of meals: full breakfast and early coffee/tea. Air conditioning, ceiling fan and cable TV in room. Fax and copier on premises. Weddings, small meetings, family reunions and seminars hosted. Antiques, fishing, parks, shopping and theater nearby. TAC10.

"I love your inn and the beautiful furnishings you have brought in."

Burton F8

Long Point Inn

RR 1 Box 86-A
Burton, TX 77835-9801
(409)289-3171

Rates: $75-125.
Payment: AX.
Innkeeper(s): Bill & Jeannine Neinast.
Circa: 1978.

Rooms: 3 rooms, 2 with PB, 1 with FP. 1 cottage.
Beds: QDT.

It might seem unusual to find a Bavarian chalet in Texas, but not when you consider that many German immigrants made the state their home after arriving in America. One of those immigrant families once lived in an 1840s log cabin that has been restored and added to the inn complex. This cabin has a stone fireplace and sleeps six. Although this inn is newer, the innkeepers patterned their dream home in Old World style, including decorating it with treasures picked up during their global travels. The home rests on a 175-acre working cattle ranch that has been in the family for four generations. So, it's at this Bavarian inn and ranch where guests enjoy the best of Texas with a touch of Europe. Rooms are a little bit Old World and a little bit country. A hearty breakfast is served underneath a German crystal chandelier on a table set with fine china. Guests might partake of a savory egg dish, homemade German sausage, potatoes, freshly baked breads and a fresh fruit compote during their morning meal. The inn is located along FM 390, the only highway in Texas to be designated a historic, scenic highway and is midway between Houston and Austin.

Breakfast and evening snack included in rates. Type of meal: gourmet breakfast. Air conditioning and ceiling fan in room. VCR on premises. 175 acres. German spoken. Antiques, parks and shopping nearby. TAC10.

Location: Midway between Houston and Austin.

"The wildflowers, Texas sunshine and the goodness of you two all created a warmth we dearly loved."

Canyon B4

Historical Hudspeth House

1905 4th Ave
Canyon, TX 79015-4023
(806)655-9800 (800)655-9809
Fax:(806)655-7457
E-mail: hudspeth@juno.com

Rates: $55-110.
Payment: MC VISA AX DS PC TC.
Innkeeper(s): Mark & Mary Clark.
Circa: 1909.

Rooms: 8 rooms with PB, 5 with FP. 2 suites. 2 conference rooms.
Beds: KQ.

TX

Artist Georgia O'Keefe was once a guest at this three-story prairie home, which serves as a bed & breakfast. The home boasts many impressive architectural features, including an expansive entry with stained glass and a grandfather clock. The parlor boasts 12-foot ceilings and antiques, other rooms include chandeliers and huge fireplaces. Guests can arrange to have a candlelit dinner in their room.

Breakfast included in rates. Type of meal: early coffee/tea. Air conditioning, ceiling fan and cable TV in room. Fax, copier and spa on premises. Amusement parks, antiques, parks, sporting events and theater nearby. TAC10.

Clifton

E7

River's Bend B&B

PO Box 228
Clifton, TX 76634-0228
(817)675-4936

Rates: $75-125.
Payment: PC.
Innkeeper(s): Helen M. Hubler & Fawn Wagner.
Circa: 1987.

Rooms: 1 room with PB, 1 with FP.
Beds: QT.

As you sit back and enjoy the scenery at this bed & breakfast, you might see deer stopping for a drink at the banks of the Bosque River. The home is rented out to one group or couple at time, allowing total privacy, surrounded by 240 peaceful acres. Covered porches are set up with swings for those who wish to enjoy the river view. The home has three bedrooms, two bathrooms, a woodburning fireplace, television, VCR and a fully equipped kitchen. The owners stock the place with homemade breads or muffins, eggs, breakfasts meats, fruit, cereals and beverages so guests can create their own morning feast. There is a fenced, one-acre yard where guests can keep a pet or horse.

Breakfast included in rates. Type of meal: full breakfast. Air conditioning and ceiling fan in room. VCR on premises. 240 acres. Antiques and fishing nearby.

Pets Allowed: One acre fenced area for outdoor animals.

Columbus

F8

Magnolia Oaks

634 Spring St
Columbus, TX 78934-2319
(409)732-2726

Rates: $80-120.
Payment: PC.
Innkeeper(s): Bob & Nancy Stiles.
Circa: 1890.

Rooms: 5 rooms with PB, 2 with FP.
Beds: KDT.

Ornate, gingerbread trim adorns the exterior of Magnolia Oaks, a charming Eastlake Victorian. A black, iron fence surrounds a yard dotted with gardens, a fountain and many magnolias and oaks. Two rooms include fireplaces, and there is an efficiency, loft apartment. During breakfasts, the host serenades guests with his guitar. The inn is within an hour drive of many attractions, including the Antique Rose Emporium. With prior notice, the innkeepers can arrange for a canoe trip down the Colorado River or create special amenities for those celebrating birthdays, honeymoons or anniversaries.

Breakfast and afternoon tea included in rates. Types of meals: full breakfast and early coffee/tea. Air conditioning, ceiling fan, cable TV and VCR in room. Bicycles and library on premises. Handicap access. Weddings, small meetings, family reunions and seminars hosted. Antiques, fishing, parks, shopping, theater and watersports nearby.

"You must know your home set an extremely high standard for all of our B&B visits to follow."

Dallas

D8

Inn on Fairmount

3701 Fairmount St
Dallas, TX 75219-4002
(214)522-2800
Fax:(214)522-2898

Rates: $80-120.
Payment: MC VISA.
Innkeeper(s): Michael C. McVay.

Rooms: 7 rooms. 1 suite.
Beds: KQT.

Located in the heart of the Oak Lawn/Turtle Creek area, this Federal-style inn is just minutes from dozens of restaurants and clubs. It's less than two minutes from the Dallas Market Center and just 10 minutes from the Arts District of Dallas. Each morning, just outside your door, freshly brewed coffee and the morning newspaper await you. The bedrooms and suites have fine furnishings, direct-dial phones and remote-control color televisions.

Breakfast and evening snack included in rates. Type of meal: continental-plus breakfast. Air conditioning, ceiling fan and cable TV in room. VCR on premises. Weddings and small meetings hosted. Amusement parks, antiques, shopping, sporting events and theater nearby.

Dayton

Audubon Lodge

PO Box 1439
Dayton, TX 77535-5439
(409)258-9141
Fax:(409)258-3058

Rates: $55-75.
Payment: VISA.
Innkeeper(s): Bob & Linda Jamison.
Circa: 1982.
Beds: KQD.

This bed & breakfast is remote, yet only a half-hour from Houston Intercontinental Airport and 45 minutes from the city. Guests are secluded on a 20-acre spread with plenty of birds and wildlife. There are three guest rooms. The bottom floor includes a fireplace, living-dining area, refrigerator, wet bar and a private deck. Second-floor guests stay either in the suite bedroom or in the loft bedroom with its two double beds. These two rooms share a full kitchen, hot tub, dining room, living room, fireplace and a deck. The decor is contemporary and elegant, but not too posh for those who seek relaxation.

Breakfast included in rates. Type of meal: continental-plus breakfast. Air conditioning and ceiling fan in room. Spa on premises. 20 acres. Small meetings hosted. Antiques, fishing, parks, shopping and theater nearby.

El Paso E1

Sunset Heights B&B

717 W Yandell Dr
El Paso, TX 79902-3837
(915)544-1743 (800)767-8513
Fax:(915)544-5119

Rates: $75-200.
Payment: MC VISA AX DS PC TC.
Innkeeper(s): R. Barnett & Ms. R. Martinez, M.D.
Circa: 1905.

Rooms: 5 rooms with PB, 1 with FP. 1 suite. 1 cottage. 1 conference room.
Beds: KQD.

This luxurious inn is accentuated by palm trees and Spanish-style arches. Inside, bedrooms are filled with antiques and boast brass and four-poster beds. Breakfast is a five- to eight-course feast prepared by innkeeper Richard Barnett. On any morning, a guest might awake to sample a breakfast with Southwestern flair, including Eggs Chillquillas and pit-smoked Machakas, a combination of smoked beef, avocado and onion. Juice, fresh coffee, tea, dessert and fresh fruits top off the meal, which might begin with caviar and quiche. Enjoy the morning meal in the dining room or spend breakfast in bed.

Breakfast included in rates. Types of meals: full breakfast and gourmet breakfast. Dinner and picnic lunch available. Air conditioning, turn-down service, ceiling fan, cable TV and VCR in room. Fax, copier, spa and swimming on premises. Weddings, small meetings, family reunions and seminars hosted. Spanish spoken. Amusement parks, antiques, parks, shopping and sporting events nearby. TAC10.

Pets Allowed: Outdoor cat.

Location: Near downtown and the university.

Publicity: *Southwest Profile.*

Special Discounts: Multiple night, multiple room.

Fort Davis F3

TX

Wayside Inn

400 W 4th St, PO Box 2088
Fort Davis, TX 79734
(915)426-3535 (800)582-7510
Fax:(915)426-3574

Rates: $65.
Payment: MC VISA AX DS PC TC.
Innkeeper(s): J.W. & Anna Beth Ward.
Circa: 1947.

Rooms: 9 rooms, 7 with PB. 3 suites. 1 cottage. 1 conference room.
Beds: KQT.

This country bed & breakfast is located at the foot of Sleeping Lion Mountain, the center piece of Fort Davis. The home is decorated in comfortable, country style with a few antiques here and there. There are several collections on hand, including quilts, hats and dolls. The historic Overland Trail is just a block away. Biscuits and gravy, bran muffins topped with apple butter, pancakes, eggs and Canadian bacon are among the treats served for breakfast.

Breakfast included in rates. Type of meal: full breakfast. Air conditioning, ceiling fan and cable TV in room. VCR and fax on premises. Small meetings and family reunions hosted. Antiques, parks and theater nearby. TAC10.

Fort Worth D8

Miss Molly's Hotel

109 1/2 W Exchange Ave
Fort Worth, TX 76106-8508
(817)626-1522 (800)996-6559
Fax:(817)625-2723

Rates: $85-150.
Payment: MC VISA AX DC CB DS PC TC.
Innkeeper(s): Mark Hancock & Alice Williams.
Circa: 1910.

Rooms: 8 rooms, 1 with PB.
Beds: TD.

An Old West flair adds charm to this hotel, which once was a house of ill repute. Miss Josie's Room, named for the former madame, is decked with elaborate wall and ceiling coverings and carved oak furniture. The Gunslinger Room is filled with pictures of famous and infamous gunsmen. Rodeo memorabilia decorates the Rodeo Room, and twin iron beds and a pot belly stove add flair to the Cowboy's Room. Telephones and TV sets are the only things missing from the rooms, as the innkeeper hopes to preserve the flavor of the past.

Breakfast included in rates. Types of meals: continental-plus breakfast and early coffee/tea. Restaurant on premises. Air conditioning and ceiling fan in room. Fax and copier on premises. Small meetings, family reunions and seminars hosted. Amusement parks, antiques, shopping, sporting events and theater nearby. TAC10.

Publicity: *British Bulldog, Arkansas Gazette, Dallas Morning News, Fort Worth Star-Telegram, Continental Profiles.*

Special Discounts: $70.00-$120.00-Sunday-Thursday excluding special events.

Fredericksburg F6

Country Cottage Inn-Nimitz Birthplace

249 E Main St
Fredericksburg, TX 78624
(210)997-8549
Fax:(210)997-8549

Rates: $80-120.
Payment: MC VISA PC.
Innkeeper(s): Mary Lou Rodriquez.
Circa: 1850.

Rooms: 11 rooms with PB, 7 with FP. 9 suites. 1 conference room.
Beds: KQD.

This beautifully preserved house was built by blacksmith and cutler Frederick Kiehne. With two-foot-thick walls, it was the first two-story limestone house in town. The Country Cottage holds a collection of Texas primitives and German country antiques, accentuated by Laura Ashley linens. Some of the baths include whirlpool tubs. The innkeepers have restored a second historic house, a block away, which is also available. Full regional-style breakfasts are brought to each room.

Breakfast included in rates. Type of meal: full breakfast. Air conditioning, ceiling fan and cable TV in room. VCR and fax on premises. Handicap access. Weddings hosted. Spanish spoken. Antiques, fishing, parks and watersports nearby. TAC10.

Publicity: *Weekend Getaway, Dallas Morning News, Glamour, Texas Highways.*

"A step back in time in 1850 style."

The Delforge Place

231 W Main St
Fredericksburg, TX 78624
(210)997-5612

Rates: $50-75.
Payment: MC VISA DS.
Innkeeper(s): Betsy Delforge.

Rooms: 3 rooms with PB. 1 suite.

The innkeeper at Delforge Place, descending from a long line of sea captains, has decorated her unique inn in a mariner's theme of different historical eras. For instance, those who stay in the Map Room will enjoy the decor of the Clipper Ship era. The Quebec Room offers a glimpse back to Revolutionary War times. Century-old costumes, trunks and atlases add to the historic ambiance.

Breakfast included in rates. Type of meal: full breakfast.

Schildknecht-Weidenfeller House

231 W Main St
Fredericksburg, TX 78624
(210)997-5612
Fax:(210)997-8282

Rates: $125-375.
Payment: MC VISA DS PC TC.
Circa: 1880.
Beds: QDT.

Beyond a gray picket fence, this pioneer German limestone house is decorated with primitive 19th-century furnishings that enhance the warm stone walls and polished pine plank floors. Located in Fredericksburg's historic district, it is among the most well-preserved of the area's limestone houses. There is a rock-floored study, a fireplace set within the thick, stone walls of the parlor and a dining area that overlooks the garden. Rockers line the front porch. Without hosts or other guests, you are free to absorb the atmosphere with complete privacy and yet still partake of a German-style breakfast left for you to enjoy whenever you please.

Breakfast included in rates. Type of meal: continental-plus breakfast. Air conditioning in room. Cable TV on premises. Small meetings and family reunions hosted. Antiques, parks and shopping nearby. TAC10.

Galveston F9

Carousel Inn

712 Tenth St
Galveston, TX 77550-5116
(409)762-2166

Rates: $80-95.
Payment: MC VISA AX DS PC TC.
Innkeeper(s): Jim & Kathy Hughes.
Circa: 1886.

Rooms: 4 rooms with PB. 1 suite.
Beds: KQD.

The Carousel Inn stands as a testament to Texas stamina. The home, located in a historic Galveston neighborhood, was one of few left standing after a fierce storm ripped through the Gulf in 1900. The inn's namesake, a hand-carved carousel horse, decorates the parlor. The guest rooms are inviting with special touches such as leaf pine walls, a private porch swing or a roomy pineapple bed. The carriage house offers the added amenity of a sitting area, private entrance and antique walnut bed. The innkeepers offer a variety of home-baked treats each morning, served up in the cheerful breakfast room. The home is near many Galveston attractions including a rail museum, a tall ship and many shops and restaurants.

Breakfast included in rates. Types of meals: continental-plus breakfast and early coffee/tea. Afternoon tea and picnic lunch available. Air conditioning and ceiling fan in room. Bicycles and library on premises. Weddings, small meetings, family reunions and seminars hosted. Spanish spoken. Amusement parks, antiques, fishing, shopping, theater and watersports nearby. TAC15.

Madame Dyer's B&B

1720 Post Office St
Galveston, TX 77550-4816
(409)765-5692

Rates: $90-125.
Payment: MC VISA PC TC.
Innkeeper(s): Linda & Larry Bonnin.
Circa: 1889.

Rooms: 3 rooms with PB, 1 with FP.
Beds: KQ.

This delightful Victorian, a highlight on the Galveston Historic Homes Tour, features wraparound verandas on each of its two stories. The guest rooms are carefully decorated with antiques and memorabilia. Ashten's Room includes carved oaks, while Corbin's Room includes a fireplace accentuated with an oak mirrored mantel. Homemade breakfasts are served in the formal dining room. Complimentary snacks and beverages are always available in the kitchen, and there are homemade cookies in the dining room. The inn is an ideal location for those who wish to explore the town's historic neighborhoods.

Breakfast included in rates. Types of meals: full breakfast and early coffee/tea. Air conditioning, turn-down service and ceiling fan in room. Cable TV, VCR and bicycles on premises. Small meetings and family reunions hosted. Antiques, fishing, shopping, theater and watersports nearby. TAC10.

Special Discounts: 15% off three consecutive nights.

"Your b&b is so quaint and romantic and your special brand of hospitality turned all that sense of history into a good feeling."

TX

The Victorian B&B Inn

511 17th St
Galveston, TX 77550-4805
(409)762-3235
Fax:(409)762-6351

Rates: $85-125.
Payment: MC VISA AX PC.
Innkeeper(s): Marcy Hanson.
Circa: 1899.

Rooms: 6 rooms, 3 with PB, 2 with FP. 2 suites. 1 cottage.
Beds: KDT.

This red brick Italianate-style house is surrounded by the original fences and gates. There is wicker furniture on one side of the wraparound porch. The inn features yellow maple floors, bird's-eye maple wainscoting, five fireplaces of carved oak with Belgian tiles and contemporary furniture. Some guest rooms have fireplaces and private balconies.

Breakfast included in rates. Types of meals: continental-plus breakfast and early coffee/tea. Air conditioning, ceiling fan and cable TV in room. Fax and library on premises. Weddings, small meetings, family reunions and seminars hosted. Antiques, fishing, parks, shopping, sporting events, theater and watersports nearby.

"The inn was great, and both of you added that little something extra that made my stay truly memorable."

Glen Rose D7

Hummingbird Lodge

FR 203 Somervell Co,
PO Box 128
Glen Rose, TX 76043
(817)897-2787
Fax:(817)897-3459

Rates: $77-115.
Payment: MC VISA PC TC.
Innkeeper(s): Sherry & Richard Fowlkes.
Circa: 1988.

Rooms: 6 rooms with PB. 1 conference room.
Beds: KQ.

For those wishing to escape the hectic pace of city life, Hummingbird Lodge may be just the place. The 140 acres offer pasture and wooded trails, streams, a waterfall and a stocked fishing pond. There are comfortable rockers set up on the porch, and also an outdoor hot tub. The interior is comfortable and inviting, the living room, highlighted by natural wood walls, exposed beams and a fireplace, is a great place to sit and relax. The living room also doubles as a small conference or meeting room. Glen Rose is seven miles down the road, offering several restaurants and a historic town square. The lodge is about an hour and a half from Dallas.

Breakfast included in rates. Type of meal: continental-plus breakfast. Air conditioning and ceiling fan in room. VCR, fax, spa and library on premises. 140 acres. Small meetings, family reunions and seminars hosted. Antiques, fishing, parks and shopping nearby. TAC10.

Special Discounts: Weekdays, Monday-Thursday: $5 off.

"The comfortable surroundings and excellent food were a great part of our success."

Ye Ole' Maple Inn

PO Box 1141
Glen Rose, TX 76043-1141
(817)897-3456

Rates: $65-80.
Payment: MC VISA AX PC TC.
Innkeeper(s): Roberta Maple.
Circa: 1950.

Rooms: 2 rooms with PB.
Beds: Q.

Pecan trees shade this comfortable home, which overlooks the Paluxy River. The interior is decorated with a variety of antiques, including a grandfather clock imported from Germany. The innkeepers also keep on display a Santa Claus collection. The fireplaced den offers a large selection of reading material. One of the bedrooms, decked in pink and gray hues, includes an iron and brass bed and wicker furnishings. The other features Victorian decor and a four-poster bed. Breakfasts feature specialties such as oatmeal waffles with pecan sauce or an egg, sausage and apple casserole. Innkeeper Roberta Maple also serves up a mouth-watering selection of evening desserts including peanut butter pie and Texas brownies.

Breakfast and evening snack included in rates. Type of meal: full breakfast. Ceiling fan in room. Cable TV, VCR and library on premises. Handicap access. Antiques, fishing, shopping, theater and watersports nearby. TAC10.

Gonzales

F7

St. James Inn

723 Saint James St
Gonzales, TX 78629-3411
(210)672-7066
Fax:(210)672-7787

Rates: $75-100.
Payment: MC VISA AX PC TC.
Innkeeper(s): Ann & J.R. Covert.
Circa: 1914.

Rooms: 5 rooms, 4 with PB, 5 with FP. 2 suites. 1 conference room.
Beds: KQ.

Ann and J.R. Covert spent three years restoring this massive Texas Hill Country mansion, once owned by a cattle baron. On the main floor is a tiled solarium, living room, reception hall, dining room, butler's pantry and kitchen. The second-floor guest rooms all have working fireplaces and porches. The top-level room is a unique wind tunnel—a long crawl space with windows on either end—which provides natural air conditioning. Gourmet candlelight dinners are available in addition to the full breakfasts.

Breakfast and afternoon tea included in rates. Types of meals: full breakfast, gourmet breakfast and early coffee/tea. Dinner, picnic lunch, lunch, gourmet lunch and banquet service available. Air conditioning, turn-down service, ceiling fan and cable TV in room. Weddings, small meetings, family reunions and seminars hosted. Antiques, fishing, parks, shopping, theater and watersports nearby.

Location: One hour east of San Antonio, one hour south of Austin.

Publicity: *Gonzales Inquirer, Houston Chronicle, Victoria Advocate, Austin American Statesman, San Antonio Express-News.*

"We had a wonderful weekend. It's a marvelous home and your hospitality is superb. We'll be back."

Granbury

D7

Dabney House B&B

106 S Jones St
Granbury, TX 76048-1905
(817)579-1260
Fax:(817)579-0426

Rates: $60-105.
Payment: MC VISA AX PC TC.
Innkeeper(s): John & Gwen Hurley.
Circa: 1907.

Rooms: 4 rooms with PB. 1 suite.
Beds: QD.

Built during the Mission Period, this Craftsman-style country manor boasts original hardwood floors, stained-glass windows and some of the original light fixtures. The parlor and dining rooms have large, exposed, wooden beams and the ceilings throughout are 10-feet high. The Dabney Suite has a private entrance into an enclosed sun porch with rattan table and chairs that allow for a private breakfast. The bedroom of this suite is furnished with a four-post tester bed with drapes and an 1800 dresser.

Breakfast and evening snack included in rates. Type of meal: full breakfast. Dinner available. Air conditioning and ceiling fan in room. VCR, spa and library on premises. Small meetings, family reunions and seminars hosted. Antiques, fishing, parks, shopping, theater and watersports nearby. TAC10.

Publicity: *Fort Worth Star Telegram, Dallas Morning News.*

Special Discounts: 10% for peace officers and fire fighters.

"Very enjoyable and certainly up among the very best of the B&Bs you are likely to find in the United Kingdom. It reminded me of staying at grandma's house. Thanks for bringing back such warm memories."

Oak Tree Farm B&B

6415 Carmichael Ct
Granbury, TX 76049-6341
(817)326-5595 (800)326-5595

Rates: $85-115.
Payment: MC VISA PC TC.
Innkeeper(s): Jeanne Bennett, Michael & Jeanette Carmichael.
Circa: 1995.

Rooms: 5 rooms with PB. 1 conference room.
Beds: KQT.

As you sit on a wicker rocking chair atop one of the covered porches at this bed & breakfast, you may see antelope or deer grazing in nearby fields. Guest rooms, decorated with many antiques, offer plenty of amenities, including tea, coffee, cookies and other treats. The innkeepers also enjoy pampering guests with a gourmet breakfast, served on bone china on the dining room's antique oak table. Guests enjoy items such as a sausage and egg strata, cinnamon French toast or perhaps biscuits and gravy. The home is set up for religious retreats, business meetings and family reunions.

Breakfast included in rates. Types of meals: gourmet breakfast and early coffee/tea. Air conditioning, turn-down service and ceiling fan in room. VCR and library on premises. 24 acres. Small meetings and family reunions hosted. Antiques, fishing, parks, shopping, theater and watersports nearby. TAC10.

"You are the most wonderful hostess and host we have encountered in our experiences with bed & breakfasts across Texas."

Pearl Street Inn B&B

319 W Pearl St
Granbury, TX 76048-2437
(817)279-PINK (888)732-7578

Rates: $59-98.
Payment: PC TC.
Innkeeper(s): Danette D. Hebda.
Circa: 1912.

Rooms: 5 rooms with PB. 1 suite.
Beds: KD.

Known historically as the B. M. Estes House, the inn is decorated with a mix of English, French and American antiques. The English Garden Suite is fashioned in a green, peach and ivy motif and features a king-size iron and brass bed, English antique furniture, airy sitting room and full bath accented by a cast iron tub and 1912 wall sink. Other guest rooms include clawfoot tubs, crystal lamps and lace.

Breakfast included in rates. Types of meals: full breakfast, gourmet breakfast and early coffee/tea. Air conditioning and ceiling fan in room. VCR and copier on premises. Weddings, small meetings and seminars hosted. Antiques, fishing, parks, shopping, theater and watersports nearby. TAC10.

Publicity: *Dallas Morning News.*

"Needless to say, we want to stay forever! We had a grand time and highly enjoyed conversations and hospitality."

Houston

F9

Angel Arbor B&B Inn

848 Heights Blvd
Houston, TX 77007-1507
(713)868-4654

Rates: $100-119.
Payment: MC VISA AX DS PC TC.
Innkeeper(s): Marguerite Swanson.
Circa: 1922.

Rooms: 4 rooms with PB. 2 suites. 1 conference room.
Beds: Q.

Each of the rooms at Angel Arbor has a heavenly name and elegant decor. The Angelique Room offers a cherry sleigh bed and a balcony overlooking the garden. Canopy or poster beds grace the other rooms and suite, named Gabriel, Raphael and Michael. The Georgian-style home is located in the historic Houston Heights neighborhood and was built by a prominent local family. The innkeeper, a cookbook author, prepares a mouthwatering homemade breakfast each morning. Ask about the innkeeper's special murder-mystery dinner parties.

Breakfast included in rates. Types of meals: full breakfast, gourmet breakfast and early coffee/tea. Afternoon tea available. Air conditioning, turn-down service, ceiling fan, cable TV and VCR in room. Fax, copier, bicycles and library on premises. Weddings, small meetings, family reunions and seminars hosted. German spoken. Amusement parks, antiques, fishing, parks, shopping, sporting events, theater and watersports nearby. TAC10.

Durham House B&B

921 Heights Blvd
Houston, TX 77008-6911
(713)868-4654 (800)722-8788
Fax:(713)868-7965

Rates: $65-95.
Payment: MC VISA AX DS PC TC.
Innkeeper(s): Marguerite & Dean Swanson.
Circa: 1902.

Rooms: 7 rooms, 6 with PB. 1 suite. 1 conference room.
Beds: QD.

Located 10 minutes from downtown Houston, this Victorian house, listed in the National Register of Historic Places, was built by the area's first fire chief. Antique furniture, a gazebo, player piano, tandem bicycle and tapes of old radio programs create an atmosphere reminiscent of the early 1900s. Breakfast in bed and romantic dining locations are available for guests, and innkeeper Marguerite Swanson offers escorted tours of the city.

Breakfast included in rates. Types of meals: continental-plus breakfast, full breakfast and early coffee/tea. Afternoon tea and evening snack available. Air conditioning, turn-down service, ceiling fan and VCR in room. Fax and library on premises. Weddings, small meetings and seminars hosted. Amusement parks, antiques, fishing, parks, shopping, sporting events, theater and watersports nearby.

Publicity: *Victorian Homes, Houston Chronicle.*

"Another comfortable, wonderful stay."

La Colombe d'Or

3410 Montrose Blvd
Houston, TX 77006-4329
(713)524-7999
Fax:(713)524-8923

Rates: Call for rates.
Innkeeper(s): Gina Bradshaw.

Rooms: 6 suites. 1 conference room.

Renowned as the "World's Smallest Luxury Hotel," the inn houses six suites having a mixture of original art and antiques. Each has its own dining room, allowing for a luxurious alternative to the public dining areas. Guests also may enjoy the romantic main dining rooms, the intimate walnut-paneled bar and cozy firelit library. Breakfast is an extra charge but can be served in your room upon request. The home originally belonged to W. W. Fondren, the founder of Humble Oil.

Gourmet lunch, banquet service, catering service and room service available. Air conditioning, turn-down service, ceiling fan and cable TV in room. VCR on premises. Weddings, small meetings, family reunions and seminars hosted. Amusement parks, antiques, shopping, sporting events and theater nearby.

Webber House B&B

1011 Heights Blvd
Houston, TX 77008-6913
(713)864-9472
Fax:(713)864-9472

Rates: $75-110.
Payment: MC VISA AX DS PC TC.
Innkeeper(s): JoAnn Jackson.
Circa: 1907.

Rooms: 4 rooms with PB, 1 with FP. 1 conference room.
Beds: KQ.

Built by a local bricksman, the inn features intricate masonry inside and outside, leaded, curved and stained glass, 11-foot-high ceilings, molasses-colored cypress woodwork and a three-level staircase anchored by large, carved posts. These many attributes were responsible for its selection as the residence of actor Glenn Ford in the movie, "Final Verdict." Each room has a television, VCR, phone and mini fridge, and one suite has a Jacuzzi tub. Tree-lined Heights Boulevard, patterned after Commonwealth Avenue in Boston, is the area's central thoroughfare with many turn-of-the-century homes and numerous antique shops.

Breakfast included in rates. Types of meals: full breakfast and early coffee/tea. Air conditioning, turn-down service, ceiling fan, cable TV and VCR in room. Fax, copier and library on premises. Weddings and small meetings hosted. Amusement parks, antiques, parks, shopping, sporting events, theater and watersports nearby. TAC10.

Special Discounts: 30% discount with Texas Travel Passport Club.

Maison Bayou: A B&B Plantation

300 Bayou St
Jefferson, TX 75657-2610
(903)665-7600
Fax:(903)665-7383

Rates: $69-135.
Payment: MC VISA PC TC.
Innkeeper(s): Jan & Pete Hochendel.
Circa: 1991.

Rooms: 11 rooms with PB, 5 with FP. 4 suites. 1 conference room.
Beds: QDT.

This Creole plantation fronts a romantic bayou complete with cypress trees and gazebo, yet it is still within the town limits of Jefferson. There are three lodging options, all of which have a private bath. Some have a fireplace, TV and kitchenette. The Antebellum cabins have a decor that suitably reflects the Creole spirit with rocking chairs, a fireplace, whitewashed wood walls and burlap curtains. The Robert E. Lee, a floating cabin, is meant to be like a steamboat. Guests can also stay in one of the two railroad cars, which offer views of Big Cypress Bayou. Finally, there are rustic and economical bunkhouse suites, overlooking the corral. Oven-baked omelets, homemade biscuits, sausage and fruit are typical breakfast fare, which is served in the Overseer's House. Crawfish boils, pig roasts and barn dances may be arranged for special occasions, weddings or company outings. The plantation's 55 acres encompass not only woodland and bayou but provide a home to peacocks, ducks, a llama, burro, horses and alligator. A short walk across a bridge takes you to the historic downtown, where you'll find antique shops, restaurants and a museum. Trolley, train and riverboat rides also are available.

Breakfast included in rates. Types of meals: full breakfast and early coffee/tea. Picnic lunch, catering service and room service available. Air conditioning and turn-down service in room. Stables on premises. Handicap access. 55 acres. Weddings, small meetings and family reunions hosted. Amusement parks, antiques, fishing, parks, shopping, theater and watersports nearby. TAC10.

Pets Allowed.

Special Discounts: Group rates available.

McKay House

306 E Delta St
Jefferson, TX 75657-2026
(903)665-7322 (800)468-2627

Rates: $80-145.
Payment: MC VISA AX PC TC.
Innkeeper(s): Joseph & Alma Anne Parker.
Circa: 1851.

Rooms: 8 rooms, 7 with PB, 6 with FP. 3 suites. 1 cottage. 1 conference room.
Beds: QD.

Both Lady Bird Johnson and Alex Haley have enjoyed the gracious Southern hospitality offered at the McKay House. Accented by a Williamsburg-style picket fence, the Greek Revival cottage features a pillared front porch. Heart-of-pine floors, 14-foot ceilings and documented wallpapers complement antique furnishings. Orange and pecan French toast or home-baked muffins and shirred eggs are served on vintage china. Victorian nightshirts and gowns await guests in each of the bedchambers. A "gentleman's" style breakfast is served.

Breakfast included in rates. Types of meals: gourmet breakfast and early coffee/tea. Air conditioning, ceiling fan and cable TV in room. Weddings, small meetings, family reunions and seminars hosted. Antiques, fishing, parks, shopping, theater and watersports nearby. TAC10.

Publicity: *Southern Accents, Dallas Morning News, Country Home, Bride.*

"The facilities of the McKay House are exceeded only by the service and dedication of the owners."

Pride House

409 Broadway
Jefferson, TX 75657
(903)665-2675 (800)894-3526
Fax:(903)665-3901

Rates: $75-110.
Payment: MC VISA PC TC.
Innkeeper(s): Carol Abernathy & Christel Frederick.
Circa: 1889.

Rooms: 10 rooms with PB, 3 with FP. 1 suite. 1 cottage.
Beds: KQDT.

Mr. Brown, a sawmill owner, built this Victorian house using fine hardwoods, sometimes three layers deep. The windows are nine-feet tall on both the lower level and upstairs. The rooms include amenities such as fireplaces, balconies, canopy beds and private entrances. Most boasts original stained-glass win-

dows. The West Room is decorated in crimson reds and features a gigantic clawfoot tub that has received an award from Houston Style Magazine for "best tub in Texas." A wide veranda stretches around two sides of the house.

Breakfast and evening snack included in rates. Types of meals: gourmet breakfast and early coffee/tea. Afternoon tea available. Air conditioning and ceiling fan in room. Handicap access. Weddings, small meetings, family reunions and seminars hosted. German spoken. Antiques, fishing, parks and theater nearby. TAC10.

Publicity: *Woman's Day, Country Home, Texas Highways, Texas Homes.*

Special Discounts: Midweek-two rooms for price of one; or two nights for one. Two people only on a space available basis.

"Like Goldilock's porridge—just right."

Johnson City F7

"A Room With A View"

Rt 1, Box 381
Johnson City, TX 78636
(210)868-7668

Rates: $65-75.
Payment: PC.
Innkeeper(s): Heather Anderson.
Circa: 1983.
Rooms: 2 suites.
Beds: Q.

More than two acres of rustic, Texas countryside surround this cottage. The grounds often are visited by wildlife, perhaps even a deer or armadillo, and guests enjoy a panoramic view of hills and a valley. The two suites are elegantly appointed in French country style. Hardwood floors and cathedral ceilings give the rooms an open, airy feel. Breakfasts include items such as orange French toast, oatmeal souffles, sausage, bacon and fresh fruit. Dinners also can be arranged. The home is near many attractions, including a 5,000-acre state park, LBJ Ranch, Fredericksburg and, of course, historic Johnson City.

Breakfast included in rates. Types of meals: full breakfast and gourmet breakfast. Air conditioning and ceiling fan in room. Weddings hosted. Antiques, fishing, parks, shopping and watersports nearby.

Dream Catcher B&B

RR 1 Box 345
Johnson City, TX 78636
(210)868-4875

Rates: $60-85.
Payment: PC.
Innkeeper(s): Lee & Peggy Arbon.
Circa: 1960.
Beds: QD.

Guests at Dream Catcher can stay either in a rustic, restored bunkhouse overlooking a creek or in a Sioux tepee. Each tepee is furnished with futons and can sleep up to five people. Although electricity, running water and toilet facilities are provided, there is no bath or shower. The bunkhouse is comfortably furnished in a Western style. It includes a bathroom and kitchenette with a small refrigerator and microwave. The bed & breakfast is 15 miles from the nearest stores, shops and restaurants, so the innkeepers also run a small gift shop.

Breakfast included in rates. Type of meal: continental-plus breakfast. Air conditioning and VCR in room. 20 acres. Antiques, fishing, parks and shopping nearby.

Pets Allowed: With permission-on leash-$10 extra.

"It's the perfect setting for a relaxing getaway!"

Kyle F7

Inn Above Onion Creek

4444 Hwy 150 W
Kyle, TX 78640
(512)268-1617 (800)579-7640
Fax:(512)268-1090

Rates: $125-225. MAP.
Payment: MC VISA AX PC TC.
Innkeeper(s): Janie & John Orr.
Circa: 1994.
Rooms: 8 rooms with PB, 8 with FP. 2 suites. 2 conference rooms.
Beds: KQ.

This inn, a posh replica of a 19th-century vernacular homestead, is a perfect respite from daily life, especially in the spring, when the bluebonnets decorate the rugged Texas countryside. Guests rooms are simple but that's not a synonym for boring. For instance, in the impressive two-story Kuykendall Suite, a four-poster is topped with a snuggly goldenrod comforter piled high with designer pillows. The bath includes a glass-enclosed shower and whirlpool tub. The suite also has a living room with a stone fireplace. All guest rooms have feather beds and fireplaces, and most have a whirlpool tub. Although the inn is new, it contains many antiques and much of the flooring is made from century-old beams. The breakfasts and dinners are gourmet treats, and both are included in the rates.

Breakfast and dinner included in rates. Types of meals: full breakfast and early coffee/tea. Picnic lunch available. MAP. Air conditioning, ceiling fan, cable TV and VCR in room. Fax, copier and swimming on premises. Handicap access. 500 acres. Weddings, small meetings, family reunions and seminars hosted. Spanish spoken. Amusement parks, antiques, fishing, parks, shopping, sporting events, theater and watersports nearby. TAC10.

"I witnessed the most beautiful sunset I have ever seen, and I've traveled far and wide."

Lake O' The Pines

McKenzie Manor

Woodland Shore,
Hwy 729, Lake O' The Pines,
TX 75630
(903)755-2240

Rates: $65-95.
Payment: MC VISA PC TC.
Innkeeper(s): Anne & Fred McKenzie.
Circa: 1964.

Rooms: 7 rooms, 5 with PB, 1 with FP. 1 suite. 1 conference room.
Beds: KQD.

Nature trails with private ponds are right outside the door of this rustic, rock lodge set on the shore of Lake O' The Pines. Guests can sit on wide decks and watch eagles soar, beavers build dams and deer graze. Relax in the gazebo or by the large rock fireplace with a good book from the private library of the innkeeper, historian and author Fred McKenzie. This four-generation family home is designed with a large meeting room, vaulted ceilings and stained-glass windows. All rooms are adjacent to sitting areas and each room is decorated in its own unique style with antiques and family possessions.

Breakfast and afternoon tea included in rates. Types of meals: continental-plus breakfast, full breakfast and early coffee/tea. Catering service available. Air conditioning and ceiling fan in room. Cable TV, swimming and library on premises. Handicap access. 400 acres. Weddings, small meetings, family reunions and seminars hosted. Antiques, fishing, shopping, theater and watersports nearby.

Lampasas E7

Historic Moses Hughes B&B

RR 2 Box 31
Lampasas, TX 76550-9601
(512)556-5923

Rates: $75-85.
Payment: PC.
Innkeeper(s): Al & Beverly Solomon.
Circa: 1856.

Rooms: 2 rooms with PB.
Beds: D.

Nestled among ancient oaks in the heart of the Texas Hill Country, this native stone ranch house rests on 45 acres that include springs, a creek, wildlife and other natural beauty. The ranch was built by Moses Hughes, the first white settler and founder of Lampasas. He and his wife decided to stay in the area after her health dramatically improved after visiting the springs. Guests can join the innkeepers on the stone patio or upstairs wooden porch for a taste of Texas Hill Country life.

Breakfast included in rates. Types of meals: full breakfast and gourmet breakfast. Air conditioning in room. VCR and library on premises. 45 acres. Weddings hosted. Antiques, fishing, parks and watersports nearby. TAC10.

Publicity: *Dallas Morning News, Spiegel Catalog, Discover.*

"What a delightful respite! Thank you for sharing your very interesting philosophies and personalities with us at this very special B&B. We hate to leave."

Lovelady

E9

Log Cabin B&B

PO Box 485
Lovelady, TX 75851-0485
(409)636-2002 (800)723-4829
Fax:(409)636-2436

Rates: $85-125.
Payment: MC VISA PC.
Innkeeper(s): Greta Hicks.
Circa: 1981.

Rooms: 3 rooms, 1 with PB. 1 suite.
Beds: KQD.

Each of the three guest rooms at this log cabin are named for prominent men in Texas history. The largest, named for Sam Houston, includes two lodge pole pine beds and a whirlpool tub. For couples traveling together, the adjacent Davy's Room (as in Crockett) joins with Sam's Room to create a suite. Stephen's Room, named for Stephen F. Austin, is a rustic tribute to the state with exposed log walls, antiques and Texas memorabilia. The cabin is located on a working ranch, and there is plenty of acreage to explore and enjoy. Guests can relax on the porch, enjoy a picnic, feed the innkeepers' loghorn cattle or curl up with a book in the living room, which offers a fireplace fashioned from native stone.

Breakfast included in rates. Type of meal: full breakfast. Air conditioning and ceiling fan in room. Library on premises. 40 acres. Family reunions hosted. Antiques, fishing, parks and watersports nearby. TAC5.

Mason

E6

Hasse House and Ranch

1221 Ischar St, PO Box 58
Mason, TX 76856
(915)347-6463

Rates: $95.
Payment: MC VISA PC TC.
Innkeeper(s): Laverne Lee.
Circa: 1883.

Rooms: 2 rooms with PB.
Beds: D.

Guests may explore the 320-acre Hasse ranch, which is a working ranch where deer, wild turkey, feral hogs and quail are common sights. After purchasing the land, Henry Hasse and his wife lived in a log cabin on the property before building the sandstone home 23 years later. Three generations of Hasses have lived here, and today it is owned by a great-granddaughter who restored the home in 1980. The inn is located in the small German village of Art, Texas, which is located six miles east of Mason. The innkeepers rent the two-bedroom National Register home out to only one group or guest at a time. The home is filled with period furniture and accessories, yet offers the modern convenience of an on-site washer and dryer and a fully stocked kitchen. The ranch grounds include a two-mile hiking trail perfect for nature lovers.

Breakfast included in rates. Type of meal: continental-plus breakfast. Air conditioning, ceiling fan and VCR in room. Library on premises. Handicap access. 320 acres. Weddings, small meetings and family reunions hosted. Antiques, fishing, parks, shopping and watersports nearby.

"We enjoyed every aspect of our stay; the atmosphere, sense of history, rustic setting with a touch of class. We would love to return the same time next year!"

Nacogdoches

E9

TX

Pine Creek Lodge

RR 3 Box 1238
Nacogdoches, TX 75964
(409)560-6282 (888)714-1414
Fax:(409)560-1675

Rates: $55-75.
Payment: MC VISA AX DS PC TC.
Innkeeper(s): The Pitts Family.
Circa: 1992.

Rooms: 9 rooms with PB. 3 conference rooms.
Beds: KQT.

Three rustic country buildings, nestled on a scenic 140-acre farm, comprise this lodge bed & breakfast. Guest rooms are stocked with amenities, including mini refrigerators stocked with beverages, baskets of fruit and candy, fluffy robes, ceiling fans, TVs and VCRs. All of the rooms have a private entrance off a porch or a deck. One of the buildings has a wraparound porch set up with swings and rockers. Guests can stroll the grounds in search of wildlife, enjoy the colors from more than 300 rose bushes, take a nap in a hammock or fish in the pond. Weekday guests are served continental-plus fare during the morning meal, and weekend guests enjoy a full breakfast. For a romantic treat, the innkeepers offer candlelit steak dinners.

Breakfast included in rates. Types of meals: continental-plus breakfast, full breakfast and early coffee/tea. Dinner, lunch and banquet service available. Air conditioning, ceiling fan and VCR in room. Fax, copier, spa and swimming on premises. 140 acres. Weddings, small meetings, family reunions and seminars hosted. East Texas Drawl spoken. Antiques, fishing, parks, shopping, sporting events, theater and watersports nearby.

"Thank you so much for warm hospitality and excellent service."

New Braunfels (Canyon Lake)

Aunt Nora's B&B

120 Naked Indian Tr
New Braunfels (Canyon Lake), TX 78132
(210)905-3989 (800)687-2887

Rates: $95-125.
Innkeeper(s): I Haley.
Circa: 1983.
Rooms: 4 rooms with PB.

Nestled on four acres, amid oak, cedar and Indian trees, this Texas country bed & breakfast has many nearby scenic areas that include a walk to the top of the hill to view Canyon Lake. The sitting room is a perfect place to relax among handmade furnishings, antiques, paintings, lacy crafts, a wood stove and natural wood floors. Enjoy the private collection of Pigtails & Lace hand-crafted dolls. The guest rooms are decorated with country curtains, natural woodwork, handmade maple and cherry wood furnishings, ceiling fans and quilts.

Breakfast included in rates. Types of meals: continental breakfast and full breakfast. Air conditioning and ceiling fan in room. Spa on premises. Weddings, small meetings, family reunions and seminars hosted. Amusement parks, shopping and sporting events nearby.

Romayor F9

Chain-O-Lakes Resort

Daniel Ranch Rd
Romayor, TX 77368
(713)592-2150
Fax:(713)592-8851

Rates: $120-150.
Payment: MC VISA AX DS PC TC.
Innkeeper(s): Jimmy & Beverly Smith.
Circa: 1982.
Rooms: 27 cottages with PB, 27 with FP.
Beds: QD.

A mix of more than two dozen log cabins dot the landscape at this 300-acre resort. The nicely appointed cabins offer romantic amenities such as fireplaces and decks with porch swings, but the resort is also the site of many conferences and business meetings, serving as a fun alternative to hotels. Swimming, hiking on nature trails, horseback riding and fishing are just a few of the activities available at Chain-O-Lakes. Occasionally, guests can enjoy horse-drawn carriage rides up to the Hilltop Herb Farm restaurant to enjoy a bountiful breakfast. The seasonal menu includes anything from banana walnut pancakes to a ham and basil quiche. Lunch and dinner are served, and there are herb gardens and cooking classes.

Breakfast included in rates. Type of meal: gourmet breakfast. Gourmet lunch available. Air conditioning, turn-down service and ceiling fan in room. Swimming and stables on premises. 300 acres. Weddings, small meetings, family reunions and seminars hosted. Amusement parks, antiques, fishing, parks, shopping, sporting events, theater and watersports nearby.

San Antonio F7

A Yellow Rose B&B

229 Madison
San Antonio, TX 78204
(800)950-9903
Fax:(210)229-1691

Rates: $85-135.
Payment: MC VISA AX DS PC TC.
Innkeeper(s): Kit Wallca & Deb Field.
Circa: 1878.
Rooms: 5 rooms with PB. 1 suite. 1 conference room.
Beds: Q.

This magnificent residence boasts some of the finest craftsmanship available, both inside and out. Visitors who lived in the house for thirty years before it was converted into a B&B have returned and stated that the home has never been as glorious. Set in the quiet, elegant King William Historic District, the home is conveniently close to travel by trolley ride and the famous San Antonio Riverwalk. Five spacious, distinctively decorated guest rooms, each with a private bath, along with covered parking and nearby restaurants and cafes, are just some of the amenities that make the stay here memorable.

Breakfast included in rates. Type of meal: gourmet breakfast. Air conditioning, ceiling fan and cable TV in room. VCR and library on premises. Small meetings, family reunions and seminars hosted. Amusement parks, antiques, parks, shopping, sporting events, theater and watersports nearby. TAC10.

Adams House B&B

231 Adams St
San Antonio, TX 78210
(210)224-4791
Fax:(210)223-5125

Rates: Call for rates.
Innkeeper(s): Betty Lancaster.
Circa: 1902.

Built in what is now known as the King William Historic District, this Georgian-style inn is a reflection of Southern tradition. Guests can partake of a hearty Southern/Texana breakfast served in the dining room or on one of the airy verandas. For your musical pleasure, a parlor has a piano and stereo equipment. A library boasts a large collection of books and records, including a law library. A short trolley ride takes you to the Alamo, Spanish Governor's Palace, Tower of the Americas and other attractions.

Air conditioning, ceiling fan and cable TV in room. VCR on premises. Weddings, small meetings and family reunions hosted. Amusement parks, antiques, shopping, sporting events and theater nearby.

Beckmann Inn & Carriage House B&B

222 E Guenther
San Antonio, TX 78204
(210)229-1449 (800)945-1449
Fax:(210)229-1061

Rates: $80-130.
Payment: MC VISA AX DC DS PC.
Innkeeper(s): Betty Jo & Don Schwartz.
Circa: 1886.

Rooms: 5 rooms with PB, 2 with FP. 2 suites.
Beds: Q.

A beautiful wraparound porch with white wicker furniture warmly welcomes guests to the main house of this Victorian inn. Through the entrance and into the living room, guests stand on an intricately designed wood mosaic floor imported from Paris. Arch-shaped pocket doors with framed opaque glass open to the formal dining room, where breakfast is served. All the guest rooms feature 12- to 14-foot ceilings with fans, tall, ornately carved queen-size antique Victorian beds, colorful floral accessories and antiques.

Breakfast included in rates. Type of meal: gourmet breakfast. Air conditioning, turn-down service, ceiling fan and cable TV in room. Fax, copier and library on premises. Family reunions hosted. Amusement parks, antiques, parks, shopping, sporting events and theater nearby.

"The Beckmann Inn & Carriage House is truly a home away from home for all who stay there. Don and Betty Jo put their heart and soul into making every guest's stay a memorable experience."

Brackenridge House

230 Madison
San Antonio, TX 78204
(210)271-3442 (800)221-1412
Fax:(210)271-3442

Rates: $80-150.
Payment: MC VISA AX DC DS PC TC.
Innkeeper(s): Bennie & Sue Blansett.
Circa: 1901.

Rooms: 5 rooms, 3 with PB. 2 suites. 1 cottage.
Beds: KQ.

Each of the guest rooms at Brackenridge House is individually decorated. Clawfoot tubs, iron beds and a private veranda are a few of the items that guests might discover. Several rooms include kitchenettes. Blansett Barn, often rented by families or those on an extended stay, includes two bedrooms, a bathroom, a full kitchen and living and dining areas. Many of San Antonio's interesting sites are nearby. The San Antonio Mission Trail begins just a block away, and trolleys will take you to the Alamo, the River Walk, convention center and more. Coffeehouses, restaurants and antique stores all are within walking distance. Small pets are welcome in Blansett Barn.

Breakfast included in rates. Types of meals: gourmet breakfast and early coffee/tea. Air conditioning, ceiling fan and cable TV in room. VCR, fax, copier and spa on premises. Family reunions hosted. Amusement parks, antiques, parks, shopping, sporting events, theater and watersports nearby. TAC10.

Pets Allowed: Small pets in carriage house.

"Innkeeper was very nice, very helpful."

The Bullis House Inn

621 Pierce St, PO Box 8059
San Antonio, TX 78208
(210)223-9426
Fax:(210)299-1479
E-mail: hisanantonio@aol.com

Rates: $49-89. AP.
Payment: MC VISA AX DS TC.
Innkeeper(s): Steve & Alma Cross.
Circa: 1906.

Rooms: 8 rooms, 2 with PB, 6 with FP. 1 suite. 4 conference rooms.
Beds: KQT.

A two-story portico supported by six massive columns accentuates the Neoclassical architecture of this home built for General Bullis who was instrumental in the capture of Chief Geronimo. Features include stairways and paneling of tiger's eye oak, marble fireplaces, chandeliers and parquet floors. There are contemporary and antique furnishings.

Breakfast included in rates. Types of meals: continental-plus breakfast, gourmet breakfast and early coffee/tea. Gourmet lunch, banquet service, catering service and catered breakfast available. AP. Air conditioning and VCR in room. Fax, copier and swimming on premises. Weddings, small meetings, family reunions and seminars hosted. French and Spanish spoken. Amusement parks, antiques, parks, shopping, sporting events and theater nearby. TAC10.

Publicity: *New York Times, Fiesta,*

Special Discounts: Weekly rates available, based on availability.

"Loved your home and your hospitality very much."

Chabot Reed House

403 Madison
San Antonio, TX 78204
(210)223-8697 (800)776-2424
Fax:(210)734-2342
E-mail: sister@txdirect.net

Rates: $125-175.
Payment: PC TC.
Innkeeper(s): Sister & Peter Reed.
Circa: 1876.

Rooms: 5 rooms with PB, 2 with FP. 2 suites. 2 cottages.
Beds: KQ.

Built by a German cotton and wool merchant, this grand Victorian mansion, a Texas landmark, is listed in the National Register and located in San Antonio's King William Historic District. The Texas landmark is situated on an acre of grounds with gardens and fountains. There are antique-filled rooms in the main house as well as two suites in the adjacent Carriage House. Gourmet quiche, fresh fruit and baskets of breads and rolls are served at breakfast, and afternoon tea is another treat. The manor is just a block from the River Walk and close to many other San Antonio sites.

Breakfast and afternoon tea included in rates. Type of meal: full breakfast. Air conditioning in room. Fax and library on premises. Spanish spoken. Amusement parks, antiques, parks, sporting events and theater nearby. TAC10.

The Columns on Alamo

1037 S Alamo St
San Antonio, TX 78210
(210)271-3245 (800)233-3364
Fax:(210)271-3245

Rates: $75-148.
Payment: MC VISA AX.
Innkeeper(s): Ellenor & Arthur Link.
Circa: 1892.

Rooms: 11 rooms with PB, 1 with FP. 1 cottage. 1 conference room.
Beds: KQ.

This bed & breakfast is located in an impressive Greek Revival home in the King William Historic District. Victorian antiques and reproductions decorate the guest rooms, including pieces such as brass beds and fainting couches. An adjacent, turn-of-the-century guest house includes a four-poster bed, gas log fireplace and a two-person Jacuzzi. The trolley stops in front of the house, transporting guests to many of San Antonio's attractions. The River Walk and the Alamo are within walking distance.

Breakfast included in rates. Types of meals: full breakfast and early coffee/tea. Room service available. Air conditioning, ceiling fan and cable TV in room. Fax, copier and library on premises. Weddings, small meetings and family reunions hosted. German spoken. Amusement parks, antiques, parks, shopping, sporting events and theater nearby. TAC10.

"The house has been an inspiration. Very friendly and helpful host and hostess."

Noble Inns-Pancoast Carriage House

102 Turner
San Antonio, TX 78204
(210)225-4045 (800)221-4045
Fax:(210)227-0877

Rates: $110-130.
Payment: MC VISA AX DS PC TC.
Innkeeper(s): Kim Harrison.
Circa: 1896.

Rooms: 3 suites, 3 with FP.
Beds: Q.

This two-story, Victorian carriage house is located in San Antonio's King William Historic District. Each of the three guest rooms is appointed in Victorian style with period antiques, a fireplace and a marble bath with clawfoot tub. The current innkeepers are the fifth generation of the Pancoast family to live on the property and are happy to share the town and family history. The kitchens are stocked with pastries, fresh fruit, cereal and beverages, so guests can prepare breakfast at their leisure. There is a swimming pool and heated spa on the premises.

Breakfast included in rates. Type of meal: continental-plus breakfast. Afternoon tea available. Air conditioning, turn-down service, ceiling fan and cable TV in room. Fax, spa and swimming on premises. Small meetings hosted. Spanish spoken. Antiques, parks, shopping, sporting events and theater nearby. TAC10.

"First impressions mean a lot, and we were delighted the moment we entered this suite."

Noble Inns-The Jackson House

107 Madison
San Antonio, TX 78204
(210)225-4045 (800)221-4045
Fax:(210)227-0877

Rates: $105-135.
Payment: MC VISA AX DS PC TC.
Innkeeper(s): Kim Harrison.
Circa: 1894.

Rooms: 6 rooms with PB, 6 with FP.
Beds: KQ.

This Victorian brick and limestone house is a sister bed & breakfast to the Pancoast Carriage House. The home, located in the King William Historic District, has been designated as a city historic structure. Rooms are decorated with Victorian antiques, fireplaces, marble baths and a clawfoot or whirlpool tub. The inn's unique gazebo, which encloses the spa, is surrounded by antique stained glass. Guests are pampered both with a full breakfast, as well as afternoon tea.

Breakfast and afternoon tea included in rates. Type of meal: full breakfast. Air conditioning, turn-down service, ceiling fan and cable TV in room. Fax, spa, swimming, bicycles and library on premises. Small meetings and family reunions hosted. Spanish spoken. Antiques, parks, shopping, sporting events and theater nearby. TAC10.

"It couldn't have been better if we dreamed it! Thank you."

The Ogé House on The River Walk

209 Washington
San Antonio, TX 78204
(210)223-2353 (800)242-2770
Fax:(210)226-5812

Rates: $135-195.
Payment: MC VISA AX DC CB DS TC.
Innkeeper(s): Sharrie & Patrick Magatagan.
Circa: 1857.

Rooms: 10 rooms with PB, 7 with FP. 1 conference room.
Beds: KQ.

This impressive antebellum mansion is a Texas Historic Landmark. It rests on the banks of the beautiful San Antonio Riverwalk on an acre-and-a-half of gardens. Shaded by graceful oak and pecan trees, the inn has a gazebo and double-tiered veranda. There are nine fireplaces. Queen- and king-size beds are provided and all the rooms are distinguished with period antiques, handsomely upholstered sofas and chairs and Oriental carpets. The trolley, convention center and the Alamo are steps away.

Breakfast included in rates. Types of meals: gourmet breakfast and early coffee/tea. Air conditioning, ceiling fan, cable TV and VCR in room. Fax and library on premises. Small meetings hosted. Amusement parks, antiques, parks, shopping, sporting events, theater and watersports nearby. TAC10.

Location: Five blocks from the Alamo on the Riverwalk.

Publicity: *Victoria, McCalls, Texas Monthly, Texas Highways, London Times, New York Times, Glamour.*

"Wonderfully relaxing weekend in an elegant home with pure Southern hospitality."

Riverwalk Inn

329 Old Guilbeau St
San Antonio, TX 78204
(210)212-8300 (800)254-4440
Fax:(210)229-9442

Rates: $89-135.
Payment: MC VISA AX DS PC TC.
Innkeeper(s): Johnny Halpenny & Tammy Hill.
Circa: 1842.

Rooms: 11 suites, 9 with FP. 1 conference room.
Beds: KQT.

With its rustic, country decor, log exterior and ideal location on the River Walk, this historic inn is a gem. The two, adjacent buildings were constructed from five log homes brought to the town from Tennessee just a few years after the battle at the Alamo. Each guest room has a fireplace and many modern amenities, such as phones with voice mail and mini-refrigerators. The innkeepers, both native Texans, serve continental breakfasts in the mornings, and desserts in the evenings.

Breakfast included in rates. Types of meals: full breakfast and early coffee/tea. Afternoon tea and evening snack available. Air conditioning, ceiling fan and cable TV in room. VCR, fax, copier and bicycles on premises. Handicap access. Weddings, small meetings, family reunions and seminars hosted. Spanish spoken. Amusement parks, antiques, fishing, parks, shopping, sporting events, theater and watersports nearby. TAC10.

Special Discounts: Ask about corporate.

The Royal Swan Guest House

236 Madison
San Antonio, TX 78204
(210)223-3776 (800)368-3073
Fax:(210)271-0373

Rates: $75-130.
Payment: MC VISA AX DS PC TC.
Innkeeper(s): Curt & Helen Skredergard.
Circa: 1892.

Rooms: 5 rooms with PB, 2 with FP.
Beds: Q.

This picture-perfect Victorian is filled with period furnishings that comfortably suit the handsome woodwork and polished floors. Crystal chandeliers, fireplaces and remarkable stained-glass windows add to the authentic atmosphere set by the foyer and a grand staircase, handsomely crafted out of pine. If you can't wait for the luscious peach or apple cobbler breakfast dessert, distract yourself with the quiche or crepes, bacon and fresh fruit, and the dessert will soon arrive. The Alamo, Riverwalk, restaurants and museums are all nearby.

Breakfast and evening snack included in rates. Types of meals: gourmet breakfast and early coffee/tea. Air conditioning, ceiling fan and cable TV in room. Fax and copier on premises. Antiques, shopping and theater nearby.

Location: In the King William Historic District.

San Augustine E9

The Wade House

202 E Livingston St
San Augustine, TX 75972
(409)275-5489
Fax:(409)275-9188

Rates: $40-80.
Payment: MC VISA PC TC.
Innkeeper(s): Nelsyn & Julia Wade.
Circa: 1940.

Rooms: 6 rooms, 4 with PB. 1 suite. 1 conference room.
Beds: KQDT.

The Wade House is a Mount Vernon-style red brick house located two blocks from the old courthouse square. Guest rooms are decorated in a mixture of contemporary and antique furnishings and are cooled by both ceiling fans and air conditioning.

Breakfast included in rates. Types of meals: continental breakfast, continental-plus breakfast and early coffee/tea. Air conditioning, ceiling fan and cable TV in room. Weddings, small meetings, family reunions and seminars hosted. Fishing and shopping nearby.

Location: Two blocks from the Central Courthouse Square.

Publicity: *San Augustine Tribune, Dallas Morning News.*

"The house is one of the most beautiful in the area. Each room is decorated to the utmost excellence."

Seabrook

F9

Pelican House B&B Inn

1302 First St
Seabrook, TX 77586-3806
(713)474-5295
Fax:(713)474-7840

Rates: $60-70.
Payment: MC VISA AX DS PC TC.
Innkeeper(s): Suzanne Silver.
Circa: 1910.

Rooms: 4 rooms with PB.
Beds: Q.

A white picket fence surrounds this early 20th-century house, painted in cheerful yellow and salmon hues. There are four guest rooms, each with bright and airy decor. The guest kitchen is decorated in a tropical fish theme and two rooms are decked in nautical style, ideal considering the waterfront, Back Bay location. Nasa is three miles away, and Galveston and Houston are nearby.

Breakfast included in rates. Types of meals: full breakfast, gourmet breakfast and early coffee/tea. Ceiling fan in room. Cable TV on premises. Antiques, fishing, parks, shopping and watersports nearby. TAC10.

Smithville

F7

The Katy House

201 Ramona St, PO Box 803
Smithville, TX 78957-0803
(512)237-4262 (800)843-5289
Fax:(512)237-2239
E-mail: thekatyh@onr.com

Rates: $56-85.
Payment: MC VISA PC TC.
Innkeeper(s): Bruce & Sallie Blalock.
Circa: 1909.

Rooms: 4 rooms with PB. 1 suite. 2 cottages.
Beds: Q.

The Italianate exterior is graced by an arched portico over the bay-windowed living room. The Georgian columns reflect the inn's turn-of-the-century origin. Long leaf pine floors, pocket doors and a graceful stairway accent the completely refurbished interior. The inn is decorated almost exclusively in American antique oak and railroad memorabilia. A leisurely 10-minute bicycle ride (innkeepers provide bikes) will take you to the banks of the Colorado River. Also available are maps that outline walking or biking tours with lists of some of the historical and interesting information of the area.

Breakfast included in rates. Types of meals: full breakfast and early coffee/tea. Air conditioning, ceiling fan and cable TV in room. VCR, fax, bicycles and pet boarding on premises. Family reunions hosted. Antiques, fishing, parks, shopping and watersports nearby.

Pets Allowed: With advance notice, in certain rooms.

Special Discounts: Weeknight discounts available.

Teague

E8

Hubbard House Inn B&B

621 Cedar St
Teague, TX 75860-1617
(817)739-2629,

Rates: $65.
Payment: VISA AX PC TC.
Innkeeper(s): John W. Duke.
Circa: 1903.

Rooms: 6 rooms.
Beds: KD.

Having served as the Hubbard House Hotel for railroad employees during part of its history, this red brick and white frame Georgian home is furnished mostly with early American antiques. There's a second-floor balcony porch with swings, which offer guests a place to relax. A country breakfast is served in the large formal dining room on a glass-topped antique pool table.

Breakfast included in rates. Type of meal: full breakfast. Air conditioning, ceiling fan and cable TV in room. VCR on premises. Handicap access. Weddings, small meetings and family reunions hosted. Antiques, fishing, parks and shopping nearby. TAC10.

Special Discounts: Three or more days 20% discount.

Texarkana C9

Mansion on Main B&B

802 Main St
Texarkana, TX 75501-5104
(903)792-1835

Rates: $60-109.
Payment: MC VISA AX PC TC.
Innkeeper(s): Lee & Inez Hayden.
Circa: 1895.

Rooms: 6 rooms with PB. 1 suite.
Beds: QD.

Spectacular two-story columns salvaged from the St. Louis World's Fair accent the exterior of this Neoclassical-style inn. Victorian nightgowns and sleepshirts are provided, and whether you are on a business trip or your honeymoon, expect to be pampered. Six bedchambers vary from the Butler's Garret to the Governor's Suite and are all furnished with antiques and period appointments. The inn is located in the downtown historic area. Enjoy a fireside cup of coffee or a lemonade on the veranda.

Breakfast included in rates. Types of meals: full breakfast, gourmet breakfast and early coffee/tea. Afternoon tea available. Air conditioning, ceiling fan and cable TV in room. Handicap access. Weddings, small meetings, family reunions and seminars hosted. Cajun spoken. Antiques, fishing, shopping and theater nearby. TAC10.

Special Discounts: Extended stay more than 3 nights-20% discount.

Turkey C5

Hotel Turkey Living Museum

3rd & Alexander, PO Box 37
Turkey, TX 79261
(806)423-1151 (800)657-7110

Rates: $69-89.
Payment: MC VISA AX PC TC.
Innkeeper(s): Gary & Suzie Johnson.
Circa: 1927.

Rooms: 15 rooms, 7 with PB. 1 suite. 1 conference room.
Beds: DT.

Guests can enjoy ranch cookouts at this historic hotel. Bob Willis, "The King of Western Swing," played in small evening concerts and dances in the dining room. The hotel is decorated with a combination of Victorian and Western design. Nearby Cuprock Canyons State Park features plenty of hiking and biking trails, and the only railroad tunnel in Texas. The hotel also offers tennis facilities.

Breakfast included in rates. Types of meals: full breakfast and early coffee/tea. Air conditioning and ceiling fan in room. VCR, copier and tennis on premises. Weddings, small meetings, family reunions and seminars hosted. Parks nearby.

Publicity: *Country, Texas Highways, Dallas Morning News, Houston Chronicle, Philadelphia Inquirer.*

Tyler D9

Chilton Grand

433 S Chilton Ave
Tyler, TX 75702-8017
(903)595-3270
Fax:(903)595-3270

Rates: $75-150.
Payment: MC VISA AX PC TC.
Innkeeper(s): Jerry & Carole Glazebrook.
Circa: 1910.

Rooms: 4 rooms with PB, 1 with FP. 2 suites. 1 cottage.
Beds: QD.

Tall pecan, maple, oak and magnolia trees shelter this red brick, Greek Revival home on a brick street in the Azalea District. (Tyler is considered by some to be the prettiest town in Texas.) Two-story columns and a crystal chandelier hanging from the front balcony and porch set the elegant tone. Inside there are antiques and romantic touches such as a Jacuzzi tub and feather beds. Ivy Cottage features a canopied queen feather bed and a two-person whirlpool tub in the Gazebo Room. Breakfast is served with silver, crystal and china. Historic mansions, Brickstreet Playhouse, the midtown Arts Center and downtown antique shops are all within walking distance.

Breakfast included in rates. Types of meals: gourmet breakfast and early coffee/tea. Air conditioning, turn-down service, ceiling fan, cable TV and VCR in room. Fax on premises. Antiques, fishing, parks, shopping, theater and watersports nearby. TAC7.

"Wow, what a beautiful place you have. The food was simply the best."

Rosevine Inn B&B

415 S Vine Ave
Tyler, TX 75702-7942
(903)592-2221
Fax:(903)593-9500

Rates: $85-150.
Payment: MC VISA AX DC CB DS PC TC.
Innkeeper(s): Bert & Rebecca Powell.
Circa: 1986.

Rooms: 6 rooms with PB, 1 with FP. 1 suite. 2 cottages.
Beds: QDT.

Located on one of Tyler's quaint brick streets, the Rosevine Inn B&B is surrounded by a white picket fence. The inn features antiques, country collectibles, fireplaces and a courtyard. There is a hot tub underneath the shady roof of the backyard pavilion near the fountain. Guest rooms are named for the area's famous flowers.

Breakfast included in rates. Types of meals: full breakfast and early coffee/tea. Picnic lunch available. Air conditioning and ceiling fan in room. Cable TV, VCR, fax, copier, spa and library on premises. Small meetings hosted. Antiques, fishing, parks, shopping, sporting events, theater and watersports nearby. TAC10.

Publicity: *Dallas Morning News, San Antonio Sunday Express-News, Country.*

"Such a dependable pleasure each time!"

Uvalde G6

Casa De Leona

1149 Pearsall Rd,
PO Box 1829
Uvalde, TX 78802
(210)278-8550
Fax:(210)278-8550

Rates: $55-150.
Payment: MC VISA AX PC TC.
Innkeeper(s): Carolyn Durr.
Circa: 1983.

Rooms: 5 rooms, 3 with PB. 2 suites. 1 cottage. 1 conference room.
Beds: QT.

This Spanish-style hacienda surrounds a courtyard and each bedroom looks out to the fountain and flower gardens. There is also a guest cottage with its own kitchenette. The local area offers many activities. Tour museums or browse through an antique mall. The Mexican border is nearby and a tour-guide service is available.

Breakfast and evening snack included in rates. Types of meals: continental breakfast, continental-plus breakfast, full breakfast, gourmet breakfast and early coffee/tea. Air conditioning, turn-down service, ceiling fan, cable TV and VCR in room. Fax on premises. Handicap access. 17 acres. Weddings, small meetings, family reunions and seminars hosted. Access to interpreters for German, Russian and Spanish spoken. Antiques, fishing, parks, shopping, sporting events, theater and watersports nearby. TAC10.

Publicity: *Innsider.*

Waco E7

The Judge Baylor House

908 Speight Ave
Waco, TX 76706-2343
(817)756-0273
Fax:(817)756-0711

Rates: $69-89.
Payment: MC VISA PC TC.
Innkeeper(s): Bruce & Dorothy Dyer.
Circa: 1940.

Rooms: 5 rooms with PB. 1 suite.
Beds: Q.

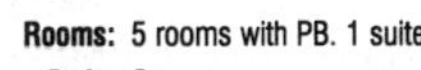

This home was built by the head of the chemistry department at Baylor University, which is just one block away. There are five well-appointed guest rooms, each decorated with English antiques. Each room has something special. In one room, guests will discover French doors leading out to a patio. In another, there is a poster bed and hand-painted pedestal sink. Aside from the university and Elizabeth Barrett & Robert Browning Library, the home is near the Brazos Riverwalk, Lake Waco, the Texas Sports Hall of Fame, antique shops, historic homes and more.

Breakfast and afternoon tea included in rates. Type of meal: full breakfast. Dinner available. Air conditioning and ceiling fan in room. Fax on premises. Small meetings hosted. Fishing, parks, sporting events and theater nearby. TAC10.

Blair House

100 Spoke Hill Rd
Wimberley, TX 78676
(512)847-1111
Fax:(512)847-8820
E-mail: blairhouse@worldnet.att.net

Rates: $135.
Payment: MC VISA AX DC DS PC TC.
Innkeeper(s): Jonnie Stansbury.

Rooms: 7 rooms with PB.
Beds: Q.

Jacuzzi tubs, fine linens, fresh flowers and chocolates are just a few of the pampering amenities. With 85 acres to explore, a sauna, a massage therapist on staff and plenty of books, movies and CDs to enjoy, guests have little trouble finding an activity. Rooms are individually decorated with elegant, romantic furnishings. The innkeeper is a well-trained chef and prepares the tempting cuisine using seasonal, organic produce. A full, gourmet breakfast, evening desserts and wine are served. On occasion, specialty dinners are prepared. A recent six-course, New Year's Eve menu started off with tiny potatoes filled with sour cream and caviar or crostini with walnut gorgonzola. For those who wish to learn her secrets, the innkeeper offers cooking school three times a year.

Types of meals: gourmet breakfast and early coffee/tea. Evening snack and catering service available. Air conditioning, turn-down service, ceiling fan and VCR in room. Fax, copier, sauna and library on premises. 85 acres. Weddings, small meetings and seminars hosted. Spanish spoken. Amusement parks, antiques, fishing, shopping, sporting events, theater and watersports nearby.

Special Discounts: $130 per person/2 in a room for retreats.

The Homestead

Ranch Rd 12 and County Rd 316
Wimberley, TX 78676
(512)847-8788 (800)918-8788
Fax:(512)847-8842
E-mail: 74372.1711@compuserve.com

Rates: $85-95.
Payment: PC.
Innkeeper(s): Clark & Sandi Aylsworth.
Circa: 1947.

Rooms: 8 cottages. 1 conference room.
Beds: QDT.

This collection of guest cottages rests along the banks of Cypress Creek on an seven-acre spread shaded by ancient cypress trees. The cottages are private enough for honeymooners to enjoy, yet all are large enough to accommodate families. The owners stock each unit with muffins, sausage, juice and coffee prior to guests arrival. Units include kitchens, linens (except beach towels for the creek) and a fireplace. There are grills, picnic tables and a spa on the premises, as well as an 800-square-foot meeting room. Pets are allowed in some cottages, at a rate of $10 per day.

Breakfast included in rates. Types of meals: continental-plus breakfast and early coffee/tea. Catering service available. Air conditioning, ceiling fan and cable TV in room. Spa and swimming on premises. Handicap access. Weddings, small meetings, family reunions and seminars hosted. Amusement parks, antiques, fishing, shopping, sporting events and theater nearby. TAC15.

Pets Allowed: Cottages 5-8, $10 per night.

Special Discounts: Five or more cottages or nights 10% discount.

Southwind

2701 Fm 3237
Wimberley, TX 78676-5511
(512)847-5277 (800)508-5277

Rates: $75-85.
Payment: MC VISA AX DS PC TC.
Innkeeper(s): Carrie Watson.
Circa: 1985.

Rooms: 5 rooms with PB, 3 with FP. 2 cottages.
Beds: KQ.

Located three miles east of the quaint village of Wimberly, this early Texas-style inn sits on 25 wooded acres. Roam the unspoiled acres and discover deer crossing your path and armadillos, raccoons and foxes skittering just beyond your footsteps. During the wet season, enjoy clear natural springs with access to swimming hole. There's a porch outside guest rooms and secluded cabins where one can sit in a rocking chair, feel gentle breezes and listen to birds sing. The parlor is a cool retreat in the summer and provides a warm fireplace in winter weather.

Breakfast included in rates. Types of meals: full breakfast and early coffee/tea. Air conditioning and ceiling fan in room. Library on premises. Handicap access. 25 acres. Weddings, small meetings, family reunions and seminars hosted. Amusement parks, antiques, fishing, parks, shopping, sporting events, theater and watersports nearby. TAC10.

Utah

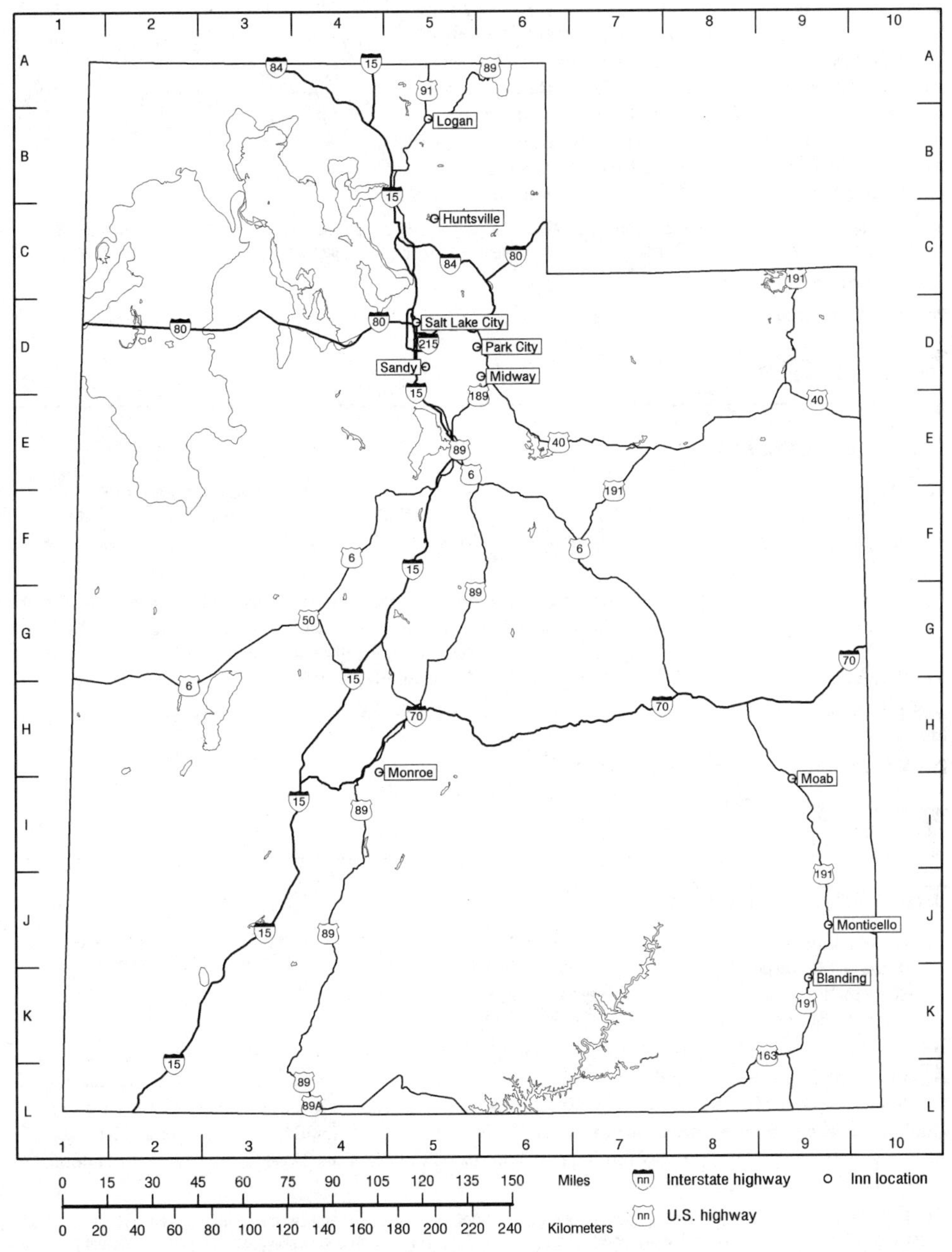
Logan
Huntsville
Salt Lake City
Park City
Sandy
Midway
Monroe
Moab
Monticello
Blanding
Miles
Kilometers
Interstate highway
U.S. highway
Inn location

UT

Blanding

K9

The Grayson Country Inn B&B

118 E 300 S
Blanding, UT 84511-2908
(801)678-2388 (800)365-0868

Rates: $42-52.
Payment: MC VISA AX.
Innkeeper(s): Dennis & Lurlene Gutke.
Circa: 1908.

Rooms: 11 rooms with PB, 1 with FP. 1 cottage.
Beds: Q.

Over the years, The Grayson Country Inn has served a number of purposes, including a small hotel and boarding house for Indian girls who attended a local school. The inn is the perfect location to enjoy the many sites in the area, and is within walking distance from a pottery factory and gift shops. The area abounds with outdoor activities, as many national parks are nearby. Edge of the Cedars State Park is only a mile from the inn. A three-bedroom cottage is available for groups and/or families.

Breakfast included in rates. Type of meal: full breakfast. Air conditioning, ceiling fan and cable TV in room. Library on premises. Small meetings and family reunions hosted. Spanish, French and Portuguese spoken. Fishing, parks, shopping and watersports nearby. TAC5.

Pets Allowed: In carriers outside.

Publicity: *Salt Lake Tribune.*

Huntsville

C5

Jackson Fork Inn

7345 E 900 S
Huntsville, UT 84317-9778
(801)745-0051 (800)255-0672

Rates: $40-110.
Payment: MC VISA AX DS PC TC.
Innkeeper(s): Vicki Petersen.
Circa: 1938.

Rooms: 8 rooms with PB.
Beds: Q.

This former dairy barn was named after the hay fork that was used to transport hay into the barn. The romantic inn now includes eight guest rooms and a restaurant. Four rooms include two-person Jacuzzi tubs, and all are cozy and comfortable. A self-serve continental breakfast is prepared each day with muffins and fresh coffee. The inn is ideal for skiers and located near Powder Mountain, Nordic Valley and Snowbasin ski resorts.

Breakfast included in rates. Dinner and lunch available. Ceiling fan in room. Weddings and small meetings hosted. Fishing, parks, shopping, downhill skiing, cross-country skiing and watersports nearby.

Pets Allowed: With $20 fee - must be kept on leash.

Midway

D6

The Inn on The Creek

375 Rainbow Ln
Midway, UT 84049
(801)654-0892
Fax:(801)654-5871

Rates: $95-475.
Payment: MC VISA AX DC PC TC.
Innkeeper(s): Joel & Becky VanLeeuwen.
Circa: 1991.

Rooms: 44 suites. 11 cottages. 1 conference room.

For golfers, this inn's location, adjacent to a championship golf course, could not be more ideal. But non-golfers will enjoy the surroundings as well. Each of the guest rooms and cottages includes a fireplace, whirlpool tub and deck featuring views of the surrounding mountains. The inn is an excellent location for families. Guest quarters offer from one to five bedrooms, and each also includes a kitchen area. There are five acres of grounds to explore and a swimming pool and spa on the premises. Breakfast is included in rates for bed & breakfast rooms only.

Breakfast included in rates. Air conditioning, cable TV and VCR in room. Fax, copier, spa and swimming on premises. Weddings, small meetings and family reunions hosted. Fishing, parks, shopping, downhill skiing, cross-country skiing, sporting events, theater and watersports nearby. TAC10.

Moab

I9

Canyon Country B&B

590 N 500 W
Moab, UT 84532-2011
(801)259-5262 (800)435-0284

Rates: $45-70.
Payment: MC VISA AX DS PC TC.
Innkeeper(s): Nelson & Christina Moyle.
Circa: 1960.

Rooms: 5 rooms, 4 with PB. 4 suites.
Beds: QDT.

Nestled between the snow-capped La Sal Mountains and the red-rock canyons of the Colorado River, this ranch-style inn offers a casual atmosphere. The inn is within walking and bicycling distance to local shops, museums, art galleries and restaurants. Special touches include a warm Southwestern decor, freshly cut flowers in each room, a mint on your pillow and an adventure travel library. Nutritious country breakfasts include freshly baked breads, muffins, bagels, waffles and whole grain cereal. Inn has mountain bike and kayak rentals for guests.

Breakfast included in rates. Type of meal: continental-plus breakfast. Air conditioning in room. Cable TV, VCR, fax, spa, bicycles and pet boarding on premises. Handicap access. Weddings, small meetings and family reunions hosted. Spanish and French spoken. Antiques, fishing, parks, shopping, cross-country skiing and watersports nearby. TAC10.

Pets Allowed.

Location: In the Canyonlands of southeast Utah.

Publicity: *Outside Magazine.*

Sunflower Hill B&B

185 N 300 E
Moab, UT 84532-2421
(801)259-2974

Rates: $50-140.
Payment: MC VISA.
Innkeeper(s): Aaron & Kim Robison.

Rooms: 11 rooms with PB.
Beds: QD.

Guests at Sunflower Hill stay either in a restored adobe farmhouse or a garden cottage. The one-and-a-half-acre grounds, dotted with gardens and wooded pathways, create a secluded environment, yet the home is only three blocks from downtown Moab. Guest rooms are decorated in country style with antiques and stenciled walls. A hearty breakfast buffet is served on an antique sideboard. Guests choose from a multitude of items, such as breakfast burritos, pancakes, muffins, fresh fruit, honey-almond granola and more. There is an outdoor hot tub on the premises.

Breakfast included in rates. Type of meal: full breakfast. Evening snack available. Air conditioning, ceiling fan and cable TV in room. Copier and spa on premises. Small meetings hosted. Fishing and watersports nearby.

Special Discounts: 10% senior rates.

"This place is awesome. We will be back."

Monroe

H4

Peterson's B&B

PO Box 142
Monroe, UT 84754-0142
(801)527-4830

Rates: $70-75.
Innkeeper(s): Mary Ann Peterson.
Circa: 1895.

Rooms: 3 rooms, 2 with PB.
Beds: KDT.

Although it appears to be a modern ranch house, this home has sections more than 100 years old. For 20 years Mary Ann has hosted bed & breakfast guests here. A former cooking teacher, she offers breakfasts of Hawaiian French toast, Pannokoken with applesauce and eggs benedict. The fenced yard is shaded by an ancient apple tree. Carport parking is offered at this inn, which is open from April through October. Visit Fremont Indian State Park and discover petroglyphs and pictographs carved into the cliffs, as well as pit dwellings of the Fremonts. Hot springs, seven blocks away, are non-sulfurous. The B&B is near five national parks. Monroe is halfway between Denver and Los Angeles.

Breakfast included in rates. Types of meals: gourmet breakfast and early coffee/tea. Air conditioning and turn-down service in room. Cable TV and VCR on premises. Fishing, parks, shopping, cross-country skiing and theater nearby.

UT

Monticello

J9

The Grist Mill Inn B&B

64 S 300 E
Monticello, UT 84535
(801)587-2597 (800)645-3762
Fax:(801)587-2579

Rates: $72-82.
Payment: MC VISA AX DC DS PC TC.
Innkeeper(s): Brenda O'Berry.
Circa: 1933.

Rooms: 10 rooms with PB, 1 with FP. 1 suite.
Beds: KQDT.

This three-story Salt Box building now houses six guest suites. There is a library on the third floor offering views of Blue Mountains. The Grainery is an addition that was moved here years ago to be used as a home. It offers three guest rooms. A gift shop features local handcrafted items in the setting of an old country store.

Breakfast included in rates. Types of meals: full breakfast, gourmet breakfast and early coffee/tea. Evening snack, catering service and catered breakfast available. Ceiling fan and cable TV in room. VCR, fax, spa and library on premises. Weddings, small meetings, family reunions and seminars hosted. Fishing, parks, shopping and cross-country skiing nearby.

Location: Southeastern corner of Utah in the four corner area, where Colorado, New Mexico, Arizona and Utah come together.

Publicity: *San Juan Happenings.*

Park City

D6

The Old Miners' Lodge - A B&B Inn

615 Woodside Ave,
PO Box 2639
Park City, UT 84060-2639
(801)645-8068 (800)648-8068
Fax:(801)645-7420

Rates: $55-245.
Payment: MC VISA AX DC CB DS PC TC.
Innkeeper(s): Susan Wynne.
Circa: 1889.

Rooms: 12 rooms with PB. 3 suites. 2 conference rooms.
Beds: KQDT.

This originally was established as a miners' boarding house by E. P. Ferry, owner of the Woodside-Norfolk silver mines. A two-story Victorian with Western flavor, the lodge is a significant structure in the Park City National Historic District. Just on the edge of the woods is a deck and a steaming hot tub.

Breakfast and evening snack included in rates. Types of meals: full breakfast and early coffee/tea. Banquet service and catering service available. Turn-down service and ceiling fan in room. Fax, copier, spa and library on premises. Small meetings, family reunions and seminars hosted. Antiques, fishing, parks, shopping, downhill skiing, cross-country skiing and theater nearby. TAC10.

Location: In the Park City Historic District.

Publicity: *Boston Herald, Los Angeles Times, Detroit Free Press, Washington Post, Ski, Bon Appetit.*

Special Discounts: Seasonal - please ask.

"This is the creme de la creme. The most wonderful place I have stayed at bar none, including ski country in the U.S. and Europe."

Washington School Inn

544 Park Ave, PO Box 536
Park City, UT 84060
(801)649-3800 (800)824-1672
Fax:(801)649-3802

Rates: $100-300.
Payment: MC VISA AX DC DS TC.
Innkeeper(s): Nancy Beaufait.
Circa: 1889.

Rooms: 12 rooms with PB, 2 with FP. 3 suites. 2 conference rooms.
Beds: KQT.

Made of local limestone, this inn was the former schoolhouse for Park City children. With its classic bell-tower, the four-story building is listed in the National Register. The inn is noted for its luxuriously appointed guest rooms. Drinks and appetizers are served each afternoon in front of an inviting fire. The inn's Jacuzzi and sauna are perfect places to relax. The hosts also offer the amenities of a concierge service and ski storage, which is helpful since the inn is only one block from ski lifts.

Breakfast, afternoon tea and evening snack included in rates. Type of meal: full breakfast. Cable TV in room. VCR, fax, spa and sauna on premises. Weddings, small meetings and family reunions hosted. Antiques, fishing, parks, shopping, downhill skiing, cross-country skiing, sporting events, theater and watersports nearby. TAC10.

Location: Park City Historic District.

Publicity: *San Diego Magazine, Arizona Daily Star, Salt Lake Tribune.*

"The end of the rainbow."

Providence

Providence Inn B&B

10 S Main
Providence, UT 84332-0099
(801)752-3432 (800)480-4943
Fax:(801)752-3482
E-mail: provinn@cache.net

Rates: $49-149.
Payment: MC VISA AX DC DS PC TC.
Innkeeper(s): Mike & Sonya Davis.
Circa: 1869.

Rooms: 14 rooms with PB, 1 with FP. 4 suites. 2 conference rooms.
Beds: KQDT.

This Georgian structure, known as the Old Rock Church, is listed in the National Register. The inn is elegant inside and out, from its manicured lawns to the king-size plantation bed decorated with ivy in the honeymoon suite. The suite also has a whirlpool tub and fireplace. Other rooms and suites also are decorated in the same refined Georgian style. Gourmet, full breakfasts are served. One specialty of the inn is a dish with flavored cream cheese layered on a boulle dipped in French toast batter, fried and then topped with raspberries, strawberries or maple syrup. The inn was selected as one of 10 sites for QVC to broadcast from, during the network's "Utah Week" series.

Breakfast included in rates. Types of meals: continental breakfast, continental-plus breakfast, full breakfast, gourmet breakfast and early coffee/tea. Picnic lunch, lunch, gourmet lunch, banquet service and catered breakfast available. Air conditioning, turn-down service, cable TV and VCR in room. Fax, copier and library on premises. Handicap access. Weddings, small meetings and seminars hosted. Spanish, German, French and Portuguese spoken. Antiques, fishing, parks, shopping, downhill skiing, cross-country skiing, sporting events, theater and watersports nearby. TAC8.

Salt Lake City

D5

The Log Cabin on The Hill B&B

2275 E 6200 S
Salt Lake City, UT 84121
(801)272-2962

Rates: $75-95.
Payment: MC VISA AX PC.
Innkeeper(s): Geri M. Symes.
Circa: 1941.

Rooms: 4 rooms with PB.
Beds: KQT.

As one might expect, this B&B is located in a log cabin on a hill. The rustic, cozy cabin is a unique contrast to the posh homes located nearby. Rooms are decorated in a Western style with a few natural wood furnishings, stenciled walls and colorful comforters. There is an outdoor hot tub for guests to enjoy. A full breakfast is served daily. One might indulge in coffee, juice, seasonal fruit, homemade strudel and a strata made from fresh-from-the-garden herbs and vegetables.

Breakfast and evening snack included in rates. Type of meal: early coffee/tea. Ceiling fan and cable TV in room. Small meetings, family reunions and seminars hosted. Amusement parks, antiques, fishing, parks, shopping, downhill skiing, cross-country skiing, sporting events and theater nearby. TAC10.

"I arrived bedraggled and road weary. I left refreshed and very well-fed."

Saltair B&B

164 S 900 E
Salt Lake City, UT 84102
(801)533-8184 (800)733-8184
Fax:(801)595-0332

Rates: $79-135.
Payment: MC VISA AX DC CB DS TC.
Innkeeper(s): Michael Harr & Karen Morrell.
Circa: 1903.

Rooms: 5 rooms, 2 with PB.
Beds: QT.

The Saltair is the oldest continuously operating bed & breakfast in Utah and a offers a prime location to enjoy Salt Lake City. The simply decorated rooms include light, airy window dresses, charming furnishings and special touches. One room includes a wood-burning stove and exposed brick. Breakfasts, especially the delicious breads, are memorable. The inn is within walking distance to four historic districts and only one block from Temple Square and the Governor's Mansion. Day trips include treks to several national and state parks and the Wasatch Front ski areas.

Breakfast and evening snack included in rates. Types of meals: continental breakfast, continental-plus breakfast, full breakfast, gourmet breakfast and early coffee/tea. Air conditioning in room. Cable TV, VCR, fax and spa on premises. Weddings, small meetings, family reunions and seminars hosted. Amusement parks, antiques, fishing, parks, shopping, downhill skiing, cross-country skiing, sporting events, theater and watersports nearby. TAC10.

Publicity: *Mobil, Logan Sun.*

"Your swing and Saltair McMuffins were fabulous."

Mountain Hollow B&B Inn

10209 Dimple Dell Rd
Sandy, UT 84092-4536
(801)942-3428 (800)757-3428

Rates: $75-150.
Payment: MC VISA AX DS PC TC.
Innkeeper(s): Doug & Kathy Larson.
Circa: 1974.

Rooms: 11 rooms, 4 with PB, 1 with FP. 2 suites.
Beds: KQDT.

Located just outside of Salt Lake City, this contemporary home is surrounded by the beautiful scenery of Little Cottonwood Canyon and the Watsatch Mountains. Ski areas are about 15 minutes away, and after a day on the slopes, guests can relax in their comfortable, country-style rooms, enjoy a soak in the outdoor hot tub or take on a round of table tennis or pool in the game room. In warm weather, the breakfasts of fresh breads, fruit, cheese, hard boiled eggs and other treats are served on the patio. In cool weather, the morning meal is presented fireside indoors.

Breakfast and evening snack included in rates. Type of meal: continental-plus breakfast. Air conditioning in room. VCR, fax, spa and library on premises. Small meetings, family reunions and seminars hosted. Amusement parks, antiques, fishing, parks, shopping, downhill skiing, cross-country skiing, sporting events, theater and watersports nearby. TAC10.

"We couldn't have asked for a better place to enjoy our honeymoon."

Gateau des Rois (12th Night Cake)

L'Auberge Provencale
White Post, Va.

4½ cups flour
¾ oz. yeast
9 T lukewarm water
1½ t salt
8 whole eggs
1 egg beaten
1 grated lemon rind
7 oz sugar
7 oz. butter, softened
½ lb. candied fruits

Place yeast and water in bowl to activate. Mix flour and sugar together and form a well on the table. Add two eggs and knead dough. Add yeast mixture and incorporate. Add eggs one at a time, alternating between the butter as you continuously knead. Add lemon rind and set aside two tablespoons of the candied fruit. Add remaining candied fruit, mix throughly.

Leave the dough which should be limp to rise over-nite.

Next day:

Knock down the dough, divide into equal parts. Shape each half in the form of a round crown. Place on buttered paper on a baking sheet and leave to rise again.

Brush dough when risen with the beaten egg.

Decorate with crystallised sugar and the remaining candied fruit.

Bake for 25 minutes at 300 degrees until top browns

Cover dough with foil and reduce heat to 250 degrees for 35 minutes.

Serve with your favorite jam.

Note: Baked in convection oven, increase regular oven temp by 25 degrees. We serve peach ginger jam made at L'Auberge Provencale.

Vermont

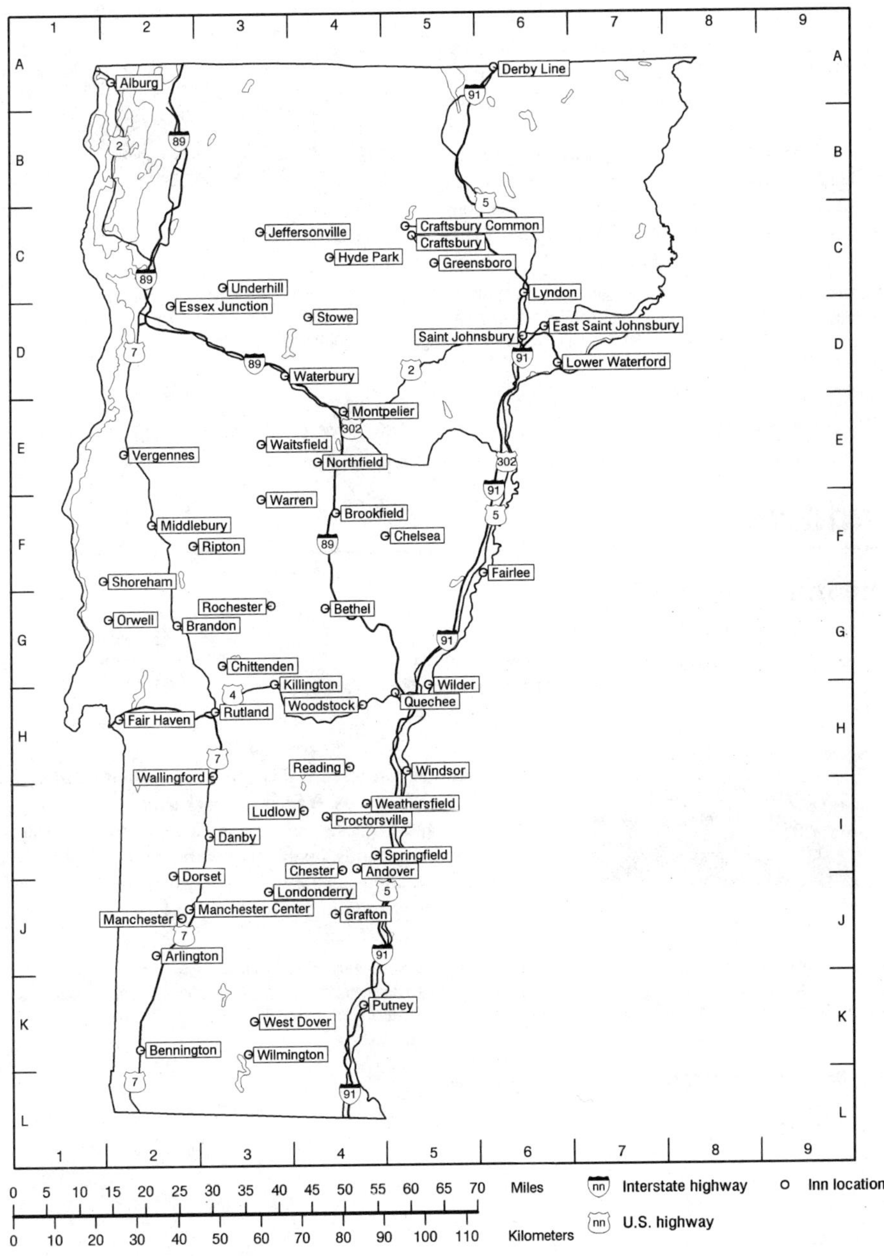

Alburg
Derby Line
Jeffersonville
Craftsbury Common
Craftsbury
Hyde Park
Greensboro
Underhill
Essex Junction
Stowe
Lyndon
East Saint Johnsbury
Saint Johnsbury
Lower Waterford
Waterbury
Montpelier
Waitsfield
Northfield
Vergennes
Warren
Brookfield
Middlebury
Chelsea
Ripton
Fairlee
Shoreham
Rochester
Bethel
Orwell
Brandon
Chittenden
Killington
Wilder
Woodstock
Quechee
Fair Haven
Rutland
Reading
Windsor
Wallingford
Weathersfield
Ludlow
Proctorsville
Danby
Springfield
Chester
Andover
Dorset
Londonderry
Manchester Center
Grafton
Manchester
Arlington
Putney
West Dover
Bennington
Wilmington
Miles
Kilometers
Interstate highway
U.S. highway
Inn location

VT

Alburg

A2

Thomas Mott Homestead B&B

Blue Rock Rd,
Rt 2 Box 149-B
Alburg, VT 05440-9620
(802)796-3736 (800)348-0843
Fax:(802)796-3736

Rates: $69-89.
Payment: MC VISA AX DC CB DS PC TC.
Innkeeper(s): Patrick Schallert.
Circa: 1838.

Rooms: 5 rooms with PB, 1 with FP. 2 suites. 3 conference rooms.
Beds: KQ.

Each room in this restored farmhouse provides a special view of Lake Champlain, yet guests often may be found enjoying the view from the sitting room as they warm by the fireplace. There are also full views of Mt. Mansfield and nearby Jay Peak. Montreal Island is one hour away. Guests are sure to enjoy the complimentary Ben & Jerry's ice cream. Patrick is a noted wine consultant, and holds Master's Degrees in criminology, sociology and the classical arts. A boat dock, extending 75 feet into the lake, recently has been added to the property. The rates include tax and gratuity.

Breakfast and evening snack included in rates. Types of meals: full breakfast, gourmet breakfast and early coffee/tea. Turn-down service and ceiling fan in room. Cable TV, fax, copier and library on premises. Weddings, small meetings, family reunions and seminars hosted. Amusement parks, antiques, fishing, parks, shopping, downhill skiing, cross-country skiing, sporting events, theater and watersports nearby. TAC10.

Location: Northwest corner of Vermont.

Publicity: *Los Angeles Times, St. Alban's Messenger, Yankee Traveler, Boston Globe, Elle, Outside, Prime Time, Vermont Life.*

"Hospitality reigns. I loved the beautiful pressed maple leaf—it is perfect and so personal."

Andover

I4

The Inn at High View

RR 1 Box 201A
Andover, VT 05143-9608
(802)875-2724
Fax:(802)875-4021

Rates: $90-135.
Payment: MC VISA.
Innkeeper(s): Gregory Bohan & Salvatore Massaro.
Circa: 1789.

Rooms: 8 rooms with PB. 2 suites. 1 conference room.
Beds: Beds: KQT.

Relaxation is stressed at this spacious farmhouse inn in the Green Mountains. A fireplace, rock garden, swimming pool and sauna add to guests' enjoyment. Cross-country ski trails are found on the grounds, hooking up with a series of others to provide up to 15 kilometers of uninterrupted skiing. The inn offers advance-reservation dinner service for its guests on weekends and specializes in Italian fare.

Breakfast included in rates. Types of meals: full breakfast and early coffee/tea. Dinner and lunch available. Turn-down service in room. VCR on premises. 72 acres. Weddings, small meetings, family reunions and seminars hosted. Italian, Spanish and English spoken. Antiques, fishing, shopping, downhill skiing, cross-country skiing and theater nearby. TAC10.

Pets Allowed: Special arrangements in suites only.

Special Discounts: Midweek and four nights plus usually 10% off.

Arlington J2

Hill Farm Inn

RR 2 Box 2015
Arlington, VT 05250-9311
(802)375-2269 (800)882-2545
Fax:(802)375-9918

Rates: $70-120.
Payment: MC VISA AX DS.
Innkeeper(s): George & Joanne Hardy, Kelly Stork.
Circa: 1790.

Rooms: 17 rooms, 10 with PB. 2 suites.
Beds: KQTD.

One of Vermont's original land grant farmsteads, Hill Farm Inn has welcomed guests since 1905 when the widow Mettie Hill opened her home to summer vacationers. The farm is surrounded by 50 peaceful acres that border the Battenkill River. Guests can relax and enjoy the simple life and 360-degree views of the mountains. Guest rooms are charming and cozy. Summer guests have the option of staying in one of four cabins. A large, country breakfast of homemade fare starts off each day.

Breakfast and afternoon tea included in rates. Types of meals: full breakfast and early coffee/tea. Dinner available. Cable TV, fax and copier on premises. 50 acres. Weddings, small meetings and family reunions hosted. Antiques, fishing, parks, shopping, downhill skiing and cross-country skiing nearby.

Pets Allowed: In cabins only.

Location: One-half mile from Historic Route 7A.

Publicity: *Providence Journal, Boston Globe, Innsider.*

"A superb location with lots to do indoors and out. Beautifully kept rooms and excellent home cooking."

Bennington K2

Molly Stark Inn

1067 Main St
Bennington, VT 05201-2635
(802)442-9631 (800)356-3076
Fax:(802)442-5224

Rates: $65-150.
Payment: MC VISA AX DS PC TC.
Innkeeper(s): Reed & Cammi Fendler.
Circa: 1890.

Rooms: 7 rooms with PB, 1 with FP. 1 cottage.
Beds: KDT.

This attractive Queen Anne Victorian inn has been serving travelers for more than 50 years. Careful restoration has enabled it to retain its Victorian charm while offering the comforts today's guests have come to expect. Features include antique furnishings, clawfoot tubs, hardwood floors, handmade quilts and a woodstove. The inn's convenient Main Street location puts it within walking distance of many restaurants and shops, and just minutes from Historic Old Bennington. The Bennington Museum boasts paintings by Grandma Moses.

Breakfast and evening snack included in rates. Types of meals: full breakfast and gourmet breakfast. Air conditioning, ceiling fan and cable TV in room. Bicycles on premises. Weddings, small meetings and family reunions hosted. Antiques, fishing, parks, shopping, downhill skiing, cross-country skiing, theater and watersports nearby. TAC10.

Bethel G4

Greenhurst Inn

River St, Rd 2, Box 60
Bethel, VT 05032-9404
(802)234-9474 (800)510-2553

Rates: $50-100. EP.
Payment: MC VISA DS PC TC.
Innkeeper(s): Lyle & Claire Wolf.
Circa: 1890.

Rooms: 13 rooms, 7 with PB, 4 with FP.
Beds: QDT.

In the National Register of Historic Places, Greenhurst is a gracious Victorian mansion built for the Harringtons of Philadelphia. Overlooking the White River, the inn's opulent interiors include etched windows once featured on the cover of Vermont Life.There are eight masterpiece fireplaces and a north and south parlor.

Breakfast included in rates. Types of meals: continental breakfast, continental-plus breakfast and early coffee/tea. EP. Air conditioning in room. Cable TV, VCR and library on premises. Weddings, small meetings, family reunions and seminars hosted. Spanish and French spoken. Antiques, fishing, parks, shopping, downhill skiing, cross-country skiing, theater and watersports nearby.

Pets Allowed: Dogs only.

Location: Midway between Boston and Montreal.

Publicity: *Los Angeles Times, Time, New York Times, Vermont Life.*

"The inn is magnificent! The hospitality unforgettable."

Brandon G2

Churchill House Inn

RR 3 Box 3265
Brandon, VT 05733-9202
(802)247-3078
Fax:(802)247-6851
E-mail: Rciatt@sover.net

Rates: $140-170. MAP.
Payment: MC VISA.
Innkeeper(s): The Jackson Family.
Circa: 1871.

Rooms: 8 rooms with PB.
Beds: QDT.

Caleb Churchill and his son, Nathan, first built a three-story lumber mill, a grist mill and a distillery here, all water powered. Later, with their milled lumber, they constructed this 20-room house. Because of its location it became a stagecoach stop and has served generations of travelers with comfortable accommodations. The inn maintains cross-country ski and hiking trails in the adjacent Green Mountain National Forest. The innkeepers also organize what are known as "inn to inn" cross-country skiing, hiking or bicycling trips. Inn guests also receive a discount off greens fees at a nearby 18-hole course.

Breakfast and dinner included in rates. Type of meal: full breakfast. Picnic lunch available. MAP. Sauna and bicycles on premises. Family reunions hosted. Antiques, parks, shopping, downhill skiing, cross-country skiing and watersports nearby.

Location: Four miles east of Brandon.

Publicity: *Country, Yankee.*

"We felt the warm, welcoming, down-home appeal as we entered the front hall. The food was uncommonly good — home cooking with a gourmet flair!"

The Lilac Inn

53 Park St
Brandon, VT 05733-1121
(802)247-5463 (800)221-0720
Fax:(802)247-5499
E-mail: lilacinn@sovernet.co

Rates: $100-250.
Payment: MC VISA AX DS PC TC.
Innkeeper(s): Michael & Melanie Shane.
Circa: 1909.

Rooms: 9 rooms with PB, 3 with FP. 1 conference room.
Beds: QT.

For some, the scenery is enough of a reason to visit Vermont. For those who need more, try the Lilac Inn. The restored inn's beautiful furnishings, polished woodwork and fireplaces add to the ambiance. Canopy beds dressed with fine linens, flowers, whirlpool tubs and sitting areas grace the guest rooms. A full, gourmet breakfast is included in the rates, but guests also should could consider taking dinner at the inn. There are two possibilities. The Tavern Room offers casual fare such as soup, sandwiches and pasta. Dinner at the Garden Room is a one-and-a-half hour, four-course experience.

Breakfast included in rates. Types of meals: full breakfast, gourmet breakfast and early coffee/tea. Afternoon tea, dinner, banquet service and catering service available. Turn-down service, ceiling fan and cable TV in room. Fax, copier, bicycles and library on premises. Handicap access. Weddings, small meetings, family reunions and seminars hosted. Antiques, fishing, parks, shopping, downhill skiing, cross-country skiing, theater and watersports nearby. TAC10.

Special Discounts: All inclusive weekend packages available.

"Tasteful, charming and personable."

Rosebelle's Victorian Inn

PO Box 370, Rt 7
Brandon, VT 05733-0370
(802)247-0098 (888)767-3235
E-mail: rosebel@vermontel.com

Rates: $75-95.
Payment: MC VISA AX PC TC.
Innkeeper(s): Ginette & Norm Milot.
Circa: 1839.

Rooms: 6 rooms, 4 with PB.
Beds: QDT.

This elegant Second Empire Victorian inn with mansard roof is listed in the National Register of Historic Places. The home was part of the Underground Railroad. Impressive both inside and out, the inn and its six guest rooms have been lovingly furnished with authentic Victorian pieces by the innkeepers. Favorite gathering spots include the comfortable common rooms and the wicker-filled porch. Guests also enjoy strolling the lush grounds where they often experience close encounters with butterflies and hummingbirds. The innkeepers, who speak French, offer gift certificates and special packages. The inn is near Middlebury College and minutes from major ski areas.

Breakfast included in rates. Type of meal: full breakfast. Ceiling fan in room. Cable TV and VCR on premises. Weddings, small meetings and family reunions hosted. Antiques, fishing, parks, shopping, downhill skiing, cross-country skiing, sporting events, theater and watersports nearby. TAC10.

Location: Heart of Vermont and only a short drive to all of Vermont's special interests.

"You have captured a beautiful part of our history."

Brookfield F4

Green Trails Inn

PO Box 494
Brookfield, VT 05036-0494
(802)276-3412 (800)243-3412
Fax:(802)276-3412
E-mail: greentrails@quest-net.com

Rates: $75-125.
Payment: MC VISA PC TC.
Innkeeper(s): Sue & Mark Erwin.
Circa: 1790.

Rooms: 14 rooms, 8 with PB, 1 with FP. 2 suites. 3 conference rooms.
Beds: QDT.

Two historic buildings, one constructed in 1790 and the other in 1830, comprise this inn. The innkeepers have an impressive clock collection, and clock restoration and repair on the premises. Many guest rooms offer views of the lake. One suite has a fireplace, another has a private Jacuzzi. The inn is across the street from Sunset Lake and the Floating Bridge. Cross-country skiing is right outside the door, and there are a number of outdoor activities nearby.

Breakfast included in rates. Types of meals: full breakfast and early coffee/tea. VCR, fax, copier, swimming, bicycles and library on premises. 17 acres. Weddings, small meetings, family reunions and seminars hosted. Antiques, fishing, parks, shopping, downhill skiing, theater and watersports nearby. TAC10.

Pets Allowed: Boarding nearby.

Publicity: *Sunday Republican.*

"The inn is really lovely, the welcome very warm and food is scrumptious."

Chelsea F5

Shire Inn

8 Main St, PO Box 37
Chelsea, VT 05038
(802)685-3031 (800)441-6908
Fax:(802)685-3871
E-mail: shireinn@sover.net

Rates: $86-210. MAP.
Payment: MC VISA DS PC TC.
Innkeeper(s): Jay & Karen Keller.
Circa: 1832.

Rooms: 6 rooms with PB, 4 with FP.
Beds: KQD.

VT

Granite lintels over the windows and a sunburst light over the entry highlight this Adams-style brick home. The inn, which is located in a 210-year-old historic village, has a grand spiral staircase ascending from wide-plank pumpkin pine floors in the entryway. Guest rooms include antique canopied beds, tall windows and 10-foot ceilings. Most have wood-burning fireplaces. Included on the property's 23 acres are granite post fencing, perennial gardens dating from the 19th century, and a broad, rocky stream spanned by a farm bridge.

Breakfast and dinner included in rates. Types of meals: full breakfast and early coffee/tea. Afternoon tea available. MAP. Fax, copier, bicycles and library on premises. 23 acres. Weddings, small meetings and family reunions hosted. Antiques, fishing, parks, shopping, downhill skiing, cross-country skiing, theater and watersports nearby. TAC10.

Publicity: *Country Inn Review, Vermont Life.*

"What an inn should be! Absolutely delicious food - great hospitality! The rooms are filled with romance."

Chester

I4

Henry Farm Inn

PO Box 646
Chester, VT 05143-0646
(802)875-2674 (800)723-8213
Fax:(802)875-2674

Rates: $55-85.
Payment: MC VISA AX PC TC.
Innkeeper(s): Barbara Bowman.
Circa: 1760.

Rooms: 7 rooms with PB.
Beds: KQT.

Fifty acres of scenic woodlands provide the setting for this handsomely restored stagecoach stop in the Green Mountains. There are original wide pine floors and carefully selected early American furnishings. A pond and river are nearby.

Types of meals: full breakfast and early coffee/tea. Afternoon tea available. VCR, fax and copier on premises. 50 acres. Weddings, small meetings and family reunions hosted. TAC10.

Location: Ten miles from I-91.

"Very comfortable and pleasant."

Hugging Bear Inn & Shoppe

Main St
Chester, VT 05143
(802)875-2412 (800)325-0519
Fax:(802)875-3823
E-mail: huggingbear@vbv-online.com

Rates: $55-95.
Payment: MC VISA AX DS PC TC.
Innkeeper(s): Georgette Thomas.
Circa: 1850.

Rooms: 6 rooms with PB.
Beds: DT.

Among the 4,000 teddy bear inhabitants of this white Victorian inn, several peek out from the third-story windows of the octagonal tower. There is a teddy bear shop on the premises and children and adults can borrow a bear to take to bed with them. Rooms are decorated with antiques and comfortable furniture. A bear puppet show is often staged during breakfast.

Breakfast included in rates. Types of meals: full breakfast and early coffee/tea. Catered breakfast available. Cable TV, VCR and library on premises. Small meetings and family reunions hosted. Antiques, fishing, parks, shopping, downhill skiing and cross-country skiing nearby.

Pets Allowed: Limited - prior conference.

Publicity: *Rutland Daily Herald, Exxon Travel, Teddy Bear Review.*

"Thanks seems to be too small of a word to describe our greatest appreciation toward all of you for all of your warmth and hospitality."

The Madrigal Inn & Fine Arts Center, Ltd.

61 Williams River Rd
Chester, VT 05143
(802)463-1339 (800)854-2208

Rates: $90.
Innkeeper(s): Raymond & Nancy Dressler.
Circa: 1992.

Rooms: 11 rooms with PB. 1 conference room.

This contemporary post-and-beam inn in the Green Mountains provides a peaceful and romantic getaway. Its guest rooms feature views of the farmland, meadows, rivers and woods of the surrounding area. Breakfasts are enjoyed in the dining room and often feature Vermont French toast with local maple syrup. For those choosing to relax at the inn, the loft library and patio are popular locations. A Steinway grand piano is available for the musically inclined and an art studio is on the premises.

Breakfast included in rates. Type of meal: early coffee/tea. Dinner and evening snack available. 60 acres. Weddings, small meetings, family reunions and seminars hosted. Shopping, downhill skiing and cross-country skiing nearby.

Publicity: *Vermont, Bellows Falls Town Crier, Retirement.*

"We're still glowing over the lovely overnight visit to your inn."

Old Town Farm Inn

RR 4, Box 383B, State Rt 10
Chester, VT 05143
(802)875-2346 (800)217-9085

Rates: $62-82.
Payment: MC VISA DS PC TC.
Innkeeper(s): Fred & Jan Baldwin.
Circa: 1861.

Rooms: 11 rooms, 5 with PB.
Beds: QDT.

This comfortable New England inn with its elegant spiral staircase was called the Town Farm of Chester because anyone who needed food and lodging were provided for, in return for a day's work on the farm. Fred R. Smith, famous as "Uncle Sam" in the '20s and '30s resided here. Artists have been inspired by the scenic views, which include a pond and meadow and woodlands inhabited by deer and wild turkey. Maple syrup from surrounding trees is served, as is the family's popular "Country Inn Spring Water."

Breakfast included in rates. Type of meal: full breakfast. Cable TV, VCR, swimming and library on premises. 11 acres. Antiques, fishing, parks, shopping, downhill skiing, cross-country skiing and theater nearby.

Publicity: *Yankee Magazine.*

"A warm haven! Very friendly and comfortable."

Chittenden G3

Tulip Tree Inn

Chittenden Dam Rd
Chittenden, VT 05737
(802)483-6213 (800)707-0017
E-mail: ttinn@sover.net

Rates: $120-269. MAP.
Payment: MC VISA PC TC.
Innkeeper(s): Ed & Rosemary McDowell.
Circa: 1830.

Rooms: 8 rooms with PB.
Beds: Q.

Thomas Edison was a regular guest here when the house was the country home of William Barstow. The inn is surrounded by the Green Mountains on three sides with a stream flowing a few yards away. The guest rooms feature antiques and Vermont country decor. Guests enjoy both breakfast and dinner at the inn. Buttermilk pancakes topped with Vermont maple syrup are typical breakfast fare, and dinners include such items as medallions of pork topped with an orange-apricot sauce and white chocolate cheesecake.

Breakfast and dinner included in rates. Types of meals: full breakfast and early coffee/tea. MAP. Library on premises. Weddings and small meetings hosted. Amusement parks, antiques, fishing, parks, shopping, downhill skiing, cross-country skiing, theater and watersports nearby. TAC10.

Publicity: *New England Getaways.*

"Tulip Tree Inn is one of the warmest, friendliest and coziest country inns you'll find in New England, New England Getaways."

Craftsbury

C5

Craftsbury Inn

Main St, Box 36
Craftsbury, VT 05826-0036
(802)586-2848 (800)336-2848

Rates: $60-150. MAP, AP.
Payment: MC VISA TC.
Innkeeper(s): Blake & Rebecca Gleason.
Circa: 1850.

Rooms: 10 rooms, 6 with PB. 1 conference room.
Beds: QDT.

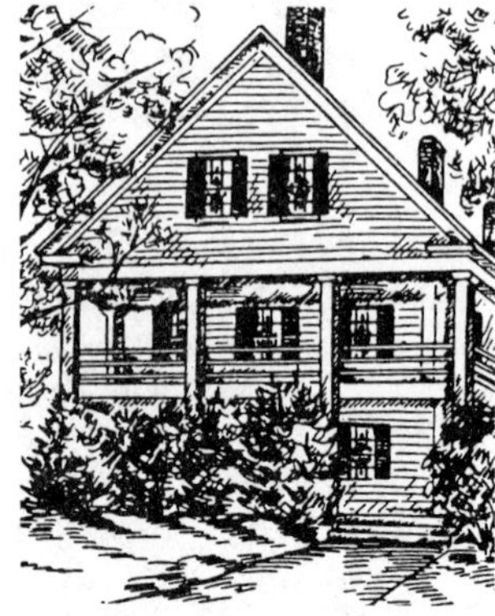

Bird's-eye maple woodwork and embossed tin ceilings testify to the history of this Greek Revival inn, which also features random-width floors with square nails. The foundation and porch steps were made of bullseye granite, quarried in town. The living room fireplace once graced the first post office in Montpelier. Guest rooms sport country antiques and handmade quilts. The dining room is open to the public by advance reservation and features four dinner seatings.

Breakfast included in rates. Type of meal: full breakfast. Dinner, picnic lunch, banquet service, catering service and catered breakfast available. MAP, AP. VCR on premises. Weddings, small meetings, family reunions and seminars hosted. Antiques, fishing, shopping, downhill skiing, cross-country skiing and watersports nearby.

Craftsbury Common

C5

The Inn on The Common

PO Box 75
Craftsbury Common, VT
05827-0075
(802)586-9619 (800)521-2233
Fax:(802)586-2249

Rates: $190-270. MAP.
Payment: MC VISA.
Innkeeper(s): Michael & Penny Schmitt.
Circa: 1795.

Rooms: 16 rooms with PB. 2 suites. 1 conference room.
Beds: KQDT.

The Inn on the Common, built by the Samuel French family, is an integral part of this picturesque classic Vermont village. With its white picket fence and graceful white clapboard exterior, the inn provides a quietly elegant retreat. Pastoral views are framed by the inn's famous perennial gardens.

Breakfast and dinner included in rates. Type of meal: full breakfast. Picnic lunch available. MAP. Fishing, downhill skiing, cross-country skiing and watersports nearby.

Pets Allowed.

Publicity: *New York Times, Craftsbury Common, Harper's Hideaway Report, Discerning Travel.*

"The closest my wife and I came to fulfilling our fantasy of a country inn was at The Inn on the Common," — Paul Grimes.

Danby

I3

Silas Griffith Inn

South Main St
Danby, VT 05739
(802)293-5567 (800)545-1509

Rates: $70-100.
Payment: MC VISA PC TC.
Innkeeper(s): Paul & Lois Dansereau.
Circa: 1891.

Rooms: 17 rooms, 14 with PB.
Beds: QT.

Originally on 55,000 acres, this stately Queen Anne Victorian mansion features solid cherry, oak and bird's-eye maple woodwork. Considered an architectural marvel, an eight-foot, round, solid-cherry pocket door separates the original music room from the front parlor.

Breakfast and afternoon tea included in rates. Types of meals: full breakfast, gourmet breakfast and early coffee/tea. Picnic lunch available. Cable TV, VCR, swimming and library on premises. 11 acres. Weddings, small meetings, family reunions and seminars hosted. Antiques, fishing, parks, shopping, downhill skiing, cross-country skiing, theater and watersports nearby.

Publicity: *Vermont Weathervane, Rutland Business Journal, Vermont, Country Magazine.*

"Never have I stayed at a B&B where the innkeepers were so friendly, sociable and helpful. They truly enjoyed their job."

Derby Line

A6

The Birchwood Bed & Breakfast

PO Box 550
Derby Line, VT 05830-0550
(802)873-9104
Fax:(802)873-9121
E-mail: birchwd@together.net

Rates: $65-70.
Payment: PC.
Innkeeper(s): Dick & Betty Fletcher.
Circa: 1920.

Rooms: 3 rooms with PB.
Beds: QDT.

Guests in search of a romantic atmosphere will have no trouble finding it at this cozy bed & breakfast. Fresh flowers, chocolates and luxury bath soaps are among the items waiting in bed chambers, which are decorated with antiques. The innkeeper also serves her gourmet breakfasts by candlelight. Derby Line, located near the Canadian border in northern Vermont, offers beautiful scenery and close access to fishing, water sports, golf and many more outdoor activities. Sleigh rides are a popular winter activity.

Breakfast included in rates. Types of meals: full breakfast and gourmet breakfast. Afternoon tea available. Cable TV, fax and library on premises. Small meetings, family reunions and seminars hosted. Antiques, fishing, parks, shopping, downhill skiing, cross-country skiing, theater and watersports nearby.

"Heaven can wait. When I die I am going to Vermont and stay much longer at The Birchwood."

Derby Village Inn

46 Main St
Derby Line, VT 05830-9203
(802)873-3604

Rates: $60-70.
Payment: MC VISA DS PC TC.
Innkeeper(s): Tom & Phyllis Moreau.
Circa: 1900.

Rooms: 8 rooms, 5 with PB.
Beds: QDT.

This stately Victorian manor is more formal than whimsical, without the abundance of gingerbread trim common to the colorful "Painted Ladies." The interior is elegant, boasting intricate wainscoting and original light fixtures. Antique-filled bedchambers are decorated with lovely wallpapers, Victorian sinks and vintage wall fixtures. The parlors are wonderful places to relax, one includes a baby grand piano and a fireplace. The inn's library also includes a fireplace. Innkeeper Phyllis Moreau's vast collection of Norman Rockwell plates decorates the high shelves that surround the kitchen. Phyllis also has designed many of the rugs and crafts found throughout the home.

Breakfast included in rates. Types of meals: full breakfast and early coffee/tea. Cable TV and library on premises. Small meetings, family reunions and seminars hosted. Antiques, fishing, parks, shopping, downhill skiing, cross-country skiing, theater and watersports nearby.

Dorset

I2

Marble West Inn

PO Box 847, Dorset West Rd
Dorset, VT 05251-0847
(802)867-4155 (800)453-7629

Rates: $90-135.
Payment: MC VISA AX PC.
Innkeeper(s): June & Wayne Erla.
Circa: 1840.

Rooms: 8 rooms with PB, 1 with FP. 1 suite.
Beds: KQDT.

This historic Greek Revival inn boasts many elegant touches, including stenciling in its entrance hallways done by one of the nation's top craftspeople. Guests also will enjoy Oriental rugs, handsome marble fireplaces and polished dark oak floors. Visitors delight at the many stunning views enjoyed at the inn, including Green Peak and Owl's Head mountains, flower-filled gardens and meadows and two trout-stocked ponds. Emerald Lake State Park is nearby.

Breakfast and afternoon tea included in rates. Type of meal: full breakfast. Turn-down service in room. Library on premises. Antiques, fishing, parks, shopping, downhill skiing, cross-country skiing, theater and watersports nearby.

"A charming inn with wonderful hospitality. The room was comfortable, immaculate, and furnished with every imaginable need and comfort."

East Saint Johnsbury

D6

Echo Ledge Farm Inn

PO Box 46, East Saint
Johnsbury, VT 05838-0046
(802)748-4750

Rates: $40-67.
Payment: MC VISA.
Innkeeper(s): Marcella & Rod Lamotte.
Circa: 1793.

Rooms: 6 rooms, 5 with PB.
Beds: DT.

Phineas Page settled here on the banks of the Moose River. Later, his son supervised the farm and made it a political meeting place where representatives were chosen for Congress. The innkeepers have created a warm, cozy atmosphere, pampering guests as if they were at Grandma's house. An all-you-can-eat breakfast is served as is afternoon tea. The inn offers plenty of opportunities for relaxation. Guests can sit on the porch and enjoy the view or stroll the grounds on walking trails and watch for moose, deer and other creatures. The area is rich for those wishing to hunt or fish. Innkeepers can also help guests find hay and sleigh rides.

Breakfast included in rates. Type of meal: full breakfast. Afternoon tea and picnic lunch available. Antiques, fishing, downhill skiing, cross-country skiing and theater nearby.

Location: Five miles east of St. Johnsbury on Rt. 2.

Publicity: *Vermont Country Sampler.*

"Great. We'll come back again! Very much like being at home."

Essex Junction

D2

Country Comfort B&B

36 Old Stage Rd
Essex Junction, VT 05452
(802)878-2589

Rates: $55-70.
Payment: MC VISA PC TC.
Innkeeper(s): Eva & Ed Blake.
Circa: 1967.

Rooms: 5 rooms, 2 with PB.
Beds: QDT.

Guests truly do enjoy a special country comfort at this bed & breakfast. Rooms are decorated with stenciling, pastel wallcoverings, quilts, antique braided rugs and a few country knickknacks or collectibles. The site of grazing sheep and the occasional cluck from one of the innkeeper's hens, adds to the bucolic charm of the place. Breakfasts include down-home fare, with a healthier twist. For instance, guests might enjoy whole-wheat pancakes topped with Vermont maple syrup, fried apples and lowfat sausage.

Breakfast included in rates. Types of meals: full breakfast and early coffee/tea. Ceiling fan in room. VCR on premises. Antiques, fishing, parks, shopping, downhill skiing, cross-country skiing, sporting events, theater and watersports nearby.

"I looked forward, each night, to return to peace, quiet and a comfortable bed."

Fair Haven

H2

Fair Haven Inn B&B

18 Main St
Fair Haven, VT 05743
(802)265-4907 (800)325-7074
Fax:(802)265-8814
E-mail: fhifhvt@sover.net

Rates: $75-85.
Payment: MC VISA AX PC TC.
Innkeeper(s): Peter & Joan Lemnotis.
Circa: 1820.

Rooms: 3 rooms with PB.
Beds: QDT.

The curved wraparound porch of this yellow and white two-story house welcomes guests to relaxed accommodations. Across the lawn is the Fair Haven Inn, a restaurant that offers a choice of fine dining, a tavern and a banquet room. A marbleized fireplace, pocket doors, a bay window in the dining room and inlaid floors are among the inn's offerings. There are four common rooms including a sitting room, den, and gym with a TV.

Breakfast included in rates. Type of meal: full breakfast. Picnic lunch available. Air conditioning and cable TV in room. VCR, fax and copier on premises. Weddings, small meetings, family reunions and seminars hosted. Amusement parks, antiques, fishing, parks, shopping, downhill skiing, cross-country skiing, sporting events and watersports nearby.

Special Discounts: November through April stay two nights, third night free (holidays excluded).

Maplewood Inn

Rt 22A S
Fair Haven, VT 05743
(802)265-8039 (800)253-7729
Fax:(802)265-8210
E-mail: maplewd@sover.net

Rates: $75-125.
Payment: MC VISA AX DC CB DS PC TC.
Innkeeper(s): Cindy & Doug Baird.
Circa: 1843.

Rooms: 5 rooms with PB, 4 with FP. 2 suites. 1 conference room.
Beds: QD.

This beautifully restored Greek Revival house was once the family home of the founder of Maplewood Dairy, Isaac Wood. Period antiques and reproductions grace the inn's spacious rooms and suites. Some rooms boast fireplaces and all have sitting areas. A collection of antique spinning wheels and yarn winders is displayed. A porch wing, built around 1795, was a tavern formerly located down the road. Overlooking three acres of lawn, the inn offers an idyllic setting. The parlor's cordial bar and evening turndown service are among the many amenities offered by the innkeepers.

Breakfast, afternoon tea and evening snack included in rates. Air conditioning, turn-down service, cable TV and VCR in room. Fax, copier and library on premises. Small meetings and family reunions hosted. Amusement parks, antiques, fishing, parks, shopping, downhill skiing, cross-country skiing, sporting events, theater and watersports nearby. TAC10.

Location: One mile south of Fair Haven village and 18 miles west of Rutland.

Publicity: *Country, Innsider, Americana, New England Getaways.*

"Your inn is perfection. Leaving under protest."

Fairlee

F6

Silver Maple Lodge & Cottages

S Main St, RR 1, Box 8
Fairlee, VT 05045
(802)333-4326 (800)666-1946

Rates: $49-74.
Payment: MC VISA AX DS PC TC.
Innkeeper(s): Scott & Sharon Wright.
Circa: 1790.

Rooms: 16 rooms, 14 with PB, 3 with FP. 8 cottages.
Beds: KQDT.

This old Cape farmhouse was expanded in the 1850s and became an inn in the '20s when Elmer & Della Batchelder opened their home to guests. It became so successful that several cottages, built from lumber on the property, were added. For 60 years, the Batchelder family continued the operation. They misnamed the lodge, however, mistaking silver poplar trees on the property for what they thought were silver maples. Guest rooms are decorated with many of the inn's original furnishings and the new innkeepers have carefully restored the rooms and added several bathrooms. A screened-in porch surrounds two sides of the house. Three of the cottages include working fireplaces and one is handicap accessible.

Breakfast included in rates. Type of meal: continental breakfast. VCR, copier and bicycles on premises. Handicap access. Small meetings and family reunions hosted. Antiques, fishing, parks, shopping, skiing, theater and watersports nearby. TAC10.

Pets Allowed: Cottage rooms only.

Location: East central Vermont.

Publicity: *Boston Globe, Vermont Country Sampler, Travel Holiday.*

Special Discounts: 10% off for corporate and senior guests.

"Your gracious hospitality and attractive home all add up to a pleasant experience."

Grafton

J4

Old Tavern at Grafton

Main St
Grafton, VT 05146
(802)843-2231 (800)843-1801
Fax:(802)843-2245
E-mail: Tavern@sover.net

Rates: $79-230. EP.
Payment: MC VISA PC TC.
Innkeeper(s): Tom List, Jr.
Circa: 1801.

Rooms: 66 rooms with PB, 6 with FP. 7 cottages. 5 conference rooms.
Beds: QDT.

This elegantly appointed hotel inn serves as a wonderful place to enjoy New England's charm and rustic atmosphere. Beautiful rooms feature antiques, traditional furnishings, four-poster beds, lace, Oriental rugs and gracious knickknacks. The innkeepers also offer six guest houses, which can sleep up to 14 people and most of the houses include full kitchens. Traditional New England fare is prepared and served up in the elegant dining room. The innkeepers offer stable facilities and the area boasts plenty of outdoor activities. Bicycles are available and the guests also can enjoy shuffleboard, billiard, pingpong, tennis and swimming. A 30-kilometer, cross-country skiing center also is on the premises. The inn often is the site for weddings, receptions and meetings.

Breakfast and afternoon tea included in rates. Types of meals: full breakfast and early coffee/tea. Dinner, picnic lunch, lunch, banquet service and catering service available. EP. Ceiling fan in room. Cable TV, fax, copier, swimming, stables, bicycles, tennis and library on premises. Handicap access. Weddings, small meetings, family reunions and seminars hosted. Dutch, German, French and Spanish spoken. Antiques, fishing, parks, shopping, downhill skiing, cross-country skiing, theater and watersports nearby. TAC10.

Publicity: *Spotlight, Boston Globe, Worchester Telegram & Gazette, Travel America, Chicago Tribune, Boston Herald, Harper's Hideaway Report.*

Special Discounts: Frequent stays (within 6 months less 5%); $95 mid-week, all rooms, Sunday-Thursday.

Greensboro

C5

Highland Lodge

RR 1 Box 1290
Greensboro, VT 05841-9712
(802)533-2647
Fax:(802)533-7494

Rates: $175-220. MAP.
Payment: MC VISA DS PC TC.
Innkeeper(s): Wilhemina & David Smith.
Circa: 1865.

Rooms: 11 cottages with PB, 11 with FP.
Beds: QDT.

With more than seven miles of lake shore and 120 acres to enjoy, guests rarely have trouble finding a way to pass the time at this lodge. The lodge is located in a mid-19th-century farmhouse, and visitors either room here in country guest rooms or in a collection of cottages. The cottages have from one to three bedrooms, a living room, bathroom and a porch. All guests are welcome to use the lodge's common areas or simply relax on the porch, but there's sailing, swimming, fishing, boating and much more on the premises. In the winter, there are plenty of cross-country ski trails. The breakfast choices might include French toast, waffles, pancakes, eggs or muffins, and at dinner, guests choose from four entrees accompanied by salad, homemade bread and dessert.

Breakfast and dinner included in rates. Types of meals: full breakfast, gourmet breakfast and early coffee/tea. Afternoon tea, picnic lunch and lunch available. MAP. Ceiling fan in room. Fax, copier, swimming, bicycles, tennis, library and child care on premises. Handicap access. 150 acres. Weddings, small meetings, family reunions and seminars hosted. Dutch spoken. Antiques, fishing, downhill skiing, cross-country skiing and theater nearby. TAC10.

Publicity: *New England Skiers Guide, Vermont Magazine, Hardwick Gazette, Rural New England Magazine, Better Homes and Gardens, Providence Sunday Journal.*

Special Discounts: Mid-week June, May, January, March, $175 per couple.

"We had a great time last weekend and enjoyed everything we did—hiking, climbing, swimming, canoeing and eating."

Hyde Park C4

Fitch Hill Inn

RFD 1 Box 1879
Hyde Park, VT 05655-9801
(802)888-3834 (800)639-2903
Fax:(802)888-7789

Rates: $69-145.
Payment: MC VISA AX PC TC.
Innkeeper(s): Richard A. Pugliese & Stanley E. Corklin.
Circa: 1797.

Rooms: 6 rooms with PB, 2 with FP. 1 suite. 1 cottage. 1 conference room.
Beds: QDT.

This Federalist-style home sits on five acres of hilltop land overlooking the village and Green Mountains. There are three lovely porches with spectacular views. The five, second-floor guest rooms share a period-furnished living room and movie library. There also is an efficiency apartment available with a whirlpool tub, fireplace, deck and kitchen. Hearty Vermont breakfasts are served in the dining room. Gourmet, candlelight dinners can be arranged by advance reservation.

Breakfast and afternoon tea included in rates. Types of meals: full breakfast, gourmet breakfast and early coffee/tea. Dinner and picnic lunch available. Air conditioning, ceiling fan, cable TV and VCR in room. Spa, bicycles and library on premises. Weddings, small meetings, family reunions and seminars hosted. English, Spanish and some French spoken. Amusement parks, antiques, fishing, parks, downhill skiing, cross-country skiing, theater and watersports nearby. TAC10.

Location: Ten miles north of Stowe.

Publicity: *Stower Reporter, Morrisville News Dispatch, Out & About Magazine, Eco-Traveller, Country Living.*

"We were very impressed with your inn, from the atmosphere to the wonderful hospitality (not to mention those killer breakfasts!). For our first visit to a B&B, it was a terrific experience. I'm sure you'll be seeing us again."

Jeffersonville C3

Jefferson House

PO Box 288, Main St
Jeffersonville, VT 05464
(802)644-2030 (800)253-9630
E-mail: jeffhouse@pwshift.com

Rates: $50-65.
Payment: DS PC TC.
Innkeeper(s): Joan & Richard Walker.
Circa: 1910.

Rooms: 3 rooms, 1 with PB.
Beds: QDT.

Three comfortable guest rooms, decorated in a country Victorian style, are the offerings at this turn-of-the-century home. As one might expect, pancakes topped with Vermont maple syrup are often a staple at the breakfast table, accompanied by savory items such as smoked bacon. Each season brings a new activity to this scenic area. In the winter, it's just a few minutes to Smugglers' Notch ski area, and Stowe isn't far. Biking or hiking to the top of Mt. Mansfield are popular summer activities.

Breakfast included in rates. Type of meal: full breakfast. Air conditioning in room. Cable TV and VCR on premises. Amusement parks, antiques, fishing, parks, shopping, downhill skiing, cross-country skiing, sporting events, theater and watersports nearby.

Pets Allowed: By prior arrangement.

Killington

G3

The Cascades Lodge & Restaurant

RR 1 Box 2848
Killington, VT 05751-9710
(802)422-3731 (800)345-0113
Fax:(802)422-3351

Rates: $50-159. MAP, EP.
Payment: MC VISA AX DS TC.
Innkeeper(s): Bob, Vickie & Andrew MacKenzie.
Circa: 1980.

Rooms: 46 rooms, 45 with PB. 6 suites.
Beds: QD.

Breathtaking views and modern amenities are found at this contemporary three-story country lodge in the heart of the Green Mountains. Guests enjoy an exercise area, indoor pool with sundeck, sauna and whirlpool. A bar and restaurant are on the premises, and the inn's amenities make it an ideal spot for meetings, reunions or weddings. Within walking distance is an 18-hole golf course and the Killington Summer Theater.

Breakfast included in rates. Types of meals: full breakfast and early coffee/tea. Dinner, picnic lunch, catering service and room service available. MAP, EP. Cable TV in room. VCR, fax, copier, spa and sauna on premises. Handicap access. Weddings, small meetings, family reunions and seminars hosted. Antiques, fishing, parks, shopping, downhill skiing, cross-country skiing and theater nearby.

Pets Allowed.

The Peak Chalet

PO Box 511,
South View Path
Killington, VT 05751-0511
(802)422-4278

Rates: $50-110.
Payment: MC VISA AX DC PC TC.
Innkeeper(s): Greg & Diane Becker.
Circa: 1978.

Rooms: 4 rooms with PB.
Beds: QT.

This contemporary chalet-style inn is located in the heart of the Killington Ski Resort. That convenience is matched by the inn's elegant accommodations and attention to detail. Guest rooms feature either a four-poster, iron, panel or sleigh bed, all queen-size. The living room, with its impressive stone fireplace and view of the Green Mountains, is a favorite gathering spot for those not on the slopes.

Breakfast and afternoon tea included in rates. Type of meal: continental-plus breakfast. Cable TV and VCR on premises. German spoken. Antiques, fishing, parks, shopping, downhill skiing, cross-country skiing, theater and watersports nearby. TAC5.

Special Discounts: January-midweek $70 DO, weekend $90 DO.

The Vermont Inn

Rt 4, Killington, VT 05751
(802)775-0708 (800)541-7795
Fax:(802)773-2440
E-mail: vtinn@aol.com

Rates: $50-185. MAP, EP.
Payment: MC VISA AX DC PC TC.
Innkeeper(s): Megan & Greg Smith.
Circa: 1840.

Rooms: 18 rooms with PB, 2 with FP.
Beds: QDT.

Surrounded by mountain views, this rambling red and white farmhouse has provided lodging and superb cuisine for many years. Exposed beams add to the atmosphere in the living and game rooms. The award-winning dining room provides candlelight tables beside a huge fieldstone fireplace.

Breakfast and afternoon tea included in rates. Types of meals: full breakfast and early coffee/tea. Banquet service available. MAP, EP. Air conditioning and ceiling fan in room. Cable TV, VCR, fax, copier, spa, swimming, sauna, tennis and library on premises. Handicap access. Weddings, small meetings, family reunions and seminars hosted. Antiques, fishing, parks, shopping, downhill skiing, cross-country skiing, theater and watersports nearby.

Publicity: *New York Daily News, New Jersey Star Leader, Rutland Business Journal, Bridgeport Post Telegram, New York Times, Boston, Vermont.*

"We had a wonderful time. The inn is breathtaking. Hope to be back."

Londonderry J3

Blue Gentian Lodge

RR 1 Box 29, Magic Mountain Rd
Londonderry, VT 05148
(802)824-5908 (800)456-2405
Fax:(802)824-3531

Rates: $50-90.
Payment: PC.
Innkeeper(s): The Alberti Family.
Circa: 1962.

Rooms: 13 rooms with PB.
Beds: KDT.

Surrounded by forests and set against picturesque Magic Mountain, Blue Gentian appears more as a European chalet than a lodge tucked in the Vermont countryside. The focus of the lodge's interior is on comfort and convenience. There is a large recreation room with table tennis, games, toys and books, and summer guests may use the inn's swimming pool. The innkeepers offer special rates for groups, family reunions and wedding parties who rent the entire lodge. Ski areas, outlet stores, art galleries and antiquing are close by.

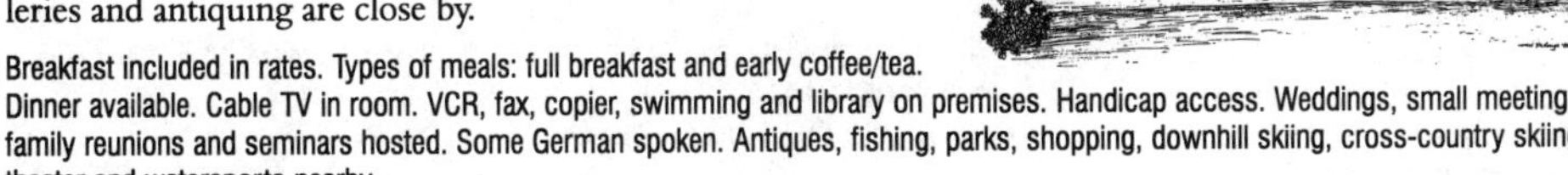

Breakfast included in rates. Types of meals: full breakfast and early coffee/tea. Dinner available. Cable TV in room. VCR, fax, copier, swimming and library on premises. Handicap access. Weddings, small meetings, family reunions and seminars hosted. Some German spoken. Antiques, fishing, parks, shopping, downhill skiing, cross-country skiing, theater and watersports nearby.

Special Discounts: Group rates.

Lower Waterford D6

Rabbit Hill Inn

Pucker St
Lower Waterford, VT 05848
(802)748-5168 (800)762-8669
Fax:(802)748-8342

Rates: $179-259.
Payment: MC VISA AX.
Innkeeper(s): John & Maureen Magee.
Circa: 1795.

Rooms: 20 rooms with PB, 5 with FP. 5 suites. 1 conference room.
Beds: KQT.

Above the Connecticut River overlooking the White Mountains, Samuel Hodby opened this tavern and provided a general store and inn to travelers. As many as 100 horse teams a day traveled by the inn. The ballroom, constructed in 1855, was supported by bent-wood construction giving the dance floor a spring effect. The classic Greek Revival exterior features solid pine Doric columns. Romance abounds in every nook and cranny. Rooms are decorated to the hilt with beautiful furnishings and linens. The Loft room, which overlooks the garden, includes cathedral ceilings and a hidden staircase. The Top-of-the-Tavern room boasts a Victorian dressing room with vintage clothing. Turndown service and afternoon tea are only a few of the amenities. Glorious breakfasts and gourmet, candlelit dinners add to a memorable stay.

Breakfast and dinner included in rates. Types of meals: full breakfast and gourmet breakfast. Picnic lunch and room service available. Copier and computer on premises. Antiques, fishing, downhill skiing, cross-country skiing and watersports nearby.

Location: Historic District.

Publicity: *New York Times, Los Angeles Herald Examiner, Today Show, Innsider, USA Today, Boston, Yankee, Bridal Guide, For the Bride, Country Living, Ski Magazine.*

"It is not often that one experiences one's vision of a tranquil, beautiful step back in time. This is such an experience. Everyone was so accommodating and gracious."

Black River Inn

100 Main St
Ludlow, VT 05149-1050
(802)228-5585 (800)844-3813

Rates: $79-125. MAP.
Payment: MC VISA AX DS PC.
Innkeeper(s): Nancy & Darwin Thomas.
Circa: 1835.

Rooms: 10 rooms, 8 with PB.
Beds: KQD.

This inn is located on the banks of the Black River, across from the gazebo at the village green. One guest room features an original copper-lined bathtub, and Abraham Lincoln is said to have slept in the 1794 walnut four-poster featured in another room. There is a two-bedroom suite available for families. A full country breakfast is served. Dinner and cocktails are available by reservation in the inn's dining room.

Breakfast included in rates. Type of meal: full breakfast. Dinner available. MAP. Antiques, fishing, shopping, downhill skiing, cross-country skiing and theater nearby.

Location: At the base of Okemo Mountain.

Echo Lake Inn

PO Box 154
Ludlow, VT 05149-0154
(802)228-8602 (800)356-6844
Fax:(802)228-3075
E-mail: echolkinn@aol.com

Rates: $99-219. MAP.
Payment: MC VISA AX DS.
Innkeeper(s): John & Yvonne Pardieu, Chip Connelly.
Circa: 1840.

Rooms: 25 rooms, 10 with PB. 1 suite.
Beds: QDT.

Just minutes from Killington and Okemo ski areas, this New England country-style inn offers gourmet candlelight dining and a full country breakfast, a library and parlor. Guests also may borrow canoes and are allowed to pick wildflowers and berries in season. Within easy driving distance, guests will find golf, horseback riding, waterfalls and wineries. The inn is located in Tyson, five miles north of Ludlow.

Breakfast and dinner included in rates. Types of meals: full breakfast and early coffee/tea. Room service available. MAP. Ceiling fan in room. Cable TV, fax, spa, swimming, sauna, tennis and library on premises. 10 acres. Weddings, small meetings, family reunions and seminars hosted. Antiques, fishing, shopping, downhill skiing, cross-country skiing, theater and watersports nearby. TAC10.

Publicity: *Bon Appetit, Gourmet.*

"Very special! We've decided to make the Echo Lake Inn a yearly tradition for our family."

Lyndon C6

Branch Brook B&B

PO Box 143
Lyndon, VT 05849-0143
(802)626-8316 (800)572-7712

Rates: $60-80.
Payment: MC VISA.
Innkeeper(s): Ted & Ann Tolman.
Circa: 1850.

Rooms: 5 rooms, 3 with PB.
Beds: KQ.

This Federal-style home is filled with charm. Exposed beams and homey rooms filled with antiques create a pleasant atmosphere. Meals are prepared at a unique English cookstove, which guests may try out. The honey and maple syrup on the breakfast table are prepared by the innkeepers and accompany items such as pancakes, French toast, bacon and eggs. Ski areas, lakes and rivers are close by, and there are antique shops, flea markets and auctions nearby.

Breakfast included in rates. Types of meals: full breakfast and early coffee/tea. Cable TV, VCR, copier and library on premises. Weddings, small meetings and family reunions hosted. Antiques, fishing, parks, shopping, downhill skiing, cross-country skiing and watersports nearby.

The Battenkill Inn

PO Box 948
Manchester, VT 05254-0948
(802)362-4213 (800)441-1628
Fax:(802)362-0975

Rates: $75-140.
Payment: MC VISA AX TC.
Innkeeper(s): Mary Jo & Ramsay Gourd.
Circa: 1840.
Rooms: 11 rooms with PB, 4 with FP.
Beds: KQDT.

There is something for everyone at this Victorian farmhouse inn. Guest rooms are filled with antiques, and four of them boast working fireplaces. Fine fishing is found in the Battenkill River on the inn's grounds, and guests also are welcome to stroll down to the pond to feed the ducks or play croquet on the lush lawns. Two sitting rooms with fireplaces are popular gathering areas. Dining and shopping experiences await visitors in Manchester Village and Emerald Lake State Park is a short drive from the inn.

Breakfast and evening snack included in rates. Types of meals: full breakfast and early coffee/tea. Air conditioning, turn-down service and ceiling fan in room. VCR, fax, copier and library on premises. Handicap access. Small meetings hosted. Antiques, fishing, parks, shopping, downhill skiing, cross-country skiing, theater and watersports nearby.

"The inn is beautiful and the atmosphere soothing. "

The Inn at Manchester

PO Box 41,
Historic Route 7A
Manchester, VT 05254-0041
(802)362-1793 (800)273-1793
Fax:(802)362-3218

Rates: $95-160.
Payment: MC VISA AX DS PC TC.
Innkeeper(s): Stan & Harriet Rosenberg.
Circa: 1880.
Rooms: 18 rooms with PB, 2 with FP. 4 suites. 1 conference room.
Beds: KQDT.

This restored Victorian and its carriage house are in the National Register. In a setting of beautiful gardens and meadows of wildflowers with a meandering brook, the inn offers an extensive art collection of old prints and paintings. Guest rooms have fine linens, bay windows and antiques. The inn was restored by the innkeepers. The guest pool is set in a secluded meadow.

Breakfast and afternoon tea included in rates. Type of meal: gourmet breakfast. Air conditioning in rooms. Cable TV, fax, copier, swimming and library on premises. Weddings and small meetings hosted. Antiques, fishing, shopping, downhill skiing, cross-country skiing and theater nearby. TAC10.

Publicity: *New York Times, Boston Globe, Travel & Leisure, Gourmet, Newsday.*

Special Discounts: Ski & Stay package, Stay & Play package.

"Spectacular! Bob Newhart — eat your heart out."

The Reluctant Panther Inn & Restaurant

1-3 West Rd
Manchester, VT 05254-0678
(802)362-2568 (800)822-2331
Fax:(802)362-2586
E-mail: panther@fover.net

Rates: $138-325. MAP.
Payment: MC VISA AX PC.
Innkeeper(s): Robert & Maye Bachofen.
Circa: 1850.
Rooms: 16 rooms with PB, 12 with FP. 4 suites. 1 conference room.
Beds: KQT.

Elm trees line a street of manicured lawns and white clapboard estates. Suddenly, a muted purple clapboard house appears, the Reluctant Panther. The well-appointed guest rooms recently have been renovated and some include fireplaces, whirlpool tubs, cable TV and air conditioning. Guests will find a collection of gracious antique furnishings in their rooms. The Greenhouse is a beautiful setting in which to enjoy a romantic dinner, on tables set with fine china and crystal. Breakfasts are served in the inn's private dining room, a bright room warmed by a crackling fire.

Breakfast and dinner included in rates. Type of meal: gourmet breakfast. Banquet service available. MAP. Air conditioning, turn-down service and cable TV in room. Fax and copier on premises. Small meetings, family reunions and seminars hosted. German, Spanish and French spoken. Antiques, fishing, shopping, downhill skiing, cross-country skiing, theater and watersports nearby. TAC10.

Publicity: *Vermont Summer, Sunday Republican, Country Inns, Gourmet, Country Accents, AAA Magazine, Discerning Traveler, Yankee, USA Today, Restaurant Business.*

"We enjoyed our stay so much that now we want to make it our yearly romantic getaway."

Manchester Center

J2

Brook-N-Hearth

Rts 11 & 30, PO Box 508
Manchester Center, VT
05255
(802)362-3604
Fax:(802)362-4694

Rates: $54-80.
Payment: MC VISA AX DS PC TC.
Innkeeper(s): Larry & Terry Greene.
Circa: 1948.

Rooms: 3 rooms with PB. 1 suite.
Beds: DT.

Simple, Colonial furnishings decorate the interior of this comfortable bed & breakfast. There are six acres surrounding this farmhouse, which include trails and a brook. Guests enjoy use of a heated swimming pool and a barbecue grill. The area offers plenty of antiquing and shopping, as well as summer and winter recreation.

Breakfast included in rates. Type of meal: full breakfast. Air conditioning in room. Cable TV, VCR, fax, copier and swimming on premises. Antiques, fishing, shopping, downhill skiing, cross-country skiing, theater and watersports nearby.

The Inn at Ormsby Hill

RR 2 Box 3264
Manchester Center, VT
05255-9518
(802)362-1163 (800)670-2841
Fax:(802)362-5176

Rates: $100-215.
Payment: MC VISA AX.
Innkeeper(s): Ted & Chris Sprague.
Circa: 1764.

Rooms: 10 rooms with PB, 9 with FP.
Beds: KQ.

This hillside Federal-style mansion offers beautiful views of the nearby Green Mountains. Inside, guests will marvel at the inn's conservatory, which was built to resemble a ship and looks out to the gardens and the mountains. Antique-filled rooms offer four-poster or canopy beds decked in fine linens. Most rooms include fireplaces and two-person whirlpool tubs. Vermont is bustling with activities, dozens of which are just a short drive from the inn.

Breakfast and afternoon tea included in rates. Air conditioning in room. Cable TV, fax and library on premises. Antiques, fishing, downhill skiing, cross-country skiing and theater nearby. TAC10.

Publicity: *Gourmet, Getaways for Gourmets.*

"After seventeen years of visiting B&B's in Vermont, we can truly say you are the best. On a scale of 1-10, you are a 12."

Manchester Highlands Inn

Highland Ave, Box 1754A
Manchester Center, VT 05255
(802)362-4565 (800)743-4565
Fax:(802)362-4028
E-mail: manhiinn@sover.net

Rates: $105-135.
Payment: MC VISA AX PC TC.
Innkeeper(s): Patricia & Robert Eichorn.
Circa: 1898.

Rooms: 15 rooms with PB.
Beds: QDT.

This Queen Anne Victorian mansion sits proudly on the crest of a hill overlooking the village. From the three-story turret, guests can look out over Mt. Equinox, the Green Mountains and the valley below. Feather beds and down comforters adorn the beds in the guest rooms. A game room with billiards and a stone fireplace are popular in winter, while summertime guests enjoy the outdoor pool, croquet lawn and veranda. Gourmet country breakfasts and home-baked afternoon snacks are served.

Breakfast and afternoon tea included in rates. Types of meals: full breakfast and gourmet breakfast. Cable TV, VCR, fax, swimming and library on premises. Weddings, small meetings, family reunions and seminars hosted. Limited French and German spoken. Antiques, fishing, parks, shopping, downhill skiing, cross-country skiing and theater nearby. TAC10.

Publicity: *Toronto Sun, Vermont, Asbury Park Press, Vermont Weathervane, Yankee Traveler.*

"We couldn't believe such a place existed. Now we can't wait to come again."

River Meadow Farm

PO Box 822
Manchester Center, VT
05255-0822
(802)362-1602

Rates: $50. MAP.
Payment: PC TC.
Innkeeper(s): Patricia J. Dupree.
Circa: 1797.

Rooms: 5 rooms.
Beds: DT.

The oldest portion of this New England farmhouse was built in the late 18th century, and in keeping with that era, Colonial-style furnishings decorate the interior. During one part of its history, the home served as Manchester Poor Farm. The living room with its grand piano and fireplace is an ideal place for those seeking relaxation. At breakfast, fresh fruit, coffee, teas and juice accompany traditional entrees such as eggs and bacon or pancakes topped with blueberries. There are 90 acres to explore at this farm, some of which borders the Battenkill River.

Breakfast included in rates. Type of meal: full breakfast. MAP. VCR and library on premises. 90 acres. Antiques, fishing, parks, shopping, downhill skiing, cross-country skiing, theater and watersports nearby.

"We really loved our stay and are planning to return as soon as possible."

Middlebury F2

Brookside Meadows

RR 3 Box 2460
Middlebury, VT 05753-8751
(802)388-6429 (800)442-9887
Fax:(802)388-1706
E-mail: rcole@brooksmeadow.com

Rates: $85-115.
Payment: MC VISA PC.
Innkeeper(s): Linda & Roger Cole.
Circa: 1979.

Rooms: 5 rooms with PB. 1 suite.
Beds: KQT.

The Green Mountains serve as a backdrop for this farmhouse, located on 20 rural acres with gardens, meadows, a pond and a brook. The guest rooms are nicely appointed in a clean, uncluttered style. One room includes a bed carved by the builder of the home, while another features a window skylight, which opens to country breezes and starry skies. The two-room suite includes a glass-front gas fireplace stove, cable TV and a private entrance. Shelburne Museum is a nearby, "must-see" attraction and both downhill and cross-country ski areas are within a 45-minute drive.

Breakfast included in rates. Type of meal: full breakfast. Air conditioning and turn-down service in room. Cable TV, VCR, fax and copier on premises. 20 acres. Family reunions hosted. Antiques, fishing, shopping, downhill skiing, cross-country skiing, sporting events and theater nearby. TAC10.

Location: at the base of Green Mountains.

Special Discounts: Corporate and midweek off season discount.

"I should like to say that their idea of hospitality gave a new meaning to the word - they are immensely valuable as ambassadors and really should be appointed as such by the State Department!"

Middlebury Inn

14 Courthouse Sq
Middlebury, VT 05753
(802)388-4961 (800)842-4666
Fax:(802)388-4563

Rates: $88-260. MAP.
Payment: MC VISA AX DS PC TC.
Innkeeper(s): Frank & Jane Emanuel.
Circa: 1827.

Rooms: 80 rooms with PB. 3 conference rooms.
Beds: QDT.

For more than 160 years this red brick, white-shuttered inn has hosted weary travelers. Guests can choose from several options when selecting a room. The grounds include three different properties aside from the Middlebury Inn, which is an amazing structure to behold. The Porter Mansion boasts a porch with wicker furnishings, marble fireplaces and a curving staircase. The Emma Willard House and Governor Weeks House offer more contemporary accommodations. At the Middlebury Inn, guests enjoy delectable afternoon teas on the veranda while enjoying the view of the Village Green. The innkeepers include plenty of special touches such as stocking rooms with books, bath soaps and lotions.

VT

Morning coffee and tea is delivered on a silver tray. The inn offers ski and bicycle storage and will help guests make arrangements for walking tours, a popular activity.

Breakfast and afternoon tea included in rates. Types of meals: continental breakfast, full breakfast and early coffee/tea. Dinner, picnic lunch, lunch and banquet service available. MAP. Air conditioning and cable TV in room. VCR, fax, copier and library on premises. Handicap access. Small meetings, family reunions and seminars hosted. Antiques, fishing, parks, shopping, downhill skiing, cross-country skiing, sporting events and watersports nearby. TAC10.

Pets Allowed: Limited, fee charges.

Publicity: *Chicago Tribune, Glamour, Burlington Free Press, New York Times.*

Special Discounts: AAA.

"The one outstanding attribute which makes your facility so outstanding is the super-plus attitude of everyone of your staff, been years since I've encountered anything like it.."

Swift House Inn

25 Stewart Ln
Middlebury, VT 05753-1248
(802)388-9925

Rates: $85-155.
Payment: MC VISA AX DC CB DS.
Innkeeper(s): John & Andrea Nelson.
Circa: 1815.

Rooms: 21 rooms with PB, 9 with FP. 1 conference room.
Beds: KQDT.

A former governor of Vermont, John Stewart, bought the elegant Swift House after Jonathan Swift's death in 1875. The governor's daughter, who married Swift's grandson, was born and lived in the mansion for 110 years, until 1981. Elaborately carved walnut and marble fireplaces and window seats grace the sitting rooms of the inn. The spacious lawns and formal gardens can be enjoyed from terraces and guest rooms.

Breakfast included in rates. Types of meals: continental breakfast, continental-plus breakfast, full breakfast and gourmet breakfast. Dinner and room service available. Fax, copier, computer, spa and sauna on premises. Handicap access. Antiques, fishing, downhill skiing, cross-country skiing, theater and watersports nearby.

Location: Corner of Rt. 7 and Stewart Lane.

Publicity: *Valley Voice, Uncommon Lodgings, Boston, New York Times, Burlington Free Press, Rutland Business Journal, Wine Spectator.*

"Fabulous wine list, great food, comfortable and relaxing atmosphere, friendly staff."

Montpelier E4

Betsy's B&B

74 E State St
Montpelier, VT 05602-3112
(802)229-0466
Fax:(802)229-5412
E-mail: betsybb@plainfield.bypass.com

Rates: $50-110.
Payment: MC VISA AX DS PC TC.
Innkeeper(s): Jon & Betsy Anderson.
Circa: 1895.

Rooms: 7 rooms with PB. 1 suite.
Beds: QDT.

Within walking distance of downtown and located in the state's largest historic preservation district, this Queen Anne Victorian with romantic turret and carriage house features lavish Victorian antiques throughout its interior. Bay windows, carved woodwork, high ceilings, lace curtains and wood floors add to the authenticity. An exercise room, hot tub and porch tempt many visitors. The full breakfast varies in content but not quality, and guest favorites include chocolate chip waffles and sourdough banana pancakes.

Breakfast included in rates. Type of meal: full breakfast. Cable TV in room. VCR, fax and spa on premises. Small meetings and family reunions hosted. Some Spanish spoken. Antiques, fishing, parks, shopping, downhill skiing, cross-country skiing, theater and watersports nearby. TAC10.

Special Discounts: $5 per night reduction for three days; seven nights for the price of six.

Northfield

E4

Northfield Inn

27 Highland Ave
Northfield, VT 05663-1448
(802)485-8558

Rates: $75-85.
Payment: MC VISA PC TC.
Innkeeper(s): Aglaia Stalb.
Circa: 1901.

Rooms: 8 rooms with PB. 2 suites.
Beds: QDT.

A view of the Green Mountains can be seen from this Victorian inn, which is set on a hillside surrounded by gardens. The picturesque inn also affords a view of the village of Northfield and historic Norwich University. Rooms are decorated with antiques and Oriental rugs, and bedrooms feature European feather bedding and brass and carved-wood beds. Many outdoor activities are available on the three-acre property, including croquet, horseshoes and sledding. Visitors may want to take a climb uphill to visit the Old Slate Quarry or just relax on one of the porches overlooking the garden with bird songs, wind chimes and gentle breezes.

Breakfast and evening snack included in rates. Type of meal: full breakfast. Turndown service, ceiling fan and cable TV in room. VCR, bicycles and library on premises. Weddings, small meetings, family reunions and seminars hosted. Greek spoken. Antiques, fishing, parks, shopping, downhill skiing, cross-country skiing, sporting events, theater and watersports nearby.

Location: Overlooking the village.

Special Discounts: Seventh night complimentary.

"Elegant as always. My second home."

Orwell

G2

Historic Brookside Farms

PO Box 36, Route 22A
Orwell, VT 05760-9615
(802)948-2727
Fax:(802)948-2015
E-mail: hbfinnvt@aol.com

Rates: $85-150. MAP, AP.
Innkeeper(s): Joan & Murray Korda.
Circa: 1789.

Rooms: 7 rooms, 2 with PB. 1 suite. 1 conference room.
Beds: DT.

Nineteen stately Ionic columns grace the front of this Neoclassical Greek Revival farmhouse, which was designed by James Lamb. This is a working farm with Hereford cattle, Hampshire sheep, maple syrup production and poultry. There are 300 acres of lush country landscape with several miles of cross-country skiing, plenty of places for hiking and a 26-acre pond for boating and fishing. Innkeeper Murray Korda is an orchestra leader/concert violinist and speaks nine languages. Downhill skiing, tennis and skating are nearby.

Breakfast and afternoon tea included in rates. Types of meals: gourmet breakfast and early coffee/tea. Dinner, evening snack, picnic lunch, lunch, gourmet lunch and banquet service available. MAP, AP. VCR, fax, copier, computer and child care on premises. Handicap access. 300 acres. Weddings, small meetings, family reunions and seminars hosted. Antiques, fishing, downhill skiing, cross-country skiing and theater nearby.

Publicity: *New York Times, Burlington Free Press, Los Angeles Times, Preservation Magazine Antiques.*

"A wonderful piece of living history."

Proctorsville

I4

The Golden Stage Inn

Depot St, PO Box 218
Proctorsville, VT 05153
(802)226-7744 (800)253-8226
Fax:(802)226-7882

Rates: $145-170. MAP.
Payment: MC VISA.
Innkeeper(s): Micki & Paul Smith-Darnauer.
Circa: 1780.

Rooms: 8 rooms with PB. 2 suites.
Beds: KQDT.

The Golden Stage Inn was a stagecoach stop built shortly before Vermont's founding. It became a link in the Underground Railroad and the home of Cornelia Otis Skinner. Extensive gardens surround the wrap-around porch as well as the swimming pool.

Breakfast, dinner and evening snack included in rates. Types of meals: full breakfast and early coffee/tea. MAP. Cable TV, VCR, fax, copier, swimming, bicycles and library on premises. Weddings, small meetings and family reunions hosted. Antiques, fishing, shopping, downhill skiing, cross-country skiing, theater and watersports nearby.

Location: Near Ludlow.

Publicity: *Journal Inquirer, Gourmet Magazine, Los Angeles Times*

"The essence of a country inn!"

Putney

K4

Hickory Ridge House

RR 3 Box 1410
Putney, VT 05346-9326
(802)387-5709

Rates: $50-90. EP.
Payment: MC VISA AX PC TC.
Innkeeper(s): Jacquie Walker & Steve Anderson.
Circa: 1808.

Rooms: 7 rooms, 3 with PB, 4 with FP. 1 suite. 2 conference rooms.
Beds: QDT.

This comely brick Federal house was originally built as an elegant farmhouse on a 500-acre Merino sheep farm. Palladian windows, and six Rumford fireplaces are original features. Rooms are painted in bright Federal colors, such as rose, salmon, blue and yellow. Weddings are popular here and innkeeper Steve Anderson often serves as justice of the peace. Hickory Ridge House is listed in the National Register of Historic Places.

Breakfast included in rates. Types of meals: full breakfast and early coffee/tea. EP. Cable TV, VCR, library and child care on premises. Handicap access. 12 acres. Weddings, small meetings, family reunions and seminars hosted. German and Russian spoken. Antiques, fishing, parks, shopping, cross-country skiing and theater nearby.

Publicity: *Philadelphia Inquirer, Boston Globe.*

Special Discounts: 10% discount for 4 or more days or stays.

"We love your serene and peaceful house and we thank you for your hospitality and warmth, good food and good company."

Mapleton Farm B&B

Rd 2 Box 510
Putney, VT 05346-9419
(802)257-5252 (800)236-5254
Fax:(802)254-1241

Rates: $79-110.
Payment: MC VISA AX.
Innkeeper(s): Linda & Jack Bisbee.
Circa: 1803.

Rooms: 5 rooms with PB.
Beds: KD.

Views of woods, meadows and a homey, country decor create a warm atmosphere at this turn-of-century (that's the 19th century) Colonial. The home was one of the first properties to be recorded in the town of Dummerston's first book of records. In the guest rooms, furnishings such as a four-poster or sleigh bed are topped with quilts and down comforters. Before breakfast, early birds can take a relaxing walk along the grounds, which include wooded trails, gardens and a pond. After communing with nature, settle down to a hearty, homemade breakfast. Guests will enjoy homemade breads, fresh fruit, savory bacon and pancakes topped with locally grown blueberries and Vermont maple syrup.

Breakfast and afternoon tea included in rates. Types of meals: full breakfast and early coffee/tea. Dinner and picnic lunch available. Air conditioning and cable TV in room. Weddings, small meetings and family reunions hosted. Antiques, fishing, parks, shopping, downhill skiing, cross-country skiing, sporting events, theater and watersports nearby.

Pets Allowed: In two rooms only. Additional charge.

Location: Southeast corner of Vermont in Connecticut River Valley.

Special Discounts: 10% discounts available.

Quechee H5

Parker House Inn

16 Main St, Box 0780
Quechee, VT 05059
(802)295-6077
E-mail: parker-house-inn@valley.net

Rates: $100-135. MAP.
Payment: MC VISA AX PC TC.
Innkeeper(s): Barbara & Walt Forrester.
Circa: 1857.

Rooms: 7 rooms with PB.
Beds: KQ.

State Sen. Joseph C. Parker built this riverside manor in 1857 and three of the guest rooms are named in honor of his family. Mornings at the inn begin with a delicious country breakfast served in the Parker House Restaurant's cozy dining rooms. The chefs are justifiably proud of their "comfort food" cuisine. Airy guest rooms feature furnishings and unique decor. Guests can stroll next door to watch the art of glass blowing, or take a walk along the Ottaquechee River. The surroundings of this historic town provide hours of activity for nature lovers and shutterbugs. Fall foliage, of course, is an autumnal delight.

Breakfast included in rates. Types of meals: full breakfast and gourmet breakfast. Dinner and banquet service available. MAP. Air conditioning and ceiling fan in room. Cable TV, VCR, fax and bicycles on premises. Weddings, small meetings, family reunions and seminars hosted. Antiques, fishing, downhill skiing, cross-country skiing, theater and watersports nearby.

Publicity: *Quechee Times.*

"The inn is lovely, the innkeepers are the greatest, excellent food and heavenly bed!"

Ripton F2

Chipman Inn

Rt 125
Ripton, VT 05766
(802)388-2390 (800)890-2390

Rates: $85-115.
Payment: MC VISA AX DS TC.
Innkeeper(s): Joyce Henderson & Bill Pierce.
Circa: 1828.

Rooms: 8 rooms with PB.
Beds: QDT.

This was the home of Daniel Chipman, a prominent legislator and founder of Middlebury College. Chipman also managed the "Center Turnpike" (now Route 125) through the Green Mountains. A replica of the tariff board stands near the inn. The inn's lounge/bar is in the original kitchen, with its old fireplace and bread oven.

Breakfast included in rates. Type of meal: full breakfast. Dinner available. Weddings, small meetings and family reunions hosted. Antiques, fishing, parks, shopping, downhill skiing, cross-country skiing and watersports nearby.

Publicity: *Gourmet, Food & Wine, New York Times, Addison County Independent.*

"Cozy, warm and friendly."

Rochester

G3

Liberty Hill Farm

RR 1 Box 158, Liberty Hill Rd
Rochester, VT 05767-9501
(802)767-3926
E-mail: libhilfarm@aol.com

Rates: $120. MAP.
Payment: PC TC.
Innkeeper(s): Robert & Beth Kennett.
Circa: 1825.

Rooms: 7 rooms.
Beds: QDT.

A working dairy farm with a herd of registered Holsteins, this farmhouse offers a country setting and easy access to recreational activities. The inn's location, between the White River and the Green Mountains, is ideal for outdoor enthusiasts and animal lovers. Barn cats, chickens, a dog, ducks, horses and turkeys are found on the grounds, not to mention the Holstein herd. Fishing, hiking, skiing and swimming are popular pastimes of guests, who are treated to a family-style dinner and full breakfast, both featuring many delicious homemade specialties.

Breakfast and dinner included in rates. Types of meals: full breakfast and early coffee/tea. MAP. VCR, fax, swimming, library and child care on premises. 106 acres. Weddings, small meetings, family reunions and seminars hosted. Antiques, fishing, parks, shopping, downhill skiing, cross-country skiing, sporting events, theater and watersports nearby.

Publicity: *New York Times, Boston Globe, Vermont Life, Family Circle, Family Fun, Woman's Day, Country Home.*

Special Discounts: Children $25.

"We had a wonderful time exploring your farm and the countryside. The food was great."

Rutland

H3

The Inn at Rutland

70 N Main St
Rutland, VT 05701-3249
(802)773-0575 (800)808-0575

Rates: $49-195.
Payment: MC VISA AX DC CB DS TC.
Innkeeper(s): Bob & Tanya Liberman.
Circa: 1890.

Rooms: 10 rooms with PB. 1 suite. 2 conference rooms.
Beds: KQD.

This distinctive Victorian mansion is filled with many period details, from high, plaster-worked ceilings to leather wainscotting in the dining room. Leaded windows and interesting woodwork are found throughout. Guest rooms have been decorated to maintain Victorian charm without a loss of modern comforts. A wicker-filled porch and common rooms are available to guests. Located in central Vermont, The Inn at Rutland is only 15 minutes from the Killington and Pico ski areas.

Breakfast included in rates. Types of meals: full breakfast and gourmet breakfast. Air conditioning, ceiling fan and cable TV in room. VCR, fax, copier and bicycles on premises. Weddings, small meetings and family reunions hosted. Antiques, fishing, parks, shopping, downhill skiing, cross-country skiing, sporting events, theater and watersports nearby.

Location: In central Vermont.

"A lovely page in the 'memory album' of our minds."

The Phelps House

19 North St
Rutland, VT 05701-3011
(802)775-4480 (800)775-4620

Rates: $50-65.
Payment: PC TC.
Innkeeper(s): Betty Phelps.
Circa: 1912.

Rooms: 6 rooms. 1 suite. 1 cottage.
Beds: QDT.

This California ranch B&B is considered the state's first Frank Lloyd Wright house. Guests will be intrigued by the custom wall murals, hand-crafted dolls and parquet floors. Children of all ages will enjoy the basement, which features pingpong and pool. The B&B's location, next door to a city playground, also will please the recreation-minded. Guests play tennis on the inn's clay court, adjacent to a barn boasting an 80-foot mural painted by the innkeeper.

Breakfast included in rates. Type of meal: full breakfast. Cable TV, VCR, tennis and library on premises. Family reunions hosted. Downhill skiing and cross-country skiing nearby.

Saint Johnsbury D6

Looking Glass Inn

Rt 18 Box 199
Saint Johnsbury, VT 05819
(802)748-3052 (800)579-3644

Rates: $60-85.
Payment: MC VISA PC TC.
Innkeeper(s): Barbara & Perry Viles.
Circa: 1850.

Rooms: 6 rooms, 2 with PB. 1 conference room.
Beds: DT.

This historic Second Empire Victorian once served travelers in the early 19th century. Visitors today enjoy the same Northeast Vermont setting and old-time hospitality, including special romantic candlelight dinners that can be arranged by reservation. Visitors start their day with a large country breakfast served in the mauve-accented dining room. Later in the day, guests are welcome to relax with a cup of tea or glass of sherry. Idyllic country roads are found throughout the surrounding area, perfect for exploring year-round.

Breakfast and afternoon tea included in rates. Types of meals: continental breakfast, continental-plus breakfast, full breakfast and early coffee/tea. Library on premises. 34 acres. Weddings, small meetings and family reunions hosted. French spoken. Antiques, fishing, parks, shopping, downhill skiing, cross-country skiing and watersports nearby. TAC8.

Publicity: *Tampa Tribune.*

Shoreham F2

Shoreham Inn & Country Store

On The Green, Main St
Shoreham, VT 05770
(802)897-5081 (800)255-5081

Rates: $85. AP.
Payment: MC VISA PC TC.
Innkeeper(s): Cleo Alter.
Circa: 1790.

Rooms: 11 rooms, 1 with PB.

Located just five miles east of Fort Ticonderoga, this Federal-style inn is a favorite of nature-lovers. Fascinating antique shops and many covered bridges are found in the area. The inn's dining room, with its large open fire, is a popular gathering spot, and guests also are drawn to the restored 19th-century sitting rooms. Guest rooms are furnished with country antiques. A country store is on the premises.

Breakfast included in rates. Types of meals: full breakfast and early coffee/tea. Dinner available. AP. Copier and library on premises. Weddings, small meetings, family reunions and seminars hosted. Antiques, fishing, parks, shopping, downhill skiing, cross-country skiing, sporting events, theater and watersports nearby.

Springfield I4

VT

Hartness House Inn

30 Orchard St
Springfield, VT 05156-2612
(802)885-2115
Fax:(802)885-2207

Rates: $82-130.
Payment: MC VISA AX PC TC.
Innkeeper(s): Eileen Gennette-Coughlin.
Circa: 1903.

Rooms: 40 rooms with PB. 1 suite. 3 conference rooms.
Beds: QDT.

There are many inns where star-gazing is a popular nighttime activity. At Hartness House, it is taken to a whole new level. The original owner not only served as the state's governor, but inventor/astronomer James Hartness also created the historic observatory that remains at the home today. Planets, stars and comets, from the historic Turret Equatorial Telescope. Aside from this uncommon amenity, the house itself is impressive. Guests who stay in the home's original portion reach their well-appointed rooms via a three-story staircase. Two newer wings also offer elegant accommodations. On weekdays, a continental breakfast is served and on weekends, full breakfast fare is available. There is a Victorian-styled dining room on the premises as well, offering dinners by candlelight. The home is often the site of weddings, receptions and parties. Country Inns magazine chose Hartness House as one of its top inns, and in another article made note of the inn's wonderful holiday decorations and festivities.

Breakfast included in rates. Types of meals: continental-plus breakfast, full breakfast and early coffee/tea. Dinner, picnic lunch and banquet service available. Air conditioning and cable TV in room. VCR, fax, copier, swimming and library on premises. 25 acres. Weddings, small meetings, family reunions and seminars hosted. Antiques, fishing, parks, shopping, downhill skiing, cross-country skiing, theater and watersports nearby. TAC10.

Special Discounts: Package plans and promotion rates.

"A wonderful place to stop and remember simple elegance and all that is important."

Stowe *D4*

Brass Lantern Inn

717 Maple St
Stowe, VT 05672-4250
(802)253-2229 (800)729-2980
Fax:(802)253-7425
E-mail: brasslantern@aol.com

Rates: $75-200.
Payment: MC VISA AX.
Innkeeper(s): Andy Aldrich.
Circa: 1810.

Rooms: 9 rooms with PB, 3 with FP.
Beds: QDT.

This rambling farmhouse and carriage barn rests at the foot of Mt. Mansfield. A recent award-winning renovation has brought a new shine to the inn from the gleaming plank floors to the polished woodwork and crackling fireplaces. Quilts and antiques fill the guest rooms and some, like the Honeymoon Room, have their own fireplace and mountain view. A complimentary afternoon and evening tea is provided along with a full Vermont-style breakfast. 1995 and 1996 winner of the Golden Fork Award from the Gourmet Dinners Society of North America.

Breakfast and afternoon tea included in rates. Types of meals: full breakfast and early coffee/tea. Air conditioning in room. VCR, fax, copier and library on premises. Weddings and small meetings hosted. Antiques, fishing, parks, shopping, downhill skiing, cross-country skiing, sporting events, theater and watersports nearby. TAC10.

Location: One-half mile from village center.

Publicity: *Vermont, Vermont Life, Innsider, Discerning Traveler, Ski.*

"The little things made us glad we stopped."

Honeywood Inn

4527 Mountain Rd
Stowe, VT 05672-4802
(802)253-4124 (800)659-6289

Rates: $44-159.
Payment: MC VISA AX DS TC.
Innkeeper(s): Carolyn & Bill Cook.
Circa: 1963.

Rooms: 13 rooms, 12 with PB, 4 with FP. 1 suite.
Beds: QDT.

A river runs through the four acres that surround Honeywood Inn. The modern home is within walking distance to the Stowe Recreation Path and just a few minutes from Mt. Mansfield and many of Stowe's restaurants and shops. Four of the guest rooms include fireplaces, and all are decorated with country-style furnishings and handmade quilts. There is an outdoor hot tub and a swimming pool.

Breakfast and afternoon tea included in rates. Type of meal: continental-plus breakfast. Air conditioning, ceiling fan and cable TV in room. VCR, copier, spa, swimming and bicycles on premises. Family reunions hosted. Antiques, fishing, parks, shopping, downhill skiing, cross-country skiing, theater and watersports nearby. TAC10.

Special Discounts: Three days, two nights: fireplace, one gourmet dinner for two, welcome wine and cheese - $99 per person double occupancy.

"We appreciated your friendliness and the way you run your lodge."

The Siebeness Inn

3681 Mountain Rd
Stowe, VT 05672-4764
(802)253-8942 (800)426-9001
Fax:(802)253-9232

Rates: $70-180. MAP.
Payment: MC VISA AX DS PC TC.
Innkeeper(s): Sue & Nils Andersen.
Circa: 1952.

Rooms: 12 rooms, 11 with PB.
Beds: KQDT.

A multi-course full breakfast enjoyed with a view of majestic Mt. Mansfield is a highlight of this New England Colonial inn. The charming village of Stowe is just a few miles away, and a free trolley shuttle takes visitors there to partake of the town's many attractions. The inn offers bicycles, an exercise room, hot tub and pool for relaxing and recreation. A fireplace, library and television are available in the inn's common areas. Favorite guest activities include tours of Ben & Jerry's Ice Cream Factory, Green Mountain Chocolate Factory and the Shelburne Museum.

Breakfast included in rates. Types of meals: full breakfast and early coffee/tea. Afternoon tea and evening snack available. MAP. Air conditioning in room. Cable TV, VCR, fax, copier, spa, swimming, bicycles and library on premises. Weddings, small meetings, family reunions and seminars hosted. Antiques, fishing, parks, shopping, downhill skiing, cross-country skiing, sporting events, theater and watersports nearby. TAC10.

Underhill — C3

Sinclair Inn B&B

RR 2 Box 35
Underhill, VT 05489-9318
(802)899-2234 (800)433-4658
Fax:(802)899-2234

Rates: $65-95.
Payment: MC VISA PC TC.
Innkeeper(s): Jeanne & Andy Buchanan.
Circa: 1890.

Rooms: 6 rooms with PB, 1 with FP. 1 conference room.
Beds: KQDT.

Enjoy the ambiance of an era gone-by at this stunning Queen Anne Victorian, which was built by carpenter Edmund Sinclair to showcase his talents. When a local hotel burned down, Sinclair added a turret to his home and opened for business, thus beginning a tradition of innkeeping. Innkeepers Jeannie and Andy Buchanan restored the home down to the last detail, preserving many original features and the home's Victorian charm. Elegant country breakfasts are served on tables set with fine linens, china and silver. The Buchanans also will create romantic amenities for your special occasions.

Breakfast included in rates. Types of meals: full breakfast and early coffee/tea. Air conditioning in room. Fax, copier and bicycles on premises. Handicap access. Weddings, small meetings, family reunions and seminars hosted. Antiques, fishing, parks, shopping, downhill skiing, cross-country skiing, sporting events, theater and watersports nearby. TAC10.

Publicity: *Burlington Free Press.*

Special Discounts: Downhill ski tickets, 1/2 price; guided cross-country.

"Coming home every night to your inn was the highlight of each day. Your generosity, warmth and kindness were extremely comforting."

Vergennes — E2

Whitford House

RR 1 Box 1490
Vergennes, VT 05491-9521
(802)758-2704 (800)746-2704
Fax:(802)758-2089

Rates: $70-165.
Payment: PC TC.
Innkeeper(s): Bruce & Barbara Carson.
Circa: 1790.

Rooms: 5 rooms, 2 with PB. 1 suite. 1 cottage.
Beds: KDT.

VT

From each guest room at this late 18th-century home, guests enjoy beautiful views of the Adirondack Mountains and surrounding valley. The interior is decorated with antiques and Mission-style furniture, as well as a few original artworks created by the innkeepers' daughter. Coffee, tea and orange juice are served in the library prior to breakfast service. Specialties such as Belgian waffles topped with that famous Vermont syrup are accompanied by items such as homemade granola or stewed apples.

Breakfast and afternoon tea included in rates. Types of meals: gourmet breakfast and early coffee/tea. Turn-down service and ceiling fan in room. VCR, fax, bicycles and library on premises. 10 acres. Weddings, small meetings, family reunions and seminars hosted. Antiques, fishing, parks, shopping, downhill skiing, cross-country skiing, sporting events and watersports nearby.

Pets Allowed: Must discuss options with owner.

"What a treat to see Vermont from your special home. . .a highlight of the weekend!"

Waitsfield

E3

1824 House Inn

Rt 100, Box 159
Waitsfield, VT 05673
(802)496-7555 (800)426-3986
Fax:(802)496-7559
E-mail: fen@madriver.com

Rates: $89-150.
Payment: MC VISA AX DS PC TC.
Circa: 1824.

Rooms: 7 rooms with PB.
Beds: KQD.

Surrounded by the Green Mountains, 1824 House Inn is a white clapboard farmhouse on 52 acres. The Mad River passes through the property and there's a private swimming hole. The inn is decorated with Oriental rugs, original art, crystal chandeliers and thick European down quilts. Guests may enjoy homemade breads, freshly squeezed orange juice and maple syrup tapped from the inn's own maples.

Breakfast and afternoon tea included in rates. Types of meals: full breakfast, gourmet breakfast and early coffee/tea. Dinner and evening snack available. Ceiling fan in room. Cable TV, VCR, fax, spa, swimming, stables, bicycles and library on premises. 23 acres. Weddings, small meetings, family reunions and seminars hosted. Antiques, fishing, parks, shopping, downhill skiing, cross-country skiing, theater and watersports nearby. TAC10.

Location: Central Vermont - near Burlington International Airport. Sugarbush and Mad River Glen resorts nearby.

Publicity: *Los Angeles Times, Miami Herald, Chicago Tribune, New York Post.*

"Established hospitality - unusual breakfast specialties."

Hyde Away Inn

Rt 17, Waitsfield, VT 05673
(802)496-2322 (800)777-4933
Fax:(802)496-7012
E-mail: hydeaway@madriver.com

Rates: $49-89.
Payment: MC VISA AX TC.
Innkeeper(s): Margaret & Bruce Hyde.
Circa: 1820.

Rooms: 12 rooms, 4 with PB, 1 with FP.
Beds: QDT.

A collection of red-roofed buildings, one dating back to the early 19th century, serves as lodging, restaurant and tavern at Hyde Away. The inn was the first such accommodation in the Mad River Valley, and offers 12 comfortable guest rooms and also serves as the location of a mountain bike touring center. Homemade breakfasts are included in the rates, and candlelight dining is available at the inn's restaurant.

Breakfast included in rates. Types of meals: continental-plus breakfast and early coffee/tea. Dinner available. Cable TV and swimming on premises. Weddings, small meetings and family reunions hosted. Antiques, fishing, shopping, downhill skiing, cross-country skiing, theater and watersports nearby. TAC10.

Pets Allowed: Only in three rooms with outside entrances, off-peak times only.

Special Discounts: 3 nights or more - 10% off; 5 nights - 20% off.

"The hospitality and warmth of your staff made me feel right at home."

Mad River Inn

Tremblay Rd, PO Box 75
Waitsfield, VT 05673
(802)496-7900 (800)832-8278
Fax:(802)496-5390

Rates: $69-125.
Payment: MC VISA AX.
Innkeeper(s): Rita & Luc Maranda.
Circa: 1860.

Rooms: 10 rooms with PB.
Beds: KQ.

Surrounded by the Green Mountains, this Queen Anne Victorian sits on seven scenic acres along the Mad River. The charming inn boasts attractive woodwork throughout, highlighted by ash, bird's-eye maple and cherry. Guest rooms feature European featherbeds and include the Hayden Breeze Room, with a king brass bed, large windows and sea relics, and the Abner Doubleday Room, with a queen ash bed and mementos of baseball's glory days. The inn sports a billiard table, gazebo, organic gardens and a Jacuzzi overlooking the mountains. Autumn visitors are free to take home a pumpkin from the inn's prolific patch.

Breakfast and afternoon tea included in rates. Type of meal: gourmet breakfast. Turn-down service and ceiling fan in room. Cable TV, VCR, fax, spa, stables and child care on premises. Weddings, small meetings and family reunions hosted. French spoken. Antiques, fishing, shopping, downhill skiing, cross-country skiing, sporting events, theater and watersports nearby. TAC10.

Publicity: *Innsider, Victorian Homes, Let's Live, Skiing, AAA Home & Away, Tea Time at the Inn, Travel & Leisure.*

"Your hospitality was appreciated, beautiful house and accommodations, great food & friendly people, just to name a few things. We plan to return and we recommend the Mad River Inn to friends & family."

The Valley Inn

Rt 1 Box 8 Rt 100
Waitsfield, VT 05673
(802)496-3450 (800)638-8466

Rates: $59-99. MAP.
Payment: MC VISA AX TC.
Innkeeper(s): Bill & Millie Stinson.
Circa: 1949.

Rooms: 20 rooms with PB. 1 conference room.
Beds: QDT.

This country inn offers guest rooms decorated with New England antiques, hand stenciled walls and beds topped with quilts. The living room is a perfect place to relax, with a woodburning stove set into its grand stone fireplace. The inn's Lone Eage Pub serves beverages and offers a variety of weekly specials. Dinner is served during ski season. For a true adventure, guests can learn how to fly a sailplane and soar over the Green Mountains with the host.

Breakfast included in rates. Type of meal: full breakfast. Dinner available. MAP. Cable TV, VCR, copier, sauna and bicycles on premises. Handicap access. Small meetings, family reunions and seminars hosted. Antiques, fishing, parks, shopping, downhill skiing, cross-country skiing, theater and watersports nearby. TAC10.

Waitsfield Inn

Rt 100, PO Box 969
Waitsfield, VT 05673
(802)496-3979 (800)758-3801

Rates: $69-119.
Payment: MC VISA AX DS PC TC.
Innkeeper(s): Ruth & Steve Lacey.
Circa: 1825.

Rooms: 14 rooms with PB.
Beds: DT.

This Federal-style home once served as a parsonage and was home to a state senator. Surrounded by a picket fence, the home's grounds boast a large garden. The old barn is now the common room and includes the original wood-planked flooring and a fireplace. Guest quarters are filled with period antiques. In the winter, freshly baked cookies and cider are served. As the inn is in the village of Waitsfield, all the town's sites are nearby. The area offers an abundance of outdoor activities throughout the year.

Breakfast included in rates. Type of meal: full breakfast. Weddings, small meetings, family reunions and seminars hosted. Antiques, fishing, shopping, downhill skiing, cross-country skiing and theater nearby.

Location: Near Sugarbush and Mad River Glen ski areas.

Wallingford H3

I. B. Munson House

7 S Main St, PO Box 427
Wallingford, VT 05773
(802)446-2600
Fax:(802)446-3336

Rates: $70-160.
Payment: MC VISA AX DS PC TC.
Innkeeper(s): Phillip & Karen Pimental.
Circa: 1856.

Rooms: 7 rooms with PB, 2 with FP. 2 suites.
Beds: QDT.

Isaac Munson might not recognize some of Wallingford anymore, but his home still would be easy enough to identify. During the restoration of the Italianate Victorian, the innkeepers preserved many original elements, such as the wood floors and the carved mantels. Period antiques and Waverly wallcoverings are featured in the guest rooms. Two include a fireplace. Wallingford is a designated historic village, so there are many interesting old homes and buildings to see. Ski areas, shops and restaurants are close by.

Breakfast included in rates. Types of meals: full breakfast and early coffee/tea. Afternoon tea available. Turn-down service and ceiling fan in room. Cable TV, VCR and fax on premises. Weddings, small meetings, family reunions and seminars hosted. Antiques, fishing, parks, shopping, downhill skiing, cross-country skiing and watersports nearby. TAC15.

Beaver Pond Farm Inn

Rd Box 306, Golf Course Rd
Warren, VT 05674
(802)583-2861
Fax:(802)583-2860

Rates: $72-96.
Payment: MC VISA AX PC.
Innkeeper(s): Robert & Elizabeth Hansen.
Circa: 1840.

Rooms: 6 rooms, 4 with PB. 1 conference room.
Beds: KQT.

This Vermont farmhouse, formerly a working dairy and sheep farm, is situated in a meadow overlooking several beaver ponds. Present owners refurbished the home, decorating the tasteful rooms with antiques and Laura Ashley wallpapers. The innkeeper holds cooking classes here. For golf lovers, the inn is located only 100 yards from the first tee of the Sugarbush Golf Course. The course is transformed into a cross-country ski center in the winter, offering miles of tracked and groomed trails. Downhill skiing is only one mile away.

Breakfast and evening snack included in rates. Types of meals: full breakfast and early coffee/tea. Dinner and picnic lunch available. VCR in room. Cable TV, fax and copier on premises. Handicap access. Weddings, small meetings, family reunions and seminars hosted. Antiques, fishing, shopping, downhill skiing, cross-country skiing, sporting events and theater nearby.

Location: Sugarbush Valley.

Publicity: *Los Angeles Times, New Woman, Innsider.*

"The inn is simply magnificent. I have not been in a nicer one on three continents. Breakfast was outrageous."

The Sugartree, A Country Inn

RR 1 Box 38
Warren, VT 05674-9708
(802)583-3211 (800)666-8907
Fax:(802)583-3203
E-mail: sugartree@madriver.com

Rates: $79-135.
Payment: MC VISA AX DS PC TC.
Innkeeper(s): Kathy & Frank Partsch.
Circa: 1960.

Rooms: 9 rooms with PB, 1 with FP.
Beds: QDT.

Ski enthusiasts not only will appreciate Sugartree's close access to downhill and cross-country slopes, but the warm, country hospitality found here as well. Rooms are inviting with canopy or brass beds topped with colorful quilts. The interior, as the name suggests, is decidedly country with needlework and Frank's woodcarvings decorating the rooms. The innkeepers' breakfasts are memorable affairs. Their recipe for ham- and pineapple-stuffed French toast has been featured in a cookbook. Every season brings a new joy to this inn and the Warren area. During the warmer months, the innkeepers decorate the exterior of their chalet-style inn with thousands of flowers. In the fall, the autumn leaves draw visitors from around the world.

Breakfast and afternoon tea included in rates. Types of meals: full breakfast and early coffee/tea. Fax and copier on premises. Weddings, small meetings, family reunions and seminars hosted. Antiques, fishing, shopping, skiing nearby. TAC10.

Special Discounts: Winter midweek, 3 nights, 4th 1/2 price, 4 nights 5th free, summer same applies midweek & weekends.

"The close proximity to the ski slopes, friendly and helpful attitude of the Innkeepers Frank and Kathy, the clean and comfortably decorated rooms, great breakfast, warm fire and the fair price made Sugartree a great find."

The Inn at Blush Hill

Blush Hill Rd, Box 1266
Waterbury, VT 05676
(802)244-7529 (800)736-7522
Fax:(802)244-7314
E-mail: innatbh@aol.com

Rates: $69-130.
Payment: MC VISA AX DS PC TC.
Innkeeper(s): Gary & Pam Gosselin.
Circa: 1790.

Rooms: 5 rooms with PB, 1 with FP.
Beds: QDT.

This shingled Cape-style house was once a stagecoach stop en route to Stowe and is the oldest Inn in Waterbury. A 12-foot-long pine farmhand's table is set near the double fireplace and the kitchen bay window, revealing views of the Worcester Mountains. A favorite summertime breakfast, served gardenside, is pancakes with fresh blueberries, topped with ice cream and maple syrup.

Breakfast, afternoon tea and evening snack included in rates. Types of meals: full breakfast, gourmet breakfast and early coffee/tea. Air conditioning, turn-down service and ceiling fan in room. Cable TV, fax and library on premises. Weddings and family reunions hosted. Antiques, fishing, parks, shopping, downhill skiing, cross-country skiing, theater and watersports nearby. TAC10.

Location: Three-quarter mile off scenic Rte 100 at I-89.

Publicity: *Vermont, Charlotte Observer, Yankee, New York Times, Ski.*

Special Discounts: Packages available.

"Our room was wonderful — especially the fireplace. Everything was so cozy and warm."

Grunberg Haus B&B and Cabins

RR 2 Box 1595-NO
Waterbury, VT 05676-9621
(802)244-7726 (800)800-7760
E-mail: grunhaus@aol.com

Rates: $55-125. MAP.
Payment: MC VISA AX DS PC TC.
Innkeeper(s): Chris Sellers & Mark Frohman.
Circa: 1972.

Rooms: 15 rooms, 10 with PB, 3 with FP. 1 suite. 4 cottages. 1 conference room.
Beds: QDT.

This hillside Tyrolean chalet was hand-built by George and Irene Ballschneider. The Grunberg Haus captures the rustic charm of country guest homes in Austria with its wall of windows overlooking the Green Mountains, a massive fieldstone fireplace and a self-service Austrian pub. Rooms are furnished with antique furniture and cozy quilts. All rooms open onto the second-floor balcony that surrounds the chalet. Attractions in Stowe, the Mad River Valley, Montpelier and the Lake Champlain region are close at hand. Innkeepers regularly entertain their guests at the Steinway Grand piano.

Breakfast and afternoon tea included in rates. Types of meals: full breakfast, gourmet breakfast and early coffee/tea. MAP. Spa, sauna, tennis and library on premises. 40 acres. Weddings, small meetings, family reunions and seminars hosted. Antiques, fishing, parks, shopping, downhill skiing, cross-country skiing, theater and watersports nearby. TAC10.

Pets Allowed: Pick up and boarding at A.K.A. pet hotel nearby.

Location: South of Waterbury on scenic route 100, between Stowe and Waitsfield.

Publicity: *Hudson Dispatch, Innsider, Ski, Toronto Globe, Vermont, Washington Times, Yankee.*

Special Discounts: Off season specials in April and November.

"You made an ordinary overnight stay extraordinary."

Old Stagecoach Inn

18 N Main St
Waterbury, VT 05676-1810
(802)244-5056 (800)262-2206
Fax:(802)244-6956

Rates: $40-110.
Payment: MC VISA AX DS PC TC.
Innkeeper(s): John & Jack Barwick.
Circa: 1826.

Rooms: 13 rooms, 10 with PB, 1 with FP. 3 suites.
Beds: KQDT.

For many years, this inn served as both a stagecoach stop and meeting house. In the 1880s, an Ohio millionaire used the home as his summer retreat. He added the Victorian touches that are still present, including the polished woodwork, stained glass and elegant fireplaces. Today, guests stay in restored rooms decorated in

Victorian style. Stowe, Sugarbush and Bolton Valley ski areas are nearby, and guests can also partake in fishing, swimming and water sports at Winooski River, Waterbury Reservoir or Lake Champlain.

Breakfast and afternoon tea included in rates. Type of meal: full breakfast. Dinner available. Air conditioning, ceiling fan and cable TV in room. Copier on premises. Weddings, small meetings and family reunions hosted. German and French spoken. Antiques, fishing, parks, shopping, downhill skiing, cross-country skiing, theater and watersports nearby. TAC10.

Pets Allowed.

Special Discounts: AAA - 10%.

"This place was first class all the way."

Thatcher Brook Inn

PO Box 490, Rt 100 N
Waterbury, VT 05676-0490
(802)244-5911 (800)292-5911
Fax:(802)244-1294

Rates: $75-185. MAP.
Payment: MC VISA AX DC DS PC TC.
Innkeeper(s): Kelly & Peter Varty.
Circa: 1899.

Rooms: 22 rooms with PB, 6 with FP. 1 suite. 1 conference room.
Beds: KQDT.

Listed in the Vermont Register of Historic Buildings, this restored Victorian mansion features a porch with twin gazebos. A covered walkway leads to the historic Wheeler House. Guest rooms are decorated in Laura Ashley-style. Six rooms have fireplaces, and some have whirlpool tubs. The inn's restaurant, Victoria's Bar and Grill, specializes in country French cuisine. Guests can dine fireside or by candlelight.

Breakfast included in rates. Type of meal: full breakfast. Evening snack and banquet service available. MAP. Ceiling fan in room. Cable TV, VCR, fax, copier and library on premises. Handicap access. Weddings, small meetings, family reunions and seminars hosted. Antiques, fishing, parks, shopping, downhill skiing, cross-country skiing, sporting events, theater and watersports nearby. TAC10.

"I'd have to put on a black tie in Long Island to find food as good as this and best of all it's in a relaxed country atmosphere. Meals are underpriced."

Weathersfield

I4

The Inn at Weathersfield

Rt 106 Box 165
Weathersfield, VT 05151
(802)263-9217 (800)477-4828
Fax:(802)263-9219

Rates: $195-220. MAP.
Payment: MC VISA AX DS.
Innkeeper(s): Diane.
Circa: 1795.

Rooms: 12 rooms with PB, 8 with FP. 3 suites. 1 conference room.
Beds: QDT.

Built by Thomas Prentis, a Revolutionary War veteran, this was originally a four-room farmhouse set on 237 acres of wilderness. Two rooms were added in 1796, and a carriage house in 1830. During the Civil War, the inn served as a station on the Underground Railroad. Six pillars give the inn a Southern Colonial look, and there are 12 fireplaces, a beehive oven, wide-plank floors and period antiques throughout.

Type of meal: early coffee/tea. Dinner, picnic lunch and room service available. MAP. Turn-down service in room. Cable TV, VCR, fax, copier, computer, sauna and child care on premises. Handicap access. 21 acres. Weddings, small meetings, family reunions and seminars hosted. Antiques, shopping, downhill skiing, cross-country skiing, sporting events and theater nearby.

Publicity: *Boston Herald, Los Angeles Times, Country Inns, Colonial Homes, Better Homes & Gardens, National Geographic Traveler.*

"There isn't one thing we didn't enjoy about our weekend with you and we are constantly reliving it with much happiness."

Austin Hill Inn

Rt 100, Box 859
West Dover, VT 05356
(802)464-5281 (800)332-7352
Fax:(802)464-1229

Rates: $90-125.
Payment: MC VISA AX DS.
Innkeeper(s): Robbie Sweeney.
Circa: 1930.

Rooms: 12 rooms with PB. 1 conference room.
Beds: KQDT.

Situated outside the historic village of West Dover, at the edge of a mountain, this completely renovated inn has walls decorated with old barn board and floral Victorian wallpapers. Old antiques and family heirlooms include family photographs dating from 1845. Most rooms have balconies and four-poster or brass beds. A full country breakfast in the fireplaced dining room is offered, as well as afternoon tea, complimentary wine and cheese.

Breakfast and afternoon tea included in rates. Type of meal: full breakfast. Catering service available. Fax, copier and computer on premises. Antiques, fishing, parks, downhill skiing, cross-country skiing and theater nearby.

Location: Mount Snow Valley.

Publicity: *Garden City Life, Newsday, Greenwich Times.*

"Another repeat of perfection."

Deerhill Inn

Valley View Rd, PO Box 136
West Dover, VT 05356-0136
(802)464-3100 (800)993-3379
Fax:(802)464-5474

Rates: $86-220. MAP.
Payment: MC VISA AX PC TC.
Innkeeper(s): Michael & Linda Anelli.
Circa: 1954.

Rooms: 15 rooms with PB, 4 with FP. 2 suites.
Beds: KQDT.

Guests who wish to ski will be happy to note that Mt. Snow and Haystack ski areas are nearby, and all will delight in the inn's panoramic views of both places as well as other mountains. Rooms are inviting as this is a place for comfort and romance. Four rooms include a fireplace. Several rooms throughout the inn are decorated with hand-painted murals. Gourmet dinners are available, and guests can select the Modified American Plan, which will include both breakfast and dinner in the rates. For the dinners, guests might start off with Portabello mushrooms stuffed with crab and lobster. From there veal medallions, grilled New York Sirloin steak or perhaps a grilled stuffed chicken breast might suffice. At breakfast, items such as pancakes, French toast or omelets with sides of potatoes, breads and bacon or sausage are served. The inn has been the site of weddings, and conference facilities are available.

Breakfast included in rates. Type of meal: full breakfast. MAP. Turn-down service and cable TV in room. VCR, fax, copier, swimming, tennis and library on premises. Handicap access. Weddings, small meetings, family reunions and seminars hosted. Antiques, fishing, parks, shopping, downhill skiing, cross-country skiing, sporting events, theater and watersports nearby.

Special Discounts: Ski, golf and fishing packages; mid-week promotions.

"A cozy fire, soft terry robes, warm flannel sheets, wonderful food and friendly innkeepers and staff - the perfect get away place to be pampered."

Shield Inn

Rt 100, Box 366
West Dover, VT 05356
(802)464-3984
Fax:(802)464-5322
E-mail: shieldinn@aol.com

Rates: $90-240.
Payment: MC VISA PC TC.
Innkeeper(s): Phyllis & Lou Isaacson.
Circa: 1959.

Rooms: 12 rooms with PB, 7 with FP. 1 suite.
Beds: KQDT.

VT

Three acres of Vermont countryside create a secluded setting at Shield Inn. Each suite is individually decorated and includes a fireplace and a Jacuzzi tub. The innkeepers are avid music lovers and schedule a variety of concerts and performances at the inn throughout the year. Guests enjoy everything from chamber music to jazz to piano recitals. The hearty breakfasts include cereals, fresh fruit, juices, breads and entrees such as

French toast or herb, vegetable and cheese omelets. During the ski season, the rates are set on a Modified American Plan (MAP), and both breakfast and dinner are included. Skiers will appreciate the close access to nearby cross-country and downhill slopes.

Breakfast included in rates. Type of meal: full breakfast. Cable TV in room. VCR, fax, copier and library on premises. Weddings, small meetings, family reunions and seminars hosted. Antiques, fishing, parks, shopping, downhill skiing, cross-country skiing, theater and watersports nearby. TAC10.

Special Discounts: Individual basis - 7 nights for price of 6, multiple room discounts.

West Dover Inn

Rt 100 Box 1208
West Dover, VT 05356
(802)464-5207
Fax:(802)464-2173

Rates: $80-205.
Payment: MC VISA AX PC TC.
Innkeeper(s): Greg Gramas & Monique Phelan.
Circa: 1846.

Rooms: 12 rooms with PB, 6 with FP. 4 suites. 1 conference room.
Beds: QDT.

This inn served originally as a stagecoach stop and has been serving guests for 150 years. Its Greek Revival structure, especially during the holidays when the exterior is illuminated with strings of lights, is what many of us might conjure up if we were to imagine a Vermont country inn. Two guest rooms and each of the four suites include a fireplace. The suites also have whirlpool tubs. Handmade quilts and antiques add to the New England country appeal. During fall foliage season, guests can opt for breakfast-only rates or choose the Modified American Plan rates, which include breakfast and dinner. Dinner at the inn's restaurant, Gregory's, is a treat. Savory appetizers, such as a Portabello with crumbled feta cheese or grilled shrimp marinated in tequila and lime, are starters. These are followed by entree selections such as mesquite grilled sirloin, poached salmon with corn and crab fritters, or perhaps marinated, grilled lamb chops.

Breakfast included in rates. Type of meal: full breakfast. Cable TV in room. VCR, fax and library on premises. Weddings, small meetings, family reunions and seminars hosted. Antiques, fishing, parks, shopping, downhill skiing, cross-country skiing, theater and watersports nearby. TAC10.

Special Discounts: Groups - 10%.

"Thank you so much for hosting our wedding. It turned out just as we had hoped."

Wilder H5

Stonecrest Farm B&B

PO Box 504, 119 Christian St
Wilder, VT 05088-0504
(802)296-2425 (800)730-2425
Fax:(802)295-1135

Rates: $105-135.
Payment: MC VISA AX PC TC.
Innkeeper(s): Gail L. Sanderson.
Circa: 1810.

Rooms: 6 rooms with PB.
Beds: QDT.

Two acres of grounds and a charming red barn create a secluded, country atmosphere at Stonecrest Farm, which is located three-and-a-half miles from Dartmouth College. The former dairy farm was owned by a prominent Vermont family and hosted notable guests such as Calvin Coolidge and Amelia Earhart. Guest rooms are decorated with antiques, and beds are topped with down comforters. The abundant breakfasts feature a different entree each morning. Orange French toast and vegetable frittatas are some of the possibilities.

Breakfast and afternoon tea included in rates. Types of meals: full breakfast and early coffee/tea. Cable TV, VCR, fax, copier and library on premises. Family reunions hosted. Limited German and French spoken. Antiques, fishing, parks, shopping, downhill skiing, cross-country skiing, sporting events, theater and watersports nearby. TAC10.

Special Discounts: Stay one week, get one night free, other rates negotiable.

"Your house is enchanting. I especially liked your grandfather clock in the hallway."

The Inn at Quail Run

HCR 63 Box 28,
106 Smith Rd
Wilmington, VT 05363-7905
(802)464-3362 (800)343-7227
Fax:(802)464-3362

Rates: $75-125.
Payment: MC VISA AX DS TC.
Innkeeper(s): Tom, Marie & Molly Martin.
Circa: 1968.

Rooms: 13 rooms with PB, 4 with FP. 1 suite. 1 cottage.
Beds: KQT.

Enjoy the serenity of the Vermont countryside at this inn surrounded by 12 private acres and mountain views. Brass and antique beds are covered with comforters perfect for snuggling. A hearty country breakfast is served each morning. Murder-mystery and Christmas Inn Vermont packages add an extra flair to vacations. Relax in the sauna after working out in the exercise room or solar-heated pool. Skiing and sleigh rides make good use of the Vermont winter. Country Theatre, flea markets and the Marlboro Music Festival are nearby attractions.

Type of meal: full breakfast. Cable TV, VCR, fax, copier, swimming, sauna and library on premises. 12 acres. Weddings, small meetings, family reunions and seminars hosted. Antiques, fishing, parks, shopping, downhill skiing, cross-country skiing, theater and watersports nearby.

The Red Shutter Inn

PO Box 636
Wilmington, VT 05363-0636
(802)464-3768

Rates: $100-170.
Payment: MC VISA AX DS PC TC.
Innkeeper(s): Renee & Tad Lyon.
Circa: 1894.

Rooms: 9 rooms with PB, 2 with FP. 2 suites.
Beds: KQD.

This colonial inn sits on a five-acre hillside amid maples, pin oaks and evergreens. Tucked behind the inn is the renovated carriage house; among its charms is a cozy fireplace suite. In the summer, guests can enjoy alfresco dining on an awning-covered porch. The Red Shutter Inn, with its woodstove in the sitting room, antique furnishings and view of a rushing river, provides a congenial atmosphere. Nearby are antique shops, galleries and craft shops.

Breakfast included in rates. Type of meal: full breakfast. Picnic lunch and banquet service available. Ceiling fan and cable TV in room. VCR, fax, copier and library on premises. Weddings, small meetings, family reunions and seminars hosted. Antiques, fishing, parks, shopping, downhill skiing, cross-country skiing and watersports nearby.

Publicity: *USA Weekend.*

Special Discounts: 10% midweek discount for multiple night stays.

"You've made The Red Shutter Inn a cozy and relaxing hideaway."

Trail's End, A Country Inn

5 Trail's End Ln
Wilmington, VT 05363-7925
(802)464-2727 (800)859-2585

Rates: $95-185.
Payment: MC VISA AX PC TC.
Innkeeper(s): Bill & Mary Kilburn.
Circa: 1956.

Rooms: 15 rooms with PB, 6 with FP. 2 suites. 1 conference room.
Beds: QDT.

The innkeepers transformed this rustic inn from its 1950s decor into a beautiful romantic bed and breakfast. The game room, where cookies and hot cider are served each day, features elegant wing-back chairs and a pool table, while the living room offers four overstuffed couches in front of a 22-foot Fieldstone fireplace. Each bedroom is decorated in a different color scheme and utilizes brass, white wicker and family heirlooms for a chic country atmosphere.

Breakfast and afternoon tea included in rates. Types of meals: full breakfast and early coffee/tea. Ceiling fan and cable TV in room. Copier, swimming, tennis and library on premises. 10 acres. Weddings, small meetings, family reunions and seminars hosted. Antiques, fishing, parks, shopping, downhill skiing, cross-country skiing, theater and watersports nearby. TAC10.

Location: Four miles north of the traffic light in Wilmington.

Publicity: *Inn Times, Snow Country, Sun Country, Changing Times.*

Special Discounts: Five day ski week, seven day summer plan.

"Thank you again for an absolutely wonderful weekend."

White House

PO Box 757
Wilmington, VT 05363-0757
(802)464-2135 (800)541-2135
Fax:(802)464-5222

Rates: $108-195.
Payment: MC VISA AX DC PC TC.
Innkeeper(s): Robert Grinold.
Circa: 1915.

Rooms: 22 rooms, 23 with PB, 9 with FP. 1 suite. 3 conference rooms.
Beds: KQD.

White House was built as a summer home for a wealthy lumber baron, and he spared no expense. The inn has 14 fireplaces, rich woodwork and hand-crafted French doors. Nine of the guest rooms include fireplaces, and some have a balcony, terrace or whirlpool tub. Seven guest rooms are located in an adjacent farmhouse. There is a swimming pool on the premises. Guests are treated to breakfast, and award-winning, gourmet dinners are available in the dining rooms. The inn has earned a four-diamond rating.

Breakfast included in rates. Types of meals: full breakfast, gourmet breakfast and early coffee/tea. Dinner and room service available. Ceiling fan in room. Cable TV, VCR, fax, copier, spa, swimming and sauna on premises. Handicap access. Weddings, small meetings, family reunions and seminars hosted. French spoken. Antiques, fishing, parks, shopping, downhill skiing, cross-country skiing, theater and watersports nearby. TAC10.

Special Discounts: Group discounts depending upon size of group.

Windsor — H5

Juniper Hill Inn

Juniper Hill Rd, RR 1 Box 79
Windsor, VT 05089
(802)674-5273 (800)359-2541
Fax:(802)674-5273

Rates: $90-140. MAP.
Payment: MC VISA DS.
Innkeeper(s): Robert & Susanne Pearl.
Circa: 1902.

Rooms: 16 rooms with PB.
Beds: QD.

This Colonial Revival mansion was built for Maxwell Evarts, who was the son of William Evarts, attorney general to Andrew Johnson. It was Maxwell's ties with the Union Pacific Railroad, which led to his familiarity with politicians and business leaders of the time. Teddy Roosevelt reportedly enjoyed the hospitality of the Evarts on a trip to Windsor. The common areas of the inn include a great hall with a massive fireplace, two dining rooms, a sitting parlor and a library.

Breakfast included in rates. Types of meals: full breakfast and early coffee/tea. Dinner available. MAP. Ceiling fan in room. VCR, fax, swimming, bicycles and library on premises. 14 acres. Weddings, small meetings, family reunions and seminars hosted. Antiques, fishing, shopping, downhill skiing, cross-country skiing and sporting events nearby. TAC10.

Publicity: *Country Inns of Vermont, Travel Holiday, Sunday Boston Globe, Bon Appetit, Spur.*

"It was the charm of your place and your personal graciousness that made it such a pleasure."

Woodstock — H4

Canterbury House

43 Pleasant St
Woodstock, VT 05091-1129
(802)457-3077 (800)390-3077

Rates: $85-150.
Payment: MC VISA AX PC.
Innkeeper(s): Fred & Celeste Holden.
Circa: 1880.

Rooms: 8 rooms with PB, 1 with FP.
Beds: KQDT.

National Geographic tabbed Woodstock as one of America's most beautiful villages, and this Victorian inn offers a lovely stopping place for those exploring the area. Visitors find themselves within easy walking distance of antique stores, art galleries, museums, restaurants and shopping. The inn has bicycles available for guest use, perfect for an outing on the area's scenic country roads. Ski lifts at Killington, Pico and Okemo are only minutes away.

Breakfast included in rates. Type of meal: gourmet breakfast. Air conditioning and cable TV in room. VCR on premises. Weddings, small meetings and family reunions hosted. Antiques, fishing, parks, shopping, downhill skiing, cross-country skiing, sporting events, theater and watersports nearby. TAC10.

Publicity: *Philadelphia Inquirer.*

Carriage House of Woodstock

15 Rt 4 W
Woodstock, VT 05091-1253
(802)457-4322
Fax:(802)457-4322

Rates: $95-135.
Payment: MC VISA AX DS PC TC.
Innkeeper(s): Dennis & Shirley Wagner.
Circa: 1850.

Rooms: 7 rooms with PB.
Beds: QT.

This century-old home has been generously refurbished and features rooms filled with period antiques and individual decor. Those in search of relaxation will find plenty of possibilities, from a hammock tucked underneath a shade tree to a porch offering a view of trees and fields. Antique shopping, the historic Billings Farm Museum and plenty of outdoor activities are found in the Woodstock area. Fall and spring bring an explosion of color, and scenic drives will take you under covered bridges.

Breakfast and afternoon tea included in rates. Types of meals: gourmet breakfast and early coffee/tea. Air conditioning and turn-down service in room. Cable TV, VCR, fax, copier, bicycles and library on premises. Weddings, small meetings, family reunions and seminars hosted. Antiques, fishing, parks, shopping, downhill skiing, cross-country skiing, sporting events, theater and watersports nearby.

Kedron Valley Inn

Rt 106 Box 145
Woodstock, VT 05071
(802)457-1473 (800)836-1193
Fax:(802)457-4469
E-mail: kedroninn@aol.com

Rates: $99-195.
Payment: MC VISA AX DS.
Innkeeper(s): Max & Merrily Comins.
Circa: 1822.

Rooms: 27 rooms with PB, 14 with FP. 2 suites. 1 conference room.
Beds: QDT.

Travelers have made this rustic, cozy inn a stopping point for more than 150 years. One of the guest buildings has a secret attic passageway and is rumored to have been a stop on the Underground Railway during the Civil War. A 60-piece quilt collection includes century-old quilts created by the hostess' great-grandmothers. Guests need not leave the grounds to enjoy a white-sand beach and swimming lake. A stable with horses is nearby. Fourteen of the rooms boast fireplaces and most rooms feature canopy beds. After feasting on a delectable breakfast, spend the day searching for antiques or viewing historic estates. The gourmet dinners are a treat.

Breakfast included in rates. Type of meal: full breakfast. Dinner available. Ceiling fan in room. Fax, copier and swimming on premises. 15 acres. Weddings, small meetings, family reunions and seminars hosted. German spoken. Antiques, fishing, parks, shopping, downhill skiing, cross-country skiing and theater nearby. TAC10.

Publicity: *Oprah Winfrey Show, Good Housekeeping, Country Living, Country Home, Yankee, Gourmet, Ski, New York Times, London Times.*

Special Discounts: Midweek discounts non-peak, plus group rates.

"It's what you dream a Vermont country inn should be and the most impressive feature is the innkeepers .. outgoing, warm and friendly."

The Lincoln Inn at The Covered Bridge

RR 2 Box 40
Woodstock, VT 05091-9721
(802)457-3312
Fax:(802)457-5808
E-mail: lincon2@aol.com

Rates: $99-139.
Payment: MC VISA DS PC TC.
Innkeeper(s): Kurt & Lori Hildbrand.
Circa: 1870.

Rooms: 6 rooms with PB. 1 conference room.
Beds: KQD.

This admirable old farmhouse sits on six acres bordered by the Lincoln Covered Bridge and the Ottauquechee River. Lawns meander to a rise overlooking the water. There's a gazebo here and nearby, a wooden swing on long chains gently sways from a tall maple. A recent renovation has revealed hand-hewn beams in the library and a fireplace in the common room. The inn's continental cuisine provides a memorable dinner.

Breakfast included in rates. Types of meals: gourmet breakfast and early coffee/tea. Dinner, evening snack, picnic lunch, lunch, banquet service and catering service available. Air conditioning in room. Cable TV, VCR, fax, copier, swimming and library on premises. Weddings, small meetings, family reunions and seminars hosted. German spoken. Antiques, fishing, parks, shopping, downhill skiing, cross-country skiing, sporting events, theater and watersports nearby.

Publicity: *Travelhost.*

"Feels like family!"

Woodstock (Reading)

Bailey's Mills B&B

PO Box 117, Bailey's Mills Rd
Woodstock
(Reading), VT 05062
(802)484-7809 (800)639-3437

Rates: $70-110.
Payment: MC VISA PC TC.
Innkeeper(s): Barbara Thaeder & Don Whitaker.
Circa: 1820.

Rooms: 3 rooms with PB, 2 with FP. 1 suite.
Beds: KQ.

This historic Federal-style inn features the architectural stylings of a Southern manor and boasts a ballroom and 11 fireplaces, with two original beehive ovens. The suite has a king bed and private sun porch. Two rooms have working fireplaces. The inn's sun porch overlooks the ruins of the old mill dam of the original house. There is a pond and stream on the premises, as well as a graveyard. The quiet country setting is perfect for bike rides and relaxing strolls, and terrific photo opportunities are found at Jenne Farm, just a few minutes away.

Breakfast included in rates. Types of meals: continental-plus breakfast and early coffee/tea. Swimming and library on premises. 48 acres. Weddings and family reunions hosted. Antiques, fishing, parks, shopping, downhill skiing, cross-country skiing and theater nearby. TAC10.

Pets Allowed: Small, polite, innkeeper approval required.

Special Discounts: Winter packages, three day special price; also coupon in brochure.

"If words could encapsulate what a wonderful weekend would be, it would have to be 'Bailey's Mills B&B.' Your home is beautiful. It is elegant yet homey."

Bruchetta

Deerhill Inn
West Dover, Vt.

- ½ loaf Italian or French bread
- 1 small purple eggplant
- 1 large red pepper roasted and peeled (divided into 4 pieces)
- 4 slices mozzarella cheese
- ¼ cup basil pesto
- 1 cup marinara sauce
- ½ cup olive oil to which 1 slivered garlic clove has been added

Slice four ¾"-thick pieces of bread from loaf. Brush one side of each with oil. Place on hot grill (may use broiler) until toasted. While browning, brush other side with oil, turn and toast. Remove from grill. Place toasted bread on a cookie sheet and top each with pesto. Slice eggplant into ½ " slices. Cook eggplant in the same manner as bread.

Remove eggplant from grill or broiler and place each slice on top of each slice of bread. Place one piece of roasted pepper on top of each slice of eggplant and one slice of mozzarella cheese on top of each pepper. Bake in 450-degree oven until cheese melts. Remove and serve at once on a bed of marinara sauce.

Serves 4.

The Lilac Inn's Banana-Rum Bread Pudding with Butter Rum Sauce

The Lilac Inn
Brandon, Vt.

Banana Bread:
(Bread can be made several days in advance and kept refrigerated until needed)
1 ¾ cups all-purpose flour
⅔ cup sugar
2 t baking powder
½ t baking soda
¼ t salt
1 ½ cups mashed ripe bananas (3-4 bananas)
⅓ cup butter
2 T half and half
3 eggs

Preheat oven to 350 degrees. Butter an 8" by 4" by 2" loaf pan.

Using an electric mixer fitted with a paddle, place the following ingredients in a large bowl: one cup of the flour, the sugar, baking powder, baking soda and salt. Add mashed banana, butter and half and half. Beat on low speed for two minutes and scrape bowl. Add eggs and remaining flour and beat on medium speed for one minute until blended.

Pour batter into prepared pan and bake for 55 to 60 minutes or until toothpick inserted near the center comes out clean. Cool in pan for 10 minutes on wire rack. Remove from pan and cool on rack thoroughly. Wrap and store overnight before using in pudding.

Pudding:
Sliced banana bread in ½ " cubes
1 quart half and half
3 T unsalted butter
1 ½ t salt
2 t pure vanilla extract
1 ¼ cups firmly packed dark brown sugar
4 large eggs
3 large egg yolks
1 cup golden raisins
¼ cup dark or light rum
2 T butter
2 T sugar
½ t cinnamon

Preheat oven to 400 degrees. Cut banana bread into ½ inch cubes leaving the crust on and put on parchment lined baking sheet. Bake in oven until golden brown and lightly crusted. Remove from oven and cool in pan.

Butter 8-by-4-by-2" loaf pan. In a medium sauce pan, heat half and half, butter, salt and vanilla over moderate heat just until hot, but not simmering. In a large bowl, whisk together sugar, eggs, egg yolks, rum and half and half in a steady stream, whisking. (Placing bowl on wet towel will help to keep it in place). Add raisins and bread cubes and toss gently. Set mixture aside until almost all liquid is absorbed into bread cubes about 1 hour.

Assembly: Reset oven to 350 degrees. Fill prepared loaf pan with mixture. Mix sugar and cinnamon. Dot pudding with butter and sprinkle cinnamon-sugar mixture on top. Place pudding pan in a baking pan with sides on middle rack of oven. Pour hot water halfway up sides of pudding pan. Bake until pudding is puffed and golden, about 40 minutes. Cool on rack until warm.

Butter Rum Sauce:
1 cup sugar
2 ¼ cups water
1 cinnamon stick or 1 t ground cinnamon
1 T unsalted butter
½ t cornstarch
2 T light or dark rum

In a medium size saucepan, combine sugar, 2 cups water, cinnamon and butter, and bring to a boil. Stir in cornstarch blended with remaining ¼ cup water and simmer, stirring, until sauce is clear. Remove from heat and add rum. Sauce will be thin.

To serve: Cut pudding into ¾" slices (heat briefly in microwave if cool) and serve with warm rum sauce. Also may be served with vanilla ice cream.

Virginia

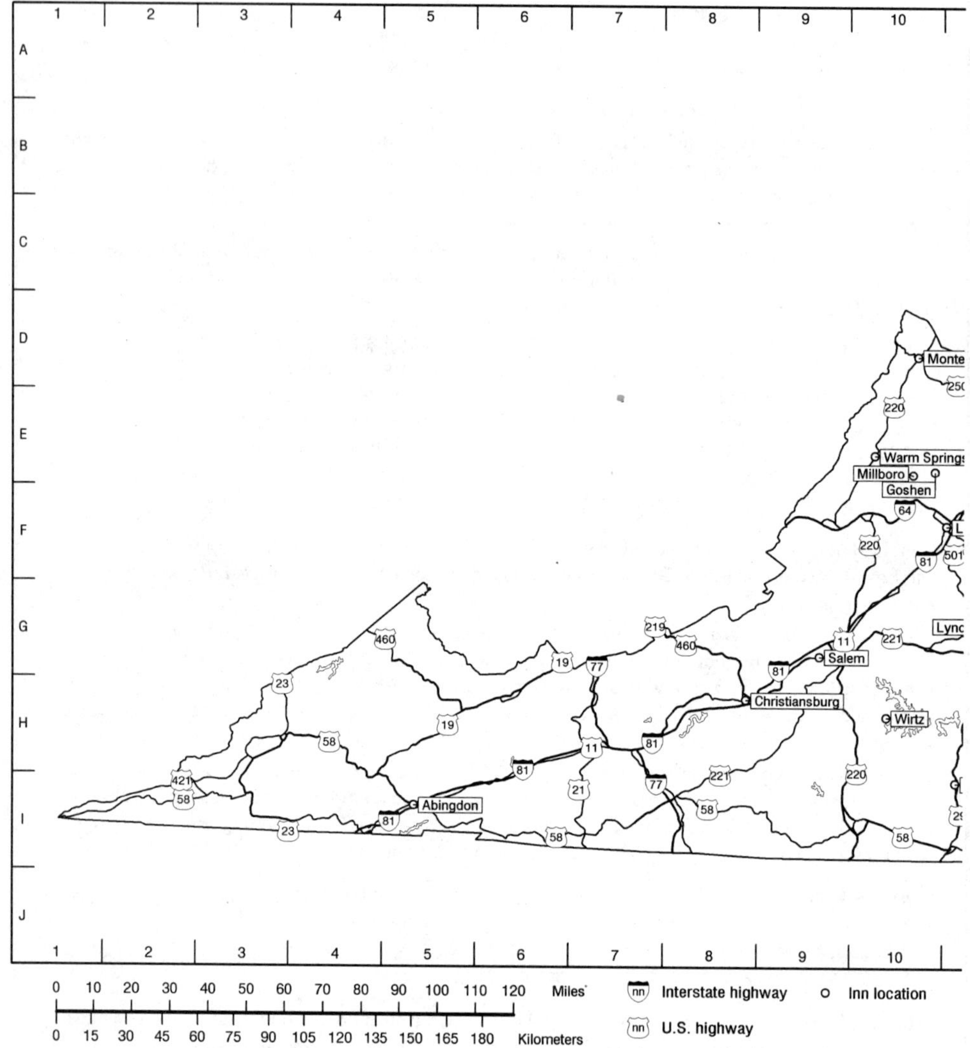

1 2 3 4 5 6 7 8 9 10
A B C D E F G H I J
Warm Springs
Millboro
Goshen
Salem
Christiansburg
Wirtz
Abingdon
0 10 20 30 40 50 60 70 80 90 100 110 120 Miles
0 15 30 45 60 75 90 105 120 135 150 165 180 Kilometers
Interstate highway
U.S. highway
Inn location

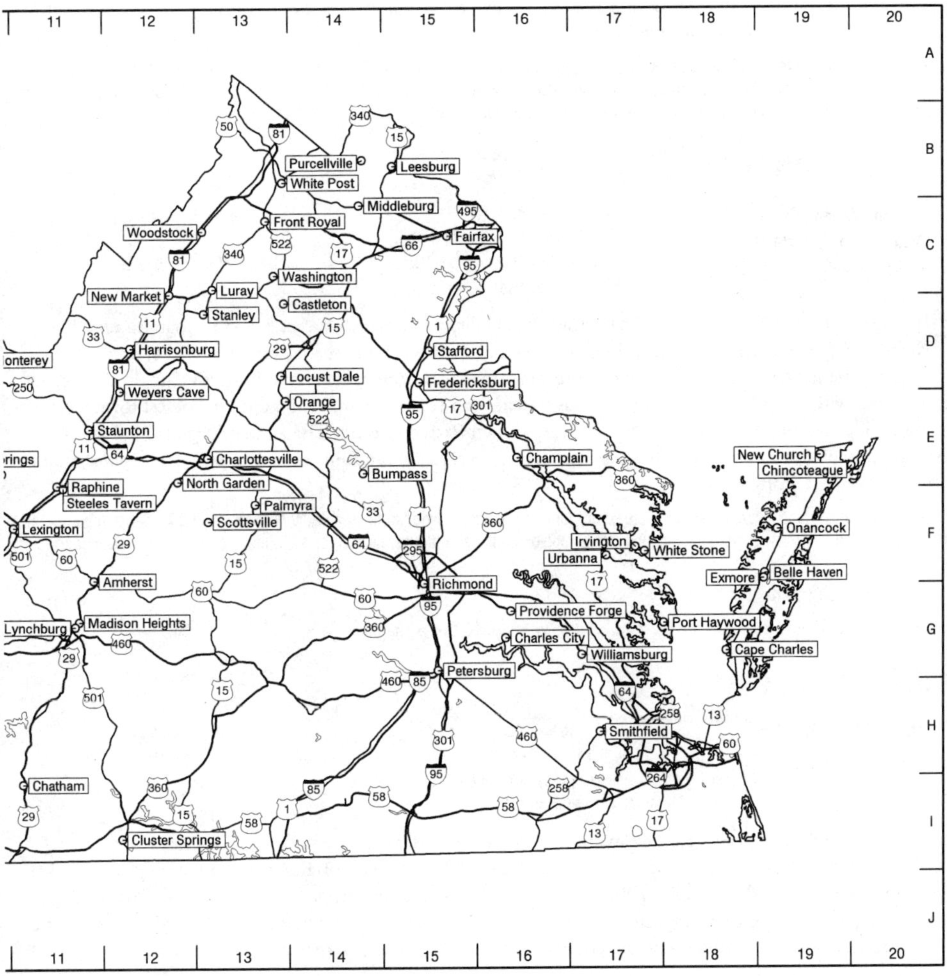

11 12 13 14 15 16 17 18 19 20

A B C D E F G H I J

Purcellville
Leesburg
White Post
Middleburg
Front Royal
Woodstock
Fairfax
Washington
New Market
Luray
Castleton
Stanley
Harrisonburg
onterey
Stafford
Locust Dale
Fredericksburg
Weyers Cave
Orange
Staunton
rings
Charlottesville
Champlain
New Church
Chincoteague
Bumpass
Raphine
North Garden
Steeles Tavern
Palmyra
Scottsville
Lexington
Onancock
Irvington
White Stone
Urbanna
Exmore
Belle Haven
Amherst
Richmond
Providence Forge
Port Haywood
Lynchburg
Madison Heights
Charles City
Williamsburg
Cape Charles
Petersburg
Smithfield
Chatham
Cluster Springs

11 12 13 14 15 16 17 18 19 20

VA

Maplewood Farm B&B

20004 Cleveland Rd
Abingdon, VA 24211-5836
(540)628-2640

Rates: $75.
Payment: TC.
Innkeeper(s): Doris Placak.
Circa: 1880.

Rooms: 3 rooms with PB.
Beds: QDT.

From the arched windows of this farmhouse, an example of Virginia Vernacular design, guests can gaze out at the wooded countryside. This site is especially picturesque during the fall foliage season. There are more than 60 acres to wander, or guests can simply take in the view of trees and a lake from the deck. The decor is elegant, but not too posh, decorated with French influences. The home rests on a working horse farm, and guests can arrange to board their own horses on the property.

Breakfast and afternoon tea included in rates. Types of meals: full breakfast, gourmet breakfast and early coffee/tea. Evening snack and picnic lunch available. Child care on premises. Handicap access. 66 acres. Weddings, small meetings, family reunions and seminars hosted. Antiques, fishing, parks, shopping, downhill skiing, cross-country skiing, sporting events, theater and watersports nearby.

Summerfield Inn

101 W Valley St
Abingdon, VA 24210
(540)628-5905 (800)668-5905

Rates: $75-125.
Payment: MC VISA AX PC TC.
Innkeeper(s): Champe & Don Hyatt.
Circa: 1923.

Rooms: 7 rooms with PB. 1 conference room.
Beds: Beds: KQDT.

Flags display the pineapple insignia that means hospitality to so many of us at post-Victorian homes. The cheerful rooms are decorated with floral touches and items such as four-poster beds, wicker and antiques. There is a guest pantry for those seeking a refreshment, and the innkeepers serve full breakfasts in the elegant dining room with freshly baked cinnamon rolls, quiche and seasonal fruit. Abingdon, the oldest town west of the Blue Ridge Mountains, is the site for the well-known Barter Theatre. The annual Virginia Highlands Festival, pleasant streets of historic houses, local arts and crafts, an old mill and many excellent restaurants add to the area's cultural offerings.

Breakfast included in rates. Type of meal: full breakfast. Air conditioning, ceiling fan and cable TV in room. VCR, bicycles and library on premises. Handicap access. Small meetings and family reunions hosted. Antiques, fishing, parks, shopping, theater and watersports nearby. TAC10.

Special Discounts: Three days 10%.

"A road-weary poet looks for a place with good vibes. Summerfield Inn is the place."

White Birches

268 White Mills Rd
Abingdon, VA 24210
(540)676-2140 (800)BIRCHES

Rates: $75.
Payment: MC VISA AX PC.
Innkeeper(s): Michael & Paulette Wartella.
Circa: 1910.

Rooms: 3 rooms with PB.
Beds: Beds: Q.

This Cape Cod-style home, painted in creamy blue hues, is decorated with an assortment of English and American antiques. Oriental rugs decorate the floors. The covered porches, complete with plants, wicker and paddle fans, are an idyllic spot for the morning meal. A koi pond completes the lush look. The meal is a formal affair, served with silver, crystal and antique china. The innkeepers often choose this spot to serve afternoon refreshments. Outlet shopping, the popular Barter Theatre and a variety of restaurants are nearby.

Breakfast and evening snack included in rates. Type of meal: full breakfast. Air conditioning, turn-down service, ceiling fan and cable TV in room. VCR on premises. Antiques, parks, shopping, downhill skiing and theater nearby.

Amherst

F11

Dulwich Manor B&B Inn

Rt 5, Box 173A, Rt 60E
Amherst, VA 24521
(804)946-7207

Rates: $69-89.
Payment: PC TC.
Innkeeper(s): Bob & Judy Reilly.
Circa: 1912.

Rooms: 6 rooms, 4 with PB, 2 with FP.
Beds: QD.

This red Flemish brick and white columned English Manor sits on five secluded acres at the end of a country lane and in the midst of 85 acres of woodland and meadow. The Blue Ridge Mountains may be enjoyed from the veranda. The entry features a large center hall and a wide oak staircase. Walls are 14 inches thick. The 18 rooms include a 50-foot-long ballroom on the third floor. The inn is decorated with a creative mix of antiques, reproductions and modern art. Your host is a professional singer and actor and your hostess was in public relations and a costumer for the theater.

Breakfast included in rates. Types of meals: full breakfast and early coffee/tea. Afternoon tea available. Air conditioning and ceiling fan in room. Spa on premises. Weddings, small meetings, family reunions and seminars hosted. Antiques, fishing, parks, shopping, downhill skiing, sporting events, theater and watersports nearby. TAC10.

Publicity: *Country Inn.*

Special Discounts: Negotiable mid-week December-March, weekly rate - 15%.

"Our experience at Dulwich Manor surpassed all of our inn visits. A truly delightful stay!"

Belle Haven

F19

Bay View Waterfront B&B

35350 Copes Dr
Belle Haven, VA 23306
(804)442-6963 (800)442-6966

Rates: $95.
Payment: PC TC.
Innkeeper(s): Wayne & Mary Will Browning.
Circa: 1800.

Rooms: 3 rooms, 1 with PB, 1 with FP.
Beds: D.

This rambling inn stretches more than 100 feet across and has five roof levels. There are heart-pine floors, high ceilings and several fireplaces. The hillside location affords bay breezes and wide views of the Chesapeake, Occohannock Creek and the inn's surrounding 140 acres. The innkeepers are descendants of several generations who have owned and operated Bay View. If you come by water to the inn's deep water dock, look behind Channel Marker 16.

Breakfast included in rates. Type of meal: full breakfast. Air conditioning in room. VCR, swimming, bicycles and library on premises. 140 acres. Weddings, small meetings and family reunions hosted. Antiques, fishing, parks, shopping, theater and watersports nearby. TAC10.

Publicity: *Rural Living, City.*

"We loved staying in your home, and especially in the room with a beautiful view of the bay. You have a lovely home and a beautiful location. Thank you so much for your hospitality."

Bumpass

E14

Rockland Farm Retreat

3609 Lewiston Rd
Bumpass, VA 23024-9659
(540)895-5098

Rates: $60-65. MAP.
Payment: AX PC.
Innkeeper(s): Roy E. Mixon.
Circa: 1820.

Rooms: 4 rooms, 3 with PB. 1 suite. 2 conference rooms.
Beds: DT.

The 75 acres of Rockland Farm includes pasture land, livestock, vineyard, crops and a farm pond for fishing. The grounds here are said to have spawned Alex Haley's "Roots." Guests can study documents and explore local cemeteries describing life under slavery in the area surrounding this historic home and 272-year-old farm.

Breakfast included in rates. Type of meal: full breakfast. Dinner, lunch, banquet service and catering service available. MAP. Air conditioning in room. VCR on premises. 75 acres. Weddings, small meetings, family reunions and seminars hosted. French and Spanish spoken. Amusement parks, antiques, fishing, parks, shopping and watersports nearby. TAC10.

Pets Allowed.

Location: Thirty minutes south of Fredericksburg, Rt 601 at Lake Anna.

Publicity: *Washington Post, Free Lance-Star.*

Cape Charles

G18

Bay Avenue's Sunset B&B

108 Bay Ave
Cape Charles, VA 23310
(804)331-2424 (888)4BAY-AVE
Fax:(804)331-4877

Rates: $75-95.
Payment: MC VISA AX DS TC.
Innkeeper(s): Albert Longo & Joyce Tribble.
Circa: 1915.

Rooms: 4 rooms with PB.
Beds: Q.

Located on waterfront Chesapeake Bay property, this B&B offers delightful breezes from its Victorian porch. Newly renovated guest rooms include eclectic decor and Hunter fans. The Victoria Room offers a queen bed, fireplace and clawfoot tub. Awake to the scent of freshly brewed coffee. After a hearty breakfast of fresh fruits, home-baked breads and delicious entrees, explore the uncrowded beach or take in a day of birdwatching, fishing or cycling.

Breakfast included in rates. Types of meals: full breakfast and early coffee/tea. Air conditioning, ceiling fan, cable TV and VCR in room. Fax and bicycles on premises. Weddings, small meetings, family reunions and seminars hosted. Antiques, fishing, parks, theater and watersports nearby. TAC10.

Publicity: *Port Folio, Southern Inns.*

"Your house is beautiful, the meals were wonderful and you really made us feel at home."

Castleton

D13

Blue Knoll Farm

Box 110 Gore Rd
Castleton, VA 22716
(540)937-5234

Rates: $95-125.
Payment: MC VISA PC TC.
Innkeeper(s): Mary & Gil Carlson.
Circa: 1850.

Rooms: 4 rooms with PB, 1 with FP.
Beds: KQ.

The original house of the Blue Knoll Farm is pre-Civil War, and many Civil War battles were fought in the area. The farmhouse is in the scenic valley of Castleton Mountain. Guest rooms feature antiques, family mementos and cozy comforters. Some rooms have fireplaces. Guests may relax on the wicker chairs on the Victorian porch.

Breakfast included in rates. Types of meals: full breakfast and early coffee/tea. Air conditioning in room. Antiques, parks, shopping and theater nearby.

Publicity: *Conde Nast Traveler.*

"Beautiful, charming inn. Delightful room, deep sleep and a delicious breakfast. Thank you. We will be back."

Champlain

E16

Linden House B&B & Plantation

PO Box 23
Champlain, VA 22438-0023
(804)443-1170 (800)622-1202

Rates: $85-135.
Payment: MC VISA AX PC TC.
Innkeeper(s): Ken & Sandra Pounsberry.
Circa: 1750.

Rooms: 8 rooms, 4 with PB, 3 with FP. 1 suite. 1 conference room.
Beds: Q.

This restored planters home is designated a state landmark and listed in the National Register. The lush grounds boast walking trails, an English garden and a gazebo. Each of the accommodations offers something special. The Carriage Suite features country decor, antiques, a private porch and a fireplace. The Robert E. Lee and Jefferson Davis rooms have a luxurious shared bath with a Jacuzzi and steam room. The fourth-floor Linden Room affords a view of the countryside and features a high back bed.

Breakfast included in rates. Types of meals: full breakfast and early coffee/tea. Afternoon tea, evening snack, banquet service, catering service and catered breakfast available. Air conditioning, turn-down service, ceiling fan and VCR in room. Stables, bicycles and library on premises. Handicap access. 204 acres. Weddings, small meetings, family reunions and seminars hosted. Amusement parks, antiques, fishing, parks, shopping, theater and watersports nearby. TAC10.

Special Discounts: AAA members 10%; 3 for 2 winter months.

Charles City

G16

Edgewood Plantation

4800 John Tyler Memorial
Hwy, Charles City, VA 23230
(804)829-6908 (800)296-3343
Fax:(804)829-2962

Rates: $100-198.
Payment: MC VISA AX.
Innkeeper(s): Dot & Julian Boulware.
Circa: 1849.

Rooms: 8 rooms, 6 with PB, 3 with FP. 2 suites. 2 cottages. 1 conference room.
Beds: KQD.

This Carpenter Gothic plantation was built by Spencer Rowland. Romantic guest rooms are furnished with antiques and old-fashioned country artifacts. There are 10 fireplaces and a winding three-story staircase. A few yards from the inn is a three-story mill with an unusual inside mill wheel built in 1725.

Breakfast included in rates. Types of meals: full breakfast, gourmet breakfast and early coffee/tea. Afternoon tea, picnic lunch and catering service available. Turn-down service, ceiling fan and VCR in room. Fax and swimming on premises. 12 acres. Weddings, small meetings, family reunions and seminars hosted. Amusement parks, antiques, fishing, parks, shopping, sporting events, theater and watersports nearby.

Location: Halfway between Williamsburg and Richmond.

Publicity: *Country Home, Southern Living, Country, Victoria.*

"A feast for the eyes and wonderful manner in which things are displayed and put together."

North Bend Plantation

12200 Weyanoke Rd
Charles City, VA 23030
(804)829-5176 (800)841-1479
Fax:(804)829-6828

Rates: $95-135.
Payment: MC VISA PC TC.
Innkeeper(s): George & Ridgely Copland.
Circa: 1819.

Rooms: 4 rooms with PB, 1 with FP. 1 suite.
Beds: QD.

Drive up beautiful old Colonial Rt. 5 to James River Plantation Country and you will discover North Bend Plantation, an experience that ought to be a highlight of your visit to Williamsburg. Here you will stay with the Copland family, fourth generation owners of this historic estate. (The innkeeper is twice great-grandson of noted agriculturist Edmund Ruffin, who is said to have fired the first shot of the Civil War at Fort Sumter.) Sheridan headquartered at North Bend and his desk is still here, one of many treasured family heirlooms. Large guest rooms are filled with antiques original to the home. Complimentary desserts are available at a nearby four-star restaurant. Guests are served refreshments upon arrival.

VA

Breakfast included in rates. Types of meals: full breakfast and early coffee/tea. Afternoon tea available. Air conditioning and ceiling fan in room. Cable TV, fax, copier, swimming, bicycles and library on premises. 250 acres. Weddings, small meetings and family reunions hosted. Amusement parks, antiques, parks and shopping nearby. TAC10.

Location: West of Colonial Williamsburg, 25 minutes.

Publicity: *New York Times, Mid-Atlantic Country, Washington Post, Travel Talk, Southern Hospitality.*

"Your hospitality, friendship and history lessons were all priceless. Your love of life embraced us in a warmth I shall never forget."

Charlottesville E13

200 South Street Inn

200 W South St
Charlottesville, VA 22902
(804)979-0200 (800)964-7008
Fax:(804)979-4403

Rates: $100-190.
Payment: MC VISA AX DC CB PC TC.
Innkeeper(s): Brendan & Jenny Clancy.
Circa: 1844.

Rooms: 20 rooms with PB, 11 with FP. 3 suites.
Beds: QT.

This house was built for Thomas Jefferson Wertenbaker, son of Thomas Jefferson's librarian at the University of Virginia. It is furnished with English and Belgian antiques. Guests may choose rooms with whirlpool baths, fireplaces and canopy beds.

Breakfast, afternoon tea and evening snack included in rates. Types of meals: continental-plus breakfast and early coffee/tea. Air conditioning and turn-down service in room. Cable TV, fax and library on premises. Handicap access. Weddings, small meetings, family reunions and seminars hosted. Antiques, fishing, parks, shopping, downhill skiing, sporting events, theater and watersports nearby. TAC10.

Location: Downtown historic district of Charlottesville.

Publicity: *New York Times, Gourmet, Vogue, Food & Wine, Los Angeles Times, Bon Appetit, Gourmet, Mid-Atlantic Country.*

"True hospitality abounds in this fine inn which is a neatly turned complement to the inspiring history surrounding it."

Clifton Country Inn

1296 Clifton Inn Dr
Charlottesville, VA 22911
(804)971-1800 (888)971-1800
Fax:(804)971-7098
E-mail: 75507.645@compuserve.com

Rates: $145-245.
Payment: MC VISA PC.
Innkeeper(s): Craig & Donna Hartman.
Circa: 1799.

Rooms: 14 rooms with PB, 14 with FP. 7 suites. 7 cottages. 2 conference rooms.
Beds: QD.

The first resident at Clifton was Thomas Mann Randolph, who served as governor of the state and was the son-in-law of Thomas Jefferson. One of the gracious guest rooms boasts a winter view of Jefferson's estate, Monticello. Elegance and a careful attention to historical detail has kept this remarkable country inn among the best in the nation, garnering award upon award for its accommodations and cuisine. In addition to the main house, guests can opt to stay in Randolph's law office, the livery or the carriage house. Aside from the abundance of history at Clifton, the innkeepers offer a variety of outdoor pursuits, including a tennis court, swimming pool, lake and 40 acres of beautiful, wooded grounds. Breakfast at Clifton is a treat with fresh fruits, lavish entrees, meat, juices and fine coffees and teas. Afternoon tea is expansive with a selection of delectable baked goods and gourmet teas. Clifton also operates a gourmet restaurant featuring five- and six- course meals prepared by innkeeper Craig Hartman and assistant Brian MacKenzie, both Culinary Institute of America graduates.

Breakfast and afternoon tea included in rates. Types of meals: continental breakfast, full breakfast, gourmet breakfast and early coffee/tea. Dinner, banquet service, catering service and catered breakfast available. Air conditioning and turn-down service in room. Fax, copier, spa, swimming, tennis, library and child care on premises. Handicap access. 40 acres. Weddings, small meetings, family reunions and seminars hosted. Antiques, fishing, parks, shopping, downhill skiing, cross-country skiing, sporting events and theater nearby. TAC10.

Publicity: *International Living, Country Inns, Washington Post, Baltimore Sun, Richmond Times Dispatch, Rural Retreats.*

"I've stayed in inns at 20 states and found this among the best. This visit has been a life time dream come true."

Silver Thatch Inn

3001 Hollymead Dr
Charlottesville, VA 22911
(804)978-4686
Fax:(804)973-6156

Rates: $110-150.
Payment: MC VISA AX DC CB.
Innkeeper(s): Rita & Vince Scoffone.
Circa: 1780.

Rooms: 7 rooms with PB, 4 with FP.
Beds: QD.

This white clapboard inn, shaded by tall elms, was built for British officers by Hessian soldiers who were prisoners during the Revolutionary War. Before its present life as a country inn, Silver Thatch was a boys' school, a melon farm and a tobacco plantation. Many additions have been made to the original house. The original 1780 section is now called the Hessian Room. The inn is filled with antiques. There are three intimate dining rooms featuring fresh American cuisine.

Breakfast included in rates. Type of meal: continental-plus breakfast. Banquet service available. Air conditioning in room. Cable TV on premises. Antiques, fishing, shopping, sporting events and theater nearby.

Publicity: *Travel & Leisure, Washington Post, Los Angeles Times, New York Magazine.*

"Everything was absolutely perfect! The room, the food and above all, the people!"

Charlottesville (Palmyra)

Palmer Country Manor

RR 1 Box 1390
Charlottesville (Palmyra), VA 22963-9801
(804)589-1300 (800)253-4306
Fax:(804)589-1300

Rates: $85-125.
Payment: MC VISA AX DC DS.
Innkeeper(s): Gregory & Kathleen Palmer.
Circa: 1830.

Rooms: 12 rooms, 10 with PB, 10 with FP.
Beds: KQ.

Each season brings a special beauty to this farmhouse surrounded by 180 wooded acres. The home and grounds originally belonged to a 2,500-acre ranch which was named Solitude, an apt title for this secluded property. Guests can opt to stay in the historic house or in one of several little cottages. Each cheery guest room is individually appointed and includes a fireplace. The hearty country breakfasts are served in a rustic room with exposed beams and brick walls. Gourmet, candlelight dinners are another romantic option available for guests. The area is full of unique activities, including white-water rafting down the James River or taking in the view on a balloon ride.

Breakfast included in rates. Type of meal: full breakfast. Afternoon tea, dinner, picnic lunch, lunch, catering service and room service available. Air conditioning in room. Bicycles on premises. 180 acres. Antiques, fishing, parks, sporting events and watersports nearby.

Chatham I11

Eldon, The Inn at Chatham

State Rd 685, Rt 1,
Box 254-B
Chatham, VA 24531
(804)432-0935

Rates: $65-80.
Payment: MC VISA PC TC.
Innkeeper(s): Joy & Bob Lemm.
Circa: 1835.

Rooms: 4 rooms, 3 with PB. 1 suite.
Beds: QDT.

Beautiful gardens and white oaks surround this former tobacco plantation home set among the backdrop of the Blue Ridge Mountains. Stroll the grounds and discover sculptures and an array of flowers and plants. Southern hospitality reigns at this charming home filled with Empire antiques. Guests rooms are light and airy and tastefully decorated with beautiful linens and traditional knickknacks. Fresh flowers accentuate the bright, cheerful rooms. A lavish, Southern-style breakfast is served up

VA

each morning, and dinners at Eldon feature the gourmet creations of Chef Joel Wesley, a graduate of the Culinary Institute of America. Eldon is a popular location for weddings and parties.

Breakfast included in rates. Types of meals: continental-plus breakfast, full breakfast, gourmet breakfast and early coffee/tea. Dinner available. Air conditioning and turn-down service in room. Swimming and library on premises. Handicap access. 13 acres. Weddings, small meetings, family reunions and seminars hosted. Antiques, parks, shopping and watersports nearby.

Publicity: *Richmond Times, Chatham Star Tribune.*

"The food, the ambiance, your wonderful hospitality made for a most charming weekend."

House of Laird

335 N Main St, PO Box 1131
Chatham, VA 24531-4405
(804)432-2523 (800)201-7335

Rates: $85-135.
Payment: MC VISA AX DS.
Innkeeper(s): Ed Laird.
Circa: 1880.

Rooms: 4 rooms. 1 suite.

This Greek Revival house is in the National Register. Lavishly appointed with handsome antiques, imported draperies, Oriental rugs and grand canopy beds, the inn offers a truly luxurious experience. Heated towels, personal bathrobes, evening turndown service and cable TV are among the amenities. Best of all is the full breakfast served in the exquisitely decorated dining room on china and silver with linen tablecloths.

Breakfast included in rates. Types of meals: full breakfast and early coffee/tea. Evening snack available. Air conditioning, turn-down service and cable TV in room. Weddings and family reunions hosted. Antiques and shopping nearby.

Chincoteague E20

The Watson House

4240 Main St
Chincoteague, VA 23336
(804)336-1564 (800)336-6787
Fax:(804)336-5776

Rates: $65-115.
Payment: MC VISA PC TC.
Innkeeper(s): Tom & Jacque Derrickson, David & Jo Anne Snead.
Circa: 1898.

Rooms: 6 rooms with PB. 2 cottages.
Beds: QD.

Situated in town, this white Queen Anne Victorian has a large front porch overlooking Main Street. The porch is a favorite spot of guests and often the location for afternoon tea and refreshments. Beach towels, chairs and bicycles are complimentary, and there is an outdoor shower for cleaning up after sunning.

Breakfast and afternoon tea included in rates. Air conditioning and ceiling fan in room. Fax and bicycles on premises. Antiques, fishing, parks, shopping and watersports nearby. TAC10.

Chincoteague (New Church) E19

The Garden and The Sea Inn

PO Box 275
New Church, VA 23415
(804)824-0672 (800)824-0672

Rates: $60-165.
Payment: MC VISA AX DS PC TC.
Innkeeper(s): Tom & Sara Baker.
Circa: 1802.

Rooms: 6 rooms with PB. 1 conference room.
Beds: Q.

Gingerbread trim, a pair of brightly colored gables and two, adjacent verandas adorn the exterior of this charming Victorian. A warm, rich Victorian decor permeates the antique-filled guest rooms, an ideal setting for romance. Several rooms include whirlpool tubs. The inn's dining room serves gourmet dinners with an emphasis on fresh catches from the waters of the Eastern shore, but many continental items are featured as well.

Breakfast included in rates. Type of meal: continental-plus breakfast. Dinner, evening snack, picnic lunch, banquet service and catering service available. Air conditioning, ceiling fan and cable TV in room. VCR, copier, library and pet boarding on premises. Handicap access. Weddings, small meetings and family reunions hosted. Antiques, fishing, parks, shopping and watersports nearby. TAC10.

Pets Allowed.

Christiansburg H8

Evergreen The Bell-Capozzi House

201 E Main St
Christiansburg, VA 24073
(540)382-7372 (800)905-7372
Fax:(540)382-4376
E-mail: evrgrninn@aol.com

Rates: $80-125.
Payment: MC VISA AX DS PC TC.
Innkeeper(s): Rocco Capozzi & Barbara Bell-Capozzi.
Circa: 1890.

Rooms: 5 rooms with PB. 1 cottage. 1 conference room.
Beds: KQ.

Enjoy the beauty of the Blue Ridge Mountains at this Victorian inn, nestled on nearly an acre of beautiful grounds. A gazebo, swings, a porch lined with rockers, flowers, wisteria, evergreens and a lighted swimming pool are all there for you to enjoy. Elegant furnishings rest on polished, heart-of-pine floors. The home still maintains original light fixtures. Hearty Southern breakfasts, which might include biscuits and gravy, cheese grits, eggs, fresh fruit, homemade jams and petite pancakes are served.

Breakfast, afternoon tea and evening snack included in rates. Types of meals: full breakfast, gourmet breakfast and early coffee/tea. Air conditioning, ceiling fan, cable TV and VCR in room. Fax, swimming and library on premises. Family reunions hosted. Italian spoken. Antiques, fishing, parks, shopping, cross-country skiing, sporting events, theater and watersports nearby. TAC10.

Cluster Springs I12

Oak Grove Plantation

PO Box 45
Cluster Springs, VA 24535
(804)575-7137

Rates: $60.
Innkeeper(s): Pickett Craddock.
Circa: 1820.

Rooms: 3 rooms.
Beds: KD.

An oak grove and 400 acres of grounds surround Oak Grove Plantation. Built by Virginia legislator Thomas Easley more than 170 years ago, this bed & breakfast is still owned by his descendants. The Blue Room features a poster bed that was handmade for the innkeeper for her seventh birthday. The inn is filled with family antiques and old family photos.

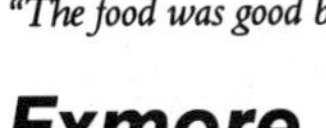

Breakfast included in rates. Type of meal: gourmet breakfast. Small meetings and family reunions hosted. Spanish spoken. Antiques, fishing, parks and watersports nearby. TAC10.

Publicity: *Gazette-Virginian, Register, Washington Post, Richmond Times Dispatch.*

"The food was good but the companionship was better. Thank you for such wonderful hospitality."

Exmore F19

The Gladstone House B&B

PO Box 296,
12108 Lincoln Ave
Exmore, VA 23350
(757)442-4614 (800)262-4837
Fax:(757)442-4678
E-mail: egan@gladstonehouse.com

Rates: $55-75.
Payment: MC VISA AX DS.
Innkeeper(s): Pat & Al Egan.

Rooms: 3 rooms with PB.

Exmore, a picturesque Eastern Shore village, is the site of this impressive brick bed & breakfast. The decor is nostalgic, a bit like stepping back in time. Guests are pampered with a four-course breakfast feast. The breakfast is an ideal start for a day exploring antique shops or enjoying the beauty of the shore, state parks and a wildlife refuge. There are bicycles available, and so that guests don't miss anything, the innkeepers have designed special bike tours of the area.

Breakfast included in rates. Types of meals: gourmet breakfast and early coffee/tea. Air conditioning, cable TV and VCR in room. Small meetings hosted. Antiques and parks nearby.

"We stayed for two days at the warm and friendly Gladstone House; and from our point of view, nothing could have been finer. What a treasure you have in your midst."

Fairfax

C15

Bailiwick Inn

4023 Chain Bridge Rd
Fairfax, VA 22030-4101
(703)691-2266 (800)366-7666
Fax:(703)934-2112

Rates: $130-295.
Payment: MC VISA AX.
Innkeeper(s): Bob & Annette Bradley.
Circa: 1800.

Rooms: 14 rooms with PB, 4 with FP. 1 suite. 1 conference room.
Beds: KQT.

Located across from the county courthouse where George Washington's will is filed, this distinguished three-story Federal brick house has recently been renovated. The first Civil War casualty occurred on what is now the inn's lawn. The elegant, early-Virginia decor is reminiscent of the state's fine plantation mansions. Ask to stay in the Thomas Jefferson Room, a replica of Mr. Jefferson's bedroom at Monticello.

Breakfast and afternoon tea included in rates. Types of meals: full breakfast, gourmet breakfast and early coffee/tea. Air conditioning and turn-down service in room. VCR, fax and copier on premises. Weddings and small meetings hosted. Antiques, parks, shopping, sporting events and theater nearby.

Publicity: *Washington Post, Journal, Fairfax Connection, Inn Times, Mid-Atlantic Country, Victoria, Country Inns.*

"A visit to your establishment clearly transcends any lodging experience that I can recall."

Fredericksburg

D15

La Vista Plantation

4420 Guinea Station Rd
Fredericksburg, VA 22408
(540)898-8444 (800)529-2823
Fax:(540)898-9414

Rates: $95.
Payment: MC VISA PC TC.
Innkeeper(s): Michele & Edward Schiesser.
Circa: 1838.

Rooms: 2 rooms with PB, 2 with FP. 1 suite. 1 cottage. 1 conference room.
Beds: KQDT.

La Vista has a long and unusual past, rich in Civil War history. Both Confederate and Union armies camped here, and this is where the Ninth Cavalry was sworn in. The house, a Classical Revival structure with high ceilings and pine floors, sits on 10 acres of pasture and woods. The grounds include a pond stocked with bass. Guest quarters include a spacious room with a king-sized, four-poster bed and Empire furniture or a four-room apartment that can accommodate up to six guests and includes a fireplace. Breakfasts include homemade egg dishes from chickens raised on the property.

Breakfast included in rates. Types of meals: full breakfast and early coffee/tea. Air conditioning in room. Copier and library on premises. 10 acres. Amusement parks, antiques, fishing, parks, shopping, sporting events, theater and watersports nearby. TAC10.

Location: Just outside historic Fredericksburg.

Publicity: *Free Lance Star, Mid-Atlantic Country.*

Special Discounts: Stay 6 days, get 7th free.

"Coming here was an excellent choice. La Vista is charming, quiet and restful, all qualities we were seeking. Breakfast was delicious."

Front Royal

C13

Chester House Inn

43 Chester St
Front Royal, VA 22630-3368
(540)635-3937 (800)621-0441
Fax:(540)636-8695
E-mail: chesthse@rma.eda

Rates: $65-180.
Payment: MC VISA AX PC TC.
Innkeeper(s): Bill & Ann Wilson.
Circa: 1905.

Rooms: 7 rooms, 5 with PB, 3 with FP. 1 suite. 1 cottage.
Beds: KQDT.

This stately Georgian-style estate rests on two acres of terraced gardens, which include vast plantings of boxwood, wisteria arbors, a fountain and brick walkways and walls. Elaborately carved marble mantels from London remain, and an original speaker tube extends from the second-floor bedroom to the kitchen. Just

down the street is the renovated village commons, the Confederate Museum and the Belle Boyd Cottage.

Breakfast, afternoon tea and evening snack included in rates. Types of meals: continental-plus breakfast and early coffee/tea. Air conditioning and turn-down service in room. Cable TV, VCR and fax on premises. Small meetings and seminars hosted. Antiques, fishing, parks, shopping, cross-country skiing, theater and watersports nearby. TAC10.

Publicity: *Winchester Star, Northern Virginia Daily, Blue Ridge Country.*

"A home of greater charm would be hard to find."

Killahevlin B&B Inn

1401 N Royal Ave
Front Royal, VA 22630-3625
(540)636-7335 (800)847-6132
Fax:(540)636-8694
E-mail: kllhvln.shentel.net

Rates: $105-175.
Payment: MC VISA AX DS PC TC.
Innkeeper(s): Susan & John Lang.
Circa: 1905.

Rooms: 6 rooms with PB, 6 with FP. 2 suites. 1 cottage. 1 conference room.
Beds: Q.

This Edwardian Mansion is in the National Register due in part to its builder, William Carson, creator of Skyline Drive, Williamsburg, Jamestown and Yorktown. Each guest room enjoys handsome decor and a working fireplace with antique mantels. Five rooms offer whirlpool tubs. Both the innkeepers share a common Irish heritage with Will Carson. Nineteenth-century Irish cottage wallpapers and Waterford crystal add to the atmosphere. In addition to views of the Blue Ridge Mountains, the inn's three acres include two restored gazebos and an ornamental fish pond with a waterfall.

Breakfast and evening snack included in rates. Types of meals: full breakfast, gourmet breakfast and early coffee/tea. Room service available. Air conditioning, turn-down service and ceiling fan in room. Cable TV, VCR, fax and library on premises. Weddings, small meetings, family reunions and seminars hosted. Antiques, fishing, parks, shopping, theater and watersports nearby. TAC10.

Special Discounts: Sunday-Thursday, less 20%.

Goshen — *E10*

The Hummingbird Inn

PO Box 147, Wood Ln
Goshen, VA 24439-0147
(540)997-9065 (800)397-3214
Fax:(540)997-0289
E-mail: hmgbird@cfw.com

Rates: $75-125.
Payment: MC VISA AX DS PC TC.
Innkeeper(s): Diana & Jeremy Robinson.
Circa: 1853.

Rooms: 5 rooms with PB, 2 with FP.
Beds: Q.

This early Victorian villa is located in the Shenandoah Valley against the backdrop of the Allegheny Mountains. Both the first and second floors offer wraparound verandas. Furnished with antiques, the inn features a library and sitting room with fireplaces. The rustic den and one guest room comprise the oldest portions of the inn, built around 1780. Four-course dinners, which include wine, are available by advance reservation. An old barn and babbling creek are on the grounds. Lexington, the Virginia Horse Center, Natural Bridge, the Blue Ridge Parkway and antiquing are all nearby.

Breakfast included in rates. Types of meals: full breakfast and early coffee/tea. Air conditioning and ceiling fan in room. VCR, fax, computer and library on premises. Handicap access. Antiques, fishing, shopping, downhill skiing, cross-country skiing and theater nearby. TAC10.

Pets Allowed: Dogs with prior arrangements.

Publicity: *Blue Ridge Country, Mid-Atlantic Getaways, Inn Spots and Special Places.*

Special Discounts: 20% corporate (Mon-Thurs); 10% AARP.

"We enjoyed our stay so much that we returned two weeks later on our way back .. for a delicious home-cooked dinner, comfortable attractive atmosphere, and familiar faces to welcome us after a long journey."

Harrisonburg

D12

Joshua Wilton House

412 S Main St
Harrisonburg, VA 22801
(540)434-4464

Rates: $100-120.
Payment: MC VISA AX PC TC.
Innkeeper(s): Roberta & Craig Moore.
Circa: 1888.

Rooms: 5 rooms with PB, 1 with FP.
Beds: Q.

This beautifully restored Victorian has served as a variety of dwellings. First a family home, it was later used by a fraternity and then converted into apartments. Today, the inn offers a wonderful glimpse back into the Victorian Era. Light, airy rooms are elegant, full of antiques, and each room includes access to a small reading area. Meals at the Wilton House are a treat. A typical breakfast at the home includes fresh fruit, pastries, delectable entrees and gourmet coffees. Guests need not stray far from their rooms to enjoy gourmet cuisine, the innkeepers run a highly recommended restaurant on the premises. Don't forget to ask about special events.

Breakfast included in rates. Types of meals: continental-plus breakfast, full breakfast, gourmet breakfast and early coffee/tea. Dinner available. Air conditioning, turn-down service and ceiling fan in room. Fax, copier and bicycles on premises. Weddings, small meetings, family reunions and seminars hosted. Amusement parks, antiques, fishing, parks, shopping, downhill skiing and sporting events nearby. TAC10.

Publicity: *Richmond Times Dispatch, Bon Appetit, Sunday New York Times, Harrisonburg Daily News Record.*

Irvington

F17

The Hope and Glory Inn

634 King Carter Dr
Irvington, VA 22480
(804)438-6053 (800)497-8228
Fax:(804)438-5362

Rates: $95-130.
Payment: PC TC.
Innkeeper(s): Joyce Barber.
Circa: 1890.

Rooms: 7 rooms with PB. 1 suite. 3 cottages.
Beds: QD.

Checkerboard wood floors and interior columns add an elegant touch to this eclectic inn, which once served as a small school. A cheerful, yellow exterior with unique windows and second-story porch is accentuated by two front doors, one for the girls and one for the boys. The decor is whimsical and romantic. One guest room features a bed dressed with a flowery comforter and a headboard that appears as a picket fence. Another room has a hidden passageway, which leads to the private bath. Tucked behind the inn are several garden cottages, and a path leading to a private outdoor shower and clawfoot tub. This unique feature is totally private and secluded. After enjoying a full breakfast, guests can partake in sailing, fishing, shopping and all the other surprises this Chesapeake Bay area town has to offer.

Breakfast included in rates. Types of meals: full breakfast and early coffee/tea. Air conditioning in room. Cable TV, VCR, fax, copier, bicycles and tennis on premises. Handicap access. Weddings, small meetings and family reunions hosted. Antiques, fishing, shopping, theater and watersports nearby.

Pets Allowed.

Kilmarnock (White Stone) F17

Flowering Fields B&B

RR 2 Box 1600
White Stone, VA 22578
(804)435-6238
Fax:(804)435-6238

Rates: $75-120.
Payment: PC TC.
Innkeeper(s): Lloyd Niziol & Susan Moenssens.
Circa: 1790.

Rooms: 5 rooms, 2 with PB. 1 suite. 1 conference room.
Beds: KQDT.

Guests will find plenty to do at this Victorian bed & breakfast. The game room is stocked with a pool table, games, darts and a fireplace. The grounds are shared by the innkeepers friendly dogs, cat and several horses. The parlor is a bit more formal,and the music room includes a baby grand piano. Guests are pampered with a selection of appetizers and beverages after check-in. Cookies and chocolates are available later in the evening, and the morning begins with a huge breakfast. Omelets, fried apples and unique items such as oyster frittatas are served, and the innkeepers will plan the meal around guests' dietary restrictions. Guest rooms include items such as a four-poster rice bed, antiques, Queen Anne chairs and Oriental rugs.

Breakfast, afternoon tea and evening snack included in rates. Types of meals: full breakfast, gourmet breakfast and early coffee/tea. Air conditioning and ceiling fan in room. Cable TV, VCR, fax, copier, bicycles and library on premises. Weddings, small meetings, family reunions and seminars hosted. Antiques, fishing, parks, shopping and watersports nearby. TAC10.

Pets Allowed: Outdoors only.

Leesburg B15

The Norris House Inn

108 Loudoun St SW
Leesburg, VA 20175-2909
(703)777-1806 (800)644-1806
Fax:(703)771-8051
E-mail: jrtp01b@prodigy.com

Rates: $75-145.
Payment: MC VISA AX DC CB DS PC TC.
Innkeeper(s): Pamela & Don McMurray.
Circa: 1760.

Rooms: 6 rooms, 3 with FP. 3 conference rooms.
Beds: QD.

The Norris brothers, Northern Virginia's foremost architects and builders, purchased this building in 1850 and began extensive renovations several years later. They used the finest wood and brick available, remodeling the exterior to an Eastlake style. Beautifully restored, the inn features built-in bookcases in the library and a cherry fireplace mantel. Evening libations are served.

Breakfast included in rates. Types of meals: full breakfast and early coffee/tea. Afternoon tea available. Air conditioning and turn-down service in room. Fax and library on premises. Weddings, small meetings, family reunions and seminars hosted. Antiques, fishing, parks, shopping and watersports nearby. TAC10.

Location: In a historic district, less than one hour from Washington, D.C.

Publicity: *New York Times, Better Homes and Gardens, Washingtonian, Country Home.*

Special Discounts: AAA, government, etc.

"Thank you for your gracious hospitality. We enjoyed everything about your lovely home, especially the extra little touches that really make the difference."

Lexington F11

Brierley Hill B&B Inn

VA

RR 2 Box 21A
Lexington, VA 24450
(540)464-8421 (800)422-4925
Fax:(540)464-8925

Rates: $80-145.
Payment: MC VISA TC.
Innkeeper(s): Barry & Carole Speton.
Circa: 1993.

Rooms: 6 rooms with PB, 2 with FP. 1 suite.
Beds: KQ.

Visitors to this inn, which is set on eight acres, enjoy a spectacular view of the Shenandoah Valley and Blue Ridge Mountains. The natural setting aside, the interior is reason enough for a stay. The rooms are decorated in light, romantic colors, reminiscent of a field of wildflowers. Antiques and poster beds blend with flowery prints, light wallpapers and knickknacks. Breakfasts, weather permitting, are served on the veranda, which offers a wonderful view.

Breakfast and afternoon tea included in rates. Types of meals: full breakfast and early coffee/tea. Air conditioning and ceiling fan in room. Cable TV, fax, copier and library on premises. Small meetings and family reunions hosted. Antiques, fishing, parks, shopping, downhill skiing, cross-country skiing, sporting events, theater and watersports nearby. TAC10.

Special Discounts: Inquire.

Maple Hall

Rt 5, Box 223
Lexington, VA 24450-8842
(540)463-2044
Fax:(540)463-6693

Rates: $95-160.
Payment: MC VISA PC.
Innkeeper(s): Don Fredenburg.
Circa: 1850.

Rooms: 21 rooms with PB, 16 with FP. 5 suites. 2 cottages. 1 conference room.
Beds: QDT.

Maple Hall is one of the Historic Country Inns of Lexington, an elegant ensemble of some of Virginia's notable mansions and homes. The red brick manor, flanked by stately columns, remained in the original owner's family until the mid-1980s. Many of the rooms include working fireplaces and all are individually decorated with antiques. A restored guest house, dating prior to the 1850 main house, includes three bedrooms, a kitchen and living room. Secluded accommodations also are available at Pond House, which includes four mini-suites and a back veranda with a view of the pond and surrounding countryside. The home rests on a 56-acre estate with boxwoods, walking trails, a fishing pond, swimming pool and tennis courts. Breakfast and evening wine is included, and gourmet dining is available at the inn's restaurant, with specialties such as lobster bisque, prime rib or poached Alaskan salmon.

Breakfast included in rates. Type of meal: continental-plus breakfast. Banquet service available. Air conditioning in room. VCR, fax, copier, swimming and tennis on premises. 56 acres. Weddings, small meetings, family reunions and seminars hosted. Antiques, fishing, parks, shopping, sporting events and theater nearby. TAC10.

Special Discounts: Offered January, February, June, July, August and first weekend of December.

"The view from the back balcony was so peaceful and serene. What a perfect weekend!"

Seven Hills Inn

408 S Main St
Lexington, VA 24450-2346
(540)463-4715
Fax:(540)463-6526

Rates: $75-125.
Payment: MC VISA AX PC TC.
Innkeeper(s): Shirley Ducommun.
Circa: 1929.

Rooms: 7 rooms, 6 with PB. 1 suite.
Beds: QDT.

This Colonial Revival house stands in the heart of the Shenandoah Valley. Carefully renovated, the inn's white columns and brick exterior are reminiscent of a Southern plantation. The guest rooms, named after area homesteads, are furnished with antiques and reproductions, and the Fruit Hill room offers a Jacuzzi tub. Within a 10-minute walk is Washington and Lee University, the Virginia Military Institute and the Lexington Visitors Center.

Breakfast included in rates. Types of meals: continental-plus breakfast and early coffee/tea. Afternoon tea and catering service available. Cable TV, VCR, fax, copier and library on premises. Weddings, small meetings and family reunions hosted. Antiques, fishing, parks, shopping, sporting events, theater and watersports nearby.

Lincoln

Springdale Country Inn

RR 2 Box 356
Lincoln, VA 20160
(540)338-1832
Fax:(540)338-1839

Rates: $95-125.
Payment: MC VISA PC.
Innkeeper(s): Nancy & Roger Fones.
Circa: 1832.

Rooms: 9 rooms, 6 with PB, 4 with FP. 2 suites. 2 conference rooms.
Beds: DT.

A National Historic Landmark, the Springdale Country Inn was once a schoolhouse, Civil War hospital and traveler's inn. The inn, with its high ceilings and windows, has richly burnished wide-board floors, reproduction wallpaper and antiques. Guest rooms have fresh flowers, stenciled walls and four-poster canopy beds. Enjoy the sun and sitting porch, pleasant gardens and local folklore of the area and the school itself.

Breakfast included in rates. Type of meal: full breakfast. Catering service available. Air conditioning in room. VCR, fax, copier and library on premises. Handicap access. Weddings, small meetings, family reunions, seminars hosted. Antiques, shopping and theater nearby. TAC8.

Publicity: *The Pamphlet, The Washington Post.*

"Quaint setting and excellent meals."

Locust Dale D13

The Inn at Meander Plantation

HC 5 Box 460A
Locust Dale, VA 22948
(703)672-4912 (800)385-4936
Fax:(703)672-4912
E-mail: meanderin@aol.com

Rates: $95-185.
Payment: MC VISA PC TC.
Innkeeper(s): Bob & Suzie Blanchard, Suzanne Thomas.
Circa: 1766.

Rooms: 8 rooms with PB, 5 with FP. 4 suites. 1 conference room.
Beds: KQD.

This elegant country estate was built by Henry Fry, close friend of Thomas Jefferson, who often stopped here on his way to Monticello. Ancient formal boxwood gardens, woodland and meadows are enjoyed by guests as well as views of the Blue Ridge Mountains from the rockers on the back porches. The mansion is decorated serenely with elegant antiques and period reproductions, including queen-size, four-poster beds. The innkeeper is a food writer and will prepare special breakfasts for individual diets. Full dinner service and picnic baskets are available with advance reservations.

Breakfast included in rates. Types of meals: full breakfast and early coffee/tea. Afternoon tea, evening snack, picnic lunch and lunch available. Air conditioning in room. VCR, fax, stables, library, pet boarding and child care on premises. 80 acres. Weddings, small meetings, family reunions and seminars hosted. Antiques, fishing, parks, shopping, downhill skiing, cross-country skiing, sporting events and theater nearby. TAC10.

Pets Allowed: In dependencies only.

Special Discounts: Weekend packages on holidays and themed weekends.

"Staying at the Inn at Meander Plantation feels like being immersed in another century while having the luxuries and amenities available today."

Luray C13

Locust Grove Inn

1456 N Egypt Bend Rd
Luray, VA 22835
(540)743-1804

Rates: $90-125.
Payment: MC VISA DS PC TC.
Innkeeper(s): Rod & Isabel Graves.
Circa: 1765.

Rooms: 5 rooms with PB, 3 with FP.
Beds: Q.

Virginia was still under Royal rule when this Colonial home was built, on what was once a Native American campsite. The first owner fought in the Revolutionary War. The Shenandoah River, which runs in front of the house, offers splendid scenery guests won't soon forget and the porches offer mountain views. The innkeepers have preserved the house's history, and although completely restored, pre-Civil War antiques and decor maintain its 18th- and early 19th-century ambiance. The inn still maintains original paint decorations and graining in the parlor and on the staircases, and unique whitewash cartoons from before 1816 decorate exposed log walls. The bedrooms display Early American antiques, offer views of the mountains, river or both, and one room has a stone fireplace. Healthy items such as crepes filled with banana and wildflower honey cream, breads and fresh fruit are served at breakfast. After the morning meal, guests can enjoy a walk on the inn's scenic 53 acres, including meadows and a mile of riverfront.

Breakfast included in rates. Type of meal: gourmet breakfast. Evening snack available. Air conditioning in room. 53 acres. Small meetings and family reunions hosted. French and Portuguese spoken. Antiques, fishing, parks, shopping and watersports nearby. TAC10.

Spring Farm B&B

13 Wallace Ave
Luray, VA 22835-9067
(540)743-4701 (800)203-2814
Fax:(540)743-7851

Rates: $75-150.
Payment: MC VISA DC DS PC TC.
Innkeeper(s): Thelma Mayes & Susan Murphy.
Circa: 1795.

Rooms: 4 rooms, 2 with PB. 1 cottage.
Beds: QD.

Spring Farm is on 10 acres two miles from Luray Caverns. Hite's Springs run through the land. The Greek Revival home has double front and back verandas. Rooms feature a mix of antique and new furnishings, and there is a fireplace in the living room. Ask the innkeepers for advice on shopping, dining and activities in the Shenandoah and they'll be happy to help you plan a getaway you'll long remember.

Breakfast, afternoon tea and evening snack included in rates. Types of meals: full breakfast and early coffee/tea. Picnic lunch available. Air conditioning in room. Cable TV, VCR and fax on premises. 12 acres. Weddings, small meetings and family reunions hosted. Spanish spoken. Antiques, fishing, parks, shopping, downhill skiing and watersports nearby. TAC10.

Woodruff House

330 Mechanic St
Luray, VA 22835
(540)743-1494
Fax:(540)743-1494

Rates: $98-165. MAP.
Payment: MC VISA DS PC TC.
Innkeeper(s): Lucas & Deborah Woodruff.
Circa: 1882.

Rooms: 6 rooms, 4 with PB, 6 with FP. 2 suites. 1 conference room.
Beds: D.

Prepare to be pampered. The Woodruffs entered the B&B business after years of experience in hotel management and have not missed a detail, ensuring a perfect, relaxing visit. The Log Cabin Suite is often the room of choice because of its interesting shape and architecture, located where the attic was before restoration. Tasteful antiques and memorabilia from years past decorate the home. Besides the extra attention and comfortable accommodations, the Woodruffs include a high tea-buffet dinner, early morning coffee or tea and a full fireside gourmet breakfast in the rates. Ask for breakfast in bed if you so desire. Candlelight sets the mood for dinner, and none of the spectacular meals are to be missed. Be sure to sample the wine-filled gourmet chocolates in the evening.

Breakfast, afternoon tea and dinner included in rates. Types of meals: gourmet breakfast and early coffee/tea. Catering service and room service available. MAP. Air conditioning and ceiling fan in room. Cable TV, VCR, fax, spa, bicycles and library on premises. Weddings, small meetings and family reunions hosted. Antiques, fishing, parks, downhill skiing, cross-country skiing and watersports nearby. TAC10.

Publicity: *Potomac Living.*

Special Discounts: Three or more night discounts available.

"The place is great. There aren't words to explain!"

Lynchburg G11

Federal Crest Inn

1101 Federal St
Lynchburg, VA 24504-3018
(804)845-6155 (800)818-6155
Fax:(804)845-1445

Rates: $85-115.
Payment: MC VISA AX DS PC TC.
Innkeeper(s): Ann & Phil Ripley.
Circa: 1909.

Rooms: 5 rooms, 4 with PB, 3 with FP. 2 suites. 1 conference room.
Beds: QD.

The guest rooms at Federal Crest are named for the many varieties of trees and flowers native to Virginia. This handsome red brick home, a fine example of Georgian Revival architecture, features a commanding front entrance flanked by columns that hold up the second-story veranda. A grand staircase, carved woodwork, polished floors topped with fine rugs and more columns create an aura of elegance. Each guest room offers something special and romantic, from a mountain view to a Jacuzzi tub. Breakfasts are served on fine china, and the first course is always a freshly baked muffin with a secret message inside.

Breakfast and evening snack included in rates. Types of meals: full breakfast, gourmet breakfast and early coffee/tea. Afternoon tea and room service available. Air conditioning, turn-down service and cable TV in room. VCR, fax, copier and library on premises. Weddings, small meetings, family reunions and seminars hosted. English spoken. Antiques, parks, shopping, downhill skiing and sporting events nearby. TAC10.

Special Discounts: 2 night special all rooms $170.00, Valentine's weekend with dinner for two $225.00.

"What a wonderful place to celebrate our birthdays and enjoy our 'last romantic getaway before the birth of our first child."

Madison Heights G11

Winridge B&B

116 Winridge Dr
Madison Heights, VA 24572
(804)384-7220
Fax:(804)384-1399

Rates: $69-85.
Payment: MC VISA PC TC.
Innkeeper(s): Lois Ann & Ed Pfister & Pfamily.
Circa: 1910.

Rooms: 3 rooms, 1 with PB.
Beds: QT.

This Colonial Revival home is surround by 14 acres and offers scenic, mountain views. The home is just five miles from Lynchburg. The Habecker Room is a favorite with its large four-poster bed, rocking chair and desk. All the rooms have ceiling fans and two have air conditioning. The host was a professional caterer and serves full breakfasts.

Breakfast included in rates. Types of meals: full breakfast and early coffee/tea. Evening snack available. Air conditioning, turn-down service and ceiling fan in room. Child care on premises. 14 acres. Weddings, small meetings, family reunions and seminars hosted. Antiques, fishing, parks, shopping, downhill skiing, sporting events, theater and water-sports nearby. TAC10.

Location: Five miles north of Lynchburg and 14 miles east of the Blue Ridge Parkway.

Publicity: *Lynchburg News & Advance, Amherst News-Era.*

Special Discounts: Brubaker Room-family rate-room is 50% off when occupied by children under 18 & rented with Walker Room.

Middleburg C14

Red Fox Inn & Mosby's Tavern

2 E Washington St
Middleburg, VA 2117-0385
(703)687-6301 (800)223-1728
Fax:(703)687-6187

Rates: $135-225.
Payment: MC VISA AX DS TC.
Innkeeper(s): F. Turner Reuter, Jr.
Circa: 1728.

Rooms: 24 rooms with PB, 3 with FP. 4 conference rooms.
Beds: KQ.

Originally Chinn's Ordinary, the inn was a popular stopping place for travelers between Winchester and Alexandria. During the Civil War, Colonel John Mosby and General Jeb Stuart met here. Guest rooms are furnished in 18th-century decor and most feature four-poster canopy beds.

Breakfast included in rates. Types of meals: continental breakfast, continental-plus breakfast, full breakfast, gourmet breakfast and early coffee/tea. Afternoon tea, dinner, evening snack, picnic lunch, lunch, gourmet lunch, banquet service, catering service, catered breakfast and room service available. Air conditioning, turn-down service and cable TV in room. VCR, fax, copier, pet boarding and child care on premises. Handicap access. Weddings, small meetings, family reunions and seminars hosted. Antiques nearby.

Pets Allowed.

Location: Thirty miles west of Washington on Route 50.

Publicity: *Washingtonian.*

Welbourne

VA

22314 Welbourne Farm Ln
Middleburg, VA 22117-3939
(703)687-3201

Rates: $85-96.
Innkeeper(s): Nathaniel Morison III.
Circa: 1775.

Rooms: 7 rooms with PB, 7 with FP. 2 suites. 1 conference room.
Beds: QT.

This seventh-generation mansion once presided over 3,000 acres. With family members starting their own estates, Welbourne now stands at 600 acres. Furnishings and carpets were collected during world travels over the past 200 years and display a faded elegance of the past. Civil War stories fill the family history book, shared with guests. In the 1930s, F. Scott Fitzgerald and Thomas Wolfe and their literary friends used the house as a setting for their writings.

Breakfast included in rates. Type of meal: full breakfast.

Location: Fifty miles west of Washington, DC.

"Furnishings portray a house and home that's been around for a long, long time. And none of it is held back from guests. Life today at Welbourne is quiet and unobtrusive. It's genteel," Philip Hayward, Country Magazine.

Millboro

E10

Fort Lewis Lodge

HCR 3 Box 21A
Millboro, VA 24460
(540)925-2314
Fax:(540)925-2352

Rates: $135-190.
Payment: MC VISA.
Innkeeper(s): John & Caryl Cowden.
Circa: 1840.

Rooms: 13 rooms with PB. 3 suites.
Beds: T.

Colonel Charles Lewis, under the command of George Washington, built one of a string of forts on this property to protect the southern pass of the Shenandoah Mountains from Indian raids. Guests at this 3,200-acre mountain farm will revel in its natural beauty. Guests can stay in the charming lodge rooms, including "sleeping in the round," in bedrooms built into a silo. The innkeepers also offer two historic hand-hewn log cabins boasting stone fireplaces. A restored 19th-century grist mill is where guests will enjoy the plentiful meals prepared by innkeeper Caryl Cowden, who serves up a variety of homemade fare. The area is full of hiking, biking, hunting and fishing possibilities.

Breakfast and dinner included in rates. Type of meal: full breakfast. Picnic lunch available. 3200 acres. Weddings, small meetings, family reunions and seminars hosted. Antiques, fishing and watersports nearby.

Publicity: *Outside, AAA Today, Mid-Atlantic Country, Tastefull, Rural Living, Country, Washington Post.*

"My husband and I have traveled the world with the military. We have stayed at many inns in France, England and Germany, none have impressed me as much as yours. You have made the most of a beautiful piece of property and I feel privileged to share it with you."

Monterey

D10

Highland Inn

Main Street, PO Box 40
Monterey, VA 24465
(540)468-2143

Rates: $49-89.
Payment: MC VISA PC.
Innkeeper(s): Michael Smith.
Circa: 1904.

Rooms: 17 rooms with PB. 4 suites.
Beds: KQD.

Listed in the National Register, this clapboard Victorian hotel has outstanding Eastlake wraparound verandas. Small-town life may be viewed from rocking chairs and swings. Guest rooms are furnished in country fashion, with iron beds and antiques. Sheep outnumber people in a pastoral setting surrounded by three million acres of National Forest.

Breakfast included in rates. Type of meal: continental-plus breakfast. Dinner available. Cable TV in room. Weddings, small meetings and family reunions hosted. Antiques, fishing, parks and shopping nearby. TAC100.

Location: Thirty-seven miles west of Staunton.

Publicity: *Washington Post, Rural Living, Richmond Times Dispatch, Roanoker.*

"The most beautiful place I've been."

New Market C12

A Touch of Country B&B

9329 N Congress St
New Market, VA 22844
(540)740-8030

Rates: $60-75.
Payment: MC VISA AX DS PC TC.
Innkeeper(s): Jean Schoellig/Dawn Kasow.
Circa: 1870.

Rooms: 6 rooms with PB.
Beds: QDT.

This white clapboard Shenandoah Valley I-frame house has a second-story pediment centered above the veranda entrance. It was built by Captain William Rice, commander of the New Market Cavalry, and the house sits on what was once a battleground of the Civil War. Rice's unit was highly praised by General Lee. Guest chambers are in the main house and in the handsome carriage house.

Breakfast included in rates. Types of meals: full breakfast and early coffee/tea. Air conditioning in room. Cable TV and VCR on premises. Antiques, fishing, parks, shopping, downhill skiing, sporting events and watersports nearby. TAC10.

Publicity: *USA Today Weekend, Country.*

"Every morning should start with sunshine, bird song and Dawn's strawberry pancakes."

Red Shutter Farmhouse B&B

RR 1 Box 376
New Market, VA 22844
(540)740-4281 (800)738-8262
Fax:(540)740-4281

Rates: $55-70.
Payment: MC VISA PC TC.
Innkeeper(s): Juanita Miller.
Circa: 1790.

Rooms: 5 rooms, 3 with PB, 3 with FP. 1 suite. 1 conference room.
Beds: KQDT.

For generations, the veranda at the Red Shutter has been the location of choice during summer to view the valley and mountains. Located on 20 acres, the inn offers large rooms and suites and a library/conference room. Breakfast is in the dining room. Enjoy drives to the many area caverns, New Market Battlefield and Skyline Drive.

Breakfast included in rates. Types of meals: full breakfast and early coffee/tea. Ceiling fan in room. VCR, fax and library on premises. 20 acres. Antiques, fishing, parks, shopping, downhill skiing, cross-country skiing, sporting events and theater nearby. TAC10.

North Garden E12

The Inn at The Crossroads

5010 Plank Rd
North Garden, VA 22959
(804)979-6452

Rates: $80-125.
Payment: MC VISA PC TC.
Innkeeper(s): Maureen & John Deis.
Circa: 1820.

Rooms: 6 rooms with PB, 6 with FP. 1 suite. 1 cottage.
Beds: KQD.

This four-story brick inn was built as a tavern on the road from Shenandoah Valley to the James River, and has been welcoming travelers since the early 19th century. The long front porch and straightforward, Federal-style architecture was common to ordinaries of that era. The four-acre grounds offer gardens of wild flowers and a swing hung under a grand oak tree, not to mention panoramic views of the foothills of the Blue Ridge Mountains. Country breakfasts are served in the inn's keeping room. The inn is nine miles south of Charlottesville, and Monticello and the University of Virginia are close by.

Breakfast and afternoon tea included in rates. Types of meals: full breakfast and early coffee/tea. Catered breakfast available. Air conditioning and ceiling fan in room. Library on premises. Weddings, small meetings, family reunions and seminars hosted. Antiques, fishing, parks, shopping, downhill skiing, cross-country skiing, sporting events, theater and watersports nearby.

Onancock

F19

The Spinning Wheel B&B

31 North St
Onancock, VA 23417-1921
(757)787-7311
Fax:(757)787-8555
E-mail: evergreen@esva.net

Rates: $75-95.
Payment: MC VISA DS PC TC.
Innkeeper(s): Karen & David Tweedie.
Circa: 1890.

Rooms: 5 rooms with PB.
Beds: Q.

This folk Victorian with its veranda and green shutters is a welcoming spot from which to enjoy the Eastern Shore. Spinning wheels and antiques are found throughout the house. You can walk to shops, restaurants and the harbor or explore even further with the tandem bicycles available from the innkeepers. Enjoy the beaches, bay and ocean or cruise to Tangier Island.

Breakfast included in rates. Type of meal: full breakfast. Air conditioning and ceiling fan in room. Fax and bicycles on premises. Small meetings and family reunions hosted. Antiques, fishing, parks, shopping, theater and watersports nearby. TAC10.

Publicity: *Pleasant Living, Washington Times.*

Orange

E13

Hidden Inn

249 Caroline St
Orange, VA 22960-1529
(540)672-3625
Fax:(540)672-5029

Rates: $79-159.
Payment: MC VISA AX PC TC.
Innkeeper(s): Barbara & Ray Lonick, Chrys Dermody.
Circa: 1880.

Rooms: 10 rooms with PB, 2 with FP. 2 cottages. 1 conference room.
Beds: KQDT.

Acres of huge old trees can be seen from the wraparound veranda of this Victorian inn nestled in the Virginia countryside. Guests are pampered with afternoon tea, and a candlelight picnic can be ordered. Monticello, Montpelier, wineries, shopping and antiquing all are nearby, and after a day of exploring the area, guests can arrange a candlelight dinner at the inn.

Breakfast and afternoon tea included in rates. Types of meals: full breakfast and early coffee/tea. Air conditioning, ceiling fan and cable TV in room. VCR, fax, copier, computer and library on premises. Weddings, small meetings, family reunions and seminars hosted. Spanish spoken. Antiques, fishing, shopping, sporting events, theater and watersports nearby. TAC10.

Location: Intersection of Rte 15 & Rte 20.

Publicity: *Forbes, Washington Post, Country Inns, Learning Channel, Inn Country USA.*

"It just doesn't get any better than this!"

Petersburg

G15

The Owl & The Pussycat B&B

405 High St
Petersburg, VA 23803-3857
(804)733-0505 (888)733-0505
Fax:(804)862-0694
E-mail: owlcat@ctg.net

Rates: $65-105.
Payment: MC VISA PC TC.
Innkeeper(s): Juliette & John Swenson.
Circa: 1895.

Rooms: 5 rooms, 3 with PB.
Beds: KQT.

Victorians have a way of standing out, and this Queen Anne is particularly unique, fashioned from creamy, yellow bricks. The innkeepers have decorated the home with Victorian antiques, such as the beds and dressers, and pieces from England. Among the impressive antiques is a carved walnut bed in the Pussycat Room and an Eastlake-style bed in the Owl Room. The home still has its original gas light fixtures and eight fireplaces, each decorated with different tiles and mantels. Midweek guests are served continental-plus fare, and weekend guests enjoy a full breakfast. English scones and Sally Lunn bread are specialties of the house. Civil War battlefields, museums, antique shops and restaurants are nearby.

Breakfast included in rates. Types of meals: continental-plus breakfast and early coffee/tea. Picnic lunch available. Air conditioning in room. Cable TV, VCR and fax on premises. Weddings, small meetings, family reunions and seminars hosted. Antiques and parks nearby. TAC10.

Pets Allowed: Small/$20.00 deposit.

Special Discounts: Sunday-Thursday $10 off rates above.

Port Haywood G18

Tabb's Creek Inn

PO Box 219 Rt 14 Matthews Co, Port Haywood, VA 23138
(804)725-5136
Fax:(804)725-5136

Rates: $125.
Payment: PC TC.
Innkeeper(s): Cabell & Catherine Venable.
Circa: 1820.

Rooms: 4 rooms with PB, 1 with FP. 2 suites.
Beds: KQD.

Surrounded by 30 acres of woods and located on the banks of Tabb's Creek, this post-Colonial farm features a detached guest cottage. There are maple, elm, magnolia trees and 150 rose bushes on the property. The suites and guest rooms feature fireplaces and antiques. Boats for rowing and canoeing, docks, a swimming pool, and private waterview porches make this an especially attractive getaway for those seeking a dose of seclusion.

Breakfast included in rates. Types of meals: full breakfast and early coffee/tea. Air conditioning, turn-down service, ceiling fan and VCR in room. Cable TV, fax, copier, swimming, bicycles and library on premises. 30 acres. Weddings, small meetings and family reunions hosted. Antiques and fishing nearby.

Pets Allowed.

Location: Mobjack Bay/Chesapeake Bay, near Yorktown/Williamsburg, Va.

"A spot of tea with a bit of heaven. Truly exceptional hosts. The best B&Bs I've happened across!"

Providence Forge G16

Jasmine Plantation B&B

4500 N Courthouse Rd
Providence Forge, VA 23140
(804)966-9836 (800)639-5368
Fax:(804)966-5679

Rates: $75-105.
Payment: MC VISA AX PC TC.
Innkeeper(s): Howard & Joyce Vogt.
Circa: 1750.

Rooms: 6 rooms, 5 with PB, 4 with FP.
Beds: QD.

Few travelers can boast that they have stayed at a mid-18th-century plantation. Jasmine Plantation is just such a place. Surrounded by more than 40 acres of Virginia countryside, it's not difficult to understand why the Morris family chose this spot for their home. The property's first dwelling was built as early as the 1680s. Several guest rooms are named for members of the Morris Family, and all are decorated with antiques. The Rose Room features furnishings from the 1930s and walls with rose stenciling. The George Morris Room includes 19th-century pieces, a fireplace and clawfoot tub. Memorabilia from multiple centuries add special charm to the place. The innkeepers have antique irons, old books and magazines and a sampling of vintage advertising signs for Philip Morris or Coca-Cola. Breakfasts are a true Southern treat with items such as sweet potato biscuits and homemade jams and jellies.

Breakfast and evening snack included in rates. Types of meals: full breakfast and early coffee/tea. Air conditioning and ceiling fan in room. Cable TV and VCR on premises. 47 acres. Weddings, small meetings, family reunions and seminars hosted. Amusement parks, antiques, fishing, parks, shopping and watersports nearby. TAC10.

"We were charmed by the plantation accommodations and the kindness of the beautiful host and hostess."

Raphine

E11

Oak Spring Farm B&B

5895 Borden Grant Tr
Raphine, VA 24472-9717
(540)377-2398 (800)841-8813

Rates: $85-95.
Payment: MC VISA PC TC.
Innkeeper(s): Celeste & John Wood.
Circa: 1826.

Rooms: 3 rooms with PB. 1 suite.
Beds: Q.

A willow tree droops gracefully over a pond at Oak Spring Farm. Guests can take a stroll through the grounds with a perennial garden, lawn and orchard. The historic plantation house features porch views of the Blue Ridge Mountains and has been pristinely renovated. Guests rooms are decorated with family heirlooms, contemporary touches and fresh flowers. Friendly exotic animals belonging to the Natural Bridge Zoo live here.

Breakfast and afternoon tea included in rates. Types of meals: gourmet breakfast and early coffee/tea. Dinner available. Air conditioning in room. 10 acres. Antiques, fishing, shopping, downhill skiing, sporting events and theater nearby. TAC10.

Location: Halfway between historic Lexington and Staunton.

Publicity: *The News-Gazette, The News and County Press, Mid-Atlantic Country.*

"The good taste, the privacy, the decor and the hosts were unbeatable!"

Richmond

F15

The Emmanuel Hutzler House

2036 Monument Ave
Richmond, VA 23220-2708
(804)353-6900
Fax:(804)355-5053

Rates: $89-145. AP.
Payment: MC VISA AX DC DS PC TC.
Innkeeper(s): Lyn M. Benson & John E. Richardson.
Circa: 1914.

Rooms: 4 rooms with PB. 2 suites.
Beds: QT.

This graciously restored Italian Renaissance home is a showcase of mahogany paneling and tastefully decorated rooms. Its 8,000 square feet includes a stunning parlor with handsome antiques, leaded-glass windows and a marble fireplace. The largest room boasts a four-poster mahogany bed, antique sofa and a private Jacuzzi tucked into an enormous bathroom. Breakfast is served in the formal dining room of this non-smoking inn. There is a resident cat at this home.

Breakfast included in rates. Types of meals: continental-plus breakfast, full breakfast and early coffee/tea. AP. Air conditioning and cable TV in room. Fax and library on premises. Small meetings hosted. Antiques, parks, sporting events and theater nearby. TAC7.

Pets Allowed.

"I'm glad there are still people like you who painstakingly restore great old houses such as this. A great job of reconstruction and beautifully decorated! Delightful hosts!"

Salem

G9

The Inn at Burwell Place

601 W Main St
Salem, VA 24153-3515
(540)387-0250 (800)891-0250
Fax:(540)387-0250

Rates: $70-110.
Payment: MC VISA AX DS PC TC.
Innkeeper(s): Cindi Lou MacMackin & Mark Bukowski.
Circa: 1907.

Rooms: 4 rooms with PB, 1 with FP. 2 suites. 2 conference rooms.
Beds: Q.

This mansion was built by a local industrialist, but the inn was named for Nathaniel Burwell, who owned the land prior to the home's construction. The home overlooks the Roanoke Valley and parts of Salem. Guest rooms feature antiques and beds dressed with down comforters and fine linens. Downtown Salem recently received a place in the National Register. The home, the site of many weddings, is a block from a restored 1890s duck pond and park.

Breakfast included in rates. Types of meals: full breakfast and early coffee/tea. Banquet service and catering service available. Air conditioning, turn-down service, ceiling fan, cable TV and VCR in room. Fax and bicycles on premises. Weddings, small meetings, family reunions, seminars hosted. Amusement parks, antiques, fishing, parks, shopping, sporting events, theater, watersports nearby. TAC10.

Special Discounts: 10% off Monday, Tuesday, Wednesday, Thursday nights.

"It was truly elegant, a day I will always remember!"

Scottsville F13

Chester

243 James River Rd
Scottsville, VA 24590
(804)286-3960

Rates: $100-130.
Payment: MC VISA PC.
Innkeeper(s): Jean & Craig Stratton.
Circa: 1847.

Rooms: 5 rooms with PB, 5 with FP.
Beds: Q.

This gracious Greek Revival house, once the home of Confederate Major Hill, is set back from the road on a large green lawn surrounded by dogwood, gardens and ancient trees. Porches are furnished with rocking chairs from which guests enjoy the inn's eight acres. Rooms are decorated with four-poster beds, wing chairs and Oriental rugs, complementing the inn's historic character. With advance notice, four- and five-course dinners are available for parties of six or more. In addition, private Civil War re-enactments are conducted on the grounds for guests.

Breakfast included in rates. Types of meals: full breakfast, gourmet breakfast and early coffee/tea. Dinner available. Air conditioning and turn-down service in room. Fax, bicycles and library on premises. Weddings, small meetings, family reunions and seminars hosted. Antiques, fishing, parks, shopping, downhill skiing, cross-country skiing, sporting events, theater and watersports nearby.

Smith Mountain Lake

The Manor at Taylor's Store B&B Country Inn

RR 1 Box 533
Smith Mountain Lake, VA
24184-9725
(540)721-3951 (800)248-6267
Fax:(540)721-5243

Rates: $85-185.
Payment: MC VISA PC TC.
Innkeeper(s): Lee & Mary Lynn Tucker.
Circa: 1820.

Rooms: 9 rooms, 8 with PB, 6 with FP. 4 suites. 1 cottage. 3 conference rooms.
Beds: QD.

Situated on 120 acres of rolling countryside, this two-story, columned manor was built on the site of Taylor's Store, a trading post just off the old Warwick Road. It served as the plantation house for a prosperous tobacco farmer, Moses Greer Booth. Guest rooms feature a variety of antiques and styles including traditional colonial and English Country. From the solarium, a wildflower trail winds through the inn's Colonial garden and green meadows where a canoe awaits those who wish to paddle across one of six ponds on the property. There's a dock for those who wish to fish.

Breakfast included in rates. Types of meals: full breakfast, gourmet breakfast and early coffee/tea. Afternoon tea, dinner, picnic lunch, gourmet lunch, banquet service and catering service available. Air conditioning and turn-down service in room. Cable TV, VCR, fax, copier, spa, swimming, stables and library on premises. 120 acres. Small meetings and seminars hosted. Antiques, fishing, parks, shopping, sporting events, theater and watersports nearby. TAC10.

Publicity: *Smith Mountain Eagle, Lake Country, Blue Ridge Country, Franklin News-Post, Southern Living, Brides.*

Special Discounts: 10% off Monday-Thursday.

"This B&B experience is a delightful one!"

Smithfield H17

Isle of Wight Inn

1607 S Church St
Smithfield, VA 23430-1831
(804)357-3176 (800)357-3245

Rates: $59-119.
Payment: MC VISA AX DS TC.
Innkeeper(s): Jackie Madrigel & Bob Hart.
Circa: 1980.

Rooms: 9 rooms with PB, 3 with FP. 2 suites. 1 conference room.
Beds: QDT.

This Colonial inn is located in a historic seaside town, boasting more than 60 homes which date back to the mid-18th century. St. Luke's Church, the oldest in the United States, dating back to 1632, is located near the inn. Antiques and reproductions fill the rooms, the suites offer the added amenities of fireplaces and

whirlpool tubs. The inn also houses a gift boutique and one of the area's finest antique shops, featuring old clocks and period furniture.

Breakfast and evening snack included in rates. Types of meals: full breakfast and early coffee/tea. Air conditioning and cable TV in room. VCR and library on premises. Handicap access. Small meetings hosted. Amusement parks, antiques, fishing, parks, shopping, theater and watersports nearby.

Stafford — D15

Renaissance Manor B&B Inn & Art Gallery

2247 Courthouse Rd
Stafford, VA 22554-5508
(540)720-3785 (800)720-3784
Fax:(540)720-3785
E-mail: renbb@aol.com

Rates: $55-150.
Payment: MC VISA AX PC TC.
Innkeeper(s): JoAnn Houser & Deneen Bernard.
Circa: 1990.

Rooms: 6 rooms, 4 with PB, 1 with FP. 2 suites. 1 conference room.
Beds: KQDT.

Although this elegant manor is a recent construction, it closely resembles Mount Vernon, the home of George Washington, which is just 20 miles away. Stroll the winding brick walkway and enjoy the site of gardens, a gazebo, fountain and rose arbors. Each of the rooms is named for a historical figure, including Martha's Retreat, in honor of America's original first lady. The room features a huge, four-poster bed and Jacuzzi tub. The breakfasts and afternoon tea are served on fine china, crystal and silver. The area offers several Civil War battlefields, national monuments and other historic sites.

Breakfast and afternoon tea included in rates. Types of meals: continental-plus breakfast and gourmet breakfast. Banquet service and catering service available. Air conditioning, turn-down service and ceiling fan in room. Cable TV, VCR, fax, copier and library on premises. Weddings, small meetings, family reunions and seminars hosted. Amusement parks, antiques, fishing, parks and shopping nearby. TAC10.

Special Discounts: AAA, military, seniors get 10%.

Stanley — D13

Jordan Hollow Farm Inn

RR 2 Box 375
Stanley, VA 22851-9538
(703)778-2285
Fax:(703)778-1759

Rates: $140-180. MAP.
Payment: MC VISA AX DC CB DS.
Innkeeper(s): Marley Beers.
Circa: 1790.

Rooms: 21 rooms with PB, 4 with FP. 1 conference room.
Beds: KQT.

Nestled in the foothills of the Blue Ridge Mountains, this delightful 45-acre horse farm is ideal for those who love riding and country living. The colonial farm house is decorated with antiques and country artifacts. Gentle trail horses are available for guests to ride for miles through the mountains and foothills. Five miles of walking trails are available on the property.

Breakfast and dinner included in rates. Type of meal: full breakfast. Picnic lunch available. MAP. Fax and copier on premises. Handicap access. Parks, cross-country skiing and watersports nearby.

Location: Shenandoah Valley, six miles south of Luray.

Publicity: *Country, Southern Living, Conde Nast, New York Times, Country Accents, Family Circle, Glamour, Vogue, Palm Beach, Washingtonian.*

"I keep thinking of my day at your lovely inn and keep dreaming of that wonderful lemon mousse cake!"

Wisteria B&B

1126 Marksville Rd
Stanley, VA 22851
(540)778-3347

Rates: $125-175. MAP.
Payment: MC VISA PC TC.
Innkeeper(s): Eric & Nicola Portch.
Circa: 1900.

Rooms: 4 rooms with PB. 2 cottages.
Beds: KQ.

This turn-of-the-century Victorian served as a post office, family home and a girl's school. The home has been restored and decorated with antiques. Guest rooms offer mountains views, and feather beds topped with down comforters. The 15 acres include hiking trails and gardens. A five-course breakfast is served, and guests choose the time. The inn is six miles from Luray, and the Luray Caverns, rafting, canoeing, golf and horseback riding are among the nearby activities.

Breakfast and evening snack included in rates. Type of meal: gourmet breakfast. Picnic lunch and room service available. MAP. Air conditioning, turn-down service and ceiling fan in room. Cable TV, VCR, spa and library on premises. 15 acres. Antiques, fishing, parks, shopping and downhill skiing nearby.

Staunton **E11**

Ashton Country House

1205 Middlebrook Ave
Staunton, VA 24401-4546
(540)885-7819 (800)296-7819

Rates: $90-125.
Payment: MC VISA PC TC.
Innkeeper(s): Dorie & Vince Di Stefano.
Circa: 1860.

Rooms: 5 rooms with PB, 4 with FP. 1 suite.
Beds: QD.

This Greek Revival home is surrounded by 25 explorable acres where cows roam and birds frolic in the trees. A mix of traditional and Victorian antiques grace the interior. Four of the guest rooms include a fireplace, and each is appointed individually. The inn's porches, where afternoon tea often is served, are lined with chairs for those who seek relaxation and the scenery of rolling hills. Woodrow Wilson's birthplace is among the town's notable attractions.

Breakfast, afternoon tea and evening snack included in rates. Types of meals: full breakfast, gourmet breakfast and early coffee/tea. Picnic lunch available. Air conditioning and ceiling fan in room. Cable TV and VCR on premises. Handicap access. 25 acres. Small meetings and family reunions hosted. Antiques, fishing, parks, shopping and watersports nearby.

Frederick House

28 N New St
Staunton, VA 24401-4306
(540)885-4220 (800)334-5575

Rates: $65-145.
Payment: MC VISA AX DC DS PC TC.
Innkeeper(s): Joe & Evy Harman.
Circa: 1810.

Rooms: 14 rooms with PB, 3 with FP. 6 suites. 1 conference room.
Beds: KQDT.

Across from Mary Baldwin College, this inn consists of five renovated town houses, the oldest of which is believed to be a copy of a home designed by Thomas Jefferson. A full breakfast is served in Chumley's Tea Room. Guest rooms are furnished with antiques and feature robes, ceiling fans, some with fireplaces. Original staircases and woodwork are highlighted throughout. Suites are available.

Breakfast and afternoon tea included in rates. Types of meals: full breakfast, gourmet breakfast and early coffee/tea. Picnic lunch and catering service available. Air conditioning, ceiling fan and cable TV in room. Library on premises. Weddings, small meetings, family reunions and seminars hosted. Antiques, fishing, parks, shopping, downhill skiing, cross-country skiing, sporting events, theater and watersports nearby. TAC10.

Location: Downtown.

Publicity: *Richmond Times-Dispatch, News Journal, Washington Post, Blue Ridge Country.*

"Thanks for making the room so squeaky-clean and comfortable! I enjoyed the Virginia hospitality. The furnishings and decor are beautiful."

The Sampson Eagon Inn

238 E Beverley St
Staunton, VA 24401-4325
(540)886-8200 (800)597-9722

Rates: $89-109.
Payment: MC VISA AX.
Innkeeper(s): Laura & Frank Mattingly.
Circa: 1840.

Rooms: 5 rooms, 3 with PB. 2 suites.
Beds: Q.

The fall leaves provide a colorful backdrop for this pre-Civil War manor. Fresh fruits, homemade bread and specialties such as melt-in-your-mouth Grand Marnier souffle pancakes fill the wonderful breakfast menu and are served with an informal Southern style and hospitality. Antiques and reproductions from the innkeepers' personal collection decorate the home. Enjoy the charm of Staunton as you visit nearby attractions such as Woodrow Wilson's birthplace and museum (one block away). Monticello is a 35-minute drive through the beautiful countryside.

Breakfast and evening snack included in rates. Types of meals: full breakfast and early coffee/tea. Air conditioning, cable TV and VCR in room. Fax, copier and library on premises. Antiques, fishing, parks, downhill skiing, sporting events and theater nearby.

Location: At the geographic center of Virginia Shenandoah Valley (I-81 and I-64).

Publicity: *Country Inns, Gourmet, Washington Post, Baltimore Sun.*

Special Discounts: Corporate and Senior Rates applicable during week only.

"Everything was special and you are the most gracious and kind hosts."

Steeles Tavern — *E11*

Steeles Tavern Manor B&B

PO Box 39
Steeles Tavern, VA 24476
(540)377-6444 (800)743-8666
Fax:(540)377-5937
E-mail: hoernlei@cfw.com

Rates: $105-140.
Payment: MC VISA PC TC.
Innkeeper(s): Eileen & Bill Hoernlein.
Circa: 1916.

Rooms: 5 rooms with PB, 2 with FP. 2 suites.
Beds: KQT.

When innkeepers Eileen and Bill Hoernlein restored and opened this romantic bed & breakfast, they were adding on to the manor's legacy of hospitality. The village of Steeles Tavern is named for David Steele, one of the area's first settlers, who hosted many guests in the town's day as a stagecoach stop. His granddaughter, Irene, was the manor's first owner, and she opened the house to tourists from its early days until the 1940s. The Hoernleins have created a cozy retreat on their 55-acre estate which boasts plenty of hiking, walking and birdwatching possibilities, as well as a stocked fishing pond. Inside, the innkeepers have placed an emphasis on romance and privacy, with quiet, cozy rooms decorated with fresh flowers, candy-filled dishes and plenty of fluffy pillows and blankets. Some rooms offer the added amenities of two-person whirlpool tubs and video libraries. An expansive country breakfast is served each morning, and the afternoon tea service offers a bounty of delightful refreshments after a day touring the area. The manor is only a few minutes from Cyrus McCormick Farm. Historic Lexington and Staunton are 15 minutes away, as is Washington & Lee University. The Blue Ridge Parkway is about a 30-minute drive. UVA, Monticello, Appamattox and Ash Lawn are a 60-minute day trip from the home.

Types of meals: full breakfast, gourmet breakfast and early coffee/tea. Afternoon tea available. Air conditioning, turn-down service, ceiling fan and VCR in room. Fax and library on premises. 55 acres. Antiques, fishing, parks, shopping, downhill skiing, cross-country skiing, sporting events, theater and watersports nearby.

Publicity: *News Gazette.*

Special Discounts: Call.

"A real winner. Excellent breakfast. Exquisite! Fabulous!"

Urbanna

F17

Hewick Plantation

VSH 602/615, Box 82
Urbanna, VA 23175
(804)758-4214
Fax:(804)758-4080
E-mail: gzkq12a@prodigy.com
and hewick1@aol.com

Rates: $95-135.
Payment: MC VISA AX DS PC TC.
Innkeeper(s): Helen & Ed Battleson.
Circa: 1678.

Rooms: 2 rooms with PB, 2 with FP.
Beds: QDT.

A driveway lined with large oak trees leads to this two-story brick Colonial located on 66 acres. There is an ancient family cemetery on the grounds, and at the rear of the house is an archaeological dig conducted by the College of William and Mary. A cross-stitch kit of Hewick Plantation, made by the Heirloom Needlecraft company, is available at the inn. The historic "Urbanna" coverlet is another unique item on display. The innkeeper is a tenth-generation descendant of Christopher Robinson, builder of Hewick Plantation and an original trustee of the College of William and Mary.

Breakfast included in rates. Type of meal: continental-plus breakfast. Air conditioning and cable TV in room. Fax and stables on premises. 66 acres. Weddings, small meetings, family reunions and seminars hosted. Spanish spoken. Amusement parks, antiques, fishing, parks, shopping and watersports nearby. TAC10.

Publicity: *Richmond Times Dispatch, Daily Press, Pleasant Living, WRIC-TV, TV-Tokyo.*

Special Discounts: 10% discount to genealogists doing research.

Warm Springs

E10

Three Hills Inn

PO Box 9
Warm Springs, VA 24484
(540)839-5381 (888)234-4557
Fax:(540)839-5199

Rates: $49-149.
Payment: MC VISA DS PC TC.
Innkeeper(s): Michael & Joann Mcbane.
Circa: 1913.

Rooms: 15 rooms, 12 with PB, 3 with FP. 7 suites. 3 cottages. 1 conference room.
Beds: KQDT.

Mary Johnston, who wrote the book "To Have and to Hold," built this inn, which rests on 38 mountainous acres. In 1917, Mary and her sisters opened the home to guests, earning a reputation for the home's view of the Allegheny Mountains and Warm Springs Gap. The innkeepers now offer lodging in the antique-filled main house or adjacent cottages. Some rooms include private decks, while others have fireplaces or clawfoot tubs. Each of the cottages include a kitchen, one has a working fireplace, another offers a woodburning stove.

Breakfast and afternoon tea included in rates. Types of meals: continental breakfast, gourmet breakfast and early coffee/tea. Picnic lunch, banquet service and catering service available. Cable TV in room. VCR, fax, copier and child care on premises. 38 acres. Weddings, small meetings, family reunions and seminars hosted. Spanish spoken. Antiques, fishing, parks, shopping, downhill skiing, cross-country skiing and theater nearby. TAC10.

Pets Allowed: Rooms with outside door.

Caledonia Farm - 1812

47 Dearing Rd (Flint Hill)
Washington, VA 22627
(540)675-3693 (800)BNB-1812
Fax:(540)675-3693

Rates: $80-140.
Payment: MC VISA DS PC TC.
Innkeeper(s): Phil Irwin.
Circa: 1812.

Rooms: 3 rooms, 2 with PB, 3 with FP. 2 suites. 1 cottage. 1 conference room.
Beds: D.

This gracious Federal-style stone house in the National Register is beautifully situated on 52 acres adjacent to Shenandoah National Park. It was built by a Revolutionary War officer, and his musket is displayed over a mantel. The house, a Virginia Historic Landmark, has been restored with the original Colonial color scheme retained. All rooms have working fireplaces and provide views of Skyline Drive and the Blue Ridge Mountains. The innkeeper is a retired broadcaster.

Breakfast and evening snack included in rates. Types of meals: gourmet breakfast and early coffee/tea. Air conditioning, turn-down service and VCR in room. Fax, copier, spa, bicycles and library on premises. 52 acres. Small meetings, family reunions and seminars hosted. German/Danish spoken. Antiques, fishing, parks, shopping, skiing, theater and watersports nearby. TAC10.

Pets Allowed: Kennel nearby.

Location: Four miles north of Washington, Va. 68 miles from Washington, DC.

Publicity: *Country, Country Almanac, Country Living, Blue Ridge Country, Discovery, Washington Post, Baltimore Sun.*

Special Discounts: Jan. 2-Sept. 15 second night free, non-holiday, Sunday-Wednesday.

"We've stayed at many, many B&Bs. This is by far the best!"

Fairlea Farm Bed & Breakfast

636 Mt Salem Ave,
PO Box 124
Washington, VA 22747
(540)675-3679
Fax:(540)675-1064

Rates: $75-125.
Payment: PC TC.
Innkeeper(s): Susan & Walt Longyear.
Circa: 1960.

Rooms: 3 rooms. 1 suite.
Beds: QT.

View acres of rolling hills, farmland and the Blue Ridge Mountains from this fieldstone house. Rooms are decorated with crocheted canopies and four-poster beds. Plants and floral bedcovers add a homey feel. The stone terrace is set up for relaxing with chairs lined along the edge. As a young surveyor, George Washington inspected the boundaries of this historic village, which is just a short walk from Fairlea Farm, which is a working sheep and cattle farm.

Breakfast and afternoon tea included in rates. Types of meals: full breakfast, gourmet breakfast and early coffee/tea. Air conditioning and turn-down service in room. VCR, fax and copier on premises. 40 acres. English and French spoken. Antiques, fishing, parks, shopping and theater nearby. TAC10.

Gay Street Inn

PO Box 237, Gay St
Washington, VA 22747
(540)675-3288

Rates: $95-135.
Payment: MC VISA AX PC TC.
Innkeeper(s): Robin & Donna Kevis.
Circa: 1855.

Rooms: 3 rooms with PB, 1 with FP, and 1 suite with three rooms
Beds: Q.

After a day of Skyline Drive, Shenandoah National Park and the caverns of Luray and Front Royal, come home to this stucco, gabled farmhouse. If you've booked the fireplace room, a canopy bed will await you. Furnishings include period Shaker pieces. The innkeepers will be happy to steer you to the most interesting vineyards, "pick-your-own" fruit and vegetable farms and Made-In-Virginia food and craft shops. Five-star dining is within walking distance of the inn. Breakfast is served in an English conservatory room.

Breakfast and afternoon tea included in rates. Types of meals: continental-plus breakfast, full breakfast, gourmet breakfast and early coffee/tea. Picnic lunch available. Air conditioning in room. Child care on premises. Handicap access. Weddings, small meetings and family reunions hosted. Antiques, fishing, parks, shopping, theater and watersports nearby. TAC10.

Pets Allowed.

"Thank you for a wonderful visit. Your hospitality was superb."

The Inn at Little Washington

PO Box 300
Washington, VA 22747-0300
(540)675-3800
Fax:(540)675-3100

Rates: $250-625.
Payment: MC VISA.
Innkeeper(s): Patrick O'Connell & Reinhardt Lynch.
Circa: 1915.

Rooms: 12 rooms with PB. 3 suites.
Beds: DT.

The restaurant at the Inn at Little Washington has received five stars and five diamonds, and guests will find the experience by which they measure all other quality dining. This two-story white clapboard inn was once a repair garage. With the assistance of English designer Joyce Conwy-Evans, fantasy and romance were created with lavish fabrics, faux woods and antiques. A garden courtyard includes a gazebo and reflecting pool.

Dinner, picnic lunch and room service available. Fax on premises. Handicap access. Antiques and fishing nearby.

Publicity: *USA Today, New York Times, San Francisco Chronicle, Virginian, Washingtonian, Washington Post, Inc., Travel & Leisure, Country Inns, Bon Appetit, Asbury Park Press, Columbus Dispatch, People, Exponent Extra, Robb Report.*

"One of the most celebrated restaurants and inns in America," — Bon Appetit.

Weyers Cave D12

The Inn at Keezletown Rd B&B

RR 1 Box 14
Weyers Cave, VA 24486
(540)234-0644

Rates: $75-95.
Payment: MC VISA PC TC.
Innkeeper(s): Sandy & Alan Inabinet.
Circa: 1896.

Rooms: 4 rooms with PB.
Beds: KQT.

This lavender pink Victorian with gingerbread trim was the grandest of several homes built by a local doctor in this quaint Shenandoah Valley village. Rooms are furnished with Oriental rugs and antiques made in the valley. The inn boasts views of the Blue Ridge Mountains; the grounds include herb and flower gardens and a goldfish pond. The full country breakfasts feature fresh eggs from the inns' chickens. The inn is close to Harrisonburg, Staunton, the airport, James Madison University and other colleges, hiking, auctions and antique shops.

Breakfast included in rates. Type of meal: full breakfast. Air conditioning, ceiling fan and cable TV in room. Small meetings hosted. Antiques, fishing, parks, shopping, downhill skiing, sporting events and theater nearby. TAC10.

Publicity: *Daily News Record.*

"A paradise in microcosm, from your Chanticleer to your Botany. Where else could one breakfast to La Boheme? You provide much more than an inn, each hour here brings reflective joy."

White Post

B13

L'Auberge Provencale

PO Box 119
White Post, VA 22663-0119
(540)837-1375 (800)638-1702
Fax:(540)837-2004

Rates: $145-250.
Payment: MC VISA AX DC DS PC TC.
Innkeeper(s): Alain & Celeste Borel.
Circa: 1753.

Rooms: 11 rooms, 10 with PB, 6 with FP. 2 suites. 1 conference room.
Beds: QD.

This farmhouse was built with fieldstones gathered from the area. Hessian soldiers crafted the woodwork of the main house, Mt. Airy. As the name suggests, a French influence is prominent throughout the inn. Victorian and European antiques fill the elegant guest rooms, several of which include fireplaces. Innkeeper Alain Borel hails from a long line of master chefs, his expertise creates many happy culinary memories guests cherish. Many of the French-influenced items served at the inn's four-diamond restaurant, include ingredients from the inn's gardens, and Alain has been hailed by James Beard as a Great Country Inn Chef.

Breakfast included in rates. Type of meal: gourmet breakfast. Dinner, evening snack, picnic lunch, banquet service and room service available. Air conditioning, turn-down service and ceiling fan in room. Fax, copier and bicycles on premises. Handicap access. 10 acres. Weddings, small meetings, family reunions and seminars hosted. French and Spanish spoken. Antiques, fishing, parks, shopping and theater nearby. TAC10.

Location: One mile south of Route 50 on Route 340.

Publicity: *Bon Appetit, Glamour, Washington Dossier, Washington Post, Baltimore, Richmond Times.*

"Peaceful view and atmosphere, extraordinary food and wines. Honeymoon and heaven all in one!"

Williamsburg

G17

Applewood Colonial B&B

605 Richmond Rd
Williamsburg, VA 23185
(804)229-0205 (800)899-2753
Fax:(804)229-9405
E-mail: apple@heartstea.net

Rates: $85-150.
Payment: MC VISA PC.
Innkeeper(s): Marty Jones.
Circa: 1929.

Rooms: 4 rooms with PB, 1 with FP. 1 suite.
Beds: QT.

This Flemish-bond brick home was built during the restoration of Colonial Williamsburg. The inn's parlor is decorated in a colonial style and features dental crown molding. A crystal chandelier hangs above the dining table where candlelight breakfasts are served. Afternoon refreshments also are served. The Colonel Vaughn suite boasts a private entrance, a fireplace and queen-size canopy bed.

Breakfast and evening snack included in rates. Types of meals: full breakfast and early coffee/tea. Air conditioning and ceiling fan in room. Cable TV, VCR, fax and library on premises. Weddings, small meetings, family reunions and seminars hosted. German spoken. Amusement parks, antiques, fishing, parks, shopping, sporting events, theater and watersports nearby. TAC10.

Publicity: *The Discerning Traveler.*

Special Discounts: Over four days, off season.

"Our accommodations were the best, and you were most kind."

Cedars

616 Jamestown Rd
Williamsburg, VA 23185
(757)229-3591 (800)296-3591

Rates: $84-165.
Payment: MC VISA PC TC.
Innkeeper(s): Carol, Jim & Brona Malecha.
Circa: 1930.

Rooms: 8 rooms with PB. 1 cottage.
Beds: KQT.

This three-story brick Georgian home is an short walk from Colonial Williamsburg and is located across from William and Mary College. Rooms are decorated with Traditional antiques, Colonial reproductions, fireplaces and four-poster or canopy beds. The bountiful breakfasts include a hearty entree, fresh fruits, breads, muffins and cereals.

Breakfast included in rates. Types of meals: full breakfast and early coffee/tea. Air conditioning and ceiling fan in room. Library on premises. Family reunions hosted. Amusement parks, parks and shopping nearby. TAC10.

Colonial Capital B&B

501 Richmond Rd
Williamsburg, VA 23185
(757)229-0233 (800)776-0570
Fax:(757)253-7667
E-mail: ccbb@tni.net

Rates: $76-135.
Payment: MC VISA AX DS PC TC.
Innkeeper(s): Barbara & Phil Craig.
Circa: 1926.

Rooms: 5 rooms with PB. 1 suite.
Beds: KQT.

This three-story Colonial Revival house features a plantation parlor with wood-burning fireplace. Nightly turn-down service is offered. Canopied beds include an antique rope bed with turned posts in the York Room. A third-floor suite offers two rooms for couples traveling together. Afternoon tea and wine are served in the parlor, porch, patio or deck. The inn has a mascot, a Golden Retriever who answers to Ginny. A gourmet breakfast is served.

Breakfast and afternoon tea included in rates. Types of meals: full breakfast, gourmet breakfast and early coffee/tea. Air conditioning, turn-down service, ceiling fan and cable TV in room. VCR, fax, copier, bicycles and library on premises. Weddings, small meetings and family reunions hosted. Amusement parks, antiques, parks, shopping, theater and watersports nearby. TAC10.

Location: Three blocks from the Colonial Williamsburg Historic District.

Publicity: *Country Inns, Mid-Atlantic.*

"This stay will always be for me a wonderful 'souvenir' thanks to Barbara and Phil."

Fox & Grape B&B

701 Monumental Ave
Williamsburg, VA 23185
(757)229-6914 (800)292-3699

Rates: $84-90.
Payment: MC VISA DS TC.
Innkeeper(s): Robert & Patricia Orendorff.
Circa: 1949.

Rooms: 4 rooms with PB.
Beds: QD.

Guests at this two-story Colonial often are found enjoying a morning cup of coffee on the home's wraparound porch. The home is decorated with antiques, folk art and other collectibles. Guest rooms feature canopy beds. Colonial Williamsburg is five blocks away.

Breakfast included in rates. Type of meal: continental-plus breakfast. Air conditioning in room. Library on premises. Amusement parks, antiques, parks and shopping nearby. TAC10.

Special Discounts: January 1-March 21 $90.00 + tax first night, second night free.

"Your home is just beautiful, and your warm, helpful and humorous manner made our trip memorable."

Indian Springs B&B

330 Indian Springs Rd
Williamsburg, VA 23185
(757)220-0726 (800)262-9165

Rates: $80-125.
Payment: VISA PC TC.
Innkeeper(s): Kelly & Paul Supplee.
Circa: 1976.

Rooms: 4 rooms with PB, 1 with FP. 3 suites. 1 cottage.
Beds: KQT.

Across from the College of William & Mary, this pristine Dutch Colonial-style house offers three guests rooms and a separate cottage. The shuttered cottage boasts a fireplace, wet bar, loft with a king-size bed and is a good selection for families with children or honeymooners. The morning meal begins with fresh fruit and homemade muffins, followed by a full breakfast.

Breakfast and afternoon tea included in rates. Types of meals: full breakfast and early coffee/tea. Air conditioning, ceiling fan, cable TV and VCR in room. Amusement parks, antiques, fishing, parks, shopping, sporting events, theater and watersports nearby. TAC10.

Liberty Rose B&B

1022 Jamestown Rd
Williamsburg, VA 23185
(804)253-1260 (800)545-1825

Rates: $100-175.
Payment: MC VISA AX.
Innkeeper(s): Brad & Sandi Hirz.
Circa: 1922.

Rooms: 4 rooms with PB, 1 with FP. 3 suites.
Beds: QT.

This cozy retreat is tucked among tall trees only a mile from Colonial Williamsburg. The owner of Jamestown constructed this two-story clapboard home. The entry porch is marked with the millstone from one of Williamsburg's old mills. Antiques and collectibles abound in each of the rooms. The innkeepers have merged modern amenities with the atmosphere of Colonial times. A gourmet country breakfast is served each morning. Each of the romantic guest rooms features something unique. Honeymooners — the inn is often full of newlyweds — will return to celebrate their anniversaries.

Breakfast included in rates. Type of meal: full breakfast. Antiques, theater and watersports nearby.

Location: One mile from Colonial Williamsburg's historic area.

Publicity: *Country Inns, Washington Post, Rural Living, Los Angeles Times, Glamour.*

"More delightful than we could possibly have imagined. Charm & romance abounds when you walk into the house."

Newport House

710 S Henry St
Williamsburg, VA 23185
(757)229-1775
Fax:(757)229-6408

Rates: $110-140.
Payment: PC TC.
Innkeeper(s): John & Cathy Millar.
Circa: 1987.

Rooms: 2 rooms with PB. 1 conference room.
Beds: QT.

This neo-Palladian house is a 1756 design by Peter Harrison, architect of rebuilt Williamsburg State House. It features wooden rusticated siding. Colonial country dancing is held in the inn's ballroom on Tuesday evenings. Guests are welcome to participate. There are English and American antiques, and reproductions include canopy beds in all the guest rooms. The host was a museum director and captain of a historic tall ship.

Breakfast included in rates. Type of meal: full breakfast. Air conditioning and VCR in room. Fax and child care on premises. Weddings, small meetings and seminars hosted. French spoken. Amusement parks, antiques, parks, shopping, theater, watersports nearby. TAC10.

Location: Five-minute walk from Colonial Williamsburg.

Publicity: *Innsider.*

"Host and hostess were charming and warm."

Piney Grove at Southall's Plantation

PO Box 1359
Williamsburg, VA 23187
(804)829-2480
Fax:(804)829-2480

Rates: $125-160.
Payment: PC.
Innkeeper(s): Gordineer Family.
Circa: 1800.

Rooms: 4 rooms with PB, 4 with FP. 1 suite. 1 conference room.
Beds: DT.

The Gordineers welcome you to their two historic homes. Piney Grove is a rare Tidewater log building in the National Register of Historic Places, located on the Old Main Road among farms, plantations, country stores and quaint churches. Ladysmith House is a modest antebellum plantation house (c. 1857). Both homes are furnished with a unique collection of artifacts and antiques that illustrates the history of the property and area. The grounds also include Ashland (1835) and Duck Church (1900). Guests also enjoy meandering among the gardens, grounds and nature trail.

Type of meal: full breakfast. Evening snack available. Air conditioning and turn-down service in room. Cable TV, VCR, fax and swimming on premises. Limited German spoken. Amusement parks, antiques, fishing, parks, shopping, sporting events, theater and watersports nearby. TAC10.

Location: James River Plantation country, outside of Williamsburg.

Publicity: *New York Times, Richmond Times-Dispatch, Washington Post, Southern Living.*

Special Discounts: AAA lodging, dining and tour packages.

"Thank you for your warm, gracious hospitality. We really enjoyed ourselves and look forward to returning."

Williamsburg Manor B&B

600 Richmond Rd
Williamsburg, VA 23185
(804)220-8011 (800)422-8011
Fax:(804)220-8011

Rates: $75-150.
Payment: MC VISA PC TC.
Innkeeper(s): Laura Sisane.
Circa: 1927.

Rooms: 5 rooms with PB.
Beds: QT.

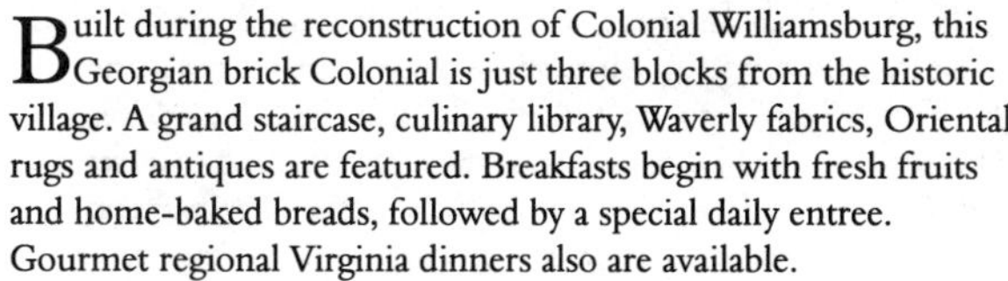

Built during the reconstruction of Colonial Williamsburg, this Georgian brick Colonial is just three blocks from the historic village. A grand staircase, culinary library, Waverly fabrics, Oriental rugs and antiques are featured. Breakfasts begin with fresh fruits and home-baked breads, followed by a special daily entree. Gourmet regional Virginia dinners also are available.

Breakfast included in rates. Types of meals: gourmet breakfast and early coffee/tea. Picnic lunch, lunch, gourmet lunch, catering service and catered breakfast available. Air conditioning, ceiling fan and cable TV in room. VCR and fax on premises. Weddings, small meetings, family reunions and seminars hosted. Amusement parks, antiques, fishing, parks, shopping, sporting events, theater and watersports nearby. TAC10.

Location: Three blocks from colonial Williamsburg.

Publicity: *Williamsburg.*

"Lovely accommodations - Scrumptious breakfast."

Williamsburg Sampler B&B

922 Jamestown Rd
Williamsburg, VA 23185
(757)253-0398 (800)722-1169
Fax:(757)253-2669

Rates: $95-140.
Payment: MC VISA PC.
Innkeeper(s): Helen & Ike Sisane.
Circa: 1976.

Rooms: 4 rooms with PB. 2 suites.
Beds: KQ.

Although this 18th-century-style home was built in the year of the bicentennial, it captures the early American spirit of Colonial Williamsburg. The rooms serve as wonderful replicas of an elegant Colonial home, with antiques, pewter and framed American and English samplers found throughout the inn. Bedchambers, which include suites with fireplaces and "Roof Top Garden," are cozy with rice-carved, four-poster beds and Colonial decor. Guests can test their skill at checkers or curl up with a book in the 1827 armchair in the Tavern Reading Room, or watch TV in the Common Keeping Room. The innkeepers term the morning meal a "skip-lunch breakfast," an apt description of the colossal menu. If they can move after this wonderful meal, guests head out for a day exploring historic Williamsburg.

Breakfast included in rates. Types of meals: full breakfast and early coffee/tea. Air conditioning, ceiling fan, cable TV and VCR in room. Fax and library on premises. Small meetings and family reunions hosted. Amusement parks, antiques, fishing, parks, shopping, sporting events, theater and watersports nearby. TAC10.

Woodstock C13

Azalea House

551 S Main St
Woodstock, VA 22664-1257
(540)459-3500

Rates: $55-75.
Payment: MC VISA AX.
Innkeeper(s): Margaret & Price McDonald.
Circa: 1892.

Rooms: 4 rooms with PB.
Beds: QD.

A white picket fence and garden archway invite guests to this Victorian house. Rooms with period antiques and parlors decorated with stenciled ceilings await guests. Caverns, vineyards, horseback riding, canoeing, Civil War sites, theaters and antiquing are nearby.

Breakfast included in rates. Types of meals: full breakfast and early coffee/tea. Air conditioning and ceiling fan in room. Cable TV and VCR on premises.

VA

Country Fare

402 N Main St Rt 11
Woodstock, VA 22664-1802
(540)459-4828

Rates: $55-65.
Payment: MC VISA PC TC.
Innkeeper(s): Bette Hallgren.
Circa: 1772.

Rooms: 3 rooms, 1 with PB.
Beds: QD.

Originally an American foursquare home, the front section of this inn has a log substructure flanked on either side by fireplaces. The home was the site of one of the Shenandoah Valley's many field houses during the Civil War, and it is one of the area's oldest homes still in use. Antiques, collectibles and original hand-stenciled designs recapture the 18th-century atmosphere of this home. Some of the rooms boast antiques that once belonged to the innkeeper's grandmother.

Breakfast included in rates. Types of meals: continental-plus breakfast and early coffee/tea. Air conditioning and ceiling fan in room. Copier on premises. Antiques, fishing, parks, shopping, downhill skiing and theater nearby.

Publicity: *Valley-Herald, Blue Ridge Country.*

"Relaxing and pleasurable as always."

The Inn at Narrow Passage

PO Box 608
Woodstock, VA 22664-0608
(540)459-8000
Fax:(540)459-8001

Rates: $85-110.
Payment: MC VISA.
Innkeeper(s): Ellen & Ed Markel.
Circa: 1740.

Rooms: 12 rooms with PB.
Beds: Q.

This log inn has been welcoming travelers since the time settlers took refuge here against the Indians. Later, it served as a stage-coach inn on the old Valley Turnpike, and in 1862, it was Stonewall Jackson's headquarters. Many guest rooms feature fireplaces and views of the Shenandoah River and Massanutten Mountains.

Breakfast included in rates. Antiques, fishing and watersports nearby.

Location: On Shenandoah River and US 11, 2-1/2 miles south of Woodstock.

Publicity: *Southern Living, Washington Post, Washington Times, Richmond Times-Dispatch.*

"We are still basking in the afterglow of our wonderful experience with you."

Skip-Lunch Breakfast

Williamsburg Sampler B&B
Williamsburg, Va.

- 3 T butter, separated
- 2 T flour
- 2 cups milk
- ½ t salt
- ⅛ t pepper
- 1 4-ounce can mushrooms, drained
- ½ cup shredded American cheese
- 1 cup chopped Canadian bacon
- ¼ cup green onions
- paprika
- 1 dozen eggs, beaten
- bread crumbs

Combine 2 tablespoons butter and flour. Blend until smooth. Cook over low heat until bubbly. Gradually stir in milk, cook until smooth and thick, stirring constantly. Add salt, pepper, cheese, heat and stir until cheese melts. Set aside. Saute bacon and onions in remaining butter until onions are tender. Add eggs; cook until set, stiring to scramble. Fold in mushrooms and cheese sauce. Spoon egg mixture into lightly greased 12-by-7 inch baking dish. Top with bread crumbs, sprinkle with paprika. Bake at 350 degrees for 30 minutes. Serves 8.

Notes: May be prepared ahead and heated to serve.

Washington

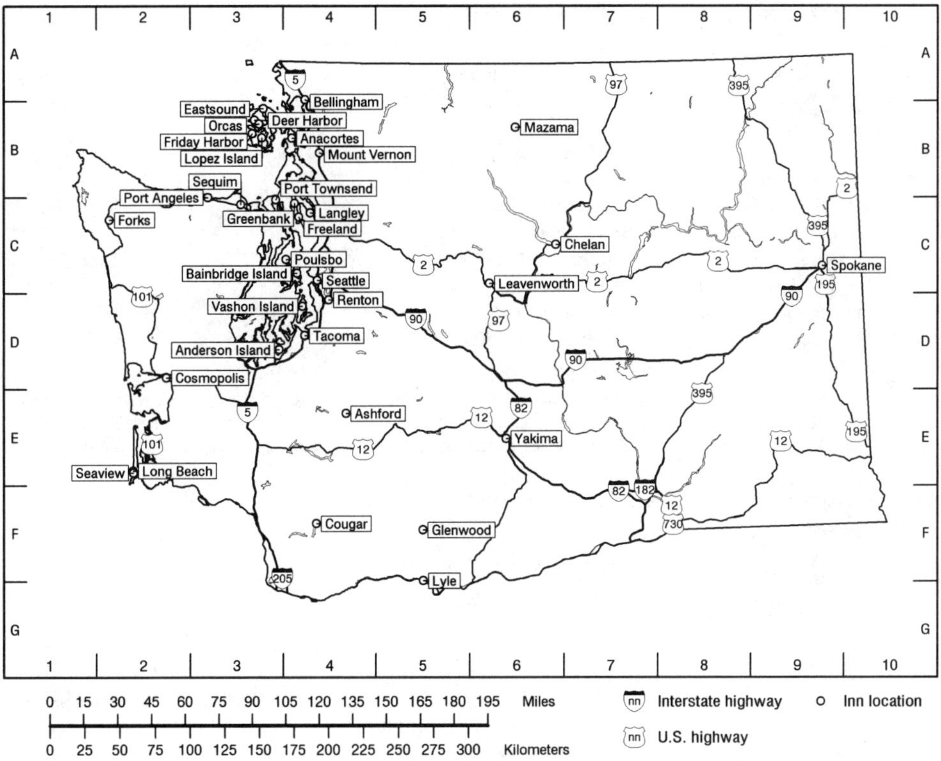

0 15 30 45 60 75 90 105 120 135 150 165 180 195 Miles
0 25 50 75 100 125 150 175 200 225 250 275 300 Kilometers

nn Interstate highway ○ Inn location
nn U.S. highway

Aberdeen (Cosmopolis)

Cooney Mansion B&B

PO Box 54, 1705 Fifth St
Aberdeen (Cosmopolis),
WA 98537-0054
(360)533-0602 (800)977-7823

Rates: $60-135.
Payment: MC VISA AX DC DS.
Innkeeper(s): Judi & Jim Lohr.
Circa: 1908.

Rooms: 8 rooms, 5 with PB, 1 with FP. 1 suite. 1 conference room.
Beds: KQDT.

This former lumber magnate's home, in a wooded setting, boasts 37 rooms. In the National Register, it was built with a ballroom in the basement, nine bedrooms and eight bathrooms. There is an intercom system with the original script still visible. Mission furnishings, original to the house, include the dining room set, sofas, desks and library tables. Weddings and corporate retreats are popular here.

Breakfast and afternoon tea included in rates. Types of meals: full breakfast and early coffee/tea. Banquet service and catering service available. Cable TV, VCR, fax, spa and sauna on premises. Weddings, small meetings, family reunions and seminars hosted. Antiques, fishing, parks, shopping, sporting events, theater and watersports nearby.

Publicity: *Daily World.*

Special Discounts: Mention this book to receive a chilled bottle of wine on arrival.

"This is an exceptional inn because of the hosts, who really care about their guests."

WA

Anacortes

B4

Albatross Bed & Breakfast

5708 Kingsway
Anacortes, WA 98221-2932
(360)293-0677 (800)622-8864

Rates: $75-90.
Payment: MC VISA AX PC TC.
Innkeeper(s): Barbie & Ken Arasim.
Circa: 1927.

Rooms: 4 rooms with PB.
Beds: KQ.

This Cape Cod-style home is one of the last remaining relics of Anacortes' booming lumber days. The current bed & breakfast was built as a home for the mill manager at the E.K. Wood Mill Company. The innkeepers have filled the home with antiques, original art and many collectibles, including a signed Norman Rockwell print. As the hosts names are Ken and Barbie, they also have included several rare "Barbie Doll" gowns created by famed designer Bob Mackie. The popular Scarlett O'Hara Room is filled with unique pieces from a 19th-century Southern mansion. The home maintains many original elements, including beaded cedar ceilings and crystal chandeliers. Skyline Marina is adjacent to the home, and the San Juan ferry boat docks just one-half mile away.

Breakfast and evening snack included in rates. Types of meals: full breakfast and gourmet breakfast. Afternoon tea available. Turn-down service in room. Cable TV, VCR, fax, copier, bicycles, tennis and library on premises. Weddings, small meetings, family reunions and seminars hosted. Antiques, fishing, parks, shopping, downhill skiing, cross-country skiing, sporting events, theater and watersports nearby. TAC10.

Location: One-half mile from ferry to the San Juan Islands and Victoria, B.C.

Publicity: *Apropos, Business Pulse.*

Special Discounts: Package offer $300.00 sailboat cruise & scenic flight & two nights.

"Our stay with you was a comfortable, enjoyable experience. Such cordiality!"

Channel House

2902 Oakes Ave
Anacortes, WA 98221-1321
(360)293-9382 (800)238-4353
Fax:(360)299-9208

Rates: $69-105.
Payment: MC VISA AX DS PC TC.
Innkeeper(s): Dennis & Pat McIntyre.
Circa: 1902.

Rooms: 6 rooms with PB, 2 with FP. 1 cottage.
Beds: KQ.

Built by an Italian count, the Channel House is designated the Krebs House by the Historical Home Tour. Guest rooms view Puget Sound and the San Juan Islands, and the ferry is minutes away. The inn has a Victorian flavor, with a library, three fireplaces, and a dining room with French doors leading out to the garden.

Breakfast and afternoon tea included in rates. Types of meals: full breakfast and early coffee/tea. Fax on premises. Antiques, fishing, parks, shopping, theater and watersports nearby. TAC10.

Location: 85 miles north of Seattle.

Publicity: *Skagit Valley Herald.*

"The house is spectacular and your friendly thoughtfulness is the icing on the cake."

Anderson Island D3

The Inn at Burg's Landing

8808 Villa Beach Rd
Anderson Island, WA 98303
(206)884-9185
Fax:(206)488-8682

Rates: $75-110.
Payment: MC VISA PC TC.
Innkeeper(s): Ken & Annie Burg.
Circa: 1987.

Rooms: 4 rooms, 2 with PB.
Beds: Q.

A short ferry trip from Steilacoom and Tacoma, this log homestead boasts beautiful views of Mt. Rainier, Puget Sound and the Cascade Mountains. The master bedroom features a skylight and a private whirlpool bath. After a full breakfast, guests can spend the day at the inn's private beach. Golf, hiking and freshwater lakes are nearby, and the area has many seasonal activities, including Fourth of July fireworks, the Anderson Island fair and parade in September and a February Sweetheart Dance and Dinner.

Breakfast included in rates. Type of meal: full breakfast. VCR in room. Spa on premises. Weddings and family reunions hosted. Amusement parks, fishing, parks, shopping and downhill skiing nearby. TAC10.

Publicity: *Sunset, Tacoma News Tribune, Portland Oregonian.*

Ashford E4

Growly Bear B&B

37311 SR 706, PO Box 103
Ashford, WA 98304
(360)569-2339 (800)700-2339

Rates: $80-105.
Payment: MC VISA AX PC TC.
Innkeeper(s): Susan Jenny Johnson.
Circa: 1890.

Rooms: 2 rooms, 1 with PB.

Guests at Growly Bear will appreciate the cozy, rustic setting of this 100-year-old mountain home located only a mile from the entrance of Mt. Rainier National Park on Highway 706. Guest rooms are large and feature comfortable furnishings, quilts and a sitting room. A full gourmet mountain country breakfast is served each morning with fresh pastries made at a nearby bakery. The breakfast is a great start to a day of hiking or cross-country skiing. The inn is an ideal location for park visitors and is four miles from the village of Ashford.

Type of meal: full breakfast. Copier on premises. 15 acres. Cross-country skiing nearby. TAC10.

Location: One mile from Mt. Rainier National Park.

"Lovely surroundings and great baked goodies."

National Park Inn

Mt Rainier Guest Services
PO Box 10
Ashford, WA 98304
(360)569-2275
Fax:(360)569-2770

Rates: $64-88. AP.
Payment: MC VISA AX DC DS PC TC.
Innkeeper(s): James R. Sproatt.
Circa: 1920.

Rooms: 25 rooms, 18 with PB.
Beds: QDT.

Mt. Rainier National Park boasts a spectacular scenery of mountains and seemingly endless forests. For more than half a century, visitors from around the world have chosen National Park Inn for their park lodging. Old hickory and twig furnishings decorate the rustic, comfortable guest rooms. Lunch and dinner service are available at the inn's dining room. From late October to May 1, rates include bed & breakfast. Breakfast is not included during the high season, from May until about Oct. 19.

Breakfast included in rates. Types of meals: continental breakfast, continental-plus breakfast and full breakfast. Afternoon tea, dinner and picnic lunch available. AP. Handicap access. Small meetings hosted. Cross-country skiing nearby. TAC5.

Location: Located in Mount Rainier National Park.

Bellingham

A4

North Garden Inn

1014 N Garden St
Bellingham, WA 98225
(360)671-7828 (800)922-6414

Rates: $45-84.
Payment: MC VISA DS PC TC.
Innkeeper(s): Frank & Barbara DeFreytas.
Circa: 1897.

Rooms: 10 rooms, 8 with PB, 1 with FP.
Beds: QDT.

Listed in the National Register, this Queen Anne Victorian originally had bars on the basement windows to keep out the bears. Guest rooms feature views of Bellingham Bay and the surrounding islands. A mahogany Steinway piano is often played for guests. The inn is within walking distance to Western Washington University.

Breakfast included in rates. Types of meals: full breakfast and early coffee/tea. Cable TV, VCR, copier and library on premises. Small meetings and family reunions hosted. French, German and Spanish spoken. Antiques, fishing, parks, shopping, skiing, sporting events, theater and watersports nearby. TAC10.

Publicity: *La Bonne Cuisine, Chocolatier, Victorian Homes, Bellingham Herald, Country.*

"Excellent everything! Room, view, hospitality, breakfast, who could ask for anything more?"

Chelan

C6

Highland Guest House

121 E Highland Ave,
PO Box 2089
Chelan, WA 98816
(509)682-2892 (800)681-2892

Rates: $50-95.
Payment: MC VISA PC.
Innkeeper(s): Marilee & Brad Stolzenburg.
Circa: 1902.

Rooms: 3 rooms, 1 with PB.
Beds: QD.

This turn-of-the-century Victorian is decorated in period style with antiques. Each of the guest rooms has its own theme. For instance, one room offers a romantic canopy bed topped with a quilt. A number of collectibles, including a spinning wheel, decorate the common areas. Strawberries and cream French toast is a typical breakfast specialty.

Breakfast included in rates. Types of meals: full breakfast and gourmet breakfast. Picnic lunch and room service available. Air conditioning and ceiling fan in room. Cable TV and library on premises. Small meetings, family reunions and seminars hosted. Amusement parks, antiques, fishing, parks, shopping, cross-country skiing, theater and watersports nearby. TAC10.

Cougar

F4

Monfort's B&B

132 Cougar Loop Rd
Cougar, WA 98616
(360)238-5229
Fax:(360)238-5229

Rates: $55-75.
Payment: MC VISA PC TC.
Innkeeper(s): Marilyn & Gary Monfort.
Circa: 1992.

Rooms: 2 rooms with PB. 1 conference room.
Beds: QT.

For those visiting the area around Mount St. Helens, Monfort's serves as a comfortable stopping place. Guests select from one of two country decorated bedrooms. One of the guest rooms includes a whirlpool tub. The owners get the morning off to a good start with a hearty breakfast, featuring specialties such as homemade caramel-nut rolls.

Breakfast included in rates. Types of meals: full breakfast, gourmet breakfast and early coffee/tea. Catered breakfast available. Ceiling fan in room. VCR and fax on premises. Handicap access. Fishing, parks, shopping, cross-country skiing and watersports nearby.

Deer Harbor B3

Palmer's Chart House

PO Box 51
Deer Harbor, WA 98243
(360)376-4231

Rates: $70.
Payment: PC TC.
Innkeeper(s): Don & Majean Palmer.
Circa: 1975.

Rooms: 2 rooms with PB. 1 cottage.
Beds: KDT.

A ferry ride will take guests from seaside Anacortes out to Orcas Island, where this bed & breakfast is located. The setting is tranquil, offering privacy and beautiful views. There are two, comfortably furnished guest rooms available. At certain times of the year, and for an extra charge, guests can book passage and tour the San Juan Islands on the Amante, a private yacht.

Breakfast included in rates. Type of meal: full breakfast. Small meetings hosted. Spanish spoken. Fishing, parks, theater and watersports nearby.

Eastsound B3

Outlook Inn on Orcas Island

PO Box 210
Eastsound, WA 98245-0210
(360)376-2200 (888)OUTLOOK
Fax:(360)376-2256

Rates: $34-225.
Payment: MC VISA AX TC.
Innkeeper(s): Jeanine McConnaughey.
Circa: 1888.

Rooms: 41 rooms, 11 with PB, 16 with FP. 16 suites.
Beds: KQT.

This inn was built as a homesteader's cabin and in the late 1800s was expanded to include a general store, barber shop and a jail. The ocean view is spectacular and the inn boasts its own private beach area. Rooms contain hand-carved beds and marble-topped dressers. A walk throughout the peaceful village is a relaxing way to spend the day. The ocean breezes and beautiful surroundings create the perfect atmosphere for weddings. The hospitality will make any bride feel pampered as she prepares for her wedding day.

Types of meals: continental breakfast, continental-plus breakfast, full breakfast, gourmet breakfast and early coffee/tea. Dinner, evening snack, picnic lunch, lunch, gourmet lunch, banquet service and room service available. Cable TV and VCR in room. Fax and copier on premises. Handicap access. Weddings, small meetings, family reunions and seminars hosted. Fishing, parks, shopping, theater and watersports nearby.

Location: Orcas Island.

"The ambiance was incredible and all due to your gracious hospitality."

Turtleback Farm Inn

Crow Valley Rd,
Rt 1 Box 650
Eastsound, WA 98245
(360)376-4914 (800)376-4914

Rates: $70-160.
Payment: MC VISA DS PC TC.
Innkeeper(s): William & Susan C. Fletcher.
Circa: 1895.

Rooms: 7 rooms with PB.
Beds: KQD.

Guests will delight in the beautiful views afforded from this wonderful farmhouse, which overlooks 80 acres of forest and farmland, duck ponds and Mt. Constitution to the east. Rooms feature antique furnishings and many boast views of the farm, orchard or sheep pasture. Beds are covered with wool comforters made from sheep raised on the property. Bon Appetit highlighted some of the breakfast recipes served at Turtlebeck; a breakfast here is a memorable affair. Tables set with bone china, silver and fresh linens make way for a delightful mix of fruits, juice, award-winning granola, homemade breads and specialty entrees. Evening guests can settle down with a game or a book in the fire-lit parlor as they enjoy sherry, tea or hot chocolate.

Breakfast included in rates. Types of meals: full breakfast and early coffee/tea. Picnic lunch available. Library on premises. Handicap access. 80 acres. Weddings and family reunions hosted. Spanish and limited French spoken. Fishing, parks, shopping, theater and watersports nearby. TAC10.

WA

Location: Six miles from ferry landing, 2 miles from Westsound.

Publicity: *Los Angeles Times, USA Today, Travel & Leisure, Contra Costa Sun, Seattle Times, Northwest Living, Sunset, Food & Wine, Gourmet, Northwest Travel, New York Times, Alaska Air.*

"A peaceful haven for soothing the soul."

Forks C2

Manitou Lodge B&B

PO Box 600
Forks, WA 98331-0600
(360)374-6295

Rates: $60-75.
Payment: MC VISA PC TC.
Innkeeper(s): Raymond & Dolores Antil.
Circa: 1972.

Rooms: 7 rooms with PB, 2 with FP. 1 cottage. 1 conference room.
Beds: KQ.

This rustic, A-frame lodge is set on 10 forest acres. The river is just a few hundred yards away, and the lodge is near national parks, the ocean and hiking trails. Guest rooms are decorated with comfortable furnishings and feature Native American touches. Two rooms include fireplaces. The innkeepers have a collection of interesting Native American pieces on hand.

Afternoon tea and picnic lunch included in rates. Types of meals: full breakfast and early coffee/tea. Evening snack, banquet service, catering service, catered breakfast and room service available. Library on premises. Handicap access. 10 acres. Weddings, small meetings, family reunions and seminars hosted. French and Mohawk spoken. Fishing, parks and shopping nearby.

Freeland C4

Cliff House & Seacliff Cottage

5440 S Windmill Rd
Freeland, WA 98249-9627
(360)331-1566

Rates: $165-485.
Payment: PC.
Innkeeper(s): Peggy Moore & Walter O'Toole.
Circa: 1981.

Rooms: 2 cottages.
Beds: KQD.

The sensual delights of forest and sea, indoor rain and sunlight, have been captured in this unusual house designed by architect Arne Bystrom. A two-story, open-air and glass-walled atrium is the focal point and part of the loft bedroom where guests can gaze at the water from a plump featherbed. A second accommodation, Sea Cliff Cottage, is also available.

Breakfast included in rates. Type of meal: continental-plus breakfast. Air conditioning, turn-down service, ceiling fan and VCR in room. Spa on premises. 12 acres. Weddings hosted. Antiques, fishing, parks, shopping, theater and watersports nearby.

Location: On Whidbey Island.

Publicity: *Sunset, Pacific Northwest Magazine.*

"It's all downhill from here. Nowhere else we go will stand a chance of matching up to Cliff House!"

Seaside Cottage

PO Box 970
Freeland, WA 98249-0970
(360)331-8455
Fax:(360)331-8636
E-mail: seaside@whidbey.com

Rates: $60-95.
Payment: DS PC TC.
Innkeeper(s): Cliff & Virginia Lindsey.
Circa: 1971.

Rooms: 1 suite. 1 cottage.
Beds: KQ.

Located on a sandy beach, Seaside Cottage provides views of the San Juan Islands and the Olympic Mountains from the living room and kitchen. You also may wish to enjoy the view without getting out of bed in the morning. A breakfast tray and easy set up is organized for you upon your arrival so you can have breakfast at your leisure. Afterwards, walk through the old-growth forest, fish from the beach or boat from the dock. Don't miss the Berry Farm Winery while on the island.

Breakfast included in rates. Types of meals: continental breakfast, continental-plus breakfast, full breakfast and early coffee/tea. Cable TV and VCR in room. Fax and copier on premises. Limited German and limited Spanish spoken. Antiques, fishing, parks, shopping, theater and watersports nearby.

Special Discounts: Nov. 1 to April 30, discount for two-night minimum, Sunday-Thursday.

Mariella Inn & Cottages

630 Turn Point Rd
Friday Harbor, WA 98250
(360)378-6868 (800)700-7668
Fax:(360)378-6822

Rates: $90-300.
Payment: MC VISA PC TC.
Innkeeper(s): Arthur & Alison Lohrey.
Circa: 1902.

Rooms: 11 rooms with PB. 8 cottages.
Beds: KQD.

This turn-of-the-century waterfront country house rests on 7.5 acres, surrounded on three sides by water. There are 11 rooms and eight waterfront cottages. An English flower garden, long stretches of lawn, a trout-filled pond, fruit orchards, moorage and kayak docks and a rocky point offer pleasant strolls. Panoramic water views are enjoyed from the dining room where breakfast is served, as well as dinner by advance reservation. For a special occasion, choose one of the waterfront cottages or one of the Solarium Suites, with a sitting room, fireplace and waterfront deck. The inn is perfect for family retreats, weddings or quiet getaways. Kayak and bicycle rentals are available.

Breakfast included in rates. Types of meals: full breakfast and gourmet breakfast. Afternoon tea and picnic lunch available. Fax, spa and bicycles on premises. Weddings, small meetings, family reunions and seminars hosted. Antiques, fishing, parks, shopping, theater and watersports nearby.

Special Discounts: Please inquire for groups.

States Inn

2039 W Valley Rd
Friday Harbor, WA 98250
(360)378-6240
Fax:(360)378-6241

Rates: $64-110.
Payment: MC VISA PC TC.
Circa: 1910.

Rooms: 9 rooms, 8 with PB, 1 with FP. 1 suite.
Beds: KQDT.

This sprawling ranch home has nine guest rooms, each named and themed for a particular state. The Arizona and New Mexico rooms, often booked by families or couples traveling together, can be combined to create a private suite with two bedrooms, a bathroom and a sitting area. The oldest part of the house was built as a country school and later used as a dance hall, before it was relocated to its current 60-acre spread. Baked French toast, accompanied by fresh fruit topped with yogurt sauce and homemade muffins are typical breakfast fare.

Breakfast and afternoon tea included in rates. Types of meals: full breakfast and early coffee/tea. Fax and stables on premises. Handicap access. 60 acres. Weddings, small meetings and family reunions hosted. Antiques, fishing, parks, shopping, theater and watersports nearby. TAC10.

Location: On San Juan Island.

Publicity: *Glamour.*

Tucker House B&B With Cottages

260 B St
Friday Harbor, WA 98250
(360)378-2783 (800)965-0123
Fax:(360)378-6437

Rates: $75-135.
Payment: MC VISA AX DS PC TC.
Innkeeper(s): Skip & Annette Metzger.
Circa: 1898.

Rooms: 5 rooms, 3 with PB. 3 cottages.
Beds: QD.

WA

Only two blocks from the ferry landing, the white picket fence bordering Tucker House is a welcome sight for guests. The spindled entrance leads to the parlor and the simply furnished five guest rooms in the house. A separate cottage next to the hot tub is popular with honeymooners.

Breakfast included in rates. Types of meals: full breakfast and gourmet breakfast. Cable TV and VCR in room. Fax and spa on premises. Family reunions hosted. Danish, German, Swedish and Norwegian spoken. Antiques, fishing, parks, shopping, theater and watersports nearby. TAC10.

Pets Allowed: Dogs under 40 pounds; $15 per evening per dog, limit two.

Location: San Juan Island.

Publicity: *Sunset, Pacific Northwest Magazine, Western Boatman.*

Special Discounts: Five days or more 10% discount.

"A lovely place, the perfect getaway. We'll be back."

Glenwood F5

Flying L Ranch-Mount Adams Country Inn & Retreat

25 Flying L Ln
Glenwood, WA 98619-9104
(509)364-3488
Fax:(509)364-3634

Rates: $56-120.
Payment: MC VISA AX PC TC.
Innkeeper(s): Darvel, Darryl & Nancy Lloyd.
Circa: 1945.

Rooms: 13 rooms, 10 with PB, 3 with FP. 1 suite. 2 cottages. 2 conference rooms.
Beds: QDT.

Star-gazing and sunsets are favorite activities from the outdoor spa of this 80-acre ranch, still in the family of the original builder. A lava fireplace and library draw guests to the common areas of the 4,000 square-foot Lodge building, where six guest rooms are located. The Guesthouse has a "water tower" observation area and five guest rooms including the Mt. Adams Suite with a queen bed, sofa, two twin beds, and fireplace. There are also two private cabins. The innkeepers cater to guests with fireplaces set and ready to light and home-made peach jam, low fat sausages, and Mr. Adams huckleberry hot cakes, served in the old-fashioned cook-house. Try moonlight skiing on the ranch trail system.

Breakfast included in rates. Types of meals: full breakfast and early coffee/tea. Dinner, lunch, catering service and room service available. VCR, fax, copier, spa, bicycles and library on premises. Handicap access. 80 acres. Weddings, small meetings, family reunions and seminars hosted. Fishing, shopping and cross-country skiing nearby. TAC10.

Publicity: *Seattle Times, Olympian, Oregonian*

Special Discounts: 20% off regular B&B rates weekdays, December-March (except holidays), two night minimum.

"The Flying L Ranch really made Christmas special for my family and me. The moonlight skiing was terrific and we had just a great time talking and singing with the other guests."

Greenbank C4

Guest House Cottages, A B&B Inn

3366 S Hwy 525,
Whidbey Island
Greenbank, WA 98253-6400
(360)678-3115
Fax:(360)321-0631

Rates: $110-285.
Payment: MC VISA AX DS PC TC.
Innkeeper(s): Don & Mary Jane Creger.

Rooms: 1 suite. 6 cottages.
Beds: KQDT.

These storybook cottages and log home are nestled within a peaceful forest on 25 acres. The Hansel and Gretel cottage features stained-glass and criss-cross paned windows that give it the feel of a gingerbread house. Two of the cottages were built in 1922. Ask for the Lodge and you'll enjoy a private setting with a pond just beyond your deck. Inside is a Jacuzzi tub, stone fireplace, king bed, antiques and an intimate hunting lodge atmosphere.

Breakfast included in rates. Type of meal: full breakfast. Air conditioning and turn-down service in room. Cable TV, VCR, fax, copier, spa, swimming and library on premises. 25 acres. French spoken. Antiques, fishing, parks, shopping, theater and watersports nearby.

Location: On Whidbey Island.

Publicity: *Los Angeles Times, Woman's Day, Sunset, Country Inns, Bride's.*

Special Discounts: 10th night free.
(No special mid-week or other discount on suite.)

"The wonderful thing is to be by yourselves and rediscover what's important."

La Conner (Mount Vernon)

The White Swan Guest House

1388 Moore Rd
La Conner (Mount Vernon), WA 98273-9249
(360)445-6805

Rates: $75-150.
Payment: MC VISA PC TC.
Innkeeper(s): Peter Goldfarb.
Circa: 1898.

Rooms: 4 rooms, 1 with PB. 1 cottage.
Beds: KQD.

Guests will marvel at innkeeper Peter Goldfarb's beautiful gardens as they wind up the driveway to reach this charming, yellow Victorian farmhouse. Inside guests are greeted with luscious home-baked chocolate chip cookies in the bright, cheery kitchen. Guest rooms are filled with comfortable, Victorian furnishings, and there's even a cozy "Garden Cottage," to stay in, complete with its own kitchen and private sun deck. Each April, the area is host to the Skagit Valley Tulip festival. La Conner, a nearby fishing village, is full of shops and galleries to explore.

Breakfast included in rates. Types of meals: continental-plus breakfast and early coffee/tea. Turn-down service in room. Family reunions hosted. Antiques, fishing, parks and shopping nearby. TAC10.

Special Discounts: Five days in cottage, 15% off, no meals.

"This has been a very pleasant interlude. What a beautiful, comfortable place you have here. We will be back."

Langley C4

Island Tyme, Bed & Breakfast Inn

4940 S Bayview Rd
Langley, WA 98260-9778
(360)221-5078 (800)898-8963

Rates: $90-140.
Payment: MC VISA AX PC TC.
Innkeeper(s): Lyn & Phil Fauth.
Circa: 1993.

Rooms: 5 rooms with PB, 2 with FP. 1 suite.
Beds: KQ.

Located on Whidbey Island, this Victorian is a whimsical mix of colors topped with gingerbread trim and a turret. The inn's 10 acres ensure solitude, and romantic amenities abound. The Heirloom Suite boasts both a fireplace and a Jacuzzi tub for two. The Turret room is tucked into the inn's tower and offers a Jacuzzi tub for two. Quilts, antiques and collectibles are found throughout the guest rooms. The dining room, where the country breakfasts are served, is located in the inn's turret.

Breakfast and evening snack included in rates. Types of meals: gourmet breakfast and early coffee/tea. Turn-down service, ceiling fan, cable TV and VCR in room. Library, pet boarding and child care on premises. Handicap access. 10 acres. Weddings, small meetings, family reunions and seminars hosted. Antiques, fishing, parks, shopping, theater and watersports nearby. TAC10.

Pets Allowed: In Keepsake Room only.

Special Discounts: 25% off two or more nights during week, off-season.

Lone Lake B&B

5206 S Bayview Rd
Langley, WA 98260-9705
(360)321-5325

Rates: $110-125.
Payment: PC TC.
Innkeeper(s): Dolores Renfrew.
Circa: 1980.

Rooms: 4 rooms, 4 with FP. 1 suite. 2 cottages.

Lone Lake guests can stay either in a suite, one of two cottages or on a sternwheel houseboat in permanent drydock. Furnishings are simple modern and Oriental pieces. Both the cottages include kitchens and fireplaces and have views of the lake. The home-built houseboat, includes a galley kitchen, tiny dining area overlooking the lake, queen-sized loft bed, a living room and a fireplace. The houseboat's bath is located on the adjacent covered deck. All accommodations include a double Jacuzzi tub. A continental breakfast is provided only for the first two days of a stay.

Breakfast included in rates. Type of meal: continental-plus breakfast. Cable TV and VCR in room. Swimming and bicycles on premises. Antiques, fishing, parks, shopping and watersports nearby.

All Seasons River Inn

PO Box 788
Leavenworth, WA 98826
(509)548-1425 (800)254-0555

Rates: $90-125.
Payment: MC VISA PC.
Innkeeper(s): Kathy & Jeff Falconer.
Circa: 1991.

Rooms: 6 rooms with PB, 3 with FP. 2 suites. 1 conference room.
Beds: Q.

Whether it be winter, summer, spring or fall, the Leavenworth area offers something for everyone and this inn is a perfect place to enjoy it all. The Cascade Mountains, Wenatchee River and surrounding forest combine for a restful, romantic setting. There are plenty of places to relax here, including the four riverfront decks or in the cozy living room, which offers a wood-burning stove and a bay window looking out to views of mountains and the river. Guest rooms, three with fireplaces, are decorated with antiques. Fishing, hiking and walking trails, golf, white water rafting and biking are among the bounty of activities. Don't forget to explore Leavenworth, a quaint Bavarian-style village offering shops, restaurants, craft fairs, festivals and more.

Breakfast and evening snack included in rates. Types of meals: full breakfast, gourmet breakfast and early coffee/tea. Picnic lunch available. Air conditioning, turn-down service and ceiling fan in room. Cable TV, VCR, swimming, bicycles and library on premises. Weddings, small meetings, family reunions and seminars hosted. Amusement parks, antiques, fishing, parks, shopping, downhill skiing, cross-country skiing, theater and watersports nearby.

Publicity: *Los Angeles Times, Northwest Travel, Oregonian, Inn Country, Spokesman Review, Outsider*

Special Discounts: Spring weekend discounts - two night stays.

"A perfect two days in what we consider a perfect B&B-wonderful hosts, food, house design, extra frills like bicycles to ride, and last but not least, the exquisite setting. We'll be back to enjoy every delightful aspect-maybe rafting or cross-country skiing next time around."

Run of The River B&B

PO Box 285
Leavenworth, WA 98826
(509)548-7171 (800)288-6491
Fax:(509)548-7547

Rates: $95-150.
Payment: MC VISA AX DS PC TC.
Innkeeper(s): Monty & Karen Turner.
Circa: 1986.

Rooms: 6 rooms with PB, 3 with FP. 1 conference room.
Beds: Q.

Situated on the banks of the Icicle River, this inn affords glorious water and mountain views. An adjacent bird sanctuary and 45 acres of wildlife refuge give each guest an ever-changing panorama of deer grazing, salmon running and bird feeding. Guest rooms feature romantic hand-made log beds and more views. Leavenworth is a Bavarian-style village in the Cascade Mountains.

Breakfast and afternoon tea included in rates. Types of meals: full breakfast and early coffee/tea. Ceiling fan and cable TV in room. Fax, copier, spa and bicycles on premises. Small meetings hosted. Spanish spoken. Antiques, parks, shopping, downhill skiing and cross-country skiing nearby. TAC10.

Publicity: *Spokesman-Review, Spokane Chronicle.*

"You certainly know how to make people comfortable and feel at home."

Long Beach

E2

Boreas Bed & Breakfast

607 N Boulevard,
PO Box 1344
Long Beach, WA 98631
(360)642-8069 (888)642-8069
Fax:(360)642-5353
E-mail: boreas@aone.com

Rates: $75-120.
Payment: MC VISA AX DC DS PC TC.
Innkeeper(s): Susie Goldsmith & Bill Verner.
Circa: 1920.

Rooms: 5 rooms. 3 suites. 1 cottage.
Beds: KQDT.

This inn started as a beach house and was remodeled eclectically with decks and a massive stone fireplace. There are two living rooms that offer views of the beach. Guest rooms all have ocean or mountain views (depending on the weather). Guests can enjoy the hot tub in the enclosed gazebo, take the path that winds through the dunes to the surf or walk to the boardwalk, restaurants and shopping. There is also a three-bedroom cottage available, and breakfast is not included in the cottage rates.

Type of meal: full breakfast. VCR, fax, spa, bicycles and library on premises. Weddings, small meetings and family reunions hosted. Limited Spanish spoken. Antiques, fishing, parks, shopping and watersports nearby.

Lopez

B4

The Inn at Swifts Bay

Rt 2, Box 3402
Lopez, WA 98261-9563
(360)468-3636
Fax:(360)468-3637
E-mail: swiftinn@aol.com

Rates: $85-225.
Payment: MC VISA AX DC DS TC.
Innkeeper(s): Robert Herrmann, Chris Brandmeir.
Circa: 1975.

Rooms: 5 rooms, 3 with PB, 3 with FP. 3 suites. 1 cottage.
Beds: Q.

This renovated country house is situated in a grove of fir trees, not too far from the ferry boats and a bike ride away from the village. Request the Attic Room for its skylights and queen-size sleigh bed topped with a lambswool comforter. A secluded hot tub is available for private star-gazing and soaking. Breakfasts delight gourmet palates.

Breakfast and evening snack included in rates. Types of meals: full breakfast and early coffee/tea. VCR in room. Fax, spa and sauna on premises. Portuguese and German spoken. Antiques, fishing, parks and watersports nearby. TAC10.

Publicity: *Brides, Vogue, San Francisco Examiner, Travel & Leisure.*

"Don't know how any future B&Bs at which we stay can top your home."

Lyle

F5

Lyle Hotel Restaurant & Bar

PO Box 838, 100 7th
Lyle, WA 98635-0838
(509)365-5953
Fax:(509)365-2668

Rates: $48.
Payment: MC VISA PC.
Innkeeper(s): Teresa Schwark.
Circa: 1911.

Rooms: 10 rooms.
Beds: KQDT.

Located one block from the mouth of the Klickitat and Columbia Rivers, this concrete and stucco structure was originally built as a railroad hotel. All the rooms have river views, including the hotel dining room. Dinner here offers specialties such as grilled halibut with cilantro citrus salsa complemented by a wide selection of Northwest brews. Nearby is a hunting preserve for game birds and prized spots for river rafting and kayaking.

Breakfast included in rates. Types of meals: continental breakfast and early coffee/tea. Dinner, picnic lunch and banquet service available. Ceiling fan in room. Cable TV, fax, spa and bicycles on premises. Weddings, small meetings, family reunions and seminars hosted. Antiques, fishing, parks, shopping, downhill skiing and watersports nearby. TAC10.

Mazama B6

Mazama Country Inn

42 Lost River Rd,
HCR 74 Box B9
Mazama, WA 98833
(509)996-2681
Fax:(509)996-2646
E-mail: mazama@methow.com

Rates: $50-175. AP.
Payment: MC VISA DS.
Innkeeper(s): George Turner.
Circa: 1985.

Rooms: 14 rooms with PB. 5 cottages.
Beds: QT.

With its log beams and cedar siding, this inn is a rustic retreat in an old mining town secluded in the beauty of the North Cascades. There are guest rooms in the inn and accommodations in cabins, a chalet and Phoenix House. Each of the latter three options are ideal for families, sleeping up to six or eight people. In the winter season, all three meals are included the rates for inn guests. A hearty breakfast is served, and guests can pack their own lunch from a selection of items, then return to the lodge in the evening for a family-style dinner. On cold nights, the lounge's huge Russian fireplace is a perfect place to relax. Guests enjoy use of a sauna and hot tub, as well.

Breakfast and picnic lunch included in rates. Types of meals: continental breakfast and full breakfast. Lunch available. AP. VCR, fax, copier, spa, sauna, stables and library on premises. Weddings, small meetings, family reunions and seminars hosted. Fishing, parks, shopping, downhill skiing, cross-country skiing and watersports nearby. TAC10.

Publicity: *New York Times*

Special Discounts: Group rates.

"Comfortable accommodations, great food, great staff-thanks!"

North Cascades Base Camp

255 Lost River Rd
Mazama, WA 98833-9700
(509)996-2334
E-mail: roberts@methow.com

Rates: $60-130. AP.
Payment: MC VISA PC TC.
Innkeeper(s): Dick & Sue Roberts.
Circa: 1980.

Rooms: 6 rooms. 1 cottage. 1 conference room.
Beds: QDT.

This rustic, contemporary home offers comfortable accommodations for those hoping to enjoy the surrounding wilderness. Hiking and nature trails, bicycle tours, mountain bike tours, horseback riding and fishing, rafting or canoeing opportunities on the Methow River are nearby. The grounds include the riverfront, a stocked trout pond, hot tub and a sandbox. Guests can opt for either bed & breakfast or full-board rates. Those choosing the full-board option have breakfast, lunch and dinner included.

Breakfast, dinner and picnic lunch included in rates. Type of meal: full breakfast. AP. Spa, bicycles and library on premises. 20 acres. Weddings, small meetings, family reunions and seminars hosted. Fishing, parks, shopping and cross-country skiing nearby.

Special Discounts: Three day midweek winter group rates.

Orcas B3

Chestnut Hill Inn B&B

PO Box 213
Orcas, WA 98280-0213
(360)376-5157
Fax:(360)376-5283
E-mail: chestnut@pacificrim.net

Rates: $105-195.
Payment: MC VISA AX DS PC TC.
Innkeeper(s): Daniel & Marilyn Loewke.
Circa: 1970.

Rooms: 5 rooms, 4 with PB, 5 with FP.
Beds: Q.

Guests enjoying an early morning walk through the 16 acres of majestic countryside that surround this inn are sure to see a variety of wildlife, including frequent deer. Four-poster canopy feather beds create an inviting atmosphere in the bedchambers, all of which boast fireplaces. Homemade breads and muffins accompany the elegant morning entree, which changes from day to day. The grounds are a perfect place to enjoy a picnic, and the innkeepers will fix up a gourmet basket for those seeking a romantic outing. In the chilly months, a cup of afternoon tea is served alongside refreshments. The gazebo adds character to the inn's garden.

Breakfast included in rates. Types of meals: gourmet breakfast and early coffee/tea. Afternoon tea and picnic lunch available. Ceiling fan in room. VCR, fax, stables and bicycles on premises. 16 acres. Parks, shopping, theater and watersports nearby. TAC10.

Port Angeles C3

Bavarian Inn B&B

1126 E 7th St
Port Angeles, WA 98362
(360)457-4098

Rates: $80-135.
Payment: MC PC TC.
Innkeeper(s): Gene & Joy Robinson.
Circa: 1982.

Rooms: 4 rooms with PB, 1 with FP. 2 suites.
Beds: KQT.

Built in the style of a Bavarian Chalet, this inn provides views of the shipping traffic to the San Juan Islands and the local ferry as it rounds the end of the Hook. Down comforters top the beds, and there are fresh flowers in the guest rooms. The innkeepers are happy to point you to special attractions in the area including mushrooming, the Olympic National Park, salmon migrations and local scenic drives.

Breakfast included in rates. Types of meals: full breakfast, gourmet breakfast and early coffee/tea. Evening snack available. Ceiling fan and VCR in room. Spa on premises. Family reunions hosted. Limited German spoken. Antiques, fishing, parks, shopping, downhill skiing, cross-country skiing, theater and watersports nearby.

Domaine Madeleine B&B

146 Wildflower Ln
Port Angeles, WA 98362
(360)457-4174
Fax:(360)457-3037

Rates: $135-165.
Payment: MC VISA AX DS PC TC.
Innkeeper(s): John Chambers.
Circa: 1947.

Rooms: 4 rooms, 5 with PB, 5 with FP. 2 suites. 1 cottage.
Beds: KQ.

This unique inn blends French with Oriental decor and offers a romantic setting on five acres and 168 feet of waterfront. The landscape includes dozens of rhododendrons, numerous wild and cultivated flowers, Douglas firs, cedars, maples and pines. Deer often browse through the property, whales can sometimes be seen off the shore and bald eagles fly above. The innkeepers take pride in helping guests plan romantic events and can pack a special lunch on request. Choosing a restaurant for dinner is made easier by browsing the inn's menu collection.

Breakfast included in rates. Type of meal: gourmet breakfast. Air conditioning, cable TV and VCR in room. Fax, copier and library on premises. Weddings and small meetings hosted. French, Spanish, German and Farsi spoken. Antiques, fishing, parks, downhill skiing, cross-country skiing and theater nearby.

Publicity: *Northwest Travel.*

"Nowhere have I found lodgings that compared to Domaine Madeleine. I consider four criteria in determining where to stay when I travel; accommodations, food, uniqueness, and hospitality. Domaine Madeleine excels in all these categories."

Tudor Inn

1108 S Oak St
Port Angeles, WA 98362
(360)452-3138

Rates: $75-120.
Payment: MC VISA AX DS PC TC.
Innkeeper(s): Jane Glass.
Circa: 1910.

Rooms: 5 rooms with PB, 1 with FP.
Beds: T.

This English Tudor inn has been tastefully restored to display its original woodwork and fir stairway. Guests enjoy stone fireplaces in the living room and study. A terraced garden with 100-foot oak trees graces the property.

Breakfast and afternoon tea included in rates. Type of meal: full breakfast. Cable TV, VCR and library on premises. Weddings hosted. Antiques, fishing, parks, shopping, skiing, theater and watersports nearby. TAC10.

Location: Eleven blocks south of the harbor with water & mountain views.

Publicity: *Seattle Times, Oregonian, Los Angeles Times, Olympic Magazine.*

"Delicious company and delicious food. Best in hospitality and warmth. Beautiful gardens!"

WA

Ann Starrett Mansion

744 Clay St
Port Townsend, WA 98368
(360)385-3205 (800)321-0644
Fax:(360)385-2976

Rates: $65-225.
Payment: MC VISA AX DS PC TC.
Innkeeper(s): Bob & Edel Sokol.
Circa: 1889.

Rooms: 11 rooms with PB, 2 with FP. 2 suites. 2 cottages. 2 conference rooms.
Beds: KQDT.

George Starrett came from Maine to Port Townsend and became the major residential builder. By 1889, he had constructed one house a week, totaling more than 350 houses. The Smithsonian believes the Ann Starrett's elaborate free-hung spiral staircase is the only one of its type in the United States. A frescoed dome atop the octagonal tower depicts four seasons and four virtues. On the first day of each season, the sun causes a ruby red light to point toward the appropriate painting.

Breakfast included in rates. Type of meal: full breakfast. Afternoon tea available. Cable TV in room. VCR, fax, copier and spa on premises. German spoken. Antiques, fishing, parks, shopping, cross-country skiing, theater and watersports nearby. TAC10.

Location: Three blocks from the business district.

Publicity: *Peninsula, New York Times, Vancouver Sun, San Francisco Examiner, London Times, Colonial Homes, Elle, Leader, Japanese Travel, National Geographic Traveller.*

"A wonderful experience for aspiring time travelers."

Holly Hill House B&B

611 Polk St
Port Townsend, WA 98368
(360)385-5619 (800)435-1454

Rates: $78-145.
Innkeeper(s): Lynne Sterling.
Circa: 1872.

Rooms: 5 rooms with PB. 1 suite.
Beds: KQT.

A unique "upside-down" century-old Camperdown elm and several holly trees surround this aptly named bed & breakfast, built by Robert C. Hill, the co-founder of the First National Bank of Port Townsend. The cozy, romantic rooms are decorated with florals and lace. Billie's Room affords a view of Admiralty Inlet and Mt. Baker, while Lizette's Room offers Victorian decor and a view of the garden. The Skyview Room includes a wonderful skylight. The spacious Colonel's Room features a picture window with water and mountain views, and the Morning Glory Room is a cozy retreat with lace-trimmed quilts. Expansive breakfasts are served in the dining room, and coffee and tea are always available for a thirsty guest. The inn's gardens are surrounded by a picket fence and nearly 200 rose bushes.

Breakfast included in rates. Type of meal: early coffee/tea. Afternoon tea, evening snack and picnic lunch available. Turn-down service in room. Cable TV and library on premises. Weddings and small meetings hosted. German spoken. Antiques, parks, shopping and theater nearby. TAC10.

Location: Two miles from Fort Worden State Park and in the heart of historic district.

Special Discounts: Mid-week-January to April - 15% discount Sunday - Thursday.

James House

1238 Washington St
Port Townsend, WA 98368
(360)385-1238 (800)385-1238

Rates: $60-150.
Payment: MC VISA AX.
Innkeeper(s): Carol McGough.
Circa: 1889.

Rooms: 12 rooms, 10 with PB, 3 with FP. 3 suites. 1 conference room.
Beds: QD.

This Queen Anne mansion built by Francis James overlooks Puget Sound with views of the Cascades and Olympic mountain ranges. The three-story staircase was constructed of solid wild cherry brought around Cape Horn from Virginia. Parquet floors are composed of oak, cherry, walnut and maple, providing a suitable setting for the inn's collection of antiques.

Breakfast included in rates. Type of meal: full breakfast. Handicap access. Antiques, fishing, cross-country skiing and theater nearby.

Location: On the bluff overlooking Port Townsend Bay.

Publicity: *Washington, Seattle Weekly, Northwest Best Places, Sunset.*

"We were enchanted by Victorian splendor and delicious breakfasts."

Old Consulate Inn F.W. Hastings House

313 Walker at Washington
Port Townsend, WA 98368
(360)385-6753 (800)300-6753
Fax:(360)385-2097

Rates: $79-185. MAP.
Payment: MC VISA AX PC TC.
Innkeeper(s): Rob & Joanna Jackson.
Circa: 1889.

Rooms: 8 rooms with PB, 1 with FP. 3 suites. 1 conference room.
Beds: KQ.

This handsome red Victorian, once the residence of the German consul, commands expansive views of Port Townsend Bay from its blufftop setting. Fine antiques, a grand piano, elegant stairway and Victorian wallcoverings create a romantic fantasy that is continued in the Tower Suite where five curved turret windows afford majestic water and mountain views. There is also a hot tub and a gazebo on the premises.

Breakfast, afternoon tea and evening snack included in rates. Types of meals: gourmet breakfast and early coffee/tea. Catering service and catered breakfast available. MAP. Turn-down service in room. Cable TV, VCR, fax, copier, spa, tennis and library on premises. Weddings, small meetings, family reunions and seminars hosted. Antiques, fishing, parks, shopping, cross-country skiing, theater and watersports nearby. TAC10.

Publicity: *Pacific Northwest, Best Places to Kiss, Seattle Weekly.*

"Beautiful in every way."

Ravenscroft Inn

533 Quincy St
Port Townsend, WA 98368
(360)385-2784 (800)782-2691
Fax:(360)385-6724

Rates: $65-165.
Payment: MC VISA AX DS PC TC.
Innkeeper(s): Leah Hammer.
Circa: 1987.

Rooms: 8 rooms with PB, 3 with FP. 2 suites. 1 conference room.
Beds: KQT.

A second suite has been added to this relaxing inn, which includes a fireplace and six-foot soaking tub. From the suite's large window seat, guests can enjoy the view of Mt. Baker.The room has an Impressionist touch, decorated in Monet colors. Other rooms are equally interesting, all individually decorated with Colonial influences. The inn is just three blocks from the water.

Breakfast included in rates. Types of meals: full breakfast, gourmet breakfast and early coffee/tea. Afternoon tea and catering service available. Cable TV, VCR, fax and library on premises. Weddings, small meetings, family reunions and seminars hosted. Antiques, fishing, shopping, cross-country skiing, theater and watersports nearby.

Special Discounts: Seasonal specials - off season rates Oct. 15-May15.

Poulsbo C4

Foxbridge B&B

30680 Hwy 3 NE
Poulsbo, WA 98370
(360)598-5599
Fax:(360)598-3588

Rates: $75-85.
Payment: MC VISA PC.
Innkeeper(s): Beverly & Chuck Higgins.
Circa: 1993.

Rooms: 3 rooms with PB.
Beds: Q.

The innkeepers at this Georgian-style home have taken the words bed & breakfast to heart. Each of the comfortable rooms has an individual theme. The Country Garden room is a floral delight with a canopy bed. The Old World room includes a sleigh bed and down comforter. The Foxhunt room is done up in masculine hues with a four-poster bed. Antiques are placed throughout the home. As for the breakfast, each morning brings a new menu. Heart-shaped waffles topped with blueberries and cream might be the fare one morning, while another day could bring eggs Benedict or a smoked-salmon quiche. All are served with cereals and a special starter, perhaps baked nectarines with cream Ambrose.

Breakfast and afternoon tea included in rates. Types of meals: gourmet breakfast and early coffee/tea. Turn-down service in room. Fax and library on premises. Weddings and family reunions hosted. Antiques, fishing, parks, shopping, cross-country skiing, theater and watersports nearby.

Renton

D4

Holly Hedge B&B

908 Grant Ave S
Renton, WA 98055-3038
(206)226-2555 (888)226-2555
Fax:(206)226-2555

Rates: $90-130.
Payment: MC VISA.
Innkeeper(s): Lynne & Marian Thrasher.
Circa: 1901.

Rooms: 1 cottage.
Beds: Q.

In 1995, Holly Hedge House received a "Country Inn Room of the Year" award from Waverly and Country Inns magazine. From its ideal hilltop location, the turn-of-the-century cottage offers majestic views of the Green River Valley and Olympic Mountain range. Guests will delight in the amenities, which include a stocked, gourmet kitchen, whirlpool tub, four-poster bed, fireplace and CD and video library. The acre of grounds also includes an outdoor hot tub and swimming pool. The cottage is within easy driving distance of the airport, Seattle, golfing and Lake Washington, yet secluded enough for honeymooners and others seeking peace and privacy.

Breakfast included in rates. Types of meals: full breakfast and early coffee/tea. Afternoon tea, evening snack, picnic lunch and room service available. Ceiling fan and VCR in room. Copier, bicycles and tennis on premises. Antiques, fishing, parks, shopping, theater and watersports nearby.

Seattle

C4

B.D. Williams House

1505 4th Ave N
Seattle, WA 98109-2902
(206)285-0810 (800)880-0810
Fax:(206)285-8526

Rates: $90-125.
Payment: MC VISA AX DC DS PC TC.
Innkeeper(s): Susan & Doug Williams & daughters.
Circa: 1905.

Rooms: 5 rooms, 3 with PB. 1 conference room.
Beds: KQT.

This inn features much original woodwork and gaslight fixtures, as well as an ornate gas fireplace. A formal parlor is accentuated with Victorian furnishings. Many of the rooms have commanding views of mountains, lakes, Puget Sound and the downtown Seattle skyline. Gardens decorate the grounds. The inn offers close access to many Seattle attractions.

Breakfast and evening snack included in rates. Type of meal: full breakfast. VCR, fax, library and child care on premises. Small meetings and seminars hosted. Amusement parks, antiques, parks, shopping, sporting events, theater and watersports nearby.

Location: Queen Anne Hill.

"Very comfortable. Excellent food and wonderful people."

Chelsea Station on The Park—A B&B Inn

4915 Linden Ave N
Seattle, WA 98103-6536
(206)547-6077 (800)400-6077
Fax:(206)632-5107

Rates: $69-119.
Payment: MC VISA AX DC DS PC TC.
Innkeeper(s): John Griffin, Karen Carbonneau.
Circa: 1929.

Rooms: 7 rooms with PB. 4 suites.
Beds: KQT.

This Federal Colonial home, a fine example of the bricklayer's art, is nestled between the Fremont Area and Woodland Park, just north of downtown Seattle. Hearty breakfasts with items such as warm date scones, fresh fruit and specialty entrees. Tea and a bottomless cookie jar are on hand throughout the day. The home's decor is predominately Mission style with antiques throughout. The zoo, Seattle Rose Garden, shops and restaurants are within walking distance.

Breakfast and afternoon tea included in rates. Types of meals: full breakfast and early coffee/tea. Fax and copier on premises. Small meetings and family reunions hosted. Amusement parks, antiques, fishing, shopping, downhill skiing, cross-country skiing, theater and watersports nearby. TAC10.

Location: Minutes north of downtown in the Fremont neighborhood. Near Greenlake & Woodland Park Zoo.

Publicity: *Seattle Post-Intelligencer, Phinney Ridge Review, Phinney Ridge Home Tour, Innviews.*

Special Discounts: Seven nights for the price of six.

"We're back ... the food and lodging remains first-class. We look forward to another visit soon!"

Pensione Nichols

1923 1st Ave
Seattle, WA 98101-1026
(206)441-7125 (800)440-7125

Rates: $85.
Payment: MC VISA AX DS TC.
Innkeeper(s): Nancy Nichols.
Circa: 1904.

Rooms: 12 rooms. 2 suites.
Beds: QDT.

The Pensione is located in a historic commercial building just above the famous Pike Place Market. European antiques, dried flowers and beds topped with quilts decorate the guest rooms, which have hosted the likes of Allen Ginsberg and The Doors' Ray Manzarek. The two suites offer views of Puget Sound, and on a sunny day, the Olympic Mountains. The inn is a convenient place to enjoy many of the shops, galleries, cafes, restaurants and night clubs Seattle has to offer.

Breakfast included in rates. Type of meal: continental breakfast. Ceiling fan in room. Small meetings and family reunions hosted. Antiques, parks, shopping, sporting events and theater nearby.

Pets Allowed: Cats and small dogs.

Special Discounts: 10% discount for stays of one week or longer.

Pioneer Square Hotel

77 Yesler Way
Seattle, WA 98104
(206)340-1234 (800)800-5514
Fax:(206)467-9424
E-mail: info@pioneersquare.com

Rates: $89-99.
Innkeeper(s): Jo Thompson.
Circa: 1914.

Rooms: 72 rooms with PB. 3 suites.
Beds: KQDT.

Seattle's founding father, Henry Yesler, built this historic waterfront hotel. The hotel is well-appointed and elegant rooms feature coordinating prints. Business travelers will appreciate the direct dial telephones with data ports, and there are individual climate controls in each room. No meals are included in the hotel's rates, but restaurants and cafes are nearby, as is Historic Pioneer Square, ferries and shopping. Pioneer Square, although historic, is run by Best Western.

Air conditioning, turn-down service and cable TV in room. Fax, copier and child care on premises. Handicap access. Weddings, small meetings, family reunions and seminars hosted. Shopping, downhill skiing, cross-country skiing, sporting events, theater and watersports nearby. TAC10.

Prince of Wales

133 13th Ave E
Seattle, WA 98102-5809
(206)325-9692 (800)327-9692
Fax:(206)322-6402
E-mail: cnorton949@aol.com

Rates: $75-110.
Payment: MC VISA AX DS PC TC.
Innkeeper(s): Carol Norton.
Circa: 1903.

Rooms: 4 rooms with PB. 2 suites.
Beds: QT.

This three-story Victorian home is within walking distance to shops, parks and local restaurants. The Prince's Retreat guest room offers a private rooftop deck, complete with telescope for viewing the Seattle skyline. There is a clawfoot tub. Early breakfasts may be accommodated by advance arrangement. Downtown is a mile and a half away.

Breakfast included in rates. Types of meals: full breakfast and early coffee/tea. Fax on premises. Some Spanish and Italian spoken. Amusement parks, antiques, fishing, parks, shopping, sporting events, theater and watersports nearby.

Location: Capitol Hill in Seattle.

Special Discounts: Special events available November-March, call for details.

WA

Roberta's B&B

1147 16th Ave East
Seattle, WA 98112-3310
(206)329-3326
Fax:(206)324-2149
E-mail: robertasbb@aol.com

Rates: $80-115.
Payment: MC VISA PC TC.
Innkeeper(s): Roberta C. Barry.
Circa: 1903.

Rooms: 5 rooms, 4 with PB. 1 suite.
Beds: Q.

This two-story Victorian home in Capitol Hill is near Volunteer Park and the Seattle Art Museum. Polished hardwood floors glisten under comfortable furnishings. The Peach Room boasts a bay window, Franklin wood stove, love seat and brass bed. Knowledgeable about Seattle, the innkeepers can help you make the most of your time with suggestions on restaurants and touring.

Breakfast included in rates. Types of meals: full breakfast and early coffee/tea. Fax and library on premises. Antiques and parks nearby.

Location: On Historic Capitol Hill near Volunteer Park.

"Thanks for all the special touches. I'm afraid you've spoiled us."

Tugboat Challenger

1001 Fairview Ave N
Seattle, WA 98109-4416
(206)340-1201
Fax:(206)621-9208

Rates: $95-200.
Payment: MC VISA AX DC DS PC TC.
Innkeeper(s): Jerry & Buffy Brown.
Circa: 1944.

Rooms: 11 rooms, 8 with PB. 3 suites.
Beds: KQD.

If you're a bit tired of the ordinary land-locked lodging, why not book a room and passage on this idyllic tugboat, docked in downtown Seattle's Chandler's Cove. The boat can sleep more than a dozen guests, in eight different cabins. The Admiral's Cabin is particularly suited to honeymooners, as it includes a four-poster bed, soaking tub and boasts city, lake and marina views. Not all rooms are as large and several main deck rooms include double or single bunks. The owners also have yachts available for renting and each can accommodate four people. Tugboat guests enjoy a full breakfast, with such items as seafood omelets and fresh fruit. The tug can be reserved for small parties and weddings.

Breakfast included in rates. Type of meal: full breakfast. Cable TV and VCR in room. Fax, copier, swimming and library on premises. Small meetings and family reunions hosted. Amusement parks, antiques, fishing, parks, shopping, sporting events, theater and watersports nearby. TAC10.

Seaview E2

Shelburne Inn

4415 Pacific Way,
PO Box 250
Seaview, WA 98644
(360)642-2442
Fax:(360)642-8904

Rates: $73-165.
Payment: MC VISA AX.
Innkeeper(s): David Campiche & Laurie Anderson.
Circa: 1896.

Rooms: 15 rooms with PB. 2 suites. 1 conference room.
Beds: QD.

The Shelburne is known as the oldest continuously operating hotel in the state of Washington, and it is listed in the National Register. The front desk at the hotel is a former church altar. Art nouveau stained-glass windows rescued from a church torn down in Morcambe, England, now shed light and color on the dining room. The guest rooms are appointed in antiques. In between the Columbia River and the Pacific Ocean, the inn is situated on Long Beach Peninsula, a 28-mile stretch of seacoast that includes bird sanctuaries and lighthouses.

Breakfast included in rates. Types of meals: full breakfast and gourmet breakfast. Dinner, picnic lunch, lunch, catering service and room service available. Fax, copier and bicycles on premises. Handicap access. Antiques and fishing nearby.

Location: Southwest Washington state.

Publicity: *Better Homes & Gardens, Bon Appetit, Conde Nast Traveler, Esquire, Gourmet, Food & Wine.*

"Fabulous food. Homey but elegant atmosphere. Hospitable service, like being a guest in an elegant home."

Sequim C3

Granny Sandy's Orchard B&B

405 W Spruce St
Sequim, WA 98382-3335
(360)683-5748
Fax:(360)683-4365

Rates: $42-77.
Payment: MC VISA PC TC.
Innkeeper(s): Sandy Ross & Paul Moore.
Circa: 1935.

Rooms: 4 rooms, 1 with PB. 1 suite.
Beds: QT.

This comfortable bed & breakfast is located in downtown Sequim on the Olympic peninsula. Rooms aren't fancy, but simple and clean with an eclectic mix of furnishings—definitely like a trip to Grandma's house. The innkeepers have a small orchard on the grounds, including plum and peach trees and bushes of blueberries and raspberries. As one might expect, many items served during the candlelight breakfasts include fresh fruit from the orchard.

Breakfast included in rates. Types of meals: full breakfast and gourmet breakfast. Cable TV, VCR, fax, copier and child care on premises. Antiques, parks, shopping, downhill skiing and theater nearby. TAC10.

Spokane C9

Marianna Stoltz House

427 E Indiana Ave
Spokane, WA 99207-2324
(509)483-4316 (800)978-6587
Fax:(509)483-6773

Rates: $65-85.
Payment: MC VISA AX DC DS PC TC.
Innkeeper(s): Phyllis & Jim Maguire.
Circa: 1908.

Rooms: 4 rooms, 2 with PB. 1 suite.
Beds: KQT.

Located on a tree-lined street, two miles from downtown Spokane, is this American four-square Victorian. It is in the local historic register and features a wraparound porch, high ceilings and leaded-glass windows. Furnishings include Oriental rugs and period pieces. Peach Melba Parfait and Stoltz House Strada are breakfast specialties.

Breakfast included in rates. Types of meals: full breakfast and early coffee/tea. Air conditioning and cable TV in room. Fax and copier on premises. Weddings, small meetings and family reunions hosted. Amusement parks, fishing, parks, shopping, downhill skiing, cross-country skiing, sporting events and theater nearby. TAC10.

Tacoma D4

Chinaberry Hill - A Victorian B&B

302 Tacoma Ave N
Tacoma, WA 98403
(206)272-1282
Fax:(206)272-1335
E-mail: wayman29@mail.idy.ne

Rates: $85-125.
Payment: MC VISA AX PC TC.
Innkeeper(s): Cecil & Yarrow Wayman.
Circa: 1889.

Rooms: 4 rooms with PB, 1 with FP. 3 suites. 1 cottage. 1 conference room.
Beds: Q.

In the 19th century, this Queen Anne was known as far away as China for its wondrous gardens, one of the earliest examples of landscape gardening in the Pacific Northwest. The home, a wedding present from a husband to his bride, is listed in the National Register. The innkeepers have selected a unique assortment of antiques and collectibles to decorate the manor. The house offers two suites and a guest room, all eclectically decorated with items such as a four-poster rice bed or a canopy bed. There are two lodging options in the Catchpenny Cottage, a restored carriage house steps away from the manor. Guests can stay either in the romantic carriage suite or the Hay Loft, which includes a bedroom, sitting room, clawfoot tub and a unique hay chute. In the mornings, as the innkeepers say, guests enjoy "hearty breakfasts and serious coffee." Not a bad start to a day exploring Antique Row or Pt. Defiance, a 698-acre protected rainforest park with an aquarium, gardens, beaches and a zoo. Seattle is 30 minutes away.

Breakfast and evening snack included in rates. Types of meals: continental breakfast, continental-plus breakfast, full breakfast, gourmet breakfast and early coffee/tea. Catered breakfast and room service available. Turn-down service in room. Cable TV, VCR, fax, copier and library on premises. Weddings, small meetings, family reunions and seminars hosted. Amusement parks, antiques, fishing, parks, shopping, sporting events, theater and watersports nearby. TAC10.

Special Discounts: 10% off on Jacuzzi suites for business travelers, Sunday-Thursday, two-night minimum, for each six consecutive days at the inn, the seventh night is free.

Commencement Bay B&B

3312 N Union Ave
Tacoma, WA 98407-6055
(206)752-8175
Fax:(206)759-4025
E-mail: greatviews@aol.com

Rates: $75-115. AP.
Payment: MC VISA AX DS PC TC.
Innkeeper(s): Sharon & Bill Kaufmann.
Circa: 1937.

Rooms: 3 rooms with PB. 1 conference room.
Beds: Q.

Watch boats sail across the bay while enjoying breakfast served with gourmet coffee at this Colonial Revival inn. Guest rooms feature bay or garden views and each is unique and individually decorated. The surrounding area includes historic sites, antique shops, restaurants, waterfront parks, wooded nature trails and Pt. Defiance Zoo and Aquarium. Relax in a secluded hot tub and deck area or in the fireside room for reading and the romantic view. The B&B is 30 miles from Seattle.

Breakfast and evening snack included in rates. Types of meals: full breakfast and early coffee/tea. AP. Cable TV and VCR in room. Fax, spa, bicycles and library on premises. Small meetings hosted. Limited Spanish spoken. Amusement parks, antiques, fishing, parks, shopping, sporting events, theater and watersports nearby. TAC10.

Location: 30 miles to Seattle.

Publicity: *Tacoma Weekly, News Tribune.*

Special Discounts: 1 night free with a week stay, excluding holidays.

"Perfect in every detail! The setting, breathtaking; the food, scrumptious and beautifully presented; the warmth and friendship here."

Vashon Island D4

The Old Tjomsland House B&B

PO Box 913,
17011 Vashion Hwy SW,
Vashon Island, WA 98070
(206)463-5275
Fax:(206)463-5275

Rates: $85-150.
Payment: MC VISA DS PC TC.
Innkeeper(s): Jan & Bill Morosoff.
Circa: 1890.

Rooms: 3 rooms. 1 suite. 1 cottage.
Beds: KQDT.

Abraham Tjomsland, Norwegian ship builder, constructed this traditional farmhouse. It reflects the small-town America atmosphere of Vashon Island. The two guest rooms on the upper floor have a separate entrance and share a common bath, large living room and kitchenette. A romantic cottage features a deck with a woodland view. A large healthy breakfast is served. Across the road is the library and a park. It's a short walk to town and local restaurants.

Breakfast included in rates. Type of meal: full breakfast. Dinner and evening snack available. Cable TV and VCR in room. Fax, copier, bicycles, library and child care on premises. German and French spoken. Antiques, fishing, parks, shopping and watersports nearby. TAC10.

Location: Twenty minutes by ferry from Seattle and Tacoma.

Publicity: *Vashon-Maury Island Beachcomber.*

Special Discounts: Business travelers get off season rates all year, senior discount 10%.

"Your house is neat as a pin, spotless. We have been at B&Bs all over the world and yours is outstanding."

Yakima E6

Birchfield Manor Country Inn

2018 Birchfield Rd
Yakima, WA 98901-9580
(509)452-1960 (800)375-3420
Fax:(509)452-2334

Rates: $80-175.
Payment: MC VISA AX DC PC TC.
Innkeeper(s): The Masset Family.
Circa: 1910.

Rooms: 11 rooms with PB, 4 with FP.
Beds: KQ.

Guests at this Prairie-style inn, once the centerpiece of a large sheep ranch, enjoy elegant decor and the tranquil scenery of seven rural acres. Four guest rooms have fireplaces, and some have double whirlpool tubs or a sauna shower. The innkeepers have won awards for their breakfasts, and for an additional charge, dinners are served on Thursday, Friday and Saturday nights.

Breakfast included in rates. Types of meals: full breakfast, gourmet breakfast and early coffee/tea. Dinner and room service available. Restaurant on premises. Air conditioning, ceiling fan and VCR in room. Swimming on premises. Handicap access. Weddings, small meetings, family reunions and seminars hosted. Antiques, fishing, parks, downhill skiing, theater and watersports nearby. TAC10.

Pets Allowed: Only in buildings with patios.

Washington, D.C.

Adams Inn

1744 Lanier Pl NW
Washington, DC 20009
(202)745-3600 (800)578-6807
Fax:(202)332-5867

Rates: $55-70.
Payment: MC VISA AX DC CB DS TC.
Innkeeper(s): Gene & Nancy Thompson, Aime Owens.
Circa: 1908.

Rooms: 24 rooms, 12 with PB.
Beds: DT.

This restored town house has fireplaces, a library and parlor, all furnished home-style, as are the guest rooms. Former residents of this neighborhood include Tallulah Bankhead, Woodrow Wilson and Al Jolson. The Adams-Morgan area is home to diplomats, radio and television personalities and government workers. A notable firehouse across the street holds the record for the fastest response of a horse-drawn fire apparatus. Located in the restaurant area, 45 restaurants and shops are within walking distance.

Breakfast included in rates. Types of meals: continental-plus breakfast and early coffee/tea. Air conditioning in room. Cable TV and library on premises. Antiques and parks nearby. TAC10.

Location: Two miles from the White House, walking distance to major hotels.

Publicity: *Travel Host.*

"We enjoyed your friendly hospitality and the home-like atmosphere. Your suggestions on restaurants and help in planning our visit were appreciated."

The Embassy Inn

1627 16th St NW
Washington, DC 20009
(202)234-7800 (800)423-9111
Fax:(202)234-3309

Rates: $69-150.
Payment: MC VISA AX DC CB TC.
Innkeeper(s): Jennifer Schroeder & Susan Stiles.
Circa: 1910.

Rooms: 38 rooms with PB.
Beds: DT.

This restored inn is furnished in a Federalist style. The comfortable lobby offers books and evening sherry. Conveniently located, the inn is seven blocks from the Adams Morgan area of ethnic restaurants. The Embassy's philosophy of innkeeping includes providing personal attention and cheerful hospitality. Concierge services are available.

Breakfast included in rates. Type of meal: continental-plus breakfast. Air conditioning and cable TV in room. Fax and copier on premises. German spoken. Antiques, parks and theater nearby. TAC10.

Location: Downtown Washington, D.C., 10 blocks north of the White House.

Publicity: *Los Angeles Times, Inn Times, Business Review.*

Special Discounts: 10% AARP; $59 weekend based on availability.

"When I return to D.C., I'll be back at the Embassy."

Morrison-Clark Inn

1015 L St NW
Washington, DC 20001
(202)898-1200
Fax:(202)289-8576

Rates: $135-185.
Payment: MC VISA AX DS.
Innkeeper(s): Michael Rawson.
Circa: 1864.

Rooms: 54 rooms with PB. 13 suites. 1 conference room.

This elegant inn is comprised of two Italianate-Victorian mansions, which once housed the Soldiers, Sailors and Marines Club from 1923 to 1983. The older part of the inn contains guest rooms with 12-foot-high ceilings and authentic period furnishings. All modern amenities are provided with many luxurious touches. Lunch and dinner are served in a beautiful, intimate dining room, which is renowned for its fine cuisine.

Types of meals: continental breakfast and early coffee/tea. Dinner, evening snack, picnic lunch, lunch, gourmet lunch, banquet service, catering service, catered breakfast and room service available. Air conditioning, turn-down service and cable TV in room. VCR, fax and copier on premises. Weddings, small meetings, family reunions and seminars hosted. Amusement parks, antiques, shopping, sporting events and theater nearby.

Location: Located in downtown Washington, D.C., three blocks from the convention center and six blocks from the White House.

Publicity: *Country Inns Magazine, Washington Post.*

Reeds B&B

PO Box 12011
Washington, DC 20005
(202)328-3510
Fax:(202)332-3885

Rates: $45-90.
Payment: MC VISA AX DC TC.
Innkeeper(s): Charles & Jackie Reed.
Circa: 1887.

Rooms: 6 rooms, 2 with FP.
Beds: QD.

This three-story Victorian townhouse was built by John Shipman, who owned one of the first construction companies in the city. The turn-of-the-century revitalization of Washington began in Logan Circle, considered to be the city's first truly residential area. During the house's restoration, flower gardens, terraces and fountains were added. Victorian antiques, original wood paneling, stained glass, chandeliers, as well as practical amenities, such as air conditioning and laundry facilities, make this a comfortable stay. There is a furnished apartment available, as well.

Breakfast included in rates. Type of meal: continental-plus breakfast. Air conditioning and cable TV in room. Computer on premises. Weddings, small meetings and family reunions hosted. French and Spanish spoken. Antiques, parks, shopping, sporting events and theater nearby. TAC8.

Location: Downtown, 10 blocks from White House.

Publicity: *Philadelphia Inquirer, Washington Gardner, Washington Post, 101 Great Choices, Washington,DC.*

"This home was the highlight of our stay in Washington! This was a superb home and location. The Reeds' treated us better than family."

The Windsor Inn

1842 16th St NW
Washington, DC 20009
(202)667-0300 (800)423-9111
Fax:(202)667-4503

Rates: $69-125.
Payment: MC VISA AX DC CB TC.
Innkeeper(s): Jennifer Schroeder & Susan Stiles.
Circa: 1910.

Rooms: 46 rooms with PB. 2 suites. 1 conference room.
Beds: QDT.

Recently renovated and situated in a neighborhood of renovated townhouses, the Windsor Inn is the sister property to the Embassy Inn. It is larger and offers suites as well as a small meeting room. The refurbished lobby is in an art deco style and a private club atmosphere prevails. It is five blocks to the Metro station at Dupont Circle. There are no elevators.

Breakfast included in rates. Type of meal: continental-plus breakfast. Air conditioning and cable TV in room. Fax and copier on premises. Weddings, small meetings and family reunions hosted. French and Spanish spoken. Antiques, parks, shopping and theater nearby. TAC10.

Location: Twelve blocks north of the White House.

Publicity: *Los Angeles Times, Inn Times, Sunday Telegram, WCUA Press Release.*

Special Discounts: Senior 10% off rack, $59 weekend rate on availability.

"Being here was like being home. Excellent service, would recommend."

West Virginia

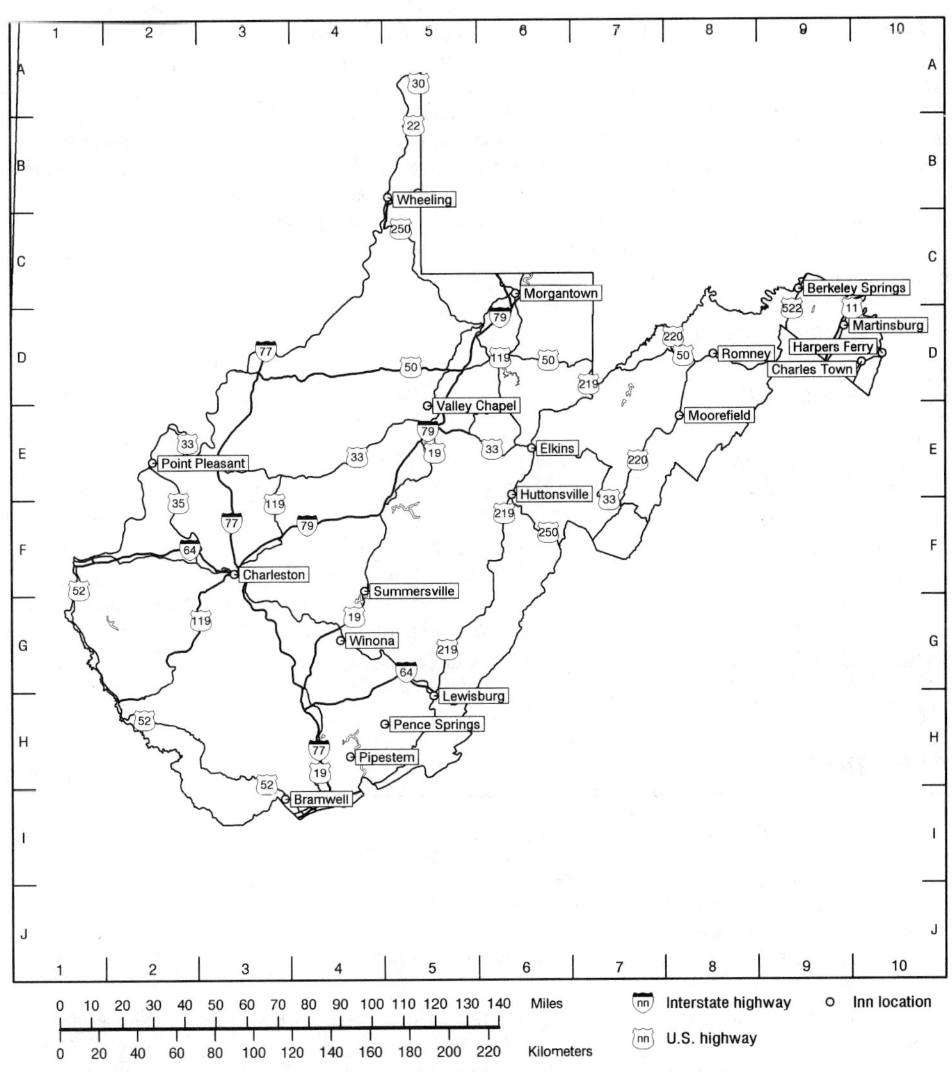

Wheeling
Morgantown
Berkeley Springs
Martinsburg
Harpers Ferry
Charles Town
Romney
Moorefield
Valley Chapel
Elkins
Huttonsville
Point Pleasant
Charleston
Summersville
Winona
Lewisburg
Pence Springs
Pipestem
Bramwell
Miles
Kilometers
Interstate highway
U.S. highway
Inn location

Berkeley Springs C9

Highlawn Inn

304 Market St
Berkeley Springs, WV
25411-1428
(304)258-5700 (800)225-5982

Rates: $83-175.
Payment: MC VISA PC TC.
Innkeeper(s): Sandra M. Kauffman.
Circa: 1897.

Rooms: 10 rooms with PB, 2 with FP. 1 suite. 1 cottage.
Beds: KQ.

Guests at this inn stay either in Highlawn Inn, a three-story Victorian, or in Aunt Pearl's, an adjacent cottage constructed in 1900. Both homes have been restored and filled with romantic furnishings and decor. The innkeeper's last addition is a suite located in the top floor of the carriage house. This idyllic retreat features double French doors leading to a rose double whirlpool tub, further decorated with tiles from a pressed tin ceiling. Exposed beams, pine floors, cathedral ceilings and a cozy library nook add ambiance to the suite. Other rooms include romantic items such as a heart-framed bed or perhaps a lattice-enclosed porch with a glider swing chair. The grounds are romantic, dotted with gardens and pebble paths. The innkeeper takes great pride in her creative breakfasts, which often feature delectables flavored with herbs from the garden. Gourmet dinners, with such items as chicken baked with rosemary, garlic and Riesling wine or cheese ravioli with Alfredo sauce, are available on Saturday night for an extra charge.

Breakfast and evening snack included in rates. Types of meals: full breakfast, gourmet breakfast and early coffee/tea. Dinner available. Air conditioning, cable TV and VCR in room. Small meetings hosted. Antiques, fishing, parks and shopping nearby.

Special Discounts: $10 per night for more than three nights (Sunday-Thursday).

The Manor Inn

415 Fairfax St
Berkeley Springs, WV 25411
(304)258-1552 (800)225-5982

Rates: $75-95.
Payment: MC VISA PC TC.
Innkeeper(s): Don & Dot Trask.
Circa: 1878.

Rooms: 4 rooms, 2 with PB. 1 suite.
Beds: QD.

In the National Register, this Second Empire Victorian features 12-foot ceilings, a mansard roof, large porch and French doors. The innkeeper collects antique quilts and is herself a quilter. George Washington is said to have bathed in the warm mineral springs in town where he owned a property a block from the Manor Inn. Roman and Turkish baths are featured in The Baths, a West Virginia State Park.

Breakfast included in rates. Types of meals: full breakfast, gourmet breakfast and early coffee/tea. Air conditioning, ceiling fan and cable TV in room. VCR on premises. Small meetings and family reunions hosted. Antiques, fishing, parks, shopping, downhill skiing, cross-country skiing, theater and watersports nearby.

Bramwell I3

Perry House B&B

Main St, PO Box 248
Bramwell, WV 24715-0248
(304)248-8145 (800)328-0248
Fax:(304)248-8145
E-mail: perryhouse@netlinkcorp.com

Rates: $40-55.
Payment: MC VISA PC TC.
Innkeeper(s): Charlie & Charlotte Sacre.
Circa: 1902.

Rooms: 4 rooms, 1 with PB. 1 cottage.
Beds: KDT.

This brick Victorian was built by a bank cashier and remained in the family for 80 years, when the current innkeepers purchased it. The rooms are decorated in period style with antiques. The innkeepers offer a private cottage with three bedrooms, a kitchen, living room and laundry facilities. Although a small village, Bramwell once was home to more than a dozen millionaires, and some of these families' homes are located on the town walking tour. The inn is listed in the National Register.

Breakfast included in rates. Types of meals: continental breakfast and early coffee/tea. Air conditioning and ceiling fan in room. Cable TV, fax, copier and library on premises. Weddings and family reunions hosted. Limited French spoken. Antiques, fishing, parks, shopping, downhill skiing, theater and watersports nearby. TAC10.

Gilbert House B&B of Middleway

PO Box 1104
Charles Town, WV 25414
(304)725-0637

Rates: $80-140.
Payment: MC VISA AX PC TC.
Innkeeper(s): Bernard F. Heiler.
Circa: 1760.

Rooms: 3 rooms with PB, 2 with FP. 1 suite.
Beds: QT.

A magnificent graystone of early Georgian design, the Gilbert House boasts the state's oldest flagstone sidewalk. During restoration, graffiti found on the upstairs bedroom walls included an 1832 drawing of President James Polk and a child's growth chart from the 1800s. Elegant appointments include fine Oriental rugs, tasteful art and antique furnishings. The inn is located in the 18th-century village of Middleway, which contains one of the country's most well-preserved collections of log houses. The village was a mill site on the original settlers' trail into Shenandoah Valley. Middleway was also the site of "wizard clip" hauntings during the last decade of the 1700s. The region was home to members of "Virginia Blues," commanded by Daniel Morgan during the American Revolutionary War.

Breakfast included in rates. Types of meals: full breakfast and gourmet breakfast. Air conditioning in room. VCR and library on premises. German & Spanish spoken. Antiques, parks, shopping and theater nearby. TAC10.

Location: Middleway historic district.

"We have stayed at inns for fifteen years, and yours is at the top of the list as best ever!"

Hillbrook Inn

Summit Point Rd,
RR 2 Box 152
Charles Town, WV 25414
(304)725-4223 (800)304-4223
Fax:(304)725-4455

Rates: $340-380. MAP.
Payment: MC VISA DS PC TC.
Innkeeper(s): Gretchen Carroll.
Circa: 1700.

Rooms: 6 rooms with PB, 2 with FP.
Beds: QD.

This graceful English Tudor inn meanders down the hillside overlooking a pond framed by daffodils and 18 acres of estate grounds that include streams, gardens and wooded walks. The land once belonged to George Washington, and although most of the current structure was built in 1920, part began in the 1700s. Decorated in a European country-house style, the inn is replete with rich dark woods and interesting pieces that demand a lengthy stay to fully enjoy. The inn is often the location for elegant events and is known for its seven-course, prix-fixe candlelight dinners served at 8 p.m.

Breakfast, afternoon tea and dinner included in rates. Types of meals: full breakfast, gourmet breakfast and early coffee/tea. Picnic lunch, lunch, gourmet lunch, catering service and room service available. MAP. Air conditioning in room. Fax and library on premises. 18 acres. Weddings, small meetings, family reunions and seminars hosted. French and German spoken. Antiques, fishing, parks, shopping, sporting events, theater and watersports nearby. TAC10.

Special Discounts: $99 B&B for same-day reservations made after 12 noon.

The Washington House Inn

216 S George St
Charles Town, WV 25414
(304)725-7923 (800)297-6957
Fax:(304)728-5150
E-mail: mnvogel@intrepid.net

Rates: $70-125.
Payment: MC VISA AX DS PC TC.
Innkeeper(s): Mel & Nina Vogel.
Circa: 1899.

Rooms: 6 rooms with PB. 1 suite. 1 conference room.
Beds: QT.

This three-story brick Victorian is said to have been built by the descendants of President Washington's brothers, John Augustine and Samuel. Carved oak mantels, fireplaces, spacious guest rooms, antique furnishings and refreshments served on the wraparound porch make the inn memorable. Harpers Ferry National Historic Park, Antietam, and the Shenandoah and Potomac rivers are all within a 15-minute drive, as is Martinsburg outlet shopping.

Breakfast, afternoon tea and evening snack included in rates. Types of meals: continental breakfast, continental-plus breakfast, full breakfast and early coffee/tea. Air conditioning, turn-down service and ceiling fan in room. Cable TV, VCR, fax, copier and bicycles on premises. Small meetings, family reunions and seminars hosted. Antiques, fishing, parks, shopping, theater and watersports nearby. TAC10.

Charleston — F3

Benedict Haid Farm

8 Hale St
Charleston, WV 25301-2806
(304)346-1054

Rates: $100.
Payment: MC VISA TC.
Innkeeper(s): Steve Jones.
Circa: 1869.

Rooms: 3 rooms. 1 cottage.
Beds: D.

Although no breakfast is served, we couldn't help including this farm on 350-mountain-top acres because it specializes in raising exotic animals that include llamas, guanacos and black mountain sheep, as well as donkeys and cows. There are two rustic cabins for those looking for an economical stay. Most will prefer the main German-built, hand-hewn log lodge, which features antique furnishings and a large screened-in deck with fireplace and hot tub. There is a stocked pond. Bring your own breakfast.

Air conditioning in room. Cable TV, VCR and bicycles on premises. 350 acres. Weddings, small meetings, family reunions and seminars hosted. Fishing and cross-country skiing nearby.

Location: Twenty-three miles northeast of Charleston.

Publicity: *Television Travel Show, One Tank Trips.*

"Like stepping back in time."

Brass Pineapple B&B

1611 Virginia St E
Charleston, WV 25311-2113
(304)344-0748 (800)225-5982
Fax:(304)344-0748

Rates: $85-115.
Payment: MC VISA AX DC PC TC.
Innkeeper(s): Sue Pepper.
Circa: 1910.

Rooms: 6 rooms with PB, 3 with FP. 1 suite.
Beds: KQT.

This elegant inn is situated in Charleston's historic district, one-half block from the Capitol Complex. Original oak paneling and leaded and stained glass are among the architectural highlights. Thoughtful amenities such as terry robes and hair dryers have been placed in each guest room. For the extended stay business traveler, there are one- and two-bedroom apartments available. Guests can enjoy a gourmet breakfast or opt for lighter, low-fat continental fare.

Breakfast, afternoon tea and evening snack included in rates. Types of meals:

continental breakfast, full breakfast and early coffee/tea. Room service available. Air conditioning, turn-down service, ceiling fan, cable TV and VCR in room. Fax, copier and bicycles on premises. Antiques, fishing, parks, shopping, sporting events, theater and watersports nearby. TAC10.

Publicity: *Mid-Atlantic Country, Charlestonian, News 8 TV, Charleston Daily Mail, Gourmet, Southern Living.*

"Many thanks for a wonderful stay. We felt like a part of a family in this dear old house."

Elkins E6

Tunnel Mountain B&B

Rt 1, Box 59-1
Elkins, WV 26241-9711
(304)636-1684

Rates: $65-75.
Payment: PC TC.
Innkeeper(s): Anne & Paul Beardslee.
Circa: 1938.

Rooms: 3 rooms with PB, 1 with FP.
Beds: QD.

Nestled on five acres of wooded land, this three-story Fieldstone home offers privacy in a peaceful setting. Rooms are tastefully decorated with antiques, collectibles and crafts. Each bedroom boasts a view of the surrounding mountains. The chestnut and knotty pine woodwork accentuate the decor. The fireplace in the large common room is a great place for warming up after a day of touring or skiing. The area is home to a number of interesting events, including a Dulcimer festival.

Breakfast included in rates. Type of meal: full breakfast. Air conditioning and cable TV in room. Antiques, fishing, parks, shopping, downhill skiing, cross-country skiing, theater and watersports nearby.

Publicity: *Blue Ridge Country.*

Special Discounts: AARP - 10%.

Harpers Ferry D10

Fillmore Street B&B

PO Box 34
Harpers Ferry, WV 25425
(304)535-2619

Rates: $75-80.
Payment: PC TC.
Innkeeper(s): Alden & James Addy.
Circa: 1890.

Rooms: 2 rooms with PB.
Beds: Q.

This two-story clapboard Victorian was built on the foundation of a Civil War structure on land deeded by Jefferson Davis, Secretary of War. The surrounding acreage was an encampment for both the Union and Confederate soldiers (at different times). Within walking distance of the inn are the national park, museums, shopping and dining.

Breakfast included in rates. Types of meals: full breakfast and early coffee/tea. Air conditioning, turn-down service and VCR in room. Library on premises. Fishing, parks, shopping and watersports nearby.

"Delightful! What superb hosts you two are. We enjoyed ourselves luxuriously."

Huttonsville E6

Richard's Country Inn

US 219, RR 1 Box 11-A-1
Huttonsville, WV 26273
(304)335-6659 (800)636-7434

Rates: $60-75.
Payment: MC VISA AX DS TC.
Innkeeper(s): Richard Brown.
Circa: 1835.

Rooms: 13 rooms, 8 with PB, 3 with FP. 1 cottage. 3 conference rooms.
Beds: QDT.

WV

This pre-Civil War home has been completely restored, including the original fireplaces and woodwork. Antiques and contemporary furnishings decorate the home. Three of the guest rooms include a fireplace. Guests also can stay in a Tudor-style cottage. There is a bar and restaurant on the premises, as well.

For breakfast, stuffed French toast is a specialty, and during dinner at the restaurant, items such as rainbow trout or New York steak are prepared.

Breakfast included in rates. Type of meal: full breakfast. Dinner, picnic lunch and lunch available. Ceiling fan in room. Weddings, small meetings, family reunions and seminars hosted. Antiques, fishing, parks, skiing, theater and watersports nearby.

Pets Allowed.

Lewisburg H5

The General Lewis

301 E Washington St
Lewisburg, WV 24901-1425
(304)645-2600 (800)628-4454
Fax:(304)645-2600

Rates: $75-125. EP.
Payment: MC VISA AX DS.
Innkeeper(s): Nan Morgan.
Circa: 1834.

Rooms: 26 rooms with PB. 2 suites.
Beds: QD.

This gracious Federal-style inn boasts a columned veranda, flower gardens and long lawns. Patrick Henry and Thomas Jefferson registered at the inn's walnut desk, which was retrieved from an old hot springs resort in the area. A stagecoach that once delivered travelers to springs on the James River and Kanawha Turnpike, rests under an arbor. American antiques are featured throughout the inn, and Memory Hall displays household items and tools once used by local pioneers. Nearby are state parks, national forests, streams and rivers, as well as sites of the Revolutionary and Civil wars.

EP. Air conditioning and cable TV in room. Fax and copier on premises. Handicap access. Weddings and family reunions hosted. Antiques, shopping and theater nearby. TAC10.

Publicity: *Southern Living, New York Times.*

"The staff is wonderful at making us feel at home, and we can be as much a part of the inn as we want."

Martinsburg D9

Aspen Hall Inn

405 Boyd Ave
Martinsburg, WV 25401
(304)263-4385

Rates: $95-125.
Payment: MC VISA AX PC TC.
Innkeeper(s): Gordon & Lou Anne Claucherty.
Circa: 1745.

Rooms: 5 rooms with PB, 1 with FP.
Beds: KDT.

This limestone Georgian manor, listed in the National Register, overlooks seven acres of lawns, gardens and a stream. The rooms are decorated in a Southern-plantation style, and there are double parlors, a library and a dining room. Second-floor guest rooms feature canopy beds and are furnished with antiques. Afternoon tea is served in the library or the garden gazebo. The property is mentioned in journals kept by George Washington, and he attended a wedding here. During the French and Indian War, Washington sent troops to protect the Quaker-owned building.

Breakfast and afternoon tea included in rates. Types of meals: full breakfast and early coffee/tea. Air conditioning, turn-down service and cable TV in room. VCR, copier and library on premises. Family reunions hosted. Antiques, fishing, parks, shopping, downhill skiing, cross-country skiing, sporting events, theater and watersports nearby.

Publicity: *Travel & Leisure, Mid-Atlantic Country.*

Special Discounts: Discounts require a three-day stay.

"We are happy to pass out your brochures to our friends with hearty recommendation."

Boydville, The Inn at Martinsburg

601 S Queen St
Martinsburg, WV 25401
(304)263-1448

Rates: $100-125.
Payment: MC VISA PC.
Innkeeper(s): LaRue Frye.
Circa: 1812.

Rooms: 6 rooms, 4 with PB, 1 with FP. 1 conference room.
Beds: QDT.

This Georgian estate was saved from burning by Union troops only by a specific proclamation from President Lincoln dated July 18, 1864. Tall maples line the long driveway leading up to the house. It is constructed of two-foot-thick stone walls covered with plaster. The entry hall retains the original wallpaper brought from England in 1812 and hand-painted murals, fireplaces, and antiques adorn the spacious guest rooms. Sunlight filters through tree tops onto estate-sized lawns and gardens.

Breakfast included in rates. Types of meals: continental-plus breakfast and early coffee/tea. Air conditioning in room. Cable TV and library on premises. 10 acres. Weddings and family reunions hosted. Antiques, shopping, downhill skiing and theater nearby.

Publicity: *Washington Post, Mid-Atlantic Country.*

Special Discounts: 10% for two night stay.

"Your gracious home, hospitality and excellent amenities were enjoyed so much. Such a fine job of innkeeping."

Moorefield E8

McMechen House Inn

109 N Main St
Moorefield, WV 26836-1154
(304)538-7173 (800)298-2466
Fax:(304)538-7841

Rates: $60-85.
Payment: MC VISA AX DC PC TC.
Innkeeper(s): Linda & Bob Curtis.
Circa: 1853.

Rooms: 7 rooms, 4 with PB. 1 suite.
Beds: D.

This handsomely restored three-story brick Greek Revival townhouse is in the National Register. There are polished pine floors, a spectacular cherry staircase winding up to the third floor, walnut doors and woodwork, cranberry glass light fixtures and indoor folding shutters. Two parlors and a library add to the gracious dining room that houses the inn's restaurant. From May through September, guests can enjoy meals outdoors Green Shutters Garden Cafe. From May through September, guests may dine at the inn's outdoor Green Shutters Cafe. There is an antique, book and gift shop on the premises. The inn is often the site of weddings and receptions.

Breakfast, afternoon tea and evening snack included in rates. Types of meals: full breakfast and early coffee/tea. Dinner, lunch, banquet service, catering service, catered breakfast and room service available. Air conditioning in room. VCR, fax, copier and library on premises. Weddings, small meetings, family reunions and seminars hosted. Antiques, fishing, parks, downhill skiing and theater nearby.

Morgantown C6

Almost Heaven B&B

391 Scott Ave
Morgantown, WV 26505
(304)296-4007 (800)225-5982
E-mail: vidman@access.mountain.net

Rates: $60-85.
Payment: MC VISA AX DC DS PC TC.
Innkeeper(s): Cookie Coombs.
Circa: 1991.

Rooms: 4 rooms with PB.
Beds: Q.

The backporch of this Federal-style inn overlooks the beautiful West Virginia Mountains. Guests can relax in the Victorian Parlor or by fireplace in the library. A large breakfast is served in the elegant dining room. Guest rooms include feather beds and ceiling fans. West Virginia University, Coopers Rock, Cheat Lake and Forks of Cheat Winery are nearby.

Breakfast included in rates. Type of meal: full breakfast. Air conditioning, ceiling fan and cable TV in room. VCR and library on premises. Antiques, fishing, parks, shopping, cross-country skiing, sporting events, theater and watersports nearby.

Pence Springs H5

The Pence Springs Hotel

Rt 3, PO Box 90
Pence Springs, WV 24962
(304)445-2606 (800)826-1829
Fax:(304)445-2204

Rates: $70-100.
Payment: MC VISA AX DC CB DS PC TC.
Innkeeper(s): D. Ashby Berkley & Rosa Lee Berkley Miller.
Circa: 1918.

Rooms: 25 rooms, 15 with PB. 3 suites. 4 conference rooms.
Beds: KDT.

This elegant brick structure has served several purposes through the years. The hotel first gained prominence as a mineral spa frequented by many wealthy guests. From there, The Pence Springs was transformed into a women's prison. But it was again refurbished into a grand getaway. Guest rooms are furnished in the art deco style, reminiscent of the hotel's heyday in the '20s. Guests enjoy full breakfasts each morning, and during the summer months, a lavish Sunday brunch is served, including vegetables grown on the hotel's 400 acres. Spend the day strolling the lush grounds or relaxing in the Cider Press lounge or on the sunporch. The area boasts many outdoor activities and plenty of antique shopping.

Breakfast included in rates. Type of meal: gourmet breakfast. Dinner, picnic lunch, banquet service, catering service and room service available. Air conditioning in room. Cable TV, VCR, fax, copier, swimming, stables, bicycles and child care on premises. Handicap access. 28 acres. Weddings, small meetings, family reunions and seminars hosted. Norwegian, German and Spanish spoken. Antiques, fishing, parks, shopping, downhill skiing, theater and watersports nearby. TAC10.

Pets Allowed: Cannot be left in room; kennel space in basement.

Publicity: *Mid-Atlantic Country, Charleston Gazette, Beckley Register-Herald, Richmond, Goldenseal, Wonderful West Virginia, Travel Host.*

"As always, I left your place rejuvenated. The property grows even more beautiful year after year."

Pipestem H4

Walnut Grove Inn

HC 78 Box 260
Pipestem, WV 25979-9702
(304)466-6119 (800)701-1237

Rates: $65.
Payment: MC VISA AX DS.
Innkeeper(s): Bonnie & Larry Graham.
Circa: 1850.

Rooms: 5 rooms with PB. 1 suite.
Beds: KQDT.

Located on 38 acres, this red shingled country farmhouse also has a century-old log barn and ancient cemetery with graves of Confederate soldiers and others prior to the Civil War. The farmhouse is decorated eclectically and the front porch is furnished with rocking chairs and a swing. Swimming, basketball, badminton and horseshoes are available. A country breakfast of biscuits and gravy, fresh eggs and homemade preserves is served in the dining room or screen room.

Breakfast, afternoon tea and evening snack included in rates. Types of meals: gourmet breakfast and early coffee/tea. Air conditioning in room. Cable TV and swimming on premises. 38 acres. Small meetings and family reunions hosted. Fishing, parks, shopping, downhill skiing, cross-country skiing, theater and watersports nearby. TAC10.

Point Pleasant E2

Stone Manor

12 Main St
Point Pleasant, WV 25550
(304)675-3442

Rates: $50.
Payment: PC.
Innkeeper(s): Janice & Tom Vance.
Circa: 1887.

Rooms: 3 rooms, 3 with FP.
Beds: QD.

This stone Victorian sits on the banks of the Kanawha River with a front porch that faces the river. Point Pleasant Battle Monument Park, adjacent to the inn, was built to commemorate the location of the first battle of the Revolutionary War. In the National Register, the inn was once the home of a family who ran a ferry boat crossing for the Ohio and Kanawha rivers. Now restored, the house is decorated with Victorian antiques and offers a pleasant garden with a Victorian fish pond and fountain.

Breakfast included in rates. Type of meal: full breakfast. Air conditioning and VCR in room. Cable TV on premises. Small meetings hosted.

Romney D8

Hampshire House 1884

165 N Grafton St
Romney, WV 26757-1616
(304)822-7171

Rates: $65-80.
Payment: MC VISA AX DC DS PC TC.
Innkeeper(s): Jane & Scott Simmons.
Circa: 1884.

Rooms: 5 rooms with PB, 3 with FP. 1 conference room.
Beds: QDT.

Located near the south branch of the Potomac River, the garden here has old boxwoods and walnut trees. The inn features ornate brickwork, tall, narrow windows, and fireplaces with handsome period mantels. A sitting room with a well-stocked library, a cozy patio and a music room with an antique pump organ are favorite places.

Breakfast included in rates. Types of meals: full breakfast and early coffee/tea. Evening snack available. Air conditioning, cable TV and VCR in room. Bicycles on premises. Small meetings hosted. Antiques, fishing, shopping and watersports nearby. TAC10.

Publicity: *Hampshire Review, Mid-Atlantic Country, Weekend Journal.*

Special Discounts: Single business rate mid-week except October $55.

"Your personal attention made us feel at home immediately."

Summersville F4

Historic Brock House B&B Inn

1400 Webster Rd
Summersville, WV 26651
(304)872-4887

Rates: $70-90.
Payment: MC VISA PC TC.
Innkeeper(s): Margie N. Martin.
Circa: 1890.

Rooms: 6 rooms, 4 with PB. 1 suite. 1 conference room.
Beds: QT.

This Queen Anne farmhouse is the second venture into the bed & breakfast business for innkeepers Margie and Jim Martin. The exterior looks friendly and inviting, perhaps because of its long history of welcoming guests. The National Register inn originally served as a hotel and later as a boarding house. Margie has a degree in design, her skills are evident in the cheerful, country rooms. Each of the guest rooms has a different color scheme and decor. One is decked in deep blue, another is appointed with flowery bedspreads and pastel curtains.

Breakfast, afternoon tea and evening snack included in rates. Types of meals: continental breakfast, full breakfast, gourmet breakfast and early coffee/tea. Dinner, gourmet lunch, banquet service, catering service and catered breakfast available. Air conditioning and turn-down service in room. Cable TV, VCR, fax and library on premises. Weddings, small meetings, family reunions and seminars hosted. Antiques, fishing, parks, shopping, theater and watersports nearby. TAC10.

Valley Chapel (Weston)

Ingeberg Acres

Millstone Rd, PO Box 199
Valley Chapel
(Weston), WV 26446-0199
(304)269-2834
Fax:(304)269-2834

Rates: $59-80.
Payment: PC TC.
Innkeeper(s): Ingeborg & John Mann.
Circa: 1981.

Rooms: 3 rooms. 1 cottage.
Beds: KDT.

Enjoy the privilege of hunting turkey, grouse and deer on private, posted land on the 450 acres of this horse and cattle farm. Wildflowers, blackberries and raspberries may be gathered as well. A pond on the property is stocked with game fish for anglers. Breakfast is served family-style and you are invited to participate in or observe everyday farm chores.

Breakfast and evening snack included in rates. Type of meal: full breakfast. Air conditioning in room. Cable TV, VCR, fax, copier, swimming, stables and library on premises. 450 acres. Small meetings and family reunions hosted. German spoken. Antiques, fishing, parks and shopping nearby.

Location: Fifteen minutes from I-79 near Weston.

Special Discounts: Children under six free in same room; special rates for hunting; 10% off for Senior citizens.

WV

Wheeling

B5

The Eckhart House

810 Main St
Wheeling, WV 26003-2526
(304)232-5439
Fax:(304)232-5439

Rates: $65-90.
Payment: MC VISA DS PC TC.
Innkeeper(s): Gretchen & Joe Figaretti.
Circa: 1892.

Rooms: 5 rooms, 3 with PB, 5 with FP.
Beds: QDT.

Eckhart House, located in a National Historic District, rests alongside a National Historic Road built in 1818. From the library, guests have a view of the river. The home is filled with Victorian elements, including a three-story staircase with delicate carvings, 10 fireplaces and stained glass. A tour of the home is included in a night's stay. All rooms include a fireplace and are decorated in Victorian style with antiques.

Breakfast included in rates. Types of meals: continental-plus breakfast and early coffee/tea. Air conditioning and ceiling fan in room. Cable TV, VCR, fax, copier and library on premises. Amusement parks, antiques, fishing, parks, shopping, downhill skiing, cross-country skiing, sporting events, theater and watersports nearby. TAC10.

Winona

G4

Garvey House

PO Box 98
Winona, WV 25942-0098
(304)574-3235 (800)767-3235

Rates: $49-61.
Payment: MC VISA TC.
Innkeeper(s): Darrell Riedesel & Christopher Terrafranca.
Circa: 1916.

Rooms: 9 rooms, 6 with PB.
Beds: DT.

Two mountainside, turn-of-the-century homes comprise this inn, which is surrounded by three lush acres decorated with trees, plants, flowers, a gazebo and goldfish pond. The main house was built by a superintendent of the Maryland New River Coal Company. Historical pictures decorate the walls, serving as the innkeepers homage to the area's coal miners and mining history. Guests sleep on antique beds, and there is an eclectic mix of antiques throughout the comfortable homes. A hearty homemade breakfast is served, and on request, dinners can be prepared. The area is known for its excellent whitewater rafting.

Breakfast included in rates. Type of meal: full breakfast. Dinner available. Ceiling fan in room. Bicycles on premises. Weddings, small meetings, family reunions and seminars hosted. Antiques, fishing, parks and shopping nearby. TAC10.

Eggs Garvey

The Garvey House
Winona, W.V.

Milk
Cream cheese
One tomato slice cut in half
Two slices bacon
Freshly chopped chives
Two fresh basil leaves
Monterey Jack cheese

In a shallow single-serving baking dish pour enough milk to cover the bottom.

Slice off three slices of cream cheese, about ¼" thick, and place side by side in the bottom of the dish. Top with two slices of cooked and drained bacon; then place the tomato slices, cut in half, on top of the bacon and crack one egg very gently in the center, or if desired place two side-by-side.

Bake at 325 degrees until done. Approximately 15 minutes for medium-cooked and 20 minutes or so for hard-cooked. Serve with toast triangles and fresh fruit.

Wisconsin

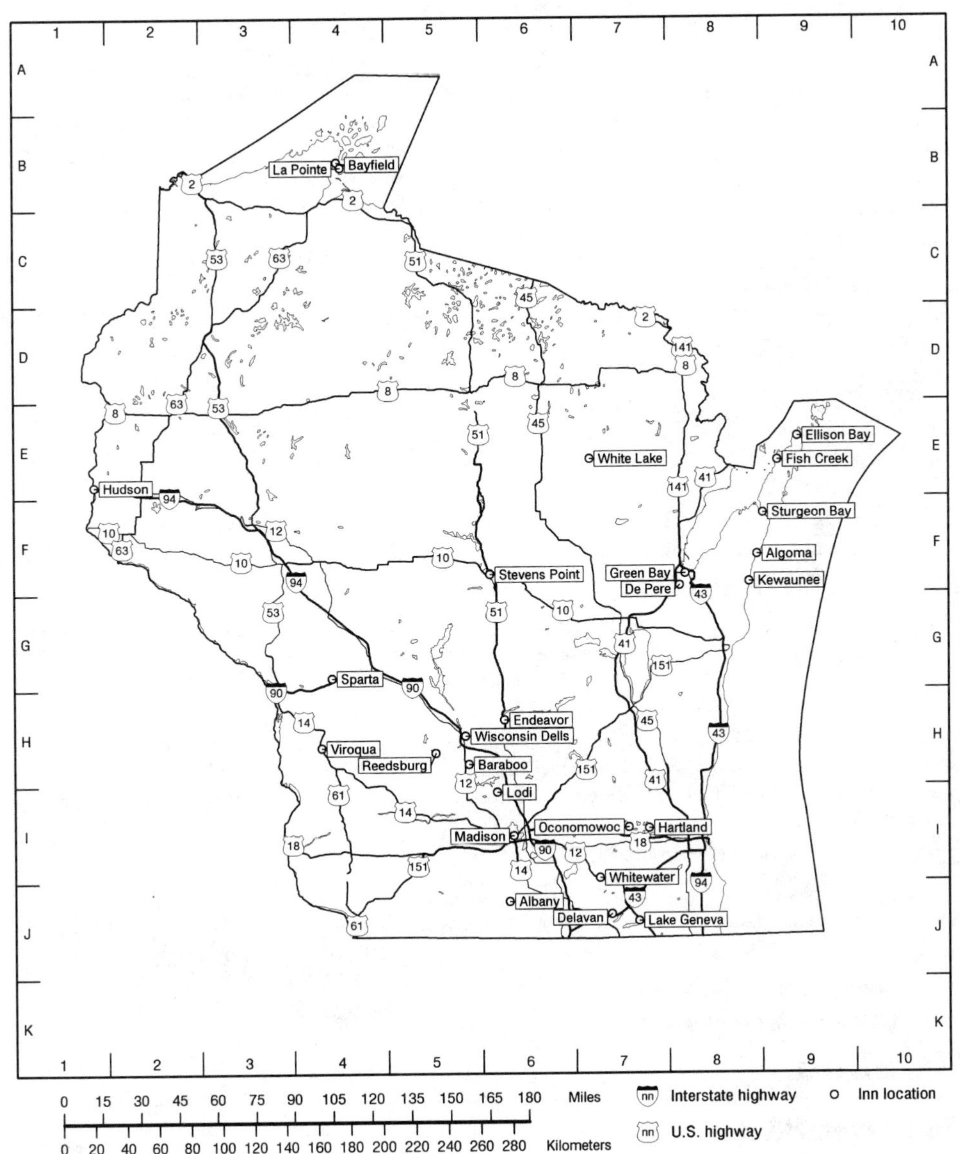
La Pointe
Bayfield
White Lake
Ellison Bay
Fish Creek
Hudson
Sturgeon Bay
Algoma
Kewaunee
Stevens Point
Green Bay
De Pere
Sparta
Endeavor
Wisconsin Dells
Viroqua
Reedsburg
Baraboo
Lodi
Oconomowoc
Hartland
Madison
Whitewater
Albany
Delavan
Lake Geneva
Miles
Kilometers
Interstate highway
U.S. highway
Inn location

Albany

J6

Albany Guest House

405 S Mill St
Albany, WI 53502-9502
(608)862-3636

Rates: $55-75.
Payment: MC VISA PC.
Innkeeper(s): Bob & Sally Braem.
Circa: 1908.

Rooms: 6 rooms, 4 with PB, 1 with FP.
Beds: KQD.

The brickwalk, red-tiled foyer, lace curtains and abundance of flowers set the comfortable tone for this three-story inn. An upright piano in the large foyer and fireplace in the living room also add to the pleasant atmosphere. The guest rooms have picture windows and hand-carved antiques. Outside, maple and black walnut trees and various gardens grace the inn's eight-acre property. Guests can tour New Glarus, a village known as America's Little Switzerland, which is a short drive away. Also, not too far away is a cheese factory that is available for tours. Guests also can enjoy a bicycle ride on the nearby Sugar River Trail.

Breakfast included in rates. Types of meals: full breakfast and early coffee/tea. Air conditioning and ceiling fan in room. VCR and library on premises. Small meetings, family reunions and seminars hosted. Antiques, fishing, parks and cross-country skiing nearby.

Publicity: *Silent Sports, Madison, Monroe Evening Times.*

Special Discounts: 10% discount for three or more consecutive weekday nights, whole house rates November-April, 15% - 1 day, 20% - 2 days.

"Was even more than I expected."

Algoma

F8

Amberwood Beach Inn

N7136 Hwy 42, Lakeshore Dr
Algoma, WI 54201
(414)487-3471

Rates: $65-95.
Payment: MC VISA PC.
Innkeeper(s): Jan Warren & George Davies.
Circa: 1925.

Rooms: 7 rooms with PB, 7 with FP. 2 suites. 2 cottages.
Beds: Beds: KQT.

Double French doors in the guest rooms open to private decks overlooking Lake Michigan. In the evening, from your room, you can hear the waves lapping ashore. Breakfast in bed is available when you book the bridal suite for a honeymoon or anniversary. A favorite activity is to picnic under the trees at the edge of the water.

Breakfast included in rates. Types of meals: full breakfast, gourmet breakfast and early coffee/tea. Ceiling fan in room. Fax, spa, swimming, sauna and library on premises. Weddings, small meetings, family reunions and seminars hosted. Amusement parks, antiques, fishing, parks, shopping, theater, watersports nearby.

Location: Lake Michigan.

Special Discounts: Seventh night free on week long stays.

"Very personable, friendly, down-to-earth."

Baraboo

H5

Pinehaven B&B

E13083 Hwy 33
Baraboo, WI 53913
(608)356-3489

Rates: $65-125.
Payment: MC VISA PC TC.
Innkeeper(s): Lyle & Marge Getschman.
Circa: 1970.

Rooms: 4 rooms with PB. 1 cottage.
Beds: KQDT.

This contemporary chalet-style home was built in 1971, and guest rooms were added 20 years later. The house is surrounded by towering pines and acres of rolling lawn. Also on the property is a private lake complete with complimentary rowboat. Scenic views can be enjoyed from the upper veranda, lower deck, and some of the bedrooms. Hosts Lyle and Marge Getschman raise Belgian draft horses, and, if time permits, Lyle will treat guests to a wagon or sleigh ride.

Breakfast included in rates. Types of meals: gourmet breakfast and early coffee/tea. Air conditioning and ceiling fan in room. VCR on premises. Amusement parks, antiques, parks, skiing and watersports nearby.

Location: On State Highway 33, 10 miles west of I 90-94 Exit 106 or three miles east of Baraboo on Highway 33.

Publicity: *Wisconsin Innkeepers, Wisconsin Trails Country.*

"Beautiful surroundings, comfy bed, marvelous breakfast, wonderful hosts and a great tour - We couldn't have wanted anything more!"

Bayfield B4

Apple Tree Inn

Rt 1, Box 251, Hwy 135
Bayfield, WI 54814-9767
(715)779-5572 (800)400-6532

Rates: $49-84.
Payment: MC VISA PC TC.
Innkeeper(s): Joanna Barningham.
Circa: 1911.

Rooms: 4 rooms with PB.
Beds: KQD.

The Apple Tree Inn is a fully restored farmhouse overlooking Lake Superior. It was once owned by a dairy farmer and landscape artist. A hearty, country-style breakfast is served in the sunroom which boasts a panoramic view of Madeline Island and Lake Superior. Guest rooms are furnished in early Americana style and three have lake views.

Breakfast included in rates. Types of meals: full breakfast, gourmet breakfast and early coffee/tea. Picnic lunch available. Air conditioning and ceiling fan in room. Cable TV, VCR, pet boarding and child care on premises. Family reunions hosted. Antiques, fishing, parks, shopping, downhill skiing, cross-country skiing, theater and watersports nearby. TAC10.

Pets Allowed: Please check with innkeeper.

Publicity: *Lake Superior.*

"You made us feel like old friends rather than guests."

De Pere F8

James St. Inn

201 James St
De Pere, WI 54115-2562
(414)337-0111 (800)537-8483
Fax:(414)337-6135

Rates: $69-139.
Payment: MC VISA AX DS PC TC.
Innkeeper(s): Kevin Flatley & Joan Pruner.
Circa: 1995.

Rooms: 30 rooms with PB, 4 with FP. 27 suites. 1 conference room.
Beds: Q.

In 1858, a flour mill sat where the James St. Inn now stands. The mill later burned and the inn was built in its place. Set alongside the Fox River, the water still flows beneath the structure as it did when it powered the mill more than a century before. The inn appears more as a creation of the 19th century than a modern building. Traditional and Shaker furnishings appear in the guest rooms. Some rooms also include whirlpool tubs, fireplaces or balconies with river views. The inn is located in the heart of downtown DePere, so there's plenty to do. Shops, restaurants, a railroad museum and the Green Bay Packer Hall of Fame are just minutes away.

Breakfast and evening snack included in rates. Types of meals: continental-plus breakfast and early coffee/tea. Air conditioning, cable TV and VCR in room. Fax and copier on premises. Handicap access. Small meetings, family reunions and seminars hosted. Amusement parks, antiques, fishing, parks, shopping, cross-country skiing, sporting events, theater and watersports nearby. TAC10.

Special Discounts: All year-two nights whirlpool suite $199. Call for seasonal promotions.

Delavan

J7

The Allyn Mansion Inn B&B

511 E Walworth Ave
Delavan, WI 53115-1209
(414)728-9090

Rates: $100.
Payment: MC VISA PC.
Innkeeper(s): Ron Markwell & Joe Johnson.
Circa: 1885.

Rooms: 8 rooms.
Beds: Q.

In the National Register and grand prize winner of the National Trust's Great American Home Awards, this ornate Queen Ann Eastlake Victorian has been meticulously restored. Rooms are filled with antiques, two grand pianos and collections suitable for its three parlors and ten marble fireplaces. Elegant guest rooms feature massive Victorian beds including a ten-foot-high Eastlake half-canopy bed and a nine-and-a-half-foot Renaissance Revival bed. Most of the private bathrooms are down the hall. A favorite breakfast speciality is Allyn Mansion's Country Quiche with four types of Wisconsin cheese. Breads and cinnamon buns are baked from scratch.

Breakfast included in rates. Type of meal: full breakfast. Evening snack available. Antiques, fishing, parks, cross-country skiing and watersports nearby.

Lakeside Manor Inn

1809 S Shore Dr
Delavan, WI 53115-3618
(414)728-5354
Fax:(414)728-2043

Rates: $79-189.
Payment: MC VISA PC TC.
Innkeeper(s): Patricia K. McCauley.
Circa: 1897.

Rooms: 7 rooms, 4 with PB, 1 with FP. 1 suite.
Beds: KQDT.

As the name suggests, this inn is located on the shores of Delavan lake. Guests can relax and take in the view from the inn's wraparound verandah, fish off the inn's private pier or curl up with a good book in the firelit parlor. Guests can opt to stay in one of six guest rooms, a honeymoon suite or a waterfront guest house. The guest house includes two bedrooms, glass-enclosed sleeping porch, living room with fireplace and efficiency kitchen. Breakfast is not included in the guest house rates.

Breakfast included in rates. Types of meals: continental-plus breakfast, full breakfast and early coffee/tea. Air conditioning, ceiling fan, cable TV and VCR in room. Fax and swimming on premises. Weddings, small meetings, family reunions and seminars hosted. Amusement parks, antiques, fishing, parks, shopping, downhill skiing, cross-country skiing, theater and watersports nearby. TAC10.

Ellison Bay

E9

The Griffin Inn & Cottages

11976 Mink River Rd
Ellison Bay, WI 54210-9705
(414)854-4306

Rates: $55-86. MAP.
Payment: PC.
Innkeeper(s): Paul Ennis & Family.
Circa: 1910.

Rooms: 14 rooms. 4 cottages.
Beds: DT.

This New England-style country inn is situated on five acres of rolling lawns and maple trees with a gazebo. There are verandas with porch swings, a gracious lobby with a stone fireplace and a cozy library. Guest rooms are furnished with antique beds and dressers and feature handmade quilts. In addition to the main house, there are four cottages. Cottage guests enjoy a continental breakfast basket, but for an extra charge, can partake of a full breakfast.

Breakfast and evening snack included in rates. Types of meals: continental breakfast, full breakfast, gourmet breakfast and early coffee/tea. Picnic lunch, lunch, banquet service and catering service available. MAP. Air conditioning and ceiling fan in room. Tennis and library on premises. Weddings, small meetings, family reunions and seminars hosted. Amusement parks, antiques, fishing, parks, shopping, cross-country skiing, theater and watersports nearby.

Location: Two blocks east of Highway 42 on the Door County Peninsula.

Publicity: *Ladies Circle, Innsider, Country Inns, Green Bay Press Gazette, Travel & Leisure, Wisconsin Trails, Country Folk Art, Midwest Living.*

Special Discounts: During winter season third night free.

"A classic bed & breakfast inn — Travel & Leisure."

Endeavor

H6

Neenah Creek Inn & Pottery

W7956 Neenah Rd
Endeavor, WI 53930-9308
(608)587-2229
Fax:(608)587-2229

Rates: $65-105.
Payment: MC VISA DS TC.
Innkeeper(s): Pat & Doug Cook.
Circa: 1900.

Rooms: 4 rooms with PB. 1 suite.
Beds: QT.

Wildlife lovers will enjoy the creekfront setting of this turn-of-the-century Portage brick farmhouse. The Circus Room honors nearby Baraboo, and features a brass queen bed. Country furnishings are found throughout the inn. Guests enjoy relaxing in the common room, on the outdoor porch, in the solarium and in the spacious dining-living room. The inn's 11 acres are filled with walking paths. Don't be shy about asking for a demonstration of the potter's wheel. Wisconsin Dells is an easy drive away.

Breakfast and evening snack included in rates. Type of meal: gourmet breakfast. Air conditioning in room. VCR, fax and copier on premises. 12 acres. Amusement parks, antiques, fishing, parks, shopping, downhill skiing, cross-country skiing and watersports nearby.

Fish Creek

E9

Thorp House Inn & Cottages

4135 Bluff Rd, PO Box 490
Fish Creek, WI 54212
(414)868-2444

Rates: $75-135.
Payment: PC TC.
Innkeeper(s): Christine & Sverre Falck-Pedersen.
Circa: 1902.

Rooms: 4 rooms with PB, 4 with FP. 6 cottages.
Beds: KQDT.

Freeman Thorp picked the site for this home because of its view of Green Bay and the village. Before his house was finished, however, he perished in the bay when the Erie L. Hackley sank. His wife completed it as a guest house. Each room has a view of the harbor, cedar forest or village. A stone fireplace is the focal point of the parlor, and four of the cottages on the property have fireplaces. Some cottages have whirlpools and all have TVs and VCRs. Everything upon which the eye might rest must be "of the era." Breakfast is not included in the rates for cottage guests.

Breakfast included in rates. Types of meals: continental-plus breakfast and early coffee/tea. Air conditioning, ceiling fan, cable TV and VCR in room. Bicycles and library on premises. Weddings hosted. Norwegian spoken. Amusement parks, antiques, fishing, parks, shopping, cross-country skiing, theater and watersports nearby.

Location: Heart of Door County, in the village of Fish Creek.

Publicity: *Madison PM, Green Bay Press-Gazette, Milwaukee Journal/Sentinel, McCall's, Minnesota Monthly.*

Special Discounts: Off season (November 1-May 1) discounts in cottages depending on length of stay.

"Amazing attention to detail from restoration to the furnishings. A very first-class experience."

Gills Rock

Harbor House Inn

12666 Hwy 42
Gills Rock, WI 54210
(414)854-5196

Rates: $49-105.
Payment: MC VISA AX.
Innkeeper(s): David & Else Weborg.
Circa: 1904.

Rooms: 14 rooms with PB.
Beds: KQT.

WI

Gills Rock, a fishing village on the northern tip of Door County, is the home of the Harbor House Inn. The inn has been in the Weborg family since its inception, and the innkeepers recently restored the home to reflect its original Victorian elegance. Also on the grounds is Troll cottage, a nautical Scandinavian dwelling. The inn's guest rooms all feature private baths, microwave ovens and refrigerators. Guests will enjoy the inn's period furniture, sauna cabin, whirlpool and gorgeous sunsets over the waters of Green Bay. A new wing recently was added, with rooms done in a Scandanavian country decor. A private beach is within walking distance.

Breakfast included in rates. Type of meal: continental-plus breakfast. Spa and sauna on premises. Fishing, theater and watersports nearby.

Pets Allowed.

Publicity: *State Journal, Travel Leisure.*

"Lovely inn. Thank you for your hospitality."

Green Bay F8

The Astor House B&B

637 S Monroe Ave
Green Bay, WI 54301-3614
(414)432-3585
E-mail: astor@exepc.com

Rates: $79-149.
Payment: MC VISA AX DC DS.
Innkeeper(s): Doug Landwehr.
Circa: 1888.

Rooms: 5 rooms with PB, 4 with FP. 3 suites.
Beds: KQDT.

Located in the Astor Historic District, the Astor House is completely surrounded by Victorian homes. Guests have their choice of five rooms, each uniquely decorated for a range of ambiance, from the Vienna Balconies to the Marseilles Garden to the Hong Kong Retreat. The parlor, veranda and many suites feature a grand view of City Centre's lighted church towers. This home is also the first and only B&B in Green Bay and received the Mayor's Award for Remodeling and Restoration. Business travelers should take notice of the private phone lines in each room, as well as the ability to hook up a modem.

Breakfast included in rates. Type of meal: continental-plus breakfast. Air conditioning, cable TV and VCR in room. Amusement parks, antiques, fishing, parks, shopping, cross-country skiing, sporting events, theater and watersports nearby.

Hartland I7

Monches Mill House

W 301 N 9430 Hwy E
Hartland, WI 53029
(414)966-7546

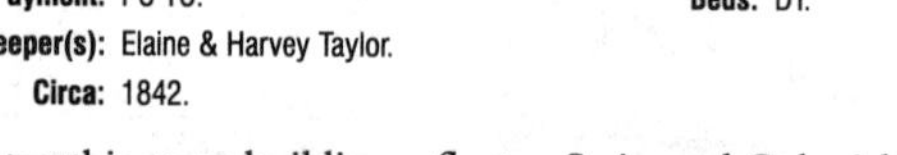

Rates: $75.
Payment: PC TC.
Innkeeper(s): Elaine & Harvey Taylor.
Circa: 1842.

Rooms: 4 rooms, 1 with PB.
Beds: DT.

This stone building reflects a Swiss and Colonial influence. Plank floors, the two-foot-thick stone walls and high ceilings create an authentic atmosphere many have tried to imitate. There is a gazebo, patio and balcony that make it easy to enjoy the millpond with its waterfall and pleasant nostalgic setting. A simple breakfast is served.

Breakfast included in rates. Type of meal: continental-plus breakfast. VCR, spa, bicycles, tennis, library and pet boarding on premises. Handicap access. Weddings, family reunions and seminars hosted. French spoken. Antiques, fishing, parks, downhill skiing, cross-country skiing, sporting events, theater and watersports nearby.

Pets Allowed.

Hudson E1

Jefferson-Day House

1109 3rd St
Hudson, WI 54016-1220
(715)386-7111

Rates: $99-169.
Payment: MC VISA AX DS PC TC.
Innkeeper(s): Tom & Sue Tyler.
Circa: 1857.

Rooms: 4 rooms with PB, 4 with FP. 1 suite.
Beds: Q.

Near the St. Croix River and 30 minutes from Mall of America, the Italianate Jefferson-Day House features guest rooms with both whirlpool tubs and gas fireplaces. Antique art and furnishings fill the rooms, and there is a formal dining room and library. Ask for the Captain's Room and you'll be rewarded with a cedar-lined bathroom, over-sized shower, antique brass bed, and a gas fireplace visible from the whirlpool tub for two. A four-course breakfast is served fireside on weekends, while continental-plus is the fare during the week.

Evening snack included in rates. Types of meals: full breakfast and gourmet breakfast. Air conditioning in room. Cable TV, VCR, spa, bicycles and library on premises. Weddings, small meetings and family reunions hosted. Amusement parks, antiques, fishing, parks, shopping, downhill skiing, cross-country skiing, sporting events, theater and watersports nearby.

Pets Allowed: Call for restrictions.

Kewaunee F8

The "Gables"

821 Dodge St
Kewaunee, WI 54216-1205
(414)388-0220

Rates: $60-75.
Payment: PC.
Innkeeper(s): Penny or Earl Dunbar.
Circa: 1883.

Rooms: 5 rooms, 1 with PB.
Beds: KQDT.

Milwaukee architect Henry Koch designed this 22-room mauve and green Queen Anne Victorian. The Windsor Room features a king-size canopy bed. Earl's garden bursts forth each spring with hundreds of daffodils, tulips and lilacs. Zelda, a Russian Blue cat, and Baron, a handsome dachshund, are the inn's mascots. Wisconsin cheeses, cherries and sausages are featured at breakfast served in the formal dining room. A secret recipe, "Cheese Cake Coffee Cake," is often served but never revealed. Penny is a dietician and teaches B&B classes. Nine miles of scenic beach start three blocks from the inn and a salmon collection station is close by.

Breakfast, afternoon tea and evening snack included in rates. Types of meals: gourmet breakfast and early coffee/tea. Turn-down service in room. Cable TV, VCR and library on premises. Small meetings and family reunions hosted. Amusement parks, antiques, fishing, parks, shopping, downhill skiing, cross-country skiing, theater and watersports nearby.

Special Discounts: We do accept state employee rates. Special rate for extended stays.

La Pointe B4

Woods Manor

Nebraska Row, PO Box 7
La Pointe, WI 54850
(715)747-3102 (800)966-3756
Fax:(715)747-2100

Rates: $89-209.
Payment: MC VISA PC.
Innkeeper(s): Nick Sellas.
Circa: 1926.

Rooms: 10 rooms with PB, 2 with FP. 1 suite. 2 cottages.
Beds: KQD.

Lake Superior's Madeline Island is home to this inn, which provides a unique setting for a romantic escape or family vacation. There are seven guest rooms in the manor and another three in the adjoining carriage house and lodge. The guest rooms vary in size and amenities, but all are comfortably appointed with antiques and family heirlooms. One of the rooms boasts a screened-in balcony with a hot tub in addition to its king bed. Guests are welcome to borrow a bicycle or canoe, or take advantage of the inn's private beach for sunbathing or swimming.

Breakfast included in rates. Type of meal: continental breakfast. VCR, fax, swimming, sauna, bicycles and library on premises. Weddings, small meetings and family reunions hosted. Antiques, fishing, parks, shopping, downhill skiing, cross-country skiing and watersports nearby.

Pets Allowed: Depends on animal & room reserved.

Lake Geneva

J7

T.C. Smith Inn B&B

865 W Main St
Lake Geneva, WI 53147
(414)248-1097 (800)423-0233
Fax:(414)248-1672

Rates: $95-350.
Payment: MC VISA AX DC DS PC TC.
Innkeeper(s): The Marks Family.
Circa: 1845.

Rooms: 8 rooms with PB, 5 with FP. 2 suites. 1 conference room.
Beds: QD.

Listed in the National Register of Historic Places, this High Victorian-style inn blends elements of Greek-Revival and Italianate architecture. The inn has massive carved wooden doors, hand-painted moldings and woodwork, a high-ceilinged foyer, an original parquet floor, Oriental carpets, museum-quality period antiques and European oil paintings. Guests may enjoy tea in the Grand Parlor by a marble fireplace or enjoy breakfast on an open veranda overlooking Lake Geneva.

Breakfast, afternoon tea and evening snack included in rates. Types of meals: full breakfast, gourmet breakfast and early coffee/tea. Room service available. Air conditioning, ceiling fan and VCR in room. Fax, copier, bicycles and child care on premises. Handicap access. Weddings, small meetings, family reunions and seminars hosted. Antiques, fishing, parks, downhill skiing, cross-country skiing, theater and watersports nearby. TAC5.

Pets Allowed: Pets allowed in specific rooms only.

Location: Forty miles from Milwaukee.

Publicity: *Keystone Country Peddler, Pioneer Press Publication.*

Special Discounts: Extended stay corporate rates.

"As much as we wanted to be on the beach, we found it impossible to leave the house. It's so beautiful and relaxing."

Lodi

I6

Victorian Treasure B&B Inn

115 Prairie St
Lodi, WI 53555-7147
(608)592-5199 (800)859-5199
Fax:(608)592-7147
E-mail: victorian@globaldialog.com

Rates: $79-169.
Payment: MC VISA PC TC.
Innkeeper(s): Todd & Kimberly Seidl.
Circa: 1893.

Rooms: 6 rooms with PB, 4 with FP. 4 suites.
Beds: Q.

Guests at Victorian Treasure stay in one of six guest rooms spread among two 19th-century Queen Anne Victorians. The interior boasts stained and leaded-glass windows, pocket doors, rich restored woods and expansive porches. Four suites include a whirlpool tub, fireplace and romantic decor with antiques. Full, gourmet breakfasts may include specialties such as eggs Florentine, an herb vegetable quiche or stuffed French toast topped with a seasonal fruit sauce.

Breakfast and evening snack included in rates. Types of meals: gourmet breakfast and early coffee/tea. Air conditioning in room. Fax, copier and library on premises. Weddings, small meetings and family reunions hosted. Antiques, parks, shopping, downhill skiing, cross-country skiing, sporting events, theater and watersports nearby. TAC10.

Publicity: *Catholic Knight, Milwaukee Sentinel, Portage Daily Register, Baraboo News Republic, Chicago Sun-Times, Wisconsin Trails, State Journal.*

Special Discounts: Weekday and corporate rates. Mention this listing for a third weeknight free in a whirlpool room. Seasonal packages.

"Wow! We have stayed in B&Bs from Maine to Virginia to California. Who would have believed we would find the best so close to home?"

Annie's Bed & Breakfast

2117 Sheridan Dr
Madison, WI 53704-3844
(608)244-2224
Fax:(608)242-9611

Rates: $74-129.
Payment: MC VISA AX.
Innkeeper(s): Anne & Larry Stuart.
Circa: 1965.

Rooms: 2 suites. 1 conference room.
Beds: KD.

This quiet, little inn is a perfect spot to get away from it all. Situated on Warner Park, with a lake close by, the home boasts a beautiful view with a romantic gazebo and butterfly gardens. Enjoy morning coffee by the terrace, before sitting down to delicious homemade breakfast in the great hall dining room, which is flanked with 18-foot-tall windows. A whirlpool tub is secluded in a special room and surrounded by plants and mirrors. The paneled library offers a wide selection of CDs and a unique Belgian woodstove.

Breakfast and evening snack included in rates. Types of meals: full breakfast and early coffee/tea. Air conditioning, ceiling fan and VCR in room. Fax, spa and library on premises. Weddings and family reunions hosted. Antiques, parks, shopping, downhill skiing, cross-country skiing, sporting events, theater and watersports nearby.

Special Discounts: Fourth week night free.

"Thank you for the immense quiet."

Arbor House, An Environmental Inn

3402 Monroe St
Madison, WI 53711-1702
(608)238-2981
Fax:(608)238-1175

Rates: $74-180.
Payment: MC VISA AX PC TC.
Innkeeper(s): John & Cathie Imes.
Circa: 1853.

Rooms: 8 rooms with PB, 2 with FP. 1 suite. 1 conference room.
Beds: Q.

Nature lovers not only will enjoy the inn's close access to a 1,280-acre nature preserve, they will appreciate the innkeepers' ecological theme. Organic sheets and towels are offered for guests as well as environmentally safe bath products. Arbor House is one of Madison's oldest existing homes and features plenty of historic features, such as romantic reading chairs and antiques, mixed with modern amenities and unique touches. The Studio Room features a skylit whirlpool tub, and the Tap Room, with its nautical theme, includes a fish tank. The innkeepers provide a computer system for business travelers. Lake Wingra is within walking distance as are biking and nature trails, bird watching and a host of other outdoor activities.

Breakfast included in rates. Types of meals: continental-plus breakfast and full breakfast. Air conditioning, ceiling fan, cable TV and VCR in room. Fax and copier on premises. Handicap access. Weddings, small meetings, family reunions and seminars hosted. Antiques, fishing, parks, shopping, cross-country skiing, sporting events and watersports nearby.

Publicity: *E.*

"What a delightful treat in the middle of Madison. Absolutely, unquestionably, the best time I spent in a hotel or otherwise. B&Bs are the only way to go! Thank you!"

Canterbury Inn

315 W Gorham at State
Madison, WI 53703
(608)258-8899 (800)838-3850

Rates: $117-290.
Payment: MC VISA PC.
Circa: 1924.

Rooms: 6 rooms with PB.

Prepare for a unique, literary experience at this unusual inn, which is dubbed a "bed, book and breakfast" by the owners. Each of the guest rooms is named for a traveler in the Canterbury Tales. Ornate stencilling and murals decorate the walls actually bringing guests into the stories. Each room is stocked with terrycloth robes, chess sets and a bookcase filled with books. The owners have won awards for the restoration of their historic building. Aside from the bed & breakfast rooms, there is a welcoming bookstore and a coffeehouse on the premises. Both the store and coffeehouse are host to many events throughout the year, including author readings, chamber music, afternoon teas, chess club meetings, readings for children and jazz ensembles.

Breakfast included in rates. Type of meal: continental breakfast. Air conditioning in room. Fax on premises.

Mansion Hill Inn

424 N Pinckney St
Madison, WI 53703-1410
(608)255-3999 (800)798-9070
Fax:(608)255-2217

Rates: $100-270.
Payment: MC VISA AX PC TC.
Innkeeper(s): Janna Wojtal.
Circa: 1858.

Rooms: 11 rooms with PB, 4 with FP. 2 suites. 1 conference room.
Beds: KQ.

The facade of this Romanesque Revival sandstone mansion boasts magnificent arched windows, Swedish railings, verandas and a belvedere. There are marble floors, ornate moldings and a magnificent mahogany and walnut staircase that winds up four stories. Lovingly restored and lavishly decorated, the inn easily rivals rooms at the Ritz for opulence. A special occasion warrants requesting the suite with the secret passageway behind a swinging bookcase.

Breakfast and evening snack included in rates. Types of meals: continental-plus breakfast and early coffee/tea. Room service available. Air conditioning, turn-down service, cable TV and VCR in room. Fax, copier and library on premises. Weddings and small meetings hosted. Fishing, parks, shopping, sporting events and theater nearby. TAC10.

Publicity: *Chicago Tribune, New York Times, Country Inns, Americana, Glamour.*

"The elegance, charm and superb services made it a delightful experience."

Oconomowoc I7

The Inn at Pine Terrace

351 E Lisbon Rd
Oconomowoc, WI 53066
(414)567-7463 (800)421-4667

Rates: $66-132.
Payment: MC VISA AX DC CB DS PC TC.
Innkeeper(s): Shirley W. Hinds & Penny A. Yakes.
Circa: 1879.

Rooms: 13 rooms with PB. 1 conference room.
Beds: T.

This inn's convenient location, midway between Madison and Milwaukee and just north of the interstate that connects them, makes it equally appealing to business travelers and those seeking a romantic retreat. Some rooms boast whirlpool tubs and visitors are welcome to use the inn's in-ground swimming pool. A conference room is available for meetings and seminars.

Breakfast included in rates. Types of meals: continental breakfast and continental-plus breakfast. Air conditioning and cable TV in room. Copier and swimming on premises. Handicap access. Weddings, small meetings, family reunions and seminars hosted. Antiques, fishing, parks, shopping, downhill skiing, cross-country skiing, sporting events, theater and watersports nearby.

Pets Allowed: Must be well behaved.

Special Discounts: November 1 through April 30 every year $65.51 second night any room.

Reedsburg H5

Parkview B&B

211 N Park St
Reedsburg, WI 53959-1652
(608)524-4333

Rates: $60-75.
Payment: MC VISA AX.
Innkeeper(s): Tom & Donna Hofmann.
Circa: 1895.

Rooms: 4 rooms, 2 with PB.
Beds: KQT.

Tantalizingly close to Baraboo and Wisconsin Dells, this central Wisconsin inn overlooks a city park in the historic district. The gracious innkeepers delight in tending to their guest's desires and offer wake-up coffee and a morning paper. The home's first owners were in the hardware business, so there are many original, unique fixtures, in addition to hardwood floors, intricate woodwork, leaded and etched windows and a suitors' window. The downtown business district is just a block away.

Breakfast included in rates. Types of meals: gourmet breakfast and early coffee/tea. Evening snack available. Air conditioning and ceiling fan in room. Cable TV on premises. Weddings hosted. Antiques, fishing, parks, shopping, skiing nearby. TAC10.

Publicity: *Reedsburg Times Press.*

Special Discounts: 25% on second night.

"Your hospitality was great! You all made us feel right at home."

Sparta G4

Just-N-Trails B&B/Nordic Ski Center

Rt 1, Box 274
Sparta, WI 54656-9729
(608)269-4522 (800)488-4521
Fax:(608)269-3280

Rates: $70-250.
Payment: MC VISA AX DS PC TC.
Innkeeper(s): Don & Donna Justin.
Circa: 1920.

Rooms: 8 rooms, 6 with PB, 3 with FP. 3 cottages. 1 conference room.
Beds: KQDT.

Nestled in a scenic valley sits this 200-acre dairy farm. Guests are welcome to share in the dairy operations and encouraged to explore the hiking and cross-country ski trails. In addition to delightfully decorated rooms in the farmhouse, there are a Scandinavian log house and plush restored granary for those desiring more privacy. The well-cared-for grounds and buildings reflect the innkeepers' pride in their home, which was built by Don's grandfather.

Breakfast included in rates. Type of meal: full breakfast. Air conditioning and ceiling fan in room. 213 acres. Weddings, small meetings, family reunions and seminars hosted. Antiques, fishing, parks, shopping, downhill skiing and cross-country skiing nearby. TAC10.

Pets Allowed: $10 per pet per day.

Location: Elroy-Sparta bike trail.

Publicity: *Milwaukee Journal, Country, Wisconsin Woman, Wisconsin Trails.*

"Everything was perfect, but our favorite part was calling in the cows."

Stevens Point F6

A Victorian Swan on Water

1716 Water St
Stevens Point, WI 54481
(715)345-0595 (800)454-9886

Rates: $55-120.
Payment: MC VISA AX DS PC TC.
Innkeeper(s): Joan Ouellette.
Circa: 1889.

Rooms: 4 rooms, 3 with PB, 1 with FP. 1 suite.
Beds: KQDT.

This Victorian is located a block and a half from the Wisconsin River. Black walnut inlays in the wood floors, crown moldings, walnut paneling and interior shutters are among the inn's architectural elements. The suite features a mural of ancient Rome, a ceiling fan, whirlpool tub, fireplace and a balcony overlooking the garden. There are antique furnishings and lace curtains. Breakfast items include rum-baked fresh pineapple and "turtle" French toast stuffed with chocolate and pecans and served with caramel sauce.

Breakfast included in rates. Types of meals: full breakfast, gourmet breakfast and early coffee/tea. Air conditioning and ceiling fan in room. Cable TV, VCR and library on premises. Weddings, small meetings, family reunions and seminars hosted. Antiques, fishing, parks, shopping, downhill skiing, cross-country skiing, sporting events, theater and watersports nearby. TAC5.

Dreams of Yesteryear B&B

1100 Brawley St
Stevens Point, WI 54481
(715)341-4525
Fax:(715)344-3047

Rates: $55-129.
Payment: MC VISA AX DS PC TC.
Innkeeper(s): Bonnie & Bill Maher.
Circa: 1901.

Rooms: 6 rooms, 4 with PB. 2 suites.
Beds: KQDT.

This elegant, three-story Queen Anne home is within walking distance of downtown, the Wisconsin River and the University of Wisconsin. The inn features golden oak woodwork, hardwood floors and leaded glass. Each guest room offers exquisite decor, the third-floor Ballroom Suite boasts a whirlpool. Gourmet breakfasts are served in the inn's formal dining room. An excellent hiking trail is just a block from the inn.

Breakfast, afternoon tea and evening snack included in rates. Types of meals: full breakfast, gourmet breakfast and early coffee/tea. Air conditioning and cable TV in room. VCR, bicycles and library on premises. Weddings, small meetings, family reunions and seminars hosted. Amusement parks, antiques, fishing, parks, shopping, downhill skiing, cross-country skiing, sporting events, theater and watersports nearby. TAC5.

Publicity: *Victorian Homes, Reach, Stevens Point Journal.*

"Something from a Hans Christian Anderson fairy tale."

48 West Oak

48 W Oak St
Sturgeon Bay, WI 54235
(414)743-4830
Fax:(414)743-9762

Rates: $90-140.
Payment: MC VISA DS PC TC.
Innkeeper(s): Jean Isaksen.
Circa: 1896.

Rooms: 2 rooms with PB, 2 with FP. 1 suite.
Beds: Q.

The decor in this Italianate inn is the proper complement to its elegant mantels and fine, carved woodwork. The Victorian furnishings include carved wood pieces, marble-topped tables and Oriental rugs. Innkeeper Henry Isaksen often passed by and admired the home as a child, and many years later, he and wife, Jean, bought it and eventually turned it into a homestay. Although breakfast is not included in the rates, one of the two suites contains a small kitchen.

Air conditioning, cable TV and VCR in room. Fax and copier on premises. Antiques, fishing, parks, shopping, cross-country skiing, theater and watersports nearby.

"This was truly the luxurious, romantic hideaway that was promised."

The Inn at Cedar Crossing

336 Louisiana St
Sturgeon Bay, WI 54235
(414)743-4200
Fax:(414)743-4422

Rates: $85-145.
Payment: MC VISA DS PC TC.
Innkeeper(s): Terry Wulf.
Circa: 1884.

Rooms: 9 rooms with PB, 6 with FP.
Beds: KQ.

This historic hotel, in the National Register, is a downtown two-story brick building that once housed street-level shops with second-floor apartments for the tailors, shopkeepers and pharmacists who worked below. The upstairs, now guest rooms, is decorated with floral wallpapers, stenciling and antiques. The Anniversary Room has a mahogany bed, fireplace and whirlpool tub. The Victorian Era dining room and pub, both with fireplaces, are on the lower level. The waterfront is three blocks away.

Breakfast and evening snack included in rates. Types of meals: continental breakfast, continental-plus breakfast, full breakfast, gourmet breakfast and early coffee/tea. Dinner, picnic lunch, lunch, gourmet lunch, catering service, catered breakfast and room service available. Air conditioning, cable TV and VCR in room. Fax, copier and library on premises. Small meetings hosted. Antiques, fishing, parks, shopping, downhill skiing, cross-country skiing, theater and watersports nearby.

Publicity: *New Month, Milwaukee Sentinel, Chicago Sun-Times, Country Inns, Bon Appetit, Gourmet, Green Bay Press Gazette, Midwest Living, Milwaukee Journal.*

Special Discounts: Special dinner packages November-April, Sunday through Thursday.

"The second year stay at the inn was even better than the first. I couldn't have found a more romantic place."

Scofield House B&B

908 Michigan St
Sturgeon Bay, WI 54235
(414)743-7727 (888)463-0204
Fax:(414)743-7727

Rates: $93-195.
Payment: PC TC.
Innkeeper(s): Bill & Fran Cecil.
Circa: 1902.

Rooms: 6 rooms with PB, 5 with FP. 3 cottages.
Beds: Q.

Mayor Herbert Scofield, prominent locally in the lumber and hardware business, built this late-Victorian house with a sturdy square tower and inlaid floors that feature intricate borders patterned in cherry, birch, maple, walnut, and red and white oak. Oak moldings throughout the house boast raised designs of bows, ribbons, swags and flowers. Equally lavish decor is featured in the guest rooms with fluffy flowered comforters and cabbage rose wallpapers highlighting romantic antique bedsteads. Door County cherry muffins are a house specialty. Modern amenities include many suites with fireplaces and double whirlpools. "Room at the Top" is a skylit 900-square-foot suite occupying the whole third floor and furnished with Victorian antiques.

Breakfast and afternoon tea included in rates. Type of meal: gourmet breakfast. Air conditioning, ceiling fan, cable TV and VCR in room. Fax and copier on premises. Amusement parks, antiques, fishing, parks, shopping, downhill skiing, cross-country skiing, sporting events, theater and watersports nearby.

Publicity: *Innsider, Glamour, Country, Wisconsin Trails, Green Bay Press Gazette, Chicago Tribune, Milwaukee Sentinel-Journal, Midwest Living, Victorian Decorating & Lifestyle, Country Inns, National Geographic Traveler.*

"You've introduced us to the fabulous world of B&Bs. I loved the porch swing and would have been content on it for the entire weekend."

Viroqua — H4

Viroqua Heritage Inn B&B's

217 & 220 E Jefferson St
Viroqua, WI 54665
(608)637-3306

Rates: $50-80.
Payment: MC VISA DS PC TC.
Innkeeper(s): Nancy Rhodes.
Circa: 1890.

Rooms: 9 rooms, 5 with PB, 1 with FP. 1 suite.
Beds: KQD.

The three-story turret of this gabled Queen Anne mansion houses the sitting rooms of a guest chamber and the formal first-floor parlor. Columns, spindles and assorted gingerbread spice the exterior, while beveled glass, ornate fireplaces and crystal chandeliers grace the interior. An antique baby grand piano and Victrola reside in the music room. Breakfast is served on the original carved-oak buffet and dining table, on the balcony or front porch.

Breakfast included in rates. Types of meals: full breakfast and early coffee/tea. Air conditioning in room. VCR, bicycles, library and child care on premises. Weddings, small meetings, family reunions and seminars hosted. Some Spanish spoken. Antiques, fishing, parks, shopping, downhill skiing, cross-country skiing, theater and watersports nearby. TAC10.

Publicity: *Milwaukee Magazine, Lax.*

"Wonderful house, great hosts."

White Lake — E7

Jesse's Wolf River Lodge

N 2119 Taylor Rd
White Lake, WI 54491
(715)882-2182

Rates: $80-150.
Payment: MC VISA PC.
Innkeeper(s): Joan Jesse.
Circa: 1929.

Rooms: 8 rooms, 4 with PB. 3 cottages.
Beds: QDT.

This rustic Northwoods lodge is made to order for outdoor-lovers. White-water river rafting, trout fishing, cross-country skiing and hiking are just a few of the available activities. Hearty homemade fare dominates the menu; crepes suzette, frozen Eskimo jam and American fried potatoes are among the breakfast favorites. Indians, French traders and loggers once populated the area, which now sports the clean, clear Wolf River as its prime attraction.

Breakfast included in rates. Types of meals: full breakfast and early coffee/tea. Dinner and picnic lunch available. Ceiling fan in room. Cable TV, VCR, fax, copier, spa, swimming, bicycles and library on premises. 12 acres. Weddings, small meetings, family reunions and seminars hosted. Antiques, fishing, parks, shopping, downhill skiing, cross-country skiing and watersports nearby. TAC10.

Pets Allowed: Advance approval.

Publicity: *New York Times, Better Homes and Gardens, Chicago Tribune, Milwaukee Journal.*

Special Discounts: 50% off third night.

"Thank you for your time, service, smiles and good food."

Whitewater I7

Victoria-On-Main B&B

622 W Main St
Whitewater, WI 53190-1855
(414)473-8400

Rates: $65-75.
Payment: MC VISA.
Innkeeper(s): Nancy Wendt.
Circa: 1895.

Rooms: 3 rooms, 1 with PB, 1 with FP.
Beds: D.

This Queen Anne Victorian is located in the heart of Whitewater National Historic District, adjacent to the University of Wisconsin. It was built for Edward Engebretson, mayor of Whitewater. Each guest room is named for a Wisconsin hardwood. The Red Oak Room, Cherry Room and Bird's Eye Maple Room all feature antiques, Laura Ashley prints and down comforters. A hearty breakfast is served and there are kitchen facilities available for light meal preparation. Whitewater Lake and Kettle Moraine State Forest are five minutes away.

Breakfast included in rates. Types of meals: full breakfast and early coffee/tea. Ceiling fan in room. Cable TV on premises. Antiques, fishing, parks, shopping, cross-country skiing, theater and watersports nearby.

Location: Between Madison and Milwaukee.

"We loved it. Wonderful hospitality."

Wisconsin Dells H5

Historic Bennett House

825 Oak St
Wisconsin Dells, WI 53965
(608)254-2500

Rates: $70-90.
Payment: PC TC.
Innkeeper(s): Gail & Rich Obermeyer.
Circa: 1863.

Rooms: 3 rooms, 1 with PB. 1 suite.
Beds: QD.

This handsomely restored Greek Revival-style home, framed by a white picket fence, housed the Henry Bennetts, whose family still operates the Bennett photographic studio, the oldest continuously operating studio in the country. Noted for the first stop-action photography, Mr. Bennett's work is displayed in the Smithsonian. The National Register home is decorated in European and Victorian styles. The grounds are decorated with sun and shade gardens.

Breakfast included in rates. Types of meals: gourmet breakfast and early coffee/tea. Air conditioning, ceiling fan, cable TV and VCR in room. Library on premises. Amusement parks, antiques, parks, shopping, theater and watersports nearby.

Publicity: *Midwest Living, Travel & Leisure, Country Life.*

"We have told everyone of your little paradise and we hope to visit again very soon."

Terrace Hill B&B

922 River Rd
Wisconsin Dells, WI 53965
(608)253-9363

Rates: $45-110.
Payment: PC TC.
Innkeeper(s): Len, Cookie, Lenard & Lynn Novak.
Circa: 1900.

Rooms: 4 rooms, 3 with PB. 1 suite.
Beds: Q.

With a park bordering one edge and the Wisconsin River just across the street, Terrace Hill guests are treated to pleasant surroundings both inside and out. The interior is a cheerful mix of Victorian and country decor. The Park View suite includes a canopy bed and a clawfoot tub, other rooms offer views and cozy surroundings. There are barbecue grills and picnic tables available for guest use. The inn is just a block and a half from downtown Wisconsin Dells.

Breakfast, afternoon tea and evening snack included in rates. Types of meals: full breakfast and early coffee/tea. Air conditioning in room. Cable TV, VCR and library on premises. Small meetings, family reunions and seminars hosted. Amusement parks, antiques, fishing, parks, shopping, downhill skiing, cross-country skiing, theater and watersports nearby.

Thunder Valley B&B Inn

W15344 Waubeek Rd
Wisconsin Dells, WI 53965
(608)254-4145

Rates: $45-80.
Payment: MC VISA PC.
Innkeeper(s): Anita, Kari & Sigrid Nelson.
Circa: 1870.

Rooms: 11 rooms with PB. 1 suite. 1 cottage.
Beds: KQDT.

As the area is full of both Scandinavian and Native American heritage, the innkeeper of this country inn has tried to honor the traditions. Chief Yellow Thunder, for whom this inn is named, often camped out on the grounds and surrounding area. The inn's restaurant is highly acclaimed. Everything is fresh, the innkeepers grind the wheat for the morning pancakes and rolls. There is a good selection of Wisconsin beers and wine, as well. Guests can stay in the farmhouse, which offers a microwave and refrigerator for guest use, or spend the night in one of two cottages. The Guest Hus features gable ceilings and a knotty pine interior. The Wee Hus, is a smaller unit, but includes a refrigerator.

Breakfast included in rates. Types of meals: full breakfast and early coffee/tea. Picnic lunch and room service available. Air conditioning, ceiling fan and VCR in room. Bicycles on premises. Handicap access. 25 acres. Weddings, small meetings, family reunions and seminars hosted. Norwegian spoken. Amusement parks, antiques, fishing, parks, shopping, downhill skiing, cross-country skiing and watersports nearby.

Publicity: *Wisconsin Trails, Country Inns, Midwest Living, Chicago Sun-Times.*

Rosemary-Cheese Bran Muffins

Ann Starrett Mansion
Port Townsend, Wash.

- 1 cup bran cereal
- 1¼ cup buttermilk
- 1 egg
- ¼ cooking oil
- ½ cup all-purpose flour
- ¼ cup sugar
- ½ t baking powder
- ½ t baking soda
- ½ t salt (optional)
- 1 cup grated cheddar cheese
- 2 t rosemary

Preheat oven to 400 degrees. Combine cereal and buttermilk in a small bowl. Beat egg until frothy, then stir in cereal mixture and oil.

Combine remaining ingredients in a large bowl. Make a well in the center and pour batter into the well.

Stir until moist, batter will be lumpy.

Fill a greased muffin pan with the batter. Bake for 20 to 25 minutes.

Makes 12 to 16 muffins.

Wyoming

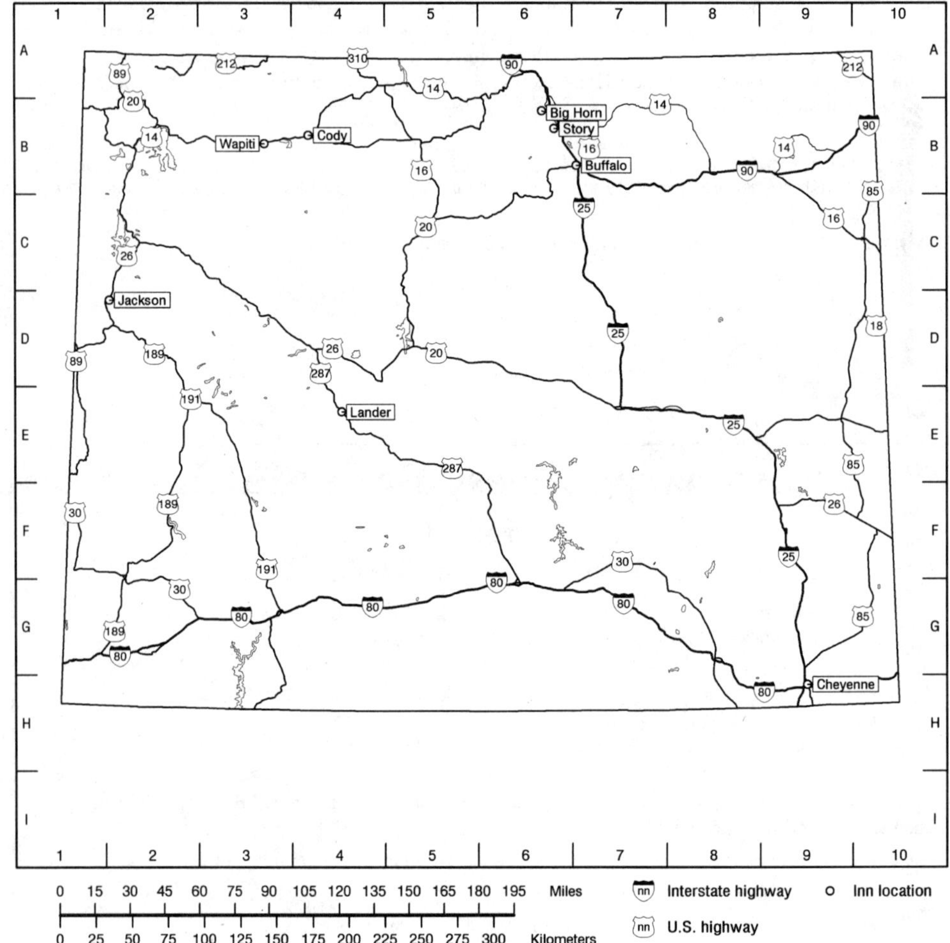

Big Horn
Story
Buffalo
Wapiti
Cody
Jackson
Lander
Cheyenne
0 15 30 45 60 75 90 105 120 135 150 165 180 195 Miles
0 25 50 75 100 125 150 175 200 225 250 275 300 Kilometers
Interstate highway
U.S. highway
Inn location

Big Horn

B6

Spahn's Bighorn Mountain B&B, LLC

70 Upper Hwy, PO Box 579
Big Horn, WY 82833-0579
(307)674-8150
E-mail: spahnbb@wave.sheridan.wy.us

Rates: $65-120.
Payment: MC VISA PC TC.
Innkeeper(s): Ron & Bobbie Spahn.
Circa: 1986.

Rooms: 4 rooms, 2 with PB, 1 with FP. 2 cottages. 1 conference room.
Beds: Q.

This towering log home and cabins sit high on the mountainside overlooking the Sheridan Valley and featuring a 100-mile view. Deer, turkey and moose roam the 40 acres and occasionally a bear or mountain lion can be spotted. Guests can make use of the three-story living room with open fire, library, piano and outside deck. Ron Spahn is a geologist and former Yellowstone Park Ranger. Cookouts and wildlife tours can be done by prior arrangement. Cabins are a five-minute walk through the forest from the Main Lodge.

Breakfast included in rates. Types of meals: full breakfast and early coffee/tea. Dinner and picnic lunch available. Cable TV, VCR, copier and child care on premises. Handicap access. 40 acres. Small meetings, family reunions and seminars hosted. Antiques, fishing, parks and cross-country skiing nearby.

Buffalo

B7

Cloud Peak Inn

590 N Burritt Ave
Buffalo, WY 82834-1610
(307)684-5794 (800)715-5794
Fax:(307)684-7653

Rates: $45-75.
Payment: MC VISA AX PC TC.
Innkeeper(s): Rick & Kathy Brus.
Circa: 1906.

Rooms: 5 rooms, 3 with PB. 1 conference room.
Beds: Beds: KQDT.

Built at the turn of the century by a wealthy rancher, this inn features a graceful staircase, elegant parlor and spacious bedrooms. At the end of the day, guests can relax in front of the "fossilized" fireplace, soak in the Jacuzzi or unwind on the porch or balcony. Arrangements can be made for dinner although there are some excellent restaurants in the area. A fine golf course is only two blocks from the inn. The innkeepers will tell you about the secret fishing spots in the mountains that are sure bets. Geologic tours of the area can be arranged with prior notice.

Breakfast and evening snack included in rates. Types of meals: full breakfast, gourmet breakfast and early coffee/tea. Banquet service and catering service available. Ceiling fan in room. Cable TV, VCR, fax, copier, spa and library on premises. Weddings, small meetings, family reunions and seminars hosted. Amusement parks, antiques, fishing, parks, shopping, downhill skiing, cross-country skiing and watersports nearby. TAC15.

Publicity: *Billings Gazette, Sheridan Press, Los Angeles Times.*

Cheyenne

H9

A. Drummonds Ranch B&B

399 Happy Jack Rd, Hwy 210
Cheyenne, WY 82007
(307)634-6042
Fax:(307)634-6042

Rates: $60-150.
Payment: MC VISA PC TC.
Innkeeper(s): Taydie Drummond.
Circa: 1990.

Rooms: 4 rooms, 2 with PB, 1 with FP. 1 suite.
Beds: QDT.

With 120 acres of Wyoming wilderness and a nearby National Forest and State Park, this Old English farmhouse offers a quiet retreat. Two hot tubs on private decks provide views of the surrounding area and for evening soakers, an unmatched night sky. Boarding is available for those traveling with horses and

pets. A. Drummonds Ranch is located half way between Cheyenne and Laramie.

Breakfast, afternoon tea and evening snack included in rates. Types of meals: full breakfast, gourmet breakfast and early coffee/tea. Dinner, picnic lunch and lunch available. Turn-down service in room. VCR, fax, copier, sauna, bicycles, library, pet boarding and child care on premises. 120 acres. Small meetings and family reunions hosted. French spoken. Fishing, parks, cross-country skiing, sporting events, theater and watersports nearby. TAC10.

Pets Allowed: Pets must be kenneled in our facilities.

Special Discounts: Stay two nights, third night 25% discount.

Cody B4

Parson's Pillow B&B

1202 14th St
Cody, WY 82414-3720
(307)587-2382 (800)377-2348

Rates: $75-85.
Payment: MC VISA PC TC.
Innkeeper(s): Lee & Eleanor Larabee.
Circa: 1902.

Rooms: 4 rooms with PB.
Beds: Q.

This historic building originally served as the Methodist-Episcopal Church. Surrounded by a picket fence and a flower-filled garden, it features a bell tower complete with the original bell donated by a cousin of Buffalo Bill. A baby grand piano sits in the parlor, once the meeting room. Guest rooms feature antiques and quilts. Early breakfasts and box lunches are available for hunters and fishermen. The Buffalo Bill Historical Center and the Cody Historic Walking Tour are nearby.

Breakfast and evening snack included in rates. Types of meals: full breakfast, gourmet breakfast and early coffee/tea. Turn-down service and ceiling fan in room. Cable TV, VCR and library on premises. Weddings, small meetings and family reunions hosted. Antiques, fishing, parks, shopping, downhill skiing and cross-country skiing nearby. TAC10.

Location: Northwest Wyoming in Cody off Hwy 14, 16 20 & 120.

Jackson D2

H.C. Richards B&B

160 W Deloney
Jackson, WY 83001
(307)733-6704
Fax:(307)733-0930
E-mail: 102173.3657@compuserve.com

Rates: $81-97.
Payment: MC VISA PC TC.
Innkeeper(s): Jackie Williams.
Circa: 1969.

Rooms: 3 rooms with PB.
Beds: QD.

Many afternoons at this ranch-style stone home are filled with the smells of baking scones, eccles cakes, crumpets or other special items from the large kitchen. Located just one-and-a-half blocks west of the town square, the inn is within walking distance to many museums, art galleries, restaurants, theaters and shops. A tennis court, basketball court and park are just out the back door and skiing is a short six blocks away. The area is a paradise for outdoor enthusiasts, as the Grand Teton and Yellowstone national parks are nearby.

Breakfast and afternoon tea included in rates. Types of meals: full breakfast, gourmet breakfast and early coffee/tea. Room service available. Turn-down service and cable TV in room. VCR and fax on premises. Antiques, fishing, parks, shopping, downhill skiing, cross-country skiing, theater and watersports nearby. TAC10.

Pets Allowed.

Rusty Parrot Lodge

175 N Jackson, PO Box 1657
Jackson, WY 83001
(307)733-2000 (800)458-2004
Fax:(307)733-5566

Rates: $98-450.
Payment: MC VISA AX DC CB DS PC.
Innkeeper(s): Ron Harrison.
Circa: 1991.

Rooms: 32 rooms with PB. 1 suite.
Beds: Q.

This four-diamond, four-star lodge is tucked in the picturesque town of Jackson Hole, just minutes from ski slopes. Rooms are beautifully appointed in a Southwestern style, and beds are topped with wool blankets and down comforters. The inn's great room offers a massive stone fireplace and plenty of comfortable places to sit and relax after a day of skiing, fly fishing or river rafting. Breakfasts are served up in "Jackson" style, which translates to homemade, hearty and delicious.

Breakfast included in rates. Types of meals: full breakfast and early coffee/tea. Cable TV in room. Antiques, fishing, downhill skiing, cross-country skiing, theater and watersports nearby.

"Perfection is not often experienced, but that is truly what we felt every day we were there."

Sassy Moose Inn

HC 362, Teton Village Rd
Jackson, WY 83001
(307)733-1277 (800)356-1277
Fax:(307)739-0793
E-mail: ckelley@wyoming.com

Rates: $109-154.
Payment: MC VISA AX DS.
Innkeeper(s): Polly Englant.
Circa: 1992.

Rooms: 5 rooms with PB.
Beds: KQT.

All of the rooms at this log-house-style inn have spectacular Teton views. The Mountain Room has a rock fireplace, queen bed and mountain cabin decor. The River Room's decor is dominated by the colors of the Snake River and accented with antiques. The inn is five minutes from Teton Village and the Jackson Hole Ski Resort. Teton Pines Golf Course and Nordic Trails are just across the road. After a day of activities, enjoy sharing your experiences over tea or relaxing in the large hot tub.

Breakfast included in rates. Types of meals: full breakfast and early coffee/tea. Afternoon tea available. Cable TV, VCR, fax, copier, spa, pet boarding and child care on premises. Weddings and family reunions hosted. Fishing, parks, shopping, downhill skiing, cross-country skiing, theater and watersports nearby. TAC10.

Pets Allowed.

Special Discounts: "Rent-The-Inn" all rooms, winter, 10% off.

Lander — E4

Blue Spruce Inn

677 S 3rd St
Lander, WY 82520-3707
(307)332-8253

Rates: $75.
Payment: MC VISA DS PC TC.
Innkeeper(s): Marvin & JoAnne Brown.
Circa: 1920.

Rooms: 4 rooms with PB.
Beds: QT.

Two blue spruce trees mark this 5,000-square-foot Arts and Crafts influenced house. Original chandeliers, stained glass, oak crown molding and woodwork add to the house's appeal. Mission-style furnishings are in keeping with the house's period. Views of the mountains may be seen from the second-floor rooms. Ask for the Spotted Elk Room for a Native American-themed accommodation. There is a sun porch and front porch, and a block away is a mountain trout stream.

Breakfast included in rates. Types of meals: full breakfast and early coffee/tea. Cable TV, VCR, bicycles and library on premises. Weddings, small meetings and family reunions hosted. Limited German spoken. Antiques, fishing, parks, shopping and cross-country skiing nearby.

Special Discounts: Three or more nights - $10 off per night.

Story

B6

Piney Creek Inn B&B

11 Skylark Ln, PO Box 456
Story, WY 82842
(307)683-2911

Rates: $50-95. MAP.
Payment: PC TC.
Innkeeper(s): Vicky Hoff.
Circa: 1956.

Rooms: 4 rooms, 2 with PB. 1 cottage.
Beds: KQDT.

There's an abundance of wildlife on the property of this secluded log-house-style inn nestled in the Big Horn Mountains. For the Old West buff, historic sites that are only minutes away include Fort Phil Kearny, Bozeman Trail, Little Big Horn Battlefield, numerous Indian battle sites and museums and galleries. Ranch experiences and trail ride packages are favorites. At the end of the day, relax on the deck or in the common area, where visitors will find a television, books, magazines and games. Guests also can relax by the campfire for conversation and viewing the stars. Historical tours, ranch adventures and trail-ride packages are available.

Breakfast and evening snack included in rates. Types of meals: continental breakfast, full breakfast and early coffee/tea. Dinner, picnic lunch and lunch available. MAP. Ceiling fan in room. Cable TV, VCR, spa and library on premises. Handicap access. Weddings, small meetings and family reunions hosted. Antiques, fishing, shopping and theater nearby.

Special Discounts: Two day special Nov. 1-May 15, $85-$155, subject to change.

Wapiti

B3

Elephant Head Lodge

1170 Yellowstone Hwy
Wapiti, WY 82450
(307)587-3980
Fax:(307)527-7922

Rates: $52-82. MAP, AP.
Payment: MC VISA AX DS PC TC.
Innkeeper(s): Phil & Joan Lamb.
Circa: 1910.

Rooms: 11 cottages with PB, 1 with FP.
Beds: QDT.

Buffalo Bill Cody's niece and her husband built the rustic main lodge using pine trees found on the property. The lodge gets its unusual name from a nearby rock formation. In addition to the main lodge, the five-acre grounds include 10 historic cabins, each with comfortable, Early American furnishings. The pioneer-style cabins include private baths and are stocked with towels, sheets and blankets. The lodge's restaurant serves breakfast, lunch and dinner. Guests may choose the American Plan rates if they wish to enjoy all three. The lodge is located just 11 miles outside of Yellowstone National Park.

Type of meal: full breakfast. Dinner and lunch available. MAP, AP. Ceiling fan in room. Cable TV, VCR, fax, copier, stables, library, pet boarding and child care on premises. Weddings, small meetings, family reunions and seminars hosted. German spoken. Antiques, fishing, parks, shopping and watersports nearby. TAC10.

Pets Allowed.

U.S. Territories

PUERTO RICO

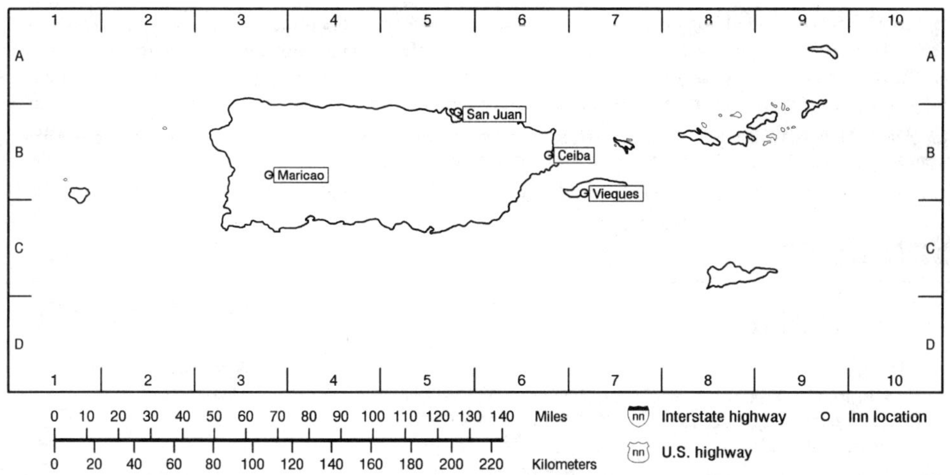

Ceiba **B6**

Ceiba Country Inn

PO Box 1067
Ceiba, PR 00735-1067
(809)885-0471
Fax:(809)885-0471

Rates: $60.
Innkeeper(s): Nicki Treat.

Rooms: 9 rooms.

A large Spanish patio is available at this tropical country inn perched on rolling, green hills. Situated 500 feet above the valley floor, the inn affords a view of the ocean with the isle of Culebra on the horizon. A continental buffet is served in the warm and sunny breakfast room. The inn is four miles from Puerto Del Rey, the largest marina in the Caribbean, and 10 miles from Luquillo Beach, which is a mile of white sand, dotted with coconut palms.

Breakfast included in rates. Type of meal: continental-plus breakfast. Air conditioning in room. 13 acres. Weddings, small meetings, family reunions and seminars hosted.

Maricao

B3

Parador La Hacienda Juanita

Road 105, PO Box 777
Maricao, PR 00606
(809)838-2550 (800)981-7575
Fax:(809)838-2551
E-mail: juanita@caribe.net

Rates: $72. MAP, EP.
Payment: MC VISA AX TC.
Innkeeper(s): Victoria E. Martinez Rivera.
Circa: 1976.

Rooms: 22 rooms, 21 with PB. 1 conference room.
Beds: KDT.

This hacienda-style building once served as the main lodge for a coffee plantation. There are 24 acres situated 1600 feet above sea level in the mountains. Antique coffee-making implements decorate the lobby and bunches of bananas usually hang from the ceiling of the veranda. Breakfast usually includes grapefruit, oranges and guavas grown on the farm. The Rain Forest Reserve and Maricao Fish Hatchery are five miles away.

Type of meal: full breakfast. Dinner, lunch, catering service and catered breakfast available. MAP, EP. Ceiling fan in room. Fax and copier on premises. Handicap access. 24 acres. Weddings, small meetings, family reunions and seminars hosted.

". . .This is the most beautiful place I've ever seen. We fell in love with your hacienda and Maricao and want to live there."

San Juan

B5

El Canario Inn

1317 Ashford Ave
San Juan, PR 00907
(787)722-3861 (800)533-2649
Fax:(787)722-0391

Rates: $70-100.
Payment: MC VISA AX DC DS.
Innkeeper(s): Jude & Keith Olson.
Circa: 1938.

Rooms: 25 rooms with PB.
Beds: Beds: DT.

This three-story inn is only a block from San Juan's glorious white-sand beaches. Rooms are decorated in a tropical theme with rattan and wicker furnishings and Bermuda ceiling fans. Relax on one of the patios or in the Jacuzzi. The inn is a charming escape from the multitude of high rise hotels along the coast. Casinos and discotheques are nearby, and sightseeing tours and boating trips can be arranged at the hotel.

Breakfast included in rates. Types of meals: continental-plus breakfast and early coffee/tea. Air conditioning, ceiling fan and cable TV in room. Fax on premises. Fishing, parks, shopping and watersports nearby. TAC10.

Publicity: *USA Today, Conde Naste Traveler.*

Vieques

B7

New Dawn Caribbean Retreat

PO Box 1512
Vieques, PR 00765-1512
(787)741-0495

Rates: $50.
Payment: PC TC.
Innkeeper(s): Gail Burchard.
Circa: 1986.

Rooms: 6 rooms. 2 cottages. 1 conference room.
Beds: Beds: QDT.

This retreat is located on secluded Vieques Island, just off Puerto Rico's coast. The modern, tropical main house was built by women taking part in carpentry courses. This rustic getaway was designed for those who enjoy the outdoors. There are six, simply furnished rooms. Those on a tight budget can bring along a tent or rent a spot in the bunkhouse. The grounds offer swings and hammocks, and guests can take in a game of volleyball, go horseback riding, take an exercise class or perhaps a relaxing nature walk. This is a female-centered retreat, but all are welcome.

Type of meal: early coffee/tea. Dinner, picnic lunch and catering service available. Ceiling fan in room. VCR, bicycles and library on premises. Handicap access. Weddings, small meetings, family reunions and seminars hosted. Limited Spanish spoken. Fishing and watersports nearby.

Special Discounts: $1,100 per week for all six guest rooms, May 15-Dec. 14.

Canada

ALBERTA

Banff

Pension Tannenhof

121 Cave Ave
Banff, AB T0L 0C0
(403)762-4636
Fax:(403)762-5660

Rates: $75-135.
Payment: TC.
Innkeeper(s): Herbert & Fannye Riedinger.
Circa: 1943.

Rooms: 10 rooms, 7 with PB, 3 with FP.
Beds: QDT.

This English country-style inn was built in the early 1940s. Parts of the home, including the inn's huge outdoor barbecue area, are made from petrified dinosaur bones. Aside from this unique feature, guests also enjoy beautiful views of the Rockies. Guest rooms are spacious and comfortably furnished. Three rooms include a fireplace. Skiing, hiking, fishing, and horseback riding are among the many nearby activities. The Cave and Basin Hot Springs are within walking distance.

Breakfast included in rates. Type of meal: full breakfast. Cable TV in room. Fax and sauna on premises. Weddings, small meetings and family reunions hosted. German, Spanish and French spoken. Fishing, parks, shopping, downhill skiing and cross-country skiing nearby.

Special Discounts: Only in low season.

BRITISH COLUMBIA

Mayne Island

Oceanwood Country Inn

630 Dinner Bay Road
Mayne Island, BC V0N 2J0
(604)539-5074
Fax:(604)539-3002

Rates: $120-295.
Payment: MC VISA TC.
Circa: 1970.

Rooms: 12 rooms with PB, 8 with FP. 1 conference room.
Beds: QT.

This Tudor-style home, located on one of British Columbia's Gulf Islands, is surrounded by 10 wooded acres and overlooks Navy Channel. The waterfront setting is a perfect catalyst for romance. There are 12 guest rooms to choose from, including the cozy Daffodil with a skylit bathroom or the posh Wisteria Suite, located in the inn's newer wing. The suite includes two private decks, one outfitted with a soaking tub. There is a sunken living room with a fireplace. Guests are pampered with a full breakfast and afternoon tea. Breakfast choices include a variety of juices, baked goods, homemade granola, yogurt, cereals and a daily entree. Dinners at the inn feature fresh ingredients and original Pacific Northwest creations. A prix-fixe menu might include chilled Roma tomato soup with pesto and avocado cream fraiche, an appetizer of roasted romaine heart with smoked salmon vinaigrette, and an entree of curried duck breast or pan-fried rainbow trout. A caramelized frozen cherry souffle finishes off this menu. Mayne Island offers fishing, boating, beaches, a museum, historic lighthouse, restaurants, shops and galleries.

Breakfast and afternoon tea included in rates. Types of meals: full breakfast and early coffee/tea. Fax, spa, swimming, sauna, bicycles and library on premises. 10 acres. Weddings, small meetings, family reunions and seminars hosted. French spoken. Fishing, parks and shopping nearby. TAC10.

North Vancouver

Sue's Victorian Guesthouse

152 E 3rd
North Vancouver,
BC V7L 1E6
(604)985-1523

Rates: $60-75.
Payment: TC.
Innkeeper(s): Gail Fowler & Jen Lowe.
Circa: 1904.

Rooms: 3 rooms, 1 with PB.
Beds: KQDT.

This turn-of-the-century home has seen more than 4,000 guests in its 10-plus years as a bed & breakfast. The home has been restored, maintaining its veranda and original staircases. Rooms are decorated with antiques, and baths have antique soaking tubs. There is a guest kitchen, and inngoers can make their own breakfast, or select from a number of local eateries.

Type of meal: early coffee/tea. Ceiling fan, cable TV and VCR in room. Amusement parks, antiques, fishing, parks, shopping, downhill skiing, cross-country skiing, sporting events, theater and watersports nearby.

Special Discounts: Seventh day free.

Peachland

Peach House B&B

4768A McLaughlin Pl
Peachland, BC V0H 1X0
(604)767-6546 (800)449-4133
Fax:(604)767-6546

Rates: $55-95.
Payment: TC.
Innkeeper(s): Debra & Pauline Stepanow.
Circa: 1972.

Rooms: 3 rooms with PB. 1 suite.
Beds: KQDT.

The Peach House is not just named so because of its Peachland location, but also the hue that decorates the exterior of the modern, ranch-style home. Each of the three guest rooms features an international theme, including English, Mexican and Egyptian. The breakfast menu varies and is always creative, with items such as whole wheat peach pancakes or the unusual Chinese eggs. Guests also enjoy a lake view from the home, which is close to wineries, beaches, skiing and golf.

Breakfast included in rates. Types of meals: full breakfast, gourmet breakfast and early coffee/tea. Turn-down service and ceiling fan in room. Cable TV, VCR and fax on premises. Limited Spanish spoken. Amusement parks, fishing, parks, shopping, downhill skiing, cross-country skiing and watersports nearby.

Special Discounts: 30% off May 1-Oct. 30, Sunday-Friday.

Salt Spring Island

Cranberry Ridge B&B

269 Don Ore Dr
Salt Spring Island,
BC V8K 2H5
(250)537-4854 (888)537-4854
Fax:(604)537-4243

Rates: $100-150.
Payment: MC VISA TC.
Innkeeper(s): Gloria Callison Lutz.
Circa: 1990.

Rooms: 3 rooms with PB, 1 with FP.
Beds: KQ.

With a panoramic view of islands, mountains and the water, many guests don't ever want to leave Cranberry Ridge. Spacious bed chambers are tastefully decorated and two have a Jacuzzi tub. The Twig Room, includes a fireplace in its sitting area; all three rooms have a private deck with a view and include locally made fine furnishings or a collection of wicker. Guests can enjoy the beautiful view from the outdoor hot tub. Coffee and juice is waiting outside your door about an hour prior to the morning meal, which is served in a dining area with a stunning view. Homemade muffins and fresh fruit are followed by a main dish such as Smoked Salmon Eggs Benedict.

Breakfast and afternoon tea included in rates. Types of meals: full breakfast, gourmet breakfast and early coffee/tea. Spa on premises. Antiques, fishing, parks, shopping, theater and watersports nearby.

Weston Lake Inn

813 Beaver Point Rd
Salt Spring Island,
BC V8K 1X9
(250)653-4311

Rates: $100-125.
Payment: MC VISA PC TC.
Innkeeper(s): Susan Evans & Ted Harrison.
Circa: 1976.

Rooms: 3 rooms with PB.
Beds: QT.

This inn is nestled on 10 acres of grounds, dotted with flowering trees and shrubs, overlooking Weston Lake. Beds are dressed with cozy, down quilts. The lounge, where a fire is often crackling, is a good spot for relaxation, and there's a hot tub, as well. Homegrown, organic produce is used to create the inn's mouthwatering breakfasts, which feature such items as fresh baked goods, berries picked on the grounds and specialty entrees.

Breakfast included in rates. Types of meals: gourmet breakfast and early coffee/tea. Afternoon tea and catered breakfast available. Ceiling fan in room. VCR, spa and library on premises. 10 acres. Small meetings, family reunions and seminars hosted. French and English spoken. Antiques, fishing, parks, shopping, theater and watersports nearby. TAC10.

Pets Allowed: Well behaved outdoor dogs.

Special Discounts: 5% to 10% for stays of seven days or more.

Sooke

Ocean Wilderness Country Inn

109 W Coast Rd, RR 2
Sooke, BC V0S 1N0
(250)646-2116 (800)323-2116
E-mail: lbj.@islandnet.com

Rates: $85-175.
Payment: MC VISA TC.
Innkeeper(s): Marion J. Rolston.
Circa: 1940.

Rooms: 9 rooms with PB.
Beds: KQT.

The hot tub of this log house inn is in a Japanese gazebo overlooking the ocean. Reserve your time for a private soak, and terry bathrobes are supplied. The innkeepers are pleased to prepare picnic lunches and arrange fishing charters, nature walks and beachcombing. Guests can enjoy wonderful seafood cookouts on Ocean Wilderness beach. Coffee is delivered to your room a half hour before breakfast is served. Rooms include antiques, sitting areas and canopy beds. Two of the rooms have hot tubs for two with spectacular ocean and Olympic Mountain views.

Breakfast included in rates. Types of meals: full breakfast and early coffee/tea. Picnic lunch and catered breakfast available. Fax and copier on premises. Handicap access. Weddings, small meetings, family reunions and seminars hosted. Amusement parks, antiques, fishing, parks, shopping and theater nearby. TAC10.

Pets Allowed: By arrangement.

Publicity: *Puget Sound Business Journal, Getaways from Vancouver.*

Special Discounts: Two nights for the price of one.

"Thank you for the most wonderful hospitality and accommodations of our entire vacation."

Sooke Harbour House Inn

1528 Whiffen Spit Rd
Sooke, BC V0S 1N0
(604)642-3421 (800)889-9688
Fax:(604)642-6988
E-mail: shh@islandnet.com

Rates: $225-295.
Payment: MC VISA AX DC TC.
Innkeeper(s): Frederique & Sinclair Philip.
Circa: 1929.

Rooms: 14 rooms, 13 with PB, 13 with FP. 1 cottage.
Beds: KQ.

The spectacular ocean views from each of the guest rooms at this farmhouse-style inn are set off by extensive flower and herb gardens and the Olympic Mountains. Ask for the Victor Newman Longhouse Room for a four-poster king-size bed, skylight, wet bar, bathtub for two overlooking an ocean view and a see-through fireplace. Each room boasts a private deck or spa. The inn's evening cuisine, proclaimed by various travel and food writers as "one of the best in British Colombia," or the "best in Canada," features locally grown produce and fresh fish and shellfish taken from local waters. There's a Japanese and French influence in the offerings. If you can tear yourself away from the captivating views and excellent meals, the innkeepers will arrange whale-watching cruises or guided nature tours.

Breakfast included in rates. Types of meals: continental breakfast and full breakfast. Picnic lunch, lunch, banquet service and room service available. Cable TV and VCR in room. Fax, copier and child care on premises. Handicap access. Weddings, small meetings, family reunions and seminars hosted. Antiques, fishing, parks, shopping and watersports nearby. TAC10.

Pets Allowed: $20.00 per day per pet.

Vancouver

Columbia Cottage

205 14th Ave W
Vancouver, BC V5Y 1X2
(604)874-5327
Fax:(604)879-2128

Rates: $80-165.
Payment: MC VISA TC.
Innkeeper(s): Susanne Salzberger & Alisdair Smith.
Circa: 1929.

Rooms: 5 rooms with PB. 1 suite.
Beds: KQDT.

This cheerful cottage is surrounded by lush gardens and is located a few minutes from downtown Vancouver. There are a few antiques here and there, and there are feather beds in the guest rooms. The suite offers a private entrance, sitting room, and the French doors in the suite's kitchen open onto the back garden and pond. The full breakfasts include such items as freshly baked scones, fresh fruit and perhaps savory basted eggs with sausages.

Breakfast included in rates. Type of meal: full breakfast. Cable TV in room. Fax and pet boarding on premises. Weddings hosted. German spoken. Antiques, parks, shopping, sporting events and theater nearby. TAC10.

Johnson Heritage House

2278 W. 34th Ave.
Vancouver, BC V6M 1G6
(604)266-4175
Fax:(604)266-4175

Rates: $70-145.
Payment: PC TC.
Innkeeper(s): Sandy & Ron Johnson.
Circa: 1920.

Rooms: 4 rooms, 2 with PB. 1 suite.
Beds: KQDT.

One of the first things guests will notice as they enter this Craftsman-style home is the ornamentation, including ornate, restored woodwork. Different patterns and a variety of woods have been used in the moldings, walls, floors and staircase. There is a pressed tin ceiling decorating the kitchen. Country antiques, Oriental rugs and collectibles also fill the whimsical interior. Brass beds, canopy beds, quilts and carousel horses are among the items guests might discover in their rooms. The suite is especially impressive and romantic with a natural wood, cathedral ceiling, canopy bed, sitting area with a loveseat, mountain views and a bathroom with a Jacuzzi tub. The grounds are decorated with gardens, and the quiet neighborhood is within walking distance of small parks, shops, city bus lines and restaurants. The University of British Columbia, Queen Elizabeth Park and the Van Dusen Gardens are nearby.

Breakfast included in rates. Type of meal: full breakfast. Ceiling fan and cable TV in some rooms. VCR, fax and library on premises. Small meetings hosted. Some French spoken. Amusement parks, antiques, fishing, parks, shopping, downhill skiing, cross-country skiing, sporting events, theater and watersports nearby. TAC10.

"We thoroughly enjoyed our four nights at your beautiful home."

Kenya Court Ocean Front Guest House

2230 Cornwall Ave
Vancouver, BC V6K 1B5
(604)738-7085

Rates: $85-100.
Payment: PC TC.
Innkeeper(s): Dr. & Mrs. H. Williams.
Circa: 1927.

Rooms: 7 rooms with PB, 4 with FP. 5 suites.
Beds: KQT.

Enjoy a piping hot cup of fresh, gourmet coffee as you gaze out over the ocean at this scenic bed & breakfast. Innkeeper Dorothy Mae Williams not only provides a delectable spread of fresh breads, croissants, cereals and fruits, she serves it in a rooftop solarium. Williams, who is in charge of the piano department at Vancouver Academy, will serenade guests with piano concerts on some days. Roomy suites feature antiques, separate entrances and boast ocean views. The home is within walking distance to the Granville Market, the planetarium and 10 minutes from the University of British Columbia. The athletically inclined will enjoy the use of tennis courts, walking and jogging trails and a heated outdoor saltwater pool across the street.

Breakfast included in rates. Types of meals: gourmet breakfast and early coffee/tea. Cable TV in room. VCR on premises. Weddings and family reunions hosted. Italian, French and German spoken. Antiques, fishing, parks, shopping, downhill skiing, cross-country skiing, sporting events, theater and watersports nearby.

Publicity: *Washington Times, Rocky Mountain News.*

"Beautiful home and enjoyed unsurpassed hospitality."

The Inn at Manor Guest House

345 W 13th Ave
Vancouver, BC V5Y 1W2
(604)876-8494
Fax:(604)876-5763

Rates: $65-160.
Payment: MC VISA TC.
Innkeeper(s): Brenda Yablon.
Circa: 1902.

Rooms: 10 rooms, 6 with PB, 1 with FP. 1 suite. 1 conference room.
Beds: KQDT.

This turn-of-the-century Edwardian still features many original elements, including carved banisters, polished wood floors and ornate wainscoting. The home is one of the city's oldest. The innkeeper has decorated the home with a collection of English antiques. The penthouse suite, which includes a bedroom, loft, deck and kitchen, boasts a view of the city. Fresh fruits, home-baked breads and specialties such as a cheese and mushroom souffle or blueberry cobbler highlight the breakfast menu.

Types of meals: full breakfast and gourmet breakfast. Cable TV in room. VCR, fax and copier on premises. Weddings, small meetings, family reunions and seminars hosted. French and German spoken. Antiques, parks, shopping, downhill skiing, sporting events, theater and watersports nearby. TAC10.

The West End Guest House

1362 Haro St
Vancouver, BC V6E 1G2
(604)681-2889
Fax:(604)688-8812

Rates: $115-210.
Payment: MC VISA AX DS.
Innkeeper(s): Evan Penner.
Circa: 1906.

Rooms: 8 rooms with PB, 2 with FP.
Beds: DT.

Among the hustle and bustle of Vancouver sits this charming, pink Victorian, which transports its guests out of the modern metropolis and back to the turn-of-the-century days. The gracious home used to house a family of musicians and photographers. Innkeeper Evan Penner has preserved their past placing lithographs and historical photos owned by the family throughout the house. Each of the rooms is individually decorated with glorious prints and beautiful antiques. The guest rooms are cozy and welcoming, the perfect place to snuggle down after a long day and sink into brass beds decked in fine linens and down comforters. Guests will enjoy relaxing on the second-story deck or strolling past the many plants and flowers in the back garden. A gourmet, country-style breakfast is served each morning, and homemade chocolates await guests as they arrive.

Breakfast included in rates. Type of meal: full breakfast. Room service available. Turn-down service, ceiling fan and cable TV in room. Small meetings hosted. Some French spoken. Amusement parks, antiques, fishing, shopping, downhill skiing, cross-country skiing, sporting events, theater and watersports nearby. TAC10.

Publicity: *New York Times, Province News.*

"Quiet, comfort, convenience, homey, delicious food and good conversations with other guests. I will do nothing but sing the praises of B&Bs from now on, and I'm sure we will meet again."

Victoria

Abigail's Hotel

906 McClure St
Victoria, BC V8V 3E7
(250)388-5363 (800)561-6565
Fax:(250)388-7787
E-mail: behune@islandnet.com

Rates: $79-199.
Payment: MC VISA AX TC.
Innkeeper(s): Daniel & Franke Behune.
Circa: 1930.

Rooms: 16 rooms with PB, 8 with FP.
Beds: KQD.

Abigail's, a Tudor-style hotel, boasts three gabled stories, stained-glass windows, crystal chandeliers and tasteful decor. Afternoon snacks are offered in the library, also a popular area for small weddings. Rooms feature a variety of amenities such as canopied beds, fireplaces, Jacuzzi baths and antiques. Smoked salmon omelets, or tomato, jack cheese, and avocado omelets are served with corn and asparagus fritters, salsa and apple sausage at breakfast.

Breakfast, afternoon tea and evening snack included in rates. Types of meals: full breakfast, gourmet breakfast and early coffee/tea. Fax, copier and library on premises. Weddings, small meetings, family reunions and seminars hosted. German spoken. Antiques, fishing, parks, shopping, theater and watersports nearby. TAC10.

Cordova Beach B&B

5137 Cordova Bay Rd
Victoria, BC V8Y 2K1
(604)658-5955

Rates: $50-110.
Payment: TC.
Innkeeper(s): Gary & Oleen Bowles.
Circa: 1976.

Rooms: 3 rooms with PB.
Beds: Q.

This ocean front homestay is built on land that slopes down to a sandy beach. The house offers views of the Haro Straits, San Juan Islands and Mount Baker. Comfortable guest rooms offer sounds of the ocean and in the morning, the aroma of home-baked scones, fresh coffee and sometimes eggs Benedict. Guests enjoy walking along the beach and enjoying the area's parks, restaurants and hiking, as well as nearby Victoria and Butchart Gardens.

Breakfast included in rates. Types of meals: full breakfast and early coffee/tea. Ceiling fan and cable TV in room. VCR on premises. Fishing, parks, shopping, sporting events and theater nearby. TAC10.

"We shall never forget the hospitality, the fabulous breakfast and the general warm feeling we received."

CAN

Dashwood Seaside Manor

Number One Cook St
Victoria, BC V8V 3W6
(604)385-5517 (800)667-5517
Fax:(604)383-1760
E-mail: reservations@dashwoodmanor.com

Rates: $75-285.
Payment: MC VISA AX DC.
Innkeeper(s): Derek Dashwood Family.
Circa: 1912.

Rooms: 14 suites.
Beds: Q.

Dashwood Manor is an Edwardian Tudor Revival mansion with a rare oceanfront location. Choose between a first-floor suite with a fireplace, chandelier and beamed ceilings, a second-story "special occasion" unit or a top-floor suite for spectacular balcony views of the ocean and the Olympic Mountains. Some units include a Jacuzzi tub. To reach downtown Victoria, take a short walk through the park.

Breakfast included in rates. Type of meal: full breakfast. Cable TV in room. Antiques, fishing, shopping and theater nearby.

Pets Allowed: Small pets with kennel.

Location: Next to world famous Beacon Hill Park.

Publicity: *San Francisco Chronicle.*

"Enchanting, very soothing."

Gregory's Guest House

5373 Patricia Bay Hwy
Victoria, BC V8Y 1S9
(250)658-8404
Fax:(250)658-4604

Rates: $55-80.
Payment: MC VISA PC TC.
Innkeeper(s): Paul & Elizabeth Gregory.
Circa: 1919.

Rooms: 3 rooms, 2 with PB.
Beds: DT.

The two acres of this historic hobby farm are just across the street from Elk Lake, six miles from Victoria near Butchart Gardens. All the rooms are decorated in antiques and lace, and they feature garden views. Lake activities include swimming, canoeing and waterskiing. A country breakfast is served. There is a veranda for guest use.

Breakfast included in rates. Type of meal: full breakfast. Fax and library on premises. Amusement parks, antiques, fishing, parks, shopping, sporting events, theater and watersports nearby. TAC10.

Location: On the east side of the highway, across from Elk Lake.

"Our family felt very welcome, loved the house and especially liked the super breakfasts."

Lilac House Victorian B&B

252 Memorial Crescent
Victoria, BC V8S 3J2
(250)389-0252

Rates: $60-85.
Payment: MC VISA TC.
Innkeeper(s): Gail Harris.
Circa: 1892.

Rooms: 3 rooms.
Beds: QD.

Located in a charming neighborhood and overlooking Moss Rocks and Ross Bay Cemetery, this restored Victorian is a wonderful way to enjoy Victoria and the Victorian Era. Rooms are decorated with antiques, wicker and original watercolors. Canadian breakfasts are served in the Pre-Raphaelite dining room. Innkeeper and poet Gail Harris is a native of Victoria and can direct guests to many interesting activities. The area boasts a variety of outdoor activities, and Lilac House affords close access to the ocean. Shopping and fine dining are nearby. Non-smoking facility.

Breakfast included in rates. Type of meal: continental-plus breakfast. Antiques, fishing, parks, shopping, theater and watersports nearby. TAC10.

Special Discounts: 10% off for stay of three or more days duration.

"Thanks for your warm hospitality. We enjoyed our stay in this old and beautiful house."

Sonia's B&B By The Sea

175 Bushby St
Victoria, BC V8S 1B5
(604)385-2700 (800)667-4489

Rates: $65-75.
Payment: TC.
Innkeeper(s): Sonia & Brian McMillan.

Rooms: 3 rooms with PB.
Beds: KQ.

A walk of about 100 yards will take guests to the shore, and this bed & breakfast offers views of the Straits of Juan de Fuca. Guests also enjoy views of the Olympic Mountains and Victoria. Both innkeepers are Vancouver Island natives (Sonia was born in Victoria), and they are happy to provide a map detailing some little-known treasures of the area. Their Tudor-style home offers three comfortable guest rooms. Breakfasts are served in a formal dining room with tables set with English china and Lennox glasswear. The bed & breakfast is open from the beginning of March until Sept. 30.

Breakfast included in rates. Shopping and watersports nearby.

Pets Allowed.

Wellington B&B

66 Wellington Ave
Victoria, BC V8V 4H5
(250)383-5976
Fax:(250)383-5976

Rates: $70-130.
Payment: MC TC.
Innkeeper(s): Inge Ranzinger.
Circa: 1912.

Rooms: 4 rooms with PB, 2 with FP. 1 suite.
Beds: KQT.

Less than one block from the ocean, this Folk Victorian inn is quiet, yet close to all the downtown activities. A nearby promenade boasts an incredible panoramic view of the ocean and Olympic Mountains. The inn is just minutes away from Beacon Hill Park and is within easy walking distance of shopping, restaurants and outdoor activities.

Breakfast included in rates. Types of meals: full breakfast and early coffee/tea. Room service available. Fax and library on premises. German spoken. Antiques, fishing, parks, shopping, theater and watersports nearby. TAC10.

"Thank you once again for an outstanding stay at Wellington."

West Vancouver

Palms Guest House

3042 Marine Dr
West Vancouver,
BC V7V 1M4
(604)926-1159 (800)691-4455
Fax:(604)926-1451

Rates: $110-225. EP.
Payment: MC VISA AX TC.
Innkeeper(s): Heidi Schmidt.
Circa: 1994.

Rooms: 4 rooms, 3 with PB, 1 with FP. 1 suite.
Beds: KQT.

This contemporary mansion offers a stunning view of the Pacific. Guest rooms are done in a mix of modern and Classical styles, with antiques. Rooms are posh, but still comfortable enough for relaxation, and each has a private balcony. Down duvets and fine linens are offered. The home's Master Suite includes walls textured with deep green fabrics, a king-size canopy bed, fireplace and a Jacuzzi tub. Freshly squeezed orange juice, piping hot croissants and a fresh fruit plate starts off the gourmet breakfast service, which might include an entree such as gravelox with dill eggs. The home is within walking distance of the beach, the Seawall, shops and eateries.

Breakfast and afternoon tea included in rates. Types of meals: full breakfast, gourmet breakfast and early coffee/tea. Room service available. EP. Air conditioning and cable TV in room. VCR, fax and library on premises. Weddings, small meetings and family reunions hosted. Spanish and German spoken. Amusement parks, antiques, fishing, parks, shopping, downhill skiing, cross-country skiing, sporting events, theater and watersports nearby. TAC10.

Whistler

Golden Dreams B&B

6412 Easy St
Whistler, BC V0N 1B6
(604)932-2667 (800)668-7055
Fax:(604)932-7055
E-mail: golden@whistler.net

Rates: $65-105.
Payment: MC VISA.
Innkeeper(s): Ann & Terry Spence.
Circa: 1986.

Rooms: 3 rooms, 1 with PB. 2 suites.
Beds: QD.

This private homestay boasts hearty vegetarian breakfasts that include homemade jam. The Victorian, Oriental and Aztec guest rooms feature duvets, sherry and slippers. Enjoy views of the mountains and the herb and flower gardens. There is a private Jacuzzi and a fireside family room, as well as a full guest kitchen. The home is a mile from ski lifts.

Breakfast included in rates. Type of meal: gourmet breakfast. Catered breakfast available. Ceiling fan in room. Cable TV, VCR, spa, bicycles, library and child care on premises. Weddings, small meetings and family reunions hosted. Fishing, parks, downhill skiing, cross-country skiing, sporting events and watersports nearby.

"Great house, great food, terrific people."

NOVA SCOTIA

Middleton

Fairfield Farm Inn

10 Main St
Middleton, NS B0S 1P0
(902)825-6989 (800)237-9896
Fax:(902)825-6989

Rates: $50-65.
Payment: MC VISA AX DC DS TC.
Innkeeper(s): Richard & Shae Griffith.
Circa: 1886.

Rooms: 5 rooms with PB. 1 conference room.
Beds: KQD.

Nova Scotia's picturesque Annapolis Valley create the peaceful surroundings at this country Victorian farmhouse. The home is located on a 110-acre spread bordered by the Annapolis River, and there are walking trails to enjoy. Guest rooms feature period antiques, as do the common areas. There is a library, parlor and solarium, as well as a guest kitchen. Guests check off breakfast selections the night before from a list that includes seasonal fruit, cereals, toast, homemade jam, eggs and beverages. A historic church, a museum, galleries, shops and restaurants all are within walking distance, and a short drive will take you to the Bay of Fundy.

Breakfast included in rates. Types of meals: full breakfast and early coffee/tea. Picnic lunch and catering service available. Air conditioning and ceiling fan in room. Cable TV, VCR, fax, copier and library on premises. 110 acres. Weddings, small meetings, family reunions and seminars hosted. French spoken. Amusement parks, antiques, fishing, parks, shopping, cross-country skiing, sporting events, theater and watersports nearby. TAC10.

Special Discounts: Government rates $54.00 and $59.

ONTARIO

Cobourg

The Victoria Inn

PO Box 180
Cobourg, ON K0K 2E0
(905)342-3261 (888)221-1131
Fax:(905)342-2798
E-mail: victorianinn@eagle.c

Rates: $80-100. MAP.
Payment: MC VISA.
Innkeeper(s): Donna & Donald Cane.
Circa: 1902.

Rooms: 9 rooms with PB, 3 with FP. 1 conference room.
Beds: QD.

This three-story inn is an architectural combination of Art Nouveau and Mission styles. Aside from the beauty of the house itself, which features turrets and stained-glass windows, the most spectacular feature is the view. Tucked just off the waters' edge, the inn boasts panoramic vistas of islands and Rice Lake. A famed

Canadian portrait painter, Gerald S. Hayward, designed this home as his summer residence. Guest rooms are well appointed, and some quarters can accommodate up to six people. Some rooms offer lake views and three have a fireplace. One room is located in the inn's turret, with a remarkable wood ceiling. Guests enjoy both breakfast and dinner, made from locally produced meats, fish and vegetables. To top it off, cuisine is served in a dining room with a view of the lake and islands. Guests can opt for vegetarian items, and those with food allergies can be accommodated.

Breakfast and dinner included in rates. Types of meals: full breakfast and early coffee/tea. Afternoon tea, evening snack, picnic lunch, lunch, banquet service, catering service, catered breakfast and room service available. MAP. Ceiling fan in room. VCR, fax and library on premises. Weddings, small meetings, family reunions and seminars hosted. Antiques, fishing, parks, shopping, cross-country skiing, theater and watersports nearby.

Pets Allowed.

Elora

Cedarbrook Farm B&B

RR 2
Elora, ON N0B 1S0
(519)843-3481

Rates: $50.
Innkeeper(s): M.I. Elste.
Circa: 1876.

Rooms: 2 rooms.

A 100-acre working farm surrounds this simple stone farm house where guests enjoy eating breakfast overlooking fields of cattle and Arabian horses. A stream and trails on the property may be explored or visit the nearby Mennonite communities of Elmira and St. Jacobs. The town of Elora and the Elora Gorge are a few minutes away. Select a full or continental breakfast or choose a vegetarian repast.

Breakfast included in rates. Types of meals: continental breakfast and full breakfast.

"Very comfortable house, lovely countryside, thank you for all of your hospitality."

Nottawa

Pretty River Valley Country Inn

RR 1
Nottawa, ON L0M IP0
(705)445-7598
Fax:(705)445-7598

Rates: $78-120.
Payment: MC VISA AX TC.
Innkeeper(s): Steve & Diane Szelestowski.
Circa: 1980.

Rooms: 8 rooms with PB, 8 with FP. 2 suites. 1 conference room.
Beds: QT.

Each of the guest rooms at this log inn includes a fireplace, and suites have the added amenity of a double whirlpool tub. The secluded, 120-acre estate offers views of the Pretty River Valley as well as the Blue Mountains. The innkeepers provide an ample breakfast, highlighted by items such as eggs Benedict. A collection of menus from local restaurants is kept on hand. Each season brings outdoor fun. Downhill and cross-country skiing, water sports on the bay and golfing are nearby, and there are plenty of antique shops to explore.

Breakfast included in rates. Type of meal: full breakfast. Air conditioning in room. Fax and spa on premises. 120 acres. Small meetings and family reunions hosted. Antiques, fishing, parks, shopping, downhill skiing, cross-country skiing and watersports nearby. TAC10.

Ottawa

Auberge McGee's Inn

185 Daly Ave
Ottawa, ON K1N 6E8
(613)237-6089 (800)262-4337
Fax:(613)237-6201

Rates: $58-150.
Payment: MC VISA.
Innkeeper(s): Anne Schutte & Mary Unger.
Circa: 1886.

Rooms: 14 rooms, 10 with PB, 2 with FP. 2 suites. 1 conference room.
Beds: KQDT.

The portico of this restored Victorian mansion is reminiscent of the McGee's Irish roots featuring pillars that were common in Dublin architecture. The home was built for John McGee, Canada's first Clerk of the Privy Council. Rooms are comfortable and decorated in soft, pleasing colors. Amenities such as stocked mini-bars and mounted hair dryers add a touch of modern convenience. For extended stays, the inn provides the use of laundry facilities and a guest kitchenette. The innkeepers celebrate ten plus years of Award Winning Hospitality. Business travelers will appreciate items such as computer modems and in-room phones with voice mail. There is no end to what guests can see and do in Ottawa. Visit the Byward Market, the many museums or 230-store Rideau center.

CAN

Breakfast included in rates. Type of meal: full breakfast. Air conditioning and cable TV in room. Fax on premises. Small meetings and family reunions hosted. Spanish, French and English spoken. Antiques, parks, shopping, downhill skiing, cross-country skiing, sporting events, theater and watersports nearby.

Publicity: *Country Inns, Ottawa Citizen, LaPressee, Ottawa.*

Special Discounts: Please inquire.

"All we could ask for."

Rideau View Inn

177 Frank St
Ottawa, ON K2P 0X4
(613)236-9309 (800)658-3564
Fax:(613)237-6842
E-mail: af540@freenet.carlton.ca

Rates: $65-80. AP.
Payment: MC VISA AX DC TC.
Innkeeper(s): George Hartsgrove, Richard Brouse & Charles Young.
Circa: 1907.

Rooms: 7 rooms, 2 with PB, 1 with FP.
Beds: QDT.

This large Edwardian home is located on a quiet residential street near the Rideau Canal. A hearty breakfast is served in the dining room. Guests are encouraged to relax in front of the fireplace in the living room.

Breakfast included in rates. Type of meal: full breakfast. AP. Air conditioning in room. Cable TV, VCR, fax and copier on premises. Small meetings and family reunions hosted. French and Spanish spoken. Antiques, parks, shopping, downhill skiing, cross-country skiing, sporting events and theater nearby. TAC10.

Location: In the center of Ottawa.

Publicity: *Ottawa Citizen.*

Special Discounts: 15-40% off nightly rate for extended stays over seven nights.

Rockport

Houseboat Amaryllis Inn

Rockport, ON K0E 1V0
(613)659-3513

Rates: $75-120.
Payment: PC.
Innkeeper(s): Pieter & Karin Bergen.
Circa: 1921.

Rooms: 4 rooms with PB. 1 suite. 1 conference room.
Beds: QDT.

Originally built as a private hunting and fishing lodge to float around the St. Lawrence and Rideau Rivers, this docked houseboat is double-decked, 100-feet long and located on its own island of 7.5 acres. Situated in the middle of 1,000 Islands, the houseboat has a large veranda deck, living room with fireplace and a dining room overlooking the water and forested shores. The atmosphere and decor are a blend of traditional and contemporary design, unique to the St. Lawrence and island area. The hosts offer tours of the area by bicycle, sailboat, walking or rowing.

Breakfast included in rates. Type of meal: full breakfast. Swimming and library on premises. Weddings, small meetings, family reunions and seminars hosted. French, German, Spanish and Estonian spoken. Amusement parks, antiques, fishing, parks, shopping, theater and watersports nearby.

Publicity: *Canadian Living, Whig Standard.*

"Beautiful houseboat. Exclusive and peaceful. Very clean. Great view and perfect atmosphere. The best nature getaway!"

St. Jacobs

Jakobstettel Guest House, Inc.

16 Isabella St
St. Jacobs, ON N0B 2N0
(519)664-2208
Fax:(519)664-1326

Rates: $105-150.
Payment: MC VISA AX PC.
Innkeeper(s): Ella Brubacher.
Circa: 1898.

Rooms: 12 rooms with PB. 1 conference room.
Beds: QT.

Coffee is always on at this Victorian inn, and guests also will find cookies in the cookie jar, juice in the fridge and a selection of teas. Common rooms include a library, game room and breakfast nook. Some of the guest rooms have a sitting room tucked into an alcove, a porch or stained-glass windows. The inn, with its five acres of trees and rose garden, is nestled in a quiet street. Around the corner, attractions include a wooded walking trail, specialty shopping in the village, restaurants, farmer's market and cultural attractions.

Breakfast, afternoon tea, evening snack and picnic lunch included in rates. Types of meals: continental-plus breakfast and early coffee/tea. Catering service available. Air conditioning in room. Cable TV, fax and bicycles on premises. Weddings, small meetings, family reunions and seminars hosted. Antiques, fishing, parks, shopping, cross-country skiing, sporting events and theater nearby.

PRINCE EDWARD ISLAND

Charlottetown

Anne's Ocean View Haven B&B Inn

Box 2044, Kinloch Rd
Charlottetown, PE C1A 7N7
(902)569-4644 (800)665-4644
Fax:(902)569-4456

Rates: $70-120.
Payment: TC.
Innkeeper(s): R. Anne Olson.
Circa: 1986.

Rooms: 5 rooms with PB. 1 suite.
Beds: KQDT.

Situated in a countryside setting with a panoramic view of Northumberland strait, this B&B offers quiet surroundings while being close to downtown. With both traditional and modern decor, the inn's guest rooms have sitting areas, refrigerators and four-piece baths. The island boasts beautiful, white sandy beaches and fertile red fields of potatoes. The beauty of the island attracts photographers from around the world and the many summer festivals provide much to do.

Breakfast and picnic lunch included in rates. Type of meal: full breakfast. Dinner available. Turn-down service, cable TV and VCR in room. Fax, copier and child care on premises. Handicap access. Family reunions hosted. Amusement parks, fishing, parks, shopping, cross-country skiing, sporting events, theater and watersports nearby.

Pets Allowed: Trained.

Special Discounts: Call for off season rates.

QUEBEC

Montreal

Auberge De La Fontaine

1301 E Rachel St
Montreal, PQ H2J 2K1
(514)597-0166 (800)597-0597
Fax:(514)597-0496

Rates: $99-175. EP.
Payment: MC VISA AX DC TC.
Innkeeper(s): Jean LaMothe & Celine Boudreau.
Circa: 1910.

Rooms: 21 rooms with PB. 3 suites. 1 conference room.
Beds: QDT.

Accommodations at this historic stone Victorian are the piece de resistance. The award-winning inn offers individually decorated, sound-proofed rooms, all in a modern style. Some rooms have exposed brick walls, sitting area, a terrace or a balcony, and the three suites include a whirlpool. Guests have access to the kitchen, where they can find a snack. Continental breakfast is served each morning. Breads, muffins, cereals, cheeses, cold cuts, yogurt and fresh fruit fill the buffet in the inn's dining room. The staff is happy to help guests find their way to attractions in Montreal, and parking at the inn is free.

Breakfast and evening snack included in rates. Type of meal: continental-plus breakfast. EP. Air conditioning and cable TV in room. VCR, fax and copier on premises. Handicap access. 80 acres. Small meetings hosted. French and English spoken. Amusement parks, antiques, fishing, parks, shopping, cross-country skiing, sporting events, theater and watersports nearby. TAC10.

B&B Apts Downtown Montreal

3523 Jeanne-Mance
Montreal, PQ H2X 2K2
(514)845-0431

Rates: $65-70.
Payment: MC VISA AX.
Innkeeper(s): Bruno Bernard.
Circa: 1885.

Rooms: 3 rooms.
Beds: Q.

The name of this lodging establishment explains the situation perfectly. Guests can stay either in bed & breakfast rooms in a renovated Victorian townhouse or apartments, all located in downtown Montreal. The apartments, located in easy walking distance from the bed & breakfast, range from one to three bedrooms and include an equipped kitchen. The decor is pleasing and comfortable, with hardwood floors and an eclectic mix of furnishings, both modern and older. The metro station is just a block away, as are shops. Restaurants, museums and the convention center all are a few minutes away.

Breakfast included in rates. Type of meal: full breakfast. Cable TV in room. Swimming and sauna on premises. French spoken. Amusement parks, parks, shopping and sporting events nearby. TAC10.

North Hatley

Cedar Gables

Box 355, 4080 Magog Rd
North Hatley, PQ J0B 2C0
(819)842-4120

Rates: $80-104.
Payment: MC VISA AX PC TC.
Innkeeper(s): Ann & Don Fleischer.
Circa: 1896.

Rooms: 5 rooms with PB, 1 with FP. 1 suite.
Beds: K.

Bordering Lake Massiwippi, this gabled home boasts a wooded country setting. The inn's dock, canoes, and rowboat are available to guests. Some bedrooms have lake views. Breakfast is served out on the veranda, weather permitting. The village is a five-minute walk from the inn.

Breakfast and afternoon tea included in rates. Types of meals: continental-plus breakfast, gourmet breakfast and early coffee/tea. Catered breakfast available. Cable TV and VCR in room. Swimming and library on premises. Handicap access. Weddings, small meetings and family reunions hosted. English & some French spoken. Antiques, fishing, parks, downhill skiing, cross-country skiing, sporting events, theater and watersports nearby. TAC10.

Pets Allowed.

Location: At lakeside on Lake Massiwippi in Quebec's eastern townships, 100 miles east of Montreal, 20 miles north of the Vermont-Quebec border.

Publicity: *Montreal Gazette.*

"We felt comfortable and at home the minute we stepped in the door."

Manoir Hovey

575 Hovey Rd, PO Box 60
North Hatley, PQ J0B 2C0
(819)842-2421 (800)661-2421
Fax:(819)842-2248
E-mail: stafford@multi-medias.ca

Rates: $145-305. MAP.
Payment: MC VISA AX DC TC.
Innkeeper(s): Steve & Kathy Stafford.
Circa: 1900.

Rooms: 40 rooms with PB. 2 cottages. 1 conference room.
Beds: KQDT.

This four-diamond inn combines posh decor and fine cuisine all on a spectacular 25-acre, lakefront resort. Built at the turn of the century, the manor was fashioned after George Washington's Mount Vernon. Guests enjoy the scents from an English garden as they wind their way down to the lakefront, where paddle-boats, kayaks, windsurfers and canoes all await. Rates include all of these activities plus use of bikes, an exercise room, a heated pool, the beach and tennis courts. Breakfast and dinner also are included, and guests enjoy haute French cuisine. Enchanting guest rooms are decorated in English country style, and serve as a perfect setting for romance.

Breakfast and dinner included in rates. Types of meals: continental breakfast, full breakfast, gourmet breakfast and early coffee/tea. Afternoon tea, picnic lunch, lunch and room service available. MAP. Air conditioning, turn-down service, ceiling fan and cable TV in room. VCR, fax, copier, swimming, bicycles, tennis and library on premises. 25 acres. Weddings, small meetings, family reunions and seminars hosted. French and English spoken. Antiques, fishing, parks, shopping, cross-country skiing, sporting events, theater and watersports nearby. TAC10.

Additional Accommodations

The following directory contains the names, cities, states and phone numbers of approximately 13,000 bed & breakfasts, country inns and additional accommodations. Every attempt has been made to be as comprehensive and as accurate as possible — however, changes are to be expected. This directory of extra inns is presented for informational purposes and is offered without warranty of any kind.

Although there are many fine inns in this list, being included does not constitute a recommendation. We suggest that if you are interested in making reservations with any of these properties that you contact them requesting brochures and rate sheets.

Alabama

Arab
Stamps Inn B&B .... (205)586-7038

Boaz
Boaz Bed & Breakfast Whitman-Hunt House .... (205)593-8031

Bon Secour
Bon Secour Inn .... (334)949-6656

Citronelle
Citronella B&B Inn .... (205)866-2849

Decatur
Dancy-Polk House .... (205)353-3579
Hearts & Treasures B&B .... (205)353-9562

Eufaula
Kendall Manor .... (334)687-8847
St. Mary's B&B .... (334)687-7195

Fairhope
Away at The Bay .... (205)928-9725
Bay Breeze Guest House ...... (334)928-8976
Church Street Inn Bed & Breakfast .... (334)928-5144
Cottages of Fairhope .... (334)990-8211
Doc & Dawn's Garden Cottage B&B .... (205)928-0253
Green House Bed & Breakfast ... (334)928-4567
The Guest House .... (334)928-6226
Touch of Class B & B .... (334)928-7499
Villa Whimsy .... (334)928-0226

Florence
Cypress Inn .... (205)760-1131
Wood Avenue Inn .... (205)766-8441

Foley
Avery Acres .... (334)943-7098

Geneva
Live Oaks Bed & Breakfast ..... (334)684-2489

Guntersville
Lake Guntersville Bed & Breakfast .... (205)505-0133

Huntsville
Dogwood Manor Bed & Breakfast .... (205)859-3946
Wandlers Inn B&B .... (205)837-6694

Lacey's Spring
Apple Jack's Inn B&B .... (205)778-7734

Loxley
Europa-Inn .... (334)964-4000

Mobile
Bradbury Inn .... (205)343-9345
Malaga Inn .... (334)438-4701
Pine Flat Plantation B&B .... (205)476-6143
Stickney's Hollow .... (205)456-4556

Montgomery
B&B Montgomery .... (205)263-1727
Colonel's Rest-East Fork Farms .. (334)215-0380
Lattice Inn Bed & Breakfast ..... (334)832-9931

Nauvoo
Old Harbin Hotel Bed & Breakfast .... (205)697-5652

Opelika
Heritage House .... (334)705-0485

Prattville
The Plantation House .... (334)361-0442

Samson
Jola Bama Guest House .... (205)898-2478

Talladega
Historic Oakwood B&B .... (205)362-0662

Troy
House of Dunns .... (334)566-9414

Valley Head
Woodhaven .... (205)635-6438

Alaska

Anchor Point
Anchor River B&B and Cabins ... (907)235-7141
Backwoods Bed & Breakfast .... (907)235-8517
Herricks Haven Bed & Breakfast . (907)235-1086
Red Door B & B .... (907)235-2730

Anchorage
12th & L Bed & Breakfast ...... (907)274-3344
A Log Home B&B .... (907)276-8527
A View With A Room B&B ..... (907)345-2781
Akxperience .... (907)346-2665
Alaska Bed & Breakfast .... (907)345-0923
Alaska Cozy Comfort B&B ..... (907)346-1957
Alaska Wildberry B&B .... (907)248-0447
Alaska's Morovia House .... (907)333-2329
Alaskan B&B, Tess's Place ..... (907)248-4704
Alaskan Bed & Breakfast ...... (907)279-3200
All The Comforts of Home ..... (907)345-4279
Alpine Woods B&B .... (907)345-5551
Always Paradise .... (907)345-2973
Anchorage B&B .... (907)333-1425
Anchorage Downtown B&B-Raspberry Meadow .... (907)278-9275
Anchorage Foothills B&B ...... (907)333-7704
Anna's .... (907)338-5331
Arctic Fox B&B Inn .... (907)272-4818
Arctic Fox Bed & Breakfast Inn .. (907)272-4818
Arctic Loon B&B .... (907)345-4935
Arctic Pines .... (907)278-6841
Arctic Poppy B&B .... (907)258-7795
Atherton Road .... (907)345-5015
Barbara's B&B .... (907)243-3095
Barry's .... (907)333-5919
Bed & Breakfast on The Park ... (907)277-0878
Beech Lane B&B .... (907)272-6228
Big Bear B&B .... (907)277-8189
Birdsong B&B .... (907)349-6325
Blackberry Bed & Breakfast .... (907)243-2557
Bonnie's B&B .... (907)345-4671
Bowery House Bed & Breakfast . (907)344-4676
Camai B&B .... (907)333-2219
Camelot Cottages .... (907)346-3039
Caribou Manor House .... (907)272-0444
Cecelia's Bed & Breakfast ...... (907)276-7309
Chelsea Inn .... (907)276-5002
Chinook Bed & Breakfast ...... (907)243-0926
Claddagh Cottage .... (907)248-7104
Coastal Trail Bed & Breakfast ... (907)243-5809
Connie's B&B .... (907)243-1606
Country Garden B&B .... (907)344-0636
Crossroads Inn Bed & Breakfast . (907)258-7378
Deals B&B .... (907)248-0331
Deveauxs' Contemporary B&B .. (907)349-8910
Double Dal Bed & Breakfast .... (907)258-5046
Down Home B&B .... (907)243-4443
Dream Catchers Bed & Breakfast (907)333-8530
Elderberry .... (907)243-6968
End of The Road .... (800)770-7799
Fancy Moose Bed & Breakfast .. (907)243-7596
Fernbrook B&B .... (907)345-6443
Gallery Bed & Breakfast .... (907)274-2567
Garden Beds .... (907)243-8880
Gingham House .... (907)276-0407
Girdwood View Bed & Breakfast Office .... (907)276-4822
Glacier Way Bed & Breakfast ... (907)337-5201
Green Bough B&B .... (907)562-4636
Grover House Bed & Breakfast .. (907)272-4381
Guesthouse .... (907)248-4493
Heart of Anchorage Bed & Breakfast .... (907)243-6814
Heidis Bed & Breakfast .... (907)563-8517
Hideaway House .... (907)346-1029
Hillcrest Haven B&B .... (907)274-3086
Hillside B & B .... (907)346-1559
Hillside Hosts .... (907)346-3096
Knollhaven B&B .... (907)258-1717
Lilac House .... (907)272-3553
Little Rabbit Creek .... (907)345-8183
Midnight Bed & Breakfast ...... (907)562-9143
Midnight Sun B&B Inn .... (907)248-6878
Missys Bed & Breakfast .... (907)338-4309
Moosewood Manor .... (907)345-8788
Northern Lights B&B .... (907)333-2666
Northwoods Guest House ...... (907)243-3249
Oceanview B&B .... (907)345-6390

Polarwise B&B .... (907)561-8227
The Potter's Inn .... (907)258-1717
Potters & Charters B&B .... (907)333-7056
Qupqugiaq Bed & Breakfast .... (907)562-5681
Ravens Nest .... (907)243-1693
Rest Assured Bed & Breakfast .. (907)344-3583
Rock Point .... (907)563-3305
At Schnell's B&B .... (907)243-2074
Siegfried's B&B .... (907)346-3152
Sixth & B B&B .... (907)279-8338
Snoozy B&B ... (907)274-9865 (800)354-0140
Snowline B&B .... (907)346-1631
Snug Harbor Inn Bed & Breakfast (907)272-6249
Swan House .... (907)346-3033
The Teddy Bear House .... (907)344-3111
The Tree House B&B .... (907)345-5421
Valley of The Moon B&B .... (907)279-7755
Walkabout Town B&B .... (907)279-2918
Welcome to Anchorage B&B .... (907)344-2323
Wesleyan House B&B .... (907)337-7383
Westcoast Int'l Inn .... (907)243-2233
The White Goose Inn .... (907)349-1022
Windflower B&B .... (907)345-2825
Wright's B&B .... (907)561-1990
Young Lodge .... (907)562-5700

Angoon

Favorite Bay Inn .... (907)788-3123
Sophies Place Bed & Breakfast .. (907)788-3194

Bethel

Bentley's Porter House B&B .... (907)543-3552
Pacifica Guest House .... (907)543-4305

Big Lake

Dollar Lake Lodging .... (907)892-7620
Jeanie's on Big Lake .... (907)892-7594

Chickaloon

Chickaloon B&B .... (907)745-1155

Chugiak

Chugiak B&B .... (907)688-2295

Clam Gulch

Clam Gulch Lodge .... (907)260-3778

Cooper Landing

Alaskan Sourdough Bed & Breakfast
.... (907)595-1541
Cooper's Landing on Kenai Lake Accomodations
.... (907)595-1281
Red Salmon Guest House ...... (907)595-1733

Cordova

Blue Heron Inn .... (907)424-3554
Cordova Rose Lodge .... (907)424-7673
Harborview Bed & Breakfast .... (907)424-5566
Oystercatcher Bed & Breakfast .. (907)424-5154
Queens Chair Bed & Breakfast .. (907)424-3000

Craig

Blue Heron-Inn of The Little .... (907)826-3606
Bucareli Bay Bed & Breakfast ... (907)826-2951

Delta Junction

Peggy's Alaskan Cabbage Patch B&B
.... (907)895-4200
Talbott's B&B .... (907)895-5025

Denali National Park

Camp Denali .... (907)683-2290
Healy Heights B&B .... (907)683-2639

Douglas

The Forecastle .... (907)364-3632
Olgas Water View Bed & Breakfast (907)364-3294
Seaview Chalet .... (907)364-3359
Windsock Inn B&B .... (907)364-2431

Eagle

Yukon Adventure B&B .... (907)547-2221

Eagle River

A Homestay at Homesteads .... (907)272-8644
Alaska Chalet .... (907)694-1528
Andy's Eagle Park B&B .... (907)694-2833
Cranberry Cliffs B&B .... (907)696-3326
The Log House .... (907)694-9231
Mountain Air B&B .... (907)696-3116
Terrace Hills B&B .... (907)694-3722

Fairbanks

1940s Age Old B&B .... (907)451-7526
7 Bridges .... (907)479-0751
7 Gables Inn .... (907)479-0751
A Cloudberry Lookout B&B ..... (907)479-7334
A Little Fox Inn .... (907)457-6539
A Pioneer B&B .... (907)452-4628
A River of Dreams Bed & Breakfast (907)474-9450
A Taste of Alaska Lodge .... (907)488-7855
Ah, Rose Marie B&B .... (907)456-2040
Alaska Golden Heart B&B ...... (907)474-9406
Alaska Heritage B&B .... (907)451-6587
Alaskan House B&B .... (907)451-9151
Alaskan Iris B&B .... (907)488-2308
Alaskan Sisters Bed & Breakfast . (907)457-5832
All Seasons B&B Inn
.... (907)451-6649 (800)770-8165
An Alaskan Viewpoint B&B ..... (907)479-7251
Cedar Creek Inn .... (907)457-3392
Arctic Igloo Inn .... (907)457-8484
Aurora Sky Fire B&B .... (907)388-7817
B&B By The River (907)474-0011 (800)474-0012
This Old House B&B .... (907)452-6343
B&R Bed and Breakfast .... (907)479-3335
Bear Paw B&B .... (907)474-4275
Beaver Bend B&B .... (907)452-3240
Becky's B&B .... (907)474-9569
Beds In Blue .... (907)479-8760
Bell House .... (907)452-3278
Beth's B&B .... (907)457-2725
Bethany House B&B .... (907)456-6589
Birch Grove B&B .... (907)479-5781
Birch Haven Inn . (907)457-2451 (800)457-2451
The Blue Goose B&B .... (907)479-6973
Blueberry Moose .... (907)456-6205
Bonnie's Abode . (907)452-7386 (800)478-2262
Bridgewater Drive B&B .... (907)456-6246
Broadmoor Bed & Bath .... (907)479-2710
Chena Homestead B&B .... (907)452-4362
Chena Pump Inn .... (907)479-6313
Chena River B&B .... (907)479-2532
Chickadee's Nest B&B .... (907)457-7887
Chocolate Rush B&B .... (907)474-8633
Chokecherry Inn .... (907)474-9381
Colette B&B .... (907)456-4850
College B&B .... (907)479-5444
Cowles St B&B .... (907)452-5252
Crestmont Manor .... (907)456-3831
Dave's B&B .... (907)457-1851
Daybreak B&B .... (907)479-2753
Eleanor's Northern Lights B&B .. (907)452-2598
Fairbanks Downtown B&B ..... (907)452-7700
Fay Creek Bed & Breakfast ..... (907)457-5494
P Geiger Haus B&B
.... (907)474-2131 (800)474-2131
Geni's B&B .... (907)488-4136
The Gray House B&B .... (907)452-7879
Hall's-With-A-View B&B .... (907)479-6020
Hillside B&B .... (907)457-2664
Husky Gardens B&B .... (907)474-8294
Jan's B&B .... (907)456-5431
Kris Kringle B&B .... (907)451-0586
Marilyn's B&B .... (907)456-1959
Meadow View B&B .... (907)457-4166
Michaels 5th Ave Bed & Breakfast (907)452-3505
Midge's Birch Lane B&B
.... (907)388-8084 (800)479-4895
Minnie St Bed & Breakfast ..... (907)456-1802
Mountain View B&B .... (907)474-9022
Mountains of Rainbows Bed & Breakfast
.... (907)456-7442
North Woods Lodge .... (907)479-6888
Plane Country B&B .... (907)479-3710
Ridgepointe B&B .... (907)479-0007
River of Dreams B&B .... (907)474-9450
Riverside Retreat (907)479-6313 (800)479-6313
Riverview B&B .... (907)474-0332
Rocking Horse Inn Bed & Breakfast (907)458-7758
Rose's Forget-Me-Not B&B ..... (907)456-5734
Scenic Loop B&B .... (907)455-6871
Sleepy Moose B&B .... (907)452-4814
Spinach Creek B&B .... (907)455-6311
Stone Frost Downtown Inn
.... (907)457-5337 (800)478-8516
Taku Gardens B&B .... (907)474-0035
The Trains Inn Guest House .... (907)474-9613
Thompson's Downtown B&B ... (907)452-5787
Three Bears B&B .... (907)457-2449
Vivian's Viewpointe B&B .... (907)479-3577
Weeks Field B&B .... (907)456-5319

Weltown

Weltown .... (907)389-2714

Fairbanks

White Fox Inn B&B .... (907)457-3867
The Wild Iris Inn .... (907)479-4062
Wildview Cabin Vacation Home .. (907)457-1154

Galena

Happy Puppy Bed & Breakfast .. (907)656-1728

Girdwood

Alyeska View B&B .... (907)783-2747
Delphinium House Bed & Breakfast (907)783-3435
Girdwood View Bed & Breakfast . (907)783-2596

Glennallen

Evergreen Lodge B&B .... (907)822-3250

Gustavus

A Puffin's B&B .... (907)697-2260
Good Riverbed & Breakfast ..... (907)697-2241
Gustavus Inn at Glacier Bay .... (907)697-3311
Tri B&B .... (907)697-2425

Haines

A Sheltered Harbor B&B .... (907)766-2741
Bed & Breakfast Fort Seward ... (907)766-2856
Cathedral Peaks Bed & Breakfast (907)766-2634
Chilkat Eagle Bed & Breakfast ... (907)766-2763
Chilkat Valley Inn .... (907)766-3331
Fort William Seward B&B ...... (907)766-2856
Officer's Inn B&B .... (907)766-2003
Riverhouse Bed & Breakfast .... (907)766-2060
The Summer Inn B&B .... (907)766-2970

Halibut Cove

Quiet Place Lodge Bed & Breakfast (907)296-2241

Healy

Beaver View Bed & Breakfast ... (907)683-2585
Dome Home B&B .... (907)683-1239
Dry Creek B&B .... (907)683-2386
Grand View Bed & Breakfast .... (907)683-2468
Homestead Bed & Breakfast .... (907)683-2575
La Hacienda Bed & Brkfst ..... (907)683-2340
Mc Kinley Wilderness Lodge .... (907)683-2277
Pat and Windell's B&B .... (907)683-2472
Rock Creek Bed & Breadkfast ... (907)683-2676

Homer

Across The Bay Cabins & Bed & Breakfast
.... (907)235-3633
Beach House .... (907)235-5945
Bear Creek Bed & Breakfast .... (907)235-8522
Beary Patch B & B .... (907)235-2483
Bed & Breakfast Chocolate Drop . (907)235-3668
Bed & Breakfast/Patchwork Farm (907)235-7368
Bed & Breakfast/Spruce Acres Cabins
.... (907)235-8388
Beeson Bed & Breakfast .... (907)235-3757
Brass Ring B&B .... (907)235-5450
Bridge Creek Bed & Breakfast ... (907)235-7590
Buffalo & Boar Bed & Breakfast . (907)235-7591
Cloudy Mt Inn .... (907)235-2254
Crestwood Manor .... (907)235-6282
Driftwood Inn .... (907)235-8019
Forest Light Cottage .... (907)235-2313
Frontier Cottages .... (907)235-8275
Halcyon Heights B & B .... (907)235-3773
Holland Days Bed & Breakfast ... (907)235-7604
Homer B&B/Seekins .... (907)235-8996
Husky Ranch Bed & Breakfast .. (907)235-6333
Island Watch Bed & Breakfast ... (907)235-2265
Kachemak Kiana Bed and Breakfast
.... (907)235-8824
Kachemak Shores Bed & Breakfast (907)235-6864
Lily Pad .... (907)235-6630
Magic Canyon Ranch Bed & Breakfast
.... (907)235-6077
Morning Glory B & B/Charter ... (907)235-8084
Old Inlet Trading Post Bed & Breakfast T
.... (907)235-7558
Room With A View .... (907)235-6955
Seaside Farm B&B .... (907)235-7850
Snuggles Harbor .... (907)235-3632
Spit Road Lodge .... (907)235-6764
Sundmarks Bed & Breakfast .... (907)235-5188
Victorian Heights Bed & Breakfast (907)235-6357
Wandering Star Bed & Breakfast . (907)235-6788
Welcome Friends Bed & Breakfast (907)235-3698
Wild Rose Bed & Breakfast ..... (907)235-8780

Hoonah

Hubbards Bed & Breakfast ..... (907)945-3414

Iliamna

Lakeview Lodge .... (907)571-1445

Juneau

Admiralty View Bed & Breakfast . (907)790-7277
Alaska House .... (907)586-2422
Big Dog Bath House .... (907)790-2244
Blueberry Lodge B&B .... (907)463-5886
Cashen Quarters .... (907)586-9863
Cozy Log Bed & Breakfast ..... (907)789-2582
Dawson's B&B .... (907)586-9708

Eagle's Nest B&B .... (907)586-6378
Glacier View Bed & Breakfast ... (907)586-2266
Jan's View B&B .... (907)463-5897
Larson's Landing B&B .... (907)789-7871
The Lost Chord .... (907)789-7296
Meander Inn .... (907)789-3944
Mullins House .... (907)586-3384
Pot Belly Bed & Breakfast ...... (907)586-1279
Sallys Bed & Breakfast .... (907)780-4708
Silverbow Inn & Restaurant ..... (907)586-4146
Sutton Place B&B .... (907)463-3232

Kasilof

Crooked Creek B&B .... (907)262-2729
Kasilof River Kabins .... (907)262-6649
Raven Mt. Farm B&B .... (907)262-9186

Kenai

Alaska Guides & Irenes Lodge .. (907)283-4501
Ashana House .... (907)283-3338
Beaver Creek Hideavay .... (907)283-7375
Beaver Creek Lodge & Guide Services
.... (907)283-7550
Chalet Bed & Breakfast .... (907)283-4528
Coyles Landing .... (907)283-3223
Daniels Lake Lodge B&B ...... (907)776-5578
Drifters Landing .... (907)283-9328
J & J Bed & Breakfast .... (907)283-4621
Kahtnu B&B .... (907)283-7152
Log Gabin Bed & Breakfast ..... (907)283-3653
Longmere Lake Bed & Breakfast . (907)262-5665
Lotties Place Bed & Breakfast ... (907)283-8707
Lyns Inn .... (907)283-8090
Marlenes Bed & Breakfast ...... (907)283-9380
Northern Comfort .... (907)283-8787
Riddles Lodge & Guide Service .. (907)283-5853
Rons Alaska Lodge .... (907)283-4333
Tower Rock House .... (907)283-3662

Ketchikan

Alaska Home Fishing B & B Lodg (907)225-6919
Alaskas First City Bed & Brea ... (907)225-7378
Alder Street B&B .... (907)247-9871
Blueberry Hill B & B .... (907)247-2583
C-Flee Beachfront Hideaway .... (907)225-9460
The Classic Stop .... (907)225-1120
Great Alaska Cedar Works Bed & Breakfast
.... (907)247-8287
House of Stewart B&B .... (907)247-3725
Innside Passage B&B .... (907)247-3700
Ketchikan Bed & Breakfast ..... (907)225-8550
Main Street B&B .... (907)225-8484
Oyster Avenue B&B .... (907)225-3449
Veldas Victorian Bed & Breakfast . (907)225-4940
Whale Tail Bed & Breakfast ..... (907)225-3380

Klawock

Klawock Bay Inn Apartment .... (907)755-2616

Kodiak

A-Wintels Bed & Breakfast ..... (907)486-6935
Baranov Bluff Oceanfront Lodgings (907)486-5407
Bear & The Bed & Breakfast .... (907)486-6154
Kodiak Bed & Breakfast .... (907)486-6567
Larch Tree Inn .... (907)486-2392
Oceanside Bed & Breakfast ..... (907)486-5835

Moose Pass

Alaska Nellies Inn Inc .... (907)288-3124
Don Dees Crown Point Bed & Breakfast
.... (907)288-3641

Nenana

Finnish Alaskan B&B .... (907)832-5628

Nikiski

Daniels Lake Lodge Bed & Breakfast
.... (907)776-5578

Ninilchik

Bluff House Bed & Breakfast .... (907)567-3605
Deep Creek Bed & Breakfast .... (907)567-3567
Double Eagle Lodge .... (907)567-3492
Drift-Inn Bed & Breakfast ...... (907)567-3448
Homestead House Bed & Breakfast (907)567-3412
Moose Haven Lodge .... (907)776-8535

Nome

Betty's Igloo B&B .... (907)443-2419
Golden Sands Guest House .... (907)443-3900
Goldies Bed & Breakfast .... (907)443-2016
Junes Bed & Breakfast .... (907)443-5984
Ocean View Manor Bed & Breakfast
.... (907)443-2133
Trails End .... (907)443-3600

North Pole

Birch Tree B&B .... (907)488-4667

Palmer

A-Lazy Acres B&B .... (907)745-6340
Byers Ranch Bed & Breakfast ... (907)745-3410
Colony Inn .... (907)745-3330
Moose Creek B&B .... (907)452-1197
Pollen's B&B .... (907)745-8920
Russell's B&B .... (907)376-7662
Tara Dells B&B .... (907)745-0407
Timberlings B&B .... (907)745-4445
The Tundra Rose .... (907)745-5854
Woodside Inn Bed & Breakfast .. (907)746-6233

Pelican

Otter Cove Bed & Breakfast ..... (907)735-2259

Petersburg

Scandia House .... (907)772-4281
Water's Edge B&B .... (907)772-3736

Port Graham

Fedoras Bed & Breakfast ...... (907)284-2239

Seldovia

Annie McKenzie's Boardwalk Hotel (907)234-7816
Crow Hill B&B .... (907)234-7410
Dancing Eagles Lodge Bed & Breakfast
.... (907)234-7627

Seward

"The Farm" B&B .... (907)224-5691
Alaskas Treenhouse Bed & Breakfast
.... (907)224-3867
Ballaine House Bed & Breakfast . (907)224-2362
Bay Vista Bed & Breakfast ..... (907)224-5880
Bear Lake Bed & Breakfast ..... (907)224-8773
Benson Bed & Breakfast .... (907)224-5290
Bluefield Bed & Breakfast ...... (907)224-8732
By-The-Sea Bed & Breakfast .... (907)224-3401
Creekside Cabins B&B .... (907)224-3834
Harborview B&B .... (907)224-3217
Korner House .... (907)224-3231
Mom Clock's B&B .... (907)224-3195
Northern Exposure B & B ...... (907)224-3211
River Valley Cabins .... (907)224-5740
Seward Bed & Breakfast .... (907)224-8787
Seward Waterfront Lodging .... (907)224-5563
Sleepy Hollow Bed & Breakfast .. (907)224-6003
Stoney Creek Inn B&B .... (907)224-3940
Swiss Chalet B&B .... (907)224-3939

Sitka

A Crescent Harbor Hideaway ... (907)747-4900
Abner's B&B .... (907)747-8779
Annahootz B&B .... (907)747-6498
Archangel B&B .... (907)747-6538
Bed & Breakfast Jamestown Bay . (907)747-5643
Biorka B&B .... (907)747-3111
By The Sea B&B .... (907)747-3993
Creek's Edge Guest House ..... (907)747-6484
Eagle's Landing B&B .... (907)747-5936
Gavan Hill B&B .... (907)747-6633
Hannah's B&B & Fishing Charters. (907)747-8309
Helga's B&B .... (907)747-5497
Jerry's Waterfront B&B .... (907)747-7265
Karras B&B .... (907)747-3978
May Mills Loft .... (907)747-6776
Mountain View B&B .... (907)747-8966
Pacific Sunset B&B .... (907)747-1020
Seaside B&B .... (907)747-6066
Seaview B&B .... (907)747-3908
Sitka House B&B .... (907)747-7460
Vonnie's on Shelikof .... (907)747-6401
Wild Strawberry Inn .... (907)747-8883

Skagway

Golden North Hotel .... (907)983-2294
Gramma's B&B .... (907)983-2312
The Historic Skagway Inn B&B .. (907)983-2289
Mile Zero B&B .... (907)983-3045
Portland House .... (907)983-2493

Soldotna

Alaskas Kenai Peninsula Bed N Breakfast/ .....
(907)262-1902
Alaskan River Rest .... (907)262-5939
Alaskas Treetop Bed & Breakfast . (907)262-6648
Casa Norte Bed & Breakfast .... (907)262-1257
Denise Lake Lodge B&B .... (907)262-1789
Eagles Nest Bed & Breakfast ..... (907)262-5396
Eagles Roost Bed & Breakfast ... (907)262-9797
Homestead Acres .... (907)262-2911
Kalifornsky Lodge .... (907)262-2535
Knight Manor Bed & Breakfast .. (907)262-2438
Lakeview B&B .... (907)262-1234
Longmere Lake Lodge B & B ... (907)262-9799
Lottie's Place .... (907)283-8707
Marlows Kenai River Bed & Breakfast
.... (907)262-5218
New Englander on The Kenai ... (907)262-5487
Posey's Kenai River Hideaway B&B Lodge
.... (907)262-7430
Ravens Nest Bed & Breakfast ... (907)260-3226
Riverside Resort B&B .... (907)262-5371
Soldotna Bed & Breakfast ...... (907)262-4779
Spruce Avenue Bed & Breakfast . (907)262-9833
Wildflower International Inn ..... (907)262-1846
Woods Hole Bed & Breakfast ... (907)262-9072

Sterling

Angler's Lodge & Fish Camp ... (907)262-1747
Kenai Moose Bed & Breadfast ... (907)262-6493
Our Point of View Bed & Breakfast (907)262-5307

Talkeetna

Alaska Log Cabin Bed & Breakfast (907)733-2584
Bays Bed & Breakfast .... (907)733-1342
Belle's Cabin .... (907)733-2414
Denali View B&B .... (907)733-2778
Fairview Inn .... (907)733-2423
North Country Bed & Breakfast .. (907)733-3981
Paradise Lodge .... (907)733-1471
River Beauty B&B .... (907)733-2741
Sunshine Creek Inn .... (907)733-1485
Talkeetna 7 Beyond B&B .... (907)733-3050
Traleika B&B .... (907)733-2700
Trapper Johns B&B .... (907)733-2354
Whistle Stop Bed & Breakfast ... (907)733-1515

Tenakee Springs

Tenakee Inn .... (907)586-1000

Thorne Bay

Deer Creek Cottage
.... (907)828-3383 (800)830-3393

Tok

Cleft of The Rock B&B
.... (907)883-4219 (800)478-5646
The Stage Stop B&B .... (907)883-5338

Trapper Creek

McKinley Foothills B&B .... (907)733-1454
North Country B&B .... (907)733-3981
Ruth Lake Lodge .... (907)495-9000

Valdez

A Touch 'O Old Town B&B ..... (907)835-4302
Alaskan Artistry B&B .... (907)835-2542
Alaskan Flower Forget-Me-Not B&B
.... (907)835-2717
Angie's Downhome B&B ...... (907)835-2832
Anna's B&B .... (907)835-2202
B&B Valdez .... (907)835-4211
Best of All B&B .... (907)835-4524
Blue Anchor B&B .... (907)835-5333
The Boathouse .... (907)835-4407
Broadmoor B&B .... (907)835-4998
Casa De La Bellezza .... (907)835-4489
Christian B&B .... (907)835-2609
Cliff House B&B .... (907)835-5244
Colonial Inn B&B .... (907)835-4929
Cooper's Cottage .... (907)835-4810
Eagle B&B .... (907)835-3831
Easy Living B&B .... (907)835-4208
Fisherman's Rack B&B .... (907)835-2073
France Inn B&B .... (907)835-4295
Gussie's Lowe St. Inn .... (907)835-4448
Headhunters Inn B&B .... (907)835-2900
Ivy Rose .... (907)835-3804
Jade Mountain B&B .... (907)835-3617
Kansas North .... (907)835-3576
L&L's B&B .... (907)835-4447
The Lake House .... (907)835-4752
Misty's .... (907)835-3865
Northern Comfort B&B .... (907)835-4649
Raven Berth and Breakfast ..... (907)835-5863
Snowtree Inn B&B .... (907)835-4399
Starrs Country Inn B&B .... (907)835-2917
Think Pink B&B .... (907)835-4367
Wendy's B&B .... (907)835-4770

Ward Cove

North Tongass B&B .... (907)247-0879

Wasilla

Alaskan Agate B&B Inn .... (907)373-2290
Arts B & B .... (907)376-1644
Bear Barn B&B .... (907)376-2082
Birchgrove B&B .... (907)376-0112
Blodgett Lake Bed & Breakfast .. (907)892-6877
Bridge Stone Cottage B&B ..... (907)376-6262

Broken Horse Shoe Ranch ..... (907)376-5478
Cat's Pajamas B&B .... (907)746-2854
Cottonwood Lake B&B .... (907)373-0300
Cottonwood Lake Island B&B ... (907)373-2578
Country Lakes Flying Service/B&B (907)373-6934
Evergreen Acres B&B .... (907)376-2608
Granny's Place .... (907)376-5971
Hunters Lakeside Lodge .... (907)376-7426
Inlet View B&B .... (907)376-7468
Lakeshore B&B .... (907)376-1380
Peak A View B&B .... (907)376-6259
Seymour Lake B&B .... (907)376-7043
Shady Acres Inn .... (907)376-3113
Southshore B&B .... (907)376-9334
Tollers' Timbers B&B Chalets ... (907)746-1438
The Viewfinder B&B .... (907)376-4704
Wasilla Bed & Breakfast .... (907)373-3600
Wasilla Lake B&B .... (907)376-5985
Win Circle Cottage B&B .... (907)373-0424

White Mountain
White Mountain Lodge .... (907)638-3431

Willow
Your Alaska Host B&B .... (907)495-6448

Wrangell
High Field House Bed & Breakfast (907)874-4000
Rooney's Roost .... (907)874-2026

Yakutat
Blue Heron Inn Bed & Breakfast . (907)784-3603

Arizona

Ajo
Guest House Inn .... (520)387-6133

Amado
Amado Inn .... (520)398-2259

Bisbee
Bisbee Grand Hotel, A B&B Inn
.... (520)432-5900 (800)421-1909
Bisbee Inn .... (602)432-5131
The Inn at Castle Rock .... (520)432-4449
The Curry Home B&B .... (520)432-4815
The Greenway House .... (602)432-7170
Mile High Court .... (520)432-4636
Oliver House .... (520)432-4286
Park Place B&B .... (520)432-3054
The White House .... (520)432-7215

Bonita
Klondyke Store & Lodge .... (520)828-3335

Cave Creek
Andora Crossing .... (602)488-3747
D-Railed Ranch .... (602)488-1855
Debra Ann's Bed & Breakfast ... (602)488-2644

Clarkdale
Flying Eagle Country Bed & Breakfast
.... (520)634-0663

Cochise
Cochise Hotel .... (602)384-3156

Douglas
Family Crest Bed & Breakfast ... (520)364-3998

Dragoon
Kellys Whistlestop Bed & Breakfast (520)586-7515

Eagar
Paisley Corner Bed & Breakfast .. (520)333-4665

Flagstaff
Arizona Mountain Inn .... (602)774-8959
Cedar B&B .... (602)774-1636
Dierker House B&B .... (520)774-3249
Haleys Hideaway .... (520)526-1780
Saginaw House .... (520)774-3929
San Francisco St Bed & Breakfast (520)779-2257

Fountain Hills
Villa Galleria B&B .... (602)837-1400

Fredonia
Jackson House Bed & Breakfast . (520)643-7702

Globe
Cedar Hills Bed & Breakfast .... (520)425-7530
Noftsger Hill Inn .... (520)425-2260
Pinal Mountain Bed & Breakfast . (520)425-2563

Greer
Red Setter Inn .... (520)735-7441

Hereford
Casa De San Pedro .... (520)366-1300
San Pedro River Inn .... (520)366-5532

Jerome
Ghost City Inn .... (520)634-4678

Lake Havasu City
Havasu Dunes .... (602)855-6626

Mount Lemmon
Aspen Trail Bed & Breakfast & Cabin Rent
.... (520)576-1558

Oracle
Triangle L Ranch B&B Retreat ... (520)896-2804
Villa Cardinale .... (520)896-2516

Page
Bed & Breakast at Lake Powell .. (520)645-2525

Paradise
George Walker House .... (520)558-2287

Patagonia
Patagonia Patio Bed & Breakfast . (520)394-2671
Sun Arrow Ranch .... (520)394-2449

Phoenix
Fountain Suites .... (602)375-1777

Pinetop
Bartrams White Mountain Bed & Breakfast
.... (520)367-1408
Coldstream Bed & Breakfast .... (520)369-0115
Meadows Inn & Dining Room ... (520)367-8200

Pomerene
Redington Land & Cattle Co at Cascabel R
.... (520)212-5555

Portal
Portal B&B .... (602)558-2223

Prescott
Briar Wreath Inn .... (520)778-6048
Lynx Creek Farm B&B .... (520)778-9573
Marks House .... (602)778-4632
Pleasant Street Inn .... (520)445-4774
The Cottages at Prescott Country Inn
.... (520)445-7991
Victorian Inn of Prescott B&B ... (520)778-2642
(800)704-2642

Safford
Olney House .... (520)428-5118

Sasabe
Rancho De La Osa .... (602)823-4257

Scottsdale
Bed & Breakfast of North Scottsdale .. (602)991-7694
Casa De Mariposa .... (602)947-9704
San Diego Yacht & Breakfast .... (602)952-9123
The Inn at The Citadel .... (800)927-8367

Sedona
A Touch of Sedona .... (520)282-6462
Briar Patch Inn .... (520)282-2342
Casa Sedona .... (520)282-2938
Cathedral Rock Lodge .... (520)282-7608
Country Elegance B&B .... (602)634-4470
Cozy Cactus B&B .... (520)284-0082
Creekside Inn at Sedona .... (520)282-4992
Garland's Oak Creek Lodge ..... (602)282-3343
Greyfire Farm B&B .... (520)284-2340
Keyes' B&B .... (602)282-6008
L'Auberge De Sedona Resort .... (602)282-7131
Moore's Music Museum B&B ... (520)282-3419
Lorie's Hideaway of Sedona .... (520)282-1944
Slide Rock Lodge & Cabins .... (602)282-3531
Wishing Well .... (520)282-4914

Springerville
Paisley Corner .... (602)333-4447

Strawberry
Strawberry House .... (520)476-2450

Tempe
Mi Casa Su Casa Bed and Breakfast
.... (602)990-0682
Valley O The Sun Bed & Breakfast (602)941-1281

Tombstone
The Buford House .... (520)457-3969
Priscilla's Bed & Breakfast ..... (520)457-3844
Tombstone Boarding House .... (520)457-3716

Tubac
Tubac Country Inn .... (520)398-3178

Tucson
Aloe Vera Inn .... (520)795-8980
Arizona Inn .... (602)325-1541
Bird In The Hand B&B .... (602)622-5428
Car-Mar's Southwest B&B ..... (520)578-1730
Casa Tierra Adobe B&B .... (520)578-3058
Congenial Quail .... (520)887-9487
Copper Bell B&B .... (520)629-9229
Desert Island Dream Bed & Breakfast
.... (520)742-0970
Desert Needlework Ranch ..... (602)885-6264
Flying V Ranch .... (602)299-4372
Horizons Bed and Breakfast .... (520)749-2955
Jeremiah Inn .... (520)749-3072
June's B&B .... (602)578-0857
La Casa De Las Bunitas .... (602)326-2973
The Peppertrees B&B Inn
.... (520)622-7167 (800)348-5763
Melissa's Desert Classic Bed & Breakfast
.... (520)744-1984
Mesquite Retreat B&B .... (602)749-4884
Paz Entera Ranch (602)744-2481 (800)726-7554
Rancho Quieto .... (520)883-3300
Rimrock West .... (602)749-8774
The Suncatcher .... (520)885-0883
The Swedish Guest House B&B . (602)742-6400
White Stallion Ranch .... (602)297-0252

Tumacacori
Valle Verde Ranch B & B .... (520)398-2246

Wickenburg
J Bar J Ranch .... (520)684-9142
Kay El Bar Ranch .... (602)684-7593

Williams
Canyon Country Inn .... (602)635-2349
Johnston Bed and Breakfast .... (520)635-2178

Yuma
Casa De Osgood Bed & Breakfast (520)342-0471

Arkansas

Arkadelphia
Buckelew's Bed & Breakfast .... (501)246-4262

Bergman
Hidden Valley B&B .... (501)741-7435

Brinkley
The Great Southern Hotel ...... (501)734-4955

Caddo Gap
River's Edge B&B .... (501)356-4864

Calico Rock
The Cedars B&B . (501)297-4197 (800)233-2777
Forest Home Lodge & Happy Lonesome Log Cabin
.... (501)297-8211
River View Hotel B&B .... (501)297-8208

Camden
Martin Carnes Milner House .... (501)836-4504
Umsted House .... (501)836-9609

Cane Hill
E. White McClellan House 1866 . (501)824-4308

Cherokee Village
Pelton Place Inn & Restaurant ... (501)257-2000

Clarksville
May House .... (501)754-6851

Conway
The Bruce House .... (501)327-2947
Olde Towne B&B .... (501)329-6989

Crossett
The Stephens Place .... (501)364-8062
The Trieschmann House .... (501)364-7592

De Valls Bluff
Palaver Place .... (800)844-4425

Deer
The Piney Inn B&B .... (501)428-5878

Eureka Springs
All Tucked Inn .... (501)253-4000
The Basin Park Hotel .... (501)253-7837
Beaver Lake B&B .... (501)253-9210
Benton Place Inn .... (501)253-7602
Bon Repos .... (501)253-6735
Brownstone Inn .... (501)253-7505
Cameo Guest Cattages .... (501)253-4944
Candlestick Cottage
.... (501)253-6813 (800)835-5184
Carriage House .... (501)253-5259
Carriage Inn at Busch Mountain . (501)253-8828
Cedarberry Cottage .... (501)253-6115
Coach House Inn .... (501)253-8099
Cobbler's Cottage .... (501)253-2650
Cobblestone Guest Cottage ..... (501)253-8175
Cottage Inn Restaurant & Lodging (501)253-5282
Country House Bed & Breakfast . (501)253-7586
Country Springs Bed & Breakfast (501)253-4027
Crescent Hotel .. (501)253-9766 (800)342-9766
Crescent Moon Townhouse ..... (501)253-9463
Dixie Cottage B&B .... (501)253-7553
Doll House Inn .... (501)253-8565
Dr. R.G. Floyd House .... (501)253-7525

Edgewood Manor Deluxe Historic Lodging
.... (501)253-6555
Ellis House at Trail's End
.... (501)253-8218 (800)243-8218
Evening Shade Inn .... (501)253-6264
Greenwood Hollow Ridge ...... (501)253-5283
Harvest House B&B Inn .... (501)253-9363
Hidden Valley Guest Ranch ..... (501)253-9777
Lake Lucerne Resort .... (501)253-8085
Lookout Cottage .... (501)253-9545
Main Street Inn .... (501)253-6042
Maison De Ville .... (800)447-7242
Maple Leaf Inn .... (501)253-6876
Four Winds Cottage .... (501)253-9169
Matterhorn Towers .... (501)253-9602
Mimosa Cottage .... (501)253-9344
Miss Annies Garden Cottages ... (501)253-8356
Tatman-Garrett House .... (501)253-7617
The Inn at More Mountain Wellspring
.... (501)253-6026
Morningstar Retreat .... (501)253-5995
Mt. Victoria/Valais Hi .... (501)253-5140
New Orleans Hotel .... (501)253-8630
Oak Crest Cottages .... (501)253-9493
The Old Homestead .... (501)253-7501
Palace Hotel & Bath House ..... (501)253-7474
Peabody House B&B .... (501)253-5376
The Piedmont House B&B
.... (501)253-9258 (800)253-9258
Pond Mountain Lodge & Resort . (501)253-5877
Primrose Place .... (501)253-9818
Redbud Manor .... (501)253-9649
Red Bud Valley Resort .... (501)253-9028
Ridgeway House B&B
.... (501)253-6618 (800)477-6618
Riverview Resort .... (501)253-8367
Rock Cottage Gardens Bed & Breakfast Inn
.... (501)253-8659
Rogues Manor at Sweet Spring .. (501)253-4911
Rose Cottage .... (501)253-7407
The Inn at Rose Hall B&B
.... (501)253-5405 (800)828-4255
Rosewood Cottage .... (501)253-7674
Scandia B&B Inn .... (501)253-8922
Singleton House B&B .... (501)253-9111
Sweet Seasons Guest Cottages .. (501)253-7603
Taylor-Page Inn .... (501)253-7315
Tweedy House .... (501)253-5435
The Victorian Rose Inn .... (501)253-8537
White Dove Manor .... (501)253-6151
White Flower Cottage .... (501)253-9636
White Houses .... (501)253-5332
White River Oaks B&B .... (501)253-9033
Willow Ridge .... (501)253-7737

Evening Shade
The Turman House B&B
.... (501)266-3405 (800)257-3405

Fayetteville
Coloniel House Bed & Breakfast . (501)582-1677
Eton House .... (501)521-6344
Hill Avenue B&B .... (501)444-0865
Oaks Manor .... (501)443-5481
Stonefence Inn .... (501)582-1087

Flippin
Fair Haven Lodge .... (501)453-2371

Fordyce
Wynne Phillips House .... (501)352-7202

Fort Smith
Beland Manor Inn B&B
.... (501)782-3300 (800)334-5052
McCartney House .... (501)782-9057
Thomas Quinn Guest House .... (501)782-0499

Gassville
Lithia Springs B&B .... (501)435-6100

Gilbert
Riverside Kitchen & Cottages ... (501)439-2288

Glenwood
Riverwood Inn .... (501)356-4567

Greenbrier
Morning Glory B&B Inn .... (501)679-4406

Harrison
The Carriage House B&B ...... (501)365-3899
Edgewood Inn B&B .... (501)741-4166
Hathaway House B&B .... (501)742-3321
Merry Otter B&B .... (501)743-2355
Mountain Pines Cabin .... (501)714-9254
Peaches N' Cream B&B .... (501)741-6527
Queen Anne House .... (501)741-1304

Helena
Foxglove B&B .... (501)338-9391
Magnolia Hill .... (501)338-6874

Hot Springs
Ann Cogburn's Inn .... (501)767-5208
The Gables .... (501)623-7576
Golden Eagle Inn .... (501)624-3641
Park Hotel .... (501)624-5323
Stitt House B&B Inn .... (501)623-2704
Wildwood 1884 B&B Inn ...... (501)624-4267
Dogwood Manor B&B .... (501)624-0896
Williams House Inn .... (501)624-4275

Hughes
Snowden Plantation B&B ...... (501)339-3414

Jasper
Arkansas House .... (501)446-5179
Brambly Hedge Cottage .... (501)446-5849
Cliff House Inn .... (501)446-2292

Jessieville
Mountain Thyme B&B .... (501)984-5428

Johnson
Johnson House B&B .... (501)756-1095

Langley
Country School Inn .... (501)356-3091

Little Rock
The Carriage House B&B ...... (501)374-7032
The Empress of Little Rock ..... (501)374-7966
Hotze House .... (501)376-6563
Pinnacle Vista Lodge .... (501)868-8905
Quapaw Inn .... (501)376-6873 (800)732-5591

Malvern
Gatewood House (501)332-6022 (800)439-6022

Mammoth Spring
Roseland Inn B&B .... (501)625-3378

Marianna
Mulberry Inn B&B .... (501)295-4200

McGehee
Magnolia House/Evans House ... (501)222-6425

Monticello
Miss Rosalind's B&B
.... (501)367-2703 (800)219-9121
Trotter House B&B .... (501)367-2703

Morrilton
Tanyard Springs .... (501)727-5200

Mountain View
Country Oaks B&B (501)269-2704 (800)455-2704
Inn at Mountain View Bed and Breakfast
.... (501)269-4200
The Lowe House .... (501)269-2191
The Inn at Mountain View ...... (501)269-4200
Owl Hollow Country Inn Bed & Breakfast
.... (501)269-8699

Norfork
Riversfork Inn .... (501)499-5391
Schroder Haus B&B .... (501)499-7775

Oark
The Bunkhouse .... (501)292-3725

Ozark
1887 Inn B&B .... (501)667-1121
The Lamplighter B&B .... (501)667-3889

Pine Bluff
Margland 11 B&B Inn .... (501)536-6000

Prescott
Pine Grove B&B .... (501)887-5682

Rogers
Arkansas Discovery B&B ...... (501)925-1744

Romance
Hammons Chapel Farm .... (501)849-2819

Salem
Lespedeza B&B .... (501)895-3061

Siloam Springs
Blue Willow B&B .... (501)524-4202
Dogwood Inn .... (501)524-6874
Vintage Inn .... (501)524-6566
Washington Street B&B .... (501)524-5669

Springdale
Faubus House on Governor's Hill (501)751-2005
Magnolia Gardens Inn .... (501)756-5744

Tyronza
Denwood B&B .... (501)537-4385

Van Buren
Old Van Buren Inn (501)474-4202 (800)474-4202

Warren
B&B of Warren "The Burnett House"
.... (501)226-2200
Colvin House B&B Inn .... (501)226-7757

Washington
Old Washington Jail B&B ...... (501)983-2461

Winslow
Sky-Vue Lodge B&B .... (501)634-2003

Wooster
Patton House B&B Inn .... (501)679-2975

Yellville
Buffalo River Lodge B&B ...... (501)439-2373
Red Raven Inn .... (501)449-5168

California

Ahwahnee
The Homestead .... (209)683-0495
Sierra Vista Bed & Breakfast .... (209)658-7050
Silver Spur Bed & Breakfast .... (209)683-2896

Alameda
Morning Rose Boat & Breakfast . (510)523-9600

Albion
Wool Loft .... (707)937-0377

Alleghany
Kenton Mine Lodge .... (916)287-3212

Alta
Crystal Springs Inn Bed & Breakfast
.... (916)389-2355

Amador City
Imperial Hotel .... (209)267-9172
Mine House Inn . (209)267-5900 (800)646-3473

Anaheim
Anaheim Country Inn .... (714)778-0150

Angels Camp
Cooper House .... (209)736-2145
Utica Mansion Inn .... (209)736-4209

Angwin
Angwin-Linda Falls Bed & Breakfast
.... (707)965-2440

Apple Valley
Beverlys Casa Del Mar Bed & Breakfast
.... (619)242-2256

Aptos
Mangels House .... (408)688-7982

Arcata
Hotel Arcata .... (707)826-0217 (800)344-1221
Lady Ann .... (707)822-2797

Arnold
Lodge at Manuel Mill B&B ..... (209)795-2622

Arroyo Grande
Crystal Rose Inn (805)481-1854 (800)767-3466
Guest House .... (805)481-9304

Auburn
Dry Creek B&B .... (916)878-0885
Lincoln House B&B .... (916)885-8880
Powers Mansion Inn .... (916)885-1166
The Victorian Hill House .... (916)885-5879

Avalon
Gull House .... (310)510-2547
Island Inn .... (213)510-1623
The Old Turner Inn .... (310)510-2236

Avila Beach
San Luis Bay Inn .... (805)595-2333

Ballard
Ballard Inn ..... (805)688-7770 (800)638-2466

Bass Lake
Bass Lake Bed & Breakfast ..... (209)642-3618

Bayside
The Robert Graham House ..... (707)822-5230

Ben Lomond
Chateau Des Fleurs .... (408)336-8943
Fairview Manor . (408)336-3355 (800)553-8840

Benicia
Captain Walsh House .... (707)747-5653
The Painted Lady .... (707)746-1646
The Union Gardens
.... (707)746-0100 (800)544-2278

Berkeley
Elmwood House B&B
.... (510)540-5123 (800)540-3050
Hillegass House .... (415)548-5517
Gramma's Rose Garden Inn .... (415)549-9281

Berry Creek
Lake Oroville Bed and Breakfast
.... (916)589-0700 (800)455-5253

Big Bear City
Big Bear B&B .... (909)585-6613
Krausmeier Haus Bavarian Lodge (909)585-2886

Big Bear Lake
Apples B&B Inn .... (909)866-0903
Cathy's Country Cottage .... (714)866-7444
Eagle's Nest B&B .... (909)866-6465
Janet K's B&B .... (800)243-7031
Knickerbocker Mansion
.... (909)866-8221 (800)785-5535
Pine Knot Guest Ranch .... (909)866-6500
Switzerland Haus .... (909)866-3729
Truffles, A Special Place .... (909)585-2772
Wainwright Inn B&B .... (909)585-6914

Big Sur
Deetjen's Big Sur Inn .... (408)667-2377
Ventana Inn .... (408)667-2331

Bishop
Chalfant House .... (619)872-1790

Blue Jay
Lake Manor .... (714)337-0914

Bodega
Estero Vista Inn .... (707)876-3300

Bodega Bay
Bayhill Mansion .... (707)875-3577
Bodega Harbor Inn .... (707)875-3594

Bolinas
Blue Heron Inn .... (415)868-1102
One Fifty Five Pine .... (415)868-2721
Rose Garden Cottage B & B .... (415)868-2209
Sharon House B & B .... (415)868-1641

Boonville
Anderson Creek Inn .... (707)895-3091
Boonville Hotel .... (707)895-2210
Toll House Inn .... (707)895-3630

Brentwood
Brentwood Oaks .... (510)634-0378

Bridgeville
Dinsmore Lodge .... (707)574-6466

Brownsville
Mountain Seasons Inn .... (916)675-2180

Burnt Ranch
Madrone Lane B&B .... (916)629-3642

Calabasas
Quail Creek Inn .... (818)222-1060

Calistoga
Brambles Bed & Breakfast ..... (707)942-4386
Brannan Cottage Inn .... (707)942-4200
Calistoga Country Lodge ...... (707)942-5555
Calistoga Enchanted Cottage .... (707)942-9463
Calistoga Inn .... (707)942-4101
Calistoga Ranch Club Resort ... (707)942-6565
Calistoga Wishing Well Inn ..... (707)942-5534
Carlin Country Cottages .... (707)942-9102
The Inn on Cedar Street .... (707)942-9244
Christopher's Inn .... (707)942-5755
Cottage Grove Inn (707)942-8400 (800)799-2482
Culver's, A Country Inn .... (707)942-4535
Dinsmoor's Wishing Well Inn ... (707)942-5534
Falcon's Nest .... (707)942-0758
Fannys .... (707)942-9491
Hillcrest Bed & Breakfast ...... (707)944-0332
La Chaumiere .... (707)942-5139
Larkmead Country Inn .... (707)942-5360
Meadowlark Country House .... (707)942-5651
Mount View Hotel .... (707)942-6877
Mountain Home Ranch .... (707)942-6616
Pine Street Inn .... (707)942-6829
The Pink Mansion (707)942-0558 (800)238-7465
Quail Mountain B&B .... (707)942-0316
Scott Courtyard .... (800)942-1515
Silver Rose Inn .... (707)942-9581
Sleepy Hollow Bed & Breakfast .. (707)942-4760
Wine Way Inn .... (707)942-0680
Wisteria Garden Bed & Breadfast . (707)942-5358
Zinfandel House .... (707)942-0733

Camarillo
Del Norte Inn .... (805)485-3999

Cambria
Beach House .... (805)927-5865
Beachside Inn .... (805)927-8723
Cambria Landing Inn .... (805)927-3136
The Cambria Pines Lodge ...... (805)927-4200
Cambria Shores Inn .... (805)927-8644
Captains Cove Lodge .... (805)927-8581
Fog Catcher Inn .... (805)927-1400
Sea Otter Inn .... (805)927-5888
Sylvia's Rigdon Hall Inn .... (805)927-5125
White Water Inn .... (805)927-1066
Windrush .... (805)927-8844

Capistrano Beach
Capistrano Seaside Inn .... (800)25B-EACH

Capitola
Monarch Cove Inn .... (408)464-1295

Carlsbad
Pelican Cove Inn .... (619)434-5995

Carmel
A Place to Stay .... (408)625-5136
Carmel Greenbriar Inn .... (408)624-2277
Cypress Inn .... (408)624-3871
Forest Lodge .... (408)624-7023
Green Lantern Inn .... (408)624-4392
Happy Landing Inn .... (408)624-7917
Holiday House .... (408)624-6267
Mission Ranch .... (408)624-6436
Monte Verde Inn .... (408)624-6046
San Antonio House .... (408)624-4334
Sea View Inn .... (408)624-8778
Sundial Lodge .... (408)624-8578
The Sunset House .... (408)624-4884
Tally Ho Inn .... (408)624-2232
Tickle Pink Inn .... (408)624-1244

Carmel By The Sea
Carmel Garden Court Inn ...... (408)624-6926
Sandpiper Inn-At-The Beach .... (408)624-6433

Carmel Valley
Country Garden Inns .... (408)659-5361
Hidden Valley Inn .... (408)659-5361
Stonepine .... (408)659-2245
Valley Lodge .... (408)659-2261

Carpinteria
Prufrock's Garden Inn .... (805)566-9696

Cassel
Clearwater House .... (916)335-5500

Castella
Castlestone Cottage Inn .... (916)235-0012

Catheys Valley
Chibchas .... (209)966-2940

Cayucos
Beachwalker Inn .... (805)995-2133

Cazadero
Cazanoma Lodge .... (707)632-5255
Timberhill Ranch .... (707)847-3477

Cedarville
Cressler-Hill House Bed & Breakfast
.... (916)279-2650

Chester
Bidwell House .... (916)258-3338
The Cinnamon Teal B&B .... (916)258-3993

Chicago Park
Bullard House .... (916)343-8020
Camelot Bed & Breakfast ...... (916)343-9164

Chico
Canyon Shadows Bed & Breakfast (916)345-5461
The Esplanade B&B .... (916)345-8084
Johnson's Country Inn .... (916)345-7829
The O'Flaherty House B&B ..... (916)893-5494
Palms of Chico .... (916)343-6868
White Sulphur Springs Bed & Breakfast
.... (916)899-1224

Clayton
Farm House at Clayton .... (510)672-8404

Clio
White Sulphur Springs Ranch
.... (916)836-2387 (800)854-1797

Cloverdale
Abrams House Inn .... (707)894-2412
Vintage Towers Inn .... (707)894-4535
Ye Olde Shelford House .... (707)894-5956

Coarsegold
Chine Creek .... (209)642-6248

Cobb
Forest Lake Inn .... (707)928-1991

Coloma
Vineyard House .... (916)622-2217

Columbia
Fallon Hotel .... (209)532-1470
Harlan House .... (209)533-4862

Colusa
O'Rourke Mansion .... (916)458-5625

Coronado
Coronado Victorian Hous ...... (619)435-2200

Coulterville
Hotel Jeffery ... (209)878-3471 (800)464-3471
Sherlock Holmes Bed & Breakfast Inn
.... (209)878-3915

Crescent City
Fernbrook Inn .... (707)458-3202
Pebble Beach Bed & Breakfast .. (707)464-9086

Crescent Mills
Crescent Hotel .... (916)284-9905

Davenport
New Davenport B&B .... (408)425-1818

Davis
Davis Bed & Breakfast Inn ..... (916)753-9611
University Inn B&B (916)756-8648 (800)756-8648

Del Mar
L'Auberge Del Mar .... (619)259-1515
Rock Haus B&B Inn .... (619)481-3764

Desert Hot Springs
Royal Palms Inn .... (619)329-7975
Traveller's Repose .... (619)329-9584

Dinuba
Country Living B&B .... (209)591-6617

Dorris
Hospitality Inn Bed & Breakfast .. (916)397-2097

Downieville
Sierra Shangri-La .... (916)289-3455

Dulzura
Brookside Farm .... (619)468-3043

Duncans Mills
Duncans Mills Lodge .... (707)865-1855
Superintendents House .... (707)865-1572

Dunsmuir
Clementine's Inn .... (916)235-4300

El Cajon
At Your Leisure Bed & Breakfast . (619)444-3124

El Granada
Harbor View Inn .... (415)726-2329
Pillar Point Inn .... (415)728-7377

Elk
Green Dolphin Inn .... (707)877-3342
Greenwood Lodge .... (707)877-3422
Greenwood Pier Inn .... (707)877-9997
Griffin House .... (707)877-3422
Harbor House - Inn By The Sea .. (707)877-3203

Elk Creek
Stony Creek Retreat .... (916)968-5178

Emigrant Gap
Emigrant Gap Inn .... (916)389-7021

Encinitas
Daphne Manor .... (619)943-1357
Sea Breeze B&B .... (619)944-0318

Escondido
De Bolton Bed & Breakfast ..... (619)741-5578

Eureka
A Weaver's Inn . (707)443-8119 (800)927-3743
Campton House B&B .... (707)443-1601
Carson House Inn .... (707)443-1601
Heuer's Victorian Inn .... (707)442-7334
Hollander House .... (707)443-2419
Nautical Nights Bed & Breakfast . (707)443-5172
Shannon House Bed & Breakfast . (707)443-8130
Waterfront Bed & Breakfast ..... (707)443-9190

Fallbrook
La Estancia Inn .... (619)723-2888

Fawnskin
The Inn at Fawnskin .... (909)866-3200
Windy Point Inn .... (909)866-2746

Felton
The Inn at Felton Crest .... (408)335-4011

Ferndale
Bartlett House Bed & Breakfast .. (707)786-9449
Ferndale Inn .... (707)786-4307
Grandmother's House B & B .... (707)786-9704
Shaw House B&B Inn .... (707)786-9958

Fish Camp
Apple Tree Inn .... (209)683-5111
Carriage House .... (209)683-8139
The Narrow Gauge Inn .... (209)683-7720
Scotty's Bed & Beakfast .... (209)683-6936
Yosemite Fish Camp .... (209)683-7426

Folsom
Plum Tree Inn .... (916)351-1541

Foresthill
Tin Roof B&B .... (916)367-4466

Forestville
Farmhouse Inn .... (707)887-3300
Quail Run .... (707)887-9077

Fort Bidwell
Ft Bidwell Hotel & Restaurant ... (916)279-6199

Fort Bragg
Jughandle Beach Country B&B Inn (707)964-1415
Claudia's Garden .... (707)964-5574
Cleone Lodge Inn .... (707)964-2788
Colonial Inn .... (707)964-9979
The Farm at Granny's Hill ...... (707)961-9600
Glass Beach B&B .... (707)964-6774
Noyo River Lodge .... (707)964-8045
Pudding Creek Inn (707)964-9529 (800)227-9529
The Rendezvous Inn & Restaurant
.... (707)964-8142 (800)491-8142
Roundhedge Inn .... (707)964-9605
Todd Farm House Bed & Breakfast (707)964-6575
Wits End .... (707)961-0775

Freestone
Green Apple Inn .... (707)874-2526

Fremont
Lord Bradley's Inn .... (510)490-0520

French Gulch
French Gulch Hotel .... (916)359-2112

Garberville
Benbow Inn .... (707)923-2125
Ranch House .... (707)923-3441

Gazelle
Hollyhock Farm Bed & Breakfast . (916)435-2627

Georgetown
American River Inn .... (916)333-4499

Geyserville
Isis Oasis Lodge .... (707)857-3524

Glen Ellen
Above The Clouds B & B ...... (707)996-7371
Beltane Ranch Bed & Breakfast .. (707)996-6501
Gaige House .... (707)935-0237
Glenelly Inn .... (707)996-6720
Jack London Lodge .... (707)938-8501
Stone Tree Ranch .... (707)996-8173

Goleta
Circle Bar B Ranch .... (805)968-1113

Grass Valley
Annie Horan's .. (916)272-2418 (800)273-7390
Domike's Inn .... (916)273-9010
Golden Ore House B&B .... (916)272-6872
Holbrooke Hotel & Purcell House (916)273-1353
Murphy's Inn ... (916)273-6873 (800)895-2488
Swan-Levine House .... (916)272-1873

Gridley
McCracken's Inn .... (916)846-2108
Thresher Mansion .... (916)846-0530

Groveland
Hotel Charlotte .... (209)962-6455

Gualala
The Inn at Getchell Cove .... (707)884-1936
Gualala Hotel .... (707)884-3441
The Old Milano Hotel & Restaurant (707)884-3256
St. Orres .... (707)884-3303
Whale Watch Inn .... (707)884-3667

Guerneville
Applewood .... (707)869-9093
Creekside Inn .... (707)869-3623
Happy Landing Guest House .... (707)869-0286
Santa Nella House .... (707)869-9488

Guernewood Park
Fern Grove Inn .. (707)869-9083 (800)347-9083

Half Moon Bay
Cypress Inn on Miramar Beach .. (415)726-6002
Half Moon Bay Lodge .... (800)368-2468
Little Creek Mansion .... (415)726-3464
Mill Rose Inn .... (415)726-7673

Happy Camp
Culverls Lodge .... (916)493-2473

Healdsburg
Belle Du Jour Farm .... (707)431-9777
Calderwood .... (707)431-1110 (800)600-5444
Frampton House .... (707)433-5084
George Alexander House ...... (707)433-1358
Healdsburg Inn on The Plaza
.... (707)433-6991 (800)431-8663
Lions Lair .... (707)431-1211
Lytton Springs Inn .... (707)431-1109
Villa Messina .... (707)433-6655

Helendale
Inn at Silver Lakes .... (619)243-4800

Hemet
Hearts Home Farm .... (909)926-3343

Homeland
Rancho Kaeru .... (714)894-5635

Homewood
Chaney House .... (916)525-7333
Rockwood Lodge .... (916)525-5273
Tahoma Meadows B&B .... (916)525-1553

Hopland
Fetzer Bed & Breakfast .... (800)846-8637

Huntington Beach
Harbour Inn at Sunset Beach ... (310)592-4770
Huntington Beach House B&B ... (714)536-7818

Hyampom
River View Inn .... (916)628-4024

Idyllwild
Cedar Street Inn .... (909)659-4789
Creekstone Inn .... (909)659-3342
Fern Valley Inn .... (909)659-2205

Indio
Palm Shadow Inn .... (619)347-3476

Inverness
Alder House .... (415)669-7218
Blackthorne Inn .... (415)663-8621
Dancing Coyote Beach .... (415)669-7200
Dunrobin Cottage .... (415)669-7170
Fairwinds Farm B&B Cottage ... (415)663-9454
Hickman House .... (415)669-7428
Hotel Inverness .... (415)669-7393
Manka's Inverness Lodge ...... (415)669-1034
The Patterson House
.... (415)669-1383 (800)690-1383
Sandy Cove Inn .... (415)669-2683

Irvine
Queen's House .... (714)380-1488

Isleton
Delta Daze Inn .. (916)777-6794 (800)585-4667

Jackson
Ann Marie's .... (209)223-1452
Broadway Hotel .... (209)223-3503
Court Street Inn . (209)223-0416 (800)200-0416
The Hughes House Inn Bed & Breakfast
.... (209)223-1117
Windrose Inn .... (209)223-3650

Jamestown
Slide Mt Ranch .... (209)984-0450

Jenner
Murphy's Jenner-By-The-Sea ... (707)865-2377
Salt Point Lodge . (707)847-3234 (800)956-3437
Stillwater Cove Ranch .... (707)847-3227

Joshua Tree
Joshua Tree Inn . (619)366-1188 (800)366-1444

Julian
Butterfield B&B . (619)765-2179 (800)379-4262
Eden Creek Orchard Guest House (619)765-2102
Fairoaks Bed & Breakfast ...... (619)765-0704
Historical House Lodging ...... (619)765-1931
Homestead Bed & Breakfast .... (619)765-1536
Julian Gold Rush Hotelp.o. Box 1 (619)765-1420
Mountain High B&B .... (619)765-1083
Oak Hill Farm Lodging .... (619)765-2356
Pine Cone Inn .... (619)765-2191
Pinecroft Manor .... (619)765-1611
Rockin' A B&B .... (619)765-2820

June Lake
Heidelberg Inn .... (619)648-7781

Kentfield
Thirty-Nine Cypress Bed & Breakfast Inn
.... (415)663-1709

Kernville
Whispering Pines .... (619)376-3733

Kings Canyon Park
Montecito-Sequoia Lodge ...... (209)565-3388

Kirkwood
Kit Carson Lodge Restaurant on Silver Lake
.... (209)258-8500

Klamath
The Requa Inn .... (707)482-8205

Knights Ferry
Knights Ferry Hotel B&B .... (209)881-3418

Kyburz
Strawberry Lodge .... (916)659-7030

La Jolla
Prospect Park Inn .... (619)454-0133

La Porte
Gold Country .... (916)675-2322

Lafayette
Donner Country Inn .... (916)587-5574

Laguna Beach
Bed & Breakfast 800 .... (714)376-0313
Eiler's Inn .... (714)494-3004
Inn at Laguna Beach .... (714)497-9722

Lake Arrowhead
Bluebelle Hosue Bed & Breakfast . (909)336-3292
Bracken Fern Manor .... (909)337-8557
The Carriage House Bed & Breakfast
.... (909)336-1400
Chateau Du Lac . (909)337-6488 (800)601-8722
Eagles Landing B&B .... (909)336-2642
Ellies Inn .... (909)337-1283
Lakeview Lodge Victorian ...... (714)337-6633
Saddleback Inn .... (714)336-3571
Sky Forest Bed & Breakfast Inn .. (909)337-4680
Willow Creek Inn .... (909)336-2008

Lake Hughes
Lake Hughes Trading Post ..... (805)724-1855

Lakeport
Arbor House .... (707)263-6444
Wooden Bridge B&B .... (707)263-9125

Laytonville
Mad Creek Inn .... (707)984-6206

Leggett
Bell Glen B&B In The Redwoods . (707)925-6425

Lemon Cove
Lemon Cove B&B Inn .... (209)597-2555

Littleriver
Glendeven .... (707)937-0083
Heritage House .... (707)937-5885
Little River Inn .... (707)937-5942
Rachel's Inn .... (707)937-0088
Stevenswood Lodge .... (707)937-2810

Lodi
Golden Era Hotel .... (209)333-8866

Loleta
Southport Landing, A B&B on Humboldt Bay
.... (707)733-5915

Long Beach
Appleton Place .... (213)432-2312
Lord Mayor's B&B Inn .... (310)436-0324

Los Angeles
Chaunessys House .... (213)664-2352
Inn at 657 .... (213)741-2200
Norja B&B Inn .... (213)933-3652
Salisbury House . (213)737-7817 (800)373-1778
Terrace Manor .... (213)381-1478

Los Gatos
La Hacienda Inn .... (408)354-9230

Los Osos
Gerarda Ondang B&B .... (805)534-0834

Lotus
Golden Lotus B&B .... (916)621-4562

Loyalton
Clover Valley Mill House .... (916)993-4819

Lucerne
Kristalberg B&B .... (707)274-8009

Malibu
Malibu Beach Inn .... (213)456-6444

Mammoth Lakes
Cinnamon Bear Inn .... (619)934-2873
Mammoth Country Inn .... (619)934-2710
Rainbow Tarns .. (619)935-4556 (800)935-4556
Snow Goose Inn .... (800)874-7368
White Horse Inn . (619)924-3656 (800)982-5657
Wildasinn House .... (619)934-3851

Manchester
Victorian Gardens .... (707)882-3606

Marina Del Rey
Mansion Inn .... (310)821-2557

Mariposa
5th Street Inn .... (209)966-6048
Bears Den .... (209)742-2327
Boulder Creek B&B .... (209)742-7729
Dick & Shirls Bed & Breakfast ... (209)966-2514
Dubord's Restful Nest .... (209)742-7127
Granny's Garden .... (209)377-8342
Little Valley Inn at The Creek .... (209)742-6204
Mariposa Hotel-Inn Downtown Mariposa
.... (209)966-4676
Meadow Creek Ranch B&B Inn .. (209)966-3843
The Pelennor B&B .... (209)966-2832
Poppy Hill B&B .... (209)742-6273
Rockwood Gardens
.... (209)742-6817 (800)859-8862
Schlageter House .... (209)966-2471
Shangri-Lab Bed & Breafkast ... (209)966-2653
Shiloh Bed & Breakfast .... (209)742-7200

Villa Monti Bed & Breakfast ..... (209)966-2439
The Whitlock House .... (209)966-5504
Winsor Farms B&B .... (209)966-5592

McCloud
Francois' Grey Squirrel Inn ..... (916)964-3105
Hogin House B&B .... (916)964-2882
Joanie's B&B .... (916)964-3106
McCloud Guest House .... (916)964-3160
McCloud River Inn .... (916)964-2130
Stoney Brook Inn .... (916)964-2300

Mendocino
Agate Cove Inn .... (707)937-0551
Ames Lodge .... (707)937-0811
B.G. Ranch & Inn .... (707)937-5322
Blue Heron Inn .... (707)947-4323
Brewery Gulch Inn .... (707)937-4752
Captain's Cove Inn .... (707)937-5150
Cypress House .... (707)937-1456
Hill House Inn .... (707)937-0554
Maccallum House Inn .... (707)937-0289
Main Street Guest House ...... (707)937-5150
McElroy's Inn .... (707)937-1734
Mendocino Farmhouse .... (707)937-0241
Mendocino Hotel (707)937-0511 (800)548-0513
Mendocino Village Cottages .... (707)937-0866
Mendocino Village Inn .... (707)937-0246
Rachel's Inn .... (707)937-0088
S.S. Seafoam Lodge .... (707)937-1827
Sea Gull Inn .... (707)937-5204
Sea Rock Bed & Breakfast Inn .. (707)937-0926
Sears House Inn .... (707)937-4076
The Stanford Inn By The Sea
.... (707)937-5615 (800)331-8884
Whitegate Inn ... (707)937-4892 (800)531-7282

Menlo Park
Stanford Park Hotel .... (415)322-1234

Merced
Peralta Farming Co .... (209)723-3991
White House .... (209)723-3991

Middletown
Big Canyon Inn .... (707)928-5631

Midpines
Homestead Guest Ranch Bed & Breakfast
.... (209)966-2820
Lions Den Guest Ranch .... (209)966-5254

Mill Valley
Mill Valley Bed & Breakfast ..... (415)389-4040
Mill Valley Inn .... (415)389-6608

Mokelumne Hill
Hotel Leger .... (209)286-1401

Montara
Farrallone Inn .... (415)728-8200

Monte Rio
Highland Dell Inn (707)865-1759 (800)767-1759
Huckleberry Springs .... (707)865-2683

Montecito
Coast Village Inn .... (805)969-3266
San Ysidro Ranch .... (805)969-5046

Monterey
Del Monte Beach Inn .... (408)649-4410
Merritt House .... (408)646-9686
Monterey Hotel .... (408)375-3184
Old Monterey Inn .... (408)375-8284
The Spindrift Inn .... (408)646-8900

Morro Bay
Coffey Break Bed & Breakfast ... (805)772-4378
Marina Street Inn .... (805)772-4016

Moss Beach
Seal Cove Inn .... (415)728-7325

Mount Shasta
Dream Inn .... (916)926-1536
Edson House .... (916)926-1754
Mount Shasta House B&B ..... (916)926-5089
Mt Shasta Cabins .... (916)926-5396
Wagon Creek Inn .... (916)926-0838

Muir Beach
Pelican Inn .... (415)383-6000

Murphys
Trade Carriage House .... (209)728-3408

Napa
1801 Inn .... (707)224-3739
Arbor Guest House .... (707)252-8144
Bowen Manor .... (707)255-8488
Brookside Vineyard Bed & Breakfast
.... (707)944-1661
The Candlelight Inn .... (707)257-3717
Cedar Gables Inn (707)224-7969 (800)309-7969
Chateau Hotel .... (707)253-7300
Coombs Residence Inn on The Park
.... (707)257-0789
The Crossroads Inn .... (707)944-0646
The Elm House .... (707)255-1831
Gallery Osgood B&B Inn .... (707)224-0100
Goodman House .... (707)257-1166
Hillview Country Inn .... (707)224-5004
Inn on Randolph .... (707)257-2886
La Belle Epoque . (707)257-2161 (800)238-8070
La Residence Country Inn ...... (707)253-0337
Oak Knoll Inn .... (707)255-2200
Sybron House .. (707)944-2785 (800)944-2785
Tall Timbers Chalets .... (707)252-7810
Trubody Ranch Bed & Breakfast . (707)255-5907

National City
Dickinson Boal Mansion .... (619)477-5363

Nevada City
Grandmere's Inn .... (916)265-4660
The Parsonage B&B .... (916)265-9478
Piety Hill Inn ... (916)265-2245 (800)443-2245

Newcastle
Victorian Manor .... (916)663-3009

Newport Beach
Doryman's Inn .... (714)675-7300
Island Cottage B&B .... (714)723-1125
Little Inn on The Bay .... (714)673-8800

Nice
Featherbed Railroad Company B&B (707)274-4434

North Hollywood
La Maida House .... (818)769-3857

Oakhurst
Ople's Guest House .... (209)683-4317
Pine Rose Inn .... (209)642-2800
Places In Paradise .... (209)683-8425

Oakland
Bedside Manor .... (510)452-4550
Rose Suite .... (510)763-1371

Occidental
Golden Apple Ranch .... (707)874-3756

Ojai
Casa De La Luna .... (805)646-4528
Ojai Manor Hotel .... (805)646-0961
The Theodore Woolsey House ... (805)646-9779
Wheeler Hot Springs .... (805)646-8131

Olema
Bear Valley Inn .... (415)663-1777
Olema Inn & Restaurant .... (415)663-9559
Point Reyes Seashore Lodge .... (415)663-9000
Roundstone Farm .... (415)663-1020

Ontario
Country Side Inn-Ontario ...... (909)986-8550
Country Suites By Ayres .... (909)390-7778

Orange
French Inn .... (714)997-5038

Orinda
Larkmead Country Inn .... (707)942-5360

Orosi
Mama Bear's Orchard B&B
.... (209)528-3614 (800)530-2327
Valley View Citrus Ranch ...... (209)528-2275

Oroville
Bed & Breakfast Jean Pratts Riverside
.... (916)533-1413
Montgomery Inn .... (916)532-1400

Pacific Grove
Gatehouse Inn .. (408)649-8436 (800)753-1881
Lighthouse Lodge .... (408)655-2111
Pacific Gardens Inns .... (408)646-9414
Pacific Grove Inn .... (408)375-2825

Palm Desert
Desert Breezes/Four Seasons ... (619)345-2637

Palm Springs
Casa De Los Ninos D'Amor .... (619)323-4733
Hedy's Hideaway .... (619)323-4413
Ingleside Inn .... (619)325-0046
Korakia Pensione .... (619)864-6411
Marquis Hotel and Villas .... (619)322-2121
Orchid Tree Inn .... (619)325-2791
Sakura, Japanese B&B
.... (619)327-0705 (800)200-0705
Villa Royale Inn .... (619)327-2314

Palo Alto
Cowper Inn .... (415)327-4475
Hotel California .... (415)322-7666

Paso Robles
Almond View Inn .... (805)238-4220
Arbor Inn .... (805)227-4673
Gillie Archer Inn .... (805)238-0879
Just Inn .... (805)238-6932
Templeton Manor .... (805)434-1529

Pescadero
Hidden Forest Cottage .... (415)879-1046
McKenzie House .... (415)879-0337

Philo
Philo Pottery Inn .... (707)895-3069
Pinoli Ranch Country Inn ...... (707)895-2550

Pine Grove
Druid House Bed & Breakfast ... (209)296-4156

Placerville
Fleming-Jones Homestead ..... (916)626-5840
Historic Combellack-Blair House . (916)622-3764
River Rock Inn .... (916)622-7640
Rupley House Inn .... (916)626-0630
Time Out .... (916)644-0314
Vineyard House Bed & Breakfast . (916)622-2217

Platina
Living Springs Farm & Guest Ranch
.... (916)352-4338

Pleasanton
Evergreen Bed & Breakfast ..... (510)426-0901
Plum Tree Inn .... (510)426-9588

Plymouth
Amador Harvest Inn .... (209)245-5512
Indian Creek Bed & Breakfast ... (209)245-4648
Plymouth House Inn .... (209)245-3298

Point Arena
Coast Guard House .... (707)882-2442
Point Arena Bed & Breakfast .... (707)882-3455
Wagner's Windhaven .... (707)884-4617

Point Reyes Station
Berry Patch Cottage .... (415)663-1942
Casa Mexicana .... (415)663-8313
Horseshoe Farm Cottage ...... (415)663-9401
Inn on Tomales Bay .... (415)663-9002
Jasmine Cottage .... (415)663-1166
Knob Hill .... (415)663-1784
London House .... (415)388-2487
Marsh Cottage Bed & Breakfast .. (415)669-7168
Pt Reyes Country Inn & Stables . (415)663-9696
Tradewinds Bed & Breakfast .... (415)663-9326
The Tree House .... (415)663-8720
Windsong Cottage Bed & Breakfast (415)663-9695

Porterville
Mountain Top Bed & Breakfast .. (209)542-2639
The Inn at Rosebed Inn .... (209)782-5580

Portola
Pullman House .... (916)832-0107

Posey
Road's End at Paso Creek ..... (805)536-8668

Princeton
Pillar Point Inn .... (800)400-8281

Quincy
New England Ranch .... (916)283-2223

Ramona
Lake Sutherland Lodge Bed & Breakfast
.... (619)789-6483
Lucys Attic .... (619)788-9543

Rancho Cucamonga
Christmas House B&B .... (909)980-6450

Red Bluff
The Jarvis Mansion .... (916)527-6901
Jefferson House .... (916)527-4133
The Jeter Victorian Inn .... (916)527-7574

Redding
Cabral House B&B .... (916)244-3766
Palisades Paradise Bed and Breakfast
.... (916)223-5305
Redding's B&B .... (916)222-2494
Tiffany House B&B Inn .... (916)244-3225

Redlands
Morey Mansion .... (909)793-7970

Redondo Beach
Villa Alegre .... (310)376-3030

Reedley
The Fairweather Inn B&B ...... (209)638-1918
Hotel Burgess .... (209)638-6315
Reedley Country Inn .... (209)638-6333

Ridgecrest
Bevlen Haus Bed & Breakfast ... (619)375-1988

Running Springs
Spring Oaks B&B .... (909)867-9636
Rutherford
Rancho Caymus Inn .... (707)963-1777
Sacramento
Amber House ... (916)552-6525 (800)755-6526
Driver Mansion Inn .... (916)455-5243
Hartley House Bed & Breakfast Inn (916)447-7829
Inn at Parkside .... (916)658-1818
River Rose .... (916)665-6550
Riverboat Delta King .... (916)444-5464
Savoyard .... (916)442-6709
Sterling Hotel .... (916)448-1300
Saint Helena
Ambrose Bierce House .... (707)963-3003
Auberge Brisebois .... (707)963-4658
Barro Station Bed & Breakfast ... (707)963-5169
Bed & Breakfast Almanac ...... (707)963-0852
Brannans Loft .... (707)963-2181
Bylund House B&B .... (707)963-9073
Chestelson House .... (707)963-2238
Creekside Inn .... (707)963-7244
Asplund Country Inn .... (707)963-4614
Erika's Hillside .... (707)944-8101
Glass Mountain Inn .... (707)963-3512
Harvest Inn .... (707)963-9463
Hilltop House Bed & Breadfast .. (707)944-0880
Hotel Saint Helena .... (707)963-4388
Hyphen Inn .... (707)942-0434
Ink House .... (707)963-3890
Judy's Ranch House .... (707)963-3081
La Fleur B&B .... (707)963-0233
Milat Bed & Breakfast .... (707)963-2612
Napa Valley Wine Country Bed & Breakfast
.... (707)963-4089
Prager Winery B&B .... (707)963-3720
Rose Garden Inn .... (707)963-4417
Rustridge Ranch .... (707)965-9353
Shady Oaks Country Inn .... (707)963-1190
Spanish Villa .... (707)963-7483
Sunny Acres Bed & Breakfast ... (707)963-2826
Vineyard Country Inn .... (707)963-1000
White Ranch .... (707)963-4635
Zinfandel Inn .... (707)963-3512
San Andreas
Robin's Nest .... (209)754-1076
Thorn Mansion Inn .... (209)754-1027
San Clemente
Casa Tropicana B&B .... (714)492-1234
San Diego
1621 Ocean Front .... (619)294-2303
Balboa Park Inn .... (619)298-0823
Beach Area Bed & Breakfast .... (619)226-4133
Bears at The Beach Bed & Breakfast
.... (619)272-2578
Bed & Breakfast-The Cottage ... (619)299-1564
Blom House Bed & Breakfast ... (619)467-0890
Britt House Bed & Breakfast .... (619)234-2926
The Cottage .... (619)299-1564
Harbor Hill Guest House .... (619)233-0638
Keating House .... (619)239-8585
Monet's Garden .... (619)464-8296
Yacht & Breakfast Charters ..... (619)297-4862
San Francisco
1818 California .... (415)885-1818
Abigail Hotel .... (415)861-9728
Adelaide Inn .... (415)441-2261
Albion House .... (415)621-0896
Alexander Inn .... (415)928-6800
Andora Inn .... (415)282-0337
Andrews Hotel .... (415)563-6877
Ansonia Cambridge Bed & Breakfast
.... (415)673-2670
Archbishop's Mansion
.... (415)563-7872 (800)543-5820
Art Center/Wamsley Gallery/B&B
.... (415)567-1526 (800)927-8236
Auberge Des Artistes .... (415)776-2530
Aurora Manor .... (415)564-2480
B G Ranch & Inn .... (415)668-1171
B&B Near The Park .... (415)753-3574
Black Stallion .... (415)863-0131
Bock's B&B .... (415)664-6842
Brady Acres .... (415)929-8033
Subtleties - Carol's Cow Hollow
.... (415)775-8295 (800)400-8295
Country Cottage B&B
.... (415)479-1913 (800)452-8249
Dakota Hotel .... (415)931-7475
Dolores Park Inn .... (415)621-0482
El Drisco Hotel .... (415)346-2880
Grove Inn .... (415)929-0780
Haus Kleebauer .... (415)821-1417
Hill Point Bed & Breakfast & Inn . (415)753-0393
Hotel David Bed & Breakfast .... (415)771-1600
The Inn on Castro .... (415)861-0321
Jackson Court .... (415)929-7670
Kensington Park Hotel .... (415)788-6400
The Mansions Hotel
.... (415)929-9444 (800)826-9398
Marina Inn B&B .... (415)928-1000
Moffatt House .... (415)753-9279
Monte Cristo .... (415)931-1875
The Nob Hill Lambourne .... (415)433-2287
Obrero Hotel & Basque Restaurant (415)989-3960
The Pacific Bay Inn .... (415)673-0234
Pensione International .... (415)775-3344
Queen Anne Hotel .... (415)441-2828
Red Victorian B&B Inn .... (415)864-1978
Sherman House .... (415)563-3600
The Tuscan-An Inn at Fisherman's Wharf
.... (415)561-1100
Union Street Inn .... (415)346-0424
Washington Square Inn
.... (415)981-4220 (800)388-0220
Willows B&B Inn .... (415)431-4770
San Jose
The Briar Rose B&B Inn .... (408)279-5999
San Juan Bautista
B&B San Juan .... (408)623-4101
San Juan Capistrano
Christian B&B of America ...... (714)496-7050
San Leandro
Best House .... (510)351-0911
San Luis Obispo
Adobe Inn .... (805)549-0321
Heritage Inn .... (805)544-7440
San Miguel
The Ranch Bed & Breakfast .... (805)463-2320
Victorian Manor B&B .... (805)467-3306
San Rafael
Blackthorne Inn .... (415)663-8621
Casa Soldavini .... (415)454-3140
Gerstle Park Inn . (415)721-7611 (800)726-7611
Jasmine Cottage .... (415)663-9449
Larkspur Bed & Breakfast ...... (415)924-5830
Laurel Ridge Cottage Inn .... (415)663-1286
Panama Hotel .... (415)457-3993
Poets Loft .... (415)453-8080
Tradewinds Bed & Breakfast .... (415)663-9326
Santa Barbara
B&B at Valli's View .... (805)969-1272
Harbour Carriage House .... (805)965-2333
El-Encanto Hotel & Garden Villas . (805)687-5000
Hacienda Motel .... (805)687-6461
Ivanhoe Inn .... (805)963-8832
The Mary May Inn .... (805)569-3398
Montecito Inn .... (805)969-7854
Mountain View Inn .... (805)687-6636
Old Mission House .... (805)569-1914
The Parsonage .. (805)962-9336 (800)775-0352
Tiffany Inn .... (805)963-2283
Bayberry Inn .... (805)682-3199
Villa D' Italia .... (805)687-6933
Villa Rosa .... (805)966-0851
Santa Cruz
The Darling House-A B&B Inn By The Sea
.... (408)458-1958
Harbor Boat & Breakfast .... (408)462-3168
Inn Laguna Creek .... (408)425-0692
Jewel By The Sea Bed & Breakfast (408)464-2665
Pleasure Point Inn .... (408)475-4657
Santa Monica
The Victorian Inn .... (310)772-7464
Santa Paula
Fern Oaks .... (805)525-7747
Glen Tavern Inn .... (805)525-6658
The White Gables Inn .... (805)933-3041
Santa Rosa
Drummond B & B Bookings .... (707)526-4828
Gee-Gee's B&B Inn .... (707)833-6667
Hilltop House B&B .... (707)944-0880
The Inn at The Belvedere ...... (707)575-1857
Sausalito
Butterfly Tree .... (415)383-8447
Scotia
The Scotia Inn .... (707)764-5683
Sea Ranch
Sea Ranch Lodge .... (707)785-2371
Seal Beach
Lamplighter Inn .... (805)547-7777
Sebastopol
Gravenstein Inn .... (707)829-0493
Shingletown
Weston House .... (916)474-3738
Sierra City
Busch & Heringlake Country Inn . (916)862-1501
High Country Inn .... (916)862-1530
Smith River
Casa Rubio .... (707)487-4313
Haight House Inn .... (707)487-9260
Soda Springs
Rainbow Lodge . (916)426-3871 (800)500-3871
Soda Springs Creekside Bed & Breakfast
.... (916)426-9308
Traverse Inn .... (916)426-3010
Solvang
Chimney Sweep Inn .... (805)688-2111
Storybook Inn Bed & Breakfast .. (805)688-1703
Tivoli Inn .... (805)688-0559
Somerset
7Up Bar Ranch .... (916)620-5450
Fitzpatrick Winery & Lodge ..... (916)620-3248
Somis
Rancho De Somis .... (805)987-8455
Sonoma
Chalet B&B .... (707)938-3129
The Hidden Oak .... (707)996-9863
Magliulo's Pensione .... (707)996-1031
Thistle Dew Inn .... (707)938-2909
Vineyard Inn .... (707)938-2350 (800)359-4667
Sonora
A Touch of Country .... (209)533-8269
Barretta Gardens Inn .... (209)532-6039
Oliver's .... (209)532-0420
Gunn House Motor Hotel ...... (209)532-3421
Hammons House Inn B&B ..... (209)532-7921
Historic Sonora Inn .... (209)532-7468
La Casa Inglesa .... (209)532-5822
Llamahall Guest Ranch .... (209)532-7264
Lulu Belle's .... (209)533-3455
Mountain View Bed & Breakfast . (209)533-0628
Rail Fence Motel .... (209)532-9191
Via Serena Ranch .... (209)532-5307
Soulsbyville
Willow Springs Country Inn ..... (209)533-2030
South Lake Tahoe
Christiana Inn .... (916)544-7337
South Pasadena
The Bissell House .... (818)441-3535
South San Francisco
Oyster Point Marina Inn .... (415)737-7633
Springville
Annie's B&B .... (209)539-3827
Stateline
Tamarack Creek Bed and & Breakfast
.... (916)659-0325
Stinson Beach
Casa Del Mar .... (415)868-2124
Ocean Court .... (415)868-0212
Redwoods Haus The B & B .... (415)868-1034
Shoreline House .... (415)868-1062
Stirling City
Stirling City Hotel Country Store & Rest
.... (916)873-0858
Stockton
The Old Victorian Inn .... (209)462-1613
Summerland
Summerland Inn .... (805)969-5225
Sunset Beach
Harbour Inn .... (310)592-4770 (800)596-4770
Harbour Inn at Sunset Beach ... (714)846-1765
Sunset B&B Inn .... (213)592-1666
Susanville
The Roseberry House .... (916)257-5675
Sutter Creek
Foxes In Sutter Creek .... (209)267-5882
Nancy & Bob's 9 Eureka Street Inn (209)267-0342
Picturebrock Inn .... (209)267-5500
Sutter Creek Inn .... (209)267-5606

Tahoe City
Chaney House .... (916)525-7333
Cottage Inn at Lake Tahoe ...... (916)581-4073
Mayfield House .... (916)583-1001
Palmer House Bed & Breakfast .. (916)581-0187
River Ranch .... (916)583-4264
Tahoe Vista
Tahoe Sands Resort .... (916)546-2592
Tahoma
The Captain's Alpenhaus ...... (916)525-5000
Norfolk Woods Inn .... (916)525-5000
Tahoma Meadows Bed & Breakfast (916)525-1553
Three Rivers
Cinnamon Creek Ranch .... (209)561-1107
Organic Gardens B&B .... (209)561-0916
Sequoia Village .... (209)561-3652
Tomales
Tomales Country Inn .... (707)878-2041
U.S. Hotel .... (707)878-2742
Trinidad
Turtle Rocks Inn .... (707)677-3707
Trinity Center
Carrville Inn B&B .... (916)266-3511
Truckee
Alta Hotel .... (916)587-6668
Bradley House .... (916)587-5388
Donner Country Inn .... (916)587-5574
Star Hotel .... (916)587-3007
Swedish House .... (916)587-0400
The Truckee Hotel .... (916)587-4444
Tuolumne
Oak Hill Ranch .... (209)928-4717
Twain Harte
Twain Harte's B&B .... (209)586-3311
Twentynine Palms
Homestead Inn .... (619)367-0030
Roughley Manor .... (619)367-3238
Ukiah
Oak Knoll B&B .... (707)462-8322
The Sanford House .... (707)462-1653
Valley Center
Lake Wohlford B&B
.... (619)749-1911 (800)831-8239
Valley Ford
The Inn at Valley Ford .... (707)876-3182
Ventura
Bella Maggiore Inn .... (805)652-0277
Visalia
Ben Maddox House B&B
.... (209)739-8381 (800)401-9800
Garden Room .... (209)561-4853
Spalding House .... (209)739-7877
Volcano
Norcross .... (209)296-4959
Walnut Creek
Diablo Mountain Inn .... (510)937-5050
Warner Springs
Lodge at Sunshine Summit ..... (619)782-3537
Watsonville
Dunmovin .... (408)722-2810
Weaverville
Granny's House .... (916)623-2756
West Covina
Hendrick Inn .... (818)919-2125
West Hollywood
San Vicente Inn .... (310)854-6915
Westminster
Wooded Hare .... (714)896-4768
Westport
Bowen's Pelican Lodge & Inn ... (707)964-5588
Dehaven Valley Farm .... (707)961-1660
Whitethorn
Shelter Cove Ocean Inn .... (707)986-7161
Williams
Wilbur Hot Springs .... (916)473-2306
Willits
The Doll House B&B .... (707)459-4055
Windsor
Country Meadow Inn .... (707)431-1276
Yosemite
The Yosemite Peregrine B&B .... (209)372-8517
Yountville
Bordeaux House . (707)944-2855 (800)677-6370
Burgundy House Country Inn ... (707)944-0889
Napa Valley Railway Inn .... (707)944-2000
Oleander House .... (707)944-8315
Sybron House .... (707)944-2785
The Webber Place .... (707)944-8384
Yreka
McFadden's Inn .... (916)842-7712
Yuba City
Harkey House B&B .... (916)674-1942
The Wicks .... (916)674-8559

Colorado

Allenspark
Allenspark Lodge .... (303)747-2552
Lazy H Guest Ranch .... (303)747-2532
Arvada
On Golden Pond B&B .... (303)424-2296
Aspen
Alpine Lodge .... (303)925-7351
The Aspen B & B Lodge .... (303)925-7650
Aspen Ski Lodge .... (303)925-3434
Christmas Inn .... (303)925-3822
Fireside Inn .... (303)925-6000
Hearthstone House .... (303)925-7632
Heatherbed Mountain Lodge .... (970)925-7077
Hotel Lenado .... (303)925-6246
Independence Square Hotel .... (303)920-2313
Innsbruck Inn .... (303)925-2980
Inverness Lodge .... (303)925-8500
Little Red Ski Haus .... (303)925-3333
Mountain House B&B .... (303)920-2550
Pomegranate Inn .... (800)525-4012
Snow Queen Lodge .... (303)925-8455
Stapleton Spurr B&B .... (303)925-7322
Tipple Inn .... (800)321-7025
Ullr Lodge .... (303)925-7696
Wolcott's .... (303)925-1064
Ault
The Adams House .... (303)834-1587
Bailey
Glen-Isle Resort .... (303)838-5461
Basalt
Altamira Ranch .... (303)927-3309
Cozy Log Home .... (303)927-4125
Shenandoah Inn .... (303)927-4991
Bayfield
Deer Valley Resorts .... (303)884-2600
Bellvue
Gypsy Terrace B&B .... (303)224-9389
Raindrop .... (719)493-0799
Sky Corral Ranch .... (303)484-1362
Berthoud
Berthoud B&B .... (970)532-4566
Beulah
Beulah House .... (719)584-3201
KK Ranch & Carriage Museum .. (303)485-3250
Black Hawk
Bed & Breakfast Inn at Blackhawk (303)582-5235
Boulder
The Alps Boulder Canyon Inn ... (303)444-5445
The Inn at Boulder Victoria ..... (303)938-1300
Gunbarrel Guest House .... (303)530-1513
The Inn on Mapleton Hill .... (303)449-6528
Pearl Street Inn .... (303)444-5584
Breckenridge
Allaire Timbers Inn .... (303)453-7530
Fireside Inn .... (303)453-6456
High Country Lodge .... (303)453-9843
Hummingbird House B&B ...... (303)453-6957
Little Mountain Lodge .... (303)453-1969
One Wellington Square .... (303)453-6196
Swiss Inn B&B .... (303)453-6489
The Walker House (303)453-2426 (800)365-6365
Williams House B&B .... (303)453-2975
Broomfield
Broomfield Guest House .... (303)469-3900
Buena Vista
Adobe Inn .... (719)395-6340
Blue Sky Inn .... (719)395-8865
Elk Mountain Ranch .... (719)395-6313
Meister House B&B
.... (719)395-9220 (800)882-1821
Trout City Inn .... (719)495-0348
Buffalo Creek
The Blue Jay Inn .... (719)395-8433
Carbondale
Aunt Grace's B&B .... (303)963-8293
Crystal River Inn .... (303)963-3902
Mt. Sopris Inn .. (970)963-2209 (800)437-8675
The Van Horn House at Lions Ridge
.... (303)963-3605
Cascade
Eastholme In The Rockies ...... (719)684-9901
Cedaredge
Cedar's Edge Llamas B&B ..... (303)856-6836
Central City
The Victorian Inn .... (303)582-0516
Winfield Scott Guestquarters B&B (303)582-3433
Chipita Park
Top of Timpa .... (719)684-2296
Clark
Home Ranch .... (303)879-1780
Coalmont
Shamrock Ranch .... (303)723-8413
Colorado Springs
Black Forest B&B (719)495-4208 (800)809-9901
Hearthstone Inn .... (719)473-4413
Katies Korner .... (719)630-3322
Keith House .... (719)630-3949
Our Hearts Inn .. (719)473-8684 (800)533-7095
The Painted Lady .... (719)473-3165
Tudor Manor .... (719)630-3433
Wedgewood Cottage B&B Inn ... (719)636-1829
Como
Como Depot .... (719)836-2594
Crawford
Sleeping Indian Mountain Lodge B&B
.... (303)921-7378
Creede
4UR Ranch .... (303)658-2202
Creede Hotel .... (719)658-2608
Crested Butte
Alpine Lace Bed & Breakfast .... (303)349-9857
Claim Jumper Inn .... (303)349-6471
Crystal Inn ..... (970)349-1338 (800)390-1338
The Elk Mountain Lodge .... (303)349-7533
Forest Queen Hotel .... (303)349-5336
Nordic Inn .... (303)349-5542
The Tudor Rose B&B .... (303)349-6253
Crestone
Rendezvous Cottage Inn .... (719)256-4821
Cripple Creek
Hotel St. Nicholas .... (800)352-5235
Over The Rainbow B&B .... (719)689-3108
Wild Bill's Pub, Gaming Parlor & B&B
.... (719)689-2707
Denver
Cafe Cartago .... (800)443-8666
Franklin House B&B .... (303)331-9106
Haus Berlin Inc . (303)837-9527 (800)659-0253
The Holiday Chalet .... (303)321-9975
Lumber Baron Inn .... (303)477-8205
The Oxford Hotel (303)628-5400 (800)228-5838
Dillon
Home & Hearth .... (303)468-5541
Divide
Silverwood B&B .... (719)687-6784
Dolores
Mountain View B&B
.... (970)882-7861 (800)228-4592
Rio Grande Southern Hotel
.... (303)882-7527 (800)258-0434
Stoner Lodge .... (303)882-7825
Durango
Blue Spruce Trading Post ...... (303)259-5657
Colorado Trails Ranch .... (800)323-DUDE
Country Sunshine .... (303)247-2853
Gable House .... (303)247-4982
Lake Mancos Ranch .... (800)325-WHOA
Penny's Place .... (303)247-8928
River House B&B .... (303)247-4775
Tall Timber .... (303)259-4813
Vagabond Inn B&B .... (303)259-5901
Eaton
The Victorian Veranda .... (970)454-3890
Edwards
The Lodge at Cordillera .... (303)926-2200
Empire
Mad Creek B&B .... (303)569-2003
Estes Park
Alpenaire Inn Inc. .... (970)586-6607
Aspen Lodge Ranch Resort
.... (303)586-4241 (800)332-6867
Big Horn Guest House
.... (303)586-4175 (800)734-0473

Emerald Manor . . . . (303)586-8050
Hearthside Inn B&B . . . . (303)586-3100
Riversong . . . . (303)586-4666
Sapphire Rose Inn . . . . (303)586-6607
Wanek's Lodge at Estes . . . . (303)586-5851
Wind River Ranch . . . . (303)586-4212

Fort Collins
Helmshire Inn . . . . (303)493-4683
West Mulberry Street B&B . . . . . (303)221-1917

Fraser
Karen's B&B . . . . (303)726-9398
Nordic B&B . . . . (303)726-8459

Frisco
Creekside Inn . . . . (970)668-5607
The Finn Inn . . . . (303)668-5108
Frisco Lodge . . . . (303)668-0195
Galena Street Mountain Inn . . . . . (303)668-3224
The Lark B&B . . . . (303)668-5237
Naomi's Nook . . . . (303)668-3730
Twilight Inn . . . . (303)668-5009
Woods Inn International, Ltd. . . . (303)668-3389

Gardner
The Malachite School & Small Farm B&B
. . . . (719)746-2412

Glen Haven
The Inn of Glen Haven . . . . (303)586-3897

Glenwood Springs
Adducci's Inn B&B . . . . (303)945-9341
Kaiser House B&B . . . . (303)945-8827
Sunlight Bavarian Inn . . . . (303)945-5225

Golden
The Dove Inn . . . . (303)278-2209
The Jameson Inn B&B . . . . (303)278-0351
Royal Scot B&B . . . . (303)526-2411

Granby
C Lazy U Ranch . . . . (303)887-3344
Drowsy Water Ranch . . . . (303)725-3456

Grand Junction
The Cider House B&B . . . . (303)242-9087
Gate House B&B . . . . (303)242-6105
Junction Country Inn . . . . (970)241-2817

Grand Lake
Hummingbird B&B . . . . (303)627-3417
Onahu Lodge . . . . (303)627-8523
The Terrace Inn . . . . (303)627-3079
Winding River Resort Village . . . . (303)627-3215

Grant
Tumbling River Ranch . . . . (303)838-5981

Greeley
Sterling House B&B Inn . . . . (303)351-8805

Green Mountain Falls
Columbine Lodge . . . . (719)684-9062

Guffey
The Spare Room . . . . (719)689-0663

Gunnison
Harmel's Ranch Resort . . . . (800)235-3402
Waunita Hot Springs Ranch . . . . (303)641-1266

Gypsum
7-W Guest Ranch . . . . (303)524-9328
Sweetwater Creek Guest Ranch . (303)524-9301

Hot Sulphur Springs
Hot Sulphur Springs . . . . (303)725-3589

Idaho Springs
St. Mary's Glacier B&B . . . . (303)567-4084

Kremmling
Latigo Ranch . . . . (800)257-9655

La Veta
1899 B&B Inn . . . . (719)742-3576

Lake City
The Adobe B&B . . . . (303)944-2642
The Cinnamon Inn B&B
. . . . (303)944-2641 (800)337-2335
Crystal Lodge . . (303)944-2201 (800)984-1234
Moncrief Mountain Ranch . . . . . . (303)944-2796
The Moss Rose B&B . . . . (303)366-4069
Old Carson Inn . . (970)944-2511 (800)294-0608
Ryan's Roost . . . . (303)944-2339

Lake George
Ute Trail River Ranch . . . . (719)748-3015

Leadville
Ana's Mountain Mansion . . . . . . (719)486-0655
Historic Delaware Hotel
. . . . (719)486-1418 (800)748-2004
The Leadville Country Inn
. . . . (719)486-2354 (800)748-2354

Peri & Ed's Mountain Hide Away
. . . . (719)486-0716 (800)933-3715

Limon
Midwest Country Inn . . . . (303)775-2373

Livermore
Cherokee Park Ranch . . . . (800)628-0949

Loveland
Jefferson House . . . . (303)669-6220
Sylvan Dale Guest Ranch . . . . . . (303)667-3915
Wild Lane B&B Inn . . . . (970)669-0303

Lyons
Peaceful Valley Lodge & Ranch Resort
. . . . (303)747-2881

Maher
Camp Stool Ranch B&B . . . . (303)921-6461

Mancos
Bauer House . . . (970)533-9707 (800)733-9707
Tucker's Mountain Meadows . . . (303)533-7664

Manitou Springs
Billy's Cottage . . . . (719)685-1828
Onaledge B&B . . . . (719)685-4265
Red Eagle Mountain B&B Inn . . . (719)685-4541
Red Stone Castle . . . . (719)685-5071
Two Sisters Inn . . . . (719)685-9684
Victoria's Keep . . (719)683-5359 (800)905-5337

Marble
The Inn at Raspberry Ridge . . . . (303)963-3025

Meredith
The Fryingpan River Ranch . . . . . (303)927-3570

Montrose
Traveler's B&B Inn . . . . (303)249-3472
Vee Broken Bracket . . . . (303)249-5609

Monument
Cross Keys Inn . . . . (719)481-2772

Morrison
Cliff House Lodge . . . . (303)697-9732

Mosca
Great Sand Dunes Country Club & Inn
. . . . (719)378-2356

Nathrop
Deer Valley Ranch . . . . (303)395-2353
Streamside B&B . . . . (719)395-2553

Norwood
Back Narrows Inn & Restaurant . (303)327-4417

Oak Creek
High Meadows Ranch . . . . (800)457-4453

Ohio City
Gold Creek Inn . . . . (303)641-2086

Ouray
Damn Yankee B&B Inn
. . . . (800)687-2926 (800)845-7512
Historic Western Hotel B&B . . . . (303)325-4645
House of Yesteryear . . . . (303)325-4277
Ouray 1898 House B&B . . . . (303)325-4871
St. Elmo Hotel . . . . (303)325-4951
Wiesbaden Hot Springs Spa & Lodge
. . . . (303)325-4347

Pagosa Springs
Davidson's Country Inn B&B . . . . (303)264-5863
Echo Manor Inn . . . . (303)264-5646

Paonia
Whistling Acres Guest Ranch . . . (800)346-1420

Parshall
Aspen Canyon Ranch . . . . (800)321-1357
Bar Lazy J Guest Ranch . . . . (303)725-3437

Powderhorn
Powderhorn Guest Ranch . . . . . . (800)786-1220

Pueblo
The Don-K Ranch . . . . (800)874-0307

Red Cliff
Plum House B&B . . . . (303)827-5881

Redstone
Avalanche Ranch . . . . (303)963-2846
Cleveholm Manor (970)963-3463 (800)643-4837

Ridgway
The Adobe Inn . . . . (303)626-5939
Chipeta Sun Lodge B&B . . . . (303)626-3737
Mactiernan's San Juan Guest Ranch
. . . . (303)626-5360

Rifle
Coulter Lake Guest Ranch . . . . . . (303)625-1473

Salida
The Gazebo Country Inn . . . . (719)539-3818
Minnie Mac's B&B (719)539-3898 (800)484-9684
Poor Farm Country Inn . . . . (719)539-3818

The Tudor Rose B&B . . . . (719)539-2002

San Luis
Casa De Oro Inn . . . . (719)672-3608
El Convento B&B . . . . (719)672-4223

Sedalia
Lost Valley Ranch . . . . (303)647-2311

Shawnee
North Fork Ranch . . . . (303)838-9873

Silver Plume
Brewery Inn . . . . (303)674-5565

Silverton
Christopher House B&B . . . . (303)387-5857
Fool's Gold . . . . (303)387-5879
Grand Imperial Hotel . . . . (303)387-5527
Smedleys B&B . . (303)387-5423 (800)342-4338
The Wyman Hotel . . . . (303)387-5372

Slater
Focus Ranch . . . . (303)583-2410

Snowmass
Starry Pines . . . . (303)927-4202

Snowmass Village
Aspen House . . . . (303)923-4300
Connables' Guest Home . . . . (303)923-5034

Steamboat Springs
Clermont Inn . . . . (303)879-3083
Crawford House . . . . (303)879-1859
Elk River Estates . . . . (303)879-7556
Grand House B&B . . . . (303)879-1939
Harbor Hotel . . . . (800)543-8888
Oak Street B&B . . . . (303)870-0484
Scandinavian Lodge . . . . (800)233-8102
The Inn at Steamboat . . . . (303)879-2600
Steamboat B&B . . . . (303)879-5724
Steamboat Llama Ranch . . . . (303)879-5767
Vista Verde Guest Ranch . . . . . . (303)879-3858

Sterling
Crest House B&B . . . . (303)522-3753

Telluride
Bear Creek B&B . . . . (303)728-6681
Dahl Haus . . . . (303)728-4158
Johnstone Inn . . . . (303)728-3316
Pennington's Mountain Village Inn (800)543-1437
Skyline Guest Ranch . . . . (303)728-3757
Victorian Inn . . . . (303)728-3684

Trinidad
Bluehouse B&B . . . . (719)846-4507

Twin Lakes
Twin Lakes Mountain Retreat . . . (719)486-2593

Vail
Antlers at Vail . . . . (303)476-2471
Black Bear Inn . . . . (303)476-1304
Columbine Chalet B&B of Vail . . . (303)476-1122

Victor
The Kessey House . . . . (719)689-2235
The Portland Inn . . . . (719)689-2102

Westcliffe
The Pines Ranch . . . . (800)446-WHOA
Rainbow Inn . . . . (719)783-2313

Wheat Ridge
Allison Manor . . . . (303)232-1002

Winter Park
Angelmark B&B . . . . (303)726-5354
Beau West B&B . . . . (303)726-5145
Engelmann Pines . . . . (303)726-4632
Outpost B&B Inn (970)726-5346 (800)430-4538
The Quilted Bear . . . . (303)726-5084
Rainbow Trout Ranch . . . . (800)633-3397

Woodland Park
The Hackman House . . . . (719)687-9851
Woodland Hills Lodge . . . . (800)621-8386

Connecticut

Barkhamsted
The Rose & Thistle . . . . (203)379-4744

Bethlehem
The Dutch Moccasin . . . . (203)266-7364

Bolton
Jared Cone House . . . . (860)643-8538

Bozrah
Fitch Claremont House . . . . (860)889-0260

Branford
Cabin In The Woods . . . . (203)488-5284

Brooklyn
Barrett Hill Farm . . . . (203)779-2686
Tannerbrook . . . . (860)774-4822

Central Village
Isaac Shepard House .... (203)564-3012
Cheshire
Inn at Ives Corne .... (203)250-7117
Colchester
Hayward House Inn .... (860)537-5772
Cornwall Bridge
Cornwall Inn & Restaurant ..... (203)672-6884
Cos Cob
Harbor House Inn .... (203)661-5845
Coventry
Millbrook Farm B&B .... (860)742-5761
Special Joys B&B .... (860)742-6359
Durham
Dan'l Merwin House B&B ...... (203)349-8415
Durham B&B .... (203)344-2779
East Haddam
The Gelston House Restaurant & Inn
.... (860)873-1411
Whispering Winds Inn .... (203)526-3055
East Hampton
Heidelberg Inn Inc .... (860)267-4228
East Windsor
The Stephen Potwine House .... (203)623-8722
Essex
Griswold Inn .... (203)767-1776
Farmington
Barney House .... (203)677-9735
Glastonbury
Udderly Wooly Acres .... (203)633-4503
Goshen
Twelve Maples .... (203)491-9316
Greenwich
Homestead Inn .... (203)869-7500
Groton
Shore Inne .... (203)536-1180
Sojourner Inn .... (860)445-1986
Hartford
The 1895 House B&B .... (860)232-0014
Mark Twain B&B .... (203)231-1475
Kent
1741 Salt Box Inn .... (860)927-4376
Chaucer House .... (860)927-4858
Constitution Oak Farm .... (203)354-6495
Country Goose Bed & Breakfast . (860)927-4746
Fife & Drum Inn .... (203)927-3509
Flanders Arms .... (203)927-3040
Mavis' B&B .... (860)927-4334
The Sam Matson's B&B .... (203)927-3643
Killingworth
Killingworth Inn .... (203)663-1103
Lakeville
Iron Masters Motor Inne .... (860)435-9844
Wake Robin Inn .... (203)435-2515
Ledyard
Abbeys Lantern Hill Inn .... (860)572-0483
Stonecroft Bed & Breakfast ..... (860)572-0771
Litchfield
College Hill Farm .... (203)672-6762
The Litchfield Inn .... (203)567-4503
Madison
Cafe Lafayette .... (203)245-7773
Dolly Madison Inn .... (203)245-7377
Madison B&B .... (203)245-0896
Madison Beach Hotel .... (203)245-1404
Middlebury
Tucker Hill Inn .... (203)758-8334
Middletown
Rowson House .... (203)346-8479
Milford
Milford Inn .... (203)878-0685
Moodus
Fowler House .... (203)873-8906
Mystic
Adams House .... (860)572-9551
Brigadoon B&B .... (860)536-3033
Comolli's Guest House .... (203)536-8723
Harbour Inn & Cottage .... (860)572-9253
House of 1833 B&B .... (860)536-6325
The Inn at Mystic .... (203)536-9604
Steamboat Inn .... (203)536-8300
New Canaan
Maples Inn .... (203)966-2927
Melba Inn .... (203)966-8413
Roger Sherman Inn .... (203)955-4541

New Hartford
Cobble Hill Farm .... (203)379-0057
New London
Lighthouse Inn .... (203)443-8411
New Milford
Buck Rock Inn .... (860)354-9831
Heritage Inn .... (203)354-8883
Homestead Inn .... (860)354-4080
Taylor Ronald & Giner .... (860)354-9831
New Preston
Hopkins Inn .... (203)868-7295
The Inn on Lake Waramaug .... (203)868-0563
Norfolk
Angel Hill B&B .... (860)542-5920
Blackberry River Inn .... (860)542-5100
The Breezes B&B .... (203)542-5920
Mountain View Inn .... (203)542-5595
Weaver's House .... (203)542-5108
North Branford
Doodys Totoket Inn .... (203)484-0588
North Stonington
Randall's Ordinary Inn .... (203)599-4540
Norwich
Norwich Inn & Spa .... (203)886-2401
Old Lyme
Hidden Meadow B&B .... (860)434-8360
Janse B&B .... (203)434-7269
Old Saybrook
Riverview Inn .... (860)388-9744
Saybrook Point Inn .... (203)395-2000
Oxford
Butterbrooke B&B .... (203)888-2000
Plainfield
French Renaissance House ..... (860)564-3277
Pomfret
Chickadee Cottage Bed Breakfast (860)963-0587
Golden Hill Farm Bed & Breakfast (860)928-5531
Pomfret Center
The Inn at Gwyn Careg .... (203)928-9352
Hillside B&B .... (203)974-3361
Portland
The Croft B&B .... (860)342-1856
Preston
Auntie Gloria's B&B .... (203)887-7114
Roseledge Farm Bed & Breakfast (860)892-4739
Putnam Heights
The Felshaw Tavern .... (203)928-3467
King's Inn .... (203)928-7961
Thurber House .... (203)928-6776
Quinebaug
Captain Parker's Inn at Quinebaug
.... (203)935-5219 (800)707-7303
Ridgefield
The Elms Inn .... (203)438-2541
Far View Manor .... (203)438-4753
Stonehenge .... (203)438-6511
Riverton
Old Riverton Inn .... (203)379-8678
Roxbury
River House Bed & Breakfast ... (860)354-1214
Salisbury
Ragamont Inn .... (203)435-2372
Wake Robin Inn-Savarin .... (860)435-2515
The White Hart .... (203)435-0030
Scotland
Nathan Fuller House .... (203)456-0687
Sharon
1890 Colonial B&B .... (203)364-0436
Fairland B & B .... (860)364-0081
Sherman
Barnes Hill Farm B&B .... (203)354-4404
Simsbury
Simsbury 1820 House
.... (203)658-7658 (800)879-1820
Somers
Hamilton House .... (203)749-4464
South Woodstock
Ebenezer Stoddard House ...... (203)974-2552
The Inn at Woodstock Hill ...... (203)928-0528
Southington
Chaffee's B&B .... (203)628-2750
Stafford Springs
Winterbrook Farm .... (203)684-5404
Stamford
A Garden House and Cottage ... (203)348-5799

Stonington
Lasbury's B&B .... (203)535-2681
Storrs
Altnaveigh Inn .... (203)429-4490
Farmhouse on The Hill .... (203)429-1400
Thompson
A Taste of Ireland B&B .... (203)923-2883
Hickory Ridge Lakefront B&B ... (203)928-9530
Lord Thompson Manor .... (203)923-3886
Samuel Watson House .... (203)923-2491
Torrington
The Yankee Pedlar Inn .... (203)489-9226
Washington
Appleyards Bed & Breakfast .... (860)868-0812
Mayflower Inn .... (203)868-0515
Washington Depot
Mayflower Inn & Restaurant .... (860)868-9466
Waterbury
Boulevard B&B .... (203)755-0314
The House on The Hill .... (203)757-9901
Seventy Hillside .... (203)596-7070
Watertown
The Clark's B&B .... (203)274-4866
The Graham House .... (860)274-2647
West Cornwall
Hilltop Haven B&B .... (203)672-6871
Westbrook
Captain Stannard House .... (860)399-4634
Talcott House .... (203)399-5020
The Welcome Inn B&B .... (203)399-2500
Westbrook Inn .... (860)399-4777
Westport
Cotswold Inn .... (203)226-3766
Longshore Inn .... (203)226-3316
The Inn at National Hall .... (203)221-1351
Wethersfield
Chester Bulkley House B&B .... (203)563-4236
Windsor
The Charles R. Hart House ..... (203)688-5555
Winsted
Provincial House .... (860)379-1631
Riverton Inn .... (860)379-8678
Woodbury
Curtis House .... (203)263-2101
Merryvale B&B .... (203)266-0800
Woodstock
Beaver Pond B&B .... (203)974-3312

Delaware

Bethany Beach
The Addy Sea .... (302)539-3707
The Sandbox .... (302)539-3354
Dover
The Inn at Meeting House Square (302)678-1242
Greenwood
Elis Country Inn .... (302)349-4265
Lewes
Blue Water House .... (302)645-7832
The Inn at Canal Square .... (302)645-8499
Kings Inn .... (302)645-6438
New Devon Inn . (302)645-6466 (800)824-8754
Savannah Inn .... (302)645-5592
New Castle
David Finney Inn .... (302)322-6367
Janvier-Black House Bed & Breakfast
.... (302)328-1339
Terry House B&B .... (302)322-2505
William Penn Guest House ..... (302)328-7736
Newark
White Clay Inn B&B .... (302)731-7469
Odessa
Cantwell House .... (302)378-4179
Rehoboth Beach
The Delaware Inn B&B .... (302)227-6031
Gladstone Inn .... (302)227-2641
Lord Baltimore Lodge .... (302)227-2855
O'Connor's .... (302)227-2419
Selbyville
Victorian Rose B&B .... (301)436-2558
Smyrna
The Main Stay .... (302)653-4293
Wilmington
Darley Manor Inn (302)792-2127 (800)824-4703
The Pink Door .... (302)478-8325
Small Wonder B&B .... (302)764-0789

Florida

Amelia Island
The 1735 House . . . . (904)261-5878
Florida House Inn . . . . (904)261-3300

Apalachicola
Gibson Inn . . . . (904)653-2191
The Pink Camellia Inn . . . . (904)653-2107

Arcadia
Sandusky Manor Bed & Breakfast (941)494-7338

Bartow
Stanford Inn . . . . (941)533-2393

Bay Harbor Islands
Bay Harbor Inn . . . . (305)868-4141

Beverly Hills
Pine Breeze Inn . . . . (352)527-1933

Big Pine Key
B & B on The Ocean-Casa Grande (305)872-2878
The Barnacle . . . . (305)872-3298
Canal Cottage . . . . (305)872-3881

Boca Grande
Gasparilla Inn . . . . (813)964-2201

Bonita Springs
Historic Shangri-La Inn & Health Spa
. . . . (941)992-3811 (800)279-3811

Bradenton Beach
Duncan House B&B . . . . (941)778-6858

Branford
Quinas Funny Farm Bed & Breakfast
. . . . (904)935-3320

Brooksville
The L&M Paso Fino Resort . . . . . (352)544-0299
Verona House . . . . (352)796-4001

Bushnell
Bed & Breakfast Cypress House . (352)568-0909
Veranda House Bed & Breakfast . (352)793-3579

Cedar Key
Cedar Key B&B . . . . (904)543-9000
Island Hotel . . . . (352)543-5111

Clewiston
The Clewiston Inn . . . . (813)983-8151

Cocoa Beach
Inn at Cocoa Beach . . . . (407)799-3460
Luna Sea Bed & Breakfast Motel . (407)783-0500

Coleman
The Son's Shady Brook & Breakfast
. . . . (352)748-7867

Crescent City
Sprague House Inn . . . . (904)698-2430

Dade City
A Personal Touch By Grace . . . . . (352)523-1773

Daytona Beach
Captain's Quarters Inn . . . . (904)767-3119
Coquina Inn B&B (904)254-4969 (800)805-7533
Live Oak Inn . . . . (904)252-4667
Mayan Inn . . . . (904)252-0584
St. Regis Hotel . . . . (904)252-8743
Three Oaks Inn . . . . (904)258-5636

Daytona Beach Shores
Bahama House . . . . (904)257-1950
Ocean Court Motel . . . . (904)253-8185

De Funiak Springs
Sunbright Manor Bed & Breakfast (904)892-0656

Deland
Deland Country Inn . . . . (904)736-4244
Eastwood . . . . (904)736-9902
The 1888 House Bed & Breakfast (904)822-4647

Destin
Henderson Park Inn . . . . (904)837-2434

Edgewater
The Colonial House . . . . (904)427-4570

Englewood
Manasota Beach Club . . . . (813)474-2614

Eustis
Dreamspinner Historic Moses Taylor Home
. . . . (352)589-8082

Everglades City
Rod & Gun Club . . . . (813)695-2101

Fernandina Beach
Addison House . . . . (904)277-1604
Allyn Graves . . . . (904)277-0948
Greyfield Inn . . . . (904)261-6408
Hoyt House . . . . (904)277-4300
The Phoenix' Nest . . . . (904)277-2129
Posada San Carlos . . . . (904)277-8744
The Taber House . . . . (904)261-6391
Walnford Inn . . . . (904)277-6660
Williams House . . . . (904)277-2328

Flagler Beach
Aitkens Olde Florida Inn . . . . (904)439-0088
Shire House . . . . (904)445-8877

Florida City
Grandma Newtons B&B . . . . (305)247-4413

Fort Lauderdale
Casa Alhambra B&B Inn . . . . (305)467-2262

Fort Myers
Drum House Inn B&B . . . . (941)332-5668
Embe's Hobby House . . . . (813)936-6378

Gainesville
Sweetwater Branch Inn B&B . . . . (352)373-6760

Havana
Gaver's B&B . . . . (904)539-5611

High Springs
Grady House Bed & Break Fast . . (904)454-2206
Lacey Country Manner . . . . (904)454-1621

Indian Shores
Meeks B&B on The Gulf Beaches (813)596-5424

Jacksonville
The Archibald . . . . (904)634-1389
Cleary-Dickert House . . . . (904)387-4762
Hospitality Inn B&B . . . . (904)777-5700
Paradise Alley . . . . (904)246-2837
The Manor Inn . . . . (904)384-4630
The San Marco Point House . . . . (904)396-1448
The Willows on The St. Johns River
. . . . (904)387-9152

Jensen Beach
Hutchinson Inn Seaside Resort . . (561)229-2000

Jupiter
Innisfail . . . . (407)744-5905

Key Largo
Largo Lodge . . . . (305)451-0424

Key West
1004 Eaton Street . . . . (305)296-8132
Alexander's . . . . (305)294-9919
Andrews Inn . . . . (305)294-7730
Angelina Guest House . . . . (305)294-4480
Artist House . . . . (305)296-3977
Author's . . . . (305)294-7381
Bottle Inn . . . . (305)294-8530
Casa Alante . . . . (305)293-0702
Cayo Hueso Cottages . . . . (305)294-4819
Center Court-Historic Inn & Cottages
. . . . (305)296-9292 (800)797-8787
Coconut Grove Guest House . . . . (305)296-5107
Colours Key West - The Guest Mansion
. . . . (305)532-9341
Conch House Heritage Inn . . . . . (305)293-0020
Douglas House . . . . (305)294-5269
Duval Gardens . . . . (305)292-3379
Duval Suites . . . . (305)293-6600
Eaton Manor Guest House . . . . . (305)294-9870
Enchanted Bed & Breakfast . . . . . (305)294-9061
Garden House . . . . (305)296-5368
Whispers B&B Inn at Gideon Lowe House
. . . . (305)294-5969
Heron House . . . (305)294-9227 (800)294-1644
The Hollinsed House . . . . (305)296-8031
Incentra Carriage House . . . . (305)296-5565
Island House . . . . (305)294-6284
L'Habitation Guest House . . . . . . (305)293-9203
La Pensione Inn . . . . (305)292-9923
Lamp Post House . . . . (305)294-7709
Lime House Inn . . . . (305)296-2978
Nancy's William Street Guesthouse (305)292-3334
Oasis Guest House . . . . (305)296-2131
Old Customs House Inn . . . . (305)294-8507
Overseas B&B . . . . (305)296-0242
Palms of Key West . . . . (305)294-3146
Pilot House Guest House
. . . . (305)294-8719 (800)648-3780
Pines of Key West . . . . (305)296-7467
The Popular House, Key West B&B
. . . . (305)296-7274 (800)438-6155
Seascape . . . . . (305)296-7776 (800)765-6438
Simonton Court . (305)294-6386 (800)944-2687
Southernmost Point Guest House (305)294-0715
Speakeasy Inn . . . . (305)296-2680
The Curry Mansion Inn
. . . . (305)294-5349 (800)253-3466
Treetop Inn Historic B&B . . . . (305)293-0712
Tropical Inn Guest House . . . . . . (305)294-9977
Walden Guest House . . . . (305)296-7161
The Watson House (305)294-6712 (800)621-9405
Westwinds . . . . (305)296-4440
White Street Inn . . . . (305)295-9599
Wicker Guest House . . . . (305)296-4275
Windsor House . . . . (305)296-6558

Kissimmee
Beaumont House . . . . (305)846-7916
Casa Coppe . . . . (407)846-7916
The Unicorn Inn English B&B . . . (407)846-1200

Lake Buena Vista
Perrihouse Bed & Breakfast Inn . . (407)876-4830

Lake City
Seven Fountains Inn & Gardens . . (904)755-5930

Lakeland
Lake Morton Bed & Breakfast . . . (941)688-6788
Magnolias In The Park . . . . (941)686-7275

Little Torch Key
Little Palm Island . . . . (305)872-2524

Madeira Beach
Lighthouse Motel Bed & Breakfast (813)391-0015

Marathon
Hopp-Inn Guest House . . . . (305)743-4118

Mayo
Jim Hollis' River Rendezvous . . . (904)294-2510

Miami
Bed and Breakfast Miami . . . . . . (305)858-3858
Hotel Sofitel . . . . (305)264-4888
Miami River Inn . . . . (305)325-0045

Miami Beach
Castle Beach Club . . . . (305)865-1500
Essex House Hotel . . . . (305)534-2700
Jefferson House . . . . (305)534-5247
Mantell Guest Inn . . . . (305)538-1821
Mermaid Guest House . . . . (305)538-5324

Micanopy
Shady Oak . . . . (352)466-3476

Minneola
Lake Minneola Inn . . . . (352)394-2232

Mount Dora
Christophers Inn Bed & Breakfast (352)383-2244
Emerald Hill Inn . . . . (352)383-2777
Raintree House . . . . (352)383-5065
Seabrook Bed & Breakfast . . . . . (352)383-4800
Simpson's B&B . . . . (352)383-2087

Myakka City
Moosy Oak Farm Bed & Breakfast (941)322-0604

New Port Richey
The Guest House . . . . (813)845-6164

New Smyrna Beach
Magnolia Inn . . . . (904)427-9120
Riverview Hotel . (904)428-5858 (800)945-7416

North Bay Village
The Inn on The Bay . . . . (305)865-7100

Ocala
Heritage Country Inn . . . . (352)489-0023
Ritz Historic Inn . . . . (352)867-7700

Orange Park
The Inn at Winterbourne . . . . (904)264-6070

Orange Springs
Orange Springs . . . . (904)546-2052

Orlando
Buckets Bermuda Bay Hideaway/A B&B
. . . . (407)896-4111
The Courtyard at Lake Lucerne . . (407)648-5188
(800)444-5289
Las Palmas Hotel . . . . (407)351-3900
Orlando Penta Hotel . . . . (407)240-1000
The Rio Pinar House . . . . (407)277-4903

Ormond Beach
Coral Sands Inn & Seaside Cottages
. . . . (904)441-1831
Ormond Inn . . . . (904)673-0950
Tea House Gardens . . . . (904)672-5557

Palm Bay
Casa Del Sol . . . . (407)728-4676

Palm Beach
Bradley House . . . . (407)832-7050
Plaza Inn . . . . (561)832-8666

Palm Beach Gardens
Heron Cay Bed & Breakfast . . . . . (561)744-6315

Palm Harbor
Sunrise Guest House . . . . (813)934-7157

Palmetto
Five Oaks Inn . . . . (941)723-1236

Pensacola
Homestead Inn .... (904)944-4816
Hospitality Inn .... (800)321-0052
Sunshine .... (904)455-6781
Yacht House Bed & Breakfast ... (904)433-3634
Plant City
Rysdon House .... (813)752-8717
Point Washington
Dolphin Inn .... (904)231-5477
Josephines Bed & Breakfast .... (904)231-1940
Sugar Beach Inn .... (904)231-1577
Pompano Beach
Atlantic Inn Motel .... (954)977-7411
Punta Gorda
Gilchrist Bed & Breakfast ...... (941)575-4129
Saint Augustine
The Agustin Inn . (904)823-9559 (800)248-7846
Casa Blanca Inn on The Bay
.... (904)829-0928 (800)826-2626
Casa De Suenos (904)824-0887 (800)824-0804
Castle Garden B&B .... (904)829-3839
Charlotte Houset .... (904)829-3819
Cordova House .... (904)825-0770
De Marin Villas .... (904)829-1725
Old City House Inn & Restaurant . (904)826-0113
Old Mansion Inn .... (904)824-1975
Old Powder House Inn .... (904)824-4149
Our House of St. Augustine ..... (904)824-9204
Penny Farthing Inn (904)824-2100 (800)395-1890
Sailor's Rest .... (904)824-3817
The Secret Garden Inn .... (904)829-3678
Segui Inn .... (904)825-2811
Victorian House B&B .... (904)824-5214
Westcott House .... (904)824-4301
The Whale's Tale .... (904)829-5901
Saint Petersburg
Gulf Front Inn .... (813)360-8844
Island's End .... (813)360-5023
Mansion House Bed & Breakfast . (813)821-9391
McCarthy Hotel .... (813)822-4141
San Mateo
Ferncourt B&B .... (904)329-9755
Sanibel
Sanibel's Seaside Inn .... (813)472-1400
Song of The Sea .... (813)472-2220
Santa Rosa Beach
A Highlands House .... (904)267-0110
Crescent Cafe & Inn .... (904)267-3333
Seaside Cottages .... (904)231-4224
Sarasota
Crescent House B&B .... (941)346-0857
Harley Sandcastle .... (813)388-2181
Mid Key Inn .... (941)346-2203
The Pepperberry House .... (813)951-0405
The Tuttles .... (813)953-5993
Wildflower Inn .... (941)346-1566
Sebastian
The Davis House B&B .... (407)589-3108
Sebring
Idyl Our Inn & Tea Room ...... (941)385-8101
Santa Rosa Inn & Cafe 1924 .... (813)385-0641
Stuart
Harborfront Inn Bed & Breakfast . (561)288-7289
The Homeplace .... (561)220-9148
Summerland Key
Knightswood .... (305)872-2246
Tallahassee
College Inn .... (904)561-0002
Governors Inn .... (904)681-6855
The Riedel House .... (904)222-8569
Tarpon Springs
East Lake B&B .... (813)937-5487
Inness Manor Bed & Breakfast .. (813)938-2900
Spring Bayou Inn .... (813)938-9333
Wakulla Springs
Wakulla Springs State Park & Lodge
.... (904)224-5950
West Palm Beach
Portside on The Inlet .... (561)842-1215
Royal Palm House .... (561)863-9836
Winter Haven
J.D.'s Southern Oaks .... (941)293-2335

Georgia

Adairsville
Old Home Place .... (706)625-3649
Albany
Beggar's Bush - Cane Mill Plantation
.... (610)388-5900
Americus
The Cottage Inn .... (912)924-9316
Guerry House 1833 Bed and Breakfast
.... (912)924-1009
Morris Manor .... (912)924-4884
The Old Parsonage .... (912)928-2124
Wise Olde Pine Plantation & Hunting Pres
.... (912)846-5491
Andersonville
A Place Away .... (912)924-1044
Athens
Hutchens-Hardeman House .... (706)353-1855
Magnolia Terrace Guesthouse
.... (706)548-3860 (800)891-1912
The Nicholson House .... (706)353-2200
Oakwood Bed & Breakfast ..... (706)546-7886
Atlanta
The 1223 at Emory .... (404)377-4987
Ansley Inn ..... (404)872-9000 (800)446-5416
Atlanta West End Manor .... (404)753-3257
Bed and Breakfast Atlanta ...... (404)875-0525
Emory Area Lodging .... (404)634-7327
Heartfield Manor .... (404)523-8633
Houston Mill House .... (404)727-7878
Inman Park B&B .... (404)688-9498
King-Keith House B&B .... (404)688-7330
Magnolia Station Bed & Breakfast (404)522-3923
Manor Grant .... (404)659-8888
Shellmont B&B Lodge .... (404)872-9290
Sugar Magnolia Bed & Breakfast . (404)222-0226
Virginia-Highland House, A B&B . (404)876-0226
Augusta
Augusta Budget Inn .... (706)722-0212
The Azalea Inn .... (706)724-3454
Oglethorpe Inn .... (706)724-9774
Perrin Guest House Inn .... (706)731-0930
Bainbridge
The White House B&B .... (912)248-1703
Blairsville
Autumn Gold B&B .... (706)745-3111
Nottely Dam Estates - Guest House
.... (706)745-7939
Misty Mountain Inn & Cottages .. (706)745-4786
Souther Country Inn .... (706)379-1603
Stonehenge B&B .... (706)745-4675
Sunrise Place .... (706)745-0624
Blakely
Camellia House .... (912)723-4378
Layside .... (912)723-8932
Blue Ridge
Harry & June's B&B .... (706)632-8846
Bowdon
The Bowdon Inn .... (706)258-5469
Brooklet
Spring Creek Lodge Inn .... (912)842-2817
Brunswick
Brunswick Manor .... (912)265-6889
Rose Manor Guest House ...... (912)267-6369
Burnswick
Scarlett House B&B .... (912)264-5902
Buena Vista
Morgan Towne House B&B ..... (912)649-3663
Yesteryear Inn .... (912)649-7307
Buford
Bona Allen Mansion .... (770)451-9001
Calhoun
Red Carpet Inn Calhoun .... (404)629-9501
Stoneleigh .... (706)629-2093
Camilla
The Davis House .... (912)336-8439
Canton
Standifer Inn .... (706)345-5805
Cartersville
Southwind Resort .... (706)917-9282
Cave Spring
Hearn Academy Inn .... (706)777-8865
Tumlin House Bed & Breakfast .. (706)777-0066
Chickamauga
Gordon-Lee Mansion B&B ..... (706)375-4728

New Dawn Farm .... (706)539-2177
Chula
Hummingbird Perch .... (912)382-5431
Clarkesville
Burns-Sutton House .... (706)754-5565
Burton Woods Cabins & Lodging (706)947-3926
Charm House Inn .... (404)754-9347
Charm House Inn .... (706)754-9347
Glen-Ella Springs Hotel .... (404)754-7295
Habersham Hollow Country Inn & Cabins
.... (706)754-5147
Laprade's .... (404)947-3312
Spring Hill .... (706)754-7094
Clarkston
The Hensler House .... (404)296-9262
Clayton
Barn Inn .... (706)782-5094
Beechwood Inn .... (706)782-5485
Old Clayton Inn .... (706)782-7722
Cleveland
Edelweiss German Country Inn .. (706)865-7371
Habersham House A Bed & Breakfast
.... (706)754-4767
Hilltop Haus .... (706)878-2388
Kellum Valley Inn .... (706)865-6379
Le Domaine Du Poulet Et De L'Oeuf B&B
.... (706)865-4730
The Lodge at Windy Acres ..... (706)865-6635
Cedar Hill .... (706)865-2666
Skelton Inn .... (706)865-6205
Tysons Homestead .... (706)865-6914
Cobb
The Hide Out .... (912)853-7250
Colquitt
Country Inn .... (912)758-5417
Tarrer Inn .... (912)758-2888
Columbus
Affaire Du Coeur .... (706)327-9567
Miss Weese's Victorian B&B .... (706)324-3349
Rothschild-Pound House B&B
.... (706)322-4075 (800)585-4075
Commerce
Magnolia Inn .... (706)335-7257
The Pittman House B&B .... (706)335-3823
Concord
Inn Scarlett's Footsteps .... (770)884-9012
Magnolia Ridge .... (770)495-9645
Conyers
The Haynes Ridge Inn .... (770)922-9151
Cordele
Marsh Pond Bed & Breakfast ... (912)273-9900
Cornelia
Robert B Lamb House .... (706)778-5262
Covington
The Inn at Inn .... (770)787-0037
Twenty One Nineteen The Inn ... (770)787-0037
Culloden
Holmes Hotel .... (912)885-2393
Miss Adell's .... (770)994-0197
Cumberland Island
The Greyfield Inn .... (904)261-6408
Dahlonega
The Blueberry Inn .... (706)396-9150
Cavender Castle Winery .... (706)864-4759
Forest Hills Mt. Resort .... (404)864-6456
Mountain Top Lodge at Dahlonega (706)864-5257
The Royal Guard Inn .... (706)864-1713
Scott's B&B .... (706)864-6472
Stanton Storehouse B&B ...... (706)864-6114
Wahsega Inn .... (706)864-2764
Worley Homestead Inn .... (404)864-7002
Dalton
Amy's Place .... (706)278-6620
Danielsville
Hony Bear Hideaway .... (706)789-2569
Danville
Magnolia Plantation .... (912)962-3988
Darien
Open Gates .... (912)437-6985
Decatur
Garden House .... (404)377-8574
Sycamore House In Old Decatur . (404)378-0685
Dillard
Dillard House Inn .... (404)746-5348
White Hall Inn .... (706)746-5511

Dublin
Vip B&B .... (912)275-3739
Eastanollee
Apple Orchard Country Inn ..... (706)779-7292
Eastman
Dodge Hill Inn .... (912)374-2644
Eatonton
Claudine's .... (706)485-0983
Crockett House .... (706)485-2248
Magnolia Hill B&B .... (706)485-0012
Rosewood B&B .... (706)485-9009
Elberton
Grenoke B&B .... (706)283-1567
Rainbow Manor .... (706)213-0314
Ellaville
Fern Brook Inn .... (912)937-5672
Ellijay
Elderberry Inn B&B Home ...... (706)635-2218
Eton
Ivy Inn .... (706)517-0526 (800)201-5477
Flowery Branch
Whitworth Inn .... (706)967-2386
Forsyth
A Country Place .... (912)994-2705
Fort Oglethorpe
Captain's Quarters B&B Inn .... (706)858-0624
Gainesville
Dunlap House .. (770)536-0200 (800)264-6992
Grantville
Bonnie Castle .... (770)583-3090
Greensboro
Early Hill .... (706)453-7876
Higdon House B&B .... (706)453-1901
Lake Oconee Inn B&B
.... (706)453-9004 (800)235-5946
Griffin
Double Cabins Plantation B&B .. (770)227-2214
Guyton
Claudette's Country Inn .... (912)772-3667
Hamilton
Annie's Log Cabin .... (706)628-5729
Magnolia Hall B&B .... (706)628-4566
Wedgwood B&B .... (404)628-5659
Hawkinsville
The Black Swan Inn .... (912)783-4466
Helen
Derdenhof Inn .... (404)878-2141
Dutch Cottage .... (706)878-3135
Greear Lodge .... (706)878-3478
Helendorf Inn .... (404)878-2271
Hilltop Haus .... (706)878-2388
Hiawassee
Blue House on West River Street . (706)896-1623
Burlesons Bed & Breakfast ..... (706)896-1331
Grahl's Comfort Zone .... (706)596-1358
Henson Cove Place B&B ...... (800)714-5542
Mountain Memories Inn of Hiawassee
.... (706)896-8439 (800)335-8439
Swan Lake B&B .... (706)896-1582
Hoboken
Blueberry Hill .... (912)458-2605
Hogansville
Fair Oaks Inn .... (706)637-8828
Fair Oaks Inn at The Grand ..... (706)637-5100
Homerville
The Helmstead .... (912)487-2222
Jackson
The Carmichale House .... (770)775-0578
Jesup
Trowell House .... (912)530-6611
Juliette
The Jarrell 1920 House .... (912)986-3972
La Grange
Thyme Away .... (706)885-9625
Lakemont
Anapauo Farm .... (404)782-6442
Lake Rabun Hotel .... (404)782-4946
Lavonia
Sleep Inn .... (706)356-2268
The Southern Trace .... (706)356-1033
Lilburn
Lilburn B&B .... (404)923-9813
Lookout Mountain
The Lookout Inn .... (706)820-2000

Madison
The Boat House .... (706)342-3061
Brady Inn .... (706)342-4400
Burnett Place .... (706)342-4034
Manchester
Sweet Dreams .... (706)655-9068
Marietta
Marlow House .... (770)426-1887
Ridgepoint .... (404)426-1883
Sixty Polk Street, A B&B
.... (404)419-0101 (800)497-2075
Mc Caysville
Maloofs Bed and Breakfast ..... (706)492-2016
Midway
The Ripely Farm .... (912)884-5450
Milledgevile
Hinson House .. (912)453-3993 (800)484-5473
Milledgeville
Mara's Tara .... (912)453-2732
Moultrie
Pinefields Plantation .... (912)985-2086
Mount Airy
Mount Airy B&B .... (706)776-2319
Mt Airy House Bed & Breakfast .. (706)776-7816
Mountain City
The York House . (706)746-2068 (800)231-9675
Newnan
Limberlost .... (706)254-8145
Magnolia Cottage .... (770)254-9754
Parrott Camp Soucy Home & Gardens
.... (404)502-0676
Rose Helen Inn .... (770)251-1539
Southern Comfort B&B Inn
.... (770)254-9266 (800)818-0066
Norman Park
Quailridge B&B .... (912)985-7262
Oxford
Hopkins House .... (770)784-1010
Palmetto
Boxwood Heights B&B .... (770)463-9966
Serenbe Bed & Breakfast ...... (770)463-2610
Parrott
217 Huckaby .... (912)623-5545
Perry
Swift Street Inn B&B .... (912)988-4477
Pine Mountain
Mountain Top Inn .... (800)533-6376
The Storms House Inn .... (706)663-9100
Plains
Plains B&B .... (912)824-7252
Quitman
White Columns B&B .... (912)263-4445
Rabun Gap
Valley of Hidden Paths .... (706)746-2278
Rome
Claremont House B&B
.... (706)291-0900 (800)254-4797
Roswell
Ten Fifty Canton Street .... (770)998-1050
Rutledge
Jones Cottage .... (404)557-2516
Saint Marys
Goodbread House .... (912)882-7490
The Historic Spencer House Inn . (912)882-1872
Riverview Hotel .... (912)882-3242
Saint Simons Island
Island Inn .... (800)673-6323
Saint Simons Inn By The Lighthouse
.... (912)638-1101
Sandersville
Saunders Inn .... (912)553-0990
Sautee
Deer Crossing B&B .... (706)878-2513
Edelweiss German Country Inn .. (706)865-7371
Sautee Nacoochee
The Glen-Kenimer-Tucker House/Grampa's Room
.... (706)878-2364
The Lumsden Homeplace ...... (706)878-2813
Nacoochee Valley Guest House .. (706)878-3830
Royal Windsor Cottage .... (706)878-1322
Savannah
118 West .... (912)234-8557
17 Hundred 90 Inn .... (912)236-7122
912 Barnard Victorian Bed & Breakfast
.... (912)234-9121

The Azalea Inn .. (912)236-2707 (800)791-9393
Ballastone Inn .... (912)236-1484
Bed & Bagel .... (912)236-1122
Broughton Street Bed & Breakfast (912)232-6633
Camellia's Tree Toad House .... (912)231-8811
Charlton Court .... (912)236-2895
Colonial Park Inn (912)232-3622 (800)799-3622
The Colophon .. (912)233-2446 (800)829-8406
Comer House .... (912)234-2923
East Bay Inn .... (912)238-1225
Eliza Thompson House .... (912)236-3620
Foley House Inn . (912)232-6622 (800)647-3708
Gastonian .... (912)232-2869
Habersham at York Inn .... (912)234-2499
Hamilton Turner Mansion Museum & Gift Shop
.... (912)233-4800
Harris House .... (912)236-4179
417 The Haslam-Fort House .... (912)233-6380
Innside Scoop Bed .... (912)238-5982
Jesse Mount House .... (912)236-1774
Joan's on Jones .... (912)234-3863
Lion's Head Inn . (912)232-4580 (800)355-5466
Magnolia Place Inn .... (912)236-7674
Mary Lee's House .... (912)232-0891
Morel House .... (912)234-4088
Olde Harbour Inn .... (912)234-4100
Planters Inn .... (912)232-5678
Presidents' Quarters .... (912)233-1600
River Street Inn .... (800)253-4229
Savannah Historic Inns .... (912)233-7666
St. Julian Street B&B .... (912)236-9939
Timmons House .... (912)233-4456
Sharpsburg
The Homeplace .... (770)253-5806
Soperton
Yellow Rose Inn .... (912)529-4912
Statesboro
Georgia's B&B .... (912)489-6330
Statesboro Inn and Restaurant
.... (912)489-8628 (800)846-9466
Stone Mountain
Silver Hill Manor .... (770)879-6800
The Village Inn B & B .... (770)469-3459
Swainsboro
Coleman House B&B .... (912)237-2822
Edenfield House Inn .... (912)237-3007
Thomaston
Hightower-Ironside House ...... (706)647-6440
Grand Oak Inn .... (706)647-2482
Woodall House .... (706)647-7044
Thomasville
1884 Paxton House .... (912)226-5197
Deer Creek B&B .... (912)226-7294
Evans House B&B .... (912)226-1343
The Grand Victoria Inn .... (912)226-7460
Our Cottage on The Park .... (912)227-0404
Susina Plantation Inn .... (912)377-9644
Thomson
1810 West Inn .. (706)595-3156 (800)515-1810
Four Chimneys B&B .... (706)597-0220
Tifton
Hummingbird's Perch B&B ..... (912)382-5431
Myon B&B .... (912)382-0959
Tignall
Holly Ridge County Inn .... (706)285-2594
Toccoa
Habersham Manor House ...... (404)886-6496
Simmons-Bond Inn .... (706)886-8411
Tybee Island
Fort Screven Inn .... (912)786-9255
The Hunter House .... (912)786-7515
Unadilla
Sugar Hill B&B .... (912)627-3557
Union Point
Penfield House & Garden ...... (706)453-9800
Valdosta
"Seven Gables" B&B .... (912)247-1567
Villa Rica
Ahava Plantation B&B
.... (770)459-2863 (800)858-3473
Twin Oaks .... (706)459-4374
Warm Springs
Hotel Warm Springs B&B Inn
.... (706)655-2114 (800)366-7616
Washington
The Belle Sterling .... (706)678-5388
Blackmon B&B .... (706)678-2278

Holly Ridge Country Inn .... (706)285-2594
Liberty Street .... (706)678-3107
Maynard's Manor .... (706)678-4303
Water Oak Cottage .... (404)678-4645

Watkinsville
Rivendell .... (706)769-4522

Waverly Hall
Raintree Farms of Waverly Hall .. (706)582-3227

Waycross
Caitlyns Courtyard .... (912)284-1755

Waynesboro
Georgia's Guest B&B .... (706)554-4863

West Point
The Nesting Place .... (706)643-8164

Winterville
The Bank B&B .... (706)788-3226
Old Winterville Inn .... (404)742-7340

Young Harris
Wild Wind Farm .... (706)379-1992

Hawaii

Aiea
Alohaland Guest House .... (808)487-0482

Captain Cook
Manago Hotel .... (808)323-2642

Haleiwa
B & B Plantation House .... (808)637-4988
Plantation Village .... (808)638-7838

Hana
Hana Hale Malamalama .... (808)248-7718
Heavenly Hana Inn .... (808)248-8442

Hanalei
Bed & Breakfast Tassa Hanalei .. (808)826-7298

Hanapepe
Hana Papahawahawa .... (808)248-8072
Hana Plantation Houses .... (808)248-7049

Hawi
Aha Hui Hawaiian Plantation .... (808)889-5523
Kohalas Guest House .... (808)889-5606

Hilo
Alii Bed & Breakfast Condo Style . (808)961-5818
Haili House Inn .... (808)969-7378
Hale Kai Bed & Breakfast ...... (808)935-6330
Hale O Panaewa .... (808)959-7432
Lannan's Lihi Kai on Hilo Bay ... (808)935-7865
Maureens Bed & Breakfast ..... (808)935-9018
Oceanfront B&B .... (808)961-5754
Wild Ginger Inn .... (808)969-1225

Holualoa
Holualoa Inn .... (808)324-1121

Honaunau
Affordable Hawaii at Pomaikai Farm
.... (808)328-2112
Da Third House .... (808)328-8410
Dragonfly Ranch .... (800)487-2159
Lions Gate .... (808)328-2335

Honokaa
Beech Linda Phd .... (808)775-7160
Luana Ola B & B Cottages ..... (808)775-7727
Waipio Wayside .... (808)775-0275

Honolulu
Bed & Breakfast Manoa .... (808)988-6333
Continental Surf Hotel .... (800)367-5004
Fairway View Bed & Breakfast ... (808)263-6439
Hale O Kahala .... (808)732-5889
Mango House .... (808)595-6682
Waikiki Royal Suites .... (800)535-0085
Waikiki Grand Hotel .... (800)535-0085
Waikiki Lanais .... (800)535-0085

Kahului
Maui Windsurfari .... (808)871-7766

Kailua
Akamai B&B .... (808)261-2227
Aloha From The Campbells ..... (808)261-4245
Sheffield House Bed & Breakfast . (808)262-0721

Kailua Kona
Adrienne's Casa Del Sol B&B Inn
.... (808)326-2272 (800)395-2272
Hale Maluhia B&B (808)329-1123 (800)559-6627
Mahana Kona .... (808)325-7117
Rosys Rest .... (808)322-7378
Three Bears B&B .... (808)325-7563

Kalaheo
Classic Vacation Cottages ...... (808)332-9201
Kauai Island B&B .... (808)332-9598
Seaview Suite Bed & Breakfast .. (808)332-9744
South Shore Vista .... (808)332-9339

Kamuela
Jennys Country Cottage .... (808)885-5663
Kamuela Inn .... (808)885-4243
Kamuelas Mauna Kea View Bed & Breakfast
.... (808)885-8425
Morningstar Meadow .... (808)885-7674
The Royal Waikoloan .... (800)733-7777

Kapaa
Aleva House .... (808)822-4606
Aloha Kauai Bed & Breakfast .... (808)822-6966
Alohilani Bed & Breakfast ...... (808)823-0128
Bed & Breakfast Ikena Nani Loa . (808)822-4010
Bed & Breakfast Kauai .... (808)822-5757
Bed & Breakfast Lampys ...... (808)822-0478
Bed & Breakfast-On The Beach .. (808)821-0885
Candys Cabin .... (808)822-5451
Fern Grotton Inn .... (808)822-2560
Hale Kohi .... (808)821-0805
Hibiscus Hollow .... (808)823-0925
Kay Barker's B&B .... (808)822-3073
Keapana Center Bed & Breakfast . (808)822-7968
Mtn View Manor .... (808)822-0406
Pono Kai Resort .... (808)822-9831
Rosewood .... (808)822-5216
Tradewinds Estate .... (808)245-7964
Wailua Country B & B & Vacation Rentals
.... (808)822-0166
Waonahele at Kupono Farms .... (808)822-7911
Winters Macnut Farm & Inn .... (808)822-3470

Kaunakakai
Kamalo Plantation .... (808)558-8236
Molokai Shores Suites .... (800)535-0085
Pau Hana Inn .... (800)367-8047

Keaau
Kakalina's B&B .... (808)822-2328
Rainforest Retreat .... (808)982-9601

Kealakekua
Rainbow Plantation .... (808)323-2393
Reggie's Tropical Hideaway .... (808)322-8888

Kihei
Affordable Accomodations Maui . (808)879-7865
Bed & Breakfast Jasmine House . (808)875-0400

Kilauea
Kauai Hideaway-Winklers' B&B .. (808)828-2828
Makai Farms .... (808)828-1874
North Country Farms .... (808)828-1513

Koloa
A Bed & Breakfast In Poipu ..... (808)742-1146
Bed & Breakfast Hale Honu at Poipu
.... (808)742-9618
Gloria's Spouting Horn B&B .... (808)742-6995
Poipu Plantation . (808)742-6757 (800)733-1632
Pua Hale (Flower Houses) ..... (808)742-1700
Sunny Poipu Villas .... (808)742-6178

Kukuihaele
Hamakua Hideaway .... (808)775-7425

Kula
Bloom Cottage B&B .... (808)878-1425
Hana Hou Hale .... (808)878-6080
Kula Lodge & Restaurant, Inc. ... (808)878-1535
Silver Cloud Ranch .... (808)878-6101

Kurtistown
Bed & Breakfast Mountain View . (808)968-7017
Butterfly Inn .... (808)966-7936

Lahaina
Garden Gate B & B .... (808)667-7999
Guest House .... (808)661-8085
House of Fountain .... (808)667-2121
The Kahili Maui . (808)669-5635 (800)786-7387
Maui Eldorado at Kaanapali ..... (800)535-0085
Old Lahaina House (808)667-4663 (800)847-0761
Paki Maui at Kaanapali .... (800)535-0085
Plantation Inn .... (800)433-6815

Lanai City
Dreams Come True .... (808)565-6961

Lihue
Bed & Breakfast A Call of Kauai . (808)822-9699

Naalehu
Beckys Bed & Breakfast .... (808)929-9690
South Point Bed & Breakfast .... (808)939-7466

Pahala
Wood Valley .... (800)854-6754

Pahoa
Huliaulea .... (808)965-9175
Ohia Inn .... (808)965-6212
Pearl's Shell B&B .... (808)965-7015
Village Inn Pahoa .... (808)965-6444

Volcano
Country Goose .... (808)967-7759
Lokahi Lodge ... (808)985-8647 (800)457-6924
My Island B&B .... (808)967-7216
Ohia Gardens .... (808)985-7051
Volcano Heart Chalet .... (808)248-7725

Waikoloa, Big Island
Waikoloa Villas .... (800)535-0085

Wailuku
Aloha Pualani .... (808)874-9265
Anuhea Bed & Breakfast Health Retreat
.... (808)874-1490
Bed Breakfast Books & Beach ... (808)879-0097
Blue Horizons .... (808)669-1965

Idaho

Ahsahka
Mule Shoe Ii Lodge .... (208)476-9980

Albion
Mountain Manor B&B .... (208)673-6642

Almo
Old Homestead .... (208)824-5521

Alta
High Country Comforts
.... (307)353-8560 (800)254-2331

Ashton
Jessen's B&B .... (208)652-3356

Blackfoot
Alder Inn B&B .... (208)785-6968

Boise
B&B at Victoria's White House .. (208)362-0507
Las Tejanas Bed and Breakfast .. (208)376-6077
Robin's Nest B&B .... (208)336-9551

Bruneau
Amsterdam Inn .... (208)543-6754
Grammy Willow Inn .... (208)543-4782
Pleasant Hill Country Inn .... (208)845-2018

Caldwell
Harvey House Bed & Breakfast .. (208)454-9874

Cambridge
Cambridge House B&B .... (208)257-3325

Cascade
Creamery .... (208)382-4621
Seasons of The Heart .... (208)382-3635

Challis
Darling Creek Bed & Breakfast .. (208)879-5222

Coeur d'Alene
Alpine Inn .... (208)664-5412
Ann & Mel's Log House B&B ... (208)667-8015
Blackwell House .... (208)664-0656
Coeur D'alene B&B .... (208)667-7527
Cricket on The Hearth B&B ..... (208)664-6926
The Gables .... (208)664-5121
Gregory's Mc Farland House .... (208)667-1232
Highwood House B&B .... (208)667-4735
Inn The First Place .... (208)667-3346
Katie's Wild Rose Inn
.... (208)765-9474 (800)371-4345
Lodgepole Pine Inn .... (208)842-2343
O'Neill B & B .... (208)664-5356
The Roosevelt Inn (208)765-5200 (800)290-3358
Silver Beach House B&B ...... (208)667-5406
Someday House B&B .... (208)664-6666
Summer House By The Lake .... (208)667-9395
The Warwick Inn .... (208)765-6565
Wolf Lodge Creek B&B .... (208)667-5902

Coolin
Old Northern Inn .... (208)443-2426

Cottonwood
Camas Prairie Inn .... (208)962-5135
Mariels Bed & Breakfast .... (208)962-5161

Deary
Eagle's Nest Lodge .... (208)877-1420

Downey
Downata Hot Springs .... (208)897-5736

Driggs
Grand Valley Lodging .... (208)354-8890
Teton Creek B&B .... (208)354-2584

Elk City
Canterbury House Inn B&B ..... (208)842-2366
Sable Trail Ranch .... (208)983-1418

Fairfield
Manard Hall Bed & Breakfast . . . (208)764-2807
Fish Haven
Bear Lake B&B . . . . (208)945-2688
Fruitland
Elm Hollow B&B . . . . (208)452-6491
Garden Valley
Champie Horse Company B&B . . (208)462-3520
Warm Springs Creek B&B . . . . . . (208)462-3516
Grangeville
Tulip House . . . . (208)983-1034
Hagerman
Cary House . . . . (208)837-4848
Hailey
Povey Pensione . . . . (208)788-4682
Harrison
Harrisons Osprey Inn . . . . (208)689-9502
Hayden Lake
Clark House on Hayden Lake
. . . . (208)772-3470 (800)765-4593
Hitching Post Manor . . . . (208)762-3126
Horseshoe Bend
Old Riverside Depot . . . . (208)793-2408
Idaho City
One Step Away Bed Breakfast & Lodging
. . . . (208)392-4938
Swan Valley B&B . . . . (208)483-4663
Idaho Falls
Little Bush Inn . . . . (208)529-0567
Irwin
McBride's B&B . . . . (208)483-4221
Swan Valley B&B . . . . (208)483-4663
Island Park
Lucky Dog Retreat . . . . (208)558-7455
Kellogg
McKinley Inn . . . . (208)786-7771
Scott's Inn . . . . . (208)786-8581 (800)767-8581
Montgomery Inn . . . . (208)786-2311
Sterling Silver Bed & Breakfast . . (208)783-4551
Ketchum
Bear Hollow B&B . . . . (208)926-7146
Busterback Ranch . . . . (208)774-2217
Lift Tower Lodge . . . . (208)726-5163
The Pinnacle Club . . . . (208)726-5601
Sessions Lodge . . . . (208)774-3366
Kooskia
Looking Glass Ranch . . . . (208)926-0855
Three Rivers Resort . . . . (208)926-4430
Laclede
Mountain View Farm B&B . . . . . . (208)265-5768
River Birch Farm B&B . . . . (208)263-3705
Lava Hot Springs
Aladdin Inn Bed & Breakfast . . . . (208)776-5357
Lava Hot Springs Inn . . . . (208)776-5830
Riverside Inn & Hot Springs
. . . . (208)776-5504 (800)733-5504
Royal Hotel B&B . . . . (208)776-5216
Lewiston
Carriage House . . . . (208)746-4506
Sheep Creek Ranch . . . . (208)746-6276
Snake River Get-A-Way . . . . (208)746-2489
Lower Stanley
Las Tejanas B&B . . . . (208)774-3301
Lowman
Martini's Mountainside B&B . . . . (208)588-2940
Mackay
Wild Horse Creek Ranch . . . . (208)588-2575
Malad City
Chantilly Bed and Breckfest . . . . (208)766-4961
McCall
1920 House B&B . . . . (208)634-4661
The Chateau B&B . . . . (208)634-4196
Hotel McCall, A Mountain Inn . . . (208)634-8105
Northwest Passage
. . . . (208)634-5349 (800)597-6658
Meridian
Home Place . . . . (208)888-3857
Moscow
Beau's Butte . . . . (208)882-4061
The Cottage B&B . . . . (208)882-0778
Paradise Ridge
Paradise Ridge B&B . . . . (208)882-5292
Moscow
Peacock Hill B&B . . . . (208)882-1423
Snow Hill Farm Bed & Breakfast . (208)882-0912

Twin Peaks Inn . . . . (208)882-4651
The Van Buren House . . . . (208)882-8531
Mountain Home
The Rose Stone Inn
. . . . (208)587-8866 (800)717-7673
Nampa
The Pink Tudor B&B . . . . (208)465-3615
New Meadows
Hartland Inn . . . . (208)347-2114
North Fork
Indian Creek Ranch . . . . (208)756-0070
Oldtown
All Aboard Bed & & Breakfast . . . (208)437-2593
Payette
Cedar Inn . . . . (208)464-2704
Pinehurst
Hillcrest House . . . . (208)682-3911
Plummer
Bonnie's B&B . . . . (208)686-1165
The Owl Chalet . . . . (208)686-1597
Pocatello
Hales Half Acre B&B . . . . (208)237-7130
Holmes Retreat . . . . (208)232-5518
Liberty Inn Victorian B&B . . . . . . (208)232-3825
Post Falls
Abel & Oliver's B&B . . . . (208)773-6925
River Cove B&B . . . . (208)773-9190
Potlatch
Rolling Hills B&B . . . . (208)668-1126
Preston
Riverdale Resort . . . . (208)852-0266
Priest Lake
Whispering Waters B&B . . . . (208)443-3229
Riggins
The Lodge B&B . . . . (208)628-3863
Sagle
Pinewoods B&B . (208)263-5851 (800)366-5851
St. Anthony
Riverview B&B . . . . (208)624-4323
Saint Maries
Birch Tree Bed & Breakfast . . . . . (208)245-2198
Ft Hemenway Manor . . . . (208)245-4568
Knoll Haus . . . . (208)245-4137
Salmon
Bilger's Place . . . . (208)756-2206
Greyhouse Inn B&B . . . .
Heritage Inn . . . . (208)756-3174
Salmon River Lodge, Inc
. . . . (208)756-6622 (800)635-4717
Syringa Lodge . . . . (208)756-3373
Sandpoint
The Inn at Angel on Lake B&B
. . . . (208)263-0816 (800)872-0816
Coit House B&B . . . . (208)265-4035
Green Gables Lodge . . . . (208)263-0257
Lakeside Inn . . . (208)263-3717 (800)543-8126
Osprey Cove . . . . (208)265-4200
Page House . . . . (208)263-6584
Serendipity Country Inn . . . . (208)265-9049
Shoshone
Governor's Mansion B&B . . . . . . (208)886-2858
Stanley
Redfish Lake Lodge . . . . (208)774-3536
Sawtooth Hotel . . . . (208)774-9947
Sun Valley
Idaho Country Inn . . . . (208)726-1019
River Street Inn . . . . (208)726-3611
Tyrolean Lodge . (208)726-5336 (800)333-7912
Wallace
21 Bank Street . . . . (208)752-1292
Jameson B&B . . . . (208)556-1554
Pine Tree Inn . . . . (208)752-4391
Weiser
Galloway Inn B&B . . . . (208)549-2659
Yellow Pine
Yellow Pine Lodge . . . . (208)382-4336

Illinois

Algonquin
Victorian Rose Garden . . . . (847)854-9667
Alorton
Jackson House . . . . (618)462-1426
Alton
Haagen House B&B . . . . (618)462-2419

Anna
The Goddard Place B&B . . . . (618)833-6256
Arcola
The Flower Patch . . . . (217)268-4876
Arthur
Favorite Brother Inn . . . . (217)543-2938
Village Inn B & B . . . . (217)543-3605
Athens
Bailey House . . . . (217)636-7695
Atwood
Harshbarger Homestead . . . . (217)578-2265
Bartlett
One Hundred Thousand Welcomes (630)289-3009
Batavia
Villa Batavia . . . . (630)406-8182
Beardstown
Nostalgia Corner B&B . . . . (217)323-5382
Belle Rive
Enchanted Crest . . . . (618)736-2647
Belleville
Farmhouse Guest Cottage . . . . . . (618)277-0964
Swans Court Bed & Breakfast . . . (618)233-0779
Victory Inn . . . . (618)277-1538
Belvidere
Victorian 1897 Herbert House B&B
. . . . (815)544-6600
Bishop Hill
Holden's Guest House . . . . (309)927-3500
Bloomington
Burr House . . . . (309)828-7686
Browning
Friddle Creek Lodge B&B . . . . . . (217)323-4232
Carlinville
Victoria Tyme Inn . . . . (217)854-8689
Carlyle
Country Haus . . . (618)594-8313 (800)279-4486
Victorian Inn . . . . (618)594-8506
Carthage
Wright Farmhouse . . . . (217)357-2421
Champaign
Alice's Place . . . . (217)359-3332
Barb's B&B . . . . (217)356-0376
Norma's Hideaway . . . . (217)359-5876
Shurts House B&B . . . . (217)367-8793
Charleston
Charleston B&B . (217)345-6463 (800)832-3366
Lincoln Land B&B . . . . (217)345-2711
Chester
Betsy's Sugarwood . . . . (618)826-2555
Chicago
Gold Coast Guest House . . . . (312)337-0361
Heritage Bed & Breakfast Registry (312)857-0800
Hyde Park House . . . . (312)363-4595
Magnolia Place Bed & Breakfast . (312)334-6860
Old Town Bed & Breakfast . . . . . (312)440-9268
Old Town Inn . . . . (312)649-9212
The Talbott Hotel (312)944-4970 (800)825-2688
Villa Toscana Guest House
. . . . (312)404-2643 (800)684-5755
Collinsville
Happy Wanderer Inn B&B . . . . . . (618)344-0477
Dallas City
1850's Guest House . . . . (217)852-3652
Danforth
Fannie's House . . . . (815)269-2145
Dixon
River View Guest House . . . . (815)288-5974
Du Quoin
Francie's B&B . . . . (618)542-6686
West Dundee
Ironhedge Inn . . . . (847)426-7777
Dwight
La Petite Voyageur . . . . (815)584-2239
East Dubuque
Captain Charles Merry Guest House
. . . . (815)747-3644
East Peoria
Amis East Inn . . . . (309)699-8646
Red Barn Bed & Breakfast . . . . . (309)694-6079
Elizabeth
Elizabeth Guest House . . . . (815)858-2533
Forget-Me-Not Bed & Breakfast . . (815)858-3744
Ridgeview B&B . . . . (815)598-3150
Elsah
Corner Nest B&B . . . . (618)374-1892

Eureka
Dickinson House Bed & Breakfast (309)467-3116
Evanston
Homestead . . . . (708)475-3300
Margarita European Inn . . . . (847)869-2273
Fairfield
Glass Door Inn . . . . (618)847-4512
Lyndas Bed & Breakfast . . . . (618)842-6343
Franklin Grove
Whitney House . . . . (815)456-2526
Freeburg
The Westerfield House . . . . (618)539-5643
Galena
Aldrich Guest House . . . . (815)777-3323
Avery Guest House . . . . (815)777-3883
Ryan Mansion Inn . . . . (815)777-2043
Belle Aire Mansion . . . . (815)777-0893
Brierwreath Manor B&B . . . . (815)777-0608
Captain Harris Guest House . . . . (815)777-1611
Chestnut Mountain Resort . . . . . (800)435-2914
Colonial Guest House . . . . (815)777-0336
Country Gardens Guest House . . (815)777-3062
Country Valley Guest Home . . . . (815)777-1915
Desoto House Hotel . . . . (815)777-0090
Farmers' Home Hotel . . . . (815)777-3456
Farster's Executive Inn . . . . (815)777-9125
Felt Manor . . . . . (815)777-9093 (800)383-2830
Four Oaks Guest House . . . . (815)777-9567
The Goldmoor . . . . (815)777-3925
Grandview Guest Home . . . . (815)777-1387
The Homestead . . . . (815)777-3536
Inn at Irish Hollow . . . . (815)777-6000
Log Cabin Guest House . . . . (815)777-2845
Mother's Country Inn . . . . (815)777-3153
Pine Hollow Inn . . . . (815)777-1071
The Queen Anne Guest House B&B (815)777-3849
Spring Street Guest House . . . . . (815)777-0354
Stillman's Country Inn . . . . (815)777-0557
Stillwaters Country Inn . . . . (815)777-0644
Victorian Mansion Guest House . (815)777-0675
The Wild Turkey . . . . (815)858-3649
Galesburg
Seacord House . . . . (309)342-4107
Geneva
The Oscar Swan Country Inn . . . (708)232-0173
Gibson City
Stolz Home . . . . (217)784-4502
Golconda
Heritage Haus . . . . (618)683-3883
The Mansion of Golconda . . . . . . (618)683-4400
Marilee's Guest House . . . . (618)683-2751
Riverview Mansion Hotel . . . . . . (618)638-3001
Grand Detour
Colonial Rose Inn . . . . (815)652-4422
Grant Park
The Bennett Curtis House . . . . . . (815)465-6025
Grayville
The Founder's Mansion Inn . . . . . (618)375-3291
Greenville
Prairie House . . . . (618)664-3003
Gurnee
Sweet Basil Hill Farm B&B Inn . . . (847)244-3333
Hanna City
Double D Country Inn, A Bed & Breakfast
. . . . (309)565-4022
Harrisburg
House of Nahum . . . . (618)252-1414
White Lace Inn . . . . (618)252-7599
Havana
McNutt Guest House . . . . (309)543-2255
Peacock House . . . . (309)543-6767
Highland
Tibbetts House . . . . (618)654-4619
Hillsboro
Red Rooster Inn . . . . (217)532-6332
Hindsboro
Breakfast In The Country . . . . . . (217)346-2739
Hopedale
Rose Manor B&B . . . . (309)449-5522
Junction
The Thomas House . . . . (618)272-7046
Kankakee
Normas Bed & Breakfast . . . . . . (815)937-1533
Keithsburg
Commercial House . . . . (309)374-2330

Knoxville
The Walnut Tree House . . . . (309)289-6933
Lanark
Standish House . (815)493-2307 (800)468-2307
Victorian Lace . . . . (815)493-2546
Lebanon
Landmark on Madison Bed & Breakfast
. . . . (618)537-9532
Lena
Sugar Maple Inn . . . . (815)369-2786
Lincoln
Prairie Fields Inn . . . . (217)732-7696
Lockport
Hotel President . . . . (815)838-1881
Macomb
The Brockway House . . . . (309)837-2375
The Pineapple Inn, Inc . . . . (309)837-1914
Maeystown
Corner George Inn . . . . (618)458-6660
Marengo
Washington Street Inn of Marengo (815)568-3442
Marion
Olde Squat Inn . . . . (618)982-2916
Marseilles
Annie Tique's Hotel . . . . (815)795-5848
Mc Leansboro
Rebecca's Guest House . . . . (618)643-3249
Mendota
Elizabeth's B&B . . . . (815)539-5555
Lord Stocking's . . . . (815)539-7905
Metropolis
Isle of View B&B . . . . (618)524-5838
Minonk
Victorian Oaks Bed & Breadfast . . (309)432-2771
Moline
River Drive Guest House . . . . (309)762-8503
Monmouth
Carr Mansion Guest House . . . . . (309)734-3654
Monticello
Linda's Country Loft . . . . (217)762-7316
Mossville
Old Church House Inn . . . . (309)579-2300
Mount Carmel
Living Legacy Homestead . . . . . . (618)298-2476
Mount Carroll
Captain's Quarters . . . . (815)244-2692
The Farm . . . . (815)244-9885
Prairie Path Guest House . . . . . . (815)244-3462
Mount Morris
Kable House Country Inn . . . . . . (815)734-7297
Mount Pulaski
Dorsey's B&B . . . . (217)792-3347
Moweaqua
Dowd House B&B . . . . (217)768-3821
Mundelein
Round-Robin Guesthouse . . . . . . (708)566-7664
Naperville
Die Blaue Gans Guesthaus . . . . . (708)355-0835
Harrison House B&B . . . . (630)420-1117
Nashville
Mill Creek Inn . . . . (618)327-8424
Nauvoo
The Ancient Pines B&B . . . . (217)453-2767
Hotel Nauvoo . . . . (217)453-2211
Mississippi Memories . . . . (217)453-2771
Parley Lane B&B . . . . (217)453-2277
Newton
Marinda Lea's . . . . (618)783-2636
Oak Park
B R Guest House Ltd . . . . (708)383-9977
Under The Ginkgo Tree . . . . (708)524-2327
Oakland
Johnson's Country Home B&B . . (217)346-3274
The Inn on The Square . . . . (217)346-2289
Oblong
Welcome Inn . . . . (618)592-3301
Olney
Richs' Inn . . . . (618)392-3821
Oregon
Lyndel Mansion . . . . (815)732-7313
Pana
Schumacher's Inn . . . . (217)562-3879
Paris
Tiara Manor . . . . (217)465-1865

Paxton
Westlawn Manor . . . . (217)379-2594
Pekin
Herget House . . . . (309)353-4025
Peoria
Ruth's B&B . . . . (309)243-5977
Wildlife Prairie Park . . . . (309)676-0998
Petersburg
Bit of Country B&B . . . . (217)632-3771
Robert Frackelton House . . . . . . (217)632-4496
Pinckneyville
Oxbow B&B . . . . (618)357-9839
Pleasant Hill
Pleasant Haven . . . . (217)734-9357
Plymouth
Plymouth Rock Roost . . . . (309)458-4444
Port Byron
The Olde Brick House . . . . (309)523-3236
Randolph
La Maison Du Rocher Country Inn (618)284-3463
Princeton
The Prairie Hill Barn B&B . . . . . . (815)447-2487
Quincy
Bueltmann Gasthaus . . . . (217)224-8428
Dashwood House . . . . (217)223-1430
The Kaufmann House . . . . (217)223-2502
Red Bud
Das Busche Haus-Guest House B & B
. . . . (618)282-2181
Richmond
Gazebo House Bed & Breakfast . . (815)678-2505
Wooden Bridge Bed & Breakfast . (815)678-4667
Robinson
The Heath Inn . . . . (618)544-3410
Rock Island
Top O' The Morning . . . . (309)786-3513
Victorian Inn . . . . (309)788-7068
Villa . . . . (309)788-4552
Rockford
The Barn . . . . (815)399-5210
Bayberry Inn B&B . . . . (815)964-7243
Rossville
The Farmhouse . . . . (217)748-6505
Rushville
Bottenberg B&B . . . . (217)322-6100
Saint Charles
Charleston Guest House . . . . (630)377-1277
Stage Coach Inn . . . . (708)584-1263
Saint Joseph
Home at Last . . . . (217)469-2402
Savanna
Granny O'Neil's River Inn . . . . . . (815)273-4726
Sesser
The Hill House . . . . (618)625-6064
Sheffield
Chestnut Street Inn . . . . (815)454-2419
Shelbyville
The Shelby Historic House and Inn
. . . . (217)774-3991 (800)342-9978
Spring Grove
Welkome Inn . . . . (815)675-1177
Springfield
Inn on Edwards Bed & Breakfast . (217)525-2660
Mischler House . . . . (217)523-5616
Stockton
Hammond House B & B . . . . (815)947-2032
Maple Lane Country Inn & Resort (815)947-3773
Memory Lane Lodge . . . . (815)947-2726
Streator
Dicus House B&B (815)672-6700 (800)262-1890
Sullivan
Little House on The Prairie . . . . . (217)728-4727
Ms. Connies B&B . . . . (217)728-8582
Sycamore
Country Charm B&B . . . . (815)895-4797
Stratford Inn . . . . (815)895-6789
Taylorville
Market Street Inn . . . . (217)824-7220
Thomasboro
Burke's Country Inn B&B . . . . . . (217)643-7257
Toulon
Rockwell's Victorian B&B . . . . . . (309)286-5201
Tuscola
Quiet Crossing Bed & Breakfast . (217)253-5637

Urbana
Lindley House .... (217)384-4800
Villa Grove
Four Oaks Inn .... (217)832-9313
Waterloo
Senator Rickert Residence B&B . (618)939-8242
Wenona
Hart of Wenona .... (815)853-4778
West Salem
Thelma's B&B .... (618)456-8401
Wheaton
Wheaton Inn .... (708)690-2600
Williamsfield
The Barn Bed & Breakfast ...... (309)639-4408
Williamsville
B&B at Edie's .... (217)566-2538
Windsor
Deerfield Bed & Breakfast ...... (217)459-2750
Winnebago
Victorian Veranda .... (815)963-1337
Winnetka
Chateau Des Fleurs .... (847)256-7272
Woodstock
The Bundling Board Inn .... (815)338-7054
Springshire Inn .... (815)337-8839
Yorkville
Silver Key B&B .. (630)553-5612 (800)246-3384

Indiana

Albion
Pathfinder Country Inn .... (219)636-2888
Alexandria
Country Gazebo Inn .... (317)754-8783
Anderson
Plum Retreat B&B .... (317)649-7586
Angola
The Chef's Nest . (219)665-9080 (800)909-9080
Hartman House . (219)665-9080 (800)909-9080
Attica
Apple Inn .... (317)762-6574
Auburn
Auburn Inn .... (219)925-6363
Hill Top Country Inn .... (219)281-2298
Yawn to Dawn B&B .... (219)925-2583
Aurora
The Aurora Inn .... (812)926-4412
Austin
Morgan's Farm .... (812)794-2536
Batesville
Sherman House Restaurant & Inn (812)934-2407
Berne
Hans Haus of Berne .... (219)589-3793
Schug House Inn .... (219)589-2303
Bloomington
The Bauer House B&B .... (812)336-4383
Grant Street Inn .... (812)334-2353
Scholars Inn ... (812)332-1892 (800)765-3466
Bluffton
Wisteria Manor .... (219)824-4619
Bristol
Milburn House .... (219)848-4026
Open Hearth B&B .... (219)825-2417
Brookville
Duck Creek Bed & Breakfast .... (317)647-6497
Duck Creek Farm B&B .... (317)647-4575
Sulina Farm .... (317)647-2955
Cannelton
Castlebury Inn .... (812)547-4714
Carbon
The Old Maple Inn .... (317)548-0228
Centerville
Historic Lantz House Inn
.... (317)855-2936 (800)495-2689
Charlestown
Trails End Farm .... (812)293-3823
Chesterton
Wingfield's Inn B&B .... (219)348-0766
Columbus
Lafayette Street B&B .... (812)372-7245
Connersville
Maple Leaf Inn B&B .... (317)825-7099
Corydon
Kintner House Inn .... (812)738-2020
Warren Cabin B&B .... (812)738-3419

Crawfordsville
Davis House .... (317)364-0461
Sugar Creek B&B .... (317)362-4095
Yount's Mill Inn .... (317)362-5864
Crothersville
Craft Colony House .... (812)793-3354
Culver
Culver B&B .... (219)842-4009
Danville
Fairhavens .... (317)745-0417
Marigold Manor .... (317)745-2347
Edinburgh
Fox Hill Retreat .... (812)526-6300
Elizabeth
Cathys Y Inn .... (812)969-2524
Evansville
The River's Inn B&B .... (812)428-7777
Fishers
The Frederick-Talbott Inn .... (317)578-3600
Fort Wayne
The Candlewyck B&B .... (219)424-2643
Maysville Manor .... (219)493-8814
Roebuck Inn .... (219)485-9619
Fowler
Pheasant Country B&B .... (317)884-0908
Franklin
Oak Haven B&B .... (317)535-9491
Goshen
Bed & Breakfast on The Farm ... (219)862-4600
Checkerberry Inn .... (219)642-4445
Country Bed & Breakfast ...... (219)862-2748
Garber's Guesthouse .... (219)831-3740
Hoover's B&B .... (219)875-5543
Indian Creek B&B .... (219)875-6606
Ol' Barn B&B .... (219)642-3222
Royer's B&B .... (219)533-1821
Spring View B&B .... (219)642-3997
Timberidge B&B .... (219)533-7133
Waterford B&B .... (219)533-6044
Whippoorwill Valley Inn .... (219)875-5746
White Birch B&B .... (219)533-3763
Grabill
Amandas Country Inn .... (219)627-2704
Grandview
Grandview Guest House & Gardens
.... (812)649-2817
River Belle B&B . (812)649-2500 (800)877-5165
Greencastle
Birdsong B&B .... (317)653-6739
Hummingbird Hill B&B .... (317)653-1531
Walden Inn .... (317)653-2761
Greenfield
Ahlbrands Inn .... (317)894-8839
Center Street Bed & Breakfast ... (317)467-0264
Greenwood
Candlestick Inn .... (317)888-3905
Persimmon Tree B&B .... (317)889-0849
Hagerstown
Teetor House ... (317)489-4422 (800)824-4319
Hartford City
De Coy's B&B .... (317)348-2164
Howe
Lasata B&B .... (219)562-3655
Indianapolis
Barn House .... (317)823-4898
Harney House Inn .... (317)636-7527
Harrison House at Ft. Harrison State Park
.... (317)543-9597
Holland House .... (317)685-9326
Le Chateau Delaware .... (317)636-9156
Stonegate B&B .... (317)887-9614
Jamestown
Oakwood B&B .... (317)676-5114
Jasper
Powers Inn B&B .... (812)482-3018
Jeffersonville
1877 House Country Inn ....
Kendallville
McCray Mansion Inn B&B ...... (219)347-3647
Kingman
Maples Bed and Breakfast ..... (317)397-7393
Knightstown
Lavendar Lady .... (317)345-2299
Old Hoosier House (317)345-2969 (800)775-5315

Kokomo
Bavarian Inn .... (317)453-4715
Laporte
Lynda's Landing .... (219)324-0956
La Porte
Pottinger House .... (219)325-0272
Ladoga
Vintage Reflections .... (317)942-1002
Lagrange
The 1886 Inn .... (219)463-4227
Atwater Century Farm .... (219)463-2743
M & N Bed & Breakfast .... (219)463-2699
Laotto
Tea Rose B&B .... (219)693-2884
Lapel
Kati-Scarlett B&B .... (317)534-4937
Laurel
Ferris Inn .... (317)698-2259
Lawrenceburg
Folke Family Farm Inn .... (812)537-4486
Leavenworth
Ye Olde Scotts Inn .... (812)739-4747
Leesburg
Prairie House B&B .... (219)658-9211
Lewisville
Cabin By The Creek .... (317)987-8204
Ligonier
Minuette .... (219)894-4494
Solomon Mier Manor .... (219)894-3668
Loogootee
Stone Ridge Manor B&B .... (812)295-3382
Madison
Autumnwood Bed & Breakfast .. (812)265-5262
The Cliff House .... (812)265-5272
Federal Inn .... (812)265-4501
Main Street B&B .... (812)265-3539
Old Madison House Bed & Breakfast
.... (812)265-6874
Schussler House B&B .... (812)273-2068
Stonefields Dream Bed & Breakfast (812)265-6856
Marion
Golden Oak B&B .... (317)651-9950
Marshall
Turkey Run Inn .... (317)597-2211
Metamora
Gingerbread House .... (317)647-5518
Grapevine Inn .... (317)647-3738
The Publick House .... (317)647-6729
The Thorpe House Country Inn .. (317)647-5425
Michigan City
Brickstone B&B .... (219)878-1819
Creekwood Inn .... (219)872-8357
Duneland Beach Inn .... (219)874-7729
Middlebury
Auer House .... (219)825-5366
Bittersweet Hill .... (219)825-5953
Bontreger Guest Rooms .... (219)825-2647
Coneygar B&B .... (219)825-5707
Country Victorian .... (219)825-2568
Empty Nest B&B .... (219)825-1042
Essenhaus Country Inn .... (219)825-9447
The Lookout B&B .... (219)825-9809
Mary's Place .... (219)825-2429
Mill Street B&B .... (219)825-5359
Patchwork Quilt Country Inn .... (219)825-2417
Rust Hollar B&B .... (219)825-1111
The Tayler House .... (219)825-7296
That Pretty Place B&B Inn
.... (219)825-3021 (800)418-9487
Theora's B&B .. (219)825-2242 (800)528-4111
Windmill Hideaway B&B .... (219)825-2939
Zimmer Haus .... (219)825-7288
Middletown
Maple Hill B&B .... (317)354-2580
Millersburg
Big House In The Little Woods .. (219)593-9076
Mishawaka
The Beiger Mansion Inn .... (219)256-0365
Kamm House ... (219)259-5789 (800)664-5790
Monon
Bestemor's B&B .... (219)253-8351
Monticello
1887 Black Dog Inn .... (219)583-8297
Beach Vue Resort .... (219)583-8918
The Knight House Inn .... (219)253-7794
Monticello Inn .... (219)583-7128

The Victoria .... (219)583-3440
Zimmer Frei Haus .... (219)583-4061

Morgantown
The Rock House .... (812)597-5100

Muncie
Elizabethan Inn .... (317)289-9449
Ole Ball Inn .... (317)281-0466

N Manchester
Fruitt Basket Inn .... (219)982-2443

Nappanee
Market Street Guest House
.... (219)773-2261 (800)497-3791
Homespun Country Inn
.... (219)773-2034 (800)311-2996
Olde Buffalo Inn . (219)773-2223 (800)272-2135
The Victorian Guest House ..... (217)773-4383

Nashville
5th Generation Farm .... (800)437-8152
Allison House .... (812)988-0814
Always Inn .... (812)988-2233
Chestnut Hill Log Home B&B ... (812)988-4995
Cornerstone Inn .... (812)988-0300
Day Star Inn .... (812)988-0430
Mindheims Inn .... (812)988-2590
Olde Magnolia House .... (812)988-4695
Plain and Fancy .... (812)988-4537
Seasons .... (812)988-2284
Wraylyn Knoll B&B .... (812)988-0733

New Castle
Catherine Winters House Bed & Breakfast
.... (317)529-5535
Country Haven Inn .... (317)533-6611

New Harmony
New Harmony Inn .... (812)682-4491
The Old Rooming House .... (812)682-4724
Raintree Inn B&B .... (812)682-5625

Newburgh
Phelps Mansion Inn .... (812)853-7766

North Vernon
North Vernon Railroad Inn ...... (812)346-7345

Paoli
Big Locust Farms .... (812)723-4856
Braxtan House Inn B&B
.... (812)723-4677 (800)627-2982

Peru
Cole House .... (317)473-7636
Rosewood Mansion .... (317)472-7151

Pleasant Lake
Sycamore Hill Bed & Breakfast .. (219)665-2690

Plymouth
Driftwood .... (219)546-2274

Poland
Wasatch Lake .... (812)986-2227

Porter
Spring House Inn .... (219)929-4600

Richland
Country Homestead .... (812)359-4870

Richmond
Hilltop Hide-A-Way Log House .. (317)935-5752
Norwich Lodge .... (317)983-1575

Rising Sun
Empire House .... (812)438-2878
The Jelley House Country Inn ... (812)438-2319

Rockport
The Rockport Inn .... (812)649-2664
Trail's End B&B .... (502)771-4723

Rockville
Billie Creek Inn .... (317)569-3430
King's Inn .... (317)569-3472
Knoll Inn .... (317)569-6345
Owl's Nest B&B .... (317)569-1803
Suits Us B&B .... (317)569-5660

Rossville
Wildwood B&B .... (317)379-2482

Rushville
Victoriana B&B .... (317)629-2274

Salem
1920 Annex .... (812)883-4858
Lanning House B&B .... (812)883-3484

San Pierre
Lomax Station .. (219)896-2600 (800)535-6629

Seymour
Country Inn .... (812)523-8172

Shipshewana
Green Meadow .... (219)768-4221
Morton Street B&B (219)768-4391 (800)447-6475

Old Carriage Inn .... (219)768-7217
Old Davis Hotel .... (219)768-7300
Weaver's Country Oaks .... (219)768-7191

South Bend
Jamison Inn .... (219)277-9682
The Inn at Saint Mary's .... (219)232-4000

Speedway
Speedway Inn B&B .... (317)487-6531

Syracuse
Anchor Inn B&B .... (219)457-4714
Victoria Bay B&B .... (219)457-5374

Taswell
White Oaks Cabins .... (812)338-3120

Terre Haute
Sycamore Farm B & B Tea Room (812)877-9288

Tippecanoe
Bessingers Wildlife Refuge ..... (219)223-3288

Topeka
Four Woods B&B .... (219)593-2021

Unionville
Possum Trot Inn .... (812)988-2964

Upland
This Old Barn ... (317)998-2520 (800)598-9121

Valparaiso
The Inn at Aberdeen .... (219)465-3753

Vernon
Raymers Bed & Breakfast ...... (812)346-5658

Vevay
Captain's Quarters B&B .... (812)427-2900

Vincennes
The Harrison Inn .... (812)882-3243

Wabash
Around Window Inn .... (219)563-6901
Lamp-Post Inn .... (219)563-3094

Walkerton
Hesters Cabin B&B .... (219)568-2105
Koontz House B&B .... (219)586-7090

Warsaw
Candlelight Inn .. (219)267-2906 (800)352-0640
White Hill Manor .... (219)269-6933

West College Corner
Doctors Inn .... (317)732-3772

Westfield
Camel Lot .... (317)873-4370

Winona Lake
Gunn Guest House .... (219)267-7552

Zionsville
The Brick Street Inn .... (317)873-9177

Iowa

Adair
Stagecoach Inn .... (515)742-3658

Anamosa
The Shaw House .... (319)462-4485

Bellevue
Mont Rest .... (319)872-4220
Spring Side Inn .... (319)782-5452

Brayton
Hallock House B&B
.... (712)549-2449 (800)945-0663

Brooklyn
Hotel Brooklyn .... (515)522-9229

Burlington
Roads-Gardner House .... (319)689-4222

Cedar Falls
Carriage House Inn B&B .... (319)277-6724
The House By The Side of The Road
.... (319)988-3691

Cedar Rapids
Gwendolyn's B&B .... (319)363-9731

Clayton
Claytonian B&B .... (319)964-2776

Clear Lake
Norsk Haus - By The Shore .... (515)357-8368

Clermont
Bushman Cozy Ranch .... (319)423-7369

Corning
Pheasants Galore .... (515)322-3749

Council Bluffs
Robin's Nest Inn B&B .... (712)323-1649

Davenport
Bishop's House Inn .... (319)324-2454
Fulton's Landing Guest House ... (319)322-4069
River Oaks Inn .. (319)326-2629 (800)352-6016

Village B&B .... (319)322-4905

Decorah
Bruvold Farm .... (319)382-4729
Montgomery Mansion .... (319)382-5088

Des Moines
Carter House Inn .... (515)288-7850

Dubuque
Collier Mansion .... (319)588-2130
Mississippi Mary's B&B .... (319)556-5466
Oak Crest Guest Homes .... (319)582-4207
Redstone Inn .... (319)582-1894
The Richards House .... (319)557-1492
Stout House .... (319)582-1890

Elk Horn
Joy's Morning Glory B&B ...... (712)764-5631
The Travelling Companion B&B .. (712)764-8932

Elkader
Little House Vacations .... (319)783-7774

Fort Madison
The Morton House .... (319)372-9517

Greenfield
The Wilson Home .... (515)743-2031

Homestead
Die Heimat Country Inn .... (319)622-3937

Iowa City
The Golden Haug .... (319)338-6452

Keosauqua
Hotel Manning .. (319)293-3232 (800)728-2718
Mason House Inn of Bentonsport (319)592-3133

Keota
Elmhurst .... (515)636-3001

Lansing
Fitzgerald's Inn B&B .... (319)538-4872

Le Claire
Mississippi Sunrise B&B .... (319)332-9203
The Monarch B&B .... (319)289-3011

Malcom
Pleasant Country B&B .... (515)528-4925

Maquoketa
Decker Hotel .... (319)652-6654

Massena
Amdor's Evergreen Inn .... (712)779-3521

Mc Gregor
Little Switzerland Inn .... (319)873-3670
River's Edge B&B .... (319)873-3501

Middle Amana
Dusk to Dawn B & B .... (319)622-3029

Missouri Valley
Midlands B&B .... (712)642-2418

Mitchellville
Whitaker Farm .... (515)967-3184

Montezuma
English Valley B&B .... (515)623-3663

Nevada
Queen Anne B&B .... (515)382-6444

Newton
La Corsette Maison Inn .... (515)792-6833

Pella
Heritage House .... (515)626-3092
Strawtown Inn .... (515)628-2681

Prescott
Maple Hill Farms .... (515)369-4874

Princeton
The Woodlands . (319)289-3177 (800)257-3177

South Amana
Babi's B&B .... (319)662-4381

Spillville
Old World Inn .... (319)562-3739

Stratford
Hook's Point Farmstead .... (515)838-2781

Swisher
Terra Verde Farm .... (319)846-2478

Thurman
Plum Creek Inn .... (712)628-2191

Tipton
Victorian House Tipton .... (319)886-2633

Walnut
Clark's Country Inn B&B .... (712)784-3010

Washington
Roses and Lace B&B .... (319)653-2462

Waukon
Allamakee B&B .... (319)568-3103

Waverly
Villa Fairfield B&B .... (319)352-0739

Webster City
Centennial Farm B&B .... (515)832-3050
Whiting
Lighthouse Marina Inn .... (712)485-2066
Williamsburg
Lucille's Country Inn .... (319)668-1185

Kansas

Abilene
Balfour's House B&B .... (913)263-4262
Dora Theay Ah's B&B .... (913)263-0226
Old Glory Guest House .... (913)263-3225
Spruce House .... (913)263-3900
Victorian Reflections B&B Inn
.... (913)263-7774 (800)279-7774
Ashland
Hardesty House .... (316)635-2911
Rolling Hills B&B .... (316)635-2859
The Slaton House .... (316)635-2290
Wallingford Inn B&B .... (316)635-2129
Atchison
The Williams House .... (913)367-1757
Atwood
The Flower Patch B&B .... (913)626-3780
Auburn
Lippincott's Fyshe House ...... (913)256-2436
Baldwin City
Grove House .... (913)594-2947
Three Sister's Inn .... (913)594-3244
Basehor
Bedknobs & Biscuits .... (913)724-1540
Bern
Lear Acres B&B .... (913)336-3903
Burlington
Victorian Memories .... (316)364-5752
Cassoday
The Sunbarger Guest House .... (316)735-4499
Cawker City
Oak Creek Lodge .... (913)454-3455
Chapman
Windmill Inn B&B .... (913)263-8755
Columbus
Meriwether House .... (316)429-2812
Concordia
Crystle's B&B .. (913)243-2192 (800)889-6373
Council Grove
The Cottage House .... (316)767-6828
Flint Hills B&B .... (316)767-6655
Dodge City
Boot Hill B&B & Guest House ... (316)225-7600
Dorrance
The Country Inn .... (913)666-4468
Dover
Sage Inn .... (913)256-6336
Elk Falls
The Sherman House .... (316)329-4425
Elkhart
The Cimarron .... (405)696-4672
Ellis
Grapevine Boarding House ..... (913)726-4173
Emporia
The White Rose Inn .... (316)343-6336
Enterprise
Ehrsam Place B&B (913)263-8747 (800)470-7774
Eureka
123 Mulberry Street B&B ...... (316)583-7515
Florence
Stone Haven B&B .... (316)878-4434
Fort Scott
Bennington House .... (316)223-1837
The Chenault Mansion .... (316)223-6800
Country Quarters .... (316)223-2889
The Courtland B&B Inn .... (316)223-0098
Lyons' House ... (316)223-0779 (800)784-8378
Fowler
Creek Side Farm B&B .... (316)646-5586
Garnett
Kirk House .... (913)448-5813
Goodland
Heart Haven Inn .... (913)899-5171
Great Bend
Peaceful Acres B&B .... (316)793-7527
Walnut Brook B&B (316)792-5900 (800)300-5901

Halstead
Heritage Inn .... (316)835-2118
Old Country Rose Inn .... (316)835-2876
Hays
Aurora Hills B&B .... (913)625-6406
Hiawatha
Pleasant Corner .... (913)742-7877
Highland
Meadowlark B&B & Tea Room .. (913)442-3727
Hill City
Pheasant Run B&B .... (913)674-2955
Pomeroy Inn .... (913)674-2098
Hillsboro
A Nostalgic B&B Place .... (316)947-3519
Holton
Dodds House B&B .... (913)364-3172
Holyrood
Hollyrood House .... (913)252-3678
Hutchinson
The Rose Garden .... (316)663-5317
Independence
Rosewood B&B .... (316)331-2221
Iola
Northrup House B&B .... (316)365-8025
Lakin
Country Pleasures B&B .... (316)355-6982
Windy Heights B&B .... (316)355-7699
Lenora
Barbeau House .... (913)567-4886
Liberal
The Bluebird Inn .... (316)624-0720
Lindsborg
Smoky Valley B&B .... (913)227-4460
Louisburg
Red Maple Inn .... (913)827-2840
Manhattan
Kimble Cliff .... (913)539-3816
Marion
Country Dreams .... (316)382-2250
Meriden
Village Inn .... (913)876-2835
Newton
Hawk House B&B .... (316)283-2045
The Old Parsonage .... (316)283-6808
Olathe
Martin Van Buren Parker B&B ... (913)780-4587
Osborne
The Loft B&B .... (913)346-5984
Oskaloosa
Stone Crest B&B .... (913)863-2166
Overbrook
Pinemoore Inn .... (913)453-2304
Paola
The Victorian Lady B&B .... (913)294-4652
Peabody
Jones Sheep Farm B&B .... (316)983-2815
Pittsburg
Victorian Gardens B&B .... (800)709-1961
Pleasanton
Cedar Crest .... (913)352-6706
Randolph
Shadow Springs Farm .... (913)293-5332
Riley
Trix's Riley Roomer .... (913)485-2654
Salina
Happy Trails .... (913)827-0190
Hunters Leigh B&B .... (913)823-6750
Seneca
Stein House B&B .... (913)336-3790
Summerfield
The Walnut Inn .... (913)244-6286
Sylvan Grove
Spillman Creek Lodge .... (913)277-3424
Syracuse
Braddock Ames B&B .... (316)384-5218
Tecumseh
Old Stone House Along The Oregon Trail
.... (913)379-5568
Topeka
Brickyard Barn Inn .... (913)235-0057
Country View Estate .... (913)862-0335
The Elderberry B&B .... (913)235-6309
Holliday Park B&B .... (913)234-8384
The Sunflower B&B .... (913)357-7509

Ulysses
Fort's Cedar View .... (316)356-2570
Valley Falls
The Barn B&B .... (913)945-3303
Victoria
Das Younger Haus .... (913)735-2760
Wakefield
The Rock House B&B .... (913)461-5732
Wakefield's Country B&B ...... (913)461-5533
Washington
The Moore-Ballard Inn .... (913)325-3292
Wathena
Carousel B&B .... (913)989-3537
Wells
Trader's Lodge .... (913)488-3930
Wichita
Castle In Riverside .... (316)263-9300
The Holiday House-Residential B&B
.... (316)721-1968
Max Paul Inn .... (316)689-8101
The Inn at Willowbend .... (316)636-4032
Winfield
The Iron Gate Inn .... (316)221-7202

Kentucky

Allensville
The Pepper Place .... (502)265-9859
Auburn
Auburn Guest House & Carriage House
.... (502)542-6019
Augusta
Augusta Landing .... (606)756-3228
Augusta White House Inn ...... (606)756-2004
Doniphan Home .... (606)756-2409
Lamplighter Inn .... (606)756-2603
The Mains House .... (606)756-3125
Bardstown
1790 House .... (502)348-7072
Amber Leann B&B .... (502)349-0014
Beautiful Dreamer B&B
.... (502)348-4004 (800)811-8312
Bruntwood 1802 .... (502)348-8218
Coffee Tree Cabin .... (502)348-1151
Kenmore Farms . (502)348-8023 (800)831-6159
The Mansion Bed & Breakfast
.... (502)348-2586 (800)399-2586
Old Talbott Tavern .... (502)348-3494
William Heavenhill House ...... (502)348-0794
Bellevue
Weller Haus B&B (606)431-6829 (800)431-4287
Benham
Schoolhouse Inn (606)848-3000 (800)391-9813
Berea
The Doctor's Inn .... (606)986-3042
Holly Tree B&B .... (606)986-2804
The Mansion House .... (606)986-9851
Morning Glory .... (606)986-8661
Blaine
The Gambill Mansion .... (606)652-3120
Bloomfield
The Vintage Rose .... (502)252-5042
Boston
The Inn at Tara Dawn Farm ..... (502)833-4553
Bowling Green
Alpine Lodge .... (502)843-4846
Walnut Lawn B&B .... (502)781-7255
Brandenburg
Doe Run Inn .... (502)422-2982
Brooksville
Guest Cottage at Swan Song ... (606)735-3551
Burkesville
Cabin Fever .... (502)737-4980
Burnside
Annies of Lake Cumberland .... (606)561-9966
Campbellsville
Della's Yesteryear .... (502)789-3961
The Yellow Cottage .... (502)789-2669
Carrollton
Historic Ghent House .... (502)347-5807
Pt. Baker House .... (502)732-4210
Cave City
Wayfarer Inn .... (502)773-3366
Covington
Amos Shinkle Townhouse ...... (606)431-2118
The Carneal House Inn .... (606)431-6130

The Claire House .... (606)491-0168

Cox's Creek

Farrell Place .... (502)241-5913

Cynthiana

Ann's B&B .... (606)484-3665
Broadwell Acres .... (606)234-4255
Seldon Renaker Inn .... (606)234-3240

Danville

The Cottage .... (606)236-9642
The Empty Nest .... (606)236-3339
Green Door Inn .... (606)238-2286
Pasick's .... (606)236-0074
Randolf House .... (606)236-9594
Twin Hollies Retreat B&B ...... (606)236-8954

Dawson Springs

Ridley House .... (502)797-2165

Elizabethtown

Olde Bethlehem Academy Inn
.... (502)862-9003 (800)662-5670

Frankfort

Capitol Manor House .... (502)227-4297
Cedar Rock Farm .... (502)747-8754
Olde Kentucke .... (502)227-7389
Taylor Compton House .... (502)227-4368

Franklin

College Street Inn .... (502)586-9352
Park Place .... (502)586-8178

Georgetown

Bourbon House Farm .... (606)987-8669
Cedar Post .... (502)863-3075
Log Cabin B&B .... (502)863-3514
Pineapple Inn .... (502)868-5453
Racer's Rest Farm .... (502)863-6342

Glasgow

B&B Country Cottage .... (502)646-2677
Four Seasons Country Inn ...... (502)678-1000

Glendale

Petticoat Junction .... (502)369-8604

Grays Knob

Three Deer Inn .... (606)573-6666

Harrodsburg

Bauer Haus .... (606)734-6289
Baxter House .... (606)734-5700
Beaumont Inn .... (606)734-3381
Canaan Land Farm B&B
.... (606)734-3984 (800)450-7607

Hazel

Outback B&B .... (502)436-5858

Henderson

L & N B&B .... (502)831-1100

Hickman

Laclede B&B .... (502)236-2902

Hindman

Quilt Maker Inn .... (606)785-5622

Hodgenville

Lakeside B&B .... (502)358-3711

Hopkinsville

Oakland Manor .... (502)885-6400

Independence

Cully Country Retreat .... (606)356-7865

Kuttawa

Davis House .... (502)388-4468
Silver Cliff Inn .... (502)388-5858

La Center

Country Style Inn .... (502)665-9903

Lancaster

Perkins Place Farm .... (606)792-6545

Lawrenceburg

Dowling Hall .... (502)839-8798

Lewisport

Hayden House .... (502)295-3335

Lexington

A True Inn .... (606)272-3957
Aaron Suites .... (606)252-3601
B&B at Sills Inn .... (606)252-3601
Cherry Knoll Farm .... (606)253-9800
Homewood .... (606)255-2814
Ms. Jesta Bell's B&B .... (606)734-7834
Sycamore Ridge .... (606)231-7714

Liberty

Liberty Greystone Manor ...... (606)787-5444
Outback Luxury B&B .... (606)787-9951

Louisville

The Columbine .... (502)635-5000
Kentucky Homes Bed & Breakfast (502)635-7341
Old Louisville B&B .... (502)636-3661
Rose Blossom .... (502)636-0295
Summer's Place .... (502)635-7341
Towne House .... (502)636-5673
Woodhaven .... (502)895-1011

Mammoth Cave

Mello Inn .... (502)286-4126

Manchester

Blair's Country Living Log Home . (606)598-2854

Marion

Bill & Sherry's Quarters .... (502)965-3114
Lafayette Club House .... (502)965-3889
Myers' B&B .... (502)965-3731 (800)965-3731
Sugar Grove .... (502)965-4342

Mayfield

Broadway B&B .... (502)623-6666
Susan B Seay's Magnolia Manor . (502)247-4108

Middlesborough

The Ridge Runner B&B .... (606)248-4299

Morehead

Appalachian House .... (606)784-5421
Kentucky Farm Inn .... (606)783-1054

Morgantown

Helm House B&B .... (502)526-2743

Mount Sterling

Trimble House .... (606)498-6561

Munfordville

The Farm Retreat .... (502)524-3697

Murray

The Diuguid House B&B .... (502)753-5470

New Concord

Outback B&B .... (502)436-5858

New Haven

The Sherwood Inn .... (502)549-3386

Newport

Gateway B&B .... (606)581-6447

Oak Grove

Tuckaway Farms .... (502)439-6255

Olive Hill

Oak Hills .... (606)286-5732

Owensboro

Weatherberry .... (502)684-8760

Paducah

1868 B&B .... (502)444-6801
Ehrhardts B&B .... (502)554-0644
Farley Place .... (502)442-2488
Fox Briar Farm Inn .... (502)554-1774
Paducah Harbor Plaza B&B
.... (502)442-2698 (800)719-7799
River City Hospitality House
.... (502)575-9987 (800)406-9795
Rosewood Inn .... (502)554-6632
Trinity Hills Farm .... (502)488-3999

Paris

Amelia's Field Country Inn ..... (606)987-5778
Pleasant Place .... (606)987-5546

Perryville

Elmwood Inn .... (606)332-2400

Princeton

Harralson House Inn .... (502)365-6872

Raywick

Blue Hill Farm B&B .... (502)465-4221

Richmond

Barnes Mill B&B Guest House . . . (606)623-5509
Jordan Hill Farm .... (606)623-8114
The Madison .... (606)623-0061

Rogers

Cliffview Resort .... (606)668-6550

Lake Cumberland

White Pillars .... (502)866-4132

Russellville

Washington House .... (502)726-7608

Sandy Hook

Charlene's Country Inn B&B .... (606)738-6674

Shelbyville

The Wallace House .... (502)633-4272

Simpsonville

The Old Stone Inn .... (502)722-8882

Smiths Grove

Cave Spring Farm .... (502)563-6941
Victorian House .... (502)563-9403

Somerset

Osborne's of Cabin Hollow ..... (606)382-5495
Shadwick House .... (606)678-4675

South Union

Shaker Tavern at South Union . . . (502)542-6801

Springfield

Glenmar Plantation B&B .... (606)284-7791
Maple Hill Manor .... (606)336-3075
McChord Carriage House Inn . . . (606)336-3290

Sulphur

Sulphur Trace Farm .... (502)743-5956

Taylorsville

Anchor Inn .... (502)477-8325
B&B at Taylorsville .... (502)477-2473
Bowling's Villa B&B .... (502)477-2636

Trenton

Woodstock Mansion .... (502)466-3506

Versailles

Derby Kentucky . (606)873-3372 (800)526-9801
Rosehill Inn .... (606)873-5957
Shepherd Place .... (606)873-7843
Tyrone Pike .... (606)873-2408
Victorian Rose .... (606)873-5252

West Point

Ditto House Inn .... (502)922-4939

Whitesburg

Salyers House .... (606)633-2532

Wilmore

Scott Station Inn .... (606)858-0121

Winchester

Windswept Farm .... (606)745-1245

Zoe

Candlelight B&B Inn .... (606)464-3992

Louisiana

Abita Springs

Trail's End B&B .... (504)867-9899

Alexandria

Matt's Cabin B&B/Inglewood Plantation
.... (318)487-8340
Tyrone Plantation .... (318)442-8528

Amite

Blythewood Plantation .... (504)345-6419
Dr. C. S. Stewart's Cottage B&B . (504)748-3700
Elliott House .... (504)748-8553

Bossier City

Beauvais House-Cottage B&B . . . (318)221-3735

Bourg

Julia's Cajun Country B&B ..... (504)851-3540
Le Jardin Sur Le Bayou .... (504)594-2722

Breaux Bridge

Bayou Boudin & Cracklin ...... (318)332-6158
Bayou Cabins .... (318)332-6158
Country Oaks Guesthouse ..... (318)332-3093

Broussard

La Grande Maison (318)837-4428 (800)829-5133
Maison D'Andre Billeaud
.... (318)837-3455 (800)960-7378

Calloway Corners

Calloway Corners B&B
.... (318)377-2058 (800)851-1088

Carencro

Belle of The Oaks .... (318)896-4965

Cheneyville

Loyd Hall Plantation .... (318)776-5641

Clinton

Brame-Bennet House .... (504)683-5241

Covington

The Guest Cottage .... (504)893-3767
Mill Bank Farms .... (504)892-1606
Riverside Hills Farm .... (504)892-1794

Cut Off

Hassell House B&B .... (504)632-8088

Darrow

Tezcuco Plantation .... (504)562-3929

Destrehan

Ormond Plantation Manor ...... (504)764-8544

Eunice

Potier's Prairie Cajun Inn ...... (318)457-0400
The Seale Guesthouse .... (318)457-3753

Gibson

Wildlife Gardens .... (504)575-3676

Hayes

La Retraite Lorrain .... (318)622-3412

Homer

Tall Timbers Lodge .... (318)927-5260

Houma

Audrey's Little Cajun Mansion . . . (504)879-3285

Capri Court B&B . . . . (800)428-8026
Crochet House B&B . . . . (504)879-3033
Grand Manor . . . . (504)876-5493

Jackson
Asphodel Plantation . . . . (504)654-6868
Milbank . . . . (504)634-5901
Old Centenary Inn . . . . (504)634-5050

Jeanerette
Alice Plantation B&B . . . . (318)276-3187
B&B on Bayou Teche . . . . (318)276-5061
Patout's Guest House . . . . (318)364-0644

Jennings
Cajun Country Craft . . . . (318)824-3145
Creole Rose Manor . . . . (318)824-3145

Kenner
7 Oaks . . . . (504)888-8649

Krotz Springs
Country Store B&B Inn . . . . (318)566-2331

Lafayette
Bois Des Chenes B&B . . . . (318)233-7816
Lafayette Inn . . . . (318)235-9442
Mouton Manor Inn . . . . (318)237-6996
Ti Frere's House . . . . (318)984-9347

Lake Charles
Adelaide's B&B . . . . (318)439-5200
Claibourne House Bed & Breakfast (318)436-6116
Ramsay-Curtis Mansion Guest House
. . . . (318)439-3859
Walter's Attic . . . . (318)439-6672

Larose
Couche Et Dejeune, Inc. . . . . (504)693-4316

Lecompte
Hardy House B&B . . . . (318)776-5896

Leesville
Huckleberry Inn . . . . (318)238-4000

Madisonville
The Magnolia House B&B . . . . . . (504)845-4922

Mandeville
The Pollyana . . . . (504)626-4053
Windy Pines B&B . . . . (504)626-9189

Metairie
Bed & Breakfast of New Orleans . (504)838-0071
Metairie Meadows . . . . (504)525-3983

Monroe
Boscobel Cottage (318)325-1550 (800)254-3529

Montegut
Amanda-Magenta Plantation House B&B
. . . . (504)594-8298

Natchez
Beau Fort Plantation . . . . (318)352-9580

Natchitoches
Breazeale House B&B . . . . (318)352-5630
Cane River House . . . . (318)352-5912
Cloutier Townhouse . . . . (800)351-7666
Dogwood Inn . . . . (318)352-9812
Fleur De Lis B&B (318)352-6621 (800)489-6621
Jefferson House B&B . . . . (318)352-5756
The Levy-East House
. . . . (318)352-0662 (800)840-0662
Martin's Roost . . . . (318)352-9215
River Oaks B&B . . . . (318)352-2776
Starlight Plantation B&B . . . . (800)866-8893
Tante Huppe Inn . . . . (318)352-5342

New Iberia
Chez Hebert . . . . (318)367-6447
Estorge-Norton House B&B . . . . (318)365-7603
La Maison Du Teche . . . . (800)667-9456
The Inn at Lerosier . . . . (318)367-5306
Masion Marceline . . . . (318)364-5922
Pourtos House Bed & Breakfast . (318)367-7045

New Orleans
A Creole House . . . . (504)524-8076
A Villa B&B . . . . (504)945-4253
Andrew Jackson Hotel . . . . (504)561-5881
Bayou St. John B&B . . . . (504)482-6677
Bed & Breakfast As You Like It . . (504)821-7716
Bougainvillia House . . . . (504)525-3983
Bourgoyne Guest House . . . . (504)524-3621
Chartres Street House . . . . (504)945-2339
Chimes Bed & Breakfast . . . . (504)899-2621
The Claiborne Mansion
. . . . (504)949-7327 (800)449-7327
Columns Hotel . . (504)899-9308 (800)445-9308
The Courtyards . (504)949-5313 (800)585-5731
Dauzat Guest House . . . . (504)524-2075
The Degas House . . . . (504)821-5009
Dufour Baldwin House . . . . (504)945-1503
Dusty Mansion . . . . (504)895-4576
The Duvigneaud House . . . . (504)948-6730
Garden District B&B . . . . (504)895-4302
Girod House . . . . (504)522-5214
Grenoble House . . . . (504)522-1331
Hotel Maison De Ville . . . . (504)561-5858
Josephine Guest House . . . . (504)524-6361
Lafitte Guest House
. . . . (504)581-2678 (800)331-7971
Longpre Garden's Guest House . . (504)561-0654
Macarty Park Guest House
. . . . (504)943-4994 (800)521-2790
Mager House . . . . (504)522-5988
Maison Esplanade (504)523-8080 (800)290-4233
Mandevilla . . . . (504)865-1000
Marigny Guest House . . . . (504)944-9700
Marquette Hotel . . . . (504)523-3014
Mazant Street Guest House . . . . . (504)944-2662
The McKendrick-Breaux House . . (504)586-1700
Mechlings Guest House . . . . (504)943-4131
Mentone B&B . . . . (504)943-3019
New Orleans First B&B . . . . (504)947-3401
New Orleans Guest House . . . . . (504)566-1177
Nicolas M. Benachi House
. . . . (504)525-7040 (800)308-7040
Nottoway Plantation Inc . . . . (504)832-2093
Old World Inn . . . . (504)566-1330
The Olivier Estate, A B&B . . . . . . (504)949-9600
PJ. Holbrooks Olde Victorian Inn . (504)522-2446
Park View . . . . (504)861-7564
Prince Conti Hotel . . . . (504)529-4172
The Prytania Park Hotel
. . . . (504)524-0427 (800)862-1984
Quarter Esplanade Guest House . (504)948-9328
Rathbone Inn . . . . (504)947-2100
The Robert Gordy House . . . . . . (504)486-9424
Rose Manor B&B Inn . . . . (504)282-8200
Royal Barracks . . . . (504)529-7269
Rue Dumaine . . . . (504)581-2802
Rue Royal Inn . . . . (504)524-3900
Soniat House . . . . (504)522-0570
Southern Comfort Bed & Breakfast (504)861-0082
St. Charles Guest House . . . . (504)523-6556
The Stone Manor Hotel . . . . (504)899-9600
Terrell House Mansion . . . . (504)524-9859
Ursuline Guest House . . . . (504)525-8509
The Victorian Guesthouse
. . . . (504)488-4640 (800)729-4640
Whitney Inn . . . . (504)521-8000

New Roads
Carruth House . . (504)638-9745 (800)749-1928
Garden Gate Manor B&B
. . . . (504)638-3890 (800)487-3890
Jubilee! B&B . . . . (504)638-8333
Mon Reve B&B . (504)638-7848 (800)644-3642
Pointe Coupee B&B . . . . (504)638-6254
River Blossom Inn . . . . (504)638-8650
Sunrise on The River . . . . (504)638-3642

Opelousas
Coteau Ridge B&B . . . . (318)942-8180

Oscar
Mon Coeur B&B . . . . (504)638-9892

Pineville
Ogeedankee B&B . . . . (318)641-9752

Plaquemine
Old Turnerville B&B . . . . (504)687-5337

Ponchatoula
Grand Magnolia . . . . (504)386-6406
The Guest House . . . . (504)386-6275

Port Sulphur
River Place Bed & Breakfast . . . . (504)564-2485

Prairieville
Tree House In The Park . . . . (800)532-2246

Rayne
Maison D'memoire . . . . (318)334-2477
Maison Daboval . . . . (318)334-3489

Reserve
Graugnard House of Terre Haute Plantation
. . . . (504)651-2889

Ruston
Melody Hills Ranch . . . . (318)255-7127

Saint Francisville
Audubon Lakes . . . . (504)635-6617
Cottage Plantation . . . . (504)635-3674
Dogwood Plantation B&B
. . . . (504)635-4790 (800)635-4790
Green Springs Plantation
. . . . (504)635-3355 (800)457-4978
Hemingbough . . . . (504)635-6617
Lake Rosemound Inn . . . . (504)635-3176
Myrtles Plantation . . . . (504)635-6277
Propinquity Bed & Breakfast . . . . (504)635-4116
Rosedown Plantation & Historic Garden
. . . . (504)635-3332
Shadetree . . . . (504)635-6116

Saint Martinville
Acorn Inn . . . . (318)394-5848
La Maison Louie B&B . . . . (318)394-1872

Shreveport
2439 Fairfield, A Bed & Breakfast (318)424-2424
The Columns on Jordan . . . . (318)222-5912
Fairfield Place . . . . (318)222-0048
Slattery House B&B . . . . (318)222-6977

Slidell
Garden Guest House . . . . (504)641-0335
Le Petite Maison . . . . (504)645-9133
Salmen-Frichie House B&B
. . . . (504)643-1405 (800)235-4168

Sunset
Chretien Point Plantation . . . . (800)880-7050

Vacherie
Bay Tree Plantation B&B
. . . . (504)265-2109 (800)895-2109
Oak Alley Plantation . . . . (504)265-2151

Vidalia
Lisburn Hall . . . . (800)972-0127

Ville Platte
Aucoin House . . . . (318)363-4228
Maison Deville . . . . (318)363-1262

Vivian
Bed & Breakfast The Rose . . . . . (318)375-5607

Washington
Camellia Cove . . . . (318)826-7362
La Chaumiere . . . . (318)826-3967

West Monroe
Rose Lee Inn . . . . (318)322-4090
Tante Marie's Bed & Breakfast . . (318)325-0186

White Castle
Nottoway Plantation Inn & Restaurant
. . . . (504)545-2730
White Castle Inn . . . . (504)545-9932

Wilson
Glencoe Plantation . . . . (504)629-5387

Winnfield
Southern Colonial Bed & Breakfast (318)628-6087

Maine

Abbot Village
Elderberry Inn . . . . (207)876-4901

Addison
Pleasant Bay B&B . . . . (207)483-4490

Alfred
Blue Door Inn . . . . (207)490-2353
Clover Hill Farm . . . . (207)490-1105
Hirams House . . . . (207)490-1126

Andover
Andover Arms Bed & Breakfast . . (207)392-4251
Pine Ellis Lodging B & B Bed & Breakfast
. . . . (207)392-4161

Anson
Hilltop Inn . . . . (207)696-0979

Athens
Hilltop Lodging . . . . (207)654-3141

Bailey Island
Driftwood Inn . . . . (207)833-5461
Johnson B&B . . . . (207)833-6053
Katie's Ketch . . . . (207)833-7785
The Lady & The Loon . . . . (207)833-6871
Log Cabin Lodging . . . . (207)833-5546

Bangor
Country Hospitality Inn . . . . (207)941-0200
Phoenix Inn . . . . (207)947-3850
Riverside Inn . . . . (207)947-3800

Bar Harbor
Bar Harbor Inn . . . . (207)288-3351
Bayview Inn & Hotel . . . . (207)288-5300
Central House . . . . (207)288-5297
Canterbury Cottage . . . . (207)288-2112
Carrying Place . . . . (207)288-8905
Castlemaine Inn . . . . (207)288-4563
Cleftstone Manor . . . . (207)288-4951
Collier House Bed & Breakfast . . (207)288-3162

Cove Fram Inn .... (207)288-5355
The Hearthside .... (207)288-4533
Heathwood Inn .. (207)288-5591 (800)582-3681
Holbrook House .... (207)288-4970
Cottage Inns of Bar Harbor ..... (207)288-9439
Kedge .... (207)288-5180
Mc Kay Lodging Rooms .... (207)288-3531
The Inn on High .... (207)288-4325
Nannau-Seaside Bed & Breakfast (207)288-5575
Primrose Inn ... (207)288-4031 (800)543-7842
Shady Maples .... (207)288-3793
Stonethrow Cottage .... (207)288-3668
Stratford House Inn .... (207)288-5189
Thornhedge .... (207)288-5398
Town Motel & Guest House .... (207)288-5548
Twin Gables Inn .... (207)288-3064
Ullikana In The Field .... (207)288-9552
The Atlantean Inn .... (207)288-5703
White Columns Inn .... (207)288-4648
The Yankee Lady Inn .... (207)288-5176

Bass Harbor

Bass Harbor Cottages & Country Inn
.... (207)244-3460
Bass Harbor Inn .... (207)244-5157
Pointy Head Inn .... (207)244-7261

Bath

1024 Washington B&B .... (207)443-5202
The Inn at Bath .... (207)443-4294
Bath Bed & Breakfast .... (207)443-4477
Front Porch Bed & Breakfast .... (207)443-5790
Morse Hall Bed & Breakfast .... (207)442-7290
Pine Hill B&B .... (207)443-2143

Belfast

Adaline Palmer House .... (207)338-5790
Fiddler's Green Farm .... (207)338-3568
Frost House B&B .... (207)338-4159
Hiram Alden Inn .... (207)338-2151
Horatio Johnson House .... (207)338-5153
Inn on Primrose Hill .... (207)338-6982
Northport House Inn .... (207)338-2740

Belgrade Lakes

Wings Hill ..... (207)495-2400 (800)509-4647

Bethel

Abbott House ... (207)824-7600 (800)240-2377
Ames Place .... (207)824-3170
Bethel Inn & Court .... (800)654-0125
Chapman Inn .... (207)824-2657
Crocker Pond House .... (207)836-2027
Douglass Place .... (207)824-2229
Hammons House .... (207)824-3170
Holidae House A Country Inn ... (207)824-3400
L'Auberge Country Inn
.... (207)824-2774 (800)760-2774
Norseman Inn .... (207)824-2002
Speckled Mountain Ranch ..... (207)836-2908
Sudbury Inn .... (207)824-2174
Sunday River Inn .... (207)824-2410

Biddeford Pool

Lodge .... (207)284-7148

Blue Hill

Arcady Down East .... (207)374-5576
Blue Hill Farm Country Inn ..... (207)374-5126
John Peters Inn .... (207)374-2116
Ken-Rose Farm Bed & Breakfast . (207)374-2468
Mountain Road House .... (207)374-2794

Boothbay

Coburn House .... (207)633-2120
Five Gables Inn .... (207)633-4551
Hodgdon Island Inn .... (207)633-7474
Seawitch .... (207)633-7804

Boothbay Harbor

Albonegon Inn .... (207)633-2521
The Anchor Watch .... (207)633-7565
The Atlantic Ark Inn .... (207)633-5690
Boothbay Harbor Inn .... (207)633-6302
Captain Sawyer's Place .... (207)633-2290
Green Shutters Inn .... (207)633-2646
Greenleaf Inn .... (207)633-7346
Hilltop House .... (207)633-3839
Howard House .... (207)633-3933
Jonathan's B&B .... (207)633-3588
Lion's Den B&B .... (207)633-7367
Waters Edge B & B .... (207)633-4251
Welch House .... (207)633-3431
Westgate Guest House .... (207)633-3552

Brewer

Brewer Lodge .... (207)989-3550

Bridgton

Bridgton House Bed & Breakfast . (207)647-0979
The Hyland Coach House ...... (207)647-8811
Tarry-A-While Resort .... (207)647-2522

Bristol

The Bristol Inn .... (207)563-1125
The Old Cape of Bristol Mills B&B (207)563-8848

Brooklin

Brooklin Inn .... (207)359-2777

Brooksville

Breezemere Farm Inn .... (207)326-8628
Buck's Harbor Inn .... (207)326-8660
Eggemoggin Reach Bed & Breakfast
.... (207)359-5073

Brownfield

Alecia's B&B .... (207)935-3969

Brownville

Carousel Bed & Breakfast ...... (207)965-7741

Brunswick

Aaron Dunning House .... (207)729-4486
Brunswick B&B .... (207)729-4914
The Captain Daniel Stone Inn ... (207)725-9898
Cupola House .... (207)725-7119
Harborgate B&B .... (207)725-5894
Harriet Beecher Stowe House ... (207)725-5543
Hazel-Bea House B&B .... (207)725-6834
Samuel Newman House .... (207)729-6959

Bryant Pond

Abbotts Mill Farm B&B .... (207)364-2697

Bucksport

L'Ermitage .... (207)469-3361
The Old Parsonage Inn .... (207)469-6477

Camden

A Little Dream .... (207)236-8742
Abigail's B&B By The Sea
.... (207)236-2501 (800)292-2501
Aubergine .... (207)236-8053
Blackberry Inn .... (207)236-6060
Blue Harbor House, A Village Inn
.... (207)236-3196 (800)248-3196
Camden Harbour Inn .... (207)236-4200
Camden River House .... (207)236-0500
Captain Swift Inn .... (207)236-8113
Chestnut House .... (207)236-6137
Elms B&B ..... (207)236-6250 (800)755-3567
Goodspeeds Guest House ..... (207)236-8077
High Tide Inn on The Ocean .... (207)236-3724
Highland Mill Inn .... (207)236-1057
Inn at Sunrise Point .... (207)236-7716
Nathaniel Hosmer Inn .... (207)236-4012
Norumbega Inn .... (207)236-4646
Owl & Turtle Harbor View Guest Rooms
.... (207)236-9014
Rockport Harbor House .... (207)236-2422
J. Sloan Inn .... (207)236-8275
Whitehall Inn ... (207)236-3391 (800)789-6565

Canton

Green Acres Inn .... (207)597-2333

Cape Neddick

Pine Hill Inn of Ogunquit .... (207)361-1004
Sea Chimes B&B .... (207)646-5378
Wooden Goose Inn .... (207)363-5673

Caratunk

The Sterling Inn .... (800)766-7238

Caribou

The Old Iron Inn .... (207)492-4766

Casco

Maplewood Inn .... (207)655-7586

Castine

Castine Inn .... (207)326-4365
Holiday House .... (207)326-4335
The Holiday House Oceanfront Inn (207)326-0900
Pentagoet Inn .... (207)326-8616

Center Lovell

Center Lovell Inn .... (207)925-1575

Chamberlain

Ocean Reefs on Long Cove ..... (207)677-2386

Chebeague Island

Chebeague Island Inn .... (207)846-5155
Chebeague Orchard Inn .... (207)846-9488
Sunset House Bed & Breakfast Inn (207)846-6568

Cherryfield

Ricker House .... (207)546-2780

China

Loons Call Inn .... (207)968-2025

Cornish

Cornish Country Inn .... (207)625-8501

Cranberry Isles

The Red House .... (207)244-5297

Crouseville

Rum Rapids Inn .... (207)455-8096

Cutler

Little River Lodge .... (207)259-4437

Damariscotta

1812 Farm .... (207)563-1812
Barnswallow B&B .... (207)563-8568
Elizabeth's B&B .... (207)563-1919
Oak Gables B&B .... (207)563-1476

Deer Isle

The Inn at Ferry Landing .... (207)348-7760
Laphroaig B&B .... (207)348-6088
Pilgrim's Inn .... (207)348-6615

Dexter

Brewster Inn of Dexter, Maine ... (207)924-3130

Dixfield

Von Simm's Victorian Inn B&B .. (207)562-4911

Dover Foxcroft

The Foxcroft .... (207)564-7720

Durham

The Bagley House (207)865-6566 (800)765-1772

East Boothbay

Linekin Village B&B .... (207)633-3681
Ocean Point Inn .... (207)633-4200
Sailmaker's Inn .... (207)633-7390
Villa By The Sea .... (203)633-2584

East Machias

East River B&B .... (207)255-8467
Mariner B&B .... (207)255-4406
Riverside Inn & Restaurant ..... (207)255-4134

East Wilton

A Victorian Rose .... (207)645-2400

Eastport

Todd House .... (207)853-2328

Edgecomb

Channelridge Farm .... (207)882-7539

Eliot

Ewenicorn Farm B&B .... (207)439-1337
Farmstead .... (207)439-5033
High Meadows B&B .... (207)439-0590
Moses Paul Inn . (207)439-1861 (800)552-6058

Ellsworth

Berry Cove House .... (207)667-7989
Capt'n N Eve's Eden .... (207)667-3109
Jordan House .... (207)667-9872
Lamoine House B&B .... (207)667-7711
Victoria's B&B .... (207)667-5893

Farmingdale

Kennedy's .... (207)582-9608

Farmington

Blackberry Farm B&B .... (207)778-2035
County Seat Inn .... (207)778-3901

Fort Fairfield

Ma Meres Bed & Breakfast ..... (207)473-7902

Fort Kent

Daigle's B&B .... (207)834-5803
Jalbert Hone .... (207)834-5595

Freeport

181 Main St .... (207)865-1226
Anita's Cottage Street Inn ...... (207)865-0932
Atlantic Seal B&B .... (207)865-6112
Bayberry Bed & Breakfast ...... (207)865-1868
Brewster House Bed & Breakfast . (207)865-4121
Harraseeket Inn . (207)865-9377 (800)342-6423
Holbrook Inn .... (207)865-6693
The Isaac Randall House
.... (207)865-9295 (800)865-9295
Maple Hill B&B .... (207)865-3730
Merrymen Inn .... (207)865-0991
Nicholson Inn .... (207)865-6404
Old Red Farm .... (207)865-4550
Porter's Landing B&B .... (207)865-4488
Stafford House Bed & Breakfast . (207)865-4490
White Cedar Inn .... (207)865-9099

Friendship

Cap'n Am's .... (207)832-5144
Friendship By The Sea .... (207)832-4386
Harbor Hill By-The-Sea .... (207)832-6646

Fryeburg

The Oxford House Inn .... (207)935-3442
Admiral Peary House .... (207)935-3365

Gorham
Country Squire B&B .... (207)839-4855
Pinecrest .... (207)839-5843
Gouldsboro
Bluff House at Osprey .... (207)963-7805
Green Hill Farm .... (207)422-3273
Oceanside Meadows .... (207)963-5557
West Gouldsboro
Sunset House .. (207)963-7156 (800)233-7156
Greenville
Devlin House .... (207)695-2229
Evergreen Lodge B&B .... (207)695-3241
Hillside Gardens .... (207)695-3386
The Lodge at Moosehead Lake .. (207)695-4400
Manitou Cottage .... (207)695-4578
Northern Pride Lodge .... (207)695-2890
Pleasant Street Inn .... (207)695-3400
The Sawyer House B&B .... (207)695-2369
Guilford
Guilford B&B .... (207)876-3477
Trebor Inn ..... (207)876-4070 (800)223-5509
Hallowell
Maple Hill Farm B&B Inn
.... (207)622-2708 (800)622-2708
Hancock
Brannoch House .... (207)422-3453
Ledomaine Restaurant & Inn .... (207)422-3916
Harpswell
Harpswell Inn .... (207)833-5509
Harrison
Tolman House Inn .... (207)583-4445
Hope
Blanchard Bed Breakfast .... (207)763-3785
Hulls Cove
Twin Gables Inn .... (207)288-3064
Islesboro
Dark Harbor House Inn .... (207)734-6669
Islesford
Kings Row Inn .... (207)348-7781
Jefferson
Jefferson House Farm B&B ..... (207)549-5768
Jonesboro
Chandler River Lodge .... (201)679-2778
Kennebunk
44 Summer Street B&B .... (207)985-4445
Alewife House .... (207)985-2118
The Brendan Inn .... (207)985-9858
Ellenberger's B&B .... (207)967-3824
Kennebunk Inn 1799 .... (207)985-3351
King's Port Inn .... (207)967-4340
William Lord Mansion .... (207)985-6213
Kennebunk Beach
Sundial Inn .... (207)967-3850
Kennebunkport
1802 House .... (207)967-5632
Breakwater .... (207)967-3118
Bufflehead Cove Inn .... (207)967-3879
Cape Arundel Inn .... (207)967-2125
The Captain Fairfield House
.... (207)967-4454 (800)322-1928
Captain Jefferds Inn .... (207)967-2311
Changing Tide .... (207)967-3993
Charrid House .... (207)967-5695
Chetwynd House .... (207)967-2235
Dock Square Inn .... (207)967-5773
English Meadows .... (207)967-5766
Farm House .... (207)967-4169
The Inn at Goose Rocks .... (207)967-5425
The Green Heron Inn .... (207)967-3315
Kilburn House .... (207)967-4762
Kylemere House 1818 .... (207)967-2780
Lake Brook Guest House ...... (207)967-4069
MacNichol's on The River ...... (207)967-3970
The Inn on Ocean Avenue ...... (207)967-3358
Old Parsonage Guest House .... (207)967-4352
Port Gallery Inn .... (207)967-3728
Schooners Inn & Restaurant .... (207)967-5333
Seaside Inn .... (207)967-4461
Tides Inn By The Sea .... (207)967-3757
Village Cove Inn .... (207)967-3993
Water's Edge .... (207)967-3948
The Welby Inn .... (207)967-4655
The White Barn Inn .... (207)967-2321
Kents Hill
Aunt Martha's B&B .... (207)897-5686

Kingfield
Herbert Inn .... (800)533-INNS
River Port Inn .... (207)265-2552
Three Stanley Avenue .... (207)265-5541
The Inn on Winter's Hill
.... (207)265-5421 (800)233-9687
Kittery
Deep Water Landing B&B ...... (207)439-0824
Enchanted Nights B&B .... (207)439-1489
Gundalow Inn .... (207)439-4040
Melfair Farm B&B .... (207)439-0320
Kittery Point
Harbour Watch B&B .... (207)439-3242
Whaleback Inn .... (207)439-9570
Lee
Dunloggins Bed & Breakfast .... (207)738-5014
Lewiston
Farnham House Bed & Breakfa .. (207)782-9495
Mom & Dads Guest House ..... (207)783-3032
Limerick
Jeremiah Mason House Bed & Breakfast
.... (207)793-4858
Limestone
Peggys Bed & Breakfast .... (207)325-4675
Lincolnville
Cedarholm Cottages .... (207)236-3886
Red House .... (207)236-4621
Sign of The Owl .... (207)338-4669
Victorian B & B .... (207)236-3785
Youngtown Inn .... (207)763-4290
Little Deer Isle
Eggemoggin Inn .... (207)348-2540
Lubec
Bayviews .... (207)733-2181
Home Port Inn .... (207)733-2077
Hugel Haus B&B .... (207)733-4965
Lubeckergasthaus B & B ...... (207)733-4385
Overview .... (207)733-2005
Peacock House .... (207)733-2403
Machias
Riverside Inn & Restaurant ..... (207)255-4134
Madison
Colony House .... (207)474-6599
Matinicus
Tuckanuck Lodge .... (207)366-3830
Bremen
Roaring Brook B&B
.... (207)529-5467 (800)660-5467
Milbridge
Birch Point Cottage .... (207)546-2955
Moonraker B&B .... (207)546-2191
Milford
A Little Bit Country .... (207)827-3036
Millinocket
Big Moose Inn Cabins & Campground
.... (207)723-8391
Sweet Lillian Bed & Breakrast ... (207)723-4894
Milo
Down Home Bed & Breakfast ... (207)943-5167
Monhegan
Monhegan House .... (207)594-7983
Mount Desert
Clover .... (207)244-5650
The Collier House .... (207)288-3162
Long Pond Inn .... (207)244-5854
The MacDonalds B&B .... (207)244-3316
Mount Vernon
Feather Bed Inn .... (207)293-2020
Naples
The Epicurean Inn .... (207)693-3839
New Harbor
Apple Tree Inn B&B .... (207)677-3491
Bradley Inn at Pemaquid Point ... (207)677-2105
Maison Suisse Inn .... (207)276-5223
Newagen
Newagen Seaside Inn .... (207)633-5242
Newcastle
The Captain's House .... (207)563-1482
Elfinhill .... (207)563-1886
Flying Cloud B&B .... (207)563-2484
Glidden House .... (207)563-1859
The Markert House .... (207)563-1309
Norridgewock
Norridgewock Colonial Inn ..... (207)634-3470
North Anson
Olde Carrabassett Inn B&B ..... (207)635-2900

North Haven
Pulpit Harbor Inn .... (207)867-2219
North New Portland
Gilman Stream B&B .... (207)628-6257
North Waterford
Olde Rowley Inn .... (207)583-4143
Northeast Harbor
Asticou Inn .... (207)276-3344
Grey Rock Inn .... (207)276-9360
Harbourside Inn .... (207)276-3272
The Maison Suisse Inn .... (207)276-5223
Oakland
Pressey House .... (207)465-3500
Ogunquit
Admirals Inn .... (207)646-7093
Beachcrest Inn .... (207)646-2156
Beauport Inn & Antiques .... (207)646-8680
Blue Shutters .... (207)646-2163
Blue Water Inn .... (207)646-5559
Colonial Inn .... (800)233-5191
Gorges Grant Hotel .... (207)646-7003
Hartwell House . (207)646-7210 (800)235-8883
Hillcrest Inn Resort .... (207)646-7776
Inn at Tall Chimneys .... (207)646-8974
Leisure Inn .... (207)646-2737
Littlefield Nellie House .... (207)646-1692
Moon Over Maine Guest House .. (207)646-6666
Morning Dove B&B .... (207)646-3891
Ogunquit House .... (207)646-2967
Old Village Inn .... (207)646-7088
Pine Hill Inn .... (207)361-1004
Puffin Inn .... (207)646-5496
Scotch Hill Inn .... (207)646-2890
Sea Chambers-The Sea Bell .... (207)646-9311
Seafair Inn .... (207)646-2181
Terrace By The Sea .... (207)646-3232
The Inn at Two Village Square ... (207)646-5779
Trellis House .... (207)646-7909
Yardarm Village Inn .... (207)646-7006
Ye Olde Perkins Place .... (207)361-1119
Old Orchard Beach
Carriage House Bed & Breakfast . (207)934-2141
Oquossoc
Horsefeather Inn .... (207)864-5465
Oquossoc's Own B&B .... (207)864-5584
Orland
Thomas Mason House .... (207)469-6318
Orono
Highlawn Bed & Breakfast ..... (207)866-2272
Orrs Island
Gulls Nest Gift Shop .... (207)833-2392
Orrs Island Bed & Breakfast .... (207)833-2940
Otter Creek
Otter Creek Inn .... (207)288-5151
Oxford
Claibern's B&B .... (207)539-2352
Inn at Little Creek .... (207)539-4046
Patten
Mt Chase Lodge & Country Inn .. (207)528-2183
Peaks Island
Kellers B&B .... (207)766-2441
Pemaquid
Little River Inn .... (207)677-2845
Phillips
The Elcourt .... (207)639-2741
Phippsburg
The Captain Drummond House .. (207)289-1394
Riverview .... (207)389-1124
Port Clyde
Copper Light .... (207)372-8510
Ocean House .... (207)372-6691
Portland
Carleton Gardens .... (207)772-3458
Danforth .... (207)879-8755
Inn at St John .... (207)773-6481
The Inn at Park Spring .... (207)774-1059
Pomegranate Inn (207)772-1006 (800)356-0408
Princeton
Mihku Lodge .... (207)796-2701
Tripps Lodge & Cabins .... (207)796-2324
Prospect Harbor
Oceanside Meadows Inn .... (207)963-5557
Rangeley
Farmhouse Inn .... (207)864-5805
Mallory's B&B Inn .... (207)864-2121
Rangeley Inn .... (207)864-3341

Raymond
North Pines Health Resort ..... (207)655-7624
Readfield
Echo Lake Lodge & Cottages ... (207)685-9550
Robbinston
Brewer House Bed & Breakfast .. (207)454-2385
Capt John Nehemiah Marks Brewer House .... (207)454-2385
Rockland
Old Granite Inn .... (207)594-9036
Lakeshore Inn Bed & Breakfast .. (207)594-4209
Lathrop House .... (207)594-5771
Limerock Inn .... (207)594-2257
Rockport
Bread & Roses B&B .... (207)236-6116
Rockport Harbor House .... (207)236-2422
Rosemary Cottage .... (207)236-3513
Sign of The Unicorn .... (207)236-8789
Twin Gables B&B .... (207)236-4717
Rockwood
Kineo House .... (207)534-8812
Rumford Point
The Last Resort .... (207)364-4986
Scarborough
Breakers .... (207)883-4820
Seal Harbor
Lighthouse Inn & Restaurant .... (207)276-3958
Searsport
Capt Albert Vinal Nichels Inn .... (207)548-6691
Carriage House Inn .... (207)548-6575
Fairwinds Captain Green Pendleton B&B .... (207)548-6523
Flowering Plum .... (207)548-2610
The Hannah Nickels House ..... (207)548-6691
Homeport Inn .... (207)548-2259
House of Three Chimneys B&B .... (207)548-6117 (800)548-6117
McGilvery House .... (207)548-6289
Sea Captain's Inn .... (800)294-5651
William and Mary Inn .... (207)548-2190
Sebasco Estates
Rock Gardens Inn .... (207)389-1161
Small Point B&B .... (207)389-1716
Skowhegan
Brick Farm B&B .... (207)474-3949
Country Cottage B&B .... (207)474-9820
Helen's B&B .... (207)474-0066
Small Point
Edgewater Farm .... (207)389-1322
Sorrento
Bass Cove Farm B&B .... (207)422-3564
South Berwick
Academy Street Inn .... (207)384-5633
Tatnic B&B .... (207)676-2209
South Casco
Migis Lodge .... (207)655-4524
South Freeport
Harborside B&B .... (207)865-3281
South Harpswell
Senter B&B .... (207)833-2874
South Thomaston
Weskeag at The Water .... (207)596-6676 (800)596-5576
Southwest Harbor
Harbour Cottage Inn .... (207)244-5738
Heron House Bed & Breakfast ... (207)244-0221
Inn at Southwest .... (207)244-3835
The Island House .... (207)244-5180
Island Watch B&B .... (207)244-7229
Kingsleigh Inn .... (207)244-5302
Lindenwood Inn .... (207)244-5335
Long Pond Inn .... (207)244-5854
Mac Donalds Bed & Breakfast ... (207)244-3316
Penury Hall .... (207)244-7102
Two Seasons .... (207)244-9627
Springfield
Old Farm Inn .... (207)738-2730
Standish
Sebago Lake Lodge & Cottages . (207)892-2698
Stockton Springs
Hichborn Inn .... (207)567-4183
Rocky Ridge Motel .... (207)567-3456
Whistlestop B&B .... (207)567-3727
Stonington
Burnt Cove B&B .... (207)367-2392
Ocean View House .... (207)367-5114

Stratton
Putt's Place B&B (207)246-4181 (800)862-6720
Widow's Walk .... (207)246-6901
Strong
Tranquillity Bed & Breakfast Inn .. (207)246-4280
Sullivan
Fieldstone Bed With Breakfast ... (207)422-3257
Island View Inn .... (207)422-3031
Sullivan Harbor
Island View Inn .... (207)422-3031
Sumner
Morrill Farm Bed & Breakfast ... (207)388-2059
Sunset
Goose Cove Lodge .... (207)348-2508
Surry
Surry Inn .... (207)667-5091
Tenants Harbor
Church Hill B&B .... (207)372-6256
Mill Pond House .... (207)372-6209
Pointed Fir B&B .... (207)372-6213
Thomaston
Captain Frost's B&B .... (207)354-8217
Gracie's B&B .... (207)354-2326
Monika's B&B .... (207)354-0944
Weskeag Inn at The Water ..... (207)596-6676
Topsham
Captain Purinton House .... (207)729-3603
Middaugh B&B .... (207)725-2562
The Walker Wilson House ...... (207)729-0715
Union
The Woodland Rose .... (207)785-2194
Van Buren
The Farrell-Michaud House ..... (207)868-5209
Vinalhaven
Fox Island Inn .... (207)863-2122
Libby House Bed & Breakfast Inn (207)863-4696
Waldoboro
The Barn B&B .... (207)832-5781
Broad Bay Inn & Gallery .... (207)832-6668 (800)736-6769
Le Vatout .... (207)832-4552
Letteney Farm Vacations .... (207)832-5143
Medomark House .... (207)832-4971
The Roaring Lion .... (207)832-4038
Washington
Windward Farm .... (207)845-2830
Waterford
Lake House .... (207)583-4182 (800)223-4182
The Parsonage House B&B and Camping Area .... (207)583-4115
Waterville
The Inn at Silver Grove .... (207)873-7724
Weld
Kawanhee Inn Lakeside Lodge & Restaurant .... (207)585-2000
Lake Webb House B&B .... (207)585-2479
Weld Inn .... (207)585-2429
Wells
Beach Farm Inn .... (207)646-7970
Grey Gull Inn .... (207)646-7501
The Haven .... (207)646-4194
Holiday Guest House .... (207)646-5582
Morning Dove .... (207)646-3891
Purple Sandpiper Guest House .. (207)646-7990
Quinney's B&B .... (207)646-8677
Rest-A-While By The Sea B&B .. (207)646-4034
Sand Dollar Inn .... (207)646-2346
Victorian House Inn .... (207)646-1210
West Bethel
Bakke B&B .... (207)442-7185
New Meadows Inn .... (207)443-3921
Speckled Mountain Ranch ..... (207)836-2908
Telemark Inn & Llama Treks .... (207)836-2703
West Forks
Crab Apple Acres .... (207)663-2218
Dead River Bed & Breakfast .... (207)663-4480
West Paris
Bradford House B&B .... (207)674-5696
Windham
Aimhi Lodge .... (207)892-6538
Sebago Lake Lodge & Cottages . (207)892-2698
Windsor
Maple Lane Farm Bed & Breakfast (207)549-3495
Winterport
Colonial Winterport Inn .... (207)223-5307

Wiscasset
The Bailey Inn & Restaurant .... (207)882-4214
The Stacked Arms .... (207)882-5436
Yarmouth
Homewood Inn .... (207)846-3351
York
Franklin Guest House .... (207)363-6075
Hannah's Loft .... (207)363-7244
Inn at Harmon Park .... (207)363-2031
Riverbank Cottage Bed & Breakfast (207)363-6811
The Wild Rose of York .... (207)363-2532
Willows Bed & Breakfast ...... (207)363-9900
York Commons Inn .... (207)363-8903
York Beach
Candle Shop Inn .... (207)363-4087
Golden Pineapple Inn .... (207)363-7837
Homestead Inn B&B .... (207)363-8952
The Inn at Katahdin Inn .... (207)363-1824
Lighthouse Inn .... (207)363-6072
Tide Watch B&B .... (207)363-4713
York Harbor
Canterbury House .... (207)363-3505
Edwards' Harborside Inn .... (207)363-3037
Riverbank Cottage on The Harbor (207)363-8333
Rivermere B&B .... (207)363-5470

Maryland

Annapolis
American Heritage B&B .... (410)280-1620
The Ark & Dove .... (410)268-6277
Charles Inn .... (410)268-1451
Chez Amis B&B .... (410)263-6631
Coggeshall House .... (410)263-5068
The College House Suites ...... (410)263-6124
Corner Cupboard Inn .... (410)263-4970
Flag House Inn B&B .... (410)280-2721
Gatehouse B&B .... (410)280-0024
Georgian House B&B .... (410)263-5618
Magnolia House B&B .... (410)268-3477
Maryrob B&B .... (410)261-2764
One-Four-Four Prince George ... (410)268-8053
The Row House .... (410)263-2187
William Page Inn B&B .... (410)626-1506
Baltimore
Society Hill Hotel .... (410)244-7227
Celie's Waterfront B&B .... (410)522-2323
The Inn at Fells Point .... (410)276-8252
The Inn at Government House ... (410)539-0566
Hargrove House .... (410)366-3480
Mr. Mole B&B .... (410)728-1179
Society Hill Hopkins .... (410)235-8600
Bel Air
Webb Hall Inn .... (410)838-8807
Berlin
Atlantic Hotel Inn & Restaurant .... (410)641-3589 (800)814-7672
Holland House .... (410)641-1956
Merry Sherwood Plantation .... (410)641-0358 (800)660-0358
Cabin John
Winslow Home .... (301)229-4654
Cambridge
Commodore's Cottages .... (410)228-6938
Glasgow B&B Inn .... (410)228-0575
Lodgecliffe .... (410)228-1760
Cascade
Inwood Guest House .... (301)241-3467
Cecilton
Anchorage Bed & Breakfast .... (410)275-1972
Centreville
The Academy B&B .... (410)758-2791
Rose Tree Bed & Breakfast ..... (410)758-3991
Chesapeake City
Bohemia House .... (410)885-3024
Inn at The Canal .... (410)885-5995
Chestertown
Claddaugh Farm B&B .... (410)778-4894 (800)328-4894
Hill's Inn ...... (410)778-4667 (800)787-4667
Homestead Tavern .... (410)778-5518
Imperial Hotel .... (410)778-5000
Parker House .... (410)778-9041
Pratt-Perry House .... (410)778-2734
Radcliffe Cross .... (410)778-5540
White Swan Tavern .... (410)778-2300
Widow's Walk Inn .... (410)778-6864

Chevy Chase
Chevy Chase B&B .... (301)656-5867
Clear Spring
Breezee Hill Farm Bed and Breakfast
.... (301)842-2608
Wilson House .... (301)582-4320
Crisfield
My Fair Lady Bed & Breakfast ... (410)968-3514
Crumpton
Cole House Bed & Bath .... (410)928-5287
Cumberland
Red Lamp Post Bed & Breakfast . (301)777-3262
Darlington
Darlington Manor .... (410)457-9021
Denton
Slo Horse Inn .... (410)634-2128
Easton
Ashby 1663 .... (410)822-4235
The Bishop's House B&B
.... (410)820-7290 (800)223-7290
Chaffinch House, A Victorian B&B (410)822-5074
The McDaniel House
.... (410)822-3704 (800)787-4667
Tidewater Inn .... (301)822-1300
Ellicott City
White Duck Bed & Breakfast .... (410)992-8994
Emmitsburg
Stonehurst Inn Bed & Breakfast .. (301)447-2880
Ewell
Ewell Tide Inn Bed & Breakfast .. (410)425-2141
Fallston
Broom Hall B&B .... (410)557-7321
Frederick
Turning Point Inn .... (301)874-2421
Tyler-Spite House (301)831-4455 (800)954-6284
Freeland
Freeland Farm .... (301)357-5364
Gaithersburg
Gaithersburg Hospitality B&B ... (301)977-7377
Galena
Rosehill Farm B&B .... (410)648-5334
Georgetown
Kitty Knight House .... (410)648-5777
Grantsville
Walnut Ridge Bed & Breakfast ... (301)895-4248
Greensboro
Riverside Hotel .... (410)482-2520
Hagerstown
Lewrene Farm B&B .... (301)582-1735
Piper House Bed & Breakfast ... (301)797-1862
Sunday's B&B .... (800)221-4828
Wingrove Manor .... (301)733-6328
Havre De Grace
Currier House .... (410)939-7886
Hughesville
Shady Oaks Bed & Breakfast ... (301)932-8864
Jefferson
Sophia's Bed & Breakfast ...... (301)371-5041
Keedysville
Antietam Overlook Farm .... (800)878-4241
Keymar
Bowling Brook Country Inn ..... (410)848-0353
Little Orleans
Town Hill Hotel .... (301)478-2794
Lutherville
Twin Gates B&B Inn .... (410)252-3131
Marlboro
Havens Rest .... (301)855-2232
Mc Henry
Country Inn .... (301)387-6694
Harley Farms B&B .... (301)387-9050
Lake Pointe Inn .... (301)387-0111
Savage River Inn .... (301)245-4440
McDaniel
Wades Point Inn on The Bay .... (410)745-2500
Middletown
Stone Manor Country Club ..... (301)473-5454
Mount Savage
The Castle .... (301)264-4645
New Market
Strawberry Inn .... (301)865-3318
North Beach
Angels In The Attic .... (301)855-2607
North East
The Mill House B&B .... (410)287-3532
North Bay B&B .... (410)287-5948
Oakland
The Oak & Apple B&B .... (301)334-9265
Red Run Inn .... (301)387-6606
Ocean City
Conners Inn Bed & Breakfast ... (410)289-7721
His Honor's Place .... (410)289-2630
Taylor House Bed & Breakfast ... (410)289-1177
Olney
The Thoroughbred B&B .... (301)774-7649
Oxford
1876 House .... (410)226-5496
Oxford Inn/Pope's Tavern
.... (410)226-5220 (800)292-5220
Pocomoke City
Littleton's Bed & Breakfast ..... (410)957-1645
Prince Frederick
Hutchins Heritage Bed and Breakfast
.... (410)535-1759
Princess Anne
Elmwood C. 1770 B&B .... (301)651-1066
Washington Hotel & Inn .... (301)651-2525
Queenstown
The House of Burgess' .... (301)827-6834
Rising Sun
Chandlee House .... (301)658-6958
Rock Hall
Bay Breeze Inn .... (410)639-2061
Black Duck Inn .... (410)639-2478
Huntingfield Manor .... (410)639-7779
The Inn at Osprey .... (410)639-2194
Moonlight Bay Marina & Inn .... (410)639-2660
Swan Point Inn .... (410)639-2500
Rockville
Aquavista .... (301)881-8028
Saint Leonard
Matoaka Cottages .... (301)586-0269
Saint Michaels
Barrett's B&B .... (410)745-3322
Dr. Dodson House .... (410)745-3691
Fox Run Farm .... (410)745-2381
Hambleton Inn .... (410)745-3350
Pasadena Inn .... (410)745-5053
The Inn at Perry Cabin .... (410)745-2200
Rigby Valliant House Bed & Breakfast
.... (410)745-3977
Tarr House .... (410)745-2175
Two Swan Inn .... (410)745-2929
Victoriana Inn .... (410)745-3368
Sharpsburg
The Inn at Antietam .... (301)432-6601
Jacob Rohrbach Inn .... (301)432-5079
Piper House on Antietam Battlefield (301)797-1862
Victoria's Hearth Bed & Breakfast (301)432-6115
Sherwood
The Moorings .... (410)745-6396
Silver Spring
Varborg .... (301)384-2842
Snow Hill
Snow Hill Inn .... (410)632-2102
Solomons
By The Bay B&B .... (410)326-3428
Davis House .... (410)326-4811
Locust Inn .... (410)326-9817
Webster House .... (410)326-0454
Spencerville
Edgewood Inn .... (301)421-5998
Stevensville
Kent Manor Inn .... (410)643-5757
Still Pond
Still Pond Inn .... (410)348-2234
Tall Timbers
Potomac View Farm .... (301)994-0418
Taneytown
Antrim 1844 .... (410)756-6812
Glenburn .... (410)751-1187
Taylors Island
The Becky Phipps Inn .... (410)397-3007
Tilghman
Chesapeake Wood Duck Inn
.... (410)886-2070 (800)956-2070
Harrison's Country Inn .... (410)886-2123
Sinclair House .... (410)886-2147
The Tilghman Island Inn .... (800)866-2141
Vienna
Tavern House .... (410)376-3347
Westminster
Glenburn .... (410)751-1187
Westminster Inn .... (410)857-4445
The Winchester Country Inn
.... (410)876-7373 (800)887-3950
Williamsport
Wolf's End Farm .... (301)223-6888
Wingate
Wingate Manor Bed & Breakfast . (410)397-8717
Wittman
The Inn at Christmas Farm ..... (410)745-3891
Woodsboro
Rosebud Inn .... (301)845-2221

Massachusetts

Adams
Bascom Lodge .... (413)743-1591
Butternut Inn .... (413)743-9394
Amherst
The Amity House .... (413)549-6446
Black Walnut Inn .... (413)549-5649
Emilys Amherst Bed & Breakfast . (413)549-0733
Lincoln Ave Bed & Breakfast .... (413)549-0517
Ivy House Bed & Breakfast ..... (413)549-7554
Parsonage Bed & Breakfast ..... (413)549-1466
Andover
Andover Inn .... (508)475-5903
Ashby
Woodside Farm B & B .... (508)386-2226
Ashfield
Apple Inn .... (413)628-4729
Bull Frog B&B .... (413)628-4493
Attleboro
Colonel Blackinton Inn
.... (508)222-6022 (800)734-2487
Barnstable
Anderson Acres .... (508)362-4395
Cobbs Cove .... (508)362-9356
Goss House B&B .... (617)362-8559
Henry Crocker House .... (508)362-8584
Thomas Huckins House .... (508)362-6379
Barre
The Jenkins House B&B Inn
.... (508)355-6444 (800)378-7373
Stevens Farm Bed & Breakfast .. (508)355-2227
Bass River
The Anchorage .... (508)398-8265
Beach House at Bass River ..... (508)394-6501
Belvedere B&B Inn .... (508)398-6674
Old Cape Inn .... (508)398-1068
The Red House .... (508)394-6501
Becket
Canterbury Farm .... (413)623-8765
Long House B&B .... (413)623-8360
Tollgate Inn .... (413)243-0715
Belchertown
Ingate Farms Bed & Breakfast ... (413)253-0440
Berlin
Ford's View B&B .... (508)838-2909
Stonehedge .... (617)838-2574
Bernardston
Falls River Inn .... (413)648-9904
Beverly
Bunny's B&B .... (508)922-2392
Beverly Farms
The Jon Larcom House .... (508)922-6074
Billerica
Billerica B&B .... (617)667-7317
Blandford
Nye Brook Inn B&B .... (413)848-2068
Bolton
Polly Wilson's B&B .... (508)779-6955
Boston
463 Beacon Street Guest House . (617)536-1302
82 Chandler St .... (617)482-0408
A Boston Harbor Bed & Breakfast (617)227-0031
A Cottage Near The Square ..... (617)254-7491
Anthony's Town House .... (617)566-3972
Bailey's Boston House-Bed & Breakfast
.... (617)262-4543
Baileys Copley Bed & Breakfast . (617)422-0646
Boston Bed & Breakfast .... (617)723-8839
Buckminster The Lodgings ..... (617)236-7050
Chandler Inn .... (617)482-3450
Eliot & Pickett Houses .... (617)248-8707

The Federal House .... (617)350-6657
John Jeffries House .... (617)367-1866
Newbury Guest House .... (617)437-7666
Nocturne B & B .... (617)247-6996
Oasis Guest House .... (617)267-2262
Quincy Adams B&B .... (617)479-6215
The Terrace Townhouse .... (617)350-6520
Victorian B&B .... (617)247-1599

Bourne
Wood Duck Inn .... (508)564-6404

Brewster
Brewster Farmhouse Inn .... (508)896-3910
Candleberry Inn .... (508)896-3300
Captain Freeman Inn .... (508)896-7481
The Chapin's .... (508)896-8210
Cobb House Inn .... (508)896-1808
High Brewster .... (508)896-3636
Isaiah Clark House (508)896-7053 (800)822-4001
Ocean Gold Cape Cod B&B ..... (800)526-3760
Old Manse Inn .... (508)896-3149
Old Sea Pines Inn .... (508)896-6114
Pepper House Inn .... (508)896-4389
The Poore House (508)896-2094 (800)233-6662
Ruddy Turnstone Bed Breakfast .. (508)385-9871
The Inn at The Egg .... (508)896-3123

Brookline
Beacon Inns .... (617)566-0088
Beacon Plaza .... (617)232-6550
Beacon Street Guest House .... (800)872-7211
Beech Tree Inn .... (617)277-1620
Brookline Manor House .... (617)232-0003
Coolidge Corner Guest House ... (617)734-4041
University Bed & Breakfast ..... (617)738-1424

Buckland
1797 House .... (413)625-2975
Scott House .... (413)625-6624

Buzzards Bay
Cape Cod Canalside B&B ...... (508)759-6564

Cambridge
A Bed & Breakfast In Cambridge . (617)868-7082
A Friendly Inn .... (617)547-7851
All New Windsor House .... (617)354-3116
Bed & Breakfast-Boston-Cambridge
.... (617)491-6107
Cambridge Bed & Muffin ...... (617)576-3166
Hamilton House A Bed & Breakfast Service
.... (617)491-0274
The Inn at Harvard .... (617)491-2222
The Irving House .... (617)547-4600
Louise Guest House .... (617)491-6108
The Mary Prentiss Inn .... (617)661-2929
Royal Sonesta Hotel Boston .... (617)491-3600

Centerville
Terrace Gardens Inn .... (508)775-4707
Allen's B&B .... (617)428-5702
Carver House .... (617)775-9414
The Inn at Fernbrook .... (508)775-4334
Long Dell Inn .... (508)775-2750
Old Hundred House .... (508)775-6166

Charlemont
Forest Way Farm .... (413)337-8321

Charlton
The Prindle House .... (508)248-3134

Chatham
Bow Roof House .... (617)945-1346
Bradford Inn .... (508)945-1030
Captains House Inn of Chatham . (508)945-0127
Carriage House Inn
.... (508)945-4688 (800)355-8868
Chatham Guest House .... (508)945-3274
Chatham Town House Inn ...... (508)945-2180
Chatham Village Inn .... (508)945-0792
Chatham Wayside Inn .... (508)945-1800
The Dolphin of Chatham .... (508)945-0070
Moses Nickerson House .... (508)945-5859
Mulberry Inn .... (508)945-2020
Oceancrest Inn .... (508)945-3128
Queen Anne Inn .... (508)945-0394

Chelmsford
Westview Landing .... (508)256-0074

Chester
Frog Hollow Farm .... (413)354-9678

Chestnut Hill
The Pleasant Pheasant .... (617)566-4178

Chilmark
Captain Flander's House .... (508)645-3123
Inn at Blueberry Hill .... (508)645-3322
Us Island County Inn .... (508)645-2720

Cohasset
On Golden Pond .... (617)383-2888
Saltmarsh Farm .... (617)383-6205

Colrain
Grandmother's House .... (413)624-3771
Maple Shade Farm B&B .... (413)624-3931
Penfrydd Farm .... (413)624-5516

Concord
Anderson-Wheeler homestead ... (508)369-3756
Colonial Inn .... (508)369-9200

Conway
The Merriams .... (413)369-4052

Cotuit
Milestones B&B .... (508)428-6764
Salty Dog B&B Inn .... (508)428-5228

Cummaquid
Anderson Acres .... (508)362-4395
Fox Glen Manor Bed & Breakfast . (508)362-4657
Waratah House . (508)362-1469 (800)215-8707

Cummington
Berkshires Hidden Brook ...... (413)634-5653
Cumworth Farm .... (413)634-5529

Dalton
Dalton House .... (413)684-3854

Danvers
Salem Village B&B .... (617)774-7851
Samuel Legro House .... (508)774-1860

Dennis
Bed & Breakfast .... (508)385-9256
The Four Chimneys Inn .... (508)385-6317

Dennis Port
By The Sea Guests .... (508)398-8685
Captain Judah Paddock .... (508)385-9959
Ruddy Turnstone Antiques ..... (508)385-9871
The Soundings .... (508)394-6561
West Wind Motel & Guest House (508)398-3015

Duxbury
Black Friar Brook Farm .... (617)834-8528
Campbell's Country B&B ...... (617)934-0862

East Falmouth
Bayberry Inn .... (508)540-2962

East Orleans
Ivy Lodge .... (508)255-0119

East Sandwich
The Azariah Snow House ...... (508)888-6677
Spring Garden .... (508)888-0710

Eastham
Eastham Windmill Bed and Breakfast
.... (508)255-8366
Kingsbury House .... (508)255-6026

Easthampton
Bloomsbury Bed & Breakfast ... (413)527-8681

Edgartown
Always Inn Bed & Breakfast .... (508)627-8947
Ashley Inn ..... (508)627-9655 (800)477-9655
Chadwick Inn .... (508)627-4435
Charlotte Inn .... (508)627-4751
Daggett House .... (508)627-4600
Dr. Shiverick House .... (508)627-8497
Edgartown Commons .... (508)627-4671
Edgartown Heritage Hotel ...... (508)627-5161
Edgartown Inn .... (508)627-4794
The Governor Bradford Inn of Edgartown
.... (508)627-9510
The Harbor View Hotel .... (508)627-7000
Harborside Inn .... (617)627-4321
Jonathan Munroe Guest House .. (508)627-5536
Katama Guest House .... (617)627-5158
The Kelley House .... (508)627-7000
Meeting House Inn .... (508)627-8626
Shiretown Inn .... (800)541-0090
Shiverick Inn .... (508)627-3797
South Water Street Inn .... (508)627-3355
Summer House .... (508)627-4857
Tuscany Inn The Lodgings ..... (508)627-5999
The Victorian Inn .... (508)627-4784
Vineyard Vines B .... (508)627-3172

Egremont
Bread & Roses .... (413)528-1099

Fairhaven
Edgewater B&B .... (508)997-5512

Fall River
Lizzie Bed & Breakfast-Museum . (508)675-7333

Falmouth
Amherst .... (617)548-2781
The Coonamessett Inn .... (508)548-2300
Elm Arch Inn .... (617)548-0133
Elms .... (508)540-7232
Falmouth Inn .... (800)255-4157
Gaslight Inn .... (508)540-8051
Gladstone Inn .... (508)548-9851
Grandview Guest House .... (508)548-4025
Hastings By The Sea .... (508)540-2887
Hawthorne Lodge .... (508)548-0389
Hewins House Bed & Breakfast .. (508)457-4363
The Moorings Lodge .... (508)540-2370
Scalloped Shell Inn .... (508)548-8245
Sea Gull Inn .... (508)540-7097
Sjoholm Inn Bed & Breakfast ... (508)540-5706
Skipper Inn .... (508)540-8089
Swan Point Inn .... (508)540-5528
The Elms B & B .... (508)540-7232
Wildflower Inn .... (508)548-9524
Worcester House .... (508)540-1592
Wyndemere House at Sippewissett (508)540-7069

Gay Head
Duck Inn .... (508)645-9018
Outermost Inn .... (508)645-3511

Gloucester
Bass Rocks Ocean Inn .... (508)283-7611
Gray Manor .... (617)283-5409
Spruce Manor Guest House .... (508)283-0614
Williams Guest House .... (508)283-4931

Goshen
The Whale Inn .... (413)268-7246

Great Barrington
A-Turn-Of-The-Century .... (413)528-6305
Bread and Roses .... (413)528-1099
Coffing-Bostwick House .... (413)528-4511
Elling's Guest House B&B ...... (413)528-4103
Greenmeadows .... (413)528-3897
Littlejohn Manor .... (413)528-2882
Red Bird Inn .... (413)229-2433
Round Hill Farm .... (413)528-3366
Thornewood Inn .... (413)528-3828
Trails End .... (413)528-3995
Turning Point Inn .... (413)528-4777
The Victorian Cottage .... (413)528-0328
Wainwright Inn .... (413)528-2062

Greenfield
Candlelight Resort Inn .... (413)772-0101
The Hitchcock House B&B ..... (413)774-7452

Groton
Wrangling Brook Farm .... (508)448-8253

Hadley
Clark Tavern Inn B&B .... (413)586-1900

Hancock
Kirkmead B&B .... (413)738-5420
Mill House Inn .... (800)497-8578

Harvard
Friendly Crossways .... (508)456-3649

Harwich
Barnaby Inn .... (508)432-6789
Victorian Inn at Harwich .... (508)432-8335

Harwich Port
The Inn on Bank Street .... (508)432-3206
The Beach House Inn .... (508)432-4444
Blueberry Inn .... (508)432-6389
Captain's Quarters (508)432-1991 (800)992-6550
The Coach House .... (508)432-9452
Country Inn Acres (508)432-2769 (800)231-1722
Eagles' Nest .... (508)430-0652
Harbor Walk .... (508)432-1675
Walker Mildred House The Bed & Breakfast
.... (508)432-6654
Wedgewood House Bed & Breakfast
.... (508)432-1378

Heath
Pen Y Bryn .... (413)376-683-

Housatonic
Christines Guest House & Bed and Breakfast
.... (413)274-6149

Huntington
Paulson B&B .... (413)667-3208

Hyannis
Captain Sylvester Baxter House .. (508)775-5611
Salt Winds Ii .... (508)790-0203
Mansfield House .... (508)771-9455
Park Square Village .... (617)775-5611
Physic Point Bed & Breakfast ... (508)790-4720
Salt Winds Guest House .... (508)775-2038
Sea Beach Inn, Inc. .... (508)775-4612

Sea Breeze By The Beach ...... (508)771-7213
The Inn on Sea Street .... (508)775-8030

Lancaster
Carter-Washburn House .... (508)365-2188
College Town Inn .... (508)368-7000

Lanesboro
Bascom Lodge .... (413)443-0011
Townry Farm .... (413)443-9285
The Tuckered Turkey .... (413)442-0260
Whippletree B&B .... (413)443-9874

Lee
1777 Greylock House .... (413)243-1717
Bedside Manor B&B .... (413)243-2746
Chambery Inn .... (800)537-4321
Juniper Hill .... (413)243-4425
The Inn at Laurel Lake .... (413)243-1436
Morgan House Inn .... (413)243-0181
The Parsonage on The Green ... (413)243-4364
Prospect Hill House .... (413)243-3460
Ramsey House .... (413)243-1598
Tollgate Inn .... (413)243-0715

Lenox
Amity House .... (413)637-4770
Apple Tree Inn .... (413)637-1477
Candlelight Inn .... (413)637-1555
Chesapeake Inn of Lenox ...... (413)637-3429
Cliffwood Inn .... (413)637-3330
Cornell House .... (413)637-0562
Cranberry Goose .... (413)637-2812
Gateways Inn .... (413)637-2532
Hilltop Inn .... (413)637-1746
Pine Acre B&B .... (413)637-2292
The Quincy Lodge .... (413)637-9750
Seven Hills Country Inn
.... (413)637-0060 (800)869-6518
Strawberry Hill .... (413)637-3381
Underledge Inn .... (413)637-0236
Village Inn ..... (413)637-0020 (800)253-0917
Wheatleigh .... (413)637-0610

Lexington
Ashley's B&B .... (617)862-6488
Halewood House .... (617)862-5404
Mary Van and Jim's This Old House B&B
.... (617)861-7057
Red Cape B&B .... (617)862-4913

Lincoln
Thoreaus Walden Bed & Breakfast (617)259-1899

Littleton
Lyttleton Inn .... (508)486-4715

Lowell
Barnes House .... (508)453-9763
Commonwealth House .... (508)452-9071
Sherman-Berry House .... (508)459-4760

Ludlow
Misty Meadows, Ltd. .... (413)583-8103

Magnolia
The White House .... (508)525-3642

Manchester
Old Corner Inn .... (508)526-4996

Marblehead
Ten Mugford Street .... (508)631-5642
A Lady Winnette's Cottage ..... (617)631-8579
Carriage House .... (617)639-1924
The Garden House .... (508)631-2324
The Golden Cod B&B .... (617)631-1846
Harbor Light Inn .... (617)631-2186
Lindsey's Garrett .... (617)631-2433
Much Ado .... (617)639-0400
The Nesting Place B&B .... (617)631-6655
Pleasant Manor Inn .... (617)631-5843
Sea Street B&B .... (617)631-1890
Seagull Inn .... (617)631-1893
Spray Cliff on The Ocean
.... (617)631-6789 (800)626-1530
State Street Inn .... (617)639-0357
Stillpoint B&B .... (617)631-1667
Tidecrest .... (508)631-4515
Victorian Rose Bed & Breakfast . . (617)631-4306

Marion
Peregrine B&B .... (508)748-0065

Martha's Vineyard
Breakfast at Tiasquam .... (508)645-3685
Twin Oaks Inn . . (508)693-8633 (800)696-8633

Mashpee
The Blackwood's .... (508)477-9252

Mattapoisett
Tall Pines B&B .... (508)758-2076

Menemsha
Beach Plum Inn . (508)645-9454 (800)528-6616
Menemsha Inn & Cottages ..... (508)645-2521

Middlefield
Strawberry Banke Farm .... (413)623-6481

Monterey
Lakeside Terrace .... (413)528-3371
Mountain Trails B&B .... (413)528-2928
Swann Lodge .... (413)528-3294

Nantucket
76 Main Street .... (508)228-2533
Anchor Inn .... (508)228-0072
Atlantic Mainstay .... (508)228-5451
Kris Van Lieu .... (508)228-2486
Beachside Resort .... (800)322-4433
Beachway Guests .... (508)228-1324
Bed 'n Breakfast on Nantucket . . (508)228-9040
Brant Point Inn .... (508)228-5442
Brass Lantern Inn .... (508)228-4064
Carriage House The Guest Hse . . (508)228-0326
Centerboard .... (508)228-9696
Centre Street Inn .... (508)228-0199
Century House .... (508)228-0530
Chatterbox Guest House .... (508)228-7576
The Chestnut House .... (508)228-0049
Claire's Bed & Breakfast .... (508)228-8966
Cliff Lodge B&B .... (508)228-9480
Cliffside Beach Club .... (508)228-0618
Cobblestone Inn .... (508)228-1987
Country Island Inn .... (508)228-0889
Easton House .... (508)228-2759
Eighteen Gardner Street Inn
.... (508)228-1155 (800)435-1450
Fair Gardens .... (508)228-4258
The Fairway .... (305)294-2887 (800)613-2276
Great Harbor Inn .... (508)228-6609
The Grey Goose .... (508)228-6597
Halliday's Nantucket House ..... (508)228-9450
The Hawthorn House .... (508)228-1468
The House of Orange .... (508)228-9287
Fair Winds .... (508)228-1998
Hussey House .... (508)228-0747
India House .... (508)228-9043
The Island Reef .... (508)228-2156
Ivy Lodge .... (508)228-7755
Jared Coffin House .... (508)228-2400
Le Languedoc Inn .... (508)228-2552
Lapetite Mansion .... (508)228-9242
Nantucket Landfall .... (508)228-0500
The Nantucket Whaler .... (508)228-6597
Parker Guest House .... (508)228-4625
Phillips House .... (508)228-9217
Quaker House .... (508)228-0400
Roberts House .... (508)228-9009
The Sherburne Inn .... (508)228-4425
Ships Inn .... (508)228-0040
Stumble Inne .... (508)228-4482
Ten Hussey .... (508)228-9863
Union Street Inn .... (508)228-9222
The Wauwinet, An Inn By The Sea (508)228-0145
West Moor Inn .... (508)228-0877
The White House .... (508)228-4677

Needham
Bay Colony Bed & Breakfast .... (617)449-5302

New Bedford
Melville House .... (508)990-1566
Victorian Mansion .... (508)993-4944

New Marlborough
Old Inn on The Green .... (413)229-3131
Millstones Guesthouse .... (413)229-8488
Red Bird Inn .... (413)229-2433

Newburyport
Clark Currier Inn . (508)465-8363 (800)360-6582
Essex Street Inn .... (508)465-3148
Garrison Inn .... (617)465-0910
Market Street Inn .... (508)465-5816
Morrill Place Inn .... (508)462-2808
Windsor House .... (508)462-3778

Newton
Lasell College Lasell Inn .... (617)965-8725
New England Bed & Breakfast . . . (617)244-2112

Newtonville
B&B Marblehead and North Shore (617)964-1606
Sage and Thyme B&B .... (617)332-0695

North Adams
Twin Sisters Inn .... (413)663-6933

North Egremont
Baldwin Grange .... (413)528-2808

North Falmouth
Captains Inn .... (508)564-6424

North New Salem
Bullard Farm B&B .... (508)544-6959

North Tisbury
Bayberry Inn-Bed & Breakfas ... (508)693-1984

Northampton
Autumn Inn .... (413)584-7660
The Knoll .... (413)584-8164
Northampton Bed & Breakfast . . . (413)586-6190

Northfield
Centennial House .... (413)498-5921
Northfield Country House ...... (413)498-2692

Oak Bluffs
Admiral Benbow Inn .... (508)693-6825
Arend's Samoset on The Sound . (508)693-5148
Attleboro House .... (508)693-4346
The Beach House .... (508)693-3955
The Beach Rose .... (508)693-6135
Capricorn House .... (508)693-2848
Circuit House .... (508)693-5033
David's Island House .... (508)693-4516
The Inn at Dockside .... (508)693-2966
Four Gables Guest House ...... (508)693-8733
Narragansett House .... (508)693-3627
Nashua House .... (508)693-0043
The Oak Bluffs Inn (508)693-7171 (800)955-6235
The Oak House .... (508)693-4187
Pequot House .... (508)693-5087
Sea Spray Inn .... (508)693-9388
Summer Place Inn .... (508)693-9908
Titticut Follies .... (508)693-4986
The Tucker Inn .... (508)693-1045

Oldsfield
The Tea House .... (413)772-2675

Orleans
185 Main Guest House .... (508)255-3397
Academy Place Bed & Breakfast . (508)255-3181
High Nauset .... (508)255-0907
Hillbourne House .... (508)255-0780
Morgan's Way B&B .... (508)255-0831
Ships Knees Inn Lodgins ...... (508)255-1312

Osterville
East Bay Lodge .... (508)428-6961
Village B&B .... (508)428-7004

Otis
Joyous Garde B&B .... (413)269-6852
Maplewood Farms 1850 Inn .... (413)269-7351
Pinnacle Bed & Breakfast ...... (413)269-7707
Stonewood Inn B&B .... (413)269-4894

Palmer
Tamarack Farm .... (413)283-8664

Paxton
Pine Hill Farm .... (508)791-1762

Peru
Chalet D'Alicia .... (413)655-8292

Petersham
Winterwood at Petersham ...... (508)724-8885

Pittsfield
Country Hearts B&B .... (413)499-3201
Greer B&B .... (413)443-3669

Plainfield
Rolling Meadow Farm .... (413)634-2166

Plymouth
Another Place Inn .... (508)746-0126
Colonial House Inn .... (508)747-4274
Halls Bed & Breakfast .... (508)746-2835
Hawthorne Hill .... (508)746-5244
In-Town B&B .... (508)746-7412
Morton Park Place .... (617)747-1730

Princeton
Harrington Farm .... (617)464-5600
Hill House .... (617)464-2061

Provincetown
1807 House .... (508)487-2173
Admiral's Landing Guest House . (508)487-9665
The Anchor Inn Beach House . . . (508)487-0432
Asheton House .... (508)487-9966
Bradford Gardens Inn .... (508)487-1616
Cape Codder Guest House ..... (508)487-0131
Captain Lysander Inn .... (508)487-2253
The Chicago House .... (508)487-0537
Clarendon House .... (508)487-1645
Ocean's Inn .... (508)487-7800

The Courtland Guesthouse ..... (508)487-2292
Elephant Walk Inn (508)487-2543 (800)889-9255
Fairbanks Inn .... (508)487-0386
Gabriel's .... (508)487-3232
The Gifford House .... (508)487-0688
Hargood House .... (508)487-1324
Lamplighter Guest House
.... (508)487-2529 (800)263-6574
Monument Guest House .... (508)487-9664
Provincetown Inn .... (508)487-9500
Red Inn .... (508)487-0050
Rose and Crown Guest House .. (508)487-3332
Sandpiper Beach House .... (508)487-1928
Somerset House .... (508)487-0383
Sunset Inn .... (508)487-9810
Three Peaks .... (508)487-1717
Trade Winds Inn .... (508)487-0138
Twelve Center Guest House ..... (508)487-0381
Victoria House .... (508)487-4455
Watership Inn ... (508)487-0094 (800)330-9413
Willows .... (508)487-0520
Windamar House .... (508)487-0599

Rehoboth
Perryville Inn .... (508)252-9239

Richmond
Cogswell Guest House .... (413)698-2750
Middlerise .... (413)698-2687
Pierson Place .... (617)698-2750
Westgate .... (413)698-2657

Rockport
Cable House .... (508)546-6383
Captain's House .... (508)546-3825
Eden Pines Inn .... (508)546-2505
Lantana House .... (508)546-3535
Mooringstone For Nonsmokers .. (508)546-2479
Old Farm Inn .... (508)546-3237
Peg Leg Inn .... (508)546-2352
Pleasant Street Inn .... (508)546-3915
Rocky Shores Inn (508)546-2823 (800)348-4003
Sally Webster Inn .... (508)546-9251
Seaward Inn .... (508)546-3471
Seven South Street Inn ...... (508)546-6708

Roslindale
A Homestay In Boston .... (617)323-9997

Worcester-Rutland
The General Rufus Putnam House (508)886-4864

Sagamore Beach
Bed & Breakfast of Sagamore Beach
.... (617)888-1559

Salem
Bullard Farm .... (508)544-6959
Coach House Inn .... (508)744-4092
Stephen Daniels House .... (508)744-5709
The Stepping Stone Inn ...... (508)741-8900
Suzannah Flint House .... (508)744-5281

Sandisfield
New Boston Inn .... (413)258-4477

Sandwich
Academy Hill B&B .... (508)888-8083
The Barclay .... (508)888-5738
The Dan'l Webster Inn .... (508)888-3622
Dillingham House .... (508)833-0065
Hawthorn Hill .... (508)888-3333
Inn at Sandwich Center ...... (508)888-6958
Sandwich B&B .... (508)888-4542
Scorton Creek .... (508)362-6267
Seth Pope House .... (508)888-5916
Six Water Street .... (508)888-6808
The Village Inn at Sandwich .... (508)833-0363
Wind Song B&B .... (508)888-3567
The Winkle House .... (508)888-5686

Scituate
Rasberry Ink .... (617)545-6629

Seekonk
Simeon's Mansion House ...... (508)336-6674

Sheffield
Bow Wow Road Inn .... (413)229-3339
Centuryhurst B&B .... (413)229-8131
The Depot Guest House .... (413)229-8894
Ivanhoe Country House .... (413)229-2143
Orchard Shade B&B .... (413)229-8463
Orchard Shade Bed & Breakfast . (413)229-8463
Race Brook Lodge .... (413)229-2916
Ramblewood Inn .... (413)229-3363
Stagecoach Hill Inn .... (413)229-8585
Staveleigh House .... (413)229-2129

Shelburne Falls
Country Comfort .... (413)625-9877
The Elmer House .... (413)625-9590
Parson Hubbard House .... (413)625-9730

Somerset
West Ossipee House .... (508)675-2246

Somerville
St James Guest House .... (617)623-0070

South Chatham
Ye Olde Nantucket House ...... (508)432-5641

South Dartmouth
Salt Marsh Farm .... (508)992-0980

South Deerfield
Deerfield B&B - The Yellow Gabled House
.... (413)665-4922
Orchard Terrace .... (413)665-3829
Sunnyside Farm .... (413)665-3113

South Egremont
Weathervane Inn .... (413)528-9580

South Hadley
Grandmarys Bed & Breakfast ... (413)533-7381

South Harwich
House on The Hill .... (508)432-4321

South Lancaster
Deershorn Manor B&B .... (508)365-9022

South Lee
Federal House Inn .... (413)243-1824

South Orleans
Hilbourne House .... (508)255-0780

South Yarmouth
Captain Farris House B&B
.... (508)760-2818 (800)350-9477
Four Winds B&B .... (508)394-4182
River Street Guest House ...... (508)398-8946

Southampton
Dianthas Garden Bed & Breakfast (413)529-0093

Spencer
Zukas Homestead Farm .... (508)885-5320

Sterling
Sterling Inn .... (508)422-6592
Sterling Orchards B&B .... (508)422-6595

Stockbridge
Berkshire Thistle Bed and Breakfast
.... (413)298-3188
Cherry Hill Farm Bed & Breakfast (413)298-5452
Inn at Stockbridge .... (413)298-3337
Olde Lamplighter B & B ...... (413)298-3053
The Red Lion Inn .... (413)298-5545
Roeder House Bed & Breakfast .. (413)298-4015
Skye House .... (413)298-5287
Taggart House .... (413)298-4303
Woodside B&B .... (413)298-4977

Stow
Amerscot House .... (508)897-0666
Stowaway Inn .... (508)897-1999

Sudbury
Arabian Horse Inn .... (508)443-9602

Taunton
The Inn at Cedar Street ...... (508)823-8966

Tisbury
Blue Goose .... (508)693-3223
Look Inn .... (508)693-6893

Townsend
B&B at Wood Farm .... (617)597-5019
The Wood Farm .... (508)597-6477

Truro
Moorlands .... (508)487-0663
Parker House B&B .... (617)349-3358
South Hollow Vineyards Bed & Breakfast
.... (508)487-6200
Summer House .... (508)487-2077

Tyringham
Golden Goose .... (413)243-3008
Sunset Farm Inn & B & B ...... (413)243-3229

Uxbridge
Capron House .... (617)278-2214

Vineyard Haven
The Aldworth Manor .... (508)693-3203
The Barn .... (508)693-3745
The Crocker House Inn .... (508)693-1151
Gazebo B&B .... (617)693-6955
Hanover House .... (508)693-1066
High Haven House .... (617)693-9204
Lothrop Merry House .... (508)693-1646
Ocean Side Inn .... (617)693-1296
The Post House .... (508)693-5337
Tuckerman House .... (508)693-0417

Waban
Boston Bed & Breakfast ...... (617)332-4199

Wakefield
Heywood Wakefield B&B ...... (617)245-2627

Waquoit
Waquoit Bay B&B .... (508)457-0084

Ware
The 1880 Country Inn .... (413)967-7847

Wareham
Little Harbor Guest House ...... (508)295-6329

Warwick
Warwick Inn .... (508)544-7802

Wellfleet
Cahoon Hollow B&B .... (508)349-6372
Holden Inn .... (508)349-3450
Surfside Colony Cottages ...... (508)349-3959

West Barnstable
Charles Hinckley House .... (508)362-9924
Gentleman Farmer Bed & Breakfast (508)362-6955
Heaven on High .... (508)362-4441
Honeysuckle Hill B&B
.... (508)362-8418 (800)441-8418

West Boylston
The Rose Cottage .... (508)835-4034

West Brookfield
Deer Meadow Farm .... (413)436-7129
Spy Room Bed & Breakfast .... (508)867-9817

West Dennis
Acadia B&B .... (800)933-6259
Bass River Guesthouse .... (508)398-6758
Beach House .... (508)398-4575
The Lighthouse Inn .... (508)398-2244

West Falmouth
Old Silver Beach B&B .... (508)540-5446
Sjoholm B&B Inn .... (508)540-5706

West Harwich
Barnaby Inn .... (508)432-6789
Cape Winds By The Sea .... (508)432-1418
The Tern Inn .... (508)432-3714

West Hawley
Stump Sprouts Guest Lodge .... (413)339-4265

West Newton
Sears-Withington House .... (617)332-8422

West Springfield
Bethany House Bed & Breakfast . (413)737-6529

West Stockbridge
Kasindorf's B&B .... (413)232-4603
Marble Inn .... (413)232-7092
Shaker Mill Tavern Inn .... (413)232-8565

West Tisbury
Farmhouse .... (508)693-5354
Old Parsonage Bed & Breakfash . (508)696-7745

Westhampton
Outlook Farm .... (413)527-0633

Whately
Sunnyside Farm .... (413)665-3113

Williamsburg
Twin Maples B&B .... (413)268-7244

Williamstown
Field Farm .... (413)458-3135
Goldberrys Bed & Breakfast .... (413)458-3935
Le Jardin .... (413)458-8032
River Bend Farm .... (413)458-3121
Steep Acres Farm .... (413)458-3774
Upland Meadow House .... (413)458-3990
The Williamstown B&B .... (413)458-9202

Worthington
The Hill Gallery .... (413)238-5914
Inn Yesterday .... (413)238-5529
Worthington Inn at Four Corners Farm
.... (413)238-4441

Yarmouth Port
Lane's End Cottage .... (508)362-5298
Liberty Hill Inn .. (508)362-3976 (800)821-3977
Old Yarmouth Inn .... (508)362-3191
Olde Captain's Inn on The Cape . (508)362-4496
Strawberry Lane Bed & Breakfast (508)362-5043
Summer House .... (508)362-8475
Village Inn .... (508)362-3182

Michigan

Adrian
Briaroaks Inn ... (517)263-1659 (800)308-7279

Alden
Torch Lake B&B .... (616)331-6424

Algonac
Linda's Lighthouse Inn .... (810)794-2992
Allegan
Castle In The Country .... (616)673-8054
Delano Inn .... (616)673-2609
Allen
The Olde Bricke House .... (517)869-2349
Alma
Granny's Garret B&B .... (517)463-3961
Saravilla .... (517)463-4078
Alpena
Fireside Inn .... (517)595-6369
Ann Arbor
Bed & Breakfast on Campus .... (313)994-9100
Gladstone House .... (313)769-0404
Reynolds House at Stonefield Farm (313)995-0301
The Urban Retreat .... (313)971-8110
Wood's Inn .... (313)665-8394
Arcadia
Watervale Inn .... (616)352-9083
Atlanta
Briley Inn .... (517)785-4784
Au Gres
Point Au Gres Hotel .... (517)876-7217
Augusta
The Lodge at Yarrow .... (616)731-2090
Bad Axe
Gray Stone Manor . (517)269-9466 (800)(80-0)()
Battle Creek
Greencrest Manor .... (616)962-8633
Old Lamplighter's Home .... (616)963-2603
Bay City
Clements Inn ... (517)894-4600 (800)442-4605
Stonehedge Inn .... (517)894-4342
Bay Port
Bayview Country Inn .... (517)656-9952
Bay View
The Florence .... (616)348-3322
The Gingerbread House .... (616)347-3538
Terrace Inn .... (616)347-2410
Beaverton
Tobacco River Ranch Resort & Range Club
.... (517)435-2080
Bellaire
Bellaire B&B .... (616)533-6077
Grass River B&B .... (616)533-6041
Benzonia
Crystal B&B .... (616)882-5741
Beulah
Windermere Inn .... (616)882-9000
Birch Run
Church Street Manor B&B ...... (517)624-4920
Black River
Silver Creek .... (517)471-2198
Blaney Park
Celibeth House .... (906)283-3409
Blissfield
Hiram D. Ellis Inn .... (517)486-3155
Boyne City
The Beardsley House-A Riverside B&B
.... (616)582-9619
Deer Lake B&B .... (616)582-9039
Duley's State Street Inn .... (616)582-7855
Boyne Falls
The Arman House .... (616)549-2764
Bridgeport
Karen's House B&B .... (517)777-7446
Brooklyn
Chicago Street Inn .... (517)592-3888
Dewey Lake Manor .... (517)467-7122
Buchanan
The Primrose Path B&B .... (616)695-6321
Buckley
A Wicklow House .... (616)269-4212
Cadillac
American Inn B&B .... (616)779-9000
Essenmacher's Bed & Breakfast . (616)775-3828
Herann's European Hotel ...... (616)775-9563
Calumet
Bostrom-Johnson House Bed & Breakfast
.... (906)337-4651
The Calumet House .... (906)337-1936
Holly Manor .... (906)337-3336
Canton
Sheldon Road Inn Bed & Breakfast (313)397-8177

Caro
Garden Gate B&B .... (517)673-2696
Caseville
Carkner House .... (517)856-3456
Country Charm Farm .... (517)856-3110
Cedar
Jarrold Farm .... (616)228-6955
Cedarville
Les Cheneaux Inn B&B .... (906)484-2007
Central Lake
Coulter Creek B&B .... (616)544-3931
Darmon Street B&B .... (616)544-3931
Lamplight Inn .... (616)544-6443
Champion
Michigamme Lake Lodge ...... (800)358-0058
Charlevoix
Aaron's Windy Hill Guest Lodge . (616)547-6100
Bay B&B .... (616)599-2570
Belvedere Inn ... (616)547-2251 (800)280-4667
Charlevoix Country Inn .... (616)547-5134
Craine Cottage .... (616)547-6781
MacDougall House B&B .... (616)547-5788
The Tallship "Appledore" .... (616)547-0024
Wildflower .... (616)547-2667
Charlotte
Schatze Manor B&B .... (517)543-4170
Chassell
Hamar House Bed and Breakfast . (906)523-4670
Palosaari's Rolling Acres B&B ... (906)523-4947
Chelsea
South House Chelsea Bed & Breakfast
.... (313)475-9300
The Whistel-Stop B&B .... (313)475-9987
Chesaning
Bonnymill Inn .... (517)845-7780
Johnston Farm B&B .... (517)845-2180
The Stone House B&B .... (517)845-4440
Clare
Doherty Hotel .... (800)525-4115
Clio
Chandelier Guest House .... (313)687-6061
Cinnamon Stick B&B .... (810)686-8391
Columbiaville
Redwing .... (313)793-4301
Conklin
Miller School Inn .... (616)677-1026
Constantine
Our Olde House B&B Inn ...... (616)435-5365
Curtis
Chamberlin's Ole Forest Inn .... (906)586-6000
Helmer House Inn .... (906)586-3204
Dearborn
The Dearborn Inn .... (313)271-2700
Detroit
Dobson House .... (313)965-1887
Dimondale
Bannicks B&B .... (517)646-0224
Douglas
Alpen Haus .... (616)857-1119
Goshorn House B&B Inn .... (616)857-1326
The Kirby House .... (616)857-2904
Kirby House .... (616)857-2904
Rosemont Inn .... (616)857-2637
Sherwood Forest Bed & Breakfast (616)857-1246
Drummond Island
Stone House Wilderness & Recreation Retreat
.... (906)493-5575
Dundee
The Dundee Guest House ...... (313)529-5706
Eagle Harbor
The Lake Breeze .... (906)289-4514
Eagle River
Eagles Nest Bed and Breakfast .. (906)337-4441
East Jordan
Jordan Inn .... (616)536-2631
Torch Lake Sunrise Bed & Breakfast
.... (616)599-2706
East Lansing
B & B Caribo .... (517)333-6751
Coleman Corners B&B .... (517)339-9360
East Tawas
East Tawas Junction B&B ...... (517)362-8006
Eastmanville
The Eastman House .... (616)837-6474

Eaton Rapids
Dusty's English Inn
.... (517)663-2500 (800)858-0598
Elberta
Summer Inn .... (616)352-7279
Elk Rapids
Cairn House .... (616)264-8994
Candlelight Inn .... (616)264-5630
Widows Walk B&B .... (616)264-5767
Ellsworth
Ellsworth House B&B .... (616)588-7001
Lake Michigan's Abiding Place .. (616)599-2808
Empire
Clipper House Inn .... (616)326-5518
Empire House B&B .... (616)326-5524
South Bar Manor .... (616)326-5304
Evart
B&B at Lynch's Dream .... (616)734-5989
Farmington Hills
The Botsford Inn .... (313)474-4800
Heron Street Company .... (810)626-3632
Locust Manor B&B .... (810)471-2278
Fennville
Grandmas House Bed & Breakfast (616)543-4706
Heritage Manor .... (616)543-4384
Hidden Pond B&B .... (616)561-2491
J. Paules' Fenn Inn .... (616)561-2836
The Porches .... (616)543-4162
Ridgeland Bed & Breadkfast .... (616)857-1633
The Witt House .... (616)561-2206
Fenton
Pine Ridge .... (313)629-8911
Flint
Avon House .... (313)232-6861
The Courtyard .... (313)238-5510
Frankenmuth
Bavarian Town B&B .... (517)652-8057
B&B at The Pines .... (517)652-9019
Home Away Lodgings .... (517)652-3383
Franklin Haus .... (517)652-3939
Johnson Haus B&B .... (517)652-8870
Keepsake Cottage Bed & Breakfast (517)652-3384
Frankfort
The Birch Haven Inn .... (616)352-4008
Chimney Corners .... (616)352-7522
Haugen's Haven B&B .... (616)352-7850
Hotel Frankfort .... (616)882-7271
Pierside Lodging .... (616)352-4778
Summer Inn .... (616)352-7279
Wayfarer Lodgings .... (616)352-9264
Fremont
Gerber House B&B .... (616)924-2829
Galesburg
Pine Arbor .... (616)746-4271
Garden
The Summer House .... (906)644-2457
Gaylord
Groveland Bed & Breakfast ..... (517)731-1184
Heritage House .... (517)732-1199
Gladstone
Willy's Place B&B .... (906)428-2278
Glen Arbor
Glen Arbor B&B .... (616)334-6789
White Gull Inn .... (616)334-4486
Glenn
Will O'Glenn Irish B&B .... (616)227-3045
Gobles
Kal-Haven B&B .... (616)628-4932
Grand Haven
Boyden House B&B .... (616)846-3538
Harbor House Inn .... (616)459-9117
Highland Park Hotel B&B ...... (616)842-6483
Washington Street Inn .... (616)842-1075
Grand Ledge
Edward's Wind Crest .... (517)627-2666
Grand Marais
Lakeview Inn .... (906)494-2612
Grand Rapids
Heald-Lear House .... (616)451-4849
Downtown B&B .... (616)454-6622
Fountain Hill .... (616)458-6621
Hampton Inn .... (616)956-9304
Peaches Bed & Breakfast ...... (616)454-8000
Urban Retreat B&B .... (616)363-1125
Grass Lake
Coppys Inn .... (517)522-4850

Grayling
Belknap's Hanson House ...... (517)348-6630
Greenville
The Gibson House .... (616)754-6691
Winter Inn .... (616)754-7108
Grosse Ile
Bishops Cottage .... (313)671-9191
Harbor Beach
Wellock Inn .... (517)479-3645
Harbor Springs
Kimberly Country Estate .... (616)526-7646
Main Street B&B .... (616)526-7782
Windy Ridge B&B .... (616)526-7650
Harrison
Carriage House .... (517)539-2500
Harrisville
Big Paw Resort .... (517)724-6326
Red Geranium Inn .... (517)724-6153
Springport Inn B&B .... (517)724-6308
The Widow's Watch B&B ...... (517)724-5465
Hart
Rooms at The Inn .... (616)873-2448
Hartland
Farmstead B&B Ltd .... (810)887-6086
Haslett
2054 The Lake .... (517)339-2283
Holland
North Shore Inn of Holland ..... (616)394-9050
The Old Holland Inn .... (616)396-6601
Reka's B&B .... (616)399-0409
Holly
Holly Crossing B&B
.... (810)634-7075 (800)556-2262
Houghton
Charleston House B&B Inn ..... (800)482-7404
Houghton Lake
Stevens White House on The Lake (517)366-4567
Hudson
Baker Hill B&B .... (517)448-8536
The Sutton's Weed Farm B&B ... (517)547-6302
Indian River
Tuscarora Historical Society B&B (616)238-9072
Interlochen
Between The Lakes B&B ...... (616)276-7751
Interlochen Aire .... (616)276-6941
Sandy Shores B&B .... (616)276-9763
Ionia
The Union Hill Inn .... (616)527-0955
Iron River
Country Garden Homestyle Inn Inc (906)265-4905
Pine Willow B&B .... (906)265-4287
Ithaca
Bon Accord Farm B&B .... (517)875-3136
Chaffin Farms B&B .... (517)875-3410
Jackson
Country Hearth Inn .... (517)783-6404
Rose Trellis B&B .... (517)787-2035
Jonesville
Munro House B&B .... (517)849-9292
Kalamazoo
Bartlett-Upjohn House .... (616)342-0230
Stuart Avenue Inn .... (616)342-0230
Kalamazoo House .... (616)343-5426
Stuart Avenue Inn Ben & Breakfast (616)342-0230
Kearsarge
Belknap's Garnet House .... (906)337-5607
Laingsburg
Seven Oaks Farm .... (517)651-5598
Lake City
B&B In The Pines .... (616)839-4876
Lake Leelanau
Centennial Inn .... (616)271-6460
Lakeside
The Pebble House .... (616)469-1416
White Rabbit Inn .... (616)469-4620
Lamont
The Stagecoach Stop B&B ..... (616)677-3940
Lanse
The Bungalow B&B .... (906)524-7595
Lansing
Cherry Hill B&B .... (517)372-9545
Maplewood B&B .... (517)372-7775
Lapeer
Hart House .... (810)667-9106

Laurium
Keweenaw House B&B .... (906)337-4822
Laurium Manor Inn B&B .... (906)337-1358
Lawrence
Oak Cove Resort .... (616)674-8228
Leland
Aspen House .... (616)256-9724
The Highlands .... (616)256-7632
Leland Lodge .... (616)256-9848
Manitou Manor B&B .... (616)256-7712
The Riverside Inn .... (616)256-9971
Snowbird Inn .... (616)256-9773
Leslie
Hampton's Guest House .... (517)589-9929
Lewiston
Gorton House .... (517)786-2764
Lakeview Hills Country Inn Resort B&B
.... (517)786-2000
Pine Ridge Lodge .... (517)786-4789
Lexington
Britannia House English B&B ... (810)359-5772
Governor's Inn .... (810)359-5770
Powell House The Bed & Breakfast (810)359-5533
Lowell
Alden Pines B&B .... (616)897-5655
McGee Homestead B&B .... (616)897-8142
Ludington
B&B at Ludington .... (616)843-9768
The Doll House Inn
.... (616)843-2286 (800)275-4616
Hamlin Lake Cottage B&B ...... (616)845-7127
Inland Sea B&B .... (616)845-7569
The Ludington House .... (616)845-7769
Welcome Home Inn .... (616)845-7699
Mackinac Island
Bay View at Mackinac .... (906)847-3295
Bogan Lake Inn .... (906)847-3439
Chippewa Hotel .... (906)847-3341
Grand Hotel .... (906)847-3331
The Island House .... (906)847-3347
Lake View Hotel .... (906)847-3384
Lilac House .... (906)847-3708
Market Street Inn .... (906)847-3811
Metivier Inn .... (906)847-6234
Murray Hotel .... (906)847-3361
Pine Cottage .... (906)847-3820
Small Point Bed & Breakfast .... (906)847-3758
Mancelona
Cedar Bend Farm .... (616)587-5709
Manistee
Inn Wick-A-Te-Wah .... (616)889-4396
The Ivy Inn .... (616)723-8881
Lake Shore B&B .... (616)723-7644
Manistee Country House ...... (616)723-2367
The Maples .... (616)723-2904
Maple City
Country Cottage B&B .... (616)228-5328
Leelanau Country Inn .... (616)228-5060
Marine City
Heather House .... (810)765-3175
Marlette
Country View B&B .... (517)635-2468
Marquette
Blueberry Ridge B&B .... (906)249-9246
The Landmark Inn (906)228-5343 (888)526-3466
Marshall
McCarthy's Bear Creek Inn ..... (616)781-8383
The National House Inn .... (616)781-7374
McMillan
Helmer House Inn .... (906)586-3204
Mears
Duneland Inn-Foster's B&B ..... (616)873-5128
Mecosta
Blue Lake Lodge .... (616)972-8391
Michigamme
Cottage-On-The-Bay B&B ...... (906)323-6191
Midland
The Bramble House B&B ...... (517)832-5082
Jay's B&B .... (517)496-2498
Milford
Hibbard Tavern .... (810)685-1435
Mio
Kilby House B&B .... (517)826-3066
Monroe
Bill & Betty's Place .... (313)457-1770

Montague
Country Haven B&B .... (616)894-4977
Old Channel Inn .... (616)893-3805
Mount Pleasant
Country Chalet .... (517)772-9259
Munising
Homestead Bed & Breakfast .... (906)387-2542
Muskegon
Blue Country B&B .... (616)744-2555
Emery House B&B .... (616)722-6978
Hackley-Holt House .... (616)725-7303
New Buffalo
Bauhaus on Barton .... (616)469-6419
Little Bohemia .... (616)469-1440
Sans Souci B&B .... (616)756-3141
Tall Oaks Inn B&B .... (616)469-0097
New Era
Needle Nook .... (616)861-4077
Okapi Inn ...... (616)861-4077 (800)726-4077
Newberry
The Macleod House .... (906)293-3841
Niles
Yesterday's Inn .... (616)683-6079
Northport
Apple Beach Inn .... (616)386-5022
Birch Brook .... (616)386-5188
North Shore Inn .... (616)386-7111
Northville
The Atchison House .... (313)349-3340
Nunica
Stonegate Inn .... (616)837-9267
Old Mission
Bowers Harbor Bed & Breakfast . (616)223-7869
Neahtawanta Inn .... (616)223-7315
Olivet
Ackerman's B&B Inn .... (616)749-9422
Omena
Frieda's B&B .... (616)386-7274
Omena B&B .... (616)386-7274
Omena Shores B&B .... (616)386-7313
Omer
Rifle River B&B .... (517)653-2543
Onaway
Stillmeadow Bed & Breakfast ... (517)733-2882
Onekama
Lake Breeze House .... (616)889-4969
Ontonagon
Northern Light Inn B & B ...... (906)884-4290
Olde Convent Bed & Breafast ... (906)884-4538
Oscoda
Huron House .... (517)739-9255
Ossineke
Cranberry Creek Cottage .... (517)471-5196
Fernwood B&B .... (517)471-5176
Owosso
Archer's Castle .... (517)723-2572
Mulberry House .... (517)723-4890
R & R Farm-Ranch .... (517)723-2553
Sylverlynd .... (517)723-1267
Victorian Splendor B&B .... (517)725-5168
Paradise
Bayview Chalet Bed & Breakfast . (906)492-3893
Parma
Hilltop Farm .... (517)531-5820
Paw Paw
Carrington's Country House .... (616)657-5321
Pentwater
The Candlewyck House B&B .... (616)869-5967
Nickerson Inn .... (616)869-8241
Pentwater Abbey .... (616)869-4094
Petoskey
Bear & The Bay .... (616)347-6077
Bear River Valley B&B .... (616)348-2046
Bed `n' Breakfast .... (616)347-6145
The Cozy Spot .... (616)347-3869
Gull's Way .... (616)347-9891
Nina's Country B&B .... (616)347-9262
Perry Hotel .... (616)347-2516 (800)456-1917
Serenity - A B&B .... (616)347-6171
Stafford's Bay View Inn
.... (616)347-2771 (800)456-1917
Pinckney
Bunn-Pher Hill .... (313)878-9236
Plymouth
Mayflower B&B Hotel .... (313)453-1620

ADDITIONAL ACCOMMODATIONS

Pontiac
Emilys Bed & Breakfast .... (810)333-7499
Port Austin
Garfield Inn .... (517)738-5254
Lake Street Manor .... (517)738-7720
Questover Inn .... (517)738-5253
Port Hope
Stafford House .... (517)428-4554
Port Sanilac
Holland's Little House In Country (810)622-9739
Raymond House Inn .... (810)622-8800
Prescott
Duncan's Country B&B .... (517)873-4237
Prudenville
Spring Brook Inn .... (517)366-6347
Rapid River
The Buck Stop Sporting Lodge and B&B
.... (906)446-3360
Reed City
Osceola Inn .... (616)832-5537
Rochester Hills
Paint Creek B&B .... (313)651-6785
Rockford
Grandma's House .... (616)866-4111
Rogers City
Rogers Ranch & Lodge .... (517)734-2178
Romeo
Country Heritage B&B .... (313)752-2879
Hess Manor B&B .... (810)752-4726
Romulus
Country Lane B&B .... (313)753-0135
Saginaw
Brockway House (517)792-0746 (800)383-5043
Heart House Inn .... (517)753-3145
Montague Inn .... (517)752-3939
Saint Clair
River House Bed & Breakfast ... (810)329-4253
William Hopkins Manor .... (810)329-0188
Saint Ignace
Colonial House Inn .... (906)643-6900
Saint James
McCann House B&B .... (616)448-2387
Saint Johns
Classic Bed & Breakfast .... (517)224-6897
Oakland Place .... (517)224-1011
Saint Joseph
The Chestnut House .... (616)983-7413
South Cliff Inn B&B .... (616)983-4881
Saline
The Homestead B&B .... (313)429-9625
Saugatuck
Bayside Inn .... (616)857-4321 (800)548-0077
Beechwood Manor B&B .... (616)857-1587
Belvedere Manor .... (616)857-5501
Fairchild House .... (616)857-5985
Four Seasons Inn .... (616)857-1962
Heritage Manor .... (616)543-4384
Ivy Inn .... (616)857-4643
Kemah Guest House
.... (616)857-2919 (800)445-3624
Maplewood Hotel .... (616)857-1771
Marywood Manor .... (616)857-4771
Moores Creek Inn .... (616)857-2411
The Newnham Inn .... (616)857-4249
Wickwood Country Inn .... (616)857-1465
Sault Sainte Marie
Ojibway Hotel .... (906)632-4100
The Water Street Inn .... (906)632-1900
Schoolcraft
Grand Street B&B .... (616)679-5697
Scottville
Eden Hill B&B .... (616)757-2023
Shelby
Elmhurst B&B .... (616)861-4846
The Shepherd's Place - B&B .... (616)861-4298
South Haven
A Country Place B&B .... (616)637-5523
Arundel House .... (616)637-4790
Carriage House .... (616)639-1776
Elmhurst Farm Inn .... (616)637-4633
The Last Resort .... (616)637-8943
North Beach Inn & Restaurant ... (616)637-6738
Rainbow's End .... (616)227-3474
The Ross .... (616)637-2256
Victoria Resort B&B
.... (616)637-6414 (800)637-5793
Yelton Manor .... (616)637-5220
Sparta
Morton House .... (616)887-7073
Spring Lake
Alberties Waterfront B&B ...... (616)846-4016
Seascape B&B .... (616)842-8409
Stephenson
Top O' The Hill .... (906)753-4757
Stockbridge
Ballacraine B&B .... (517)851-7437
Sturgis
Christmere House .... (616)651-8303
Suttons Bay
Century Farm .... (616)271-2421
The Cottage B&B .... (616)271-6348
Garthe Guest House .... (616)271-3776
Lee Point Inn on West Grand Traverse Bay
.... (616)271-6770
Morning Glory Beach .... (616)271-6048
Open Windows .. (616)271-4300 (800)520-3722
Swartz Creek
Pink Palace Farms .... (810)655-4076
Tecumseh
Boulevard Inn .... (517)423-5169
Stacy Mansion .... (517)423-6979
Traverse City
Bowers Harbor B&B .... (616)223-7869
Cherryland Lodge .... (616)922-7330
Cider House B&B .... (616)947-2833
Fairview Inn .... (616)922-7120
Grainary .... (616)946-8325
Hannah Beach House .... (616)947-8778
Linden Lea on Long Lake ...... (616)943-9182
Tall Ship Malabar .... (616)941-2000
Neahtawanta Inn .... (616)223-7315
Painted Pony Inn .... (616)947-9117
Peninsula Manor .... (616)929-1321
Queen Anne's Castle .... (616)946-1459
Rafael's B&B .... (616)946-4106
The Stonewall Inn .... (616)223-7800
Warwickshire Inn .... (616)946-7176
The Wooden Spool .... (616)947-0357
Trenton
Bear Haven .... (313)675-4844
Union City
Victorian Villa .... (517)741-7383
Union Pier
Garden Grove B&B (616)469-6346 (800)613-2872
Gordon Beach Inn .... (616)469-0800
Pumpernickle Inn .... (616)469-9000
Rivers Edge Bed & Breakfast ... (616)469-6860
Vermontville
Stoney Hill Farm B&B .... (517)726-0711
Wakefield
The Medford House .... (906)229-5057
Walled Lake
Villa Hammer .... (313)624-1071
Walloon Lake
Masters House B&B .... (616)535-2944
Walloon Lake Inn .... (616)535-2999
Wayland
Roughys Resort-Gun Lake ..... (616)792-2219
Webberville
Basic Brewer B&B .... (517)468-3970
West Bloomfield
Wren's Nest .... (810)624-6874
West Branch
Green Inn .... (517)345-0334
The Rose Brick Inn .... (517)345-3702
White Cloud
Crow's Nest B&B (616)689-0088 (800)354-0850
Shack Country Inn .... (616)924-6683
White Pigeon
River Haven .... (616)483-9104
Whitehall
White Swan Inn .... (616)894-5169
Williamsburg
Zum Tannenblick (Pine View) ... (616)267-9302
Williamston
Wheatfield House Bed & Breakfast (517)655-4327

Minnesota

Afton
Afton's Mulberry Pond on River Road
.... (612)436-8086
Dee's Country B&B .... (612)436-6964
The Historic Afton House Inn ... (612)436-8883
Albert Lea
Fountain View Inn .... (507)377-9425
The Victorian Rose Inn .... (507)373-7602
Alexandria
Carrington House on The Lake .. (320)846-7400
The Robard's House .... (612)763-4073
Annandale
Thayer Inn .... (320)274-8222
Anoka
Bendemere on The Mississippi .. (612)427-1815
Askov
The Governor's House .... (612)838-3296
Austin
Rebecca's Bed & Breakfast ..... (507)437-8219
Battle Lake
Page House B&B .... (218)864-8974
Baudette
Rainy River Lodge .... (218)634-2730
Blooming Prairie
Pine Springs Inn .... (507)583-4411
Blue Earth
Fering's Guest House .... (507)526-5054
Brainerd
Sherwood Forest Lodge .... (218)963-2516
Brooklyn Center
The Inn on The Farm .... (612)569-6330
Caledonia
The Inn on The Green .... (507)724-2818
Cannon Falls
Candlewick Country Inn .... (507)263-0879
The Hart House Inn .... (507)263-3617
Quill & Quilt .... (507)263-5507 (800)488-3849
Chaska
Bluff Creek Inn .... (612)445-2735
Chatfield
Lund's Guest House .... (507)867-4003
Cold Spring
Pillow, Pillar & Pine Guest House (612)685-3828
Cook
Muskego Point Resort and Bed & Breakfast
.... (218)666-5696
Swanson's Point Estate .... (218)666-5641
Crookston
The Elm Street Inn (218)281-2343 (800)568-4476
Crosby
Hallett House .... (218)546-5433
Crosslake
Birch Hill Inn Bed & Breakfast ... (218)692-4857
Lo-Kiandy Inn .... (218)692-2714
Deerwood
Walden Woods B&B
.... (612)692-4379 (800)892-5336
Detroit Lakes
Idlewood By The Lake .... (218)847-1229
Duluth
Barnum House .... (218)724-5434
The Ellery House .... (218)724-7639
Fitger's Inn .... (218)722-8826
Manor on The Creek .... (218)728-3189
The Mansion .... (218)724-0739
Mathew S. Burrows 1890 Inn ... (218)724-4991
Olcott House Bed & Breakfast ... (218)728-1339
Spinnaker Inn Bed and Breakfast . (218)525-9292
Stanford Inn .... (218)724-3044
Wiess A Charles Inn .... (218)724-7016
Ely
Blue Heron Bed & Breakfast .... (218)365-4720
Our Mom's B&B Inn .... (218)365-2620
Sandemar Lodge .... (218)365-2769
Three Deer Haven B&B .... (218)365-6464
Trezona House .... (218)365-4809
Embarrass
Finnish Heritage Homestead
.... (218)984-3318 (800)863-6545
Excelsior
Christopher Inn .... (612)474-6816
Clark James H House .... (612)474-0196
Falcon Heights
The Rose B&B .... (612)642-9417
Faribault
Cherub Hill B&B Inn
.... (507)332-2024 (800)332-7254

Finlayson
Giese B&B Inn .... (612)233-6429
Franklin
Maple Hill Cottage .... (507)557-2403
Garvin
Glenview B&B .... (507)629-4808
Graceville
Lakeside B&B .... (612)748-7657
Grand Marais
Dreamcatcher B&B .... (800)682-3119
East Bay Hotel .... (218)387-2800
Gunflint Lodge .... (218)388-2294
MacArthur House Bed & Breakfast (218)387-1840
Pin Cushion Mountain Bed & Breakfast
.... (218)387-1276
The Superior Overlook B&B ..... (218)387-1571
Young's Island B&B .... (218)388-4487
Grand Rapids
A Seagrens Bed & Breakfast .... (218)326-9040
Judge Thwing House .... (218)326-5618
Hastings
A Country Rose .... (612)436-2237
Hearthwood Bed & Breakfast ... (612)437-1133
Rosewood Bed & Breakfast Inn .. (612)437-3297
Thorwood & Rosewood Historic Inns
.... (612)437-3297 (800)992-4667
Hendricks
Lil Farm Bed & Breakfast Farm .. (507)275-3740
Triple L Farm .... (507)275-3740
The Wahlstrom House .... (507)275-3769
Herman
Lawndale Farm .... (612)677-2687
Houston
Addie's Attic .... (507)896-3010
The Bunkhouse Lodge B&B .... (507)896-2080
Hovland
Trovall's Inn .... (218)475-2344
Jackson
Burnham House The Bed & Breakfast
.... (507)847-4327
Moorlands Country Inn .... (507)847-4707
Old Railroad Inn .... (507)847-5348
Jordan
Nicolin Inn .... (612)492-3608
Kasson
Jacob's Inn .... (507)634-4920
Kenyon
Grandfather's Woods .... (507)789-6414
Lake City
Evergreen Knoll Acres .... (612)345-2257
Pepin House .... (612)345-4454
Red Gables Inn .... (612)345-2605
The Victorian B&B .... (612)345-2167
Lanesboro
Birch Knoll Ranch R&R .... (612)467-2418
Cady Hayes House .... (507)467-2621
Carrolton Country Inn .... (507)467-2257
Cottage House .... (507)467-2577
Galligan House Bed & Breakfast . (507)467-2299
Historic Scanlan House
.... (507)467-2158 (800)944-2158
Mrs. B's Historic Lanesboro Inn . (507)467-2154
Le Sueur
The Cosgrove .... (507)665-2763
Lester Prairie
Prairie Farm Bed & Breakfast ... (320)395-2055
Lindstrom
The Boathouse B&B .... (612)257-9122
Little Falls
Pine Edge Inn .... (612)632-6681
Little Marais
Stone Hearth Inn B&B .... (218)226-3020
Lutsen
Caribou Lake B&B .... (218)663-7489
The Woods B&B .... (218)663-7144
Mankato
The Butler House .... (507)387-5055
Mantorville
Grand Old Mansion .... (507)635-3231
Marine on St Croix
Asa Parker House .... (612)433-5248
Marshall
Blanchford Inn B&B .... (507)532-5071
McGregor
Savanna Portage Inn B&B
.... (218)426-3500 (800)428-6108

Minneapolis
1900 Dupont .... (612)374-1973
Braisie House .... (612)377-5946
Coe Mansion Carriage House ... (612)871-4249
Elmwood House .... (612)822-4558
Evelo's B&B .... (612)374-9656
Heatherwood Bed & Breakfast .. (612)870-4610
Nicollet Island Inn .... (612)331-1800
Wales House .... (612)331-3931
Minnetonka
Special Places .... (612)938-3326
Monticello
Rand House .... (612)295-6037
Mora
Williams House Bed & Breakfast Inc
.... (320)679-9931
Morgan
Circle R.W. Ranch .... (507)249-3439
Morris
The American House .... (320)589-4054
New Prague
Schumacher's New Prague Hotel (612)758-2133
New Ulm
Buck Thorn Inn .... (507)359-2319
New York Mills
Whistle Stop Inn B&B .... (218)385-2223
Nisswa
Victorian Villa .... (218)963-3953
North Branch
Red Pine B&B .... (612)583-3326
Northfield
Archer House .... (507)645-5661
Dr. Joseph Moses House B&B .. (507)663-1563
Oak Park Heights
Cover Park Manor .... (612)430-2955
Olivia
Sheep Shedde Inn .... (612)523-5000
Ottertail
Wildwood Flower B&B .... (218)367-2117
Owatonna
Northrop-Offendahl House ..... (507)451-4040
Park Rapids
Grammas Bed & Breakfast ..... (218)732-0987
Heartland Trail Inn B & B ...... (218)732-5305
Red Bridge Inn .... (218)732-0481
Pelican Rapids
Prairie View Estate .... (218)863-4321
Pequot Lakes
Stonehouse B&B .... (218)568-4255
Pipestone
Calumet Inn .... (507)825-5871
Preston
Sunnyside Cottage at Forestville . (507)765-3357
Princeton
Oakhurst Inn B&B (612)389-3553 (800)443-2258
Red Lake Falls
Sleepy Hollow .. (218)253-2921 (800)210-2022
Red Wing
The Candlelight Inn .... (612)388-8034
Pratt-Taber Inn .... (612)388-5945
Redwood Falls
Country Oaks Inn .... (507)644-3111
Stanhope .... (507)644-2882
Round Lake
The Prairie House on Round Lake (507)945-8934
Rush City
Grant House .... (612)358-3661
Rushford
River Trail Inn .... (507)864-7886
Saint Charles
Victorian Lace Inn .... (507)932-4496
Saint Joseph
Lamb's B&B .... (612)363-7924
Saint Paul
Chatsworth B&B .... (612)227-4288
Como Villa B&B .... (612)647-0471
Prior's on Desoto .... (612)774-2695
University Club of St. Paul ..... (612)222-1751
Saint Peter
Park Row B&B .... (507)931-2495
Sanborn
Sod House on The Prairie ...... (507)723-538-
Sauk Centre
Palmer House Hotel .... (612)352-3431

Shafer
Country B&B .... (612)257-4773
Shakopee
Apple Hill B&B .... (612)445-4487
Sunny Morning Manor .... (612)496-1482
Side Lake
McNairs Bed & Breakfast ...... (218)254-5878
Silver Bay
Gowdys Inn Bed & Breakfast ... (218)226-4614
Guest House B&B .... (218)226-4201
Norsk Kubbe Hus .... (218)226-4566
The Inn at Palisade .... (218)226-3505
Slayton
Golden K Bed & Breakfast ...... (507)836-8077
Sleepy Eye
The Woodland Inn .... (507)794-5981
Spicer
Green Lake Inn .... (320)796-6523
Spicer Castle Bed & Breakfast Inn (320)796-5870
Spring Grove
Touch of The Past .... (507)498-5146
Spring Lake
Anchor Inn .... (218)798-2718
Spring Valley
Chase's .... (507)346-2850
Stacy
Kings Oakdale Park Guest House . (612)462-5598
Stephen
Grandma's House .... (218)478-2743
Stillwater
Anne Bean House .... (612)430-0355
The Brunswick Inn .... (612)430-2653
Elephant Walk .... (612)430-0528
Heirloom Inn B&B .... (612)430-2289
James A. Mulvey Residence Inn . (612)430-8008
Lowell Inn .... (612)439-1102
Lumber Barons .... (612)439-6000
Outing Lodge at Pine Point ..... (612)439-9747
Rivertown Inn .. (612)430-2955 (800)562-3632
William Sauntry .... (612)430-2653
Taopi
The Dusty Farmhouse .... (507)582-3697
Taylors Falls
Cottage Bed & Breakfast .... (612)465-3595
Two Harbors
Bryan House-B & B .... (218)834-2950
Wabasha
Anderson House .... (612)565-4524
Bridgewater B&B .... (612)565-4208
Cottonwood Inn .... (612)565-2466
The Parsonage House .... (612)565-2466
Wabasso
Victorian Lady B&B .... (507)747-2170
Walker
Chase on The Lake Lodge & Motor Inn
.... (218)547-1531
Peacecliff .... (218)547-2832
Tianna Farms B&B (218)547-1306 (800)842-6620
Warroad
Hospital Bay B&B (218)386-2627 (800)568-6028
Welch
Hungry Point Inn .... (612)437-3660
Whalan
Bestas Hus B & B & Tea Room .. (507)467-2630
Willmar
The Buchanan House B&B ..... (612)235-7308
Winona
Carriage House B&B .... (507)452-8256
Windom Park Bed & Breakfast .. (507)457-9515

Mississippi

Aberdeen
Huckleberry Inn .... (601)369-7294
Bay Saint Louis
Bay Town Inn .... (601)466-5870
Palm House .... (601)467-1665
Belzoni
Magnolia Inn .... (601)247-4932
Biloxi
Father Ryan House Bed & Breakfast Inn
.... (601)435-1189
River Bed & Breakfast .... (601)396-9725
Brookhaven
Edgewood .... (601)833-2001

Church Hill
Cedars Plantation .... (601)445-2203
Columbus
Amzi Love B&B .... (601)328-5413
Cartney-Hunt House .... (601)329-3856
Columbus Historic Foundation ... (601)329-3533
Highland House .... (601)327-5577
Temple Heights .... (601)329-3533
White Arches B&B .... (601)328-7576
Corinth
Madison Inn .... (601)287-7157
Robbins Nest Bed & Breakfast .. (601)286-3109
Fayette
Historic Springfield Plantation ... (601)786-3802
French Camp
French Camp B&B .... (601)547-6835
Greenville
Azalea House Bed & Breakfast .. (601)335-0507
Victorian Inn .... (601)335-6000
Gulfport
Old Oaks Inn .... (601)896-5049
Old South Guesthouse .... (601)864-7759
Hattiesburg
Tally House .... (601)582-3467
Hernando
Shadow Hill Bed & Breakfast ... (601)449-0800
Houston
Harmon Hall .... (601)456-2131
Iuka
East Port Inn .... (601)423-2511
Jackson
Kirkhaven .... (601)982-7381
Kirkland Homes .... (601)982-7381
Millsaps-Buie House .... (601)352-0221
Lorman
Canemont Plantation
.... (601)877-3784 (800)423-0684
Magnolia
Coney House .... (601)783-3000
McComb
The Governor's House B&B .... (601)684-4307
Meadville
The Hancock House .... (601)384-5080
Natchez
Aunt Clara's Cottage .... (601)442-1344
The Briars Inn .. (601)446-9654 (800)634-1818
Camellia Gardens .... (601)446-7944
Clifton Height B&B .... (601)446-8047
D'evereux .... (601)446-6631
Dixie .... (601)442-2525
Dorsey House .... (601)442-5845
The Governor Holmes House ... (601)442-2366
Guest House of Natchez .... (601)445-6000
Harper House .... (601)445-5557
Hope Farm .... (601)445-4848
Linden .... (601)445-5472
Lytle House .... (601)442-2906
Mark Twain Guest House ...... (601)446-8023
Mount Repose .... (800)647-6742
Pleasant Hill .... (601)442-7674
Ravenna .... (601)445-8516
Ravennaside .... (601)442-8015
Riverside .... (601)446-5730
Russell House .... (601)445-7499
Shield's Townhouse .... (601)442-7680
Sweet Olive Tree Mnor .... (601)445-2010

Texada .... (601)445-4283
Trosclair House .... (601)442-2989
Twin Oaks .... (601)446-6631
Vandyke House .... (601)445-4516
Wensel House .... (601)445-8577
Weymouth Hall .... (601)445-2304
White Wings .... (601)442-2757
The Wigwam .... (601)442-2600
William Harris House .... (601)445-2003
Ocean Springs
Magnolia House Bed & Breakfast (601)875-7269
Oak Shade B & B .... (601)875-1050
Wilson House Inn .... (601)875-6933
Olive Branch
Country Goose Inn .... (601)893-2644
Oxford
Isom Place .... (601)236-5600
Oliver-Britt House .... (601)234-8043
Puddin Place .... (601)234-1250

Pass Christian
The Harbour Oaks Inn .... (601)452-9399
Inn at The Pass .... (601)452-0333
Port Gibson
Cane Mount Plantation .... (601)877-3784
Gibson Landing .... (601)437-3432
Oak Square Plantation
.... (601)437-5300 (800)729-0240
Rosswood Plantation .... (601)437-4215
Satartia
No Mistake Plantation .... (601)746-6579
Slate Spring
Doler-Doolittle B&B .... (601)637-2695
Starkville
Caragen House .... (601)323-0340
The Cedars B&B .... (601)324-7569
The Cotton District B&B .... (601)323-5132
Tunica
Tunica Levee Inn .... (601)363-2002
Tupelo
The Mockingbird Inn B&B ...... (601)841-0286
Vicksburg
Balfour House .. (601)638-7113 (800)294-7113
Cherry Street Cottage .... (601)636-7086
Columns .... (601)634-4751
The Duff Green Mansion/Inn .... (601)636-6968
Gray Oaks .... (601)638-4424
The Vicksburg .... (601)636-4146
Water Valley
Town Creek Inn B&B .... (601)473-1010
West
Alexander House Bed & Breakfast (601)967-2266
Woodville
Neals Magnolia Inn .... (601)888-4826

Missouri

Arrow Rock
Borgman's B&B .... (816)837-3350
Down Over Holdings .... (816)837-3268
Miss Nelle's B&B (816)837-3280 (800)795-2794
Bethany
Unicorn Lodge B&B .... (816)425-3676
Bonne Terre
Mansion Hill Country Inn ...... (314)358-5311
Boonville
Morgan Street Repose B&B
.... (816)882-7195 (800)248-5061
Bourbon
Meramec Farm Bed and Board .. (573)732-4765
Branson
Branson Hotel B&B Inn .... (417)335-6104
Branson House .... (417)334-0959
The Brass Swan B&B .... (417)334-6873
Cameron's Crag For A Bird's Eye View
.... (417)335-8134 (800)935-8529
Emory Creek B&B and Gift Shop . (417)334-3805
The Inn at Fall Creek
.... (417)336-3422 (800)280-3422
Gaines Landing B&B .... (417)334-2280
The Lodge at We Lamb Farm ... (417)334-1485
Schroll's Lakefront B&B .... (417)335-6759
Camdenton
Ramblewood B&B .... (314)346-3410
Cape Girardeau
Bellevue B&B ... (573)335-3302 (800)768-6822
Carthage
Brewer's Maple Lane Farm B&B . (417)358-6312
Grand Avenue Inn .... (417)358-7265
The Leggett House .... (417)358-0683
Concordia
Fannie Lee B&B Inn .... (816)463-7395
Defiance
Country Porch B&B .... (314)798-2546
Dixon
Rock Eddy Bluff . (314)759-6081 (800)335-5921
Eminence
Eminence Cottages B&B .... (314)226-3642
Hawkins House .... (314)226-3793
Maple Tree Inn .... (314)226-3644
River's Edge .... (314)226-3233
Ethel
Recess Inn .... (816)486-3328
Excelsior Springs
Crescent Lake Manor
.... (816)637-2958 (800)897-2958

Fulton
Loganberry Inn .... (314)642-9229
Hannibal
Fifth Street Mansion B&B
.... (573)221-0445 (800)874-5661
Hermann
Bide-A-Wee B&B .... (314)486-3961
Birk's Goethe Street Gasthaus ... (314)486-2911
Captain Wohlt Inn .... (314)486-3357
Das Brownhaus .... (314)486-2911
William Klinger Inn .... (314)486-2030
Hermann Hill Vineyard & Inn .... (314)486-4455
Reiff House B&B (573)486-2994 (800)482-2994
Schmidt Guesthouse .... (314)486-2146
Seven Sisters B&B Cottage ..... (314)486-3717
White House Hotel B&B .... (314)486-3200
Independence
House of Hoyt .... (816)461-7226
Woodstock Inn .... (816)833-2233
Jackson
Trisha's B&B .... (314)243-7427
Jefferson City
Peacock Inn .... (314)659-4444
Joplin
Visages .... (417)624-1397
Kansas City
Dome Ridge .... (816)532-4074
Milford House B&B .... (816)753-1269
Pridewell .... (816)931-1642
Kimberling City
Cinnamon Hill B&B .... (417)739-5727
Kimmswick
Kimmswick Korner Inn & Gift Shop (314)467-1028
Kirkwood
Fissy's Place .... (314)821-4494
Lathrop
Parkview Farm .... (816)664-2744
Lesterville
Wilderness Lodge .... (314)637-2295
Liberty
James Inn .... (800)781-3677
Lockwood
Prairie Chicken .... (417)232-4925
Louisiana
Louisiana Guest House .... (314)754-6366
Serando's House (314)754-4067 (800)754-4067
Macon
St. Agnes Hall B&B .... (816)385-2774
Marthasville
Gramma's House B&B .... (314)433-2675
Mexico
Hylas House .... (314)581-2011
Mountain View
Jack's Fork Country Inn .... (417)934-1000
Merrywood Guest House ...... (417)934-2210
Nevada
Red Horse Inn .. (417)667-7796 (800)245-3685
Ozark
Country Lane Cabin B&B
.... (417)581-7372 (800)866-5903
Platte City
Basswood Country Inn Resort
.... (816)858-5556 (800)242-2775
Pleasant Hill
Pleasant Stay Inn .... (816)987-5900
Poplar Bluff
The Stuga .... (314)785-4085
Potosi
The Bust Inn ... (573)438-4457 (800)431-4457
Rocheport
Roby River Run, A B&B .... (314)698-2173
Yates House B&B .... (314)698-2129
Saint Charles
Boone's Lick Trail Inn
.... (314)947-7000 (800)366-2427
Lococo House Ii .... (314)946-0619
The Saint Charles House ...... (314)946-6221
Saint Joseph
Harding House .... (816)232-7020
Saint Louis
Doelling Haus .... (314)894-6796
Geandaugh House .... (314)771-5447
Inn on Midland .... (314)726-2707
Mansion Hill Inn and 1909 Depot B&B
.... (314)731-5003

Seven Gables Inn .... (314)863-8400
Soulard Manor B&B .... (314)664-9738

Sainte Genevieve
Hotel Saint Genevieve .... (314)883-2737

Sedalia
Sedalia House .... (816)826-6615

Shell Knob
Shore Hollow B&B .... (417)858-2415

Sullivan
Whip Haven Farm B&B .... (314)627-3717

Tecumseh
The Farmhouse B&B .... (417)284-3699

Van Buren
Inn at Park Place .... (314)323-4642
Skyline Lodge and Supper Club .. (314)323-4144

Versailles
The Hilty Inn .... (314)378-2020

Warrensburg
The Camel Crossing .... (816)429-2973

Washington
Schwegmann House
.... (314)239-5025 (800)949-2262
Washington House B&B Inn .... (314)239-2417

West Plains
Blue Spruce Inn .... (417)256-3209

Weston
Benner House B&B .... (816)386-2616
The Hatchery .... (816)386-5700

Zanoni
Zanoni Mill Inn .... (417)679-4050

Montana

Absarokee
Oliver's .... (406)328-4813

Big Sandy
Raven Crest .... (406)378-3121
Sky View B&B .... (406)378-2549

Big Sky
Lone Mountain Ranch .... (406)995-4644
Rainbow Ranch B&B .... (406)995-4132

Big Timber
The Grand .... (406)932-4459
Lazy K Bar Ranch .... (406)537-4404

Bigfork
Big Fork Inn .... (406)837-6680
Cherry Way Inn .... (406)837-6803
Flathead Lake Lodge .... (406)837-4391
Gustin Orchard .... (406)982-3329
Jubilee Orchards Lake Resort B&B (406)837-4256
O'Duachain Country Inn
.... (406)837-6851 (800)837-7460
Schwartz's B&B .... (406)837-5463

Billings
The Sanderson Inn .... (406)656-3388

Boulder
Boulder Hot Springs B&B ...... (406)225-4339

Bozeman
Bergfeld B&B .... (406)586-7778
Brackett Creek Inn .... (406)686-4440
Lehrkind Mansion .... (406)586-1214
Lindley House .. (406)587-8403 (800)787-8404
Millers-Montana B&B .... (406)763-4102
Sun House B&B .... (406)587-3651

Cameron
Cliff Lake Lodge .... (406)682-4982

Choteau
Country Lane .... (406)466-2816
Harvest Home B&B .... (406)466-5809
Pine Butte Guest Ranch .... (406)466-2158
Seven Lazy P Ranch .... (406)466-2044

Columbia Falls
Bad Rock Country B&B
.... (406)892-2829 (800)422-3666
Plum Creek House (406)892-1816 (800)682-1429
Turn In The River .... (406)257-0724

Condon
Holland Lake Lodge .... (406)754-2282

De Borgia
Hotel Albert B&B (406)678-4303 (800)678-4303

Dodson
Stage Road Inn .... (406)383-4410

Emigrant
The Gate House .... (406)333-4613

Ennis
9T9 Ranch .... (406)682-7659

Essex
Izaak Walton Inn .... (406)888-5700

Eureka
Trail's End .... (406)889-3486

Fort Benton
Cottonwood .... (406)622-5675

Fortine
Laughing Water Ranch .... (406)882-4680

Gallatin Gateway
Gallatin Gateway .... (406)763-4672

Gold Creek
LH Ranch B&B .... (406)288-3436

Great Falls
The Chalet B&B Inn
.... (406)452-9001 (800)786-9002
Murphy's House B&B .... (406)452-3598
Old Oak Inn .... (406)452-0032
The Sarah .... (406)452-5906
Three Feathers Inn .... (406)453-0519

Hamilton
The Bavarian Farmhouse B&B ... (307)358-2033
Deer Crossing B&B
.... (406)363-2232 (800)763-2232

Hardin
Kendrick House .... (406)665-3035

Harlowton
Star Hotel & Cafe .... (406)632-4786

Helena
The Barrister B&B .... (406)443-7330
Upcountry Inn .... (406)442-1909

Huson
Whispering Pines .... (406)626-5664

Kalispell
Brick Farmhouse B&B .... (406)756-6230
Demersville School B&B .... (406)756-7587
Serendipity House .... (406)755-0331
Still Water Inn B&B (406)755-7080 (800)398-7024
Switzer House Inn (406)257-5837 (800)257-5837

Lakeside
Shoreline Inn .... (406)844-3222

Laurel
Riverside Bed & Breakfast ..... (406)628-7890
(800)768-1580

Libby
Bobtail B&B .... (406)293-3926
The Kootenai Country Inn ...... (406)293-7878

Livingston
Davis Creek B&B .... (406)333-4353
Talcott House .... (406)222-7699

Manhattan
Station House .... (406)284-6094

Marion
Hargrave Ranch . (406)858-2284 (800)933-0696

Missoula
Colonial House .... (406)258-6787

Noxon
Bighorn Lodge .... (406)847-5597

Polson
Bayview B&B .... (406)883-6744
Borchers of Finley Point .... (406)887-2500
Hammond's B&B .... (406)887-2766
Hawthorne House .... (406)883-2723
Ruth's B&B .... (406)883-2460

Pony
The Lodge at Potosi Hot Springs . (406)685-3594

Pray
Rizzotto Ranch .... (406)333-4763

Red Lodge
Willows Inn .... (406)446-3913

Roundup
Ryan's Homestead Inn .... (406)323-2347

Saint Ignatius
Mandorla Ranch .... (406)745-4500

Seeley Lake
The Emily A. B&B (406)677-3474 (800)977-4639

Sheridan
King's Rest .... (406)842-5185

Somers
Osprey Inn .... (406)857-2042

Stevensville
Country Caboose .... (406)777-3145

Sula
Camp Creek Inn .... (406)821-3508

Swan Lake
Stoney Creek Ranch .... (406)886-2002

Three Forks
Sacajawea Inn .. (406)285-6515 (800)821-7326

Townsend
The Bedford Inn .... (406)266-3629
Hidden Hollow Hideaway ...... (406)266-3322

Troy
Bull Lake Guest Ranch .... (406)295-4228

Virginia City
Just An Experience .... (406)843-5402
Nevada City Hotel .... (406)843-5377
The Stonehouse Inn .... (406)843-5504
Virginia City Country Inn .... (406)843-5515

West Yellowstone
Sportsman's High B&B .... (406)646-7865

Westby
Hilltop House B&B .... (406)385-2533

Wht Sphr Spgs
The Columns .... (406)547-3666
Foxwood Inn .... (406)547-3918
Gillett's Elkhorn Lodge .... (406)547-2260

Whitefish
Crenshaw House (406)862-3496 (800)453-2863
Duck Inn .... (406)862-3825
Garden Wall Inn B&B .... (406)862-3440
Kandahar Lodge .... (406)862-6098

Wolf Creek
Missouri River Trout Shop ...... (406)235-4474

Wolf Point
Forsness Farm B&B .... (406)653-2492

Nebraska

Ainsworth
Ainsworth Inn .... (402)387-0408

Bartley
Pheasant Hill Farm .... (308)692-3278

Beemer
Behrens Inn .... (402)528-3212

Berwyn
1909 Heritage House .... (308)935-1136

Big Springs
Phelps Hotel .... (308)889-3447

Blair
Nostalgia Inn B&B .... (402)426-3280

Brewster
Eliza's Cottage .... (308)547-2432
Sandhills Country Cabin .... (308)547-2460
Uncle Buck's Lodge .... (308)547-2210

Broken Bow
Pine Cone Lodge .... (308)872-6407

Brownville
Thompson House .... (402)825-6551

Burwell
Raven's Roost .... (308)346-4026

Callaway
Chesley's Lodge .... (308)836-2658

Cedar Rapids
River Road Inn .... (308)358-0827

Central City
The Popcorn Palace .... (308)946-2751

Chadron
The Olde Main Street Inn ...... (308)432-3380

Chappell
The Cottonwood Inn .... (308)874-3250

Cody
Cody's Country Cabin .... (402)823-4182

Columbus
Valley View B&B .... (402)563-2454

Crawford
Butte Ranch .... (308)665-2364

Crofton
Historic Argo Hotel (402)388-2400 (800)607-2746

Crookston
Two Rivers Ranch .... (402)425-3353

Dannebrog
Bedstemor's Hus .... (308)226-2403
The Heart of Dannebrog .... (308)226-2303
Nestle Inn .... (308)226-8252

Dixon
The George Farm .... (402)584-2625

Fairbury
Parker House B&B .... (402)729-5516
Personett House .... (402)729-2902

Fremont
B&B of Fremont .... (402)727-9534

ADDITIONAL ACCOMMODATIONS

Funk
Uncle Sam's Hilltop Lodge ..... (308)995-5568
Gering
Monument Heights B&B .... (308)635-0109
Gordon
Meadow View Ranch B&B Bunkhouse
.... (308)282-0679
Horse Thief Cave Ranch .... (308)282-1017
Grant
Prairie Jean's B&B .... (308)352-2355
Greeley
The Rutledge Inn .... (308)428-5000
Gretna
Bundy's B&B .... (402)332-3616
Hastings
Grandma's Victorian B&B ...... (402)462-2013
Hemingford
Hansen Homestead B&B ...... (308)487-3805
Holdrege
The Crow's Nest .... (308)995-5440
Hooper
Empty Nest B&B .... (402)664-2715
Howells
Beran B&B .... (402)986-1358
Prairie Garden .... (402)986-1251
Hyannis
Verde Valley Guest Ranch ...... (308)458-2220
Kearney
The George W. Frank, Jr. House B&B
.... (308)237-7545
Laurel
Kraemer Estates B&B .... (402)256-3585
Lexington
Memories .... (308)324-3290
Lincoln
The Atwood House B&B .... (402)438-4567
Capitol Guesthouse B&B .... (402)476-6669
The Dutch Pillow .... (402)435-0225
Rogers House .... (402)476-6961
Simple Pleasures Inn .... (402)435-7208
Sweet Dream .... (402)438-1416
Yellow House on The Corner .... (402)466-8626
Long Pine
Pine Valley Resort .... (402)273-4351
Loup City
Enchanted Retreat .... (308)745-0850
Madrid
Clown 'n Country B&B .... (308)326-4378
Marquette
Timberlake Ranch Camp .... (308)946-3871
McCook
Park House Guest House ...... (308)345-6057
Merna
The Country Nest .... (308)643-2486
Merriman
Twisted Pine Ranch B&B Whitetail Hunting
.... (308)684-3482
Minden
Home Comfort B&B
.... (308)832-0533 (800)318-0533
Murdock
Farm House B&B .... (402)867-2062
Nebraska City
Le Bleu Bonnet .... (402)873-5590
Whispering Pines .... (402)873-5850
North Bend
Platte Valley Guernsey B&B .... (402)652-3492
North Platte
Knoll's Country Inn
.... (308)368-5634 (800)337-4526
Ogallala
Denim to Lace B&B .... (308)284-6200
Omaha
The Jones's .... (402)397-0721
Mary Mahoney's Thissen House B&B
.... (402)553-8366
Orchard
Diamond E Trout Resort
.... (402)893-3002 (800)658-3244
Ord
The Shepherd's Inn .... (308)728-3306
Osmond
Willow Way B&B .... (402)748-3593
Pawnee City
My Blue Heaven B&B .... (402)852-3131

Paxton
Gingerbread Inn B&B .... (308)239-4265
Plainview
Rose Garden Inn .... (402)582-4708
Potter
B&B of Potter .... (308)879-4418
Ravenna
Aunt Betty's B&B .... (308)452-3739
Saint Libory
The Quiet Country Farmhouse ... (308)687-6207
Sidney
Snuggle Inn B&B .... (308)254-0500
Sparks
Buffalo Creek Ranch .... (402)376-2985
Springview
Big Canyon Inn . (402)497-3170 (800)437-6023
Larrington's Guest Cottage ..... (402)497-2261
St. Paul
Miss Lizzie's Boardin' House ... (308)754-4137
Steinauer
Convent House .... (402)869-2276
Sutton
Maltby House .... (402)773-4556
Table Rock
Hill Haven Lodge .... (402)839-2023
Tekamah
Deer Run B&B .... (402)374-2423
Trenton
Blue Colonial B&B .... (308)276-2533
Flying A Ranch B&B Hunting Lodge
.... (308)334-5574
Valentine
Boardman Springs Ranch ...... (402)376-1498
Elysian B&B .... (402)376-3210
Stone House Inn .... (402)376-1942
Town and Country B&B .... (402)376-2193
Verdigre
The Verdigre Inn .... (402)668-2277
Wayne
Swanson's B&B .... (402)584-2277
Wilber
Hotel Wilber .... (402)821-2020 (800)609-4663

Nevada

Baker
Border Inn .... (702)234-7300
Beatty
Burro Inn .... (702)553-2225
Phoenix Inn .... (702)553-2250
Boulder City
Nevada Inn .... (702)293-2044
Western Inn .... (702)294-0393
Carson City
Bliss Mansion Bed & Breakfast .. (702)887-8988
Deer Run Ranch B&B .... (702)882-3643
Mill House Inn .... (702)882-2715
Round House Inn .... (702)882-3446
Royal Crest Inn .... (702)882-1785
Silver Queen Inn .... (702)882-5534
Warren Inn .... (800)331-7700
Westerner Inn .... (702)883-6565
Elko
Shilo Inn Elko .... (702)738-5522
Ely
Fireside Inn .... (702)289-3765
Great Basin Inn .... (702)289-4468
Rustic Inn .... (702)289-4404
Eureka
Parsonage House B&B .... (702)237-5756
Fallon
Tania's Bedn Breakfast .... (702)423-8999
Fernley
Truck Inn .... (702)789-1000
Gardnerville
Adaven Hotel Victorian Inn ..... (702)782-8720
The Nenzel Mansion .... (702)782-7644
Sierra Spirit Ranch .... (702)782-7011
Genoa
Genoa House Inn .... (702)782-7075
Orchard House .... (702)782-2640
Wally's Hot Springs Resort ..... (702)782-8155
Incline Village
The Inn at Incline & Condominiums (702)831-1052
Jarbidge
Tsawhawbitts B&B .... (702)488-2338

Lamoille
Breitenstein House .... (702)753-6356
Lovelock
Cadillac Inn .... (702)273-2798
Lovelock Inn .... (702)273-2937
Metropolis
Canyon Pheasant Club .... (702)752-3065
Minden
Carson Valley Inn .... (702)782-9711
Palomino Valley
Stone House Country Inn ...... (702)578-3530
Reno
H Bar B Farms .... (702)475-0100
Silver City
Hardwicke House .... (702)847-0215
Smith
Windybrush Ranch .... (702)465-2481
Sparks
Blue Fountain B&B .... (702)359-0359
Virginia City
Chollar Mansion B&B .... (702)847-9777
Crooked House .... (702)847-0521
Gold Hill Hotel .... (702)847-0111
Spargo House .... (702)847-7455
Wellington
Hoyes Mansion Bed & Breakfast . (702)465-2959
Wells
Old West Inn .... (702)752-3888
Yerington
Harbor House .... (702)463-2991
Robric Ranch .... (702)463-3515

New Hampshire

Alexandria
Stone Rest B&B .... (603)744-6066
Alstead
Darby Brook Farm .... (603)835-6624
Alton
Brook & Bridel Inn .... (603)569-2707
Andover
Andover Arms Guest House .... (603)735-5953
The English House .... (603)735-5987
Highland Lake Inn .... (603)735-6426
Antrim
Antrim Inn .... (603)588-8000
Steele Homestead Inn .... (603)588-6772
Uplands Inn .... (603)588-6349
Ashland
Country Options .... (603)968-7958
Haus Trillum .... (603)968-2180
Ashuelot
Crestwood .... (603)239-6393
Bartlett
Notchland Inn .... (603)374-6131
Bedford
The Bedford Village Inn
.... (603)472-2001 (800)852-1166
Wayfarer Inn .... (603)622-3766
Bethlehem
The Gables at Park & Main B&B . (603)869-3111
The Highlands Inn .... (603)869-3978
Mulburn Inn .... (603)869-3389
Sherman Inn ... (603)869-2457 (800)336-8344
Wayside Inn & Motel .... (603)869-3364
Bradford
Andrew Brook Lodge .... (603)938-2920
Candlelite Inn .... (603)938-5571
Mountain Lake Inn .... (603)938-2136
Village House at Sutton Mills .... (603)927-4765
Bristol
Pleasant View Bed and Breakfast (603)744-5547
Victorian B&B Inn .... (603)744-6157
Thornton (campton)
Amber Lights Inn B&B .... (603)726-4077
Campton
Bridge House Inn .... (603)726-9853
Campton Inn .... (603)726-4449
Osgood Inn B&B .... (603)726-3543
Scandinavi-Inn .... (603)726-3737
Canaan
The Inn on Canaan Street ...... (603)523-7310
The Towerhouse Inn .... (603)523-7244
Center Conway
Lavender Flower Inn .... (800)729-0106
Merrill Farm Resort .... (603)447-3866

Center Harbor
Dearborn Place .... (603)253-6711
Kona Carriage House Inn ...... (603)253-9954
Kona Mansion Inn .... (603)253-4900
Red Hill Inn .... (603)279-7001 (800)573-3445
Watch Hill Bed & Breakfast ..... (603)253-4334

Center Ossipee
Effingham Inn .... (603)539-2141
Hitching Post Village Inn .... (603)539-3360
Mount Whittier Motel .... (603)539-4951

Center Sandwich
Corner House Inn (603)284-6219 (800)832-7829
Overlook Farm B&B .... (603)284-6485

Charlestown
Indian Shutters Inn .... (603)826-4445

Chichester
Hitching Post B&B .... (603)798-4951

Chocorua
The Farmhouse .... (603)323-8707
Mt. Chocorua View House ..... (603)323-8350
Staffords-In-The-Field .... (603)323-7766

Colebrook
The Balsams Resort
.... (603)255-3400 (800)255-0600
Monadnock B&B .... (603)237-8216

Concord
A Touch of Europe B&B .... (603)226-3771

Conway
B & B Beside The River .... (603)447-6468
The Darby Field Inn
.... (603)447-2181 (800)426-4147
Foothills Farm B&B .... (207)935-3799

Cornish
Barberry House .... (603)675-2802
Chase House B&B Inn
.... (603)675-5391 (800)401-9455
Home Hill Country Inn .... (603)675-6165

Danbury
The Inn at Danbury .... (603)768-3318

Deerfield
Isabels Bed & Breakfast .... (603)463-7522

Dover
Highland Farm .... (603)743-3399

Dublin
Dubliner Bed & Breakfast ...... (603)563-8700
Trinitarian Parsonage .... (603)563-8889

Durham
Deweys Hannah House .... (603)659-5500
Hannah House B&B .... (603)659-5500
Helgas Guest House .... (603)659-6856
Hickory Pond Inn & Golf Course . (603)659-2227
University Guest House .... (603)868-2728

East Andover
Highland Lake Inn B&B .... (603)735-6426

East Wakfield
Lake Ivanhoe Inn .... (603)522-8824

Eaton Center
The Inn at Crystal Lake
.... (603)447-2120 (800)343-7336
Rockhouse Mountain Farm Inn .. (603)447-2880

Elkins
Limner Haus .... (603)526-6451

Enfield
Boulder Cottage on Crystal Lake . (603)632-7355
Kluge's Sunset Hill Inn .... (603)632-4335
Mary Keane House .... (603)632-4241
Shaker Farm B&B (603)632-7664 (800)613-7664

Epsom
The Quiet Place B&B Antiques .. (603)736-9696

Etna
Moose Mountain Lodge .... (603)643-3529

Fitzwilliam
Fitzwilliam Inn .... (603)585-9000
The Hannah Davis House ...... (603)585-3344

Francestown
The Inn at Crotched Mountain ... (603)588-6840
The Francestown B&B .... (603)547-6333

Franconia
Blanche's B&B .... (603)823-7061
Horse and Hound Inn .... (603)823-5501
Lovett's Inn .... (603)823-7761
Pinestead Farm Lodge .... (603)823-5601
Sugar Hill Inn .... (603)823-5621
Sunset Hill House .... (603)823-5522

Franklin
Paige House Bed & Breakfast ... (603)934-6535

Strolling Woods on Webster Lake (603)934-9809
Webster Lake Inn .... (603)934-4050

Freedom
Freedom House Bed & Breakfast . (603)539-4815
Knob Hill B&B .... (603)539-6576

Gilford
Cartway House Inn .... (603)528-1172
Gunstock Country Inn .... (603)293-2021
The Inn at Smith Cove .... (603)293-1111

Gilmanton
The Historic Temperance Tavern . (603)267-7349

Glen
Covered Bridge House B&B
.... (603)383-9109 (800)232-9109

Gorham
The Gorham House Inn
.... (603)466-2271 (800)453-0023

Goshen
Back Side Inn .... (603)863-5161
Cutter's Loft .... (603)863-5306

Greenland
Ayres Homestead Bed & Bekfast (603)436-5992
Captain Folsom Inn .... (603)436-2662

Guild
Drum Inn & Restaurant .... (603)863-3881

Hampstead
Stillmeadow B&B at Hampstead . (603)329-8381

Hampton
The Curtis Field House .... (603)929-0082
Elmdale Guest House .... (603)926-2507
Griffin House Bed & Breadfas ... (603)926-2868
Lamie's Inn & Tavern .... (603)926-0330
The Oceanside .... (603)926-3542
The Roy Family B&B .... (603)926-7893
Victoria Inn .... (603)929-1437

Hancock
Westwinds of Hancock .... (603)525-6600

Hanover
Trumbull House B & B .... (603)643-2370

Harrisville
Harrisville Squire's Inn .... (603)827-3925

Haverhill
Haverhill Inn .... (603)989-5961
Westgate House .... (603)989-3311

Henniker
Henniker House .... (603)428-3198

Hill
Snowbound .... (603)744-9112

Hillsborough
Stonebridge Inn .... (603)464-3155

Holderness
Chase Mary Inn Bed & Breakfast . (603)968-9454
Curmudg Inn .... (603)968-4417
Manor on Golden Pond .... (603)968-3348

Hopkinton
The Country Porch B&B .... (603)746-6391
Windyledge B&B .... (603)746-4054

Intervale
New England Inn .... (603)356-5541
Old Field House .... (603)356-5478
Riverside, An Elegant Country Inn (603)356-9060

Jackson
Blake House .... (603)383-9057
Carter Notch Inn . (603)383-9630 (810)794-9434
Christmas Farm Inn .... (603)383-4313
Jackson House B&B
.... (603)383-4226 (800)338-1268
Paisley & Parsley B&B .... (603)383-0859
Wildcat Inn .... (603)383-4245

Jaffrey
B&B on Board .... (603)532-8083
Galway House B&B .... (603)532-8083
Gould Farm .... (603)532-6996
Lilac Hill Farm .... (603)532-7278
Jaffrey Manor Inn .... (603)532-8555
Mill Pond Inn .... (603)532-7687

Jaffrey Center
Monadnock Inn .... (603)532-7001

Jefferson
Swag Hollow Inn .... (603)586-4598

Kearsarge
Isaac Merrill House Inn
.... (603)356-9041 (800)328-9041

Keene
289 Court .... (603)357-3195
Carriage Barn Guest-House .... (603)357-3812

Laconia
Ferry Point House .... (603)524-0087
Kings Grant Inn .... (603)293-4431
Tin Whistle Inn .... (603)527-1010

Lancaster
White House Bed & Breakfast & Cabins
.... (603)788-4090

Lebanon
Bed & Breakfast of Bank St ..... (603)448-2041

Lincoln
Red Sleigh Inn .... (603)745-8517

Lisbon
Ammonoosuc Inn .... (603)838-6118

Littleton
1895 House .... (603)444-5200
Ravens Inn Inc .... (603)444-1348
Thayers Inn .... (603)444-6469

Loudon
Lovejoy Farm B&B .... (603)783-4007

Lyme
Alden Country Inn (603)795-2222 (800)794-2296
The Dowds' Country Inn .... (603)795-4712
Loch Lyme Lodge .... (603)795-2141
Lyme Inn .... (603)795-2222

Madison
Madison Carriage House ...... (603)367-4605
Maple Grove House .... (603)367-8208
Snowvillage Inn . (603)447-2818 (800)447-4345

Meredith
The Inn at Mill Falls .... (603)279-7006
New Hampshire Bed & Breakfast . (603)279-8348
The Nutmeg Inn .... (603)279-8811
The Tuckernuck Inn .... (603)279-5521

Milford
Ram In The Thicket .... (603)654-6440
Zahn's Alpine Guesthouse. ..... (603)673-2334

Mont Vernon
Zahns Alpine Guest House ..... (603)673-2334

Mount Sunapee
Blue Goose Inn .... (603)763-5519

New Boston
Colburn Homestead Bed & Breakfast & Gift
.... (603)487-5250

New Castle
Great Islander Bed & Breakfast .. (603)436-8536

New Ipswich
The Inn at New Ipswich .... (603)878-3711

New London
Colonial Farm Inn (603)526-6121 (800)805-8504
Hide-Away Inn .. (603)526-4861 (800)457-0589
Maple Hill Farm .... (603)526-2248
New London Inn .... (603)526-2791

Newport
Backside Inn .... (603)863-5161
The Eagle Inn at Coit Mountain
.... (603)863-3583 (800)367-2364

North Conway
1768 Country Inn (603)356-3836 (800)639-6572
By The Brook Inn .... (603)356-2874
Cabernet Inn, "A Vintage B&B"
.... (603)356-4704 (800)866-4704
Center Chimney - 1787 .... (603)356-6788
Country Inns In The White Mountains
.... (603)356-9460
Eastman Inn .... (800)626-5855 (800)626-5855
The Farm By The River B&B .... (603)356-2694
Old Red Inn & Cottages
.... (603)356-2642 (800)338-1356
Recompense Bed & Breakfast ... (603)356-5276
Scottish Lion Inn .... (603)356-6381
Sunny Side Inn .... (603)356-6239
Victorian Harvest Inn
.... (603)356-3548 (800)642-0749
Wildflowers Guest House ...... (603)356-2224
Wyatt House Country Inn
.... (603)356-7977 (800)527-7978

North Sutton
Follansbee Inn .... (603)927-4221
Village House at Sutton Mills .... (603)927-4765

North Woodstock
The Birches B&B .... (603)745-6603
Cascade Lodge .... (603)745-2722
Rivers Edge Bed & Breakfast ... (603)745-2208
Wilderness Inn .... (603)745-3890
Woodstock Inn .... (603)745-3951

Northwood
Aviary .... (603)942-7755
Lake Shore Farm .... (603)942-5921
Meadow Farm B&B .... (603)942-8619
Nostalgia B&B .... (603)942-7748
Orford
White Goose Inn . (603)353-4812 (800)358-4267
Ossipee
Acorn Lodge .... (603)539-2151
West Ossipee House .... (603)539-2874
Peterborough
Apple Gate B&B .... (603)924-6543
Peterborough Manor .... (603)924-8304
Piermont
Piermont Inn .... (603)272-4820
Pittsfield
Appleview Bed & Breakfast ..... (603)435-7641
Dame Homestead .... (603)798-5446
Plymouth
Crab Apple Inn .... (603)536-4476
Northway House .... (603)536-3438
Portsmouth
Theatre Inn .... (603)431-7760
The Inn at Christian Shore ...... (603)431-6770
Governor's House B&B .... (603)431-6546
Leighton Inn .... (603)433-2188
Martin Hill Inn .... (603)436-2287
Meadowbrook Inn (603)436-2700 (800)370-2727
Oracle House Inn .... (603)433-8827
Sise Inn .... (603)433-1200
The Inn at Strawbery Banke .... (603)436-7242
Rindge
Grassy Pond House .... (603)899-5166
Rochester
Governor's Inn .... (603)332-0107
Rye
The Cable House .... (603)964-5000
Rock Ledge Manor B&B .... (603)431-1413
Shelburne
Philbrook Farm Inn .... (603)466-3831
Lake Spofford
Tower Light Inn .... (603)363-8154
Stark
Stark Village Inn .... (603)636-2644
Strafford
Province Inn .... (603)664-2457
Stratham
Maple Lodge B&B .... (603)778-9833
Stratham Hill Farm .... (603)772-3999
Sugar Hill
Foxglove, A Country Inn .... (603)823-8840
The Inn at Skunk Hollow .... (603)823-8532
Sunapee
Dexter's Inn .... (603)763-5571 (800)232-5571
Old Governor's House .... (603)763-9918
Seven Hearths Inn .... (603)763-5657
The Inn at Sunapee
.... (603)763-4444 (800)327-2466
Suncook
Suncook House .... (603)485-8141
Tamworth
Highland House .... (603)323-7982
Red Horse Hill Farm .... (603)323-7275
Tamworth Inn ... (603)323-7721 (800)642-7352
Whispering Pines B&B .... (603)323-7337
Temple
Birchwood Inn .... (603)878-3285
Tilton
The Black Swan Inn .... (603)286-4524
Country Place .... (603)286-8551
Troy
The Inn at East Hill Farm
.... (603)242-6495 (800)242-6495
Twin Mountain
Fieldstone Country Inn .... (603)846-5646
Walpole
The Josiah Bellows House ..... (603)756-4250
Warner
Jacob's Ladder B&B .... (603)456-3494
Warren
The Black Iris B&B .... (603)764-9366
Waterville Valley
Silver Squirrel Inn .... (603)236-8325
Snowy Owl Inn .... (603)236-8383

Weare
Weare-House B & B .... (603)529-2660
Wentworth
Hilltop Acres .... (603)764-5896
Hobson House .... (603)764-9460
Wentworth Inn & Art Gallery .... (603)764-9923
West Chesterfield
Chesterfield Inn .... (603)256-3211
West Ossipee
Phoenix .... (603)539-2874
West Springfield
Wonderwell .... (603)763-5065
Whitefield
The 1875 Mountain Inn .... (603)837-2220
General Lagayette Country Inn .. (603)837-9300
Kimball Hill Inn .... (603)837-2284
Maxwell Haus .... (603)837-9717
Winnisquam
Tall Pines Inn .... (603)528-3632
Wolfeboro
Brook & Bridle Inn .... (603)569-2707
Tuc' Me Inn B&B .... (603)569-5702
The Wolfeboro Inn .... (603)569-3016

New Jersey

Alloway
Josiah Reeve House .... (609)935-5640
Andover
Crossed Keys .... (201)786-6661
Hudson Guide Farm .... (201)398-2679
Asbury Park
Hermitage Guest House B&B ... (908)776-6665
Avalon
Sealark B&B .... (609)967-5647
Avon
Avon-By The-Sea Bed & Breakfast Inns (908)774-8444
Avon By The Sea
The Avon Manor B&B Inn ...... (908)774-0110
Cashelmara Inn .... (908)776-8727
Ocean Mist Guest House ...... (908)775-9625
The Sands B&B Inn .... (908)776-8386
The Summer House .... (908)775-3992
Victoria Hotel .... (908)988-9798
Barnegat
The Dynasty .... (609)698-1566
Bay Head
Bay Head Gables .... (908)892-9844
Bay Head Harbor Inn .... (908)899-0767
Bay Head Sands .... (908)899-7016
Bentley Inn .... (908)892-9589
Conover's Bay Head Inn .... (908)892-4664
Grandville Hotel & Resturant .... (908)892-3100
Beach Haven
Amber Street Inn .... (609)492-1611
Barque .... (609)492-5216
Magnolia House .... (609)492-2226
Pierrot By The Sea .... (609)492-4424
Victoria Guest House .... (609)492-4154
Belmar
Carols Guest House .... (908)681-9671
House By The Sea .... (908)681-8386
The Seaflower B&B .... (908)681-6006
The Inn at The Shore .... (908)681-3762
Bernardsville
Bernards Inn .... (908)766-0002
Bradley Beach
Bradley Inn .... (908)774-7000
Bridgeton
Bacon's Grant .... (609)453-9537
Cape May
The Inn at 22 Jackson
.... (609)884-2226 (800)452-8177
Abigail Adams B&B .... (609)884-1371
Albert G. Stevens Inn
.... (609)884-4717 (800)890-2287
Angel of The Sea .... (609)884-3369
Annabel Lee Guest House ...... (609)898-1109
Belvidere Guest House .... (609)884-8713
Buttonwood Manor .... (609)884-4070
Cliveden Inn .... (609)884-4516
Colvmns By The Sea .... (609)884-2228
Delsea .... (609)884-8540
Fairthorne B&B . (609)884-8791 (800)438-8742
Frog Hollow Inn .... (609)884-1426

Heather Inn .... (609)884-5329
Holly House .... (609)884-7365
Jeremiah Hand Guest House .... (609)884-1135
John F. Craig House .... (609)884-0100
Kelly's Celtic Inn .... (609)898-1999
Leith Hall Historic Seashore Inn .. (609)884-1934
The Manor House .... (609)884-4710
Manse Inn .... (609)884-0116
The Mason Cottage
.... (609)884-3358 (800)716-2766
Mayors Hearth .... (609)898-0017
The Mission Inn . (609)884-8380 (800)800-8380
Mooring .... (609)884-5425
Open Hearth Inn .... (609)884-4933
Peter Shields Inn .... (609)884-9090
Pharos Guest House .... (609)884-9380
The Primrose B&B .... (609)884-8288
The Prince Edward .... (609)884-2131
Rhythm of The Sea
.... (609)884-7788 (800)498-6888
Saltwood House .... (609)884-6754
Sand Castle Guest House ...... (609)884-5451
Sevilla .... (609)884-4530
Springside .... (609)884-2654
Summer Cottage Inn .... (609)884-4948
Twin Gables .... (609)884-7332
Victorian Lace Inn .... (609)884-1772
Brass Bed Inn .... (609)884-8075
White House Inn .... (609)884-5329
Wilbraham Mansion .... (609)884-2046
The Wooden Rabbit .... (609)884-7293
Woodleigh House (609)884-7123 (800)399-7123
Cape May Courthouse
Doctors Inn .... (609)463-9330
Chatham
Parrot Mill Inn .... (201)635-7722
Chester
Publick House Inn .... (201)879-6878
Closter
Crown Point B&B .... (201)768-4008
Dover
Silver Lining B&B .... (201)361-9245
Franklin
Sullivans Gas Light Inn .... (201)209-9723
Fredon
Natalie's Country Inn .... (201)383-9577
Frenchtown
The Hunterdon House .... (908)996-3632
National Hotel .... (201)996-4871
Haddonfield
Queen Anne Inn .... (609)428-2195
Highlands
Seabird Inn .... (908)872-0123
Seascape Manor .... (908)291-8467
Hope
Millers Cottage at Sunrise Farms . (908)459-5622
Island Heights
Studio of John F. Peto .... (908)270-6058
Lambertville
Bridge Street House .... (609)397-2503
Coryell House .... (609)397-8292
Inn of The Hawke .... (609)397-9555
York Street House .... (609)397-3007
Long Valley
Neighbor House .... (908)876-3519
Longport
Winchester House .... (609)822-0623
Lyndhurst
The Jeremiah J. Yereance House . (201)438-9457
Manahawkin
Goose N. Berry Inn .... (609)597-6350
Mays Landing
Abbott House .... (609)625-4400
The Inn at Sugar Hill .... (609)625-2226
Medford
Main Stay Bed & Breakfast ..... (609)654-7528
Milford
Chesnut Hill .... (201)995-9761
Millville
Country Inn .... (800)456-4000
Montclair
The Marlboro Inn .... (201)783-5300
Ocean City
Barnagate B&B .... (609)391-9366
Beach End Inn B&B .... (609)398-1016
Beachfront Bed & Breakfast .... (609)399-0477

Bradbury's . . . . (609)398-1008
Bryn Mawr B & B . . . . (609)399-8744
Delancy Manor . . . . (609)398-9831
Ebbie Guest & Apartment House . (609)399-4744
The Enterprise B&B . . . . (609)398-1698
Laurel Hall . . . . (609)399-0800
Manor The Guests . . . . (609)399-4509
Mayfair Guest House . . . . (609)399-2728
New Brighton Inn . . . . (609)399-2829
Seahorse Bed & Breakfast . . . . . (609)398-4889
Susanne's Victorian Summer Cottages . . . . (609)399-9550
Terrace The Rooming House . . . . (609)399-4246
Top O' the Waves . . . . (609)399-0477

Ocean Grove

Carol Inn . . . . (908)502-0303
House By The Sea . . . . (908)774-9639
Keswick Inn . . . . (908)877-7506
The Manchester Inn B&B . . . . . . (908)775-0616
Ocean Park Inn Bed & Breakfast . (908)988-5283
Ocean Plaza . . . . (908)774-6552
Park View Inn . . . . (908)775-1645
Pine Tree Inn . . . . (908)775-3264

Pittstown

Seven Springs Farm B&B . . . . . . (908)735-7675

Point Pleasant

Steepleview B & B Cottage . . . . . (908)899-8999

Point Pleasant Beach

Gull Point . . . . (908)899-2876
Pier House Guests . . . . (908)295-0180

Princeton

Bed & Breakfast of Princeton . . . (609)924-3189
Peacock Inn . . . . (609)924-1707

Red Bank

Shaloum Guest House . . . . (201)530-7759

Salem

Ma' Bowman's B&B . . . . (609)935-4913
Woodnutt House . . . . (609)935-4175

Sea Girt

Beacon House . . . . (908)449-5835
Holly Harbor Guest House . . . . . (908)974-8389

Sea Isle City

The Colonnade Inn . . . . (609)263-0460

Spring Lake

Carriage House . . . . (908)449-1332
Classic Inns of The Garden Coast (908)449-9799
Hamilton House Inn . . . . (908)449-8282
The Hewitt-Wellington Hotel . . . . (908)974-1212
Hollycroft B&B . . . . (908)681-2254
Johnson House . . . . (908)449-1860
Kenilworth . . . . (908)449-5327
Lauberge Chalakani . . . . (908)449-9019
The Moulton House . . . . (908)449-5177
The Normandy Inn . . . . (908)449-7172
Sea Crest By The Sea . . . . (908)449-9031
Spring Lake Hotel . . . . (908)449-2010
Villa Park . . . . (908)449-9698
Walden on The Pond . . . . (908)449-7764
Warren Hotel . . . . (908)449-8800
White Lilac Inn . . . . (908)449-0211

Stewartsville

Stewart Inn . . . . (908)479-6060

Stockton

The Stockton Inn, Colligan's . . . . (609)397-1250

Stone Harbor

Holiday Manor Guest House . . . . (609)368-1133

Upper Greenwood Lake

Willow Brook Inn . . . . (201)853-7728

Whitehouse Station

Holly Thorn House . . . . (908)534-1616

Wildwood

Angelas Place Inc . . . . (609)729-2631
Beach House . . . . (609)729-1800
Craig House . . . . (609)522-8140
Highland House . . . . (609)898-1198
Moffitt House . . . . (609)898-0915
Stuarts Once Upon A Time Bed & Breakfast . . . . (609)523-1101

Wildwood Crest

Mount Vernon Hotel . . . . (609)522-7010

New Mexico

Albuquerque

Adobe and Roses B&B . . . . (505)898-0654
Casa De Granjero (505)897-4144 (800)701-4144
Casas De Suenos Old Town B&B Inn . . . . (505)247-4560
Casita Chamisa . . . . (505)897-4644
Las Palomas Inn (505)345-7228 (800)909-3683
The Inn at Paradise . . . . (505)898-6161
Sarabande . . . . (505)345-4923
W.E. Mauger Estate . . . . (505)242-8755
The Windmill Ranch . . . . (505)898-6864

Alto

Sierra Mesa Lodge . . . . (505)336-4515

Angel Fire

The Inn at Angel Fire . . . . (800)666-1949

Artesia

Heritage Inn . . . . (505)748-2552

Canoncito

Apache Canyon Ranch B&B Inn . (505)836-7220

Capitan

La Pobiana . . . . (505)354-2583

Chama

Corkins Lodge . . . . (505)588-7261
Enchanted Deer Haven B&B . . . . (505)588-7535
Jones House B&B . . . . (505)756-2908

Chimayo

Casa Escondida . . . . (505)351-4805
Hacienda Rancho De Chimayo . . (505)351-2222
La Posada De Chimayo . . . . (505)351-4605

Cimarron

St. James Hotel . . . . (505)376-2664

Cloudcroft

The Lodge at Cloudcroft . . . . (505)682-2566

Continental Divide

Stauder's Navajo Lodge . . . . (505)862-7553

Corrales

Casa La Resolana (505)898-0203 (800)884-0203
Corrales Inn B&B . . . . (505)897-4422
Sandhill Crane B&B . . . . (505)898-2445 (800)375-2445

Costilla

Costilla B&B . . . . (505)586-1683

Espanola

Casa Del Rio . . . . (505)753-2035
La Puebla House . . . . (505)753-3981

Estancia

The Roundhouse . . . . (505)384-5370

Glenwood

Los Olmos Guest Ranch . . . . (505)539-2311

Hillsboro

The Enchanted Villa . . . . (505)895-5686

Jemez Springs

Jemez River B&B Inn . . . . (505)829-3262

Kingston

The Black Range Lodge . . . . (505)895-5652

Las Cruces

Hilltop Hacienda . . . . (505)382-3556
Lundeen Inn of The Arts . . . . (505)526-3326
Trh Smith Mansion B&B . . . . (505)524-8227

Las Vegas

Carriage House B&B . . . . (505)454-1784

Lincoln

Wortley Hotel (Country Inn) . . . . (505)653-4500

Los Alamos

Casa Del Rey . . . . (505)672-9401
Orange Street Inn . . . . (505)662-2651

Los Ojos

Casa De Martinez . . . . (505)588-7858

Nogal

Monjeau Shadows Inn . . . . (505)336-4191

Ojo Caliente

The Inn & Mercantile at Ojo . . . . (505)583-9131

Placitas

Hacienda De Placitas . . . . (505)867-3775

Portales

Morning Star Inn . . . . (505)356-2994

Ramah

The Vogt Ranch B&B . . . . (505)783-4362

Ranchos De Taos

Adobe & Pines Inn . . . . (505)751-0947
Don Pascual Martinez B&B . . . . . (505)758-7364
Ranchos Ritz B&B . . . . (505)758-2640

Raton

Red Violet Inn . . (505)445-9778 (800)624-9778

Red River

El Western Lodge . . . . (505)754-2272

San Juan Pueblo

Chinguague Compound . . . . (505)852-2194

Santa Fe

Adobe Abode . . . . (505)983-3133
Adobe Guest House . . . . (505)983-9481
The Inn on Alameda . . . . (505)984-2121 (800)289-2122
Arius Compound . . . . (505)982-8859
Dancing Ground/Sun . . . . (505)986-9797
Don Gaspar Compound . . . . (505)986-8664
Dos Casas Viejas . . . . (509)831-636-
Four Kachinas Inn (505)982-2550 (800)397-2564
Grant Corner Inn . . . . (505)983-6678
Hotel St. Francis . . . . (505)983-5700
Inn of The Animal Tracks . . . . . . (505)988-1546
Jean's Place . . . . (505)471-4053
La Posada De Santa Fe . . . . (800)621-7231
Open Sky . . . . (505)471-3475
Preston House . . . . (505)982-3465
Rancho Encantado . . . . (505)982-3537
Sunset House . . . . (505)983-3523
The Inn at The The Anasazi . . . . . (505)988-3030
Triangle Inn-Santa Fe . . . . (505)455-3375
Water Street Inn . . . . (505)984-1193

Taos

American Artists Gallery House . . (505)758-4446
Brooks Street Inn . . . . (505)898-7027
Casa Benavides . . . . (505)758-1772
Casa De Las Chimeneas . . . . (505)758-4777
Casa Encantada . (505)758-7477 (800)223-TAOS
Casa Feliz . . . . (505)758-9790
Dasburg House & Studio . . . . . . (505)758-9513
El Rincon . . . . (505)758-4874
Gallery House West . . . . (505)758-8001
Harrison's B&B . . . . (505)758-2630
The Suite Retreat . . . . (505)758-3960
Taos Country Inn . . . . (505)758-4900
Taos Hacienda Inn . . . . (505)758-1717
The Taos Inn . . . (505)758-2233 (800)826-7466

Taos Ski Valley

Amizette Inn . . . . (505)265-6777

Truchas

Rancho Arriba B&B . . . . (505)689-2374

New York

Acra

Mountain View Bed & Breakfast . (518)622-2300

Adams Basin

Canalside Inn . . . . (716)352-6784

Addison

Mose Country Home . . . . (607)359-3903

Afton

Jericho Farm Inn . . . . (607)639-1842

Albany

Mansion Hill Inn . . . . (518)465-2038
State Street Mansion Bed & . . . . (518)462-6780

Alexandria Bay

Bach's Alexandria Bay Inn . . . . . (315)482-9697

Alpine

Fontainebleau . . . . (607)594-2008

Altamont

Appel Inn . . . . (518)861-6557

Amagansett

Amagansett House Bed & Breakfa (516)267-3808
Bluff Cottage . . . . (516)267-6172

Amenia

Hilltop Bed & Breakfast . . . . (914)373-9568

Andes

Open Studios Bed & Breakfast . . (914)676-3538

Angelica

Angelicas Guest House . . . . (716)466-3706

Ashland

Ashland Farmhouse B&B . . . . . . (518)734-3358
Country Suite Bed & Breakfast . . (518)734-4079

Ashville

Chestnut Hill on The Lake . . . . . . (716)789-5371

Athens

Stewart House . . . . (518)945-1357

Auburn

Springside Inn . . . . (315)252-7247

Aurora

Aurora Inn . . . . (315)364-8888

Austerlitz

Harvey Mountain Inn . . . . (518)392-7094
Twenty-Two Green River . . . . (518)392-6676

Avoca

Patchwork Peace B&B . . . . (607)566-2443

Avon
Charlton Bed & Breakfast Inn . . . (716)226-2838
Mulligan Farm . . . (716)226-3780

Bainbridge
Berry Hill Farm B&B
. . . (607)967-8745 (800)497-8745

Baldwinsville
Pandora's Getaway . . . (315)635-9571

Barneveld
Sugarbush B&B . . . (315)896-6860

Barryville
All Breeze Guest Farm . . . (914)557-6485

Bath
Wheeler B&B . . . (607)776-6756

Beaver Falls
Beaver Inn . . . (315)346-6301

Belfast
Belfast Bed & Breakfast . . . (716)365-2692

Bellport
Great South Bay Inn . . . (516)286-8588

Bemus Point
Bemus Point Lakeside Cottages . (716)386-2535

Berkshire
Kinship B&B . . . (607)657-4455 (800)493-2337

Berlin
Sedgwick Inn . . . (518)658-2334

Binghamton
Pickle Hill B&B . . . (607)723-0259
South Mountain Bed & Breakfast . (607)723-0149

Blue Mountain Lake
Blue Mountain Lake Inn . . . (518)352-7600

Bolton Landing
Hilltop Cottage B&B . . . (518)644-2492

Branchport
Four Seasons B&B . . . (607)732-5581

Brant Lake
Tumble Brook Farm . . . (518)494-3020

Bridgewater
The White House Berries Inn . . . (315)822-6558

Brockport
Bed & Breakfast at The White Farm (716)637-0459
Clarkson Corners Bed & Breakfast (716)637-0340
The Portico B&B . . . (716)637-0220
The Victorian B&B (716)637-7519 (800)836-1929

Brookfield
Bivona Hill Bed and Breakfast . . . (315)899-8921
Gates Hill Homestead . . . (315)899-5837

Brooklyn
Brooklyn B&B . . . (718)383-3026

Brooktondale
Dutch Touch B&B . . . (607)539-7091

Buffalo
Beau Fleuve B&B Inn . . . (716)882-6116
Bryant House . . . (716)885-1540
Rainbow Hospitality Bed & Breakfast
. . . (716)873-4262
Warnick's Village B&B . . . (716)875-5860

Burdett
Country Gardens . . . (607)546-2272
The Red House Country Inn . . . (607)546-8566

Cadyville
Martins' B&B . . . (518)293-7006

Callicoon
Tonjes Farm B&B . . . (914)482-5357

Cambridge
Maple Ridge Inn . . . (518)677-3674

Camillus
Green Gate Inn . . . (315)672-9276
The Re Family B&B . . . (315)468-2039

Canaan
Inn at Silver Maple Farm . . . (518)781-3600
The Inn at Shaker Mill Farm . . . (518)794-9345
Woodbine . . . (518)781-4748

Canandaigua
Clawson's B&B . . . (716)396-1947
Cricket Club Tearoom . . . (716)229-5343
Finagan's Llama Farm B&B . . . (716)394-1603
Habersham Country Inn . . . (716)394-1510
Nottingham Lodge B&B . . . (716)374-5355
Oliver Phelps Country Inn . . . (716)396-1650

Canaseraga
The Country House . . . (607)545-6439

Canastota
Goldie Days Bed & Breakfast . . . (315)697-3802

Candor
The Edge of Thyme, A B&B Inn
. . . (607)659-5155 (800)722-7365

Caroga Lake
Nick Stoner Inn . . . (518)835-8000

Castile
Glen Iris Inn . . . (716)493-2622
Meadowood Acres . . . (716)493-2940

Catskill
Friar Tuck Inn . . . (518)678-2271

Cazenovia
Brae Loch Inn . . . (315)655-3431
Country Bumpkin . . . (315)655-8084
Lincklaen House . . . (315)655-3461

Central Valley
Gasho Inn . . . (914)928-2277

Chappaqua
Crabtree's Kittle House . . . (914)666-8044

Chateaugay
Banner House . . . (518)425-3566

Chatham
Rosehill Bed & Breakfast . . . (518)392-3060
Wolfe's Inn Bed & Breakfast . . . (518)392-5218

Chautauqua
Longfellow Inn . . . (716)357-2285

Chazy
Grand-Vue B&B . . . (518)298-5700

Cherry Creek
Cherry Creek Inn . . . (716)296-8957

Chestertown
Balsam House Inn (518)494-2828 (800)441-6856
Chester Inn . . . (518)494-4148
Landon Hill Bed & Breakfast . . . (518)494-2599

Clarence
Coventry Tea Room . . . (716)759-8101
Village Haven Motel . . . (716)759-6845

Claverack
Berl Soll . . . (518)851-5405

Clayton
Thousand Islands Inn . . . (315)686-3030

Clinton
Hedges . . . (315)859-5909

Clinton Corners
Center at High Valley . . . (914)266-2309

Cobleskill
The Gables . . . (315)733-0040 (800)941-2337

Cohocton
Button's Creekside Farm B&B . . . (607)566-2406

Cohoes
Century House Inn & Conference Center
. . . (518)785-0931

Cold Spring
One Market Street . . . (914)265-3912
Pig Hill . . . (914)265-9247
Village Victorian . . . (914)265-9159

Cold Spring Harbor
Swan View Manor . . . (516)367-2070

Colden
Back of The Beyond . . . (716)652-0427

Conesus
Bluestone B&B . . . (716)346-6929
Conesus Lake B&B . . . (716)346-6526

Cooperstown
Adalaide Bed & Breakfast . . . (607)547-1215
Angelholm . . . (607)547-2483
Bassett House Inn . . . (607)547-7001
The Inn at Brook Willow Farm . . . (607)547-9700
Brown-Williams House . . . (607)547-5569
Otesaga Hotel . . . (607)547-2567
Creekside B&B . . . (607)547-8203
Hickory Grove Inn . . . (607)547-8100
The J. P. Sillhouse . . . (607)547-2633
Jones House . . . (607)547-5547
Litco Farms B&B . . . (607)547-2501
Main Street Bed & Breakfast . . . (607)547-9755
Moon Dreams . . . (607)547-9432
Overlook Bed & Breakfast . . . (607)547-2019
Thistlebrook . . . (607)547-6093
Tunnicliff Inn . . . (607)547-9611

Corfu
Hens Nest . . . (716)599-6417

Corinth
The Inn at The Edge of The Forest
. . . (518)654-6656 (800)654-3343

Corning
1865 White Birch B&B . . . (607)962-6355
Delevan House . . . (607)962-2347
Rosewood Inn . . . (607)962-3253
Victoria House . . . (607)962-3413

Croton Hudson
Alexander Hamilton House . . . (914)271-6737

Cuba
33 South B&B . . . (716)968-1387
Rocking Duck Inn . . . (716)968-3335

Deposit
Alexander's Inn . . . (607)467-6023
The White Pillars Inn . . . (607)467-4191

Dover Plains
Old Drovers Inn . . . (914)832-9311

Downsville
Adams Farm House B & B . . . (607)363-2757
Juniper Hill . . . (607)363-7647
The Victoria Rose B&B . . . (607)363-7838

Dryden
Sarah's Dream Village Inn . . . (607)844-4321
Serendipity B&B . . . (607)844-9589
Spruce Haven . . . (607)844-8052

Dundee
The 1819 Red Brick Inn . . . (607)243-8844
South Glenora Tree Farm B&B . . . (607)243-7414
Willow Cove . . . (607)243-8482

Durhamville
Towering Maples Bed & Breakfast (315)363-9007

Eagle Bay
Big Moose . . . (315)357-2042

East Aurora
Green Glen . . . (716)652-1394
Shepherd Hill Farm Bed & Breakfast
. . . (716)652-3452

East Chatham
Milk & Honey B & B . . . (518)392-7594

East Durham
Carriage House B&B . . . (518)634-2284
Gavin's Golden Hill House . . . (518)634-2582
Golden Harvest B&B . . . (518)634-2305
Kennedy's B&B . . . (518)622-2075

East Hampton
132 North Main . . . (516)324-9771
1770 House . . . (516)324-1770
Centennial House . . . (516)324-9414
Hedges House . . . (516)324-7100
Huntting Inn . . . (516)324-0410
Maidstone Arms . . . (516)324-5006
The Pink House . . . (516)324-3400

East Rochester
Acorn Inn . . . (716)586-4720

Eden
Eden Inn Bed & Breakfast . . . (716)992-2624

Edmeston
Owls Nest Inn . . . (607)965-8720

Elizabethtown
Old Mill Studio . . . (518)873-2294
Stoneleigh Bed & Breakfast . . . (518)873-2669

Elka Park
The Cottage B&B . . . (518)589-6496
The Redcoat's Return . . . (518)589-9858

Ellenburg Depot
The McGregor House B&B . . . (518)594-7673

Ellicottville
The Jefferson Inn of Ellicottville . . (716)699-5869

Elmira
Strathmont . . . (607)733-1046

Essex
Blockhouse Farm B&B . . . (518)963-8648
Cabins By The Lake . . . (518)963-7374
Essex House B&B . . . (518)963-7739
The Essex Inn . . . (518)963-8821
Little Brick House . . . (518)963-4199
The Stone House . . . (518)963-7713
Sunburst Tea Garden B&B . . . (518)963-7482

Fair Haven
Brown's Village Inn B&B . . . (315)947-5817
Frost Haven B&B Inn . . . (315)947-5331
Pleasant Beach Inn . . . (315)947-5592
Whispering Pines Inn Bed & Breakfast
. . . (315)947-6666

Fairport
Bed & Breakfast at Woods Edge . (716)223-8877

Fayetteville
Beard Morgan House B&B . . . (315)448-0088

Collin House A Bed & Breakfast . (315)637-4671
Craftsman Inn .... (315)637-8000

Ferndale

Country Inn B&B .... (914)292-6993

Fleischmanns

Highland Fling Inn .... (914)254-5650

Fly Creek

Breezy Knoll .... (607)547-8362

Franklin

Magnolia Guest House .... (607)829-3102

Fredonia

The White Inn .... (716)672-2103

Freehold

Olde Country Inn .... (518)634-7636

Freeville

Lopinto Farm Lodge
.... (607)347-6556 (800)551-5806

Fulton

Aunt T's B&B .... (315)592-2425
Doney's Bed & Breakfast ...... (315)593-7419

Gardiner

Schaibles Serendipity Bed & Breakfast
.... (914)255-5667

Garrison

The Golden Eagle Inn .... (914)424-3067

Geneseo

Macphail House Bed & Breakfast (716)346-5600
Oak Valley Inn .... (716)243-5570
Some Place Else .... (716)243-9440

Geneva

The Inn at Belhurst Castle ...... (315)781-0201
The Cobblestones .... (315)789-1896
Virginia Deane's B&B .... (315)789-6152

Germantown

Fox Run Bed & Breakfast ...... (518)537-6945

Gilbertsville

Leatherstocking Trails .... (607)783-2757

Gilboa

Windy Ridge B&B .... (607)588-6039

Glen Wild

M&M's Country House .... (914)434-2716

Glenfield

Keystone Manor .... (315)376-8326

Goshen

Anthony Dobbins Stage Coach Inn (914)294-5526

Gowanda

The Teepee .... (716)532-2168

Great Bend

Grand View Bed & Breakfast .... (315)493-1089

Greenhurst

Sheldon Hall Bed & Breakfast ... (716)664-4691
Spindletop B&B .... (716)484-2070

Greenport

Fordham House Bed & Breakfast . (516)477-8419
Watsons By The Bay Bed & Breakfast
.... (516)477-0426
White Lions B&B .... (516)477-8819

Greenville

The Homestead Victorian B&B .. (518)966-4474

Groton

Austin Manor .... (607)898-5786
Benn Conger Inn .... (607)898-5817

Guilford

Tea & Sympathy Bed & Breakfast (607)895-6874

Hadley

Saratoga Rose .. (518)696-2861 (800)942-5025

Hague

Locust Inn .... (518)543-6035

Haines Falls

Brookside B&B .... (518)589-6548
Settle Inn .... (518)589-7140

Halcottsville

Lake Wawaka Guest House ..... (607)326-4694

Hamden

Bella Vista Ridge B&B .... (607)746-2553

Hammondsport

Another Tyme B&B .... (607)569-2747
Blushing Rose B&B .... (607)569-3483
The Bowman House .... (607)569-2516
Bully Hill B&B .... (607)868-3226
Cedar Beach B&B .... (607)868-3228
Country Barn B&B .... (607)292-3559
J.S. Hubbs B&B .... (607)569-2440
Laufersweiler .... (607)569-3402
Park Inn Hotel .... (607)569-9387

Hampton Bays

Castaways Cottage Garden ..... (516)728-3769
House on The Water .... (516)728-3560

Hancock

Cranberry Inn .... (607)637-2788
Silver Lake Lodge .... (607)467-5390

Hannibal

Stone Manor Inn Bed & Breakfast (315)564-5850

Hector

Peach Orchard Bed & Breakfast . (607)546-2593
Seneca Springs .... (607)546-4066

Hempstead

Tara Ii B&B .... (516)292-0332

Henderson

Dobson House Bed & Breakfast . (315)938-5901

Hensonville

Point Lookout Mountain Inn .... (518)734-3381

Herkimer

Bellinger Woods .... (315)866-2770

High Falls

Captain Schoonmaker's House .. (914)687-7946
House on The Hill .... (914)687-9627
Locktender Cottage .... (914)687-7700

Hillsdale

Creek at Hillsdale .... (518)325-6334
The Inn at Green River .... (518)325-7248
Linden Valley .... (518)325-7100

Homer

David Harum House .... (607)749-3548

Honeoye

Aubins Lodgings In The Pines ... (716)367-3774
The Greenwoods B&B Inn ...... (716)229-2111

Hopewell Junction

Bykenhulle House .... (914)226-3039
Le Chambord Inn .... (914)221-1941

Houghton

Inn at Houghton Creek .... (716)567-8400

Hudson

Hudson House B&B .... (518)828-1942
Inn at Blue Stores .... (518)537-4277

Hunter

Dew Drop Inn B&B .... (518)263-4189
Fitch House B&B .... (518)263-5032
Gannon's Inn .... (518)263-4860
Sedgwick House .... (518)263-3871
Washington Irving Lodge ...... (518)589-5560
The Xenia .... (518)263-4700

Hurleyville

Whispering Spruce .... (914)434-7899

Hyde Park

Fala B&B .... (914)229-5937

Inlet

Cinnamon Bear Bed & Breakfast . (315)357-6013

Interlaken

Silver Strand .... (607)532-9595

Irvington on Hudson

Shadowbrook B&B .... (914)591-9291

Ithaca

Bed & Breakfast at The Foot Of .. (607)272-6767
Buttermilk Falls B&B .... (607)272-6767
Hound & Hare .... (607)257-2821
Lily Hill .... (607)273-7128
Mac Intire's Cottage .... (607)273-8888
The Peirce House B&B .... (607)273-0824
Peregrine House .... (607)272-0919
Rita's Country B&B .... (607)257-2499
Thomas Farm .... (607)539-7477

Jacksonville

Pleasant Grove .... (607)387-5420

Jamesville

High Meadows B&B .... (315)492-3517

Jeffersonville

The Griffin House .... (914)482-3371

Johnstown

Home Again Bed and Breakfast .. (518)736-4663
Knox Mansion Bed & Breakfast .. (518)762-5669

Keeseville

Bosworth Tavern .... (518)834-5401

Kent

Ward's Farm House .... (716)682-3037

Kinderhook

Kinderhook Bed & Breakfast .... (518)758-1850

Kingston

Cordts Mansion Bed & Breakfast . (914)331-3921
Miss Gussie Bugs .... (914)334-9110
Rondout B&B .... (914)331-2369

Lake Placid

Adirondack Loj .... (518)523-3441
Blackberry Inn .... (518)523-3419
Highland House Inn
.... (518)523-2377 (800)342-8101
South Meadow Farm Lodge .... (518)523-9369
Spruce Lodge B&B .... (518)523-9350
The Stagecoach Inn
.... (518)523-9474 (800)520-9474

Lake Pleasant

Hummingbird Hill .... (518)548-6386

Lansing

The Bay Horse B&B .... (607)533-4612

Lawyersville

Stone House Bed & Breakfast ... (518)234-2603

Leeds

Leeds Country Inn B&B .... (518)943-2099

Leicester

National Hotel .... (716)382-3130

Leroy

Edson House .... (716)768-8579

Lew Beach

Beaverkill Valley Inn .... (914)439-4844

Lewiston

John Lasher House .... (716)754-9291
The Kelly House .... (716)754-8877
The Little Blue House B&B ..... (716)754-9425

Lexington

Carpathia House B&B .... (518)989-6622

Lisbon

Tilden Stage at Iroquois Farm ... (315)393-4346

Lisle

Dorchester Farm B&B .... (607)692-4511

Little Falls

Gansevoort House .... (315)823-1833

Livingston Manor

Clarke's Place In The Country ... (914)439-5442
Lanza's Country Inn .... (914)439-5070
R.M. Farm .... (914)439-5511

Livonia

The Cobblestone House B&B ... (716)346-2805

Lockport

National Centennial House ..... (716)434-8193

Lodi

Maxsom's Bed and Breakfast ... (607)582-6248

Long Eddy

The Rolling Marble Guest House . (914)887-6016

Long Lake

Mountain View Farm of Long Lake (518)624-2521

Loon Lake

Conways Lake Manor .... (518)494-2211
Inn at Loon Lake .... (518)891-6464

Lowville

Hill Top B&B .... (315)376-6364
Hinchings Pond B&B Inn .... (315)376-8296

Lyons

Roselawne .... (315)946-4218

Lyons Falls

River Valley Inn .... (315)348-4480

Macedon

Iris Farm .... (315)986-4536

Madison

Abigail's Straw Hat B & B ...... (315)893-7077

Malone

Kilburn Manor .. (518)483-4891 (800)454-5287

Margaretville

Margaretville Mountain Inn B&B . (914)586-3933

Mayville

Plumbush B&B at Chautauqua .. (716)789-5309

Medina

Crafts B&B .... (617)735-7343

Meridale

Old Stage Line Stop .... (607)746-6856

Mexico

Loons Nest Lodge .... (315)963-4704

Middleport

Canal Country Inn .... (716)735-7572

Milford

The 1860 Spencer House ...... (607)286-9402
Middlefield Guest House .... (607)286-7056

Millbrook

A Cat In Your Lap .... (914)677-3051

Millerton

Simmons' Way Village Inn ..... (518)789-6235

Montauk
Greenhedges Oceanside Villa . . . (516)668-5013
Monticello
Gabriels Haven Inc . . . . (914)796-3456
Mount Morris
Allan's Hill B&B . . . . (716)658-4591
Allegiance Inn . . . . (716)658-2769
Mount Tremper
Mount Tremper Inn . . . . (914)688-5329
Mumford
Genesee Country Inn
. . . . (716)538-2500 (800)697-8297
Naples
The Maxfield Inn . . . . (716)374-2510
Naples Valley B&B . . . . (716)374-6397
Nottingham Lodge Bed & Breakfast (716)374-5355
The Vagabond Inn . . . . (716)554-6271
Narrowsburg
Narrowsburg Inn . . . . (914)252-3998
Nelliston
The Historian B&B . . . . (518)993-2233
New Paltz
Jingle Bell Farm . . . . (914)255-6588
Mohonk Mountain House . . . . . . (914)255-4500
Nieuw Country Lloft . . . . (914)255-6533
Ujjala's B&B . . . . (914)255-6360
New York
The 412 House . . . . (212)744-6157
A Stella Marina Enterprises Bed & Breakfast
. . . . (212)475-6092
Chelsea Inn . . . . (212)645-8989
Incentra Village House . . . . (212)206-0007
The Inn at Irving Place . . . . (212)533-4600
The Gracie Inn . . . . (212)628-1700
Newark
Chapman's Blue Brick Inn . . . . . . (315)331-3226
Twin-Steeples Farm B&B . . . . . . (315)597-2452
Niagara Falls
An Old Niagara House . . . . (716)285-9408
Linen 'n Lace B&B Inn . . . . (716)285-3935
Park Place Bed & Breakfast . . . . (716)282-4626
Rainbow Guest House Inn . . . . . (716)282-1135
Red Coach Inn . . . . (716)282-1459
Nichols
River Tree B&B . . . . (607)699-7484
Nicholville
Chateau L'esperance . . . . (315)328-4669
North Chili
Daisy House . . . . (716)889-2497
North Creek
Goose Pond Inn B & B . . . . (518)251-3434
Highwinds Inn . . . . (518)251-3760
Pascales North Acres Bed & Breakfast
. . . . (518)251-4296
North Granville
Chateau . . . . (518)642-1511
North Hudson
Pine Tree Inn B&B (518)532-9255 (800)645-5605
North River
Garnet Hill Lodge . . . . (518)251-2821
Highwinds Inn . . (518)251-3760 (800)241-1923
Toags Lodge Bed & Breakfast . . . (518)251-2496
North Rose
Lake Bluff Inn Bed & Breakfast . . (315)587-2421
Northville
Trailhead Lodge . . . . (518)863-2198
Nunda
Butternut B&B . . . . (716)468-5074
Oak Hill
Hill House B&B . . . . (518)239-4772
Ocean Beach
Four Seasons B&B . . . . (516)583-8295
Ogdensburg
Maple Hill . . . . (315)393-3961
Olcott
Bayside Guest House . . . . (716)778-7767
Old Chatham
Depot Lane Bed & Breakfast . . . . (518)794-8336
Locust Tree House . . . . (518)794-8671
Old Forge
Waters Edge Inn & Conference Cetner
. . . . (315)369-2484
Olean
The Old Library Inn . . . . (716)373-9804
White House . . . . (716)373-0505
Oneida
Governors House Bed & Breakfast (315)363-5643
The Pollyanna . . . . (315)363-0524
Oneonta
Cathedral Farms Restaurant & Inn (607)432-7483
Christopher's Country Lodge . . . (607)432-2444
Ontario
The Tummonds House . . . . (315)524-5381
Oswego
Chestnut Grove Inn . . . . (315)342-2547
Owego
The Pumpelly House B&B . . . . . . (607)687-0510
Painted Post
Dannfield . . . . (607)962-2740
Palenville
Palenville House B&B . . . . (518)678-5649
Parksville
Kenslee Cottage . . . . (914)292-4299
Pawling
Pawling Guest House . . . . (914)855-1420
Penn Yan
Finton's Landing . . . . (315)536-3146
Fox Inn . . . . (315)536-1100
Fox Run Vineyards B&B . . . . (315)536-2507
The Heirlooms . . . . (315)536-7682
On The Beach . . . . (315)536-4646
The Wagener Estate B&B . . . . . . (315)536-0010
Phoenix
Main Street House B&B . . . . (315)695-5601
Pine Bush
Jane Whiteman B&B . . . . (914)733-1324
Pine City
Rufus Tanner House . . . . (607)732-0213
Pine Hill
Birchcreek Inn . . . . (914)254-5222
Pine Plains
The Pine . . . . (518)398-7677
Piseco
Irondequoit Inn . . . . (518)548-5500
Pittsford
Oliver Loud's Inn . . . . (716)248-5000
Plattsburgh
C & Ls Graystone Manor . . . . . . (518)566-0629
Marshall House . . . . (518)566-8691
Sunny Side Up B&B . . . . (518)563-5677
Port Henry
Elk Inn . . . . (518)546-7024
Kings Inn . . . . (518)546-7633
Port Jefferson
A Reasonable Alternative . . . . . . (516)928-4034
Terryville
Captain Hawkins House . . . . (516)473-8211
Port Jefferson
Compass Rose Bed & Breakfast . (516)474-1111
Port Jervis
Educators Inn East . . . . (914)856-5543
Portageville
Genesee Falls Hotel . . . . (716)493-2484
Poughkeepsie
Alumnae House: The Inn at Vassar College
. . . . (914)437-7100
The Inn at The Falls B&B . . . .
Pulaski
18 80 House . . . . (315)298-6088
Grindstone Creek Lodge . . . . (315)298-7226
Salmon River Anglers Lodge . . . . (315)298-3044
Schoolhouse Inn . . . . (315)298-3367
Shillelaghs & Shamrocks Bed & Breakfast
. . . . (315)298-7040
Pulteney
Bully Hill Vineyards Farm House
. . . . (607)868-3337
Queensbury
The Crislip's B&B . . . . (518)793-6869
Sanford's Ridge B&B . . . . (518)793-4923
Randolph
Highland View Farm B&B . . . . . . (716)358-2882
Ransomville
Capt Jim Evans: Providence Charter/Lodge
. . . . (716)791-4784
Red Hook
Grand Dutchess Bed & Breakfast (914)758-5818
Lombards Antiques & Bed & Breakfast
. . . . (914)758-3805
The Red Hook Inn . . . . (914)758-8445
Redfield
Fort Jeronimo Sports Lodge . . . . (315)599-7761
Remsen
The Winnes . . . . (315)831-5443
Rensselaer
The Tibbitts House . . . . (518)472-1348
Rexford
Rexford Crossings B&B . . . . (518)399-1777
Rhinebeck
Beekman Arms . . . . (914)876-7077
Mansakenning Carriage House . . (914)876-3500
Veranda House B&B . . . . (914)876-4133
Whistle Wood Farm . . . . (914)876-6838
Richfield Springs
Country Manor B&B . . . . (315)858-2561
Country Spread B&B . . . . (315)858-1870
Jonathan House . . . . (315)858-2870
Summerwood B&B . . . . (315)858-2024
Rochester
"428 Mt. Vernon" - A B&B Inn
. . . . (716)271-0792 (800)836-3159
The Rose Mansion & Gardens . . . (716)546-5426
Strawberry Castle B&B . . . . (716)385-3266
Swan Walk . . . . (716)865-7552
Woods Edge . . . . (716)223-8877
Rock City Falls
The Mansion . . . . (518)885-1607
Rock Hill
Stonewall Acres . . . . (914)791-9474
Rome
The Little Schoolhouse . . . . (315)336-4474
Maplecrest B&B . . . . (315)339-2107
Wright Settlement B&B . . . . (315)337-2417
Roscoe
The Baxter House . . . . (607)498-5811
Baxter House Bed & Breakfast . . (607)498-5811
Huff House . . . . (914)482-4579
The Open Door B&B . . . . (607)498-5772
Reynolds House Inn . . . . (607)498-4772
The Open Door B & B . . . . (607)498-5772
Rosendale
Astoria Hotel . . . . (914)658-8201
Roxbury
Scudder Hill House . . . . (607)326-4215
Rushford
Klartag Farms B&B . . . . (716)437-2946
Rushville
Lakeview Farm B&B . . . . (716)554-6973
Salem
Bunker Hill Inn . . . . (518)854-9339
Salt Point
Mill at Bloomvale Falls . . . . (914)266-4234
Sandy Creek
Pink House Inn . . . . (315)387-3276
Tug Hill Lodge . . . . (315)387-5326
Sandy Pond
Angler's Roost Bed & Breakfast . (315)387-5690
Saranac Lake
Doctors Inn . . . . (518)891-3464
The Point . . . . . . (518)891-5674 (800)678-8946
Sunday Pond Bed & Breakfast . . . (518)891-1531
Ballston Spa
Apple Tree B&B . . . . (518)885-1113
Saratoga Springs
The Inn on Bacon Hill B&B . . . . . (518)695-3693
Batcheller Mansion Inn . . . . (518)584-7012
Browns Beach . . . . (518)587-8280
Brunswick Bed & Breakfast . . . . . (518)583-4177
Chestnut Tree Inn . . . . (518)587-8681
The Inn at Saratoga . . . . (518)583-1890
Union Gables B&B . . . . (518)584-1558
Westchester House B&B
. . . . (518)587-7613 (800)587-7613
Saugerties
The Evergreen Country Inn . . . . . (914)247-0015
High Woods Inn . . . . (914)246-8655
House on The Quarry . . . . (914)246-8584
Sauquoit
Hayfield House B&B . . . . (315)737-6102
Schroon Lake
Schroon Lake Inn . . . . (518)532-7042
Schuylerville
Fish Creek Inn . . . . (518)581-0297
Marshall House . . . . (518)695-3765
Scio
Scio House Victorian B&B . . . . . (716)593-1737

Seaview
Place In The Sun .... (516)583-5716
Severance
The Red House .... (518)532-7734
Shandaken
Two Brooks B&B .... (914)688-7101
Sharon Springs
Edgefield .... (518)284-3339
Roses 'n' Lace .... (518)284-2335
Shelter Island
Azalea House .... (516)749-4252
Belle Crest Inn .... (516)749-2041
Chequit Inn .... (516)749-0018
Shelter Island Resort .... (516)749-2001
Shelter Island Heights
Olde Country Inn .... (516)749-1633
Sherburne
Lok N Logs Bed & Breakfast .... (607)674-6227
Sherman
Miller House Bed & Breakfast ... (716)761-6795
Weises The Inn-Between ...... (716)761-6255
Skaneateles
The Gray House .... (315)685-0131
Sodus Point
Carriage House Inn
.... (315)483-2100 (800)292-2990
Lakecrest Guest House .... (315)483-6090
Lakeside Inn Bed & Breakfast ... (315)483-0206
Silver Waters Guest House ..... (315)483-8098
South Dayton
Town & Country B&B .... (716)988-3340
South Otselic
Northwest Corners B&B .... (315)653-7776
Southampton
Concord Resort .... (516)283-6100
Mainstay .... (516)283-4375
Village Latch Inn .... (516)283-2160
Speculator
The Inn at Speculator .... (518)548-3811
Spencertown
Spencertown Guests .... (518)392-2358
Springville
The Franklin House .... (716)592-7877
Gaffneys Bed & Breakfast ...... (716)592-0240
Staatsburg
Belvedere Country Inn .... (914)889-8000
Staten Island
Jean's B&B .... (718)948-1731
Victorian B&B .... (718)273-9861
Stephentown
Keepsake Inn .... (518)733-6277
Kirkmead .... (518)733-5420
Mill House Inn .... (518)733-5606
Mountain Changes .... (518)733-6923
Stillwater
The Farm House .... (518)584-7576
Lee's Deer Run B&B .... (518)584-7722
Stone Ridge
Baker's B&B .... (914)687-9795
The Inn at Stone Ridge .... (914)687-0736
Stony Brook
Three Village Inn .... (516)751-0555
Stow
Stuart Manor Bed & Breakfast ... (716)789-9902
Syracuse
Bed & Breakfast Wellington
.... (315)471-2433 (800)724-5006
Benedict House B&B .... (315)476-6541
Boone Manor B&B .... (315)422-0698
Giddings Garden Bed & Breadfast (315)492-8542
Tannersville
Deer Mountain Inn .... (518)589-6268
The Eggery Inn .... (518)589-5363
Greene Mountain View Inn ..... (518)589-5511
Kennedy House .... (518)589-6082
Snowed Inn .... (518)589-5492
Thendara
Moose River House B&B ...... (315)369-3104
Van Aukens Inne .... (315)369-3033
Trumansburg
Archway .... (607)387-6175
Cretser House Bed & B .... (607)387-9666
The Pillars .... (607)387-3628
Sage Cottage B&B .... (607)387-6449
Taughannock Farm .... (607)387-7711
Westwind .... (607)387-3377

Tupper Lake
Green Gables Bed & Breakfast .. (518)359-7815
Turin
Towpath Inn .... (315)348-8122
Ulster Park
Rennie House Bed & Breakfast .. (914)331-5560
Utica
The Iris Stonehouse .... (315)732-6720
Valley Falls
Maggie Towne's B&B .... (518)663-8369
Vernon
Taylor Creek Inn .... (315)829-4663
Victor
Golden Rule B&B .... (716)924-0610
Safari House Bed & Breakfast Deluxe
.... (716)924-0250
Sugar Tree Inn B & B .... (716)742-3170
Wallkill
Audreys Farmhouse B&B ...... (914)895-3440
Walton
Aching Acres Bed & Breakfast .. (607)865-8569
Carriage House Bed & Breakfast . (607)865-4041
Warrensburg
The Bent Finial Manor .... (518)623-3308
White House Lodge .... (518)623-3640
Warwick
Peach Grove Inn .... (914)986-7411
Warwick Valley Bed & Breakfast . (914)987-7255
Waterloo
Art Barn B&B .... (315)789-2075
The Historic James R. Webster Mansion
.... (315)539-3032
Waterloo House .... (315)539-9739
Watertown
Starbuck House B&B .... (315)788-7324
Watkins Glen
Castel Grisch Estate .... (607)535-9614
Glen Manor House Bed & Breakfast
.... (607)535-9737
The Rose Window B&B .... (607)535-4687
Seneca Watch B&B .... (607)535-4488
The Victorian .... (607)535-6582
Vintage View B&B .... (607)535-7909
Webster
Country Schoolhouse B&B ..... (716)265-4720
Weedsport
Mansard on The Erie .... (315)834-2262
Wells
Abner Greenfields Country Inn ... (518)924-2206
West Kill
Marie's Dream House Country Inn (518)989-6565
Schwarzenegger's Sunshine Valley House
.... (518)989-6500
West Shokan
Glen Atty Farm .... (914)657-8110
Westfield
Westfield House .... (716)326-6262
Westhampton Beach
Inn on Main .... (516)288-8900
White Plains
Soundview Manor .... (914)421-9080
Whitehall
Apple Orchard Inn .... (518)499-0180
Ash Rose Inn .... (518)499-0010
Willet
Woven Waters .... (607)656-8672
Williamsville
Heritage House Country Inn .... (716)633-4900
Willsboro
1852 Inn B&B .... (518)963-4075
Champlain Vistas .... (518)963-8029
Windham
Christman's Windham House ... (518)734-4230
Country Suite B&B .... (518)734-4079
Windsor
Country Haven B & B/Crafts .... (607)655-1204
Woodstock
Ivy Farm Inn .... (914)679-9045
Youngstown
Cameo Inn Bed & Breakfast .... (716)692-3162
Ontario House .... (716)745-7557
Yulan
Bear Paw Lodge .... (914)557-6002

North Carolina

Aberdeen
The Inn at Bryant House
.... (910)944-3300 (800)453-4019
Page Manor House B&B .... (910)944-5970
Andrews
Bradley Inn Bed Breaakfast & Antiques
.... (704)321-2391
The Cover House .... (704)321-5302
Howard Haus .... (704)321-4103
Old Bradley Hotel/Inn .... (704)321-2391
The Walker Inn of Old Valleytown (704)321-5019
Asheboro
The Doctor's Inn .... (910)625-4916
Asheville
A Bed of Roses .... (704)258-8700
Abbington Green B&B .... (704)251-2454
Aberdeen Inn .... (704)254-9336
Beaufort House Victorian B&B .. (704)254-9935
Black Walnut B&B .... (704)254-3878
Bois d'Arc Bed & Breakfast ..... (704)253-4345
Bridle Path Inn .... (704)252-0035
Cairn Brae .... (704)252-9219
Carolina B&B .... (704)254-3608
Chestnut Street Inn .... (704)285-0705
The Colby House .... (704)253-5644
Flint Street Inn .... (704)253-6723
The Grove Park Inn & Country Club (704)252-2711
Johnson Inn .... (704)258-2868
The Lion & The Rose
.... (704)255-7673 (800)546-6988
Miller's Mountain Lodge .... (704)299-3542
North Lodge .... (704)252-6433
Ray House .... (704)252-0106
The Resting Place .... (704)298-8500
The Scarlett Inn .... (704)253-7888
Sourwood Inn .... (704)255-0690
Atkinson
Hawes House B&B .... (910)283-5600
Avon
Cape Hatteras Bed & Breakfast .. (919)995-4511
Bald Head Island
Theodosia's B&B .... (910)457-6563
Balsam
Balsam Lodge .... (704)456-6528
Balsam Mountain Inn
.... (704)456-9498 (800)224-9498
Hickory Haven Inn .... (704)452-1106
Banner Elk
Archers Mountain Inn .... (704)898-9004
The Banner Elk Inn B&B .... (704)898-6223
Crows Nest B&B .... (704)963-7771
Hummingbird Lodge B&B ...... (704)963-7210
Manning House .... (704)898-9669
Tufts House Inn .... (704)898-7944
Wapiti Lodge B&B .... (704)898-5611
Bat Cave
Cave Inn .... (704)625-0222
Old Mill Inn .... (701)625-4256
Original Hickory Nut Gap Inn .... (704)625-9108
Bath
Bath Guest House .... (919)923-6811
Beaufort
Beaufort Inn .... (919)728-2600
Captains' Quartersbed & Biscuit . (919)728-7711
Cedars at Beaufort .... (919)728-7036
Cousins B&B .... (919)504-3478
Inlet Inn .... (919)728-3600
Langdon House B&B .... (919)728-5499
The Shotgun House .... (919)728-6248
Beech Mountain
Top of The Beech Inn .... (704)387-2252
Belhaven
Amble Inn B&B .... (919)943-3500
Belhaven Inn B&B .... (919)943-6400
The Duck Blind B&B .... (919)943-6399
River Forest Manor (919)943-2151 (800)346-2151
Black Mountain
Black Mountain Inn .... (704)669-6528
The Blackberry Inn .... (704)669-8303
Friendship Lodge .... (704)669-9294
Red Rocker Country Inn .... (704)669-5991
Blowing Rock
Brookside Inn .... (704)295-3380
Cottage Inn .... (704)295-0069

ADDITIONAL ACCOMMODATIONS

Crippen's Country Inn & Restaurant
.... (704)295-3487
Gideon Ridge Inn .... (704)295-3644
The Lindridge House .... (704)295-7343
Meadowbrook Inn .... (704)295-9341
Rocking Horse Inn B&B .... (704)295-3311
Stone Pillar B&B .... (704)295-4141
Sunshine Inn .... (704)295-3487
Victorian Inn .... (704)295-0034

Boone
Gragg House .... (704)264-7289
The Lion's Den .... (800)963-5785
Overlook Lodge .... (704)963-5785
Window Views Bed and Breakfast (704)963-8081

Brevard
Patton House .... (704)877-3700
Pines Country Inn .... (704)877-3131
Red House Inn .... (704)884-9349
Womble Inn .... (704)884-4770

Bryson City
Fisher House B&B .... (704)497-5921
Governors Island Bed & Breakfast (704)488-2924
Hemlock Inn .... (704)488-2885
Irene's B&B .... (704)488-8742
Mountain Laurel B&B .... (704)488-2055
West Oak Bed & Breakfast ..... (704)488-2438

Burnsville
A Little Bit of Heaven .... (704)675-5379
Celo Inn .... (704)675-5132
Estes Mountain Retreat .... (704)682-7264
Hamrick Inn B&B .... (704)675-5251
Terrell House B&B .... (704)682-4505

Candler
Owl's Nest Inn at Engadine
.... (704)665-8325 (800)665-8868

Cape Carteret
Harborlight Guest House
.... (919)393-6868 (800)624-8439

Carolina Beach
Bayberry Inn By-The-Sea ...... (910)458-9663
Davy Crockett Inn .... (910)458-6244
Harbour Lodge .. (910)458-3644 (800)458-3645

Carthage
The Blacksmith Inn B&B .... (910)947-1692

Cashiers
Innisfree Victorian Inn .... (704)743-2946

Cedar Mountain
The Sassy Goose .... (704)966-9493

Chadbourn
Magnolia Manor Bed & Breakfast Accommodations
.... (910)654-5138

Chapel Hill
Hillcrest House .... (919)942-2369

Charlotte
601 Poplar Street B&B .... (704)358-1464
Cricket Inn .... (704)597-8500
The Elizabeth B&B .... (704)358-1368
The Homeplace B&B .... (704)365-1936
The Inn Uptown .... (704)342-2800
Overcarsh House .... (704)334-8477
Philemon Inn on Lake Wylie .... (704)393-0707
Roswell Inn B&B .... (704)332-4915
Still Waters .... (704)399-6299

Chimney Rock
The Dogwood Inn .... (704)625-4403

Clemmons
Manor House at Tanglewood .... (910)766-0591

Clinton
The Courthouse Inn
.... (910)592-2634 (800)463-9817

Clyde
Mountain Sunset Inn .... (704)627-1400
Windsong: A Mountain Inn ..... (704)627-6111

Columbia
Heart's Delight B&B .... (919)796-1778

Concord
Country Walk B&B .... (704)938-4550
The Red Door B&B .... (704)784-1830

Creston
Peak Inn Bed & Breakfast ...... (910)385-9826

Crumpler
Glendale Springs Inn & Restaurant (910)982-2103

Cullowhee
Cullowhee B&B .... (704)293-5447

Davidson
Davidson Village Inn .... (704)892-8044

Dillsboro
Applegate Inn B&B .... (704)586-2397
Dillsboro Inn .... (704)586-3898
Jarrett House .... (704)586-9964
Olde Towne Inn .... (704)586-3461
Squire Watkins Inn .... (704)586-5244

Eagle Springs
The Inn at Eagle Springs .... (910)673-2722

Edenton
Captain's Quarters Inn
.... (919)482-8945 (800)482-8945
Dram Tree Inn .... (919)482-4038
Governor Eden Inn B&B .... (919)482-2072
Leigh House .... (919)482-3184
Mulberry Hill .... (800)348-1405
Trestle House Inn .... (919)482-2282

Elizabeth City
Culpepper Inn .... (919)335-1993

Elizabethtown
Warwick House B&B .... (910)862-4970

Ellerbe
Ellerbe Springs Inn .... (910)652-5600

Emerald Isle
The Inn at Emerald Isle Inn and B&B By Sea
.... (919)354-3222

Everetts
Ocean Side .... (919)792-4548

Faison
Magnolia Hall B&B .... (910)267-9241

Fayetteville
MacPherson House Inn .... (910)323-0081

Flat Rock
Flat Rock Inn ... (704)696-3273 (800)266-3996

Fletcher
Tudor House .... (704)687-7604

Franklin
Heritage Inn .... (704)524-4150
Hickory Knoll Lodge .... (704)524-9666
Lullwater Farmhouse Inn .... (704)524-6532
Snow Hill The Inn .... (704)369-2100
The Summit Inn .... (704)524-2006

Fuquay Varina
Baileywick Bed & Breakfa ...... (919)552-4891

Gastonia
Falls Ridge B&B Inn .... (704)865-4502
York Chester B&B (704)853-2700 (800)327-5067

Glendale Springs
Lee's Country Inn .... (910)982-3289
Mountain View Lodge and Cabins (910)982-2233

Grassy Creek
River House .... (910)982-2109

Greensboro
Greenwich Inn .... (910)272-3474
The Troy-Bumpass Inn (910)370-1660 (800)370-9070

Hatteras
Outer Banks B&B .... (919)986-2776
Risa Inn .... (919)986-1111

Hayesville
Broadax Inn .... (704)389-6987

Henderson
La Grange Plantation Inn .... (919)438-2421

Hendersonville
Apple Inn .... (704)693-0107
Echo Mountain Inn .... (704)692-4008
Fairfield House .... (704)687-0534
Havenshire Inn .... (704)692-4097
Mountain Home Bed & Breakfast . (704)697-9090
Stillwell House .... (704)693-6475
Stonehearth Inn .... (704)625-4027
Teneriffe Bed & Breakfast ...... (704)698-8178
Westhaven B&B .... (704)693-8791
Woods House Inn .... (704)749-9562

Hertford
1812 on The Perquimans B&B Inn (919)426-1812
Beechtree Inn .... (919)426-7815

High Point
The Premier B&B .... (910)889-8349

Highlands
4 1/2 Street Inn .... (704)526-4464
The Guest House .... (704)526-4536
Highlands Inn .... (704)526-9380
Lakeside Bed & Breakfast ...... (704)526-4498
The Laurels: Freda's B&B ...... (704)526-2091
Lees Inn .... (704)526-4746
Long House Bed & Breakfast ... (704)526-4394
Mirror Lake Lodge .... (704)526-5947
Old Edwards Inn .... (704)526-5036
Phelp's House .... (704)526-2590

Hillsborough
Colonial Inn .... (919)732-2461
Hillsborough House Inn
.... (919)644-1600 (800)616-1660
The Inn at Teardrop .... (919)732-1120

Hot Springs
Duckett House Inn & Farm
.... (704)622-7621 (800)306-5038

Kenansville
The Murray House .... (910)296-1000

Kill Devil Hills
Ye Olde Cherokee Inn .... (919)441-6127
The Figurehead B&B .... (919)441-6929

Kinston
The Bentley .... (919)523-2337

Kitty Hawk
3 Seasons Guest House
.... (919)261-4791 (800)847-3373
Sanderling Inn Resort .... (919)261-4111

Kure Beach
The Ocean Princess Inn
.... (910)458-6712 (800)762-4863

Lake Junaluska
Lagoalinda .... (704)456-3620
Providence Lodge .... (704)456-6486
Sunset Inn .... (704)456-6114

Lake Lure
Hickory Nut Gap Lnn .... (704)625-9108

Lake Toxaway
Earthshine Mountain Lodge .... (704)862-4207
Sassy Goose .... (704)966-9493
Twin Streams B&B .... (704)883-3007

Lake Waccamaw
B&B By The Lake .... (910)646-4744
Lake Shore Lodge .... (910)646-3748

Laurel Springs
Doughton Hall B&B Inn .... (910)359-2341

Lexington
Lawrences .... (704)249-1114

Little Switzerland
Alpine Inn .... (704)765-5380
Big Lynn Lodge .... (704)765-4257
Switzerland Inn .... (704)765-2153

Littleton
Littletons Maplewood Manor Bed & Breakfast
.... (919)586-4682

Louisburg
The Hearthside Inn B&B .... (919)496-6776

Madison
The Boxley B&B . (910)427-0453 (800)429-3516

Maggie Valley
Cataloochee Ranch .... (704)926-1401
The Ketner Inn & Farm
.... (704)926-1511 (800)714-1397
Mountainbrook Inn .... (704)926-3962

Magnolia
Magnolia Inn .... (910)289-4050

Manteo
Booth's Guest House .... (919)473-3696
Roanoke Island Inn .... (919)473-5511
Scarborough Inn .... (919)473-3979
The Tranquil House Inn .... (919)473-1404
The White Doe Inn (919)473-9851 (800)473-6091

Marion
The Inn at Blue Ridge .... (704)756-7017

Mars Hill
Baird House B&B .... (704)689-5722

Marshall
Marshall House .... (704)649-9205
The Mashburn House B&B ..... (704)649-3509

Mebane
The Inn at Old Place B&B Log Cabin
.... (910)563-1733

Milton
Woodside Inn .... (919)234-8646

Mooresville
24 Spring Run B&B .... (704)664-6686

Morehead City
The Dill House B&B .... (919)726-4449
Lighthouse Inn .... (919)247-3133

Morganton
Burleson House .... (704)437-5356

Mount Airy
Merritt House B&B (910)786-2174 (800)290-6290
Pine Ridge Inn .... (919)789-5034
Mountain Home
Courtland Manor .... (704)692-1133
Murfreesboro
Winborne House .... (919)398-5224
Murphy
Hilltop House .... (704)837-8661
Hoover House .... (704)837-8734
Stone Manor Inn Bed & Breakfast (704)837-8676
Nags Head
Carefree Cottages .... (919)441-2343
Nebo
Merry Heart Cabin .... (704)584-6174
Robardajen Woods .... (704)584-3191
New Bern
The Aerie .... (919)636-5553
The Magnolia House .... (919)633-9488
New Berne House (919)636-2250 (800)842-7688
Newland
Chinquapin Inn .... (704)765-0064
Newton
Trotthouse Inn .... (704)465-0404
Ocracoke
Blackbeard's Lodge .... (919)928-3421
Crew's Inn B&B .... (919)298-7011
Eugenia's B&B .... (919)928-1411
Island Inn .... (919)928-4351
The Lightkeeper's Inn .... (919)928-1821
Oscar's House .... (919)928-1311
Ship's Timbers .... (919)928-4061
Old Fort
The Inn at Old Fort .... (704)668-9384
Magnolia Inn .... (704)668-9051
Oriental
The Cartwright House B&B ..... (919)249-1337
Oxford
General B S Royster B&B ...... (919)690-1228
Penland
Chinquapin Inn .... (704)765-0064
Pilot Mountain
Pilot Knob-A B&B Inn .... (919)325-2502
Pinehurst
Magnolia Inn .... (919)295-6900
Pine Crest Inn .... (919)295-6121
Pinnacle
Scenic Overlook B&B .... (910)368-9591
Pisgah Forest
Key Falls Inn .... (704)884-7559
Plymouth
Four Gables Bed & Breakfast Inn . (919)793-6696
Raleigh
The Oakwood Inn .... (919)832-9712
The William Thomas House .... (919)755-9400
Ridgecrest
Mote's Mountain View .... (704)669-4714
Roaring Gap
Roaring Gap Guest House ...... (910)363-1234
Robbinsville
Blue Boar Lodge .... (704)479-8126
Thunderbird Mountain Resort ... (704)479-6442
Rocky Mount
Sunset Inn B&B . (919)446-9524 (800)786-7386
Rutherfordton
Carrier Houses .... (704)287-4222
Pinebrae Manor B&B .... (704)286-1543
Saluda
Bear Creek Lodge .... (704)749-2272
Four Oaks B&B .... (803)249-1871
The Oaks .... (704)749-9613
Orchard Inn .... (704)749-5471 (800)581-3800
Saluda Inn .... (704)749-9698
Sapphire
Sapphire Valley Resort .... (704)743-3441
Woodlands Inn of Sapphire ..... (704)966-4709
Scaly Mountain
Oak View Inn .... (704)526-4446
Shallotte
Breakfast Creek B&B .... (910)754-3614
Goose Creek B&B .... (910)754-5849
Shelby
The Inn at Webbley .... (704)481-1403
Siler City
B&B at Laurel Ridge .... (919)742-6049

Southern Pines
Jefferson Inn .... (910)692-8300
Southport
Cape Fear Inn .... (910)457-5989
Dosher Plantation House B&B ... (919)457-5554
Indian Oak Inn .... (910)457-0209
Sparta
Bald Knob Farm House .... (910)372-4191
Harmony Hill Bed & Breakfast ... (910)372-6868
Mountain Hearth .... (910)372-8743
Red Roof Farm .... (910)372-8785
Turby Villa .... (919)372-8490
Spruce Pine
Fairway Inn .... (704)765-4917
Inn at Plumtree .... (704)765-8364
Ansley Richmond Inn B&B ..... (704)765-6993
Statesville
Aunt Mae's .... (704)873-9525
Madelyn's B&B .... (704)872-3973
Stokes
Sheppard Mill Farm B&B .... (919)757-0992
Sugar Grove
Olde Cobblestone Chimney Inn B&B
.... (704)297-5111
The Sugar Grove Inn .... (704)297-3336
Supply
Doe Creek B&B Inn .... (910)754-7736
Surf City
The Gillies B&B .... (910)328-3087
The Pink Palace of Topsail ..... (910)328-5114
Swan Quarter
Cutrell Inn B&B .... (919)926-9711
Swansboro
Mt. Pleasant B&B .... (919)326-5106
Scott's Keep B&B (910)326-1257 (800)348-1257
Sylva
Mountain Brook .... (704)586-4329
Olde Towne Inn .... (704)586-3461
Tapoco
Tapoco Lodge .... (704)498-2435
Tarboro
Barracks Inn .... (919)641-1614
Lady Ann of Historic Tarboro B&B (919)641-1438
Little Warren .... (919)823-1314
Main Street Inn .... (919)823-2560
Traphill
Swaringen Inn B&B .... (910)957-2159
Tryon
Pine Crest Inn .. (704)859-9135 (800)633-3001
Stone Hedge Inn .... (704)859-9114
Valle Crucis
River Valley Inn .... (704)297-3820
The Inn at The Taylor House .... (704)963-5581
Vass
Amble Inn B&B .... (910)245-7175
Wadesboro
Sullivan Place .... (704)694-2511
Wanchese
C.W. Pugh's B&B .... (919)473-5466
Island House of Wanchese B&B . (919)473-5619
Queen Annes Revenge Restrnt .. (919)473-5466
Warrenton
Olde Christmas Inn .... (919)257-2727
Warsaw
The Squire's Vintage Inn ....
The Vintage Inn .... (910)296-1727
Washington
Acadian House B&B .... (919)975-3967
Pamlico House .... (919)946-7184
Waynesville
Haywood Street Inn .... (704)456-9831
Heath Lodge Mountain Inn
.... (704)456-3333 (800)432-8499
Herren House .... (704)452-7837
Ketner Inn & Farm .... (704)926-1511
Laurels Bed and Breadfast ..... (704)456-7186
Mountain Creek Inn .... (704)456-5509
The Palmer House B&B .... (704)456-7521
Snuggery .... (704)456-3660
The Swag .... (704)926-0430
Ten Oaks ...... (704)452-4373 (800)563-2925
Way Inn .... (704)456-3788
Wynne's Creekside Bed & Breakfast Lodge
.... (704)926-8300
Yellow House .... (704)452-0991

Weaverville
Carter Hill Farm .... (704)626-3852
Dry Ridge Inn ... (704)658-3899 (800)839-3899
Freedom Escape Lodge .... (704)658-0814
The Inn on Main Street .... (704)645-3442
Weaverville Featherbed & Breakfast (704)645-7594
West Jefferson
Nations Inn .... (910)246-2080
Ransom's B&B .... (910)246-5177
Rocking Chair Inn .... (910)246-3060
Whittier
Mountain Creek Chalets .... (704)586-6042
Williamston
Big Mill B&B .... (919)792-3036
Wilmington
Anderson Guest House .... (910)343-8128
Camelia Cottage B&B .... (910)763-9171
French House .... (910)763-3337
Front Street Inn .... (910)762-6442
Grayston Guesthouse .... (910)763-2000
Hoge-Wood House .... (910)762-5299
Inn on Orange .... (910)815-0035
The Kingsley House .... (910)763-6603
Market Street B&B .... (910)763-5442
Rosehill Inn .... (910)815-0250 (800)815-0250
The Inn at St. Thomas Court
.... (910)343-1800 (800)525-0909
Wine House The Bed & Breakfast (910)763-0511
Worth House - A Victorian Inn .. (910)762-8562
Winnabow
Funston Farm House .... (919)253-5643
Winston-Salem
Brookstown Inn B&B
.... (910)725-1120 (800)845-4262
Fairview Cottage .... (910)761-1548
Henry F Shaffner House .... (910)777-0052
Hylehurst B&B Inn .... (910)722-7873
Lowe-Alston House .... (919)727-1211
Mickle House B&B .... (910)722-9045
The Thomas-Welch House ..... (910)723-3586
Wachovia B&B .... (910)777-0332

North Dakota

Bismarck
White Lace B&B .... (701)258-4142
Bowman
Logging Camp B&B .... (701)279-5702
Carrington
Blue Swan Inn .... (701)652-3978
Center
Bobb B&B .... (701)794-3288
Devils Lake
Dakotah Friend B&B Inn .... (701)662-6327
Dickinson
Joyce's Home Away From Home B&B
.... (701)227-1524
Fargo
Bohlig's B&B .... (701)235-7867
Glen Ullin
Kohler's B&B .... (701)348-3830
Goodrich
Sheyenne Valley Lodge .... (701)884-2432
Grand Forks
511 Reeves B&B .... (701)772-9663
Lord Bryon B&B Inn .... (701)775-0194
Merrifield House .... (701)775-4250
Kenmare
Farm Comfort .... (701)848-2433
Leonard
Lady Bird B&B .... (701)645-2509
Lidgerwood
Kaler B&B .... (701)538-4848
Linton
Umber B&B .... (701)254-4134
Luverne
Grandma's House Farm Vacation (701)845-4994
Minnewaukan
Minnewaukan B&B .... (701)473-5731
Minot
Broadway Inn B&B .... (701)838-6075
D Over L B&B .... (701)722-3326
Dakotah Rose .... (701)838-3548
The Muffin House .... (701)852-1488
New Salem
Prairie View B&B .... (701)843-7236

Northwood
Twin Pine Farm B&B .... (701)587-6075
Oakes
House of 29 .... (701)742-2227
Reeder
Rocking Chair B&B .... (701)587-2204
Regent
Dancing Dakota .... (701)563-4631
Fin & Feather Farmstead .... (701)563-4499
The Old West B&B .... (701)563-4542
Scranton
Historic Jacobson Mansion ..... (701)275-8291
Stanley
Triple T Ranch .... (701)628-2418
Tower City
Tower City Inn B&B .... (701)749-2660
Velva
Hagenhus .... (701)338-8262
Wahpeton
Adam's Fairview Bonanza Farm B&B
.... (701)274-8262
Wing
Eva's B&B .... (701)943-2461
Zahl
Pheasant Run Lodge .... (701)694-6585

Ohio

Akron
O'Neil House .... (330)867-2650
Albany
Albany House .. (614)698-6311 (800)600-4941
Alliance
Aleida's B&B .... (216)823-1470
Anderson
Apple Homestead Bed & Breakfast (513)474-4717
Archbold
Murbach House .... (419)445-5195
Ashland
Winfield Bed & Breakfast ...... (419)281-5587
Ashtabula
Michael Cahill B&B .... (216)964-8449
Atwater
The Buckeye Lady B&B Home .. (216)947-3932
Avon
A French Creek House .... (216)934-5195
Barnesville
Georgian Pillars B&B
.... (614)425-3741 (800)525-3741
Bellefontaine
Whitmore House .... (513)592-4290
Bellevue
Britannia Bed & Breakfast ...... (419)483-4597
Bellville
Frederick Fitting House .... (419)886-2863
Belmont
Victorian B&B .... (614)484-4872
Berlin
Amish Country Inn .... (330)893-3000
Shaver's Bed & Breakfast ...... (330)893-3061
Townhouse Bed & Breakfast .... (330)893-2353
Birmingham
The House of Seven Hearths ... (216)965-5503
Blue Rock
McNutt Farm/Outdoors Lodge ... (614)674-4555
Bowerston
Lloyd's Tearoom & B&B .... (614)269-1715
Bryan
Elegant Inn Bed & Breakfast .... (419)636-2873
Bucyrus
Hide Away B&B .... (419)562-3013
Caldwell
Harkins House Inn .... (614)732-7347
Cambridge
Clare Inn .... (614)439-1178
Misty Meadow Farm .... (614)439-5135
Morning Glory Bed & Breakfast .. (614)439-2499
Centerburg
Otter Fork Hills .... (614)893-2467
Centerville
Yesterday B&B .... (513)433-0785
Chagrin Falls
Inn of Chagrin Falls .... (216)247-1200
Charm
Charm Countryview Inn .... (216)893-3003
Guggisberg Swiss Inn .... (330)893-3600
Chillicothe
Blair House Bed & Breakfast .... (614)774-3140
Chillicothe B&B .... (614)772-6848
The Greenhouse B&B .... (614)775-5313
Old McDill-Anderson Place ..... (614)774-1770
Sulphur Lick Springs Hotel/Country Inn
.... (614)772-2422
The Canal House .... (614)775-7384
Vanmeter B&B .... (614)774-3510
Victoria Manor B&B .... (614)775-6424
Cincinnati
Cooper Woods .... (513)984-3867
Neil House .... (513)961-4805
The Parker House B&B of Clifton . (513)579-8236
Prospect Hill B&B .... (513)421-4408
The Victoria Inn of Hyde Park ... (513)321-3567
Circleville
Braeburn Farm B&B .... (614)474-7086
Castle Inn .... (614)477-3986
The Fireside Inn .... (614)474-6640
Cleveland
The Baricelli Inn .... (216)791-6500
Clyde
Pine Rose Inn .... (419)547-9707
Columbus
Belmont B&B .... (614)421-1235
Dorrian's B&B .... (614)228-7479
Harrison House B&B .... (614)421-2202
Hausfrau Haven-In German Village (614)443-3680
The House of The Seven Goebels (614)761-9595
Lincoln Hotel .... (614)291-5056
Victorian B&B .... (614)299-1656
Conesville
Log House B&B .... (614)829-2757
Canneaut
Bridgeview B&B .... (216)593-6767
Conneaut
Buccia B&B .... (216)593-5976
Campbell Braemar .... (216)599-7362
Homestead B&B .... (216)599-2237
Lakeland Colonial B&B .... (216)599-8139
Liberty Inn .... (216)593-6767
Coshocton
1890 Bed & Breakfast .... (614)622-1890
Apple Butter Inn .... (614)622-1329
Roscoe Village Inn .... (614)622-2222
Dayton
Candlewick B&B .... (513)223-9297
Prices' Steamboat House B&B .. (513)223-2444
De Graff
Rollicking Hills B&B .... (513)585-5161
Delaware
Miracle House Bed & Breakfast .. (614)369-4017
Olentangy River Valley B&B .... (614)885-5859
Van Deman Bed & Breakfast .... (614)363-2963
Dellroy
Pleasant Journey Inn .... (330)735-2407
Whispering Pines B&B
.... (216)735-2824 (800)890-3811
Dover
Olde World Bed & Breakfast .... (330)343-1333
Dresden
Adams House Inn .... (614)754-4004
Hemlock House Bed & Breakfast . (614)754-4422
Village Victorian Bed & Breakfast . (614)754-2231
East Liverpool
Granny's Shanty Bed & Breakfast (330)385-7722
Fayette
Red Brick Inn .... (419)237-2276
Findlay
The Ponds Country Suites ..... (419)422-6640
Fort Recovery
Main Street Inn B&B .... (419)375-4955
Fostoria
Corporate Etc. Bed & Breakfast .. (419)435-4567
Fredericktown
Heartland Country Resort
.... (419)768-9300 (800)230-7030
Fremont
Buckland Bed & Breakfast ..... (419)332-5187
Fresno
Valley View Inn .... (330)897-3232
Gahanna
The Lily Stone .... (614)476-1976
Galion
The Rose of Sherron .... (419)468-3973
Gambier
Gambier House .... (614)427-2668
Garrettsville
Blueberry Hill B&B .... (216)527-5068
Geneva
The Last Resort Bed & Breakfast (216)466-6500
Glouster
Country Line Farm B&B .... (614)767-4185
Grand Rapids
Mill House Bed & Breakfast .... (419)832-6455
Grand River
Boatel Boat & Breakfast .... (216)352-8122
Granville
Bed & Breakfast of Granville .... (614)587-4764
Buxton Inn .... (614)587-0001
Follett-Wright House B & B ..... (614)587-0941
Granville Inn .... (614)587-3333
Granville Manor .... (614)587-4677
Porch House Bed & Breakfast ... (614)587-1995
Greenfield
Mertz Place .... (513)981-2219
Hanoverton
Crystal Springs B&B .... (216)223-2198
The Spread Eagle Tavern & Inn .. (216)223-1583
Hillsboro
The Victoria House .... (513)393-2743
Huron
Captain Montague's B&B ...... (419)433-4756
Jackson
Bowman House .... (614)286-1916
The Maples .... (614)286-6067
Johnstown
Pudding House B&B For Writers . (614)967-6060
Kelleys Island
Cricket Lodge .... (419)746-2263
Eagles Nest .... (419)746-2708
Fly Inn B&B .... (419)746-2525 (800)359-4661
House on Huntington Lane ..... (419)746-2765
The Inn on Kelleys Island ...... (419)746-2258
South Shore B&B .... (419)746-2409
Southaven .... (419)746-2784
Sweet Valley Inn .... (419)746-2750
Zettlers Lakefront B&B .... (419)746-2315
Kent
Eidson House B&B .... (216)673-5544
Kings Mills
King's Manor Inn B&B .... (513)459-9959
Kinsman
Hidden Hollow .... (216)876-8686
Lakeside
Rothenbuler's Guest House .... (419)798-5656
Lakeside Marblehead
Ivy House Bed & Breakfast ..... (419)798-4944
Lakeview Historic Inn .... (419)798-5845
Lakeville
Quiet Country B&B .... (216)378-2291
Lancaster
Butterfly Inn .... (614)654-7654
Shaw's Inn .... (614)654-1842
Laurelville
Hocking House B&B
.... (614)332-1655 (800)477-1541
Lebanon
Burl Manor .... (513)932-1266
Golden Lamb .... (513)932-5065
White Tor .... (513)932-5892
Lewisville
Grandma Betty's B&B .... (614)567-3456
Lexington
The White Fence Inn .... (419)884-2356
Wittmers Country Acres .... (419)884-2846
Lodi
Squirrel's Run B&B .... (216)948-3026
Logan
Bartholomew .... (614)385-8363
Critter Ridge .... (614)385-4941
Johnson's B&B .... (614)385-4488
The Rainbow's End .... (614)385-2537
London
Wintchester House .... (614)852-0499
Loudonville
Blackfork Inn .... (419)994-3252

Louisville
The Mainstay B&B .... (216)875-1021
Lucas
Stillmeadow Inn .... (419)892-3197
Lucasville
The Olde Lamplighter .... (614)259-3002
Manchester
Three Islands Bed & Breakfast .. (513)549-2149
Mansfield
The B&B at Willow Pond .... (419)522-4644
Marblehead
Victoria Manor B&B .... (419)734-5611
Marietta
Larchmont B&B .... (614)376-9000
Marion
Olde Towne Manor (614)382-2402 (800)341-6163
Victoriana Bed & Breakfast ..... (614)382-2430
Martins Ferry
Mulberry Inn B&B .... (614)633-6058
McConnelsville
The Outback Inn . (614)962-2158 (800)542-7171
Medina
Livery Building .... (216)722-1332
Miamisburg
English Manor B&B
.... (513)866-2288 (800)676-9456
Middle Bass
Middle Bass Island Inn .... (419)285-3802
Milan
The Coach House Inn B&B ..... (419)499-2435
Gastier Farm B&B .... (419)499-2985
Millersburg
A Touch of Time .... (330)674-4311
Blue Moon .... (330)674-5119
Das Gasthaus Bed & Breakfast .. (330)893-3089
Indiantree Farm Bed & Breakfast . (330)893-2497
Monroeville
Heymann House .... (419)465-2633
Mount Gilead
Holiday House .... (419)947-8804
Mount Vernon
The Accent House .... (614)392-6466
Mount Vernon House .... (614)397-1914
Oak Hill B&B .... (614)393-2912
The Russell-Cooper House ..... (614)397-8638
The Stauffer House .... (614)397-9594
Nashville
Quiet Country Bed & Breakfast .. (330)378-2291
New Bremen
Grandmas House .... (419)629-3925
New Matamoras
Archers Fork Manor .... (614)865-3670
North Ridgeville
St. George House .... (216)327-9354
Norwalk
Boos Family Inn B&B .... (419)668-6257
Carriage House Bed & Breakfast . (419)663-5700
Old Inn B&B .... (419)668-6422
Norwood
Arlenes Stone Porch Bed & Breakfast
.... (513)531-4204
Oberlin
The Ivy Tree Inn & Garden ..... (216)774-4510
The Oberlin College Inn .... (216)775-1111
Oxford
The Alexander House .... (513)523-1200
Barker's 1848 Guest Home ..... (513)523-1107
Duck Pond .... (513)523-8914
Painesville
Rider's 1812 Inn .... (216)354-8200
Peebles
The Bayberry Inn .... (513)587-2221
Pettisville
Tudor Country Inn .... (419)445-2531
Philo
Salt Creek Bed & Breakfast ..... (614)674-7299
Pickerington
Central House .... (614)837-0932
Plain City
Wood's B&B .... (614)873-8332
Pomeroy
Holly Hill Inn .... (614)992-5657
Port Clinton
Dragonfly .... (419)734-6370
Five Bells Inn .... (419)734-1555
Island House Hotel .... (419)734-2166
McKenna's Inn .... (419)797-9619
Rock Ledge Inn & Cottages .... (419)734-3265
Put In Bay
Arlington House .... (419)285-2844
Bay House B&B .... (419)285-2822
Fether B&B .... (419)285-5511
The Vineyard .... (419)285-6181
Ripley
Baird House B&B .... (513)392-4918
Hoskins Manor .... (513)392-4741
Rittman
Crawford House Bed & Breakfast (330)925-1977
Rockbridge
Glenlaurel Inn ... (614)385-4070 (800)809-7378
Spencer House .... (614)385-8187
Rossburg
St Clair Bed & Breakfast .... (513)548-9533
Waring House .... (513)548-3448
Rushville
Stoney Ridge B&B .... (614)743-2611
Sagamore Hills
The Inn at Brandywine Falls .... (216)467-1812
Saint Marys
Grand Lake St Marys Bed & Breakfast
.... (419)394-1138
Saint Paris
Azorean Bed & Breakfast ...... (513)663-5448
Sandusky
The Cottage Rose .... (419)625-1285
Pipe Creek .... (419)626-2067
The Red Gables .... (419)625-1189
The Sanduskian .... (419)626-6688
Smith's Cottage House .... (419)627-8552
Tearose Tearoom-Bed & Breakfast (419)627-2773
Sardinia
Chamberhouse-Bed & Breakfast . (513)446-4146
Sharon Center
Hart & Mather B&B
.... (216)239-2801 (800)352-2584
Shelby
Gamble Street Inn .... (419)347-3360
Smithville
The Smithville B&B
.... (330)669-3333 (800)869-6425
Somerset
Somer Tea B&B .... (614)743-2909
South Amherst
Birch Way Villa .... (216)986-2090
South Bloomingville
Deep Woods .... (614)332-6084
South Charleston
Houstonia B&B .... (513)462-8855
Sugarcreek
Bed & Breakfast Barn .... (330)852-2337
Marbeyo B&B .... (216)852-4533
Thornville
Wal-Mec Farm B&B .... (614)246-5450
Tiffin
Fort Ball Bed & Breakfast ...... (419)447-0776
Mad River Railroad Bed & Breakfast
.... (419)447-2222
Zelkova Inn .... (419)447-4043
Toledo
Mansion View .... (419)244-5676
Troy
H.W. Allen Villa B&B .... (513)335-1181
Urbana
At Home In Urbana .... (513)653-8595
Barnett Hill Bed & Breakfast .... (513)653-7010
Valley City
Reutters Roost Bed & Breakfast . (330)483-4145
Vermilion
Captain Gilchrist .... (216)967-1237
Walnut Creek
Indiantree Farm .... (216)893-2497
Troyer's Country View B&B .... (216)893-3284
Walnut Creek Carlisle Village Inn . (330)893-3636
Warren
Twin Maples Bed & Breakfast ... (330)399-7768
Warsaw
Mary Harris House Bed & Breakfast
.... (614)824-4141
Waverly
Governor's Lodge .... (614)947-2266
Waynesville
Sugar Camp Cottage .... (513)382-6075
Waynesville Guest .... (513)897-3811
West Alexandria
Twin Creek Country B&B ...... (513)787-3990
West Liberty
Liberty House B&B
.... (513)465-1101 (800)437-8109
West Milton
Locust Lane Farm .... (513)698-4743
West Union
Murphin Ridge Inn .... (513)544-2263
West Unity
Barn House Bed & Breakfast .... (419)924-5603
Westerville
Cornelia's Corner B&B
.... (614)882-2678 (800)745-2678
Priscilla's B&B .... (614)882-3910
Williamsport
Elys Grist Mill .... (614)986-6365
Wilmington
Cedar Hill B&B In The Woods ... (513)383-2525
Historic South St. House ...... (513)382-7978
Wilmot
Cranberry Cottage .... (216)359-5171
Wooster
Howey House B&B .... (330)264-8231
Leila Belle Inn .... (330)262-8866
The Wooster Inn .... (216)264-2341
Worthington
A.M. House B&B .... (614)885-5580
Worthington Inn .... (614)885-2600
Xenia
Allendale Inn .... (513)372-1856
Yellow Springs
Morgan House .... (513)767-7509
Zanesfield
Myeerah's Inn B&B .... (513)593-3746
Zanesville
Mrs Smiths Country Living ..... (614)450-1838
Rag A Muffin Manor .... (614)452-7242
Zoar
Cider Mill .... (330)874-3240
Cobbler Shop Inn .... (216)874-2600
The Inn at Cowger House ...... (216)874-3542
Garden Gate Bed & Breakfast ... (330)874-2693
Weaving Haus .... (216)874-2646

Oklahoma

Bartlesville
White Swan .... (918)336-3519
Buffalo
Buffalo Trails .... (405)735-2301
Claremore
Country Inn .... (918)342-1894
Clayton
Clayton Country Inn .... (918)569-4165
Coalgate
Memories .... (405)927-3590
Coweta
Sandhill .... (918)486-1041
El Reno
The Goff House Inn .... (405)262-9334
Guthrie
Harrison House .... (405)282-1000
Guymon
Prairie View B&B .... (405)338-3760
Keota
Overstreet-Kerr Living History Farm (918)966-3282
Ketchum
Clark's B&B .... (918)782-3851
Marietta
Lake Country B&B .... (405)276-5175
McAlester
Bay Side Inn of Elmpoint ...... (918)426-4456
Muskogee
The Graham-Carroll House ..... (918)683-0100
Miss Addie's B&B .... (918)682-1506
Queen's House .... (918)687-6767
Rowsey Mansion .... (918)683-0100
Norman
The Dickenson House .... (405)321-2096
Oklahoma City
Chisholm Springs .... (405)942-5193

Country House . . . . (405)794-4008
Flora's B&B . . . . (405)840-3157

Park Hill

The Lord & Taylor's B&B . . . . . . (918)696-3147

Pawhuska

Inn at Woodyard Farms . . . . (918)287-2699

Ponca City

Davarnathey Inn . . . . (405)765-9922
The White House . . . . (405)767-1113

Poteau

Kerr Country Mansion & Conference Center
. . . . (918)647-8221

Ramona

Jerrett Farm Country Inn . . . . (918)371-9868

Stillwater

Thomasville B&B . . . . (405)372-1203

Sulphur

The Artesian . . . . (405)622-5254

Tulsa

The Lantern Inn . . . . (918)747-5878
Old English Inn . . . . (918)494-0063
The Robin's Nest . . . . (918)446-8700

Oregon

Albany

Brier Rose Inn B&B . . . . (541)926-0345

Aloha

The Brautigam House . . . . (503)649-8033

Arch Cape

St. Bernards B&B (503)436-2800 (800)436-2848

Ashland

Adams Cottage B&B . . . . (800)345-2570
Albion Inn . . . . (541)488-3905
All's Well Guest House . . . . (541)488-0874
Anne Bole Inn . . . . (541)482-5944
Antique Rose Inn . . . . (541)482-6285
Arden Forest Inn . . . . (541)488-1496
Ashberry Inn . . . (541)488-8000 (800)460-8076
Ashland Guest Villa . . . . (503)488-1508
Ashland's Main Street Inn . . . . . . (503)488-0969
Ashland's Victory House . . . . . . (541)488-4428
Auburn Street Cottage . . . . (503)482-3004
Bayberry Inn . . . . (541)488-1252
Buckhorn Springs . . . . (541)488-2200
Cadbury Cottage . . . . (541)488-5970
Chanticleer B&B Inn
. . . . (503)482-1919 (800)898-1950
Clarity Cottage . . . . (541)488-2457
Colonel Silsbys Bed & Breakfast . (541)488-3070
Columbia Hotel . . . . (503)482-3726
Coolidge House B&B
. . . . (541)482-4721 (800)655-5522
Country Willows Inn . . . . (541)488-1590
Cowslip's Belle . (541)488-2901 (800)888-6819
Drovers Inn . . . . (541)482-6280
Eagle Mill Bed & Breakfast . . . . . (541)488-4482
Ann Hathaway's Cottage
. . . . (541)488-1050 (800)643-4434
Fiddle Family Inn . . . . (541)482-1956
Fox House Inn . . . . (541)488-1055
Grapevine Inn . . . . (503)482-7944
Hersey House . . . . (541)482-4563
Highland Acres . . . . (503)482-2170
Jessel House . . . . (541)488-0588
Laurel Street Inn . (541)488-2222 (800)541-5485
Lithia Rose Lodging . . . . (541)482-1882
Lithia Springs Inn (541)482-7128 (800)482-7128
McCall House . . . . (541)482-9296
Mousetrap Inn . . (541)482-9228 (800)460-5453
Neil Creek House . . . . (541)482-6443
Nightingail's Inn . (541)482-7373 (800)460-8037
Oak Hill Country B&B . . . . (503)482-1554
Oak Street Station . . . . (541)482-1726
Parkside . . . . (541)482-2320
Peerless Hotel . . (541)488-1082 (800)460-8758
Pelton House . . . . (541)488-2293
Pinehurst Inn at Jenny Creek . . . . (503)488-1002
Queen Ann . . . . (541)482-0220
The Redwing B&B . . . . (541)482-1807
Romeo Inn . . . . (541)488-0884
Royal Carter House . . . . (503)482-5623
Scenic View B&B . . . . (503)482-2315
Studios Inn . . . . (541)488-5882
Waterside Inn . . . . (541)482-3315
Wimer Street Inn (541)488-2319 (800)460-2211
Winchester Inn . . . . (503)488-1113
Wolfe Manor Inn . (541)488-3676 (800)801-3676
The Woods House B&B
. . . . (503)488-1598 (800)435-8260

Astoria

Astoria Inn . . . . (503)325-8153
Benjamin Young Inn
. . . . (503)325-6172 (800)201-1286
Clementine's B&B . . . . (503)325-2005
Columbia River Inn B&B . . . . (503)325-5044
Franklin Street Station . . . . (503)325-4314
Inn-Chanted B&B (503)325-5223 (800)455-7018
Rosebriar Inn . . . . (503)325-7427
Windover House . (503)325-8093 (800)990-9330

Athena

Dudley House . . . . (541)566-3719

Aumsville

Meadow View Inn B&B . . . . (503)749-1344

Aurora

The Inn at Aurora . . . . (503)678-1932

Baker City

A Demain "Until Tomorrow" B&B (541)523-2509
Powder River Tackle Co & Bed & Breakfast
. . . . (541)523-7143
York's B&B . . . . (541)523-5360

Bandon

Bailey's Cedar House B&B . . . . . (541)347-3356
Dreamcatchers . . . . (541)347-1413
Lighthouse B&B . . . . (541)347-9316
Pacific House B&B . . . . (541)347-9526
Riverboat B&B . . . . (541)347-1922

Beaverton

Yankee Tinker B&B (503)649-0932 (800)846-5377

Bend

Avonlea Farm Bed & Breakfast . . (541)385-5224
Farewell Bend B&B . . . . (541)382-4374
The Guest Cottage at Heritage Antiques
. . . . (503)382-9451
Juniper Acres B&B . . . . (541)389-2193
Lara House B&B . . . . (541)388-4064
Mill Inn . . . . (541)389-9198
Mirror Pond House . . . . (503)389-1680
Mountain View Lodge at Bend . . . (541)388-3855
The Sather House B&B . . . . (541)388-1065
The Country Inn The City . . . . . . (541)385-7639
Three Sisters B&B . . . . (503)382-5884

Boring

Lariat Gardens B&B . . . . (503)663-1967

Bridal Veil

Bridal Veil Lodge B&B . . . . (503)695-2333

Bridgeport

Bruno Ranch Bed & Breakfast & Primitive
. . . . (541)446-3468

Brightwood

Brightwood Guesthouse . . . . (503)622-5783

Brookings

Casa Rubio . . . . (707)487-4313
Chart House B&B (541)469-3867 (800)290-6208
Holmes Sea Cove . . . . (541)469-3025
Lowden's Beachfront B&B
. . . . (541)469-7045 (800)453-4768
Oceancrest House B&B
. . . . (541)469-9200 (800)769-9200
Pacific View B&B (541)469-6837 (800)461-4830
Sea Dreamer Inn . . . . (541)469-6629

Camp Sherman

Metolius Inn Bed & Breakfast . . . (541)595-6445

Cannon Beach

Cannon Beach Hotel . . . . (503)436-1392
Stephanie Inn . . . . (503)436-2221
Tern Inn . . . . (503)436-1528
The Waves . . . . (503)436-2205

Carver

Kipling Rock Farm B&B . . . . (503)658-5056

Cascade Locks

Shahala Inn1280 Ne Forest Lane . (503)374-8222

Cave Junction

Oregon Caves Chateau . . . . (503)592-3400

Central Point

Colonial House B & B . . . . (541)770-2783

Charleston

Talavar Inn . . . . (541)888-5280

Cloverdale

Hudson House B&B Inn . . . . (503)392-3533
Sandlake Country Inn . . . . (503)965-6745

Coburg

Wheeler's B&B . . . . (503)344-1366

Coos Bay

Blackberry Inn B&B . . . . (541)267-6951
Coos Bay Manor . . . . (541)269-1224
Itty Bitty Inn . . . . (541)756-6398
The Old Tower House B&B . . . . . (541)888-6058
River Star Ranch . . . . (541)267-7394
This Olde House B&B . . . . (503)267-5224
The Upper Room Chalet . . . . (541)269-5385

Coquille

Barton House . . . (541)396-5306 (800)972-7948
Coquille Bed & Breakfast . . . . . . (541)396-5272

Corbett

Chamberlain House Bed & Breakfast
. . . . (503)695-2200

Corvallis

A Bed & Breakfast at Sparks' Hearth
. . . . (541)757-7321
The Ashwood . . . (541)757-9772 (800)306-5136
Chapman House Bed & Breakfast (541)929-3059
Courtyard Inn . . . . (541)754-7136
The Hanson Country Inn . . . . (541)752-2919
Harrison House . . . . (541)752-6248
MacPherson Inn . . . . (541)753-2955
Mellon House . . . . (541)753-7725

Cottage Grove

Apple Inn . . . . . . (541)942-2393 (800)942-2393
Deermeadow Inn B&B . . . . (503)942-4878
Hillcrest Dairy B&B . . . . (503)942-0205
Ivanoffs' Inn . . . . (541)942-3171
Lily of The Field B&B . . . . (541)942-2049
River Country Inn . . . . (541)942-9334

Crescent Lake

Willamette Pass Inn
. . . . (541)433-2211 (800)301-2218

Creswell

The Country House B&B . . . . (541)895-3924

Dallas

Woodridge Haven B&B . . . . (503)623-6924

Dayville

Fish House Inn . . . . (541)987-2124

Depoe Bay

Channel House . . . . (503)765-2140
Gracie's Landing . . . . (503)765-2322
Pirate's Cove B&B . . . . (503)765-2477

Detroit

Repose & Repast . . . . (503)854-3204

Elkton

Elkqua Lodge . . . . (541)584-2161

Elmira

The Dome Bed & Breakfast . . . . . (503)935-3138
McGillivray's Log Home B&B . . . (541)935-3564

Enterprise

The George Hyatt House B&B Inn (541)426-0241
Lozier's Country Loft . . . . (503)426-3271
Outbound Inn & Breakfast House . (541)426-6457

Eugene

A Morning Rose B&B Inn . . . . . . (503)683-0605
Backroads B&B . . . . (503)484-4602
Camille's B&B . . . . (541)344-9576
Campus Cottage . . . . (503)342-5346
Coyote Creek B&B . . . . (541)343-8605
The Farmer's Daughter B&B . . . . (503)688-4229
Gable's View . . . . (503)686-8422
Lorane Valley B&B . . . . (503)686-0241
Timewarp Inn . . . . (503)344-5556
Van Buren House B&B . . . . (503)687-1074

Florence

Edwin K Bed & Breakfast . . . . . . (541)997-8360
The Johnson House
. . . . (503)997-8000 (800)768-9488
Oak Street B&B . . . . (541)997-4000

Forest Grove

Main Street B&B . . . . (503)357-9812

Frenchglen

Frenchglen Hotel . . . . (503)493-2565

Gardiner

Gardiner By Sea . . . . (503)271-4005

Garibaldi

Hill Top House B&B . . . . (503)322-3221
Pelican's Perch B&B . . . . (503)322-3633

Glendale

Mt. Reuben Inn . . . . (541)832-2653

Glide

Steelhead Run Bed & Breakfast . . (541)496-0563

Gold Beach

Endicott Gardens . . . . (541)247-6513

Heather House B&B .... (503)247-2074
The Tale Spinner B&B .... (503)247-4115
Tu Tu Tun Lodge .... (503)247-6664

Gold Hill

Willowbrook Inn .... (541)582-0075

Government Camp

Mt Hood Manor .... (503)272-3440

Grants Pass

Chriswood Inn .... (541)474-9733
The Clemens House B&B Inn ... (541)476-5564
Fiery Manor .... (541)476-3591
Home Farm B&B .... (541)582-0980
Martha's House . (503)476-4330 (800)261-0167
Paradise Ranch Inn .... (503)479-4333
The Washington Inn .... (541)476-1131

Halfway

Birch Leaf Farm .... (503)742-2990

Hammond

Hammond House .... (503)861-3454
Officers Inn Bed & Breakfast .... (503)861-0884

Hillsboro

Pleasant View Farms of Schools B&B Guest
.... (503)628-1065

Hood River

The Beryl House .... (541)386-6767
Brown's B&B .... (541)386-1545
Brun Fir Mountain Ranch ...... (541)354-2753
Casa Baja .... (541)386-5462
Cascade Avenue B&B .... (541)387-2377
The Cottage .... (541)386-7747
Cottonwood B&B .... (541)386-1310
Gorge View Bed & Breakfast .... (541)386-5770
Hackett House .... (541)386-1014
Inn at The Gorge-B & B .... (541)386-4429
Lake Cliff Estate .... (541)386-7000
Panorama Lodge .... (541)387-2687
State Street Inn .... (541)386-1899
The Upper Rooms on Avalon B&B (541)386-2560

Idleyld Park

Idleyld Park Lodge & Restaurant . (541)496-0088

Independence

Davidson House .... (503)838-3280
Out of The Blue B&B .... (503)838-3636

Jacksonville

Colonial House B&B .... (503)770-2783
Meadow Lark .... (503)899-8963
Jacksonville Inn .... (503)899-1900
McCully House Inn .... (541)899-1942
The Old Stage Inn .... (541)899-1776
Orth House B&B .... (503)899-8665
Reames House .... (541)899-1868
Touvelle House . . (503)899-8938 (800)846-8422

Joseph

Chandler's Inn . . (541)432-9765 (800)452-3781
Tamarack Pines Inn .... (541)432-2920

Junction City

Black Bart Bed & Breakfast ..... (503)998-1904

Kerby

Kerbyville Inn .... (541)592-4689

Kimberly

Land's Inn B&B .... (503)934-2333

Klamath Falls

Boarding House Inn Bed & Breakfast
.... (541)883-8584
Klamath Manor B&B
.... (503)883-5459 (800)956-5459
Thompsons' B&B .... (541)882-7938

La Grande

Cottonwoods Bed & Breakfast ... (541)963-8432
Pitcher Inn B&B .... (541)963-9152
Somerset Guest House .... (541)963-5054
Stang Manor Inn .... (541)963-2400

Langlois

Floras Lake House By The Sea . . (541)348-2573

Leaburg

Marjon B&B Inn .... (541)896-3145

Lebanon

Historical Booth House B&B .... (503)258-2954

Lincoln City

Brey House "Ocean View" B&B . . (541)994-7123
Pacific Rest B&B .... (503)994-2337
Inlet Garden B&B .... (541)994-7932
Portlands Whitehouse .... (541)994-8414
Rose Lodge Bed & Breakfast ... (541)994-5305
The Rustic Inn .... (541)994-5111
Young's B&B, Tastes of Yesterday (541)994-6575

Madras

Madras .... (503)475-2345

Manzanita

The Arbors at Manzanita .... (503)368-7566
The Inn at Manzanita .... (503)368-6754

Maupin

C and J Lodge B&B .... (503)395-2404

McMinnville

Alderstreet Bed & Breakfast .... (503)472-8418
Baker Street B&B (503)472-5575 (800)870-5575
Garden Cottage B & B .... (503)434-2842
Orchard View Inn B&B .... (503)472-0165
Steiger Haus B&B .... (503)472-0821
Williams House B&B
.... (503)434-9016 (800)441-2214

Medford

Carpenter Hill Inn .... (541)535-4147
Under The Greenwood Tree ..... (541)776-0000
Waverly Cottage Bed & Breakfast (541)779-4716

Mill City

Ivy Creek B&B .... (503)897-2001
Morrison Cottage .... (503)897-3371

Milton-Freewater

Birch Tree Manor .... (503)938-6455

Milwaukie

Dana Estate B & B .... (503)653-0018
Gray Gables .... (503)654-0470
Historic Broetje House .... (503)659-8860
Lo Stivale Italian B & B .... (503)655-1832

Monmouth

Howell's B&B .... (503)838-2085

Monroe

The Valley Grand B&B .... (541)847-5523

Mosier

Cherry Hill .... (541)478-4455

Mount Hood Parkdale

Mt Hood Bed & Breakfast ...... (541)352-6885
Pear Ridge Bed & Breakfast .... (541)352-6637

Myrtle Creek

Sonka's Sheep Station Inn ..... (503)863-5168

Newberg

The Partridge Farm .... (503)538-2050
Belanger's Secluded B&B ...... (503)538-2635
Smith House .... (503)538-1995
Springbrook Hazelnut Farm
.... (503)538-4606 (800)793-8528

Newport

Ocean House B&B .... (541)265-6158
Sea Cliff B&B .... (541)265-6664
Sylvia Beach Hotel .... (541)265-5428
Tyee Lodge Oceanfront .... (541)265-8953

North Bend

Dunes Bed & Breakfast .... (541)756-5088
Highlands .... (503)756-0300
Sherman House B&B .... (503)756-3496

Oakland

The Beckley House .... (503)459-9320
Pringle House .... (503)459-5038

Oceanside

Sea Haven Inn .... (503)842-3151
Three Capes B&B .... (503)842-6126

Oregon City

Ainsworth House Bed & Breakfeast (503)655-5172
The Inn of The Oregon Trail ..... (503)650-9322
Hydrangea Bed & Breakfast .... (503)650-4421
Tolle House Bed & Breakfast .... (503)655-4325

Otis

Lake Side B&B .... (541)996-8938
Salmon River B&B .... (541)994-2639

Otter Rock

The Inn at Otter Crest .... (503)765-2111

Pacific City

Eagle's View B&B .... (503)965-7600
Pacific View B&B .... (503)965-6498
Sandlake Country Inn .... (503)965-6745

Pendleton

A Place Apart B&B Inn .... (541)276-0573
Dories Inn .... (541)276-1519
Graham's B&B .... (541)278-1743
Parker House Bed & Breakfast . . (541)276-8581
Swift Station Inn B&B .... (541)276-3739
Working Girls Old Hotel .... (541)276-4767

Pleasant Hill

Glendale Resort B&B .... (503)726-2064

Port Orford

Home By The Sea B&B .... (503)332-2855
Steelblue Chameleon Lodge .... (541)332-3140

Portland

A Tudor House B&B .... (503)287-9476
A Victorian Rose .... (503)223-7673
Abernathy's B&B .... (503)243-7616
Allenhouse B&B .... (503)227-6841
Cape Cod B&B .... (503)246-1839
The Clinkerbrick House .... (503)281-2533
Garden House Inn .... (503)236-0794
Gedney Gardens .... (503)226-6514
General Hooker's House
.... (503)222-4435 (800)745-4135
Georgian House B&B .... (503)281-2250
Heron Haus .... (503)274-1846
Holladay House .... (503)282-3172
Hostess House Bed & Breakfast . (503)282-7892
Irvington Inn .... (503)280-2299
Knott Street Inn B&B .... (503)249-1855
The Lion and The Rose .... (503)287-9245
MacMaster House .... (503)223-7362
Old Country Farmhouse Bed & Breakfast
.... (503)690-9009
Pittock Acres B&B .... (503)226-1163
Plum Tree B&B .... (503)280-0679
Portland Guest House .... (503)282-1402
Portland's White House .... (503)287-7131
Sauvie Island B&B .... (503)621-3216
Sullivan's Gulch B&B .... (503)331-1104
3 B's at Market .... (503)232-1554
Westlund's River Edge B&B .... (503)621-9856

Prairie City

Riverside School House Bed & Breakfast
.... (541)820-4731
Strawberry Mountain Inn ...... (800)545-6913

Prineville

The Historic Elliott House ...... (541)416-0423

Redmond

Llast Camp Llamas .... (541)548-6828

Roseburg

Hokanson's Guest House ...... (541)672-2632
House of Hunter .... (541)672-2335
Oak Ridge B&B .... (503)672-2168
The Umpqua House B&B ...... (503)459-4700
The Woods .... (503)672-2927

Saint Helens

Hopkins House B&B .... (503)397-4676

Salem

Bethel Heights Farm Bed & Breakfast
.... (503)364-7688
Cottonwood Cottage B&B ...... (503)362-3979
Eagle Crest Bed & Breakfast .... (503)364-3960
Hampshire House Bed & Breakfast (503)370-7181
Harbison House .... (503)581-8118
Marquee House .... (503)391-0837
State House B&B .... (503)588-1340

Sandy

Auberge Des Fleurs .... (503)663-9449
Fernwood at Alder Creek .... (503)622-3570

Scappoose

Malarkey Ranch Inn B & B ..... (503)543-5244

Seal Rock

Blackberry Inn .... (541)563-2259

Seaside

10th Avenue Innbed & Breakfast (800)569-1114
The Anderson's Boarding House
.... (503)738-9055 (800)995-4013
Baileys Bide-A-Wee Bread & Breakfast
.... (503)738-3711
Beachwood B&B .... (503)738-9585
Custer House B&B .... (503)738-7825
Gaston's Beachside B&B ...... (503)738-8320
The Gilbert Inn, B&B .... (503)738-9770
Chateau on The River
.... (503)738-8800 (800)789-7287
Riverside Inn .... (503)738-8254
Sea Side Inn .... (503)738-6403
Summer House .... (503)738-5740

Sheridan

Thre'pence B&B .... (503)843-4984

Silverton

Abiqua Creek Farms B&B ...... (503)873-6878
The Egg Cup Inn B&B .... (503)873-5497

Sisters

Cascade Country Inn .... (541)549-4666
Hospitality House .... (541)549-4909
Squaw Creek B&B (541)549-4312 (800)930-0055

Sixes
Sixes River Hotel & Farm
. . . . (541)332-3900 (800)828-5161
Spray
Pioneer B&B . . . . (503)462-3934
Stayton
Bird and Hat Inn-B & B . . . . (503)769-7817
The Inn at Gardner House Bed & Breakfast
. . . . (503)769-6331
Horncroft . . . . (503)769-6287
The Stayton House . . . . (503)769-4342
Steamboat
Steamboat Inn . . . . (503)498-2411
Sublimity
Silver Mountain B&B
. . . . (503)769-7127 (800)952-3905
Summer Lake
Summer Lake B&B Inn
. . . . (541)943-3983 (800)261-2778
Sun River
Diamondstone Guest Lodge & Gallery
. . . . (541)536-6263 (800)600-6263
The Dalles
Bigelow B&B . . . . (503)298-8239
Boarding House . . . . (541)296-5299
The Columbia House . . . . (541)298-4686
Captain Gray's Guest House
. . . . (541)298-8222 (800)448-4729
The Heimrich-Seufert House . . . . (541)298-4321
Williams House Inn . . . . (503)296-2889
Windrider Inn . . . . (541)296-2607
Tigard
The Woven Glass Inn . . . . (503)590-6040
Tillamook
Whiskey Creek B&B . . . . (503)842-2408
Troutdale
Riverview Farm B&B . . . . (503)695-5847
Tualatin
Stafford Road Country Inn
. . . . (503)638-0402 (800)360-7806
Vernonia
Handulah Inn . . . . (503)429-0409
Vida
Eagle Rock Lodge . . . . (541)822-3962
McKenzie River Inn . . . . (541)822-6260
Waldport
Colleens Country Bed & Breakfast (541)563-2301
The Sanderling Bed & Breakfast . (541)563-4752
Wallowa
The McCrae House, A Country Inn (503)886-4352
Welches
Doublegate Inn B&B . . . . (503)622-4859
Mountain Shadows B&B . . . . (503)622-4746
Old Welches Inn B&B . . . . (503)622-3754
West Linn
Rose Cottage Bed & Breakfast . . (503)650-6053
Swift Shore Chalet . . . . (503)650-3853
Walden House Bed & Breakfast . . (503)655-4960
Westfir
Westfir Lodge, A B&B Inn . . . . . . (541)782-3103
Weston
Tamarack Inn B&B . . . . (541)566-9348
Westport
King Salmon Lodge . . . . (503)455-2400
Wolf Creek
Wolf Creek Tavern . . . . (503)866-2474
Woodburn
The Carriage House B&B . . . . . . (503)982-1543
Yachats
Adobe . . . . (503)547-3141
Amaroo Inn-B & B . . . . (541)547-3639
Burd's Nest Inn B&B . . . . (541)547-3683
Kittiwake B&B . . . . (541)547-4470
Morning Star Gallery, B&B at The Beach
. . . . (541)547-4412
New England House B&B
. . . . (541)547-4799 (800)508-6455
Oregon House Inn . . . . (503)547-3329
The Sanderling B&B . . . . (541)563-4752
Serenity B&B . . . . (541)547-3813
Ziggurat . . . . (541)547-3925
Yamhill
Flying M Ranch . . . . (503)662-3222
Messina Manor . . . . (503)662-4466

Pennsylvania

Aaronsburg
Brick House . . . . (814)349-8795
Abbottstown
The Altland House . . . . (717)259-9536
Adamstown
Amethyst Inn . . . . (717)484-0500
Addison
Abram Augustine Homestead . . . (814)395-5827
Akron
Bella Vista B&B . . . . (717)859-4227
The Boxwood Inn . . . . (800)238-3466
Springhouse Inn B&B . . . . (717)859-4202
Alexandria
Hearthwood House . . . . (814)669-4386
Allentown
Coachaus . . . . (215)821-4854
Hamilton House B&B . . . . (610)433-3919
Annville
Shutter Cupboard . . . . (717)867-4449
Ardmore
The Shamrock House B&B . . . . . (215)642-2655
Arendtsville
Hartzel Haven . . . . (717)677-4849
Aspers
Clover Hill Inn Bed & Breakfast . . (717)677-9727
Atglen
Umble Rest . . . . (215)593-2274
Avondale
Windswept Bed & Breakfast . . . . (610)869-2512
Bangor
Hurray Back River House . . . . . . (610)498-2131
Beach Lake
East Shore House B&B . . . . (717)729-8523
Evergreen Lodge . . . . (717)729-8404
Bear Creek
Bischwind . . . . (717)472-3820
Bedford
Jean Bonnet Tavern . . . . (814)623-2250
Bellefonte
Aunt Junes Bed & Breakfast . . . . (814)355-1135
The Garret . . . . (814)355-3093
Selgate House . . . . (814)353-1102
Yocum's Victorian B&B . . . . (814)355-5100
Benton
Red Poppy B&B . . . . (717)925-5823
Berlin
Vietersburg Inn B&B . . . . (814)267-3696
Berwick
Tom & Becky's Place . . . . (717)752-3362
Bethlehem
The Bethlehem Inn . . . . (215)867-4985
Salisbury House . . . . (215)791-4225
Biglerville
Mulberry Farm Bed & Breakfast . (717)334-5827
Birchrunville
Flowing Springs Inn . . . . (610)469-0899
Bird-In-Hand
Graystone Manor B&B . . . . (717)393-4233
Mill Creek Homestead B&B
. . . . (717)291-6419 (800)771-2578
Birdsboro
Brooke Mansion Victorian Inn
. . . . (610)582-9775 (800)544-1094
Blakeslee
Blue Berry Mountain Inn . . . . (717)646-7144
Bloomsburg
Irondale Inn B&B . . . . (717)387-0203
Magee's Main Street Inn
. . . . (717)784-3500 (800)331-9815
The Inn at Turkey Hill . . . . (717)387-1500
Blossburg
Mountain Laurel Bed & Breakfast (717)638-3588
The John Deming House . . . . . . (717)638-3011
Boalsburg
The House on Top of The Hill . . . (814)466-2070
Summer House B&B . . . . (814)466-3304
The Wagon Shed at Nittany Meadow Farm
. . . . (814)466-7550
Boiling Springs
The Garmanhaus . . . . (717)258-3980
Highland House B&B . . . . (717)258-3744
Yellow Breeches House B&B
. . . . (717)258-8344 (800)258-1639

Boyertown
The Enchanted Cottage . . . . (610)845-8845
Little House of Oley B&B . . . . . . (610)689-4814
Twin Turrets Inn . . . . (610)367-4513
Brackney
Indian Mountain Inn B&B . . . . . . (717)663-2645
Linger Longer at Quaker Lake . . . (717)663-2844
Bradford
Fisher Homestead B&B . . . . (814)368-3428
Brockway
Humphreys Homestead . . . . (814)265-0162
Buck Hill Falls
Buck Hill Inn . . . . (800)233-8113
Buffalo Mills
Buffalo Lodge . . . . (814)623-2207
Bushkill
Pocmont Resort . . . . (717)588-6671
Saw Creek Estates . . . . (818)588-6614
Butler
Horizons Plus . . . . (412)865-2545
Cambridge Springs
Bethany Guest House . . . . (814)398-2046
Rider Hill Inn Bed & Breakfast . . . (814)398-4249
Canadensis
Dreamy Acres . . . . (717)595-7115
Frog Town Inn . . . . (717)595-6282
Laurel Grove . . . . (717)595-7262
Nearbrook . . . . (717)595-3152
Pine Knob Inn . . . . (717)595-2532
Pump House Inn . . . . (717)595-7501
Carlisle
Kellerhaus . . . . (717)249-7481
Line Limousin Farm House B&B . (717)243-1281
Village Farm . . . . (717)249-7827
Cedar Run
Cedar Run Inn . . . . (717)353-6241
Center Valley
Fogelhaus . . . . (215)797-4379
Centre Hall
Nittany Meadow Farm . . . . (814)466-7550
Chalfont
Sevenoaks Farm . . . . (215)822-2164
Simon Butler Mill House B&B . . . (215)822-3582
Chambersburg
Falling Spring Inn . . . . (717)267-3654
The Ragged Edge Inn . . . . (717)261-1195
Shultz Victorian Mansion B&B . . . (717)263-3371
Churchtown
The Foreman House B&B . . . . . . (717)445-6713
Clarion
Clarion House B&B
. . . . (814)226-4996 (800)416-3297
Clark
Tara . . . . (800)782-2803
Clarks Summit
The Inn at Nichols Village . . . . . . (800)642-2215
Clifford
Wiffy Bog Farm Bed & Breakfast . (717)222-9865
Coburn
Feathered Hook . . . . (814)349-8757
Cochranton
Smith Mills Coach Stop . . . . (814)425-2377
Confluence
Hannahouse Inn Bed & Breakfast (814)395-5151
Point Guest Rooms . . . . (814)395-3082
Ruths Garden Cottage . . . . (814)395-5857
Conneaut Lake
Roe's Lakeside B&B . . . . (814)382-7363
Cooksburg
Clarion River Lodge
. . . . (814)744-8171 (800)648-6743
Gateway Lodge & Cabins . . . . . . (814)744-8017
Corry
Day Lily Inn Bed & Breakfast . . . . (814)664-9047
Coudersport
Lush Victoiran Bed & Breakfast . . (814)274-7557
Cowansville
Garrott's B&B . . . . (412)545-2432
Cranberry Township
Cranberry Bed & Breakfa . . . . . . (412)776-1198
Cranesville
Historic Zion's Hill B&B . . . . (814)774-2971
Cresco
Crescent Lodge . . . . (717)595-7486
La Anna Guest House . . . . (717)676-4225

Cresson
Station Inn . . . . (814)886-4757
Danville
The Pine Barn Inn . . . . (717)275-2071
Delaware Water Gap
Mountain House . . . . (717)424-2254
Shepard House . . . . (717)424-9779
Denver
Cocalico Creek B&B . . . . (717)336-0271
Dillsburg
The Peter Wolford House . . . . . . (717)432-0757
Donegal
Mountain View B&B & Antiques . (412)593-6349
Douglassville
Yellow House Hotel . . . . (610)689-9410
Dover
Danmar House . . . . (717)292-5128
Detters Acres B&B . . . . (717)292-3172
Downingtown
Glen Isle Farm . . (610)269-9100 (800)269-1730
Doylestown
Doylestown Inn . . . . (215)345-6610
The Inn at Fordhook Farm . . . . . . (215)345-1766
Highland Farms Bed & Breakfast . (215)340-1354
Lambertville House . . . . (215)348-7166
Pine Tree Farm . . . . (215)348-0632
Duncansville
Sunbrook Mansion Bed & Breakfast
. . . . (814)695-6664
Dushore
Cherry Mill Lodge . . . . (717)928-8978
Heritage Guest House . . . . (717)928-7354
Eagles Mere
Crestmont Inn . . (717)525-3519 (800)522-8767
Eagles Mere Flora Villa Inn . . . . . (717)525-3245
Shady Lane B&B (717)525-3394 (800)524-1248
East Berlin
Lion and The Lamb . . . . (717)259-9866
East Brady
Clark House . . . . (412)526-5022
East Mc Keesport
Gate House B&B . . . . (412)824-9399
East Petersburg
The George Zahm House . . . . . . (717)569-6026
East Stroudsburg
The Inn at Meadowbrook . . . . . . (717)629-0296
Easton
The Lafayette Inn . . . . (215)253-4500
Ebensburg
Noon-Collins Inn . . . . (814)472-4311
Edinboro
Rooster Ridge B&B . . . . (814)756-5135
Elizabethtown
West Ridge Guest House
. . . . (717)367-7783 (800)367-7783
Elizabethville
The Inn at Elizabethville . . . . (717)362-3476
Elkland
Marigold Manor Bed & Breakfast . (814)258-7144
Elliottsburg
Reapsome House at Willow Spring (717)582-2064
Elm
Elm Country Inn . . . . (717)664-3623
Elverson
Rocky Side Farm . . . . (215)286-5362
Elysburg
Crab Apple Cove . . . . (717)672-2078
Latorre House B&B . . . . (717)672-7243
Emigsville
Emig Mansion . . . . (717)764-2226
Emlenton
Apple Alley B&B . . . . (412)867-9636
Barnard House . . . . (412)867-2261
Emmaus
Leibert Gap Manor (215)967-1242 (800)964-1242
Emporium
Emporium Victorian . . . . (814)486-3932
Ephrata
The 1777 House at Doneckers . . (717)738-9502
Bed & Breakfast at Wissler's . . . . (717)738-1322
Clearview Farm . . . . (717)733-6333
Covered Bridge Inn . . . . (717)733-1592
Gerhart House B&B . . . . (717)733-0263
Hackman's Country Inn . . . . (717)733-3498
The Inn at Donecker . . . . (717)738-9502
Kimmell House . . . . (717)733-6358
Red Maple Overnite Guests . . . . . (717)733-9405
Equinunk
Hills Twin Spruce Lodge . . . . (717)224-6044
Erie
Carroll Inn . . . . (814)455-2022
Royal Acre Retreat . . . . (814)838-7928
Spencer House B&B
. . . . (814)454-5984 (800)890-7263
Erwinna
Isaac Stover House . . . . (215)294-8044
Everett
Newry Manor . . . . (814)623-1250
Exton
Duling Kurtz House . . . . (215)524-1830
Fairfield
Christiansen Old Barn B&B . . . . . (717)642-5711
Windborne Farm . . . . (717)642-5436
Falls
Taylor Sisters Bed & Breakfast . . (717)388-6335
Farmington
Quiet House B&B . . . . (412)329-8120
Fogelsville
Glasbern . . . . (215)285-4723
Franklin
Lamberton House . . . . (814)432-7908
Quo Vadis B&B . . . . (814)432-4208
Choconut
Addison House B&B . . . . (717)553-2682
Gaines
Rough Cut Lodge . . . . (814)435-2192
Gap
Belmont View B&B . . . . (717)442-5269
Ben-Mar Farm B&B . . . . (717)768-3309
Farm View Guest House B&B . . . (717)442-9055
Gardenville
Maplewood Farm B&B . . . . (215)766-0477
Gettysburg
The Gaslight Inn . . . . (717)337-9100
Dobbin House Tavern . . . . (717)334-2100
The Herr Tavern & Publick House
. . . . (717)334-4332 (800)362-9849
Historic Farnsworth House . . . . . (717)334-8838
Brierfield B&B . . . . (717)334-8725
Kings Water Gardens & Pond Supplies
. . . . (717)334-2321
Swinn's Lodging . . . . (717)334-5255
The Tannery B&B . . . . (717)334-2454
Tiber House Bed & Breakfast . . . (717)334-0493
Gilbert
Tobias House B&B . . . . (610)681-4854
Gillett
Gillett House B & B . . . . (717)596-4428
Glen Mills
Crier In The Country . . . . (610)358-2411
Sweetwater Farm . . . . (215)459-4711
Glen Riddle Lima
Hamanassett B&B . . . . (610)459-3000
Glen Rock
Dogwood House at Spoutwood Farm
. . . . (717)235-6610
Glen Rock Mill Inn . . . . (717)235-5918
Glenmoore
Conestoga Horse B&B . . . . (215)458-8535
Gordonville
Colonial Ridge B&B
. . . . (717)768-8507 (800)777-7274
Eby's Pequea Tourist Farm . . . . . (717)768-3615
Hat Tavern Farm . . . . (717)768-3909
Old Leacock Road B&B . . . . (717)768-3824
The Osceola Mill House . . . . (717)768-3758
Grand Valley
In The Woods Bed & Breakfast and Mini-Co
. . . . (814)436-7343
Greencastle
Phaeton Farm B&B . . . . (717)597-8656
Welsh Run Inn . . . . (717)328-9506
Greensburg
Huntland Farm B&B . . . . (412)834-8483
Mountain View Inn . . . . (412)834-5300
Grove City
Snow Goose Inn (412)458-4644 (800)317-4644
Hallstead
Log Cabin B&B . . . . (717)879-4167
Hanover
Beechmont B&B Inn
. . . . (717)632-3013 (800)553-7009
Country View Acres . . . . (717)637-8992
Harford
9 Partners Inn . . . . (717)434-2233
Harmony
Neff House . . . . (412)452-7512
Harrisburg
Abide With Me B&B . . . . (717)236-5873
Harrisville
Gillray Inn . . . . (412)735-2274
Harveys Lake
The Duck Inn . . . . (717)639-2605
Hatfield
Der Stone Farmhouse . . . . (215)723-9158
Hawley
Morning Glories . . . . (717)226-0644
Woodloch Pines Resort . . . . (717)685-7121
Hazleton
Forest Hills Inn . . . . (717)459-2730
Hershey
Horetsky's Tourist Home . . . . (800)533-5783
Pinehurst Inn B&B . . . . (717)533-2603
Union Canal House Country Inn . (717)566-0054
Hesston
Aunt Susies Country Vacation . . . (814)658-3638
Hickory
Shady Elms Farm B&B . . . . (412)356-7755
Hillsgrove
Renningers Country Store . . . . . . (717)924-3505
The Tannery House . . . . (717)924-3505
Holicong
Ash Mill Farm . . . . (215)794-5373
Hollidaysburg
The Jackson Inn . . . . (814)695-1232
Parris House B&B . . . . (814)696-2849
Hollsopple
Stone Ridge Bed & Breakfast . . . (814)288-3931
Holtwood
Country Cottage . . . . (717)284-2559
Drytown Inn . . . . (717)284-4816
Honesdale
Hotel Wayne . . . . (717)253-3290
Olver's B&B . . . . (717)253-4533
Honey Brook
Waynebrook Inn . . . . (610)273-2444
Honey Grove
McCullochs Mills Inn . . . . (717)734-3628
Howard
Howard Homestead B&B . . . . . . (814)625-2506
Hummelstown
Tea Cozy . . . . (717)566-9976
Huntingdon
Ripka's Cottages . . . . (814)643-4206
Solvang The Inn At . . . . (814)643-3035
Yoder's B&B . . . . (814)643-3221
Indiana
Blosser Art Studio B&B . . . . (412)465-7052
Jacobus
Past Purr-Fect B&B . . . . (717)428-1634
James Creek
Zeigler House . . . . (814)658-2633
Jamestown
Willowood Inn B&B . . . . (412)932-3866
Jennerstown
Thee Olde Stagecoach B&B . . . . (814)629-7440
Jersey Shore
Ye Olde Library B&B . . . . (717)398-1571
Jim Thorpe
Ritz on Broadway . . . . (717)325-3677
Victoria Ann's B&B . . . . (717)325-8107
Kempton
Hawk Mountain B&B . . . . (610)756-4224
Orchard Creek Inn B&B . . . . (610)756-4324
Kennett Square
Buttonwood Farm . . . . (215)444-0278
The Inn at Lightedholly . . . . (215)444-9246
Longwood Inn . . . . (215)444-3515
Scarlett House . . (610)444-9592 (800)820-9592
Kintnersville
Bucksville House . . . . (215)847-8948
Light Farm . . . . (610)847-3276
Kinzers
Groff Farm Home Lodging . . . . . (717)442-8223

Sycamore Haven Farm . . . . (717)442-4901

Knox

Mitchell Ponds Inne . . . . (814)797-1690
Wolfs Den B&B . . . . (814)797-1103

Kutztown

Around The World B&B . . . . (610)683-8885
Crystal B&B . . . . (610)777-4422
New Smithville Country Inn . . . . . (610)285-2987

Lahaska

Golden Plough Inn . . . . (215)794-4004
Lahaska Hotel . . . . (215)794-0440
Mill Creek Farm Bed & Breakfast . (215)794-0776

Lake Harmony

Harmony Lake Shore Inn . . . . . . (717)722-0522

Lakeville

Caesars Cove Haven . . . . (800)233-4141

Lancaster

90 Greenfield . . . . (717)299-5964
Buena Kotte B&B . . . . (717)295-2597
Equestrian Estates Horse Farm B&B . . . . (717)464-2164
Hollinger House . . . . (717)464-3050
Landyshade Farms . . . . (717)898-7689
Maison Rouge . . . . (717)399-3033
Meadowview Guest House . . . . . (717)299-4017
New Life Homestead B&B . . . . . . (717)396-8928
Nissley's Lancaster City Inns-Apt Suites . . . . (717)392-2311
Patchwork Inn . . . . (717)394-5522

Landenberg

Daybreak Farm Bed & Breakfast . (610)255-0282

Laughlintown

Ligonier Country Inn . . . . (412)238-3651

Lebanon

Inn 422 . . . . (717)274-3651
Zinns Mill Homestead . . . . (717)272-1513

Leesport

The Loom Room . . . . (215)926-3217

Leetsdale

Whistlestop Bed & Breakfast . . . . (412)251-0852

Lewisberry

Dutch Country Inn B & B . . . . . . (717)938-8191

Lewisburg

Brookpark Farm B&B . . . . (717)523-0220
The Inn on Fiddler's Tract . . . . . . (717)523-7197
Pineapple Inn . . . . (717)524-6200

Liberty

Hill-Top Haven . . . . (717)324-2608

Ligonier

Campbell House B&B-Gift Parlour (412)238-9812
Grant House B&B . . . . (412)238-5135
Old Kiln Place . . . . (412)238-2524
Woolley Fox . . . . (412)238-3004

Lititz

Banner House B&B . . . . (717)626-REST
Carter Run Inn B&B . . . . (717)626-8807
Cricket Hollow B&B . . . . (717)626-4083
General Sutter Inn . . . . (717)626-2115
Sleepy Mill Farm . . . . (717)626-6629
Spahr's Century Farm B&B . . . . . (717)627-2185

Lock Haven

Farmhouse . . . . (717)748-8099
Roger's By The River . . . . (800)237-8688
Victorian Inn B&B . . . . (717)748-8688

Loganville

Market Sleigh B&B . . . . (717)428-1440

Lumberville

1740 House . . . . (215)297-5661
Black Bass Hotel . . . . (215)297-5770

Lykens

Mausers Bed & Breakfast . . . . . . (717)453-9449

Macungie

Sycamore Inn . . . . (610)966-5177

Malvern

General Warren Inne . . . . (610)296-3637

Manchester

The Garden House B&B . . . . (717)266-6205

Manheim

Country Pines Farm & Cottage . . (717)665-5478
Herr Farmhouse Inn . . . . (717)653-9852 (800)584-0743
Jonde Lane Farm . . . . (717)665-4231
Landis Farm . . . . (717)898-7028
The Inn at Mt.hope . . . . (717)664-4708
Penn's Valley Farm & Inn . . . . . . (717)898-7386

Rose Manor B&B and Herbal Gift Shop . . . . (717)664-4932 (800)666-4932
Stone Haus Farm . . . . (717)653-5819
Wenger's B&B . . . . (717)665-3862

Marietta

Morning Meadows Farm . . . . (717)426-1425
The Noble House . . . . (717)426-4389
Olde Fogie Farm . . . . (717)426-3992
Vogt Farm B&B . (717)653-4810 (800)854-0399

Markleysburg

Kamps Personal Care Home . . . . (412)329-1020

Marshalls Creek

Mountain Manor Inn & Golf Club . (717)223-8098

Matamoras

Riverview Inn Inc . . . . (717)491-2173

McKeesport

Butlers Golf Course John Butler House- . . . . (412)751-6670

McClure

The Water Company Farm . . . . . (717)658-3536

McConnellsburg

Market Street Inn . . . . (717)485-5495

Meadville

Azalea House B & B . . . . (814)337-8883
Fountainside B&B . . . . (814)337-7447

Mechanicsburg

Moores Mountain Inn . . . . (717)766-3412

Mercer

The Magoffin Inn (412)662-4611 (800)841-0824
Stranahan House B&B . . . . (412)662-4516

Mercersburg

Fox Run Inn . . . . (717)328-5707
Guest Farm . . . . (717)328-9049
Maplebrow Bed & Breakfast . . . . (717)328-3172
The Mercersburg Inn . . . . (717)328-5231
The Steiger House . . . . (717)328-5757

Mertztown

Longswamp B&B . . . . (610)682-6197

Middlebury

Woods Rustic Inn Bed & Breakfast (717)376-3331

Milford

Black Walnut Inn . . . . (717)296-6322
Pine Hill Farm B&B . . . . (717)296-7395
Tom Quick Inn . . . . (717)296-6514
The Vines . . . . (717)296-6775

Millersburg

Victorian Manor Inn . . . . (717)692-3511

Millersville

Walnut Hill B&B . . . . (717)872-2283

Milton

Pau-Lyn's Country B&B . . . . (717)742-4110
Teneriff Farm B&B . . . . (717)742-9061
Tomlinson Manor B&B . . . . (717)742-3657

Mohnton

Sananda's Retreat . . . . (610)856-1585

Montoursville

Governor Shulze House Bed & Breadfast . . . . (717)368-8966

Montrose

Addison House Bed & Breakfast . (717)553-2682
The Montrose House . . . . (717)278-1124

Mount Gretna

Mt Gretna Inn . . . . (717)964-3234

Mount Jewett

Silverside Inn . . . . (814)778-5991

Mount Joy

Brenneman Farm B&B . . . . (717)653-4213
Cameron Estate Inn . . . . (717)653-1773
Country Gardens Farm . . . . (717)426-3316
Donegal Mills Plantation & Inn . . . (717)653-2168
Green Acres Farm . . . . (717)653-4028
Nolt Farm Guest Home . . . . (717)653-4192
Olde Country Log House Farm . . (717)653-4477
Rocky Acre Farms . . . . (717)653-4449

Mount Pocono

Farmhouse B&B . . . . (717)839-0796

Mountville

Mountville Antique B&B . . . . (717)285-5956

Muncy

Walton House Bed & Breakfast . . (717)546-8114

Myerstown

Tulpehocken Manor Inn & Plantation . . . . (717)866-4926

Narvon

Ironstone Acres . . . . (717)354-8547

Jeric Inn . . . . (717)445-6840

Churchtown

The Inn at Twin Linden . . . . (717)445-7619

Nazareth

Classic Victorian B&B . . . . (610)759-8276

New Albany

Waltman's B&B . . . . (717)363-2295

New Bloomfield

Tressler House B&B . . . . (717)582-2914

New Cumberland

Farm Fortune . . . . (717)774-2683

New Holland

Smucker's Farm Guest House . . . (717)354-4374

New Hope

1740 House . . . . (215)297-5661
Backstreet Inn of New Hope . . . . (215)862-9571
Centre Bridge Inn . . . . (215)862-2048
Hacienda Inn . . . . (215)862-2078
Hollyhedge B&B . . . . (215)862-3136
Hotel Du Village . . . . (215)862-9911
Lexington House . . . . (215)794-0811
The Inn at Phillips Mill . . . . (215)862-2984
The Mansion Inn . . . . (215)862-1231
The Wedgwood Collection of Historic Inns . . . . (215)862-2570

New Kingstown

Kanaga House B&B . . . . (717)697-2714

New Oxford

Adam's Apple B&B . . . . (717)624-3488
Flaherty House . . (717)624-9494 (800)217-0618
Kehrs Corner Cupboard Bed & Breakfast . . . . (717)624-3054

New Wilmington

Beechwood Inn . . . . (412)946-2342
Behms Bed & Breakfast . . . . (412)946-8641
Gabriel's B&B . . . . (412)946-3136
The Tavern & Tavern Lodge . . . . . (412)946-2020

Newtown

Ye Olde Temperance House . . . . . (215)860-0474

Newville

Nature's Nook Farm . . . . (717)776-5619
Quaint Occasion Bed & Breakfast (717)776-6575

North Bend

North Bend Bed & Breakfast . . . . (717)923-2927

North East

Brown's Village Inn . . . . (814)725-5522
Vineyard B&B . . . . (814)725-5307

North Wales

Joseph Ambler Inn . . . . (215)362-7500

Northumberland

Campbell's B&B . . . . (717)473-3276

Numidia

Fair Haven Bed & Breakfast . . . . . (717)799-0264

Oakmont

The Inn at Oakmont . . . . (412)828-6079

Oley

Reiff Farm B&B . . . . (610)987-6216

Orrtanna

Hickory Bridge Farm . . . . (717)642-5261
Mt Carmel Inn . . . . (717)642-6598

Ottsville

Frankenfield Farm . . . . (610)847-2771

Oxford

Hershey's Log House Inn B&B . . (610)932-9257

Palmyra

Shepherd's Acres . . . . (717)838-5899

Paradise

Maple Lane Farm . . . . (717)687-7479
Neffdale Farm . . . . (717)687-7837
Frogtown Acres B&B Inn & Amish Gift Shop . . . . (717)768-7684
Verdant View Farm . . . . (717)687-7353

Patton

Nationality House . . . . (814)674-2225

Paupack

Lampost B&B . . . . (717)857-1738

Peach Bottom

Pleasant Grove Farm . . . . (717)548-3100

Philadelphia

Abigail Adams' B&B . . . . (215)546-7336
Antique Row Bed & Breakfast . . . (215)592-7802
Appels Society Hill B & B . . . . . . (215)925-5460
Bag & Baggage Bed & Breakfast . (215)546-3807
Gables Bed & Breakfast . . . . (215)662-1918
Shippen Way Inn (215)627-7266 (800)245-4873

Society Hill Hotel . . . . (215)925-1919
Steele Away B&B . . . . (215)242-0722
Village Guest House . . . . (215)755-9770

Phoenixville
Almost Like Home . . . . (610)935-0935
Amsterdam Bed & Breakfast . . . . (610)983-9620

Pine Bank
Cole's Log Cabin B&B . . . . (412)451-8521

Pittsburgh
Appletree Bed & Breakfast . . . . . (412)661-0631
La-Fleur Bed & Breakfa . . . . (412)921-8588
Oakwood . . . . (412)835-9565
Pittsburgh Bed & Breakfa . . . . . . (412)431-3344
The Priory . . . . (412)231-3338
The Shadyside B&B . . . . (412)683-6501

Plumsteadville
Maplewood Farm . . . . (215)766-0477
Plumsteadville Inn . . . . (215)766-7500

Port Clinton
Union House B&B . . . . (610)562-3155

Port Matilda
Martha Furnace House . . . . (814)692-4393

Pottstown
Coventry Forge Inn . . . . (215)469-6222
Fairway Farm B&B . . . . (215)326-1315

Quarryville
Bright Pine Hollow Farm . . . . (717)299-4501

Reading
The Inn at Centre Park . . . . (215)374-8557
The House on The Canal B&B . . . (610)921-3015
Hunter House . . . . (215)374-6608

Red Lion
Red Lion B&B . . . . (717)244-4739
Fairmount B&B . . . . (717)244-0165

Rehersburg
Kurr House . . . . (717)933-8219

Reinholds
Brownstone Corner B&B . . . . (717)484-4460

Rexmont
Rexmont Inn . . . . (800)717-274-

Ridgway
Faircroft B&B . . . . (814)776-2539
Post House . . . . (814)772-2441

Riegelsville
Riegelsville Hotel . . . . (215)749-2469

Roaring Spring
Spring Garden Farm B&B . . . . . . (814)224-2569
Spring Manor B&B . . . . (814)224-5820

Rockwood
Trenthouse Inn . . . . (814)352-8492

Ronks
Cherry-Crest Dairy Farm . . . . (717)687-6844
Florys Cottages & Camping . . . . (717)687-6670
Melody Lawn Farm Tourist Home (717)684-0951

Saint Marys
Old Charm Bed & Breakfast . . . . (814)834-9429

Saint Thomas
Rice's White House Inn . . . . (717)369-4224

Saxonburg
Main Stay Teh . . . . (412)352-9363

Saxton
Weaver's Ridge Resort . . . . (814)635-3730

Sayre
Park Place Bed & Breakfast . . . . (717)888-5779

Schellsburg
Bedford's Covered Bridge Inn . . . (814)733-4093

Scottdale
Pine Wood Acres B&B . . . . (412)887-5404

Selinsgrove
The Blue Lion Inn . . . . (717)374-2929
Unicorn Bed & Breakfast . . . . . . (717)374-5616

Shamokin
Lengthening Years . . . . (717)648-4101

Shartlesville
Haag's Hotel . . . . (215)488-6692

Shawnee on Delaware
Eagle Rock Lodge . . . . (717)421-2139

Shelocta
Charbert Farm B&B
. . . . (412)726-8264 (800)475-8264

Shippensburg
Candlelight Bed & Breakfast . . . . (717)532-5846
McLean House B&B . . . . (717)530-1390
Thornbury Farm . . . . (717)776-5617
Wilmar Manor Bed & Breakfast . . (717)532-3784

Shohola
Pegasus B&B . . . . (717)296-4017

Shrewsbury
Kolter House B&B . . . . (717)235-5528

Sinnamahoning
Karen Maries Bed & Breakfast . . . (814)546-2635

Slippery Rock
Applebutter Inn . . . . (412)794-1844
Creekside Village . . . . (412)530-6347

Smethport
Blackberry Inn B&B . . . . (814)887-7777
Christmas Inn . . . . (814)887-5665

Smoketown
Old Road Guest Home . . . . (717)393-8182
Smoketown Village Tourist Home (717)393-5975

Solebury
Rambouillet at Hollyhedge Estate . (215)862-3136

Somerset
Bayberry Inn B&B . . . . (814)445-8471
The Inn at Georgian Place . . . . . . (814)443-1043
Glades Pike Inn . . . . (814)443-4978
Somerset Country Inn . . . . (814)443-1005

South Sterling
The French Manor . . . . (717)676-3244
Sterling Inn . . . . (717)676-3311

Spring City
French Creek Falls . . . . (610)469-0899

Spring Mills
General Potter Farm at Potters Mills
. . . . (814)238-1484

Springdale
Maggie West Bed & Breakfast . . . (412)274-8906

Spruce Creek
The Dell's B&B at Cedar Hill Farm (814)632-8319
Spruce Creek B&B . . . . (814)632-3777

Starlight
The Inn at Starlight Lake
. . . . (717)798-2519 (800)248-2519

Starrucca
Matta Streamside Manor . . . . (717)727-2330

State College
Carnegie House . . . . (814)234-2424
The Vincent Douglas House . . . . (814)237-4490
Windswept Farm . . . . (814)355-1233

Strasburg
Coventry Cottage B&B . . . . (717)687-6986
Limestone Inn B&B . . . . (717)687-8392
The Red Caboose . . . . (717)687-6646
Strasburg Village Inn
. . . . (717)687-0900 (800)541-1055

Stroudsburg
Academy Hill House . . . . (717)476-6575
Country Inns of The Poconos . . . (717)421-5791
Country Roots . . . . (717)992-5557
Stroudsmoor Country Inn . . . . . . (717)421-6431

Sumneytown
Kaufman House . . . . (215)234-4181

Susquehanna
April Valley Bed & Breakfast . . . . (717)756-2688

Swiftwater
Britannia Country Inn & Antlers Restaurant
. . . . (717)839-7243
Holiday Glen . . . . (717)839-7015

Thompson
Ararat Lodge Inc . . . . (717)727-3174
Burchman House . . . . (717)727-3200

Thompsontown
General Evans Inn . . . . (717)535-5678

Three Springs
Aughwick House B&B . . . . (814)447-3027

Tionesta
Country Kitchen Catering Bed & Breakfast
. . . . (814)755-3636

Titusville
McMullen House B&B . . . . (814)827-1592

Topton
The Victorian Inn B&B . . . . (610)682-6846

Towanda
Victorian Guest House . . . . (717)265-6972

Troy
Holcomb House Bed & Breakfast (717)297-2460
Silver Oak Leaf B&B
. . . . (717)297-4315 (800)326-9834

Tunkhannock
Annmarie's Gazebo B&B . . . . (717)836-5730
Weeping Willow . . . . (717)836-5877

Tyler Hill
Tyler Hill B&B . . . . (717)224-6418

Ulster
Failte Inn . . . . (717)358-3899
Misty Meadow Farm . . . . (717)596-4077

Union Dale
Hollymont Bed & Breakfast . . . . . (717)679-2600
Stone Bridge Inn & Restaurant . . (717)679-9200

Unionville
Whitethorne . . . . (215)793-1748

Upland
Cheshire House - 1716 Mansion . (610)876-5355

Upper Black Eddy
Bridgeton House . . . . (215)982-5856
Tara . . . . (215)982-5457

Valley Forge
Bed & Breakfast of Valley Forge . (610)783-7838

Valley Forge (Linfield)
Shearer Elegance (610)495-7429 (800)861-0308

Verona
Inn at Oakmont . . . . (412)828-0410

Volant
Candleford Inn . . . . (412)533-4497

Walnutport
Anchor Inn Bed & Breakfast . . . . (610)767-0575

Warminster
Apple Bucket Country Inn . . . . . . (215)674-1799

Warren
Acorn Bed & Breakfast . . . . (814)723-3632
Jefferson House & Pub . . . . (814)723-2268

Washington Crossing
Woodhill Farms Inn . . . . (215)493-1974

Waterville
English Center Bed & Breakfast . . (717)634-3104

Waynesburg
Greene Gables . . . . (412)627-4391

Wellsboro
Auntie M's B&B . . . . (717)724-5771
Bed & Breakfast Stop Light . . . . . (717)724-2290
Foxfire B&B . . . . (717)724-5175
Four Winds B&B . . . . (717)724-6141

Wellsville
Warrington Farm B&B . . . . (717)432-9053

West Chester
The Barn . . . . (215)436-4544
Faunbrook B&B . . . . (610)436-5788
Franklin House B & B . . . . (610)696-7727
Highland Manor B&B . . . . (215)686-6251
Monument House . . . . (610)793-2986

West Reading
Nine-Patch B&B . . . . (610)777-4422

Westline
Westline Inn . . . . (814)778-5103

Westport
Bucktail Lodge on Kettle Creek . . (717)923-2472

Williamsport
Snyder House Victorian Bed & Breakfast
. . . . (717)326-0411
Thomas Lightfoote Inn . . . . (717)326-6396

Willow Street
The Apple Bin Inn . . . . (717)464-5881
Cook's Guest House . . . . (717)464-3273
Green Gables B&B . . . . (717)464-5546

Woodbury
Waterside Inn . . . . (814)766-3776
Woodbury Inn . . . . (814)766-3647

Woodward
Woodward Inn . . . . (814)349-8118

Wrightstown
Aberdare B&B . . . . (215)598-3896

Wyalusing
Wyalusing Hotel . . . . (717)746-1204

Wysox
Beemans Bed & Breakfast & Antiques
. . . . (717)265-8798

York
Briarwold B&B . . . . (717)252-4619
Friendship House B&B . . . . (717)843-8299
Olde Mill Manor . . . . (717)757-6164
Smyser-Bair House . . . . (717)854-3411
Sunstar Bed & Breakfast . . . . (717)755-7511

Zelienople
Benvenue Manor Bed & Breakfast (412)452-1710
The Inn on Grandview . . . . (412)452-0469

Rhode Island

Block Island
1661 Inn & Hotel Manisses
. . . . (401)466-2421 (800)626-4773
The Barrington Inn . . . . (401)466-5510
Capt Willis House . . . . (401)466-5113
Dewey Cottage . . . . (401)466-3155
Driftwind Guests . . . . (401)466-5548
Estas at Old Harbor . . . . (401)466-2651
Gables Inn . . . . (401)466-2213
The Gothic Inn . . . . (401)466-2918
Guest House . . . . (401)466-2676
Hardy Smith House . . . . (401)466-2466
High View Hotel . . . . (401)466-5912
The Island Home . . . . (401)466-5944
Island Manor Resort . . . . (401)466-5567
Mill Pond Cottages . . . . (401)466-2423
New Shoreham House
. . . . (401)466-2651 (800)272-2601
The Inn at Old Harbour . . . . (401)466-2212
Old Town Inn . . . . (401)466-5958
Sea Breeze Inn . . . . (401)466-2275
Seacrest Inn . . . . (401)466-2882
Sullivan House . . . . (401)466-5020
Adrian . . . . (401)466-2693
Islander . . . . (401)466-2897
Willow Grove . . . . (401)466-2896

Bristol
Bradford-Dimond-Norris House . . (401)253-6338

Carolina
Brenda's B&B . . . . (401)364-3608

Charlestown
General Stanton Inn . . . . (401)364-0100
Hart's-On The Pond . . . . (401)364-3148
Inn The Meadow . . . . (401)789-1473
One Willow By The Sea B&B . . . . (401)364-0802
The Place Called Hathaways B&B (401)364-6665

East Greenwich
The 1873 House . . . . (401)884-9955
Vincent House . . . . (401)885-2864

East Providence
The Last Resort . . . . (401)433-1577

Green Hill
Fairfield-By-The-Sea . . . . (401)789-4717

Harrisville
Willingham Manor . . . . (401)568-2468

Hopkinton
The General Thurston House-1763 (401)377-9049

Jamestown
Calico Cat Guest House . . . . (401)423-2641
Lionel Champlin House . . . . (401)423-2782

Kingston
The Farmer Brown House . . . . . . (401)783-5477

Lincoln
Whipple-Cullen Farmstead Bed & Breakfast
. . . . (401)333-1899

Little Compton
Ballyvoreen . . . . (401)635-4396
Lands End B&B . . . . (401)635-9557
Sakonnet Vineyards B & B Guest House
. . . . (401)635-8407

Middletown
Artful Lodger . . . . (401)847-3132
Atlantic House . . . . (401)847-7259
Bartram's B&B . . . . (401)846-2259
Bed & Breakfast 'n More . . . . (401)846-3646
Bliss Mine Road House . . . . (401)846-2979
The Briar Patch . . . . (401)841-5824
The Country Goose B&B . . . . (401)846-6308
Easton's Inn on The Beach . . . . . (401)846-0310
Green End Gardens . . . . (401)849-0309
Hedgegate B&B . . . . (401)846-3906
Maude Kerr's B&B . . . . (401)847-5997
Peckham's Guest Home . . . . (401)846-2382

Middleltown
Rhea's B&B . . . . (401)841-5560 (800)474-1194

Middletown
Sea Breeze . . . . (401)847-5626
Seaview Inn . . . . (401)846-5000
Stone Towers . . . . (401)846-3227
Stoneyard . . . . (401)847-0494
Wolcott House By-The-Sea . . . . . (401)846-9376

Misquamicut
Andrea Hotel . . . . (401)348-8788
Ocean View . . . . (401)596-7170

Narragansett
23 Perkins . . . . (401)783-9158

Naragansett
The Canterbury . . . . (401)783-0046

Narragansett
Chestnut House . . . . (401)789-5335
Four Gables . . . . (401)789-6948
Ilverthorpe Cottage . . . . (401)789-2392
Kenyon Farms . . . . (401)783-7123
Louis Sherry Cottage . . . . (401)783-8626
Maison Bienvenue . . . . (401)783-1190
Mon Reve . . . . (401)783-2846
Murphy's B&B . . . . (401)789-1824
Nansea's By The Bay . . . . (401)783-4045
The Old Clerk House . . . . (401)783-8008
Phoenix House . . . . (401)783-1918
Richards' Guest House . . . . (401)783-6895
Regina Cottage . . . . (401)783-1875
The Richards . . . . (401)789-7746
Sea Gull Guest House . . . . (401)783-4636
Seafield Cottage . . . . (401)783-2432
Southwest Wind Acres . . . . (401)783-5860
Starr Cottage . . . . (401)783-2411
Stone Lea . . . . (401)783-9546
The Tower House B&B . . . . (401)783-8628
White Rose B&B . . . . (401)789-0181

Newport
1812 House Bed & Breakfast . . . (401)847-1188
503 Spring Street . . . . (401)847-3132
Admiral Farragut Inn . . . . (401)846-4256
Guest House International . . . . . . (401)849-0051
Beachstone . . . . (401)849-3839
Beech Tree Inn . . . . (401)847-9794
Bellevue House . . . . (401)847-1828
Black Duck Inn . . . . (401)841-5548
Blue Stone . . . . (401)846-5408
The Burbank Rose B&B . . . . (401)849-9457
The Inn at Castle Hill . . . . (401)849-3800
Chambord Bed & Breakfast . . . . . (401)849-9223
Clarkeston . . . . (401)848-5300
Cliff Walk Manor . . . . (401)847-1300
Corner House Bed & Breakfast . . (401)847-8888
Covell Guest House . . . . (401)847-8872
Culpeper House . . . . (401)846-4011
Elm Tree Cottage . . . . (401)849-1610
Flag Quarters . . . . (401)849-4543
Flower Garden Guests . . . . (401)846-3119
Francis Malbone House . . . . (401)846-0392
Gingerbread B&B . . . . (401)846-3037
Gull House . . . . (401)849-3550
Hammett House Inn
. . . . (401)848-0593 (800)548-9417
Harborside Inn . . . . (401)846-6600
Hydrangea House (401)846-4435 (800)945-4667
Ivy Lodge . . . . (401)849-6865
Jenkins Guest House . . . . (401)847-6801
Banister John House . . . . (401)846-0059
La Forge Cottage . . . . (401)847-4400
Labrador House . . . . (401)849-8660
Mariner House . . . . (401)847-6938
Marshall Slocum Guest House
. . . . (401)841-5120 (800)372-5120
Merritt House Guest . . . . (401)847-4289
Mill Street Inn . . . (401)849-9500 (800)392-1316
Moulton-Weaver House . . . . (401)847-0133
Mount Vernon Inn . . . . (401)846-6314
Oceancliff . . . . (401)847-7777
On The Point B&B . . . . (401)846-8377
Pine Steet Inn . . . . (401)849-6500
Queen Anne Inn . . . . (401)846-5676
Rhode Island House . . . . (401)848-7787
Sarah Kendall House . . . . (401)846-3979
Serendipity Cottage . . . . (401)847-7080
Seven Waites Wharf . . . . (401)847-7777
Spring Street Inn . . . . (401)847-4767
Stella Maris Inn . . . . (401)849-2862
Sunnyside Mansion . . . . (401)849-3114
Tucked Away Inn . . . . (401)847-7158
Victorian Angel . . . . (401)842-0390
Victorian Ladies . . . . (401)849-9960
Wayside . . . . (401)847-0302
William Fludder House . . . . (401)849-4220
Willows of Newport . . . . (401)846-5486
Yankee Peddler Inn . . . . (401)846-1323
Yellow Cottage . . . . (401)847-6568

North Kingstown
The John Updike House . . . . (401)294-4905

Providence
Cady House . . . . (401)273-5398
Charles Hodges House . . . . (401)861-7244

Tiverton
Fort Barton House . . . . (401)624-2533

Wakefield
B&B at Highland Farm . . . . (401)783-2408
Gooseberry Marina B&B . . . . (401)789-5431

Warren
Nathaniel Porter Inn . . . . (401)245-6622

Watch Hill
Watch Hill Inn . . . . (401)348-8912

Weekapaug
J. Livingston's Guest House By The Sea
. . . . (401)322-0249
Weekapaug Inn . . . . (401)322-0301

West Kingston
The Stone Cottage B&B . . . . (401)789-0039

Westerly
Pauls Westerly House . . . . (401)348-9966
Shelter Harbor Inn (401)322-8883 (800)468-8883
The Shore Inn at Misquamicut . . . (401)348-8637
White Rose Inn . . . . (401)596-9449
Woody Hill B&B . . . . (401)322-4003

Wickford
The Holloway House . . . . (401)295-1200
Meadowland . . . . (401)294-4168

South Carolina

Abbeville
Abbewood B&B . . . . (803)459-5822
The Hitching Post Inn
. . . . (803)459-2959 (800)459-2959
The Painted Lady . . . . (864)459-8171
The Vintage Inn . (864)459-4784 (800)890-7312

Aiken
The Chancellor Carroll House . . . (803)649-5396
The Briar Patch . . . . (803)649-2010
Hollie Berries Inn . . . . (803)648-9952
Pine Knoll Inn . . . . (803)649-5939

Anderson
Centennial Plantation . . . . (803)225-4448
Evergreen Inn . . . . (803)225-1109
The Jefferson House . . . . (864)224-0678
River Inn . . . . (864)226-1431

Bamberg
General Bamberg Inn . . . . (803)245-5904

Batesburg
Batcheler's B & B . . . . (803)532-2926

Beaufort
Bay Street Inn . . . . (803)522-0050
Old Point Inn . . . . (803)524-3177
The Rhett House Inn . . . . (803)524-9030
Trescot Inn . . . . (803)522-8552
Twelve Oaks Inn . . . . (803)525-1371

Belton
Belton Inn B&B . . . . (803)338-6020

Bishopville
The Foxfire B&B . . . . (803)484-5643
Law Street Inn . . . . (800)253-5474

Blacksburg
The White House Inn . . . . (864)839-3000

Blackville
Miss Lillian's . . . . (803)284-3736

Camden
Aberdeen . . . . (803)432-2524
Bloomsbury . . . . (803)432-9714
Carolina Oaks . . . . (803)432-2366
The Carriage House . . . . (803)432-2430
The Coach House Inn . . . . (803)432-0986
The Greenleaf Inn . . . . (803)425-1806
McLeans 1890 House . . . . (803)425-1806

Central
Heritage House B&B . . . . (803)639-1506

Charleston
36 Meeting Street B&B . . . . (803)722-1034
Historic Charleston B&B . . . . (803)577-3583
The Anchorage Inn . . . . (803)723-8300
Ann Harper's B&B . . . . (803)723-3947
Ansonborough Inn . . . . (803)723-1655
Ashley Inn B&B . . . . (803)723-1848
Barksdale House Inn . . . . (803)577-4800
Battery Carriage House Inn
. . . . (803)727-3100 (800)775-5575
Bed, No Breakfast . . . . (803)723-4450
Belle Blanc . . . . (803)853-3825

Brasington House . . . . (803)722-1274
Cannonboro Inn . . . . (803)723-8572
Capers-Motte House . . . . (803)722-2263
Charleston Bed & Breakfast . . . . (803)722-6606
Charleston Society B&B . . . . (803)723-4948
Church Street Inn . . . . (803)722-3420
East Bay B&B . . . . (803)722-4186
Harbor View . . . . (803)762-4900
Indigo Inn . . . . (803)577-5900
Jasmine House . . . . (803)577-5900
King's Inn . . . . (803)577-3683
Lodge Alley Inn . (803)722-1611 (800)845-1004
Maison Du Pre . . (803)723-8691 (800)844-4667
Meeting Street Inn . . . . (803)723-1882
Middleton Inn . . . . (803)556-0500
Opus 11 . . . . (803)723-2165
Palmer Home . . . . (803)723-1574
Sweet Grass Inn . . . . (803)723-9980
Sword Gate Inn . . . . (803)723-8518
Vendue Inn . . . . (803)577-7970

Cheraw
505 Market Street B&B . . . . (803)537-9649
501 Kershaw . . . . (803)537-7733
Spears Guest House Red Bed and Breakfast . . . . (803)537-1097

Clemson
Nord-Lac . . . . (803)639-2939

Clio
Henry Bennett House . . . . (803)586-2701

Columbia
Chesnut Cottage B&B . . . . (803)256-1718
Claussen's Inn . . (803)765-0440 (800)622-3382
Richland Street B&B . . . . (803)779-7001
Royal Inn . . . . (803)750-5060

Conway
The Cypress Inn . . . . (803)248-2273

Darlington
Croft Magnolia Inn . . . . (803)393-1908

Dillon
Magnolia Inn B&B . . . . (803)774-0679

Due West
Somewhere In Time . . . . (803)379-8671

Edgefield
Cedar Grove Plantation/Edgefield . (803)637-3056
The Inn on Main . . . . (803)637-9915
The Village Inn . . . . (803)637-3789

Edgemoor
The Country House at Rose Haven (803)789-5845

Edisto Island
Cassina Point Plantation . . . . (803)869-2535

Ehrhardt
Broxton Bridge Plantation . . . . . . (800)437-4868
Ehrhardt Hall . . . . (803)267-2020

Estill
The John Lawton House . . . . (803)625-3240

Eutawville
Little Mount Vernon . . . . (803)492-9718

Fair Play
Yoder's Farm B&B . . . . (803)972-3133

Florence
Colonial Inn . . . . (803)662-1486

Fort Mill
Pleasant Valley B&B . . . . (803)548-5671

Gaffney
Jolly Place, A B&B Inn . . . . (803)489-4638

Georgetown
"Shipwright's" B&B . . . . (803)869-2535
Ashfield Manor . . . . (803)546-0464
Dozier House . . . . (803)527-1350
Walton House . . . . (803)527-1114
Mansfield Plantation . . . . (803)546-6961 (800)355-3223
The Merritt House . . . . (803)546-2903

Greenwood
Grace Place B&B . . . . (864)229-0053

Greer
Arlington House B&B . . . . (803)877-3201

Hartsville
Missouri Inn B&B . . . . (803)383-9553

Hilton Head Island
Ambiance . . . . (803)671-4981
Home Away B&B . . . . (803)671-5578
Main Street Inn . . . . (803)681-3001

Honea Path
Sugarfot Castle . . . . (803)369-6565

Johnston
The Cox House Inn . . . . (803)275-2707

Lancaster
Homeplace . . . . (803)285-7773

Landrum
Country Mouse Inn . . . . (864)457-4061
Mountain High . . . . (803)457-4010

Latta
Abingdon Manor . (803)752-5090 (800)392-0819
Bailie Hall B&B . . . . (803)752-7376

Laurens
Sterling Rose Inn . . . . (803)984-4880

Leesville
The Able House Inn . . . . (803)532-2763

Lexington
Lake Murray House . . . . (803)957-3701

Liberty
Liberty House . . . . (864)843-9696

Little River
Stella's Guest House . . . . (803)249-1871

Long Creek
Chauga River House Inn . . . . (803)647-9587

Marion
Montgomery's Grove . . . . (803)423-5220
Rosewood Manor . . . . (803)423-5407

Mayesville
Windsong . . . . (803)453-5004

Mc Cormick
Fannie Kate's Inn (803)465-0061 (800)965-0061

McClellanville
McClellan's B&B . . . . (803)887-3371
Village B&B Inn . . . . (803)887-3266

Montmorenci
Annie's Inn . . . . (803)649-6836

Mount Pleasant
Charleston East B&B League . . . . (803)884-8208
Guilds Inn . . . . (803)881-0510
Sailmaster's House . . . . (803)884-8208
Sunny Meadows . . . . (803)884-7062
Tara Oaks B&B . . . . (803)884-7082

Mullins
O'hara's . . . . (803)464-7287
Webster Manor . . . . (803)464-9632

Myrtle Beach
Brustman House . . . . (803)448-7699
Cain House B&B . . . . (803)448-3063
Serendipity Inn . . . . (803)449-5268

Newberry
Barklin House . . . . (803)321-9155
Gildercrest B&B Cottages . . . . . . (803)321-2348

North Augusta
Bloom Hill . . . . (803)593-2573

Pendleton
195 East Main . . . . (803)646-5673
Liberty Hall Inn - 1840 . . . . (800)643-7944 (800)643-7944

Pickens
The Schell Haus . . . . (803)878-0078

Prosperity
Stewart House Inc . . . . (803)364-0558

Ridgeland
Lakewood Plantation . . . . (802)726-5141

Rock Hill
The Book and The Spindle . . . . . (803)328-1913
East Main Guest House . . . . (803)366-1161
Park Avenue Inn . . . . (803)325-1764

Saint Matthews
East Bridge Inn . . . . (803)874-4017

Saluda
Cree Hall B&B . . . . (803)445-7029

Starr
The Gray House . . . . (803)352-6778
Upland Growers . . . . (864)352-6778

Sullivans Island
The Palmettos . . . . (803)883-3389

Summerville
B&B of Summerville . . . . (803)871-5275
Camellia Walk . . . . (803)871-3553
Gadsden Manor Inn . . . . (803)875-2602
Linwood . . . . (803)871-2620
Woodlands . . . . (803)875-2600 (800)774-9999

Sumter
The Bed and Breakfast of Sumter (803)773-2903
Magnolia House . . . . (803)775-6694

Union
Juxa Plantation . . . . (803)427-8688

Vance
Dantzler House . . . . (803)492-9499

Walhalla
Liberty Lodge . . . . (803)638-8639

Walterboro
Mt. Carmet Farm B&B . . . . (803)538-5770

Winnsboro
Brakefield B&B . . . . (803)635-4242
Carriage House at Boycelynn . . . (803)635-9714
Songbird Manor . . . . (803)635-6963

South Dakota

Batesland
Wakpamni B&B . . . . (605)288-1800

Belle Fourche
Candlelight B&B . (605)892-4568 (800)469-7572

Beresford
Ryger's Union House . . . . (605)763-2460

Bruce
Re-Klein Inn . . . . (605)627-9200

Chamberlain
B&B Riverview Ridge . . . . (605)734-6084

Corsoca
Country Corner B&B . . . . (605)946-5852

Custer
The Rose Garden . . . . (605)673-2714

Desmet
Prairie House Manor B&B . . . . . . (605)854-9131

Deadwood
Aunt Sophia's B&B . . . . (605)578-3257
Our House B&B . . . . (605)578-1438
Strawberry B&B . . . . (605)578-2149

Dell Rapids
Rose Stone Inn . . . . (605)428-3698

Draper
Cedar Canyon Rand B&B . . . . . . (605)669-2356

Emery
Emery House B&B . . . . (605)449-4855

Flandreau
Talk of The Town B&B . . . . (605)997-5170

Gettysburg
Harer Lodge B&B (605)765-2167 (800)283-3356

Gregory
Gray House Inn B&B . . . . (605)835-8479

Hermosa
Behrens' Ranch B&B . . . . (605)342-1441
The Bunkhouse . . . . (605)342-5462
J-D Guest Ranch B&B . . . . (605)255-4700 (800)261-3329

Hill City
Country Manor B&B . . . . (605)574-2196
Deerview B&B . . . . (605)574-4204
High Country Ranch B&B Trail Rides . . . . (605)574-9003
White Pines Inn B&B . . . . (605)574-2583

Hot Springs
Cascade Ranch . . . . (605)745-3397
Rocking G B&B . . . . (605)745-3698

Keystone
The Anchorage B&B . . . . (605)574-4740 (800)318-7018
Battle Creek Lodge B&B . . . . (605)666-4800
Bed & Breakfast Inn . . . . (605)666-4490

Kimball
Red Barn Inn . . . . (605)778-6332

Lead
Blackstone Manor B&B . . . . (605)584-3270
Cheyenne Crossing B&B . . . . (605)584-3510
Collins House B&B . . . . (605)584-1736
Homestake Mansion B&B . . . . . . (605)584-1166

Lemmon
The 49'er B&B Inn . . . . (701)376-3280

Milesville
Fitch Farms . . . . (605)544-3227

Oelrichs
Dakota Prairie Ranch B&B . . . . . (605)535-2001

Philip
Triangle Ranch B&B . . . . (605)859-2122

Piedmont
Valley View B&B . . . . (605)787-4425

Platte
Grandma's House B&B . . . . (605)337-3589

Presho
Sweeney's B&B . . . . (605)895-2586
Rapid City
Abigail's Garden B&B . . . . (605)343-6530
Anemarie's Country B&B . . . . . . (605)343-9234
Black Forest Inn B&B Lodge . . . . (605)574-2000
The Carriage House . . . . (605)343-6415
Flying B Ranch B&B . . . . (605)342-5324
Hayloft B&B . . . . (605)343-5351
Madison Ranch B&B . . . . (605)342-6997
Raspberry Oaks B&B . . . . (605)342-5519
The Rimrock . . . . (605)348-5124
Willow Springs Cabin . . . . (605)342-3665
Scenic
Circle View Ranch . . . . (605)433-5355
Sioux Falls
Hemphrey's B&B . . . . (605)338-9310
Spearfish
Aunt Apple's Inn . . . . (605)642-1619
Lown House Restaurant B&B . . . (605)642-5663
Tamarack Inn B&B . . . . (605)642-8660
Sturgis
Old Stone House B&B . . . . (605)347-3007
Vale
Dakota Shepherd B&B . . . . (605)456-2836
Vermillion
The Goebel House B&B . . . . (605)624-6691
Vivian
Rafter L Bar Ranch B&B . . . . (605)895-2202
Wessington Springs
Winegar Farms Sky Country Lodge (605)539-1594
Whitewood
Rockinghorse B&B . . . . (605)269-2625

Tennessee

Alcoa
Duck Inn . . . . (423)984-0632
Allardt
Charlo B&B . . . . (615)879-8056
The Old Allardt Schoolhouse . . . . (615)879-8056
Altamont
The Manor, 1885 B&B . . . . (615)692-3153
Woodlee House B&B . . . . (615)692-2368
Ashland City
Bird Song Country Inn B&B . . . . . (615)792-4005
Baxter
Hummingbird Hill B&B . . . . (615)858-2598
Bell Buckle
Spindle House B&B . . . . (615)389-6766
Belvidere
Falls Mill B&B . . . . (615)469-7161
Benton
Southern Memories B&B . . . . . . (615)388-4351
Blountville
Woodland Place B&B . . . . (423)323-2848
Bolivar
Magnolia Manor . . . . (901)658-6700
Brentwood
English Manor B&B Inn & Catering Service
. . . . (615)373-4627 (800)332-4640
Sunny Hill Farm B&B . . . . (615)373-1514
Bristol
New Hope Bed & Breakfast . . . . . (423)989-3343
Bulls Gap
Pittman's Country Inn . . . . (423)235-2455
Carthage
Hospitality House Bed & Breakfast (615)735-3369
Chattanooga
Bluff View Inn . . . . (423)265-5033
The Chattanooga Choo-Choo Inn . (615)266-5000
Lookout Lake B&B . . . . (423)821-8088
Lookout Mountain Guest House . (615)821-8307
McElhattan's Owl Hill B&B . . . . . (615)821-2040
Clarksville
Hachland Hill Inn . . . . (615)647-4084
Cleveland
Brown's Manor B&B . . . . (615)476-8029
Clifton
Hidden Hollow Farm-Log Cabin . . (615)676-5295
College Grove
Peacock Hill Country Inn
. . . . (615)368-7727 (800)327-6663
Columbia
Locust Hill B&B . . . . (615)388-8531
Oak Springs Inn & Gallery . . . . . . (615)388-7539
Cookeville
Scarecrow Country Inn . . . . (615)526-3431
Cordova
The Bridgewater House . . . . (901)384-0080
Covington
Havenhall Guest House . . . . (901)476-7359
Crossville
An-Jen Inn . . . . (615)456-0515
Culleoka
Sweetwater Inn B&B . . . . (615)987-3077
Dandridge
Combs Crest Farms, Inc. . . . . . . (615)397-3045
Mill Dale Farm . . . . (615)397-3470
Sugar Fork B&B . . . . (615)397-7327
Sweet Basil & Thyme B&B . . . . . (423)397-7128
Dayton
Rose House . . . . (615)775-3311
Dickson
East Hills Bed & Breaksfast Inn . . (615)441-9428
The Inn on Main Street . . . . (615)441-6879
Duck River
McEwen Farm Log Cabin B&B . . (615)583-2378
Ducktown
Ducktown's Cozy Corner Guest House
. . . . (615)496-3399
Elizabethon
Old Main Manor . . . . (423)543-6423
Erin
Country Cedar Cabin B&B . . . . . . (615)289-3209
Erwin
Tumbling Creek Mountain Inn . . . (615)743-5308
Fairview
Sweet Annie's B&B and Barn . . . (615)799-8833
Fayetteville
Fayetteville Bed & Breakfast . . . . (615)433-9636
Franklin
Blueberry Hill . . . . (615)791-9947
Carothers House B&B . . . . (615)794-4437
Franklin House B&B . . . . (615)794-0848
Inn Towne B&B . . . . (615)794-3708
Lyric Springs B&B . . . . (615)329-3385
Magnolia House B&B . . . . (615)794-8178
Namaste Acres Barn B&B . . . . . . (615)791-0333
Gallatin
Hancock House . . . . (615)452-8431
Gatlinburg
Brevard Inn B&B . . . . (615)436-7233
The Colonel's Lady . . . . (615)436-5432
Cornerstone Inn B&B . . . . (615)430-5064
Eight Gables Inn . . . . (423)430-3344
Hippensteal Inn . . . . (615)436-5761
Leconte Lodge . . . . (615)436-4473
Mountainbrook Inn . . . . (800)251-2811
Goodlettsville
Woodshire B&B . . . . (615)859-7369
Gordonsville
Pride Hollow B&B . . . . (615)683-6396
Gray
Boone's Creek B&B . . . . (615)753-6070
Greenbrier
Triple Springs B&B . . . . (615)643-1127
Greeneville
East Tennessee B&B Inns and Lodges Assoc
. . . . (615)638-2917
Nolichuckey Bluffs . . . . (800)842-4690
Oak Hill Farm B&B . . . . (615)639-5253
The Inn at Pigeon Creek Farm . . . (615)638-7990
Hohenwald
Armstrong Bakery Bed & Breakfast (615)796-7591
Jackson
Highland Place B&B . . . . (901)427-1472
Moss Rose Inn and Cafe . . . . . . (901)423-4777
Jamestown
Wildwood Lodge B&B . . . . (615)879-9454
Jefferson City
Branner-Hicks House . . . . (615)475-2302
Joelton
Hachland Hill Inns . . . . (615)876-1500
Johnson City
A Touch of Thyme B&B Inn . . . . . (615)926-7570
Hart House B&B . . . . (423)926-3147
Jonesborough
Aiken-Brow House . . . . (615)753-9440
Bowling Green Inn B&B . . . . (423)753-6356
Bugaboo B&B . . . . (615)753-9345
Countryside B&B . . . . (615)753-3252
Hawley House B&B . . . . (423)753-8869
Jonesborough . . . . (615)753-9223
Sheppard Springs B&B . . . . (615)753-6471
Kingsport
C J's Place . . . . (423)378-3517
Shadowilde Manor . . . . (615)323-3939
Kingston
Whitestone . . . . (423)376-0113
Knoxville
Bays Mountain Country Club . . . . (423)577-8172
Blakely Hotel . . . . (423)523-0000
Langskomen B&B Country Home (615)693-3797
Maple Grove Inn . . . . (423)690-9565
The Middleton . . . . (423)524-8100
Windy Hill B&B . . . . (615)690-1488
Kodak
Grandma's House . . . . (615)933-3512
Lafollette
Blue Moon B&B . . . . (615)566-1550
Dogwood Acres B&B Inn . . . . . . (615)566-1207
Mountain-Ayer . . . . (615)562-7334
Lawrenceburg
The Granville House . . . . (615)762-3129
Lebanon
Campbell Country Inn B&B . . . . . (615)449-7713
Lewisburg
Bryant Station B&B . . . . (615)359-5142
Lyles
Silver Leaf 1815-Country Inn . . . (615)670-3048
Lynchburg
Cedar Lane B&B . . . . (615)759-6891
Maryville
High Court Inn . . . . (423)981-2966
Sports Haven B&B . . . . (615)982-8382
McEwen
White Oak Creek B&B . . . . (615)582-3827
Memphis
Bridgewater House . . . . (901)384-0080
Cedarwood Farms . . . . (901)794-7000
Greystone Inn B&B . . . . (901)278-7897
The Peabody . . . . (901)529-4000
Monteagle
North Gate Lodge . . . . (615)924-2799
Morristown
Victoria Rose B&B . . . . (615)581-9687
Mountain City
Hidden Acres Farm B&B . . . . (615)727-6564
Newcomb Place B&B . . . . (615)727-5392
Mulberry
Mulberry House B&B . . . . (615)433-0583
Murfreesboro
The Cedar Thicket . . . . (615)893-4015
Clardy's Guest House . . . . (615)893-6030
Nashville
Ann Deol's B&B . . . . (615)255-2411
Apple Brook B&B and Barn . . . . . (615)646-5082
Miss Anne's B&B . . . . (615)885-1899
Mitchell Blue House B&B . . . . . . (615)383-3128
Ms Rickie's B&B . . . . (615)269-3850
Savage House Inn . . . . (615)244-2229
Tanglewood Lodge B&B . . . . (615)262-9859
Normandy
Parish Patch Farm & Inn . . . . (615)857-3017
Orlinda
Aurora Inn B&B . . . . (615)654-4266
Pelham
Wonder Cave B&B . . . . (615)467-3041
Pigeon Forge
Day Dreams Country Inn . . . . . . (615)428-0370
Evergreen Cottage Inn . . . . (615)453-4000
Town Villas Luxury Suites
. . . . (615)428-3333 (800)346-5553
Pikeville
Colonial Bed & Breakfast . . . . . . (423)447-7183
Red Boiling Springs
Armours Red Boiling Springs Hotel (615)699-2180
Donoho Hotel . . . . (615)699-3141
Rockford
Wayside Manor . (423)970-4823 (800)675-4823
Rogersville
Hale Springs Inn . . . . (615)272-5171
Rugby
Grey Gables B&B . . . . (615)628-5252
Savannah
Ross House B&B . . . . (901)925-8353

Sevierville
The Gallery House .... (615)428-6937
Huckleberry Inn .... (615)428-2475
Jenny Lind B&B .... (615)428-6719
Persephone's Retreat B&B ..... (615)428-3904
Place of The Blue Smoke B&B .. (615)453-6355
Shelbyville
Bottle Hollow Lodge B&B ...... (615)695-5253
Cinnamon Ridge B&B .... (615)685-9200
Flat Creek Farm B&B .... (615)695-5144
Home of Mrs. Robert B. Fort, Jr. B&B
.... (615)684-5163
Signal Mountain
Phyllis Charlet B&B .... (615)886-4880
Stone House .... (615)886-2531
Smithville
Evins Mill Retreat .... (615)597-2088
Somerville
Magnolia Place .... (901)465-3906
Springfield
Oak House Bed & Breakfast .... (615)382-2187
Sweetwater
Flow Blue Inn .... (615)442-2964
The Fox Trot Inn .... (615)337-4236
Talbott
Arrow Hill .... (615)585-5777
Tiptonville
Backyard Birds Lodge .... (901)253-9064
Townsend
Smoky Bear Lodge .... (615)448-6442
Triune
Xanadu Farm B&B .... (615)395-4771
Tullahoma
Jenny's B&B .... (615)455-9496
Vonore
Edna's B&B Home .... (615)295-2354
Walland
Crikett Lane B&B .... (615)983-1322
Wartrace
Log Cabin Inn Bed & Breakfast .. (615)389-6020
Walking Horse Hotel & Restaurant (615)389-6407
Watertown
Watertown B&B .... (615)237-9999
Waynesboro
Waynesboro Inn .... (615)722-7321
Wincester
The Antebellum Inn .... (615)967-5550
Winchester
Country Manor Bed & Breakfast . (615)962-0541

Texas

Abilene
Bolin's Prairie House B&B
.... (915)675-5855 (800)673-5855
Albany
The Ole Nail House Inn .... (915)762-2928
Virginia's B&B .... (915)762-2013
Allen
Blee Cottage .... (214)390-1884
Alpine
Holland Hotel .... (915)837-3455
Alto
Lincrest Lodge .... (409)858-2223
Amarillo
Auntie's House B&B .... (806)371-8054
Galbraith House B&B .... (806)374-0237
Archer City
The Spur Hotel .... (817)574-2501
Athens
Carriage House at Hickory Hill .. (903)677-3939
Aubrey
Country Place of Crossroads ... (817)440-3331
Austin
Brook House .... (512)459-0534
Driskill Hotel .... (512)474-5911
The Gardens on Duval Street .... (512)477-9200
Lake Travis B&B .... (512)266-3386
Triple Creek Ranch Resort ..... (512)264-1371
Ballinger
Miz Virginia's B&B (915)365-2453 (800)344-0781
Bandera
Bald Eagle Ranch, Inc. .... (210)460-3012
Bandera Creek B&B .... (210)796-3518
Cool Water Acres .... (210)796-4866
Horseshoe Inn .... (512)796-3105
Mayan Dude Ranch .... (512)796-3312
Bastrop
The Colony B&B .... (512)303-1234
Pfeiffer House .... (512)321-2100
Bellville
High Cotton Inn . (409)865-9796 (800)321-9796
Townsquare Inn .... (409)865-9021
Ben Wheeler
Wild Briar .... (214)852-3975
Blessing
Hotel Blessing .... (512)588-9579
Boerne
Borgman's Sunday House B&B .. (512)249-9563
Guadalupe River Ranch .... (312)336-2048
Windmill Hill B&B .... (210)510-6736
Brazoria
River House B&B .... (713)493-0754
Brenham
The Brenham House .... (409)830-0477
Captain Clay B&B .... (409)836-1916
Far View B&B .... (409)836-1672
Heartland Country Inn B&B and Retreat
.... (409)836-1864
James Walker Homestead B&B .. (409)836-6717
Mariposa Ranch B&B .... (409)836-4712
Nueces Canyon B&B .... (409)289-5600
Vernon's B&B .... (409)836-6408
Broaddus
The Cole House Sam Rayburn Lake B&B
.... (409)872-3666
Country Inn "A Motel" .... (409)872-3691
Buchanan Dam
Mystic Cove B&B .... (512)793-6642
Burnet
Airy Mount .... (512)756-4149
Rocky Rest B&B .... (512)756-2600
Williams Point .... (512)756-2074
Burton
The Cottage at Cedar Creek .... (409)278-3770
Knittel Homestead .... (409)289-5102
Canton
Buffalo Beal's Boardin' House ... (903)567-4892
Canyon
Country Home B&B
.... (806)655-7636 (800)664-7636
Canyon Lake
Holiday Lodge .... (210)964-3693
Carmine
Sugar Hill Retreat B&B .... (409)278-3039
Cat Spring
Southwind B&B .... (409)992-3270
Center
Pine Colony Inn .... (409)598-7700
Center Point
Marianne's B&B .... (210)634-7489
Chappell Hill
The Browning Plantation .... (409)836-6144
The Mulberry House .... (409)830-1311
Stagecoach Inn .... (409)836-9515
Chireno
Gingerbread House .... (409)362-2365
Cleburne
Anglin Queen Anne B&B .... (817)645-5555
Cleburne House .... (817)641-0085
Hotel Santa Fe B&B .... (817)517-5529
Columbus
The Cabin In The Woods ...... (409)732-6319
The Gant Guest House .... (409)732-5135
The Victorian B&B .... (409)732-2125
Comanche
The Guest House at Heritage Hill . (915)356-3397
Comfort
B&B on Cypress Creek .... (210)995-2479
The Comfort Common .... (210)995-3030
Haven River Inn .... (210)995-3834
Idlewilde .... (210)995-3844
Commerce
Bois D'arc B&B .... (903)886-7705
Conroe
Heather's Glen . . . A B&B
.... (409)441-6611 (800)665-2643
Corsicana
The Ashmore Inn .... (903)872-7311
Crockett
Warfield House .... (409)544-4037
Crosbyton
Smith House Inn .... (806)675-2178
Cuero
Reiffert-Mugge Inn .... (512)275-2626
Dallas
The Adolphus .... (214)742-8200
The American Dream B&B ..... (214)357-6536
Hotel St. Germain .... (214)871-2516
The Rose B&B .... (214)298-8586
The Stoneleigh Hotel .... (214)871-7111
Del Rio
The Foster House .... (210)775-9543
Denison
Ivy Blue B&B ... (903)463-2479 (888)489-2583
Denton
Redbud Inn .... (817)565-6414
Dripping Springs
Country Air B&B Guest House ... (512)858-4535
Eagle Lake
Farris 1912 .... (409)234-2546
Edgewood
Crooked Creek Farm B&B
.... (903)896-1284 (800)766-0790
Texas Star B&B .... (903)896-4277
Edom
Red Rooster Square .... (214)852-6774
El Paso
Gardner Hotel .... (915)532-3661
Elgin
Nana's B&B .... (512)285-3243
Fayetteville
The Live Oak Street Guest Cottage (409)968-8787
Floydada
Lamplighter Inn B&B .... (806)983-3035
Fort Davis
The Hotel Limpia (915)426-3237 (800)662-5517
Indian Lodge .... (915)426-3254
Old Texas Inn .... (915)426-3118
The Veranda B&B .... (915)426-2233
Fort Worth
Medford House .... (817)924-2765
Stockyards Hotel .... (817)625-6427
Texas White House B&B .... (817)923-3597
Fredericksburg
Alfred's & The Granary at Giles M (210)990-8400
Allegani's Sunday Haus .... (210)997-7448
John Walter House .... (210)997-5612
B&B Fredericksburg .... (512)997-4712
Baron's Creek Inn .... (512)997-9398
Bell Cottage .... (512)997-4712
Block Creek Ranch .... (512)997-7227
The Nevels House .... (512)997-4712
Das College Haus .... (512)997-9047
Delforge Place & Weber Farm House
.... (210)997-6212 (800)494-4678
East of The Sun-West of The Moon
.... (210)997-4981 (800)865-9668
Ernestine's B&B .... (512)997-5645
Fredericksburg Bed & Brew ..... (210)997-1646
Fredericksburg Inn on The Square (512)997-7083
Fredericksburg Victorian House
.... (210)997-0288 (800)997-0288
Gasthaus Bed & Breakfast Lodging Service
.... (512)997-4712
Haus Gusti .... (512)997-4712
The Herb Haus at Fredericksburg Farm
.... (210)997-8615
Hill Country Lodging .... (210)990-8455
Hoerster Bldg, Chemist Loft .... (512)997-8615
Immel Cottage .... (512)997-4712
Inn on The Creek .... (512)997-9585
J Bar K Ranch B&B .... (512)669-2471
Judy Ferles Harris Haus & Art Studio
.... (512)997-3860
Knopp Haus .... (512)997-4712
The Log Cabin .... (512)997-7227
The Luckenback Inn .... (210)997-2205
Magnolia House . (210)997-0306 (800)880-4374
Town Creek B&B (512)997-7928 (800)466-8651
Old Pedernales School House ... (512)997-5612
Our House .... (512)997-4712
Palo Alto Creek Farm .... (210)997-5612
Claus Haus .... (512)997-5612
Vogel Sunday House .... (512)997-4712
Watkins Hill Guest House ...... (210)997-6739
The White House of Fredericksburg (210)997-5612

Freeport
Anchor B&B .... (409)239-3543
Galveston
1887 Coppersmith Inn .... (409)763-7004
The Inn on The Strand .... (409)762-1653
Gilded Thistle B&B .... (409)763-0194
Hazelwood House B&B Inn ..... (409)762-1668
Key Largo .... (800)833-0120
Michael's B&B .. (409)763-3760 (800)776-8302
Tremont House .... (409)763-0300
Trube Castle Inn .... (409)765-4396
Garland
Capture The Moment .... (214)414-8201
Catnap Creek B&B .... (214)530-0819
Georgetown
Clairbourne House .... (512)930-3934
Page House .... (512)863-8979
Gladewater
Honeycomb Suites .... (900)594-2253
Primrose Lane .... (903)845-5922
Glen Rose
Bussey's Something Special B&B (817)897-4843
The Hideaway Country Log Cabins (817)823-6606
Lilly House .... (817)897-9747
The Lodge at Fossil Rim .... (817)897-2960
The Inn on The River
.... (214)424-7119 (800)575-2101
The Wild Rose Inn .... (817)897-4112
Goliad
The Dial House .... (512)645-3366
Gonzales
Houston House B&B .... (210)672-6940
Granbury
Nutt House .... (817)573-5612
Grand Saline
Bailiteal Farm .... (903)962-4475
Saline Creek Farm B&B .... (903)829-2709
Hamilton
Hamilton Guest House .... (817)386-8977
Harlingen
The Ross Haus .... (512)425-1717
Haskell
The Bevers House on Brick St B&B (817)864-3284
Hemphill
Sunset-Sunrise B&B .... (409)579-3265
Hico
Indian Mountain Ranch B&B .... (817)796-4060
Hillsboro
Tarlton House of 1895 .... (817)582-7216
Houston
Bed & Breakfast Society of Texas (713)868-4654
The Highlander .. (713)861-6110 (800)807-6110
The Lovett Inn .... (713)522-5224
The Oaks Cottage B&B .... (713)520-0226
Patrician B&B Inn (713)523-1114 (800)553-5797
Robin's Nest ... (713)528-5821 (800)622-8343
Sara's B&B Inn . (713)868-1130 (800)593-1130
Hunt
Joy Spring Ranch B&B .... (512)238-4531
River Bend B&B . (210)238-4681 (800)472-3933
Huntsville
Nelson's Blue Bonnet B&B ..... (409)294-0787
The Whistler B&B .... (409)295-2834
Jacksonville
The English Manor .... (903)586-9821
Jasper
Belle-Jim Hotel B&B .... (409)384-6923
Jefferson
Azalea Inn .... (903)665-2051
The Back Door Inn .... (903)665-2401
The Bluebonnet Inn of Jefferson . (903)665-8572
Captain's Castle B&B .... (903)665-2330
Cottonwood Inn .... (903)665-2080
Davanna House .... (903)665-8238
Excelsior House .... (903)665-2513
The Faded Rose .... (903)665-2716
Falling Leaves .... (903)665-8803
Holcomb Lodge .... (903)665-3236
Home Sweet Home Cottage .... (903)665-2493
Hotel Jefferson .... (903)665-2631
La Casa De Las Flores .... (903)665-2215
Line Street Guest House .... (903)665-2447
The Lodge on Busy B Ranch .... (903)665-7448
The Magnolias .... (903)665-2754
Pecan Place .... (903)665-8481
Queen Anne's Lace .... (903)665-2483
Roseville Manor .... (903)665-7273
Rowell House .... (903)665-2634
Stillwater Inn .... (903)665-8415
The Terry House .... (903)665-2644
The Turner House .... (903)665-8616
Twin Oaks Country Inn .... (903)665-3535
William Clark House .... (903)665-8880
Wise Manor .... (903)665-2386
Johnson City
B&B of Johnson City .... (210)868-4548
Hoppe's Guest House .... (512)868-7359
Smith's Tin House on The Square (512)868-4548
Karnack
Mimosa Hall .... (903)679-3632
Kemah
Captains Quarters .... (713)474-2042
Kingsville
B Bar B Ranch Inn .... (512)225-6333
Kyle
New Tracks Ranch B&B .... (512)268-3211
La Coste
Swan & Railway Country Inn ... (512)762-3742
La Grange
Blue Caboose .... (409)968-5053
Lago Vista
Shores at Lake Travis .... (512)267-7181
Lakehills
Wandering Aengus B&B .... (210)751-3345
Leakey
Whiskey Mountain Inn .... (210)232-6797
Ledbetter
Ledbetter Hotel .... (409)249-3066
Llano
Badu House .... (915)247-4304
Fraser House B&B .... (915)247-5183
Pecan Creek Cottage .... (915)247-4074
Pecan Tree Inn & Antiques ..... (915)247-3502
Mabank
Heavenly Acres B&B .... (800)283-0341
Marathon
The Gage Hotel .... (915)386-4205
Granite Shoals
La Casita B&B .. (210)598-6443 (800)798-6443
Marfa
The Lash-Up B&B .... (915)729-4487
Marshall
The Lily Pad .... (903)938-4325
Mandalay .... (903)938-8860
Weisman-Hirsch-Beil Home .... (903)938-5504
Wood Boone Norrell House ..... (903)935-1800
Martindale
Countryside Inn .... (512)357-2550
Mason
Bridges House .... (915)347-6440
The Humming Bird .... (915)347-5148
Mason Square B&B
.... (915)347-6398 (800)369-0405
Mc Gregor
Lighthouse B&B .... (817)840-2683
McAllen
Casa De Palmas .... (512)631-1101
McKinney
D'armond Hotel & Restaurant ... (214)562-1102
Meridian
Rose Hill Terrace .... (817)435-6257
Midland
B&B of Midland .... (915)683-8224
Mineola
Beckham Hotel .... (903)569-9914
Munzesheimer Manor .... (903)569-6634
Sellers' Corner .... (214)569-6560
Montgomery
Honeysuckle Rose .... (409)760-3744
Nacogdoches
Haden Edwards Inn .... (409)564-9999
Little House B&B .... (409)564-2735
Llano Grande Plantation .... (409)569-1249
Navasota
The Castle .... (409)825-8051
New Braunfels
Antik House .... (512)629-6666
Comfort Common .... (512)995-3030
Hill Country Haven .... (512)629-6727
Historic Danville School & Waldrip Haus
.... (210)625-8372
Karbach Haus .... (512)625-2131
Lillian B's B&B .... (512)629-0750
Prince Solms Inn .... (512)625-9169
River Haus .... (512)625-6411
Riverside Haven .... (512)625-5823
The Rose Garden B&B .... (210)629-3296
Paint Rock
Chaparral Ranch B&B .... (915)732-4225
Lipan Ranch B&B .... (915)468-2571
Palacios
Moonlight Bay B&B .... (512)972-2232
Palestine
Ash-Bowers Residence .... (903)729-1935
Bailey Bunkhouse .... (903)549-2028
Country Christmas Tree Farm B&B (903)549-2671
Wiffletree Inn .... (903)723-6793
Paris
Magnolia House B&B .... (903)785-5593
Pipe Creek
Lightning Ranch .... (210)535-4096
Pittsburg
Texas Street B&B .... (903)856-7552
Port Arthur
Cajun Cottages .... (409)982-6050
Port Isabel
Queen Isabel Inn .... (210)943-1468
Port O'Connor
Port O'Connor Fishing Club ..... (512)983-2897
Post
Hotel Garza B&B .... (806)495-3962
Pottsboro
Yacht-O-Fun .... (903)786-8188
Rainbow
Rainbow's End .... (817)897-2238
Rio Frio
Rio Frio B&B .... (512)232-6633
Rio Grande City
La Borde House .... (210)048-5101
Rockdale
Rainbow Courts .... (512)446-2361
Rockport
Blue Heron Inn .... (512)729-7526
Round Rock
St. Charles B&B .... (512)244-6850
Round Top
Heart of My Heart Ranch B&B .. (800)327-1242
The Royers' Inn at Heritage Farm (800)624-7437
Royse City
Country Lane B&B (214)636-2600 (800)240-8757
Salado
Country Place B&B .... (817)947-9683
The Inn on Creek .... (817)947-5554
Halley House B&B .... (817)947-1000
Rose Mansion .... (817)947-5999
San Antonio
A Victorian Lady Inn
.... (210)224-2524 (800)879-7116
The Academy House of Monte Vista
.... (210)731-8393 (888)731-8393
B&B on The River .... (210)225-6333
Beauregard House B&B .... (210)222-1198
Belle of Monte Vista .... (210)732-4006
The Blansett Barn (210)226-3139 (800)356-1605
Bonner Garden .. (210)733-4222 (800)396-4222
Brookhaven Manor .... (210)733-3939
Classic Charms . (210)271-7171 (800)209-7171
The Fairmount Hotel .... (512)224-8800
Falling Pines B&B Inn .... (800)880-4580
Gatlin Guesthouse (210)223-6618 (800)317-7143
Linden House B&B .... (210)224-8902
Menger Hotel .... (210)223-4361
Sheraton Gunter Hotel .... (210)227-3241
Adelynne's Summit Haus ...... (210)736-6272
Terrell Castle .... (512)271-9145
Victorian Lace .... (210)492-3929
San Augustine
Captain E.d. Downs House ..... (409)275-5305
San Marcos
Aquarena Springs Inn .... (512)396-8901
Crystal River Inn .... (512)396-3739
Finer Things B&B/Crockett House (512)353-2908
Seguin
Weinert House B&B .... (210)372-0422
Shiner
The Old Kasper House .... (512)594-4336

Smithville
Lakeview Cottage at Indian Hills . (512)237-4792
South Padre Island
Brown Pelican Inn .... (210)761-2722
Moonraker B&B .... (210)761-2206
Spring
McLachlan Farm B&B .... (713)350-2400
Stephenville
Oxford House .... (817)965-6885
Sunnyvale
Durant Star Inn B&B .... (214)226-2412
Terlingua
Lajitas on Rio Grande .... (915)424-3471
Texarkana
Main House .... (903)793-5027
Tomball
Frey Ranch B&B .... (713)351-4477
Tyler
Bed of Roses Country Inn ...... (800)256-7673
The Carousel House Complex-Fireside Inn
.... (903)845-6830
Mary's Attic B&B .... (903)592-5181
The Woldert-Spence Manor .... (903)533-9057
Uncertain
Caddo Cottage .... (903)679-3988
Utopia
Blue Bird Hill B&B .... (512)966-3525
Utopia on The River .... (512)966-2444
Van Alstyne
Durning House B&B .... (903)482-5188
Vanderpool
Tubbs Heritage House .... (512)966-3510
Victoria
Friendly Oaks B&B .... (512)575-0000
Santa Rosa Oaks B&B .... (512)578-1605
Waxahachie
Bonnynook Inn .. (214)938-7207 (800)486-5936
The Chaska House .... (214)937-3390
Rose of Sharon B&B .... (214)938-8833
Weatherford
Derrick-Hoffman Farm B&B .... (817)573-9952
Victorian House B&B .... (817)599-9600
Weslaco
The Fortress .... (210)565-6325
Rio Grande B&B .... (512)968-9646
West
Zachary Davis House .... (817)826-3953
Wichita Falls
Guest House B&B .... (817)322-7252
Harrison House B&B
.... (817)322-2299 (800)327-2299
Wimberley
B&B of Wimberley .... (512)847-9666
Bandit's Hideaway .... (512)874-9088
Dancing Waters Inn .... (512)847-9391
Eagles' Nest B&B .... (512)847-3921
Heart House .... (512)847-1414
The Inn Above Onion Creek ..... (512)268-1617
J.R. Dobie House .... (800)525-8683
Old Oaks Ranch B&B .... (512)847-9374
Over The Moon .... (512)847-5661
Rancho Cama .... (512)847-2596
Stars at Night B&B .... (800)424-1292
Wide Horizon .... (512)847-3782
Winnsboro
Yesteryear B&B .... (903)342-3024
Wolfforth
Country Place B&B .... (806)863-2030
Woodville
Antique Rose B&B (409)283-8926 (800)386-8926
Yoakum
Our Guest House B&B .... (512)293-3482

Utah

Alta
Chalet Valhalla .... (801)742-3100
Alton
Pinewoods Restaurant & Inn .... (801)682-2512
American Fork
American Fork B&B .... (801)756-5122
Blanding
Rogers House Bed & Breakfast Inn (801)678-3932
Bluff
Bluff B&B .... (801)672-2220
Recapture Lodge .... (801)672-2281
The Scorup House .... (801)672-2272
Boulder
Boulder Mountain Guest Ranch .. (801)335-7480
Boulder Pines B&B Inn .... (801)335-7375
Brighton
Das Alpen Haus .... (801)649-0565
Cedar City
Bard's Inn .... (801)586-6612
Meadeau View Lodge .... (801)682-2495
Paxman's House B&B .... (801)586-3755
Road Creek Ranch .... (801)586-7502
The Theater B&B .... (801)586-0404
Willow Glen Inn .... (801)586-3275
Coalville
Dearden Bedn Breakfast Home Home
.... (801)336-5698
Cottonwood
Grandmothers House Bed & Breakfast
.... (801)943-0909
Eden
The Snowberry Inn .... (801)745-2634
Ephraim
Ephraim Homestead .... (801)283-6367
W. Pherson House B&B .... (801)283-4197
Escalante
Rainbow Country Tours & Bed & Breakfast
.... (801)826-4567
Fillmore
Suite Dreams .... (801)743-6862
Garden City
Inn of The Three Bears at Bear Lake
.... (801)946-8590
Glendale
The Homeplace .... (801)648-2194
Smith Hotel .... (801)648-2156
Green River
Bankurz Hatt B&B .... (801)564-3382
Hanksville
Joy's B&B .... (801)542-3252
Hatch
Calico House B&B .... (801)735-4382
Heber City
The Cottage B&B .... (801)654-2236
Helper
Kenilworth Inn .... (801)472-3221
Hurricane
Pah Tempe Hot Springs B&B .... (801)635-2879
Kamas
Patricia's Country Manor ...... (801)783-2910
Kanab
Judd House Bed & Breakfast ... (801)644-2936
Miss Sophie's B&B .... (801)644-5952
Nine Gables Inn .... (801)644-5079
La Sal
La Sal Mountain Guest Ranch ... (801)686-2223
Mt Peale Bed & Breakfast & Country Store
.... (801)686-2284
Liberty
Vue De Valhalla .... (801)745-2558
Loa
Road Creek Inn .... (801)836-2485
Logan
Alta Manor Suites .... (801)752-0808
Beaver Creek Lodge & Recreation (801)753-1076
Center Street B&B .... (801)752-3443
Logan House Inn (801)752-7727 (800)478-7459
Manti
Brigham House Inn B&B .... (801)835-8381
Heritage House .... (801)835-5050
Manti House Inn .... (801)835-0161
Manti Old Grist Mill Inn .... (801)835-6455
Yardley's Inn .... (801)835-1861
Marysvale
Moores Old Pine Inn .... (801)326-4565
Mexican Hat
Lee Ranch .... (801)683-2292
Midway
Kastle Inn .... (801)654-2689
The Homestead .... (800)327-7220
Moab
Sistelita .... (801)259-6012
Desert Chalet .... (801)259-5793
Kane Creek B&B .... (801)259-7345
Matterhorn Heights Guest House . (801)259-8352
Mayor's House B&B .... (801)259-6015
Millcreek Inn .... (801)259-8524
Pack Creek Ranch, A Country Inn (801)259-5505
Rockland Ranch Inn .... (801)259-2048
Sandi's Family Homestyle B&B .. (801)259-6359
Shiloh B&B .... (801)259-8684
Slick Rock Inn .... (801)259-2277
Westwood Guesthouse
.... (801)259-7283 (800)526-5690
Mt. Carmel
Sugar Knoll B&B .... (801)648-2335
Mount Pleasant
Mansion House B&B .... (801)462-3031
Nephi
The Whitmore Mansion B&B .... (801)623-2047
Oakley
Graystone Lodge & Guest House (801)783-5744
Orderville
Hummingbird B&B .... (801)648-2415
Panguitch
William Prince Inn .... (801)676-2525
Park City
Angel House Inn .... (801)647-0338
Goldener Hirsch Inn & Restaurant (801)649-7770
The Imperial Hotel (801)649-1904 (800)669-8824
Old Town Guest House .... (801)649-2642
Owl's Roost .... (801)649-6938
The Snowed Inn .... (801)649-5713
Parowan
Adams Historic Home B&B ..... (801)477-8295
Grandma Bess' Cottage B&B ... (801)477-8224
Janetlynn House Bed & Breakfast (801)477-1133
Richfield
The Old Church B&B .... (801)896-6705
Rockville
The Blue House B&B .... (801)772-3912
Dream Catcher Inn Lc .... (801)772-3600
The Handcart House B&B ...... (801)772-3867
Hummingbird Inn .... (801)772-3632
Serenity House Bed & Breakfast . (801)772-3393
Saint George
Aunt Annies Inn .... (801)673-5504
Greene Gate Village Historic B&B Inn
.... (801)628-6999 (800)350-6999
Horseman Inn Bed & Breakfast .. (801)634-9494
Morris Mulberry Inn .... (801)673-7383
St. George
Penny Farthing Inn & B&B ..... (801)673-7755
Saint George
Seven Wives Inn .... (801)628-3737
Salina
The Victorian Inn (801)529-7342 (800)972-7183
Salt Lake City
The Anton Boxrud B&B
.... (801)363-8035 (800)524-5511
Armstrong Mansion Inn
.... (801)531-1333 (800)708-1333
Brambles .... (801)521-6830
Brigham Street Inn .... (801)364-4461
Carlton Hotel .... (801)355-3418
Dave's Cozy Cabin Inn .... (801)278-6136
Mother Karen's B&B .... (800)733-0771
Pinecrest B&B Inn .... (801)583-6663
The Spruces B&B .... (801)268-8762
Wildflowers B&B (801)466-0600 (800)569-0009
Sandy
Quail Hills B&B .... (801)942-2858
Scofield
Winter Quarters Inn .... (801)448-9253
Spanish Fork
Escalante B&B .... (801)798-6652
Spring City
Horseshoe Mountain Bed & Breakfast Inn
.... (801)462-2871
Springdale
Harvest House B&B .... (801)772-3880
Morning Glory Inn .... (801)772-3301
Nove House Inn at Zion .... (801)772-3650
O'Toole's Under The Eaves ..... (801)772-3457
Red Rock Inn .... (801)772-3139
Zion House B&B .... (801)772-3281
Springville
Kearns Hotel .... (801)489-0737
Sterling
Cedar Crest Inn .... (801)835-6352
Teasdale
Cockscomb Inn B&B .... (801)425-3511

Toquerville
Your Inn Toquerville .... (801)635-9964
Torrey
Sky Ridge B&B .... (801)425-3222
Tropic
Bryce Point B&B .... (801)679-8629
Fox's Bryce Trails B&B .... (801)679-8688
Francisco's B&B .... (801)679-8721
Half House B&B .... (801)679-8643
Vernal
Hillhouse B&B .... (801)789-0700
Virgin
Snow Family Guest Ranch Bed & Breakfast
.... (801)635-2500
Zion's Blue Star B&B .... (801)635-3828

Vermont

Albany
The Village House Inn .... (802)755-6722
Alburg
Auberge Alburg .... (802)796-3169
Ransom Bay Inn B&B
.... (802)796-3399 (800)729-3393
Arlington
The Arlington Inn (802)375-6532 (800)443-9442
Arlington Manor House B&B .... (802)375-6784
Arlingtons West Mountain Inn ... (802)375-6516
Country Guest House .... (802)375-9928
Country Willows B&B
.... (802)375-0019 (800)796-2585
The Inn on Covered Bridge Green (802)375-9489
The Evergreen Inn .... (802)375-2272
The Inn at Sunderland .... (802)362-4213
Inn on Covered Bridge Green ... (802)375-9489
Ira Allen House .... (802)362-2284
Keelan House B&B .... (802)375-9029
Macauley House .... (802)375-1178
Shenandoah Farm .... (802)375-6372
West Mountain Inn .... (802)375-6516
Whimsy Farm B&B .... (802)375-6654
Willow B&B .... (802)375-9773
Bakersfield
Village Bed & Breakfast .... (802)827-3206
Barnard
Maple Leaf Inn .... (802)234-5342
The Silver Lake House .... (802)234-9957
Twin Farms .... (802)234-9999
Brnet
The Inn at Maplemont Farm
.... (802)633-4880 (800)230-1617
Barre
The Hollow Inn .... (802)479-9313
Woodruff House .... (802)476-7745
Barton
Anglin' B&B .... (802)525-4548
The Barton Inn .... (802)525-4721
Fox Hall B&B ... (802)525-6930 (800)566-6930
Lafont's B&B .... (802)755-6127
Our Village Inn & Antique Shop .. (802)525-3380
Paupers Manse B&B .... (802)525-3222
Rosebrae B&B .. (802)525-4912 (800)628-3677
Tranquility B, B&B .... (802)525-3646
Bellows Falls
Blue Haven Christian B&B
.... (802)463-9008 (800)228-9008
Horsefeathers B&B .... (802)463-9776
River Mist B&B .... (802)463-9023
Belmont
The Leslie Place .... (802)259-2903
Bennington
Alexandra B&B .... (802)442-5619
Apple Valley Inn & Cafe .... (802)442-6588
Bennington Haus .... (802)447-7972
Bennington Orchard Inn .... (802)447-1185
Four Chimneys Inn .... (802)447-3500
Hubbell House B&B .... (802)447-3361
Safford Manor B&B .... (802)442-5934
South Shire Inn .... (802)447-3839
Sugar Maple Inne .... (802)442-2529
Bethel
Eastwood House .... (802)234-9686
Bolton
Bolton Mountain Resort
.... (802)434-2131 (800)451-3220
Bomoseen
Edgewater Resort .... (802)468-5251

Bondville
Alpenrose Inn .... (802)297-2750
Bromley View Inn (802)297-1459 (800)297-1459
Red Fox Inn .... (802)297-2488 (800)870-3424
Bradford
Merry Meadow Farm .... (802)222-4412
Brandon
The Adams .... (802)247-6644
Brandon Inn .... (802)247-5766 (800)639-8685
Fort Vengeance .... (802)483-2136
The Gazebo Inn .... (802)247-3235
Hivue B&B Tree Farm
.... (802)247-3042 (800)880-3042
Moffett House .. (802)247-3843 (800)752-5794
Old Mill Inn .... (802)247-8002
Brattleboro
"40 Putney Road" B&B .... (802)254-6268
Brattleboro Inn .. (802)254-8701 (800)286-8701
Green River Homespun .... (802)257-7275
Meadowlark Inn .... (802)257-4582
The Tudor B&B .... (802)257-4983
Bridgewater
The Corners Inn & Restaurant ... (802)672-9968
Bridgewater Corners
October Country Inn .... (802)672-3412
Bristol
Crystal Palace Victorian B&B ... (802)453-4131
Firefly Ranch .... (802)453-2223
Long Run Inn .... (802)453-3233
Maplewood Farm B&B .... (802)453-2992
Mary's at Baldwin Creek .... (802)453-2432
Brookfield
Birch Meadow Luxury Log Cabins & B&B
.... (802)276-3156
Brookline
Massey Farm .... (802)365-4716
Brownsville
Mill Brook B&B .... (802)484-7283
The Inn at Mt. Ascutney .... (802)484-7725
The Pond House .... (802)484-0011
South View B&B .... (802)484-7934
Burlington
Allyn House B&B .... (802)863-0379
Burlington B&B .... (802)862-3646
Burlington Redstone B&B ...... (802)862-0508
Howden Cottage B&B .... (802)864-7198
Tetreault House .... (802)862-2781
Cabot
Creamery Inn .... (802)563-2819
Calais
Evergreens Chalet .... (802)223-5156
The Fitch House .... (802)223-5617
Cambridge
4 Pause B&B .... (802)899-3927
Cavendish
Cavendish Inn .... (802)226-7329
Charlotte
The Inn at Charlotte .... (802)425-2934
Charlotte's Web B&B .... (802)425-3341
Vermont Wildflower Farm ...... (802)425-3500
Chester
Chester House .... (802)875-2205
Glen Finerte Farm .... (802)875-2160
Greenleaf Inn .... (802)875-3171
Inn Victoria and Tea Pot Shoppe
.... (802)875-4288 (800)732-4288
The Inn at Long Last .... (802)875-2444
Rowell's Inn .... (802)875-3658
Second Wind B&B .... (802)875-3438
Stone Village B&B .... (802)875-3914
Chittenden
Mountain Top Inn & Resort
.... (802)483-2311 (800)445-2100
Colchester
On The Lamb B&B .... (802)879-1179
Cornwall
Cornwall Orchards .... (802)462-2272
Coventry
Heermansmith Farm .... (802)754-8866
Craftsbury
Brassknocker B&B .... (802)586-2814
Finchingfield Farm B&B .... (802)586-7763
Gary Meadow Dairy Farm ...... (802)586-2536
Cuttingsville
Maple Crest Farm .... (802)492-3367

Danby
Quail's Nest B&B .... (802)293-5099
Danville
Danvillle Restaurant Inn .... (802)684-3484
Raspberry Patch .... (802)684-3971
Dorset
Barrows House .... (802)867-4455
Cornucopia of Dorset .... (802)867-5751
Dorset Hollow B&B .... (802)867-5993
Dorset Inn .... (802)867-5500
Dovetail Inn .... (802)867-5747
The Little Lodge at Dorset ...... (802)867-4040
East Burke
Das German Haus .... (802)626-8568
Garrison Inn .... (802)626-8329
Holiday Haven .... (802)626-9810
Mountain View Creamery ...... (802)626-9924
Nutmegger .... (802)626-5205
Old Cutter Inn .... (802)626-5152
The Village Inn of East Burke .... (802)626-3161
East Charleston
Echo Lake B&B .... (802)723-5951
East Dorset
Christmas Tree B&B .... (802)362-4889
East Dover
Cooper Hill Inn .... (802)348-6333
East Hardwick
Brick House Guests .... (802)472-5512
East Haven
Hansel & Gretel Haus .... (802)467-8884
East Middlebury
The Annex B&B .... (802)388-3233
By The Way B&B .... (802)388-6291
October Pumpkin .... (802)388-9525
Robert Frost B&B .... (802)388-6042
East Montpelier
Cherry Tree Hill B&B .... (802)223-0549
East Warren
The Soft Landing .... (802)496-6531
Enosburg Falls
Berkson Farms .... (802)933-2522
Essex Junction
The Inn at Essex Junction ...... (802)878-1100
Landon House .... (802)878-9588
Mrs. B's B&B .... (802)878-5439
Tandys Bed & Breakfast .... (802)878-4729
Varnum's .... (802)899-4577
Willey's Farm B&B .... (802)878-4666
The Wilson Inn .... (802)879-1515
Fair Haven
Vermont Marble Inn .... (802)265-8383
Fairfax
Buck Hollow Farm .... (802)849-2400
Wagner Road Bed & Breakfast .. (802)849-6030
Fairfield
Tetreault's Hillside View Farm ... (802)827-4480
Fairlee
Aloha Manor .... (802)333-4478
Lake Morey Inn .... (800)423-1211
Rutledge Inn & Cottages .... (802)333-9722
Fayston
Slide Brook Meadows .... (802)496-4039
Tucker Hill Lodge & Restaurant .. (802)496-3983
White Horse Inn .... (802)496-3260
Franklin
Fair Meadows Farm .... (802)285-2132
Gaysville
Cobble House Inn .... (802)234-5458
Laolke Lodge .... (802)234-9205
Glover
Gloverview Inn B&B .... (802)525-3836
The Willow Garden .... (802)525-6695
Goshen
Judith's Garden B&B .... (802)247-4707
Grafton
Brandywine B&B .... (802)869-2777
Eaglebrook of Grafton .... (802)843-2564
The Farmhouse 'round The Bend . (802)843-2515
The Hayes House .... (802)843-2461
Woodchuck Hill Farm .... (802)843-2398
Grand Isle
Farmhouse on The Lake
.... (802)372-8849 (800)372-8849
Graniteville
Quarry House B&B .... (802)476-7164

Greensboro
Greensboro House B&B .... (802)533-7155

Guildhall
Guildhall B&B .... (802)676-3720

Hancock
Kincraft Inn .... (802)767-3734

Hardwick
Carolyn's Victorian Inn .... (802)472-6338
Kahagon at Nichols Pond .... (802)472-6446
The Marshall House .... (802)472-6006
Somerset House B&B .... (802)472-5484 (800)838-8074

Hartford
House of Seven Gables .... (802)295-1200
The Williamson House .... (802)295-2765

Highgate Springs
Country Essence B&B .... (802)868-4247
Tyler Place .... (802)868-3301

Hinesburg
By The Old Mill Stream .... (802)482-3613

Hyde Park
Ten Bends .... (802)888-2827

Irasburg
Brick House B&B .... (802)754-2108

Island Pond
Clyde River Hotel .... (802)723-5663
The Island Pond Snowed Inn B&B (802)723-6569
Jeannine's B&B .... (802)723-6673

Isle La Motte
Ruthcliffe Lodge & Restaurant ... (802)928-3200
Terry Lodge of Isle La Motte .... (802)928-3264

Jacksonville
Candlelight B&B . (802)368-7826 (800)992-2635

Jamaica
Three Mountain Inn .... (802)874-4140

Jay
Jay Village Inn .... (802)988-2643
Schneehutte Inne .... (802)988-4020
Woodshed Lodge .... (802)988-4444

Jeffersonville
The Keresey House .... (802)644-2761
Sterling Ridge Inn .... (802)644-8265
Three Mountain Lodge ....
Windridge Inn .... (802)644-5556

Jericho
Bechard's Mill Brook B&B .... (802)899-3846
Birds Nest .... (802)899-3993
Henry M. Field Victorian House B&B .... (802)899-3984
Homeplace B&B .... (802)899-4694
Maple Corner Farm B&B .... (802)899-2026
Milliken's .... (802)899-3993
Minterhaus B&B .... (802)899-3900

Johnson
The Dodge House B&B .... (802)635-7622
The Homestead B&B .... (802)635-7354

Killington
Alpenhof Lodge .... (802)422-9787
Chalet Killington . (802)422-3451 (800)451-4105
Cortina Inn .... (800)451-6108
Grey Bonnet Inn .... (800)342-2086
Killington Village Inn .... (802)422-3301
Little Buckhorn Lodge .... (802)422-3314
The Inn at Long Trail .... (802)775-7181 (800)325-2540
Mountain Meadows Lodge .... (802)775-1010
Mountain Morgans .... (802)422-3096
Mountain Sports Inn .... (802)422-3315
The Red Rob Inn .... (802)422-3303
Sherburne Valley Inn .... (802)422-9888
The Inn at The Six Mountains ... (802)422-4302
Snowed Inn .... (802)422-3407
Summit Lodge .. (802)422-3535 (800)635-6343
Trailside Lodge .... (802)422-3532
Whispering Pines Lodge .... (802)422-3014

Landgrove
The Landgrove Inn (802)824-6673 (800)669-8466
Nordic Inn .... (802)824-6444

Londonderry
Greenmount Lodge .... (802)824-5948
The Highland House .... (802)842-3019

Landgrove
White Pine Lodge .... (802)824-3442

Londonderry
Viking Guest House .... (802)824-3933

Lower Waterford
Yankee Woods B&B .... (802)748-5420

Ludlow
The Andrie Rose Inn .... (802)228-4846 (800)223-4846
Combes Family Inn .... (802)228-8799
Fletcher Manor B&B .... (802)228-3548
The Governor's Inn .... (802)228-8830
Jewell Brook Inn .... (802)228-8926
Okemo Inn .... (802)228-8834
Old Farm House Inn & Tavern ... (802)228-8700
St Joseph's Dwelling Place .... (802)228-4952
The Winchester Inn .... (802)228-3841

Lyndonville
Wheelock Inn B&B .... (802)626-8503
The Wildflower Inn .... (802)626-8310

Manchester
1811 House .... (802)362-1811
Birch Hill Inn ... (802)362-2761 (800)372-2761
Pinnacle Sun & Ski Lodge .... (802)824-6608 (800)899-8768
Suttons Guest House .... (802)362-1165
Village Country Inn (802)362-1792 (800)370-0300
Wilburton Inn ... (802)362-2500 (800)648-4944
Worthy Inn .... (802)362-1792

Manchester Center
Butternut Country House .... (802)362-3371
Seth Warner Inn .... (802)362-3830
The Inn at Willow Pond .... (802)362-4733

McIndoe Falls
McIndoe Falls Inn .... (802)633-2240

Middlebury
A Point of View .... (802)388-7205
Bonnie's B&B .... (802)388-7134
By The Way B & B .... (802)388-6291
Elizabeth's October Pumpkin .... (802)388-9525 (800)237-2007
Fairhill B&B .... (802)388-3044
Ferland's B&B .... (802)388-1703
Linens & Lace .... (802)388-0832
Middlebury B&B .... (802)388-4851
Stevenson House .... (802)462-2866

Middletown Springs
Priscilla's Victorian Inn .... (802)235-2299

Montgomery
Black Lantern Inn (802)326-4507 (800)255-8661
Kate's Suite .... (802)326-4434

Montgomery Center
Eagle Lodge .... (802)326-4518
Phineas Swan B&B .... (802)326-4306
The Inn on Trout River .... (802)326-4391 (800)338-7049

Montpelier
Gambles .... (802)229-4810
The Inn at Montpelier .... (802)223-2727
Montpelier B&B .... (802)229-0878
Wayside B&B .... (802)223-6202

Moretown
Honeysuckle Inn .... (802)496-6200
Schultzes' Village Inn .... (802)496-2366

Morgan
Seymour Lake Lodge .... (802)895-2752

Morrisville
Lepines Inn By The Brook .... (802)888-5862
Moore's-By-The-Brook .... (802)253-8366
Randolph House .... (802)888-7300

Mount Holly
Austria Haus .... (802)259-2441
Hortonville Inn .... (802)259-2587
Hound's Folly .... (802)259-2718

Mount Snow
Kitzhof Lodge ... (802)464-8310 (800)388-8310

New Haven
Horn Farnsworth B&B .... (802)388-2300
New Haven Hills B&B .... (802)453-5495

Newbury
A Century Past .... (802)866-3358
Sleepers Meadow .... (802)866-5676

Newfane
Four Columns Inn .... (802)365-7713
Old Newfane Inn .... (802)365-4427
West River Lodge .... (802)365-7745

Newport City
Family Guest House @ Thursday (802)766-2915

North Bennington
Cold Spring Farm B&B .... (802)442-5535

North Ferrisburg
Dunn-Inn .... (802)425-2902

North Hero
Charlie's Northland Lodge .... (802)372-8822
North Hero House .... (802)372-8237
Shore Acres Inn & Restaurant ... (802)372-8722

North Thetford
Stone House Inn .... (802)333-9124

North Troy
1893 House B&B .... (802)988-9614
North Troy Inn .... (802)988-2527
Rose Apple Acres Farm .... (802)988-4300

Northfield
Long Way Inn .... (802)485-3559
Margaret Holland Inn .... (802)485-9867

Northfield Falls
Four Bridges Inn .... (802)485-8995

Norton
Swanson Oldfarm B&B, Antique Barn .... (802)822-5221

Orleans
Valley House Inn (802)754-6665 (800)545-9711

Orwell
Buckswood B&B .... (802)948-2054
Country Road B&B .... (802)948-2129
Lake Ledge Farm B&B .... (802)948-2347

Perkinsville
Gwendolyn's B&B .... (802)263-5248

Peru
Russell Inn .... (802)824-6631
Wiley Inn .... (802)842-6600

Pittsfield
Fleur De Lis Lodge .... (802)746-8949
Stockbridge Inn Bed & Breakfast . (802)746-8165
Stonewood Inn .... (802)746-8881
Swiss Farm Lodge .... (802)746-8341

Plainfield
Northview B&B .... (802)454-7191

Plymouth
The Hawk Inn & Mountain Resort (802)672-3811
Plymouth Towne Inn .... (802)672-3059

Post Mills
Lake House Inn .... (802)333-4025

Poultney
Stonebridge Inn . (802)287-9849 (800)308-7001
Tower Hall B&B . (802)287-4004 (800)894-4004

Pownal
Inn at Oak Hill Bed & Breakfast .. (802)823-7849

Proctorsville
Castle Inn .... (802)226-7222
Depot Corner Inn and Restaurant .... (802)226-7970 (800)487-8576
Okemo Lantern Lodge .... (802)226-7770
Whitney Brook B&B .... (802)226-7460

Putney
Misty Meadows B&B .... (802)722-9517 (800)566-4789
The Inn at Pittsfield .... (802)746-8943

Quechee
Country Garden Inn B&B .... (802)295-3023 (800)859-4191
Hamilton Bed & Breakfast .... (802)295-1649
Quechee B&B .... (802)295-1776
Quechee Gorge Friendship Inn ... (802)295-7600
Sugar Pine Farm B&B .... (802)295-1266

Randolph
Emerson's B&B .... (802)728-4972
Foggy Bottom Farm B&B .... (802)728-5782
The Three Stallion Inn .... (802)728-5575

Reading
Greystone B&B .... (802)484-7200
The Peeping Cow B&B .... (802)484-5036

Readsboro
Old Coach Inn .... (802)423-5394

Richford
Troy Street B&B .... (802)848-3557

Richmond
Black Bear Inn .... (802)434-2126
Crosscreek B&B .... (802)434-3091
Mama Bower's B&B .... (802)434-2632
Rich Mound Acres B&B .... (802)434-2454
The Richmond Victorian Inn .... (802)434-4440

Rochester
Harvey's Mountain View Inn .... (802)767-4273
The New Homestead .... (802)767-4751
Tupper Farm Lodge .... (802)767-4243

Roxbury
The Inn at Johnnycake Flats .... (802)485-8961
Royalton
Fox Stand Inn & Restaurant ..... (802)763-8437
Rutland
Hillcrest Guest House .... (802)775-1670
Saint Albans
Bayview B&B .... (802)524-5609
Bellevue .... (802)527-1115
Old Mill River Place .... (802)524-7211
Reminisce B&B .... (802)524-3907
Wagner Road B&B (802)849-6030 (800)842-6030
Saint Johnsbury
Broadview Farm B&B .... (802)748-9902
Echo Ledge Farm Inn .... (802)748-4750
Heart 'n Hand .... (802)748-4487
Rabbit Hill Inn .. (802)748-5185 (800)213-8180
Sleepy Hollow .. (802)748-8066 (800)213-8180
Salisbury
Plumb's B&B .... (802)352-4551
Saxtons River
Red Barn Guest House .... (802)869-2566
Saxtons River Inn .... (802)869-2110
Three Chimney House .... (802)869-2524
Shaftsbury
Country Cousin Bed & Breakfast . (802)375-6985
Shaftsbury Guest House .... (802)447-0907
Sharon
Baxter Mountain House .... (802)763-8824
Shelburne
Best Friends B&B .... (802)985-8185
Elliott House B&B .... (802)985-1412
The Inn at Shelburne Farms .... (802)985-8686
Shoreham
Quiet Valley B&B .... (802)897-7887
Shrewsbury
Crown Point Inn . (802)492-3589 (800)492-8089
High Pastures B&B (802)773-2087 (800)584-4738
South Burlington
Anchorage Inn .... (802)863-7000
Lindenwood .... (802)862-2144
Willow Pond Farm B&B .... (802)985-8505
South Hero
Paradise Bay B&B .... (802)372-5393
South Londonderry
1830 Inn on The Green .... (802)824-6789
Londonderry Inn .... (802)824-5226
Three Clock Inn .... (802)824-6327
South Newbury
Peach Brook Inn .... (802)866-3389
South Newfane
The Inn at South Newfane ...... (802)348-7191
South Pomfret
Rosewood Inn B&B .... (802)457-4485
South Strafford
Watercourse Way B&B .... (802)765-4314
South Wallingford
Green Mountain Tea Room ..... (802)446-2611
Springfield
Baker Road Inn .... (802)886-2304
Bull Run Farm B&B .... (802)886-8470
Starksboro
Millhouse B&B .... (802)453-2008
North Country B&B .... (802)453-3911
Stockbridge
Chase Inn .... (802)746-8972
Stockbridge Inn B&B
.... (802)746-8165 (800)588-8165
The Wild Berry Inn .... (802)746-8141
Stowe
The 1860 House .... (802)253-7351
Andersen Lodge-An Austrian Inn . (802)253-7336
Baas' Gastehaus .... (802)253-8376
Bittersweet Inn .... (802)253-7787
Buccaneer Country Lodge ..... (802)253-4772
Butternut Inn .... (802)253-4277
Candlelight Cottage .... (802)253-8592
Charbonneau Guest House ..... (802)253-7701
Fiddler's Green Inn .... (802)253-8124
Fountain House .... (802)253-9285
Foxfire Inn .... (802)253-4887
Gables Inn .... (802)253-7730
Green Mountain Inn .... (802)253-7301
Grey Fox Inn .... (802)253-8921
Guest House Horman .... (802)253-4846
Hadleigh House .... (802)253-7703
Hob Knob Inn .... (802)253-8549
Innsbruck Inn ... (802)253-8582 (800)225-8582
Logwood Inn .... (802)253-7354
Miguel's Stowe Away .... (802)253-7574
The Inn at The Mountain
.... (802)253-3000 (800)253-4754
Plum Door ..... (802)253-9995 (800)258-7586
The Raspberry Patch B&B ..... (802)253-4145
The Salzburg Inn .... (802)253-8541
Scandinavia Inn . (802)253-8555 (800)544-4229
Ski Inn .... (802)253-4050
Stowe Inn at Little River
.... (802)253-4836 (800)227-1108
Stowe-Bound Lodge .... (802)253-4515
Stowehof Inn .... (802)253-9722
Ten Acres Lodge .... (802)327-7357
Timberholm Inn .... (802)253-7603
Topnotch at Stowe Resort & Spa (800)451-8686
Trattoria La Festa/Toscana Inn ... (802)253-9776
Trapp Family Lodge .... (802)253-8511
The Inn at Turner Mill .... (802)253-2062
Walkabout Creek Lodge .... (802)253-7354
Wilkins House B&B
.... (802)253-4469 (800)994-5546
Woodchip Inn .... (802)253-9080
Ye Olde England Inne
.... (802)253-7558 (800)477-3771
Stratton Mountain
Birkenhaus .... (802)297-2000
Taftsville
The Maitland-Swan House ..... (800)959-1404
Townshend
Boardman House .... (802)365-4086
Old Brick Tavern .... (802)365-4527
Redwing Farm B&B .... (802)365-4656
Townshend Country Inn
.... (802)365-4141 (800)569-1907
Troy
Frietlich Haus .... (802)744-6113
Underhill
Henry M Field House .... (802)899-3984
Rolling Meadows Farm Guest Rooms
.... (802)899-4062
Underhill Center
A Mansfield View B&B .... (802)899-4793
Haus Kelley B&B .... (802)899-3905
Vergennes
Emersons' Guest House .... (802)877-3293
Strong House Inn .... (802)877-3337
Woodman Hill House B&B ..... (802)877-2720
Vershire
The Risley House .... (802)685-4417
Waitsfield
Finchingfield Farm .... (802)496-7555
Carpenters Farm Country Inn ... (802)496-3433
Featherbed Inn .... (802)496-7151
Knoll Farm Country Inn .... (802)496-3939
Lareau Farm Country Inn
.... (802)496-4949 (800)833-0766
The Inn at Mad River Barn ..... (802)496-3310
Millbrook Inn ... (802)496-2405 (800)477-2809
Mountain View Inn .... (802)496-2426
Olde Tymes Inn .... (802)496-3875
Romantic Little B & B Inns ..... (802)496-4667
The Inn at Round Barn Farm .... (802)496-2276
Snuggery Inn .... (802)496-2322
Wait Farm Motor Inn .... (802)496-2033
Weathertop Lodge .... (802)496-4909
Wallingford
White Rocks Inn .... (802)446-2077
Warren
Christmas Tree Inn & Condos
.... (802)583-2211 (800)535-5622
Golden Lion Riverside Inn ...... (802)496-3084
The Guest House .... (802)496-5306
Hamilton House . (802)583-1066 (800)760-1066
Pepper's Lodge . (802)583-2202 (800)638-7369
Pitcher Inn .... (802)496-3831
Powderhound Inn .... (802)496-5100
Sugar Lodge .... (802)583-3300
Sugarbush Inn .. (802)583-2381 (800)451-4320
West Hill House .... (802)496-7162
Waterbury Center
The Black Locust Inn .... (802)244-7490
Wells River
Long Meadow Inn .... (802)757-2538
West Arlington
Four Winds Country Inn .... (802)375-6734
Mountainside Lodge B&B ...... (802)375-2238
West Brattleboro
Dalem's Chalet .... (802)254-4323
West Burke
Old Time B&B .... (802)467-3129
West Dover
Doveberry Inn .... (802)464-5652
The Gray Ghost Inn .... (802)464-2474
Mount Snow Mountaineer Inn
.... (802)464-5404 (800)682-4637
The Inn at Mt Snow .... (802)464-3300
The Inn at Sawmill Farm .... (802)464-8131
Weathervane Lodge .... (802)464-5426
Whippletree at Mount Snow .... (802)464-5485
Yankee Doodle Lodge .... (802)464-5591
West Glover
Rodgers Country Inn .... (802)525-6677
West Hartford
The Half Penney Inn B&B ...... (802)295-6082
West Townshend
Windham Hill Inn (802)874-4080 (800)944-4080
Westmore
Fox Hall Inn .... (802)525-6930
Willoughvale Inn & Restaurant ... (802)525-4123
Weston
The Colonial House Inn .... (802)824-6286
Darling Family Inn .... (802)824-3223
Simple Living Inn .... (802)824-5946
The Inn at Weston (802)824-6789 (800)754-5804
Wilder Homestead Inn .... (802)824-8172
White River Junction
Anthony Field Gallery B&B ..... (802)295-2922
Stonecrest Farm Bed & Breakfast (802)296-2425
Williamstown
Autumn Crest Inn (802)433-6627 (800)339-6627
Rosewood Inn .... (802)433-5822
Williamsville
Brook Acres B&B .... (802)348-7709
The Country Innwilliamsville .... (802)348-7148
Willimasville
Mugwump Farm B&B .... (802)348-7761
Williston
Partridge Hill B&B .... (802)878-4741
Susse Chalet Inn of Burlington .. (802)879-8999
Wilmington
Brookbound B&B .... (802)464-3511
Hermitage Inn .... (802)464-3511
Horizon Inn .... (802)464-2131
Misty Mountain Lodge .... (802)464-3961
Nordic Hills Lodge .... (802)464-5130
Nutmeg Inn .... (802)464-3351
Old Red Mill Inn . (802)464-3700 (800)843-8483
On The Rocks Lodge .... (802)464-8364
Shearer Hill Farm B&B .... (802)464-3253
Slalom Lodge .... (802)464-3783
Windsor
What Not House .... (802)674-2752
The Inn at Windsor (802)674-5670 (800)754-8668
Winooski
Windflower B&B .... (802)655-4611
Wolcott
Golden Maple Inn .... (802)888-6614
Woodbury
Hidden Pines .... (802)472-6262
Kahabon B&B .... (802)472-6446
Woodstock
The 1830 Shire Town Inn ...... (802)457-1830
Applebutter Inn .... (802)457-4158
Ardmore Inn .... (802)457-3887
Barr House .... (802)457-3334
Cambria House .... (802)457-3077
Charleston House .... (802)457-3843
Deer Brook Inn .... (802)672-3713
Jackson House .... (802)457-2065
Maitland Swan House .... (802)457-5181
Sugarbush Farm .... (802)457-1757
Thomas Hill Farm B&B .... (802)457-1067
Three Church Street .... (802)457-1925
Village Inn of Woodstock ...... (802)457-1255
The Winslow House .... (802)457-1820
Woodstock House B&B .... (802)457-1758
Woodstocker B&B (802)457-3896 (800)457-3896

Virginia

Abingdon
Cabin on The River . . . . (703)623-1267
Litchfield Hall . . . . (703)628-9317
Martha Washington Inn . . . . (703)628-3161
Mason Place B&B . . . . (703)628-2887
River Garden Bed & Breakfast . . . (540)676-0335
Silversmith Inn . . . . (540)676-3924
The Inn on Town Creek . . . . (703)628-4560
Victoria & Albert B&B . . . . (540)676-2797

Accomac
Drummond Town Inn . . . . (804)787-3679

Afton
Afton House . . . .
Looking Glass House . . . . (703)456-6844

Alberta
Englewood . . . . (804)949-0111

Aldie
Little River Inn . . . . (703)327-6742

Alexandria
The Little House . . . . (703)548-9654
Morrison House . . . . (703)838-8000

Altavista
Castle to Country House . . . . (804)369-4911

Amherst
Fairview Bed & Breakfast . . . . . . (804)277-8500
Rutledge Inn . . . . (804)946-7670

Appomattox
Appomattox Court House Inn . . . (804)352-5001

Arlington
Memory House . . . . (703)534-4607
Swedish Inn . . . . (703)524-4682

Ashland
The Henry Clay Inn
. . . . (804)798-3100 (800)343-4565

Banco
Olive Mill B&B . . . . (703)923-4664

Bedford
Elmo's Rest . . . . (703)586-3707
Otter's Den Bed & Breakfast . . . . (540)586-2204
Peaks of Otter Lodge . . . . (703)586-1081

Berryville
Battletown Inn . . . . (540)955-4100
Berryville Bed & Breakfast . . . . . (540)955-2200
Blue Ridge B&B . (703)955-1246 (800)296-1246

Blacksburg
Per Diem B&B . . . . (540)953-2604
Brush Mountain Inn . . . . (540)951-7530
L'Arche B&B . . . . (540)951-1808
Sycamore Tree B&B . . . . (703)381-1597
Twin Porches B&B . . . . (540)552-0930

Blackstone
Epes House B&B . . . . (804)292-7941
Grey Swan Inn . . (804)292-3199 (800)509-3567

Bland
Willow Bend Farm B&B . . . . (703)688-3719

Boston
Thistle Hill B&B . . . . (703)987-9142

Bowling Green
Mansion View B&B
. . . . (804)633-4377 (800)251-9335

Boyce
River House . . . . (703)837-1476

Brandy Station
Blue Haven B&B . . . . (540)825-0716

Bridgewater
Bear & Dragon B&B . . . . (703)828-2807

Bristol
Glencarin Manor . . . . (540)466-0224

Brodnax
Sherwood Manor Inn . . . . (804)848-0361

Brookneal
Staunton Hill Country Inn . . . . . . (804)376-4048

Buena Vista
Noahs Ark Bed & Breakfast . . . . . (540)261-5301

Burkeville
Hyde Park Farm . . . . (804)645-8431

Cape Charles
Cape Charles House . . . . (804)331-4920
Nottingham Ridge B&B . . . . (804)331-1010
Pickett's Harbor B&B . . . . (804)331-2212
Sea Gate . . . . (804)331-2206

Castlewood
Greystone B&B . . . . (540)762-0559

Charles City
Piney Grove at Southall's Plantation
. . . . (804)829-2480

Charlottesville
The 1817 Antique Inn
. . . . (804)979-7353 (800)730-7443
Carrsbrook . . . . (804)973-8177
Chester Bed & Breakfast . . . . (804)286-3960
English Inn . . . . (804)295-7707
Longhouse . . . . (804)979-7264
The Inn at Monticello . . . . (804)979-3593
The Inn at Sugar Hollow Farm . . . (804)823-7086
The Inn at Sunnyfields . . . . (804)296-9005

Chatham
Sims-Mitchell House B&B
. . . . (804)432-0595 (800)967-2867

Chesapeake
Fairfield Inn . . . . (804)420-1300
Hampton Inn . . . . (804)420-1550

Chesterfield
Bellmont Manor B&B . . . . (804)745-0106

Chilhowie
Clarkcrest B&B . . . . (703)646-3707
Pendleton House Inn . . . . (540)646-2047

Chincoteague
Channel Bass Inn . . . . (804)336-6148
Duck Haven Cottages . . . . (804)336-6290
Island Manor House . . . . (804)336-5436
Main Street House B&B . . . . (804)336-6030
Miss Molly's Inn . (804)336-6686 (800)221-5620

Christiansburg
The Oaks Bed & Breakfast Inn . . . (540)381-1500

Churchville
Buckhorn Inn . . . . (703)337-6900

Clarksville
Kinderton Manor Inn . . . . (804)374-8407
Needmoor Inn . . . . (804)374-2866
Noreen's Nest . . . . (804)374-0603
Simply Southern B&B Inn . . . . . . (804)374-9040

Clifton Forge
Longdale Inn . . . (540)862-0892 (800)862-0386

Colonial Beach
Potomac Inn . . . . (804)224-7711
Quiet Water Cove Bread & Breakfast
. . . . (804)224-7410

Columbia
Upper Byrd Farm B&B . . . . (804)842-2240

Copper Hill
Bent Mountain Lodge . . . . (703)929-4979

Covington
Milton Hall B&B Inn . . . . (540)965-0196

Culpeper
Fountain Hall B&B (703)825-8200 (800)298-4748
Hazel River Inn . . . . (540)937-5854

Dabneys
Bare Castle Farm B&B . . . . (804)749-3950

Daleville
Baileywick Farm B&B . . . . (703)992-2022

Danville
Broad Street Manor . . . . (804)792-0324
Gold Leaf Inn . . . . (804)793-1433
Bright Leaf House . . . . (804)799-4644

Deltaville
River Place-At-Deltaville . . . . (804)776-9153

Dillwyn
Buckingham Springs Plantation . . (804)392-8770

Draper
Claytor Lake Homestead Inn
. . . . (540)980-6777 (800)676-5253

Dublin
Bell's B&B . . . . (703)674-6331

Edinburg
Edinburg Inn B&B Ltd. . . . . (540)984-8286
Hatch The-A Bed & Breakfast . . . (540)984-8939

Elkton
Spotswood Inn Bed & Breakfast . (540)298-2088

Etlan
Dulaney Hollow at Old Rag Mountain B&B
. . . . (703)923-4470

Exmore
Martha's Inn . . . . (804)442-4641

Fairfield
Angel's Rest Farm . . . . (540)377-6449

Fancy Gap
The Inn at Orchard Gap . . . . (703)398-3206

Farmville
Linden B&B . . . . (804)223-8443
Tranquility Farm Bed & Breakfast . (804)392-4456

Flint Hill
The School House . . . . (703)675-3030
Stone House Hollow . . . . (703)675-3279

Floyd
Brookfield Inn B&B . . . . (703)763-3363

Forest
Summer Kitchen . . . . (804)525-0923

Franktown
Stillmeadow Inn B&B
. . . . (804)442-2431 (800)772-8397

Fredericksburg
Fredericksburg Colonial Inn . . . . . (703)371-5666
Mary Josephine Ball B&B . . . . . . (703)373-7674
The Richard Johnston Inn . . . . . . (540)899-7606

Front Royal
Constant Spring Inn . . . . (540)635-7010

Glasgow
Anderson Street B&B . . . . (540)258-2123

Gloucester
The Willows B&B . . . . (804)693-4066

Gordonsville
Norfields Farm B&B . . . . (703)832-5939
Rabbit Run B&B . . . . (540)832-2892
Ridge Top Country Cottage . . . . . (540)832-2946
Rocklands . . . . (703)832-7176
Sleepy Hollow Farm B&B
. . . . (703)832-5555 (800)215-4804
Tivoli . . . . (703)832-2225 (800)840-2225

Gore
Rainbow's End . . . . (703)858-2808

Goshen
Hummingbird Inn . . . . (540)997-9065

Hamilton
Stonegate B&B . . . . (703)338-9519

Hardyville
River's Rise B&B . . . . (804)776-7521

Hillsville
Bray's Manor B&B Inn
. . . . (703)728-7901 (800)753-2729

Hot Springs
King's Victorian Inn . . . . (703)839-3134

Independence
River View B&B . . . . (703)236-4187

Irvington
Kendall Hall Inn . . . . (804)438-6927
King Carter Inn . . . . (804)438-6053

Keswick
Ashley House/Keswick Estate . . . (804)979-3440

Lancaster
The Inn at Levelfields
. . . . (804)435-6887 (800)238-5578

Leesburg
Colonial Inn . . . . (703)777-5000
Fleetwood Farm B&B . . . . (703)327-4325
Laurel Brigade Inn . . . . (703)777-1010

Lexington
Asherowe B&B . . . . (540)463-4219
Blue and Grey B&B . . . . (540)463-6260
D & D Bed & Breakfast . . . . (540)463-6298
Fassifern B&B . . . . (703)463-1013
Historic Country Inns of Lexington (540)463-2044
Howland House at Stoneridge . . . (540)463-4090
Lavender Hill Farm B&B . . . . (703)464-5877
Llewellyn Lodge at Lexington
. . . . (540)463-3235 (800)882-1145
Mountain View B&B . . . . (540)463-6619
Stoneridge B&B . (540)463-4090 (800)491-2930
The Inn at Union Run
. . . . (703)463-9715 (800)528-6466

Lincoln
Creek Crossing Farm . . . . (703)338-7550
Oakland Green Farm . . . . (703)338-7628
Springdale Country Inc . . . . (540)338-1832

Louisa
Ginger Hill B&B . . . . (540)967-3260
Whistle Stop B&B . . . . (540)967-2911

Luray
Brookside Cabins . . . . (540)743-5698
Hawksbill Retreat B&B . . . . (703)778-2780
Mayneview . . . . (540)743-7921
The Mimslyn Inn . . . . (800)296-5105
Mountain View House B&B . . . . . (703)743-3723
Riverview at Kauffman's Mill . . . . (540)743-5653

The Ruffner House . . . . (540)743-7855
Shenandoah Countryside B&B . . (703)743-6434
Shenandoah River Inn . . . . (540)743-1144
Shenandoah River Roost . . . . . . (703)743-3467

Lynchburg
Fort Early Bed & Breakfast . . . . . (804)846-3628
Langhorne Manor (804)846-4667 (800)851-1466
Lynchburg Mansion Inn B&B . . . . (804)528-5400 (800)352-1199
The Madison House B&B . . . . . . (804)528-1503
Once Upon A Time Bed & Breakfast . . . . (804)845-3561

Madison
Shenandoah Springs Inn . . . . (703)923-4300

Mathews
Ravenswood Inn . . . . (804)725-7272
Riverfront House & Cottage . . . . (804)725-9975

McGaheysville
Shenandoah Valley Farm & Inn . . (703)289-5402

McKenney
Cedar Green Farm Bed & Breakfast (804)478-5784

Middleburg
Briar Patch at Middleburg . . . . . . (703)327-4455
Middleburg Country Inn . . . . (703)687-6082
Middleburg Inn & Guest Suites . . (703)687-3115

Middletown
Wayside Inn Since 1797 . . . . (703)869-1797

Millboro
River Ridge Guest Ranch . . . . . . (703)996-4148

Millwood
Brookside B&B . . . . (703)837-1780

Mineral
Littlepage Inn . . . (540)854-9861 (800)248-1803

Mollusk
Greenvale Manor . . . . (804)462-5995

Moneta
The Holland-Duncan House at Smith Mtn Lake . . . . (703)721-8510

Montebello
Dutch Haus Geselligkeit . . . . (540)377-2119

Monterey
Bobbie's Bed & Breakfast . . . . . . (703)468-2308

Montross
Montross Inn & Restaurant . . . . . (800)321-0979
The Wine Seller . . . . (804)493-9097

Morattico
Holly Point . . . . (804)462-7759

Mount Holly
Mt. Holly Steamboat Inn . . . . (804)472-3336

Mount Jackson
Widow Kip's Country Inn . . . . . . (540)477-2400 (800)478-8714

Natural Bridge
Burger's Country Inn . . . . (540)291-2464
Red Mill Inn B&B . . . . (540)291-1704
Braford Cottage B&B . . . . (540)291-2217

Nellysford
Acorn Inn . . . . (804)361-9357
The Mark Addy . (804)361-1101 (800)278-2154
The Meander Inn . . . . (804)361-1121
Trillium House . . (804)325-9126 (800)325-9126
Upland Manor . . . . (804)361-1101

New Market
Cross Roads Inn B&B . . . . (540)740-4157

Norfolk
Page House Inn . . . . (804)625-5033

North
Cedar Point Country Inn . . . . (804)725-9535

Occoquan
Rockledge B&B . . . . (703)690-3377

Onancock
76 Market Street B&B . . . . (804)787-7600

Orange
The Holladay House . . (540)672-4893 (800)358-4422
The Shadows B&B Inn . . . . (540)672-5057
Willow Grove Inn (703)672-5982 (800)349-1778

Palmyra
Danscot House . . . . (804)589-1977

Pamplin
Sleepy Lamb B&B . . . . (804)248-6289

Paris
The Ashby Inn . . . . (703)592-3900

Penn Laird
Hearth N' Holly Inn . . . . (703)434-6766

Petersburg
Mayfield Inn . . . . (804)861-6775

Pocahontas
Laurel Inn Bed & Beakfast . . . . . . (540)945-2787

Port Republic
Busy Bee Bed & Breakfast . . . . . (540)289-5480

Pratts
Colvin Hall B&B . . . . (703)948-6211

Pulaski
The Count Pulaski B&B and Garden . . . . (540)980-1163 (800)980-1163

Pungoteague
Evergreen Inn . . . . (804)422-3375

Purcellville
Creek Crossing Farm . . . . (540)338-4548
Dandongreen Manor . . . . (703)338-4202
The Log House . . . . (703)668-9003

Radford
Alleghany Inn . . . . (540)731-4466
Hideaway B&B . . . . (703)731-3126

Raphine
Willow Pond Farm B&B . . . . (540)348-1310

Rapidan
Eastern View B&B . . . . (703)854-4924

Reedville
Cedar Grove B&B Inn . . . . (804)453-3915
The Morris House . . . . (804)453-7016
Magnolia Tree Bed & Breakfast . . (804)453-4720

Richmond
Abbie Hill Guest Lodging . . . . . . (804)355-5855
Be My Guest B&B . . . . (804)358-9901
Bensonhouse . . . . (804)353-6900
The Jefferson . . . . (804)788-8000
The Leonine Experience . . . . (804)349-1952
Lions Inn . . . . (804)355-7265
Mr. Patrick Henry's Inn . . . . (804)644-1322
The West-Bocock House . . . . . . (804)358-6174
The William Catlin House B&B Inn (804)780-3746

Roanoke
Lone Oaks B&B . . . . (703)989-9599
Walnuthill Bed & Breadfast . . . . . (540)427-3312

Rochelle
Dawson's Country Place B&B . . . (703)948-7013

Rocky Mount
The Claiborne House B&B . . . . . (540)483-4616

Rosedale
Rosedale Country Inn Bed & Breakfast . . . . (540)880-1268

Round Hill
Poor House Farm B&B . . . . (703)554-2511

Salem
Old Manse . . . . (703)389-3921

Scottsville
Belle Meade Bed & Breakfast . . . (804)286-2665
Deerfield Bed & Breakfast . . . . . . (804)286-6306
High Meadows Vineyard & Mtn Sunset Inn . . . . (804)286-2218 (800)232-1832

Smithfield
Four Square Plantation . . . . (804)365-0749
Smithfield Station Inn and Marina (804)357-7700

Sperryville
Apple Hill Farm B&B . . . . (703)987-9454

Spotsylvania
Roxbury Mill B&B . . . . (703)582-6611

Stanardsville
Edgewood Farm B&B . . . . (804)985-3782

Stanley
River's Bend Ranch . . . . (800)672-7726

Staunton
Belle Grae Inn . . . . (540)886-5151
Kenwood . . . . (540)886-0524
Hilltop House . . . . (540)886-0042
Thornrose House at Gypsy Hill . . . . (540)885-7026 (800)861-4338

Steeles Tavern
The Osceola Mill Country Inn . . . . (703)377-6455 (800)242-7352

Strasburg
Hotel Strasburg . . . . (540)465-9191
Sonner House Bed & Breakfast . . (540)465-4712
Vesper Hall . . . . (703)465-5192

Surry
Seward House B&B . . . . (804)294-3810
Surrey House . . . . (804)294-3191

Swoope
Lambsgate B&B . . . . (703)337-6929

Syria
Grave's Mountain Lodge . . . . (703)923-4231

Tangier
Sunset Inn . . . . (804)891-2535

Toano
Blue Bird Haven . . . . (804)566-0177

Trevilians
Prospect Hill . . . . (703)967-0844

Trout Dale
Fox Hill Inn . . . . (703)677-3313

Upperville
1763 Inn . . . . . . (703)592-3848 (800)669-1763

Urbanna
Atherston Hall B&B . . . . (804)758-2809
The Town House . . . . (804)758-3521

Vesuvius
Irish Gap Inn . . . . (804)922-7701

Virginia Beach
Barclay Cottage B&B . . . . (804)422-1956
Church Point Manor House . . . . . (804)460-2657

Wachapreague
The Burton House . . . . (804)787-4560
Hart's Harbor House B&B . . . . . . (804)787-4848

Warm Springs
Anderson Cottage B&B . . . . (703)839-2975
The Inn at Gristmill Square . . . . . (703)839-2231
Hidden Valley B&B . . . . (703)839-3178
Meadow Lane Lodge . . . . (703)839-5959

Washington
The Foster-Harris House . . . . (540)675-3757 (800)666-0153
Heritage House B&B . . . . (703)675-3207
Middleton Inn . . . (540)675-2020 (800)816-8157
Sunset Hills Farm . . . . (703)987-8804
Sycamore Hill House & Gardens . (703)675-3046
Withrow House . . . . (540)463-2044

Waterford
The Pink House . . . . (703)882-3453

Waynesboro
Redwood Lodge . . . . (540)943-8765
The Iris Inn . . . . (540)943-1991

Williamsburg
Alice Person House . . . . (804)220-9263
Candlewick Bed & Breakfast . . . . (804)253-8693
Erika's Cottage . . . . (804)229-6421
Governor's Trace B&B . . . . (804)229-7552
Greenwoode Inn . . . . (804)566-8800
The Hite House . . . . (804)229-4814
Holland's Lodge . . . . (804)253-6476
Homestay B&B . (804)229-7468 (800)836-7468
Magnolia Manor . (804)220-9600 (800)462-6667
Princess Anne . . . . (804)229-2455
Second Street Inn . . . . (804)253-6450
War Hill Inn . . . . (804)565-0248
Wood's Guest Home . . . . (804)229-3376

Willis Wharf
Ballard House Bed N Breakfast . . (804)442-2206

Wolftown
Tax Hollow Hill . . . . (703)948-5235

Woodstock
The Candlewick Inn . . . . (703)459-8008
River'd Inn . . . . . (540)459-5369 (800)637-4561

Woolwine
Mountain Rose B&B . . . . (703)930-1057

Wytheville
Boxwood Inn B&B . . . . (540)228-8911

Yorktown
York River Inn Bed & Breakfast . . (804)887-8800

Washington

Aberdeen
Aberdeen Mansion Inn . . . . (360)533-7079

Acme
River Valley B&B . . . . (206)595-2686

Anacortes
A Burrows Bay B&B . . . . (360)293-4792
Blue Rose B&B . . . . (206)293-5175
Campbell House . (206)293-4910 (800)484-9596
Cap Sante Court B&B . . . . (206)293-8088
Dutch Treat House . . . . (206)293-8154
Hasty Pudding House . . . . (360)293-5773 (800)368-5588
Lowman House . . . . (360)293-0590

Nantucket Inn .... (360)293-6007
Old Brook Inn . . . (360)293-4768 (800)503-4768
Outlook Bed & Breakfast .... (360)293-3505
Skyline B&B .... (206)293-5780
Sunset Beach B&B (206)293-5428 (800)359-3448

Anderson Island
Beach Home Bed & Breakfast . . . (206)884-4045
Hideaway House .... (206)884-4179

Ariel
Speelyai Ridge Bed & Breakfast . (360)231-4334

Ashford
Alexander's Country Inn .... (206)569-2300
Ashford Mansion .... (206)569-2739
The Hershey Homestead .... (206)569-2674
Jasmer's at Mt. Rainer .... (360)569-2682
Mountain Meadows Inn B&B .... (360)569-2788
Wild Mint B&B .... (206)569-2235

Auburn
Blomeen House B&B .... (206)939-3088

Bainbridge Island
A Crystal House Bed & Breakfast (206)842-5070
Agate Pass Waterfront Bed & Breakfast
.... (206)842-1632
Bainbridge House B&B .... (206)842-1599
Bainbridge Inn .... (206)842-7564
Beach Cottage .... (206)842-6081
The Captain's House .... (206)842-3557
Cedar Meadow .... (206)842-6530
Contemporary B&B .... (206)842-2431
Country Haus Bed & Breakfast .. (206)842-8425
Hunter House .... (206)842-7777
Mary's Farmhouse .... (206)842-4952
Rockaway Beach Guest House .. (206)780-9427
Rose Cottage .... (206)842-6248
Sabine's B&B .... (206)780-9211
Marith's Place .... (206)842-1427
The Woodsman .... (206)842-7386

Battle Ground
Pheasant Run Bed & Breakfast .. (360)687-0942

Beaver
Eagle Point Inn .... (206)327-3236

Belfair
Country Garden Inn .... (360)275-3683
North Bay Inn .... (206)275-5378

Bellevue
A Cascade View Bed & Breakfast (206)883-7078
Bellevue B&B .... (206)453-1048
Bridle Trails Bed & Breakfast .... (206)861-0700
Petersen B&B .... (206)453-1435

Bellingham
Anderson Creek Lodge B&B
.... (206)966-2126 (800)441-5585
De Cann House B&B .... (360)734-9172
Big Trees B&B .... (360)647-2850
The Castle B&B .... (360)676-0974
The Secret Garden .... (206)671-5327
Shawmanee B&B .... (206)676-9109
Springcrest Farm .... (206)966-7272
Stratford Manor .... (360)715-8441
Sunrise Bay B&B .... (360)647-0376

Benton City
Palmer House B&B .... (509)588-3701

Bingen
Bingen Haus .... (509)493-4888
The Grand Old House .... (509)493-2838

Birch Bay
Birch Bay B&B .... (206)325-3500

Bow
Alice Bay B&B .... (206)766-6396
Benson Farmstead .... (360)757-0578
Samish Point By The Bay ...... (360)766-6610

Bremerton
Highland Cottage .... (360)373-2235
Willcox House .... (360)830-4492

Buckley
Buckley Bed & Breakfast ...... (360)829-4150

Burton
Harbor Inn B&B .... (206)463-6794

Camano Island
The Inn at Barnum Point .... (206)387-2256
Salal Hill B&B .... (206)387-3763
Willcox House B&B .... (360)629-4746

Camas
Washingtonia Inn .... (206)834-7629

Carnation
Idyl Inn on The River .... (206)868-2000

Carson
Carson Hot Springs Hotel ...... (509)427-8292

Cashmere
Cashmere Country Inn .... (509)782-4212
Grandview Orchard Inn .... (509)782-2340
Warm Hearth B&B .... (509)782-1553

Castle Rock
Rocks Hideaway .... (360)274-3101

Cathlamet
Cathlamet Hotel .... (360)795-3122
Country Keeper B&B Inn .... (206)795-3030
The Gallery B&B at Little Cape Horn
.... (360)425-7395

Centralia
Candalite Mansion .... (360)736-4749

Chehalis
Rivergarden .... (360)748-6737
Whispering River B&B .... (206)262-9859

Chelan
Brickhouse Inn .... (509)682-4791
Holden Village B&B .... (509)687-9695
Mary Kay's Whaley Mansion .... (509)682-5735
(800)729-2408

Chimacum
Summer House .... (206)732-4017
Windridge Cottage .... (360)732-4575

Clallam Bay
Winter Summer Inn .... (206)963-2264

Clarkston
Highland House .... (509)758-3126
Suite Dreams Bed & Breakfast .. (509)758-8213
Swallowhaven Bed & Breakfast .. (509)758-8357

Clinton
A Room With A View .... (360)321-6264
The Beach House .... (206)321-4335
Cape Cod Cottage .... (360)321-2964
Home By The Sea .... (206)321-2964
Kittleson Cove .... (206)221-2734
Sweetwater Cottage .... (360)341-1604

Colville
Care Free Quest Ranch Bed & Breakfast
.... (509)684-4739
Maple at Sixth B&B .... (509)684-5251

Concrete
Cascade Mountain Inn .... (206)826-4333

Coulee City
The Main Stay .... (509)632-5687

Coulee Dam
Four Winds Guest House ...... (509)633-3146

Coupeville
Anchorage Inn .... (206)678-5581
Captain Whidbey Inn
.... (360)678-4097 (800)366-4097
Colonel Crockett Farm .... (360)678-3711
The Compass Rose B&B ...... (360)678-5318
Coupeville Inn of Penn Cove .... (360)678-6668
Fort Casey Inn .... (360)678-8792
Old Morris Farm .... (360)678-6586
The Inn at Penn Cove
.... (206)678-8000 (800)688-2683
The Victorian B&B .... (360)678-5305

Darrington
Hemlock Hills B&B .... (206)436-1274
Sauk River Farm .... (206)436-1794

Davenport
A Victorian House B&B .... (509)725-0308

Dayton
Baker House B&B .... (509)382-4764
The Purple House (509)382-3159 (800)486-2574
Weinhard Hotel .... (509)382-4032

Deer Harbor
Deep Meadow Farm B&B ...... (360)376-5866
Deer Harbor Inn .... (206)376-4110

Deming
The Guest House .... (206)592-2343

Dockton
Angels of The Sea B&B .... (206)463-6980
Castle Hill B&B .... (206)463-5491

Duvall
The Victorian .... (206)788-1671

Eastsound
Blue Heron .... (360)376-5259
Cabin on The Point .... (206)376-4114
Double Mountain Bed & Breakfast (360)376-4570
Kangaroo House .... (206)376-2175
Laerie Bed & Breakfast .... (360)376-4647
Rosario Resort Hotel .... (206)376-2222
The Whale Watch House .... (206)376-4793

Eatonville
Old Mill House B&B .... (206)832-6506

Edmonds
Dayton B&B .... (206)778-3611
Driftwood Lane .... (206)776-2686
Harrison House .... (206)776-4748
Hudgens Haven .... (206)776-2202
Maple Tree B&B .... (206)774-8420

Ellensburg
Carriage House Cottage .... (509)925-2108
The Treehouse B&B .... (509)925-4620
The Willows .... (509)962-2839

Enumclaw
The Homestead B&B .... (206)825-7816
Stillmeadow Bed & Breakfast ... (206)825-6381
White Rose Inn .... (360)825-7194

Everett
Vintage Lady Bed & Breakfast ... (206)252-9334

Everson
Applewood Farm B&B .... (206)966-5183
Wilkin's Farm B&B .... (206)966-7616

Fall City
The Colonial Inn .... (206)222-5191

Ferndale
Slater Heritage House B&B ..... (206)384-4273

Forks
Brightwater House B & B ...... (360)374-5453
Fisherman's Widow Bed & Breakfast
.... (360)374-5693
Miller Tree Inn .... (206)374-6806
River Inn .... (360)374-6526
Shirley's Rain Country Inn ..... (206)374-5607

Fox Island
The Beach Place .... (206)549-2555
Beachside B&B .... (206)549-2524
Island Escape B&B .... (206)549-2044

Freeland
Bush Point Wharf B&B .... (206)321-0405
Double Bluff Bed & Breakfast ... (360)321-0502
Uncle John's Cottage .... (360)331-5623
Viewhaven Beach Getaway ..... (360)331-1242
Where Ships Pass Bed & Breakfast (360)331-8214

Friday Harbor
Argyle House B&B .... (360)378-4084
Blair House B&B .... (360)378-5907
Duffy House B&B .... (360)378-5604
Friday's Historical Inn .... (360)378-5848
Harrison House Suites .... (360)378-3587
Jensen Bay Pines Bed & Breakfast (360)378-5318
The Meadows B&B .... (360)378-4004
Old English Roses Manor ...... (360)378-6484
Olympic Lights .... (360)378-3186
Orcinus Inn .... (360)378-4060
Panacea Bed & Breakfast ...... (360)378-3757
San Juan Inn B&B (360)378-2070 (800)742-8210
Tower House B&B .... (360)378-5464
Trumpeter Inn . . (360)378-3884 (800)826-7926
Westwinds B&B .... (206)378-5283

San Juan Island
Wharfside B&B .... (360)378-5661

Gardiner
Diamond Point Inn .... (360)797-7720

Garfield
R.C. McCroskey House .... (509)635-1459

Gig Harbor
The Fountain's B&B .... (206)851-6262
Hillside Gardens B&B .... (206)851-5007
Inn The Woods .... (206)857-4954
Johnsons Scandanavian B&B ... (206)265-2247
Krestine, A Tall Ship .... (206)858-9395
Lagoon Lodge .... (206)858-8827
Marys Bed & Breakfast .... (206)858-2424
No Cabbages B&B .... (206)858-7797
The Parsonage B&B .... (206)851-8654
The Pillars B&B .... (206)851-6644
Rosedale B&B .... (206)851-5420
Waters Edge .... (206)851-3890

Glenoma
St. Helens Manor House .... (360)497-2090
(800)551-3290

Goldendale
Victorian House Bed & Breakfast . (509)773-5338

Graham
Country House B&B .... (206)846-1889

ADDITIONAL ACCOMMODATIONS

Granger

An English B&B ... (509)854-2272
Rinehold Cannery Homestead ... (509)854-2508

Grapeview

Llewop B&B ... (206)275-2287

Greenbank

Smugglers Cove Haven ... (360)678-7100

Hamilton

The Smith House ... (206)826-4214

Harrington

Harrington Inn ... (509)253-4728

Hoquiam

Lytle House ... (360)533-2320 (800)677-2320

Ilwaco

Chick A Dee Inn at Ilwaco ... (360)642-8686
Kola House B&B ... (206)642-2819

Index

A Stones Throw ... (360)793-0100
Bush House ... (206)793-2312
Wild Lily Ranch ... (360)793-2103

Indianola

Indianola B&B ... (206)297-2107

Ione

Driscolls Bed & Beakfast Inn ... (509)442-3442

Issaquah

Mountains & Plains B&B ... (206)392-8068

Kalama

Blackberry Hill B&B ... (206)673-6299

Kent

Victorian Gardens 1888 Bed & Breakfast
... (206)850-1776

Kettle Falls

My Parents' Estate ... (509)738-6220

Kirkland

Shumway Mansion ... (206)823-2303

La Conner

An English Cottage ... (360)466-2067
Heather House ... (360)466-4675
Heron In La Conner ... (360)466-4626
Katy's Inn ... (360)466-3366 (800)914-7767
La Conner Country Inn ... (360)466-3101
Lighthouse Inn ... (360)466-3147
Rainbow Inn Bed & Breakfast ... (360)466-4578
Ridgeway B&B .. (206)428-8068 (800)428-8068
The Wild Iris ... (360)466-1400

Lake Stevens

Lake Stevens Peony House ... (206)334-1046

Langley

Beach & Bluff Bed & Breakfast .. (360)221-5292
The Blue House Inn ... (360)221-8392
Chanticleer House ... (360)221-5494
Christy's Country Inn ... (360)321-1815
Country Cottage of Langley ... (360)221-8709
The Courtyard B&B ... (360)321-0911
Drakes Landing ... (360)221-3999
Eagles Nest Inn ... (360)221-5331
Edgecliff Cottage ... (360)221-8857
Garden Path Inn ... (360)221-5121
Grampa Art's Place ... (360)321-1838
Island Palms ... (360)221-8173
The Inn at Langley ... (360)221-3033
Log Castle B&B ... (360)221-5483
Maxwelton Manor ... (360)221-5199
The Orchard ... (360)221-7880
Pine Cottage ... (360)730-1376
Primrose Path Cottage ... (360)221-3722
Sally's B&B Manor ... (360)221-8709
Twickenham House B&B Inn ... (360)221-2334
Whidbey House ... (360)221-7115
Whispering Woods Farm & Guest House
... (360)221-1007

Leavenworth

Abendblume Pension ... (509)548-4059
Autumn Pond B&B (509)548-4482 (800)222-9661
Bavarian Meadows B&B ... (509)548-4449
Bindlestiff's Riverside ... (509)548-5015
Bosch Garten B&B ... (509)548-6900
Country Cottage Inn B&B ... (509)548-4591
Edel Haus B&B ... (509)548-4412
Fromms Mountain Home Ranch . (509)548-5770
Haus Lorelei Inn ... (509)548-5726
Haus Rohrbach Pension
... (509)548-7024 (800)548-4477
Hotel Europa ... (509)548-5221
Leavenworth Village Inn ... (509)548-6620
Leirvangen B&B ... (509)548-5165
Mc Clain's B&B ... (509)548-7755
Moonlight and Roses Bed & Breakfast Inn
... (509)548-6766
Morgan's Serendipity ... (509)548-7722
Mountain Home Lodge ... (509)548-7077
Nelsons Creekside Bed & Breakfast
... (509)548-8102
Old Blewett Pass B&B ... (509)548-4475
Phippens Bed & Breakfast ... (509)548-7755
Pine River Ranch ... (509)763-3959
Ponderosa Country Inn ... (509)548-4550

Long Beach

Edgewood Inn ... (360)642-8227
Land's End B&B ... (360)642-8268
Scandinavian Gardens Inn
... (360)642-8877 (800)988-9277

Longmire

National Park Inn ... (206)569-2565

Longview

The Mansion B&B ... (206)636-5611
Traveller's Rest B&B ... (206)423-6515

Lopez

Aleck Bay Inn ... (360)468-3535
Edenwild Inn ... (360)468-3238
Island Farmhouse ... (206)468-2864

Lopez Island

Lopez Farm & Cottages ... (360)468-3555
Mackaye Harbor Inn ... (360)468-2253
Village Guest House ... (360)468-2191

Lummi Island

Deer Creek Farm B&B ... (360)758-2678
Loganita, A Villa By The Sea ... (360)758-2651
West Shore Farm ... (360)758-2600
Willows Inn ... (360)758-2620

Lynden

Stap's B&B ... (360)354-2609

Manson

Hubbard House B&B ... (509)687-3058
Proctor House .. (509)687-6361 (800)441-1233

Maple Falls

Country Hill B&B ... (206)599-2407
Thurston House B&B ... (206)599-2261

Maple Valley

Maple Valley B&B ... (206)432-1409

Mercer Island

Mercer Island Hideaway ... (206)232-1092
Mole House B&B ... (206)232-1611

Montesano

The Abel House . (360)249-6002 (800)235-2235
Sylvan Haus ... (360)249-3453

Moses Lake

Carriage House Bed & Breakfast . (509)766-7466

Mossyrock

Botzer House B&B ... (360)983-3792

Mount Vernon

Fulton House B&B ... (360)336-2952
Hill Crest House ... (360)336-6810
Ridgeway Bed & Breakfast ... (360)428-8068
Thirteen Firs Bed & Breakfast ... (360)445-3571
Whispering Firs B&B ... (360)428-1990

Moxee City

The Desert Rose ... (509)452-2237

Mukilteo

McNab-Hogland House ... (206)742-7639

Naches

The Cozy Cat B&B ... (509)658-2953
The Hopkinson House ... (509)454-9431

Nahcotta

Moby Dick Hotel & Oyster Farm . (360)665-4543
Our House In Nahcotta B&B ... (360)665-6667

Newport

Burroughs House B&B ... (509)447-2590

North Bend

Hillwood Gardens ... (206)888-0799
Roaring River Bed & Breakfast .. (206)888-4834

Oak Harbor

A Country Pillow ... (360)675-8505
Elfreeda's Place ... (360)679-2770
Harbor Pointe B&B ... (360)675-3379
John Quincy Adams Country B&B (360)675-7108
Maranatha Sea Horse B&B ... (360)679-2075
North Island Bed & Breakfast ... (360)675-7080

Oakesdale

The Hanford Castle ... (509)285-4120

Ocean Park

Caswells on The Bay ... (360)665-6535
The Coast Watch B&B ... (360)665-6774

Olalla

Olalla Orchard ... (206)857-5915

Olga

Buck Bay Farm ... (360)376-2908
Sand Dollar Inn ... (360)376-5696
Spring Bay Inn ... (360)376-5531

Olympia

Britt's Place ... (360)264-2764
Forest Haven Bed & Breakfast ... (360)956-7800
Harbinger Inn ... (360)754-0389
Kennedy's B&B ... (360)459-3628
Puget View Guesthouse ... (360)459-1676

Orcas

Liberty Call B&B ... (360)376-5246
Orcas Hotel ... (360)376-4300
Windsong B&B ... (360)376-2500

Orting

Sierra-Rainier B&B ... (206)893-6422

Pateros

Amy's Manor B&B ... (509)923-2334
French House B&B ... (509)923-2626

Peshastin

Mt Valley Vista ... (509)548-5301

Point Roberts

Cedar House Inn Bed & Breakfast (360)945-0284

Port Angeles

Anniken's B&B ... (360)457-6177
Bayton's On-The-Bluff B&B ... (360)457-5569
Clarks' Harbor View B & B ... (360)457-9891
Country Cottage Bed & Breakfast (360)452-7974
Crescent Bay Inn ... (360)928-3694
Elwha Ranch B&B ... (360)457-6540
Freshwater Bay Inn ... (360)928-2181
Glimberg House ... (360)457-6579
Haven Bed & Breakfast ... (360)452-6373
House of The Mermaid B&B Inn . (360)457-4890
Klahhane Bed & Breakfast ... (360)417-0260
Lake Crescent Lodge ... (360)928-3211
Maple Rose Inn . (360)457-7673 (800)457-4661
Nice Touch B&B ... (800)598-3007
Our House B&B ... (360)452-6338

Port Ludlow

Nantucket Manor ... (360)437-2676

Port Orchard

"Reflections" - A B&B Inn ... (360)871-5582
Cedar Hollow ... (360)876-4585
Laurel Inn ... (360)769-9544
Northwest Interlude ... (360)871-4676
Ogle's B&B ... (360)876-9170

Port Townsend

A Rose Cottage B&B
... (360)385-6944 (800)232-6944
Annapurna Inn ... (360)385-2909
Arcadia Country Inn ... (360)385-5245
Baker House ... (360)385-6673
Bishop Victorian Guest Suites ... (360)385-6122
The Cabin ... (360)385-5571
Chanticleer Inn .. (360)385-6239 (800)858-9421
Discovery Gardens ... (360)385-4313
The English Inn . (360)385-5302 (800)254-5302
Heritage House Inn ... (360)385-6800
Horse Haven Inn ... (360)385-7784
Hunt Manor Guest House ... (360)379-9241
Lincoln Inn ... (360)385-6677
Lizzie's ... (360)385-4168 (800)700-4168
Manresa Castle . (360)385-5750 (800)732-1281
Palace Hotel ... (360)946-5176
Port Townsend Inn & Spa ... (360)385-2211
Salmon Berry Farm ... (360)385-1517
Trenholm House ... (360)385-6059

Poulsbo

Edgewater Beach B&B ... (360)779-3004
Haven House Guest Cottage ... (360)779-9544
Manor Farm Inn ... (360)779-4628
Murphy House Bed & Breakfast . (360)779-1600
Solliden Guest House ... (360)779-3969

Prosser

Cottage Court B&B ... (509)786-1430
Wine Country Inn ... (509)786-2855

Pullman

Ash Street House Bed & Breakfast (509)332-3638
Carstens Bed & Breakfast ... (509)332-6162
Country B&B ... (509)334-4453

Puyallup

Artful Lodger Bed & Breakfeast .. (206)770-3387
Tayberry House B&B ... (206)848-4594

Quinault
Lake Quinault Lodge .... (206)288-2571
Randle
Hampton House B&B .... (206)497-2907
Raymond
Log Cabin Tree Farm B&B ...... (360)942-6111
Riverview Inn Bed & Breakfast .. (360)942-5271
Redmond
Cottage Creek Manor B&B ..... (206)881-5606
Ritzville
The Portico Victorian B&B ..... (509)659-0800
Roslyn
Coal Country Inn .... (509)649-3222
Hummingbird Inn .... (509)649-2758
Roslyn B&B .... (509)649-2463
Salkum
The Shepherd's Inn B&B .... (360)985-2434
Seabeck
Summer Song .... (360)830-5089
Tides End Cottage .... (360)692-8109
The Walton House .... (360)830-4498
Seattle
A Traditional Breakfast at Mant's . (206)782-7900
Allison House B&B .... (206)242-3717
Bed & Breakfast Capitol Hill .... (206)325-0320
Bed & Breakfast on Broadway ... (206)329-8933
Beech Tree Manor .... (206)281-7037
Bellevue Place Bed & Breakfast .. (206)325-9253
Blue Willow Bed & Breakfast .... (206)284-4240
Broadway Guest House .... (206)329-1864
Capitol Hill House .... (206)322-1752
Capitol Hill Inn .... (206)323-1955
Cat's Eye Lodge .... (206)935-2229
Cedar Haven Lodging .... (206)322-9203
Chambered Nautilus B&B Inn ... (206)522-2536
College Inn Guest House ...... (206)633-4441
Colonial Manor .... (206)938-3381
Continental Inn Bed & Breakfast . (206)324-9511
Corner House B & B .... (206)328-2865
Galer Place .... (206)282-5339
Gaslight Inn .... (206)325-3654
Green Gables Guesthouse
.... (206)282-6863 (800)400-1503
Hainsworth House .... (206)938-1020
Hill House B&B .... (206)720-7161
Houseboat Hideaway .... (206)323-5323
Inn at Queenanne .... (206)282-7357
Lake Union B&B .... (206)547-9965
Landes House .... (206)329-8781
Mildred's B&B .... (206)325-6072
Queen Anne Hill B&B .... (206)284-9779
Salisbury House .... (206)328-8682
Scandia House .... (206)725-7825
Shafer-Baillie Mansion B&B .... (206)322-4654
The Stimson Green Mansion .... (206)624-0474
Three Tree Point Bed & Breakfast (206)669-7646
Villa Heidelberg .... (206)938-3658
Vincent's Guest House .... (206)323-7849
Seaview
Gumm's B&B Inn (360)642-8887 (800)662-1046
Sequim
Brigadoon B&B .... (360)683-2255
Greywolf Inn .... (360)683-5889
Groveland Cottage .... (360)683-3565
Hidden Meadow Inn .... (360)681-2577
The Inn at Margie's Inn on Bay Bed & Breakfast
.... (360)683-7011
Shelton
Abby's Angel Inn B&B .... (206)426-9307
Pickle Ball Cottage .... (206)426-8190
Twin River Ranch B&B .... (206)426-1023
Silverdale
Seabreeze Beach Cottage ...... (360)692-4648
Silverlake
B-G's B&B .... (360)274-8573
Snohomish
Country Manner B&B .... (206)568-8254
Eddy's B&B .... (206)568-7081
The Redmond House B&B ..... (206)568-2042
Victorian Rose .... (206)568-9472
Snoqualmie
Old Honey Farm .... (206)329-4628
Snoqualmie Pass
Wardholm West B&B .... (206)434-6540
South Bend
Maring's B&B .... (206)875-6519
South Cle Elum
Moore House Country Inn ...... (509)674-5939
Spokane
Angelicas Mansion .... (509)624-5598
Blakely Estate B&B .... (509)926-9426
Fotheringham House .... (509)838-1891
The Georgian .... (509)624-7107
Hillside House .... (509)534-1426
Oslos Bed & Breakfast .... (509)838-3175
Riverside Bed & Breakfast ..... (509)459-9396
Shakespeare Inn .... (509)534-0935
Spokane Room B&B .... (509)467-9804
Town & Country Cottage .... (509)466-7559
Waverly Place B&B .... (509)328-1856
Starbuck
F & R Farms .... (509)399-2287
Starbuck Country Bread & Breakfast
.... (509)399-2287
Stehekin
Silver Bay Inn .... (509)682-2212
Stevenson
Evergreen Inn .... (509)427-4303
Snug Harbor Lodge .... (509)427-4287
Sojourner Inn .... (509)427-7070
Sultan
Krebs Mansion .... (360)793-0447
Sumner
Carlsen's .... (206)863-4557
Sunnyside
Sunnyside Inn B&B
.... (509)839-5557 (800)221-4195
Von Hellstrum .... (509)839-2505
Tacoma
Blount's Guest House .... (206)759-4534
Devoe Mansion Bed & Breakfast . (206)539-3991
Evelines Old World B & B ...... (206)383-0595
Green Cape Cod Bed & Breakfast (206)752-1977
Keenan House .... (206)752-0702
Lucius R Manning House Bed & Breakfast
.... (206)272-8031
Oakes Street Barn Bed & Breakfast (206)475-7047
Sally's Bear Tree Cottage ...... (206)475-3144
Traudel's Haus B&B .... (206)535-4422
Villa A Mediteranian Renaissance Mansion
.... (206)572-1157
Tekoa
Touch O' Country B&B .... (509)284-5183
Tonasket
Orchard Country Inn .... (509)486-1923
Trout Lake
The Farm Bed & Breakfast ..... (509)395-2488
Huckleberry Ridge Bed & Breakfast (509)395-2965
Uniontown
Churchyard Inn .... (509)229-3200
Usk
River Bend Inn .... (509)445-1476
Vancouver
Country Heart Bend & Breakfast . (360)896-8316
Vashon
Back Bay Inn B&B .... (206)463-5355
Colvos Passage B&B .... (206)567-5102
Crown and Sceptre B&B .... (206)463-2697
Edson House Overlooking Quartermastrer
.... (206)463-2646
Island Within Bed & Breakfast ... (206)567-4177
Maury Garden Cottage .... (206)463-3034
Mimis Cottage By The Sea ..... (206)567-4383
Old Mill Cottage .... (206)463-1670
Paradise Farm .... (206)463-9815
Shepards Loft .... (206)463-2544
Smyth Beach House .... (206)567-4049
Towering Cedars .... (206)463-9030
Tramp Harbor Inn B&B .... (206)463-5794
Van Gelders Retreat .... (206)463-1774
Wee Bit Oireland .... (206)463-3881
Vashon Island
Ayh Ranch & Summer Hostel ... (206)463-2592
Sweetbriar B&B .... (206)463-9186
Walla Walla
Green Gables Inn .... (509)525-5501
The Sicyon Gallery & Sculpture Garden B&B
.... (509)525-2964
Stone Creek Inn .... (509)529-8120
Washtucna
Gray's Country B&B .... (509)646-3482
Waterville
Tower House B&B .... (509)745-8320
Wenatchee
Airport Inn Bed and Breakfast ... (509)884-4130
Cherub Inn .... (509)662-6011
Coventry Inn B&B .... (509)662-6771
The Pink House .... (509)663-1911
Stonehouse B&B .... (509)663-8409
Warm Springs Inn Bed & Breakfast (509)662-8365
Westport
Glenacres B&B .... (206)268-9391
White Salmon
Llama Ranch B&B (509)395-2786 (800)800-5262
Orchard Hill Inn .... (509)493-3024
Winthrop
Dammann's B&B .... (509)996-2484
Farmhouse Inn .... (509)996-2191
Mountain View B&B .... (509)996-3234
Woodinville
Bear Creek Inn .... (206)881-2978
By The Creek Bed & Breakfast .. (206)885-0639
Woodland
Grandmass House Bed & Breakfast
.... (360)225-7002
Yacolt
Fir N Fin Bed & Breakrast ...... (360)686-3064
Yakima
'37 House .... (509)965-5537
A Touch of Europe Inn .... (509)454-9775
Irish House B&B .... (509)453-5474
Meadowbrook B&B .... (509)248-2387
Tudor Guest House B&B .... (509)452-8112
Yelm
Salsich Mansion Guest Lodging . (360)458-7741

Washington, D.C.

Brenton .... (202)332-5550
Capitol Hill Guest House .... (202)547-1050
Hereford House .... (202)543-0102
Kalorama Guest House .... (202)667-6369
Little White House Bed & Breakfast (202)583-4074
Meg's International Guest House . (202)232-5837
New Hampshire Suites .... (202)832-8600
Normandy Inn .... (202)483-1350
Sign of The Cat .... (202)966-4145
The St. James .... (202)457-0500
Tabard Inn .... (202)785-1277
Washington Court on Capitol Hill . (202)628-2100

West Virginia

Athens
Concord Church Inn .... (304)384-5084
Aurora
Cabin Lodge .... (304)735-3563
Beaver
House of Grandview .... (304)763-4381
Beckley
Erma's Garden .... (304)253-5987
Beckwith
Woodcrest B&B .... (304)574-3870
Berkeley Springs
Oak Lee B&B .... (304)258-4079
Cacapon Bed & Breakfast ...... (304)258-1442
Folkestone B&B .... (304)258-3743
Glens Country Estate .... (304)258-4536
Maria's Garden & Inn .... (304)258-2021
On The Banks Guest House .... (304)258-2134
Bramwell
The Bluestone Inn .... (304)248-7402
Buckhannon
Deer Park Country Inn & Lodge .. (304)472-8430
Henderson House B&B .... (304)472-1611
Post Mansion Inn Bed & Breakfast (304)472-8959
Burlington
Shelly's Homestead .... (304)289-3941
Cairo
Bias Farm B&B .... (304)643-4517
Hilltop Manor .... (304)628-3711
Cass
Shay Inn .... (304)456-4652
Charles Town
The Carriage Inn .... (304)728-8003
The Cottonwood Inn .... (304)725-3371
Magnus Tate's Kitchen .... (304)725-8052

Charleston
Historic Charleston B&B
.... (304)345-8156 (800)225-5982
Chloe
Pennbrooke Farm B&B .... (304)655-7367
Clarksburg
Main Street Bed & Breakfast .... (304)623-1440
Clendenin
Erics Beech Tree Inn .... (304)548-4521
Crawley
Oak Knoll B&B .... (304)392-6903
Daniels
Edelweiss Inn .... (304)763-3391
Davis
Meyers House B&B .... (304)259-5451
Twisted Thistle B&B .... (304)259-5389
Durbin
Cheat Mountain Club .... (304)456-4627
Elizabeth
Burning Sprigs Bed & Breakfast . (304)275-6699
Elkins
Cheat River Lodge .... (304)636-2301
Lincoln Crest B&B .... (304)636-8460
Marian's Guest House .... (304)636-9883
The Retreat at Buffalo Run ..... (304)636-2960
Warfield House Bed & Breakfast . (304)636-6120
The Wayside Inn .... (304)636-1985
Fairmont
Acacia House .. (304)367-1000 (800)225-5982
Tichnell's Tourist Home .... (304)366-3811
Fayetteville
County Seat B&B .... (304)574-0823
Morris Harvey House
.... (304)574-1179 (800)225-5982
White Horse B&B .... (304)574-1400
Frankford
High Meadow B&B .... (304)497-2585
Franklin
Candlelight Inn .... (304)358-3025
McCoy's Mill B&B .... (304)358-7893
Gerrardstown
Prospect Hill Farm .... (304)229-3346
Glen Ferris
Glen Ferris Inn .... (304)632-1111
Harpers Ferry
Between The Rivers B&B ...... (304)535-2768
Harpers Ferry Guest House ..... (304)535-6955
Lee-Stonewall Inn .... (304)535-2532
Ranson-Armory House Bed & Breakfast
.... (304)535-2142
The View B&B .... (304)535-2688
Harrisville
Apple Alley B&B .... (304)643-2272
Heritage Inn .... (304)643-2938
Helvetia
Beekeeper Inn .... (304)924-6435
Hillsboro
Yew Mountain Lodge .... (304)653-4821
Hinton
Historic Hinton Manor .... (304)466-3930
Sunset .... (304)466-3740
Huntington
Nicotera B&B .... (304)523-5118
Huttonsville
The Cardinal Inn .... (304)335-6149
Hutton House .... (304)335-6701
Jane Lew
West Fork Inn .... (304)745-4893
Kearneysville
The Daniel Fry House B&B ..... (304)728-6400
Keyser
The Candlewyck Inn .... (304)788-6594
Kingwood
The Preston County Inn .... (304)329-2220
Lewisburg
Hide Away B&B .... (304)645-7718
Lynn's Inn B&B .... (304)645-2003
Logan
Manor Haus .... (304)752-5824
Lookout
Midland Trail B&B .... (304)574-3285
Lost Creek
Country Corner .... (304)745-3017
Lost River
Guest House .... (304)897-5707
Inn at Lost River .... (304)897-6788
Malden
Rose Cottage B&B .... (304)925-6568
Marlinton
Carriage House Inn .... (304)799-6706
Jerico B&B .... (304)799-6241
Old Clark Inn .... (304)799-6377
Martinsburg
Pulpit & Palette Inn .... (304)263-7012
Mathias
Valley View Farm .... (304)897-5229
Milton
Wine Cellar Bed & Breakfast .... (304)743-5665
Montrose
White Oak B&B .... (304)478-4705
Moorefield
Hickory Hill Farm .... (304)538-2511
Morgantown
Appelwood Bed & Breakfast .... (304)296-2607
Chestnut Ridge School .... (304)598-9595
The Maples B&B .... (304)594-1122
Maxwell B&B .... (304)594-3041
New Creek
Maplewood Manor .... (304)749-8208
Orlando
Kilmarnock Farm .... (304)452-8319
Parkersburg
Harmony House B&B Inn ...... (304)485-1458
Paw Paw
Paw Paw Patch B&B .... (304)947-7496
Petersburg
Smoke Hole Lodge .... (304)242-8377
Philippi
Stoney Creek Cottage .... (304)457-4799
Tygart River Lodge .... (304)457-2792
Princeton
Sans Souci B&B .... (304)425-4804
Ravenswood
Hemlock Farm B&B .... (304)273-5572
Shepherdstown
Bavarian Inn & Lodge .... (304)876-2551
Belle Vue B&B .... (304)876-0889
The Little Inn .... (304)876-2208
Shang-Ra-La B&B .... (304)876-2391
Stonebrake Cottage .... (304)876-6607
Thomas Shepherd Inn Bed & Breakfast
.... (304)876-3715
Slatyfork
Willis Farm .... (304)572-3771
Snowshoe
Whistlepunk Inn .... (304)572-1126
Valley Head
Nakiska Chalet B&B
.... (304)339-6309 (800)225-5982
Wellsburg
Dovers Inn .... (304)737-0188
Elmhurst Manor .... (304)737-3675
Times Past B&B .... (304)737-0592
West Liberty
The Atkinson Guest House ..... (304)336-7577
White Sulpher Springs
The James Wylie House B&B ... (304)536-9444

Wisconsin

Albany
Oak Hill Manor .... (608)862-1400
Sugar River Inn .... (608)862-1248
Algoma
King Olaf's Pub & Inn .... (414)487-2090
Allenton
Addison House .... (414)629-9993
Alma
The Gallery House .... (608)685-4975
Laue House .... (608)685-4923
Appleton
Franklin Street Inn .... (414)739-3702
The Queen Anne .... (414)739-7966
Arkdale
Silver Maples Bed & Breakfast .. (608)564-2388
Ashland
Hotel Chequamegon .... (715)682-9095
Augusta
Park House Inn .... (715)286-5345
Avoca
Prairie Rose .... (608)532-6878 (800)409-7673
Baileys Harbor
Blacksmith Inn .... (414)839-9222
The Potters Door .... (414)839-2003
Baldwin
Kaleidoscope Inn .... (715)684-4575
Baraboo
The Clark House .... (608)356-2191
Cranberry Cottage B&B .... (608)356-5727
Garden Gate B&B .... (608)356-0963
Gollmar Guesthouse .... (608)356-9432
Victorian Rose B&B .... (608)356-7828
Barnes
Sunset Resort B&B Lodge ..... (715)795-2449
Barneveld
Garden B&B .... (608)924-2108
Bayfield
Baywood Place .... (715)779-3690
Cooper Hill House .... (715)779-5060
Greunke's Inn .... (715)779-5480
The Morning Glory B&B .... (715)779-5621
Old Rittenhouse Inn .... (715)779-5111
Pinehurst Inn .... (715)779-3676
Thimbleberry Inn B&B .... (715)779-5757
Vincent Taylor Lodging .... (715)779-5905
Beaver Dam
Tiffany Inn .... (414)426-1000
Victorian B&B .... (414)885-9601
Belleville
Abendruh B&B Swiss Style ..... (608)424-3808
Cameo Rose B&B .... (608)424-6340
Beloit
Church Street Bed & Breakfa .... (608)362-6585
Richardson House .... (608)365-1627
Birchwood
Cobblestone B&B .... (715)354-3494
Farm B&B .... (715)354-3367
Black Creek
Old Coach Inn B&B .... (414)984-3840
Bloomer
Tee Pee Lodge .... (715)568-4136
Brantwood
Palmquist Farm .... (715)564-2558
Brodhead
Brodhead Plumb House B&B ... (608)897-2044
Buckskin Lodge B&B .... (608)897-2914
Browntown
Four Seasons .... (608)966-1680
Old School Inn B&B .... (608)966-1848
Burlington
Hillcrest B&B .... (414)763-4706
Cable
Connors B&B .... (715)798-3661
Cambridge
Bison Trail B&B .... (414)648-5433
Cambridge House B&B .... (608)423-7008
The Night Heron B&B .... (608)423-4141
Camp Douglas
Sunny Field Farm .... (608)427-3686
Campbellsport
Mielke-Mauk House .... (414)533-8602
Newcastle Pines .... (414)533-5252
Cascade
Timberlake Inn .... (414)528-8481
Cashton
Cannondalen B&B (608)269-2886 (800)947-6261
Cassville
The Geiger House .... (608)725-5419
River View B&B .... (608)725-5895
Cedarburg
Stagecoach Inn B&B .... (414)375-0208
The Washington House Inn
.... (414)375-3550 (800)554-4717
Chetek
The Annandale Inn .... (715)837-1974
Canoe Bay Inn & Cottages ..... (800)568-1995
Trails End B&B .... (715)924-2641
Chilton
East Shore Inn .... (414)849-4230
Chippewa Falls
McGilvray's Victorian B&B ..... (715)720-1600
Pleasant View B&B .... (715)382-4401
Clayton
Shady Rest Inn .... (715)948-2020

Cochrane
The Rosewood B&B .... (608)248-2940
Colfax
Clearview Hills B&B .... (608)255-4230
Son-Ne-Vale Farm B&B .... (715)962-4342
Columbus
By The Okeag .... (414)623-3007
The Dering House .... (414)623-2015
Maple Leaf Inn B&B .... (414)623-5166
Red Bud Rooms Bed & Breakfast (414)623-4823
Cornucopia
The Village Inn .... (715)742-3941
Crandon
Courthouse Square B&B .... (715)478-2549
Cross Plains
The Enchanted Valley Garden ... (608)798-4554
Past & Present Inn .... (608)798-4441
Cuba City
Country Blue Inn .... (608)744-3757
Cumberland
The Rectory .... (715)822-3151
Curtiss
Thompson's Inn .... (715)223-6041
Dane
Dunroven House .... (608)592-4560
De Forest
Circle B B&B .... (608)846-3481
De Pere
Birch Creek Inn .... (414)336-7575
Delavan
Autumn House Bed & Breadfast . (414)728-2550
Denmark
Dansk Hus B&B .... (414)863-3138
Downsville
Creamery .... (715)664-8354
Dresser
Lessards on The Lake .... (715)294-2447
Drummond
Chequamegon House .... (715)739-6665
Durand
Ryan House .... (715)672-8563
Eagle
Eagle Centre House B&B ...... (414)363-4700
Novels B&B Art & Antique Gallery (414)594-3729
Eagle River
Brennan Manor .... (715)479-7353
The Inn at Pinewood .... (715)479-4114
East Troy
Mitten Farm .... (414)642-5530
Pine Ridge B&B .... (414)594-3269
Eau Claire
Apple Tree Inn .. (715)836-9599 (800)347-9598
Fanny Hill Inn ... (715)836-8184 (800)292-8026
Otter Creek Inn .... (715)832-2945
Edgerton
Olde Parsonage B&B .... (608)884-6490
Egg Harbor
Country Gardens B&B .... (414)743-7434
Harbor Point Inn .... (414)868-2234
Elkhart Lake
Eastlake Bed & Breakfast ...... (414)876-2272
Siebken's .... (414)876-2600
Elkhorn
Ye Olde Manor Houuse .... (414)742-2450
Ellison Bay
A Country Woods B&B .... (414)854-5706
Hotel Disgarden .... (414)854-9888
Elroy
East View B&B .... (608)463-7564
Stillested B&B .. (608)462-5633 (800)462-4980
Waarvik Century Farm B&B ..... (608)462-8595
Elton
Dehart's Section House & Evergreen Inn
.... (715)882-4781
Ephraim
Eagle Harbor Inn .... (414)854-2121
The Ephraim Inn .... (414)854-4515
French Country Inn of Ephraim .. (414)854-4001
Hillside Hotel B&B (414)854-2417 (800)423-7023
Prairie Garden B&B .... (414)854-2555
Waterbury Inn .... (414)854-2821
Evansville
Holmes Victorian Inn .... (608)882-6866
Fennimore
Gazebo B&B .... (608)822-3928

Fish Creek
Birchwood B&B .... (414)868-3214
Juniper Inn .... (414)839-2629
Whistling Swan Inn .... (414)868-3442
White Gull Inn .... (414)868-3517
Florence
Lakeside B&B .... (715)528-3259
The Lodge at River's Edge ..... (715)696-3406
Fontana
Lazy Cloud Lodge Bed & Breakfast (414)275-3322
Strawberry Hill .... (414)275-5998
Fort Atkinson
La Grange B&B .... (414)563-1421
Lamp Post Inn .... (414)563-6561
Frederic
Seven Pines Lodge .... (715)653-2323
Friendship
Friendship Inn .... (608)339-3112
Galesville
The Clark House B&B .... (608)582-4190
Gays Mills
Miss Molly's B&B .... (608)735-4433
Glen Haven
Parson's Inn B&B .... (608)794-2491
Grand View
Hummingbird B&B .... (715)763-3214
Green Bay
Stonewood Haus .... (414)499-3786
Green Lake
McConnell Inn .... (414)294-6430
Oakwood Lodge .... (414)294-6580
Strawberry Hill B&B .... (414)294-3450
Greenwood
Mead Lake B&B .... (715)367-6264
Gresham
Nightsong B&B .... (715)787-4472
Hammond
Summit Farm B&B .... (715)796-2617
Hartford
Jordan House .... (414)673-5643
Hayward
Edgewater Inn .... (715)462-9412
Joyces Bed & Breakfast .... (715)634-8559
Lumberman's Mansion Inn ..... (715)634-3012
Mustard Seed .... (715)634-2908
Spider Lake Lodge B&B .... (715)462-3793
Hazel Green
Ambrosia Inn .... (608)854-2000
De Winters of Hazel Green ..... (608)854-2768
Percival's Country Inn .... (608)854-2881
Wisconsin House Stagecoach Inn (608)854-2233
Hazelhurst
Hazelhurst Inn .... (715)356-6571
Herbster
Okkonen House B&B .... (715)774-3411
Hillsboro
Edgecombe Inn .... (608)489-2915
Mascione's Hidden Valley ...... (608)489-3443
Tiger Inn .... (608)489-2918
Hixton
Triple R Resort .... (715)964-8777
Hollandale
The Old Granary Inn .... (608)967-2140
Houlton
Shady Ridge Farm B&B .... (715)549-6258
Hudson
Boyden House .... (715)386-7435
Grapevine Inn B&B .... (715)386-1989
The Phipps Inn .... (715)386-0800
Stageline Inn Bed & Breakfast ... (715)386-5203
Iola
Iris Inn .... (715)445-4848
Taylor House B&B .... (715)445-2204
Irma
Swan Song B&B .... (815)453-1173
Iron River
Iron River Trout Haus .... (715)372-4219
Janesville
Antique Rose B&B .... (608)754-8180
Jackson Street Inn .... (608)754-7250
Juneau
Country Retreat on Primrose .... (414)386-2912
Kansasville
The Linen & Lace B&B .... (414)534-4966

Kendall
Cabin at Trails End .... (608)427-3877
Dusk to Dawn B&B .... (608)463-7547
Kenosha
The Manor House .... (414)658-0014
Kewaskum
Country Ridge Inn B&B .... (414)626-4853
Doctors Inn .... (414)626-2666
Kewaunee
Chelsea Rose B&B .... (414)388-2012
Duvall House .... (414)388-0501
Kewaunee House .... (414)388-1017
Kiel
River Terrace B&B .... (414)894-2032
La Crosse
Country Manor Bed & Breakfast . (608)787-1719
The Martindale House .... (608)782-4224
La Farge
Trillium .... (608)625-4492
Lake Delton
The Swallow's Nest B&B ...... (608)254-6900
Lake Geneva
Eleven Gables Inn on The Lake .. (414)248-8393
Elizabethian Inn .... (414)248-9131
French Country Inn on The Lake . (414)245-5220
The Geneva Inn on The Lake .... (414)248-5680
Lawrence House B&B
.... (414)248-4684 (800)530-2262
Pederson Victorian B&B .... (414)248-9110
Red House Inn .... (414)248-1009
Roses, A B&B .... (414)248-4344
The Oaks Inn .... (414)248-9711
Two Akers of England .... (414)248-4826
Lake Mills
The Bayberry Inn .... (414)648-3654
Lake Nebagamon
Lawn Beach Inn & Supper Club .. (715)374-3511
Lancaster
Maple Harris Guest House ..... (608)723-4717
Martha's B&B .... (608)723-4711
Lewis
Seven Pines Lodge .... (715)653-2323
Livingston
Oak Hill Farm .... (608)943-6006
Lodi
Prairie Garden B&B (608)592-5187 (800)380-8427
Loganville
Shanahan's B&B .... (608)727-2507
Lomira
The White Shutters .... (414)269-4056
Luxemburg
Bit of The Bay .... (414)866-9901
Madison
The Collins House .... (608)255-4230
Monona
The Lake House on Monona .... (608)222-4601
Madison
The Livingston, A Victorian Inn .. (608)257-1200
Stoney Oaks .... (608)278-1646
University Heights B&B .... (608)233-3340
Maiden Rock
Eagle Cove B&B .... (715)448-4302
Harrisburg Inn .... (715)448-4500
Manawa
Ferg Haus Inn .... (414)596-2946
Victorian Acres .... (414)596-3643
Manitowich Waters
Friar's Tuckaway B&B .... (715)543-8231
Manitowoc
Arbor Manor B&B .... (414)684-6095
The Holmestead .... (414)692-0434
Jarvis House B&B .... (414)682-2103
Mahloch's Cozy B&B .... (414)775-4404
Marinette
Lauerman Guest House .... (715)732-7800
Marshfield
Evergreen Inn B&B .... (715)387-1644
Mauston
Edward's Estates .... (608)847-5246
Mayville
The Audubon Inn .... (414)387-5858
J & R's Sherm Inn .... (414)387-4642
Menomonee Falls
Dorshel's B&B Guest House .... (414)255-7866
Hitching Post B&B .... (414)255-1496

Menomonie
Cedar Trail Guesthouse . . . . (715)664-8828
Mequon
American Country Farm . . . . (414)242-0194
The Homestead of Mequon . . . . . (414)242-4174
Sonnenhof Inn . . . . (414)375-4294
Merrill
The Brick House . . . . (715)536-3230
Candlewick Inn . . (715)536-7744 (800)382-4376
Middleton
The Middleton Beach Inn . . . . . . (608)831-6446
Milton
Chase on The Hill . . . . (608)868-6646
Milwaukee
Bed & Breakfast of Milwaukee . . . (414)277-8066
Guest House of 819 . . . . (414)271-1979
Lakeside Inn Cafe . . . . (414)276-1577
Marie's . . . . (414)483-1512
Mineral Point
Cothren House Bed & Breakfast . (608)987-2612
Duke Guest House B&B . . . . (608)987-2821
Jones House . . . . (608)987-2337
Knudson's Guest House . . . . (608)987-2733
The Walker House . . . . (608)987-3794
Wilson House Inn . . . . (608)987-3600
Minocqua
Kinsale B&B . . . . (715)356-3296
Whitehaven B&B . . . . (715)356-9097
Mishicot
Victorian Blue B&B . . . . (414)755-4907
Monroe
The Nathaniel Treat House . . . . . (608)325-5656
Victorian Garden B&B . . . . (608)328-1720
Montello
Country Peddler Guest House . . . (414)295-0100
Westmont Farms . . . . (414)293-4456
Mount Horeb
The H.B. Dahle House B&B Inn . . (608)437-8894
Mountain
Winter Green . . . . (715)276-6885
Neillsville
The Morgan House . . . . (715)743-6887
New Auburn
Jacks Lake B&B . . . . (715)967-2730
New Glarus
Jeanne-Marie's B&B . . . . (608)527-5059
Spring Vlley Creek B&B . . . . (608)527-2314
Zentner Haus . . . . (608)527-2121
New Holstein
Krupp Farm Homestead . . . . (414)782-5421
Norwalk
The Convent House . . . . (608)823-7992
Lonesome Jake's Devil's Hole Ranch
. . . . (608)823-7585
Oconomowoc
The Victorian Belle . . . . (414)567-2520
Ogema
Timm's Hill B&B . . . . (715)767-5288
Onalaska
Lumber Barron Inn . . . . (608)781-8938
Ontario
The Inn at Wildcat Mountain - B&B (608)337-4352
Osceola
Pleasant Lake Inn (715)294-2545 (800)294-2545
St. Croix River Inn . . . . (715)294-4248
Oxford
Halfway House . . . . (608)586-5489
Pardeeville
Gator Gully B&B . . . . (608)429-2754
Pepin
A Summer Place . . . . (715)442-2132
Harbor Hill Inn B B . . . . (715)442-2002
Pepin Prairie Winds Bed & Breakfast
. . . . (715)442-2149
Phelps
Hazen Inn . . . . (715)545-3600
Limberlost Inn . . . . (715)545-2685
Phillips
East Highland School House B&B (715)339-3492
Plain
Attic Treasures Country Estate B&B
. . . . (608)546-4371
Bettinger House B&B . . . . (608)546-2951
The Kraemer House B&B Inn . . . (608)546-3161

Plainfield
Johnson Inn . . . . (715)335-4383
Platteville
The Cunningham House . . . . (608)348-5532
Plymouth
B. L. Nutt Inn . . . . (414)892-8566
Beverly's Log Guest House . . . . . (414)892-6064
Hillwind Farm B&B . . . . (414)892-2199
Spring Farm Cottage . . . . (414)892-2101
Yankee Hill Inn B&B . . . . (414)892-2222
Port Washington
Grand Inn . . . . (414)284-6719
The Inn at Old Twelve Hundred . . (414)268-1200
Port Washington Inn . . . . (414)284-5583
Portage
Breese Waye B&B . . . . (608)742-5281
Riverbend Inn . . . . (608)742-3627
Poynette
Jamieson House . . . . (608)635-4100
Prairie Du Chien
Neumann House B&B . . . . (608)326-8104
Prairie Du Sac
Graff House B&B . . . . (608)643-6978
Prescott
Arbor Inn . . . . (715)262-4522
The Oak Street Inn B&B . . . . (715)262-4110
Princeton
The Ellisons' Gray Lion Inn . . . . . (414)295-4101
Racine
College Avenue B&B . . . . (414)637-7870
Linen & Lace B&B . . . . (414)534-4966
Lochnaiar Inn . . . . (414)633-3300
The Mansards-On-The-Lake . . . . (414)632-1135
Rhinelander
Cranberry Hill B&B . . . . (715)369-3504
Richland Center
Candlewood "A Cabin In The Woods"
. . . . (608)647-6865
Lambs Inn B&B . . . . (608)585-4301
Littledale . . . . (608)647-7118
The Mansion . . . . (608)647-2808
Ripon
The Farmer's Daughter Inn . . . . . (414)748-2146
Thorne Apple Inn . . . . (414)748-7726
River Falls
Trillium Woods . . . . (715)425-2555
Saint Germain
Stonehouse B&B . . . . (715)542-3733
Shawano
Prince Edward . . . . (715)526-2805
Sheboygan
Scheele House Tourist Lodging . . (414)458-0998
Sheboygan Falls
The Rochester Inn . . . . (414)467-3123
Siren
Forgotten Tymes Country Inn . . . (715)349-5837
Sister Bay
Church Hill Inn . . . . (414)854-4885
The White Apron . . . . (414)854-5107
The Wooden Heart Inn . . . . (414)854-9097
Soldiers Grove
Old Oak Inn & Acorn Pub . . . . . . (608)624-5217
South Milwaukee
Riley House B&B . . . . (414)764-2521
Sparta
Briar Patch B&B . . . . (608)269-1026
The Franklin Victorian
. . . . (608)269-3894 (800)845-8767
Strawberry Lace Inn B&B . . . . . . (608)269-7878
Spooner
Aunt Martha's Guest House B&B (715)635-6857
Green Valley Inn B&B . . . . (715)635-7300
Spring Green
Deer Acres B&B . . . . (608)588-7299
Hill Street B&B . . . . (608)588-7751
The Silver Star . . . . (608)935-7297
Spring Green . . . . (608)588-2042
Spring Valley
Pahl's B&B . . . . (608)435-6434
Springbrook
The Stout Trout B&B . . . . (715)466-2790
Stanley
Roe House Bed & Breakfast . . . . (715)644-5611
Starlake
Whippoorwill Inn . . . . (715)542-3333

Stevens Point
The Birdhouse . . . . (715)341-0084
Marcyanna's B&B . . . . (715)341-9922
Stockholm
Great River Farm . . . . (715)442-5656
Hyggelig Hus . . . . (715)442-2086
Pine Creek Lodge . . . . (715)448-3203
Stone Lake
Lake House . . . . (715)865-2811
New Mountain B&B . . (715)865-2486 (800)639-6822
Stoughton
Stokstad's Century Farm B&B . . . (608)884-4941
Strum
The Crystal Lake House . . . . (715)693-3519
Sturgeon Bay
The Barbican . . . . (414)743-4854
The Bare's B&B . . . . (414)823-2525
Bay Shore Inn . . . . (414)743-4551
Chadwick Inn . . . . (414)743-2771
Chanticleer Guest House . . . . . . (414)746-0334
Cozy Quilt Bed-Brkfst Accomdtn . (414)743-3020
Gandt's Haus . . . . (414)743-1238
Gray Gables . . . . (414)743-7667
Gray Goose B&B . . . . (414)743-9100
Hearthside B&B Inn . . . . (414)746-2136
Hillside Orchards Retreat Bed-Brkfst Acc
. . . . (414)743-9160
Pembrooke Inn . . . . (414)746-8811
Quiet Cottage . . . . (414)743-3362
Van Clay Guest House . . . . (414)743-6611
White Lace Inn . . . . (414)743-1105
Whitefish Bay Farm B&B . . . . (414)743-1560
Superior
Crawford House Bed & Breakfast (715)394-5271
Gull Wing Inn Bed & Breakfast . . (715)398-3986
Two Rivers
Abba's Inn B&B . . . . (414)793-1727
The Red Forest B&B . . . . (414)793-1794
Verona
Beet Road Farm . . . . (608)437-6500
Riley Tavern B&B . . . . (608)845-9150
Viola
The Inn at Elk Run (608)625-2062 (800)729-7313
Viroqua
Eckhart House . . . . (608)637-3306
Serendipity Farm . . . . (608)637-7708
Wabeno
Crystal Bell Bed & Breakfast . . . . (715)473-2202
Walworth
Arscott House B&B . . . . (414)275-3233
Warrens
Cranberry Hide-Away . . . . (608)378-4459
Washington Island
Island House B&B . . . . (414)847-2779
Waterford
River View Inn . . . . (414)534-5049
Waterloo
Carousel . . . . (414)478-2536
Watertown
Brandt Quirk B&B . . . . (414)261-7917
Karlshuegel Inn . . . . (414)261-3980
Waukesha
Joanie's B&B . . . . (414)542-5698
Mill Creek Farm B&B . . . . (414)542-4311
Waupaca
Crystal River B&B . . . . (715)258-5333
Thomas Pipe Inn . . . . (715)824-3161
Walker's Barn B&B . . . . (715)258-5235
Whippoorwill Acres B&B . . . . . . (715)256-0373
White Horse B&B . . . . (715)258-6162
Waupun
The Rose Ivy Inn . . . . (414)324-2127
Wausau
Everest Inn . . . . (715)848-5651
Rosenberry Inn . . . . (715)842-5733
Stewart Inn . . . . (715)848-2864
Wausaukee
Hotel Wausaukee . . . . (715)856-5627
Wautoma
Kristine Ann's Inn . . . . (414)787-4901
West Bend
Mayer-Pick Haus . . . . (414)335-1524
West Salem
Wolfway Farm . . . . (608)486-2686

Westby
Westby House .... (608)634-4112
Westfield
Millpond B&B .... (608)296-1495
White Lake
Pilsners Bear Paw Inn .... (715)882-3502
Whitehall
Augustine House .... (715)538-4749
Whitewater
The Greene House Country Inn .. (414)495-8771
Hamilton House B&B .... (414)473-1900
Wild Rose
Birdsong B&B .... (414)622-3770
Williams Bay
Bailey House .... (414)245-9149
Wilton
Foothills .... (608)435-6877
Rice's Whispering Pines B&B ... (608)435-6531
Trail-Side Bed & Breakfast ..... (608)435-6525
Winter
Chippewa River Inn Bed & Breakfast .. (715)266-2662
Wisconsin Dells
The Dells Carver Inn .... (608)254-4766
Hawk's View .... (608)254-2979
Sherman House .... (608)253-2721
Thomson House .... (608)253-9363
Wisconsin Rapids
The Nash House .... (715)424-2001
Wittenberg
Willow Springs Bed & Breakfast . (715)253-3010

Wyoming

Alcova
Sand Creek Ranch .... (307)234-9597
Arvada
Powder River Experience ...... (307)736-2402
Beulah
Windy Acres Ranch B&B ...... (307)283-2664
Big Horn
Blue Barn B&B .... (307)672-2381
Buffalo
Paradise Guest Ranch .... (307)684-7876
South Fork Inn .... (307)684-9609
TA Guest Ranch .... (307)684-7002
V Bar F Cattle Ranch .... (307)758-4382
Casper
Bessemer Bend B&B .... (307)265-6819
Durbin Street Inn B&B .... (307)577-5774
Centennial
Brooklyn Lodge .... (307)742-6916
Cheyenne
Adventurers' Country B&B Raven Cry Ranch
.... (307)632-4087
Bit-O-Wym Ranch B&B .... (307)638-8340
Porch Swing .... (307)778-7182
Rainsford Inn B&B .... (307)638-BEDS
Pueblo Storyteller B&B .... (307)634-7036
Terry Bison Ranch .... (307)634-4171
Windy Hills Guest House ...... (307)632-6423
Cody
Buffalo Bill's Cody House ...... (307)587-2528
Bunkhouse B&B .... (307)527-5132
Casual Cove B&B .... (307)587-3622
Goff Creek Lodge .... (307)587-3753
Hidden Valley Ranch .... (307)587-5090
Hunter Peak Ranch .... (307)587-3711
The Lockhart B&B Inn
.... (307)587-6074 (800)377-7255
Rimrock Dude Ranch .... (307)587-3970
Rockwell Ranch B&B .... (307)587-8223
Seven D Ranch .... (307)587-3997
Shoshone Lodge Resort .... (307)587-4044
Valley Ranch .... (307)587-4661
Wind Chimes Cottage B&B ..... (307)527-5310
Douglas
Akers Ranch .... (307)358-3741
Carriage House B&B .... (307)358-2752
Cheyenne River Ranch .... (307)358-2380
Deer Forks Ranch .... (307)358-2033
Two Creek Ranch .... (307)358-3467
Wagonhound Ranch
.... (307)358-5439 (800)528-5439
Dubois
Dunloggin B&B .... (307)455-2445
Geyser Creek B&B .... (307)455-2702
Jakey's Fork Homestead .... (307)455-2769
MacKenzie Highland Ranch ..... (307)455-3415
Wapiti Ridge Ranchbed & Breakfast
.... (307)455-2219
Encampment
Grand & Sierra Lodge .... (307)327-5200
Platt's Rustic Mountain Lodge ... (307)327-5539
Evanston
Pine Gables B&B .... (307)789-2069
Gillette
Skybow Castle Ranch .... (307)682-3228
Glenrock
Hotel Higgins ... (307)436-9212 (800)458-0144
Opal's Bed & Breakfast .... (307)436-2626
Greybull
Historic Hotel Greybull
.... (307)765-2012 (800)417-1115
Guernsey
Annette's White House .... (307)836-2148
Hulett
Diamond L Guest Ranch
.... (307)467-5236 (800)851-5909
Jackson
Alpine House ... (307)739-1570 (800)753-1421
Bentwood B&B .... (307)739-1411
Buckrail Lodge .... (307)733-2079
Don't Fence Me In .... (307)733-7979
The Huff House Inn .... (307)733-4164
Moose Meadows B&B .... (307)733-9510
Nowlin Creek Inn (307)733-0882 (800)533-0882
The Painted Porch B&B .... (307)733-1981
Powderhorn Ranch .... (307)733-3845
Twin Mountain River Ranch B&B . (307)733-1168
Jelm
El Rancho Pequeno .... (307)745-9567
Old Glendevey Ranch .... (303)435-5701
Rawah Ranch .... (303)435-5715
Kaycee
Graves B&B .... (307)738-2319
Kelly
Red Rock Ranch .... (307)733-6288
Lagrange
Bear Mountain Back Trails ..... (307)834-2281
Lander
Black Mountain Ranch .... (307)332-6442
Bunk House B&B .... (307)332-5624
Country Fare B&B .... (307)332-9604
Edna's Bed & Breakfast .... (307)332-3175
The Empty Nest .... (307)332-7516
The Outlaw B&B .... (307)332-3011
Piece of Cake B&B (307)332-7608 (800)251-6080
Whispering Winds B&B .... (307)332-9735
Laramie
Annie Moore's Guest House
.... (307)721-4177 (800)552-8992
Prairie Breeze B&B .... (307)745-5482
Vee Bar Guest Ranch .... (307)745-7036
Lusk
Mill Iron 7 Ranch .... (307)334-2951
Manderson
Harmoney Ranch Cottage ...... (307)568-2514
Moran
Box K Ranch .... (307)543-2407
The Inn at Buffalo Fork
.... (307)543-2010 (800)260-2010
Diamond D Ranch-Outfitters .... (307)543-2479
Fir Creek Ranch .... (307)543-2416
Jenny Lake Lodge .... (307)733-4677
Newcastle
Eva-Great Spirit Ranch B&B .... (307)746-2537
Parkman
Foothills Ranch B&B .... (307)655-9362
Pinedale
The Chambers House .... (307)367-2168
Pole Creek Ranch B&B .... (307)367-4433
Window on The Winds .... (307)367-2600
Powell
I Can Rest B&B . (307)754-4178 (800)452-9462
The Joann Ranch .... (307)899-1573
Ranchester
Historic Old Stonehouse B&B ... (307)655-9239
Rawlins
Ferris Mansion .... (307)324-3961
Riverton
Cottonwood Ranch B&B .... (307)856-3064
Rock River
Dodge Creek Ranch .... (307)322-2345
Rock Springs
Sha Hol Dee B&B .... (307)362-7131
Saratoga
Far Out West B&B .... (307)326-5869
Hood House .... (307)326-8901
Wolf Hotel .... (307)326-5525
Savery
Antelope Retreat Center & Ranch (307)383-2625
Savery Creek Thoroughbred Ranch (307)383-7840
Shell
Clucas Ranch B&B .... (307)765-2946
Trapper's Rest B&B .... (307)765-9239
Sheridan
Old Croff House B&B .... (307)672-0898
Ponderosa Pines .... (307)751-4210
Sundance
The Canfield Ranch .... (307)283-2062
Thermopolis
Broadway Inn B&B .... (307)864-2636
Faye's B&B .... (307)864-5166
Out West B&B .... (307)864-2700
Wapiti
The Lodge at June Creek
.... (307)587-2143 (800)295-6343
Wheatland
The Blackbird Inn .... (307)322-4540
Wilson
Fish Creek B&B .... (307)733-2586
Heck of A Hill Homestead ...... (307)733-8023
Teton Tree House .... (307)733-3233
Teton View B&B .... (307)733-7954

U.S. Territories

Puerto Rico

Carolina
The Duffys' Inn .... (809)726-1415
Culebra
Posada La Hamaca .... (809)742-3516
Villa Arynar, B&B .... (809)742-3145
Luquillo
Parador Martorell .... (809)889-2710
San German
Parador Oasis .... (809)892-1175
San Juan
Buena Vista By-Sea .... (809)726-2796
El Prado Inn .... (809)728-5526
Green Isle Inn .... (809)726-4330
La Casa Mathiesen .... (809)727-3223
La Condesa Inn .... (809)727-3698
Tres Palmas Guest House ...... (809)727-4617
Wind Chimer .... (809)727-4153
Vieques
La Casa Del Frances .... (809)741-3751

Virgin Islands

Frederiksted
The Prince Street Inn .... (809)772-9550
Saint Croix
Pink Fancy ..... (809)773-8460 (800)524-2045
Saint John
Estate Zootenvaal .... (809)776-6321
Intimate Inn of St. John .... (809)776-6133
Cruz Inn .... (809)776-7449
Saint Thomas
Calico Jack's Courtyard Inne ... (809)774-7555
Danish Chalet Inn .... (809)774-5764
Galleon House .... (809)774-6952
Hotel 1829 .... (809)776-1829
The Inn at Mandahl .... (809)775-2100
Pavillions & Pools Hotel .... (800)524-2001
Villa Elaine .... (809)774-0290
The Villas at Fort Recovery Estate
.... (800)367-8455 (800)367-8455

Canada

Alberta

Banff
Kananaskis Guest Ranch ...... (403)673-3737
Calgary
A Good Knight B&B .... (403)270-7628
Aileen's B&B .... (403)244-3739
B&B at Harrisons' .... (403)274-7281
Bratton's B&B .... (403)282-4894
Connie & Lou's B&B .... (403)275-1613
The Cozy Nest .... (403)286-7041
Evelyn's B&B .... (403)286-5979
Janet's B&B .... (403)284-3615
Leota's B&B .... (403)282-6592
Linkside B&B .... (403)288-9495
Lions Park B&B .... (403)282-2728
Mrs. Buroker's B&B .... (403)282-2479
The Robin's Nest .... (403)931-3514
Rosedale House B&B .... (403)284-0010
Silver Springs B&B .... (403)288-3208
Sweet Dreams & Scones ...... (403)289-7004
Turgeon's B&B .... (403)288-0494
Canmore
Cougar Creek Inn .... (403)678-4751
Lady MacDonald Country Inn ... (406)678-3665
Cardston
Historic Granite Inn .... (403)653-3157
West-Wind B&B .... (403)653-1882
Claresholm
Creekside B&B .... (403)625-2187
Cochrane
Dickens Inn B&B .... (403)932-3945
Dewinton (Calgary)
Chickadee Hollow .... (403)256-6980
Edmonton
Alberta's Gem B&B .... (403)434-6098
Barratt House B&B .... (403)437-2568
Grande Prairie
Field Stone Inn B&B .... (403)532-7529
Granum
Dimm's Ranch B&B .... (403)687-2274
Willow Lane Ranch .... (403)687-2284
High River
Rita's Repose B&B .... (403)652-3413
Sexsmith House .... (403)652-3797
Lethbridge
Chelisea House .... (403)381-1325
Forsyth House .... (403)320-5344
Millarville
Hilltop B&B .... (403)931-3356
Three Point Creek Ranch B&B ... (403)931-3217
Monarch
Bluebird B&B .... (403)553-2332
Mountain View
Mountain View B&B .... (403)653-1882
Nanton
Broadway Farm B&B .... (403)646-5502
Okotoks
The Ranch B&B .... (403)938-5109
Welcome Acres B&B .... (403)933-7529
Pincher Creek
Allandale Lodge & Retreat ...... (403)627-5598
Allison House .... (403)627-3739
Priddis
Dwelling Place B&B .... (403)931-2639
South Edmonton
Norma's Place B&B .... (403)434-6832
Taber
Berlin House B&B .... (403)233-9406
Turner Valley
Rose's Rest B&B .... (403)933-4174

British Columbia

Armstrong
Turningpoint Farms .... (604)546-3515
Atlin
The Noland House B&B .... (604)651-7585
Black Creek
Grey Mouse B&B .... (604)337-5795
Brentwood Bay
Brentwood Bay B&B .... (604)652-2012
Campbell River
April Point .... (604)285-2222
Campbell River Lodge and Fishing Resort
.... (604)287-7446
Clinton
Kelly Lake Ranch B&B .... (604)000-0000
Cobble Hill
Kirribilli Farm B&B .... (604)743-2021
Coquitlam
Gabriela's .... (604)464-4239
Cowichan Bay
Blackberry Inn .... (604)748-4665
Dawson Creek
B&B Inn Margaree .... (604)782-4148
Northern Lights B&B .... (604)782-3197
Willow Creek Farms B&B ...... (604)843-7253
Delta
Primrose Hill Guest House ..... (604)940-8867
Duncan
Fairburn Farm Country Manor ... (604)746-4637
Pathways .... (604)748-4458
Fort Nelson
Fort Nelson .... (604)774-6050
Home on The Hill B&B .... (604)744-3000
Snuggle Inn B&B .... (604)774-2493
Galiano Island
Casa De Edrie Holloway .... (250)539-2581
Woodstone Country Inn .... (604)539-2022
Gibsons
Bonniebrook Lodge .... (604)886-2887
Honeymoon Bay
Honeymoon Bay Lakeside Bed & Breakfast
.... (604)749-3316
Kelowna
The Gables Country Inn .... (604)768-4468
Homeplace Guest House B&B ... (604)765-2449
Ladysmith
Manana Lodge and Marina ..... (604)245-2312
Yellow Point Lodge .... (604)245-7422
Mill Bay
Pine Lodge Farm B&B .... (604)743-4083
Nelson
Meadows Inn B&B .... (604)354-1993
New Aiyansh
Miles Inn on The T'seax .... (604)633-2636
New Denver
Sweet Dreams Guest House .... (604)358-2415
North Vancouver
Grand Manor .... (604)988-6719
Helen's B&B .... (604)985-4869
Laburnum Cottage B&B .... (604)988-4877
The Platt's B&B .... (604)987-4100
Vickeridge B&B .... (604)985-0338
Penticton
Memory Inn B&B .... (604)493-9368
Riordan House .... (604)493-5997
Powell River
Cedar Lodge .... (604)483-4414
Prince George
Prince George B&B .... (604)561-2337
Prince Rupert
Eagle Bluff B&B .... (604)627-4955
Rose's B&B .... (604)624-5539
Salt Spring Island
Wisteria Guest House .... (604)537-5899
Saturna
Boot Cove Lodge & Restaurant .. (604)539-2254
Shawnigan Lake
Hipwood House B&B .... (604)743-7855
Marifield Manor, An Edwardian B&B
.... (604)743-9930
Smithers
Cranberry Hill B&B .... (604)847-3468
Kathlyn Creek B&B .... (604)847-8947
Sorrento
Evergreens B&B .... (604)675-2568
Valemount
Rainbow Retreat B&B .... (604)566-9747
Vancouver
The Albion Guest House .... (604)873-2287
Brighton House B&B .... (604)253-7175
Diana's Luxury B&B .... (604)321-2855
Lakewood House B&B .... (604)251-2242
Whitehead House Bed & Breakfast (604)736-3050
Vernon
Coldstream Cottage B&B ...... (604)545-2450
Idyll Times B&B .... (604)558-3344
Pleasant Valley B&B .... (604)545-9504
Tuck Inn B&B .... (604)545-3252
Vernon National Hotel Ltd. ..... (604)545-0731
Victoria
Anna Lea's .... (604)381-1195
Battery Street Guesthouse ..... (604)385-4632
The Beaconsfield Inn .... (604)384-4044
Benders B&B .... (604)477-6804
Cadboro Bay B&B .... (250)477-6558
The Captain's Palace .... (604)388-9191
Carriage Stop B&B .... (604)383-6240
Claddagh House B&B .... (604)370-2816
Dogwood House .... (604)652-2137
Elk Lake Lodge .... (604)658-8879
Glyn House .... (604)598-0664
The Haterleigh .... (604)384-9995
Heritage House .... (604)479-0892
Herma's B&B .... (604)721-3683
Holland House Inn .... (604)384-6644
Joan Brown's B&B Inn .... (604)592-5929
Maridou House .... (604)360-0747
Oak Bay Guest House .... (604)598-3812
Portage Inlet House .... (604)479-4594
The Prior House .... (604)592-8847
The Red Door B&B .... (604)595-6715
Rose Cottage B&B .... (604)381-5985
Scholefield House B&B
.... (604)385-2025 (800)661-1623
Seaview B&B .... (604)383-7098
Sunnymeade House Inn .... (604)658-1414
Top O'Triangle Mountain .... (604)478-7853
West Vancouver
Beachside B&B .... (604)922-7773
Park Royal Hotel .... (604)926-5511
Whistler
Brio Haus B&B .... (604)932-3313
Durlacher Hof Pension-Inn ..... (604)932-1924
Stancliff House .... (604)932-2393
Williams Lake
Soda Creek Acres Bed, Bales, & Breakfast
.... (604)297-6418

Manitoba

Brandon
Casa Maley B&B .... (204)728-0812
Winnipeg
Chestnut House B&B .... (204)772-9788

New Brunswick

Albert Co
Cail'swick Babbling Brook ...... (506)882-2079
Campobello
The Owen House .... (506)752-2977
Fredericton
Happy Apple Acres .... (506)472-1819
Grand Manan Island
Grand Harbour Inn .... (506)662-8681
Shorecrest Lodge .... (506)662-3216
Plaster Rock
Northern Wilderness Lodge .... (506)356-8327
Sackville
The Different Drummer B&B .... (506)536-1291
Saint Andrews
Rossmount .... (506)529-3351
Saint Martins
The Quaco Inn .... (506)833-4772
York Co
Chickadee Lodge .... (506)363-2759

Nova Scotia

Chester
Mecklenburgh Inn .... (902)275-4638
Liverpool
Lane's Privateer Inn & B&B
.... (902)354-3456 (800)794-3332

Ontario

Alma
Washa Farms .... (519)846-9788

Almonte
Countryside Wildwest Vacation Farm
. . . . (613)257-2771
Kilmorie B&B . . . . . (613)253-7005
Menzies House 1853 B&B . . . . . (613)256-2055
Old Burnside B&B . . . . . (613)256-2066
Alton
Cataract Inn . . . . . (519)927-3033
Hockley & Area B&B . . . . . (519)942-4737
The Millcroft Inn . . . . . (519)941-8111
Alymer
Ye Olde Apple Yard B&B . . . . . (519)765-2708
Amherstburg
Honors' B&B . . . . . (519)736-7737
Amhert Island
Poplar Dell . . . . . (613)389-2012
Ancaster
Duck Tail Inn . . . . . (905)648-3596
Apsley
Catherine's B&B . . . . . (705)656-3149
Ariss
Parklawn Place . . . . . (519)767-0812
Athens
Apple Grove B&B . . . . . (613)924-1463
Atwood
Country Corner B&B . . . . . (519)356-2755
Ayton
Eastcliff Farm . . . . . (519)327-8518
Baden
Northridge Farm . . . . . (519)634-8595
Balderson
Perth Town and Country B&B . . . (613)267-1493
Woodrow Farm . . . . . (613)267-1493
Bampton
Kumar B&B . . . . . (905)453-6497
Barrie
Round Table B&B . . . . . (705)739-0193
Barry's Bay
Barry's Bay B&B . . . . . (613)756-1023
Bayfield
Little Inn . . . . . (519)565-2611
Beamsville
Maaike's Homestead . . . . . (416)563-4335
Belwood
Baumdale Farm . . . . . (519)855-6320
The Brown's Myrtle McArthur . . . (519)843-3368
De Herberg Farm . . . . . (519)843-7552
Bloomfield
Cornelius White House . . . . . (416)393-2282
Bonfield
Ravenhill . . . . . (705)776-1247
Bracebridge
Bourdages B&B Ptl Maple Syrup Farm
. . . . (705)645-3711
Heron Blue B&B . . . . . (705)645-2746
Tree Tops . . . . . (705)645-6271
Bradford
Gorelea Acre Farm . . . . . (905)775-3585
Brantford
Helm House . . . . . (519)759-4762
On The Grand B&B . . . . . (519)752-2972
Brighton
Applecrest House . . . . . (613)475-0538
Heritage House . . . . . (613)475-3531
Main Street B&B . . . . . (613)475-0351
Sanford House . . . . . (613)475-3930
Britt
B&B In Britt . . . . . (705)383-2441
Brockville
Robertson House Inn . . . . . (613)345-7378
Burce Mines
North Shore B&B . . . . . (705)785-3510
Burlington
Cactus Flower . . . . . (905)632-1996
Cambridge
Langdon Hall . . . . . (519)740-2100
Spruceview Century Farm . . . . . (519)621-2769
Campbellford
Linden House B&B . . . . . (705)653-4406
Campbellville
Windrush Farm . . . . . (519)856-9761
Winklewood Lane B&B . . . . . (905)854-0527
Canfield
Shady Maples Farm . . . . . (905)774-4413
Cargill
Cornerbrook Farm . . . . . (519)366-2629
Carleton Place
Hudson House B&B . . . . . (613)257-8547
Stewart's Landing . . . . . (613)257-1285
Carrying Place
The Quinte Anchorage . . . . . (613)394-5593
Chatsworth
Hidden Valley Farm . . . . . (519)794-3727
Cherry Valley
Burrowood Jersey Farm . . . . . (613)476-2069
Clarksburg
Maple Home Farms . . . . . (519)599-2699
The Walton's Country Home . . . . (519)599-3898
Cogourg
MacKechnie House . . . . . (905)372-6242
Victoria View . . . . . (905)372-3437
Woodlawn Terrace Inn . . . . . (905)372-2235
Colborne
The Maples B&B . . . . . (905)355-2059
Coldwater
Inn The Woods B&B . . . . . (705)835-6193
Collingwood
Beild House Inn . . . . . (705)444-1522
Consecon
Stouffer Wellers View B&B . . . . . (613)392-2079
Consecon East
Fox & Frog B&B . . . . . (613)965-1029
Deep River
Settlers Inn . . . . . (613)584-2721
Delta
The Denaut Mansion . . . . . (613)928-2588
Demorestville
Roblin Homestead . . . . . (613)476-3619
Dobbinton
Grandma Pheobe's B&B . . . . . (519)934-2230
Dorion
Wolf Den B&B . . . . . (807)857-2913
Drayton
The McIsaac's . . . . . (519)638-2190
Dundalk
Arburn Farm . . . . . (519)923-6952
Dundas
Glenwood B&B . . . . . (905)627-5096
Dutton
Dunwich Farm B&B . . . . . (519)762-3006
Eagle Lake
Sir Sam's Inn . . . . . (800)361-2188
Eganville
Hilltop Treasure . . . . . (613)628-3485
Lakeview Tourist Home B&B . . . . (613)625-2318
Stonehedge . . . . . (613)628-6901
Elgin
The Opinicon . . . . . (613)359-5233
Elk Lake
Montreal River B&B . . . . . (705)678-2105
Elmira
Teddy Bear B&B Inn . . . . . (519)669-2379
Elora
Desert Rose B&B . . . . . (519)846-0685
Eastep Farms . . . . . (519)846-5874
Elora Mill Country Inn . . . . . (519)846-5356
Gingerbread House . . . . . (519)846-0521
Lakeview Farm . . . . . (519)846-9218
Embro
Harrington House In The Pines . . (519)475-4760
Essex
Ridgeview B&B . . . . . (519)839-5587
Falconbridge
Brier Patch . . . . . (705)693-5034
Fanelon Falls
Olde Rectory B&B . . . . . (705)887-9796
Fenelon Falls
Eganridge Inn & Country Club . . . (705)738-5111
Gazebo Corner . . . . . (705)887-6800
Fergus
4-Eleven B&B . . . . . (519)843-5107
Laplacia B&B . . . . . (519)843-3115
Maplecrest Farm . . . . . (519)787-1849
Flesherton
Highland Hill Farm . . . . . (519)924-2892
Frankville
Gibbons Family Farm . . . . . (613)275-2893
Gananoque
Leanhaven Farms . . . . . (613)382-2698
Manse Lane B&B . . . . . (613)382-8642
Trinity House . . . . . (800)265-4871
Georgetown
Pegasus B&B . . . . . (905)877-3440
Victorian Rose B&B . . . . . (905)702-0166
Goderich
Benmiller Inn . . . . . (800)265-1711
La Brassine . . . . . (519)524-6300
Maison Tanguay . . . . . (519)524-1930
The Inn at Port . . . . . (519)529-7986
Gorrie
Walk-A-Bott Creek . . . . . (519)335-3234
Grafton
St. Anne's . . . . . (416)349-2493
Gravenhurst
Allen's B&B . . . . . (705)687-7368
Ameliorative Place . . . . . (705)687-6889
Cunningham's B&B . . . . . (705)687-4511
The Griffith House . . . . . (705)687-1311
Milnes' B&B . . . . . (705)687-4395
Haliburton
Domain of Killien . . . . . (705)457-1100
Sunnyside B&B . . . . . (705)457-9173
Hamer
Loonsnest . . . . . (705)969-9852
Hamilton
Haddo House . . . . . (905)524-0071
Inchbury Street B&B . . . . . (905)522-3520
Harriston
The Country Place . . . . . (519)323-1008
Hastings
Spring Valley Farm . . . . . (705)696-2878
Hearst
The Benefits of Nature . . . . . (705)362-8783
Northwinds B&B . . . . . (705)362-4531
Rejeanne's B&B . . . . . (705)362-4442
Hillier
Jamka Farm . . . . . (613)399-2796
Hillsburgh
Coningsby Brae B&B . . . . . (519)855-4685
Hunta
Country Haven . . . . . (705)272-6802
Huntsville
Edelweis House Betty's B&B . . . . (705)789-5455
Tulip Country Inn . . . . . (705)789-4001
Ignace
Sunset Country B&B . . . . . (807)934-2597
Indian River
Elm Lodge Farm . . . . . (705)295-6960
Idyllwood Farm . . . . . (705)295-4227
Ingersoll
Elm Hurst . . . . . (519)485-5321
Iroquois
Blue Heron Bleu . . . . . (613)652-2601
Jackson's Point
The Briars . . . . . (800)465-2376
Jarvis
Roth Acres Farm . . . . . (905)779-3346
Kakabeka Falls
Cedar Haven . . . . . (807)577-8452
Kaliburton
All-Hart B&B . . . . . (705)457-5272
Kamaniskey Lake
Inglenook . . . . . (613)756-0727
Kenora
Heritage Place . . . . . (807)548-4380
Island Paradise . . . . . (807)548-4778
Keswick
Lismore . . . . . (905)476-7427
The Yorke Farm . . . . . (905)476-4402
Kimberly
Lamont Guest House . . . . . (519)599-5905
Kincardine
Porcupine Run . . . . . (519)395-3744
Kindcardine
Hanks Heritage House . . . . . (519)396-7991
King City
Tannery Hill . . . . . (905)859-0999
Kingston
1878 B&B . . . . . (613)547-1878
Hochelaga Inn . . . . . (613)549-5534
Joy's B&B . . . . . (613)544-3580
The North Nook B&B . . . . . (613)547-8061
O'Brien House B&B . . . . . (613)542-8660
Reveille Island B&B . . . . . (613)659-3026

- Rideau En Ville .... (613)544-9274
- Riverview B&B .... (613)546-7707
- Rosemount B&B Inn .... (613)531-8844

Kirkfield
- Sir William MacKenzie Inn .... (705)438-1278

Kitchener
- Why Not B&B .... (519)748-4577

Kleinburg
- Humber House .... (905)893-9108

Komoka
- Cudney Homestead .... (519)657-0228

Lakefield
- Windmere .... (705)652-6292 (800)465-6327

Lanark
- Eagle's Rest Farm .... (613)259-3306
- Linden Meadow Farm .... (613)259-2693

Lancaster
- MacPine Farms .... (613)347-2003

Lansdowne
- Hart Country Estate .... (613)659-2873

Leamington
- Home Suite Home B&B .... (519)326-7169

Lion's Head
- Home to Home B&B .... (519)795-7525

Listowel
- Maplevue .... (519)291-2949

London
- Anderson, Dorita's Place .... (519)472-6083
- Annigan's .... (519)439-9196
- Chiron House .... (519)673-6878
- Clermont Place .... (519)672-0767
- Cosy Corners .... (519)673-4598
- Dillon's Place .... (519)439-9666
- Eileen's .... (519)471-1107
- Halina Koch B&B .... (519)434-4045
- Hilltop .... (519)681-7841
- Idlewyld Inn .... (519)433-2891
- McLellan Place .... (519)686-3590
- Overdale .... (519)641-0236
- The Pink Chestnut .... (519)673-3963
- The Rose House .... (519)433-9978
- Serena's Place .... (519)471-6228
- Trillium .... (519)453-3801
- Vail .... (519)432-9942

Lucan
- Hindhope .... (519)227-4514

Lucknow
- Evergreen Lane .... (519)528-5953
- Lee View Farms .... (519)528-3812

Lynden
- Cluny Lodge Farm .... (905)627-4591

Madawaska
- Riverland Camp and B&B .... (613)637-5338

Madoc
- Camelot Country Inn .... (613)473-0441

Manotick
- Brownlee House .... (613)826-2201
- Long Island B&B .... (613)692-2042
- Olde Virginia Manor B&B .... (613)692-4329

Markdale
- Rocky Glen Farm .... (519)369-5110

Marrickville
- Millisle B&B .... (613)269-3627

Massey
- Pinecrest Farm .... (705)865-2249

Mattawa
- Bear Creek Farm .... (705)744-2423

Maxville
- Dorishaven Farms .... (613)527-3021

McKellar
- The Inn at Manitou .... (800)571-8818

Meaford
- Franro Farm .... (519)538-4597
- Inverurie B&B .... (519)538-5525
- Irish Mountain B&B .... (519)538-2803
- Philappleis Guest Home .... (519)538-1928
- Scotch Mountain Guest House .... (519)538-1420

Merlin
- Country Comfort .... (519)682-0513

Merrickville
- Sam Jakes Inn .... (613)269-3711 (800)567-4667

Milford
- Jackson's Falls Schoolhouse B&B (613)476-8576

Millbank
- Honeybrook Farm .... (519)595-4604

Millbrook
- Bellcrest Farms .... (705)932-5485
- Westmacott House .... (705)932-2957

Mindemoya
- Mindemoya Lake View Farm B&B (705)377-5714

Minden
- Grey Manor .... (705)286-3702
- Hunter Creek Inn .... (705)286-3194
- Mill B&B .... (705)489-3024
- Minden House .... (705)286-4450
- Stone Hedge Farm .... (705)286-1709
- The Stone House .... (705)286-1250

Mississauga
- Glenerin Inn .... (905)828-6103

Morrisburg
- Upper Canada B&B .... (613)543-3336

Mount Albert
- Thorcrest .... (905)473-1028

Murillo
- Sunrise Farms .... (807)935-2824

Napanee
- Beechwood Farm .... (613)354-5770
- Century Farm B&B .... (613)354-1028
- Sherwood House Guest Home and B&B .... (613)354-2287

Navan
- Bearbrook Farm .... (613)835-2227

New Hamburg
- Brimstock Farm .... (519)656-3268
- Glenalby Farms .... (519)625-8353
- The Station House .... (519)662-2957

Newboro
- Newboro House B&B .... (613)272-3181
- Stagecoach Inn .... (613)272-2900

Newcastle
- Welcome Home .... (905)987-1296

Niagara Falls
- Bedham Hall .... (905)374-8515
- Butterfly Manor .... (416)358-8988
- Gretna Green .... (416)357-2081
- Park Place B&B .... (416)358-0279

Niagara-On-The-Lake
- All Seasons Guest Homes .... (905)468-7007
- Blaney House B&B .... (905)468-5362
- Brockamour Manor .... (905)468-5527
- Charming Victoria Cottage .... (905)468-2570
- Dietsch'e Empty Nest .... (905)468-3906
- House on The Park .... (905)468-7555
- The Kings Way B&B .... (905)468-5478
- Linden House B&B .... (905)468-3923
- Northumbria Guest Home .... (905)468-5428
- Oban Inn .... (905)468-2165
- Pillar & Post .... (905)468-2123
- Queen's Landing Inn .... (905)468-2195
- Waverley .... (905)684-0949
- Wren House .... (905)468-4361

Nobel
- Maple Rock Farm .... (705)342-9662

Norland
- Moore Lake Inn .... (705)454-1753

North Gower
- Carsonby Manor .... (613)489-3219

Oakville
- Oakville Hideaway .... (905)844-5513

Orilla
- The Pinnacle .... (705)325-9368

Orillia
- Betty & Tony's Waterfront B&B .... (705)326-1125
- Cavana House .... (705)327-7759
- Pine Tree House .... (705)329-0518

Orrville
- Malkin House .... (705)732-2994

Ottawa
- Albert House .... (613)236-4479
- Beatrice Lyon Guest House .... (613)236-3904
- Blue Spruce .... (613)236-8521
- Bye-The-Way .... (613)232-6840
- Cartier House Inn .... (613)236-4667
- Gasthaus Switzerland Inn .... (613)237-0335
- Ottawa House B&B .... (613)789-4433
- Waverley House .... (613)233-0427

Owen Sound
- Sunset Farms B&B .... (519)371-4559

Paisley
- Rosewood Forest .... (519)353-5462

Pakenham
- Carnivic Lodge .... (613)624-5453
- Gillanderry Farms .... (613)832-2317
- Kia Ora B&B .... (613)256-2116

Paris
- The Grahams .... (519)442-2375

Parry Sound
- Otter Lake B&B .... (705)378-2812

Penetanguishene
- No. 1 Jury Drive B&B .... (705)549-6851

Perth
- Drummond House .... (613)264-9175
- House on The Corner .... (613)264-0901
- Rivendell B&B .... (613)264-2742
- Woodrow Farm .... (613)267-1493

Peterborough
- Blue Willow B&B .... (705)742-0433
- The Elizabeth Davidson House .... (705)749-6960
- King Bethune Guest House .... (705)743-4101

Petersborough
- Armour Road Studio B&B .... (705)745-2071

Picton
- Butternut Cupboard .... (613)476-7744
- Ginkgo Tree Place .... (613)476-7275
- Isaiah Tubbs Resort .... (613)393-2090
- Log House B&B .... (613)476-5978
- Maple Ridge Farms .... (613)476-2838
- Marysburg House B&B .... (613)476-7125
- Picton House B&B .... (613)476-1911
- The Poplars .... (613)476-3513
- Rosemere B&B .... (613)476-1473
- Travellers' Tales Bed, Breakfast & Books .... (613)476-1885
- Wilhome Farmhouse B&B .... (613)393-5630
- Woodville Farm .... (613)476-5462

Plantagenet
- Willowbank Farm .... (613)673-4875

Port Carling
- Sherwood Inn .... (800)461-4233

Port Dover
- B&B By The Lake .... (519)583-1010

Port Lambton
- The Willows .... (519)677-4035

Port Stanley
- Kettle Creek Inn .... (519)782-3388

Portland
- Wendigo Acres B&B .... (613)272-2597

Powassan
- Satis House B&B .... (705)724-2187

Puslinch
- Esperanza B&B .... (519)763-6385

Renfrew
- Meadowview Farm .... (613)432-6798
- Red Door Ranch .... (613)432-8767

Richards Landing
- Anchorage B&B .... (705)246-2221
- Rainbow Ridge Farm .... (705)246-2683
- Rains Homestead Century Farm .... (705)246-2556
- See View Cottage B&B .... (705)246-3277
- Windsong Meadows .... (705)246-1807

Ripley
- Quiet Country Home .... (519)395-2815

Rockwood
- The Colonel Strange House .... (519)856-2138
- Country Spirit .... (519)856-9879
- Northwood Farm .... (519)855-6286

Rodney
- Serene Acres .... (519)785-0218

Rossport
- Rossport Inn .... (807)824-3213

Saint Jacobs
- The Carpenter's House .... (519)664-2451

Sarsfield
- Canaan Ridge Farm .... (613)835-2457

Sault Ste Marie
- Hillsview B&B .... (705)759-8819
- Top O' The Hill B&B .... (705)253-9042

Schomberg
- Puck's Farm .... (905)939-7036

Seaforth
- Holmsted House .... (519)527-2040

Sharbot Lake
- Lakeside B&B .... (613)279-2580

Singhampton
- Rob Roy 1853 Farm .... (519)922-2706

Sioux Lookout
Tumble Inn .... (807)737-2631
South Gillies
Captain's Quarters B&B .... (807)475-5630
Unicorn Inn & Restaurant ...... (807)475-4200
South Mountain
Turn of The Century .... (613)989-3220
Sparta
Loma Linda .... (519)773-3335
St. Catharines
Cripps' Cosy Corner .... (416)688-2306
St. Marys
Westover Inn .... (519)284-2977
Stratford
Ambassador B&B Guest Homes . (519)271-5385
Deacon House .... (519)273-2052
Duggan Place B&B Inn .... (519)273-7502
Glenwood .... (519)273-5930
The Maples .... (519)273-0810
The Queen's Inn .... (800)461-6450
Stone Maiden Inn .... (519)271-7129
Sutton
Rotherwood B&B .... (905)722-3478
Tavistock
Hendershot House .... (519)665-2540
Stockwill Farm .... (519)462-2678
Tehkummah
Happy Acres B&B .... (705)859-3453
Thedford
Donview Farms B&B .... (519)786-5469
Thornbury
The Mill Pond .... (519)599-6717
Thorndale
Cove B&B .... (519)461-0125
Thunder Bay
At Your Leisure B&B .... (807)767-6834
Mount Forest B&B .... (807)473-9336
Park Haven .... (807)623-7175
Totem B&B .... (807)939-1354
Tillsonburg
The English Robin .... (519)842-8605
Tobermory
Hidden Valley Lodge .... (519)596-2610
Toronto
The Admiral/St. George B&B .... (416)921-1899
Amblecote B&B .... (416)927-1713
Annex House .... (416)920-3922
Ashleigh Heritage Homes ...... (416)535-4000
Beaconsfield B&B .... (416)535-3338
Beverley Place .... (416)977-0077
Burken Guest House .... (416)920-7842
Daisy's B&B .... (416)532-3217
Feathers B&B .... (416)534-1923
Mayfair B&B .... (416)769-1558
Orchard View B&B .... (416)488-6826
Queen West B&B .... (416)340-7707
Trenton
Devonshire House B&B .... (613)394-4572
The Smithrim House .... (613)394-5001
Tweed
Black River Country Inn .... (613)478-1465
Utopia
Harvey House .... (705)424-9771
Utterson
Rowntree Cottage .... (705)769-3640
Uxbridge
Willo' Wind .... (416)852-3787
Woodlawn .... (905)852-7944
Vermilion Bay
The Blue Lake B&B .... (807)227-5400
Vernon
Gruen Valley Farm .... (613)821-2579
Verona
Blueroof Farm .... (613)374-2147
Vittoria
Plantation House .... (519)426-0849
Waldhof
Eagle Ridge B&B .... (807)227-2340
Wallenstein
Glenna Guesthouse .... (519)638-2470
Westar Farm .... (519)638-5745
Walton
Mitchell's Country B&B .... (519)887-6697
Warsaw
The McMullen Farm .... (705)652-3024

Wasaga Beach
Deerview B&B .... (705)429-6498
Waterford
Round Plains Plantation .... (519)443-5847
Wawa
Goose Down B&B .... (705)856-7003
Lakeshore B&B .... (705)856-1709
Welland
Martha's B&B .... (905)732-3170
Wellington
Devonshire Inn on The Lake .... (613)399-1851
Shamrock B&B .... (613)399-2261
Tara Hall B&B .... (613)399-2801
Wendover
Wendover B&B .... (613)673-1615
Westbrook
Limestone & Lilacs B&B .... (613)545-0222
Westmeath
Saxony Farm .... (613)587-4403
Westport
A Bit of Gingerbread B&B ...... (613)273-7848
The Cove .... (613)273-3636
Stepping Stone .... (613)273-3806
Wheatley
La Marsh House 1865 B&B .... (519)825-3929
Royal Harbour View .... (519)825-7955
Whitby
Ezra Annes House .... (905)430-1653
Wiarton
Bruce Gables .... (519)534-0429
The Green Door B&B .... (519)534-4710
Lovaloon B&B .... (519)534-4066
Wilberforce
The House In The Village B&B Guest Home
.... (705)448-3161
Williamstown
Caron House .... (613)347-7338
Winchester
Harkhaven Farm .... (613)774-3418
Windsor
Branteaney's B&B .... (519)966-2334
Ye Olde Walkerville B&B ...... (519)254-1507
Woodham
Country Haven .... (519)229-6416
Woodstock
Heritage Guest House .... (519)456-8721
Wyebridge
Hackney Horse B&B .... (705)322-1339
Yarker
Hollow Tree Farm .... (613)377-6793
Zephyr
High Fields Farm .... (905)473-6132

Prince Edward Island

Bay Fortune
The Inn at Bay Fortune .... (902)687-3745
Bonshaw
Strathgartney Country Inn ...... (902)675-4711
Brackley Beach
North Shore B&B (902)672-2242 (800)661-9575
Windsong Farm B&B .... (902)672-2874
Cape Traverse
Glennhaven B&B .... (902)855-2729
Cardigan
Roseneath B&B .... (902)838-4590
Carleton
Carleton Cove Farm B&B ...... (902)855-2795
Carleton Siding
MacCallum B&B .... (902)855-2229
Cavendish
Kindred Spirits Country Inn ..... (902)963-2434
MacLure B&B .... (902)963-2239
Central Bedeque
Pine-Lawn B&B .... (902)887-2270
Charlottetown
Allix's B&B .... (902)892-2643
An Island Rose B&B
.... (902)569-5030 (800)775-5030
Anchors Aweigh B&B .... (902)892-4319
Barachois Inn .... (902)963-2194
Birch Hill B&B .... (902)892-4353
Bye-The-Shore B&B .... (902)569-2548
Campbells Maple B&B .... (902)894-4488
Court B&B .... (902)894-5871
Cutcliffe's B&B .... (902)894-9361

The Duchess of Kent Inn
.... (902)566-5826 (800)665-5826
Dunstaffnage Heights B&B ..... (902)628-1715
Elmwood Heritage Inn .... (902)368-3310
Fitzroy Hall .... (902)368-2077
Heritage Harbour House Inn
.... (902)892-6633 (800)660-6633
MacInnis B&B .... (902)892-6725
Orient Hotel .... (902)658-2503
Tea Hill B&B .... (902)569-2366
Charlottetown West
Chez-Nous (A Tender Treasure) B&B
.... (902)566-2779 (800)566-2779
Churchill
Churchill B&B .... (902)675-2481
Cornwall
Century Kennels and Farm B&B
.... (902)566-2110 (800)393-2110
Oak Lane Farm B&B
.... (902)675-3945 (800)276-5197
Pye's Village Guest Home ...... (902)566-2026
Ellerslie
Burleigh's B&B .... (902)831-2288
Hilltop Acres B&B .... (902)831-2817
Frenchfort
Miller's Farm B&B .... (902)629-1509
Hampton
Bradway Inn B&B .... (902)658-2178
Harrington
Wilbert's B&B .. (902)368-8145 (800)847-8145
Kensington
Sea Breeze B&B .... (902)836-5275
Knutsford
Smallman's B&B .... (902)859-3469
Lady Fane
Empty Nest B&B .... (902)658-2013
Little Pond
Little Pond Country Store B&B .. (902)583-2892
Murray River
Bayberry Cliff Inn B&B .... (902)962-3395
Marshfield
Rosevale Farm B&B .... (902)629-1341
Woodmere B&B . (902)628-1783 (800)747-1783
Mill River
Thomas B&B .... (902)859-3209
Millview
Drake's Farm B&B .... (902)651-2039
Smith's Farm B&B (902)651-2728 (800)265-2728
Milton
Miltonvale B&B .... (902)368-1085
Montague
Boudreault's "White House" B&B (902)838-2560
Parker's B&B .... (902)838-3663
Partridge's B&B .... (912)838-4687
The Pines B&B .... (902)838-3675
Morell
A Village B&B .... (902)961-2394
Kelly's B&B .... (902)961-2389
Murray Harbour
The Morning Glory B&B
.... (902)962-3150 (800)881-3150
Murray Harbour North
Lady Catherine's B&B .... (902)962-3426
New Perth
Van Dykes' B&B .... (902)838-4408
Nine Mile Creek
Laine Acres B&B .... (902)675-2402
North Bedeque
"The Island Way" Farm B&B
.... (902)436-7405 (800)361-3435
Blue Heron Country B&B ...... (902)436-4843
Country at Heart B&B
.... (902)436-9879 (800)463-9879
Rice Point
Straitview Farm B&B .... (902)675-2071
Richmond
Mom's Bed 'n' Breakfast ...... (902)854-2419
Seven Mile Bay
The Captain's Lodge B&B ...... (902)855-3106
Souris
The Matthew House Inn .... (902)687-3461
Spring Brook
Dunevue B&B .... (902)886-2557
St. Peter's Bay
Cable Head B&B .... (902)961-3275

Crab 'n' Apple B&B .... (902)961-3165

Stanley Bridge

Gulf Breeze B&B .... (902)886-2678

Summerside

Silver Fox Inn .... (902)436-4033
The Smallman's B&B .... (902)886-2846

Tignish

Maple St. Inn - B&B .... (902)882-3428

Tyne Valley

The Doctor's Inn B&B .... (902)831-2164

Uigg

Dunvegan Farm B&B .... (902)651-2833

Victoria

Dunrovin Lodge & Farm B&B ... (902)658-2375

West Point

The West Point Lighthouse Inn
.... (902)859-3605 (800)764-6854

West Royalty

A Country Home (Hall's)
.... (902)368-2340 (800)265-4255

Wilmot Valley

Birchvale Farm B&B
.... (902)436-3803 (800)463-3803

Winsloe

Larter's Country Inn .... (902)368-1070
MacPherson's Farm Tourist Deligh (902)621-0078

Wood Islands West

Baba's House Guests B&B ..... (902)962-2772

Woodville

Woodlands Country Inn .... (902)583-2275

Quebec

Amqui

Domaine Du Lac Matapedia .... (418)629-5004

Ayer's Cliff

Ripplecove Inn .. (819)838-4296 (800)668-4296

Bic

Aux Cormorans .... (418)736-8113

Deschambault

Auberge du Roy .... (418)286-6958
Maison de la Veuve Grolo ...... (418)286-6831

Fulford, Lac Brome

Le Tu-Dor .... (514)534-3947

Ile d'Orleans

Ferme Lachance .... (418)829-3259

Kamouraska

Gite Aux Portes du Palais ...... (418)492-9273

L'Islet Sur Mer

La Marguerite .... (418)247-5454

Mansonville

B&B Le Pied-A-Terre .... (514)292-5684

Montreal

Armor Inn .... (514)285-0140
Manoir Ambrose .... (514)288-6922

New Richmond

Gite Les Bouleaux .... (418)392-4111

North Hatley

Auberge Hatley .... (819)842-2451
La Montagnarde .... (819)842-2576
North Hatley Trillium .... (819)842-2269
Sunset View .... (819)842-2560

Quebec City

Aumanoir Ste. Genevieve ...... (418)694-1666
Battlefields B&B .... (418)527-0481
Le Chateau De Pierre .... (418)694-0429

Saint Antoine

Auberge Saint-Antoine .... (418)692-2211

Saint-Irenee

Auberge Des Sablons .... (418)452-3594

St Honore

Le Gite Beauceron .... (418)485-6510

St Irenee Charlevoix

Desroches Farm .... (418)452-3209

St Marc Sur Richelie

Hostellerie Les Trois Tilleuls .... (514)584-2231

St-Antoine-De-Tilly

Auberge Manoir De Tilly .... (418)886-2407

Ste Petronille

Auberge La Goeliche Inn .... (418)828-2248

Val David

Auberge Charme De Suisse .... (819)322-3434

Yukon Territory

Dawson City

Bonanza House B&B .... (403)993-6909
Patridge Creek Farm B&B ...... (403)667-1068
White Ram Manor B&B .... (403)993-5772

Mayo

Country Charm B&B .... (403)996-2918
Mayo B&B .... (403)996-2221

Watson Lake

Heritage House .... (403)536-2400

Whitehorse

Blue Gables B&B .... (403)668-2840
The Drifters B&B .... (403)633-5419
Scandia B&B .... (403)633-5421

Alaska

Anchorage

Alaska Available B&B Reservation Service .... (907)337-3400

Alaska Sourdough B&B Assoc. .... (907)563-6244

Stay With A Friend ..... (907)258-1717

Homer

B&B By The Sea .... (907)235-7886

Juneau

Alaska Bed and Breakfast. (907)586-2959

Wasilla

Statewide Reservation Services .... (907)376-4405 (800)376-4405

Arizona

Fountain Hills

Arizona Trails .... (602)837-4284 (888)799-4284

Prescott

B&B Scottsdale and The West .... (520)776-1102

Scottsdale

Bed & Breakfast In Arizona (602)995-2831

Tempe

Mi Casa-Su Casa Reservation Service .... (602)990-0682

Tucson

Old Pueblo Homestays... (602)790-2399

Arkansas

Calico Rock

Arkansas Ozarks B&B Reservation Service .... (501)297-4197 (800)233-2777

Eureka Springs

Assoc. of B&Bs, Cabins & Cottages .... (501)253-6767

Bed & Breakfast Reservations .... (501)253-9111

California

Albany

B&B International ...... (415)525-4569

Altadena

Eye Openers B&B Reservations .... (818)797-2055

Calistoga

B&B Exchange .... (707)942-5900

Cambria

B&B Homestay .... (805)927-4613

Carmel

Carmel Tourist Valley .... (408)624-1711

Fullerton

B&B of Southern California (714)738-8361

Garden Grove

Rent-A-Room International (714)638-1406

Laguna Beach

California Riviera 800.... (800)621-0500

Napa

Napa Valley's Finest Lodging .... (707)224-4667

San Francisco

B&B International ...... (415)696-1690

B&B San Francisco America Family Inn .... (415)931-3083

San Luis Obispo

Megan's Friends B&B Reservations .... (805)544-4406

Tarzana

California Houseguests International .... (818)344-7878

Westlake Village

B&B of Los Angeles .... (818)889-7325

Whittier

Co-Host, America's B&B . (213)699-8427

Colorado

Vail

Vail B&B .... (303)949-1212

Connecticut

Guilford

B&B/Inns of New England Res. Service .... (603)279-8348 (800)582-0853

Norfolk

Covered Bridges Conn. Res. .... (860) 542-5944

North Stonington

Antiques & Accommodations .... (860)535-1736

Delaware

Wilmington

Bed & Breakfast of Delaware .... (302)479-9500

Florida

Miami

B&B Company .... (305)661-3270

Saint Augustine

R.S.V.P. .... (904)471-0600

Saint Petersburg

B&B Suncoast Accommodations .... (813)786-6667

Tallahassee

Bed & Breakfast Scenic Florida .... (904)386-8196

Georgia

Atlanta

Atlanta Hospitality ...... (404)493-1930

B&B Atlanta .... (404)875-0525

Georgia B&B .... (404)493-1930

Hawaii

Hana

Hana Plantation Houses . (808)248-7248

Honolulu

B&B Honolulu Statewide.. (808)595-7533

Kapaa

B&B Hawaii .... (808)822-7771

Idaho

Boise

B&B of Idaho .... (208)342-8066

Illinois

Chicago

Bed & Breakfast/Chicago . (312)951-0085

Heritage B&B .... (312)857-0800

Hoffman Estates

B&B Midwest Reservations (800)342-2632

Kentucky

Louisville

Kentucky Homes B&B ... (502)635-7341

Versailles

Bluegrass B&B .... (606)873-3208

Louisiana

Baton Rouge

B&B Travel .... (800)926-4320

New Orleans

B&B Exclusive Registry of New Orleans .... (800)729-4640

Bed & Breakfast, Inc. ... (504)488-4640

New Orleans B&B ...... (504)838-0071

Maine

Falmouth

B&B of Maine .... (207)781-4528

Franklin

B&B Down East .... (207)338-9761

Massachusetts

Boston

B&B Agency of Boston .. (617)720-3540

B&B Associates Bay Colony Ltd. .... (617)449-5302

Brookline

Greater Boston Hospitality (617)277-5430

Cambridge

B&B Cambridge & Greater Boston .... (617)576-1492

Newton Centre

New England B&B ...... (617)244-2112

Orleans

Orleans B&B Associates . (508)255-3824

Osterville

Destinnations New England .... (508)428-5600 (800)333-4667

Revere
Golden Slumber Accommodations
. . . . (617)289-1053
West Hyannisport
B&B Cape Cod . . . . (508)775-2772
Williamsburg
Berkshire Bed & Breakfast Homes
. . . . (413)268-7244

Michigan

Saugatuck
B&B Dirctory - Michigan . (800)832-6657
Traverse City
B&B Connection . . . . (616)943-9182

Mississippi

Meridian
Bed & Breakfast Mississippi
. . . . (601)482-5483

Missouri

Saint Louis
River Country B&B of St Louis
. . . . (314)965-4328

Nebraska

Gothenburg
Swede Hospitality B&B . . (308)537-2680

New Jersey

Princeton
B&B of Princeton . . . . . . (609)924-3189

New Mexico

Santa Fe
Bed & Breakfast of New Mexico
. . . . (505)982-3332

New York

Buffalo
Rainbow Hospitality . . . . (800)373-8797
Edmeston
Central New York Hospitality
. . . . (607)965-8076
New York
Adobe B&B Ltd.
. . . . (212)472-2000 (800)835-8880
New World Bed & Breakfast, Ltd.
. . . . (212)675-5600
Urban Ventures . . . . (212)594-5650
Port Jefferson
A Reasonable Alternative . (516)928-4034
Saratoga Springs
Saratoga B&B . . . . (518)584-0920

North Carolina

Everetts
B&B In The Albemarle . . . (919)335-3491

Ohio

Cleveland
Private Lodging . . . . (216)321-3213
Powell
Buckeye Bed & Breakfast . (614)548-4555

Oregon

Portland
B&B Oregon . . . . (503)245-0642
Northwest Bed and Breakfast Travel
. . . . (503)243-7616

Pennsylvania

Gettysburg
Inns of The Gettysburg Area
. . . . (800)247-2216
Hershey
Hershey B&B . . . . (717)533-2928
Philadelphia
Bed & Breakfast Center City
. . . . (215)735-1137
Bed & Breakfast of Philadelphia
. . . . (800)220-1917
Pine Grove Mills
Rest & Repast B&B Reservation Service
. . . . (814)238-1484
Valley Forge
Bed & Breakfast of Valley Forge
. . . . (800)344-0123

Rhode Island

Newport
Anna's Victorian Connection
. . . . (401)624-6621
Bed & Breakfast of Rhode Island, Inc
. . . . (800)828-0000
Guest House Association of Newport
. . . . (401)849-7645

South Carolina

Beaufort
Bay Street Accommodations
. . . . (803)524-7720
Charleston
Historic Charleston Bed & Breakfast
. . . . (803)722-6606

Tennessee

Hampshire
Natchez Trace B&B Reservation Service
. . . . (615)285-2777
Memphis
Bed & Breakfast In Memphis
. . . . (800)458-2421
Nashville
Bed & Breakfast Adventures
. . . . (615)383-6611 (800)947-7404
Bed & Breakfast Hospitality-TN
. . . . (615)331-5244

Texas

Corpus Christi
Sand Dollar Hospitality B&B
. . . . (512)853-1222
Dallas
Bed & Breakfast Texas Style
. . . . (800)899-4538
Fredericksburg
Gastehaus Schmidt Reservation Service
. . . . (210)997-5612
Historic Hotel Assoc. of Texas
. . . . (512)997-3980
Jefferson
Book-A-Bed-Ahead . . . . . (903)665-3956
San Antonio
Bed & Breakfast Hosts of San Antonio
. . . . (210)824-8036

Vermont

East Fairfield
Vermont Bed & Breakfast (802)827-3827
Essex
Vermont Center Point . . . (800)449-2745
Saint Albans
American Bed & Breakfast In New England
. . . . (802)524-4731

Virginia

Charlottesville
Guesthouses . . . . (804)979-7264
Norfolk
Bed & Breakfast of Tidewater Virginia
. . . . (804)627-1983

Washington

Mercer Island
Travellers' Bed & Breakfast
. . . . (206)232-2345
Seattle
Pacific Bed & Breakfast . . (206)784-0539
Tacoma
Greater Tacoma B&B Reservations
. . . . (206)759-4088

Washington, D.C.

Bed 'n Breakfast Ltd. of Washington DC
. . . . (202)328-3510

CANADA

British Columbia

Victoria
Garden City B&B . . . . (604)479-9999

Ontario

Toronto
Toronto B&B . . . . (416)588-8800

Alabama

Alabama B&B Assoc. . . . . (334)687-8847

Alaska

Alaska B&B Assoc. . . . . . (907)243-2074

Wasilla

Bed & Breakfast Assoc. of Alaska Mat-Su Ch . . . . (907)376-4461 (800)401-7444

Arizona

Arizona Association of B&B Inns . . . . (800)284-2589

Arkansas

Bed & Breakfast Assoc. of Arkansas . . . . (800) NATURAL

California

Coloma

Historic Country Inns of The Mother Lode . . . . (916)622-6919

Dana Point

American Historic Inns Inc. (714)499-8070

Ferndale

B&B Inns of Humbolt County . . . . (707)786-4000

Guerneville

Country Inns of The Russian River . . . . (800)927-4667

Inverness

Inns of Point Reyes . . . . . (415)662-1420

Mariposa

Yosemite, Mariposa B&B Association . . . . (209)742-7666

Mendocino

Mendocino Coast Innkeepers Association . . . . (707)964-6725

Placerville

El Dorado County Innkeepers Association . . . . (916)626-5840

Sacramento

Sacramento Innkeepers Association . . . . (916)441-5007

Santa Barbara

B&B Innkeepers Guild of Santa Barbara . . . . (408)425-8212

Professional Assoc. of Innkeepers International . . . . (805)569-1853

Santa Cruz

B&B Innkeepers of Santa Cruz . . . . (408)425-8212

Sonora

B&B Inns of The Gold Country . . . . (916)644-2740

Gold Country Inns of Toulomne County . . . . (209)532-9024

Soquel

California Association of B&B Inns . . . . (209)533-1441

Temecula

B&B Innkeepers of Southern California . . . . (714)676-7047

Colorado

B&B Innkeepers of Colorado . . . . (719)473-3165

Estes Park

Assoc. of Historic Hotels of Rocky Mtns. (970)586-3371

Distinctive Inns of Colorado . . . . (800)866-0621

Tabernash

Colorado Dude & Guest Ranch Association . . . . (303)887-3128

Florida

Inn Route . . . . (800)524-1880

High Springs

B&B Association of High Springs Florida . . . . (904)454-4040

Georgia

Great Inns of Georgia . . . (404)843-0471

Hawaii

Hawaii Island B&B Assoc. (808)329-5773

Kailua

B&B Homestay Proprietors, Association Of . . . . (808)261-1059

Idaho

Coeur d'Alene

Accommodations Coeur d'Alene & Vicinity . . . . (209)667-5081

Illinois

Illinois B&B Association . . (815)777-3638

Rock Island

B&B of the QCA Association . . . . (309)788-7068

Indiana

Chesterton

Indiana B&B Association . (219)926-5781

Iowa

Des Moines

Iowa Bed & Breakfast Innkeeper's Assoc. (800)888-4667

Newton

Iowa Bed & Breakfast Innkeepers Assoc. (515)792-6833

Kansas

Kansas B&B Association (888)8KS-INNS

Kentucky

Covington

B&B Association of Kentucky . . . . (800)292-2632

Louisiana

Baton Rouge

Louisiana B&B Association . . . . (504)346-1857

Carencro

Louisiana B&B Association . . . . (318)896-6529

Maryland

Annapolis

Annapolis Association . . . . (301)263-6418

Cambridge

B&B Inns of The Eastern Shore . . . . (301)228-0575

Frederick

Inns of The Blue Ridge . . . (301)663-8703

Massachusetts

Buckland

In The Country B&B Association . . . . (413)625-2975

Stockbridge

Independent Innkeepers Association . . . . (413)243-0303

West Hyannisport

Association of Massachusetts Reservation . . . . (508)775-2772

Worthington

Hampshire Hills B&B Association . . . . (413)296-4363

Michigan

Marshall

Independent Innkeepers' Association . . . . (800)344-5244

New Buffalo

Lake to Lake B&B Association of Michigan . . . . (800)832-6657

Minnesota

Minnesota B&B Guild . . . (612)424-8238

Mississippi

B&B Assoc. of Mississippi (601)435-1189

Missouri

Bed & Breakfast Inns of Missouri . . . . (800)213-5642

Montana

Montana B&B Association (406)892-2829

Nebraska

Elgin

Nebraska Association of B&B
. . . . (402)466-8626

New Hampshire

North Hampton

New England Innkeepers Association
. . . . (603)964-6792

New Jersey

B&B Innkeepers Association of New Jersey
. . . . (908)449-3535

Avon By The Sea

Inns Along The Coast . . . (201)776-8727

New Mexico

New Mexico B&B Association
. . . . (800)661-6649

Taos

Taos B&B Association . . . (800)876-7857

New York

Penn Yan

Finger Lakes B&B Association
. . . . (800)695-5590

Syracuse

B&B Association of New York State
. . . . (315)474-3641

North Carolina

North Carolina Bed & Breakfast & Inns
. . . . (800)849-5392

North Carolina B&B Assoc. (704)693-9193

Ohio

Columbus

Ohio B&B Association . . . (800)BUCKEYE

Oklahoma

Norman

Oklahoma Bed & Breakfast Association
. . . . (405)321-6221

Oregon

Oregon B&B Guild . . . . . . (800)944-6196

Ashland

Ashland B&B Network . . . (541)482-2337

Hood River

Columbia River Gorge B&B Association
. . . . (503)386-5566

Portland

Portland Metro Innkeepers (503)222-4435

Pennsylvania

Pennsylvania Travel Council
. . . . (717) 232-8880

Doylestown

B&B Association of Delaware River Valley
. . . . (215)766-0477

Lewisburg

North Central Pennsylvania Association
. . . . (717)524-7733

New Hope

B&B Association of Pennsylvania
. . . . (215)794-5254

Willow Street

Lancaster County B&B Inns Association
. . . . (717)464-5881

York

White Rose Area B&B . . . (717)854-3411

Rhode Island

Newport

Newport Historic Inns . . . (401)846-4435

South Carolina

Columbia

South Carolina B&B Association
. . . . (803)869-2535

Rock Hill

The Book & The Spindle . . (803)328-1913

South Dakota

B&B Innkeepers of South Dakota
. . . . (800)642-9812

Philip

Old West & Badlands B&B (605)859-2120

Tennessee

Kodak

Tennessee's True B&B . . . (423)933-3512

Nashville

Tennessee B&B Innkeeper's Assoc.
. . . . (800)820-8144

Texas

Historic Accommodations of Texas
. . . . (210)997-3980

Houston

B&B Society of Texas . . . . (713)523-1114

Utah

B&B Inns of Utah . . . . (801)628-6999

Vermont

Arlington

Historic Inns of Norman Rockwell's Vt.
. . . . (802)375-2269

Virginia

Bed & Breakfast Assoc. of Virginia
. . . . (703) 672-0870

Irvington

Inns of The Northern Neck
. . . . (804)438-6053

Staunton

Virginia Inns of Shenandoah
. . . . (804)379-2222

Washington

Bed & Breakfast Guild . . . (509) 838-1891

Anacortes

Fidalgo Island B&B Guild . (206)293-4792

Friday Harbor

B&B Association of San Juan Island
. . . . (360)378-5464

Langley

Whidbey Island B&B Association
. . . . (206)678-3115

Leavenworth

Leavenworth Area B&B Association
. . . . (509)548-7171

Lopez

Island B&B Inns of Distinction
. . . . (206)468-2253

Maple Valley

Suburban Seattle B&B Association
. . . . (206)432-1409

Seattle

Seattle B&B Association . . (206)522-2536

Spokane

B&B of Spokane Association
. . . . (509)624-3776

West Virginia

Parkersburg

B&B Network of West Virginia
. . . . (304)485-1458

Wisconsin

Delavan

Wisconsin B&B Homes and Historic Inns
. . . . (715)536-2507

Merrill

Wisconsin Bed & Breakfast Association
. . . . (715)536-2507 (800)432-8747

Sparta

B&B Innkeepers Assoc. of Wisconsin
. . . . (608)269-3894

Wyoming

Wyoming Homestay/Outdoor Adventure
. . . . (307) 358-2380

Jackson

Jackson Hole B&B Association
. . . . (800)542-2632

CANADA

Western Canada

B&B Innkeepers Association
. . . . (604) 255-9199

The Road Best Traveled's Top 50 Inns

These selections were made by the Road Best Traveled® newsletter. The only distinction made is between the top 20 and the next 30.

The Top 20

The Inn at Little Washington
Washington, Va.

Spencer House
San Francisco, Calif.

Great Oak Manor
Chestertown, Md.

Fairview
Jackson, Miss.

The Queen Victoria
Cape May, N.J.

King's Cottage
Lancaster, Penn.

La Colombe D'or
Houston, Texas

Beaufort Inn
Beaufort, S.C.

John Rutledge House Inn
Charleston, S.C.

Shelburne Inn
Seaview, Wash.

Dairy Hollow House
Eureka Springs, Ark.

The Inn at Mitchell House
Chestertown, Md.

Rose Inn
Ithaca, N.Y

The Fearrington House
Pittsboro, N.C.

L'Auberge Provencale
White Post, Va.

Guest House Cottages, A B&B Inn
Whidbey Island, Greenbank, Wash.

The Scofield House B&B
Sturgeon Bay, Wis.

Chateau du Sureau
Oakhurst, Calif.

The Mainstay Inn
Cape May, N.J.

Maison Fleurie
Yountville, Calif.

. . . the next 30

The Inn on Mt. Ada
Avalon, Calif.

Carter House Inn
Eureka, Calif.

Green Gables
Pacific Grove, Calif.

The Coombs House Inn
Apalachicola, Fla.

Madewood Plantation
Napoleonville, La.

Gross Coate Plantation
Easton, Md.

A Cambridge House
Cambridge, Mass.

Mountain Timbers Lodge
West Glacier, Mont.

Richmond Hill Inn
Asheville, N.C.

Thomas Bond House
Philadelphia, Pa.

Bailiwick Inn
Fairfax, Va.

Williamsburg Sampler
Williamsburg, Va.

Channel Road Inn
Santa Monica, Calif

Blue Lake Ranch
Hesperus (Near Durango), Colo.

Boulders Inn
New Preston, Conn.

Manor House
Norfolk, Conn.

Poipu Bed & Breakfast
Poipu Beach, Kauai, Hawaii

Historic Pinehill B&B
Oregon, Ill.

The Inn at Buckeystown
Buckeystown, Md.

Windflower Inn
Great Barrington, Mass.

St. James Hotel
Red Wing, Minn.

The White Oak Inn
Danville, Ohio

Campbell House Inn
Eugene, Ore.

The Inn at Weathersfield
Weathersfield, Vt.

The Whitehall Inn
New Hope, Penn.

Cliffside Inn
Newport, R.I.

The Inn at Depot Hill
Capitola-by-the-Sea, Calif.

Grand Victorian B&B Inn
Bellaire, Mich.

White Swan Inn
San Francisco, Calif.

The Keeper's House
Isle Au Haut, Maine

The Road Best Traveled's Most Romantic Inns

These selections were made by the Road Best Traveled® newsletter. The inns are listed randomly.

10 Most Romantic Inns for 1996

The Inn at Depot Hill
Capitola-by-the-Sea, Calif.

School House B&B Inn
Rocheport, Mo.

Durham House B&B
Houston, Texas

Manor House
Norfolk, Conn.

Maison Fleurie
Yountville, Calif.

L'Auberge Provencale
White Post, Va.

Rose Inn
Ithaca, N.Y.

Mainstay Inn
Cape May, N.J.

Ann Starrett Mansion
Port Townsend, Wash.

St. James Hotel
Red Wing, Minn.

10 Most Romantic Inns for 1995

The Inn at Canoe Point
Bar Harbor, Maine

Blantyre
Lenox, Mass.

The Fearrington House
Pittsboro, N.C.

Kings Courtyard Inn
Charleston, S.C.

Ravenwood Castle
New Plymouth, Ohio

Anchuca Mansion
Vicksburg, Miss.

Casa Europa
Taos, N.M.

The Inn on Mt. Ada
Avalon, Calif.

The Lost Whale Inn
Trinidad, Calif.

Lahaina Inn
Maui, Hawaii

Best Waterfront Inns

12 of the Best Waterfront Inns

Whether you are looking to escape the winter chill or you are trying to find the perfect romantic interlude, the waterfront rarely fails. The Road Best Traveled® newsletter searched the country for 12 waterfront properties that are special places to rest the mind, body and soul.

Elizabeth Pointe Lodge
Amelia Island, Fla.

Canoe Bay Inn & Cottages
Chetek, Wis.

Blue Lantern Inn
Dana Point, Calif.

Great Oak Manor
Chestertown, Md.

Crescent House B&B
Sarasota, Fla.

The Club Continental Suites
Orange Park, Fla.

Kailua Plantation House
Kailua, Kona, Hawaii

The Inn at Harbor Head
Kennebunkport, Maine

Steamboat Inn
Steamboat, Ore.

Cliff House & Seacliff Cottage
Freeland, Wash.

Green Gables Inn
Pacific Grove, Calif.

Harrison House
Edmonds, Wash.

SUMMER ON THE CAPE: Beaches, quaint villages, cafes attract thousands.

One thing to note is that high season in these Massachusetts hot spots, runs from about mid-May to Columbus Day. During low season, many shops, restaurants, inns and B&Bs shut down, and the population of the towns drop by the thousands.

Cape Cod

Cape Cod is located on a 70-mile stretch of peninsula in southern Massachusetts. If you check out a state map, you'll recognize it as the land that jets off the coast like a hook. Located within Cape Cod are many little villages and towns, as well as Pilgrim's Heights, where the Mayflower actually landed.

It is quite fashionable to "summer" on the Cape, and the history, beauty and beaches are three reasons why guests flock here.

Check out these cities, for where to stay in Cape Cod: Barnstable, Chatham, Dennis, East Orleans, East Sandwich, Eastham, Falmouth, Falmouth Heights, Harwich Port, Hyannis Port, Orleans, Provincetown, Sandwich, South Dennis, Wellfleet, West Harwich, West Yarmouth, Woods Hole and Yarmouth.

Recommended Restaurants

Note: For the northern end of the Cape, one innkeeper commented that during the high season, there are more than 300 restaurants open from hot dog stands to elegant dining. In fact, throughout the Cape, more than 500 restaurants are open during the high season, which is more restaurants per capita than anywhere else in the United States. So these are just a few of the many, many, many choices. Comments were made by Cape Cod innkeepers.

Landfall (Woods Hole)
(508) 548-1758

Comment: Wonderful reputation with a well-rounded menu.

Martin House (Provincetown)
(508) 487-1327

Comment: Located in the second oldest house in town. Quaint New England austere setting and best dessert in town.

Oysters Too (Falmouth)
(508) 548-9191

Comment: This restaurant, located on Rt. 28, has a spectacular new chef. Cuisine is in the medium price bracket.

Shucker's (Falmouth)
(508) 540-3850.

Comment: As 80 percent of the seating here is outdoors, this eatery is open from mid-May to Columbus Day only. Overlooks the harbor and yacht basin. Also billed as "world famous."

Activities

Note: Each little town on the Cape offers something. Shops, restaurants, museums and galleries are scattered along the way. You'll find much of the Cape is charming with a lot of New England flavor. Hyannis is the most urban of the cities, and it's here that you can find malls, fast food and other bastions of suburban life.

Cape Cod Factory Stores (Sagamore)
(508) 888-8417

This is the Cape's largest factory outlet, open seven days a week. From Monday to Saturday, the hours are 9:30 a.m. to 9 p.m. On Sunday, hours are 10 a.m. to 6 p.m.

Cape Cod National Seashore

Beautiful (albeit chilly) beaches, guided and self-guided walks, a museum and gift shop all are to be found at this seashore located on Rt. 6 in Eastham. The shore is open from 9 a.m. to 6 p.m. from late June to Labor Day, and 9 a.m. to 4:30 p.m. daily in the off-season times. The shore is open only on weekends in January and February.

Christmas Tree Shops

With locations in Falmouth, Hyannis, Orleans, Sagamore, West Dennis, West Yarmouth and Yarmouth, it's the place to go for bargains on housewares, Chinese porcelain and more.

Plimoth Plantation (Plymouth)

(508) 746-1622

OK, this isn't actually on Cape Cod. It's close (unless you're staying in Provincetown) and worth a trip, especially for those who opt to stay in the Woods Hole, Falmouth, Sandwich parts of Cape Cod. The plantation, which is also close to Plymouth Rock, is an authentic recreation of the actual 1627 Pilgrim settlement. Guests also can walk a ways and tour Wampanoag and view how Native Americans lived prior to the Pilgrims' arrival. Don't forget the Mayflower II, a replica of the famous ship that took the Pilgrims on their famous voyage to the New World.

The staff at Plimoth Plantation suggests setting aside three to four hours for your tour and an additional hour for a tour of Mayflower II.

Hours: The plantation is not open all year, but during its season, the hours are 9 a.m. to 5 p.m. Monday to Sunday.

Tickets: Admission to Plimoth Plantation is $15 for adults and $9 for youth; admission to Mayflower II is $5.50 for adults and $3.75 for youth. For admission to both, the price is $18.50 for adults and $11 for youth. Youth ages are from 6 to 17. Children 5 and younger get in for free.

Whale Watching

Several companies can take you out to view the many varieties of cetaceans that also enjoy Cape Cod's waters.

Portuguese Princess Whale Watch of Provincetown (Provincetown)

(508) 487-2651 or (508) 487-3901

The Dolphin Fleet of Provincetown (Provincetown)

(800) 826-9300

Whale Watcher Cruises

(508) 362-6088

Martha's Vineyard

Martha's Vineyard is an island south of the edge where Cape Cod joins with the rest of Massachusetts. On a trip to The Vineyard, you'll be refreshingly free of fast-food joints and tourist boutiques. Instead, you'll find an idyllic assortment of seaside villages with many a country inn or bed & breakfast. As only one ferry out to the island takes autos, some tourists opt to rent a car at the airport. The Vineyard is packed during the summer, so if you plan to stay during this peak season, be sure to make reservations for lodging and car rentals many months in advance. There are shuttles on the island, so you probably can do well without a car.

Check out these cities, for where to stay in Martha's Vineyard: Chilmark, Edgartown, Oak Bluffs, Gay Head, Menemsha, Vineyard Haven and West Tisbury.

How to Get There

By air, one can book passage aboard Cape Air at (800) 352-0714, which has flights from Boston, New Bedford, Hyannis and Nantucket. Air New England at (508) 693-8899 also offer flights from select cities.

By sea, there are ferries from Falmouth (508) 548-9400; Hyannis (508) 548-9400; New Bedford (508) 997-1688; and Woods Hole (508) 477-8600.

Note: The Woods Hole ferry is the only one that allows cars, and in the summer, make car ferry reservations well in advance or you probably will be out of luck.

Recommended Restaurants

Black Dog Tavern (Vineyard Haven)

(508) 693-9223

Comment: The most popular restaurant on the island, everyone buys a Black Dog T-shirt.

The Home Port (Menemsha)

(508) 645-2679

Comment: Seafood extraordinaire.

Lola's (Oak Bluffs)

(508) 645-2679

Comment: One of the most popular, serves Southern Creole cuisine.

Outermost Inn (Gay Head)
(508) 645-3511

Comment: Dining room at this inn offers dinners Spring through Fall, cuisine with a Continental flavor.

Activities

Note: For 4th of July fireworks, two spots in Oak Bluffs spring to mind. One, the Ocean Park Gazebo and the other, State Beach.

The Beach

Many are private, so check with your innkeeper as he or she will probably be in the know as to which beaches are open to the public and which are the best.

Chicamo Vineyards (West Tisbury)
(508) 693-0309

What would a trip to "The Vineyard" be without a visit to its only commercial vineyard and winery. Open from Memorial Day to Columbus Day.

The Flying Horses (Oak Bluffs)
(508) 693-9481

This is the oldest operating carousel in the United States and was hand-carved in 1876. The carousel is open from 10 a.m. to 10 p.m. every day from Memorial Day until Labor Day. From then, it is open weekends only until Columbus Day.

Oak Bluffs Harbor (Oak Bluffs)

In the summer, more than 4,000 boats crowd the harbor. The boardwalk offers a selection of shops.

Shopping

If you want commercialism, head back to the mainland. What you'll find in Martha's Vineyard is few stores, but ones that display fine craftsmanship.

The Vincent House (Edgartown)
(508) 627-8619

This museum is the oldest house in The Vineyard, and offers a look at three centuries of life on the island. Also consider a tour at the adjacent Daniel Fisher House.

Vineyard Museum (Edgartown)
(508) 627-4441

Maritime and whaling exhibits are among the items to see at this museum, which is open all week from July 5 to Labor Day, 10 a.m. to 4:30 p.m. During the rest of the year, the museum is open from 1 p.m. to 4 p.m. on Wednesday through Friday and 10 a.m. to 4 p.m. on Saturday.

West Tisbury

With its old-fashioned general store and town hall, this is a good place to experience what a quaint New England village is all about.

HOT SPOTS—CAPE MAY, N.J.

ON THE SHORE: Visit a Victorian paradise on the New Jersey coast.

Just a few miles down the coast from the bright lights and casinos of Atlantic City, visitors will find Cape May, an almost magical Victorian town.

Although some might complain of the commercialism found in the souvenir shops, the hand of modern tourism does not extend its reach to the rows of restored Victorian houses, which line Cape May's streets. The homes are like rainbows, painted in every imaginable color, from purple to green to aquamarine.

We arrived one early September morning on the Cape May-Lewes Ferry, which runs, much as the name suggests from Lewes, Del., to Cape May and vice-versa. Lewes has the distinction of being the oldest town in the oldest state. The ferry carries both cars and walk-on passengers, and has a small snack bar and souvenir shop and video arcade. We bypassed the arcade and souvenir shop to sample hot dogs and count the jellyfish along the 70-minute ride.

For those planning a trip to Cape May, the truly difficult part is deciding at which bed & breakfast to stay. Many of the restored Victorians have been transformed into graciously appointed inns. Competition for guests is fierce, so the quality remains fairly high and consistent among the inns. Note: Parking is sometimes hard to find. Most inns offer parking to load and unload cars, but guests must find on-street parking elsewhere.

There's plenty to do and see in Cape May. It's always bustling in the summer, and again at Christmas, which is a beautiful sight.

Attractions

The Beach: For those unfamiliar with New Jersey, guests must have a pass in order to visit the actual beach. Some innkeepers provide these for their guests.

Cape May-Lewes Ferry
(800) 64-FERRY

The one-way fare for cars, minivans and small trucks is $18, which includes the driver's fare. Motorcycle drivers must pay $15, and bicyclists pay $5. Additional passengers age 12 and older pay $4.50 each. Tickets for children ages six to 12 cost $2.25. Children five and younger ride for free.

Emlen Physick Estate
1048 Washington St.

Tours are available of this Victorian house museum, which was built in 1879.

Mid-Atlantic Center for the Arts
1048 Washington St. (609) 884-5404

This is a good starting point. Visitors can receive maps and tour information. Be sure to ask about special events. With so much going on, it's also wise to call ahead and request a calendar of events.

The Nature Center of Cape May
1600 Delaware Ave. (609) 884-9590

Children often enjoy visits here. The center offers classes, workshops, walking tours and features exhibits.

Cape May Point Lighthouse and State Park
(609) 884-8656.

This completely restored 1859 lighthouse is a popular attraction. The lighthouse, a short drive from the main village, is open from May to November.

DOWN SOUTH: History abounds in this majestic Carolina town.

Charleston, in South Carolina's picturesque Low Country, has long been recognized as one the nation's top cities. Conde Nast Traveler readers have rated Charleston not only as a top U.S. city, but as one of the world's best. With its multitude of attractions from historic sites to golf, as well as fine restaurants and outstanding inns, it's little wonder why it's a top vacation spot.

Recommended Restaurants

Anson
(803) 577-0551

Comment: Located in the old city market, specializes in fresh, local seafood.

Bocci's Italian Restaurant
(803) 720-212

Comment: For excellent, Northern Italian fare.

Magnolia's-Uptown/Down South
(803) 577-7771

Comment: Good Low Country food.

Mint Juleps Fine Southern Dining
(803) 853-6468

Comment: More good Low Country food.

Planters Café
(803) 723-0700

Comment: This is the restaurant at the four-diamond rated Planters Inn.

Activities

Note: In addition to regular public transportation, the downtown area is served by the Downtown Area Shuttle (DASH), a fleet of trolley car-like trams. A one-day pass is $2 and a three-day pass is $5. Maps are available through the visitors bureau and at many inns and hotels.

African-American National Heritage Museum

Four different sites comprise this museum.

The Slave Mart Museum, (803) 724-7395, is located in Charleston's historic district. Slave auctions were held here, and the museum now serves to recognize the contribution and struggle of African Americans from the time of their arrival in 1670 to the Civil Rights Movement.

McCleod Plantation, (803) 723-1623, on James Island offers a glimpse of life on a plantation. More than 70 slaves worked here, producing one of the South's largest cotton crops.

The Aiken-Rhett House, (803) 723-1159, was the governor's residence as the first Civil War shots were fired at Fort Sumter.

Avery Research Center, (803) 727-2009, was established more than a decade ago out of what was the Avery Normal Institute, a school established just after the Civil War ended to educate young African Americans.

Fort Sumter

(803) 722-1691

Visit the spot where the Civil War began back in 1861. The fort is located on a manmade island at the entrance to Charleston Harbor. Fort Sumter Tours offers trips aboard sightseeing yachts to the fort from the City Marina and Patriots Point. The 2-hour and 15-minute trip includes a tour of the fort and harbor.

Tickets are $10 for adults and $4.25 for children under 12. Children six and younger tour for free.

Gardens

The South is known for its beautiful gardens and Charleston is no exception. For half a century, the annual Festival of Houses and Gardens has drawn visitors during the spring. Other options include the Cypress Gardens, Magnolia Plantation and Gardens, and Middleton Place.

Cypress Gardens: Visitors here can enjoy what once was part of an important rice plantation. Explore the swamp by boat or roam the colorful gardens. Admission rates are subject to change, for more information, call (803) 553-0515.

Magnolia Plantation: The plantation, built in the 17th century, is listed in the National Register of Historic Places and was occupied by the original family for 10 generations. There is an herb garden, Biblical garden, horticultural maze and a topiary garden. A newer addition is the Audubon Swamp Garden. For more information, call (803) 571-1266.

Middleton Place: Enjoy America's oldest landscaped gardens, dating back more than 250 years. The gardens are located on an 18th-century plantation. For more information, call (803) 556-6020.

The Ghosts of Charleston

(803) 723-1670 or (800) 854-1670.

Visitors can take a unique tour of haunted Charleston, led by local supernatural researchers. Among the ghostly sites are several haunted bed & breakfasts. The cost is $12 per person, and tours are available in the morning, early evening or, as the brochure states, "under the veil of darkness, (insert evil laugh here now)." The tour may not be appropriate for children under 10.

Golfing

Charleston was the site of the first U.S. golf course, established in 1786. Two centuries later, there are many, many courses. Several of which are ranked as top golfing picks by the likes of Golf magazine and Golf Digest.

For a guide to Low Country golfing, call Charleston Golf, Inc. at (800) 774-4444.

Historic Homes

There are dozens of historic city homes, buildings and plantations in Charleston. For sites in historic Charleston, call the Historic Charleston Foundation at (803) 723-1623. Also check out the Charleston section in this guide, as many of the inns have fascinating histories. The Charleston Trident Convention and Visitors Bureau, (803) 853-8000, also has information about historic homes and Low Country plantations. One can also receive a hefty visitors packet from this bureau.

OZARK RETREAT: This eclectic little town offers hot springs, variety of B&Bs

If you're looking for a place to immerse yourself in the Victorian era, Eureka Springs just might be the right place for you.

The town's early beginnings were of a place known for the healing waters that bubbled from its springs. Early Native Americans called the area "Sacred Ground."

Because of its early popularity, the town grew at an accelerated pace, undergoing 25 years of normal 19th-century building and civic growth in only two years.

After a period of no growth, the town was revitalized and became listed in the National Register of Historic Places.

Nearly all of the town is part of the historic district with Victorian homes and other structures dating back to the late 1800s.

The hand-hewn stone hotels, bathhouses, churches, civic and commercial buildings still serve the town.

Once in town, stepping back in time is quite easy. Horse-drawn carriage rides go up and down Eureka Springs' famed boulevard with its stately homes. An oil burning train leaves the Eureka Springs depot and winds its way through the Ozark Mountains.

Back in town, a first stop for the traveler might be the Eureka Springs Historical Museum, which was built in 1889 and turned into a museum in 1971.

Walking tours are another way to get a good feel for the town. Maps and brochures are available at the Chamber of Commerce, which is located at the downtown trolley depot.

If you'd like to take a little of the town home with you, exploring the antique shops just might be for you.

For watersport enthusiasts, Eureka Springs is surrounded by lakes, prime for fishing and boating. Or for the more adventurous, rent a canoe and paddle down the White River.

Rounding out a trip to Eureka Springs would be a stay at one of the town's many bed & breakfasts. Some 50 inns serve travelers.

Phyllis Becker, innkeeper at the Crescent Cottage also offered these notable restaurants for Eureka Springs visitors. The first three offer more elegant surroundings. Center St. South is considered funky and eclectic, while Autumn Breeze is a good place for lunch and desserts.

Recommended Restaurants

Cottage Inn
(501) 253-5282

Ermillios
(501) 253-8806

Chez Charles
(501) 253-9509

Center St. South
253-8100

Autumn Breeze
(501) 253-7734

HOT SPOTS—LANCASTER COUNTY, PENN.

AMISH COUNTRY: Barn raisings and buggies will take you into a quieter era.

For much of Lancaster County it's as if time stood still. Here, in the heart of Pennsylvania Dutch Country, the Amish people still travel by horse and buggy and still dress in the plain costumes of the many generations that came before.

Besides the Amish, there are Mennonite and Brethren people who also live in Lancaster County. Their farm markets, county auctions and home businesses often are open to those interested in getting a glimpse of their lifestyle.

Although the image of an Amish buggy traveling gently down a rolling country road is an image burned on the minds of many of us familiar with Lancaster County, the area is a place rich in American history.

The county once became known as the "Gateway to the West" because the Old Philadelphia Pike passed through for those traveling west to the Allegheny Mountains. To accommodate travelers, inns were built every few miles.

Today, many of the inns still serve travelers looking to get in touch with the history of the land.

Many historic towns and villages comprise Lancaster County including Adamstown, Bird-in-Hand, Columbia, Ephrata, Intercourse, Lancaster, Lititz, Paradise and Strasburg.

Columbia is a 200-year-old community established by an English Quaker. The Quaker settled by the banks of the Susquehanna River to preach to the Native Americans.

Columbia was two votes shy of becoming the capitol of the United States. The Columbian, which is an inn in town, has a brochure that describes the town like this, "It is a 'porch-sitting' town where you can still get a vanilla coke or a malted at the local drugstore."

It seems only fitting that a visitor to Lancaster County find respite at a place of history. There are a myriad of choices from simple farmhouses to manor houses to historic inns.

Aside from the many inns and bed & breakfasts listed below, travelers also can stay in a variety of B&Bs run by Mennonite families. For a list of such places or more information, call the Mennonite Information Service at (717) 299-0954.

Attractions

In addition to the following attractions, there are dozens of antique stores, shops, restaurants and museums in the area. Our list doesn't even begin to scratch the surface of all there is to see and do in the area.

To obtain a visitors' package, call the Pennsylvania Dutch Convention & Visitor's Bureau at (800) PA-DUTCH, ext. 2474.

The Bridges of Lancaster Country

There are 28 historic, covered bridges in Lancaster County, and a map marking these picturesque sites can be obtained by contacting the visitor's bureau.

Lancaster

This historic village served as the U.S. Capitol for one day when the Continental Congress met here in 1777 to escape British troops.

Among its interesting sites are Fulton Opera House, the nation's oldest theater in continuous operation; a circa 1850 prison designed to look like an English castle; and Trinity Lutheran Church, which dates back to 1729, and until 1800, its steeple was the tallest structure west of Philadelphia.

The Central Market

Located in Lancaster, this market has been open every Tuesday and Friday since the mid-1700s. Visitors will find a variety of goods at this historic gathering of farmers, butchers and bakers.

The Amish Farm & Home

This 1805 home is located just outside of Lancaster on Rt. 30 East. The home and surrounding working farm offer a glimpse of the lifestyle of the Old Order Amish.

There also is a gift shop and museum on the premises. Tickets are $5 for adults and $3 for children ages 5 to 7.

For more information, call (717) 394-6185.

The Strasburg Railroad

Enjoy a ride aboard one of the nation's oldest steam trains. Amish farms are among the sites along the way.

For more information, call (717) 687-7522.

MONTEREY PENINSULA:
To many, its rugged coastline is an unsurpassed sight.

Half a day's drive north of Los Angeles and just four hours south of San Francisco, set along the rugged central California coast, lies the area immortalized in John Steinbeck's "Cannery Row." While today's Cannery Row is decidedly a different one from the days when people toiled long hours packing fish, there is something surreal about this place.

Jagged coastline, forested hills and quaint, timeless villages are surrounded by old Victorians, Spanish-style haciendas, million-dollar estates and a collection of quirky, California cottages. For years, the Carmel Valley, has been a welcoming place for the rich and famous, eager to escape Hollywood or the corporate world.

Today, the towns of Carmel, Monterey and Pacific Grove welcome hundreds of thousands of travelers each year, many opting for the multitude of charming, memorable bed & breakfast inns that line the coast. Golfers, shoppers, artists, Epicureans and naturalists alike should have no trouble filling a long weekend.

Recommended Restaurants

Dominico's On The Wharf (Monterey)
(408) 372-3655

El Crocodrilo (Pacific Grove)
(408) 655-3311

Fandangoes (Pacific Grove)
(408) 372-3456

Fishwise (Pacific Grove)
(408) 375-7107

Fresh Cream (Monterey)
(408) 375-9798

The Gallery (Monterey)
(408) 649-5127

Kincaid's (Carmel)
(408) 624-9626

Montrio (Monterey)
(408) 648-8880

Old Bath House (Pacific Grove)
(408) 375-5195

Paradiso Trattoria (Monterey)
(408) 375-4155

Pasta Mia (Pacific Grove)
(408) 375-7709

Rio Grill (Carmel)
(408) 625-5436

Attractions

Cannery Row (Monterey)
(408) 649-6690.

Monterey Bay Aquarium (Monterey)
(408) 648-4888.

This is a terrific aquarium and an ideal stopping point for families, conveniently located in Cannery Row.

Seventeen Mile Drive

This drive, around the Monterey Peninsula, costs $6 and begins at Lighthouse Avenue in Pacific Grove or off Highway 1 and North San Antonio Avenue in Carmel.

Monterey State Historic Park (Monterey)
(408) 649-7118.

Point Lobos State Reserve
(408) 624-4909.

Big Sur

Just south of Carmel is a breathtaking 26-mile drive down the coast.

WINE COUNTRY: Hundreds of vineyards await your tastebuds.

When one thinks of Napa, just a short hour drive from San Francisco, wine springs to mind and perhaps Steinbeck's "Grapes of Wrath." Whatever the image, this much is true, the wines of Napa Valley are some of the world's finest. The French may scoff, but critics around the world agree that the vineyards deserve recognition.

To be fair, the true wine country encompasses Napa and Sonoma counties, as well as a bit of Mendocino county. Within this space is the fertile soil that has encouraged hundreds of wineries to develop and prosper.

Check out these cities for where to stay in the wine country: Angwin, Calistoga, Geyserville, Guerneville, Healdsburg, Napa, Petaluma, Saint Helena, Santa Rosa, Sonoma and Yountville.

Recommended Restaurants

Napa, where a branch of the famed Culinary Institute of America is located (the main one is in Hyde Park, N.Y.), offers dozens and dozens of restaurant choices. Some innkeepers keep a selection of menus on hand to narrow down the vast array of eateries.

Bistro Don Giovanni's (Napa)
(707) 224-3300

Comment: Excellent food, innkeeper tested and approved.

La Boucan French Grill (Napa)
(707) 253-1177

Comment: Small restaurant serving excellent French cuisine.

Compadre's (Yountville)
(707) 944-2406

Comment: For good Mexican cuisine.

Domaine Chandon (Yountville)
(707) 944-8844

Comment: This restaurant is owned by the vineyard, a producer of sparkling wines. Advance reservations recommended.

The French Laundry (Yountville)
(707) 944-2380

Try this for a fine, elegant special occasion. Definitely make advance reservations.

Mustards Grill (Yountville)
(707) 944-2424

Comment: Although a fairly casual place, reservations are highly recommended.

Ristorante Piatti (Yountville)
(707) 944-2070

Comment: Good Italian choice, homemade pastas and pizzas.

Rutherford Grill (Rutherford)
(707) 963-1792

Wine Spectator Greystone Restaurant (St. Helena)
(707) 967-1010

Comment: A newer restaurant, run by the Culinary Institute of America's Napa Valley campus. Mediterranean cuisine.

Activities

Balloon Rides

Several companies offer scenic rides over the Napa Valley. Above the West, (800) 627-2759, offers a pre-flight breakfast before your trip, which costs $185 per person. At Balloon Aviation of Napa Valley, (800) 367-6272, guests enjoy pre-flight coffee and pastries, the trip itself and a post-flight champagne brunch all for $165 per person. Adventures Aloft, (800) 944-4408, also offers pre-flight goodies, the trip and a post-flight breakfast for $175 per person.

Napa Valley Wine Train (Napa)
(707) 253-2111, (800) 427-4124

Take a three-hour, 36-mile trek through this vast land of vineyards. Rates include anything from a basic deli lunch to a multi-course dinner. Wine and spirits are extra. Rates range from $24 per person for a trip with a deli lunch to $99 per person for the murder-mystery dinner theater.

Old Faithful Geyser
(807) 942-6463

One of the three Old Faithfuls, this geyser erupts approximately every 40 minutes. Located two miles from Calistoga.

Petrified Forest
(707) 942-6667

Millions of years ago volcanic ash covered some of California's beautiful redwoods, and now we can see the petrified results. Located six miles from Calistoga.

Russian River
(800) 253-8800

Swimming, fishing, canoeing, tubing and boating all are available here.

Wineries

There are dozens and dozens of vineyards and wineries here, producing some of the world's finest vintages. Tours and tastings are available at many, many, many of these wineries. For information, contact the Napa Convention and Visitors Bureau or try the Internet at napa-online.com, which lists the wineries and gives addresses, phone numbers and tour information.

SAN FRANCISCO: The city by the bay offers a little something for everyone.

San Francisco, created during the gold rush days, has long been considered one of the world's finest cities. From its intimidating hilly streets to its cable cars to its assortment of architecture, San Francisco is a place like no other. You'll find hundreds of great restaurants, an array of wonderful B&Bs and inns and plenty to see and do.

Recommended Restaurants

San Francisco is definitely one of the world's great food capitols. There are many, many great restaurants here, but these are few innkeeper recommendations.

Beetelnut
(415) 929-8855

Comment: Fantastic food, very unusual, refined Asian cuisine.

Boulevard
(415) 543-6084

Comment: An eclectic upper-end restaurant.

The Dining Room at the Ritz-Carlton
(415) 296-7465

Comment: For a formal dinner, a top-of-the-list choice.

Fleur de Lis
(415) 673-7779

Comment: A good place for a romantic and expensive treat.

House of Nanking
(415) 421-1429

Comment: Great Chinese, kind of a hole-in-the-wall establishment.

Masa's
(415) 989-7154

Comment: Considered one of the city's best, unique Chinese and French cuisine.

Oriental Pearl

Comment: Good for authentic Chinese, wonderful dim sum.

Postrio
(415) 776-7825

Comment: Popular with guests, one of Wolfgang Puck's creations (chef/owner of L.A.'s popular Spago and Chinois on Main).

Rose Pistola
(415) 399-0499

Comment: In North Beach, Italian done by one of the city's premier restaurateurs.

Rubicon
(415) 434-4100

Comment: Excellent, California-Mediterranean cuisine.

Activities

Alcatraz Island

(415) 546-2882

Be sure to reserve a ferry ride to "the Rock" well in advance. Al Capone and Machine Gun Kelly were two of the many inmates at this infamous high-security prison. Included in a tour is the ferry ride, an introduction with national park rangers about the prison, a slide show and self-guided cassette tour. The cassettes are available in six languages. It is recommended to plan two and a half hours for the complete tour.

Ferries to the island depart from Pier 41. On Monday through Friday, ferries depart at 9:30 a.m. and every 45 minutes until 2:45 p.m.. On Saturday, Sundays and holidays, ferries depart at 9:30 a.m. and continue every 30 minutes until 2:15 p.m.

Tickets for adults are $10, seniors age 62 and older pay $8.25, and for children ages five to 11, the cost is $4.75. Some group rates are available, and ferry departure times are subject to change. Tickets are non-refundable and non-exchangeable.

The ferry company, Red and White Fleet, also offers tours to Muir Woods and Golden Gate Bridge Park.

California Academy of Sciences

(415) 750-7145

This wonderful museum includes a planetarium, natural history museum and aquarium all in one. The museum is open 365 days a year from 10 a.m. to 5 p.m. This one is terrific for the entire family, and there is always a special featured exhibit. The museum is located in Golden Gate Park.

Chinatown

No longer is the influence strictly Chinese in the unique ethnic neighborhood. An influx of immigrants from Southeast Asia has added to the flavor of streets lined with restaurants, shops, markets and vegetable stands. Enter at the Grant Avenue entrance, flanked by the famous Chinatown Gate. At Grant Avenue and Stockman Street, you'll find Chinatown's busiest area. At Grant and Jackson, visit the city's largest tea emporium.

Coit Tower

(415) 362-0808

In Chicago it's Sears Tower, in New York it's the Empire State Building, in San Francisco, the place to catch a great view of the city is Coit Tower. Tickets are $3.

Fisherman's Wharf

Touristy, but a necessity for those new to the city. Restaurants and shops line the way, and it is here where one catches a ride to Alcatraz. On a cool, foggy day, we recommend a stop at the Buena Vista for an Irish coffee. Or even on a bright, sunny day, we recommend an Irish coffee at the Buena Vista.

The Wharf begins at Pier 39 and continues on to Ghiradelli Square with shops and restaurants lining the way. At Pier 39, you'll find plenty of family fare from sea lions to the Cable Car Company to Underwater World.

Golden Gate Park

Among the notables in this 1,000-acre park are a Victorian crystal palace, the Asian Art Museum (415) 668-7855 and the Japanese Tea Garden (415) 752-1171. The California Academy of Sciences (above) also is located here, as are gardens and a children's park.

North Beach

Chinese immigrants created Chinatown and Italian immigrants created North Beach. This is the place for Italian food, a cup of espresso and nightlife. Although some of the nightclubs make this a not-so appropriate place for kids, it's full of adult fun.

San Francisco Museum of Modern Art

(415) 357-4000

Whether it be paintings or sculpture, there's always something new and exciting to see at this museum, which displays works from some of the world's best modern artists. The museum is closed on Mondays.

The hours Tuesday, Wednesday and Friday are 11 a.m. to 6 p.m. On Thursday, the hours are 11 a.m. to 9 p.m. On weekends, the museum is open from 11 a.m. to 6 p.m.

Our detailed articles on hot spots are just a few of the areas where you'll find a large assortment of fine bed & breakfasts or country inns. There are plenty of other cities that are not only fun to visit, but offer many wonderful B&B and inn choices.

Victoria, B.C.

With its plethora of historic buildings, the Butchart Gardens, Parliament buildings and Craigdarroch Castle, a trip to Victoria is a bit reminiscent of Europe with the added bonus of the West Coast's spectacular scenery. There are an abundance of turn-of-the-century and early 20th-century homes and buildings to enjoy, some of which now are inns and B&Bs.

Eureka, Calif.

As the lumber industry grew, Eureka boomed with it. Historic homes, including many stunning Victorians are what you'll find, as well as the grand redwood forests.

Julian, Calif.

Julian is Southern California's only gold rush town, and here you can pan for gold or visit a gold mine. Julian also is famous for its apples, and there are plenty of places to enjoy an apple pie.

Key West, Fla.

The beach is the big draw at this tropical paradise, but museums, the Hemingway House, the Little White House, the historic district, shops and restaurants are other draws.

St. Augustine, Fla.

This, the nation's oldest city, was founded in 1565. St. Augustine has a distinctly Spanish flavor and many historic sites, from museums to the Fountain of Youth.

Stillwater, Minn.

A collection of picturesque Victorians, many of which are bed & breakfast inns, make this Midwestern town a charming place to visit. Christmas, albeit cold, is an especially nice time here with all the decorations and the annual Christmas Tour and Tea, where visitors get a glimpse of historic homes while sampling gourmet tidbits.

Natchez, Miss.

This historic Southern town is a perfect place to begin a journey up the Natchez Trace, a road which leads from the Deep South into Tennessee. Plantations and historic homes line the way, and the Mississippi River is another draw to this town.

Santa Fe, N.M.

Although the West has long been thought of as a baby by Easterners who stepped off the Mayflower, Santa Fe is the second oldest city in the nation. Santa Fe's Native American, Mexican and Spanish influences are clearly evident, from the architecture to the cuisine. Its rich history, beautiful scenery and great skiing are three reasons why travelers flock here every year.

Taos, N.M.

Taos, an unpretentious little town of 5,000, is known for many things. Writer D.H. Lawrence helped put the community on the map as a colony for writers and artists. Its Spanish and Native American tradition have made it a place of history, including the Taos Pueblo, a designated World Heritage Site. Its mountains beckon thousands of skiers each year.

Newport, R.I.

Millionaires flocked to this seaside town, building what now is known as the Newport Mansions. Aside from that the harbor, Tennis Hall of Fame, museums, shops, restaurants, historic sites and the Untied States' oldest operating tavern draw thousands of visitors each year.

San Antonio, Texas

Texans always have known that rustic San Antonio was a treasure. In the last decade or so, the rest of the country has been discovering the town. Many of the city's inns and B&Bs are located in the King William Historic District. The Alamo, Fort Sam Houston, museums, restaurants and the Riverwalk are some of the popular attractions.

NEW CAREER: Homework is essential in order to pass the innkeeping test.

Nearly everyone who visits inns has entertained notions of being an innkeeper at some time in their lives. It often happens when people first stay at a really well-run bed & breakfast. They take in the beautiful, serene surroundings, meet their cordial, seemingly unruffled innkeeper, and think dreamily, "I could do this."

Well, you probably can. Innkeeping is one of the few sought-after professions that requires very little formal training. Ask innkeepers what their occupations were before they started running an inn and you'll get all kinds of answers — corporate work, computer company owners, playwrights, bankers, nursing, teaching, sales — anything, usually, but hotel management. Most innkeepers have made their escape from a high-powered, high-stress job or a nine-to-five office and commuting grind. When your work day begins by going downstairs to the kitchen and turning on the coffee machine — well, it's easy to understand the lure.

Yes, you can do it. And if you have a dream, it can crystallize into something that becomes, as Crescent Dragonwagon of the Dairy Hollow House says, "is much more joy than we imagined...". And she continues, "It is a rare privilege to be able to offer something that is better than people had imagined, to watch them melt on the floor with pleasure and surprise that such a thing can be..." [1]

It is also "much more work ...than we imagined" she says. But it can be done — if you love being around people all the time, don't mind long hours, hard physical work, very little money or time to yourself and wearing many hats at once. If you have carpentry, gardening, cooking and business-marketing skills, it's also a good start. An innkeeper is much like the director of a film and guests are the audience — they see only the finished product, not all of the work and sweat that went into making it look that way.

Today, however, it's not enough to reel out the same old "film." With more than 15,000 bed & breakfast inns and country inns and 10,000 homestays across the nation, it will not be easy to rise above the competition. B&Bs and country inns now comprise 25 percent of all lodging properties. In a crowded B&B market, innkeepers who are making it financially are those who offer exceptional quality and character and know how to make themselves known.

When B&Bs were first opening 15 or 20 years ago, there were hardly any learning resources for the aspiring innkeeper — you just jumped into it and learned as you went along. Now, however, innkeeping is taken much more seriously, and the only way to stay ahead of the game is to view it as a professional business. Take a look at any successful inn today and you'll find an innkeeper who has done more than his or her share of homework.

Beginning your research

Where do you start? Begin by reading books and trade journals on the subject (see the resource list at the end of this article) to get an overview of the profession. Take innkeeping classes or workshops. If you're still not sure whether innkeeping is for you, try interning as an innkeeper at a nearby inn.

Before, and even after, you have started your own B&B, visit as many other inns — successful inns — as you can. Traveling to a well-conceived inn is like taking a mini-course in innkeeping — it gives one a better awareness of what appeals to guests and

---

[1] The Dairy Hollow House cookbook, Crescent Dragonwagon, Jan Brown, Macmillan Publishing Co., New York, NY. c. 1986

what satisfies their needs, such as amenities, projecting a sense of hospitality, special services and the many tiny details that go into creating a great lodging experience. Not only can you pick up countless new ideas at other inns, but playing the role of the guest is something all innkeepers should practice now and then.

Types of Bed & Breakfasts

Next, you should decide what type of B&B you want — a homestay, a bed & breakfast inn, urban inn or country inn — and clearly define your goals.

Here are some characteristics of the different types of bed & breakfasts:

HOMESTAY:

—Individually decorated.
—One to five guest rooms.
—Advertising may be prohibited.
—Signage often not allowed.
—Hobby business to produce extra income. Owners usually work outside the B&B.
—Owner operated.
—Primarily functions as owner's home.
—Low occupancy and frequent closures.

BED & BREAKFAST INN:

—Individually decorated.
—May or may not have TVs, phones in the room.
—Usually has a common room.
—Continental or full breakfast is included in rates.
—A commercial business that can be sold.
—Can advertise and signage is allowed.
—Full-time occupation, not a hobby business.
—Two to 30 rooms.
—Usually collects bed tax and meets all local license requirements.
—Usually owner-operated.

URBAN INN:

—Similar to B&B inn.
—Centrally located in a city location.
—Often offers business traveler amenities.

COUNTRY INN:

—Similar to B&B inn.
—Generally implies a dining room and offers both breakfast and dinner.
—Breakfasts may or may not be included in the rates.

Location

The most important aspect of starting an inn is choosing a location. If you simply want to preserve your great-grandmother's house no matter what it takes, then there is no decision on location. Likewise, if you've inherited the property, and there is no mortgage payment to meet. (However, you may be better off to sell the inherited building and buy a more appropriate property.) If you envision a hobby type business and you have another source of income, this is also the case. However, if you plan to make a career of innkeeping, choosing a location is the most important decision you will make.

In a nationwide survey of innkeepers, we asked "With the knowledge you have now, what would you do differently at your inn if you could start over?"

The most frequent answers given were "picking a better location" and "having more rooms."

But innkeepers went on to describe the better location. They said they needed to be closer to the theater district, within walking distance of the most popular attraction in town, be lakefront instead of across the street from the water, or be on the main street in town. Some wished they would have picked an area that had more year-round traffic and less seasonal business. In retrospect, most wished they could have paid the extra price for a better location.

Consultant and innkeeper Carl Glassman in an article for the *The Journal for Innkeepers,* says, "Indeed, certain destinations ... are approaching saturation. However, there are many other geographic areas in the country that are ripe for inn lodgings, such as mid-size destination cities ... In addition, new inns serving distinct, well-researched market segments continue to open and thrive even in established destinations."

In an article from Norm Strasma's *Inn Marketing*, Dec. '96 issue, titled "Hottest Hotel Markets in the United States," attributes of the top 10 hotel markets included the following:

—Most were in the largest population centers in their state.
—Each was a major commercial center.

—Some were major port cities.
—Attractions included prominent cultural and educational institutions; some had professional sports teams.
—Five were centers for high-technology and computer research.
—Each of the 10 had multiple natural, historical and recreational attractions.

We offer a location test that we developed during our years of teaching "How to Start a Bed & Breakfast" in the California University system. This is one way to begin to evaluate a location. For the most accurate results, objectivity is important.

Location test

Score points and half-points and add up your total at the end.

Population centers. If the inn is within a two-hour drive of a large population area, score one point per million. For population centers farther away — within a four-hour drive — score a half a point per million population.

If there are other B&Bs and country inns within five miles, score a half point for each. If there are none, deduct four points.

If occupancy rates are 60 percent year-round in small hotels and motels in the area, add two points.

If the occupancy rate is more than 70 percent, add two additional points.

Have occupancy rates dropped in last year? Deduct two points for each percentage drop. (Information about occupancy can be derived from transient bed tax collected by local authorities.)

Do you have a solid source of referral business? Add four points.

Is there a short tourist season? If the season is less than five months subtract two points.

Is there a long tourist season? If more than five months add a half point per month for each month over five.

Is there a university or large hospital within walking distance? Add two points.

Is the property close to local attractions? If it's a short walk, add five points. For a long walk add three points. If there is more than one major attraction, add one point.

Are you within a mile of a major interstate? Add two points.

Has there been a decline in traffic count or tourism? Subtract two points.

Are you in a town that will offer you heavy business traveler traffic? Add three points.

Is there a major flaw in your prospective location? Subtract 10 points (next to a gas station, difficult to reach, on the wrong part of town, etc.).

See the graphic to find your results.

Here's how to score the inn location:

1-5	Forget it.
6-10	Only if you have money and time to spare.
11-15	Marginal. Have another job to supplement.
16-20	Possible, but count on long build up time. Concentrate on promotion, hold back on over spending on refurbishing. Don't quit your job.
21-25	Good location but plan on working hard on marketing.
26-35	Choice location. Plan on two to four years for high occupancy. Work on promotion and inn personality.
36+	Prime location if you can afford it. Don't blow it. Decorate and market professionally.

Financial Matters

When you are gathering your material to take to a bank, you will need to prepare a business plan/prospectus of the property you wish to buy, whether it is an existing inn or a property to be converted.

In it you will need sections on location, area occupancy rates, your projected occupancy, room rates of nearby lodging, floor plans, expansion plans, marketing plans, etc. If you hire an inn buying consultant, a commercial contractor or a hotel/inn appraiser, they will help you pull this piece together. A detailed projection of expected financial results and actual cash requirements for at least three years should be included. Using discounted cash flow calculations, it is possible to determine an approximate value for your inn.

Appraising a property to determine its true worth is not a job for amateurs. Your local residential Realtor will do you a disservice if he or she tries. Get the expertise of an experienced inn consultant, a hotel appraiser or other professional. In most cases, these days, you will be making very serious financial decisions and you will want the most professional help available.

In our innkeeper survey mentioned previously, we asked for financing advice for perspective innkeepers when dealing with the special needs of small inns. The most frequent suggestion given was to work with your local bank.

Many innkeepers had taken their prospectus around to downtown banks in larger cities near them, only to be turned down time and time again. One innkeeper had 12 interviews with loan officers at 12 different banks, only to finally find his local banker willing to finance his package. "Become friends with your local banker," is advice that applies to owners of all types of companies. Although financing lodging properties is not a specialty of most local banks, many consider it good business to try to accommodate their local customer base and to extend this type of financing.

Many inns are now finding Small Business Administration loans nationally through The Money Store. According to Nancy Davis, Vice President and Regional Sales Manager at the company's Sacramento, Calif. headquarters, The Money Store offers an alternative that is very popular for the innkeeping community. A Small Business Administration lender since 1983, one of its specialties is in owner-occupied businesses, such as doctors' practices and small inns. Davis states, "The popularity of the program is due to its long-term loan payback of 25 years and its low down payment. Customarily, an 80 percent loan-to-value loan is made." A typical bed & breakfast loan for The Money Store is in the area of $300,000-$600,000, but it can go as high as $1.5 million. If you are planning on building your inn from scratch and are putting together a start-up operation, however, you will need 30 percent down figured on the entire cost of the start-up, including furniture and fixtures, etc.

Creating a unique inn

One element that has changed recently in the B&B business are the guests themselves. Travelers today are much more sophisticated and discerning than in the early B&B days. A weekend at a cute little inn doesn't always fill their expectations. Nowadays, inngoers want a more memorable experience in exchange for their hard-earned dollar — something really exceptional and different. It's not enough to have a run-by-the-book, generic, chain-style B&B. You will need to create ways to set yourself apart from everyone else and be noticed.

Find a certain style or theme that you feel comfortable with and play it up as much as possible. Begin by using the advantages that already exist naturally. Take the building itself, for example: Is there something unique about its history, style or architecture? Can you accentuate these features with a certain decor, menu or interesting collection? What if your inn is Victorian — the most common perception of a B&Bs around? Then do something slightly different with your interior, like branching off into an Arts and Crafts or Jacobean decor.

No matter what style you choose, you can further establish a sense of originality by adding your own whimsical decorating touches. Create a lamp out of an old-fashioned fitting form; use a fishing tackle basket to hold the tissue box; put some quirky surprise in the closet.

Perhaps you have an absolutely fabulous location, with river frontage, wildlife, scenic acreage or vineyards. But if not, what is unique about the general region you live in?

If your B&B is in the Southwest, for example, you can play up the Southwestern theme with chile baskets, and spicy dishes. Is there bird watching in your area? Then emphasize a bird theme at your inn with birding books, extra binoculars and bird feeders outside the windows of the breakfast room. Is the wine country nearby? Don't just name your rooms after grapes — feature wine-tastings and special wine seminars for your guests.

To further establish a unique identity, more and more inns are creating guest rooms with novel motifs, such as specific historic and nostalgic themes, international themes and storybook themes.

Incorporate your own interests, whether it's the opera or rabbits, and make this your theme. This is a perfect opportunity-to convey a sense of whimsy and humor to your guests. Take The Jabberwock, for example — a Lewis Carroll-inspired inn in Monterey. Your stay begins with a welcome note that has to be held up to a mirror to be read; some of the clocks are backwards, and guest rooms have names like Mimsey and Wabe. Innkeeper Jim Allen has incorporated his love of storytelling (he reads to local school children) into the breakfast time — he captivates guests with stories while they enjoy dishes such as "snorkleberry flumptious" and "phantasmagoria."

Though a fantastic location and incredible luxury always help make an inn stand out, not every inn owner has the resources to sink into oceanfront acreage, Egyptian cotton towels or individual hot tubs. A more important factor — and one that can make your guests feel very pampered — is attention to detail. Decorate the breakfast plates with little edible flowers. Leave a handwritten welcome note for your guests.

Provide lots of special little amenities: hot-out-of-the-oven cookies upon check-in; a basket of emergency goodies in the bathroom; a nice decanter of water by the bed; something more clever than the usual chocolate at turndown. (One health-oriented hotel in San Francisco places a beta-carotene tablet on the pillow with a philosophical goodnight thought.) Instead of one rubber ducky by the tub, give guests a whole basket of bathtub toys. Send your guests off with a little gift when they check out. It's these little surprises that they're going to remember later and tell their friends about.

Ripley Hotch and Carl Glassman, authors of *How to Start & Run Your Own Bed & Breakfast*, have summed up the key to successful innkeeping quite succinctly: "Heed this. Avoid the stereotype. In order to be a success, you have to be idiosyncratic, maybe even eccentric. You have to be, above all, more than people expect. If at least one guest a week doesn't say that, or something like it, you're not sufficiently different."

Marketing

Once you have created the idiosyncratic inn of your dreams — or as close to it as your budget will allow — you'll need to find ways to make yourself known and fill those rooms. That means you must sell your unique inn concept to people just as anyone would a new product. In every marketing move you make, focus on how you can promote your inn as more than just another face in the crowd.

There are a few crucial investments you'll need to make right from the beginning: The first and most important is an attractive, well-written brochure. As you design your brochure, remember that this is the only visual and verbal impression of your inn that most guests will have before they arrive; and this is the No. 1 item that media people will keep from your press kit and refer to when they write copy for their guidebooks and articles. Give them something to write about. Thousands of inn brochures have been written with the same well-worn phrases that give no idea of the inn's unique character. If you don't feel up to writing a creative, distinctive brochure, then hire a professional to do it.

A good line drawing of your inn, plus some professional-quality color slides are also essential in your marketing strategy. These can be used for all kinds of publicity, including your own brochure. Remember — these few visual images may make or break a decision to come and stay with you, so it's important for them to be good.

Next, join whatever professional organizations would be advantageous for you on an international, state and local level. (The Professional Association of Innkeepers

International has great resources for both aspiring and established innkeepers.) Invite groups like AAA, Mobil, the American Bed & Breakfast Association, and state associations of country inns to come and rate your inn. Use these names in your publicity to give your inn more credibility.

When you are ready to make your "debut," send out press kits to the media, including guidebook authors, magazines and newspapers — your richest sources of free publicity. Go to several bookstores, see what B&B guidebooks are getting the best exposure, and find out how to get in them. Some guidebooks charge a fee ranging from about $50 to $100. If the book and publishers have a proven track record it should be worthwhile depending on what markets you are trying to target.

Many innkeepers say that guidebooks provide their single largest source of referrals. Eventually, a good inn will then turn these guidebook customers into repeats who will refer additional people and your circle of fame will spread. However, keep in mind that you will always need to have new customers to make up for those who move away or no longer travel.

Other creative ways to fill your rooms include special promotions (such as a frequent stayer program or the American Historic Inns Buy-One-Night-Get-One-Night-Free programs), special events (such as mystery weekends or seasonal open houses), offering a toll-free phone number, and cooperative advertising with other inns.

The latter is especially beneficial if you are in an area where there is a high concentration of inns. You may find greater strength in numbers by banding together with group marketing, referrals, events and brochures. A lot of innkeepers are afraid of losing their individuality by doing this, and they prefer to remain insular, pretending that they're the only inn around. But this kind of myopic vision usually does more harm than good. Cooperating with other inns can only give your inn an image of greater integrity.

Innkeepers in some areas spend as much as 20 hours a week on marketing activities. Lynn Montgomery, former owner of Gold Mountain Manor, is an Emmy award winner and continues to write screenplays and movies. When she ran her inn in Big Bear a few years ago, she found that whenever she let up on her marketing activities she saw a decrease in occupancy within a few weeks. Being in a mountain area two hours from Los Angeles (and a saturated area for B&Bs, cabin and house rentals) presented a huge challenge.

Montgomery spent hours each week on the phone trying to interest editors in stories and themes about the area mountains. Members of the Big Bear Chamber of Commerce told her that whenever they saw press on Big Bear they knew she had been the one to generate the interest.

Marketing is critical for an inn's success unless your favorite uncle owns the packed four-star historic hotel a block down the street, with 80 percent occupancy. (We recently met innkeepers benefitting from this precise situation.)

One of the most efficient ways to fill your rooms is to make your guests happy — so happy that they are motivated enough to return and tell their friends about your inn. To make them happy, you will need to find out what they want and don't want at an inn.

Some "wants" are universal: Every guest wants to feel welcome and comfortable and special; to be greeted with warmth and genuine enthusiasm at the door; to be oriented to the inn personally by the innkeeper. The amount of privacy guests need varies. Most guests want some attention from the innkeepers — usually at check-in or during breakfast — but they don't want the innkeepers hovering.

What do guests want in their bedroom? Counter space — lots of it — good reading lights, a firm, comfortable bed with nice linens, some written information about the inn and its policies (because they won't remember everything you tell them at check-in), and lots of little amenities, like flowers, snacks and refreshments. Of course, it goes without saying that everyone expects their room to be super clean and fresh.

B&Bs are tending toward more sophisticated luxuries, and private baths are a bigger priority than ever. Not just a private bathroom, but a nice, spotless bathroom with lots of fluffy towels and pampering toiletries. Jacuzzi tubs for two have also been a popular trend in recent years.

What people want from breakfast can be tricky because it depends on the layout of your inn and the types of inngoers you draw. A growing trend is to let the guests choose the time and place (in their own room or in the dining area), or to offer a serve-yourself buffet breakfast during a certain time range. Most guests look forward to an artfully presented, gourmet breakfast.

What do guests not want? Most guests don't care for too much froo froo, fuss and frills. They don't like finding personal items in the closets, or any reminders that they are intruding in someone's private home. Most guests feel uncomfortable with a don't-touch environment, where everything is so formal that they feel compelled to tip-toe around and whisper. And no guest likes being given a list of too many things they can't do.

Business travelers are a market that more inns are catering to — especially single travelers who want a homelike environment while away on business — and their needs can be very different from the vacationer. They'll probably want a phone in their room, desk space, early morning coffee and breakfast on the run.

Some inns, especially those in cities, are pulling out all the stops for business travelers, offering meeting rooms, fax machines and computers.

Other niches that more innkeepers are targeting include retirees (one of the fastest growing travel groups), people with children and those who travel with their pets. Entertaining groups such as weddings, business meetings, retreats and other events can be a great source of income for your inn, but it's a lot of work and often intrusive for your other guests. You'll have to decide if your inn can handle the special needs of these niches. Don't try to be all things to all people.

To further understand what your guests need, spend a night in each of your guest rooms, trying them out personally. Pretend you are the guest — unpack luggage, use the shower, sleep and read in the bed. You'll be amazed at how enlightening this can be.

Hotch and Glassman write: "Taking care of people for an innkeeper means showing a kind of care that will surprise the guest. And as long as inns offer what many marketers call high touch (warmth and genuine hospitality, personal service, and attention to detail) to their guests, who live and work in an increasingly high-tech world, they will continue to grow and prosper."

Just make sure it's your own singular style of high touch.

Our favorite innkeepers are those who have something of themselves to give, some wonderful quirky interest or warm, yet eccentric part of their personality that they extend into innkeeping. Some are naturally charismatic, great storytellers or quiet, sensitive caretakers.

Some philosophers say the highest art is living well. To us the best innkeepers live their own beautifully creative lives. They renew and restore themselves instead of being swallowed up by the ever-enlarging work loads that can tempt them in this career. One exceptionally creative, nationally recognized innkeeper I admire is not always available to her guests — she trades work days with her husband. Each has three or four days a week to pursue their writing and community affairs. They keep their own individual passions alive and it is this energy makes their inn a lively, joyful, celebratory place.

RESOURCES:

Publications

How to Open and Operate a Bed & Breakfast Home

Jan Stankus, The Globe Pequot Press.

How to Start & Run Your Own Bed & Breakfast Inn

Ripley Hotch and Carl Glassman, Stackpole Books.

Lodging Listing Requirements & Diamond Rating Guidelines by American Automobile Association

1000 AAA Drive, Heathrow, FL 32746-5063

This is an excellent resource for building an inn or expanding a property to a three- or four-diamond standing. This booklet has a guest service section that clearly describes levels of hospitality and reveals what seasoned travelers expect when they travel.

Traveling Through Time: Restoring Historic Homes as B&B Inns

PO Box 1776, Atlanta, GA 30301; 404/656-0779

So...You Want to be an Innkeeper

Mary Davies, Pat Hardy, Jo Ann Bell and Susan Brown, Chronicle Books.

Consultants:

Concept Consultant Services

Norman D. Kinney, PO Box 151, Marshall, MI 49068; 616/781-2494

Insurance

Bed & Breakfast Insurance Specialists

PO Box 65788, Salt Lake City, UT 84165; 800/356-6517

Brown, Schuck, Townsend Associates, Susan Breischer

1735 Jefferson Davis Hwy #900, Arlington, VA 23202

Professional Association of Innkeepers International

PO Box 90710, Santa Barbara, CA 93190; 805/569-1835, 25-page report demystifies inn insurance.

Potter, Leonard & Cahan Inc, Michael Dunkin

PO Box 82840, Kenmore, WA 98028; 800/548-8857

SP Tarantino Insurance Broker

490 Jefferson St, San Francisco, CA 94109; 415/397-0261

James W. Wolf Insurance, James W. Wolf

PO Box 510, Elicott City, MD 21041; 800/488-1135; Fax 410/750-0322

Magazines & Newsletters

Aspiring Innkeepers Kit

Includes innkeeping newsletter, "So ... You Want to Be an Innkeeper?," Coping with the IRS-Special Report, Professional Inn Guide, Business Planning Guide and an actual business plan of a country inn, $125.

Country Inns Publications, Inc.

PO Box 182, South Orange, NJ 07079; 201/762-7090, Fax 201/762-1491

Future Innkeepers' Packet

Ten Questions to Ask Yourself Before Buying an Inn and a List of the Ten Best Resources to Guide You to Success, Professional Association of Innkeepers International, PO Box 90710, Santa Barbara, CA 93190; 805/569-1853

"innkeeping" Newsletter

Professional Association of Innkeepers International, PO Box 90710, Santa Barbara, CA 93190; 805/569-1835, $65 per year or included in PAII membership.

Inn Marketing Newsletter

Norm Strasma, Publisher, PO Box 1789, Kankakee, IL 60901; 815/939-3509; Fax 815/933-8320. The trade journal for B&B innkeepers giving industry news with emphasis on marketing ideas and creative promotions.

InnQuest

Oates & Bredfeldt, PO Box 1162, Brattleboro, VT 05302; 802/254-5931. Published four times per year, $30 for a subscription of six issues.

The Inn Times, Innkeeping Business News and B&B Features

2101 Crystal Plaza Arcade, Suite 246, Arlington, VA 22202; 202/363-9305, published six times per year, $14.95 per year.

The Journal for Innkeepers B&B

Virgo Publishing, Inc., 3300 N Central Ave, Suite 2500, Phoenix, AZ 85012; 602/990-1101. on year subscription $29.95.

Real Estate

Michael Yovino-Young

2716 Telegraph Ave, Berkeley, CA 94705; 510/548-1210; Fax 510/548-3110

Classes

Brophy, Marie, Isaiah Hall B&B Inn
PO Box 1007, Dennis, MA 02638; 617/385-9928

Buelow, Carol Jean
PO Box 5666, Madison, WI 53705; 608/238-6776

Caples, David J., Lodging Resources Workshops
PO Box 1210, Amelia Island, FL 32034; 904/277-4851

Glassman, Carl, Wedgwood Inn
111 W Bridge Street, New Hope, PA 18938; 215/862-2570

Inn at Manchester
Box 41, Manchester, VT 05254; 802/362-1793

Innkeeping Consultants
PO Box 79, Okemos, MI 48805; 800/926-4667

Kay, Ron, TwoSuns Limited
1705 Bay Street, Beaufort, SC 29902; 800/532-4244 or 803/522-1122

Mid-Atlantic Center for the Arts
PO Box 340, Cape May, NJ 08204; 800/275-4278 or 609/884-5404

Oates & Bredfeldt
PO Box 1162, Brattleboro, VT 05302; 802/254-5931.
Web site: http://www.webrover.com/oates
Offers eight seminars a year.

Petty, Lynda & Joe, Park House B&B
888 Holland St, Saugatuck, MI 49453; 616/857-4535

Phillips, Mary & Jerry, Old Rittenhouse Inn
PO Box 584, Bayfield, WI 54814; 715/799-5111

Riley, Kit, Sage Blossom Consluting
PO Box 17193, Boulder, CO 80308; 303/440-4227; Fax 303/786-7716

Ryan, Barb & Jerry, Arrowhead Inn B&B
106 Mason Rd, Durham, NC 27712; 919/477-8430

School of Hotel Administration
Cornell University, Statler Hall, Ithaca, NY 14853; 607/256-4990

BED AND BREAKFAST SALES, 1994-1996

DESCRIPTION	SALE DATE	# OF ROOMS	SALE PRICE	GROSS SALES	PRICE PER ROOM	TIMES GROSS	COMMENTS
Active Berkshires Town	Oct-96	20	1,265,000	231,881	63,250	5.46	Partial Owner Financing
Elegant Savannah	Oct-96	16	2,200,000	700,000	137,500	3.14	SBA 504 Financing
Maine Coastal Village	Sep-96	15	1,100,000	235,082	73,333	4.68	Owner Financing
Maine, Mt. Desert	Apr-96	12	875,000	180,000	72,917	4.86	Bank, 15% Owner
Camden, ME	Nov-95	8	850,000	111,449	106,250	7.63	8th Rm Added; Owner Financing
Coastal Maine	Nov-95	16	925,000	177,222	57,813	5.22	Owner Financing
Coast Village Maine	Nov-95	13	355,000	133,269	27,307	2.66	Cmplt Renovation; Owner Financing
In Town Coastal Maine	Oct-95	10	980,000	215,687	98,000	4.54	SBA, No Owner
Vermont Resort Town	Sep-95	5	950,000	130,777	190,000	7.26	5 rooms added, Owner financing
Asheville North Carolina	Aug-95	5	635,000	135,000	127,000	4.70	
Maine Mt. Desert	Aug-95	8	485,000	76,000	60,625	6.38	Bank, SBA, 5% Owner
North Carolina Resort Town	Jun-95	7	250,000	135,000	35,714	1.85	
Maine Mt. Desert	Apr-95	6	425,000	72,000	70,833	5.90	Bank, 7% Owner
Maine Mt. Desert	Mar-95	9	550,000	100,000	61,111	5.50	
Asheville North Carolina	Mar-95	4	495,000	80,000	123,750	6.19	
Cape Cod Massachusetts	Feb-95	6	185,000	n/a	30,833	n/a	Distress Sale
Asheville North Carolina	Jan-95	6	520,000	n/a	86,667	n/a	
Coastal Resort New Jersey	Jan-95	9	850,000	245,416	94,444	3.46	Bank and Owner Financing
Vermont Ski Town	Dec-94	7	460,000	77,234	65,714	5.96	Bank
Urban Inn Savannah GA	Aug-94	20	1,020,000	374,428	51,000	2.72	Bargain; SBA 504
Cape Cod Massachusetts	Jul-94	7	755,000	158,000	107,857	4.78	SBA & The Money Store
Urban Inn Savannah GA	Jun-94	13	810,000	189,325	62,308	4.28	Bargain; Owner Financing
Hamptons New York	Mar-94	8	650,000	131,944	81,250	4.93	Bank Financing
Vermont Rural	Feb-94	10	375,000	88,722	37,500	4.23	Bank Financing
Overage Average 1994-1996		**10.00**	**748,542**	**180,838**	**74,854**	**4.14**	
Average 18 Inns 1992-1994		**10.61**	**720,278**	**157,109**	**68,545**	**4.91**	
Average 12 Inns 1990-1992		**9.67**	**653,917**	**134,999**	**63,809**	**4.84**	

Source Oates and Bredfeldt Brattleboro, VT.

GOURMET: Country inns offer some of the nation's finest cuisine.

As the scent of freshly ground coffee brewing wafts gently upward to your room, two thoughts enter your head. Either you are in a coffee commercial or snuggled deep beneath a down comforter on a four-poster bed at your favorite country inn.

All things considered, take the country inn.

After all, those in a coffee commercial only get a cup of coffee. Guests at many country inns and bed & breakfasts receive much more.

For instance, guests at the Blue Spruce Inn in Soquel, Calif., always wake on the right side of the bed. Why not? A lavish breakfast awaits them in the dining room.

Imagine a beginning course of burgundy poached pears with raspberry sauce, followed by buttermilk nutbread with homemade honey butter and country granola with a choice of toppings. The main course is a succulent sundried tomato and Brie frittata adorned with a dash of sour cream and slices of perfectly ripe avocado.

At the Spencer House in San Francisco, chef Tracy Weber serves up specialties such as a poached eggs over polenta with a rose green pepper sauce or perhaps a warm bread pudding with currants. The scones, muffins and breads are flavored with fresh herbs from the inn's garden.

Multi-course, gourmet feasts are served at many inns and B&Bs. At some inns, fine linen, crystal and china decorate tables warmed with candlelight. At others, guest dine al fresco on a veranda or in a courtyard, where the sound of a waterfall is music to the ears.

Guests at the Inn at Little Washington in Washington, Virg., experience not only five-diamond accommodations, but five-diamond cuisine, as well. The inn's restaurant has been a AAA five-diamond recipient for eight years.

One has the option of sampling light continental fare, such as freshly baked croissants, breads, pastries and fresh fruit or take on a gourmet meal with a lobster omelet or perhaps scrambled eggs accompanied by smoked salmon in a potato nest.

For most, patrons and food critics alike, it's the dinners at the inn that truly are an Epicurean delight.

Executive chef Patrick O'Connell creates a creative selection of savory, seasonal cuisine, using an abundance of local produce.

A typical four-course dinner at the inn is anything but typical. Guests might start off with risotto with shrimp, oyster mushrooms and country ham or perhaps foie gras with poached pears, sauternes jelly and pear butter toasts.

From here, guests select either an icy lemon-rosemary sorbet as a palate cleanser or a salad of watercress and Belgian endive tossed with walnuts, bacon, pears and bleu cheese.

The menu unfolds into a stunning and artfully presented main course. Traditional items such as a grilled beef tenderloin are stuffed with truffles and winter vegetables. Local rabbit braised in freshly pressed apple cider is served with garlic mashed potatoes and wild mushrooms. Maine lobster finds a perfect home in tomato minestrone with just a hint of Peranod.

Whatever the choice, don't forget to save a little room for dessert. You might select a warm rhubarb pizza topped with ginger ice cream, custard bread pudding with Jack Daniel's sauce or maybe a simple serving of strawberries with a Grand Marinier Sauce.

After enjoying this feast, guests retire to beautifully appointed guest rooms or perhaps take a stroll and enjoy a star-filled sky in the Virginia countryside.

Even if your choice of bed & breakfast isn't five-star, you're sure to sample fine cuisine. Many innkeepers, despite their lack of Cordon Bleu credentials, are aces in the kitchen. After all, these are people who wake at the crack of dawn, grind up the gourmet coffee, mix the muffin batter, prepare fresh fruit salads, crack the eggs for the omelets, sprinkle powdered sugar on the French toast, set the table with fine china and serve the guests, all the while regaling their patrons with interesting stories about the house or community. And most make it look easy.

For those who seek out the breakfast as much as the bed (or perhaps the dinner, too), do a little homework before booking a room at an inn.

Check your country inn guidebook, and highlight inns that describe gourmet meals. Call the inn and ask for a brochure and information about the food.

If you have your heart set on a morning feast, ask whether the inn serves full, continental or continental-plus breakfasts. Full usually includes breads or muffins, fresh fruit and main dish or perhaps a breakfast buffet or maybe a large selection of eggs, bacon, homemade breads, fruits, cereals, etc., served family style.

A continental breakfast usually means a selection of breads, donuts or muffins and juice and coffee. Continental-plus fare expands on this, with breads, pastries, fruit and maybe yogurt or cereals.

Bed & breakfasts typically serve only breakfast included in the rates, but many also offer afternoon tea. Special dinners often can be arranged at bed & breakfasts, perhaps even a candlelight feast served in the privacy of your room. The meal may be catered by a fine restaurant or created by your innkeeper. In some areas, laws prohibit bed & breakfasts from serving meals other than breakfast. They still might provide a light afternoon tea or evening snack, but no lunch or dinner is available.

Country inns often serve dinner, and many have restaurants on the premises. Some country inns offer rates on what is known as the Modified American Plan. This means that both breakfast and dinner is included in the rates. Not all country inns serve dinner, so be sure to ask.

Some country inns, lodges, ranches or resorts offer American Plan rates, which means that all three meals are included in the rates.

Our best tip for those in search of fine cuisine is to ask the innkeeper. The innkeepers that truly enjoy creating a memorable breakfast or dinner are usually happy to describe the meals in fine detail. If you have food allergies or health restrictions, be sure to mention this when you make a reservation. Most innkeepers are more than happy to accommodate your needs, but everybody works better with advance notice.

If you're still unsure, which inns offer top cuisine, here are some lists to help. This is just the tip of the iceburg. We receive hundreds of recommendations each year from inngoers, and most include a glowing review of the food.

Inns with Top Cuisine:

Dairy Hollow House

Eureka Springs AR

Chef catered President Clinton's inaugural brunch.

Zosa Ranch

Escondido, CA

The innkeeper is an accomplished chef, and her cuisine has been featured on the TV Food Network, as well as in Bon Appetit.

Spencer House

San Francisco, CA

Chef was a graduate of hotel and restaurant management at Boston University.

The Lovelander B&B Inn

Loveland, CO

The inn's cuisine has been featured on the TV shows "Inn Country USA" and "Inn Country Chefs."

The Old Mill Inn B&B

Somesville, CT

One innkeeper is an accomplished chef and professional cake decorator.

Chalet Suzanne Country Inn & Restaurant

Lake Wales, FL

The inn's restaurant received the Craig Claiborne award as one of the 121 best restaurants in the world.

Kilauea Lodge
Volcano, HI

The innkeepers' cuisine has been featured in Bon Appetit.

Inn at Bethlehem
Bethlehem, IN

Innkeeper is an accomplished chef; prix-fixe, multi-course gourmet dinners are served on weekends.

Arundel Meadows Inn
Kennebunk, ME

Innkeeper Mark Bachelder studied under Madeleine Kamman, a popular chef on PBS.

Palmer House Inn
Falmouth, MA

Cuisine has been featured in Gourmet and Bon Appetit.

The Cranberry Rose
Wareham, MA

Innkeeper's recipe for Cranberry Bars was featured in Bon Appetit.

The Inn at Duck Creeke
Welfleet, MA

The inn's restaurant Sweet Seasons won Cape Cod Life's annual award for "Best Fine Dining."

Bernerhof Inn
Glen, NH

Inn has an award-winning restaurant. The inn offers a "Taste of the Mountains Cooking School."

Hacienda Antigua B&B
Albuquerque, NM

One of the inn's recipes appeared in Culinary Trends magazine.

Salsa del Salto B&B Inn
El Prado, NM

Chef holds cooking schools and is a cookbook author.

The Irish Rose
Auburn, NY

The innkeeper is a former head chef.

Old Chatham Sheepherding Company
Old Chatham, NY

Chef graduated first in her class at the Culinary Institute of America.

Albergo Allegria
Windham, NY

Innkeepers own "LaGriglia," a gourmet restaurant across the street.

The Fearrington House Inn
Fearrington, NC

Both the inn and restaurant are five-diamond recipients.

Morning Star Inn
Highlands, NC

One of the innkeepers is a culinary school graduate, cooking classes sometimes are available.

Snowbird Mountain Lodge
Robbinsville, NC

One innkeeper is a trained chef, cooking seminars are offered.

Railroad House Restaurant B&B
Marietta, PA

Some of the restaurant's innovative recipes have been featured in Bon Appetit.

Planters Inn
Charleston, SC

Recipes from this four-diamond inn's restaurant, Planters Café, have been featured in Gourmet and Bon Appetit.

Villa de la Fontaine
Charleston, SC

Chef's recipe for cornmeal waffles appeared in a Better Homes & Gardens cookbook.

Blair House
Wimberly, TX

Innkeeper is a trained chef and teaches cooking classes.

Rabbit Hill Inn
Lower Waterford, VT.

The inn's dining room is a four-diamond recipient.

Eldon, The Inn at Chatham
Chatham, VA

Chef Joel Wesley is a graduate of the Culinary Institute of America.

Clifton Country Inn
Charlottesville, VA

Innkeeper and assistant chef both graduated from the Culinary Institute of America.

L'Auberge Provencale
White Post, VA

Innkeeper & chef Alain Borel is a fourth generation chef from Avignon, France. The restaurant is a five-time recipient of the four-diamond award. Borel has been hailed by James Beard as a Great Country Inn Chef.

The Inn at Little Washington
Washington, VA

Both the inn and restaurant have received a five-diamond award.

Williamsburg Manor
Williamsburg, VA

The innkeeper, whose parents also run a successful B&B in town, was director of Catering at Ford's Colony Country Club. The dining room at the country club is a five-diamond recipient.

Turtleback Farm Inn
Eastsound, WA

Bon Appetit highlighted some of the breakfast recipes served at Turtleback. Recipe for granola has won awards.

The Shelburne Inn
Seaview, WA

Inns' cuisine has been ranked as some of the Pacific Northwest's best by Bon Appetit and Gourmet.

Inns with Cookbooks:

Canyon Villa
Sedona, AZ

"Red Rocks and Cinnamon Rolls"

Dairy Hollow House
Eureka Springs, AR

"The Dairy Hollow House Cookbook"

"The Dairy Hollow House Soup & Bread Cookbook"

Heartstone Inn & Cottages
Eureka Springs,. AR

"Heartstone Inn Breakfast Cookbook"

Four Sisters Inns

"Four Sisters Inns Cookbook"
Note: Includes recipes from five of this excellent collection of inns, including the Cobblestone Inn, Carmel, CA; Green Gables Inn, Pacific Grove, CA; Gosby House Inn, Pacific Grove, CA; Petite Auberge, San Franscisco, CA; and White Swan Inn, San Francisco, CA.

Campbell Ranch Inn
Geyserville, CA

"Campbell Ranch Inn Cookbook"

Old Yacht Club Inn
Santa Barbara, CA

"Old Yacht Club Inn Cookbook"

Blue Spruce Inn
Soquel, CA

"A Taste of Blue Spruce Inn"

Lovelander B&B
Loveland, CO

"Recipes from the Lovelander"

Varns Guest House
Middlebury, IN

"Varns Guest House Cookbook"

Dockside Guest Quarters
York, ME

"Recipes from Dockside"

Garth Woodside Mansion
Hannibal, MO

"Breakfast Inn Bed"

Mainstay Inn
Cape May, NJ

"Breakfast at Nine – Tea at Four"

Sea Holly Inn
Cape May, NJ

"Sea Holly Bed and Breakfast: A Sharing of Secrets"

The William Seward Inn
Westfield, NY

"Favorite Recipes of The William Seward Inn"

The Fearrington House
Fearrington, NC

"Fearrington House Cookbook"

Mast Farm Inn
Valle Crucis, NC

"Mast Farm Inn – Family Style"

Grandview Lodge
Waynesville, NC

"Recipes from Grandview Lodge"

White Oak Inn
Canville, OH

"By Request, The White Oak Cookbook"

Settler's Inn
Hawley, PA

"Recipes From Our Breakfast Basket"

Hill Farm Inn
Arlington, VT

"Recipes from the Kitchen of"

Black River Inn
Ludlow, VT

"Entertaining Black River Inn Style"

Trail's End, A Country Inn
Wilmington, VT

"Trail's End Cookbook"

Hidden Inn
Orange, VA

"Welcome to the Hidden Inn"

The Inn at Little Washington
Washington, VA

"The Inn at Little Washington Cookbook: A Consuming Passion"

Ravenscroft Inn
Port Townsend, WA

"Something's Cooking"

Sheburne Inn
Seaview, WA

"Shelburne Breakfasts"

FAMILY: More and more inns are catering to the needs of parents and children.

Many bed & breakfasts, which more often are thought of as exclusive honeymoon retreats and romantic hideaways, now are changing their tune in order to accommodate the growing number of American families who hit the road together.

Family vacation options no longer may be limited to either motor homes or staying at hotels. More and more, a viable alternative is bonding with family at a B&B or country inn.

A survey of 1,200 innkeepers revealed that 66 percent of B&Bs and country inns nationwide consider themselves family-oriented.

"During the '80s, B&Bs were heavily oriented towards couples," said Maine innkeeper Rick Litchfield. "But in the last four or five years we've seen an increase in the number of families coming to our inn."

Litchfield said that the percentage of family stays at his Kennebunkport inn, The Captain Lord Mansion, have increased from 5 to 25 percent in a four- or five-year period.

Litchfield recognized this trend early, and although his 1812 colonial inn, with elegant antiques, four-story spiral staircase and bedroom fireplaces personifies romance, he purchased several twin beds that were placed in almost every room.

"Both my wife and I recognize that the customer's needs are what's important to meet," Litchfield said. "Besides buying the beds we had to change our attitude."

At The Captain Lord Mansion, where rates begin at $149 per room, children between 5 and 8 years old are an additional $10 per room as opposed to an adult charge of $25 extra. Litchfield said the charges for older children are the same as adults, and younger children stay for free.

The extent to which families' needs are taken care of has a lot to do with the attitude of the innkeepers.

Lindsay Copeland, another innkeeper in Kennebunkport, said he doesn't just welcome children but believes they make the whole guest experience at the Maine Stay Inn & Cottages better.

"We have two small children of our own, so we are pretty sensitive to families' needs," said Copeland, who has managed the inn with his wife for more than five years. "Attitude is very important, including when you first talk to the guest on the phone.

"Instead of just saying 'yes' on the phone in answer to the question of children, I say 'absolutely'."

The Maine Stay Inn & Cottages is physically set up to accommodate families in cottages that have two double beds in addition to the king or queen bed and a kitchen. Sitting rooms in the suites of the main building have double pull-out sofas.

"A family with children may feel out of place in an inn geared toward couples," Copeland said. "I know they certainly don't feel that here.

"We really do enjoy having children. Along with our hot breakfasts we also have Frosted Flakes and Cheerios because children may be used to that."

For those times when parents just have to break away, Copeland said he can arrange for a baby-sitter.

Some innkeepers recognize the trend but want to continue the traditional image of a peaceful, quiet, and romantic B&B.

In the survey, 86 percent of the innkeepers said they accepted children, but 20 percent of those did not consider their inn family-oriented. Legally, many states disallow the exclusion of children at lodging establishments.

Copeland said that although many inns must legally accept children, setting rules like "two-to-a-room" to dissuade parents from bringing their children is something travelers may have to accept.

"Discouraging families from bringing their children may be appropriate for some inns that aren't equipped or do not have the proper atmosphere," he said. "There are enough choices out there."

Tom Taylor, former innkeeper of the 29-room Blue Lantern Inn, which is located in Dana Point, Calif., said guests sometimes are a bit cautious when asking about whether his inn accepts children.

"I think some people are used to the response (when inquiring) of some of the more traditional B&Bs where there are no-children policies," Taylor said "They act out of courtesy when asking. Our response is that we welcome children and we say, 'We're sure they are well behaved'."

B&Bs that are changing with the times and making their inn children-friendly have improved their inns' soundproofing, placed smaller beds and cribs into rooms, laid carpeting on stairs and wooden floors, installed kitchenettes and built cottages or converted other structures.

Many innkeepers, especially those with children of their own, appreciate the needs of families and stock the inn with games and toys. B&Bs on farms and dude ranches often welcome children. The ranches sometimes have special programs and activities designed for children of various ages.

The best advice is to always remember that not all inns and bed & breakfasts can accommodate your needs, so ask the innkeeper whether or not they do welcome children. More and more, you'll find that the answer is yes.

Remember, approximately two-thirds of innkeepers consider their inns "family oriented." Although, we've tried to highlight whether an inn is ideal for children or families in each inn's description, always inquire with innkeeper.

Inns for the Business Traveler

BIG CITIES: From faxes to dry cleaning, innkeepers are ready for business guests.

It may seem like an oxymoron, but business travelers and bed & breakfasts do mix.

While hotels and motels in the middle of business and convention zones continue courting business people, growing numbers of executive types are switching to bed & breakfasts for a good night's sleep.

Why are these normally structured "suits" suddenly breaking away from the traditional fare?

"People are tired of the high rises," said Atlanta innkeeper Mit Amin. "Checking in is such a long process before you get to your room. At my inn, it can be done in five minutes."

Amin is the innkeeper of the Beverly Hills Inn, an 18-room inn built in 1929. It is located only five minutes from downtown Atlanta and in the residential area of Buckhead, a financial district and popular night spot.

There are other differences that make bed & breakfast stays more attractive, Amin says.

"Staying at an inn is more personal," he said. "At a hotel, you get lost among the hundreds of people."

The flow of business travelers to the Beverly Hills Inn has grown dramatically in the last few years – from 35 percent to 65 percent, Amin said.

In addition to staying the night, business groups are holding meetings and luncheons at the inn. Fortune 500 companies are among Amin's regular clientele.

"I have a saying," Amin said. "If you sleep in a better environment, you work better."

Guests at the Beverly Hills Inn can come to the breakfast room and have access to two computers and a copy machine. Also available is a fax machine and phones with modem links.

Innkeepers at The Bertram Inn in Brookline, Mass., say about one-fifth of their guests are business travelers. The inn's Boston-area location is a convenient respite from the city.

The turn-of-the-century Greek Revival inn is located on a peaceful tree-lined street. Among its old English stylings and authentic antiques, guests find modern amenities such as fax services.

Guests at Castle Marne in Denver, Colo., are located in an urban setting, yet the luxurious surroundings and Richardsonian Romanesque architecture could make anyone forget a day of high-stress meetings.

But if you must work, there are both a Macintosh and PC computer available, as well as a fax machine and copier. Corporate guests also may receive a 5 percent discount, and like all other guests, they enjoy a homemade breakfast and afternoon tea.

Kansas City's Country Club Plaza is one of its most picturesque areas, and it's here you'll find Southmoreland on the Plaza. Aside from four-star accommodations and a full, gourmet breakfast, business travelers can make free local calls, use a copier or fax, grab a copy of the day's paper and request cable TV in their rooms.

The rates also include an early evening wine and cheese reception and membership privileges at the Rockhill Tennis Club. Corporate rates are offered, and the inn is within minutes of downtown Kansas City.

Fleur-de-Lys Inn, Mansion at the Park, is one of St. Louis' newer lodging options. The four-room inn is designed for both business travelers or those seeking romance.

Discounted corporate rates are available, and business travelers enjoy a host of amenities. An executive center with fax, copying and printing services is available, as well as same-day dry cleaning, a selection of local and national newspapers, in-room desks and good lighting.

For those in search of something different in the Big Apple, try Broadway B&B Inn. Located above an Irish pub in Times Square, this 40-room inn offers comfortable rooms with a homier atmosphere than most big city hotels.

A continental breakfast is included, and a fax and copier is available.

The Midtown location offers close access to theaters and restaurants, so there is plenty to see and do after the meetings end.

Montreal's Auberge de la Fontaine offers a more personal environment for the business traveler. Each room offers in-room phones, cable TV and desks. There is a copier and fax machine available, as well. The inn's location, overlooking Parc de la Fontaine, offers close access to the heart of the city.

Something else to consider, bed & breakfast inns typically experience their highest occupancy on the weekends. So to fill rooms, discounts sometimes are provided for corporate and midweek guests. Be sure to ask about special corporate and midweek rates when you book a room.

Inns and B&Bs that offer fax service, copiers and conference facilities are indicated throughout the Bed & Breakfast Encyclopedia. Also check out the inn's description for more details about amenities for the business traveler.

LIVING HISTORY: Immerse yourself in the past at these unique inns.

Have you ever dreamed of stepping back in time to the early part of the century, or the Civil War era, or even the colonial days? Our nation has thousands of historic inns that give us at least a taste of the past, yet very few go the extra length to fully transport their guests to another era. A special few, however, are not only steeped in history but actively encourage their guests to immerse themselves in the past.

Some innkeepers greet their guests in Victorian costume, others decorated their inns in authentic period style, paying careful attention to the tiniest details. The following are a few samples where innkeepers have gone out of their way to provide a truly historic getaway.

The Red Castle Inn in California's Gold Country is a prime example of a bed & breakfast that has truly captured another sense of time and place. Resembling a gingerbread house with its white icicle wood trim, the 1860 inn is one of only two Gothic Revival brick buildings built on the West Coast. Perched on Prospect Hill above the historic district of Nevada City, each of the four stories has its own veranda or balcony hung with patriotic bunting in the summer.

Innkeepers Mary Louise and Conley Weaver have remained delightfully impervious to the modernizing trends of most other bed & breakfasts. There are no televisions in the rooms, and the only telephone is a single turn-of-the-century model. Each room is layered with authentic Victorian heirlooms, rich fabrics, vases of peacock feathers (popular in Victorian times), and some personal, whimsical touches. Here, you will feel thoroughly cocooned from any 20th-century abrasiveness. But if you feel like venturing out, you can board a horse-drawn carriage and descend into the historic district for a tour. Nevada City is one of the most delightful gold towns in California.

Afternoon tea is a special treat at the Red Castle Inn, and not just because of their melt-in-your-mouth heirloom recipes. A Mark Twain look-alike often makes impromptu appearances and carries on conversations with the guests just as he would have in the 1800s. Lola Montez also drops by on occasion and might even do a toned-down version of her famous spider dance for you.

From the moment you enter "An Elegant Victorian Mansion" in Eureka, Calif., you leave the present day behind. Innkeepers Doug and Lily Vieyra, a friendly, vivacious couple, love dressing in turn-of-the-century costumes. Chances are, in fact, that Doug will greet you at the door in his butler costume. "I'm Jeeves, your impeccable butler," he says, with a twinkle in his eye.

"An Elegant Victorian Mansion," certainly lives up to its name. The downstairs parlors are exquisitely detailed with hand-painted moldings, intricately pieced Bradbury and Bradbury wallpaper, rich draperies with century-old trim and Oriental rugs. As Doug leads you on a tour of their richly decorated mansion, he might crank up the gramophone and play popular tunes of the era. All 200 of their cassettes feature period music, and their 500 videos (some of which are silent) all have vintage themes. The books are all about Victorian housekeeping or architecture; the newspaper or magazine on the table might be dated 1905. Upstairs, the guest rooms are named after 19th-century notables, including Lillie Langtry and Leland Stanford Jr., who once stayed in these namesake rooms. Outside, you can play croquet, ride around the historic district on bicycles, or go for a spin in Doug's Model A Ford.

At breakfast, the dining room table is set formally as a Victorian table would be. You could descend the stairs dressed in old-fashioned costumes and feel right at home.

In the East, Civil War buffs can immerse

themselves in the 1860s with an overnight at The Doubleday Inn, which sits directly on the Gettysburg Battlefield. The colonial-style inn has nine guest rooms decorated with antiques and country quilts. Breakfast is a candlelit affair.

The Doubleday Inn also has a collection of over 500 volumes devoted exclusively to the Battle of Gettysburg. On some evenings, guests can participate in discussions with a Civil War historian who brings the battle alive with accurate accounts, authentic memorabilia and weaponry. Staying here is an education in American history as well as a trip to the past.

At Longfellow's Wayside Inn in Sudbury, Mass., guests can stay in a painstakingly restored inn, which dates back to 1708. One can still enjoy a drink in the original tavern. The inn was immortalized by Henry Wadsworth Longfellow's "Tales of the Wayside Inn."

Among the impressive historical features are a grist mill restored in the 1920s by Henry Ford. All of the wheat for the inn's hearty breads and muffins are stone ground at this mill.

The innkeeper employs a full staff, including two curators, a miller and a schoolteacher. For groups of schoolchildren, the teacher will lead classes in the turn-of-the-19th-century schoolhouse

Those who wish to be transported back to a "Gone With The Wind"-style era should try the Cedar Grove Mansion Inn in the Mississippi town of Vicksburg. This grand antebellum estate was built in 1840 by John Klein as a wedding present for his bride.

Unlike many other Vicksburg homes, the house survived destruction because Klein's wife was a cousin of Union commander William T. Sherman. Nonetheless, a cannonball is still lodged in the parlor wall, serving as a reminder of how close the Union armies came.

Some of the 24 guest rooms contain their original furnishings. The Grant Room, for instance, has a bed thought to have been used by the general during the 47-day siege at Vicksburg when he and his troops lived in the lower part of the house. Scarlet's Room is highlighted by a double canopy bed and fainting couch.

Tours of the Cedar Grove Mansion Inn, the ballroom, and its four acres of gardens, fountains, and gazebos are conducted by hostesses dressed in 19th-century costumes. Guests can sip mint juleps on the wrought-iron terraces, while overlooking a magnificent view of the Mississippi River.

Some inns are not only pieces of living history in themselves, but are also ideally situated within historic villages or parks. The whole village of Deerfield, Mass., for example, has been designated a National Historic Landmark. Settled in 1670, the earth here still reveals occasional bones and ax heads from an ancient Indian massacre.

Fifty beautifully restored colonial and Federal homes line mile-long The Street, considered by many to be the loveliest street in New England. Fourteen of these houses are museums that display historic textiles, silver and period homes.

Also located on The Street and owned by the Historic Deerfield organization is the Deerfield Inn, built in 1884. The New England-style country inn is filled with antiques from historic Deerfield's remarkable collection. Most of the 23 rooms are decorated in historic Deerfield patterns from the late 1700s. The inn offers all meals, including afternoon tea.

Another attractive and well-preserved historic town is Fredericksburg, Texas. This fertile area was first settled by German farmers who arrived in 1846. German bakeries, cafes and old stone houses line Main Street, offering a comforting reminder of the town's German heritage. There are also many B&B's and guest houses in Fredericksburg, including Country Cottage Inn and Delforge Place.

Country Cottage Inn actually consists of two separate historic houses, the Nimitz Birthplace and the Kiehne House. Built in the 1850s and 1860s, both buildings are constructed of two-foot-thick stone walls and large stone fireplaces. The Kiehne House was the first two-story limestone house in town. The Nimitz Birthplace has the added interest of being the birthplace of Fleet Admiral Chester W. Nimitz. The little room where he was born is now a guest room, with letters and mementos hung on the walls. Both houses are largely unchanged, decorated with a vast collection of rustic antiques such as a blacksmith bellows, cheese press and flint threshing board. The only obvious updates are the bathrooms, which have romantic whirlpool tubs for two. The Mountain Laurel Room features an old-fashioned, eight-foot copper tub.

Both cottages are self-catering, which gives guests an ideal private setting in which to indulge and immerse themselves in the past. But those who prefer the hosting of an innkeeper will enjoy the Delforge Place.

Innkeeper Betsy Delforge, who comes from a long line of sea captains, has decorated every one of her guest rooms in a different time period and corresponding mariner's theme. The Map Room highlights the clipper ship era; the American Room sports a Civil War theme; and the Quebec Suite features the American Revolution. The second level is built to resemble a ship's prow, complete with a ship's wheel on the outside. The Victorian-style house and its seafaring touches are a delight for history buffs. 19th-century costumes, paintings, atlases, trunks, and quilts offer guests an intriguing glimpse of the past. Betsy's antiques change frequently because they are kept circulating through museums.

Staying in the Amish country of Ohio, Indiana or Pennsylvania is another way to transport yourself back to a gentler time. Holmes County, Ohio, boasts the world's largest Amish settlement, and the Bigham House, in historic Millersburg, is one of several inns that are close to the Amish. Innkeepers John and Janice Ellis can arrange a three-hour tour through the back roads of the Amish country, visiting a cheese factory, farms and bakery.

The two-story brick house was built in 1869 by an army surgeon of the Civil War. Its four guest rooms evoke the feeling of days gone by with period pieces, some Amish furnishings, floral wall coverings, and ceiling fans. John, who is British-born, also runs an English tea room that is open to the public.

Bringing "Inn" the Holiday Cheer

HOLIDAYS: Innkeepers deck the halls with extraordinary decorations.

If chilly weather and icy roads keep your mind far from a winter getaway to your favorite inn, imagine taking a horse-drawn sleigh ride across a snowy meadow or carolers gathered in the town square for a holiday concert.

Many bed & breakfasts and country inns across the country celebrate the winter season with a host of special events.

Some inns become an active part of communities that relive a sense of history and association with warm, simple holiday celebrations of a different era. These towns relish the days when families weren't struck with a barrage of high-pressure commercials pitching video games as the perfect Christmas present, and parents didn't have to comb the stores in search of the ever illusive Power Ranger gift item.

You'll find that visions of Christmas past come alive at these special places.

"An Elegant Victorian Mansion" Eureka, Calif.

To accent and cover all the lines of this Gingerbread Victorian with Christmas lights and strings of bulbs takes a long time, and the final result is a very elaborate display, innkeeper Doug Vieyra said.

The inn and the seaport town have a strong Victorian feel all year round and during Christmas, "another layer" of what the 1890s was like is added.

The interior, which is a living museum, includes many decorations and a Christmas tree with candles that are lit for short periods of time during special occasions. (Vieyra is also a firefighter and takes necessary precautions). Stockings hung at the fireplace are crocheted and knitted by

Vieyra's wife, Lily.

The Vieyras can arrange horse-drawn carriage rides and the inn has its own collection of horseless carriages that are used for Victorian tours and special events. The town is bustling with Christmas-related activities including caroling, Santa's arrival and tree-lighting ceremonies.

Guests at the inn can enjoy eggnog and hot cider drinks in the evening.

"This town has a very deep sense of the Victorian experience," Vieyra said. "I haven't found anyplace else like this on the West Coast."

Bridgeford House
Eureka Springs, Ark.

Innkeeper Denise McDonald said her inn is decorated "to the hilt" and that pretty much describes the rest of Eureka Springs during the holidays. The chamber of commerce puts out a booklet entitled "Share the Spirit of Christmas Past," in which a schedule of events includes activities for every weekend in December and then some. The Christmas Home Tour includes a walk through the historic district and its many Victorian structures.

On weekends, the Christmas Caroling bus travels the historic loop, picking up carolers at the Bridgeford House and at other stops along the way. After an evening of holiday activities around town, guests are treated to hot chocolate and snacks.

Every year, although the McDonalds always string red lights, they choose a different decorating theme for their inn. One year, candy canes were the primary inspiration for their home, which is decorated inside and outside.

"We try to be different," McDonald said. "We're also easy to find because of all our red lights."

Carriages pulled by horses outfitted in Christmas splendor are available every day, as well as a trolley that's also decorated appropriately.

The Hardy House
Georgetown, Colo.

Chosen for its unique atmosphere at the base of the Rocky Mountains, Georgetown was the site for the filming of The Christmas Gift, a movie starring John Denver. For more than 20 years, the town, which includes 200 Victorian buildings, has celebrated the holidays with Christmas Market Weekends, a festive array of activities, decorated homes and stores.

Guests staying at The Hardy House during the holidays are in for numerous treats. A carriage or hay ride meanders through this picturesque, former silver-mining town year-round, but at no other time are the buildings as dressed up.

The Hardy House is no exception. A white picket fence in front of this red and white inn is decorated with garlands, red bows, wreaths and lights. All the guest rooms have a Christmas tree.

Every weekend, the nearby Hamil House Museum is host to an open house Christmas party where music, poetry and tree-lighting ceremonies abound.

Innkeeper Michael Wagner said guests at the inn really become a part of his family's holiday.

"Last year, we had guests for Christmas Eve and Day and we cooked a big turkey," Wagner said. "We really got into the spirit."

For information on town activities, call the Visitors Center at (303) 569-2555 or the Chamber of Commerce at (303) 569-2888.

Commonwealth Cottage
Sturbridge, Mass.

This 16-room Queen Anne Victorian is included as an "Afternoon Tea" stop in Worcester County's Christmas event program named "Chain of Lights."

"We've decked the halls," said innkeeper Wiebke Gilbert. "There are lots of greens, ribbons and bows in all rooms."

In the parlor and dining room, the fireplaces are decorated with garlands, lights and a variety of family treasures, such as nutcrackers, angels, Santas and music boxes.

The outside of the house is decorated with wreaths and garlands spanning the 40-foot front gazebo porch and bows.

Guests are invited to a tree-trimming party that usually takes place the weekend before Christmas. A "very fat and tall" tree is decorated with glass ornaments that belonged to Gilbert's German grandmother, ones made by the innkeepers' children, and those given to the family for special occasions. All ornaments have a special story.

Other "Chain of Lights" activities include a Gingerbread House Contest at a local restaurant, a Yule Log Celebration and Breakfast with Santa at the Publick House Historic Inn and horse-drawn wagon or sleigh rides through Old Sturbridge Village.

To receive a calendar of events from the Tri-Community (Sturbridge, Southbridge and Charlton) Chamber of Commerce call (800) 628-8379.

The Queen Victoria
Cape May, N.J.

If you plan to come to Cape May during the holidays, book early. Christmas is a special festival in this beautiful, Victorian town often referred to as the "Bed & Breakfast Capitol of the United States." Tree-trimming workshops, Charles Dickens feasts and costumed carolers crowd the calendar.

Innkeeper Dane Wells said that years ago, the holiday season was a slow time in Cape May for tourism business. Now, December is "almost like the summer."

"There are more house tours in December than any other time of the year," Wells said. "The inns tend to tell a story about Christmas rather than just be decorated."

Afternoon tea at The Queen Victoria includes a discussion on the evolution of the Victorian Christmas celebration. Wells has done research on the subject and includes a talk on Santa. He also uses the three trees displayed at the inn, which represent different periods of the Victorian era, to help illustrate the topic.

"About 15 to 20 inns are heavily involved in presenting and interpreting Christmas," Wells said. "Also, a local actors group, called the 'Cape May Christmas Troupe,' does a Christmas show involving song, drama and audience participation."

Outside, the inn is decorated with 4,000 lights. "For this area, (the amount of lights) is run-of-the-mill," Wells said. "I wouldn't call it out-of-the-ordinary."

Adding to the town's holiday spirit, horses pulling carriages wear sleigh bells.

Williamsburg Manor B&B
Williamsburg, Va.

Built during the reconstruction of Colonial Williamsburg, this Georgian brick Colonial is three blocks from the historic village.

Unlike many historic towns that dress up for the holidays, Williamsburg keeps the decorations low-key and observes the holidays in an 18th-century Colonial style. The town is decorated with natural materials and overflows with music, dancing, caroling and banquets.

On Tuesdays, there are free organ recitals on the magnificent, albeit 20th-Century, organ at Bruton Parish Church. The Williamsburg Lodge hosts a Groaning Board Banquet, which is held five times during the season. Wreaths and garlands of fruits and greens go up on the doors and stair rails of the restored brick and clapboard houses and shops. Instead of strings of lights, solitary candles illuminate windows.

Williamsburg ushers in the season on the first Sunday in December by sending off canon salvos at dusk followed by a fireworks display. Up to 25,000 locals and visitors line the streets for the Grand Illumination. After the fireworks, balladeers in Colonial dress, dancers and fiddlers perform on stages illuminated by the glow of bonfires and tall cressets—hanging baskets of burning pine pitch.

While indulging on local food, save room for dining at the manor, where the innkeeper is a culinary professional who delight guests with seasonal fare.

For more information on the town's activities contact: Christmas Events, Colonial Williamsburg, PO Box 1776, Williamsburg, Va., 23187-1776. Phone: (804) 221-8950.

St. James Hotel
Red Wing, Minn.

It takes only moments after arriving in the historic town of Red Wing to feel transported back in time. This river town with many red brick buildings, small parks and quaint shops is nestled along the banks of the Mississippi River.

Rooms at the historic St. James offer a view of the river or of Red Wing, which is especially decked out for the holidays and almost assured of a white Christmas.

An eight-foot poinsettia tree adorns the entry way of the hotel and a 14-foot Christmas tree is found in the lobby. All of the windows are lined with electric candles and garlands. Ribbons and bows are everywhere.

Santa's house, lighted reindeers and trees are across the street in a multi-level city park. Buildings in the town are outlined in clear lights.

Many guests arrive at the 60-room hotel on Christmas Eve and stay one or two days. After checking in, guests will find a small bottle of champagne, a tray of assorted Christmas cookies and a box of chocolates in their rooms.

A Christmas Eve dinner, which has grown in popularity, includes a buffet. A local theater group gives a presentation in the lobby area at 8:30 p.m. Afterwards, a sweets table is offered in the Victorian dining room.

Special meals are also served on Christmas morning and afternoon. Guests departing on Boxing Day are given a small gift. Those who come for New Year's Eve can enjoy an elegant dinner that includes a show given by another local arts group and later, guests can bring on the New Year with dancing.

For further information on activities planned in Red Wing, call the Chamber of Commerce at (612) 388-4719.

Grand Victorian B&B Inn
Bellaire, Mich.

This Queen Anne Victorian dresses up for the holidays with rows of tiny lights and garlands accenting the gables, square corner towers, bays and overhangs.

Innkeeper Jill Watson said she hosts several local groups' parties and afternoon Christmas teas are served on Sundays in December. Guests are treated to holiday baked goods and classical Christmas music.

One of the many Bellaire events scheduled each year includes Santa's arrival at the Autrim County Airport, located in the downtown area. Window decorating contests are held, making this Victorian town come alive with holiday spirit.

In the shopping area of Bellaire, Christmas music can be heard from outdoor speakers and antique Victorian lamp posts are decorated festively.

"This is real small town America," Watson said. "Around the holidays it's like a little fairy town."

The Grand Victorian, which is located at the end of the main street, is a common stop for curiosity seekers wanting to get a glimpse of a uniquely decorated inn.

Stress-Free Travel

STRESS: These tips help ensure a more peaceful, easy vacation.

The plane isn't on time. You forgot to pack your swimsuit. The taxi fares are outrageously high priced. You're about to pull out your hair and the vacation has barely started.

Relaxation may not always be the by-product of a vacation — especially for the traveler whose expectations don't match with reality. Or vacationers who don't really have a gameplan for their trip.

Taking time off from work, leaving home and breaking from your daily routine, do not necessarily mean that you're ready for a stress-free vacation.

Some things are out of your control, but there are other circumstances that can be avoided:

Not knowing where you're going to spend the night.

Avoid unnecessary stress by having your vacation pre-planned. Get as many things prearranged and have an itinerary before you go.

It is especially important to make almost all arrangements before you travel to another country.

"I've seen a lot of couples go over to

Europe and say, 'we'll just stay where we can, as we go,'" said Jeanne Epping, of the American Society of Travel Agents. "More couples go over and do that and come back and get a divorce."

Epping, who also runs a travel agency in Santa Cruz, Calif., said it is her responsibility as her clients' travel consultant to not send them on a trip to Europe without anything more than airplane and car rental reservations.

Recently, a family asked her to do simply that and she refused. "I told them 'you won't be a happy family when you come back,'" she said. "In some cases, if my clients insist, then I will recommend that they make lodging reservations in key places, like the beginning and end of a trip."

Selecting a suitable trip.

Choosing a vacation that fits your needs can be difficult. Some travelers prefer a tour, where everything is pre-arranged. Others prefer to strike out on their own and see where a little adventure will get them.

Often, one person in your traveling group will be a tour person and another will be a little more free-wheeling. Try to come to an itinerary agreement before embarking on your vacation.

Not being able to check-in to your inn or hotel upon arrival.

Frustration levels can run high if you've arrived at your destination and all you can do is wait for the check-in time before you can get your room.

Make a call to the inn to find out about check-in time. You may want to arrange your arrival close to check-in (times vary from noon to 3 p.m.). Or, if you are early, plan to hit a couple of the local attractions before checking in. Many places can make arrangements for your bags.

The physical and mental toll of long flights.

There are several steps to take that will help you deal with long flights.

"The key is to completely relax for as long as possible on a long flight," Epping said. "Take a good book. Drink lots of water (to avoid dehydration). It's not a good idea to drink alcohol.

"Take a walk every one or two hours," she said. "These things will make you relax and not have a tendency to be stressed."

Theft.

Crime continues to be a growing problem everywhere. You should not assume that you won't be a victim.

At airports, never check luggage that contains valuables. Some baggage handlers know how to open all types of luggage.

Do not leave luggage unattended, even for a brief moment. If your briefcase contains money or important documents, don't put it down. Lock your luggage and be sure it's well identified as being yours.

Forgotten necessary items.

Make a check list of personal things you can't be without and then pack them into a convenient place ... always within close reach. Don't wait until the last minute to pack.

Always have your medication handy. If you wear glasses, it's a good idea to bring an extra pair.

Bored travel companions.

Nothing can be more frustrating than sharing a vacation with someone who can't or really doesn't want to do the same things you do.

If you're going with children, make sure there are activities at your destination that will be enjoyable for them. If you can arrange time for yourself to do the things you want to, then do so. Everyone must understand that not everything is of interest to all.

Research your destination and share your information with everyone going on your trip. Visualize what you will do once you get there. Get a good understanding of how your days will be spent.

Maybe the best advice is to "pack your common sense," Epping said.

Know the areas in which you're traveling. Always carry a map, but don't make yourself easily identifiable as a tourist.

"We don't say 'travel in the '90s can be

stressful' we say 'living in the '90s can be stressful'," she said. "Don't do anything that you wouldn't do at home."

For bed & breakfasts guests, here are some specific tips to keep in mind:

Will there be a private bath?

While Europeans are a bit more accustomed to the shared-bath situation, Americans are not. Some bed & breakfasts have a limited number of private baths, and a few have no private baths at all. This is more common in Europe than the United States, but you'll still find that a percentage of bed & breakfasts in North America have bathrooms that are shared.

This may be fine if you are sharing a bathroom with family or friends, but if you want to make sure you're getting a private bath, tell the innkeeper prior to making the reservation.

Dietary needs.

Most innkeepers are happy to accommodate special dietary needs, but they must be aware of those needs in advance. Again, it's best to ask the innkeeper if she or he can make a special breakfast for you when you make your reservation.

Handicap access.

As many inns and B&Bs are located in old (sometimes centuries old) buildings, there are rarely the elevators you'll find in a modern hotel. If you have trouble walking up stairs, be sure to ask about reserving a first-floor guest room. Also, there may not be someone there to carry your luggage, so be prepared to lug it.

Check-in.

At hotels, you often can check in at odd hours. At country inns and more likely at a B&B, there may not be someone on-site to meet you if you arrive very late at night. If you know that you will be arriving late, be sure to make arrangements with the innkeeper.

Know what to expect.

Bed & breakfasts and country inns are much different from hotels. Chances are you'll be treated to some extra attention by an innkeeper whose goal is to make you feel as welcome as possible.

You may be eating breakfast side-by-side with other guests. Frankly, eating with the innkeeper and other guests is one of the best ways to find out about where to go and what to do.

Some innkeepers strive to take you away from hectic, everyday life, so you may not have a TV or telephone in your room.

Sometimes because of the abundance of antiques or because the innkeeper wants a more romantic ambiance geared toward couples, it may be an uncomfortable environment for family travelers. So, inquire if the inn is appropriate for children, and ask if they have cribs or rooms that can accommodate families.

Ask the innkeeper to send you a brochure, these usually give a description of the inn, rates, cancellation policies and information about activities in the community. This way, you can gauge which inn best meets your needs.

An Impressive Guest Register

WHO SLEPT HERE?: Stay where the famous have dined, danced and dreamt.

After his beloved wife Carole Lombard died in a plane crash, actor Clark Gable found solace at a Tuscon, Ariz., hideaway. That 1930 home now serves as the aptly named The Gable House. Within its walls are spacious, airy guest rooms decorated with Santa Fe Pueblo and Mexican influences. It's not hard to understand why Gable chose this rustic home as a place for reflection.

Gable was no stranger to cozy hideaways. He and Carole honeymooned at the Gold Mountain Manor, a romantic inn tucked away in mountainous Big Bear, Calif. This retreat hosted many of the rich and famous.

For those of us who frequent bed & breakfasts or country inns, the myriad of statesmen, writers, actors and other such adorned personalities who once visited these places is one of many characteristics that make the whole experience so unique.

For instance, guests staying at the opulent John Rutledge House Inn in Charleston, S.C., may proclaim not only that George Washington once dined there, but that first drafts of the U.S. Constitution were drawn up in the mansion's ballroom. The home's builder, John Rutledge, was no slouch himself in the context of American history. Rutledge, was not only a writer and signer of the Constitution, he also served as South Carolina's first governor and a Supreme Court justice. A stay at Rutledge's home is to experience a little piece of American history.

Much of our nation's history is preserved at inns and bed & breakfasts. Presidents Andrew Jackson, James Polk and Andrew Johnson stayed at the Rogersville, Tenn., inn now known as Hale Springs Inn. On the town square, this is the oldest continually operating inn in the state. The structure itself was built in 1824. McKinney Tavern, as it was known then, served as Union headquarters during the Civil War.

Authors Samuel Clemens and Jack London, as well as President Theodore Roosevelt were among the famous guests at the Vichy Hot Springs Resort & Inn in Ukiah, Calif. Although the lodging facilities have been updated, the 1860s naturally sparkling mineral baths remain unchanged. As you relax in a mineral bath, it's not hard to imagine the days when guests were able to discuss "Tom Sawyer," or "The Call of the Wild," with the authors.

In its heyday, Eureka, Calif., was a booming, Victorian-era lumber town. One of its leading lumber barons fashioned a gracious mansion in town, drawing the likes of entertainers Lillie Langtry and Sarah Bernhardt, as well as a multitude of senators and representatives. Today, the home serves as the bed & breakfast, "An Elegant Victorian Mansion." Guests at the mansion are treated to an authentic, Victorian experience, complete with hosts and a butler decked in full, period attire.

Doric columns adorn The Veranda, a 9,000-square-foot hotel, built at the turn of the century in Senoia, Ga. Georgia veterans of the Civil War held their annual reunion at the hotel, and Margaret Mitchell of "Gone With the Wind" fame came here once to interview the former soldiers. William Jennings Bryan was another famous guest at this Southern hotel.

It was at the Wooden Rabbit in Cape May, N.J., that Robert E. Lee brought his wife to help ease her arthritis, and coincidently, this sea captain's home was also part of the Underground Railroad.

Robert E. Lee also was a guest at what is now Rocklands, an executive retreat owned by the same family since 1926. Although the Georgian Revival home was built in 1905, the significance of the property dates back to the Civil War when a battle broke out between Union and Confederate soldiers. Lee was a guest at one of the early buildings on the property.

It's not surprising that many an artist visited Hacienda del Sol, an 1810 adobe home located in Taos, N.M. Among the famous guests were Georgia O'Keefe, who painted here, and D.H. Lawrence. The home is a restful place, set among huge cottonwoods, blue spruce and Ponderosa pines, with an uninterrupted view of the mountains across 95,000 acres of Native American lands.

Naturalist and author John James Audubon enjoyed the hospitality of Jonathan Weston and his family while awaiting passage to Labrador at the Weston's home, which overlooks the Passamaquoddy Bay. The home now serves as Weston House, a charming bed & breakfast furnished with antiques and Oriental rugs. The innkeepers have named a room for Audubon and this special place offers views of the bay and gardens, just the way John Audubon would have wanted it.

Witmer's Tavern, a pre-Revolutionary War inn is the sole survivor of 62 inns that once lined the old Lancaster-to-Philadelphia turnpike.

History buffs will enjoy seeing the Native American escape tunnel entrance and knowing that President John Adams once stayed here.

At The General Lewis, a stagecoach that once delivered travelers to the springs on the James River and Kanawha Turnpike, rests under an arbor. Patrick Henry and Thomas Jefferson registered at this 1834 inn's walnut desk, which was retrieved from an old hot springs resort in the area.

Henry Fry, a close friend of Thomas Jefferson, built what is now The Inn at Meander Plantation in Locust Dale, Va. Jefferson often stopped at this 1766 home on his way to Monticello.

From the grounds, which feature ancient formal boxwood gardens, woodland, meadows and views of the Blue Ridge Mountains, one can almost picture Jefferson and Fry engaged in a discussion of politics as they strolled the lawn after a gourmet dinner.

Many of these historic hotels, bed & breakfasts and country inns would be worthy of interest and historic recognition even without the famous guests. But it's always nice for travelers to reminisce their journeys with the knowledge that George Washington did indeed once sleep here.

For a further listing of inns that were host to presidents, actors, writers and other famous folk, check out the Inns of Interest section.

Dude Ranches

RIDE THE RANGE: Rustic vacation spots often provide fun for the whole family.

Even though it's been several years since the release of "City Slickers" and the ensuing wave of urbanites who headed to dude ranches, the popularity of this alternative form of vacationing has not died down.

Many ranches have developed into full-blown resorts, and while not all offer guests the opportunity to actually work with the ranch hands, most give the chance to be a part of the ranch experience. Horseback rides, hay rides and cook-outs are the norm.

These days, dude ranches have become an ideal place for family vacations, many even offer full programs for children.

Rates often are quoted by the week. Many ranches include all three meals, and many activities also may be included. Some offer overnight campouts, entertainment, hikes, canoe trips and more.

If you are looking for a ranch, it's important to know exactly what you want and ask for specifics when calling or writing to a ranch for information. Although the programs differ, all ranches have horseback riding as a main activity.

Some ranches offer walking rides, while others offer trotting and faster paced riding. Some working cattle ranches allow guests to assist with ranch chores or cattle drives.

"About one-third of our callers ask about a working ranch," said Jim Futterer, who is the executive director of the Dude Ranchers' Association. "A recent trend seems to be that people are asking for more upscale ranches. They are looking for diverse programs that might include white-water rafting and are also asking about whether the ranches serve upscale meals."

The Dude Ranchers' Association has 109 ranches as members, and one-third are working ranches, Futterer said. Even though you might be herding cattle during the day, chances are your accommodations will not be in the "roughing it" category.

If you need help with deciding on a ranch, you may want to call the Dude Ranchers' association at (970) 223-8440. They can send you a guide detailing activities and rates at many North American ranches.

The following is a sample of what you might find at a dude ranch:

Three Bars Cattle & Guest Ranch
3 Site 19 62 DRA
Cranbrook BC VIC 6H3
(604) 426-5230

Guests are invited to "share an experience

of a lifetime" at this Canadian ranch, which is located in the southeastern corner of British Columbia in the Canadian Rockies.

Aside from the 350 head of cattle, which keep the ranch hands busy, activities include fly fishing, river rafting, hiking to a nearby waterfall, tennis and volleyball. The ranch also offers a heated pool and outdoor whirlpool spa.

Hunewill Circle "H" Ranch

PO Box 368
Bridgeport, CA 93517
(619) 932-7710

This ranch started operating in 1861, and cattle ranching has always been the main business.

Situated on 4,400 acres and with more than 2,000 cattle, there's an opportunity to do some cattle-work and plenty of ranch activities.

Should you decide to take some time off from the ranch work, there's hiking, swimming in a stream that's on the property, breakfast rides, cookouts, picnics, trout fishing and car trips to deserted mining towns.

Aspen Canyon Ranch

13206 Country Road #3, Star Route
Parshall, CO 80468
(800) 321-1357

There's plenty of instruction for guests on aspects of ranching and rodeo. Roping, barrels and other aspects are taught in the ranch's rodeo arena. At the end of the week, guests can enjoy a professional rodeo.

A river flows right next to cabins, which have a fireplace, refrigerator, coffeemaker and a stocked cookie jar. Other activities include a breakfast ride, fishing and hunting. Also, there's excellent biking and hiking trails.

Flathead Lake Lodge & Dude Ranch

Box 248, Big Fork, MT 59911
(406) 837-4391

Guests of this 2,000-acre ranch are welcome to learn all aspects of ranching from riding or roping to daily chores around the corrals. The ranch also offers a diverse set of activities, including whitewater rafting, sailing, water skiing and fishing. Flathead Lake Lodge has a four-star rating.

Lost Fork Ranch

11-12 Hwy. 287
Madison Valley, MT 59720
(406) 682-7690

Beginners and experts at horseback riding are accommodated at this ranch with horses to suit your style.

The ranch's program includes riding instruction, rodeo arena work, moving cattle, team penning and a weekly rodeo for the children.

Hargrave Cattle & Guest Ranch

300 Thompson River Valley
Marion, MT 59925
(406) 858-2284

National forests surround this 87,000-acre ranch.

In the summer, guests are invited to ride and work real cattle jobs or ride through tall timber and on meadow trails. Also, included are overnight campouts, skeet or target shooting, archery and lake canoeing. In the evening, entertainment consists of cowboy music around the campfire.

Hartley Guest Ranch

HCR 73, Box 55
Roy, NM 87743
(800) OUR DUDE

At this ranch, guests can explore the 200 miles of trails that go through forests of juniper, oak and pine and circle the rims of red-rock canyons, either on horseback or by ATV.

Activities include working cattle, branding (in season), fishing, hiking and cowboy campouts.

Guests also can explore ancient Indian sites, search for dinosaur bones and view interesting geological formations located on the ranch.

Brush Creek Guest Ranch

Star Route, Box Ten
Saratoga, WY 82331
(800) RANCH WY

Roping and branding lessons are among the fun activities for guests at this ranch, which is situated at the base of the Snowy Range Mountains. Besides horseback riding through beautiful terrain, guests can chose to get "hands-on" experience moving cattle.

Airlines

Aeromexico .... (800) 237-6639
Air Canada........... (800) 776-3000
Alaska Air............ (800) 426-0333
America Airlines....... (800) 433-7300
America West Airlines... (800) 235-9292
Canadian Airlines Int'l... (800) 426-7000
Continental Airlines..... (800) 525-0280
Delta Airlines .... (800) 221-1212
Mexicana Airlines...... (800) 531-7921
Midway Airlines .... (800) 446-4392
Midwest Express ...... (800) 452-2022
Northwest Airlines ..... (800) 225-2525
Reno .... (800) 736-6247
Southwest Airlines ..... (800) 435-9792
Tower Air............ (800) 221-2500
United Airlines .... (800) 241-6522
USAir............... (800) 428-4322
ValuJet.............. (800) 825-8538

Complaints & Compliments

American Airlines...... (817) 967-2000
America West......... (800) 235-9292
Continental Airlines..... (800) 932-2732
Delta Airlines .... (404) 715-1450
Northwest Airlines ..... (612) 726-2046
Southwest Airlines ..... (214) 904-4223
United Airlines .... (847) 952-6796
USAir............... (910) 661-0061
U.S. Department of Transportation
.... (202) 366-2220

Car Rentals

Advantage Rent-A-Car... (800) 777-5500
Alamo Rent-A-Car...... (800) 327-9633
Avis Rent-A-Car....... (800) 331-1212
Budget Rent-A-Car..... (800) 527-0700
Dollar Rent-A-Car...... (800) 800-4000
Enterprise............ (800) 325-8007
Hertz Rent-A-Car...... (800) 654-3131
National Car Rental..... (800) 328-4567
Payless Car Rental..... (800) 729-5377
Rent A Wreck......... (800) 535-1391
Sears/Budget Rent-A-Car (800) 527-0770
Thrifty Car Rental...... (800) 367-2277
Value Rent-A-Car...... (800) 468-2583

Railroad

Amtrak.............. (800) USA-RAIL

State/U.S. Territory Tourist Offices

Alabama Bureau of Tourism & Travel
.... (800) 252-2262
Alaska Division of Tourism (907) 465-2012
Arizona Office of Tourism (800) 842-8257
Arkansas Department of Parks & Tourism
.... (800) 872-1259
California Division of Tourism
.... (800) GO CALIF
Colorado- Denver Metro Convention & Visitors Bureau........ (800) 645-3446
Connecticut- State of Connecticut Tourism Division...... (800) CT BOUND
Delaware Tourism Office. (800) 441-8846
District of Columbia- Washington, D.C. Convention and Visitors Association
.... (202) 789-7000
Florida Division of Tourism (904) 487-1462
Georgia Department of Industry, Trade & Tourism........ (800) VISIT-GA
Hawaii Visitors Bureau .. (808) 923-1811
In NYC: (212) 947-0717
Idaho Dept. of Commerce-Div. of Tourism
.... (800) 635-7820
Illinois Bureau of Tourism (800) 2 CONNECT
Indiana Department of Commerce, Tourism Development... (800) 382-6771
Iowa Division of Tourism. (800) 345-IOWA
Kansas Travel & Tourism. (800) 2-KANSAS
Kentucky Dept. of Travel Dev.
.... (800) 225-8747
Louisiana Office of Tourism (800) 334-8626
Maine- Office of Tourism. (800) 533-9595
Maryland- Office of Tourism Dev.
.... (410) 333-6611
Massachusetts Office of Travel & Tourism
.... (800) 227-MASS
Michigan Travel Bureau . (800) 543-2-YES
Minnesota Office of Tourism
.... (800) 657-3700
Mississippi Division of Tourism Development......... (800) WARMEST
Missouri Division of Tourism
.... (800) 535-3210
Montana Travel Promotion Division
.... (800) 548-3390
Nebraska Travel & Tourism (800) 228-4307
Nevada Commission on Tourism
.... (800) NEVADA-8
New Hampshire Office of Travel and Tourism............. (800) FUN-INNH
New Jersey Division of Travel & Tourism
.... (800) JERSEY7
New Mexico Dept. of Tourism
.... (800) 545-2070
New York Convention & Visitors Bureau
.... (800) 692-8474
North Carolina Division of Travel & Tourism.............. (800) VISIT NC
North Dakota Tourism Department
.... (800) 435-5663
Ohio Division of Travel and Tourism
.... (800) BUCKEYE
Oklahoma Travel & Tourism Division
.... (800) 652-4552
Oregon Tourism Division. (800) 547-7842
Pennsylvania Travel Council (800) 237-4363
Puerto Rico .... (800) 874-1230
Rhode Island Tourism Division
.... (800) 556-2484
South Carolina Dept of Tourism
.... (800) 868-2492
South Dakota Tourism... (800) 732-5682
Tennessee Tourist Development
.... (800) 741-9065
Texas Div. of Travel and Information
.... (800) 452-9292
U.S. Virgin Islands ..... (202) 293-3707
Utah Travel Council..... (800) 200-1160
Vermont Dept. of Travel & Tourism
.... (800) VERMONT
Virginia Division of Tourism (804) 786-2051
Washington State Tourism Division
.... (800) 544-1800
West Virginia Division of Tourism & Parks
.... (800) CALL-WVA
Wisconsin Division of Tourism
.... (800) 432-TRIP
Wyoming Div. of Tourism. (800) 225-5996

Canadian Tourist Offices

Alberta Economic Division & Tourism
.... (800) 661-8888
Tourism British Columbia. (800) 663-6000
Travel Manitoba .... (800) 665-0040
New Brunswick Dept. of Tourism
.... (800) 561-0123
Newfoundland/Labrador Tourism
.... (800) 563-6353
Northwest Territories Tourism
.... (800) 661-0788
Nova Scotia Mktg Agency (800) 341-0000
Ontario Ministry of Culture, Tour & Recreation ...... (800) ONTARIO
Prince Edward Island Tourism
.... (800) 463-4PEI
Tourism Quebec....... (800) 363-7777
Tourism Saskatchewan .. (306) 787-5282
Tourism Yukon .... (403) 667-5340

International Tourism Offices

Antigua & Barbuda..... (212) 541-4117
Argentina Govt Tourism . (213) 930-0681
Australia Tourist Commission
.... (310) 552-1988
Austrian National Tourist Office
.... (212) 944-6880
Bahamas Tourist Office. (800) 4-BAHAMA
Bermuda Dept of Tourism (800) 223-6106
British Virgin Islands Tourist Board
.... (800) 835-8530
Cayman Islands .... (213) 738-1968
China National Tourist Office
.... (212) 760-9700
Egyptian Tourist Authority (312) 280-4666
French Govt Tourist Office. (212) 725-1125
Germany National Tourist Office
.... (212) 661-7200
Great Britain.......... (800) GO2-BRIT
Greece National Tourist Organization
.... (212) 626-6696
Hong Kong Tourist Assoc (310) 208-4582
Irish Tourist Board..... (800) 223-6470
Israel Government Tourist Office
.... (212) 560-0600
Italian Government Tourist Office
.... (212) 245-4822
Japan National Tourist Organization
.... (212) 757-5640
Mexican Govt Tourism... (312) 565-2778
New Zealand Tourism Board (800) 388-5494
Polish National Tourist Office (212) 338-9412
Portuguese National Tourist Office
.... (212) 354-4403
Singapore Tourist Promotion Board
.... (212) 302-4861
Spain Tourist Office..... (212) 759-8822
Switzerland .... (212) 757-5944

AAA Bed & Breakfast: Britain
American Automobile Association
ISBN 156251-0681 $14.95

AAA Bed & Breakfast: Europe
American Automobile Association
ISBN 156251-069X $14.95

Australian Bed & Breakfasts
Thomas, J.
ISBN 156554-1987 $15.95

Bed & Breakfast Australia
Schonberger
ISBN 089815-3409 $14.95

Bed & Breakfast: Caribbean
Reid
ISBN 0671-899287 $16.00

Bed & Breakfast Ireland
Dillard, Elsi
ISBN 08118-11581 $13.95

Bed & Breakfast Lithuania
Zalatorius, G.
ISBN 09640496-00 $12.00

Britain Bed & Breakfast
Stilwell Publications
ISBN 09521909-74 $18.95

Canadian Bed & Breakfast
Pantel, Gerda
ISBN 014-0257519 $13.95

Great British Bed & Breakfasts 1996
ISBN 0952280736 $13.95

Guide to French Bed & Breakfasts
Sawday, Alist
ISBN 09521954-10 $21.95

Ireland Bed & Breakfasts
Stilwell, Staf
ISBN 09521909-82 $11.95

Irish Country Inns & Cottages
Brown, June
ISBN 0930328-183 $12.95

New Zealand Bed & Breakfast
Thomas, J.
ISBN 156554-0107 $14.95

Nova Scotia Pictorial Country Inns
Hines, Sherma
ISBN 0921128-355 $12.95

Scotland Bed & Breakfasts
Stilwell, Staf
ISBN 09521909-66 $11.95

The Irish Bed & Breakfast
Sullivan
ISBN 156554-0344 $12.95

Timpson's English Country Inns
Timpson, John
ISBN 07472-08263 $35.00

Wales Bed & Breakfast 1993
Welsh Tourist Organization
ISBN 185013-0493 $6.95

Water-Mill Inns of France
Luther, Marv
ISBN 09649085-49 $16.95

Books by Karen Brown

California: Charming Inns & Itineraries
ISBN 093032842-6 $17.95

Austria: Charming Inns & Itineraries
ISBN 093032841-8 $17.95

England, Wales & Scotland: Charming Hotels & Itineraries
ISBN 093032843-4 $17.95

England: Charming Bed & Breakfasts
ISBN 093032844-2 $16.95

France: Charming Inns & Itineraries
ISBN 093032850-7 $17.95

Germany: Charming Inns & Itineraries
ISBN 093032852-3 $17.95

Ireland: Charming Inns & Itineraries
ISBN 093032853-1 $17.95

Italy: Charming Inns & Itineraries
ISBN 093032854-X $17.95

Italy: Charming Bed & Breakfasts
ISBN 093032855-8 $16.95

Spain: Charming Inns & Itineraries
ISBN 093032856-6 $17.95

Switzerland: Charming Inns & Itineraries
ISBN 093032857-4 $17.95

To order books by Karen Brown, call (415) 342-9117 or fax (415) 342-9153

Inns of Interest

African-American History

Bird-In-Hand . . . . Coventry, Conn.
Inn at Bethlehem . . . . Bethlehem, Ind.
Wingscorton Farm Inn . . . . East Sandwich, Mass.
Troutbeck . . . . Amenia, N.Y.
The Old Post House . . . . Southampton, N.Y.
The Signal House . . . . Ripley, Ohio
Rosebelle's Victorian Inn . . . . Brandon, Vt.
The Inn at Weathersfield . . . . Weathersfield, Vt.
1790 House B&B Inn . . . . Georgetown, S.C.
The Inn at Weathersfield . . . . Weathersfield, Vt.
Kedron Valley Inn . . . . Woodstock, Vt.
The Golden Stage Inn . . . . Proctorsville, Vt.
Rockland Farm Retreat . . . . Bumpass, Va.

Associated with Literary Figures

Louisa May Alcott, Ralph Waldo Emerson, Nathaniel Hawthorne
Hawthorne Inn . . . . Concord, Mass.
Henry Beston
Over Look Inn . . . . Eastham (Cape Cod), Mass.
F. Scott Fitzgerald, Thomas Wolfe
Welbourne . . . . Middleburg, Va.
D.H. Lawrence
Hacienda del Sol . . . . Taos, N.M.
Jack London
Vichy Hot Springs Resort & Inn . . . . . . Ukiah, Calif.
Margaret Mitchell
The Veranda . . . . Senoia, Ga.
Jonathon Swift
Swift House Inn . . . . Middlebury, Vt.
Mark Twain (Samuel Clemens)
Captain Josiah Mitchell House . . . . . Freeport, Maine
Garth Woodside . . . . Mansion Hannibal, Mo.
Vichy Hot Springs Resort & Inn . . . . . . Ukiah, Calif.
Lew Wallace (wrote screenplay for "Ben Hur")
Esmeralda Inn . . . . Chimney Rock, N.C.
Edith Wharton
The Gables Inn . . . . Lenox, Mass.

Barns

Brannon-Bunker Inn . . . . Damariscotta, Maine
Cornerstone B&B Inn . . . . Landenberg, Pa.
Waitsfield Inn . . . . Waitsfield, Vt.

Bordellos (Former, of course)

Cheyenne Canon Inn . . . . . Colorado Springs, Colo.
Oar House . . . . Newport, Ore.

Castle

Ravenwood Castle . . . . New Plymouth, OH

Churches

The Beechcroft Inn . . . . Brewster, Mass.
Parson's Pillow . . . . Cody, Wyo.

Civil War

Culpeper House . . . . Senoia, Ga.
Myrtledene B&B . . . . Lebanon, Ky.
Rosswood Plantation . . . . Lorman, Miss.
Dunleith . . . . Natchez, Miss.
Anchuca . . . . Vicksburg, Miss.
Cedar Grove Mansion Inn . . . . Vicksburg, Miss.
Lindenwald Haus . . . . Elmira, N.Y.
Churchtown Inn B&B . . . . Churchtown, Pa.
Baladerry Inn . . . . Gettysburg, Pa.
Brafferton Inn . . . . Gettysburg, Pa.
The Doubleday Inn Gettysburg . . . . . Gettysburg, Pa.
Baladerry Inn . . . . Gettysburg, Pa.
King's Inn at Georgetown . . . . Georgetown, S.C.
La Vista Plantation . . . . Fredericksburg, Va.
Springdale Country . . . . Inn Lincoln, Va.
A Touch of Country . . . . New Market, Va.
Country Fare . . . . Woodstock, Va.
The Inn at Narrow Passage . . . . Woodstock, Va.
Boydville, Inn at Martinsburg . . . . Martinsburg, W.V.

Farms/Orchards/Vineyards

Ramsey Canyon Inn . . . . Hereford, Aria.
Fool's Cove Ranch B&B . . . . Kingston, Ariz.
Apple Blossom Inn B&B . . . . Ahwahnee, Calif.
Apple Lane Inn . . . . Aptos, Calif.
Scarlet's Country Inn . . . . Calistoga, Calif.
The Inn at Shallow Creek Farm . . . . . . Orland, Calif.
Howard Creek Ranch . . . . Westport, Calif.
Apple Orchard Inn . . . . Durango, Colo.

Maple Hill Farm . . . . Coventry, Conn.
Applewood Farms Inn . . . . Ledyard, Conn.
Kealakekua Bay B&B . . . . Kealakekua, Hawaii
Kingston 5 Ranch . . . . Kingston, Idaho
Cottage at Amber Creek . . . . Galena, Ill.
Hedrick's Exotic Animal Farm . . . . . Nickerson, Kan.
Jordan Farm . . . . Georgetown, Ky.
Baldwin Hill Farm B&B. . . . Great Barrington, Mass.
On Cranberry Pond B&B. . . . . . . Middleboro, Mass.
Gilbert's Tree Farm B&B . . . . Rehoboth, Mass.
Wingscorton Farm Inn . . . . Sandwich, Mass.
Wades Point Inn on The Bay . . . Saint Michaels, Md.
Crane House . . . . Fennville, Mich.
Bluebird Trails . . . . Hillsdale, Mich.
Horse & Carriage B&B . . . . Jonesville, Mich.
Four Columns Inn . . . . Sherburn, Minn.
Old Pioneer Garden Guest Ranch . . . Unionville, Nev.
Colby Hill Inn . . . . Henniker, N.H.
Ellis River B&B . . . . Jackson, N.H.
Beal House Inn . . . . Littleton, N.H.
Olde Orchard Inn . . . . Moultonborough, N.H.
Apple Valley Inn and Antiques . . . . . Glenwood, N.J.
Agape Farm B&B . . . . Cornith, N.Y.
Breezy Acres Farm B&B . . . . Hobart, N.Y.
Old Chatham Sheepherding
Company Inn . . . . Old Chatham, N.Y.
Cedar Hill Farm B&B . . . . Statesville, N.C.
Volden Farm . . . . Lucerne, N.D.
Cedarbrook Farm B&B . . . . Elora, Ont.
Mattey House . . . . McMinnville, Ore.
Youngberg Hill Vineyard . . . . McMinnville, Ore.
Weatherbury Farm . . . . Avella, Pa.
Mill Creek Farm B&B . . . . Buckingham, Pa.
Ponda-Rowland B&B Inn . . . . Dallas, Pa.
Meadow Spring Farm . . . . Kennett Square, Pa.
Cedar Hill Farm . . . . Mount Joy, Pa.
Field & Pine B&B . . . . Shippensburg, Pa.
B&B at Skogland Farm . . . . Canova, S.D.
Hotel Turkey Living Museum . . . . Turkey, Texas
Hill Farm Inn . . . . Arlington, Vt.
Old Town Farm Inn . . . . Chester, Vt.
Historic Brookside Farms . . . . Orwell, Vt.
Liberty Hill Farm . . . . Rochester, Vt.
Just-N-Trails B&B/Nordic Ski Center. . . Sparta, Wis.
Benedict Haid Farm . . . . Charleston, W.V.
Ingeberg Acres . . . . Valley Chapel (Weston) W.V.

French and Indian War

Aspen Hall Inn . . . . Martinsburg, W.V.

Gold Mines & Gold Panning

Pearson's Pond Luxury Inn . . . . Juneau, Alaska
Julian Gold Rush Hotel . . . . Julian, Calif.
Dunbar House 1880 . . . . Murphys, Calif.
Hotel Nipton . . . . Nipton, Calif.

Inns Built Prior to 1799

1637 York Harbor Inn . . . . York Harbor, Maine
1678 Hewick Plantation . . . . Urbanna, Va.
1690 The Great Valley
House of Valley Forge . . . . Malvern, Pa.
1699 Ashley Manor Inn . . . . Barnstable, Mass.
1700 Hacienda Vargas. . . . . Algodones, N.M.
1700 Hollileif B&B . . . . Newtown, Pa.
1709 The Woodbox Inn . . . Nantucket Island, Mass.
1710 The Robert Morris Inn. . . . . Oxford, Md.
1720 Butternut Farm . . . . Glastonbury, Conn.
1723 Corner House . . . . Nantucket, Mass.
1725 Witmer's Tavern -
Historic 1725 Inn . . . . Lancaster, Pa.
1730 Colonial House Inn . . . . Yarmouth, Mass.
1731 Maple Hill Farm B&B . . . . . . Coventry, Conn.
1732 Under Mountain Inn. . . . . . . Salisbury, Conn.
1732 The Cookie Jar B&B . . . . Wyoming, R.I.
1738 Brown's Historic Home B&B . . . . Salem, N.J.
1740 Red Brook Inn Old . . . . Mystic, Conn.
1740 Henry Ludlam Inn . . . . Woodbine, N.J.
1740 Evermay-on-the-Delaware . . . . . . Erwinna, Pa.
1740 Barley Sheaf Farm . . . . Holicong, Pa.
1740 Tattersall Inn Point . . . . Pleasant, Pa.
1740 The Inn at Narrow Passage. . . . Woodstock, Va.
1743 The Inn at Mitchell House . . Chestertown, Md.
1750 Isaac Hilliard House B&B . . . Pemberton, N.J.
1750 Galisteo Inn. . . . . Galisteo, N.M.
1750 House on the Hill B&B
. . . . Lake George/Warrensburg, N.Y.
1750 The Melville House . . . . Newport, R.I.
1750 Henry Farm Inn. . . . . Chester, Vt.
1751 Penny House Inn . . . . Eastham, Mass.
1753 Maplehedge B&B. . . . . Charlestown, N.H.
1753 L'Auberge Provencale . . . . White Post, Va.
1754 Crocker Tavern B&B. . . . . . . Barnstable, Mass.
1756 Bee and Thistle Inn . . . . Old Lyme, Conn.
1757 Wingscorton Farm Inn . . East Sandwich, Mass.

1760 Henry Ludlam Inn.......... Woodbine, N.J.
1760 Gilbert House B&B of Middlebury
.... Charles Town, Va.
1761 The Bird & Bottle Inn........ Garrison, N.Y.
1763 Smithton Inn................. Ephrata, Pa.
1763 John Rutledge House....... Charleston, S.C.
1765 Captain Samuel Eddy House... Auburn, Mass.
1765 The Carlisle House .. Nantucket Island, Mass.
1765 Bankhouse B&B .... West Chester, Pa.
1766 The Inn at Meander Plantation
.... Locust Dale, Va.
1769 Thomas Bond House .... Philadelphia, Pa.
1770 Silvermine Tavern.......... Norwalk, Conn.
1770 The Parsonage Inn....... East Orleans, Mass.
1770 Garden Gables Inn............ Lenox, Mass.
1775 Colonel Roger Brown House.. Concord, Mass.
1775 Arrowhead Inn .... Durham, N.C.
1775 Welbourne................ Middleburg, Va.
1776 The Inn at Chester.......... Chester, Conn.
1779 Captain Josiah Mitchell House
.... Freeport, Maine
1779 Miles River Country Inn .... Hamilton, Mass.
1780 The 1780 Egremont Inn
.... South Egremont, Mass.
1780 Silver Thatch Inn .... Charlottesville, Va.
1781 Haan's 1830 Inn...... Mackinac Island, Mich.
1785 The 1785 Inn .... North Conway, N.H.
1786 Silvermine Tavern.......... Norwalk, Conn.
1786 Gibson's Lodgings .... Annapolis, Md.
1786 Kenniston Hill Inn......... Boothbay, Maine
1786 The Wayside Inn..... Greenfield Center, N.Y.
1786 The Brafferton Inn.......... Gettysburg, Pa.
1787 Nereledge Inn & White Horse Pub
.... North Conway, N.H.
1787 The Lords Proprietors' Inn .... Edenton, N.C.
1789 Captain Josiah Mitchell House
.... Freeport, Maine
1789 The Hancock Inn........... Hancock, N.H.
1789 The Inn at High View.......... Andover, Vt.
1789 Historic Brookside Farms........ Orwell, Vt.
1790 Fairhaven Inn .... Bath, Maine
1790 Packard House............... Bath, Maine
1790 Crown 'N' Anchor........ Newcastle, Maine
1790 Tuck Inn .... Rockport, Mass.
1790 Olde Orchard Inn....... Moultonboro, N.H.
1790 Pheasant Field B&B .... Carlisle, Pa.
1790 Field & Pine B&B......... Shippensburg, Pa.
1790 King George Inn & Guests... Charleston, S.C.
1790 1790 House .... Georgetown, S.C.
1790 Silver Maple Lodge & Cottages.... Fairlee, Vt.
1790 Shoreham Inn & Country Store
.... Shoreham Village, Vt.
1790 The Inn at Blush Hill......... Waterbury, Vt.
1790 Red Shutter Farmhouse ..... New Market, Va.
1791 St. Francis Inn .... Saint Augustine, Fla.
1791 The Inn on Cove Hill....... Rockport, Mass.
1793 Cove House......... Kennebunkport, Maine
1793 Echo Ledge Farm Inn .. East St. Johnsbury, Vt.
1794 The Inn at Maplewood Farm.. Hillsboro, N.H.
1795 The Acorn Inn............ Canadaigua, N.Y.
1795 Maplewood Inn .... Fair Haven, Vt.
1795 Rabbit Hill Inn .... Lower Waterford, Vt.
1795 The Inn at Weathersfield.... Weathersfield, Vt.
1795 Spring Farm B&B .... Luray, Va.
1796 Babbling Brook B&B Inn... Santa Cruz, Calif.
1796 National Pike Inn .... New Market, Md.
1797 Bay View Waterfront B&B ... Belle Haven, Va.

Jailhouses

Jailer's Inn...................... Bardstown, Ky.
The Jail House Historic Inn........ Preston, Minn.
Casa de Patron.................... Lincoln, N.M.
Jailhouse Inn .... Newport, R.I.

Lighthouses

East Brother Light Station... Point Richmond, Calif.
The Keeper's House .... Isle Au Haut, Maine
Chesapeake Bay Lighthouse B&B ... Annapolis, Md.
The Big Bay Point Lighthouse B&B.. Big Bay, Mich.

Log Cabins/Houses

Ocean Wilderness Country Inn........ Sooke, B.C.
Anniversary Inn................ Estes Park, Colo.
Sandusky House & O'Neal Log Cabin B&B
.... Nicholasville, Ky.
The Log House .... Russellville, Ky.
Lingren's B&B.................... Lutsen, Minn.
The Log House & Homestead .... Vergas, Minn.
Trout House Village Resort........... Hague, N.Y.
Inn at Cedar Falls.................. Logan, Ohio
Chain-O-Lakes Resort .... Romayor, Texas
The Log Cabin on the Hill..... Salt Lake City, Utah
Fort Lewis Lodge.................. Millboro, Va.
The Inn at Burg's Landing ... Anderson Island, Wash.

Natural Hot Springs

Vichy Hot Springs Resort & Inn . . . . . . Ukiah, Calif.
Idaho Rocky Mountain Ranch . . . . Stanley, Idaho

Old Mills

Silvermine Tavern. . . . . Norwalk, Conn.
Arbor Rose B&B. . . . . Stockbridge, Mass.
Twin Gables Country Inn . . . . Saugatuck, Mich.
The Inn at Millrace Pond . . . . Hope, N.J.
Asa Ransom House . . . . Clarence, N.Y.

Old Taverns

Red Brook Inn . . . . Old Mystic, Conn.
Birchwood Inn. Lenox, Mass.
Bird & Bottle . . . . Garrison, N.Y.
Smithton Inn . . . . Ephrata, Pa.
Witmer's Tavern - Historic 1725 Inn . . Lancaster, Pa.
Field & Pine B&B . . . . Shippensburg, Pa.
The Inn at the Crossroads . . . . . . North Garden, Va.
Rabbit Hill Inn . . . . Lower Waterford, Vt.
The Wayside Inn. . . . . Greenfield Center, N.Y.

Oldest Continuously Operated Inns

Historic National Hotel . . . . Jamestown, Calif.
Julian Gold Rush Hotel . . . . Julian, Calif.
The Cranberry Inn at Chatham . . . . Chatham, Mass.
Wakefield Inn . . . . Wakefield, N.H.
The Bellevue House . . . . Block Island, R.I.
The Bark Eater . . . . Keene, N.Y.
Kedron Valley Inn . . . . Woodstock, Vt.
Shelburne Inn . . . . Seaview, Wash.

On the Grounds of a U.S. National Memorial

Cathedral House B&B . . . . Rindge, N.H.

Partially Constructed with Dinosaur Bones

Pension Tannenhof. . . . . Banff, Alberta

Plantations

Kirkwood Plantation . . . . Eutaw, Ala.
Samples Plantation . . . . Greenville, Ga.
Little St. Simons Island . . . . . . St. Simons Island, Ga.
Haikuleana B&B Inn. . . . . Haiku, Hawaii
Poipu B&B Inn & Gallery . . . . Kauai, Hawaii
The House on Bayou Road . . . . . . New Orleans, La.
Mostly Hall B&B . . . . Falmouth, Mass.
Gross' Coate Plantation 1658 . . . . Easton, Md.
Rosswood Plantation . . . . Lorman, Miss.
Dunleith . . . . Natchez, Miss.
Sunrise Farm B&B . . . . Salem, S.C.
Maison Bayou: A B&B Plantation . . . Jefferson, Texas
Jasmine Plantation B&B. . . . . . Providence Forge, Va.
Hewick Plantation . . . . Urbana, Va.

Ranches

Grapevine Canyon Ranch. . . . . Pearce, Ariz.
B&B at Saddle Rock Ranch. . . . . Sedona, Ariz.
Random Oaks Ranch . . . . Julian, Calif.
Howard Creek Ranch . . . . Westport, Calif.
Wit's End Guest Ranch. . . . . Bayfield, Colo.
The Lazy Ranch B&B . . . . Edwards, Colo.
Plum Bear Ranch. . . . . Springfield, Colo.
Elk Echo Ranch Country B&B . . . . Stoneham, Colo.
Idaho Rocky Mountain Ranch . . . . Stanley, Idaho
Wine Country Farm . . . . Dayton, Ore.
Spring Creek Llama Ranch B&B . . . . Newberg, Ore.
Whippletree Inn & Farm . . . . Emelton, Pa.
Buck Valley Ranch . . . . Warfordsburg, Pa.
Hasse House and Ranch . . . . Mason, Texas

Revolutionary War

The Robert Morris House . . . . Oxford, Md.
Captain Samuel Eddy House . . . . Auburn, Mass.
Ashley Manor Inn. . . . . Barnstable, Mass.
Crocker Tavern B&B . . . . Barnstable, Mass.
Colonel Roger Brown House . . . . . . Concord, Mass.
Village Green Inn. . . . . Falmouth, Mass.
Crown Point B&B . . . . Crown Point, N.Y.
Pace One Restaurant & Country Inn . . Thornton, Pa.
The Culpeper House . . . . Newport, R.I.
The Melville House . . . . Newport, R.I.
John Rutledge House Inn . . . . Charleston, S.C.
The Kitchen House . . . . Charleston, S.C.
Loundes Grove Inn . . . . Charleston, S.C.
The Inn at Weathersfield . . . . Weathersfield, Vt.
Silver Thatch Inn . . . . Charlottesville, Va.
Gilbert House B&B of Middleway. . Charles Town, Va.

Schoolhouses

The Anderson House Inn. . . . . . Heber Springs, Ark.

Tollgate Hill Inn .... Litchfield, Conn.
School House B&B Inn .... Rocheport, Mo.
Schoolhouse & Teacherage .... Huson, Mont.
The Inn at Bingham School ..... Chapel Hill, N.C.
Washington School Inn .... Park City, Utah

SPACE SHUTTLE LAUNCHES

The Higgins House .... Sanford, Fla.

SPEAKEASY

Mary Monroe's B&B .... North River, N.Y.

STAGECOACH STOPS

Fensalden Inn .... Albion, Calif.
The Dorrington Hotel & Restaurant
.... Dorrington, Calif.
Simpson House Inn .... Santa Barbara, Calif.
Melitta Station Inn .... Santa Rosa, Calif.
Ski Tip Lodge .... Keystone, Colo.
Tidewater Inn .... Madison, Conn.
John Dill House .... Fort Gaines, Ga.
Egremont Inn .... South Egremont, Mass.
Merrell Historic Inn Stockbridge .. (South Lee), Mass.
Mendon Country Inn .... Mendon, Mich.
The Inn at Blush Hill .... Waterbury, Vt.
Hancock Inn .... Hancock, N.H.
Wakefield Inn .... Sanbornville N.H.
Hacienda Antigua B&B........ Albuquerque, N.M.
Hacienda Vargas .... Algondones, N.M.
The Wayside Inn.......... Greenfield Center, N.Y.
The Bark Eater Inn .... Keene, N.Y.
Mary Monroe's B&B........... North River, N.Y.
The Inn at Bingham School ..... Chapel Hill, N.C.
Mountain Home B&B ..... Mountain Home, N.C.
Penguin Crossing B&B .... Circleville, Ohio
Ye Kendall Inn .... Boerne, Texas
Churchill House Inn .... Brandon, Vt.
Henry Farm Inn.................... Chester, Vt.
The Golden Stage Inn .... Proctorsville, Vt.
Old Stagecoach Inn .... Waterbury, Vt.
Inn at Blush Hill .... Waterbury, Vt.
West Dover Inn .... West Dover, Vt.
Steele's Tavern Manor .... Steele's Tavern, Va.
The Inn at Narrow Passage .... Woodstock, Va.
The General Lewis .... Lewisburg, W.V.

STILL IN THE FAMILY

Oakland House Seaside Inn & Cottages
.... Brooksville, Maine
Cape Neddick House Cape .... Neddick, Maine
The Grey Havens .... Georgetown, Maine
Horse & Carriage B&B .... Jonesville, Mich.
Cedarcroft Farm .... Warrensburg, Mo.
The Sanders - Helena's B&B .... Helena, Mont.
Chalfonte .... Cape May, N.J.
Northern Plantation B&B .... Urbanna, Ohio
Cedar Hill Farm .... Mount Joy, Pa.
Hasse House and Ranch .... Mason, Texas
Bay View Waterfront B&B .... Belle Haven, Va.
North Bend Plantation........... Charles City, Va.
Welbourne .... Middleburg, Va.
Hewick Plantation .... Urbanna, Va.
Flying L Ranch - Mt. Adams Country Inn
.... Glenwood, Wash

THREE-SEAT OUTHOUSE

Maple Hill Farm B&B .... Coventry, Conn.

TRAIN STATIONS & RENOVATED RAIL CARS

The Inn at Depot Hill .. Capitola-By-The-Sea, Calif.
Melitta Station Inn .... Santa Rosa, Calif.
Varner's Caboose............... Montpelier, Iowa

TUNNELS, CAVES, SECRET PASSAGEWAYS

Wingscorton Farm .... East Sandwich, Mass.
Colonel Spencer Inn .... Plymouth, N.H.
Witmer's Tavern - Historic 1725 Inn .. Lancaster, Pa.
Kedron Valley Inn .... South Woodstock, Vt.

UNUSUAL ARCHITECTURE

Haan's 1830 Inn .... Mackinac Island, Mich.

UNUSUAL SLEEPING PLACES

Above a gold mine
Chichester-McKee House B&B ... Placerville, Calif.
In a blacksmith's shop
The Cookie Jar B&B.............. Wyoming, R.I.
In a water tower
John Doughtery House .... Mendocino, Calif.

INNS OF INTEREST

On a houseboat
Houseboat Amaryllis Inn .... Rockport, Ontario
Lone Lake B&B .... Langley, Wash.
On a Yacht
Dockside Boat & Bed .... San Francisco, Calif.
Tugboat Challenger .... Seattle, Wash.
On or next to an archaeological dig
Hewick Plantation .... Urbanna, Va.
Under water
Jules' Undersea Lodge .... Key Largo, Fla.

WATERFALLS

Fall Creek Falls B&B .... Pikeville, Tenn.

WHO STAYED/VISITED HERE

John James Audubon
Lincoln House Country Inn .... Dennysville, Maine
Henry Bennett, photographer
Historic Bennett House ...... Wisconsin Dells, Wis.
Sarah Bernhardt, Lillie Langtry
"An Elegant Victorian Mansion" ...... Eureka, Calif.
The Bigelow Family
Stonehurst Manor .... North Conway, N.H.
Billy the Kid
Casa de Patron B&B Inn .... Lincoln, N.M.
Billy The Kid, Doc Holliday, Big Nose Katy
Plaza Hotel .... Las Vegas, N.M.
Clara Bow
Hotel Nipton .... Nipton, Calif.
William Jennings Bryan
The Veranda .... Senoia, Ga.
Grover Cleveland, Woodrow Wilson
The Cordova .... Ocean Grove, N.J.
Calvin Coolidge
Lehmann House B&B .... St. Louis, Mo.
Calvin Coolidge, Amelia Earhart
Stonecrest Farm B&B .... Wilder, Vt.
Calvin Coolidge, Dwight D. Eisenhower
State Game Lodge .... Custer, S.D.
Calvin Coolidge, Warren Harding, Wrigley Family
The Inn on Mt. Ida .... Avalon, Calif.
Jefferson Davis
Anchuca .... Vicksburg, Miss.
Thomas Edison, Henry Ford, Eleanor Roosevelt
Avon Inn .... Avon, N.Y.
Douglas Fairbanks, Mary Pickford, Gloria Swanson
Esmeralda Inn .... Chimney Rock, N.C.
Clark Gable
Gable House .... Tucson, Ariz.
Esmeralda Inn .... Chimney Rock, N.C.
Clark Gable, Carole Lombard
Gold Mountain Manor Historic B&B. . Big Bear, Calif.
Cary Grant, Barbara Hutton, The Woolworth Family
The Mulburn Inn .... Bethlehem, N.H.
Alexander Hamilton, Lafayette
The Bird & Bottle Inn .... Garrison, N.Y.
Lillian Hellman, Marx Brothers
Barley Sheaf Farm .... Holicong, Pa.
Patrick Henry, Thomas Jefferson
The General Lewis .... Lewisburg, W.V.
Herbert Hoover
The Carriage House at Stonegate . . Montoursville, Pa.
Thomas Jefferson
The Inn at Meander Plantation .... Locust Dale, Va.
Kellogg Family
Village Country Inn .... Manchester Village, Vt.
Abraham Lincoln
Black River Inn .... Ludlow, Vt.
Mercedes McCambridge
The Dairy Hollow House ..... Eureka Springs, Ark.
President McKinley
Chesire Cat Inn .... Santa Barbara, Calif.
Karl Menninger
Heritage House .... Topeka, Kan.
Georgia O'Keefe
Hacienda del Sol .... Taos, N.M.
Norman Rockwell
Card Lake Inn .... West Stockbridge, Mass.
Theodore Roosevelt
Vichy Hot Springs Resort & Inn ...... Ukiah, Calif.
Lehmann House B&B .... St. Louis, Mo.
Troutbeck .... Amenia, N.Y.
Loundes Grove Inn .... Charleston, S.C.
Lillian Russell
Bayview Hotel B&B Inn .... Aptos, Calif.
Babe Ruth
Cranmore Mt. Lodge .... North Conway, N.H.
William Seward
The William Seward Inn .... Westfield, N.Y.
Fred R. Smith (A.K.A. "Uncle Sam")
Old Town Farm Inn .... Chester, Vt.
William H. Taft
Lehmann House B&B .... St. Louis, Mo.
Greenwood B&B .... Greensboro, N.C.
George Washington
The Bird & Bottle Inn .... Garrison, N.Y.
John Rutledge House Inn .... Charleston, S.C.
Aspen Hall Inn .... Martinsburg, Va.
Stanford White
The Inn at Jackson .... Jackson, N.H.

WORLD WAR II

Kilauea Lodge .... Volcano, Hawaii

Publications From American Historic Inns

The Bed & Breakfast Encyclopedia

By Deborah Edwards Sakach & Tiffany Crosswy

Our latest creation! This massive guide is the most comprehensive guide on the market today. Packed with detailed listings to more than 2,000 bed & breakfasts and country inns, the Encyclopedia also includes an index to an additional 13,000 inns, detailed state maps and more than 900 illustrations. Recipes, helpful phone numbers, information about reservation services and informative articles about bed & breakfast hot spots, the best bed & breakfasts, inns of interest, how to start your own B&B and much, much more.

If you're planning a getaway, this all-inclusive guide is a must!

960 pages, paperback **Price $16.95**

Bed & Breakfast and Country Inns, Eighth Edition

By Deborah Edwards Sakach

Imagine the thrill of receiving this unique book with its FREE night certificate as a gift. Now you can let someone else experience the magic of America's country inns with this unmatched offer. *Bed & Breakfasts and Country Inns* is the most talked about guide among inngoers.

This fabulous award-winning guide features more than 1,600 inns from across the United States and Canada. Best of all, no other bookstore guide offers a FREE night certificate.* This certificate can be used at any one of the featured Inns.

American Historic Inns, Inc. has been publishing books about bed & breakfasts since 1981. Its books and the FREE night offer have been recommended by many travel writers and editors, and featured in: *The New York Times, Washington Post, Boston Globe, Chicago Sun Times, USA Today, Good Housekeeping, Cosmopolitan, Consumer Reports* and more.

*With purchase of one night at the regular rate required. Subject to limitations.

544 pages, paperback, 500 illustrations **Price $21.95**

The Official Guide to American Historic Inns

Completely Revised and Updated, Fifth Edition

By Deborah Edwards Sakach

Open the door to America's past with this fascinating guide to Historic Inns that reflect our colorful heritage. From Dutch Colonials to Queen Anne Victorians, these bed & breakfasts and country inns offer experiences of a lifetime.

This special edition guide includes certified American Historic Inns that provide the utmost in hospitality, beauty, authentic restoration and preservation.

With inns dating back as early as 1637, this guide is filled with treasures waiting to be discovered. Full descriptions, illustrations and guest comments all are included to let you know what's in store for you before choosing to stay at America's Historic Inns.

528 pages, paperback, 800 illustrations **Price $15.95**

the Road Best Traveled – Monthly Newsletter

Here's the only way to make sure you don't get left out of the latest bed & breakfast and country inn promotions. This travel newsletter is packed with information about more FREE night offers, huge discounts on lodgings and family vacation opportunities.

And that's not all! *The Road Best Traveled* is your one-stop travel shopping source to help you plan your next vacation. This outstanding publication includes the latest hotel bargains, methods to get the cheapest air fare, unbelievable cruise deals and affordable excursion packages to exotic and far off places.

Wait, there's more! As a special offer to readers of this book, you'll receive a special edition of *Bed & Breakfasts and Country Inns* FREE with your subscription. This book includes a FREE night certificate! A great gift for a friend or another FREE night for you!

One-year subscription (12 issues) **(Reg. $48.00)** **Special price $39.95**
Special two-year subscription (Reg. $96.00) **Special price $69.95**

Bed & Breakfast and Country Inn Travel Club

Membership From American Historic Inns, Inc.

SAVE! SAVE! SAVE! Now, for the first time ever, we offer an exclusive discount club that lets you enjoy the excitement of bed & breakfast and country inn travel again and again. As a member of this once-in-a-lifetime offer you'll receive benefits that include savings of 25% to 50% off every night's stay!

The best part of being an American Historic Inns Travel Club Member is that the card can be used as many times as you like.

In addition to your card, you will get a FREE night's stay certificate—truly a club membership that's hard to pass up!

All travel club members receive:

- Travel club card entitling holder to 25% to 50% off lodging.
- FREE night's stay certificate.
- Guide to more than 1,100 participating inns across America.
- Sample issue of *The Road Best Traveled,* a monthly newsletter with discount updates.

Membership is good for one year only. Free night's stay with purchase of one night at the regular rate. Discount and certificate cannot be combined. Other restrictions may apply.

Introductory price with full benefits (Reg. $59.95) **$49.95**

How To Start & Run Your Own Bed & Breakfast Inn

By Ripley Hotch & Carl Glassman

In this book you'll discover the secrets of the best inns. Learn how to decide whether owning or leasing an inn is right for you. Find out what business strategies characterize a successful inn and learn how to incorporate them in your own business.

If you've always dreamed of owning a Bed & Breakfast, then this book is for you!

182 pages, paperback **Price $14.95**

PO Box 669
Dana Point
California
92629-0669
(714) 499-8070
Fax (714) 499-4022

Order Form

Date: __/__/__ Shipped: __/__/__

Name: __________

Street: __________

City/State/Zip: __________

Phone: (___) ___-____

QTY.	Prod. No.	Description	Amount	Total
___	AHIE1	Bed & Breakfasts Encyclopedia	$16.95	___
___	AHI8	Bed & Breakfasts and Country Inns	$21.95	___
___	AHIH5	The Official Guide to American Historic Inns	$15.95	___
___	AHIN1	The Road Best Traveled Newsletter (one year; includes free-night guide and Shipping)	$39.95	___
___	AHIN2	The Road Best Traveled Newsletter (two years; includes free-night guide and Shipping)	$69.95	___
___	AHIC2	Bed & Breakfast and Country Inn Travel Club (Includes sample issue of The Road Best Traveled)	$49.95	___
___	CB03	How to Start Your Own B&B	$14.95	___
			Subtotal	___
			California buyers add 7.75% sales tax	___
			Shipping and Handling on Book and Travel Club Orders 4th Class Book Rate (10-20 days): $2.25 for the first book. 75¢ each additional copy. Priority Mail (2-4 days): $3.75 for one copy. $5.50 – two copies. $6.50 – three copies.	___
			TOTAL	___

❑ Check/Money Order ❑ Mastercard ❑ Visa ❑ American Express

Account Number __________ Exp. Date __/__

Name on card __________

Signature __________

INN EVALUATION FORM

Please copy and complete this form for each stay and mail to the address shown. Since 1981 we have maintained files that include thousands of evaluations from inngoers who have sent this form to us. This information helps us evaluate and update the inns listed in this guide.

Name of Inn: ______________________________

City and State: ______________________________

Date of Stay: ______________________________

Your Name: ______________________________

Address: ______________________________

City/State/Zip: ______________________________

Phone: (___) ___-____

Please use the following rating scale for the next items.
1: Outstanding. 2: Good. 3: Average. 4: Fair. 5: Poor.

Location	1	2	3	4	5
Cleanliness	1	2	3	4	5
Food Service	1	2	3	4	5
Privacy	1	2	3	4	5
Beds	1	2	3	4	5
Bathrooms	1	2	3	4	5
Parking	1	2	3	4	5
Handling of reservations	1	2	3	4	5
Attitude of staff	1	2	3	4	5
Overall rating	1	2	3	4	5

Comments on Above: ______________________________

____

____

____

____

MAIL THE COMPLETED FORM TO:
American Historic Inns, Inc.
PO Box 669
Dana Point, CA 92629-0669
(714) 499-8070

Notes